EIGHTH EDITION

PSYCHOLOGY

Lester M. Sdorow
Arcadia University

Cheryl A. Rickabaugh
University of Redlands

Adrienne J. Betz
Quinnipiac University

Academic Media Solutions
Affordable - Quality Textbooks, Study Aids, & Custom Publishing

To Les Sdorow.

To Gail and Barbara, with love.

To my family, past, present, and future, for supporting me and keeping things in perspective.

Psychology, 8th Edition, Sdorow/Rickabaugh/Betz

Paperback (black/white):	ISBN–13: 978-1-942041-62-7
	ISBN–10: 1-942041-62-4
Paperback (color):	ISBN–13: 978-1-942041-63-4
	ISBN–10: 1-942041-63-2
Loose-leaf version:	ISBN–13: 978-1-942041-64-1
	ISBN–10: 1-942041-64-0
Online version:	ISBN–13: 978-1-942041-65-8
	ISBN–10: 1-942041-65-9

Copyright © 2019 by Academic Media Solutions. All Rights Reserved.

No part of this publication may be reproduced, stored in a retrieval system, or transmitted, in any form or by any means, electronic, mechanical, photocopying, recording, Web distribution, information storage and retrieval systems, or otherwise, without the prior written permission of the publisher.

Printed in the United States of America by Academic Media Solutions.

Brief Contents

Boxed Features x

Gender/Diversity and Biopsychology Coverage xi

Preface xiv

About the Authors xx

1 The Nature of Psychology 1

2 Psychology as a Science 25

3 Biopsychological Bases of Behavior 60

4 Human Development 107

5 Sensation and Perception 151

6 Consciousness 198

7 Learning 237

8 Memory 270

9 Thought and Language 308

10 Intelligence 343

11 Motivation 375

12 Emotion 413

13 Personality 443

14 Psychological Disorders 480

15 Therapy 529

16 Psychology, Health, and Stress 561

17 Social Psychology 595

Answers to Section Review Questions Ans-1

Answers to Chapter Quiz Questions Ans-14

Key Contributors KC-1

Glossary G-1

References R-1

Name Index I-1

Subject Index I-32

Contents

Boxed Features x
Gender/Diversity and Biopsychology Coverage xi
Preface xiv
About the Authors xx

1 The Nature of Psychology 1

The Historical Context of Psychology 2
The Roots of Psychology 2
The Founding Schools of Psychology 5
The Growth of Psychology 8

Contemporary Perspectives in Psychology 13
The Humanistic Perspective 13
The Cognitive Perspective 14
The Biopsychological Perspective 14
The Sociocultural Perspective 16

The Scope of Psychology 17
Academic Fields of Specialization 18
Professional Fields of Specialization 19

Chapter Summary 22 *Key Terms* 22
Chapter Quiz 23 *Thought Questions* 24

2 Psychology as a Science 25

Sources of Knowledge 25
Common Sense 25
Science 27

Goals of Scientific Research 30
Description 30
Prediction 31
Control 32
Explanation 32

Methods of Psychological Research 33
Descriptive Research 33
Correlational Research 38
Experimental Research 39

Statistical Analysis of Research Data 46
Descriptive Statistics 46
Correlational Statistics 48
Inferential Statistics 49

Ethics of Psychological Research 52
Ethical Treatment of Research Data 52
Ethical Treatment of Human Participants 52
Ethical Treatment of Animal Subjects 54

Chapter Summary 56 *Key Terms* 57
Chapter Quiz 57 *Thought Questions* 59

3 Biopsychological Bases of Behavior 60

Nature versus Nurture 61
Evolutionary Psychology 62
Behavioral Genetics 62

Biological Communication Systems 67
The Nervous System 67
The Endocrine System 68

Neuronal Activity 71
The Structure of the Neuron 72
The Neural Impulse 72
Synaptic Transmission 75

Brain Functions 80
Techniques for Studying Brain Functions 80
Functional Organization of the Brain 84
Cerebral Hemispheric Lateralization 93
Neural Plasticity 99

Chapter Summary 103 *Key Terms* 104
Chapter Quiz 105 *Thought Questions* 106

4 Human Development 107

Research Methods in Developmental Psychology 108
Longitudinal Research 108
Cross-Sectional Research 109
Cohort-Sequential Research 109

Prenatal Development 110
The Germinal Stage 110
The Embryonic Stage 110
The Fetal Stage 111

Infant and Child Development 112
Physical Development 112
Perceptual Development 113
Cognitive Development 114
Psychosocial Development 118

Adolescent Development 129
Physical Development 129
Cognitive Development 131
Psychosocial Development 132

Adult Development 136
Physical Development 136
Cognitive Development 137
Psychosocial Development 141

Chapter Summary 147   Key Terms 148
Chapter Quiz 149   Thought Questions 150

5 Sensation and Perception 151

Sensory Processes 152
Sensory Thresholds 152
Sensory Adaptation 155

Visual Sensation 156
Light Waves 156
Vision and the Eye 157
Vision and the Brain 160
Basic Visual Processes 160

Visual Perception 165
Form Perception 165
Depth Perception 167
Perceptual Constancies 169
Visual Illusions 171
Experience, Culture, and Perception 173

Hearing 174
Sound Waves 175
The Auditory System 175
Auditory Perception 177

Chemical Senses 181
Smell 181
Taste 183

Skin Senses 184
Touch 184
Pain 185

Body Senses 188
The Kinesthetic Sense 188
The Vestibular Sense 189

Extrasensory Perception 190
Alleged Paranormal Abilities 191
Problems with Paranormal Research 192
The Status of Parapsychology 193

Chapter Summary 194   Key Terms 195
Chapter Quiz 196   Thought Questions 197

6 Consciousness 198

The Nature of Consciousness 199
The Stream of Consciousness 199
Attention 200
The Unconscious 201

Sleep 204
Biological Rhythms and the Sleep-Wake Cycle 204
Patterns of Sleep 205
The Functions of Sleep 209
Sleep Disorders 211

Dreams 214
The Content of Dreams 215
The Purpose of Dreaming 217

Hypnosis 219
Hypnotic Induction and Susceptibility 220
Effects of Hypnosis 221
The Nature of Hypnosis 222

Psychoactive Drugs 224
Depressants 227
Stimulants 228
Other Psychoactive Drugs 230
Entactogens 232

Chapter Summary 234   Key Terms 234
Chapter Quiz 235   Thought Questions 236

7 Learning   237

Classical Conditioning   238
- Principles of Classical Conditioning   239
- Applications of Classical Conditioning   242
- Biological Constraints on Classical Conditioning   246

Operant Conditioning   247
- Principles of Operant Conditioning   247
- Applications of Operant Conditioning   255
- Biological Constraints on Operant Conditioning   259

Cognitive Learning   260
- Cognitive Factors in Associative Learning   261
- Latent Learning   262
- Observational Learning   263

Chapter Summary 266   Key Terms 267
Chapter Quiz 267   Thought Questions 269

8 Memory   270

Information Processing and Memory   271

Sensory Memory   272

Short-Term Memory   273

Long-Term Memory   276
- Encoding   276
- Storage   278
- Retrieval   281
- Forgetting   283

Memory, Forgetting, and Eyewitness Testimony   290
- Children as Eyewitnesses   291
- Questioning the Eyewitness   294

Improving Your Memory   294
- Using Effective Study Habits   294
- Using Mnemonic Devices   296

The Biopsychology of Memory   298
- The Neuroanatomy of Memory   298
- The Neurochemistry of Memory   301

Chapter Summary 304   Key Terms 305
Chapter Quiz 306   Thought Questions 307

9 Thought and Language   308

Thought   309
- Concept Formation   310
- Problem Solving   312
- Creativity   316
- Decision Making   320
- Artificial Intelligence   322

Language   324
- The Structure of Language   326
- The Acquisition of Language   328
- The Relationship Between Language and Thought   332
- Language in Apes   335

Chapter Summary 339   Key Terms 340
Chapter Quiz 341   Thought Questions 342

10 Intelligence   343

Intelligence Testing   345
- The History of Intelligence Testing   345
- Standardization in Intelligence Testing   347

Extremes of Intelligence   351
- Intellectual Disabilities   351
- Mental Giftedness   355

Theories of Intelligence   357

Factor-Analytic Theories of Intelligence   357

Sternberg's Triarchic Theory of Intelligence   360

Gardner's Theory of Multiple Intelligences   360

Nature, Nurture, and Intelligence   362
- Early Studies of Women   362
- Early Studies of Immigrants   363
- The Influence of Heredity and Environment on Intelligence   364

Chapter Summary 371   Key Terms 372
Chapter Quiz 372   Thought Questions 374

11 Motivation   375

The Nature of Motivation   376
- Sources of Motivation   376
- Maslow's Hierarchy of Needs   378

The Hunger Motive 379
- The Physiology of Hunger 379
- Obesity 381
- Eating Disorders 385

The Sex Motive 389
- Biopsychological Factors in Sexual Behavior 390
- Psychosocial Factors in Sexual Behavior 391
- Sexual Dysfunctions 393
- Gender Identity 394
- Sexual Orientation 395

The Arousal Motive 399
- Optimal Arousal 399
- Sensory Deprivation 400
- Sensation Seeking 401

The Achievement Motive 402
- Need for Achievement 403
- Goal Setting 404
- Intrinsic Motivation 404

The Role of Motivation in Sport 406
- The Arousal Motive and Sport 406
- The Achievement Motive and Sport 407

Chapter Summary 409 Key Terms 410
Chapter Quiz 411 Thought Questions 412

12 Emotion 413

The Biopsychology of Emotion 414
- The Autonomic Nervous System and Emotion 414
- The Brain and Emotion 415
- The Chemistry of Emotion 420

The Expression of Emotion 422
- Vocal Qualities and Emotion 422
- Body Movements and Emotion 423
- Facial Expressions and Emotion 423

The Experience of Emotion 426
- Happiness 427
- Humor 429

Theories of Emotion 431
- Biopsychological Theories of Emotion 432
- The Facial-Feedback Theory of Emotion 434
- Cognitive Theories of Emotion 436

Chapter Summary 440 Key Terms 440
Chapter Quiz 441 Thought Questions 442

13 Personality 443

The Psychoanalytic Approach to Personality 444
- Freud's Psychosexual Theory 444
- Adler's Theory of Individual Psychology 447
- Horney's Theory of Feminine Psychology 449
- Jung's Theory of Analytical Psychology 449
- Psychoanalytic Assessment of Personality 450
- Status of the Psychoanalytic Approach 451

The Dispositional Approach to Personality 452
- Type Theories 452
- Trait Theories 454
- Dispositional Assessment of Personality 455
- Status of the Dispositional Approach 457

The Cognitive-Behavioral Approach to Personality 460
- Social-Cognitive Theory 460
- Schema Theory 461
- Cognitive-Behavioral Assessment of Personality 462
- Status of the Cognitive-Behavioral Approach 463

The Humanistic Approach to Personality 465
- The Self-Actualization Theory of Personality 466
- The Self Theory of Personality 467
- The Humanistic Assessment of Personality 468
- Status of the Humanistic Approach 469

The Biopsychological Approach to Personality 470
- The Relationship Between Physique and Personality 471
- The Relationship Between Heredity and Personality 473
- Biopsychological Assessment of Personality 473
- Status of the Biopsychological Approach 474

Chapter Summary 476 Key Terms 477
Chapter Quiz 478 Thought Questions 479

14 Psychological Disorders 480

- Characteristics of Psychological Disorders 480
  - Criteria for Psychological Disorders 481
  - Viewpoints on Psychological Disorders 482
  - Classification of Psychological Disorders 488
- Anxiety Disorders 489
  - Generalized Anxiety Disorder 491
  - Panic Disorder 492
  - Phobias 494
- Obsessive-Compulsive Disorder 496
  - Characteristics of Obsessive-Compulsive Disorder 497
  - Causes of Obsessive-Compulsive Disorder 497
- Somatic Symptom and Related Disorders 498
  - Illness Anxiety Disorder 498
  - Conversion Disorder 499
- Dissociative Disorders 500
  - Dissociative Amnesia and Fugue 500
  - Dissociative Identity Disorder 501
- Major Depressive Disorder and Related Disorders 503
  - Major Depressive Disorder 503
  - Seasonal Affective Disorder 506
  - Suicide and Major Depressive Disorder 508
- Bipolar Disorder 509
  - Characteristics of Bipolar Disorder 510
  - Causes of Bipolar Disorder 510
- Schizophrenia 511
  - The Nature of Schizophrenia 512
  - Causes of Schizophrenia 513
- Personality Disorders 517
  - Borderline Personality Disorder 518
  - Antisocial Personality Disorder 519
- Developmental Disorders 520
  - Autism Spectrum Disorder (ASD) 521
  - Attention Deficit Hyperactivity Disorder (ADHD) 522

Chapter Summary 525 *Key Terms* 526
Chapter Quiz 527 *Thought Questions* 528

15 Therapy 529

- The History of Therapy 530
  - Ancient Practices 530
  - Medieval and Renaissance Approaches 530
  - 18th- and 19th-Century Reforms 530
  - The Mental Health Movement 531
- The Psychoanalytic Orientation 532
  - The Nature of Psychoanalysis 532
  - Techniques in Psychoanalysis 532
  - Offshoots of Psychoanalysis 533
- The Behavioral Orientation 533
  - Classical Conditioning Therapies 534
  - Operant-Conditioning Therapies 536
  - Social-Learning Therapies 538
- The Cognitive Orientation 538
  - Rational-Emotive Behavior Therapy 538
  - Cognitive Therapy 540
- The Humanistic Orientation 540
  - Person-Centered Therapy 540
  - Gestalt Therapy 541
- The Social-Relations Orientation 542
  - Group Therapy 542
  - Family Therapy 543
- The Biological Orientation 544
  - Psychosurgery 544
  - Electroconvulsive Therapy 545
  - Drug Therapy 546
- Community Mental Health 548
  - Deinstitutionalization 548
  - Prevention of Psychological Disorders 548
- The Rights of the Therapy Client 549
  - The Rights of Hospitalized Patients 549
  - The Right to Confidentiality 550
- Finding the Proper Therapy 551
  - Selecting the Right Therapist 551
  - Bibliotherapy as an Alternative 552
- The Effectiveness of Psychotherapy 552
  - Evaluation of Psychotherapy 553
  - Factors in the Effectiveness of Psychotherapy 554

Chapter Summary 557 *Key Terms* 558
Chapter Quiz 559 *Thought Questions* 560

16 Psychology, Health, and Stress 561

Psychological Stress and Stressors 562
 Life Changes 562
 Daily Hassles 564

The Biopsychology of Stress and Illness 566
 General Adaptation Syndrome 567
 Stress and Cardiovascular Disease 567
 Stress and Immune Functioning 570
 Stress and Cancer 573

Factors That Moderate the Stress Response 574
 Physiological Reactivity 574
 Cognitive Appraisal 575
 Explanatory Style 575
 Perceived Control 576
 Psychological Hardiness 577
 Social Support 578

Coping with Stress 579
 Emotional Release and Stress Management 580
 Stress-Inoculation Training 580
 Exercise and Stress Management 580
 Relaxation and Stress Management 581

Health-Promoting Habits 582
 Practicing Safe Sex 582
 Keeping Physically Fit 583
 Maintaining a Healthy Diet and Body Weight 585
 Avoiding Tobacco Products 586

Reactions to Illness 588
 Seeking Treatment for Health Problems 588
 Relieving Patient Distress 589
 Encouraging Adherence to Medical Regimens 590

Chapter Summary 592   Key Terms 592
Chapter Quiz 592   Thought Questions 594

17 Social Psychology 595

Social Cognition 596
 Causal Attribution 596
 Person Perception 598

Interpersonal Attraction 601
 Liking 601
 Romantic Love 603

Attitudes 606
 The Formation of Attitudes 607
 The Art of Persuasion 608
 Attitudes and Behavior 610
 Prejudice 612

Group Dynamics 615
 Group Decision Making 615
 Group Effects on Performance 617
 Social Influence 619

Aggression 622
 Theories of Aggression 622
 Group Violence 625

Prosocial Behavior 626
 Altruism 626
 Bystander Intervention 627

Chapter Summary 631   Key Terms 632
Chapter Quiz 632   Thought Questions 634

Answers to Section Review Questions Ans-1
Answers to Chapter Quiz Questions Ans-14
Key Contributors KC-1
Glossary G-1
References R-1
Name Index I-1
Subject Index I-32

Boxed Features

Critical Thinking About Psychology

Does Melatonin Have Beneficial Physical and Psychological Effects? 26
What Can We Infer from the Size and Shape of the Brain? 82
Are There Significant Psychological Gender Differences? 138
Can We Be Controlled by Subliminal Messages? 155
Does Television Influence Children's Behavior? 264
Should We Trust "Recovered Memories" of Childhood Abuse? 287
How Should We Respond to *The Bell Curve*? 364
Is There a Gay Brain? 397
Do Lie Detectors Tell the Truth? 416
How Effective Is Psychological Profiling in Identifying Criminals? 464
Does the Insanity Defense Let Many Violent Criminals Escape Punishment? 486

Psychology versus Common Sense

Can We Reliably Detect When Someone Is Drunk? 28
Is Being Left-Handed a Pathological Condition? 96
Can Baseball Batters Really Keep Their Eyes on the Ball? 162
Is Sleep Necessary for Good Health? 212
Can Leading Questions Alter Our Memories of Vivid Events? 292
Can Rewarding Creative Behavior Inhibit Creativity? 318
Are Faster Brains More Intelligent Brains? 358
Will Rewarding a Behavior Always Increase Our Desire to Perform It? 405
Do Emotional Experiences Depend on Physical Responses to Emotional Situations? 433
Is Personality Consistent from One Situation to Another? 458
Can Mentally Healthy People Be Recognized in a Mental Hospital? 490

The Research Process

Can Experimenter Expectancies Affect the Behavior of Laboratory Rats? 44
Has Evolution Influenced Gender Differences in Romantic Jealousy? 63
When Do Infants Develop Depth Perception? 116
Are There Cultural Differences in the Painfulness of Childbirth? 187
Is Hypnosis an Altered State of Consciousness? 224
Can Classical Conditioning Help Maintain the Appetites of Children Undergoing Chemotherapy? 245
Do We Form Sensory Memories of All the Information That Stimulates Our Sensory Receptors? 274
Does Language Influence Children's Conceptions of Gender Roles? 334
What Is the Fate of Childhood Geniuses? 356
How Satisfied Are Men and Women with Their Bodies? 386
Do Emotions Depend on Our Attribution of a Cause for Our Physiological Arousal? 437
How Similar Are the Personalities of Identical Twins Reared Apart? 474
Are People Who Ruminate About Their Problems More Likely to Develop Major Depressive Disorder? 507
Do Endorphins Mediate the Effect of Systematic Desensitization on Phobias? 536
Can the Immune Response Be Altered by Classical Conditioning? 573
Would You Harm Someone Just Because an Authority Figure Ordered You To? 622

Experiencing Psychology

What Are the Locations and Functions of Brain Structures? 103
An Analysis of Children's Toys 147
A Personal Study of Sleep and Dreams 233
Shaping the Professor's Behavior—A Case Study 265
Does the Pegword Method Improve Memory Performance? 304
Will the Replication of a Classic Research Study on Mental Sets Produce Similar Findings Today? 338
What Would You Include in an IQ Test? 371
Can Mental Imagery Improve Sport Performance? 409
Are Humorous Professors More Effective Teachers? 439
Are Amazing Similarities in Personality Just the Result of Coincidence? 476
How Do the Media Portray Psychological Disorders? 525
How Do the Media Portray Drug Therapy? 557
Increasing Exercise Adherence 591
A Study of Personal Advertisements 630

Gender/Diversity and Biopsychology Coverage

Gender/Diversity Coverage

Chapter 1
Women's role in history of psychology 8
Cross-cultural, cultural, and ethnic psychology and issues 16

Chapter 2
Interpretation of group differences and individual differences 51–52

Chapter 3
Gender differences and similarities in jealousy (with acknowledgment of cultural factors) (The Research Process feature) 63
Gender similarities in prolactin secretion of expectant parents 69
Cultural factors in handedness 94–97
Gender differences in cerebral lateralization 94, 95

Chapter 4
Sociocultural factors in teratogens 111–112
Cross-cultural differences and similarities in correlates of attachment 119–121
Paternal attachment 120
Cross-cultural factors influencing nature of parenting behaviors 122
Gender, culture, and childhood friendship 124
Cultural similarities in familial conflict 123–124
Ethnic identity 133–134
Relationship dissolution among heterosexual, gay, and lesbian couples 143–144

Chapter 5
Color-blindness as sex-linked trait 165
Cross-cultural and gender differences in olfaction 181

Chapter 6
Cross-cultural similarities in sleep deficit (with mention of gender) 207–209
Gender and ethnic differences in sleep cycle 208

Chapter 8
Study of Turkish residents who had/had not experienced Marmara earthquake 270

Effect of gender schemas on memory 281
Cross-cultural differences and similarities in eyewitness testimony 291
Gender differences in emotional memory 299
Research on effect of estrogen and testosterone on age-related memory deficits 303

Chapter 9
Cross-cultural research on perception of click consonants 326
Cognitive linguistics and cross-cultural variation in language 334
Hyde's research on nonsexist language (The Research Process feature) 334

Chapter 10
Sociohistorical influences on gifted women (The Research Process feature) 356
Early studies of gender differences in intelligence 362–363

Chapter 11
Chapter-opening story of Mother, a sexual minority 375–376
Gender, ethnicity, and sexual orientation—differences and similarities in prevalence of eating disorders 387–389
Study of gender identity 394–395
Cultural factors influencing sexual orientation (including gender) 394–398

Chapter 12
Cross-cultural differences in emotional expression 422
Gender stereotypes and perceived gender differences in emotionality 424–425
Gender differences in smiling 424–425
Cross-cultural differences in experience of positive and negative emotions 434

Chapter 13
Cross-cultural research on five-factor theory 454–455
Collective efficacy 461
Gender and cross-cultural differences in self-esteem 468

Chapter 14
Sociocultural influences on psychological disorders 485–487
Gender and cross-cultural differences/similarities in generalized anxiety disorder 491

Gender and cross-cultural differences/similarities in panic disorder 492–493

Gender and cross-cultural differences/similarities in phobias 494–496

Gender and cross-cultural differences/similarities in obsessive-compulsive disorder (OCD) 497

Gender and cross-cultural differences/similarities in somatic symptom and related disorders 498–500

Gender and ethnic differences in major depressive disorder 503–506

Cross-cultural research on attributional model of major depressive disorder 504–506

Cultural influences on major depressive disorder 504–506

Gender differences in suicide 508–509

Gender differences in bipolar disorder 510

Cross-cultural differences in course of schizophrenia 512–513

Gender differences in antisocial personality disorder 519

Chapter 15
Cultural competence in psychotherapy 531
Ethnic match in psychotherapy 555

Chapter 16
Gender and ethnic differences in life events 562–563
Tend-and-befriend response 566
Poverty and learned helplessness 576
Gender and cross-cultural differences in the expressed need for social support 578–579
Gender differences in smoking relapse 587
Gender, ethnic differences in use of health care delivery system 588–589

Chapter 17
Gender differences in evaluation of self-handicappers 598–599
Gender and first impressions (handshakes) 599
Cross-cultural differences in romantic love 603–604
Influence of gender and sexual orientation in mate selection (also Experiencing Psychology feature) 606, 630
Conformity and cultural values related to uniqueness 619–620
Gendered aggression 622–625

Biopsychology Coverage

Chapter 2
Effect of melatonin vs. placebo on sleep 40

Chapter 3
Possible evolutionary basis of gender differences in romantic jealousy (The Research Process feature) 63
Shared historical context of Galvani's views on the electrical nature of neural conduction and Mary Shelley's use of "galvanism" in *Frankenstein* 73

Otto Loewi's discovery of the chemical basis of neural transmission in a dream 76
Whether left-handedness is a pathological condition (Psychology versus Common Sense feature) 96–97
Neural plasticity, including neural transplantation 99–102

Chapter 4
Research study indicating that fetuses form memories of smells experienced in the womb 114

Chapter 5
Case of a man who mistook his wife for a hat as an example of sensation vs. perception 151–152
Pupil dilation as a measure of snake phobia 157–158
Prosthetic vision via direct stimulation of the visual cortex 160
Sign language activating the auditory cortex of "listeners" deaf since birth 177
Effects of listening to personal stereos and rock concerts on hearing loss (Meyer-Bisch, 1996) 179
Research indicating that our response to the sound of a fingernail scratching on a blackboard might be genetically based because that sound is similar to the warning cry of a macaque monkey 180
A basis for the incest taboo based on the aversion of fathers and daughters and brothers and sisters to each others' odors 182
MRI study indicating that simply anticipating pain activates pain-relevant brain regions 186

Chapter 6
Superiority of phase delay to phase advance in rotating shifts 205
Beneficial effects of sleep on the immune response (Psychology versus Common Sense feature) 212
Positive effect of REM sleep on memory 218–219
Research study indicating that hypnosis might not be an altered state of consciousness (The Research Process feature) 224

Chapter 7
Conditioned taste aversion to prevent coyotes from killing sheep 237–238
Use of classical conditioning in the control of nocturnal enuresis 240–241
Role of classical conditioning in drug overdoses 243–244
Classical conditioning to help children undergoing chemotherapy maintain their appetites (The Research Process feature) 245

Chapter 8
Marijuana and state-dependent memory 289–290
Controversy over research on the chemical transfer of memories 301
Role of NMDA receptors in rats' recognition of the smell of other rats' breath 302

Chapter 10
Role of heredity in intelligence of identical twins reared as fraternal and fraternal twins reared as identical 366

Role of heredity in intelligence of "virtual twins" 366–367

Chapter 11
Role of heredity in dietary preferences of identical twins reared apart 379

Inhibitory effect of cholecystokinin on hunger 380

Research study on World War II famine, showing role of early nutrition in later body weight 383–384

Gender differences in body images (The Research Process feature) 386

Changes in sexual values as indicated by publication of article submitted in 1899 in 1983 issue of the *Journal of the American Medical Association* 392

Penis size differences between gay and straight men, indicating possible role of hormones in sexual orientation 396

The "gay brain" (Critical Thinking About Psychology feature) 397

Role of optimal arousal in playing basketball 406–407

Chapter 12
The validity of the lie detector (Critical Thinking About Psychology feature) 416–418

Effect of lateralized brain damage on positive and negative emotions 419–420

Hemispheric specialization for positive and negative emotions in infants 420

Role of endorphins in emotional experience of music-concert audience members 421

Role of right hemisphere in the emotional tone of speech, using the Wada test 422

Role of body movements in the perception of emotion, using lights on body joints in the dark 423

Facial-feedback theory of emotion 434–435

Chapter 13
Personality similarities in identical twins reared apart (The Research Process feature) 474

Chapter 14
Why a viral explanation of schizophrenia might explain why one identical twin may be afflicted and the other not 515

Role of lateral ventricles in schizophrenia from meta-analysis of MRI studies 516

Chapter 15
Role of endorphins in systematic desensitization (The Research Process feature) 536

Chapter 16
Effects of hassles and uplifts on the immune response 564–565

Classical conditioning of the immune response (The Research Process feature) 573

Effect of social support on the immune response of students undergoing exam stress 578

Effect of writing about emotional issues on the immune response 580

Effect of exercise on health in students under stress 580

Preface

From psychology's inception as a separate discipline, authors of introductory psychology textbooks have been confronted with the need to convey a broad discipline to students in a book of reasonable length. To accomplish all that Les Sdorow originally intended in the first edition of *Psychology*, the book could easily have been twice as long as it is now. More than a century ago, William James, disturbed at the length of his now-classic *Principles of Psychology*, gave his own stinging review of it. He called it, among other things, "a bloated tumescent mass." Though this comment might have been written during one of James's frequent bouts with depression, it indicates the challenge of synthesizing a vast quantity of information. Given that psychology has become an even broader discipline and has accumulated an enormous information base, Les quickly discovered that he would somehow have to produce a textbook that adequately covered the discipline of psychology without becoming what textbook reviewers refer to as, perhaps euphemistically, "encyclopedic."

If you have not adopted this book in the past, we believe that you will find that your students will be eager to read it and to learn from it. You will find that the book achieves interest and readability while also accomplishing the following goals:

- Portraying psychology as a science
- Demonstrating the superiority of science over common sense
- Showing that psychological research occurs in a sociocultural context
- Illustrating the relevance of psychology to everyday life
- Encouraging critical thinking in all aspects of life, particularly in regard to the media
- Placing psychology in its intellectual, historical, biographical, and sociocultural contexts

To ensure that students will find the book appealing, we have made every effort to write clearly and concisely and to include interesting content. To make our prose as clear as possible, we have taken care that every sentence, paragraph, and section in the book presents a crisp, logical flow of ideas. To make the content more interesting, we have included many engaging examples of concepts and issues throughout the book. Because more readable textbooks provide vivid examples of the concepts and issues they cover, we have included concrete examples from psychological research and from virtually every area of life.

A textbook should be readable, but for students to respect psychology as a science, the textbook they use also must be scholarly. Though popular examples are provided throughout this text, they do not substitute for evidence provided by scientific research. If you skim the References section at the end of the book, you will note that it is as up-to-date as possible in its coverage of research studies, yet does not slight classic studies.

Themes Guiding *Psychology*

The eighth of *Psychology* includes special features that advance the five main themes of this text.

Psychology Is a Science

Over the years, several of our colleagues have expressed frustration that many people—including students—do not realize that psychology is a science, instead believing that it is based on common sense and the opinions of experts called "psychologists." Because of this misconception, one of our primary goals in this book is to show the student reader that psychology is indeed a science. Psychologists do have opinions, but as scientists, they try their best to hold opinions that do not come out of thin air but, rather, are supported by empirical data.

Yet, a psychology textbook should provide students with more than research findings. It should discuss "how we know" as well as "what we know." To give students enough background to appreciate the research process, in Chapter 2 we introduce psychology as a science, the methods of psychological research, and the statistical analysis of research data. The chapter includes a concrete example of the scientific method that shows how it relates to an interesting classic research study on interpersonal attraction. The chapter also includes data from a hypothetical experiment on the effects of melatonin on sleep and explains how to calculate descriptive statistics using that data.

Beginning with Chapter 2, each chapter features an in-depth discussion of a research study. This feature, ***The Research Process***, highlights the rationale, methods, results, and interpretation of research studies in a manner accessible to beginning psychology students. The studies have been chosen for both their appeal and their ability to illustrate the scientific method. These studies include the following:

- David Buss and colleagues' (1992) evolutionary psychology study of emotional and sexual jealousy (Chapter 3)
- Nicholas Spanos and Erin Hewitt's (1980) study of hypnosis as an altered state of consciousness (Chapter 6)
- Lewis Terman's longitudinal study, the Genetic Studies of Genius (Chapter 10)

Psychology Is Superior to Common Sense

Many psychology professors we have known have stressed the need to demonstrate that psychology is more than formalized common sense. Though common sense is often correct and functionally useful, unlike science it is not self-correcting. False commonsense beliefs might survive indefinitely—and might be held tenaciously by introductory psychology students—despite being wrong. The text provides numerous examples of the failure of commonsense beliefs to stand up to scientific challenge. For example, Chapter 2 provides research evidence contradicting the commonsense belief that students should not change their answers on multiple-choice tests.

To demonstrate the superiority of the scientific approach, most chapters include the feature **Psychology versus Common Sense**. This feature challenges widely held commonsense beliefs by evaluating them scientifically.

- Chapter 2 presents a study that showed how scientific research has countered the commonsense belief (upheld even in high-court decisions) that we can reliably determine if someone is legally drunk by observing their behavior.
- Chapter 5 discusses a research study indicating that it might be impossible for baseball players to follow the commonsense directive to "keep your eye on the ball" when they are at bat.
- Chapter 6 presents evidence that supports the commonsense belief that we need to sleep in order to maintain our physical health.

Psychology Is Relevant to Everyday Life

This textbook contains concrete examples that illustrate concepts while providing relief from the typically sober material often presented in psychology textbooks. Our examples—showing the relevance of psychology to everyday life—clarify concepts and make the material more interesting. These examples come from many areas of life, including art, sport, history, politics, biography, literature, entertainment, and student life, and are interwoven into the body of the text. Among these many examples are the following:

- Research-based suggestions for overcoming insomnia (Chapter 6)
- How operant conditioning is used to train animals (Chapter 7)
- Ways to improve one's memory and study habits (Chapter 8)

Psychology Improves Critical Thinking

If students learn nothing else from the introductory psychology course, they should learn to think more critically—that is, to be skeptical rather than gullible or cynical. Chapter 2 describes formal steps in thinking critically, and critical thinking is encouraged throughout the book. Students will find that the ability to think critically benefits them in their daily lives when confronted with claims made by friends, relatives, politicians, advertisers, or anyone else. Every chapter of the book gives the student repeated opportunities to critically assess popular claims portrayed in the media, provide alternative explanations for research findings, and think of possible implications of research findings.

In a senior seminar course that Les has taught over the years, entitled "Current Issues in Psychology," students read many journal articles and some popular articles on a host of controversial topics, which they then discuss or debate. Because of the success of this course—students enjoy sinking their teeth into controversial issues—we have adapted its rationale in the **Critical Thinking About Psychology** features throughout the book. The topics chosen for this feature promote critical thinking by showing that psychologists use reason and empirical data to tackle controversies. Some of the topics include the following:

- The furor over Einstein's preserved brain (Chapter 3)
- The validity of "recovered memories" of childhood abuse (Chapter 8)
- The controversy over *The Bell Curve* (Chapter 10)

Psychology Has a Variety of Contexts

Psychology does not exist in a vacuum. It must consider sociocultural factors; it has an intellectual heritage; it reflects its times; and it is the product of individual human lives. That is, psychology has a variety of contexts: sociocultural, intellectual, historical, and biographical. This contextual variety is stressed throughout the book.

Psychology's Sociocultural Context Throughout the text, cross-cultural, ethnic, and gender differences are discussed within the context of human universals. Critical thinking about group differences must include consideration of the magnitude of these differences as well as the variables on which groups do not differ appreciably. For example, Chapter 2 includes a discussion of a research study that found that responses to rating scales might depend in part on one's cultural background. Students from North America were more willing to use the extremes of the scales than were students from East Asia. The discussion considers the possible cultural basis for this difference in the students' response tendencies. And Chapter 6 reports gender and ethnic differences in some aspects of the sleep cycle, noting that these differences may be attributable to variables that are correlated with gender and ethnicity, such as

Preface

stress levels and sleep environments. Chapter 12 describes studies that report cross-cultural differences in the experience and socialization of emotion along with studies that report remarkable cross-cultural similarity in self-reported happiness and well-being. Moreover, the power of gender roles is emphasized in many discussions of gender differences. For example, in Chapters 11 and 17 we discuss the influence of gender roles on body satisfaction, eating disorders, physical attractiveness, and mate selection among heterosexual women and men, lesbians, and gay men.

Psychology's Intellectual Context Students need to realize that psychology is not intellectually homogeneous. Psychologists favor a variety of perspectives, including the psychoanalytic, the behaviorist, the cognitive, the humanistic, the biopsychological, and the sociocultural. Our text's attention to each of these perspectives reflects our belief that an introductory psychology textbook should introduce students to a variety of perspectives rather than reflect the author's favored one. That is, the introductory psychology textbook should be fair in representing psychology's intellectual context—while being critical of the various perspectives when research findings merit it. Students are introduced to the major psychological perspectives in Chapter 1 and continue to encounter them throughout the book, most obviously in the chapters on personality, psychological disorders, and therapy.

The text explains the different approaches to particular topics that are taken by psychologists who represent different perspectives. For example, Chapter 14's discussion on the possible causes of depression presents the differing views of psychologists who favor the psychoanalytic, behavioral, cognitive, humanistic, biopsychological, and sociocultural perspectives.

Psychology is diverse not only in its intellectual perspectives but also in its intellectual fields. Our students often express amazement at the breadth of psychology. One psychologist might devote a career to using fMRI techniques in studying cerebral hemispheric functions; another might devote a career to studying the relationship of childhood attachment patterns to adult romantic relationships. And whereas one member of a psychology department studies the causes of human aggression, another studies the nature of so-called flashbulb memories. Because of this breadth, we were forced to be selective in the topics, studies, and concepts presented in the book. Nonetheless, we believe that this book includes a representative sampling of the discipline of psychology.

Psychology's Historical Context An article dealing with psychology and the liberal arts curriculum in the June 1991 issue of the *American Psychologist* stressed that an essential goal in undergraduate psychology education is to provide students with the historical context of psychology. Introductory psychology textbooks should not present psychology as though it developed in ivory towers divorced from a historical context. Throughout this book, you will find many ways in which topics are given a historical grounding. Chapter 1 includes a discussion of the contributions made by female psychologists to the early growth of psychology—as well as the obstacles they faced. By drawing a connection between Galvani's work on electricity, Mary Shelley's *Frankenstein*, and views on the nature of neural conduction, Chapter 3 reveals how, over the centuries, activity in one area of scientific endeavor can influence theorizing in another. And Chapter 10 traces the nature-nurture debate regarding intelligence back to the work of Francis Galton in the late 19th century. And, though this book is grounded in the history of psychology, studies throughout have been updated to reflect the current status of research in the field. Most notably, Chapter 14 has been extensively revised to reflect changes with the publication of the *DSM-5*.

Psychology's Biographical Context Psychology is influenced not only by the intellect of the psychologist but also by his or her own life experiences. Throughout this text, we show evidence that psychology is a human endeavor, practiced by people with emotions as well as intellects, and that scientific progress depends on serendipity as well as on purposeful scientific pursuits. For example, Chapter 3 points out that the first demonstration of the chemical basis of communication between nerve cells came to Otto Loewi in a dream. And Chapter 7 explains why the name *Pavlov* rings a bell but the name *Twitmyer* does not. Students tend to find this biographical information engaging, making them more likely to read assigned material in the text.

Pedagogical Features

Chapter Openers

We have made a special effort to include chapter openers that engage the student and promote interest in reading the chapter. Among the chapter openers are the following:

- **Chapter 1** begins with a description of the shootings at Columbine High School, which then is addressed later in the chapter through the lenses of the different psychological perspectives.
- **Chapter 4** begins with the story of Hulda Crooks, a 91-year-old mountain climber, which illustrates that people do not necessarily deteriorate in old age.
- **Chapter 7** begins with a discussion of the use of conditioned taste aversion to prevent coyotes from killing sheep, which indicates how basic research findings can be applied to practical problems.
- **Chapter 11** begins with the story of the life of "Mother" Joseph Cavellucci, a gay transvestite, which

anticipates later coverage of theory and research on gender identity and sexual orientation.
- **Chapter 12** begins with a report of the use—and misuse—of the polygraph test to protect nuclear weapons secrets, which shows psychology's relationship to important current events.
- **Chapter 14** begins with the story of Norton I, Emperor of the United States, a man with schizophrenia who was renowned in 19th-century San Francisco, which demonstrates that even people with serious mental illnesses may live full lives.
- **Chapter 17** begins with a description of the Heaven's Gate mass suicide, which anticipates later text coverage of conformity, compliance, and obedience.

Running Marginal Glossary

A running marginal glossary is integrated throughout the book. This feature eliminates the need for us to torture our prose into the formal tone of a dictionary definition when we introduce new concepts. Terms that are printed in boldface are defined in the margins and listed as Key Terms at the end of the chapter. The marginal definitions are also collected in the ***Glossary*** at the end of the book, which provides a handy tool for students when they encounter those terms in other chapters and when they are studying for exams.

Section Review Self-Quizzes

Each of the major sections within the chapters ends with a self-quiz called ***Section Review***. These quizzes encourage students to pause and assess whether they can recall and comprehend important information from the relevant section. The quizzes include factual, conceptual, and applied questions. Answers to all the questions are provided at the end of the book and in the Online Edition.

Illustrations

We selected or helped design all the illustrations in this book. In doing so, we tried to make each of them serve a sound pedagogical purpose. Though the illustrations make the book aesthetically more appealing, they were chosen chiefly because their visual presentations complement material discussed in the text. The illustrations include beautifully executed drawings, graphs of research data, and many interesting photographs of people and events that students will recognize.

Chapter Summary

Each chapter ends with a bulleted ***Chapter Summary*** that captures the essential points made in the major sections of the chapter. The summaries provide a quick overview that will help students master what they have read.

Key Terms

Each chapter includes a list of ***Key Terms*** that were discussed in the chapter. The list is arranged alphabetically and according to each chapter's first-level headings and indicates the pages on which the terms were discussed. The list will help students in reviewing and studying for exams.

Experiencing Psychology

We have designed ***Experiencing Psychology*** activities to engage students in critical thinking about topics discussed in the text. These projects may be adapted for use as in-class activities or as out-of-class assignments. Activities include:

- Assessing the effectiveness of a mnemonic technique (Chapter 8)
- Replicating a classic study of the effects of mental sets on problem solving (Chapter 9)
- Testing the hypothesis that humorous professors are more effective educators (Chapter 12)
- Assessing the media's portrayal of mental illness (Chapter 14)
- Applying behavior modification techniques to increase adherence to an exercise regimen (Chapter 16)

Chapter Quiz and Thought Questions

Each chapter concludes with a multiple-choice ***Chapter Quiz*** and open-ended ***Thought Questions*** about material covered in the chapter. Answers for the quiz questions are provided at the end of the book and in the Online Edition, and possible answers for the Thought Questions are provided in the Instructor's Manual.

Online and in Print

Student Options: Print and Online Versions

This edition of *Psychology* is available in multiple versions: online and in print as either a paperback or loose-leaf text. The most affordable version is the online book, with upgrade options including the online version bundled with a print version. What's nice about the print version is that it offers you the freedom of being unplugged—away from your computer. The people at Academic Media Solutions recognize that it's difficult to read from a screen at length and that most of us read much faster from a piece of paper. The print options are particularly useful when you have extended print passages to read.

The online edition allows you to take full advantage of embedded digital features, including search and notes. Use the search feature to locate and jump to discussions anywhere in the book. Use the notes feature to add personal comments or annotations. You can move out of the book to follow Web links. You can navigate within and between chapters using a clickable table of contents. These features allow you to work at your own pace and in your own style, as you read and surf your way through the material. (See "Harnessing the Online Version" for more tips on working with the online version.)

Appendixes

Three appendixes are available online and can be downloaded in PDF format and printed:

Appendix A Majoring in Psychology

Appendix B Industrial/Organizational Psychology

Appendix C Statistics

Harnessing the Online Version

The online version of *Psychology* 8e offers the following features to facilitate learning and to make using the book an easy, enjoyable experience:

- *Easy-to-navigate/clickable table of contents*—You can surf through the book quickly by clicking on chapter headings, or first- or second-level section headings. And the Table of Contents can be accessed from anywhere in the book.
- *Key terms search*—Type in a term, and a search engine will return every instance of that term in the book; then jump directly to the selection of your choice with one click.
- *Notes and highlighting*—The online version includes study apps such as notes and highlighting. Each of these apps can be found in the tools icon embedded in the Academic Media/Textbook Media's online eBook reading platform (http://www.academicmediasolutions.com).
- *Upgrades*—The online version includes the ability to purchase additional study apps and functionality that enhance the learning experience.

Instructor Supplements

In addition to the student-friendly features and pedagogy, the variety of student formats available, and the uniquely affordable pricing options, *Psychology* 8e comes with the following teaching and learning aids:

- *Test Item File*—An extensive set of multiple-choice, short answer, and essay questions for every chapter for creating original quizzes and exams.
- *Instructor's Manual*—An enhanced version of the book offering assistance in preparing lectures, identifying learning objectives, developing essay exams and assignments, and constructing course syllabi.
- *PowerPoint Presentations*—Key points in each chapter are illustrated in a set of PowerPoint files designed to assist with instruction.
- *Online Video Labs with Student Worksheets*—A collection of high-quality, dynamic, and sometimes humorous video segments (contemporary and classic) produced by a variety of news, entertainment, and academic sources, accessed via the web. Organized by chapter, the video segments illustrate key topics/issues discussed in the chapters. Each video segment is accompanied by a student worksheet that consists of a series of discussion questions that help students connect the themes presented in the video segment with key topics discussed in the specific chapter. Instructors are provided with suggested answers for each worksheet (for questions not based on student opinion).

Student Supplements and Upgrades (Additional Purchase Required)

- *Lecture Guide*—This printable lecture guide is designed for student use and is available as an in-class resource or study tool. *Note:* Instructors can request the PowerPoint version of these slides to use as developed or to customize.
- *Quizlet Study Set*—Quizlet is an easy-to-use online learning tool built from all the key terms from the textbook. Students can turbo charge their studying via digital flashcards and other types of study apps, including tests and games. Students are able to listen to audio, as well as create their own flashcards. Quizlet is a cross-platform application and can be used on a desktop, tablet, or smartphone.
- *Study Guide*—A printable version of the online study guide is available via downloadable PDF chapters for easy self-printing and review.

Acknowledgments

Because of their professionalism, good humor, and extensive knowledge of academic publishing, our editors at Academic Media Solutions have made writing this edition of our text a smooth, pleasurable process. We also would like to thank our production team at Putman Productions, especially Victoria Putman, for providing us with their superb expertise and personal support throughout the process—while always being fun to work with.

Cheryl thanks her colleagues at the University of Redlands, especially Susan Goldstein, who cheerfully shared her expertise in cross-cultural psychology, and Sandi Richey, who helped in researching the text. Cheryl also thanks her sister, Gail Rickabaugh; her sister outlaw, Barbara Bridges; and her friends Kym Bennett, Jill Borchert, Dan Conte, Emily Culpepper, Susanne Pastuschek, and Judy Tschann for their respect, love, and support. And a special thanks to Oscar, who will always be her best friend and help her keep things in perspective.

Adrienne would like to thank her amazingly supportive family and friends. Without them, she would not be able to balance it all. She would also like to thank her colleagues at Quinnipiac University across all departments, but most especially the Department of Psychology. She would also like to thank John Salamone for his unwavering support.

We hope that you enjoy the process of learning from our text. If you have any comments or questions, please contact Academic Media Solutions at info@academicmedia solutions.com or contact us directly at cheryl_rickabaugh@redlands.edu or adrienne.betz@quinnipiac.edu.

Reviewers

Thanks to the many reviewers of the various editions of this text.

Rahan S. Ali, *Pennsylvania State University*

Ronald Baenninger, *Temple University*

Ute Johanna Bayen, *University of North Carolina, Chapel Hill*

Robert C. Beck, *Wake Forest University*

Bethany Neal-Beliveau, *Indiana University–Purdue University Indianapolis*

John Benjafield, *Brock University*

Robert D. Boroff, M.D., *Modesto Junior College*

Linda Brannon, *McNeese State University*

Robert Paul Brown, *Jefferson Community College*

Dennis Cogan, *Texas Technical University*

John B. Connors, *Canadian Union College*

Stanley Coren, *University of British Columbia*

Randolph Cornelius, *Vassar College*

Verne C. Cox, *University of Texas at Arlington*

Jeffrey Ratliff-Crain, *University of Minnesota, Morris*

Ken Cramer, *University of Windsor*

Richard Cribs, *Motlow State Community College*

Hank Davis, *University of Guelph*

Scott Dickman, *University of Massachusetts, Dartmouth*

Deanna L. Dodson, *Lebanon Valley College*

Donald K. Freedheim, *Case Western Reserve University*

Larry Fujinaka, *Leeward Community College*

Preston E. Garraghty, *Indiana University*

Janet Gebelt, *University of Portland*

Ajaipal S. Gill, *Anne Arundel Community College*

Sandy Grossman, *Clackamas Community College*

Morton G. Harmatz, *University of Massachusetts, Amherst*

Debra L. Hollister, *Valencia Community College*

Daniel Houlihan, *Mankato State University*

Lera Joyce Jonson, *Centenary College*

Deanna Julka, *University of Portland*

Stanley K. Kary, *St. Louis Community College at Florrissant Valley*

Karen Kopera-Frye, *University of Akron*

Janet L. Kottke, *California State University, San Bernardino*

Gary LaBine, *Edinboro University of Pennsylvania*

Joan B. Lauer, *Indiana University–Purdue University Indianapolis*

Ting Lei, *Borough of Manhattan Community College*

Richard Lippa, *California State University, Fullerton*

Dennis Lorenz, *University of Wisconsin*

Gerald McRoberts, *Stanford University*

Ralph Miller, *State University of New York, Binghamton*

Joel Morgovsky, *Brookdale Community College*

James Mottin, *University of Guelph*

Ian Neath, *Purdue University*

Christopher Pagano, *Clemson University*

Richard Pisacreta, *Ferris State University*

Karen Quigley, *Pennsylvania State University*

Robert W. Ridel, *Maryhurst University*

Linda Robertello, *Iona College*

Sonya M. Sheffert, *Central Michigan University*

NC Silver, *University of Nevada, Las Vegas*

Brent D. Slife, *Brigham Young University*

Michael D. Spiegler, *Providence College*

George T. Taylor, *University of Missouri, St. Louis*

Lisa Valentino, *Seminole Community College*

Frank Vattano, *Colorado State University*

Benjamin Wallace, *Cleveland State University*

Wilse Webb, *University of Florida, Gainesville*

Amy Wilkerson, *Stephen F. Austin State University*

Ian Wishaw, *University of Lethbridge*

Michael Zicker, *Bowling Green University*

About the Authors

Les Sdorow was chairperson of the Department of Psychology at Arcadia University (formerly Beaver College). He received his B.A. from Wilkes College and his M.A. and Ph.D. from Hofstra University. He was chairperson of the Department of Behavioral Science at St. Francis College (Pa.) and the Department of Psychology at Allentown College (now DeSales University). Les was named Outstanding Educator at St. Francis College and Teacher of the Year at Allentown College. He also cofounded (with the late Richmond Johnson of Moravian College) the Annual Lehigh Valley Undergraduate Psychology Research Conference (one of the oldest such conferences in North America) and served as president of the Pennsylvania Society of Behavioral Medicine and Biofeedback. Les's research interests were in psychophysiology, sport psychology, and health psychology. His main teaching interests included introductory psychology, research methods, sport psychology, health psychology, and history of psychology. Les made numerous presentations on the teaching of psychology at local, regional, and national conferences. He also was invited to contribute a chapter to the first book published by NITOP (2005), *Voices of Experience: Memorable Talks from the National Institute on the Teaching of Psychology*, copublished by the American Psychological Society.

Cheryl A. Rickabaugh is professor of psychology at the University of Redlands. She received her B.A. from California State University, Los Angeles, and her M.A. and Ph.D. in social-personality psychology at the University of California, Riverside. She has received two Outstanding Faculty Awards for teaching during her 26 years at the University of Redlands. Cheryl teaches introductory psychology, research methods, social psychology, and psychology of gender, in addition to a travel abroad course, Jews, Muslims & Basques: Their sociocultural contributions to Spain. She also teaches an interdisciplinary course—women, wellness, and sport—in the University of Redlands Women and Gender Studies program. She has published research in social psychology, health psychology, psychology of gender, and the teaching of undergraduate psychology, and is the author of *Sex and Gender: Student Projects and Exercises*, 2nd ed. (2005). Believing that one is never too old to learn, she is taking Spanish classes at the University of Redlands and El Instituto de Cervantes. She lives in Spain during her summer breaks.

Adrienne J. Betz is a member of the Department of Psychology at Quinnipiac University. She received her B.A. from University of Connecticut in psychology. Her M.A. and Ph.D., also from University of Connecticut, were in behavioral neuroscience in the Psychology Department under the supervision of John D. Salamone. After receiving her Ph.D., she was a post-doctoral and associate at Yale School of Medicine in molecular psychiatry under the supervision of Jane R. Taylor. She is currently the Director of Behavioral Neuroscience at Quinnipiac University and organizes a regional neuroscience conference, NEURON, which supports undergraduate and graduate research in neuroscience. Adrienne's main teaching interests include physiological psychology, senior thesis, and research methods in behavioral neuroscience. Her research, published in journals such as *Psychopharmacology, Frontiers in Behavioral Neuroscience, Neuroscience, Pharmacology*, and *Biochemistry & Behavior*, focuses on changes that occur in the brain after experiencing stress.

The Nature of Psychology

Chapter 1

On April 20, 1999, Americans were horrified when two students went on a shooting rampage at Columbine High School in Jefferson County, Colorado. The students were Eric Harris, age 18, and Dylan Klebold, age 17. Armed with pistols, rifles, shotguns, and homemade bombs they held their fellow students and teachers hostage. Over the course of several hours, they systematically killed one teacher and 12 students and wounded 23 other students. The two then committed suicide. It took days for the police to defuse about 30 bombs Harris and Klebold had planted in the school to maim or kill would-be rescuers. Harris and Klebold were members of a group known as the Trench Coat Mafia, a group of students who always wore black clothing and ridiculed so-called jocks and students who conformed to traditional social norms.

The issue of school violence has become a pervasive one in the United States. The Columbine High School incident was but one in a series of similar incidents at schools in towns such as Pearl, Mississippi; West Paducah, Kentucky; Jonesboro, Arkansas; and Springfield, Oregon. In 2007, the fatal shooting of 32 people by a student at Virginia Tech University became the largest school massacre in American history. School violence of all kinds is of concern to psychologists. What would lead two intelligent teenagers from apparently stable, affluent families to commit a heinous act like the one at Columbine High School? How can we prevent other incidents like it? How can we help survivors cope with such incidents? The Columbine massacre, for example, led school districts across the United States to ask school psychologists to develop violence-prevention programs and crisis counseling programs for those affected by school violence (Crepeau-Hobson, Filaccio, & Gottfried, 2005).

The science of *psychology* seeks answers to questions about violence and all other aspects of human and animal behavior. Can the effects of brain damage be overcome by the transplantation of brain tissue? Do attachment patterns in infancy predict attachment patterns in adolescent and adult romantic relationships? Do eyewitnesses give accurate testimony? Can chimpanzees learn to use language? Do lie detectors really detect lies? Is there a heart-attack-prone personality? What factors promote interpersonal attraction? These are some of the many questions about human and animal behavior answered in this book.

But what is psychology? The word *psychology* was coined in the 16th century from the Greek terms *psyche,* meaning "soul" or "mind," and *logos,* meaning "the study of a subject." Thus, the initial

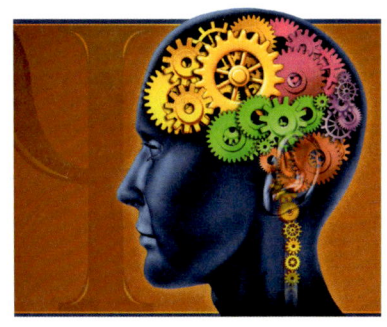

Source: CLIPAREA/Custom media/Shutterstock.com.

Chapter Outline

The Historical Context of Psychology

Contemporary Perspectives in Psychology

The Scope of Psychology

meaning of *psychology* was "the study of the soul or mind" (Brozek, 1999). This definition reflected the early interest of theologians in topics that are now considered the province of psychologists. Psychology has continued to be defined by its subject matter, which has changed over time. By the late 19th century, when psychology emerged as a science, it had become "the Science of Mental Life" (James, 1890/1981, Vol. 1, p. 15).

Beginning in the 1910s, many psychologists—believing that a true science could study only directly observable, measurable events—abandoned the study of the mind in favor of the study of overt behavior. Psychologists moved from studying mental experiences, such as thirst or anger, to studying their observable manifestations, such as drinking or aggression. Consequently, by the 1920s, psychology was commonly defined as "the scientific study of behavior." This definition was dominant until the 1960s, when there was a revival of interest in studying the mind. As a result, **psychology** is now more broadly defined as "the science of behavior and cognitive processes."

psychology The science of behavior and cognitive processes.

What makes psychology a science? Psychology is a science because it relies on the *scientific method* (Holmes & Beins, 2009). Sciences are "scientific" because they share a common method, not because they share a common subject matter. Physics, chemistry, biology, and psychology differ in what they study, yet each uses the scientific method. Whereas a biochemist might use the scientific method to study the unhealthful effects of toxic pollutants on plants or animals, a psychologist might use it to study the behavior or cognitive experiences of a person suffering from severe depression. The role of the scientific method in psychology is discussed at length in Chapter 2.

The Historical Context of Psychology

Psychologists stress the importance of knowing the history of their discipline, with the vast majority of academic psychology departments offering a course devoted to the history of psychology (Fuchs & Viney, 2002). Like any other science, psychology has evolved over time. It has been influenced by developments in other disciplines and by its social, cultural, and historical contexts. To appreciate the state of psychology today, you should understand its origins (Danziger, 1994).

The Roots of Psychology

Psychology's historical roots are in philosophy and science. When psychologists of the late 19th century began to use the scientific method to study the mind, psychology became an independent scientific discipline (Hatfield, 2002). Though scientists and philosophers alike rely on systematic observation and reasoning as sources of knowledge, philosophers rely more on reasoning. For example, a philosopher might use reasoning to argue whether we are ever truly altruistic (that is, completely unselfish) in helping other people, whereas a psychologist might approach this issue by studying the cognitive, emotional and situational factors that determine the circumstances in which one person will help another (see Chapter 17).

Plato (c. 428-347 B. C.)
Plato introduced the concepts of nativism and rationalism.
Source: Antonio Abrignani/Shutterstock.com.

The Philosophical Roots of Psychology
The philosophical roots of psychology reach back to the philosophers of ancient Greece, most notably Plato (c. 428–347 B.C.) and his pupil Aristotle (384–322 B.C.), who were especially interested in the origin of knowledge. Plato noted that our senses can deceive

Chapter 1 The Nature of Psychology

us, as in illusions such as the apparent bending of a straight stick partly immersed in a pool of water. Downplaying knowledge gained through the senses, Plato believed that people enter the world with inborn knowledge—a philosophical position called **nativism**. Plato also believed that we can gain access to inborn knowledge through reasoning, a philosophical position called **rationalism**.

Though Aristotle accepted the importance of reasoning, he was more willing than Plato to accept sensory experience as a source of knowledge—a philosophical position called **empiricism**. Yet, he recognized the frailty of sensory data, as in "Aristotle's illusion." To experience this illusion for yourself, cross a middle finger over an index finger and run a pen between them. You will feel two pens instead of one. Aristotle was one of the first thinkers to speculate on psychological topics, as indicated by the titles of his works, including *On Dreams, On Sleep and Sleeplessness, On Memory and Reminiscence,* and *On the Senses and the Sensed.*

During the early Christian and medieval eras, answers to psychological questions were given more often by theologian philosophers than by secular philosophers like Plato or Aristotle. The dominant Western authority was Saint Augustine (354–430), who lived almost all of his life in what is now Algeria. Augustine wrote of his views on memory, emotion, and motivation in the self-analysis he presented in his classic autobiographical *Confessions.* He also speculated extensively on the nature of dreams (Sirridge, 2005) and anticipated Sigmund Freud by providing insight into the continual battle between our human reason and our animal passions, especially the powerful sex drive (Gay, 1986).

During the Middle Ages, when the Christian West was guided largely by religious dogma and those who dared to conduct empirical studies risked punishment, scientific research became almost the sole province of Islamic intellectuals. The most noteworthy of these was the Persian scientist, physician, and philosopher Abu Ibn Sina (980–1037)—better known in the West as Avicenna—who kept alive the teachings of Aristotle (Afnan, 1958/1980). Avicenna also contributed to our knowledge of medicine, even putting forth a theory of the cause of migraine headaches similar to one of the most influential theories today (Abokrysha, 2009). With the revival of Western intellectual activity in the late Middle Ages, scholars who had access to Arabic translations of the Greek philosophers rediscovered Aristotle. But most of these scholars limited their efforts to reconciling Aristotle's ideas with Christian teachings.

With the coming of the Renaissance, extending from the 14th to the 17th centuries, Western authorities once again relied less on theology and more on philosophy to provide answers to psychological questions. The spirit of the Renaissance inspired René Descartes (1596–1650), the great French philosopher-mathematician-scientist. Descartes, the first of the modern rationalists, insisted that we should doubt everything that is not proven to be self-evident by our own reasoning. In fact, in his famous statement, "I think, therefore I am," Descartes went to the extreme of using reasoning to prove to his own satisfaction that he existed. Descartes contributed to the modern intellectual outlook, which opposes blind acceptance of proclamations put forth by authorities— religious, political, scientific, or otherwise—unless they are supported by logical arguments (Kisner, 2005). Church leaders felt so threatened by Descartes's challenge to their authority that they put his works on their list of banned books.

Other intellectuals, though favoring empiricism instead of rationalism, joined Descartes in rejecting the authority of theologians to provide answers to scientific questions. Chief among these thinkers was the English politician-philosopher-scientist Francis Bacon (1561–1626). Bacon inspired the modern scientific attitude that favors skepticism, systematic observation, and verification of scientific claims by other observers (Hearnshaw, 1985). He also was a founder of applied science, which seeks practical applications of research findings. In support of applied science, Bacon asserted, "to be useless is to be worthless." Ironically, his interest in the application of scientific findings might have cost him his life. While studying the possible use of refrigeration to preserve food, he experimented by stuffing a chicken with snow in frigid weather—and came down with a fatal case of pneumonia.

nativism The philosophical position that heredity provides individuals with inborn knowledge and abilities.

rationalism The philosophical position that true knowledge comes through correct reasoning.

empiricism The philosophical position that true knowledge comes through the senses.

René Descartes (1596–1650)
René Descartes was the first of the modern rationalists.
Source: Georgios Kollidas/Shutterstock.com.

Francis Bacon (1561–1626)
Francis Bacon inspired the modern scientific attitude that favors skepticism, systematic observation, and verification of scientific claims by other observers.
Source: Georgios Kollidas/Shutterstock.com.

John Locke (1632–1704)

According to John Locke, each of us is born with a blank slate, or *tabula rasa*.
Source: Georgios Kollidas/Shutterstock.com.

Following in Francis Bacon's empiricist footsteps was the English philosopher John Locke (1632–1704). According to Locke (borrowing a concept from Aristotle), each of us is born with a blank slate—or *tabula rasa*—on which are written the life experiences we acquire through our senses. Whereas nativists such as Descartes believe that much of our knowledge is inborn, empiricists such as Locke believe that knowledge is acquired solely through life experiences (Gaukroger, 2009). Concern about the relative importance of heredity and life experiences is known as the *nature versus nurture* issue.

Because Locke's views were incompatible with the belief in the inborn right of certain people to be rulers over others, you can appreciate why Locke's writings helped inspire the American and French Revolutions. The nature versus nurture issue, a recurring theme in psychological theory and research, appears later in this book in discussions about a host of topics, including language, intelligence, personality, and psychological disorders.

The German philosopher Immanuel Kant (1724–1804) offered a compromise between Descartes's extreme rationalism and Locke's extreme empiricism. Kant was the ultimate "ivory tower" intellectual, never marrying and devoting his life to philosophical pursuits. Despite his international acclaim, he never left his home province—and probably never saw an ocean or a mountain (Paulsen, 1899/1963).

Kant taught that knowledge is the product of inborn cognitive faculties that organize and interpret sensory input from the physical environment (Slife, 2005). For example, though your ability to speak a language depends on inborn brain mechanisms, the specific language you speak (whether English or another) depends on experience with your native tongue (Newcombe, 2002).

The Physiological Roots of Psychology

By the 19th century, physiologists were making progress in answering questions about the nature of psychological processes that philosophers were having difficulty answering. As a consequence, intellectuals began to look more and more to physiology for guidance in the study of psychological topics. For example, in the mid-19th century, popular belief, based on reasoning, held that nerve impulses travel the length of a nerve as fast as electricity travels along a wire—that is, almost instantaneously—and were too fast to measure. This claim was contradicted by research conducted by the German physiologist Hermann von Helmholtz (1821–1894), one of the premier scientists of the 19th century (Cahan, 2006). In studying nerve impulses, Helmholtz found that they took a measurable fraction of a second to travel along a nerve. In one experiment, he had participants release a telegraph key as soon as they felt a touch on the foot or thigh. A device recorded their reaction time. Participants reacted more slowly to a touch on the foot than to a touch on the thigh. Helmholtz attributed this difference to the longer distance that nerve impulses must travel from the foot to the spinal cord and then on to the brain. This experiment indicated that nerve impulses are not instantaneous. In fact, Helmholtz found that human nerve impulses traveled at the relatively slow speed of 50 to 100 meters per second. Chapter 5 describes Helmholtz's pioneering theories on the psychology of vision and hearing.

Helmholtz's scientific contemporaries made important discoveries about brain functions that likewise could not have been discovered by philosophical speculation. The leading brain researcher was the French physiologist Pierre Flourens (1794–1867), the founder of scientific research on the localization of brain functions (Pearce, 2009). He found, for example, that damage to the cerebellum, a large structure at the back of the brain, caused motor incoordination. Animals with damage to the cerebellum would walk as though they were drunk. This study led him to conclude, correctly, that the cerebellum helps regulate the coordination of movements.

Other 19th-century scientists were more interested in the scientific study of cognitive processes apart from the brain structures that served them. The most notable of these researchers was the German mystic-physician-scientist Gustav Fechner (1801–1887). In his scientific research, Fechner used the methods of **psychophysics**, which was the intellectual offspring of the German physicist Ernst Weber (1795–1878), whose writings influenced Fechner (Marshall, 1990). Fechner, inspired to do so by a daydream, used

Hermann von Helmholtz (1821–1894)

Through experimentation, Hermann von Helmholtz developed pioneering theories on vision and hearing.
Source: Nicku/Shutterstock.com.

psychophysics The study of the relationship between the physical characteristics of stimuli and the conscious psychological experiences that are associated with them.

psychophysical methods to quantify the relationship between physical stimulation and the mental experience of sensation (Heidelberger, 2004).

Psychophysics considers questions such as these: How much change in the intensity of a light is necessary for a person to experience a change in its brightness? And how much change in the intensity of a sound is necessary for a person to experience a change in its loudness? Psychophysics contributed to psychology's maturation from being a child of philosophy and physiology to being an independent discipline with its own subject matter, and it has had important applications. For example, the researchers who perfected television relied on psychophysics to determine the relationship between physical characteristics of the television picture and the viewer's mental experience of qualities such as color and brightness (Baldwin, 1954).

Psychologists of the late 19th century also were influenced by the theory of evolution put forth by the English naturalist Charles Darwin (1809–1882). Darwin announced his theory in *The Origin of Species* (Darwin, 1859/1975), which described the results of research he conducted while studying the plants and animals he encountered during a five-year voyage around the world on HMS *Beagle*. Though thinkers as far back as ancient Greece had proposed that existing animals had evolved from common ancestors, Darwin, along with fellow English naturalist Alfred Russell Wallace (Padian, 2008), was the first to propose a process that could account for it. According to Darwin, through *natural selection* physical characteristics that promote the survival of the individual are more likely to be passed on to offspring because individuals with these characteristics are more likely to live long enough to reproduce.

Darwin's theory had its most immediate impact on psychology through the work of his cousin, the English scientist Francis Galton (1822–1911). In applying Darwin's theory of evolution, Galton argued that natural selection could account for the development of human abilities. Moreover, he claimed that individuals with the most highly developed abilities, such as vision and hearing, would be the most likely to survive long enough to reproduce. This belief led him to found the field of **differential psychology** (Buss, 1976), which studies variations among people in physical, personality, and intellectual attributes. Galton's impact on the study of intelligence is discussed in Chapter 10.

Differential psychology was introduced to North America by the psychologist James McKeen Cattell (1860–1944), who studied with Galton in England. In 1890 Cattell coined the term *mental test,* which he used to describe various tests of vision, hearing, and physical skills that he administered to his students. After being banished from academia for opposing America's entrance into World War I, Cattell started his own business, the Psychological Corporation, which to this day is a leader in the development of tests that assess abilities, intelligence, and personality. Thus, Cattell was a pioneer in the development of psychology as both a science and a profession (Landy, 1997).

differential psychology The field of psychology that studies individual differences in physical, personality, and intellectual characteristics.

The Founding Schools of Psychology

James McKeen Cattell became the first psychology professor in the world (that is, he was the first person to hold such a position independent of an academic biology or philosophy department) when he took a position at the University of Pennsylvania in 1889. Because he assumed his professorship more than a century ago, this supports a remark made by Hermann Ebbinghaus (1850–1909), a pioneer in psychology: "Psychology has a long past, but only a short history" (quoted in Boring, 1950, p. ix). By this, Ebbinghaus meant that though intellectuals have been interested in psychological topics since the era of ancient Greece, psychology did not become a separate discipline until the late 19th century.

Psychologists commonly attribute the founding of this new discipline to the German physiologist Wilhelm Wundt (1832–1920). In 1875 Wundt set up a psychology laboratory at the University of Leipzig in a small room that had served as a dining hall for impoverished students. Wundt's request for a more impressive laboratory had been rejected by the school's administrators, who did not want to promote a science they believed would drive students crazy by encouraging them to scrutinize the contents of their minds (Hilgard, 1987). Beginning in 1879 Wundt's laboratory became the site of formal research

Wilhelm Wundt (1832–1920)

Wilhelm Wundt established the first psychology laboratory at the University of Leipzig in 1875.

Source: Nicku/Shutterstock.com.

conducted by many students who later became some of the most renowned psychologists in the world. Wundt and his students conducted research on topics such as attention, sensation, and reaction time. More than 30 American psychologists, including Cattell, took their PhDs with Wundt (Benjamin, Durkin, Link, Vestal, & Acord, 1992). These students also included G. Stanley Hall (1846–1924), who founded the American Psychological Association in 1892. The growth of the new science was marked by the rise of competing intellectual schools of psychology championed by charismatic leaders, who often were trained in both philosophy and physiology. The earliest schools were *structuralism* and *functionalism.*

Structuralism

structuralism The early psychological viewpoint that sought to identify the components of the conscious mind.

The first approach—**structuralism**—arose in the late 19th century, championed by European psychologists inspired by the efforts of biologists, chemists, and physicists to analyze matter into cells, molecules, and atoms. Following the lead of these scientists, structuralists tried to analyze the mind into its component elements and discover how the elements interact. Structuralism was named and popularized by Wundt's student Edward Titchener (1867–1927). Titchener, an Englishman, introduced structuralism to the United States after receiving his PhD from Wundt in 1892 and then joining the faculty of Cornell University later that year.

analytic introspection A research method in which highly trained participants report the contents of their conscious mental experiences.

To study the mind, he had his participants use **analytic introspection**, a procedure aimed at analyzing complex mental experiences into what he believed were the three basic mental elements: images, feelings, and sensations. In a typical study using analytic introspection, Titchener would present a participant with a stimulus (for example, a repetitious sound produced by a metronome) and then ask the participant to report the images, feelings, and sensations evoked by it. Based on his research, Titchener concluded that there were more than 40,000 mental elements, with the great majority of them visual in nature (Lieberman, 1979).

Among Titchener's contributions was research on the sense of taste, which found that even complex tastes are mixtures of the four basic tastes of sour, sweet, salty, and bitter (Webb, 1981). Despite Titchener's renown, structuralism declined in its influence. This decline was, in part, because structuralism was limited to the laboratory. In fact, Titchener frowned on psychologists who tried to apply the new science of psychology to everyday life (White, 1994).

But the demise of structuralism owed more to its reliance on introspection, which limited it to the study of conscious mental experience in relatively intelligent adults with strong verbal skills. Psychologists also found introspection to be unreliable, because introspective reports in response to a particular stimulus by a given participant were inconsistent from one presentation of the stimulus to another. Similarly, introspective reports in response to the same stimulus were inconsistent from one participant to another. Though the shortcomings of analytic introspection made it fade into oblivion, some psychologists today rely on the related research procedure of having their participants give verbal reports of their mental experience—without necessarily trying to analyze them into their components.

Functionalism

functionalism The early psychological viewpoint that studied how the conscious mind helps the individual adapt to the environment.

Functionalism arose in America chiefly as a response to structuralism. Functionalists criticized the structuralists for limiting themselves to analyzing the contents of the mind. The functionalists preferred, instead, to study how the mind affects what people do. Whereas structuralists might study the mental components of tastes, functionalists might study how the ability to distinguish different tastes affects behavior. This approach reflected the influence of Darwin's theory of evolution, which stressed the role of inherited characteristics in helping the individual adapt to the environment. The functionalists assumed that the mind evolved because it promoted the survival of the individual. Your conscious mind permits you to evaluate your current circumstances and select the best course of action to adapt to them. Recall a time when you tasted food that had gone bad. You quickly spit it out, vividly demonstrating the functional value of the sense of taste.

The most prominent functionalist was the American psychologist and philosopher William James (1842–1910). In his approach to psychology, James viewed the mind as a stream, which, like a stream of water, cannot be meaningfully broken down into discrete elements. Thus, he believed that the mind—or *stream of consciousness*—is not suited to the kind of analytic study favored by structuralists. In 1875, the same year that Wundt established his laboratory at Leipzig, James established a psychology laboratory at Harvard University. But unlike Wundt, James used the laboratory for demonstrations, not for experiments. Instead, he urged psychologists to study how people function in the world outside the laboratory. James and Wundt were so influential that a survey of several major Canadian universities found that half of their psychology faculty members could trace their intellectual lineage through key faculty members back to one of the two (Lubek, Innis, Kroger, McGuire, Stam, & Herrmann, 1995).

Though he conducted few experiments, James made several contributions to psychology. His classic textbook, *The Principles of Psychology* (James, 1890/1981), highlighted the interrelationship of philosophy, physiology, and psychology. The book is so interesting, informative, and beautifully written that it is one of the few psychology books more than a century old still in print. An abridged version of the book, *Psychology: Briefer Course* (James, 1892/1985), became a leading introductory psychology textbook. William James also contributed a theory of emotion (discussed in Chapter 12) that is still influential today (Palencik, 2007). And his views influenced later theories and research in self psychology (Coon, 2000), which is discussed in Chapter 13.

As a group, the functionalists broadened the range of subjects and participants used in psychological research by including animals, children, and people with psychological disorders. The functionalists also expanded the subject matter of psychology to include such topics as memory, thinking, and personality. And unlike the structuralists, who limited their research to the laboratory, the functionalists, in the tradition of Francis Bacon, applied their research to everyday life. The functionalist John Dewey (1859–1952) applied psychology to the improvement of educational practices and remains an influential intellectual figure in educational and developmental psychology (Fallace, 2010). The functionalist who founded the field of applied psychology itself was Hugo Münsterberg (1863–1916), who became a tragic figure in the history of psychology.

In 1892 William James, tiring of the demands of running the psychology laboratory at Harvard, hired Münsterberg, who had earned his PhD under Wilhelm Wundt in 1885 and had become a renowned German psychologist, to take over the laboratory. Münsterberg quickly gained stature in America. During the first decade of the 20th century, Münsterberg was second only to James in his fame as a psychologist. Ironically, though he was hired to run the Harvard psychology laboratory, Münsterberg's main contributions were in applied psychology (Van de Water, 1997). He conducted research, wrote books, and gave talks describing how psychology could be applied to law, industry, education, psychotherapy, and even the study of motion pictures (Bruno, 2009). But Münsterberg experienced extreme stress after being ostracized by his colleagues for trying to promote good relations between America and Germany during the years leading up to World War I (Spillmann & Spillmann, 1993). He died after suffering a stroke he experienced during a class lecture. Because Münsterberg and his functionalist colleagues dared to move psychology out of the laboratory and into the everyday world, they felt the wrath of structuralists, such as Titchener, who insisted that psychology could be a science only if it remained in the laboratory. Titchener established an organization called the Society of Experimentalists in part as a reaction against what he and his supporters saw as the American Psychological Association's movement away from the laboratory (Goodwin, 1985). Despite Titchener's criticisms, most psychologists today would applaud William James and the functionalists for increasing the kinds of research topics, methods, participants, and settings in psychological research (Yanchar, 1997).

James also helped open the door for the entry of women into the discipline of psychology. Most notably, he championed the career of Mary Whiton Calkins (1863–1930), the first prominent female psychologist. In 1903 Calkins, along with Margaret Floy

Washburn, the leading animal psychologist of her time, and Christine Ladd-Franklin, who put forth an early theory of color vision, was included in James McKeen Cattell's influential list of the 50 most eminent American psychologists (O'Connell & Russo, 1990). But being one of James's students did not guarantee Calkins an easy path to a career as a psychologist (Furumoto, 1980).

Though Harvard did not permit women to enroll as matriculated students, Calkins's father, an influential Protestant minister, convinced its president to permit Calkins to audit courses. In her autobiography, Calkins describes being the only student in a course with William James (Calkins, 1930). Evidently, the male students dropped the course rather than attending it with a woman. Though Calkins completed all the coursework and the doctoral dissertation required for a doctoral degree, Harvard's administration refused the recommendation of her faculty sponsor, Hugo Münsterberg, that she be awarded the PhD in 1896. James had even called her oral defense of her doctoral dissertation "the most brilliant examination for the PhD that we have had at Harvard." Psychologists and student activists have continued to submit proposals to the Harvard administration for a posthumous PhD to be awarded to Calkins but to date have not been successful (Boatwright & Nolan, 2005).

Despite never receiving her doctorate, Calkins became a successful psychologist. She founded the psychology laboratory at Wellesley College, began the scientific study of dreams, invented the paired-associate technique of assessing memory, and wrote one of the first introductory psychology textbooks (Calkins, 1901). She spent most of her career developing her theory of self psychology, which viewed psychology as the empirical study of the person in conscious interaction with the environment (McDonald, 2007). In 1905 she became the first female president of the American Psychological Association. In 1918, Calkins, also a renowned philosopher, became the first female president of the American Philosophical Association. Calkins would be pleased that today many women earn doctoral degrees in psychology each year. In fact, more women than men now earn doctoral degrees in psychology (Denmark, 1998).

The Growth of Psychology

Structuralism and functionalism were soon joined by other intellectual schools of psychology, which included *Gestalt psychology, psychoanalysis,* and *behaviorism.* These schools broadened the subject matter, methodology, and applications of psychology. Though they were somewhat influenced by structuralism and functionalism, they became more influential than those two founding schools.

Gestalt Psychology

Gestalt psychology The early psychological viewpoint that claimed that we perceive and think about wholes rather than simply combinations of separate elements.

The structuralists' attempt to analyze the mind into its component parts was countered by the German psychologist Max Wertheimer (1880–1943), who founded **Gestalt psychology**. Wertheimer used the word gestalt, meaning "form" or "shape," to underscore his belief that we perceive wholes rather than combinations of individual elements. A famous tenet of Gestalt psychology asserts that "the whole is different from the sum of its parts" (Wertheimer & King, 1994). Because of this basic assumption, Wertheimer ridiculed structuralism as "brick-and-mortar psychology" for its attempt to analyze mental experience into discrete elements.

phi phenomenon Apparent motion caused by the presentation of different visual stimuli in rapid succession.

The founding of Gestalt psychology can be traced to a train trip taken by Wertheimer in 1912, when he daydreamed about the **phi phenomenon**, which involves seeing apparent motion in the absence of actual motion (as in a motion picture at a movie theater). At a stop, Wertheimer left the train and bought a toy stroboscope, which, like a motion picture, produces the illusion of movement by rapidly presenting a series of pictures that are slightly different from one another. On returning to his laboratory, he continued studying the phi phenomenon by using a more sophisticated device called a tachistoscope, which flashes visual stimuli for a fraction of a second. Wertheimer had the tachistoscope flash two lines in succession, first a vertical one and then a horizontal one. When the interval between flashes was just right, a single line appeared to move from a vertical to a horizontal orientation.

According to Wertheimer, the phi phenomenon shows that the mind does not respond passively to discrete stimuli, but instead organizes stimuli into coherent wholes. Thus, perception is more than a series of individual sensations. This conclusion is in keeping with Immanuel Kant's notion of the mind as an active manipulator of environmental input. If your mind only responded passively to discrete stimuli, when you observed Wertheimer's tachistoscope demonstration, you would first see the vertical line appear and disappear and then see the horizontal line appear and disappear. Gestalt psychology gave a new direction to psychology by stressing the active role of the mind in organizing sensations into meaningful wholes (Feest, 2007).

Though Wertheimer founded Gestalt psychology, it was popularized by his colleagues Kurt Koffka (1886–1941), the most prolific and influential writer among the Gestalt psychologists, and Wolfgang Köhler (1887–1967), who promoted Gestalt psychology as a natural science (Henle, 1993) and applied it to the study of problem solving. Koffka and Köhler introduced Gestalt psychology to the United States after fleeing Nazi Germany. Köhler, a Christian college professor, had provoked the Nazis by writing and speaking out against their persecution of his Jewish colleagues (Henle, 1978). He became a respected psychologist and in 1959 was elected president of the American Psychological Association.

Psychoanalysis

Unlike the other early approaches to psychology, which originated in universities, **psychoanalysis** originated in medical science. Sigmund Freud (1856–1939), the founder of psychoanalysis, was an Austrian neurologist who considered himself "a conquistador of the mind" (Gay, 1988). Freud noted that his theory, which views the human species as animals first and foremost, owed a debt to Darwin's theory of evolution. Psychoanalysis grew, in part, from Freud's attempts to treat patients suffering from physical symptoms, such as paralyzed legs, inability to speak, or loss of body sensations, that had no apparent physical causes. Based on his treatment of patients suffering from such symptoms of conversion hysteria, Freud concluded that the disorder was the result of unconscious psychological conflicts about sex caused by early sexual trauma or cultural prohibitions against sexual enjoyment (Guttman, 2006). These conflicts were "converted" into the physical symptoms seen in conversion hysteria, which might even provide the patient with an excuse to avoid engaging in the taboo behaviors.

Freud's case studies led him to infer that unconscious conflicts, usually related to repressed sexual or aggressive feelings that might elicit disapproval from one's self or

psychoanalysis The early school of psychology that emphasized the importance of unconscious causes of behavior.

"It goes back to being pulled out of the hat."

Psychoanalysis

Sigmund Freud established psychoanalysis.
Source: Cartoonresource/Shutterstock.com.

psychic determinism The Freudian assumption that all human behavior is influenced by unconscious motives.

others, were prime motivators of human behavior. Freud believed that all behavior—whether normal or abnormal—was influenced by psychological motives, often unconscious ones. This belief is called **psychic determinism**. In his book *The Psychopathology of Everyday Life,* Freud (1901/2011) explained how even apparently unintentional behaviors could be explained by psychic determinism. Psychic determinism explains misstatements, popularly known as "Freudian slips," that arise when an unconscious wish overcomes the desire not to reveal it, as in the case of the radio announcer who began a bread commercial by saying, "For the breast in bed . . . I mean, for the best in bread . . . ." As a leading psychologist observed, the concept of psychic determinism meant that "the forgotten lunch engagement, the slip of the tongue, the barked shin could no longer be dismissed as accident" (Bruner, 1956, p. 465).

In addition to shocking the public of the Victorian era by claiming that people are motivated chiefly by unconscious—often sexual—motives, Freud made the controversial claim that early childhood experiences were the most important factors in personality development. Freud believed that memories of early childhood experiences stored in the unconscious mind continue to affect behavior throughout one's life. According to Freud, these unconscious influences explain the irrationality of much human behavior and the origins of psychological disorders.

Freudian psychoanalysis was so extraordinarily influential that a survey of chairs of graduate psychology departments found that they considered Freud to be the most important figure in psychology's first century (Davis, Thomas, & Weaver, 1982). Nonetheless, critics have pointed out that the unconscious mind can be too easily used to explain any behavior for which there is no obvious cause. William James had expressed this concern even before Freud's views had become known. James warned that the unconscious "is the sovereign means for believing whatever one likes in psychology and of turning what might become a science into a tumbling ground for whimsies" (James, 1890/1981, Vol.1, p.166).

Psychoanalysis also has been subjected to criticism for failing to provide adequate research evidence for its claims of the importance of sexual motives, unconscious processes, and early childhood experiences (Dufresne, 2007). Other critics claim that Freud's theory focuses on the male experience and thus has less relevance to women's lives (Masling, Bornstein, Fishman, & Davila, 2002). Moreover, Freud never tested his theory experimentally. Instead, he based his theory on notes written after seeing patients, which made his conclusions subject to his own memory lapses and personal biases. Moreover, Freud violated good scientific practice by generalizing to all people the results of his case studies of a relative handful of people with psychological disorders.

Despite these shortcomings, Freud's views have influenced the psychological study of topics as diverse as dreams, creativity, motivation, development, personality, psychopathology, and psychotherapy. Freud's views have also inspired the works of artists, writers, and filmmakers, including Eugene O'Neill's play *Mourning Becomes Electra* (1931) and the classic science fiction film *Forbidden Planet* (1956). Freud's contributions to a variety of psychological topics are discussed in several other chapters.

The decline of strictly Freudian psychoanalysis began when two of Freud's followers, Carl Jung (1875–1961) and Alfred Adler (1870–1937), developed psychoanalytic theories that contradicted important aspects of Freud's theory. Jung, Adler, and other so-called neo-Freudians placed less emphasis on the biological drives of sex and aggression and more emphasis on the importance of social relationships. Jung developed his own theory of personality, which included the concepts of the inner-directed *introvert* and the outer-directed *extravert.* Adler based his personality theory on his belief that each of us tends to compensate for natural childhood feelings of inferiority by striving for superiority, as in the case of students who study long hours to earn the necessary grades for admission to medical school, or athletes who train for Olympic competition. Other neo-Freudians also contributed to the psychoanalytic approach. Anna Freud (1895–1982), Sigmund Freud's daughter, was a leader in the field of child psychoanalysis, as was her intellectual rival Melanie Klein (1882–1960), who developed the technique of play therapy. The views of influential neo-Freudians are discussed in later chapters, particularly in Chapters 13.

Behaviorism

In 1913 a leading functionalist published an article entitled "Psychology as the Behaviorist Views It." It included the following proclamation:

> Psychology as the behaviorist views it is a purely objective experimental branch of natural science. Its theoretical goal is the prediction and the control of behavior. Introspection forms no essential part of its methods, nor is the scientific value of its data dependent on the readiness with which they lend themselves to interpretation in terms of consciousness. (Watson, 1913, p. 158)

This bold statement by the American psychologist John B. Watson (1878–1958) heralded the rise of **behaviorism**, an approach to psychology that dominated the discipline for half a century. He was influenced by Russian physiologist Ivan Pavlov (1849–1936), whose work he helped introduce to North American psychology (Buckley, 1989). Watson rejected the position shared by structuralists, functionalists, Gestalt psychologists, and psychoanalysts that the mind is the proper object of study for psychology. He and other behaviorists were emphatic in their opposition to the study of mental experience. Though Watson was fascinated by Freud's theory, like William James, he rejected the notion that unconscious cognitive processes could motivate human behavior.

behaviorism The psychological viewpoint that rejects the study of mental processes in favor of the study of overt behavior.

To Watson, the proper subject matter for psychological research was observable behavior. Unlike mental experiences, overt behavior can be recorded and subjected to verification by other scientists. For example, some psychologists might study the mental experience of hunger, but behaviorists would prefer to study the observable behavior of eating. Though Watson denied that cognitive processes could cause behaviors, he did not deny the existence of the mind. Thus, he would not have denied that people have the mental experience called "hunger," but he would have denied that the mental experience of hunger causes eating (Moore, 1990). Instead, he would have favored explanations of eating that placed its causes in the body (such as low blood sugar) or in the environment (such as a tantalizing aroma) instead of in the mind (such as feeling famished or craving a specific food).

Watson impressed his fellow psychologists enough to be elected president of the American Psychological Association in 1915. Watson was an attractive and charismatic person who popularized his brand of psychology by giving speeches and writing books and articles. Though he wrote about both heredity and environment, he placed great faith in the effect of environmental stimuli on the control of behavior, especially children's behavior (Horowitz, 1992). His "stimulus-response" psychology placed him firmly in the empiricist tradition of John Locke and is best expressed in his famous pronouncement on child development:

> Give me a dozen healthy infants, well-formed, and my own specified world to bring them up in and I'll guarantee to take any one at random and train him to become any type of specialist I might select—doctor, lawyer, artist, merchant-chief and, yes, even beggar man and thief, regardless of his talents, penchants, tendencies, abilities, vocations, and race of his ancestors. (Watson, 1930, p. 104)

Apparently, no parents rushed to offer their infants to be trained by Watson. Nonetheless, his views on child rearing became influential. Despite some of their excessive claims, behaviorists injected optimism into psychology by fostering the belief that people are minimally limited by heredity and easily changed by experience. In favoring nurture over nature, behaviorists assumed that people, regardless of their hereditary background, could improve themselves and their positions in life. Watson and his fellow behaviorists were more than willing to suggest ways to bring about such improvements. Watson even hoped to establish a utopian society based on behavioristic principles (Morawski, 1982).

Behaviorism dominated psychology through the 1960s (O'Neil, 1995). In fact, from 1930 to 1960 the term *mind* rarely appeared in psychological research articles (Mueller, 1979). But since then, the mind has returned as a legitimate object of study. The weakened influence of orthodox behaviorism is also shown by renewed respect for the constraints that heredity places on learning (a topic discussed in Chapter 7).

Watson's intellectual descendent was the American psychologist B. F. Skinner (1904–1990). As a young man, Skinner pursued a career as a writer and even spent six months living in Greenwich Village, New York, to soak up its creative Bohemian atmosphere. After discovering that he was not cut out to be a fiction writer and after being excited by the writings of John B. Watson, Skinner decided to become a psychologist (Keller, 1991). Though he eventually became a prominent figure in 20th-century psychology, second only to Sigmund Freud (Rutherford, 2000), it took many years for him to achieve that standing. His landmark book, *The Behavior of Organisms* (which had been published in 1938), sold only 80 copies by the end of World War II in 1945.

Like Watson, Skinner urged psychologists to ignore mental processes and to limit psychology to the study of observable behavior. He and other behaviorists insisted that psychology could not be on a scientific par with other natural sciences if psychologists tried to make it the study of mental experiences. Many behaviorists still refuse to treat verbal reports of mental experiences as appropriate subject matter for psychological research.

In contrast to Watson, Skinner stressed the role of the consequences of behavior, rather than environmental stimuli, in controlling behavior. He noted that animals and people tend to repeat behaviors that are followed by positive consequences. Consider your performance in school. If your studying (a behavior) pays off with an A on an exam (a positive consequence), you will be more likely to study in the future. In Skinner's terms, your behavior has been "positively reinforced."

Skinner, like Watson, was a utopian. In 1948 Skinner—showing that he did, in fact, have the ability to write fiction—published *Walden Two*, a novel that describes an ideal society based on behaviorist principles. In Skinner's utopia, benevolent behaviorists control the citizens by providing positive consequences for desirable behaviors. Several communities, most notably Twin Oaks in Louisa, Virginia, and Los Horcones near Hermosillo, Mexico, were founded on principles presented in *Walden Two* (Kuhlmann, 2005). Though there is still no behavioral utopia, the behavioral perspective has contributed to improvements in education, child rearing, industrial productivity, and therapy for psychological disorders. These topics are discussed in later chapters.

Despite Skinner's efforts, the influence of orthodox behaviorism has faded in recent years in the face of growing dissatisfaction with the lack of attention orthodox behaviorists give to cognitive processes. This dissatisfaction has prompted some behaviorists to study the relationship between cognitive processes such as thoughts or mental images, which cannot be directly observed, and overt behavior, which can. These psychologists are called cognitive behaviorists. One of their most influential leaders has been Albert Bandura (2001), who has noted that we can learn by observing as well as by doing. The views of Skinner and Bandura are discussed further in Chapter 7. Despite the rise of cognitivism, behaviorism remains a powerful force in psychology (Leigland, 2000).

Table 1-1 summarizes the major characteristics of the early perspectives of psychology.

TABLE 1-1 Major Psychological Perspectives

Perspective	Object of Study	Goal of Study	Method of Study
Structuralism	Conscious experience	Analyzing the structure of the mind	Analytic introspection
Functionalism	Conscious experience	Studying the functions of the mind	Introspection and testing
Gestalt	Conscious experience	Demonstrating the active, holistic nature of the mind	Introspection and demonstrations
Psychoanalysis	Unconscious motivation	Studying unconscious motives of behavior	Clinical case studies
Behaviorism	Observable behavior	Controlling behavior	Observation and experiments

> **Section Review:** The Historical Context of Psychology
>
> 1. How did the work of 19th-century scientists lead to the emergence of psychology as a science?
> 2. What were the contributions of functionalism to psychology?
> 3. What was Gestalt psychology's main criticism of structuralism?
> 4. What prompted the emergence of behaviorism?

Contemporary Perspectives in Psychology

According to Thomas Kuhn (1970), an influential philosopher of science, as a science matures, it develops a unifying **scientific paradigm**, or model, that determines its appropriate goals, methods, and subject matter. Though, as you have just read, psychology has been influenced by different approaches, the discipline still lacks a unifying scientific paradigm to which most psychologists would subscribe (Shapiro, 2005). Instead, diverse psychological perspectives exist, in addition to the psychoanalytic, behavioristic, and humanistic perspectives. The past half century has seen the emergence of three highly influential new perspectives—the *humanistic perspective,* the *cognitive perspective,* and the *biopsychological perspective*—as well as, more recently, the *sociocultural perspective.*

scientific paradigm A model that determines the appropriate goals, methods, and subject matter of a science.

The Humanistic Perspective

Because it provided the first important alternative to the highly influential psychoanalytic and behavioral perspectives, the **humanistic perspective** has been called the "third force" in psychology (Cosgrove, 2007). It was founded in the 1950s by the American psychologists Abraham Maslow (1908–1970) and Carl Rogers (1902–1987) to promote the idea that people have free will and are not merely pawns in the hands of unconscious motives or environmental stimuli. Maslow, who served as president of the American Psychological Association in 1967, had begun as a behaviorist but later rejected what he saw as behaviorism's narrow focus on observable behavior and the effects of the environment. He stressed people's natural tendency toward *selfactualization,* which was his term for the fulfillment of one's potentials.

humanistic perspective The psychological viewpoint that holds that the proper subject matter of psychology is the individual's subjective mental experience of the world.

Rogers echoed Maslow, and both assumed that the subject matter of psychology should be the individual's unique subjective mental experience of the world. In favoring the study of mental experience, Maslow and Rogers showed their intellectual kinship to William James. Though Maslow and Rogers considered subjective mental experience to be one of several important aspects of humanistic psychology, the study of subjective mental experience is the overriding focus of the branch of humanistic psychology called **phenomenological psychology**. For example, phenomenological psychologists might study the mental experience of depression (Slavik & Croak, 2006) as opposed to behaviors exhibited by depressed people or the brain factors or unconscious motives that may underlie depression. And humanistic psychology's assumption that people have free will is central to **existential psychology**. This branch of humanistic psychology favors the study of how people respond to the basic givens of reality, including the responsibility of personal freedom, the isolation of one person from another, the need to find meaning in one's life, and the realization that we eventually will die.

phenomenological psychology A branch of humanistic psychology primarily concerned with the study of subjective mental experience.

existential psychology A branch of humanistic psychology that studies how individuals respond to the basic philosophical issues of life, such as death, meaning, freedom, and isolation.

Humanistic psychology has been a prime mover in the field of psychotherapy, most notably through the efforts of Carl Rogers. His person-centered therapy, one of the chief kinds of psychotherapy, is discussed in Chapter 15. Though person-centered therapy has been the subject of extensive scientific research, other aspects of humanistic psychology, such as techniques that promote personal "growth experiences" and "consciousness raising," have been criticized for having little scientific support (Wertheimer, 1978). This lack of scientific rigor might be one reason why humanistic psychology has had only a relatively minor impact on academic psychology, a fact lamented by Rogers (1985) near the end of his life. Despite its scientific shortcomings, humanistic psychology has made a valuable contribution in promoting the study of positive aspects of human experience, including love, altruism, and healthy personality development. Moreover, many humanistic psychologists have become more willing to use experimentation to test their theories (Koole, Greenberg, & Pyszczynski, 2006)

The Cognitive Perspective

In his presidential address to the American Psychological Association, Wolfgang Köhler (1959) urged Gestalt psychologists and behaviorists to create a psychology that included the best aspects of both their schools. Psychologists who favor the *cognitive approach* have followed Köhler's advice, beginning with the "cognitive revolution" in psychology that began in the late 1950s. This revolution was largely provoked by the perceived shortcomings of behaviorism (Proctor & Kim-Phuong, 2006))—leading to the emergence of a **cognitive perspective**, which combines aspects of Gestalt psychology and the behavioral perspective (Simon, 1995). Like Gestalt psychologists, cognitive psychologists stress the active role of the mind in organizing perceptions, thinking, forming memories, and interpreting experiences. And like behavioral psychologists, cognitive psychologists stress the need for objective, well-controlled, laboratory studies. Thus, cognitive psychologists infer the presence of cognitive processes from observable responses without relying on verbal reports alone. But unlike strict behavioral psychologists, who claim that cognitive processes such as thoughts cannot affect behavior, many cognitive psychologists believe they can.

The cognitive perspective is illustrated in the work of the Swiss biologist-psychologist Jean Piaget (1896–1980), who put forth a cognitive theory of the child's mental development based on his interviews with children as they solved various problems. For example, he studied developmental changes in children's understanding of physical causality (Chandler, 2009). Piaget's research is discussed in Chapter 4. The cognitive perspective also has been influenced by the computer revolution that began in the 1950s, which stimulated research on the human brain as an information processor. A leader in this field was Herbert Simon (1916–2001), a psychologist who won the 1978 Nobel Prize in economics, the field in which he worked early in his career (Anderson, 2001). Some cognitive psychologists use computer programs to create models of human thought processes; others use their knowledge of human thought processes to improve computer programs, like those for computer chess games.

Beginning about 1980, the cognitive perspective surpassed the behavioral perspective and the psychoanalytic perspective in its influence on psychology (Robins, Gosling, & Craik, 1999). As you will realize while reading upcoming chapters, the cognitive perspective pervades almost every field of psychology. For example, the concept of cognitive schemas, or specialized knowledge structures, has been applied to the study of human development, memory, thought and language, social behavior, and personality.

The Biopsychological Perspective

Though several of the early approaches to psychology had their roots in 19th-century physiology, until relatively recently there was never a strictly biopsychological approach to psychology. But growing interest in the biological basis of behavior and cognitive processes, combined with the development of sophisticated research equipment, has led to the emergence of a **biopsychological perspective**. Psychologists who favor this perspective are interested in studying the brain, the hormonal system, and the effects of heredity on psychological functions. Though most biopsychology researchers rely on animals as subjects, some of their most important studies have used human participants. For example, in the course of surgery on the brains of epilepsy victims to reduce their seizures, the Canadian neurosurgeon Wilder Penfield (1891–1976) mapped the brain by using weak

---

cognitive perspective The psychological viewpoint that favors the study of how the mind organizes perceptions, processes information, and interprets experiences.

biopsychological perspective The psychological viewpoint that stresses the relationship of physiological factors to behavior and mental processes.

Left brain versus right brain

Human and animal brains have somewhat different psychological functions.
Source: Macrovector/Shutterstock.com.

electrical currents to stimulate points on its surface. He found that stimulation of particular points on one side of the brain caused movements of particular body parts on the opposite side.

One branch of the biopsychological perspective is cognitive neuroscience, which studies topics such as the neurological bases of emotional memory (Labar & Cabeza, 2006), mental giftedness (Kalbfleisch, 2008), and attention deficit hyperactivity disorder (Vaidya & Stollstorff, 2008). Use of functional MRI (fMRI) to provide scans of ongoing brain activity has helped advance research in cognitive neuroscience (Poldrack & Wagner, 2008). In 1981 the American biopsychologist Roger Sperry (1913–1994) was awarded a Nobel Prize for his studies of the functions of the left and right brain hemispheres of epilepsy patients whose hemispheres had been surgically separated to reduce their seizures (Berlucchi, 2006). In conducting research on the brain in the 1960's, Sperry and his colleagues found that each hemisphere was somewhat superior to the other in performing particular psychological functions. Results indicated that the left side of the brain is somewhat better at performing analytical and verbal tasks whereas the right side of the brain is somewhat better at performing spatial abilities and perceiving complex sounds such as music. Chapter 3 describes the research of Penfield, Sperry, and other contributors to biopsychology. Because of the increasing influence of this perspective, psychology might be moving toward an even broader definition as "the science of behavior and cognitive processes, and the physiological processes underlying them."

Some biopsychologists work in the field of **behavioral genetics**, which studies the relative influence of hereditary and environmental factors on human and animal behavior, such as the genetic bases of autism (Moy & Nadler, 2008) and psychological depression (Crowley & Lucki, 2006). Chapter 3 discusses the use of behavioral genetics in explaining differences in human intelligence and personality. Many of those who study the role of heredity rely on Charles Darwin's theory of evolution as the inspiration for their research. They champion the relatively new approach, based upon Darwinian principles and descended from functionalism, called **evolutionary psychology** (Barker, 2006). For example, evolutionary psychologists interpret some gender differences in social behavior to be the product of natural selection (Nicolson, 2002), in which traits and behaviors that have had survival value for men and women are passed from generation to generation. According to evolutionary psychology, men tend to be more physically aggressive than women in large part because physical aggression has had greater survival value for men than for women. Chapter 3 presents a study by evolutionary psychologist David Buss and his colleagues (1992) on the possible evolutionary basis of gender differences in sexual and emotional jealousy. And Chapter 17 considers evolutionary psychology's explanation

behavioral genetics The study of the relative effects of heredity and life experiences on behavior.

evolutionary psychology The study of the evolution of behavior through natural selection.

Chapter 1 The Nature of Psychology

of gender differences in the attributes that women and men find attractive in potential romantic partners.

The Sociocultural Perspective

Though Wilhelm Wundt is most famous for founding psychology as a laboratory science, he stressed the importance of considering sociocultural influences on human psychology (Cahan & White, 1992). In fact, his 10-volume *Folk Psychology,* which was published during the years 1900 to 1920, anticipated the **sociocultural perspective**. This perspective has developed as a reaction against what its proponents believe is the unfortunate tendency to presume that psychological research findings, obtained chiefly from research conducted in Europe and North America, are always generalizable to other cultures and other social groups. As two leading sociocultural psychologists have commented:

> The typical psychology text contains hundreds of concepts, terms, and theories. . . . Most of these abstractions are used as if it has already been established that they are applicable everywhere. This is a premature if not dangerous assumption to make. (Lonner & Malpass, 1994, p. 2)

sociocultural perspective The psychological viewpoint that favors the scientific study of human behavior in its sociocultural context.

Throughout this text you will read about studies that have attempted to determine whether research findings obtained in one culture are, in fact, applicable to other cultures. Also, you will read about studies of the influence of sociocultural variables such as gender, ethnicity, and sexual orientation on the many aspects of human behavior and thought processes studied by psychologists. Harry Triandis (1990), one of the founders of the sociocultural perspective, takes a position that would be favored by functionalists. He suggests that we avoid ethnocentrism (viewing other cultures by using our own as the ideal standard of comparison) and, instead, view each culture as the outcome of attempts by its members to adapt to particular ecological niches. Then we would realize that, had we been born in another culture, our behavior and our views about what is normal and desirable might fit that culture's norms.

What has accounted for the relatively recent surge of interest in the sociocultural perspective? Perhaps the greatest influence has been the "shrinking" of our planet. Today people on opposite sides of the world can communicate instantly with one another using a variety of means, including telephone, radio, television, and the Internet. Other factors include tourism, immigration, international trade, and ethnic conflict. Thus, it behooves people from different cultures to be less ethnocentric so they can better understand one another.

cross-cultural psychology An approach that tries to determine the extent to which research findings about human psychology hold true across cultures.

But supporters of the sociocultural perspective take a variety of approaches to conducting their research. Some study **cross-cultural psychology**. Cross-cultural psychologists employ research methods designed to compare two or more cultures in an attempt to discover the degree to which psychological principles can be generalized across cultures. Cross-cultural psychologists study topics such as sociocultural factors involved in eating habits (Rozin, 2005), attitudes toward psychotherapy (Digiuni, Jones, & Camic, 2013), and psychological disorders such as depression in elderly women and men (Tiedt, 2013). Related to this topic is one of the central issues in cross-cultural psychology: *relativism* versus *universalism.* Whereas relativists stress the importance of identifying psychological differences across cultures and tend to support tolerance of differences, universalists stress the importance of identifying psychological commonalities across cultures and tend to stress universal phenomena.

multicultural psychology The field that studies psychological similarities and differences across the subcultures that commonly exist within individual countries.

The sociocultural perspective also has given rise to **multicultural psychology**, which studies psychological similarities and differences across the subcultures that commonly exist within individual countries. For example, the American Psychological Association and the American Counseling Association formally support the desirability of psychological counselors to have multicultural competencies to be able to deal effectively with clients from diverse cultural backgrounds (Cokley & Rosales, 2005).

cultural psychology An approach that studies how cultural factors affect human behavior and mental experience.

Other psychologists believe that human behavior and cognitive processes are so molded by culture that we should be most concerned with studying how culture influences human behavior and cognitive processes. This approach is called **cultural psychology**, which includes, for example, research on how culture influences child development (Quintana et al., 2006). A related field, **ethnic psychology**, employs sociocultural methods to describe the experience of members of groups that have been historically underrepresented in psychology. For example, ethnic psychologists Mamie Phipps Clark, Kenneth B. Clark, and William E. Cross Jr. have studied the relationship between African Americans' self-concept and their mental health (Lal, 2002).

ethnic psychology The field that employs culturally appropriate methods to describe the experience of members of groups that historically have been underrepresented in psychology.

Section Review: Contemporary Psychological Perspectives

1. In what way does the cognitive approach combine aspects of Gestalt psychology and behaviorism?
2. What are three areas of interest to psychologists who favor the biopsychological perspective?
3. Why has the sociocultural perspective become influential?

The Scope of Psychology

As psychology has evolved as a science, its fields of specialization have multiplied, and its educational and training requirements have become formalized. Today psychologists work in a wide variety of academic and professional settings (see Figure 1-1). Psychologists are so committed to the study of human behavior that some even study the factors associated with choosing to become an academic psychologist devoted mainly to teaching and research or a professional psychologist devoted mainly to applying psychology in practical settings (Leong, Zachar, Conant, & Tolliver, 2007).

But how does one go about becoming a psychologist? Psychologists first earn a bachelor's degree, preferably, but not necessarily, in psychology. Earning a master's-level degree takes up to two years of additional schooling. Those who pursue a doctorate (PhD or PsyD) in psychology generally take 6 years or so beyond the bachelor's degree to do so. Those who pursue doctorates in clinical or counseling psychology complete internships and typically

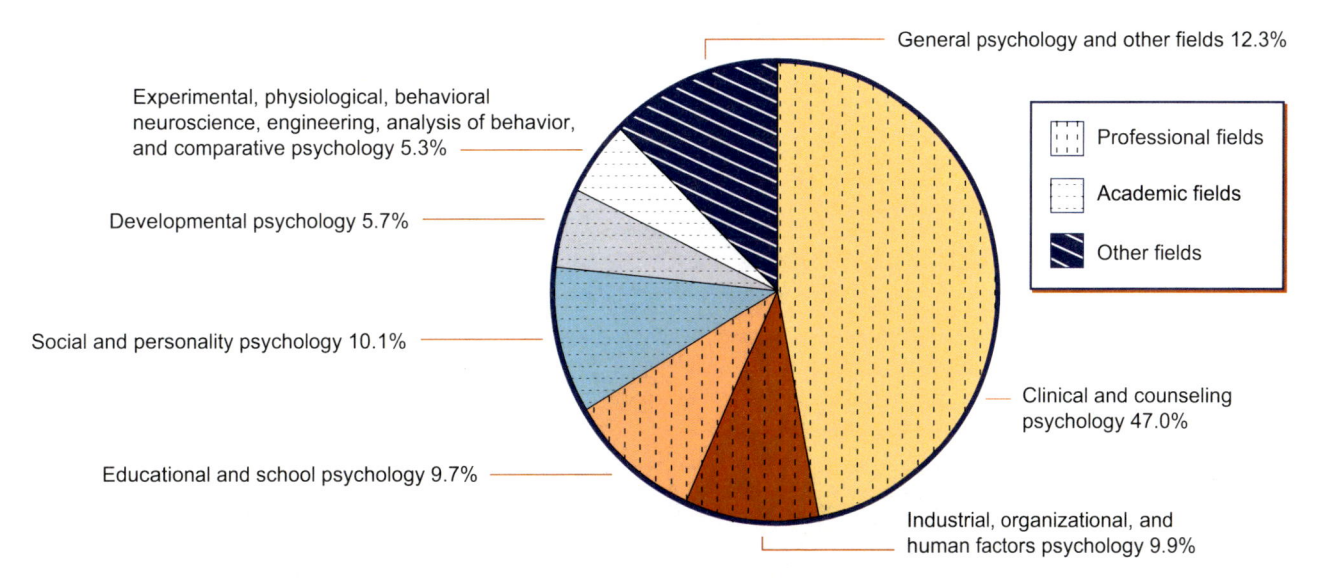

FIGURE 1-1 Fields of Specialization in Psychology

This graph presents the percentages of members of the American Psychological Association working in major fields of specialization.

Source: Data from the American Psychological Association (2014). Division Profiles by Division [Online] http://www.apa.org/about/division/officers/services/profiles.aspx

Chapter 1 The Nature of Psychology

Behavioral Neuroscience

Psychologists in the field of behavioral neuroscience study the biological bases of behavior and cognitive processes.

Source: withGod/Shutterstock.com.

basic research Research aimed at finding answers to questions out of theoretical interest or intellectual curiosity.

applied research Research aimed at improving the quality of life and solving practical problems.

experimental psychology The field primarily concerned with laboratory research on basic psychological processes, including perception, learning, memory, thinking, language, motivation, and emotion.

behavioral neuroscience The field that studies the physiological bases of human and animal behavior and mental processes.

comparative psychology The field that studies similarities and differences in the physiology, behaviors, and abilities of different species of animals, including human beings.

write a dissertation based on an original research study that they conduct. Some undergraduate psychology departments offer courses devoted to discussing career options in psychology and planning how to pursue a career in psychology (Macera & Cohen, 2006).

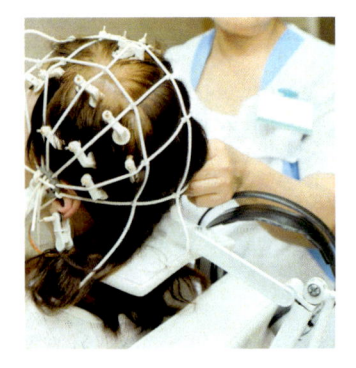

Academic Fields of Specialization

Most of the chapters in this book discuss academic fields of specialization in psychology, usually practiced by psychologists working at colleges or universities. In fact, colleges and universities are the main employment settings for psychologists. Because each field of psychology contains subfields, which in turn contain sub-subfields, a budding psychologist has hundreds of potential specialties from which to choose. For example, a psychologist specializing in the field of sensation and perception might be interested in the subfield of vision, with special interest in the sub-subfield of color vision.

Psychology researchers typically conduct either **basic research**, which is aimed at contributing to knowledge, or **applied research**, which is aimed at solving a practical problem. Note that basic research and applied research are not mutually exclusive, and many psychologists conduct both kinds of research. Findings from basic research can often be applied outside the laboratory. For example, psychologists have taken basic research findings on the interactive effects of alcohol and nicotine as the basis for treatment programs for individuals who are dependent on both alcohol and nicotine (Rohsenow, 2005).

The largest field of academic specialization in psychology is **experimental psychology**. Experimental psychologists restrict themselves chiefly to laboratory research on basic psychological processes, including perception, learning, memory, thinking, language, motivation, and emotion. Though this field is called experimental psychology, it is not the only field that uses experiments. Psychologists in almost all fields of psychology conduct experimental research.

Consider some of the topics tackled by experimental psychologists that will be discussed in upcoming chapters. Chapter 5 describes how perception researchers determine whether people can identify other individuals by their odor. Chapter 8 explains how memory researchers assess the effect of people's moods on their ability to recall memories. And Chapter 12 discusses how emotion researchers demonstrate the effect of facial expressions on emotional experiences.

Psychologists in the field of **behavioral neuroscience** study the biological bases of behavior and cognitive processes. Chapter 3 discusses research by behavioral neuroscientists on the effects of natural opiates in the brain and the differences in functioning between the left and right hemispheres of the brain. In Chapter 6 you will learn of research by behavioral neuroscientists on the effects of psychoactive drugs on mind and behavior.

The related field of **comparative psychology** studies similarities and differences in the physiology, behaviors, and abilities of animals, including the human species. The field

Comparative Psychology

The field of comparative psychology is particularly concerned with studying how evolution has led to animals adapting their behavior to different ecological niches.
Source: Tratong/Shutterstock.com.

is particularly concerned with studying how evolution has led to animals adapting their behavior to different ecological niches (Tobach, 2006). Comparative psychologists study motives related to eating, drinking, aggression, courtship, sexual behavior, and parenting. Chapter 9 discusses how comparative psychologists study whether apes can learn to use language.

The field of **developmental psychology** is home to psychologists who study the factors responsible for physical, cognitive, and social changes across the life span. Research in developmental psychology has found, for example, that undergraduate students who report having had a lack of affectionate touching by parents in childhood are more prone to depression and problems in romantic relationships (Takeuchi et al., 2010). Chapter 4 presents research showing that infants are born with better perceptual skills than you might assume and that many gender differences might be smaller than is commonly believed.

Personality psychology is concerned with differences in behavior among individuals. As noted in Chapter 13, this field seeks answers to questions such as these: Are our personalities determined more by nature or by nurture? And to what extent do people behave consistently from one situation to another? Personality psychologists also devise tests for assessing personality, such as the famous Rorschach "inkblot test."

Psychologists in the field of **social psychology** study the effects people have on one another and the power of social situations. In Chapter 17 you will learn how social psychologists study the factors that influence interpersonal attraction, the problem of "groupthink" in making important decisions, and the reasons why people are often all too willing to follow orders to harm others.

Professional Fields of Specialization

Professional psychologists commonly work in settings outside college or university classrooms and laboratories. Undergraduates are often surprised at the variety of professional fields of psychology (Stark-Wroblewski, Wiggins, & Ryan, 2006). Two of the largest are **clinical psychology** and **counseling psychology**, which deal with the causes, prevention, diagnosis, and treatment of psychological disorders. Counseling psychologists tend to deal with problems of everyday living related to career planning, academic performance, and personal relationships. In contrast, clinical psychologists typically treat more serious disorders, including phobias, alcoholism, drug abuse, and severe depression. Chapter 15

developmental psychology The field that studies physical, perceptual, cognitive, and psychosocial changes across the life span.

personality psychology The field that focuses on factors accounting for the differences in behavior and enduring personal characteristics among individuals.

social psychology The field that studies how the actual, imagined, or implied presence of other people affects one another's thoughts, feelings, and behaviors.

clinical psychology The field that applies psychological principles to the prevention, diagnosis, and treatment of psychological disorders.

counseling psychology The field that applies psychological principles to help individuals deal with problems of daily living, generally less serious ones than those treated by clinical psychologists.

Clinical and Counseling Psychology

Counseling psychologists tend to deal with problems of everyday living; clinical psychologists typically treat more serious disorders.

Source: wavebreakmedia/Shutterstock.com.

Chapter 1 The Nature of Psychology

discusses the various techniques used by clinical and counseling psychologists as well as research concerning this important question: Is psychotherapy effective?

Clinical psychology and counseling psychology are distinctly different from the medical field of **psychiatry**. A psychiatrist is not a psychologist but a physician (with either an M.D. or a D.O.) who has served a residency in psychiatry, which takes a medical approach to the treatment of psychological disorders. Because psychiatrists are physicians, they may prescribe drugs or other biomedical treatments. Some clinical psychologists practicing in the state of New Mexico may undergo additional training and prescribe drugs. This controversial change has been made due to New Mexico's residents having comparatively less access to medical care than other Americans (Raw, 2003). Chapter 15 considers the various biopsychological treatments, including drugs to treat schizophrenia and electroconvulsive therapy to relieve depression. Some psychiatrists also offer psychotherapy to their clients.

Those who practice **health psychology** apply psychological principles to the maintenance of health and coping with illness. The major areas of health psychology include the relationship between stress and illness, the effects of behavior on health and illness, the individual's reaction to illness, and the role of psychology in serious and terminal illness. Health psychologists also develop interventions that reduce health-impairing habits, such as overeating and sedentary lifestyles (Baban & Cracian, 2007). Chapter 16 presents a comprehensive discussion of research findings and applications in health psychology.

Psychologists who practice **industrial/organizational psychology** work to increase productivity in businesses, industries, government agencies, and virtually any other kind of organization. They do so by improving working conditions, methods for hiring and training employees, and management techniques used by administrators. Some industrial/organizational psychologists stress the importance of improving the quality of workers' lives, not just productivity (Zickar, 2003).

One of the oldest professional fields of specialization is **school psychology**. School psychologists work in elementary schools, middle schools, and high schools. They help improve students' academic performance and school behavior. For example, school psychologists take part in programs to improve students' reading acquisition (Bramlett, Murphy, Johnson, Wallingsford, & Hall, 2002). Today, school psychologists have been forced to also deal with serious issues, such as the prevention of suicide and the aftermath of suicides by schoolchildren (Debski, Spadafore, Jacob, Poole, & Hixson, 2007) and the plague of bullying, including cyber bullying via the Internet (Diamanduros, Downs, & Jenkins, 2008).

The allied field of **educational psychology** tries to improve the educational process, including curriculum, teaching, and the administration of academic programs. For example, educational psychologists help school teachers understand the challenges faced by students with dyslexia (Regan & Woods, 2000). They also assess the effectiveness of inclusive programs versus traditional programs on the progress of students with intellectual or physical disabilities (Lindsay, 2007). There has been an influential movement in educational psychology to use only practices that have been supported by sound scientific research rather than simply relying on traditional practices or the opinions of educators (Stoiber & Waas, 2002). Educational psychologists usually are faculty members at colleges or universities.

Sport psychology applies psychology to the acquisition of athletic skills, the improvement of athletic performance, and the maintenance of exercise programs. Sport psychologists typically work with elite collegiate, Olympic, or professional athletes to help them achieve excellence in performance. Some sport psychologists work with injured athletes to help them cope with the rehabilitation process (Hamson-Utley, Martin, & Walters, 2009) or wheelchair athletes to help them adjust to their physical disability while performing to their optimal level (Page, Martin, & Wayda, 2001). Chapter 11 discusses the relationship between motivation and sport performance.

---

psychiatry The field of medicine that diagnoses and treats psychological disorders by using medical or psychological forms of therapy.

health psychology The field that applies psychological principles to the prevention and treatment of physical illness.

industrial/organizational psychology The field that applies psychological principles to improve productivity in businesses, industries, and government agencies.

school psychology The field that applies psychological principles to improve the academic performance and social behavior of students in elementary, middle, and high schools.

educational psychology The field that applies psychological principles to help improve curriculum, teaching methods, and administrative procedures.

sport psychology The field that applies psychological principles to help amateur and professional athletes improve their performance.

Environmental Psychology

Environmental psychologists work with a host of environmental settings and design exhibition centers, such as zoos and museums, to provide effective educational environments.
Source: Andrev Burmakin/Shutterstock.com.

Psychologists who practice **forensic psychology** apply psychology to the legal system. The topics they study include the jury deliberation process and the best ways to select jurors. Forensic psychologists also help train police to handle domestic disputes, negotiate with hostage takers, and cope with job-related stress. And they seek to determine the fairest ways to present lineups of criminal suspects for identification by eyewitnesses (Kebbell, 2000), assess the competency of children to testify in court (Bala, Kang, Lindsay, & Talwar, 2010), develop training programs for law enforcement leaders (Miller, Watkins, & Webb, 2009), and conduct risk assessments of sex offenders being considered for parole (Freeman, Palk, & Davey, 2010). Chapter 8 describes another issue of interest to forensic psychologists: What is the best way to obtain accurate eyewitness testimony from children?

Environmental psychology studies the effect of the physical environment on human behavior, including how to design environments that improve the quality of life. Environmental psychologists work with a host of environmental settings and engage in activities as diverse as designing capsule habitats for exploring outer space, the deep sea, and the polar regions (Suedfeld & Steel, 2000) and designing exhibition centers, such as zoos and museums, to provide effective educational environments (Bitgood, 2002). Environmental psychologists also contribute to our knowledge of the role of changes in ambient light levels and other environmental factors implicated in seasonal affective disorder (discussed in Chapter 14), which is marked by the development of severe depression during a particular season of the year—typically the winter (Tonello, 2008).

One of the newest fields of applied psychology is **peace psychology**, which aims at reducing conflicts and maintaining peace. Though the field is comparatively new, it became a formal subdiscipline during the Cold War, which began at the conclusion of World War II and ended in the early 1990s. During this time the world was threatened by nuclear annihilation as the then-Soviet Union and Western nations engaged in an escalating nuclear arms race (Christie, 2006). However, psychologists have long been interested in applying psychology to the promotion of peace. During the decade leading up to World War II, there was a symposium on the psychology of peace and war (Glover & Ginsberg, 1934). And near the end of that war, psychologists discussed ways of applying psychology to the coming peace and reconstruction (Lerner, 1943). Today, peace psychologists are particularly interested in finding ways to reduce tensions that promote ethnic conflicts and terrorism (Wagner, 2006).

forensic psychology The field that applies psychological principles to improve the legal system, including the work of police and juries.

environmental psychology The field that applies psychological principles to help improve the physical environment, including the design of buildings and the reduction of noise.

peace psychology The field that applies psychological principles to reducing conflict and maintaining peace.

> **Section Review:** Professional Fields of Specialization
>
> 1. What is the difference between basic and applied research?
> 2. How does psychiatry differ from psychology?
> 3. What is the nature of peace psychology?

Chapter Summary

The Historical Context of Psychology

- Psychology is the scientific study of behavior and cognitive processes.
- The roots of psychology are in philosophy and physiology.
- The commonly accepted founding date for psychology is 1879, when Wilhelm Wundt established the first formal psychology laboratory.
- Structuralism sought to analyze the mind into its component parts.
- Functionalism favored the study of how the conscious mind helps the individual adapt to the environment.
- Gestalt psychology favored the study of the mind as active and the study of perception as holistic.
- Psychoanalysis studies the influence of unconscious motives on behavior.
- Behaviorism rejects the study of the mind in favor of the study of observable behavior.

Contemporary Perspectives in Psychology

- To date, psychology has no unifying scientific paradigm, only competing psychological perspectives.
- The humanistic perspective, which favors the study of conscious mental experience and accepts the reality of free will, arose in opposition to psychoanalysis and behaviorism.
- The cognitive perspective views the individual as an active processor of information.
- The biopsychological perspective favors the study of the biological bases of behavior, mental experiences, and cognitive processes.
- The sociocultural perspective insists that psychologists must study people in their social and cultural contexts.

The Scope of Psychology

- Academic fields of specialization are chiefly concerned with conducting basic research.
- Professional fields of specialization in psychology are chiefly concerned with applying psychological research findings.

Key Terms

psychology (p. 2)

The Historical Context of Psychology

analytic introspection (p. 6)
behaviorism (p. 11)
differential psychology (p. 5)
empiricism (p. 3)
functionalism (p. 6)
Gestalt psychology (p. 8)
nativism (p. 3)
phi phenomenon (p. 8)
psychic determinism (p. 10)
psychoanalysis (p. 9)
psychophysics (p. 4)
rationalism (p. 3)
structuralism (p. 6)

Contemporary Perspectives in Psychology

behavioral genetics (p. 15)
biopsychological perspective (p. 14)
cognitive perspective (p. 14)
cross-cultural psychology (p. 16)
cultural psychology (p. 16)
ethnic psychology (p. 17)
evolutionary psychology (p. 15)
existential psychology (p. 13)
humanistic perspective (p. 13)
multicultural psychology (p. 16)
phenomenological psychology (p. 13)
scientific paradigm (p. 13)
sociocultural perspective (p. 16)

The Scope of Psychology

applied research (p. 18)
basic research (p. 18)
behavioral neuroscience (p. 18)
clinical psychology (p. 19)
comparative psychology (p. 18)
counseling psychology (p. 19)
developmental psychology (p. 19)
educational psychology (p. 20)
environmental psychology (p. 21)
experimental psychology (p. 18)
forensic psychology (p. 21)
health psychology (p. 20)
industrial/organizational psychology (p. 20)
peace psychology (p. 21)
personality psychology (p. 19)
psychiatry (p. 20)
school psychology (p. 20)
social psychology (p. 19)
sport psychology (p. 20)

Chapter Quiz

Note: Answers for the Chapter Quiz questions are provided at the end of the book.

1. If you insisted that "seeing is believing," you would show your belief in
   a. nativism.
   b. empiricism.
   c. rationalism.
   d. psychic determinism.

2. The main difference between a psychiatrist and a clinical psychologist is that the psychiatrist
   a. is a physician.
   b. might analyze dreams.
   c. relies strictly on Freudian theory.
   d. deals with more serious kinds of disorders.

3. When you watch a cartoon in a movie theater, you are experiencing (the)
   a. phi phenomenon.
   b. Zeigarnik effect.
   c. psychic determinism.
   d. analytic introspection.

4. A psychologist would be most likely to
   a. prescribe drugs to treat anxiety.
   b. study the ability of apes to learn language.
   c. provide evidence for or against the existence of God.
   d. treat depression by administering electroshock therapy.

5. The philosopher who would most approve of Hugo Münsterberg's founding of applied psychology would be
   a. Plato.
   b. Saint Augustine.
   c. Immanuel Kant.
   d. Francis Bacon.

6. Darwin's theory of evolution had its greatest impact on
   a. structuralism.
   b. functionalism.
   c. Gestalt psychology.
   d. cognitive psychology.

7. Biology and psychology are both sciences because they
   a. study the brain.
   b. rely on statistics.
   c. share a common method.
   d. require specialized education.

8. Strict determinism would most likely be rejected by a
   a. psychoanalyst.
   b. biopsychologist.
   c. behavioral psychologist.
   d. humanistic psychologist.

9. The psychological perspective that is interested in studying the brain, the hormone system, and the effects of heredity on behavior is the
   a. differential perspective.
   b. neurochemical perspective.
   c. cerebrocortical perspective.
   d. biopsychological perspective.

10. The discussion of women in the early history of psychology noted that, since the early 20th century, psychology has been
    a. more hospitable to women than to men.
    b. more hospitable to women than other sciences have been.
    c. less hospitable to women than other sciences have been.
    d. about as hospitable to women as other sciences have been.

11. A research study on the effectiveness of psychological counseling techniques in helping Olympic athletes reach their potential would be an example of
    a. pure research.
    b. basic research.
    c. applied research.
    d. psychic determinism.

12. The discovery of possible universal psychological truths is central to
    a. parapsychology.
    b. cultural psychology.
    c. humanistic psychology.
    d. cross-cultural psychology.

13. If a psychologist insisted that a person's recent fall down a flight of stairs was more attributable to unconscious self-loathing than to clumsiness, she would be supporting the Freudian notion of
    a. stimulus control.
    b. psychic determinism.
    c. positive reinforcement.
    d. psychophysical parallelism.

14. Near the end of his life, Carl Rogers lamented that humanistic psychology had little impact on mainstream psychology, in part because it
    a. lacked scientific rigor.
    b. was too concerned with sex.
    c. likened the human mind to a computer.
    d. stressed unconscious motivation instead of conscious experience.

15. Neither behaviorism nor psychoanalysis
    a. studies the mind.
    b. uses case studies.
    c. considers the environment.
    d. focuses on the conscious mind.

16. Research in differential psychology, a field founded by Francis Galton, would be most likely to
    a. use placebo control groups.
    b. determine the effect of exercise on academic performance.
    c. study factors that make certain individuals more stress-resistant than others.
    d. assess changes in the personality of a single subject across various life stages.

17. A behaviorist would be most likely to agree with the belief that leaders
    a. are made, not born.
    b. are born, not made.
    c. use will power to dominate other people.
    d. are motivated by an unconscious desire for control.

18. An interest in the unconscious mind would be most characteristic of
    a. behaviorism.
    b. psychoanalysis.
    c. humanistic psychology.
    d. cognitive psychology.

19. B. F. Skinner would be most likely to attribute your desire to pursue a college education to
    a. your drive for self-actualization.
    b. an unconscious need to prove yourself.
    c. your past success in academic courses.
    d. intellectual interests inherited from your parents.

20. If a psychologist is interested in helping you to feel more self-actualized in your life, she is probably a(n)
    a. forensic psychologist.
    b. cognitive psychologist.
    c. humanistic psychologist.
    d. experimental psychologist.

21. The main employment settings of psychologists are
    a. private practices.
    b. businesses and industries.
    c. colleges and universities.
    d. governmental research laboratories.

22. Cognitive psychology can be viewed as the offspring of
    a. psychoanalysis and functionalism.
    b. behaviorism and Gestalt psychology.
    c. structuralism and humanistic psychology.
    d. biopsychology and differential psychology.

23. The idea that the proper subject matter of psychology should be a person's conscious mental experience was put forth by
    a. Ivan Pavlov.
    b. Roger Sperry.
    c. B. F. Skinner.
    d. Abraham Maslow.

24. According to philosopher Thomas Kuhn, as a science matures, it develops a paradigm shared by most scientists. Today, psychology
    a. lacks a unifying scientific paradigm.
    b. is dominated by the humanistic paradigm.
    c. is dominated by the behavioristic paradigm.
    d. is dominated by the psychoanalytic paradigm.

25. The first psychological laboratory was established in 1879 by
    a. Sigmund Freud.
    b. Wilhelm Wundt.
    c. John B. Watson.
    d. Edward Titchener.

Thought Questions

1. How would nativists and empiricists differ in their opinion of early childhood intervention projects, such as Head Start?

2. In the late 19th and early 20th centuries, many Americans believed that women's and men's lives should be lived in "separate spheres." How did this notion limit women's contributions to psychology?

3. Suppose you find that your professor is an unusually "happy" person—smiling, cracking jokes, and complimenting students on their brilliant insights. How would the different psychological perspectives explain this behavior?

Psychology as a Science

Chapter 2

As discussed in Chapter 1, psychology is the science that studies human and animal behavior and cognitive processes. Psychology deals with topics of great interest to people, making them also of particular interest to the media. But the media at times are more interested in attracting readers, viewers, and listeners than in the objective reporting of scientific findings. This focus often leads the media to exaggerate or sensationalize research findings. Consider the media's coverage of the supposed effects of the hormone melatonin on the next page.

In discussing psychology as a science, this chapter will answer questions such as these: Why do psychologists use the scientific method? What are the goals of psychological research? How do psychologists employ the scientific method in their research? What techniques do psychologists rely on to analyze their data? And what ethical principles guide psychological research? The answers to these questions will help you appreciate the scientific basis of the issues, theories, research findings, and practical applications presented throughout this book.

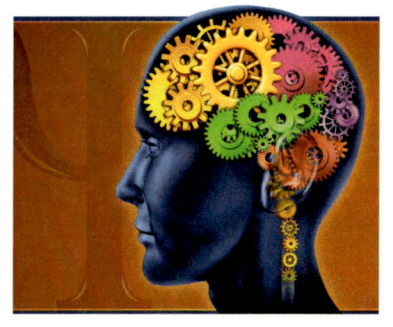

Source: Lightspring/Shutterstock.com.

Chapter Outline

Sources of Knowledge
Goals of Scientific Research
Methods of Psychological Research
Statistical Analysis of Research Data
Ethics of Psychological Research

Sources of Knowledge

Psychologists and other scientists favor the scientific method as their means of obtaining knowledge, such as knowledge about the effects of melatonin. To appreciate why they do, you need to understand the shortcomings of the everyday alternative to the scientific method: *common sense*.

Common Sense

When you rely on common sense, you assume that the beliefs you have obtained from everyday life are trustworthy. Commonsense knowledge has a variety of sources, including statements by recognized authorities, your own reasoning about things, and observations from your personal experience. Many college students view psychology as little more than common sense—until they are presented with examples of how scientific research has demonstrated that their commonsense beliefs are false (Osberg, 1993).

As an example of the frailty of common sense, consider sports fans' belief in the "hot hand," especially in professional basketball. According to this belief, a player's performance will temporarily improve following a string of successful shots. The accuracy of this commonsense belief was examined in a study of NBA Long Distance Shootout contests from 1994 through 1997.

Critical Thinking About Psychology

Does Melatonin Have Beneficial Physical and Psychological Effects?

In November 1995, *Newsweek* magazine's cover story reported a craze inspired by the supposed beneficial physical and psychological effects of a "natural wonder drug": the hormone melatonin (Cowley, 1995). Melatonin, secreted by the pineal gland (located in the center of the brain), was touted in the article as a cure for aging, insomnia, and jet lag. And *Newsweek* was not alone. Reports by magazines, newspapers, radio stations, and television networks across the United States stimulated public excitement about melatonin.

The effects of the media reports were so powerful that many health-food stores could not keep up with consumer demand for melatonin. At the time the *Newsweek* article was published, a book praising the effects of melatonin was third on the *New York Times* best-seller list. Though the craze has subsided since 1995, the media still include periodic reports on the effects of melatonin—and the Internet is brimming with Web sites that praise the alleged benefits of melatonin, while they just so happen to offer it for sale online.

Should readers have accepted the claims about melatonin's alleged beneficial effects simply because they appeared in a popular news weekly that relied mainly on testimonials from people who used or marketed it? Psychologists, being scientists, do not accept such claims unless they are supported by sound scientific research findings—such as more recent research indicating that melatonin might indeed have beneficial psychological effects. Research studies have found that melatonin can be effective in treating insomnia (Wade et al., 2010) and cancer (Mills, Wu, Seely, & Guatt, 2005), countering jet lag (Paul et al., 2010), preventing heart disease (Veneroso, Tuñón, González-Gallego, & Collado, 2009), and slowing aging of the brain (Carretero et al., 2009). As you read this chapter, you will learn how a psychologist might use the scientific method to conduct an experiment to test the effects of melatonin. But you must first understand the nature of psychology as a science.

Science versus Pseudoscience

Should we accept media reports as strong evidence for popular claims, such as melatonin's alleged ability to promote sleep, overcome jet lag, and slow the aging process? Scientists require more rigorous standards of evidence than that.
Source: tab62/Shutterstock.com.

Analyses of videotaped free throws revealed that—contrary to common sense—players did *not* perform better following a "streak" of successes. In fact, players performed at about their base rate following a sequence of successful shots (Koehler & Conley, 2003). Thus, the best predictor of basketball players' next shots is their average performance, not the perception that they have "hot hands."

Even the judicial system, which strives for objectivity in courtroom deliberations, at times relies more on common sense than on scientific research to settle important issues, such as judges' and jurors' faith in the accuracy of eyewitness testimony (Benton, Ross, Bradshaw, Thomas, & Bradshaw, 2006). But we should not automatically discount the possibility that commonsense beliefs might be true. According to Harold Kelley (1921–2003), a leading researcher on commonsense thinking, "Discarding our commonsense psychology baggage would require us needlessly to separate ourselves from the vast sources of knowledge gained in the course of human history" (Kelley, 1992, p. 22). In other words, common sense may inspire scientific research, even though it cannot substitute for it—as in the research study inspired by a major social problem discussed in the "Psychology versus Common Sense" box on page 28.

Common Sense

Should you change your answers on multiple-choice tests? Student common sense would say no. You probably have heard the folk wisdom, "Don't change your answers on exams, because you'll be more likely to change a correct wrong answer to a wrong answer than a wrong answer to a correct answer." You might be surprised that scientific research has consistently found that students are slightly more likely to change a wrong answer to a correct answer than a correct answer to a wrong answer (N. F. Skinner, 1983).
Source: Tyler Olson/Shutterstock.com.

Science

Because of the weaknesses of common sense and the need for a more objective, self-correcting source of knowledge, scientists prefer the scientific method, which is based on certain assumptions and follows a formal series of steps. The fact that the scientific method is the dominant research method in psychology owes much to its origins in 19th-century natural science, particularly physiology.

Assumptions of Science

Scientists share some basic assumptions that guide their thinking about physical reality. Two of the most important of these assumptions are determinism and skepticism.

Determinism and Lawfulness Albert Einstein was fond of saying, "God does not play dice with the universe." In using the scientific method, psychologists and other scientists share his belief that there is order in the universe, meaning that the relationships among events are lawful rather than haphazard. In looking for these lawful relationships, scientists also share the assumption of **determinism**, which holds that every event has physical, possibly measurable, causes. Determinism rules out free will and supernatural influences as causes of behavior.

Yet, as pointed out more than a century ago by William James, scientists might be committed to determinism in conducting their research, while being tempted to assume the existence of free will in their everyday lives (Immergluck, 1964). They might succumb to this temptation because, if carried to its logical extreme, the assumption of strict determinism would lead them to unpalatable conclusions (Holton, 2009)—for example, that Mother Teresa did not deserve praise for her work with the poor and that Adolph Hitler did not deserve blame for his acts of genocide, because neither was free to choose otherwise. This logical extreme also means that strict determinism is incompatible with the legal system, which, because it assumes the existence of free will, holds criminals responsible for their actions.

Despite centuries of philosophical debate, neither side of the determinism versus free will debate has won. Even William James, after pondering this issue for many years,

determinism The assumption that every event has physical, potentially measurable, causes.

Chapter 2 Psychology as a Science   27

Psychology versus Common Sense

Can We Reliably Detect When Someone Is Drunk?

In the landmark 1961 *Zane* decision, a New Jersey court stated, "Whether the man is sober or intoxicated is a matter of common observation not requiring special knowledge or skill" (Langenbucher & Nathan, 1983, p. 1071). This assumption is an important one because state laws in the United States, based on the commonsense belief that drunkenness is easily detected, hold people such as party hosts and tavern owners legally responsible for the actions of people who become drunk at their homes or businesses. The ability to detect drunkenness was tested in a scientific study by researchers James Langenbucher and Peter Nathan (1983).

Langenbucher and Nathan had 12 bartenders, 49 social drinkers, and 30 police officers observe drinkers and judge whether they were legally drunk or sober. The drinkers in each case were two male and two female young adults. Each drinker consumed one of three drinks: tonic water, moderate doses of vodka (but not enough to become legally drunk), or high doses of vodka (enough to become legally drunk). A Breathalyzer ensured that the desired blood-alcohol concentrations were achieved for participants in the two vodka conditions.

The bartenders observed their participants being interviewed in a cocktail lounge. The social drinkers observed their participants being interviewed in the Alcohol Behavior Research Laboratory at Rutgers University. And the police officers observed their participants in a simulated nighttime roadside arrest in which they were given 3 minutes to determine whether the motorist they had pulled over was drunk or sober.

Langenbucher and Nathan found that the observers correctly judged the drinkers' level of intoxication only 25 percent of the time. Not a single legally drunk person was identified as such by a significant number of the observers. Of the 91 persons who served as judges, only five were consistently accurate—and all of them were members of a New Jersey State Police special tactical unit for the apprehension of drunk drivers. Those five police officers had received more than 90 hours of training in the detection of drunkenness. The results implied that, without special training, even people with extensive experience in observing drinkers might be unable to determine whether a person is legally drunk or sober.

The social implication of these findings is that common sense is wrong in the assumption that people with experience in observing drinkers can detect whether someone is drunk. We are even more confident in the findings of this study because they were supported by the results of a different experiment conducted by a different researcher, using different participants, in a different research setting (Beatty, 1984). Perhaps bartenders, police officers, and habitual party givers should obtain special training similar to that given to the five police officers who performed well in the study.

The Detection of Drunkenness

Scientific research contradicts the commonsense belief that we can easily detect when someone is legally drunk.
Source: Andresr/Shutterstock.com.

---

failed to find enough evidence to favor either side of the determinism versus free will debate (Bricklin, 1999). This controversy is one that neither psychologists nor philosophers have been able to resolve, though some still try by resorting to soft determinism, which asserts that determinism generally governs events though at times we can impose free will on our actions (Clarke, 2010).

Skepticism and Critical Thinking Aside from assuming that the universe is an orderly place in which events—including behaviors—are governed by determinism, scientists today, like René Descartes and Francis Bacon before them (see Chapter 1), insist that open-minded **skepticism** is the best intellectual predisposition when judging the merits of any claim. Open-minded skepticism requires the maintenance of a delicate balance between cynicism and gullibility. As Mario Bunge, a leading philosopher of science, has noted, skeptics "do not believe anything in the absence of evidence, but they are willing to explore bold new ideas if they find reasons to suspect that they have a chance" (Bunge,

skepticism An attitude that doubts all claims not supported by solid research evidence.

1992, p. 380). This skeptical attitude requires supportive evidence before accepting any claim. The failure to maintain a skeptical attitude leads to the acceptance of phenomena, such as ESP, that lack sufficient scientific support (Bartholomew & Radford, 2003). Nonetheless, researchers who accept the possible existence of ESP argue that critics tend to be more cynical than skeptical by not even considering sound scientific evidence supporting its existence (Radin, 2007).

Skepticism also is important in psychology because many psychological "truths" are tentative, in part because psychological research findings may depend on the times and places in which the research takes place. What generally is true of human behavior in one era or culture might be false in another era or culture. For example, gender differences in behavior in Western cultures have changed dramatically over the past few decades, and gender differences observed in Western cultures might be unlike those in non-Western cultures. More than two decades before the sociocultural perspective (see Chapter 1) achieved widespread acceptance in North American psychology, Anne Anastasi (1908–2001), in her presidential address to the American Psychological Association, showed foresight in urging psychologists not to confuse their ethnocentric personal beliefs and values with scientific "truths" (Anastasi, 1972).

Skepticism is valuable not only for scientists but for all of us in our everyday lives, as we evaluate information presented in academic courses, media reports, and Web sites. Skepticism also is the basis of *critical thinking*—the systematic evaluation of claims and assumptions. Students who major in psychology tend to become particularly adept at critical thinking by their senior year (Lawson, 1999). The following steps in critical thinking will serve you well as you evaluate claims encountered in your everyday life:

1. Identify the claim being made. Ask yourself whether it is based on empirical data (which would be subject to scientific evaluation) or on personal values, opinions, or religious beliefs (which would be less subject to scientific evaluation).
2. Examine the evidence in support of the claim. Try to assess whether the evidence has merit.
3. If the evidence does have merit, determine whether it logically supports the claim. The evidence might have merit in itself without necessarily being logically connected to the claim.
4. Consider possible alternative explanations of the claim. Perhaps there is a better explanation than the one that has been given.

Steps in Conducting Scientific Research

Because psychologists are skeptical about claims not supported by research findings, they employ the **scientific method** as their means of gaining knowledge. Though scientists vary in their approach to the scientific method, ideally they follow a formal series of steps:

Step 1: Provide a *rationale* for the study. The scientist identifies the problem, reviews the relevant research literature, decides on the research method to use, and states the research **hypothesis**. A hypothesis (from the Greek word for "supposition") is a testable prediction about the relationship between two or more events or characteristics.

Step 2: Conduct the study. The scientist carries out the research procedure and collects data.

Step 3: Analyze the data. The scientist usually uses mathematical techniques called *statistics* and discusses the implications of the research findings.

Step 4: Communicate the research findings. The scientist may present the research study at a professional meeting and publish an article describing the study in a professional journal. In doing so, the scientist includes the rationale for the research, the exact method that was used, the results of the research, and a discussion of the implications of the results.

Step 5: Replicate the study. **Replication** involves repeating the study, exactly or with some variation. Either the original researcher or other researchers may replicate

scientific method A source of knowledge based on the assumption that knowledge comes from the objective, systematic observation and measurement of particular variables and the events they affect.

hypothesis A testable prediction about the relationship between two or more events or characteristics.

replication The repetition of a research study, usually with some alterations in its methods or setting, to determine whether the principles derived from that study hold up under similar circumstances.

the study. Successful replications of research studies strengthen confidence in their findings.

These steps were used by psychologist Donn Byrne and his colleagues (Byrne, Ervin, & Lamberth, 1970) in a classic research study of interpersonal attraction: Do opposites attract? Or do birds of a feather flock together? In this study, the problem concerned the relationship between interpersonal similarity and interpersonal attraction. After reviewing the research literature relevant to the problem, Byrne decided to conduct a *field experiment* that studied college students in a real-life setting instead of in a laboratory. In fact, his experiment was a replication conducted to determine whether the results of previous laboratory studies on the effects of attitude similarity on interpersonal attraction would generalize to a field setting.

Based on his review of the research literature, Byrne hypothesized that heterosexual men and women with similar attitudes would be more likely to be attracted to each other than would those with dissimilar attitudes. Byrne had his research participants complete a 50-item questionnaire that assessed their attitudes as part of a computer-dating service. He told them that their responses would be used to pair them with a student who shared their attitudes. But the students were actually paired so that some partners were similar in attitudes and others were dissimilar. Their similarity on the questionnaire provided a concrete definition of "similarity." The 44 heterosexual couples, selected from 420 volunteers, then were sent to the student union for a 30-minute get-acquainted date. Several weeks later, participants were asked to rate their partners, which provided Byrne with his research data.

Like almost all researchers, Byrne used statistics to summarize his data and to determine whether his hypothesis was supported. In this case, Byrne found that the data did support the hypothesis. Partners who were similar in attitudes were significantly more likely to recall each other's name, to have talked with each other since the date, and to desire to date each other again. Thus, in this study, the use of the scientific method found that birds of a feather tend to flock together.

Byrne communicated his findings by publishing them in a professional journal. He also might have shared his findings by presenting them at a research conference. Even undergraduate psychology researchers can present the results of their research studies at psychology research conferences—including undergraduate conferences—held each year.

Section Review: Sources of Knowledge

1. What are the basic assumptions of science?
2. What is critical thinking?
3. What are the formal steps in the scientific method?

Goals of Scientific Research

In conducting their research, psychologists and other scientists share common goals. They pursue the goals of description, prediction, control, and explanation of behavior and cognitive processes (Green & Powell, 1990).

Description

To a scientist, description involves noting the observable characteristics of an event, object, or individual. For example, we might note that participants who take daily doses of melatonin sleep longer. Psychologists, following in the intellectual tradition of Francis Bacon discussed in Chapter 1, are systematic in what they describe. Instead of arbitrarily describing everything that they observe, they describe only things that are relevant to their research topic. Thus, good observational skills are essential to psychologists. The need to be systematic in what you describe is expressed well in a statement about criminal investigations made by the fictional detective Sherlock Holmes to his friend Dr. Watson:

> A fool takes in all the lumber [facts] that he comes across, so that the knowledge which might be useful to him gets crowded out, or at best is jumbled up with a lot of other things . . . It is of the highest importance, therefore, not to have useless facts elbowing out the useful ones. (Doyle, 1930)

In science, descriptions must be more than systematic; they must be precise. Precise descriptions are concrete rather than abstract, and typically involve **measurement**, which is the use of numbers to represent events or characteristics. According to Francis Galton, one of the pioneers of psychology, "Until the phenomena of any branch of knowledge have been submitted to measurement . . . it cannot assume the status and dignity of a science" (quoted in Cowles, 1989, p. 2). Thus, describing a friend as "generous" would be acceptable in everyday conversation but would be too imprecise for scientific communication.

Scientists solve this problem by using **operational definitions**, which define behaviors or qualities in terms of the procedures used to measure or produce them (Feest, 2005). Donn Byrne did this when he defined *similarity* according to participants' responses to a questionnaire in his study of interpersonal attractiveness. More than a century ago, Galton, in studying audience behavior at plays and lectures, operationally defined *boredom* by recording the number of fidgets by audience members. You might operationally define *generous* as "donating more than 5 percent of one's salary to charity." And a common operational definition of being *legally drunk* is "a blood-alcohol concentration of at least 0.08 percent." Though operational definitions are desirable, psychologists sometimes find it difficult to agree on acceptable ones. For example, a series of journal articles argued about how best to operationally define "suicide attempt" (Kidd, 2003). Perhaps the main value of an operational definition is that it promotes more precise communication among scientists.

measurement The use of numbers to represent events or characteristics.

operational definition The definition of behaviors or qualities in terms of the procedures used to measure or produce them.

Prediction

Psychologists are not content just to describe things. They also make predictions in the form of hypotheses about changes in behavior, cognitive experiences, or physiological activity. A hypothesis is usually based on a **theory**, which is a set of statements that summarize and explain research findings and from which research hypotheses can be derived. For example, Sigmund Freud's theory of psychoanalysis integrates many observations he had made of the characteristics of people suffering from psychological disorders. Theories provide coherence to scientific research findings and suggest applications of research findings, making science more than the accumulation of isolated facts (Kukla, 1989).

theory An integrated set of statements that summarizes and explains research findings and from which research hypotheses can be derived.

Because we cannot know all the factors that affect a person or an animal at a given time, psychologists never are certain about the predictions made in their research hypotheses. In fact, it would be pointless to conduct a research study for which the outcome was certain. Moreover, scientific predictions about human participants or animal subjects usually are more accurate when applied to many people or animals than when applied to a specific case. For example, your automobile insurance company can more accurately predict the percentage of people in your age group who will have an accident this year than it can predict whether you will have one. Likewise, though melatonin might prove effective in treating insomnia for most people, we would be unable to predict with certainty whether a particular person would benefit from it.

Psychology has nothing to apologize for in being limited to probabilistic prediction because this situation is no different in the other sciences, which likewise are limited to making predictions that scientists are not 100 percent certain are correct (Hedges, 1987). Your physician might prescribe an antibiotic that, based on medical research, is effective 98 percent of the time in treating pneumonia, but she or he cannot guarantee that it will cure your pneumonia. Similarly, flood forecasters know that regions along certain rivers are more likely to flood (Reggiani & Weerts, 2008) and earthquake forecasters know that regions along geological faults are more likely to experience earthquakes (Molchan & Keilis-Borok, 2008), but they cannot accurately predict well in advance the day, or even the year, that a flood or an earthquake will occur in a given region.

For example, the U.S. Geological Survey has estimated that there is a 76 percent chance that before 2030, a powerful earthquake measuring 6.7 or more on the seismic scale will occur in northern California (Perlman, 1999). But seismologists are far from being able to predict that "a magnitude 7.3 earthquake will strike 18 miles northeast of San Francisco in the spring of 2020." In the same vein, in regard to interpersonal attraction, people with similar attitudes will probably—but not always—be more attracted to each other than are people with dissimilar attitudes. We cannot predict with certainty whether two specific people with similar attitudes will be attracted to each other.

Control

Psychologists go beyond describing and predicting changes in behavior, cognitive processes, and physiological activity. They also try to influence those changes by controlling factors that affect them. The notion of control is used in two ways (Cowles, 1989). First, as you will read later in the chapter, control is an essential ingredient in the conduct of experiments. Second, psychologists try to apply their research findings to the control of behavior in everyday life (Smith, 2002). Thus, melatonin might be prescribed to control insomnia by promoting sleep, and young adults might be advised to find romance by seeking people who share their values and interests. Psychologists seek to help individuals gain control over phenomena as diverse as psychological disorders (Mansell & Carey, 2009) and Type 2 diabetes (Gonzales, Salas, & Umpierrez, 2011).

Explanation

The ultimate goal of psychology is explanation—the discovery of the causes of overt behaviors and cognitive processes. If it is demonstrated that people who ingest melatonin consistently overcome insomnia, the next step might be to explain how melatonin affects the brain to trigger sleep. Likewise, even though we know that attitude similarity promotes interpersonal attraction, we still would need to explain why we prefer people who have similar attitudes.

As discussed in Chapter 1, psychologists' favored perspectives determine where they look for explanations of psychological phenomena, such as psychological disorders (Lam, Salkovskis, & Warwick, 2005). Psychologists who favor the cognitive, humanistic, or psychoanalytic perspective will look for causes in the mind. Psychologists who favor the behavioral perspective will look for causes in the environment. Psychologists who favor the biopsychological perspective will look for causes in the brain or hormonal system. And psychologists who favor the sociocultural perspective will look for causes in the social or cultural context of the event.

Section Review: Goals of Scientific Research

1. Why do scientists use operational definitions?
2. In what way are psychology and other sciences probabilistic?
3. What is the nature of scientific explanation in psychology?

TABLE 2-1 The Goals and Methods of Psychology

Goal	Research Method	Relevant Question
Description	Descriptive	What are its characteristics?
Prediction	Correlational	How likely is it?
Control	Experimental	Can I make it happen?
Explanation	Experimental	What causes it?

Methods of Psychological Research

Given that psychologists favor the scientific method as their primary source of knowledge, how do they use it in their research? And once they have collected their data, how do they make sense of it? As shown in Table 2-1, psychologists use research methods that permit them to describe, predict, control, or explain relationships among variables. *Descriptive research* pursues the goal of description, *correlational research* pursues the goal of prediction, and *experimental research* pursues the goals of control and explanation.

Descriptive Research

Descriptive research is descriptive because researchers simply record what they have systematically observed. Descriptive research methods include *naturalistic observation, case studies, surveys, psychological testing,* and *archival research*.

Naturalistic Observation

In **naturalistic observation**, people or animals are observed behaving in their natural environment. Researchers who use naturalistic observation study topics as diverse as the ability to find where one has parked one's car (Lutz, Means, & Long, 1994), peer reactions to the bullying of children in school playgrounds (Hawkins, Pepler, & Craig, 2001), and factors related to smiling or laughing during group interactions (Mehu & Dunbar, 2008). To make sure that their observations represent natural behavior, observers refrain as much as possible from influencing the individuals they are observing. In other words, the observer remains unobtrusive. If you were studying the eating behavior of students in your school cafeteria, you would not announce your intention over a loudspeaker. Otherwise, your participants might behave unnaturally; a person who normally gorged on cake, ice cream, and chocolate pudding for dessert might eat fruit instead.

Naturalistic observation also is useful in studying animal behavior. Some of the best-known studies employing naturalistic observation were conducted by Jane Goodall, who spent decades observing chimpanzees in Gombe National Park in Tanzania (Crain, 2009). To prevent newly encountered chimpanzees from acting unnaturally because of her presence, Goodall spent her initial observation periods letting them get used to her.

The study of animal behavior in the natural environment, as in Goodall's research, is called **ethology**. One of the advantages of an ethological approach is the potential discovery of behaviors not found in more artificial settings, such as zoos and laboratories. Goodall reported observations concerning mundane chimpanzee behavior, such as "fishing" for ants with sticks (O'Malley, Wallauer, Murray, & Goodall, 2012) and observations of chimpanzee behavior that have not been made in captivity, including cannibalism, infanticide, and unprovoked killing of other chimpanzees (Goodall, 1990). But researchers who use naturalistic observation, like those who use other research methods, must not be hasty in generalizing their findings. Even the generalizability of Jane Goodall's observations must be qualified. The behavior of the Gombe chimpanzees differs from the behavior of chimpanzees in the Mahali Mountains of western Tanzania. For example,

descriptive research Research that involves the recording of behaviors that have been observed systematically.

naturalistic observation The recording of the behavior of people or animals in their natural environments, with little or no intervention by the researcher.

ethology The study of animal behavior in the natural environment.

Naturalistic Observation

Jane Goodall's naturalistic observations of chimpanzees in the wild have contributed to our understanding of their everyday habits, many of which had never been observed in zoos or laboratories.
Source: Tinseltown/Shutterstock.com.

female Mahali chimpanzees hunt more often than female Gombe chimpanzees do (Takahata, Hasegawa, & Nishida, 1984).

Naturalistic observation cannot determine the causes of the observed behavior because there are simply too many factors at work in a natural setting. So you could not determine *why* female chimpanzees hunt more in one part of Tanzania than in another. Is it due to differences in prey, in climate, in topography, or in another factor or some combination of factors? It would be impossible to tell just by using naturalistic observation.

Case Study

case study An in-depth study of an individual.

Another descriptive research method is the **case study**—an in-depth study of a person, typically conducted to gain knowledge about a particular psychological phenomenon that is relatively rare, such as psychosocial factors related to pathological hoarding of items (Koretz & Gutheil, 2009), or that would be unethical to study experimentally, such as psychosocial factors related to fibromyalgia (Griffies, 2010). The case-study researcher obtains as much relevant information as possible about a host of factors, perhaps including the person's thoughts, feelings, life experiences, and social relationships. The case study often is used in clinical studies of people suffering from psychological disorders. In fact, Sigmund Freud based his theory of psychoanalysis on data he obtained from clinical case studies, which are still a staple of psychoanalytic research (Midgley, 2006).

Most recently, the case study method has been used to gain insight into factors related to a rash of student shootings of their teachers and classmates. Researchers conducted case studies of 15 shooting incidents between 1995 and 2001 to examine the possible role of social rejection. Ostracism, bullying, or romantic rejection was present in all but two of the cases. The shooters also tended to have one or more of the following three risk factors: an interest in guns or explosives, a fascination with death or Satanism, or psychological problems involving depression, impulse control, or sadistic tendencies (Leary, Kowalski, Smith, & Phillips, 2003).

Because a person's behavior is affected by many variables, the case study method cannot determine the particular variables that caused the behavior being studied. Though it might seem reasonable to assume that the shooters' experiences of rejection caused them to lash out at their teachers and fellow students, that assumption might be wrong. Other factors, unrelated to social rejection, might have caused the violence. It even is conceivable that the shooters' peers rejected them only *after* discovering their fascination with death, Satanism, or guns.

Another shortcoming of the case study is that the results of a single case study, no matter how dramatic, cannot be generalized to all people. Even if the shooters lashed out at their teachers and students in response to social rejection, other people who commit violent acts might not have experienced social rejection. For example, as you will learn in Chapter 14, numerous studies have shown that both biopsychological and psychosocial factors play a role in violence.

Survey

survey A set of questions related to a particular topic of interest administered to a sample of people through an interview or questionnaire.

When psychologists wish to collect information about behaviors, opinions, attitudes, life experiences, or personal characteristics of many people, they use a descriptive research method called the survey. A **survey** asks participants a series of questions about the topic of interest, such as product preferences or political opinions. Surveys deal with topics as varied as factors related to condom use (French & Holland, 2013), purchasing habits of students using school vending machines (Rose, 2011), occupational stress experienced by university professors (Slišković, Seršić, & Burić, 2011), and psychological symptoms related to video-game dependency (Rehbein, Kleimann, & Mödle, 2010). Surveys commonly are in the form of personal interviews or written questionnaires—sometimes presented over the Internet, as in product marketing surveys.

You probably have been asked to respond to several surveys in the past year, whether enclosed in the "You May Have Already Won!" offers that you receive in the mail or conducted by your student government association to get your views on campus policies.

34 Chapter 2 Psychology as a Science

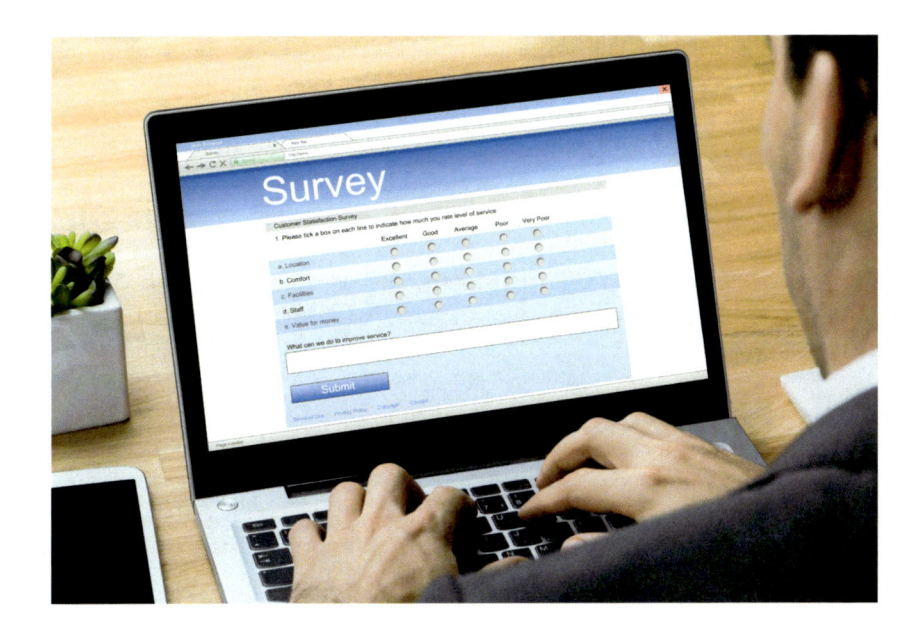

Surveys

The Internet is a fruitful area for conducting survey research. Some advantages for researchers are increased access to unique populations and saving time and money. Some disadvantages are the lack of random sampling due to the fact that Internet access might not be available to all potential participants.
Source: Andrey_Popov/Shutterstock.com.

The prevalence of surveys, and the annoyance they may induce, is not new. More than a century ago, William James (1890/1981) was so irritated by the seeming omnipresence of surveys that he called them "one of the pests of life." Today, the most ambitious of these "pests" is the U.S. census, which is conducted every 10 years. Others you might be familiar with include the Gallup public opinion polls, the Pew Research Center surveys, and Harris polls.

High-quality surveys use clearly worded questions that do not bias respondents to answer in a particular way. But surveys are limited by respondents' willingness to answer honestly and by social desirability—the tendency to give socially appropriate responses. You can imagine the potential effect of social desirability on responses to surveys on delicate topics such as child abuse, academic cheating, or sexual practices.

Still another issue to consider in surveys is the effect of sociocultural differences between test takers. You certainly are familiar with questionnaires that ask you to respond on a scale from, say, 1 to 7, with 1 meaning "strongly agree" and 7 meaning "strongly disagree." A cross-cultural study of high school students found that they differed in the degree to which they were willing to use the extreme points on scales like this. Students from Japan and Taiwan were more likely to use the midpoint than were students from Canada and the United States. This finding might be attributable to the greater tendency toward individualism in North American cultures and the greater tendency toward collectivism in East Asian cultures (Chen, Lee, & Stevenson, 1995). Consequently, survey researchers who use these kinds of scales should consider the cultural backgrounds of their participants when interpreting their findings.

Because of practical and financial constraints, surveys rarely include everyone of interest. Instead, researchers administer a survey to a **sample** of people who represent the target **population**. In conducting a survey at your school, you might interview a sample of 100 students. But for the results of your survey to be generalizable to the entire student population at your school, your sample must be representative of the student body in age, sex, and any other relevant characteristics. Generalizable results are best achieved by **random sampling**, which makes each member of the population equally likely to be included in the sample. Surveys that have used random sampling have, for example, increased our knowledge of to the relationship between pornography and men's acceptance of violence against women (Malamuth, Hald, & Koss, 2012) and the relationship between religious orientation and health-relevant behaviors in residents of the greater Syracuse, New York, region (Masters & Knestel, 2011). Failure to achieve a random sample of respondents might produce bias because those selected to participate might be different from those not selected to participate in regard to the topic of the survey (Menachemi, 2011).

sample A group of participants selected from a population.

population A group of individuals who share certain characteristics.

random sampling The selection of a sample from a population so that each member of the population has an equal chance of being included.

Chapter 2 Psychology as a Science

The need for a sample to be representative of its population was dramatically demonstrated in a notorious poll conducted by the *Literary Digest* during the 1936 U.S. presidential election. Until then, the *Literary Digest*'s presidential poll, based on millions of responses, had accurately predicted each presidential election from 1916 through 1932. In 1936, based on that poll, the editors predicted that Alf Landon, the Republican candidate, would easily defeat Franklin Roosevelt, the Democratic candidate. Yet, Roosevelt defeated Landon in a landslide.

What went wrong with the poll? Evidently, the participants included in the survey were a *biased sample,* not representative of those who voted. Many of the participants were selected from telephone directories or automobile registration lists in an era—the Great Depression—when telephones and automobiles were luxuries to many people, and those who had telephones or automobiles tended to be wealthier than those who did not. Because Republican candidates attracted wealthier voters than did Democratic candidates, people who had telephones or automobiles were more likely to favor the Republican (Landon) over the Democrat (Roosevelt). The previous polls did not suffer from this bias because economic differences among voters did not significantly affect their party allegiances until the 1936 election.

Psychological Testing

psychological test A formal sample of a person's behavior, whether written or performed.

A widely used descriptive research method is the **psychological test**, which is a formal sample of a person's behavior, whether written or performed. The advantage of good tests is that they help us make less-biased decisions about individuals. There are many psychological tests, including tests of interests, attitudes, abilities, creativity, intelligence, and personality. Psychological testing has a variety of uses, including helping to decide child custody in divorce cases (Hagan & Hagan, 2008), determining law-enforcement leadership potential (Miller, Watkins, & Webb, 2009), and assessing the relationship of environmental lead exposure to cognitive, perceptual, and motor performance (Kmiecik-Małecka, Małecki, Pawlas, Woźniakova, & Pawlas, 2009). As noted by Anne Anastasi (1985), who was an influential authority on psychological testing for several decades (Hogan, 2003), a good test reflects important principles of test construction: *standardization, reliability,* and *validity.*

standardization 1. A procedure ensuring that a test is administered and scored in a consistent manner.
2. A procedure for establishing test norms by giving a test to large samples of people who are representative of those for whom the test is designed.

norm A score, based on the test performances of large numbers of participants, that is used as a standard for assessing the performances of test takers.

There are two major aspects of **standardization**. The first ensures that the test will be administered and scored in a consistent manner. In giving a test, all test administrators must use the same instructions, the same time limits, and the same scoring system. If they do not, test takers' scores might misrepresent their individual characteristics. The second establishes **norms**, which are the standards used to compare the scores of test takers. Without norms, a score on an intelligence test would be a meaningless number. Norms are established by giving the test to samples of hundreds or thousands of people who are representative of the people for whom the test is designed. If a test is to be used in North America, samples might include representative proportions of homosexual and heterosexual men and women; people from all ethnic groups; lower-, middle-, and upper-class individuals; and urban, rural, and suburban dwellers. Standardized norms have been established for tests that measure things such as factors involved in developmental changes in attention in children (Vakil, Blachstein, Sheinman, & Greenstein, 2009) and intelligence test scores of American and Canadian children (Reddon, Whipplet, & Reddon, 2007).

The use of testing norms became popular in North America in the early 20th century, in part because of the introduction of the Stanford-Binet Intelligence Scale in 1916 by Lewis Terman. In one case, Terman (1918) used the scale's norms to prevent the execution of a young man with intellectual disability who had committed a heinous murder. Should he have been tried as an adult and, therefore, be held responsible for his actions? Or was he so intellectually limited that he should not have been held responsible? The man's score on the Stanford-Binet indicated that his mental age was equivalent to that of a 7-year-old child. Terman testified as a defense witness in opposition to the prosecution's expert witness, who claimed that the young man could perform various activities that only an adult could perform. But the expert witness presented no evidence, only his personal opinion. Terman convinced the jury, using his intelligence scale's norms as objective evidence, that the activities noted by the prosecution witness could easily be performed by a child of 7 or 8 years of age. The jury, convinced by Terman, accepted that the man suffered from an intellectual disability and ruled out the death penalty in his case (Dahlstrom, 1993). The importance of standardized testing for grade school placement, college admissions, and other purposes increased throughout the 20th century. Today, standardized testing to ensure that children are progressing satisfactorily in school is mandatory in the United States under the widely publicized No Child Left Behind legislation (Mattai, 2002).

An adequate psychological test also must be *reliable.* The **reliability** of a test is the degree to which it gives consistent results over time and across administrators. Suppose you took an IQ test and scored 105 (average) one month, 62 (intellectually disabled) the next month, and 138 (mentally gifted) the third month. Because your level of intelligence would not fluctuate that much in 3 months, you would argue that the test is unreliable. Likewise, you would doubt the reliability of a test that produced different results depending on who administered it.

One way to determine whether a test is reliable is to use the *test-retest method,* in which the same test is given to a group of people on two occasions. The greater the consistency of the scores on the tests from one occasion to the other, the higher the reliability of the test. Another way to determine a test's reliability is to determine its inter-rater reliability by assessing how strongly the results obtained by different administrators with the same test takers correlate with one another. The Preschool Behavioral and Emotional Rating Scale, for example, has both strong test-retest reliability and strong inter-rater reliability (Epstein & Synhorst, 2008).

A reliable test would be useless if it were not also valid. **Validity** is the extent to which a test measures what it is supposed to measure. An important kind of validity, *predictive validity,* indicates that the test accurately predicts behavior related to what the test is supposed to measure. A test of mechanical ability with predictive validity would accurately predict who would perform better as an automobile mechanic. The behavior or characteristic that is being predicted by a test, whether baking, automobile repair, or academic performance, is called a *criterion.*

One of the first studies of the predictive validity of a formal test was conducted by Francis Galton. He collected the civil service exam scores of hundreds of Englishmen who had taken the test in 1861 and compared them to their salaries 20 years later. He found that the exam had good predictive validity, in that those who had scored higher had higher salaries (the criterion) than did those who had scored lower. More recently, a large-scale review of the predictive validity of the Graduate Record Examination (GRE) found that it is a valid predictor of graduate school performance, as measured by first-year grade-point average (Kuncel, Hezlett, & Ones, 2001). That is, those who score high on the GRE tend to do better in graduate school than those who score low on it.

The sociocultural perspective has inspired greater interest in assessing the extent to which psychological tests, typically developed in North America, have cross-cultural reliability and validity. Tests that have shown cross-cultural reliability and validity include the Portuguese version of the Dental Anxiety Scale (Hu, Gorenstein, & Fuentes, 2007), the Japanese version of the Social Phobia Inventory (Nagata, Nakajima, Teo, Yamada, & Yoshimura, 2013), the Turkish version of the Beck Depression Inventory-II (Canel-Çınarbaş, Cui, & Lauridsen, 2011), and the Korean version of the Panic Disorder Severity Scale (Lee, Kim, & Yu, 2009). However, it is important to ensure that the research materials, samples, and participants' familiarity with the research task are culturally equivalent, or appropriate for the cultures under study (Allen & Walsh, 2000).

Archival Research

The largest potential source of knowledge from descriptive research is **archival research**, which examines collections of letters, manuscripts, tape recordings, video recordings, or

reliability The extent to which a test gives consistent results.

validity The extent to which a test measures what it is supposed to measure.

archival research The systematic examination of collections of letters, manuscripts, tape recordings, video recordings, or other records.

Archival Research

The Internet has become a fruitful area for archival research in addition to survey research. Since archival research does not permit causal statements, a researcher can ask questions such as "assuming that this hypothesis is true, in what ways is it manifested in the world?"

Source: Goritza/Shutterstock.com.

similar materials. The uses of archival research are virtually without limit. For example, archival research discussed in Chapter 3 attempts to answer the following controversial question: Do right-handed people live longer than left-handed people? An archival study of North American comic books found that their number of authoritarian themes increased during times of high perceived national social and economic threat and decreased during times of low perceived national social and economic threat (Peterson & Gerstein, 2005). And consider this question: Do women and men have different or similar physical fitness goals? In one archival study, researchers conducted Google Image searches for four consecutive years for the terms "burn fat" and "build muscle." They also recorded whether a woman, man, or no people appeared in the image. The researchers found that, regardless of the year, images of women were associated with the term "burn fat" and images of men were associated with the term "build muscle." This finding indicates that there are indeed gender differences in physical fitness goals (Salvatore & Maracek, 2010).

Archives also are valuable sources of historical information about psychology itself. Through the efforts of John Popplestone and Marion McPherson (Benjamin, 2002), the Archives of the History of American Psychology at The University of Akron has become the main repository of records related to the development of American psychology. The Archives provide insight into the major issues, pioneers, and landmark events in the history of American psychology (Popplestone & McPherson, 1976).

But note that, as is true of all descriptive research, archival research does not permit conclusive causal statements about its findings. For example, archival research cannot conclusively determine why women are more interested in burning fat than building muscle. Nor can archival research, by itself, explain why comic book themes become more authoritarian during times of perceived national social and threat.

Correlational Research

When psychologists want to predict changes in one variable based on changes in another, rather than simply describe something, they turn to **correlational research**. A **correlation** refers to the degree of relationship between two or more *variables*. A **variable** is an event, behavior, condition, or characteristic that has two or more values. Examples of possible variables include age, height, temperature, and intelligence.

correlational research Research that studies the degree of relationship between two or more variables.

correlation The degree of relationship between two or more variables.

variable An event, behavior, condition, or characteristic that has two or more values.

positive correlation A correlation in which variables tend to change values in the same direction.

negative correlation A correlation in which variables tend to change values in opposite directions.

causation An effect of one or more variables on another variable.

Kinds of Correlation

A **positive correlation** between two variables indicates that they tend to change values in the same direction. That is, as the first increases, the second increases, and as the first decreases, the second decreases. For example, as hours of studying increase, grade-point average tends to increase. A **negative correlation** between two variables indicates that they tend to change values in opposite directions. For example, as age increases in adulthood, visual acuity tends to decrease. Correlations range in magnitude from zero, meaning that there is no systematic relationship between the variables, to 1.00, meaning that there is a perfect relationship between them. Thus, a perfect positive correlation would be +1.00, and a perfect negative correlation would be −1.00.

Consider the relationship between obesity and exercise. The more people exercise, the less they tend to weigh. This relationship indicates a negative correlation between exercise and body weight: As one increases, the other decreases. But it is essential to realize that when two variables are correlated, one can be used to *predict* the other, but the first does not necessarily have a causal relationship with the other (Brigham, 1989). That is, *correlation* does not necessarily imply **causation**. Even though it is plausible that exercise causes lower body weight, it is also possible that the opposite is true: Lower body weight might cause people to exercise. Lighter people might exercise more because they find it less strenuous, less painful, and less embarrassing than heavier people do. Nonetheless, correlational research plays an important role when experimental research is either unethical or impractical to conduct, as is often true in certain settings, such as education (Thompson, Diamond, McWilliam, Snyder, & Snyder, 2005).

Causation versus Correlation

As another example of the need to distinguish between causation and correlation, consider the positive correlation between educational level and the likelihood of developing a deadly form of skin cancer called malignant melanoma ("Melanoma Risk and Socio-Economic Class," 1983). This positive correlation means that as educational level rises, the probability of getting the disease also rises. You would be correct in predicting that people who attend college will be more likely, later in life, to develop malignant melanoma than will people who never go beyond high school.

But does this finding mean that you should drop out of school today to avoid the disease? The answer is no, because the positive correlation between educational level and malignant melanoma does not necessarily mean that attending college causes the disease. Other factors common to people who attend college might cause them to develop the disease. Given that extensive exposure to the sun is a risk factor in malignant melanoma (Ivry, Ogle, & Shim, 2006), perhaps people who attend college increase their risk of malignant melanoma by exposing themselves to the sun more frequently than do those who have only a high school education. College students might be more likely to spend spring breaks in Florida, find summer jobs at beach resorts, or go on frequent Caribbean vacations after graduating, and finding higher-paying, full-time jobs. Instead of dropping out of college to avoid the disease, students might be wiser to spend less time in the sun.

Psychologists are careful not to confuse causation and correlation. They are aware that if two variables are positively correlated, the first might cause changes in the second, the second might cause changes in the first, or another variable might cause changes in both. Because of the difficulty in distinguishing causal relationships from mere correlational ones, correlational research has stimulated controversies in important areas of research. Does televised violence cause real-life aggression? A review of research on that question found a significant positive correlation between watching televised violence and exhibiting aggressive behavior. But this correlation does not indicate that televised violence *causes* aggressive behavior (Freedman, 1984). Perhaps people who are aggressive for other reasons simply prefer to watch violent television programs. Nonetheless, as discussed in Chapter 7, there have been a number of experimental studies that do support a causal link between media violence and viewer aggression (Bushman & Anderson, 2001).

Experimental Research

The research methods discussed so far do not enable you to discover causal relationships between variables. Even when there is a strong correlation between variables, you cannot presume a causal relationship between them. To determine whether there is a causal relationship between variables, scientists use the **experimental method**. Psychologists have relied on the experimental method ever since the discipline finally completed its separation from philosophy in the late 19th century (Hatfield, 2002).

Experimental Method

Like the components of correlational research, the components of an experiment are called variables. Every experiment includes at least one *independent variable* and one *dependent variable*. The **independent variable** is manipulated by experimenters, which means that they determine its values before the experiment begins. The **dependent variable** shows any effects of the independent variable. In terms of cause-and-effect relationships, the independent variable would be the *cause* and changes in the dependent variable would be the *effect*. Thus, in a hypothetical experiment on the effects of drinking on driving, the independent variable of alcohol intake would be the cause of changes in the dependent variable of, say, steering accuracy.

The simplest experiment uses one independent variable with two values (an experimental condition and a control condition) and one dependent variable. A group of participants, the **experimental group**, is exposed to the experimental condition, and a second

Causation versus Correlation

People who exercise regularly tend to be thinner than those who do not. But is exercise the cause of thin physiques? Perhaps not. Thin people might simply be more likely to exercise than people who are overweight. So, a negative correlation between exercise and body weight does not imply that exercise causes weight loss. Only experimental research can determine whether there is such a causal relationship.
Source: Flashon Studio/Shutterstock.com.

experimental method Research that manipulates one or more variables, while controlling other factors, to determine the effects on one or more other variables.

independent variable A variable manipulated by the experimenter to determine its effect on another, dependent, variable.

dependent variable A variable showing the effect of the independent variable.

experimental group Participants in an experiment who are exposed to the experimental condition of interest.

Chapter 2 Psychology as a Science   39

control group The participants in an experiment who are not exposed to the experimental condition of interest.

field experiment An experiment that is conducted in real life as opposed to laboratory settings.

placebo An inactive substance that might induce some of the effects of the drug for which it has been substituted.

group of participants, the **control group**, is exposed to the control condition. The control condition is often simply the absence of the experimental condition. For example, the experimental condition might be exposure to a particular advertisement, and the control condition might be nonexposure to the advertisement. The dependent variable might be the number of sales of the advertised product. The control group provides a standard of comparison for the experimental group. If you failed to include a control group in the suggested experiment on the effects of advertising, you would be unable to determine whether the advertising accounted for changes in the volume of sales.

This example illustrates the **field experiment**, which is conducted in real life, as opposed to laboratory settings. Another example of a field experiment is one in which salesclerks had their moods altered by how alleged shoppers acted (that is, after interacting with a "shopper" trained by the experimenter—also called a *confederate*—which induced a positive or negative mood in the salesclerk). The salesclerks were then asked by another alleged shopper for help finding an item that the department store did not carry. The study found that the manipulation affected the extent to which inexperienced employees helped, but not the extent to which experienced employees helped. Positive mood induction led to more helping and negative mood induction led to less helping only among inexperienced salesclerks (Forgas, Dunn, & Granland, 2008).

To appreciate the nature of the experimental method, imagine you are a psychologist interested in conducting an experiment on the effect of melatonin on nightly sleep duration. A basic experiment on this topic is illustrated in Table 2-2. Assume that introductory psychology students volunteer to be participants in the study. Members of the experimental group receive the same dose of melatonin nightly for 10 weeks, while members of the control group receive a **placebo**, which has no demonstrated effect on sleep. As the experimenter, you would try to keep constant all other factors that might affect the two groups. By treating both groups the same except for the condition to which the experimental group is exposed, you would be able to conclude that any significant difference in average sleep duration between the experimental group and the control group was probably caused by the experimental group's receiving doses of melatonin. Without the use of a control group, you would have no standard of comparison and would be less secure in reaching that conclusion.

In the experiment on melatonin and nightly sleep duration, the independent variable (drug condition) has two values: melatonin and placebo. The experimenter is interested in the effect of the independent variable on the dependent variable. The dependent variable in this case is nightly sleep duration, with many possible values: 6 hours and 2 minutes, 7 hours and 48 minutes, and so on.

As an experimenter, you would try to hold constant all factors other than the independent variable, so that the effects of those factors are not confused with the effect of the independent variable. In the melatonin experiment, you would not want differences between the experimental group and the control group in diet, drugs, and other relevant factors to cause changes in the dependent variable that you would mistakenly attribute to the independent variable.

The effectiveness of melatonin in treating insomnia was, in fact, supported by a double-blind, placebo study of children with insomnia. Forty children, ages 6 to 12 years, with chronic difficulty falling asleep were randomly assigned to groups that received doses of

TABLE 2-2 A Basic Experimental Research Design

Group	Independent Variable	Dependent Variable
(Randomly assigned)	(Drug condition)	(Sleep)
Experimental group	Take melatonin	Hours of sleep
Control group	Take placebo	Hours of sleep

melatonin or a placebo at 6 p.m. for four weeks. Thus, drug condition was the independent variable. The dependent variables included the time when the children turned the lights off in their bedrooms, the time when they fell asleep, and how long they slept. Those who received a placebo showed no significant change on these variables. In contrast, those who received doses of melatonin turned their lights off an average of 34 minutes earlier, fell asleep an average of 75 minutes earlier, and slept an average of 41 minutes longer (Smits, Nagtegaal, van der Heijden, & Coenen, 2001). Placebo control groups are essential in research on drug therapy, as in research on the effectiveness of drugs for treating depression (Hughes, Gabay, Funnel, & Dowrick, 2012) or anxiety (Bidzan, Mahableshwarkar, Jacobsen, Yan, & Sheehan, 2012).

Internal Validity

An experimenter must do more than simply manipulate an independent variable and record changes in a dependent variable. The experimenter must also ensure the **internal validity** of the experiment by *controlling* any extraneous factors whose effects on the dependent variable might be confused with those of the independent variable (Christ, 2007) in order to show a cause-and-effect relationship. Such extraneous factors are called **confounding variables**, because their effects are confused, or *confounded*, with those of the independent variable. A confounding variable might be associated with the experimental situation, participants, or experimenters involved in an experiment.

Situational Variables In carrying out the procedure in the melatonin experiment, you would not want any confounding variables to affect nightly sleep duration. You would want the participants to be treated the same, except that those in the experimental group would receive the same dose of melatonin nightly over a 10-week period. But suppose that some participants in the experimental group decided to take sleeping pills, to exercise more, or to practice meditation. If, at the end of the study, the experimental group had a longer nightly sleep duration than the control group, the results might be attributable not to the melatonin but to confounding variables—that is, differences between the groups in the extent to which they used sleeping pills, exercised, or practiced meditation.

As an example of the importance of controlling potential confounding procedural variables, consider what happened when the Pepsi-Cola company conducted a "Pepsi Challenge" taste test, an example of *consumer psychology* ("Coke-Pepsi Slugfest," 1976). Coca-Cola drinkers were asked to taste each of two unidentified cola drinks and state their preference. The drinks were Coca-Cola and Pepsi-Cola. The brand of cola was the independent variable, and the preference was the dependent variable. To keep the participants from knowing which cola they were tasting, they were given Pepsi-Cola in a cup labeled M and Coca-Cola in a cup labeled Q. To the delight of Pepsi-Cola stockholders, most of the participants preferred Pepsi-Cola.

The Pepsi-Cola company proudly—and loudly—advertised this finding as evidence that even Coca-Cola drinkers preferred Pepsi-Cola. But knowing the pitfalls of experimentation, the Coca-Cola company replicated the experiment, this time filling both cups with Coca-Cola. Most of the participants still preferred the cola in the cup labeled M. Evidently, the Pepsi Challenge had not demonstrated that Coca-Cola drinkers preferred Pepsi-Cola. It had demonstrated only that Coca-Cola drinkers preferred the letter M to the letter Q. The effect of the letters on the dependent variable (the taste preference) had been confounded with that of the independent variable (the kind of cola).

If you were asked to design a more scientifically sound Coke-Pepsi taste challenge, how would you control the effect of the letter on the cup? Pause to think about this question before reading on. One way to control it would be to use cups without letters. Of course, the experimenter would have to keep track of which cup contained Coke and which contained Pepsi. A second way to control the effect of the letter would be to label each of the colas M on half of the taste trials and Q on the other half. Thus, two ways to control potential confounding procedural variables are to eliminate them or to ensure that they affect all conditions equally.

internal validity The extent to which changes in a dependent variable can be attributed to one or more independent variables rather than to a confounding variable.

confounding variable A variable whose unwanted effect on the dependent variable might be confused with that of the independent variable.

Consumer Psychology: Example of a Blind Taste Test

How could you control for the effect of labeling each of the three products?
Source: John T Takai/Shutterstock.com.

Chapter 2 Psychology as a Science   41

Participant Variables Experimenters must likewise control potential confounding participant variables that might produce effects that would be confused with those of the independent variable. Suppose that in the melatonin experiment the participants in the experimental group initially differed from the participants in the control group on several variables, including their nightly sleep duration, psychoactive drug habits, and daily exercise practices. These differences might carry over into the experiment, affecting the participants' nightly sleep duration during the course of the study and giving the false impression that the independent variable (melatonin versus no melatonin) caused a significant difference on the dependent variable (nightly sleep duration) between the two groups.

Experimenters increase the chance that the experimental group and the control group will be initially equivalent on as many participant variables as possible by relying on *random assignment* of participants to groups (Enders, Laurenceau, & Stuetzle, 2006). In **random assignment**, participants are as likely to be assigned to one group as to another. Given a sufficiently large number of participants, random assignment will make the two groups initially equivalent on many, though not necessarily all, relevant participant variables.

After randomly assigning participants to the experimental group and the control group, you still would have to control other participant variables. One of the most important of these is **participant bias**, the tendency of people who know they are participants in a study to behave differently than they normally do. As in the case of naturalistic observation, you might choose to be unobtrusive, exposing people to the experimental condition without their being aware of it. If this were impossible, you might choose to misinform the participants about the true purpose of the study. (The ethical issues involved in using deception are discussed in the section entitled "Ethics of Psychological Research.") Placebos are used in conjunction with random assignment so that participants do not succumb to demand characteristics of the experimental situation, in which knowledge of the experimental hypothesis leads them to perform in a manner that supports it—even more so when they like the experimenter (Nichols & Maner, 2008).

Experimenter Variables Experimenters must control not only potential confounding variables associated with the research procedure or the research participants but also potential confounding variables associated with themselves. *Experimenter effects* on dependent variables can be caused by the experimenter's personal qualities, actions, and treatment of data. Experimenter effects have been studied most extensively by Robert Rosenthal and his colleagues, who have demonstrated them in many studies since the early 1960s. Rosenthal has found that the experimenter's personal qualities—including sex, attire, and attractiveness—can affect participants' behavior (Barnes & Rosenthal, 1985).

Also of concern is the effect of the experimenter's actions on the recording of data or on the participants' behavior, as in the **experimenter bias effect**. This occurs when the results are affected by the experimenter's expectancy about the outcome of a study, which is expressed through her or his unintentional actions. The tendency of participants to behave in accordance with experimenter expectancy is called *self-fulfilling prophecy*. Actions that might promote self-fulfilling prophecy include facial expressions (perhaps smiling at participants in one group and frowning at those in another), mannerisms (perhaps shaking hands with participants in one group but not with those in another), or tone of voice (perhaps speaking in an animated voice to participants in one group and speaking in a monotone to those in another). Self-fulfilling prophecy is especially important to control in studies of psychotherapy, because therapist expectancies, rather than therapy itself, might affect the outcome of therapy (Harris, 1994).

In a study of self-fulfilling prophecy that became widely publicized, Rosenthal found that elementary school teachers' expectancies for the performance of their students affected how well the children performed. Students whose teachers were led to believe they were fast learners performed better than did students whose teachers were led to believe they were slow learners. Yet, the students did not differ in their initial ability (Rosenthal & Jacobson, 1968). This finding became known as the *Pygmalion effect*, after the story in

---

random assignment The assignment of participants to experimental and control conditions so that each participant is as likely to be assigned to one condition as to another.

participant bias The tendency of people who know they are participants in a study to behave differently than they normally would.

experimenter bias effect The tendency of experimenters to let their expectancies alter the way they treat their participants.

which an uneducated woman improves herself because of her mentor's faith in her. The Pygmalion effect also can occur between parents and children, therapists and patients, and employers and workers (McNatt, 2000). The classic research study discussed in "The Research Process" box demonstrated that experimenter expectancies can even affect the behavior of animal subjects.

How might experimenter bias affect the results of the hypothetical melatonin experiment? The experimenter might act more friendly and encourage the participants in the experimental group, perhaps motivating them to sleep better than they would have otherwise. Participants with a higher need for social approval would be especially susceptible to experimenter expectancy effects such as this special treatment (Hazelrigg, Cooper, & Strathman, 1991). One way to control experimenter bias would be to have those people who interact with the participants be unaware of the research hypothesis, eliminating the influence of the experimenter's expectancies on the participants' performance.

At times, both participant bias and experimenter bias might become confounding variables. This possibility might prompt experimenters to use the **double-blind technique**, in which neither the experimenter nor the participants know the conditions to which the participants have been assigned. This technique is common in studies of the effectiveness of drug treatments for psychological disorders. Consider a study on the effectiveness of nicotine-replacement therapy for smoking cessation. In a double-blind study, experimental groups received either nicotine gum or a nicotine inhaler, while the control group received a placebo. Participants in the nicotine replacement condition were significantly more likely to smoke fewer cigarettes or stop smoking altogether than the participants in the placebo condition (Kralikova, Kozak, Rasmussen, Gustavsson, & Le Houezec, 2009). In a double-blind melatonin experiment, instead of giving one group melatonin and the other nothing, it would be wise to give one group melatonin and the other a placebo. Neither the experimenter nor the participants would know which participants received the melatonin and which received the placebo.

Self-Fulfilling Prophecy
Can teacher expectations affect student performance?
Source: Andresr/Shutterstock.com.

double-blind technique A procedure that controls experimenter bias and participant bias by preventing experimenters and participants from knowing which participants have been assigned to particular conditions.

External Validity

Though experimenters are chiefly concerned with matters of internal validity, they also are concerned with matters of **external validity**—the extent to which they can generalize their research findings to other populations, settings, and procedures. Experiments may have strong internal validity yet have inadequate external validity. Researchers in the field of alcoholism treatment, for example, note that treatment studies with excellent internal validity often bear little relationship to what is actually done in normal clinical practice, thus potentially limiting their external validity (Sterling, 2002). In other words, the circumstances under which treatment studies are carried out often bear little relationship to the actual treatment provided by clinicians in different treatment settings and with different clients. Similarly, laboratory experiments on consumer behavior often have strong internal validity but may lack external validity in regard to consumer behavior in everyday life, making those who run marketing campaigns unsure of whether consumer behavior that occurs in the laboratory will occur in everyday life too (Winer, 1999). Likewise, the external validity of experiments on automobile driving behavior using laboratory driving simulators depends on the simulation being relevant to real-life driving behavior (Araújo, 2007).

Because psychology relies heavily on college students as research participants, external validity is an important consideration (Blanton & Jaccard, 2008). One must ask if college students represent the sample population of what is being studied. In addition, those who volunteer to participate in experiments may differ in important characteristics from those who choose not participate, possibly weakening the external validity of experimental findings—as in experiments on smoking cessation programs aimed at finding techniques to use with smokers in general (Graham et al., 2008). Generalizability is enhanced when the characteristics of the sample used in the experiment are similar to those of the population it represents (Hughes & Callas, 2010).

external validity The extent to which the results of a research study can be generalized to other people, animals, or settings.

Chapter 2 Psychology as a Science

The Research Process

Can Experimenter Expectancies Affect the Behavior of Laboratory Rats?

Rationale

Robert Rosenthal noted that in the early 20th century, Ivan Pavlov had found that each succeeding generation of his animal subjects learned tasks faster than the preceding one. At first, Pavlov presumed that this improvement supported the (since-discredited) notion of the inheritance of acquired characteristics. But he eventually came to believe that the animals' improvement was caused by changes in the way in which his experimenters treated them. Rosenthal decided to determine whether experimenter expectancies could likewise affect the performance of laboratory animals.

Method

Rosenthal and his colleague Kermit Fode had 12 students act as experimenters in a study of maze learning in rats conducted at Harvard University (Rosenthal & Fode, 1963). Six of the students were told that their rats were specially bred to be "maze bright," and six were told that their rats were specially bred to be "maze dull." In reality, the rats did not differ in their inborn maze-learning potential. Each student was given five albino rats to run in a T-shaped maze, with one horizontal arm of the maze painted white and the other painted gray. The rats received a food reward whenever they entered into the gray arm. The arms were interchanged on various trials so that the rats had to learn to respond to the color gray rather than to the direction left or right. The students ran the rats 10 times a day for five days and recorded how long it took them to reach the food.

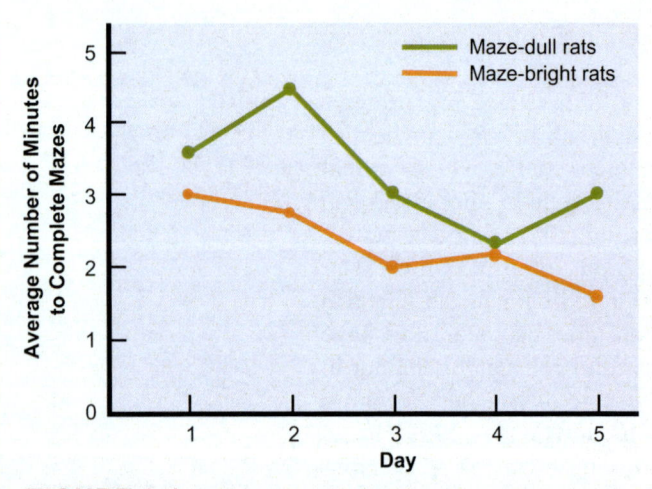

Source: sextoacto/Shutterstock.com.

Results and Discussion

As shown in Figure 2-1, the results indicated the apparent influence of experimenter expectancy: On average, the "maze-bright" rats ran mazes faster than the "maze-dull" rats did. Because there was no evidence of cheating or misrecording of data by the students, the researchers attributed the results to experimenter expectancy. The students' expectancies apparently influenced the manner in which they trained or handled the rats, somehow leading the rats to perform in accordance with the expectancies. For example, those who trained "maze-bright" rats reported handling them more, and more gently, than did those who trained "maze-dull" rats. Confidence in the experimenter expectancy effect with animal subjects was supported in a replication study by a different researcher, using different rats, and involving a different learning task (Elkins, 1987). These findings indicate that those responsible for handling animals during an experiment should, if possible, be kept unaware of any presumed differences among the animals.

FIGURE 2-1 Experimenter Bias

The graph shows the results of the Rosenthal and Fode (1963) experiment, which found that allegedly maze-bright rats ran mazes faster than allegedly maze-dull rats did, depending on the experimenters' expectations.

Source: Data from Rosenthal and Fode (1963), "The Effect of Experimenter Bias on the Performance of the Albino Rat" in *Behavioral Science, 8,* 183–189.

Moreover, as stressed by Stanley Sue (1999) and other psychologists who favor the sociocultural perspective, the results of a research study done in one culture will not necessarily be generalizable to another culture or ethnic group. Researchers must identify the specific populations to which their research findings may be applied. An archival study of 14 psychology journals over a five-year period found that only 61 percent of 2,536 articles related to applied psychology reported participants' ethnicity. Of those that did, the ethnic breakdown of the samples was generally representative of the population estimates provided by the U.S. Census Bureau. However, Latinos—for whom English may be a second language—were underrepresented. The generalizability of research findings from those studies to non-English speakers is limited (Case & Smith, 2000).

But cross-cultural replications of research sometimes do demonstrate the possible universality of findings. Research has found cross-cultural similarities in coping strategies employed by Canadian and New Zealand women with a history of child sexual abuse (Barker-Collo, Read, & Cowie, 2012). Another study found that the same sociocultural factors that were associated with body self-image and eating disorders in American women also were found in Japanese women (Yamamiya, Shroff, & Thompson, 2008). And, researchers have found that marital discord also is associated with depression in both American and Brazilian women (Hollist, Miller, Falceto, & Fernandes, 2007).

Replication to assess external validity is not only important in experimental research but in other kinds of research as well. A national American survey found that about the same percentage of people had obsessions or compulsions as several previous national surveys had found (Ruscio, Stein, Chiu, & Kessler, 2010). A study that used psychological testing of self-esteem replicated prior research by showing that a major factor in overall self-esteem is one's perceived appraisal by significant others such as parents, teachers, and friends (Stephan & Maiano, 2007). And a study on the effectiveness of a high school suicide prevention program found results similar to that found by a previous study in regard to changing undesirable attitudes toward suicide and in decreasing reluctance to seek mental health treatment (Ciffone, 2007).

Another problem affecting external validity is the use of volunteer participants. People who volunteer to take part in a given experiment might differ from people who fail to, possibly limiting the generalizability of the research findings. In a study using volunteer participants, male and female undergraduates were given the choice of participating in either a study in which they would be given a sexual interview or a study in which they would watch an explicit sexual video. When compared with students who refused to volunteer, students who volunteered for either of the studies were more sexually experienced, held less traditional sexual attitudes, and scored higher on measures of sexual esteem and sexual sensation seeking. These findings indicate that people who participate in sexual research might not be representative of people in general, limiting the confidence with which sex researchers can generalize their findings (Wiederman, 1999).

Of course, differences between volunteers and nonvolunteers do not automatically mean that the results lack external validity. The best way to determine whether the results of research studies do in fact have external validity is to replicate them. Replication also enables researchers to determine whether the results of laboratory studies will generalize to the world outside the laboratory. Most replications are approximate; they rarely use the same setting, participants, or procedures. For example, confidence in the Pygmalion effect was strengthened when it was replicated by different researchers, using different teachers, with different students, in a different school (Meichenbaum, Bowers, & Ross, 1969). The ideal would be to replicate studies systematically several times, varying one aspect of the study each time (Hendrick, 1990). Thus, you would be more confident in your ability to generalize the findings of the melatonin experiment if people with insomnia, of a variety of ages, in several different cultures, succeeded in sleeping longer after habitually taking melatonin before bedtime.

Now that you have been introduced to the descriptive, correlational, and experimental methods of research, you should be able to recognize them as you read about research studies described in later chapters. As you read particular studies, try to determine which kind of method was used as well as its possible strengths and weaknesses—most notably, any potential confounding variables and any limitations on the generalizability of the research findings. You now are ready to learn how psychologists analyze the data generated by their research methods.

> ### Section Review: Methods of Psychological Research
> 1. Why is it important to use unbiased samples in surveys?
> 2. What is validity in psychological testing?
> 3. What is an independent variable?
> 4. What is internal validity?

Statistical Analysis of Research Data

How would you make sense out of the data generated by the hypothetical melatonin experiment? In analyzing the data, you would have to do more than simply state that Ann Lee slept 9.1 hours, Steve White slept 7.8 hours, Sally Ramirez slept 8.2 hours, and so on. You would have to identify overall patterns in the data and whether the data support the research hypothesis that inspired the experiment.

As mentioned earlier, to make sense out of their data, psychologists rely on statistics. The term *statistics* was originally used to refer to the practice of recording quantitative political and economic information about European nation-states (Cowles, 1989). During the 20th century, the use of statistics to analyze research data became increasingly more prevalent in articles published in psychology journals (Parker, 1990). Psychologists use *descriptive statistics* to summarize data, *correlational statistics* to determine relationships between variables, and *inferential statistics* to test their experimental research hypotheses. Appendix C (available in the Online Edition) presents an expanded discussion of statistics and their calculation.

Descriptive Statistics

descriptive statistics Statistics that summarize research data.

You would summarize your data by using **descriptive statistics**. An early champion of the use of descriptive statistics was Florence Nightingale (1820–1910), one of the founders of modern nursing. She urged that hospitals keep medical records on their patients. As a result, she demonstrated statistically that British soldiers during times of war were more likely to die from disease and unsanitary conditions than from combat. She also was a pioneer in the use of graphs to support her conclusions. Her work led to reforms in nursing and medicine and to her being made a fellow of the Royal Statistical Society and an honorary member of the American Statistical Association (Viney, 1993). Descriptive statistics include *measures of central tendency* and *measures of variability*.

Measures of Central Tendency

measure of central tendency A statistic that represents the "typical" score in a set of scores.

mode The score that occurs most frequently in a set of scores.

median The middle score in a set of scores that have been ordered from lowest to highest.

A **measure of central tendency** is a single number used to represent a set of scores. The measures of central tendency include the *mode,* the *median,* and the *mean.* Psychological research uses the mode least often, the median somewhat more often, and the mean most often.

The **mode** is the most frequent score in a set of scores. As shown in Table 2-3, in the melatonin experiment the mode for the experimental group is 8.6 hours and the mode for the control group is 8.9 hours. The **median** is the middle score in a set of scores that have been arranged in numerical order. Thus, in the melatonin experiment the median score for each group is the fifth score after the scores are put in rank order. The median for the

46 Chapter 2 Psychology as a Science

TABLE 2-3 Descriptive Statistics from a Hypothetical Experiment on the Effect of Melatonin on Average Nightly Sleep Duration

Experimental Group (Melatonin)				**Control Group (No Melatonin)**			
Participant	Duration	d	d^2	Participant	Duration	d	d^2
1	9.1	0.2	0.04	1	7.4	−0.5	0.25
2	8.6	−0.3	0.09	2	8.2	0.3	0.09
3	8.6	−0.3	0.09	3	9.5	1.6	2.56
4	8.8	−0.1	0.01	4	8.9	1.0	1.00
5	7.8	−1.1	1.21	5	6.7	−1.2	1.44
6	9.9	1.0	1.00	6	8.9	1.0	1.00
7	8.6	−0.3	0.09	7	7.5	−0.4	0.16
8	9.7	0.8	0.64	8	6.2	−1.7	2.89
9	9.0	0.1	0.01	9	7.8	−0.1	0.01
	Sum = 80.1		Sum = 3.18		Sum = 71.1		Sum = 9.40

Mode = 8.6 hours

Median = 8.8 hours

Mean = $\frac{80.1}{9}$ = 8.9 hours

Range = 9.9 − 7.8 = 2.1 hours

Variance = $\frac{\text{sum of } d^2}{\text{no. of participants}} = \frac{3.18}{9} = 0.35$

Standard deviation = $\sqrt{\text{Variance}}$
= $\sqrt{0.35}$
= 0.59 hours

Mode = 8.9 hours

Median = 7.8 hours

Mean = $\frac{71.1}{9}$ = 7.9 hours

Range = 9.5 − 6.2 = 3.3 hours

Variance = $\frac{\text{sum of } d^2}{\text{no. of participants}} = \frac{9.40}{9} = 01.04$

Standard deviation = $\sqrt{\text{Variance}}$
= $\sqrt{1.04}$
= 1.02 hours

Note: d = deviation from the mean.

experimental group is 8.8 hours and the median for the control group is 7.8 hours. You are most familiar with the **mean**, which is the arithmetic average of a set of scores. You use the mean when you calculate your exam average, batting average, or average gas mileage. In the melatonin experiment, the mean for the experimental group is 8.9 hours and the mean for the control group is 7.9 hours.

mean The arithmetic average of a set of scores.

One of the problems in the use of measures of central tendency is that they can be used selectively to create misleading impressions. Suppose you had the following psychology exam scores: 23, 23, 67, 68, 69, 70, 91. The mode (the most frequent score) would be 23, the median (the middle score) would be 68, and the mean (the average score) would be 58.7. In this case, you would prefer the median as representative of your performance. But what if you had the following scores: 23, 67, 68, 69, 70, 91, 91? The mode would be 91, the median would be 69, and the mean would be 68.43. In that case, you would prefer the mode as representative of your performance.

Product advertisers, government agencies, and political parties also are prone to this selective use of measures of central tendency, as well as other statistics, to support their claims. But the use of statistics to mislead is not new. Its prevalence in the 19th century prompted British Prime Minister Benjamin Disraeli to declare, "There are three kinds of

Chapter 2 Psychology as a Science

lies: lies, damned lies, and statistics." Even a basic understanding of statistics will make you less likely to be fooled by claims based on their misleading use.

Measures of Variability

measure of variability A statistic describing the degree of dispersion in a set of scores.

range A statistic representing the difference between the highest and lowest scores in a set of scores.

To represent a distribution of scores, psychologists do more than report a measure of central tendency. They also report a **measure of variability**, which describes the degree of dispersion of the scores. That is, do the scores tend to bunch together, or are they scattered? Commonly used measures of variability include the range and the standard deviation. The **range** is the difference between the highest and the lowest score in a set of scores. In Table 2-3 the range of the experimental group is 9.9 – 7.8 = 2.1 hours, and the range of the control group is 9.5 – 6.2 = 3.3 hours. But the range can be misleading because one extreme score can create a false impression. Suppose that a friend conducts a similar experiment and reports that the range of sleep duration among the 15 participants in his experimental group is 4 hours, with the longest duration being 9.3 hours and the shortest duration being 5.3 hours. You might conclude that there was a great deal of variability in the distribution of scores. But what if he then reported that only one participant slept less than 9.1 hours? Obviously, the scores would bunch together at the high end, making the variability of scores much less than you had presumed.

standard deviation A statistic representing the degree of dispersion of a set of scores around their mean.

variance A measure based on the average deviation of a set of scores from their group mean.

Because of their need to employ more meaningful measures of variability than the range, psychologists prefer to use the standard deviation. The **standard deviation** represents the degree of dispersion of scores around their mean and is the square root of a measure of variability called the *variance*. The **variance** is a measure based on the average deviation of a set of scores from their group mean. Table 2-3 shows that the standard deviation of the experimental group is 0.59 hours, whereas the standard deviation of the control group is 1.02 hours. Thus, the distribution of scores in the experimental group has a larger mean, but the distribution of scores in the control group has a larger standard deviation.

Correlational Statistics

coefficient of correlation A statistic that assesses the degree of association between two or more variables.

If you were interested in predicting one set of scores from another, you would use a measure of correlation. The concept of correlation was put forth in 1888 by Francis Galton, who wanted a way to represent the relationship between parents and offspring on factors, such as intelligence, presumed to be affected by heredity. Whereas the mean and standard deviation are useful in describing individual sets of scores, a statistic called the coefficient of correlation is useful in quantifying the degree of association between two or more sets of scores. The **coefficient of correlation** was devised by the English mathematician Karl Pearson (1851–1926) and is often called *Pearson's r* (with the *r* standing for "regression," another name for correlation).

As you learned earlier, a correlation can be positive or negative and can range from zero to +1.00 or –1.00. In a *positive correlation* between two sets of scores, relatively high scores on one set are associated with relatively high scores on the other, and relatively low scores on one set are associated with relatively low scores on the other (Branch, 1990). For example, there is a positive correlation between height and weight and between high school and college grade-point averages. In a *negative correlation* between two sets of scores, relatively high scores on one set are associated with relatively low scores on the other. For example, there is a negative correlation between driving speed and gas mileage. A *zero correlation* indicates that there is no relationship between one set of scores and another. You would find an approximately zero correlation between the intelligence levels of two groups of randomly selected strangers. The types of correlations are illustrated graphically in Figure 2-2.

The higher the correlation between two variables, the more accurately the scores on one variable will predict the scores on the other. For example, suppose you found a correlation of .83 between the number of milligrams of melatonin that people take each night and their nightly sleep duration. This strong correlation would make you fairly confident

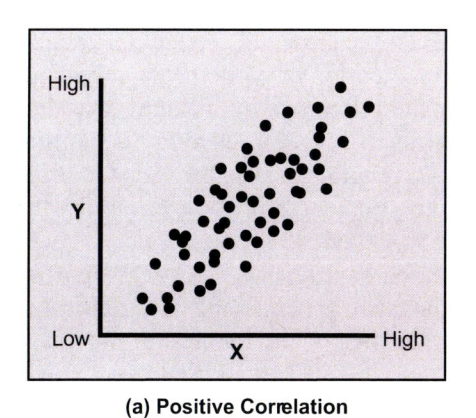

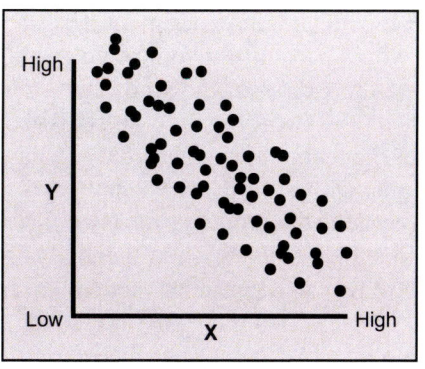

FIGURE 2-2
Correlations

(a) In a *positive correlation*, scores on the variables increase and decrease together. An example is the relationship between SAT verbal scores and college grade-point average. (b) In a *negative correlation*, scores on one variable increase as scores on another variable decrease. An example is the relationship between age and nightly sleep. (c) In a *zero correlation*, scores on one variable are unrelated to scores on another. A possible example is the relationship between the number of times people brush their teeth each day and the number of houseplants they have to water.

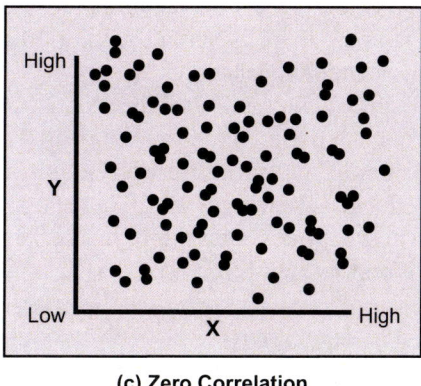

(a) Positive Correlation

(b) Negative Correlation

(c) Zero Correlation

in predicting that as the dose of melatonin increases, the average nightly duration of sleep would increase. If, instead, you found a weak correlation of .17, you would have less confidence in making that prediction.

Inferential Statistics

In the melatonin experiment, the experimental group had a longer average nightly sleep duration than the control group. But is the difference in average nightly sleep duration between the two groups large enough for you to conclude with confidence that melatonin was responsible for the difference? Perhaps the difference happened by chance—that is, because of a host of random factors unrelated to melatonin. To determine whether the independent variable, rather than chance factors, caused the changes in the dependent variable, psychologists use **inferential statistics**. By permitting psychologists to determine the causes of events, inferential statistics help them achieve the goal of explanation. Inferential statistics are "inferential" because they enable experimenters to make inferences from the samples used in their experiment to the populations of individuals they represent.

inferential statistics Statistics used to determine whether changes in a dependent variable are caused by an independent variable.

Statistical Significance

If there is a low probability that the difference between groups on the dependent variable is attributable to chance (that is, to random factors), the difference is statistically significant and is attributed to the independent variable. The concept of **statistical significance** was first put forth by the English mathematician Ronald Fisher (1890–1962) when he sought a way to test a noblewoman's claim that she could tell whether tea or milk had been added to her cup first (Tankard, 1984). Though he never carried out the demonstration, he proposed presenting her with a series of cups in which tea was sometimes added first and milk was sometimes added first. He assumed that if she could report the correct order at a much greater than chance level, her claim would be verified. To rule out simple lucky guessing, she would have to be correct significantly more than 50 percent of the time—the chance level of guessing between two events.

statistical significance A low probability (usually less than 5 percent) that the results of a research study are due to chance factors rather than to the independent variable.

Chapter 2 Psychology as a Science

In the melatonin experiment described previously, you would expect that chance factors would account for some changes in the sleep duration of participants in both groups during the course of the study. As a result, for the difference in average sleep duration between the two groups to be statistically significant, it would have to be significantly larger than would be expected by chance alone. Psychologists usually accept a difference as statistically significant when there is less than a 5 percent (5 in 100) probability that the difference is the product of chance factors—the so-called .05 level.

Nonetheless, even when the analysis of research data reveals statistical significance, the best way to determine whether research findings are generalizable is to replicate them (Falk, 1998). Two real experiments did, in fact, "replicate" the findings of the imaginary melatonin experiment described earlier. These experiments, which used the double-blind technique, found that participants who took melatonin slept longer than did participants who took the placebo—regardless of whether the participants were normal sleepers (Waldhauser, Saletu, & Trinchard, 1990) or insomnia sufferers (MacFarlane, Cleghorn, Brown, & Streiner, 1991). Thus, there is scientific support for the claims made in the *Newsweek* cover story that opened this chapter.

Another issue is the need to distinguish between statistical significance and clinical significance. Participants in an experimental group may differ on the target measure from participants in the control group, but the difference might not be large enough to produce meaningful clinical effects. Likewise, a small, but statistically significant difference between the experimental and control group might not be large enough to have practical significance outside the laboratory (Wijk, 2009).

Meta-analysis

meta-analysis A technique that combines the results of many similar studies to determine the effect size of a particular kind of independent variable.

Still another approach to assessing generalizability is to use the relatively new statistical technique called **meta-analysis**. Meta-analysis combines research findings from many, typically dozens, of related studies and goes beyond simply determining statistical significance. After gathering the studies under analysis, the researcher computes a statistic, d or *Cohen's d*, for each study in the analysis. This statistic compares the difference between the mean scores of each group and the distribution of scores (using the standard deviation) within each group. In other words, group differences are considered relative to individual differences. Then, the d statistic is averaged across all studies to compute the average size of the effect of the independent variable. As a general rule, effect sizes are described as small ($d = .20$), moderate ($d = .50$), or large ($d = .80$) (Cohen, 1969).

Because meta-analyses consider a large number of published, and sometimes unpublished studies, other factors influencing research findings may be evaluated in addition to effect sizes (Rosenthal & DiMatteo, 2002). For example, a meta-analysis of altruism found that men were more likely than women to help in risky situations, particularly when others were present (Eagly & Crowley, 1986). Thus, this gender difference might be attributable to the male gender role. Meta-analyses also enable psychologists to compare effect sizes across time, thus assessing the effect of sociocultural change. Two metaanalyses of gender differences in verbal and mathematical ability compared the effect sizes of studies published before and after 1973 (Hyde, Fennema, & Lamon, 1990; Hyde and Linn, 1988). In both analyses, the size of gender differences declined over the years.

Meta-analyses have been useful to psychologists interested in distilling the results of a large number of studies. However, the use of meta-analyses cannot overcome the methodological limitations of the studies on which they are based. Most important, studies that rely on selective recruitment of participants and poor assessment procedures are not improved by the use of meta-analysis (Halpern, 1995). Proponents such as Janet Shibley Hyde (1948–) (1994) assert that meta-analyses are helpful in understanding group differences, the effect of social roles and other situational factors on people's behavior, and how variables such as gender and ethnicity may influence each other. Psychologists have used the results of meta-analyses to shed light on a number of topics, including the psychological and physical health of elderly caregivers (Pinquart & Soerensen, 2003), gender differences and similarities in smiling (LaFrance, Hecht, &

Paluck, 2003), and gender differences and similarities in the quality of romantic attachment (Del Giudice, 2011).

Meta-analysis has been applied to many research topics, including some that even might be interesting to nonscientists. A meta-analysis of studies involving 3,401 participants found that the infamous commonsense "freshman 15"—a gain of 15 pounds—that supposedly marks the first year of college is off the mark. The meta-analysis found that there is an average weight gain of about 4 pounds during the first year—closer to a "freshman 5" (Vella-Zarb & Elgar, 2009). Chocolate lovers who are concerned about high blood pressure will appreciate that a meta-analysis of relevant studies found that eating dark chocolate significantly reduces high blood pressure (Ried, Sullivan, Fakler, Frank, & Stocks, 2010).

As you read the research studies discussed in later chapters, keep in mind that almost all were analyzed by one or more descriptive statistics, correlational statistics, or inferential statistics. You should also note that statistical significance does not necessarily imply practical or social significance (Favreau, 1997; Rachman, 1993). For example, a number of studies have reported small but consistent gender differences in social influence (Eagly, 1983). Though studies have found statistically significant differences in women's and men's behavior, these differences might not be of practical significance. In other words, they might not be large enough to account for the observed differences in men's and women's lives. Some journals that contain reports of research in counseling now require statements of not just statistical significance but also practical or clinical significance (Thompson, 2002).

Group Differences versus Individual Differences

When psychologists report gender, ethnic, or cross-cultural differences in research studies, they are describing group differences on the dependent variable. For example, one study might conclude that boys are more aggressive than girls. This conclusion is based on tests of inferential statistics—the mean for the sample of boys was greater than the mean for the sample of girls. And the difference between these two means was statistically significant. Thus, on average, boys were more aggressive than girls.

A statement about group differences—as in this case of gender differences in aggression—does not mean that the behavior of all the male participants differed from that of all the female participants. When frequency distributions of gender, ethnic, or cross-cultural group scores are plotted, there usually is overlap between the two curves. It is extremely unlikely that each participant in one group scored higher than each participant in the other group.

A statistically significant gender difference in aggression also might be smaller than individual differences in aggression. In this example, it is important to consider the magnitude of within-group variability. As you can see in Figure 2-3, many of the boys and

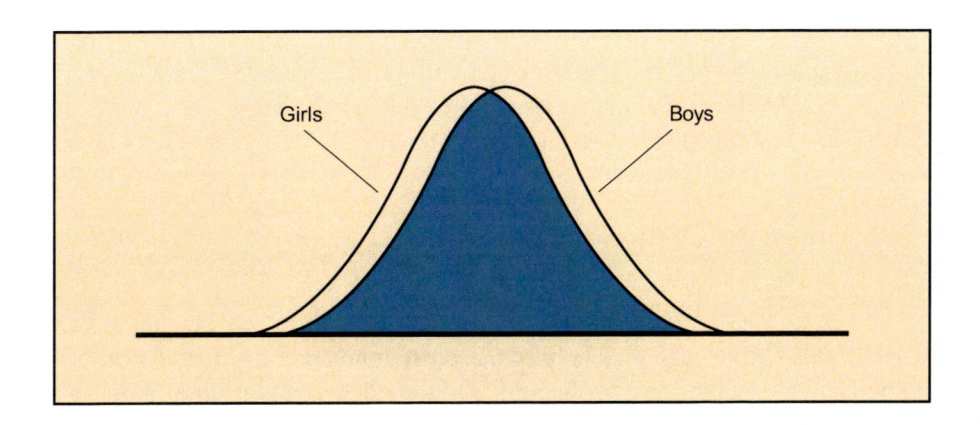

FIGURE 2-3
Statistically Significant Gender Differences

These overlapping curves represent frequency distributions of aggressiveness in a sample of girls and boys. Though these curves represent a statistically significant gender difference in aggressiveness, note that many of the boys and girls did not differ in their aggressiveness (the shaded area of the overlapping curves).

Chapter 2 Psychology as a Science

girls in these two samples did not differ in their aggressiveness. The areas shared by the overlapping curves represent this similarity. Moreover, some boys were not very aggressive at all whereas some girls were very aggressive. As you can see, the variability of the girls' and boys' scores—the spread of each curve—is greater than the distance between the two group means.

It is important, then, to understand that though there might be average group differences, it also is likely that there are considerable individual differences. And when individual differences are greater in magnitude than group differences, it is difficult to predict a particular person's behavior on the basis of group differences. Suppose a researcher reports significant cross-cultural differences between European American and Asian American participants in parenting behaviors. It would be a mistake to conclude from these findings that all European American parents treat their children differently than all Asian Americans. And the difference between two European American parents is likely to be greater in magnitude than the average cross-cultural difference.

Section Review: Statistical Analysis of Research Data

1. What are measures of central tendency?
2. What are measures of variability?
3. What is statistical significance?
4. How does meta-analysis summarize the results of many research studies?

Ethics of Psychological Research

Psychologists must be as concerned with the ethical treatment of their data and human participants and animal subjects as they are with the quality of their research methods and statistical analyses. Academic psychology departments place a premium on teaching their students the necessity of conducting ethically responsible research (Fisher, Fried, & Feldman, 2009).

Ethical Treatment of Research Data

A serious ethical violation in the treatment of data is falsification. Thus, in the hypothetical melatonin experiment, you would have to record your data accurately—even if it contradicted your hypothesis. During the past century, there have been several notorious cases in which researchers in physics, biology, medicine, or psychology have been accused of falsifying their data (Park, 2008). Chapter 10 discusses a prominent case in psychology in which Sir Cyril Burt, an eminent psychologist, was so intent on demonstrating that intelligence depends on heredity that he apparently misrepresented his research findings (Tucker, 1997). Though occasional lapses in the ethical treatment of data have provoked controversy, there has been even greater concern about the ethical treatment of people and animals in psychological research.

Ethical Treatment of Human Participants

The first code of ethics for the treatment of human participants in psychological research was developed in 1953, largely in response to the Nuremberg war crimes trials following World War II (Miller, 2003). The trials disclosed the cruel medical experiments performed by Nazi physicians on prisoners of war and concentration camp inmates. Today, the U.S. government requires institutions that receive federal research grants to establish a committee—known as an Institutional Review Board (IRB)—that reviews research proposals to ensure the ethical treatment of human participants and animal subjects (McGaha & Korn, 1995).

APA Code of Ethics

The code of ethics of the American Psychological Association (APA) contains specific requirements for the treatment of human participants and has published books detailing the ethical treatment of volunteers in experiments (Sales & Folkman, 2000).

1. The researcher must inform potential participants of all aspects of the research procedure that might influence their decision to participate. In the melatonin experiment, you would not be permitted to tell participants that they will be given melatonin and then give them a placebo instead unless they had been informed of the possibility. This requirement, *informed consent,* can be difficult to ensure because participants might be unable to give truly informed consent. Perhaps the participants are children (Vitiello, 2008), are prisoners (Regehr, Edward, & Bradford, 2000), or have schizophrenia (Beebe & Smith, 2010) or intellectual disabilities such as dementia (Cubit, 2010), and cannot comprehend the language used on informed consent documents.
2. Potential participants must not be forced to participate in a research study, which could become a problem with prisoners or hospitalized patients who fear the consequences of refusing to participate (Rosenthal, 1995). Though sometimes forcing the individual to undergo therapy, as in the case of adolescents with anorexia nervosa (a disorder marked by self-starvation), can be lifesaving (Manley, Smye, & Srikameswaran, 2001), it is not ethically permissible in research studies.
3. Participants must be permitted to withdraw from a study at any time. Of course, when participants withdraw, it can adversely affect the study because those who remain might differ from those who drop out. The loss of participants can therefore limit the ability to generalize research findings from those who complete the study to the desired target population (Trice & Ogden, 1987).
4. The researcher must protect the participants from physical harm and mental distress. Again, the use of deception might violate this provision by inducing mental distress. Certain research practices themselves might raise ethical concerns because of the distress they produce, such as contacting recently bereaved relatives to recruit them to participate in research on bereavement (Steeves, Kahn, Ropka, & Wise, 2001).
5. If a participant does experience harm or distress, the researcher must try to alleviate it. But some critics argue that it is impossible to routinely determine whether attempts to relieve distress produce long-lasting benefits (Norris, 1978).
6. Information gained from participants must be kept confidential. Confidentiality becomes a major issue when participants reveal information that indicates they might be in danger, such as children or adolescents being abused by parents (Wiles, Crow, Heath, & Charles, 2008).

Deception in Research

Despite their code of ethics, psychologists sometimes confront ethical dilemmas in their treatment of human participants, as in the use of deception to reduce participant bias. Psychologists might fail to inform people that they are participating in a study or might misinform participants about the true nature of a study. This deception is of concern, in part, because it violates the ethical norm of informed consent. Recall that the computer-dating study by Donn Byrne and colleagues (Byrne et al., 1970) used deception by falsely claiming that all participants would be matched with partners who shared their attitudes. Today, for this study to be considered ethical, the researcher would have to demonstrate to the IRB that the experiment could not be conducted without the use of deception and that its potential findings are important enough to justify the use of deception (Fisher & Fyrberg, 1994). Moreover, at the completion of the study, each participant would have

debriefing A procedure, after the completion of a research study, that informs participants of the purpose of the study and aims to remove any physical or psychological distress caused by participation.

to be debriefed. In **debriefing** participants, the researcher explains the reasons for the deception and tries to relieve any distress that might have been experienced (Benham, 2008). Some commentators insist that debriefing should be a component of nondeceptive research as well (Sharpe & Faye, 2009).

Some psychologists worry that deceptive research will make potential participants distrust psychological research (Hertwig & Ortmann, 2008). And Diana Baumrind (1985), a critic of deceptive research, argues that not even the positive findings of studies that use deception outweigh the distress of participants who learn that they have been fooled. Arguments against deceptive research have been countered by psychologists who argue that it would be unethical not to conduct deceptive studies that might produce important findings (Christensen, 1988). Still others urge psychologists not only to weigh the costs and benefits of using deception but also to inform participants that deception might be used as part of the study (Pittenger, 2002).

Whereas some psychologists argue about the use of deception, others try to settle the debate over deceptive research by using the results of empirical research. In one study, undergraduates who had participated in deceptive experiments rated their experience as more positive than did those who had participated in nondeceptive ones. Moreover, those in deceptive experiments did not rate psychologists as less trustworthy. Any negative emotional effects reported by participants seemed to be relieved by debriefing. The researchers concluded that debriefing eliminates any negative effects of deception, perhaps because the participants learn the importance of the research study (Smith & Richardson, 1983).

But this interpretation of the findings has been criticized. You might wish to pause to see if you can think of an alternative explanation for why participants in deceptive experiments responded more positively. One possibility is that the procedures used in deceptive experiments are more interesting and enjoyable than those used in nondeceptive ones (Rubin, 1985). Remembering that psychology, as a science, resolves issues through empirical research instead of through argument alone, how might you conduct a study to determine whether this assumption is correct? One way would be to conduct experiments whose procedures have been rated as equally interesting, and use deception in only half of them. If the participants still rate the deceptive experiments more positively, then the results would support Smith and Richardson (1983). If the participants rate the deceptive experiments less positively, then the results would support Rubin (1985).

Ethical Treatment of Animal Subjects

At the 1986 annual meeting of the American Psychological Association in Washington, D.C., animal rights advocates picketed in the streets and disrupted talks, including one by the prominent psychologist Neal Miller (1909–2002), a defender of the use of animals in psychological research (Miller, 1985). The present conflict between animal rights advocates and psychologists who study animals is not new. In the early 20th century, animal rights activists attacked the work of leading psychologists, including John B. Watson and G. Stanley Hall. In 1925, in part to blunt these attacks, the American Psychological Association's Committee on Precautions in Animal Experimentation established a code of regulations for the use of animals in research (Dewsbury, 1990).

Animal Rights versus Animal Welfare

Many *animal rights* advocates oppose all laboratory research using animals, regardless of its scientific merit or practical benefits. Thus, they would oppose testing the effects of melatonin on animal subjects. A survey of demonstrators at an animal rights march in Washington, D.C., in 1990 found that almost 80 percent of animal rights advocates valued animal life at least as much as human life, and 85 percent wanted to eliminate all animal research (Plous, 1991). Some animal rights advocates even have vandalized laboratories that conduct animal research to intimidate researchers and interfere with their research (Hadley, 2009).

Scientists Pro-Test in Support of Animal Research
In response to animal rights activists, scientists have begun to demonstrate their support for lifesaving medical research using animals.
Source: Professor David Jentsch. Used with permission.

Animal rights advocates go beyond *animal welfare* advocates, who would permit laboratory research on animals as long as the animals are given humane care and the potential benefits of the research outweigh any pain and distress caused to the animals (Wolfensohn & Maguire, 2010). Thus, they would be more likely to approve the use of animals in testing the effects of melatonin on sleep. Bernard Rollin, an ethicist who has tried to resolve the ethical conflict between animal researchers and animal rights advocates, would permit animal research but urges that when in ethical doubt, experimenters should err in favor of the animal (Bekoff, Gruen, Townsend, & Rollin, 1992).

The current ethical standards of the American Psychological Association and other professional organizations, such as the Society for Neuroscience, for the treatment of animals are closer to those of animal welfare advocates than to those of animal rights advocates. The standards require that animals be treated with respect, housed in clean cages, and given adequate food and water. Researchers also must ensure that their animal subjects experience as little pain and distress as possible; when it is necessary to kill the animals, researchers must do so in a humane, painless way. Moreover, all institutions that receive research grants from the U.S. government must have approval from review boards (similar to IRBs) that judge whether research proposals for experiments using animal subjects meet ethical standards (Holden, 1987). The Canadian government likewise regulates the treatment of research animals in universities, government laboratories, and commercial institutions (Rowsell, 1988).

Reasons for Using Animals in Research

But with so many people available, why would psychologists be interested in studying animals? Advocates point to a number of benefits derived from animal research (Carroll & Overmier, 2001).

1. Some psychologists are simply intrigued by animal behavior and wish to learn more about it. To learn about the process of echolocation of prey, you would have to study animals such as bats rather than college students.
2. It is easier to control potential confounding variables that might affect the behavior of an animal. You would be less likely to worry about participant bias effects, for instance, when studying pigeons.
3. Developmental changes across the life span can be studied more efficiently in animals. If you were interested in the effects of the complexity of the early childhood environment on memory in old age, you might take 75 years to complete an experiment using human participants but only 3 years to complete one using rats.
4. Research on animals can generate hypotheses that are then tested using human participants. B. F. Skinner's research on learning in rats and pigeons stimulated research on learning in people.
5. Research on animals can benefit animals themselves. For example, as described in Chapter 7, psychologists have developed techniques to make coyotes feel nauseated by the taste of sheep; perhaps these techniques can someday be used to protect sheep from coyotes and coyotes from angry sheep ranchers.
6. Based on the assumption that animals do not have the same moral rights as people (Baldwin, 1993), certain procedures that are not ethically permissible with human participants are ethically permissible under current standards using animal subjects. Thus, if you wanted to conduct an experiment in which you studied the effects of surgically damaging a particular brain structure, you would be limited to the use of animals (Caminiti, 2009). But some critics of animal research note that the use of primates in invasive brain research because they most closely resemble people provides an argument against such research (Crum, 2009). Recent media attention has been drawn to the National Institute of Health's (NIH) decision to phase out much of its research on chimpanzees. As is common with any ethical dilemma, sound arguments can be raised for both sides regarding the use of animals in research. Often there is no resolution that is fully satisfactory to advocates of both sides.

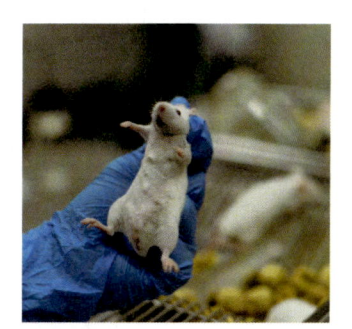

Research on Animals Is Beneficial

Source: panyawat bootanom/Shutterstock.com.

Section Review: Ethics of Psychological Research

1. Why has the use of deception in research provoked controversy?
2. What is debriefing in psychological research?
3. How do animal rights and animal welfare advocates differ from one other?

Chapter Summary

Sources of Knowledge

- Psychologists prefer the scientific method to common sense as a source of knowledge.
- The scientific method is based on the assumptions of determinism and skepticism.
- In using the scientific method to conduct research, a psychologist first provides a rationale for the research, then conducts the research study, analyzes the resulting data, and finally, communicates the results to other researchers.
- Replication of research studies is an important component of the scientific research process.

Goals of Scientific Research

- In conducting research, psychologists pursue the goals of description, prediction, control, and explanation.
- Scientific descriptions are systematic and rely on operational definitions.
- Scientific predictions are probabilistic, not certain.
- Scientists exert control over events by manipulating the factors that cause them.
- Scientific explanations state the probable causes of events.

Methods of Psychological Research

- Psychologists use descriptive, correlational, and experimental research methods.
- Descriptive research methods pursue the goal of description through naturalistic observation, case studies, surveys, psychological testing, and archival research.
- Correlational research pursues the goal of prediction by uncovering relationships between variables.
- When using correlational research, psychologists avoid confusing correlation with causation.
- Experimental research pursues the goals of control and explanation by manipulating an independent variable and measuring its effect on a dependent variable.
- Experimenters promote internal validity by controlling confounding variables whose effects might be confused with those of the independent variable.
- Confounding variables might be associated with the experimental situation, the participants in the experiment, or the experimenter.
- Random assignment is used to make the experimental group and control group equivalent before exposing them to the independent variable.
- Experimenters also must control for participant bias and experimenter bias.
- Another concern of experimenters is external validity—whether their results are generalizable from their participants and settings to other participants and settings.
- Experimenters rely on replication to determine whether their research has external validity.

Statistical Analysis of Research Data

- Psychologists typically make sense of their data by using mathematical techniques called statistics.
- Psychologists use descriptive statistics to summarize data, correlational statistics to determine relationships between variables, and inferential statistics to test their experimental hypotheses.
- Descriptive statistics include measures of central tendency (including the mode, median, and mean) and measures of variability (including the range, variance, and standard deviation).
- Correlational statistics let researchers use the values of one variable to predict the values of another.
- Inferential statistics examine whether numerical differences between experimental and control groups are statistically significant.
- Meta-analysis involves computation of the average effect size across a number of related studies.
- Statistical significance does not necessarily indicate social or practical significance. The magnitude of individual differences must be considered when examining group differences.

Ethics of Psychological Research

- American and Canadian psychologists have ethical codes for the treatment of human participants and animal subjects.
- In research using human participants, researchers must obtain informed consent, not force anyone to participate, let participants withdraw at any time, protect participants from physical harm and mental distress,

- alleviate any inadvertent harm or distress, and keep information obtained from the participants confidential.
- The use of deception in research has been an especially controversial issue.
- The use of animals in research also has been controversial.
- Many animal rights supporters oppose all research on animals.
- Animal welfare supporters approve of research on animals as long as the animals are treated humanely and the potential benefits of the research outweigh any pain and distress caused to the animals.
- Most psychologists support the use of animals in research because of the benefits of such research to both people and animals.

Key Terms

Sources of Knowledge
determinism (p. 27)
hypothesis (p. 29)
replication (p. 29)
scientific method (p. 29)
skepticism (p. 28)

Goals of Scientific Research
measurement (p. 31)
operational definition (p. 31)
theory (p. 31)

Methods of Psychological Research
archival research (p. 37)
case study (p. 34)
causation (p. 38)
confounding variable (p. 41)
control group (p. 40)
correlation (p. 38)
correlational research (p. 38)
dependent variable (p. 39)
descriptive research (p. 33)
double-blind technique (p. 43)
ethology (p. 33)
experimental group. (p. 39)
experimental method (p. 39)
experimenter bias effect (p. 42)
external validity (p. 43)
field experiment (p. 40)
independent variable (p. 39)
internal validity (p. 41)
naturalistic observation (p. 33)
negative correlation (p. 38)
norm (p. 36)
participant bias (p. 42)
placebo (p. 40)
population (p. 35)
positive correlation (p. 38)
psychological test (p. 36)
random assignment (p. 42)
random sampling (p. 35)
reliability (p. 37)
sample (p. 35)
standardization (p. 36)
survey (p. 34)
validity (p. 37)
variable (p. 38)

Statistical Analysis of Research Data
coefficient of correlation (p. 48)
descriptive statistics (p. 46)
inferential statistics (p. 49)
mean (p. 47)
measure of central tendency (p. 46)
measure of variability (p. 48)
median (p. 46)
meta-analysis (p. 50)
mode (p. 46)
range (p. 48)
standard deviation (p. 48)
statistical significance (p. 49)
variance (p. 48)

Ethics of Psychological Research
debriefing (p. 54)

Chapter Quiz

Note: Answers for the Chapter Quiz questions are provided at the end of the book.

1. The scientist is governed by an attitude of
   a. dualism.
   b. cynicism.
   c. dogmatism.
   d. skepticism.

2. Typically, for a statistical difference between the performances of experimental and control groups to be significant, its probability of occurring by chance must be less than
   a. 3 percent.
   b. 5 percent.
   c. 10 percent.
   d. 50 percent.

3. The prediction that "People high in psychological hardiness will be less likely to become ill than will people low in psychological hardiness" is an example of
   a. a fact.
   b. a hypothesis.
   c. inductive reasoning.
   d. an operational definition.

4. Deception is usually used in social psychological research to
   a. reduce participant bias.
   b. reduce experimenter bias.
   c. assess the reactions of people to being fooled.
   d. prevent potential participants from finding out about the experimental procedure in advance.

5. The more you smoke, the more likely you are to develop lung cancer. This demonstrates that smoking
   a. causes cancer.
   b. is caused by cancer.
   c. is positively correlated with cancer.
   d. is negatively correlated with cancer.

6. If people who score high on a test of mechanical ability perform better on tasks such as fixing a typewriter, building a bookcase, and replacing shock absorbers, this indicates that the test might have
   a. reliability.
   b. predictive validity.
   c. satisfactory norms.
   d. no relationship to mechanical ability.

7. You conduct an experiment to investigate the effect of meditation on the level of stress in men and women who vary in their religiosity. The dependent variable in your study is
   a. meditation.
   b. religiosity.
   c. sex of participants.
   d. level of stress.

8. Scientific predictions are
   a. invariably correct.
   b. probabilistic statements.
   c. based on the researcher's intuition.
   d. always made in the form of syllogisms.

9. Determinism is
   a. a procedure for ensuring that experimental and control groups are equivalent.
   b. a scientific assumption that every event has physical, potentially measurable causes.
   c. a means of finding out whether a confounding variable affected the dependent variable.
   d. a statistical technique for deciding whether research findings are statistically significant.

10. The most likely author of the statement "Never accept anything as true unless your own reasoning tells you it is true" is
    a. John Locke.
    b. B. F. Skinner.
    c. John B. Watson.
    d. René Descartes.

11. If the standard deviation of a set of scores is 4, the variance is
    a. 2.
    b. 4.
    c. 16.
    d. impossible to determine.

12. The best example of an operational definition would be defining
    a. *happy* as "being content with one's life."
    b. *beautiful* as "being physically attractive."
    c. *expert* as "being knowledgeable in one's own field."
    d. *strong* as "being able to bench-press one's body weight."

13. A child psychologist spends three hours a week watching and recording the play patterns of 3-year-old children in a nursery school. This is an example of (a)
    a. case study.
    b. archival research.
    c. experimental research.
    d. naturalistic observation.

14. The study discussed in the textbook that found that only 5 of 91 persons could identify a drunken person demonstrated the shortcomings of
    a. science.
    b. common sense.
    c. deductive reasoning.
    d. systematic observation.

15. A psychologist's favored perspective will determine where he or she looks for explanations of psychological events. For example, a humanistic psychologist will look for the causes of depression in the
    a. brain.
    b. environment.
    c. conscious mind.
    d. unconscious mind.

16. A psychologist who has designed a personality test administers it to a group of people on two occasions and determines how consistent the performances are. This is a procedure used to assess a test's
    a. reliability.
    b. validity.
    c. norms.
    d. criterion.

17. Both participant bias and experimenter bias can be controlled by
    a. using the double-blind technique.
    b. using more than one independent variable.
    c. replicating research studies several times.
    d. random assignment of participants to the experimental and control groups.

18. If you study the childhood diaries of adults you are seeing as psychotherapy clients to determine factors that are associated with adult emotional problems, then you are engaging in
    a. survey research.
    b. archival research.
    c. experimental research.
    d. naturalistic observation.

19. The "Pepsi Challenge" controversy discussed in the textbook revealed that
    a. Pepsi tastes better than Coke.
    b. Coke tastes better than Pepsi.
    c. taste preferences depended on a confounding variable.
    d. taste preferences cannot be determined by experiments.

20. The largest of the following correlations is
    a. .37
    b. .00
    c. −.01
    d. −.93

21. Cause is to effect as
    a. dependent variable is to independent variable.
    b. independent variable is to dependent variable.
    c. dependent variable is to confounding variable.
    d. confounding variable is to independent variable.

22. The generalizability of research findings is best determined by
    a. replication.
    b. common sense.
    c. archival research.
    d. deductive reasoning.

23. Given the numbers 2, 3, 22, 10, 3, 7, 9, the median is
    a. 3.
    b. 7.
    c. 8.
    d. 10.

24. Jane Goodall's research on chimpanzees in the wild is an example of
    a. ethology.
    b. evolutionary psychology.
    c. experimentation.
    d. archival research.

25. Every member of the population of interest has an equal chance of being selected in a
    a. quota sample.
    b. random sample.
    c. stratified sample.
    d. systematic sample.

Thought Questions

1. How would a skeptical attitude toward ESP, UFOs, and similar topics differ from either a cynical or a gullible attitude?

2. How would the four goals of scientific research influence research on violence?

3. In what way are medical treatments, weather forecasting, horse-race handicapping, college admissions decisions, and psychological child-rearing advice "probabilistic"?

4. Why is the experimental method considered a better means of determining causality than nonexperimental methods?

CHAPTER 3

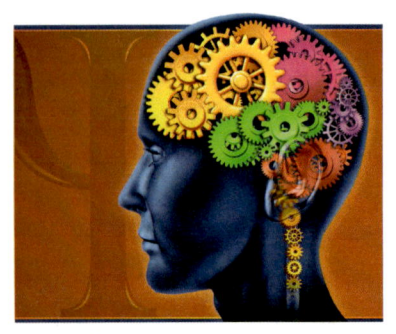

Biopsychological Bases of Behavior

Source: Lightspring/Shutterstock.com.

Chapter Outline

Nature versus Nurture
Biological Communication Systems
Neuronal Activity
Brain Functions

unilateral neglect A disorder, caused by damage to a parietal lobe, in which the individual acts as though the side of her or his world opposite to the damaged lobe does not exist.

A 64-year-old, right-handed man was awakened by the sense that there was something strange in his bed. Opening his eyes, he observed to his horror that there was a strange arm reaching toward his neck. The arm approached nearer, as if to strangle him, and the man let out a cry of terror. Suddenly, he realized that the arm had on its wrist a silver-banded watch, which the man recognized to be his own. It occurred to him that the arm's possessor must have stolen his watch sometime during the night. A struggle ensued, as the man attempted to wrestle the watch off of the arm. During the struggle, the man became aware that his own left arm was feeling contorted and uncomfortable. It was then that he discovered that the strange arm in fact was his own. The watch was his, and it was on his left wrist. He was wrestling with his own arm (Tranel, 1995, p. 885)!

What could account for such bizarre behavior? It was caused by a stroke that damaged the right side of the man's brain. This made him exhibit **unilateral neglect**, in this case making it difficult for the man to attend to the left side of his body and immediate environment (Osawa & Maeshima, 2010). A person with unilateral neglect, associated with right-brain damage, often acts as though the left side of his or her world, including his or her body, does not exist. A man with unilateral neglect might shave the right side of his face, but not the left, and might eat the pork chop on the right side of his plate but not the potatoes on the left. If the plate is turned for him, he might be surprised to see the food from the left side and deny it was ever there. About 25–30 percent of stroke victims develop unilateral neglect, with much functional recovery occurring during the first 2–3 months post-stroke. But large brain lesions usually lead to long-term impairment (Kerkhoff & Rossetti, 2006). Though more than 90 percent of cases of unilateral neglect are found after damage to the right side of the brain, it sometimes is found in people with damage to the left side of the brain; they show neglect for objects in the right half of their spatial world (Corbetta, Kincades, Lewis, Snyder, & Sapir, 2005).

Such profound effects of brain damage on physical and psychological functioning indicate that abilities we often take for granted require a properly functioning brain. If you have an intact brain, as you read this page your eyes inform your brain about what you are reading. At the same time, your brain interprets the meaning of that information and stores some of it in your memory. When you reach the end of a right-hand page, your brain will direct your hand to turn the page.

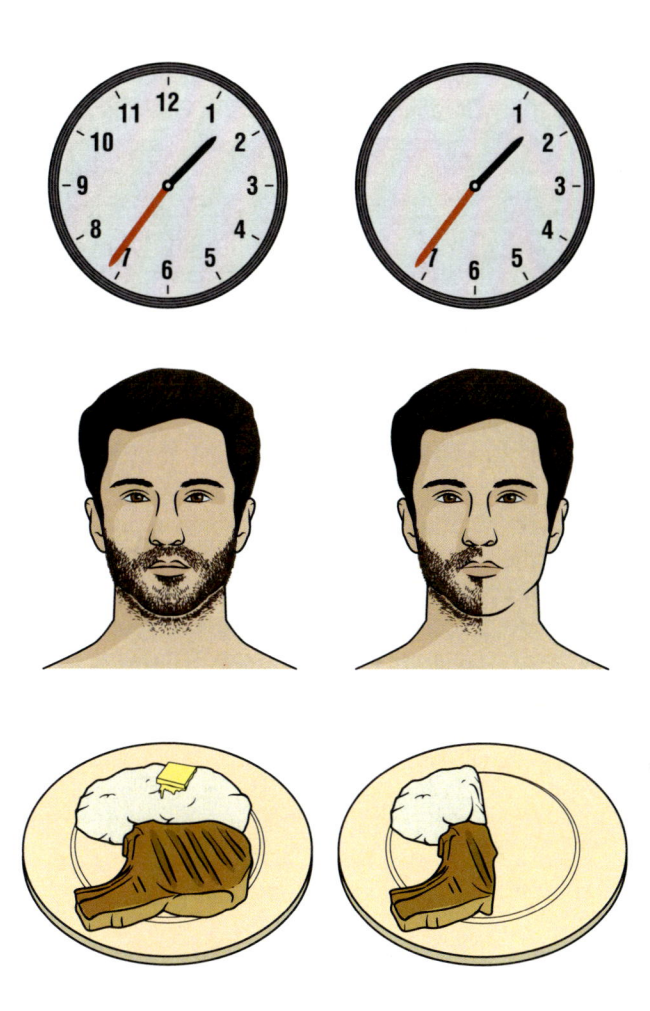

Unilateral Neglect

Representative drawings (*left column*) and the copies made of them by patients with left unilateral neglect (*right column*). Left unilateral neglect is a consequence of damage to the parietal cortex of the *right* hemisphere of someone's brain.

But how do your eyes inform your brain about what you are reading? How does your brain interpret and store the information it receives? And how does your brain direct the movements of your hand? The answers to these questions are provided by the field of **behavioral neuroscience**, which studies the relationship between neurological processes (typically, brain activity) and psychological functions (such as memory, emotion, and perception). More than a century ago William James (1890/1981), in his classic textbook, *The Principles of Psychology*, stressed the close association between physiology and psychology. James declared, "I have felt most acutely the difficulties of understanding either the brain without the mind or the mind without the brain" (quoted in Bjork, 1988, p. 107).

behavioral neuroscience The field that studies the physiological bases of human and animal behavior and mental processes.

Nature versus Nurture

William James was influenced by Charles Darwin's (1859/1975) theory of evolution, which holds that individuals who are biologically well adapted to their environment are more likely to survive, reproduce, and pass on their physical traits to succeeding generations through their genes. Thus, the human brain has evolved into its present form because it helped people throughout history adapt successfully to their surroundings and survive long enough to reproduce. Our brain is remarkably flexible in helping us adapt to different circumstances and environments. For example our brain helped ancient people

Chapter 3 Biopsychological Basis of Behavior

survive without automobiles, grocery stores, or electric lights. It helps people today survive in the arctic, outer space, and adapt to our current environments.

To what extent are you the product of your heredity, and to what extent are you the product of your environment? This issue of "nature versus nurture" (Sameroff, 2010) has been with us since the era of ancient Greece, when Plato championed nature and Aristotle championed nurture. Plato believed we are born with some knowledge; Aristotle believed that at birth our mind is a blank slate (or *tabula rasa*) and that life experiences provide us with knowledge.

Evolutionary Psychology

In modern times, the nature-nurture issue became even more heated after Charles Darwin (1859/1975) put forth his theory of evolution in the mid-19th century. Darwin noted that animals and people vary in their physical traits. Given the competition for resources (including food and water) and the need to foil predators (by avoiding them, defeating them, or escaping from them), animals and people with physical traits best adapted to these purposes would be the most likely to survive long enough to produce offspring, who would likely also have those traits. As long as particular physical traits provide a survival advantage, those traits will have a greater likelihood of showing up in succeeding generations. Darwin called this process *natural selection*.

evolutionary psychology The study of the evolution of behavior through natural selection.

Psychologists who champion **evolutionary psychology** employ Darwinian concepts in their research and theorizing (Ploeger, van der Maas, & Raijmakers, 2008). For example, research findings indicate that it is easier to condition fear responses to aversive stimuli than to neutral stimuli (Phelps & LeDoux, 2005). For example, natural threats such as snakes were more likely to elicit a fear response such as freezing (at the sight of one) as opposed to viewing a neutral stimuli, such as a house (Öhman, 2009). The possible role of evolution in human social relationships inspired a study by evolutionary psychologist David Buss and his colleagues Randy Larsen, Drew Westen, and Jennifer Semmelroth (1992) at the University of Michigan (see "The Research Process" box on the following page).

Behavioral Genetics

behavioral genetics The study of the relative effects of heredity and life experiences on behavior.

Beginning in the 1970s, psychology has seen the growth of **behavioral genetics**, which studies how heredity affects behavior. In humans, this information is gathered through family, twin, and adoption studies. Research in behavioral genetics has found evidence of a hereditary basis for characteristics as diverse as delinquency (Taylor, Iacono, & McGue, 2000), prosocial behavior (Gregory, Light-Häusermann, Rijsdijk, & Eley, 2009), marital satisfaction (Spotts et al., 2005), and antisocial personality disorder (Gunter, Vaughn, & Philibert, 2010). Antisocial personality disorder is discussed in Chapter 16.

Nonetheless, it is crucial to note that behavioral genetics does not presume that heredity is the most important factor in the development of these characteristics. All behavior is determined by interactions between people's genes and their environment. For most psychological traits, the proportion of individual variability attributable to heredity is less than 50 percent, so personal characteristics are almost always influenced more by environmental factors than by hereditary (Plomin & Asbury, 2001). Moreover, children reared in the same family tend to be less influenced by shared environmental factors than by nonshared environmental factors. This may help account for why children reared in the same family can turn out to be so different from one another. Perhaps they are treated somewhat differently by their parents and are subject to different outside environmental influences from their peers and other people they encounter in everyday life (Plomin, Asbury, & Dunn, 2001).

To appreciate behavioral genetics, you should have a basic understanding of genetics itself. The cells of the human body contain 23 pairs of *chromosomes*, which are long strands of *deoxyribonucleic acid (DNA)* molecules. (Unlike the other body cells, the egg cell and sperm cell each contain 23 single chromosomes.) DNA molecules are ribbon-like structures composed of segments called *genes*. Genes direct the synthesis of *ribonucleic*

Chapter 3 Biopsychological Basis of Behavior

> ### The Research Process
>
> **Has Evolution Influenced Gender Differences in Romantic Jealousy?**
>
> **Rationale**
>
> Buss and his colleagues believe that evolution has left its mark on human behavior, even in the area of romance. Because women can be sure that their newborns are truly theirs, whereas men cannot, Buss hypothesized that men would exhibit more sexual jealousy than emotional jealousy. Because prehistoric women were, on the average, physically weaker and more responsible for caring for their children and depended on men to support them while pregnant and after giving birth, the researchers hypothesized that women would exhibit more emotional jealousy than sexual jealousy. The researchers believed that these differences were the product of thousands of generations of natural selection.
>
> **Method**
>
> Participants were 202 male and female undergraduate students. They were asked which of the following two dilemmas would distress them more: their romantic partner forming a deep emotional attachment to someone else or that partner enjoying passionate sexual intercourse with someone else. The participants also were asked to respond to a similar dilemma in which their romantic partner either fell in love with another person or tried a variety of sexual positions with that person.
>
> **Results and Discussion**
>
> The results showed that for the first dilemma 60 percent of the male participants reported greater jealousy over their partner's potential sexual infidelity. In contrast, 83 percent of the female participants reported greater jealousy over their partner's potential emotional infidelity. This pattern of responses was repeated in response to the second dilemma. Buss and other colleagues provided additional support for these findings in later research studies. For example, in an archival study, they examined 345 cases in which women were murdered by their husbands as part of lovers' triangles. They found that younger women, as compared with older women, were more likely to be killed by jealous husbands. The researchers noted that evolutionary psychology would have predicted this. Given that younger women have more reproductive potential than older women, evolutionary psychologists would predict more intense jealousy regarding the sexual infidelity of younger women than that of older women (Shackelford, Buss, & Weekes-Shackelford, 2003).
>
> Of course, other interpretations of these findings—not dependent on evolutionary psychology—are possible. One alternative explanation has been put forward by Christine Harris (2003), who reviewed the relevant research. The most consistent evidence for gender differences in jealousy is found when researchers ask respondents to consider a hypothetical relationship. When participants are surveyed about their responses to personal experiences of sexual infidelity, gender differences disappear. And when the base rates for murders are taken into account, men are not proportionately more likely to murder their wives in a jealous rage. But evolutionary psychologists had pointed to research supporting the commonness of gender differences in sexual and emotional jealousy as evidence of its possible hereditary basis. And Buss and his colleagues' findings regarding gender differences in jealousy have been replicated in some research studies across different cultures (Wiederman & Kendall, 1999).
>
> But the degree of the difference in female and male responses to sexual and emotional infidelity varies across cultures and ideologies. In one study, for example, gender differences in the two kinds of jealousy were stronger in the United States than in Germany or the Netherlands (Buunk, Angleitner, Oubaid, & Buss, 1996). Another study found that gender differences in sexual and emotional jealousy were greater among undergraduates who believed in gender inequality (Pratto & Hegarty, 2000). As you can see, research findings on gender differences in jealousy might be compatible with an evolutionary interpretation or a sociocultural interpretation (Wood & Eagly, 2000).

acid (RNA). RNA, in turn, directs the synthesis of proteins, which are responsible for the structure and function of our tissues and organs.

Though our genes direct our physical development, their effects on our behavior are primarily indirect. There are, for example, no "zipline daredevil genes." Instead, genes influence physiological factors, such as hormones, neurotransmitters, and brain structures. These factors, in turn, make people somewhat more likely to engage in particular behaviors. Perhaps people destined to become zipline daredevils inherit a less physiologically reactive nervous system for arousal, making them experience less anxiety in dangerous situations. Likewise, perhaps people destined to become zipline daredevils inherit a more physiologically reactive nervous system for arousal, making them experience

Our Cells Make Genes

The nucleus of our cells contains chromosomes. A gene is a length of DNA that codes for a specific protein. Your genotype is unique to you and is made up of different DNA sequences. Genotypes, along with environmental and developmental factors, will determine your phenotype.

Source: Designua/Shutterstock.com.

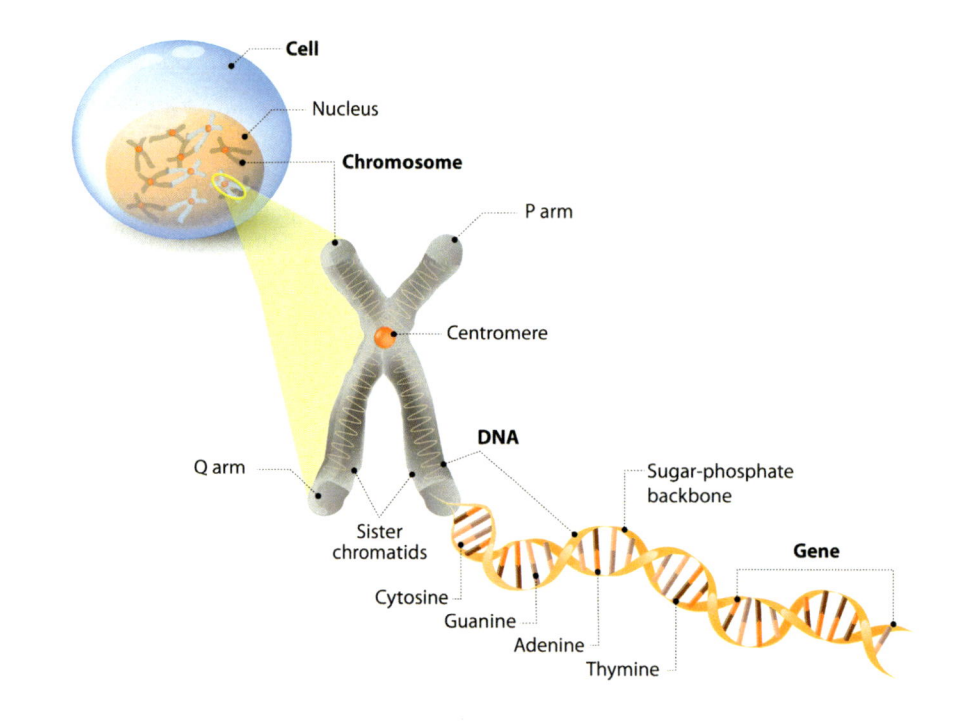

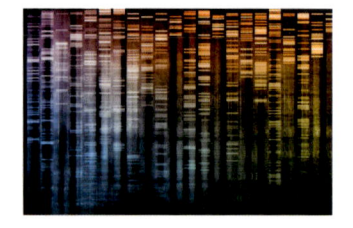

Human Genome

A digital representation of a human genome.

Source: kentoh/Shutterstock.com.

genotype An individual's genetic inheritance.

phenotype The overt expression of an individual's genotype (genetic inheritance) in his or her appearance or behavior.

heritability The proportion of variability in a trait across a population attributable to genetic differences among members of the population.

thrill seeking in dangerous situations. Moreover, given current trends in molecular genetics, behavioral geneticists are on the threshold of identifying genes that affect specific behaviors. For example, the ambitious Human Genome Project has identified more than 20,000 human genes (van Ommen, 2005). Most researchers in behavioral genetics prefer to search for the effects of interactions among these genes, rather than single-gene effects, as influences on behavior (Wahlsten, 1999). This research also holds promise for the prevention and treatment of physical and psychological disorders that have possible genetic bases, such as obesity (see Chapter 11) and schizophrenia (see Chapter 16).

Our outward appearance and behavior might not indicate our exact genetic inheritance. In recognition of this, scientists distinguish between our genotype and our phenotype. Your **genotype** is your genetic inheritance. Your **phenotype** is the overt expression of your inheritance in your appearance or behavior. For example, your eye color is determined by the interaction of a gene inherited from your mother and a gene inherited from your father. The brown-eye gene is *dominant*, and the blue-eye gene is *recessive*. Dominant genes take precedence over recessive genes. Traits carried by recessive genes show up in phenotypes only when recessive genes occur together. If you are blue-eyed, your genotype includes two blue-eye genes (both recessive). If you have brown eyes, your genotype may include two brown-eye genes (both dominant) or one brown-eye gene (dominant) and one blue-eye gene (recessive).

In contrast to simple traits like eye color, most characteristics are governed by more than one pair of genes—that is, they are *polygenic*. With rare exceptions, this is especially true of genetic influences on human behaviors and abilities. Your athletic, academic, and social skills depend on the interaction of many genes as well as your life experiences. For example, your muscularity (your phenotype) depends on both your genetic endowment (your genotype) and your dietary, health, and exercise habits (your life experiences).

To appreciate research studies that try to determine the relative contributions of heredity and environment to human development, you should understand the concept of heritability. **Heritability** refers to the proportion of variability in a trait across a population attributable to genetic differences among members of the population (Turkheimer, 1998). For example, people differ in their intelligence (as measured by IQ tests). To what extent is this variability caused by heredity, and to what extent is it caused by experience? Heritability values range from 0.0 to 1.0. If heritability accounted for none of the variability in intelligence, it would have a value of 0.0. If heritability accounted for all of the variability in intelligence, it would have a value of 1.0. In reality, the heritability of intelligence, as measured by IQ tests, is estimated to be between .50 (Chipuer, Rovine, & Plomin, 1990) and .70 (Bouchard, Lykken, McGue, Segal, & Tellegen, 1990). This indicates that the variability in intelligence is strongly, but not solely, influenced by heredity. Environmental factors also account for much of the variability. Moreover, note that heritability applies to groups, not to individuals. Heritability cannot be used, for example, to determine the relative contributions of heredity and environment to your own intelligence. Research procedures that assess the relative contributions of nature and nurture involve the study of relatives. These include studies of families, adoptees, and identical twins reared apart.

Family Studies

Family studies investigate similarities between relatives with varying degrees of genetic similarity. These studies find that the closer the genetic relationship (that is, the more genes that are shared) between relatives, the more alike they tend to be on a variety of traits. For example, the siblings of a person who has schizophrenia are significantly more likely to have schizophrenia than are the person's cousins. Though it is tempting to attribute this to their degree of genetic similarity, one cannot rule out that it is actually due to their degree of environmental similarity (Althoff, Faraone, Rettew, Morley, & Hudziak, 2005).

The best kind of family study is the *twin study*, which compares identical (or *monozygotic*) twins to fraternal (or *dizygotic*) twins. This kind of study was introduced by Francis Galton (1822–1911), who found more similarity between identical twins than between fraternal twins—and attributed this to heredity. Identical twins, because they come from the same fertilized egg, have identical genes. For this reason, they have the same genetic inheritance. Moreover, they are of the same sex. Fraternal twins, because they come from different fertilized eggs, do not have identical genes. Therefore, fraternal twins can be the same or other sex. They have merely the same degree of genetic similarity as ordinary siblings do.

Moreover, twins, whether identical or fraternal, are born at the same time and share more similar environments than other siblings do. Because research has found that identical twins reared in similar environments are more psychologically similar than fraternal twins reared in similar environments, it is reasonable to attribute the greater similarity of identical twins to heredity. Twin studies have been consistent across cultures in supporting the heritability of psychological characteristics, as in studies of obsessive-compulsive disorder in twins (van Grootheest, Cath, Beekman, & Boomsma, 2005), sexual orientation and conformity to gender roles in Australian twins (Bailey, Dunne, & Martin, 2000), and childhood aggression in twins (Porsch et al., 2016). Nonetheless, there is an alternative, environmental explanation. Perhaps identical twins become more psychologically similar because they are treated more alike than are fraternal twins.

Monozygotic Twins

Monozygotic twins develop from the same fertilized egg.
Source: SvetlanaFedoseyeva/Shutterstock.com.

Adoption Studies

Another way to examine heritability is to study adopted children. *Adoption studies* measure the correlation in particular traits between adopted children and their biological parents and between those same children and their adoptive parents. Adoption studies have found that adoptees tend to be more similar to their biological parents than to their adoptive parents in characteristics such as drug abuse (Cadoret et al., 1995), vocational interests (Lykken, Bouchard, McGue, & Tellegen, 1993), and religious values (Waller, Kojetin, Bouchard, & Lykken, 1990). These findings indicate that with regard to such characteristics, the genes that adoptees inherit from their biological parents affect their development more than does the environment they are provided with by their adoptive parents.

Yet, the environment cannot be ruled out as an explanation for the greater similarity between adoptees and their biological parents. As you will see in Chapter 4, prenatal experiences can affect children's development. Perhaps adoptees are more like their biological parents not because they share the same genes but because during prenatal development the adoptees were subject to their mother's drug habits, health habits, nutritional intake, or other environmental influences. Moreover, their experiences with their biological parents in early infancy, before they were adopted, might likewise affect their development, possibly making them more similar to their biological parents.

Biological versus Adoptive Relatives: A Real-Life Experiment

Adoption creates two groups: genetic relatives and environmental relatives.
Source: DNF Style/Shutterstock.com.

Chapter 3 Biopsychological Basis of Behavior

Studies of Identical Twins Reared Apart

Perhaps the best procedure is to study identical twins reared apart. Research on a variety of traits has consistently found higher positive correlations between identical twins reared apart than between fraternal twins reared together. Because identical twins share identical genes, virtually identical prenatal environments, and highly similar prenatal environments, this research provides strong evidence in favor of the nature side of the debate. In keeping with this, a widely publicized ongoing study conducted at the University of Minnesota under the leadership of Thomas Bouchard has examined similarities between identical twins who were separated in infancy and reunited later in life. As part of the University of Minnesota study of twins reared apart, researchers administered a personality test to 71 pairs of adult identical and 53 pairs of adult fraternal twins reared apart and 99 pairs of adult identical and 99 pairs of adult fraternal twins reared together. The results found that the heritability estimate for personality was 0.46, indicating that heredity plays an important, but not dominant, role in personality (Bouchard, McGue, Hur, & Horn, 1998). Other studies of identical twins reared apart have found that the heritability of personality is approximately .40 (Bouchard & Loehlin, 2001).

The University of Minnesota twin studies have found some uncanny similarities in the habits, abilities, and physiological responses of the reunited twins. For example, one pair of twins at their first reunion discovered that they "both used Vademecum toothpaste, Canoe shaving lotion, Vitalis hair tonic, and Lucky Strike cigarettes. After that meeting, they exchanged birthday presents that crossed in the mail and proved to be identical choices, made independently in separate cities" (Lykken, McGue, Tellegen, & Bouchard, 1992).

But some of these similarities might be due to coincidence or being reared in similar environments or having some contact with each other before being studied. In fact, research on even unrelated people sometimes shows surprising similarities in their personality traits (Wyatt, 1993). Moreover, identical twins look the same and might elicit responses from others that indirectly lead to their developing similar interests and personalities. Consider how people might treat identical twins who are obese, muscular, attractive, or acne prone. Thus, identical twins who share certain physical traits might become more similar than ordinary siblings who do not share such traits—even when reared in different cultures (Ford, 1993). As you can see, no kind of study is flawless in demonstrating the superiority of heredity over environment in guiding development.

Regardless of the influence of heredity on development, behavioral genetics researcher Robert Plomin reminds us that life experiences also are important. In one study, personality test scores of identical and fraternal twins were compared at an average of 20 years of age and then at an average of 30 years of age. Plomin concluded that the stable core of personality is strongly influenced by heredity but that personality change is overwhelmingly influenced by environment (McGue, Bacon, & Lykken, 1993). Thus, heredity might have provided you with the personality traits needed to become a Nobel Prize winner, but without adequate academic experience in childhood, you might not perform well enough even to graduate from college. In fact, heredity and environment interact in influencing characteristics such as social smiling (Jones, 2008), childhood obesity (Levin, 2009), drug addiction (Agrawal & Lynskey, 2008), gender differences in religiosity (Bradshaw & Ellison, 2009), and psychological disorders (Wermter et al., 2010).

Section Review: Nature versus Nurture

1. What is evolutionary psychology?
2. Why are the greater physical, cognitive, and personality similarities among relatives than among nonrelatives not enough evidence to demonstrate conclusively that they are the product of heredity?

Biological Communication Systems

Biopsychological activity is regulated by two major bodily communication systems: the *nervous system* and the *endocrine system*. These systems regulate biopsychological functions as varied as hunger, memory, sexuality, and emotionality.

The Nervous System

The brain is part of the **nervous system**, the chief means of communication within the body. The basic unit of the nervous system is the **neuron**, a cell that is specialized for the transmission and reception of information. As illustrated in Figure 3-1, the two divisions of the nervous system are the *central nervous system* and the *peripheral nervous system*.

The Central Nervous System

The **central nervous system** comprises the *brain* and the *spinal cord*. The **brain**, protectively housed in the skull, is so important in psychological functioning that most of this chapter and many other sections of this book are devoted to it. As you will learn, the brain is intimately involved in learning, thinking, language, memory, emotion, motivation, body movements, social relationships, psychological disorders, perception of the world, and even immune-system activity.

The **spinal cord**, which runs through the bony, protective spinal column, provides a means of communication between the brain and the body. Motor output from the brain travels down the spinal cord to direct activity in muscles and certain glands. Sensory input from pain, touch, pressure, and temperature receptors in the body travels up the spinal cord to the brain, informing it of the state of the body. As discussed in the chapter section "Neuronal Activity," the spinal cord also plays a role in limb reflexes. A **reflex** is an automatic, involuntary motor response to sensory stimulation. Thus, when you step on a sharp, broken shell at the beach, you immediately pull your foot away. Your response occurs at the level of the spinal cord; it does not require input from the brain.

Damage to the spinal cord can have catastrophic effects. You might know people who have suffered a spinal-cord injury in a diving, vehicular, or contact-sport accident, causing them to lose the ability to move their limbs or feel bodily sensations below the point of the injury. Longitudinal studies show that 30–40 percent of people with spinal-cord injuries suffer from depression and anxiety (Kennedy & Rogers, 2000). Successful adjustment to

nervous system The chief means of communication in the body.

neuron A cell specialized for the transmission of information in the nervous system.

central nervous system The division of the nervous system consisting of the brain and the spinal cord.

brain The structure of the central nervous system that is located in the skull and plays important roles in sensation, movement, and information processing.

spinal cord The structure of the central nervous system that is located in the spine and plays a role in bodily reflexes and in communicating information between the brain and the peripheral nervous system.

reflex An automatic, involuntary motor response to sensory stimulation.

FIGURE 3-1
The Nervous System

The nervous system comprises the central nervous system (brain and spinal cord) and the peripheral nervous system (nerves).

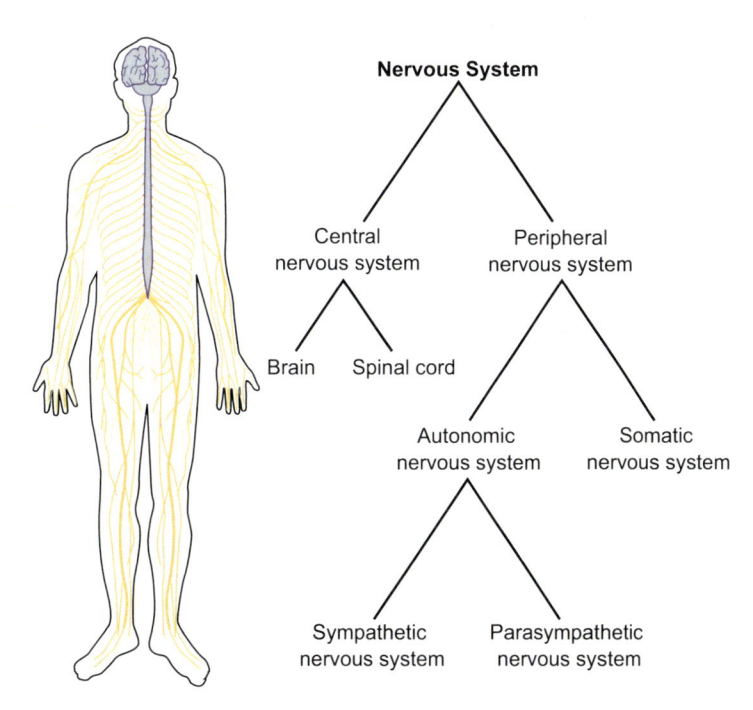

Chapter 3 Biopsychological Basis of Behavior

spinal-cord injury is promoted by participating in physical activities to the extent possible (Ginis, Jetha, Dack, & Hetz, 2010) and by finding a purpose in life despite one's disability (Thompson, Coker, Krause, & Henry, 2003). Emotional reactions to spinal-cord injuries show the influence of gender and culture. Two studies of people with spinal-cord injuries in southern California found that men reported more distress over interpersonal problems than women did (Krause, 1998). Moreover, severe depression was more common among Latinos than among European Americans or African Americans (Kemp, Krause, & Adkins, 1999). As discussed in greater depth later in the chapter, research on the transplantation of healthy nerve tissue into damaged spinal cords of animals indicates that scientists may be on the threshold of discovering effective means of restoring motor and sensory functions to people who have suffered spinal-cord injuries (Kim et al., 1999).

The Peripheral Nervous System

The **peripheral nervous system** contains the **nerves**, which provide a means of communication between the central nervous system and the sensory organs, skeletal muscles, and internal bodily organs. The peripheral nervous system comprises the *somatic nervous system* and the *autonomic nervous system*. The **somatic nervous system** includes *sensory nerves*, which send messages from the sensory organs to the central nervous system, and *motor nerves*, which send messages from the central nervous system to the skeletal muscles. The **autonomic nervous system** controls automatic, involuntary processes (such as sweating, heart contractions, and intestinal activity) through the action of its two subdivisions: the *sympathetic nervous system* and the *parasympathetic nervous system*. The **sympathetic nervous system** arouses the body to prepare it for action, and the **parasympathetic nervous system** calms the body to conserve energy.

Imagine that you are playing a tennis match. Your sympathetic nervous system would speed up your heart rate to pump more blood to your muscles, make your liver release sugar into your bloodstream for quick energy, and induce sweating to keep you from overheating. As you cool down after the match, your parasympathetic nervous system would slow your heart rate and constrict the blood vessels in your muscles to divert blood for use by your internal organs. Chapter 12 describes the role of the autonomic nervous system in emotional responses and includes a diagram (Figure 12-1) illustrating its effects on various bodily organs. Chapter 13 explains how chronic activation of the sympathetic nervous system can contribute to the development of stress-related diseases. The peripheral nervous system is particularly subject to sport- and exercise-related injuries that produce temporary or chronic physical disability (Toth, McNeil, & Feasby, 2005).

The Endocrine System

The glands of the **endocrine system**, the other major means of communication within the body, exert their functions through hormones (Bauer, 2005). **Hormones** are chemicals that affect physical or psychological processes or both. The endocrine glands secrete hormones into the bloodstream, which transports them to their site of action. The actions of the endocrine system are slower, longer lasting, and more diffuse than those of the nervous system. Endocrine glands differ from *exocrine glands*, such as the sweat glands and salivary glands, which secrete their chemicals onto the body surface or into body cavities. Endocrine secretions have many behavioral effects, but exocrine secretions have few. Figure 3-2 illustrates the locations of major endocrine glands. Hormones can act directly on body tissues, serve as neurotransmitters, or modulate the effects of neurotransmitters.

The Pituitary Gland

The **pituitary gland**, an endocrine gland protruding from underneath the brain, regulates many of the other endocrine glands by secreting hormones that affect their activity. This is why the pituitary is known as the "master gland." The pituitary gland, in turn, is regulated by the brain structure called the *hypothalamus*. Feedback from circulating hormones stimulates the hypothalamus to signal the pituitary gland to increase or decrease their secretion (Charlton, 2008).

---

peripheral nervous system The division of the nervous system that conveys sensory information to the central nervous system and motor commands from the central nervous system to the skeletal muscles and internal organs.

nerve A bundle of axons that conveys information to or from the central nervous system.

somatic nervous system The division of the peripheral nervous system that sends messages from the sensory organs to the central nervous system and messages from the central nervous system to the skeletal muscles.

autonomic nervous system The division of the peripheral nervous system that controls automatic, involuntary, physiological processes.

sympathetic nervous system The division of the autonomic nervous system that arouses the body to prepare it for action.

parasympathetic nervous system The division of the autonomic nervous system that calms the body and performs maintenance functions.

endocrine system The physiological system whose glands secrete hormones into the bloodstream.

hormones Chemicals, secreted by endocrine glands, that play a role in a variety of functions, including synaptic transmission.

pituitary gland An endocrine gland that regulates many of the other endocrine glands by secreting hormones that affect the secretion of their hormones.

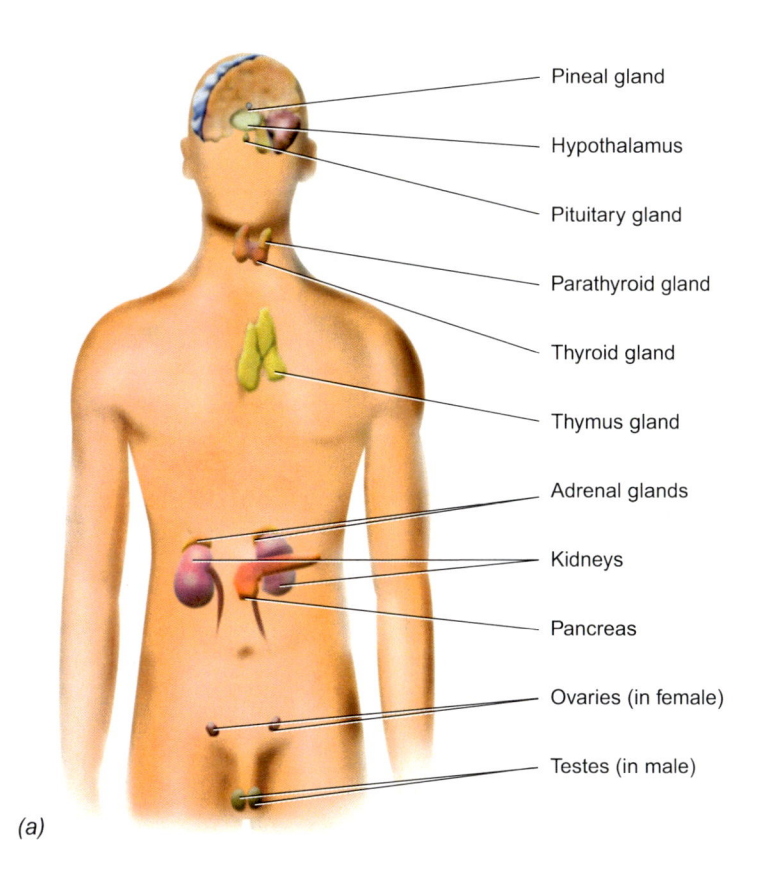

FIGURE 3-2
The Endocrine System

(a) Hormones secreted by the endocrine glands affect behavior, mood, cognitive activity, and a host of other physical and psychological processes.
(b) Crosssection of the brain showing major structures of the endocrine system.

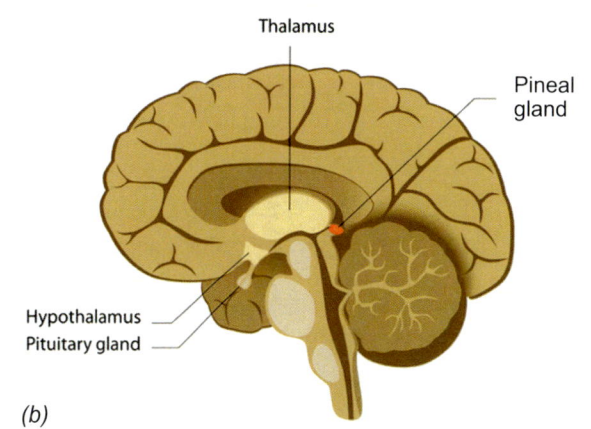

Labels (a): Pineal gland, Hypothalamus, Pituitary gland, Parathyroid gland, Thyroid gland, Thymus gland, Adrenal glands, Kidneys, Pancreas, Ovaries (in female), Testes (in male)

Labels (b): Thalamus, Pineal gland, Hypothalamus, Pituitary gland

Pituitary hormones also exert a wide variety of direct effects. For example, *prolactin* levels increase in pregnant women—as well as in expectant fathers—shortly before childbirth (Storey, Walsh, Quintin, & Wynne-Edwards, 2000). Because an elevated prolactin level is also associated with both infertility (Grattan et al., 2001) and psychological stress (Sonino et al., 2004), prolactin might be involved in stress-related infertility. Women who are highly anxious about their inability to become pregnant might enter a vicious cycle in which their anxiety increases the level of prolactin, which in turn makes them less likely to conceive.

Growth hormone, another pituitary hormone, aids the growth and repair of bones and muscles. A child who secretes too much growth hormone might develop *giantism*, marked by excessive growth of the bones. A child who secretes insufficient growth hormone might develop *dwarfism*, marked by stunted growth. Giantism and dwarfism do not impair intellectual development. Children with growth-hormone deficiency may respond to growth hormone treatment (Rosenwald, 2009). Though it might seem logical to administer growth hormone to increase the height of extremely short children who are not diagnosed with dwarfism, this is unwise because the long-term side effects exposing children to hormone treatment for years are unknown (Tauer, 1994).

Adults who secrete high levels of growth hormone, often caused by a pituitary gland tumor, may develop *acromegaly*. This produces unusual enlargement of the hands, feet, jaw, and brow ridge. Because acromegaly increases the risk of mortality due to cardiovascular, cerebrovascular, or pulmonary dysfunction, it is treated by surgery, radiation, and medications (Melmed, 2009). Some competitive athletes take growth hormone alone or in combination with anabolic steroids to improve strength and stamina. Of course, they risk the effects of growth hormone overdose, much akin to acromegaly (Guhu, Sönksen, & Holt, 2010). Moreover, there is inconsistent evidence to support the effectiveness of growth hormone administration in improving athletic performance (Liu et al., 2008).

Other Endocrine Glands

Among the other psychologically important endocrine glands are the *adrenal glands* and the *gonads*. The **adrenal glands**, which lie on the kidneys, secrete important hormones.

adrenal gland An endocrine gland that secretes hormones that regulate the excretion of minerals and the body's response to stress.

Chapter 3 Biopsychological Basis of Behavior

The *adrenal cortex*, the outer layer of the adrenal gland, secretes hormones, such as *aldosterone*, that regulate the excretion of sodium and potassium, which contribute to proper neural functioning. The adrenal hormone *cortisol* helps the body respond to stress by stimulating the liver to release sugar. Firefighters participating in simulated firefighting exercises show marked increases in cortisol secretion (Perroni et al., 2009). Cortisol levels decrease about 30 percent after massage therapy, providing evidence that massage therapy reduces stress (Field, Hernandez-Reif, Diego, Schanberg, & Kahn, 2005). Cortisol levels in premature infants are reduced by maternal touch, indicating that maternal touch might help relieve infants' stress (Gitau et al., 2002).

Moreover, cortisol levels have been found to be related to the levels of stress experienced by heterosexual couples who discuss the transition to marriage. In one study, cortisol levels were assessed in the laboratory after couples discussed the possibility of marriage. Cortisol levels were lower among couples who had previously discussed marriage during the course of their relationship. In contrast, higher levels of cortisol were found among couples who had not previously discussed marriage during the course of their relationships, and for whom the idea of being married was more novel, and presumably, more stressful (Loving, Gleason, & Pope, 2009).

In response to stimulation by the sympathetic nervous system, the *adrenal medulla*, the inner core of the adrenal gland, secretes *epinephrine* and *norepinephrine*, which function as both hormones and neurotransmitters. Epinephrine and norepinephrine play a role in stress-related responses. For example, spouses (especially wives) show increases in epinephrine and norepinephrine during marital conflict (Kiecolt-Glaser et al., 1996). Positive moods are associated with lower levels of cortisol and norepinephrine (Brummett, Boyle, Kuhn, Siegler, & Williams, 2009).

gonads The male and female sex glands.

testes The male gonads, which secrete hormones that regulate the development of the male reproductive system and secondary sex characteristics.

ovaries The female gonads, which secrete hormones that regulate the development of the female reproductive system and secondary sex characteristics.

The **gonads**, the sex glands, affect sexual development and regulate the structure and organization of brain areas that control reproductive behavior. The **testes**, the male gonads, secrete *testosterone*, which regulates the development of the male reproductive system and secondary sex characteristics. Testosterone also stimulates sexual arousal in both males and females (Apperloo, Van Der Stege, Hoek, Schultz, & Willibrord, 2003). The **ovaries**, the female gonads, secrete *estrogen*, which regulates the development of the female reproductive system and secondary sex characteristics. The ovarian hormone *progesterone* regulates changes in the uterus that help maintain pregnancy. Physicians may administer progesterone to prevent premature delivery (Majhi, Bagga, Kalra, & Sharma, 2009). During prenatal development, sex hormones also affect certain structures and functions of the brain. The effects of sex hormones on human development and sexual behavior are discussed in Chapters 4 and 11.

Anabolic steroids, synthetic forms of testosterone, have provoked controversy during the past two decades. They have been used by athletes, bodybuilders, and weight lifters to promote muscle development, increase endurance, and boost athletic self-confidence (Wright, Grogan, & Hunter, 2000). Yet, studies have shown inconsistent effects of steroids on physical strength. It is unclear whether anabolic steroids directly increase strength or do so through a placebo effect in which users work out more regularly and more vigorously simply because they have faith in the effectiveness of steroids (Maganaris, Collins, & Sharp, 2000). Moreover, a dangerous side effect of anabolic steroid use is increased aggressiveness in some users (Beaver, Vaughn, DeLisi, & Wright, 2008).

Section Review: Biological Communication Systems

1. What are the divisions of the nervous system?
2. What is the difference between exocrine glands and endocrine glands?

Chapter 3 Biopsychological Basis of Behavior

Neuronal Activity

You are able to read this page because *sensory neurons* are relaying input from your eyes to your brain. You will be able to write down information from this page because *motor neurons* from your spinal cord are sending commands from your brain to the muscles of your hand. A **sensory neuron** sends messages to the brain or spinal cord. A **motor neuron** sends messages to a gland, the cardiac muscle, or a skeletal muscle, as well as to a smooth muscle of an artery, small intestine, or other internal organ.

Many motor neurons in the brain not only respond when a person initiates a movement but also when the person observes that movement being performed by another person. These are known as *mirror neurons* (Dushanova & Donoghue, 2010), and they play an important role in observational learning (see Chapter 7). Illnesses that destroy motor neurons, such as *amyotrophic lateral sclerosis* (also known as Lou Gehrig's disease, after the great baseball player struck down by it), cause muscle paralysis and eventual death from respiratory muscle paralysis (Beleza-Meireles & Al-Chalabi, 2009).

Within the nervous system, about 10 percent of the cells are neurons and 90 percent are *glial cells* (Colon-Ramos & Shen, 2008). A **glial cell** may serve one of a number of functions, such as providing a physical support structure for the neurons (*glial* comes from the Greek word for "glue"), neurons with nutrients, removing neuronal metabolic waste materials, guiding interneuronal connections, and helping regenerate damaged neurons in the peripheral nervous system. The three main types of glial cells are *astrocytes*, *microglia*, and *oligodendrocytes*. Glial cells even facilitate the transmission of messages by neurons (Cras, 2007) and play a role in learning and memory (Hertz & Chen, 2016; Yates, 2016). One of the most serious kinds of cancer is *glioblastoma*, a malignant glial cell tumor of the brain. It is treated by surgery, radiation, and chemotherapy. A recent addition to the treatment arsenal is monoclonal antibody therapy aimed at preventing angiogenesis—the development of blood vessels that nourish the tumor (Moen, 2010).

To appreciate the role of neurons in communication within the nervous system, consider the functions of the spinal cord. Neurons in the spinal cord convey sensory messages from the body to the brain and motor messages from the brain to the body. In 1730 the English scientist Stephen Hales demonstrated that the spinal cord also plays a role in limb reflexes. He decapitated a frog (to eliminate any input from the brain) and then pinched

sensory neuron A neuron that sends messages from sensory receptors to the central nervous system.

motor neuron A neuron that sends messages from the central nervous system to smooth muscles, cardiac muscles, or skeletal muscles.

glial cell A kind of cell that provides a physical support structure for the neurons, supplies them with nutrition, removes neuronal metabolic waste materials, facilitates the transmission of messages by neurons, and helps regenerate damaged neurons in the peripheral nervous system.

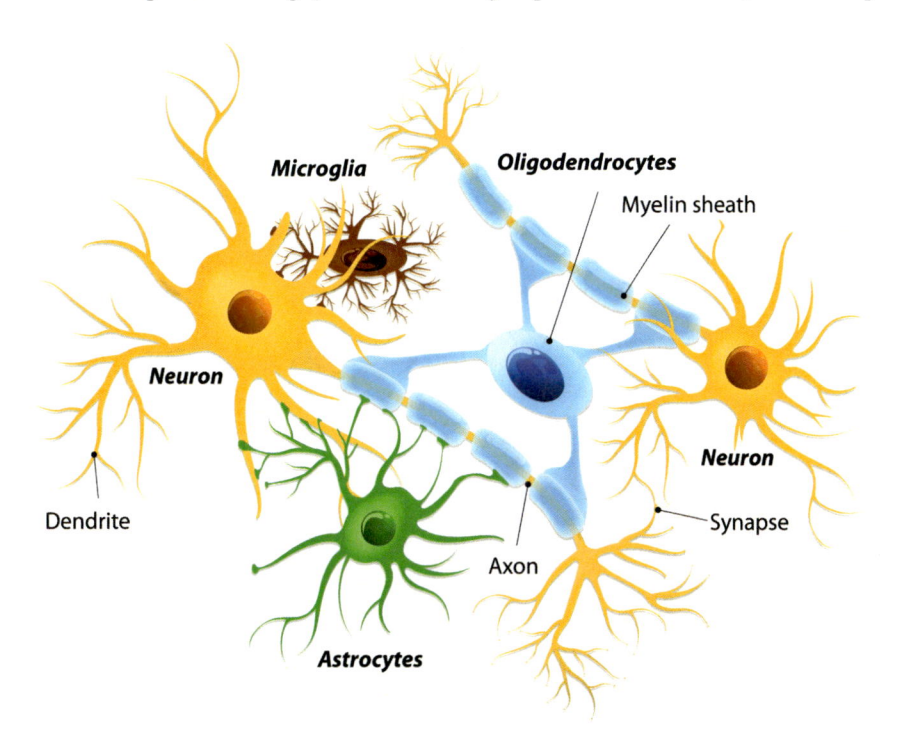

Glial Cells

Supporting our billons of nerve cells are glial cells. The three main types of glial cells are astrocytes, microglia, and oligodendrocytes.
Source: Chepko Designua/Shutterstock.com.

Chapter 3 Biopsychological Basis of Behavior

one of its legs. The leg reflexively pulled away. Hales concluded that the pinch had sent a signal to the spinal cord, which in turn sent a signal to the leg, eliciting its withdrawal. We now know that this limb-withdrawal reflex involves sensory neurons that convey signals from the site of stimulation to the spinal cord, where they transmit their signals to *interneurons* in the spinal cord (McCrea, 1992). An **interneuron** conveys messages between neurons in the brain or spinal cord. The interneurons then send signals to motor neurons, which stimulate flexor muscles to contract and pull the limb away from the source of stimulation—making you less susceptible to pain and injury.

interneuron A neuron that conveys messages between neurons in the brain or spinal cord.

The Structure of the Neuron

To understand how neurons communicate information, you should first become familiar with the structure of the neuron (see Figure 3-3). The **soma** (or cell body) contains the nucleus, which directs the neuron to act as a nerve cell rather than as a fat cell, a muscle cell, or any other kind of cell. The **dendrites** (from the Greek word for "tree") are short, branching fibers that receive neural impulses. The dendrites are covered by bumps called *dendritic spines*, which provide more surface area for the reception of neural impulses from other neurons (Grutzendler, Kasthuri, & Gan, 2002) and play a critical role in learning and memory (Kasai, Fukuda, Watanabe, Hayashi-Takagi, & Noguchi, 2010). The **axon** is a single fiber that sends neural impulses. Axons range from a tiny fraction of an inch (as in the brain) to more than 3 feet in length (as in the legs of a 7-foot-tall basketball player). Just as bundles of wires form telephone cables, bundles of axons form the nerves of the peripheral nervous system and tracks in the central nervous system. A nerve can contain motor neurons or sensory neurons, or both.

soma The cell body, which is the neuron's control center.

dendrites The branchlike structures of the neuron that receive neural impulses.

axon The part of the neuron that conducts neural impulses to glands, muscles, or other neurons.

The Neural Impulse

How does the neuron convey information? It took centuries of investigation by brilliant minds to find the answer. In the 17th century, René Descartes (1596–1650) was intrigued by moving statues in the royal gardens of King Louis XIII that were controlled hydraulically by fluid-filled tubes activated when visitors stepped on hidden levers. Descartes speculated that the body is controlled in a similar way by fluids, which he called vital spirits, flowing through the nerves. He assumed that our limbs move when vital spirits expand the muscles that control them.

Descartes was wrong about how muscles function. Though they shorten and thicken when contracted, their overall size remains the same. By the mid-18th century, an alterna-

FIGURE 3-3
The Neuron

The main structures of the neuron are the dendrites, the soma, and the axon. The dendrites receive neural impulses from other neurons, the soma regulates neuronal functions, and the axon conveys signals to other neurons, skeletal muscles, or internal organs. When a neuron receives sufficient stimulation from other neurons, it transmits an electrical-chemical neural impulse along its entire axon.

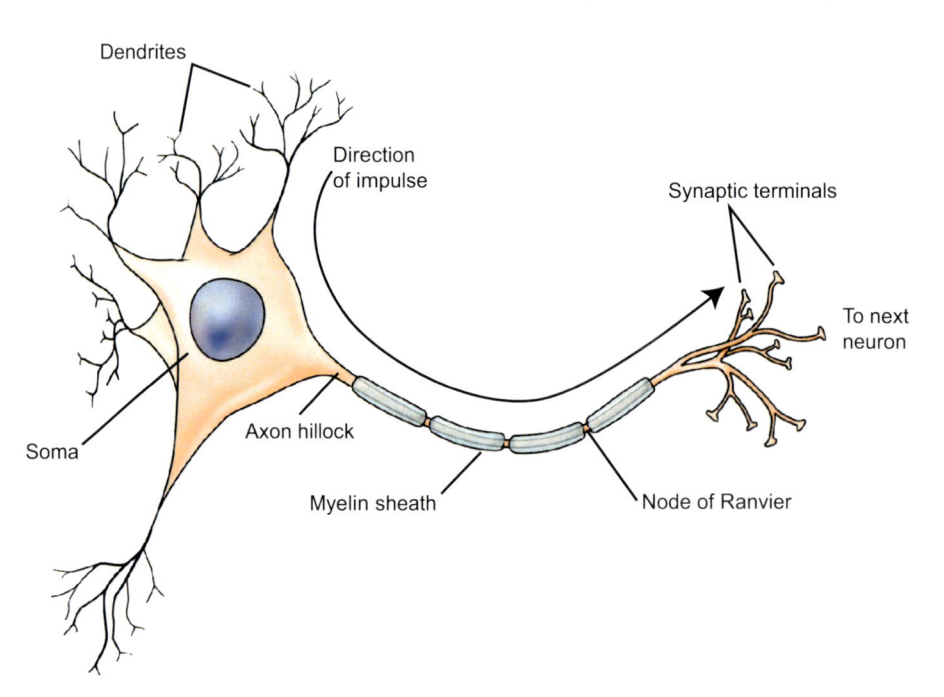

Chapter 3 Biopsychological Basis of Behavior

tive explanation, put forth by the great scientist Isaac Newton, replaced Descartes's explanation (Wallace, 2003). Newton, who studied the nature of vibrating strings, believed that nerves communicated by vibrating. Thus, for example, a motor nerve would vibrate faster when we lift a heavy object than a light object. Newton's explanation was discredited by anatomical research, which found that nerves do not vibrate.

The first significant discovery regarding nerve conduction came in 1786, when demonstrations by the Italian physicist Luigi Galvani (1737–1798) hinted that the nerve impulse is electrical in nature. Galvani found that by touching the leg of a freshly killed frog with two different metals, such as iron and brass, he could create an electrical current that made the leg twitch. He believed he had discovered the basic life force—electricity. Some of Galvani's followers, who hoped to use electricity to raise the dead, obtained the fresh corpses of hanged criminals and stimulated them with electricity. To the disappointment of these would-be resurrectionists, they failed to induce more than the flailing of limbs (Hassett, 1978). Not much later, another of Galvani's contemporaries, Mary Shelley, applied what she called "galvanism" (apparently, the use of electricity) to revive the dead in her classic novel *Frankenstein.*

Though Galvani and his colleagues failed to demonstrate that electricity was the basic life force, they put scientists on the right track toward understanding how neural impulses are conveyed in the nervous system. But it took almost two more centuries of research before scientists identified the exact mechanism. We now know that neuronal activity, whether involved in hearing a doorbell, throwing a softball, or recalling a childhood memory, depends on electrical-chemical processes, beginning with the *resting potential*.

The Resting Potential

In 1952, English scientists Alan Hodgkin and Andrew Huxley discovered the electrical-chemical nature of the processes that underlie **axonal conduction**, the transmission of a *neural impulse* along the length of the giant squid axon (Huxley, 1959). In 1963 Hodgkin and Huxley won the Nobel Prize for physiology or medicine for their discovery (Lamb, 1999). Hodgkin and Huxley found that in its inactive state, the neuron maintains an electrical **resting potential**, produced by differences between the *intracellular fluid* inside the neuron and the *extracellular fluid* outside the neuron. These fluids contain *ions*, which are positively or negatively charged molecules. In regard to the resting potential, the main positive ions are *sodium* and *potassium,* and the main negative ions are *proteins* and *chloride*.

The *neuronal membrane*, which separates the intracellular fluid from the extracellular fluid, is selectively permeable to ions. This means that some ions pass back and forth through tiny *ion channels* in the membrane more easily than do others. Because ions with like charges repel each other and ions with opposite charges attract each other, you might assume the extracellular fluid and intracellular fluid would end up with the same relative concentrations of positive ions and negative ions. But, because of several complex processes, the intracellular fluid ends up with an excess of negative ions, and the extracellular fluid ends up with an excess of positive ions. This makes the inside of the resting neuron negative relative to the outside, so the membrane is said to be *polarized*, just like a battery. For example, at rest, the inside of a motor neuron has a charge of –70 millivolts relative to its outside. (A millivolt is one-thousandth of a volt). In other words, when a neuron is at rest (not firing), it has an electrical charge.

axonal conduction The transmission of a neural impulse along the length of an axon.

resting potential The electrical charge of a neuron when it is not firing a neural impulse.

The Action Potential

When a neuron is sufficiently stimulated by other neurons or by a sensory organ, it stops "resting." The neuronal membrane becomes more permeable to positively charged sodium ions, which, attracted by the negative ions inside, rush into the neuron. This movement makes the inside of the neuron less electrically negative relative to the outside, a process called *depolarization*. As sodiumcontinue to rush into the neuron, and the inside becomes less and less negative, the neuron reaches its *firing threshold* (about –55 millivolts in the case of a motor neuron), and an *action potential* occurs at the point where the axon leaves the cell body, the axon hillock. Figure 3-4 illustrates the phases of the action potential.

Chapter 3 Biopsychological Basis of Behavior

FIGURE 3-4
The Action Potential

(a) Sodium ions flow into the axon, causing a *depolarization* (i.e., a more positive charge inside the cell). *(b)* Shortly after sodium flows into the axon, potassium ions flow out of the axon.

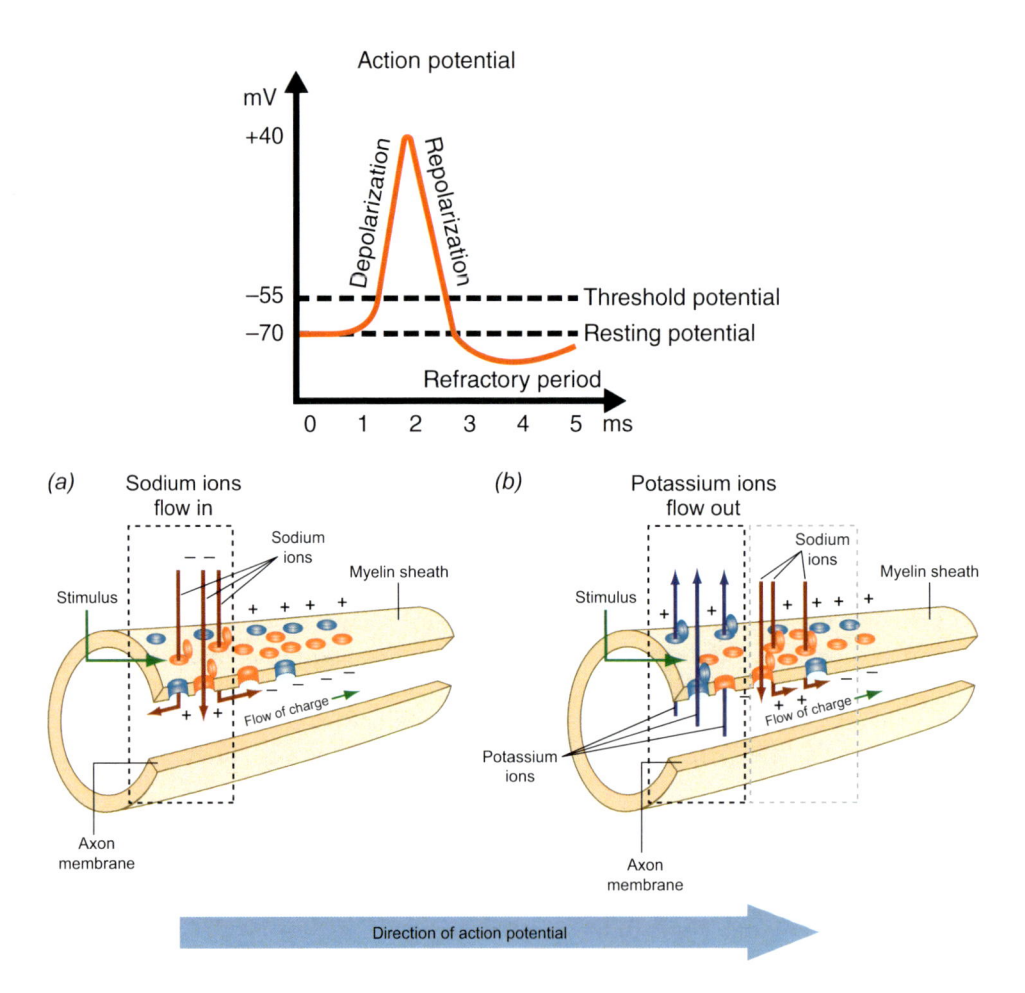

action potential A series of changes in the electrical charge across the axonal membrane that occurs after the axon has reached its firing threshold.

all-or-none law The principle that once a neuron reaches its firing threshold, a neural impulse travels at full strength along the entire length of its axon.

An **action potential** is a change in the electrical charge across the axonal membrane, with the inside of the membrane becoming more electrically positive than the outside and, in the case of a motor neuron, reaching a charge of +40 millivolts. Once an action potential has occurred, that point on the axonal membrane immediately restores its resting potential through a process called *repolarization*. This occurs, in part, because the sudden excess of positively charged sodium ions inside the axon repels the positive potassium ions, driving many of them out of the axon. This loss of positively charged ions helps return the inside of the axon to its negatively charged state relative to the outside. The restored resting potential also is maintained by chemical "pumps" that transport sodium and potassium ions across the axonal membrane, helping return them to their original concentrations.

If an axon fails to depolarize enough to reach its firing threshold, no action potential occurs—not even a weak one. If you have ever been under general anesthesia, you became unconscious because you were given a drug that prevented the axons in your brain that are responsible for the maintenance of consciousness from depolarizing enough to fire off action potentials (Nicoll & Madison, 1982). When an axon reaches its firing threshold and an action potential occurs, a neural impulse travels the entire length of the axon at full strength, as sodium ions rush in at each successive point along the axon. This result is known as the **all-or-none law**. It is analogous to firing a gun: If you do not pull the trigger hard enough, nothing happens; but if you do pull the trigger hard enough, the gun fires and a bullet travels down the entire length of its barrel.

Thus, when a neuron reaches its firing threshold, a neural impulse travels along its axon, as each point on the axonal membrane depolarizes (producing an action potential) and then repolarizes (restoring its resting potential). This process of depolarization/repolarization is so rapid that an axon might conduct up to 1,000 neural impulses a second. The loudness of sounds you hear, the strength of your muscle contractions, and the

74 Chapter 3 Biopsychological Basis of Behavior

level of arousal of your brain all depend on the number of neurons involved in those processes and the rate at which they conduct neural impulses.

The speed at which the action potential travels along the axon varies from less than 1 meter per second in certain neurons to more than 100 meters per second in others. The speed depends on several factors, most notably whether sheaths of a fatty white substance called **myelin** (which is produced by one type of glial cells, oligodendrocytes) are wrapped around the axon. At frequent intervals along myelinated axons, tiny areas are nonmyelinated. These areas are called *nodes of Ranvier*, after Louis-Antoine Ranvier, the French physiologist who identified them in the 19th century (Barbara, 2007). In myelinated axons, such as those forming much of the brain and spinal cord as well as the motor nerves that control our muscles, the action potential jumps from node to node instead of traveling from point to point along the entire axon. We call this phenomenon saltatory conduction (from the Latin word, *saltare*, which means "to dance"). This explains why myelinated axons conduct neural impulses faster than nonmyelinated axons. This increased speed allows humans and animals to think and react faster.

If you were to look at a freshly dissected brain, you would find that the inside appears mostly white and the outside appears mostly gray because the inside contains many more myelinated axons, whereas the outside contains more cell bodies. You would be safe in concluding that the brain's white matter conveys information faster than its gray matter. Some neurological disorders are associated with abnormal myelin conditions. In the autoimmune demyelinating disease *multiple sclerosis (MS)*, portions of the myelin sheaths surrounding axons in the brain and spinal cord are destroyed, causing muscle weakness, sensory disturbances, memory loss, impaired reasoning, and other cognitive deterioration as a result of the disruption of normal axonal conduction (DeSousa, Albert, & Kalman, 2002).

To summarize, a neuron maintains a *resting potential* during which the inside is electrically negative relative to the outside. Stimulation of the neuron makes positive sodium ions rush in and *depolarize* the neuron (that is, make the inside less negative relative to the outside). If the neuron depolarizes enough, it reaches its *firing threshold*, and an *action potential* occurs. During the action potential, the inside of the neuron becomes electrically positive relative to the outside. Because of the *all-or-none law*, a *neural impulse* is conducted along the entire length of the axon at full strength. Axons covered by a *myelin sheath* conduct impulses faster than other axons. After an action potential has occurred, the axon *repolarizes* and restores its resting potential.

myelin A fatty white substance that forms sheaths around certain axons and increases the speed of neural impulses.

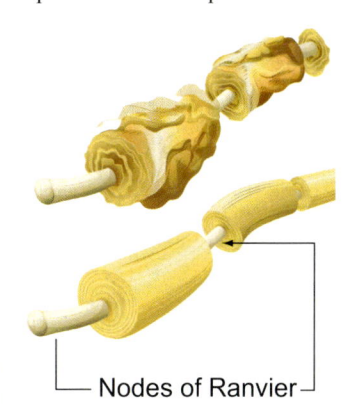

Damaged and Healthy Myelin Sheaths

The top image shows damage to the myelin of a section of a neuron associated with multiple sclerosis. The bottom image is of a healthy neuron. Arrows point to the nodes of Ranvier.
Source: BlueRingMedia/Shutterstock.com.

Synaptic Transmission

If all the neuron did was conduct a series of neural impulses along its axon, we would have an interesting but useless phenomenon. The reason we can enjoy a movie, feel a mosquito bite, think about yesterday, or ride a bicycle is because neurons can communicate with one another by the process of **synaptic transmission**—communication across gaps between neurons. Many psychological processes, such as detecting the direction of a sound by determining the slight difference in the arrival time of sound waves at the two ears, require rapid and precisely timed synaptic transmission (Sabatini & Regehr, 1999).

The question of how neurons communicate with one another provoked a heated debate in the late 19th century. The Spanish anatomist Santiago Ramón y Cajal (1852–1934) argued that neurons were separate from one another (Koppe, 1983), whereas the Italian scientist Camillo Golgi (1843–1926) thought nervous tissue was a single system, not made up of separate cells. Ramón y Cajal won the debate by showing that neurons are units that form a network (Ramón y Cajal, 1937/1966). His finding led to the modern *neuron doctrine*, which views the neuron as the basic unit of nerve function, with the neurons physically separated by gaps (Albright et al., 2001). In 1897, the English physiologist Charles Sherrington (1857–1952) coined the term **synapse** (from the Greek word for "junction") to refer to the gaps that exist between neurons. You should note that synapses also exist between neurons and glands, between neurons and muscles, and between neurons and sensory organs.

synaptic transmission The conveying of a neural impulse between a neuron and a gland, muscle, sensory organ, or another neuron.

synapse The junction between a neuron and a gland, muscle, sensory organ, or another neuron.

Chapter 3 Biopsychological Basis of Behavior

Mechanisms of Synaptic Transmission

As is usually the case with scientific discoveries, the observation that neurons were separated by synapses led to still another question: How could neurons communicate with one another across these gaps? At first, some scientists assumed that the neural impulse simply jumped across the synapse, just as sparks jump across the gap in a spark plug. But the correct answer came in 1921—in a dream (Loewi, 1960).

The dreamer was Otto Loewi (1873–1961), an Austrian physiologist who had been searching without success for the mechanism of synaptic transmission. Loewi awoke from his dream and carried out the experiment it suggested. He removed the beating heart of a freshly killed frog, along with the portion of the *vagus nerve* attached to it, and placed it in a solution of salt water. By electrically stimulating the vagus nerve, he made the heart beat slower. He then put another beating heart in the same solution. Though he had not stimulated its vagus nerve, the second heart also began to beat slower. If you had made this discovery, what would you have concluded? Loewi concluded, correctly, that the vagus nerve of the hearts had released a chemical into the solution. He named the chemical "vagus stuff." It was this chemical, which other researchers identified as *acetylcholine* (Brown, 2006), that slowed the beating of both hearts (Sourkes, 2009). In 1936 Loewi and British physiologist Henry Dale were co-recipients of the Nobel Prize in physiology or medicine for their research identifying the chemical basis of synaptic transmission (Todman, 2008).

neurotransmitter Chemicals secreted by neurons that provide the means of synaptic transmission.

Acetylcholine is a **neurotransmitter**, a chemical that transmits neural impulses across synapses. Neurotransmitters are stored in round packets called *synaptic vesicles* in the intracellular fluid of *synaptic terminals* (bumps at the end of the axon; sometimes called *synaptic buttons*) that project from the end branches of axons. The discovery of the chemical nature of synaptic transmission led to a logical question: How do neurotransmitters facilitate this transmission? Subsequent research revealed the processes involved (see Figure 3-5):

1. When a neural impulse reaches the end of an axon, it induces a chemical reaction that makes some synaptic vesicles release neurotransmitter molecules into the synapse.
2. The molecules diffuse across the synapse and reach the dendrites of another neuron.
3. The molecules attach to tiny areas on the dendrites called *receptor sites*.
4. The molecules interact with the receptor sites to excite the neuron; this slightly depolarizes the neuron by permitting sodium ions to enter it. But for a neuron to depolarize enough to reach its firing threshold, it must be excited by neurotransmitters released by many neurons. To further complicate the process, a neuron also can be affected by neurotransmitters that inhibit it from depolarizing. Thus, a neuron will fire an action potential only when the combined effects of *excitatory neurotransmitters* sufficiently exceed the combined effects of *inhibitory neurotransmitters*.
5. Neurotransmitters do not remain attached to the receptor sites, continuing to affect them indefinitely. Instead, after the neurotransmitters have done their job, they either are broken down by chemicals called *enzymes* or taken back into the neurons that released them—in a process called *reuptake*.

Neurotransmitters and Drug Effects

Neurotransmitters affect our moods and are responsible for the mental and behavioral effects of psychoactive drugs. In fact, four of the main neurotransmitters out of the perhaps 100 that have been identified account for the effects of just about all psychoactive drugs (Snyder, 2002). Of the neurotransmitters, acetylcholine is the best understood and the first discovered. In the peripheral nervous system, it is the neurotransmitter at synapses between the neurons of the parasympathetic nervous system and the organs they control, such as the heart. Acetylcholine also is the neurotransmitter at synapses between motor neurons and muscle fibers, where it stimulates muscle contractions. *Curare*, a poison that Amazon Indians put on the darts they shoot from their blowguns into prey, par-

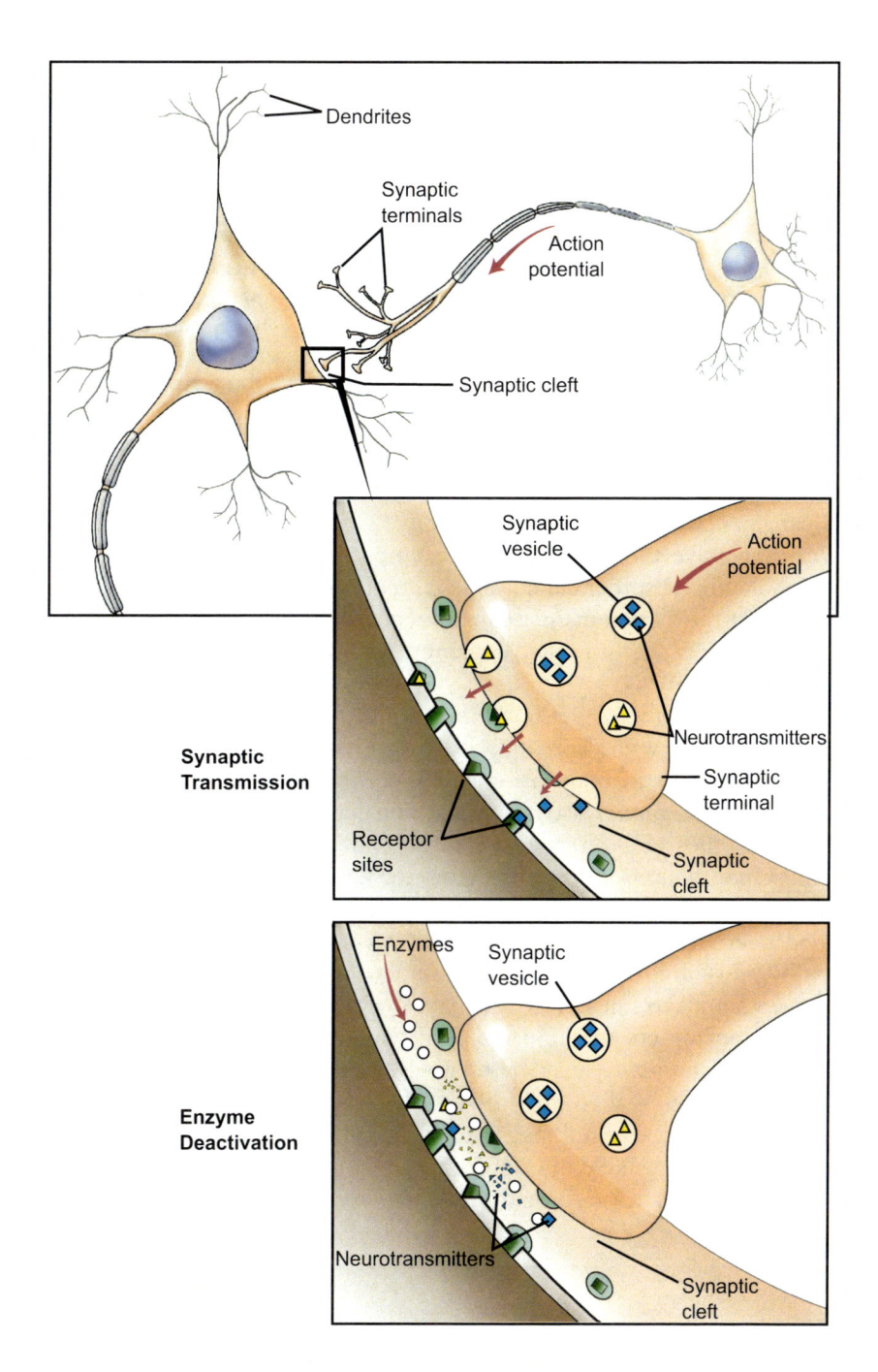

FIGURE 3-5

Mechanisms of Synaptic Transmission

When a neural impulse reaches the end of an axon, it stimulates synaptic vesicles to release neurotransmitter molecules into the synaptic cleft. The molecules diffuse across the fluid in the synaptic cleft and interact with receptor sites on another neuron. The molecules then disengage from the receptor sites and are either broken down by enzymes or taken back into the axon in a process called reuptake.

alyzes muscles by preventing acetylcholine from attaching to receptor sites on muscle fibers. The resulting paralysis of muscles, including the breathing muscles, causes death by suffocation. In the autoimmune disease *myasthenia gravis*, the immune system attacks and destroys acetylcholine receptor sites on muscle fibers, causing muscle weakness that tends to wax and wane over time (Carr, Cardwe, McCarron, & McConville, 2010).

In the brain, acetylcholine helps regulate memory processes (Levin & Simon, 1998). The actions of acetylcholine can be impaired by drugs or diseases. For example, chemicals in marijuana inhibit acetylcholine release, which is crucial in memory processes, so marijuana smokers might have difficulty forming new long-term memories (Domino, 1999). **Alzheimer's disease**, a progressive brain disorder that strikes in middle or late adulthood, destroys acetylcholine neurons in the brain. Alzheimer's disease is associated with the inability to form new memories and with severe intellectual and personality deterioration. Though we have no cure for Alzheimer's disease, treatments that increase levels of acetylcholine in the brain—most notably drugs that do so by preventing its breakdown

Alzheimer's disease A brain disorder characterized by difficulty in forming new memories and by general mental deterioration.

Chapter 3 Biopsychological Basis of Behavior

Parkinson's disease A degenerative disease of the dopamine pathway, which causes marked disturbances in motor behavior.

and deactivation in synapses—delay the mental deterioration that it induces (Sabbagh & Cummings, 2011).

Since the discovery of acetylcholine, many other neurotransmitters have been identified. Your ability to perform smooth voluntary movements depends on brain neurons that secrete the neurotransmitter *dopamine*. **Parkinson's disease**, first described by physician James Parkinson in 1817 (Cranwell-Bruce, 2010), is a disorder, characterized by decreased mobility and tremors, caused by the destruction of dopamine neurons in the brain. Drugs, such as levodopa (L-dopa), that increase dopamine levels provide some relief from Parkinson's disease symptoms. Genetic research is now aimed at increasing dopamine production and at converting other kinds of neurons into dopamine-producing neurons (Feng & Maguire-Zeiss, 2010). There also are research programs aimed at preventing neurodegeneration and restoring neural functioning in Parkinson's disease (Giovanni, 2008).

Dopamine has psychological as well as physical effects. Positive moods are maintained in part by activity in dopamine neurons (Kumari, Hemsley, Cotter, Checkley, & Gray,1998). Excessively high levels of dopamine activity are commonly found in the serious psychological disorder called *schizophrenia*. Drugs that block dopamine activity alleviate some of the symptoms of schizophrenia (Meizenzahl et al., 2007), and drugs, such as amphetamines, that stimulate dopamine activity may induce symptoms of schizophrenia (Adeyemo, 2002a).

Our moods vary with the level of the neurotransmitter *norepinephrine* in the brain. A low level is associated with depression. Some antidepressant drugs work by increasing norepinephrine levels in the brain (Dremencov, el Mensari, & Blair, 2009). A low level of the neurotransmitter *serotonin* also is implicated in depression. In fact, people who become so depressed that they commit suicide typically have unusually low levels of serotonin (Purselle & Nemeroff, 2003). Drugs that boost the level of serotonin in the nervous system relieve depression (Meisenzahl, Schmitt, Scheuerecker, & Möller, 2010). Antidepressant drugs called *selective serotonin reuptake inhibitors*, such as fluoxetine (Prozac), relieve depression by preventing the reuptake of serotonin into the axons that release it, thereby increasing serotonin levels in serotonin synapses (Racagni & Brunello, 1999).

Some neurotransmitters are amino acids. The main inhibitory amino acid neurotransmitter is *gamma aminobutyric acid* (or GABA). GABA promotes muscle relaxation and reduces anxiety. So-called tranquilizers, such as lorazepam (Ativan), relieve anxiety (Kalueff & Nutt, 2007) and insomnia (Winsky-Sommerer, 2009) by promoting the action of GABA. As discussed in Chapter 8, the main excitatory amino acid neurotransmitter, *glutamate*, helps in the formation of memories (Gravius, Pietraszek, Dekundy, & Danysz, 2010).

Endorphins

Another class of neurotransmitters comprises small proteins called *neuropeptides*. *Neuropeptide Y* promotes the deposit of abdominal fat, particularly in response to stressors (Kuo et al., 2007). The neuropeptide *substance P* has sparked interest because of its apparent role in the transmission of pain impulses (Ruiz, 2009), as in sciatic nerve pain (Malmberg & Basbaum, 1998), and following the accidental loosening of a hip replacement (Qian, Zeng, Zhang, & Jiang, 2008). During the past few decades, neuropeptides called **endorphins** have generated much research and publicity because of their possible roles in relieving pain and inducing feelings of euphoria.

endorphins Neurotransmitters that play a role in pleasure, pain relief, and other functions.

The endorphin story began in 1973, when Candace Pert and Solomon Snyder of Johns Hopkins University discovered opiate receptors in the brains of animals (Pert & Snyder, 1973). Opiates are pain-relieving drugs (or *narcotics*)—including morphine, codeine, and heroin—derived from the opium poppy. Snyder and Pert became interested in conducting their research after finding hints in previous research studies by other scientists that animals might have opiate receptors. They took samples of brain tissue from mice, rats, and guinea pigs and treated them with radioactive morphine and naloxone, a chemical similar in structure to morphine that blocks morphine's effects. A special device detected whether the morphine and naloxone had attached to receptors in the brain tissue.

Pert and Snyder found that the chemicals had bound to specific receptors (opiate receptors). If you had been a member of Pert and Snyder's research team, what would you have inferred from this observation? Pert and Snyder inferred that the brain must manufacture its own opiate-like chemicals. This would explain why it had evolved opiate receptors, and it seemed a more likely explanation than that the receptors had evolved to take advantage of the availability of opiates such as morphine and codeine in the environment. Pert and Snyder's findings inspired the search for opiate-like chemicals in the brain.

The search bore fruit in Scotland when Hans Kosterlitz and his colleagues found an opiate-like chemical in brain tissue taken from animals (Hughes et al., 1975). They called this chemical *enkephalin* (from Greek terms meaning "in the head"). Enkephalin and similar chemicals discovered in the brain were later dubbed "endogenous morphine" (meaning "morphine from within"). This term was abbreviated into the now-popular term *endorphin*. Endorphins function as both neurotransmitters and *neuromodulators*—neurochemicals that affect the activity of other neurotransmitters. For example, endorphins serve as neuromodulators by inhibiting the release of substance P, thereby blocking pain impulses.

Once researchers had located the receptor sites for the endorphins and had isolated endorphins themselves, they then wondered, *Why has the brain evolved its own opiate-like neurochemicals?* Perhaps the first animals blessed with endorphins were better able to function in the face of pain caused by diseases or injuries, making them more likely to survive long enough to reproduce and pass this physical trait on to successive generations (Levinthal, 1988). Evidence supporting this speculation has come from both human and animal experiments.

In one experiment, researchers first recorded how long mice would allow their tails to be exposed to radiant heat from a light bulb before the pain made them flick their tails away from it. Those mice then were paired with more aggressive mice, which attacked and defeated them. The losers' tolerance for the radiant heat was then tested again. The results showed that the length of time the defeated mice would permit their tails to be heated had increased, which suggests that the aggressive attacks had raised their endorphin levels. But when the defeated mice were given naloxone, which blocks the effects of morphine, they flicked away their tails as quickly as they had done before being defeated. The researchers concluded that the naloxone had blocked the pain-relieving effects of the endorphins (Miczek, Thompson, & Shuster, 1982). Other studies have found that the endorphins likewise are associated with pain relief in people (Spinella, Znamensky, Moroz, Ragnauth, & Bodnar, 1999). And increases in pain may be associated with reductions in endorphin levels. Premenstrual pain, for example, is associated with low endorphin levels (Straneva et al., 2002).

Endorphin levels may rise in response to vigorous exercise (Harbach et al., 2000), perhaps accounting for the "exercise high" reported by many athletes, including runners, swimmers, and cyclists. This hypothesis was supported by a study that found increased endorphin levels after aerobic dancing (Pierce, Eastman, Tripathi, & Olson, 1993). Further support came from a study of bungee jumpers. After jumping, their feelings of euphoria showed a positive correlation with increases in their endorphin levels (Hennig, Laschefski, & Opper, 1994).

The Runner's High

The euphoric "exercise high" experienced by long-distance runners might be caused by the release of endorphins.
Source: HUAJI/Shutterstock.com.

Section Review: Neuronal Activity

1. What are the major structures of the neuron?
2. What is the basic process underlying neural impulses?

Brain Functions

"Tell me, where is fancy bred, in the heart or in the head?" (*The Merchant of Venice*, act 3, scene 2). The answer to this question from Shakespeare's play might be obvious to you. You know that your brain, and not your heart, is your feeling organ—the site of your mind. But you have the advantage of centuries of research, which has made the role of the brain in all psychological processes obvious even to nonscientists. Of course, the cultural influence of early beliefs may linger. Just imagine the response of someone who received a gift of Valentine's Day candy in a box that was brain-shaped instead of heart-shaped.

The ancient Egyptians associated the mind with the heart and discounted the importance of the apparently inactive brain. In fact, when the pharaoh Tutankhamen ("King Tut") was mummified to prepare him for the afterlife, his heart and other bodily organs were carefully preserved, but his brain was discarded. The Greek philosopher Aristotle (384–322 B.C.) also believed that the heart was the site of the mind, because when the heart stops, mental activity stops (Laver, 1972). But the Greek physician-philosopher Hippocrates (460–377 B.C.), based on his observations of the effects of brain damage, did locate the mind in the brain:

> Some people say that the heart is the organ with which we think and that it feels pain and anxiety. But it is not so. Men ought to know that from the brain and from the brain alone arise our pleasures, joys, laughter, and tears. (quoted in Penfield, 1975, p. 7)

Techniques for Studying Brain Functions

Later in this chapter, you will learn about the function of the different substructures of the brain. But how did scientists discover them? They have relied on *clinical case studies, experimental manipulation, recording of electrical activity*, and *brain imaging*. But pause first to consider an alternative, commonsense approach to studying brain functions that dominated the 19th century and in various forms continued into the 20th century (see "Critical Thinking About Psychology" box).

Clinical Case Studies

For thousands of years, people have noticed that when individuals suffer brain damage from injuries, they may experience physical and psychological changes. Physicians and scientists sometimes conduct *clinical case studies* of such people to assess the acute and chronic effects of brain damage, as well as patterns of recovery following it (Muccio et al., 2009). For example, in the section "Functional Organization of the Brain," you will read about a clinical case study of Phineas Gage, a man who survived the tragic experience of having a 3-foot-long metal rod pierce his brain. The late neurologist Oliver Sacks wrote several books based on clinical case studies of patients who suffered brain damage that produced unusual—even bizarre—symptoms, including a man who lost the ability to recognize familiar faces. This disorder, *prosopagnosia*, is discussed in Chapter 5.

Experimental Manipulation

Clinical case studies involve individuals who have suffered brain damage from illness or injury. In contrast, techniques that involve *experimental manipulation* involve purposely damaging the brain, electrically or chemically stimulating the brain, or observing the effects of drugs on the brain.

When scientists use brain lesioning, they destroy specific parts of animal brains and, after the animal has recovered from the surgery, look for changes in behavior. Since the early 19th century, when the French anatomist Pierre Flourens formalized this practice, researchers who employ this technique have learned much about the brain. As described in Chapter 11, for example, researchers in the late 1940s demonstrated that destroying a specific part of the brain structure called the *hypothalamus* would make a rat starve itself even in the presence of food, whereas destroying another part of the hypothalamus would make a rat's appetite insatiable, and the rat would overeat until it became obese.

Some researchers, instead of destroying parts of the brain to see its effects on behavior, use electrical stimulation of the brain (ESB). They use weak electrical currents to stimulate highly localized sites in the brain and observe any resulting changes in behavior. Perhaps the most well-known research using ESB was conducted by neurosurgeon Wilder Penfield, who, in the course of operating on the brains of people with severe epilepsy, meticulously stimulated the surface of the brain. As a result, as discussed in the section "Brain Functions," Penfield discovered that specific sites on the brain control specific body movements and that specific sites are related to sensations from specific body sites.

The relatively new technique (first developed in the mid-1980s) of **transcranial magnetic stimulation (TMS)** involves electrically stimulating the cerebral cortex of the brain by using pulsed magnetic fields administered near the scalp. TMS has been used in cognitive studies of memory, language, and learning (Bailey, Karhu, & Ilmoniemi, 2001). Moreover, TMS has shown promise for reducing migraine headaches (McComas & Upton, 2009), clinical depression (Fitzgerald, Hoy, Daskalakis, & Kulkarni, 2009), and auditory hallucinations (Bagati, Nizamie, & Prakash, 2009).

Whereas some experimental researchers assess the effects of ESB or TMS, others observe the behavioral effects of drugs on the brain. In the section "Synaptic Transmission," you learned how animal subjects, when given the drug naloxone, do not show the same reduction in pain that they do when given a placebo. Because naloxone blocks the effects of opiates, this finding supported research implicating endorphins as the body's own natural opiates. Later in this chapter, you will learn of a technique that involves injecting a barbiturate into an artery serving either the left or right side of the brain and then observing any resulting effects. When the drug affects the left side of the brain, but rarely when it affects the right side, the person will lose the ability to speak. This result supports research indicating that the left half of the brain regulates speech in most people.

> **transcranial magnetic stimulation (TMS)** An experimental manipulation of the brain that involves electrically stimulating the cerebral cortex of the brain by using pulsed magnetic fields administered near the scalp.

Recording Electrical Activity

Consider the **electroencephalograph (EEG)**, which records the patterns of electrical activity produced by neuronal activity in the brain. The EEG has a peculiar history, going back to a day near the turn of the 20th century when an Austrian scientist named Hans Berger fell off a horse and narrowly escaped serious injury. That evening he received a telegram informing him that his sister felt he was in danger. The telegram inspired Berger to investigate the possible association between *mental telepathy* (the alleged, though scientifically unverified, ability of one mind to communicate with another by extrasensory means) and electrical activity from the brain (La Vaque, 1999). In 1924, after years of experimenting on animals and his son Klaus, Berger succeeded in perfecting a procedure for recording electrical activity in the brain. He attached small metal disks called *electrodes* to Klaus's scalp and connected them with wires to a device that recorded changes in the patterns of electrical activity in his brain.

> **electroencephalograph (EEG)** A device used to record patterns of electrical activity produced by neuronal activity in the brain.

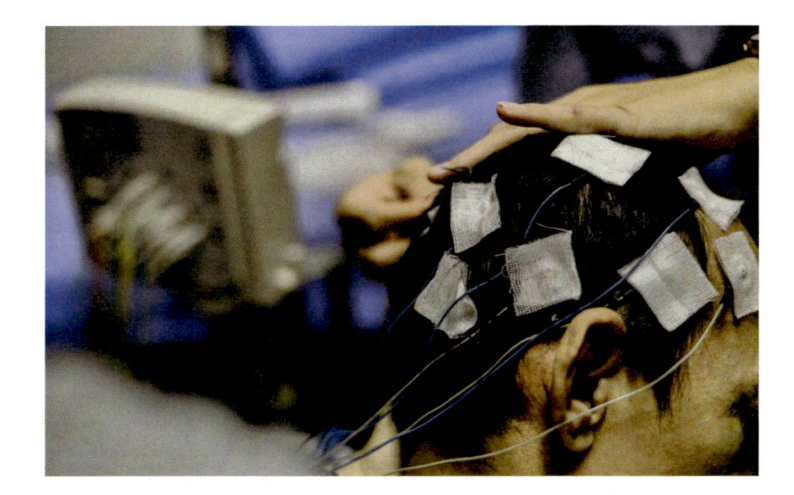

EEG

An EEG records momentary changes in electrical activity. The person must wear electrodes placed close to the scalp.
Source: Chaikom/Shutterstock.com.

Chapter 3 Biopsychological Basis of Behavior

Critical Thinking About Psychology

What Can We Infer from the Size and Shape of the Brain?

"Research on Einstein's Brain Finds Size Does Matter" (*CBC Newsworld*, 6/19/99)

"Peek into Einstein's Brain" (*Discovery* Online, 6/18/1999)

"Einstein Was Bigger Where It Counts, Analysis Shows" (*Sydney Morning Herald*, 6/18/1999)

"The Roots of Genius" (*Newsweek*, 6/24/1999)

"Part of Einstein's Brain 15 Percent Bigger Than Normal" (NPR, 6/18/1999)

As you can gather from the preceding headlines, the international media responded with excitement when researchers at McMaster University in Ontario, Canada, announced that the brain of scientific genius Albert Einstein was anatomically distinct. That is, a particular region of it, the parietal lobe, was larger than that same region tended to be in other people. The media reports were based on a study of Einstein's preserved brain published in *The Lancet*, a respected British medical journal. Einstein, who conceived the theory of relativity, is considered one of the outstanding scientists in history. The reports attributed his scientific genius to that unusually large region of his brain—a region associated with spatial and mathematical ability. It seemed to be a matter of common sense; if you know the function of a brain structure, and that structure is unusually large in a particular person, then that person must have excelled in that function. But attempts to assess intellectual and personality functions by studying the size or shape of specific areas of the brain are not new—and typically have been fruitless, as in the case of the pseudoscience practice known as **phrenology** (Greek for "science of the mind").

"You need to have your head examined!" is a refrain heard by many people whose ideas and behavior upset other people. Today, this comment is simply a figure of speech, but for most of the 19th century and well into the early 20th century, it was common practice for people to—literally—have their heads examined for career counseling, contributing to the founding of that human service field (Hershenson, 2008). The pseudoscience of phrenology was perhaps the most dramatic example of the commonsense practice of inferring personal characteristics from the size and shape of the brain.

Phrenology began when the respected Viennese physician-anatomist Franz Joseph Gall (1758–1828) proclaimed that particular regions of the brain controlled specific psychological functions (Simpson, 2005). Gall not only believed that specific brain sites controlled specific mental faculties, he assumed that the shape of specific sites on the skull indicated the degree of development of the brain region beneath it. To Gall it was simply a matter of common sense to assume that a bumpy site would indicate a highly developed brain region; a flat site would indicate a less developed brain region.

But what did Gall use as evidence to support his practice? Much of his evidence came from his own casual observations. For example, as a child he noted, with some envy, that classmates with good memories had bulging eyes. He concluded that their eyes bulged because excess brain matter behind them pushed them out of their sockets, which led him to the commonsense conclusion that memory is controlled by the region of the brain just behind the eyes. Thus, phrenology was supported by commonsense reasoning about isolated cases, which is frowned on by scientists because of its unreliability.

Though phrenology had its scientific shortcomings and disappeared in the early 20th century, it sparked interest in the localization of brain functions (Miller, 1996). But what of Einstein's brain? If it did not make scientific sense to infer the size of brain areas and the

---

phrenology A discredited technique for determining intellectual abilities and personality traits by examining the bumps and depressions of the skull.

Though Berger failed to find physiological evidence in support of mental telepathy, he found that specific patterns of brain activity are associated with specific mental states, such as coma, sleep, and wakefulness (Gloor, 1994). He also identified two distinct rhythms of electrical activity. He called the relatively slow rhythm associated with a relaxed mental state the *alpha rhythm* and the relatively fast rhythm associated with an alert, active mental state the *beta rhythm*. Berger also used the EEG to provide the first demonstration of the stimulating effect of cocaine on brain activity. He found that cocaine increased the relative proportion of the beta rhythm in EEG recordings (Herning, 1985).

Berger's method of associating EEG activity with psychological processes is still used today. For example, the EEG has been used to record changes in infants' brain-wave

Critical Thinking About Psychology

What Can We Infer from the Size and Shape of the Brain? *continued*

degree of development of their associated functions from the shape of the skull, are inferences about brain functions from the size of particular structures any more scientifically credible?

When Einstein died in 1955 at the age of 76 in Princeton, New Jersey, his body was cremated and his ashes spread across the nearby Delaware River, but his brain was removed and kept by the pathologist, Thomas Harvey, who did the autopsy. Harvey took the brain with him when he moved to Wichita, Kansas, where he kept it in two mason jars. Most of it had been cut into sections that looked like cubes of tofu.

Over the years, Harvey had mailed small sections of the brain to scientists who wished to study its microscopic structure. But the 1999 study was the first to examine the structure of the brain as a whole. The researchers compared Einstein's brain with the preserved brains of 35 men and 56 women who were of presumably normal intelligence when they died. Einstein's brain was the same weight and overall size as those of the other men, including eight who were similar in age at the time of death. Though Sandra Witelson, the neuroscientist who led the research team, found that Einstein's brain was normal in size, she found specific differences between Einstein's brain and those of the other men. The lower portion of the parietal lobe was 15 percent wider than normal. This led Witelson to conclude there might have been more neural connections in that region of Einstein's brain. A more recent analysis of his brain has revealed that his corpus callosum (a band of axons connecting the two hemispheres of the brain) was thicker than both younger and age-matched controls (Men et al., 2014).

"That kind of shape was not observed in any of our brains and is not depicted in any atlas of the human brain," noted Witelson (Ross, 1999, p. A-1). Because research has indicated that the parietal region is involved in spatial and mathematical functions, Witelson inferred that the larger size might account for Einstein's superiority as a physicist and mathematician—especially since Einstein always insisted that he did his scientific thinking spatially, not verbally.

But what can we make of this research report? Though some researchers have found that brain size on average is positively correlated with intellectual ability (Rushton & Ankney, 2009), Witelson warned that overall brain size is not a valid indicator of differences in intelligence between particular individuals. But she noted that the more specific anatomical differences between Einstein's brain and the others might indicate that mathematical genius is, at least to some extent, inborn. "What this is telling us is that environment isn't the only factor" (Ross, 1999, p. A-1). Nonetheless, Witelson added that she would not discount the importance of the environment in governing brain development. Perhaps Einstein was born with a brain similar to those of the people his was compared to, but a lifetime of thinking scientifically and mathematically (not to mention other experiences, such as diet and personal health habits) altered his brain and created distinctive anatomical differences between it and the others.

The media tend to seek the most interesting, controversial research studies to report. Scientific consumers are well advised to go beyond popular reports and articles and think critically about what they claim, perhaps even reading some of the scientific literature itself when it relates to topics of personal importance. One of the goals of this book is to make you that kind of critical consumer of information—whether presented by a scientist or a journalist.

---

patterns during their first year in response to music (Schmidt, Trainor, & Santesso, 2003) and in adults in response to aerobic exercise (Bailey et al., 2008) and the aroma of incense (Iijima, Osawa, Nishitan, & Iwata, 2009). Moreover, the EEG has been used clinically to assess patterns of brain activity associated with autism spectrum disorder (Bosl, Tierney, Tager-Rusberg, & Nelson, 2011), epilepsy (Vulliemoz, Lemieux, Daunizeau, Michel, & Duncan, 2010), and stages of sleep (Bersagliere & Achermann, 2010). **Magnetoencephalography (MEG)**, a newer way of measuring brain activity, detects changes in the patterns of magnetic fields produced by neural activity. MEG has been used to map brain areas involved in speech disorders (Breier, Randle, Maher, & Papanicolaou, 2010), music perception (Brattico et al., 2009), clinical depression (Takei et al., 2009), and Alzheimer's disease (Abatzoglou, Anninos, Tsalafoutas, & Koukourakis, 2009).

magnetoencephalography (MEG) A functional neuroimaging technique to measure brain activity using magnetic fields. MEG is useful to map brain changes across time and is often used together with fMRI.

Brain Imaging

The computer revolution has given rise to a major breakthrough in the study of the brain: brain-imaging techniques. Brain imaging involves scanning the brain to provide pictures of brain structures or "maps" of ongoing activity in the brain (Cacioppo, Berntson, & Nussbaum, 2008). One of the most important kinds of brain scan to psychologists is **positron-emission tomography (PET)**, which lets them measure ongoing activity in particular regions of the brain. In using the PET scan, researchers inject radioactive glucose (a type of sugar) into a participant. Because neurons use glucose as a source of energy, the most active region of the brain takes up the most radioactive glucose. The amount of radiation emitted by each region is measured by a donut-shaped device that encircles the head. This information is analyzed by a computer, which generates color-coded pictures showing the relative degree of activity in different brain regions. PET scans are useful in revealing the precise patterns of brain activity during the performance of motor, sensory, and cognitive tasks. For example, PET scans have been used to study brain activity of individuals while they smoked marijuana (Mathew et al., 2002) or played music in an ensemble (Satoh, Takeda, Nagata, Hatazawa, & Kuzuhara, 2001).

Two other brain-scanning techniques, which are more useful for displaying brain structures than for displaying ongoing brain activity, are **computed tomography (CT)** and **magnetic resonance imaging (MRI)**. The CT scan takes many X-rays of the brain from a variety of orientations around it. Detectors then record how much radiation has passed through the different regions of the brain. A computer uses this information to compose a picture of the brain. The MRI scan exposes the brain to a powerful magnetic field, and the hydrogen atoms in the brain align themselves along the magnetic field. A radio signal then disrupts the alignment. When the radio signal is turned off, the atoms align themselves again. A computer analyzes these changes, which differ from one region of the brain to another, to compose an even more detailed picture of the brain. Traditional CT and MRI scans have been useful in detecting structural abnormalities. For example, localized brain degeneration in adults with Alzheimer's disease has been verified by MRI scans (Appel et al., 2010).

A technique called **functional magnetic resonance imaging (fMRI)** has joined the PET scan as a tool for measuring ongoing activity in the brain. This ultrafast version of the traditional MRI detects increases in blood flow to active brain regions. Functional MRI has been used to study brain activity involved in pain (Yuan et al., 2010), orgasm (Komisaruk & Whipple, 2005), meditation (Engstrom & Söderfeldt, 2010), smelling odors (Katata et al., 2009), and mild cognitive impairment (Ries et al., 2008). Figure 3-6 illustrates images produced by functional MRI. A more recent version of computed tomography, **single photon emission computed tomography (SPECT)**, does more than provide images of brain structures. It creates images of regional cerebral blood flow. SPECT has been used in assessing brain activity in substance abuse (Amen, 2010), Alzheimer's disease (Habert et al., 2000), and epileptic seizures (Huberfeld et al., 2006).

Functional Organization of the Brain

The human brain's appearance does not hint at its complexity. Holding it in your hands, you might not be impressed by either its 3-pound weight or its walnut-like surface. You might be more impressed to learn that it contains billions of neurons. And you might be astounded to learn that any given brain neuron might communicate with thousands of others, leading to an enormous number of pathways and networks for messages to follow in the brain. Moreover, the brain is not homogeneous. It has many separate structures that interact to help you perform the myriad of activities that let you function in everyday life. When discussing the functions of the brain, it is customary to divide it into three major regions: the *brain stem*, the *limbic system*, and the *cerebral cortex* (see Figure 3-7).

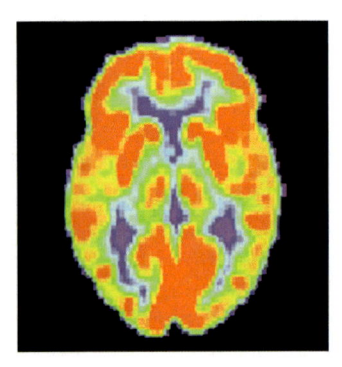

PET Scan

Positron-emission tomography (PET) scans are a technique to record brain activity by injecting a radioactive substance called a tracer into humans or animals. This PET scan shows the brain activity of a healthy person. Red indicates the highest activity during some task, followed by yellow, green, and blue.
Source: Courtesy Alzheimer's Disease Education and Referral Center, a service of the National Institute on Aging.

positron-emission tomography (PET) A brain-scanning technique that produces color-coded pictures showing the relative activity of different brain areas.

computed tomography (CT) A brain-scanning technique that relies on X-rays to construct computer-generated images of the brain or body.

magnetic resonance imaging (MRI) A brain-scanning technique that relies on strong magnetic fields to construct computer-generated images of the brain or body based on blood flow.

functional magnetic resonance imaging (fMRI) A brain-scanning technique that relies on strong magnetic fields to construct computer-generated images of physiological activity in the brain or body.

single photon emission computed tomography (SPECT) A brain-imaging technique that creates images of cerebral blood flow.

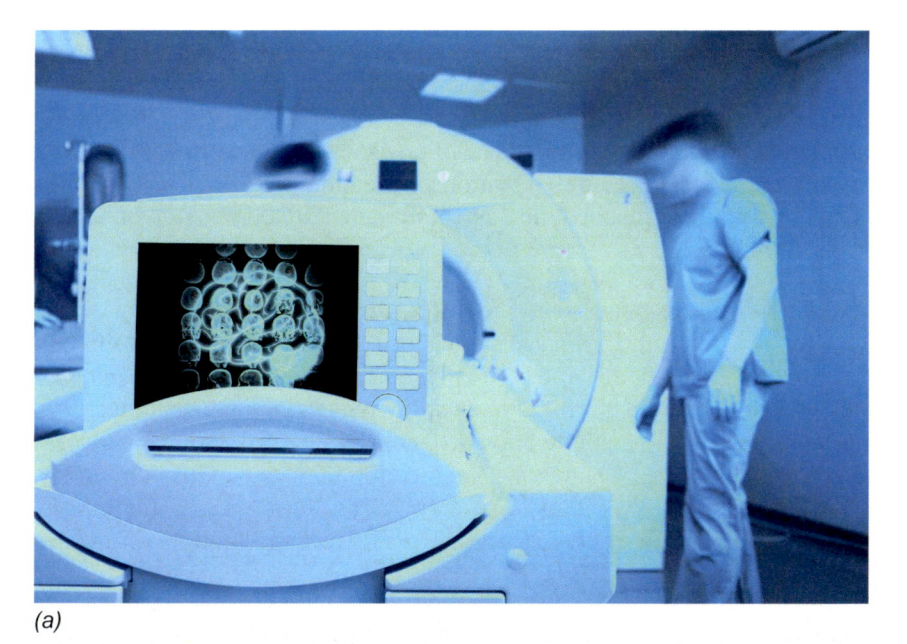

(a)

(b)

FIGURE 3-6
Functional MRI

(a) Functional magnetic resonance imaging (fMRI) is a technique that uses magnetic detectors outside the head to measure metabolism in different parts of the brain. *(b)* Researchers can thereby infer activity levels in various brain areas. Participants can perform cognitive tasks while in a fMRI scanner, and the areas that are most active are generally represented in red and areas least activated are represented in blue.

Sources: (a) sfam_photo/Shutterstock.com, (b) U.S. Department of Health and Human Services: National Institute of Mental Health.

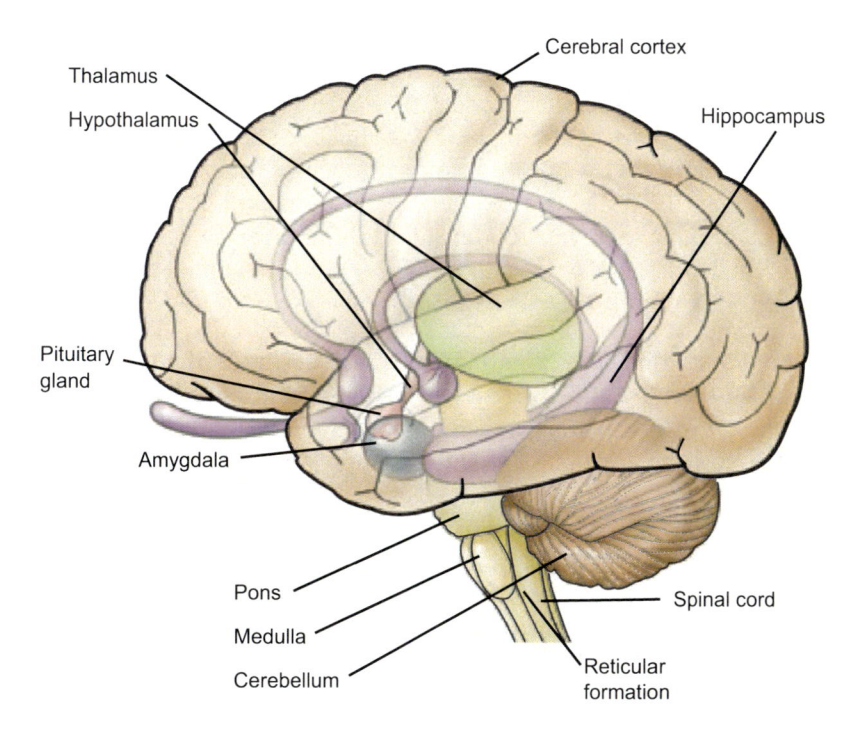

FIGURE 3-7
The Structure of the Human Brain

The structures of the brain serve a variety of life-support, sensory, motor, and cognitive functions.

Chapter 3 Biopsychological Basis of Behavior 85

The Brain Stem

brain stem A group of brain structures that provide life-support functions.

Your ability to survive from moment to moment depends on your **brain stem**, located at the base of the brain. The brain stem includes the *medulla*, the *pons*, the *cerebellum*, the *reticular formation*, and the *thalamus*. The brain stem plays the primary role in maintaining breathing and consciousness. Cessation of breathing and loss of consciousness are components of what physicians define as "brain death" (Connie, Kelvin, Chung, Diana, & Gilberto, 2008).

medulla A brain stem structure that regulates breathing, heart rate, blood pressure, and other life functions.

The Medulla Of all the brain stem structures, the most crucial to your survival is the **medulla**, which connects the brain and spinal cord. At this moment, your medulla is regulating your breathing, heart rate, and blood pressure. When called upon, your medulla also stimulates sneezing, coughing, vomiting, swallowing, and even hiccupping. By inducing vomiting, for example, the medulla prevents people who drink too much alcohol too fast from poisoning themselves. Damage to the medulla may cause difficulty in swallowing (Oku & Okada, 2008). The medulla also is important in regulating the transmission of pain impulses from the body to appropriate regions of the brain (Porreca & Gebhart, 2002).

pons A brain stem structure that regulates the sleep-wake cycle.

The Pons Just above the medulla lies the bulbous structure called the **pons** (which means "bridge" in Latin), which likewise plays a role in regulating breathing. As explained in Chapter 6, the pons helps regulate the sleep-wake cycle through its effect on consciousness (Datta, 2002). Surgical anesthesia induces unconsciousness by acting on the pons (Ishizawa, Ma, Dohi, & Shimonaka, 2000) and other brain regions. And if you have ever been the unfortunate recipient of a blow to the head that knocked you out, your loss of consciousness was caused by the blow's effect on your pons (Hayes et al., 1984). In more extreme cases, such as damage to the pons produced by a stroke, individuals might enter a comatose state in which they are unconscious and unresponsive to the environment (Claassen & Rao, 2008).

cerebellum A brain stem structure that controls the timing of well-learned movements.

The Cerebellum The pons connects the **cerebellum** (meaning "little brain" in Latin) to the rest of the brain. The cerebellum controls the timing and coordination of well-learned sequences of movements that are too rapid to be controlled consciously (Schmitt, Bitoun, & Manto, 2009), as in running a sprint, singing a song, playing the piano, or even throwing a ball (Timmann, Lee, Watts, & Hore, 2008). As you know from your own experience, conscious efforts to control normally automatic sequences of movements such as these can disrupt them. Pianists who think of each key they are striking while playing a well-practiced piece would be unable to maintain proper timing. Research indicates that the cerebellum may even affect the smooth timing and sequencing of mental activities, such as the use of language (Fabbro, 2000). Damage to the cerebellum can disrupt the ability to perform skills that we take for granted, such as using one's fingers to retrieve tiny objects (Glickstein, Waller, Baizer, Brown, & Timmann, 2005) and the tongue and oral muscles in speaking (Schweizer, Alexander, Gillingham, Cusimano, & Stuss, 2010). Moreover, cerebellar damage may lead to difficulty maintaining balance while walking and an increased risk of falls (Marsden, 2011).

reticular formation A diffuse network of neurons, extending through the brain stem, that helps maintain vigilance and an optimal level of brain arousal.

The Reticular Formation The brain stem also includes the **reticular formation**, a diffuse network of neurons that helps regulate vigilance and brain arousal. It also affects sleep, particularly dreaming (Blanco-Centurian & Salin-Pascual, 2001). The role of the reticular formation in maintaining vigilance is shown by the "cocktail party phenomenon," in which you can be engrossed in a conversation but still notice when someone elsewhere in the room says something of significance to you, such as your name. Thus, the reticular formation acts as a filter, letting you attend to an important stimulus while ignoring irrelevant ones (Haykin & Chen, 2005). Experimental evidence supporting the role of the reticular formation in brain arousal came from research by Giuseppe Moruzzi and Horace Magoun in which they awakened sleeping cats by electrically stimulating the reticular formation (Moruzzi & Magoun, 1949).

The Thalamus Capping the brain stem is the egg-shaped **thalamus**. The thalamus functions as a sensory relay station, sending taste, bodily, visual, and auditory sensations on to other areas of the brain for further processing. The only sensory information that is *not* relayed through the thalamus is related to smell. Sensory information from smell receptors in the nose goes directly to areas of the brain that process odors. The visual information from this page is being relayed by your thalamus to areas of your brain that process vision. And your thalamus is processing impulses that will inform your brain if part of your body feels cold (Davis et al., 1999) or is in pain (Narita et al., 2008). Research indicates that the thalamus also might take part in other psychological functions, including language (Whelan, Murdoch, Theodoros, Silburn, & Hall, 2002), memory (Hampstead, 2009), and attention (Dantzer, 2006).

thalamus The brain stem structure that acts as a sensory relay station for taste, body, visual, and auditory sensations.

The Limbic System

Surrounding the thalamus is a group of structures that comprise the **limbic system**. The word *limbic* comes from the Latin for "border," indicating that the limbic structures form a border between the higher and lower structures of the brain. The limbic system interacts with other brain structures to promote the survival of the individual and, as a result, the continuation of the species by engaging in functionally adaptive behaviors (Feinstein et al., 2010). Major components of the limbic system include the *hypothalamus*, the *amygdala*, and the *hippocampus*.

limbic system A group of brain structures that, through their influence on emotion, motivation, and memory, promote the survival of the individual and, as a result, the continuation of the species.

The Hypothalamus Just below the thalamus, on the underside of the brain, lies the **hypothalamus**. (In Greek, the prefix *hypo-* means "below.") The hypothalamus helps regulate numerous functions, including eating, drinking, emotion, sexual behavior, blood pressure, and body temperature (Caqueret, Yang, Duplin, & Boucher, 2005). It exerts its influence by regulating the secretion of hormones by the pituitary gland and by signals sent along neurons to bodily organs controlled by the autonomic nervous system. The hypothalamus is especially important in stress because it regulates hormones secreted by both the pituitary gland and the adrenal glands (Armario, 2006). The hypothalamus also plays a role in sexual arousal, as demonstrated by a recent fMRI study of women's and men's responses to erotic stimuli. Whereas all participants were aroused by the erotica, as assessed by self-report and physiological measures, the researchers found significantly greater activation of the hypothalamus among male participants (Karama et al., 2002). As you will read in this book, gender differences and similarities are attributable to complex interactions of physiological and social-cultural factors.

hypothalamus A limbic system structure that, through its effects on the pituitary gland and the autonomic nervous system, helps regulate aspects of motivation and emotion, including eating, drinking, sexual behavior, body temperature, and stress responses.

The importance of the hypothalamus in emotionality was discovered by accident. Psychologists James Olds and Peter Milner (1954) of McGill University in Montreal inserted fine wire electrodes into the brains of rats to study the effects of electrical stimulation of the reticular formation. They had already trained the rats to press a lever to obtain food rewards. When a wired rat now pressed the lever, it obtained mild electrical stimulation of its brain. To the experimenters' surprise, the rats, even when hungry or thirsty, ignored food and water in favor of pressing the lever—sometimes thousands of times an hour—until they dropped from exhaustion up to 24 hours later (Olds, 1956). Olds and Milner examined brain tissue from the rats and discovered that they had mistakenly inserted the electrodes near the hypothalamus and not into the reticular formation. They concluded they had discovered a "pleasure center." But we now know that the hypothalamus is but one structure in an interconnected group of brain structures that induce feelings of pleasure when stimulated.

The Amygdala The **amygdala** of the limbic system, located in the temporal lobe, continuously evaluates information from the immediate environment and contributes to the formation of memories of emotionally significant events, particularly of stressful situations (Roozendaal, McEwen, & Chattarji, 2009; Phelps & LeDoux, 2005). The amygdala is most notably important in regulating our responses to the social environment—such as facial expressions, tone of voice, and even laughing and crying—and helps elicit appropriate emotional and behavioral responses (Sander, Brechmann, & Scheich, 2003). If you

amygdala A limbic system structure that evaluates information from the immediate environment, contributing to feelings of fear, anger, or relief.

Chapter 3 Biopsychological Basis of Behavior

saw a pit bull running toward you, your amygdala would help you quickly decide whether the dog was friendly, vicious, or simply roaming around. Depending on your evaluation of the situation, you might feel happy and pet the dog, feel afraid and jump on top of your desk, or feel relief and go back to studying. Research shows that the amygdala stimulates the profuse emotional sweating that some people exhibit when under extreme stress (Asahina, Suzuki, Mori, Kanesaka, & Hattori, 2003).

A functional MRI study of people with social anxiety disorder found that they experienced exaggerated amygdala responses to angry faces compared to people without that disorder (Evans et al., 2008). Amygdala responses to facial expressions also are influenced by culture. A functional MRI study of Japanese and American participants found greater activation of the amygdala in response to facial fear expressed by members of their own ethnic group. This makes sense from an evolutionary perspective; given that one would presume that fear expressed by a member of one's own ethnic group would indicate a greater threat to other members of the same group (Chiao et al., 2008).

In the late 1930s, Heinrich Klüver and Paul Bucy (1937) found that lesions of the amygdala in monkeys led to "psychic blindness," an inability to evaluate environmental stimuli properly. The monkeys indiscriminately examined objects by mouth, tried to mate with members of other species, and acted fearless when confronted by a snake. People who suffer amygdala damage also may exhibit symptoms of Klüver-Bucy syndrome (Unal et al., 2007).

The Hippocampus Whereas your amygdala helps you evaluate emotional information from your environment, the limbic system structure that is particularly important in helping you form memories of that information (including what you are now reading) is the **hippocampus** (Axmacher, Lenz, Haupt, Elger, & Fell, 2010). Much of what we know about the hippocampus comes from case studies of people who have suffered damage to it. The most famous study is of Henry Gustav Molaison (1926–2008), widely known as "H. M." (Scoville & Milner, 1957), whose hippocampus was surgically removed in 1953—when he was 27—to relieve his uncontrollable epileptic seizures. Following the surgery, H. M. formed few new memories, though he could easily recall events and information from before his surgery. It wasn't until his death in 2008, that H. M.'s identity was revealed. He was a Connecticut resident and played a critical role in the development of cognitive neuropsychology theories that explain the link between brain function and *memory*. You can read more about the implications of his case in regard to memory in Chapter 8. Damage to the hippocampus has been implicated in the memory loss associated with Alzheimer's disease. Victims of this disease suffer from degeneration of the neurons that serve as pathways between the hippocampus and other brain areas (Perl, 2010).

The Cerebral Cortex

Covering the brain is the crowning achievement of brain evolution—the **cerebral cortex**. Cortex means "bark" in Latin. And just as the bark is the outer layer of the tree, the cerebral cortex is the thin, 3-millimeter-thick outer layer of the uppermost portion of the brain called the *cerebrum*. The human cerebral cortex and that of other mammals has evolved folds called *convolutions*, which give it the appearance of kneaded dough. The convolutions permit more cerebral cortex to fit inside the skull. This is necessary because evolution has assigned so many complex brain functions to the mammalian cerebral cortex that the brain has, in a sense, outgrown the skull in which it resides. If the cerebral cortex were smooth (like other species) instead of convoluted, the human brain would have to be enormous to permit the same amount of surface area. The brain would be encased in a skull so large that it would give us the appearance of extraterrestrial creatures from science fiction movies.

The cerebrum is divided into left and right halves called the **cerebral hemispheres**. Figure 3-8 shows that the cerebral cortex covering each hemisphere is divided into four regions, or *lobes*: the *frontal lobe*, the *temporal lobe*, the *parietal lobe*, and the *occipital lobe*. The lobes have *primary cortical areas*. A **primary cortical area** serves motor or

hippocampus A limbic system structure that contributes to the formation of memories.

cerebral cortex The outer covering of the brain.

cerebral hemispheres The left and right halves of the cerebrum.

primary cortical area Regions of the cerebral cortex that serve motor or sensory functions.

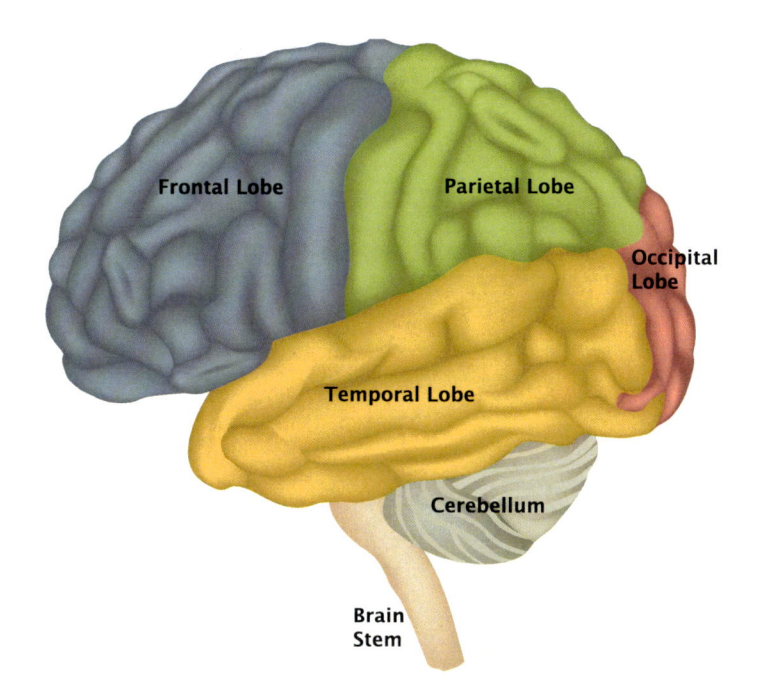

FIGURE 3-8
The Lobes of the Brain

The cerebral cortex covering each cerebral hemisphere is divided into four lobes: the frontal lobe, the temporal lobe, the parietal lobe, and the occipital lobe.
Source: Yoko Design/Shutterstock.com.

sensory functions. The lobes also have *association areas*. An **association area** integrates information from the primary cortical areas and other brain areas in activities such as speaking, problem solving, and recognizing objects.

Motor Cortex Your tour of the cerebral cortex begins in 1870, when the German physicians Gustav Fritsch and Eduard Hitzig (1870/1960) published their findings that electrical stimulation of a strip of cerebral cortex along the rear border of the right or left **frontal lobe** of a dog induces limb movements on the opposite side of the body. This phenomenon is known as *contralateral control*. The area they stimulated is called the **motor cortex**. They were probably the first to demonstrate conclusively that specific sites on the cerebral cortex control specific body movements (Gross, 2007).

Figure 3-9 presents a "map" of the motor cortex of the frontal lobe, represented by a *motor homunculus*. (*Homunculus* is a Latin term meaning "small human.") Each area of the motor cortex controls a particular contralateral body movement. Certain neurons on the motor cortex are related to particular aspects of movement, such as velocity (Stark, Drori, Asher, Ben-Shaul, & Abeles, 2007), and certain sites on the motor cortex even show activity merely in anticipation of particular body movements (Hyland, 1998). Note that the motor homunculus is upside down, with the head represented at the bottom and the feet represented at the top.

You also might be struck by the disproportionate sizes of the body parts on the motor homunculus—each body part is represented in proportion to the precision of its movements, not in proportion to its actual size. Because your fingers move with great precision in manipulating objects, the region of the motor cortex devoted to your fingers is disproportionately large relative to the regions devoted to body parts that move with less precision, such as your arms. An fMRI study of professional piano players found that they showed less activity than nonmusicians did in their motor cortical areas while doing a finger tapping task. As we become proficient at using our finger muscles, we employ more and more precise motor cortical areas, which eliminate even slightly irrelevant movement (Jaencke, Shah, & Peters, 2000).

Sensory Cortex The primary cortical areas of the frontal lobes control movements; the primary cortical areas of the other lobes process sensory information. You will notice in Figure 3-8 that the primary cortical area of the **parietal lobes** runs parallel to the motor cortex of the frontal lobes. This area is called the **somatosensory cortex** because it processes information related to skin senses (Zhu, Disbrow, Zumer, McGonigle, & Nagarajan,

association area Region of the cerebral cortex that integrates information from the primary cortical areas and other brain areas.

frontal lobe A lobe of the cerebral cortex responsible for motor control and higher mental processes.

motor cortex The area of the frontal lobes that controls specific voluntary body movements.

parietal lobe A lobe of the cerebral cortex responsible for processing bodily sensations and perceiving spatial relations.

somatosensory cortex The area of the parietal lobes that processes information from sensory receptors in the skin.

Chapter 3 Biopsychological Basis of Behavior

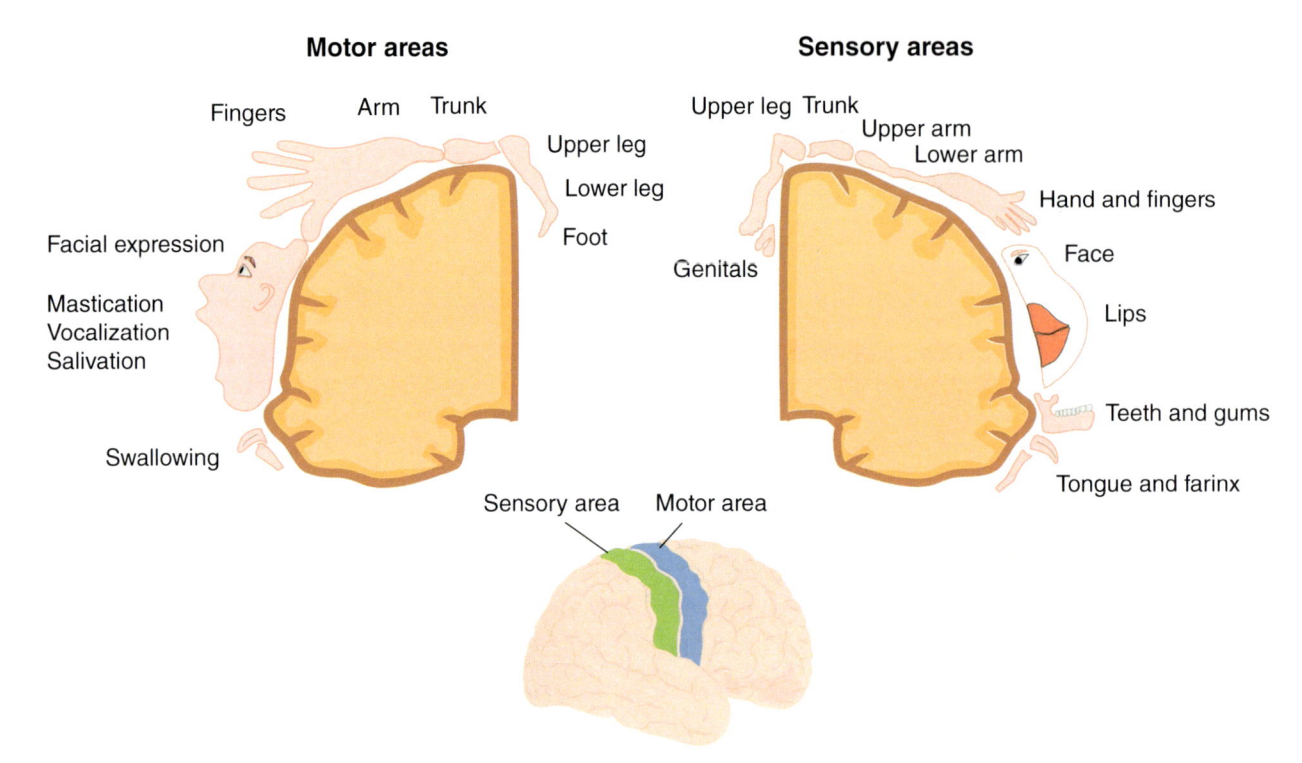

FIGURE 3-9 The Motor Cortex and the Somatosensory Cortex

Both the motor cortex and the somatosensory cortex form distorted, upside-down maps of the contralateral side of the body. Activity in the motor cortex of a cerebral hemisphere produces contralateral movement. Touching a spot on one side of the body produces activity in the contralateral somatosensory cortex.
Source: ellepigrafica/Shutterstock.com.

2007), such as pain, touch, and temperature. Like the motor cortex, the somatosensory cortex forms a distorted, upside-down homunculus of the body and receives input from the opposite side of the body. Each body part is represented on the *sensory homunculus* in proportion to its sensory precision rather than its size. This is why the region devoted to your highly sensitive lips is disproportionately large relative to the region devoted to your less sensitive back.

How do we know that a motor homunculus and a sensory homunculus exist on the cerebral cortex? We know because of research conducted by neurosurgeon Wilder Penfield (1891–1976) of the Montreal Neurological Institute in the course of brain surgery to remove defective tissue causing epileptic seizures. Of his many contributions, his most important was the "Montreal procedure" for surgically removing scar tissue that caused epilepsy. In applying the procedure, he made the first use of Hans Berger's EEG by comparing brain activity before and after surgery to see if it had been successful in abolishing the abnormal brain activity that had triggered his patients' seizures.

In using the Montreal procedure, Penfield made an incision through the scalp, sawed through a portion of the skull, and removed a large flap of bone—exposing the cerebral cortex. His patients required only a local anesthetic at the site of the scalp and skull incisions because incisions in the brain itself do not cause pain. A local anesthetic applied at the site of the skull incision allowed the patients to remain awake during surgery and to converse with him.

Penfield then administered a weak electrical current to the exposed cerebral cortex. He did so for two reasons. First, he wanted to induce an *aura* that would indicate the site that triggered the patient's seizures. An aura is a sensation (such as an unusual odor) that precedes a seizure. Second, he wanted to avoid cutting through parts of the cerebral cortex that serve important functions.

Penfield found that stimulation of a point on the right frontal lobe might make the left forefinger rise and that stimulation of a point on the left parietal lobe might make the patient report a tingling feeling in the right foot. After stimulating points across the entire cerebral cortex of many patients, Penfield found that the regions governing movement and bodily sensations formed the distorted upside-down maps of the body shown in Figure 3-8 (Rasmussen & Penfield, 1947). His discovery has been verified by research on animals as well as on people. For example, stimulation of points on the motor cortex of baboons produces similar distorted motor "maps" of the body (Waters, Samulack, Dykes, & McKinley, 1990).

The **temporal lobes** have their own primary cortical area, the **auditory cortex**. Particular regions of the auditory cortex are responsible for processing sounds of particular frequencies (Menéndez-Colino et al., 2007), which enables the temporal lobes to analyze all kinds of sounds, including speech (Binder, JRao, Hammeke, & Yetkin, 1994) and music (Zatorre, Belin, & Penhune, 2002). There also is evidence from magnetoencephalography that an area of the temporal cortex involved in music perception is larger and responds faster in professional musicians than in amateur musicians (Schneider et al., 2002).

At the back of the brain are the **occipital lobes**, which contain the **visual cortex**. This region integrates input from your eyes into a visual "map" of what you are viewing (Swindale, 2000). Because of the nature of the pathways from your eyes to your visual cortex, visual input from objects in your *right visual field* is processed in your left occipital lobe, and visual input from objects in your *left visual field* is processed in your right occipital lobe. Certain neurons in the visual cortex process facial recognition (Pourtois, Schwartz, Seghier, Lazeyras, & Vuilleumier, 2009), and others process object movements (Mercier, Schwartz, Michel, & Blanke, 2009). Damage to a portion of an occipital lobe can produce a blind spot in the contralateral visual field (Trevethan & Sahraie, 2003). In some cases, damage can produce visual hallucinations, such as the perception of parts of objects that are not actually present (Anderson & Rizzo, 1994).

Association Cortex In reading about the brain, you might have gotten the impression that each area functions independently of the others. That is far from the truth. Consider the association cortex that composes most of the cerebral cortex. These areas combine information from other areas of the brain. For example, the association cortex of the frontal lobes integrates information involved in thinking, planning, and problem solving. The unusually large association cortex of the human cerebral cortex provides more area for processing information, which contributes to the human species' greater flexibility than other animals in adapting to diverse circumstances (Semendeferi, Lu, Schenker, & Damasio, 2002). The frontal lobes also play a role in motivated behavior. Research has found that college students who crave playing videogames on the Internet, as opposed to players who do not crave playing, show frontal lobe activity similar to people who are

---

temporal lobe A lobe of the cerebral cortex responsible for processing hearing.

auditory cortex The area of the temporal lobes that processes sounds.

occipital lobe A lobe of the cerebral cortex responsible for processing vision.

visual cortex The area of the occipital lobes that processes visual input.

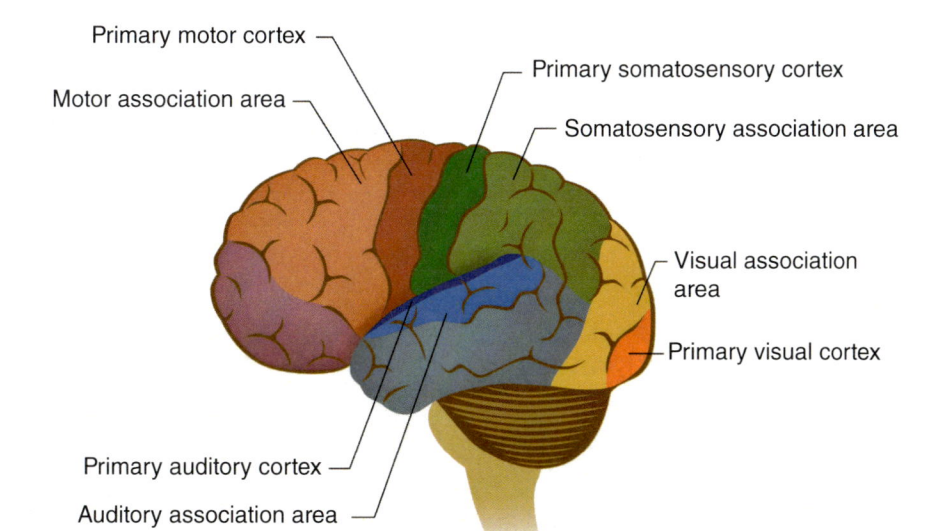

Association Cortex

The association cortex involved in higher-order mental functions such as judgment, memory, and facial recognition.
Source: Alila Medical Media/Shutterstock.com.

- Primary motor cortex
- Motor association area
- Primary somatosensory cortex
- Somatosensory association area
- Visual association area
- Primary visual cortex
- Primary auditory cortex
- Auditory association area

Chapter 3 Biopsychological Basis of Behavior

substance abusers in response to stimuli associated with the substances (Han, Kim, Lee, Min, & Renshaw, 2010).

Some of the evidence supporting the importance of the association areas of the frontal lobes in emotion and personality has come from case studies of people with damage to it, most notably the case of Phineas Gage (Harlow, 1993). On a fall day in 1848, Gage, the 25-year-old foreman of a Vermont railroad crew laying track, was clearing away rocks. While he was using an iron tamping rod to pack a gunpowder charge into a boulder, a spark ignited the gunpowder. The resulting explosion hurled the rod into Gage's left cheek, through his frontal lobes, and out the top of his skull. Miraculously, Gage survived, recuperated, and lived 12 more years, with little impairment of his intellectual abilities. But there were dramatic changes in his personality and emotionality. Instead of remaining the friendly, popular, hardworking man he had been before the accident, he became an ornery, disliked, irresponsible bully. Gage's friends believed he had changed so radically that "he was no longer Gage."

The case study of Phineas Gage implies that the frontal lobe structures damaged by the tamping rod might be important in emotion and personality. But, as explained in Chapter 2, it is impossible to determine causality from a case study. Perhaps Gage's emotional and personality changes were caused not by the brain damage itself, but instead by Gage's psychological response to his traumatic accident or by changes in how other people responded to him. Nonetheless, the frontal lobe's importance in emotion and personality has been supported by subsequent scientific research (Stuss, Gow, & Hetherington, 1992). As in the case of Phineas Gage, damage to the frontal lobes typically causes the person to become uninhibited, emotionally unstable, unable to plan ahead, and prone to socially inappropriate behavior (Macmillan, 2000). The association areas of the frontal lobes are especially important in helping us adapt our emotions and behavior to diverse situations. A case study of a 50-year-old man with frontal lobe damage similar to Gage's showed that he had intact cognitive abilities but had difficulty inhibiting his behavior and trouble behaving responsibly (Dimitrov, Phipps, Zahn, & Grafman, 1999).

Language Cortex The integration of different brain areas underlies many psychological functions. Consider the process of speech, one of the most distinctly human abilities. Speech depends on the interaction of the association cortex of the frontal and temporal lobes. In most left-handed people and almost all right-handed people, the left cerebral hemisphere is superior to the right in processing speech. The speech center of the frontal lobe, **Broca's area**, is named for its discoverer, the French surgeon and anthropologist Paul Broca (1824–1880). In 1861 Broca treated a 51-year-old man named Leborgne, who was given the nickname "Tan" because he had a severe speech disorder that made *tan* the only syllable he could pronounce clearly. After Tan died of an infection, Broca performed an autopsy and found damage to a defined area of the left frontal lobe of his brain. Broca concluded that this area controls speech. Tan's speech disorder is now called *Broca's aphasia*. (*Aphasia* is the Greek word for "speechless.") Broca's observation was confirmed in later autopsies of the brains of people who had speech disorders similar to Tan's. CT scans have also verified that damage to Broca's area is, indeed, associated with Broca's aphasia (Breathnach, 1989).

What is the nature of Broca's aphasia? Though its victims retain the ability to comprehend speech, they speak in a telegraphic style that can be comprehended only by listeners who pay careful attention. For example, when one victim of Broca's aphasia was asked about a family dental appointment, he said, "Monday . . . Dad and Dick . . . Wednesday nine o'clock . . . doctors and teeth" (Geschwind, 1979, p. 186). The speaker expressed the important thoughts but failed to express the connections between them. Nonetheless, you probably got the gist of the statement.

Speech also depends on a region of the temporal lobe cortex called **Wernicke's area**, named for the German physician Karl Wernicke. In contrast to Broca's area, which controls the production of speech, Wernicke's area controls the meaningfulness of speech. In 1874, Wernicke reported that patients with damage to the rear margin of the left temporal

Broca's area The region of the frontal lobe responsible for the production of speech.

Wernicke's area The region of the temporal lobe that controls the meaningfulness of speech.

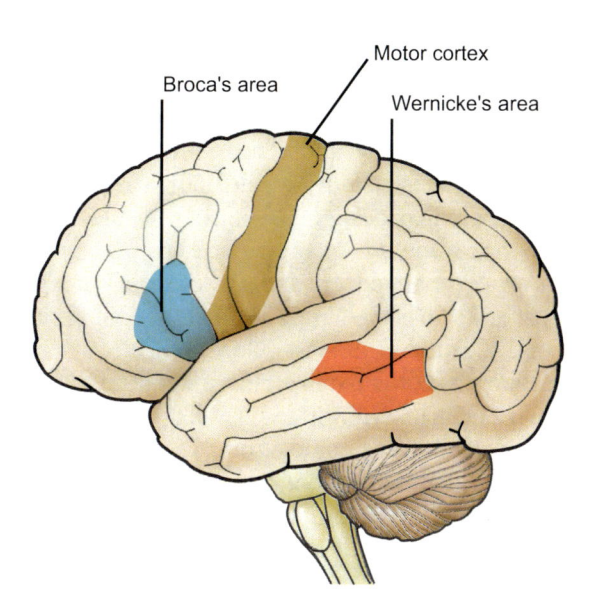

FIGURE 3-10
Speech and the Brain

Wernicke's area, Broca's area, and the motor cortex interact in producing speech.

lobe spoke fluently but had difficulty comprehending speech and made little or no sense to even the most attentive listener. This disorder became known as *Wernicke's aphasia*.

Consider the following statement by a victim of Wernicke's aphasia that describes a picture of two boys stealing cookies behind a woman's back: "Mother is away here working her work to get her better, but when she's looking the two boys looking in the other part. She's working another time" (Geschwind, 1979, p. 186). The statement seems more grammatical than the telegraphic speech of the victim of Broca's aphasia, but it is impossible to comprehend—it is almost meaningless.

The consensus among researchers is that, as presented in Figure 3-10, speech production requires the interaction of Wernicke's area, Broca's area, and the motor cortex (Geschwind, 1979). Wernicke's area selects the words that will convey your meaning and communicates them to Broca's area. Broca's area then selects the muscle movements to express those words and communicates them to the region of the motor cortex that controls the speech muscles. Finally, the motor cortex communicates these directions through motor nerves to the appropriate muscles, and you speak the intended words. As you can see, speaking phrases as simple as "let's go out for pizza" involves the interaction of several areas of your brain.

Cerebral Hemispheric Lateralization

You may have noted reports in the popular media alleging that the cerebral hemispheres control different psychological functions, leading to the notion of "left-brained" and "right-brained" people. Though most researchers would not assign complete responsibility for any psychological function to just one hemisphere, they have reached agreement on some of the psychological functions at which each hemisphere excels. The left hemisphere is somewhat superior at performing verbal, mathematical, analytical, and rational functions, and the right hemisphere is somewhat superior at performing nonverbal, spatial, holistic, and emotional functions (Springer & Deutsch, 1998). Some researchers believe we have evolved hemispheric lateralization because it makes us more efficient in carrying out multiple activities at the same time, such as speaking while remaining vigilant to potential threats (Rogers, 2000). Though each hemisphere has its own strengths, the hemispheres do not work in isolation. For example, the left hemisphere generally controls the production of speech, but the right hemisphere gives speech its appropriate emotional intonation (Snow, 2000).

Brain imaging has revealed that the area of the primary motor cortex that serves the dominant hand is larger on that side of the brain than on the other, providing people with the opportunity to learn to perform more precise movements (Hammond, 2002).

Because about 90 percent of people are right-handed and, as a consequence, the manufactured environment favors right-handers, left-handers have more trouble functioning in the everyday world. For example, left-handers have difficulty operating control panels designed for right-handers, especially under stressful conditions that can cause confusion, as in airplane cockpits. Because of this difficulty, human-factors engineers must consider left-handed people when designing control consoles (Garonzik, 1989). Nonetheless, left-handedness has some advantages. For example, a disproportionate number of competitive athletes are left-handed, apparently because it provides a tactical and positional advantage (a left-handed baseball hitter is closer to first base) in sport competitions (Grouios, Tsorbatzoudis, Alexandris, & Barkoukis, 2000).

Because right-handedness is prevalent in almost all cultures, heredity evidently is more important than life experiences in determining handedness and cerebral lateralization of functions. Additional evidence of this comes from research findings that even newborns show evidence of cerebral lateralization of psychological functions (Fein, 1990), and most fetuses show a preference for sucking their right thumb while in the womb (Hepper, Shahidullah, & White, 1991). Yet, cultural factors can override hereditary tendencies, as revealed in a survey of natives of the Amazon region of Colombia. All of the persons in the survey reported that they were right-handed. The researchers who did the survey concluded that those who had been born with initial tendencies toward left-handedness became right-handed as a result of cultural pressures to do so (Bryden, Ardila, & Ardila, 1993). Some researchers have found no relationship between heredity and handedness in twin studies comparing handedness similarities (Bishop, 2001). Yet, other researchers believe they have identified a gene that may influence handedness, though this has not been confirmed by other researchers (McManus, Nicholls, & Vallortigara, 2009).

Perhaps the most controversial issue in recent decades regarding handedness is whether right-handed people tend to live longer than left-handed people. No controversy exists about this one fact: There are proportionately fewer left-handers among older adults than among younger adults in North America. Two of the main proponents of the belief that left-handers do in fact die sooner have been Stanley Coren and Diane Halpern (see the "Psychology versus Common Sense" box).

In addition to their interest in handedness, cerebral-laterality researchers study the psychological functions of the left and right hemispheres. They do so by studying the damaged brain, the intact brain, and the split brain.

Evidence of Hemispheric Lateralization from the Damaged Brain

As you read earlier in the chapter, the earliest source of knowledge about cerebral hemispheric lateralization was the study of unilateral brain damage—that is, damage to one cerebral hemisphere. If damage to one hemisphere of the brain produces symptoms that differ from symptoms produced by damage to the other hemisphere, researchers conclude that the damaged hemisphere plays more of a role in that function than does the other hemisphere.

Paul Broca, after finding that a specific kind of language disorder consistently followed damage to the left hemisphere, concluded that language depended more on the left hemisphere than on the right hemisphere (Harris, 1999). More recent research on brain damage has found that both hemispheres are involved in language but that their particular roles differ. For example, though the left hemisphere is more important for the production and comprehension of speech, the right hemisphere is more important for processing aspects of speech unrelated to the spoken words themselves. Damage to the right hemisphere produces greater deterioration in the ability to interpret the speaker's emotional tone of voice than does damage to the left hemisphere (Ross, Thompson, & Yenkosky, 1997).

Evidence of Hemispheric Lateralization from the Intact Brain

Psychologists interested in hemispheric lateralization have devised several methods for studying the intact brain. One of the chief methods has participants perform tasks while an EEG or brain scan measures the relative activity of their cerebral hemispheres. A study using fMRI found that people produce greater activity in certain areas of the left hemisphere while performing a verbal task and greater activity in certain areas of the right hemisphere while performing visual-spatial tasks (Stephan et al., 2003). Research using fMRI has demonstrated activity in the language areas of the left hemisphere even in people using American Sign Language. But American Sign Language also involves greater involvement of the right hemisphere than does English (Bavelier et al., 1998).

Another approach, the **Wada test**, studies human participants in whom a hemisphere has been anesthetized in the course of brain surgery to correct a neurological defect, often one that induces epileptic seizures. The Wada test is named for Juhn Wada, who introduced it in 1949 (Emde Boas, 1999). This procedure is done by injecting sodium amytal into either the right or the left carotid artery, which provides oxygenated blood to the associated cerebral hemisphere. The injection anesthetizes that hemisphere. As you might expect, anesthetization of the left hemisphere, but only rarely of the right hemisphere, induces temporary aphasia—the patient has difficulty speaking. Recent research and meta-analysis indicates that the use of fMRI may be preferable to the invasive Wada test in assessing lateralization of language (Abou-Khalill, 2007; Dym, Burns, Freeman, & Lipton, 2011).

Wada test A technique in which a cerebral hemisphere is anesthetized to assess hemispheric lateralization.

Considerable controversy surrounds gender differences in cerebral lateralization. Whereas some studies have demonstrated gender differences in the structure of the two hemispheres, such as the number of convolutions in the cortex of each hemisphere (e.g., Luders, Narr, Bilder, Szaszko, Gurbani, & Hamilton, 2008), other researchers have investigated gender differences in the extent to which males and females exhibit cerebral lateralization and the extent to which gender differences in cerebral lateralization are correlated with cognitive abilities and performance. For example, two meta-analyses of research studies of the lateralization of spatial and verbal abilities found that male participants were slightly more lateralized than female participants (Medland, Geffen, & McFarland, 2002; Vogel, Bowers, & Vogel, 2003). Moreover, the size of the gender difference varies as a function of the laboratory task (Kansaku & Kitazawa, 2001) and test-taking strategy (Voyer & Flight, 2001). These inconsistent results are not surprising, as you will learn when you read about research described in Chapter 4. Whereas prenatal hormones do have an effect on brain structure and function, the observed gender differences in verbal and spatial skills generally are small and variable—especially for visual-spatial skills. So what accounts for the elusive "now you see it; now you don't" gender differences in hemispheric lateralization? One hypothesis is based on brain size. Larger brains are more lateralized. Because male brains are on average larger than female brains, gender differences in lateralization may be attributable to differences in brain size (Jancke & Steinmetz, 2003).

An alternative hypothesis emphasizes the interaction of sociocultural factors with biological factors such as hemispheric lateralization (Eviatar, 2000). Neuroscientists studying cross-cultural differences in the relation between thought and language provide support for this hypothesis (see Chapter 9). For example, one cross-cultural study tested the relationship between hemispheric laterality and the direction of written language (left to right in Italian and right to left in Arabic). The results indicated that performance on visual imaging tasks was influenced both by hemispheric lateralization and visual scanning (Maass & Russo, 2003).

Evidence of Hemispheric Lateralization from the Split Brain

Studies of damaged brains and intact brains have provided most of the evidence regarding cerebral hemispheric lateralization, but the most fascinating approach has been **split-brain research**. This research involves people whose hemispheres have been surgically separated from each other. Though split-brain research is only a few decades old, the idea was entertained in 1860 by Gustav Fechner, who was introduced in Chapter 1 as a founder of psychology. Fechner claimed that people who survived the surgical separation of their cerebral hemispheres would have two separate minds in one head (Springer & Deutsch, 1998). Decades later English psychologist William McDougall argued that such an operation would not divide the mind, which he considered indivisible. McDougall

split-brain research A research technique for the study of cerebral hemispheric lateralization that involves people whose hemispheres have been surgically separated from each other.

Psychology versus Common Sense

Is Being Left-Handed a Pathological Condition?

Stanley Coren, a psychologist at the University of British Columbia, and Diane Halpern, a psychologist at Claremont McKenna College in California, pointed to earlier studies indicating that the percentage of right-handers was greater in older age groups (Coren & Halpern, 1991). Note that by age 80 there are virtually no left-handers in the population! To assess this handedness effect, Halpern and Coren (1988) conducted an archival study of longevity in professional baseball players, using the *Baseball Encyclopedia* as their source of data on more than 2,000 players. They found that, on the average, right-handers lived eight months longer than left-handers. This finding inspired them to replicate that study to determine if their findings would generalize to people other than baseball players.

Coren and Halpern sent brief questionnaires to the next of kin of 2,875 persons who recently had died in two southern California counties. The questionnaires asked about the deceased's handedness regarding writing, drawing, and throwing. Each person's age at death was obtained from death certificates. Despite the apparent intrusion of the questionnaires into the lives of grieving relatives, 1,033 questionnaires were returned. Of these, 987 were usable. Coren and Halpern determined whether the deceased had been right-handed or left-handed.

The results were startling: Right-handers lived an average of 9 years longer than left-handers. Thus, this study found a much larger longevity gap than the study of baseball players had found. Coren and Halpern attributed the gap to the earlier deaths of left-handers (the *elimination hypothesis*) rather than to cultural pressures to become right-handed (the *modification hypothesis*) that affected older generations more than younger ones. Coren and Halpern found that the most important factors accounting for this longevity gap were a greater tendency for left-handers to have accidents, immune disorders, and evidence of neurological defects. In an archival study of 975 women and 741 men, Coren found that non-right-handers are more susceptible to broken bones (Coren & Previc, 1996). Moreover, there is a somewhat greater risk of the sometimes fatal disease multiple sclerosis in left-handers than in right-handers (Gardener, Munrer, Chitnis, Spiegelman, & Ascherio, 2009). Left-handers are also more prone to clinical depression (Denny, 2009), which is associated with higher risk of mortality from suicide and illnesses exacerbated by depression. And in a study of more than 1,200 college students, Coren found that left-handed people find it more difficult to fall asleep and stay asleep (Coren & Searleman, 1987). This finding is important because (as explained in Chapter 6) sleep is necessary for proper functioning of the immune system and optimal daytime alertness.

But research findings from other studies have not consistently supported Coren and Halpern's findings. Even the allegedly longer life spans of right-handed baseball players have been called into question. In fact, a study of more than 5,000 professional baseball players found that left-handers actually lived an average of 8 months longer than right-handers (Hicks, Johnson, Cuevas, & Debaro, 1994). Coren and Halpern's explanations for the apparent longevity difference favoring right-handers also have been disputed. For example, a study in the Netherlands found no relationship between accident proneness and handedness among undergraduate students (Merckelbach, Muris, & Kop, 1994). Moreover, research has been inconsistent on the relationship between handedness and immune disorders, with some studies even showing that right-handers are more susceptible to them (Bryden, 1993). And there is conflicting evidence about the greater likelihood of neurological disorders in left-handers, to which some researchers attribute the slightly higher rate of left-handedness in men (Bishop, 1990; Corballis, 2001).

One of the main reasons for the inconsistent findings regarding the susceptibility of left-handers to disease and injury may be inconsistency in how research studies have defined handedness. In one study of more than 5,000 deaths, instead of dividing handedness into either right-handed or left-handed, the researchers divided the deceased into extremely right-handed, generally right-handed, ambidextrous, generally left-handed, and extremely left-handed. The researchers found that only generally left-handed people died significantly younger than other people (Ellis & Engh, 2000).

The strongest response to Coren and Halpern has come from Lauren Harris (1993) of Michigan State University, who believes that the modification hypothesis is a better explanation for the decline in left-handers across the life span. According to Harris, today's older adults grew up at a time when left-handers were forced to use their right hands or simply chose to conform

continued

Psychology versus Common Sense

Is Being Left-Handed a Pathological Condition? *continued*

to a right-handed world. In contrast, over the past few decades left-handedness has lost its stigma, resulting in more left-handers remaining left-handed.

Harris's hypothesis was supported by a study in Norway. In keeping with Coren and Halpern's findings, the researchers found that 15.2 percent of 21- to 30-year-olds were left-handed and that only 1.7 percent of those more than 80 years old were left-handed. But the researchers found that the apparent decline in left-handedness across the life span was, in reality, due to the fact that many left-handers in earlier generations had switched to being right-handed (Hugdahl, Satz, Mitrushina, & Miller, 1993). Despite these findings, which contradict their position, Halpern and Coren (1993) insist that most scientifically sound studies support their belief that left-handers tend to die younger.

Halpern and Coren's research findings prompted widespread interest and animosity. Halpern and Coren responded to critics of their research by noting that scientific research findings should not be affected by whether they please or displease particular groups of people. Instead, those who oppose research studies should criticize their methodology and, if possible, present research findings that contradict them (Halpern, Gilbert, & Coren, 1996).

In regard to the issue at hand, several questions remain to be answered, but the main one is this: If we follow groups of young people as they grow older, will the left-handers tend to die sooner than the right-handers? If they do, it would support Coren and Halpern's explanation. If they do not, it would support Harris's explanation. Of course, this determination would take many decades. In any case, as you can now appreciate, the commonsense belief that there are significantly fewer left-handers than right-handers in late adulthood because left-handers die younger may be wrong.

FIGURE 3-11 Left-Handedness Has Lost Its Stigma

Over the past few decades, left-handedness has lost its stigma. This has resulted in more left-handers remaining left-handed.

Source: DmitriMaruta/Shutterstock.com.

The Corpus Callosum

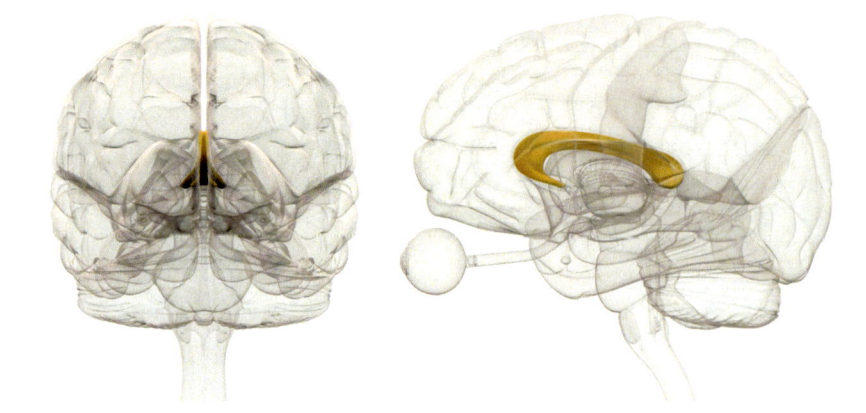

A frontal and lateral view of the brain showing the location and shape of the corpus callosum (Latin for "tough body") within the brain. The corpus callosum is a wide band of axons that connects the right and left hemispheres.

Source: decade3d—anatomy online/Shutterstock.com.

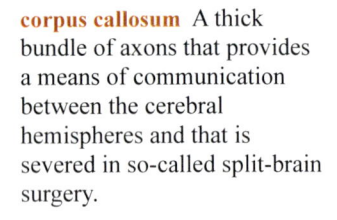

corpus callosum A thick bundle of axons that provides a means of communication between the cerebral hemispheres and that is severed in so-called split-brain surgery.

even volunteered to test Fechner's claim by having his own cerebral hemispheres surgically separated if he ever became incurably ill.

Though McDougall never had split-brain surgery, it was performed on patients in the early 1960s, when neurosurgeons Joseph Bogen and Phillip Vogel severed the **corpus callosum** of epileptic patients to reduce seizure activity that had not responded to drug treatments. The corpus callosum is a thick bundle of axons that provides the means of communication of information between the cerebral hemispheres (Pearce, 2007). Split-brain surgery works by preventing seizure activity in one hemisphere from spreading to the other. Split-brain patients function normally in their everyday lives, but special testing procedures have revealed an astonishing state of affairs: Their left and right hemispheres can no longer communicate with each other (Gazzaniga, 2005). Each acts independently of the other, as though each has its own independently functioning mind (Sperry, 1984). In *callosal agenesis*—the so-called natural split brain—the corpus callosum fails to develop prenatally, causing some of the same effects seen following split-brain surgery (Lassonde & Sauerwine, 2003).

Roger Sperry (1982) and his colleagues, most notably Jerre Levy and Michael Gazzaniga, have been pioneers in split-brain research. In a typical study, information is presented to one hemisphere and the participant is asked to give a response that depends more on one hemisphere than on the other. In a classic study (Gazzaniga, 1967), a split-brain patient performed a block-design task in which he had to arrange multicolored blocks so that their upper sides formed a pattern that matched the pattern printed on a card in front of him. Our left hands are controlled by the right hemisphere, and our right hands are controlled by the left hemisphere. The experimental task is illustrated in Figure 3-12. When the participant performed with his left hand, he did well, but when he performed with his right hand, he did poorly. Can you explain why that happened?

Because the left hand is controlled by the right hemisphere, which is superior in perceiving spatial relationships, such as those in designs, he performed well with his left hand. And because the right hand is controlled by the left hemisphere, which is inferior in perceiving spatial relationships, he performed poorly with his right hand—even though he was right-handed. At times, when his right hand was having a hard time completing the design, his left hand would sneak up on it and try to help. This led to a bizarre battle for control of the blocks—as if each hand belonged to a different person. A similar conflict between competing behaviors has been observed in subsequent research on patients with damage to the corpus callosum (Nishikawa et al., 2001).

Despite the dramatic findings of split-brain studies, Jerre Levy (1983) has claimed that researchers, including Gazzaniga (1983), have exaggerated the extent to which each hemisphere regulates particular psychological processes, especially the supposed superiority of the left hemisphere. As always, only continued scientific research will resolve the Levy-Gazzaniga debate, which, you might note, is an example of the continual controversy over the degree to which psychological functions are localized in particular areas of the brain. The extent to which split-brain surgery produces two separate consciousnesses is controversial. Some commentators believe split-brain surgery leaves the patient with

FIGURE 3-12
A Split-Brain Study

Gazzaniga (1967) had a split-brain patient arrange multicolored blocks to match a design printed on a card in front of him. The patient's left hand performed better than his right because the left hand is controlled by the right hemisphere, which is superior at perceiving spatial relationships. You would be able to perform a block-design task equally well with either your right or your left hand because your intact corpus callosum would let information from your spatially superior right hemisphere help your left hemisphere control your right hand.

Right hand | Left hand
Block pattern

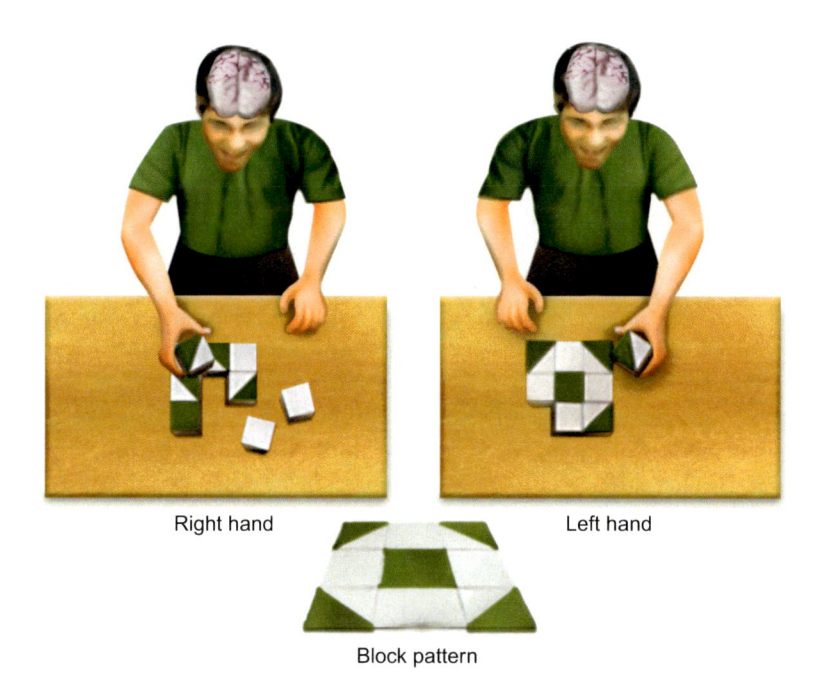

two complete, separate minds (Schechter, 2012). Others believe split-brain surgery leaves the patient with a complete stream of consciousness in the left hemisphere but only a primitive one in the right hemisphere, in part because the right hemisphere generally lacks language ability, which plays a crucial role in self-awareness (Morin, 2001).

Neural Plasticity

The human brain is remarkable in its ability to learn from experience and to promote adaptive behavior. In doing so, the brain shows **neural plasticity**—that is, it is not completely "hardwired" at birth. Plasticity is shown by the elimination of excess synaptic connections (Huttenlocher, 1990) in childhood and the formation of new synaptic connections throughout life (Rosenzweig & Bennett, 1996). The biggest challenge to the plasticity of the brain is brain damage, whether caused by a stroke, a blow to the head, or a disease such as Alzheimer's or Parkinson's. Natural processes in response to brain damage promote a limited degree of recovery. More recently, a technique formerly relegated to science fiction—the transplantation of neural tissue—has shown promise as a means of encouraging greater recovery from brain damage and spinal-cord damage.

neural plasticity The brain's ability to learn from experience and to promote adaptive behavior.

Recovery from Neural Damage

Brain and spinal-cord damage can produce devastating effects, including paralysis, sensory loss, memory disruption, and personality deterioration. But what are the chances of recovering from such damage? It depends on the location of the damage and the kind of animal that has been damaged. Certain species of fish and amphibians, such as frogs (Krishnan, Sankar, & Muthusamy, 2001), can recover from spinal-cord damage by regenerating functional connections, but mammals—including people—do not.

People can regenerate damaged axons to regain lost functions only in the peripheral nervous system. Have you ever gotten a severe paper cut on your finger? The tingling sensation as it heals is the regeneration of peripheral nervous system axons. The regeneration is instigated, in part, by chemical signals that promote regrowth of the damaged axons (Vrbova et al., 2009). The possible effectiveness of a chemical called nerve growth factor in restoring neural functioning in the brain or spinal cord has been demonstrated in animal studies. For example, the administration of nerve growth factor has been effective in restoring functions after damage to the brain stem of rats (Alto et al., 2009). Glial cells in the peripheral nervous system form tunnels that guide the regrowth of damaged axons. In contrast, molecules released by glial cells in the brain and spinal cord block

Chapter 3 Biopsychological Basis of Behavior

regeneration of axons (Bolsover, Fabes, & Anderson, 2008). This is why damage to your axons in your central nervous system can lead to paralysis. Christopher Reeve (1952–2004), the actor who played Superman in a series of motion pictures, was thrown from his horse in 1995 during an equestrian competition. Tragically, he landed on his head. The resulting injury to his spinal cord rendered him a quadriplegic, and he required a wheelchair and breathing assistance for the rest of his life.

In mammals, perhaps the most important factor in the recovery of functions that have been lost because of brain damage is the ability of intact brain areas to take over the functions of damaged ones (Johnston, 2009). In one experiment, researchers surgically destroyed portions of the motor cortex and somatosensory cortex that served one of the hind limbs of rats. The researchers found that the motor and somatosensory cortical "maps" representing those portions gradually shifted to intact adjacent areas of the cortex and to contralateral cortical areas, restoring the ability of the limb to function (Abo, Chen, Lai, Reese, & Bjelke, 2001). This likewise occurred in a case study of a boy who had suffered frontal lobe damage at age 7 due to an arterial rupture but showed remarkable recovery of functions over the years. The researchers found that fMRIs at age 24 indicated that undamaged cortical areas had taken over the processing of cognitive activities normally controlled by the damaged areas (Thompson et al., 2009).

collateral sprouting The process in which branches from the axons of nearby healthy neurons grow into the pathways normally occupied by the axons of damaged neurons.

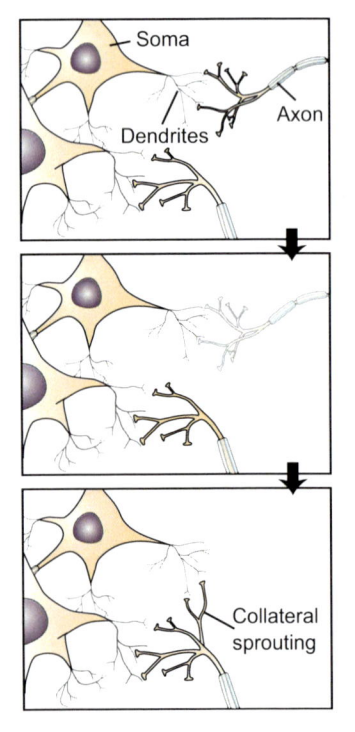

Possible mechanisms by which spinal-cord injuries can be treated to regain some function include regeneration of axons and *collateral sprouting*, among others (Bradbury & McMahon, 2006). Through **collateral sprouting** (illustrated in Figure 3-13), branches from the axons of nearby healthy neurons grow into the pathways normally occupied by the axons of the damaged neurons. Ideally, the healthy neurons will take over the functions of the damaged ones. The younger the individual, the more likely collateral sprouting is to occur.

Neural plasticity following central nervous system damage, as in the spinal cord, is also promoted by exercise rehabilitation programs (Martinez, Brezun, Zennou-Azogui, Baril, & Xerri, 2009), particularly if there is incomplete severing of the spinal cord (Gregory et al., 2007). Apparently this occurs in part because it stimulates activity of neural stem cells that produce neuronal generation (Foret et al., 2010). Current cutting-edge research aims to activate endogenous neural stem cells to create new, fully functioning brain or spinal-cord neurons. Nonetheless, technical issues need to be worked out to make sure that newly generated neurons are functionally effective, given that haphazard regeneration can produce failure or even negative neurological effects (Okano, Sakaguchi, Ohki, & Suzuki, 2007).

It should be noted that people's responses to brain or spinal-cord injury are not simply the product of the extent of injury and degree of recovery. Psychosocial factors also play a role. For example, recovery depends in part on cognitive interpretations and emotional reactions to injury. In fact, research indicates that variability in physical recovery after mild traumatic brain injury is more related to factors such as pain and depression than to the brain injury itself (Mooney, Speed, & Sheppard, 2005).

FIGURE 3-13
Collateral Sprouting

When an axon dies and its connections to the dendrites of other neurons degenerate, adjacent axons may sprout branches that form synapses with the vacated sites.

Another psychosocial factor in rehabilitation from spinal-cord injury is the culture's approach to medical care for people with neurological disabilities. A comparative study found that American spinal care medical professionals stress the desirability of getting patients into wheelchairs as soon as possible, whereas their colleagues in Italy and Canada are more concerned with attempting to restore as much self-ambulation as possible. The differences appear to be related to medical insurance policies. In the United States, to save on financial reimbursement, insurance providers direct physicians to move patients with brain or spinal-cord damage out of intensive rehabilitation as soon as they show even a minimal amount of mobility, whether while in a wheelchair or becoming self-ambulatory. Given that wheelchair functioning tends to come easier and faster, this may explain why American medical personnel favor wheelchair use as a primary goal. In contrast, in Italy and Canada, insurance providers permit patients to receive lengthy treatment aimed at maximizing their self-functioning before being released from intensive rehabilitation (Ditunno et al., 2006).

Chapter 3 Biopsychological Basis of Behavior

Neural Transplantation

Though plasticity might restore some lost functions, most people who have suffered brain or spinal-cord damage do not recover completely. This has led to research on possible ways to repair damaged brains and spinal cords, including attempts to administer chemicals that promote regeneration of neural connections (Santucci, Gluck, Kanof, & Haroutunian, 1993) or to stimulate the same processes that permit axons of the peripheral nerves to regenerate (Bertelli, Orsal, & Mira, 1994). The most widely publicized, and controversial, way has been to use **neural grafting**—the transplantation of healthy tissue into damaged nerves, brains, or spinal cords. For example, transplantation of retinal ganglion cells (which comprise the optic nerves) to treat damaged ganglion cells in rats restored the rats' ability to respond to light, though their visual acuity remained impaired (Kittlerova & Valouskova, 2000).

Transplantation of human embryonic stem cells that are neuronal precursors has been successful in restoring some motor and sensory functioning in rats with brain damage, leading to greater interest in the possible use of this technique in people with similar damage (Hicks et al., 2009). Animal research also shows that transplantation of peripheral nerve grafts can help restore some motor function in rats with complete spinal-cord damage (Nordblom, Persson, Svensson, & Mattsson, 2009). A particularly promising preliminary study of people with ALS involved transplanted stem cells from the individual's blood into the motor cortex. Those who received the transplants showed improved functioning and longer survival than comparable ALS patients who received only typical medical treatment (Martinez et al., 2009).

Studies have reported a variety of successful applications of neural grafting in treating central nervous system disorders. Epileptic seizures that have been experimentally induced by surgically created brain damage in rats have been reduced by the transplantation of inhibitory GABA neurons from fetal rat brains (Fine, Meldrum, & Patel, 1990). And researchers have successfully used embryonic brain-tissue grafts to reduce epileptic seizures in people (Akimova et al., 2000). Neuroscientist Jacqueline Sagen works with the Miami Project to Cure Paralysis to help victims of spinal-cord injuries recover lost functions, potentially by using neural grafts to promote functional recovery.

Given the success of some experiments on fetal transplants in animals, it is natural to consider the possibility of using such transplants in people. Some studies in which fetal brain tissue has been transplanted to human patients with brain damage have produced significant, long-lasting restoration of lost functions. For example, more than 20 years ago, researchers in Sweden reported success in reducing symptoms of Parkinson's disease by using fetal cell transplants (Lindvall et al., 1990). Today, we know that such treatments are variable but can be as effective as levodopa (L-dopa). If these treatments are used early in the disease, they could substantially reduce the amount of medication a patient would need. What has yet to be determined is if early intervention with fetal transplants will significantly alter the course of the disease (Barker, Barrett, Mason, & Björklund, 2013). If such neural grafts are perfected, brain damage caused by strokes, tumors, diseases, or accidents might be treated by brain-tissue transplants. One application, which appears to be promising in the future but has yet to be tested in humans, is neural transplants for the treatment of Alzheimer's disease. Researchers who study animal models of Alzheimer's disease have used neural transplants containing acetylcholinergic neurons and transplanted them into the hippocampus of rodents. Once there, the acetylcholinergic neurons became anatomically and functionally incorporated into the hippocampus and delivered acetylcholine (Tarricone et al., 1996). Neural transplants appear to achieve their beneficial effects by secreting neurotransmitters that the damaged structure normally secretes (Becker, Curran, & Freed, 1990), by forming new neural circuits to replace damaged ones (Nunn & Hodges, 1994), or by secreting substances that promote neural regeneration (Lescaudron & Stein, 1990).

Pioneering research has produced promising findings, which indicate that the 21st century might see the cure of brain and spinal-cord damage. Adrenal-gland transplants in rats and mice have reduced symptoms akin to those found in Parkinson's disease (Espejo

---

neural grafting The transplantation of healthy tissue into damaged nerves, brains, or spinal cords.

Quadriplegia and Quality of Life

The quality of life for people with spinal-cord injury increases over time, especially in the first year post-injury. Christopher Reeve lived almost 10 years after his spinal cord injury in 1995, and was an advocate for individuals with physical disabilities living fulfilling lives.
Source: Firma V/Shutterstock.com.

Fetal Stem Cells

Fetal stem cells, once harvested, cannot become embryos but can be coaxed into developing into any type of cell in the body. Though their use is controversial when they are obtained from a terminated pregnancy or collected from fertilization clinics, stem cells have helped advance treatment options for people with Parkinson's disease.

Source: Designua/Shutterstock.com.

et al., 2001) and Huntington's disease (Jousselin-Hosaja et al., 2001) and have reduced memory loss caused by hippocampus damage (Tarricone, Simon, Li, & Low, 1996) and movement disturbances caused by cerebellum damage (Triarhou, 1995). Moreover, gene therapy designed to increase dopamine production in people with Parkinson's disease shows initial promise (Wakeman, Dodiya, & Kordower, 2011) and will likely replace invasive procedures such as fetal transplants.

Before becoming too optimistic about neural transplants, you should realize that many attempts at them have failed (Swenson, Danielsen, Klausen, & Erlich, 1989). And even "successful" transplants might not have the intended effects. The enhanced secretion of a neurotransmitter or the formation of new neural circuits might disrupt existing activity or neural pathways, creating even more functional deterioration, though recent research indicates that this might potentially be overcome by technical improvements in methodology (Politis, 2010). Though neural grafts have yet to demonstrate their everyday practical worth, research still might pay off with breakthroughs that will restore functions that have been lost as the result of brain or spinal-cord damage (Baisden, 1995). Recent research on transplantation of bone marrow stem cells from rats into regions of brain damage in those rats has produced neural generation and functional recovery. It remains for this to be applied in clinical trials with human participants (Bonilla et al., 2009).

Section Review: Brain Functions

1. What are the major functions of the brain stem, the limbic system, and the cerebral cortex?
2. What roles do Broca's area and Wernicke's area play in speech production?
3. What evidence is there for hemispheric lateralization based on split-brain research?

Chapter 3 Biopsychological Basis of Behavior

> **Experiencing Psychology**
>
> ### What Are the Locations and Functions of Brain Structures?
>
> Using pencils of different colors, modeling clay of different colors, and any reference material you require, draw or sculpt the following brain structures. Use different colors for the different structures. Write a description of the functions of each of the structures. This exercise will reinforce what you have learned from class lectures and the chapter by providing you with two-dimensional or three-dimensional, as well as verbal understanding of the major brain structures and their functions.
>
> **Cerebral Cortex Structures**
>
> The language areas
> The sensory areas
> The motor areas
>
> **Limbic System Structures**
>
> The hippocampus
> The amygdala
> The hypothalamus
>
> **Brain Stem Structures**
>
> The thalamus
> The cerebellum
> The pons
> The medulla

Chapter Summary

Nature versus Nurture

- Psychologists who champion evolutionary psychology employ Darwinian concepts in their research and theorizing.
- Scientists who study behavioral genetics are interested in how heredity affects behavior.
- Heritability refers to the proportion of variability in a trait across a population attributable to genetic differences among members of the population.
- Research procedures that assess the relative contributions of nature and nurture involve studies of families, adoptees, and identical twins reared apart.

Biological Communication Systems

- The field of behavioral neuroscience studies the relationships between physiological processes and psychological functions.
- The nervous system is composed of cells called neurons and serves as the main means of communication within the body.
- The nervous system is divided into the central nervous system, which comprises the brain and the spinal cord, and the peripheral nervous system, which comprises the nerves of the somatic nervous system and the autonomic nervous system.
- The autonomic nervous system is subdivided into the sympathetic nervous system, which arouses the body, and the parasympathetic nervous system, which conserves energy.
- Hormones, secreted into the bloodstream by endocrine glands, also serve as a means of communication within the body.
- Hormones participate in functions as diverse as sexual development and responses to stress. Most endocrine glands are regulated by hormones secreted by the pituitary gland, which in turn is regulated by the hypothalamus.

Neuronal Activity

- The nervous system carries information along sensory neurons, motor neurons, and interneurons, as in the limb-withdrawal reflex mediated by the spinal cord.
- The neuron generally receives signals through its dendrites and sends signals along its axon.
- The axon maintains a resting potential during which it is electrically negative on the inside relative to its outside, as a result of a higher concentration of negative ions inside.
- Sufficient stimulation of the neuron causes the axon to depolarize (become less electrically negative) and reach its firing threshold.
- Depolarization produces an action potential, which causes a neural impulse to travel along the entire length of the axon.
- The neural impulses stimulate the release of neurotransmitter molecules into the synapse.
- The molecules cross the synapse and attach to receptor sites on glands, muscles, or other neurons.
- These molecules exert either an excitatory or an inhibitory influence.
- In recent years, the neurotransmitters known as endorphins have inspired research because of their role in pain relief and euphoria.

Chapter 3 Biopsychological Basis of Behavior

Brain Functions
- The functions of the brain have been revealed by clinical case studies, experimental manipulation, recording of electrical activity, and brain-imaging techniques.
- The medulla regulates vital functions, such as breathing; the pons regulates arousal and attention; and the cerebellum controls the timing of well-learned sequences of movements.
- The reticular formation regulates brain arousal and helps maintain vigilance.
- The thalamus relays sensory information (except smell) to various regions of the brain for further processing.
- Within the limbic system, the hypothalamus regulates the pituitary gland as well as emotion and motives, such as eating, drinking, and sex.
- The amygdala continuously evaluates the immediate environment for potential threats, and the hippocampus processes information into memories.
- The cerebral cortex covers the brain and is divided into the frontal, temporal, parietal, and occipital lobes.
- Well-defined areas of the lobes regulate movements and process sensory information.
- Most areas of the cerebral cortex are association areas devoted to integrating information from different brain areas, such as those devoted to speech.
- Brain imaging techniques, including positron-emission tomography (PET), functional magnetic resonance imaging (fMRI), and single photon emission computed tomography (SPECT), have contributed to our understanding of the functions of different areas of the brain.
- Researchers historically have disagreed about the extent to which particular psychological functions are localized in particular areas of the brain.
- Each cerebral hemisphere has psychological functions at which it excels, though both hemispheres influence virtually all functions.
- Studies of the degree of activity in each hemisphere, of the effects of damage to one hemisphere, and of people whose hemispheres have been surgically disconnected show that the left hemisphere is typically superior at verbal tasks and the right hemisphere is typically superior at spatial tasks.
- Scientists have been making progress in treating brain and spinal-cord damage.
- One of the most promising, though controversial, treatments for brain and spinal-cord damage is neural grafting.

Key Terms

Biopsychological Bases of Behavior
behavioral neuroscience (p. 61)
unilateral neglect (p. 60)

Nature versus Nurture
behavioral genetics (p. 62)
evolutionary psychology (p. 62)
genotype (p. 64)
heritability (p. 64)
phenotype (p. 64)

Biological Communication Systems
adrenal gland (p. 69)
autonomic nervous system (p. 68)
brain (p. 67)
central nervous system (p. 67)
endocrine system (p. 68)
gonads (p. 70)
hormones (p. 68)
nerve (p. 68)
nervous system (p. 67)
neuron (p. 67)
ovaries (p. 70)
parasympathetic nervous system (p. 68)
peripheral nervous system (p. 68)
pituitary gland (p. 68)
reflex (p. 67)
somatic nervous system (p. 68)
spinal cord (p. 67)
sympathetic nervous system (p. 68)
testes (p. 70)

Neuronal Activity
action potential (p. 74)
all-or-none law (p. 74)
Alzheimer's disease (p. 77)
axon (p. 72)
axonal conduction (p. 73)
dendrites (p. 72)
endorphins (p. 78)
glial cell (p. 71)
interneuron (p. 72)
motor neuron (p. 71)
myelin (p. 75)
neurotransmitter (p. 76)
Parkinson's disease (p. 78)
resting potential (p. 73)
sensory neuron (p. 71)
soma (p. 72)
synapse (p. 74)
synaptic transmission (p. 75)

Brain Functions
amygdala (p. 87)
association area (p. 89)
auditory cortex (p. 91)
brain stem (p. 86)
Broca's area (p. 92)
cerebellum (p. 86)
cerebral cortex (p. 88)
cerebral hemispheres (p. 88)
collateral sprouting (p. 100)
computed tomography (CT) (p. 84)
corpus callosum (p. 98)
electroencephalograph (EEG) (p. 81)
frontal lobe (p. 89)
functional magnetic resonance imaging (fMRI) (p. 84)
hippocampus (p. 88)
hypothalamus (p. 87)
limbic system (p. 87)
magnetic resonance imaging (MRI) (p. 84)
magnetoencephalography (MEG) (p. 83)
medulla (p. 86)
motor cortex (p. 89)
neural grafting (p. 101)
neural plasticity (p. 99)
occipital lobe (p. 81)
parietal lobe (p. 89)
phrenology (p. 82)
pons (p. 86)
positron-emission tomography (PET) (p. 84)

primary cortical area (p. 88)
reticular formation (p. 86)
single photon emission computed tomography (SPECT) (p. 84)
somatosensory cortex (p. 89)
split-brain research (p. 95)
temporal lobe (p. 91)
thalamus (p. 87)
transcranial magnetic stimulation (TMS) (p. 81)
visual cortex (p. 91)
Wada test (p. 95)
Wernicke's area (p. 92)

Chapter Quiz

1. The central nervous system comprises the
   a. brain and spinal cord.
   b. nerves and spinal cord.
   c. somatic and autonomic nervous systems.
   d. sympathetic and parasympathetic nervous systems.

2. Mary Shelley wrote the novel *Frankenstein* at about the same time that the possible electrical nature of nerve impulses was demonstrated by
   a. Isaac Newton.
   b. Luigi Galvani.
   c. René Descartes.
   d. Charles Sherrington.

3. A football player is tackled and knocked unconscious. The blow probably affected his
   a. pons.
   b. thalamus.
   c. hippocampus.
   d. hypothalamus.

4. The convolutions of the cerebral cortex
   a. integrate sensory and motor information.
   b. act as biological radiators to cool the brain.
   c. permit more cerebral cortex to fit inside the skull.
   d. provide a means of communication between the hemispheres.

5. Myelinated axons conduct neural impulses faster because they
   a. contain nodes of Ranvier.
   b. tend to have smaller synaptic clefts.
   c. make impulses leap from one neuron to another.
   d. tend to be smaller in diameter than other neurons.

6. The nerves compose the
   a. brain.
   b. spinal cord.
   c. peripheral nervous system.
   d. reticular activating system.

7. An arrow from a careless archer pierces the brain of a bystander. The victim survives, recalls events from before the accident, but cannot form new memories. The arrow probably destroyed the
   a. pons.
   b. hippocampus.
   c. hypothalamus.
   d. parietal lobes.

8. If a split-brain patient were to draw a map, she would probably perform
   a. better with her left hand.
   b. better with her right hand.
   c. equally well with both hands.
   d. better using a foot rather than a hand.

9. Phrenology was based on the mistaken assumption that
   a. heredity affected brain development.
   b. brain neurons could regenerate after injury.
   c. brain structure could be determined by bumps on the skull.
   d. all psychological functions are processed bilaterally in the brain.

10. A classical pianist suffers a stroke and can no longer play the piano with proper timing, though she can use all of her fingers to strike the correct keys. The stroke probably affected her
    a. cerebellum.
    b. motor cortex.
    c. corpus callosum.
    d. somatosensory cortex.

11. The Wada test is used to
    a. measure the speed of neural conduction.
    b. identify the site of injury in stroke victims.
    c. determine the lateralization of particular psychological functions.
    d. assess the relative concentrations of extracellular and intracellular fluid.

12. Damage to the temporal cortex would most likely cause
    a. inability to move a body part.
    b. loss of sensation from a body part.
    c. a blind spot in the contralateral visual field.
    d. impaired ability to perceive sounds of certain pitches.

13. The sensory relay station of the brain is the
    a. thalamus.
    b. hypothalamus.
    c. corpus callosum.
    d. reticular activating system.

Chapter 3 Biopsychological Basis of Behavior

14. In Otto Loewi's demonstration of the chemical basis of neurotransmission in his study of frog hearts, he found that the chemical involved was
    a. dopamine.
    b. endorphins.
    c. acetylcholine.
    d. norepinephrine.

15. Electrical stimulation of the rear portion of the frontal lobe would most likely
    a. evoke an old memory.
    b. make a body part move.
    c. create images of lights or colors.
    d. cause a touch sensation from a body part.

16. The case study of railroad foreman Phineas Gage provided evidence that factors related to emotionality and personality are regulated by the
    a. limbic system.
    b. brain stem.
    c. frontal lobes.
    d. corpus callosum.

17. The probable existence of gaps between neurons was first demonstrated by
    a. Otto Loewi.
    b. Camillo Golgi.
    c. Luigi Galvani.
    d. Santiago Ramon y Cajal.

18. A stroke victim uses grammatically correct, but meaningless, speech. She most likely suffered damage to
    a. Broca's area.
    b. Wernicke's area.
    c. parietal association areas.
    d. occipital association areas.

19. In the 18th century, Stephen Hales's research on decapitated frogs demonstrated that they could still
    a. make croaking sounds.
    b. negotiate a water maze.
    c. form memories of visual events.
    d. respond reflexively to leg pinches.

20. A victim of a gunshot wound to the head dies immediately. The bullet most likely damaged the
    a. cerebellum.
    b. frontal lobes.
    c. corpus callosum.
    d. medulla.

21. A detective investigates a murder by poisoning in which the victim's skeletal muscles are completely relaxed. The detective suspects that the poison was
    a. curare.
    b. strychnine.
    c. tetanus toxin.
    d. acetylcholine.

22. The cell that is specialized for the transmission and reception of information is the
    a. soma.
    b. neuron.
    c. synapse.
    d. neuroglia.

23. Because of his views on the site of psychological functions, the philosopher who would most appreciate hearing the song "I Left My Heart in San Francisco" and receiving Valentine's Day candy in a heart-shaped box would be
    a. Plato.
    b. Socrates.
    c. Aristotle.
    d. Hippocrates.

24. A diving accident completely severs the spinal cord of a diver at mid-chest level. He would most likely experience
    a. initial leg paralysis, which would gradually disappear over time.
    b. permanent leg paralysis and permanent loss of feeling in the legs.
    c. almost immediate death due to destruction of control centers for breathing and heart rate.

25. The endocrine system would be most likely to be affected by a tumor of the
    a. tectum.
    b. amygdala.
    c. hypothalamus.
    d. corpus callosum.

Thought Questions

1. How do psychologists interested in behavioral genetics use studies of identical twins reared apart to assess the role of heredity in human development?

2. How would you determine whether the joy of a student who earns a 4.0 grade-point average is associated with an increase in endorphin levels?

3. Why do some psychologists believe that phrenology was an important but misguided approach to the localization of brain functions?

4. How does split-brain research provide evidence that the left cerebral hemisphere is somewhat superior in processing speech and the right cerebral hemisphere is somewhat superior in perceiving spatial relations?

Human Development

CHAPTER 4

In 1987 Hulda Crooks climbed Mount Whitney in the Sierra Nevada Mountains of California for the 23rd time. This would be a noteworthy feat for any person, given that at 14,495 feet, Mount Whitney is the tallest mountain in the contiguous 48 states. What made it more impressive was that Hulda was 91 years old at the time, making her the oldest person ever to reach the summit. That year she also became the oldest woman to climb Mount Fuji, the tallest mountain in Japan. The Japanese sponsors of her ascent honored her with a banner reading "Grandma Fuji."

The following year Hulda decided to add the U.S. Capitol to her long list of conquests. She barely worked up a sweat as she ascended the 350-step staircase in the building's dome in just 30 minutes. Hulda, a physical fitness proponent who also held eight Senior Olympics world records in track and field at the time, made the climb to celebrate National Women in Sports Day (Connors, 1988).

In 1991 a peak near Mount Whitney was named Crooks Peak in Hulda's honor. "You have not only highlighted the importance of physical fitness for all Americans, but also served as a role model for senior citizens everywhere," wrote President George H. W. Bush in a letter recognizing her accomplishments. At the ceremony naming the peak, Hulda observed, "It's never too late to change your lifestyle if you realize it's not appropriate. I want to impress to young people that they're building their old age now" (Kuebelbeck, 1991).

Hulda, who died in 1997 at the age of 101, was a vegetarian who took up hiking in her 40s following a bout with pneumonia. She did not scale her first peak until she was 66, when many people are content to lead a more sedentary life. Hulda advocated a sparse diet, vigorous exercise, and avoiding caffeine and alcohol. She also credited her healthy life to her spirituality as a devout member of the Seventh Day Adventist Church. Hulda published her memoirs, *Conquering Life's Mountains*, as a testament to the importance of mental, physical, and spiritual well-being. At a book signing, she was treated as a celebrity. Mountaineers lined up to have her sign their copies. One of them laughed when he realized that he had retired from mountain climbing at 55, when he was more than 10 years younger than Hulda was when she began her climbing career (Fieckenstein, 1996).

Hulda Crooks' accomplishments in old age contradict the stereotype of the elderly as frail and lacking in vitality. Psychologists who study the aging process find that severe mental and physical decline is not

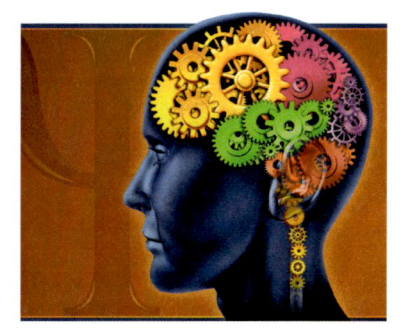

Source: Lightspring/Shutterstock.com.

Chapter Outline

Research Methods in Developmental Psychology
Prenatal Development
Infant and Child Development
Adolescent Development
Adult Development

developmental psychology The field that studies physical, perceptual, cognitive, and psychosocial changes across the life span.

maturation The sequential unfolding of inherited predispositions in physical and motor development.

necessarily a characteristic of old age. As Hulda noted, by keeping mentally and physically active in adulthood we can have rich, rewarding lives throughout our later years. **Developmental psychology** is the study of the physical, perceptual, cognitive, and psychosocial changes that take place across the life span. Though opinions about the nature of human development can be found in the writings of ancient Greek philosophers, the scientific study of human development did not begin until the 1870s. That decade saw the appearance of the "baby biography," usually written by a parent, which described the development of an infant. Though much of infant development depends on learning, it also is guided by physical **maturation**—the sequential unfolding of inherited predispositions (as in the progression from crawling to standing to walking). Developmental psychologists recognize that most aspects of human development depend on the interaction of genetic and environmental factors (Belsky & Pluess, 2009). The 1890s saw the beginning of research on child development after infancy (White, 1990), most notably at Clark University by G. Stanley Hall (1844–1924). Hall based his views on Darwin's theory of evolution, earning him the title of "the Darwin of the mind." He applied research findings to the improvement of education and child rearing, and today he is recognized as the founder of *child psychology*. Until the 1950s the study of human development was virtually synonymous with child psychology. During that decade, psychologists began to study human development across the life span. More recently, psychologists have come to realize the importance of considering social-cultural factors in human development.

Research Methods in Developmental Psychology

Though developmental psychologists often use the same research methods as other psychologists, they also rely on methods that are unique to developmental psychology. These include *longitudinal research*, *cross-sectional research*, and *cohort-sequential research*, which enable researchers to study age-related differences and changes in their participants.

Longitudinal Research

longitudinal research A research design in which the same group of participants is tested or observed repeatedly over a period of time.

Longitudinal research follows the same participants over a period of time, typically ranging from months to years. The researcher looks for changes in particular characteristics, such as language, personality, intelligence, or perceptual ability. Suppose you wanted to study changes in the social maturity of college students. If you chose to use a longitudinal design, you might assess the social maturity of an incoming class of first-year students and then note changes in their social maturity across their 4 years in college. Longitudinal research has been used to study numerous topics, such as factors associated with the development of creativity in children and adolescents (Weller, 2012), the relationship between identity, intimacy, and well-being in midlife (Sneed, Whitbourne, Schwartz, & Huang, 2012), and older adults' evaluations of their physical health as they age (Sargent-Cox, Anstey, & Luszcz, 2010).

Though longitudinal research has the advantage of permitting us to study individuals as they change across their life spans, it has major weaknesses. First, the typical longitudinal study takes months, years, or even decades to complete. This often requires ongoing financial support and continued commitment by researchers—neither of which can be guaranteed. Second, the longer the study lasts, the more likely it is that participants will drop out. They might refuse to continue or move away or even die. If those who drop out differ in important ways from those who remain, the results of the research might be less generalizable to the population of interest (Feng, Silverstein, Giarrusso, McArdle, & Bengtson, 2006). For example, a 14-year longitudinal study of changes in adult intelligence found that those who dropped out had scored lower on intelligence tests than did those who remained. This made it unwise to generalize the study's findings to all adults. Including only those who remained in the study would have led to the erroneous conclusion that as adults age they show a marked increase in intelligence (Schaie, Labouvie, & Barrett, 1973).

Cross-Sectional Research

The weaknesses of longitudinal research are overcome by **cross-sectional research**, which compares groups of participants of different ages at the same time. Each of the age groups is called a **cohort**. If you chose to use a cross-sectional design to study age-related differences in social maturity of college students, you might compare the current social maturity of four cohorts: first-year students, sophomores, juniors, and seniors. A cross-sectional research design was used in a study of differences in male sexuality across adulthood. The researchers compared samples of men in their 30s through 90s. The stereotypical view of old age as a time of asexuality was countered by the finding that all of the participants in the oldest groups reported feelings of sexual desire (Mulligan & Moss, 1991). Cross-sectional research designs have been used to study topics as varied as differences in attitudes about love, sex, and "hooking up" among students during their first year of college (Katz & Schneider, 2013) and the relationship between medical education and differences in moral reasoning across four years of medical school (Self & Baldwin, 1998).

cross-sectional research A research design in which groups of participants of different ages are compared at the same point in time.

cohort A group of people of the same age group.

Like longitudinal research, cross-sectional research has its own weaknesses. The main one is that cross-sectional research can produce misleading findings if a cohort in the study is affected by circumstances unique to that cohort (Fullerton & Dixon, 2010). Thus, cross-sectional studies can identify differences between cohorts of different ages, but those differences might not hold true if cohorts of those ages were observed during another era. Suppose that you conduct a cross-sectional study and find that older adults are more prejudiced against minorities than are younger adults. Does this mean that we become more prejudiced with age? Not necessarily. Perhaps, instead, the cohort of older adults was reared at a time when prejudice was more acceptable than it is today. Members of the cohort might simply have retained attitudes that they developed in their youth.

Cohort-Sequential Research

One way to deal with the shortcomings of longitudinal and cross-sectional research is to use **cohort-sequential research**, which begins as a cross-sectional study by comparing different cohorts and then follows the cohorts longitudinally. As an example, consider how a cohort-sequential research design was employed in a study of alcohol use in old age. Healthy cohorts ranging in age from 60 to 86 years were first compared cross-sectionally. The results showed a decline in the percentage of drinkers with age. The cohorts then were followed longitudinally for 7 years. The results remained the same: as the drinkers aged, they drank less. This made it more likely that the decline in drinking with age was related to age rather than to life experiences peculiar to particular cohorts (Adams, Garry, Rhyne, & Hunt, 1990). Another cohort-sequential study found that participation in sports, athletics, or exercising was related to lower levels of substance abuse by teenagers and young adults rather than merely being associated with different patterns of substance abuse for different age cohorts (Terry-McElrath & O'Malley, 2011).

cohort-sequential research A research design that begins as a cross-sectional study by comparing different cohorts and then follows the cohorts longitudinally.

Cohort-sequential research designs also may reveal age differences that are cohort effects rather than being age-related effects. This was the case in the Seattle Longitudinal Study. Cognitive abilities of participants in the longitudinal aspect of the study were measured in 1956, 1963, 1970, and 1977. At each of those times, the cognitive abilities of participants of different ages were compared cross-sectionally. The findings showed that there was a larger cognitive decline in the cross-sectional comparisons than in the longitudinal comparisons. This indicates that observed differences in cognitive ability at

Chapter 4 Human Development

different ages is more related to factors affecting particular cohorts than to changes that naturally accompany aging (Williams & Klug, 1996).

Longitudinal research, cross-sectional research, and cohort-sequential research have long been staples of research on development from birth to death. Today, technology permits developmental psychologists to study ongoing developmental processes even before birth, during the prenatal period.

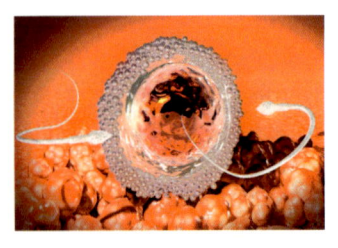

Section Review: Research Methods in Developmental Psychology

1. What is maturation?
2. What are the strengths and weaknesses of cross-sectional and longitudinal research designs?

The Germinal Stage

The germinal stage begins with conception, when one sperm penetrates the outer layer of the egg in a fallopian tube. Once this occurs, cells divide until a multi-cell clump, called a blastocyst, which continues on its journey to the uterus.
Source: Ralwel/Shutterstock.com.

germinal stage The prenatal period that lasts from conception through the second week.

embryonic stage The prenatal period that lasts from the end of the second week through the tenth week.

Prenatal Development

All of us began life as a single cell. The formation of that cell begins the prenatal period, which lasts about 9 months and is divided into the germinal stage, the embryonic stage, and the fetal stage.

The Germinal Stage

The **germinal stage** begins with conception, which occurs when a *sperm* from the man unites with an egg (or *ovum*) from the woman, usually in one of her two *fallopian tubes*, forming a one-celled *zygote*. The zygote contains 23 pairs of chromosomes, one member of each pair coming from the ovum and the other coming from the sperm. The chromosomes, in turn, contain genes that govern the development of the individual. The zygote begins a trip down the fallopian tube, during which it is transformed into a larger, multicelled ball, called a *blastocyst*, by repeated cell divisions. By the end of the second week, the blastocyst attaches to the wall of the uterus. This marks the beginning of the embryonic stage.

The Embryonic Stage

The **embryonic stage** lasts from approximately the end of the second week through approximately the tenth week of prenatal development. The embryo, nourished by nutrients that cross the placenta, increases in size and begins to develop specialized organs, including the eyes, heart, and brain. What accounts for this rapid, complex process? The development and location of bodily organs is regulated by genes, which determine the kinds of cells that will develop and also control the actions of *cell-adhesion molecules*. These molecules direct the movement of cells and determine which cells will adhere to one another, thereby determining the size, shape, and location of organs in the embryo (Rungger-Brändle, Ripperger, Steiger, Soltanieh, & Rungger, 2010). By the end of the embryonic stage, development has progressed to the point at which the heart is beating and the approximately one-inch-long embryo has facial features, limbs, fingers, and toes.

But what determines whether an embryo becomes a female or a male? The answer lies in the 23rd pair of chromosomes, the sex chromosomes, which are designated *X* or *Y*. Embryos that inherit two X chromosomes are genetic females, and embryos that inherit one X and one Y chromosome are genetic males. The presence of a Y chromosome directs the development of the testes; in the *absence* of a Y chromosome, the ovaries differentiate. Near the end of the embryonic period, the primitive gonads of male embryos secrete the hormone *testosterone*, which stimulates the development of male sexual organs. And the primitive gonads of female embryos secrete the hormones *estrogen* and *progesterone*,

Human Embryonic and Fetal Development

Fertilized egg   2-cell stage   4-cell stage   8-cell stage   16-cell stage   Blastocyst

Fetus - 4 weeks   Fetus - 10 weeks   Fetus - 16 weeks   Fetus - 20 weeks

Prenatal Development

Human prenatal development is the process in which a fertilized egg becomes an embryo and develops as a fetus until birth. In the fetal stage, many organs are formed.
Source: BlueRingMedia/Shutterstock.com.

which stimulate the development of female sexual organs. Thus, the hormonal environments of female and male fetuses differ at the embryonic stage of development.

Prenatal hormones direct the differentiation of sexual organs and the brain, especially the hypothalamus (see Chapter 3). The secretion of testosterone by the male fetus directs the differentiation of the male sexual organs. In cases where testosterone is absent, female sexual organs differentiate. There is evidence, though, that estrogen plays a greater role in sexual differentiation of the female fetus than has been estimated in the past (Collaer, Geffner, Kaufman, Buckingham, & Hines, 2002).

The Fetal Stage

The presence of a distinctly human appearance marks the beginning of the **fetal stage**, which lasts from the beginning of the third prenatal month until birth. By the fourth month, pregnant women report movement by the fetus. And by the seventh month, all of the major organs are functional, which means that an infant born even 2 or 3 months prematurely has a chance of surviving. The final 3 months of prenatal development are associated with most of the increase in the size of the fetus.

The fetus also develops rudimentary sensory and cognitive abilities, including the ability to hear sounds and form long-term memories. In one study, 143 fetuses were exposed to a series of conditions. First, there was 2 minutes of silence. Second, there was a tape recording of their mother reading a story. The recording was played for 2 minutes through a speaker held about 4 inches from the mother's abdomen. Then, they were exposed to another 2 minutes of silence. Fetal heart rate increased in response to the mother's voice and decreased when they were exposed to silence. This indicates that the fetus can perceive and form a memory of its mother's voice (Kisilevsky & Haines, 2011).

Premature infants tend to be smaller and less physically and cognitively mature than full-term infants. For example, when an object approaches the eyes of a premature infant, the infant might not exhibit normal defensive blinking (Pettersen, Yonas, & Fisch, 1980). Moreover, though prenatal development usually produces a healthy infant, in some cases genetic defects produce distinctive physical and psychological syndromes. The chromosomal disorder called Down syndrome (discussed in Chapter 10), for example, is associated with intellectual disabilities and abnormal physical development. Other sources of prenatal defects are **teratogens**, which are noxious substances or other factors that can disrupt prenatal development and prevent the individual from reaching her or

fetal stage The prenatal period that lasts from the end of the eighth week through birth.

teratogen A noxious substance, such as a virus or drug, that can cause prenatal defects.

Chapter 4 Human Development

his inherited potential. (The word *teratogen* was coined from Greek terms meaning "that which produces a monster.")

Most teratogens affect prenatal development by first crossing the placenta. A potent teratogen is the German measles (rubella) virus, which can cause defects of the eyes, ears, and heart—particularly during the first 3 months of prenatal development. Many drugs, both legal and illegal, can cross the placenta and cause abnormal physical and psychological development. These drugs include nicotine (Piper, Gray, & Birkett, 2012) and marijuana (Keegan, Parva, Finnegan, Gersen, & Belden, 2010). And alcohol consumption during pregnancy is associated with **fetal alcohol syndrome**. Fetal alcohol syndrome is associated with facial deformities, intellectual disabilities, attentional deficits, and poor impulse control. Researchers have demonstrated the striking teratogenic effect of alcohol in animal studies. When pregnant rats were given alcohol during the embryo stage, their offspring had physical deformities and behavioral deficits similar to those seen in humans (Sulik, Johnston, & Webb, 1981).

fetal alcohol syndrome A disorder, marked by physical defects and intellectual disability, that can afflict the offspring of women who drink alcohol during pregnancy.

Factors that are correlated with parental substance abuse also may have harmful long-term effects. Recreational drug use has adverse effects on the father's health, including damaged DNA that results in abnormal sperm (Pollard, 2000). Parents with a history of substance abuse also are more likely to have turbulent relationships. One study found that women who were heavy cocaine users were more likely to report that the father of the child abused alcohol or other drugs. And fathers with a history of a drug or alcohol problems were more likely to subject their partner to physical or mental abuse during her pregnancy (Frank, Brown, Johnson, & Cabral, 2002). Sadly, children with a history of prenatal drug exposure also are at risk of receiving poor-quality parental care after birth (Eiden, Schuetze, & Coles, 2011). Thus, teratogens not only have a direct effect upon prenatal development, they also may harm the child indirectly by contributing to an environment that fails to ensure the child's well-being.

Section Review: Prenatal Development

1. What are cell-adhesion molecules?
2. What are the symptoms of fetal alcohol syndrome?

Infant and Child Development

Childhood extends from birth until puberty and begins with **infancy**, a period of rapid physical, cognitive, and psychosocial development, extending from birth to age 2 years. Many developmental psychologists devote themselves to studying the changes in physical, perceptual, cognitive, and psychosocial development that occur during childhood.

childhood The period that extends from birth until the onset of puberty.

infancy The period that extends from birth through 2 years of age.

Physical Development

Newborn infants exhibit reflexes that promote their survival, such as blinking to protect their eyes from an approaching object and rooting (searching) for a nipple when their cheeks are touched. Through maturation and learning, the infant quickly develops motor skills that go beyond mere reflexes. The typical infant is crawling by 6 months and walking by 13 months. Though infant motor development follows a consistent sequence, the timing of motor milestones varies somewhat from one infant to another. Figure 4-1 depicts the major motor milestones.

Infancy also is a period of rapid brain development, when many connections between brain cells are formed and many others are eliminated. Though some of these changes are governed by maturation, research studies by Marian Diamond and her colleagues over the past few decades have demonstrated that life experiences can affect brain development (Diamond, 1988). One of these studies determined the effect of enriched and impover-

FIGURE 4-1
Motor Milestones

Infancy is a period of rapid motor development. The infant begins with a set of motor reflexes and, over the course of little more than a year, develops the ability to manipulate objects and move independently through the environment. The ages at which healthy children reach motor milestones vary somewhat from child to child, but the sequence of motor milestones does not.

ished environments on the brain development of rats (Camel, Withers, & Greenough, 1986). A group of infant rats spent 30 days in an enriched environment and another group spent 30 days in an impoverished environment. In the enriched environment, the rats were housed together in two large, toy-filled cages, one containing water and one containing food, which were attached to the opposite ends of a maze. The pattern of pathways and dead ends through the maze was changed daily. In the impoverished environment, the rats were housed individually in small, empty cages.

Microscopic examination of the brains of the rats found that those exposed to enriched environments had longer and more numerous dendrites (see Chapter 3) on their brain neurons than did those exposed to the impoverished environment. The increased size and number of dendrites would provide the rats exposed to the enriched environment with more synaptic connections among their brain neurons. The benefits of enriched environments on neural development also have been replicated in studies of children (Bryck & Fisher, 2012).

After infancy, the child's growth rate slows, and most children grow two or three inches a year until puberty. The child's motor coordination also improves. Children gradually learn to perform more sophisticated motor tasks, such as using scissors, tying their shoes, and riding bicycles. The development of motor skills even affects the development of cognitive skills. For example, children's ability to express themselves through language depends on the development of motor abilities that permit them to speak and to write.

Perceptual Development

Over a century ago, in describing what he believed was the chaotic mental world of the newborn infant, William James (1890/1981, Vol. 1, p. 462) claimed, "The baby, assailed by eyes, ears, nose, skin, and entrails at once, feels it all as one great blooming, buzzing confusion." But subsequent research has shown that newborn infants have more highly developed sensory, perceptual, and cognitive abilities than James believed. For example, though newborns cannot focus on distant objects, they can focus on objects less than a

Chapter 4 Human Development 113

foot away—as though nature has programmed them to focus at the distance of the face of a person who might be holding them (Aslin & Smith, 1988). Newborn infants can use their sense of touch to discriminate between objects with different surface textures (Molina & Jouen, 1998). Newborns also have a more sophisticated sense of smell than James would have presumed. In one study, infants were exposed to either the odor of amniotic fluid (which they experienced while in the womb) or another odor they had not been exposed to before. The results showed that the infants were more likely to turn their heads toward the odor of amniotic fluid than toward the other odor (Schaal, Marlier, & Soussignan, 1998).

Ingenious studies have permitted researchers to infer what infants perceive by recording changes in their eye movements, head movements, body movements, sucking behavior, or physiological responses (such as changes in heart rate or brain-wave patterns). For example, a study of newborn American infants found that they could discriminate between Japanese words with different pitch patterns as indicated by their sucking harder on a rubber nipple in response to particular patterns (Nazzi, Floccia, & Bertoncini, 1998). Infant preferences can be determined by recording which targets they look at longer or by presenting them with a stimulus, waiting for them to *habituate* to it (that is, stop noticing it—as indicated by, for example, a stable heart rate), and then changing the stimulus. If they notice the change, they will show alterations in physiological activity, such as a *decrease* in heart rate.

Studies using these techniques have found that infants have remarkably well-developed sensory-perceptual abilities. Tiffany Field has demonstrated that infants less than 2 days old can imitate sad, happy, and surprised facial expressions (Field, Woodson, Greenberg, & Cohen, 1982). Nonetheless, other studies have been inconsistent in their findings regarding neonatal imitation of facial expressions. The most consistent finding has been that neonates will respond to models who stick out their tongues by sticking out their own (Anisfeld, 1996).

The Research Process box illustrates one of the ways in which psychologists study infant perceptual development. The study made use of a "visual cliff" to test infant depth perception.

Infants also have good auditory abilities, including the ability to localize sounds. Between the ages of 8 and 28 weeks, infants can localize sounds that shift in location by only a few degrees, as indicated by head turns or eye movements in response to the shifts (Morrongiello, Fenwick, & Chance, 1990). Infants can even match the emotional tone of sounds to the emotional tone of facial expressions. In one study, 7-month-old infants were shown a sad face and a happy face. At the same time, they were presented with tones that either increased or decreased in pitch. When presented with a descending tone, they looked longer at a sad face than a happy face, as if they were equating the lower tones with a sad mood and the higher tones with a happy mood (Phillips, Wagner, Fells, & Lynch, 1990). As the preceding studies attest, infants are perceptually more sophisticated than William James presumed.

Cognitive Development

Infancy also is a time of rapid cognitive development, during which infants show the unfolding of inborn abilities and their talent for learning. In regard to inborn abilities, for example, newborn infants can distinguish groups of objects that differ in number (Wynn, 1995). In regard to learning, by 4 or 5 months of age, an infant's response to the sound of its own name differs from its response to hearing other names (Mandel, Jusczyk, & Pisoni, 1995).

Jean Piaget (1896–1980), a Swiss biologist and psychologist, put forth the most influential theory of cognitive development. Piaget (1952) proposed that children pass through four increasingly sophisticated cognitive stages of development (see Table 4-1). According to Piaget, a child is more than an ignorant adult; the child's way of thinking is qualitatively different from the adult's. Moreover, infants are not passive in developing their cognitive views of the physical world. Instead, their views depend on their active interpretation of objects and events in the physical world.

TABLE 4-1 Piaget's States of Cognitive Development

Stage	Age	Description	Developmental Outcome
Sensorimotor	Birth–2 Years	Infants learn to integrate sensory input and motor output and begin to use symbolic thought.	Object permanence
Preoperational	2–7 Years	Children become more sophisticated in their use of language and symbolic thought, but they have difficulty in reasoning logically.	Loss of egocentrism
Concrete operational	7–11 Years	Children become proficient in reasoning logically about concrete situations, such as the ability to make transitive inferences.	Conservation
Formal operational	11–15 Years	Many adolescents learn to use abstract reasoning and to form hypotheses about future events based on relevant current knowledge.	Abstract reasoning and hypothesis testing

Though Piaget assumed that complete passage through one stage is a prerequisite for success in the next one, research suggests that children can achieve characteristics of later stages without completely passing through earlier ones (Berninger, 1988). The issue of whether human cognitive development is continuous (gradual and quantitative) or discontinuous (in stages and qualitative) remains unresolved (Fischer & Silvern, 1985). The stages put forth by Piaget are the *sensorimotor stage*, *preoperational stage*, *concrete operational stage*, and *formal operational stage*. Some psychologists have criticized Piaget's theory for its assumption that cognitive development follows a universal pattern (Elkind, 1996). Cross-cultural research indicates that children throughout the world do tend to pass through these stages in the same order, though the timing varies (Segall, Dasen, Berry, & Poortings, 1990).

Sensorimotor Stage

Piaget called infancy the **sensorimotor stage**, during which the child learns to coordinate sensory experiences and motor behaviors. Infants learn to interact with the world by sucking, grasping, crawling, and walking. In little more than a year, they change from being reflexive and physically immature to being purposeful, locomoting, and language-using. By the age of 9 months, for example, sensorimotor coordination becomes sophisticated enough for the infant to grasp a moving object by aiming her or his reach somewhat ahead of the object—using its speed and direction—instead of where the object appears to be at that moment (Keen, Carrico, Sylvia, & Berthier, 2003).

Piaget claimed that experiences with the environment help the infant form **schemas**, which are cognitive structures incorporating the characteristics of persons, objects, events, procedures, or situations. This means that infants do more than simply gather information about the world. Their experiences actively change the way in which they think about the world. Schemas permit infants to adapt their behaviors to changes in the environment. But what makes schemas persist or change? They do so as the result of the interplay between **assimilation** and **accommodation**. We *assimilate* when we fit information into our existing schemas and *accommodate* when we revise our schemas to fit new information.

Young infants, prior to 6 months old, share an important schema in which they assume that the removal of an object from sight means that the object no longer exists. If an object is hidden by a piece of cloth, for example, the young infant will not look for it, even after watching the object being hidden. To the young infant, out of sight truly means out of mind. As infants gain experience with the coming and going of objects in the environment, they accommodate and develop the schema of **object permanence**—the

sensorimotor stage The Piagetian stage, from birth through the second year, during which the infant learns to coordinate sensory experiences and motor behaviors.

schema A cognitive structure that guides people's perception and information processing that incorporates the characteristics of particular persons, objects, events, procedures, or situations.

assimilation The cognitive process that interprets new information in light of existing schemas.

accommodation 1. The cognitive process that revises existing schemas to incorporate new information. 2. The process by which the lens of the eye increases its curvature to focus light from close objects or decreases its curvature to focus light from more distant objects.

object permanence The realization that objects exist even when they are no longer visible.

The Research Process

When Do Infants Develop Depth Perception?

Rationale

One of the most important perceptual abilities is depth perception. It lets us tell how far away objects are from us, preventing us from bumping into them and providing us with time to escape from potentially dangerous ones. But how early can infants perceive depth? This was the subject of a classic study by Eleanor Gibson (1910–2002) and Richard Walk (Gibson & Walk, 1960).

Method

Gibson and Walk used a "visual cliff" made from a piece of thick, transparent glass set about four feet off the ground (see Figure 4-2). Just under the "shallow" side was a red and white checkerboard pattern. The same pattern was placed at floor level under the "deep" side. The sides were separated by a one-foot-wide wooden board. The participants were 36 infants, aged 6 to 14 months. The infants were placed, one at a time, on the wooden board. The infants' mothers called to them, first from one side and then from the other.

Results and Discussion

When placed on the board, 9 of the infants refused to budge. The other 27 crawled onto the shallow side toward their mothers. But only 3 of the 27 crawled onto the deep side. The remaining ones instead cried or crawled away from it. This indicated that the infants could perceive the depth of the two sides—and feared the deep side. It also demonstrated that depth perception is present by 6 months of age. Replications of the study using a variety of animals found that depth perception develops by the time the animal begins moving about on its own—as early as the first day after birth for chicks and goats. This is adaptive, because it reduces their likelihood of being injured. More recent research on human infants, using decreases in heart rate as a sign that they notice changes in depth, indicates that rudimentary depth perception is present in infants as young as 4 months (Aslin & Smith, 1988). But research findings indicate that human infants will not fear heights until they have had several weeks of crawling experience. Infants will not avoid the deep side of the visual cliff until they have been crawling for at least 12 weeks (Kretch & Adolph, 2013).

FIGURE 4-2 The Visual Cliff

Eleanor Gibson and Richard Walk (1960) developed the *visual cliff* to test infant depth perception. The visual cliff consists of a thick sheet of glass placed on a table. The shallow end of the visual cliff has a checkerboard surface just below the glass. The deep end of the visual cliff has a checkerboard surface a few feet below the glass. Infants who have reached the crawling stage will crawl from the center of the table across the shallow end, but not across the deep end, to reach their mothers. This finding indicates that by 6 months infants can perceive depth. Of course, this study does not preclude the possibility that infants can perceive depth even before they can crawl.

realization that objects not in view may still exist. Infants generally fail to search for objects that are suddenly hidden from view until they are about 8 months old (Munakata, McClelland, Johnson, & Siegler, 1997). But researchers have questioned Piaget's explanation that young infants fail to search for hidden objects because they lack a schema for object permanence. Perhaps, instead, they simply forget the location of an object that has been hidden from view (Bjork & Cummings, 1984).

After the age of 8 months, most infants demonstrate their appreciation of object permanence by searching at other places for an object they have seen being hidden from view. At this point in their development, they can retain a mental image of a physical object even after it has been removed from their sight, and they realize that the object might be elsewhere. This also signifies the beginning of representational thought—the use of symbols to stand for physical objects. But Piaget might have placed the development of object permanence too late, because infants as young as 6 months have been found to show an appreciation of it (Shinskey, 2012).

Preoperational Stage

According to Piaget, when the child reaches the age of 2 years and leaves infancy, the sensorimotor stage gives way to the **preoperational stage**, which lasts until about age 7. The stage is called preoperational because the child cannot perform what Piaget called *operations*—mental manipulations of reality. For example, before about the age of 5 the early preoperational child cannot perform mental addition or subtraction of objects. During the preoperational stage, however, the child improves in the use of language, including a rapid growth in vocabulary and a more sophisticated use of grammar. Thus mental development sets the stage for language development. Unlike the sensorimotor-stage child, the preoperational-stage child is not limited to thinking about objects that are physically present.

preoperational stage The Piagetian stage, extending from 2 to 7 years of age, during which the child's use of language becomes more sophisticated but the child has difficulty with the logical mental manipulation of information.

During the preoperational stage, the child also exhibits what Piaget called **egocentrism**, the inability to perceive reality from the perspective of another person. Egocentrism declines between 4 and 6 years of age (Ruffman & Olson, 1989). Children display egocentrism when they draw a picture of their family but fail to include themselves in the drawing. In some capital criminal cases, lawyers might gain a reduced sentence for a child defendant if they can convince the jury that the child had not progressed beyond egocentrism and therefore was unaware of the effect of the criminal act on the victim (Ellison, 1987).

egocentrism The inability to perceive reality from the perspective of another person.

Concrete Operational Stage

At about the age of 7, the child enters what Piaget calls the **concrete operational stage**, which lasts until about the age of 11. The child learns to reason logically but is at first limited to reasoning about physical things. For example, when you first learned to do arithmetic problems, you were unable to perform mental calculations. Instead, until perhaps the age of 8, you counted by using your fingers or other objects. An important kind of reasoning ability that develops during this stage is the ability to make **transitive inferences**—the application of previously learned relationships to infer new ones. For example, suppose that a child is told that Pat is taller than Lee, and that Lee is taller than Terry. A child who can make transitive inferences will correctly conclude that Pat is taller than Terry. Though Piaget claimed that the ability to make transitive inferences develops by age 8, research has shown that children as young as 4 can make them—provided they are given age-appropriate tasks (Andrews & Halford, 1998).

concrete operational stage The Piagetian stage, extending from 7 to 11 years of age, during which the child learns to reason logically about objects that are physically present.

transitive inference The application of previously learned relationships to infer new relationships.

By the age of 8, the child in the concrete operational stage also develops what Piaget called **conservation**—the realization that changing the form of a substance or the arrangement of a set of objects does not change the amount. Suppose that a child is shown two balls of clay of equal size. One ball is then rolled out into a snake, and the child is asked if either piece of clay has more clay. The child who has not achieved conservation will probably reply that the snake has more clay because it is longer. Figure 4-3 shows a classic

conservation The realization that changing the form of a substance does not change its amount.

FIGURE 4-3
Conservation

During the concrete operational stage, children develop an appreciation of conservation. They come to realize that changing the form of something does not change its amount. For example, they realize that pouring water from a tall, narrow container into a short, wide container does not change the amount of water.

Conservation of Liquid

When shown the same amount of water being poured into two identical glasses, a child will report that both glasses contain the same amount.

If the water from one of the glasses is poured into a shorter, wider container, a child who has achieved conservation of liquid probably will report that the container contains the same amount of water as the glass.

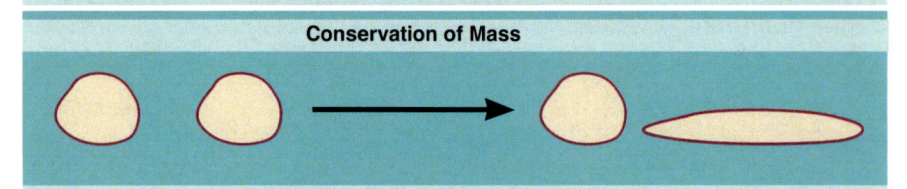

Conservation of Mass

When shown two identical balls of clay, a child will report that the balls contain the same amount.

If one of the balls is rolled out so that it becomes longer, a child who has achieved conservation of mass probably will report that it contains the same amount of clay as the ball of clay.

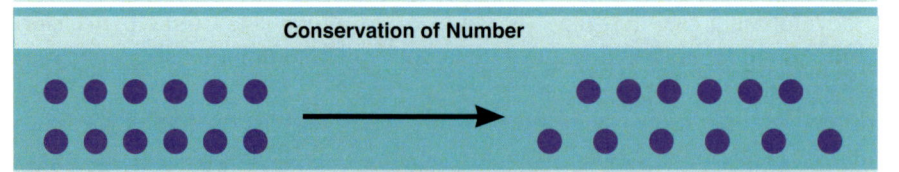

Conservation of Number

When shown two identical rows of coins, a child will report that the rows are identical.

If the coins in one row are spread farther apart, a child who has achieved conservation of number probably will report that the number of coins has not changed.

means of testing whether a child has developed the schema of conservation. Conservation has implications for children as eyewitnesses. Children who have achieved conservation are less susceptible to leading questions than are children who have not achieved it (Muir-Broddus, King, Downey, & Petersen, 1998).

The effect of sociocultural experiences on the timing of conservation was demonstrated in a study of children in a Mexican village whose parents were pottery makers. The children who normally helped their parents in making pottery acquired conservation (at least of mass) earlier than other children did (Price-Williams, Gordon, & Ramirez, 1969). Moreover, certain nonverbal variations of the conservation of liquid volume problem show that children might develop conservation earlier than indicated by studies that have used the traditional verbal demonstration procedure (Wheldall & Benner, 1993).

In early adolescence, the concrete operational stage might give way to the formal operational stage, which is discussed in the section of this chapter devoted to adolescent development.

Psychosocial Development

Just as Piaget believed that the child passes through stages of cognitive development, psychoanalyst Erik Erikson (1902–1994) believed that the child passes through stages of psychosocial development. Erikson observed that we go through eight distinct stages across the life span. Each stage is marked by a conflict that must be overcome, as described in Table 4-2. Research has supported Erikson's belief that we pass through the stages

Chapter 4 Human Development

TABLE 4-2 Erikson's Stages of Psychosocial Development

Age	Social Conflict	Successful Resolution of Conflict
Birth–1 year	Trust vs. mistrust	A sense of security and attachment with caregivers.
2 years	Autonomy vs. shame and doubt	A sense of independence from caregivers.
3–5 years	Initiative vs. guilt	The ability to control impulses while still being spontaneous
6 years–puberty	Industry vs. inferiority	A sense of competence in regard to a variety of everyday activities
Adolescence	Identity vs. role confusion	A mature sense of self characterized by living according to one's own values, interests, and goals
Young adulthood	Intimacy vs. isolation	The establishment of mature relationships characterized by personal commitment and emotional attachment
Middle adulthood	Generativity vs. stagnation	An investment in others and concern about their well-being.
Late adulthood	Integrity vs. despair	A sense of acceptance from reflecting on a meaningful life.

sequentially—though people differ in the ages at which they pass through them (Vaillant & Milofsky, 1980). Erikson also was one of the first researchers to consider sociocultural differences in psychosocial development, noting that the society, not just the family, affects the child's development (Eagle, 1997). This view was influenced by Erikson's studies of children in Sioux, Yurok, and other Native American cultures.

You also should be aware that there might be sociocultural differences among peoples we normally might consider to be members of a homogenous cultural group. In Central Africa, for example, infants have markedly different experiences among Ngandu farmers and neighboring Aka hunter-gatherers. Aka infants are more likely to be held, and Nkandu infants are more likely to be left alone, possibly contributing to early behavioral differences that are observed between them (Hewlett, Lamb, Shannon, Leyendecker, & Schoelmerich, 1998).

Social Attachment and Interpersonal Relationships

Erikson found that the major social conflict of the first year of infancy is **trust versus mistrust**. One of the most important factors in helping the infant develop trust is **social attachment**, a strong emotional relationship between an infant and a caregiver that develops during the first year. Beginning in the 1930s, British psychiatrist John Bowlby (1907–1990) became interested in the effects of early maternal loss or deprivation on later personality development. Much of his theorizing was based on his study of orphans whose parents were killed in World War II. Bowlby favored an evolutionary viewpoint, suggesting that infants have evolved an inborn need for attachment because their survival depends on adult caregivers (Bowlby, 1988). Thus, infants seek to maintain physical proximity and evoke responses from adults through crying, cooing, smiling, and clinging. Similarly, Sigmund Freud assumed that an infant becomes attached to his or her mother for a functional reason—she provides nourishment through nursing.

Freud's assumption was contradicted by research conducted by Harry Harlow and his colleagues on social attachment in rhesus monkeys. Harlow separated infant monkeys from their parents and peers and raised them for 6 months with two "surrogate mothers." The surrogates were wire monkeys with wooden heads. One surrogate was covered with terry cloth and the other was left bare. Harlow found that the monkeys preferred to cling to the cloth-covered surrogate, even though milk was available only from a bottle attached to the bare-wire surrogate. Harlow concluded that physical contact is a more important factor than nourishment in promoting infant attachment (Harlow & Zimmerman, 1959).

trust versus mistrust Erikson's developmental stage in which success is achieved by having a secure social attachment with a caregiver.

social attachment A strong emotional relationship between an infant and a caregiver.

Harlow's research findings inspired interest in the possible role of attachment in human psychosocial development. Of course, today's ethical standards would prevent the replication of Harlow's experiment with human infants (and perhaps even with infant monkeys). Much of what we know about attachment in human infants comes from research by Mary Ainsworth (1913–1999) on the mother-infant relationship. She was inspired by her long-time collaboration with Bowlby. Ainsworth conducted her first studies of infant-mother attachment patterns after visiting Uganda. Though cross-cultural studies have found differences in infant behaviors and maternal behaviors and beliefs, the importance of infant-mother attachment patterns has been found to generalize across many cultures (Pierrehumbert et al., 2009).

In assessing attachment, Ainsworth made a distinction between *securely attached* and *insecurely attached* infants. This becomes an especially important issue at about 8 months of age, when infants show a strong preference for their mothers over strangers and show separation anxiety. To test this, Ainsworth developed the Strange Situation: The mother and infant are in a room together; the mother leaves the room, a stranger enters the room, the stranger then leaves, and the infant's response to the mother is assessed when she then returns to the room. The securely attached infant seeks physical contact with the mother, yet, despite mildly protesting, freely leaves her to play and explore, using the mother as a secure base. In contrast, the insecurely attached infant clings to the mother, acts either apathetic or highly anxious when separated from her, and is either unresponsive or angry when reunited with her.

A meta-analysis of 21 studies using the Strange Situation with more than 1,000 infants found a moderately strong relationship between the mother's sensitivity and the infant's attachment security (De Wolff & van IJzendoorn, 1997). An infant whose mother is more sensitive, accepting, and affectionate will become more securely attached. Infants who are securely attached, in turn, have better relationships with their peers in childhood and adolescence than infants who are insecurely attached (Gorrese & Ruggieri, 2012). And research indicates that the relationship between maternal responsiveness and the quality of infant attachment generalizes across cultures. Cultural differences have been observed, though, in the maternal and infant behaviors observed in the Strange Situation, especially in measures of visual referencing—infants' willingness to play at a distance while keeping mothers within eyesight—and physical proximity seeking, such as clinging and cuddling (Leyendecker, Lamb, Fracasso, Schölmerich, & Larson, 1997; Zach & Keller, 1999).

Until recently, research on attachment has been limited to use of the Strange Situation in assessing the quality of attachment with the infant's primary caregiver—typically the mother (Field, 1996). Researchers investigating the role of the father in social development have found that paternal interaction also promotes secure attachment in infants. Moreover, families may be described as reflecting a system of attachments between infants, young children, and family members who provide care and engage them in social interaction (van IJzendoorn & DeWolff, 1997).

One study assessed the quality of attachment between mothers, fathers, and two of their children. The Strange Situation was used to measure attachment in the younger children (aged 18 to 24 months), and a questionnaire was used to measure attachment in older children (4 to 5 years of age). Parental caregiving was assessed through naturalistic observation and questionnaires. Results indicated that the majority of the children had developed secure attachments with both parents. Moreover, the quality of parental care-giving predicted secure attachment in only one case: between mothers and their younger children. Maternal caregiving was unrelated to the quality of attachment in older children. And paternal caregiving was unrelated to the quality of attachment of younger and older children (Schneider-Rosen & Burke, 1999). These findings suggest that caregiving is only one avenue by which parents, usually mothers, contribute to the development of a secure attachment in infancy. Moreover, the quality of attachment in older children appears to be related to other aspects of family interaction, such as the quality of parent-child play (Grossmann, Grossmann, Kremmer-Bombik, Scheuerer-Englisch, &

Zimmerman, 2002). And, though neglected by early research in attachment, fathers do contribute to the development of attachment in infancy and early childhood.

Researchers also have investigated the stability of attachment security across the life span. Two longitudinal studies found that attachment security is remarkably stable from infancy through adolescence (Beijersbergen, Juffer, Bakermans-Kranenburg, & van IJzendoorn, 2012) and early adulthood (Fraley, Roisman, Booth-LaForce, Owen, & Holland, 2013). In these studies, attachment category had been assessed in infancy. Later, participants completed questionnaires assessing the quality of their attachment or were interviewed by raters blind to their original classification. In both studies, the majority of the securely attached participants' classification was unchanged. But what predicts changes in attachment security? Attachment security can be adversely affected by negative life events that disrupt a family's functioning and the psychological well-being of adults in the household—and in turn their responsiveness and sensitivity to their offspring (Waters, Weinfield, & Hamilton, 2000).

According to Erikson, during the second year the child experiences a conflict involving **autonomy versus shame and doubt**. The child explores the physical environment, begins to learn self-care skills, such as feeding, and tries out budding motor and language abilities. In doing so, the child develops a greater sense of independence from her or his parents. This might account for the popular notion of the "terrible twos," when the child enjoys behaving in a contrary manner and saying no to any request. Parents who stifle efforts at reasonable independence or criticize the child's awkward efforts will promote feelings of shame and doubt. Elementary and high school teachers who support autonomy in their students have a more positively motivating style of teaching (Reeve, Bolt, & Cai, 1999).

autonomy versus shame and doubt Erikson's developmental stage in which success is achieved by gaining a degree of independence from one's parents.

At 3 years of age, the child enters the stage that involves the conflict Erikson calls **initiative versus guilt**. The child shows initiative in play, social relations, and exploration of the environment. The child also learns to control his or her impulses, feeling guilt for actions that go beyond limits set by parents. So, at this stage, parents might permit their child to rummage through drawers but not to throw clothing around the bedroom. Thus, the stage of initiative versus guilt deals with the development of a sense of right and wrong.

initiative versus guilt Erikson's developmental stage in which success is achieved by behaving in a spontaneous but socially appropriate way.

At about the age of 6, and continuing until about the age of 12, Erikson observed, the child faces the conflict of **industry versus inferiority**. The industrious child who achieves successes during this stage is more likely to feel competent. This is important, because children who feel academically and socially competent are happier than other children and have more positive relationships with their peers (Mouratidis & Michou, 2011). A child who develops a sense of inferiority may lose interest in academics, avoid social interactions, or fail to participate in sports. Successful resolution of the conflict over industry versus inferiority also leads to more positive feelings of vocational competence in high-school students (Gribble, 2000). The importance of this stage in psychosocial development has been demonstrated in both Western and non-Western countries, including the People's Republic of China (Zhang & Nurmi, 2012).

industry versus inferiority Erikson's developmental stage in which success is achieved by developing a sense of competency.

Parent-Child Relationships

One of the most important factors in psychosocial development is the approach that parents take to child rearing. This is especially important, given the increasingly diverse family configurations within the United States. Stepparents, for example, who try to develop a friendship with their stepchildren before marrying and who continue their friendship after marrying have relationships with their stepchildren that are more likely to be marked by liking and affection. Stepparents who, instead, try to control their stepchildren are less likely to develop a positive relationship (Ganong, Coleman, Fine, & Martin, 1999). And a frequently expressed concern is whether the children of gay or lesbian parents will suffer from personal or social adjustment problems. An extensive review of research studies found no differences between the children of gay and lesbian parents and those of heterosexual parents on a number of measures of psychosocial adjustment (Wainright, Russell, & Patterson, 2004).

Parenting Style Psychologist Diana Baumrind (1966) distinguished three parenting styles: *permissive*, *authoritarian*, and *authoritative*. Permissive parents set few rules and rarely punish misbehavior. Permissiveness is undesirable because children will be less likely to adopt positive standards of behavior. At the other extreme, authoritarian parents set strict rules and rely on punishment. They respond to questioning of their rules by saying, "Because I say so!"

Authoritarian parenting, likewise, is undesirable. Authoritarian parents exert coercive power over their children, which is arbitrary and domineering (Baumrind, 2010), and which may lead to emotional abuse (Hamarman, Pope, & Czaja, 2002). Authoritarian parents also are more likely to resort to physical discipline—perhaps escalating to physical abuse. Aside from the potential for injury to the child, physical child abuse is associated with lasting emotional effects on the target of the abuse. Abused children have lower self-esteem and are more depressed (Leeson & Nixon, 2011), they tend to be more aggressive (Barry, Lochman, Fite, Wells, & Colder, 2012), and they are more likely to develop behavior problems in adolescence (Thompson, Hollis, & Richards, 2003).

Another form of physical and emotional child abuse is sexual abuse—in many cases by a parent or close family member. A review of research studies published between 1989 and 1999 found that about 10 percent of child abuse cases involve sexual abuse and about 17 percent of women and 8 percent of men had histories of sexual abuse as children (Putnam, 2003). The scourge of child sexual abuse makes it imperative that children be taught to avoid situations that might make them potential targets of sex abusers. Of great concern is the vicious cycle in which abused children become abusive parents. However, though most child abusers were abused as children, only one-third of abused children become abusers—a far cry from claims that being an abused child automatically makes one a future child abuser (Putnam, 2003). So, if you were unfortunate enough to have a history of child abuse, you may very well be able to break the vicious cycle when rearing your own children.

Baumrind has found that the best approach to child rearing is **authoritative parenting** (Baumrind, 1983). Authoritative parents tend to be warm and loving, yet insist that their children behave appropriately. They encourage independence within well-defined limits, show a willingness to explain the reasons for their rules, and permit their children to express verbal disagreement with them. By maintaining a delicate balance between freedom and control, authoritative parents help their children internalize standards of behavior.

Children of authoritative parents report better physical and psychological well-being than children of authoritarian or permissive parents Children who have authoritative parents are more likely to be socially competent, independent, and responsible. They are less likely to drink alcohol or smoke (Piko & Balázs, 2012), more likely to perform well in school (Mattanah, Pratt, Cowan, & Cowan, 2005), and more likely to be autonomous and display a mastery orientation, which is essential for motivation (Kudo, Longhofer, & Floersch, 2012). But, as cautioned in Chapter 2, be wary of concluding that parenting style causes these effects. Remember that only experimental, not correlational, research permits statements about causality. Perhaps the direction of causality is the opposite of what one would assume. For example, children who behave properly might evoke authoritative parenting.

Research tends to support a positive relationship between authoritative parenting and children's competence. But we still do not know how or why it does so (Darling & Steinberg, 1993). Though the relationship between authoritative parenting and healthy child development appears to be a universal phenomenon (Zhou et al., 2008), we must be aware of cultural differences in child rearing—both between and within societies. Cultural differences in beliefs about parental and child roles and the nature of child rearing influence parents' interactions with their children (Rudy & Grusec, 2001). For example, Chinese parenting may be seen as authoritarian and controlling. Chinese cultural beliefs about parenting stress the concept of *chiao shun*, or training the child to meet social expectations. Thus, parental control may have different meanings in cross-cultural contexts (Chao, 1994; 2001).

authoritative parenting An effective style of parenting in which the parent is warm and loving yet sets well-defined limits that he or she enforces in an appropriate manner.

Day Care Another important, and sometimes controversial, factor in child rearing is day care. The number of American children placed in day care increased during the 1990s, with more than half of infants and toddlers spending at least 20 hours per week in the care of adults other than their parents (Singer, Fuller, Keiley, & Wolf, 1998). Though day care, overall, seems to have neither strong benefits nor strong detrimental effects (Lamb, 1996), research findings are contradictory in regard to the effects of day care on infants. On the negative side are studies finding that infant day care of more than 20 hours a week in the first year of life is associated with insecure attachment during infancy and greater noncompliance and aggressiveness in early childhood (Hill, Wadlfogel, Brooks-Gunn, & Han, 2005) and that children who enter day care before age 2 later perform more poorly in high school than do children who enter day care after age 2 (Ispa, Thornburg, & Gray, 1990). Of course, we can never be sure about the cause and effect from studies such as these. On the positive side are studies finding that infants in day care do not become insecurely attached (Burchinal, Bryant, Lee, & Ramey, 1992) and that they later do well in school and act less aggressively than other children do (Field, 1991). And a longitudinal study that examined preschoolers' behavior before and after their mothers returned to work showed no negative outcomes (Chase-Lansdale et al., 2003). These contradictory findings reflect the complex nature of the issue, which involves numerous variables, including the characteristics of the infants, their parents, their caretakers, and the day-care settings.

Because many working parents have no choice but to place their infants in day care, it is reassuring to know that research indicates that high-quality infant day care is probably not harmful (Maccoby & Lewis, 2003). According to findings of the National Institute of Child Health and Human Development Study of Early Child Care, "high-quality" means that the number of children and the adult-child ratio are small, the adults practice nonauthoritarian caregiving, and the environment is safe, clean, and stimulating (NICHD Early Child Care Research Network, 1997). Some researchers have found that high-quality daycare can have long-term benefits on children's cognitive and social emotional development (Peisner-Feinberg et al., 2001). High-quality day care has been found to be especially influential in the prevention of behavior problems in low-income boys and African American children (Votruba-Drzal et al., 2010). Though, overall, day care has neither positive nor negative effects on infants or children, poor day care and lack of a stable care provider tend to have a negative effect (Lamb, 1996). But the cost of high-quality day care—if it is, in fact, available—makes it unaffordable to many families. Nonetheless, even day care that is not optimal tends not to have damaging effects on most children. Heredity and home environment tend to outweigh the effects of day care, even when it is not of high quality (Scarr, 1998).

Parental Conflict Children are affected not only by parenting styles and day-care practices but also by the quality of their parents' relationship. A meta-analysis of relevant studies found that parental discord spills over into negative parent-child relationships (Erel & Burman, 1995). Moreover, marital discord can undermine the child's feeling of emotional security and lead to adjustment problems in childhood and adolescence (Klahr, Rueter, McGue, Iacono, & Alexander, 2011) and marital discord in adulthood (Davies & Cummings, 1994).

In some cases marital discord leads to divorce. Because about half of all marriages in the United States end in divorce, many children spend at least part of their childhood primarily with one parent. Though it is easier for two adults to meet the stressful demands of providing the consistent, responsive caregiving that promotes children's well-being, research on single parents indicates that one responsible, emotionally available adult can provide the social and emotional bond that is essential to optimal childhood development (Silverstein & Auerbach, 1999). More than one-third of American children born in the past three decades will experience parental divorce. And they will be more likely to suffer emotional problems, particularly depression (Aseltine, 1996). The long-term effects of divorce on children include greater personal distress and more problems in intimate relationships in adulthood (Christensen & Brooks, 2001).

Because divorce involves so many variables, including the age and economic status of the parents, the age of the children, and the custody arrangements, different combinations of these variables can have different effects on the children (Lamb, 2012). The effects of each combination remain to be determined. It should be noted, however, that children from divorced families have a greater sense of well-being than children from intact families with intense parental conflict (Amato & Keith, 1991). Moreover, divorce itself might induce less distress in children than parental conflict prior to the divorce. A meta-analysis of research studies published during the 1990s on the well-being of children of divorce versus children from intact families found that children of divorce were worse off on variables such as self-esteem, personal conduct, psychological adjustment, interpersonal relationships, and academic performance. These differences were slightly greater in later studies than those reported in studies conducted during the 1980s (Reifman, Villa, Amans, Rethinam, & Telesca, 2001).

Interaction with Peers

Children are affected by their relationships with friends and siblings as well as those with their parents. Friendships provide the context for social and emotional growth (Newcomb & Bagwell, 1995). Secure attachment to both mothers and fathers provides a solid basis for friendships (Verissimo et al., 2011). And childhood friendships may have a bearing on adult emotional well-being. Consider a study that compared young adults who had a best friend in fifth grade and young adults who had no friends in fifth grade. Those who had a best friend had higher self-esteem than those who had no friends. And those who had no best friend were more likely to have symptoms of psychological disorders (Bagwell, Newcomb, & Bukowski, 1998). Of course, you must be careful not to assume that there is a causal relationship in which friendships promote healthy personalities. Perhaps, instead, children with certain personalities are simply more likely to make friends and to have higher self-esteem.

Few children develop friendships before the age of 3, and 95 percent of childhood friendships are between children of the same sex (Hartup, 1989). Girls tend to have fewer, but more intimate, friendships than do boys (Berndt & Hoyle, 1985). A meta-analysis of children's peer relations found that socially and academically competent children are popular with their peers. In contrast, children who are withdrawn, aggressive, or academically deficient tend to be rejected by their peers (Newcomb, Bukowski, & Pattee, 1993).

Peer relationships in childhood involve play. A classic study (Parten, 1932) found that the interactive play of children gradually increased between 2 and 4 years of age, but that throughout this period, children engaged mainly in parallel play, as when two children in a sandbox play separately from each other with pails and shovels. Parallel play provides a transition into social play, in which children play interactively, with children as old as 4 years alternating between the two (Anderson, 2001). There also are cultural differences in play. For example, whereas gender-segregated play appears to be a universal phenomenon, there are cultural differences in the extent to which children engage in cross-sex play (Aydt & Corsaro, 2003).

Gender-Role Development

One of the most frequently studied aspects of psychosocial development in childhood is the development of **gender roles**, which are behavior patterns that are considered appropriate for men or women in a given culture. The first formal theory of gender-role development was put forth by Sigmund Freud. He assumed that the resolution of what he called the Oedipus (in the case of boys) and Electra (in the case of girls) complexes (discussed in Chapter 13) at age 5 or 6 led the child to internalize the gender role of the same-sex parent. The Oedipus and Electra complexes begin with the child's sexual attraction to the other-sex parent. According to Freud, because the child fears punishment for desiring the other-sex parent, the child comes to identify with the same-sex parent. But studies of children show that children develop gender roles even when they live in single-parent

gender roles Behaviors that are considered appropriate for women or men in a given culture.

households. Because of the lack of research support for Freud's theory, most researchers favor more recent theories of gender-role development.

Social learning theory stresses the importance of observational learning, rewards, and punishment. Thus, social learning theorists assume that the child learns gender-relevant behaviors by observing gender-role models and by being rewarded for appropriate, and corrected or punished for inappropriate, gender-role behavior. This process of gender typing begins on the very day of birth and continues through the life span. In one study, new parents were interviewed within 24 hours of the birth of their first child. Though there are no observable differences in the physical appearance of male and female newborns whose genitals are covered, newborn daughters were more likely to be described by their parents as cute, weak, and uncoordinated than newborn sons were (Rubin, Provenzano, & Luria, 1974). But an influential review of research by Eleanor Maccoby found that parents reported that they did not treat their sons and daughters differently (Maccoby & Jacklin, 1974). Of course, parents might believe that they treat their daughters and sons the same, while actually treating them differently. A meta-analysis, however, supported Maccoby by finding that gender-role development seems, at best, weakly related to differences in how parents rear their sons and daughters (Lytton & Romney, 1991).

Parents are not the only social influences contributing to gender-role development. As noted earlier in this chapter, children tend to socialize with same-sex peers and engage in sex-segregated play. Children reward each other for engaging in gender-appropriate activities and punish or exclude children who engage in cross-gender behavior. Moreover, this peer pressure is stronger for boys than for girls. Considering the inconsistent evidence for the role of differential parental reinforcement of children's behaviors, it is very likely that peers may wield a stronger influence on gender-role development than do parents (Bussey & Bandura, 1999). One such factor is the sex of one's siblings. A large-scale study of 3-year-olds found that both boys and girls with an older brother were more masculine and less feminine. Boys with an older sister were more feminine but not less masculine. And girls with an older sister were less masculine but not more feminine (Rust, Golombok, Hines, Johnston, & Golding, 2000).

An alternative to the social learning theory of gender-role development is Sandra Bem's (1981) **gender schema theory**, which combines elements of social learning theory and the cognitive perspective. Bem's theory holds that people differ in the schemas they use to

social learning theory A theory of learning that assumes that people learn behaviors mainly through observation and mental processing of information.

gender schema theory A theory of gender-role development that combines aspects of social learning theory and the cognitive perspective.

Gender Roles

According to social learning theory, children learn gender-role behaviors by being rewarded for performing those behaviors and by observing adults, particularly parents, engaging in them.
Source: XiXinXing/Shutterstock.com.

Chapter 4 Human Development

organize their social world. People may have schemas relevant to age, ethnicity, gender, occupations, or any number of social categories. *Gender schemas* are specialized cognitive structures that assimilate and organize information about women and men. Children are *gender schematic* if they categorize people, behavior, activities, and interests as masculine or feminine. In contrast, *gender aschematic* children do not categorize these types of information into masculine and feminine categories. Gender schematic individuals are likely to notice, attend to, and remember people's behavior and attributes that are relevant to gender. For example, one study found that gender schematic adults recalled more gender-stereotypic information than did gender aschematic adults (Renn & Calvert, 1993).

Gender schemas develop early. One study found that toddlers were able to label same-sex toys—operationally defined as touching a masculine or feminine toy—as early as 2 years of age (Levy, 1999). Social experiences can modify the development of gender schema, though, as shown in studies of traditional and egalitarian families. A meta-analysis of 48 studies found that parents' gender schemas were correlated with their children's gender schemas. Though the effect size was small, traditional parents were more likely than nontraditional parents to have children who thought about themselves and others in gender-typed ways (Tenenbaum & Leaper, 2002). Gender schema theory provides a glimpse into the development of gender stereotypes and how gender stereotypes influence social behavior (Deaux & Major, 1987).

Moral Development

American psychologists have researched and tested the development of morality in children and adults for more than a century (Wendorf, 2001). Today, the most influential theory of moral development is Lawrence Kohlberg's (1981) cognitive-developmental theory.

Kohlberg's Theory of Moral Development Kohlberg's theory, formulated in the 1960s, is based on Piaget's (1932) proposal that a person's level of moral development depends on his or her level of cognitive development. Piaget found that children, in making moral judgments, are at first more concerned with the consequences of actions. Thus, a young child might insist that accidentally breaking ten dishes is morally worse than purposely breaking one dish. As children become more cognitively sophisticated, they base their moral judgments more on a person's intentions than on the consequences of the person's behavior. Kohlberg assumed that as individuals become more cognitively sophisticated, they reach more complex levels of moral reasoning. Research findings indicate that adequate cognitive development is, indeed, a prerequisite for each level of moral reasoning (Walker, 1986).

Kohlberg, agreeing with Piaget, developed a stage theory of moral development based on the individual's level of moral reasoning. Kohlberg determined the individual's level of moral reasoning by presenting a series of stories, each of which includes a moral dilemma. The person must suggest a resolution of the dilemma and give reasons for choosing that resolution. The person's stage of moral development depends not on the resolution, but instead on the reasons given for that resolution. What is your response to the following dilemma proposed by Kohlberg? Your reasoning in resolving it would reveal your level of moral development:

> In Europe, a woman was near death from a very bad disease, a rare kind of cancer. There was one drug that the doctors thought might save her. It was a special form of radium that a druggist in the same town had recently discovered. The drug was expensive to make, but the druggist was charging 10 times what the drug cost him to make. He paid 200 dollars for the radium and charged two thousand dollars for a small dose of the drug. The sick woman's husband, Heinz, went to everyone he knew to borrow the money, but he could get together only about one thousand dollars, which was half of what it cost. He told the druggist that his wife was dying and asked him to sell it cheaper or let him pay later. But the druggist said, "No, I discovered the drug, and I am going to make money from it." So Heinz got desperate and broke into the man's store to steal the drug for his wife. (Kohlberg, 1981, p. 12)

TABLE 4-3 Kohlberg's Theory of Moral Development

Level of Moral Development	Stage of Moral Development
Preconventional level: Concern with consequences of behavior for oneself	**Stage 1:** Moral choices made to avoid punishment
	Stage 2: Moral choices made to gain rewards
Conventional level: Concern with social laws and values	**Stage 3:** Moral choices made to gain social approval
	Stage 4: Moral choices made to fulfill duty, respect authority, and maintain social order
Postconventional level: Concern with moral principles, agreed-upon laws, and human dignity	**Stage 5:** Moral choices made to follow mutually agreed-upon principles and ensure mutual respect of others
	Stage 6: Moral choices made to uphold human dignity and one's own ethical principles

The levels of moral development represented by particular responses to this dilemma are presented in Table 4-3. Kohlberg has identified three levels: the *preconventional*, the *conventional*, and the *postconventional*. Each level contains two stages, making a total of six stages of moral development. As Piaget noted, as we progress to higher levels of moral reasoning, we become more concerned with the actor's motives than with the consequences of the actor's actions. This was supported by a study of moral judgments about aggressive behavior, which found that high school and college students at higher stages of moral reasoning were more concerned with the aggressor's motivation than were students at lower stages (Berkowitz, Mueller, Schnell, & Padberg, 1986).

People at the **preconventional level** of moral reasoning, which typically characterizes children up to 9 years old, are mainly concerned with the consequences of moral behavior to themselves. In stage 1, the child has a punishment and obedience orientation, in which moral behavior serves to avoid punishment. In stage 2, the child has an instrumental-relativist orientation, in which moral behavior serves to get rewards or favors in return, as in "you scratch my back and I'll scratch yours."

People at the **conventional level** of moral reasoning, usually reached in late childhood or early adolescence, uphold conventional laws and values by favoring obedience to parents and authority figures. Kohlberg calls stage 3 the good boy/nice girl orientation because the child assumes that moral behavior is desirable because it gains social approval, especially from parents. Kohlberg calls stage 4 the society-maintaining orientation, in which the adolescent views moral behavior as a way to do one's duty, show respect for authority, and maintain the social order. These four stages have even been used to show differences in moral reasoning among members of the U.S. Congress about political issues (Shapiro, 1995).

At the end of adolescence, some of those who reach Piaget's formal operational stage of cognitive development also reach the **postconventional level** of morality. At this level of moral reasoning, people make moral judgments based on ethical principles that might conflict with their self-interest or with the maintenance of social order. In stage 5, the social-contract orientation, the person assumes that adherence to laws is in the long-term best interest of society but that unjust laws might have to be violated. The U.S. Constitution is based on this view. Stage 6, the highest stage of moral reasoning, is called the universal ethical principle orientation. The few people at this stage assume that moral reasoning must uphold human dignity and their conscience—even if that brings them into conflict with their society's laws or values. Thus, an abolitionist who helped runaway American slaves flee to Canada in the 19th century would be acting at this highest level of moral reasoning.

preconventional level In Kohlberg's theory, the level of moral reasoning characterized by concern with the consequences that behavior has for oneself.

conventional level In Kohlberg's theory, the level of moral reasoning characterized by concern with upholding laws and conventional values and by favoring obedience to authority.

postconventional level In Kohlberg's theory, the level of moral reasoning characterized by concern with obeying mutually agreed-upon laws and by the need to uphold human dignity.

Criticisms of Kohlberg's Theory Kohlberg's theory has received mixed support from research studies. Children do appear to proceed through the stages he described in the order he described (Walker, 1989). And a study of adolescents on an Israeli kibbutz found that, as predicted by Kohlberg's theory, their stages of moral development were related to their stages of cognitive development (Snarey, Reimer, & Kohlberg, 1985). But Kohlberg's theory has been criticized on several grounds. First, the theory explains moral reasoning, not moral action. A person's moral actions might not reflect her or his moral reasoning. Yet some research supports a positive relationship between moral reasoning and moral actions. For example, one study found that college students who believed that the use of illegal drugs was morally wrong based on principle were, in fact, less likely to use drugs than peers who believed that illegal drug use was a matter of simple personal choice (Abide, Richards, & Ramsay, 2001).

A second criticism is that the situation, not just the person's level of moral reasoning, plays a role in moral decision making and moral actions. This was demonstrated in a study of male college students who performed a task in which their goal was to keep a stylus above a light moving in a triangular pattern—a tedious, difficult task. When provided with a strong enough temptation, even those at higher stages of moral reasoning succumbed to cheating (Malinowski & Smith, 1985).

Other critics insist that Kohlberg's theory might not be generalizable beyond Western cultures, with their greater emphasis on individualism (Sachdeva, Singh, & Medin, 2011). This criticism has been countered by Kohlberg and his colleagues. They found that when people in other cultures are interviewed in their own languages, using moral dilemmas based on situations that are familiar to them, Kohlberg's theory holds up well. Moreover, in other cultures, the stages of moral reasoning unfold in the order claimed by Kohlberg. For example, a study of Taiwanese children and young adults found that they progressed through the moral stages in the order and at the rate found in Americans (Lei, 1994). Nonetheless, postconventional moral reasoning is not found in all cultures (Snarey, Reimer, & Kohlberg, 1985).

Still another criticism of Kohlberg's theory is that it is biased in favor of a male view of morality. The main proponent of this criticism has been Carol Gilligan (1982). She points out that Kohlberg's theory was based on research on male participants, and she claims that Kohlberg's theory favors the view that morality is concerned with detached, legalistic justice (an allegedly masculine orientation) rather than with involved, interpersonal caring (an allegedly feminine orientation).

Thus, Gilligan believes that women's moral reasoning is colored by their desire to relieve distress, whereas men's moral reasoning is based on their desire to uphold rules and laws. Because Kohlberg's theory favors a male view, women are unfairly considered lower in moral development. Despite some research support for Gilligan's position (Garmon, Basinger, Gregg, & Gibbs, 1996), there does not appear to be a moral chasm between men and women—there are no significant differences between men and women in their use of justice and care orientations. For example, a recent study lent only mixed support to Gilligan's position. More than 200 men and women rated hypothetical mixed (containing elements of both care and justice orientations) and real-life (conflicts they had personally experienced) moral dilemmas. As Gilligan would predict, women scored higher on care reasoning and men scored higher on justice reasoning on the hypothetical mixed dilemmas. However, there were no gender differences in the ratings of the real-life moral dilemmas. Regardless of participant sex, real-life moral dilemmas involving ongoing personal relationships elicited care reasoning. And real-life moral dilemmas concerning the self or casual acquaintances elicited justice reasoning (Skoe, Cumberland, Eisenberg, Hansen, & Perry, 2002). Moreover, a meta-analysis found that females exhibit a care orientation only slightly more than males, and males exhibit a justice orientation only slightly more than females (Jaffee & Hyde, 2000).

Other critics claim that both Kohlberg's and Gilligan's theories are simplistic and do not consider enough of the factors that influence moral development. These critics believe that an adequate theory of moral development must consider the interaction of cultural, religious, and biological factors (Woods, 1996).

> **Section Review:** Infant and Child Development
>
> 1. What has research discovered about infant depth perception?
> 2. What are Piaget's basic ideas about cognitive development?
> 3. What has research found about the importance of infant attachment to a caregiver?
> 4. What are the differences between permissive, authoritarian, and authoritative parenting?

Adolescent Development

Change marks the entire life span, though it is more dramatic at certain stages than at others. Biological factors have a more obvious influence during adolescence and late adulthood than during early and middle adulthood. Social factors exert their greatest influence through the **social clock**, which includes major events that occur at certain times in the typical life cycle in a given culture. In Western cultures, for example, major milestones of the social clock include graduation from high school, leaving home, finding a job, getting married, having a child, and retiring from work. Being late in reaching these milestones can cause emotional distress (Rook, Catalano, & Dooley, 1989).

There also is some evidence for cross-cultural and cohort differences in young adults' beliefs about the timing of life events. For example, one study of Australian undergraduates found that the "best" ages associated with adult milestones differed from American age norms of the 1960s. Moreover, participants suggested later ages for marriage and grandparenthood and a wider age range for retirement (Peterson, 1996).

Cultural and historical factors can have different effects on different cohorts. Depending on your cohort, your adolescent and adult experiences might differ from those of other cohorts. A Swiss study compared young adult participants born between World Wars I and II (the "Between the Wars" cohort) participants born in the years immediately after World War II (the "Early Baby Boomers" cohort) and participants born in the early 1970s (the "Generation X" cohort) regarding their views concerning the main tasks of young adulthood. The largest difference was between the "Between the Wars" cohort and the "Generation X" cohort. Whereas the "Between the Wars" cohort placed relatively more value on work and family, the "Generation X" cohort placed relatively more value on higher education and leisure-time activities (Bangerter, Grob, & Krings, 2001). Thus, as you read, keep in mind that although common biological factors and social clocks might make generations somewhat similar in their development, cultural and historical factors that are unique to particular cohorts can make them somewhat different from cohorts that precede or succeed them.

Adolescence is unknown in many developing countries. Instead, adulthood begins with the onset of puberty and is commonly celebrated with traditional rites of passage. With the advent of universal free education and child labor laws in Western countries, children, who otherwise would have entered the adult work world by the time they reached puberty, entered a period of life during which they developed an adult body yet maintained a childlike dependence on parents. Formal study of **adolescence**, the transitional period between childhood and adulthood, began with the work of G. Stanley Hall (1904).

Physical Development

Recall your own adolescence. What you might recall most vividly are the rapid physical changes associated with **puberty** (from the Latin word for "adulthood"). As illustrated in Figure 4-4, puberty is marked by a rapid increase in height; girls show a growth

---

social clock The typical or expected timing of major life events in a given culture.

adolescence The transitional period lasting from the onset of puberty to the beginning of adulthood.

puberty The period of rapid physical change that occurs during adolescence, including the development of the ability to reproduce sexually.

Girls

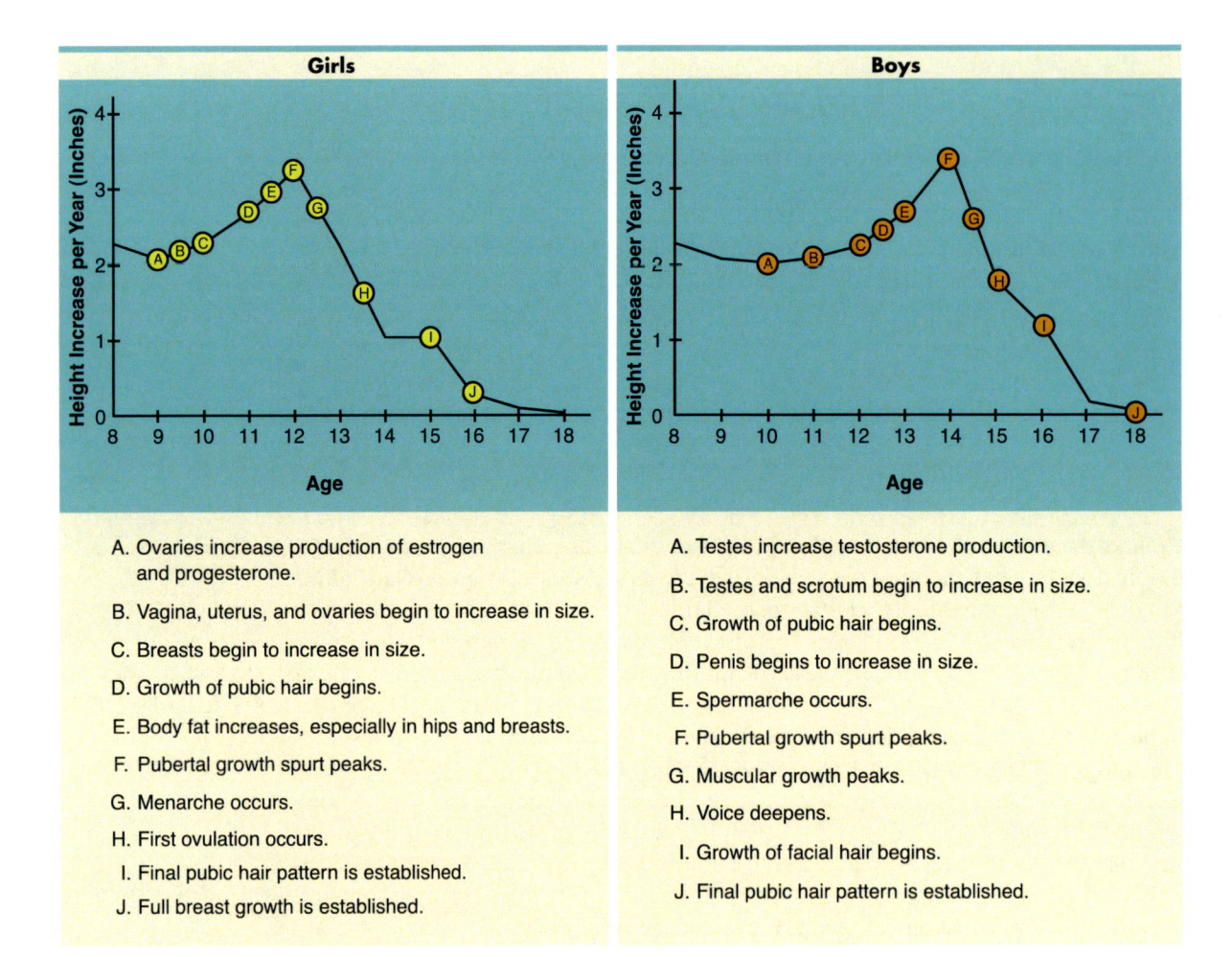

A. Ovaries increase production of estrogen and progesterone.
B. Vagina, uterus, and ovaries begin to increase in size.
C. Breasts begin to increase in size.
D. Growth of pubic hair begins.
E. Body fat increases, especially in hips and breasts.
F. Pubertal growth spurt peaks.
G. Menarche occurs.
H. First ovulation occurs.
I. Final pubic hair pattern is established.
J. Full breast growth is established.

Boys

A. Testes increase testosterone production.
B. Testes and scrotum begin to increase in size.
C. Growth of pubic hair begins.
D. Penis begins to increase in size.
E. Spermarche occurs.
F. Pubertal growth spurt peaks.
G. Muscular growth peaks.
H. Voice deepens.
I. Growth of facial hair begins.
J. Final pubic hair pattern is established.

FIGURE 4-4 The Adolescent Growth Spurt and Pubertal Change

The onset of puberty is associated with a rapid increase in height. The growth spurt of girls occurs earlier than that of boys. Note that the ages given for the timing of particular physical changes during puberty are based on averages. Individual pubertal changes may vary from these averages without falling outside the range of normal development.

spermarche The first ejaculation, usually occurring between the ages of 13 and 15.

menarche The beginning of menstruation, usually occurring between the ages of 11 and 13.

spurt between the ages of 10 and 12, and boys show a growth spurt between the ages of 12 and 14. The physical changes of puberty also include the maturation of primary and secondary sex characteristics. Primary sex characteristics are hormone-induced physical changes that enable us to engage in sexual reproduction. These changes include growth of the penis and testes in males and the vagina, uterus, and ovaries in females. Secondary sex characteristics are stimulated by sex hormones but are unrelated to sexual reproduction. Pubertal males develop facial hair, deeper voices, and larger muscles. Pubertal females develop wider hips, larger breasts, and more rounded physiques, caused in part by increased deposits of fat.

These physical changes are triggered in girls by a spurt in the secretion of the sex hormone estrogen between ages 10 and 11 and in boys by increased levels of the sex hormone testosterone between ages 12 and 13. Boys generally experience **spermarche**, their first ejaculation, between the ages of 13 and 15, typically while asleep (so-called nocturnal emissions). Girls exhibit earlier physical maturation than boys and generally experience **menarche**, their first menstrual period, between the ages of 11 and 13 (Paikoff & Brooks-Gunn, 1991). The average age at menarche is lower than in the past; this decline in the age of menarche has been attributed to improved health and nutrition. For example, the average age of menarche declined from 16.5 to 13.7 years over a span of 40 years in two rural counties of China. During this period of modernization, the health and living conditions of the rural Chinese population improved dramatically (Graham, Larsen, & Xu, 1999). And increasing rates of obesity across the globe are associated with a decline in the

Puberty

Because adolescents enter puberty at different ages, groups of young adolescents include individuals who vary greatly in height and physical maturity. As a consequence, a typical middle-school class might appear to include a wider age range than it actually does.
Source: Tracy Whiteside/Shutterstock.com.

average age of menarche. The Health Behavior in School-Aged Children study assessed the relationship between obesity and the average age of menarche among girls in 34 countries. The researchers concluded that most cross-cultural differences in the average age of menarche were attributable to childhood obesity (Currie et al., 2012).

Though the dramatic physical changes of puberty are caused by hormonal changes, adolescent mood swings are not necessarily the by-products of hormones run wild. Hormone fluctuations affect the adolescent's moods, but life events have a greater effect (Brooks-Gunn & Warren, 1989). Of course, the physical changes of puberty, including acne, rapid growth, and physical maturation, can themselves produce emotional distress. This is especially true if the adolescent is unprepared for them or is made to feel self-conscious by peers or parents. Boys find it difficult enough to deal with scruffy facial hair, unwanted penile erections, and voices that crack, without being made more anxious about those changes. Girls, likewise, find it difficult enough to discover suddenly that they have enlarged breasts, a monthly menstrual cycle, and possibly tower several inches above many of their male peers.

The timing of puberty may influence how adolescents respond to these physical changes. Research findings on the relative effects of early versus late puberty have been inconsistent, in part because of the different methodologies that have been used. Cross-sectional research findings indicate that late maturation is, overall, more negative for both males and females in regard to behavior and personal adjustment, but longitudinal research findings indicate that the timing of puberty, overall, has neither positive nor negative effects on adolescents (Dorn, Susman, & Ponirakis, 2003). Nonetheless, at times early maturation may bring with it certain problems. For example, boys and girls who enter puberty early drink more alcohol and become intoxicated more often than their peers who do not mature early. This correlation is stronger for boys than for girls (Kaltiala-Heino, Koivisto, Marttunen, & Fröjd, 2011).

Cognitive Development

Adolescent cognitive development is less dramatic, with no obvious surge in mental abilities to match the surge in physical development. According to Piaget's theory, at about 11 years of age, some adolescents pass from the concrete operational stage to the **formal operational stage**. A person who reaches this stage is able to reason about abstract, not just concrete, situations. The adolescent who has reached the formal operational stage can apply abstract principles and make predictions about hypothetical situations. In contrast, an adolescent still in the concrete operational stage would rely more on blind trial and error than on a formal approach to problem solving.

formal operational stage The Piagetian stage, beginning at about age 11, marked by the ability to use abstract reasoning and to solve problems by testing hypotheses.

To appreciate this, imagine that you are given four chemicals and are asked to produce a purple liquid by mixing them—but it is left up to you to discover the proper mixture. People at the concrete operational level would approach this task in an unsystematic manner, hoping that through trial and error they would hit upon the correct combination of chemicals. In contrast, people at the formal operational level would approach it systematically, perhaps by mixing each possible combination of two of the chemicals, then each possible combination of three, and finally all four. Thus, people who reach the formal operational stage perform better on more complex intellectual pursuits. A study of seventh and eighth graders found that those in transition between the concrete operational stage and the formal operational stage showed better understanding of abstract concepts presented in a physics textbook than did those still in the concrete operational stage (Renner, Abraham, Grzybowski, & Marek, 1990).

Piaget found that so few people reach the formal operational stage that he gave up his earlier belief that it was universal. Those who reach that stage are more likely to have been exposed to scientific thinking in their academic courses (Rogoff & Chavajay, 1995). Though educational interventions have been effective in fostering the development of formal operational thought in developing countries such as Pakistan (Iqbal & Shayer, 2000), people from cultures that do not stress science in their school curricula are less likely to achieve the formal operational stage.

Psychosocial Development

Erik Erikson noted that psychosocial development continues through adolescence into adulthood and old age. Perhaps the most important psychosocial tasks of adolescence are the formation of a personal identity and the development of healthy relationships with peers and parents.

Identity Achievement

identity versus role confusion
Erikson's developmental stage in which success is achieved by establishing a sense of personal identity.

According to Erikson (1963), the most important feat of adolescence is the resolution of the conflict of **identity versus role confusion**. The adolescent develops a sense of identity by adopting her or his own set of values and social behaviors. Erikson believed this is a normal part of finding answers to questions related to one's identity, such as these: What do I believe is important? What are my goals in life?

Erikson's emphasis on the importance of the identity crisis might reflect, in large part, his own life history. He was born in Germany, the child of a Danish Christian mother and father. Erik's father abandoned his mother while she was pregnant with him. She then married a Jewish physician, Theodore Homburger. Erik was given his new father's surname, making him Erik Homburger. But it was not until Erik reached adolescence that he was told that Homburger was not his biological father (Hopkins, 1995).

Erikson, uncomfortable among Jews and Christians alike, sought to find himself by traveling in European artistic and intellectual circles, as many young adults did in the 1920s. Eventually he met Anna Freud, Sigmund's daughter and an eminent psychoanalyst herself. Erikson underwent psychoanalysis with her almost daily for 3 years. In 1933 Erikson changed his name to Erik Homburger Erikson and left to pursue a career in the United States. His long, rich life was a testament to his success in finding his identity as a husband, writer, teacher, and psychoanalyst.

To appreciate the task that confronts the adolescent in developing an identity, consider the challenge of having to adjust simultaneously to a new body, a new mind, and a new social world. The adolescent body is larger and sexually mature. The adolescent mind can question the nature of reality and consider abstract concepts regarding ethical, political, and religious beliefs. The social world of the adolescent requires achieving a balance between childlike dependence and adultlike independence. This also manifests itself in the conflict between parental and peer influences. Children's values mirror their parents', but adolescents' values oscillate between those of their parents and those of their peers. Adolescents move from a world guided by parental wishes to a world in which they are confronted by a host of choices regarding sex, drugs, friends, schoolwork, and other things. Erikson's theory of adolescence has received support from longitudinal studies showing that, in fact, adolescents typically move from a state of role confusion to a state of identity achievement (Streitmatter, 1993). Among the factors that are related to successful identity achievement are positive parental involvement with the adolescent and active interest in the adolescent's school performance and social relationships (Brittain & Lerner, 2013).

There also is some evidence that Erikson's theory may generalize to adolescents' experiences across cultures. One study found that Hong Kong adolescents who achieved a sense of identity were more prosocial and exhibited fewer antisocial behaviors than adolescents who had not (Ma, Shek, Cheung, & Oi, 2000). And African adolescents who achieved a sense of identity reported more extensive exploration of career options and held broader vocational interests than adolescents who had not (Schmitt-Rodermund & Vondracek, 1999). Successful identity achievement is positively related to personal adjustment (Hunsberger, Pratt, & Pancer, 2001). Failure to achieve a sense of identity is associated with emotional distress, including feelings of emptiness and depression (Taylor & Goritsas, 1994).

But Carol Gilligan (1982) believes that Erikson's theory applies more to male than to female adolescents. She points out that Erikson based his theory on studies of men, who tend to place a greater premium on the development of self-sufficiency than do women, who tend to place a greater premium on intimate relationships in which there is mutual caring. Thus, female adolescents who fail to develop an independent identity at the same time as their male age peers might unfairly be considered abnormal. One recent study compared self-descriptions and personality attributes of male and female undergraduates. Self-descriptions of men and women who had achieved identity were more similar than the self-descriptions of men and women who had not. However, gender differences were found in the relationship of personality variables that have been thought to contribute to identity development (Cramer, 2000). Though intimate relationships are important to both men's and women's well-being, psychologists studying gender differences in identity development believe that women's identity development emphasizes the self in relation to others.

Psychologists also have investigated the nature of ethnic identity, particularly among immigrants and members of ethnic minority groups (Phinney, 1990). Studies of ethnic and American identity in multi-ethnic samples have found that ethnic identity is positively correlated with self-esteem—regardless of participants' ethnicities. Thus, positive attitudes toward one's ethnic group contribute to high self-esteem. Ethnic and American identity, however, tend to be strongly correlated only for European American participants (Phinney, Cantu, & Kurtz, 1997). Ethnic identity was found to be positively correlated with many measures of psychological adjustment, including optimism, mastery, and coping, in a multi-ethnic sample of over 5,400 American adolescents (Roberts et al., 1999).

Identity Formation

During adolescence our peers play a large role in the development of our sense of identity. Generation after generation, this has distressed North American parents—though, as adolescents, their stylistic choices may have upset their own parents.

Sources: Left: Gina Smith/Shutterstock.com. *Right:* marcogarrincha/Shutterstock.com.

Chapter 4 Human Development

This research has important implications for members of ethnic minority groups, many of whom consider themselves to be bicultural. One study assessed ethnic identity and measures of acculturation among 1,367 American undergraduates, most of whom were of Mexican origin. Ethnic identity was strongest for first-generation and less acculturated participants. And higher levels of acculturation were associated with a diminished sense of ethnic identity and belongingness. More positive outcomes were associated with participants who were high in biculturalism—that is, feeling a part of both majority American and traditional Mexican cultures. Participants who scored high on a measure of biculturalism had higher ethnic identity scores and were more socially oriented than participants who scored low on biculturalism (Cuellar, Roberts, Nyberg, & Maldonado, 1997).

Once again, this demonstrates the importance of considering the cultural context of theoretical positions. For example, the Inuit people of Canada see personal identity as inseparable from the physical, animal, and human environments. The Inuits would find it maladaptive if members of their culture formed more individualistic identities (Stairs, 1992).

Social Relationships

Because the adolescent is dependent on parents while seeking an independent identity, adolescence has traditionally been considered a period of conflict between parents and children, or what G. Stanley Hall called a period of "storm and stress." Parents might be shocked by their adolescent's preferences in dress, music, and slang. In trying out various styles and values, adolescents are influenced by the cohort to which they belong. Thus, male adolescents shocked their parents by wearing pompadours in the 1950s, shoulder-length hair in the 1970s, spiked haircuts in the 1990s, and piercings and tattoos at the turn of the 21st century. Though parental conflict, moodiness, and a tendency for engaging in risky behavior are more common in adolescence, there are considerable cross-cultural differences. Adolescents in traditional cultures tend to maintain traditional values and practices—even those experiencing the rapid pace of modernization and globalization. Moreover, there are considerable individual differences in behavioral and mood disruptions among adolescents (Arnett, 1999).

Despite the normal conflicts between parental values and adolescent behaviors, most adolescents have positive relations with their parents. In general, adolescence is a time of only slightly increased parent-child conflict. Though the emotional intensity of parent-child conflicts is somewhat higher at puberty, the rate of parent-child conflict declines over the adolescent years (Laursen, Coy, & Collins, 1998) as both adolescents and their parents adopt more positive conflict resolution styles (Van Doom, Branje, & Meeus, 2011).

Adolescents' increasing autonomy and involvement with their peers often leads to disagreements with their parents about family obligations. For example, Jean Phinney and Anthony Ong assessed beliefs about family obligations in a large sample of Vietnamese-American and European-American adolescents and their parents. Regardless of socioeconomic status or cultural background, disagreement over family obligations was negatively correlated with the adolescent participants' life satisfaction (Phinney & Ong, 2003). Conflicts also may be more frequent among first-generation immigrants and their children due to differential rates of acculturation within the family. Compared to non-immigrant families, immigrant Armenian, Vietnamese, and Mexican parents were more likely to stress family obligations than their children. Moreover, among immigrant families, intergenerational discrepancies in familial values increased as a function of time spent living in the United States (Phinney, Ong, & Madden, 2000).

In regard to their friendships, adolescents have more intimate friendships than do younger children, possibly because they are more capable of sharing their thoughts and feelings and understanding those of others. Adolescents who fail to develop intimate friendships are especially prone to loneliness. In fact, adolescent friendships are more important than relationships with family members in preventing loneliness (Ciftci Uruk & Demir, 2003). Though the level of intimate feelings expressed by boys and girls when interacting with their same-sex friends does not differ, there are gender differences in the ways adolescents establish and experience intimate friendships. Adolescent girls tend to establish intimacy through self-disclosure and discussion, whereas adolescent boys tend to establish intimacy through shared activities (McNelles & Connolly, 1999).

Adolescence is associated with an important biologically based psychosocial conflict between the powerful urge to engage in sexual relations and societal values against premarital sex. The proportion of sexually active American adolescents increased steadily from the 1930s, when less than 10 percent had premarital sex, to today, when most older adolescents engage in it. But the sexes differ in their sexual attitudes. Male adolescents are more willing to engage in casual sex, whereas female adolescents are more likely to prefer sex as part of a committed relationship, though this gender difference is not large and gender similarities in sexual attitudes have increased over time (Petersen & Hyde, 2010; also see Chapter 11).

Psychologists recently have begun correcting the one-dimensional view of adolescent erotic relationships as consisting solely of sexual behavior. More researchers are focusing on the nature of adolescent romance, not just sexual behavior, including parental influences and changes in the nature of adolescent romance (Furman, 2002). A study of over 200 college students found that the quality of their romantic relationships was related to the nature of their relationships with their parents. Students who felt a low degree of trust, communication, and closeness in their relationships with their parents tended to feel devalued, disrespected, and emotionally controlled by their current romantic partner. Moreover, students who were unhappy in their current romantic relationship reported that their past relationships with their parents were marked by frequent, intense, and poorly resolved conflicts. A key factor moderating the relationship between their past negative relationships with their parents and their current romantic relationships was the expectation that their romantic partner would ultimately reject them. Such a pessimistic expectation may lead individuals to engage in behaviors that harm their romantic relationships (Gray, 2001).

Adolescence also is a period often involving experimentation with, or chronic use of, psychoactive drugs, including alcohol, nicotine, cocaine, and marijuana. Adolescent drug use, such as smoking, is influenced more by peers than by parents (Bauman, Carver, & Gleiter, 2001). But parental involvement, including monitoring their children's behavior, can help counter the possibility of the adolescent's being initiated into smoking by peers (Simons-Morton, 2002). The importance of avoiding unwise use of psychoactive drugs is highlighted by the association of adolescent smoking and drug use with risky sexual behavior, particularly engaging in sexual intercourse without using a condom (Wu, Witkiewitz, McMahon, & Dodge, 2010).

Drug use also has a negative effect on academic performance. A survey of more than 18,000 American adolescents assessed the relationship between using cigarettes, marijuana, alcohol, and cocaine and academic achievement. The main factors related to poor academic achievement were smoking cigarettes, getting drunk, and being under the influence of alcohol while at school. Cocaine use had a negligible relationship to academic achievement, perhaps because few adolescents reported being under the influence of cocaine while at school (Jeynes, 2002). Today, alcohol is the main drug of choice among adolescents in many countries. A survey of more than 2,600 Canadian adolescents found that alcohol use was associated with more problem behaviors than was the use of other drugs (Gfellner & Hundleby, 1994). Fortunately, despite the risks associated with sexual irresponsibility and drug and alcohol abuse, almost all adolescents enter adulthood relatively unscathed.

Section Review: Adolescent Development

1. Why should adolescence researchers be concerned with cohort effects?
2. What is the formal operational stage?
3. According to Erikson, how does identity formation manifest itself in adolescents?

Adult Development

adulthood The period beginning when the individual assumes responsibility for her or his own life.

In Western cultures, **adulthood** begins when adolescents become independent of their parents and assume responsibility for themselves. Interest in adult development accelerated in the 1950s after being inspired by Erikson's theory of life-span development (Levinson, 1986) and brought an increased realization that physical, cognitive, and psychosocial changes take place across the entire life span.

Physical Development

Adults reach their physical peak in their late twenties and then begin a slow physical decline that does not accelerate appreciably until old age. Most athletes peak in their twenties, as is shown by the ages at which world-class athletes achieve their best performances (Schulz & Curnow, 1988). Beginning in our twenties, our basal metabolic rate (the rate at which the body burns calories when at rest) also decreases, accounting in part for the tendency to gain weight in adulthood. This makes it especially important for adults to pay attention to diet and exercise, which are associated with healthier cardiovascular functioning in middle age and old age (Sawatzky & Naimark, 2002). Physical exercise also is associated with better cognitive functioning in old age (Colcombe & Kramer, 2003). Of course, one must be careful not to presume that exercise *causes* improved cardiovascular or cognitive functioning. Perhaps, for example, having a healthier cardiovascular system or good cognitive functioning makes individuals more likely to exercise.

menopause The cessation of menstruation, usually occurring between the ages of 40 and 55.

andropause The gradual decline of testosterone experienced by men after the age of 40.

The aging process is marked by hormonal changes in women and men. Typically, women experience **menopause**—the cessation of their menstrual cycle between the ages of 40 and 55. This is associated with a reduction in estrogen secretion, cessation of ovulation, and consequently the inability to become pregnant. The reduction in estrogen can cause sweating, hot flashes, and brittle bones, as well as atrophy of the vaginal tissue, uterus, and mammary glands (Freedman, 2002). Typically, men experience **andropause**—a gradual decline of testosterone after the age of 40. As testosterone levels decline, men produce fewer and fewer sperm and experience changes in their sexual response, such as slower erections and delayed or less frequent orgasms. However, they still can father children into old age (Morley, 2001).

Midlife hormonal changes do not signal an end to sexuality. Postmenopausal women still have fulfilling sex lives and social lives. A survey of 16,000 American women from five ethnic groups (European American, African American, Japanese American, Chinese American, and Latino) found that women's attitudes toward menopause were neutral to positive and that health status, not menopausal status, predicted the happiness of women in midlife (Sommer et al., 1999). Attitudes toward menopause, however, can vary by culture and social class. For example, one cross-cultural study found that French women generally reported positive attitudes toward menopause. However, Tunisian women, especially poor Tunisian women, reported more negative attitudes and physical symptoms than the French (Delanoë et al., 2012). Moreover, though the prevalence of erectile dysfunction does increase with age, many older men have satisfying sex lives. One large survey of more than 1,000 men aged 58 to 94 years found that positive sexual attitudes, good health, and a responsive sexual partner were associated with continued sexual activity (Bortz, Wallace, & Wiley, 1999).

Middle-aged adults tend to become farsighted and require reading glasses, as evidenced by an increasing tendency to hold books and newspapers at arm's length. But marked changes in physical abilities usually do not occur until late adulthood. The older adult exhibits deterioration in heart output, lung capacity, reaction time, muscular strength, and motor coordination (Maranto, 1984). Old age also brings a decline in hearing, particularly of high-pitched sounds.

Eventually, no matter how well we take care of our bodies, all of us reach the ultimate physical change—death. Though the upper limit of the human life span seems to be about 120 years, few people live to even 100 years of age. But why is death inevitable? Death seems to be genetically programmed into our cells by limiting their ability to repair or reproduce themselves (Hayflick, 1980). Animal research indicates that aging can be slowed by the reduction of daily caloric intake, which prevents the buildup of certain metabolic by-products that promote aging. For example, a study of rats found that those who ate a low-calorie diet lived longer (Masoro, Shimokawa, Higami, & McMahan, 1995). The effects of low-calorie diets on human aging and longevity remain unclear, but ongoing research with human participants suggests that there are positive benefits in reducing caloric intake (Roth & Polotsky, 2012). Longevity also is influenced by physical activity. One longitudinal study of 70-year-old residents of western Jerusalem found that mortality rates were significantly lower for participants who reported engaging in regular exercise. Moreover, walking as little as four hours per week was linked to increased survival in this sample (Stessman, Maaravi, Hammerman-Rozenberg, & Cohen, 2000).

We do know, however, that the mere act of continuing to work is associated with slower aging. In a study supporting this, elderly people who continued to work or who retired but participated in regular physical activities showed a constant level of cerebral blood flow over a 4-year period. In contrast, elderly retirees who did not participate in regular physical activities showed a significant decline in cerebral blood flow. Those who continued to work also scored better on cognitive tests than did the inactive retirees (Rogers, Meyer, & Mortel, 1990). One 30-year longitudinal study found that adults who were employed in occupations that required complex work—requiring thought and independent decision making—demonstrated higher levels of intellectual functioning compared to adults who were employed in less demanding occupations. Moreover, the beneficial effect of complex work was more pronounced in late adulthood compared to young adulthood (Schooler, Mulatu, & Oates, 1999). There is even evidence that individuals who engage in complex activities can generate new synapses in the brain, partly countering some of the negative effects of aging (Black, Isaacs, & Greenough, 1991). Thus, whereas physical aging is inevitable, people who maintain an active lifestyle might age at a slower rate. Note that these results do not conclusively demonstrate that activity causes a slowing of the effects of aging. Perhaps, instead, people who age more slowly are more likely to stay active.

Aging and Physical Health
These adults show that diet and exercise can contribute to a healthy old age.
Source: Lisa F. Young/Shutterstock.com.

Cognitive Development

One of the most controversial issues in developmental psychology is the pattern of adult cognitive development, particularly intellectual development. Early studies showed that we experience a steady decline in intelligence across adulthood. But this apparent decline is found more often in cross-sectional studies than in longitudinal studies. Longitudinal studies have found that a marked decline in intelligence does not begin until about age 60. This indicates that the decline in intelligence across adulthood found in cross-sectional studies might be a cohort effect (perhaps due to differences in early educational experiences) rather than an aging effect (Schaie & Hertzog, 1983). Moreover, the intellectual decline in old age does not encompass all facets of intelligence. Instead, it holds for fluid intelligence but not for crystallized intelligence (Ryan, Sattler, & Lopez, 2000). **Fluid intelligence** reflects the ability to reason and to process information; **crystallized intelligence** reflects the ability to gain and retain knowledge.

But what accounts for the decline in fluid intelligence in old age? The Seattle Longitudinal Study of 1,620 adults between 22 and 91 years of age conducted by K. Warner Schaie (1989) found that the speed of information processing slows in old age. This has been replicated in other research studies (Zimprich & Martin, 2002). This slowing is especially detrimental to short-term memory (Salthouse, 1991), which is the stage of memory that involves the conscious, purposeful mental manipulation of information. But the decline in fluid intelligence can be slowed. The Seattle Longitudinal Study found that a group of older adults who were given cognitive training did not show the same decline in fluid intelligence shown by older adults who were not given such training (Saczynski, 2002).

Older adults tend to do more poorly than adolescents and young adults on cognitive tasks. One factor that explains why is that they have been out of school for many years. This was the finding of a study that compared the recall ability of college students of

fluid intelligence The form of intelligence that reflects reasoning ability, memory capacity, and speed of information processing.

crystallized intelligence The form of intelligence that reflects knowledge acquired through schooling and in everyday life.

Critical Thinking About Psychology

Are There Significant Psychological Gender Differences?

In the 19th century, scientific interest in gender differences was stimulated by Darwin's theory of evolution and promoted by Francis Galton, whose views were influenced by sexist attitudes of the Victorian era (Buss, 1976). Galton assumed that women and men had evolved physical and psychological differences that help them function in particular roles, and he insisted that they should remain in those roles (Shields, 1975). As discussed in Chapter 10, views like his were countered by some psychologists, such as Leta Stetter Hollingworth (1886–1939), who insisted that gender differences were due to social factors and did not denote the inferiority of women.

The first major review of gender differences was published by Eleanor Maccoby and Carol Jacklin (1974). They reported that women were superior in verbal abilities and men were superior in spatial and mathematical abilities. They also found that men were more aggressive than women. Nonetheless, they found fewer differences, and generally smaller differences, than were commonly believed to exist. Today, researchers who study gender differences are particularly concerned with cognitive abilities and psychosocial variables. Many of these researchers have used the statistical technique meta-analysis, which enables them to assess the size of gender differences and situational or sociocultural factors that influence these effect sizes (see Chapter 2).

Cognitive Abilities

In studying cognitive differences between women and men, researchers have studied differences primarily in three kinds of abilities. They ask, Are there gender differences in verbal abilities? spatial abilities? mathematical abilities?

Verbal Abilities

Research on children supports the popular belief in the verbal superiority of girls and women. Girls tend to be superior to boys in speaking, spelling, vocabulary, and reading comprehension. Yet the size of these differences decreases by adolescence. Overall, gender differences in verbal abilities have declined in size in recent decades until they are virtually negligible (Hyde & Plant, 1995). But what about talkativeness, which the popular stereotype holds to be the province of women? Research indicates that, contrary to the stereotype, men are consistently more talkative than women (Hyde & Linn, 1988).

Spatial Abilities

Research has tended to consistently find a large gender difference in one test of spatial abilities. Men are superior in the rotation of mental images (Hyde, Fennema, & Lamon, 1990). Gender differences in other spatial abilities, though, tend to be smaller and inconsistent. Moreover, a meta-analysis of research studies of gender differences in spatial abilities found that the sizes of the differences have decreased in recent years (Voyer, Voyer, & Bryden, 1995). However, gender differences in spatial abilities are observed in early childhood (Levine, Huttenlocher, Taylor, & Langrock, 1999) and in many nonlaboratory settings. For example, when providing directions, women are more likely to rely upon landmarks, whereas men are more likely to refer to north-south-east-west strategies (Halpern & LeMay, 2000). A recent study revealed, though, that gender differences also may be influenced by regional differences. In the Midwest and Western United States and in regions characterized by a grid-like pattern of roads, *both* men and women were more likely to refer to compass or left-right directions (Lawton, 2001). Thus, social experiences can influence spatial abilities.

Mathematical Abilities

Perhaps the most strongly established cognitive gender difference is that adolescent and adult men have higher average scores than adolescent and adult women on standardized mathematics tests. A national talent search by Camilla Benbow and Julian Stanley (1983) found that among seventh- and eighth-graders who took the mathematics subtest of the Scholastic Aptitude Test (SAT), the average score for boys was higher than the average score for girls. In fact, among those scoring higher than 700 (out of 800), boys outnumbered girls by a ratio of 13 to 1. Could this be attributable to boys having more experience in mathematics? Benbow and Stanley say no, having found little difference in the number of mathematics courses taken by females and males. And because they found no other life experiences that could explain their findings, Benbow and Stanley concluded that heredity probably accounts for the difference. This explanation has received some support from other researchers (Thomas, 1993).

But it has also provoked controversy. Critics argue that the gender differences in mathematical abilities reported by Benbow and Stanley might be attributable to as yet unidentified differences in girls' and boys' experiences with mathematics. Also, boys do not have a higher average score than girls on all measures of mathematical ability. Though boys have higher average scores on mathematics achievement tests, which stress problem solving, girls receive higher grades in mathematics courses (Halpern, 2000). A recent meta-analysis of 242 studies published between 1997 and

Chapter 4 Human Development

> **Critical Thinking About Psychology**
>
> ### Are There Significant Psychological Gender Differences? *continued*
>
> 2007 based upon more than 1,200,000 participants found, overall, no gender differences in mathematical performance (Lindberg, Hyde, Peterson, & Linn, 2010).
>
> It also is important to consider that gender differences in mathematics achievement are smaller than cross-cultural or ethnic differences in achievement (Kimball, 1995). In fact, the greatest gender difference in mathematics ability is found among European American samples (Hyde, Fennema, & Lamon, 1990). In cultures with comparatively smaller gender differences, parents are more likely to encourage academic achievement and advanced study in mathematics—for both sons and daughters (Hanna, Kundiger, & Larouche, 1990). Moreover, gender differences in mathematics are larger in countries where women do not share economic, social, and political power with men (Else-Quest, Hyde, & Linn, 2010).
>
> As discussed in Chapter 17, people's beliefs about group differences may lead to a self-fulfilling prophecy, which ultimately influences their behavior. And research has shown that women's and men's beliefs about gender and ethnic differences can affect their performance on mathematics tests (Smith & White, 2002). Thus, stereotypes about women's and men's cognitive abilities may contribute to gender differences in mathematics achievement.
>
> ### Psychosocial Variables
>
> Researchers also study gender differences in psychosocial behavior. They have been especially concerned with differences in personality and aggression.
>
> #### *Personality*
>
> Meta-analyses of research studies on personality differences have found that men are more assertive where-as women are slightly more extraverted ($d = -.14$) and more anxious, trusting, and, especially, tender-minded (that is, more caring and nurturing). These differences tended to be consistent across all ages and educational levels of participants, as well as across a variety of different cultures (Feingold, 1994). A recent meta-analysis found that male participants score slightly higher on standardized measures of self-esteem than do female participants. The size of this small gender difference does increase—at least temporarily—in adolescence (Kling, Hyde, Showers, & Buswell, 1999). And a recent meta-analysis (Else-Quest, Hyde, Goldsmith, & Van Hulle, 2006) found that girls score much higher on measures of self-control than do boys ($d = -1.01$), whereas there is a moderate gender difference favoring boys on factors related to rough-and-tumble play, such as activity level ($d = .30$) and the intensity of their emotional experiences ($d = .33$).
>
> **Gender Differences and Similarities**
> Physiological and sociocultural factors play an important role in girls' and boys' cognitive abilities.
> *Source:* Zurijeta/Shutterstock.com.
>
> *continued*

Critical Thinking About Psychology

Are There Significant Psychological Gender Differences? *continued*

Researchers also have studied a variety of other personality variables with the use of meta-analysis. For example, do women reveal more of their private thoughts, feelings, and experiences than men do? Contrary to popular belief, women are only marginally more likely to self-disclose than men are (Dindia & Allen, 1992). But consistent with popular views, males are slightly more likely than females to take risks across a variety of situations (Byrnes, Miller, & Shafer, 1999) and women and girls are slightly more able than men and boys to delay gratification (Silverman, 2003). But what of the popular belief that women are more empathetic than men? This apparent gender difference depends on how empathy is measured. When asked to report on their level of empathy, women score higher than men. But when empathy is measured by physiological arousal or overt behavior, gender differences disappear. Evidently, social expectations that women will be more emotionally sensitive than men create differences in their subjective views of themselves but not necessarily in their actual behavior or physiological responses (Eisenberg & Lennon, 1983). This hypothesis was tested in a recent meta-analysis that found women's empathy scores were higher than men's only when participants were aware that their empathy was being assessed. This gender difference disappeared in experimental situations that lacked this demand characteristic (Ickes, Gesn, & Graham, 2000).

One recent study provided more evidence of gender similarities in basic values. Over 11,000 participants were surveyed in eight cultures (Chinese East Asia, Eastern Europe, Finland, France, Israel, Japan, Latin America, and the United States). Whereas some cross-cultural differences were found, results indicated that there were no consistent gender differences in the meaning of personal values across cultures (Struch, Schwartz, & van der Kloot, 2002).

Aggression

Just as women are reputed to be more empathetic than men, men are reputed to be more aggressive than women. Research has found that men are somewhat more physically aggressive than are women (Eagly & Steffen, 1986). Moreover, gender differences in aggression might be the product of gender roles. This was the conclusion of a study in which male and female participants were tested in the laboratory. When they were singled out as individuals, men were more aggressive than women. When they were deindividuated (that is, made to feel anonymous), men and women did not differ in aggression. The researchers attributed this difference to the power of gender roles: When we feel that we are being noticed, we behave according to gender expectations (Lightdale & Prentice, 1994). Moreover, as discussed in Chapter 17, when operational definitions of aggression are broadened to include behaviors that are more stereotypically female—such as indirect aggression—gender differences in aggression are minimized.

Explanations for Possible Gender Differences

If psychological gender differences exist, what might account for them? Researchers point to physiological factors and sociocultural factors.

Physiological Factors

Because of the obvious physical differences between men and women, researchers have looked to physiological factors to explain psychological gender differences. David Buss believes that men and women inherit certain behavioral tendencies as a product of their long evolutionary history. According to Buss, "Men and women differ . . . in domains in which they have faced different adaptive problems over human evolutionary history. In all other domains, the sexes are predicted to be psychologically similar" (Buss, 1995, p. 164). Thus, men are more aggressive and women more nurturing because prehistoric males were more likely to be hunters and prehistoric females were more likely to be caregivers. They do not differ in traits unrelated to their prehistoric roles as males and females.

But how might heredity affect psychological gender differences? Evidence supporting the biological basis of gender differences in social behavior implicates hormonal factors. Girls whose adrenal glands secrete high prenatal levels of testosterone are more likely to become "tomboys" who prefer rough play and masculine activities (though most tomboys do not have this adrenal disorder). These girls' genitals look more similar to those of boys at birth (though they are usually modified by surgery), and this might make parents treat them as though they were boys, yet parents usually report that they treat these girls the same as parents treat girls without the disorder (Berenbaum & Hines, 1992). There is some evidence, though, for a hormonal basis for cognitive gender differences (Kimura & Hampson, 1994). There also is evidence of a hormonal basis for gender differences in play behavior in childhood and fairly strong evidence for its influence on gender differences in physical aggression (Collaer & Hines, 1995).

A second way that heredity might affect gender differences is through brain development. But efforts to associate specific cognitive differences with differences in brain structures have produced mixed results. As

> **Critical Thinking About Psychology**
>
> **Are There Significant Psychological Gender Differences?** *continued*
>
> discussed in Chapter 3, some studies have found that men's brains may be more lateralized than women's brains. Studies of people with brain damage have found that damage to men's left cerebral hemisphere is associated with impaired verbal skills, and damage to men's right cerebral hemisphere is associated with impaired nonverbal skills. In contrast, women's verbal and nonverbal skills do not seem to be influenced by the side of the brain damaged (Springer & Deutsch, 1998). Other studies, though, have failed to find gender differences in hemispheric lateralization (e.g., Snow & Sheese, 1985). And there are large individual differences in brain organization; biological sex is only one of many variables influencing brain organization (Kimura, 1987).
>
> *Sociocultural Factors*
>
> The possibility that gender differences in cognitive abilities are influenced more by sociocultural factors than by physiological factors is supported by studies that have found a narrowing of gender differences in cognitive abilities between North American male and female participants during the past 40 years (Hyde & Plant, 1995; Lindberg, Hyde, Peterson, & Linn, 2010). This might be explained in part by the cultural trend to provide girls and boys with somewhat more similar treatment and opportunities (Jacklin, 1989). Even Camilla Benbow (1988) agrees that environmental, as well as hereditary, factors play an important role in cognitive abilities such as mathematics. For example, minimal gender differences have been found among participants from the study of Mathematically Precocious Youth who had gone on to graduate study in math and sciences. The profiles of female and male participants included attributes that are critical to achieving excellence in these fields—exceptional quantitative abilities, scientific interests and values, and persistence in seeking out educational opportunities (Lubinski, Benbow, Shea, Eftekhari-Sanjani, & Halvorson, 2001).
>
> After decades of extensive research, no gender differences have emerged that are large enough to predict with confidence how individual men and women will behave (Deaux, 1985). This has provoked a controversy about whether we should continue to study gender differences. Some psychologists, such as Roy Baumeister (1988), argue that we should no longer study them. Why study differences that are too few or too small to have practical significance? And why study gender differences when reports of even small differences might support sex discrimination? But Baumeister's view was countered by gender difference researchers Alice Eagly (1995) and Diane Halpern (1994), who believe that objective scientific research on gender differences should continue, even if it might find differences that some people would prefer did not exist.
>
> A compromise position has been put forth by Janet Shibley Hyde, who favors studying gender differences but warns against relying on the results of studies that have not been replicated, interpreting gender differences as signs of female deficiencies, and automatically attributing such differences to inherited biological factors. She favors acknowledging the fact that gender similarities are the rule and that the few gender differences that have been found can be attributed primarily to sociocultural factors (Hyde, 2007).

traditional age, their peers not attending college, and older people not attending college. The average age of the younger groups was 22, and the average age of the older group was 69. The three groups were equal in their level of intelligence.

The results showed that the recall ability of the college group was better than that of the other two groups. But there was no difference in the performance of the groups of older persons and younger persons who were not attending college. This indicates that it might be the failure to use one's memory, rather than simply brain deterioration accompanying aging, that accounts for the inferior performance of the elderly on tests of recall. When it comes to the maintenance of cognitive abilities, such as memory, the adage "Use it or lose it" might have some validity (Hultsch, Hertzog, Small, & Dixon, 1999). One of the more intriguing longitudinal studies of cognitive aging and Alzheimer's disease is the Nun Study, which has involved following a large sample of Catholic religious sisters for more than 60 years—through the deaths of many of them (Santa Cruz et al., 2011).

Psychosocial Development

Social development continues through early, middle, and late adulthood. Keeping in mind that these divisions are somewhat arbitrary, assume that early adulthood extends from age 20 to age 40, middle adulthood from age 40 to age 65, and late adulthood from age 65

Back to School

The myth that intellectual decline is a normal aspect of aging is countered by the increasing number of older adults who enroll in undergraduate degree programs. In the case of memory and other cognitive abilities, the adage "use it or lose it" seems to have validity.

Source: bikeriderlondon/Shutterstock.com.

on. The similarities exhibited by people within these periods are related to the common social experiences of the "social clock." In recent decades, the typical ages at which some of these experiences occur have varied more than in the past. A graduate student might live at home with his parents until his late twenties, a woman working toward her medical degree might postpone marriage until her early thirties, and a two-career couple might not have their first child until they are in their late thirties. Of course, events that are unique to each person's life can also play a role in psychosocial development. Chance encounters in our lives, for example, contribute to our unique development (Bandura, 1982). You might reflect on chance encounters that influenced your choice of an academic major or that helped you meet your current boyfriend, girlfriend, husband, or wife.

Early Adulthood

Though Sigmund Freud paid little attention to adult development, he did note that normal adulthood is marked by the ability to love and to work. Erik Erikson agreed that the capacity for love is an important aspect of early adulthood, and he claimed that the first major task of adulthood is facing the conflict of **intimacy versus isolation**. Intimate relationships involve a strong sense of emotional attachment and personal commitment. The Rochester Adult Longitudinal study of a community sample supported Erikson's belief that the development of the capacity for intimacy depends on the successful formation of a psychosocial identity in adolescence. The achievement of identity during adolescence contributed to the development of intimacy in young adulthood. Participants who were capable of developing both identity in adolescence and a high degree of intimacy in young adulthood reported more successful romantic relationships and greater life satisfaction in midlife (Sneed, Whitbourne, Schwartz, & Huang, 2012).

intimacy versus isolation
Erikson's developmental stage in which success is achieved by establishing a relationship with a strong sense of emotional attachment and personal commitment.

Establishing Intimate Relationships About 95 percent of young adults eventually experience the intimate relationship of marriage. Of course there is a variety of family arrangements. And at any given time many adults are unmarried—they are either widowed, divorced, not ready, or committed to remaining single. However, the results of a longitudinal study of six countries (Austria, Germany, the Netherlands, Great Britain, Ireland, and the United States) found that men's and women's attitudes are shifting away from the norms of traditional marriage. Participants reported a remarkable diversity of lifestyles and individual differences in the timing of marriage and parenthood (Gubernskay, 2010).

A strong and consistent positive correlation has been found between marriage and psychological well-being. The World Values Survey, a survey of 159,169 adults in 42 countries, found that married women and men reported higher levels of life satisfaction than cohabiting couples, single adults, and divorced or separated adults. Though there were significant cross-cultural differences, these differences were negligible. And men and women derive similar benefits from marriage (Diener, Gohm, Suh, & Oishi, 2000). These results recently have been replicated in nationally representative samples from Australia, Germany, and Great Britain (Luhmann, Lucas, Eid, & Diener, 2013). Unmarried status is correlated with greater physical and psychological risks, especially for men. A survey of more than 18,000 men conducted in England found that unmarried middle-aged men of all kinds—single, widowed, divorced, or separated—had higher mortality rates than did married men (Ben-Shlomo, Smith, Shipley, & Marmot, 1993). One reason for this is a lower risk of illness in the married, especially if their partner is responsive to their needs (Selcuk & Ong, 2013).

What characteristics do adults look for in potential mates? As you might expect, both women and men tend to seek partners who are kind, loyal, honest, considerate, intelligent, interesting, and affectionate. But men tend to be more concerned than women with the potential spouse's physical attractiveness, and women tend to be more concerned than men with the potential spouse's earning capacity (Buss et al., 1990). As discussed in Chapter 17, psychologists argue whether these preferences reflect the influence of evolution or of cultural norms that differentially affect men's and women's marital expectations.

What determines whether a relationship will succeed? An important factor is similarity—in age, religion, attitudes, ethnicity, personality, intelligence, and educational level (O'Leary & Smith, 1991). Willingness to talk about problems is another important factor, as found in a 2-year longitudinal study of newlyweds. Those couples who believed that conflicts should be discussed openly reported greater marital happiness than those who believed they should be ignored (Crohan, 1992). A 4-year longitudinal study found that high-quality, positive communication between couples was associated with higher levels of marital satisfaction. Moreover, marital dissolution was associated with marital conflict and aggression—especially if present early in the marriage (Rogge & Bradbury, 1999).

Communication is essential to marital satisfaction. One study examined videotapes of 78 married or cohabiting couples discussing a conflict they were having. Positive interruptions (agreement with what the partner was saying) were positively correlated with the couples' feelings about the conversation and their relationship satisfaction. Negative interruptions (disagreement with what the partner was saying) were negatively correlated with the couples' feelings about the conversation and their relationship satisfaction (Daigen & Holmes, 2000). Research indicates that marital satisfaction is greater when partners take a collaborative approach to resolving conflicts than when one or both take a competitive approach (Greeff & de Bruyne, 2000).

Dissolving Intimate Relationships Unfortunately, for many couples, happiness is elusive, and they may eventually seek to end their relationship. In the United States, about half of first marriages are so unhappy that they end in divorce. In fact, the United States has the highest divorce rate of any industrialized country (O'Leary & Smith, 1991). A study that interviewed over 1,300 persons found that divorce has increased not because marriages were happier in the "good old days," but instead because barriers to divorce (such as conservative values or shared social networks) have fallen and alternatives to divorce (such as a wife's independent income or remarriage prospects) have increased. Thus, the threshold of marital happiness that will trigger divorce is lower than it was several decades ago.

The barriers to relationship dissolution associated with marriage are important in understanding the higher rate of relationship dissolution among gay and lesbian couples. One study compared relationship satisfaction and dissolution rates among heterosexual, gay, and lesbian couples. Heterosexual married couples' satisfaction with their relationship was similar to that reported by cohabiting gay and lesbian couples. Whereas relationship satisfaction declined among all three groups, gay and lesbian couples were more likely to have ended their relationships over the 5 years of the study. These results are attributed to the fact that gay and lesbian couples perceived fewer barriers to ending their relationship—for example, the cost of divorce or the loss of insurance or health benefits (Kurdek, 1998).

There are a variety of specific factors that contribute to divorce. One of the hallmarks of an unhappy marriage is the tendency of spouses to consistently offer negative explanations for their spouse's behavior (Karney & Bradbury, 2000). In dual-wage-earner marriages, perceived inequality in doing housework—particularly by wives—appears to contribute to divorces (Frisco & Williams, 2003). And even the nature of commitment may predict relationship dissolution. Couples who display avoidant commitment (that is, those who want to avoid the negative consequences of breaking up) are more likely than committed couples who display approach commitment (that is, those who want to retain the positive consequences of staying together) to break up (Frank & Brandstaetter, 2002).

Yet there is evidence that people might remain committed to spouses or partners who treat them poorly. You probably have known someone who sticks with a romantic partner who treats that person in a manner that you would not tolerate. Consider a study of 86 pairs of married couples from central Texas, with an average age of 32 years and an average length of marriage of 6 years (Swann, Hixon, & De La Ronde, 1992). The spouses took personality tests measuring their self-concepts. They also measured how the spouses appraised each other and how committed they were to each other. The results revealed that the degree of commitment to one's spouse depended on the degree of congruence between one's self-concept and how one was viewed by one's spouse. That is, those with positive self-concepts felt more committed when their spouses viewed them positively. Likewise, those with negative self-concepts felt more committed when their spouses viewed them negatively.

What could account for this finding, which runs counter to the commonsense notion that we all wish to be admired and treated well? The researchers found that though we might insist on being treated well in casual relationships, we insist on being treated in accordance with our self-concept within the intimacy of marriage. That is, we want our spouses to verify our self-concept so we are not confused about ourselves or about how other people will treat us. In addition, we will trust spouses more who do not try to "snow" us by telling us we're attractive when we feel ugly, intelligent when we feel stupid, and personally appealing when we feel socially inept. Moreover, whereas people with positive self-concepts might welcome high expectations of them, people with negative self-concepts might fear unrealistically high expectations that they could not meet.

Parenthood For most couples, parenthood is a major component of marriage. Raising children can be one of the greatest rewards in life, but it can also be one of life's greatest stresses. Because women still tend to be the primary caregiver, their parental responsibilities tend to be especially stressful. But couples who share childcare responsibilities are more likely to successfully weather the stress of becoming new parents (Belsky & Hsieh, 1998). Overall, parents who live with their biological children show greater declines in marital happiness over time than do married, childless couples or married couples living with stepchildren (Kurdek, 1999). Of course, some couples remain childless. They are not necessarily unhappy. In fact, especially if they are voluntarily childless, they might be as happy as couples with children. This is attributable, in part, to the fact that they do not have the stress that parents experience from money woes, children's illnesses, loss of sleep, and lack of recreational outlets. Women who are childless by choice show higher levels of psychological well-being than women who are involuntarily childless (Jeffries & Konnert, 2002).

But what of single parents? In the 1960s and 1970s, divorce was the chief cause of single parenting. This has been joined by planned or unplanned childbearing outside of marriage. Though single parents are usually women, one in five is male. Many single parents, given social and financial support, are successful in rearing children. For example, one study of single parents serving in the U.S. military found that mothers and fathers readily used social, financial, and organizational resources to balance their family and work obligations (Heath & Orthner, 1999). But according to the U.S. Bureau of the Census, single-parent families, on the average, suffer disadvantages in regard to income, health, and housing conditions. The most disadvantaged are families consisting of children and a never-married mother (Bianchi, 1995).

Middle Adulthood

In 1850 few Americans lived beyond what we now call early adulthood; the average life span was only 40 years (Shneidman, 1987). But improved nutrition, sanitation, and health care have almost doubled that life span. What was the end of the life span more than a century ago is today simply the beginning of middle adulthood. Daniel Levinson (1978) found that during the transition to middle adulthood, men commonly experience a midlife crisis, in which they realize that the "dream" they had pursued in regard to their life goals will not be achieved or, even if achieved, will seem transient in the face of the inevitability of death. Other studies indicate, however, that the midlife crisis is less intense than Levinson found in his research (Fagan & Ayers, 1982). Moreover, the life dreams of women tend to be more complex than the life dreams of men. Whereas men typically focus on their careers, women focus on marriage and children, as well as their careers (Kittrell, 1998).

According to Erik Erikson, the main task of middle adulthood is the resolution of the conflict of **generativity versus stagnation**. Those who achieve generativity become less self-absorbed and more concerned about being a productive worker, spouse, and parent (Slater, 2003). They are more competent, continue to strive for achievement, and are more altruistic and trusting (Cox, Wilt, Olson, & McAdams, 2010). They also are more satisfied with their lives (McAdams, de St. Aubin, & Logan, 1993). One way of achieving generativity is to serve as a mentor for a younger person. This lets mentors realize their life dreams vicariously and know that their dreams will continue even after their own deaths (Westermeyer, 2004).

Middle adulthood also brings transitions affected by one's parental status. You might be surprised to learn that parents become more distressed and experience more marital unhappiness after their first child leaves home than after their last child leaves home. In fact, after the last child has left home, parents tend to be relieved and experience improved marital relations (Harris, Ellicott, & Holmes, 1986). Perhaps the notion of an "empty nest syndrome" (after the last child has left home) should be replaced by the notion of a "partly empty nest syndrome" (after the first child has left home). Moreover, a growing trend in North America is the "revolving-door nest," caused by the return home of young adults who find it personally or financially difficult to live on their own (Dennerstein, Dudley, & Guthrie, 2002).

Late Adulthood

Now that more people in developed countries are living into their 70s and beyond, developmental psychologists have become more interested in studying late adulthood. In 1900 only one person in thirty was over 65. By 2020 one person in five will be over 65 (Eisdorfer, 1983). Though this increase in the elderly population, including many more retired people, will create more concern about physical well-being in old age, it also will create more concern about psychosocial development in old age. Research has provided inconsistent findings regarding whether retirement generally has positive, negative, or no effects on psychological well-being (Kim & Moen, 2001).

Erikson claimed that the main psychosocial task of late adulthood is to resolve the crisis of **integrity versus despair**. A sense of integrity results from reflecting back on a meaningful life through a "life review." In fact, Erikson claimed that pleasurable reminiscing is essential to satisfactory adjustment in old age. This was supported by a study of nursing home residents aged 70 to 88 years. Participants in the experimental group received a visitor who encouraged them to reminisce and engage in a life review. Participants in the control group received a friendly visit. Participants who engaged in a life review scored higher on a questionnaire that measured their level of ego integrity, as long as 3 years after the intervention (Haight, Michel, & Hendrix, 2000). Older adults who are able to review and accept their past are more likely to develop a sense of coherence and experience more positive psychological development (Wiesmann & Hannich, 2011).

And old age is not necessarily a time of physical decay, cognitive deterioration, and social isolation. For many, it is a time of physical activity, continued education, and

Generativity
According to Erik Erikson, people who successfully resolve the midlife conflict of generativity versus stagnation become less self-absorbed and more concerned with the well-being of the next generation.
Source: Pressmaster/Shutterstock.com.

generativity versus stagnation
Erikson's developmental stage in which success is achieved by becoming less self-absorbed and more concerned with the well-being of others.

integrity versus despair
Erikson's developmental stage in which success is achieved by reflecting back on one's life and finding that it has been meaningful.

rewarding social relations (Whitbourne & Hulicka, 1990). Many elderly adults optimize their cognitive and physical functioning by capitalizing on their strengths and compensating for their weaknesses. For example, they may allot more time to perform tasks, practice old skills, or learn new skills. The use of these strategies by elderly adults has been found to be associated with successful aging, characterized by more positive emotions, enhanced feelings of well-being, and less loneliness (Freund & Baltes, 1998).

Eventually, many adults must confront one of the greatest psychosocial challenges of old age—the death of a mate. During the period immediately following the death of their spouse, bereaved spouses are more likely to suffer depression, illness, or death than are their peers with living spouses. An increase in morbidity, mortality, and psychological well-being tends to be found among surviving spouses. This might stem from the loss of the emotional and practical support previously provided by the now-deceased spouse. One study tested this hypothesis with a sample of recently bereaved spouses. Widowers were more likely to experience greater deterioration in physical and mental health and receive less social support than were widows. However, there was no evidence that the loss of social support reported by widowers mediated this gender difference (Stroebe, Stroebe, & Abakoumkin, 1999). Thus, it is likely that other factors contribute to the poorer health and negative psychological outcomes experienced by bereaved widowers. For example, a study of older German adults found that widowers tend to be lonelier than widows (Pinquart, 2003). A variety of techniques have been used to aid the bereavement process, with varying success (Durland, 2000). In one study, 44 college students who had lost a loved one were randomly assigned to write about either their bereavement experience or about a trivial, unrelated topic. The results indicated that writing about one's bereavement experience helped reduce feelings of distress (Range, Kovac, & Marion, 2000). Similar findings were reported in a study in which college students wrote about their bereavement experience regarding a loved one who had committed suicide in the prior two years (Kovac & Range, 2000).

Though, as Benjamin Franklin observed in 1789, "in this world nothing's certain but death and taxes," we can at least improve the way in which we confront our own mortality. In old age, successful resolution of the crisis of ego integrity versus despair is associated with less fear of death (Goebel & Boeck, 1987). And a survey of 200 adults found that those with strong religious convictions and a greater belief in an afterlife have lower death anxiety (Alvarado, Templer, Bresler, & Thomas-Dobson, 1995).

Prior to the 20th century, death was accepted as a public part of life. People died at home, surrounded and comforted by loved ones. Today, people commonly die alone, in pain, in hospital rooms, attached to life-support systems. One of the most important developments to counter this approach to death and dying is the **hospice movement**, founded in 1958 by the British physician Cicely Saunders. She was motivated to do so by her colleagues' failure to respond sensitively to dying patients and their families. Hospices provide humane, comprehensive care for the dying patient in a hospital, residential, or home setting, with attention to alleviating the patient's physical, emotional, and spiritual suffering (Saunders, 1996). A study comparing hospices to traditional nursing homes found that elderly dying cancer patients received more effective pain relief and better quality of life during their time spent in hospice (Black et al., 2011).

hospice movement The providing of care for the dying patient with attention to alleviating the patient's physical, emotional, and spiritual suffering.

Section Review: Adult Development

1. What is the apparent relationship between caloric intake and aging?
2. What does research indicate about changes in intelligence in old age?
3. How do adults successfully resolve Erikson's conflict involving generativity versus stagnation?

Experiencing Psychology

An Analysis of Children's Toys

Rationale

As discussed in this chapter, children as young as toddlers learn to classify toys as masculine or feminine. In fact, toys are examples of how social and cultural factors influence gender-role development. In this exercise you will examine a selection of toys, observe any gender-specific messages or gender typing, and discuss your work in the context of what you learned from reading this chapter.

Procedure

Find a local toy store that has a well-stocked selection of toys for boys and girls of different ages. Before you make your trip, consider the ways that gender typing may be reflected in a toy's attributes. For example, you might consider colors of the toys or pictures of children playing with the toys on packaging materials. Other factors to consider might be indicators that toys are for girls or boys. Some packages might indicate that the toy is appropriate for boys of a certain age range. Or, the store might group toys that girls would be interested in together.

Spend about an hour in the store, examining the toys, their packaging, and their placement in the store and make notes of any evidence of gender typing. Summarize your findings by answering the following questions:

1. Could you find toys that were easily identifiable as boys' toys? What types of toys? What type of play or activities do they encourage?
2. Could you find toys that were easily identifiable as girls' toys? What types of toys? What type of play or activities do they encourage?
3. Could you find any gender-neutral toys—that is toys, that were neither boys' nor girls' toys? What types of toys? What type of play or activities do they encourage?

Results and Discussion

Describe your findings. Did you find evidence of gender typing during your observation? As discussed in the chapter, cultural trends have indicated more similar treatment of boys and girls. Do your results support what you read in the chapter? Were there any other conclusions you reached after summarizing your observations?

Chapter Summary

Research Methods in Developmental Psychology

- Developmental psychology is the field that studies the physical, perceptual, cognitive, and psychosocial changes that take place across the life span.
- Research designs typical of developmental psychology include longitudinal research, cross-sectional research, and cohort-sequential research.

Prenatal Development

- The prenatal period is divided into the germinal, embryonic, and fetal stages.
- Cell-adhesion molecules direct the size, shape, and location of organs in the embryo.
- Teratogens can impair prenatal development.
- Women who drink alcohol, a teratogen, during pregnancy might have offspring who suffer from fetal alcohol syndrome.

Infant and Child Development

- Childhood extends from birth until puberty.
- The first 2 years of childhood are called infancy.
- Motor development follows a consistent sequence, though the timing of motor milestones varies somewhat among infants.
- Jean Piaget found that children pass through distinct cognitive stages of development.
- During the sensorimotor stage, the infant learns to coordinate sensory experiences and motor behavior, and forms schemas that represent aspects of the world.
- The preoperational stage is marked by egocentrism. In the concrete operational stage, the child learns to make transitive inferences and to appreciate conservation.
- Erik Erikson put forth an influential theory of psychosocial development. He believed that the life span consists of eight distinct stages, each associated with a crisis that must be overcome.
- An important factor in infant development is social attachment, a strong emotional relationship between an infant and a caregiver.
- Permissive and authoritarian child-rearing practices are less effective than authoritative ones.
- Children who receive high-quality day care do not appear to suffer ill effects from being separated from their parents, though this might not be true of infants.
- Research on the effects of divorce on children has produced inconsistent results, with some studies finding

- no effects, others finding negative effects, and still others finding positive effects.
- Though the causes of gender-role development are still unclear, social learning theory and gender-schema theory try to explain it.
- The most influential theory of moral development has been Lawrence Kohlberg's cognitive-developmental theory, which is based on Piaget's belief that a person's level of moral development depends on his or her level of cognitive development.
- Kohlberg proposes that we pass through preconventional, conventional, and postconventional levels of moral development.
- Carol Gilligan argues that Kohlberg's theory is biased toward a masculine view of morality. Research has provided mixed support for Kohlberg's theory.

Adolescent Development

- Adolescence is a transitional period between childhood and adulthood that begins with puberty.
- In regard to physical development, the adolescent experiences the maturation of primary and secondary sex characteristics.
- In regard to cognitive development, some adolescents enter Piaget's formal operational stage, meaning that they can engage in abstract, hypothetical reasoning.
- And, in regard to psychosocial development, adolescence is a time of identity formation, an important stage in Erik Erikson's theory of development.
- The adolescent also is increasingly influenced by peer values, especially in regard to fashion, sexuality, and drug use.
- Research on sex differences has found no consistent differences in male and female brains.
- Girls and boys differ little in their gross motor abilities until puberty, when boys begin to outperform girls.
- Women tend to have better verbal abilities, while men tend to have better spatial and mathematical problem-solving abilities.
- Men also tend to be more physically aggressive than women.
- Research on gender differences is controversial because of fears that its findings might be used to promote and legitimate discrimination.
- Gender differences are based on group averages, and most are so small that they should not be used to make decisions about individuals.

Adult Development

- Adulthood begins when adolescents become independent from their parents.
- In regard to physical development, adults reach their physical peak in their late twenties, at which point they begin a gradual decline that does not accelerate appreciably until old age.
- Middle-aged women experience menopause, which, contrary to popular belief, is rarely a traumatic event, and middle-aged men experience andropause.
- In regard to cognitive development, though aging brings some slowing of cognitive processes, people who continue to be mentally active show less cognitive decline than do their peers who do not stay active.
- In regard to social development, Erik Erikson saw the main task of early adulthood as the establishment of intimacy, typically between a husband and wife. About 95 percent of adults marry, but half of North American marriages will end in divorce.
- The most successful marriages are those in which the spouses discuss, rather than avoid, marital issues.
- Erikson saw the main task of middle adulthood as the establishment of a sense of generativity, which is promoted by parenting.
- After the last child leaves home, parents typically improve their emotional and marital well-being.
- Erikson saw the final stage of life as ideally promoting a sense of integrity in reflecting on a life well lived.
- Eventually, all people must face their own mortality.
- The hospice movement, founded by Cicely Saunders, has promoted more humane, personal, and homelike care for the dying patient.

Key Terms

developmental psychology (p. 108)
maturation (p. 108)

Research Methods in Developmental Psychology

cohort (p. 109)
cohort-sequential research (p. 109)
cross-sectional research (p. 109)
longitudinal research (p. 108)

Prenatal Development

embryonic stage (p. 110)
fetal alcohol syndrome (p. 112)
fetal stage (p. 111)
germinal stage (p. 110)
teratogen (p. 111)

Infant and Child Development

accommodation (p. 115)

assimilation (p. 115)
authoritative parenting (p. 122)
autonomy versus shame and doubt (p. 121)
childhood (p. 112)
concrete operational stage (p. 117)
conservation (p. 117)
conventional level (p. 127)
egocentrism (p. 117)

gender roles (p. 124)
gender schema theory (p. 125)
industry versus inferiority (p. 121)
infancy (p. 112)
initiative versus guilt (p. 121)
object permanence (p. 115)
postconventional level (p. 127)
preoperational stage (p. 117)
preconventional level (p. 127)
schema (p. 115)
sensorimotor stage (p. 115)

social attachment (p. 119)
social learning theory (p. 125)
transitive inference (p. 117)
trust versus mistrust (p. 119)

Adolescent Development

adolescence (p. 129)
formal operational stage (p. 131)
identity versus role confusion (p. 132)
menarche (p. 130)
puberty (p. 129)

social clock (p. 129)
spermarche (p. 130)
andropause (p. 136)
adulthood (p. 136)
crystallized intelligence (p. 137)
fluid intelligence (p. 137)
generativity versus stagnation (p. 145)
hospice movement (p. 146)
integrity versus despair (p. 145)
intimacy versus isolation (p. 142)
menopause (p. 136)

Chapter Quiz

Note: Answers for the Chapter Quiz questions are provided at the end of the book.

1. A child who first believes that changing the form of something changes its amount, but eventually realizes that changing the form of something does not change its amount, would be exhibiting
   a. assimilation.
   b. accommodation.
   c. transitive inference.
   d. transductive reasoning.

2. In regard to the pubertal growth spurt,
   a. boys and girls typically show a spurt at about the same age.
   b. boys typically show a spurt about two years earlier than girls.
   c. girls typically show a spurt about two years earlier than boys.
   d. boys and girls a century ago typically showed a spurt several years earlier than boys and girls today.

3. A junior high school student shows excellent ability in designing and conducting experiments to test basic principles regarding the movement of objects. The student has probably reached what Piaget called the
   a. sensorimotor stage.
   b. preoperational stage.
   c. formal operational stage.
   d. concrete operational stage.

4. An important reason that adults tend to put on weight is that
   a. their appetite tends to increase.
   b. their basal metabolic rate slows.
   c. they reduce their secretion of insulin.
   d. they increase their secretion of insulin.

5. According to Erikson, the main psychosocial conflict of adolescence involves
   a. intimacy versus isolation.
   b. industry versus inferiority.
   c. identity versus role confusion.
   d. generativity versus stagnation.

6. A child who realizes that pouring all of the soda from a short, wide glass into a tall, narrow glass does not change the amount of soda is exhibiting an appreciation of
   a. object permanence.
   b. conservation.
   c. transitive inference.
   d. transductive reasoning.

7. Mary Ainsworth has contributed to our knowledge of infant
   a. social attachment.
   b. cognitive abilities.
   c. physical maturation.
   d. perceptual development.

8. Elderly persons would be most likely to show a decline in fluid intelligence if, for example, they
   a. lost the ability to swim.
   b. forgot the names of old friends.
   c. could no longer solve algebra problems.
   d. could no longer form new memories of daily events.

9. The "visual cliff" is used to test infant
   a. visual acuity.
   b. depth perception.
   c. movement detection.
   d. balance and coordination.

10. The sperm normally fertilizes the egg in the
    a. ovary.
    b. vagina.
    c. uterus.
    d. fallopian tube.

11. According to Diana Baumrind, authoritative parents
    a. prohibit "back talk."
    b. often rely on physical punishment.
    c. explain the reasons for their rules.
    d. often have children who become juvenile delinquents.

12. According to Sigmund Freud, resolution of the Oedipus and Electra complexes influences the development of
    a. weaning.
    b. gender roles.
    c. aggressiveness.
    d. social attachment.

13. In regard to moral development, Gilligan believes that girls and women
    a. favor justice more than caring.
    b. favor caring more than justice.
    c. favor caring and justice equally.
    d. are superior to males as children but not as adults.

14. According to Jean Piaget, assimilation and accommodation determine the infant's
    a. schemas.
    b. sensory acuity.
    c. motor maturation.
    d. social attachment.

15. A psychologist compares the language ability of a group of 12-month-olds, a group of 15-month-olds, and a group of 18-month-olds. This is an example of
    a. longitudinal research.
    b. cross-sectional research.
    c. cohort-sequential research.
    d. quasi-experimental research.

16. Research indicates that divorce has increased in the United States because
    a. barriers to divorce have fallen.
    b. marriages were happier in the past.
    c. children have become more burdensome.
    d. the age of first marriages continues to decline.

17. Jim is older than Phil. Susan is younger than Phil. A child who correctly concludes that Jim is older than Susan would be exhibiting
    a. conservation.
    b. transitive inference.
    c. preoperational thought.
    d. transductive reasoning.

18. According to Kohlberg, students who do not cheat on exams because they fear the teacher will punish them are at the
    a. concrete level of moral development.
    b. conventional level of moral development.
    c. preconventional level of moral development.
    d. postconventional level of moral development.

19. Teratogens
    a. may cause prenatal defects.
    b. guide embryonic development.
    c. depend on the individual's genotype.
    d. do not have effects until the last three months before birth.

20. According to Erikson the main conflict of old age is
    a. integrity versus despair.
    b. intimacy versus isolation.
    c. industry versus inferiority.
    d. generativity versus stagnation.

21. The average infant walks at age
    a. 5 months.
    b. 9 months.
    c. 13 months.
    d. 18 months.

22. The sequential unfolding of inherited predispositions is called
    a. eugenics.
    b. phylogeny.
    c. maturation.
    d. predeterminism.

23. In regard to gender differences in empathy, on the average,
    a. women report they are more empathetic than do men.
    b. women behave more empathetically than men.
    c. women show physiological changes indicating that they are more empathetic than men.
    d. men and women are equally empathetic on all measures of empathy.

24. The fact that college students who experienced the "Reagan revolution" of the 1980s might differ from those who experienced the "Woodstock era" of the 1960s may limit a psychologist to making only tentative conclusions about the psychological development of college students. This limitation would be most likely to affect the conclusions drawn from
    a. longitudinal research.
    b. cross-sectional research.
    c. naturalistic observation.
    d. quasi-experimental research.

Thought Questions

1. How would you use a longitudinal research design, a cross-sectional research design, and a cohort-sequential research design to study whether college students become more tolerant of ethnic groups that are not their own between their admission to college and their senior year?

2. A child insists on going out to play without first doing his homework. How might parents respond differently in using authoritarian parenting, permissive parenting, and authoritative parenting?

3. What are some of the major biological and sociocultural factors that contribute to the development of gender differences?

4. How might an adult successfully meet each of the last three crises in Erikson's theory of psychosocial development?

Sensation and Perception

CHAPTER 5

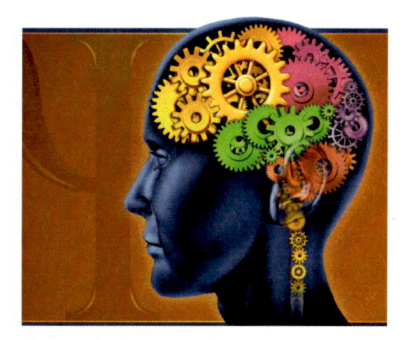

He reached out his hand and took hold of his wife's head, tried to lift it off, to put it on. He had apparently mistaken his wife for a hat! (Sacks, 1985, p. 10)

This bizarre scene was described in a case study presented in a bestselling book, *The Man Who Mistook His Wife for a Hat*, by the late neurologist Oliver Sacks. In the book, Sacks used case studies to illustrate the sometimes extraordinary effects of brain damage on human behavior. The man who mistook his wife for a hat, whom Sacks called "Dr. P.," was a talented singer and musician who taught at a music school. But his students began to notice that he could not recognize their faces. Yet, when they spoke, he identified them immediately. Dr. P. also saw people where they did not exist. As he strolled down a street, for example, he would kindly pat the tops of water hydrants and parking meters, mistaking them for the heads of children. At first people laughed and thought he was just joking—after all, he was known for his quirky sense of humor.

Did Dr. P. have a problem with his eyes? An eye examination found that he had good vision. Puzzled, the ophthalmologist sent him for a neurological examination by Dr. Sacks. After examining him, Sacks said, "His visual acuity was good: he had no difficulty seeing a pin on the floor" (Sacks, 1985, p. 9). But given that Dr. P. had normal vision, what accounted for his inability to recognize faces? Over time Sacks put the clues together to solve the mystery of Dr. P.'s peculiar problem. On one occasion, when Dr. P. perused an issue of *National Geographic*, he could identify individual details in scenes but not the scenes as a whole. When Sacks asked him to identify photographs of his family members, he could not—though he could identify their facial features. He identified his brother, Paul, based on his unusually large teeth. But Dr. P. did not recognize Paul's face. He simply inferred that it was Paul based on the size of the teeth.

Eventually, Sacks realized that Dr. P. suffered from brain damage (perhaps from an undetected stroke) that produced visual agnosia and prosopagnosia. In **visual agnosia**, the individual can see objects and identify their features, but cannot recognize them (Behrmann & Kimchi, 2003). When, for example, Dr. P. was shown a glove, he described it as being continuously curved, but he could not recognize it as a glove—until he put it on and used it. A person with **prosopagnosia** (a form of visual agnosia) can identify details of faces but cannot recognize them as a whole (de Gelder & Rouw, 2000).

Source: Lightspring/Shutterstock.com.

Chapter Outline
Sensory Processes
Visual Sensation
Visual Perception
Hearing
Chemical Senses
Skin Senses
Body Senses
Extrasensory Perception

visual agnosia A condition in which an individual can see objects and identify their features but cannot recognize the objects.

prosopagnosia A condition in which an individual can recognize details in faces but cannot recognize faces as a whole.

151

sensation The process that detects stimuli from the body or surroundings.

perception The process that organizes sensations into meaningful patterns.

sensory receptors Specialized cells that detect stimuli and convert their energy into neural impulses.

sensory transduction The process by which sensory receptors convert stimuli into neural impulses.

psychophysics The study of the relationship between the physical characteristics of stimuli and the conscious psychological experiences that are associated with them.

absolute threshold The minimum amount of stimulation that an individual can detect through a given sense.

FIGURE 5-1
Sensation and Perception

Do you see anything in this picture? Though *sensation* lets you see the pattern of light and dark in the picture, *perception* lets you organize what you sense into a meaningful pattern—a person riding a horse.

Source: Dallenbach, K. M. (1951). A puzzle picture with a new principle of concealment. *American Journal of Psychology, 54*, 431–433.

Imagine a man with prosopagnosia. He might fail to recognize his wife's face, yet still recognize her voice. Every time they met, she would have to speak so he could identify her.

Functional MRI reveals that when individuals with prosopagnosia look at familiar faces, they exhibit lower activity in a strip of association cortex (see Chapter 3) running along the underside of the occipital and temporal lobes of the brain (Hadjikhani & de Gelder, 2002). Visual agnosia and prosopagnosia illustrate the difference between **sensation**, the process that detects stimuli from the environment, and **perception**, the process that organizes sensations into meaningful wholes.

Sensory Processes

The starting point for both sensation and perception is a stimulus (plural, stimuli), a form of energy (such as light waves or sound waves) that can affect sensory organs (such as the eyes or the ears). Visual sensation lets you detect the black marks on this page; visual perception lets you organize the black marks into letters and words. To appreciate the difference between sensation and perception, try to identify the picture in Figure 5-1. Most people cannot identify it because they sense the light and dark marks on the page but fail to perceive a meaningful pattern.

Sensation depends on specialized cells called **sensory receptors**, which detect stimuli and convert their energy into neural impulses. This process is called **sensory transduction**. Receptors serve our visual, auditory, smell, taste, skin, and body senses. But some animals have receptors that serve unusual senses. The blind cave salamander has electroreceptors that detect electrical fields produced by prey (Schlegel & Roth, 1997). Because whales and dolphins navigate by using receptors sensitive to the earth's magnetic field (Walker, Dennis, & Kirschvink, 2002), disruption of this sense might account for some of the periodic strandings of whales and dolphins on beaches.

Sensory Thresholds

How intense must a sound be for you to detect it? How much change in light intensity must occur for you to notice it? Questions like these are the subject matter of **psychophysics**, the study of the relationship between the physical characteristics of stimuli and the corresponding psychological responses to them. Psychophysics was developed by the German scientists Ernst Weber (1795–1878) and Gustav Fechner (1801–1887). Fechner, after the publication of his classic *Elements of Psychophysics* in 1860, devoted the rest of his life to studying the relationship between physical stimulation and cognitive experiences. Psychophysics has been used to assess, among other things, differences in digital video quality (Moore, 2002), infants' ability to detect differences between colors (Adams & Courage, 2002), and the ability of monkeys and baboons to detect changes in the sweetness of sugar solutions (Laska, Scheuber, Sanchez, & Luna, 1999).

Absolute Threshold

The minimum amount of stimulation that a person can detect is called the **absolute threshold**, or *limen*. For example, a cup of coffee would require a certain amount of sugar before you could detect a sweet taste. Weber used fine bristles to measure touch sensitivity by bending them against the skin. Because the absolute threshold for a particular sensory experience varies, psychologists operationally define the absolute threshold as the minimum level of stimulation that can be detected 50 percent of the time when a stimulus is presented. Thus, if you were presented with a low-intensity sound 30 times

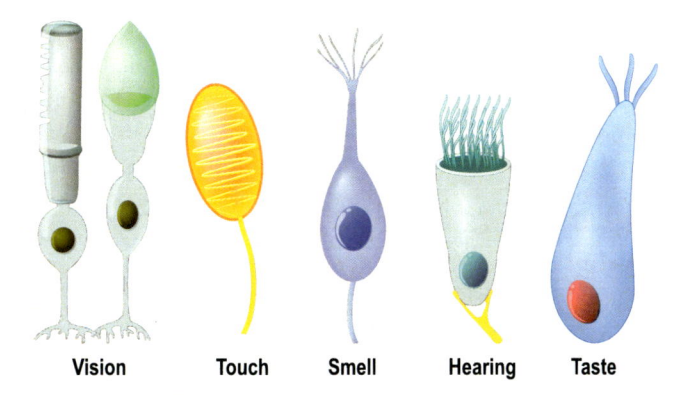

Sensory Receptors

Receptor cells: Rod and cone (vision), Meissner's corpuscle (touch), olfactory receptor (smell), hair cell (hearing), and gustatory cell (taste).
Source: Designua/Shuterstock.com.

Vision Touch Smell Hearing Taste

and you detected it 15 times, that level of intensity would be your absolute threshold for that stimulus. The absolute thresholds for certain senses are remarkable. For example, you can detect the sweetness from a teaspoon of sugar dissolved in two gallons of water, the odor of one drop of perfume diffused throughout a three-room apartment, the wing of a bee falling on your cheek from a height of one centimeter, the ticking of a watch under quiet conditions at a distance of 20 feet, and the flame of a candle seen from a distance of 30 miles on a clear, dark night (Galanter, 1962). The absolute threshold is used, for example, in testing the ability of people with hearing impairments to detect speech (Nejime & Moore, 1998).

Signal-Detection Theory The absolute threshold also is affected by factors other than the intensity of the stimulus. Because of this, researchers, inspired by Fechner's work, have devised **signal-detection theory**, which assumes that the detection of a stimulus depends on both its intensity and the physical and psychological state of the individual. One of the most important psychological factors is *response bias*—how ready the person is to report the presence of a particular stimulus. Imagine you are walking down a street at night. Your predisposition to detect a sound would partly depend on your estimate of the probability of being mugged, so you would be more likely to perceive the sound of footsteps in a neighborhood that you believe to be dangerous than in a neighborhood you believe to be safe.

Signal-detection researchers study four kinds of reports that a person might make in response to a stimulus. A *hit* is a correct report of the presence of a target stimulus. A *miss* is a failure to report the presence of a target stimulus that is, in fact, present. A *false alarm* is a report of the presence of a target stimulus that is not, in fact, present. And a *correct rejection* is a correct report of the absence of a target stimulus. Consider these four kinds of reports in regard to walking down a dark street at night. A hit would be perceiving footsteps when they actually occur. A miss would be failing to perceive footsteps when they actually occur. A false alarm would be perceiving footsteps when they do not occur. And a correct rejection would be failing to perceive footsteps when they do not occur.

Signal-detection theory has important applications to crucial tasks, such as identifying bombs put through airport X-ray machines. It has been used to assess differences in drivers' reactions to potentially dangerous situations, including merging into traffic and approaching a yellow traffic light (Rosenbloom & Wolf, 2002). Even caregivers' responses to infants' cries may depend on their response biases. In one study, 38 mothers were presented with taped cries of infants that they had been told were "easy" or "difficult." In reality, one of the labels was randomly assigned to each infant. Cries of supposedly "difficult" infants elicited greater detection sensitivity, such as response time and heart rate changes from the mothers (Donovan, Leavitt, & Walsh, 1997).

Subliminal Perception Research on **subliminal perception** investigates whether participants can unconsciously perceive stimuli that do not exceed the absolute threshold. In other words, such stimuli are below threshold detection. Though this remains a controversial topic in psychology, the existence of subliminal perception is no longer disputed.

signal-detection theory The theory holding that the detection of a stimulus depends on both the intensity of the stimulus and the physical and psychological state of the individual.

subliminal perception The unconscious perception of stimuli that are too weak to exceed the absolute threshold for detection.

Chapter 5 Sensation and Perception

What is debated, however, is the proper way to design, measure, and replicate convincing studies of this type of nonconscious processing of stimuli (Kouider & Dehaene, 2007). A recent review of functional magnetic resonance imaging (fMRI) studies showed that subliminal stimuli activate the amygdala and hippocampus areas in the visual cortex, though participants were not consciously aware of the stimuli (Brooks et al., 2012). Assuming that we might be able to perceive subliminal stimuli, could manufacturers make us buy their products by bombarding us with subliminal advertisements? This question is the heart of a controversy that arose in the late 1950s after a marketing firm subliminally flashed the words "Eat Popcorn" and "Drink Coca-Cola" during movies shown at a theater in Fort Lee, New Jersey. After several weeks of this subliminal advertising, popcorn sales had increased 50 percent and Coke sales had increased 18 percent (McConnell, Cutler, & McNeil, 1958). Marketing executives expressed glee at this potential boon to advertising, but the public feared that subliminal perception might be used as a means of totalitarian mind control.

Psychologists, however, pointed out that the uncontrolled conditions of the study made it impossible to determine the actual reason for the increase in sales. Perhaps sales increased because better movies, hotter weather, or more appealing counter displays attracted more customers during the period when subliminal advertising was used. Another problem is that the limen varies from trial to trial for each participant. This variation makes it difficult to assess when stimulation has truly been subliminal (Miller, 1991). Thus, perhaps moviegoers were, at times, consciously aware of the supposedly subliminal messages about Coke and popcorn. Moreover, there even is evidence that the original study just might have been a fabrication created by an overeager advertising executive (Pratkanis, 1992).

But some more recent controlled studies have provided support for the possible effectiveness of subliminal advertising. In one study, participants watched an episode of *The Simpsons* during which stimuli related to thirst were presented subliminally. A control group watched the episode without being exposed to the subliminal material. The results showed that those who had been exposed to the subliminal thirst stimuli became thirstier than the control group and thirstier than they had been before watching the episode (Cooper & Cooper, 2002). Despite studies like this one, a meta-analysis of subliminal advertising studies found that it is generally ineffective in influencing consumers' product choices (Trappey, 1996).

But what of the popular subliminal self-help audiotapes that supposedly help you to improve yourself? Producers of subliminal self-help audiotapes claim that they can help listeners do everything from smoke less to improve their study habits. People who listen to these audiotapes typically hear soothing music or nature sounds. Messages (such as "Study harder") presented on audiotapes below the auditory threshold supposedly motivate the listener to improve in the desired area. Consider an experiment that examined the effectiveness of subliminal audiotapes (Froufe & Schwartz, 2001). Young adults were randomly assigned to one of four conditions. One group listened to audiotaped music with both supraliminal (above threshold detection) and subliminal self-esteem messages. A second group listened to music with only subliminal self-esteem messages. A third group listened to music, though they were told that the audiotape contained subliminal messages. And a fourth group did not listen to an audiotape. Each participant was given a self-esteem scale before and after each of the conditions had been administered. Whereas each of the first three groups showed an increase in self-esteem, the fourth group did not. This indicated that any improvements in self-esteem were no more than placebo effects.

Difference Threshold

In addition to detecting the presence of a stimulus, we must be able to detect changes in its intensity. The minimum amount of change in stimulation that can be detected is called the **difference threshold**. For example, you would have to increase or decrease the intensity of the sound from your CD player a certain amount before you could detect a change in its volume. Like the absolute threshold, the difference threshold for a particular sensory

difference threshold The minimum amount of change in stimulation that can be detected.

> ### Critical Thinking About Psychology
>
> **Can We Be Controlled by Subliminal Messages?**
>
> Since the 1950s, the media periodically have created alarm by sensationalizing claims that we can be influenced by stimulation that does not exceed the absolute threshold—subliminal stimulation. This attention has provoked fears among citizens and government officials that subliminal stimulation could be used to control people's behavior. Over the years, concern has been raised in the media about subliminal messages presented in movies, on television, on audiotapes, in advertisements, and in rock music recordings. Subliminal stimulation even became part of the 2000 U.S. presidential election when Democrats complained that Republicans had superimposed the subliminal message "RATS" over a televised campaign advertisement attacking candidate Al Gore's Medicare plan. Given an unusually close election like that one, might subliminal messages sway enough voters to determine who wins?
>
> As another example, after the John Travolta movie *Phenomenon* was released in 1996, the *Globe* tabloid (Richard Baker, September 3, 1996) quoted two disc jockeys from Flint, Michigan, as saying that the movie was filled with subliminal messages about Travolta's belief in Scientology. These messages were supposedly conveyed through *backmasking*—the superimposing of a soundtrack backwards over a forward one.
>
> This controversy even merited attention on the television tabloid show *Extra*. The show claimed, for example, that the movie's theme song, "I Have the Touch," sung by Peter Gabriel, included the words, "Don't you miss Ron?" when played backward. Some people took this phrase as a reference to L. Ron Hubbard, the founder of Scientology and author of *Dianetics*, the book that popularized it. Might a message like this be effective in encouraging readers to want to learn more about Scientology?
>
> Parents likewise have expressed concerns about the alleged subliminal messages in rock music recordings, such as Led Zeppelin's "Stairway to Heaven," that supposedly can be heard clearly when the recording is played backward. Despite the lack of evidence that such messages exist, fear that they might cause crime, suicide, Satanism, and sexual promiscuity led California and other states to pass laws requiring warnings on recordings that allegedly contain subliminal messages. Yet, even if recordings (or movies) contain subliminal messages, there is no evidence that listeners will obey them like zombies any more than they will obey messages they are aware of (Vokey & Read, 1985). That is, subliminal *stimulation* should not be confused with subliminal *persuasion*.

experience varies from person to person and from occasion to occasion. Therefore, psychologists formally define the difference threshold as the minimum change in stimulation that can be detected 50 percent of the time by a given person. The difference threshold has practical applications, as in a study of passengers' perception of differences in the comfort level of automobile rides based on changes in the intensity of vehicle vibrations (Mansfield & Griffin, 2000).

Weber and Fechner referred to the difference threshold as the **just noticeable difference (jnd)**. They found that the amount of change in intensity of stimulation needed to produce a jnd is a constant fraction of the original stimulus. This fraction became known as **Weber's law** (Droesler, 2000). For example, because the jnd for weight is about 2 percent if you held a 50-ounce weight, you would notice a change only if there was at least a 1-ounce change in it. But a person holding a 100-ounce weight would require the addition or subtraction of at least 2 ounces to notice a change. Research indicates that Weber's law holds better for mid-range stimuli than for stimuli at either the low or high extreme. Other factors also may play a role. For example, the jnd for two-dimensional bar graphs is smaller than for three-dimensional bar graphs. This means that three-dimensional bar graphs require larger differences between the heights of bars for those differences to be noticed (Hughes, 2001).

just noticeable difference (jnd) Weber and Fechner's term for the difference threshold.

Weber's law The principle that the amount of change in stimulation needed to produce a just noticeable difference is a constant proportion of the original stimulus.

Sensory Adaptation

Given that each of your senses is constantly bombarded by stimulation, why do you notice only certain stimuli? One reason is that if a stimulus remains constant in intensity, you will gradually stop noticing it. For example, on entering a friend's dormitory room, you might be struck by the repugnant stench of month-old garbage. A few minutes later,

Chapter 5 Sensation and Perception

sensory adaptation The tendency of the sensory receptors to respond less and less to a constant stimulus.

though, you might not notice it at all. This tendency of sensory receptors to respond less and less to an unchanging stimulus is called **sensory adaptation**.

Sensory adaptation lets us detect potentially important changes in our environment while ignoring unchanging aspects of it. For example, when vibrations repeatedly stimulate your skin, you stop noticing them (Hollins, Delemos, & Goble, 1991). And once you have determined that the swimming pool water is cold, it would serve little purpose to continue noticing it—especially when more important changes might be taking place elsewhere in your surroundings. Of course, you will not adapt completely to extremely intense sensations, such as severe pain or freezing cold. This continuation of response also is adaptive, because to ignore such stimuli might be harmful or even fatal.

Section Review: Sensory Processes

1. What is the difference between sensation and perception?
2. What is psychophysics?
3. What is sensory adaptation?

Visual Sensation

Because of our reliance on vision, psychologists have conducted more research on it than on all the other senses combined. **Vision** lets us sense objects by the light reflected from them into our eyes.

vision The sense that detects objects by the light reflected from them into the eyes.

Light Waves

visible spectrum The portion of the electromagnetic spectrum that we commonly call light.

Light is the common name for the **visible spectrum**, a narrow band of energy within the *electromagnetic spectrum* (depicted in Figure 5-2). The wavelength of light corresponds to its *hue*, the perceptual quality that we call color. The wavelength is the distance between two wave peaks, measured in nanometers (billionths of a meter). Visible light varies in wavelength from about 350 nanometers to about 750 nanometers. A light composed of short wavelengths of light appears violet; a light composed of long wavelengths appears red. We see these wavelengths because we have receptors in our central nervous system that respond to them.

Though people have visual receptors that sense only the visible spectrum, certain animals have visual receptors that detect other forms of electromagnetic energy. Bats, for example, though they rely primarily on echolocation for detecting objects, also have

FIGURE 5-2
The Visible Spectrum

The human eye is sensitive to only a narrow slice (from about 400 to 700 nanometers) of the electromagnetic spectrum. This visible spectrum appears in rainbows, when sunlight is broken into its component wavelengths as it passes through raindrops in the atmosphere.

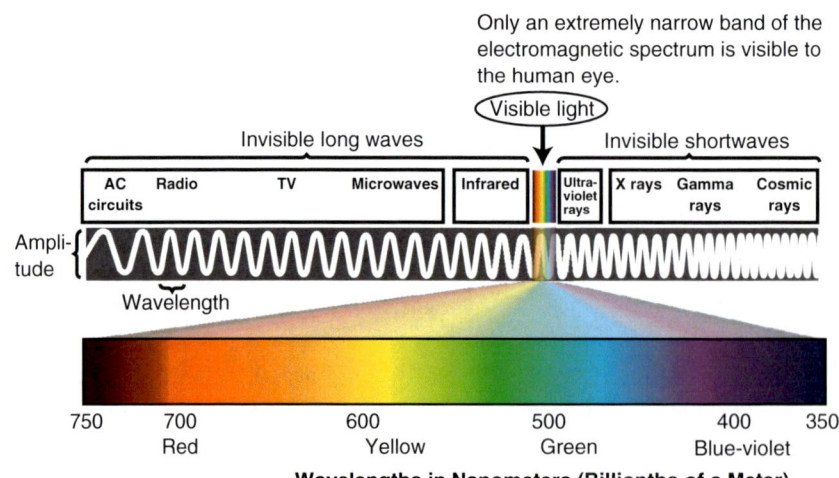

Only an extremely narrow band of the electromagnetic spectrum is visible to the human eye.

Invisible long waves | Visible light | Invisible shortwaves

AC circuits | Radio | TV | Microwaves | Infrared | Ultraviolet rays | X rays | Gamma rays | Cosmic rays

750 Red — 700 — 600 Yellow — 500 Green — 400 Blue-violet — 350

Wavelengths in Nanometers (Billionths of a Meter)

visual receptors that are sensitive to the relatively short wavelengths of ultraviolet light, which affects people chiefly by causing sunburn (Winter, Lopez, & von Helversen, 2003). Pythons have receptors located in pits below their eyes that are sensitive to the relatively long wavelengths of infrared light, which conveys heat. This capability lets them hunt at night by detecting the heat emitted by nearby prey (Grace, Woodward, Church, & Calisch, 2001). Police and soldiers may use special infrared scopes and goggles to provide vision in the dark (Rabin & Wiley, 1994).

Returning to the visible spectrum, the height, or *amplitude*, of light waves determines the perceived intensity, or *brightness*, of a light. When you use a dimmer switch to adjust the brightness of a light bulb, you change the amplitude of the light waves emitted by it. The purity of a light's wavelengths determines its *saturation*, or vividness. The narrower the range of wavelengths, the more saturated the light. A highly saturated red light, for example, would seem "redder" than a less saturated one.

Vision and the Eye

Vision depends on the interaction of the eyes and the brain. The eyes sense light reflected from objects and convey this information to the brain, where visual perception takes place. The eye (see Figure 5-3) is a fluid-filled sphere. The "white" of your eye is a tough membrane called the **sclera**, which protects the eye from injury. At the front of the sclera is the round, transparent **cornea**, which focuses light into the eye. Are you blue-eyed? brown-eyed? green-eyed? Your eye color is determined by the color of your iris, a donut-shaped band of muscles behind the cornea. At the center of the iris is an opening called the pupil. The iris controls the amount of light that enters the eye by regulating the size of the pupil, dilating it to let in more light and constricting it to let in less. Your pupils dilate when you enter a dimly lit room and constrict when you go outside into sunlight.

You can demonstrate the pupillary response to light by first noting the size of your pupils in your bathroom mirror. Next, turn out the light for 30 seconds. Then turn on the light and look in the mirror. Notice how much larger your pupils have become and how quickly they constrict in response to the light.

The size of the pupil also is affected by a variety of psychological factors. When we are psychologically aroused, the sympathetic nervous system makes our pupils dilate. For example, the pupils dilate in response to emotional stimuli. In one study, young adults listened to negative sounds (such as a baby crying), positive sounds (such as a baby laughing), and neutral sounds (such as common office sounds). The participants' pupils became significantly larger in response to the negative and positive sounds than to the neutral sounds (Partala & Surakka, 2003). Because pupil dilation is a sign of emotional arousal, psychotherapists have used it to monitor the effectiveness of therapy, as in the treatment of snake phobia (that is, an intense fear of snakes that interferes with everyday

sclera The tough, white, outer membrane of the eye.

cornea The round, transparent area in the front of the sclera that allows light to enter the eye.

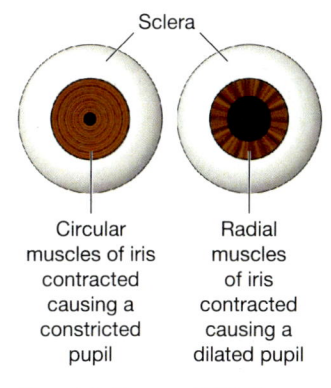

Circular muscles of iris contracted causing a constricted pupil

Radial muscles of iris contracted causing a dilated pupil

Constriction and Dilation of Pupil

The iris adjusts the amount of light entering the pupil by controlling the size of the pupil.

Source: Blamb/Shutterstock.com.

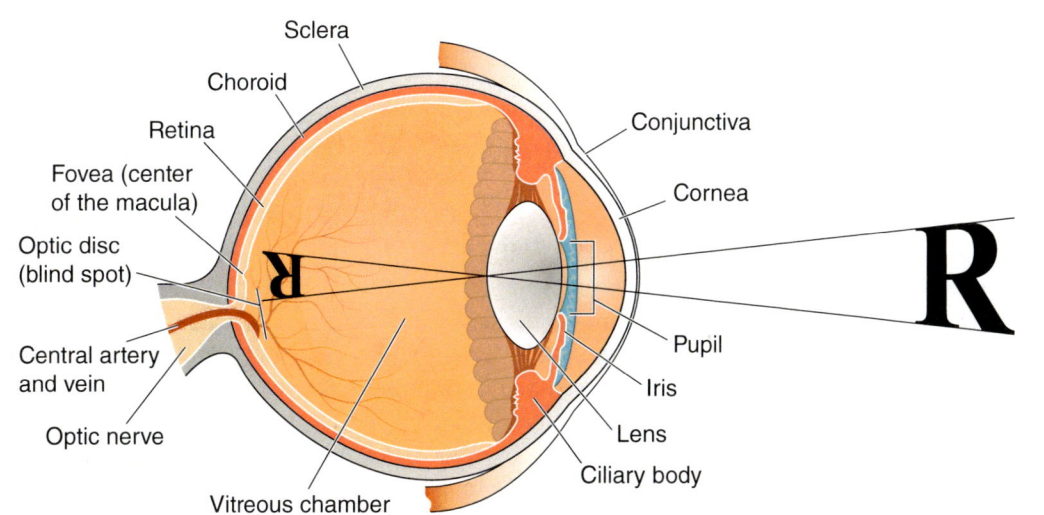

FIGURE 5-3
The Human Eye

The lens (from the Latin word *lentil*) is behind the pupil and focuses light onto the retina in this cross section of the eye. The letter R is in the visual field and is projected upside down onto the retina. Our brain interacts with the visual system and corrects the flip, and we perceive a letter R in front of us.

Source: Blamb/Shutterstock.com.

Chapter 5 Sensation and Perception

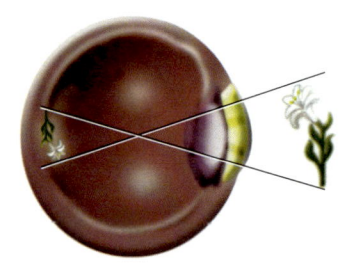

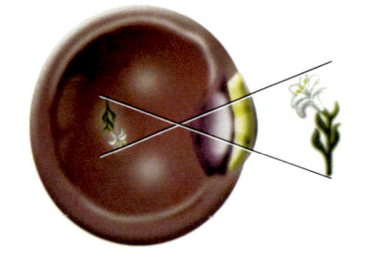

(a) Normal Vision (b) Myopia (c) Hyperopia

FIGURE 5-4 Visual Acuity

(a) In normal vision, the lens clearly focuses images on the retina. *(b)* In myopia, the lens focuses images in front of the retina. *(c)* In hyperopia, the lens focuses images at a point that would fall behind the retina.

lens The transparent structure behind the pupil that focuses light onto the retina.

retina The light-sensitive inner membrane of the eye that contains the receptor cells for vision.

accommodation 1. The cognitive process that revises existing schemas to incorporate new information. 2. The process by which the lens of the eye increases its curvature to focus light from close objects or decreases its curvature to focus light from more distant objects.

myopia Visual nearsightedness, which is caused by an elongated eyeball.

hyperopia Visual farsightedness, which is caused by a shortened eyeball.

rods Receptor cells of the retina that play an important role in night vision and peripheral vision.

cones Receptor cells of the retina that play an important role in day vision and color vision.

optic nerve The nerve, formed from the axons of ganglion cells, that carries visual impulses from the retina to the brain.

functioning). As the participants' anxiety decreases, their pupils dilate less when they look at a snake (Sturgeon, Cooper, & Howell, 1989).

Regardless of the psychological phenomena associated with the pupil, its primary function is to regulate the amount of light that enters the eye. After passing through the pupil, light is focused by the **lens** onto the **retina**, the light-sensitive inner membrane of the eye. Tiny muscles connected to the lens control **accommodation**, the process by which the lens increases its curvature to focus light from close objects or decreases its curvature to focus light from more distant objects. Sustained accommodation, as when working at a computer monitor for a prolonged period, produces accommodation fatigue, which may reduce visual acuity (Hasebe, Graf, & Schor, 2001).

Today we know that the image cast on the retina is upside down. This phenomenon is illustrated in Figures 5-3 and 5-4. In the 15th century, Leonardo da Vinci (1452–1519) had rejected this possibility because he could not explain how the brain saw a right-side-up world from an upside-down image. Why, then, do we not see the world upside down? The neural pathways in the brain simply "flip" the image to make it appear right side up.

Disruption of normal accommodation has important effects. As we age, the lens loses its elasticity, making it less able to accommodate when focusing on near objects. Adults typically discover this in their early 40s, when they find themselves holding books and newspapers at arm's length to focus the print more clearly on their retinas. Many people, whether young or old, have conditions that make them unable to focus clear images on the retina. The two most common conditions are illustrated in Figure 5-4. In **myopia**, or *nearsightedness*, the lens focuses images of near objects on the retina, but focuses images of far objects at a point in front of the retina. In **hyperopia**, or *farsightedness*, the lens focuses images of far objects on the retina, but focuses images of near objects at a point that would fall behind the retina. Both of these conditions often are corrected with prescription eyeglasses or contact lenses.

The Retina

As shown in Figure 5-5, the retina contains specialized neurons called *photoreceptors*, which respond when stimulated by light. There are two kinds of photoreceptors, **rods** and **cones**, whose names reflect their shapes. Each eye has about 120 million rods and about 6 million cones. The rods and cones stimulate *bipolar cells*, which in turn stimulate *ganglion cells*. The axons of the ganglion cells form the **optic nerve** of each eye, which conveys visual information to the brain.

The rods are especially important in night vision and peripheral vision; the cones are especially important in color vision and detailed vision. Rod vision and cone vision depend on different pathways in the brain (Hadjikhani & Tootell, 2000). The rods are more prevalent in the periphery of the retina, and the cones are more prevalent in the center. You can demonstrate this arrangement for yourself by taking small pieces of colored paper and selecting one without looking at it. Hold it beside your head, and slowly move

158 Chapter 5 Sensation and Perception

Structure of the Retina

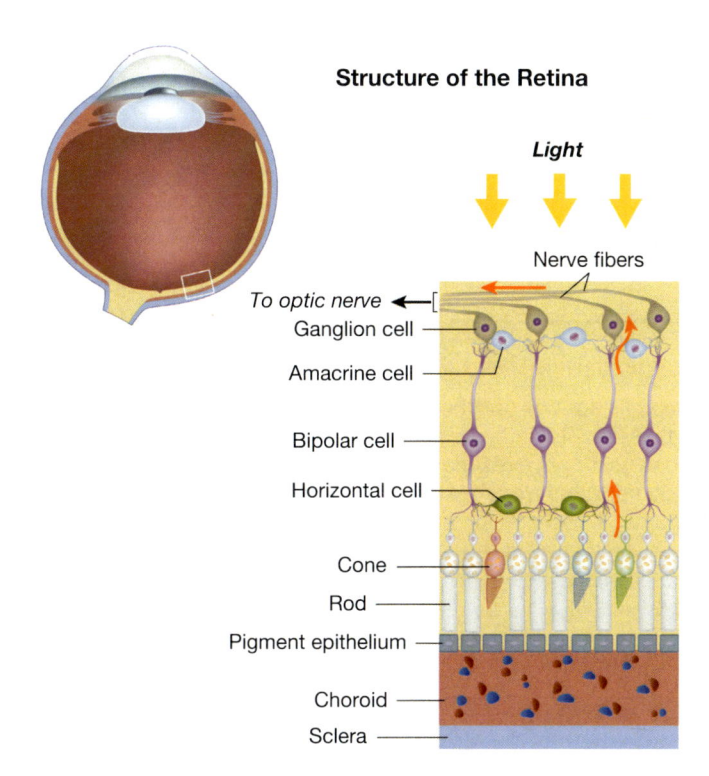

FIGURE 5-5
The Cells of the Retina

Light must first pass through layers of ganglion cells and bipolar cells before striking the rods and cones. The rods and cones transmit neural impulses to the bipolar cells, which in turn transmit neural impulses to the ganglion cells. The axons of the ganglion cells form the optic nerves, which transmit neural impulses to the visual processing areas of the brain.
Source: Alila Medical Media/Shutterstock.com.

it forward while staring straight ahead. Because your peripheral vision depends on your rods and your color vision depends on your cones, you will notice the paper before you can identify its color. Peripheral vision has survival value. For example, we rely on it to help avoid traffic hazards when crossing a street (David, Foot, & Chapman, 1990). Also, since rods are more sensitive to faint light, it is easier to see a faint star in the sky if you look slightly to the side of it instead of directly at it.

A small area in the center of the retina, the **fovea**, contains only cones. One reason why people differ in their visual acuity is that they vary in the number of foveal cones (Curcio, Sloan, Packer, Hendrickson, & Kalina, 1987). Because the fovea provides our most acute vision, we try to focus images on it when we want to see fine details. As you read this sentence, words focused on your cone-rich fovea look clear. Meanwhile, words focused on the cone-poor area around your fovea look blurred. One reason foveal vision is more acute is that each cone transmits neural impulses to one bipolar cell. In other words, the exact retinal site of input from a given cone is communicated along the visual pathway. In contrast, neural impulses from an average of 50–100 rods are sent to a single bipolar cell (Cicerone & Hayhoe, 1990). Thus, the exact retinal site of stimulation of a given rod is lost. But in dim light the many rods sending their output to a given bipolar cell help make rod vision more sensitive than cone vision. A ganglion cell may receive input from many rods and cones in a given area of the retina. The area of the retina that feeds input to a ganglion cell is called its *receptive field*. Some ganglion cells increase their activity when light strikes inside the relevant receptive field and reduce their activity when light strikes outside it. Other ganglion cells increase their firing when light strikes outside the relevant receptive field and reduce their activity when light strikes inside it. This variation in reaction makes the brain especially responsive to differences in adjacent lighter and darker areas, helping it distinguish one object from another by emphasizing each object's borders. Ganglion cells also respond to motion. A particular ganglion cell might respond to motion in a given direction but not in any other direction (Taylor & Vaney, 2003).

The retinal images of the words you read, or of any object on which your eyes are focused, are coded as neural impulses sent to the brain along the optic nerves. In the 17th century, the French scientist Edmé Mariotte demonstrated the existence of the *blind spot*, the point at which the optic nerve leaves the eye (Riggs, 1985). He placed a small disk on a screen, closed one eye, stared at the disk, and moved his head until the image of the

fovea A small area at the center of the retina that contains only cones and provides the most acute vision.

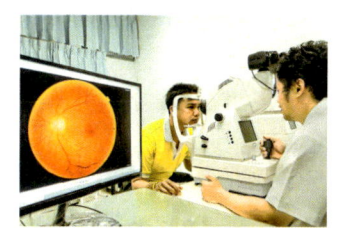

The Fovea

Many ophthalmologists use fundus cameras when conducting eye examinations. These retinal photographs help to monitor, diagnose, and treat eye diseases. The fovea can be seen as a dark orange spot in this image.
Source: Armon Thongkonghan/Shutterstock.com.

Chapter 5 Sensation and Perception   159

FIGURE 5-6 Finding Your Blind Spot

Because your retina has no rods or cones at the point where the optic nerve leaves the eye, the retina is "blind" at that spot. To find your blind spot, keep your eyes about an arm's length away from the figure, close your right eye, and focus your left eye on the black dot. Move your head slowly toward the figure. When your head is about a foot away, the image of the mouse should disappear. It disappears when it becomes focused on your blind spot. You do not normally notice your blind spot because your eyes see different views of the same scene, because your eyes constantly focus on different parts of the scene, and because your brain fills in the missing portion of the scene.

disk disappeared. It disappeared when it fell on the blind spot. The blind spot is "blind" because it contains no rods or cones. We do not normally notice the blind spot because the visual system fills in the missing area (Lou & Chen, 2003). To repeat Mariotte's demonstration, follow the procedure suggested in Figure 5-6.

Eye Movements

smooth pursuit movements Eye movements controlled by the ocular muscles that keep objects focused on the fovea.

We use **smooth pursuit movements** to keep moving objects focused on the foveae. One of the dangers of drinking and driving is that alcohol disrupts the ocular muscles, which control smooth pursuit movements (Freivalds & Horii, 1994). The "Psychology versus Common Sense" box illustrates how scientists studied these movements in testing commonsense belief about hitting a baseball.

Vision and the Brain

optic chiasm The point under the frontal lobes at which some axons from each of the optic nerves cross over to the opposite side of the brain.

visual cortex The area of the occipital lobes that processes visual input.

Figure 5-7 traces the path of neural impulses from the eyeballs into the brain. The optic nerves travel under the frontal lobes of the brain and meet at a point called the **optic chiasm**. At the optic chiasm in people, axons from the half of each optic nerve toward the nose cross to the opposite side of the brain. Axons from the half of each optic nerve nearer the ears travel to the same side of the brain as they began on. Some axons of the optic nerves go to the specialized neurons in the brain that control visual reflexes like blinking. Most axons of the optic nerves go to the *thalamus* (see Chapter 3), which transmits visual information to the **visual cortex** of the *occipital lobes*. Retinal information about objects in the right visual field is processed in the left occipital lobe, and retinal information about objects in the left visual field is processed in the right occipital lobe. The visual cortex integrates visual information about objects, including their shape (Buechel, Price, Frackowiak, & Friston, 1998) and distance (Dobbins, Jeo, Fiser, & Allman, 1998) as well as their color (Engel, 1999), brightness (Rossi, Rittenhouse, & Paradiso, 1996), and movement (Moore & Engel, 1999). Functional MRI has shown that particular regions of the visual cortex also display distinctive patterns of activity in response to particular categories of objects, such as faces, houses, and chairs (Ishai, Ungerleider, Martin, & Haxby, 2000).

Basic Visual Processes

photopigments Chemicals, including rhodopsin and iodopsin, that enable the rods and cones to generate neural impulses.

People with normal vision can see because of processes taking place in their retinas. Visual sensations depend on chemicals called **photopigments**. Rod vision depends on the photopigment *rhodopsin*, and cone vision depends on three kinds of photopigments called *iodopsin*. Until the late 19th century, when the role of photopigments was first discovered,

Chapter 5 Sensation and Perception

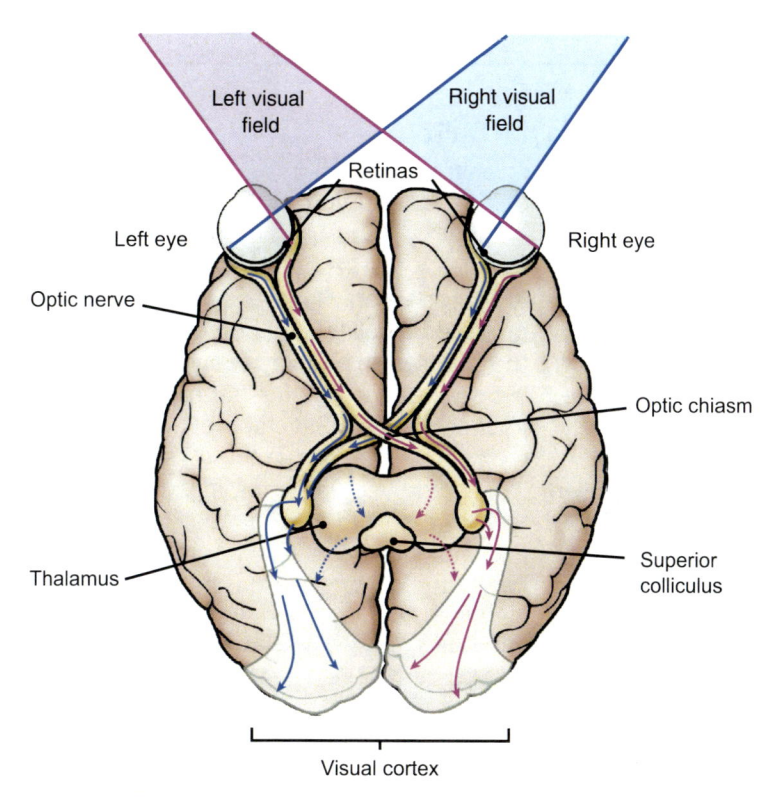

FIGURE 5-7 The Visual Pathway

This illustration of a horizontal section of the brain shows that images of objects in the right visual field are focused on the left side of each retina, and images of objects in the left visual field are focused on the right side of each retina. This information is conveyed along the optic nerves to the optic chiasm and then on to the thalamus. The thalamus then relays the information to the visual cortex of the occipital lobes. Because of the nature of the visual pathway, images of objects in the right visual field are processed by the left occipital lobe, and images of the objects in the left visual field are processed by the right occipital lobe. Also note that a secondary visual pathway goes to the superior colliculus, a structure that contributes to visual reflexes, such as blinking when an object rapidly approaches your eyes.

prominent scientists, including Thomas Young, claimed that vision depended on light rays striking the retina, making the optic nerves vibrate (Riggs, 1985).

Today we know that when light strikes the rods or cones, it breaks down their photopigments. This breakdown begins the process by which neural impulses are eventually sent along the optic nerves to the brain. After being broken down by light, the photopigments are resynthesized—more rapidly in dim light than in bright light. The cones function better than the rods in normal light, but the rods function better than the cones in dim light. Because of this difference, in normal light we try to focus fine details on the fovea. But if you were to look directly at a star in the night sky, you would be unable to see it because it would be focused on the fovea. To see the star, you would have to turn your head slightly, thereby focusing the star on the rod-rich periphery of the retina. The photoreceptors are also important in the processes of *dark adaptation* and *color vision*.

Dark Adaptation

When you enter a darkened movie theater, you have difficulty finding a seat because your photoreceptors have been bleached of their photopigments by the light in the lobby. But your eyes adapt by increasing their rate of synthesis of iodopsin and rhodopsin, gradually increasing your ability to see the seats and people in the theater. The cones reach their maximum sensitivity after about 10 minutes of dim light. But your rods continue to adapt to the dim light, reaching their maximum sensitivity in about 30 minutes. So, you owe your ability to see in dim light to your rods. **Dark adaptation** is the process by which the

dark adaptation The process by which the eyes become more sensitive to light when under low illumination.

Chapter 5 Sensation and Perception

Psychology versus Common Sense

Can Baseball Batters Really Keep Their Eyes on the Ball?

Professional athletes make faster smooth pursuit eye movements than amateurs do (Harbin, Durst, & Harbin, 1989). This characteristic is important because, for example, a professional baseball batter might have to track a baseball thrown by a pitcher at more than 90 miles an hour from a distance of only 60 feet. Ted Williams, arguably the greatest hitter in the history of baseball, called hitting a baseball the most difficult single task in any sport. Given this difficulty, is there any scientific support for the commonsense suggestion to batters, "Keep your eye on the ball"? Take a look at a study by Terry Bahill and Tom LaRitz (1984), of the University of Arizona, in which they sought the answer to this question. Bahill and LaRitz rigged a device that propelled a ball toward home plate along a string at up to 100 miles an hour on a consistent path. A photoelectric device recorded the batter's eye movements as he tracked the ball. Several professional baseball players took part in the study.

Eye-movement recordings indicated that the batters were able to track the ball until it was about 5 feet from home plate. Over the last few feet they could not keep the ball focused on their foveae—it simply traveled too fast over those last few degrees of visual arc. Thus, the commonsense advice to keep your eye on the ball is well intentioned, but it is impossible to follow the ball's movement all the way from the pitcher's hand to home plate. The reason some hitters, including Ted Williams, claim they can see the ball strike the bat is that, based on their extensive experience in batting, their brains automatically calculate both the speed and the trajectory of the ball. This calculation allows them to anticipate the point in space at which the bat will meet the ball and make a final eye movement to that exact point. Years later Bahill likewise presented research evidence contradicting the commonsense belief that fastballs can "rise" (Bahill & Karnavas, 1993). To baseball players, as well as other people, "seeing is believing." Nonetheless, scientists insist that objective evidence from research is superior to common sense as a source of knowledge.

Keeping Your Eye on the Ball

The commonsense idea that batters can "keep their eye on the ball" is contradicted by scientific research. Professional hitters anticipate the point in space where the bat will meet the ball and make a final eye movement to that point.
Source: Peter Kim/Shutterstock.com.

---

eyes become more sensitive to light. Impaired dark adaptation, which accompanies aging (Jackson, Owsley, & McGwin, 1999), has been implicated in the disproportionate number of nighttime driving accidents that involve older adults. Dark adaptation also explains why motorists should dim their high beams when approaching oncoming traffic and why passengers should not turn on the dome light to read maps. High beams shining into the eyes or dome lights illuminating the inside of the vehicle bleach the rods, impairing the driver's ability to see objects that might be ahead. You also should note that the cones are most sensitive to the longer wavelengths of the visible spectrum (which produce the experience of red) and the rods are most sensitive to the medium wavelengths (which produce the experience of green). This fact explains why at dusk (when we shift from cone vision to rod vision) a red jacket looks dull while a patch of green grass looks vibrant.

Color Vision

Color enhances the quality of our lives, as manifested by our concern with the colors of our clothing, furnishings, and automobiles. Color also contributes to our survival, as exemplified by the orange or yellow life rafts used at sea that make search and rescue easier (Donderi, 1994). Primates such as apes, monkeys, and people have good color vision because they have three types of cones. Most other mammals, including dogs, cats, and

A *Green* Fire Truck?

Because the rods are more sensitive to the green region of the visible spectrum than to the red region, green objects look brighter than red objects in dim light. As a result, though red fire trucks look bright in the daylight, they look grayish in dim light. This finding has prompted some fire departments to increase the evening visibility of their vehicles by painting them a yellowish green color.
Source: Gary Paul Lewis/Shutterstock.com.

cows, have poor color vision. They lack a sufficient number or variety of cones. Most birds and fish have good color vision. But fish that live in the dark depths of the ocean lack color vision, which would be useless to them because cones function well only in bright light (Levine & MacNichol, 1982).

Theories of Color Vision What processes account for color vision? One answer was offered in 1802 when British physicist Thomas Young presented the **trichromatic theory** of color vision, which was championed in the 1850s by German scientist Hermann von Helmholtz (1821–1894). Helmholtz's theories continue to influence research on the senses. Young and Helmholtz found that red, green, and blue lights could be mixed into any color, leading them to conclude that the brain pools the input of three receptors. Today the trichromatic theory is also called the *Young-Helmholtz theory*. It assumes that the retina has three kinds of receptors (which we now know are cones), each of which is maximally sensitive to red, green, or blue light (Chichilnisky & Wandell, 1999).

A century after Helmholtz put forth his theory, George Wald (1964) provided evidence for it in research that earned him a Nobel Prize. Wald found that some cones respond maximally to red light, others to green light, and still others to blue light. The colors we experience depend on the relative degree of stimulation of the cones. Figure 5-8 illustrates the principles of mixing colored lights and mixing colored pigments, which differ from each other. Mixing colored lights is an additive process: Wavelengths added together stimulate more cones. For example, mixing red light and green light produces yellow. Mixing pigments is a subtractive process: Pigments mixed together absorb more wavelengths than does a single pigment. For example, mixing blue paint and yellow paint subtracts those colors and leaves green to be reflected into the eyes. More recent research has lent support to the trichromatic theory (Jacobs, Neitz, Deegan, & Neitz, 1996).

In the 1870s, the German physiologist Ewald Hering (1834–1918) proposed an alternative explanation of color vision (Hurvich, 1969), the **opponent-process theory**. He did

trichromatic theory The theory that color vision depends on the relative degree of stimulation of red, green, and blue receptors.

opponent-process theory
1. The theory that color vision depends on red-green, blue-yellow, and black-white opponent processes in the brain.
2. The theory that the brain counteracts a strong positive or negative emotion by evoking an opposite emotional response.

FIGURE 5-8
The Three Primary Colors of Light

By mixing the three primary colors of light—red, green, and blue—you can create any color. For example, mixing red and green produces yellow, and mixing all three together produces white.

Chapter 5 Sensation and Perception 163

afterimage An image that persists after the removal of a visual stimulus.

so in part to explain the phenomenon of color **afterimages**—images that persist after the removal of a visual stimulus. If you stare at a red or blue surface for a minute and then stare at a white surface, you will see an afterimage that is the complementary color. For example, staring at red will produce a green afterimage, and staring at blue will produce a yellow afterimage. See Figure 5-9 for a demonstration of an afterimage.

The opponent-process theory assumes that there are *red-green*, *blue-yellow*, and *black-white* opponent processes (with the black-white opponent process determining the lightness or darkness of what we see). Stimulation of one process inhibits its opponent. When stimulation stops, the inhibition is removed and the complementary color is seen as a brief afterimage. This theory explains why staring at red leads to a green afterimage and staring at blue leads to a yellow afterimage. It also explains why we cannot perceive reddish greens or bluish yellows: Complementary colors cannot be experienced simultaneously because each inhibits the other.

Psychologist Russell de Valois and his colleagues (de Valois, Abramov, & Jacobs, 1966) provided evidence that supports the opponent-process theory. For example, certain ganglion cells in the retina and certain cells in the thalamus send impulses when the cones that send them input are stimulated by red and stop sending impulses when the cones that send them input are stimulated by the complementary color, green. Other ganglion cells and cells in the thalamus send impulses when the cones that send them input are stimulated by green and stop sending impulses when the cones that send them input are stimulated by red.

color blindness The inability to distinguish between certain colors, most often red and green.

Color Deficiency The opponent-process theory also explains another phenomenon that the trichromatic theory cannot explain by itself: **color blindness**. People with full color vision are *trichromats*—they have three kinds of iodopsin (red, blue, and green). Most people with color blindness are *dichromats*—they have a normal number of cones but lack one kind of iodopsin (Shevell & He, 1997). The most common form of color blindness is the inability to distinguish between red and green. People with red-green color blindness have cones with blue iodopsin, but their red and green cones have the same iodopsin, usually green. Because many people suffer from red-green color blindness, traffic lights always have the red light on top so that people with red-green color blindness will know when to stop and when to go. Figure 5-10 presents an example of one of the ways of testing for color blindness, the Ishihara color test (Birch, 1997). Interestingly, special lenses developed for medical professionals to view the blood vessels of the eye have demonstrated a potential use for treating color blindness. These lenses amplify the

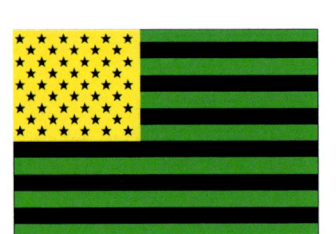

FIGURE 5-9 Color Afterimages

If you stare at this image for a minute and then stare at a white surface (such as a sheet of printer paper), you will see an afterimage in which the flag appears in familiar colors—red, white, and blue. This color afterimage comprises colors that are complementary to the ones in the original image.

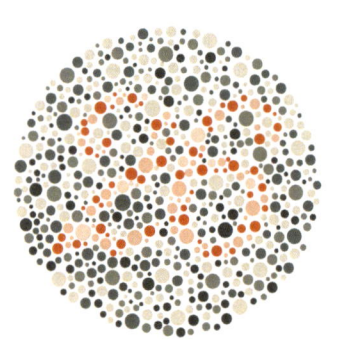

FIGURE 5-10 Color Deficiency

This figure provides an informal test for red-green color blindness. A person with red-green color blindness would not be able to read the number (26) contained in this design. Instead, he or she would see only scattered dots of different sizes. These reproduced figures are not appropriate for clinical use and only original plates with a qualified medical professional should be used for testing red-green color blindness.

Chapter 5 Sensation and Perception

weak red-green sensitivity, allowing individuals with certain color blindness to distinguish colors for the first time.

Color blindness is a *sex-linked trait*. Genes on the sex chromosomes control the expression of sex-linked traits. Because color blindness is a recessive trait carried on the X chromosome, men are more likely than women to be color-blind. Approximately 1 in 15 men are color-blind (Bowmaker 1998). For traits carried on the X chromosome, a woman would inherit two genes (one on each X chromosome) controlling the trait. Men, because they have only one X chromosome, inherit a single gene controlling the trait. The Y chromosome is small relative to the X chromosome and lacks the gene controlling this trait. A woman must inherit two recessive genes to be color-blind. If a man inherits only one recessive gene on his single X chromosome, he will be color-blind. Few dichromats have blue-yellow color blindness. And even fewer people are *monochromats*—completely color-blind.

But how does color blindness support the opponent-process theory? It does so because, though dichromats cannot distinguish between the complementary colors of red and green or blue and yellow, they never fail to distinguish between red and blue, red and yellow, green and blue, or green and yellow. Today the trichromatic theory and the opponent-process theory are combined in explaining color vision this way (Boynton, 1988): Impulses from the red, green, and blue cones of the retina are sent to the opponent-process ganglion cells and then further integrated in the thalamus and visual cortex.

Section Review: Visual Sensation

1. What structures do light waves pass through on their way from the cornea to the retina?
2. What is the trichromatic theory of color vision?

Visual Perception

Visual sensations provide the raw materials that are organized into meaningful patterns by *visual perception*. Do we have to learn through experience to convert sensations into accurate perceptions? This is the basic assumption of the *constructionist theory* of Hermann von Helmholtz. Or, instead, does visual perception depend mainly on inborn mechanisms that automatically convert sensations into perceptions of stimuli? This is the basic assumption of the *direct perception theory* of James J. Gibson (1904–1979). According to Gibson (1979), evolution has endowed us with brain mechanisms that create perceptions directly from information provided by the sense organs. Thus, we do not need to rely on experience to help us perceive this information properly (Nakayama, 1994). Research, discussed in Chapter 4, on the sophisticated inborn perceptual abilities of newborn infants supports Gibson's theory. But most perception researchers believe that we "construct" our perceptions based on what Helmholtz called *unconscious inferences* that we make from our sensations (Wagemans et al., 2012a). These inferences are based on our experience with objects in the physical environment.

Form Perception

To perceive *forms* (meaningful shapes or patterns), we typically must distinguish a figure (an object) from its *ground* (its surroundings), though there is some evidence that form perception can precede the segmentation into figure and ground (Peterson & Gibson, 1994).

Figure-Ground Perception
Research on the monkey visual cortex has found cells that respond more to a stimulus when it is perceived as a figure than to a stimulus when it is perceived as a ground (Lamme,

figure-ground perception The distinguishing of an object (the figure) from its surroundings (the ground).

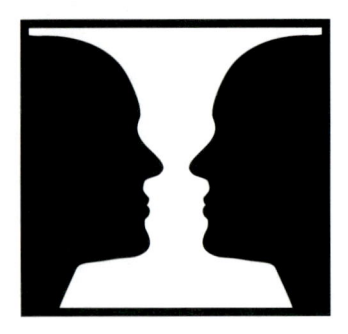

FIGURE 5-11
Figure-Ground Perception

As you view this picture, you will see that it seems to reverse. At one moment you see a vase, and at the next moment you see the profiles of two faces. What you see depends on what you perceive as figure and what you perceive as ground.

1995). Gestalt psychologist Edgar Rubin (1886–1951) called this process **figure-ground perception**. The words on this page are figures against the ground of the white paper. Gestalt psychologists stress that form perception is an active rather than a passive process. Your expectancies might affect what you see in an ambiguous figure, for example (Davis, Schiffman, & Greis-Bousquet, 1990). If you first were shown pictures of pottery and then were shown Figure 5-11, you would be more likely to perceive a vase; if you first were shown pictures of faces, you would be more likely to perceive two profiles. The idea that our expectations impose themselves on sensations to form perceptions (so-called *top-down processing*) runs counter to the idea that we construct our perceptions strictly by mechanically combining sensations (so-called *bottom-up processing*). In fact, participants do not spontaneously reverse ambiguous figures. They must have experience with reversible figures or be informed that the figures are reversible before they will reverse them (Rock, Gopnik, & Hall, 1994). There is evidence that top-down and bottom-up processes interact in producing figure-ground perception (Wagemans et al., 2012b).

Gestalt Principles

Gestalt psychologists, including Max Wertheimer, Kurt Koffka, and Wolfgang Köhler, were the first to study the principles that govern form perception. Research has shown that these principles are more relevant to perceiving complex figures (Gillam, 1992). The principle of *proximity* states that stimuli that are close together tend to be perceived as parts of the same form. The principle of *closure* states that we tend to fill in gaps in forms. The principle of *similarity* states that stimuli similar to one another tend to be perceived as parts of the same form. And the principle of *continuity* states that we tend to group stimuli into forms that follow continuous lines or patterns. These principles are illustrated in Figure 5-12. The principles only recently have been subjected to experimental research, with initial support for the role of similarity, continuity, and proximity in grouping stimuli into coherent patterns (Pomerantz & Portillo, 2011).

According to Gestalt psychologists, forms are perceived as wholes rather than as combinations of features (Westheimer, 1999). This might prompt you to recall the famous Gestalt saying, mentioned in Chapter 1, that "the whole is different from the sum of its parts." Thus, in Figure 5-13 you see an image of a giraffe rather than a bunch of black marks.

FIGURE 5-12
Gestalt Principles of Form Perception

These patterns illustrate the roles of *(a)* closure, *(b)* proximity, *(c)* similarity, and *(d)* continuity in form perception.

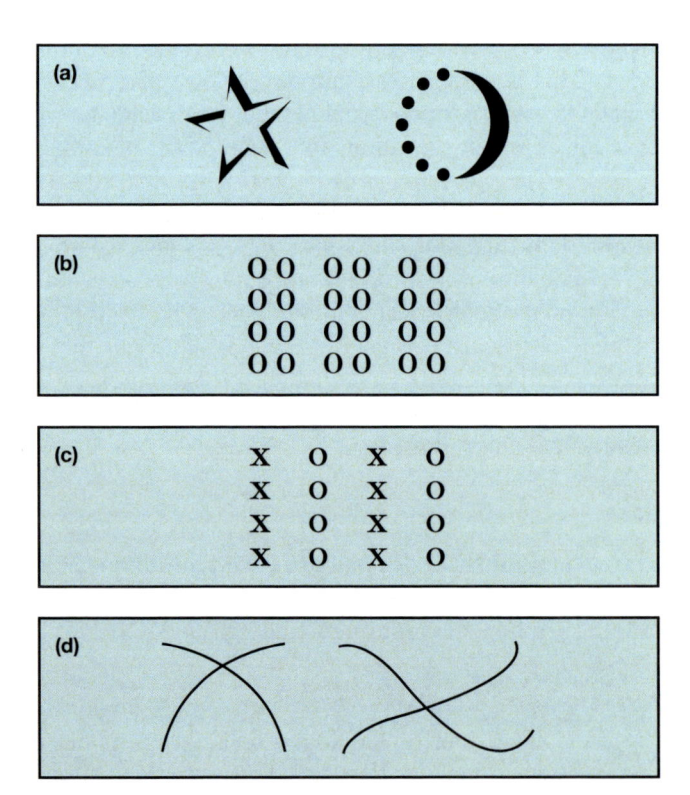

To a Gestalt psychologist, you see a picture of a giraffe instead of a random grouping of black marks (bottom-up processing) because your brain, based on your experience seeing real giraffes and pictures of giraffes, imposes organization on what it perceives (top-down processing). A person who has never seen a picture of a giraffe might fail to perceive the marks as a meaningful form. How does your perception of the giraffe depend on each of the Gestalt principles of similarity, proximity, closure, and continuity?

Feature Analysis

Though some research findings support the Gestalt position that forms are perceived holistically (Wagemans et al., 2012b), other research findings suggest that forms can be perceived through the analysis of their features (Oden, 1984). Consider the letter A. Do we perceive it holistically as a single form or analytically as a combination of lines of various lengths and angles? Gestalt psychologists would assume that we perceive it holistically. But the **feature-detector theory** of David Hubel and Torsten Wiesel (1979) assumes that we construct it from its components. Hubel and Wiesel base their theory on studies in which they implanted microelectrodes into single cells of the visual cortex of cats and then presented the cats with lines of various sizes, orientations, and locations. Certain cells responded to specific features of images on the retina, such as a line of a certain length, a line at a certain angle, or a line in a particular location. Hubel and Wiesel concluded that we construct our visual perceptions from activity in such feature-detector cells. For their efforts, Hubel and Wiesel won a Nobel Prize in 1981. More recent studies indicate that whereas some *feature-detector cells* respond to component features of forms, others respond to whole forms (Wenderoth, 1994). Other neurons combine input from feature detectors into more complex patterns, such as letters, faces, or objects. Figure 5-14 illustrates Hubel and Wiesel's procedure for identifying feature-detector cells in the visual cortex.

Some feature-detector cells in the visual cortex respond to remarkably specific combinations of features. Feature-detector cells in the visual cortex even provide an anatomical basis for the **illusory contours** shown in Figure 5-15 because the cells respond to nonexistent contours as if they were the edges of real objects (Pan et al., 2012).

Depth Perception

If we lived in a two-dimensional world, form perception would be sufficient. Because we live in a three-dimensional world, we have evolved **depth perception**—the ability to judge the distance of objects.

Given that images on the retina (such as the image of a helicopter landing pad) are two-dimensional, how can we perceive depth? That is, how can we determine the distance of an object (the *distal stimulus*) from the pattern of stimulation on our retinas (the *proximal stimulus*)? Researchers in the tradition of Helmholtz's constructionist theory maintain that depth perception depends on the use of *binocular cues* (which require two eyes) and *monocular cues* (which require one eye).

Binocular Depth Cues

The two kinds of **binocular cues** involve the interaction of both eyes. A study of accidents involving Canadian taxi drivers found that those with binocular depth perception problems tended to be involved in more crashes than those without such problems (Maag, Vanasse, Dionne, & Laberge-Nadeau, 1997).

One binocular cue is *binocular disparity*, the degree of difference between the images of an object that are focused on the two retinas. The closer the object, the greater the binocular disparity. To demonstrate binocular disparity for yourself, point a forefinger vertically between your eyes. Look at the finger with one eye closed. Then look at it with the other closed. You will notice that the background shifts as you view the scene with different eyes. This demonstration shows that the two eyes provide different views of the same stimulus. The "Viewmaster" device, a stereoscopic toy common in the 1960s and 1970s, creates the impression of visual depth by presenting slightly different images to

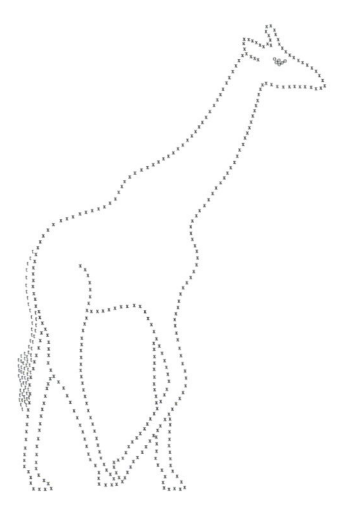

FIGURE 5-13
The Whole Is Different from the Sum of Its Parts

According to Gestalt psychologists, you see a picture of a giraffe instead of a random grouping of marks because your brain imposes organization on what it perceives. Your perception of the giraffe depends on the Gestalt principles of similarity, proximity, closure, and continuity. As discussed later in this chapter, your perception of the giraffe also depends on your prior experience. A person from a culture unfamiliar with giraffes might fail to perceive the dots as a meaningful form.

feature-detector theory The theory that we construct perceptions of stimuli from activity in neurons of the brain that are sensitive to specific features of those stimuli.

illusory contours The perception of nonexistent contours as if they were the edges of real objects.

depth perception The perception of the relative distance of objects.

binocular cues Depth perception cues that require input from the two eyes.

Chapter 5 Sensation and Perception 167

FIGURE 5-14
Feature Detectors

David Hubel and Torsten Wiesel implanted microelectrodes in the visual cortex of cats. The scientists found that specific cells responded to lines with certain features, such as lines that were tilted at a particular angle. An oscilloscope, a device used to display varying levels of electric potentials measured in voltages, was used to display increases in the activity of these feature-detector cells.

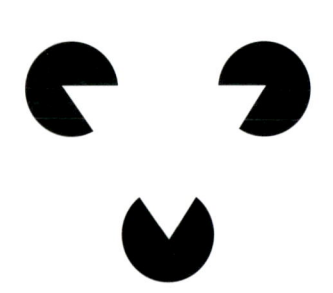

FIGURE 5-15
Illusory Contours

Seeing a complete triangle when only its corners are displayed is an example of the Gestalt principle of closure. Feature-detector cells in the visual cortex respond to such illusory contours as if they were real. This finding supports the Gestalt position that the brain imposes organization on stimuli.
Source: Based on an image from the Wikimedia Commons: Kanizsa, G. (1955).

monocular cues Depth perception cues that require input from only one eye.

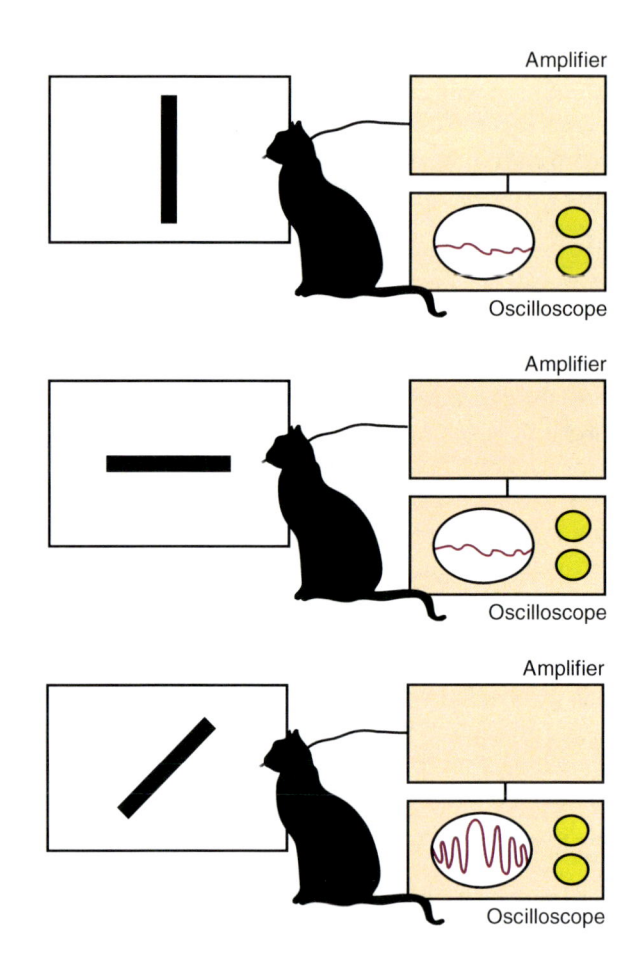

the eyes at the same time—mimicking binocular disparity. Binocular disparity is greater when an object is near you than when it is farther away from you. Certain cells in the visual cortex detect the degree of binocular disparity, which the brain uses to estimate the distance of an object focused on the retinas (Minnini, Parker, & Bridge, 2010).

The second binocular cue to depth is *convergence*, the degree to which the eyes turn inward to focus on an object. As you can confirm for yourself, the closer the object, the greater the convergence of the eyes. Hold a forefinger vertically in front of your face and move it toward your nose. You should notice an increase in ocular muscle tension as your finger approaches your nose. Neurons in the cerebral cortex translate the amount of muscle tension into an estimate of the distance of your finger (Takagi, Yoshizawa, & Hara, 1992). Using a computer monitor for hours can induce eye fatigue caused by continuous convergence (Watten, Lie, & Birketvedt, 1994).

Monocular Depth Cues

There are many more monocular cues than binocular cues. **Monocular cues** require only one eye, so even people who have lost the sight in one eye still can have good depth perception. One monocular cue is *accommodation* (Meehan & Day, 1995), which, as explained earlier, is the change in the shape of the lens to help focus the image of an object on the retina. Specialized brain neurons respond so that the greater the accommodation of the lens, the closer the object appears (Judge & Cumming, 1986).

A second monocular cue is *motion parallax*, the tendency to perceive ourselves as passing objects faster when they are closer to us than when they are farther away. This phenomenon occurs because when you fix your eyes on the horizon, images of objects that are close to you move across your retinas faster than do images of objects that are far away from you (McDougal, Crowe, & Holland, 2003). Animal research indicates that particular brain cells might respond to motion parallax. For example, the pigeon's brain has specialized cells that code motion parallax (Xiao & Frost, 2013).

The remaining monocular cues are often called *pictorial cues* (see Figure 5-16) because artists use them to create depth in their drawings and paintings. They include occlusion, relative size, linear perspective, elevation, shading patterns, aerial perspective, and texture gradient. The ability of infants to make use of pictorial cues, such as linear perspective and texture gradient, appears at 22 to 28 weeks of age (Kavšek, Yonas, & Granrud, 2012).

Leonardo da Vinci formalized pictorial cues in the 15th century in teaching his students how to use them to make their paintings look more realistic (Haber, 1980). He noted that an object that overlaps another object will appear closer, a cue called occlusion (Anderson, 2003). Because your psychology professor overlaps the blackboard or whiteboard, you know she or he is closer to you than the board. Comparing the relative size of familiar objects also provides a cue to their distance (Higashiyama & Kitano, 1991). If you know that two people are about the same height and one casts a smaller image on your retina, you will perceive that person as farther away.

You probably have noticed that parallel objects, such as railroad tracks, seem to get closer together as they get farther away (and farther apart as they get closer). This pictorial cue is called *linear perspective*. During World War II, naval aviation cadets flying at night sometimes crashed into airplanes ahead of them, apparently because of a failure to judge the distance of those planes. Taking advantage of linear perspective solved the problem. Two taillights set a standard distance apart replaced the traditional single taillight. As a result, when pilots noticed that the taillights of an airplane appeared to move farther apart, they realized that they were getting closer to it (Fiske, Conley, & Goldberg, 1987). Figure 5-17 shows another example of linear perspective.

An object's *elevation* provides another cue to its distance. Objects that are higher in your visual field seem to be farther away. If you paint a picture, you can create depth by placing more distant objects higher on the canvas. *Shading patterns* provide cues to distance because we tend to assume that light is striking objects from above (Lovell, Bloj, & Harris, 2012) and areas in shadow tend to recede, whereas areas in light tend to stand out. Painters use shading to make balls, balloons, and oranges appear round. *Aerial perspective* refers to the fact that objects that are closer to us seem clearer than more distant ones. A distant mountain will look hazier than a near one (O'Shea, Govan, & Sekuler, 1997).

The final monocular cue, the *texture gradient*, affects depth perception because the nearer an object, the more details we can make out, and the farther an object, the fewer details we can make out. When you look across a field, you can see every blade of grass near you, but only an expanse of green far away from you. Recent research has identified particular cortical neurons that respond to the texture gradient (Tsutsui, Sakata, Naganuma, & Taira, 2002).

Perceptual Constancies

The image of a given object focused on your retina may vary in size, shape, and brightness. Yet, because of *perceptual constancy*, you will continue to perceive the object as stable in size, shape, and brightness. There is evidence that size and shape constancy are present at birth (Slater, 1992). Perceptual constancy is adaptive because it provides you with a more visually stable world, making it easier for you to function in it.

Size Constancy

Size constancy is the perceptual process that makes an object appear to remain the same size despite changes in the size of the image it casts on the retina. The size of the object on your retina does not, by itself, tell you how far away it is. As an object gets farther away from you, it produces a smaller image on your retina. If you know the actual size of an object, size constancy makes you interpret a change in its retinal size as a change in its distance rather than as a change in its size. When you see a car a block away, it does not seem smaller than one that is half a block away, even though the more distant car produces a smaller image on your retina. Size constancy can be disrupted by alcohol. In one study, young adults drank alcohol and then were asked to estimate the size of an object. They consistently underestimated its size. Disruption of size constancy might be

size constancy The perceptual process that makes an object appear to remain the same size despite changes in the size of the image it casts on the retina.

(a) (b) (c) (d) (e) (f)

FIGURE 5-16 Pictorial Cues to Depth

Artists make use of pictorial cues to portray depth in their drawings and paintings. These cues include *(a)* occlusion, *(b)* aerial perspective, *(c)* linear perspective, *(d)* texture gradient, *(e)* elevation, and *(f)* shading patterns.

Sources: (a) Dmitrydesign/Shutterstock.com. *(b)* behindlens/Shutterstock.com. *(c)* Viktor Gladkov/Shutterstock.com. *(d)* Haryadi CH/Shutterstock.com. *(e)* littlewormy/Shutterstock.com. *(f)* salajean/Shutterstock.com.

FIGURE 5-17
Linear Perspective from the Driver's Seat

Linear perspective is an important factor in everyday depth perception, as when you are determining the distance of a vehicle that you are following at night. As the two taillights of the vehicle you are following appear to move farther apart, you perceive yourself as getting closer to the vehicle. In contrast, as the two taillights appear to move closer together, you perceive yourself as getting farther from the vehicle.
Source: Brian A. Jackson/Shutterstock.com.

one way in which alcohol intoxication promotes automobile accidents (Farrimond, 1990). This should be a reminder that driving under the influence is dangerous.

Shape Constancy

Shape constancy ensures that an object of known shape will appear to maintain its normal shape regardless of the angle from which you view it. Pick up a book and hold it at various orientations relative to your line of sight. Unless you look directly at the cover when it is on a plane perpendicular to your line of vision, it will never cast a rectangular image on your retinas, yet you will continue to perceive it as rectangular. Shape constancy occurs because your brain compensates for the slant of an object relative to your line of sight (Wallach & Marshall, 1986).

Shape constancy is subject to top-down processes in that viewers' expectations can affect it. This effect is especially true for young children, as in a study in which 4- to 7-year-old children viewed a luminous circular disc oriented at a slant and presented in a darkened chamber. The children tended to overestimate the circularity of the disc when they knew the object was really a circle. This effect was greater in the younger children. In contrast, children who viewed an identical shape that they knew was an actual ellipse did not overestimate its circularity. Thus, the children's expectations affected their perception of the figure (Mitchell & Taylor, 1999).

shape constancy The perceptual process that makes an object appear to maintain its normal shape regardless of the angle from which it is viewed.

Brightness Constancy

Though the amount of light reflected from a given object can vary, we perceive the object as having a constant brightness. This phenomenon is called **brightness constancy**. A white shirt appears equally bright in dim light or bright light, and a black shirt appears equally dull in dim light or bright light. But brightness constancy is relative to other objects. If you look at a white shirt in dim light in the presence of nonwhite objects in the same light, it will maintain its brightness. But if you look at the white shirt by itself, perhaps by viewing a large area of it through a hollow tube, it will appear dull in dim light and brighter in sunlight.

brightness constancy The perceptual process that makes an object maintain a particular level of brightness despite changes in the amount of light reflected from it.

Visual Illusions

You may have heard of so-called antigravity hills, which have been the subject of sensationalized media coverage. An antigravity hill is a short stretch of road, away from buildings, and surrounded by low-lying hills. When a car is put into neutral at one of these

Chapter 5 Sensation and Perception

FIGURE 5-18
The Ponzo Illusion

Though the two horizontal lines are the same length in both *(a)* and *(b)*, the line that appears more distant appears longer. These illusions are the product of our perceptual assumption that if a more distant object produces the same size image on our retinas as a closer object, then the more distant object must be larger.
Source: (b) kenkistler/Shutterstock.com.

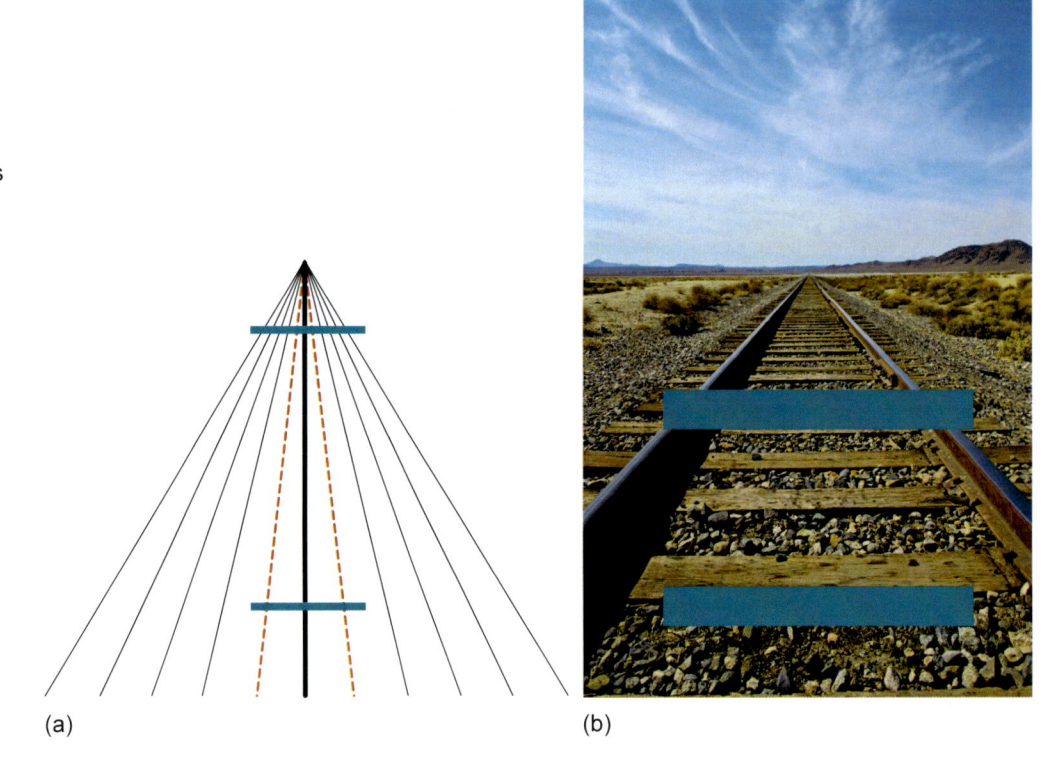

(a)   (b)

visual illusion A misperception of physical reality usually caused by the misapplication of visual cues.

moon illusion The misperception that the moon is larger when it is at the horizon than when it is overhead.

locations, it seems to roll uphill—an apparent violation of the law of gravity. This example shows how the misperception of visual cues can produce a **visual illusion**, in this case a false perception regarding the slope and horizon of the road. Visual illusions provide clues to the processes involved in normal visual perception (Gordon & Earle, 1992).

As with most illusions, the Ponzo illusion (see Figure 5-18) is caused by the misapplication of perceptual cues. As you read earlier, linear perspective is a cue to depth. Because the train tracks appear to come together in the distance, the horizontal bar higher in the figure appears to be farther away than the one lower in the figure. If you measure the bars, you will find that they are equal in length. Because the bars produce images of equal length on your retinas, the bar that appears to be farther away seems to be longer.

As another example, from ancient times to modern times, people have been mystified by the **moon illusion**, in which the moon appears larger when it is at the horizon than when it is overhead. This is an illusion because the moon is the same distance from us at the horizon as when it is overhead. Thus, the retinal image it produces is the same size when it is at the horizon as when it is overhead. In the 2nd century the Greek astronomer Ptolemy put forth the earliest explanation of the moon illusion. His explanation, based on the principle of size constancy, is called the *apparent-distance hypothesis* (Kaufman & Rock, 1962). Ptolemy assumed that we perceive the sky as a flattened dome, with the sky at the horizon appearing *farther* away than it does overhead. Because the image of the moon on the retina is the same size whether the moon is overhead or at the horizon, the brain assumes the moon must be *larger* at the apparently more distant location—the horizon. But modern research has found that under certain conditions the sky can look farther away overhead than at the horizon. So if the apparent-distance hypothesis were correct, the moon under those conditions would appear larger overhead than it does at the horizon (Baird & Wagner, 1982). Moreover, researchers have found that a variety of factors interact to create the moon illusion, so it remains to be seen whether researchers will find a single satisfactory explanation for it (Schmid, 2003).

Figure 5-19 depicts the Müller-Lyer illusion, another illusion that has stimulated many research studies. This illusion, developed more than a century ago by Franz Müller-Lyer, is perhaps the most widely studied of all illusions. Look at the two vertical lines with normal arrowheads and inverted arrowheads on the left in the figure. The line on the right

172 Chapter 5 Sensation and Perception

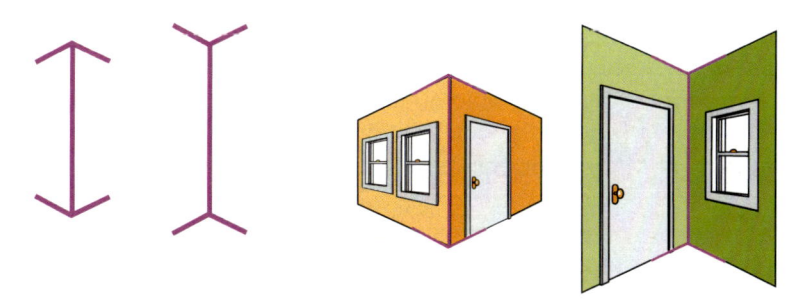

FIGURE 5-19 The Müller-Lyer Illusion

Perhaps the most widely studied illusion was developed more than a century ago by Franz Müller-Lyer. Note that the vertical line on the right appears longer than the one on the left. If you take a ruler and measure the lines, you will find that they actually are equal in length. Though no explanation has achieved universal acceptance (Mack, Heuer, Villardi, & Chambers, 1985), a favored one relies on size constancy and the resemblance of the figure on the right to the inside corner of a room and the resemblance of the figure on the left to the outside corner of a building. Given that the lines project images of equal length onto the retina, the line that appears farther away will be perceived as longer. Because an inside corner of a room appears farther away than an outside corner of a building, the line on the right appears farther away and therefore longer than the line on the left (Gillam, 1980).

should appear longer than the one on the left. If you take a ruler and measure the lines, you will find they are actually equal in length. The Müller-Lyer illusion may even impair our accuracy in estimating driving distances while reading maps when roads form patterns similar to those found in the illusion (Binsted & Elliott, 1999).

Experience, Culture, and Perception

As you have just read, visual perception depends on the interaction of the eyes and the brain. But it also depends on experience. Even the visual pathways themselves can be altered by life experiences, as demonstrated by the following study.

The Effect of Experience on Perception

As discussed in the section "Form Perception," David Hubel and Torsten Wiesel found that feature detectors in the visual cortex respond to lines of particular orientations. Other researchers (Hirsch & Spinelli, 1970) reared kittens with one eye exposed to vertical stripes and the other eye exposed to horizontal stripes. When the kittens later were exposed to lines of either orientation with one eye, certain feature-detector neurons in their visual cortexes responded only to lines of the orientation to which that eye had been exposed. But what would occur if kittens were reared in an environment that exposed both eyes to either only vertical or only horizontal stripes? This question was addressed in a study by Colin Blakemore and Graham Cooper (1970) of Cambridge University in England. Blakemore and Cooper reared kittens from the age of 2 weeks to the age of 5 months in darkness, except for 5 hours a day in a lighted, large cylinder with walls covered by either vertical or horizontal black and white stripes. Because the kittens also wore large saucer-shaped collars, they could not even see their own legs or bodies. This restriction prevented their being exposed to lines other than the vertical or horizontal stripes.

After 5 months, the kittens' vision was tested under normal lighting by waving a rod in front of them, sometimes vertically and sometimes horizontally. Kittens that had been exposed to vertical lines swatted at the vertical rod but not at the horizontal rod. And kittens that had been exposed to horizontal lines swatted at the horizontal rod but not at the vertical rod. Recordings of the activity in certain neurons in the visual cortex showed that particular neurons acted as feature detectors by responding to either vertical or horizontal lines, depending on the stripes to which the kittens had been exposed during the previous 5 months (Blakemore & Cooper, 1970). Later studies indicated that neurons in the visual cortex that are responsive to lines of different orientations are present at birth. But in an individual who is not exposed to lines of a particular orientation, the neurons responsive to that orientation will degenerate (Swindale, 1982).

Another source of evidence for the effect of experience on perception comes from studies of people blind from birth who have gained their sense of vision years later. The German physiologist Marius von Senden (1932–1960) reviewed all the studies of people who had been born blind because of lens cataracts and who gained their vision after surgical removal of the cataracts. He found that the newly sighted were immediately able to distinguish colors and to separate figure from ground, but had difficulty visually recognizing objects they had learned to identify by touch. They did, however, show gradual improvement in visual object recognition (von Senden, 1960).

Cultural Influences on Perception

Visual perception also can be influenced by cultural factors. This influence was demonstrated by the anthropologist Colin Turnbull (1961), who studied the Bambuti Pygmies of central Africa. Turnbull drove one of the Pygmies, Kenge, who lived in a dense forest, to an open plain. Looking across the plain at a herd of grazing buffalo, Kenge asked Turnbull to tell him what kind of insect they were. Turnbull responded by driving Kenge toward the herd. As the image of the "insects" got bigger and bigger on his retinas, Kenge accused Turnbull of witchcraft for turning the insects into buffaloes. Because he had never experienced large objects at a distance, Kenge had a limited appreciation of size constancy. To him the tiny images on his retinas could only be insects. Because of his understandable failure to apply size constancy appropriately, Kenge mistook the distant buffalo for a nearby insect.

Experiences with monocular cues to depth, such as linear perspective, even affect responses to the Ponzo illusion (Fujita, 1996). Rural Ugandan villagers, who have little experience with monocular cues in two-dimensional stimuli, are less susceptible to the Ponzo illusion than are Ugandan college students, who have more experience with such cues in art, photographs, and motion pictures (Leibowitz & Pick, 1972). Cross-cultural researchers have found substantial variability among populations in the susceptibility to visual illusions (Henrich, Heine, & Norenzayan, 2010). But research finding that infant monkeys respond to pictorial depth cues indicates that learning from exposure to these Western forms of depth representation is not necessary to produce such illusions (Gunderson, Yonas, Sargent, & Grant-Webster, 1993). Moreover, even pigeons and horses (Timney & Keil, 1996) are affected by the Ponzo illusion, making it less likely that it is simply the product of being exposed to Western art (Fujita, Blough, & Blough, 1993).

Section Review: Visual Perception

1. What are the Gestalt principles of form perception?
2. What are two binocular cues to depth perception?

Hearing

audition The sense of hearing.

Like the sense of vision, the sense of hearing (or **audition**) helps us function by informing us about objects at a distance from us. Unlike vision, audition informs us about objects we cannot see because they are behind us, hidden by darkness, or blocked by another object. On average, women have better hearing sensitivity and experience greater deterioration from exposure to high-frequency noise. Men are better at sound localization and detecting specific sounds from among other sounds. Because these gender differences are not found in women who have a male twin, they have been attributed to prenatal exposure to male sex hormones, which may androgenize the auditory system of the female twin (McFadden, 1998, 2002).

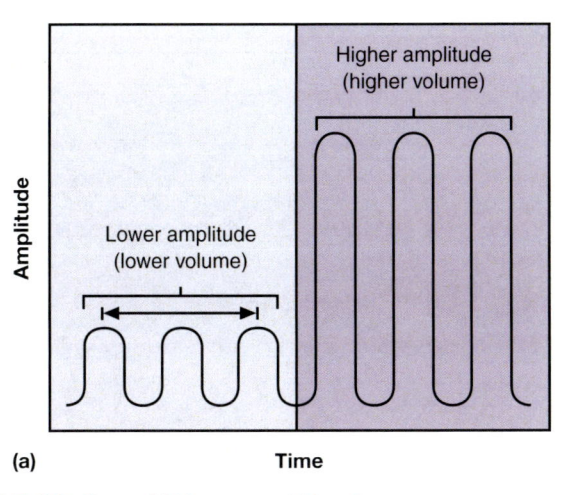

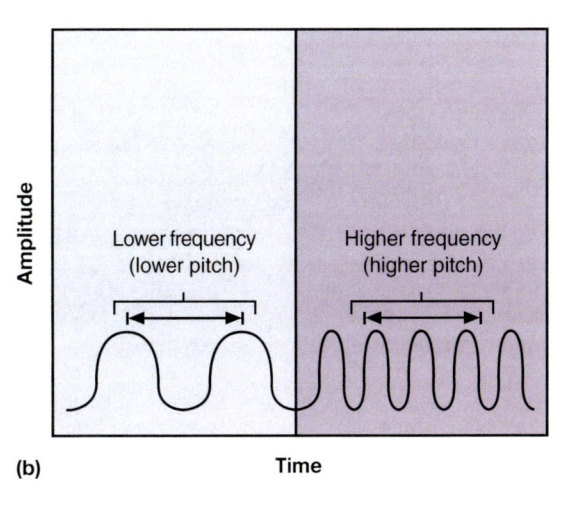

FIGURE 5-20 Sound Waves and Hearing

(a) The amplitude of a sound wave primarily affects loudness (volume), and *(b)* its frequency primarily affects pitch.
Source: Based on Seely, Stephens, and Tate, *Anatomy and Physiology*, 4th ed., McGraw-Hill, 1998.

Sound Waves

Sound is produced by vibrations carried by air, water, or other mediums. Because sound requires a medium through which to travel, it cannot travel in a vacuum. Sound vibrations create a successive bunching and spreading of molecules in the sound medium. A sound wave is composed of a series of these bunching-spreading cycles. The height of a sound wave is its *amplitude*, and the number of sound-wave cycles that pass a given point in a second is its *frequency*. Sound-wave frequency is measured in *hertz (Hz)*, named for the 19th-century German physicist Heinrich Hertz. A 60-Hz sound would have a frequency of 60 cycles a second. Figure 5-20 illustrates the main properties of sound waves that affect perceived pitch and loudness.

The Auditory System

Sound waves are sensed and perceived by the auditory system, which begins at the ear. The structure of the ear is illustrated in Figure 5-21. The ear is divided into an outer ear, a middle ear, and an inner ear.

The Outer Ear

The *outer ear* includes the *pinna*, the oddly shaped flap of skin and cartilage that we commonly call the "ear." Though the pinna plays a small role in human hearing, some animals, such as cats and deer, have large, movable pinnae that help them detect and locate faint sounds (Populin & Yin, 1998). Sound waves gathered by the pinna pass through the *external auditory canal* and reach the **tympanic membrane**, better known as the *eardrum*. Sound waves make the eardrum vibrate, and our hearing is responsive to even the slightest movement of the eardrum. If our hearing were any more acute, we would hear the air molecules that are constantly bouncing against the eardrum (Békésy, 1957).

A recent study found that temperature differences between the right and left tympanic membranes are associated with emotionality. That is, a warmer left tympanic membrane was associated with a more positive emotional state, and a warmer right tympanic membrane was associated with a more negative emotional state. As discussed in Chapter 12, positive emotions are associated with relatively greater activity in the left cerebral hemisphere, and negative emotions are associated with relatively greater activity in the right cerebral hemisphere. Thus, measurement of tympanic membrane temperature might help in assessing children who are at risk for emotional problems (Boyce et al., 2002).

tympanic membrane The eardrum; a membrane separating the outer ear from the middle ear that vibrates in response to sound waves that strike it.

FIGURE 5-21
The Human Ear

The human ear is divided into an outer ear, middle ear, and inner ear. Sound waves pass through the outer ear and strike the eardrum, making it vibrate. This action produces vibrations in the bones (ossicles) of the middle ear (the hammer, the anvil, and the stirrup), which in turn convey the vibrations to the oval window of the inner ear. Vibrations of the oval window produce waves that travel through the fluid of the cochlea. The waves cause bending of hair cells that protrude from the basilar membrane, which stimulates the transmission of neural impulses along the neurons that form the auditory nerve. These impulses travel to the auditory cortex of the temporal lobes as well as to other regions of the brain involved in hearing.

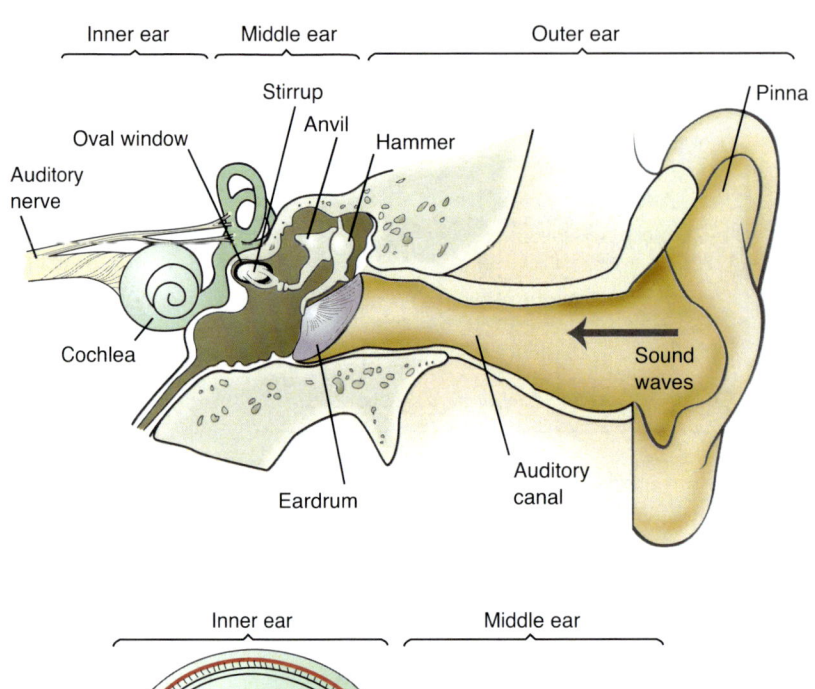

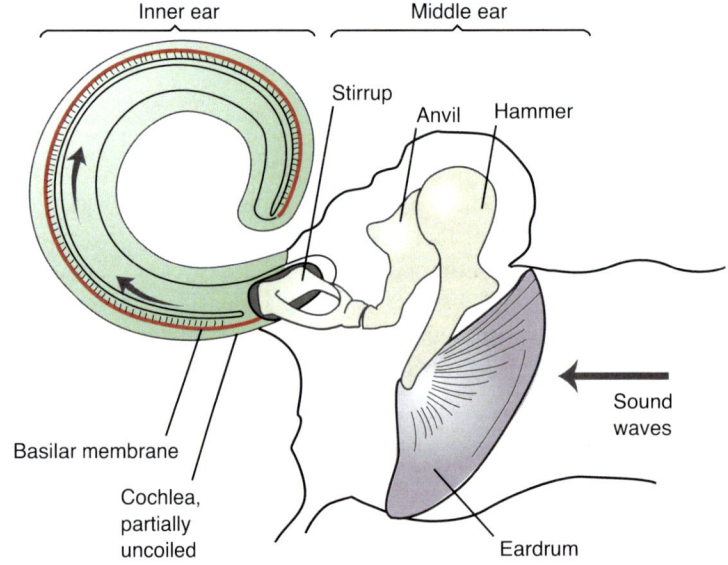

The Middle Ear

The eardrum separates the outer ear from the *middle ear*. Vibrations of the eardrum are conveyed to the bones, or ossicles, of the middle ear. The ossicles are three tiny bones connected to one another by ligaments. The Latin names of the ossicles reflect their shapes: the *malleus* (hammer), the *incus* (anvil), and the *stapes* (stirrup). Infections of the middle ear must be taken seriously; in children they can produce hearing losses that adversely affect cognitive development, though most children recover within a few years (Johnson et al., 2000).

Connecting the middle ear to the back of the throat are the *eustachian tubes*, which permit air to enter the middle ear to equalize air pressure on both sides of the eardrum. You might become painfully aware of this function during airplane descents, when the pressure increases on the outside of the eardrum relative to the inside. Chewing gum can help open the eustachian tubes and equalize the pressure.

The Inner Ear

Vibrations of the stapes are conveyed to the *oval window* of the *inner ear*. The oval window is a membrane in the wall of a spiral structure called the **cochlea** (from a Greek word meaning "snail") (Figure 5-22). Vibrations of the oval window send waves through

cochlea The spiral, fluid-filled structure of the inner ear that contains the receptor cells for hearing.

176   **Chapter 5** Sensation and Perception

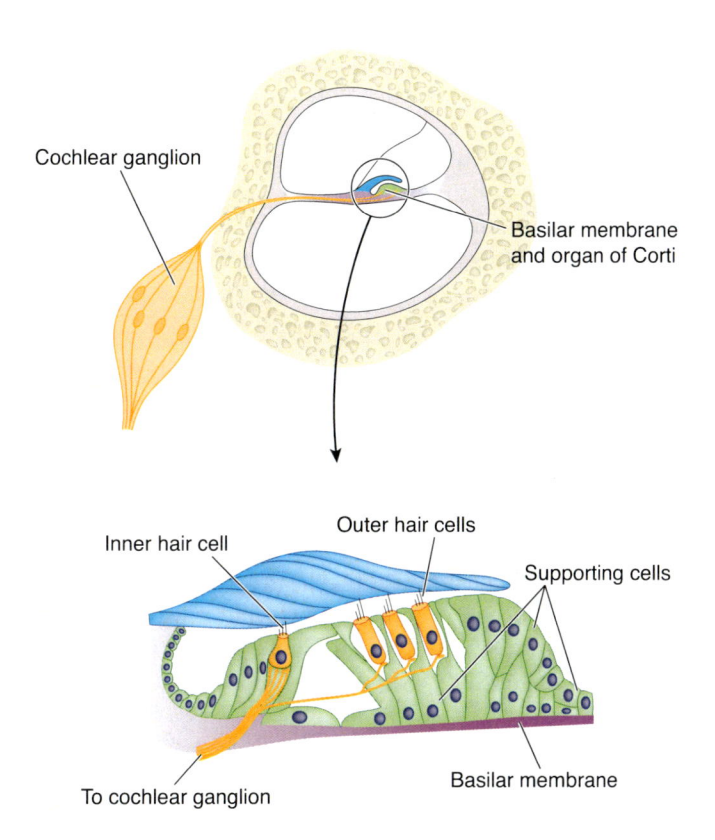

FIGURE 5-22
The Cochlea

The cochlea contains the organ of Corti, a specialized layer of cells that contains the inner and outer hair cells, on the basilar membrane.
Source: Blamb/Shutterstock.com

a fluid-filled chamber that runs the length of the cochlea. These waves set in motion the **basilar membrane**, which also runs the length of the cochlea. The movement of the basilar membrane causes bending of **hair cells** that protrude from it. The bending triggers impulses that travel along the axons of the neurons that form the **auditory nerve**. Auditory impulses eventually reach the thalamus, where some processing takes place (Edeline & Weinberger, 1991). Input to the thalamus is then relayed to the **auditory cortex** of the temporal lobes of the brain, the ultimate site of sound perception (Hirata, Kuriki, & Pantev, 1999).

People with schizophrenia who experience auditory hallucinations show increased activity in their auditory cortex (David, Woodruff, Howard, & Mellers, 1996). Likewise, in functional MRI (fMRI) studies, when we read words silently, the auditory cortex becomes more active, perhaps indicating that it plays a role in reading even when there is no auditory input (Haist et al., 2001). And PET scans reveal increased activity during sign language communication even in the auditory cortex of the temporal lobes of "listeners" who have been deaf since birth (Nishimura et al., 1999). The effects of damage to the auditory cortex depend on the precise location of the damage. Damage that spares the perception of speech and environmental sounds, for example, might profoundly impair the perception of tunes and voices (Peretz, Kolinsky, Tramo, & Labrecque, 1994).

basilar membrane A membrane running the length of the cochlea that contains the auditory receptor (hair) cells.

hair cell A sensory receptor of the auditory system located in the organ of Corti of the cochlea.

auditory nerve The nerve that conducts impulses from the cochlea to the brain.

auditory cortex The area of the temporal lobes that processes sounds.

Auditory Perception

How do vibrations conveyed to the basilar membrane (the proximal stimulus) create a complex auditory experience regarding their source (the distal stimulus)? Your ability to perceive sounds of all kinds depends on *pitch perception, loudness perception, timbre perception,* and *sound localization.*

Pitch Perception

The frequency of a sound is the main determinant of its perceived pitch, whether the low-pitched sounds of a tuba or the high-pitched sounds of a flute. When you use the tone control on a CD player, you alter the frequency of the sound waves produced by the vibration of the speakers. This in turn alters the pitch of the sound. People and other animals vary

Chapter 5 Sensation and Perception

in the range of frequencies they can hear. People hear sounds that range from 20 Hz to 20,000 Hz. Because elephants can hear sounds only up to 10,000 Hz, they cannot hear higher-pitched sounds that people can hear. Dogs can hear sounds up to about 45,000 Hz (Heffner, 1983). Because dog whistles produce sounds between 20,000 and 45,000 Hz, they are audible to dogs but not to people. People with *absolute pitch* can identify and produce tones of a specific pitch. This ability appears to be learned best before the age of 6 and becomes difficult or impossible to develop afterward (Crozier, 1997). The potential to develop absolute pitch appears to be present from birth, provided that infants are presented with verbal labels for specific pitches (Deutsch, 2002).

Place Theory What accounts for **pitch perception**? In 1863 Hermann von Helmholtz put forth **place theory**, which assumes that particular points on the basilar membrane vibrate maximally in response to sound waves of particular frequencies. Georg von Békésy (1899–1972), a Hungarian scientist, won a Nobel Prize in 1961 for his research on place theory. He took the cochleas from the ears of guinea pigs and human cadavers, stimulated the oval window, and, using a microscope, noted the response of the basilar membrane through a hole cut in the cochlea. He found that as the frequency of the stimulus increased, the point of maximal vibration produced by the traveling wave on the basilar membrane moved closer to the oval window. And as the frequency of the stimulus decreased, the point of maximal vibration moved farther from the oval window (Békésy, 1957).

Frequency Theory But place theory fails to explain pitch perception much below 1,000 Hz because such low-frequency sound waves do not make the basilar membrane vibrate maximally at any particular point. Instead, the entire basilar membrane vibrates equally. Because of this limitation, perception of sounds below 1,000 Hz is explained best by a theory first put forth by the English physicist Ernest Rutherford (1861–1937) in 1886.

His **frequency theory** assumes that the basilar membrane vibrates as a whole in direct proportion to the frequency of the sound waves striking the eardrum. The neurons of the auditory nerve will in turn fire at the same frequency as the vibrations of the basilar membrane. But because neurons can fire only up to 1,000 Hz, the frequency theory holds only for sounds up to 1,000 Hz.

Volley Theory Still another theory, the **volley theory** of psychologist Ernest Wever (Wever & Bray, 1937), explains pitch perception between 1,000 Hz and 5,000 Hz. Volley theory assumes that sound waves in this range induce certain groups of auditory neurons to fire in volleys. Though no single neuron can fire at more than 1,000 Hz, the brain might interpret the firing of volleys of particular auditory neurons as representing sound waves of particular frequencies up to 5,000 Hz (Zwislocki, 1981). For example, the pitch of a sound wave of 4,000 Hz might be coded by a particular group of five neurons, each firing at 800 Hz. Though there is some overlap among the theories, frequency theory best explains the perception of low-pitched sounds, place theory best explains the perception of high-pitched sounds, and volley theory best explains the perception of medium-pitched sounds.

Loudness Perception

Sounds vary in intensity, or loudness, as well as in pitch. The loudness of a sound depends mainly on the amplitude of its sound waves. When you use the volume control on a CD player, you alter the amplitude of the sound waves leaving the speakers. **Loudness perception** depends on both the number and the firing thresholds of hair cells on the basilar membrane that are stimulated. Because hair cells with higher firing thresholds require more intense stimulation, the firing of hair cells with higher thresholds increases the perceived loudness of a sound. A region of the auditory cortex processes differences in the intensity of sounds (Röhl, Kollmeier, & Uppenkamp, 2011).

The unit of sound intensity is the *decibel (dB)*. The decibel is one-tenth of a Bel, a unit named for Alexander Graham Bell, who invented the telephone. The faintest detectable sound has an absolute threshold of 0 dB. For each change of 10 decibels, the perceived

---

pitch perception The subjective experience of the highness or lowness of a sound, which corresponds most closely to the frequency of the sound waves that compose it.

place theory The theory of pitch perception that assumes that hair cells at particular points on the basilar membrane are maximally responsive to sound waves of particular frequencies.

frequency theory The theory of pitch perception that assumes that the basilar membrane vibrates as a whole in direct proportion to the frequency of the sound waves striking the eardrum.

volley theory The theory of pitch perception that assumes that sound waves of particular frequencies induce auditory neurons to fire in volleys, with one volley following another.

loudness perception The subjective experience of the intensity of a sound, which corresponds most closely to the amplitude of the sound waves composing it.

TABLE 5-1 Decibel Levels of Some Everyday Sounds

General Effect	Decibel Level	Example
Possible Hearing Loss	140	Jet airplane on runway
	130	Pain threshold
	120	Propeller airplane on runway
	110	Rock concert
	100	Jackhammer
Annoyingly Noisy	90	City street with traffic
	80	Downtown city apartment
	70	Active business office
Relatively Quiet	60	Normal conversation
	50	Suburban street
	40	Rural farm
	30	Soft whisper
	20	Quiet residence
	10	Fluttering leaf
	0	Hearing threshold

Source: Olivier Le Moal/Shutterstock.com.

Image Sources: Shutterstock.com. (*Top*) frank_peters, (*middle*) welcomia, (*bottom*) Polarpx.

loudness doubles. Thus, a 70-dB sound is twice as loud as a 60-dB sound. Table 5-1 presents the decibel levels of some everyday sounds. Exposure to high-decibel sounds promotes hearing loss. Chronic exposure to loud sounds first destroys hair cells nearest the oval window, which respond to high-frequency sound waves. A study of the effects of loud music found significant hearing loss among participants who listened to personal stereos for more than 7 hours a week. In addition, two-thirds of the participants who attended rock concerts at least twice monthly exhibited symptoms of hearing loss (Meyer-Bisch, 1996). Older Americans, after a lifetime of exposure to loud sounds, tend to have poor high-frequency hearing. In contrast, the typical 90-year-old in rural African tribes, whose surroundings only occasionally produce loud sounds, has better hearing than the typical 30-year-old North American (Raloff, 1982).

In extreme cases, individuals can lose more than their high-frequency hearing. They can become deaf. In **conduction deafness**, a mechanical problem in the outer or middle ear interferes with hearing. The auditory canal might be filled with wax, the eardrum might be punctured, or the ossicles might be fused and inflexible. Conduction deafness caused by deterioration of the ossicles can be treated by surgical replacement with plastic ossicles. Conduction deafness is more often overcome by hearing aids, which amplify sound waves that enter the ear.

In **nerve deafness**, there is damage to the basilar membrane, the auditory nerve, or the auditory cortex. Victims typically lose the ability to perceive sounds of certain frequencies. Nerve deafness responds poorly to surgery or hearing aids. But cochlear implants, which provide electronic stimulation of the neurons leaving the basilar membrane, promise to restore at least rudimentary hearing in people with nerve deafness caused by the destruction of basilar membrane hair cells. More than 20,000 children worldwide have had successful cochlear implants, which have improved their hearing, language ability,

conduction deafness Hearing loss usually caused by blockage of the auditory canal, damage to the eardrum, or deterioration of the ossicles of the middle ear.

nerve deafness Hearing loss caused by damage to the hair cells of the basilar membrane, the axons of the auditory nerve, or the neurons of the auditory cortex.

and social relationships (Balkany et al., 2002). Nonetheless, cochlear implants have provoked controversy between those who believe they are an important means of correcting a disability and those who believe that routine practice of cochlear implants reflects a judgment that people who are deaf are inferior to those who can hear (Levy, 2002).

Timbre Perception

timbre The subjective experience that identifies a particular sound and corresponds most closely to the mixture of sound waves composing it.

Sounds vary in timbre as well as in pitch and loudness. **Timbre** is the quality of a sound, which reflects a particular mixture of sound waves. Timbre is especially apparent, for example, in the complex sounds produced in orchestral music (Tardieu & McAdams, 2012). Middle C on the piano has a frequency of 256 Hz, but it has a distinctive timbre because of overtones of varying frequencies. Timbre lets us identify the source of a sound, whether a voice, a musical instrument, or even—to the chagrin of students—a fingernail scratching across a chalkboard. The timbre of that spine-chilling sound is similar to that of the warning cry of macaque monkeys. Perhaps our squeamish response to it reflects a vestigial response inherited from our common distant ancestors who used it to signal the presence of predators (Halpern, Blake, & Hillerbrand, 1986).

The cortical areas that process differences in timbre, as between a violin and a trumpet, are more responsive in trained musicians than in non-musicians. Moreover, those cortical areas are even more responsive to the sound of the instrument on which professional musicians have been trained. Thus, the relevant cortical areas of violinists respond more strongly to the sound of a violin, and the relevant cortical areas of a trumpeter respond more strongly to the sound of a trumpet (Pantev, Roberts, Schulz, Engelien, & Ross, 2001).

Sound Localization

sound localization The process by which the individual determines the location of a sound.

We need to localize sounds as well as identify them. **Sound localization** involves discerning where sounds are coming from. People have an acute ability to localize sounds, whether of voices at a crowded party or of instruments in a symphony orchestra. Some animals have especially impressive sound localization ability. A barn owl can capture a mouse in the dark simply by following the faint sounds produced by its movements (Knudsen, 1981). The ability to localize sound is important for our survival, as in judging the distance of approaching vehicles. This aspect is especially important for young children, who are not proficient at detecting approaching vehicles from their sounds (Pfeffer & Barnecutt, 1996).

We are aided in localizing sounds by having two ears. Sounds that come from points other than those equidistant between our two ears, for example from behind you, reach one ear slightly before they reach the other. Our auditory system then determines the direction and source of the sound by comparing the messages from each ear. Such sounds also are slightly more intense at the ear closer to the sound source because it receives the sound waves first. The auditory cortex has cells that respond to these differences in intensity and arrival time, permitting the brain to determine the location of a sound (McAlpine & Grothe, 2003). Even sounds that come from points equidistant between our ears can be located because the irregular shape of the pinna alters sounds differently, depending on the direction from which they enter the ear (Middlebrooks & Green, 1991). The pinna is angled forward to help catch sounds coming toward you best. And the parietal cortex aids the auditory cortex in localizing sounds, in keeping with its role in spatial perception (Zatorre, Bouffard, Ahad, & Belin, 2002).

Section Review: Hearing

1. What are the major structures of the outer, middle, and inner ear?
2. What is the place theory of pitch perception?
3. What are the basic processes in sound localization?

Chemical Senses

The chemical senses of smell and taste let us identify things on the basis of their chemical content. These senses also provide us with both pleasure and protection.

Smell

Helen Keller (1880–1968), though deaf and blind from infancy, could identify her friends by their smell and could even tell whether a person had recently been in a kitchen, garden, or hospital room by his or her odor (Ecenbarger, 1987). Though most of us do not rely on smell to that extent, the sense of smell (or **olfaction**) is important to all of us. It warns us of dangers, such as fire, deadly gases, or spoiled food, and lets us enjoy the pleasant odors of food, nature, and other people.

olfaction The sense of smell, which detects molecules carried in the air.

North Americans find odors so important that they spend millions of dollars on perfumes, colognes, and deodorants to make themselves more socially appealing. Workers also might feel more motivated when in the presence of a pleasant fragrance. This reaction was demonstrated in a study in which men wore cologne for 10 days and reported their moods twice daily on those days as well as on 2 baseline days. The results showed that their moods while wearing cologne were improved over their moods during the 2 baseline days (Schiffman, Suggs, & Sattely-Miller, 1995). This finding was replicated in a study in which women exposed to pleasant odors had enhanced moods in response to them (Schiffman, Sattely-Miller, & Suggs, 1995). The possible influence of fragrances on moods has led some business owners to diffuse scents into their stores to gain a competitive advantage. Nonetheless, few research studies have supported the effectiveness of this technique (Spangenberg, Crowley, & Henderson, 1996).

Our responses to odors are influenced by culture, gender, and even disease states. Cultural differences in the perceived intensity and pleasantness of particular odors appear to be attributable to cultural differences in people's experience with different odors (Ayabe-Kanamura et al., 1998). For example, a study of Mexican, German, and Japanese women found that participants rated familiar odors to be more intense and more pleasant than unfamiliar odors (Distal et al., 1999). Women tend to outperform men when detecting and identifying odors. This finding may be attributable to gender differences in experience and thus familiarity with various odors (Brand & Millot, 2001). In another experiment, patients with early-stage Alzheimer's disease were tested, with their eyes closed, for their ability to detect an odor, one nostril at a time. There were measurable distance differences in detection between Alzheimer's patients and a control group matched by age and gender (Stamps, Bartoshuck, & Heilman, 2013). This study reveals a non-invasive and inexpensive test that appears to be sensitive to identifying patients with early-stage Alzheimer's.

The ability of odors to affect our moods has led to the advent of so-called *aromatherapy*, which attempts to use different fragrances to enhance cognitive abilities or psychological well-being. In one experiment, groups of adults were exposed to either an alerting aroma (rosemary) or a relaxing odor (lavender) and were asked to perform mathematical calculations. The rosemary group showed heightened alertness as measured by self-reports and brain waves. Both groups increased their speed of calculations, but only the lavender group showed improved accuracy of calculations (Diego et al., 1998). In another experiment, agitated patients with Alzheimer's disease were randomly assigned to have either lemon-scented oil or a placebo oil rubbed on their arms and face twice a day for 4 weeks. The results showed that those who received lemon-scented oil became significantly calmer than those who received the placebo oil (Ballard, O'Brien, Reichelt, & Elaine, 2002). Despite some positive research findings regarding aromatherapy, some studies have failed to support its effectiveness (Lee, Choi, Posadzki, & Ernst, 2012). Consumers should remain skeptical of some of the extreme claims made for its effectiveness by those who stand to profit from aromatherapy products and services.

What accounts for our ability to smell odors? In part because of the practical difficulty of gaining access to the olfactory pathways, we have relatively limited knowledge of

FIGURE 5-23
The Olfactory System

Inhaled molecules attach to receptor cells high up in the nasal passages. This action stimulates neural activity in the olfactory bulbs, which generates olfactory-nerve impulses that are sent to brain regions that process smell sensations.

Source: ellepigrafica/Shutterstock.com.

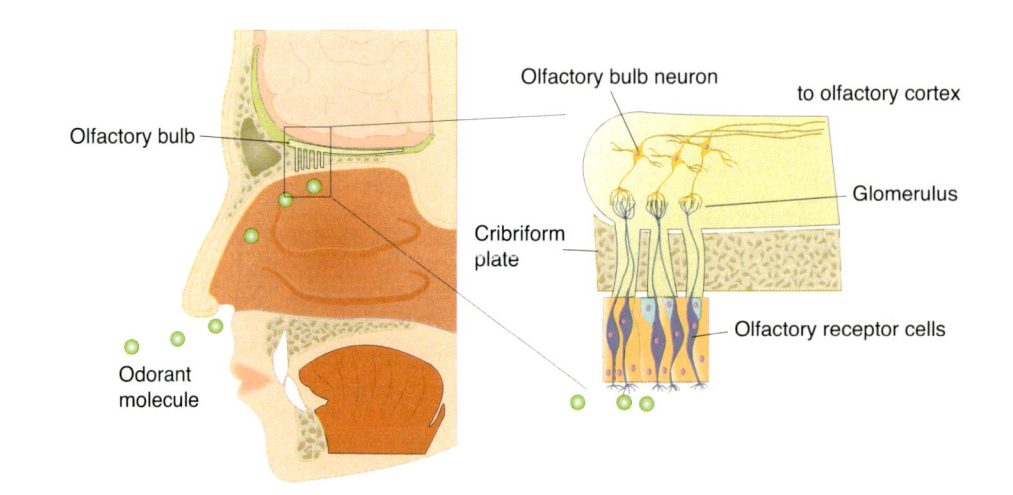

how olfactory anatomy affects the detection and recognition of odors. We do know that molecules carried in inhaled air stimulate smell receptor cells on the olfactory epithelium high up in the nasal passages. Figure 5-23 illustrates the major structures of the olfactory system.

Today, research findings indicate that molecules that reach the olfactory epithelium alter the resting potential and firing frequency of receptor cells, stimulating some and inhibiting others. Distinctive patterns in the firing of receptor cells evoke particular odors. Leading olfaction researcher Linda Bartoshuk has found that regardless of the exact mechanisms by which this occurs, olfaction depends on stimulation of different receptors, composed of proteins, on the olfactory epithelium by specific airborne chemicals (Bartoshuk & Beauchamp, 1994).

Neural impulses from the receptor cells travel along the short *olfactory nerves* to the frontal lobes of the brain. Smell is the only sense that is not processed first in the thalamus before being processed in other olfactory centers in the brain. The *limbic system*, a structure of the brain that is important in the experience of emotion, discussed in Chapter 3, receives many neural connections from the olfactory nerves. These connections might account for the powerful emotional effects of certain odors that evoke vivid memories of important events, places, or persons (Vermetten & Bremner, 2003). In one study, participants were exposed to 20 different odors and were asked to rate the odors and report whether they evoked a personal memory. In keeping with popular belief, memories evoked by the odors tended to be rare, vivid, emotional, and relatively old (Herz & Cupchik, 1992). And happiness, disgust, and to a lesser extent, anxiety, are reliably elicited by odors (Croy, Olgun, & Joraschky, 2011).

Our sense of smell has a remarkably low absolute threshold; we can detect minute amounts of chemicals diffused in the air. For example, *National Geographic* needed only 1 ounce of an odorous chemical to include a sample of it with 11 million copies of a smell survey (Gibbons, 1986). Our ability to identify familiar odors was highlighted in a study of college students who showered themselves, put on fresh T-shirts, and used no soap, deodorant, or perfume for 24 hours. Participants then sniffed the shirts, one at a time, through an opening in a bag. Of the 29 participants, 22 correctly identified their own shirts (Russell, 1976). A more recent study assessed the reactions of participants to the odors of their relatives. The only odor aversions were between fathers and daughters and between brothers and sisters. The researchers concluded that odor aversion might contribute to the maintenance of the incest taboo (Weisfeld, Czilli, Phillips, Gall, & Lichtman, 2003).

Though smell is important to people, it is more important to many other animals. For example, salmon have an amazing ability to travel hundreds of miles to their home streams to spawn, following the familiar odors of the soil and plants on the banks of the waterways that mark the correct route home (Gibbons, 1986). Researchers have been especially interested in the effects of secretions called **pheromones**, intraspecies chemical signals, on the sexual behavior of animals. For example, *aphrodisin*, a vaginal phero-

pheromone An odorous chemical secreted by an animal that affects the behavior of other animals.

182 Chapter 5 Sensation and Perception

mone released by female hamsters, stimulates copulation when inhaled by male hamsters (Singer & Macrides, 1990). Recent research indicates there may be human pheromones that affect emotions and behavior. For example, in one study, exposure to the pheromone *androstadienone*, which is primarily secreted by men, improved women's moods (Lundstrom, Goncalves, Esteves, & Olsson, 2003). But research results regarding the ability of any supposed human pheromone to consistently produce a particular effect are inconclusive (Hays, 2003). You should be wary of companies offering to sell you pheromones that they "guarantee" will help your romantic life.

Taste

Our other chemical sense, taste (or **gustation**), protects us from harm by preventing us from ingesting poisons and enhances our enjoyment of life by letting us savor food and beverages. Taste depends on thousands of **taste buds**, which line the grooves between bumps called *papillae* on the surface of the tongue. The taste buds contain receptor cells that send neural impulses when stimulated by molecules dissolved in saliva (Smith & Margolis, 1999). Taste sensitivity also varies with the density of taste buds. One of the reasons that children prefer sweet tastes more than adults do is their greater density of papillae in areas of the tongue that are particularly sensitive to sweet tastes (Segovia, Hutchinson, Laing, & Jinks, 2002). Taste buds die and are replaced every few days, so the taste buds destroyed when you burn your tongue with hot food or drink are quickly replaced. But because replacement of taste buds slows with age, elderly people may find food less flavorful than they did earlier in life. Older adults often prefer foods with more intense flavors (de Graaf, Polet, & van Staveren, 1994).

In the 11th century, the Arab scientist Avicenna proposed that there were four basic tastes: sweet, sour, salty, and bitter. In 1891, Hjalmar Ohrwall provided support for Avicenna's proposal. Ohrwall tested the sensitivity of the papillae by applying a variety of chemicals, one at a time, to different papillae. Some papillae responded to one taste and some to more than one. But overall, he found that particular papillae were maximally sensitive to sweet, sour, salty, or bitter substances (Bartoshuk, Cain, & Pfaffmann, 1985). The front of the tongue is most sensitive to sweet and salty, the sides are most sensitive to sour and salty, and the back is most sensitive to bitter (Figure 5-24). All other tastes are combinations of these basic tastes and depend on the pattern of stimulation of the taste receptors (Sato & Beidler, 1997).

Gustation depends in part on the shape and size of molecules that stimulate the taste receptors. Taste researchers use this knowledge when they develop artificial sweeteners. Taste receptors in different areas of the tongue are maximally sensitive to molecules of particular shapes. Animal research has shown that different clusters of nerve fibers in pathways from the tongue to the brain (so-called labeled lines) serve the senses of sweet, salty, and bitter (Hellekant, Ninomiya, & Danilova, 1998). There also are taste receptors that are sensitive to the presence of particular nutrients, such as fats and umami, the

gustation The sense of taste, which detects molecules of substances dissolved in the saliva.

taste buds Structures lining the grooves of the tongue that contain the taste receptor cells.

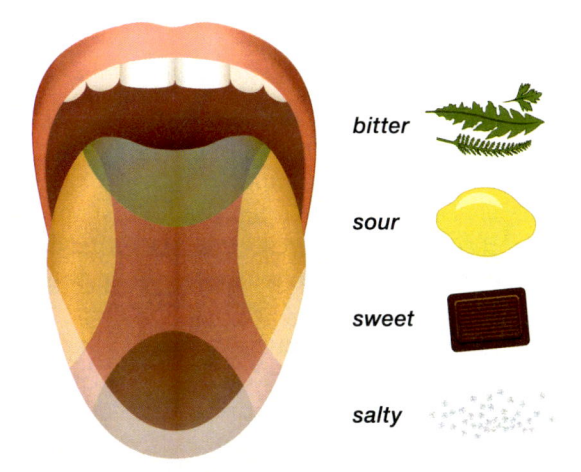

FIGURE 5-24
The Four Basic Tastes

All regions of the tongue are sensitive to each of the four basic tastes, but certain regions are more sensitive to particular ones. Sweet receptors line the tip of the tongue, sour and salty receptors line the sides, and bitter receptors line the back.
Source: Peter Hermes Furian/Shutterstock.com.

Chapter 5 Sensation and Perception

Flavor

Have you ever noticed that when you have a head cold, food can sometimes lack flavor?

Source: CHAjAMP /Shutterstock.com.

pleasurable taste elicited by monosodium glutamate, a common ingredient in Asian foods (Bellisle, 1999). Different regions of the somatosensory cortex respond more to certain tastes than to others (Kobayakawa et al., 1999).

Do not confuse taste with flavor, which is more complex. Whereas taste depends on sensations from the mouth, flavor relies on both taste and smell as well as on texture, temperature, and even pain—as in chili peppers (Bartoshuk, 1991). If you closed your eyes and held your nose, you would have trouble telling the difference between a piece of apple and a piece of potato placed in your mouth. Because smell is especially important for flavor, you might find that when you have a head cold that interferes with your ability to smell, food lacks flavor. In fact, people who lose their sense of smell because of disease or brain damage (a condition known as anosmia) find food less appealing (Ferris & Duffy, 1989).

Section Review: Chemical Senses

1. What are pheromones?
2. Why might a head cold affect your ability to enjoy the flavor of food?

Skin Senses

skin senses The senses of touch, temperature, and pain.

We rely on our **skin senses** of touch, temperature, and pain to identify objects, communicate feelings, and protect us from injury. Though there are a variety of receptors that produce skin sensations, there is no simple one-to-one relationship between specific kinds of receptors and specific skin senses. For example, there is only one kind of receptor in the cornea, but it is sensitive to touch, temperature, and pain. The pattern of stimulation of receptors, not the specific kind of receptor, determines skin sensations. Neural impulses from the skin receptors reach the thalamus, which relays them to the **somatosensory cortex** of the brain (see Chapter 3). Now consider what research has discovered about the senses of touch and pain.

somatosensory cortex The area of the parietal lobes that processes information from sensory receptors in the skin.

Touch

Your sense of *touch* lets you identify objects rapidly and accurately even when you cannot see them, as when you find your house key while fumbling with a key chain in the dark. Touch also helps us maintain our balance and equilibrium. Touch receptors on the soles of our feet, for example, help us maintain an upright posture while moving about (Roll, Kavounoudias, & Roll, 2002). Touch also is important in our social attachments, whether between lovers or between parent and child (Hertenstein, 2002), and in our well-being, as in helping physicians conduct medical examinations (Thompson & Lambert, 1995). Touch sensitivity depends on the concentration of receptors. The more sensitive the area of skin (such as the lips or fingertips), the larger is its representation on the somatosensory cortex. Touch sensitivity declines with age, perhaps because of the loss of touch receptors (Gescheider, Beiles, Checkosky, & Bolanowski, 1994) or alterations in the somatosensory cortex (Spengler, Godde, & Dinse, 1995).

The sense of touch is so precise that it can be used as a substitute for vision. In 1824 a blind Frenchman named Louis Braille invented the Braille system for reading and writing, which uses patterns of raised dots to represent letters. Blind adults who have used Braille for reading are superior to sighted adults in using their fingers to recognize fine details on objects. This sensitivity may be the result of a lifetime of using their fingers for reading (Van Boven, Hamilton, Kauffman, Keenan, & Pascual-Leone, 2000). The Braille concept has been extended to provide a substitute for vision. The blind person wears a camera on special eyeglasses and a special computer-controlled electronic vest covered with a grid of tiny Teflon cones. Outlines of images provided by the camera are impressed onto the skin by vibrations of the cones. People who have used the device have been able to identify familiar objects (Hechinger, 1981).

Pain

The sense of *pain* (or *nociception*) protects us from injury or even death. People born without a sense of pain, or who lose it through nerve injuries, may harm themselves without realizing it. Pain also interferes with functioning, as in back pain or headaches. Back pain is especially debilitating to certain professionals, such as truck drivers who commonly develop chronic lower back pain (Lyons, 2002). About 5 percent of the population experiences chronic daily headaches (Lake & Saper, 2002). In the United States, headaches account for 18 million visits to physicians and the loss of more than 150 million workdays each year (Smith, 2000). Migraine headaches are generally more painful and debilitating than are tension headaches (Martins & Parriera, 2001). Migraine headaches are caused by dilation of arteries of the scalp, inflammation of nerves of the scalp, and decreased inhibition of pain transmission in the brain (Spierings, 2003). Based on the answers of almost 30,000 individuals who responded to a large-scale U.S. survey, 18.2 percent of female and 6.5 percent of male respondents reported having migraine headaches. European Americans are more likely to have migraines than African Americans, and migraines are more common among people of lower socioeconomic status. The frequency of migraines tends to increase through early adulthood and decline beginning in middle adulthood (Lipton, Stewart, Diamond, Diamond, & Reed, 2001).

Because acute pain can be extremely distressing and chronic pain is severely depressing (Banks & Kerns, 1996), researchers are studying the factors that cause pain and possible ways of relieving it.

Pain Factors

An injury or intense stimulation of sensory receptors induces pain. So, bright lights, loud noises, hot spices, and excessive pressure, as well as cuts, burns, and bruises are painful. Heredity plays a role in the pain response (Lariviere et al., 2002). The main pain receptors (or *nociceptors*) are free nerve endings in the skin. Two kinds of neuronal fibers, or sensory neurons, transmit pain impulses: *A-delta fibers* carry sharp or pricking pain, and *C fibers* carry dull or burning pain (Mengel, Stiefenhofer, Jyvasjarvi, & Kniffki, 1993). Many pain receptor neurons transmit pain impulses by releasing the neuropeptide substance P from their axons (Meert, Vissers, Geenen, & Kontinen, 2003). For example, the intensity of arthritis pain varies with the amount of *substance P* released by neurons that convey pain impulses, and analgesics that reduce levels of substance P reduce arthritis pain intensity (Torri, Cecchettin, Bellometti, & Galzigna, 1995). Two substances implicated in pain are *bradykinin*, a chemical that accumulates at the site of an injury or inflammation (Banik, Kozaki, Sato, Gera, & Mizumura, 2001) and the neurotransmitter glutamate, which affects pain receptors in the brain, the spinal cord, and the body (Fundytus, 2001).

A brain region called the *periaqueductal gray* is an important pain-inhibiting center (Zanoto de Luca, Brandao, Motta, & Landeira-Fernandez, 2003). And pathways to the limbic system appear to affect emotional responses to pain (Giesler, Katter, & Dado, 1994). Painful stimulation of the skin triggers neural impulses that travel to the thalamus (Treede, 2002) and then are relayed to sites on the somatosensory cortex (Kanda et al., 2000).

The most influential theory of pain is the **gate-control theory**, formulated by psychologist Ronald Melzack and biologist Patrick Wall (1965). The theory assumes that pain impulses from the limbs or body pass through a part of the spinal cord that provides a "gate" for pain impulses, perhaps involving substance P neurons (Holland, Goldstein, & Aronstam, 1993). Stimulation of neurons that convey touch sensations "closes" the gate, preventing input from neurons that convey pain sensations. This theory might explain why rubbing a shin that you have banged against a table will relieve the pain. The closing of the pain gate is stimulated by the secretion of *endorphins* (Anderson, Sheth,

gate-control theory The theory that pain impulses can be blocked by the closing of a neuronal gate in the spinal cord.

Bencherif, Frost, & Campbell, 2002), which (as described in Chapter 3) are the brain's natural opiates. Endorphins might close the gate by inhibiting the secretion of substance P (Ruda, 1982). And exercise increases endorphin levels and reduces pain sensitivity (Sadigh-Lindell et al., 2001). The gate-control theory remains the most comprehensive, widely accepted theory of pain (Sufka & Price, 2002).

The pain gate also is affected by neural impulses that originate in the brain (Gilbert, 2003). In fact, merely anticipating pain increases activity in brain regions that process pain. In one study, participants were told that they would be given either painful or non-painful stimulation of the foot. Cortical responses, as measured by fMRI, indicated that both kinds of stimulation increased activity in the area devoted to the foot, but the activity was more intense in response to anticipation of pain (Porro et al., 2002). This finding might explain why anxiety, relaxation, and other psychological factors can affect pain perception (Melzack, 1993). Cognitive factors are particularly important in moderating pain. Catastrophizing about pain, for example, by magnifying it and ruminating about it tends to intensify it (France, France, al'Absi, Ring, & McIntyre, 2002). And a feeling of control over pain's effects on one's life and over one's pain helps reduce people's distress (Tan et al., 2003). Thus, cognitive processes can affect physiological processes related to pain (Pincus & Morley, 2001).

Sociocultural factors, likewise, have been found to influence the perception of pain. A metaanalysis of experimental studies found that women report higher levels of pain sensitivity than do men. Moreover, effect sizes ranged from large to moderate depending on the type of painful stimulus (Riley, Robinson, Wise, Myers, & Fillingim, 1998). Women and men do appear to respond to some painful stimuli and analgesia differently, a difference that is attributable to biological, cognitive, and social factors (Miaskowski, 1999; Racine et al., 2012). African Americans and European Americans also respond to painful stimuli differently. This difference may be attributable to sociocultural factors, such as beliefs and attitudes, and psychological factors, such as coping strategies (Rahim-Williams, Riley, Williams, & Fillingim, 2012). Cross-cultural research has found that women find it more socially appropriate to admit to experiencing pain than do men (Nayak, Shiflett, Eshun, & Levine, 2000). And cultural factors can influence pain perception and responses to pain treatments (Goldberg & Remy-St. Louis, 1998), as in cross-cultural differences in the interpretation and expression of pain (Rollman, 1998) and research on reactions to childbirth of women from different cultures (see "The Research Process: Are There Cultural Differences in the Painfulness of Childbirth?" on the following page).

Pain Control

Chronic pain afflicts millions of Americans. The pain of cancer, surgery, injuries, headaches, and backaches makes pain control an important topic of research in both medicine and psychology. The most popular approach to the relief of severe pain relies on drugs such as morphine, a highly effective pain reliever, which affects endorphin receptors in the brain. Even **placebo** "sugar pills," which are supposedly inactive substances that are substituted for pain-relieving drugs, can relieve pain. One study found that patients with chronic pain who respond to placebos produce higher levels of endorphins than do those who fail to respond (Lipman et al., 1990). But other studies have failed to find a role for endorphins in the placebo effect (Montgomery & Kirsch, 1996).

Other techniques that do not rely on drugs or placebos also relieve pain by stimulating the release of endorphins. For example, the technique of **acupuncture**, popular in China for thousands of years, relies on the insertion of fine needles into various sites on the body. *Naloxone*, a drug that blocks the effects of opiates, inhibits the analgesic effects of acupuncture. This finding provides evidence for the role of endorphins in acupuncture (Murray, 1995), perhaps by blocking impulses at the pain gate in the spinal cord (Lee & Beitz, 1992). Research using functional MRI of the brain found that acupuncture might exert its pain-relieving effects in part by affecting the limbic system (Hui et al., 2000).

Acupuncture has been effective in reducing a variety of kinds of pain, including chronic neck pain (Irnich et al., 2002) and pain during labor (Nesheim et al., 2003). It has been

placebo An inactive substance that might induce some of the effects of the drug for which it has been substituted.

acupuncture A pain-relieving technique that relies on the insertion of fine needles into various sites on the body.

The Research Process

Are There Cultural Differences in the Painfulness of Childbirth?

Childbirth is both a physiological and cultural event of major importance in many women's lives. Italian researchers Alda Scopesi, Mirella Zanobini, and Paolo Carossino (1997), of the University of Genoa, wondered to what extent cultural factors would affect women's reactions to childbirth, including the degree of pain they experienced during labor and delivery. They decided to study the reactions of women in comparable cities in four different cultures.

Method

The research study was carried out in 18 hospitals in four industrialized cities: Boston in the United States, Genoa in Italy, Cologne in Germany, and Reims in France. Of the 414 women in the study, 93 were from Boston, 109 from Genoa, 107 from Cologne, and 105 from Reims. The women were asked to respond to a questionnaire with 29 questions about the course of their pregnancy and their subjective reactions to childbirth.

Results and Discussion

The results indicated that there was no statistically significant difference between the groups regarding pain during labor. But there was a statistically significant difference in their degree of pain during delivery. Most of the women in each city reported that delivery was bearable, but significantly fewer women in Genoa (only 6 percent reported that delivery was unbearably painful. Boston and Reims had the highest percentage of women (22 percent in each city) reporting that delivery was unbearably painful.

The authors concluded that women in Genoa were less likely to experience delivery as unbearable because childbirth there is more likely to be considered a medical event in which pain is expected. This interpretation agrees with research findings that our expectations can affect our responses to pain. If we can predict that we will experience pain, we will experience it as less intense than if severe pain is not considered a part of delivery.

Another potentially important finding was that women who reported that pain during delivery was unbearable also tended to report that they experienced a greater degree of joy afterward. This phenomenon, in which a positive emotional experience follows a powerful negative one, is discussed in Chapter 12. This study provided evidence that women in different cultures will respond differently to the pain of childbirth. But it will take more cross-cultural studies like this one to determine the factors that account for this difference, including the reasons why women in four different cultures would differ in their subjective level of pain during delivery but not during labor. One possible explanation for these differences is the influence of the medical staff's expectations and treatment of their patients. Cross-cultural studies indicate that women's responses during labor might indeed be affected by the attitudes of their hospital caregivers (Sheiner, Sheiner, Shoham-Vardi, Mazor, & Katz, 1999).

---

particularly effective in treating chronic lower back pain. In one study, participants debilitated by lower back pain were randomly assigned to receive either acupuncture or a placebo treatment. After three months, the acupuncture group reported a significantly greater decrease in pain. Moreover, they used less pain medication, had better quality sleep, and were more likely to have returned to work (Carlsson & Sjoelund, 2001). Though most studies on the use of acupuncture in treating pain have produced positive findings, the quality of acupuncture research needs to be improved in order to provide stronger evidence of its effectiveness (Ezzo et al., 2000). Some recent animal studies have shed light on the potential mechanism of acupuncture in decreasing pain. One researcher found that acupuncture or electrical stimulation applied to certain body sites can facilitate the release of endorphins (Han, 2003). Another researcher found that an endorphin involved in pain relief was released in mice who experienced acupuncture treatment (Fleckenstein et al., 2010). Though fewer clinical studies of humans demonstrate similar findings, this type of research likely will contribute to the theoretical controversy regarding the effect of acupuncture on pain.

A similar, more modern technique for pain relief relies on **transcutaneous electrical nerve stimulation (TENS)**, which involves electrical stimulation of sites on the body. TENS has proved effective in relieving many kinds of pain, including back pain (Marchand, Charest, & Chenard, 1993) and headache pain (Solomon & Guglielmo, 1985). A survey of chronic-pain patients who used TENS found that the patients had a significant reduction in their use of pain-killing drugs (Chabal, Fishbain, Weaver, & Heine, 1998).

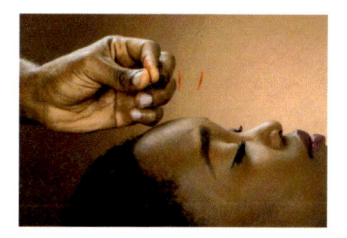

Acupuncture

Acupuncture appears to achieve its pain-relieving effects by stimulating the release of endorphins.
Source: Andrey_Popov/Shutterstock.com.

transcutaneous electrical nerve stimulation (TENS) The use of electrical stimulation of sites on the body to provide pain relief, apparently by stimulating the release of endorphins.

Chapter 5 Sensation and Perception

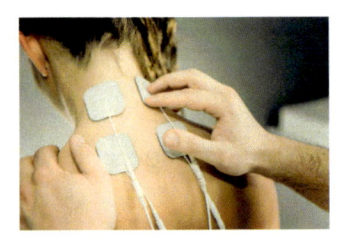

Back Pain

Transcutaneous electrical nerve stimulation (TENS) devices are used in noninvasive nerve stimulation intended to reduce pain by stimulating the release of endorphins.

Source: Microgen/Shutterstock.com.

As in the case of placebos and acupuncture, TENS might relieve pain by stimulating the release of endorphins because its effects are blocked by naloxone (Wang, Mao, & Han, 1992). TENS also might inhibit activity in the pain gate in the spinal cord (Garrison & Foreman, 1994).

Still another technique, hypnosis, is effective in relieving pain (Hawkins, 2001). For example, it has helped relieve pain experienced by burn victims (Patterson, Adcock, & Bombardier, 1997) and cancer patients (Liossi & Hatira, 2003). But unlike other pain-relieving techniques, hypnosis does not appear to work by stimulating the release of endorphins. Studies have found that hypnosis might exert its effects by sending neural impulses that block pain impulses at the spinal-cord pain gate (Kiernan, Dane, Phillips, & Price, 1995), by reducing attention to pain sensations (Crawford, Knebel, & Vendemia, 1998), or by inducing a state of consciousness in which the individual feels disconnected from the pain (Freeman, Barabasz, Barabasz, & Warner, 2000).

Pain victims also can control their pain by using distracting thoughts or distracting stimuli (Tsao, Fanurik, & Zeltzer, 2003). In a study of dental patients, participants distracted by music during procedures experienced less pain and distress than did participants in a control group who were not exposed to music (Anderson, Baron, & Logan, 1991). And a meta-analysis found that distraction is effective in reducing children's pain and distress during medical procedures (Kleiber & Harper, 1999). One mechanism by which distraction reduces pain is by stimulating activity in the periaqueductal gray, which receives sensory input from the cortex, limbic system, and brain stem as measured by fMRI (Tracey et al., 2002).

Section Review: Skin Senses

1. How has the sense of touch been used to provide an electronic substitute for vision?
2. What is the gate-control theory of pain?
3. How is naloxone used to determine whether a pain-relieving technique works by stimulating endorphin activity?

Body Senses

Just as your skin senses let you judge the state of your skin, your body senses tell you the position of your limbs and help you maintain your equilibrium. The body senses—the *kinesthetic sense* and the *vestibular sense*—often are taken for granted and have inspired less research than the other senses. But they are crucial to everyday functioning.

The Kinesthetic Sense

kinesthetic sense The sense that provides information about the position of the joints, the degree of tension in the muscles, and the movement of the arms and legs.

The **kinesthetic sense** informs you of the position of your joints, the tension in your muscles, and the movement of your arms and legs. This information is provided by special receptors in your joints, muscles, and tendons. Kinesthetic receptors in your muscles let you judge the force as well as the path of your limb movements. Limb movements produce activity in specific regions of the somatosensory cortex (Prud'homme, Cohen, & Kalaska, 1994).

If your leg has ever "fallen asleep" (depriving you of kinesthetic sensations) and collapsed when you stood up, you realize that the kinesthetic sense helps you maintain enough tension in your legs to stand erect. Your kinesthetic sense also protects you from injury. If you are holding an object that is too heavy, kinesthetic receptors signal you to put it down to prevent injury to your muscles and tendons. Alcohol intoxication interferes with kinesthetic feedback, impairing movement by disrupting the sense of limb position

(Wang, Nicholson, Mahoney, & Li, 1993). Athletes may benefit from using mental imagery of kinesthetic sensations to improve their performance on tasks that demand precise timing and coordination of movements (Fery, 2003).

Imagine losing your kinesthetic sense permanently, as happened to a woman described in a case study by the neurologist Oliver Sacks (1985). This robust, athletic young woman developed a rare inflammatory condition that affected only her kinesthetic neurons. She lost all feedback from her body, making it impossible for her to sit, stand, or walk. Her body became as floppy as a rag doll, and she reported feeling like a disembodied mind. She was able to compensate only slightly by using her sense of vision to regulate her body posture and movements. Thus, our kinesthetic sense, which we usually take for granted, plays an important role in our everyday motor functioning, such as writing (Teasdale, Forget, Bard, & Paillard, 1995).

As in the case of other senses, kinesthetic perception is subject to top-down processes, as in its ability to judge the weight of objects. This finding was demonstrated in a study that compared the ability of golfers and non-golfers to judge the weights of practice golf balls and real golf balls. Though practice balls are normally heavier than real balls, the balls used in this study were equal in weight. The golfers, whose experience told them that practice balls are heavier than real balls, judged the practice balls to be heavier. The non-golfers, who had no experience with golf balls, correctly judged the balls to be equal in weight. Thus, the golfers' experience with golf balls affected their kinesthetic perception of the balls' comparative weights (Ellis & Lederman, 1998).

The Body Senses

The kinesthetic sense and the vestibular sense provide gymnasts, dancers, athletes, and other performers, with exquisite control over their body movements.
Source: Tutti Frutti/Shutterstock.com.

The Vestibular Sense

Whereas the kinesthetic sense informs you of the state of your body parts, your **vestibular sense**, which depends on organs in the inner ear, informs you of your head's position in space, helping you maintain your balance and orientation.

vestibular sense The sense that provides information about the head's position in space and helps in the maintenance of balance.

The Vestibular Organs

The **otolith organs** (the saccule and the utricle) detect horizontal or vertical linear movement of the head and help you orient yourself in regard to gravity. The other vestibular organs are the **semicircular canals**, which are three fluid-filled tubes oriented in different planes. Their location is indicated in Figure 5-25. When your head moves in a given direction, the jellylike fluid in the semicircular canal oriented in that direction at first lags behind the movement of the walls of the canal. This makes hair cells protruding into the fluid bend in the direction opposite to the direction of head movement. The bending of hair cells triggers neural impulses that are relayed to your cerebellum, to help you maintain your balance.

otolith organs The vestibular organs that detect horizontal or vertical linear movement of the head.

semicircular canals The curved vestibular organs of the inner ear that detect rotary movements of the head in any direction.

Motion Sickness

Though the vestibular sense helps you maintain your equilibrium, it also can induce motion sickness, particularly in the case of slow, rolling motions (Howarth & Griffin, 2003). Fortunately, repeated exposure to situations that induce motion sickness tends to produce tolerance (Hu & Stern, 1999), and a study of paratroopers found that two-thirds had motion sickness on their first jump but only one-quarter had it on their fifth jump (Antunano & Hernandez, 1989). Moreover, motion sickness is reduced by a sense of personal control—which might explain why you are less likely to develop motion sickness when you are driving an automobile than when you are a passenger in one (Golding, Bles, Bos, Haynes, & Gresty, 2003).

The mechanisms that underlie motion sickness are still debated, but an influential view holds that motion sickness is induced by conflict between visual and vestibular sensations. Suppose you are in a windowless cabin aboard a ship in a rough sea. Your eyes tell you that you are stationary in relationship to one aspect of your environment—your cabin. Yet your vestibular sense tells you that you are moving in relationship to another aspect of your environment—the ocean. But this view does not explain why conflict between visual

FIGURE 5-25
The Vestibular Organs

When your head moves, fluid movement in the vestibular organs of the inner ear causes hair cells to bend, generating neural impulses that travel along the vestibular nerve to the brain. The semicircular canals detect tilting or rotation of your head. The otolith organs (the saccule and the utricle) detect linear movements of the head.

Source: Alexilusmedical/Shutterstock.com.

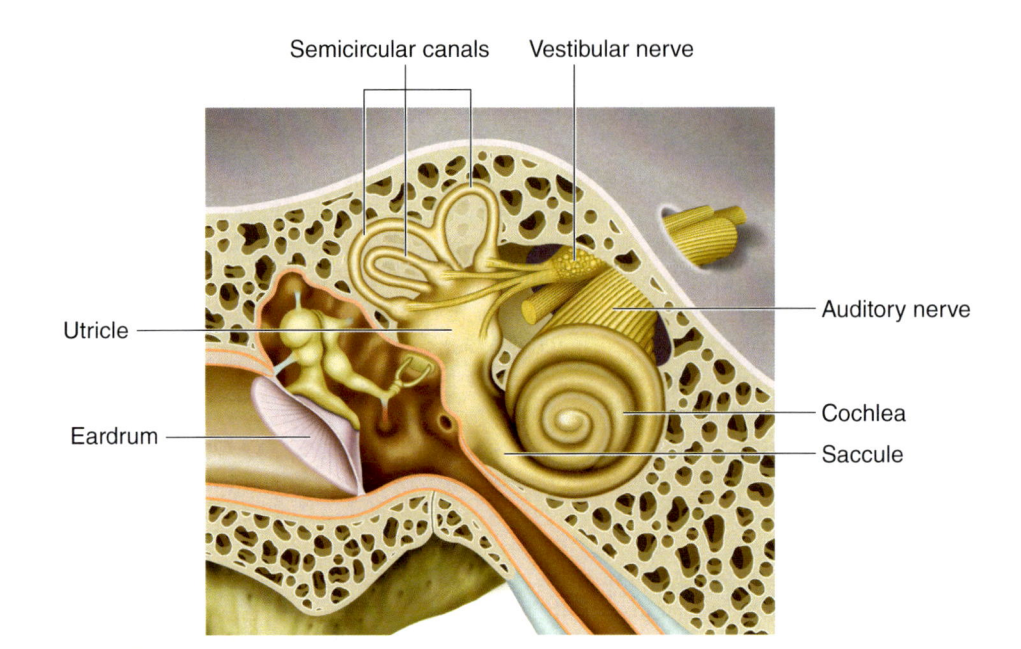

and vestibular sensations induces nausea. One hypothesis is that the motion-induced disruption of the normal association between visual and vestibular sensations is similar to the disruption produced by toxins, such as those in spoiled food, that induce nausea. As a result, motion induces nausea (Warwick-Evans, Symons, Fitch, & Burrows, 1998). As mentioned earlier, motion sickness is reduced by a sense of personal control—which might explain why if you look at the horizon while aboard a ship, you are less likely to develop motion sickness.

Section Review: Body Senses

1. What is the kinesthetic sense?
2. What is the role of the vestibular sense in motion sickness?

Extrasensory Perception

As you have just read, perception depends on the stimulation of sensory receptors by various kinds of energy. But you have certainly heard claims that support the possibility of perception independent of sensory receptors, so-called **extrasensory perception (ESP)**. The field that studies ESP and related phenomena is called **parapsychology** (*para-* means "besides"). The name indicates its failure to gain widespread acceptance within mainstream psychology. Parapsychological abilities are typically called *paranormal*. During the past decade, scientific interest in paranormal research has spread beyond Europe and North America, particularly into Latin American countries such as Brazil (Zangariand & Machado, 2001), Mexico (Ledezma & Monroig, 1997), Argentina (Parra, 1997), and China (Li & Zheng, 2015).

Despite scientific skepticism about paranormal abilities, a survey found that more than 99 percent of American college students believed in at least one paranormal ability and that more than 65 percent claimed a personal experience with at least one (Messer & Griggs, 1989). Moreover, mainstream journals in psychology, philosophy, and medicine periodically publish articles on paranormal abilities. Popular belief in paranormal abilities was exemplified in a 1986 lawsuit in which a Philadelphia woman who made a living as a psychic sued a hospital, insisting that a CT scan of her head made her lose her

extrasensory perception (ESP) The alleged ability to perceive events without the use of sensory receptors.

parapsychology The study of extrasensory perception, psychokinesis, and related phenomena.

ESP abilities. A jury, impressed by the testimony of police officers who claimed she had helped them solve crimes by using ESP, awarded her $988,000 for the loss of her livelihood (Tulsky, 1986). (The jury's decision was later overturned on appeal.) Despite such widespread public acceptance of paranormal abilities, most psychologists are skeptical (Bem & Honorton, 1994). Before learning why they are, consider several of the paranormal abilities studied by parapsychologists.

Alleged Paranormal Abilities

More than three decades ago, members of the Grateful Dead rock band had their audiences at a series of six concerts in Port Chester, New York, try to transmit mental images of slides of art prints to a person asleep in a dream laboratory miles away at Maimonides Hospital in Brooklyn. When the sleeper awoke, he described the content of his dreams. Independent judges rated his dream reports as more similar to the content of the slides than were the dream reports of another person who had not been designated to receive the images (Ullman, Krippner, & Vaughan, 1973). It was reported as a successful demonstration of **mental telepathy**, the alleged ability to perceive the thoughts of others. This experiment was part of a series of ESP-dream studies carried out at Maimonides Hospital by Stanley Krippner and his colleagues (Krippner, 1993). Krippner is recognized as one of the contemporary leaders in the scientific approach to paranormal phenomena ("Stanley C. Krippner," 2003).

Dream-ESP studies conducted since the Maimonides studies have been less successful (Sherwood & Roe, 2003). One study of dream telepathy had a "sender" advertise in a national newspaper that he would send a dream telepathy image between midnight and 10 a.m. on a specified night. Different images were "sent" every 2 hours. More than 500 readers submitted dream reports and the times they "received" the images. Judges blind to the target sequence decided whether the reports matched the pictures. Unlike the results of the Grateful Dead demonstration, these judges' assessments provided no support for dream telepathy—the reports did not match the images that were sent (Hearne, 1989).

Related to mental telepathy is **clairvoyance**, the alleged ability to perceive objects or events without any sensory contact (Steinkamp, Milton, & Morris, 1998). You might be considered clairvoyant if you could identify all the objects in your psychology professor's desk drawer without looking in it. Many colleges host psychic entertainers, such as "the Amazing Kreskin," who impress their audiences by giving demonstrations such as "reading" the serial number of a dollar bill in an audience member's wallet. Reports that clairvoyant psychics have solved crimes by leading police to bodies or stolen items are exaggerated. A survey of police departments in the 50 largest American cities found not a single report of a clairvoyant who had solved a crime for them (Sweat & Durm, 1993).

Whereas mental telepathy and clairvoyance deal with the present, **precognition** is the alleged ability to perceive events in the future. An example would be predicting the next spin of a roulette wheel, one of the common ways of measuring precognitive ability (Kugel, 1990–1991). In regard to precognition about future events that come true, researchers must be aware that people who believe that they have had a precognitive experience might by their own behavior bring about the event that they predict (Steinkamp, 2000). Parapsychologists who are open to the possibility that precognition does exist are left with the daunting scientific problem of explaining how minds that exist in the present can perceive events that take place in the future (Randall, 1998).

Do not confuse precognition with **déjà vu**, an uncanny feeling that you have experienced a present situation in the past and that you can anticipate what will happen in the next few moments. There are four major viewpoints regarding the nature of déjà vu experiences. First, the *dual-processing* view holds that two cognitive processes are momentarily out of synchronization. Second, the *neurological* view holds that there is a momentary disruption in neurological transmission. Third, the *memory* view holds that we may be unconsciously aware of unfamiliar stimuli. Fourth, the *attention* view holds that we first perceive something without attending to it and then shortly thereafter perceive it while

mental telepathy The alleged ability to perceive the thoughts of others.

clairvoyance The alleged ability to perceive objects or events without any sensory contact with them.

precognition The alleged ability to perceive events in the future.

déjà vu A feeling that you have experienced a present situation in the past and that you can anticipate what will happen next.

psychokinesis (PK) The alleged ability to control objects with the mind alone.

attending to it. There is not enough scientific evidence to strongly support or refute any of these views (Brown, 2003).

Closely allied with ESP is **psychokinesis (PK)**, the alleged ability to control objects with the mind alone. In an early experiment on PK, a person who supposedly had PK ability used a cup to throw six dice 2,376 times while trying to make a particular face come up. Each of the six possible faces was used as the designated face an equal number of times. The individual produced significantly more "hits" than would be expected by chance. The researchers concluded that this experiment provided evidence for the existence of PK (Herter & Rhine, 1945). More recent research has assessed people's ability to influence computer games (Broughton & Perlstrom, 1992) or a laser beam (Stevens, 1998–99). But a report by the National Academy of Sciences found no basis for any kind of paranormal ability (Palmer, Honorton, & Utts, 1989).

Problems with Paranormal Research

Parapsychology has attracted many prominent supporters. Mark Twain, William James, and G. Stanley Hall were members of the Society for Psychical Research, with James serving a term as president and Hall a term as vice president. James even established standards for research design in parapsychology, insisting that the scientific method was the only adequate means to determine whether paranormal phenomena were real (Schmeidler, 1993). Credit for the attempt to make parapsychology a legitimate area of scientific research to some scientists goes to J. B. Rhine (1895–1980) of Duke University, who began a program of experimentation on paranormal phenomena in the 1930s (Matlock, 1991). His wife, Louisa Rhine, likewise became a leading parapsychologist (Feather, 1983). Several prestigious British universities also have lent credibility to parapsychology by sponsoring paranormal research. Edinburgh University in Scotland even set up the first faculty chair in parapsychology with a $750,000 grant from the estate of author Arthur Koestler (Dickson, 1984).

Despite the popular acceptance of parapsychology, most psychologists remain skeptical (Wesp & Montgomery, 1998). One reason is that many supposed instances of paranormal phenomena turn out to be the result of poorly controlled demonstrations (Schmidt & Walach, 2000). In a case reported by the magician James "The Amazing" Randi, a woman claimed she could influence fish by PK. Every time she put her hand against one side of an aquarium, the fish swam to the opposite side. Randi responded, "She calls it psychic; I call it frightened fish." He suggested she put dark paper over a side of the aquarium and test her ability on that side. After trying Randi's suggestion and finding that the fish no longer swam to the opposite side, she exclaimed, "It's marvelous! The power doesn't penetrate brown paper!" (Morris, 1980, p. 106). You might recognize her comment as an example of Piaget's concept of assimilation (see Chapter 4).

Supporters of parapsychology might also too readily accept chance events as evidence of paranormal phenomena (Brugger & Taylor, 2003). For example, at some time you probably have decided to call a friend, picked up the phone, and found your friend already on the other end of the line. Did mental telepathy make you call each other at the same time? Not necessarily. Perhaps the occurrence is simply due to coincidence, or perhaps you and your friend call each other often and at about the same time of day, so on occasion you might coincidentally call each other at exactly the same moment.

Another blow against the credibility of parapsychology is that some impressive demonstrations later have been found to involve fraud (Rhine, 1974). In a widely publicized case, the noted psychic Tamara Rand claimed to have predicted the 1981 assassination attempt on U.S. president Ronald Reagan in a videotape made before the attempt and later shown on the *Today* show. This case was considered evidence of precognition—until James Randi discovered that she had made the videotape after the assassination attempt ("Psychic Watergate," 1981).

Magic tricks also are often passed off as paranormal phenomena. In 1979 James McDonnell, chairman of the board of the McDonnell-Douglas corporation, gave $500,000 to Washington University in St. Louis to establish a parapsychology research laboratory.

A respected physics professor took charge of the project and invited alleged psychics to be tested there. Randi sent two magicians, aged 17 and 18, to be tested as psychics. After demonstrating their PK "abilities" during 120 hours of testing over a 3-year period, the two were proclaimed the only participants with PK ability.

But both had relied on magic—in some instances, beginner's-level magic. For example, they demonstrated PK by moving a clock across a table through the use of an ultra-thin thread held between their thumbs. Because of demonstrations like this one, Randi has urged parapsychologists to permit magicians to observe their research so that magic tricks are not mistaken for paranormal phenomena (Cox, 1984). Since 1965, Randi has offered a reward—now amounting to $1 million—to anyone who can demonstrate a true paranormal ability under well-controlled conditions. No one has done so.

Parapsychologists defend their research and insist that critics often reject positive findings by assuming they are impossible and therefore must be caused by some other factor, such as poor controls, magic tricks, or outright fraud (Child, 1985). Thus, opposition to paranormal research might reflect the current scientific paradigm as much as it does any methodological weaknesses in paranormal research (Krippner, 1995). Moreover, parapsychologists argue, paranormal abilities might be so subtle that they cannot be demonstrated at will or require highly motivated individuals to demonstrate them. For example, believers in paranormal abilities perform better on paranormal tests than do nonbelievers (Schmeidler, 1985). Likewise, experimenters who believe in paranormal abilities are more likely than nonbelievers to conduct research studies that produce positive findings. Gertrude Schmeidler (1997), a leading parapsychologist, notes that experimenter bias might account for the poor performance of some participants in ESP or PK studies. She insists that experimenters who are cynical about ESP or PK might inhibit talented people from performing well in research studies.

But even many parapsychologists agree that, from a scientific standpoint, the main weakness of research studies on paranormal abilities is the difficulty in replicating them (Galak, LeBoeuf, Nelson, & Simmons, 2012). As discussed in Chapter 2, scientists discredit events that cannot be replicated under similar conditions. Yet some parapsychologists insist that positive research findings related to paranormal phenomena have been replicated more often than critics of parapsychology will acknowledge (Roig, 1993), that meta-analyses show effects that are greater than those expected by chance alone (Storm, Tressoldi, & DiRisio, 2010), and that paranormal phenomena are so subtle that they are more likely to occur spontaneously in everyday life than on demand in a laboratory setting (Alvarado, 1996).

A final criticism of parapsychology is that there is no satisfactory explanation of paranormal phenomena (Fassbender, 1997). Their acceptance might require the discovery of new forms of energy. Evidence for the role of some sort of energy force comes from the finding that research studies conducted during periods of low geomagnetic activity have been associated with the most positive ESP research findings (Krippner, Vaughan, & Spottiswoode, 2000). But attempts to detect any unusual form of energy radiating from people with supposed paranormal abilities have failed (Balanovski & Taylor, 1978).

The Status of Parapsychology

Parapsychologists point out, however, that failure to know the cause of something does not mean that the phenomenon does not exist (Rockwell, 1979). They remind psychologists to be skeptical rather than cynical because many phenomena that are now scientifically acceptable were once considered impossible and unworthy of study. For example, scientists used to ridicule reports of stones falling from the sky and refused to investigate them. In 1807, after hearing of a report by two Yale University professors of a stone shower in Connecticut, President Thomas Jefferson, a scientist himself, said, "Gentlemen, I would rather believe that those two Yankee professors would lie than to believe that stones fell from heaven" (quoted in Diaconis, 1978). Today, even young children know that such stones are meteorites and that they indeed fall from the sky. Even William James, perhaps reflecting his being one of the most open-minded of scientists, believed at the end of his life that there was something to psychic phenomena but that he had still not found any convincing evidence of it. Nonetheless, because alleged paranormal abilities are so unusual, seemingly inexplicable, and difficult to demonstrate reliably, even open-minded psychologists will continue to discount them unless they receive more compelling evidence. The extraordinary claims made by parapsychologists will require extraordinary evidence for mainstream psychologists to accept their validity (Grey, 1994).

> **Section Review:** Extrasensory Perception
>
> 1. What are the four alleged paranormal abilities?
> 2. What are the major shortcomings of paranormal research?

Chapter Summary

Sensory Processes

- Sensation is the process that detects stimuli from one's body or environment.
- Perception is the process that organizes sensations into meaningful patterns.
- Psychophysics is the study of the relationships between the physical characteristics of stimuli and the conscious psychological experiences they produce.
- The minimum amount of stimulation that can be detected is called the absolute threshold.
- According to signal-detection theory, the detection of a stimulus depends on both its intensity and the physiological and psychological state of the receiver.
- Research on subliminal perception investigates whether participants can unconsciously perceive stimuli that do not exceed the absolute threshold.
- The minimum amount of change in stimulation that can be detected is called the difference threshold.
- Weber's law states that the amount of change in stimulation needed to produce a just noticeable difference is a constant proportion of the original stimulus.
- The tendency of our sensory receptors to be increasingly less responsive to an unchanging stimulus is called sensory adaptation.

Visual Sensation

- Vision lets us sense objects by the light reflected from them into our eyes.
- The lens focuses light onto the rods and cones of the retina.
- Visual input is transmitted by the optic nerves to the brain, ultimately reaching the visual cortex.
- During dark adaptation the rods and cones become more sensitive to light, with the rods becoming significantly more sensitive than the cones.
- The trichromatic theory of color vision considers the interaction of red, green, and blue cones.
- The opponent-process theory assumes that color vision depends on activity in red-green, blue-yellow, and black-white ganglion cells and cells in the thalamus.
- Color blindness is usually caused by an inherited lack of a cone pigment.

Visual Perception

- Form perception depends on distinguishing figure from ground.
- In studying form perception, Gestalt psychologists identified the principles of proximity, similarity, closure, and continuity.
- Whereas Gestalt psychologists claim that we perceive objects as wholes, other theories claim that we construct objects from their component parts.
- Depth perception lets us determine how far away objects are from us.
- Binocular cues to depth require the interaction of both eyes.
- Monocular cues to depth require only one eye.
- Experience in viewing objects contributes to size constancy, shape constancy, and brightness constancy.
- The misapplication of depth perception cues and perceptual constancies can contribute to visual illusions.
- Sensory experience and cultural background both affect visual perception.

Hearing

- The sense of hearing (audition) detects sound waves produced by the vibration of objects.
- Sound waves cause the tympanic membrane to vibrate.
- The ossicles of the middle ear convey the vibrations to the oval window of the cochlea, which causes waves to travel through fluid within the cochlea.
- The waves bend hair cells on the basilar membrane, sending neural impulses along the auditory nerve.
- Sounds are ultimately processed by the auditory cortex of the temporal lobes.

- The frequency of a sound determines its pitch.
- Pitch perception is explained by place theory, frequency theory, and volley theory.
- The intensity of a sound determines its loudness.
- People may suffer from conduction deafness or nerve deafness.
- The mixture of sound waves determines a sound's quality, or timbre.
- Sound localization depends on differences in a sound's arrival time and intensity at the two ears.

Chemical Senses

- The chemical senses of smell and taste detect chemicals in the air we breathe or the substances we ingest.
- The sense of smell (olfaction) depends on receptor cells on the nasal membrane that respond to particular chemicals.
- Odorous secretions called pheromones affect the sexual behavior of animals.
- The sense of taste (gustation) depends on receptor cells on the taste buds of the tongue that respond to particular chemicals.
- The basic tastes are sweet, salty, sour, and bitter.

Skin Senses

- Skin senses depend on receptors that send neural impulses to the somatosensory cortex.
- Touch sensitivity depends on the concentration of receptors in the skin.
- Pain depends on both physical and psychological factors.
- According to the gate-control theory of pain, stimulation of touch neurons closes a spinal gate, which inhibits neural impulses underlying pain from traveling up the spinal cord.
- Pain-relieving techniques such as placebos, acupuncture, and transcutaneous nerve stimulation relieve pain by stimulating the release of endorphins.
- Hypnosis appears to relieve pain by distracting the hypnotized person.

Body Senses

- Your body senses make you aware of the position of your limbs and help you maintain your equilibrium.
- The kinesthetic sense informs you of the position of your joints, the tension in your muscles, and the movement of your arms and legs.
- The vestibular sense informs you of your position in space, helping you maintain your equilibrium.
- The vestibular organs comprise the otolith organs (the saccule and the utricle) and the semicircular canals.
- An influential theory of motion sickness attributes it to conflict between the visual and vestibular senses.

Extrasensory Perception

- Most members of the lay public accept the existence of paranormal phenomena such as extrasensory perception and psychokinesis; most psychologists do not.
- Psychologists are skeptical because research in parapsychology has been marked by sloppy procedures, acceptance of coincidences as positive evidence, fraudulent reports, use of magic tricks, failure to replicate studies, and inability to explain paranormal phenomena.
- Supporters of parapsychology claim that their research has been subjected to unfair criticism.

Key Terms

perception (p. 152)
prosopagnosia (p. 151)
sensation (p. 152)
visual agnosia (p. 151)

Sensory Processes

absolute threshold (p. 152)
difference threshold (p. 154)
just noticeable difference (jnd) (p. 155)
psychophysics (p. 152)
sensory adaptation (p. 156)
sensory receptors (p. 152)
sensory transduction (p. 152)
signal-detection theory (p. 153)
subliminal perception (p. 153)
Weber's law (p. 155)

Visual Sensation

accommodation (p. 158)
afterimage (p. 164)
color blindness (p. 164)
cones (p. 158)
cornea (p. 157)
dark adaptation (p. 161)
fovea (p. 159)
hyperopia (p. 158)
lens (p. 158)
myopia (p. 158)
opponent-process theory (p. 163)
optic chiasm (p. 160)
optic nerve (p. 158)
photopigments (p. 160)
retina (p. 158)
rods (p. 158)
sclera (p. 157)
smooth pursuit movements (p. 160)
trichromatic theory (p. 163)
visible spectrum (p. 156)
vision (p. 156)
visual cortex (p. 160)

Visual Perception

binocular cues (p. 167)
brightness constancy (p. 171)
depth perception (p. 167)
feature-detector theory (p. 167)
figure-ground perception (p. 166)
illusory contours (p. 167)
monocular cues (p. 168)
moon illusion (p. 172)
shape constancy (p. 171)
size constancy (p. 169)
visual illusion (p. 172)

Hearing

audition (p. 174)
auditory cortex (p. 177)
auditory nerve (p. 177)
basilar membrane (p. 177)
cochlea (p. 176)
conduction deafness (p. 179)
frequency theory (p. 178)
hair cell (p. 177)
loudness perception (p. 178)
nerve deafness (p. 179)
pitch perception (p. 178)

place theory (p. 178)
sound localization (p. 180)
timbre (p. 180)
tympanic membrane (p. 175)
volley theory (p. 178)

Chemical Senses

gustation (p. 183)
olfaction (p. 181)
pheromone (p. 182)
taste buds (p. 183)

Skin Senses

acupuncture (p. 186)
gate-control theory (p. 185)
placebo (p. 186)
skin senses (p. 184)
somatosensory cortex (p. 184)
transcutaneous electrical nerve stimulation (TENS) (p. 187)

Body Senses

kinesthetic sense (p. 188)

otolith organs (p. 189)
semicircular canals (p. 189)
vestibular sense (p. 189)

Extrasensory Perception

clairvoyance (p. 191)
dèjá vu (p. 191)
extrasensory perception (ESP) (p. 190)
mental telepathy (p. 191)
parapsychology (p. 190)
precognition (p. 191)
psychokinesis (PK) (p. 192)

Chapter Quiz

Note: Answers for the Chapter Quiz questions are provided at the end of the book.

1. Conflict between visual and vestibular sensations may induce
   a. psychokinesis.
   b. motion sickness.
   c. auditory dominance.
   d. mental dissociation.

2. The study of visual restriction in kittens (Blakemore & Cooper, 1970) found that kittens not exposed to lines of a particular orientation will
   a. fail to grow neurons responsive to that orientation.
   b. show degeneration of neurons responsive to that orientation.
   c. overcompensate by growing more neurons responsive to that orientation.
   d. show degeneration of neurons responsive to that orientation and perpendicular orientations.

3. A Viewmaster (a stereoscopic) toy creates a 3-D image by taking advantage of
   a. convergence.
   b. motion parallax.
   c. binocular disparity.
   d. linear perspective.

4. Smells may evoke powerful emotional responses because of pathways from the olfactory nerves to the
   a. brain stem.
   b. limbic system.
   c. corpus callosum.
   d. medulla.

5. Accommodation in the eye
   a. helps focus images on the retina.
   b. provides binocular depth perception.
   c. regulates the amount of light striking the retina.
   d. lets it rebound to its normal curvature after being poked by a finger or other object.

6. The kinesthetic sense enables one to
   a. perceive the movement of objects.
   b. detect the position of one's limbs.
   c. allegedly move objects with one's mind.
   d. sense changes in the temperature of objects.

7. While studying in the library you are, at first, distracted by the constant hum of the heating system. But you eventually stop noticing it. This is an example of
   a. synesthesia.
   b. sublimation.
   c. habituation.
   d. sensory adaptation.

8. Pheromones
   a. account for color vision.
   b. may explain motion sickness.
   c. affect the behavior of other animals.
   d. enable bats to locate prey by their echoes.

9. A hearing aid would be LEAST useful in treating deafness caused by damage to the
   a. pinna.
   b. eardrum.
   c. ossicles.
   d. auditory nerve.

10. A person suffers a wound that damages the temporal lobe. He would most likely experience difficulty in
    a. moving.
    b. seeing.
    c. hearing.
    d. smelling.

11. The study that used professional baseball players found that batters can keep their eyes on the ball
    a. only when it is about to hit their bat.
    b. only after it is about halfway to home plate.
    c. from the pitcher's hand until it reaches a few feet from home plate.
    d. from the pitcher's hand all the way to the point it makes contact with the bat.

12. The fact that the inner corner of a room looks farther away than the outer corner of a building provides one explanation of the
    a. Ponzo illusion.
    b. Ames room illusion.
    c. Poggendorf illusion.
    d. Müller-Lyer illusion.

13. If you could get the answers to this quiz by reading your professor's mind, you would demonstrate
    a. precognition.
    b. clairvoyance.
    c. psychokinesis.
    d. mental telepathy.

14. If a person's left optic nerve is completely severed, she would be
    a. blind in her left eye.
    b. blind in her left visual field.
    c. blind in her right visual field.
    d. able to detect objects, but not identify them, with her left eye.

15. The gate-control theory explains
    a. pain perception.
    b. taste perception.
    c. touch perception.
    d. pitch perception.

16. Papillae are found on the
    a. skin.
    b. tongue.
    c. basilar membrane.
    d. olfactory epithelium.

17. After observing that naval aviators sometimes crashed into airplanes ahead of them, researchers decided to set their taillights a standard distance apart. This improved depth perception by taking advantage of
    a. convergence.
    b. motion parallax.
    c. linear perspective.
    d. aerial perspective.

18. Advocates of top-down processing assume that the
    a. ability to perceive forms is based on heredity.
    b. mind is active, rather than passive, in perceiving forms.
    c. visual system composes perceptions mechanically from raw sensations.
    d. visual system processes the upper portions of objects and then proceeds to lower portions.

19. The frequency theory of hearing is best for sounds
    a. above 5,000 Hz.
    b. up to 1,000 Hz.
    c. between 1,000 and 5,000 Hz.
    d. within the range of human hearing.

20. Credit for trying to make ESP a legitimate topic of scientific interest is generally given to
    a. Uri Geller.
    b. J. B. Rhine.
    c. James Randi.
    d. Tamara Rand.

21. You should dim your high beams to oncoming traffic at night and not turn on the dome light to read a map because those actions would interfere with
    a. synesthesia.
    b. afterimages.
    c. color vision.
    d. dark adaptation.

22. The technical name for the "eardrum" is the
    a. pinna.
    b. oval window.
    c. basilar membrane.
    d. tympanic membrane.

23. The saying "the whole is different from the sum of its parts" would be most closely associated with
    a. John Locke.
    b. Ernst Weber.
    c. Max Wertheimer.
    d. Hermann von Helmholtz.

24. Touch sensations would most likely be disrupted by damage to the
    a. frontal lobes.
    b. temporal lobes.
    c. parietal lobes.
    d. occipital lobes.

25. An engineer designing a new television finds that for the middle ranges of light intensity a perceived change in brightness is a constant fraction of the original intensity. This is an example of
    a. Wundt's law.
    b. Weber's law.
    c. Young's law.
    d. Helmholtz's law.

Thought Questions

1. Why is it conceivable that creatures elsewhere in the universe have evolved sensory receptors that detect radio and television waves?

2. How does the opponent-process theory of color vision explain afterimages?

3. Why are both frequency theory and place theory needed to explain pitch perception?

4. Why do psychologists tend to discount the existence of paranormal abilities?

CHAPTER 6

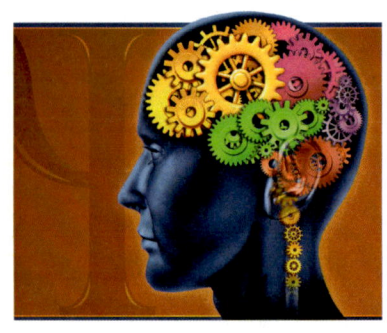

Consciousness

Source: Lightspring/Shutterstock.com.

Chapter Outline

The Nature of Consciousness
Sleep
Dreams
Hypnosis
Psychoactive Drugs

If you are like many students, you have experienced the dreaded "all-nighter"—staying awake through the night to write a paper or study for an exam. You probably felt exhausted the next night, collapsed into bed, slept a bit longer than usual, and awoke refreshed—none the worse for your experience. But what would happen to you if you stayed awake for several days? Would you suffer cognitive and physical deterioration? Would any negative effects be long-lasting?

Though research on prolonged sleep deprivation began in the 1890s, the first study to gain widespread attention took place in 1959. On January 21, Peter Tripp, a popular disc jockey in New York City, began a radiothon to raise money for the March of Dimes fight against polio. He decided to proceed despite anecdotal reports about animals and people who had died after prolonged sleep deprivation. He chose to believe, instead, other anecdotal reports about explorers and military troops who had survived bouts of extended sleep deprivation (Coren, 1996).

During his radiothon, Tripp stayed awake for 200 hours (more than 8 days), each evening broadcasting his 5 to 8 p.m. radio show from an Army recruiting booth in Times Square. He did this for the publicity and to permit passersby to look through the windows of the booth and verify that he was awake. Tripp periodically left the booth to go to the Astor Hotel across the street to wash up, use the toilet, change his clothes, and undergo medical examinations. Physicians and researchers monitored several of his physiological responses during the radiothon for his safety and to obtain scientific data about the effects of sleep deprivation.

As the days passed, Tripp showed signs of psychological deterioration. After 4 days he could not focus his attention well enough to do simple tasks, and he began experiencing hallucinations, such as seeing a rabbit run across the booth and flames shooting out of a drawer in his hotel room. Some accounts of Tripp's radiothon note that after 5 days he began taking a stimulant to stay awake (Luce & Segal, 1966). On the 8th and final day, he displayed delusional thinking, insisting that his physician was an undertaker coming to prepare him for burial. Tripp became so paranoid that he refused to undergo requested tests and insisted that unknown enemies were trying to force him to fall asleep by putting drugs in his food and drink. After his ordeal, Tripp slept 13 hours and quickly returned to his customary level of psychological well-being.

Did Tripp's experience demonstrate that we need to sleep to maintain healthy psychological functioning and that a single night's sleep can overcome any ill effects of sleep deprivation? Possibly—but possibly not. First, Tripp's experiences were those of a single participant. His reactions to sleep deprivation might have been unique and not necessarily true of other people. Second, as you will learn later in the chapter, the delusions Tripp displayed near the end of his ordeal might have been caused by the stimulants he took to stay awake and not by his lack of sleep. Our knowledge of the effects of sleep deprivation and the effects of stimulants comes from research by psychologists and other scientists interested in the study of *consciousness*.

The Nature of Consciousness

What is consciousness? In 1690 John Locke wrote that "consciousness is the perception of what passes in a man's own mind" (Locke, 1690/1959, p. 138). Today psychologists share a similar view of **consciousness**, defining it as the subjective awareness of one's own cognitive activity, including thoughts, feelings, sensations, and surroundings.

consciousness Awareness of one's own cognitive activity, including thoughts, feelings, and sensations.

The Stream of Consciousness

Two hundred years after Locke offered his definition of consciousness, William James (1890/1981) noted that consciousness is personal, selective, continuous, and changing. Consider your own consciousness. It is *personal* because you feel that it belongs to you—you do not share it with anyone else. Consciousness is *selective* because you can attend to certain things while ignoring other things. Right now you can shift your attention to a nearby voice, the first word in the next sentence, or the feel of clothing touching your body. Consciousness is *continuous* because its contents blend into one another—the mind cannot be broken down into meaningful segments. And consciousness is *changing* because its contents are in a constant state of flux, with one cognitive state following another in rapid succession. Because of this, you cannot focus on one thing more than momentarily without other thoughts, feelings, or sensations drifting through your mind.

Because consciousness is both continuous and changing, James likened it to a stream (Natsoulas, 1997–98). Your favorite stream remains the same stream even though the water at a particular site is continuously being replaced by new water. Even as you read this paragraph, you might notice irrelevant thoughts, feelings, and sensations passing through your own mind. Some might grab your attention; others might quickly fade away. If you were to write them down as they occurred, a person reading what you had written might think you were confused or even that you were mentally ill. The disjointed nature of stream-of-consciousness writing makes it hard to follow without knowing the context of the story. You can appreciate this by trying to make sense of the opening passage from James Joyce's *A Portrait of the Artist as a Young Man*:

> Once upon a time and a very good time it was there was a moocow coming down along the road and this moocow that was coming down along the road met a nicens little boy named baby tuckoo. . . .
>
> His father told him that story: his father looked at him through a glass: he had a hairy face.
>
> He was baby tuckoo. The moocow came down the road where Betty Byrne lived: she sold lemon platt.
>
> *O, the wild rose blossoms*

Chapter 6 Consciousness

On the little green place.

He sang that song. That was his song.

O, the green wothe botheth.

When you wet the bed first it is warm then it gets cold. His mother put on the oilsheet. That had the queer smell.

His mother a nicer smell than his father. She played on the piano the sailor's hornpipe for him to dance. (Joyce, 1916/1967, p. 171)

As a functionalist, William James believed that consciousness is an evolutionary development that enhances our ability to adapt to the environment. James declared, "It seems reasonable to suppose that, unless consciousness served some useful purpose, it would not have been superadded to life" (quoted in Rieber, 1980, p. 205). That is, consciousness helps us function. Consciousness provides us with a cognitive representation of the world that permits us to try out courses of action in our mind before acting on them. This makes us more reflective and more flexible in adapting to the world, thereby reducing our tendency to engage in aimless, reckless, or impulsive behavior.

Attention

attention The process by which the individual focuses awareness on certain contents of consciousness while ignoring others.

Today researchers are especially interested in an aspect of consciousness identified by James: its *selectivity*. We refer to the selectivity of consciousness as **attention**, which functions like a tuner to make us aware of certain stimuli while blocking out others. This selectivity is adaptive because it prevents our consciousness from becoming a chaotic jumble of thoughts, feelings, and sensations. For example, while you are reading this paragraph, it would be maladaptive for you to also be aware of irrelevant stimuli, such as the shoes on your feet or people talking. Of course, it would be adaptive to shift your attention if your shoes are too tight or someone yelled "Fire!" outside your room. The functional advantage of selective attention is demonstrated by the greater tendency of children with a history of physical abuse to notice angry facial expressions (Pollak & Tolley-Schell, 2003), and by people with schizophrenia who display deficits in selective attention (Ferchiou, Schühoff, Bulzacka, Leboyer, & Szöke, 2010).

Experimental research, as well as everyday experience, illustrates the selectivity of attention. Consider a study in which participants watched two videotapes superimposed on each other (Neisser & Becklen, 1975). One videotape portrayed two people playing a hand-slapping game, and the other portrayed three people bouncing and throwing a basketball. Participants were told to watch one of the games and to press a response key whenever a particular action occurred. Those watching the hand game had to respond whenever the participants slapped hands with each other. Those watching the ball game had to respond whenever the ball was thrown. The results showed that participants made few errors. But when they were asked to watch both games simultaneously, using their right hand to respond to one game and their left hand to respond to the other, their performances deteriorated, and they made significantly more errors than when they attended to just one of the games.

What determines whether we will attend to a given stimulus? Functional MRI indicates that your frontal lobe governs the ability to divide one's attention during divided-attention tasks (Loose, Kaufmann, Auer, & Lange, 2003). Among the many stimulus factors that affect attention are whether the stimulus is important, changing, shifting, or novel. We tend to notice stimuli that are personally important. You have certainly experienced the "cocktail party phenomenon," in which you might be engrossed in one conversation at a party yet notice that your name has been mentioned in another conversation. A change in stimulation is likely to attract our attention. When watching television, you are more likely to pay attention to a commercial that is much louder or quieter than the program it interrupts. The importance of attention in everyday life—and survival—is illustrated in

Multitasking
Driving while multitasking is dangerous.
Source: wavebreakmedia/Shutterstock.com.

the controversy regarding the use of cellular telephones in motor vehicles. Research indicates that using a cellular telephone while driving distracts drivers from possibly dangerous situations that they should respond to (Garcia-Larrea, Perchet, Perrin, & Amenedo, 2001). This recent rise in cellular phone use while driving has prompted researchers to investigate divided attention and simulated driving in the laboratory setting. Researchers have found that text messaging and speaking on a cellular phone decrease reaction time and impair driving performance (Drews, Yazdani, Godfrey, Cooper, & Strayer, 2009; Horrey & Wickens, 2006).

Though William James and other psychology pioneers stressed the importance of attention and other aspects of consciousness, interest in these topics declined after John B. Watson stated that "the time seems to have come when psychology must discard all references to consciousness" (Watson, 1913, p. 163). The renewed interest in studying altered states of consciousness during the past few decades (Nelson, 1996) reflects James's observation that "normal waking consciousness, rational consciousness as we call it, is but one special type of consciousness, whilst all about it, parted from it by the filmiest of screens, there lie potential forms of consciousness entirely different" (James, 1902/1992, p. 388).

The Unconscious

In the late 19th century, William James (1890/1981), in his classic psychology textbook, included a section entitled "Can States of Mind Be Unconscious?" which presented 10 arguments answering yes and 10 answering no. Today the extent to which we are affected by unconscious influences still provokes animated debate. But the notion of the unconscious involves any of three different concepts: (1) *perception without awareness*, the unconscious perception of stimuli that normally exceed our absolute threshold (see Chapter 5) but that fall outside our focus of attention; (2) the *Freudian unconscious*, a region of the mind containing thoughts and feelings that motivate us without our awareness; and (3) *subliminal perception*, the unconscious perception of stimuli that are too weak to exceed the absolute threshold for detection. For a lengthier discussion of subliminal perception, see Chapter 5.

Perception Without Awareness

There is substantial evidence that we can be affected by stimuli that are above the normal absolute threshold but to which we are not attending at the time. At the turn of the 20th century, the existence of such **perception without awareness** (Merikle, Smilek, & Eastwood, 2001) led some psychologists to assume that suggestions given to people while they sleep might help children study harder or adults quit smoking (Jones, 1900). But subsequent research has failed to support such sleep learning. Any learning that does take place apparently occurs during brief awakenings (Wood, Bootzin, Kihlstrom, & Schacter, 1992). So, if you decide to study for your next psychology exam by playing an audiotape of class lectures while you are asleep, you will be more likely to disrupt your sleep than to learn significant amounts of material. Though there is no evidence that we can form memories while asleep, there is evidence that when we are awake, we can form memories of events and information that we are unaware of (Czyzewska, 2001). The formation of such *implicit memories* is discussed in Chapter 8.

perception without awareness The unconscious perception of stimuli that normally exceed the absolute threshold but fall outside our focus of attention.

Dichotic Listening Research on attention also has demonstrated the existence of perception without awareness. Consider studies of *dichotic listening*, in which the participant, wearing headphones, repeats—or "shadows"—a message being presented to one ear while another message is being presented to the other ear (Cherry, 1953). Dichotic listening is illustrated in Figure 6-1. By shadowing one message, the participant is prevented from consciously attending to the other one. Though participants cannot recall the unattended message, they might recall certain qualities of it, such as whether it was spoken in a sad, angry, happy, or neutral tone (Voyer & Rodgers, 2002). These studies

FIGURE 6-1
Dichotic Listening

In studies of dichotic listening, participants repeat a message presented to one ear while a different message is presented to the other ear.

"They drove to Florida for spring break and camped on the…"

"He went to the bank to get the loan, which he had…"

"They drove to Florida for spring break and camped on the…"

demonstrate that our brain can process incoming stimuli that exceed the normal absolute threshold even when we do not consciously attend to them.

Blindsight Perception without awareness also is supported in studies of brain damage. Consider *prosopagnosia*, the inability to recognize faces. The disorder, also called face-blindness, typically is caused by damage to a particular region of the cerebral cortex (see Chapter 5). In one study, two women with prosopagnosia were shown photographs of strangers, friends, and relatives while their galvanic skin response (a measure of arousal based on changes in the electrical activity of the skin due to moisture levels from sweat) was recorded. Though the women were unable to recognize their friends and relatives from the photographs, their galvanic skin responses to those photographs were larger compared to their galvanic skin responses to the photographs of strangers. Intact visual pathways in the brain had distinguished between the familiar and the unfamiliar faces without the women's conscious awareness (Tranel & Damasio, 1985). The phenomenon of blindsight occurs for visual stimuli other than faces. People who are blind in a portion of their visual field because of brain damage may still identify a particular target object in that field at greater than a chance level—even though they are not consciously aware of seeing it (Brogaard, 2011).

Controlled versus Automatic Processing Of course, "awareness" is usually not an all-or-none phenomenon. For example, there is a continuum between controlled processing and automatic processing of information (Strayer & Kramer, 1990). At one extreme, when we focus our attention on one target, we use **controlled processing**, which involves more conscious awareness (attention) and cognitive effort and interferes with the performance of other activities. At the other extreme, when we do one thing while focusing our attention on another, we use **automatic processing**, which requires less conscious awareness and cognitive effort and does not interfere with the performance of other activities. Reading, for example, requires an interplay of controlled and automatic processing. We use controlled processing to read unfamiliar words or difficult passages and automatic processing to read familiar words or easy passages (Walczyk, 2000). Figure 6-2 illustrates the difference between controlled and automatic processing.

As we practice a task, we devote less and less attention to it because we move from controlled processing to automatic processing (Bargh, 1992). Think back to when you first learned to write in script or cursive in elementary school. You depended on controlled processing, which required you to focus your complete attention on forming each

---

controlled processing
Information processing that involves conscious awareness and cognitive effort and that interferes with the performance of other ongoing activities.

automatic processing
Information processing that requires less conscious awareness and cognitive effort and that does not interfere with the performance of other ongoing activities.

conscious mind The level of consciousness that includes the cognitive experiences that we are aware of at a given moment.

preconscious mind The level of consciousness that contains feelings and memories that we are unaware of at the moment but can become aware of at will.

unconscious mind The level of consciousness that contains thoughts, feelings, and memories that influence us without our awareness and that we cannot become aware of at will.

letter. Today, after years of practice, you make use of automatic processing. You can write notes in class while focusing your attention on the professor's lecture rather than on the movements of your pen. Automatic processing also is involved in *implicit attitudes*—attitudes that we are not consciously aware of (Cunningham, Preacher, & Banaji, 2001). The importance of implicit attitudes in prejudice is discussed in Chapter 17.

Automatic processing can, at times, interfere with controlled processing. Consider the Stroop effect, named for its discoverer, John Ridley Stroop (1897–1979), illustrated in Figure 6-3. Record the time it takes you to read the words. Then record the time for how long it takes you to name the colors of the words. You probably performed the first task faster, presumably because of your extensive experience in reading. But the automaticity of reading words interfered with your ability to name the colors, a task that you are rarely called on to do (Davidson, Zacks, & Williams, 2003). Thus, even when you try to name the colors and ignore the words, automatic, unconscious processes make it difficult for you not to read the words. Thus, the Stroop effect refers to your tendency to read the words rather than naming the color of the words.

The Freudian Unconscious

During the 1988 National League baseball playoffs between the New York Mets and the Los Angeles Dodgers, relief pitcher Brian Holton of the Dodgers became so nervous that he could not grip the baseball. Suddenly he found himself singing the lyrics to a folk song, "You take the high road and I'll take the low road." This surprised him because he believed he had never heard the song. Yet, for some reason, singing it relaxed him enough to enable him to grip the baseball. When he told his mother about this mysterious behavior, she informed him that his father had comforted him by singing the song to him when he was a young child.

Levels of Consciousness Psychoanalytic theorists use anecdotal reports such as Holton's to support the existence of the Freudian unconscious. Sigmund Freud divided consciousness into three levels: the conscious, the preconscious, and the unconscious (see Figure 6-4). As had William James, Freud viewed the **conscious mind** as the awareness of fleeting images, feelings, and sensations. The **preconscious mind** contains memories of which we are unaware at the moment but of which we can become aware at will. And the **unconscious mind** contains repressed feelings, memories, and response tendencies of which we are unaware. Through what Freud called *psychic determinism*, these unconscious factors affect our behavior. Perhaps psychic determinism explains why we instantly like or dislike someone for no apparent reason or why we commit a "Freudian slip," in which we replace intended words with sexual or aggressive ones. Whereas psychologists who favor the reality of the Freudian unconscious point to evidence that our behavior can be influenced by unconscious emotional and motivational states, psychologists who accept the reality of a cognitive unconscious but not a Freudian unconscious point to a lack of evidence supporting the influence of unconscious emotional and motivational states (Ruys & Aarts, 2012).

Based on the foregoing discussion of unconscious influences, you should now realize that solid scientific evidence indicates that we can be affected by stimuli of which we are unaware. Some of the more extreme claims for unconscious influences on our moods and behaviors, however, have tainted an otherwise legitimate topic for psychological research.

Section Review: The Nature of Consciousness

1. What is the difference between automatic and controlled processing?
2. What is the cocktail party phenomenon?

FIGURE 6-2 Controlled Processing versus Automatic Processing

(a) When we learn a new task, we depend on controlled processing, which makes us focus our attention on each aspect of the task. With experience, we depend less on automatic processing. *(b)* Eventually, we may be able to perform the task while focusing our attention on other activities.

Sources: *(a)* szefei/Shutterstock.com. *(b)* Warren Goldswain/Shutterstock.com.

PINK   RED
BLUE   GREEN

FIGURE 6-3
The Stroop Effect

You will find it easier to read the words than to name the colors. Evidently, after years of daily reading, the reading of words has become so automatic that you cannot completely inhibit that tendency even when you try. In contrast, the naming of colors is a less common task that requires controlled processing.

FIGURE 6-4
Levels of Consciousness

According to Sigmund Freud, there are three levels of consciousness. The conscious level contains thoughts, images, and feelings that we are aware of. The preconscious level contains memories that we can retrieve at will. And the unconscious level contains repressed motives and memories that would evoke intense feelings of anxiety if we became aware of them.

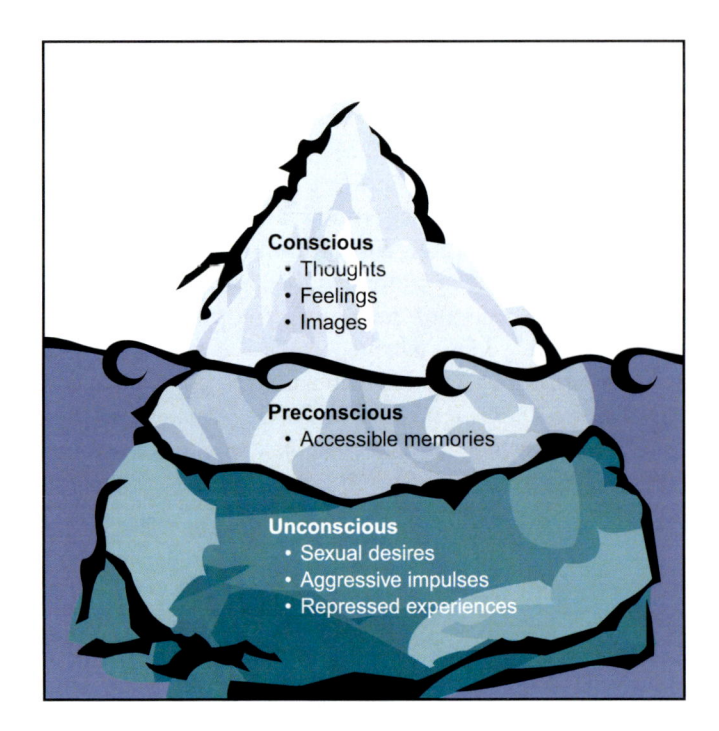

Conscious
- Thoughts
- Feelings
- Images

Preconscious
- Accessible memories

Unconscious
- Sexual desires
- Aggressive impulses
- Repressed experiences

---

biological rhythms Repeating cycles of physiological changes.

circadian rhythms Twenty-four-hour cycles of physiological changes, most notably the sleep-wake cycle.

pineal gland An endocrine gland that secretes a hormone that has a general tranquilizing effect on the body and that helps regulate biological rhythms.

Circadian Rhythms

Circadian rhythms (from the Latin words *circa* and *diem*) are 24-hour cycles of changes in physiological processes.
Source: cobalt88/Shutterstock.com.

Sleep

Perhaps the most obvious alternative to waking consciousness is *sleep*. The daily sleep-wake cycle is one of our **biological rhythms**, which are cyclical changes in physiological processes. Other examples of biological rhythms are the menstrual cycle in women and the annual cycle of waking and hibernation in bears. Be sure not to confuse biological rhythms, a legitimate topic of scientific research, with "biorhythms," a topic better left to pop psychology. Those who believe in biorhythms claim that each of us is born with physical, emotional, and intellectual cycles that stay constant in length and govern us for the rest of our lives. No scientifically worthy research supports these claims (Hines, 1998).

Biological Rhythms and the Sleep-Wake Cycle

The daily sleep-wake cycle is the most obvious of our **circadian rhythms**, which are 24-hour cycles of changes in physiological processes. Our circadian rhythm of body temperature parallels our circadian rhythm of brain arousal, with most people beginning the day at low points on both and rising on them through the day. College roommates who are out of phase with each other in their circadian rhythms are more likely to express dissatisfaction with their relationship (Watts, 1982). A student who is a "morning person"—already warmed up and chipper at 7 a.m.—might find it difficult to socialize with a roommate who can barely crawl out of bed at that time.

Moreover, there is some evidence that these individual differences in circadian rhythm are established early in childhood (Cofer et al., 1999). Human and animal studies have demonstrated that a set of genes that are thought to be involved in circadian rhythms (Bunney et al., 2015; Li et al., 2013; Osiel, Golumbek, & Ralph, 1998).

Factors in Biological Rhythms

What governs our circadian rhythms? A chief factor is a part of the hypothalamus called the *suprachiasmatic nucleus* (Schaap & Meijer, 2001), which controls body temperature (Murphy & Campbell, 1997) and regulates the secretion of the hormone *melatonin* by the **pineal gland**, an endocrine gland in the center of the brain. The suprachiasmatic nucleus, which is our body's main "clock," receives neural input from the eyes, making it sensi-

204 Chapter 6 Consciousness

tive to changes in light levels. As a result, melatonin secretion varies with light levels, decreasing in daylight and increasing in darkness (Caldwell, 2000).

When people are cut off from cues related to the day-night cycle, perhaps by living in a cave or a windowless room for several weeks, a curious thing happens. For unknown reasons, their sleep-wake cycle changes from 24 hours to 25 hours in length. They go to bed slightly later and get up just a few minutes later each successive day (Lavie, 2000). You may have experienced this phenomenon during vacations from work and school. Perhaps you find yourself going to bed later and later and, as a result, awakening later and later.

Jet Lag and Shift Work

The natural tendency for the sleep-wake cycle to lengthen might explain why jet lag is more severe when we fly west to east than when we fly east to west. The symptoms of jet lag, caused by a disruption of the normal sleep-wake cycle, include fatigue, insomnia, irritability, and difficulty concentrating (Waterhouse, Reilly, Atkinson, & Edwards, 2007). Eastbound travel shortens the sleep-wake cycle (**phase advance**), countering its natural tendency to lengthen. In contrast, westbound travel lengthens the sleep-wake cycle (**phase delay**), which agrees with its natural tendency to lengthen. So, phase advance requires more adjustment by travelers. Thus, people traveling eastbound suffer from jet lag more than people traveling westbound. So, if you have just flown a few time zones east and are not sleepy, studies have shown that both melatonin and exposure to bright sunlight in the morning can help reduce the feeling of jet lag (Crowley & Eastman, 2013).

Workers on rotating shifts, including airline personnel, factory workers, and police officers, often find their sleep-wake cycles disrupted. A meta-analysis of research studies on the effects of rotating shifts found that workers with slowly rotating shifts slept longer than workers with rapidly rotating shifts. Adjustment to rotating shifts depended on an interaction between the nature of the job, the direction of rotation, the rapidity of rotation, and other factors (Pilcher, Lambert, & Huffcutt, 2000). Given the natural tendency of the sleep-wake cycle to increase in length, workers on rotating shifts might respond better to phase delay than to phase advance. This hypothesis was demonstrated in a study of industrial workers. Those on a phase-delay schedule moved from the night shift (12 midnight to 8 a.m.) to the day shift (8 a.m. to 4 p.m.) to the evening shift (4 p.m. to 12 midnight). Those on a phase-advance schedule moved in the opposite direction, from the night shift to the evening shift to the day shift. The results showed that workers on a phase-delay schedule had better health, greater satisfaction, higher productivity, and lower turnover (Czeisler, Moore-Ede, & Coleman, 1982). Nonetheless, some research studies—particularly ones involving air-traffic controllers—have failed to find that phase delay is superior to phase advance in improving adjustment to rotating shifts (Cruz, Boquet, Detwiler, & Nesthus, 2003).

phase advance Shortening the sleep-wake cycle, as occurs when traveling from west to east.

phase delay Lengthening the sleep-wake cycle, as occurs when traveling from east to west.

Shift Work

Workers on rotating shifts might become less alert on the job. This could be especially dangerous in occupations such as law enforcement that require vigilance.
Source: John Roman Images/Shutterstock.com.

Patterns of Sleep

In 1960, four leading introductory psychology textbooks made no mention of sleep, and the most extensive coverage in any introductory textbook was two pages (Webb, 1985). Today, in contrast, all introductory psychology textbooks include (usually extensive) coverage of sleep. This increased coverage indicates the explosion of scientific interest in the study of sleep since the 1960s. Two of the main topics of interest regarding sleep patterns are the sleep cycle and the duration of sleep.

A Typical Night's Sleep

Imagine that you are participating in a sleep study. You would first sleep a night or two in a sleep laboratory to get accustomed to the novel surroundings. You would then sleep several nights in the laboratory while special devices recorded changes in your brain waves, eye movements, heart rate, blood pressure, body temperature, breathing rate, muscle tension, and respiration rate. Your behavior, including any utterances you made, would be recorded on videotape and audiotape.

FIGURE 6-5

The Stages of Sleep

Studies of participants in sleep laboratories have found that the stages of sleep are associated with distinctive patterns of brainwave activity. As we drift into deeper stages of sleep, our brain waves decrease in frequency and increase in amplitude. When we are in rapid eye movement (REM) sleep, our brainwave patterns resemble the patterns of our waking state. Sometimes this is called paradoxical sleep.

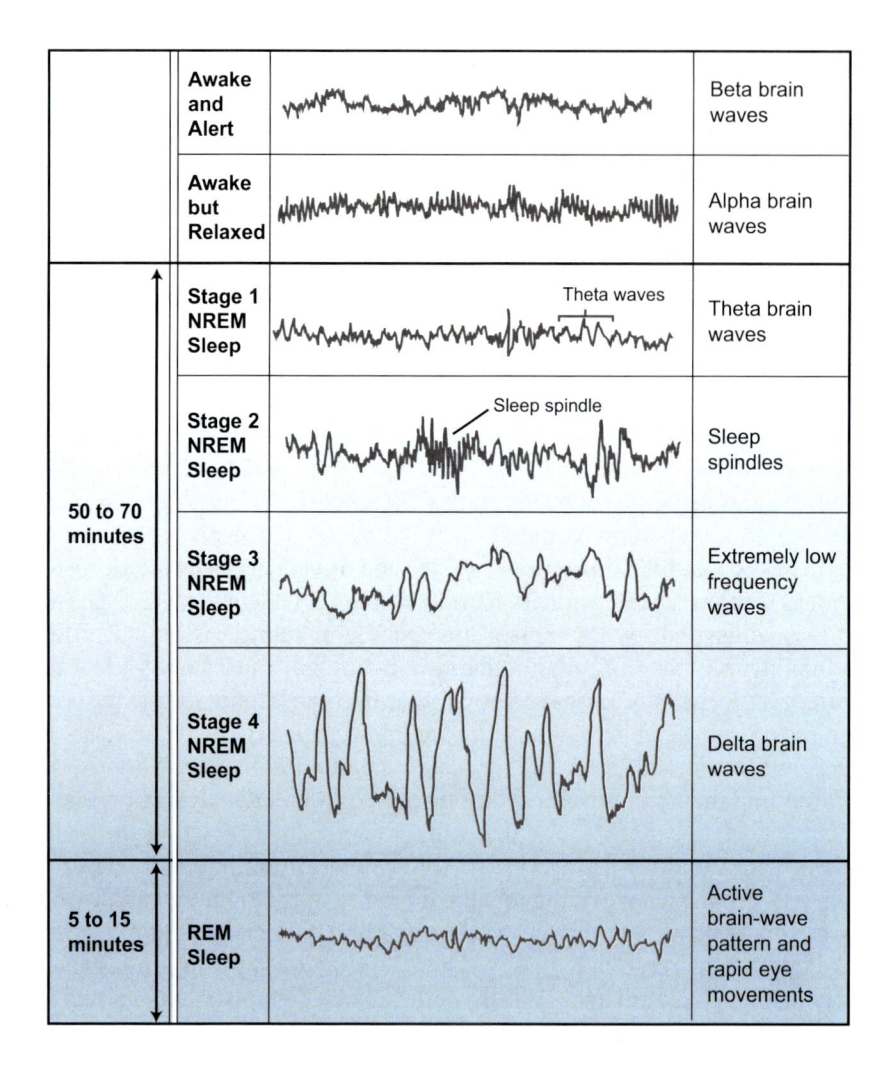

	Awake and Alert		Beta brain waves
	Awake but Relaxed		Alpha brain waves
50 to 70 minutes	Stage 1 NREM Sleep	Theta waves	Theta brain waves
	Stage 2 NREM Sleep	Sleep spindle	Sleep spindles
	Stage 3 NREM Sleep		Extremely low frequency waves
	Stage 4 NREM Sleep		Delta brain waves
5 to 15 minutes	REM Sleep		Active brain-wave pattern and rapid eye movements

The physiological recordings would reveal that you do not simply drift into deep sleep, stay there all night, and suddenly awaken in the morning. Instead, they would show that you pass through repeated sleep cycles, which are biological rhythms marked by variations in the depth of sleep as defined by particular brain-wave patterns. Figure 6-5 illustrates these patterns, which were first identified in the 1930s through the use of the electroencephalograph (EEG) (Loomis, Harvey, & Hobart, 1937).

Falling Asleep As you lie in bed with your eyes closed, an EEG recording would show that your brain-wave pattern changes from primarily high-frequency *beta waves* (14 to 30 cycles a second), which mark an alert cognitive state, to a higher proportion of lower-frequency *alpha waves* (8 to 13 cycles a second), which mark a relaxed, introspective cognitive state. As you drift off to sleep, you would exhibit slow, rolling eye movements, and your brainwave pattern would show a higher proportion of *theta waves* (4 to 7 cycles a second), which have a lower frequency than alpha waves. You also would exhibit a decrease in other signs of arousal, including heart rate, breathing rate, muscle tension, and respiration rate.

The cessation of the rolling eye movements would signify the onset of sleep (Ogilvie, McDonagh, Stone, & Wilkinson, 1988). This initial light stage of sleep is called *stage 1*. After 5 to 10 minutes in stage 1, you would enter the slightly deeper *stage 2*, associated with periodic bursts of higher-frequency (12 to 16 cycles a second) brain waves known as sleep spindles. After 10 to 20 minutes in stage 2, you would enter *stage 3*, marked by the appearance of extremely low-frequency (1/2 to 3 cycles a second) *delta waves*. When at least 50 percent of your brain waves are delta waves, you would be in *stage 4*, the deepest stage of sleep. After remaining in stages 3 and 4 for 30 to 40 minutes, you would drift up

206 Chapter 6 Consciousness

through stages 3, 2, and 1 until, about 90 minutes after falling asleep, you would reach the REM stage of sleep.

The NREM-REM Cycle **REM sleep** gets its name from the darting eye movements that characterize it. You probably have seen these movements under the eyelids of sleeping people—or even a sleeping pet dog, or cat. Because stages 1, 2, 3, and 4 are not characterized by these eye movements, they are collectively called *non-REM*, or **NREM sleep**. NREM sleep is characterized by slow brain waves, deep breathing, regular heart rate, and lower blood pressure. After an initial 10-minute period of REM sleep, you would again drift down into NREM sleep, eventually reaching stage 4.

The NREM-REM cycles take an average of 90 minutes, meaning that you pass through four or five cycles in a typical night's sleep. Adults normally spend about 25 percent of the night in REM sleep, 5 percent in stage 1, 50 percent in stage 2, and 20 percent in stages 3 and 4. As shown in Figure 6-6, the first half of your night's sleep has relatively more NREM sleep than the second half, whereas the second half has relatively more REM sleep than the first half. You might not even reach stages 3 and 4 during the second half of the night.

While you are in REM sleep, your heart rate, respiration rate, and brain-wave frequency increase, making you appear to be awake. But you also experience flaccid paralysis of your limbs, making it impossible for you to shift your position in bed. Given that you become physiologically aroused, yet immobile and difficult to awaken, REM sleep is also called *paradoxical sleep*. Because we are paralyzed during REM sleep, sleepwalking (or *somnambulism*) occurs only during NREM sleep, specifically stages 3 and 4. In fact, sleepwalkers spend a greater proportion of their sleep in stages 3 and 4 than nonsleepwalkers do (Blatt, Peled, Gadoth, & Lavie, 1991). Sleepwalking is also more common in children than in adults. A survey of 5,000 people aged 18 years or older found that 2 percent engaged in sleepwalking (Bjorvatn, Grønli, & Pallesen, 2010).

Despite warnings to the contrary, sleepwalkers may be awakened without fear of doing physical or psychological harm to them. Of course, the habitual sleepwalker should be protected from injury by keeping doors and windows locked. Sleepwalking has been used successfully as a legal defense in criminal cases, as in the case of a man who was caught walking outside naked during the night (Thomas, 1997).

Another characteristic of REM sleep is erection of the penis and clitoris. Erection occurs spontaneously and is not necessarily indicative of a sexual dream. Clinicians use REM erections to determine whether men with erectile dysfunction are suffering from a physical or a psychological disorder. If a man has erections while in REM sleep, his problem is psychological, not physical (Mann, Pankok, Connemann, & Roeschke, 2003).

REM sleep is associated with dreaming. We know this because of research conducted in the early 1950s by Eugene Aserinsky and Nathaniel Kleitman (1953) of the University

REM sleep The stage of sleep associated with rapid eye movements, an active brain-wave pattern, and vivid dreams.

NREM sleep The stages of sleep not associated with rapid eye movements and marked by relatively little dreaming.

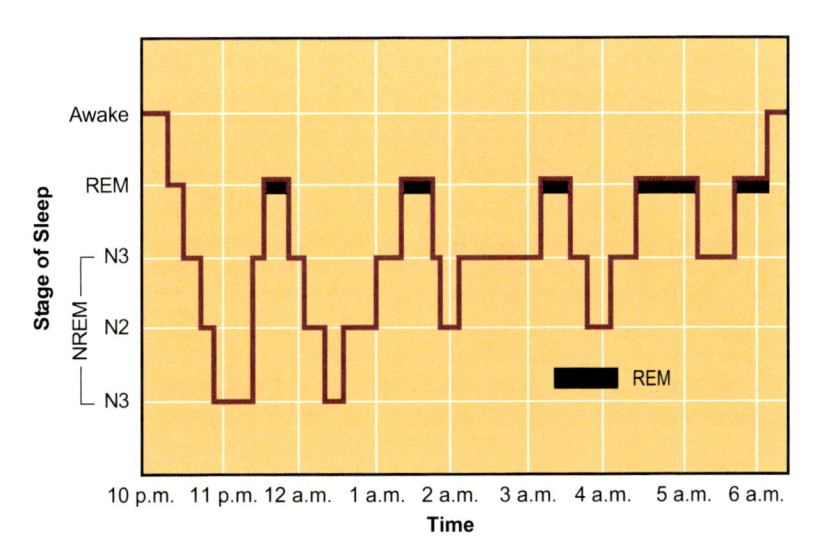

FIGURE 6-6
A Typical Night's Sleep

During a typical night's sleep, we pass through cycles that involve stages of NREM sleep and the stage of REM sleep. Note that we obtain our deepest sleep during the first half of the night and that the periods of REM sleep become longer with each successive cycle (Cartwright, 1978).

Source: Based on *A Primer on Sleep and Dreaming* by Rosalind Cartwright. Copyright © 1978 Addison-Wesley.

Chapter 6 Consciousness 207

Sleep Deprivation

Many people, particularly college students burdened by academic responsibilities, suffer from sleep deprivation and snatch moments of sleep whenever they can. Sleep deprivation can impair the ability to perform academically, vocationally, and socially.

Source: Arieliona/Shutterstock.com.

of Chicago. When they awakened sleepers displaying rapid eye movements, the sleepers usually reported that they had been dreaming. In contrast, sleepers awakened during NREM sleep rarely reported that they had been dreaming. Because the longest REM period occurs during the last sleep cycle of the night, you often find yourself in the middle of a dream when your alarm clock wakes you in the morning. You might be tempted to infer that rapid eye movements reflect the scanning of dream scenes, but Aserinsky and his colleagues (1985) have found that they do not—so if you were dreaming about, say, a tennis match, your rapid eye movements would not have been following the ball's flight.

Researchers are learning more and more about the physiological bases of the sleep cycle. Brain structures that help regulate sleep include the pons, thalamus, hypothalamus, and reticular formation. Neurotransmitters that help regulate sleep include serotonin, norepinephrine, and acetylcholine, with sleep onset related to a reduction in their secretion (Sharpley, 2002). More recently, the peptide neurotransmitter *orexin* (also called *hypo-cretin*), which is secreted by the hypothalamus, has been implicated in the sleep-wake cycle. Higher levels of orexin are associated with wakefulness, and lower levels of it are associated with sleep (Scammell, 2001; Lee, Hassani, & Jones, 2005). Hence, orexin helps people stay awake.

Though sleep patterns are similar across cultures, there is some evidence for ethnic and gender differences in some aspects of the sleep cycle. A recent meta-analysis of 14 studies found small-to-moderate differences in the sleep cycles of African Americans compared to European Americans. African Americans experienced poorer quality sleep, including sleeping less, spending more time in stage 2 sleep and less time in stage 3 and 4 sleep. African Americans also awoke more frequently during the night (Ruiter, DeCoster, Jacobs, & Lichstein, 2011). Sleep continuity and duration were found to be influenced by biopsychosocial factors, whereas the differences in stages of sleep were not. And a study of elementary school students found that girls slept longer than boys and exhibited more "motionless sleep." However, there were no gender differences in the perceived quality of sleep (Sadeh, Raviv, & Gruber, 2000). Additionally, this study highlights different sleep patterns across childhood and indicates that older children (6th grade versus 2nd grade) go to bed later yet report increased daytime sleepiness. Sociologists have found that women self-report sleeping slightly longer than men, a difference that may be attributed to women's greater likelihood of being engaged in unpaid work and enjoying less high-quality leisure time than men (Burgard, & Ailshire, 2013). On the other hand, these findings could be attributed to different family responsibilities, such as caregiving for children, differences in napping, or other unknown factors. As you will read later in this chapter, there are many situational factors that affect sleep patterns, sleep continuity, and sleep disorders. These differences in the sleep-wake cycle may be attributable to factors such as stress levels, sleep environments, work and family responsibilities and other variables that are correlated with ethnicity and gender.

The Duration of Sleep

Sleep not only is cyclical but also varies in duration. People are moderately long sleepers, with young adults averaging 8 hours of sleep a day. In contrast, some animals, such as elephants, sleep as little as 2 hours a day, whereas other animals, such as bats, sleep as much as 20 hours a day. Efforts to wean people from sleep indicate that it cannot be reduced much below 4 hours without inducing extreme drowsiness and severe mood alterations (Webb, 1985). Our daily need for sleep varies across the life span. At one extreme, infants typically sleep 16 hours a day and spend a significant portion of their sleep time in REM. At the other extreme, elderly people typically sleep 6 hours a day. Of course, you might need to sleep more or less than your age peers. This variability in normal sleep duration and sleep characteristics is different in children and adults and appears to have a hereditary basis (Barclay & Gregory, 2013). Researchers often have wondered about the contribution of genetic factors to sleep duration and quality. A recent longitudinal study using an adult twin cohort over the course of 15 years found that although genetic factors do play a stable and modest role in sleep stability and length, health issues and other environmental factors play stronger or more important roles (Hublin, Partinen, Koskenvuo, & Kaprio, 2013). This study implies that individuals experiencing short bouts of sleep or problematic sleep—for example, individuals suffering from insomnia—might gain relief from interventions such as sleep medications.

Regardless of how much sleep they need, North Americans habitually get less than their ideal quota. They might stay awake to watch television, do schoolwork, work on a computer, check social media, or perform other activities. You might go to bed when you want to (perhaps after watching the late movie) and awaken when you have to (perhaps in time for an 8 a.m. class), making you chronically sleep deprived. According to sleep researcher William Dement, "Most Americans no longer know what it feels like to be fully alert" (Toufexis, 1990, p. 79). His conclusion is supported by the results of a survey of over 4,000 Long Island, New York, mass-transit commuters. More than 50 percent of the respondents reported experiencing problems with sleep and wakefulness (Walsleben, Norman, Novak, O'Malley, Rapoport, & Strohl, 1999). Cross-cultural research, too, suggests that the proportion of Japanese adults who suffer from inadequate sleep is comparable to that reported in surveys of American samples (Liu et al., 2000). Moreover, in another study the prevalence of excessive daytime sleepiness among Japanese female workers was almost double that of Japanese male workers. The researchers attributed this difference to the additional family responsibilities that women face at the beginning and end of the workday (Doi & Minowa, 2003).

Difficulty in getting a good night's sleep has been increasing among college students. In a replication of an earlier study, a survey of college students published in 1992 found that they reported sleeping less and being less satisfied with their sleep than college students had reported in a survey conducted in 1978 (Hicks, Johnson, & Pellegrini, 1992). A common problem in regard to young adults' sleep patterns is the tendency to get too little sleep during the week because of staying up late and rising early, followed by sleeping late on Saturday and Sunday mornings. This tendency leads to "Sunday night insomnia" followed by "Monday morning blues." That is, young adults tend to report poorer moods and exhibit poorer cognitive performance on Monday mornings (Yang & Spielman, 2001).

Many people try to overcome the effects of inadequate nighttime sleep by taking daytime naps. Some cultures, typically in hot climates, even incorporate siestas as part of everyday life. Stores and businesses shut down for part of the afternoon so that individuals can rest or nap for an hour or two instead of being worn out by working during the hottest time of the day. With the growth of the European Union, though, many corporations in Mediterranean countries are adopting the workday schedules of their European neighbors. One recent survey conducted in Spain found that only 24 percent of the population were regular siesta takers. Moreover, anecdotal reports of chronic fatigue were on the rise (Boudreaux, 2000). However, many students and executives in non-siesta cultures have come to value their "power naps." They are being wise because an afternoon nap can increase alertness and improve task performance (Horne & Reyner, 1996). One study found that a 1-hour nap while on the night shift markedly improved workers' alertness and motivation for the rest of the shift (Bonnefond et al., 2001). And research findings indicate that an afternoon nap improves alertness and driving performance in long-haul truck drivers (Macchi, Boulos, Ranney, Simmons, & Campbell, 2002).

The Functions of Sleep

Assuming that you live to be 90, you will have spent about 30 years asleep. Are you wasting one-third of your life, or does sleep serve important functions for you? Among the many hypothesized functions of sleep, scientists have identified two that are the most prominent: *sleep as physical restoration* and *sleep as adaptive inactivity*.

Sleep as Physical Restoration

The most commonsense view of sleep holds that it restores the body and the mind after the wear and tear imposed by waking activities. Why else would we have a mechanism that forces us to spend at least one-third of our lives sleeping? Perhaps sleep repairs body tissues, removes metabolic waste products, and replenishes brain neurotransmitters (Inouye, Honda, & Komoda, 1995). One recent hypothesis suggests that sleep may help the brain sweep itself clean of toxins. Dr. Nedergaard and colleagues (Xie et al., 2013) discovered this while studying sleeping mice. The researchers noticed that the sleeping brain allowed for its cells to shrink and the fluid surrounding the brain to increase. This brain-cleaning process has yet to be observed in humans but could help us understand disorders such as Alzheimer's disease that are linked to sleep disorders. Alzheimer's disease is associated with an increase in a protein waste product called beta amyloid, and proper sleep can help clear the brain of it. Formal as well as anecdotal research has provided evidence of the detrimental effects of sleep loss and the restorative effects of sleep. Sleep deprivation is associated with a decline in the ability to perform physical and cognitive tasks (Quigley, Green, Morgan, Idzikowski, & King, 2000). For example, a survey of college students found a negative correlation between length of sleep and grade point average. That is, the fewer hours students slept each night, the lower their grade point averages tended to be (Kelly, Kelly, & Clanton, 2001).

The longer we stay awake, the more we crave sleep. In the case of Peter Tripp, sleep deprivation apparently produced hallucinations and delusional thinking, which disappeared after a single night's sleep. In a similar case in 1965, Randy Gardner, a 17-year-old San Diego high school student, stayed awake 264 hours (11 days) as his contribution to a science fair. He hoped to get his name in the Guinness Book of World Records. Two of his friends alternated shifts to keep him from falling asleep. Gardner stayed awake by remaining physically active—talking, walking, and playing games. He found it easier to stay awake during the daytime than at night—a finding in keeping with his natural circadian rhythm. At various times during the 11 days, Gardner had trouble focusing his eyes, suffered incoordination, became moody, showed memory deterioration, had difficulty concentrating, thought a street sign was a person, and experienced the delusion that he (though a person of European background) was a famous African American football player who was being oppressed by racism.

During the last 4 days, William Dement monitored Gardner's behavioral and physiological reactions to his prolonged sleep deprivation. When the media began covering Gardner near the end of his feat, he seemed to become more motivated. On the last night, he even defeated Dement in 100 consecutive games of pinball. Gardner also performed well at a press conference at the end of the eleventh day. When a reporter asked him how he managed to stay awake so long, he simply replied, "It's just mind over matter" (Dement, 1976, p. 12). Gardner then slept 14 hours, 40 minutes, and awoke practically recovered—recovering completely after a second night's sleep (Gulevich, Dement, & Johnson, 1966). Gardner's remarkable physical performance was attributed to his excellent physical condition, strong motivation, and support from those around him. But some scientists noted that he might have gained a boost from so-called microsleeps, which are repeated periods of sleep lasting only but a few seconds (which you might have experienced when exhausted and fighting to stay awake during a boring lecture). Microsleeps can be especially dangerous when performing tasks that require constant attention such as driving. The cumulative effect of these ultra-short "naps" might have helped Gardner combat the effects of sleep deprivation.

Another source of evidence for the restorative function of sleep is research on the effects of vigorous physical activity on subsequent sleep patterns. Sleep, especially deep sleep, increases on the nights after vigorous exercise (Vein, Sidorov, Martazaev, & Karlov, 1991). This finding was supported by a study of runners who participated in a 57-mile ultramarathon race. They experienced an increase in the duration of sleep, particularly stage 3 and stage 4, on the first two nights after the race (Shapiro, Bortz, Mitchell, Bartel, & Jooste, 1981). Though we still do not know exactly what, if anything, sleep restores, one explanation for the increase in deep sleep after vigorous exercise concerns the secretion of growth hormone, which increases during deep sleep. Growth hormone promotes the synthesis of proteins needed for the repair of muscles and other body tissues.

Sleep as Adaptive Inactivity

An alternative view, championed by Wilse Webb (1992), is that sleep evolved because it protected the sleeper from harm and prevented the useless expenditure of energy.

Sleep as Protection from Harm Our prehistoric ancestors who slept at night were less likely to gain the attention of hungry nocturnal predators. The limb paralysis accompanying REM sleep may have evolved because it prevented cave dwellers from acting out their dreams, when they might have bumped into trees, fallen off cliffs, or provided dinner for saber-toothed tigers. Evidence for this protective function of REM sleep comes from studies of cats. Destruction of a portion of the pons that normally induces REM paralysis in cats produces stalking and attacking movements during sleep, as though the cats are acting out their dreams (Morrison, 1983).

Further support for the protective function of sleep comes from studies showing that animals with little to fear while asleep (either because they are predators or because they sleep in safe places) sleep for much of the 24-hour day. In contrast, animals that have much to fear while asleep (either because they are prey or because they sleep in exposed places) sleep for relatively little of the 24-hour day. Thus, cats, which are predators, sleep much longer (15 hours) than rabbits (8 hours), which are prey. Likewise, bats, which sleep in caves, sleep much longer (20 hours) than horses (3 hours), which sleep in the open.

Sleep as a Conserver of Energy Another reason to believe that sleep might be a period of adaptive inactivity is that it conserves energy (Berger & Phillips, 1995). Evidence supportive of this view comes from studies of the food-finding habits of different species. Because the length of sleep for a given species is negatively correlated with how long it takes members of that species to find their daily food, perhaps animals stay awake only long enough to eat sufficient food to meet their energy needs. Animals might have evolved sleep in part to conserve energy the remainder of the time. Thus, the typical young adult's need for about 8 hours of nightly sleep might mean that our prehistoric ancestors needed about 16 hours to find their daily food (Cohen, 1979).

According to Wilse Webb (1992), both the restorative theory and the adaptive-inactivity theory must be included in an adequate theory of sleep. The restorative theory explains why sleepiness increases as sleep loss increases. The adaptive inactivity theory explains why sleep follows a circadian rhythm. You may have experienced this phenomenon if you have ever pulled an all-nighter while studying for exams. If you fight your sleepiness and force yourself to stay awake all night, you might be surprised to find yourself less sleepy in the morning (when your circadian rhythm would make you more alert). Later, you would find yourself becoming sleepy when your normal bedtime approaches again.

One Cause of Insomnia
Stimulation from computer monitors can delay sleep onset.
Source: Romanchuck Dimitry/Shutterstock.com.

Sleep Disorders

You might take sleep for granted, but many people do not. They suffer from sleep disorders such as *insomnia*, *sleep apnea*, and *narcolepsy*.

Insomnia

Twenty to 30 million Americans suffer from **insomnia** (Roth, 1995), chronic difficulty in sleeping. There are two major forms of insomnia. People who suffer from *sleep-onset insomnia* have trouble falling asleep. You have experienced sleep-onset insomnia if you have ever lain in bed, perhaps for hours, fruitlessly waiting to drift off to sleep. Those who experience *sleep-maintenance insomnia* fall asleep normally but find themselves awakening repeatedly—typically during the second half of the night (Narita, Echizenya, Takeshima, Inomata, & Shimizu, 2011).

If you suffer from insomnia, what should you do? Many people with insomnia resort to sedative drugs, including alcohol and barbiturates, to fall asleep. Though sedatives will, at least initially, help you fall asleep, they do so at a cost. First, they interfere with the normal sleep cycle, most notably by reducing REM sleep. Second, they eventually lose

insomnia Chronic difficulty in either falling asleep or staying asleep.

Psychology versus Common Sense

Is Sleep Necessary for Good Health?

Your parents may have repeatedly urged you to go to bed at a reasonable hour to maintain your health. Is this just another example of a well-intentioned but erroneous commonsense belief, or is it a commonsense belief with scientific backing? As mentioned in Chapter 2, commonsense beliefs are sometimes true, but scientists insist that they be supported by research findings before accepting them. But what of the effects of sleep deprivation on health? It seems that in this case, common sense might be right—sleep is necessary for proper functioning of the immune system. Many students anecdotally report that after obtaining only a few hours' sleep night after night during final exams, they often become ill a few days after their exams are over. And when we become ill, we tend to sleep more—perhaps because sleep promotes the immunological response to invading microorganisms (Majde & Krueger, 2005). One study that investigated the health effects of chronic sleep loss in people aged 18–34 found that participants suffered from increased daytime sleepiness and inflammatory cytokines (Pejovic et al., 2013). Inflammatory cytokines are a family of molecules produced by your immune system that help your body fight threats such as inflammation, stress, or infections. Thus, people who fail to get an optimal night's sleep for extended periods may become less healthy and secrete higher levels of stress hormones and inflammatory markers, which can lead to illness. Thankfully, studies also show that these effects can be reversed with extended sleep.

Consider natural killer cell (NKC) activity. NKCs are lymphocytes—white blood cells—that help defend the body against cancer cells. Many studies have found that sleep loss is associated with a reduction in NKC activity. In one study, 29 persons, aged 40 to 78 years, spent three nights in a sleep laboratory. NKC activity was positively correlated with how long they slept (Hall et al., 1998). But additional research is needed to determine whether this reduction in NKC activity makes sleep-deprived people more susceptible to cancer by impairing the ability of NKCs to destroy cancer cells before they can reproduce and form invasive tumors.

Moreover, as noted in Chapter 2, scientists caution against confusing causation and correlation. The positive correlation between hours of sleep and NKC activity does not necessarily mean that sleep deprivation causes a reduction in NKC activity. Other factors might account for the relationship between sleep and NKC activity. In fact, it is conceivable that the presumed direction of causality is just the opposite: immunological activity might promote sleep, thereby accounting for the positive correlation between the two (Karnovsky, 1986).

Because of the possibility of misinterpretation, scientists rely on experimental rather than correlational research to determine causal relationships between variables. Experiments that have used hours of sleep as the independent variable and immunological activity as the dependent variable consistently have shown that depriving people and animals of sleep does in fact reduce immunological activity. In one experiment, laboratory rats were deprived of sleep for 8 hours. They showed a significant reduction in their immunological responses to foreign cells (Brown, Price, King, & Husband, 1989). Moreover, when animals are purposely subjected to infections, those who obtain more deep sleep are more likely to survive (Toth & Krueger, 1990).

In an experiment with human participants, 23 healthy men, aged 22 to 61 years, were prevented from obtaining a full night's sleep. Eighteen of the men showed a decrease in NKC activity, with a statistically significant reduction to 72 percent of their average baseline levels of NKC activity. After just a single full night's sleep, their NKC activity returned to baseline levels (Irwin et al., 1994).

These findings supporting the role of sleep in immune responses have practical implications. To prevent illness, make sure you get enough sleep. When you are ill, make sure to get more sleep than usual. Perhaps hospital patients, who need their immune systems to function optimally, should not be awakened to receive medication or have blood drawn. Table 6-1 offers you an opportunity to determine whether you are getting enough sleep.

---

their effectiveness, leaving you with the same problem you began with. And third, they have harmful side effects, including drug dependence. Instead of turning to sedatives, insomnia victims can use psychological techniques to obtain a good night's sleep. If you suffer from insomnia, you should reduce your presleep arousal by avoiding exercise; stimulation from television, computer, or cellular phone screens; and caffeine too close to bedtime. A relatively new area of research addresses the effects of sleep and technology use. For example, researchers have found that LED-backlit device use or bright environmental light can contribute to sleep problems by inducing delayed bedtimes and shorter sleep time (NSF, 2011; Adams & Kisler, 2013). Another example that can help

> **Psychology versus Common Sense**
>
> ### Is Sleep Necessary for Good Health? *continued*
>
> **TABLE 6-1** Are You Getting Enough Sleep?
>
> As discussed earlier, the amount of sleep you need every night decreases with age. The Centers for Disease Control and Prevention and the National Sleep Foundation have provided the following recommendations for the hours of sleep necessary for good physical and psychological health across the life span.
>
> | Age Group | | Recommended Hours of Sleep Per Day |
> |---|---|---|
> | Newborn | 0–3 months | 14–17 hours (National Sleep Foundation)[1]
 No recommendation (American Academy of Sleep Medicine)[2] |
> | Infant | 4–12 months | 12–16 hours per 24 hours (including naps)[2] |
> | Toddler | 1–2 years | 11–14 hours per 24 hours (including naps)[2] |
> | Preschool | 3–5 years | 10–13 hours per 24 hours (including naps)[2] |
> | School age | 6–12 years | 9–12 hours per 24 hours[2] |
> | Teen | 13–18 years | 8–10 hours per 24 hours[2] |
> | Adult | 18–60 years | 7 or more hours per night[3] |
> | | 61–74 years | 7–9 hours[1] |
> | | 65 years and older | 7–8 hours[1] |
>
> [1]Hirshkowitz M, Whiton K, Albert SM, Alessi C, Bruni O, et al. The National Sleep Foundation's sleep time duration recommendations: methodology and results summary. *Sleep Health*. 2015;1(1):40–43.
>
> [2]Paruthi S, Brooks LJ, D'Ambrosio C, Hall WA, Kotagal S, Lloyd RM, et al. Recommended amount of sleep for pediatric populations: a consensus statement of the American Academy of Sleep Medicine. *J Clin Sleep Med*. 2016;12(6):785–786.
>
> [3]Watson NF, Badr MS, Belenky G, et al. Recommended amount of sleep for a healthy adult: a joint consensus statement of the American Academy of Sleep Medicine and Sleep Research Society. *Sleep*. 2015;38(6):843–844.
>
> Source: "How Much Sleep Do I Need?" Centers for Disease Control and Prevention. https://www.cdc.gov/sleep/about_sleep/how_much_sleep.html. Retrieved 6/21/17.

aid in sleep is practicing progressive muscle relaxation, which involves tensing and then relaxing major muscle groups in sequence (Taylor & Roane, 2010). It also is advisable to avoid napping. If you nap during the day, you might not feel sleepy enough to fall asleep at your desired bedtime. Because trying to suppress thoughts that might be racing through your mind as you lie in bed tends to promote insomnia (Harvey, 2003), you might even benefit from *paradoxical intention*, in which you try to stay awake while lying in bed. This method can, paradoxically, induce sleep by preventing fruitless, anxiety-inducing efforts to fall asleep. Another technique, *stimulus control*, requires arranging your bedtime situation to promote sleep. First, go to bed only when you feel sleepy. Second, to ensure that you associate lying in bed with sleep and not with being awake, do not eat, read, watch television, use your computer or phone, or listen to music while lying in bed. Third, if you toss and turn, get out of bed and return only when you are sleepy (Arnold, Miller, & Mehta, 2012).

Sleep Apnea

Imagine that you stopped breathing hundreds of times every night and awakened each time in order to breathe. You would be suffering from **sleep apnea** (*apnea* means the absence of breathing). Victims of sleep apnea have repeated episodes throughout the night in which they fall asleep and then stop breathing for up to a minute or more. This cessation of

sleep apnea A condition in which a person awakens repeatedly in order to breathe.

breathing produces a decrease in blood oxygen that stimulates the brain to awaken them, permitting them to start breathing again. People with sleep apnea typically feel chronically sleepy during the day, yet do not recall their repeated nighttime awakenings. They also may lie in bed for 8–10 hours per night but get less than half of that time as quality sleep.

There are two major causes of sleep apnea. One is a neurological dysfunction of brain stem structures that regulate breathing (Gilman et al., 2003). Cases with this cause sometimes respond to drug therapy (Mendelson, Maczaj, & Holt, 1991). The second major cause is the collapse of the breathing passage, which is more common in people who are obese (Fogel et al., 2003). The treatment of choice in 80 percent of these cases is *continuous positive airway pressure*—the use of a device that pumps a steady flow of air through a breathing mask worn by the sleeper. This apparatus helps prevent the breathing passage from collapsing, yet compliance with its use is challenging (Olsen, Smith, Simon, Oei, & Douglas, 2012).

Narcolepsy

narcolepsy A condition in which an awake person suffers from repeated, sudden, and irresistible REM sleep attacks.

Whereas victims of sleep apnea find it impossible to stay asleep at night, victims of **narcolepsy** find it impossible to stay awake all day. If you suffered from narcolepsy, you would experience repeated, irresistible sleep attacks. During these attacks, you would immediately fall into REM sleep for periods lasting from a few minutes to a half hour. Because of its association with REM sleep, narcolepsy is typically accompanied by a sudden loss of muscle tone (*cataplexy*) that causes the victim to collapse. You can imagine how dangerous narcolepsy is for people performing hazardous activities. For example, many people with narcolepsy fall asleep while driving (Aldrich, 1992).

Because narcoleptic attacks such as cataplexy can be instigated by strong emotions, victims try to maintain a bland emotional life, avoiding both laughing and crying, which interferes with victims' sex lives, work performance, and social relationships (Goswami, 1998). The cause of narcolepsy is unknown, but given that it runs in families, we know that there is a strong genetic basis, and researchers have identified specific genes involved in the development of narcolepsy (Singh, Mahlios, & Mignot, 2013). The sleep disturbances of narcolepsy are caused by degeneration of neurons that secrete orexin (also known as hypocretin), which promotes wakefulness (Scammell, 2003). People with narcolepsy have fewer normal neurons that produce orexin. Though there is no cure for narcolepsy, stimulants and antidepressants drugs help reduce daytime sleep attacks (Littner et al., 2001). And one study found that the combination of taking daytime naps and maintaining a regular nightly bedtime is effective in reducing daytime sleep attacks in people with narcolepsy (Rogers, Aldrich, & Lin, 2001). Currently there are no available medications that target orexin specifically. In the future, it is very likely that research will discover such treatments.

Section Review: Sleep

1. What cycles take place during a typical night's sleep?
2. What evidence supports the view that sleep is a form of adaptive inactivity?
3. What helpful tips would you give to a person suffering from sleep-onset insomnia?

Dreams

dream A storylike sequence of visual images, usually occurring during REM sleep.

The most dramatic aspect of sleep is the **dream**, a story-like sequence of visual images that commonly evoke strong emotions. Though dreaming can occur during any sleep stage, intense dreaming is thought to occur during REM sleep (Hobson, Pace-Schott, & Stickgold, 2000). Actions that would be impossible in real life may seem perfectly normal in dreams. In a dream, you might find it reasonable to hold a conversation with a dinosaur or to leap across the Grand Canyon. But what are the major characteristics of dreams? This question was addressed in a classic study conducted more than a century ago by Mary Whiton Calkins (1893).

Though Sigmund Freud is famous for making the analysis of dreams an important part of psychoanalysis, beginning with the publication of *The Interpretation of Dreams* in 1900, he was not the first person to study them formally. An article published by Mary Whiton Calkins (1893) described a dream study she conducted with her colleague, Edmund Clark Sanford. The study is noteworthy because Freud referred to it in his book and its findings have held up well. It also shows the transition in late 19th-century psychology from philosophical speculation about psychological topics, such as dreams, to empirical research on them. This is a landmark study because Sanford presented a paper on it in 1892 at the first meeting of the American Psychological Association.

Calkins recorded her own dreams for 55 nights, and Sanford recorded his for 46 nights. They used alarm clocks to awaken themselves at various times during the night in order to jot down any dreams they were having. Calkins observed dream characteristics that later research has confirmed. One researcher, J. Allan Hobson (1988), credits Calkins with anticipating modern approaches to dream research and pioneering the intensive study of dreams over many nights with the use of dream diaries and reports. Her findings included the following:

- *We dream every night.* On several nights, Calkins believed she had not dreamed—only to find that she had written down several dreams during the night. Calkins hypothesized that we forget our dreams because of a lack of congruity between dreaming and the waking states of consciousness. This finding anticipated interest in *state-dependent memory*, which has inspired research studies only in the past few decades and is discussed in Chapter 8.
- *We have about four dreams a night.* Calkins recorded 205 dreams on 55 nights, and Sanford 170 on 46 nights. This finding agrees with modern research indicating that we have four or five REM periods on a typical night.
- *As the night progresses, we are more likely to be dreaming.* Calkins found that most dreams occurred during the second half of the night. Her conclusion agrees with later research findings, obtained with physiological recording equipment, that successive REM periods increase in length across the night. In other words, we have more dreams closer to when we wake in the morning.
- *Most dreams are mundane and refer to recent life events.* We might not realize that dreams are usually mundane because we tend to recall only the most dramatic ones.
- *Dreams can incorporate external stimuli.* In one of her dreams, Calkins found herself struggling to crawl from an elevator through a tiny opening into an eighth-floor apartment. She awoke to find herself in a cramped position with a heavy blanket over her face.
- *What Calkins called "real thinking" occurs during sleep.* This finding anticipated research findings that NREM sleep is marked by ordinary thinking, as opposed to the fantastic images and events common to REM dreaming.
- *We can reason while dreaming and even, to an extent, control our dreams.* This finding anticipated research on lucid dreaming, a serious topic of research only in the past decade that is discussed in the following section, "The Content of Dreams."
- *Dreams can disguise their true meaning.* This finding anticipated Freud's belief that dreams can use symbols to represent their true—often sexual—meaning.

The Content of Dreams

People have long been intrigued by dreams; references to the content of dreams are found on Babylonian clay tablets dating from 5000 B.C. As just described, Mary Whiton Calkins

Dreaming

As discussed earlier in this chapter compared to adults, infants spend more time in REM sleep—and dreaming.

Source: KieferPix/Shutterstock.com.

Nightmares

Nightmares are especially common in young children who spend more time in REM sleep than do adults.

Source: Anna Grigorjeva/Shutterstock.com.

nightmare A frightening dream occurring during REM sleep.

night terror A frightening NREM experience, common in childhood, in which the individual may suddenly sit up, let out a bloodcurdling scream, speak incoherently, and quickly fall back to sleep, yet usually fails to recall it on awakening.

(1893) found that we tend to dream about mundane personal matters. This finding was supported by the research of Calvin Hall (1966), who analyzed the content of thousands of dreams reported by his participants, and by more recent studies that indicate that our dreams reflect recent events that affect us emotionally. For example, a study of individuals who regularly recorded their dreams compared their last 10 dreams before the suicide airliner attacks on the United States on September 11, 2001, and their first 10 dreams after the attacks found that the intensity of the dreams was markedly greater after the attacks (Hartmann & Basile, 2003). But what of people who have recurrent dreams? A study of 52 college students who recorded their dreams over a 14-day period found that recurrent dreamers tended to report more stress in their lives, lower levels of psychological well-being, and more negative content in their dreams (Zadra, O'Brien, & Donderi, 1998).

Dream content also is associated with sociocultural factors. Though Hall noted several gender-related differences in dreams, these differences have been decreasing. In fact, a recent study of the dreams of 40 male and 40 female college students found greater similarity in their dream content than would have been true several decades ago (Bursik, 1998), though there is some evidence that the content of males' dreams is somewhat more aggressive than that of females' dreams (Blume-Marcovici, 2010). A study of the relationship between culture and dream content examined the dreams of 205 children aged 7 to 12 years from peaceful Finland, from violence-prone regions of Gaza, and from relatively violence-free regions of Gaza. The children recorded their dreams each morning for 7 days. The results showed that the children exposed to violence had more vivid dreams, incorporating more themes of persecution and aggression (Punamaecki & Joustie, 1998).

When you have a frightening dream, you are experiencing a **nightmare**. Children as young as two to three years of age report having nightmares (Byars, Yolton, Rausch, Lanphear, & Beebe, 2012), which are more common in children with high levels of anxiety (Mindell & Barrett, 2002). Nightmares tend to occur when we feel emotionally distressed. Frequent nightmares have been reported in studies of military personnel who have experienced intense combat (Long et al., 2011), people who have been exposed to terrorism (Soffar-Dudek & Shahar, 2010), and women who have been sexually assaulted (Karkow et al., 2002).

Do not confuse a nightmare, which is a frightening dream that occurs during REM sleep, with a **night terror**, which occurs during NREM sleep stages 3 and 4. The person experiencing a night terror will suddenly sit upright in bed, feel intense fear, let out a bloodcurdling scream, exhibit a rapid pulse and breathing rate, and speak incoherently. After a night terror, the person typically falls right back to sleep and does not recall the experience the next morning. As a result, a night terror can be more disturbing to the family members who are rudely awakened by it than to the person who has experienced it. Though night terrors are more common in children, especially those experiencing stress (Talarczyk, 2011), they can afflict adults as well (Llorente, Currier, Norman, & Mellman, 1992). A survey of almost 5,000 people aged 15 to 100 years found that 2 percent experienced night terrors (Ohayon, Guilleminault, & Priest, 1999).

As noted by Mary Whiton Calkins (1893), the content of dreams can be affected by immediate environmental stimuli. Even before Calkins made this observation, it was portrayed by Herman Melville in his novel *Moby Dick* in describing the effect of Captain Ahab's peg leg on the dreams of his ship's sailors. Melville wrote, "To his weary mates, seeking repose within six inches of his ivory heel, such would have been the reverberating crack and din of that bony step that their dreams would have been of the crunching teeth of sharks." Similarly, you might find yourself dreaming of an ice cream truck ringing its bell, only to awaken suddenly and discover that your dream had been stimulated by the ringing of your telephone.

Such anecdotal reports of the incorporation of stimuli into dreams have inspired laboratory experiments. In one of the first of these, researchers sprayed sleepers with a water mist when they were in REM sleep; on being awakened, many of the participants reported dreams with watery themes, such as a leaky roof or being caught in the rain (Dement & Wolpert, 1958). Experiments also have found that sleeping participants who are touched

Night Terror

Night terrors typically occur in children between 3 and 12 years of age. Night terrors occur during non-REM sleep, whereas nightmares occur during REM sleep.
Source: Yuganov Konstantin/Shutterstock.com.

on their bodies (Nielsen, 1993) or rocked in a hammock (Leslie & Ogilvie, 1996) might incorporate that stimulation into their dreams. Despite these positive findings, stimuli that we experience when we are asleep are not always incorporated into our dreams. For example, a study of sleep apnea patients found no increase in dream content related to breathing problems (Gross & Lavie, 1994).

Mary Whiton Calkins (1893) also noted that we might be able to control our ongoing dreams. In **lucid dreaming**, an approach devised by Stephen LaBerge (Kahan & LaBerge, 1994), sleeping individuals learn how to be aware while dreaming and how to direct their dreams. Lucid dreamers report an enhanced sense of well-being (Wolpin, Marston, Randolph, & Clothier, 1992), though the reasons for this feeling are unclear. Lucid dreaming has been used to alleviate depression (Taits, 2011) and help people with recurrent nightmares alter aspects of their dreams to make them less frightening (Zadra & Pihl, 1997).

lucid dreaming The ability to be aware that one is dreaming and to direct one's dreams.

The Purpose of Dreaming

REM sleep—dream sleep—is important. Participants who have been deprived of sleep, and then are allowed to sleep as long as they like, show an increase in REM sleep (Dement, 1960). This phenomenon is known as the *REM rebound effect* and indicates that dream sleep serves important functions. But what are the functions of dreams? People have pondered this question for thousands of years, and cultures vary in the significance and value they place on dreams (Wax, 1999). Native American cultures tend to make less of a demarcation between waking and dreaming realities and view dreams as messages from another realm that can enlighten the dreamer (Krippner & Thompson, 1996). The ancient Hebrews, Egyptians, and Greeks believed that dreams brought prophecies from God or the gods, as in the Pharaoh's dream that was interpreted by Joseph in the Old Testament of the Bible and in dreams described in Homer's *Iliad* and *Odyssey*. But Aristotle, who at first accepted the divine origin of dreams, later rejected this belief, claiming that it is merely coincidental when prophetic dreams come true.

Dreaming as Wish Fulfillment

Sigmund Freud (1900/1990) provided the first formal view of dreaming as wish fulfillment. Freud claimed that dreams function as the "royal road to the unconscious" by serving as safe outlets for unconscious sexual or aggressive impulses that we cannot act on while we are awake because of cultural prohibitions against them. Freud distinguished between a dream's **manifest content**, which is the dream as recalled by the dreamer, and its **latent content**, which is the dream's hidden, underlying meaning. Thus, the manifest content of a dream hides its latent content. But why do we not dream about the latent content directly? If we dreamed directly about emotionally charged sexual or aggressive material, we might repeatedly awaken ourselves from our sleep.

manifest content Sigmund Freud's term for the verbally reported dream.

latent content Sigmund Freud's term for the true, though disguised, meaning of a dream.

Chapter 6 Consciousness   **217**

But how can we uncover a dream's latent content from its manifest content? According to Freud, a dream's manifest content consists of symbols that disguise its latent sexual or aggressive content. Thus, in our dreams, trees, rifles, or skyscrapers might act as phallic symbols representing unconscious sexual impulses. The manifest content of a dream reported by a person is translated into its latent content during the process of psychoanalysis, which is discussed in Chapter 15. Nonetheless, even Freud said that "sometimes a cigar is just a cigar"—meaning that sometimes the manifest content is not symbolic but instead is the true content of the dream. Additionally, this approach to dream interpretations is difficult to study empirically; thus, Freud's approach to dream analysis in treatment settings is on the decline.

Dreaming as Problem Solving

The failure of psychoanalysts to provide convincing research support for dreaming as a form of disguised wish fulfillment (Fisher & Greenberg, 1985) led researchers to study other possible functions of dreams, such as problem solving. Anecdotal reports have long supported the view that dreaming serves the function of problem solving. For example, Elias Howe completed his invention of the sewing machine only after gaining insight from a dream. And there is research evidence that events we are concerned about from the previous day are more likely to be included in our dreams (Cipolli, Bolzani, Tuozzi, & Fagioli, 2001). Rosalind Cartwright (1978), a leading dream researcher, has conducted formal studies of the possible role of dreaming in solving practical and emotional problems.

According to Cartwright, dreaming provides a more creative approach to problem solving because it is freer and less constrained by the more logical thinking of waking life. In a study of people in the process of divorcing their spouse, Cartwright (1991) found that those who dreamed about their relationship with their spouse while they were going through the divorce were less depressed and better adjusted to single life a year later. This finding was particularly true of those who had highly emotional dreams. Note, however, that this study revealed a positive correlation between dreaming and emotional adjustment. It did not provide evidence that dreaming *caused* better emotional adjustment. Another experimental study found that participants who were directed to dream about particular problems later reported less distress and a reduction in the problems compared to participants who had not been directed to do so (White & Taytroe, 2003). Likewise, lucid dreamers who were directed to dream about a "guru" who knew the answers to particular problems later reported more creative solutions than did participants who were not lucid dreamers (Stumbrys & Daniels, 2010). Because these studies were experimental rather than correlational, it provides more convincing evidence that dreaming might play a role in helping us deal with personal problems.

Dreaming as an Aid to Memory

Do you ever stay up all night to study for exams? If so, you might be impairing your ability to memorize the material you have studied. Decades of research indicate that sleep can help you form long-term memories (Fenn, Nusbaum, & Margoliash, 2003), particularly emotional memories (Wagner, Gais, & Born, 2001). REM sleep appears to be even more beneficial to memory than NREM sleep. Researchers studying mice have found that the signaling molecules that are activated during memory processing in the hippocampus are also active during REM but not NREM sleep (Luo, Phan, Yang, Garelick, & Storm, 2013). Consider a study in which undergraduates learned a story during the day and then were awakened periodically to deprive them of equal periods of either REM sleep or stage 4 sleep. The next day they were asked to recall the story they had learned the day before. Participants who had been deprived of REM sleep showed poorer recall than participants who had been deprived of stage 4 sleep (Tilley & Empson, 1978).

Additional evidence for the importance of REM sleep comes from research findings that the more REM sleep we have during a night's sleep, the better our memory will be for material learned during the day before. In one study, undergraduates learned Morse code just before bedtime on three consecutive nights. After awakening, they were given a Morse code test. The results revealed a positive correlation between the length of REM sleep and their performance on the test (Mandai, Guerrien, Sockeel, & Dujardin, 1989). However, some researchers have pointed out that the evidence for the role of sleep in the formation of long-term memories is inconsistent (Vertes & Eastman, 2000). Thus, sleep may play a role in memory consolidation, and some researchers hypothesize that dreaming may enhance memory by facilitating a storehouse of memories that are unique to each individual (Oudiette & Paller, 2013).

Dreaming as the By-Product of Random Brain Activity

The **activation-synthesis theory** of J. Allan Hobson and Robert McCarley (1977) holds that dreams are the by-products of the cortex's attempt to make sense of activity generated by the brain stem during REM sleep. That is, the cortex interprets brain activation and *synthesizes* it into a dream. As an example, consider a dream in which you are being chased but feel that you cannot run away. According to the activation-synthesis theory, this dream might reflect the cortex's attempt to explain the failure of signals from the motor areas of the brain to stimulate limb movements during the paralysis that accompanies REM sleep—paralysis produced by activity in the brain stem. The inability of the cortex to make logical sense of patterns of random brain stem activity might explain why our REM dreams tend to be more bizarre than our daydreams (Williams, Merritt, Rittenhouse, & Hobson, 1992).

The activation-synthesis theory does not discount the influence of psychological factors on one's dreams. That is, the theory accepts that the cortex's interpretation of random brain stem activity presumably reveals something about the personality and experiences of the dreamer. The theory simply assumes that dreams are generated by random brain stem activity, not by unconscious wishes or emotional conflicts. Indeed, recent research indicates that dreams are not merely the meaningless by-products of brain activity (Colace, 2003). Psychological factors come into play only *after* the onset of brain stem activity (Rittenhouse, Stickgold, & Hobson, 1994). One problem with this theory is that there is no way to make clear testable hypotheses if a researcher were to design an experiment to test it. For example, there may be plenty of extraneous sounds or stimuli present while a person is sleeping, but a dream might only occasionally incorporate them. Also, consider if you have ever had a dream about a salient joyful or worrisome event that occurred long ago. Both examples would be difficult to explain using the activation-synthesis theory alone. Despite more than a century of research, no single dream theory has been clearly shown to be superior at explaining the functions of dreams. One of the difficulties in dream research is that the same dream can be explained equally well by different theories. This possibility is illustrated in Figure 6-7.

activation-synthesis theory The theory that dreams are the by-products of the cortex's attempt to make sense of the spontaneous changes in physiological activity generated by the brain stem during REM sleep.

Section Review: Dreams

1. In what ways did Mary Whiton Calkins's 1893 study of dreams anticipate later research findings?
2. What is Freud's theory of dreaming?

Hypnosis

Whereas sleep is a naturally occurring state of consciousness, **hypnosis** is an induced state of consciousness in which one person responds to suggestions by another person to alter perception, thinking, feelings, and behavior. Hypnosis originated in the work of the Viennese physician Franz Anton Mesmer (1734–1815), who claimed that he could cure illnesses by transmitting to his patients a form of energy he called *animal magnetism*, a process that became known as *mesmerism*. In the late 18th century, Mesmer—a charismatic

hypnosis An induced state of consciousness in which one person responds to suggestions by another person for alterations in perception, thinking, and behavior.

FIGURE 6-7
One Dream, Three Explanations

The Dream: The person dreams that he is running in place and can neither move from the spot nor stop running.
Theoretical Explanations:
(a) Freud's wish fulfillment theory requires that the manifest content (the dream as reported) be interpreted to find its latent content (its true meaning). The dream might be interpreted as meaning that the dreamer has a conflict about his wish for sex (symbolized by his desire to move from the spot) and his guilty feelings about that wish (symbolized by his wish to stop running).
(b) Cartwright's problem-solving theory assumes that dreaming helps us solve real-life problems. Perhaps the dreamer has been concerned with recent excessive weight gain but has been unable to decide on the best course of action for losing weight. The dream might be directing him to take up aerobic exercise.
(c) Hobson and McCarley's activation-synthesis theory attributes dreaming to brain activity while we are asleep. During REM sleep, the pons generates neural impulses that activate random regions of the cerebral cortex. Perhaps it has activated the region of the motor cortex that controls leg movements. Because the sleeper's legs are paralyzed during REM sleep, he might synthesize the cortical arousal and leg paralysis into a dream about running in place without being able to move or stop.

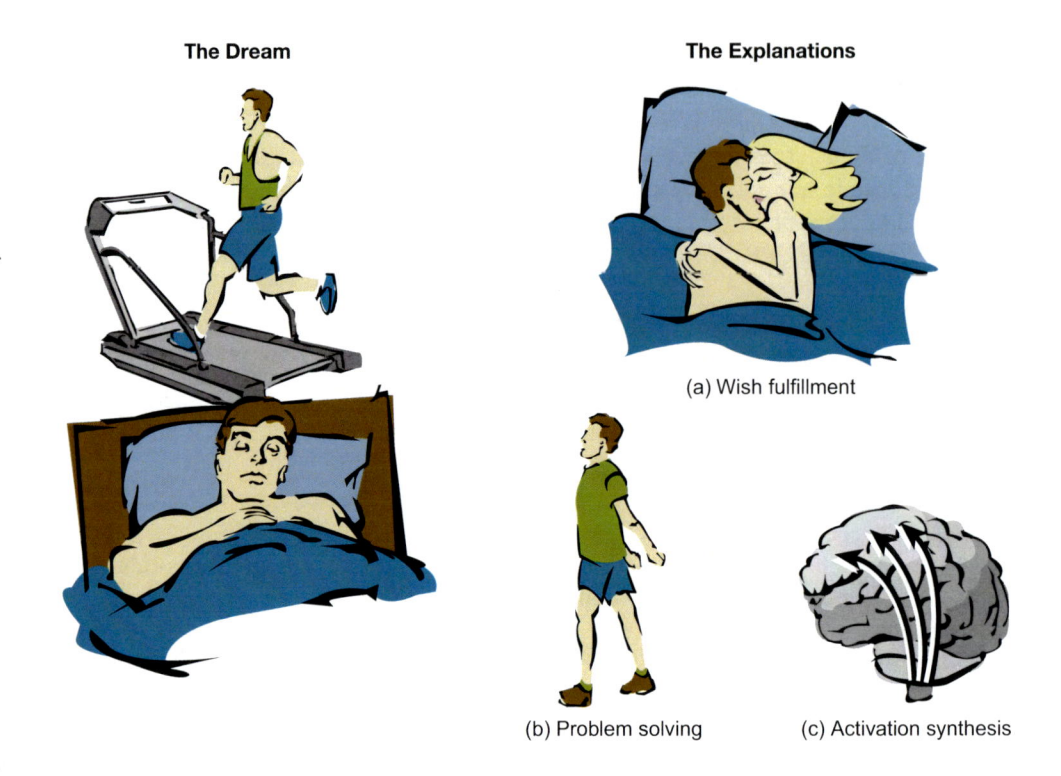

The Dream

The Explanations

(a) Wish fulfillment

(b) Problem solving   (c) Activation synthesis

man—became the rage of Paris, impressing audiences with his demonstrations of mesmerism (Musikantow, 2011). Today we still use the word *mesmerized* to describe a person in a trancelike state and *animal magnetism* to describe people with charismatic personalities.

Mesmer's flamboyance and extravagant claims, as well as the professional jealousy of other physicians, provoked King Louis XVI to appoint a commission to investigate mesmerism. The commission was headed by Benjamin Franklin and included Antoine Lavoisier (the founder of modern chemistry) and J. I. Guillotin (the inventor of the infamous decapitation device, the guillotine). The commission completed its investigation in 1784, concluding that there was no evidence of animal magnetism and that the effects of mesmerism were attributable to the power of suggestion and people's active imagination (Franklin et al., 1784/2002). In 1842 the English surgeon James Braid (1795–1860) used mesmerism in his practice as an anesthetic and concluded that it induced a sleeplike state. He renamed mesmerism *hypnotism*, from Hypnos, the Greek god of sleep.

Hypnotic Induction and Susceptibility

How do hypnotists induce a hypnotic state? The process depends less on the skill of the hypnotist than on the suggestibility of the individual. Highly hypnotizable people have a superior ability to vividly and uncritically imagine things suggested to them and to become completely absorbed in what they are doing (Enea & Dafinoiu, 2013). Thus, these characteristics could be considered a cognitive trait associated with the responsiveness to suggestions. And perhaps of greatest importance, highly hypnotizable people tend to have strong empathy, or the ability to recognize other people's feelings (Wickramasekera & Szlyk, 2003).

Psychologists have developed tests of hypnotizability, such as the Stanford Hypnotic Susceptibility Scale (Weitzenhoffer & Hilgard, 1962) and more recently the Spanos Attitudes Toward Hypnosis Questionnaire (Milling, 2012). These tests determine the extent to which participants will comply with hypnotic suggestions after a brief hypnotic induction. A simple suggestion, to test for some susceptibility, might direct you to hold your hands in front of you and move them apart. A more difficult suggestion, to test for high susceptibility, might direct you to produce handwriting similar to that of a child. Regardless of their susceptibility, people cannot be hypnotized against their will (Lynn, Rhue, & Weekes, 1990).

The aim of hypnotic induction is to create a relaxed, passive, highly focused state of mind. During hypnotic induction the hypnotist might have you focus your eyes on a spot on the ceiling. The hypnotist might then suggest that you notice your eyelids closing, feet warming, muscles relaxing, and breathing slowing—events that would take place even without hypnotic suggestions. You would gradually relinquish more and more control of your perceptions, thoughts, and behaviors to the hypnotist.

Effects of Hypnosis

Research studies have demonstrated a variety of impressive effects of hypnosis. These include physical, perceptual, cognitive, and behavioral effects.

Physical Effects of Hypnosis

Many extreme claims about remarkable physical effects of hypnosis have been discredited by experimental research. Perhaps you have heard the claim that hypnotized people who are given the suggestion that their hand has touched red-hot metal will develop a blister—a claim first made over two centuries ago (Gauld, 1990). Experiments have shown that such hypnotic suggestions can, at best, merely promote warming of the skin by increasing the flow of blood to it (Spanos, McNeil, & Stam, 1982). Nonetheless, there is evidence that hypnosis can have highly specific physical effects. One study found that postsurgical patients who received hypnotic suggestions for wound healing showed wound healing superior to that of patients who received supportive attention or usual medical care (Ginandes, Brooks, Sando, Jones, & Aker, 2003). Another study assessed the effect of hypnosis on the immune response. Dental and medical students were randomly assigned to receive either hypnosis or no hypnosis prior to a major exam. The results showed that those who received hypnosis did not show the normal stress-related decline in the immunological response (Kiecolt-Glaser, Marucha, Atkinson, & Glaser, 2001). At best, hypnosis might subtly inhibit pain pathways. Remember from Chapter 5 that pain is comprised of both sensory and emotional components.

Perceptual Effects of Hypnosis

Stage hypnotists commonly use hypnosis to induce alterations in perception, such as convincing participants that a vial of water is actually ammonia. Participants will jerk their heads away after smelling it. But the most important perceptual effect of hypnosis is in pain relief. In the mid-19th century, the Scottish surgeon James Esdaile (1808–1859) used hypnosis to induce anesthesia in more than 300 patients undergoing surgery for the removal of limbs, tumors, or cataracts (Ellenberger, 1970).

A recent meta-analysis of laboratory and biomedical research studies (Montgomery, DuHamel, & Redd, 2000) found that hypnosis has a moderate to large effect in relieving pain, as in cancer pain (Shea, 2003), pain during labor and childbirth (Landolt & Milling, 2011), or postoperative pain (Lew, Kravits, Garberoglio, & Williams, 2011). But how does hypnosis produce its analgesic effects? As discussed in Chapter 5, one way is by using suggestions that help distract sufferers from their pain (Farthing, Venturino, & Brown, 1984). A second way is by sending neural impulses from the brain down the spinal cord that block the transmission of pain impulses from the body to the spinal cord (Holroyd, 1996). This method is in keeping with the gate-control theory of pain (see Chapter 5).

Cognitive Effects of Hypnosis

In 1976, 26 elementary schoolchildren and their bus driver were kidnapped in Chowchilla, California, and imprisoned in a buried tractor trailer. The bus driver and two of the children dug their way out and got help. The driver, Frank Ray, had seen the license plate number of the kidnappers' van but was unable to recall it. After being hypnotized and told to imagine himself watching the kidnapping unfold on television, he was able to recall all but one of the digits of the number. His recollection enabled the police to track down the kidnappers (Smith, 1983).

hypermnesia The hypnotic enhancement of recall.

The Chowchilla case was a widely publicized example of one of the chief cognitive applications of hypnosis—**hypermnesia**, the enhancement of memory. Though many memories retrieved by hypnosis are accurate (Ewin, 1994), hypnosis also can create inaccurate memories, or pseudomemories (Spanos, Burgess, Burgess, Samuels, & Blois, 1999). In fact, one of the most common misconceptions that the American public holds about hypnosis is its role in restoring accurate memories (Johnson & Hauck, 1999). Because of the possibility of inaccuracy, the use of hypnosis in legal cases to enhance eyewitness memories is controversial, and its use is limited.

One problem is that hypnotized eyewitnesses feel more confident about the memories they recall under hypnosis—regardless of their accuracy (Weekes, Lynn, Green, & Brentar, 1992). In one study, 27 participants were hypnotized and then given the suggestion that they had been awakened by a loud noise one night during the preceding week. Later, after leaving the hypnotized state, 13 of the participants claimed that the suggested event had actually occurred. Even after being informed of the hypnotic suggestion, 6 participants still insisted that they had been awakened by the noise (Laurence & Perry, 1983). These findings indicate the potential danger of hypnotically enhanced eyewitness testimony, particularly because juries put more trust in confident eyewitnesses (Sheehan & Tilden, 1983) and hypnotized eyewitnesses (Wagstaff, Vella, & Perfect, 1992).

Behavioral Effects of Hypnosis

Though hypnosis can help some people, a debate has raged for more than a century about whether hypnosis can be used to induce harmful behavior (e.g., Liegois, 1899). Martin Orne and Frederick Evans (1965) demonstrated that hypnotized people could be induced to commit dangerous acts. Their study included a group of hypnotized participants and a group of participants who simulated being hypnotized. When instructed to do so, participants in both groups plunged their hands into what they were told was a nitric acid solution, threw the liquid in another person's face, and tried to handle a poisonous snake. Of course, the experimenters protected the participants (by immediately washing off the liquid, by actually having them throw water instead of acid, and by stopping them from touching the snake). Because both groups engaged in apparently dangerous acts, the research setting, rather than hypnosis, might have accounted for the results. In any case, there is no evidence that hypnotized people become mindless zombies who blindly obey orders to commit harmful acts (Gibson, 1991).

Similarly, some of the effects of stage hypnosis might have less to do with hypnosis than with the setting in which they occur. For example, you might have seen a stage hypnotist direct a hypnotized volunteer from the audience to remain as rigid as a plank while lying extended between two chairs. But highly motivated, non-hypnotized persons also can perform this "human plank" trick. According to researcher Theodore Barber, even the willingness of hypnotized participants to obey suggestions to engage in bizarre behaviors, such as clucking like a chicken, might be more attributable to the theatrical "anything goes" atmosphere of stage hypnosis than to the effect of hypnosis itself (Meeker & Barber, 1971).

The Nature of Hypnosis

In the late 19th century, most notably in France, practitioners of hypnosis disagreed whether hypnosis induced an altered, or trance, state of consciousness. One group argued that hypnosis induces a trancelike state called **dissociation**, in which parts of the mind become separated from one another and form independent streams of consciousness. Many distance runners use dissociation to divorce their conscious minds from possibly distressful bodily sensations while still remaining consciously aware of the racecourse ahead of them (Masters, 1992). Another group of French hypnotists argued that hypnosis does not induce a trance state. Instead, they insisted that it just induces a state of heightened suggestibility. This debate lingers on; some researchers view hypnosis as an altered state of consciousness, and others view it as a normal state of waking consciousness.

dissociation A state in which the mind is split into two or more independent streams of consciousness.

Hypnosis as a Dissociated State

Cognitive psychologists have become interested on the effects of attention and suggestion on hypnosis (Halligan & Oakley, 2013). Today, the main theory of hypnosis as an altered state is **neodissociation theory**, This theory originated in a classroom demonstration of hypnotically induced deafness by Ernest Hilgard (1904–2001), who directed a hypnotized blind student to raise an index finger if he heard a sound. When blocks were banged near his head, the student did not even flinch. But when asked if some part of his mind had actually heard the noise, his finger rose. Hilgard called this part of the mind the **hidden observer** (Hilgard, 1978). Hilgard helped make hypnosis scientifically legitimate when he founded his laboratory for hypnosis research at Stanford University in 1957 (Bowers, 1994).

Hilgard used the concept of the hidden observer to explain hypnotically induced pain relief. He relied on the cold pressor test, in which participants submerge an arm in ice water and are asked every few seconds to estimate their degree of pain. Though hypnotized participants who are told that they will feel less pain report that they feel little or no pain, the hidden observer, when asked, reports that it has experienced intense pain (Hilgard, 1973).

Additional evidence in favor of hypnosis as an altered state comes from experiments in which hypnotized participants experience physiological changes in response to hypnotic suggestions. In one study, highly hypnotizable participants learned lists of words and were given **posthypnotic suggestions** to forget them. Those who reported *posthypnotic amnesia* (their inability to recognize the words they had read) showed changes in components of their brain-wave patterns that are related to attention and recognition. This evidence indicates that posthypnotic amnesia is possibly related to selective attention rather than a state of heightened suggestibility (Allen, Iacono, Laravuso, & Dunn, 1995). Research studies using PET scans have shown that hypnosis is associated with activity in distinct regions of the brain that play critical roles in regulating consciousness (Rainville, Hofbauer, Bushnell, Duncan, & Price, 2002). More recent data using MRI have shown that hypnotic-susceptible individuals do in fact show activation of distinct brain circuits related to attention. These circuits mimic the same circuits that are responsive during placebo analgesic effects (Huber, Lui, & Porro, 2013).

Hypnosis as Role-Playing

The claim that hypnosis is an altered state of consciousness has not gone unchallenged. Critics insist that hypnotically induced effects are only responses to personal factors, such as the participant's motivation, and situational factors, such as the hypnotist's wording of suggestions. By arranging the right combination of factors, the hypnotist increases the likelihood that the participant will comply with hypnotic suggestions.

Evidence that hypnosis is a state of heightened suggestibility has also come from studies of hypnotic **age regression**, in which hypnotized participants are told to return to childhood. A hypnotized adult might use baby talk or play with an imaginary teddy bear. But a published review of research on hypnotic age regression found that adults do not adopt the true cognitive, behavioral, and physiological characteristics of children; they just act as though they were children (Nash, 1987). For example, in a classic study, Martin Orne (1927–2000) hypnotized college students and suggested that they regress back to their sixth birthday party. He then asked them to describe the people and activities at the party, which they did in great detail. When Orne asked the participants' parents to describe the same birthday party, he found that many of the participants' "memories" had been fabrications. They reported people and events they presumed would have been at their own sixth birthday party. There was no evidence that they actually reexperienced their sixth birthday party (Orne, 1951).

Neither side in the debate about the nature of hypnosis has provided sufficient evidence to discount the other side completely. As noted by William James more than a century ago, both sides might be correct: Hypnosis might be a dissociated state of consciousness that can be shaped by the social context and hypnotic suggestions (Kihlstrom & McConkey, 1990). After decades as a leading hypnosis researcher, Theodore Barber (2000) concluded

Hypnosis

Hypnotherapists make use of posthypnotic suggestions in the treatment of conditions such as chronic pain or anxiety.
Source: wavebreakmedia/Shutterstock.com.

neodissociation theory The theory that hypnosis induces a dissociated state of consciousness.

hidden observer Ernest Hilgard's term for the part of the hypnotized person's consciousness that is not under the control of the hypnotist but is aware of what is taking place.

posthypnotic suggestions Suggestions directing people to carry out particular behaviors or to have particular experiences after leaving hypnosis.

age regression A hypnotic state in which the individual apparently behaves as she or he did as a child.

The Research Process

Is Hypnosis an Altered State of Consciousness?

Rationale

In an experiment conducted by Nicholas Spanos (1942–1994) and Frin Hewitt of Carleton University in Ottawa, the hidden observer was made to give contradictory reports, depending on the hypnotist's suggestions (Spanos & Hewitt, 1980).

Method

The experiment recruited undergraduate participants who scored high on a hypnotizability scale and were then given suggestions for hypnotic analgesia. Two groups of participants were given contradictory suggestions. One group was told that the hypnotized part of their minds would have little awareness of the pain, while a hidden part would be more aware of the actual intensity of the pain. Another group was told that the hypnotized part of their minds would have little awareness of the pain, while a hidden part would be even less aware of the pain. Participants were asked to place a forearm in ice water, which induces pain. They were told to have the hypnotized parts of their minds state their level of pain on a scale from 0 to 20 every 5 seconds for 60 seconds. They also were told to hold a forearm in ice water while having their hidden observer report their level of pain (from 0 to 20) by tapping out a simple code on a response key every 5 seconds for 60 seconds.

Results and Discussion

When asked to report the intensity of the pain, the hidden observer reported what the participants had been led to expect. It experienced more pain than the hypnotized part when told it would be more aware and less pain when told it would be less aware. Thus, the hidden observer might simply be a result of the participant's willingness to act as though he or she has experienced suggested hypnotic effects. Spanos found that this willingness is not a case of faking but probably reflects the well-established ability of people to distract themselves from their pain. Moreover, the hidden observer never appears spontaneously—it appears only when explicitly asked to. This study, as well as others by Spanos, indicates that the hidden observer is a product not of the dissociation of consciousness, but instead of the participant's willingness to follow the hypnotist's suggestions.

---

that the all-or-none debate is fruitless. Instead, he believes researchers should study the three kinds of people he has identified as susceptible to hypnosis. The first are people who have had active fantasy lives since childhood. The second are people who are prone to dissociation and tend to repress undesirable thoughts, emotions, and memories. The third are people who are motivated to play the role of hypnotized participants.

Section Review: Hypnosis

1. How would you induce a state of hypnosis?
2. What are the benefits and risks of using hypnosis in enhancing the recall of memories?
3. Why do some researchers believe that hypnosis is not an altered state of consciousness?

Psychoactive Drugs

psychoactive drugs Chemicals that induce changes in mood, thinking, perception, and behavior by affecting neuronal activity in the brain.

Normal waking consciousness also can be altered by **psychoactive drugs**, which are chemicals that induce changes in mood, thinking, perception, and behavior by affecting neuronal activity. People seem drawn to psychoactive drugs. Many people consume alcohol to reduce social anxiety, take barbiturates to fall asleep, use narcotics to feel euphoric, drink coffee to get going in the morning, or smoke marijuana to enrich their perception of music.

Psychoactive drugs exert their effects by altering synaptic transmission, by either promoting or inhibiting it. But the effects of psychoactive drugs depend on a host of factors. These include the drugs' dosage, the user's experience with them, the user's expectations about their effects, and the setting in which they are taken.

Many psychoactive drugs can cause *psychological dependence*—an intense desire to achieve the intoxicated state induced by the drug. Most psychoactive drugs also can cause *physical dependence* (or *addiction*). That is, after people use the drug for a period of time, they develop a physiological need for the drug and experience withdrawal. As people use physically addicting drugs, they develop *tolerance*—a decrease in physiological responsiveness to the drug. As a result, they require increasingly higher doses to achieve the desired effect. If you are concerned that you might have a problem with substance abuse, complete the questionnaire in Table 6-2.

When people stop taking the drug they are addicted to, they experience *withdrawal symptoms*. The pattern and severity of withdrawal symptoms is specific to the kind of drug to which the person is addicted. Common withdrawal symptoms include craving, chills, headache, fatigue, nausea, insomnia, depression, convulsions, and irritability. A possible consequence of psychoactive drug use is a *drug overdose*, which can be fatal. An ironic finding is that drug overdoses are common following drug detoxification. This occurs because detoxification produces a loss of drug tolerance, and when former addicts return to drug use, they may use a dangerously high dose (Strang et al., 2003). As shown in Table 6-3, the psychoactive drugs can be divided into general categories: *depressants*, *stimulants*, *hallucinogens*, and *entactogens*.

TABLE 6-2 Are You Abusing a Drug?

Instructions: Listed below are eight criteria that the American Psychiatric Association uses to diagnose drug abuse (also known as *substance dependence*) in the DSM-5. If three or more of the following criteria describe your own behavior, you may have a problem with drug abuse.

Yes	No	
___	___	1. You take the drug in larger amounts or over a longer period than intended.
___	___	2. You have a persistent desire, or have made one or more unsuccessful efforts, to cut down or control drug use.
___	___	3. You spend a great deal of your time in activities necessary to get the drug (for example, theft), taking the drug (for example, chain smoking), or recovering from its effects (for example, alcohol hangovers) and do this while you are expected to fulfill obligations at work, school, or home, or when drug use is physically dangerous (for example, driving when intoxicated).
___	___	4. You experience strong urges for the drug that can occur anywhere but can be more intense in the context in which the drug is obtained or used (for example, intense craving where the individual cannot think of anything else but the drug).
___	___	5. You give up or reduce in frequency important social, occupational, or recreational activities because of drug use.
___	___	6. You continue to use the drug despite recognizing its harmfulness to your social or interpersonal life.
___	___	7. You need increased amounts of the drug (at least 50 percent more) to achieve the desired effect and/or you experience a decreased effect with continued use of the same amount (tolerance).
___	___	8. You often take the drug to relieve or avoid withdrawal symptoms.

Source: Adapted from the American Psychiatric Association (2013).

TABLE 6-3 Psychoactive Drugs and Their Effects on the Brain

Category	Drugs	Effects on the Brain	Sites of Action in Brain
Depressants	Alcohol (low doses inhibit anxiety; high doses produce sedation)	Removes social inhibitions Relieves anxiety Induces sleep Impairs judgment Causes disorientation and lack of coordination	Block glutamate receptors and facilitate GABA receptors
	Barbiturates	Remove social inhibitions Relieve anxiety Induce sleep Impair judgment Cause disorientation	Facilitate GABA receptors
	Benzodiazepines	Relieve anxiety Induce sleep Reduce seizures Relax muscles	Facilitate GABA receptors
	Opiates	Induce feelings of euphoria Relieve pain Induce sleep	Stimulate opiate receptors
Stimulants	Caffeine	Stimulates alertness Promotes wakefulness	Blocks adenosine receptors
	Nicotine	Stimulates alertness Relieves anxiety	Stimulates acetylcholine receptors
	Amphetamine and methamphetamine	Stimulate alertness Promote wakefulness and insomnia Create an overblown sense of confidence Induce feelings of elation Can cause symptoms of paranoia	Stimulate release of dopamine and norepinephrine
	Cocaine	Induces feelings of euphoria Creates an overblown sense of confidence	Blocks reuptake of dopamine and thus increases dopamine in the brain
Other Psychoactive Drugs	LSD	Causes visual hallucinations Creates a sense of oneness and timelessness Induces seemingly mystical insights	Stimulates serotonin receptors
	Marijuana	Induces relaxation Removes social inhibitions Intensifies sensory experience Interferes with memory formation	Stimulates cannabinoid receptors Stimulate release of serotonin
	Entactogens or empathogens (MDE, MDMA)	Induce relaxation Induce positive mood Create a sense of interpersonal closeness Enhance emotional sensitivity and feelings Alter perceptions of the time and physical environment	

Depressants

Depressants reduce arousal by inhibiting activity in the central nervous system. This section discusses several kinds of depressants: *alcohol, barbiturates, benzodiazepines,* and *opiates* which have unique effects.

Alcohol

Ethyl alcohol (or **ethanol**), an addictive drug, has been used—and abused—for thousands of years. Even the ancient Romans had to pass laws against drunk driving—of chariots (Whitlock, 1987). Drunk drivers are dangerous because they suffer from impaired judgment, perceptual distortions, decreased reaction times and motor incoordination. Alcohol is involved in 50 percent of traffic accidents in the United States (Matthews, Best, White, Vandergriff, & Simon, 1996). Chronic alcoholics often lose their jobs, homes, and families and create a large toll on society. Many alcoholics die from cirrhosis of the liver or chronic diseases associated with poor living conditions. Women who abuse alcohol while pregnant run the risk of giving birth to babies with fetal alcohol syndrome. This condition is characterized by malformations of the head and brain abnormalities and is accompanied by intellectual disabilities (see Chapter 4).

Alcohol facilitates the actions of the neurotransmitter GABA, which inhibits neuronal transmission in the brain (Korpi, 1994), and blocks glutamate, which excites neuronal transmission in the brain. Given that the typical person metabolizes about one ounce of alcohol an hour, a person who drinks faster than that will become intoxicated. Men, due to their greater muscle mass and lower proportion of body fat, metabolize alcohol more efficiently than women do, so a woman might become intoxicated on less alcohol than it would take to intoxicate a man (Mumenthaler, Taylor, O'Hara, & Yesavage, 1999). Women also experience less activity of *alcohol dehydrogenase*, an enzyme that metabolizes alcohol (Baraona et al., 2001). This also might contribute to this gender difference.

You probably have seen shy people become the life of the party, proper people become sexually indiscreet, or mild people become verbally or physically aggressive after a few drinks. Intoxicated men are less able to determine when sexual advances are unwelcome, perhaps contributing to the incidence of "acquaintance rape" (Marx, Gross, & Adams, 1999). One 15-month longitudinal study of men entering alcoholism and domestic violence treatment programs found that their wives and partners were significantly more likely to be physically assaulted on the days that the men drank (Fals-Stewart, 2003). And alcohol has been implicated in verbal and physical aggression among female and male heterosexual college students involved in abusive dating relationships (Shook et al., 2000). But the demonstration of an association between drinking alcohol and engaging in violence does not necessarily indicate a causal relationship between the two. Perhaps people who drink alcohol are more likely to be around other people, making aggressive encounters more likely. Or perhaps people who tend to be aggressive may prefer to drink more alcohol than do people who are not aggressive.

Evidence of a causal relationship between alcohol and aggression comes from experimental rather than correlational research. For example, experiments indicate that participants are, in fact, more likely to be aggressive after drinking alcohol than after drinking a placebo that merely tastes like alcohol (Dougherty, Cherek, & Bennett, 1996). Aside from alcohol's power to make people less inhibited by its direct effects on the brain, psychologists have identified other factors that account for alcohol's ability to weaken our inhibitions and increase risk-taking behavior. Alcohol researcher Claude Steele points to "alcohol myopia"—the inability of intoxicated people to foresee the negative consequences of their actions—as one reason why they will fail to inhibit undesirable behaviors (Steele & Josephs, 1990). For example, when college men are intoxicated, they report a greater willingness to engage in sexual intercourse without wearing condoms (MacDonald, MacDonald, Zanna, & Fong, 2000). Other researchers have found that because we are aware of alcohol's reputation for removing social inhibitions, we also might use it as an excuse for engaging in questionable behavior (Hull & Bond, 1986). This use is known as self-handicapping (see

depressants Psychoactive drugs that inhibit activity in the central nervous system.

ethyl alcohol (ethanol) A depressant found in beverages and commonly used to reduce social inhibitions.

Chapter 14). If we can attribute our silliness, sexuality, or aggression to alcohol, we might feel less guilt and embarrassment for our actions when we sober up.

Barbiturates and Benzodiazepines

barbiturates Depressants used to induce sleep or anesthesia.

benzodiazepines Depressants used to relieve anxiety and nervousness.

opiates Depressants, derived from opium, used to relieve pain or to induce a euphoric state of consciousness.

Barbiturates, also known as *major tranquilizers*, are derived from barbituric acid and are the oldest sedative-hypnotics. They produce effects similar to those of alcohol and likewise work by facilitating the actions of GABA (Yu & Ho, 1990) to promote inhibition. Because of this, these drugs are extremely dangerous to combine with alcohol and can lead to coma or death. The barbiturate Seconal, which acts quickly to induce drowsiness, is used as a sleeping pill. This drug class is known to induce sleep, but it is worth noting that the sleep is abnormal, with a reduced amount of REM-stage sleep. The barbiturate Pentothal is used as a general anesthetic in surgery. Because mild doses of Pentothal induce a drunken, uninhibited state in which the intoxicated person is more willing to reveal private thoughts and feelings, it is popularly known as "truth serum," though it does not guarantee that the information revealed will be true. Finally, there is a large abuse potential for this class of drug.

Benzodiazepines, also known as *minor tranquilizers*, and are synthetically made. They were first developed in the 1950s and are considered much safer than barbiturates. The first drug was made by Leo Sternbach in 1955 and was called Librium (Lader, 1991). Other common benzodiazepines are Valium, Xanax, and Ativan. For short-term use, these drugs are considered safe. However, long-term use and large doses can be dangerous. Rohypnol is a benzodiazepine that has gained popularity for misuse (Saum & Inciardi, 1997) and become known as the "date-rape drug."

Opiates

Opium Poppy
Opium is extracted from the seed pods of the plant opium poppy.
Source: ljansempoi/Shutterstock.com.

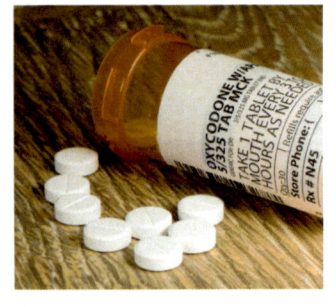

The opium poppy is the source of **opiates**, which include opium, morphine, heroin, and codeine. The opiates have been prized since ancient times for their ability to relieve pain and to induce euphoria. Sumerian clay tablets from about 4000 B.C. refer to the opium poppy as "the plant of joy" (Whitlock, 1987). Some 19th-century artists and writers used opiates to induce altered states of consciousness. Samuel Taylor Coleridge wrote his famous poem "Kubla Khan" under the influence of opium.

In the early 1860s, physicians used morphine, the main active ingredient in opium, to ease the pain of wounded soldiers in the American Civil War. Morphine was named after Morpheus, the Greek god of dreams, because it induces a state of blissful oblivion. In 1898 scientists used opium to derive a more potent drug—heroin. Heroin was named after the Greek god Hero because it was welcomed as a powerful painkiller and cure for morphine addiction. But physicians soon found that heroin simply replaced morphine addiction with heroin addiction. By the early 20th century, so many Americans had become addicted to opiates that in 1914 Congress passed the Harrison Narcotic Act banning their nonmedical use. Today, morphine, codeine, and the synthetic opiates demerol and oxycodone, are routinely prescribed to relieve severe pain. Paul Offit, a leading pediatrician, has suggested that the heroin epidemic in the United States may be a result of physicians overprescribing opioid-based painkillers which have increased significantly between 1991 and 2011 (NIDA, 2014). The euphoric and pain-relieving effects of the opiates are caused by their binding to endorphin receptors, which act to block pain impulses and stimulate the brain's pleasure centers (Levinthal, 1988). This is also the mechanism that facilitates addiction.

Oxycodone
Oxycodone is a semi-synthetic opioid similar to morphine. Manufacturers are trying to make tamper-proof pills to curb its potential for abuse.
Source: PureRadiancePhoto/Shutterstock.com.

Stimulants

stimulants Psychoactive drugs that increase central nervous system activity.

Whereas depressants reduce arousal, stimulants increase it. **Stimulants** include caffeine, nicotine, amphetamines, methylphenidate, and cocaine.

Caffeine

caffeine A stimulant used to increase mental alertness.

Few of us go a day without ingesting the addictive drug **caffeine**, which is found in a variety of products, including coffee, tea, soft drinks, chocolate, cold pills, diet pills, energy drinks, and stimulant tablets. The mind-altering effects of caffeine have made it a popular drug for centuries. Chocolate, for example, was considered a gift from the gods by the Aztecs of Mexico, who drank cocoa during their religious rituals. In the late 19th century, Americans' use of coffee accelerated after the introduction of the first commercial mix of coffee beans at a Nashville hotel called Maxwell House (Ray, 1983).

Today, caffeine is a popular means of maintaining cognitive alertness, apparently by stimulating the release of the excitatory neurotransmitter glutamate (Silinsky, 1989) and blocking the neurotransmitter adenosine. Caffeine reduces fatigue, improves attention, and facilitates information processing (Lorist & Tops, 2003). Unfortunately, caffeine's ability to enhance physiological arousal can interfere with nightly sleep, even if the coffee is ingested only early in the day (Landolt, Werth, Borbely, & Dijk, 1995). Because of its ability to increase alertness, caffeine is beneficial to night-shift workers. In one study, workers received either caffeinated or decaffeinated coffee for several nights during a simulated 8.5-hour night shift. The results showed that the caffeine group had decreased sleepiness and enhanced performance on an assembly-line task (Muehlbach & Walsh, 1995). If you are a habitual caffeine user and suddenly stop using it, you will find that caffeine withdrawal is marked by headaches and drowsiness (Hughes et al., 1991).

Coffea, the Source of Caffeine
Coffee is made from the seeds of the flowering plant *Coffea*.
Source: S_Photo/Shutterstock.com.

Nicotine

"If you can't send money, send tobacco" read a 1776 appeal from General George Washington (Ray, 1983). Washington's troops actually craved **nicotine**, a powerful addictive drug contained in tobacco. Nicotine works by stimulating certain acetylcholine receptors, which might increase the efficiency of information processing in the brain (Pritchard et al., 1995), a point not lost on students who smoke. And many smokers rely on nicotine to reduce anxiety (Kassel & Unrod, 2000). The World Health Organization estimates that 50 percent of smokers begin using this drug during adolescence. Adults who continue to smoke are at risk of experiencing smoking-related death or illness. Nicotine in combination with the other substances found in cigarettes can cause cancers of the lung, mouth, throat, and esophagus. Recently, there has been a rise in the use of "electronic" or e-cigarettes. These smokeless cigarettes vaporize the nicotine with a battery-powered device. There currently is a legislative debate about the regulation of their use; moreover, there is no scientific evidence of their safety or efficacy. They are being marketed as a smoking cessation tool (Brown, Beard, Kotz, Michie, & West, 2014); however, many health professionals are still advising the use of traditional nicotine replacement such as transdermal patches.

nicotine A stimulant used to regulate physical and cognitive arousal.

In regard to its addictiveness, nicotine is comparable to the addictiveness of cocaine, heroin, and alcohol (Stolerman & Jarvis, 1995) and has been attributed to more deaths than the so-called "hard drugs." But why is it that some people get quickly addicted to nicotine, others smoke only occasionally, and still others avoid it totally? There seems to be a genetic basis for this variability. The more responsive users are to nicotine, the more quickly they develop tolerance and become dependent on it (Pomerleau, 1995). And nicotine is associated with intense withdrawal symptoms, which also may impair cognitive performance (Giannakoulas, Katramados, Melas, Diamantopoulos, & Chimonas, 2003). You can read more about the effects, treatment, and prevention of smoking in Chapter 16.

Tobacco
Many products containing nicotine are made from dried tobacco leaves.
Source: PunyaFamily/Shutterstock.com.

Amphetamines

Amphetamines—including Benzedrine, Dexedrine, and Methedrine—are addictive synthetic stimulants that are popularly known as "speed" and are more powerful than caffeine and nicotine. They exert their effects by stimulating the release of dopamine and norepinephrine and inhibiting their reuptake by the neurons that secrete them. In the 1930s, truck drivers discovered that amphetamines would keep them alert during long hauls, letting them drive for many hours without sleeping. For several decades, college students have used amphetamines to stay awake while cramming for final exams. Amphetamines even were used during Operation Desert Storm by the U.S. Air Force Tactical Air Command to stay alert during the Persian Gulf War against Iraq (Emonson & Vanderbeek, 1995). Because amphetamines also suppress appetite and increase the basal metabolic rate, they

amphetamines Stimulants used to maintain alertness and wakefulness.

are commonly used as diet pills. But people who ingest high doses of amphetamines may develop symptoms of schizophrenia, including delusions, hallucinations, and thought disorders (Adeyemo, 2002). Methamphetamines are more potent forms of amphetamine and therefore have one of the highest potentials for abuse. These drugs damage dopamine neurons (Ares-Santos, Granado, & Moratalla, 2013) and serotonin neurons and cause the death of brain cells (Cadet, Jayanthi, & Deng, 2005).

Cocaine

cocaine A stimulant used to induce cognitive alertness and euphoria.

During the 1980s, **cocaine**, an extract from the coca leaf, became the stimulant of choice for people who desired the brief but intense feeling of exhilaration and self-confidence that it induces. Cocaine prevents the reuptake of dopamine and norepinephrine by the neurons that secrete them (Gawin, 1991) and by facilitating activity at serotonin synapses (Aronson, Black, McDougle, & Scanley, 1995). Users snort or sniff cocaine in powdered form, smoke it in crystal form ("crack"), or inject it in solution form. The most common form of abuse is through sniffing, which allows the cocaine to come into contact with the nasal mucosa. This delivers the drug to the brain very rapidly.

People of the Andes have chewed coca leaves for more than a thousand years to induce euphoric feelings and to combat fatigue. In the 19th century, Sir Arthur Conan Doyle made his fictional character Sherlock Holmes a cocaine user. And Robert Louis Stevenson relied on cocaine to stay alert while taking just 6 days to write two drafts of *The Strange Case of Dr. Jekyll and Mr. Hyde*. In 1886, an Atlanta druggist named John Pemberton contributed to cocaine's popularity by introducing a stimulant soft drink that contained both caffeine and cocaine, which he named Coca-Cola.

Unfortunately, cocaine causes harmful side effects, as discovered by Sigmund Freud, who used it himself in part to help him function more efficiently (Karmel, 2003). In the 1880s, Freud praised cocaine as a wonder drug for combating depression, inducing local anesthesia, relieving asthmatic symptoms, and curing opiate addiction. But Freud stopped using and prescribing cocaine after discovering its ability to cause addiction, paranoia, and hallucinations (Freud, 1974). In the early 20th century, the dangers of cocaine use also led to its removal as an ingredient in Coca-Cola. Cocaine can stimulate the heart (Foltin, Fischman, & Levin, 1995), which may account for instances of sudden death in persons with cardiac dysfunctions.

The Source of Cocaine
Extraction of cocaine from the coca plant requires many chemicals.
Source: Dr. Morley Read/Shutterstock.com.

Other Psychoactive Drugs

Hallucinogens

hallucinogens Psychoactive drugs that induce extreme alterations in consciousness, including visual hallucinations, a sense of timelessness, and feelings of depersonalization.

The **hallucinogens** induce extreme alterations in consciousness and interpretations of sensations. Users might experience visual hallucinations, a sense of timelessness, and feelings of depersonalization. It has been difficult to determine whether adverse personality changes associated with hallucinogens are caused mainly by the powerful effects of the drugs or by the tendency of people with psychological instability to use them (Strassman, 1984). The hallucinogens can induce psychological dependence, but there is little evidence that they can induce physical dependence. They exert their effects primarily by affecting serotonin neurons, stimulating some and inhibiting others (Glennon, 1990). The most commonly used hallucinogens include psilocybin, a chemical present in certain mushrooms, mescaline, a chemical in the peyote cactus, and phencyclidine, a synthetic drug better known as "PCP" or "angel dust." But perhaps the best-known hallucinogen is lysergic acid diethylamide (LSD).

LSD

LSD A hallucinogen derived from a fungus that grows on rye grain.

On April 19, 1943, Albert Hofmann, director of research for the Sandoz drug company in Switzerland, accidentally experienced the effects of a microscopic amount of the chemical lysergic acid diethylamide (**LSD**). He evidently absorbed it through his skin. Hofmann reported that he felt as though he was losing his mind: "in a twilight state with my eyes closed . . . I found a continuous stream of fantastic images of extraordinary vividness and intensive kaleidoscopic colours" (Julien, 1981, p. 151). Hofmann found it a horrifying experience. Because many people in the 1960s and 1970s used LSD recklessly, Hofmann (1983) titled his autobiography *LSD: My Problem Child*.

LSD seems to exert its effects by affecting brain receptors for serotonin, most likely by inhibiting their activity (Aghajanian, 1994). A dose of LSD induces a "trip" that lasts up to 12 hours. The trip includes visual hallucinations, such as shifting patterns of colors, changes in the shapes of objects, and distortions in the sizes of body parts. Many people who use LSD believe that it provides them with personal and philosophical insights and extreme perceptual changes (Prepeliczay, 2002). Even **synesthesia** is possible. This phenomenon occurs when stimulation of sensory receptors triggers sensory experiences that characterize another sense (Cytowic, 1989). Thus, someone listening to music while on an LSD trip might report seeing the notes as different colors. Users of LSD might also report a sense of timelessness, a feeling of oneness with the universe, and at times, mystical insights into the meaning of life. Nonetheless, mystical experiences induced by LSD are different from those induced by nondrug means (Smith & Tart, 1998).

The effects of LSD are so powerful that users can have "bad trips," in which the alteration in their consciousness is so disturbing that it induces feelings of panic (Miller & Gold, 1994). People who are more likely to have a bad trip are those who have unstable personalities, who are not told what to expect, or who are in stressful circumstances (McWilliams & Tuttle, 1973). LSD users also may report flashbacks (or hallucinogen persisting perception disorder), in which aspects of the trip are experienced long after the immediate effects of the drug have worn off (Lerner et al., 2002). Hofmann (1983), appalled by the indiscriminate use of LSD and the psychological harm it might do, questioned whether the human mind should be subjected to such extreme alteration. After all, the brain evolved to help us function by letting us perceive reality in a particular way, unaffected by hallucinogens like LSD.

synesthesia The process in which an individual experiences sensations in one sensory modality that are characteristic of another.

Marijuana

The most widely abused psychoactive drug is marijuana. Its active ingredient is **tetrahydrocannabinol (THC)**, present in the hemp plant *Cannabis sativa*. People eat or smoke marijuana and potent hashish (another product from the plant) to induce an altered state of consciousness. Marijuana is a combination of the crushed stems, leaves, and flowers of the plant, and hashish is its dried resin. Marijuana and hashish exert their effects by stimulating THC receptors in the brain (Herkenhahn, Lynn, deCosta, & Richfield, 1991).

Marijuana has been used for thousands of years as a painkiller; the earliest reference to that use is in a Chinese herbal medicine book from 2737 B.C. (Julien, 1981). Marijuana relieves pain, inhibits vomiting, stimulates appetite (especially highly palatable foods), and reduces fluid pressure in the eye related to glaucoma (Nahas et al., 2002). Today, most marijuana smokers use it for its mind-altering effects, which are related to its concentration of THC. Cancer patients use marijuana to reduce nausea produced by chemotherapy drugs. Moderately potent marijuana makes time seem to pass more slowly and induces rich sensory experiences in which music seems fuller and colors seem more vivid. Highly potent marijuana can induce visual hallucinations in which objects may appear to change their size and shape.

In 1937, after centuries of unregulated use, marijuana was outlawed in the United States because of claims that it induced bouts of wild sexual and aggressive behavior. Contrary to its popularity as an alleged aphrodisiac, marijuana at best causes disinhibition of the sex drive, which itself might be a placebo effect caused by its reputation as an aphrodisiac (Powell & Fuller, 1983). Moreover, marijuana does not promote aggression and might even inhibit it (Myerscough & Taylor, 1985). Today, while still illegal and considered a Schedule 1 drug at the federal level, some states have supported the regulated use of marijuana. This is highly controversial, and regulations for its use vary state by state.

tetrahydrocannabinol (THC) The psychoactive ingredient found in the *Cannabis sativa* plant.

Cannabis sativa

The dried flowers and surrounding leaves of the *Cannabis sativa* plant are the most widely consumed form of marijuana.
Source: RomboStudio/Shutterstock.com.

Chapter 6 Consciousness

Nevertheless, it would be unwise to drive or to operate machinery while under the influence of marijuana—or any other psychoactive drug. This is because marijuana impairs coordination (Navarro, Fernandez-Ruiz, de Miguel, & Hernandez, 1993) and the ability to concentrate on tasks without being distracted (Solowij, Michie, & Fox, 1995). And marijuana can disrupt memory formation by reducing acetylcholine levels in the hippocampus (Nava, Carta, Colombo, & Gessa, 2001). In fact, a review of high-quality research studies on the negative effects of marijuana found that the only consistently supported negative finding is that marijuana inhibits the formation of new long-term memories (Grant, Gonzalez, Carey, Natarajan, & Wolfson, 2003). Marijuana smokers also may exhibit amotivational syndrome (Cherek, Lane, & Dougherty, 2002), in which they prefer doing nothing rather than working or studying. But this finding raises the issue of causation versus correlation. That is, though marijuana smoking might produce the syndrome, it is just as logical to assume that unmotivated people are drawn to marijuana.

Entactogens

entactogens A new category of psychoactive drugs that have unique effects intermediate to those associated with hallucinogens and stimulants.

The **entactogens**, also known as empathogens, are a new category of psychoactive drugs that have unique effects intermediate to those associated with hallucinogens and stimulants and produce distinct social and emotional effects. Drugs in this category include *methylenedioxyethylamphetamine* (*MDE* or "Eve") and *methylenedioxymethamphetamine* (*MDMA* or "Ecstasy").

The unique effects of the entactogen substance group were investigated in a study comparing doses of MDE, psilocybin, and methamphetamine in three groups of volunteer participants (Gouzoulis-Mayfrank et al., 1999). Participants who ingested MDE reported a sense of contentment, relaxation, peacefulness, and interpersonal closeness. In addition, some stimulant and hallucinogenic effects were observed as well—though the hallucinations were weaker than those reported by the participants in the psilocybin group. Similar effects have been reported by participants who receive a single dose of MDMA. These effects include a feeling of closeness with others, altered perceptions, enhanced mood and well-being, and increased emotional sensitivity (Vollenweider, Gamma, Liechti, & Huber, 1998). Though the two drugs are metabolized differently and have slightly different effects (Kovar, 1998), they appear to promote the release of the neurotransmitters dopamine, serotonin, norepinephrine, and acetylcholine. The euphoric effects of MDMA are associated with its stimulation of dopamine neurons, and its hallucinatory effects are associated with its stimulation of serotonin neurons (Liechti & Vollenweider, 2001).

The side effects of MDE and MDMA are difficult to assess. The results of animal studies indicate that serotonin levels are disrupted, and damage to the hippocampus and areas of the cortex are observed (Boot, McGregor, & Hall, 2000). Researchers who assess the effects on people conduct two types of studies: the effects of a single dose on nonusers and the cumulative effects of the drugs on long-term users. Not surprisingly, human studies of long-term use indicate more serious side effects, typically memory impairment (Verbaten, 2003). But because MDMA use is commonly associated with the use of marijuana—which impairs memory—it is impossible to determine the relative influence of MDMA and marijuana on the memory deficits displayed by MDMA users (Gouzoulois-Mayfrank, Becker, Pelz, Tuchtenhagen, & Daumann, 2002).

Entactogens have become known as "club drugs" because their use is common among young adults who attend raves and other social activities associated with polydrug use. Three surveys of users in Europe and Australia conclude that the side effects reported by users may be due to these confounding variables (Hammersley, Ditton, Smith, & Short, 1999; Pedersen & Skrondal, 1999; Topp, Hando, Dillon, Roche, & Solowij, 1999). What is certain, though, is that tolerance to these drugs develops rapidly (Boot, McGregor, & Hall, 2000).

Experiencing Psychology

A Personal Study of Sleep and Dreams

Much of this chapter was devoted to a discussion of sleep and dreams. As noted earlier, formal scientific interest in the nature of sleep and dreams goes back to the 1890s, when Mary Whiton Calkins (1893) conducted her classic study. In this exercise you will record data about your sleep and dreams, analyze it statistically, and discuss it in the context of what you learned from reading this chapter. The student participants should agree on hypotheses about what they will find.

Method

Participants

The participants will be students from your introductory psychology course. The more who participate, the more secure you will be in drawing conclusions from your findings. But, as stressed in the discussion of research ethics in Chapter 2, participation must be voluntary, and any personal data must be kept strictly confidential.

Materials

All participants will maintain an anonymous daily sleep and dream diary on a one-page form created by the student participants. The form should include spaces for identifying the participant's sex, time of sleep onset, time of awakening in the morning, total amount of nightly sleep, number of awakenings during the night, any nap periods, and number of dreams recalled in part or whole. The form also should include spaces for recording responses to the following:

1. Was the dream about the previous day? How many of the dreams were about the previous day?
2. Was the dream about a personal problem or conflict? How many of the dreams were about a personal problem or conflict?
3. How many men and how many women were in the dream?
4. Did the dream seem to incorporate any external stimuli?

If other aspects of sleep and dreams interest the participants, feel free to add them to the daily recording form.

Procedure

The participants will record their data for 7 days. On awakening in the morning, they should record their data on a separate form. To avoid influencing each other, participants should avoid discussing their sleep and dreams during the 7 days of the study.

Results

Each participant should calculate her or his mean for aspects of the data that are of interest to the participants, including the average length of nightly sleep, number of nightly awakenings, and number of dreams. The data from all the participants should be pooled, and group means for their data should be calculated. Group means should be used to create a graph showing both the average hours of sleep and the average number of dreams each night. (See Chapter 2 and Appendix C—available in the Online Edition.) Also use the data to calculate means for all the men and all the women.

Discussion

Discuss whether your results agree with your hypotheses. Do the results support what you read in the chapter, such as Calkins's (1893) findings from her classic research study? Do the results support any of the theories discussed in the chapter? Were there any differences between men and women? Are there any other conclusions that can be reached from the data?

As a researcher, you should also note any shortcomings of the study and things you would change to improve it. Finally, you should suggest a research study that would be a logical offshoot of this study.

Section Review: Psychoactive Drugs

1. What are the symptoms of physical dependency on drugs?
2. What are the effects and side effects of cocaine?
3. What are the effects and side effects of marijuana?
4. What are the effects and side effects of entactogens?

Chapter Summary

The Nature of Consciousness

- Consciousness is the awareness of one's own cognitive activity.
- William James noted that consciousness is personal, selective, continuous, and changing.
- The selectivity of consciousness is the basis of research on attention.
- Perception without awareness is the unconscious perception of stimuli that exceed the absolute threshold but fall outside our focus of attention.
- We might experience perception without awareness whenever we use automatic rather than controlled processing of information.
- The Freudian unconscious is a portion of the mind containing thoughts and feelings that influence us without our awareness.
- Subliminal psychodynamic activation provides a means of scientifically studying the Freudian unconscious.

Sleep

- The sleep-wake cycle follows a circadian rhythm.
- The pineal gland and the suprachiasmatic nucleus help regulate circadian rhythms.
- The depth of sleep is defined by characteristic brainwave patterns.
- REM sleep is associated with dreaming.
- Our nightly sleep duration and the percentage of time we spend in REM sleep decrease across the life span.
- The functions of sleep are still unclear. One theory views sleep as restorative.
- A second theory views it as adaptive inactivity, either because it protects us from danger when we are most vulnerable or because it conserves energy.
- The major sleep disorders include insomnia, sleep apnea, and narcolepsy.

Dreams

- Though we might fail to recall our dreams, everyone dreams.
- Most dreams deal with familiar people and situations.
- REM sleep can be disturbed by nightmares; NREM sleep can be disturbed by night terrors.
- In some cases we might incorporate into our dreams stimuli from the immediate environment.
- The major theories of dreaming view it as wish fulfillment, as problem solving, as an aid to memory, or as a by-product of spontaneous brain activity.

Hypnosis

- Hypnosis is a state in which one person responds to suggestions by another person for alterations in perception, thinking, feeling, and behavior.
- Hypnosis had its origin in mesmerism, a technique promoted by Franz Anton Mesmer to restore the balance of what he called animal magnetism.
- Hypnotic induction aims at the creation of a relaxed, passive, highly focused state of mind.
- Hypnosis may be useful in treating pain.
- Under certain conditions, hypnotized people—like nonhypnotized people—might obey suggestions to perform dangerous acts.
- The effects of stage hypnosis might result as much from the theatrical atmosphere as from being hypnotized.
- Researchers debate whether hypnosis is an altered state of consciousness or merely role-playing.
- Ernest Hilgard put forth the concept of the hidden observer to support his neodissociation theory of hypnosis as an altered state.
- Neodissociation theory was challenged by Nicholas Spanos and his colleagues, who believe that hypnosis is a kind of role-playing.

Psychoactive Drugs

- Psychoactive drugs induce changes in mood, thinking, perception, and behavior by affecting neuronal activity.
- Depressants reduce arousal by inhibiting activity in the central nervous system.
- The main depressants are alcohol, barbiturates, and opiates.
- Stimulants, which increase arousal, include caffeine, nicotine, amphetamines, methamphetamine, and cocaine.
- Hallucinogens induce extreme alterations in consciousness, including hallucinations, a sense of timelessness, and feelings of depersonalization.
- The main hallucinogens are psilocybin, mescaline, phencyclidine, LSD, and marijuana.
- Entactogens induce altered perceptions, a sense of well-being, and closeness with others.
- Common entactogens include MDE and MDMA.

Key Terms

The Nature of Consciousness

attention (p. 200)
automatic processing (p. 202)
conscious mind (p. 203)
consciousness (p. 199)
controlled processing (p. 202)
perception without awareness (p. 201)
preconscious mind (p. 202)
unconscious mind (p. 202)

Sleep

biological rhythms (p. 204)
circadian rhythms (p. 204)
insomnia (p. 211)
narcolepsy (p. 214)

NREM sleep (p. 207)
phase advance (p. 205)
phase delay (p. 205)
pineal gland (p. 204)
REM sleep (p. 207)
sleep apnea (p. 213)

Dreams
activation-synthesis theory (p. 219)
dream (p. 214)
latent content (p. 217)
lucid dreaming (p. 217)
manifest content (p. 217)
night terror (p. 216)
nightmare (p. 216)

Hypnosis
age regression (p. 223)
dissociation (p. 222)
hidden observer (p. 223)
hypermnesia (p. 222)
hypnosis (p. 219)
neodissociation theory (p. 223)
posthypnotic suggestions (p. 223)

Psychoactive Drugs
amphetamines (p. 229)
barbiturates (p. 228)
benzodiazepines (p. 228)
caffeine (p. 228)

tetrahydrocannabinol (THC) (p. 231)
cocaine (p. 230)
depressants (p. 227)
entactogens (p. 232)
ethyl alcohol (ethanol) (p. 227)
hallucinogens (p. 230)
LSD (p. 230)
nicotine (p. 229)
opiates (p. 228)
psychoactive drugs (p. 224)
stimulants (p. 228)
synesthesia (p. 231)

Chapter Quiz

Note: Answers for the Chapter Quiz questions are provided at the end of the book.

1. Heroin's original purpose was to
   a. cure morphine addiction.
   b. help people overcome insomnia.
   c. induce mystical states of consciousness.
   d. enable truck drivers to make long hauls without sleeping.

2. The "cocktail party phenomenon" inspired research on
   a. attention.
   b. stage hypnosis.
   c. alcohol effects.
   d. biological rhythms.

3. Research has found that shift workers perform best when they move from the night shift to the day shift to the swing shift. In regard to biological rhythms, this is an example of phase
   a. delay.
   b. advance.
   c. inversion.
   d. acceleration.

4. Delta brain waves are most characteristic of
   a. stage 1 sleep.
   b. stage 2 sleep.
   c. stage 3 sleep.
   d. REM sleep.

5. Between infancy and adulthood, the percentage of a night's sleep spent in REM sleep
   a. decreases.
   b. increases.
   c. stays the same.
   d. increases and decreases unpredictably.

6. William James noted that the main qualities of consciousness are that it is changing, personal, selective, and
   a. cosmic.
   b. vestigial.
   c. continuous.
   d. superficial.

7. You would be most likely to be interrupted in the middle of a dream if you were awakened by a phone call
   a. shortly after falling asleep.
   b. in the middle of a night's sleep.
   c. just before you would wake up.
   d. about a half hour after falling asleep.

8. If you are experiencing a night terror, you are most likely to be in
   a. REM sleep.
   b. stage 1 sleep.
   c. stage 2 sleep.
   d. stage 4 sleep.

9. The term *animal magnetism* had its origin in
   a. mesmerism.
   b. neodissociation theory.
   c. transcendental meditation.
   d. research on biological rhythms.

10. The "hidden observer" is related to
    a. astral projection.
    b. hypnosis-induced dissociation.
    c. peyote-evoked hallucinations.
    d. subliminal psychodynamic activation.

11. A person has surgery to remove a brain tumor and experiences disruption of his circadian rhythm. The surgery most likely affected his
    a. thymus gland.
    b. thyroid gland.
    c. adrenal gland.
    d. pineal gland.

12. Research (Hull & Bond, 1986) indicates that people may ingest alcohol because
    a. they are fixated at the oral stage.
    b. we have evolved an inborn liking for the taste of alcohol.
    c. it provides them with an excuse to engage in socially disapproved behaviors.
    d. it acts as a central nervous system stimulant to make them more alert and energetic.

Chapter 6 Consciousness

13. A man shows all the symptoms of drunkenness, but has not ingested alcohol. He has mostly likely ingested
    a. LSD.
    b. cocaine.
    c. an amphetamine.
    d. a barbiturate.

14. If you dreamed of flying like a bird, a psychoanalyst might interpret it to mean that you would like to be less socially inhibited. According to Sigmund Freud, the dream of your flying like a bird, itself, would be the
    a. latent content.
    b. abstract content.
    c. concrete content.
    d. manifest content.

15. A person is rushed to an emergency room experiencing hallucinations. Given that she is not schizophrenic, she probably is a heavy user of
    a. opiates.
    b. amphetamines.
    c. barbiturates.
    d. marijuana.

16. A person suffering from a "bad trip" probably ingested the drug
    a. cocaine.
    b. amphetamine.
    c. nitrous oxide.
    d. LSD.

17. Somnambulism does not occur during REM sleep because
    a. somnambulism is a myth.
    b. dreaming is distracting.
    c. we are blind during REM sleep.
    d. our limbs are paralyzed during REM sleep.

18. A habitual drug user is suffering from an inability to recall classroom and textbook material. He probably has been ingesting
    a. LSD.
    b. cocaine.
    c. marijuana.
    d. phencyclidine.

19. Research on dichotic listening and the Stroop effect most strongly supports
    a. subliminal advertising.
    b. perception without awareness.
    c. subliminal psychodynamic activation.
    d. Freud's notion of the motivated unconscious.

20. The deepest level of sleep tends to occur
    a. just before one normally arises.
    b. during the first half of a night's sleep.
    c. during the second half of a night's sleep.
    d. as much during the first half as during the second half of a night's sleep.

21. The sleep-deprivation experiences of Peter Tripp and Randy Gardner indicated that extended sleep loss
    a. has no apparent effects.
    b. proves that sleep in human beings is merely vestigial.
    c. produces symptoms that disappear after a night's sleep.
    d. induces personality changes that last for weeks afterwards.

22. Paradoxical intention has been used to
    a. help people overcome insomnia.
    b. induce obedience to subliminal messages.
    c. support the "trance" theory of hypnosis.
    d. explain the apparent mystical experiences induced by LSD.

23. The use of unconscious messages to stimulate unconscious fantasies is called
    a. hypnagogia.
    b. hypermnesia.
    c. preconscious processing.
    d. subliminal psychodynamic activation.

24. According to the activation-synthesis theory, dreams are
    a. wish fulfillments.
    b. prophecies from God.
    c. aids to problem solving.
    d. by-products of brain activity.

25. An example of hypermnesia would be the use of
    a. hypnosis to have a person recall a phone number.
    b. subliminal perception to affect consumer behavior.
    c. depressant drugs to induce a profound, coma-like state.
    d. hypnosis to help a person forget a traumatic experience.

Thought Questions

1. How does research on people with brain damage support the existence of perception without awareness?
2. Given the nature of our circadian rhythms, why is it easier for people to travel across time zones going from east to west than going from west to east?
3. What evidence is there for the beneficial physical effects of sleep?
4. What would be the difference between Freudian theory and the activation-synthesis theory in explaining a sexual dream?
5. How did the experiment by Spanos and Hewitt (1980) demonstrate that hypnosis might be role-playing and not an altered state of consciousness?
6. What are the neurotransmitter mechanisms by which cocaine and amphetamines exert their effects?

Learning

CHAPTER 7

Growing up in Utah, Carl Gustavson (1946–1996) learned to love the wolves, coyotes, and other predators that abounded in his home state. Later, after becoming a wildlife psychologist (the application of psychological science to the protection of wildlife), he sought ways to ensure their survival. Coyotes in particular had long drawn the fury—and bullets—of sheep ranchers for their habit of preying on sheep. In 1974 Gustavson began research on psychological methods of fostering the survival of both coyotes and sheep (Gustavson, Garcia, Hawkins, & Rusiniak, 1974). Gustavson took advantage of the coyote's natural aversion to eating things that make it feel nauseous (Garcia & Gustavson, 1997). He inserted lithium chloride, a chemical that causes nausea, into sheep carcasses. When coyotes ate the tainted meat, they became nauseous. Gustavson predicted that the coyotes would associate the nausea with eating sheep and would stop killing them. He hoped this method would provide a happy compromise between ranchers who want to kill coyotes and conservationists who want to save them.

Gustavson began his research program in zoos, using captured coyotes, wolves, and a cougar. To his delight, the animals refused to eat meat from the kind of prey that had been associated with nausea; what psychologists refer to as a conditioned taste aversion was developed. More important, the predators also tended to shy away from the live animals themselves. Wolves and coyotes that had eaten tainted lamb and sheep meat avoided live lambs and sheep. Coyotes that had eaten tainted rabbit meat no longer attacked rabbits.

Other researchers successfully replicated this research using other predators, including hawks and ferrets. In one program, researchers scattered sheep meat laced with lithium chloride on a sheep range in Washington. This action was followed by a significant reduction in the killing of lambs by predators. Following the introduction of a similar program in southern California's Antelope Valley, the number of sheep kills was reduced to zero. The success of the method led to its adoption as the means of choice for controlling predators in Saskatchewan, Canada.

Despite its success in several field settings, Gustavson's method met with opposition from those with vested interests in killing coyotes. These included trappers who kill coyotes for fees and pelts and pilots who take hunters on flights to shoot coyotes from airplanes. Moreover, many sheep ranchers—more concerned with protecting their sheep than with the survival of coyotes—are reluctant to use the technique, preferring instead to simply eradicate the coyotes (Reese, 1986). Thus,

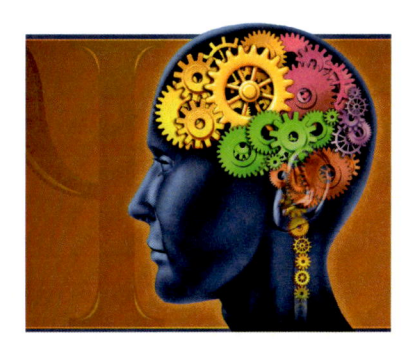

Source: Lightspring/Shutterstock.com.

Chapter Outline
Classical Conditioning
Operant Conditioning
Cognitive Learning

a procedure that is scientifically feasible is not always one that will be practical.

Moreover, as is at times the case in scientific research, some researchers failed to replicate Gustavson's findings. For example, insertion of lithium chloride into meat inhibited some predators from eating, but not killing, their prey (Timberlake & Melcer, 1988). In a more recent study, two Alaskan Husky dogs that were given sheep meat laced with lithium chloride shunned sheep meat but still attacked sheep (Hansen, Bakken, & Braastad, 1997).

Regardless of the extent of its practicality and reliability, Gustavson's method illustrates the importance of **learning**, which is a relatively permanent change in knowledge or behavior that results from experience. What you learn is relatively permanent; it can be changed by future experience. This chapter will answer questions about the role of learning in a variety of areas, including these: How can children learn to stop bed-wetting? How can children receiving cancer chemotherapy learn to maintain their appetites? How do animal trainers apply learning principles in their work? How might psychological depression depend on learning?

> **learning** A relatively permanent change in knowledge or behavior resulting from experience.

Do not confuse learning with reflexes, instincts, or maturation. A *reflex* is an inborn, involuntary response to a specific kind of stimulus, such as automatically withdrawing your hand after touching a hot pot. An *instinct* is an inborn complex behavior found in members of a species (such as nest building in birds). And *maturation* is the sequential unfolding of inherited predispositions (such as walking in human infants, see Chapter 4). Moreover, because learning is more flexible, it enables us to adapt to ever-changing circumstances.

Psychologists began the scientific study of learning in the late 19th century. In keeping with Charles Darwin's theory of evolution, they viewed learning as a means of adapting to the environment. Because Darwin stressed the continuity between animals and human beings, psychologists became interested in studying learning in animals, hoping to identify principles that also might apply to human learning (Purdy, Harriman, & Molitorisz, 1993). As you will read, many of the principles of learning do indeed apply to both animals and people.

Psychologists have identified three kinds of learning. *Classical conditioning* considers the learning of associations between stimuli and responses. *Operant conditioning* considers the learning of associations between behaviors and their consequences. *Cognitive learning* considers learning as the acquisition of information.

Classical Conditioning

Classical conditioning grew out of a tradition that can be traced back to Aristotle, who believed that learning depended on contiguity—the occurrence of events close together in time and space (such as lightning and thunder). British philosophers of the 17th and 18th centuries, most notably John Locke and David Hume, became known as associationists because they agreed with Aristotle's view that learning depends on associating contiguous events with one another.

In the early 20th century, the research of Ivan Pavlov (1849–1936) stimulated worldwide scientific interest in the study of *associative learning* (Delamater, 2011), which involves associating contiguous events with each other. Pavlov, a Russian physiologist, won a Nobel Prize in 1904 for his research on digestion in dogs, which attracted the interest of scientists around the world (Windholz & Kuppers, 1990). In his research, Pavlov would place meat powder on a dog's tongue, which stimulated reflexive salivation. He collected the saliva from a tube attached to one of the dog's salivary glands. He found that after repeated presentations of the meat powder, the dog would salivate in response to stimuli (that is, environmental events) associated with the meat powder. A dog would salivate at the sight of its food dish, the sight of the laboratory assistant who brought the food, or the sound of the assistant's footsteps. At first Pavlov was distressed by this phenomenon, which he called "psychic reflexes" or "conditional responses," because he could no longer control the onset of salivation by his dogs. But he eventually became so intrigued by the phenomenon that he devoted the rest of his career to studying it.

Pavlov was not alone in discovering this phenomenon, which was well known to scientists during the 19th century (Logan, 2002). Moreover, at the annual meeting of the American Psychological Association in 1904, the same year that Pavlov received his Nobel Prize, Edwin Twitmyer (1873–1943), an American graduate student at the University of Pennsylvania, reported the results of a study on the "knee jerk" reflex. As you may know from a past physical examination, when a physician strikes you with a rubber hammer on your patellar tendon just below your bent knee, your lower leg reflexively extends. In his study, Twitmyer rang a bell as a warning that the hammer was about to strike. After repeated trials in which the sound of the bell preceded the hammer strike, the sound of the bell alone caused extension of the lower leg (Twitmyer, 1974). But, to his disappointment, Twitmyer's presentation was met with indifference. In fact, William James, who chaired Twitmyer's session, was so bored (or hungry) that he adjourned the session for lunch—without providing the customary opportunity for discussion (Coon, 1982). North American psychologists did not begin to take serious note of this kind of learning until John B. Watson described Pavlov's research in his presidential address at the annual meeting of the American Psychological Association in 1914. Because of Pavlov's extensive early research on "conditional responses," the phenomenon earned the name of classical conditioning.

Principles of Classical Conditioning

As Pavlov first noted, in **classical conditioning** a stimulus comes to elicit (that is, bring about) a response (either an overt behavior or a physiological change) that it does not normally elicit. But how does this occur? It must be acquired.

Acquisition of the Classically Conditioned Response

To demonstrate classical conditioning (see Figure 7-1), you must first identify a stimulus that already elicits a reflexive response. The stimulus is called an **unconditioned stimulus (UCS)**, and the response is called an **unconditioned response (UCR)**. You then present several trials in which the UCS is preceded by a neutral stimulus—a stimulus that does not normally elicit the UCR. After one or more pairings of the neutral stimulus and the UCS, the neutral stimulus itself elicits the UCR. At that point the neutral stimulus has become a **conditioned stimulus (CS)**, and the response to it is called a **conditioned response (CR)**. Pavlov used the UCS of meat powder to elicit the UCR of salivation. He then used a tone as the neutral stimulus. After several trials in which the tone preceded the meat powder, the tone itself became a CS that elicited the CR of salivation. But does the CS directly elicit the CR? On the contrary, research indicates that the CS activates a memory trace representing the UCS, which then elicits the CR (Jacobs & Blackburn, 1995).

Higher-Order Conditioning In **higher-order conditioning**, a neutral stimulus can become a CS after being paired with an existing CS. In this case, the existing CS functions like a UCS. If the neutral stimulus precedes the existing CS, it elicits a CR similar to that elicited by the existing CS. Higher-order conditioning explains how neutral stimuli that have not been paired with a biological UCS such as food or other cues in our environment can gain control over our behavior. Higher-order conditioning might explain why music in commercials (such as those advertising fast-food restaurants) can affect our

classical conditioning A form of learning in which a neutral stimulus comes to elicit a response after being associated with a stimulus that already elicits that response.

unconditioned stimulus (UCS) In classical conditioning, a stimulus that automatically elicits a particular unconditioned response.

unconditioned response (UCR) In classical conditioning, an unlearned, automatic response to a particular unconditioned stimulus.

conditioned stimulus (CS) In classical conditioning, a neutral stimulus that comes to elicit a particular conditioned response after being paired with a particular unconditioned stimulus that already elicits that response.

conditioned response (CR) In classical conditioning, the learned response given to a particular conditioned stimulus.

higher-order conditioning In classical conditioning, the establishment of a conditioned response to a neutral stimulus that has been paired with an existing conditioned stimulus.

FIGURE 7-1
Classical Conditioning

Before Conditioning
Before conditioning, the unconditioned stimulus (UCS) (meat) elicits the unconditioned response (UCR) (salivation), but the neutral stimulus (tone) does not elicit salivation.

Neutral stimulus (tone) → No response

Unconditioned stimulus (meat) → Unconditioned response (salivation)

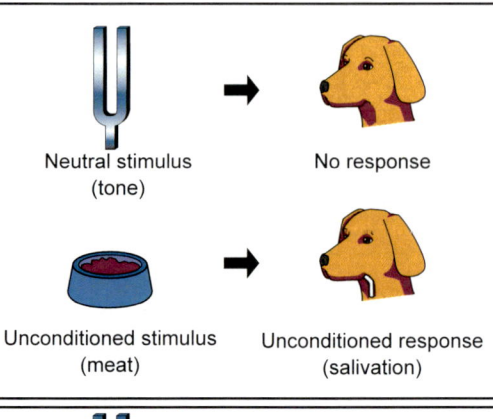

During Conditioning
During conditioning, the neutral stimulus (tone) is repeatedly presented just before the UCS (meat), which continues to elicit the UCR (salivation).

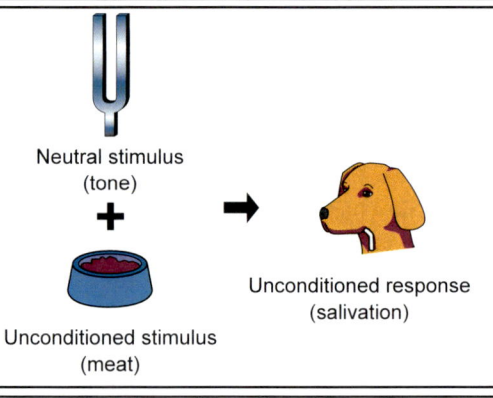

Neutral stimulus (tone) + Unconditioned stimulus (meat) → Unconditioned response (salivation)

After Conditioning
After conditioning, the neutral stimulus (tone) becomes a conditioned stimulus (CS) that elicits a conditioned response (CR) (salivation).

Conditioned stimulus (tone) → Conditioned response (salivation)

---

semantic conditioning In classical conditioning, the use of words as conditioned stimuli.

attitudes toward the products presented in the commercials (Blair & Shimp, 1992). The classical conditioning of an emotional response to a product is important in enhancing its appeal to consumers (Kim, Lim, & Bhargava, 1998).

Among the most important conditioned stimuli are words. This phenomenon is known as **semantic conditioning**. In a clever classroom demonstration of this, a college professor used the word *Pavlov* as a neutral stimulus (Cogan & Cogan, 1984). Student participants said "Pavlov" just before lemonade powder was placed on their tongues. The UCS of lemonade powder naturally elicited the UCR of salivation. After repeated pairings of "Pavlov" and the lemonade powder, *Pavlov* became a CS that elicited the CR of salivation. Classical conditioning might account, in part, for the power of words to elicit emotional responses. Perhaps the mere mention of the name of someone with whom you have a romantic relationship makes your heart flutter. Similarly, if someone repeatedly says something, such as "tickle, tickle," before tickling the sole of your foot, you might eventually learn to jerk away your foot as soon as you hear the words "tickle, tickle" (Newman, O'Grady, Ryan, & Hemmes, 1993).

Even bed-wetting, or *nocturnal enuresis*, in childhood can be controlled by classical conditioning. An effective technique, devised more than half a century ago (Mowrer & Mowrer, 1938), uses an electrified mattress pad that consists of a cloth sheet sandwiched between two thin metal sheets. The upper metal sheet contains tiny holes. When a drop of urine penetrates that sheet and soaks through the cloth sheet, the moisture completes an electrical circuit between the two metal sheets. This electrical circuit sets off a battery-powered alarm, which wakes the child, who then goes to the toilet. The alarm serves as a UCS, which elicits awakening as a UCR. After repeated trials, bladder tension, which precedes the alarm, becomes a CS, which then elicits awakening as a CR. The child eventually responds to bladder tension by awakening and going to the toilet instead of urinating in bed. This technique has become one of the most effective methods of treating nocturnal enuresis (Mellon & McGrath, 2000).

Factors Affecting Classical Conditioning What factors affect classical conditioning? In general, the greater the intensity of the UCS and the greater the number of pairings of the CS and the UCS, the greater will be the strength of conditioning. The time interval between the CS and the UCS also affects acquisition of the CR. In *delayed conditioning*, the CS is presented first and remains *at least* until the onset of the UCS. An interval of about 1 second between the CS and the UCS is often optimal in delayed conditioning (Rescorla & Holland, 1982), though it varies with the kind of CR. In delayed conditioning using Pavlov's procedure, the tone is presented first and remains on at least until the meat powder is placed on the dog's tongue. Thus, the CS and UCS overlap. In *trace conditioning*, the CS is presented first and ends *before the onset* of the UCS. Trace conditioning requires that a memory trace of the CS be retained until the onset of the UCS—the brain structure most likely involved is the hippocampus (Flesher, Butt, & Kinney-Hurd, 2011). In trace conditioning using Pavlov's procedure, the tone is presented and then turned off just before the meat powder is placed on the dog's tongue. In *simultaneous conditioning*, the CS and UCS begin together. In simultaneous conditioning using Pavlov's procedure, the tone and the meat powder are presented together. And in *backward conditioning*, the onset of the UCS precedes the onset of the CS. In backward conditioning using Pavlov's procedure, the meat powder is presented first, followed immediately by the tone. In general, delayed conditioning produces strong conditioning, trace conditioning produces moderately strong conditioning, and simultaneous conditioning produces weak conditioning. Backward conditioning generally produces no conditioning, though it sometimes is used successfully (Washio, Hayes, Hunter, & Pritchard, 2011).

Stimulus Generalization and Stimulus Discrimination in Classical Conditioning

In classical conditioning, the CR can occur in response to stimuli that are similar to the CS. This phenomenon is called **stimulus generalization**. A person who learns to fear a particular stimulus might come to fear similar ones (Glenn et al., 2012). For example, a child who undergoes a painful dental procedure might develop a fear of all dentists or the sound of any drill. Likewise, the dog that salivates to a particular bell might eventually salivate to other bells, such as a doorbell. Marketing research has found that, through stimulus generalization, generic brands of products that are similar in name to nationally known products may elicit similar responses from consumers (Till & Priluck, 2000). Thus, a cola soft drink manufactured by a small company may elicit a favorable response from people simply because they are familiar with the more famous national brand colas.

If a child undergoes painless dentistry with other dentists, she will eventually become afraid only of the dentist with whom she associated pain. This example is an instance of **stimulus discrimination**, in which the person or animal responds to the CS but not to stimuli that are similar to the CS. Similarly, the dog might eventually salivate only in response to the dinner bell if it learns that the other bells are not followed by food.

Extinction

In Pavlov's procedure, will a dog conditioned to salivate in response to a dinner bell do so forever? Not necessarily. If a CS is repeatedly presented without the UCS being presented, the CR will diminish and eventually stop occurring. This process is called **extinction**. A dog that has learned to salivate to a dinner bell (the CS) will eventually stop doing so unless presentations of the dinner bell are periodically followed by presentations of food (the UCS). Likewise, an animal that comes to fear a tone after it has been repeatedly followed by an electric shock will eventually stop acting fearful if the tone is repeatedly presented without being followed by the electric shock.

stimulus generalization In classical conditioning, giving a conditioned response to stimuli similar to the conditioned stimulus.

stimulus discrimination In classical conditioning, giving a conditioned response to the conditioned stimulus but not to stimuli similar to it.

extinction
1. In classical conditioning, the gradual disappearance of the conditioned response when the conditioned stimulus is repeatedly presented without being paired with the unconditioned stimulus.
2. In operant conditioning, the gradual disappearance of a response that is no longer followed by a reinforcer.

FIGURE 7-2

Processes in Classical Conditioning

During acquisition of the CR, repeatedly presenting the CS just before the UCS strengthens the CR. After acquisition of the CR, if the CS is repeatedly presented without being followed by the UCS, extinction of the CR occurs. Then, following a rest period during which neither the CS nor the UCS is presented, spontaneous recovery of the CR occurs. But extinction immediately takes place again, even more rapidly than the first time.

spontaneous recovery
1. In classical conditioning, the reappearance after a period of time of a conditioned response that has been subjected to extinction.
2. In operant conditioning, the reappearance after a period of time of a behavior that has been subjected to extinction.

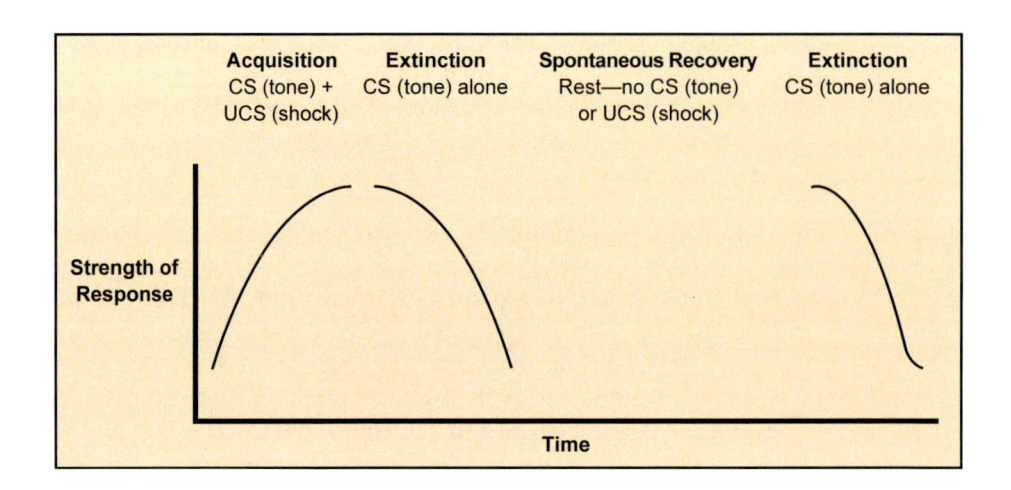

Though extinction inhibits the CR, it does not eliminate it (Bouton & Swartzentruber, 1991). In fact, after a CR has been subjected to extinction, it can reappear if the CS is reintroduced. For example, suppose you produce extinction of the CR of salivation by no longer presenting the dog with food after ringing the dinner bell. If you rang the dinner bell a few days later, the dog might respond again by salivating. This process, by which a CR that has been subjected to extinction will again be elicited by a CS, is called **spontaneous recovery**. In spontaneous recovery, however, the CR is weaker and extinguishes faster than it did originally. Thus, after spontaneous recovery the dog's salivation to the dinner bell will be weaker and subject to faster extinction than it was originally. Likewise, consider rats that have been conditioned to fear a tone that has repeatedly preceded an electric shock. If the tone is repeatedly presented without the electric shock, their fear of the tone will extinguish. But if the tone is again presented after a few days, they might exhibit complete spontaneous recovery; that is, they will display the same degree of fear of the tone as they had before extinction (Quirk, 2002). Figure 7-2 illustrates the acquisition, extinction, and spontaneous recovery of a classically conditioned response.

Applications of Classical Conditioning

In his 1932 novel *Brave New World*, Aldous Huxley warned of a future in which classical conditioning would mold people into narrow social roles. In the novel, classical conditioning is used to make children who have been assigned to become workers repulsed by any interests other than work. This repulsion is achieved by giving the children electric shocks (the UCS) in the presence of forbidden objects, such as books or flowers (the CS). Despite such fears of diabolical use, classical conditioning has, in reality, been applied in less ominous and often beneficial ways. Classical conditioning prepares the body for likely events and has been used to explain phobias, drug dependence, and learned taste aversions.

Classical Conditioning and Phobias

More than three centuries ago, John Locke (1690/1956) observed that children who had been punished in school for misbehaving became fearful of their books and other stimuli associated with school. Today we would say these children had been classically conditioned to develop school phobias. A phobia is an unrealistic or exaggerated fear, and a phobia was the subject of a classic research investigation of classical conditioning.

The study was conducted by John B. Watson and his graduate student Rosalie Rayner (Watson & Rayner, 1920). The participant was an 11-month-old boy, Albert B., later known as "Little Albert," who enjoyed playing with animals, including tame white rats. Watson and Rayner hoped to provide scientific evidence for the classical conditioning of emotional responses. This evidence would provide an alternative to the Freudian idea that phobias are symbolic manifestations of unconscious conflicts that arise from early child-

Classical Conditioning and Advertising

Advertisers know that they can make products more appealing to consumers by pairing them with sexual stimuli.
Source: Goran Bogicevic/Shutterstock.com.

hood sexual conflicts (see Chapter 14). On several trials, just as Albert touched a white rat, Watson made a loud noise behind Albert's head by banging a steel bar with a hammer. Albert responded to the noise (the UCS) with fear (the UCR). He jumped violently, fell forward, and buried his face. After seven pairings of the rat and the noise (twice on the first day and five times a week later), Albert responded to the rat (the CS) with fear (the CR) by crying and showing distress.

When tested later, Albert showed stimulus generalization. He responded fearfully to other fur-like objects, including a dog, a rabbit, cotton wool, and a sealskin fur coat. Two months later he even showed fear of a Santa Claus mask. He had not shown fear of any of these objects at the age of 9 months. Watson and Rayner hypothesized that pleasurable stimulation paired with a feared object would reduce Albert's phobia. But Albert left the experiment before they had the opportunity to try that technique. As discussed in Chapter 15, Watson's student, Mary Cover Jones (1924), who became a prominent psychologist, used it a few years later to relieve a child's animal phobia.

Current ethical standards of psychological research (see Chapter 2) would prevent the experimental induction of phobias in children. Though this study lacked the experimental control necessary for a convincing demonstration of a classically conditioned phobia, it led to sounder research studies demonstrating that fears and phobias can indeed be learned through classical conditioning (McAllister & McAllister, 1994). For example, a study found that breast cancer patients responded with anxiety to a distinctive stimulus that had been presented before each chemotherapy session (Jacobsen, Bovbjerg, Schwartz, & Hudis, 1995).

Classical Conditioning and Drug Dependence

Classical conditioning might even explain dependence on psychoactive drugs. For example, one reason that cigarette smokers find it difficult to quit is that their smoking has become a conditioned response to various environmental stimuli (Austin & Duka, 2012). Smokers might light up when the telephone rings, when they finish a meal, or under a host of other conditions.

Consider another example of the role of classical conditioning in drug dependence. When a psychoactive drug (the UCS) such as heroin is administered, it produces characteristic physiological effects (the UCR). With continued use, higher and higher doses of the drug are required to produce the same physiological effects. This tolerance might be, in part, the product of classical conditioning (Deffner-Rappold, Azorlosa, & Baker, 1996). Stimuli associated with the administration of certain drugs act as conditioned stimuli that elicit conditioned physiological responses opposite to those of the drug. For example, though heroin induces respiratory depression, stimuli associated with its administration induce respiratory excitation. Why would stimuli associated with drug taking elicit effects opposite to those of the drug itself? Perhaps it is an adaptive, compensatory mechanism that prevents the physiological response to the drug from becoming too extreme.

Consider heroin addiction and the phenomenon of tolerance. Tolerance to heroin might occur because stimuli associated with its administration, such as hypodermic needles and particular settings, can act as conditioned stimuli to counter the physiological effects produced by the drug. Tolerance might explain why heroin addicts sometimes die of respiratory failure from an "overdose" after injecting themselves with their normal dose of heroin in a setting different from that in which they normally administer the drug. By doing so, they remove the conditioned stimuli that elicit conditioned physiological responses that normally counter the unconditioned physiological responses elicited by the drug. As a consequence, their conditioned tolerance is reduced. The unconditioned physiological responses, particularly respiratory depression, to a normal dose might be stronger than usual—in some cases strong enough to be fatal (Siegel, Baptista, & Kim, 2000). This notion is supported by work with laboratory animals and often observed in people.

Classical Conditioning and Taste Aversions

Have you ever eaten something, by coincidence contracted a virus several hours later, become nauseated, and later found yourself repulsed by what you had eaten? If so, you have experienced a **conditioned taste aversion**—the classical conditioning of an aversion to a taste that has been associated with a noxious stimulus. The research program of Carl Gustavson that was described at the beginning of the chapter, in which he used classical conditioning to make coyotes nauseated by the taste of sheep meat, was an application of conditioned taste aversion. Research on conditioned taste aversion was prompted by the need to determine the effects of atomic radiation subsequent to the extensive atomic bomb testing of the 1950s. One of the leading researchers in that effort was John Garcia. Garcia and his colleagues exposed rats to radiation in special cages. He found that the rats failed to drink water in the radiation cages, yet drank normally in their own cages. They continued to refrain from drinking in the radiation cages even when they were no longer exposed to radiation in them. Garcia concluded that the plastic water bottles lent a distinctive taste to the water in the radiation cages, which created a conditioned taste aversion after being paired with radiation-induced nausea. Because the water bottles in the rats' own cages were made of glass, the rats did not associate the taste of water from them with nausea (Garcia, Kimeldorf, Hunt, & Davies, 1956).

Garcia also found that conditioned taste aversions could occur even when the animal did not become nauseous until hours after being exposed to the taste. In responding to Garcia's finding that a taste aversion could be learned even when the taste preceded feelings of nausea by hours, psychologists at first were shocked by this apparent violation of contiguity in classical conditioning, and many of them simply dismissed his findings as impossible (Garcia, 1981). How could the taste of food be associated with nausea that occurs hours later? (Tastes do not linger long enough for the contiguity of taste and nausea to be an explanation.) Through the persistence of Garcia and his colleagues, who

conditioned taste aversion A taste aversion induced by pairing a taste with gastrointestinal distress.

Taste Aversion

If a taste or smell is associated with the development of nausea, sickness, or vomiting, a conditioned taste aversion will occur. Humans and animals seem to be prepared to associate taste and smell with illness, and some scientists refer to this as *biological preparedness*.

Source: Photographee.eu/Shutterstock.com.

244   Chapter 7 Learning

The Research Process

Can Classical Conditioning Help Maintain the Appetites of Children Undergoing Chemotherapy?

Rationale

Ilene Bernstein (1991), of the University of Washington, has conducted a program of research on taste aversion in chemotherapy patients. In one study, Bernstein (1978) determined whether children receiving chemotherapy would associate a novel taste with the nausea induced by chemotherapy.

Method

Bernstein assigned children receiving chemotherapy to one of three groups. The first group ate "Mapletoff" ice cream, which has a novel maple-walnut flavor, before each chemotherapy session. The second group ate Mapletoff on days when they did not receive chemotherapy. And the third group never ate Mapletoff. From 2 to 4 weeks later, the children were given the choice of eating Mapletoff or playing with a game. Later, at an average of 10 weeks after the first session, the children were asked to select Mapletoff or another novel-tasting ice cream.

Results and Discussion

As illustrated in Figure 7-3, when given the option of playing with a game or eating Mapletoff, 67 percent of the children who never ate Mapletoff and 73 percent of the children who ate it only on days when they did not receive chemotherapy chose Mapletoff. In contrast, only 21 percent of the children who ate Mapletoff on days they received chemotherapy chose Mapletoff. When given the option of choosing Mapletoff or another novel ice cream flavor, only 25 percent of those in the Mapletoff-plus-chemotherapy group chose Mapletoff, while 50 percent of the Mapletoff-only group and 66 percent of the no-Mapletoff group chose it. Thus, children exposed to Mapletoff plus chemotherapy developed a taste aversion to Mapletoff.

Based on these findings, and on findings that taste aversion is stronger in response to novel-tasting foods than to familiar-tasting foods (Kimble, 1981), perhaps cancer patients should be given a novel-tasting food before receiving chemotherapy. This practice might lead them to experience taste aversion in response only to the novel "scapegoat" food instead of to familiar foods, thereby helping them maintain their appetite for familiar, nutritious foods. Bernstein has, in fact, accomplished this conditioning with children receiving chemotherapy by using candies with unusual flavors (such as coconut) as scapegoats (Broberg & Bernstein, 1987).

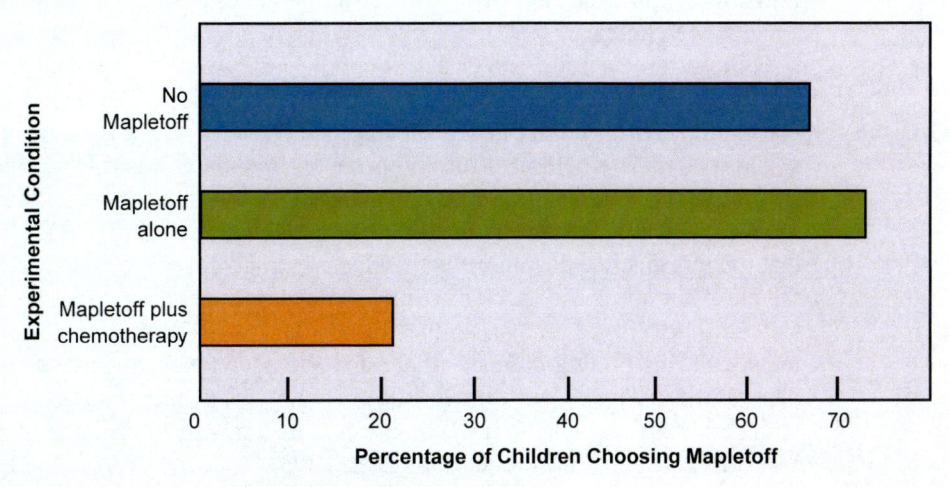

FIGURE 7-3 Chemotherapy and Conditioned Taste Aversion

Ilene Bernstein (1978) found that children undergoing cancer chemotherapy developed conditioned taste aversions to a novel flavor of ice cream (Mapletoff) eaten on the same days that they underwent treatment. The children might have developed the aversion to the flavor because it became associated with the nausea induced by the treatment. As the graph shows, when later given the choice of eating Mapletoff or playing a game, children who had eaten Mapletoff on the days they received treatment were less likely to choose Mapletoff than were children who had never eaten it or who had eaten it on days when they did not receive treatment.

Source: Data from Ilene L. Bernstein, "Learned Taste Aversions in Children Receiving Chemotherapy" in *Science*, 200: 1302–1303, American Association for the Advancement of Science, 1978.

replicated his findings, the conditioning of a taste aversion using a long interval between the CS and the UCS is now an accepted psychological phenomenon. Moreover, there even is evidence that learned taste aversions are more likely to occur when there is a longer interval between the CS and UCS than when there is a shorter interval. For example, a 30-minute interval is superior to a 10-second interval between presentation of a distinctive taste and presentation of a nausea-inducing chemical in the classical conditioning of an aversion to the taste (Schafe, Sollars, & Bernstein, 1995). One other special attribute of conditioned taste aversion is that it can occur, reliably and powerfully, with single trials or single experiences. If you have no previous experience with a food and then become ill after eating it, you will likely avoid that food in the future.

Had Garcia been less persistent, we might have been denied a potentially useful tool for combating the nausea-induced loss of appetite experienced by cancer patients undergoing chemotherapy. Their loss of appetite makes them eat less and lose weight, weakening them and impairing their ability to fight the disease.

Biological Constraints on Classical Conditioning

According to Ivan Pavlov (1928, p. 88), "Every imaginable phenomenon of the outer world affecting a specific receptive surface of the body may be converted into a conditioned stimulus." Until the past few decades, learning theorists agreed with Pavlov's proclamation. They assumed that any stimulus paired with an unconditioned stimulus could become a conditioned stimulus. But we now know that there are inherited biological constraints, perhaps the product of evolution, on the ease with which particular stimuli can be associated with particular responses. These constraints were demonstrated in an early study that tried to replicate Watson and Rayner's study on conditioned fear by using an opera glass instead of a white rat. The opera glass did not become a fear-inducing conditioned stimulus after being paired with an unconditioned stimulus that induced fear (Valentine, 1930). Nonetheless, as discussed in Chapter 14, some research studies have failed to support the role of biological preparedness in the development of phobias (de Jong & Merckelbach, 1997).

Biological constraints on classical conditioning were demonstrated in a study of classically conditioned taste aversion in which two groups of rats were presented with a CS consisting of three components: saccharin-flavored water, a flash of light, and a clicking sound (Garcia & Koelling, 1966). For one group the CS was followed by a strong electric shock (the UCS) that induced pain (the UCR). For another group the CS was followed by X-rays (the UCS) that induced nausea and dizziness (the UCR). The results indicated that the rats that had been hurt by the electric shock developed an aversion to the light and the click but not to the saccharin-flavored water. In contrast, the rats that had been made to feel ill developed an aversion to the saccharin-flavored water but not to the light and the click. This finding indicates that rats have a tendency, apparently inborn, to associate nausea and dizziness with tastes but not with sights and sounds, and to associate pain with sights and sounds but not with tastes. Thus, not all stimuli and responses are equally associable (Weiss, Panlilio, & Schindler, 1993).

Section Review: Classical Conditioning

1. How would you use classical conditioning to make a pet cat come running at the sound of a can opener?

2. How does Ilene Bernstein suggest using classical conditioning to help chemotherapy patients retain their appetite for nutritious foods by using scapegoat foods?

3. In what way did John Garcia demonstrate biological constraints on classical conditioning?

FIGURE 7-4
Puzzle Boxes

Edward Thorndike, working under a limited budget, used Heinz shipping crates to create puzzle boxes for the conditioning of cats. In this example, the cat is prevented from escaping by panes of glass between the slats.

Operant Conditioning

In the late 1890s, while Russian physiologists were studying the relationship between stimuli and responses, an American psychologist named Edward Thorndike (1874–1949) was studying the relationship between actions and their consequences. While pursuing a doctoral degree at Harvard University, Thorndike studied learning in chicks by rewarding them with food for successfully negotiating a maze constructed of books. After his landlady objected to Thorndike's raising the chicks in his bedroom, William James, one of his professors, agreed to raise the chicks in his basement—much to the delight of the James children (Thorndike, 1961).

Thorndike left Harvard and completed his studies at Columbia University. At Columbia he conducted research using cats in so-called puzzle boxes (Hearst, 1999), which were constructed from wooden Heinz shipping crates (see Figure 7-4). In a typical puzzle box study, Thorndike (1898) put a hungry cat in the box and a piece of fish outside it. A sliding latch kept the door to the box closed. The cat could escape by stepping on a pedal or pulling a string that released the latch. At first the cat performed ineffective actions, such as biting the wooden slats or trying to squeeze between them. Eventually the cat accidentally performed the correct action, thereby releasing the latch, opening the door, and gaining access to the fish. Thorndike repeated this experiment for several trials and found that as the trials progressed, the cat took less and less time to escape, eventually escaping as soon as it was placed in the box.

The results of his puzzle box studies led Thorndike to develop the **law of effect**, which states that a behavior followed by a "satisfying" state of affairs is strengthened and a behavior followed by an "annoying" state of affairs is weakened. In the puzzle box experiments, behaviors that let the cat reach the fish were strengthened, and behaviors that kept it in the box were weakened. Because Thorndike studied the process by which behaviors are instrumental in producing certain consequences, the process became known as **instrumental conditioning**.

Principles of Operant Conditioning

Thorndike's work inspired B. F. Skinner (1904–1990), perhaps the best-known psychologist during the decades following World War II. In the 1930s Skinner called instrumental conditioning **operant conditioning**, because animals and people learn to "operate" on the environment to produce desired consequences instead of just responding reflexively (for example, salivation) to stimuli, as in classical conditioning. Following in Thorndike's footsteps, Skinner used chambers, now known as **Skinner boxes** or operant boxes, to study learning in animals—in particular, rats learning to press levers to obtain food

law of effect Edward Thorndike's principle that a behavior followed by a satisfying state of affairs is strengthened and a behavior followed by an annoying state of affairs is weakened.

instrumental conditioning A form of learning in which a behavior becomes more or less probable, depending on its consequences.

operant conditioning B. F. Skinner's term for instrumental conditioning, a form of learning in which a behavior becomes more or less probable, depending on its consequences.

Skinner box An enclosure that contains a bar or key that can be pressed to obtain food or water and that is used to study operant conditioning in rats, pigeons, or other small animals.

FIGURE 7-5
The Skinner Box

Rats placed in Skinner boxes, now more often referred to as operant boxes, learn to obtain food by pressing a bar, and pigeons placed in Skinner boxes learn to obtain food by pecking a lighted disk.

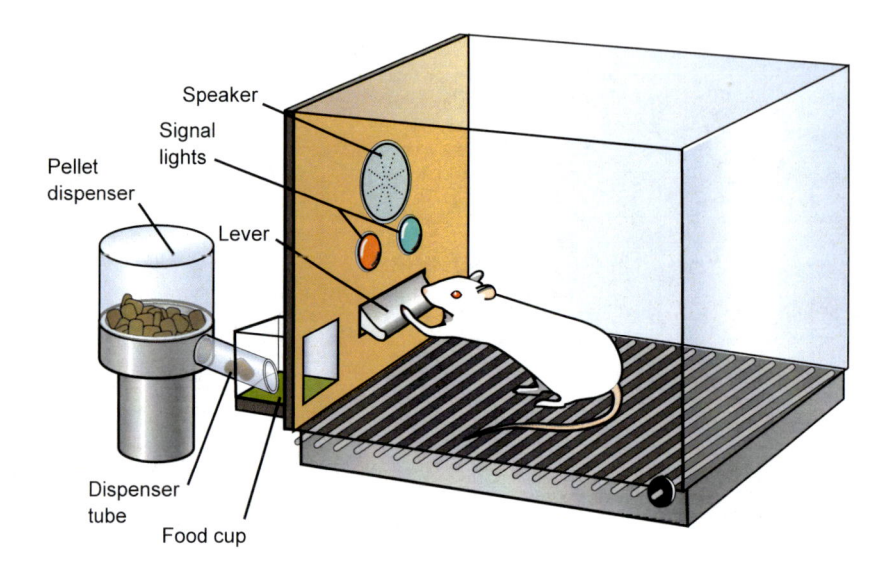

Positive Reinforcement

pellets and pigeons learning to peck at lighted disks to obtain grain (see Figure 7-5). Skinner devoted his career to studying the relationships between behaviors and their consequences, which he called **behavioral contingencies**: positive reinforcement, negative reinforcement, extinction, and punishment (Lattal, 1995).

Over two centuries ago, while leading a fort-building expedition, Benjamin Franklin increased the likelihood of attendance at daily prayer meetings by withholding his men's rations of rum until they had prayed (Knapp & Shodahl, 1974). This action showed Franklin's appreciation of the power of reinforcement. A reinforcer is a consequence of a behavior that increases the likelihood that the behavior will occur again. In **positive reinforcement** a behavior (for example, praying) that is followed by the presentation of a desirable stimulus (for example, rum) becomes more likely to occur in the future. Skinner called the desirable stimulus a positive reinforcer. You certainly are aware of the effect of positive reinforcement in your own life. For example, if you find helping your parents or caregivers with household chores earns you their praise, you are more likely to help them in the future. Positive reinforcement has been used to condition bees to make specific antenna movements (Kisch & Erber, 1999) and to make police officers and staff more courteous (Wilson, Boni, & Hogg, 1997). However, what serves as a reinforcer for one person might not for another.

A handy approach to determining what will be an effective positive reinforcer is provided by the **Premack principle**, named for its discoverer, David Premack. Premack (1965) pointed out that a behavior that has a higher probability of occurrence can be used as a positive reinforcer for a behavior that has a lower probability. Parents use the Premack principle with their children when they make viewing television or using other electronic devices a positive reinforcer for the completion of homework. Even animals are trained using the Premack principle. For example, a study using rats as subjects successfully used wheel running, a higher-probability behavior, as a positive reinforcement for lever pressing, a lower-probability behavior (Iversen, 1993). Keep in mind that according to the Premack principle, something that is reinforcing to one individual might be less so to another (Timberlake & Farmer-Dougan, 1991). Parental praise might be a positive reinforcer to you, yet have little effect on your friend's behavior.

In general, positive reinforcement is strengthened by increasing the magnitude of the reinforcer, decreasing the interval between the behavior and the reinforcer, and increasing the number of pairings of the behavior and the reinforcer. There are two classes of positive reinforcers. A **primary reinforcer** is biological and unlearned, such as oxygen, food, water, and warmth. In contrast, a **secondary reinforcer** (also known as a conditioned reinforcer) is learned and becomes reinforcing by being associated with a primary rein-

---

behavioral contingencies Relationships between behaviors and their consequences, such as positive reinforcement, negative reinforcement, extinction, and punishment.

positive reinforcement In operant conditioning, an increase in the probability of a behavior that is followed by a desirable consequence.

Premack principle The principle that a more probable behavior can be used as a reinforcer for a less probable one.

primary reinforcer In operant conditioning, an unlearned reinforcer that satisfies a biological need such as food, water, or oxygen.

secondary reinforcer In operant conditioning, a neutral stimulus that becomes reinforcing after being associated with a primary reinforcer.

forcer. Secondary reinforcers were demonstrated in a classic study in which chimpanzees could obtain grapes by inserting tokens into a vending machine (Wolfe, 1936). After using tokens to obtain grapes from the "chimp-o-mat," the chimps would steal tokens and hoard them. The tokens had become secondary reinforcers. Among the most powerful secondary reinforcers to people are praise, money, and prestige. How much time do you spend working for secondary reinforcers?

Why do behaviors that have been positively reinforced not occur continually? One reason is that behavior is controlled by discriminative stimuli, a process that Skinner calls stimulus control. A **discriminative stimulus** cues an individual when a behavior is likely to be reinforced. You would be silly to dial a telephone number on your landline if you did not first hear a dial tone, which acts as a discriminative stimulus to signal to you that dialing might result in positive reinforcement—reaching the person whom you are calling. Stimulus control even plays a role in drug abuse. Specific stimuli associated with drug use make drug use more likely in their presence (Falk, 1994), which explains, in part, why drug users who have undergone successful treatment often relapse when they return to the people and surroundings associated with their former drug use. Therapists emphasize the importance of addicts minimizing their exposure to situations, locations, and people that may elicit cravings for a particular drug.

A second reason that reinforced behaviors do not occur continually is the individual's relative degree of satiation in regard to the reinforcer. Reinforcement is more effective when the individual has been deprived of the reinforcer. In contrast, reinforcement is ineffective when the individual has been satiated by having free access to the reinforcer. So, water is more reinforcing to a thirsty person, food to a hungry person, and praise is more reinforcing to a person who is rarely praised.

Shaping and Chaining Positive reinforcement is useful in increasing the likelihood of behaviors that are already in an individual's repertoire. But how can we use positive reinforcement to promote behaviors that rarely or never occur? Consider the trained dolphins you have seen jump through hoops held high above the water. You cannot reinforce a behavior until it occurs. The trainer who simply waits until a dolphin jumps through a hoop held above the water might wait forever; dolphins do not naturally jump through hoops held above the water.

Animal trainers rely on a technique called **shaping** to train rats, dolphins, and other animals to perform actions that they would rarely or never perform naturally. In shaping, the individual is reinforced for successive approximations of the target behavior and eventually reinforced for the target behavior itself. A dolphin trainer might begin by giving a dolphin a fish for turning toward a hoop held underwater and then, successively, for moving toward the hoop, for coming near the hoop, and for swimming through the hoop. The trainer then would gradually raise the hoop and continue to reward the dolphin for swimming through it. Eventually the trainer would reward the dolphin for swimming through the hoop when it was held partly out of the water, then for jumping through the hoop when it was held slightly above the water, and finally, for jumping through the hoop when it was held several feet above the water. Shaping is also the process by which rats are taught to press levers and pigeons to peck at disks in Skinner boxes.

Shaping occurs naturally in the wild and may explain why wild rats living next to the Po River in Italy will dive to the river bottom to get shellfish to eat despite their inherent disinterest in swimming, whereas similar wild rats living next to other rivers will not (Galef, 1980). See Figure 7-6 for an illustration of the rats' behavior.

Shaping is not limited to animals. It also is useful in training people to perform novel behaviors. The successful application of what we now call shaping was reported as long ago as the 7th century, when it was used in England to help a mute person learn to speak (Cliffe, 1991). In a much more recent application, shaping was used to train a child with Down syndrome to jump over a hurdle in preparation for the Special Olympics (Cameron & Cappello, 1993).

What if you wish to teach an individual or animal to perform a series of behaviors rather than single behaviors? You might use **chaining**, which involves the reinforcement

discriminative stimulus In operant conditioning, a stimulus that indicates the likelihood that a particular response will be reinforced.

shaping An operant conditioning procedure that involves the positive reinforcement of successive approximations of an initially improbable behavior to eventually bring about that behavior.

chaining An operant conditioning procedure used to establish a desired sequence of behaviors by positively reinforcing each behavior in the sequence.

FIGURE 7-6

Shaping in the Wild on the Po River

Shaping might explain why wild rats living near the Po River in northern Italy will dive to the river bottom to get shellfish to eat, whereas similar wild rats living next to other rivers will not. The Po River experiences radical changes in depth. *(a)* At times, the rats living next to the Po can scamper across exposed areas of its bed to get shellfish. *(b)* As the water rises, the rats wade into the river and submerge their heads to get shellfish. *(c)* Eventually, when the water becomes deeper, they swim about in the river and dive to get shellfish. Thus, the natural changes in the depth of the river shape the rats' behavior by positively reinforcing them with shellfish for successive approximations of diving—until they are able to do full-fledged diving (Galef, 1980).

of each behavior in a series. For example, in one study, chaining was used successfully to train adults with intellectual disabilities to perform the 18 separate steps required to make a corsage (Hur & Osborne, 1993). In *forward chaining*, a sequence of actions is taught by reinforcing the first action in the chain and then working forward, each time adding a behavioral segment to the chain, until the individual performs all the segments in sequence. Forward chaining has been successful in areas as diverse as teaching the use of a musical keyboard (Ash & Holding, 1990) and training children with autism spectrum disorders to speak more frequently (Taylor, Levin, & Jasper, 1999).

In *backward chaining*, a sequence of actions is taught by reinforcing the final action in the chain and then working backward until the individual performs all the segments in sequence (Hagopian, Farrell, & Amari, 1996). For example, a father could use chaining to teach his child to put on a shirt. The father would begin by putting the shirt on the child, leaving only the top button open. He then would work backward, first reinforcing the child for buttoning the top button, then for buttoning the top two buttons, and so on, until the child could perform the sequence of actions necessary for putting on a shirt. Even flight-training programs for pilots are more successful when they have trainees practice individual segments of a chain of actions they are to learn and combine them together through backward chaining (Wightman & Lintern, 1984).

Schedules of Reinforcement Once an individual has been conditioned to perform a behavior, the performance of the behavior is influenced by its schedule of reinforcement—the pattern of reinforcements given for a desired behavior. In a **continuous schedule of reinforcement**, every instance of a desired behavior is reinforced. A rat in a Skinner box that receives a pellet of food each time it presses a bar is on a continuous schedule of reinforcement. Similarly, candy vending machines put you on a continuous schedule of reinforcement. Each time you insert the correct change, you receive a package of candy. If you do not receive the candy, you might pound on the machine, but you would, at best, insert coins only one more time. This example illustrates another characteristic of continuous schedules of reinforcement—they are subject to rapid extinction when reinforcement stops. Extinction is the decline in the probability of a behavior and its eventual disappearance as a result of its no longer being followed by a reinforcer.

In **partial schedules of reinforcement** (also known as intermittent schedules), reinforcement is given for only some instances of a desired behavior. Because partial schedules produce less predictable reinforcement, they are more resistant to extinction than are continuous schedules. Skinner (1956) discovered partial schedules by accident when he ran short of food pellets and decided not to reinforce each response but instead to reinforce responses only every so often. The rats kept responding and showed resistance to extinction. Partial schedules are further divided into ratio schedules and interval schedules. In a ratio schedule of reinforcement, reinforcement is provided after the individual makes a certain number of desired responses.

There are two kinds of ratio schedules: fixed and variable. A **fixed-ratio schedule of reinforcement** provides reinforcement after a specific number of desired responses. A rat in a Skinner box might be reinforced with a pellet of food after every five bar presses. Suppose a garment worker is paid with a voucher after every three shirts sewn. That person, too, would be on a fixed-ratio schedule. In one experiment, a fixed-ratio schedule of reinforcement increased the length of time exercisers rode stationary bicycles. In this case, 25-second video clips were presented after the riders completed a fixed number of pedal rotations (Cohen, Chelland, Ball, & LeMura, 2002). Fixed-ratio schedules produce high, steady response rates, with a brief pause in responding immediately after each reinforcement.

Unlike a fixed-ratio schedule, a **variable-ratio schedule of reinforcement** provides reinforcement after an unpredictable number of desired responses. The number of responses required will vary around an average. For example, a rat in a Skinner box might be reinforced with a food pellet after an average of 7 bar presses—perhaps 5 presses one time, 10 presses a second time, and 6 presses a third time. People playing slot machines are on a variable-ratio schedule because they cannot predict how many times they will have to play before they win. Even the archerfish, which hunts insects by spitting water at them as they fly by, continues to hunt that way (despite missing many times) because it is on a variable-ratio schedule of reinforcement (Goldstein & Hall, 1990).

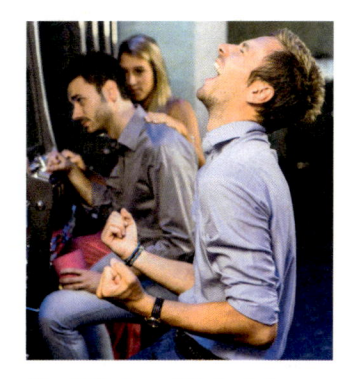

Variable-ratio schedules produce high, steady rates of responding that are more resistant to extinction than are those produced by any other schedule of reinforcement. In fact, by using a variable-ratio schedule of reinforcement, Skinner conditioned pigeons to peck a lighted disk up to 10,000 times to obtain a single pellet of food. Variable-ratio schedules also offer one reason compulsive gamblers find it so difficult to quit—eventually they will receive positive reinforcement, though their reinforcement history is unpredictable (Horsley, Osborne, Norman, & Wells, 2012) and resistant to extinction.

Whereas ratio schedules of reinforcement provide reinforcement after a certain number of desired responses, interval schedules of reinforcement provide reinforcement for the first desired response after a period of time. As in the case of ratio schedules, there are two kinds of interval schedules: fixed and variable. A **fixed-interval schedule of reinforcement** reinforces the first desired response after a set period of time. For example, a rat in a Skinner box might be reinforced with a food pellet for its first bar press after intervals of 30 seconds. Bar presses that occur during the intervals would not be reinforced.

A fixed-interval schedule produces a drop in responses immediately after reinforcement and a gradual increase in responses as the time for the next reinforcement approaches.

---

continuous schedule of reinforcement A schedule of reinforcement that provides reinforcement for each instance of a desired response.

partial schedule of reinforcement A schedule of reinforcement that reinforces some, but not all, instances of a desired response.

fixed-ratio schedule of reinforcement A partial schedule of reinforcement that provides reinforcement after a set number of desired responses.

variable-ratio schedule of reinforcement A partial schedule of reinforcement that provides reinforcement after varying, unpredictable numbers of desired responses.

fixed-interval schedule of reinforcement A partial schedule of reinforcement that provides reinforcement for the first desired response made after a set length of time.

Gambling and Schedules of Reinforcement

Gamblers are on variable-ratio schedules of reinforcement, which makes their gambling highly resistant to extinction. This is one of the reasons why compulsive gambling is so difficult to treat.

Source: William Perugini/Shutterstock.com.

Variable-Interval Schedule of Reinforcement

Since you receive email at varying times during the day, you are on a variable-interval schedule of reinforcement. You cannot predict how long you will have to wait to receive your next email.

Source: Spectruminfo/Shutterstock.com.

Suppose that you have a biology exam every 3 weeks. You would study before each exam to obtain a good grade—a positive reinforcer. But you would probably stop studying biology immediately after each exam and not begin studying it again until a few days before the next exam.

A **variable-interval schedule of reinforcement** provides reinforcement for the first desired response made after periods of time, which vary around an average. For example, a rat might be reinforced for its first bar press after 19 seconds, then after 37 seconds, then after 4 seconds, and so on, with the interval averaging 20 seconds. When you are fishing, you are on a variable-interval schedule of reinforcement because you cannot predict how long you will have to wait until a fish bites. Variable-interval schedules produce relatively slow, steady rates of responding that are highly resistant to extinction. An individual might continue to fish even if the fish are few and far between. And teachers who give periodic surprise quizzes make use of variable-interval schedules to promote more consistent studying by their students.

Ratio schedules produce faster response rates than do interval schedules because the number of responses, not the length of time, determines the onset of reinforcement. Variable schedules produce steadier response rates than do fixed schedules because the pattern of reinforcement is unpredictable. Figure 7-7 illustrates differences in response patterns under different schedules of reinforcement.

variable-interval schedule of reinforcement A partial schedule of reinforcement that provides reinforcement for the first desired response made after varying, unpredictable lengths of time.

FIGURE 7-7
Schedules of Reinforcement

The hash marks show the delivery of reinforcement Fixed-ratio and variable schedules of reinforcement have steeper slopes, which indicates higher rates of responding.

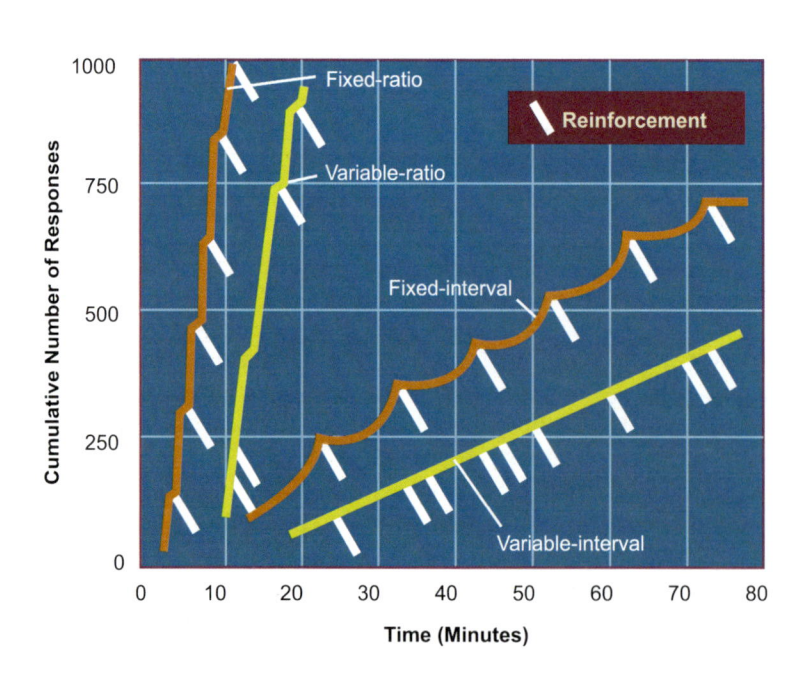

252 Chapter 7 Learning

Negative Reinforcement

In **negative reinforcement**, a behavior that brings about the removal of an aversive stimulus becomes more likely to occur in the future. Note that both positive and negative reinforcement increase the likelihood of a behavior. Consider the boring lecture. Because daydreaming lets you escape from boring lectures, you are likely to daydream whenever you find yourself listening to one. This form of negative reinforcement is called **escape learning**—learning to end something aversive. For example, you can terminate an irritating warning buzzer by putting on your automobile seat belt.

Of course your class might be so boring that you stop attending it. This form of negative reinforcement is called **avoidance learning**—learning to prevent something aversive. Thus, you can avoid the sound of a warning buzzer by buckling up before you start your automobile engine. And dormitory students at some schools quickly learn to scamper out of the shower when they hear a toilet being flushed to avoid being scalded when cold water is diverted to the toilet (Reese, 1986).

But if negative reinforcement involves engaging in a behavior that removes an aversive stimulus, how could avoidance learning (which only prevents an aversive stimulus) be a form of negative reinforcement? That is, what is the aversive stimulus that is being removed? Evidently, what is being removed is an internal aversive stimulus—the emotional distress caused by your anticipation of the aversive event, such as a boring class or a scalding shower. Thus, in escape learning, the aversive stimulus itself is removed, whereas in avoidance learning, the emotional distress caused by anticipation of that stimulus is removed (Mowrer, 1947). Even relatively simple animals engage in avoidance learning. For example, bees that get caught in spider webs—and are fortunate enough to escape—may learn to avoid them in the future (Craig, 1994).

Extinction

As in classical conditioning, behaviors learned through operant conditioning are subject to **extinction**. Skinner discovered extinction by accident. In one of his early studies, he conditioned a rat in a Skinner box to press a bar to obtain pellets of food from a dispenser. On one occasion he found that the pellet dispenser had become jammed, preventing the release of pellets. Skinner noted that the rat continued to press the bar, though at a diminishing rate, until it finally stopped pressing at all. Extinction might occur when a student who raises her hand is no longer called on to answer questions. Because she is no longer being positively reinforced for raising her hand, she would eventually stop doing so.

When extinction begins, there is typically a burst in the response. This phenomenon is important in behavior therapy techniques that use extinction because the techniques might, at first, seem to be ineffective. Experienced therapists are aware of this burst and might promote appropriate behavior by reinforcing it while an undesired behavior is undergoing extinction (Lerman & Iwata, 1995). Extinction therapy is useful for individuals with phobias.

---

negative reinforcement In operant conditioning, an increase in the probability of a behavior that is followed by the removal of an aversive stimulus.

escape learning Learning to perform a behavior that terminates an aversive stimulus, as in negative reinforcement.

avoidance learning Learning to prevent the occurrence of an aversive stimulus by giving an appropriate response to a warning stimulus.

extinction
1. In classical conditioning, the gradual disappearance of the conditioned response when the conditioned stimulus is repeatedly presented without being paired with the unconditioned stimulus.
2. In operant conditioning, the gradual disappearance of a response that is no longer followed by a reinforcer.

Extinction

Extinction involves the removal of reinforcement. If you ignore a temper tantrum, this should, eventually, result in extinction of the behavior.
Source: wavebreakmedia/Shutterstock.com.

spontaneous recovery
1. In classical conditioning, the reappearance after a period of time of a conditioned response that has been subjected to extinction. 2. In operant conditioning, the reappearance after a period of time of a behavior that has been subjected to extinction.

punishment In operant conditioning, the process by which an aversive stimulus decreases the probability of a response that precedes it.

Also, as with classical conditioning, a behavior that has been subjected to extinction can show **spontaneous recovery**—it might reappear after a period of time. Spontaneous recovery provides a functional advantage. For example, suppose that wild animals that visit a certain water hole normally obtain positive reinforcement by finding water. If they visit the water hole on several successive occasions and find that it has dried up, their behavior will undergo extinction; they will stop visiting the water hole. But after a period of time, the animals might exhibit spontaneous recovery, again visiting the water hole—in case it had become refilled with water.

Punishment

Still another way of reducing the probability of behaviors is through **punishment**, in which the consequence of a behavior decreases its likelihood. Do not confuse punishment with negative reinforcement. Negative reinforcement is "negative" because it involves the removal of an aversive stimulus; it does not involve punishment. Negative reinforcement increases the probability of a behavior by removing something undesirable as a consequence of that behavior; punishment decreases the probability of a behavior by presenting something undesirable (*positive punishment*) as a consequence of that behavior or by removing something desirable (*negative punishment*) as a consequence of that behavior. For example, a driver who gets a speeding ticket—an example of positive punishment—is less likely to speed in the future. Likewise, a teenager who is not allowed to use the family car because of speeding—an example of negative punishment—also will be less likely to speed again.

Punishment is useful in animals, as well as in people. For example, social animals punish underlings who threaten group well-being. They use punishment to discipline offspring, promote cooperation, and maintain dominance hierarchies (Clutton-Brock & Parker, 1995). Though punishment can be an effective means of reducing undesirable behaviors, it often is ineffective. Consider some effective and ineffective ways of using punishment to discipline children (Walters & Grusec, 1977).

- Punishment for misbehavior should be immediate so that the child will associate the punishment with the misbehavior. A parent should not resort to threats of "wait until your father [mother] gets home," which might separate the misbehavior and punishment by hours.
- Punishment should be strong enough to stop the undesirable behavior but not excessive. You might punish a child for throwing clothes about his room by making him clean the room, but you would be using excessive punishment if you made him clean every room in the house. Punishment that is excessive induces resentment aimed at the person who administers the punishment.
- Punishment should be consistent. If parents truly want to reduce a child's misbehavior, they must punish the child each time it occurs. Otherwise the child learns only that her parents are unpredictable—that is, the child is on a variable-ratio schedule of reinforcement (which is highly resistant to extinction).
- Punishment should be aimed at the misbehavior, not at the child. For example, a child who is repeatedly called "stupid" for making mistakes while playing softball might feel incompetent and lose interest in softball and other sports.
- Punishing undesirable behavior merely suppresses the behavior in response to a specific discriminative stimulus, such as the parent who administers punishment and only teaches the child what not to do. To make sure that the child learns what to do, positive reinforcement of desirable behavior should also be used.

One of the main controversies concerning punishment is the use of physical punishment (Gershoff, 2002). Children imitate parental models. If they observe that their parents rely on physical punishment, they might rely on it in dealing with their friends, siblings, and eventually, their own children. Though physical punishment of children can suppress misbehavior in the short run, in the long run it is associated with problems such as juve-

TABLE 7-1 Behavioral Contingencies

Contingency	Behavioral Consequence	Probability of Behavior	Example
Positive reinforcement	Brings about something desirable	Increases	You study for an exam and receive an A, which makes you more likely to study in the future.
Negative reinforcement	Removes something undesirable	Increases	You go to the dentist to have a cavity filled. This eliminates your toothache, which makes you more likely to visit the dentist in the future when you have a toothache.
Extinction	Fails to bring about something desirable	Decreases	You say hello to a person who repeatedly fails to greet you in return. This leads you to stop saying hello.
Punishment	Brings about something undesirable	Decreases	You overeat at a party and suffer from a severe upset stomach. In the future you become less likely to overeat.

nile delinquency and adult criminality (Straus, 1991). Being physically punished as a child also is associated with subsequent adult depression, suicidal tendencies, alcohol and spousal abuse (Straus & Kantor, 1994), and children resorting to physical violence during interpersonal disputes with their peers (Simons & Wurtele, 2010). Table 7-1 summarizes the differences among the behavioral contingencies of positive reinforcement, negative reinforcement, extinction, and punishment.

Applications of Operant Conditioning

B. F. Skinner (1986) claimed that many of our everyday problems could be solved by more widespread use of operant conditioning. As one example, consider the problem of injuries and deaths caused by automobile accidents. Operant conditioning has been effective in teaching children to use seat belts, thereby reducing their risk of injury (Roberts & Fanurik, 1986). Now consider several other ways in which operant conditioning has been applied to everyday life.

Operant Conditioning and Animal Training

Skinner and some of his colleagues have been pioneers in the use of shaping and chaining to train animals to perform novel behaviors (Lukas, Marr, & Maple, 1998). Zoos rely on positive reinforcement, as in a popular otter-training program that was open to the public at Zoo Atlanta (Anderson, Kelling, Pressley-Keough, Bloomsmith, & Maple, 2003). Perhaps Skinner's most noteworthy feat in animal training occurred during World War II in "Project Pigeon." In this secret project, Skinner (1960) trained pigeons to guide missiles toward enemy ships by training them to peck at an image of the target ship shown on a display to obtain food pellets. Though this guidance system proved feasible, it was never used in combat.

More recently, pigeons have been trained to serve as air-sea rescue spotters in the Coast Guard's "Project Sea Hunt" (Stark, 1981). The pigeons are reinforced with food pellets for responding to red, orange, or yellow objects—the common colors of flotation devices. Three pigeons are placed in a compartment under a search plane so that they look out of windows oriented in different directions. When a pigeon spots an object floating in the sea, it pecks a key, which sounds a buzzer and flashes a light in the cockpit. Pigeons are superior to human spotters because they have the ability to focus over a wider area and to scan the sea for longer periods of time without becoming fatigued.

In another beneficial application of operant conditioning, psychologists have trained capuchin monkeys to serve as aides to physically disabled people (Mack, 1981). These monkeys act as extensions of the disabled person—bringing drinks, turning pages in books, changing television channels, and performing a host of other services. The person directs the monkey by using an optical pointer that focuses a beam of light on a desired object.

Operant Conditioning and Child Rearing

In 1945, Skinner shocked the public when he published the article "Baby in a Box," which described how he and his wife had reared an infant daughter in an enclosure called an *air crib*. The air crib filtered and controlled the temperature of the infant's air supply. Instead of diapers, it used a roll of paper that permitted sections to be placed under the baby and discarded when dirty. The parents could even pull down a shade over the front window of the air crib when the baby was ready to go to sleep. Skinner claimed that the air crib was a more convenient way to rear infants and allowed more time for social interaction with them. Critics disagreed with Skinner, claiming that his treatment of his daughter was dehumanizing. Over the past few decades, rumors have claimed that Skinner's daughter's experience with the air crib eventually led her to sue her father, to become mentally ill, or to commit suicide. In reality, she had a happy childhood and has pursued a successful career as an artist (Langone, 1983).

The air crib provoked fears of impersonal child rearing, and it was never widely used. Skinner had tried, unsuccessfully, to market the air crib under the clever brand name *Heir Conditioner* (Benjamin & Neilsen-Gammon, 1999). Nonetheless, operant conditioning has proved useful in child rearing. For example, parents have used extinction to eliminate their child's tantrums. When parents ignore the tantrums rather than give in to the child's demand for toys, candy, or attention, the tantrums might at first intensify but eventually will stop (Williams, 1959).

Operant Conditioning and Educational Improvement

Teachers likewise have used positive reinforcement to improve their students' classroom performance. For example, verbal praise has been used to increase participation in classroom discussions (Smith, Schumaker, Schaeffer, & Sherman, 1982), and positive reinforcement in the form of token economies has been used to promote desirable classroom behaviors (Swiezy, Matson, & Box, 1992). In a **token economy**, teachers use tokens to reward students for proper conduct and academic excellence. The students then use the tokens to purchase items such as toys or privileges such as extra recess time. Token economies have been used to increase classroom participation by college students (Boniecki & Moore, 2003) and appropriate behavior by adolescents in a drug and alcohol rehabilitation (Taylor & Mudford, 2012).

Perhaps the most distinctive contribution that operant conditioning has made to education has been **programmed instruction**, which had its origin in the invention of the teaching machine by Sidney Pressey of Ohio State University in the 1920s. His machines provided immediate knowledge of results and a piece of candy to reward correct answers (Benjamin, 1988). But credit for developing programmed instruction is generally given to B. F. Skinner for his invention of a teaching machine that takes the student through a series of questions related to a particular subject, gradually moving the student from simple to more complex questions. After the student answers a question, the correct answer is revealed.

The teaching machine failed to catch on in the 1950s and 1960s because of fears that it would be dehumanizing, that it could teach only certain narrow subjects, and that teachers would lose their jobs. Nonetheless, supporters note that programmed instruction has several advantages over traditional approaches to education (Vargas & Vargas, 1991). Programmed instruction provides immediate feedback of results (positive reinforcement for correct answers and only mild punishment for incorrect answers), eliminates the need for anxiety-inducing exams, and permits the student to go at her or his own pace. Skinner (1984) claimed that if schools adopted programmed instruction, students would learn twice as much in the same amount of time.

Today's use of **computer-assisted instruction** (Skinner, 1989) is a descendant of Skinner's programmed instruction. Computer programs take the student through a graded

token economy An operant conditioning procedure that uses tokens as positive reinforcers in programs designed to promote desirable behaviors, with the tokens later used to purchase desired items or privileges.

programmed instruction A step-by-step approach, based on operant conditioning, in which the learner proceeds at his or her own pace through more and more advanced material and receives immediate knowledge of the results of each response.

computer-assisted instruction The use of computer programs to provide programmed instruction.

Computer-Assisted Instruction

Students may benefit from computer-assisted instruction because it permits them to go at their own pace, receive immediate feedback on their progress, and, in some cases, obtain remedial help in areas of weakness.
Source: Robert Kneschke/Shutterstock.com.

series of items at the student's own pace. The programs even branch off to provide extra help on items that the student finds difficult. Though teaching machines and computers have not replaced teachers, they have added another teaching tool to the classroom. Computer-assisted instruction has proved useful, whether teaching academic skills to elementary school students (Christmann & Badgett, 2003), nursing skills to caregivers of elderly adults (Ponpaipan et al., 2010), or introductory psychology to college students (Pear & Crone-Todd, 1999). Computer-assisted instruction also is useful with special populations, such as children with autism spectrum disorder (Ploog, Scharf, Nelson, & Brooks, 2013), learning disabilities (Hall, Hughes, & Filbert, 2000), or intellectual disabilities (Patra & Rath, 2000).

Operant Conditioning and Psychological Disorders

Operant conditioning has enhanced our understanding of psychological disorders, particularly depression. The concept of **learned helplessness** has gained influence as an explanation for depression through the work of Martin Seligman (see Chapter 14). In his original research, Seligman exposed dogs restrained in harnesses to electric shocks. One group of dogs could turn off the shock by pressing a switch with their noses. A second group could not. The dogs then were tested in a shuttle box, which consisted of two compartments separated by an easily hurdled divider. A warning tone was sounded, followed a few seconds later by an electric shock. Dogs in the first group escaped by jumping over the divider into the other compartment. In contrast, dogs in the second group whimpered but did not try to escape (Seligman & Maier, 1967).

Though replications of various versions of this study have produced inconsistent support for learned helplessness in animals (Klosterhalfen & Klosterhalfen, 1983), it is a model that is commonly used to elicit behaviors that resemble symptoms of depression and post-traumatic stress disorder (PTSD) in humans. Moreover, these behavioral changes respond to treatment with antidepressant medications (Hammack, Cooper, & Lezak, 2012). This study, as well as others, has demonstrated the effectiveness of this intervention in animals. However, it is not possible to use this method with people (Winefield, 1982). Nevertheless, the possibility that learned helplessness is a factor in depression has inspired hundreds of studies (Deuser & Anderson, 1995) and contributed to our understanding of the neurobiology that underlies the relationship between stress and depression. Depressed people experience less control over obtaining positive reinforcers and avoiding punishments. As a consequence, they are less likely to try to change their life situations—which further contributes to their feelings of depression. Consider adults whose everyday functioning can be reduced by uncontrollable pain. They might become depressed, reduce their activities even more, and perhaps become housebound (Kropp et al., 2012).

learned helplessness A feeling of futility caused by the belief that one has little or no control over events in one's life, which can make one stop trying and experience depressed mood.

Operant conditioning also has been used to change maladaptive behaviors. This use is known as *behavior modification*. For example, token economies have been useful in training mental hospital patients to care for themselves (Morisse, Batra, Hess, & Silverman, 1996). Patients are trained to dress themselves, to use toilets, to brush their teeth, and to eat with utensils. They use the tokens to purchase merchandise or special privileges.

Operant Conditioning and Biofeedback

One day, more than three decades ago, the eminent learning researcher Neal Miller stood in front of a mirror trying to teach himself to wiggle one ear. By watching his ear in the mirror, he eventually was able to make it wiggle (Jonas, 1972). The mirror provided Miller with visual *feedback* of his ear's movement. This experience convinced him that people might learn to control physiological responses that are not normally subject to voluntary control if they were provided with feedback of those responses. Since the 1960s Miller and other psychologists have developed a technique called biofeedback to help people learn to control normally involuntary responses such as brain waves, blood pressure, and intestinal contractions.

biofeedback A form of operant conditioning that enables an individual to learn to control a normally involuntary physiological process or to gain better control of a normally voluntary one when provided with visual or auditory information indicating the state of that response.

Biofeedback is a form of operant conditioning that enables an individual to learn to control a normally involuntary physiological response or to gain better control of a normally voluntary one when provided with visual or auditory information indicating the state of that response. The feedback acts as a positive reinforcer for changes in the desired direction. The feedback might be provided by a light that changes in brightness as heart rate changes, a tone that changes in pitch as muscle tension changes, or any of a host of other visual or auditory stimuli that vary with changes in the target physiological response.

Biofeedback was popularized in the late 1960s by reports of participants who learned to control their alpha brain-wave patterns, which, as described in Chapter 6, are associated with a relaxed state of mind. But biofeedback did not become scientifically credible to many psychologists until Neal Miller reported success in training rats to gain voluntary control over physiological responses normally controlled solely by the autonomic nervous system. In his studies, Miller used electrical stimulation of the brain's reward centers (positive reinforcement) or, in some cases, escape or avoidance of shock (negative reinforcement) to train rats to increase or decrease their heart rate, intestinal contractions, urine production, or blood pressure. Because Miller was an eminent, hard-nosed researcher (Coons, 2002), serious scientists became more willing to accept the legitimacy of biofeedback. Ironically, for unknown reasons, attempts at replicating his rat studies generally have failed (Dworkin & Miller, 1986).

Disappointment at the failure to replicate Miller's rat studies and of biofeedback to fulfill early promises to induce mystical states of consciousness led to skepticism about its merits. But even though biofeedback has not proven to be an unqualified success, it has not proven to be a failure. Hundreds of studies have demonstrated the effectiveness of biofeedback in helping people learn to control a variety of physiological responses, such as chronic headaches (Blume, Brockman, & Breuner, 2012). Clinical applications have included reducing arrhythmia by training patients to regulate their own heart rates (Wheat & Larkin, 2010) and helping people with painfully cold hands to warm them by increasing blood flow (Sedlacek & Taub, 1996).

One of biofeedback's main uses has been in training people to gain better control of their skeletal muscles. For example, biofeedback has been used to train people with physical disabilities to maintain their balance (Milosevic & McConville, 2011), children with cerebral palsy to control their body movements (Bloom, Przekop, & Sanger, 2010), and people with panic disorder to reduce their symptoms by regulating their breathing (Meurat, Wilhelm, & Roth, 2001). Figure 7-8 shows how biofeedback can be used to control muscle tension.

Though biofeedback is widely used by psychologists and health professionals, it is not a panacea. In fact, there is controversy about its effectiveness and practicality. To demonstrate the effectiveness of biofeedback, one must show that self-regulation of physiological responses is caused by the feedback and not by extraneous factors (Heywood

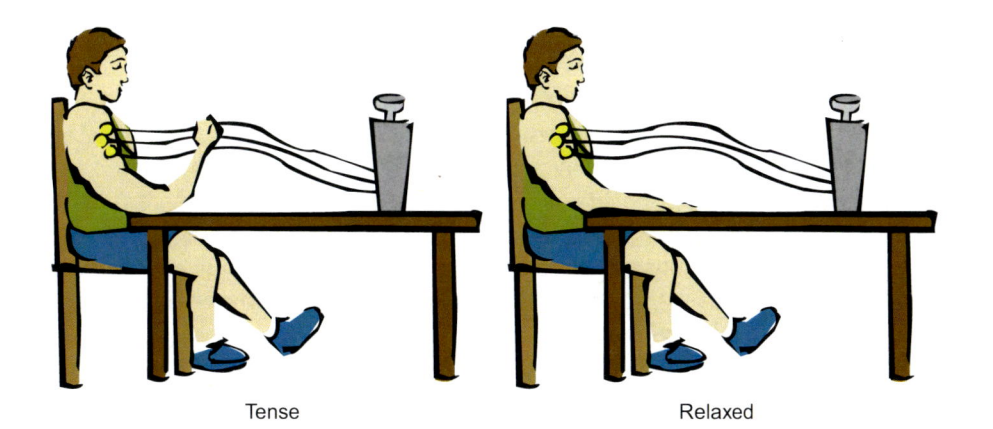

FIGURE 7-8
Biofeedback

People who are provided with feedback of physiological processes may gain some control over normally involuntary ones, such as blood pressure, or gain improved control over normally voluntary ones, such as muscle tension during physical rehabilitation. The individual shown here is undergoing physical rehabilitation using muscle biofeedback.

Tense   Relaxed

& Beale, 2003). For example, early biofeedback studies showed that feedback of alpha brain waves could increase them and induce a state of relaxation. But replications of those early studies showed that the effects were caused by the participants' sitting quietly with their eyes closed. The brain-wave feedback added nothing (Plotkin, 1979). Even when the results of a biofeedback study can be attributed to the feedback, the technique still might not be of practical use. Why?

- The typical biofeedback device costs hundreds or even thousands of dollars. Thus, clinicians must decide whether the benefits of biofeedback justify its cost, especially when other equally effective, less expensive treatments are available. Yet overall, treatment programs that include biofeedback have proved cost-effective in enhancing the quality of life and in reducing physician visits, medication use, medical care costs, hospital stays, and mortality (Schneider, 1987).

- Laboratory experiments on biofeedback can produce results that are statistically significant (a concept discussed in Chapter 2) and merit being reported but that are too small to be of practical use in clinical settings (Steiner & Dince, 1981). For example, biofeedback might produce a *statistically significant* reduction in blood pressure in hypertensive persons that is too small to be *clinically meaningful*.

- Biofeedback training in a clinician's office might produce results that do not last much beyond the training sessions. That is, there is a need for research on how to promote long-term maintenance of biofeedback-induced changes (McGrady, 2002). One way to promote the generalization of benefits from clinical training sessions to everyday life is to use portable biofeedback devices (Harrison, Gavin, & Isaac, 1988).

- The results of laboratory studies might not be applicable to the clinical setting. The therapist who uses biofeedback typically achieves success by combining biofeedback with other therapeutic approaches. Thus, biofeedback does not achieve its clinical effects by itself, as an antibiotic might do in curing a bacterial infection. That is, though it would be scientifically sound to compare a psychotherapy-plus-biofeedback group to a psychotherapy-alone group, it would be scientifically unsound to compare a psychotherapy-alone group to a biofeedback-alone group. As in other forms of therapy, emotional and cognitive factors play a role in the effectiveness of biofeedback therapy (Shahab, West, & McNeill, 2011).

Biological Constraints on Operant Conditioning

Around the turn of the 20th century, Edward Thorndike put forth the concept of *belongingness* to explain why he found it easier to train cats to escape from his puzzle boxes by stepping on a pedal than by scratching themselves. Thorndike observed that evolution seemed to have endowed animals with inherited tendencies to associate the performance of certain behaviors with certain consequences. Cats are more predisposed to escape by performing actions that affect the environment, such as stepping on a pedal, than by performing actions that affect their bodies, such as scratching themselves.

Thorndike's observation had little influence on his contemporaries, and it was not until the 1950s that psychologists rediscovered what he had observed. Among the first psychologists to make this rediscovery were Keller and Marian Breland, former students of B. F. Skinner who became renowned animal trainers (Timberlake, 2003). Since its founding in 1947, their Animal Behavior Enterprises in Hot Springs, Arkansas, trained animals to perform in zoos, fairs, movies, circuses, museums, amusement parks, department stores, and television commercials.

Despite their success in training animals, the Brelands were distressed by the tendency of some animals to "misbehave" (Breland & Breland, 1961). Their misbehavior was actually a reversion to behaviors characteristic of their species, which the Brelands called **instinctive drift**. For example, they used operant conditioning to train a chicken to hit a baseball by pulling a string to swing a miniature bat and then run to first base for food. Sometimes, instead, the chicken chased after the ball and pecked at it. This "misbehavior" of animals has distressed animal trainers, but it demonstrates that animals sometimes may revert back to species-specific behaviors even when being reinforced for other behaviors.

After considering instinctive drift and related problems in operant conditioning, psychologist Martin Seligman (1970) concluded that there is a continuum of **behavioral preparedness** for certain behaviors. For example, a hamster more easily learns to dig than to wash its face to obtain positive reinforcement (Shettleworth & Juergensen, 1980). The continuum of behavioral preparedness ranges from *prepared* to *unprepared* to *contraprepared*. Behaviors for which members of a species are prepared have evolved because they have survival value for them and are easily learned by members of that species. Behaviors for which members of a species are *unprepared* have no survival value for them and are difficult to learn for members of that species. And behaviors for which members of a species are *contraprepared* have no survival value for them and are impossible to learn for members of that species. For example, human beings are prepared, chimpanzees are unprepared, and dogs are contraprepared to use language. Human beings can learn to speak, read, write, and use sign language. Chimpanzees can learn to use sign language. And dogs cannot learn any of these language skills.

instinctive drift The reversion of animals to behaviors characteristic of their species even when being reinforced for performing other behaviors.

behavioral preparedness The degree to which members of a species are innately prepared to learn particular behaviors.

Section Review: Operant Conditioning

1. In what way was Edward Thorndike's instrumental conditioning the forerunner of B. F. Skinner's operant conditioning?

2. How would you use shaping to train children to straighten up their rooms?

3. In what ways are positive reinforcement and negative reinforcement similar, and in what ways are they different?

Cognitive Learning

Both classical conditioning and operant conditioning traditionally have been explained by the principle of contiguity—the mere association of events in time and space. Contiguity has been used to explain the association of a conditioned stimulus and an unconditioned stimulus in classical conditioning and the association of a behavior and its consequence in operant conditioning. Over the past few decades, the associationistic explanation of learning has been criticized for viewing human and animal learners as passive reactors to "external carrots, whips, and the stimuli associated with them" (Boneau, 1974, p. 308). These critics, influenced by the "cognitive revolution" in psychology, favor the study of cognitive factors in classical conditioning and operant conditioning, as well as the study of learning by observation, which had routinely been ignored by learning researchers (Wasserman, 1997).

Cognitive Factors in Associative Learning

The traditional view of classical conditioning and operant conditioning is that they are explained by contiguity alone. But evidence has accumulated that mere contiguity of a neutral stimulus and an unconditioned stimulus is insufficient to produce classical conditioning, and mere contiguity of a behavior and a consequence is insufficient to produce operant conditioning. This evidence has led to cognitive interpretations of associative learning, as in the case of operant conditioning. For example, secondary reinforcers traditionally have been thought to gain their reinforcing ability through mere contiguity with primary reinforcers. Cognitive theorists believe, instead, that secondary reinforcers gain their reinforcing ability because they have reliably *predicted* the occurrence of primary reinforcers (Rose & Fantino, 1978).

Suppose that you are using treats as positive reinforcers to train your dog to "shake hands." Just before giving your dog a treat, you might offer praise by saying "Good dog!" If you did so every time that your dog shook hands, the words "Good dog!" might become a secondary reinforcer. The traditional view of operant conditioning would claim that the praise became a secondary reinforcer by its mere *contiguity* with food. In contrast, the cognitive view would claim that the praise became a secondary reinforcer because it had become a good *predictor* of the food reward.

Psychologists also have provided cognitive explanations of classical conditioning that rule out mere contiguity as a sufficient explanation. The most influential of these explanations states that classical conditioning will occur only when the conditioned stimulus permits the individual to reliably predict the occurrence of the unconditioned stimulus (Siegel & Allan, 1996). The better the conditioned stimulus is as a predictor, the stronger the conditioning will be. Conditioning involves learning relations, or contingencies, among events in the environment (Rescorla, 1988).

Prediction was demonstrated by Robert Rescorla (1968), who favors a cognitive explanation of conditioning. In one experiment, he paired a buzzer (the neutral stimulus) with an electric shock (a UCS), which he administered to rats. All the rats received the same number of pairings of the buzzer and the electric shock. But some of the rats were given additional shocks not preceded by a buzzer. According to the traditional contiguity-based explanation of classical conditioning, because the buzzer and the electric shock had been paired an equal number of times for all the rats, the buzzer should have become an equally strong CS, eliciting a CR, for all of them. Yet, those for whom the buzzer always preceded the electric shock showed stronger conditioning.

Rescorla would explain this result cognitively—that is, in terms of the rats' knowledge of the relationship between the buzzer and the electric shock (Rescorla, 2003). The rats that always received an electric shock after the buzzer developed a stronger expectancy that an electric shock would follow the buzzer than did the rats that sometimes did and sometimes did not receive an electric shock after the buzzer. Consider this explanation in regard to Pavlov's studies of salivation in dogs. The dog learns that a tone is followed by meat powder. The more consistently the tone precedes the meat powder, the more predictable the relationship will be and, as a consequence, the stronger the conditioning will be.

Another source of evidence that supports the cognitive explanation of classical conditioning is the phenomenon of **blocking**, in which a neutral stimulus paired with a CS that already elicits a CR will fail to become a CS itself (Blaisdell, Gunther, & Miller, 1999). Blocking is illustrated in Table 7-2. Suppose that you have conditioned a dog to salivate to the sound of a bell by repeatedly presenting the bell before presenting meat powder. If you then repeatedly paired a light with the bell before presenting the meat powder, the principle of contiguity would make you expect that the light, too, would gain the ability to elicit salivation. But it will not. Instead, the CS (the bell) "blocks" the neutral stimulus (the light) from becoming a conditioned stimulus. According to the cognitive explanation, blocking occurs because the neutral stimulus (the light) adds nothing to the predictability

blocking The process by which a neutral stimulus paired with a conditioned stimulus that already elicits a conditioned response fails to become a conditioned stimulus.

Chapter 7 Learning

TABLE 7-2 Blocking

In this example, in phase 1, rats in the experimental group are presented with a tone (the CS) immediately followed by an electric shock (the UCS), while rats in the control group receive neither stimulus. In phase 2, both groups are exposed to a tone and light, followed by a shock. In phase 3, both groups show fear (the CR) in response to the tone, but only the control group shows fear in response to the light. Because the tone already served as a reliable predictor of the shock for the experimental group, the tone blocked the light from becoming a CS for the rats in that group. That is, the light remained a neutral stimulus for the experimental group.

	Phase 1	Phase 2	Phase 3
Experimental Group	CS (tone) + UCS (shock)	CS (tone + light) + UCS (shock)	CS (tone)→CR (fear) Neutral stimulus (light)→No CR
Control Group	No training	CS (tone + light) + UCS (shock)	CS (tone)→CR (fear) CS (light)→CR (fear)

of the UCS (the meat powder). The CS (the bell) already predicts the occurrence of the UCS. Blocking has been demonstrated in animals (Urushihara & Miller, 2010) and people (Hinchy, Lovibond, & Ter-Horst, 1995).

Still another source of evidence against a strictly contiguity-based view of classical conditioning comes from research on conditioned taste aversion. As you learned earlier, individuals who suffer gastrointestinal illness hours after eating novel food might avoid that food in the future. This finding contradicts the notion that events must be contiguous for us to learn to associate those events with each other.

Latent Learning

The "cognitive revolution" in psychology also has produced a trend to view learning less in terms of changes in overt behavior, as in classical or operant conditioning, and more in terms of the acquisition of knowledge (Greeno, 1980). Learning can occur without revealing itself in observable behavior. For example, suppose that after studying many hours and mastering the material for a psychology exam, you fail the exam. Should your professor conclude that you had not learned the material? Not necessarily. Perhaps you failed the exam because the questions were ambiguous or because you were so anxious that your mind went blank. Your performance on the exam did not reflect how well you had learned the material.

But some researchers were interested in cognitive factors in learning decades before the onset of the cognitive revolution, even in regard to animal learning (Dewsbury, 2000). The first psychologist to stress the distinction between learning and performance was Edward Tolman (1932), who pointed out that learning can occur without rewards being given for overt actions, a process that he called **latent learning**. In latent learning, learning is not immediately revealed in performance but is revealed later when a reward is provided for performance. In a classic study, Tolman had three groups of rats run individually through a maze once a day for 10 days. One group received food as a positive reward for reaching the end of the maze, and the other two groups did not. The rewarded rats quickly learned to run through the maze with few wrong turns, while the nonrewarded rats did not. Beginning on the eleventh day, one of the groups of nonrewarded rats also was positively rewarded with food for reaching the end of the maze. The next day that group ran the maze as efficiently as the previously rewarded group did, while the remaining, still nonrewarded group continued to perform poorly. Tolman's study demonstrated latent learning. The rats that were not rewarded until the eleventh day had learned the route to

latent learning Learning that occurs without the reinforcement of overt behavior.

the end of the maze, but they revealed this learning only when rewarded for doing so (Tolman & Honzik, 1930).

More recent research has provided additional support for latent learning. In one study, rats given an opportunity to observe a water maze before swimming through it for a food reward performed better than did rats that were not given such an opportunity (Keith & McVety, 1988). This experiment provided evidence that rats can form what Tolman called "cognitive maps"—mental representations of physical reality. But they use their cognitive maps only when rewarded for doing so. Nonetheless, some researchers have found that in similar experiments rats might be guided in their swimming not by cognitive maps but instead by visual cues in their environment (Prados, Chamizo, & MacKintosh, 1999).

Observational Learning

In the 1960s, research on latent learning stimulated interest in **observational learning**, in which an individual learns a behavior by watching others (models) perform it. That is, learning occurs without any overt behavior by the learner. Research on observational learning in animals dates back to at least 1881 (Robert, 1990). Observational learning has been demonstrated in a variety of animals, including cattle (Veissier, 1993), pigeons (Zentall, Sutton, & Sherburne, 1996), sea gulls (Obozova, Smirnova, & Zorina, 2011), horses (Ahrendt, Christensen, & Ladewig, 2012), dogs (Kupán, Miklósi, Gergely, & Topál, 2011), and even octopuses (Fiorito & Scotto, 1992). Consider rats. A rat that observes other rats eating foods will be more likely to eat those foods (Galef, 1993), infant rats that observe older rats opening pine cones will learn to do so themselves (Aisner & Terkel, 1992), and rats that observe other rats pushing a joystick in a particular direction to get food will learn to push it in that direction themselves (Heyes, Dawson, & Nokes, 1992).

There are numerous examples of observational learning in people (Ferrari, 1996). A few examples include basketball, baseball, ice hockey, and soccer players and their coaches learning athletic skills (Hancock, Rymal, & Ste-Marie, 2011), and students learning to behave properly by observing other students doing so (Hallenbeck & Kauffman, 1995). And in one study, 2-month-old infants watched a video of a woman responding positively or negatively to an object. Afterward, those who had seen the model respond negatively to the object tended to avoid it and to respond to it with negative emotionality (Mumme & Fernald, 2003).

Observational learning is central to Albert Bandura's **social learning theory**, which assumes that behavior is learned chiefly through observation and the mental processing of information. What accounts for observational learning? Bandura (1986) has identified four factors: First, you must pay attention to the model's actions; second, you must remember the model's actions; third, you must have the ability to produce the actions; and fourth, you must be motivated to perform the actions. Consider a gymnast learning to perform a flying dismount from the uneven bars. She might learn to perform this feat by first paying attention to a gymnast who can already perform it. To be able to attempt the feat, the learner would have to remember what the model did. But to perform the feat, the learner must have the strength to swing from the bars. Assuming that she paid attention to the model, remembered what the model did, and had the strength to perform the movement, she still might be motivated only to perform the feat in important competitions.

We are beginning to understand the neural circuits that might be responsible for observational learning and the imitation of others' actions. The neurons involved are called **mirror neurons**. The exact location of mirror neurons and their networks in the frontal and parietal cortex remains controversial (Hickok, 2009), and studies in both monkeys and humans are helping us understand more. In monkeys or humans, these neurons fire during the observation of the same actions or behaviors done by other individuals. For example, this system might be useful for infants learning to express emotion and mimic their mothers, or these neurons might provide feedback for us to help us understand how people feel. Consider if you have ever mimicked someone's facial expression if they are telling you a sad story or you have felt empathy toward that person. Neurological disorders such as stroke, autism spectrum disorder and schizophrenia are also providing

observational learning Learning produced by observing the consequences that others receive for performing particular behaviors.

social learning theory A theory of learning that assumes that people learn behaviors mainly through observation and mental processing of information.

mirror neurons Neurons that appear to be involved in the neural circuits responsible for observational learning.

Critical Thinking About Psychology

Does Television Influence Children's Behavior?

Research on observational learning has contributed to concerns about the effects of the media on viewers, particularly children. For example, one study of children's television shows broadcast in the Los Angeles area found that 70 percent contained physical aggression, compared to 60 percent of nonchildren's shows. Moreover, children's shows contained three times more incidents of physical aggression than did nonchildren's shows (Wilson, Smith, Potter, Kunkel, Linz, Colvin, & Donnerstein, 2002). Concern about the effects of television on behavior is not new. It has existed ever since television became a popular medium in the 1950s (Carpenter, 1955). The first congressional report on the effects of television was a 1954 report on its impact on juvenile delinquency. Since then, reports on the social effects of television appeared in 1972 and 1982. Both reports found that violence on television led to aggressive behavior in children and adolescents and recommended a decrease in televised violence (Walsh, 1983). But critics of these reports claimed that, on the one hand, the results of laboratory experiments on the effects of televised violence might not generalize to real life and, on the other hand, field studies on the effects of televised violence failed to control all the other variables that might encourage violence (Fisher, 1983).

In a classic experiment by Bandura (1965) on the effect of television viewing on children, three groups of preschool children watched a film of an adult punching and verbally abusing a blow-up Bobo doll. Each group saw a different version of the film. In the first version the model was rewarded with candy, soda, and praise by another adult. In the second version the other adult scolded and spanked the model. And in the third version there were no consequences to the model. The children then played individually in a room with a Bobo doll and other toys. Those who had seen the model being rewarded for being aggressive were more aggressive in their play than were those who had seen the other two versions of the film. This experiment demonstrated that operant conditioning can occur vicariously, simply through observing others receiving positive reinforcement for engaging in the target behavior.

Over the past four decades, research and field studies have presented a complex picture of the effects of televised violence. A recent meta-analysis of relevant research studies found that there is a positive, significant correlation between televised violence and aggressive behavior (Paik & Comstock, 1994). Another meta-analysis found a causal relationship in which viewing televised aggression led to small increases in viewer aggression. This effect was stronger in cultures outside the United States (Hogben, 1998).

Children who watch television are exposed not only to antisocial models but also to prosocial models. Whereas children who watch violent programs tend to be more aggressive, children who watch altruistic programs such as *Mister Rogers' Neighborhood* tend to engage in more prosocial behaviors (Huston, Watkins, & Kunkel, 1989). In a recent study, Lawrence Rosenkoetter (1999) assessed whether elementary school-aged children understood the moral lessons in two situation comedies from the late 1980s and early 1990s, *The Cosby Show* and *Full House*. One-third of the first graders and one-half of the third graders in his sample were able to describe the prosocial theme of each show. Moreover, children's prosocial behavior was positively correlated with the frequency with which they viewed prosocial programs. This relationship was even stronger for the children who understood the underlying moral of the programming. Thus, children who watched such programs *and* understood their underlying messages engaged in more prosocial behavior.

As discussed in Chapter 4, television is only one of many influences on children's social development. The time children spend watching television is influenced by school and homework schedules, playing with other children, and other activities. One recent study of an ethnically diverse sample of children from low- and middle-income families found that participants who lived in more stimulating home environments and who had better educated mothers spent more of their television viewing time watching educational programming (Huston, Wright, Marquis, & Green, 1999). Thus, many psychologists believe that caregivers can exert considerable influence on children's viewing habits by using TV rating information to regulate television viewing and discussing program content with children (Abelman, 1999).

evidence for mirror neurons. Some researchers hypothesize that the social deficits seen in autism spectrum disorder and schizophrenia may arise from dysfunctional mirror-neuron networks (Datko, Pineda, & Müller, 2017). And in stroke patients, the action of observation followed by imitation is a useful approach for rehabilitation of disabilities (Small, Buccino, & Solodkin, 2012).

Observational learning can promote undesirable as well as desirable behavior. For example, we can develop phobias vicariously through observing people who exhibit them

> **Experiencing Psychology**
>
> ### Shaping the Professor's Behavior—A Case Study
>
> Shaping has proved to be a powerful tool in conditioning behaviors that have little or no chance of occurring spontaneously. Shaping has contributed to areas as diverse as industry, parenting, education, animal training, athletic training, and treating mental hospital patients. This activity will provide you with experience in shaping to condition the behavior of your introductory psychology professor.
>
> ### Method
> #### Participant
> The participant will be your introductory psychology professor. Because you will be using shaping to condition your professor's behavior, the students should inform the professor that they intend to shape an unidentified but nonembarrassing behavior.
>
> #### Materials
> You will need a pen and a sheet of paper to record each of your professor's behaviors and each time he or she receives a positive reinforcer.
>
> #### Procedure
> The students should agree on a behavior to shape. Some possibilities include having the professor touch his or her face, lecture toward one side of the room, or lecture from a particular spot in the room. Feel free to choose another (nonembarrassing) behavior. Do not inform your professor of the specific behavior you will be shaping. Of course, you must first obtain your professor's permission to do this demonstration.
>
> After you have obtained permission and have identified a behavior to shape, you must decide on the positive reinforcer to use. Possible positive reinforcers include smiling at the professor, making eye contact with the professor, raising one's hand to make a comment, and appearing to be studiously taking notes. Once you have decided on the positive reinforcer to use, the students should agree on the sequence of behaviors to positively reinforce as successive approximations of the target behavior. Then proceed to shape your professor's behavior during a class lecture. The students must reinforce each successive behavior immediately after it occurs.
>
> The students should try to be subtle in providing positive reinforcement. If all the students suddenly smile or make eye contact or perform some other simultaneous action, it might become too obvious to the professor. Thus, it would be advisable to have only certain students assigned to provide the positive reinforcer. Continue this procedure for as many class sessions as it takes to achieve the target behavior.
>
> Record how many reinforcements are required to establish the target behavior. Also record how long the professor engages in the target behavior during the class session after the one in which it first occurs. On the class session following the one in which the target behavior is established, stop the positive reinforcement. Measure how long the professor engages in the target behavior during the next three sessions.
>
> ### Results
> Using data recorded by each of the students and finding the mean, note how many sessions and reinforcements were needed to condition the target behavior. Also using the data recorded from each of the students and finding the mean, note how long the professor engaged in the target behavior on the day after it first appeared. Again using the data recorded from each of the students and finding the mean, note the average length of time the professor engaged in the behavior on the three nonreinforced sessions.
>
> ### Discussion
> Discuss how successful the students were in shaping the target behavior as well as any difficulties you encountered. Would you do anything different if you repeated this exercise? Did the professor become aware of the target behavior? If so, do you think that it helped or hindered the shaping of the target behavior? Suggest a related follow-up demonstration you would be interested in doing.

(Rachman, 1991). In fact, a study of people with spider phobia found that 71 percent traced it to observational learning, 57 percent to classical conditioning, and 45 percent to their knowledge of spiders (Merckelbach, Arntz, & de Jong, 1991). Even monkeys can develop fears through observing other monkeys (Mineka & Cook, 1993). For example, in a study that also found support for the concept of preparedness in the development of phobias through observation, rhesus monkeys watched videotapes of model monkeys showing fear of presumably fear-relevant stimuli (toy snakes or a toy crocodile) or presumably fear-irrelevant stimuli (flowers or a toy rabbit). The monkeys developed fears of the fear-relevant but not the fear-irrelevant stimuli (Cook & Mineka, 1989). Perhaps they are prepared by evolution to do so because such fears have survival value.

> ### Section Review: Cognitive Learning
>
> 1. How do experiments on blocking support a cognitive interpretation of classical conditioning?
> 2. In what ways do latent learning and observational learning support a cognitive view of learning?
> 3. How might mirror neurons help individuals empathize with emotions of other people?

Chapter Summary

Classical Conditioning

- Learning is a relatively permanent change in knowledge or behavior resulting from experience.
- In the kind of learning called classical conditioning, a stimulus (the conditioned stimulus) comes to elicit a response (the conditioned response) that it would not normally elicit. It does so by being paired with a stimulus (the unconditioned stimulus) that already elicits that response (the unconditioned response).
- In stimulus generalization, the conditioned response occurs in response to stimuli that are similar to the conditioned stimulus.
- In stimulus discrimination, the conditioned response occurs only in response to the conditioned stimulus.
- In extinction, the conditioned stimulus is repeatedly presented without the unconditioned stimulus, causing the conditioned response to diminish and eventually stop.
- In spontaneous recovery, a conditioned response that has been extinguished will reappear after the passage of time.
- Classical conditioning has been applied in many ways, as in explaining phobias, drug dependence, and learned taste aversions.
- Research has shown that in classical conditioning there are biological constraints on the ease with which particular stimuli can be associated with particular responses.

Operant Conditioning

- Operant conditioning involves learning the relationship between behaviors and consequences.
- There are four behavioral contingencies between behaviors and consequences: positive reinforcement, negative reinforcement, extinction, and punishment.
- In shaping, positive reinforcement involving successive approximations of the desired behavior is used to increase the likelihood of a behavior that is not in an individual's repertoire.
- In chaining, positive reinforcement is used to teach an individual to perform a series of behaviors.
- In operant conditioning, behavior is affected by schedules of reinforcement.
- In a continuous schedule, every instance of a desired behavior is reinforced.
- In partial schedules, reinforcement is not given for every instance.
- Partial schedules include ratio schedules, which provide reinforcement after a certain number of responses, and interval schedules, which provide reinforcement for the first desired response after a certain interval of time.
- In negative reinforcement, a behavior followed by the removal of an aversive stimulus becomes more likely to occur in the future.
- Negative reinforcement is implicated in avoidance learning and escape learning.
- When a behavior is no longer followed by reinforcement, it is subject to extinction.
- But after a period of time the behavior might reappear, in so-called spontaneous recovery.
- In punishment, an aversive consequence of a behavior decreases the likelihood of the behavior.
- To be effective, punishment should be immediate, firm, consistent, aimed at the misbehavior rather than the individual, and coupled with reinforcement of desirable behavior.
- Operant conditioning has even more diverse applications than does classical conditioning; these include animal training, child rearing, educational improvement, and understanding and treating psychological disorders.
- Biofeedback is a form of operant conditioning that enables an individual to learn to control a normally involuntary physiological response or to gain better control of a normally voluntary physiological response when provided with visual or auditory feedback of the state of that response.

- Like classical conditioning, operant conditioning is subject to biological constraints because members of particular species are more evolutionarily prepared to perform certain behaviors than to perform others.

Cognitive Learning
- Cognitive psychologists have shown that contiguity might not be sufficient to explain learning.
- Mere contiguity of a neutral stimulus and an unconditioned stimulus is insufficient to produce classical conditioning, and mere contiguity of a behavior and a consequence is insufficient to produce operant conditioning.
- Instead, for learning to occur, active cognitive assessment of the relationship between stimuli or the relationship between behaviors and consequences appears to be essential.
- In latent learning, learning is revealed in overt behavior only when reinforcement is provided for that behavior.
- Albert Bandura's social learning theory considers how individuals learn through observing the behavior of others.
- Mirror neurons may play a role in observational learning.
- There is a relationship between watching television and aggression and prosocial behavior.
- But the extent to which this relationship is causal is unclear.

Key Terms

Classical Conditioning
classical conditioning (p. 239)
conditioned response (CR) (p. 239)
conditioned stimulus (CS) (p. 239)
conditioned taste aversion (p. 244)
extinction (p. 241)
higher-order conditioning (p. 239)
learning (p. 238)
semantic conditioning (p. 240)
spontaneous recovery (p. 242)
stimulus discrimination (p. 241)
stimulus generalization (p. 241)
unconditioned response (UCR) (p. 239)
unconditioned stimulus (UCS) (p. 239)

Operant Conditioning
avoidance learning (p. 253)
behavioral contingencies (p. 248)
behavioral preparedness (p. 260)
biofeedback (p. 258)
chaining (p. 249)
computer-assisted instruction (p. 256)
continuous schedule of reinforcement (p. 251)
discriminative stimulus (p. 249)
escape learning (p. 253)
extinction (p. 253)
fixed-interval schedule of reinforcement (p. 251)
fixed-ratio schedule of reinforcement (p. 251)
instinctive drift (p. 260)
instrumental conditioning (p. 247)
law of effect (p. 247)
learned helplessness (p. 257)
negative reinforcement (p. 253)
operant conditioning (p. 247)
partial schedule of reinforcement (p. 251)
positive reinforcement (p. 248)
Premack principle (p. 248)
primary reinforcer (p. 248)
programmed instruction (p. 256)
punishment (p. 254)
secondary reinforcer (p. 248)
shaping (p. 249)
Skinner box (p. 247)
spontaneous recovery (p. 254)
token economy (p. 256)
variable-interval schedule of reinforcement (p. 252)
variable-ratio schedule of reinforcement (p. 251)

Cognitive Learning
blocking (p. 261)
latent learning (p. 262)
mirror neurons (p. 263)
observational learning (p. 263)
social learning theory (p. 263)

Chapter Quiz

Note: Answers for the Chapter Quiz questions are provided at the end of the book.

1. You wear a new jacket and receive many compliments, which makes you more likely to wear the jacket. This is an example of
   a. extinction.
   b. spontaneous recovery.
   c. positive reinforcement.
   d. negative reinforcement.

2. You have a toothache, which motivates you to go to the dentist. The dentist fills a cavity, eliminating your pain. When you have a toothache in the future, you will be more likely to go to the dentist. This is an example of
   a. extinction.
   b. punishment.
   c. positive reinforcement.
   d. negative reinforcement.

3. A psychologist decides to teach a child with an autism spectrum disorder how to cook a meal. She uses pieces of a chocolate chip cookie to reinforce the child for each of the steps in cooking a meal, until the child is able to perform each of the steps in sequence. This technique is called
   a. latent learning.
   b. behavioral chaining.
   c. programmed instruction.
   d. intermittent reinforcement.

4. You meet someone who reminds you of a former romantic partner and your heart "flutters." This is an example of
   a. response discrimination.
   b. stimulus discrimination.
   c. response generalization.
   d. stimulus generalization.

Chapter 7 Learning

5. According to the classical conditioning explanation of drug overdoses, they occur when the
   a. drug dose is preceded by a bell.
   b. unconditioned stimulus is no longer presented to the person.
   c. person self-administers a drug dose in unfamiliar circumstances.
   d. environment contains stimuli that are typically present when the individual self-administers a drug dose.

6. A particular child is more likely to draw pictures than to practice the piano. The child's parent does not permit him to draw until he has practiced the piano. This is an application of (the)
   a. chaining.
   b. latent learning.
   c. Premack principle.
   d. negative reinforcement.

7. A pigeon is reinforced for its first peck at a lighted disc after varying lengths of time. The pigeon is on a
   a. fixed-ratio schedule.
   b. fixed-interval schedule.
   c. variable-ratio schedule.
   d. variable-interval schedule.

8. A psychologist conditions a person to salivate to the word "Pavlov" by saying the word and then immediately placing lemon powder on the person's tongue. The lemon powder induces salivation. After several pairings of "Pavlov" and the lemon powder, the person salivates to the word "Pavlov" itself. The psychologist then presents the word "Skinner" before "Pavlov" and the lemon powder for several trials. Despite this, "Skinner" fails to elicit salivation. This is an example of
   a. blocking.
   b. extinction.
   c. latent learning.
   d. stimulus discrimination.

9. A child who plays with electrical outlets receives an electric shock, making her less likely to play with them in the future. In operant conditioning, this is an example of
   a. punishment.
   b. latent learning.
   c. spontaneous recovery.
   d. negative reinforcement.

10. A health psychologist conducts an experiment on the classical conditioning of the immune response to an allergen in guinea pigs. After she injects the guinea pigs with an allergen, they display an allergic (immune) response. She then presents a distinctive odor to the guinea pigs on several trials just before giving them the injection. The guinea pigs eventually display an allergic response to the odor. The odor is the
    a. conditioned response.
    b. conditioned stimulus.
    c. unconditioned response.
    d. unconditioned stimulus.

11. A child is reinforced with praise by his parents on some occasions that he brings home an "A" on a spelling test. Sometimes they praise the child, sometimes they do not—in a completely unpredictable manner. The child is on a
    a. fixed-ratio schedule.
    b. fixed-interval schedule.
    c. variable-ratio schedule.
    d. variable-interval schedule.

12. Each time you turn the ignition key in your car, the car starts. This means that you are on a
    a. continuous schedule of reinforcement.
    b. fixed-interval schedule of reinforcement.
    c. variable-ratio schedule of reinforcement.
    d. variable-interval schedule of reinforcement.

13. A form of operant conditioning that enables a person to learn to control a normally involuntary physiological process is called
    a. chaining.
    b. biofeedback.
    c. latent learning.
    d. spontaneous recovery.

14. When you see a green traffic light, you know that it is safe to drive across an intersection. According to B. F. Skinner, the light serves as a(n)
    a. primary reinforcer.
    b. unconditioned stimulus.
    c. discriminative stimulus.
    d. intermittent reinforcer.

15. A biopsychologist tries to condition constriction of the blood vessels of the skin in response to a tone. She sounds a tone, which is turned off before she directs a blast of cold air at the subject's right hand (which makes its peripheral vessels constrict). This would be an example of
    a. trace conditioning.
    b. delayed conditioning.
    c. backward conditioning.
    d. simultaneous conditioning.

16. Computer-assisted instruction, a descendant of teaching machines and programmed instruction, is most closely associated with
    a. latent learning.
    b. operant conditioning.
    c. classical conditioning.
    d. social-learning theory.

17. A child who normally throws temper tantrums in toy stores, and is reinforced by having his parents give in and buy him a toy, stops the tantrums when the parents no longer give in to them. But on visiting a toy store, after going three months without visiting one, the child again throws a tantrum. In operant conditioning, this is an example of
    a. punishment.
    b. latent learning.
    c. spontaneous recovery.
    d. negative reinforcement.

18. A relatively permanent change in knowledge or behavior resulting from experience is called
    a. instinct.
    b. learning.
    c. maturation.
    d. habituation.

19. A person decides to teach her dog to roll over. She uses dog treats to reinforce any slight rolling movement, then only larger rolling movements, and, eventually, only a complete roll. This technique makes use of
    a. shaping.
    b. latent learning.
    c. programmed instruction.
    d. secondary reinforcement.

20. Your friend, who drives a standard-shift car, suffers a leg injury and cannot drive home. Though you have only driven automatic-shift cars, you have observed other people drive cars with standard shifts. As a result, you succeed, despite shifting roughly, in driving your friend to the emergency room. This would be an example of
    a. blocking.
    b. latent learning.
    c. instinctive drift.
    d. learning without awareness.

21. A student calls her boyfriend every night just after 10 p.m., when he has returned home from his evening job. If she calls before 10, he is never home. If she calls after 10, she always reaches him. She is on a
    a. fixed-ratio schedule.
    b. fixed-interval schedule.
    c. variable-ratio schedule.
    d. variable-interval schedule.

22. You train a raccoon to take a tiny basketball and "dunk" it in a hoop. But, at times, the raccoon stops to wash the ball in a nearby puddle, much as it would wash food in the wild. This would be an example of
    a. extinction.
    b. latent learning.
    c. instinctive drift.
    d. spontaneous recovery.

23. The procedure in which a conditioned response is given to a neutral stimulus that has been paired with an existing conditioned stimulus is called
    a. shaping.
    b. chaining.
    c. instinctive drift.
    d. higher-order conditioning.

24. A dog learns that immediately after its owner opens the front door on returning home from work, food is placed in its food dish. The dog eventually salivates in response to the opening of the door. But the owner changes the dog's feeding schedule, placing food in the food dish an hour after returning home. The dog gradually stops salivating to the opening of the door. This is called
    a. shaping.
    b. extinction.
    c. spontaneous recovery.
    d. spontaneous remission.

25. On a quiz show, contestants are reinforced with $1000 after every three correct answers in a row. The contestants are on a
    a. fixed-ratio schedule.
    b. fixed-interval schedule.
    c. variable-ratio schedule.
    d. variable-interval schedule.

Thought Questions

1. How would you use shaping to teach a child to ride a tricycle?

2. What are the shortcomings of research on the use of conditioned taste aversion to prevent predators from killing sheep?

3. How does the phenomenon of blocking support a cognitive interpretation of classical conditioning?

4. How would you use the Premack principle to get a child to clean his room?

5. Why do researchers still disagree about the existence of a causal relationship between televised violence and real-life aggression?

CHAPTER 8

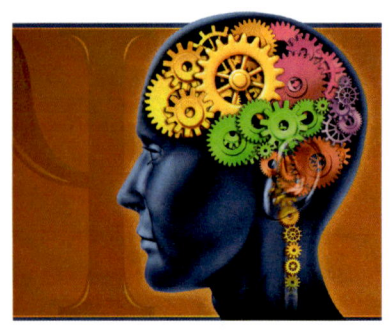

Memory

Source: Lightspring/Shutterstock.com.

Chapter Outline

Information Processing and Memory
Sensory Memory
Short-Term Memory
Long-Term Memory
Memory, Forgetting, and Eyewitness Testimony
Improving Your Memory
The Biopsychology of Memory

flashbulb memory A vivid, long-lasting memory of a surprising, important, emotionally arousing event.

In 1898, a survey of 179 middle-aged and elderly Americans asked, "Do you recall where you were when you heard that Lincoln was shot?" Of those surveyed, 127 claimed they could recall exactly where they were and what they were doing at that moment on April 14, 1865 (Colegrove, 1899). Such a vivid, long-lasting memory of an important, surprising, emotionally arousing event is called a **flashbulb memory** (Brown & Kulik, 1977). People with flashbulb memories of an event might recall who told them about it, where they were, and trivial things that occurred at the time.

Perhaps you have a flashbulb memory of your first kiss or an award you received. Depending on your age, you might have a flashbulb memory of the suicide airline attacks of September 11, 2001, the death of John F. Kennedy Jr., the massacre at Columbine High School in Colorado, or the death of Princess Diana (Hornstein, Brown, & Mulligan, 2003). Older adults might have a flashbulb memory from November 22, 1963, when they heard that President John F. Kennedy had been assassinated. A survey of over 600 Turkish residents found that flashbulb memories were more prevalent among participants who had personally experienced the 1999 Marmara earthquake than participants who had learned about the earthquake on the news. This finding supports research indicating that the formation of a flashbulb memory requires that an event be important and charged with emotion (Er, 2003).

What accounts for flashbulb memories? The answer is unclear and psychologists disagree on the mechanism responsible for this type of memory. You can imagine how hard it would be to simulate a surprising event in a laboratory setting that would result in such a memory. Some psychologists believe that flashbulb memories are the product of normal memory processes, such as thinking more often and more elaborately about such experiences (McCloskey, Wible, & Cohen, 1988). Likewise, other psychologists insist that the emotional nature of flashbulb memories can explain the phenomenon (Lanciano, Curci, & Semin, 2010).

One study tested the common belief that flashbulb memories are more accurate than everyday memories. On September 12, 2001, undergraduates completed questionnaires about their memories of the suicide airliner attacks on the United States and an unrelated event that occurred a few days before the attacks. One group of participants was retested 1 week later, a second group was retested 6 weeks later, and a third group was retested 32 weeks later. The accuracy of students' memories of the attacks and the everyday memories did not differ

Flashbulb Memories

Memory researchers are searching for explanations of flashbulb memories of momentous events, such as the devastating earthquake that occurred in the Philippines in October 2013.
Source: Richard Whitcomb/Shutterstock.com.

significantly; both memories declined with time. However, participants were significantly more confident about their memories of the attacks. These results indicate that flashbulb memories might seem special not because of a special mechanism but because of the undue confidence we place in them (Talarico & Rubin, 2003). Moreover, a survey of more than 3,000 residents of Great Britain regarding two major, unexpected events found that flashbulb memories might not be as vivid as commonly believed (Wright, Gaskell, & O'Muircheartaigh, 1998).

The exact nature of flashbulb memories will be discovered by research on **memory**, the process by which information is acquired, stored in the brain, later retrieved, and eventually possibly forgotten. As William James noted more than a century ago, memory provides our consciousness with its continuity over time. In the section "The Neuroanatomy of Memory," you will read about Henry Molaison, referred to before his death as H. M. for the purpose of participant anonymity, who suffered from brain damage that impaired his ability to maintain this continuity of consciousness. Memory also enables us to adapt to situations by letting us call on skills and information gained from our relevant past experiences. Your abilities to drive a car, to perform well on an exam, and to serve as a witness at a trial all depend on memory. Moreover, memory enriches our emotional lives. Your memory lets you re-experience events from your past, such as an uplifting family gathering.

In studying memory, psychologists consider several major "how" questions: How are memories formed? How are memories stored? How are memories retrieved? How are brain anatomy and brain chemistry related to memories? How dependable are eyewitness memories? This chapter addresses these questions.

memory The process by which information is acquired, stored in the brain, later retrieved, and eventually possibly forgotten.

Information Processing and Memory

During the past three decades, memory research has been driven by the "cognitive revolution" in psychology, which views the mind as an information processor. This predominance is reflected in the most influential model of memory, developed by Richard Shiffrin and Richard Atkinson (1969). Their model assumes that memory involves the processing of information in three successive stages: *sensory memory*, *short-term memory*, and *long-term memory*. **Sensory memory**, also known as the *sensory register*, is the first stage

sensory memory The stage of memory that briefly (for at most a few seconds) stores exact replicas of sensations.

Chapter 8 Memory 271

FIGURE 8-1
Memory Processes

The information-processing model of memory assumes that information (such as a seven-digit phone number) passes from sensory memory to short-term memory to long-term memory. Information might also pass from long-term memory to short-term memory. Each of the stages involves information encoding, storage, and retrieval.
Source: ImageFlow/Shutterstock.com.

short-term memory The stage of memory that can store a few items of unrehearsed information for up to about 20 seconds.

long-term memory The stage of memory that can store a virtually unlimited amount of information relatively permanently.

encoding The conversion of information into a form that can be stored in memory.

storage The retention of information in memory.

retrieval The recovery of information from memory.

forgetting The failure to retrieve information from memory.

information-processing model The view that the processing of memories involves encoding, storage, and retrieval.

of memory. In this stage, sensory information from the world around you is taken in by sensory receptors (see Chapter 5) and processed by the central nervous system. Sensory memories last for a brief period—from less than 1 second to several seconds. There are three types of sensory memory that have been studied: iconic (visual), haptic (touch), and echoic (auditory). When you attend to information in sensory memory, it is transferred to **short-term memory**, which stores it for about 20 seconds unless you maintain it through mental rehearsal—as when you repeat a phone number to yourself long enough to dial it. Information transferred from short-term memory into **long-term memory** can be stored for up to a lifetime. Your ability to recall old memories indicates that information also passes from long-term memory into short-term memory.

The handling of information at each memory stage has been compared to information processing by a computer, which involves encoding, storage, and retrieval. **Encoding** is the conversion of information into a form that can be stored in memory. When you strike the keys on a computer keyboard, your actions are translated into a code that the computer understands. Similarly, information in your memory is stored in codes that your brain can process. **Storage** is the retention of information in memory. Computers typically store information on hard drives or CDs. In human and animal memory, information is stored in the brain. **Retrieval** is the recovery of information from memory. When you strike certain keys, you provide the computer with cues that make it retrieve the information you desire. Similarly, we often rely on cues to retrieve memories that have been stored in the brain. We are also subject to **forgetting**—the failure to retrieve information from memory. Forgetting is analogous to the erasing of information on a hard drive. Figure 8-1 summarizes this **information-processing model** of memory. Though some psychologists question the existence of separate information-processing stages for sensory memory, short-term memory, and long-term memory, there is strong evidence in support of them (Cowan, 1988).

Section Review: Information Processing and Memory

1. What evidence is there that flashbulb memories are not the product of a special brain mechanism?
2. How do sensory memory, short-term memory, and long-term memory differ from one another?

Sensory Memory

Think back to the last movie you saw. It was actually a series of frames, each containing a picture slightly different from the one before it. So why did you see smooth motion instead of a rapidly presented series of individual pictures? You did so because of your *visual sensory memory*, which stores images for up to a second. Visual sensory memory is called **iconic memory**; an image stored in it is called an *icon* (from the Greek word for "image"). The movie projector presented the frames at a rate (commonly 24 frames a second) that made each successive frame appear just before the previous one left your iconic memory, blending together the successive images and creating the impression of smooth motion. You can demonstrate iconic memory by rapidly swinging a pen back and forth. Notice how iconic memory lets you see a blurred image of the path taken by the pen. But how much of the information that stimulates our visual receptors is stored in iconic memory? That question inspired the classic experiment discussed in "The Research Process" box.

Auditory sensory memory serves a purpose analogous to that of visual sensory memory, blending together successive pieces of auditory information. Auditory sensory memory is called **echoic memory** because sounds linger in it. Echoic memory stores information longer than iconic memory does, normally holding sounds for 3 or 4 seconds but perhaps as long as 10 seconds (Samms, Hari, Rif, & Knuutila, 1993). The greater persistence of information in echoic memory lets you perceive speech by blending together successive spoken sounds that you hear (Ardila, Montanes, & Gempeler, 1986). A good demonstration of your echoic memory is when someone says something to you that you do not become aware of until a few seconds after it was said. Suppose that while you are enthralled by a television show a friend asks, "Where did you put the can opener?" After a brief delay, you might say, "What? . . . Oh, it's in the drawer to the left of the sink." Researchers have identified a precise region in the primary auditory cortex that processes echoic memories (Lu, Williamson, & Kaufman, 1992).

Tactile sensory memory is based upon the sense of touch. Tactile sensory memory is called **haptic memory** and might be used when gripping familiar objects or assessing features or textures of novel objects. Information from the sensory receptors in the skin travels along sensory neurons to the spinal cord and ultimately to the somatosensory cortex in the parietal lobe of the brain. Recent evidence has shown that cells in the somatosensory cortex work together with cells in the visual and auditory cortex (Wang et al., 2015; Zhou & Fuster, 2004) to coordinate sensory memory. Studies such as these are helping to clarify the neural mechanisms that coordinate memory.

Based on Sperling's study and subsequent research, we know that sensory memory can store virtually all the information provided by our sensory receptors and that this information fades rapidly (though the fade rate varies among the senses). Nonetheless, we can retain information that is in sensory memory by attending to it and transferring it into short-term memory.

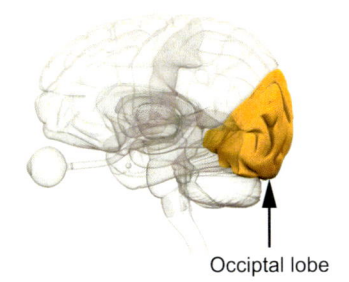

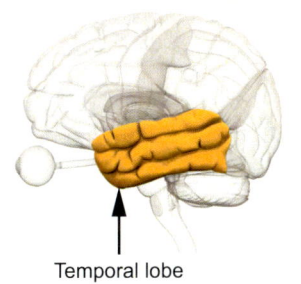

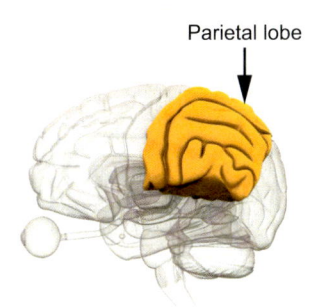

Occipital lobe

Temporal lobe

Parietal lobe

Locations of Sensory Memory

Animal studies have shown that the cells in the visual cortex (occipital lobe), auditory cortex (temporal lobe), and somatosensory lobe (parietal lobe) all contribute to sensory memory. Scientists are particularly interested in how these areas work together to create memories.

Source: decade3d - anatomy online/Shutterstock.com.

iconic memory Visual sensory memory, which lasts up to about a second.

echoic memory Auditory sensory memory, which lasts up to 4 or more seconds.

haptic memory Tactile sensory memory, which lasts up to 2 seconds.

Section Review: Sensory Memory

1. How did George Sperling demonstrate that iconic memory stores more information than commonly believed?
2. How does the relatively long duration of echoic memory help us perceive speech?

Short-Term Memory

When you pay attention to information in your sensory memory or information retrieved from your long-term memory, the information enters your short-term memory, which has a limited capacity and holds information for about 0.2 to 60 seconds. Because you are paying attention to this sentence, it has entered your short-term memory. In contrast, other information in your sensory memory, such as the feeling of your tongue touching your teeth, will not enter your short-term memory until your attention is directed to it. And note that you are able to comprehend the words in this sentence because you have

The Research Process

Do We Form Sensory Memories of All the Information That Stimulates Our Sensory Receptors?

Rationale
Though we have a sensory register for each of our senses, most research on sensory memory has been concerned with iconic memory. The classic experiment on iconic memory was carried out by a Harvard University doctoral student named George Sperling (1960). Sperling used an ingenious procedure to test the traditional wisdom that sensory memory stores only a small amount of the information that stimulates our sensory receptors.

Method
Sperling's procedure is illustrated in Figure 8-2. Participants, tested individually, stared at a screen on which Sperling projected sets of 12 letters, arranged in three rows of 4. Each presentation lasted for only 0.05 second—a mere flash. Sperling then asked the participants to report as many of the letters as possible. He found that the participants could accurately report an average of only 4 or 5 letters. Participants claimed, however, that they had briefly retained an image of the 12 letters, but by the time they had reported a few of them the remaining ones had faded away.

Rather than dismiss these claims, Sperling decided to test them experimentally by using a variation of this task. Instead of using whole report (asking participants to report as many of the 12 letters as possible), he used partial report (asking participants to report as many of the 4 letters as possible from a designated row). The task again included displays of 12 letters arranged in three rows of 4. But this time, at the instant the visual display was terminated, one of three different tones was sounded that indicated which row of letters was to be recalled.

Results and Discussion
When participants gave partial reports, they accurately reported an average of 3.3 of the 4 letters in a designated row. Because the participants did not know which row would be designated until after the display was terminated, the results indicated that, on the average, 9.9 of the 12 letters were stored in iconic memory. Sperling concluded that virtually all the information from visual receptors is stored as an image in iconic memory, but as his participants had claimed, the image fades rapidly.

These results inspired Sperling to seek the answer to another question: How fast does the information in iconic memory fade? He found the answer by repeating his partial-report procedure, but this time delaying the tone that signaled the participant to give a partial report. He varied the period of delay from 0.1 second to 1.0 second. As the delay lengthened, the participants' ability to recall letters in a designated row declined more and more. Sperling found that when the delay reached 1.0 second, the number of letters that could be recalled was about the same as when a whole report was used. Subsequent research has found that the typical duration of iconic memory is closer to 0.3 seconds than to 1.0 second (Loftus, Duncan, & Gehrig, 1992).

Fixation	Stimulus	Signal	Participant Report
+	D G P R X S M T C H Z L	High-pitched tone Medium-pitched tone Low-pitched tone	D G P R X S M T C H Z L

Time →

FIGURE 8-2 Testing Sensory Memory

In Sperling's (1960) study of sensory memory, the participant fixated on a cross on a projection screen. A display of letters was then flashed briefly on the screen. This procedure was repeated with many different displays. At varying times after a display had been flashed, a tone signaled the participant to report the letters in a particular row. These reports enabled Sperling to determine how many of the letters were stored in sensory memory. By delaying the tone for longer and longer intervals, Sperling also was able to determine how quickly images in sensory memory fade.

Source: G. Sperling, *Psychological Monographs*, 74 (whole no. 498), 1960.

retrieved their meanings from your long-term memory. Because we use short-term memory to think about information provided by either sensory memory or long-term memory, it also is called *working memory*. Though some cognitive psychologists prefer to distinguish between short-term memory and working memory (Kail & Hall, 2001), they have yet to agree on the characteristics that would differentiate the two.

Information stored in short-term memory is encoded as sounds or visual images and then manipulated in working memory (Logie, 1999). We typically encode information as sounds—even when the information is visual. This phenomenon was demonstrated in a study in which participants were shown a series of 6 letters and immediately were asked to try to recall them. The participants' errors showed that they more often confused letters that sounded alike (for example, T and C) than letters that looked alike (for example, Q and O). The letters, though presented visually, had been encoded according to their sounds (Conrad, 1962).

In comparison to sensory memory or long-term memory, short-term memory has a relatively small storage capacity. You can demonstrate this for yourself by performing this exercise: Read the following numerals one at a time, and then (without looking at them) write them down in order on a sheet of paper: 6, 3, 9, 1, 4, 6, 5. Next, read the following numerals one at a time and write them down from memory: 5, 8, 1, 3, 9, 2, 8, 6, 3, 1, 7. If you have average short-term memory storage capacity, you were probably able to recall the 7 numbers in the first set but not the 11 numbers in the second set.

The normal limit of seven items in short-term memory was the theme of a famous article by psychologist George Miller (1956) entitled "The Magical Number Seven, Plus or Minus Two." Miller noted that short-term memory can hold, on the average, seven "chunks" of information, with a range of five to nine chunks. His observation has received support from other research studies (Logie, 2012), though some researchers have found that the normal range of capacity is greater than five to nine chunks (H. V. Smith, 1992). A *chunk* is a meaningful unit of information, such as a date, a word, or an abbreviation. For example, to a college student familiar with American culture, a list that includes the meaningful chunks CBS, NFL, and FBI would be easier to recall than a list that includes the meaningless combinations of letters JOL, OBS, and CWE.

Miller noted that the ability to chunk individual items of information can increase the amount of information stored in short-term memory (Baddeley, 1994). For example, after a 5-second look at the positions of pieces on a chessboard, expert chess players are significantly better than novice chess players at reproducing the positions of the pieces. Chess experts have a greater ability to chunk chess pieces into thousands of familiar configurations (Chase & Simon, 1973). Thus, though chess experts do not store more memory chunks in their short-term memory than novices do, their memory chunks contain more information (Gobet & Simon, 1998).

Given that about 7 chunks is the typical amount of information in short-term memory, how long will it remain stored? Without **maintenance rehearsal** (that is, without repeating the information to ourselves), we can store information in short-term memory for no more than about 20 seconds. But if we use maintenance rehearsal, we can store it in short-term memory indefinitely. You could use maintenance rehearsal to remember the items on a short grocery list long enough to select each of them at the store.

Early evidence that unrehearsed information in short-term memory lasts perhaps 20 seconds came from a study conducted by Lloyd and Margaret Peterson (1959) in which they orally presented trigrams that consisted of three consonants (for example, VRG) to their participants. Their procedure is presented in Figure 8-3. To distract the participants and prevent them from engaging in maintenance rehearsal of the trigrams, immediately after a trigram was presented a light signaled the participant to count backward from a 3-digit number by threes (for example, "657, 654, 651, . . ."). Following an interval that varied from 3 seconds to 18 seconds, a light signaled that the participants were to recall the trigram. The longer the interval, the less likely the participants were to recall the trigram. And when the interval was 18 seconds, the participants rarely could recall the trigram. Thus, the results indicated that unrehearsed information normally remains in short-term memory for no longer than about 20 seconds.

maintenance rehearsal
Repeating information to oneself to keep it in short-term memory.

FIGURE 8-3

The Duration of Short-Term Memory

Peterson and Peterson (1959) demonstrated that the information in short-term memory lasts no more than 20 seconds. A warning light signaled that a trial was to begin. The participant then heard a 3-letter trigram and a 3-digit number. To prevent rehearsal of the trigram, the participant counted backward by threes from the number. After a period of 3 to 18 seconds, a light signaled the participant to recall the trigram. The longer the delay between presentation and recall of the trigram, the less likely the participant was to recall it accurately.

Source: L. R. Peterson and M. J. Peterson, "Short-Term Retention of Individual Items" in *Journal of Experimental Psychology*, 58: 193–198, 1959.

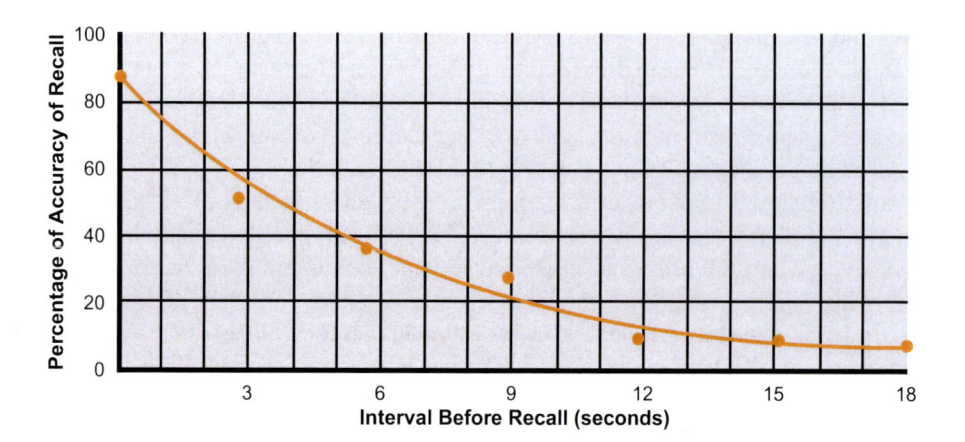

Information stored in short-term memory is commonly lost when other information interferes with it. For example, students who study while having the television playing in the background (Armstrong & Chung, 2000) often experience this loss. Background sounds interfere with the material that they have stored in short-term memory and prevent it from reaching long-term memory. Even low-volume irrelevant background sounds can markedly interfere with cognitive performance. Thus, simply turning down the volume will not be as beneficial as turning off the television.

Section Review: Short-Term Memory

1. Why do psychologists believe that visual information tends to be stored acoustically in short-term memory?
2. How did Lloyd and Margaret Peterson demonstrate that short-term memories last about 20 seconds?

Long-Term Memory

As mentioned earlier, information moves back and forth between short-term memory and long-term memory. Information processing in long-term memory has been compared to the workings of a library. Information in a library is encoded in materials such as books or magazines, stored on shelves in a systematic way, retrieved via cues given by online catalogs, and forgotten when it is misplaced or its computer record is erased. Similarly, information in long-term memory is encoded in several ways, stored in an organized manner, retrieved via cues, and forgotten because of a failure to store it adequately or to use appropriate retrieval cues.

Encoding

William James (1890/1981, Vol. 1, p. 646) noted, "A curious peculiarity of our memory is that things are impressed better by active than by passive repetition." To appreciate James's claim, try to draw the face side of a U.S. penny from memory. Next, look at the drawings of pennies in Figure 8-4. Which one is accurate? Even if you have handled thousands of pennies over the years and realize that the front of a penny has a date and a profile of Abraham Lincoln, you probably were unable to draw every detail. And even when presented with several drawings to choose from, you still might have chosen the wrong one. If you had difficulty, you are not alone. A study of adult Americans found that few could draw a penny from memory, and less than half could recognize the correct drawing of one (Nickerson & Adams, 1979).

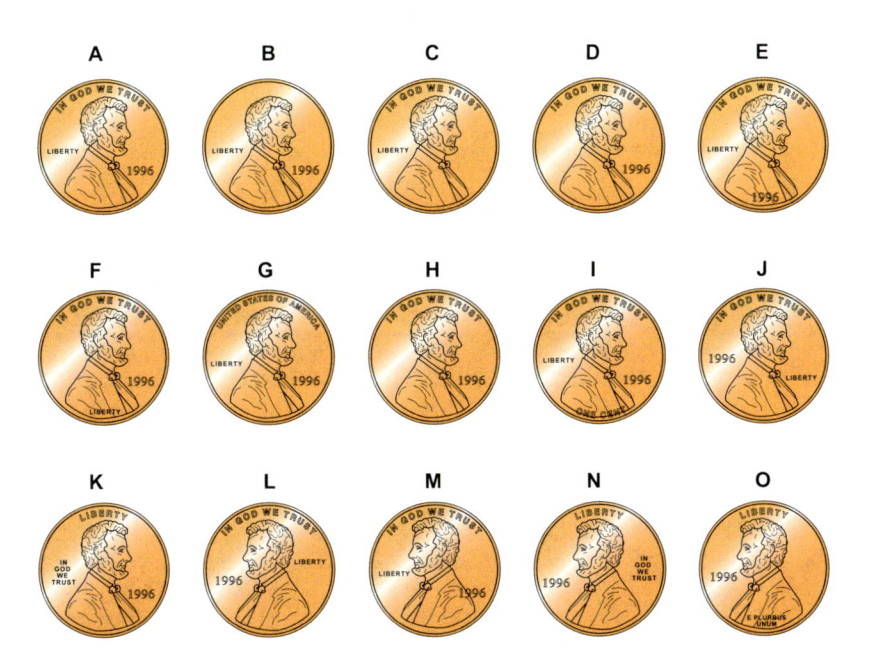

FIGURE 8-4

Can You Identify the Real Penny?

What accounts for our failure to remember an image that is a common part of everyday life? The answer depends in part on the distinction between *maintenance rehearsal* and *elaborative rehearsal*. As noted earlier, in using maintenance rehearsal, we simply hold information in short-term memory without trying to transfer it into long-term memory, as when we remember a phone number just long enough to dial it. In **elaborative rehearsal**, we actively organize information and integrate it with information already stored in long-term memory, as when studying material from this chapter for an exam. Though maintenance rehearsal can encode some information (such as the main features of a penny) into long-term memory (Wixted, 1991), elaborative rehearsal encodes more information (such as the exact arrangement of the features of a penny) into long-term memory (Greene, 1987).

You can experience the benefits of elaborative rehearsal when you are confronted by new concepts in a textbook. If you try to understand a concept by integrating it with information already in your long-term memory, you will be more likely to encode the concept firmly into your long-term memory. For example, when the concept "flashbulb memory" was introduced at the beginning of this chapter, you would have been more likely to encode the concept into long-term memory if it provoked you to think about your own flashbulb memories. Elaborative rehearsal also has important practical benefits. In one study, sixth graders who were taught cardiopulmonary resuscitation showed better retention of what they learned if they used elaborative rehearsal (Rivera-Tovar & Jones, 1990).

The superior encoding of information through elaborative rehearsal supports the **levels of processing theory** of Fergus Craik and Robert Lockhart (1972), which originally was presented as an alternative to the information-processing model of memory. Craik and Lockhart believe that the level, or "depth," at which we process information determines how well it is encoded and, as a result, how well it is encoded in memory (Lockhart & Craik, 1990). When you process information at a shallow level, you attend to its superficial, sensory qualities—as when you use maintenance rehearsal of a telephone number. In contrast, when you process information at a deep level, you attend to its meaning—as when you use elaborative rehearsal of textbook material. Similarly, if you merely listen to the sound of a popular song over and over on the radio—a relatively shallow level of processing—you might recall the melody but not the lyrics. But if you listen to the lyrics and think about their meaning (perhaps even connecting them to personally significant events)—a deeper level of processing—you might recall both the words and the melody. Functional MRI and PET scans have provided support for the levels of processing theory by revealing that different brain regions are more active during shallow information processing than during deeper, more semantic information processing (Nyberg, 2002).

elaborative rehearsal Actively organizing new information to make it more meaningful and integrating it with information already stored in long-term memory.

levels of processing theory The theory that the "depth" at which we process information determines how well it is encoded, stored, and retrieved.

Chapter 8 Memory

FIGURE 8-5
Levels of Processing

Craik and Tulving (1975) found that words that were processed at a deeper level were better remembered. Encoding words according to their meaning produced better recognition of them than did encoding them according to their sound or appearance.

Source: Data from F. I. M. Craik and E. Tulving, *Journal of Experimental Psychology: General*, 104: 268–294, American Psychological Association, 1975.

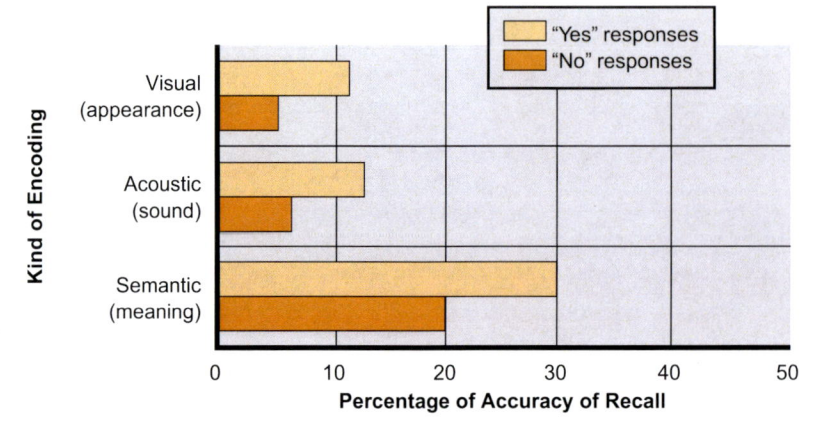

Level of Processing	Question	Answer Yes	Answer No
Visual (appearance)	Is the word presented in lowercase letters?	sofa	SOFA
Acoustic (sound)	Does the word rhyme with "look"?	book	DESK
Semantic (meaning)	Would the word fit in the sentence: "She left a _____ unlocked"?	DOOR	open

In a study that supported the levels of processing theory, researchers induced participants to process words at different levels by asking them different kinds of questions about each word just before it was flashed on a screen for a fifth of a second (Craik & Tulving, 1975). Imagine that you are replicating the study, and one of the words is *bread*. You could induce a shallow, *visual* level of encoding by asking how the word *looks*—for instance, "Is the word written in capital letters?" You could induce a somewhat deeper, *acoustic* level of encoding by asking how the word *sounds*—"Does the word rhyme with head?" And you could induce a much deeper, *semantic* level of encoding by asking a question related to what the word *means*—"Does the word fit in the sentence 'The boy used the ___ to make a sandwich'?" After repeating this procedure with several words, you would present participants with a list of words and ask them to identify which of the words had been presented before.

Craik and Tulving (1975) found that the deeper the level at which a word had been encoded, the more likely it was to be correctly identified (see Figure 8-5). Thus, the deeper the level at which information is encoded, the better it will be remembered. This conclusion has been supported by research showing that participants exhibited better recognition of previously presented words when they had attended to the words' meanings than when they had attended to the words' sounds (Ferlazzo, Conte, & Gentilomo, 1993). But some research findings indicate that the strength of the levels of processing effect depends on the nature of the material that is being processed in memory (Challis, Velichovsky, & Craik, 1996).

Storage

There are several major viewpoints on the nature of memory storage. Memory researchers look to *memory systems*, *semantic networks*, and *cognitive schemas* to explain the storage of memories.

Memory Systems

According to influential memory researcher Endel Tulving (1985), we store information in two kinds of long-term memory: **Procedural memory** includes memories of how to perform behaviors, such as making an omelet or using a computer; **declarative memory** includes memories of facts. Declarative memory and procedural memory also are referred

procedural memory The long-term memory system that contains memories of how to perform particular actions.

declarative memory The long-term memory system that contains memories of facts.

Chapter 8 Memory

to, respectively, as **explicit memory** and **implicit memory** (Schacter, 1992). Implicit memory for odors can influence human behavior, as in a study of adults who performed creative, counting, and mathematical tests in unscented rooms or rooms weakly scented with jasmine or lavender. Though none of the participants reported smelling either odor, the results showed that jasmine hurt performance and lavender helped performance (Degel & Koester, 1999). Research on advertising has found that it can produce effects on both implicit and explicit memory. That is, we may be affected by memories of information that we may not be aware of (Northrup & Mulligan, 2013).

Tulving (1993) subdivides declarative memory into *semantic memory* and *episodic memory*. **Semantic memory** includes memories of general knowledge, such as the definition of an omelet or the components of a personal computer. **Episodic memory** includes memories of personal experiences tied to particular times and places, such as the last time you made an omelet or used your computer.

Some memory researchers believe that the brain evolved different memory systems for storing these different kinds of memory into declarative memory for facts and events and procedural memory for skills, habits, and conditioned responses (Eichenbaum, 1997). There is evidence that brain-wave activity distinguishes different memory systems. Participants in one study were presented with a series of pairs of words and had to judge whether members of the pairs were related in meaning (semantic memory) or whether they had been presented with specific pairs before (episodic memory). The semantic memory task was associated with an abundance of alpha brain waves, and the episodic memory task was associated with an abundance of slower theta brain waves (Klimesch, 2012).

The main line of evidence in support of multiple memory systems in human beings comes from studies of people with brain damage. For example, either implicit or explicit memory can be intact while the other is impaired (Gabrieli Fleischman, Keane, & Reminger, 1995). In one case study (Schacter, 1983), a victim of Alzheimer's disease, which is a degenerative brain disorder marked by severe memory impairment, was able to play golf (procedural memory) and had good knowledge of the game (semantic memory) but could not find his tee shots (episodic memory). Though semantic memory and episodic memory are both forms of declarative memory, they may involve different brain systems. This conclusion is supported by PET scan studies that have found that different brain regions are involved in the performance of semantic and episodic memory tasks (Viard, Chételat, Lebreton, Desgranges, Landeau, de la Sayette, Eustache, & Piolino, 2011). Figure 8-6 illustrates the relationship of the different memory systems.

explicit memory Conscious recollection of general information or personal experiences.

implicit memory Recollection of previous experiences demonstrated through behavior rather than through conscious, intentional remembering.

semantic memory The subsystem of declarative memory that contains general information about the world.

episodic memory The subsystem of declarative memory that contains memories of personal experiences tied to particular times and places.

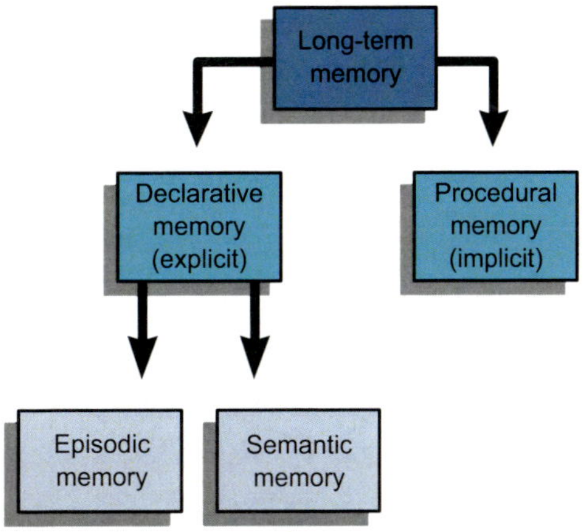

FIGURE 8-6 Memory Systems

Some memory researchers believe that there is sufficient behavioral and physiological evidence for the existence of memory systems that store different kinds of information. The declarative memory system stores explicit memories, which involve factual information that can be consciously recalled. Whereas the semantic memory system stores general information, the episodic memory system stores information about personal experiences. The procedural memory system stores implicit memories, which involve behavioral tendencies that can occur without conscious recollection of their origins. These memories include skills, habits, and conditioned responses.

Nonetheless, some theorists believe that the selective loss of procedural, semantic, or episodic memories does not necessarily mean that we have separate memory systems (Horner, 1990). The question that many memory researchers seek to answer is this: Do different brain systems serve the different kinds of memory, or does a single brain system serve all of them? Regardless of how many memory systems we have, long-term memories must be stored in a systematic way. Unlike short-term memory, in which a few unorganized items of information can be stored and retrieved efficiently, long-term memory requires that millions of pieces of information be stored in an organized rather than arbitrary manner. Otherwise, you might spend years searching your memory until you retrieved the memory you wanted, just as you might spend years searching the Library of Congress for William James's *The Principles of Psychology* if the library's books were shelved randomly. The better we are at organizing our memories, the better our recall of them is (Bjorklund & Buchanan, 1989). For example, a study of a server who could take 20 complete full-course dinner orders without writing them down found that he did so by quickly categorizing the items into meaningful groupings. When he was prevented from doing so, he was unable to recall all the orders (Ericsson & Polson, 1988).

Semantic Networks

semantic network theory The theory that memories are stored as nodes interconnected by links that represent their relationships.

A theory that explains how semantic information is meaningfully organized in long-term memory is the **semantic network theory**, which assumes that semantic memories are stored as nodes interconnected by links (see Figure 8-7). A *node* is a concept such as "pencil," "green," "uncle," or "cold," and a *link* is a connection between two concepts. More related nodes have shorter (that is, stronger) links between them. Even young children organize memories into semantic networks. For example, preschool children who enjoy playing with toy dinosaurs and listening to their parents read to them about dinosaurs may organize their knowledge of dinosaurs into semantic networks (Chi & Koeske, 1983). The dinosaurs would be represented as nodes (for example, "Brontosaurus" or *"Tyrannosaurus rex"*), and their relationships would be represented by links. The retrieval of a dinosaur's name from memory would activate nodes with which it is linked. So, retrieval of *Brontosaurus* would be more likely to activate nodes that contain the names of other plant-eating dinosaurs than nodes that contain the names of meat-eating dinosaurs, such as *Tyrannosaurus rex*. Deterioration of semantic networks may help account for the memory and language disruption seen in many people with schizophrenia (Brébion, et al., 2013) or Alzheimer's disease (Chan, Salmon, & De La Pena, 2001).

Cognitive Schemas

schema theory The theory that long-term memories are stored as parts of schemas, which are cognitive structures that organize knowledge about events or objects.

An alternative to the semantic network theory of memory organization is **schema theory**, which is used to explain both episodic memory and semantic memory. Schema theory

FIGURE 8-7
A Semantic Network Model

According to Collins and Loftus (1975), our long-term memories are organized into semantic networks in which concepts are interconnected by links. The shorter the link between two concepts, the stronger the association between them. After a retrieval cue has activated a concept, related concepts will also be activated and retrieved from long-term memory.

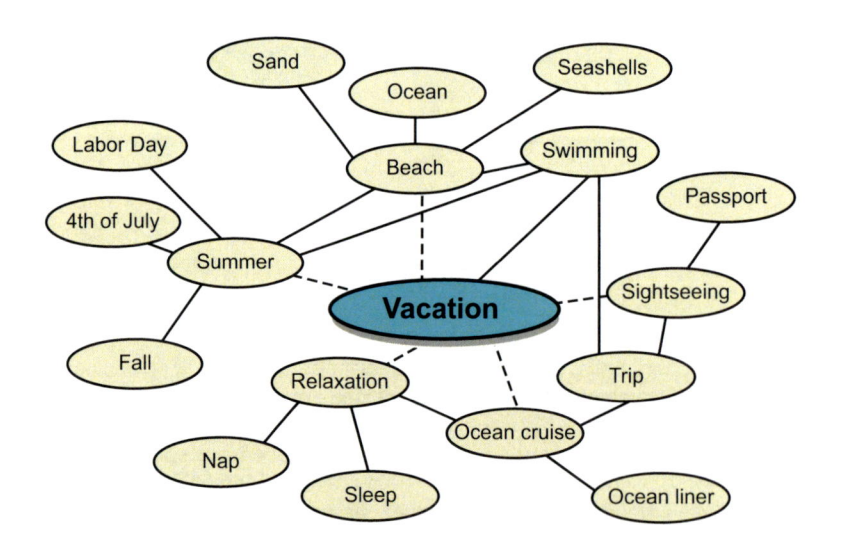

280 Chapter 8 Memory

was put forth decades ago by the English psychologist Frederic Bartlett (1932), who found that long-term memories are stored as parts of schemas. A *schema* is a cognitive structure that organizes knowledge about an event or an object and that affects the encoding, storage, and retrieval of information related to it (Alba & Hasher, 1983). Examples of schemas include "birthday party," "class clown," and "Caribbean vacation."

In a classic study, Bartlett instructed British college students to read a Native American folktale that told about a warrior fighting ghosts and later to write the story from memory. He found that the participants recalled the theme of the story but added, eliminated, or changed details to fit their own story schemas. For example, the participants added a moral, left out an event, or altered an aspect (such as changing a canoe to a boat). The reconfiguration of details in memory has received some support from more recent experiments (Ahlberg & Sharps, 2002).

Cultural schemas, which include the experiences, conventions, and expectations particular to one's culture, also can influence memory for stories. In a similar study, children from Papua, New Guinea, and the United States were read two fables ("The Boy Who Cried Wolf" and "Stone Soup"). Like the participants in Bartlett's study, the children changed many of the details in their retelling of the stories. Moreover, there were significant cross-cultural differences in the retelling of these stories, which were attributed to cultural differences in story schemas (Invernizzi & Abouzeid, 1995). Schema theory also has been used to explain gender differences in memory. In one study, children were taken to a playroom where they played with toys for 2 minutes. Half the toys were male-stereotyped (e.g., a space shuttle and train), and half were female-stereotyped (e.g., a Barbie doll and a tea set). Later, each child was asked to identify the toys from the playroom from a set of picture cards provided by the experimenter. Though there were no gender differences in the number of items identified, both girls and boys recognized more toys that were traditionally associated with their sex (Cherney & Ryalls, 1999). These results are consistent with studies that have reported similar biases in memory of masculine and feminine behaviors and female and male characters in children's literature (Signorella, Bigler, & Liben, 1997).

Other researchers have begun to investigate the influence of gender schemas on autobiographical memory in adults and children. In a series of studies, Penelope Davis (1999) found that women and girls reported more childhood memories—and accessed these memories more rapidly—than did men and boys. This gender difference was observed for events that were associated with both positive and negative emotions. In other words, female participants were more likely to recall incidents in which they, or others, were happy, sad, or fearful. Moreover, this gender difference also has been observed for everyday life events that are not associated with strong emotions (Seidlitz & Diener, 1998). The results of these studies have been attributed to gender differences in the socialization of emotional expression in men and women that influence the encoding of life events (Bauer, Stennes, & Haight, 2003).

Retrieval

Memory researchers are not only interested in how we encode and store memories but also in how we retrieve them. Psychologists who favor the semantic network theory study the role of *spreading activation*, and psychologists who favor schema theory study the role of *constructive recall*.

Spreading Activation

> In short, we may search in our memory for forgotten ideas, just as we rummage our house for a lost object. In both cases, we visit what seems to us the probable neighborhood of that which we miss. We turn over the things under which, or within which, or alongside which, it may possibly be; and if it lies near them, it soon comes to view. But these matters, in the case of a mental object sought, are nothing but its *associatives*. (James, 1890/1981, Vol. 1, p. 615)

The semantic network theory of memory agrees with William James's statement that the retrieval of memories from long-term memory begins by searching a particular region of memory and then tracing the associations among nodes (memories) in that region, rather than by haphazardly searching through information stored in long-term memory. The retrieval of a node from memory stimulates activation of related nodes, so-called *spreading activation* (Collins & Loftus, 1975). This process is analogous to looking for a book in a library. You would use the online catalog to give you a retrieval cue (a book number) to help you locate the book you want. Similarly, when you are given a memory retrieval cue, the relevant stored memories are activated, which in turn activate memories with which they are linked (Anderson, 1983). In keeping with this phenomenon, advertisers incorporate distinctive retrieval cues in their advertisements for specific products so that the repetition of those cues will evoke recall of those products. For example, a study found that the use of a visual cue helped children recall advertised cereal better and made them more likely to ask their parents to buy the cereal (Macklin, 1994).

To illustrate retrieval from a semantic network, suppose that you were given the cue "sensory memory." If your semantic network were well organized, the cue might activate nodes for "Sperling," "iconic," and "partial report." But if your semantic network were less well organized, the cue might also activate nodes for "amnesia," "chunks," or "Alzheimer's." And if your semantic network were poorly organized, the cue might activate nodes completely unrelated to sensory memory, such as "hallucination," "sensory deprivation," or "extrasensory perception."

Research findings indicate that spreading activation is important in a variety of contexts. The retrieval of mathematical facts depends on spreading activation within an arithmetic memory network (Niedeggen & Roesler, 1999). Word retrieval, as in the case of translation, among bilingual speakers also depends on spreading inactivation with the two language networks (Zhou & Li, 2013). And a study of radiologists found that their ability to make correct diagnoses from X-ray films depended in part on how well their relevant semantic networks facilitated spreading activation (Raufaste, Eyrolle, & Marine, 1998).

Constructive Recall

In contrast to semantic network theory, schema theory assumes that when we retrieve memories we might alter them to make them consistent with our schemas. An example of the schematic nature of memory retrieval, taken from testimony about the 1972 Watergate burglary that led to the resignation of President Richard Nixon, was provided by the eminent memory researcher Ulric Neisser (1981). Neisser described how a schema influenced the testimony of John Dean, former legal counsel to President Nixon, before the Senate Watergate Investigating Committee in 1973. Dean began his opening testimony with a 245-page statement in which he recalled the details of dozens of meetings that he had attended over a period of several years. Dean's apparently phenomenal recall of minute details prompted Senator Daniel Inouye of Hawaii to ask skeptically, "Have you always had a facility for recalling the details of conversations which took place many months ago?" (Neisser, 1981, p. 1).

Neisser found that Inouye's skepticism was well founded. In comparing Dean's testimony with tape recordings (secretly made by Nixon) of those conversations, Neisser found that Dean's recall of their themes was accurate, but his recall of many of the details was inaccurate. Neisser took this finding as evidence for Dean's reliance on a schema to retrieve memories. The schema reflected Dean's knowledge that there had been a cover-up of the Watergate break-in. Neisser (1984) used this analysis to support his conclusion that, in recalling real-life events, we rely on constructive recall more often than literal recall.

constructive recall The distortion of memories by adding, dropping, or changing details to fit a schema.

What Neisser called **constructive recall** is the distortion of memories by adding or changing details to fit a schema (Schacter, Norman, & Koutstaal, 1998). Schemas in the form of scripts for particular events even can affect eyewitness testimony. For example, the scripts we have for different crimes can affect our recall of events related to them. We might recall things that did not actually occur during a robbery if they fit our script for that kind of robbery (Garcia-Bajos & Migueles, 2003). Constructive recall might even explain why honest people have reported being abducted by aliens in UFOs. These people's memories might be constructed from nightmares, media attention, hypnotic suggestions during therapy, and support for their claims by alien-abduction groups (Clancy, 2007). But neither schema theory nor semantic network theory has yet emerged as the best explanation of the storage and retrieval of long-term memories. Perhaps a complete explanation requires both.

Forgetting

According to William James (1890/1981, Vol. 1, p. 640), "If we remembered everything, we should on most occasions be as ill off as if we remembered nothing." James believed that forgetting is adaptive because it rids us of useless information that might impair our recall of useful information. But as you are sometimes painfully aware of when taking exams, even useful information that has been stored in memory is not always retrievable. The inability to retrieve previously stored information is called *forgetting*.

Measuring Forgetting

The first formal research on forgetting was conducted by the German psychologist Hermann Ebbinghaus (1885/1913). Ebbinghaus (1850–1909) made a purposeful decision to do for the study of memory what Gustav Fechner had done for the study of sensation—subject it to the scientific method (Postman, 1985). Ebbinghaus studied memory by repeating lists of items over and over until he could recall them in order perfectly. The items he used were called *nonsense syllables* (consisting of a vowel between two consonants, such as VEM) because they were not real words. He used nonsense syllables instead of words because he wanted a "pure" measure of memory, unaffected by prior associations with real words. Despite this effort, he discovered that even nonsense syllables varied in their meaningfulness, depending on how similar they were to words or parts of words.

Ebbinghaus found that immediate recall is worse for items in the middle of a list than for those at the beginning and end of a list (see Figure 8-8). This differential forgetting is called the **serial-position effect** (Korsnes, Magnussen, & Reinvang, 1996). The better memory for items at the beginning of a list is called the *primacy effect*, and the better memory for items at the end of a list is called the *recency effect*. Thus, in memorizing a list of terms from this chapter, you would find it harder to memorize terms from the middle of the list than terms from the beginning or end of the list. The serial-position effect can even influence our memory for television commercials. A consumer psychology study demonstrated that when participants watched blocks of television commercials, their recall was worse for commercials in the middle of the blocks than at the beginning (especially) and end of the blocks. Television advertisers need to consider the relative placement of their advertisements for maximum impact on viewers' memories (Pieters & Bijmolt, 1997).

serial-position effect The superiority of immediate recall for items at the beginning and end of a list.

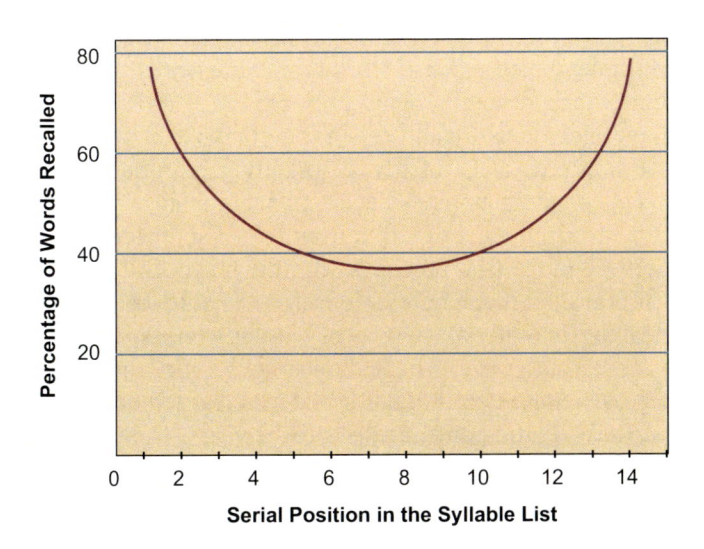

FIGURE 8-8
The Serial-Position Effect

This typical serial-position curve shows that items in the middle of a list are the most difficult to recall.

What accounts for the serial-position effect? The primacy effect seems to occur because the items at the beginning of a list are subjected to more rehearsal as a learner memorizes the list, firmly placing those items in long-term memory. And the recency effect seems to occur because items at the end of the list remain readily accessible in short-term memory. In contrast, items in the middle of the list are neither firmly placed in long-term memory nor readily accessible in short-term memory. Note that this explanation supports Shiffrin and Atkinson's distinction between short-term memory and long-term memory. Before Ebbinghaus's work, knowledge of memory was based on common sense, anecdotal reports, and reasoning, with little supporting empirical evidence. Ebbinghaus moved memory from the philosophical realm into the psychological realm, making it subject to scientific research.

method of savings The assessment of memory by comparing the time or number of trials needed to memorize a given amount of information and the time or number of trials needed to memorize it again at a later time.

Ebbinghaus also introduced the **method of savings**, which is commonly called *relearning*, as a way to assess memory. In using the method of savings, Ebbinghaus memorized items in a list until he could recall them perfectly, noting how many trials he needed to achieve perfect recall. After varying intervals, during which he naturally forgot some of the items, Ebbinghaus again memorized the list until he could recall it perfectly. The delay varied from 20 minutes to 31 days. He found that it took him fewer trials to relearn a list than to learn it originally. He called the difference between the number of original trials and the number of relearning trials *savings* because he relearned the material more quickly the second time. The phenomenon of savings demonstrates that even when we cannot recall information, much of it still remains stored in memory, even though it is inaccessible to recall. If it were not still stored, we would take just as long to relearn material as we took to learn it originally.

When you study for a cumulative final exam, you experience savings. Suppose that your psychology course lasts 15 weeks, and you study your notes and readings for 6 hours a week to perform at an A level on exams given during the semester. You will have studied for a total of 90 hours. If you then studied for a cumulative final exam, you would not have to study for 90 hours to memorize the material to your original level of mastery. In fact, you would have to study for only a few hours to master the material again. Savings occurs because relearning improves the retrieval of information stored in memory (MacLeod, 1988).

Relearning is a method of testing implicit memory because it assesses information that has been retained without necessarily being accessible to conscious awareness prior to relearning. As another example of an implicit memory test, consider the word-stem completion test. Suppose you are exposed in passing to a list of words that includes *telephone*. Later, despite having no recollection of having seen the word, you would be more likely to take the word stem *tele-* and form the word *telephone* than if you had not been exposed to that word earlier.

You are more familiar with tests of explicit memory. A *recognition test* measures your ability to identify information that you have been exposed to previously when it is presented again. Recognition tests that you might encounter in college include matching, true/false, and multiple-choice exams. A *recall test* measures your ability to remember information without the information being presented to you. Recall tests that you might encounter in college include essay and fill-in-the-blanks exams. Ebbinghaus also found that once we have mastered a list of items, forgetting is initially rapid and then slows (see Figure 8-9). This phenomenon has been replicated many times (Wixted & Ebbesen, 1991). So, if you memorized a list of terms from this chapter for an exam, you would do most of your forgetting in the first few days after the exam. But in keeping with the concept of levels of processing, meaningless nonsense syllables are initially forgotten more rapidly than is meaningful material, such as psychology terms.

forgetting curve A graph showing that forgetting is initially rapid and then slows.

Ebbinghaus's **forgetting curve**, which shows rapid initial forgetting followed by less and less forgetting over time, even holds for material learned decades before, as demonstrated in a recent study. Participants, aged 11 to 70 years, were former pupils of an elementary school in the Molenberg neighborhood of Heerlen in the Netherlands. Though some of the participants had not lived in the neighborhood for 50 years, they showed sur-

FIGURE 8-9
The Forgetting Curve

The graph presents the results of a study by Ebbinghaus on memory for nonsense syllables. It shows that forgetting is initially rapid and then levels off.

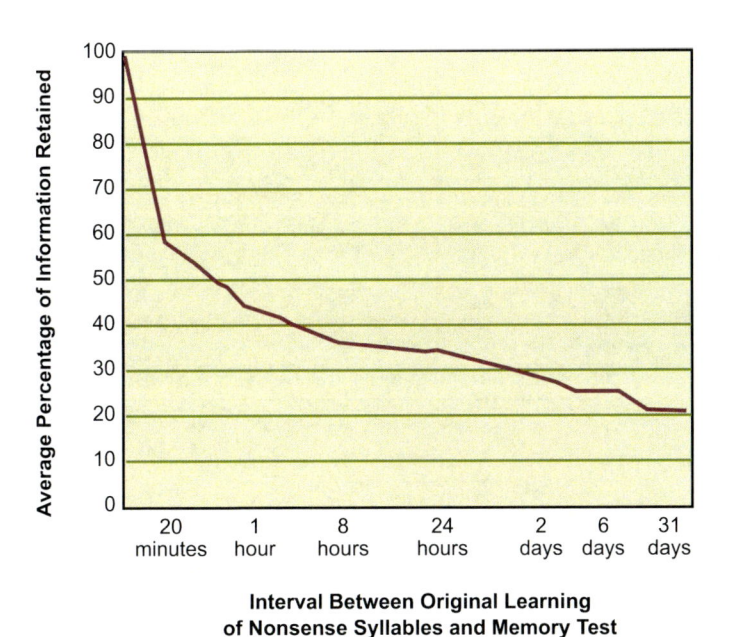

prisingly good retention of the street names. Their forgetting was rapid in the first 5 years after leaving the neighborhood, but then it stabilized for more than 40 years after leaving. After a certain amount of time, memories that have not been forgotten can become permanently held, in a kind of "permastore" (Schmidt et al., 2000).

Explanations of Forgetting

During the past century, psychologists have provided several explanations of forgetting. These include *trace decay, interference, motivation,* and *encoding specificity*.

Trace Decay Plato, anticipating **decay theory**, likened memory to an imprint made on a block of soft wax: Just as soft-wax imprints disappear over time, memories fade over time. But decay theory has received little research support, and a classic study provided evidence against it. John Jenkins and Karl Dallenbach (1924) had participants memorize a list of 10 nonsense syllables and then either stay awake or immediately go to sleep for 1, 2, 4, or 8 hours. At the end of each period, the participants tried to recall the nonsense syllables. The researchers wondered whether sleep would prevent waking activities from interfering with the memories.

The graph in Figure 8-10 shows that participants had better recall if they slept than if they remained awake. There was some memory loss during sleep, providing modest support for decay theory, but if decay theory were an adequate explanation of forgetting, participants should have shown the same level of recall whether they remained awake or slept. Jenkins and Dallenbach concluded that participants forgot more of the nonsense syllables if they remained awake because experiences they had while awake interfered with their memories. In contrast, participants had forgotten fewer nonsense syllables after sleeping because they had few experiences while asleep that could interfere with their memories for the nonsense syllables. The durability of many childhood memories throughout adulthood, such as memories of your childhood neighborhood held in "permastore," also provides evidence against the decay theory.

Interference Since Jenkins and Dallenbach's classic study contradicting decay theory, psychologists have come to favor interference as a better explanation of forgetting. **Interference theory** assumes that forgetting results from particular memories' interfering with the retrieval of other memories. Interference occurs, for example, when we try to recall advertisements for the myriad of products we are exposed to in everyday life (Kumar, 2000). In **proactive interference**, old memories interfere with new memories (if you move to a new home, for instance, your memory of your old phone number might

decay theory The theory that forgetting occurs because memories naturally fade over time.

interference theory The theory that forgetting results from some memories interfering with the ability to recall other memories.

proactive interference The process by which old memories interfere with the ability to recall new memories.

Chapter 8 Memory 285

FIGURE 8-10
Interference and Recall

Jenkins and Dallenbach (1924) found that when participants learned a list of nonsense syllables and then slept, they forgot fewer of the nonsense syllables than when they stayed awake.

Source: J. G. Jenkins and K. M. Dallenbach, "Obliviscence During Sleeping and Waking" in *American Journal of Psychology*, 35: 605–612, 1924.

FIGURE 8-11
Proactive and Retroactive Interference

Forgetting takes place, in part, because memories interfere with each other. In proactive interference, old memories interfere with new memories. In retroactive interference, new memories interfere with old memories.

retroactive interference The process by which new memories interfere with the ability to recall old memories.

repression In psychoanalytic theory, the defense mechanism that involves banishing threatening thoughts, feelings, and memories into the unconscious mind.

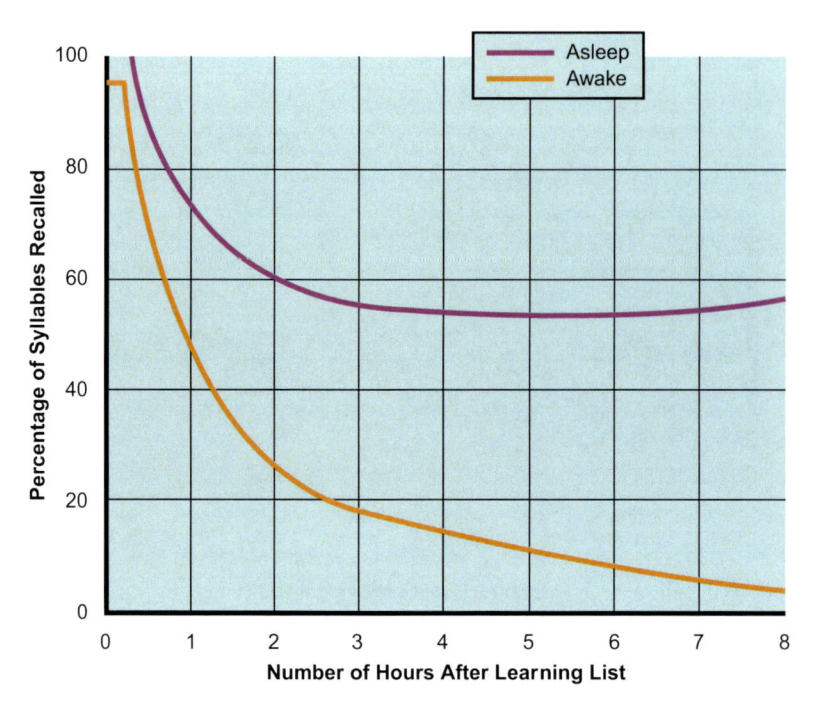

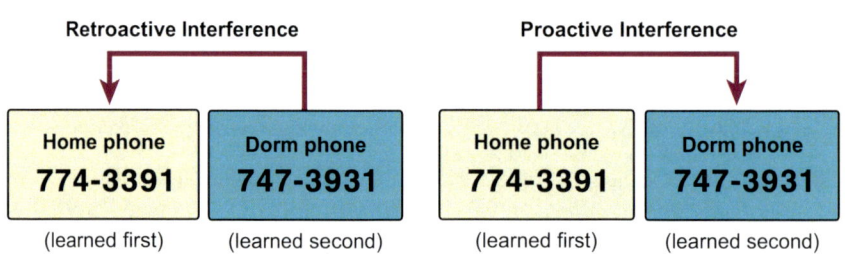

interfere with your ability to recall your new one). Proactive interference has been used to demonstrate that sign language and spoken language may be stored separately in human memory. A study found that there is less proactive interference in memory when old and new materials are each presented in a different language (that is, sign language and spoken language) than if both are presented in the same language (Hoemann & Keske, 1995). In **retroactive interference**, new memories interfere with old ones (your memory of your new phone number might interfere with your memory of your old one). Retroactive interference explains why learning a second language may interfere with our ability to retrieve words from our first language (Isurin & McDonald, 2001). Figure 8-11 illustrates the difference between proactive interference and retroactive interference.

You certainly have experienced both kinds of interference when taking an exam. Material you have studied for other courses sometimes interferes with your memories of the material on the exam. And interference is stronger when the materials are similar. Thus, biology material will interfere more than computer science material with your recall of psychology material. Because of the great amount of material you learn during a semester, proactive interference might be a particularly strong influence on your later exam performance (Dempster, 1985). So it would be best to study different subjects as far apart as possible rather than studying a bit of each every day. Moreover, be sure to study before going to sleep and right before your exam to reduce the effect of retroactive interference on your retrieval of relevant memories during the exam.

Motivation Sigmund Freud (1901/1965) claimed that we can forget experiences through **repression**, the process by which emotionally threatening experiences, such as witnessing a murder, are banished to the unconscious mind. Though research findings tend to

Chapter 8 Memory

Critical Thinking About Psychology

Should We Trust "Recovered Memories" of Childhood Abuse?

One day in 1989, Eileen Franklin-Lipsker looked into her 7-year-old daughter's eyes and was overcome by a horrible memory. Twenty years earlier, as an 8-year-old child, she had witnessed her father sexually assault and bludgeon to death her best friend, Susan Nason. Eileen recalled that her father, George Franklin, had warned her that he would kill her if she told anyone about the murder. Her attorney claimed that she had been so emotionally overwhelmed that she repressed the event for two decades—until the look in her daughter's eyes evoked the same feelings she had when looking into the eyes of Susan as she was being attacked. In 1990, George Franklin was convicted of murder (MacLean, 1993). The case was widely publicized by the media and was the basis of a made-for-television movie. In 1996, George Franklin's conviction was overturned on appeal because of a legal technicality.

Psychologists agree that most people with a history of childhood sexual assault remember all or part of their traumatic experiences. However, in a minority of cases, childhood memories of sexual abuse have resurfaced in adulthood. The media have become more skeptical in their treatment of such cases after finding that memory researchers are divided about whether to accept the validity of recovered memories. Researchers who support their validity believe that childhood trauma may result in total or partial amnesia and that memories may be recovered many years later (Alpert, Brown, & Courtois, 1998). Other researchers warn either that recovered memories are scientific fictions or that even if one accepts that phenomena such as dissociation or repression exists, therapists might purposely or unwittingly manipulate their clients into recalling vivid memories of events that never took place (Orenstein, Ceci, & Loftus, 1998). This manipulation becomes even more of an issue when therapists engage in "memory work" or in inappropriate use of techniques such as hypnosis to help their clients recover past memories. Hypnotized people are especially susceptible to forming memories of events that never took place (Wagstaff & Frost, 1996).

Researchers who believe there is little or no support for the validity of recovered memories call this phenomenon *false memory syndrome*. A national False Memory Syndrome Foundation in Philadelphia acts as a resource for people who claim they have been falsely accused of crimes based on recovered memories. People who claim they have been accused of crimes based on false recovered memories are suing therapists for implanting memories and convincing their clients of the reality of those memories. The notion that false memories may be created by therapists has a long history. In fact, the first documented creation of such a memory was reported in 1889 by the renowned French hypnotist Hippolyte Bernheim. Bernheim convinced a person that an extremely traumatic event had occurred, which led to the person's believing that this false memory was true (Rosen, Sageman, & Loftus, 2004). Nonetheless, supporters of the validity of recovered memories note that opposition to their existence comes primarily from memory researchers rather than from clinicians. Some clinicians insist that even though laboratory research has provided little support for this phenomenon, clinical experience with clients has convinced them that some cases of recovered memory are true (Critchlow, 1998). For example, clinicians have reported cases in which World War II veterans have recovered memories of traumatic, independently verified wartime experiences many years later—and obtained emotional relief by doing so (Karon & Widener, 1998).

But some memory researchers counter that these clinical reports are not reliable enough to support the validity of recovered memories (Lilienfeld & Loftus, 1998). Supporters of the validity of recovered memories point to scientific research indicating that recovered memories of childhood abuse can occur and that they are just as accurate as memories of abuse that have been recalled continuously from the time the events took place (Brown, Scheflin, & Whitfield, 1999). Other researchers claim that the memory processes of maltreated and healthy children are more similar than different (Howe, Toth, & Cicchetti, 2011), Memory researchers and clinicians do agree, though, that more research is necessary to identify the psychological processes that affect memory of childhood sexual abuse.

Expert memory researcher Elizabeth Loftus studies the fallibility of human memory. She insists that we might hold dearly to memories of events that never took place if we are led to believe they truly occurred through situations such as interviews conducted with leading questions. She stresses the need to protect both the accused and the accuser—a delicate balance, indeed. No one wants to see abusers or murderers go free. But no one wants to see innocent people convicted of acts they did not commit. Aside from concern that innocent people might be falsely accused based on therapist-induced memories, child advocates warn that such cases, when exposed, might undermine support for cases involving survivors of actual childhood sexual abuse (Lindsay, 1994).

Motivated Forgetting

According to Sigmund Freud, a person (such as children who experience trauma such as physical assault, warfare, or natural disasters) might forget a traumatic event by repressing its memory to the unconscious mind.

Source: kitty/Shutterstock.com.

contradict Freudian repression as an explanation of forgetting (Abrams, 1995), some studies suggest that we are more motivated to forget emotionally upsetting experiences than other kinds of experiences. Yet other studies find that there is no difference in recall of pleasant or unpleasant experiences (Bradley & Baddeley, 1990).

In an experiment that possibly demonstrated motivated forgetting, participants were shown one of two versions of a training film for bank tellers that depicted a simulated bank robbery. In one version, a shot fired by the robbers at pursuers hit a boy in the face. The boy fell to the ground, bleeding profusely. In the other version, instead of showing the boy being shot, the bank manager was shown talking about the robbery. When asked to recall details of the robbery, participants who had seen the violent version had poorer recall of the details of the crime than did participants who had seen the nonviolent version. One possible explanation is that the content of the violent version motivated participants to forget what they had seen (Loftus & Burns, 1982). However, in some cases, memory of traumatic events will be superior to memory of ordinary events (Christianson & Loftus, 1987).

Encoding Specificity Because the retrieval of long-term memories depends on adequate retrieval cues, forgetting sometimes can be explained by the failure to have or to use those cues. For example, odors that we associate with an event can aid our recall of it (Smith, Standing, & de Man, 1992). This explanation is known as *cue-dependence theory*. At times we might fail to find an adequate cue to activate the relevant portion of a semantic memory network. Consider the **tip-of-the-tongue phenomenon**, in which you cannot quite recall a familiar word—though you feel that you know it (Schwartz & Smith, 1997). As a demonstration, you might induce a tip-of-the-tongue experience by trying to recall the names of the seven dwarfs in the Snow White fairy tale. You might fail to recall one or two of them, yet still feel that you know them (Miserandino, 1991). The tip-of-the-tongue phenomenon indicates that when we speak, we might retrieve the meaning of a word before we retrieve its sound pattern (Vigliocco, Vinson, Martin, & Garrett, 1999). The frequency of tip-of-the-tongue experiences and the time that it takes to resolve them by retrieving the correct word increase with age (Heine, Ober, & Shenaut, 1999).

A study of the tip-of-the-tongue phenomenon presented college students with the faces of 50 celebrities and asked them to recall their names. The results indicated that the students searched for the names by using cues associated with the celebrities. The students tried to recall their professions, where they usually performed, and the last time they had seen them. Characteristics of the names also served as cues for recalling them. These cues included the first letters of the names, the first letters of similar-sounding names, and the number of syllables in the names (Yarmey, 1973). This study supports the concept of **encoding specificity**, which states that recall will be best when cues that were associated with the encoding of a memory are also present during attempts at retrieving the memory (Tulving & Thomson, 1973). Researchers interested in the role of encoding specificity in forgetting study *context-dependent memory* and *state-dependent memory*.

tip-of-the-tongue phenomenon The inability to recall information that one knows has been stored in long-term memory.

encoding specificity The principle that recall will be best when cues that were associated with the encoding of a memory are also present during attempts at retrieving it.

Context-Dependent Memory In an unusual experiment on encoding specificity, scuba divers memorized lists of words while either underwater or on a beach, and then tried to recall the words while either in the same location or in the other location (Godden & Baddeley, 1975). The participants communicated with the experimenter through a special intercom system. The results indicated that when participants memorized and recalled the words in different locations, they recalled about 30 percent fewer than when they memorized and recalled the words in the same location. This tendency for recall to be best when the environmental context present during the encoding of a memory also is present during attempts at retrieving it is known as **context-dependent memory**. The findings of the study even have practical implications. Instructions given to scuba divers should be given underwater as well as on dry land, and if divers are making observations about what they see underwater, they should record them there and not wait until they get on dry land (Baddeley, 1982).

When you return to your old school or neighborhood, long-lost memories might come flooding back, evoked by environmental cues that you had not been exposed to for years. This effect of environmental context on recall is not lost on theater directors, who hold dress rehearsals in full costume amid the scenery that will be used during actual performances. Similarly, even your academic performance can be affected by environmental cues (Parker & Gellatly, 1997), as in a study in which college students read an article in either noisy or silent conditions and then were tested on their comprehension of it in either noisy or silent conditions (Grant et al., 1998). They performed better when they read the article and were tested under the same conditions (noisy-noisy or silent-silent) than when they did so under different conditions (noisy-silent or silent-noisy). Likewise, college students may perform worse when their exams are given in classrooms other than their normal ones (Abernethy, 1940). Perhaps you have noticed this phenomenon when you have taken a final exam in a strange room. If you find yourself in that situation, you might improve your performance by mentally reinstating the environmental context in which you learned the material (Smith, 1984).

There is controversy among memory researchers about whether the environmental context is important when *recall* is required but not when *recognition* is required. In other words, your performance on an essay exam might be impaired if you took the exam in a strange room, but your performance on a multiple-choice test would not. Perhaps tasks that require recognition include enough retrieval cues of their own, making environmental retrieval cues relatively less important (Eich, 1980). But some research indicates that even recognition memory is affected by environmental context. In one study, participants observed a person and then were asked to identify the individual in a photo lineup. Some participants had to identify the individual under the same environmental context, and some under different contexts. Recognition was better under the same context. In fact, participants who simply imagined the original context improved their recognition performance (Smith & Vela, 1992).

State-Dependent Memory Our recall of memories depends not only on cues from the external environment but also on cues from our internal states. The effect on recall of the similarity between a person's internal state during encoding and during retrieval is called **state-dependent memory**. For example, memories encoded while the person is in a psychoactive drug-induced state will be recalled better when the person is in that state. A variety of drugs induce state-dependent memory, a fact first noted in 1835 (Overton, 1991). These drugs include alcohol (Nakagawa & Iwasaki, 1996), benzodiazepines (Sanday, Zanin, Patti, Tufkik, & Frussa-Filho, 2012), and barbiturates (Kumar, Ramalingam, & Karanth, 1994). Likewise, people who learn material while exercising on a bicycle ergometer will recall the material better if they do so while exercising on a bicycle ergometer (Miles & Hardman, 1998). Given this phenomenon, perhaps people who discuss business deals during aerobic exercise might have some difficulty recalling what they discussed when they return to their offices.

In a government-sponsored study on the possible state-dependent effects of marijuana (Eich, Weingartner, Stillman, & Gillin, 1975), one group of participants memorized a list of words after smoking marijuana, and a second group memorized the same list after smoking

context-dependent memory The tendency for recall to be best when the environmental context present during the encoding of a memory is also present during attempts at retrieving it.

state-dependent memory The tendency for recall to be best when one's emotional or physiological state is the same during the recall of a memory as it was during the encoding of that memory.

State-Dependent Memory

Memory retrieval is most efficient when you are in the same emotional or physiological state as when the memory was encoded.

Source: Rommel Canlas/Shutterstock.com.

a placebo that tasted like marijuana. Participants were "blind"; that is, they did not know whether they were smoking marijuana or a placebo. Four hours later, half of each group smoked either marijuana or a placebo and then tried to recall the words they had memorized. Recall was better either when participants smoked the placebo on both occasions or when they smoked marijuana on both occasions than when they smoked marijuana on one occasion and the placebo on the other. You should *not* conclude that marijuana smoking improves memory. As noted in Chapter 6, marijuana actually impairs memory. And indeed, in this study the group who smoked the placebo on both occasions performed *better* than the groups who smoked marijuana on either occasion or both occasions.

Our internal states also involve our moods, which can play a role in a form of state-dependent memory called *mood-dependent memory*, in which our recall of information that has been encoded in a particular mood will be best when we are in that mood again. If you study material while listening to music that evokes a particular mood and then are tested on the material later, you might perform better if you are tested while listening to music that evokes a similar mood (Balch, Myers, & Papotto, 1999). Mood appears to act as a cue for the retrieval of memories. In one study, one group of undergraduates memorized a word list while in a state of fear, and a second group memorized a word list while in a state of relaxation. Recall was better for participants who learned and recalled the word lists in the same emotional state (Robinson & Rollings, 2011). Thus, if you have an emotional experience, you might be more likely to recall details of that experience when you are again experiencing the same emotion.

> ### Section Review: Long-Term Memory
>
> 1. How does the superiority of elaborative rehearsal, compared to maintenance rehearsal, support the levels of processing theory of long-term memory encoding?
>
> 2. What is the difference between procedural memory and declarative memory?
>
> 3. What is the difference between proactive and retroactive interference?
>
> 4. What evidence is there to support the notion of state-dependent memory?

Memory, Forgetting, and Eyewitness Testimony

In August 1979, Father Bernard Pagano went on trial for a series of armed robberies. Eyewitnesses had identified him as the so-called gentleman bandit, a polite man who had robbed several convenience stores in Wilmington, Delaware. Father Pagano was arrested after several people who knew him told the police that he resembled published drawings of the bandit. Seven eyewitnesses, who were shown photographs in which Father Pagano wore his clerical collar, identified him as the robber. They might have been influenced by previous police reports that indicated that the perpetrator looked like a clergyman. Fortunately for Father Pagano, while he was on trial, another man, Ronald Clouser, confessed to the crimes (Rodgers, 1982).

There was little resemblance between Father Pagano and Ronald Clouser. The possibility of convicting innocent people or of exonerating guilty people based on inaccurate eyewitness testimony has led psychologists to study the factors that affect eyewitness memories. This concern is not new. Hugo Münsterberg (1908), a pioneer in the study of psychology and the law, warned us to consider the imperfections of human memory when evaluating the accuracy of **eyewitness testimony**. At about the same time, Alfred Binet, who gained fame for developing the first IQ test, championed the scientific study of eyewitness testimony. He introduced the *picture-description test*, which required participants to examine a picture of a scene and, after varying lengths of time, to recall as much as possible about the picture or to answer questions about it posed by an interrogator. Binet

eyewitness testimony
Witnesses' recollections about events, most notably about criminal activity.

found that eyewitness testimony usually included inaccuracies and that testimony under questioning was less accurate than spontaneous testimony (Postman, 1985).

During the past few decades, psychologists have conducted many research studies of the factors that affect the accuracy of eyewitness testimony (Frenda, Nichols, & Loftus, 2011). Research on eyewitness memories shows that they are not like mental tape recordings that record and play back exact representations of events. Instead, eyewitness recollections are reconstructive, somewhat altering the events that they represent. For example, cognitive schemas can influence eyewitness testimony. When eyewitnesses are presented with an ambiguous crime schema, they are more likely to insert schema-consistent information that had not been present than schema-inconsistent information (Tuckey & Brewer, 2003).

The misidentification of Father Pagano would not surprise psychologists who study eyewitness testimony. They know that misidentifications from lineups of suspects are the single leading cause of wrongful criminal convictions (Lindsay & Pozzulo, 1999). Moreover, law enforcement and court procedures can contribute to misidentification of suspects. These procedures include the wording of questions, instructions for viewing lineups and mug shots, and exposing witnesses to information after the event (Kassin, Tubb, Hosch, & Memon, 2001).

The fragility of eyewitness testimony has been supported cross-culturally. In a study conducted in Japan based on a real-life event, customers (confederates of the researcher) visited stores and bought items from professional sales clerks. Three months later each clerk was asked to identify from a photograph the customer who had bought the items. Half the sales clerks recalled details of the event and the customer, but only two-thirds of those details were accurate. Of the two-thirds who claimed they could identify the customer from a photograph, only 14 percent were accurate (Naka, Itsukushima, & Itoh, 1996). And cross-cultural differences can influence eyewitness testimony. This finding was demonstrated in a study using 48 Spanish and 48 English undergraduates. Participants were shown two films, one of an event common in Spanish culture and one of an event common in English culture. Later they were asked to recall what they had seen. Perhaps contrary to common sense, recall accuracy was greater for the event that was not from the participants' own culture (Davies & Alonso-Quecuty, 1997).

A number of studies have found that recall is even less accurate when eyewitnesses are asked to recognize persons from other ethnic groups (Bothwell, Brigham, & Malpass, 1989). In one study, European American and African American participants were more accurate when they identified suspects from their own ethnic group (Devine & Malpass, 1985). These findings have been replicated with Latino (Platz & Hosch, 1988) and Asian samples (Ng & Lindsay, 1994). Two of the main topics of interest regarding eyewitness testimony are the accuracy of children's eyewitness testimony and the effects of questioning on eyewitness testimony.

Children as Eyewitnesses

An issue that has concerned psychologists since the beginning of the 20th century is whether the testimony of children is trustworthy (Ceci & Bruck, 1993). As first demonstrated by the German psychologist William Stern, children tend to be less accurate than adults in their eyewitness accounts of crimes, in part because they are more suggestible—that is, they are more susceptible to leading questions (Templeton & Wilcox, 2000). Concerns about children as eyewitnesses have been supported by research indicating that misleading information about events can distort children's memories of them. In an experiment that tested this finding, children aged 3 to 12 years listened to a story about a girl who had a *stomachache* after eating *eggs* too fast. When asked questions about the story, the children answered correctly almost all the time. But when asked if they remembered the story of a little girl who got a *headache* because she ate her *cereal* too fast, the children typically responded that they had. The effect of misleading questions was greater on the younger children than on the older ones (Ceci, Ross, & Toglia, 1987).

Other studies likewise have found that the younger the children, the less accurate their testimony tends to be. In one such study, children 3 to 4 years old or 6 years old were interviewed

Psychology versus Common Sense

Can Leading Questions Alter Our Memories of Vivid Events?

One of the main factors potentially affecting eyewitness testimony is the wording of questions. If you saw an automobile accident and you were questioned about the automobile's speed, color, and direction, you probably would assume that your responses would be independent of these questions. Common sense tells you that being asked questions about your memory does not change your memories. In fact, a survey of university students found that they believed their own common sense was their single best source of information about eyewitness testimony (Shaw, Garcia, & McClure, 1999).

But Elizabeth Loftus, an expert on human memory and a contemporary pioneer in experimental research on eyewitness testimony, would disagree. Many of her research studies on eyewitness testimony have demonstrated that eyewitnesses might not only be subject to normal memory lapses but also to alterations in their memories produced by questioning by lawyers, prosecutors, and police officers. Judges and lawyers are taught to beware of leading questions, which can affect the testimony of eyewitnesses. Nonetheless, clever lawyers use subtle wording to influence testimony. In a dramatic study, Elizabeth Loftus and John Palmer (1974) examined the effect of leading questions regarding eyewitness accounts of an automobile accident.

Forty-five undergraduate participants viewed one of 7 driver education films of two-car automobile accidents lasting 5 to 30 seconds. Some participants were asked, "About how fast were the cars going when they smashed into each other?" Other participants were asked a similar question, with the word *smashed* replaced by *contacted*, *hit*, *bumped*, or *collided*. In a similar version of the experiment, another sample of 150 undergraduates likewise viewed films of two-car automobile accidents. Participants in one group were asked, "About how fast were the cars going when they smashed into each other?" and participants in a second group were asked, "About how fast were the cars going when they hit each other?" A week later, participants were asked, "Did you see any broken glass?" To avoid sensitizing participants to its purpose, the question was embedded in a list of 10 questions. In reality, there was no broken glass at the accident scene.

Participants' estimates of the speed of the cars in the first part of the study were influenced by the severity of the word used in the question. The average estimates for *contacted*, *hit*, *bumped*, *collided*, and *smashed* were, respectively, 31.8, 34.0, 38.1, 39.3, and 40.8 miles per hour. In the second part of the study, though there had been no broken glass, participants in both groups recalled seeing some. But participants who had been given the question containing the word

Elizabeth Loftus

"One reason most of us, as jurors, place so much faith in eyewitness testimony is that we are unaware of how many factors influence its accuracy."
Source: Courtesy Elizabeth Loftus.

about real and fictitious events and were asked whether the events had happened to them. The younger children were more likely than the older ones to claim they had experienced an event that they had only thought about. Such studies might help explain some cases in which young children have falsely claimed they were sexually abused only after being interviewed in some detail about the alleged abuse (Ceci, Huffman, & Smith, 1994).

Children also are more likely to guess when testifying, as in a study in which kindergartners viewed a slide show of a staged theft and then were asked to identify the perpetrator from a lineup. Many identified a person in the lineup even when the perpetrator was not in the lineup. Moreover, some children who had made correct identifications when the perpetrator was present in the lineup later identified a person in a lineup in which the perpetrator was absent. Children may have a tendency to guess or make up answers when they testify repeatedly about the same event (Ackil & Zaragoza, 1998; Beal, Schmitt, & Dekle, 1995). In fact, children are more reliable eyewitnesses when they are given an option to say that they are not sure when they are providing their testimony (Brewer, Keast, & Sauer, 2010).

> **Psychology versus Common Sense**
>
> **Can Leading Questions Alter Our Memories of Vivid Events?** *continued*
>
> *smashed* were significantly more likely to report having seen broken glass than were participants who had been given the question containing the word *hit*.
>
> Loftus's findings have been replicated in other studies. In one study, college students were shown a videotaped mock crime. One week later they read a passage that described the crime. The passage contained leading, misleading, or control (no supplemental) information. When asked to recall the crime they had witnessed, the participants placed more confidence in the biased information presented by the experimenter than in their own memories (Ryan & Geiselman, 1991).
>
> Studies like these demonstrate that the memories of eyewitnesses can be reconstructions, instead of exact replicas, of the events witnessed. Eyewitness memories can be altered by inaccurate information introduced during questioning. That is, "under some conditions misleading postevent information can impair the ability to remember what was witnessed and can lead people to believe that they witnessed things that they did not" (Lindsay, 1993, p. 86). To avoid such situations, leading questions are barred in courtroom proceedings. Though leading questions can affect the recall of eyewitnesses, research indicates that eyewitnesses might be less susceptible to them than had been suggested by earlier research (Kohnken & Maass, 1988).
>
> Eyewitness memory can be improved by relatively simple procedures. One procedure, based on the principle of encoding specificity, improves recall by mentally reinstating the physical setting of the event. In one study, store clerks were asked to identify a previously encountered customer from an array of photographs. The original context was reinstated by providing physical cues from the encounter and by instructing the clerk to mentally recall events that led up to the customer's purchase. As discussed earlier, mentally reinstating the context in which you learned something can improve your recall of it. In this study, the reinstatement of the original context led to a significant increase in the accuracy of identifications (Krafka & Penrod, 1985).
>
> We also can prevent misleading information from influencing the memories of eyewitnesses by warning them about that possibility. This was the finding of a study in which participants were warned just prior to the presentation of misleading information about a simulated crime. Participants viewed slides of a wallet being snatched from a woman's purse and then read descriptions of the crime. Participants who had been given warnings showed greater resistance to misleading information in the descriptions (Greene, Flynn, & Loftus, 1982). But some psychologists argue that informing jurors of the unreliability of eyewitness testimony might make already skeptical jurors too skeptical, perhaps leading to the exoneration of guilty persons (McCloskey & Egeth, 1983).
>
> Regardless of the exact extent to which eyewitness testimony can be influenced by misleading information and the reasons for that influence, Elizabeth Loftus believes that eyewitness testimony is, in fact, too easily affected by such information. She expressed this belief in a statement that was a takeoff on John B. Watson's claim (quoted in Chapter 1) regarding his ability to condition infants to become any kind of person one desired. Loftus remarked:
>
>> Give us a dozen healthy memories, well-informed, and our own specified world to handle them in. And we'll guarantee to take any at random and train it to become any type of memory that we might select—hammer, screwdriver, wrench, stop sign, yield sign, Indian chief—regardless of its origin or the brain that holds it. (Loftus & Hoffman, 1989, p. 103)

Not only are young children more fallible in their testimony than older children are, but also children tend to be less accurate in their testimony than adults. One study compared adults and children in the accuracy of their memories for an event they experienced 2 years earlier. The children were less accurate in responding to yes/no questions and open-ended questions and were more likely to fabricate responses to a question about a man's occupation. This fallibility might have an effect on court cases that take a long time to reach trial (Poole & White, 1993).

Of course, especially because of the prevalence of child sexual and physical abuse, courts must achieve a delicate balance between believing children's testimony and being skeptical of it (Goodman & Schaaf, 1997). Fortunately, children can give accurate testimony provided that they are not given leading questions and provided that the questions are worded so that the children can understand them (Brooks & Siegel, 1991). To promote accuracy in children's testimony, the questioning of children should be done by neutral parties rather than by individuals who are biased either toward or against believing the

Chapter 8 Memory

children's stories of abuse. Failure to do so might induce children to testify in a manner consistent with the questioner's personal agenda.

Questioning the Eyewitness

Though issues regarding the accuracy of children's eyewitness testimony have important social consequences, there has been even more research on the effects of questioning on adult eyewitness testimony. Because jurors attribute greater accuracy to the testimony of eyewitnesses who display confidence, an important factor in eyewitness testimony is how confident eyewitnesses are about their memories. In the 1972 case of *Neil v. Biggers*, the U.S. Supreme Court even ruled that one of the criteria that juries should use in judging the accuracy of an eyewitness's testimony is the degree of confidence expressed by the eyewitness. But this ruling might be misguided because eyewitnesses' level of confidence generally is unrelated to the accuracy of their testimony (Wells & Lindsay, 1985), and hypnotized witnesses may be subject to the formation of inaccurate "pseudomemories" (Green, Lynn, & Malinoski, 1998). As a consequence, it can be unwise for jurors to assume that a confident eyewitness is necessarily an accurate eyewitness.

Misinformation Effect

One reason police officers try to keep eyewitnesses separated while being questioned at the scene of a crime or accident is because of the misinformation effect.
Source: Photographee.eu/Shutterstock.com.

Section Review: Memory, Forgetting, and Eyewitness Testimony

1. What has research discovered about the accuracy of children's eyewitness testimony?
2. What concerns Elizabeth Loftus about the accuracy of eyewitness testimony?

Improving Your Memory

More than a century ago William James (1890/1981) criticized those who claimed that memory ability could be improved by practice. To James, memory was a fixed, inherited ability and not subject to improvement. He concluded this after finding that practice in memorizing did not decrease the time it took him and other participants to memorize poetry or other kinds of literature. Regardless of the extent to which memory ability is inherited, we certainly can make better use of the ability we have by improving our study habits and by using *mnemonic devices*. For example, expert taxi drivers make good use of memory techniques to help them recall street names (Kalakoski & Saariluoma, 2001).

Using Effective Study Habits

Given two students with equal memory ability, the one with better study habits probably will perform better in school (Sanghvi, 1995). To practice good study habits, you would begin by setting up a schedule in which you would do the bulk of your studying when you are most alert and most motivated—whether in the early morning, in the late afternoon, or at some other time. You also should study in a quiet, comfortable place, free of distractions. If you study in a dormitory lounge with students milling around and holding conversations, you might find yourself distracted from the information being processed in your short-term memory, making it more difficult for you to transfer the information efficiently into your long-term memory. As for particular study techniques, you might consider using the *SQ3R method*, *overlearning*, and *distributed practice*.

The SQ3R Method

SQ3R method A study technique in which the student surveys, questions, reads, recites, and reviews course material.

In the **SQ3R method** (Robinson, 1970), SQ3R stands for Survey, Question, Read, Recite, and Review. This method has proved helpful to students in college (Carlston, 2011) and elementary school (Darch, Carnine, & Kameenui, 1986). It requires elaborative rehearsal, in which you process information at a relatively deep level. This process is distinct from

Effective Study Habits

Good study habits include setting up a schedule and studying in a quiet place free of distractions.

Source: wavebreakmedia/Shutterstock.com.

rote memorization, in which you process information at a relatively shallow level. If you have ever found yourself studying for hours yet doing poorly on exams, it might be the consequence of failing to use elaborative rehearsal. For example, in one study students used either rote memory, writing down unfamiliar terms and their definitions, or elaborative rehearsal, writing down how the words might or might not describe them. One week later, students who had used elaborative rehearsal recalled significantly more definitions than did students who had used rote memory (Flannagan & Blick, 1989).

Suppose that you decide to use the SQ3R method to study the final section of this chapter. You would follow several steps:

- *Survey* the main headings and subheadings to create an organized framework in which to fit the information you are studying.
- As you survey the sections, ask yourself *questions* to be answered when you read them. For example, you might ask yourself, What is the physiological basis of memory?
- *Read* the material carefully, trying to answer your questions as you move through each section. In memorizing new terms, you might find it especially helpful to say them out loud. A study found that participants who read terms out loud remembered more of them than did participants who read them silently, wrote them down, or heard them spoken by someone else (Gathercole & Conway, 1988).
- After reading a section, *recite* information from it to see whether you understand it. Do not proceed to the next section until you understand the one you are studying.
- Periodically (perhaps every few days) *review* the information in the entire section by quizzing yourself on it and then rereading anything you fail to recall. Asking questions of yourself as you read can increase elaborative rehearsal and the depth of processing, thereby improving your memory for the material (Andre, 1979). You also will find yourself experiencing savings; each time you review the material, it will take you less time to reach the same level of mastery.

Overlearning Material

You also might wish to apply other principles to improve your studying. Take advantage of **overlearning**. That is, study the material until you feel you know all of it—and then go over it several more times. A meta-analysis of research studies found that overlearning significantly improves the retention of material (Driskell, Willis, & Copper, 1992). Overlearning appears to work by making you less likely to forget material you have studied and more confident that you know it (Nelson, Leonesio, Shimamura, Landwehr, & Narens, 1982). This method might improve your exam performance by making you less anxious. The power of overlearning is revealed by the amazing ability people show for recognizing the names and faces of their high school classmates decades after graduation. This ability is attributable to their having overlearned the names and faces during their years together in school (Bahrick, Bahrick, & Wittlinger, 1975).

overlearning Studying material beyond the point of initial mastery.

Chapter 8 Memory 295

Distributed Practice

distributed practice Spreading out the memorization of information or the learning of a motor skill over several sessions.

massed practice Cramming the memorization of information or the learning of a motor skill into one session.

Use **distributed practice** instead of **massed practice**. The advantage of distributed practice over massed practice is especially important in studying academic material (Benjamin & Tullis, 2010). If you can devote a total of 5 hours to studying this chapter, you would be better off studying for 1 hour on five different occasions than studying for 5 hours on one occasion. Moreover, longer breaks between practice sessions have been found to facilitate memory in more complex tasks (Donovan & Radosevich, 1999). You might recognize this method as a suggestion to avoid cramming for exams. Note how the following explanation by William James for the negative effects of cramming anticipated recent research into the effects of elaborative rehearsal, overlearning, environmental cues, and semantic networks on memory:

> The reason why *cramming* is such a bad mode of study is now made clear. . . . Things learned thus in a few hours, on one occasion, for one purpose, cannot possibly have formed many associations with other things in the mind. . . . Speedy oblivion is the almost inevitable fate of all that is committed to memory in this simple way. . . . Whereas on the contrary, the same information taken in gradually, day after day, recurring in different contexts, considered in various relations, associated with other external incidents, and repeatedly reflected on, grow into a fabric, lie open to so many paths of approach, that they remain permanent possessions. (James, 1890/1981, Vol. 1, pp. 623–624)

Even students who are learning English as a second language can benefit from distributed practice, as in a study of economics and business students whose native language was Malay. The students were assigned to groups that received a total of 5 study sessions that consisted of 3 daily sessions over the period of a week or a session every 14 days. The students were tested on their understanding of English syntax 7 days after the training and 2 months later. The group that had received distributed practice performed significantly better on both occasions. The results indicate that those who teach languages to non-native speakers might be wise to divide long sessions into shorter ones (Bird, 2011).

Using Mnemonic Devices

mnemonic device Techniques for organizing information to be memorized to make it easier to remember.

acronym A mnemonic device that involves forming a term from the first letters of a series of words that are to be recalled.

Mnemonic devices are techniques for organizing information and providing memory cues to make it easier to recall, such as learning the names of U.S. presidents (Mastropieri, Scruggs, & Whedon, 1997) or learning the names of unfamiliar animals (Carney & Levin, 2001). These devices are named after Mnemosyne, the Greek goddess of memory. You are familiar with certain mnemonic devices, such as *acronyms*. An **acronym** is a term formed from the first letters of a series of words. Examples of acronyms include *USA*, *NFL*, and even *SQ3R*. Many students have used the acronym *Roy G Biv* to help them recall the colors of the rainbow. Acronyms also have proved useful to psychiatrists, helping them recall the diagnostic criteria for psychological disorders (Pinkofsky, 1997).

You probably are familiar with the use of rhymes as mnemonic devices, as in "*I* before *e* except after *c*" and "Thirty days has September. . . ." Though rhymes are useful mnemonic devices, they sometimes can impair memory. In one study, children who listened to stories presented in prose had better recall of them than did children who listened to the stories presented in verse. Evidently, the children who listened to verse processed the stories at a shallow level, as sounds, whereas the children who listened to prose processed the stories at a deeper level, in terms of their meaning (Hayes, Chemelski, & Palmer, 1982). The possible negative effect of using rhyming to help children learn academic material has been replicated in other research studies (Hayes, 1999). Moreover, a study in which adults listened to radio advertisements and then were randomly assigned to use either a rhyming mnemonic or no rhyming mnemonic found no difference in their ability to remember the advertisements a week later (Smith & Phillips, 2001). The major mnemonic devices include the *method of loci*, the *pegword method*, and the *link method*.

296 Chapter 8 Memory

The Method of Loci

About 2,500 years ago the Greek poet Simonides stepped outside the banquet hall where he was to recite a poem in honor of a nobleman. While Simonides was outside, the hall collapsed, killing all the guests and maiming them beyond recognition. Yet, by recalling where each guest had been sitting, Simonides was able to identify each of them. He called this the **method of loci** (*loci* means "place" in Latin), which he recommended to orators because papers and pens were too expensive to waste on writing routine speeches (Bower, 1970). The method of loci is useful for memorizing lists of items. You might memorize concrete terms from this chapter by associating them with places and landmarks on your campus and then retrieving them while taking a mental walk across it. The method of loci has proved helpful in training patients who have undergone cardiac surgery to improve their memory and attention skills (Tourney-Jetté, Dupuis, Denault, Carter, & Bherer, 2012). Even the places on a Monopoly board have been used successfully to help students employ the method of loci (Schoen, 1996).

method of loci A mnemonic device in which items to be recalled are associated with landmarks in a familiar place and then recalled during a mental walk from one landmark to another.

The Pegword Method

A mnemonic device that relies on both imagery and rhyming is the **pegword method**, which begins with memorizing a list of concrete nouns that rhyme with the numbers 1, 2, 3, 4, 5, and so on. For this method to work well, the image of the pegword object and the image of the object to be recalled should interact rather than just be paired with each other (Wollen, Weber, & Lowry, 1972). Suppose that you wanted to remember the grocery list presented in Figure 8-12. You might imagine, among other things, sugar being poured from a shoe, bees in a hive brushing their teeth, and a hen drinking from a soda bottle. To recall an item, you would simply imagine the pegword that is paired with a particular number, which would act as a cue for retrieving the image of the object that interacted with that pegword. Thus, if you imagined a shoe, you would automatically retrieve an image of sugar being poured from it. The pegword method has proved successful even when used by young children to learn nouns (Krinsky & Krinsky, 1996). The effectiveness of the pegword method also was demonstrated in a study in which one group of undergraduates memorized lists of facts such as the world's 10 highest mountains using the pegword method and a second group of undergraduates memorized the list without using

pegword method A mnemonic device that involves associating items to be recalled with objects that rhyme with the numbers 1, 2, 3, and so on to make the items easier to recall.

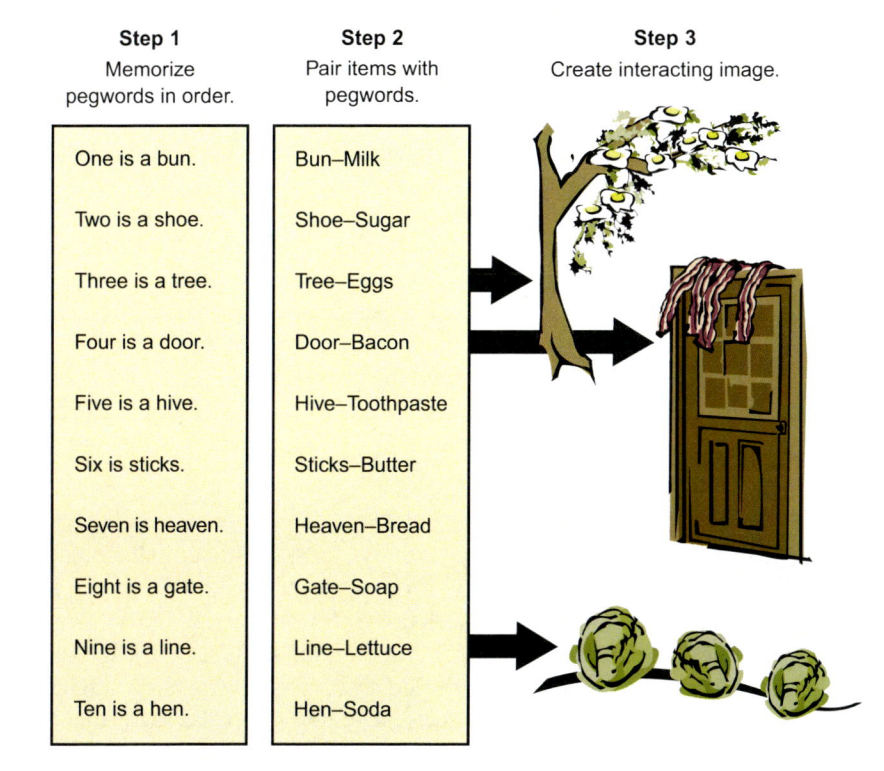

FIGURE 8-12
The Pegword Method

The pegword method can be used to recall a grocery list. Each grocery item is paired with a pegword. Thus, the retrieval of a pegword will cue the retrieval of the associated grocery item.

Step 1 Memorize pegwords in order.

One is a bun.
Two is a shoe.
Three is a tree.
Four is a door.
Five is a hive.
Six is sticks.
Seven is heaven.
Eight is a gate.
Nine is a line.
Ten is a hen.

Step 2 Pair items with pegwords.

Bun–Milk
Shoe–Sugar
Tree–Eggs
Door–Bacon
Hive–Toothpaste
Sticks–Butter
Heaven–Bread
Gate–Soap
Line–Lettuce
Hen–Soda

Step 3 Create interacting image.

Chapter 8 Memory

it. When asked to recall the list immediately and 2 days later, the group that used the pegword method performed significantly better than the other group (Carney & Levin, 2011).

The Link Method

link method A mnemonic device that involves connecting, in sequence, images of items to be memorized, to make them easier to recall.

Still another mnemonic device that makes use of imagery is the **link method**, which takes images of the items to be memorized and connects them in sequence. One version of the link method is the *narrative method*, in which unrelated items are connected to one another in a story. In a study that showed the effectiveness of the narrative method, two groups of participants memorized 12 lists of 10 nouns. One group used the narrative method to memorize the nouns; the other group used ordinary mental rehearsal. Both groups showed nearly perfect immediate recall. But when later asked to recall all the lists, the narrative group recalled an average of 93 percent of the words, whereas the mental rehearsal group recalled an average of only 13 percent (Bower & Clark, 1969). More recent research has replicated the effectiveness of this technique (Hill, Allen, & McWhorter, 1991).

Ironically, despite the usefulness of mnemonic devices, a survey of college professors found that memory researchers were no more likely than other professors to use formal mnemonic devices. Instead, memory researchers and other professors alike recommended that memory be improved by writing things down, by organizing material to be learned, or by rehearsing material to be remembered (Park, Smith, & Cavanaugh, 1990). Like physicians who smoke, memory researchers might not practice what they preach.

Section Review: Improving Your Memory

1. What are some suggestions for improving your study habits?
2. How would you use the pegword method to recall lists of objects?

The Biopsychology of Memory

Though study habits and mnemonic devices depend on overt behavior and mental processes, they ultimately work by affecting the encoding, storage, and retrieval of memories in the brain. Today, research on the neuroanatomy and neurochemistry of memory is revealing more and more about its biological bases.

The Neuroanatomy of Memory

During the first half of the 20th century, psychologist Karl Lashley (1890–1958) carried out an ambitious program of research aimed at finding the sites where individual memories are stored in the brain. Lashley trained rats to run through mazes to obtain food rewards. He then destroyed small areas of their cerebral cortex and noted whether this procedure made a difference in their maze performance. To Lashley's dismay, no matter what area he destroyed, the rats still negotiated the mazes, showing at most a slight decrement in performance. Lashley concluded that he had failed in his lifelong search for the *memory trace*, which he had assumed was the basis of memories (Lashley, 1950).

The Memory Trace

But many scientists remained undaunted by Lashley's pessimistic conclusion and continued to search for the site of a memory trace. This persistence paid off decades later when a team of researchers began studying the sea snail *Aplysia* (Kandel, 2001). This creature has relatively few but large neurons, making it a simpler subject of study than animals with complex brains. Researchers have identified a neuronal event formed when *Aplysia* is classically conditioned to withdraw its gills in response to the movement of water (Kandel & Schwartz, 1982). This withdrawal (the conditioned response) occurs after sev-

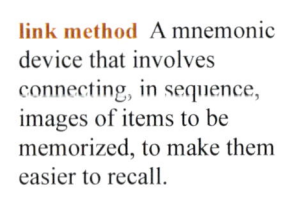

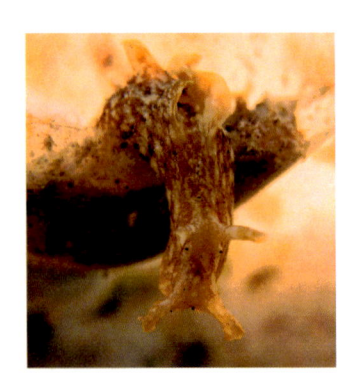

Aplysia
The sea slug, aplysia, is a model organism to study learning and memory because it has approximately 20,000 neurons.
Source: LauraD/Shutterstock.com.

eral trials in which the movement of the water (the conditioned stimulus) has preceded an electric shock (the unconditioned stimulus) that automatically elicits gill withdrawal (the unconditioned response). Eric Kandel, along with several colleagues, won the Nobel Prize in 2000 for studying memory in this approach. His work set the stage for understanding the biochemical changes in neurons associated with learning and memory.

Evidence for the localization of memory traces in more complex animals comes from research that has identified neural substrates in the cerebellum (see Chapter 3), a brain structure that plays a role in both memory and the maintenance of equilibrium. The researchers classically conditioned rabbits to blink in response to a tone. Presentations of the tone (the conditioned stimulus) were followed by puffs of air (the unconditioned stimulus) directed at the rabbit's eyes, which elicited blinking (the unconditioned response). After several pairings of the tone and puffs of air, the tone itself elicited blinking (the conditioned response). After conditioning, the researchers found that electrical stimulation of a tiny site in the cerebellum of the rabbit elicited the conditioned eyeblink, whereas destruction of the site eliminated it—but not the unconditioned response. Thus, they had succeeded in locating a neural substrate for a classically conditioned memory (Krupa, Thompson, & Thompson, 1993)—undoubtedly, not the only site.

The Synapse

As for human memory, in 1894 Sigmund Freud and Santiago Ramón y Cajal independently speculated that learning produces changes in the efficiency of synaptic connections between neurons and that these changes might be the basis of memory formation. Ramón y Cajal, speculated that neurons do not directly connect; rather they are separated by a microscopic synaptic gap. This speculation has been supported by research findings that the formation of memories is associated with synaptic changes, including increases in the number of dendritic branches and the number of *dendritic spines* at certain sites (Martin & Morris, 2002). Recent research indicates that memory also might depend on the facilitation of neural impulses across synapses in the brain. The most widely studied phenomenon related to the facilitation of neural impulses is **long-term potentiation**, in which synaptic transmission of impulses between two neurons is made more efficient by brief electrical stimulation of specific neural pathways (Thompson, 2000). This phenomenon, discovered in the hippocampus and only demonstrated in animals, is viewed as a possible basis for long-term memory because long-term potentiation induced by specific experiences might strengthen synaptic connections in specific pathways (Martinez & Derrick, 1996). Long-term memories also depend on the actions of proteins that strengthen particular synaptic connections (Steward & Worley, 2002).

The Hippocampus

Researchers who study long-term potentiation are particularly interested in the *hippocampus*, which lies deep within the temporal lobes and helps consolidate memories (Norman & O'Reilly, 2003). Figure 8-13 illustrates the location of the hippocampus and other brain structures important in memory, including the thalamus (Van Der Werf et al., 2003), the amygdala (Seidenbecher et al., 2003), and as mentioned earlier, the cerebellum (Linden, 2003). The amygdala is particularly important in the formation of emotional memories (Pare, Collins, & Guillaume Pelletier, 2002).

Long-term potentiation in the hippocampus apparently promotes the storage of new memories but is required for only a limited period of time after a learning experience. Evidence for this finding comes from animal studies in which the hippocampus is purposely damaged at varying times after learning. The longer the delay before hippocampal damage, the less effect it has on the storage of the new memories (Zola-Morgan & Squire, 1990). More evidence for the importance of the hippocampus in the formation of long-term memories comes from research on Alzheimer's disease, which is marked by degeneration of neural pathways from the hippocampus (Teipel et al., 2003). Victims of Alzheimer's disease have a progressively more difficult time forming new long-term memories, particularly declarative memories (Davis et al., 2002). Alzheimer's disease

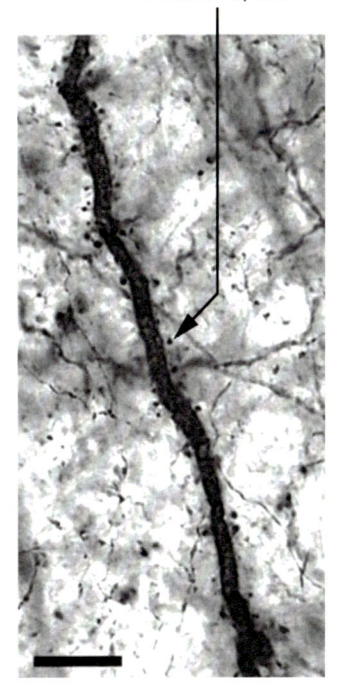

long-term potentiation A phenomenon related to the facilitation of neural impulses in which synaptic transmission of impulses is made more efficient by brief electrical stimulation of specific neural pathways.

Dendritic Spines

A photomicrograph of dendritic spines. A single neuron can contain hundreds to thousands of dendritic spines, thus allowing for increased contacts in the synapse between other neurons.
Source: Raddy Ramos.

FIGURE 8-13
Anatomy of Memory

The brain contains no distinct memory center. Instead, memory depends on the integration of activity in several areas of the brain, including the thalamus, the amygdala, the cerebellum, and especially the hippocampus.

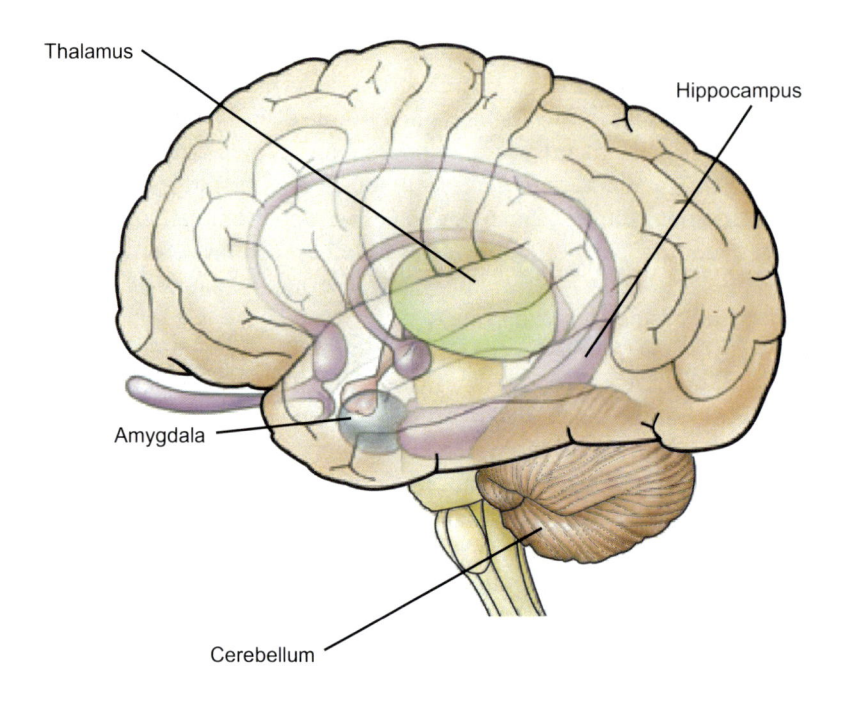

also is characterized by the buildup of wanted proteins called *beta-amyloid* plaques. In animal models of Alzheimer's disease using transgenic mice with extra beta-amyloid, long-term potentiation is difficult to induce (Kimura, MacTavish, Yang, Westaway, & Jhamandas, 2012). Recently, advances were made in studying long-term potentiation-like events in humans using transcranial magnetic stimulation, a technique that places a magnetic field over the head. Researchers found that patients with Alzheimer's disease had impaired long-term potentiation signal events in their brains (Koch et al., 2012). This indicates that this deficit accounts for the lack of plasticity and potential for learning and forming new memories. Nevertheless, we know that the hippocampus plays a role in the consolidation of short-term memory into long-term memory, but the exact sites of memory storage are unknown.

The hippocampus might provide an explanation for *infantile amnesia*, the inability to recall declarative memories from early childhood. A study of college students found that their earliest childhood memories were from age 2 for a hospitalization or the birth of a sibling and from age 3 for the death of a family member or a family move to a new home. If these events occurred earlier, the students were unable to recall them (Usher & Neisser, 1993). Perhaps infantile amnesia occurs because the hippocampus is too physically immature during infancy to consolidate short-term declarative memories into long-term ones. Note that we show perfectly good retention of procedural memories from infancy. Such memories, which involve skills, habits, and conditioned responses, do not seem to depend on the hippocampus.

The most celebrated single source of evidence for the role of the hippocampus and adjacent medial temporal lobe structures in memory comes from the case study of Henry Molaison (1926–2008), better known as H. M. H. M. was studied most notably since the mid-1950s by Brenda Milner of the Montreal Neurological Institute (Scoville & Milner, 1957) and since the early 1960s by her former graduate student Suzanne Corkin of the Massachusetts Institute of Technology. H. M. had formed few new declarative memories since undergoing brain surgery in 1953, when he was 27 years old. The surgery, performed to relieve uncontrollable epileptic seizures, removed almost all of his hippocampus. As a result, H. M. developed anterograde amnesia, marked by the partial or complete inability to form new long-term declarative memories. After his surgery, H. M. was able to form several new semantic memories, but no episodic memories (Corkin, 2004). Because he could not recall events since his surgery, he felt that each moment of his life was like waking from a dream—short-term memories continually entered his consciousness and then faded away. H. M. and his condition inspired the film *Memento*.

H. M. could recall declarative memories from before his surgery, but because of his inability to convert short-term memories into long-term memories, he would read the same magazine over and over without realizing that he had read it before. He would meet the same person on repeated occasions, yet have to be reintroduced each time. Though H. M. had found it almost impossible to form new declarative memories, he could form new procedural and other nondeclarative memories. After undergoing classical conditioning of an eye-blinking response, he retained this non-declarative memory for 2 years, yet he could not recall the experimenters, instructions, or methodology that had been used to condition the response—each of which involves declarative memory (Woodruff-Pak, 1993).

Corkin used magnetic resonance imaging (MRI) to specify the extent of the damage H. M.'s surgery did to his brain. The MRI found that, in fact, he had lost much of his hippocampus in each temporal lobe, as well as most of his amygdala and portions of other structures (Corkin et al., 1997). Corkin is one of many neuroscientists who are using brain-scanning techniques to refine our knowledge of the specific roles of brain structures in memory processes. For example, memory researchers using MRI have found that memories of faces and names are encoded by the front region and retrieved by the rear region of the hippocampus (Zeineh et al., 2003). Other neuroscientists have found that the hippocampus is, indeed, involved in the formation of declarative but not procedural memories (Teng & Squire, 1999). Research findings strongly implicate the hippocampus in semantic and episodic as well as spatial memory (Adeyemo, 2002).

The Neurochemistry of Memory

In 1959, James McConnell and his colleagues stunned the scientific world by reporting the results of an unusual experiment (McConnell, Jacobson, & Kimble, 1959). They had classically conditioned flatworms to contract their bodies in response to a light by repeatedly pairing presentations of the light with mild electric shocks. They then cut the flatworms in half. Because flatworms can regenerate themselves, both halves grew into whole flatworms. They then were retrained to contract in response to a light. As expected, the flatworms that had regenerated from the head (brain) ends showed memory savings—they took fewer trials to learn to respond to the light than had the original flatworms, which provided evidence that prior learning had been retained by the brain end. But to the researchers' surprise, the flatworms that had regenerated from the tail ends learned to respond to the light as fast as those that had regenerated from the brain ends. The memory of the classically conditioned response may have been encoded chemically and transported to the tail ends.

These findings led to a series of even more unusual experiments by a variety of researchers that seemed to demonstrate that memories could be transferred from one animal to another (Setlow, 1997). In one study, rats were trained to run to a lighted compartment instead of to a dark compartment (which they would normally favor) by shocking them whenever they entered the dark compartment. When extracts from the brains of these rats were injected into mice, the mice spent less time in the dark compartment than they normally would have. The researchers later isolated the proteinlike substance apparently responsible for this effect, which they called *scotophobin*, meaning "fear of the dark" (Unger, Desiderio, & Parr, 1972).

As you might assume, the results of successful memory transfer studies created controversy, leading 23 researchers to write a letter to the influential journal *Science* in which they reported their failure to produce memory transfer in 18 studies in seven laboratories (Byrne et al., 1966). Failure to replicate memory transfer studies became the main reason to reject those studies that found positive results (Rilling, 1996). But a few years later a published review of the research literature concluded that hundreds of studies of flatworms, goldfish, chickens, mice, rats, and hamsters had demonstrated the transfer of memories (Smith, 1974). Yet, because of the failure of other researchers to replicate those studies and to identify a physiological basis for the chemical transfer of memories, interest in the study of memory transfer has waned.

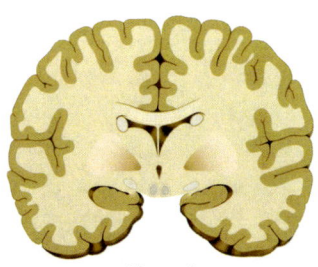

Normal

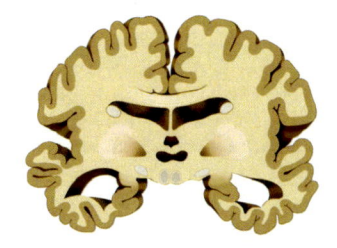

H. M.'s Brain

H. M.'s Brain

H. M.'s seizures increased with such frequency that his hippocampus and amygdala were surgically removed. This resulted in a form of amnesia called anterograde amnesia.
Source: Alexilusmedical/Shutterstock.com.

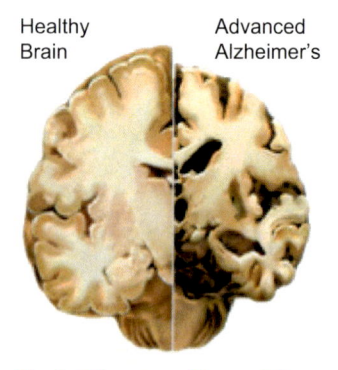

Brain Changes Caused by Alzheimer's Disease

Advanced Alzheimer's disease causes massive cell loss changes in the whole brain. This image shows a crosswise "slice" through the middle of the brain between the ears.

Source: © 2013 Alzheimer's Association. www.alz.org. All rights reserved. Illustrations by Stacy Jannis.

Perhaps interest has declined in part because the very notion of memory transfer seems better suited to science fiction than to science. Scientists in all disciplines, including biology, chemistry, and physics, tend to avoid topics that appear to violate accepted scientific paradigms (see Chapter 2). In contrast with the conflict generated by research on the chemical transfer of memories, there is no controversy about whether certain other neurochemical processes play a role in memory. Neuroscientists have concentrated their efforts on studying roles of the neurotransmitter *acetylcholine*, NMDA receptors from the amino acid neurotransmitter glutamate, *hormones*, and levels of blood *glucose* in memory.

Acetylcholine and Memory

The neurotransmitter that is most strongly implicated in memory processes is *acetylcholine* (Gold, 2003). Acetylcholine, the first neurotransmitter discovered, might be more important in the formation of declarative memories than in the formation of procedural memories. This relationship was implied by the results of a study in which one group of adult participants received a drug that blocked the effects of acetylcholine, and another group received a placebo (Nissen, Knopman, & Schacter, 1987). Those who received the active drug showed a reduced ability to recall and recognize stimuli presented previously (declarative memory) but no reduction in their ability to perform a reaction-time task they had learned previously (procedural memory).

But the most striking evidence of the role of acetylcholine in memory comes from studies of victims of Alzheimer's disease. Autopsies of victims of Alzheimer's disease show degeneration of acetylcholine neurons that connect the hippocampus to other brain areas (Crews, 1994). In fact, when healthy participants are given drugs that inhibit the activity of acetylcholine neurons, they show memory losses similar to those seen in victims of Alzheimer's disease (McKinney & Richelson, 1984). Given this finding, it would seem logical that treatments aimed at elevating brain levels of acetylcholine would improve the ability of Alzheimer's victims to form new memories. One approach has been to administer *choline*—the dietary substance from which acetylcholine is synthesized and that is found in milk and eggs. Unfortunately, administration of high doses of choline has been only marginally effective in improving the cognitive functioning of Alzheimer's victims (Davidson et al., 1991). Evidently the degeneration of acetylcholine neurons prevents the additional choline from having a beneficial effect, just as adding gasoline to the empty tank of a car with no spark plugs would not make it more likely to start.

NMDA Receptors and Memory

Perhaps the most exciting area of current research on the chemical basis of memory concerns N-methyl-D-aspartate (NMDA) receptors that often are found on the dendritic spines (Steele, Stewart, & Rose, 1995). NMDA itself is an amino acid compound that acts on the receptor for which it was named, the NMDA receptor. When NMDA is injected into animals, it acts like glutamate and binds to NMDA receptors in the hippocampus and enhances the efficiency of synaptic transmission along particular neural pathways. Blocking NMDA receptors in the amygdala prevents the formation of fear memories (Lee & Kim, 1998).

Consider a study of food preferences in rats. Rats, which are wary of unfamiliar foods, learn to prefer the foods eaten by neighboring rats—by smelling the scent of the food on another rat's breath. "Observer" rats were housed with a "demonstrator" rat that had eaten food laced with one of four spices (celery seed, anise, cloves, or marjoram). The experimental group received a dose of a drug that blocked NMDA receptors; the control group received a placebo injection. Then, each rat was provided with two sources of food. The familiar food was laced with the spice eaten by the demonstrator rat. The novel food was laced with one of the other spices. Both groups of rats preferred the familiar food shortly after the experimental procedure. When tested 72 hours later, the experimental group showed no food preference; the control group still preferred the familiar food. This study supports the role of NMDA receptors in the maintenance of long-term memory (Roberts & Shapiro, 2002). Additional support for the role of NMDA receptors in long-term memory consolidation comes from research on Alzheimer's disease. In the brains of victims of the disease, neural degeneration occurs in pathways rich in NMDA receptors (Maragos et al., 1987).

Hormones and Memory

Even hormones play a role in memory formation. The hormone *epinephrine* might have a special function in ensuring that we recall emotionally arousing events (McGaugh & Roozendaal, 2002). For example, in one study, participants were given injections of either an epinephrine blocker or a placebo. An hour later, they watched a series of slides accompanied by a neutral or an emotional story. When tested 1 week later, participants who received the epinephrine blocker had poorer recall of the emotional story than of the neutral story (Cahill et al., 1994). Given such findings, perhaps, if flashbulb memories are a real phenomenon, epinephrine plays a role in their formation. The effectiveness of epinephrine in promoting memory formation is independent of its role in stimulating the release of glucose from the liver (Gamaro et al., 1997).

Sex hormones, too, play a role in the formation of memory. Some studies have shown that estrogen replacement therapy promotes long-term memory and may reduce the risk of developing Alzheimer's disease in postmenopausal women (Zec & Trivedi, 2002). Other studies have found that testosterone replacement therapy has a similar effect on older men's long-term memory (Cherrier et al., 2001). The Women's Health Initiative Memory Study, a double-blind clinical trial with a sample of more than 4,500 postmenopausal women, is the most comprehensive study of the effect of hormone replacement therapy on women's memory to date. The results indicated that hormone replacement therapy had no effect on participants' long-term memory and *doubled* the risk of Alzheimer's disease and stroke (Shumaker et al., 2003; Yaffe, 2003). The increased health risks were due to the therapy regimen: estrogen prescribed with progestins, which are combined to reduce women's risk of uterine cancer (Brinton & Nilsen, 2003). And the long-term effects of testosterone replacement therapy on men's health are unknown (Morley & Perry, 2003). Thus, memory researchers are faced with the challenge of devising an effective treatment for age-related memory loss that does not increase older adults' health risks.

Glucose and Memory

Still another topic of research interest regarding the chemical basis of memory is the effect of blood sugar, or glucose. There is a positive correlation between blood glucose levels and memory performance. For example, studies indicate that college students' performance on memory tasks is improved more by having a glucose drink than by having a placebo drink (Benton, Owens, & Parker, 1994). Dietary supplements of glucose also might improve memory in the elderly. In one study, adults at least 60 years old received doses of either glucose or saccharin (a placebo) before or after memorizing a brief prose passage. Their recall of the passage was tested 24 hours later. Those who had ingested glucose before or after memorizing the passage showed significantly better recall than those who had ingested saccharin. Evidently, the glucose promoted the storage of the prose passages in memory (Manning, Parsons, & Gold, 1992). Nonetheless, students should not conclude that it would be wise to ingest massive amounts of glucose. On the contrary, the greatest enhancement of memory is produced by moderate doses of glucose (Parsons & Gold, 1992).

As you can see, research on the biopsychology of memory cannot be divorced from the psychology of memory. And biopsychological research promises to discover ways of improving memory. Memory improvement would be a boon both to people with intact brains and to people with damaged brains.

Experiencing Psychology

Does the Pegword Method Improve Memory Performance?

Research has found that we can improve our memory for lists of terms by connecting those terms to information we already have stored in memory. The pegword method, described in the section "Using Mnemonic Devices," involves memorizing a list of nouns that rhyme with numbers and then connecting terms to be learned to the nouns. In this exercise you will use the pegword method to memorize a grocery list.

Method

Participants

There should be at least 10 adult male and female participants (more would be even better) selected from among your friends, classmates, and relatives.

Materials

You will provide all the participants with two sheets, each with its own list of 10 grocery items to be memorized. One sheet will contain only a list of 10 items; the other sheet will contain a different list of 10 items and a list of pegwords paired with the numbers 1 through 10. Feel free to create your own number-pegword pairs or use the following: 1-bun, 2-shoe, 3-tree, 4-door, 5-hive, 6-sticks, 7-heaven, 8-gate, 9-line, and 10-hen.

Procedure

Have half the participants memorize the first list of grocery items for 2 minutes—without using any mnemonic devices. Have the other half memorize the same list of grocery items paired with pegwords, also for 2 minutes. Those using the pegword method should create vivid images of the pegwords and the items interacting together. At the end of 2 minutes, have the participants turn over their lists and immediately write down as many of the items as they can recall. They will have 2 minutes to do so. Then, using the second list of grocery items, have the two groups switch their methods in memorizing and then recalling the new list. Have the participants record the number of items they recalled correctly under each method.

Results and Discussion

Calculate the mean number of correct items under each of the two conditions of memorization. Draw a bar graph (see Appendix C in the Online Edition) representing these two means. Did the two memorization conditions produce markedly different results in the average number of items that were correctly recalled? Why would it be better to use an inferential statistic (see Chapter 2 and Appendix C in the Online Edition) to make that judgment? Could any extraneous variables have accounted for your results? Could the results have had anything to do with the nature of the participants or the grocery lists themselves?

Section Review: The Biopsychology of Memory

1. How did researchers demonstrate the presence of a classically conditioned memory trace in the cerebellum?
2. How does the case of H. M. support the role of the hippocampus in the consolidation of long-term memories?
3. Why do researchers believe that acetylcholine plays an important role in long-term memory?

Chapter Summary

Information Processing and Memory

- Memory research has been influenced by the cognitive revolution in psychology.
- The most widely accepted model of memory assumes that memory processing involves the stages of sensory memory, short-term memory, and long-term memory.
- At each stage the processing of memories involves encoding, storage, retrieval, and forgetting.

Sensory Memory

- Stimulation of sensory receptors produces sensory memories.
- Visual sensory memory is called iconic memory, and auditory sensory memory is called echoic memory.
- George Sperling found that iconic memory contains more information than had been commonly believed and permanent.

Short-Term Memory

- Short-term memory is called working memory because we use it to manipulate information provided by either sensory memory or long-term memory.
- We tend to encode information in short-term memory as sounds.
- We can store an average of seven chunks of information in short-term memory without rehearsal.
- Memories in short-term memory last about 20 seconds without rehearsal.
- Forgetting in short-term memory is caused by decay and displacement of information.

Long-Term Memory

- Memories stored in long-term memory are relatively permanent.
- Elaborative rehearsal of information in short-term memory is more likely to produce long-term memories than is maintenance rehearsal.
- The levels of processing theory assumes that information processed at deeper levels will be more firmly stored in long-term memory.
- Researchers distinguish between procedural, semantic, and episodic memories.
- Semantic network theory assumes that memories are stored as nodes interconnected by links.
- Schema theory assumes that memories are stored as cognitive structures that affect the encoding, storage, and retrieval of information related to them.
- Hermann Ebbinghaus began the formal study of memory by employing the method of savings.
- Ebbinghaus identified the serial-position effect and the forgetting curve.
- The theories of forgetting include decay theory, interference theory, motivation theory, and encoding specificity theory.
- The main versions of encoding specificity theory are context-dependent memory and state-dependent memory.

Memory, Forgetting, and Eyewitness Testimony

- Research by Elizabeth Loftus and her colleagues has shown that eyewitness testimony often can be inaccurate.
- An important research finding is that eyewitnesses' confidence in their memories is not a good indicator of their accuracy.
- Another important finding is that leading questions can alter the recall of memories by eyewitnesses.
- Of special concern is the need for care in determining the accuracy of children's eyewitness testimony.

Improving Your Memory

- You can improve your memory by practicing good study habits and by using mnemonic devices.
- A useful study technique is the SQ3R method, in which you survey, question, read, recite, and review.
- Overlearning and distributed practice are also useful techniques.
- Mnemonic devices are memory aids that organize material to make it easier to recall.
- The main mnemonic devices include acronyms, the method of loci, the pegword method, and the link method.

The Biopsychology of Memory

- Though Karl Lashley failed in his search for the exact location of a memory trace, researchers have discovered some of the anatomical and chemical bases of memory.
- The hippocampus plays an important role in converting short-term memories into long-term memories.
- Research on NMDA receptors promises to contribute to our understanding of the physiological bases of memory.
- Neurotransmitters, particularly acetylcholine, and hormones play crucial roles in memory formation.
- Even blood glucose can facilitate memory formation.

Key Terms

flashbulb memory (p. 270)
memory (p. 271)

Information Processing and Memory

encoding (p. 272)
forgetting (p. 272)
information-processing model (p. 272)
long-term memory (p. 272)
retrieval (p. 272)
sensory memory (p. 271)
short-term memory (p. 272)
storage (p. 272)

Sensory Memory

echoic memory (p. 273)

haptic memory (p. 273)
iconic memory (p. 273)

Short-Term Memory

maintenance rehearsal (p. 275)

Long-Term Memory

constructive recall (p. 282)
context-dependent memory (p. 289)
decay theory (p. 285)
declarative memory (p. 278)
elaborative rehearsal (p. 277)
encoding specificity (p. 288)
episodic memory (p. 279)
explicit memory (p. 279)

forgetting curve (p. 284)
implicit memory (p. 279)
interference theory (p. 285)
levels of processing theory (p. 277)
method of savings (p. 284)
proactive interference (p. 285)
procedural memory (p. 278)
repression (p. 286)
retroactive interference (p. 286)
schema theory (p. 280)
semantic memory (p. 279)
semantic network theory (p. 280)
serial-position effect (p. 283)
state-dependent memory (p. 289)
tip-of-the-tongue phenomenon (p. 288)

Memory, Forgetting, and Eyewitness Testimony
eyewitness testimony (p. 290)

Improving Your Memory
acronym (p. 296)
distributed practice (p. 296)
link method (p. 298)
massed practice (p. 296)
method of loci (p. 297)
mnemonic device (p. 296)
overlearning (p. 295)

pegword method (p. 297)
SQ3R method (p. 294)

The Biopsychology of Memory
long-term potentiation (p. 299)

Chapter Quiz

Note: Answers for the Chapter Quiz questions are provided at the end of the book.

1. Certain drugs or hormones may enhance memory indirectly by stimulating the liver to release
   a. glucose.
   b. vitamin C.
   c. bile salts.
   d. hemoglobin.

2. "Working memory" is another name for
   a. encoding.
   b. sensory memory.
   c. long-term memory.
   d. short-term memory.

3. Your knowledge that the primary color pigments are red, blue, and yellow is an example of
   a. semantic memory.
   b. episodic memory.
   c. schematic memory.
   d. procedural memory.

4. The benefits of elaborative rehearsal provide support for the
   a. engram.
   b. decay theory.
   c. use of rote memorization.
   d. levels of processing theory.

5. In regard to eyewitness testimony, the confidence of eyewitnesses
   a. tends to be unrelated to their accuracy.
   b. is higher for female than male eyewitnesses.
   c. has no impact on jurors' perceptions of their accuracy.
   d. has been outlawed by the U.S. Supreme Court as a criterion of accuracy in jury decision making about guilt or innocence.

6. A partygoer drinks alcohol and becomes inebriated. After sobering up, she forgets where she put her car keys. After drinking enough to become inebriated again, she recalls where she put them. This is an example of
   a. mnemonic memory.
   b. schematic memory.
   c. state-dependent memory.
   d. context-dependent memory.

7. After suffering a stroke, a person recovers and learns how to cook gourmet meals, but forgets ever having learned how to cook them. This shows the difference between
   a. semantic memory and procedural memory.
   b. procedural memory and episodic memory.
   c. semantic memory and declarative memory.
   d. episodic memory and declarative memory.

8. Research by Elizabeth Loftus indicates that the accuracy of eyewitness recall may be affected by
   a. hypnosis.
   b. repression.
   c. leading questions.
   d. alcohol intoxication.

9. The blurring of a motion picture when the projector presents frames too fast is a phenomenon of
   a. mnemonics.
   b. sensory memory.
   c. long-term memory.
   d. short-term memory.

10. If you studied a list of concepts from this chapter until you went through the list perfectly once and then went through the list five more times perfectly, you would be taking advantage of
    a. overlearning.
    b. massed practice.
    c. distributed practice.
    d. maintenance rehearsal.

11. Many Americans have unusually vivid memories of the circumstances in which they heard that the World Trade Center had been attacked on September 11, 2001. These memories are called
    a. memory traces.
    b. mnemonics.
    c. echoic memories.
    d. flashbulb memories.

12. A person suffers damage to the hippocampus. She would be LEAST likely to have difficulty
    a. recalling where she had breakfast earlier today.
    b. remembering the names of people she met yesterday.
    c. studying this textbook chapter and taking an exam on it.
    d. learning how to use a CD player and retaining that ability later.

13. Your ability to use a word processor would be an example of
    a. semantic memory.
    b. episodic memory.
    c. procedural memory.
    d. declarative memory.

14. A football quarterback memorizes his team's playbook by studying 2 hours a day for 10 days, rather than trying to master it in one 20-hour session. He would be making use of
    a. overlearning.
    b. massed practice.
    c. distributed practice.
    d. maintenance rehearsal.

15. Under the condition of immediate partial report, George Sperling found that
    a. we can recall less information than under the condition of whole report.
    b. our preconscious mind can store much more information than our unconscious mind.
    c. we store virtually all available sensory information in sensory memory.
    d. we store only a tiny fraction of available sensory information in sensory memory.

16. If you were asked to recall your last visit to a beach, you might incorrectly recall certain events that are commonly associated with that activity (such as building a sand castle), but that you did not actually perform. This would support
    a. schema theory.
    b. state-dependent memory.
    c. semantic network theory.
    d. levels of processing theory.

17. Your memory of your first day in this class is an example of
    a. semantic memory.
    b. episodic memory.
    c. procedural memory.
    d. short-term memory.

18. If you tried to memorize a list of grocery items by associating it with a sequential list of places in your home, you would be making use of the
    a. method of loci.
    b. pegword method.
    c. in situ method.
    d. method of localization.

19. On Monday you study for a biology test. On Tuesday you study for a psychology test. On Wednesday you take a psychology test. If material you studied on Monday interferes with your ability to recall information you studied on Tuesday, you would experience
    a. retrograde amnesia.
    b. anterograde amnesia.
    c. proactive interference.
    d. retroactive interference.

20. The normal number of items that can be stored in short-term memory ranges from
    a. 3 to 5.
    b. 5 to 9.
    c. 9 to 12.
    d. 10 to 15.

21. The facilitation of certain neural pathways is called
    a. overlearning.
    b. neurotransmission.
    c. elaborative rehearsal.
    d. long-term potentiation.

22. Because of the serial-position effect, in studying a list of terms from this chapter, you should place
    a. the easiest words at the end of the list.
    b. the easiest words in the middle of the list.
    c. the easiest words at the beginning of the list.
    d. half of the easiest words at the beginning of the list and half at the end of the list.

23. You are introducing a new acquaintance to one of your friends, only to be embarrassed by your failure to recall the new person's name—despite your feeling that you know the name and your ability to conjure up the first letter. This is an example of the
    a. mnemonic effect.
    b. overlearning effect.
    c. schematic phenomenon.
    d. tip-of-the-tongue phenomenon.

24. A person witnesses a horrible accident in which people are maimed and killed. Weeks later he cannot recall the accident. According to Freud, he forgot the accident because of
    a. decay.
    b. decoding.
    c. expunging.
    d. repression.

25. A person suffers a stroke and can no longer form new memories. The stroke most likely affected the person's
    a. frontal lobes.
    b. parietal lobes.
    c. temporal lobes.
    d. occipital lobes.

Thought Questions

1. How might the notion of mood-congruent memory explain the difficulty that depressed people often have in getting rid of their depressed mood?

2. How would you use the concept of levels of processing to improve your memory for material you learn in your introductory psychology course?

3. Why should we be wary about the accuracy of eyewitness testimony?

4. What does the case of H. M. indicate about the role of the hippocampus in memory?

CHAPTER 9

Thought and Language

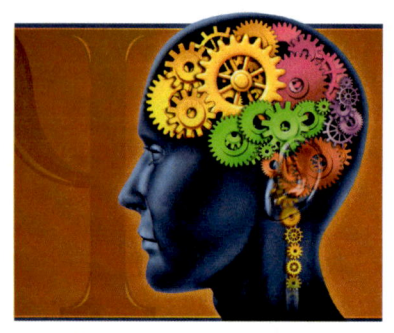

Source: Lightspring/Shutterstock.com.

Chapter Outline

Thought
Language

critical period A period in childhood when experience with language produces optimal language acquisition.

In 1800, a boy who appeared to be about 12 years old emerged from a forest near Aveyron, France, apparently having survived for many years without human contact (Hunter, 1993). The boy, named Victor by physician Jared Itard, became known as the "Wild Boy of Aveyron." Victor learned to use gestures, comprehend speech, and read and write on a basic level. Though Itard made an intensive effort to teach him to speak French, the only word Victor learned to say was "lait" (milk). Similar reports have provided evidence of a **critical period** for language acquisition that extends from infancy to adolescence, during which language learning is optimal. If people are not exposed to a language until after childhood, they might never become proficient in speaking it (Grimshaw, Adelstein, Bryden, & MacKinnon, 1998). There also seems to be a critical period for the acquisition of fluent sign language (Newman, Bavelier, Corina, Jezzard, & Neville, 2002).

A more recent and well-documented case described an American girl, Genie, who had been raised in isolation. In 1970, 13-year-old Genie was discovered by welfare workers in a room in which her father had kept her restrained in a harness and away from social contact—and language—since infancy. He communicated with her by barking and growling and beat her whenever she made a sound. By 1981, more than a decade after returning to society and undergoing intensive language training, Genie had acquired a large vocabulary but only a limited ability to speak. Like Victor, Genie might have been past her critical period for language acquisition when she returned to society (Pines, 1981).

Though the cases of Victor and Genie, as well as those of other children who have been reared in social isolation (Kenneally, Bruck, Frank, & Nalty, 1998), support the view that there is a critical period for language acquisition, you may recall from Chapter 2 that it is unwise to generalize too freely from case studies. For example, some children who have lived for years in social isolation, such as Kaspar Hauser, who was discovered in Nuremberg, Germany, in 1828 at age 17, have been able to learn language well even after reaching adolescence (Simon, 1979). Perhaps other factors could account for the findings in the cases of Victor and Genie. For example, suppose that Victor and Genie were born with brain disorders that interfered with their ability to acquire language. Even if they had been reared from birth in normal family settings, they still might have failed to acquire mature language.

Research on the acquisition of language and other topics related to how the brain processes information fall within the domain of *cognitive psychology*—perhaps the most influential field of psychology in recent years. In fact, the 1950s and 1960s saw a "cognitive revolution" in which the behaviorist perspective was countered by increased concern with the study of the mind (Miller, 2003). This revolution was inspired by an explosion of interest in the study of computer and cognitive sciences, cognitive processes, and language acquisition.

Cognitive psychology combines William James's concern with mental processes and John B. Watson's concern with observable behavior. Cognitive psychologists accomplish this combination by using techniques that permit them to infer cognitive processes from overt behavior (Greenwood, 1999). Cognitive psychologists who are interested in the neurological bases of cognitive processes pursue their research interests in **cognitive neuroscience**. A cognitive neuroscientist might, for example, use PET scans or functional MRI to assess brain activity that accompanies the performance of cognitive tasks such as language, memory, creativity, or decision making.

Thought and language are different, yet interrelated, cognitive activities. Chapter 8 describes the cognitive activity of memory, which permits you to store and retrieve information. Like memory, thought and language help you profit from experience and adapt to your environment. Your ability to think and to use language will enable you to comprehend the information conveyed in this chapter and to apply some of it, perhaps in your everyday life.

cognitive psychology The field of psychology that studies cognitive processes such as thought and language.

cognitive neuroscience The study of the neurological bases of cognitive processes.

Thought

Forming concepts. Solving problems. Being creative. Making decisions. Each of these processes depends on **thought**, which is the purposeful cognitive manipulation of words and images. Yet in 1925, John B. Watson, the founder of behaviorism and the psychologist who conducted the controversial "Little Albert" experiment described in Chapter 7, claimed that thought is not a mental activity. Instead, he insisted that it was no more than subvocal speech—activity of the speech muscles that is too subtle to produce audible sounds. Margaret Floy Washburn (1916), Watson's contemporary, made a similar claim in her *motor theory of thought*. There is an intuitive appeal to this claim because you might sometimes find yourself engaging in subvocal speech—perhaps even while reading this chapter. Moreover, physiological recordings of activity in the speech muscles have shown that some people do subvocalize while thinking (McGuigan, 1970).

thought The cognitive manipulation of words and images, as in concept formation, problem solving, and decision making.

But these findings do not necessarily support Watson's claim that subvocal speech *is* thought. Convincing evidence against Watson's claim came from a study in which a physician, Scott Smith, had himself paralyzed for half an hour by the drug that blocks acetylcholine—curare (Smith, Brown, Toman, & Goodman, 1947). He did so to assess its possible use in the induction of general anesthesia. Because curare paralyzes the skeletal muscles (see Chapter 3), including the breathing muscles, Smith was put on a respirator. After the curare wore off, he was able to report conversations that had taken place while he had been paralyzed. Because Smith was able to think and form memories while his speech muscles were paralyzed, thought does not depend on subvocal speech.

Most behaviorists did not equate thought with subvocal speech, but they agreed with Watson's position that cognitive processes were not the proper objects of study for psychologists. By the 1960s, though, dissatisfaction with the inability of strict behaviorism to explain memory, thought, and certain other psychological processes contributed to the cognitive revolution. This dissatisfaction reintroduced the study of mental processes, or "cognition," to psychology (Mandler, 2002). One of the basic cognitive processes is concept formation, the next topic in this chapter.

> **Section Review: Thought**
>
> 1. What is meant by a critical period for language acquisition in human development?
> 2. In what way does cognitive psychology show the influence of William James and John B. Watson?
> 3. What evidence contradicts the motor theory of thought?

Concept Formation

If you encountered a snake while hiking, you would be more willing to pick up and hold a nonpoisonous snake than a poisonous snake. Similarly, you might be willing to pluck and eat a nonpoisonous mushroom but not a poisonous mushroom. Your actions would show that you understood the concepts "poisonous" and "nonpoisonous." A **concept** represents a category of objects, events, qualities, or relations whose members share certain features. For example, poisonous objects share the ability to make you ill or kill you. During your life you have formed thousands of concepts, which provide the raw materials for thinking. Concepts enable us to respond to events appropriately and to store memories in an organized way. Cognitive psychologists distinguish between *logical concepts* (sometimes called *artificial concepts*) and *natural concepts* (Kalish, 2002).

concept A category of objects, events, qualities, or relations that share certain features.

Logical Concepts

How do we form concepts? Consider the case of a **logical concept**, which is formed by identifying the specific features possessed by all things to which the concept applies. "Great Lakes state" is a logical concept. Each of its members has the features of being a state and of bordering one or more of the Great Lakes. The book of Leviticus in the Old Testament of the Bible provides two of the oldest examples of logical concepts. Leviticus distinguishes between "clean" animals, which may be eaten, and "unclean" animals, which may not. As one example, "clean" sea animals have fins and scales, whereas "unclean" sea animals do not. Bass and trout are "clean" animals, and clams and lobsters are "unclean" animals (Murphy & Medin, 1985).

logical concept A concept formed by identifying the specific features possessed by all things to which the concept applies.

Logical concepts like those found in Leviticus refer to real-life concepts and have typically not been the kinds studied in the laboratory. Instead, laboratory studies generally have used logical concepts created by the researcher. The use of logical concepts lets the researcher exert more precise control over the definitions of particular concepts. An experiment on the formation of a logical concept might present participants with a series of symbols varying in size, shape, and color. The participant's task is to discover the features that define the concept. For example, a symbol might have to be large, square, and blue to be considered an example of the particular concept. Participants determine the features of the concept by testing hypotheses about its possible defining features on successive examples that are labeled as either positive or negative instances of it. A positive instance would include the defining features of the concept (in this case, large, square, and blue), whereas a negative instance would lack at least one of the defining features (for example, large, square, and red). Try to identify the concept presented in Figure 9-1.

Natural Concepts

Is baseball a sport? How about table tennis? fishing? foosball? golf? chess? mountain biking? professional wrestling? You have an intuitive sense of how "sportlike" each of these activities is. "Sport" is an example of a **natural concept**, a concept formed through everyday experience rather than by testing hypotheses about particular features that are common to all members of the concept. We might be unable to identify the defining features of natural concepts such as "sport." That is, natural concepts have "fuzzy borders."

natural concept A concept, typically formed through everyday experience, whose members possess some, but not all, of a common set of features.

FIGURE 9-1
Concept Formation

Laboratory studies of the formation of logical concepts present participants with a series of examples varying on specific features. The participant's task is to identify the features that compose the concept. The figures in this example can vary in size (small or large), symbol (crescent or star), color (red or blue), or number (one or two). Given that the odd-numbered cards are members of the concept and the even-numbered cards are not, see how quickly you can identify the concept. (Answer is below.)

Answer: large stars.

prototype The best representative of a concept.

Such concepts include "love" (Regan, Kocan, & Whitlock, 1998), "emotion" (Russell, 1991), "moral" (Hart, 1998), "pleasure" (Dube & Le Bel, 2003), and "prejudice" (Inman & Baron, 1996). Even Saint Augustine, in the fifth century, noted that a natural concept can have fuzzy borders when he remarked, "I know what 'time' is until someone asks me to define it" (Chadwick, 1986, p. 70).

The difficulty in defining natural concepts led psychologist Eleanor Rosch (1975) to propose that they are related to prototypes. A **prototype** is considered to be the best representative of a concept. According to Rosch, the more similarity between an example and a prototype, the more likely we are to consider the example to be a member of the concept represented by the prototype. A robin is a more prototypical bird than a penguin. Both have wings and feathers and hatch from eggs, but only the robin can fly. In regard to the concept "sport," baseball is more prototypical than golf, which in turn is more prototypical than foosball. The fuzziness of natural concepts can lead to arguments about whether a particular example is a member of a given concept (Medin, 1989). This problem was evident in 1988 in a series of letters to the editor of *The Sporting News* either supporting or opposing its coverage of Wrestlemania, the Indianapolis 500, and the World Chess Championship. Supporters considered these events to be examples of the concept "sport"; opponents did not.

Subsequent research has indicated that we do form concepts by creating prototypes of the relevant objects, events, qualities, or relations (Nosofsky, 1991). In regard to the concept "commitment," one experiment found that commitment is better understood from the prototype perspective than from the logical concept perspective. Commitment to friends, family, and spouse was considered most prototypical of "commitment"; commitment to one's work, education, or more distant relationships was considered less so (Fehr, 1999). Reliance on prototypes also can have practical benefits. Clinicians and trained laypeople can diagnose certain personality disorders when given a prototype of the disorder as well, if not better, than when they use the DSM-5 (see Chapter 14), a standardized reference of psychological disorders (Westen, DeFife, Bradley, & Hilsenroth, 2010).

Influenced by the work of Rosch, psychologists have become more interested in conducting laboratory studies of natural concept formation—the formation of concepts without logically testing hypotheses about their defining features. Consider the following study of the identification of artistic styles (Hartley & Homa, 1981). Participants who were naïve about artistic styles were shown works by the painters Manet, Renoir, and Matisse. Later, the participants were shown more paintings by these artists and by other artists, without being told the artists' identities. After viewing the second set of paintings, participants accurately matched particular paintings with the styles of the artists whose works they had seen in the first set of paintings. Participants used the first set to form concepts representing the styles of the three artists: a "Manet," a "Renoir," and a "Matisse." These results could not be explained as an example of logical concept formation because participants were unable to identify a set of features that distinguished a Manet from a Renoir from a Matisse. Similar approaches have been successful in teaching artistically naïve persons how to comprehend works of art (Seifert, 1996).

Other research studies have demonstrated that birds can form concepts of musical styles, as in a study in which one group of sparrows was reinforced for perch sitting only when music by Bach was played and a second group was reinforced for perch sitting only when music by Schoenberg was played. When presented with other music by those composers, the Bach group tended to perch in response to music by Bach and the Schoenberg group tended to perch in response to music by Schoenberg. Later, when presented with music by Vivaldi and Carter, the birds showed generalization. The Bach group tended to perch in response to music by Vivaldi. Both are classical music composers. The Schoenberg group tended to perch in response to music by Carter. Both are modern music composers. Thus, even birds may form concepts of artistic styles (Watanabe & Sato, 1999).

Section Review: Concept Formation

1. What is the difference between a logical concept and a natural concept?
2. In what way do concepts such as "love" and "sport" have fuzzy borders?

Problem Solving

problem solving The thought process by which an individual overcomes obstacles to reach a goal.

One of the most important uses of concepts is in **problem solving**, the thought process that enables us to overcome obstacles to reach goals. Suppose that your car will not start. In looking for a solution to your problem, you might follow a series of steps commonly used in solving problems (Kramer & Bayern, 1984). First, you *identify the problem*: My car won't start. Second, you *gather information* relevant to the problem: Am I out of gas? Is my battery dead? Are my ignition wires wet? Third, you *try a solution*: I'm not out of gas, so I'll dry off the wires. Finally, you *evaluate the result*: The car started, so the wires were indeed wet. If the solution fails to work, you might try a different one: Drying off the wires didn't work, so I'll try a jump start.

Approaches to Problem Solving

Problem solving commonly involves one of several strategies, including *trial and error*, *insight*, *algorithms*, and *heuristics*.

trial and error An approach to problem solving in which the individual tries one possible solution after another until one works.

Trial and Error A common strategy for solving problems is **trial and error**, which involves trying one possible solution after another until one works. Ivan Pavlov, though best known for his research on classical conditioning, was one of the first scientists to stress the importance of trial and error (Windholz, 1992). Even the humble *E. coli* bacterium navigates by trial and error (Marken & Powers, 1989), and spiders pursue prey by using trial and error (Jackson, Carter, & Tarsitano, 2001). For an example of trial and error in human problem solving, imagine that your psychology professor asks you to get a timer from a laboratory and gives you a ring with 10 keys on it. Suppose that on reaching the laboratory you realize that you don't know which key opens the door to the laboratory. You would immediately identify the problem: finding the correct key. After assessing your situation, you probably would decide to use trial and error to solve the problem. You would try one key after another until you found one that opened the door.

Though trial and error often is effective, it is not always efficient. For example, a study of novice computer programmers found that the slower learners relied too much on trial and error (Green & Gilhooly, 1990). If your professor gave you a ring with 50 keys on it, you might find it more efficient to return and ask your professor to identify the correct key rather than waste time trying one key after another. Even worse, imagine learning how to use computer software by trying various combinations of keystrokes until you hit on the correct ones to perform desired functions (such as centering a line of text). It might take you years to complete even a brief term paper.

Insight In the third century B.C., the Greek physicist Archimedes was asked to solve a problem: Was King Hiero's new crown made of pure gold, or had the goldsmith cheated

Trial and Error
You would likely use trial and error to figure out which key opens a specific door.
Source: DmitriMaruta/Shutterstock.com.

him by mixing cheap metals with the gold? Archimedes discovered a way to solve this problem when he noticed that if he sat in his bathtub, the water level rose. After shouting "Eureka!" he decided to submerge the crown in water and measure the volume of water it displaced. Reasoning that the volume of water displaced is proportionate to the weight of the object displacing it, he would compare the volume displaced by the crown to the volume displaced by an equal amount of metal that he knew to be pure gold. Archimedes found that the crown was indeed pure gold. To make this discovery, he relied on **insight**, an approach to problem solving that depends on cognitive manipulation of information rather than on overt trial and error.

Insight also is characterized by an "Aha!" moment or experience—the sudden realization of the solution to a problem (Topolonski & Reber, 2010)—as found in research by Janet Metcalfe. In a typical experiment, every 10 seconds Metcalfe asks participants working on either insight problems or non-insight problems (such as algebra) how "warm" they feel—that is, how close they feel they are to the correct solution. She has found that those working on insight problems are less accurate, indicating that solutions to non-insight problems are incremental and predictable, whereas solutions to insight problems are sudden and unpredictable (Metcalfe & Wiebe, 1987). Nonetheless, her interpretations of her research findings have been countered by recent research that suggests that what we call insight might seem to be sudden and unpredictable, but it is the product of the gradual accumulation of knowledge as one works on a problem (Hamel & Elshout, 2000; Novick & Sherman, 2003).

Assuming that insight does exist, can animals use it to solve problems? The classic study of insight in animals was conducted by Gestalt psychologist Wolfgang Köhler (1887–1967) on the island of Tenerife in the Canary Islands during World War I. Köhler (1925) presented a chimpanzee named Sultan with bananas, hanging them from the top of Sultan's cage, well out of his reach. But his cage also contained several crates. After trying fruitlessly to reach the bananas by jumping, Sultan suddenly hit on the solution. He piled the crates on top of one another, quickly climbed to the top, and grabbed a banana—just as the shaky structure came tumbling down.

The assumption that Sultan displayed insight was challenged more than a half century later by several behaviorists (Epstein, Kirshnit, Lanza, & Rubin, 1984). In a tongue-in-cheek study analogous to the one involving Sultan, they used food rewards to train a pigeon to first perform the separate acts of moving a tiny box, standing on the box, and pecking a plastic, miniature banana. When later confronted with the banana hanging out of reach from the top of its cage, the pigeon at first seemed confused but then suddenly moved the box under the banana, climbed on the box, and pecked at the banana to get a food reward. According to the researchers, if a pigeon can perform supposedly insightful behavior, then perhaps insight in animals—and even in people—is no more than the chaining together of previously rewarded behaviors (see Chapter 7). However, more recent research has found that birds, rats, and chimpanzees can demonstrate insight in laboratory tasks (Shettleworth, 2012; Panksepp & Panksepp, 2013).

It has long been known that nonhuman primates can display other complex emotions, such as empathy and insight, but can other species, such as rats? Electrophysiological studies performed by Durstewitz and colleagues (2010) with laboratory rats have demonstrated that groups of cells in the prefrontal cortex are activated during complex decision making that could be related to insight. The rats were trained in an instrumental conditioning set-shifting task and rewarded for pressing one of two levers that was illuminated by a light. After the rats learned this rule, the researchers then shifted the required response to press a lever in a specific location. This shift, from a visual to spatial cue, was the new rule the rat had to learn in order to receive a reward and was accompanied by changes in neuronal activation in the prefrontal cortex. The rat had to develop a new strategy and abandon an old strategy. This is related to insight because, as humans, we are faced with changes that require shifts in strategy, such as how to solve a difficult problem, that are distinct from trial-and-error processes.

Algorithms If you use the formula "length multiplied by width," you will obtain the area of a rectangle. A mathematical formula is an example of a problem-solving strategy called

insight An approach to problem solving that depends on cognitive manipulation of information rather than overt trial and error and produces sudden solutions to problems.

algorithm A problem-solving rule or procedure that, when followed step by step, ensures that a correct solution will be found.

an algorithm. An **algorithm** is a rule that, when followed step by step, ensures that a solution to a problem will be found. Many physicians use algorithms to diagnose disorders, such as sexual dysfunctions, by noting specific combinations of symptoms and personal characteristics of patients (Hatzichristou, Bertero, & Goldstein, 1994). Researchers also have developed algorithms for the diagnosis of autism spectrum disorder (Kamp-Becker et al., 2013) and the most effective treatment strategies for anxiety disorders (Culpepper, 2003). But some critics fear that the recent trend toward medical insurance providers requiring the use of algorithm-based treatments for psychological disorders—which at this time do not lend themselves to standardized treatments to the same extent that many medical illnesses do—is motivated more by the providers' desire to reduce costs than by their desire to ensure the provision of high-quality therapy (Slayton, 1998).

The notion of an algorithm is an offshoot of research in computer science by cognitive psychologists Allen Newell and Herbert Simon (1972). Many computer programs rely on algorithms to process information accurately. But, like trial and error, an algorithm can be an inefficient means of finding the solution to a problem. To appreciate this inefficiency, imagine that you are in the middle of a chess game. An algorithm for finding your best move would require tracing all possible sequences of moves from the current position. Because there is an average of 35 different moves that can be made in any single position in the middle of a chess game, you would need literally millions of years to find the best move by tracing all possible sequences of moves. Even using an algorithm to follow all possible sequences of just the next 3 moves in the middle of a chess game would require the analysis of an average of 1.8 billion moves (Waltz, 1982). Because a formal chess match has a typical time limit of 5 hours, even world chess champions do not rely on algorithms. Instead, they rely on problem-solving strategies called heuristics.

heuristic A general principle that guides problem solving, though it does not guarantee a correct solution.

Heuristics A **heuristic** is a general principle, or rule of thumb, that guides problem solving in everyday life and in scientific fields, such as biology (Baker & Dunbar, 2000). Unlike an algorithm, a heuristic does not guarantee a solution. But a heuristic can be more efficient because it rules out many useless alternatives before they are even attempted. A chess player might rely on heuristics, such as trying to control the center of the board or trading weaker pieces for stronger ones. A heuristic for studying and getting good grades might be to set aside at least 2–3 hours per class per week for reviewing class material.

Impediments to Problem Solving

Researchers who study problem solving are interested in obstacles that interfere with it. Two of the major obstacles are *mental sets* and *functional fixedness*.

Mental Sets Before reading on, try to solve the six problems presented in Figure 9-2, in which you must use three jars to measure out exact amounts of water. If you are like most research participants, you could easily solve the first five problems but ran into difficulty with the sixth. In an early study using the water-jar problem, participants quickly realized that the solution to the first problem was to fill jar B, pour enough water from it to fill jar A, and then pour enough water from jar B to fill jar C twice. These steps left the desired amount in jar B. The participants then found that the same strategy worked for each of the next four problems. But when they reached the sixth problem, two-thirds of them were unable to solve it. Those who failed to solve it had developed a strategy that was effective in solving previous examples but made the simple solution to problem 6 difficult to discover. In contrast, of participants who were asked to solve only the sixth problem, few had difficulty discovering the simple solution: fill jar A and pour enough water from it to fill jar C, leaving the desired amount in jar A (Luchins, 1946).

mental set A tendency to use a particular problem-solving strategy that has succeeded in the past but that may interfere with solving a problem requiring a new strategy.

This study demonstrated that we sometimes are hindered by a **mental set**, a problem-solving strategy that has succeeded in the past but that can interfere with solving a problem that requires a new strategy. In one study, expert computer programmers and novice computer programmers were given a programming problem that could be solved by using a simple programming strategy that is more often used by novices. The results showed that the novices were more likely than the experts to solve the problem because the experts

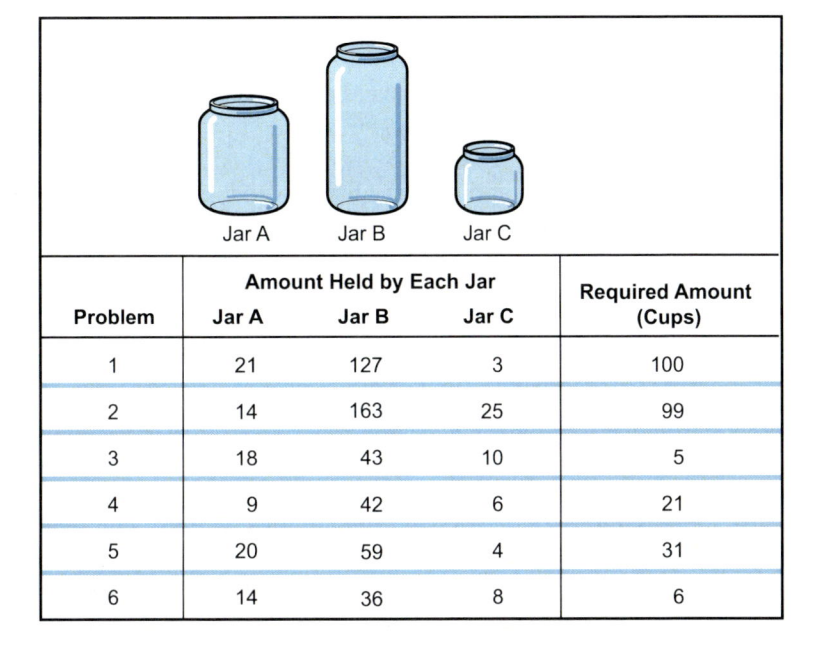

FIGURE 9-2
Mental Sets

Luchins (1946) asked participants to use jars with the capacities shown in columns A, B, and C to obtain the amounts required in the right column. The first five problems led participants to overlook a simpler solution in the sixth problem.

Problem	Amount Held by Each Jar			Required Amount (Cups)
	Jar A	Jar B	Jar C	
1	21	127	3	100
2	14	163	25	99
3	18	43	10	5
4	9	42	6	21
5	20	59	4	31
6	14	36	8	6

tried to use a more sophisticated but ineffective strategy that they had adopted during their careers as computer programmers. In other words, the experts had developed a mental set that blinded them to the simpler solution (Adelson, 1984). The possibility that expertise may create mental sets that blind problem solvers to simple solutions has been replicated in other research studies (Wiley, 1998). Even the bestseller book, *The Da Vinci Code*, contains an example of how a mental set can hamper an expert's ability to solve a problem that a novice might solve easily. In the novel, Sophie, an expert cryptographer, scolds herself for her failure to decipher a coded message that might help uncover an astounding biblical secret:

> Her shock over the anagram was matched only by her embarrassment at not having deciphered the message herself. Sophie's expertise in complex cryptanalysis had caused her to overlook simplistic word games, and yet she knew she should have seen it. After all, she was no stranger to anagrams—especially in English. (Brown, 2003, p. 99)

How can you overcome a mental set? One way is to make assumptions opposite to those you normally make. This approach might have helped the expert computer programmers who were unable to solve the problem that the novices were able to solve.

Functional Fixedness Another way in which past experience can impede our ability to solve problems is through **functional fixedness**, the inability to realize that a problem can be solved by using a familiar object in an unusual way. The term *functional fixedness* was coined by Gestalt psychologist Karl Duncker (1903–1940), who was a leader in the study of insight learning (Behrens, 2003). The role of functional fixedness in problem solving was demonstrated in a classic study (Maier, 1931) in which each participant was asked to perform the simple task of tying together two long strings hanging from a ceiling. The problem was that the two strings were too far apart for the participant to grasp them both at the same time. The room contained a variety of objects, including a table, a chair, an extension cord, and a pair of pliers.

Participants were given 10 minutes to solve the problem. Each time the participant identified a solution, the experimenter said, "Now do it a different way." One solution was to tie the extension cord to one string, grasp the other string, pull the strings toward one another, and then tie them together. Participants who discovered the solution that the experimenter was interested in tied the pliers to one of the strings and started it swinging like a pendulum. They then grabbed the other string, walked toward the swinging pliers, and tied the two strings together (Maier, 1931). To discover that solution, the participants had to realize that the pliers could be used as a weight and not solely as a tool. Only 39.3 percent of the participants discovered this solution on their own. More participants

functional fixedness The inability to realize that a problem can be solved by using a familiar object in an unusual way.

Chapter 9 Thought and Language

discovered it when the experimenter provided a hint by subtly setting one of the strings in motion.

As with mental sets, functional fixedness can be overcome. One of the best ways is to change or ignore the names of familiar objects. In a study that used this technique, participants were given a bulb, some wire, a switch, a wrench, and batteries. The participants were told to create a circuit that would light the bulb, even though they had too little wire to complete the circuit. The solution was to use the wrench to complete it. Participants who were told to use nonsense names such as "jod" to refer to the wrench were more likely to solve the problem than were participants who called the wrench a "wrench" (Glucksberg & Danks, 1968). By using nonsense words to refer to the wrench, participants were less likely to think of it as just a mechanical tool.

More recently, researchers have facilitated this process by designing the *generic parts technique*. Using the above example, participants would be asked two questions. The first question, "Can this be decomposed further?" asks participants to break objects into subparts that might be useful in solving the problem. Thus, participants might think of pliers or wrenches as weights rather than tools to remove bolts or pins. The second question, "Does this imply a use?" asks participants to create descriptions of uses based on attributes of the object, such as shape or form. Thus, participants might think of pliers as creating a swing when tied to string or wrenches as providing additional metal to complete a circuit. One study found that participants trained in this method solved 67 percent more problems that generated functional fixedness than a control group (McCaffrey, 2012).

Section Review: Problem Solving

1. Why might heuristics be both superior and inferior to algorithms?
2. How do mental sets hamper problem solving in everyday life?

Creativity

In 1950, in his final address as president of the American Psychological Association, creativity researcher J. P. Guilford (1897–1987) expressed disappointment that of the more than 100,000 psychological studies published up until then, fewer than 200 dealt with creativity. Following Guilford's address, and influenced by the cognitive revolution, there was a striking increase in the number of scientific studies of creativity (Simonton, 2000). And this increase has not been limited to the United States. Scientific studies of creativity have spread around the world (Kaufman, 2010).

But what is creativity? Like other natural concepts, creativity cannot be defined by a specific set of features—that is, it has fuzzy borders. We might be able to distinguish between creative and noncreative behavior without being able to identify exactly what makes one example creative and another noncreative. Psychologists generally define **creativity** as a form of problem solving characterized by finding solutions that are novel as well as useful or socially valued (Mumford & Gustafson, 1988), whether practical, artistic, or scientific.

creativity A form of problem solving that generates novel, socially valued solutions to problems.

Of course, the works of many creative geniuses were not socially valued in their time. The exhibition of works by the French artist Paul Cézanne (1839–1906) that toured the world in 1996 drew millions of visitors to museums, attracted by the allure of an artist whom many authorities believe inspired the development of modern art. Yet, in his own time, Cézanne was considered a technically inadequate artist whose paintings had little appeal to critics and laypeople alike. What is considered creative in one era or one culture might be considered inept in another.

Thus, in his time, Cézanne's works were considered novel but were not valued—novelty is not sufficient to demonstrate creativity (Epstein, 1991). Said the French mathe-

Expressions of Creativity?
Art may be socially valued. Which of these paintings are examples of creativity?
Source: Shutterstock (*left*) hybridtechno, (*middle*) Kostantyn Ivanyshen, (*right*) Moolkum.

matician Henri Poincaré (1948, p. 16), "To create consists precisely in not making useless combinations and in making those which are useful and which are only a small minority. Invention is discernment, choice." Thus, if you gave a monkey a canvas, a paintbrush, and a pallet of paint, it might produce novel paintings, but they would not be considered examples of creativity. Among the leading tools for measuring creativity are the Torrance Tests of Creative Thinking. These tests, developed by E. Paul Torrance, assess creativity using words or pictures (Palaniappan & Torrance, 2001).

Characteristics of Creative People

What characteristics are associated with creativity? Though creative people tend to have above-average intelligence, you do not have to be a genius to be highly creative (Nicholls, 1972). For example, a study of undergraduates found that their scores on a test of intelligence and a test of creative thinking correlated .24, indicating a positive but weak relationship between the two (Rushton, 1990). And a study of children found a positive correlation between their intelligence and their creativity up to an IQ of 120 (above average but not in the gifted range), but no relationship beyond that level of intelligence (Fuchs-Beauchamp, Karnes, & Johnson, 1993).

Creative people also tend to exhibit certain personality characteristics (Simonton, 1999). They tend to prefer novelty, favor complexity, and make independent judgments (Barron & Harrington, 1981). Creative people attend to stimuli that other people might screen from consciousness as being irrelevant to the task at hand (Carson, Peterson, & Higgins, 2003). They also tend to have a wide range of interests, be open to new experiences, and be nonconformists and unconventional (Simonton, 1999). For example, a recent study of university undergraduates investigated the relationship of multicultural experiences to creativity. The sample included three groups of participants. One group had studied abroad, another group had planned to study abroad, and the last group did not plan to study abroad. The participants who had studied abroad outperformed the other two groups on a standardized test of creativity as well as a culture-specific test (Lee, Therriault, & Linderholm, 2012). And creative people tend to be more creative when they are engaged in creative behavior for its own sake rather than to obtain some kind of reward (de Jesus, Rus, Lens, & Imaginário, 2013).

Creativity and the Sociocultural Environment

Psychologists also have studied the extent to which socialization and culture influence the development and expression of creativity in individuals. For example, historical eras characterized by political unrest or warfare tend to dampen creative expression and productivity (Simonton, 1984). Cultures, too, differ in the extent to which they encourage the expression of individuality and originality. One study compared musical innovation

Chapter 9 Thought and Language **317**

> **Psychology versus Common Sense**
>
> ### Can Rewarding Creative Behavior Inhibit Creativity?
>
> Common sense might lead us to presume that we can encourage people to become more creative by rewarding them when they engage in creative activities. But this commonsense bit of wisdom has been called into question by scientific research on creativity. According to creativity researcher Teresa Amabile (1989), creative people are more motivated by their intrinsic interest in creative tasks than by extrinsic factors such as fame, money, or approval. In fact, when people are presented with extrinsic reasons for performing intrinsically interesting creative tasks, they can lose their motivation to perform them. Amabile's 1985 study, presented here, provided further evidence of this loss of motivation.
>
> Participants were recruited through advertisements asking for writers to participate in a study of people's reasons for writing. Most of the respondents were undergraduate or graduate students in English or creative writing. All the participants were asked to write two brief poems on designated themes (the first on snow, and the second on laughter). Each participant was assigned to one of three groups. After the participants wrote the first poem, one group completed a questionnaire that focused on intrinsic reasons for writing, such as the opportunity for self-expression, whereas a second group completed a questionnaire that focused on extrinsic reasons for writing, such as gaining public recognition. The third group served as a control group and was not given a questionnaire. Twelve experienced poets judged the creativity of the poems on a 40-point scale.
>
> When the first poems were judged for their creativity, the three groups did not differ. However, when the second poems were judged for their creativity, the poems written by the group exposed to the questionnaire that focused on extrinsic reasons for writing were judged less creative than those written by the other two groups; the intrinsic-reasons group and the control group showed no change in creativity from the first poem to the second, but the extrinsic-reasons group showed a significant decrease. Thus, though concentrating on intrinsic reasons for creative writing did not improve creativity, concentrating on extrinsic reasons for creativity impaired it. Even the mere expectation of having one's performance evaluated will hamper creativity (Amabile, Goldfarb, & Brackfield, 1990). These findings agree with the experience of the noted American poet Sylvia Plath, who believed that her persistent writer's block was caused by her excessive concern about an extrinsic reason for writing—the recognition of her work by publishers, critics, and the public. Perhaps, given students who enjoy writing, teachers should avoid pointing out the extrinsic rewards for it, such as obtaining a better job or being accepted into graduate school. Chapter 11 discusses theories that explain the negative effects of extrinsic motivation on people's performance.
>
> The example above supports the notion that psychology as a science is important and can rule out commonsense explanations. All sciences use an empirical approach. The empirical approach allows psychologists to use careful observation and experiments to gather facts and evidence.

among dancers in four cultures. In two cultures, Samoan and Balinese, dancers are expected to emphasize their individuality as a form of artistic expression. In two other cultures, Japanese and Omaha Indian, individual expression is discouraged in favor of perfecting traditional form and style. Musical innovation was found to be more common in the Samoan and Balinese cultures (Colligan, 1983). Thus, cultural norms encouraging the expression of individualized style may support the expression of individual creativity. However, it also is important to remember that there are cultural differences in how creativity is conceptualized, the extent to which creativity is encouraged, and as in this instance, the nature of artistic and creative processes (Lubart, 1999).

Cross-cultural psychologists recently have investigated theories of creativity and the level of creative expression in Western and Asian cultures to assess both culture-specific and universal aspects of creativity. A recent review of cross-cultural studies revealed that Western and Asian participants have similar—but not identical—conceptions of creativity. And Western and Asian samples differ on some measures of creativity (Niu & Sternberg, 2002). The extent of these differences, however, is not as large as one would expect. In a recent study, 50 European American and 48 Chinese participants created original drawings of geometric shapes, a creative task that should be unaffected by cultural differences in artistic style. Six European American and eight Chinese judges were trained to evaluate the creativity expressed in the drawings. The judges demonstrated remarkable consensus in judging the creativity of the drawings created by European American and Chinese undergraduates. And there were no cross-cultural differences in the level of participants' creativity (Chen et al., 2002).

Creativity and Divergent Thinking

How many ways can you use a brick? If you could think of only such uses as "to build a house" or "to build a fireplace," you would exhibit convergent thinking. According to Guilford, **convergent thinking** focuses on finding conventional "correct" solutions to problems. If you also thought of less conventional "correct" uses for a brick, such as "to prop open a door" or "to save water by putting it in a toilet tank," you would be engaging in divergent thinking. **Divergent thinking**, a hallmark of creativity (Guilford, 1984), involves freely considering a variety of potential solutions to artistic, literary, scientific, or practical problems. The importance of divergent thinking in creativity was noted as long ago as the mid-18th century (Puccio, 1991).

Overemphasis on convergent thinking can impair divergent thinking and, as a result, inhibit creativity (Reddy & Reddy, 1983). One way of inducing divergent thinking is brainstorming, in which thinkers are encouraged to conjure up as many solutions as possible to a problem. Brainstorming in small groups may result in more creative ideas than individual brainstorming, especially if the group is composed of diverse members and the exchange of ideas is encouraged (Brown & Paulus, 2002). Moreover, brainstorming is most effective in cases where the group is strongly committed to solving the problem (Litchfield, Fan, & Brown, 2011).

Performance on tests of divergent thinking correlates moderately highly with creative behavior (Runco, 1993). But creative ability in one area, such as writing poetry, might not correlate highly with creativity in another, such as writing stories. That is, divergent thinking might not be a general trait but instead might be limited to specific creative domains. This finding was illustrated in a study of seventh graders in which half were given divergent-thinking training in writing poetry and half were not. The students later were asked to write poems and short stories. Experts judged that the students who had received divergent-thinking training wrote more creative poetry than the ones who had not received special training. Moreover, the trained students showed greater creativity in their poems than in their short stories. Training in divergent thinking might affect performance on targeted tasks without affecting performance on presumably related tasks (Baer, 1996).

Divergent thinking can be cultivated. It is promoted by parents who raise their children to be open to a wide variety of experiences (Harrington, Block, & Block, 1987). Even adults can learn to use divergent thinking. This idea is not lost on industrial leaders, many

convergent thinking The cognitive process that focuses on finding conventional solutions to problems.

divergent thinking The cognitive process by which an individual freely considers a variety of potential solutions to artistic, literary, scientific, or practical problems.

Creativity

Creative people tend to be more creative when they are engaged in creative behavior for its own sake rather than to obtain some kind of reward, such as this woodcrafter in Indonesia.
Source: Dima Fadeev/Shutterstock.com.

Chapter 9 Thought and Language

of whom have their employees attend seminars so they can learn to think more creatively by engaging in divergent thinking (Basadur, Wakabayashi, & Takai, 1992). Divergent thinking also is promoted by positive emotional states (Vosburg, 1998). When you are anxious, for example, you are more likely to engage in convergent thinking (Byron & Khazanchi, 2011). Thus, teachers who evoke positive emotions in their students, and managers who evoke positive emotions in their employees, can encourage creative academic or vocational problem solving. For example, a study of physicians found that when positive emotions were induced in participants, they became more creative than control participants (Estrada, Isen, & Young, 1994).

Section Review: Creativity

1. What are some personal characteristics associated with creativity?
2. How did Amabile's study demonstrate that extrinsic rewards can impair creativity?

Decision Making

decision making A form of problem solving in which one tries to make the best choice from among alternative judgments or courses of action.

Each of our days is filled with decisions. They can be minor, such as deciding whether to take along an umbrella when leaving home, or major, such as deciding which college to attend. **Decision making** is a form of problem solving in which we try to make the best choice from among alternative courses of action to produce a desired outcome. Studies in the 1970s found that decision making also is subject to biases that can keep us from making objective decisions. Biases in decision making have been studied most extensively by two cognitive psychologists: Amos Tversky and Nobel Prize winner Daniel Kahneman. These researchers have found that our decision making often is biased by our reliance on heuristics (Kahneman, 2003). Judges, for example, sometimes use heuristics in making judicial decisions, such as setting the amount of bail in a criminal case (Dhami, 2003). Psychologists also understand that the biological basis of decision making and cognitive control is governed by the prefrontal cortex. This part of your brain helps govern self-control, self-restraint, and planning complex behavior. Human imaging studies using fMRI have shown that patients with lesions in the ventral portion of the prefrontal cortex perform worse on tasks associated with value-based decision making than healthy participants (Gläscher et al., 2012). These studies suggest that it is likely that your prefrontal cortex helps guide your use of heuristics.

Heuristics in Decision Making

Kahneman and Tversky have identified several kinds of heuristics involved in decision making. Two that have been widely studied are the *representativeness heuristic* and the *availability heuristic*.

representativeness heuristic In decision making, the assumption that a small sample is representative of its population.

The Representativeness Heuristic In using the **representativeness heuristic**, we assume that a small sample is representative of its population (Kahneman & Tversky, 1973). For example, we use the representativeness heuristic when we eat at a fast-food restaurant and assume that other restaurants in the chain will be that good (or bad). Even young children use the representativeness heuristic (Davidson, 1995). Because a sample might not accurately represent its population, the use of the representativeness heuristic does not guarantee that our decisions will be correct ones. We may make unwise decisions under emotional stress because we are more likely to rely on the representativeness heuristic when we are in stressful situations (Shaham, Singer, & Schaeffer, 1992).

Consider a study of the effect of the representativeness heuristic in relation to undergraduates' perception of the timing of historic events (Moshinsky & Bar-Hillel, 2002). Hebrew University students were given lists of important events in American and European history from 1750 to 1961. The lists contained pairs of events, one American and one European. Half the pairs included an American event that occurred earlier than the European event, and half included a European event that occurred earlier than the American event. Participants were asked to mark the event that occurred earlier. Responses were correct 58 percent of the time, but the researchers analyzed the incorrect responses. Results indicated that when the earlier event occurred in America, the error rate was 36 percent. However, when the earlier event occurred in Europe, the error rate was 47 percent. The researchers concluded that participants were biased by thinking about America as the "New World" and Europe as the "Old World." Apparently, we assume that European historical events are representative of a longer history than American historical events. The representativeness heuristic guides decisions as varied as choosing a lottery ticket number (Holtgraves & Skeel, 1992), buying or selling stocks on the stock market (Andreassen, 1988), and judging the musical tastes of strangers based on a brief description (Lonsdale & North, 2012).

The Availability Heuristic To appreciate another kind of heuristic, answer the following question: In English, is the letter *k* more likely to be the first letter or the third letter of a word? Though the letter *k* is more likely to be the third letter, most people decide that it is more likely to be the first. This result is explained by what Tversky and Kahneman (1973) call the **availability heuristic**, which is the tendency to estimate the probability of an event by how easily instances of it come to mind. The more easily an instance comes to mind, the more probable we assume the event will be. But the ease with which instances come to mind might not reflect their actual probability. Instead, instances might come to mind because they are vivid, recent, or important. Thus, because it is easier to recall words that begin with *k*, such as *kick* or *kiss*, than words that have *k* as their third letter, such as *make* or *hike*, we conclude that more words have *k* as their first letter than as their third letter.

availability heuristic In decision making, the tendency to estimate the probability of an event by how easily relevant instances of it come to mind.

In a study of the impact of the availability heuristic, undergraduates were given lists containing equal numbers of male and female names of famous people and nonfamous people and were then asked to estimate whether the lists contained more male or female names. The students' estimates depended on whether the male names or the female names were more famous. Apparently, the availability heuristic affected the students' judgment of the relative number of names—even though the number of male and female names was always equal (McKelvie & Drumheller, 2001). A similar study found that children judged the names of famous people and cartoon characters to be more common than they actually are, presumably because they come to mind more easily than other names (Davies & White, 1994).

The practical effect of the availability heuristic was shown in a study in which participants estimated the prevalence of cheating by welfare recipients. Participants who first read a vivid case of welfare cheating overestimated its prevalence (Hamill, Wilson, & Nisbett, 1980). This finding reflects our tendency to respond to rare but vivid news reports of instances of welfare recipients living in luxurious comfort by overestimating the likelihood of welfare cheating. In fact, when we lack the information required for making an objective judgment, the availability of even a single instance of an event can make us overestimate the probability of other occurrences of that event (Lewicki, 1985). This tendency holds true when judging the prevalence of drug use (Eisenman, 1993), the probability of product failures (Folkes, 1988), and the likelihood of a person contracting HIV (Triplet, 1992). It also might explain why, until recently, New York City, though usually not one of the top 10 American cities in violent crime statistics, has the reputation of being the most dangerous American city. Perhaps the national media coverage given to horrible rapes and murders in New York creates, through the availability heuristic, the belief that individuals are more likely to become victims of violent crimes there than they actually are.

Framing Effects in Decision Making

Consider the following statements: "Dr. Jones fails 10 percent of his students" and "Dr. Jones passes 90 percent of his students." Though both statements report the same reality,

framing effects Biases introduced into the decision-making process by presenting an issue or situation in a certain manner.

you might be more inclined to enroll in Dr. Jones's course after hearing the second comment than you would be after hearing the first. Your inclination is an example of what Kahneman and Tversky call *framing effects*, biases introduced in the decision-making process by presenting a situation in a particular manner. Judges, lawyers, and prosecutors are aware of framing effects in the form of leading questions, which can bias jury decisions. Research also indicates that the manner in which television news coverage portrays social protests can create powerful framing effects that influence viewer decisions about the merits of the protesters' causes (McLeod & Detenber, 1999).

Framing effects also influence our everyday decisions. In one study (Levin, Schnittjer, & Thee, 1988), undergraduates rated the incidence of cheating at their school higher when told that "65 percent of students had cheated at some time in their college career" than when told that "35 percent of the students had never cheated." The undergraduates also were more likely to rate a medical treatment as more effective, and were more apt to recommend it to others, when they were told it had a "50 percent success rate" than when told it had a "50 percent failure rate." A similar study found that undergraduates rated meat more highly when it was labeled "75 percent lean" than when it was labeled "25 percent fat" (Donovan & Jalleh, 1999). Note that in each study both statements present the same fact and differ only in how they frame the information. A recent meta-analysis of 136 studies found the overall effect size of framing on decision making to be small to moderate (Kuehberger, 1998).

To further appreciate framing effects, consider the following study by Kahneman and Tversky (1982), in which people were asked one of the following two questions: "If you lost a pair of tickets to a Broadway play for which you paid $40, would you purchase two more?" or "If you lost $40 on your way to purchase tickets at the box office, would you still purchase tickets?" Though in each case the participant would be $40 poorer, more participants answered yes to the second question. Thus, the way in which the questions were framed, not the amount of money the participants would lose, influenced their decision. Their subjective evaluation was more important than the objective situation. Framing effects influence a variety of decisions, including investment decisions (van de Heijden, Klein, Müller, & Potters, 2012), the choice of appropriate medical procedures for treating illnesses (Wang & Johnston, 1995), and decisions to engage in healthier behaviors, such as practicing regular breast self-examinations (Williams, Clarke, & Borland, 2001) and smoking cessation (Schneider et al., 2001). Framing effects even influence evaluations of a potential romantic partner as well as the anticipated success of the relationship (Knee & Boon, 2001).

Section Review: Decision Making

1. What is the availability heuristic?
2. How does the framing of leading questions influence decision making?

Artificial Intelligence

Two centuries ago a Hungarian inventor named Wolfgang von Kempelen toured Europe with the Maezel Chess Automaton, a chess-playing machine. The Automaton defeated almost all the people who dared play against it. One of its admirers was the noted American author Edgar Allen Poe, who wrote an essay speculating—incorrectly—on how it worked. After years of defeating one challenger after another, the Automaton's mechanism was finally revealed. Inside it was a legless Polish army officer named Worouski, who was a master chess player ("Program Power," 1981).

During the past few decades, computer scientists have developed computer programs that actually can play chess. Computer chess programs are the offshoot of studies in **artificial intelligence (AI)**, a field founded by Nobel Prize winner Herbert Simon that

artificial intelligence (AI) The field that integrates computer science and cognitive psychology in studying information processing through the design of computer programs that appear to exhibit intelligence.

Chapter 9 Thought and Language

integrates computer science and cognitive psychology. Researchers who study AI try to simulate or improve on human thought by using computer programs. For example, computer scientists have developed a program that answers political questions as though it were either a politically liberal or a politically conservative person (Abelson, 1981). Perhaps more important, some researchers in the field of peace psychology are now using AI to predict conflicts between countries and to promote successful conflict resolution (Hergovich & Olbrich, 2002).

Computer science and artificial intelligence researchers also are using artificial *neural networks*, which mimic human brain functioning, to help solve practical problems. For example, neural networks have been used in Milan, Italy, to help assess and prevent vehicular accidents at particular sites in that city (Mussone, Ferrari, & Oneta, 1999). Other applications of neural networks include diagnosing pancreatic cancer (Gorunescu, Gorunescu, Saftoiu, Vilmann, & Belciug, 2011), modeling insect navigation (Dale & Collett, 2001), and assessing the IQ of people with intellectual disabilities (Di Nuovo, Nuovo, & Buono, 2012). One of the central goals of this type of research is to improve the way we live our lives by pursuing innovative technologies.

Expert Systems

Many AI researchers are interested in developing computer programs, so-called **expert systems**, that display expertise in specific domains of knowledge. Computer chess programs have led the way in these efforts—and have contributed to the development of cognitive psychology itself (Charness, 1992). The first computer chess programs were developed in the 1950s at Los Alamos Laboratory in New Mexico and improved steadily during the next two decades until they finally began defeating expert chess players. In 1978 David Levy, the chess champion of Scotland, got a scare when a computer chess program defeated him in the fourth game of a six-game chess match. Levy had made a $2,500 bet that no chess program could defeat him in a match. But Levy won or drew the other five games and renewed his bet (Ehara, 1980). Despite his victory, Levy and world chess champions were doomed to eventual defeat by computer chess programs. An ominous sign occurred in 1979 at a backgammon match in Monte Carlo, when a computer program defeated the world backgammon champion, Luigi Villa of Italy. This was the first time a computer program had defeated a human world champion in an intellectual game ("Teaching a Machine the Shades of Gray," 1981).

In 1981, at the Virginia Open Chess Tournament, a computer chess program named Belle took fourth place in competition against master chess players ("Program Power," 1981). The only rating above master is grand master, the level achieved by the best chess players in the world. Whereas other computer chess programs relied on algorithms—searching for all possible sequences of moves, several moves deep—to find the best move in a given position, Belle took a more sophisticated, human approach by using heuristics. Though Belle could follow potential sequences of moves four moves deep, it did not follow each sequence to its conclusion. Instead, Belle stopped following a sequence as soon as it proved inferior to another that had already been identified. This heuristic approach made Belle perform faster and examine more potentially effective moves in a given time span than did other computer chess programs (Peterson, 1983). Expert computer programs have made great strides since the era of Belle. One chess program, KnightCap, achieved human master's level after only 3 days of online play on the Internet (Baxter, Tridgell, & Weaver, 2000). And in 1997, IBM's computer chess program Deep Blue defeated world chess champion Gary Kasparov. This was the first time that a computer chess program defeated a human world champion.

Though computer chess programs are the best known of expert systems, computer scientists have developed a variety of other systems. Among these expert systems, Mycin has helped physicians diagnose infectious diseases, Prospector has helped mining companies decide where to dig for minerals, and Dipmeter has helped analyze geological data from oil-well drillings (Davis, 1986). Expert systems also can help in the diagnosis and treatment of eating disorders (Todd, 1996). The program ES-MR helps select the best

Artificial Intelligence and Competitive Chess

Computer scientists can program a computer to play chess.
Source: maxuser/Shutterstock.com.

expert systems Computer programs that display expertise in specific domains of knowledge.

rehabilitation treatment for patients with stroke, brain injuries, and dementia (Man, Tam, & Hui-Chan, 2003), and the program Sexpert helps in the assessment and treatment of sexual dysfunctions (Ochs & Binik, 1998). Expert systems are helpful because in narrow domains of knowledge, they can analyze data more quickly and more objectively than human experts can.

Robotics

Though expert systems can analyze data more efficiently than can humans, AI researchers believe that an important difference between expert systems and human problem solving is that the latter occurs in the "real world." Experimental studies are being conducted with a new approach that uses robotics—machines operating within a physical environment rather than software programs that manipulate data. AI researchers interested in this approach believe that problem solving must be modeled with an embodied entity that is embedded in a physical context and, most important, exhibits actions that are modifiable by feedback based on the consequences of these actions (Ekbia, 2008).

The study of robotics is based on the design of robots that interact with the physical environment through sensors as well as behavioral feedback. A network of systems guides the robot's actions by sensing obstacles and avoiding collisions and enables the robot to wander the environment. Another system may, for example, allow the robot to match features of objects in the environment to perceptual categories that have been programmed into the system. The machine receives feedback from yet another system. For example, if the machine grasps the incorrect object for the task, it may receive the feedback "failure; retry." Darwin VII is one robotic machine that has a complex neural network organization. It visually explores the environment, avoids obstacles during locomotion, and tracks and grips objects. Moreover, Darwin VII displays a simulated tasting process that is sensitive to learning. Pleasant tastes are sought out more frequently, and unpleasant tastes are avoided (Krichmar & Edelman, 2002). Thus, this new approach combines cognitive psychology with behaviorist principles to more effectively model everyday human problem solving. A more recent example of intuitive robotics is that of the daVinci Surgical System. This technology is being utilized by doctors to perform delicate and complex surgeries with tiny incisions and a precise robotic arm (Renaud et al., 2013).

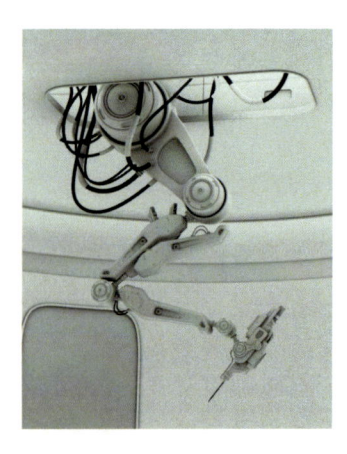

Robotics and Surgery
Today, many surgeries are performed with the assistance of programmable robots.
Source: Ociacia/Shutterstock.com.

Section Review: Artificial Intelligence

1. Why are expert systems now capable of defeating the best chess players in the world?
2. How does the robotics approach differ from that of expert systems?

Language

Arguing about politics. Reading a book. Using sign language. Each of these is made possible by **language**, a formal system of communication involving symbols—whether spoken, written, or gestured—and rules for combining them. In using language, we rely on spoken symbols to communicate through speech, written symbols to communicate through writing, and gestured symbols to communicate through sign language. We use language to communicate with other people, to store and retrieve memories, and to plan for the future.

But what makes a form of communication "language"? The world's several thousand languages share three characteristics: semanticity, generativity, and displacement. **Semanticity** is the conveying of the communicator's thoughts in a meaningful way to those who understand the language. For example, you know that *anti-* at the beginning of

language A formal system of communication involving symbols—whether spoken, written, or gestured—and rules for combining them.

semanticity The characteristic of language marked by the use of symbols to convey thoughts in a meaningful way.

Language

The ability of people to use language makes us much more flexible than any other animal in communicating with one another. We can communicate complex thoughts through spoken language or written language as well as sign language.
Source: Vladimir Mucibabic/Shutterstock.com.

a word means being against something and *-ed* at the end of a word means past action. As discussed in Chapter 14, the language spoken by people with schizophrenia often lacks semanticity; it can be meaningless to other people.

Generativity is the combining of language symbols in novel ways, without being limited to a fixed number of combinations. In fact, each day you probably say or write things that have never been said or written by anyone before. This generativity of language accounts for baby talk, rap music, Brooklynese, and the works of Shakespeare.

Displacement is the use of language to refer to objects and events that are not present. The objects and events can be in another place or in the past or future. Thus, you can talk about someone in China, your fifth birthday party, or who will win the World Series next year.

Language is only one form of communication. Many animals, ourselves included, can communicate without using language. For example, researchers allowed dogs to witness a toy or treat being placed where the dogs could not access it. When their owners were present, the dogs would alternate their gaze between their owner and the unavailable object (Miklosi, Polgardi, Topal, & Csanyi, 2000). But are dogs using language? No, the only characteristic of language that dogs display is semanticity. Dogs do not exhibit generativity or displacement in their communications.

Other animals also communicate without using true language. A bee can communicate the location of nectar-containing flowers to residents of its hive. When a bee returns to its hive after finding nectar less than 50 yards away, it performs a "circle dance" on the wall of the hive. If the nectar is farther away, the bee does a "waggle dance," moving in a figure-eight pattern. The angle of the straight line in the figure-eight pattern relative to the sun indicates the direction to the nectar, and the duration of the dance indicates the distance to the nectar—the longer the duration, the farther away it is (Dyer, 2002). But these dances are merely a form of communication, not language. They have semanticity and displacement, but they lack generativity—they are not used to indicate anything other than the location of nectar.

Consider also how monkeys use different alarm calls to signal the presence of particular kinds of predators. In one study, researchers presented Vervet monkeys with tape recordings of alarm calls that signified the presence of an eagle, a boa constrictor, or a leopard. The monkeys responded to eagle alarms by looking up, to boa constrictor alarms by looking down, and to leopard alarms by climbing up into trees (Seyfarth, Cheney, & Marler, 1980). Though monkeys use alarm calls to communicate, they do not use true language. Their calls have semanticity because they communicate the presence of a particular kind of predator, but they lack generativity and displacement. Monkeys neither combine their calls in novel ways nor use them to refer to animals that are not present.

generativity The characteristic of language marked by the ability to combine words in novel, meaningful ways.

displacement The characteristic of language marked by the ability to refer to objects and events that are not present.

Chapter 9 Thought and Language

In contrast to dogs, bees, and monkeys, people use true language. Without language, we would be severely limited in our ability to communicate with one another. You would not even be reading this book; books would not exist. Even the book of Genesis from the Old Testament recognizes the importance of language. In the story of the Tower of Babel, God punishes people for their pride by having them speak different languages—restricting their ability to communicate and to engage in cooperative projects, such as building a tower to heaven.

The Structure of Language

English and all other languages have structures governed by rules known as **grammar**. The components of grammar include *phonology*, *syntax*, and *semantics*.

grammar The set of rules that governs the proper use and combination of language symbols.

Phonology

phoneme The smallest unit of sound in a language.

phonology The study of the sounds that compose languages.

All spoken languages are composed of **phonemes**—the basic sounds of a language. The study of phonemes is called **phonology**. Languages use as few as 20 and as many as 80 phonemes. English contains about 40—the number varies with the dialect. Each phoneme is represented by either a letter (such as the *o* sound in *go*) or a combination of letters (such as the *sh* sound in *should*). Words are combinations of phonemes, and each language permits only certain combinations. A native speaker of English would realize that the combination of phonemes in *cogerite* forms an acceptable word in English even though there is no such word. That person also would realize that the combination of phonemes in *klputng* does not form an acceptable word in English. There is some evidence that women recognize and process phonemes faster than do men (Majeres, 1999).

One language might not include all the phonemes found in another language, and people learning to speak a foreign language might have more difficulty pronouncing the phonemes in the foreign language that are not in their native language. For example, native speakers of Japanese who learn English as adults have difficulty in distinguishing between *r* sounds, as in *rock*, and *l* sounds, as in *lock*. This difficulty may be due to differences in how phonemes are processed by the brain and early childhood experience with language—though providing training and feedback to native speakers of Japanese improves their ability to distinguish between the two sounds (McClelland, Fiez, & McCandliss, 2002). Catherine Best and Robert Avery investigated American and African adults' perception of *click consonants*—sounds produced by creating suction in the mouth and then releasing with the tongue, producing a sound that is similar to a "tsk" with an abrupt stop. English speakers process clicks acoustically—that is, as nonspeech sounds. In some African languages, clicks have linguistic significance and are perceived as consonants. Participants in the study were native speakers of English and Zulu and Xhosa, two African tone languages with click consonants. The experimental task involved identifying and matching click consonants and nonsense syllables. Results indicated that native Zulu and Xhosa speakers demonstrated more accurate performance on the experimental tasks, and the researchers attributed this finding to the fact that African tone language speakers processed the clicks linguistically rather than acoustically (Best & Avery, 2000).

morpheme The smallest meaningful unit of language.

Individual phonemes and combinations of phonemes form **morphemes**, the smallest meaningful units of language. Words are composed of one or more morphemes. For example, the word *book* is composed of a single morpheme. In contrast, the word *books* is composed of two morphemes: *book*, which refers to an object, and *-s*, which indicates the plural of a word. One of the common morphemes that affect the meaning of words is the *-ing* suffix, which indicates ongoing action. Note that the 40 or so phonemes in English build more than 100,000 morphemes, which in turn build almost 500,000 words. Using these words, we can create a virtually infinite number of sentences. One of the outstanding characteristics of language is, indeed, its generativity.

Chapter 9 Thought and Language

Syntax

In addition to rules that govern the acceptable combinations of sounds in words, languages have **syntax**—rules that govern the acceptable arrangement of words in phrases and sentences. Because you know English syntax, you would say "She ate the ice cream" but not "She the ice cream ate" (though poets do have a "license" to violate normal syntax). And syntax varies from one language to another. The English sentence *John hit Bill* would be translated into its Japanese equivalent as *John Bill hit*. The normal order of the verb and the object in Japanese is the opposite of their normal order in English (Gliedman, 1983). As for adjectives, in English they usually precede the nouns they modify, whereas in Spanish adjectives usually follow the nouns they modify. The English phrase *the red book* would be *el libro rojo* in Spanish. Therefore, a Spanish-speaker learning English might say "the book red," whereas an English-speaker learning Spanish might say "el rojo libro."

syntax The rules that govern the acceptable arrangement of words in phrases and sentences.

Semantics

Not only must words be arranged appropriately in phrases and sentences, they must be meaningful. The study of how language conveys meaning is called **semantics**. Psycholinguist Noam Chomsky has been intrigued by our ability to convey the same meaning through different phrases and sentences. Consider the sentences *The boy fed the horse* and *The horse was fed by the boy*. Both express the same meaning, but they use different syntax. Moreover, the meaning expressed by these sentences can be expressed in French, Chinese, Swahili, and so on, though the sentences used to express it in those languages would be different from the English sentences.

semantics The study of how language conveys meaning.

To explain this ability to express the same meaning using different phrases or different languages, Chomsky distinguishes between a language's deep structure and its surface structure. The **deep structure** is the underlying meaning of a statement; the **surface structure** is the word arrangements that express the underlying meaning. Our ability to discern the deep structure of literary works, for example, lets us appreciate the motives of the main characters. **Transformational grammar** is the term that Chomsky gives to the rules by which languages generate surface structures out of deep structures, and deep structures out of surface structures. Language comprehension involves transforming the surface structure, which is the verbal message, into its deep structure, which is its meaning. Thus, the sentences *The boy fed the horse* and *The horse was fed by the boy* are transformed into the same deep structure, or meaning.

deep structure The underlying meaning of a statement.

surface structure The word arrangements used to express meaning.

transformational grammar The rules by which languages generate surface structures out of deep structures and deep structures out of surface structures.

The meaning of a statement depends not only on its words and their arrangement but also on the social context in which the statement is made (Paradis, 1998). The branch of semantics that is concerned with the relationship between language and its social context is called **pragmatics**. To appreciate the relationship between language and its social context, consider the following statement made by a student about an upcoming meal in the cafeteria: "I can't wait to have dinner tonight." If spoken in an enthusiastic voice during Thanksgiving week, the statement might mean that the student expects to enjoy a delicious turkey dinner. Yet, if spoken in a sarcastic voice during a normal school week, the same statement might mean that the student expects to be confronted by the cafeteria's notorious "mystery meat." Language pragmatics are based upon the cultural knowledge of native speakers (Reeder & Shapiro, 1993). Cross-cultural differences in the pragmatics that characterize Western and Asian languages include turn-taking (Lerner & Takagi, 1999) and directness of speech (Holtgraves, 1997). And in African postcolonial cultures such as Cameroon it is considered disrespectful to call certain people by their names rather than their roles in the culture, such as father-in-law or co-wife (Anchimbe, 2011).

pragmatics The relationship between language and its social context.

The importance of pragmatics also is exemplified by the difficulty scientists have had in developing computer programs that can truly converse with people (Saygin & Cicekli, 2002). A program capable of comprehending speech would have to consider characteristics of the message, the speaker, and the situation. The difficulty in employing pragmatics in developing computer programs that can comprehend speech is illustrated

Chapter 9 Thought and Language

in the following conversation (Gorman, 1985, p. 65) between a news reporter (R) and a computer "therapist" called Eliza (E):

R: Row, row, row your boat

E: What about your own boat?

R: Gently down the stream

E: Why do you say that?

R: Merrily, merrily, merrily, merrily

E: I am not sure I understand you fully.

R: Life is but a dream.

E: What does the dream suggest to you?

Section Review: The Structure of Language

1. What roles do semanticity, generativity, and displacement play in language?
2. What is the relationship between transformational grammar and the deep structure and surface structure of language?

The Acquisition of Language

What accounts for a child's ability to progress from a crying, gurgling infant to a talkative 3-year-old? The process of language acquisition seems to be universal, with infants in all cultures acquiring language in similar ways as they pass through distinct stages (Rice, 1989). Though the timing of the stages can vary among infants, the order does not.

Language Milestones

For the first few months after birth, infants are limited to communicating vocally through cooing, gurgling, and crying, which they use to indicate that they are content, happy, distressed, hungry, or in pain. Between 4 and 6 months of age, infants enter the babbling stage. When infants babble, they repeat sequences of phonemes, such as ba-ba-ba. Infants in all cultures begin babbling at about the same age and produce the same range of phonemes, including some that are not part of their parents' language (Roug, Landberg, & Lundberg, 1989). This similarity in phonemes might account for the prevalence of the words *mama*, *papa*, and *dada* to refer to parents in a variety of cultures. Even deaf infants begin babbling at the same age as infants who can hear, though their babbling is different from that of infants who can hear (Oller & Eilers, 1988). The universality of the onset and initial content of babbling indicates that it is a product of the maturation of an inborn predisposition, rather than a product of experience. Nonetheless, by the age of 9 months, infants begin to show the influence of experience, as they limit their babbling to the phonemes of the language, or languages, that they hear in their social environment.

When infants are about 1 year old, they begin to say their first words. Their earliest words typically refer to objects that interest them. Thus, common early words include *milk* and *doggie*. In using words, older infants exhibit **overextension**, applying words too broadly (Behrend, 1988). Consider an infant who refers to her cat as "kitty." If she also refers to dogs, cows, horses, and other four-legged animals as "kitty," she would be exhibiting overextension. In contrast, if she refers to her cat, but to no other cats, as "kitty," she would be exhibiting **underextension**—applying words too narrowly (Caplan & Barr, 1989). As infants gain experience with objects and language, they rapidly learn to apply their words to the correct objects.

After learning to say single words, infants begin using them in **holophrastic speech**, which is the use of single words to represent whole phrases or sentences. For example,

overextension The tendency to apply a word to more objects or actions than it actually represents.

underextension The tendency to apply a word to fewer objects or actions than it actually represents.

holophrastic speech The use of single words to represent whole phrases or sentences.

Language Milestones

If this child refers to her cat as "kitty" and all other animals as "kitty," she would exhibit overextension. When she only refers to her cat—but no other cats—as "kitty," she would be exhibiting underextension.
Source: Oksana Kuzmina/Shutterstock.com.

an infant might say "car" on one occasion to indicate that the family car has pulled into the driveway and on another occasion to indicate that he would like to go for a ride. Between the ages of 18 and 24 months, infants go beyond holophrastic speech by speaking two-word phrases, typically including a noun and a verb in a consistent order. The infant is now showing a rudimentary appreciation of proper syntax, as in "Baby drink" or "Mommy go." Because, in the two-word stage, infants rely on nouns and verbs and leave out other parts of speech (such as articles and prepositions), their utterances are called **telegraphic speech**. To save time and money, people who used to write telegrams left out connecting parts of speech yet still communicated meaningful messages.

Until they are about 2 years old, infants use words to refer only to objects that are located in their immediate environment. At about age 2, children begin speaking sentences that include other parts of speech in addition to nouns and verbs. They also begin to exhibit displacement, as when a 2-year-old asks, "Grandma come tomorrow?" After age 2, children show a rapid increase in their vocabulary and in the length and complexity of their sentences. Psychologist Roger Brown (1973) invented a unit of measurement, the **mean length of utterance (MLU)**, to assess children's level of language maturation. The MLU is calculated by taking samples of a child's statements and finding their average length in morphemes. The MLU increases rapidly in early childhood, though there is some variability from one child to another. The MLU is a better predictor of overall language ability at younger ages than in later childhood (Scarborough, Rescorla, Tager-Flusberg, Fowler, & Sudhalter, 1991). The use of the MLU has proved useful in assessing language development with a variety of native languages, including Icelandic (Thordardottir & Weismer, 1998). The MLU also has been used to assess the language development of children with intellectual disabilities (Pattison & Robertson, 2016).

The increased sophistication that young children show in their use of language is partly attributable to their application of language rules, which they learn from listening to the speech of those around them. From the day of their birth, infants are exposed to sophisticated language. In fact, studies have found that, contrary to popular impressions, staff members in hospital nurseries do not rely solely on baby talk and soothing sounds when speaking to newborn infants. Instead, staff members spend much of the time speaking to the infants with normal, though perhaps simple, phrases and sentences (Rheingold & Adams, 1980). The language rules that children in European American cultures learn are strongly influenced by their parents' speech—especially mothers' (Leaper, Anderson, & Sanders, 1998). In most non-Western cultures, however, children acquire language through interacting with a number of adults and other children (Mohanty & Perregaux, 1997).

Many languages, like English, have exceptions to grammatical rules. This inconsistency might explain the phenomenon of **overregularization**—the application of grammatical rules without making necessary exceptions (Maratsos, 2000). For example, at

telegraphic speech Speech marked by reliance on nouns and verbs while other parts of speech, including articles and prepositions, are omitted.

mean length of utterance (MLU) A unit of measurement that assesses children's level of language maturation.

overregularization The application of a grammatical rule without making necessary exceptions to it.

Chapter 9 Thought and Language

first children using the past tense will, correctly, say words such as *did*, *went*, and *brought*, which violate the *-ed* rule for forming the past tense. They learn these words by hearing the speech of older children and adults. But as children learn the *-ed* rule, they say words such as *doed*, *goed*, or *bringed*. Later, when they realize that grammatical rules have exceptions, they learn not to apply the *-ed* rule to irregular verbs, and again say *did*, *went*, and *brought* (Kolata, 1987). Thus, children tend at first to use correct wording, then begin to overregularize, and finally realize when to follow grammatical rules and when to break them (Marcus, 1995).

How do we know that infants learn rules rather than a series of specific instances of correct grammar? One source of evidence is a study by Jean Berko (1958), who reasoned that if children use correct grammar when confronted with words they have never heard, then they must be relying on rules, not rote memory. To test her assumption, Berko developed the "Wug test," which included drawings of imaginary creatures called "wugs." Berko found that children would, indeed, apply grammatical rules to novel words. For example, when shown a picture identified as a "wug" and then a picture with two of them, children completed the statement "There are two ____" with the word *wugs*. This finding shows that they have learned to use the *-s* ending to indicate the plural.

Is There a Critical Period for Language Acquisition?

As described at the beginning of the chapter, many language researchers believe that there is a critical period for the acquisition of language during childhood. Children who are kept isolated from contact with language and not intensively exposed to language until adolescence—typically because they live in an abusive household—usually have great difficulty becoming proficient in their use of language. But such case studies do not permit us to know for certain whether these children would have shown normal language development had they been exposed to language beginning in infancy in a nurturing household.

Another, perhaps stronger, line of research on critical periods is concerned with adults who learn second languages. Second languages become progressively more difficult to learn as we get older (Birdsong & Molis, 2001). Support for this finding came from a study in which older Korean and Chinese immigrants to the United States found it more difficult to learn English than did younger immigrants—even though the groups were intellectually equal (Johnson & Newport, 1989). Nonetheless, this finding must be viewed with caution in light of the many other factors that could account for differences in the ease with which younger and older immigrants learn a new language.

Theories of Language Acquisition

Language researchers debate this question: Is language acquired solely through learning, or is it strongly influenced by the maturation of an inherited predisposition to develop language? Those who favor the learning position assume that if it were possible to raise two infants together with no exposure to language, they would not develop true language. In contrast, those who favor the view that language emerges from an inherited predisposition assume that the two infants might develop a rudimentary form of language marked by semanticity, generativity, and displacement. According to this position, learning normally determines only which language an infant will speak, whether English, French, or Navajo.

Language as the Product of Learning B. F. Skinner (1957) claimed that language is acquired solely through learning, chiefly through the positive reinforcement of appropriate speech. For example, a 1-year-old child might learn to say "milk" because her parents give her milk and praise her when she says "milk." Similarly, a 2-year-old child named Jane might be given a cookie and praise for saying "Give Jane cookie" but not for saying "Jane cookie give." As you can see, Skinner assumed that vocabulary and grammar are learned through positive reinforcement. In a study supportive of Skinner's position, two groups of infants between 2 and 7 months old were positively reinforced for producing

Modeling Language

The modeling of language by parents is an important factor in the acquisition of a particular language by children.
Source: rSnapshotPhotos/Shutterstock.com.

different phonemes. The infants were reinforced by smiles, *tsk* sounds, and light stroking of the abdomen. One group was reinforced for making vowel sounds, whereas the other group was reinforced for making consonant sounds. The infants responded by increasing their production of the phonemes that were reinforced. This study showed that positive reinforcement can affect language acquisition (Routh, 1969). Of course, it does not indicate that language is acquired *solely* through learning.

Albert Bandura (1977), the influential cognitive-behavioral psychologist, stresses the role of observational learning in language acquisition. He assumes that children develop language primarily by imitating the vocabulary and grammatical constructions used by their parents and others in their everyday lives. In a study that supported his position, adults replied to statements made by 2-year-old children by purposely using slightly more complex syntax than the children normally would. After 2 months, the children had developed more complex syntax than did children who had not been exposed to the adult models (Nelson, 1977). Additional support for the effect of modeling comes from findings that 2-year-olds whose parents read to them acquire language more rapidly than do 2-year-olds whose parents do not (Whitehurst, Falco, Lonigan, Fischel, DeBaryshe, Valdez-Menchaca, & Caulfield, 1988). Yet, we cannot discount the possibility that other differences between the two groups of parents produced this effect.

Language as an Inherited Predisposition The assumption that language is acquired solely through learning has been challenged by the American linguist and scientist Noam Chomsky and his followers (Rondall, 1994). Chomsky insists that infants are born with the predisposition to develop language. He believes they inherit a *language acquisition device*—a hypothetical place in the brain that makes them sensitive to phonemes, syntax, and semantics. Chomsky has since refined this idea to the theory of *universal grammar*, which suggests that the ability to learn language is hard-wired, does not need to be taught, and is common to all humans. In analyzing the interactions of parents and children, Chomsky has found that children in different cultures progress through similar stages and learn their native languages without formal parental instruction. Children say things that adults never say, and their parents do not positively reinforce proper grammar (or correct improper grammar) in any consistent manner. Modeling, too, cannot explain all language learning because observations of children show that they vary greatly in the extent to which they imitate what their parents say (Snow, 1981).

What evidence is there to support Chomsky's position? One source of evidence comes from the Human Genome Project. In 2001, scientists discovered that the gene FOXP2 plays an important role in our ability to acquire spoken language (Marcus & Fisher, 2003). Another source of evidence is the universality in the basic features of language and the stages of language acquisition (Miller, 1990), which indicates that the tendency to develop language is inborn. Studies of deaf children and children of deaf parents support

Chomsky's position. One study observed deaf children who were neither rewarded for using sign language nor exposed to a model who used it. Nonetheless, the children spontaneously developed their own gestural system in which they communicated by using signs with the characteristics of true language (Goldin-Meadow & Mylander, 1998). And infants born to deaf parents develop unique rhythmic hand movements that reflect the rhythmic patterns of language (Petitto, Holowka, Sergio, & Ostry, 2001).

Despite the evidence favoring language as innate and contradicting learning as an explanation for language acquisition, research has provided some support for the learning position (Stemmer, 1990). One study tested the claim made by those who favor Chomsky's position that adults typically ignore children's speech errors and fail to correct their ungrammatical statements. The study found that language acquisition does depend in part on feedback provided by adults who correct specific instances of improper grammar. Adults do so by repeating a child's grammatically incorrect statements in grammatically correct form or by asking the child to clarify his or her statements (Bohannon & Stanowicz, 1988).

It seems that the positions of Chomsky, Skinner, and Bandura must be integrated to explain how language is acquired. We appear to be born with a predisposition to develop language, which provides us with an innate sensitivity to grammar. But we might learn our specific language, including its grammar, mainly through operant conditioning and observational learning.

> ### Section Review: The Acquisition of Language
>
> 1. What are the main characteristics of the stages of language development during infancy?
> 2. How do the theories of Skinner and Chomsky differ in regard to language development?

The Relationship Between Language and Thought

In his novel *1984*, George Orwell (1949) envisioned a totalitarian government that controlled citizen's thoughts by regulating their language. By adding, removing, or redefining words, the government used *Newspeak* to ensure that citizens would not think rebellious thoughts against their leader, "Big Brother." For example, in Newspeak the word *joycamp* referred to a forced labor camp. And the word *free* was redefined to refer only to physical reality, as in *The dog is free from lice*, rather than to political freedom. Even democratic government officials will, at times, resort to euphemisms reminiscent of Newspeak. For example, to reduce public outrage about deceptive government practices, American officials coined the word *misinformation* to replace the word *lying*. Businesspeople also understand the power of language to shape thought, as when used-car dealers refer to their vehicles as *previously owned* instead of *used*.

The Linguistic Relativity Hypothesis

linguistic relativity hypothesis
Benjamin Whorf's hypothesis that one's perception of the world is molded by one's language.

Orwell's view of the influence of language on thought was shared by the linguist-anthropologist Benjamin Lee Whorf (1897–1941), who expressed it in his **linguistic relativity hypothesis**, which assumes that our perception of the world is determined by the particular language we speak (Smith, 1996). Whorf (1956) pointed out that Inuit (once called "Eskimo") languages have several words for snow (such as words that distinguish between falling snow and fallen snow), whereas the English language has only one. According to the linguistic relativity hypothesis, the variety of words for snow in an Inuit language causes people who speak it to perceive differences in snow that people who speak English do not.

Critics argue that, on the contrary, thought determines language. Perhaps the greater importance of snow in their culture led the Inuits to coin several words for snow, each referring to a different kind. Moreover, English speakers to whom snow is important, such as avid skiers, use different adjectives to describe different kinds of snow. Their ability to distinguish between crusty, powdery, and granular snow indicates that even English speakers can perceive wide variations in the quality of snow. And the number of words for snow in Inuit languages might have been exaggerated in the early reports that influenced Whorf and other linguistic relativity theorists (Pullum, 1991).

What does formal research have to say about the linguistic relativity hypothesis? In an early study bearing on Whorf's hypothesis (Carmichael, Hogan, & Walter, 1932), participants were presented with ambiguous drawings of objects that were given either of two labels (see Figure 9-3). When later asked to draw the objects, participants drew pictures that looked more like the object that had been named than like the object they had seen. These results supported Whorf's hypothesis, at least in that language appeared to influence the participants' recall of objects.

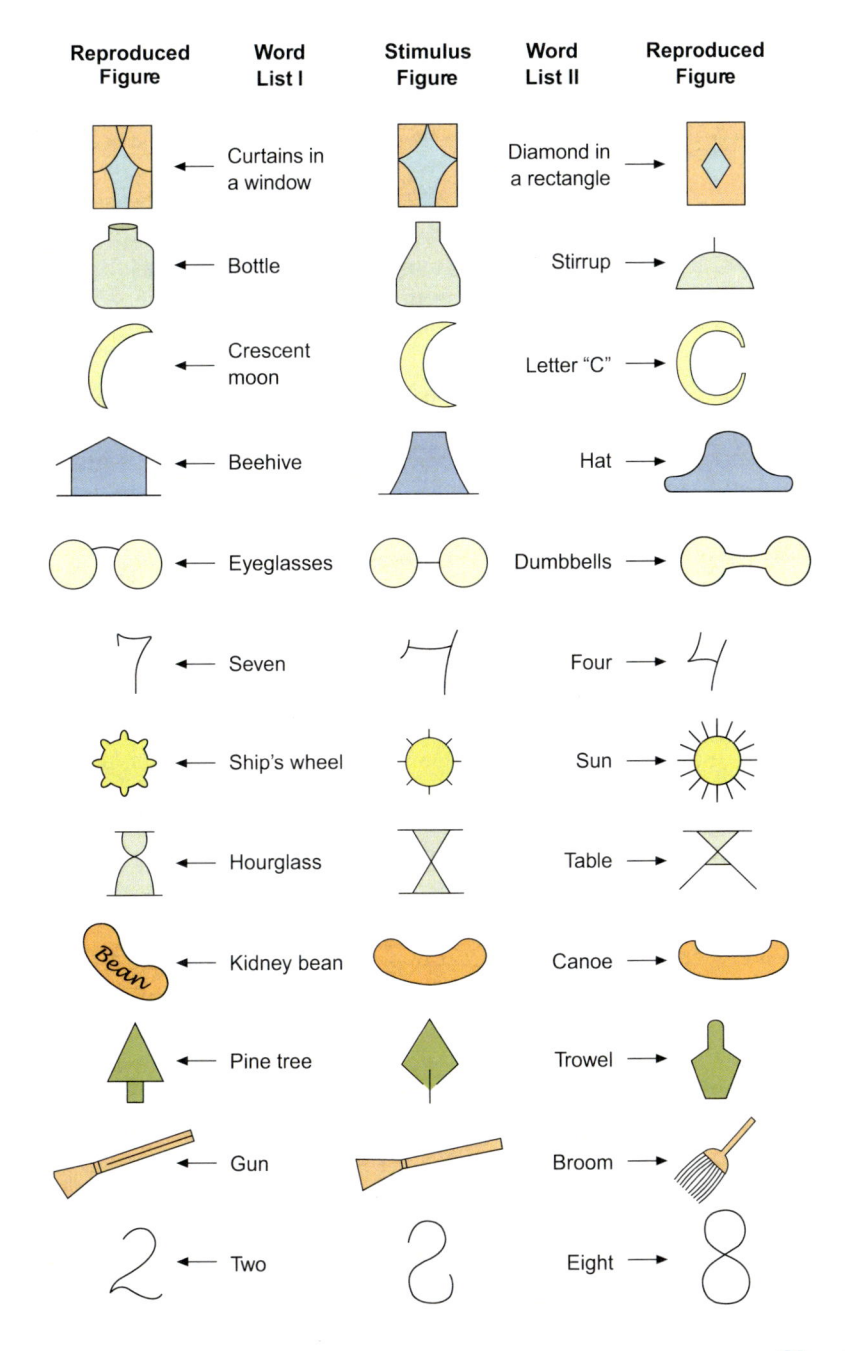

FIGURE 9-3
The Effect of Labels on Recall

Participants were shown the pictures in the middle column with one of two different labels. When later asked to draw what they had seen, the participants drew pictures that were consistent with the labels, not with the pictures. This finding indicates that language can affect how we think about the world even though it might not affect how we perceive the world.

Source: Carmichael, L., Hogan, H. P., & Walter, A. (1932). An experimental study of the effect of language on the reproduction of visually perceived forms. *Journal of Experimental Psychology, 15*, 73–86.

> ## The Research Process
>
> ### Does Language Influence Children's Conceptions of Gender Roles?
>
> **Rationale**
>
> Janet Shibley Hyde (1984) conducted a classic study to test the effects of gendered pronouns on children's stereotypes about women and men.
>
> **Method**
>
> The participants in Hyde's study were 132 male and female third and fifth graders. All children read a story about a fictitious occupation: *wudgemaker*. Four versions of the story were prepared. In each version, the description of wudgemakers was identical; only the pronouns used in each story differed. One group read stories with *he* for the pronoun, the second read stories with *they*, the third read stories with *he or she*, and the fourth read stories with *she*. After reading the stories, the children were asked to provide two ratings: how well men could do the job and how well women could do the job.
>
> **Results and Discussion**
>
> Children's ratings of the male wudgemakers' competence were not affected by the pronouns they read in their stories. Male wudgemakers were seen as equally competent, regardless of the pronouns used in the stories. However, pronouns did have an effect on mean ratings of the female wudgemakers. The group who read stories with *he* as a pronoun rated female wudgemakers as "just O.K." In contrast, the other three groups rated female wudgemakers as significantly more competent. The highest rating was obtained for the group who read stories with *she* as a pronoun. Hyde concluded that pronoun use did have an influence on children's gender-role stereotypes.
>
> These findings have been supported by more recent empirical research. Mykol Hamilton and her colleagues conducted three studies in which they asked children and adults to tell stories about sex-neutral stuffed animals (e.g., a dog, deer, or mouse). Most participants, regardless of age or sex, referred to the animals as "he" (Lambdin, Greer, Jibotian, Wood, & Hamilton, 2003). Because our use of language can affect the way we think about gender roles as well as other aspects of everyday life, the linguistic relativity hypothesis might have some merit, as long as it is used to recognize that though language influences thought, it does not determine it (Davies, 1998).

Eleanor Rosch (1975) conducted a classic study to test whether language influences the perception of colors. She hypothesized that if the linguistic relativity hypothesis were correct, people who speak a language that has many color words would perceive colors differently than would people who speak a language with few color words.

When Rosch visited the Dani people of New Guinea, she found that the Dani language has two basic color words: *mili* for dark, cool colors, and *mola* for light, warm colors. In contrast, English has eleven basic color words: *black*, *white*, *red*, *green*, *yellow*, *blue*, *brown*, *purple*, *pink*, *orange*, and *gray*. To describe these colors, the Dani use relatively long phrases. Rosch wondered whether these differences in language would be associated with differences in the perception of colors. She decided to test this hypothesis by using "focal" colors, which are considered the best representatives of each of the colors (for example, "fire-engine red" for red), and nonfocal colors.

Dani and American participants were given a series of trials on which they were first shown a colored plastic chip for 5 seconds. After another 30 seconds, they were asked to select the chip from among 160 colored chips. Both the American participants and the Dani participants performed better when the chip to be recalled was a focal color than when it was a nonfocal color. These results contradicted Whorf's hypothesis because, though the Dani use only two color names, they are as capable as English-speaking people of perceiving all the focal colors in the English language. Perhaps we are genetically prepared to perceive these focal colors regardless of whether our language takes special note of them.

During the past decades, though, interest in the relationship between language and thought has been spurred by recent research in cognitive linguistics. Cognitive linguistics researchers have found that language may influence cross-cultural variation in a number of ways, including noun-verb relations, conversational and story-telling patterns, cultural scripts that encourage or discourage particular ways of thinking, encoding of the meaning of words, and theories of the self (Goddard, 2003). For example, one study investigated 39 languages spoken in 71 cultures. Cultures with "pronoun drop languages"—languages that omit personal pronouns (*I* and *you*) in conversation—are less individualistic than are cultures with languages that include personal pronouns (Kashima & Kashima, 1998).

Linguistic Relativity and Sexist Language

Though language does not determine how we think about the world, it might influence how we think about the world (Hoffman, Lau, & Johnson, 1986). This presumption is the basis of the current concern about the traditional use of masculine pronouns, such as *his* and *him*, to refer to persons when no sexual identification is intended (Prentice, 1994). Critics of this practice claim that it makes people think that such statements refer primarily to men. Perhaps repeated exposure to such use of the male pronoun to refer to both women and men promotes the belief that certain gender-neutral activities are more suitable for men than for women, the topic discussed in "The Research Process" box above.

Section Review: The Relationship Between Language and Thought

1. How does Orwell's concept of Newspeak embody the belief that language affects thought?
2. How are concerns about sexist language related to the linguistic relativity hypothesis?

Language in Apes

In the early 17th century, the philosopher René Descartes argued that language was the critical feature that distinguished people from other animals. Interest in teaching animals cognitive skills, such as language, that normally are associated with people was stimulated by the case of "Clever Hans," a horse who impressed onlookers by solving arithmetic problems in Germany in the early 20th century. Hans was trained to count out the answers to arithmetic problems by tapping one of his hooves until he reached the correct answer. He counted anything present, including persons, hats, or umbrellas. But a psychologist named Oskar Pfungst showed that Hans stopped counting when he noticed tiny movements of his questioner's head, which cued the initiation and termination of counting. When the questioner knew the answer, Hans was correct almost all the time. But when the questioner did not know the answer, Hans was wrong all the time. So, Hans might have been clever, but he had no idea how to perform arithmetic (Davis & Memmott, 1982).

As interest waned in teaching animals to perform arithmetic, interest in teaching them language grew. As you read earlier in the chapter, animals as diverse as bees, dogs, and monkeys can communicate in limited, stereotyped ways. But they do not use true language, which is characterized by semanticity, generativity, and displacement. Research on language learning in dolphins (Herman & Uyeyama, 1999) and sea lions (Gisiner & Schusterman, 1992) is promising but has yet to provide conclusive findings. A much larger body of research supports the belief that there is at least one kind of nonhuman animal capable of acquiring true language—the ape (Williams, Brakke, & Savage-Rumbaugh, 1997).

Teaching Chimpanzees to Use Language

More than 50 years ago, Winthrop and Luella Kellogg (1933) published a book about their experiences raising a chimpanzee named Gua with their infant son, Donald. Even after being exposed to speech as a member of the family, Gua could not speak a single word. Another couple, Cathy and Keith Hayes (Hayes, 1951), had only slightly better

Can Chimpanzees Acquire Language?

Studying chimpanzees has helped us learn about the nature of language.

Source: underworld/Shutterstock.com.

results with Viki, a chimpanzee they too raised as a member of their family. Despite their intensive efforts over a period of several years, Viki learned to say only four words: *mama*, *papa*, *cup*, and *up*. The Hayeses concluded that the vocal anatomy of apes is not designed for producing speech.

In 1925 the primatologist Robert Yerkes, wondering whether apes have lots to say but no way of saying it, suggested teaching them to use sign language instead of speech. His suggestion was not carried out until 1966, when Allen and Beatrix Gardner (1969) of the University of Nevada began teaching American Sign Language (ASL) to a 1-year-old chimpanzee named Washoe. They raised Washoe in a trailer next to their house. To encourage her to use ASL, they never spoke in her presence; instead, they signed to each other and Washoe, using simple words about various objects and everyday events (Dewsbury, 1996). They also asked Washoe simple questions, praised her correct signs, and tried to comply with her requests, just as parents do with young children. After 4 years of training, Washoe, had a repertoire of 132 signs, which she used to name objects and to describe qualities of objects. The Gardners later replicated their work with four other apes, teaching each to use sign language (Gardner, Gardner, & Van Cantfort, 1989).

Washoe also displayed the ability to generalize her signs to refer to similar things. For example, she used the sign for *open* to refer to doors on a car, a house, and a refrigerator. Washoe even seemed to show an important characteristic of true language—generativity. On seeing a swan for the first time, Washoe made the signs for *water bird*. And in a chimpanzee colony in Washington State, Washoe taught ASL to a young chimpanzee named Loulis, whom she had "adopted" (Cunningham, 1981). After 5 years, Loulis had acquired a vocabulary of more than 50 signs, which he could have learned only from Washoe and other chimpanzees, since all human signing was forbidden when Loulis was present (Gardner, Gardner, & Van Cantfort, 1989).

During the past few decades, several other apes have been taught to use sign language or other forms of language. Ann and David Premack taught a laboratory chimpanzee named Sarah to use plastic chips of different shapes and colors to represent words (Premack, 1971). Sarah learned to answer questions by arranging the chips in different sequences on a board to form sentences. Duane Rumbaugh taught a chimpanzee named Lana to use a computer to create sentences by pressing large keys marked by lexigrams—geometric shapes representing particular words (Rumbaugh, Gill, & von Glasersfeld, 1973). Lana formed sentences by pressing keys in a particular order. Lana's language was called "Yerkish," in honor of Robert Yerkes. When Lana made grammatically correct requests, she was rewarded with food, toys, music, or other things she enjoyed.

Controversy About Ape-Language Research

Have Washoe, Sarah, and Lana learned to use true language? Do they exhibit semanticity, generativity, and displacement? That is, can they communicate meaningfully, create novel combinations of signs, and refer to objects that are not present? Columbia University psychologist Herbert Terrace, who once believed that apes can use language, says no (Terrace, Petitto, Sanders, & Bever, 1979). Terrace taught a chimpanzee named Nim Chimpsky to use sign language. (Nim was named after Noam Chomsky, who believes that apes cannot learn true language.) After 5 years of training, Nim had mastered 125 signs. At first, Terrace assumed that Nim had learned true language. But after analyzing videotapes of conversations with Nim and videotapes of other apes that had been taught sign language, he concluded that Nim and the other apes did not display true language.

On what did Terrace base his conclusion? He found that apes merely learned to make signs, arrange forms, or press computer keys in a certain order to obtain rewards. In other words, their use of language was no different from that of a pigeon that learns to peck a sequence of keys to get food rewards. So, the ability of an ape to produce a string of words does not indicate that the ape has learned to produce a sentence. Terrace also claims that the apparent generativity of ape language might be a misinterpretation of their actions. For example, Washoe's apparent reference to a swan as a "water bird" might have been a reference to two separate things—a body of water and a bird.

As additional evidence against ape language, Terrace claims that many instances of allegedly spontaneous signing by chimpanzees are actually responses to subtle cues from trainers. Terrace found that Nim communicated primarily in response to prompting by his trainer or by imitating signs recently made by his trainer. Thus, he did not use language in an original or spontaneous way, and his signs were simply gestures prompted by cues from his trainer that produced consequences he desired—a kind of operant conditioning (Terrace, 1985).

Terrace's attack has not gone unchallenged. Francine Patterson taught a gorilla named Koko to use more than 300 signs ("Ape Language," 1981). Koko even displays generativity, as in spontaneously referring to a zebra as a "white tiger." Patterson criticized Terrace for basing his conclusions on his work with Nim and on isolated frames he has examined from films of other apes using ASL. She claimed that Nim's inadequate use of language might stem from his being confused by having 60 different trainers, which could account for Nim's failure to use sign language in a spontaneous way. In contrast, Patterson reported that Koko had only one primary trainer and used signs more spontaneously than Nim did. For example, Koko responded to a velvet hat by signing "that soft" (Patterson, Patterson, & Brentari, 1987).

In recent years, the strongest evidence in support of ape language comes from studies by Duane Rumbaugh and Sue Savage-Rumbaugh of the Language Research Center at Georgia State University. They trained two chimpanzees, Austin and Sherman, to communicate through Yerkish, the language used earlier by Lana. Austin and Sherman use language in a more sophisticated way than previous chimpanzees. In one study, Austin, Sherman, and Lana were taught to categorize three objects (an orange, a beancake, and a slice of bread) as "edible" and three objects (a key, a stick, and a pile of coins) as "inedible." When given other objects, Austin and Sherman, but not Lana, were able to categorize them as edible or inedible. Perhaps Lana could not learn this task because she had been trained to use language to associate labels with specific objects rather than to understand the concepts to which the labels referred (Savage-Rumbaugh, Rumbaugh, Smith, & Lawson, 1980).

Even when housed in different rooms, Austin and Sherman can request objects from each other. This ability was demonstrated when one of the chimpanzees was given a box from which he could obtain food or drink only by using a tool located in the other chimpanzee's room. The chimpanzee in the room with the food indicated the tool he needed by striking a specific series of keys on a computer keyboard. The chimpanzee in the room with the tools then passed that tool to the other chimpanzee (Marx, 1980).

More recently, Sue Savage-Rumbaugh and her colleagues (1986) described their work with two pygmy chimpanzees, Kanzi and Mulika, who have achieved language ability superior to that of previous apes. Savage-Rumbaugh and her researchers exposed the chimpanzees to human language during everyday activities rather than as part of an

Experiencing Psychology

Will the Replication of a Classic Research Study on Mental Sets Produce Similar Findings Today?

In the section titled "Problem Solving," you read about the cognitive impediment to problem solving called a mental set. A mental set is a predisposition to rely on an approach to solving a problem that has worked so well in the past that it blinds you to an effective solution to a current problem. The classic water-jar study supporting the negative effect of mental sets on problem solving was conducted more than 50 years ago (Luchins, 1946). In this exercise, you will conduct an approximate replication of the water-jar study to determine whether the original findings will hold up today.

Method
Participants
The participants will be 30 "naïve" fellow male and female students—that is, students who have not taken introductory psychology. Using students who have taken introductory psychology might threaten the validity of your study by including some who have learned about mental sets, perhaps even reading about the classic water-jar study.

Materials
You will use three versions of the water-jar problem discussed earlier in the chapter. You will need to present these problems to the participants in a written format or on a computer screen.

Procedure
Create three versions of the water-jar problem. One version should be identical to that described earlier in the chapter: The first five problems will be solvable by the same approach, and the sixth problem will not be solvable by that approach—though it will be solvable by a simpler approach. The second version should just present the sixth problem. The third version, added here to control for the possible effect of working on five problems before attempting the sixth, should present the same five problems as in the original study but the sixth problem should be solvable by the approach used in solving the first five.

Tell the participants that they will be participating in a study on problem solving, without revealing its exact purpose. Give 10 students the first version of the task, 10 students the second version, and 10 students the third version. To avoid biasing students who will be participating in the study later, ask your participants not to discuss the study with anyone else until it has been completed.

Results and Discussion
Count the number of correct responses to the problem in the second version and the sixth problem in the other two versions. Draw a bar graph (see Appendix C in the Online Edition) comparing the number of correct answers to those three problems.

Note how your results compare with those of Luchins (1946). Do the results appear to support the influence of a mental set? If not, try to explain why. Were there any confounding variables that might have adversely affected your study? Why would the use of an inferential statistic (see Chapter 2 and Appendix C in the Online Edition) have been preferable to subjectively judging the size of the differences between the three groups? Think of another study you could conduct to assess the effects of mental sets on problem solving.

---

artificial training program (Menzel, Savage-Rumbaugh, & Menzel, 2002). Kanzi learned Yerkish spontaneously by observing people and other chimpanzees (including his mother) pressing appropriate lexigrams on a keyboard (Savage-Rumbaugh, 1990). He also can identify symbols referred to in human speech. Previous apes depended on their own particular language system to comprehend human communications. Kanzi can even form requests in which other individuals are either the agent or the recipient of action—which reflects his appreciation of syntax (Savage-Rumbaugh, Murphy, Sevic, & Brakke, 1993). Before, apes such as Nim made spontaneous requests only in which they were the targets of a suggested action. Moreover, Kanzi shows displacement, using lexigrams to refer to things that are not present (Savage-Rumbaugh, 1987).

Nonetheless, some critics insist that even Kanzi does not display all the characteristics of true language (Kako, 1999). Savage-Rumbaugh has responded to this criticism by asking critics to stress the important language skills that Kanzi has exhibited rather than continually seeking to identify the relatively minor aspects of language that he has failed to exhibit (Shanker, Savage-Rumbaugh, & Taylor, 1999). Moreover, Allen Gardner has reported that Washoe and other language-trained chimpanzees who are living together in retirement converse with one another and with people in a manner similar to that of human children (Jensvold & Gardner, 2000).

Perhaps future studies using pygmy chimpanzees will succeed where others have failed in demonstrating convincingly that apes are capable of using true language. But even if apes can use true language, no ape has gone beyond the language level of a 3-year-old child. Is that the upper limit of ape language ability, or is it just the upper limit using current training methods? Research soon might provide the answer. In any case, we do know that apes are capable of more complex communication than simply grunting to convey crude emotional states.

Section Review: Language in Apes

1. What evidence is there that apes such as Washoe demonstrate the characteristics of true language?
2. Why do critics doubt that these apes have acquired true language?

Chapter Summary

Thought
- The past few decades have seen a cognitive revolution in psychology, with increased interest in the study of thought.
- Thought is the purposeful mental manipulation of words and images.

Concept Formation
- Thought depends on concepts, which are categories of objects, events, qualities, or relations whose members share certain features.
- A logical concept is formed by identifying specific features possessed by all members of the concept.
- A natural concept is formed through everyday experiences and has fuzzy borders.
- The best representative of a concept is called a prototype.

Problem Solving
- One of the most important uses of concepts is in problem solving, the thought process that enables us to overcome obstacles to reach goals.
- A basic method of solving problems is trial and error, which involves trying one possible solution after another until finding one that works.
- The problem-solving strategy called insight depends on the mental manipulation of information.
- An algorithm is a rule that, when followed step by step, ensures that a solution to a problem will be found.
- A heuristic is a general principle that guides problem solving but does not guarantee the discovery of a solution.
- A mental set is a problem-solving strategy that has succeeded in the past but that can interfere with solving a problem that requires a new strategy.
- Our past experience also can impede problem solving through functional fixedness, the inability to realize that a problem can be solved by using a familiar object in an unusual way.

Creativity
- Creativity is a form of problem solving characterized by novel solutions that also are useful or socially valued.
- Creative people tend to have above-average intelligence and are able to integrate different kinds of thinking.
- Creative people are more motivated by their intrinsic interest in creative tasks than by extrinsic factors.
- Sociocultural factors also may influence the development and expression of creativity.
- Creativity also depends on divergent thinking, in which a person freely considers a variety of potential solutions to a problem.

Decision Making
- In decision making, we try to make the best choice from among alternative courses of action.
- In using the representativeness heuristic, we assume that a small sample is representative of its population.
- In using the availability heuristic, we estimate the probability of an event by how easily instances of it come to mind.
- We are also subject to framing effects, which are biases introduced in the decision-making process by presenting a situation in a certain manner.

Artificial Intelligence
- Artificial intelligence is a field that integrates computer science and cognitive psychology to try to simulate or improve on human thought by using computer programs.

- Computer programs called expert systems display expertise in specific domains of knowledge.
- Computer scientists are studying human performance by creating robots that engage in problem solving and intuitive movement while exploring and mapping the environment.

Language

- In using language, we rely on spoken symbols to communicate through speech, written symbols to communicate through writing, and gestured symbols to communicate through sign language.
- We use language to communicate with other people, to store and retrieve memories, and to plan for the future.

The Structure of Language

- True language is characterized by semanticity, generativity, and displacement.
- The rules of a language are its grammar.
- Phonemes are the basic sounds of a language, and morphemes are its smallest meaningful units.
- A language's syntax includes rules governing the acceptable arrangement of words and phrases.
- Semantics is the study of how language conveys meaning.
- Noam Chomsky calls the underlying meaning of a statement its deep structure and the words themselves its surface structure.
- We translate between the two structures by using transformational grammar.
- The branch of semantics concerned with the relationship between language and its social context is called pragmatics.

The Acquisition of Language

- Infants in all cultures progress through similar stages of language development.
- They begin babbling between 4 and 6 months of age and say their first words when they are about 1 year old.
- At first they use holophrastic speech, in which single words represent whole phrases or sentences.
- Between the ages of 18 and 24 months, infants begin speaking two-word sentences and use telegraphic speech.
- As infants learn their language's grammar, they may engage in overregularization, in which they apply grammatical rules without making necessary exceptions.
- There might be a critical period for language acquisition that extends from infancy to adolescence.
- B. F. Skinner and Albert Bandura believe that language is acquired solely through learning, whereas Noam Chomsky believes we have an innate predisposition to develop language.

The Relationship Between Language and Thought

- Benjamin Lee Whorf's linguistic relativity hypothesis assumes that our view of the world is determined by the particular language we speak.
- But research has shown that though language can influence thought, it does not determine it.

Language in Apes

- Researchers have taught apes to communicate by using sign language, form boards, and computers.
- The most well-known of these apes include the gorilla Koko and the chimpanzees Washoe, Sarah, and Lana.
- Herbert Terrace, the trainer of Nim Chimpsky, claims that apes have not learned true language; instead, they have learned to give responses that lead to rewards, just as pigeons learn to peck at keys to obtain food.
- Francine Patterson, Duane Rumbaugh, and Sue Savage-Rumbaugh have countered by providing evidence that the apes have indeed learned true language characterized by semanticity, generativity, and displacement.

Key Terms

cognitive neuroscience (p. 309)
cognitive psychology (p. 309)
critical period (p. 308)

Thought
thought (p. 309)

Concept Formation
concept (p. 310)
logical concept (p. 310)
natural concept (p. 310)
prototype (p. 311)

Problem Solving
algorithm (p. 314)
functional fixedness (p. 315)
heuristic (p. 314)

insight (p. 313)
mental set (p. 314)
problem solving (p. 312)
trial and error (p. 312)

Creativity
convergent thinking (p. 319)
creativity (p. 316)
divergent thinking (p. 319)

Decision Making
availability heuristic (p. 321)
decision making (p. 320)
framing effects (p. 322)
representativeness heuristic (p. 320)

Artificial Intelligence
artificial intelligence (AI) (p. 322)
expert systems (p. 323)

Language
displacement (p. 325)
generativity (p. 325)
language (p. 324)
semanticity (p. 324)

The Structure of Language
deep structure (p. 327)
grammar (p. 326)
morpheme (p. 326)
phoneme (p. 326)
phonology (p. 326)

pragmatics (p. 327)
semantics (p. 327)
surface structure (p. 327)
syntax (p. 327)
transformational grammar (p. 327)

The Acquisition of Language
holophrastic speech (p. 328)
mean length of utterance (MLU) (p. 329)
overextension (p. 328)
overregularization (p. 329)

telegraphic speech (p. 329)
underextension (p. 328)

The Relationship Between Language and Thought
linguistic relativity hypothesis (p. 332)

Chapter Quiz

Note: Answers for the Chapter Quiz questions are provided at the end of the book.

1. A computer program that could conduct psychotherapy would be an example of
    a. a heuristic.
    b. a prototype.
    c. an algorithm.
    d. an expert system.

2. A child who says "cup" whenever he is hungry would be exhibiting
    a. overextension.
    b. telegraphic speech.
    c. overregularization.
    d. holophrastic speech.

3. A computerized statistical program that always gives correct answers if numbers are entered into it properly is an example of
    a. a prototype.
    b. an algorithm.
    c. a heuristic.
    d. a mental set.

4. The speech of people with schizophrenia often is marked by incomprehensibility, arbitrary word orders, and bizarrely novel combinations of words. Given this, the characteristic of true language most often found in the speech of people with schizophrenia is
    a. syntax.
    b. semanticity.
    c. generativity.
    d. overregularization.

5. An experienced chess player who could checkmate her opponent in two moves fails to notice that opportunity and instead continues to follow a less effective approach that has worked in similar situations in the past. This failure to show flexibility in problem solving is an example of the influence of a
    a. prototype.
    b. mental set.
    c. expert system.
    d. framing effect.

6. A prime number can be evenly divided only by itself or one. "Prime number" is an example of
    a. an algorithm.
    b. a heuristic.
    c. a natural concept.
    d. a logical concept.

7. A child who says "I eated the lunch" or "I throwed the ball" would be exhibiting
    a. overextension.
    b. underextension.
    c. overregularization.
    d. holophrastic speech.

8. Though music by Alice in Chains or the Rolling Stones would be universally classified as rock, it might be difficult to agree on the classification of other music as rock. This difficulty indicates that "rock" is
    a. an algorithm.
    b. a heuristic.
    c. a logical concept.
    d. a natural concept.

9. The difficulty that computer programs such as Eliza have in comprehending speech is mainly related to
    a. syntax.
    b. pragmatics.
    c. holophrastic speech.
    d. linguistic relativity.

10. People high in creativity also are likely to
    a. combine different ways of thinking.
    b. filter out irrelevant stimuli to attend to the task at hand.
    c. display extrinsic motivation.
    d. be geniuses.

11. The linguistic relativity hypothesis is most relevant to
    a. George Orwell's *1984*.
    b. Joan Rivers's *Still Talking*.
    c. Mary Shelley's *Frankenstein*.
    d. J. D. Salinger's *The Catcher in the Rye*.

12. If you more easily recall media reports of street crime in city A than in city B, you may decide that city A is more crime-ridden than city B—even though city B may actually be the more crime-ridden city. This thinking would be an example of the
    a. availability heuristic.
    b. error of overextension.
    c. representative heuristic.
    d. fundamental attribution error.

13. The sentence "John the book gave to Jane" violates proper English
    a. syntax.
    b. semantics.
    c. pragmatics.
    d. displacement.

Chapter 9 Thought and Language

14. A man, trying to reach a wristwatch that has been swept out of his reach under a couch, searches in vain for a long, thin object that would enable him to reach it. He fails to realize that he could obtain such an object by untwisting a wire coat hanger and straightening it into a single long wire. His oversight would show the influence of
    a. underextension.
    b. overregularization.
    c. divergent thinking.
    d. functional fixedness.

15. Baseball strategies such as intentionally walking a good hitter in order to pitch instead to a weaker hitter and using a sacrifice bunt to move a runner from first base to second base are examples of
    a. prototypes.
    b. algorithms.
    c. heuristics.
    d. logical concepts.

16. An automobile company finds that customers are more likely to purchase one of its cars when it is advertised as being "safer than 18 of the top 20 sellers" than when it is advertised as being "safer than all but 2 of the top 20 sellers." This wording is an example of
    a. framing effects.
    b. the availability heuristic.
    c. the representative heuristic.
    d. the fundamental attribution error.

17. A child who enjoys playing the piano begins to play less often after his parents begin giving him five dollars every time he practices. His loss of interest was most likely the product of
    a. pragmatics.
    b. overextension.
    c. overregularization.
    d. extrinsic motivation.

18. The sentence "Yesterday, he zorked the brem in Antarctica" is most lacking in
    a. syntax.
    b. morphemes.
    c. semanticity.
    d. displacement.

19. If you meet three members of an ethnic group who act shy and soft-spoken and you decide that most members of that group share those traits, you would be exhibiting the
    a. availability heuristic.
    b. error of overextension.
    c. representative heuristic.
    d. fundamental attribution error.

20. A baby cries when it is in pain. The cry mainly exhibits
    a. syntax.
    b. semanticity.
    c. displacement.
    d. generativity.

21. The statement "They look great for their age" could be interpreted as either sarcasm or flattery, depending on its social context and the speaker's tone of voice. This interpretation is an example of
    a. syntax.
    b. pragmatics.
    c. generativity.
    d. linguistic relativity.

22. An infant's father has a beard. Because of this, she calls all men with beards "daddy." Her behavior is an example of
    a. generativity.
    b. overextension.
    c. overregularization.
    d. holophrastic speech.

23. Psychologists have been most successful in training apes to communicate by using
    a. speech.
    b. sign language.
    c. simple writing.
    d. facial expressions.

24. According to Noam Chomsky, language is acquired primarily through
    a. watching people model the use of language.
    b. an inborn biological language acquisition device.
    c. positive reinforcement of correct use of language.
    d. higher-order conditioning using words as conditioned stimuli.

25. The difficulty that people have in learning to pronounce certain words in a foreign language is related to
    a. syntax.
    b. phonemes.
    c. morphemes.
    d. pragmatics.

Thought Questions

1. Why might people be more likely to argue whether bowling is a true sport than whether tennis is a true sport?

2. How might heuristics contribute to ethnic prejudice?

3. How might calling people "senior citizens" rather than "elderly" and calling people "intellectually disabled" as opposed to "mentally retarded" be related to the linguistic relativity hypothesis?

4. What issues must be confronted by researchers who wish to demonstrate the acquisition of true language in apes?

Intelligence

CHAPTER **10**

In the 1988 movie *Rain Man*, which won an Academy Award for best picture, Dustin Hoffman portrays Raymond Babbitt, a man with **autism spectrum disorder (ASD)** who could perform amazing mental feats, such as memorizing restaurant menus, recalling the telephone number of anyone in the telephone book, and rapidly calculating complicated mathematical problems in his head. Raymond refuses to fly, basing his decision on the many airplane crashes he can recall, including the dates and fatalities of each one. Hoffman's performance won him the Academy Award for best actor. The film depicts a cross-country journey of self-discovery for his younger brother, Charlie, a self-centered young man whose father dies and leaves his $3 million estate to Raymond—a brother that Charlie never knew he had and whom he "kidnaps" from an institution, hoping to ransom him for half the money. Along the way, Raymond uses his unusual memory ability to help Charlie win almost $100,000 playing blackjack in Las Vegas. Charlie learns to be less self-centered and to accept—and even love—someone who is different from him.

The film is likewise a journey of discovery for viewers, who come to understand some aspects of ASD (see Chapter 14). For example, as is typical in ASD Raymond follows a strict routine—even insisting that pancake syrup always be put on the table before the pancakes arrive. He also shows the compulsive repetition of phrases and the difficulty in connecting emotionally to other people that is common. *ASD* is a term for a group of psychological disorders that are characterized by difficulties with social relationships, impaired language and communication, and repetitive behaviors.

Raymond not only suffers from ASD but also exhibits abilities that once would have had him labeled an *idiot savant* (French for "learned fool"). To avoid the negative connotation of the word *idiot*, idiot savants are now called *autistic savants*, or people with savant syndrome (Miller, 1999). An autistic savant is a person with ASD and below-average general intelligence but who has hyperdeveloped cognitive skills—typically in art (Hou et al., 2000), music (Heaton, Hermelin, & Pring, 1998), mechanics, or calculating (Kelly, Macaruso, & Sokol, 1997). These talents are developed beyond the person's level of functioning in other areas, and all involve exceptional memory ability. Studies suggest that 10 percent of individuals with ASD have savant skills (Bolte & Poustka, 2004; Corrigan, Richards, Treffert, & Dager, 2012).

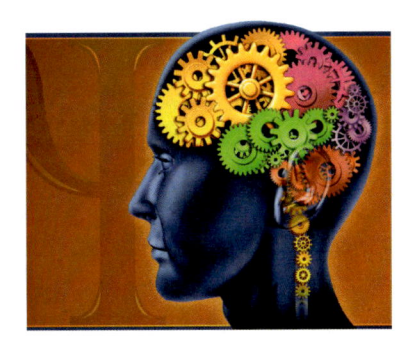

Source: Lightspring/Shutterstock.com.

Chapter Outline
Intelligence Testing
Extremes of Intelligence
Theories of Intelligence
Nature, Nurture, and Intelligence

autism spectrum disorder (ASD) A group of psychological conditions characterized by poor social relationships, impaired communication, and repetitive behaviors.

343

What we now call the savant syndrome was first noted in 1751 in a German magazine article that described the case of an uneducated farmhand with an extraordinary memory (Foerstl, 1989). In 1887, the phenomenon was named the idiot savant condition by John Langdon Down, the physician who also identified what we now call Down syndrome. In a much more recent case, a 12-year-old autistic savant could play unfamiliar piano pieces after listening to them once (Young & Nettelbeck, 1995). In another case, an autistic savant could give the day of the week for any date in the 20th century (Hurst & Mulhall, 1988). He had spent many hours memorizing the day of the week of each date, just as Dustin Hoffman's character spent many hours memorizing the telephone book. Because autistic savants tend to be socially isolated and persistent at tasks, they can spend the many hours needed to memorize large amounts of material (Heavey, Pring, & Hermelin, 1999) but also have the ability to retrieve the information at "lightning speed." Their feats are beyond the ability of children who memorize statistics from the backs of hundreds of baseball cards and then recall any statistic for any player.

The savant syndrome occurs in about 10 percent of people with ASD and six times more often in males than in females. Autistic savants vary in their ability to function in everyday life. Not all savants function at the level that Dustin Hoffman did in *Rain Man*. Though there are many autistic savants, fewer than 100 *prodigious savants*—the kind celebrated by the media—have been identified. A prodigious savant is a person with ASD who has a talent so highly developed that it would be remarkable even in a person of normal intellectual ability (Treffert, 1989).

There is no single accepted cause of the savant syndrome, but research findings implicate overdevelopment of certain structures of the right cerebral hemisphere that govern particular talents (Corrigan, Richards, Treffert, & Dager, 2012). Some speculation remains as to the exact underlying mechanisms of savant syndrome due to the inability to perform large-scale neuroimaging studies on these individuals. Nevertheless, researchers consistently find anatomical and neurochemical abnormalities within regions of the brain associated with learning and memory. The talents exhibited by autistic savants seem to be processed by implicit rather than explicit memory. As discussed in Chapter 8, the implicit memory system deals with memories that are processed without the conscious intention to do so. The outstanding talents of prodigious savants are probably strongly affected by heredity because their remarkable knowledge of the rules of art, music, or mathematics does not appear to be the product of practice alone (Treffert, 1989).

An autistic savant who memorizes enormous amounts of material is displaying *intelligence*. You certainly recognize intelligent behavior when you see it: someone getting an A on a calculus exam, or composing a great symphony, or discovering a cure for a disease. Recognizing intelligent behavior, though, is easier than defining intelligence itself. The word *intelligence* comes from the Latin word meaning "to understand," but the concept of intelligence is broader than that. Finding a universally acceptable definition of intelligence is difficult because intelligence is a natural concept. Natural concepts have "fuzzy borders"—they are not easily defined by a distinct set of features (see Chapter 9).

Decades ago, David Wechsler (1958), a leading intelligence researcher, put forth an influential definition of intelligence. He called **intelligence** the global capacity

intelligence The global capacity to act purposefully, to think rationally, and to deal effectively with the environment.

to act purposefully, to think rationally, and to deal effectively with the environment. In other words, intelligence reflects how well we *function*. This definition is in the spirit of the early school of psychology called functionalism (see Chapter 1), which stressed the importance of adaptive behavior in everyday life.

Intelligence Testing

Modern interest in the study of intelligence began with the development of tests of cognitive abilities, which include achievement tests, aptitude tests, and intelligence tests. An **achievement test** assesses knowledge of a particular subject. For decades, New York State has required students to pass the Regents Exams, which are achievement tests designed to measure students' knowledge of major academic areas such as English, history, and mathematics. An **aptitude test** predicts your potential to benefit from instruction in a particular academic or vocational setting. Of course, an aptitude test is partly an achievement test—your performance on it depends on your previous experience with the material covered by the test. Aptitude tests are commonly used to screen job applicants and college applicants. In applying to colleges, you may have submitted the results of your performance on either the Scholastic Assessment Test (SAT) or the American College Test (ACT). These scores help admissions committees determine whether applicants have the potential to succeed in college. An **intelligence test**, the main topic of this section, is a kind of aptitude test that assesses overall mental ability, which influences our functioning in a variety of areas of life, including school and work (Brody, 1999).

achievement test A test that measures knowledge of a particular subject.

aptitude test A test designed to predict a person's potential to benefit from instruction in a particular academic or vocational setting.

intelligence test A test that assesses overall mental ability.

The History of Intelligence Testing

The use of tests of mental abilities has been traced back to 2200 B.C., when the Chinese appear to have used them to select talented individuals to serve as civil servants (Fox, 1981). But ability testing did not become the subject of scientific study until more than a century ago, when the English scientist Francis Galton (1822–1911) set up his Anthropometric Laboratory at the 1884 International Health Exhibition in London.

Francis Galton and Anthropometry

The word *anthropometric* means "human measurement." More than 9,000 visitors to Galton's laboratory paid to be measured on a variety of physical characteristics, including head size, grip strength, visual acuity, and reaction time to sounds (Morse, 1999). Galton was inspired by his cousin, Charles Darwin, and his theory of evolution. According to Darwin, individuals who are the most physically well adapted to their environment are the most likely to survive long enough to produce offspring, who would be likely to also have those physical characteristics. Galton similarly assumed that people with superior physical abilities, especially sensory and motor abilities, are better adapted for survival. He viewed such people as more intelligent than those with average or inferior physical abilities.

Galton's interest in studying physical differences reflected his interest in studying all sorts of individual differences, including the relative beauty of women from different countries. In a possible instance of experimenter bias, Galton found that the women of England, his home country, were the most beautiful. His research on individual differences established the field of **differential psychology**, which is concerned with the study of cognitive and behavioral differences among individuals. Differential psychology differs from traditional psychology in that modern psychologists study groups rather than individuals. Galton's anthropometric method was introduced to the United States by James McKeen Cattell (1860–1944), who administered Galton's tests—which Cattell called mental tests—to American students (Cattell, 1890). But anthropometry proved fruitless as a way of measuring general intelligence because many anthropometric measurements, such as grip strength, proved to have little or no relationship to mental measures of

differential psychology The field of psychology that studies individual differences in physical, personality, and intellectual characteristics.

intelligence, such as reasoning ability. As discussed in the "Psychology Versus Common Sense" box, on page 358, however, more recent research has demonstrated a relationship between mental measurements and physical measures such as reaction time.

Alfred Binet, Theodore Simon, and the IQ Test

The first formal test of general intelligence—the *Binet-Simon scale* (and later modified and renamed the *Stanford-Binet IQ Test)*—appeared in 1905. It grew out of an 1881 French law that required all children to attend school even if they could not profit from a standard curriculum (Levine, 1976). This ruling led the French minister of public education to ask psychologist Alfred Binet (1857–1911) to develop a test to identify children who required special classes for slow learners. Binet collaborated with psychiatrist Theodore Simon (1873–1961) to develop a test that could assess children's ability to perform in school. Binet and Simon began by administering many questions related to language, reasoning, and arithmetic to elementary schoolchildren of all ages. Binet and Simon eliminated questions that tended to be answered the same by children of all ages. Questions that were answered correctly by more and more children at each successive age were retained and became the Binet-Simon scale.

The test was administered to children who needed to be placed in school. Each student was assigned a *mental age*, based on the number of test items she or he passed—the greater the number of items passed, the higher the mental age. A student with a mental age significantly below his or her chronological age was considered a candidate for placement in a class for slow learners. Binet urged that his test be used solely for class placement. He disagreed with those who claimed that the test measured a child's inherited level of intelligence or that a child's level of intelligence could not be improved by education.

The Binet-Simon scale proved useful, but the measure of mental age occasionally proved misleading. Suppose that a 10-year-old child had a mental age of 8 and a 6-yearold child had a mental age of 4. Both would be 2 years below their chronological ages, but the 6-year-old would be proportionately farther behind her or his age peers than the 10-year-old. This problem was solved by German psychologist William Stern (1871–1938), who recommended using the ratio of mental age to chronological age to determine a child's level of intelligence (Kreppner, 1992). A 10-year-old with a mental age of 8 has a ratio of 8/10 = 0.80, and a 6-year-old with a mental age of 4 has a ratio of 4/6 = 0.67. The 6-year-old is relatively further behind his or her age peers. Stanford University psychologist Lewis Terman eliminated the decimal point by multiplying the ratio by 100. Thus, 0.80 becomes 80, and 0.67 becomes 67. The formula (mental age/chronological age × 100) became known as the **intelligence quotient (IQ)**. As you can see, a child whose mental and chronological ages are the same has an IQ of 100, and a child who has a higher mental than chronological age has an IQ above 100.

intelligence quotient (IQ)
Originally, the ratio of mental age to chronological age; that is, mental age/chronological age × 100.

Lewis Terman and American Intelligence Testing

The Binet-Simon scale was translated into English and first used in the United States by the American psychologist Henry Goddard (1866–1957) in New Jersey at the Vineland Training School, which served children with intellectual disabilities (formerly referred to as mental retardation). In 1916, Lewis Terman (1877–1956) published a revised version of the Binet-Simon scale that was more suitable for children reared in American culture. The American version became known as the *Stanford-Binet Intelligence Scale* and still is used today. Terman also redesigned the Stanford-Binet to make it suitable for testing both children and adults. The test has been revised several times since 1916.

Because the Stanford-Binet is given individually and can take an hour or more to administer, it is not suitable for testing large groups of people in a brief period of time. The time factor became a problem during World War I, when the U.S. Army sought a way to assess the intelligence of large groups of recruits. The army wanted to reject recruits who did not have the intelligence to perform well and to identify recruits who would be good officer candidates. Terman and several other prominent psychologists provided the solution to this problem. They developed two group tests of intelligence—the Army

Alpha Test and the Army Beta Test. The Army Alpha Test was given in writing to those who could read English, and the Army Beta Test was given orally to those who could not read English. The tests, reflecting their functionalist heritage, viewed intelligence as the ability to adapt to the environment (Mayrhauser, 1989). Descendants of these group intelligence tests include the Otis-Lennon Mental Abilities Tests and the Armed Forces Qualification Test.

David Wechsler and the Deviation IQ

After World War I, the Stanford-Binet became the most widely used intelligence test. But the ratio IQ devised by Stern, which was adequate for representing the intelligence of children, proved inadequate for representing the intelligence of adults. Because growth in mental age slows markedly after childhood, the use of the ratio IQ led to the absurdity of people with average or above-average intelligence becoming below average simply because their chronological age increased. For example, consider a 15-year-old girl with a mental age of 20. She would have an IQ of $(20/15) \times 100 = 133$. This score would put her in the mentally gifted range (that is, above 130). Suppose that at age 40 she had retained the mental age of 20. She would then have an IQ of $(20/40) \times 100 = 50$. This score would put her well within the range of intellectual disabilities (that is, below 70). Yet she might be a successful lawyer, physician, or professor.

This inadequacy of the ratio IQ was overcome by David Wechsler (1896–1981). He replaced Stern's ratio IQ with a deviation IQ, which compares a person's intelligence test score with the mean score of his or her age peers. Those persons who perform at exactly the mean of their age peers receive an IQ of 100, those who perform above the mean of their age peers receive an IQ above 100, and those who perform below the mean of their age peers receive an IQ below 100.

In 1939 Wechsler developed his own intelligence test. While working as chief psychologist at Bellevue Hospital in New York City, he sought a way to assess the intelligence of adult psychiatric patients with low verbal ability (Boake, 2002). Because the Stanford-Binet stressed verbal ability and was geared toward testing children, it was not suitable for that purpose. Wechsler was led to develop an adult intelligence test that tested nonverbal as well as verbal ability, which he called the *Wechsler-Bellevue Intelligence Scale.*

Wechsler later developed versions of his test for use with different age groups, beginning with the *Wechsler Intelligence Scale for Children (WISC),* for ages 6 to 16; followed by the *Wechsler Adult Intelligence Scale (WAIS),* for ages from late adolescence through adulthood; and concluding with the *Wechsler Preschool and Primary Scale of Intelligence (WPPSI),* for ages 4 to 6-1/2. The Wechsler scales have been revised periodically; for example, the fifth edition of the WICS (WISC-V) was released in 2014. Each of the Wechsler intelligence scales contains 11 subtests that measure different aspects of verbal and nonverbal intelligence. The test taker receives a verbal IQ, a performance (nonverbal) IQ, and an overall IQ. Research has supported the usefulness of distinguishing, as measured by the Wechsler scales, these three kinds of intelligence (LoBello & Gulgoz, 1991).

Standardization in Intelligence Testing

Formal tests must be standardized, reliable, and valid (see Chapter 2). *Standardization* refers to both the establishment of performance norms on a test and uniformity in how the test is administered and scored. When an intelligence test is standardized, the mean performance of the standardization group for each age range is given a score of 100, with a standard deviation of 15. The standard deviation is a measure of how variable a group of scores are around their mean. Figure 10-1 shows that IQ scores fall along a *normal curve.* For the Wechsler scales, about 68 percent of test takers will score between 85 and 115, and about 95 percent will score between 70 and 130. Average intelligence falls between 85 and 115. IQs below 70 fall in the range of intellectual disabilities, and IQs above 130 fall in the mentally gifted range. Though the word "standardized" can conjure up emotions of anxiety, imagine if a test of intelligence was not standardized. The opposite of a standardized test is unstandardized—a test with no clear questions or administered and

FIGURE 10-1
The Normal Distribution of IQ Test Scores

Scores on standardized tests, such as the Wechsler intelligence scales, form what is known as a normal distribution (also called a "bell-shaped curve"). Given that the mean of the Wechsler scales is set at 100 and the standard deviation is 15, we can determine the percentage of individuals who fall above or below particular IQ scores and the percentage who fall between any two IQ scores.

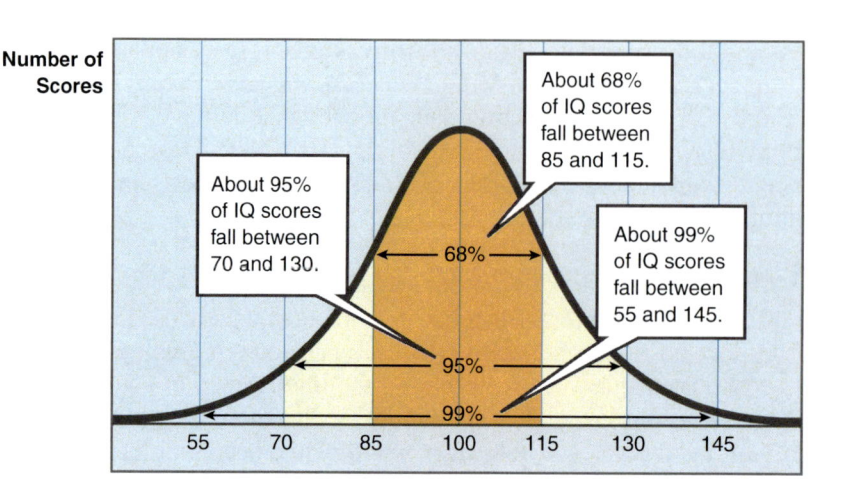

[Figure shows a bell curve with Number of Scores on the y-axis and IQ scores (55, 70, 85, 100, 115, 130, 145) on the x-axis. Annotations indicate: About 68% of IQ scores fall between 85 and 115. About 95% of IQ scores fall between 70 and 130. About 99% of IQ scores fall between 55 and 145.]

scored under different conditions. The consistency provided by standardization can permit a reliable comparison of all test takers.

The Reliability of Intelligence Tests

You would have confidence in an intelligence test only if it were reliable. The *reliability* of a test is the degree to which it gives consistent results—or in other words, the repeatability of its scores. Suppose you took an IQ test and scored 102 (average) one month, 53 (within the range of intellectual disabilities) the next month, and 146 (mentally gifted) the third month. Your level of intelligence normally would not fluctuate that much in 3 months, and you would argue that the test is unreliable. Because the test-retest reliability correlation coefficients for the Stanford-Binet and Wechsler scales are at least .90 (out of a maximum of 1.00), the tests are reliable.

Though standardized IQ tests are reliable in the short run, an individual's IQ score can change over a period of years. The Berkeley Growth Study, conducted at the University of California at Berkeley, contradicted the once-popular belief that intelligence does not change during childhood. The study found that mental ability increases through adolescence and then levels off at about the age of 20 (Bayley, 1955). The nature of intellectual change later in life is discussed in Chapter 4.

The Validity of Intelligence Tests

A reliable test is not necessarily a valid one. A test's *validity* depends on whether the test measures what it is supposed to measure. The validity of IQ tests can be assessed by comparing their results to each other. A study of 40 children aged 6 to 16 years found a high correlation between their scores on the Stanford-Binet Intelligence Scale and on the Wechsler Intelligence Scale for Children, as well as no statistically significant difference in the mean scores on the two tests (Lavin, 1996). The two tests are indeed measuring the same thing: "intelligence."

College Admissions Tests *Predictive validity* is especially important. Consider the SAT's ability to predict school performance. A published review of research on the SAT reported that the SAT correlated .41 with first-year college grade-point average. This correlation means that the SAT is a moderately good predictor. But high school grade-point average, which correlated .52 with first-year college grade-point average, is an even better predictor. Moreover, the combination of the SAT and high school grade-point average was a still better predictor, correlating .58 with first-year college grade-point average (Linn, 1982).

Claims that students with access to SAT preparation courses have an unfair advantage over students who do not might be unfounded. Such courses produce modest gains that are far less than promised by many of the organizations that offer SAT preparation courses (Powers & Rock, 1999). An increase of just 20 to 30 points on the verbal and mathematics subtests would require hours of study almost equivalent to full-time schooling (Messick & Jungeblut, 1981). The modest effects of preparatory courses appear to hold true across cultures, as in a study of the predictive validity of the Israeli Psychometric Entrance Exam. Students were randomly assigned to receive either preparatory coaching or no preparatory coaching. The results showed no difference in the predictive validity of the exam for the two groups of students regarding their subsequent performance in college (Allalouf & Ben-Shakhar, 1998).

Bias in Testing The Stanford-Binet and Wechsler scales correlate between .40 and .75 with school performance, depending on the aspect of school performance being measured (Aiken, 1982). These correlations indicate that the tests are good—but far from perfect—predictors of school performance. Because the correlations are less than a perfect 1.00, factors other than those measured by the SAT or IQ tests also contribute to school performance. The existence of other factors has made the fairness of intelligence tests one of the most controversial issues in contemporary psychology.

Critics argue that IQ tests and other tests of mental ability might be unfair to minority groups in the United States, most notably African Americans (Bender, Ponton, Crittenden, & Word, 1995), who score an average of 10 to 15 points lower than European Americans. A review of research on ethnic differences in intelligence found that environmental factors, such as socioeconomic status, had a stronger influence on IQ scores and might contribute to the disparity. There also has been a similar long-standing difference in scores on achievement tests between African Americans and European Americans. But this gap has been declining slowly in recent decades (Nisbett et. al., 2012). Critics of IQ testing allege that because African Americans are less likely to have the same cultural and educational experiences as European Americans, they tend, on the average, to perform more poorly on IQ tests that assume that both groups share common cultural and educational experiences (Brooks-Gunn, Klebanov, & Duncan, 1996). For example, one study found that European American participants outperformed African Americans in general vocabulary knowledge. However, this ethnic difference disappeared when participants were tested on newly learned words (Fagan & Holland, 2002). But does this finding mean that IQ tests are *biased* against African Americans?

The issue of the validity of IQ tests for African Americans reached the courts in the 1970s. In 1979, Judge Robert Peckham of the Federal District Court in San Francisco ruled that, without court approval, California schools could no longer base class placement of African American schoolchildren on IQ tests. His ruling came in the case of *Larry P. v. Wilson Riles* (Riles was the California superintendent of education), which was brought on behalf of six African American children in San Francisco who had been placed in classes for what was then called the educable mentally retarded (that is, those with mild intellectual disabilities). After hearing 10,000 pages of testimony from experts and advocates on both sides of the issue, Peckham ruled that the use of IQ tests violated the civil rights of African American children because a proportionately greater number of these children than European American children were being placed in classes for children with intellectual disabilities. His decision convinced school districts in several other states to abandon the use of IQ tests for determining the school placement of African American children (Taylor, 1990).

But Peckham's decision also was met by arguments that IQ tests are not biased against African Americans because the tests have good predictive validity—they accurately predict the performance of both African American children and European American children in elementary school classes (Hunter & Schmidt, 2000). The differences in IQ scores between the two groups of children may reflect the fact that African American children might be more likely to be reared in socially disadvantaged circumstances that do not provide them with the opportunity to gain experiences that are important in doing well on IQ tests and in school (Lambert, 1981). A committee of scholars from several academic fields reported to the National Academy of Science that standardized tests are accurate predictors of school and job performance for all groups and therefore are not biased

Reliable, not valid

Low validity, low reliability

Not reliable, not valid

Both reliable and valid

Bull's Eye Example of Reliability and Validity

The principles of validity and reliability are displayed in this archery bull's-eye as an example of their roles in experimental design. Experimental findings should be both reliable and valid to be accepted.

Chapter 10 Intelligence

against any particular group ("NAS Calls Tests," 1982). This conclusion was supported by a study of Native American high school students that showed that their performance on the ACT accurately predicted their college performance (House, 1998). Thus, the consensus appears to be that tests of intellectual ability are not biased (Brown, Reynolds, & Whitaker, 1999).

Nonetheless, the issue has become as political as it is scientific. On the one side are the people, such as Judge Peckham, who believe that biased tests of cognitive abilities are being used to perpetuate discrimination against African American children by placing more of these children in slower classes and by preventing African American adults from obtaining desirable jobs. Peckham and his supporters favor outlawing the use of such tests. On the other side are those people who believe that blaming IQ tests for revealing the negative consequences of deprived upbringings is like killing the messenger who brings bad news. They favor changing the conditions that contribute to the lower average IQ test performance of African Americans and certain other minority groups (Elliott, 1988).

Culturally Unbiased Tests One possible solution to this controversy presents a compromise: Use tests that are not affected by the test taker's cultural background. The desirability of culturally unbiased tests has inspired research in a variety of cultures, including India (Misra, Sahoo, & Puhan, 1997) and South Africa (Claassen, 1997). But efforts to develop "culture-free" tests, beginning in the 1940s (Cattell, 1940), and "culture-fair" tests, beginning in the 1950s (Davis & Eels, 1953), produced disappointing results. These tests presented test takers with items that emphasized perceptual and spatial abilities rather than verbal abilities and avoided the use of items that would presume an extensive background in a particular culture. Figure 10-2 presents an example of the Raven Progressive Matrices, a nonverbal intelligence test that some educators have favored over the Stanford-Binet or Wechsler scales (Colom & Garcia-Lopez, 2003). But just like on traditional intelligence tests, people of higher socioeconomic status perform better on these nonverbal tests than do people of lower socioeconomic status (Jensen, 1980). And European Americans typically perform better than African Americans on tests of cognitive ability even when the tests are reworded to make them more comfortable to African American test takers (DeShon, Smith, Chan, & Schmitt, 1998).

Moreover, members of one culture may even perform the same on intelligence tests developed in another culture as they do on ones developed in their own culture. This finding was demonstrated in a study in which more than 600 grade school children from India and more than 1,000 grade school children from Holland were given two IQ tests, one developed in each country. The tests were slightly modified when given to students from the other country. The results showed that the students' performances were comparable on the two tests, indicating that cultural biases did not affect their IQ test performances (Bleichrodt, Hoksbergen, & Khire, 1999).

Stereotype Threat and IQ Test Performance According to psychologist Claude Steele, self-fulfilling prophecy may account for the poorer performance of African Americans on intelligence tests because of what he calls *stereotype threat* (Steele & Aronson, 2004). As discussed in Chapter 2, research has found that teachers' expectancies can help or hinder students' academic performance. Steele's twist is that in certain situations you become aware of others' expectations about your own stereotyped group; in turn, this awareness affects your performance. Because African Americans are aware of the negative stereotypes related to their academic abilities and achievement as early as middle childhood (McKown & Weinstein, 2003), they may become anxious and not perform as well on intelligence tests. In one study, Steele administered a verbal ability test to African American and European American college students approximately equal in their intellectual ability. Half of each group was told that the test simply served to assess how people solve problems. The other half was told that the test measured verbal reasoning ability.

The performance of African American and European American participants did not differ under the first condition, but African American participants performed worse than European American participants under the second condition. Steele concluded that under

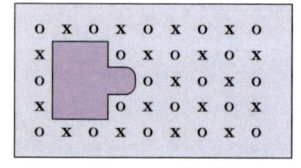

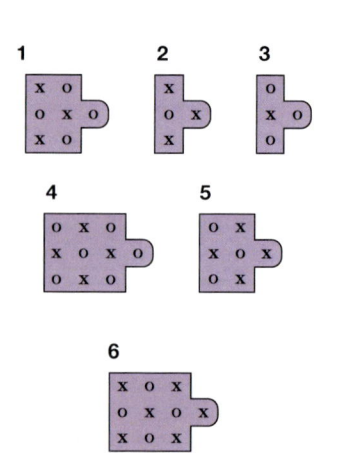

FIGURE 10-2
Raven Progressive Matrices

This figure is an example of the kind of matrix used in the Raven Progressive Matrices. In this "culture-fair" test, the person is presented with a series of incomplete matrices and must complete each by selecting the appropriate pattern from an accompanying group of patterns.

the second condition, African American participants succumbed to stereotype threat, became anxious, and thus performed more poorly (Steele & Aronson, 1995). Other research studies have found that stereotype threat has been shown to impair performance on cognitive tasks by increasing physiological arousal (O'Brien & Crandall, 2003) and reducing working memory capacity (Schmader & Johns, 2003) among participants from stigmatized groups.

Imagine how Alfred Binet would have reacted to the controversy that has arisen over the use of standardized tests, considering that he saw testing as an unbiased means of assessing students' abilities. In fact, despite the shortcomings of standardized tests, no alternative is as unbiased in assessing individuals without regard to irrelevant characteristics such as sex or ethnic background (Reilly & Chao, 1982). As Richard Weinberg, a leading intelligence researcher, has noted:

> In light of the effectiveness of current IQ tests to predict school performance, it is ironic that tests have been outlawed for the very purpose for which they were designed—to prevent subjective judgment and prejudice from being the basis for assigning students to special classes or denying them certain privileges. (Weinberg, 1989, p. 100)

Section Review: Intelligence Testing

1. What is an autistic savant?
2. How was Galton's view of intelligence influenced by his cousin Charles Darwin's theory of evolution?

Extremes of Intelligence

Another controversial issue regarding intelligence is the classification and education of people who fall at either extreme of the range of intelligence. As you learned in the section "Standardization in Intelligence Testing," 95 percent of the population score between 70 and 130 on IQ tests. Of the remaining 5 percent, half score below 70 and half score above 130. Those who score 70 or below fall in the range of intellectual disabilities, and those who score 130 or above fall in the mentally gifted range—though the classification of a person as having an intellectual disability or being mentally gifted is not based on IQ scores alone.

Intellectual Disabilities

Depending on the criteria used to define **intellectual disabilities**, from slightly more than 3 million to almost 7 million Americans have an intellectual disability. The estimate varies because a person's level of adaptive behavior, and not just level of intelligence, needs to be assessed before the person is classified as having an intellectual disability. In fact, the trend in classification has been to rely more on the person's everyday functioning and less on his or her IQ score (Haywood, Meyers, & Switzky, 1982).

intellectual disabilities
Intellectual deficiency marked by an IQ of 70 or below and difficulties performing in everyday life.

Classification of Intellectual Disabilities

We have come a long way in our use of terms to classify persons with the condition once referred to as mental retardation. In the early 20th century, such persons were sorted into three categories, in terms of increasing degrees of mental retardation: moron (from a Greek word meaning "foolish"), imbecile (from a Latin word meaning "weak-minded"), and idiot (from a Greek word meaning "ignorant"). Fortunately, professionals no longer use these terms, but as you are well aware, they have become terms of disparagement in everyday language. In fact, because the term *mental retardation* itself has spawned disparaging terms and negative connotations, the American Association on Mental Retardation recently changed its name to the American Association on Intellectual and Developmental Disabilities, and the term has been changed to *intellectual disabilities*.

To be classified as having an intellectual disability, a person must have an IQ of 70 or below and, beginning in childhood, difficulties performing in everyday life (Landesman & Ramey, 1989)—including difficulties in self-care (such as eating and dressing), schoolwork (such as reading and arithmetic), and social relationships (such as conversing and developing friendships). Moreover, before a person can be classified as having an intellectual disability, alternative causes of the person's low IQ score and performance difficulties must be ruled out. These alternative causes include physical illness, impairment of vision or hearing, and coming from a family of people who are not native speakers of the language in which the IQ test was administered.

People with an intellectual disability suffer from varying degrees of cognitive deficits (Detterman, 1999). One of the most common deficits that they exhibit is inadequate use of language, in part related to difficulty with pragmatics. As described in Chapter 9, pragmatics is the aspect of language that involves using the sociocultural context of speech to help us give meaning to speech (Hatton, 1998). That is, people with an intellectual disability often interpret speech too literally, making them miss some of the subtleties of what is being said. Today, there are four categories of intellectual disabilities (American Psychiatric Association, 2013). Persons with IQs of 50 to 70 have *a mild intellectual disability* and constitute 85 percent of persons with intellectual disabilities. They are able to care for themselves, reach a sixth-grade level of education, hold responsible jobs, be married, and serve as adequate parents. Those with IQs of 35 to 49 have *a moderate intellectual disability* and constitute 10 percent of persons with intellectual disabilities. They might be trained to care for themselves, reach a second-grade level of education, and hold menial jobs, often in sheltered workshops, but they have difficulty maintaining social relationships, and they rarely marry.

Those with IQs between 20 and 34 have a *severe intellectual disability* and constitute 3 to 4 percent of persons with intellectual disabilities. They can learn rudimentary language and work skills but might be unable to care for themselves, benefit from schooling, hold jobs, or maintain normal social relationships. And those with IQs below 20 have a *profound intellectual disability* and constitute 1 to 2 percent of persons with intellectual disabilities. They have so few skills that they might spend their lives in institutions that provide them with no more than custodial care.

Causes of Intellectual Disabilities

In 1912, Henry Goddard traced the descendants of a Revolutionary War soldier he called Martin Kallikak. The soldier produced two lines of descendants. One line arose from his affair with a tavern maid who had what was described then as mental retardation. The other line arose from his marriage to a respectable woman of normal intelligence. Goddard found that the descendants of the tavern maid included many derelicts, prostitutes, and persons with mental retardation. In contrast, the descendants of his wife included few such people.

The differences between the two lines of descendants account for Goddard's use of the name *Kallikak*. The name is a combination of the Greek words *kalos* (meaning "good") and *kakos* (meaning "bad"). Goddard concluded that the descendants of the soldier's wife inherited the tendency to be moral and intelligent, whereas the descendants of the tavern maid inherited the tendency to be immoral and of lower intelligence. He discounted the effects of the markedly different sociocultural environments into which the children in each branch of the family were born as the probable causes of the differences.

Though some cases of intellectual disabilities may be linked to genetic factors (Winnepenninckx, Rooms, & Kooy, 2003), about 75 percent of cases of intellectual disabilities are caused by sociocultural deprivation. In fact, almost all persons with a mild intellectual disability come from such backgrounds. Their families might fail to provide them with adequate intellectual stimulation, such as discussing current events with them, encouraging them to read, helping them with homework, and taking them on trips to zoos, museums, and other educational settings. They also are more likely to attend inferior schools, to suffer from malnutrition, and to lack adequate medical care—each of which can impair intellectual growth.

Though some cases of intellectual disabilities are caused by sociocultural deprivation, many cases are caused by brain damage, which we can now identify by using modern brain-scanning techniques (Schaefer & Bodensteiner, 1999) such as MRI and PET. Brain damage in people with intellectual disabilities is often seen in the hippocampus, a structure associated with memory processes (see Chapter 8), and the cerebellum, a structure associated with motor coordination (Pulsifer, 1996). The brain damage that produces an intellectual disability is commonly caused by harmful environmental factors, sometimes related to parental health habits (Bryant & Maxwell, 1999) or prenatal environments. For example, pregnant women who ingest drugs or alcohol can cause brain damage in their offspring. And pregnant women who have certain diseases, such as the virus *rubella* (German measles) during the first 3 months of pregnancy (often referred to as the first trimester), also have a greater risk of giving birth to offspring with an intellectual disability. Pregnant women whose immune systems are activated due to bacterial or viral infections are at risk of their infants being diagnosed with ASD (Zerbo et al., 2013).

Women who suffer from severe malnutrition during their pregnancies can give birth to infants with an intellectual disability and other neurodevelopmental disorders because of irreversible effects occurring at critical developmental periods. Animal studies have shown that the hippocampus and parts of the cortex are particularly vulnerable to malnutrition in early pregnancy (Penido et al., 2012). Additionally, studies have shown that *in utero* malnutrition can have long-lasting effects and affect individuals later in life. Prenatal exposure to X-rays can impair the normal migration of brain cells, increasing the possibility of intellectual disabilities (Schull, Norton, & Jensh, 1990). And a newborn infant who fails to breathe for several minutes after birth will experience *hypoxia*, a lack of oxygen to the brain. Hypoxia can cause the brain damage that characterizes **cerebral palsy**, a motor disorder often—but not always—accompanied by intellectual disabilities (Johnson, 2002; Maenner et al., 2016).

Intellectual disabilities also are caused by genetic factors (Simonoff, Bolton, & Rutter, 1996), as in the case of **phenylketonuria (PKU)**. PKU is caused by an inherited lack of the enzyme required to metabolize the amino acid *phenylalanine*, which is found in milk and other common foods. This deficiency produces chemical changes that block the ability of brain cells to produce myelin (see Chapter 3), which leads to brain dysfunction and, as a result, an intellectual disability (Dyer, 1999). Fortunately, routine screening of newborns in the United States and other countries can detect PKU early enough to protect infants from brain damage by putting them on a diet that eliminates almost all their intake of phenylalanine (Sullivan & Chang, 1999).

Some cases of intellectual disabilities are produced by genetic defects that cause abnormal development during gestation, as in the case of **Down syndrome**. John Langdon Down identified the disorder in 1866 (Merrick, 2000). People normally have 23 pairs of chromosomes, with one member of each pair coming from each parent. A person with Down syndrome has an extra, third chromosome on the 21st pair. The extra chromosome can come from either the mother or the father. The chances of having a child with Down syndrome increase with age, being more common in middle-aged parents than in younger ones.

Down syndrome usually is characterized by moderate intellectual disability and distinctive physical characteristics. These characteristics include small ears and hands; short necks, feet, and fingers; protruding tongues; and a fold over the eyes, giving them an almond-shaped, Asian appearance. Because of this appearance, Down syndrome was originally called "mongolism." This term reflected the 20th-century Western belief that people with the disorder failed to develop beyond what was then presumed by Westerners to be the more primitive physical and intellectual level of Asians, such as Mongolians

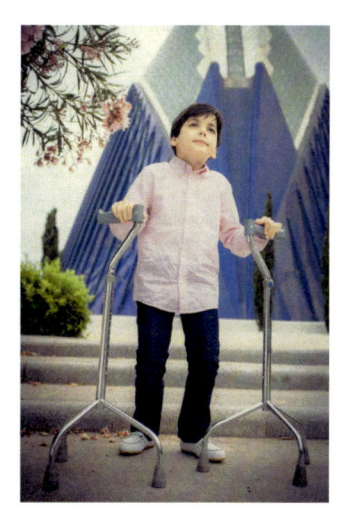

Cerebral Palsy

Cerebral palsy, which is characterized by motor dysfunction and may be accompanied by intellectual disabilities, can result from hypoxia after birth.
Source: sweetmonster/Shutterstock.com

cerebral palsy A movement disorder that is caused by brain damage and is often accompanied by intellectual disabilities.

phenylketonuria (PKU) A hereditary enzyme deficiency that, if left untreated in the infant, causes intellectual disabilities.

Down syndrome A form of intellectual disability, associated with certain physical deformities, that is caused by an extra, third chromosome on the 21st pair.

Down Syndrome

Down syndrome usually is characterized by moderate intellectual disability and distinctive physical characteristics. The risk of having a child with Down syndrome increases with age and is more common among middle-aged parents than among younger parents.
Source: Photo of Gertie Munholland, courtesy of Global Down Syndrome Foundation.

(Gould, 1981). Cognitive disorders often are associated with a loss or gain of functioning during development. For example, individuals with PKU are missing an enzyme and individuals with Down syndrome have an extra chromosome.

Education of People with Intellectual Disabilities

Over the centuries, people with an intellectual disability have been treated as everything from children of God who were believed to bring good luck, to subhumans who, it was believed, should be locked up as dangerous (Wolfensberger, 1972). Today, psychologists interested in persons with an intellectual disability stress their potential to benefit from education and training. One reason why people with an intellectual disability do not perform as well as other people is that they fail to use effective methods of information processing. For example, when people with an intellectual disability are given a series of words or pictures to remember, they tend not to rehearse the items or group them into chunks—techniques that are commonly used by people who do not have an intellectual disability (Campione & Brown, 1979). As explained in Chapter 8, memory is enhanced by the rehearsal and chunking of information.

Today, people with a mild intellectual disability are called "educable," and persons with a moderate intellectual disability are called "trainable." From the 1950s to the 1970s, persons who were categorized at the time as being educable mentally retarded were placed in special classes in which they received teaching tailored to their level of ability. But in the 1970s, dissatisfaction with the results of this approach led to mainstreaming, which places children with intellectual disabilities in as many normal classes as possible and encourages them to participate in activities with children who do not have intellectual disabilities. To promote mainstreaming in America, the Education for All Handicapped Children Act of 1975 mandated that children with intellectual disabilities be given instruction in the most normal academic setting that is feasible for them (Sussan, 1990).

The educational needs of individuals with intellectual disabilities are not limited to academic subjects. They also might need training in self-care skills (including eating, toileting, hygiene, dressing, and grooming), home management skills (including home maintenance, clothing care, food preparation, and home safety), consumer skills (including telephone use, money management, and shopping), and community mobility skills (including pedestrian safety and use of public transportation). Behavior modification has been especially useful in teaching self-care to people with intellectual disabilities (Huang

The Mentally Gifted

Children and adolescents who are mentally gifted, like those who have an intellectual disability, benefit from special education programs to help them develop their skills.
Source: CREATISTA/Shutterstock.com.

& Cuvo, 1997). For example, behavior modification has been used successfully in training such persons to shower themselves (Matson, DiLorenzo, & Esveldt-Dawson, 1981).

A movement that has paralleled mainstreaming is *normalization*, the transfer of individuals with intellectual disabilities from large institutional settings into community settings so that they can live more normal lives. Given adequate support services, even people with severe and profound intellectual disabilities can progress in settings other than large, custodial institutions, with the greatest benefit shown in their ability to care for themselves (Lynch, Kellow, & Willson, 1997). But in too many instances, normalization has simply created smaller custodial settings rather than ones that truly encourage independent living (Sinson, 1994).

Mental Giftedness

The study of intellectual disabilities has been accompanied by interest in the study of **mental giftedness**. Francis Galton (1869) began the study of the mentally gifted in the late 19th century. Lewis Terman considered Galton himself to be mentally gifted. Terman based his assessment on Galton's early accomplishments, including his ability to recite the alphabet when he was 18 months old and read classical literature when he was 5 years old (Terman, 1917). Today, the mentally gifted are people with IQs of 130 or above and with exceptionally high scores on achievement tests in specific subjects, such as mathematics (Fox, 1981). Ever since Leta Stetter Hollingworth founded the practice of special education for gifted students (Klein, 2000), the special needs of the mentally gifted generally have received less attention than those of persons with intellectual disabilities. Many gifted children feel isolated and unchallenged in their classes (Swiatek & Lupkowski-Shoplik, 2003). In the United States, there has been a decline in funding for research on the gifted and a lack of funding for the education of gifted children (Sternberg, 1996). One positive trend has been a greater attempt to identify gifted ethnic-minority children (Scott, Deuel, Jean-Francois, & Urbano, 1996). Perhaps the best-known organization dedicated to meeting the needs of the mentally gifted is MENSA (Serebriakoff, 1985), which limits its membership to those who are above age 14 and score in the top 2 percent on a standardized intelligence test.

mental giftedness Intellectual superiority marked by an IQ of 130 or above and exceptionally high scores on achievement tests in specific subjects, such as mathematics.

The Study of Mathematically Precocious Youth

Perhaps the best-known recent study of mentally gifted children is the longitudinal Study of Mathematically Precocious Youth by Camilla Benbow and Julian Stanley (1983) at Johns Hopkins University. Benbow and Stanley provided special programs for young

The Research Process

What Is the Fate of Childhood Geniuses?

Rationale

Terman began his study in 1921, and it continued long after his death. He had hoped to counter the common-sense belief that being too intelligent too early led to later failure.

Method

Terman used the Stanford-Binet Intelligence Scale to identify California children with IQs above 135. He found 1,528 such children between the ages of 8 and 12. Their average IQ was 150. Reports on Terman's gifted children appeared periodically during the 20th century. After Terman's death in 1956, Robert Sears (who was a member of the original sample) and Pauline Sears of Stanford University continued the study.

Results and Discussion

The Terman Genetic Studies of Genius longitudinal study has shown that mentally gifted children tend to become socially, physically, vocationally, and academically superior adults. They are healthier and more likely to attend college, to have professional careers, and to have happy marriages. The 1972 report on Terman's participants, then at an average age of 62, found that they generally were satisfied with life, combining successful careers with rewarding family lives (Sears, 1977). Moreover, more recent follow-up studies found that participants who reported having lived up to their intellectual potential at age 49 were more satisfied with their work and family lives than were those who felt they had not realized their potential (Holahan, Holahan, & Wonacott, 1999).

Of course, Terman's study is not without certain weaknesses. Perhaps participants' awareness of being in such an important study affected how they performed in life—a kind of self-fulfilling prophecy. Also, could socioeconomic status, and not solely intelligence, have been a contributing factor? A follow-up study of samples of men from the original study found that those who maintained better health, had more stable marriages, and pursued more lucrative careers were less likely to come from families in which there was divorce, alcoholism, or other major family problems (Oden, 1968). Evidently, even for geniuses, the family environment is related to their success in life. A less ambitious replication of the Terman study involved 156 adults (aged 35 to 50 years) who had graduated from an elementary school for gifted children. As did their counterparts in the Terman study, these gifted individuals showed superior social, physical, and vocational well-being (Subotnik, Karp, & Morgan, 1989).

Opportunities for educational and occupational achievement differed for the men and women who participated in the Terman study. Two-thirds of the Terman women graduated from college—an astounding proportion considering they reached college age during the Great Depression of the 1930s—but only approximately half of the women were employed outside the home at some point in their adult lives (Tomlinson-Keasey, 1990). It is important to remember, though, that women of their generation were expected to devote themselves to their spouses and family, and the social context provided fewer professional opportunities for women than for men. Most (63 percent) of the Terman women expected to be wives and mothers, and many of them contributed to their spouse's career, worked in traditionally female occupations (typically teaching) after their children were grown, or dedicated themselves to volunteer organizations or the arts. Educational and employment opportunities for gifted women have improved over the last 50 years, however, and later studies find that the majority of gifted women—single or married—are employed in professional occupations. Nonetheless, a comparison of the Terman women, born in 1910, and a younger sample, born in 1940, revealed no differences in life satisfaction (Schuster, 1990).

Other studies have added to our understanding of mentally gifted people. A study of mathematically gifted adolescents supported the conclusions of Terman's study by finding that mentally gifted people are more socially competent (McCallister, Nash, & Meckstroth, 1996) and more psychologically well adjusted (Parker, 1996) than other people. Another study found that gifted high school students were more perfectionistic than other students, as shown by a greater need for order and more demands placed on themselves (Orange, 1997). Despite their high level of intelligence, mentally gifted people—as in Terman's study—rarely become recognized for extraordinarily creative achievements. Outstanding creativity involves skills and personality traits different from those of the typical mentally gifted person (Winner, 2000).

adolescents who scored above 700 (out of a maximum of 800) on the mathematics subtest of the SAT. The programs offered intensive summer courses in science and mathematics, accelerated courses at universities, and counseling for parents to help them meet the academic and emotional needs of their gifted children (Barnett & Corazza, 1998). A 25-year follow-up found that participants in the study had many outstanding educational achievements and successful careers, particularly in the sciences, technology, engineering, and mathematics (Wai, Lubinski, Benbow, & Steiger, 2010). And contrary to popular belief, the participants also did not suffer academic burnout from their demanding course work (Swiatek, 1993). A 20-year follow-up of the adolescents involved in this program found that they tended to be high achievers and highly satisfied with their careers (Benbow, Lubinski, Shea, & Eftekhari-Sanji, 2000). Moreover, there is no evidence that gifted children are prone to the personal and social problems that plagued William James Sidis. In fact, a program such as the ones provided by Benbow and Stanley might have helped Sidis pursue a rewarding career as a mathematician instead of fading into obscurity.

Section Review: Extremes of Intelligence

1. What are some possible causes of intellectual disabilities?
2. In what way did Terman's Genetic Studies of Genius counter the notion of "early ripe, early rot"?

Theories of Intelligence

Is intelligence a general characteristic that affects all facets of behavior, or are there different kinds of intelligence, each affecting a specific facet of behavior? Today, intelligence researchers tend to assume that there are several kinds of intelligence (Sternberg & Wagner, 1993). Consider, for example, a study of men who spent much of their recreational time at racetracks betting on horse races. The results indicated that the men's ability to handicap races accurately was unrelated to their scores on a test of general intelligence. Handicapping horse races taps a specific kind of mental ability (Ceci & Liker, 1986).

Factor-Analytic Theories of Intelligence

At about the same time that Alfred Binet was developing his intelligence test, the British psychologist Charles Spearman (1863–1945) was developing a theory of intelligence. He considered intelligence a general ability that underlies most behaviors.

Spearman's Theory of General Intelligence

In 1927, after more than two decades of research, Spearman published his conclusions about the nature of intelligence. He developed a statistical technique called **factor analysis**, which determines the degree of correlation between performances on various tasks (Bartholomew, 1995). If performances on certain tasks have a high positive correlation, then they are presumed to reflect the influence of a particular underlying factor. For example, if performances on a vocabulary test, a reading test, and a writing test correlate highly, they might reveal the influence of a "verbal ability" factor.

In using factor analysis, Spearman first gave a large group of people a variety of mental tasks. He found that scores on the tasks had high positive correlations with one another. In other words, participants tended to score high *or* moderate *or* low on all the tests. Spearman concluded that performance on all the tasks depended on the operation of a single underlying factor. He called this factor *g*—a general intelligence factor.

But because the correlations between the tasks were less than a perfect 1.00, Spearman concluded that performance on each task also depended, to a lesser extent, on its

factor analysis A statistical technique that determines the degree of correlation between performances on various tasks to determine the extent to which they reflect particular underlying characteristics, which are known as factors.

> **Psychology versus Common Sense**
>
> **Are Faster Brains More Intelligent Brains?**
>
> We sometimes refer to people as being "quick-witted" or "fast thinkers," or being mentally swift in some other way. Common sense presumes that the faster our brains are at processing information, the more intelligent we are. Though we could argue about this commonsense belief—pro or con—by simply presenting arguments why we do or do not accept it, psychologists prefer to base their beliefs on empirical research findings. Many research studies have indeed found that people who score high on intelligence tests tend to be relatively faster in cognitive processing (Baumeister, 1998; Holm, Ullén, & Madison, 2011). For example, studies consistently have found a negative correlation between intelligence and reaction time (Neubauer, Riemann, Mayer, & Angleitner, 1997). That is, faster reaction times are associated with higher intelligence, and slower reaction times are associated with lower intelligence. One explanation for this relationship is that intelligence might partially depend on the speed of neural impulse conduction (Barrett, Daum, & Eysenck, 1990). Perhaps one can indeed be "quick-witted."
>
> Researchers who support information-processing speed as a measure of intelligence have provoked criticism. This criticism has been particularly intense because one of the leading researchers whose research has supported a relationship between intelligence and information processing speed has been Arthur Jensen, who has attributed this relationship to heredity (Vernon, 1998). Jensen's belief that inherited ethnic differences in intelligence favor people of European descent over people of African descent has led some scientists to brand him a racist. This controversy is discussed in the section "The Influence of Heredity and Environment on Intelligence."
>
> A major criticism of the research on the relationship between intelligence and information-processing speed is that researchers who claim a strong relationship between intelligence and the speed of information processing have exaggerated the implications of generally modest correlations between the two. A second criticism is that researchers have failed to explain the meaning of significant correlations between intelligence and the speed of information processing (Stankov & Roberts, 1997). In addition, the relationship between intelligence and reaction time varies in its strength across cultures. One study found, for example, that the size of the relationship between intelligence test scores and reaction time is smaller and in fact relatively weaker in rural Guatemalans than in residents from more urbanized environments (Choudhury & Gorman, 1999). It might be unwise to make sweeping statements about the importance of information-processing speed in intelligent behavior.
>
> Still another, somewhat humorous, source of criticism comes from research comparing the information processing-speed of animals and humans. In one study, rhesus monkeys demonstrated faster reaction times on an information-processing task than human participants did (Washburn & Rumbaugh, 1997). But few people would use this finding to jump to the conclusion that monkeys are more intelligent than they are. At this time, the commonsense belief that people who are faster at information processing tend to be more intelligent than other people has some research backing, but the extent to which intelligence depends on information-processing speed remains to be determined.

own specific factor, which he called *s*. For example, Spearman explained that scores on vocabulary tests and arithmetic tests tended to have a high positive correlation with each other because vocabulary ability and arithmetic ability are both influenced by a general intelligence factor. But because scores on vocabulary tests and arithmetic tests are not perfectly correlated, each ability must also depend on its own intelligence factor. Nonetheless, Spearman believed that the general intelligence factor was more important than any specific intelligence factor in governing a given ability. The existence of the factor *g* has received some research support. It appears to be associated mainly with activity in the frontal lobes of the brain (Duncan et al., 2000). Given that most intellectual tasks require attention and working memory, we know that neural networks in the frontal lobe are activated during cognitive processing. Researchers can attempt to study the neuroanatomical correlates of intelligence. In recent studies, 104 young adults were given 21 psychological tests of intelligence and then were placed in MRI scanners. Results indicated that tests of intelligence, working memory, attention, and processing speed all showed activation of portions of the frontal cortex as opposed to other cortical areas. This suggests that intelligence and cognitive factors are correlated, in part, due to shared specific regions in the brain (Colom et al., 2013).

Thurstone's Theory of Primary Mental Abilities

Like Spearman, Louis Thurstone (1887–1955) used factor analysis to determine the nature of intelligence. But unlike Spearman, Thurstone (1938) concluded that there was no general intelligence factor. Instead, based on a battery of tests that he gave to college students, he identified seven factors, which he called *primary mental abilities*: reasoning, word fluency, perceptual speed, verbal comprehension, spatial visualization, numerical calculation, and associative memory.

Though scores on tests measuring these abilities had moderately high positive correlations with one another, they did not correlate highly enough for Thurstone to assume the existence of a general underlying intelligence factor. Suppose that you took tests to assess your abilities in reasoning, verbal comprehension, and numerical calculation. Thurstone would insist that your performance on any single test would reflect, not the influence of a general intelligence factor, but instead the influence of a specific intelligence factor related to the particular ability assessed by that test. Like Thurstone, J. P. Guilford (1897–1987) rejected the notion of a general intelligence factor (Guilford, 1959). Instead of the mere seven factors in Thurstone's theory, though, Guilford identified 120 factors through the use of factor analysis. By the end of his life, Guilford (1985) had increased the number of factors to 180.

Horn and Cattell's Two-Factor Theory of Intelligence

A more recent theory of intelligence based on factor analysis was developed by John Horn and Raymond Cattell (1966), who identified two intelligence factors. **Crystallized intelligence** reflects the acquisition of skills and knowledge through schooling and everyday experience. Horn and Cattell found that crystallized intelligence increases or remains the same in late adulthood. **Fluid intelligence** reflects thinking ability, memory capacity, and speed of information processing. Whereas the ability to apply learned solutions to new problems depends on crystallized intelligence, the ability to find novel solutions to problems depends on fluid intelligence (Hunt, 1997). Short-term memory (discussed in Chapter 8) is strongly associated with fluid intelligence (Martínez et al., 2011).

Horn and Cattell found that fluid intelligence is largely inherited, is affected little by training, and declines in late adulthood. Recent research studies confirm that fluid intelligence declines across late adulthood (Schretlen et al., 2000). Fluid intelligence has much in common with Spearman's notion of a general intelligence factor (Duncan, Burgess, & Emslie, 1995). Changes in fluid intelligence and crystallized intelligence across the life span are illustrated in Figure 10-3.

It remains for psychologists to determine which, if any, of the factor-analytic theories of intelligence is the best. Perhaps a more telling criticism of factor-analytic theories of intelligence is that they assume that intelligence primarily reflects those cognitive abilities related to academic performance. A more encompassing theory of intelligence would consider a broader range of abilities (Frederiksen, 1986). Theories proposed by Robert Sternberg and Howard Gardner have done so.

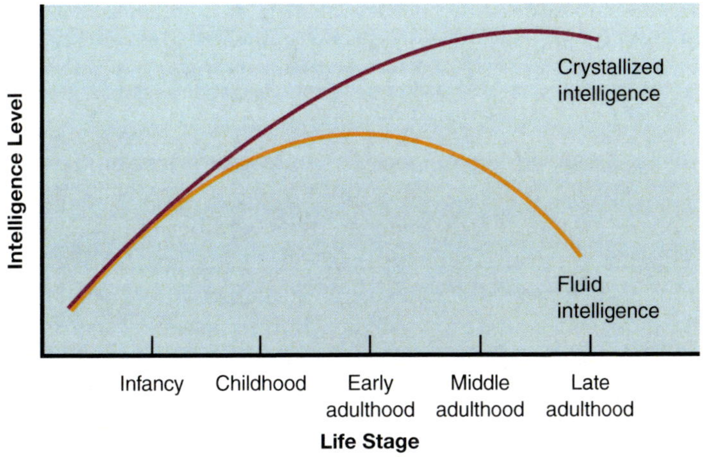

crystallized intelligence The form of intelligence that reflects knowledge acquired through schooling and in everyday life.

fluid intelligence The form of intelligence that reflects reasoning ability, memory capacity, and speed of information processing.

FIGURE 10-3

Life-Span Change in Intelligence

Whereas fluid intelligence tends to decline in old age, crystallized intelligence tends to increase.

Source: From J. L. Horn and G. Donaldson, "On the Myth of Intellectual Decline in Adulthood" in *American Psychologist*, 31: 701–719. Copyright © 1976 by the American Psychological Association.

Sternberg's Triarchic Theory of Intelligence

As a child, Robert Sternberg performed poorly on IQ tests and suffered from severe test anxiety, yet he later earned a Ph.D. and became a leading researcher in cognitive psychology. His experience contributed to his belief that intelligence comprises more than the abilities measured by traditional intelligence tests (Trotter, 1986). To determine the views of laypersons on the nature of intelligence, Sternberg and his colleagues (1981) surveyed people reading in a college library, entering a supermarket, or waiting for a train. The participants were asked to list what they believed were the main characteristics of intelligent people. The results showed that respondents assumed that intelligent people had good verbal skills, social judgment, and problem-solving abilities.

Beginning in the early 1980s, Sternberg developed a **triarchic theory of intelligence**, which claims that intelligence comprises three kinds of abilities similar to those reported by the people in his earlier survey (Sternberg, 2000). He based his theory on his observations of how people process information. *Componential intelligence* is similar to the kind of intelligence considered by traditional theories of intelligence. It primarily reflects our information-processing ability, which helps in academic performance. *Experiential intelligence* is the ability to combine different experiences in insightful ways to solve novel problems based on past experience. In part, it reflects creativity, as exhibited by an artist, composer, or scientist. Creative geniuses, such as Leonardo da Vinci and Albert Einstein, had especially high levels of experiential intelligence. *Contextual intelligence* is the ability to function in practical, everyday social situations. It reflects "street smarts," as in negotiating the price of a new car. Though many situations require the use of all three kinds of intelligence, some people are better at using one kind than at using the other two (Sternberg & Clinkenbeard, 1995).

The triarchic theory recognizes that we must be able to function in settings other than school. According to Sternberg (1999), the triarchic theory of intelligence is a better basis for developing intelligence tests that account for cultural factors more than conventional intelligence tests do. Sternberg has developed the Sternberg Triarchic Abilities Test to assess the three kinds of intelligence, and he believes that each kind can be improved by special training (Sternberg, Castejon, Prieto, Hautamaeki, & Grigorenko, 2001). The triarchic theory received some support from a study of intellectually gifted adolescent students. They were superior to nongifted adolescent students in the cognitive abilities that are encompassed by componential intelligence. For example, they were more sophisticated and efficient in solving decision-making problems (Ball, Mann, & Stamm, 1994). Though Sternberg's theory goes beyond traditional theories by considering creative intelligence and practical intelligence as well as academic intelligence, more research is needed to determine its merits. In one of the few experimental studies of the triarchic theory, classroom instructional methods based on that theory (which involved analytical, creative, and practical instruction) produced better student performance among third graders and eighth graders on a variety of tests than was produced by traditional instructional methods (Sternberg, Torff, & Grigorenko, 1998). Sternberg more recently renamed his triarchic theory the *theory of successful intelligence*. He changed the name to stress his belief that intelligence is the ability to achieve success, given one's personal standards and sociocultural context (Sternberg, 2003).

Gardner's Theory of Multiple Intelligences

Whereas Sternberg based his theory on his study of information processing, Howard Gardner (1983) based his **theory of multiple intelligences** on his belief that the brain has evolved separate systems for different adaptive abilities that he calls "intelligences." According to Gardner, there are seven types of intelligence, each of which is developed to a different extent in each of us: linguistic, logical-mathematical, spatial, musical, bodily-kinesthetic, intrapersonal, and interpersonal. Gardner assumes that certain brain structures and pathways underlie the intelligences and that brain damage interferes with one or more of them. For example, damage to speech centers interferes with linguistic intelligence, and damage to the cerebellum interferes with bodily-kinesthetic intelligence.

---

triarchic theory of intelligence
Robert Sternberg's theory of intelligence, which assumes that there are three main kinds of intelligence: componential, experiential, and contextual.

theory of multiple intelligences
Howard Gardner's theory of intelligence, which assumes that the brain has evolved separate systems for seven kinds of intelligence.

Several of Gardner's kinds of intelligence are assessed by traditional intelligence tests. *Linguistic intelligence* is the ability to communicate through language. If you are good at reading textbooks, writing term papers, and presenting oral reports, you are high in linguistic intelligence. A person with high *logical-mathematical intelligence* is good at analyzing arguments and solving mathematical problems. And a person with high *spatial intelligence*, such as a skilled architect or carpenter, is good at perceiving and arranging objects in the environment.

The remaining kinds of intelligence are assessed little, if at all, by traditional intelligence tests. *Musical intelligence* is the ability to analyze, compose, or perform music. A person with good *bodily-kinesthetic intelligence* is able to move effectively, as in dancing or playing sports, or to manipulate objects effectively, as in using tools or driving a car. If you have high *intrapersonal intelligence*, you know yourself well and understand what motivates your behavior. For example, emotionally depressed people high in intrapersonal intelligence might be more likely to find ways to relieve their depression. And if you have high *interpersonal intelligence*, you function well in social situations because you are able to understand the needs of other people and to predict their behavior. People high in interpersonal intelligence are better at judging, for example, whether other people are trustworthy (Yamagishi, Kikuchi, & Kosugi, 1999).

Gardner's list of multiple intelligences has much in common with the kinds of intelligence targeted by the ancient Chinese educational program called the Six Arts (Chongde & Tsingan, 2003). According to Gardner, our ability to succeed in life depends on the degree to which we develop the kinds of intelligence that are needed to function well in our culture. For example, for most people in the United States, success depends more on linguistic intelligence than on musical intelligence. Success in a culture that relies on hunting skills would put a greater premium on spatial intelligence and bodily-kinesthetic intelligence. Gardner's theory has failed to generate sufficient scientific research to determine its merits, particularly research demonstrating valid means of assessing multiple intelligences (Plucker, Callahan, & Tomchin, 1996). But it is potentially superior to traditional theories of intelligence in its attention to the kinds of abilities needed to function in both academic and nonacademic settings. The theory has been used to determine the relationship between multiple intelligences and academic performance among high school students (Snyder, 2000). Unfortunately, the theory sometimes has been used to develop academic programs in schools simply based on the assumption that programs that seem logically related to the theory will be effective—with little research evidence to support that belief (Mettetal, Jordan, & Harper, 1997).

A recent area of interest to intelligence researchers has been the concept of *emotional intelligence*, which overlaps intrapersonal intelligence and interpersonal intelligence. People who are high in emotional intelligence are more empathic (Davies, Stankov, & Roberts, 1998), more socially skilled (Schutte et al., 2001), better able to manage their emotional states (Ciarocchi, Chan, & Caputi, 2000), and more satisfied with their lives and less prone to depression (Martinez-Pons, 1997). But some researchers have criticized Gardner's theory for leaving out important intelligences. Psychologist Robert Emmons (2000) believes that, for example, the theory of multiple intelligences also should include spiritual intelligence. Gardner (2000) considers this proposal interesting but believes more research is needed before he would be willing to accept spirituality as an intelligence.

Section Review: Theories of Intelligence

1. What is the difference between Spearman's and Thurstone's factor-analytic theories of intelligence?
2. According to Gardner's theory of multiple intelligences, what kinds of intelligence are there?

Musical Intelligence

According to Gardner's theory of multiple intelligences, an accomplished pianist would be high in musical intelligence.

Source: Kiselev Andrey Valerevich/Shutterstock.com.

Nature, Nurture, and Intelligence

In the 1983 movie *Trading Places*, two upper-class men argued about whether our social positions are determined more by heredity or by environment. They agreed to settle their argument by manipulating a rich European American (portrayed by Dan Ackroyd) and a poor African American (portrayed by Eddie Murphy) into trading homes (a mansion versus the street), vocations (big business versus panhandling), and financial status (wealth versus poverty). This movie illustrates the popular concern with the issue of nature versus nurture.

In the 1870s, Francis Galton popularized the phrase *nature versus nurture* (Fancher, 1984). As a follower of his cousin Charles Darwin, Galton (1869) concluded that intelligence is inherited, after finding that eminent men had a higher proportion of eminent relatives than did other men. This conclusion led Galton to champion **eugenics** (Rabinowitz, 1984), the practice of encouraging supposedly superior people to reproduce while preventing supposedly inferior people from reproducing. Scientists today still argue about whether research on the relative contributions of nature and nurture will benefit humanity or instead have dehumanizing consequences (Turkheimer, 1998). Even at the turn of the 21st century, many people still believed in the practice of eugenics (Ouimet & de Man, 1998).

eugenics The practice of encouraging supposedly superior people to reproduce while preventing supposedly inferior people from reproducing.

Early Studies of Women

Gender differences in mental abilities were studied as early as 1900 when Helen Bradford Thompson (1874–1947)—later known by her married name, Helen Thompson Woolley—compared 25 men and 25 women on measures of motor and sensory abilities, intellect, and emotion. She concluded that the gender differences that she observed were due to socialization rather than to biological differences between women and men (Milar, 2000). In a later review of the psychological research on gender differences, she concluded, "There is perhaps no field aspiring to be scientific where flagrant personal bias, logic martyred in the cause of supporting a prejudice, unfounded assertions, and even sentimental rot and drivel, have run riot to such an extent as here" (Woolley, 1910, p. 340).

Despite this empirical evidence—and the fact that women were entering higher education in record numbers—belief in the superiority of the male intellect was unshaken. Differential psychologists turned to the *variability hypothesis* (Shields, 1982). The **variability hypothesis** was derived from evolutionary theory. It stated that men, as a group, are more variable than women. Variability within a group was seen as adaptive because it was thought to enable the species to evolve and adapt to changing circumstances. Thus, whereas groups of women and men might be equivalent on average—as Wooley's review reported—only men will be found at the extremes of human attributes. The variability hypothesis was used to explain why there were more men with extraordinary intellects—and more men with intellectual deficits—than women.

variability hypothesis The prediction that men, as a group, are more variable than women.

The variability hypothesis was tested in a series of studies by Leta Stetter Hollingworth (1886–1939). In 1912 and 1913, she studied 1,000 female and male residents of the Clearing-House for Mental Defectives, where she administered Binet-Simon intelligence tests. She found that men and boys were admitted more frequently, but these data were biased. Male residents were admitted at an earlier age than female residents, which she attributed to the fact that women were identified as "mentally deficient" less often. In contrast, boys' deficits in intellectual abilities and functioning were more readily apparent. She concluded that many women escaped institutionalization because they could perform menial domestic tasks (Hollingworth, 1914). In another study, Helen Montague and Hollingworth (1914) examined the birth records of 2,000 infants in the New York Infirmary for Women and Children. They found that though male infants were larger than females, there were no gender differences in the variability of physical characteristics. Hollingworth's empirical research and her conclusion that social factors played an important role in the observed differences between women's and men's lives strongly influenced her contemporaries. By the 1920s the variability hypothesis was discredited, and prominent psychologists such as Lewis Terman began to consider the role of social discrimination in women's intellectual achievement (Benjamin & Shields, 1990).

Early Studies of Immigrants

In 1912 Henry Goddard became director of testing the intelligence of immigrants arriving at Ellis Island in New York Harbor. Goddard (1917) made the astonishing claim that 79 percent of Italians, 80 percent of Hungarians, 83 percent of Jews, and 87 percent of Russians scored in the "feebleminded" range on the Binet-Simon scale, which today we would call the range of mild intellectual disabilities. Even after later reevaluating his data, he claimed that an average of "only" 40 percent of these groups were "feebleminded" (Gelb, 1986). Goddard, following in the footsteps of Galton, concluded that these ethnic groups were by nature intellectually inferior.

You probably realize that Goddard discounted possible environmental causes for the poor test performance of immigrants. He failed to consider a lack of education, a long ocean voyage below deck, and anxiety created by the testing situation as causes of their poor performance. Moreover, even though the tests were translated into the immigrants' native languages, the translations were often inadequate. Despite the shortcomings of the tests, low test scores were used as the basis for deportation of many supposedly "feebleminded" immigrants. Ironically, at the 1915 meeting of the American Psychological Association in Chicago, a critic of Goddard's program of intelligence testing reported that the native-born mayor of Chicago had taken an IQ test and had scored in the feebleminded range (Gould, 1981).

Further support for Goddard's position was provided by the army's intelligence-testing program during World War I, headed by Robert Yerkes (1876–1956). One of Yerkes's colleagues, Carl Brigham (1923), published the results of the testing program. He found that immigrants scored lower on the IQ tests than their American-born counterparts did. Brigham attributed these differences in IQ scores to differences in heredity. The U.S. Congress passed the Immigration Act of 1924, which restricted immigration from eastern and southern Europe. There is disagreement among researchers who believe that Brigham's findings influenced passage of the act (McPherson, 1985) and those who believe that they did not (Snyderman & Herrnstein, 1983).

Regardless, in 1930, Brigham stated that he had been wrong in assuming that the poorer performance of immigrants was overwhelmingly attributable to heredity. He noted that in their everyday lives, immigrants—living in their original cultures—might not have had the opportunity to encounter much of the material in the army IQ tests. To appreciate Brigham's

Immigration and Intelligence Testing

Newly arrived European immigrants at Ellis Island in 1921, many of whom were assessed by the Binet-Simon scale.

Source: Everett Historical/Shutterstock.com.

Critical Thinking About Psychology

How Should We Respond to *The Bell Curve*?

Few books have provoked controversy in both professional journals and the popular media the way *The Bell Curve: Intelligence and Class Structure in American Life* did after it was published in 1994. For a while it was impossible to go a day without being confronted by media coverage of the controversy surrounding the book, which spent 15 weeks on *The New York Times* best-seller list and sold more than 500,000 copies within a few months of its publication. Reaction to *The Bell Curve* was in keeping with an earlier controversy over a book with a similar message, Arthur Jensen's (1980) *Bias in Mental Testing*. *The Bell Curve* provoked an even more intense and widespread controversy, inspiring hundreds of articles by critics and supporters of its content, implications, and scientific adequacy.

Books were published just to counter *The Bell Curve*'s claims, such as Steven Fraser's (1995) *The Bell Curve Wars*, a collection of commentaries on *The Bell Curve*. The controversy made the cover of *Newsweek* and *The New York Times Magazine*. And radio and television programs, including *Nightline*, *Charlie Rose*, and the *McNeil-Lehrer News Hour*, pitted the book's supporters and detractors against each other. But what was it about *The Bell Curve*—a book about intelligence—that created this furor?

The furor was created primarily by a conclusion implied by psychologist Richard Herrnstein and political scientist Charles Murray, the authors of *The Bell Curve*. They implied, without formally stating it, that research studies had convincingly demonstrated significant ethnic differences in intelligence, with people of European descent being intellectually superior to those of African descent. They also concluded that because intelligence is largely inherited, efforts to improve the intellectual abilities of children with lower socioeconomic status, such as Project Head Start, will have little effect. The authors urged that instead of fruitless efforts to improve the status of people who cannot improve, we should simply place people in the social positions for which they are genetically well suited.

Many academics who opposed the book's premise accused its authors of basing their conclusions on flawed statistical analyses (Darlington, 1996) and weak scientific evidence (Poston & Winebarger, 1996). Some critics accused Herrnstein and Murray of using poor science to support their own unadmitted racist social and political agendas (Alderfer, 2003). Even the American Psychological Association established a task force on intelligence to assess the claims made in *The Bell Curve* (Neisser et al., 1996).

Other scholars noted that the authors, in tracing the history of attempts to examine the hereditary basis of intelligence, left out any instances in which claims of ethnic differences in intelligence were based on scientific fraud or biased interpretations of data (Samelson, 1997). In the early 20th century, these claims were often used to support prejudice and discrimination against ethnic minorities that were considered intellectually inferior. Yet some of these groups, such as Jews and Asians, have since surpassed the American average on IQ scores. The increases in intelligence from one generation to the next in many ethnic groups around the world was noted by Thomas Sowell, who offered perhaps the most intellectually balanced re-

point, consider the following multiple-choice items from the Army Alpha Test: "Crisco is a: patent medicine, disinfectant, toothpaste, food product [the correct answer]"; and "Christy Mathewson is famous as a(n): writer, artist, baseball player [the correct answer], comedian" (Gould, 1981). Similarly, the poorer performance of African Americans on IQ tests was attributed to sociocultural deprivation caused by segregation (Rury, 1988).

The Influence of Heredity and Environment on Intelligence

After three decades of relative indifference to it, the issue of nature versus nurture reemerged in the 1960s when President Lyndon Johnson began Project Head Start, which provides preschool children from deprived socioeconomic backgrounds with enrichment programs to promote their intellectual development. Head Start was stimulated in part by the finding that African Americans scored lower than European Americans on IQ tests (Kagan, 2002). Supporters of Head Start attributed this difference to the poorer socioeconomic conditions in which African American children were more likely to be reared.

But in 1969 an article by psychologist Arthur Jensen questioned whether programs such as Head Start could significantly boost the intellectual level of deprived children. Jensen's doubts were based on the notion of **heritability**, the extent to which the variabil-

heritability The proportion of variability in a trait across a population attributable to genetic differences among members of the population.

Critical Thinking About Psychology

How Should We Respond to *The Bell Curve*? *continued*

view of *The Bell Curve* in his article "Ethnicity and IQ" in *The American Spectator* (February 1, 1995). Moreover, there is evidence that the consistent 15-point difference, on average, between European Americans and African Americans is the product of environment, not heredity. A study by psychologist Jeanne Brooks-Gunn and colleagues found that factors related to socioeconomic status explained the difference in intelligence test scores between European American and African American children. They found no evidence that the difference was attributable to heredity (Brooks-Gunn, Klebanov, & Duncan, 1996).

Though *The Bell Curve* received more criticism than support, some scholars have praised its scientific merits (Weidman, 1997) and conclusions (Carroll, 1997). Supporters accused the book's critics of ignoring strong evidence favoring its claims in order to support their own sociopolitical agendas (Rushton, 1997). In response to the widespread criticism of *The Bell Curve*, 52 international scholars in the field of intelligence signed a statement entitled "Mainstream Science on Intelligence" that was published in *The Wall Street Journal* (December 13, 1994) and that supported a number of the book's scientific conclusions. Few of the signees had ever been accused of letting racism guide their scientific practices. They refrained from endorsing some of the more inflammatory claims made in the book. Though supporting the reality of a genetic basis for IQ differences, they made no claims about the contribution of heredity to IQ differences among ethnic groups.

Perhaps the most astounding argument put forth by a psychologist in favor of the book's premise—to those who oppose it—is that many of the book's critics, especially college professors, are genetically predisposed to express moral outrage at it! According to this view, people who are genetically programmed to be more altruistic are drawn to helping occupations, such as education. This tendency, according to the argument, inclines them toward more liberal sociopolitical positions—such as opposing any evidence of a genetic basis for social status in favor of insisting that environmental manipulations can have profound effects on people's upward mobility (Ellis, 1998).

What is one to conclude? Though scientists, ideally, would use meticulous methodology, objective gathering of data, appropriate statistical analysis, and rational conclusions drawn from their research studies, they are limited because they are people with biases, emotions, and unique life histories. Thus, in regard to controversies about complicated topics—such as the possibility of inherited ethnic differences in intelligence—intelligent people easily can find reasons to support the position that agrees with their own biases and assumptions about human nature. Relatively few people would be able to approach such issues with an open mind (Rogers, 1996). In his highly critical article, noted naturalist Stephen Jay Gould (1994) concluded that, given what he believed to be the scientific impossibility of determining whether there are hereditary ethnic differences in intelligence, the best position to take is one of intellectual agnosticism toward the issue—though he believed that intellectuals should be free to study that and virtually any other topic.

---

ity in a characteristic within a population can be attributed to heredity. Jensen claimed that intelligence has a heritability of .80, which would mean that 80 percent of the variability in intelligence among the members of a group can be explained by heredity. He concluded that the IQ gap between European American and African American children was mainly attributable to heredity (Rushton & Jensen, 2003). But he was accused of making an unwarranted inference. Just because intelligence might have high heritability within a group does not mean that IQ differences between groups, such as African Americans and European Americans, are caused by heredity. Moreover, research has found that the heritability of intelligence is closer to .50 than to .80 (Casto, DeFries, & Fulker, 1995). Jensen's article led to accusations that he was a racist and to demonstrations against him when he spoke on college campuses, illustrating the tension between academic freedom and social sensitivity.

In the tradition of eugenics, one of Jensen's chief supporters, William Shockley (1972), urged that the federal government pay Americans with below-average IQ scores (who would be disproportionately African American) to undergo sterilization. He recommended paying them $1,000 for each point by which their IQ scores were less than 100. Though Shockley was not a psychologist or even a social scientist, he gained media attention because he had won a 1956 Nobel Prize for inventing the transistor. Shockley and several other Nobel Prize winners even deposited their sperm in a sperm bank in California for use by women of superior intelligence who wished to produce highly intelligent offspring ("Superkids?" 1980).

A vigorous response to those who claimed that intelligence is chiefly the product of heredity came from Leon Kamin (1974). Kamin reported that important data supporting the hereditary basis of intelligence had been falsified. Cyril Burt (1883–1971), a British psychologist, had published findings from three studies showing that the positive correlation in IQ scores between identical twins reared apart was higher than the correlation in IQ of fraternal twins reared together. Because identical twins reared apart have the same genes but different environments, the data supported the greater influence of heredity on intelligence.

In each of his studies, supposedly using different sets of twins, Burt reported that the correlation in intelligence between identical twins reared apart was .771. But, as Kamin observed, the odds against finding the same correlation to three decimal places in three different studies are so high as to defy belief. Burt's findings were literally too good to be true. Even Burt's official biographer, who began as an admirer and who believed that Burt had not falsified his data, grudgingly concluded that the data were indeed fraudulent (Hearnshaw, 1979). These findings have not prevented others from coming to Burt's defense, trying to explain away his apparent falsification of data as the product of carelessness rather than the wholesale fabrication of data (Joynson, 2003). Whatever the explanation, Burt's data are not trustworthy (Butler & Petrulis, 1999). Ironically, less than a decade after Kamin's critique of Burt's research, the Minnesota Study of Twins Reared Apart found that identical twins reared apart had a correlation of .710 in their intelligence—not very different from what Burt had reported (Lykken, 1982).

Family Studies of Intelligence

Though the publicity generated by the discovery of Cyril Burt's deception struck a blow against the hereditary view of intelligence, other researchers have conducted legitimate family studies of intelligence. As shown in Figure 10-4, the closer the genetic relationship between relatives, the more similar they are in intelligence (Bouchard & McGue, 1981). But the closer the genetic relationship between relatives, the more likely they also are to share similar environments. Consequently, the size of the correlation in intelligence between relatives of varying degrees of genetic similarity is, by itself, inadequate to determine whether this similarity is caused primarily by hereditary factors or by environmental factors. But support for the relatively weak effect of environment on intelligence comes from "virtual twin" studies, in which unrelated children are reared in the same family from early infancy. A study of 90 pairs of virtual twins found that though there was a

FIGURE 10-4
Heredity versus Environment

The correlation in IQ between relatives increases as their hereditary or environmental similarity increases.

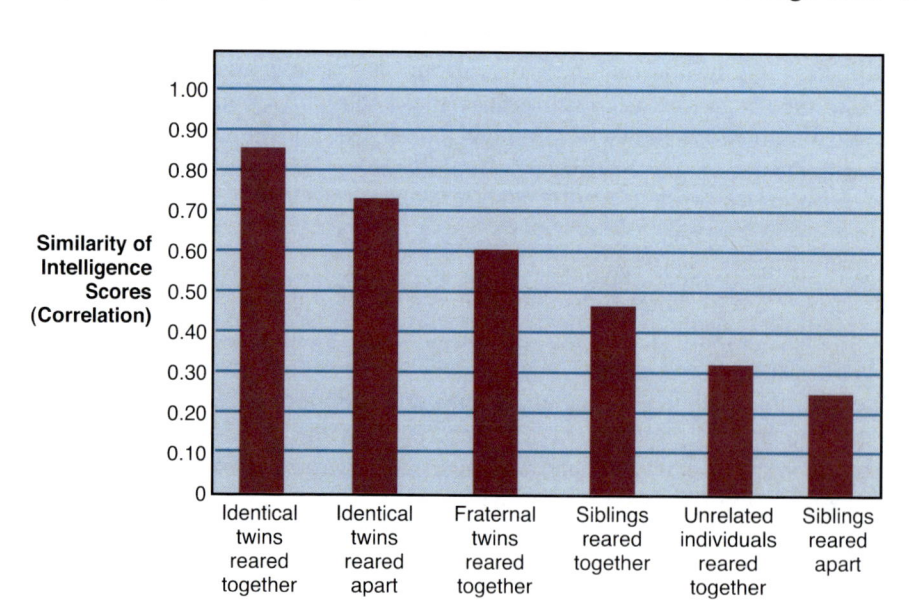

statistically significant correlation in their intelligence ($r = .26$), which indicates that the environment affects intelligence, their correlation in intelligence is lower than the correlation between nontwin siblings reared in the same family ($r = .50$). This finding indicates that heredity also affects intelligence (Segal, 2000).

Twin Studies Perhaps the higher correlation in intelligence between identical twins reared together than between fraternal twins reared together might be attributable to the more similar treatment received by identical twins. But research findings have provided strong evidence against this interpretation. When identical twins are mistakenly reared as fraternal twins, they become as similar in intelligence as identical twins who are reared as identical twins. Moreover, fraternal twins who are mistakenly reared as identical twins become no more similar in intelligence than do fraternal twins reared as fraternal twins (Scarr & Carter-Saltzman, 1979). These findings indicate that the similarity in intelligence between twins is determined more by their genetic similarity than by their environmental similarity.

Adoption Studies To separate the effects of heredity and environment, researchers have turned to adoption studies. Some of these studies compare the correlation in intelligence between adopted children and their adoptive parents to the correlation in intelligence between adopted children and their biological parents. A published review of adoption studies found the positive correlation in intelligence between adoptees and their biological parents is larger than the positive correlation between adoptees and their adoptive parents (Loehlin, Horn, & Willerman, 1994). This finding supports a genetic basis of intelligence; the genes inherited from the natural parents appear to exert a stronger influence on adoptees than does the environment provided by their adoptive parents (Bouchard & McGue, 1981).

Both the Colorado Adoption Project (Coon, Fulker, DeFries, & Plomin, 1990) and the Texas Adoption Project (Loehlin, Horn, & Willerman, 1994) have provided strong support for a hereditary component in intelligence. The influence of heredity on the variability in intelligence among children *increases* from infancy through childhood. For example, the Colorado Adoption Study has found that the heritability of intelligence is only .09 at age 1 but .36 at age 7 (Fulker, DeFries, & Plomin, 1988). As children spend more years in their home environment, the environment—counter to what common sense would predict—decreases in its influence on the variability in intelligence.

In addition to their support for the influence of heredity on intelligence, adoption studies have provided support for the effect of the environment on intelligence. If nature dominates nurture, then children from lower socioeconomic classes who are adopted by parents from higher socioeconomic classes should show little or no gain in IQ when compared to equivalent children who remain with their biological parents. This possibility was tested by Sandra Scarr and Richard Weinberg (1976) in the Minnesota Adoption Study. The study included African American children who had been adopted by European American couples of higher socioeconomic status than the children's biological parents. The study found that the children who had been adopted had an average IQ of 110. The environment had a strong effect on their intelligence because the adoptees scored about 20 points higher than the average IQ of African American children of the same socioeconomic status reared by their biological parents. These findings indicate that nurture as well as nature is important in intellectual development because children adopted into families of higher socioeconomic status have IQs that are higher than those of their biological parents, though lower than those of their adoptive parents (Weinberg, Scarr, & Waldman, 1992).

A study of adopted children in France found that these findings also held for European children. Participants in the study were 32 children who had been abandoned at birth by their lower-socioeconomic-class parents and adopted at an average age of 4 months by higher-socioeconomic-class professionals. When compared with their siblings who were reared by their biological parents, the adoptees scored an average of 14 points higher in intelligence and were less likely to be left back in school (Schiff, Duyme, Dumaret, &

The Nurturing of Intelligence

(a) Children from high socioeconomic backgrounds will be more likely than (b) children from lower socioeconomic backgrounds to receive the intellectual enrichment they need to reach their intellectual potential.

Sources: (a) Monkey Business Images/Shutterstock.com; *(b)* Nolte Lourens/Shutterstock.com.

(a)   (b)

Tomkiewicz, 1982). A more recent study in France included 87 adolescents given up at birth and adopted before 3 years of age into different socioeconomic classes. The results showed a significant negative correlation of –.37 between the social class of the adoptive families and the likelihood of repeating a grade in school. That is, as the socioeconomic class of the adoptive families increased, the likelihood of the adoptee having to repeat a grade decreased. This finding supported the importance of the environment in determining intellectual performance (Duyme, 1988). But other researchers have found that adopted children reared in families of higher socioeconomic status than that of their biological families show a smaller enhancement in intelligence than had been reported in previous studies (Locurto, 1990). Based on their review of adoption studies, Scarr and Weinberg (1983) concluded that intelligence is influenced by both heredity and environment, with neither dominating the other.

Family Configuration Studies An alternative source of support for the influence of the environment on intelligence comes from family configuration studies. A survey of 400,000 19-year-old men in the Netherlands found that the larger their families and the later they were in the birth order, the less intelligent they tended to be (Belmont & Marolla, 1973). This finding has been explained by Robert Zajonc's (1986) **confluence model**, which assumes that each child is born into an intellectual environment that depends on the intelligence level of his or her parents and siblings. The greater the number of children and the smaller the average interval between births, the lower will be what Zajonc calls the average intellectual environment into which a child is born (Zajonc & Mullally, 1997). One of the reasons for this drop may be the inevitable reduction in the attention parents give to each of their children after the birth of another child (Gibbs, Teti, & Bond, 1987).

In a bold gesture, Zajonc (1976) used the confluence model to predict that the decline in SAT scores that had begun in 1963 would stop in 1980 and then begin to rise. Zajonc based his prediction on the fact that high school students who took the SAT between 1963 and 1980 had been born into increasingly larger families during the post–World War II baby boom. But after 1980, high school students who would take the SAT would come from smaller and smaller families. Zajonc's prediction was supported: SAT scores continued to decline until 1980 and then began to rise. Of course, the decline could have a host of other explanations, including greater numbers of academically poor students taking the test (Astin & Garber, 1982).

Though Zajonc (1993) continues to present evidence supporting the confluence model, other researchers present evidence contradicting it (Barbut, 1993). For example, data from a study by the National Institutes of Health, which included 47,000 women and their 53,000 children, failed to find a relationship between the intelligence of the children and the average interval between the births in their families (Brackbill & Nichols, 1982). Moreover, the confluence model has demonstrated, at best, a *correlational* rather than a

confluence model Robert Zajonc's model of environmental influences on intelligence, which assumes that each child is born into an intellectual environment related to birth order and to the number and differences in age of her or his siblings.

368   Chapter 10   Intelligence

causal relationship between family configuration and intelligence (Rodgers, Cleveland, van den Oord, & Rowe, 2000). That is, even if the relationship is real, perhaps other unidentified factors account for it.

Intellectual Enrichment Programs

Further support for the influence of the environment on intelligence comes from the finding that the difference between European American and African American performance on the SAT narrowed between 1976 and 1983 (Jones, 1984). Moreover, the difference between African American and European American children in IQ test scores is declining, possibly because more African American children have gained access to better educational and economic resources (Vincent, 1991). Access to enrichment programs such as Project Head Start also might play a role. Head Start ensures that poor children get medical care, helps their families gain access to social services, finds employment for parents, serves nutritious meals, provides intellectual stimulation, and helps children develop the social competence necessary to succeed in school (Zigler, 1999). Socioeconomically deprived children who attend Head Start show an average gain of 10 points in their IQ scores (Zigler, Abelson, Trickett, & Seitz, 1982) and greater improvement in their cognitive abilities compared to those not in such programs. This finding contradicts Jensen's (1969) prediction that Head Start would have no significant effect on intellectual growth. Unfortunately, the gains achieved by children in preschool enrichment programs often decline during grade school (Locurto, 1991), perhaps in part because these children typically attend inferior schools (Lee & Loeb, 1995). This finding indicates the need to continue enrichment programs beyond the preschool years.

Preschool enrichment programs other than Head Start also can have beneficial effects, as shown in a study of disadvantaged African American children who attended Head Start, other preschool, or no preschool programs. Children in the Head Start and other preschool programs showed greater improvement in several intellectual abilities than did those who did not attend either kind of program. This result could not be attributed to initial differences in intellectual abilities because the children were statistically matched on various relevant characteristics (Lee, Brooks-Gunn, Schnur, & Liaw, 1990).

Other countries also have found that intellectual enrichment programs can be beneficial. One of the most ambitious of all enrichment programs took place from 1979 to 1983 in Venezuela, under its minister of state for the development of intelligence (Gonzalez, 1989). The program provided good prenatal care and infant nutrition, as well as sensory stimulation of preschoolers and special training in cognitive skills. New mothers

Project Head Start

Intellectual enrichment programs, such as Project Head Start, provide a stimulating preschool environment that better prepares children for success in elementary school.
Source: Olesya Feketa/Shutterstock.com.

watched videocassettes on proper child rearing while in their hospital rooms, schoolchildren attended "learning to think" classes, and television commercials promoted the need to develop the minds of Venezuelan children (Walsh, 1981). The more than 400 Venezuelan seventh graders who participated in a program to teach thinking skills (such as reasoning, problem solving, and decision making) achieved better academic performance than comparable control students who had not participated (Herrnstein, Nickerson, de Sanchez, & Swets, 1986).

Even more evidence of the influence of the environment on intelligence comes from the finding that IQ scores have increased from 5 to 25 points in 14 nations during the past few decades, apparently because of better nutrition, education, and health care (Flynn, 1987). And both Galton and Goddard would be surprised to find that today the Japanese, whom they considered intellectually inferior, score significantly higher than Americans on IQ tests that have been standardized on Americans. Japanese children score about 10 points higher than American children (Lynn, 1982). The Japanese increase in IQ scores parallels that country's increased emphasis on education, with children going to school more hours, attending school more days, and studying more hours than do American children. It is difficult to attribute this increase in IQ scores to accelerated evolution of Japanese brains.

Even the academic achievements of Asian Americans surpass those of European Americans and African Americans. What might account for this finding? Stanley Sue, a cross-cultural psychologist, insists that it is wrong to attribute these achievements to either an inborn intellectual superiority or a culture that places a high value on education. Instead, Sue looks to simple adaptive behavior. According to Sue, because Asian Americans have had cultural and discriminatory barriers to their upward mobility in careers that place less emphasis on education (such as sports, politics, entertainment, and corporate leadership), they have sought to pursue careers that provide fewer barriers. These more accessible alternatives (such as science, mathematics, and engineering) typically place a premium on academic excellence (Sue & Okazaki, 1990). Sue's hypothesis has not yet been adequately tested.

Some psychologists have suggested that it might not be in our best interest to study the relative importance of nature and nurture in intellectual development (Sarason, 1984). To do so might discover little of scientific import while providing apparent scientific support for discrimination against racial or ethnic minorities. Instead of examining the relative importance of nature versus nurture, it might be better to do what Anne Anastasi (1958), an authority on psychological testing, suggested more than three decades ago: determine *how* both achieve their effects (Turkheimer, 1991).

Section Review: Nature, Nurture, and Intelligence

1. What have adoption studies (especially studies of identical twins reared apart) discovered about the role of nature and nurture in intelligence?

2. What effects do programs such as Head Start have on deprived children's intellectual abilities?

> ### Experiencing Psychology
>
> **What Would You Include in an IQ Test?**
>
> **Rationale**
>
> Traditional IQ tests are descendants of the Binet-Simon Scale, which was designed to help place students in appropriate classes in French schools in the early 20th century. Because of their original use, as discussed in the sections "Sternberg's Triarchic Theory of Intelligence" and "Gardner's Theory of Multiple Intelligences," traditional IQ tests have been criticized for assessing narrow aspects of intelligence, primarily those related to verbal ability. Such criticisms have motivated some intelligence researchers to develop intelligence tests based on broader conceptions of intelligence, most notably Robert Sternberg's triarchic theory of intelligence and Howard Gardner's theory of multiple intelligences.
>
> **Assignment**
>
> Based on what you have learned about Sternberg's triarchic theory and Gardner's theory of multiple intelligences, write a proposal describing your own intelligence test. The test should assess more than the abilities necessary for performing well academically.
>
> Describe the rationale and the components of your test (that is, the kinds of talents and abilities that it would assess). Also, discuss how you would standardize the test, determine its reliability, and establish its validity. Describe any similarities or differences between your test and traditional intelligence tests, such as the Wechsler and Stanford-Binet intelligence scales. Include a discussion of a relevant journal article that you found in Psychological Abstracts, perhaps by using *PsycInfo*.

Chapter Summary

Intelligence Testing

- Intelligence is the global capacity to act purposefully, to think rationally, and to deal effectively with the environment.
- An achievement test assesses knowledge of a particular subject, an aptitude test predicts the potential to benefit from instruction in a particular academic or vocational setting, and an intelligence test is a kind of aptitude test that assesses overall mental ability.
- Francis Galton began the study of mental abilities in the late 19th century and founded the field of differential psychology.
- The first formal test of general intelligence was the Binet-Simon scale, which was developed to help place children in school classes.
- The American version of the test became known as the Stanford-Binet Intelligence Scale.
- Today, the Stanford-Binet Intelligence Scale and the Wechsler Intelligence Scales are the most popular intelligence tests.
- Tests must be standardized so that they are administered in a uniform manner and so that test scores can be compared with norms.
- A test must also be reliable, giving consistent results over time.
- And a test must be valid, meaning that it measures what it is supposed to measure.
- Controversy has arisen over whether intelligence testing is fair to minority groups, particularly African Americans.
- Opponents of intelligence testing claim that because African Americans, on the average, score lower than European Americans do, the tests are biased against African Americans.
- Proponents of intelligence testing claim that the tests accurately predict the academic performance of both African Americans and European Americans and typically attribute the differences in performance to the deprived sociocultural backgrounds that are more common among African American children.
- Attempts to develop tests that are not affected by the test taker's sociocultural background have failed.

Extremes of Intelligence

- To be classified as having an intellectual disability, a person must have an IQ of 70 or below and, beginning in childhood, difficulties performing in everyday life.
- The four categories of intellectual disabilities are mild intellectual disability, moderate intellectual disability, severe intellectual disability, and profound intellectual disability.
- Though most cases of intellectual disabilities are caused by sociocultural factors, some are caused by brain damage.
- Most people with an intellectual disability can benefit from education and training programs.
- To be classified as mentally gifted, a person must have an IQ of 130 or above and demonstrate unusual ability in at least one area, such as art, music, or mathematics.
- Lewis Terman's Genetic Studies of Genius have demonstrated that mentally gifted children tend to become successful in their academic, social, physical, and vocational lives.

- Social change and increased occupational opportunity for women are reflected in generational differences in gifted women's achievement.
- Benbow and Stanley's Study of Mathematically Precocious Youth identifies children with outstanding mathematical ability, provides them with special programs, and counsels their parents about how to help them reach their potential.

Theories of Intelligence

- Theories of intelligence traditionally have depended on factor analysis, a statistical technique for determining the abilities that underlie intelligence.
- The theories differ in the extent to which they view intelligence as a general factor or a combination of different factors.
- The most recent factor-analytic theory distinguishes between fluid intelligence and crystallized intelligence.
- Robert Sternberg's triarchic theory of intelligence (recently renamed the theory of successful intelligence) is based on his research on information processing.
- Sternberg's theory distinguishes between componential (academic) intelligence, experiential (creative) intelligence, and contextual (practical) intelligence.
- Sternberg also believes that people can be taught to process information more effectively, thereby increasing their level of intelligence.
- Howard Gardner's theory of multiple intelligences is a biopsychological theory, which assumes that the brain has evolved separate systems for different adaptive abilities that he calls "intelligences": linguistic, logicalmathematical, spatial, musical, bodily-kinesthetic, intrapersonal, and interpersonal intelligences.
- Each of us varies in the degree to which we have developed each of these kinds of intelligence.

Nature, Nurture, and Intelligence

- One of the most controversial issues in psychology has been the extent to which intelligence is a product of heredity or of environment.
- Early studies of women addressed gender differences and variability in physical and mental attributes.
- Few gender differences were observed, and the variability hypothesis was not supported.
- Early studies of immigrants concluded that many were "feebleminded."
- The examiners attributed this "feeblemindedness" to hereditary factors rather than to a host of cultural and environmental factors that actually accounted for that finding.
- Arthur Jensen created a stir by claiming that heredity is a much more powerful determinant of intelligence than is environment.
- Studies of twins, adopted children, family configuration effects, and enrichment programs indicate that neither heredity nor environment is a significantly more important determinant of intelligence.
- Though intelligence might be highly heritable, there is no widely accepted evidence that differences in intelligence among particular racial or ethnic groups are caused by heredity.

Key Terms

autism spectrum disorder (ASD) (p. 343)
intelligence (p. 344)

Intelligence Testing
achievement test (p. 345)
aptitude test (p. 345)
differential psychology (p. 345)
intelligence quotient (IQ) (p. 346)
intelligence test (p. 345)

Extremes of Intelligence
cerebral palsy (p. 353)
Down syndrome (p. 353)
intellectual disabilities (p. 351)
mental giftedness (p. 355)
phenylketonuria (PKU) (p. 353)

Theories of Intelligence
crystallized intelligence (p. 359)

factor analysis (p. 357)
fluid intelligence (p. 359)
theory of multiple intelligences (p. 360)
triarchic theory of intelligence (p. 360)

Nature, Nurture, and Intelligence
confluence model (p. 368)
eugenics (p. 362)
heritability (p. 364)
variability hypothesis (p. 362)

Chapter Quiz

Note: Answers for the Chapter Quiz questions are provided at the end of the book.

1. So-called culture-fair tests and culture-free tests have proved
   a. more biased than traditional IQ tests.
   b. less biased than traditional IQ tests.
   c. easier for people of lower socioeconomic status than of higher socioeconomic status.
   d. easier for people of higher socioeconomic status than of lower socioeconomic status.

2. Cerebral palsy, which sometimes involves intellectual disabilities, is associated with
   a. schizophrenia.
   b. movement disorders.
   c. interhemispheric interference.
   d. inability to form new memories.

3. According to the theory of multiple intelligences, if you realized why you had a short temper when confronted with minor frustrations, you would exhibit
   a. experiential intelligence.
   b. componential intelligence.
   c. interpersonal intelligence.
   d. intrapersonal intelligence.

4. According to the triarchic theory of intelligence, if you were a renowned abstract painter, you would be high in
   a. innate intelligence.
   b. contextual intelligence.
   c. componential intelligence.
   d. experiential intelligence.

5. Intellectual disabilities caused by phenylketonuria (PKU) can be prevented by
   a. dietary control.
   b. avoiding hypoxia at birth.
   c. Caesarean delivery.
   d. not exposing the fetus to rubella.

6. William Stern's formula for calculating IQ was inadequate when applied to
   a. adults.
   b. adolescents.
   c. people whose chronological age was greater than their mental age.
   d. people whose mental age was greater than their chronological age.

7. David Wechsler devised his first intelligence test to assess
   a. immigrants.
   b. army recruits.
   c. schoolchildren.
   d. psychiatric patients.

8. A test designed to predict your ability to benefit from training as a chef would be an
   a. aptitude test.
   b. expertise test.
   c. achievement test.
   d. intelligence test.

9. David Wechsler's definition of intelligence is in the spirit of
   a. structuralism.
   b. cognitivism.
   c. functionalism.
   d. psychoanalysis.

10. According to the triarchic theory of intelligence, if you can change a flat tire, feel at ease when meeting new people, and perform well when interviewing for a job, you are high in
    a. innate intelligence.
    b. contextual intelligence.
    c. componential intelligence.
    d. experiential intelligence.

11. Francis Galton was inspired by
    a. Cyril Burt's theory of eugenics.
    b. Charles Darwin's theory of evolution.
    c. Henry Goddard's theory of innate intelligence.
    d. Robert Sternberg's triarchic theory of intelligence.

12. Given a mental age of 8 and a chronological age of 16, a child would have an IQ of
    a. 2.
    b. 8.
    c. 50.
    d. 128.

13. A formal test of fans' knowledge of the rules, players, history, and all-time records in professional sports would be
    a. an aptitude test.
    b. an achievement test.
    c. a commonsense test.
    d. an intelligence test.

14. The case of *Larry P. v. Wilson Riles*
    a. outlawed federal funding for eugenics.
    b. ordered mainstreaming for elementary students with intellectual disabilities.
    c. provided special advanced classes for the mentally gifted.
    d. found that IQ tests violated the civil rights of African American children.

15. The original purpose of the intelligence test was to
    a. identify geniuses.
    b. find potential officer candidates for the military.
    c. place students in classes according to their ability.
    d. demonstrate the innate superiority of certain racial and ethnic groups.

16. You develop a new test of social intelligence and establish norms by administering it to groups varying in their sex, age, income, educational level, and geographic location. This procedure is an aspect of
    a. normalization.
    b. homogenization.
    c. standardization.
    d. factor analysis.

17. The extent to which variability in a characteristic within a group can be attributed to heredity is called
    a. eugenics.
    b. heritability.
    c. polygenicity.
    d. differential psychology.

18. To be classified as having an intellectual disability, a person must have a low IQ and
    a. lack the ability to communicate.
    b. medically verified brain damage.
    c. difficulty functioning in everyday life.
    d. complete dependence on others for self-care.

19. If you were an excellent problem solver and could rapidly perform mental arithmetic calculations, you would demonstrate excellent
    a. fluid intelligence.
    b. structural intelligence.
    c. experiential intelligence.
    d. crystallized intelligence.

20. A championship contestant on the television quiz show *Jeopardy* has acquired a great deal of knowledge from schooling and everyday life. This fund of information characterizes the kind of intelligence that increases across the life span, which is better known as
    a. fluid intelligence.
    b. structural intelligence.
    c. experiential intelligence.
    d. crystallized intelligence.

21. On a standardized intelligence test with a standard deviation of 15, the proportion of people who score between 70 and 130 is about
    a. 60%.
    b. 68%.
    c. 95%.
    d. 99%.

22. The belief that intelligence reflects both a general ability and several specific abilities was held by
    a. J. P. Guilford.
    b. Louis Thurstone.
    c. Raymond Cattell.
    d. Charles Spearman.

23. According to Robert Zajonc, the most intelligent child would probably be a 10-year-old girl with
    a. a 9-year-old sister and an 11-year-old sister.
    b. an 8-year-old brother and a 14-year-old sister.
    c. a 1-year-old brother and an 18-year-old sister.
    d. a 12-year-old brother and a 16-year-old brother.

24. If you claimed that only elite athletes and people who score above 1400 on the SAT should be permitted to reproduce, you would favor
    a. eugenics.
    b. polygenetics.
    c. evolutionary confluence.
    d. environmental determinism.

25. Research studies indicate that there is a larger positive correlation in intelligence between
    a. unrelated children reared together than between identical twins reared apart.
    b. fraternal twins reared together than between identical twins reared apart.
    c. adoptees and their biological parents than between adoptees and their adoptive parents.
    d. adoptees and their adoptive parents than between adoptees and their biological parents.

Thought Questions

1. In what ways have science, politics, and sociocultural factors become part of the debate on the relative roles of nature and nurture in intelligence?

2. Why do some psychologists believe that Gardner's theory of multiple intelligences might lead to intelligence tests that are superior to traditional ones?

3. How did Terman's longitudinal study of geniuses revise people's thinking about extremely intelligent people?

Motivation

CHAPTER 11

On a beautiful spring day in 2000, hundreds of residents of the popular arts community comprising New Hope, Pennsylvania, and Lambertville, New Jersey, attended the funeral of a beloved man who had been known as "Mother" since he arrived in 1949, looking for work as a female impersonator. Mother, born Joseph Cavellucci in New York City in 1925, "came out of the closet" regarding his homosexuality as a teenager growing up in Philadelphia.

Mother's death left a void in the lives of those who were used to seeing him—dressed in female attire—on his daily walk, wearing pink slippers or high heels, across the bridge from his home in New Hope to do his grocery shopping in Lambertville. His death left a larger void in the lives of those who sought his wisdom and practical assistance (which accounted for his being called "Mother"). Cavellucci, who accepted being called either "he" or "she," never turned down a request to perform at an event to raise money for someone in need.

Mother was so beloved and well known that *The Philadelphia Inquirer* published a major obituary for him, calling him an icon of the gay community. His local daily newspaper, the Doylestown *Intelligencer Record*, called him "larger than life" and said, "Cavellucci achieved something many of us aspire to—he lived life on his own terms" (Duffy, 2000, p. A-1). Mother often behaved like a curmudgeon with a sense of humor. On one occasion, while working as a server (his long-time profession) at a canal-side restaurant, Mother responded to a woman who complained that her companion had one more shrimp than she had by simply tossing one of her partner's shrimp into the canal. He added, "Now you both have the same number."

As one of Mother's "family" remarked after his death, "She was truly the town's mother. She embraced everyone no matter what. But she could care for you and put you in your place at the same time" (Duffy, 2000, p. A-4). Mother's "children"—gay, lesbian, and straight—repaid his kindness by holding several fundraisers to pay for his long battle against cancer. They even kept paying the rent on his apartment, never giving up hope that he would one day return home. In his last days, Mother lived at Buckingham Valley Nursing Home, which he naturally renamed "Buckingham Palace," with himself as both king and queen. "I am the reigning man and woman," he announced. The nurses took turns putting on Mother's makeup and nail polish and styling his hair.

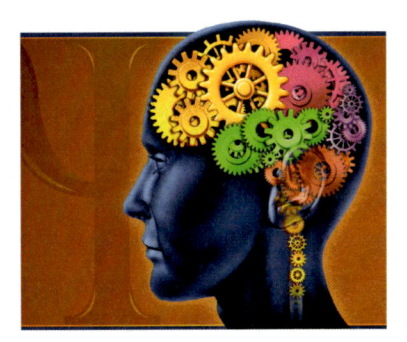

Source: Lightspring/Shutterstock.com.

Chapter Outline

The Nature of Motivation
The Hunger Motive
The Sex Motive
The Arousal Motive
The Achievement Motive
The Role of Motivation in Sport

Mother frequently worked as a female impersonator, appearing in extravaganzas throughout the United States, including the Gay Miss U.S.A. pageant. He loved dressing in shimmering gowns and wearing makeup, nail polish, and a bouffant hairdo when performing. He would bring down the house with his vocal stylings of "Hello, Dolly" and "God Bless America." A soulful rendition of the latter accompanied the long procession following his coffin out of St. John's Church in Lambertville. In eulogizing Mother, New Hope's mayor, Laurence Keller, recognized him as a pioneer for gay rights. (Mother was fond of saying, "Honey, I put the 'G' in gay.") Keller tearfully concluded his eulogy by saying, "I'll always remember the grand dame of New Hope" (Duffy, 2000, p. A-4).

After reading this brief passage on the life of Joseph "Mother" Cavellucci, you might ask: Why would a person born male be sexually attracted to other men? Why would a man prefer dressing in women's clothing? And why would a man claim to be both male and female? Possible answers to these questions are presented in the section on human sexuality. The chapter also discusses other kinds of human *motivation*, including hunger, arousal, and achievement.

The Nature of Motivation

motivation The psychological process that arouses, directs, and maintains behavior toward a goal.

Motivation is the psychological process that arouses, directs, and maintains behavior toward a goal. The hunger motive, for example, normally arouses us to take action, directs us to find food, and makes us eat until our hunger subsides. Because we cannot directly observe people's motivation, we must infer it from their behavior. We might infer that a person who drinks a quart of water is motivated by a strong thirst and that a person who becomes dictator of a country is motivated by a strong need for power. The concept of motivation also is useful in explaining fluctuations in behavior over time (Atkinson, 1981). If yesterday morning you ate three stacks of pancakes but this morning you ate only a piece of toast, your friends would not attribute your change in behavior to a change in your personality. Instead, they would attribute it to a change in your degree of hunger—your motivation.

Sources of Motivation

What are the main sources of motivation? In seeking answers to this question, psychologists have implicated *genes*, *drives*, and *incentives*.

Genes and Motivation

instinct A complex, inherited behavior pattern characteristic of a species.

In the early 20th century, many psychologists, influenced by Charles Darwin's theory of evolution and led by William McDougall (1871–1938), attributed human and animal motivation to inherited *instincts*. An **instinct** is a complex, inherited (that is, unlearned) species-specific behavior pattern. Instincts are at work when birds build nests, spiders weave webs, and salmon swim upstream to their spawning grounds. But what of human instincts? McDougall (1908) claimed that people are guided by a variety of instincts, including instincts for "pugnacity," "curiosity," and "gregariousness." As discussed in Chapter 13, McDougall's contemporary, Sigmund Freud, based his theory of personality on instincts that supposedly motivate sex and aggression. And William James (1890/1981) claimed that humans are motivated by more instincts than any other animal.

In the 1920s, psychologists, influenced by behaviorist John B. Watson, rejected instincts as factors in human motivation. Watson believed that human behavior depended on learning, not heredity. One reason why instinct theorists lost scientific credibility was that they had attempted to explain almost all human behavior as instinctive, in some cases compiling lists of thousands of alleged human instincts (Cofer, 1985). You might say, for example, that people paint because of an "aesthetic instinct" or play sports because of a "competitive instinct." A second reason why instinct theorists fell out of favor was their failure to explain the behaviors they labeled as instinctive. Consider the following hypothetical dialogue about an alleged "parenting instinct":

- Why do parents take care of their children?
- Because they have a parenting instinct.
- But how do you know parents have a parenting instinct?
- Because they take care of their children.

Such circular reasoning neither explains why parents take care of their children nor provides evidence of a parenting instinct. Each assertion is simply used to support the other. For these reasons, psychologists prefer not to refer to human instincts.

Though instinct theory, as applied to humans, has fallen into disfavor, some scientists believe that human social behavior does in fact have a genetic basis (Hoffman, 1995). The chief proponents of this belief work in the field of **sociobiology**, founded by Edward O. Wilson in the 1970s, which studies the hereditary basis of human and animal social behavior within the framework of evolution (Wilson, 1975). Sociobiological principles have been recognized for centuries in different cultures, as in the Japanese novel *The Tale of Genji*, written a millennium ago. This story is filled with sociobiological themes regarding human motivation (Thiessen & Umezawa, 1998).

But sociobiology has been criticized for overestimating the role of heredity in human social behavior (Hood, 1995). Critics fear that acceptance of sociobiology would lend support to the status quo, making us less inclined to change what many people believe has been "ordained by God or nature," such as the since-discredited theory of racial differences in criminality, social status, sexual behavior, and child neglect and abuse (Peregrine, Ember, & Ember, 2003). Nonetheless, research on personality and other topics lends support to some sociobiological notions. In fact, some personality researchers still see a role for evolutionary principles in the study of personality (Millon, 2003).

Drives and Motivation

Following the decline of the instinct theory of human motivation, the **drive-reduction theory** of Clark Hull (1884–1952) dominated psychology in the 1940s and 1950s (Webster & Coleman, 1992). According to Hull (1943), a **need** caused by physiological deprivation, such as a lack of food or water, induces a state of tension called a **drive**, which motivates the individual to reduce it. The thirst drive motivates drinking, the hunger drive motivates eating, and the sex drive motivates sexual behavior. Even the alleviation of a drug craving by the ingestion of a drug can be interpreted as an example of drive reduction (McMillan & Katz, 2002).

Drive reduction aims at the restoration of **homeostasis**, a steady state of physiological equilibrium. Consider your thirst drive. When your body loses water, as when you perspire, receptor cells in your hypothalamus (see Chapter 3) respond and make you feel thirsty. Thirst arouses you, signaling you that your body lacks water, and directs you to drink. By drinking, you reduce your thirst and restore homeostasis by restoring your body's normal water level. Undoubtedly, we are motivated to reduce drives such as thirst, hunger, and sex, but drive reduction cannot explain all human motivation. In some cases, we perform behaviors that do not reduce physiological drives, as in the case of Jim Abbott, who had only one hand yet pursued a successful career as a major league baseball pitcher.

Incentives and Motivation

Whereas a drive is an internal state of tension that "pushes" you toward a goal, an **incentive** is an external stimulus that "pulls" you toward a goal. Through experience, we learn that certain stimuli (such as a puppy) are desirable and should be approached,

Instincts
An instinct, or innate behavior, is a complex, inherited species-specific behavior pattern.
Source: Kristaps K/Shutterstock.com.

sociobiology The study of the hereditary basis of human and animal social behavior.

drive-reduction theory The theory that behavior is motivated by the need to reduce drives such as sex or hunger.

need A motivated state caused by physiological deprivation, such as a lack of food or water.

drive A state of psychological tension induced by a need.

homeostasis A steady state of physiological equilibrium.

incentive An external stimulus that pulls an individual toward a goal.

Chapter 11 Motivation

making them *positive* incentives. We also learn that other stimuli (such as elevator music) are undesirable and should be avoided, making them *negative* incentives. Thus, we are pulled toward positive incentives and away from negative ones. Incentives often are used by teachers and employers to motivate students (Rassuli, 2012) and employees (Jeffrey & Adomdza, 2011).

Incentives often are associated with drives. For example, your thirst drive motivates you to replenish your body's water, but incentives determine what you choose to drink. Your thirst would push you to drink, but your favorite flavor would pull you toward a particular beverage. As with all incentives, your favorite flavor would partly depend on learning, which in this case would depend on your past experience with a variety of flavors. In the case of airline passengers who survived a crash in the Andes years ago and cannibalized the bodies of passengers who had died, a strong hunger drive made them respond to a weak incentive, human flesh (Read, 1974). The opposite can occur in your everyday life. Despite not feeling hungry, you might be motivated to eat in response to a strong incentive, such as an ice cream sundae.

Maslow's Hierarchy of Needs

If forced to make a choice, would you prefer enough food to eat or straight As in school? Would you prefer to have a warm home or close friends? In each case, though both options are appealing, you probably would choose the first; this quiz shows that some motives have priority over others. The fact that we have such preferences led the humanistic psychologist Abraham Maslow (1970) to develop a **hierarchy of needs** (see Figure 11-1), which ranks important needs by their priority. Maslow used the term *need* to refer to both physiological and psychological motives. According to Maslow, you must first satisfy your basic *physiological* needs, such as your needs for food and water, before you will be motivated to meet your higher needs for *safety* and *security*, and so on up the hierarchy from the need for *belongingness and love*, through the need for *esteem*, and ultimately to the needs for *self-actualization* (achievement of all your potentials). Unpublished works from Maslow's later years (Koltko-Rivera, 2006) describe a sixth need he termed *transcendence* (spiritual fulfillment and altruism). Though his theory has been criticized for its basis on Western and individualistic views on personal growth (Hanley & Abell, 2002), Maslow's concept of a hierarchy of needs has much in common with views of human motivation that are widely accepted in India (Satapathy, 2001).

Maslow believed that because most people are unable to satisfy all their lower needs, few people reach the two highest levels. Nonetheless, success in meeting lower-level needs in the hierarchy is positively correlated with psychological well-being (Lester, 1990). Though Maslow died before conducting much research on people who had reached transcendence, he did study the lives of people he considered self-actualized, including Abraham Lincoln and Eleanor Roosevelt (see Chapter 13).

hierarchy of needs Maslow's arrangement of needs in the order of their motivational priority, ranging from physiological needs to the needs for self-actualization and transcendence.

FIGURE 11-1
Maslow's Hierarchy of Needs

Abraham Maslow assumed that our needs are arranged in a hierarchy, with our most powerful needs at the bottom. We will be weakly motivated by higher needs until our lower needs are met.

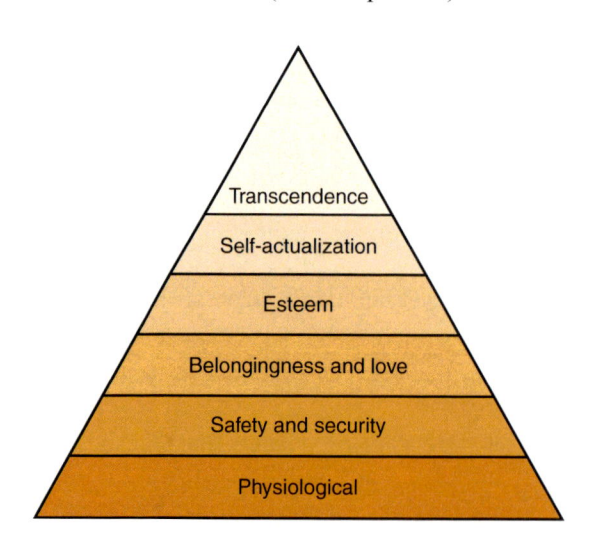

Pyramid (bottom to top): Physiological; Safety and security; Belongingness and love; Esteem; Self-actualization; Transcendence.

Though some research on Maslow's hierarchy of needs—such as a study of the satisfaction of those needs in 88 countries from 1960 to 1994 (Hagerty, 1999)—has supported his sequence of need achievement, we do not always place a higher priority on lower-level needs (Goebel & Brown, 1981). This finding was supported by a study in which a survey given to 150 college students asked them to identify which of the needs in Maslow's hierarchy was most important to them. Both male and female undergraduates chose being in love as more important than any other need (Pettijohn, 1996). Moreover, martyrs such as Mahatma Gandhi will starve themselves for the sake of social justice. Now consider the biological motives of *hunger*, *sex*, and *arousal*; the social motive of *achievement*; and the role of motivation in sport.

Section Review: The Nature of Motivation

1. Why do some scientists criticize sociobiological explanations of human behavioral differences?
2. What are the different levels in Maslow's hierarchy of needs?

The Hunger Motive

The *hunger* motive impels you to eat to satisfy your body's need for nutrients. If you have just eaten, food might be the last thing on your mind. But if you have not eaten for a few days—or even for a few hours—food might be the only thing on your mind.

The Physiology of Hunger

Research on hunger and eating has grown in recent decades, largely because of concerns about the health risks associated with the increase in obesity and eating disorders in industrialized countries. One factor involved in body weight is heredity, which plays a role in the regulation of eating (De Castro, 1999). Much of this evidence has come from twin studies. The Minnesota Study of Twins Reared Apart compared monozygotic (identical) twins reared apart, dizygotic (fraternal) twins reared apart, and nontwins in regard to their dietary preferences. The results showed that the participants' dietary preferences were more strongly related to their degree of hereditary similarity than to their degree of environmental similarity (Hur, Bouchard, & Eckert, 1998). Though some researchers study the hereditary basis of eating regulation, most study bodily, brain, or environmental factors.

Bodily Factors and Hunger

The main bodily mechanisms that regulate hunger involve the mouth, the stomach, the small intestine, the liver, and the pancreas. Taste receptors on the tongue play a role in hunger by sending taste sensations to the brain, allowing you to perceive the taste of food. Though sensations from your mouth affect hunger, they are not its sole source. Your stomach also plays a role in hunger. In 1912, physiologist Walter Cannon (1871–1945) had his assistant Arthur Washburn swallow a balloon, which inflated in his stomach. The balloon was connected by a tube to a device that recorded stomach contractions by measuring changes they caused in the air pressure inside the balloon. Whenever Washburn felt a hunger pang, he pressed a key, producing a mark next to the recording of his stomach contractions. The recordings revealed that Washburn's hunger pangs were associated with stomach contractions, prompting Cannon and Washburn (1912) to conclude that stomach contractions cause hunger. Walter Cannon also coined the term "fight-or-flight" (see Chapter 12), an animal's response to threat, which can include changes in hunger.

Might they have interpreted their findings about hunger and stomach contractions in another way? Perhaps the opposite was true: Washburn's hunger might have caused the stomach contractions. Or, given that we now know that stomach contractions occur when the stomach contains food, perhaps the balloon itself caused Washburn's stomach contractions. Moreover, later research revealed that hunger sensations are not entirely dependent on the stomach; even people whose stomachs have been removed because of cancer or severe ulcers can experience hunger (Ingelfinger, 1944). Therefore, hunger also is regulated by other mechanisms.

Though the stomach is not necessary for the regulation of hunger, it does play an important role. Receptor cells in the stomach detect the amount of food it contains. After gorging yourself on a Thanksgiving dinner, you might become all too aware of the stretch receptors in your stomach that respond to the presence of food (Stricker & McCann, 1985). These receptors inform the brain of the amount of food in the stomach by sending neural impulses along the vagus nerve to the brain, reducing your level of hunger.

Food stored in the stomach eventually reaches the small intestine, the main site of digestion, where it stimulates the secretion of the hormone *cholecystokinin*, which in turn stimulates the vagus nerve to send neural impulses to the brain, reducing your level of hunger (Gosnell & Hsiao, 1984). In a study demonstrating the inhibitory effect of cholecystokinin on hunger, men received doses of either cholecystokinin or a saline placebo. Those who received doses of cholecystokinin reported less hunger than those who received the placebo (Greenough, Cole, Lewis, Lockton, & Blundell, 1998). Though the mouth, stomach, and small intestine each play a role in regulating hunger and eating, optimal regulation depends on the combination of signals from the three of them (Cecil, 2001).

Of special importance in the regulation of hunger are the hormones *insulin*, *ghrelin*, *melanocortin*, and *cholecystokinin* (see Table 11-1). Insulin is secreted by the pancreas. It helps blood sugar enter body cells for use in metabolism, promotes the storage of fat, and induces feelings of hunger. Ghrelin is produced by cells in your stomach and released when your stomach is empty—in other words, when you are hungry. Ghrelin is considered an appetite-regulating hormone and hunger signal. In fact, hunger depends on interplay of several physiological feedback systems. For example, *glucose* is another important factor in the regulation of hunger. Glucose is a simple sugar that is absorbed directly into your bloodstream during digestion. It is the most important source of energy for your body and brain. Researchers have conducted studies in which the level of blood sugar was held constant by a continuous infusion of glucose while insulin levels were permitted to rise. Participants in those studies reported increased levels of hunger (Rodin, 1985).

Brain Factors and Eating

How does your brain decide when and what to eat? Signals from the body regulate hunger by their effects on the brain. In 1902, Viennese physician Alfred Fröhlich reported that patients with tumors of the pituitary gland (see Chapter 3) often became obese. Fröhlich concluded that the pituitary gland regulates hunger. But later research found that, in reality, the tumors influenced hunger by affecting the *hypothalamus*, which lies just above the pituitary gland. The neurotransmitter norepinephrine promotes eating by stimulating receptors in the hypothalamus (Towell, Muscat, & Willner, 1989).

Insulin and Hunger

The mere sight of rich, delicious food can stimulate your pancreas to secrete insulin, making you more hungry and, as a consequence, more likely to eat the food.

Source: cowardion/Shutterstock.com.

TABLE 11-1 Hormones Related to Hunger and Body Weight

Hormone	Function
Insulin	Promotes the storage of fat and induces feelings of hunger
Ghrelin	Regulates appetite and serves as a hunger signal
Melanocortin	Regulates feelings of satiety
Cholecystokinin	Inhibits feelings of hunger

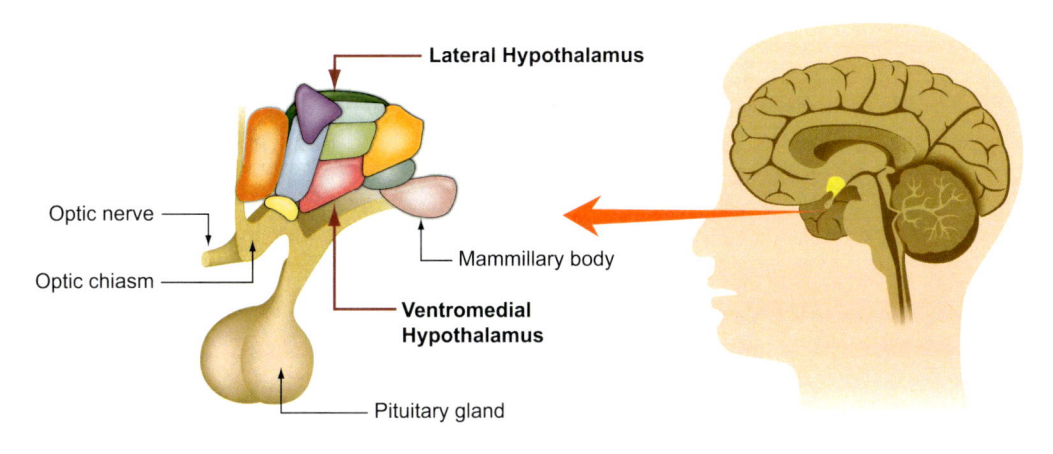

FIGURE 11-2

The Hypothalamus and Hunger

The hypothalamus, located below the thalamus, is a portion of the brain that contains a number of small nuclei with a variety of functions, including regulating hunger. Each side of the brain has this grouping of nuclei. This image shows one side of the brain with the lateral hypothalamus on the outside edge and ventromedial hypothalamus in the bottom middle. These two areas are especially important in the regulation of hunger.

Source: Adapted from Alila Medical Media/Shutterstock.com.

Two areas of the hypothalamus are especially important in the regulation of hunger (see Figure 11-2). Electrical stimulation of the *ventromedial hypothalamus (VMH)*, an area at the lower middle of the hypothalamus, inhibits eating, and its destruction induces eating. Rats whose VMH has been destroyed will eat until they became grossly obese and then eat enough to maintain their new, higher level of weight (Hetherington & Ranson, 1942). They have continuously high levels of insulin in their blood and store their meals as fat. They may weigh up to three times as much as a normal rat. Whereas the VMH has been implicated in reducing hunger, the *lateral hypothalamus (LH)*, comprising areas on both sides of the hypothalamus, has been implicated in increasing it. Research findings indicate that one way in which cholecystokinin suppresses hunger is by inhibiting neuronal activity in the LH and stimulating it in the VMH (Shiraishi, 1990). Electrical stimulation of the LH promotes eating, whereas its destruction inhibits eating. Rats whose LH has been destroyed will stop eating and starve to death even in the presence of food (Anand & Brobeck, 1951). Though early experiments led to the conclusion that the LH acts as our "hunger center" and the VMH acts as our "satiety center," later experiments have shown that these sites are merely important components in the brain's complex system for regulating hunger and eating (Stricker & Verbalis, 1987).

But how does damage to the hypothalamus affect hunger? It does so in part by altering the body's **set point**—that is, its normal weight (Michel & Cabanac, 1999). People and animals maintain a fairly constant weight across their lifetime. Your set point depends on the level of *leptin*, a hormone that regulates energy intake and expenditure. Leptin receptors are located in the hypothalamus. Damage to the LH lowers the set point, reducing hunger and making the animal eat less to maintain a lower body weight. In contrast, damage to the VMH raises the set point, increasing hunger and making the animal eat more to maintain a higher body weight (Keesey & Powley, 1986). Whereas signals from the body regulate changes in hunger from meal to meal, the set point regulates changes in hunger over months or years. Nonetheless, some researchers insist that there is relatively weak evidence of a role for a bodily set point in hunger and eating (Pinel, Assanand, & Lehman, 2000).

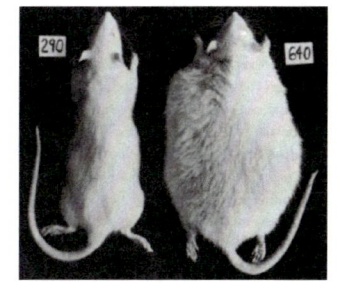

Sociocultural Influences That Regulate Hunger

Hunger, especially in humans, is regulated by external as well as internal factors. Food can act as an incentive to make you feel hungry. The taste, smell, sight, sound, and texture of food can pull you toward it. But how can the mere sight of food induce feelings of hunger? One way is by increasing the level of insulin in your blood. In fact, even daydreaming about food can stimulate your pancreas to release insulin, making you hungry and possibly sending you on a hunt for cake, candy, or ice cream (Rodin, 1985).

Obesity

Obesity is a medical condition characterized by an excessive accumulation of body fat. It is defined by the ratio of lean body mass to fat (the body mass index [BMI]; see

The VMH Rat

Destruction of the ventromedial hypothalamus induces overeating and gross obesity. A rat whose ventromedial hypothalamus has been destroyed might eat until it becomes three times its normal weight.

Source: From P. Teitelbaum, Appetite, *Proceedings of the American Philosophical Society, 108*, 1964, 464–473.

set point A specific body weight that the brain tries to maintain through the regulation of diet, activity, and metabolism.

obesity An unhealthy condition in men who have more than 25 percent body fat and women who have more than 30 percent body fat.

Chapter 11 Motivation   **381**

FIGURE 11-3
Calculating Your Body Mass Index

One way of estimating the ratio of lean body mass to fat is by calculating the body mass index (BMI). BMI scores are positively correlated with body fat percentages. However, two people may have the same BMI and have different percentages of body fat. For example, a bodybuilder would have a lower percentage of body fat than a sedentary person with the same BMI. The correlation between BMI scores and body fat percentage also varies by age and sex. Thus, your BMI score is an estimation of your lean body mass to fat ratio and should be taken into consideration with other factors, such as your level of physical activity.

$$\text{BMI} = \frac{\text{Weight in pounds}}{(\text{Height in inches}) \times (\text{Height in inches})} \times 703$$

Figure 11-3). Men with more than 25 percent body fat and women with more than 30 percent body fat are considered to be obese. More than 60 percent of American adults are overweight, and more than one-third are clinically obese. Obesity is associated with health risks—notably, stroke, diabetes, heart disease, and some cancers (Ogden, Carroll, Kit, & Flegal, 2012)—and costs Americans approximately $147 billion a year in medical expenses (Finkelstein, Trogdon, Cohen, & Dietz, 2009).

In recent decades, obesity has been increasing among American adults, regardless of socioeconomic status (Ljungvall & Zimmerman, 2012). Obesity also has been increasing in other countries, particularly industrialized countries, though less than in the United States. Common sense and scientific opinion attribute the worldwide increase in obesity to higher calorie diets, larger portion sizes, and a decline in physical activity, but research evidence indicates that these are not the sole factors (Taubes, 1998). Obesity appears to depend on the interaction of several biopsychological and behavioral factors.

Biopsychological Factors in Obesity

Research studies are providing more and more evidence that obesity is prompted by several biopsychological factors. They include heredity and genetics, the body's set point, and basal metabolic rate.

Heredity and Obesity Thinness runs in families; research findings support a genetic basis for food and physical activity preferences (Wardle, Guthrie, Sanderson, Birch, & Plomin, 2001). Heredity influences our caloric intake (Faith, Rha, Neale, & Allison, 1999) and our degree of preference for fatty foods and sweet-tasting carbohydrates, all of which promote obesity (Reed, Bachmanov, Beauchamp, & Tordof, 1997). Twin, adoption, and family studies show that a person's obesity risk increases when he or she has obese relatives. The heritability of obesity is about 86 percent (Bulik, Sullivan, & Kendler, 2003). The role of heredity in obesity has been supported by studies of identical twins. Identical twins who have been reared together show a correlation of .75 in their amount of body fat. Even when identical twins have been reared apart, they show only a slightly lower correlation in their amount of body fat (Price & Gottesman, 1991). Evidence that heredity helps determine body weight also was provided by archival research on Danish adoption records. The results (see Figure 11-4) revealed a strong positive correlation between the weights of adoptees and the weights of their biological parents, but little relationship between the weights of adoptees and those of their adoptive parents. Heredity plays a more important role in obesity than do habits learned from the family in which one is reared (Stunkard, Stinnett, & Smoller, 1986).

Recent genetic studies in both humans and animals have linked the hormone *melanocortin* to body weight (see Table 11-1). People with melanocortin mutations are unable to feel full (a lack of satiety) and have severe early-onset obesity (Fani, Bak, Delhanty, van Rossum, & van den Akker, 2013). Mice that have mutated such that they lack melanocortin receptors become obese despite being born at normal weights. As they advance in age,

FIGURE 11-4 Heredity and Obesity

Data from Danish adoption records indicate a positive relationship between the weight of adopted children and that of their biological parents, but no relationship between the weight of adopted children and that of their adoptive parents. The graph illustrates the relationship between adoptees and their biological and adoptive mothers. The relationship also holds true for adoptees and their biological and adoptive fathers.

Source: Data from A. J. Stunkard et al., *New England Journal of Medicine*, 314: 193–198, Massachusetts Medical Society, 1986.

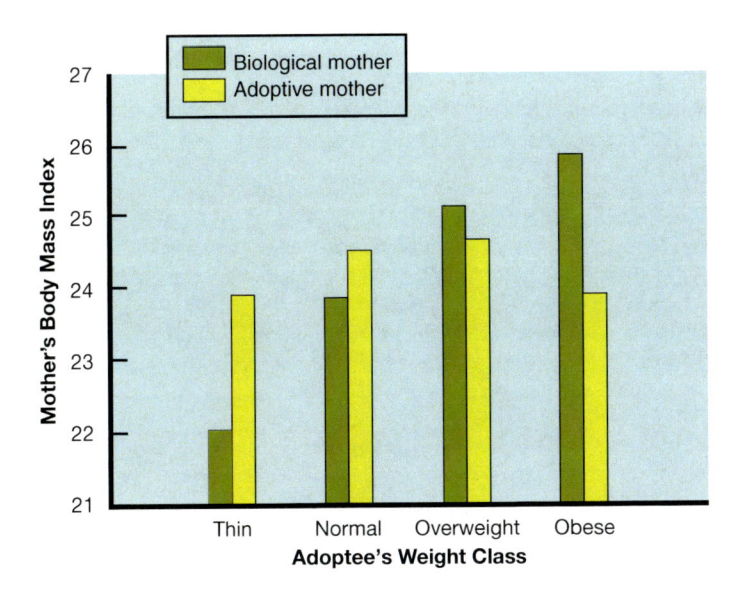

they become extremely obese on a diet of regular rodent chow, though there are negligible differences in food intake between mutant and control mice. These mutant mice have increased fat tissue and leptin levels (Asai et al., 2013). It can be concluded that the gene for melanocortin contributes to body weight regulation in humans and animals; however, most cases of obesity are related to the combination of genes and the environment.

Set Point and Obesity An important factor in obesity is the body's set point, which reflects the amount of fat stored in the body. Though fat cells can increase in number and can increase or decrease in size, they cannot decrease in number. Once you have fat cells, they are yours forever. Obese people can lose weight only by shrinking the size of their fat cells. Because this effort induces constant hunger, it is difficult to maintain weight loss for an extended period of time (Kolata, 1985).

The set point seems to be affected by early nutrition, as shown by the results of an archival study of 300,000 men who years earlier had been exposed to a famine in Holland during World War II. Men who had been exposed to the famine during a critical period of development, which encompassed the third trimester of pregnancy and the first month after birth, were less likely to become obese than were men who had been exposed to the famine at other times during their early development (Ravelli, Stein, & Susser, 1976). The men exposed to the famine during the critical period might have developed lower set points than the other men. Even the results of the study of weight in Danish adoptees (Stunkard, Stinnett, & Smoller, 1986) might be explained by prenatal nutrition rather than by heredity. Perhaps adopted offspring are more similar in body weight to their biological mothers not because they share genes but because they spent their prenatal period in their mothers' wombs, where they were subjected to environmental influences such as nutrients provided by their mothers. These prenatal influences might affect their later body weight (Bonds & Crosby, 1986).

Basal Metabolic Rate and Obesity Another important factor in obesity is the **basal metabolic rate**, the rate at which the body burns calories just to keep itself alive. The basal metabolic rate typically accounts for 65 to 75 percent of the calories that your body ingests (Shah & Jeffery, 1991). Ever wonder why one of your friends can habitually ingest a milkshake, two hamburgers, and a large order of french fries yet remain thin, whereas another gains weight by habitually ingesting a diet cola, a hamburger without a bun, and a few french fries? Your first friend might have a basal metabolic rate high enough to burn a large number of calories; your second friend might have a basal metabolic rate too low to burn even a modest number of calories, which forces the body to store much of the

basal metabolic rate The rate at which the body burns calories just to keep itself alive.

Chapter 11 Motivation   **383**

Basal Metabolic Rate (BMR)

Basal metabolic rate is the rate at which the body burns calories while at rest. BMR is influenced by several factors, including age and sex.
Source: designer491/Shutterstock.com.

ingested food as fat. One way that aerobic exercise promotes weight loss is by elevating the basal metabolic rate (Davis, Sargent, Brayboy, & Bartoli, 1992).

Behavioral Factors in Obesity

The chief behavioral factors in promoting obesity are having easy access to food, eating large portions, eating foods high in fat, and failing to engage in regular physical activity (Hill & Peters, 1998). Scientists interested in the role of behavioral factors in obesity are particularly interested in studying the effects of physical inactivity, responsiveness to external food cues, and stress-related eating patterns.

Inactivity and Obesity Though Americans are modifying their eating habits, obesity continues to rise. One possible cause is physical inactivity (Sallis, Carlson, Mignano, Lemes, & Wagner, 2013). Sedentary children are more likely to become obese. Moreover, girls are less physically active than boys throughout childhood, thus increasing their risk of obesity (Prentice-Dunn & Prentice-Dunn, 2012). But the commonsense assumption that lack of exercise causes obesity is not necessarily correct. People who are obese might, as a result of being obese, engage in less physical activity. Moreover, some studies have found that the health risks associated with obesity might be related more to a lack of physical activity than to excess body fat (Wickelgren, 1998). And the tendency to be physically inactive appears to have a hereditary basis (Hewitt, 1997).

As discussed in Chapter 16, the relationship between obesity and physical inactivity is why exercise is a component of weight-reduction programs (Foster-Schubert et al., 2012). These programs have to counter a prime culprit in physical inactivity: television watching. Watching television instead of participating in physical activities is associated with obesity throughout America, whether in children (Centers for Disease Control and Prevention, 2011) or adult Pima Indians, a population with an unusually high incidence of obesity (Andersen, Crespo, Bartlett, Cheskin, & Pratt, 1998). Some exercise programs use the lure of television watching to promote physical activity in children by using the Premack principle (see Chapter 7) to make television watching a reward for physical activity (Jason & Brackshaw, 1999).

Eating Cues and Obesity Some researchers also have linked obesity to differences in responsiveness to external food cues. Because a series of studies in the 1960s indicated that obese people feel hungrier and eat more in the presence of external food cues, Stanley Schachter (1971) concluded that obese people are more responsive to those cues. Subsequent studies have provided some support for this belief. One study found that overweight children were more likely to overeat after being exposed to the enticing smell of tasty food or eating one bite of an appetizing snack. In fact, compared to lean children, overweight children salivated more in response to the smell and taste of food (Aspen,

Stein, & Wilfley, 2012). Though studies like these support the belief that obese people are more responsive to food cues, the "externality" of obese people does not seem to cause their obesity. Instead, their obesity might cause their externality. How? Many obese people are constantly dieting, so they might be in a chronic state of hunger (Lowe, Foster, Kerzhnerman, Swain, & Wadden, 2001). Moreover, obesity researcher Judith Rodin (1981) has found that obese people may have chronically high levels of insulin, making them hungrier and, as a result, more responsive to food cues. This responsiveness gives the false impression that obese people become obese because they are more external than nonobese people.

In addition, an important environmental factor in eating involves the kinds of foods we eat when we are hungry. We tend to like foods more when we are hungry than when we are not, but this effect is stronger for fatty foods (Lozano, Crites, & Aikman, 1999). Perhaps people who are prone to obesity, being chronically hungry, are more motivated to eat fatty foods.

Stress and Obesity Another external factor—stress—can induce hunger and overeating (Sinha & Jastreboff, 2013). Stressful situations can induce negative emotions, such as anger, boredom, depression, and loneliness, and obese people are more likely than nonobese people to overeat when under stress (Laitinen, Ek, & Sovio, 2002). But how does stress induce overeating? One possibility is that stress stimulates the brain to secrete endorphins. As discussed in Chapters 3 and 5, endorphins are neurotransmitters that relieve pain. They also stimulate eating. One study found that endorphin levels were higher in obese women than in lean women (Perfetto, Piluso, Cagnacci, & Tarquini, 2002). Because endorphin levels increase when we are under stress, endorphins might contribute to stress-related overeating (Morley & Levine, 1980). Perhaps obese people eat more under stress than nonobese people do because stress induces greater increases in their endorphin levels. Stress also activates the *hypothalamic-pituitary-adrenal (HPA) axis*. The hormones of the HPA axis play an important role in regulating food intake, and dysregulation of the HPA axis may lead to the development of overeating.

Yet, stress does not always provoke overeating. A study of 95 adults who recorded their stress level and eating behavior for 12 weeks found a negative correlation between the two: As stress increased, eating decreased. This tendency was more pronounced in women than in men (Stone & Brownell, 1994). Thus, more research is needed to identify the conditions under which stress provokes overeating and the conditions under which it inhibits it.

Eating Disorders

Are you pleased with your physical appearance? As revealed by the study in the "Research Process" box, your answer might depend in part on whether you are a woman or man. Your satisfaction with your body also might influence the likelihood that you will develop an eating disorder. The ideal that women should be thin has permeated the Western media (Thompson & Heinberg, 1999). A recent study of the body measurements of female *Playboy* centerfolds found that the size of centerfold models has continued to decrease since the 1980s (Owen & Laurel-Seller, 2000). And another study compared the muscularity of male *Playgirl* centerfolds from 1973 to 1997. Whereas female centerfolds are becoming thinner, male centerfolds are becoming more muscular (Leit, Pope, & Gray, 2001).

Recent research indicates that the internalization of an ideal body type is a risk factor for distorted body image and eating disorders (Thompson & Stice, 2001). In one study, for example, children aged 6 through 12 were shown pictures of thin women in sexualized poses and muscular men with bare torsos. Girls and boys responded positively to the images of their own gender, but the effect was more pronounced for the girls (Murnen, Smolak, Mills, & Good, 2003). And among women and men, reading beauty or body-building magazines, respectively, is related to concerns about physical appearance, internalization of body ideals, and eating (Morry & Staska, 2001). Thus, internalization of unrealistic media images may be a powerful sociocultural influence on body satisfaction and the development of eating disorders.

The Research Process

How Satisfied Are Men and Women with Their Bodies?

Rationale
Some researchers believe that eating disorders, which are more common in women, can be promoted by distorted body images. This hypothesis inspired researchers April Fallon and Paul Rozin (1985) to examine the issue empirically.

Method
College students were presented with a set of nine drawings of body figures that ranged from very thin to very heavy. The participants were asked to indicate which figures were closest to their current physique, their ideal physique, and the physique they felt was most attractive to the other sex.

Results and Discussion
As shown in Figure 11-5, for men the current, the ideal, and the most attractive physiques were almost identical. For women, the current physique was heavier than the most attractive, and the most attractive was heavier than the ideal. The women also thought men liked women thinner than the men actually reported. Moreover, women tended to be less satisfied with their own physiques than men were with their own physiques.

A study that replicated the essence of these findings found that adolescent girls preferred to be thinner than the average for their age and were more dissatisfied with their own bodies than adolescent boys. Moreover, underweight adolescent boys were more dissatisfied with their own bodies than boys of average weight (Mäkinen, Puukko-Viertomies, Lindberg, Siimes, & Aalberg, 2012).

Perhaps this dissatisfaction contributes to women's greater tendency to develop eating disorders marked by excessive concern with weight control. In fact, people who disparage their own bodies for being fat, whether or not it is objectively true that they are fat, are more likely to develop eating disorders (Hsu & Sobkiewicz, 1991).

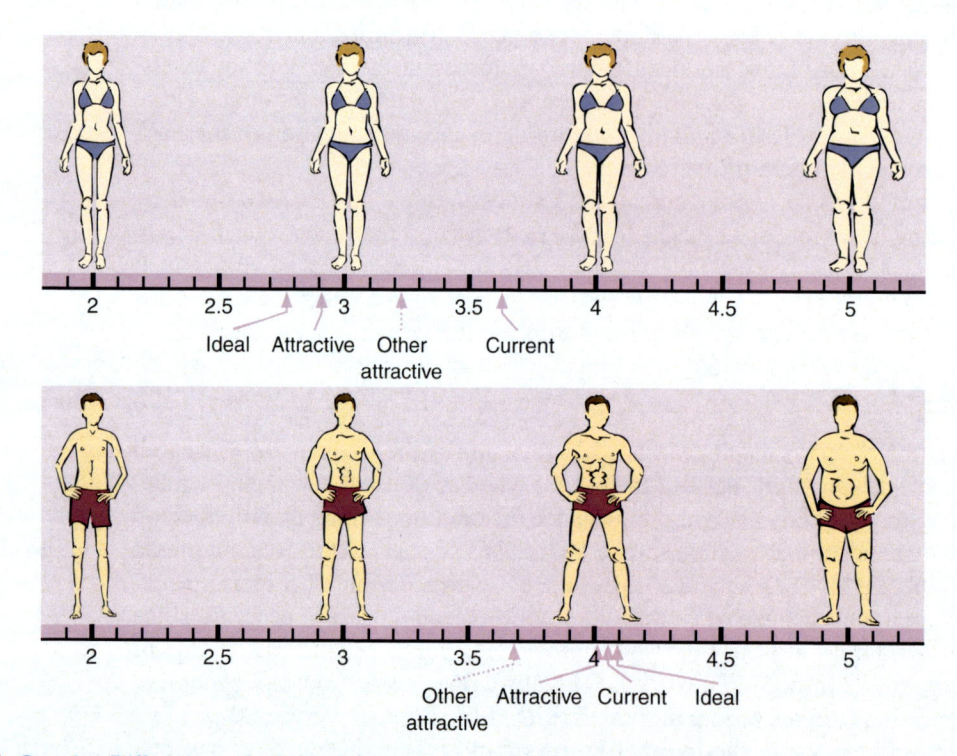

FIGURE 11-5 Gender Differences in Body Images

Fallon and Rozin (1985) found that for men (lower illustration), their self-perceived physique ("Current"), the physique that they believed was ideal ("Ideal"), and the physique that they believed was most attractive to women ("Attractive") were almost identical. The physique that they believed women preferred ("Attractive") was heavier than the one that women actually preferred ("Other attractive"). In contrast, for women (upper illustration), their self-perceived physique ("Current") was heavier than the physique that they believed was ideal ("Ideal") and the physique that they believed was most attractive to men ("Attractive"). Moreover, the physique that they believed men preferred ("Attractive") was thinner than the one that men actually preferred ("Other attractive").

Source: Fallon, A. E., & Rozin, P. (1985). Sex differences in perceptions of desirable body shape. *Journal of Abnormal Psychology, 94,* 102–105.

As Western culture exerts greater influence over other cultures, eating disorders among women have increased in those cultures—perhaps because they too have adopted Western ideals. For example, researchers studied eating attitudes and behaviors in Fijian adolescents. Participants' eating behaviors and attitudes were assessed before the introduction of television to the region, one month later, and three years later. Rates of binge eating and self-induced vomiting were significantly higher at the three-year follow-up. Moreover, participants reported a greater interest in losing weight in an attempt to look more like the television actors (Becker, Burwell, Herzog, Hamburg, & Gilman, 2002). Acculturation also has been found to be related to body dissatisfaction among Guatemalan American female college students and Chinese women and girls living in the United States (Davis & Katzman, 1999; Franko & Herrera, 1997).

A review of research conducted during the second half of the 20th century found that gender differences in body image had increased, with women showing progressively more negative body images over that time period (Feingold & Mazzella, 1998). Though eating disorders are more prevalent among girls and women (Hoek & van Hoeken, 2003), the rate of male admissions to inpatient facilities for treatment of eating disorders between 1984 and 1997 increased (Braun, Sunday, Huang, & Halmi, 1999). Gender interacts with other sociocultural variables such that some groups are more at risk than others. For example, African American women are slightly less likely to develop eating disorders than are European American women (O'Neill, 2003). Research studies have found that African American women are more satisfied with their bodies than European American women (Walsh & Devlin, 1998) and are less likely to disparage large women, especially large African American women (Hebl & Heatherton, 1998).

Sexual orientation also influences the incidence of dissatisfaction with one's body and of eating disorders. Lesbians report greater satisfaction with their bodies, less frequent dieting, and fewer eating disorders than do heterosexual women (Lakkis, Ricciardelli, & Williams, 1999). The results of recent research suggest that lesbians are less likely than heterosexual women to have internalized cultural norms for thinness (Bergeron & Senn, 1998). In contrast, gay men express more dissatisfaction with their bodies and are more likely to engage in disordered eating than are heterosexual men (Lakkis, Ricciardelli, & Williams, 1999). The comparatively high rate of eating disorders among both gay men and heterosexual women may be due to a shared desire to attract men. One study found that heterosexual and gay men place a higher priority on physical appearance when judging a potential romantic partner than do heterosexual or lesbian women (Siever, 1994).

Though eating disorders are associated with sociocultural differences, they are influenced by many other factors. One factor is heredity. Though the heritability of many eating disorders has yet to be firmly established (Fairburn, Cowen, & Harrison, 1999), twin studies provide evidence that some people have a genetic predisposition to develop an eating disorder (Klump, McGue, & Iacono, 2002). Stressful life experiences also are important. Women who are under high psychological stress are more prone to eating disorders than are women who are under low psychological stress (Ball & Lee, 2000). Even personality factors are important. One study found that male and female university students who scored high on a measure of perfectionism were especially prone to eating disorders (Boone, Soenens, Vansteenkiste, & Braet, 2012).

Anorexia Nervosa

In 1983, the popular singer Karen Carpenter died of heart failure caused by starvation—despite having access to all the food she could want. She suffered from **anorexia nervosa**, a sometimes fatal disorder in which the victim is so desperate to lose weight that he or she goes on a starvation diet and becomes emaciated. People with anorexia nervosa view themselves as fat, even when they are objectively thin (as was Carpenter), and they are preoccupied with food—talking about it, cooking it, and urging others to eat it. Anorexia nervosa has a prevalence rate of 0.3 percent and is more common in young women (Hoek & Van Hoeken, 2003). Anorexia typically develops during late childhood and adolescence. Some women and men who participate in sports or activities that stress weight control

anorexia nervosa An eating disorder marked by self-starvation.

(such as dancing, modeling, or wrestling) are more prone to develop eating disorders (Pierce & Daleng, 1998). Moreover, a recent meta-analysis of the relationship of athletic participation to eating disorders among women concluded that elite athletes were most at risk. Among nonelite and high school athletes, however, sport served as a protective factor that reduced the risk of eating disorders among women (Smolak, Murnen, & Ruble, 2000).

Possible Causes of Anorexia Nervosa Possible causes of anorexia nervosa include heredity (Klump, Miller, Keel, McGue, & Iacono, 2001), excessive secretion of cholecystokinin (Cuntz et al., 2013), an emotionally enmeshed and critical family (Polivy & Herman, 2002), an excessive desire for self-control of eating (Fairburn, Shafran, & Cooper, 1999), obsessiveness and dependency (Rogers & Petrie, 2001), and a reaction to the tendency to accumulate unwanted body fat during puberty (Attie & Brooks-Gunn, 1989). Certain genes such as those that encode for leptin and melanocortin have been implicated in the development of anorexia nervosa. However, a recent metaanalysis indicated that genes did not play a significant role in its development (Hinney & Volckmar, 2013). Thus, researchers still have to discover a clear mechanism for this disorder.

Treatment of Anorexia Nervosa Because many people with anorexia nervosa are unwilling to seek treatment, their families often have to force them to receive it (Russell, 2001). Treatment of severe anorexia nervosa commonly begins with the provision of high-calorie nourishment (Agostino, Erdstein, & Di Meglio, 2013), often through intravenous feeding or feeding through a nasogastric tube. Therapists then typically use cognitive-behavioral therapy to promote more adaptive ways of eating, thinking about food, and perceiving one's body (Hay, Touyz, & Sud, 2012). Given that anorexia nervosa is associated with maladaptive family relationships, family therapy sometimes is included as a component of its treatment (Levitt, 2001).

Bulimia Nervosa

Persons with the related, more common, disorder called **bulimia nervosa** go on repeated eating binges in which they ingest thousands of calories at a time—they might eat a half gallon of ice cream, a two-pound box of chocolates, and other high-carbohydrate foods—but they maintain normal weight by then ridding themselves of the food by self-induced vomiting. People with bulimia nervosa tend to evaluate themselves in terms of their body weight and shape and to think obsessively about food. They also tend to have poor impulse control, binging in response to the presence of tempting food, and then purging to compensate for the binge (Polivy & Herman, 2002). The prevalence rates for bulimia nervosa are 1 percent of young women and 0.7 percent of young men (Hoek & Van Hoeken, 2003). Whereas the prevalence of anorexia is consistent across cultures, there are considerable cross-cultural differences in the prevalence of bulimia nervosa. Compared to anorexia nervosa, bulimia nervosa may be more influenced by sociocultural factors (Keel

Anorexia Nervosa

People with anorexia nervosa see themselves as fat, though they are actually thin.
Source: PutilichD/Shutterstock.com.

bulimia nervosa An eating disorder marked by binging and purging.

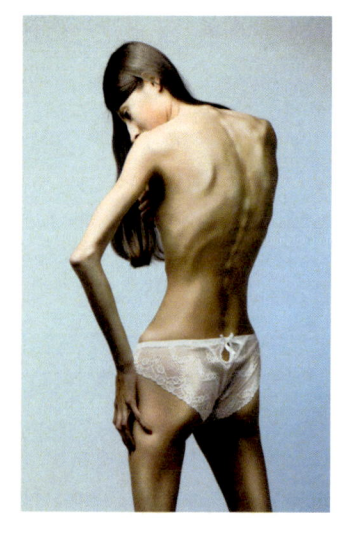

Bulimia Nervosa

Bulimia nervosa is an eating disorder marked by a binge-and-purge cycle.
Source: michaelheim/Shutterstock.com.

& Klump, 2003), and women and girls with bulimia nervosa recover earlier than those with anorexia nervosa (Eddy et al., 2017).

Possible Causes of Bulimia Nervosa There is some evidence that people with bulimia nervosa have a genetic predisposition to develop the disorder (Rowe, Pickles, Simonoff, Bulik, & Silberg, 2002). Another possible cause of bulimia nervosa is a low level of the neurotransmitter serotonin, which is associated with depression (Pichika et al., 2012). People with bulimia nervosa often try to elevate their moods or cope with stress by eating. Eating then leads to shame and guilt, which then is relieved by purging. The person becomes trapped in a vicious binge-and-purge cycle (Alpers & Tuschen-Caffier, 2001). This hypothesis is supported by research showing that antidepressant drugs that increase serotonin levels are useful in treating bulimia nervosa (Zhu & Walsh, 2002). In one study, women with bulimia nervosa were given fluoxetine (Prozac), an antidepressant that inhibits the reuptake of serotonin by the neurons that secrete it. While on the drug, participants snacked less frequently and ate less at each meal. Moreover, the drug inhibited binge eating (Wilcox, 1990).

Factors other than brain chemistry also play a role in bulimia nervosa. People who pursue activities that emphasize weight control are more likely to develop the disorder. For example, men with bulimia nervosa are often dancers, jockeys, or collegiate wrestlers (Striegel-Moore, Silberstein, & Rodin, 1986). People with bulimia nervosa tend to be perfectionistic (Boone et al., 2012), to have suffered a recent family disruption (Welch, Doll, & Fairburn, 1997), and to come from families who are critical, intrusive, and coercive (Polivy & Herman, 2002). And people with bulimia tend to respond to unhappy or stressful interpersonal experiences with self-criticism and negative moods (Steiger, Gauvin, Jabalpurwala, Séguin, & Stotland, 1999).

Treatment of Bulimia Nervosa The most common psychological treatment for bulimia nervosa is cognitive-behavioral therapy. This approach aims at changing irrational thinking about eating and body weight and altering maladaptive behaviors, particularly bingeing and purging. Research reviews consistently have found that cognitive-behavioral therapy is effective in treating bulimia nervosa (Wilson, Fairburn, Agras, Walsh, & Kraemer, 2002).

A medical approach to the treatment of bulimia nervosa is the use of antidepressants, an approach based on the finding that bulimia nervosa is commonly associated with lower levels of serotonin (Freeman, 1998). Drugs such as Prozac that increase levels of serotonin have achieved some success in treating bulimia (Narash-Eisikovits, Dierberger, & Westen, 2002). But cognitive-behavioral therapy is superior to drug therapy in treating the disorder (Whittal, Agras, & Gould, 1999). What about treatments that combine drug therapy and cognitive-behavioral therapy? Research findings are inconsistent about whether the combination is (Agras, 1997) or is not (Goldbloom et al., 1997) more effective than cognitive-behavioral therapy alone.

Section Review: The Hunger Motive

1. What is the role of the hypothalamus in eating?
2. What evidence is there for a hereditary basis of obesity?
3. What are some possible explanations for the greater incidence of eating disorders among heterosexual women and gay men?

The Sex Motive

Though some individuals, such as religious celibates, can live long lives without engaging in sexual intercourse, the survival of the species requires that many individuals engage in it. Had sexual intercourse not evolved into an extremely pleasurable behavior, we would have no inclination to seek it. But what factors account for the power of the sex motive?

Biopsychological Factors in Sexual Behavior

Sexual behavior is influenced by biopsychological factors. Many sex researchers study the physiological factors that affect human and animal sexual behavior. Some of these researchers focus on the physiology of the human sexual response cycle.

Physiological Factors and Sex

Important physiological factors in sexual motivation are sex hormones secreted by the **gonads**, the sex glands. The secretion of sex hormones is controlled by hormones secreted by the pituitary gland, which in turn is controlled by the hypothalamus. Sex hormones direct sexual development as well as sexual behavior (see Chapter 4). Though hormones exert a direct effect on human sexual development, they are less influential motivators of sexual behavior in humans than they are in animals. Research indicates that testosterone motivates both male and female sexual behavior (Apperloo et al., 2003), though women secrete less of it than men do.

gonads The male and female sex glands.

The Sexual Response Cycle

Many Americans were shocked in the 1960s by reports of research conducted by William Masters and Virginia Johnson. Masters and Johnson were not content with just asking people about their sexual motivation and behavior. Instead, they studied ongoing sexual behavior and recorded physiological changes that accompanied it in hundreds of men and women. To study the human sexual response, they even invented devices that measured physiological changes in the penis and vagina during sexual arousal.

Based on their study of more than 10,000 orgasms experienced by more than 300 men and 300 women, Masters and Johnson (1966) identified four phases in the **sexual response cycle**: excitement, plateau, orgasm, and resolution (see Figure 11-6). During the *excitement phase*, mental or physical stimulation causes sexual arousal. In men the penis becomes erect as it becomes engorged with blood. In women the nipples become erect, the vagina becomes lubricated, and the clitoris protrudes as it too becomes engorged with blood in response to both direct stimulation and vaginal stimulation (Lavoisier, Aloui, Schmidt, & Watrelot, 1995).

sexual response cycle During sexual activity, the phases of excitement, plateau, orgasm, and resolution.

During the *plateau phase*, heart rate, blood pressure, muscle tension, and breathing rate increase. In men the erection becomes firmer, and the testes are drawn closer to the body to prepare for ejaculation. Drops of semen, possibly containing sperm (and capable of

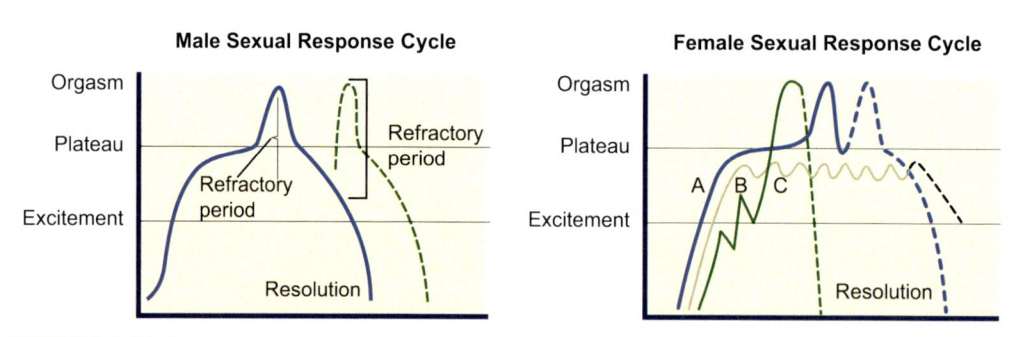

FIGURE 11-6 The Human Sexual Response Cycle

Masters and Johnson found that men and women have sexual response cycles comprising four phases: excitement, plateau, orgasm, and resolution. After reaching orgasm, men cannot achieve another orgasm until they have passed through a refractory period. In contrast, pattern A shows that women might experience more than one orgasm during a single cycle. Pattern B shows a cycle during which a woman has reached the plateau stage without proceeding to orgasm. Pattern C shows a cycle during which a woman has reached orgasm quickly. Men, too, may experience pattern B and pattern C.

causing pregnancy), may appear at the tip of the penis. In women the body flushes, lubrication increases, the clitoris retracts, and the breasts swell around the nipples (making the nipples seem to shrink).

The excitement and plateau phases compose the period of sexual foreplay. Men and women differ in the importance they assign to foreplay. A survey of young adults found that women chose foreplay as more important than either intercourse or afterplay, whereas men chose intercourse as most important. Women also preferred to spend more time on foreplay and afterplay than did men. Women reported more than men did that they enjoyed the verbal and physical affection of sexual behavior (Denney, Field, & Quadagno, 1984).

During the *orgasm phase*, heart rate and breathing rate reach their peak, men ejaculate semen (a fluid containing sperm), and both men and women experience intensely pleasurable sensations induced by rhythmic muscle contractions. There is evidence that the pleasure of orgasm might be caused by the release of *prolactin*, a hormone that targets the mammary glands, in men and women (Krueger, Haake, Hartmann, Schedlowski, & Exton, 2002). The subjective experience of orgasm also is similar for women and men. One study asked undergraduate participants to describe their most recent orgasmic experience on two occasions: during masturbation and during sex with a partner. Male and female participants' ratings of the physical sensations of their orgasmic experiences in both settings did not differ. But women and men rated their orgasms experienced with a partner as more pleasurable, ecstatic, and emotionally intimate than their orgasms experienced when alone. Whereas the physical experience of orgasm is unaffected by the circumstances in which it occurs, women and men find orgasms experienced with a partner as more emotionally and sexually satisfying (Mah & Binik, 2002).

Following the orgasm phase, the person enters the *resolution phase*, as blood leaves the genitals and sexual arousal lessens. This phase is associated with a *refractory period*, lasting from minutes to hours, during which the man cannot achieve orgasm. For many women, however, continued sexual stimulation can induce multiple orgasms. A survey of 720 women found that 43 percent had experienced multiple orgasms (Darling, Davidson, & Jennings, 1991).

Masters and Johnson's research has made a remarkable contribution to our understanding of human sexuality. However, it is not without controversy. Critics have pointed to the selective nature of their sample—primarily sexually experienced married men and women who were willing to engage in sexual activity in the laboratory. Perhaps more important, they failed to study individuals who had difficulty in experiencing orgasm and failed to consider individual differences in sexual responses and sexual desire (Tiefer, 1995). But their research has provided an important basis for the scientific study of the physiology of human sexuality.

Psychosocial Factors in Sexual Behavior

Though human sexuality is affected by biopsychological factors, it is strongly influenced by psychosocial factors as well. Researchers who study psychosocial factors in sexuality are particularly interested in the role of culture in sexual behavior. We know much about sexual behavior in American culture from surveys that have been carried out since the mid-20th century.

Culture and Sexual Behavior

Sex hormones are the main motivators of animal sexual behavior, but human sexual behavior depends more on sociocultural factors. Because in most animals sexual motivation is rigidly controlled by hormones, members of a given species vary little in their sexual behaviors. In contrast, because human sexual motivation is influenced more by sociocultural factors, we vary greatly in our sexual behavior. For example, breast caressing is a prelude to sexual intercourse among the Marquesan islanders of the Pacific but not among the Sirionian Indians of Bolivia (Klein, 1982).

In Western cultures, acceptable sexual behavior has varied over time. The ancient Greeks viewed bisexuality as normal and masturbation as a desirable way for youth to relieve their

Human Sexual Behavior

Human sexual behavior is guided by sex hormones, but even more important are sociocultural factors.
Source: Nina Vaclavova/Shutterstock.com.

sexual tensions. In contrast, most Americans and Europeans of the Victorian era in the 19th century believed that all sexual activity should be avoided except when aimed at procreation. The Victorian emphasis on sexual denial led John Harvey Kellogg to invent what he claimed was a nutritional "cure" for masturbation—cornflakes (Money, 1986).

The liberalization of attitudes toward sexual behavior in Western industrialized countries during the 20th century was shown in 1983 when the *Journal of the American Medical Association* published an article on human sexuality. This event would not be noteworthy except that the article had been submitted for publication in 1899, near the end of the Victorian era. The article, based on a paper presented by gynecologist Denslow Lewis (1899/1983) at the annual meeting of the American Medical Association, concerned female sexuality. Lewis described the female sexual response, the need for sex education, the importance of sex for marital compatibility, and techniques for overcoming sexual problems. Lewis even made the radical (for his time) suggestion that wives be encouraged to enjoy sex as much as their husbands did. At the time, the editor of the journal refused to publish the paper, which a prominent physician called "filth" and another editor feared would bring charges of sending obscene material through the mail (Hollender, 1983).

Surveys of Human Sexual Behavior

Denslow Lewis's critics would have been even more upset by research in human sexuality that has taken place in the past few decades, particularly the research studies of Masters and Johnson and Alfred Kinsey. Shortly after World War II, Kinsey (1894–1956), a biologist at Indiana University, found that he was unable to answer his students' questions about human sexual behavior because of a lack of relevant information. This dearth inspired him to conduct surveys to gather information on the sexual behavior of men (Kinsey, Pomeroy, & Martin, 1948) and women (Kinsey, Pomeroy, Martin, & Gebhard, 1953).

Kinsey's Findings Kinsey obtained his data from interviews with thousands of men and women and published his findings in two best-selling books. Kinsey's books (which contained statistics but no pictures) shocked the public because Kinsey reported that masturbation, oral sex, premarital sex, extramarital sex, homosexuality, and other sexual behaviors were more prevalent than commonly believed. Many Americans considered Kinsey's reports to be attacks on the moral order. J. Edgar Hoover, the FBI director, ordered that a dossier be compiled on Kinsey to determine whether he was a threat to the United States (Jones, 1997).

Among Kinsey's many findings were that most of the men and almost half of the women engaged in premarital sexual intercourse, and most of the women and almost all of the men masturbated. The public was particularly startled to learn that about one-third of men had engaged in at least one sexual act with another man to orgasm and that about 10 percent had more than casual homosexual relations. Kinsey concluded that most people were neither homosexual nor heterosexual but instead fit along a continuum that he developed (the *Kinsey Scale*) from exclusively heterosexual (0) to exclusively homosexual (6). Kinsey's survey of women was noteworthy because it challenged the widely held belief that women were uninterested in sex (Bullough, 1998).

Sex Surveys Since Kinsey Scientists warned that care should be taken in generalizing Kinsey's findings to all Americans because his sample was not representative of the American population; the sample included primarily European American, well-educated easterners and midwesterners who were willing to be interviewed about their sexual behavior. Moreover, what is true of people in one generation might not be true of those in another. For example, from the 1950s to the 1980s, premarital sexual activity in the United States increased. In the 1980s, however, premarital sexual activity with multiple partners tapered off because of increased fears about incurable sexually transmitted diseases, including AIDS, which is fatal, and genital herpes, which is painful and can harm romantic relationships (Gerrard, 1987). The transmission and prevention of AIDS are discussed in Chapter 16.

Changes in sexual behavior since Kinsey's day indicate that sexual norms do indeed depend on the time period during which they are studied. However, some gender differences in human sexual behavior appear to be unchanged despite considerable sociocultural change. Peterson and Janet Shibley Hyde (2010) conducted a meta-analysis of 730 research studies of 1,419,807 male and female participants from 87 countries on six continents published between 1993 and 2007. Of the 30 effect sizes computed, no large gender differences emerged. Four gender differences that were moderate in size were found: Men were somewhat more likely to use pornography, masturbate, have more positive attitudes toward casual sex, and engage in more casual sex than were women. To consider the size of these differences, you might want to contrast the effect sizes with those for the gender differences in cognitive abilities and social behavior reported in Chapter 4. Moreover, these effect sizes held steady regardless of the year of publication. The remaining gender differences were small to negligible. For example, men report more permissive attitudes toward extramarital sex and tend to have more permissive attitudes about sex overall. Moreover, men report having had more sex partners than do women, but these effect sizes are small. Gender similarities were the rule for a number of variables, such as sexual satisfaction, attitudes about masturbation, and incidence of some sexual behaviors other than sexual intercourse.

Sexual Dysfunctions

After Masters and Johnson had identified the phases of the human sexual response cycle, they became interested in studying **sexual dysfunctions**, which are chronic problems at phases in the sexual response cycle. Sexual dysfunctions are common among both sexes, with estimates ranging from 10 percent to 52 percent of men and 25 percent to 63 percent of women in the United States (Laumann, Paik, & Rosen, 1999). Sexual dysfunctions are associated with discord and conflict among partners (Metz & Epstein, 2002).

sexual dysfunction A chronic problem at a particular phase of the sexual response cycle.

Kinds of Sexual Dysfunctions

The most common male sexual dysfunctions include *erectile dysfunction* and *premature ejaculation*. About 5 percent to 10 percent of men suffer from an erectile dysfunction—failing either to attain an erection or to maintain it through the arousal phase (Spector & Carey, 1990). Causes of erectile dysfunction include physical factors, such as diabetes, and psychological factors, such as depression (Seidman, 2003). About one-third of all men experience premature ejaculation (Spector & Carey, 1990). Premature ejaculation is caused by psychological factors, such as performance anxiety or relationship problems, or physical factors, such as nerve damage, prostate inflammation, or withdrawal from certain drugs, particularly narcotics (Carver, 1998).

Among women, the most common sexual dysfunctions include *orgasmic disorder*, *dyspareunia*, and *vaginismus*. A woman with orgasmic disorder, present in 5 percent to 10 percent of women, is unable to reach the orgasm phase. Women who experience orgasmic disorder tend to have greater sexual guilt, difficulty discussing sexual activities, and more negative attitudes toward masturbation (Kelly, Strassberg, & Kircher, 1990). Women who suffer from dyspareunia experience pain during or after sexual intercourse, and those with vaginismus experience involuntary muscle spasms around the opening of the vagina. Dyspareunia and vaginismus appear to be caused by a complex interplay of genital pain, fear of pain, and history of abusive or distressing sexual experiences (Pukall, Payne, Binik, & Khalif, 2003; Reissing, Binik, Khalife, Cohen, & Amsel, 2004).

Treating Sexual Dysfunctions

Based on their research findings, Masters and Johnson (1970) concluded that the psychological causes of sexual dysfunctions are usually sexual guilt, sexual ignorance, or anxiety about sexual performance. Masters and Johnson's sex therapy is based on counseling clients to help them overcome their sexual guilt; educating them about sexual anatomy, sexual motivation, and sexual behavior; and teaching them specific ways of reducing performance anxiety.

sensate focusing A technique, pioneered by Masters and Johnson, in which partners are urged to concentrate on their pleasurable feelings instead of striving for erections and orgasms.

The main technique in Masters and Johnson's sex therapy is **sensate focusing**, in which the partners first participate in nongenital caressing and only later proceed to genital stimulation, and finally engage in sexual intercourse. The partners at first are urged to concentrate on their pleasurable feelings instead of striving for erections and orgasms. They also are instructed to tell each other what kinds of stimulation they enjoy and what kinds they do not enjoy.

Therapists trained in Masters and Johnson's sex therapy also teach their clients other techniques. In treating premature ejaculation, they might have the man's partner repeatedly stimulate his penis just to the point before orgasm to teach him to gain control over its timing. They might have a woman with an orgasmic disorder practice masturbating to orgasm as a step toward reaching orgasm during sexual intercourse, a more difficult feat. Another technique to promote female orgasm during heterosexual intercourse is to teach the couple ways of aligning their bodies to maximize penile stimulation of the clitoris.

Masters and Johnson (1970) reported that more than two-thirds of their sex therapy clients showed improvement. But they were criticized for not operationally defining what they meant by "improvement" and for failing to conduct follow-up studies of their clients to determine whether the positive effects of therapy were long lasting. Masters and Johnson also have been criticized for stressing sexual intercourse as a physical act and for ignoring factors such as sexual desire, love, and cultural differences in sexuality (Tiefer, 1994).

Some sexual dysfunctions respond well to medical as well as psychological treatments. Perhaps the best known of these medical treatments is the drug *sildenafil*, better known by its trade name, Viagra. Viagra is being studied as a potential treatment for sexual dysfunctions associated with the use of antidepressants in both men and women (Salerian et al., 2000). However, critics argue that such treatment neglects the social, psychological, and emotional factors in relationships, especially among older adults (Barnett, Robleda-Gomez, & Pachana, 2012). Thus, because sexual dysfunctions can affect self-esteem and romantic relationships, orgasmic dysfunctions might require both psychological and drug treatments (Zajecka et al., 2002).

gender identity One's self-perceived sex.

sexual orientation A person's pattern of erotic attraction to persons of the same sex, other sex, or both sexes.

During the past few decades, Masters and Johnson joined with other sex researchers in studying two other major topics in sexuality. These topics are **gender identity** (one's self-perceived sex) and **sexual orientation** (one's pattern of erotic attraction—whether to persons of one's own sex or of the other sex or both).

Gender Identity

In 1966, a 7-month-old boy lost most of his penis in a surgical accident. After consultation with sex researcher John Money, the 17-month-old child underwent sex reassignment surgery that involved castration, the removal of the remaining penile tissue, and the construction of a vagina. His parents were instructed to change his name, hairstyle, and clothing, and to raise him as a girl. Because the child had an identical twin brother who had not undergone surgery, Money was able to compare the development of the two children. Initial reports suggested that the child adopted feminine interests and behaviors and thought of herself as a girl, whereas the twin brother continued to think of himself as a boy. Based on these observations, Money concluded that gender identity was more strongly influenced by socialization than by genetic or hormonal factors (Money & Ehrhardt, 1972).

As the child entered puberty, however, it became clear that the sex reassignment was a failure. The teenager rejected hormonal therapy and began living as a young man, eventually marrying a woman and becoming a father to her young children (Colapinto, 2001; Diamond & Sigmundson, 1997). More recent research suggests that the development of gender identity involves a complex interaction of sociocultural and biopsychological influences. A sample of 16 genetic males aged 5 to 16 were treated at Johns Hopkins University for a rare congenital disorder that results in an absent penis and other medical problems. Fourteen children underwent sex reassignment surgery and were raised as girls; parents of two of the boys refused the surgery.

To date, the children and their families have been followed for 34 to 98 months. At the last reassessment, 6 of the 14 children who had been reassigned and raised as girls were living as boys—as were the two boys who had not undergone surgery. Five children were successfully living as girls. The remaining child angrily refused to be interviewed (Reiner & Gearhart, 2004). The results of this study are provocative and provide important information about the development of gender identity. These results suggest that sex reassignment may be successful in some cases but not in others. Moreover, as seen in the cases of the two children whose parents rejected sex reassignment, surgical correction of genitalia might not be necessary for the healthy establishment of gender identity.

Sexual Orientation

Gender identity should not be confused with sexual orientation, one's pattern of erotic attraction. For example, though Mother lived life as a man/woman, his sexual orientation would best be described as homosexual. *Homosexuals*—gay men or lesbians—are attracted to persons of the same sex; *heterosexuals* are attracted to persons of the other sex. And *bisexuals* have erotic feelings toward persons of both sexes. Today, attitudes toward homosexuality and bisexuality vary both among and within cultures. Moreover, there is considerable cross-cultural variation in same-sex behaviors and the expression of sexual orientations (Lippa & Tan, 2001).

Biopsychological Factors in Sexual Orientation

Given that our evolutionary history, reproductive anatomy, and contemporary cultural norms favor heterosexuality, why are an estimated 1 percent of women and 3 percent of men self-identified as homosexual (Laumann, Gagnon, Michael, & Michaels, 1994; Gates, 2013)? Theories of sexual orientation abound, and none has gained universal acceptance. Biopsychological theories of homosexuality implicate hereditary and physiological factors.

Heredity, the Brain, and Sexual Orientation Homosexuality runs in families, providing circumstantial evidence for the role of genetic factors (Bailey, Dunne, & Martin, 2000). For example, lesbians are more likely than nonlesbians to have lesbians among their sisters, daughters, and nieces (Pattatucci & Hamer, 1995). Of course, it is impossible to determine, based on this evidence alone, whether this pattern is caused more by hereditary similarities or environmental similarities. Likewise, identical twins are more likely to both be homosexual than are fraternal twins, but again, the extent to which this difference is due to shared genetic or shared environmental influences is unclear. Moreover, the strength of sexual attraction and concordance rates differ for men and women (Bailey, Dunne, & Martin, 2000).

Stronger support for the hereditary basis of homosexuality comes from research showing the following regarding identical twins (who have the same genes) who have been adopted as infants by different families: If one of the twins is homosexual, the other twin

Sexual Orientation

Whereas attitudes toward homosexuality and bisexuality vary both among and within cultures, there is considerable cross-cultural variation in same-sex behaviors and the expression of sexual orientations.
Source: Grigoriev Rusian/Shutterstock.com.

has a higher likelihood of also being homosexual than does a nontwin sibling reared together in the same family with a homosexual sibling (Eckert, Bouchard, Bohlen, & Heston, 1986). And a study of 40 families containing two nontwin homosexual brothers indicated that 26 of the sibling pairs (64 percent) shared genetic markers on the X chromosome (Hamer, Hu, Magnuson, & Hu, 1993). These findings have been countered by researchers who believe that the evidence is not strong enough to connect homosexuality to a specific genetic factor (Risch, Squires-Wheeler, & Keats, 1993). For example, if homosexuality were completely genetically determined, then when one identical twin is homosexual, the other would always be homosexual.

It is well established that there are hormonal, functional, and structural differences between male and female brains. Researchers are just beginning to examine the neural correlates of gender identity and sexual orientation. The most well-studied region is a portion of the anterior hypothalamus called the INAH-3 that plays a role in the regulation of male sexual behavior. This region was examined in deceased adult men who died of AIDS. LeVay (1991) and colleagues found this region to be twice as large in heterosexual men than homosexual men (see the box "Critical Thinking About Psychology"). Given the inherent difficulty with studies of deceased persons, researchers have begun utilizing neuroimaging studies to examine sexual orientation. In one study, 26 healthy homosexual men and 26 age-matched healthy heterosexual men were assessed using MRI technology to assess functional connectivity, brain morphology, and neural activity. The participants' sexual orientation was evaluated using the Kinsey Scale (see page 392). The researchers found that homosexual men had reduced gyri and temporal lobe homogeneity. Regional homogeneity refers to the strength with which a particular brain region communicates with its immediate neighbors (Hu, 2013). Studies such as these will help us understand the neural basis of sexual orientation.

Prenatal Development and Sexual Orientation Male and female fetuses differ in hormonal concentrations as early as 8 weeks *in utero*. Additional support for the physiological basis of homosexuality comes from research on prenatal development—though some researchers warn against concluding that a correlation between prenatal hormonal exposure and later sexual orientation necessarily indicates a causal relationship between the two (Doell, 1995). Women exposed prenatally to excessively high levels of estrogens are more likely to be lesbians or bisexuals (Meyer-Bahlburg et al., 1995). Male homosexuality is associated with hormonal activity during a critical period between the second and the fifth month after conception that differs from that of heterosexual men. This hormonal activity might affect the development of the hypothalamus, which helps regulate sexual orientation, in a way that predisposes some men toward a homosexual orientation (Ellis & Ames, 1987).

An interesting hypothesis about the possible origin of brain differences in homosexual and heterosexual men implicates birth order. Researchers have hypothesized that pregnant women develop an immune response to H-Y antigens produced by the male fetus. With each male conception, the maternal immune response to the H-Y antigen, a substance foreign to her body, increases. One study found that homosexual men with older brothers had lower birth weights than heterosexual men with older brothers. The researchers concluded that a strong maternal immune response reduces the boy's birth weight and increases the likelihood of homosexuality (Blanchard & Ellis, 2001). Of course, this hypothesis fails to explain why many gay men are firstborns. Moreover, the theory does not explain the development of homosexuality in women.

An unusual piece of evidence of a possible prenatal influence on sexual orientation comes from a sample of almost 1,000 homosexual men and more than 4,000 heterosexual men interviewed by the Kinsey Institute between 1938 and 1963. The survey found that homosexual men, on average, had larger penises than heterosexual men. This finding supports the possibility that differences in prenatal hormone levels or other factors affecting the development of reproductive organs might affect sexual orientation (Bogaert & Hershberger, 1999). Also, a recent meta-analysis of 20 studies reported that gay men and lesbians had a 39 percent greater likelihood of being non-right-handed than heterosexual women and men, a difference also attributed to the influence of prenatal hormones (Lalu-

Critical Thinking About Psychology

Is There a Gay Brain?

In 1991, Simon LeVay, then a neuroanatomist at the Salk Institute in La Jolla, California, published research findings indicating specific structural differences between the brains of homosexual and heterosexual men. As part of his study, LeVay examined hypothalamic tissue from 19 gay men (all of whom had died of AIDS), 16 heterosexual men (6 of whom had died of AIDS), and 6 heterosexual women (1 of whom had died of AIDS). LeVay (1991) found that a region of the anterior hypothalamus was significantly larger in heterosexual men than in gay men.

Because LeVay's report provided evidence that men's sexual orientation might be determined by localized brain differences—perhaps genetically based—it created a media sensation. For several years after the publication of LeVay's report, there was a flood of television stories and magazine and newspaper articles about the possible genetic basis of sexual orientation. The excitement generated by his research is reflected in the titles of some of these articles, which included "Hypothalamus Study Stirs Social Questions" in the *APA Monitor* (Adler, 1991), "Does DNA Make Some Men Gay?" in *Newsweek* (Begley & Hager, 1993), "Search for the Gay Gene" in *Time* (Thompson, 1995), and "The X Factor: The Battle Over the Ramifications of a Gay Gene" in *The New Yorker* (Kevles, 1995).

LeVay's report also attracted a mountain of commentary on its scientific weaknesses and social implications. Scientists criticized LeVay's study on several grounds. Isn't it possible, critics noted, that the presumed direction of causality might be opposite to what common sense would presume? That is, perhaps brain differences do not cause differences in sexual orientation, but instead, perhaps a lifetime of being homosexual, bisexual, or heterosexual produces the differences in hypothalamic structures that LeVay found. Moreover, LeVay's research failed to account for lesbians' sexual orientation.

Scientific critics also noted that the differences in the brains of the homosexual and heterosexual men in LeVay's study might have been the product of AIDS, which afflicted all of the gay men in his sample but only a few of the heterosexual men. Neuro-anatomist William Byne reported that many men with AIDS suffer testicular atrophy before death, and animal research shows that certain gonadal hormones affect the size of hypothalamic structures. Because of these findings, Byne wondered whether LeVay's research would have produced the same results if he had compared the brains of homosexual and heterosexual men who had not died of AIDS (Byne, 1997). LeVay responded to this criticism by pointing out that the hypothalamic structure of interest was larger in the heterosexual men who had died of AIDS than in the gay men who had died of AIDS. If testicular atrophy related to AIDS in turn caused atrophy of that structure, it should have done so in both gay and heterosexual men. Ironically, Byne has conducted research indicating that differences in the structure of the hypothalamus are not the product of AIDS. Nonetheless, Byne cautions that we have little solid evidence of a causal relationship between specific brain structures and sexual orientation because most studies on the biological bases of sexual orientation are correlational, have not been replicated, or have been based on animal research that may not be generalizable to human beings.

Many gay men and lesbians were overjoyed by LeVay's research because it indicated that sexual orientation is not the product of a freely chosen lifestyle but instead is determined by brain differences—perhaps as the result of heredity. If so, this genetic basis would counter the contention of many conservative religious leaders and their followers that homosexuality is a matter of free choice and would weaken their claim that homosexual behavior is a sin. But other homosexual activists warned that LeVay's contention that sexual orientation is produced by brain differences—possibly genetically based—might provide fuel to those who would use it to support their belief that homosexuality is the product of a genetic defect. They fear that this conclusion might lead to demands that scientists seek ways to "cure" gay men and lesbians of their brain disorder, perhaps by tinkering with a "gay gene" that might be identified. They also fear that many parents would choose to abort fetuses that they were told had a "gay gene." LeVay responded to these fears by noting that public opinion polls have found that people who believe sexual orientation is the product of free choice are more likely to be biased against lesbians and gay men than are people who believe sexual orientation is biologically determined.

miere, Blanchard, & Zucker, 2000). However, it is important to be cautious in interpreting the results of studies that report physiological differences that vary by sexual orientation. Many researchers have studied a number of physical correlates of sexual orientation, most recently the structure and function of the cochlea (McFadden & Pasanen, 1999) and finger length patterns (Williams et al., 2000). Not only is it difficult to ascertain the direction of causality, but also critics assert that studies that report findings consistent with stereotypes about gender and sexual orientation may be more easily accepted by the scientific and lay communities than are studies that do not (Carroll, 1998).

Psychosocial Factors in Sexual Orientation

Traditional psychosocial explanations of sexual orientation have been influenced by psychoanalytic views of child development. They emphasize the family environment and early childhood experience.

Childhood Upbringing and Sexual Orientation The traditional view favored the Freudian notion that sexual orientation is determined by mothers' and fathers' relations with the preschool-aged children. However, there is no evidence that any particular pattern of childhood experiences alone determines one's sexual orientation (Bell, Weinberg, & Hammersmith, 1981). In addition, the importance of the family environment in determining sexual orientation is contradicted by research findings that the great majority of children who are raised in lesbian families develop a heterosexual orientation (Golombok & Tasker, 1996).

Gender and Sexual Orientation The patterns and development of sexual orientation among women do appear to differ from those of men. Lisa Diamond is conducting a longitudinal study investigating the determinants of sexual orientation, sexual attraction, and sexual behavior among lesbian, bisexual, and "unlabeled" adolescents and young women. Her research counters the notion that sexual orientation is stable and established in childhood—at least among women. A majority of her respondents reported that their sexual attractions varied over time and across situations, and they failed to consider themselves to be exclusively attracted to other women (Diamond, 1998). In a follow-up study two years later, she found that the vast majority of the 80 participants had changed their self-described sexual orientation at least once. Changes were more likely to be reported by bisexual and unlabeled women. Sexual behaviors also varied, with one quarter of the lesbians reporting having sex with men (Diamond, 2005).

The results of research investigating gender differences in women's and men's sexuality has prompted psychologist Roy Baumeister (2000) to suggest that women's sexuality is more flexible than men's. He suggests that women—lesbian, bisexual, or heterosexual—exhibit more variability in sexual behaviors and attractions and are more strongly influenced by situational and cultural influences than men. Perhaps most controversial is his assertion that women's sex drive may be weaker than men's (Baumeister, Catanese, & Vohs, 2001). Though his theory has been met with criticism—perhaps most notably that he neglects to consider the extent to which gender differences in sexual behavior and attitudes are far outweighed by gender similarities (Anderson, Cyranowski, & Aarestad, 2000) and that gender roles have a profound influence on women's sexual experiences (Hyde & Durik, 2000)—his theory provides intriguing hypotheses for future research in the sociocultural determinants of women's sexuality.

Current Status of Theories of Sexual Orientation

Despite numerous studies on the origins of sexual orientation, none has identified any physiological or social factor that by itself explains why one person develops a heterosexual orientation and another develops a homosexual orientation. As suggested by Alfred Kinsey more than 50 years ago, it might even be mistaken to view homosexuality and heterosexuality as mutually exclusive categories (Haslam, 1997). This was the finding of a study in which homosexual men and heterosexual men rated their degree of homosexuality-heterosexuality and the size of their penile erections was measured while they watched brief movie clips of nude men and nude women. The men's self-ratings and penile responses showed a positive correlation. As you might expect, the more homosexual their self-rating, the greater their penile response to nude men; and the more heterosexual their self-rating, the greater their penile response to nude women. Yet, both the gay men and the heterosexual men tended to respond at least somewhat both to nude men and nude women (McConaghy & Blaszcynski, 1991).

According to John Money (1987), sexual orientation is affected by the interaction of biological, psychological, and sociocultural factors, the relative influences of which vary. Money points, as an example, to the Sambia tribe of New Guinea, in which boys and young men between the ages of 9 and 19 are encouraged to engage in same-sex sexual behavior to become more manly. At age 19 the young men marry and switch to a heterosexual orientation. Thus, a complete explanation of human sexual orientation probably will have to include biological, psychological, and sociocultural factors (e.g., Bem, 2000; Diamond, 2003b).

Section Review: The Sex Motive

1. According to Masters and Johnson, what are the four phases of the human sexual response cycle?
2. Why were Kinsey's sex surveys controversial, and what are the best-established gender differences and similarities in sexual behavior and attitudes?
3. What biopsychological factors have been implicated in the development of sexual orientation?

The Arousal Motive

Though the hunger motive and the sex motive seem to dominate North American culture, people also are influenced by another biological motive, the **arousal motive**. *Arousal* is the general level of physiological activation of the brain and body. As noted in Chapter 3, the reticular formation regulates brain arousal, and the autonomic nervous system and endocrine system regulate bodily arousal. Three of the main areas of research interest regarding the arousal motive are *optimal arousal*, *sensory deprivation*, and *sensation seeking*.

arousal motive The motive to maintain an optimal level of physiological activation.

Optimal Arousal

In 1908, researchers reported that mice learned tasks best at moderate levels of external stimulation and that the more complex the task, the lower the level of optimal stimulation (Yerkes & Dodson, 1908). Later researchers, led by Donald Hebb (1955) of McGill University in Montreal, showed that people perform best at a moderate level of arousal, with performance deteriorating under excessively high or low arousal levels. This relationship between arousal and performance, represented by an inverted U-shaped curve (see Figure 11-7), became known as the **Yerkes-Dodson law**, after the researchers who had conducted the earlier animal study—even though that study dealt with the level of external stimulation rather than with the level of arousal (Teigen, 1994).

Yerkes-Dodson law The principle that the relationship between arousal and performance is best represented by an inverted U-shaped curve.

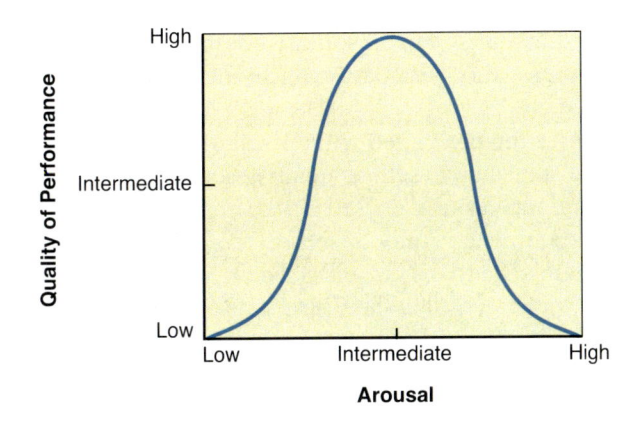

FIGURE 11-7
The Yerkes-Dodson Law

The graph depicts the relationship between arousal level and task performance. Note that the best performance occurs at a moderate level of arousal. Performance declines when arousal is below or above that level.

Chapter 11 Motivation 399

Hebb found that optimal arousal is higher for simple tasks than for complex tasks. For example, the optimal level of arousal for doing a simple addition problem would be higher than for doing a complex geometry problem. Hebb also found that optimal arousal is higher for well-learned tasks than for novel tasks. Your optimal level of arousal for reading is higher now than it was when you were first learning to read. Perhaps, when studying bores you, you find that playing music in the background helps you raise your level of brain arousal enough for you to maintain your concentration (Patton, Routh, & Stinard, 1986).

But how does arousal level affect performance? According to Hebb, it lets us concentrate and attend to tasks, such as exams. If you are underaroused, your mind might wander to irrelevant details, like when you make careless errors, such as darkening the letter C when you meant to darken the letter B on a multiple-choice exam. But if you are overaroused, your focus of attention might become too narrow, reducing your ability to shift to other details that might help you solve a problem, as when you find yourself so anxious that you stare at a particular exam question for several minutes. Overarousal impairs performance in part by interfering with the retrieval of information in short-term memory (Anderson, Revelle, & Lynch, 1989).

Though some research studies based on the Yerkes-Dodson law have tended to be methodologically flawed and inconsistent in their findings (Muse, Harris, & Feild, 2003), many studies have supported the notion of an optimal level of arousal for task performance (Robazza, Bortoli, & Nougier, 1998). In a study of arithmetic performance in third and fourth graders under time pressure, low-anxious children performed better than did moderately anxious or high-anxious children (Plass & Hill, 1986). How could the concept of optimal arousal explain these findings? Assume that before performing arithmetic, the low-anxious children began below their optimal level of arousal, the moderately anxious children began at their optimal level, and the high-anxious children began above their optimal level. The additional arousal induced by the arithmetic task might have boosted the arousal of the low-anxious children to their optimal level and the arousal of the moderately anxious children above their optimal level, while the arousal of the high-anxious children might have been boosted even further above their optimal level.

Though research has supported the notion of an optimal level of arousal for task performance, it has been inconsistent in supporting the belief that the optimal level of arousal will be lower for more difficult tasks than for easier tasks (Watters, Martin, & Schreter, 1997). Moreover, for any given task, there is no single optimal level of arousal; the optimal level varies from person to person (Ebbeck & Weiss, 1988). So an outstanding math student would have a higher optimal level of arousal for performing arithmetic than would a poor math student. As a consequence, the outstanding math student might have to "psych up" before an exam, and the poor math student might have to relax—each in an effort to reach an optimal arousal level.

Sensory Deprivation

Though people differ in the amount of arousal they prefer, they require at least a minimal amount for their brains to function properly. Anecdotal reports from Arctic explorers, shipwrecked sailors, and prisoners in solitary confinement made early psychologists aware that people require sensory stimulation for proper perceptual, cognitive, and emotional functioning.

Sensory deprivation is the prolonged withdrawal of normal levels of external stimulation. When people are subjected to sensory deprivation, they may experience delusions, hallucinations, and emotional arousal caused by the brain's attempt to restore its optimal level of arousal. The experimental study of sensory deprivation began in the early 1950s when the Defense Research Board of Canada asked Donald Hebb to find ways of countering the "brainwashing" techniques that the Chinese communists used on prisoners during the Korean War. During brainwashing, prisoners were deprived of social and physical stimulation. This experience became so unpleasant that it motivated them to cooperate with their captors just to receive more stimulation (Hebb, 1958).

sensory deprivation The prolonged withdrawal of normal levels of external stimulation.

Hebb and his colleagues conducted studies of sensory deprivation in which each participant was confined to a bed in a soundproof room with only the monotonous hum of a fan and an air conditioner. The participants wore translucent goggles to reduce visual sensations, and cotton gloves and cardboard tubes over their arms to reduce touch sensations. They were permitted to leave the bed only to eat or to use the toilet. They stayed in the room for as many days as they could tolerate.

After many hours of sensory deprivation, some participants experienced hallucinations, emotional instability, and intellectual deterioration. Though the students who volunteered for the study were paid $20 a day (a tidy sum at the time) for participating, most quit within 48 hours. They found the lack of sensory stimulation so aversive that they preferred to forego the monetary incentive in favor of sensory stimulation (Bexton, Heron, & Scott, 1954).

Research on sensory deprivation demonstrates that inadequate external stimulation might motivate us to seek external stimulation or to generate our own stimulation through alterations in brain activity. This situation is especially true of people who perform monotonous tasks in relative isolation, such as those who drive long-distance trucking hauls or live for extended periods in outer space. And, as you are certainly aware, even college students seek external stimulation to combat boring classes and dull campus life (Weinstein & Almaguer, 1987).

A form of sensory deprivation called flotation restricted environmental stimulation (flotation REST), developed by Peter Suedfeld, has been effective in reducing arousal without causing distress or cognitive impairment (Norlander, Kjellgren, & Archer, 2000–2001). In flotation REST, participants float in a dark, soundproof tank filled with warm saltwater. Flotation REST has proved successful in eliminating the use of drugs such as nicotine (Suedfeld, 1990). Flotation REST also has been applied successfully in a variety of other ways, particularly in situations that call for a reduction in arousal. These applications include the treatment of high blood pressure (McGrady, Turner, Fine, & Higgins, 1987) and the relief of chronic back and neck pain (Kjellgren, Sundequist, Norlander, & Archer, 2001). Though flotation REST produces feelings of relaxation and even euphoria, the exact physiological basis of these effects remains to be determined (Schulz & Kaspar, 1994).

Sensation Seeking

Would you prefer to ride a roller coaster or lie on a beach? Would you prefer to attend a lively party or have a quiet conversation? Your preferences would depend in part on your degree of **sensation seeking**, which is your motivation to pursue sensory stimulation. People high in sensation seeking prefer activities that increase their arousal levels; those low in sensation seeking prefer activities that decrease their arousal. A study of personal relationships, Internet usage, and music preferences in college students found that those who scored higher in sensation seeking had more casual and close friends; used the Internet to download pornography, play games, and chat with friends; and preferred punk, heavy metal, and reggae music than did those who scored lower in sensation seeking (Weisskirch & Murphy, 2004). Another study of college students from 14 different countries who had studied in a foreign country as part of California State University's International Program found that they scored higher in sensation seeking than a control group with no study-abroad experience (Schroth & McCormack, 2000).

Sensation seeking varies by age, gender, and culture. Perhaps not surprisingly, younger people score higher in sensation seeking than do older people (Ball, Farnill, & Wangeman, 1984). Men, on average, have higher sensation-seeking scores than women, particularly on subscales that measure disinhibition and thrill and adventure seeking (Zuckerman, Eysenck, & Eysenck, 1978). Also, one cross-cultural study has found that Chinese respondents scored lower on sensation seeking than did Western samples (Wang et al., 2000).

Sensation seeking also is related to risky behavior. Those who score high in sensation seeking are more likely to gamble (Barrault & Varescon, 2013), engage in binge drinking and smoking marijuana (Moreno et al., 2012), and engage in risky behaviors such as Alpine skiing and snowboarding without a helmet (Ruedl, Abart, Ledochowski, Burtscher, & Kopp, 2012). The relationship between sensation seeking and risky behavior can be deadly.

sensation seeking The motivation to pursue sensory stimulation.

Sensation Seeking

(a) People low in sensation seeking prefer activities that decrease their arousal levels. *(b)* People high in sensation seeking prefer activities that increase their arousal levels.
Sources: (a) Dudarev Mikhail/Shutterstock.com. *(b)* Vitalii Nesterchuk/Shutterstock.com.

(a)   (b)

Sensation seeking is positively correlated with the frequency of risky sexual behavior such as cruising and casual sex among gay men (Bancroft et al., 2003) and men who have sex with prostitutes and other sex workers (Xantidis & McCabe, 2000). There is evidence that many people who are high in sensation seeking pursue such activities because of a desire to counteract a chronic inability to experience pleasure in their daily lives (Pierson, le Houezec, Fossaert, Dubal, & Jouvent, 1999). As discussed in Chapter 2, correlation does not necessarily imply causation. In this case, the association between sensation seeking and risky behaviors does not necessarily mean that sensation seeking in itself causes those behaviors.

Section Review: The Arousal Motive

1. How would the Yerkes-Dodson law explain poor exam performance by students who are either too relaxed or too anxious?
2. What evidence is there to support the effectiveness of flotation REST?

The Achievement Motive

People are motivated by social as well as physiological needs. Interest in studying social motivation was stimulated in the 1930s and 1940s by the work of Henry Murray (1938), who identified a variety of important social motives, including dominance, achievement, and affiliation. Since Murray's pioneering research, psychologists, led by John Atkinson and David McClelland, have been especially interested in studying the **achievement motive**, which is the desire for mastery, excellence, and accomplishment. In the context of Maslow's hierarchy of needs, the need for achievement would be associated with one of the higher levels, the need for esteem. This association means that the need for achievement would be stronger in cultures in which most people have satisfied their lower needs, such as in Canada and the United States. But even in the United States, the relative importance of the need for achievement has changed over time. Consider an archival study of children's readers published between 1800 and 1950 that found that the number of achievement themes in the readers increased until about 1890 and then decreased through 1950. This change was accompanied by a parallel change in the number of patents issued, indicating that changes in a country's achievement motivation can affect its practical achievements (DeCharms & Moeller, 1962). Nonetheless, it is not certain from the data that changes in achievement motivation caused changes in practical achievements. You will recall that a positive correlation between two variables does not necessarily mean that changes in one cause changes in the other. Of course, it does not preclude the possibility of a causal relationship, either.

achievement motive The desire for mastery, excellence, and accomplishment.

Historical trends in the achievement motive also differ for men and women. From the late 1950s to the late 1970s, American men showed no change in their achievement motivation, whereas American women showed a marked increase. This increase has been attributed to the contemporary feminist movement of the past few decades, which encouraged women to pursue personal achievement outside traditional women's domains, such as homemaking (Veroff, Depner, Kulka, & Douvan, 1980).

Need for Achievement

Henry Murray (1938) referred to the achievement motive as the *need for achievement*, which reveals itself in efforts to meet high standards of performance or to compete successfully against other people. How do psychologists measure the need for achievement? The most common means has been the *Thematic Apperception Test (TAT)*, developed by Murray and his colleague, Christiana Morgan (Morgan & Murray, 1935). The TAT is based on the assumption that our fantasies reveal our motives. The test consists of a series of drawings of people in ambiguous situations. Participants are asked to tell what is happening in the picture, what led up to it, how the people feel, and how the situation turns out. The responses are scored for any consistent themes. Individuals with a high need for achievement tend to tell stories in which people overcome obstacles, work hard to reach goals, and accomplish great things.

What do we know about people who score high on the need for achievement? Research shows that they persist at tasks in the face of difficulties, delay gratification in the pursuit of long-term goals, and are more successful than people with a low need for achievement. They also select moderately difficult challenges, neither so easy that they guarantee success nor so difficult that they guarantee failure (McClelland, 1985). One research team investigated the relation of the achievement motive to migration in a sample of over 1,000 college students in Albania, the Czech Republic, and Slovenia. They found that students who wished to leave their country of birth scored higher on achievement motivation than did students who wished to stay. These results were replicated in a sample of American college students (Boneva, Frieze, Ferligoj, Pauknerova, & Orgocka, 1998).

Though the importance of achievement motivation in situations such as academic courses has been demonstrated in different cultures (Jegede, Jegede, & Ugodulunwa, 1997), the achievement motive appears to be multidimensional and culture specific. In individualistic cultures, the achievement motive primarily is expressed in terms of individual achievement. In collectivist cultures, which value interdependence, achievement primarily is expressed through the family and other social groups (Niles, 1998). Moreover, bicultural individuals may express both motives. Angela Lew and her colleagues (1998) found that acculturation among Asian American college students was positively correlated with the achievement motive. However, students who endorsed both American

The Achievement Motive

The social nature of the achievement motive is demonstrated not only by this boy's delight over his achievement, but also his mother's love and pride.
Source: Creativa/Shutterstock.com.

The Thematic Apperception Test

What is happening in this picture? What led up to it? How does the person feel? How will it turn out? Your responses to several ambiguous pictures like this one might contain themes revealing the strength of your need for achievement.
Source: Library of Congress.

incentive value The perceived rewards that accompany success in a particular area.

expectancy 1. The strength of the individual's beliefs about whether a particular outcome is attainable.
2. The perceived probability of success in a particular area.

and Asian values also had higher scores in individual-oriented and, to a lesser extent, social-oriented achievement.

The need for achievement varies with the achievement situation. People with a high need for achievement rarely seek success in more than a few areas of life. So your achievement behavior depends on more than just the strength of your general need for achievement. Your achievement behavior also depends on **incentive value**, the perceived rewards that accompany success in a particular area, and **expectancy**, the perceived probability of success in a particular area (Eccles & Wigfield, 1995). The combination of expectancy and incentive value even affects the choice of a college major by students (Sullins, Hernandez, Fuller, & Tashiro, 1995).

Consider your achievement motivation in regard to your achievement behavior in a psychology course. If you are high in achievement motivation, if you find that a good grade in the course has high incentive value for you, and if you expect that studying hard is likely to result in a good grade, you are more likely to work hard in the course. Yet, if you are high in achievement motivation but do not value a high grade in psychology (perhaps because it is only an elective course) or believe that you have little chance of success in the course (perhaps because the professor is a notoriously hard grader), you might not work as hard.

Research also has shown that the need for achievement can interact with arousal to determine a person's performance. As noted earlier, we perform best at our optimal level of arousal for a given task. In an arousing situation, such as giving a speech to a class, a student with a low need for achievement might perform well because the situation raises the student to her optimal level of arousal. In the same situation, a student with a high need for achievement and already at an optimal level of arousal might perform poorly because the situation raises the student beyond his optimal level (Humphreys & Revelle, 1984).

Goal Setting

goal setting The use of goals to increase motivation and improve performance by providing incentives.

Suppose that you are high in the need for achievement in academics, sports, or some other area. How should you seek to fulfill that need? Hundreds of studies have demonstrated the importance of **goal setting**. Goals increase motivation and improve performance by providing incentives. Goal setting has been especially useful in business and industry in stimulating productivity (Nordstrom, Lorenzi, & Hall, 1990). Management by objectives, in which employees participate in setting goals, has been especially effective. Of 70 studies included in a review of research on the effectiveness of management by objectives, 68 found that it increased productivity (Rodgers & Hunter, 1991). Goal setting is useful in a variety of other circumstances as well. These include improving adult health behavior (Pierson, 2012), students' writing ability (Page-Voth & Graham, 1999), and college students' exam performance (Fleming, 2002).

But how should you set your goals? Research findings by Edwin Locke and his colleagues provide several suggestions (Locke & Latham, 2002). Specific, challenging goals (such as "I will increase my studying by one hour a night") produce better performance than do vague goals (such as "I will increase the time I spend studying"), easy goals (such as "I will increase my studying by 10 minutes a week"), or mere encouragement to do your best. Feedback on your progress (such as keeping a record of how much time you spend studying) will help you reach that goal. And a goal that you set yourself will motivate you more than a goal imposed on you (as when a parent forces a child to stay home and study every day after school). Though goal setting improves task performance, goal setting paired with performance feedback is superior to goal setting alone (McCalley & Midden, 2002). Thus, workers and students who set goals will tend to perform better if given feedback about their job or school performance.

Intrinsic Motivation

If you have ever written a term paper just to obtain a grade, you can appreciate William James's distress at having to complete his now-classic 1890 textbook for an extrinsic reason. According to Edward Thorndike (1961, p. 267), "James wrote the *Principles* with

> **Psychology versus Common Sense**
>
> ### Will Rewarding a Behavior Always Increase Our Desire to Perform It?
>
> Until the 1970s, most psychologists agreed with B. F. Skinner that rewards will increase the probability of behavior or, at worst, have no effect on it. But then research began to contradict this commonsense belief. In one of the first experiments on intrinsic motivation, children were given a period of time during which they could draw. Some of them were then given a certificate as a reward for having drawn. When given a subsequent chance to draw, students who had been rewarded for drawing spent less time at it than did students who had not been rewarded (Lepper, Greene, & Nisbett, 1973). A meta-analysis of 128 studies concluded that extrinsic rewards had a moderate detrimental effect on intrinsic motivation. Moreover, extrinsic rewards were more likely to undermine children's intrinsic motivation than young adults' intrinsic motivation (Deci, Koestner, & Ryan, 1999).
>
> Keep in mind that despite consistent research findings showing the negative effect of external rewards on motivation, research findings on intrinsic versus extrinsic motivation have been based almost solely on studies in Western, individualistic cultures. Cross-cultural research indicates that the effects of extrinsic motivation might be culturally dependent. A study on the effect of free choice on intrinsic motivation in task performance found that European American students showed greater intrinsic motivation after making their own choices than after the choices were made for them by trusted others. In contrast, Asian American students—from more interdependent cultures—showed greater intrinsic motivation after the choices were made for them by trusted others than after making their own choices (Iyengar & Lepper, 1999).

wailing and gnashing of teeth to fulfill a contract with a publishing firm." Though James enjoyed writing, he did not enjoy writing for money. He was not unusual because research has shown that receiving extrinsic rewards for performing intrinsically rewarding activities can reduce the motivation to perform them.

Intrinsic motivation is the desire to perform a behavior for its own sake. In contrast, **extrinsic motivation** is the desire to perform a task to gain external rewards, such as praise, grades, or money. For example, you might take a psychology course because you find it interesting (an intrinsic reason) or because it is a graduation requirement (an extrinsic reason).

Given the everyday observation that extrinsic rewards can increase achievement motivation, especially in people who initially have little or no motivation in a particular area (Cameron, Banko, & Pierce, 2001), why do extrinsic rewards sometimes decrease achievement motivation? Two theories provide possible answers.

Overjustification Theory

Overjustification theory assumes that an extrinsic reward decreases intrinsic motivation when a person attributes his or her performance to the extrinsic reward. For example, in the "Psychology versus Common Sense" box, the students who were rewarded for drawing might have attributed their behavior to the reward rather than to their interest in drawing. Overjustification occurs when there is high intrinsic interest and the reward is perceived as more than adequate justification for performing the act. In a study of first and second graders, children played with an interesting or uninteresting toy and were rewarded or not rewarded. Rewards reduced the motivation to play with the interesting toy but not the uninteresting toy (Newman & Layton, 1984). A meta-analysis found strong support for over-justification theory (Tang & Hall, 1995), though some research studies indicate that it has limitations as an explanation for decreases in intrinsic motivation (Pittenger, 1996).

Cognitive-Evaluation Theory

An alternative theory, **cognitive-evaluation theory**, holds that a reward perceived as providing information about a person's competence in an activity will increase her or his intrinsic motivation to perform that activity (Deci, Nezlek, & Sheinman, 1981). But a reward perceived as an attempt to control a person's behavior will decrease his or her

---

intrinsic motivation The desire to perform a behavior for its own sake.

extrinsic motivation The desire to perform a behavior in order to obtain an external reward, such as praise, grades, or money.

overjustification theory The theory that an extrinsic reward will decrease intrinsic motivation when a person attributes her or his performance to that reward.

cognitive-evaluation theory The theory that a person's intrinsic motivation will increase when a reward is perceived as a source of information but will decrease when a reward is perceived as an attempt to exert control.

intrinsic motivation to perform that activity. The more controlling and less informative that students perceive a teacher to be, the lower will be the students' intrinsic motivation (Guay, Boggiano, & Vallerand, 2001).

Consider a student whose teacher rewards her for doing well in drawing. If the student believes that the reward is being used to provide information about her competence, her intrinsic motivation to perform that activity may increase. But if she believes that the reward is being used to control her behavior (perhaps to make her spend more time drawing), her intrinsic motivation to perform may decrease. Though there is strong research support for cognitive-evaluation theory (Rummel & Feinberg, 1988), some research findings have contradicted it (Carton, 1996).

> ### Section Review: The Achievement Motive
>
> 1. What are some basic rules for the effective use of goal setting?
> 2. What is the difference between overjustification theory and cognitive-evaluation theory in explaining the negative effects of extrinsic motivation?

The Role of Motivation in Sport

sport psychology The field that applies psychological principles to help amateur and professional athletes improve their performance.

Near the end of the 19th century, Indiana University psychologist Norman Triplett (1898) observed that bicyclists rode faster when competing against other bicyclists than when competing against time. This study was perhaps the first in **sport psychology**, the field that studies the relationship between psychological factors and sport performance. Though Triplett began the scientific study of sport performance, magazines devoted to sport had advanced the desirability of a psychological approach to sport in the late 19th century (King, Raymond, & Simon-Thomas, 1995). One of the first celebrated participants in sport psychology research was baseball star Babe Ruth. In 1921, he performed tasks in a laboratory at Columbia University to help researchers discover what accounted for his extraordinary ability to hit home runs. The researchers hoped to use what they learned to help identify future baseball stars (Fuchs, 1998). Today, in studying motivation in sport, researchers are especially interested in the arousal motive and the achievement motive.

The Arousal Motive and Sport

Your arousal motive influences your sport performance. Of particular importance are your level of sensation seeking and your level of optimal arousal.

Sensation Seeking and Sport

Your level of sensation seeking might affect your choice of sports to pursue. People who score high on tests of sensation seeking are more likely to participate in risky activities such as skydiving, hang gliding, mountain climbing, and automobile racing (Jack & Ronan, 1998). And rugby and lacrosse players score higher in sensation seeking than do rowers and soccer players (Schroth, 1995).

Optimal Arousal and Sport

The arousal motive also is important to athletes in regard to their maintaining an optimal level of arousal for their sport performance. If you have ever played a competitive sport, you know what it is to choke—to be so anxious that you perform below your normal level of ability. Choking occurs when your anxiety makes you attend to the normally automatic movements involved in playing a sport. If you consciously attend to those movements, they will be disrupted (Baumeister, 1984). Consider the shooting of free throws in basketball. If you attend to each movement of your arm and hand as you shoot a free throw, you will disrupt the smooth sequence of movements that free-throw shooting requires. Athletes at an optimal level of arousal are less likely to be undermotivated or to choke, as shown in a study of female collegiate basketball players. Those with a moderate level of pregame anxiety performed better than did those with a low or high level (Sonstroem & Bernardo, 1982).

As mentioned earlier, the optimal level of arousal is lower for complex tasks than for simple tasks. This finding also is true in sports (Gardner, 1986). Your optimal level of arousal while hitting a golf ball (a relatively complex task) would be lower than your optimal level while playing shuffleboard (a relatively simple task). Moreover, the more skilled the athlete, the higher her optimal level of arousal will be. The golfer who makes a putt on the green to win the U.S. Open might be so skillful that he has a higher optimal level of arousal than does the golfer who chokes in the same situation. When teaching beginners to play golf, to ride a bicycle, or to serve a volleyball, you should try to keep their arousal levels from becoming too high. To avoid excess arousal, beginners should refrain from competition and not practice while being watched by people other than the coach or instructor.

One technique for achieving optimal arousal in athletes is flotation REST. Flotation REST has helped competitive archers maintain relaxed hand muscles (Norlander, Bergman, & Archer, 1999). And in a study of the effects of flotation REST on recreational basketball performance, college students who practiced flotation REST reported greater confidence and performed better than controls who did not practice it (Suedfeld & Bruno, 1990).

The Achievement Motive and Sport

On June 4, 1986, six weeks after setting the collegiate record for the 10,000-meter run, Kathy Ormsby, running among the leaders, veered off the track midway through the final race at the NCAA championships in Indianapolis. She left the stadium, ran to the nearby White River Bridge, and leaped 50 feet to the riverbank. The fall fractured her spine and paralyzed her from the waist down. Besides excelling at running, Ormsby had been her high school's valedictorian (with an average of 99 percent) and was a premedical student at North Carolina State University. Ormsby was certainly high in her motivation to succeed.

Ormsby had been overcome periodically by anxiety strong enough to force her to drop out of races. Though her high need for achievement certainly motivated her to compete, she apparently succumbed to her anxiety, finding it more and more difficult to motivate herself to compete against other elite athletes. Kathy Ormsby's tragic story shows that the achievement motive can be a powerful force in athletic competition as it is in other areas of life.

Need for Achievement and Sport

Athletes with a high need for achievement are motivated to seek competition that provides a fair test of their abilities. Early evidence for this finding came from a study in which college students played a game of ringtoss. Participants with a high need for achievement were more likely to stand at an intermediate distance from the peg, whereas participants with a low need for achievement were more likely to stand either close to the peg or far from it (Atkinson & Litwin, 1960). Similarly, if you were high in your need for achievement in tennis, you would probably choose to play someone of your own ability. In contrast, a person low in the need for achievement might prefer to play either someone who barely knows how to grip a racket, which would ensure success, or a professional tennis player, which would ensure that losing would be attributable to the professional opponent's excellence rather than to personal incompetence.

One way in which superior athletes make competition against lesser athletes more motivating is by giving themselves a handicap, making the competition a moderate challenge rather than a guaranteed success (Nicholls, 1984). If you are an excellent table tennis player, you might provide a moderate challenge for yourself by giving a lesser opponent 10 points in a 21-point game. Similarly, in the 1960s, Wilt Chamberlain, perhaps the most physically imposing athlete in history (who once averaged 50 points a game for a whole season in the National Basketball Association), developed a fadeaway jump shot to show that he could score even when giving up his greatest asset, his ability to score from near the basket because of his great strength and height (7 feet, 1 inch tall). By doing so, he made scoring a moderate rather than easy challenge for himself—often to the distress of his coaches.

Motivation in Sport

Athletes' motivation can involve both the arousal motive and the achievement motive.
Source: Pete Saloutos/Shutterstock.com.

Chamberlain's use of intentional *self-handicapping* (see Chapter 13) is common among athletes in a variety of sports, including collegiate swimming and wrestling (Bailis, 2001).

Goal Setting and Sport

As in other areas of life, goal setting is important in sport motivation. A survey of 185 male and 143 female Olympic athletes found that all of them used goal setting to help enhance their performance and that they found it to be effective (Burton, Gillham, Weinberg, Yukelson, & Wiegand, 2013). A study of the effects of goal setting on college sharpshooters' performance found that sharpshooters who set specific goals improved more than those who set do-your-best goals (Boyce, 1992). Athletes whose performance can be improved by goal setting include football players (Ward & Carnes, 2002), gymnasts (Lambert, Moore, & Dixon, 1999), and tennis players (Harwood & Swain, 2002).

Studies have demonstrated that goal setting is particularly useful in basketball. One study used what is known as an A-B-A design with multiple baselines to assess the effect of mental imagery and goal setting on the free-throw shooting of female collegiate basketball players. The participants were given several baseline sessions (A) during which they shot free throws. The length of the baseline sessions varied from one participant to another. The researchers varied the length of the baseline sessions to reduce the likelihood that another event (for example, the beginning of a new workout program on the very day that the participants began the test sessions that followed) could account for changes between the baseline sessions and the test sessions.

The participants then were given several test sessions (B) during which four participants used imagery, four used goal setting, and four used both imagery and goal setting to improve their free-throw shooting. The study concluded with another series of baseline sessions (A) during which the participants shot free throws without using imagery or goal setting. The results indicated that goal setting by itself produced the best results (Lerner et al., 1996).

Intrinsic Motivation and Sport

Athletes also are more motivated by intrinsic rewards than by extrinsic rewards (Vallerand & Losier, 1999). For example, a recent study found higher intrinsic motivation among Division I athletes who perceived that their coach's feedback focused on positive and informational feedback rather than control (Amorose & Horn, 2001). In terms of cognitive-evaluation theory, discussed earlier, rewards that are perceived as a means of control can decrease intrinsic motivation, and rewards that are perceived as a means of providing information about competence can increase intrinsic motivation (Ryan, 1980).

Intrinsic motivation also is important in adherence to exercise programs. A study of participants in aerobics, weight training, or tae kwon do found that those who were more motivated by intrinsic factors, such as enjoyment, social interaction, and improved competence, tended to adhere to their programs. In contrast, those who were more motivated by extrinsic factors, such as a desire to become more fit or attractive, tended not to adhere to their programs sooner (Ryan, Frederick, Lepes, Rubio, & Sheldon, 1997).

As you can see, motivational factors that are important in other areas of life also are important in sport. Athletes perform best at an optimal level of arousal, which varies with the individual, the sport, and the task. And athletes are influenced by their achievement motive; their level of motivation is enhanced by their need for achievement, proper use of goal setting, and reliance on intrinsic rewards.

Section Review: The Role of Motivation in Sport

1. How does the concept of optimal arousal explain why athletes perform differently in practice and in real competition?

2. Why would an athlete high in the need for achievement prefer an opponent of similar ability rather than one of much lower or much higher ability?

Experiencing Psychology

Can Mental Imagery Improve Sport Performance?

Rationale
Sport performance depends on several factors, including athletic ability, training techniques, physical conditioning, and personal motivation. A popular approach to improving performance is the use of mental imagery, which can improve technique and motivation. This activity will be an experiment comparing the effectiveness of two kinds of visual imagery in improving basketball free-throw shooting performance. The first kind of visual imagery, *internal imagery*, involves perceiving the task as though looking out through one's own eyes. The second kind of visual imagery, *external imagery*, involves perceiving the task as though looking through the eyes of an observer. Experiments have found that external imagery is superior to internal imagery for sport activities in which form is especially important, including karate, gymnastics, and rock climbing (Hardy & Callow, 1999).

Method
Participants
In this experiment you will need 30 female and male college students; 10 will be randomly assigned to each of three groups. The first group will use internal imagery, the second group will use external imagery, and the third group—the control group—will use no mental imagery. Be sure to include equal numbers of male and female participants in each group.

Materials
The participants will use the same basketball. You will need a data sheet to record the number of free throws made by each of the 30 participants.

Procedure
Each participant will take 20 free throws on an indoor basketball court, with those in the imagery groups using mental imagery before each free throw. Those in the internal imagery group will be told to close their eyes and imagine themselves shooting a successful free throw from their own visual perspective. Those in the external imagery group will be told to close their eyes and imagine themselves shooting a successful free throw from the perspective of someone observing them. Those in the no-imagery group will be told simply to try their best. Record the number of free throws made by each participant.

Results and Discussion
Calculate the mean number of free throws made for each of the three groups. Using these means, draw a bar graph (see Appendix C in the Online Edition). Are there any large differences between the means of the three groups? What do you conclude about the effectiveness of the imagery techniques? Why would scientists prefer to use inferential statistics (see Chapter 2 and Appendix C in the Online Edition) instead of subjective judgments of the differences between the means? What confounding variables might have affected the experiment? Among the possible factors to consider are the basketball, the setting, and the instructions given to participants.

If you were to perform the experiment again, how would you improve it? Given that research studies have provided some evidence that internal imagery is more effective for experts and external imagery is more effective for nonexperts, suggest an experiment that might test that hypothesis.

Chapter Summary

The Nature of Motivation
- Motivation is the psychological process that arouses, directs, and maintains behavior.
- The main sources of motivation include genes, drives, and incentives.
- Though William McDougall's instinct theory failed to achieve scientific credibility, interest in the hereditary basis of social behavior remains alive today in the field of sociobiology.
- Instinct theories gave way to the drive-reduction theory of Clark Hull, which assumes that physiological deprivation causes a need, which induces a state of tension called a drive.
- Drive reduction aims at restoring a steady state of physiological equilibrium called homeostasis.
- A drive "pushes" you toward a goal, whereas an incentive is an external stimulus that "pulls" you toward a goal.
- Abraham Maslow categorized human needs in a hierarchy, with the pursuit of higher needs contingent on the satisfaction of lower ones.

The Hunger Motive
- Hunger impels you to eat to satisfy your body's need for nutrients.
- Hunger is regulated by bodily, brain, and environmental factors.
- Areas of the hypothalamus regulate hunger by responding to signals from the blood and internal organs.

Chapter 11 Motivation

- External food-related cues also influence hunger and eating.
- The most common eating problem is obesity.
- Men with more than 25 percent body fat and women with more than 30 percent body fat are considered to be obese.
- Obesity depends on one's set point, basal metabolic rate, responsiveness to external cues, chronic level of blood insulin, and reactions to stress.
- Two of the most prevalent eating disorders are anorexia nervosa, which involves self-starvation, and bulimia nervosa, which typically involves binging and purging.

The Sex Motive

- Sex serves as both a drive and an incentive.
- Sex hormones direct sexual development and sexual behavior.
- Unlike in other animals, sexual behavior in human adults is controlled more by sociocultural factors than by sex hormones.
- Formal research on human sexuality began with surveys on men's and women's sexual behavior conducted by Alfred Kinsey and his colleagues.
- Later research by William Masters and Virginia Johnson showed that women and men have similar sexual response cycles.
- Masters and Johnson also developed sex therapy techniques that have been successful in helping men and women overcome sexual dysfunctions, which are chronic problems at phases in the sexual response cycle.
- Gender identity is one's self-perceived sex.
- Sexual orientation is one's pattern of erotic attraction.
- Gender identity and sexual orientation are influenced by biopsychological and sociocultural factors.

The Arousal Motive

- Arousal is the general level of physiological activation of the brain and body.
- The Yerkes-Dodson law holds that there is an optimal level of arousal for the performance of a given task, with the optimal level becoming lower as the task becomes more complex.
- Studies of sensory deprivation by Donald Hebb and his colleagues show that people are motivated to maintain at least a minimal level of sensory stimulation.
- Flotation REST has been successful in improving human physical and psychological functioning.
- People also differ in their degree of sensation seeking, which is the motivation to seek high or low levels of sensory stimulation.

The Achievement Motive

- The achievement motive is the desire for mastery, excellence, and accomplishment.
- Henry Murray and Christiana Morgan introduced the Thematic Apperception Test as a means of assessing the need for achievement.
- People with a high need for achievement persist at tasks in the face of difficulties, delay gratification in the pursuit of long-term goals, and achieve greater success than do people with a low need for achievement.
- People with a high need for achievement also prefer moderately difficult challenges.
- People's actual achievement behavior in a given situation depends on the strength of their need for achievement, the incentive value of success for them, and their expectancy of success.
- Goal setting increases motivation and improves performance by providing incentives.
- The best goals are specific and challenging, and feedback is useful for monitoring progress toward goals.
- The intrinsic motivation to engage in an activity can be reduced by extrinsic rewards.
- Overjustification theory and cognitive-evaluation theory provide different explanations for the detrimental effects of extrinsic rewards.

The Role of Motivation in Sport

- Sport psychology is the field that studies the relationship between psychological factors and sport performance, particularly the influence of motivation.
- To keep from choking during competition, athletes must learn to keep from rising above their optimal level of arousal.
- Athletic performance also is affected by other motivational factors, including the need for achievement, goal setting, and intrinsic motivation.

Key Terms

The Nature of Motivation
drive (p. 377)
drive-reduction theory (p. 377)
hierarchy of needs (p. 378)
homeostasis (p. 377)
incentive (p. 377)
instinct (p. 376)

motivation (p. 376)
need (p. 377)
sociobiology (p. 377)

The Hunger Motive
anorexia nervosa (p. 387)
basal metabolic rate (p. 383)

bulimia nervosa (p. 388)
obesity (p. 381)
set point (p. 381)

The Sex Motive
gender identity (p. 394)
gonads (p. 390)

sensate focusing (p. 394)
sexual dysfunction (p. 393)
sexual orientation (p. 394)
sexual response cycle (p. 390)

The Arousal Motive
arousal motive (p. 399)
sensation seeking (p. 401)

sensory deprivation (p. 400)
Yerkes-Dodson law (p. 399)

The Achievement Motive
achievement motive (p. 402)
cognitive-evaluation theory (p. 405)
expectancy (p. 404)
extrinsic motivation (p. 405)

goal setting (p. 404)
incentive value (p. 404)
intrinsic motivation (p. 405)
overjustification theory (p. 405)

The Role of Motivation in Sport
sport psychology (p. 406)

Chapter Quiz

Note: Answers for the Chapter Quiz questions are provided at the end of the book.

1. If you were high in your need for achievement, you would most likely seek to play basketball against
   a. an 8-year-old child.
   b. an Olympic basketball player.
   c. a person 6 inches shorter than you.
   d. a person similar in ability to you.

2. One of the criticisms of sociobiology is that it
   a. may simply support the status quo.
   b. favors "politically correct" science.
   c. has only been successful in explaining altruism.
   d. emphasizes social experiences over biological endowment.

3. Alfred Kinsey suggested viewing homosexuality and heterosexuality as
   a. genetically ordained.
   b. points on a continuum.
   c. products of free choice.
   d. mutually exclusive categories.

4. A person with anorexia nervosa
   a. engages in self-starvation.
   b. becomes morbidly overweight.
   c. binges on food and then vomits.
   d. exhibits conditioned taste aversions.

5. The Yerkes-Dodson law states that the relationship between arousal and performance is best represented by
   a. a U-shaped curve.
   b. an inverted U-shaped curve.
   c. a negatively accelerated curve.
   d. a positively accelerated curve.

6. Stress-related overeating is related to secretion of
   a. glucose.
   b. glucagon.
   c. endorphins.
   d. cholecystokinin.

7. Your self-perceived sex is your
   a. gender identity.
   b. sexual response.
   c. sexual orientation.
   d. gender role.

8. The notion that an extrinsic reward will decrease intrinsic motivation when a person attributes his or her performance to that reward is called
   a. overextension theory.
   b. overjustification theory.
   c. overregularization theory.
   d. cognitive-evaluation theory.

9. The thirst motive is regulated by the
   a. hypothalamus.
   b. aqueous humor.
   c. substantia nigra.
   d. medulla.

10. Reports of brainwashing during the Korean War inspired research on
    a. autism spectrum disorder.
    b. hypnosis.
    c. starvation.
    d. sensory deprivation.

11. Maslow's arrangement of motives in order of their motivational priority, ranging from physiological needs to the need for self-actualization and transcendence, is called the
    a. expectancy theory.
    b. intrinsic motives.
    c. hierarchy of needs.
    d. drive-reduction theory.

12. Hunger is reduced by the secretion of the hormone
    a. renin.
    b. thyroxin.
    c. cholecystokinin.
    d. prolactin.

13. Flotation REST is a kind of
    a. paraphilia.
    b. sex therapy.
    c. sensory deprivation.
    d. timeout used to enhance achievement motivation.

14. The set point is the
    a. body's normal weight.
    b. subject of research in sport psychology.
    c. degree of achievement that one finds satisfactory.
    d. amount of stimulation needed to trigger an orgasm.

15. Denslow Lewis's article, which he submitted to the *Journal of the American Medical Association*, was controversial because it
    a. promoted pedophilia.
    b. advocated premarital sex.
    c. encouraged women to enjoy sex.
    d. contained drawings of the sex organs.

16. The binge eating seen in bulimia nervosa may be an attempt to relieve feelings of
    a. mania.
    b. anxiety.
    c. depression.
    d. depersonalization.

17. According to Masters and Johnson, the order of phases in the human sexual response cycle is
    a. plateau, excitement, orgasm, resolution.
    b. excitement, plateau, orgasm, resolution.
    c. excitement, orgasm, resolution, plateau.
    d. excitement, orgasm, plateau, resolution.

18. The optimal level of arousal would probably be lowest for
    a. lifting weights.
    b. throwing a football.
    c. serving a tennis ball.
    d. making a shot on a pool table.

19. Controversial research by Simon LeVay has attributed one's sexual orientation to differences in
    a. early childhood rearing.
    b. part of the hypothalamus.
    c. genes on the X chromosome.
    d. prenatal hormone exposure.

20. The study of Danish adoption records by Stunkard et al. (1986) found that the body weight of adoptees is
    a. unrelated to the body weight of either the biological mother or the adoptive mother.
    b. more related to the body weight of the biological mother than the adoptive mother.
    c. more related to the body weight of the adoptive mother than the biological mother.
    d. more related to the body weight of the adoptive mother than the adoptive father.

21. You and several friends finish a meal and feel full. A server then gives a description of several delicious chocolate desserts, prompting an obese friend to order one. This reaction would most likely be a response to the secretion of
    a. glucose by the liver.
    b. insulin by the pancreas.
    c. glucagon by the pancreas.
    d. cholecystokinin by the small intestine.

22. One of the main criticisms of Kinsey's research is that
    a. it promoted the double standard.
    b. he used questionnaires instead of interviews.
    c. he observed people while they were engaged in sex.
    d. his sample of participants was not representative of the general population.

23. A man who would be most likely to develop bulimia nervosa would be a
    a. chef.
    b. psychologist.
    c. newspaper editor.
    d. collegiate wrestler.

24. The rate at which the body burns calories just to keep itself alive is called the
    a. set point.
    b. rate of homeostasis.
    c. basal metabolic rate.
    d. optimal caloric rate.

25. When you eat a meal, stretch receptors in your stomach reduce your hunger by sending impulses to the brain along the
    a. vagus nerve.
    b. gustatory nerve.
    c. trochlear nerve.
    d. trigeminal nerve.

Thought Questions

1. Given the factors that regulate hunger and eating, what are some ways to maintain a healthy body weight?

2. In what ways are sexual dysfunctions associated with different phases of the sexual response cycle?

3. How would the concept of optimal arousal explain your performance on an English exam?

4. How might research findings on the roles of intrinsic and extrinsic motivation explain why professional athletes who are paid millions of dollars to play games that children enjoy playing for free lose their desire to play?

Emotion

CHAPTER 12

On September 16, 1999, CNN reported that U.S. Energy Secretary Bill Richardson had taken a polygraph test—popularly known as a lie detector test—during which he was asked if he had ever been a spy or met with foreign espionage agents. No results were made public, but it was presumed that he passed the test. Richardson took the test not because he was suspected of being a spy, but to demonstrate to nuclear weapons scientists that they had nothing to fear from mandatory polygraph testing. Following evidence of Chinese spying and lax security at weapons laboratories, Richardson urged that 5,000 scientists working for the Department of Energy submit to polygraph tests about security matters. Scientists with access to top-secret information about nuclear weapons were to be asked if they had ever illegally disclosed classified information; contacted foreign intelligence services without authorization; or committed espionage, sabotage, or terrorism. If they failed even one question, they would be subject to an FBI investigation.

Richardson's proposal was met by outrage from scientists, who claimed it threatened their sense of honor and violated their right to privacy. Scientists at the Lawrence Livermore National Laboratory in Livermore, California, argued that polygraph testing is neither valid nor reliable. Scientists at Los Alamos National Laboratory in New Mexico threatened to form a union to oppose the testing program.

In response, Richardson said, "I took the test. It was administered effectively, efficiently. It's easy and I believe scientifically sound. I respect the views of some of the lab scientists. But I think they have nothing to worry about." The U.S. Congress, backing Richardson and disregarding the scientists, passed a law permitting polygraph testing of employees with access to top-secret information. Directors of national laboratories insisted that the threat of this practice was hurting their efforts to recruit top scientists. Did scientists have good reason to fear the polygraph test? This question will be addressed later in the chapter. But to understand the nature and effectiveness of polygraph testing, it would be helpful to begin by learning about *emotion*.

How do you feel? Are you *anxious* about an upcoming exam, *depressed* by a recent loss, in *love* with a wonderful person, *angry* at a personal affront, or *happy* about your favorite team's performance? Such feelings are emotions. The word *emotion* comes from a Latin word meaning "to set in motion," and like motives (such as sex and hunger), emotions (such as love and anger) motivate behavior that helps us adapt to different situations (Ekman, 1992a). Though it is

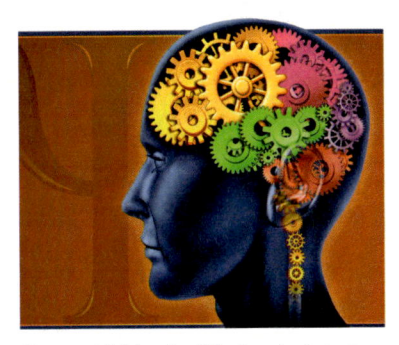

Source: Lightspring/Shutterstock.com.

Chapter Outline

The Biopsychology of Emotion
The Expression of Emotion
The Experience of Emotion
Theories of Emotion

413

easy to recognize an emotion, especially one that is a pure, prototypical example (such as extreme anger or intense romantic love), it is difficult to provide a formal definition of the concept itself (Russell, 1991). This difficulty led two prominent emotion researchers to observe, "Everyone knows what an emotion is, until asked to give a definition" (Fehr & Russell, 1984, p. 464).

Despite the difficulty of precisely defining the concept of emotion, most psychologists agree that an **emotion** is a motivated state that is marked by physiological arousal, expressive behavior, and cognitive experience. Emotions also vary in their intensity and pleasantness/unpleasantness (Buck, 1985). Consider an angry man. His heart might pound (a sign of physiological arousal), he might grit his teeth (an expressive behavior), and he might feel enraged (an intense, unpleasant mental experience). Emotions have evolved to motivate us to respond adaptively to changing environmental circumstances (Lang, Bradley, & Cuthbert, 1998). In trying to explain emotion, some psychologists prefer to study the biological level (the biopsychology of emotion), others the behavioral level (the expression of emotion), and still others the cognitive level (the experience of emotion).

emotion A motivated state marked by physiological arousal, expressive behavior, and cognitive experience.

The Biopsychology of Emotion

What are the physiological bases of emotion? To answer this question, psychologists study the autonomic nervous system, the brain, and neurochemicals.

The Autonomic Nervous System and Emotion

Both your emotional expression and your emotional experience depend on physiological arousal, which reflects activity in your *autonomic nervous system* (ANS). The system is called "autonomic" because it was thought to function independently, without the need for conscious, voluntary regulation by the brain. We now know that the brain and the spinal cord regulate the ANS; it does indeed operate below the level of consciousness. However, we still refer to the "autonomic" nervous system. Figure 12-1 illustrates the functions of the two branches of the autonomic nervous system: the *sympathetic nervous system* and the *parasympathetic nervous system*. The interplay of these two systems contributes to the ebb and flow of emotions and controls our internal organs such as the heart and intestines. The sympathetic nervous system relies on the neurotransmitter *norepinephrine* to regulate its target organs; the parasympathetic nervous system relies on the neurotransmitter *acetylcholine* to regulate its target organs.

Activation of the sympathetic nervous system can stimulate the **fight-or-flight response**, which evolved because it enabled our prehistoric ancestors to meet sudden physical threats (whether from nature, animals, or people) by either confronting them or running away from them. After a threat has been met or avoided, the sympathetic nervous system becomes less active and the parasympathetic nervous system becomes more active, calming the body. This system has been referred to as rest-and-digest. Yet, because the sympathetic nervous system stimulates the secretion of epinephrine and norepinephrine from the adrenal glands into the bloodstream, physiological arousal may last for a while after the threat has disappeared.

fight-or-flight response A state of physiological arousal that enables us to meet sudden threats by either confronting them or running away from them.

The fight-or-flight response is triggered not only by physical threats but also by psychological threats—such as academic demands that we feel are beyond our abilities. To appreciate the role of the autonomic nervous system in the emotional response to a psychological threat, imagine that you are about to give a classroom presentation for which you did not prepare adequately. As you walk to your class, you experience anxiety associated with physiological arousal induced by your sympathetic nervous system.

Chapter 12 Emotion

FIGURE 12-1

The Autonomic Nervous System and Its Two Branches

Emotional responses involve the interplay of the two branches of the autonomic nervous system: the sympathetic nervous system, which tends to arouse us, and the parasympathetic nervous system, which tends to return us to a calmer state. The black lines represent clusters of neurons and their distribution to the organs. Both branches are constantly active, though one system can dominate depending on your arousal state.

Parasympathetic Nervous System
- **Eyes:** Pupils constrict.
- **Salivary glands:** Salivation is increased.
- **Sweat glands:** Perspiration is not affected.
- **Bronchioles:** Bronchioles constrict; respiration decreases.
- **Heart:** Heart rate and force decrease.
- **Stomach:** Digestion resumes.
- **Adrenal glands:** Epinephrine and norepinephrine secretion is not affected.
- **Liver:** Sugar release is not affected.
- **Small intestine:** Contractions are stimulated.
- **Bladder:** Sphincter relaxes.
- **Rectum:** Anal sphincter relaxes.

Sympathetic Nervous System
- **Eyes:** Pupils dilate.
- **Salivary glands:** Salivation is reduced.
- **Sweat glands:** Perspiration increases.
- **Bronchioles:** Bronchioles dilate; respiration increases.
- **Heart:** Heart rate and force increase.
- **Stomach:** Digestion slows.
- **Adrenal glands:** Epinephrine and norepinephrine are secreted.
- **Liver:** Sugar is released into bloodstream.
- **Small intestine:** Contractions are inhibited.
- **Bladder:** Sphincter constricts.
- **Rectum:** Anal sphincter constricts.

As you enter the classroom, you become more alert and energetic as your circulatory system diverts blood rich in oxygen and other nutrients normally destined for your stomach and intestines to your brain and skeletal muscles. Your energy increases as your liver releases sugar into your bloodstream. Your heart pounds rapidly and strongly in response to epinephrine secreted by your adrenal glands. Your bronchioles dilate to permit more oxygen-rich air to enter your lungs, and you breathe more rapidly as your lungs work harder to expel carbon dioxide. A classmate might notice your pupils dilating, which improves your vision by letting more light into your eyes. And you might notice your mouth becoming dry, goose bumps appearing on your arms, and beads of perspiration forming on your forehead. Your dry mouth reflects a marked reduction in salivation. Your goose bumps are caused by hairs standing on end—a remnant of threat displays made by our furry prehistoric ancestors. And your perspiration provides a means of cooling off your aroused body.

Fight or Flight

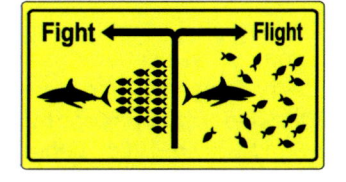

The fight-or-flight response is stimulated when the sympathetic division of the ANS is activated.

Source: Sangoiri/Shutterstock.com.

Suppose that as you sit in class in this anxious, aroused state, your professor announces that a surprise guest speaker will lecture for the entire class period. You immediately feel relieved at not having to give your presentation; your arousal subsides partly because of activity in your autonomic nervous system. Your brain becomes less alert, your muscles less energetic, your heartbeat less noticeable, and your breathing more regular. Your pupils constrict to their normal size, your mouth becomes moist again, your goose bumps disappear, and you stop sweating. You might become so profoundly relaxed and relieved that you fall asleep during the guest speaker's lecture.

The Brain and Emotion

Though bodily arousal plays a role in emotionality, the brain is ultimately in control of emotional responses (LeDoux, 1995). Emotion researchers are especially interested in the roles of the limbic system and cerebral hemispheric lateralization in emotionality.

Critical Thinking About Psychology

Do Lie Detectors Tell the Truth?

At times in the 1980s and again in the 1990s, hardly a week went by without the media reporting a controversy about the use of the polygraph test, or lie detector test. The chapter opened with a summary of a 1999 controversy about Department of Energy Secretary Bill Richardson's proposal to subject nuclear scientists to polygraph testing to ensure that they have not passed top-secret information to foreign spies. The media also reported on the role of polygraph testing in several high-profile legal cases, including the O. J. Simpson murder trial and the Bill Clinton–Monica Lewinsky sex scandal. But the media tend to report disagreements about the use of polygraph testing without reporting what scientific research says about its validity. One is left with the impression that these disagreements are simply clashes of opinions regarding its validity, with little scientific evidence to back up any of the competing claims. Consider what scientific research, as opposed to personal opinion, says about the polygraph as a means of identifying liars and truth tellers.

If you have ever detected a phony smile from a salesperson or politician, you probably noted certain cues indicating that the smile was insincere. Perhaps the smile lasted too long. Or perhaps you noticed that the smile was asymmetrical. Phony expressions, including smiles, will usually be more pronounced on the left side of the face than on the right side (Rinn, 1984). Nonetheless, in everyday life most people are poor at detecting deceit from facial expressions. One exception is U.S. Secret Service agents, who learn to attend to nonverbal cues in their efforts to protect the president from attack (Ekman & O'Sullivan, 1991). Other groups that are better than average at detecting deception from a person's demeanor include psychologists and law enforcement officers (Ekman, O'Sullivan, & Frank, 1999).

The detection of lies through interpretation of expressive behavior has a long history. The Old Testament describes a case in which King Solomon resolved a dispute between two women who claimed to be the mother of the same infant. Solomon wisely proposed cutting the infant in half, then giving one half to each woman. Whereas one of the women calmly agreed to this, the other pleaded with Solomon to give the infant to her adversary. Solomon reasoned that the pleading woman had to be the real mother because she was willing to lose the infant rather than see the child killed.

King Solomon inferred lying from expressive behavior, but lie detection has historically been based on the assumption that liars display increased physiological arousal. In the 15th century, interrogators for the Inquisition required suspected heretics to swallow pieces of bread and cheese. If the food stuck to the person's palate, he or she was considered guilty. As you will recall, the arousal of the sympathetic nervous system that accompanies emotionality reduces salivation, leading to a dry mouth. A dry mouth would make it more difficult to swallow certain foods. As you can imagine, people brought before the Inquisition would experience increased arousal—whether or not they were heretics—and would be convicted of heresy.

The Polygraph Test

Modern lie detection began in the 1890s with the work of Cesare Lombroso, an Italian criminologist who questioned suspects while recording their heart rate and blood pressure. He assumed that if they showed marked fluctuations in heart rate and blood pressure while responding to questions, they were lying (Kleinmuntz & Szucko, 1984b). Today, the lie detector test, or **polygraph test**, typically measures breathing patterns, heart rate, blood pressure, and electrodermal activity. Electrodermal activity reflects the amount of sweating; greater emotionality is associated with more sweating. Though the polygraph test is used to detect lying, no pattern of physiological responses by itself indicates lying. Instead, the test detects physiological arousal produced by activation of the sympathetic nervous system. As David Lykken, an expert on lie detection, has said, "The polygraph pens do no special dance when we are lying" (Lykken, 1981, p. 10).

Given that no pattern of physiological responses indicates lying, how is the recording of physiological arousal used to detect lies? The typical polygraph test given to a criminal suspect begins with an explanation of the test and the kinds of questions to be asked. The suspect is then asked *control questions*, which are designed to provoke lying about minor transgressions common to almost everyone. For example, the suspect might be asked, "Have you ever stolen anything from an employer?" It is a rare person who has not stolen at least an inexpensive item, yet many people would answer no, creating an increase in physiological arousal; and even suspects who answer yes to a control question would probably experience some increase in physiological arousal in response to that question.

The suspect's physiological response to control questions is compared to her or his physiological response to *relevant questions*, which are concerned with facts about the crime, such as "Did you steal money from the bank safe?" Polygraphers assume that a guilty person will show greater physiological arousal in response to relevant questions and that an innocent person will show greater physiological arousal in response to control questions. Figure 12-2 shows a polygraph printout of differences in arousal in response to the different questions. The typical polygraph test asks about 12 relevant questions, which are repeated three or four times.

Critical Thinking About Psychology

Do Lie Detectors Tell the Truth? *continued*

Issues in Lie Detection

Polygraph testing has provoked controversy because it is far from being a perfect measure of lying. One difficulty is that the accuracy of the polygraph test depends in part on the suspect's physiological reactivity. People with low reactivity exhibit a smaller difference between their responses to control questions and their responses to relevant questions than do people with high reactivity. This difference might cause an unemotional criminal to be declared innocent and an emotional innocent person to be declared guilty (Waid, Wilson, & Orne, 1981). Moreover, tranquilizers reduce the detectability of lying by reducing physiological arousal (Waid & Orne, 1982).

Criminals also are aware of countermeasures that can make them appear innocent on a polygraph test. Consider the case of Floyd Fay, an innocent man convicted in 1978 of murdering his best friend and sentenced to life in prison after failing a polygraph test that he had taken voluntarily. Two years later, a public defender tracked down the real murderer. While in prison, Fay became an expert on lie detection and taught prisoners how to beat the polygraph test. Of 27 inmates who had admitted their guilt to him, 23 passed their polygraph tests (Kleinmuntz & Szucko, 1984a). One technique for fooling the polygraph test uses the properly timed induction of pain. For example, suppose that during control questions you bite your tongue or step on a tack hidden in your shoe. This would increase your level of physiological arousal in response to control questions, thereby reducing the difference between your physiological responses to control questions and relevant questions (Honts, Hodes, & Raskin, 1985).

Though aware that criminals can fool the polygraph machine, critics of the test are more concerned with the possibility that the polygraph will find innocent people guilty. In the 1980s, millions of Americans were subjected to polygraph tests in criminal cases, employment screening, employee honesty checks, and security clearances (Kleinmuntz & Szucko, 1984b). In 1983, President Reagan gave an executive order to use the polygraph test to identify federal employees who reveal classified information. But a report commissioned by Congress found that the polygraph test was invalid in the situations favored by Reagan. The report concluded that the only justifiable use of the polygraph test is in criminal cases (Saxe, Dougherty, & Cross, 1985). Though the test might not be valid, it can elicit confessions from suspects who believe in its effectiveness (Simpson, 1986). Thus, the unreliability of the polygraph test makes its use to detect deception questionable (Fiedler, Schmid, & Stahl, 2002).

In June 1988 President Reagan, confronted with overwhelming opposition to the unrestricted use of polygraph tests, signed the Polygraph Protection Act banning their use for preemployment screening by private employers. But the law still permitted the use of polygraph tests in ongoing investigations of specific incidents. And drug companies, security services, government agencies, and private companies that have contracts with government intelligence agencies were exempted from the ban on using polygraph tests in employment screening (Bales, 1988).

What evidence led to the widespread opposition to the unrestricted use of the polygraph? Supporters of the polygraph test claim accuracy rates of 90 percent or

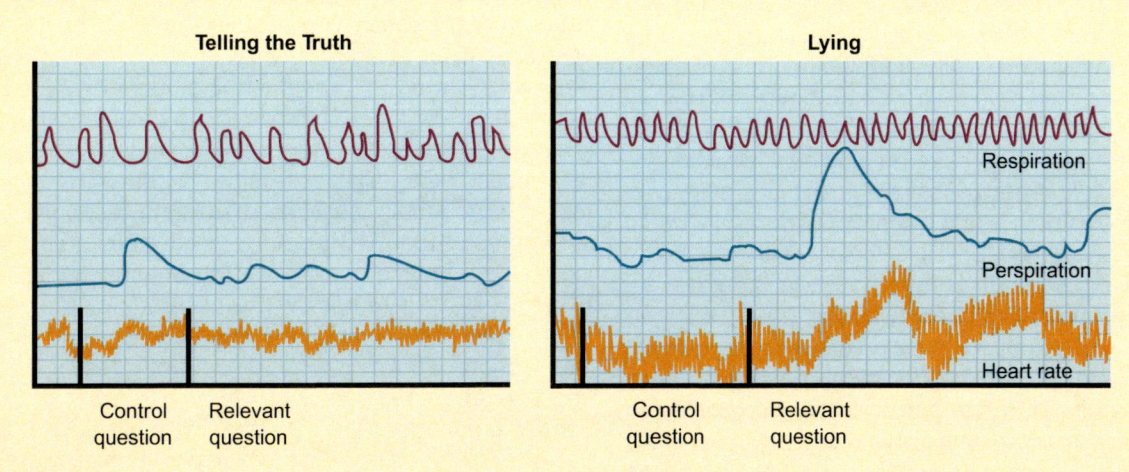

FIGURE 12-2 Relevant Questions Versus Control Questions

The polygraph test compares physiological responses to relevant and control questions. The record on the left is of a person who responded less strongly to a question relevant to a crime than to an emotionally arousing control question not relevant to the crime. Such responses indicate to the examiner that the person is telling the truth. The record on the right is of a person who responded more strongly to a question relevant to a crime than to an emotionally arousing control question not relevant to the crime. Responses such as this one indicate to the examiner that the person is lying.

Chapter 12 Emotion

Critical Thinking About Psychology

Do Lie Detectors Tell the Truth? *continued*

better (Raskin & Podlesny, 1979). But research findings indicate that it is much less accurate than that, as revealed by the following study (Kleinmuntz & Szucko, 1984a). The polygraph printouts of 50 thieves and 50 innocent people were presented to six highly trained professional polygraphers. They were asked questions about real thefts. The results showed that the polygraphers correctly identified 76 percent of the guilty persons and 63 percent of the innocent persons. Though their performance was better than chance, these results also meant that they incorrectly identified 24 percent of the guilty persons as innocent and 37 percent of the innocent persons as guilty. The tendency of the polygraph test to produce unacceptably high rates of false positives (that is, identifying innocent persons as guilty) has been replicated in other studies (Horowitz, Kircher, Honts, & Raskin, 1997). The polygraph test's high rate of false positives can have tragic consequences for those who are unjustly denied jobs, fired from jobs, or prosecuted for crimes.

The Guilty Knowledge Test

A possible improvement over the control-question test is the **Guilty Knowledge Test**, developed by David Lykken (1974). If you have ever played the board game *Clue*, you have some understanding of the test. In contrast to the control-question test, Lykken's test assesses knowledge about a transgression rather than alleged anxiety about it. The Guilty Knowledge Test is useful only when details of the transgression are known to the transgressor but not to others who take the test. Consider its use in interrogating suspects in a bank robbery. A suspect would be asked questions about the victim, the site of the crime, and the commission of the crime. Instead of being asked, "Did you steal money from the bank safe?" the suspect would be asked, "Was the money stolen from the ____?" This question would be asked several times, each time with different words completing the statement. In this case, the words might be *bank safe*, *teller's drawer*, and *armored car*.

The Guilty Knowledge Test assumes that a guilty person (who knows details of the crime), but not an innocent person, will show more physiological arousal in response to the relevant words than in response to the irrelevant words (Verschuere, Crombez, & Koster, 2004). If a person shows greater physiological reactivity to the relevant words in a *series* of statements (a single positive instance would be insufficient), that person would be considered guilty. Of course, examiners should not know any details of the crime. Otherwise, they might affect the suspect's physiological response to relevant words (Elaad, 1997), perhaps by saying those words louder or softer. Researchers are developing a version of the Guilty Knowledge Test that would measure changes in brain-wave patterns to determine when a person has information that he or she is trying to conceal (Allen & Iacono, 1997).

A laboratory test in which undergraduates committed mock murders supported the assumption that guilt could be detected by differential physiological responses to relevant and irrelevant stimuli (Timm, 1982). In its first use in a study of real criminals, the Guilty Knowledge Test was given to 50 innocent and 48 guilty participants. The results supported the effectiveness of the test, particularly its ability to avoid false positives. Judges correctly classified 94 percent of the innocent and 65 percent of the guilty (Elaad, 1990). Research findings indicate that the Guilty Knowledge Test is biased toward false negatives, whereas control-question tests are biased toward false positives (McCauley & Forman, 1988). So, people more interested in protecting the innocent would favor the Guilty Knowledge Test, whereas those more interested in ferreting out transgressors would favor the control-question test.

Lykken, recognizing the merits of the Guilty Knowledge Test, urges its widespread adoption (Lykken, 1988). But research support for the superiority of the Guilty Knowledge Test has not been universal. Though one study found that it was effective in detecting individuals with knowledge relevant to a crime (Elaad, 1994), another study found that participants with guilty knowledge might not be detected reliably (Bradley & Warfield, 1984). Still another study found no difference in the success of the control-question test and Guilty Knowledge Test in detecting lying (Podlesny & Raskin, 1978). There also is evidence that guilty people can defeat the Guilty Knowledge Test by recalling emotional scenes from their past during the presentation of irrelevant items. This reduces differences in their physiological responses to relevant and irrelevant items, making them appear to have no more knowledge of relevant items than irrelevant ones (Ben-Shakhar & Dolev, 1996). Nonetheless, a meta-analysis of 80 experimental studies of the Guilty Knowledge Test found that it tends to be highly effective in detecting deception (Ben-Shakhar & Elaad, 2003).

Researchers are assessing whether modifying testing procedures, such as measuring response time (Seymour, Seifert, Shafto, & Mosmann, 2000) and asking multiple-choice questions (Ben-Shakhar, Gronau, & Elaad, 1999), may improve the accuracy of the Guilty Knowledge Test. So even though the Guilty Knowledge Test is more promising than the control-question test, it has not yet gained sufficient research support to merit complete confidence in it. In fact, there is evidence that use of a Guilty Actions Test (which presents actions that were performed by the perpetrator) might be superior to the Guilty Knowledge Test (Bradley, MacLaren, & Carle, 1996). Moreover, scientists have had some initial success in using brain-scanning techniques, such as functional MRI, to detect patterns of brain activity that are associated with deceptive responses (Lee et al., 2002).

The Limbic System and Emotion

As discussed in Chapter 3, autonomic nervous system arousal is regulated by the brain structure called the *hypothalamus*, a component of the *limbic system*, which also includes the *amygdala*, the *olfactory bulbs*, the *fornix*, the *septum*, and other structures. Among other things, the hypothalamus helps control changes in breathing and heart output during the fight-or-flight response (Spyer, 1989). The septum (a neural relay center in the brain) suppresses aversive emotional states. For example, electrical stimulation of the septum in rats reduces their tendency to avoid fear-inducing stimuli (Thomas, 1988).

The amygdala prompts us to react emotionally to environmental circumstances, enabling us to respond adaptively and to form memories of emotional situations (Pare, Collins, & Pelletier, 2002). The amygdala plays more of a role in recognizing unpleasant stimuli evoking emotionally negative feelings, such a fear or anger, than in recognizing pleasant stimuli evoking emotionally positive feelings (Hamann, Ely, Hoffman, & Kilts, 2002). Evidence supporting this finding comes from research on the effects of damage to the amygdala on the recognition of emotions. One study reported the case of a 54-year-old woman with amygdala damage who experienced difficulty in interpreting facial expressions of emotion. However, her ability to encode facial expressions of fear and other basic emotions was unaffected (Anderson & Phelps, 2000). In electrophysiological studies using animals, single neurons in the amygdala can become active when fearful stimuli are presented or retrieved from memory (Courtin, Karalis, Gonzalez-Campo, Wurtz, & Herry, 2013). These studies indicate the importance of the amygdala in processing information about environmental threats. The main limbic system structures are illustrated in Figure 12-3.

Hemispheric Lateralization and Emotion

Though the limbic system is important in the processing of emotions (Servan-Schreiber & Perlstein, 1998), the *cerebral cortex*, which covers the cerebral hemispheres, is important for our subjective experience of emotion. For example, though the limbic system tends to trigger rapid, automatic emotional reactions to stimuli, the frontal cortex modulates these reactions so that they are not excessive (Hariri, Bookheimer, & Mazziotta, 2000). Thus, a sudden noise might make you instantly experience fear generated by activity in your limbic system, but if you immediately realize that the noise was produced by your pet dog, your frontal cortex would prevent you from running away screaming or grabbing an object with which to defend yourself. Research findings indicate that the cerebral hemispheres play different roles in emotion. For example, PET scans indicate that the right hemisphere is more active than the left when we try to assess emotional states from facial expressions (Nakamura et al., 1999). Research findings also suggest that each cerebral

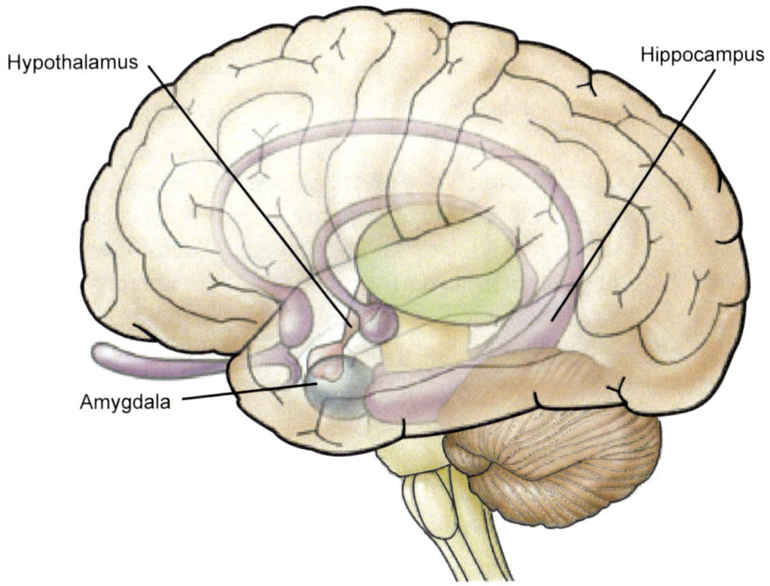

polygraph test The lie detector test, which assesses lying by measuring changing patterns of physiological arousal in response to particular questions.

Guilty Knowledge Test A method that assesses lying by comparing physiological arousal in response to information that is relevant to a transgression and physiological arousal in response to information that is irrelevant to that transgression.

FIGURE 12-3
The Limbic System

A lateral view of the brain showing the limbic structures deep within the brain. Our emotional responses are regulated by activity in the limbic system, particularly in the amygdala, hippocampus, and hypothalamus.

hemisphere is specialized to process different emotions, with the left hemisphere more involved in positive emotions and the right hemisphere more involved in negative emotions (Marosi et al., 2002). But keep in mind that particular emotions are not processed *solely* in one hemisphere or the other. Both cerebral hemispheres play a role in all emotional experience (Danko, Bechtereva, Shemyakina, & Antonova, 2003).

Much of our knowledge about the role of each hemisphere in emotional experience comes from studies, particularly those conducted by Richard Davidson, that have measured the relative degree of activity in each hemisphere during emotional arousal. For example, excessive activation of the left hemisphere is associated with euphoria, and excessive activation of the right hemisphere is associated with depression (Flor-Henry, 1983). One study measured electrical activity while participants watched emotionally positive or negative film clips to evoke positive or negative emotions in them. Those who experienced positive emotion had higher left-hemisphere activity; those who experienced negative emotion had higher right-hemisphere activity (Wheeler, Davidson, & Tomarken, 1993). A study that recorded electrical activity from the brains of 10-month-old infants found that hemispheric differences in the processing of emotions appear early in life. Greater activation of the left hemisphere was associated with a pleasant facial expression and a tendency to approach people. In contrast, greater activation of the right hemisphere was associated with an unpleasant facial expression and a tendency to withdraw from people (Fox & Davidson, 1988). Nonetheless, a published review of the relevant research literature found that the right hemisphere plays a greater role than the left hemisphere in regulating facial expressions of emotion (Borod, Haywood, & Koff, 1997).

The *Wada test*, which involves selective anesthesia of one cerebral hemisphere to determine hemispheric functions (particularly the site of the speech center), also has provided evidence of the lateralization of emotionality. In the Wada test, the anesthetic sodium amobarbital is injected into the left or right carotid artery of patients who are about to undergo brain surgery. Because the carotid arteries supply blood to the brain, injection of sodium amobarbital into one of them will anesthetize the associated hemisphere. Research using the Wada test shows that laughter and elation (positive emotionality) are more frequent after right-hemisphere anesthesia, whereas crying (negative emotionality) is more frequent after left-hemisphere anesthesia (Lee, Loring, Meader, & Brooks, 1990).

Further evidence that the left hemisphere is more related to positive emotions and the right hemisphere more related to negative emotions has been provided by studies of brain damage. Because each cerebral hemisphere inhibits the emotional activity of the other, we normally experience neither intensely positive nor intensely negative emotions. But damage to one hemisphere can release the other from its inhibition. Damage to the right hemisphere, releasing the left hemisphere from inhibition, leads to laughing, elation, optimism, and other signs of positive emotion. In contrast, damage to the left hemisphere, releasing the right hemisphere from inhibition, leads to crying, worry, pessimism, and other signs of negative emotion (Leventhal & Tomarken, 1986).

The Chemistry of Emotion

When we say that there is "good chemistry" or "bad chemistry" between people, we mean that they have positive or negative emotions in response to each other. Research has shown that our emotional responses do indeed depend on chemistry—hormones and neurotransmitters that convey emotion-related impulses from one neuron to another or between neurons and body organs (Baum, Grunberg, & Singer, 1992). For example, abnormal levels of the neurotransmitters norepinephrine and serotonin have been implicated in psychological disorders (see Chapter 14), such as severe depression (Curzon, 1982).

Hormones and Emotion

As noted earlier (see Chapter 11), stressful situations cause HPA axis activation and the secretion of the hormones such as epinephrine and norepinephrine, which also serve as neurotransmitters. In a study of psychologists and physicians, levels of these hormones were measured on a day when participants gave a public speech and on a day when they did not. Public speaking was associated with an increase in the level of both epinephrine and norepinephrine. Epinephrine increases glucose metabolism allowing for energy expenditure. Moreover, there was a rise in blood cholesterol on days when participants gave speeches relative to days when they did not. Perhaps stress hormones, by stimulating an increase in low-density lipoproteins (which are implicated in cardiovascular disease), provide one of the mechanisms by which emotional responses to stressful situations contribute to the development of cardiovascular disease (Bolm-Audorff, Schwammle, Ehlenz, & Kaffarnik, 1989). Another important hormone that regulates the stress response is *cortisol*. Cortisol is a glucocorticoid secreted from the adrenal glands in response to stress. The hypothalamus signals to the adrenal gland to increase or decrease production of cortisol and other hormones. There are glucocorticoid receptors in many parts of the brain, and activation of the receptors contributes to our neural response to stress. This interplay of hormonal and neural regulation is considered a feedback loop.

Endorphins and Emotion

Endorphins, a class of neurotransmitters discussed in Chapters 3 and 5, contribute to emotional experiences by providing pain relief and evoking feelings of euphoria. For example, blood levels of endorphins rise markedly after bungee jumping and correlate positively with resulting feelings of euphoria (Hennig, Laschefski, & Opper, 1994). Even the emotional thrill we experience from a concert, a motion picture, or a dance performance may depend on endorphin activity. This finding was demonstrated in a study of college students who listened to a musical passage and then received an injection of either naloxone (a drug that blocks the effects of endorphins) or a placebo (in this case, a saline solution that does not block the effects of endorphins). Neither the participants nor the experimenter knew whether participants had received naloxone or a placebo (you might recognize this application of the *double-blind procedure* that was described in Chapter 2); the double-blind procedure prevented participant bias or experimenter bias from affecting the results. After receiving the injection, participants again listened to the musical passage. When asked to estimate the intensity of their emotional thrill in response to the music, participants who had received naloxone reported a significant decrease in intensity. Participants who had received a placebo reported no such decrease. Because naloxone blocks the effects of endorphins, but a placebo does not, the findings support the role of endorphins in positive emotional experiences (Goldstein, 1980).

Endorphins and Emotion

The emotional thrills experienced by fans at concert festivals might be caused by the release of endorphins in their brains.
Source: Franz Pfluegl/Shutterstock.com.

> **Section Review:** The Biopsychology of Emotion
>
> 1. What evidence is there that positive and negative emotions are processed primarily in different brain hemispheres?
> 2. What evidence is there that endorphins are involved in feelings of euphoria?

The Expression of Emotion

How do you know how your fellow students feel? Because our emotional experiences are private, they cannot be directly observed by other people. Instead, emotions are inferred from descriptions of them or from expressive behaviors. Behaviors that express emotions include vocal qualities, body movements, and facial expressions. The expression of emotion varies across cultures. For example, people from collectivist cultures, such as Costa Rica, are less comfortable expressing negative emotions than are people from individualistic cultures, such as the United States (Stephan, Stephan, & de Vargas, 1996). Yet, there are basic facial expressions of emotion that are recognizable across cultures (Izard, 1994). Research studies also indicate that there might be gender differences in emotional expression. This research is discussed in Chapter 14.

Vocal Qualities and Emotion

prosody The vocal features of speech other than the words themselves.

When you speak, both your words and your voice convey emotion (Pell, Jaywant, Monetta, & Kotz, 2011). The vocal features of speech other than the words themselves are called **prosody**. Prosodic features include rate, pitch, and loudness. You can use the same spoken words to express different emotions by simply altering the prosodic features of your speech—the same statement can sound sincere or sarcastic depending on its vocal qualities. When you are happy, your voice goes up in pitch (just recall the last time you heard the voices of two people greeting each other after a long separation). Changes in vocal qualities indicative of changes in emotion tend to be consistent from one person to another and from one culture to another (Frick, 1985). Perhaps these common vocal patterns evolved in our prehistoric, prelanguage ancestors as a universal means of communicating emotional states in everyday social interaction.

Voice quality also affects social relations. Sometimes it can cause social rejection, as in a study in which undergraduates rated depressed or nondepressed fellow undergraduates who differed in how they spoke. Depressed participants were more likely to be rejected, in part because they spoke in soft, flat voices, with long pauses. This finding is important, because unappealing prosodic features can create a vicious cycle in which the depressed person alienates others, thereby reducing the likelihood of positive social interactions that might help the person overcome his or her depression (Paddock & Nowicki, 1986).

The prosodic features of speech are regulated primarily by the right cerebral hemisphere (Gandour, Larsen, Dechongkit, & Ponglorpisit, 1995), both when we speak (Graves & Landis, 1990) and when we listen to a speaker (Herrero & Hillix, 1990). Evidence for the role of the right hemisphere in prosody comes from studies of stroke victims and patients undergoing the Wada test. Patients with right-hemisphere strokes might retain their ability to speak but might speak with abnormal emotional tone (Gorelick & Ross, 1987). A study in which the Wada test was given to patients about to undergo brain surgery to relieve their epilepsy found that when the patients received injections of sodium amobarbital in the left carotid artery, they lost their ability to speak. When it was injected in their right carotid artery, they retained their ability to speak but lost the ability to impart emotion to their speech (Ross, Edmondson, Seibert, & Homan, 1988). In essence, it seems that "the left hemisphere provides the text [words], while the right hemisphere plays the accompaniment [emotional tone]" (Merewether & Alpert, 1990, p. 325). Though most research studies on the lateralization of prosody support a greater role for the right hemisphere, some also have found similar role for the left hemisphere (Pell, 1998). Pell (1999) suggests that damage to either the left or the right hemisphere can produce emotional prosody deficits. A recent functional MRI study also found evidence for bilateral processing of emotion in language (Kotz et al., 2003). Nevertheless, many newer fMRI studies point to a significant and distinct role for the right hemisphere in decoding emotional prosody (Wildgruber et al., 2005).

Body Movements and Emotion

If you have observed the gestures of impatient drivers in heavy traffic on a hot summer day, you know that body movements can convey emotions. Even movements of the whole body can do so. The performance of basketball player Michael Jordan was especially appealing because his movements conveyed emotions.

But how do we know that we are responding to people's movements rather than simply to their facial expressions or physical appearances? The importance of body movements in expressing emotion has been demonstrated in studies that have eliminated other nonverbal emotional cues. In one study (Walk & Homan, 1984), college students watched a videotape of people performing dances that portrayed various emotions. To eliminate the influence of facial expressions and physical appearance, the dancers wore lights on their joints and danced in total darkness. Thus, participants saw only the movement of lights. Nonetheless, they accurately identified the emotions represented by the dances. This study indicates that the emotional cues provided by body movements are distinct from those provided by facial expressions or physical appearance.

The ability to decode nonverbal behavior is important in social interaction, as exemplified by the following research findings. Women are superior to men in decoding emotional states from body movements (Sogon & Izard, 1987). Elementary school children who are better at decoding nonverbal emotional cues are more popular (Nowicki & Duke, 1992). College roommates rate their relationship more positively when both are high in nonverbal decoding ability than when one or both are low in it (Hodgins & Zuckerman, 1990). And psychological counselors might be more effective when they are skillful in noting changes in their clients' nonverbal behavior (Hill & Stephany, 1990). The ability to recognize specific emotions from particular patterns of body movements develops across early childhood, with the ability to recognize basic emotions—including fear, anger, sadness, and happiness—present by age 8 (Boone & Cunningham, 1998).

We seem to prefer an optimal level of nonverbal interaction in everyday social interactions. We like people who are neither too nonverbally aloof nor too nonverbally intrusive. In a study that supported this finding, people who were walking on a college campus were asked to respond to a survey. During the brief interaction, they were randomly exposed to one of four conditions related to the interviewer's behavior: (1) eye contact and a momentary touch; (2) eye contact and no touch; (3) no eye contact and a momentary touch; or (4) no eye contact and no touch. At the end of the interaction, the interviewer dropped several folded questionnaires. Participants in the second or third conditions were more likely to help pick up the papers than were participants in the first or fourth. Thus, in agreement with the notion that there is an optimal level of nonverbal communication, participants responded more positively to a moderate level of nonverbal interaction (Goldman & Fordyce, 1983).

Body Movements

Emotional cues from body movements are distinct from those provided by facial expressions and physical appearance.
Source: ostill/Shutterstock.com.

Facial Expressions and Emotion

Philip D. Chesterfield, an 18th-century British statesman, noted that our faces give away our emotions: "Look in the face of the person to whom you are speaking if you wish to know his real sentiments, for he can command his words more easily than his countenance." Chesterfield's observation may explain in part how teachers' expectations create the Pygmalion effect (see Chapter 2). Though teachers might believe that they are unbiased when speaking to their students, their facial expressions can communicate their true feelings, whether positive or negative, about particular students (Babad, Bernieri, & Rosenthal, 1989). But our recognition of facial expressions might depend on the social context. In one study, participants who displayed facial expressions of anger while in a frightening situation were judged to be afraid (Carroll & Russell, 1996).

Research has shown that facial expressions convey both the intensity and the pleasantness of our emotional states. Infants can express the emotions of joy and surprise as early as 4 months of age (Bennett, Bendersky, & Lewis, 2002). However, children's ability to recognize emotions from facial expressions develops more gradually. One study found that 5-month-old infants were able to discriminate between a smile and facial expressions of fear (Bornstein & Arterberry, 2003). And in another study, children aged 2 to 5 years were asked to identify and label facial expressions of basic emotions. The participants' ability to identify emotions improved with age. Whereas younger participants could reliably identify expressions of happiness, anger, and sadness, the older participants could more accurately identify expressions of fear, surprise, and disgust (Widen & Russell, 2003). As in the recognition of emotions from body movements, women are superior to men in recognizing emotions from facial expressions (Giovannini & Ricci Bitti, 1981)—a gender difference that emerges as early as infancy (McClure, 2000). Moreover, though men and women tend to respond empathetically by mimicking facial expressions, women do so more demonstratively (Lundqvist, 1995).

Does women's greater nonverbal expressivity reflect greater emotionality? One of the most consistent, long-standing gender stereotypes states just that—women are the emotional sex (e.g., Williams & Best, 1990). Two studies tested the relationship between gender role stereotypes and the interpretation of emotional expression in women (Plant, Hyde, Keltner, & Devine, 2000). A sample of 117 female and male undergraduates completed a questionnaire assessing the frequency with which men and women experienced 19 emotions. Participants believed that most of these emotions (awe, embarrassment, fear, distress, happiness, guilt, sympathy, sadness, love, surprise, shame, and shyness) were experienced more frequently in women than in men. Men were thought to experience only two emotions more frequently—pride and anger.

Another sample of over 150 male and female undergraduates then was asked to rate slides of two men and two women trained to pose facial expressions of four emotions. In two of the slides unambiguous emotions were posed; that is, pure expressions of anger and sadness. In two of the slides ambiguous emotions were posed; that is, facial expressions were a blend of anger and sadness.

Results indicated that gender-role stereotypes influenced ratings of emotional expression by female stimuli. Participants rated women expressing ambiguous emotions as both sadder and less angry than men. This effect also was observed for the two slides depicting women posing unambiguous facial expressions of anger—participants rated these stimuli as a blend of anger and sadness. Thus, it appears that observers' interpretation of men's and women's emotional expression can be influenced by gender-role stereotypes. Women were perceived to be expressing greater sadness, a female-stereotyped emotion, whereas men were perceived to be expressing more anger, a male-stereotyped emotion.

Actors who feel the emotions they are portraying facially produce performances that are more emotionally convincing to audiences (Gosselin, Kirouac, & Dore, 1995). Knowledge of the relationship between facial expressions and emotions has enabled researchers to distinguish honest emotional expressions from fake ones. For example, the face reveals when smiles are sincere or false. Sincere smiles include muscular activity around the eyes, causing the skin to wrinkle, and around the mouth, causing the corners of the lips to rise (Quagflieg, Vermuelen, & Roisson, 2013). This natural smile is called the *Duchenne smile*. In contrast, when people display insincere smiles, perhaps to hide their negative emotional state, the corners of their lips are drawn downward and their upper lip curls up. In one experiment, participants were more likely to display the Duchenne smile when they watched a pleasant film than when they watched an unpleasant film. They also reported more positive emotions when they exhibited the Duchenne smile, verifying it as a sign of a pleasant emotional state (Ekman, Davidson, & Friesen, 1990).

Researchers studying smiling also have investigated the relationship between gender roles and emotional expression. In one creative study, school yearbooks—from kindergarten to college—were collected, and photographs of students, staff, and faculty were coded for the presence or absence of smiling. Gender differences were small to nonexistent until 4th grade—at which point girls smiled more frequently than did boys. This gender difference increased until 9th grade and remained steady through adulthood, a difference that the researchers attributed to gender-role socialization (Dodd, Russell, & Jenkins, 1999).

Heredity and Facial Expressions

Charles Darwin (1872/1965) believed that facial expressions evolved because they promoted survival by communicating emotions and helping individuals distinguish friend from foe. For example, the human facial expression of contempt might be a modification of the snarl found in dogs, apes, and our prehistoric ancestors (Izard & Haynes, 1988). Darwin's belief was supported in an experiment that measured how quickly participants could detect an angry face or a happy face in a crowd (Hansen & Hansen, 1988). Participants reported that a single angry face seemed to pop out of the crowd faster than a single happy face. The results supported the participants' impressions—they were able to detect an angry face faster than a happy face. Likewise, a more recent study has found that participants detect angry postures in a crowd faster than happy postures. Thus, angry faces and postures "pop out" from a crowd and are more quickly detected by people. Why might we have evolved the ability to detect angry faces and postures more quickly than other faces and postures? A possible reason is that it promotes our survival by motivating us to take more immediate action to confront or to escape from a person displaying an angry face (Gilbert, Martin, & Coulson, 2011).

Research by Carroll Izard (1990a) and his colleagues supports Darwin's view that facial expressions for basic emotions are inborn and universal. One line of research has found that even people who are blind from birth can use facial expressions to accurately communicate their emotional states to others (Galati, Miceli, & Sini, 2001). An early case study involved a 10-year-old girl who had been born deaf and blind. Despite her inability to see normal facial expressions or to receive spoken instructions on how to form them, she displayed appropriate facial expressions for the basic emotions, which include fear, anger, disgust, sadness, and surprise (Goodenough, 1932). Nonetheless, blind infants exhibit a more limited repertoire of facial expressions than do sighted infants (Troster & Brambring, 1992).

A second line of research support for the inborn, universal nature of facial expressions comes from studies showing that young infants produce facial expressions for the basic emotions (Izard, Huebner, Risser, McGinnes, & Dougherty, 1980). In one study, newborn infants were given solutions of sugar or quinine (which tastes bitter). Despite having no prior experience with those tastes, their facial expressions showed pleasure or displeasure, depending on which solution they had tasted. And the intensity of their facial expressions varied with the strength of the solutions (Ganchrow, Steiner, & Daher, 1983). Though infants can produce facial expressions for the basic emotions, their degree of expressiveness varies across cultures. Chinese infants are less facially expressive in smiling and crying than are Japanese or European American infants (Camras et al., 1998).

Culture and Facial Expressions

Further support for Darwin's evolutionary view of facial expressions comes from studies showing that facial expressions for the basic emotions are universal across cultures (Ekman, 1993; Izard, 1994). The research participants in one study were members of the Fore tribe of New Guinea, who had almost no contact with European Americans prior to the study (Ekman & Friesen, 1971). The tribe members listened to descriptions of a series of emotion-arousing situations representing joy, fear, anger, disgust, sadness, or surprise. The descriptions included situations such as "He is looking at something that smells bad" and "Her friends have come, and she is happy." After each description, the tribe members viewed a set of three photographs of European American faces expressing different emotions, from which they selected the face portraying the emotion of the person in the description they had just heard.

The tribe members correctly identified expressions portraying joy, anger, sadness, and disgust but failed to distinguish between expressions portraying fear and surprise. Perhaps the tribe members' expressions for fear and surprise did not differ because similar situations (such as an enemy or a wild animal suddenly appearing from out of the jungle) evoke both fear and surprise in their culture. This study was replicated, with similar results, in a more recent study of people in 10 different cultures from around the world (Ekman et al., 1987). A meta-analysis of 97 studies supported the universality of certain emotional expressions. In more than 95 percent of the samples, emotions were universally recognized at levels greater than chance. The average cross-cultural accuracy rate was 58 percent. However, the cross-cultural accuracy rate was influenced by a number of factors. Recognition of facial expression of emotion was superior among members of the same national, ethnic, or regional group. This finding suggests that whereas there is remarkable universality in the facial expression of emotion, people are able to identify emotional expressions within their own cultural group with greater accuracy. However, this in-group advantage was found to be greater in culturally isolated groups. Thus, geographic proximity and cross-cultural interaction can reduce this ingroup advantage (Elfenbein & Ambady, 2002).

Nonetheless, some researchers have found that cross-cultural differences in the detection of universal facial expressions of emotion vary as a function of the methodology used in the studies (Frank & Stennett, 2001; Haidt & Keltner, 1999). And other researchers question whether research showing cross-cultural consistency in recognition of facial expressions has been sound enough to merit accepting the findings (Russell, 1994). That is, there are cross-cultural differences in the subjective feelings, physiological responses, and expressive behavior associated with emotions (Scherer & Wallbott, 1994). For example, one survey of more than 4,000 male and female participants in 30 countries investigated the influence of culture on people's moods after crying. The results indicated that the emotional response to a crying episode depended on cultural norms of emotional expression. In cultures where crying was common, participants reported feeling better after a cry. In cultures where crying was uncommon, participants reported feeling worse after a cry. As you might expect, cross-cultural differences in the frequency of crying were related to shameful feelings about shedding tears. Thus, crying in cultures that discourage such expressions of emotion is accompanied by a feeling of shame and a worsening of mood. And crying in cultures that encourage such expressions of emotion is accompanied by emotional relief (Becht & Vingerhoets, 2002).

Section Review: The Expression of Emotion

1. What gender differences have been found in nonverbal expressivity?
2. What evidence is there that certain emotional facial expressions are universal?

The Experience of Emotion

Though we have hundreds of words for emotions, there seem to be only a few basic emotions, from which all others are derived. One model of emotion, devised by Robert Plutchik (1980), considers joy, fear, anger, disgust, sadness, surprise, acceptance, and anticipation to be the basic emotions. More complex emotions arise from mixtures of these basic ones.

Charles Darwin assumed that the basic emotions evolved because they promoted our survival. For example, disgust (which means "bad taste") might have evolved because it prevented our ancient ancestors from ingesting poisonous substances. People in all cultures exhibit an early feeling of disgust at the sight and smell of feces—the "universal disgust object" (Rozin & Fallon, 1987). Note that disgust involves each of the major aspects of emotion: physiological change (stomach contractions causing nausea), expressive behavior (a contorted face), and cognitive experience (a feeling of revulsion). And the facial expression of disgust now has a social meaning as well, expressing revulsion at something that someone has said or done.

Folk wisdom holds that just as certain people are prone to experience unpleasant emotions, certain days—particularly so-called blue Mondays—are more likely to induce unpleasant emotions. In a study of the blue Monday effect, researchers asked that people who insisted their moods were lowest on Mondays keep daily diaries of their emotional states (Stone, Hedges, Neale, & Satin., 1985). The results indicated that a given person's emotional states tended to be similar on Monday, Tuesday, Wednesday, and Thursday. But as you might expect, the person's emotional state on weekend days—Friday, Saturday, and Sunday—tended to be more positive than on weekdays. It might be that our blue Mondays owe their blueness to the contrast of returning to our normal weekday emotional state rather than to something unique about Mondays. In essence, we might have blue Mondays, but we also have equally blue Tuesdays, Wednesdays, and Thursdays. We simply notice more the contrast between bright Sunday and blue Monday. There also is evidence that the expectation that Mondays will be blue might account in part for individuals reporting less positive moods on Mondays (Croft & Walker, 2001). Older and retired participants also are less likely to report changes in mood over the course of the week (Stone, Schneider, & Harter, 2012).

The experience of emotion varies in both its intensity and its pleasantness. People who tend to experience intensely pleasant emotions (such as elation) also tend to experience intensely unpleasant emotions (such as despair). People who tend to experience mildly pleasant emotions (such as gladness) also tend to experience mildly unpleasant emotions (such as disappointment). This variation might be one reason why our happiness depends more on the frequency than on the intensity of our positive emotional experiences. A second reason is that intensely positive events can make less intense positive events seem even less positive. And a third reason is that the happier you are when you succeed at a task, the unhappier you will be when you fail at it (Diener, Colvin, Pavot, & Allman, 1991).

There is evidence, however, that culture influences the experience of positive and negative emotions. One study compared self-reported emotional experiences in a number of situations in samples of undergraduates recruited from the University of Michigan and the University of Beijing. Positive and negative emotions were negatively correlated in the American sample. Thus, in situations that American participants experienced as very joyful and loving, they reported experiencing *less* sadness and fear. In contrast, ratings of positive and negative emotions were positively correlated in the Chinese sample. In situations that Chinese participants experienced as very joyful and loving, they reported experiencing *more* sadness and fear. Though gender differences were observed across cultures—the correlation for women in both samples was stronger than that for men—the researchers attributed these findings to cultural differences in the interpretation of positive and negative events. Americans appear to adopt an optimistic *or* pessimistic perspective, depending on the circumstances. In Chinese culture, successes are not celebrated with elation, because things might not turn out so well in the future. And the blow of failure may be softened by the thought that things might turn out better next time (Bagozzi, Wong, & Yi, 1999).

People tend to view pleasant emotions, such as happiness, as normal, and unpleasant emotions, such as depression, as abnormal (Sommers, 1984). Yet, until the past few decades, psychologists had conducted many more studies of unpleasant emotions. In fact, *Psychological Abstracts*, traditionally the main research tool of psychologists, first published in the 1920s, did not include the term *happiness* in its index until 1973 (Diener, 1984). Another perusal of *Psychological Abstracts* found that it contained more emotion-related references under the category of "pathology" than under any other category (Whissell, 1984). To counter the traditional overemphasis placed on unpleasant emotions, and because unpleasant emotions such as anxiety and depression are discussed in later chapters, this chapter discusses the topics of happiness and humor.

Happiness

Many philosophers have considered happiness, what researchers in the field now call *subjective well-being*, the highest good (Diener, Suh, Lucas, & Smith, 1999). Thomas Jefferson even made happiness a central issue in the Declaration of Independence. Most people—

regardless of age, nationality, or gender—report being at least moderately happy (Myers, 2000). Factors that correlate with happiness in cultures around the world include political systems that promote human rights and societal and economic equality (Diener, 2013). Financial satisfaction is positively correlated with life satisfaction—but only if it is associated with financial satisfaction and optimism (Diener, Tay, & Oishi, 2013). Happiness is positively correlated with intelligence, social skills, and family support (Diener & Fujita, 1995). Physical attractiveness has a positive correlation with happiness. But this relationship does not necessarily mean that physical attractiveness causes happiness. Perhaps happy people make themselves more physically attractive. For example, happy people are more likely to wear attractive clothing, jewelry, and hairstyles (Diener, Wolsic, & Fujita, 1995).

Happiness also is related to marital status. A cross-cultural study found that married people were, on average, happier than unmarried people. This finding held equally true for men and women. Happiness was more weakly associated with simply living together unmarried. The role of marriage in promoting happiness was linked to improved health and financial security (Stack & Eshleman, 1998), but the two most important factors in happiness are, first, one's state of health and, second, one's personality (DeNeve, 1999). Personality factors that correlate highly with happiness are trust, extraversion, agreeableness, self-esteem, emotional stability, and a sense of personal control (DeNeve & Cooper, 1998). Happiness is strongly related to what has been called *stable extraversion*, that is, being outgoing but not out of control (Steel & Ones, 2002). The association between extraversion and happiness has gained support from studies not only in Western cultures but also in non-Western cultures, such as China (Lu & Shih, 1997). And cross-cultural research has found that happy people place more emphasis on the best and most satisfying aspects of their lives when evaluating their levels of happiness (Diener, Lucas, Oishi, & Suh, 2002).

Cultural differences are found, though, in what makes people feel good. One research study investigated the correlates of positive emotions in a sample of 283 American and 630 Japanese male and female undergraduates. Results indicated that among Japanese participants—who live in a culture that values interdependence—positive emotions were correlated with social emotions (such as feeling friendly toward others). In contrast, among American participants—who live in a culture that values independence—positive emotions were correlated with personal emotions (such as feeling pride in a personal accomplishment) (Kitayama, Markus, & Kurokawa, 2000). As you will see in Chapter 13, these differences may be attributable to how the self is construed in individualistic and collectivistic cultures.

Social-Comparison Theory

Our happiness depends on comparisons we make between ourselves and others and between our current circumstances and our past circumstances (Diener, Oishi, & Lucas, 2003). Charles Montesquieu, an 18th-century French philosopher, noted: "If one only wished to be happy, this could be easily accomplished; but we wish to be happier than other people, and this is always difficult, for we believe others to be happier than they are." One of the most influential theories of happiness—**social-comparison theory**—shares Montesquieu's assumption about the nature of happiness. This theory considers happiness to be the result of estimating that one's life circumstances are more favorable than those of others (VanderZee, Buunk, & Sanderman, 1996), such as when you discover that your grade is one of the highest in the class. In one study, college students felt happier about themselves when in the presence of another person who was relatively worse off (Strack, Schwarz, Chassein, & Kern, 1990). Thus, you can make yourself happier with your own life by purposely comparing it with the lives of those who are less fortunate.

One factor in social comparison that is less important than commonly believed is wealth. Though there is an association between economic well-being and happiness (Schyns, 1998), wealth does not necessarily bring greater happiness. According to happiness researcher Edward Diener (1984), wealthy Americans are no happier than nonwealthy Americans, provided that the nonwealthy people have at least the basic necessities of life, such as a job, home, and family. Though this finding holds true in the United States,

social-comparison theory The theory that happiness is the result of estimating that one's life circumstances are more favorable than those of others.

it does not hold true in all cultures. For example, a study of people in 39 other countries found a stronger relationship between high income and happiness than in the United States (Diener, Sandvik, Seidlitz, & Diener, 1993). Overall, based on surveys in countries throughout the world, Diener concludes that with the possible exception of people living in impoverished societies, most people are happy (Diener & Diener, 1996). In fact, most people believe they are happier than the average person, apparently because we attend to our own level of contentment more than other people's (Klar & Giladi, 1999).

Adaptation-Level Theory

Adaptation-level theory holds that happiness depends not on comparing yourself with other people but on comparing yourself with yourself. Thus, your current happiness depends in part on comparing your present circumstances and your past circumstances. Your present state of happiness is governed more by the most recent events in your life than by the more distant events (Suh, Diener, & Fujita, 1996). But as your circumstances improve, your standard of happiness becomes higher. This increase can have surprising emotional consequences for people who gain sudden financial success. Life's small pleasures might no longer make them happy—their standards of happiness might become too high, as revealed by a study of Illinois state lottery winners (Brickman, Coates, & Janoff-Bulman, 1978). Despite winning from $50,000 to $1 million, these winners were no happier than they had been in the past. In fact, they found less pleasure in formerly enjoyable everyday activities, such as watching television, shopping for clothes, or talking with a friend. So, though comparing our circumstances with those of less-fortunate people can make us happier, improvements in our own circumstances might make us adopt increasingly higher standards of happiness—making happiness more and more elusive. Recognizing this problem, the 19th-century clergyman Henry Van Dyke remarked, "It is better to desire the things we have than to have the things we desire."

adaptation-level theory The theory that happiness depends on comparing one's present circumstances with one's past circumstances.

Humor

Happiness is enhanced by humor, whether offered by friends, funny movies, situation comedies on television, or stand-up comedians in nightclubs. Psychologists have only recently begun to study humor scientifically. Research findings support the importance of humor in our everyday lives. Humor promotes romance (Lundy, Tan, & Cunningham, 1998), defuses interpersonal conflict (Brown & Keegan, 1999), contributes to effective teaching (Wanzer & Frymier, 1999), creates positive patient-physician rapport (Sala, Krupat, & Roter, 2002), and reduces the effects of stress (Abel, 2002), psychological distress, and anxiety (Szabo, 2003). Advertisers make good use of humor, realizing that viewers show better recall of humorous than nonhumorous advertisements (Krishnan & Chakravarti, 2003). And restaurant servers who display a sense of humor tend to get larger tips from customers (Guègen, 2002).

Money Does Not Necessarily Buy Happiness

If you buy lottery tickets because you believe that winning the jackpot would make you happy, you might be in for a disappointment should you someday win. Lottery winners often are no happier after they win than when they were broke. In fact, they might no longer gain satisfaction from life's little pleasures.
Source: Ilya Shapovalov/Shutterstock.com.

Chapter 12 Emotion

One surprising finding has been that humorous people might not feel as extraverted as they act. Consider the class clown, who sees humor in everything. Though that person might be popular, she might not be as sociable as you might expect; she might, instead, use humor as a way to avoid close personal relationships. For example, a study of humorous adolescents found that they often used humor to maintain their social distance from other people (Prasinos & Tittler, 1981). You may have been frustrated at one time or another by such people, who joke about everything, rarely converse in a serious manner, and never disclose their personal feelings. Evidence that some people use humor to maintain their social distance might explain anecdotal reports that many comedians, who might appear socially outgoing in public performances, are socially reclusive in their private lives. Johnny Carson, who retired in 1992 after 30 years as host of the *Tonight Show*, was humorous and engaging on stage but relatively somber and socially aloof off stage.

Granted that humorous people might not be as gregarious as they seem, we are still left with the question: What makes their humor amusing? The brain, particularly the right hemisphere, plays an important role. For example, damage to the right frontal lobe disrupts humor appreciation, including diminished smiling and laughing, more than damage to other parts of the brain (Shammi & Stuss, 1999). Though the brain is important in humor appreciation, we know more about psychological factors that affect our reactions to humor. For example, there are cross-cultural commonalities as well as differences in what people view as humorous, as demonstrated in a study of German and Italian adults' reactions to jokes and cartoons. The participants gave similar rankings for the quality of the jokes and cartoons, but Germans, compared to Italians, rated nonsense humor as funnier and sexual humor as less funny (Ruch & Forabosco, 1996). Another factor is the social context, such as night clubs, in which humor is expressed. To people who are inebriated, comedians who use blunt, simple humor will seem funnier than comedians who use subtle, complex humor (Weaver, Masland, Kharazmi, & Zillman, 1985). Thus, if you drank a few beers, you would probably find a Three Stooges movie more amusing and a Dennis Miller monologue less amusing. But what accounts for our responses to humor while in a sober state? The most popular theories are *disparagement theory*, *incongruity theory*, and *release theory* (Berger, 1987).

Disparagement Theory

disparagement theory The theory that humor is amusing when it makes one feel superior to other people.

According to C. L. Edson, a 20th-century American newspaper editor, "We love a joke that hands us a pat on the back while it kicks the other fellow down the stairs." Edson's comment indicates that he favored the **disparagement theory** of humor, first put forth by the 17th-century English philosopher Thomas Hobbes. Hobbes claimed that we feel amused when humor makes us feel superior to other people (Nevo, 1985). One study found that political conservatives found anti-left wing jokes as funnier and political liberals found anti-right wing jokes as funnier than jokes that disparaged members of their own political orientation (Braun & Preiser, 2013). Research supporting Hobbes's position has found that we are especially amused when we dislike those to whom we are made to feel superior (Wicker, Barron, & Willis, 1980). Satirists, newspaper columnists, and television commentators take this approach by disparaging certain commonly disliked groups, such as greedy lawyers, crooked politicians, and phony evangelists.

We also like disparaging humor better when we like the person doing the disparaging. Consider David Letterman, former host of the *Late Show*. Why is his disparaging humor perceived as funny? It is funny, in part, because many people find him likable. In a study in which students were presented with examples of Letterman's disparaging humor, those who found him likable rated his humor as funnier (Oppliger & Sherblom, 1992).

Incongruity Theory

incongruity theory The theory that humor is amusing when it brings together incompatible ideas in a surprising outcome that violates one's expectations.

In the 18th century, the German philosopher Immanuel Kant put forth an alternative theory of humor, **incongruity theory**. Incongruous humor brings together incompatible ideas in a surprising outcome that violates our expectations (Perlmutter, 2002), a technique commonly used in television commercials (Alden, Mukherjee, & Hoyer, 2000). Incongruous jokes tend to be perceived as more humorous than other jokes (Hillson &

Martin, 1994). Incongruity theory explains why many jokes require timing and may lose something on the second hearing—bad timing or repetition can destroy the incongruity (Kuhlman, 1985). The appreciation of incongruous humor varies with age and conservatism. A study of more than 4,000 participants aged 14 to 66 found that older people and more conservative people preferred incongruous humor more, and nonsense humor less, than did younger people and more liberal people (Ruch, McGhee, & Hehl, 1990).

Release Theory

Another theory of humor, **release theory**, is based on Sigmund Freud's claim that humor is a cathartic outlet for anxiety caused by repressed sexual or aggressive energy, as explained in his book *Jokes and Their Relationship to the Unconscious* (Freud, 1905). Humor can raise your level of anxiety—and then suddenly lower it, providing you relief so pleasurable that it can make you laugh (McCauley, Woods, Coolidge, & Kulick, 1983). Consider a study in which students were told they would be handling or taking blood samples from rats. As they approached the rats, they suddenly discovered that the rats were toys. The students then responded to questionnaires about their reactions to the situation. The more anxious and the more surprised they had been, the funnier they found the situation, thereby supporting release theory (Shurcliff, 1968). Release theory explains the popularity of humor that plays on our sexual anxieties by weaving a story that ends with a punch line that relieves our tension (Schill & O'Laughlin, 1984).

In a study bearing on the release theory of humor in regard to aggression, high school students were given a frustrating exam. Afterward, they were more likely to respond aggressively to a subsequent frustrating situation. But students who were exposed after the exam to a humorous situation that provoked laughter became less likely to respond aggressively to the later frustration. According to release theory, the students' laughter provided a cathartic experience, which released energy that would have provoked later aggression (Ziv, 1987).

A recent study tested another prediction from Freud's theory—that hostility toward women may underlie sexist humor. A sample of college undergraduates completed a series of attitude and personality inventories and rated 10 sexist cartoons on perceived funniness. Enjoyment of the sexist cartoons was positively correlated with rape-related beliefs and psychological, physical, and sexual aggression among men but not women. That is, men who were more tolerant of rape and were more aggressive also found the sexist cartoons to be more enjoyable. Women found the cartoons to be less acceptable and less enjoyable than men did—though women were not less likely to retell them (Ryan & Kanjorski, 1998). The results of this study suggest that despite some research supportive of release theory, sexual or aggressive humor does not usually reduce sexual or aggressive tendencies (Nevo & Nevo, 1983).

The field of humor research is relatively young, and more research is needed to uncover the factors that make people find amusement in one kind of humor but not in another. Such research might explain, for example, why advertisers in some cultures employ humor in some cultures whereas advertisers in other cultures do not (Laroche, Nepomuceno, Huang, & Richard, 2011).

release theory The theory that humor relieves anxiety caused by sexual or aggressive energy.

Section Review: The Experience of Emotion

1. What factors are associated with personal happiness?
2. What are the disparagement theory, the incongruity theory, and the release theory of humor?

Theories of Emotion

How do we explain emotional experience? Theories of emotion vary in their attention to physiology, behavior, and cognition.

Biopsychological Theories of Emotion

Though most theories of emotion recognize the importance of physiological factors, certain theories stress them.

The James-Lange Theory of Emotion

In the late 19th century, the American psychologist William James (1884) claimed that physiological changes precede emotional experiences. Because a Danish physiologist named Carl Lange (1834–1900) made the same claim at about the same time, it became known as the **James-Lange theory** (see Figure 12-4). Note that the theory violates the commonsense belief that physiological changes follow emotional experiences (see the "Psychology versus Common Sense" box).

James-Lange theory The theory that specific patterns of physiological changes evoke specific emotional experiences.

The Cannon-Bard Theory of Emotion

After rejecting the James-Lange theory of emotion, Walter Cannon (1927) and Philip Bard (1934) put forth their own theory, giving equal weight to physiological changes and cognitive processes. The **Cannon-Bard theory** (see Figure 12-4) claims that an emotion is produced when an event or object is perceived by the thalamus, a brain structure that conveys this information simultaneously to the cerebral cortex and to the skeletal muscles and sympathetic nervous system.

Cannon-Bard theory The theory that an emotion is produced when an event or object is perceived by the thalamus, which conveys this information simultaneously to the cerebral cortex and the skeletal muscles and sympathetic nervous system.

The cerebral cortex then uses memories of past experiences to determine the nature of the perceived event or object, providing the subjective experience of emotion. Meanwhile, the muscles and sympathetic nervous system provide the physiological arousal that prepares the individual to take action to adapt to the situation that evoked the emotion. Unlike the James-Lange theory, the Cannon-Bard theory assumes that different emotions are associated with the same state of physiological arousal. The Cannon-Bard theory has failed to gain research support, because the thalamus does not appear to play the role the researchers envisioned. But if the theory is recast in terms of the limbic system instead of the thalamus, it is supported by research findings. For example, though the thalamus might not directly cause emotional responses, it does relay sensory information to the amygdala, which then processes the information. This transfer can occur even when the cerebral cortex is removed; in one study, rats whose visual cortexes had been destroyed still learned to fear visual stimuli associated with pain (LeDoux, Romanski, & Xagoraris, 1989).

Research on victims of spinal cord damage has provided support for the Cannon-Bard theory while contradicting the James-Lange theory. Studies have found that even people with spinal cord injuries that prevent them from perceiving their bodily arousal experience distinct emotions just as intensely as people with intact spinal cords do (Cobos, Sanchez, Garcia, Vera, & Vila, 2002). This finding violates the James-Lange theory's assumption that emotional experience depends on the perception of bodily arousal, and supports the Cannon-Bard theory's assumption that emotional experience depends on the brain's perception of ongoing events. Of course, as you will learn later, research on victims of spinal cord damage does not rule out sensations from one's own facial expressions as a factor in emotional experience.

FIGURE 12-4
Theories of Emotion

According to the James-Lange theory, specific patterns of physiological changes evoke specific emotional experiences. According to the Cannon-Bard theory, activity in the thalamus precedes both arousal and emotional experience.

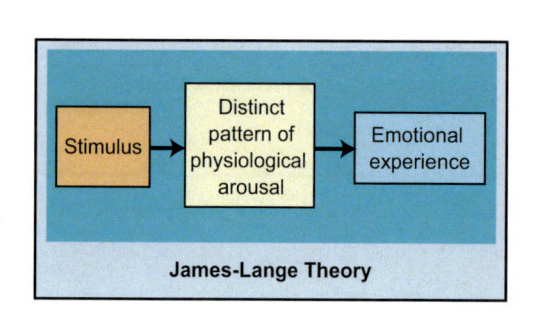

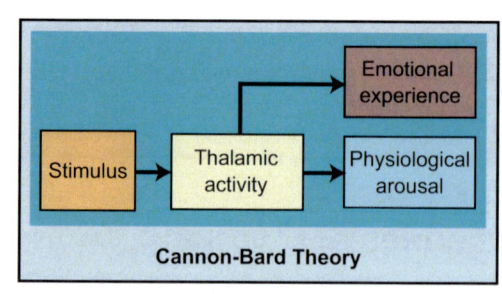

James-Lange Theory: Stimulus → Distinct pattern of physiological arousal → Emotional experience

Cannon-Bard Theory: Stimulus → Thalamic activity → Emotional experience / Physiological arousal

Psychology versus Common Sense

Do Emotional Experiences Depend on Physical Responses to Emotional Situations?

The main implication of the James-Lange theory is that particular emotional events stimulate specific patterns of physiological changes, each evoking a specific emotional experience (Lang, 1994). According to James (1890/1981, Vol. 2, p. 1065),

> Commonsense says, we lose our fortune, are sorry and weep; we meet a bear, are frightened and run; we are insulted by a rival, are angry and strike . . . the more rational statement is that we feel sorry because we cry, angry because we strike, afraid because we tremble.

Your own experience might provide evidence in support of this theory. If you have ever barely avoided an automobile accident, you may have noticed your pulse racing and your palms sweating, and then a moment later found yourself overcome by fear.

The James-Lange theory provoked criticism from the American physiologist Walter Cannon (1927). One of his criticisms was based on his assumption that individuals are unable to perceive many of the subtle physiological changes induced by the sympathetic nervous system. How could the perception of physiological changes be the basis of emotional experiences when we cannot perceive many of those changes? In part because of Cannon's criticisms, the James-Lange theory fell into disfavor for several decades.

But recent research has lent some support to the James-Lange theory (Barbalet, 1999). One line of support for the theory comes from research studies showing that fear can be evoked by threatening situations before we are consciously aware of them. We will react behaviorally to fear-inducing situations before we experience the emotion consciously. This process might have evolved because it is an adaptive, potentially life-saving process that permits us to react more quickly to confront or flee from a threat than we would if we had to first become consciously aware of it (Robinson, 1998). Other sources of evidence that we can react to emotional stimuli without being consciously aware of them (Mayer & Merckelbach, 1999) are discussed in Chapters 5 and 6.

Cannon also noted that different emotions are associated with the same pattern of physiological arousal. How could different emotions be evoked by the same pattern of arousal? In a study that supported the basic assumptions of the James-Lange theory, participants were directed to adopt facial expressions representing fear, anger, disgust, sadness, surprise, and happiness (Ekman, Levenson, & Friesen, 1983). Participants were told which muscles to contract or relax but were not told which emotions they were expressing. Recordings of heart rate and skin temperature were taken as they maintained the facial expressions. The results supported the assumption that the physiological changes underlying emotional responses to situations can occur before we consciously experience an emotion.

The results also supported the assumption that different behavioral reactions can induce different patterns of physiological activity. The facial expression of fear induced a large increase in heart rate and a slight decrease in finger temperature, whereas the facial expression of anger induced a large increase in both heart rate and finger temperature. Finger temperature varies with the amount of blood flow: A decrease in blood flow causes a decrease in temperature, and an increase in blood flow causes an increase in temperature. The presence of different patterns of autonomic activity for different emotions has been replicated in Western cultures (Christie & Friedman, 2004) and non-Western cultures, such as West Sumatra (Levenson, Ekman, Heider, & Friesen, 1992).

Note our everyday language: When we are afraid, we have "cold feet," and when we are angry, our "blood is boiling." The difference in the patterns of physiological arousal between fear and anger supports the assumption of the James-Lange theory that particular emotions are associated with particular patterns of physiological arousal. More recent studies have lent further support to the specificity of autonomic nervous system responses in different emotions. In one study, children watched the film *E.T., The Extraterrestrial* while being monitored physiologically. Scenes that evoked sadness were associated with greater variability in heart rate and blood oxygenation than were scenes that evoked happiness (Miller & Wood, 1997). In another study, participants had six of their autonomic nervous system responses, including heart rate and skin blood flow, monitored after inhaling five fragrances that produced different emotional responses. As predicted by the James-Lange theory, each of the fragrances was associated with its own pattern of autonomic activity (Alaoui-Ismaieli, Vernet-Maury, Dittmar, Delhomme, & Chanel, 1997).

opponent-process theory The theory that the brain counteracts a strong positive or negative emotion by evoking an opposite emotional response.

facial-feedback theory The theory that particular facial expressions induce particular emotional experiences.

The Opponent-Process Theory of Emotion

In anticipating another theory of emotion, Plato, in the Phaedo, states:

> How strange would appear to be this thing that we call pleasure! And how curiously it is related to what is thought to be its opposite, pain! The two will never be found together in a man, and yet if you seek the one and obtain it, you are almost bound always to get the other as well, just as though they were both attached to one and the same head. . . . Wherever the one is found, the other follows up behind. So, in my case, since I had pain in my leg as a result of the fetters, pleasure seems to have come to follow it up.

If Plato were alive today, he might favor the **opponent-process theory** of emotion (see Figure 12-5), which holds that the mammalian brain has evolved mechanisms that counteract strong positive or negative emotions by evoking an opposite emotional response to maintain homeostasis. According to Richard Solomon (1980), who first put forth the theory, the opposing emotion begins sometime after the onset of the first emotion and lasts longer than the first emotion. If we experience the first emotion on repeated occasions, the opposing emotion grows stronger, and the emotion that is experienced becomes a compromise between the two opposing emotional states.

Suppose that you took up skydiving. The first time you parachuted from an airplane you would probably feel terror. After surviving the jump, your feeling of terror would be replaced by a feeling of relief. As you jumped again and again, you would feel anticipation instead of terror as you prepared to jump. And your initial post-jump feeling of relief might intensify into a feeling of exhilaration.

The opponent-process theory might help explain the "baby blues" that often follow the joy of childbirth or the euphoria that often follows the anxiety of final exams week. It might even explain why some blood donors become seemingly "addicted" to donating blood. When a person first donates blood, she might experience fear—but afterward might experience a pleasant feeling known as the "warm glow" effect. If the person repeatedly donates blood, the warm glow strengthens, leading the person to donate blood in order to induce that feeling (Piliavin, Callero, & Evans, 1982).

The opponent-process theory implies that our brains are programmed against hedonism, because people who experience intense pleasure are doomed to experience intense displeasure. This theory provides support for those who favor the "happy medium"—moderation in everything, including emotional experiences.

The Facial-Feedback Theory of Emotion

Benjamin Franklin claimed, "A cheerful face is nearly as good for an invalid as healthy weather." Have you ever received the advice "Put on a happy face" or "Keep a stiff

FIGURE 12-5
The Opponent-Process Theory

According to the opponent-process theory, when we experience an emotion (A), an opposing emotion (B) will counter the first emotion, dampening the experience of that emotion (as indicated by the steady level of A being lower than the peak of A). As we experience the first emotion (A') on repeated occasions, the opposing emotion (B') becomes stronger and the first emotion weaker, which leads to an even weaker experience of the first emotion (as indicated by the steady level of A' being lower than the peak of A'). For example, the first time you drove on a highway you might have experienced fear, followed by a feeling of relief. As you drove on highways on repeated occasions, your feeling of fear eventually gave way to a feeling of mild arousal.

Source: From R. L. Solomon, "The Opponent-Process Theory of Acquired Motivation: The Costs of Pleasure and Benefits of Pain" in *American Psychologist*, 35: 691–712. Copyright © 1980 by the American Psychological Association. Reprinted with permission.

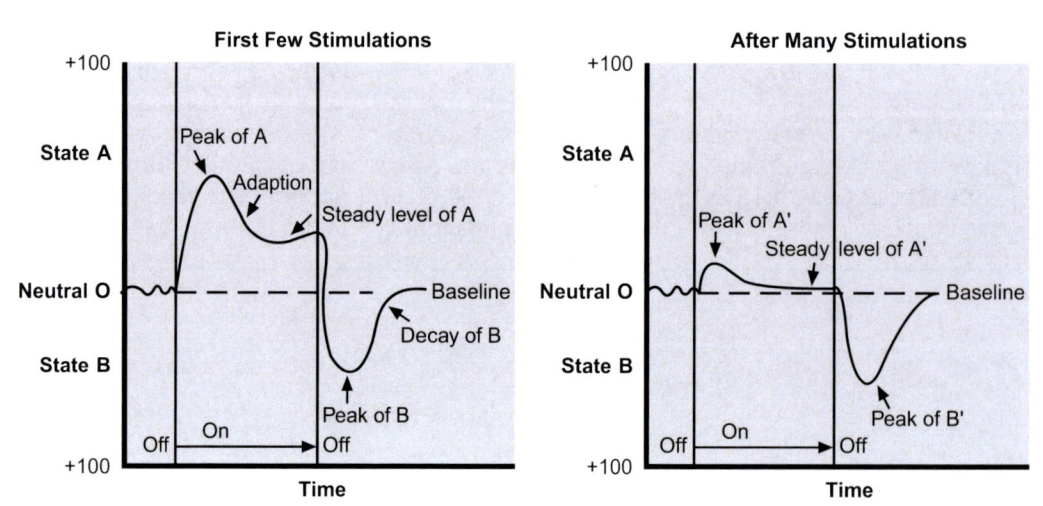

upper lip" from people trying to help you overcome adversity? Both these bits of advice are commonsense versions of the **facial-feedback theory** of emotion (see Figure 12-6), which holds that our facial expressions affect our emotional experiences. Because it assumes that emotional experience is caused by the perception of physiological changes, the James-Lange theory inspired the facial-feedback theory (Izard, 1990b). As you learned in the discussion of the James-Lange theory, adopting a facial expression characteristic of a particular emotion can induce that emotion (Ekman, Levenson, & Friesen, 1983). But unlike the James-Lange theory, which primarily is concerned with the effects of autonomic nervous system activity on emotion, the facial-feedback theory is limited to the effects of facial expressions.

The facial-feedback theory was put forth in 1907 by the French physician Israel Waynbaum and recently has been restated in various versions. Waynbaum assumed that particular facial expressions alter the flow of blood to particular regions of the brain, thereby evoking particular emotional experiences. For example, smiling might increase the flow of blood to regions of the brain that elevate mood (Zajonc, 1985). A descendant of Waynbaum's theory, called the vascular theory, assumes that changes in facial expressions affect the volume of air flow through the nose, which alters brain temperature and, as a result, influences emotional states. The theory assumes that increased airflow cools the brain and induces positive moods, whereas decreased airflow warms the brain and induces negative moods. The theory received support from a study in which participants who adopted negative facial expressions had reduced nasal airflow and experienced more negative moods (McIntosh, Zajonc, Vig, & Emerick, 1997). Because the vascular theory is relatively new, more research is needed to assess its validity.

Most contemporary facial-feedback theorists, led by Paul Ekman (1992b), assume that evolution has endowed us with facial expressions that provide different patterns of sensory feedback of muscle tension levels to the brain, thereby evoking different emotions. Support for the theory has come from studies that have found that emotional experiences follow facial expressions rather than precede them, and that sensory neurons convey information from facial muscles directly to the hypothalamus, which plays an important role in emotional arousal (Zajonc, 1985).

But the facial-feedback theory has not received unqualified support. Though there is a positive association between particular facial expressions and particular emotional experiences (Adelmann & Zajonc, 1989), the effect of facial feedback on emotional experience tends to be small (Matsumoto, 1987). Some studies also have found that emotional experience depends more on feedback from autonomic nervous system organs than on feedback from facial muscles (Buck, 1980). Another study found that facial feedback *and* body posture contributed to participants' emotional experience (Flack, Laird, & Cavallaro, 1999). And a case study of a woman with facial paralysis revealed that though she was unable to generate facial expressions of emotion, her self-reported responses to emotional stimuli did not differ from a healthy control sample (Keillor, Barrett, Crucian, Kortenkamp, & Heilman, 2002). Apparently, feedback from facial expressions is just one of several factors that govern our emotional experiences.

Though facial expressions might not be the sole cause of emotions, they can affect the intensity of ongoing emotions and induce emotions (McIntosh, 1996), with positive facial expressions inducing positive moods and negative facial expressions inducing negative moods (Kleinke, Peterson, & Rutledge, 1998). Try smiling and then frowning, and note the subtle differences they induce in your mood. For example, participants who respond with a genuine Duchenne smile to pleasant stimuli report more positive affect—and different pat-terns of autonomic arousal—than participants who view the same stimuli with pursed lips (Soussignan, 2002). In one study, heterosexual female participants were asked to imagine three pleasant scenes and three unpleasant scenes (McCanne & Anderson, 1987). The three pleasant scenes were "You get a 4.0 grade point average," "You inherit a million dollars," and "You meet the man of your dreams." The three unpleasant scenes were "Your mother dies," "You lose a really close friendship," and "You lose a limb in an accident."

Fear and Euphoria

According to the opponent-process theory of emotion, the fear that this skier experienced when he first learned to ski eventually gave way to a feeling of euphoria.
Source: lm_photo/Shutterstock.com.

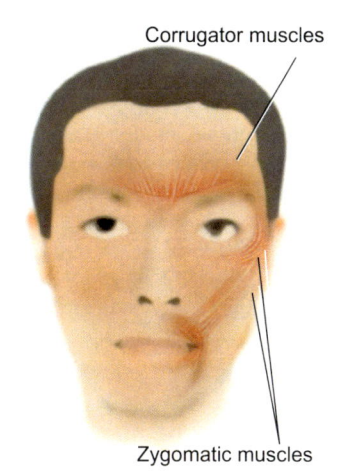

FIGURE 12-6
The Facial-Feedback Theory

According to the facial-feedback theory of emotion, particular patterns of sensory feedback from facial expressions evoke particular emotions. Thus, sensory feedback from the corrugator muscles, which are active when we frown, might contribute to unpleasant emotional experiences. Similarly, sensory feedback from the zygomatic muscles, which are active when we smile, might contribute to pleasant emotional experiences.

Participants imagined each scene three times. The first time they simply imagined the scene. The second time they imagined the scene while maintaining increased muscle tension in one of two muscle groups: either muscles that control smiling or muscles that control frowning. Through the use of biofeedback (see Chapter 7), participants learned to tense only the target muscles. The third time they imagined the scene, participants were instructed to suppress muscle tension in either their smiling muscles or their frowning muscles. On each occasion, participants were asked to report the degree of enjoyment or distress they experienced while imagining the scene. The results provided some support for the facial-feedback theory. Participants reported less enjoyment when imagining pleasant scenes while suppressing activity in their smiling muscles, and they reported less distress when imagining unpleasant scenes while suppressing activity in their frowning muscles.

Cognitive Theories of Emotion

More recent theories of emotion emphasize the importance of cognition. They assume that our emotional experiences depend on our subjective interpretation of situations in which we find ourselves.

The Two-Factor Theory of Emotion

two-factor theory The theory that emotional experience is the outcome of physiological arousal and the attribution of a cause for that arousal.

Stanley Schachter and Jerome Singer's **two-factor theory** (see Figure 12-7) views emotional experience as the outcome of two factors: physiological arousal and the attribution of a cause for it (see "The Research Process" box).

The Cognitive-Appraisal Theory of Emotion

cognitive-appraisal theory The theory that our emotion at a given time depends on our interpretation of the situation we are in at that time.

Though Schachter and Singer's two-factor theory has failed to gain strong support, it has stimulated interest in the cognitive basis of emotion. The purest cognitive theory of emotion is the **cognitive-appraisal theory** of Richard Lazarus (1993a). Unlike the two-factor theory, the cognitive-appraisal theory downplays the role of physiological arousal. Like the two-factor theory, the cognitive-appraisal theory assumes that our emotion at a given time depends on our interpretation of the situation we are in at that time. If we develop inflexible, maladaptive ways of appraising situations, we may develop emotional disorders (Lazarus, 1995). The cognitive appraisal of specific kinds of situations is consistent across different cultures, though cognitive appraisals vary somewhat from the norm in certain cultures. This conclusion was supported by a study of almost 3,000 people in 37 countries who had been asked to recall their cognitive appraisal of recent events associated with feelings of joy, fear, shame, guilt, anger, disgust, and sadness (Scherer, 1997).

This cognitive view of emotion is not new. In *Hamlet*, Shakespeare wrote: "There is nothing either good or bad, but thinking makes it so." Cognitive appraisal can affect your emotions as you prepare for an exam. One study tracked college undergraduates' emotional states and appraisals of an upcoming exam. Compared to participants who appraised the exam as a threat, participants who appraised the exam as a challenge were more confident about their coping ability and experienced more positive emotions prior to the exam (Skinner & Brewer, 2002). People whose jobs require them to confront human pain, illness, and death find that cognitively reappraising situations, perhaps by finding meaning even in the worst disasters, helps them cope emotionally (McCammon, Durham, Allison, & Williamson, 1988).

FIGURE 12-7
The Two-Factor Theory

According to Schachter and Singer's two-factor theory, physiological arousal and a causal attribution combine to produce emotional experiences.

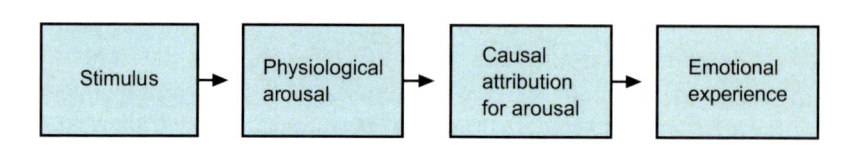

Stimulus → Physiological arousal → Causal attribution for arousal → Emotional experience

The Research Process

Do Emotions Depend on Our Attribution of a Cause for Our Physiological Arousal?

Rationale
According to Schachter and Singer, when you experience physiological arousal, you search for its source. Your attribution of a cause for your arousal determines the emotion that you experience. For example, if you experience intense physiological arousal in the presence of an appealing person, you might attribute your arousal to that person and, as a result, feel that you are attracted to him or her.

The two-factor theory resembles the James-Lange theory in assuming that emotional experience follows physiological arousal (Winton, 1990). But it is different from the James-Lange theory in holding, as does the Cannon-Bard theory, that all emotions involve similar patterns of physiological arousal. But the Cannon-Bard theory assumes that emotional experience and physiological arousal occur simultaneously; the two-factor theory assumes instead that emotion follows the attribution of a cause for one's physiological arousal.

Method
The original experiment on the two-factor theory provided evidence that when we experience physiological arousal, we seek to identify its source, and that what we identify as the source in turn determines our emotional experience (Schachter & Singer, 1962). Male college student volunteers participated one at a time and were told that they were getting an injection of a new vitamin called "Suproxin" to assess its effect on vision. In reality, they received an injection of the hormone epinephrine, which activates the sympathetic nervous system. The epinephrine caused hand tremors, a flushed face, a pounding heart, and rapid breathing. Some participants (the informed group) were told to expect these changes. Some participants (the misinformed group) were told to expect itching, numb feet, and headache, and some (the uninformed group) were told nothing about the effects. Other participants received a placebo injection of a saline solution instead of an injection of epinephrine and were told nothing about its physiological effects.

The participant then waited in a room with the experimenter's accomplice, a man who acted either happy or angry. When acting happy, the accomplice was cheerful and threw paper airplanes, played with a Hula Hoop, and shot wads of paper into a wastebasket. When acting angry, the accomplice acted upset, stomped around, and complained about a questionnaire given by the experimenter, which included questions about the bathing habits of the respondent's family and the sex life of his mother. The participant's emotional response to the accomplice was assessed by observing him through a one-way mirror and by having him complete a questionnaire about his feelings.

Results and Discussion
The results showed that the informed participants were unaffected by the accomplice's behavior, whereas the misinformed participants and uninformed participants expressed and experienced emotions similar to those of the accomplice. But the placebo group also expressed and experienced situation-appropriate emotions despite the lack of drug-induced physiological arousal. Schachter and Singer concluded that the informed participants attributed their arousal to the injection and did not experience situation-appropriate emotions. In contrast, the misinformed participants and the uninformed participants attributed their physiological arousal to the situation they were in, responding positively when the accomplice acted happy and responding negatively when the accomplice acted angry. Schachter and Singer assumed that the placebo participants became physiologically aroused in response to the emotional display of the accomplice and interpreted their own feelings as congruent with those of the accomplice.

Since the original studies of the two-factor theory in the early 1960s, research has produced inconsistent findings. Consider the theory's assumption that unexplained physiological arousal can just as well provoke feelings of joy as provoke feelings of sadness, depending on the person's interpretation of the source of the arousal. This assumption was contradicted by a study in which participants received injections of epinephrine without being informed of its true effects. The participants tended to experience negative emotions regardless of their immediate social environment. Even those in the presence of a happy person tended to experience unpleasant emotions (Marshall & Zimbardo, 1979). A review of research on Schachter and Singer's two-factor theory concluded that the only assumption of the theory that has been consistently supported is that physiological arousal misattributed to an outside source will intensify an emotional experience. There is little evidence that such a misattribution will cause an emotional experience (Reisenzein, 1983). More recent research has likewise provided mixed support for the two-factor theory (Mezzacappa, Katkin, & Palmer, 1999; Neumann, 2000).

An early study by Lazarus and his colleagues supported the cognitive-appraisal theory of emotion (Speisman, Lazarus, Mordkoff, & Davison, 1964). The participants watched a film about a tribal ritual in which incisions were made on adolescents' penises. Participants' level of emotional arousal was measured by recording their heart rate and skin conductance an increase in the electrical conductivity of the skin, caused by sweating). Each participant watched the same film but heard different sound tracks. Those in the *silent group* saw the film without a sound track. Those in the *trauma group* were told that the procedure was extremely painful and emotionally distressing. Those in the *intellectualization group* were told about the procedure in a detached, matter-of-fact way, with no mention of feelings. And those in the *denial group* were told that the procedure was not painful and that the boys were overjoyed because it signified their entrance into manhood.

Recordings of the participants' physiological arousal showed that the trauma group experienced greater arousal than the silent group, which in turn experienced greater arousal than the denial and intellectualization groups. These findings indicate that subjective appraisal of the situation, rather than the objective situation itself, accounted for participants' emotional arousal. Lazarus (1993b) has applied his theory of cognitive appraisal in helping individuals cope with stressful situations—a topic discussed in Chapter 16. More recent studies provide additional support for the assumption that your interpretation of a situation affects your emotional state (Wolgast, Lundh, & Viborg, 2011). Consider a situation that is all too familiar to people who fly frequently—lost luggage. A study of more than 100 airline passengers who had reported that their luggage was lost found that their emotional response to the loss depended on their cognitive appraisal of it (Scherer & Ceschi, 1997).

Moreover, there are cultural differences in the cognitive appraisal of personal experiences of success and failure. Participants were 67 European American students at the University of Michigan and 58 Japanese students at Kanazawa University. Participants rated their emotional responses to a situation involving personal success or failure (for example, getting a grade that was better or worse than usual) or social success or failure (for example, getting along well with someone versus not getting along well with someone). Results indicated that American participants felt proud of their successes and angry or unlucky when they failed. Japanese participants felt lucky when they succeeded and shameful when they failed. The researchers attributed these findings to cross-cultural differences in appraisals about the meaning of success and failure to the self. American participants attributed their successes to themselves and their failures to the situation or other external factors, whereas Japanese participants attributed their successes to the situation and their failures to themselves (Imada & Ellsworth, 2011). As you will read in Chapters 13 and 17, this is consistent with cross-cultural differences in construals of the self and causal attributions.

But the cognitive-appraisal theory has been challenged by Robert Zajonc (1984) and others, who insist that cognitive appraisal is not essential to the experience of emotion. For example, you probably have taken an instant liking or disliking to a person without knowing why. And, as noted in Chapter 6, research findings show that we can respond emotionally to stimuli we are unaware of (Dimberg, Thunberg, & Elmehed, 2000). This and other evidence indicates that emotional experience can take place without conscious cognitive appraisal (Izard, 1993).

There even is physiological evidence for this phenomenon, because of the direct pathways from the thalamus (which relays sensory input to other brain regions) to the limbic system (which plays an important role in emotional processing). These pathways bypass the cerebral cortex, the involvement of which seems required for conscious cognitive appraisal (see Figure 12-8). Thus, we can have emotional reactions to stimuli of which we are unaware (LeDoux, 1986).

What can we conclude from the variety of contradictory theories of emotion? The best we can do is to realize that none of them is sufficient to explain emotion, though each describes a process that contributes to it. Moreover, the theories illustrate the importance of the physiological, expressive, and experiential components of emotion.

FIGURE 12-8
Pathways for Emotion

This schematic drawing of a lateral view of the brain shows structures involved in the control and generation of emotion. The thalamus receives sensory input and relays information to the amygdala or cortex. Rapid responses of emotion, such as fear, are channeled through the amygdala. This pathway does not have cortical processing, which may explain why some emotions occur before any conscious appraisal. More careful assessment of emotions uses cortical circuits.

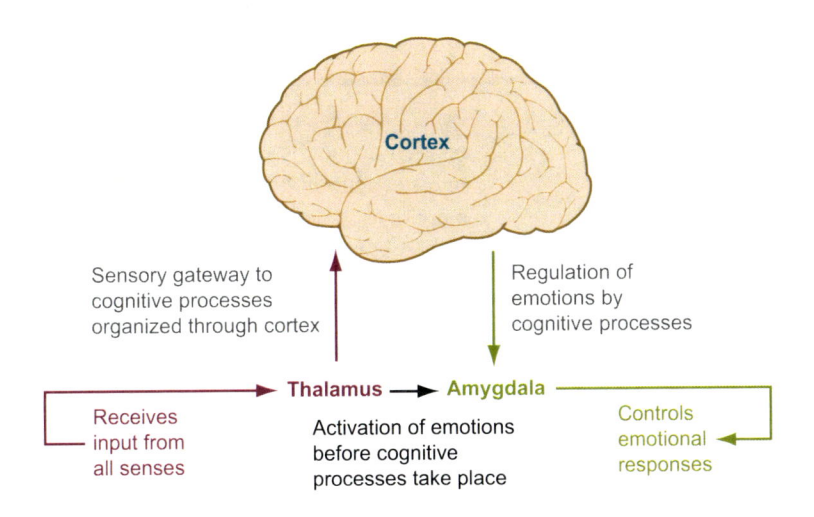

Section Review: Theories of Emotion

1. What evidence is there for and against the James-Lange theory of emotion?
2. How has research supported the facial-feedback theory of emotion?
3. What does research conducted since Schachter and Singer's classic study say about their two-factor theory of emotion?

Experiencing Psychology

Are Humorous Professors More Effective Teachers?

Rationale

As mentioned in the chapter section "Humor," research has found that humor is related to teaching effectiveness. To test this claim, you will be asked to conduct a study of the relationship between professors' use of humor and students' performance on exams. Feel free to alter the proposed study to suit your own circumstances.

Method

Participants

The participants will be college students and their professors. The more participants you use, the better. Be sure to ask your introductory psychology professor about ethical issues that will have to be addressed before conducting the study. These issues include deception, confidentiality, informed consent, and post-study debriefing.

Materials

The students will record instances of professorial humor during their lectures. You will have to agree on the kinds of behavior that will be considered examples of humor and create data sheets to record them.

Procedure

Have each student record instances of professorial humor (including bad humor) for three class lectures with each of the professors they have for lecture courses. No student should use data from the same professor. Add up the number of instances of humor for each class session. Also have the students write down their latest exam score (as a percentage) in each of their lecture classes. All data should be anonymous in regard to the names of the students and the names of the professors.

Results and Discussion

Find the mean number of instances of humor for each professor. Calculate a Pearson's correlation (see Appendix C in the Online Edition) pairing each professor's mean number of instances of humor and the associated student exam score. Draw a scattergram (see Appendix C in the Online Edition) of the relationship between in-stances of humor and student exam scores.

How strong is the correlation? What do you infer from that? What is the direction of the correlation? What do you infer from that? Would a large, positive correlation mean that professorial humor *causes* better student grades? Note any shortcomings of the study and suggest how to improve it.

Chapter 12 Emotion

Chapter Summary

The Biopsychology of Emotion

- Emotion is a motivated state marked by physiological arousal, expressive behavior, and cognitive experience.
- Emotional arousal depends on activity in the autonomic nervous system and the limbic system.
- The lie detector, or polygraph, test assumes that differences in physiological arousal in response to control questions and relevant questions can be used to determine whether a person is lying.
- Critics point out that the polygraph test can be fooled and that it has poor validity because it finds a large proportion of guilty people innocent and an even larger proportion of innocent people guilty.
- A promising alternative to the traditional polygraph test is the Guilty Knowledge Test, which depends on the guilty person's physiological arousal to important facts about his or her transgression.
- The left cerebral hemisphere plays a greater role in positive emotions; the right cerebral hemisphere plays a greater role in negative emotions.
- Neurotransmitters, including endorphins, alter our moods by affecting neuronal activity.

The Expression of Emotion

- We express our emotions behaviorally through changes in vocal qualities, body movements, and facial expressions.
- Charles Darwin believed that facial expressions evolved because they communicate emotions and help individuals distinguish friend from foe.
- The hereditary basis of facial expressions is supported by research showing cross-cultural similarity in the positive association between particular facial expressions and particular emotions.

The Experience of Emotion

- Robert Plutchik considers the basic emotions to be joy, fear, anger, disgust, sadness, surprise, acceptance, and anticipation.
- Emotions vary in their intensity and pleasantness; people who tend to experience intensely pleasant emotions are also likely to experience intensely unpleasant emotions.
- Psychologists have only recently begun to study pleasant emotions, such as happiness and humor-induced amusement, to the same extent as unpleasant emotions.
- According to social-comparison theory, happiness is the result of estimating that one's life circumstances are more favorable than those of others.
- According to adaptation-level theory, happiness depends on estimating that one's current life circumstances are more favorable than one's past life circumstances.
- Humor is explained by disparagement theory, incongruity theory, and release theory.

Theories of Emotion

- The James-Lange theory assumes that physiological changes precede emotional experiences and that different patterns of physiological arousal are associated with different emotions.
- The Cannon-Bard theory claims that the thalamus perceives an event and communicates this information to the cerebral cortex (which provides the subjective experience of emotion) and stimulates the physiological arousal characteristic of emotion.
- According to the opponent-process theory, the brain has evolved mechanisms that counteract strong positive or negative emotions by evoking an opposite emotional response.
- If the first emotion is repeated, the opposing emotion gradually strengthens and the first emotion gradually weakens, until a more moderate response becomes habitual.
- According to the facial-feedback theory, different emotions are caused by sensory feedback from different facial expressions.
- The two-factor theory views emotional experience as the consequence of attributing physiological arousal to a particular aspect of one's immediate environment.
- Cognitive-appraisal theory ignores the role of physiological arousal and considers emotional experience to be solely the result of a person's interpretation of her or his current circumstances.

Key Terms

emotion (p. 414)

The Biopsychology of Emotion

fight-or-flight response (p. 414)
Guilty Knowledge Test (p. 418)
polygraph test (p. 416)

The Expression of Emotion

prosody (p. 422)

The Experience of Emotion

adaptation-level theory (p. 429)
disparagement theory (p. 430)
incongruity theory (p. 430)
release theory (p. 431)
social-comparison theory (p. 428)

Theories of Emotion

Cannon-Bard theory (p. 432)
cognitive-appraisal theory (p. 436)
facial-feedback theory (p. 435)
James-Lange theory (p. 432)
opponent-process theory (p. 434)
two-factor theory (p. 436)

Chapter Quiz

Note: Answers for the Chapter Quiz questions are provided at the end of the book.

1. A vicious dog runs after you. You run for your front door, pull it open, and escape into your home—just before the dog reaches you. You notice that you are sweating and breathing heavily and that your heart is beating rapidly. Only then do you notice that you feel terrified. This experience would provide circumstantial evidence for the
   a. James-Lange theory.
   b. Cannon-Bard theory.
   c. facial-feedback theory.
   d. opponent-process theory.

2. A study of the polygraph printouts of 50 thieves and 50 innocent people (Kleinmuntz & Szucko, 1984a) found that the polygraph test was
   a. equally good in detecting guilty and innocent people.
   b. better at detecting guilty people than innocent people.
   c. better at detecting innocent people than guilty people.
   d. no better than flipping a coin in detecting whether a person is guilty or innocent.

3. The bodily arousal that underlies emotional experience is associated mainly with activity in the
   a. central nervous system.
   b. somatic nervous system.
   c. autonomic nervous system.
   d. extrapyramidal motor system.

4. A person suffers a bullet wound of the brain and begins to respond inappropriately to threatening situations, often showing no concern for her own safety. The bullet probably damaged her
   a. amygdala.
   b. cerebellum.
   c. basal ganglia.
   d. medulla.

5. A construction worker is accidentally struck on the head by an iron beam. After recovering, he seems to always be happy and laughs at almost everything. The accident probably damaged his
   a. superior colliculus.
   b. inferior colliculus.
   c. left cerebral hemisphere.
   d. right cerebral hemisphere.

6. An emotion comprises mental experience, physiological arousal, and
   a. drive reduction.
   b. expressive behavior.
   c. affective vacillation.
   d. unconscious motivation.

7. An Olympic-class runner finds it difficult to be happy, because every time she improves her performance her standard of happiness becomes higher. This phenomenon is best explained by
   a. incongruity theory.
   b. disparagement theory.
   c. adaptation-level theory.
   d. social-comparison theory.

8. A study of the blue Monday effect (Stone et al., 1985) found that
   a. there is a general blue weekday effect.
   b. we tend to be bluer on Monday than on other weekdays.
   c. weekend days make us feel even bluer than does Monday.
   d. moods tend to be more positive on Monday than on any other day.

9. You return home and realize that your parents are angry with you—because of the rate, pitch, and loudness of their speech—even though the words they are using are not angry words. You are basing your judgment of their emotional state on
   a. prosody.
   b. kinesics.
   c. proxemics.
   d. physiognomy.

10. A victim of an automobile accident suffers a brain injury that disrupts her fight-or-flight response to stressful situations. The accident probably injured her
    a. hypothalamus.
    b. basal ganglia.
    c. occipital lobe.
    d. adrenal glands.

11. When you are physiologically aroused, epinephrine is secreted by your
    a. hypothalamus.
    b. adrenal glands.
    c. thyroid gland.
    d. pituitary gland.

12. Goldstein (1980) injected subjects with naloxone or a placebo and asked them to estimate the intensity of their emotional thrill in response to a musical passage. Because the placebo group experienced more intense feelings, his findings indicated that the positive feelings evoked by music may be related to the secretion of
    a. dopamine.
    b. endorphins.
    c. glutamic acid.
    d. acetylcholine.

Chapter 12 Emotion   441

13. Research indicates that negative emotions are primarily associated with activity in the
    a. thalamus.
    b. brainstem.
    c. left cerebral hemisphere.
    d. right cerebral hemisphere.

14. Target organs in the sympathetic nervous system are regulated by
    a. dopamine.
    b. epinephrine.
    c. acetylcholine.
    d. norepinephrine.

15. A scientist using sophisticated recording equipment finds that when you are happy you exhibit a consistent, specific pattern of physiological changes that slightly precede your emotional experience. This finding would support the
    a. two-factor theory.
    b. James-Lange theory.
    c. Cannon-Bard theory.
    d. opponent-process theory.

16. After a harrowing automobile ride to school over icy roads, you arrive physiologically aroused. You notice a fellow student whom you find to be more romantically attractive than you have in the past. The best explanation for your emotion would be provided by the
    a. two-factor theory.
    b. James-Lange theory.
    c. Cannon-Bard theory.
    d. opponent-process theory.

17. The Duchenne smile
    a. indicates lying.
    b. is a natural smile.
    c. indicates possible brain damage.
    d. is used in threat displays by animals.

18. The first time you canoe through white water on a river, you may be terrified. If you go white-water canoeing repeatedly, you will eventually instead feel exhilarated. This emotional experience would be explained best by the
    a. two-factor theory.
    b. James-Lange theory.
    c. Cannon-Bard theory.
    d. opponent-process theory.

19. "There is nothing either good or bad, but thinking makes it so." This line from Shakespeare's *Hamlet* bears a kinship to the
    a. James-Lange theory.
    b. Cannon-Bard theory.
    c. opponent-process theory.
    d. cognitive-appraisal theory.

20. The Polygraph Protection Act of 1988
    a. totally bans the use of the polygraph test.
    b. limits the use of the polygraph test to criminal cases.
    c. permits the use of the polygraph test by government intelligence agencies.
    d. protects polygraphers from being sued by suspects who are incorrectly accused of lying.

21. When you are physiologically aroused, sugar is released into your bloodstream by the
    a. liver.
    b. spleen.
    c. stomach.
    d. pancreas.

22. The interacting set of brain structures that regulate emotional arousal composes the
    a. basal ganglia.
    b. limbic system.
    c. superior colliculi.
    d. cerebral ventricles.

23. The Wada test is used for determining the
    a. validity of the lie detector.
    b. role of cerebrospinal fluid in emotionality.
    c. functions of the cerebral hemispheres in emotionality.
    d. relation between hormone levels and emotional intensity.

24. The importance of facial expressions in promoting survival was first noted by
    a. Sigmund Freud.
    b. Wilhelm Wundt.
    c. Charles Darwin.
    d. John B. Watson.

25. The study of Illinois state lottery winners (Brickman, Coates, & Janoff-Bulman, 1978) found that
    a. sudden wealth brings happiness.
    b. their reactions did not support adaptation-level theory.
    c. only winners who donated much of their winnings to charity felt happy.
    d. sudden wealth may make everyday sources of happiness less pleasurable.

Thought Questions

1. Why is it technically incorrect to refer to the polygraph test as a lie detector test?

2. What are the main sources of evidence supporting hemispheric lateralization of emotion?

3. How does research on implicit or unconscious processing support the James-Lange theory?

CHAPTER 13

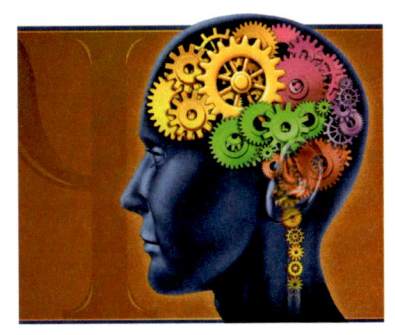

Personality

Years ago, a researcher placed a newspaper advertisement that offered a free, personalized astrological profile. Of the 150 persons who responded and received their personality profiles, 141 (94 percent) later said they had recognized their own personalities in the "personalized" profiles. The purpose of the study was to see how gullible people can be regarding astrological descriptions of personalities. Each of the respondents actually had received the same personality profile—the profile of a mass murderer who had terrorized France (Waldrop, 1984). Take a moment to see if you recognize yourself in the following personality profile:

> You have a strong need for other people to like and admire you. You have a tendency to be critical of yourself. You have a great deal of unused capacity, which you have not turned to your advantage.... Disciplined and controlled on the outside, you tend to be worrisome and insecure inside.... At times you are extraverted, affable, and sociable; at other times, you are introverted, wary, and reserved. (Ulrich, Stachnik, & Stainton, 1963)

Study after study has shown that when people are given personality tests and then presented with a mock personality description like this one, they tend to accept their description as accurate. They do so because their description *is* accurate. But it—like the one used in the astrology study—is accurate because it contains traits that are shared by almost everyone; it says nothing that distinguishes one person from another. The acceptance of personality descriptions that are true of almost everyone is known as the "Barnum effect" (Meehl, 1956). This term reflects P. T. Barnum's saying that "There's a sucker born every minute." We are more likely to succumb to the Barnum effect when the personality description is flattering (MacDonald & Standing, 2002). The Barnum effect demonstrates that to be useful, personality descriptions must distinguish one person from another. You should no more accept a personality profile that fails to recognize your distinctive combination of personality traits than you would accept a physical description that merely states that you have a head, a torso, two eyes, ten toes, and other common physical characteristics.

Many times we refer to people as having a "good personality" or a "bad personality." But what exactly is personality? The word *personality* comes from the Latin word *persona*, meaning "mask." Just as masks distinguished one character from another in ancient Greek and Roman plays, your personality distinguishes you from other people. Your **personality** is your unique, relatively consistent pattern of thinking, feeling, and behaving.

Source: Lightspring/Shutterstock.com.

Chapter Outline

The Psychoanalytic Approach to Personality

The Dispositional Approach to Personality

The Cognitive-Behavioral Approach to Personality

The Humanistic Approach to Personality

The Biopsychological Approach to Personality

personality An individual's unique, relatively consistent pattern of thinking, feeling, and behaving.

443

Given that each of us has a unique personality, how do we explain our distinctive patterns of thinking, feeling, and behaving? Personality theorists favor several approaches to this question. In reading about them, you will see that the theorists' own life experiences often color their personality theories (Atwood & Tomkins, 1976). The approaches to the study of personality differ on several dimensions, including the influence of unconscious motivation, the extent to which we are molded by learning, the role of cognitive factors, the importance of subjective experience, and the effects of biological factors.

The Psychoanalytic Approach to Personality

The *psychoanalytic approach* to personality is rooted in medicine and biology. Sigmund Freud, the founder of psychoanalysis, was a physician who hoped to find the biological basis of the psychological processes contained in his psychosexual theory.

Freud's Psychosexual Theory

Freud (1856–1939) was born in Moravia (a region in the Czech Republic) to Jewish parents; the family moved to Vienna when he was 4 years old. Though Freud desired a career as a physiology professor, anti-Semitism limited his choice of professions to law, business, or medicine. He chose medicine and practiced as a neurologist. Freud remained in Vienna until the Nazis threatened his safety. In 1938 he emigrated to England, where he died the following year after suffering for many years from mouth cancer.

Early in his career, Freud became interested in the effects of the mind on physical symptoms. He had studied with the French neurologist Jean Charcot, who demonstrated the power of hypnosis in treating *conversion hysteria*, a disorder characterized by physical symptoms such as deafness, blindness, or paralysis without a physical cause. Freud also was intrigued by a report that psychiatrist Josef Breuer had successfully used a "talking cure" to treat conversion hysteria. Breuer found that by encouraging his patients to talk freely about whatever came to mind, they became aware of the psychological causes of their physical symptoms and, as a result, experienced emotional release, or *catharsis*. Catharsis led to the disappearance of the symptoms.

Freud's personality theory reflected his time—the Victorian era of the late 19th century. The Victorians valued rationality and self-control of physical drives as characteristics that separated people from animals. Freud attributed the symptoms of conversion hysteria to unconscious sexual conflicts, which were symbolized in the symptoms. For example, paralyzed legs might represent a sexual conflict. Freud's claim that sexuality was an important determinant of human behavior shocked and disgusted many of his contemporaries (Rapp, 1988). After the carnage of World War I, Freud expanded his theory to include aggression as a central human motive. He claimed that we are motivated by both a life instinct, *Eros*, which promotes personal growth and development, and a death instinct, *Thanatos*, which promotes personal deterioration and destructiveness.

Levels of Consciousness

As described in Chapter 6, Freud divided the mind into three levels. The *conscious mind* is merely the "tip of the iceberg," representing a tiny region of the mind. The contents of the conscious mind are in a constant state of flux as feelings, memories, and perceptions enter and leave. Just below the conscious mind lies the *preconscious mind*, which includes accessible memories, that is, memories we can recall at will. The *unconscious mind*, the bulk of the mind, lies below both the conscious mind and the preconscious mind. It contains material we cannot recall at will.

Freud claimed that threatening thoughts or feelings are subject to *repression*, the banishment of conscious material into the unconscious. Because Freud assumed that unconscious thoughts and feelings are the most important influences on our behavior, he proclaimed: "The theory of repression is the cornerstone on which the whole structure of psychoanalysis rests" (Freud, 1914/1957, p. 16). The notion of repressed thoughts and feelings led to the concept of *psychic determinism*, which holds that all behavior is influenced by unconscious motives. Psychic determinism is exhibited in *Freudian slips*, unintentional statements that might reveal our repressed feelings (Reason, 2000). For instance, the slip "I loathe you . . . I mean, I love you" might reveal repressed hostility.

The Structure of Personality

As illustrated in Figure 13-1, Freud distinguished three structures of personality: the *id*, the *ego*, and the *superego*. The **id** is unconscious and consists of our inborn biological drives. In demanding immediate gratification of drives, most notably sex and aggression, the id obeys the **pleasure principle**.

The word *id* is Latin for "it," reflecting the id's impersonal nature. The classic 1950s science fiction movie *Forbidden Planet* portrays the amoral nature of the id: The id of a mad scientist is transformed into a being of pure energy that runs amok on an alien planet, blindly killing anyone in its path.

Through life experiences we learn that acting on every sexual or aggressive impulse is socially maladaptive. As a consequence, each of us develops an **ego**, Latin for "I." The ego obeys the **reality principle**, directing us to express sexual and aggressive impulses in socially acceptable ways. Suppose that a professor refuses to change your grade on an exam that was graded with an incorrect answer key. Your ego would encourage you to argue with the professor instead of punching him or her.

The **superego** (Latin for "over the I") counteracts the id, which is concerned only with immediate gratification, and the ego, which is concerned only with adapting to reality. The superego acts as our moral guide. It contains the *conscience*, which makes us feel guilty for doing or thinking wrong, and the *ego ideal*, which makes us feel good for doing or thinking right. To Freud, your personality is the outcome of the continual battle for dominance among the id, the ego, and the superego.

Defense Mechanisms

The ego might resort to **defense mechanisms**, which distort reality, to protect itself from the anxiety caused by id impulses, particularly those of sex and aggression. The ego also may use defense mechanisms to relieve the anxiety caused by unacceptable personal characteristics and unpleasant personal experiences, including traumatic experiences such as torture experienced by political prisoners (Punamaeki, Kanninen, Quota, & El-Sarr, 2002). Each of us uses defense mechanisms to varying extents, which contributes

---

id In Freud's theory, the part of the personality that contains inborn biological drives and that seeks immediate gratification.

pleasure principle The process by which the id seeks immediate gratification of its impulses.

ego In Freud's theory, the part of the personality that helps the individual adapt to external reality by making compromises between the id, the superego, and the environment.

reality principle The process by which the ego directs the individual to express sexual and aggressive impulses in socially acceptable ways.

superego In Freud's theory, the part of the personality that acts as a moral guide telling us what we should and should not do.

defense mechanism In Freud's theory, a process that distorts reality to prevent the individual from being overwhelmed by anxiety.

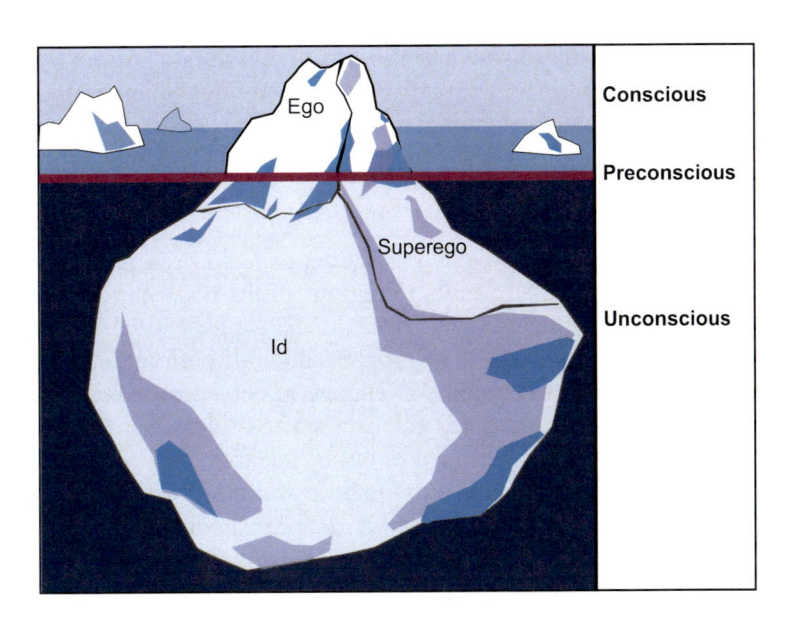

FIGURE 13-1
The Structure of Personality

Freud divided personality into the id, ego, and superego. The id is entirely unconscious and demands immediate gratification of its desires. The ego is partly conscious and partly unconscious. This permits it to balance the id's demands with the external demands of reality and the moralistic demands of the superego, which also is partly conscious and partly unconscious.

to the distinctiveness of our personalities. Researchers studying the role of unconscious processes in stress and coping have renewed scientific interest in defense mechanisms (P. Cramer, 2003). And as noted in Chapter 14, Freudians believe that excessive reliance on defense mechanisms contributes to the development of psychological disorders.

Because all defense mechanisms involve *repression*, we are not aware when we are using them. The memory of a traumatic event, such as an auto accident, might be repressed to relieve the anxiety that the memory produces. As discussed in Chapter 8, the defense mechanism of repression has become a controversial topic in the mass media because of the rise in reports of adults recalling apparently recovered memories of sexual abuse in early childhood (Loftus, Joslyn, & Polage, 1998).

We sometimes rely on immature kinds of defense mechanisms. In using *denial*, we simply refuse to admit a particular aspect of reality. For example, terminally ill patients might initially reduce their anxiety by denying they have a fatal disease. In resorting to the defense mechanism of *regression*, the individual displays immature behaviors that have relieved anxiety in the past. A child might respond to physical abuse by bed-wetting or refusing to be parted from a comforting stuffed toy (Finzi, Har-Even, & Weizman, 2003).

Other defense mechanisms rely on changing our perception of reality. When we resort to *rationalization*, we provide socially acceptable reasons for our inappropriate behavior. For example, a student whose semester grades include one D and four Fs might blame the four Fs on studying too much for the course in which he received a D. People who use *intellectualization* reduce anxiety by reacting to emotional situations in a detached, unemotional way. Instead of reacting to the death of a loved one by crying, they might react by saying, "Everyone must die sometime."

In some cases, defense mechanisms direct sexual or aggressive drives in safer directions. A person who fears the consequences of expressing her or his feelings toward a particular person might express them toward someone less threatening. This defense mechanism is known as *displacement*. For example, a worker who hates his boss but fears criticizing him might instead abuse his children with his hostility. If we cannot accept our own undesirable feelings, we might resort to *projection*, attributing our undesirable feelings to others. One experiment found, for example, that when people project onto other people their own feelings of anger or their belief that they are dishonest, they report that they feel less anger and believe that they are less dishonest (Schimel, Greenberg, & Martens, 2003). *Reaction formation* involves countering undesirable feelings by acting in a manner opposite to them. Samuel Johnson, the 18th-century writer and dictionary editor, reported a classic example of reaction formation. A pair of proper ladies who met him at a literary tea commented, "We see, Dr. Johnson, that you do not have those naughty words in your dictionary." Johnson replied, "And I see, dear ladies, that you have been looking for them" (Morris & Morris, 1985, p. 101).

According to Freud, the most successful defense mechanism is *sublimation*, the expression of sexual or aggressive impulses through indirect, socially acceptable outlets. The sex drive can be sublimated through creative activities (Kim, Zeppenfield, & Cohen, 2013), such as painting, ballet dancing, or composing music. And the aggressive drive can be sublimated through sports such as football, soccer, or field hockey.

Psychosexual Development

Freud assumed that personality development depended on changes in the distribution of sexual energy, which he called **libido**, in regions of the body he called *erogenous zones*. Stimulation of these regions produces pleasure. Thus, he was concerned with stages of *psychosexual development*. Failure to progress smoothly through a particular stage can cause *fixation*, a tendency to continue to engage in behaviors associated with that stage. Freud called the first year of infancy the **oral stage** of development, because the infant gains pleasure from oral activities such as biting, sucking, and chewing. An infant inadequately weaned, because of too much or too little oral gratification, might become fixated at the oral stage. Fixation might lead to an *oral-dependent* personality, marked by passivity, dependency, and gullibility. The person will "swallow anything" and might become a

Sublimation
According to Freud, the aggressive drive can be sublimated through participating in sports such as boxing.
Source: Sergey Nivens/Shutterstock.com.

libido Freud's term for the sexual energy of the id.

oral stage In Freud's theory, the stage of personality development between birth and age 1 year, during which the infant gains pleasure from oral activities and faces a conflict over weaning.

"sucker." Or fixation might lead to an *oral-aggressive* personality, marked by cruelty and sarcastic, "biting" remarks.

At the age of 1 year, children enter the **anal stage**. They now obtain pleasure from defecation and experience an important conflict regarding toilet training. Freud claimed that inadequate toilet training, either premature or delayed, can lead to fixation at the anal stage.

Freud claimed that between the ages of 3 and 5, the child passes through the **phallic stage**, in which pleasure is gained from genital stimulation. This stage is associated with the **Oedipus complex**, in which the child sexually desires the parent of the other sex while fearing punishment from the parent of the same sex. Freud noted this conflict in Sophocles' play *Oedipus Rex*, in which Oedipus, abandoned as an infant, later kills his father and marries his mother—without knowing they are his parents.

Freud believed that the Oedipus story reflected a universal truth—the sexual attraction of each child to the other-sex parent. Resolution of the conflict leads to identification with the same-sex parent. The boy gives up his desire for his mother because of his *castration anxiety*—his fear that his father will punish him by removing his genitals. The girl, because of *penis envy*, becomes angry at her mother, whom she believes caused her to be born without a penis, and becomes attracted to her father. This stage is now known as the **Electra complex**, named by Carl Jung after a Greek character who had her mother killed (Kilmartin & Dervin, 1997). But, fearing the loss of maternal love, the girl identifies with her mother, hoping to still attract her father. Through the process of *identification*, boys and girls adopt parental values, develop a superego, and establish their gender identity and sexual orientation.

Freud called the period between age 5 and puberty the **latency stage**. He was relatively uninterested in this stage because he believed that the child experiences little psychosexual development during it. Instead, the child develops social skills and friendships. Finally, during adolescence, the child reaches the **genital stage** and becomes sexually attracted to other people. To Freud, the first three stages are the most important determinants of personality development. He assumed that personality is essentially fixed by the age of 5. Table 13-1 summarizes these psychosexual stages of development.

Because Freud's intellectual descendants modified his theory in developing their own, they became known as *neo-Freudians*. For example, a central concept of Erich Fromm's theory (1941) is the conflict between the need for freedom and the anxiety that freedom brings. And Harry Stack Sullivan (1953) emphasized the importance of healthy interpersonal relationships to personality development.

Adler's Theory of Individual Psychology

One of the most influential of Freud's followers was Alfred Adler (1870–1937). In 1902, Adler, a Viennese physician, joined the discussions of psychoanalysis at Freud's home and became a devoted disciple. But in 1911, Adler broke with Freud, downplaying the importance of sexual motivation and the unconscious mind. Adler (1927) developed his own theory, which he called *individual psychology*. The popularity of Adler's theory provoked Freud to complain, "I made a pygmy great" (Hergenhahn, 1984, p. 65).

Adler's childhood experiences inspired his theory of personality. He was a sickly child who saw himself as inferior to his stronger and healthier older brother. Adler assumed that because children feel small, weak, and dependent on others, they develop an *inferiority complex*. This complex motivates them to compensate by *striving for superiority*—that is, developing certain abilities to their maximum potential. Perhaps Adler compensated for his childhood frailty by becoming an eminent psychoanalyst.

Adler believed that striving for superiority is healthiest when it promotes active concern for the welfare of both oneself and others, which he called *social interest* (Adler, 1994). For example, both a physician and a criminal strive for superiority, but the physician expresses this motive in a socially beneficial way. Cohesive, emotionally expressive families with low levels of conflict promote the development of social interest (Johnson, Smith, & Nelson, 2003). One study found that adolescent mentors with high social interest were more likely to continue as a mentor after the first year, to choose more

Fixation

Is it too early or late for this child for toilet training? According to Freud, if this process is interrupted it could lead to a fixation.
Source: ARZTSAMUI/Shutterstock.com.

anal stage In Freud's theory, the stage of personality development between ages 1 and 3, during which the child gains pleasure from defecation and faces a conflict over toilet training.

phallic stage In Freud's theory, the stage of personality development between ages 3 and 5, during which the child gains pleasure from the genitals and must resolve the Oedipus complex.

Oedipus complex In Freud's theory, a conflict, during the phallic stage, between the child's sexual desire for the parent of the other sex and fear of punishment from the same-sex parent.

Electra complex A term used by some psychoanalysts, but not by Freud, to refer to the Oedipus complex in girls.

latency stage In Freud's theory, the stage between age 5 and puberty, during which there is little psychosexual development.

genital stage In Freud's theory, the last stage of personality development, associated with puberty, during which the individual develops erotic attachments to others.

TABLE 13-1 The Stages of Psychosexual Development

Stage	Age	Characteristics
Oral	Birth to 1	Gratification from oral behaviors, such as sucking, biting, and chewing Conflict over weaning
Anal	1 to 3	Gratification from defecation Conflict over toilet training
Phallic	3 to 5	Gratification from genital stimulation Resolution of the Oedipus or Electra complex
Latency	5 to puberty	Sexual impulses repressed Development of friendships
Genital	Puberty on	Gratification from genital stimulation Development of intimate relationships

Photo sources: Oral—Oksana Kuzmina/Shutterstock.com; Anal—Jamie Hooper/Shutterstock.com; Phallic—Rob Marmion/Shutterstock.com; Latency—Monkey Business Images/Shutterstock.com; Genital—swissmacky/Shutterstock.com.

challenging mentees, and to feel more connected with their school (Karcher & Lindwall, 2003). According to Adler, in striving for superiority we develop a *style of life* based on *fictional finalism*, which he referred to as the "guiding self ideal" (Watts & Holden, 1994). We are motivated by beliefs that might not be objectively true. A person guided by the belief that "nice guys finish last" might exhibit a ruthless, competitive style of life. In contrast, a person guided by the belief that "it is more blessed to give than to receive" might exhibit a helpful, altruistic style of life.

Horney's Theory of Feminine Psychology

Though Karen Horney (1885–1952) never studied with Freud she was a prominent neo-Freudian. She challenged many of his theoretical assumptions, beginning with a ground-breaking paper that she presented at the Seventh International Psychoanalytic Congress in 1922—at a session chaired by Freud. The paper was the first of a series of papers that ultimately formed the basis for her theory of feminine psychology (Horney, 1924). She criticized a number of Freud's concepts, such as penis envy and the Oedipal and Electra complexes. Most important, she believed that Freudian psychoanalytic theory neglected the role of sociocultural factors in personality development. She was an early advocate of a cross-cultural approach to psychology, and in her later years worked on integrating psychoanalysis and concepts from Zen Buddhism (Morvay, 1999).

Zen

Zen is a school of Buddhism developed in China as early as the 6th century. This statue is located in Tian Tan.
Source: Blue Sky Studio/Shutterstock.com.

Horney believed that psychoanalytic theory was *androcentric*, using male personality development as the norm by which to explain the development of women's personalities. In particular, she critiqued Freud's emphasis on penis envy, noting that men were just as likely to experience *womb envy*. In support of this notion, she pointed out that children often are in awe of women's ability to give birth (Horney, 1926/1967). She also believed that Freud overemphasized sexuality in the phallic stage. Horney asserted that girls were not envious of boys' genitalia but rather the fact that men held superior—and more powerful—positions in society (O'Connell, 1990). In her later work, she continued to emphasize the importance of gender roles, interpersonal power, and sociocultural factors influencing women's personality (Miletic, 2002).

Like Adler, Horney's childhood experiences are reflected in her theory. She was an anxious child who felt unwanted and struggled to gain her parents' love and approval. Later, in self-analysis, she realized that she felt hostile toward her parents, especially her authoritarian father. Horney theorized that children develop *basic anxiety* because of their emotional and physical dependency on adults—who have the power to give or withhold love. Basic anxiety leads to *basic hostility*, an emotional response that children must suppress to gain love and security from their parents. To combat these intense feelings of anxiety and hostility and to gain a sense of security, a child develops one of three coping styles: *moving toward others*, in which the child becomes compliant and affectionate; *moving against others*, in which the child becomes aggressive; or *moving away from others*, in which the child becomes detached and aloof (Coolidge, Moor, Yamazaki, Stewart, & Segal, 2001). These coping styles become part of one's personality. Neurotic people rigidly rely on one style; mentally healthy people are flexible and use each style when appropriate (Horney, 1950).

Basic Anxiety

According to Horney, children develop basic anxiety because of their emotional and physical dependency on adults.
Source: Stuart Monk/Shutterstock.com.

Jung's Theory of Analytical Psychology

Freud's favorite disciple was Carl Jung (1875–1961). Though Jung, a native of Switzerland, came from a family in which the men traditionally pursued careers as Protestant pastors, he was inspired to become a psychoanalyst after reading Freud's *The Interpretation of Dreams* (1900/1990). Beginning in 1906, Freud and Jung carried on a lively correspondence, and Freud hoped that Jung would become his successor as head of the psychoanalytic movement. But in 1914 they parted over revisions Jung made in Freud's theory, especially Jung's de-emphasis of the sex motive. Jung called his version of psychoanalysis *analytical psychology*.

Though Jung agreed with Freud that we each have our own unconscious mind (the **personal unconscious**), he claimed that we also share a common unconscious mind—the **collective unconscious**. Jung held that the collective unconscious contains inherited

personal unconscious In Jung's theory, the individual's own unconscious mind, which contains repressed memories.

collective unconscious In Jung's theory, the unconscious mind that is shared by all people and that contains archetypal images passed down from our prehistoric ancestors.

The Mandala

Balanced, circular paintings such as these have been found in cultures throughout history and throughout the world. Jung claimed that they represent the complete congruence of the self and the persona.

Sources: (top) krishnasomya/Shutterstock.com; (bottom) OkPic/Shutterstock.com.

archetypes In Jung's theory, inherited images that are passed down from our prehistoric ancestors and that reveal themselves as universal symbols in art, dreams, and religion.

extravert A person who is socially outgoing and prefers to pay attention to the external environment.

introvert A person who is socially reserved and prefers to pay attention to his or her private cognitive experiences.

projective test A psychoanalytic personality test based on the assumption that individuals project their unconscious feelings when responding to ambiguous stimuli.

memories passed down from generation to generation. He called these memories **archetypes**, which are images that represent important aspects of the accumulated experience of humanity (McDowell, 2001). Jung claimed that archetypes influence our dreams, religious symbols, and artistic creations.

Jung (1959/1969) even connected the archetype of God to UFO sightings that began to be reported in the late 1940s, following the horrors of World War II and the advent of the atomic bomb. According to Jung, these sightings stemmed from the desire of people, inspired by the archetype of God, to have a more powerful force than themselves save humanity from self-destruction. Even the round shape of the flying saucer represented the archetypal image of godlike unity and perfection of the archetype of the *self*. Beginning in the 1950s with the movie *The Day the Earth Stood Still* and continuing with movies such as *Close Encounters of the Third Kind*, science fiction movies have reflected the Jungian theme of powerful aliens arriving in flying saucers to save us from ourselves.

The *persona* is another archetype related to the self. Whereas the self is the true, private personality, the persona is the somewhat false social "mask" that we wear in public. According to Jung, the persona and self of a psychologically healthy individual are fairly congruent. Jung also distinguished between the *anima*, the feminine archetype in men, and the *animus*, the masculine archetype in women. According to Jung, a psychologically healthy person, whether female or male, must maintain a balance between masculinity and femininity. A "macho" man who acts tough and rarely expresses tender emotions would be unhealthy, as would a "prissy" woman who acts passive and has little control over her emotions.

Jung even contributed to our everyday language by distinguishing between two personality types. **Extraverts** are socially outgoing and pay more attention to the surrounding environment; **introverts** are socially reserved and pay more attention to their private cognitive experiences. Jung applied this concept in his own life, viewing Freud as an extravert and Adler as an introvert (Monte, 1980).

Psychoanalytic Assessment of Personality

More than a century ago, Sir Arthur Conan Doyle popularized the use of handwriting analysis, or *graphology*, by having his fictional detective Sherlock Holmes use it to solve crimes. Graphology was an ancestor of psychoanalytic personality tests. Graphology is based on the assumption that because all children in a given culture learn to form written letters and words the same way, any deviations from the original prototypes reflect in part one's distinctive personality. Given the lack of experimental evidence in support of graphology, few psychologists today use it to assess personality.

Graphology has the same rationale as modern psychoanalytic assessment techniques, which are called **projective tests**. They are based on the assumption that we will "project" our repressed feelings and conflicts onto ambiguous stimuli. It is especially important that those who are interpreting responses to projective tests do not let their own preconceptions about the test takers affect their interpretations (Wiederman, 1999). Today, the most popular projective tests are the *Rorschach test* and the *Thematic Apperception Test*.

The Rorschach Test

Have you ever seen animal shapes in cloud formations? Have you ever argued about images in abstract paintings? If so, you will have some appreciation for the *Rorschach test*, which asks participants to report what they see in inkblots. The Rorschach test was introduced in 1921 by the Swiss psychiatrist Hermann Rorschach (1884–1922), who died before he was able to conduct much research with it. The test consists of 10 bilaterally symmetrical inkblots. Some of the inkblots are in black and white, and the others include colors.

In responding to the inkblots, the person tells what he or she sees in each one and then reports the features of the inkblot that prompted the response. After scoring each response, based on formal criteria, the examiner uses clinical judgment and one of several available scoring systems to write a profile of the person's motives and conflicts. Such profiles have been used for purposes as diverse as diagnosing suicide risk among adolescents and young adults (Blasczyk-Schiep, Kazén, Kuhl, & Grygielski, 2011) and distinguishing between the personalities of murderers and nonviolent criminals (Coram, 1995). And a recent meta-analysis found some validity of the test in assessing cognitive and perceptual abilities (Mihura, Meyer, Dumitrascu, & Bombel, 2013).

The Thematic Apperception Test

The Thematic Apperception Test (TAT) (Morgan & Murray, 1935) was created by the American psychoanalyst Henry Murray and his associate Christiana Morgan (Morgan, 2002). The TAT consists of 1 blank card and 19 cards containing black-and-white pictures of people in ambiguous situations. The examiner asks several questions about each one: What is happening in the card? What events led up to that situation? Who are the people in the card? How do they feel? How does the situation turn out? Murray and Morgan assumed that people's responses would reveal their most important needs, such as the need for sex, power, achievement, or affiliation. The TAT is a moderately good predictor of real-life achievement, such as career success (Spangler, 1992). The TAT also has been used to measure changes in the use of defense mechanisms as a result of psychotherapy (Cramer, 1999).

Status of the Psychoanalytic Approach

Of all the psychoanalytic theories of personality, Freud's has been the most influential, but it has received limited support for its concepts (Fisher & Greenberg, 1985). As described in Chapter 6, there is substantial evidence demonstrating the effect of unconscious processes on human behavior (Dixon & Henley, 1991). And as described in Chapter 8, there is support for the Freudian view of repression from research showing that people are less likely to recall emotionally unpleasant personal experiences (Sparks, Pellechia, & Irvine, 1999), though the notion of total repression of traumatic emotional experiences has received only weak support (Bowers & Farvolden, 1996). Some research has supported the existence of several defense mechanisms, including projection and reaction formation. However, there is little support for certain other defense mechanisms, including displacement and sublimation (Baumeister, Dale, & Sommer, 1998).

There also has been little support for some of Freud's other concepts. For example, there is little evidence to support Freud's belief that resolution of the Oedipus and Electra complexes is essential for gender identity, sexual orientation, and superego development (Schrut, 1994). Perhaps the greatest weakness of Freudian theory is that many of its terms refer to processes that are neither observable nor measurable. Who has ever seen or measured an id? As noted in Chapter 2, we cannot conduct experiments on concepts that are not operationally defined.

Despite the limited support for certain psychoanalytic concepts, the psychoanalytic approach has contributed to our understanding of personality. It has revealed that much of our behavior is governed by motives of which we are unaware, as revealed in dreams, and it has stimulated interest in studying sexual behavior and sexual development. It has demonstrated the importance of early childhood experiences, such as infant attachment; it has contributed to the emergence of formal psychological therapies; and it has inspired research into the effects of psychological factors on illness. It also has influenced the works of artists, writers, and filmmakers (Highet, 1998).

Adler's theory of personality has influenced cognitive psychology and humanistic psychology (Watts & Critelli, 1997) through its emphasis on the importance of our subjective experiences of reality. Of the Adlerian concepts that impressed humanistic psychologists, the most influential were the concepts of social interest and style of life (Ansbacher, 1990). Moreover, his concept of a style of life that reflects our striving for superiority has an important descendant in the current interest in *Type A behavior*, which is discussed at length in Chapter 16 as a possible factor in coronary heart disease. Despite Adler's influence on humanistic and cognitive approaches to personality and psychotherapy, however, interest in individual psychology itself has declined in recent years (Freeman, 1999).

Horney's conceptualization of neurosis made a lasting contribution to American psychology and psychoanalysis (Ingram, 1985). Though there is little research directly testing Horney's theory, her work on human neurosis contributed to many of the principles

The Rorschach Test

The basic assumption of the Rorschach test is that what we report seeing in a series of inkblots will reveal our unconscious motives and conflicts.

Source: michaeljung/Shutterstock.com.

and techniques of cognitive therapy and the treatment of anxiety and depression (see Chapter 15). Like Adler, Horney influenced other psychological theorists. For example, her idea of basic anxiety is similar to Erikson's concept of basic trust-mistrust explained in Chapter 4. Moreover, her emphasis on sociocultural determinants of women's personality was carried forward in the work of contemporary feminist psychoanalytic theorists, such as Nancy Chodorow (1978), who explore the relation of gender roles, family relationships, and power to women's personality development.

And what of Jung's theory? Jung's concept of personality types has received research support. One study compared the styles of extraverted painters and introverted painters. Extraverted painters tended to use realistic styles, reflecting their greater attention to the external environment. In contrast, introverted painters tended to use abstract styles, reflecting their greater attention to private mental experience (Loomis & Saltz, 1984). Jung's concept of the archetype has been criticized because it violates known mechanisms of inheritance in its assumption that memories can be inherited. Nonetheless, research findings support the possibility that hereditary tendencies akin to archetypes affect human behavior (Neher, 1996). Evidence for this finding comes from research, explained in Chapter 14, showing that we have an inborn predisposition to develop phobias about snakes, heights, and other situations that were dangerous to our prehistoric ancestors. Thus, what Jung called archetypes might be inborn behavioral tendencies rather than inherited memories.

As for projective tests of personality, the Rorschach test and the TAT are frequently used by clinical and forensic psychologists. However, a recent review of the literature concluded that neither test has been shown to have greater validity than objective personality tests, such as the Minnesota Multiphasic Personality Inventory (MMPI), which is discussed in the section, "Dispositional Assessment of Personality." Moreover, it is unclear whether scoring procedures and norms for these tests are generalizable to different cultures and racial or ethnic groups (Lilienfeld, Wood, & Garb, 2000).

Section Review: The Psychoanalytic Approach to Personality

1. What does the Barnum effect indicate about the study of personality?
2. What is the relationship between the three structures of personality in Freud's theory?
3. What are the basic tenets of Adler's theory?
4. How did Horney broaden psychoanalytic theory to include social and cultural forces?
5. According to Jung, how do the collective unconscious and its archetypes affect our lives?

The Dispositional Approach to Personality

Personality theorists have traditionally assumed that personality is stable over time and consistent across situations. The *dispositional approach* to personality attributes this apparent stability and consistency to relatively enduring personal characteristics called *types* and *traits*.

Type Theories

In his book *Characters*, the Greek philosopher Theophrastus (ca. 372–ca. 287 B.C.) wondered why Greeks differed in personality despite sharing the same culture and geography. He concluded that personality differences arise from inborn predispositions to develop particular personality *types* dominated by a single characteristic. Like Theophrastus, we rely on personality typing when we call someone a "morning person" or an "evening person" (Mecacci & Rocchetti, 1998).

Today the most influential theory of personality types is Hans Eysenck's *three-factor theory* (Eysenck, 1990). Eysenck (1916–1997), a German psychologist, fled to England after refusing to become a member of Hitler's secret police. Eysenck used the statistical technique of factor analysis (see Chapter 10) in identifying three dimensions of personality. By measuring where a person falls on these dimensions, we can determine his or her personality type.

The dimension of *neuroticism* measures a person's level of stability/instability. Stable people are calm, even-tempered, and reliable; unstable people are moody, anxious, and unreliable. One study of moderate to heavy drinkers found that participants high in neuroticism engaged in more solitary drinking on days during which they had more negative interpersonal experiences than did participants low in neuroticism (Mohr et al., 2001). The dimension of *psychoticism* measures a person's level of tough-mindedness/tender-mindedness. Tough-minded people are hostile, ruthless, and insensitive, whereas tender-minded people are friendly, empathetic, and cooperative. Juvenile delinquents score high in psychoticism (Furnham & Thompson, 1991).

The dimension of *extraversion* measures a person's level of introversion/extraversion. Extraverts try to have fun, connect with other people, and tend to experience positive emotional states (McCabe & Fleeson, 2012). This dimension, first identified by Jung, has stimulated the most research interest. For example, studies have shown that there are proportionately more introverts among expert chess players than in the general population. Because introverted chess champions may be uncomfortable in social situations, they prefer to avoid victory parties, press conferences, and autograph hounds. They might even feel compelled to leave the chess scene itself. In 1972, the American, Bobby Fischer, generated unprecedented interest in chess with his brilliant play in winning the World Chess Championship, only to retire into seclusion soon after (Olmo & Stevens, 1984). Figure 13-2 illustrates the interaction of the dimensions of introversion/extraversion and stability/instability.

There is evidence that the dimensions in Eysenck's theory have a biological basis (Loehlin & Martin, 2001). For example, research on twins indicates that neuroticism, psychoticism, and extraversion have genetic bases. Heredity might explain why introverts are more physiologically reactive than are extraverts (Stelmack, 1990). This reactivity might in turn explain behavioral differences between introverts and extraverts. The greater physiological reactivity of introverts might explain why extraverts can work better than introverts under distracting conditions. Consider students who, perhaps like yourself, study

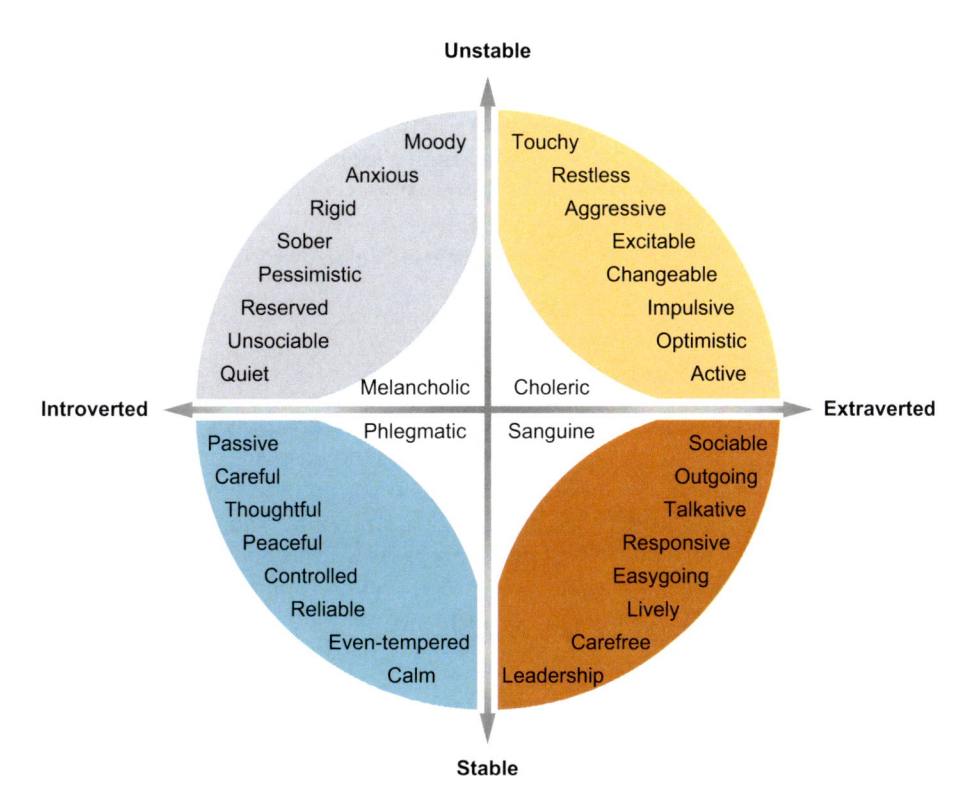

FIGURE 13-2
Eysenck's Personality Dimensions

The drawing shows the interaction of Eysenck's personality dimensions of introversion/extraversion and stability/instability.

Source: Based on Eysenck, S. B. G., & Eysenck, J. J. (1963). "The validity of questionnaire and rating assessments of extraversion and neuroticism, and their factorial stability" from *British Journal of Psychology, 54,* 51–62.

while music is playing in the background. One study compared the effect of background music, office noise, and silence on reading comprehension, recall, and mental arithmetic tasks. Extraverts performed better while listening to background music or office noise, and introverts performed better in the silent condition. Thus, an introverted student would be wise to study in the library, whereas an extraverted student may study effectively while listening to music (Furnham & Strbac, 2002).

Another observable behavioral difference that can be measured is social withdrawal, which is related to introversion. Modern methods make it possible to search for genes associated with behavior characteristic of social withdrawal. Researchers collected genetic information from 551 six- to eighteen-year-olds in 187 families after administering two behavioral scales related to social withdrawal, the Child Behavior Checklist and the Withdrawn Behavior Subscale. The results indicated that genes regulating serotonin were associated with shyness and inhibition. And this relationship was particularly pronounced in young children (Rubin et al., 2013). This study and others indicate that some personality dimensions are biologically hereditable. But other researchers believe that people's personalities are as a result of environmental influences.

Trait Theories

Instead of describing personality in terms of single types, trait theorists describe personality in terms of distinctive combinations of personal dispositions (McCrae & Costa, 1995). A **trait** is a relatively enduring, cross-situationally consistent personality characteristic that is inferred from a person's behavior. Eysenck's theory can be viewed as either a type theory or a trait theory, because the personality types in his theory are products of the interaction of certain trait dimensions. The most influential trait theory is that of Gordon Allport (1897–1967), who was a leader in making personality an important area of American psychological research in the 1920s and 1930s (Lombardo & Foschi, 2002).

trait A relatively enduring, cross-situationally consistent personality characteristic that is inferred from a person's behavior.

Allport's Trait Theory

Early in his career, Allport had a brief meeting in Vienna with Sigmund Freud that convinced him that psychoanalysis was not the best approach to the study of personality. Confronted with a silent Freud, Allport broke the silence by describing a boy he had met on a train who had complained of dirty people and whose mother had acted annoyed at his behavior. Freud responded, "And was that little boy you?" Based on this meeting, Allport concluded that Freud was too concerned with finding hidden motives for even the most mundane behaviors (Allport, 1967).

Allport began his research by identifying all the English words that refer to personal characteristics. In 1936, Allport and his colleague, Henry Odbert, using an unabridged dictionary, counted almost 18,000 such words. By eliminating synonyms and words referring to temporary states (such as *hungry*), they reduced the list to about 4,500 words. Allport then grouped the words into less than 200 clusters of related words, which became the original personality traits in his theory.

Allport distinguished three kinds of traits, the differences depending on how important they are in a given person's life. *Cardinal traits* are similar to personality types in that they affect every aspect of the person's life. For example, altruism was a cardinal trait in the personality of Mother Teresa. Because cardinal traits are rare, you probably know few people whose lives are governed by them. *Central traits* affect many aspects of our lives but do not have the pervasive influence of cardinal traits. When you refer to someone as kind, humorous, or conceited, you are usually referring to a central trait. The least important traits are *secondary traits*, because they affect relatively narrow aspects of our lives. Preferences for wearing cuffed pants, reading mysteries, or eating chocolate ice cream reflect secondary traits. One study looked at the relative influence of cardinal, central, and secondary traits on consumers' tendency to bargain or to complain (Harris & Mowen, 2001).

The Five-Factor Model

The most influential personality research of the past few decades indicates that there are five basic personality traits (McCrae & Costa, 1997). These traits are commonly known as "The Big Five." *Extraversion* resembles Eysenck's factor of introversion/extraversion, and *neuroticism* resembles his factor of stability/instability. *Agreeableness* indicates whether a person is warm, good-natured, and cooperative. *Conscientiousness* indicates whether a person is ethical, reliable, and responsible. And *openness to experience* indicates whether a person is curious, imaginative, and interested in intellectual pursuits.

The five-factor model of personality has been used successfully in predicting achievement orientation (Ross, Rausch, & Canada, 2003), alcohol consumption and grade-point average (Paunonen, 2003), religiosity (McCullough, Tsang, & Brion, 2003), job strain (Tömroos et al., 2013), and personal values (Roccas, Sagi, Schwartz, & Knafo, 2002). The five-factor model has been applied to a wide range of behaviors, and it recently has been tested in many cultures. One study investigated the distribution of personality traits in more than 27,000 participants from 36 cultures. Personality traits were unrelated to most geographic variables, such as distance from the equator and average temperature. However, personality profiles of cultures in close proximity were more similar than those of distant cultures. And the researchers found differences between European American and Asian cultures similar to individualist and collectivist orientations. Whereas European American cultures scored higher in extraversion and openness to experience, Asian cultures scored higher on agreeableness (Allik & McCrae, 2004).

Dispositional Assessment of Personality

The dispositional assessment of personality relies on tests of personality types or traits. These tests are called *objective tests* because they present participants with straightforward statements rather than with ambiguous stimuli, as in projective tests.

Tests of Personality Types

One of the most popular objective tests is the *Myers-Briggs Type Indicator* (Briggs & Myers, 1943). The test assesses various personality characteristics, including personality types derived from Jung's analytical theory of personality. The participant is presented with pairs of statements and selects the statement in each pair that is closest to how she or he usually acts or feels. A typical item would be "At parties, do you (a) sometimes get bored or (b) always have fun?" An introvert would be more likely to select *a* and an extravert *b*. The test has satisfactory reliability (Capraro & Capraro, 2002) and validity (Murray, 1990) and has been used in a variety of research studies. One study found that psychological well-being, life satisfaction, and self-consciousness are related to specific personality profiles on the test (Harrington & Loffredo, 2001). A study that administered the Myers-Briggs Type Indicator to more than 1,000 participants found that the American population is equally divided into introverts and extraverts (Hammer & Mitchell, 1996).

Tests of Personality Traits

Researchers recently have developed personality tests based on the five-factor model of personality. These tests include the Five Factor Personality Inventory (Hendriks, Hofstee, & DeRaad, 1999) and the NEO Personality Inventory, which has been used to study relationships between personality traits and attitudes or behaviors, such as musical preferences (Rawlings & Ciancarelli, 1997). But the most widely used of all personality tests is the *Minnesota Multiphasic Personality Inventory (MMPI)*, which measures personality traits.

The MMPI was developed at the University of Minnesota by psychologist Starke R. Hathaway and psychiatrist John C. McKinley (1943) to diagnose psychological disorders. Hathaway and McKinley used the *empirical method* of test construction, which retains only those questions that discriminate between people who differ on the characteristics of interest. Hathaway and McKinley collected 1,000 statements, which they administered to 700 people, including nonpatients, medical patients, and psychiatric patients. Participants responded "True," "False," or "Cannot Say" to each statement, depending on whether it was true of them. Hathaway and McKinley kept those statements that tended to be answered the same way by people with particular psychiatric disorders. For example, they included the statement "Nothing in the newspaper interests me except the comics" solely because significantly more depressed people than nondepressed people responded "True" to that statement (Holden, 1986).

TABLE 13-2 Scales of the MMPI-2

Scales	Content
Clinical Scales	
Hypochondriasis	Items identifying people who are overly concerned with bodily functions and symptoms of physical illness
Depression	Items identifying people who feel hopeless and who experience slowing of thought and action
Hysteria	Items identifying people who avoid problems by developing mental or physical symptoms
Psychopathic deviate	Items identifying people who disregard accepted standards of behavior and have shallow emotional relationships
Masculinity-femininity	Items identifying people with stereotypically male or female interests
Paranoia	Items identifying people with delusions of grandeur or persecution who also exhibit pervasive suspiciousness
Psychasthenia	Items identifying people who feel guilt, worry, and anxiety and who have obsessions and compulsions
Schizophrenia	Items identifying people who exhibit social withdrawal, delusional thoughts, and hallucinations
Hypomania	Items identifying people who are overactive, easily excited, and recklessly impulsive
Social introversion	Items identifying people who are emotionally inhibited and socially shy
Validity Scales	
Cannot say	Items that are not answered, which may indicate evasiveness
Lie	Items indicating an attempt to make a positive impression
Frequency	Items involving responses that are rarely given by normal people, which may indicate an attempt to seem abnormal
Correction	Items revealing a tendency to respond defensively in admitting personal problems or shortcomings

Source: Clinical Scales and sample of Validity Scales taken from the MMPI®-2 (Minnesota Multiphasic Personality Inventory®-2) Manual for Administration, Scoring, and Interpretation, Revised Edition. Copyright © 2001 by the Regents of the University of Minnesota. Used by permission of the University of Minnesota Press. All rights reserved. "MMPI" and "Minnesota Multiphasic Personality Inventory" are trademarks owned by the Regents of the University of Minnesota.

As shown in Table 13-2, the MMPI has 10 clinical scales that measure important personality traits. For example, *hypochondriasis* measures concern with bodily functions and symptoms, and *paranoia* measures suspiciousness and delusions of persecution. The MMPI also has four *validity scales* that test for evasiveness, defensiveness, lying to look good, and faking to look bad. For example, the Lie scale contains statements that describe common human failings to which almost all people respond "True." So, a person who responded "False" to statements such as "I sometimes have violent thoughts" might be lying to create a good impression (Rogers et al., 2003).

Psychologists commonly use the MMPI to screen applicants for positions in which people with serious psychological disorders might be dangerous, such as law enforcement. The MMPI has proved to be a valid means of diagnosing psychological disorders (Parker, Hanson, & Hunsley, 1988). But researchers found that by the 1980s the test was diagnosing a higher proportion of people as psychologically disordered than it did when it was first adopted. Did this finding mean that more people had psychological disorders than in the past? Or did it mean that the MMPI's norms were outdated? The latter seemed to be the case. As one critic noted more than three decades ago, "Whoever takes the MMPI today is being compared with the way a man or woman from Minnesota endorsed those items in the late 1930s and early 1940s" (Herbert, 1983, p. 228).

Because of this problem, the MMPI was restandardized in the 1980s. The revised 567-item MMPI (the MMPI-2) has added, deleted, or changed many statements. It also has new norms based on a more representative sample of the American population in regard to age, sex, ethnic background, educational level, and region of the country. These changes make the MMPI-2, though still imperfect, an improvement over the MMPI (Helmes & Reddon, 1993).

Uses of the MMPI-2 have included measuring social introversion (Ward & Perry, 1998), identifying sex offenders (Grover, 2011), evaluating parents in child custody and parental competency cases (Resendes & Lecci, 2012), and determining the relationship of personality to spirituality (MacDonald & Holland, 2003). Research findings indicate that the MMPI-2 is valid across many ethnic groups, including African Americans (Hall, Bansal, & Lopez, 1999) and Latinos (Fantoni-Salvador & Rogers, 1997), though there is some evidence that acculturation appears to influence Asian Americans' scores on nine subscales (Tsai & Pike, 2000). Translated versions of the MMPI have been found to be culturally equivalent and valid for use with diverse samples such as Vietnamese refugees (Dong & Church, 2003) and Latino adolescents (Scott, Butcher, Young, & Gomez, 2002).

Status of the Dispositional Approach

Though the dispositional approach to personality has been useful in *describing* personality differences, it is less successful in *explaining* those differences. Suppose that the results of testing with the Myers-Briggs Type Indicator reveal that one of your friends is an extravert. Someone might ask, "Why is she an extravert?" You might respond, "Because she likes to socialize." The person might then ask, "Why does she like to socialize?" To which you might reply, "Because she is an extravert." This circular reasoning would not explain why your friend is an extravert.

One of the few dispositional theories that tries to explain personality is Eysenck's three-factor theory. The existence of the three personality factors identified by Eysenck has been verified by other researchers (Zuckerman, Joireman, Kraft, & Kuhlma, 1999), and it has some support from cross-cultural research (Eysenck, Barrett, & Barnes, 1993). The introversion/extraversion dimension has received especially strong research support. One of Eysenck's assumptions is that a person's degree of introversion/extraversion depends on his or her customary level of physiological reactivity. As noted in the section, "Type Theories," introverts are more physiologically reactive to stimulation than extraverts are. As explained in Chapter 11, we have a tendency to try to adopt a moderate level of arousal. This tendency might explain why introverts avoid stimulation and extraverts seek it. For example, introverted students prefer to work in quieter conditions than extraverted students do (Geen, 1984), and extraverts are more likely than introverts to seek help from others in coping with stress (Swickert, Rosentreter, Hittner, & Mushrush, 2002).

There also is support for the possible universality of the five-factor model of personality (McCrae, Costa, Del Pila, Rolland, & Parker, 1998). One study found that the model, developed in the United States, holds up even when applied to personality profiles of people from China, Korea, Japan, Israel, Portugal, and Germany (McCrae & Costa, 1997). Nonetheless, psychologists who agree that there are five basic personality factors often fail to agree on their nature. Some researchers, for example, have failed to find support for the openness-to-experience factor (McKenzie, 1998). Other researchers have found the need to add a sixth factor: hedonism/spontaneity (Becker, 1999).

Section Review: The Dispositional Approach to Personality

1. What are the basic characteristics of Allport's trait theory of personality?
2. In what way is the MMPI based on an empirical approach to personality test construction?
3. What evidence is there that personality is more consistent across situations than Mischel believed?

Psychology versus Common Sense

Is Personality Consistent from One Situation to Another?

You might recall that the definition of personality includes the word *consistent*. But do people really behave consistently from one situation to another? Professors who write letters of recommendation for students assume so when they refer to their students as "mature," "friendly," and "conscientious." But will a student who has been mature, friendly, and conscientious in college necessarily exhibit those traits in a job or in graduate school? The degree of cross-situational consistency in personality has been one of the most controversial issues in personality research. Until the late 1960s, commonsense belief among psychologists and nonpsychologists alike held that personality is consistent across different situations, with few researchers questioning that belief. But then some psychologists began reporting research findings indicating that personality might not be as cross-situationally consistent as was commonly believed.

Personality as Inconsistent

The debate over the consistency of personality began in 1968 with the publication of a book by the social-cognitive psychologist Walter Mischel. He reported that personality is much less consistent from one situation to another than was commonly believed. Mischel found that the correlation between any two behaviors presumed to represent the same underlying personality trait rarely exceeded a relatively modest .30. This finding means that we could not predict with confidence whether a person who scored high on the trait of generosity would behave in a generous manner in a given situation. For example, a person who scored high on a test measuring generosity might donate to a local charity but might not pick up the check in a restaurant—though both behaviors presumably would reflect the trait of generosity. Based on his review of research findings, Mischel concluded that our behavior is influenced more by the situations in which we find ourselves than by our personality characteristics. Though Mischel stimulated the recent debate over the issue of personality consistency, the issue is not new. Forty years before Mischel published his findings, psychologists reported research showing that children's honesty was inconsistent across situations. A child might cheat on a test but not in an athletic event, or lie at school but not at home (Hartshorne & May, 1928).

If personality is inconsistent across situations, why do we perceive it to be consistent in our everyday lives?

- We might confuse the consistency of behavior in a given situation over time with the consistency of that behavior across different situations (Mischel & Peake, 1982). If a student is consistently humorous in your psychology class, you might mistakenly infer that she is humorous at home, at parties, and in the dormitory.
- We tend to avoid situations that are inconsistent with our personalities (Snyder, 1983). If you view yourself as even-tempered, you might avoid situations that might make you lose your temper, such as a discussion about the abortion issue.
- Our first impression of a person can make us discount later behavior that is inconsistent with it (Hayden & Mischel, 1976). If someone is friendly to you the first time you meet but is rude to you the next time you meet, you might say that he was "not himself" at the second meeting.
- Our perception of cross-situational consistency in others might reflect a powerful situational factor—our presence in their environment (Lord, 1982). If others adapt their behavior to our presence, we might erroneously infer that they are consistent across situations.

Personality as Consistent

These attacks on cross-situational consistency have provoked responses from researchers who claim that there is more cross-situational consistency than Mischel and his allies believe (Kenrick & Funder, 1988).

- Individuals do show consistency on certain traits. But how do we know *which* traits? One way to find out is to ask. People who claim to be consistent on a given trait tend to exhibit behaviors reflecting that trait across situations (Zuckerman et al., 1988). In one study, students were asked to judge how consistent they were on the trait of friendliness. Those who claimed to be friendly across situations were, in fact, more consistently friendly than were students who did not claim to be—as verified by their peers, parents, and other observers (Bem & Allen, 1974).
- Cross-situational consistency in behavior depends on whether a person is a *high self-monitor* or a *low self-monitor*. High self-monitors are concerned about how people perceive them and adapt their behaviors to fit specific situations, whereas low self-monitors are less concerned about how people perceive them and do not adapt their behaviors as much to fit specific situations. This difference means that low self-monitors show greater cross-situational consistency in their behaviors than do high self-monitors (Gangestad & Snyder, 1985), though this effect is stronger among individualistic cultures than among collectivistic cultures (Church et al., 2006).

Psychology versus Common Sense

Is Personality Consistent from One Situation to Another? *continued*

- Many of the studies that Mischel reviewed were guaranteed to find low cross-situational consistency because they either correlated trait test scores with single instances of behaviors or correlated single instances of behaviors with each other. This situation would be like trying to predict your exact score on your next psychology test from your score on the Scholastic Assessment Test or from your score on a biology test. The prediction would most likely be wrong, because many factors influence your performance on any given academic test. Similarly, many factors other than a given personality trait influence your behavior in a given situation.

Psychologists have achieved greater success in demonstrating cross-situational consistency by using *behavioral aggregation*. In aggregating behaviors, you would observe a person's behavior across several situations. You then would determine how the person *typically*, but not necessarily *always*, behaves—much in the same way that you would find your average on several exams to determine your typical performance in a course. A "humorous" person would be humorous in many, but not all, situations. When we predict how a person will typically behave instead of how that person will behave in a specific situation, the correlation between traits and behaviors becomes a relatively high .60 or more (Epstein & O'Brien, 1985). The importance of behavioral aggregation in determining personality consistency was demonstrated in the following classic study.

When behavioral aggregation was applied to the Hartshorne and May (1928) study, the correlation between the trait of honesty and honest behaviors rose considerably. Consider a similar study by George Dudycha (1936), which examined personality consistency in regard to punctuality. Dudycha noted that some people have reputations for always being punctual and others for always being late. He decided to study the phenomenon of punctuality in everyday life rather than set up artificial situations in which punctuality would be measured. Participants were 307 male and female undergraduates at Ripon College during the 1934–1935 academic year. Their punctuality was assessed on many occasions in six situations: 8 A.M. classes; dinnertime at a dining hall; conference appointments with professors; extracurricular activities (college band and college singers); church services; and entertainment programs (basketball, plays, and concerts). There were a total of 15,360 observations.

When correlations were computed between any two of these situations, students were inconsistent. This finding seemed to indicate that the situation, not personality traits, accounted for punctuality. But, as in the Hartshorne and May (1928) study, when behavioral aggregation was applied to the Dudycha study, college students showed much greater cross-situational consistency in their punctuality. Thus, though personality traits might not predict our behavior in particular situations, they might predict our typical behavior across a variety of related situations.

The cross-situational consistency debate has died down. Researchers now tend to agree that the best approach is to consider the interaction of the person and the situation in assessing cross-situational consistency (Mischel, Shoda, & Mendoza-Denton, 2002). Even Gordon Allport, the noted trait researcher, viewed human behavior as the product of those factors, with different traits aroused to different degrees by different situations (Zuroff, 1986). Of course, some situations (such as being in a worship service) are so powerful that almost all people—regardless of their personalities—will behave the same way in them (Monson, Hesley, & Chernick, 1982).

"Dad, I have commissioned my buddy to study your behaviour patterns."

Behavioral Aggregation

In aggregating behaviors, you would observe a person's behavior across several situations.
Source: Cartoonresource/Shutterstock.com.

The Cognitive-Behavioral Approach to Personality

Researchers who favor the *cognitive-behavioral approach* to personality discount biological factors, unconscious influences, and dispositional traits. Instead, they stress the importance of cognitive and situational factors (Staats, 1994). The cognitive-behavioral approach was influenced by B. F. Skinner (1953), whose operant conditioning theory is described in Chapter 7. He saw no use for concepts invoking biological predispositions, unconscious motives, personality traits, and the like. What we call *personality*, in Skinner's view, is simply a person's unique pattern of behavior, tied to specific situations (Skinner, 1974).

According to Skinner, we are what we do. And what we do in a particular situation depends on our experiences in that situation and similar situations. We tend to engage in behaviors that have been positively or negatively reinforced and to avoid engaging in behaviors that have been punished or extinguished. Thus, Skinner might assume that a gregarious person has a history of receiving attention or anxiety relief for being socially outgoing in a variety of situations. In contrast, a shy person might have a history of being criticized or ignored for being socially outgoing in a variety of situations.

Social-Cognitive Theory

Social-cognitive theory builds a bridge between Skinner's strict behavioral approach and a more cognitive approach to personality. Social-cognitive theory is similar to traditional behavioral theories in stressing the role of reinforcement and punishment in the development of personality. But it is different from traditional behavioral theories in arguing that behavior is affected by cognitive processes. That is, our interpretation of our own personal characteristics and environmental circumstances affects our behavior (Bandura, 1989).

Social-cognitive theory was developed by Albert Bandura (b. 1925), who was reared in Canada but became a professor in the United States and served as president of the American Psychological Association in 1974. Other social-cognitive theories have been developed by Julian Rotter and Walter Mischel. Bandura's theory of personality grew out of his research on observational learning, which also is described in Chapter 7. According to Bandura, we learn many of our behavioral tendencies by observing other people receiving rewards or punishments for particular behaviors. For example, children learn altruistic behavior from adults who behave in a helpful manner.

Bandura's (1986) theory of personality also stresses the concept of **reciprocal determinism**, which reflects his belief that neither personal dispositions nor environmental factors can by themselves explain behavior. You will note that reciprocal determinism differs from environmental determinism, which was favored by Skinner, and psychic determinism, which was favored by Freud. Environmental determinism assumes we are pawns controlled by external stimuli, and psychic determinism assumes we are pawns controlled by unconscious motives. Instead, as illustrated in Figure 13-3, Bandura assumes that cognitive factors, environmental factors, and overt behavior affect one another.

Research studies have found that reciprocal determinism can explain many kinds of behaviors, such as why depression is so difficult to overcome (Teichman & Teichman, 1990). A depressed person's negative thoughts and emotions might induce gloomy statements, sad facial expressions, and aloof social behavior. These outward indications might make other people avoid or respond negatively toward the depressed person. This social response would promote continued negative thoughts and emotions in the depressed person, thereby completing a vicious cycle that is difficult to break.

According to Bandura, one of the most important cognitive factors in reciprocal determinism is **self-efficacy**. Self-efficacy is the extent to which a person believes that she or he can perform behaviors that are necessary to bring about a desired outcome. Self-efficacy determines our choice of activities, our intensity of effort, and our persistence in the face of obstacles and unpleasant experiences, in part by reducing the anxiety that might interfere with engaging in the activity (Bandura, Reese, & Adams, 1982). Self-efficacy promotes motivation and the attainment of performance goals (Bandura & Locke, 2003), adherence to physical exercise programs (Short, Vendelanotte, Rebar, & Duncan, 2013),

---

reciprocal determinism Bandura's belief that cognitive factors, environmental factors, and overt behavior affect each other.

self-efficacy In Bandura's theory, a person's belief that she or he can perform behaviors that are necessary to bring about a desired outcome.

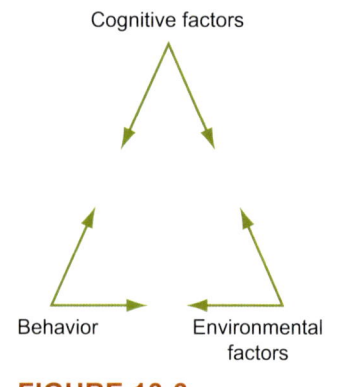

FIGURE 13-3
Reciprocal Determinism

Bandura's concept of reciprocal determinism considers the mutual influence of the person's cognitive factors, behavior, and environment. Each of the three factors can affect the other two.

performance in academic courses (Robbins, Lauver, Davis, Langley, & Carlstrom, 2004), and adherence to addiction treatment regimens (Kelly & Greene, 2013) and chronic pain (da Menezes Costa, Maher, McAuley, Hancock, & Smeets, 2011).

But what determines whether you will have a feeling of self-efficacy in a given situation? The first determinant is *previous success*. You will have a greater feeling of self-efficacy in your psychology course if you have done well in previous courses. The second determinant is *vicarious experience*. You will have a greater feeling of self-efficacy if you know other students who have succeeded in the course. The third determinant is *verbal persuasion*. You will have a greater feeling of self-efficacy if you give yourself pep talks or your advisor convinces you that you have the ability to do well in the course. And the fourth determinant is *physiological arousal*. You will have a greater feeling of self-efficacy if you are at an optimal level of arousal (see Chapter 11).

Bandura (2000) has continued to develop the concept of self-efficacy, noting that with increased interdependence between people, communities, and nations that individuals often have to work together to obtain a desired outcome. **Collective efficacy** refers to people's perception that with collaborative effort the group will obtain its desired outcome. Thus, whereas self-efficacy refers to the perception that "I think *I* can do it," collective efficacy refers to the perception that "I think *we* can do it." Collective efficacy has been found to predict family functioning and satisfaction with family life (Bandura, Caprara, Barbaranelli, Regalia, & Scabini, 2011), to predict engagement and performance in work groups (Salanova, Llorens, Cifre, Martinez, & Schaufeli, 2003), and to be higher among cohesive rugby teams (Kozub & McDonnell, 2000). Collective efficacy also has been used to explain the "home-court advantage" of basketball teams playing on their home court (Bray & Widmeyer, 2000).

collective efficacy People's perception that with collaborative effort the group will obtain its desired outcome.

Though collective efficacy is a relatively new concept and has not been subjected to rigorous empirical research as has the concept of self-efficacy, it provides a promising avenue by which researchers may investigate cultural variations in perceptions of control (Bandura, 2002) and the avenues by which people improve their lives through political activism and promotion of social change. For example, American bank tellers who scored high in personal control and high in self-efficacy experienced fewer stress-related health symptoms and lower job turnover than did tellers high in personal control and low in self-efficacy. A similar relationship was found for personal control and collective efficacy in a sample of bank tellers from Hong Kong. Tellers who scored high in personal control and high in collective efficacy experienced fewer stress-related health symptoms and lower job turnover than did tellers who scored high in personal control and low in collective efficacy (Schaubroeck, Lam, & Xie, 2000). Thus, perceptions of control and the belief that one can meet the demands of the job may reduce stress in individualistic cultures. And perceptions of control and the belief that with collaboration and cooperation the group can meet the demands of the job may reduce stress in collectivist cultures.

Schema Theory

During the past three decades cognitive theories of personality have moved toward an information-processing model, employing the concept of *schemas*. Schemas are cognitive structures that guide people's perception, organization, and processing of social information (see Chapters 4 and 9). Individual differences in personality are thought to be related to the different schemas people use to process information—in this case, about the self.

According to psychologist Hazel Markus (1977), **self-schemas** are specialized cognitive structures about the self. They develop through social experience and serve to organize and guide the processing of social information. Your self-schema consists of aspects of your life and behavior that are important to you (see Figure 13-4). Because each of us has different experiences and interests, not everything we do becomes part of our self-schema (Markus, 1983). For example, two college students may both be avid cyclists and fans of foreign cinema. But both activities may not be part of their self-schemas. If one student is training for a triathlon and describes herself as a serious recreational athlete, then cycling may be a part of her self-schema. If the other student has career aspirations

self-schema In schema theory, specialized cognitive structures about the self.

FIGURE 13-4
Self-Schema

Your self-schema is a specialized cognitive structure about the self. It consists of aspects of your life and behavior that are important to you.

to become an accomplished film director, then studying cinematography and attending foreign films may be part of his self-schema. Thus, activities, interests, and behaviors that are relevant to the self may become part of the self-schema.

Schema theory has been useful in research investigating the relationship between self-schemas and individual differences in a number of variables, including children's willingness to share and help others (Froming, Nasby, & McManus, 1998); women's attitudes toward mathematics (Oswald & Harvey, 2003); recovery from breast cancer surgery (Yurek, Farrar, & Andersen, 2000); adherence to exercise regimens (Whaley, 2003); the development of sexual identity among heterosexual men (Elder, Brooks, & Morrow, 2012); and gender differences in the impact of parenting on self-schemas (Morfei, Hooker, Fiese, & Cordeiro, 2001).

Schema theory has provided a glimpse into the cultural determinants of personality, especially the dimension of individualism versus collectivism (Triandis, 1989). Hazel Markus and Shinobu Kitayama (1991) have proposed that there are cross-cultural differences in the construal of self-schemas in individualistic and collectivistic cultures. These differences involve the concept of independence versus interdependence. Western cultures emphasize individual aspects of the self. People in Western cultures strive to be unique, engage in self-expression, and promote individual goals. In contrast, Asian cultures emphasize interdependent aspects of the self. People in Asian cultures value being part of a group, cooperating, and pursuing group goals. In this way, cultural values and social experiences become integrated into the self-schema. For example, cross-cultural differences in the nature of autobiographical memory (Wagar & Cohen, 2003) and consumers' responses to advertising (Forehand, Deshpande, & Reed, 2002; Wang, Briston, Mowen, & Chakraborty, 2000) have been attributed to cultural differences in self-schemas.

Cognitive-Behavioral Assessment of Personality

There are two main behavioral approaches to the assessment of personality. One approach examines overt behavior; the other examines cognitions that are closely tied to overt behavior.

Experience Sampling

Theorists who favor the examination of overt behavior believe that we should note what people actually do or say they would do in specific situations rather than simply record their responses to personality tests. One form of behavioral assessment uses the *experience-sampling method*. The person carries a beeper that is activated at random times, and on

Chapter 13 Personality

hearing the beep the person reports his or her experiences and behaviors at that time. This method reveals relationships between specific situations and the person's thoughts, feelings, and behaviors (Hormuth, 1986). Several studies have demonstrated the practical usefulness of experience sampling, such as studying depression (Telford, McCarthy-Jones, Corcoran, & Rowse, 2012), work-related stress and fatigue in medical residents (Zohar, Tzischinski, & Epstein, 2003), and cross-cultural differences in emotional experiences (Oishi, 2002). A study of elementary school children assessed their mental self-talk while they worked at their seats. Whenever the children heard a buzzer, they recorded their self-talk. The results showed that children who engaged in positive self-talk had higher academic achievement and more appropriate social behavior, whereas children who engaged in negative self-talk had poorer academic achievement and less appropriate social behavior (Manning, 1990). Of course, only experimental research could determine whether self-talk *causes* differences in academic achievement or social behavior.

The Locus of Control Scale

As an example of the cognitive assessment of personality, consider the *Internal-External Locus of Control Scale*, which was developed by Julian Rotter (1966) to measure what he calls the locus of control. Your *locus of control* is the degree to which you expect that you are in control of the outcomes of your behavior or that those outcomes are controlled by factors such as fate, luck, or chance (Rotter, 1990). In the former case you would have an internal locus of control, and in the latter case you would have an external locus of control. Rotter's concept of the locus of control has been so influential that his original study is one of the most frequently cited studies in the recent history of psychology (Sechrest, 1984).

The scale contains 29 pairs of statements, including 6 that serve to disguise the purpose of the test. A typical relevant pair would be similar to the following: "The more effort you expend, the more likely you are to succeed" and "Luck is more important than hard work in job advancement." Your responses would reveal whether you have an internal or an external locus of control. Just as your sense of self-efficacy might affect your behavior in everyday life, your locus of control might determine whether you try to exert control over real-life situations.

Locus of control has been the subject of numerous studies. People with an internal locus of control are less fatalistic, which makes them more likely to seek medical attention for their physical symptoms (Strickland, 1989). People with an internal locus of control are more likely to take protective action when warned of an impending natural disaster, such as an earthquake (McLure, Walkey, & Allen, 1999). An internal locus of control also is associated with higher job satisfaction and productivity, apparently because employees with an internal locus of control are more motivated and feel more competent (Erez & Judge, 2001; Judge & Bono, 2001). Drivers with an internal locus of control have fewer fatal accidents, perhaps because they are more cautious, attentive, and adept at avoiding dangerous situations (Montag & Comrey, 1987). And people reared in individualistic cultures, such as the United States, tend to be higher in their internal locus of control than are people from collectivist cultures (Rawdon, Willis, & Ficken, 1995), though some studies have found smaller differences when culture-specific measures are employed (e.g., Spector, Sanchez, Sui, Salgado, & Ma, 2004). Moreover, cross-cultural differences in locus of control may be attributed to the fact that in collectivist cultures an external locus of control may be more functional than in individualistic cultures (Cheng, Cheung, Chio, & Chang, 2013).

Status of the Cognitive-Behavioral Approach

B. F. Skinner's operant conditioning theory of personality has been praised for making psychologists more aware of the influence of environmental factors on personality. But the theory has been criticized by Hans Eysenck (1988) for ignoring the influence of heredity on individual differences in personality. The social-cognitive theorists have responded by recognizing the importance of cognitive and environmental factors. But traditional behavioral theorists argue that thoughts do not *cause* behavior. And psychoanalytic theorists criticize cognitive theories for ignoring the irrational, emotional bases of behavior.

> ### Critical Thinking About Psychology
>
> **How Effective Is Psychological Profiling in Identifying Criminals?**
>
> Over the years, you probably have read books or articles or seen television shows about FBI profilers, who provide descriptions of wanted criminals—typically serial killers or terrorists—with the hope of helping investigators narrow the range of potential suspects. Psychological profiling began in the mid-1970s at the FBI training center in Quantico, Virginia. There even was a television series in the 1990s, *Profiler*, that portrayed the exploits of an FBI profiler played by Robert Davi.
>
> But how accurate are psychological profilers? Though the media might publicize individual cases in which psychological profiles have apparently helped solve crimes, there are other cases in which profilers have been inaccurate, sometimes even identifying the wrong person as a suspect. In December 1996, for example, security guard Richard Jewell won a settlement of more than $500,000 from NBC. Nightly news anchor Tom Brokaw had mentioned that Jewell was a suspect in the widely publicized bombing incident at the 1996 Summer Olympic Games in Atlanta that killed one person and injured more than 100 others. Brokaw noted that investigators believed that Jewell fit the psychological profile of other bombers. Nonetheless, investigators eventually cleared Jewell of any responsibility for the bombing.
>
> More recently, with the rash of school shootings across the United States, psychological profiling is being used to help educators identify students at risk of violence (Drummond, 1999). But this application has led to claims that students who are not potential mass murderers are unfairly being brought under suspicion because they fit that psychological profile. In a widely publicized case in late 1999, nuclear scientist Wen Ho Lee accused the government of racism for imprisoning him after accusing him of spying for China and stealing military secrets while working at Los Alamos Laboratory in New Mexico. Lee claimed that he was the victim of overzealous psychological profiling.
>
> If you are interested in learning how detectives develop formal psychological profiles of criminals, you might want to read the *Crime Classification Manual* by John Douglas, Ann Burgess, Allen Burgess, and Robert Ressler (1997). Richard Jewell hired Ressler, a renowned FBI profiler, to support his claim that he was the victim of an inappropriate use of FBI profiling. Ressler claimed that legal authorities were under so much pressure to find the Atlanta bomber that they arrested the first person they thought might be guilty.
>
> Ressler, director of Forensic Behavioral Services, has his own website that describes his 30 years of investigative experience, including 20 with the FBI, and has written an autobiography, *Whoever Fights Monsters* (Ressler & Shachtman, 1992), which describes his work with violent serial and sexual criminals. His work influenced the creators of the book and movie *Silence of the Lambs* and the television series *The X Files*. Ressler and other profilers gained media attention regarding their views in the murder of JonBenet Ramsey, a child

Bandura's concept of self-efficacy has been supported by research findings in a variety of areas in addition to those already mentioned. One study found that high school students' feelings of self-efficacy in mathematics were positively correlated with final exam scores (Pietsch, Walker, & Chapman, 2003). Another study found that people with feelings of self-efficacy for long-distance running are more likely to enter marathon races, train hard for those races, and continue running despite the pain and fatigue they experience (Okwumabua, 1985). A meta-analysis of more than 100 studies involving more than 21,000 participants found that self-efficacy is positively correlated with performance on work-related tasks (Stajkovic & Luthans, 1998). And the concept of collective self-efficacy has broadened our understanding of cross-cultural beliefs in the nature of control, motivation, and agency (Bandura, 2000).

Schema theory also has stimulated research investigating a range of topics such as the relationship of chronic pain, illness, and the self (Pincus & Morley, 2001), development of the self through adulthood (Cross & Markus, 1991), attributions about relapse from exercise regimens (Kendzierski, Sheffield, & Morganstein, 2002), and gender differences in perceptions of political leadership and power (Lips, 2000). Though some cross-cultural psychologists have disputed Markus and Kitayama's model (Matsumoto, 1999), self-schema theory has provided an important theoretical perspective for cross-cultural research investigating personality and motivation (Hernandez & Iyengar, 2001).

> **Critical Thinking About Psychology**
>
> **How Effective Is Psychological Profiling in Identifying Criminals?** *continued*
>
> who was murdered December 26, 1996, in her Boulder, Colorado, home. Her parents, John and Patsy Ramsey, called on Gregg McCrary, a former FBI criminal profiler and colleague of Ressler's, to support their claim that they could not have committed the crime. After he refused to take their case, they hired John Douglas (Brennan, 1997a). McCrary claimed that Douglas's profile was vague and contained characteristics that could be true of many people. Ressler added, "It doesn't in any way resemble an FBI profile. In a nutshell, the profile is bogus. It has very little pertinence to what's going on here. It's so general, it could fit half of Boulder" (Brennan, 1997b). You might note this situation as a possible instance of the Barnum effect, discussed at the beginning of the chapter.
>
> Given the popularity of psychological profiling, researchers are conducting research and publishing articles on it in professional journals. One reason for supporting psychological profiling is that some courts let prosecutors and defense attorneys consider the psychological state of the defendant (Cochran, 1999). Though personality profiling in criminal cases has gained media attention, its validity remains to be established (Kocsis, 2013). Nonetheless, there is evidence that specially trained FBI profilers do produce more accurate profiles than other people do. But even people who support the usefulness of psychological profiling insist that it should be used to generate leads and direct investigations and that it should not be used by itself to identify particular suspects (Palermo, 2002). Moreover, the reasoning ability of profilers might be more important than the amount of experience that they have. In one study, for example, police detectives and undergraduate chemistry majors were presented with information about an actual homicide that an individual had been convicted of committing. Participants were asked to compose criminal profiles of the perpetrator. Contrary to what common sense would have predicted, the chemistry majors outperformed the police detectives—including detectives with many years of homicide investigative experience (Kocsis, Hayes, & Irwin, 2002).
>
> Researchers are trying to provide a more scientific grounding for psychological profiling. In one study, profilers successfully developed psychological profiles that were useful in distinguishing between distinctly different kinds of arsonists (Kocsis, Irwin, & Hayes, 1998). Scientists now are attempting to develop psychological profiles that distinguish different kinds of burglars, (Fox & Farrington, 2012), child sex offenders (Marsa et al., 2004), stranger murderers (Salfati & Canter, 1999), and rapist-murderers (Keppel & Walter, 1999; Schlesinger & Revitch, 1999). The media certainly will continue to celebrate psychological profiling, but it will be up to science to determine whether psychological profiling is a valid technique.

Section Review: The Cognitive-Behavioral Approach to Personality

1. How does the social-cognitive theory of personality differ from the operant conditioning theory?
2. What is reciprocal determinism?
3. How does schema theory explain cross-cultural differences in individualism and collectivism?
4. How do psychologists use experience sampling in the assessment of personality?

The Humanistic Approach to Personality

The *humanistic approach* to personality, which emerged in the 1950s, holds that people are naturally good. This approach contrasts with psychoanalytic personality theorists, who believe that people are predisposed to be selfish and aggressive, and behavioral personality theorists, who believe that people are neither naturally good nor naturally evil.

The humanistic approach also contrasts with the psychoanalytic approaches in accepting subjective mental experience (*phenomenological experience*) as its subject matter. This acceptance makes the humanistic approach similar to the cognitive-behavioral approach, though more concerned with emotional experience. Moreover, the humanistic approach assumes that we have free will, meaning that our actions are not compelled by id impulses or environmental stimuli.

The Self-Actualization Theory of Personality

The first humanistic theory of personality was that of Abraham Maslow (1970), whose theory of motivation is discussed in Chapter 11. Maslow, reared in Brooklyn, was urged by his parents to attend law school. One day he found himself in a course in which he had no interest, and he bolted from the classroom.

Maslow never returned to law school. Instead, against his parents' wishes, he decided to pursue a career in psychology. This willingness to fulfill one's own needs rather than trying to please other people became a hallmark of humanistic theories of personality. As discussed in Chapter 11, Maslow believed we have a need for **self-actualization**, the predisposition to try to reach our potentials. The concept of self-actualization is a descendant of Adler's concept of striving for superiority (Crandall, 1980).

But who is self-actualized? Maslow presented several candidates, including President Abraham Lincoln, psychologist William James, and humanitarian Eleanor Roosevelt. Table 13-3 presents a list of characteristics shared by self-actualized people. Maslow decided on these characteristics after testing, interviewing, or reading the works of individuals he considered self-actualized. Our psychological well-being is related in part to the extent to which we are self-actualized. For example, it seems that one of the reasons why extraverted people tend to be happier than other people is that they are more self-actualized than are more introverted people (Lester, 1990). Parents who score high on measures of self-actualization tend to practice authoritative parenting (Dominguez & Carton, 1997), a parenting style that is superior to permissive parenting and authoritarian parenting. These parenting styles are discussed in Chapter 4.

self-actualization In Maslow's theory, the individual's predisposition to try to fulfill her or his potentials.

TABLE 13-3 Characteristics of Self-Actualized People

- Desire for privacy in certain personal areas of life
- Concern with solving problems more than serving selfish interests
- Nonconformist approach to life
- Means not confused with ends
- Nonhostile sense of humor
- Ability to be sociable while maintaining individual identity
- Objective, realistic outlook on life and others
- Accepting of self and others
- Egalitarian attitude toward others
- Interest in improving the lives of others
- Spontaneous, rather than constricted, in interpersonal relations
- Creative in relating to others and the world
- Preference for several intimate relationships rather than many superficial ones
- Spiritual, though not necessarily religious, experiences

Source: Data from A. H. Maslow (1971), *The Farther Reaches of Human Nature.* New York: Viking Press.

The Self Theory of Personality

Carl Rogers (1902–1987) was born near Chicago to a devoutly religious family. His religious upbringing led him to enter Union Theological Seminary in New York City. But Rogers left the seminary to pursue a career in psychology, eventually serving as president of the American Psychological Association in 1946.

The Self

Rogers pointed out that self-actualization requires acceptance of one's *self* or *self-concept*, which is your answer to the question "Who are you?" But each of us experiences some incongruence between the self and personal experience. We might learn to deny our feelings, perhaps claiming that we are not angry or embarrassed even when we are. This denial might make us feel phony or, as Rogers would say, not genuine. This incongruence between our self and our experience causes us anxiety, which in turn motivates us to reduce the incongruence by altering the self or reinterpreting the experience. Though complete congruence between the self and experience is impossible and would be maladaptive (we would have no motivation to improve the self if we did not experience some incongruence), people who have a great incongruence between the self and experience may develop psychological disorders (see Chapter 14).

How does incongruence between the self and experience develop? According to Rogers, children who do not receive *unconditional positive regard*—that is, complete acceptance—from their parents will develop incongruence by denying aspects of their experience. To gain acceptance from parents, a child might express thoughts, feelings, and behaviors that are acceptable to them. For example, a boy whose parents insist that "boys don't cry" might learn to deny his own painful physical and emotional experiences in order to gain parental approval. Such *conditions of worth* lead children to become rigid and anxious because of a failure to accept their experiences. Instead of becoming self-actualizing, such children may adopt a lifestyle of conformity and ingratiation (Baumeister, 1982). Rogers, like other personality theorists, reveals his own life experiences in his theory. He recalled that as a child he felt that his parents did not love him for himself apart from his accomplishments (Dolliver, 1995).

As shown in Figure 13-5, psychologically healthy people have greater congruence between the *actual self* (Rogers's *self*) and the *ideal self* (the person they would like to be). The more self-actualized the person, the less the incongruence between the person's actual self and ideal self and, as a result, the greater the person's self-esteem (Garcia & Hoskins, 2001). People with a great incongruence between their actual self and their ideal self have more self-doubts and fewer social skills. A study of undergraduates found that as the congruence between their actual and their ideal selves increased, their happiness increased (Drigotas, 2002).

Self-Handicapping

One way to protect the actual self is by *self-handicapping*, in which people claim that a task is too difficult or that factors beyond their control might contribute to their less-than-ideal behavior or performance (Jones & Berglas, 1978). People are more likely to engage in self-handicapping when their self-concept is threatened by potential failure. As you have certainly observed, self-handicapping is common among athletes (Gibson, Sachau, Doll, & Shumate, 2002) and students (Martin, Nejad, Colmar, & Liem, 2013). Thus, a student walking into class for a test might remind his classmates that the need to console a friend the night before prevented him from studying enough. Given these excuses, possible failure on the test would be less of a blow to the actual self. And if the student performs well on the test, the actual self would be elevated. One study found that undergraduates who were high self-handicappers reduced their study time and experienced more stress prior to an introduction to psychology exam. As you might expect, high self-handicappers received lower scores on the exam than did low self-handicappers. Nevertheless, despite their poor exam performance, high self-handicappers believed that

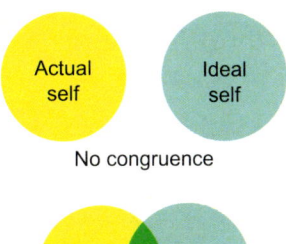

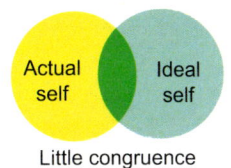

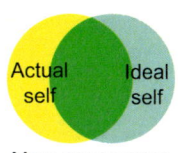

FIGURE 13-5
The Relationship of the Actual and Ideal Self

These diagrams show different degrees of congruence between the actual and ideal self. The more self-actualized the person, the less the incongruence between the actual and ideal self.

they had the ability to do well in psychology, because they attributed their poor exam scores to lack of preparation rather than lack of ability (McCrea & Hirt, 2001).

Self-Esteem

Childhood experiences have a marked influence on *self-esteem*, a person's sense of self-worth (Rosenberg, 1965). Children with warm, nurturant parents are higher in self-esteem (Pawlak & Klein, 1997). One study found that children and their mothers with low self-esteem felt less loved by one another than did children and mothers with high self-esteem (DeHart, Murray, Pelham, & Rose, 2003). And women who believe they have received unconditional positive regard from their fathers have higher self-esteem and less fear of intimate relationships (Scheffler & Naus, 1999). There also is hope for children who have low self-esteem. A meta-analysis found that formal programs aimed at enhancing children's self-esteem can be effective (Haney & Durlak, 1998).

Self-esteem also has important implications for adults. A longitudinal study found that children who had positive relationships with their parents during their transition into adulthood had higher self-esteem then and 20 years later (Roberts & Bengtson, 1996). The quality of romantic relationships is positively related to self-esteem (D. Cramer, 2003). And a study of adult romantic attachment styles found that those with secure or dismissive styles were higher in self-esteem than were those with fearful or preoccupied styles (Bylsma, Cozzarelli, & Sumer, 1997). Moreover, a recent meta-analysis of more than 100 longitudinal studies found that low self-esteem has been found to be correlated with both anxiety and depression across the life span (Sowislo & Orth, 2013).

According to *terror management theory*, self-esteem serves a protective function against death anxiety. People live their lives with an awareness of their own mortality and the inevitability of death. Numerous research studies have found that people high in self-esteem experience lower levels of anxiety. Likewise, people respond to reminders of their own mortality by bolstering their self-esteem (Pyszczynski, Greenberg, Solomon, & Arnst, 2004). Moreover, close relationships serve an additional protective function against death anxiety (Mikulincer, Florian, & Hirschberger, 2003). One study found that participants with secure attachment styles did not exhibit self-defensive responses when reminded of their own mortality. Instead, securely attached participants responded by desiring higher levels of intimacy than did anxious-ambivalent and avoidant participants (Mikulincer & Florian, 2000).

Self-esteem also is related to sociocultural factors. A meta-analysis of studies that included about 145,000 participants found that men tend to have a slightly higher level of self-esteem than women, though the overall effect size is small. The gender difference in self-esteem is greatest at late adolescence, which may be due in part to the increased influence of gender roles, dating, and cultural emphasis on physical appearance (Kling, Hyde, Showers, & Buswell, 1999). People from individualistic cultures tend to have higher self-esteem than do people from collectivist cultures. People from individualistic cultures also are more responsive to positive and negative social interactions than are people from collectivist cultures. Thus, the self-esteem of people from individualistic cultures will fluctuate more than the self-esteem of people from collectivist cultures in response to everyday social interactions (Tafarodi & Walters, 1999).

The Humanistic Assessment of Personality

How do humanistic psychologists assess personality? Two of the main techniques are the *Personal Orientation Inventory* and the *Q-sort*.

The Personal Orientation Inventory

Psychologists who wish to assess self-actualization commonly use the *Personal Orientation Inventory (POI)* (Shostrom, 1962). The POI determines the degree to which a person's values and attitudes agree with Maslow's description of self-actualized people, such as being governed by one's own motives and principles. The inventory contains items that force the person to choose between options, such as (a) "Impressing others is most important" and (b) "Expressing myself is most important." One study found POI scores were higher among older adults—who had mastered more developmental tasks—than among younger adults (Ivtzan, Gardner, Bernard, Sekhon, & Hart, 2013). A newer test of self-actualization, the Brief Index of Self-Actualization (Sumerlin & Bundrick, 1996), has yet to generate enough research to determine its usefulness.

The Q-Sort

The *Q-sort*, derived from Rogers's self theory, is used to measure the degree of congruence between a person's actual self and her or his ideal self. If you took a Q-sort test, you would be given a pile of cards with a self-descriptive statement on each. A typical statement might be "I feel comfortable with strangers." You would put the statements in several piles, ranging from a pile containing statements that are most characteristic of your actual self to a pile containing statements that are least characteristic of your actual self. You would then follow the same procedure for your ideal self, creating a second set of piles. The greater the degree of overlap between the two sets of piles, the greater the congruence between your actual self and your ideal self. Psychotherapists have used the Q-sort method to determine whether therapy has increased the congruence between a client's actual self and ideal self (Leaf, Krauss, Dantzig, & Alington, 1992). The Q-sort also has been used to assess developmental trends in psychological health from adolescence through old age (Jones & Meredith, 2000) and to predict international graduate students' acculturation and integration into university life (Bang & Montgomery, 2013).

Status of the Humanistic Approach

Research has produced mixed support for Maslow's concept of self-actualization. For example, a study of students who scored low in self-actualization on the POI at the beginning of a university preparatory course found they increased in self-actualization by the end of the course (Fogarty, 1994). But there have been inconsistent findings regarding the assumption that self-actualization increases with age. A cross-sectional study (see Chapter 4) of women aged 19 to 55 found an increase in their sense of autonomy. That is, older participants were more motivated by their own feelings than by the influence of other people—a characteristic of self-actualized people (Hyman, 1988). Yet a cross-sectional study of faculty members aged 30 to 68 found that their self-actualization did not increase with age (Hawkins, Hawkins, & Ryan, 1989). Researchers are working on cross-cultural approaches to identifying the universal characteristics of self-actualization and to develop a valid measure of it (Leclerc, Lefrancois, Dube, Hebert, & Gaulin, 1998).

There has been relatively more research on the self, per se, than on self-actualization. In fact, there has been a sprouting of a variety of "selves." A view of the self put forth by E. Tory Higgins (1987) considers the relationship between three selves: the *actual self*, the *ideal self*, and the *ought self*. Incongruence between the actual self and the ideal self will make a person feel depressed. Incongruence between the actual self and the ought self (which is similar to Freud's ego ideal in representing beliefs about one's moral duties) will make a person feel anxious (Strauman & Higgins, 1988). We are motivated to alleviate our personal distress by reducing the incongruence between these selves (Higgins, 1990).

The humanistic approach has been praised for countering psychologists' tendency to study the negative aspects of human experience by encouraging them to study love, creativity, and other positive aspects of human experience. The humanistic approach also has renewed interest in studying conscious mental experience, which was the original subject matter of psychology over a century ago (Singer & Kolligian, 1987). Moreover, the humanistic approach might best reflect popular views of personality. A survey of people in everyday life found that most people believe that others would know them best if others knew their private mental experiences rather than their overt behavior (Andersen & Ross, 1984). The humanistic approach also has contributed to the recent interest in self-development, including beginning a health and fitness regimen when faced with one's mortality (Arndt, Schimel, & Goldenberg, 2003).

But the humanistic approach has not escaped criticism. Critics accuse it of divorcing the person from both the environment and the unconscious mind and for failing to operationally define and experimentally test abstract concepts such as self-actualization (Daniels, 1982). And the assumption of the innate goodness of humanity has been called naïve even by the influential humanistic psychologist Rollo May (1982), who believes that innately good people would not have created the evil that the world has known. Moreover, cross-cultural psychologists question whether positive self-regard is a universal human need. For example, a self-critical focus is more characteristic of Japanese society than American culture (Heine, Lehman, Markus, & Kitayama, 1999), and self-enhancement is more characteristic of American culture (Taylor & Brown, 1988).

Maslow and Rogers have been accused of unintentionally promoting selfishness by stressing the importance of self-actualization without placing an equal emphasis on social responsibility (Geller, 1982). Critics assert that Maslow's model of self-actualization represents a Western model of individualistic growth at the expense of interpersonal relatedness (Hanley & Abell, 2002). But this accusation is countered by research showing that people who have developed a positive self-regard tend to have a greater regard for others than do people with a negative self-regard (Epstein & Feist, 1988). Thus, we must be careful not to confuse self-regard with self-centeredness.

Other researchers have questioned the importance and benefits of high self-esteem. Whereas self-esteem is positively correlated with many measures of mental health and negatively correlated with depression (Taylor & Brown, 1988), the direction of causality is unclear. Moreover, there are instances when high self-esteem may be related to psychological and interpersonal problems—including aggression and antisocial behavior (Baumeister, Campbell, Krueger, & Vohs, 2003). Some researchers have investigated the correlates of inflated self-esteem, as assessed by comparing participants' self-descriptions with those of trained raters and their peers. People who self-aggrandize—that is, regard themselves more positively than others see them—tend to have poor social skills and exhibit some indices of psychological maladjustment (Colvin, Block, & Funder, 1995).

Though the humanistic approach to personality has received its share of criticism, Rogers has been widely praised for his contributions to the advancement of psychotherapy, which is discussed in Chapter 15. Today, no single approach to personality dominates the others. Each makes a valuable contribution to our understanding of personality.

Section Review: The Humanistic Approach to Personality

1. What are the principal characteristics of humanistic theories of personality?
2. What are some of the topics in research on the "self"?
3. How would you use the Q-sort to assess someone's personality?

The Biopsychological Approach to Personality

Personality researchers who favor the *biopsychological approach* warn that "any theory that ignores the evidence for the biological underpinnings of human behavior is bound to be an incomplete one" (Kenrick & Dantchik, 1983, p. 302). The biological basis of personality has been recognized by ancient and modern thinkers alike. The Greek physician-philosopher Hippocrates (460–377 B.C.) presented an early biological view of personality, which was elaborated on by the Greek physician Galen (A.D. 130–200). Hippocrates and Galen claimed that **temperament**, a person's predominant emotional state, reflects the relative levels of body fluids they called *humors*. They associated blood with a cheerful, or *sanguine*, temperament; phlegm with a calm, or *phlegmatic*, temperament; black bile with a depressed, or *melancholic*, temperament; and yellow bile with an irritable, or *choleric*, temperament. Research has failed to find a humoral basis for personality,

temperament A person's characteristic emotional state, first apparent in early infancy and possibly inborn.

Temperament

Infants are born with different temperaments, which form the basis of personality.
Source: Hannamariah/Shutterstock.com.

though differences in temperaments show some relationship to specific patterns of brain activity (Robinson, 2001) and hormonal secretion (Gerra et al., 2000). But as discussed in section 13-2a, "Type Theories," Hans Eysenck's research supports the existence of these four basic temperaments (Stelmack & Stalikas, 1991).

Differences in fetal movement and heart rate are associated with differences in temperament in infancy. More active fetuses become more difficult and unadaptable infants than do less active fetuses. In other words, temperamental differences exist even prenatally (Dipietro et al., 2002). Thus, infants are born already differing in their temperaments. The personality you have today is the indirect product of your temperament as an infant (Rothbart, Ahadi, & Evans, 2000). Your behavior and the reactions of those around you when you were an infant were molded by your temperament. Infants who respond with distress to unfamiliar stimuli tend to become more fearful and subdued in childhood and adolescence (Kagan, 1997). Early life temperament also plays an important role in adult life. An fMRI study found that adults who had an inhibited temperament at 2 years of age had a greater amygdalar response (see Chapter 12, section 12-1b, "The Brain and Emotion") to unfamiliar faces than did adults who had been uninhibited children (Schwartz, Wright, Shin, Kagan, & Rauch, 2003). Likewise, some researchers think that this brain region, along with the hippocampus, might be responsible for influencing personality differences that contribute to temperament. Another fMRI study examined 39 participants that were separated into two groups: extremely inhibited or uninhibited temperaments. Participants were shown neutral faces on a screen while in a fMRI. In contrast to participants with uninhibited temperaments, the amygdala and hippocampus failed to habituate to novel faces in participants with inhibited temperaments (Blackford, Allen, Cowan, & Avery, 2013). Thus, people with inhibited temperaments may be hypervigilant to strangers and social situations.

The humoral theory of personality was dominant until the late 18th century, when it was joined by phrenology and physiognomy. As described in Chapter 3 (see "Thinking Critically About Psychology"), *phrenology* is the study of the contours of the skull. Phrenologists assumed that specific areas of the brain controlled specific personality characteristics and that the bumps and depressions of the skull indicated the size of those brain areas. Those who believed in *physiognomy*, the study of physical appearance, held that personality was revealed by the features of the face.

Research failed to support phrenology and physiognomy. Like astrology, they were subject to the Barnum effect. Phrenologists did, however, spark interest in the study of the biological bases of personality, particularly the role of heredity (Hilts, 1982). The early 20th century saw biologically inclined personality researchers begin to study the relationship between physique and personality.

The Relationship Between Physique and Personality

The scientific study of the relationship between physique and personality began with the work of the German psychiatrist Ernst Kretschmer (1888–1964). Kretschmer (1925) measured the physique of hundreds of mental patients and found a relationship between thin physiques and schizophrenia and between rounded physiques and manic depression. But the researcher who did the most to advance the scientific study of the physique-personality relationship was the American physician and psychologist William Sheldon

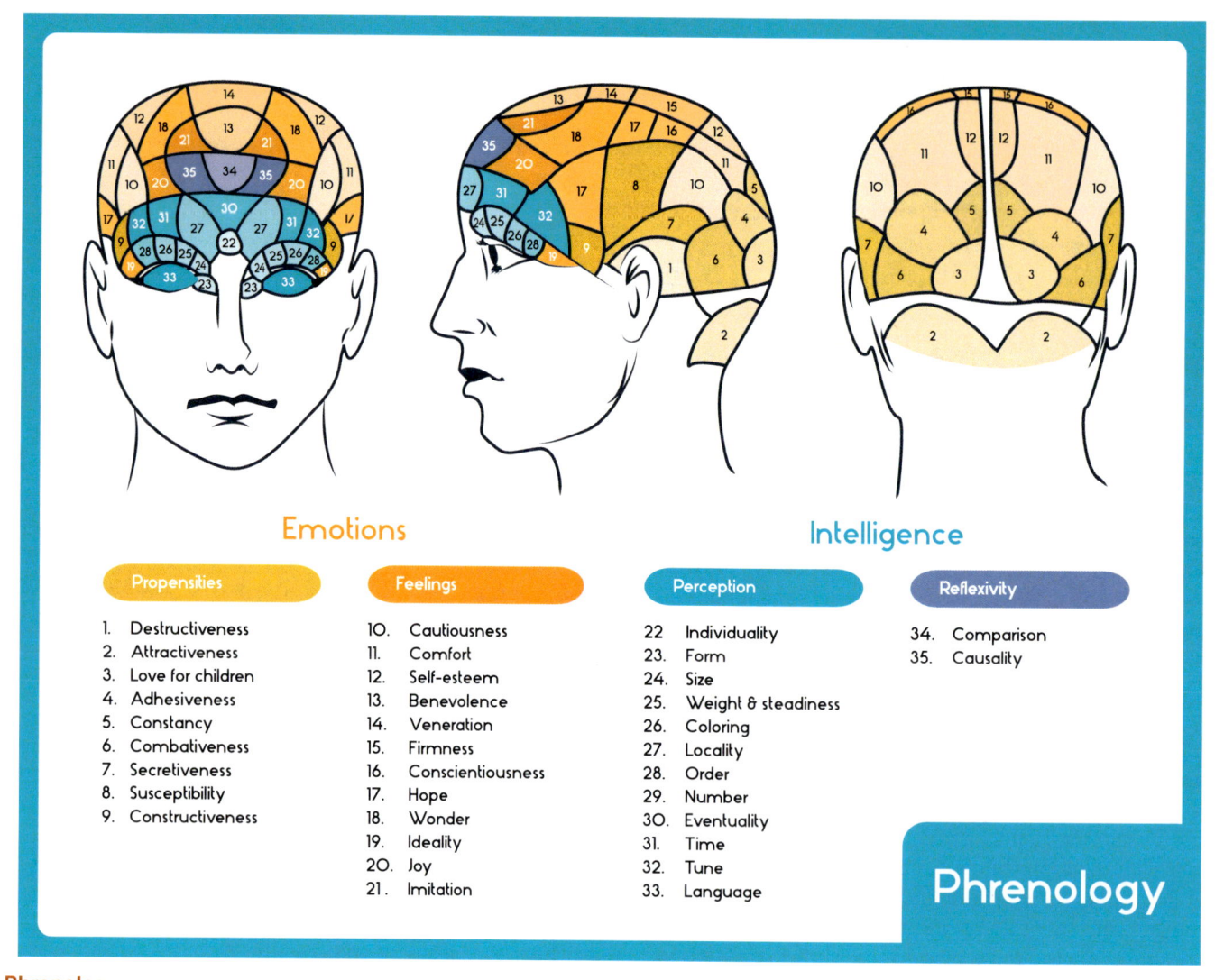

Phrenology

Emotions

Propensities
1. Destructiveness
2. Attractiveness
3. Love for children
4. Adhesiveness
5. Constancy
6. Combativeness
7. Secretiveness
8. Susceptibility
9. Constructiveness

Feelings
10. Cautiousness
11. Comfort
12. Self-esteem
13. Benevolence
14. Veneration
15. Firmness
16. Conscientiousness
17. Hope
18. Wonder
19. Ideality
20. Joy
21. Imitation

Intelligence

Perception
22. Individuality
23. Form
24. Size
25. Weight & steadiness
26. Coloring
27. Locality
28. Order
29. Number
30. Eventuality
31. Time
32. Tune
33. Language

Reflexivity
34. Comparison
35. Causality

Phrenology

Phrenology was a pseudoscience that studied the contours of the skull.
Source: Polina Kudelkina/Shutterstock.com.

(1898–1977), whose inspiration to become a psychologist came from having William James as his godfather (Hilgard, 1987).

In formulating his *constitutional theory* of personality, Sheldon examined photographs of thousands of young men. He identified three kinds of physiques, each of which represents a different **somatotype**. The *ectomorph* has a thin, frail physique; the *mesomorph* has a muscular, strong physique; and the *endomorph* has a soft, rounded physique. Because Sheldon recognized that few people were pure somatotypes, he rated participants on a scale of 1 to 7 for each of the three kinds of physiques. Sheldon also administered personality tests to his research participants. He found that each somatotype was associated with a particular temperament. He called the shy, restrained, and introspective temperament of the ectomorph *cerebrotonia*; the bold, assertive, and energetic temperament of the mesomorph *somatotonia*; and the relaxed, sociable, and easygoing temperament of the endomorph *viscerotonia* (Sheldon & Stevens, 1942).

But how might somatotypes affect personality? Sheldon reasoned that their own somatotypes might affect people's behavior and the behavior of others toward them. For example, one study found that heterosexual women found mesomorphic men to be most sexually attractive, followed by ectomorphic and endomorphic men (Dixson, Halliwell, East, Wignarajah, & Anderson, 2003). Sheldon's theories, with some exceptions, are con-

somatotype In Sheldon's theory, a physique associated with a particular temperament.

sidered to be outdated. Today, psychologists who are interested in the biological bases of personality are more likely to study the effects of heredity and how heredity interacts with social experience.

The Relationship Between Heredity and Personality

More than a century ago Francis Galton insisted that "nature prevails enormously over nurture" (Holden, 1987, p. 598). Today, researchers like Galton who believe that heredity molds personality assume that evolution has provided us with inborn behavioral tendencies that differ from person to person (Bouchard & Loehlin, 2001). The field that studies the relationship between heredity and behavior is called *behavioral genetics* (see Chapters 3 and 4). For example, a behavioral genetics study found that the inherited tendency to be highly emotional is an important risk factor in regard to divorce (Jocklin, McGue, & Lykken, 1996).

Behavioral geneticists also study the manner in which heredity interacts with the environment. For example, mutations, in the gene that codes for the enzyme Monoamine Oxidase A (MAO-A), have been strongly associated with antisocial behavior. MAO-A is important for serotonin, norepinephrine, and dopamine signaling in brain regions associated with emotional processing. One recent study examined MAO-A as a marker for this behavioral trait. The researchers found that 7-year-old British boys with low MAO-A activity later developed mental health problems and that these individuals might be more susceptible to environmental stress (Kim-Cohen et al., 2006). Likewise, another recent study examined the same MAO-A mutation and the relationship between parenting and infant temperament. Participants, mothers and infants, were given assessments to examine maternal sensitivity and anger proneness, respectively. What researchers found was that low levels of MAO-A activity were dependent on both decreased maternal sensitivity and increased infant anger proneness (Pickles, 2013). MAO-A activity is an important mediator for predicting poor mental health outcomes for anger-prone individuals. This study and others contribute to our understanding of heredity and how heredity interacts with social experience.

How might these initial differences in temperament contribute to the development of differences in personality? They might affect how infants respond to other people and, in turn, how other people respond to them. For example, a placid infant would be less responsive to other people. As a consequence, others would be less responsive to the infant. This early lack of response might predispose the infant to become less sociable later in childhood, laying the groundwork for an introverted personality. Inherited differences in temperament contribute to the development of differences in specific personality characteristics, such as self-esteem (Kendler, Gardner, & Prescott, 1998). And as discussed above, genetics can affect behavior and can interact with social experience.

Biopsychological Assessment of Personality

In general, the closer the genetic relationship is between two persons, the more alike they will be in personality characteristics. But this relationship might reflect common life experiences rather than common genetic inheritance. For example, identical twins might respond similarly to personality tests because they are exposed to more similar environments than are fraternal twins (Schonemann & Schonemann, 1994). Because of the difficulty in separating genetic effects and environmental effects in studies of relatives who share similar environments, researchers have resorted to adoption studies. The Texas Adoption Project found that, in regard to personality, children tend to resemble their biological parents more than their adoptive parents (Loehlin, Horn, & Willerman, 1990). Such findings indicate that parent-child personality similarity is influenced more by common heredity than by common life experiences, as supported by the study described in "The Research Process: How Similar Are the Personalities of Identical Twins Reared Apart?"

One of the newer biopsychological approaches to personality assessment involves the measurement of brain activity. Much of the research has involved correlating brain

The Research Process

How Similar Are the Personalities of Identical Twins Reared Apart?

Rationale

Since 1979, psychologist Thomas Bouchard of the University of Minnesota has conducted the most comprehensive study of identical twins reared apart and then reunited later in life. He has found amazing behavioral similarities between some of the twins. Consider the case of Oskar Stohr and Jack Yufe, who were born in Trinidad to a Jewish father and a Catholic mother. The twins were separated shortly after birth and reared in vastly different life circumstances. While Oskar was reared in Germany as a Nazi by his maternal grandmother, Jack was reared in Trinidad as a Jew by his father. Decades later, when they arrived at the airport in Minneapolis to take part in Bouchard's study, both Jack and Oskar sported mustaches, wire-rimmed glasses, and two-pocket shirts with epaulets. Bouchard found that they both preferred sweet liqueurs, stored rubber bands on their wrists, flushed the toilet before using it, read magazines from back to front, and dipped buttered toast in their coffee (Holden, 1980). Though there are probably no "flush toilet before using" genes, the men's identical genetic inheritance might have provided them with similar temperaments that predisposed them to develop certain behavioral similarities. In fact, Bouchard and his colleagues have found that the rearing environment has relatively little influence on the development of personality (Bouchard & McGue, 1990).

Studies of identical twins reared apart provide the strongest support for the hereditary basis of personality. Identical twins have 100 percent of their genes in common, whereas fraternal twins are no more alike genetically than nontwin siblings. Their shared genes might explain why identical twins who are adopted and reared by different families are more similar in personality than fraternal twins who are reared by their biological parents—even three decades after adoption (Tellegen et al., 1988).

Method

Participants were volunteers in the Minnesota Twin Study between 1970 and 1984. There were 217 identical twin pairs reared together, 114 fraternal twin pairs reared together, 44 identical twin pairs reared apart, and 27 fraternal twin pairs reared apart. The twins who had been reared apart had been separated, on the average, more than 30 years. Participants were given the Multidimensional Personality Questionnaire, which measures basic personality traits.

Results and Discussion

The results indicated that identical twins reared together and identical twins reared apart were highly similar in intelligence. Identical twins reared apart also were more similar than fraternal twins reared together. Overall, the heritability of personality was .48. (The heritability of personality is a population's proportion of the variability in personality that is caused by heredity.) Thus, the participants' personalities were strongly, though not solely, influenced by heredity.

---

activity with introversion and extraversion. One study found differences in the electrical activity of the brain, between extraverts and introverts in their response to emotional stimuli (Bartussek, Becker, Diedrich, & Naumann, 1996). Studies that have used the PET scan also have found differences in patterns of brain activity between introverts and extraverts (Fischer, Wik, & Fredrikson, 1997; Johnson et al., 1999). Studies using fMRI have examined the relationship between brain structure and personality as well. Researchers have found that amygdalar volume and cortical thickness and the way in which these structures communicate are positively correlated with externalizing behavior in children (Ameis et al., 2013). Further, extroverts with disorders such as oppositional defiant disorder or conduct disorder have problems making moral decisions. Imaging studies have shown that this might also be related to communication between structures such as the amygdala and cortex (Marsh et al., 2011). Therefore, brain structure and connectivity may contribute to personality traits.

Status of the Biopsychological Approach

Research has failed to find the strong relationship between somatotype and personality reported by Sheldon. One of the main problems with Sheldon's research was that *he* rated both the somatotypes and the temperaments of his participants. His close involvement provided room for experimenter bias, perhaps making his ratings support his theory more than they should have. Nonetheless, there is a modest relationship between physique and personality. For example, as predicted by Sheldon, mesomorphic men are more extraverted, self-confident, and emotionally stable (Tucker, 1983). But a study in which staff members rated the personalities of children at a day-care center found no relationships between their physiques and their personalities (Lester, Kaminsky, & McGovern, 1993).

Even positive findings do not indicate that physique differences *cause* personality differences. Perhaps, instead, personality differences affect dietary and exercise habits, thereby causing differences in physique. Another possibility is that hereditary factors cause a relationship between physique and personality due to the interaction of heredity and social experience. For example, a study found that newborn ectomorphic infants were more emotionally responsive than infants with other physiques (Lester & Wosnack, 1990). This finding supported Sheldon's notion that the same genes might determine both physique and temperament (Sheldon & Stevens, 1942).

Putting aside the question of the relationship between physique and personality, how heritable is personality? Research has been mostly consistent, though results vary, in finding that the heritability of personality is about .30 to .60 (Benjamin, Ebstein, & Belmaker, 1997; Bouchard & Hur, 1998; Plomin, Corley, Caspi, Fulker, & DeFries, 1998). Moreover, there is some cross-cultural support for these estimates of the heritability of personality (Jang, McCrae, Angleitner, Riemann, & Livesley, 1998; Borkenau, Riemann, Angleitner, & Spinath, 2001). Studies in behavioral genetics have found, for example, genetic influences on the likelihood of marrying (Johnson et al., 2004), the degree of job satisfaction (Ilies & Judge, 2003), and the tendency to experience social anxiety (Stein, Jang, & Livesley, 2002). Research on the human genome has begun to identify specific genes associated with particular personality traits, including aggressiveness (Rujescu, Giegling, Gietl, Hartmann, & Moeller, 2003), and social detachment (Joensson et al., 2003).

As for environmental influences on personality, research findings have contradicted the commonsense belief that shared environmental experiences play a major role in personality similarity between close relatives. Research findings have consistently demonstrated that non-shared environmental experiences outweigh the effects of shared environmental experiences in affecting personality development (Hur, McGue, & Iacono, 1998; Saudino et al., 1999; Vernon, Jang, Harris, & McCarthy, 1997). Nonetheless, some personality traits, such as religious orthodoxy, do show substantial relationships to shared environmental experiences (Beer, Arnold, & Loehlin, 1998).

And what of Bouchard's research on identical twins reared apart? Care must be taken in drawing conclusions from the amazing behavioral similarities in some of the twins he has studied. Imagine that you and a fellow student were both asked thousands of questions (as Bouchard asks his participants). Undoubtedly you would find some surprising similarities between the two of you, even though you were not genetically related. This result was demonstrated in a study that found many similarities between pairs of strangers. For example, one pair of women were both Baptists, nursing students, active in tennis and volleyball, fond of English and mathematics, not fond of shorthand, and partial to vacations at historic places (Wyatt et al., 1984). Of course, by comparing twins' performances on formal personality tests, Bouchard does more than simply report selected instances of amazing similarities between certain ones. Given the evidence for both genetic and environmental influences, the best bet is to accept that they both strongly—apparently about equally—affect the development of personality.

Section Review: The Biopsychological Approach to Personality

1. What weaknesses are there in research on somatotypes and personality?
2. How do studies of identical twins who have been reunited provide evidence supporting the role of heredity in personality development?

Experiencing Psychology

Are Amazing Similarities in Personality Just the Result of Coincidence?

Rationale

As discussed in "The Research Process: How Similar Are the Personalities of Identical Twins Reared Apart?", amazing psychological and behavioral similarities between identical twins who were separated in infancy and reunited years later have provoked interest in the possible hereditary basis of personality. But researchers typically ask the reunited twins hundreds or even thousands of questions. Perhaps the amazing similarities we hear about have been research report examples selected by the media to support claims that personality development depends more on one's heredity than on one's environment. If, instead, we asked unrelated people many questions about themselves, we would find equally amazing similarities among them (Wyatt, Posey, Walker, & Seamonds, 1984).

Method

Participants

The participants will be the members of your introductory psychology class.

Materials

You and your classmates will complete the "Identical Twins Reunited Questionnaire" that accompanies this exercise. The questionnaire asks (not terribly personal) questions about behaviors, relationships, and personal characteristics.

Procedure

Have the students take the questionnaire anonymously. Go through the questionnaire responses to determine whether any pair of questionnaires has remarkable similarities in responses.

Results and Discussion

Describe your class findings. Were any similarities between students truly startling? If so, how might this finding affect your judgment of media reports of astounding similarities between identical twins reunited later in life? Why do research reports of similarities in personality between identical twins reared apart not suffer from the selection bias that might plague media reports of the same research?

Identical Twins Reunited Questionnaire

Give your responses to each of the following questions. If you prefer not to answer particular questions, feel free to leave them blank.

1. Academic major:
2. Favorite musical group/performer:
3. Mother's first name:
4. Favorite dessert:
5. Boyfriend's/girlfriend's first name:
6. Favorite television show:
7. Political affiliation (Dem/Rep/Indep/Other):
8. Favorite food:
9. Favorite actor:
10. Favorite actress:
11. Favorite movie:
12. Favorite hobby:
13. Favorite sport to watch:
14. Favorite sport to play:
15. Favorite professional sports team:
16. Favorite author:
17. Father's first name:
18. Most distinctive habit:
19. Favorite politician:
20. Favorite professional athlete:
21. Most disliked food:
22. Favorite automobile:
23. Favorite kind of pet animal:
24. Professional goal:
25. Most recent noncourse book read:

Chapter Summary

The Psychoanalytic Approach to Personality

- Your personality is your unique, relatively consistent pattern of thoughts, feelings, and behaviors.
- Freud's psychosexual theory emphasizes the conflict between biological drives and sociocultural prohibitions in the development of personality.
- Freud divided the mind into conscious, preconscious, and unconscious levels.
- Freud distinguished between the personality structures called the id, the ego, and the superego.
- According to Freud, we progress through oral, anal, phallic, latency, and genital stages of development.
- We may use defense mechanisms to protect us from being overwhelmed by anxiety.

- Freud's intellectual descendants altered his theory, generally downplaying the importance of sexuality and emphasizing the importance of social relationships.
- Alfred Adler's theory of individual psychology assumes that personality develops from our attempts to overcome early feelings of inferiority.
- Karen Horney's theory emphasized the role of social and cultural factors in personality development.
- Carl Jung's theory of analytical psychology assumes that we are influenced by both a personal unconscious and the archetypes in a collective unconscious.
- The Rorschach test and the Thematic Apperception Test are two of the main psychoanalytic assessment techniques.

The Dispositional Approach to Personality

- The dispositional approach to personality attributes the consistency we see in personality to relatively enduring personality attributes.
- Hans Eysenck's three-factor theory sees personality as dependent on the interaction of three dimensions: stability/instability, tough-minded/tender-minded, and introversion/extraversion.
- In his trait theory of personality, Gordon Allport distinguished three kinds of traits: cardinal traits, central traits, and secondary traits.
- Personality types are measured by tests such as the Myers-Briggs Type Indicator, and personality traits are measured by tests such as the MMPI.
- Walter Mischel provoked controversy by claiming that situations are more important determinants of behavior than are personality traits.
- Mischel based this conclusion on studies finding that individuals' behavior is not consistent across different situations.
- Research indicates that personality is neither as inconsistent as Mischel originally claimed nor as consistent as personality theorists had previously claimed.

The Cognitive-Behavioral Approach to Personality

- B. F. Skinner's operant conditioning theory assumes that what we call personality is simply a person's unique pattern of behavior.
- Albert Bandura's social-cognitive theory argues that cognitive factors influence behavior.
- Bandura's concept of reciprocal determinism points out the mutual influence of cognitive factors, overt behaviors, and environmental factors.
- One of the most important personality characteristics is self-efficacy, the extent to which a person believes that she or he can perform behaviors that are necessary to bring about a desired outcome.
- Self-schemas are cognitive structures about the self. Cross-cultural differences may be reflected in the construal of self-schemas.
- Behavioral assessment is accomplished through the experience-sampling method.
- Julian Rotter's Internal-External Locus of Control Scale is one of the main cognitive-behavioral assessment techniques.

The Humanistic Approach to Personality

- Abraham Maslow's self-actualization theory is based on his hierarchy of needs.
- Maslow assumes that we have a need to develop all of our potentials, a process he called self-actualization.
- Maslow identified the characteristics of eminent people whom he believed were self-actualized.
- Carl Rogers's self theory holds that psychological well-being depends on the congruence between one's self and one's experience.
- Other researchers point to the importance of congruence between the actual self, the ideal self, and the ought self.
- Self-actualization is measured by the Personal Orientation Inventory.
- Congruence between the actual self and the ideal self is measured by the Q-sort.

The Biopsychological Approach to Personality

- Closely related to personality is temperament, a person's most characteristic emotional state.
- Sheldon's constitutional theory holds that different temperaments are associated with different physiques, or somatotypes.
- Research in behavioral genetics has found evidence of the hereditary basis of temperament and other aspects of personality.
- Heredity and its interaction with social experience play a role in personality development.

Key Terms

personality (p. 443)

The Psychoanalytic Approach to Personality

anal stage (p. 447)
archetypes (p. 450)
collective unconscious (p. 449)
defense mechanism (p. 445)
ego (p. 445)
Electra complex (p. 447)
extravert (p. 450)
genital stage (p. 447)
id (p. 445)
introvert (p. 450)
latency stage (p. 447)
libido (p. 446)
Oedipus complex (p. 447)
oral stage (p. 446)

personal unconscious (p. 449)
phallic stage (p. 447)
pleasure principle (p. 445)
projective test (p. 450)
reality principle (p. 445)
superego (p. 445)

The Dispositional Approach to Personality

trait (p. 454)

The Cognitive-Behavioral Approach to Personality

collective efficacy (p. 461)
reciprocal determinism (p. 460)
self-efficacy (p. 460)
self-schema (p. 461)

The Humanistic Approach to Personality

self-actualization (p. 466)

The Biopsychological Approach to Personality

somatotype (p. 472)
temperament (p. 470)

Chapter Quiz

Note: Answers for the Chapter Quiz questions are provided at the end of the book.

1. A student is tempted to cheat on an exam, but feels guilty and resists the impulse. A Freudian would attribute this to a strong
   a. id.
   b. ego.
   c. superego.
   d. archetype.

2. A person's characteristic emotional state, first apparent in early infancy, is called (the)
   a. ego.
   b. archetype.
   c. personality.
   d. temperament.

3. A researcher studies the hunger motive by providing participants with a buzzer randomly throughout the day. In response to the buzzer, the participants jot down the situation they are in and any of their immediate thoughts or feelings about food. This is an example of
   a. experience sampling.
   b. behavioral observation.
   c. reciprocal determinism.
   d. situational interviewing.

4. The role of self-esteem in protecting us from death anxiety is a central concept in
   a. self-schema theory.
   b. psychoanalytic theory.
   c. terror management theory.
   d. individual psychology.

5. A person who acts in a loud, boisterous manner in all situations would be low in
   a. somatotonia.
   b. extraversion.
   c. self-efficacy.
   d. self-monitoring.

6. The dimensions in Hans Eysenck's three-factor theory of personality are neuroticism, extraversion, and
   a. eroticism.
   b. psychoticism.
   c. obsessiveness.
   d. hypochondriasis.

7. According to William Sheldon, a person with an endomorphic physique has a temperament that he called
   a. adipotonia.
   b. somatotonia.
   c. cerebrotonia.
   d. viscerotonia.

8. The five-factor theory of personality includes the traits of extraversion, neuroticism, agreeableness, openness to experience, and
   a. melancholia.
   b. romanticism.
   c. aggressiveness.
   d. conscientiousness.

9. The view that personality is a person's unique pattern of behavior tied to specific situations would most likely be held by
   a. B. F. Skinner.
   b. Abraham Maslow.
   c. Raymond Cattell.
   d. Harry Stack Sullivan.

10. A student who responds to the stress of final exams by sucking on lollipops, playing on a seesaw, and watching children's cartoon shows on television would most likely be resorting to the defense mechanism of
    a. denial.
    b. projection.
    c. regression.
    d. rationalization.

11. Carl Jung used the archetype of God to explain the
    a. Oedipus complex.
    b. striving for superiority.
    c. need for self-actualization.
    d. reports of flying saucers after World War II.

12. Walter Mischel (1968) argued that personality is not consistent because the correlation between behaviors that presumably represent the same trait rarely exceeded about
    a. .05.
    b. .10.
    c. .30.
    d. .60.

13. According to Hazel Markus and Shinobu Kitayama, people in Western cultures have a self-schema that is characterized by
    a. interdependence.
    b. independence.
    c. reciprocal determinism.
    d. constructive alternativism.

14. In Albert Bandura's theory, a person's belief that he or she can perform behaviors that are necessary to bring about a desired outcome is called
    a. self-efficacy.
    b. self-actualization.
    c. psychic determinism.
    d. reciprocal determinism.

15. According to Carl Rogers, personality development is affected by the degree of incongruence between the self and personal experience, which is affected by the degree of parental
    a. fixation.
    b. self-actualization.
    c. reciprocal determinism.
    d. unconditional positive regard.

16. According to researchers such as Gordon Allport, a relatively enduring, cross-situationally consistent personality characteristic is called a(n)
    a. trait.
    b. archetype.
    c. defense mechanism.
    d. personal construct.

17. One of the strongest criticisms of Freudian personality theory is that it
    a. does not operationally define its terms.
    b. has had little influence outside of psychotherapy.
    c. lacks any research support for unconscious motivation.
    d. gives more importance to adolescent experiences than to childhood experiences.

18. The Minnesota Multiphasic Personality Inventory (MMPI) was designed to
    a. reveal unconscious motives.
    b. diagnose psychological disorders.
    c. identify patterns of personal constructs.
    d. trace changes in personality across the life span.

19. The word *personality* comes from the Latin word for
    a. mask.
    b. character.
    c. individual.
    d. temperament.

20. According to Karen Horney, a person exhibiting a neurotic coping style might be submissive, aggressive, or
    a. manic.
    b. humorous.
    c. reclusive.
    d. extraverted.

21. According to Freud, the cornerstone of his theory is
    a. libido.
    b. free will.
    c. repression.
    d. early childhood experiences.

22. A psychologist shows you a series of pictures of people in ambiguous situations and asks you to tell her the story behind each. She is using the
    a. Q-sort.
    b. TAT.
    c. MMPI.
    d. Rorschach test.

23. In Alfred Adler's theory, the healthiest way of striving for superiority is expressed through
    a. sublimation.
    b. social interest.
    c. obeying one's archetypes.
    d. constructive alternativism.

24. The conflict between the need for freedom and the anxiety that freedom brings is a core concept in the personality theory of
    a. Erich Fromm.
    b. Karen Horney.
    c. Erik Erikson.
    d. Harry Stack Sullivan.

25. In his personality theory, Harry Stack Sullivan stressed the importance of
    a. somatotypes.
    b. behavioral consistency.
    c. healthy social relationships.
    d. sufficient numbers of personal constructs.

Thought Questions

1. How might Karen Horney's concept of basic anxiety explain the three major trends that she observed in how people relate to one another?

2. What are the arguments in favor of the cross-situational consistency of personality traits?

3. How might self-handicapping be used in everyday life in work, school, and sports?

CHAPTER **14** | # Psychological Disorders

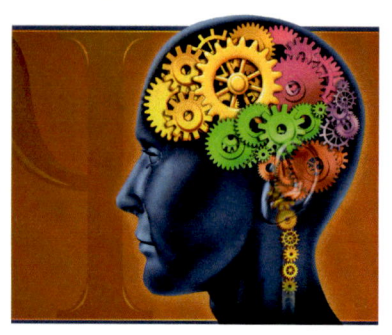

Source: Lightspring/Shutterstock.com.

Chapter Outline

Characteristics of Psychological Disorders
Anxiety Disorders
Obsessive-Compulsive Disorder
Somatic Symptom and Related Disorders
Dissociative Disorders
Major Depressive Disorder and Related Disorders
Bipolar Disorder
Schizophrenia
Personality Disorders
Developmental Disorders

You might be surprised to learn that the United States once had a self-proclaimed emperor, the Emperor Norton I. He began his life as Joshua Norton, a man who left his family farm and built the first rice mill in California. Norton became a respected, seemingly normal San Francisco merchant. But after losing a hard-earned fortune of $40,000 and going bankrupt, in 1859 he deteriorated psychologically and placed an advertisement in *The San Francisco Bulletin* proclaiming himself Norton I, Emperor of the United States and Protector of Mexico. For the next two decades, he wore an officer's uniform and a beaver hat with a feather. He also carried a saber as he strolled the streets of the city, lifting the spirits of his "subjects." Though an emperor, he lived in an inexpensive rooming house, paying 50 cents a day for rent. Nonetheless, in his role as emperor, he abolished Congress and dissolved the United States.

The Emperor Norton (as he was affectionately known to his subjects) also declared streetcars to be free and issued bonds and collected taxes, which actually were donations to support him given by friendly bankers and shopkeepers. Norton became a renowned figure in the San Francisco Bay area. Though Jewish, he was welcomed into a different Christian church each Sunday—as part of his effort to prevent his subjects from believing that he favored one faith over another.

Norton received free meals at the finest restaurants, and he saw audiences rise in his honor when he arrived at the theater. And he did his best to protect his subjects. On one occasion, he prevented a frenzied crowd from attacking Chinese citizens by reciting the Lord's Prayer—shaming them into silence and freezing them in their place. He was so popular that when he was arrested for vagrancy, newspapers published editorials criticizing the police for their treatment of San Francisco's first citizen.

Though Norton was talkative, many of his speeches were virtually incomprehensible, consisting of his delusional thinking about the state of the country. Yet, some of his ideas were farsighted. In 1869 he placed an announcement in the *Oakland Daily News*, ordering the construction of a bridge across the bay. He was ridiculed for proposing such a "foolish" venture, an endeavor that was considered impossible at the time.

At the time of his death in 1880, the Emperor Norton had become the most famous and beloved person in San Francisco. But he died a pauper, his meager financial resources comprising $5.50 in coins and several Bonds of the Empire. The day after Norton's death, the *San Francisco Chronicle* carried the headline "Le Roi Est Mort" ("The King Is Dead"). Well-to-do friends paid for an elaborate funeral—fit for an emperor—attended by many thousands of Norton's subjects. Several years later, Robert Louis Stevenson wrote that his favorite San Franciscan had been the Emperor Norton (McDonald, 1980). At Norton's final resting place, his friends erected a marble tombstone that read:

Norton I

Emperor of the United States and Protector of Mexico

Joshua A. Norton, 1819–1880

Aside from demonstrating that San Francisco has long been hospitable to people with unusual lifestyles, the story of Joshua Norton is an example of a person with the psychological disorder called *schizophrenia*, which often is marked by language problems, hallucinations, peculiar behavior, and delusions of grandeur, such as believing that one is a rich, famous, or powerful person. It also demonstrates that even a person with schizophrenia might be able to live a fulfilling life.

Characteristics of Psychological Disorders

How do psychologists determine whether a person has a psychological disorder? What are the causes of psychological disorders? And how are psychological disorders classified and diagnosed? Answers to these questions are provided by professionals with expertise in **psychopathology**—the study of psychological disorders. A diagnosis of a psychological disorder may interfere with a person's daily life, and many professionals are qualified to treat psychological disorders.

psychopathology The study of psychological disorders.

Criteria for Psychological Disorders

An ambitious study called the National Comorbidity Survey Replication (NCS-R) examined the prevalence of psychological disorders in the United States. This survey of more than 9,000 persons ages 15 to 54 years found that 32.4 percent had at least one psychological disorder within the past year (Kessler, Chiu, Demler, Merikangas, & Walters, 2005) and 48 percent had at least one during their lifetime (Kessler et al., 2004). You probably know people whose patterns of moods, thoughts, and actions make you suspect that they too suffer from a psychological disorder. But what are the criteria for determining that a person has a disorder? The main criteria are *abnormality*, *maladaptiveness*, and *personal distress*.

The Criterion of Abnormality

Abnormal behavior deviates from the behavior of the "typical" person—the *norm*. A norm can be qualitative or quantitative. *Qualitatively abnormal* behavior deviates from culturally accepted standards, perhaps even seeming bizarre. A railroad conductor who announces train stops would be normal. But a passenger who announces train stops would be abnormal. *Quantitatively abnormal* behavior deviates from the statistical average. A woman who washes her hands 3 times a day would be normal. But a woman who washes her hands 30 times a day would be abnormal.

By itself, abnormality is not a sufficient criterion for determining the presence of a psychological disorder. If qualitative abnormality were sufficient, then artistic innovators, political dissidents, and people who achieve rare accomplishments, such as a Nobel Prize winner or your student government president, would be considered psychologically disordered. And if quantitative abnormality were sufficient, then even a physician who washes her hands 30 times a day in the course of seeing patients would be considered psychologically disordered. Thus, the sociocultural context in which "abnormal" behavior occurs must be considered before deciding that it is symptomatic of a psychological disorder.

The Criterion of Maladaptiveness

According to the criterion of *maladaptiveness*, you would have a psychological disorder if your behavior seriously disrupted your social, academic, or vocational life. As an example, consider a person with the anxiety disorder called *agoraphobia*, which is the fear of being in public places. Such a person might be afraid to leave home and might consequently alienate friends, fail in school, and lose a job. Similarly, a person who uses drugs or alcohol excessively would be considered psychologically disordered because such behavior would interfere with everyday functioning. But maladaptive behavior is not always a sign of a psychological disorder. Though cramming for exams, failing to eat fruits and vegetables, and driving 90 miles an hour on a busy highway are maladaptive behaviors, they would not necessarily be symptomatic of a psychological disorder.

The Criterion of Personal Distress

The criterion of *personal distress* assumes that our subjective feeling of anxiety, depression, or other unpleasant emotions determines whether we have a psychological disorder. Nonetheless, personal distress might not be a sufficient criterion for determining the presence of a psychological disorder (Widiger & Trull, 1991). Some people, like the notorious John Wayne Gacy—a Chicago man who killed 33 boys and young men in the 1970s but expressed no guilt about it—might have a psychological disorder without feeling any distress.

Behavior that is abnormal, maladaptive, or personally distressing might indicate that a person has a psychological disorder. But there is no single point at which a person moves from being psychologically healthy to being psychologically disordered. Each of us varies on each of the criteria. Thus, there is a degree of subjectivity in even the best answers to the question of how abnormal, maladaptive, or personally distressing a person's behavior must be before we determine that he or she has a psychological disorder.

Viewpoints on Psychological Disorders

Even when psychologists agree on the presence of a particular psychological disorder, they may disagree on its causes. That is, they favor different viewpoints regarding the causes of psychological disorders. Since ancient times, people have tried to explain the unusual or distressing behavior patterns that we now call psychological disorders. Many ancient Greek authorities assumed that the gods inflicted psychological disorders on people to punish them for their misdeeds. But the Greek physician Hippocrates (ca. 460–ca. 377 B.C.) argued instead that psychological disorders had natural causes.

Despite the efforts of Hippocrates and his followers, supernatural explanations existed alongside naturalistic ones until the 19th century. The 16th-century Swiss physician Paracelsus (1493–1541) rejected the supernatural viewpoint. Instead of attributing unusual behavior to demons, he attributed it to the moon. Paracelsus called the condition *lunacy* and the people who exhibited it *lunatics*. These terms were derived from the Latin word for "moon." You probably have heard someone say, on an evening when people are acting oddly, "There must be a full moon tonight." Yet contrary to popular belief, the moon does not affect the incidence of crime, mental illness, or other abnormal behavior (Rotton & Kelly, 1985). This finding holds across countries. For example, a study of admissions to emergency psychiatric centers in Iran found no relationship between a full moon and the number of admissions (Kazemi-Bajestani, Amirsadri, Samari, & Akbar, 2011).

Current viewpoints on psychological disorders attribute them to natural factors. As shown in Table 14-1, the viewpoints differ in the extent to which they attribute psychological disorders to biological, mental, or environmental factors. But no single viewpoint provides an adequate explanation of psychological disorders. This lack of an explanation has led to the emergence of the **biopsychosocial model** (Figure 14-1), which holds that psychological disorders are the result of an interaction of biological, psychological, and social factors (Johnson, 2013). Often, professionals will have expertise in one aspect of this model, but very few would deny that all three aspects are important.

biopsychosocial model The model that considers that psychological disorders are the result of an interaction of biological, psychological, and social factors.

TABLE 14-1 The Major Viewpoints on Psychological Disorders

Viewpoint	Causes of Psychological Disorders
Biopsychological	Inherited or acquired brain disorders involving imbalances in neurotransmitters or damage to brain structures
Psychoanalytic	Unconscious conflicts over impulses such as sex and aggression, originating in childhood
Behavioral	Reinforcement of inappropriate behaviors and punishment or extinction of appropriate behaviors
Cognitive	Irrational or maladaptive thinking about one's self, life events, and the world in general
Humanistic	Incongruence between one's actual self and public self as a consequence of trying to live up to the demands of others
Sociocultural	Sociocultural factors that influence psychological symptoms and the prevalence of psychological disorders

According to the biopsychosocial model, there can be many individual differences in the development of psychological disorders. For example, a person with a low sense of personal control might succumb to relatively low levels of stress due to factors such as a romantic breakup or academic failure. This person would be unlikely to cope well with most stressful situations. Likewise, a person with a high sense of personal control might not succumb to even moderate levels of stress, due to these same factors. This person would be likely to cope well with stressful situations by engaging in proactive strategies, such as recruiting the support of friends and family. Researchers often want to know what makes one person vulnerable to stress while another person is resilient to stress. Research findings indicate that the biopsychosocial model can explain the interaction of biological, psychological, and social factors to cause some psychological disorders, such as major depressive disorder (Schotte, Van Den Bossche, De Doncker, Claes, & Cosyns, 2006) and substance abuse that results from social anxiety (Buckner, Heimberg, Ecker, & Vinci, 2013). A core concept of this model is that all three features—biological, psychological, and social factors—interact with each other.

Biological Factors
- Genetics
- Neurotransmitter levels
- Environmental toxins
- Immune response

Psychological Factors
- Learning history
- Stress
- Emotional responses
- Personality
- Habits

Social Factors
- Social support
- Interpersonal problems
- Health education
- Medical care

Psychological Disorders

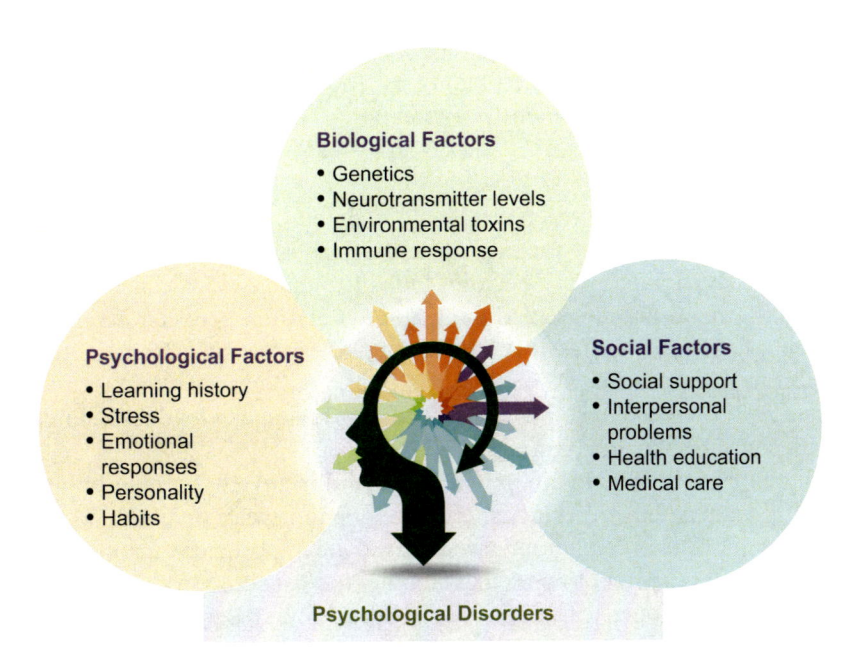

FIGURE 14-1

The Biopsychosocial Model

According to the biopsychosocial model, psychological disorders are the result of an interaction of biological, psychological, and social factors.

Source: (center image) art4all/Shutterstock.com.

The Biopsychological Viewpoint

More than a century ago, Sigmund Freud remarked, "In view of the intimate connection between things physical and mental, we may look forward to a day when paths of knowledge will be opened up leading from organic biology and chemistry to the field of neurotic phenomena" (Taulbee, 1983, p. 45). As a physician and biologist, Freud might have approved of the *biopsychological viewpoint*, which favors the study of the biological causes of psychological disorders.

Modern interest in the biological causes of psychological disorders was stimulated in the late 19th century when early researchers discovered that a disorder called general paresis, marked by severe mental deterioration, was caused by brain damage due to untreated syphilis. Researchers in the 19th century also found that toxic chemicals could induce psychological disorders. In fact, the Mad Hatter in the book *Alice in Wonderland* exhibits psychological symptoms caused by exposure to the mercury that was used in making felt hats. This phenomenon was the origin of the phrase "mad as a hatter" (O'Carroll, Masterton, Dougall, Ebmeier, & Goodwin, 1995). We now know that mercury poisoning can cause neurocognitive disorders and other psychological symptoms due to the accumulation of heavy metals in the brain. Examples of the biological roots of psychological disorders include heredity, atypical brain development, excessive or deficient neurotransmitter activity, and variations in hormone levels. Some other contributing factors that might be dependent on these biological roots are sleep disturbances, substance abuse, poor nutrition, and infectious diseases.

Today, biopsychological researchers are interested in how psychological factors interact with the biological roots of psychological disorders. Research supporting the possible role of heredity in the development of psychological disorders has found that monozygotic (identical) twins show higher correlations than dizygotic (fraternal) twins in traits that indicate psychopathology (Eaves et al., 1997). Moreover, monozygotic twins reared apart show higher correlations than ordinary siblings reared together in traits that indicate psychopathology (DiLalla, Carey, Gottesman, & Bouchard, 1996). Several recent studies examined the neural networks related to agoraphobia, a type of anxiety disorder in which people experience panic attacks in public or open spaces. Using fMRI, 72 participants with agoraphobia and their healthy matched controls were scanned while being shown images of open spaces. Researchers found that participants with agoraphobia had increased brain activity in regions associated with panic attacks, such as portions of the basal ganglia that connect to the limbic system, while viewing images or even anticipating viewing the images (Wittmann et al., 2014). Studies such as these contribute to our understanding of both the biology (brain activity) and psychology (perceptual processes) that contribute to the development of agoraphobia. Moreover, they will help researchers develop innovative treatments. Understanding psychological disorders is not a matter of biology versus psychology, but rather the interaction of both.

The Psychoanalytic Viewpoint

The *psychoanalytic viewpoint*, which originated in medicine, grew out of the biopsychological viewpoint. But instead of looking for underlying biological causes of psychological disorders, the psychoanalytic viewpoint looks for unconscious causes. As discussed in Chapter 13, Sigmund Freud stressed the continual conflict between inborn biological drives, particularly sex and aggression, which demand expression, and the norms of society that inhibit their expression. According to Freud, conflicts about sex and aggression can be repressed into the unconscious mind. This repression can lead to feelings of anxiety caused by pent-up sexual or aggressive energy.

Freud claimed that we might gain partial relief of this anxiety by resorting to defense mechanisms. If your defense mechanisms are either too weak or too rigid, you might develop psychological disorders. Freud also stressed the importance of anxiety-provoking childhood experiences in promoting the development of psychological disorders. A major study, the NCS-R mentioned earlier in this chapter, found that some disorders were, in fact, associated with adverse experiences during childhood. For example, the more adverse events children experienced, the more likely they were to experience adult psychopathology. Additionally, there were gender differences in the development of adult psychological disorders. Among adult women, psychological disorders were related to childhood sexual abuse, whereas among adult men, psychological disorders were related to economic hardship in the family (Putnam, Harris, & Putnam, 2013).

The Behavioral Viewpoint

The *behavioral viewpoint* arose in opposition to psychological viewpoints that looked for mental causes of behavior. In the tradition of B. F. Skinner, psychologists who favor the behavioral viewpoint look to the environment and to the learning of maladaptive behaviors as the causes of psychological disorders. A psychological disorder might arise when a person is reinforced for inappropriate behavior or has appropriate behavior punished or extinguished. Social-cognitive behaviorists, such as Albert Bandura, would add that we might develop a psychological disorder by observing other people's behavior. For example, a person might develop a phobia (an unrealistic fear) of dogs after either being bitten by a dog or observing someone else being bitten by a dog.

Those who favor the behavioral viewpoint, with its emphasis on environmental factors, also would be more likely to consider the negative effects of socioeconomic conditions on psychological well-being. For example, poverty is a predisposing factor in a variety of psychological disorders. A survey found that poverty is associated with a higher risk of almost all psychological disorders. This finding holds true for young and old, men and women, and African Americans and European Americans (Bruce, Takeuchi, & Leaf, 1991). Moreover, a recent study found that psychiatric symptoms among children from families who moved out of poverty fell to the level of those who had never experienced poverty (Costello, Compton, Keeler, & Angold, 2003).

The Cognitive Viewpoint

The Greek Stoic philosopher Epictetus (A.D. ca. 60–ca. 120) taught that "men are disturbed not by things, but by the views which they take of things." This statement is the central assumption of the *cognitive viewpoint*, which holds that psychological disorders arise from maladaptive ways of thinking about oneself and the world. Many cognitive theorists assume that people with psychological disorders hold irrational beliefs that lead to emotional disturbances and maladaptive behaviors. For example, major depressive disorder is associated with a negative self-schema (see Chapter 13) and is exacerbated when people ruminate over their negative self-views (Dozois & Dobson, 2003; Sheppard & Teasdale, 2004). Yet, studies indicate that people with moderate levels of depression, termed *dysphoria*, may think more rationally and objectively than other people about themselves and the world (Taylor & Brown, 1988) and likely ruminate less. That is, if you are mentally healthy, you might be unrealistically optimistic and view the world through rose-colored glasses.

The Humanistic Viewpoint

As described in Chapter 13, psychologists who favor the *humanistic viewpoint*, most notably Carl Rogers and Abraham Maslow, stress the importance of self-actualization, which is the fulfillment of one's potential. According to Rogers and Maslow, psychological disorders occur when people fail to reach their potential, perhaps because others, especially their parents, discourage them from expressing their true desires, thoughts, and interests. This *conditional positive regard* may lead the person to develop a public self-image that is favorable to others but markedly different from his or her actual, private self. The distress caused by the failure to behave in accordance with one's own desires, thoughts, and interests can lead to the development of a psychological disorder.

The Sociocultural Viewpoint

One of the main influences on human diversity is culture, a factor that psychologists generally overlooked until the past 30 years. Psychologists who stress the importance of cultural influences on psychological disorders favor the *sociocultural viewpoint*. Instead

Critical Thinking About Psychology

Does the Insanity Defense Let Many Violent Criminals Escape Punishment?

More than 2,000 years ago, Plato noted that "someone may commit an act when mad or afflicted with disease . . . let him pay simply for the damage; and let him be exempt from other punishment" (quoted in Carson & Butcher, 1992, p. 32). Today, Plato would face opposition from those who argue against the insanity defense. Spurred by the media's coverage of the successful insanity plea of John Hinckley Jr. following his attempted assassination of President Ronald Reagan and the plea by Dan White after the murders of San Francisco mayor George Moscone and city supervisor Harvey Milk, critics believe that the insanity defense is a miscarriage of justice (Szasz, 1980). But do these and other cases portrayed in the media indicate that many people have gotten away with murder by using the insanity defense?

The Volitional Rule

A person who did not know what he or she was doing at the time of the crime could still use the insanity defense.
Source: Noel Powell/Shutterstock.com.

Characteristics of the Insanity Defense

Insanity is a legal, not a psychological or psychiatric, term attesting that a person is not responsible for his or her own actions. In criminal cases, insanity is usually determined by a jury. The insanity defense was formalized in 1843 in the case of Daniel M'Naghten, a man with schizophrenia who had tried to murder the English prime minister Robert Peel, whom he believed was persecuting him. But M'Naghten killed Peel's secretary, Edward Drummond, by mistake. After a controversial trial that was sensationalized in magazines and newspapers, M'Naghten was ruled not guilty by reason of insanity and was committed to a mental hospital. The *M'Naghten rule* became a guiding principle in English law. The rule states that a person is not guilty if, at the time of a crime, the person did not know what she or he was doing or did not know that it was wrong.

Today, the most widely used standard for determining insanity in the United States is that of the American Law Institute. The standard comprises two rules. First, the *cognitive rule*, similar to the M'Naghten rule, says that a person was insane at the time of a crime if the person did not know what he or she had done or did not know that it was wrong. Based on this rule, some defendants who have killed a person while sleepwalking have been acquitted of murder charges (Thomas, 1997).

Second, the *volitional rule* says that a person was insane at the time of a crime if the person was not in voluntary control of her or his behavior. In 1857, in an early use of the volitional rule, Abraham Lincoln—then an attorney in Illinois—prosecuted a case in which defense attorneys claimed that a defendant was insane at the time he committed a murder because he was under the influence of chloroform, a drug that can induce anesthesia (Spiegel & Suskind, 1998).

Controversy Concerning the Insanity Defense

In recent decades, several cases involving the insanity defense, including that of John Hinckley Jr., have provoked controversy. For example, in October 2002, John Allen Muhammad and Lee Boyd Malvo killed 10 people during a 3-week period of random attacks in the Washington, D.C., area. The pair stalked people going about their daily lives in highways, shopping malls, and gas stations and then shot the victims with military precision using long-distance firearms. Muhammad, a 43-year-old Gulf War veteran, was sentenced to death by a Virginia court in March 2004. Malvo, who

---

insanity A legal term attesting that a person is not responsible for his or her own actions, including criminal behavior.

of presuming that psychological disorders are identical in their prevalence and symptoms across cultures, these psychologists note that, though some disorders are universal, others are unique to particular cultures, and still others occur in most, but not all, cultures (Thakker, Ward, & Strongman, 1999). There is some cross-cultural universality in the symptoms of certain disorders, such as major depressive disorder and schizophrenia, but less universality in other disorders. Most psychological disorders show the influence of social, ethnic, and cultural factors (Draguns & Tanaka-Matsumi, 2003). For example, hunger, low-paid work under dangerous conditions, and chronic domestic violence are the social root of many mental health problems experienced by women worldwide. A recent study that examined over 5,500 Canadian Americans found an alarming relationship between

Critical Thinking About Psychology

Does the Insanity Defense Let Many Violent Criminals Escape Punishment? *continued*

was 17 at the time of the shootings, pleaded not guilty by reason of insanity, claiming that Muhammad had brainwashed him while acting as his surrogate father. Nonetheless, Malvo was found guilty of his crimes and was sentenced to life in prison.

Despite media-driven concern about alleged abuses of the insanity defense, it rarely is used in felony crimes and is generally successful only with the most obviously disturbed persons. For example, an archival study of felony cases adjudicated in New York County from 1988 to 1997 found that less than 1 percent involved any type of insanity defense (Kirschner & Galperin, 2001). Even when the insanity defense is successful, the person is usually confined for an extended period (Lymburner & Roesch, 1999). This finding holds true in the United States as well as in other countries, such as Ireland (Gibbons, Mulryan, & O'Connor, 1997).

Guilty but Mentally Ill

The notoriety of cases such as those of John Hinckley, Dan White, and Lee Boyd Malvo prompted a reevaluation of the insanity defense by state legislatures and professional organizations. Some states have abandoned the insanity defense entirely, whereas others have adopted a rule of *guilty but mentally ill*. This rule requires that an insane person who committed a crime be placed in a mental hospital until she or he is no longer mentally ill, at which time the person would serve the remainder of the sentence in prison. This compromise verdict has provoked controversy regarding its wisdom (Melville & Naimark, 2002).

The American Psychiatric Association, the American Psychological Association, and the American Bar Association have their own positions regarding the insanity defense. The American Psychiatric Association position states that the insanity defense is a legal and moral question, not a psychiatric one, and that psychiatrists should testify only about a defendant's mental status—not about a defendant's responsibility for a crime (Herbert, 1983).

The American Psychological Association took a more cautious approach, calling for research on the effects of the insanity defense before deciding to eliminate it or replace it with a plea of guilty but mentally ill (Mervis, 1984). The past few decades have, in fact, seen a series of studies on the insanity defense. In an experiment on the effect of the guilty-but-mentally-ill verdict option, undergraduates participated as jurors in a mock trial. They then answered questions about the case. Participants who were given the guilty-but-mentally-ill verdict option showed a two-thirds reduction in the verdicts of either guilty or not guilty by reason of insanity when compared to participants not given that option (Poulson, 1990).

The American Bar Association would retain the cognitive rule but would eliminate the volitional rule in the insanity defense. A person who did not know what he or she was doing could still use the insanity defense. That is, someone who knowingly stole a smartphone, for example, would be legally responsible even if he believed that the smartphone was issuing instructions to him from Mars. Mental illness would be a defense only if a person were so psychotic that he thought he was squeezing an orange when he was strangling a child (Holden, 1983).

The volitional rule has come under especially strong attack because it might be impossible to determine whether a person has acted from free will or from an irresistible impulse. For example, in 1994 Lorena Bobbitt, in a celebrated case in which she cut off her husband Wayne's penis, was ruled not guilty by reason of insanity. Though she claimed that she had been driven to it after years of physical abuse, the prosecution claimed she should still be held criminally responsible for her act.

It remains to be seen whether legislatures will completely overturn our long tradition of not holding people with severe psychological disorders responsible for criminal actions. Both science and politics will determine the outcome of this issue, reflecting the battle between empiricism and emotionalism in regard to the insanity defense (Rogers, 1987).

---

the lack of food and psychological disorders (Muldoon, Duff, Fielden, & Anema, 2013). Similarly, the social disruption, unemployment, and culture shock experienced by young male immigrants are risk factors for substance abuse (López & Guarnaccia, 2000).

In some cases, behavior that is considered disordered in one culture is considered normal in another. For example, Ethiopian immigrants who exhibit an altered state called *Zar*, which is considered normal in Ethiopia, have mistakenly been diagnosed as suffering from obsessive-compulsive disorder and treated with drug therapy by Western psychiatrists (Grisaru, Budowski, & Witztum, 1997). Given the importance of culture, it is desirable that the diagnosis of psychological disorders consider the individual's cultural background (Parron, 1997).

The Sociocultural Viewpoint

According to the sociocultural viewpoint, most psychological disorders show the influence of sociocultural factors, such as hunger.

Source: Stanislav Tiplyashin/Shutterstock.com.

Classification of Psychological Disorders

Over the centuries, authorities have distinguished a variety of psychological disorders, each with its own set of symptoms. In 1883 German psychiatrist Emil Kraepelin (1856–1926) devised the first modern classification system (Weber & Engstrom, 1997). Today, the most widely used system of classification of psychological disorders is the fifth edition of the *Diagnostic and Statistical Manual of Mental Disorders (DSM-5)*, published by the American Psychiatric Association. The *DSM-5* and all of its previous iterations have helped health care practitioners create a standardized system of diagnosing psychological disorders. This is useful because when a person is diagnosed with, for example, generalized anxiety disorder, it means approximately the same thing to different other practitioners. On a more practical level, a diagnosis from this manual helps guide important decisions about what insurers cover and what special services a child might receive in school.

The DSM

The *DSM-5*, published in 2013, is a revised version of the *DSM-IV*, which was published in 1994 (and revised in 2007 as the *DSM-IV-TR*). They were preceded by the *DSM-III*, which was published in 1980 (and revised in 1987 as the *DSM-III-R*), the *DSM-II*, which was published in 1968, and the *DSM-I* in 1952. The *DSM* provides a means of communication among mental health practitioners, offers a framework for research on the causes of disorders, and helps practitioners diagnose and choose the best treatment for particular disorders (Clark, Watson, & Reynolds, 1995).

The *DSM-I* and the *DSM-II*, which were based on psychoanalytic theory, divided disorders into neuroses and psychoses. A neurosis involved anxiety, moderate disruption of social relations, and relatively good contact with reality. A psychosis involved thought disturbances, bizarre behavior, severe disruption of social relations, and relatively poor contact with reality. The *DSM-III*, *DSM-IV*, and *DSM-5* dropped this psychoanalytic orientation and, consistent with the biopsychosocial model, consider the interaction of biological, psychological, and social factors in the diagnosis of psychological disorders.

The *DSM-IV* provided five axes for diagnosing psychological disorders. Axis I contained 16 major categories of psychological disorders. Axis II contained personality disorders and mental retardation, or as described in Chapter 10, intellectual disability disorder. Axis III contained medical conditions that might affect the person's psychological disorder. Axis IV contained social and environmental sources of stress that the person has been under recently. And Axis V contained an estimate of the person's level of functioning. The *DSM-5* introduced a major change in this system, noting that the multi-axial system was not necessary for the diagnosis of mental disorders. Instead, the *DSM-5* has adopted the World Health Organization's International Classification of Diseases (ICD). In addition to the ICD, clinicians must consider the psychological and environmental factors that an individual must face (Axis IV of the *DSM-TR*), and the World Health

488 Chapter 14 Psychological Disorders

Organization's Disability Assessment Schedule (WHODAS) has been included—subject to future research—to replace Axis V.

Though the *DSM-5* has been recently published, there is a growing body of research examining its reliability and validity. The reliability of a diagnosis refers to the extent to which different evaluators make the same diagnosis. For example, will several clinical psychologists independently agree that a given person has schizophrenia? The validity of a diagnosis refers to the extent to which a diagnosis is accurate. For example, does a person who has been diagnosed as schizophrenic truly have schizophrenia? Though some critics accuse the *DSM-5* of having poor reliability and unknown validity (Jones, 2012), research indicates that the *DSM-5* has good to very good reliability (Narrow et al., 2013). Research trials assessing the validity of the *DSM-5* and various disorders are currently ongoing. Nevertheless, many psychologists agree that the *DSM-5* is an improvement over the *DSM-IV-TR* (Freedman et al., 2013). Moreover, though the *DSM-5* has been praised for being more culturally sensitive and gender-fair in diagnosing disorders (Kupfer, Kuhl, & Regier, 2013), it also has been criticized for not going far enough in doing so (e.g., Hinton & Lewis-Fernández, 2011; Swartz, 2013).

One advancement is the noticeable shift in considering gender-related issues. In the *DSM-5*, gender identity disorder has been replaced with the diagnosis *gender dysphoria*, which refers to transgender individuals whose gender identity is not consistent with their sex assigned at birth (see Chapter 11). Other notable changes include an intent to avoid inconsistencies and improve reliability in the diagnosis of autism spectrum disorder (ASD). For example, Asperger's syndrome, which is characterized by impaired social interactions, was once a subcategory of ASD. Now, it is diagnosed as ASD. As the *DSM* is a "living document," it is likely to change again in the future. This is evidenced by the purposeful change from Roman numerals to Arabic numbers. The next version will be *DMS-5.1* and so on.

Criticisms of the Diagnosis of Psychological Disorders

Despite the widespread reliance on the *DSM*, some professionals criticize the potential negative effects of the diagnosis of psychological disorders. This critical attitude was inspired in part by the classic study on the effects of diagnosis that is described in the "Psychology versus Common Sense" feature.

Section Review: Characteristics of Psychological Disorders

1. How do the various viewpoints regarding the causes of psychological disorders differ from one another?

2. What is the difference between the cognitive rule and the volitional rule in regard to the insanity defense?

3. What is the main implication of Rosenhan's study of the diagnosis of psychological disorders?

Anxiety Disorders

You certainly have experienced anxiety when learning to drive, taking an important exam, or going on a first date. *Anxiety* is a feeling of apprehension accompanied by sympathetic nervous system arousal, which increases sweating, heart rate, and breathing rate and produces other physiological responses. Though anxiety is a normal and beneficial part of everyday life, warning us about potential threats, in **anxiety disorders**, it becomes intense, chronic, and disruptive of everyday functioning. About 33 percent of adult Americans suffer from anxiety disorders (Kessler, Petukhova, Sampson, Zaslavsky, & Wittchen, 2012), which briefly include *generalized anxiety disorder*, *panic disorder*, and *phobias*, such as *specific phobias*, *social anxiety disorder*, and *agoraphobia*.

anxiety disorder A psychological disorder marked by persistent and unrealistic worry that disrupts everyday functioning.

Chapter 14 Psychological Disorders

Psychology versus Common Sense

Can Mentally Healthy People Be Recognized in a Mental Hospital?

This classic study was conducted by psychologist David Rosenhan (1973). He wondered whether we should accept the commonsense belief that mentally healthy people, complaining of symptoms of schizophrenia, could gain admission to a mental hospital and, once admitted, be discovered by the staff. Rosenhan had eight apparently healthy persons, including himself, gain admission to mental hospitals by calling the hospitals for appointments and then complaining of hearing voices that said "empty, hollow, thud." Hearing imaginary voices is a symptom of schizophrenia.

The eight pseudopatients were admitted to 12 hospitals in five states; their stays ranged from 7 to 52 days. During their stays, they behaved normally, did not complain of hearing voices, and sometimes wrote hundreds of pages of notes about their experiences in the hospitals. Though no staff members discovered that the pseudopatients were faking, several real patients accused them of being journalists or professors investigating mental hospitals. Rosenhan concluded that the diagnosis of psychological disorders is influenced more by preconceptions and by the setting in which we find a person than by any objective characteristics of the person. According to his findings, the commonsense belief that professionals can easily determine whether someone has a psychological disorder is mistaken.

But Rosenhan's study provoked criticism from psychiatrist Robert Spitzer, who helped revise the *DSM* and who felt that Rosenhan had misinterpreted the results (Spitzer, 1975). First, the admission of the pseudopatients to the mental hospitals was justified because people who report hearing imaginary voices may have schizophrenia. Second, people with schizophrenia can go long periods of time without displaying obvious symptoms of the disorder. Thus, the staff members who observed the pseudopatients during their stays had no reason to conclude that they were faking.

Nonetheless, the suggestion that the label "mentally ill" has the power to color our judgment of a person was supported by another study. When participants observed people labeled as mental patients (who actually were not) or similar people not given that label, they were more likely to rate the alleged mental patients as being "unusual" (Piner & Kahle, 1984). The diagnosis of psychological disorders also can be influenced by social class and gender role stereotypes. In two studies, clinicians (Landrine, 1987) and undergraduate psychology students (Landrine, 1989) read descriptions of women and men of different social classes and were asked to assign diagnoses to each case. Participants were cautioned that the descriptions might be of normal cases. Patterns of diagnosis varied by gender and social class. For example, descriptions of lower-class men were more likely to be labeled antisocial, and descriptions of married middle-class women were more likely to be labeled dependent. Thus, both clinicians and undergraduate psychology students perceived gender and social class patterns associated with psychopathology.

The leading critic of diagnostic labels is psychiatrist Thomas Szasz (1960), who has gone so far as to call mental illness, including schizophrenia, a "myth" (Dammann, 1997). He believes that the behaviors that earn the label of mental illness are "problems in living." According to Szasz, labeling people as mentally ill wrongly blames their maladaptive functioning on an illness. He believes that the notion of mental illness is a two-edged sword. On the one hand, it might excuse heinous behavior committed by those labeled mentally ill. On the other hand, it might enable governments to oppress nonconformists by labeling them mentally ill. Szasz's claim that mental illness is a myth has provoked critical responses from other mental health practitioners (Bentall & Pilgrim, 1993), as indicated in the following comment:

> This myth has a seductive appeal for many persons, especially if they do not have to deal clinically with individuals and their families experiencing the anguish, confusion, and terror of schizophrenia. Unfortunately, informing schizophrenics and their relatives that they are having a mythological experience does not seem to be appreciated by them and is not particularly helpful. (Kessler, 1984, p. 380)

The many mental health professionals who helped create the *DSM-5* do not view the psychological disorders it describes as myths. Among the most important categories of psychological disorders are *anxiety disorders, somatic symptom and related disorders, dissociative disorders, major depressive disorder and related disorders, schizophrenic disorders, personality disorders,* and *developmental disorders*. Figure 14-2 indicates the prevalence of several important psychological disorders in the United States.

Psychology versus Common Sense

Can Mentally Healthy People Be Recognized in a Mental Hospital? *continued*

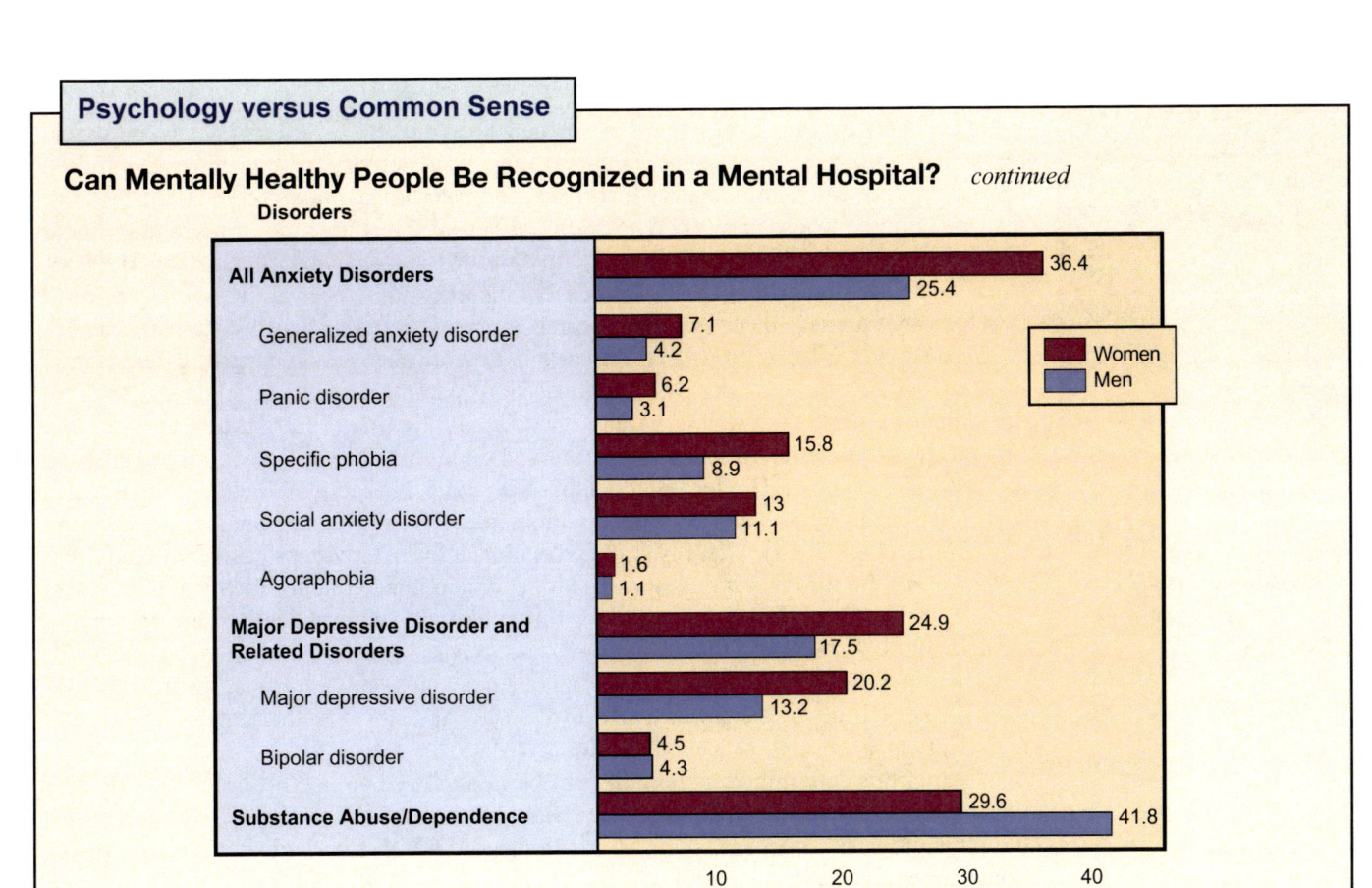

Disorders

Disorder	Women	Men
All Anxiety Disorders	36.4	25.4
Generalized anxiety disorder	7.1	4.2
Panic disorder	6.2	3.1
Specific phobia	15.8	8.9
Social anxiety disorder	13	11.1
Agoraphobia	1.6	1.1
Major Depressive Disorder and Related Disorders	24.9	17.5
Major depressive disorder	20.2	13.2
Bipolar disorder	4.5	4.3
Substance Abuse/Dependence	29.6	41.8

Percentage of Americans Who Have Had This Disorder During Their Lifetime

FIGURE 14-2 Prevalence of Some Major Psychological Disorders in the United States

Source: Data from Kessler, R. C., Berglund, P. A., Demler, O., Jin, R., Merikangas, K. R., and Walters, E. E. (2005). Lifetime prevalence and age-of-onset distributions of *DSM-IV* disorders in the National Comorbidity Survey Replication (NCS-R). *Archives of General Psychiatry, 62*(6), 593–602.

Generalized Anxiety Disorder

Though people normally experience anxiety in response to stressful situations, the person with a **generalized anxiety disorder** is in a continual state of worry that exists independent of any particular stressful situation. In essence, anxiety becomes one of the individual's cardinal personality traits (Rapee, 1991).

generalized anxiety disorder An anxiety disorder marked by a persistent state of worry that exists independently of any particular stressful situation and often interferes with daily functioning.

Characteristics of Generalized Anxiety Disorder

The central feature of generalized anxiety disorder is extreme and habitual worry. The person worries constantly about almost everything, including work, school, finances, and social relationships. About 6 percent of Americans suffer from sometime during their lifetime, with the disorder being more common in women than in men (Kessler, Petukhova, Sampson, Zaslavsky, & Wittchen, 2012). This gender difference emerges as early as age 6, with girls being twice as likely as boys to experience an anxiety disorder (Lewinsohn, Gotlib, Lewinsohn, Seeley, & Allen, 1998), though the size of the gender difference varies by culture (Gater et al., 1998). The experience of anxiety appears to be universal, though there are cross-cultural differences in symptoms and their meaning. For example, a common expression of anxiety among Latinos is *ataque de nervios*, characterized by fear, trembling, and bodily symptoms. These symptoms usually are related to disrupted family relationships and are socially acceptable manifestations of feeling "out of control" (López & Guarnaccia, 2000).

Childhood Anxiety

Childhood anxiety has been linked to an increased risk for the development of mood and anxiety disorders later in life.

Source: Tomsickova Tatyana/Shutterstock.com.

Causes of Generalized Anxiety Disorder

What accounts for the development of a generalized anxiety disorder? Biopsychological researchers look to heredity, neurochemistry, and brain activity for answers. The children of parents who suffer from anxiety disorders are seven times more likely to develop them than are children whose parents do not. Samuel Turner, a leading anxiety researcher, spent years examining the factors that make people prone to anxiety disorders. His early work suggested a possible genetic basis for anxiety disorders; however, it did not permit us to conclude that anxiety disorders are affected more by heredity than by life experiences (Turner, Beidel, & Costello, 1987). Turner's later work focused on parenting behavior as he studied the children of anxious and nonanxious parents. His results suggested that the "emotional climate" that anxious parents create in families may contribute to the increased risk for the development of anxiety disorders in children (Turner, Beidel, Roberson-Nay, & Tervo, 2003; Turner, Beidel, & Roberson-Nay, 2005). In fact, fFMI studies have found that enlarged amygdalas are associated with anxiety in children as young as seven years of age (Qin et al., 2014). There is stronger evidence for a hereditary basis of anxiety disorders comes from research that shows a higher concordance rate for identical twins, who share 100 percent of their genes, than for fraternal twins, who typically share 50 percent of their genes (Torgersen, 1983). The *concordance rate* is the likelihood that a person will develop a psychological disorder given that a particular relative has that disorder. Moreover, the heritability of generalized anxiety disorder appears to be the same in women and men (Hettema, Prescott, & Kendler, 2001).

Whether it is determined by heredity or not, generalized anxiety disorder is associated with an unusually strong stress response (Brawman-Mintzer & Lydiard, 1997) and unstable physiological responses, such as breathing rate (Wilhelm, Trabert, & Roth, 2001). Some genes also have been implicated in the development of anxiety disorder. For example, researchers have studied the role of the *MANEA* gene in the development of both panic disorder and social anxiety disorder (Jensen et al., 2014). Like most complex disorders, the probability of identifying one causal gene is low. However, this study and others may lead to effective treatments tailored to the unique genetic makeup of people with generalized anxiety disorder.

Psychoanalytic theorists view anxiety as the consequence of *id* impulses that threaten to overwhelm *ego* controls. Cognitive-behavioral theorists find that people with generalized anxiety disorder are more prone than other people to worry about finances, personal competence and achievement, and interpersonal relations. Moreover, they experience more distress over their worries because they perceive their worries to be more threatening and less controllable than do other people (Hazlett-Stevens & Craske, 2003). This continual worrying places the person in a constant fight-or-flight state of arousal. There is evidence that the higher prevalence of generalized anxiety disorder among women is due to the stress they experience related to gender role demands, interpersonal relationships, and adverse life events (Shear, Feske, & Greeno, 2000). Humanistic psychologists believe that anxiety arises from a discrepancy between the actual self and the ought self (Strauman & Higgins, 1988), as described in Chapter 13.

According to the humanistic perspective, people might develop generalized anxiety disorder when they feel that they have failed to live up to desirable standards of behavior. Despite the differing viewpoints of cause and effect, generalized anxiety disorders respond well to both antidepressant treatments such as Prozac (Baldwin, Woods, Lawson, & Taylor, 2011) and cognitive-behavioral therapy (Mitte, 2005). In fact, Mitte (2005) found that overall dropout rates were lower for individuals receiving cognitive behavioral therapy, which suggests that this treatment is better tolerated by patients than drug therapy alone.

Panic Disorder

In describing the motivation for his painting *The Scream*, Norwegian artist Edvard Munch (1863–1944) remarked, "I was walking . . . and I felt a loud, unending scream piercing nature" (Blakemore, 1977, p. 155). The image in this painting conveys the intense anxiety and terror characteristic of a *panic attack*, which is a symptom of **panic disorder**.

panic disorder An anxiety disorder marked by sudden, unexpected attacks of overwhelming anxiety, often associated with the fear of dying or "losing one's mind."

Characteristics of Panic Disorder

Another refinement of the *DSM-5* is that panic disorder is no longer linked to agoraphobia and is considered to be its own anxiety disorder. Panic disorder is marked by sudden attacks of overwhelming anxiety, accompanied by dizziness, trembling, cold sweats, heart palpitations, shortness of breath, fear of dying, and fear of going crazy. People experiencing panic attacks also might feel detached from their own bodies or feel that other people are not real. These panic attacks are now categorized as expected and unexpected. Though panic attacks usually last only a few minutes, they are so distressing that more people seek therapy for panic disorder than for any other psychological disorder (Boyd, 1986). About 2 percent of Americans experience panic disorder sometime in their lives, with women more likely to develop the disorder than men (Kessler et al., 2012), though there is evidence that men are less willing to report experiencing panic (Birchall, 1995). And symptoms of panic disorder differ by culture and gender. Women tend to report more respiratory symptoms, which have been attributed to gender differences in sensitivity to carbon dioxide levels (Sheikh, Leskin, & Klein, 2002). Japanese people with panic disorder, for example, show different patterns of symptoms than Americans with panic disorder (Shioiri, Murashita, Kato, & Fujii, 1996). Moreover, Taiwan has a much lower prevalence of panic disorder than does the United States (Carter, Mitchell, & Sbrocco, 2012; Weissman, Bland, Canino, & Faravelli, 1997).

Causes of Panic Disorder

Biopsychological researchers note that panic disorder runs in families, with a concordance rate among family members of about 20 percent (Crowe, 1990). The concordance rate is higher for identical twins than for fraternal twins (Stein, Jang, & Livesley, 1999). Again, these findings strongly suggest, but do not guarantee, a genetic predisposition for panic disorder. As mentioned earlier, a biopsychological factor that has gained substantial support is that people with panic disorder are hypersensitive to carbon dioxide levels in their blood. Instead of responding by breathing normally to reduce their carbon dioxide levels, they might at times respond as though they are being suffocated or hyperventilating—and experience a panic attack (van Beek et al., 2003). As discussed earlier, the *MANEA* gene has been found to have a relationship to the development of both panic disorder and social anxiety disorder (Jensen et al., 2014). And levels of enzymes related to dopamine and norepinephrine differ in people with panic disorder and healthy people (Shimada-Sugimoto, Otowa, & Hettema, 2015). Likewise, an imbalance of serotonin activity could be related to panic symptoms. A number of studies have linked variations in the enzyme *tryptophan hydroxylase 2*, which controls serotonin, to anxiety disorders, often in a gender-specific way. Researchers have recently studied men and women with panic disorder and found that women are particularly sensitive to the effect of tryptophan hydroxylase 2 (Maron et al., 2007). One of the most consistent findings related to anxiety is the involvement of the amygdala, which plays an important role in emotional regulation. A recent meta-analysis found that all anxiety disorders are correlated with an abnormally high fear response in the amygdala (Etkin & Wager, 2007).

Psychoanalytic theorists have had relatively little to say about panic disorder. Psychoanalytic theorists who consider panic disorder look to early childhood experiences as influences on its development (Vuksic-Mihaljevic, Mandic, Barkic, & Mrdenovic, 1998). For example, a meta-analysis of 25 studies found that adults with panic disorder tend to have experienced separation anxiety in childhood (Kossowsky et al., 2013). Separation anxiety evoked by recalling an important person in one's life whom one has lost is especially likely to instigate a panic attack (Horesh, Amir, Kedem, Goldberger, & Kotler, 1997). According to cognitive theorists, panic disorder results from faulty thinking. People prone to panic disorders engage in catastrophic thinking, misattributing physical symptoms of arousal caused by factors such as caffeine, exercise, mild stress, or emotional memories, to a serious mental or physical disorder (Schmidt, Lerew, & Jackson, 1999).

Phobias

phobia An anxiety disorder marked by excessive or inappropriate fear.

The word **phobia** comes from *Phobos*, the name of the Greek god of fear, and refers to the experience of excessive or inappropriate fear. People with a phobia realize that their fear is irrational but cannot prevent it.

Characteristics of Phobias

A subcategory of anxiety disorders includes phobias. Phobias can have maladaptive consequences. People with *claustrophobia* (the fear of enclosed places), for example, are sometimes too terrified to undergo diagnostic MRIs, which might require them to lie still in a cylinder for up to an hour or more (Kilborn & Labbe, 1990). The major classes of phobias are *specific phobias*, *social anxiety disorder*, and *agoraphobia*.

specific phobia A phobia of a specific object or situation.

Specific Phobias A **specific phobia** is an intense, irrational fear of a specific object or situation, such as a spider or a height. Former television football announcer John Madden's flying phobia was so intense that to broadcast a game, he crossed the country in his own bus, even when forced to travel between the East Coast and the West Coast. In another case, a 14-year-old boy feared crickets so much that his fear hampered his academic performance (Jones & Friman, 1999). People with specific phobias might go to great lengths to avoid the object or situation they fear despite realizing that their fears are irrational. Specific phobias are more common among women than men, and men and women differ in the likelihood of specific phobias and have a lifetime prevalence of over 15.8 percent (Kessler et al., 2012). Table 14-2 lists common specific phobias.

social anxiety disorder A phobia of situations that involve social evaluation.

Social Anxiety Disorder People with a **social anxiety disorder**, which affects about 12 percent of Americans (Kessler et al., 2012), fear social evaluation, which might lead them to avoid playing sports, making telephone calls, or performing music in public (Cox & Kenardy, 1993). The most common social anxiety disorder is the fear of public speaking (Kessler, Stein, & Berglund, 1998). Women are more likely than men to have social anxiety disorder, and women also experience more severe symptoms (Turk et al., 1998).

TABLE 14-2 Specific Phobias

Phobia	Feared Object or Situation
Acrophobia	High places
Ailurophobia	Cats
Algophobia	Pain
Aquaphobia	Water
Arachnophobia	Spiders
Astraphobia	Lightning storms
Claustrophobia	Enclosed places
Cynophobia	Dogs
Hematophobia	Blood
Monophobia	Being alone
Mysophobia	Dirt
Nyctophobia	Darkness
Ocholophobia	Crowds
Thanatophobia	Death
Triskaidekaphobia	Number 13
Xenophobia	Strangers
Zoophobia	Animals

Acrophobia

A person with acrophobia might feel anxiety just looking at this photograph of a roller coaster.

Source: SIHASAKPRACHUM/Shutterstock.com.

This gender difference holds true across different cultures, as shown in a study that compared social anxiety disorder rates in Korea, Canada, Puerto Rico, and the United States (Weissman et al., 1996).

A large proportion of the social anxiety disorders reported by East Asians comprises a culture-specific category: offensive social anxiety disorders. One type of offensive social anxiety disorder common among Koreans, for example, is characterized by a fear of being with others due to a pervasive sense that one's body odors are offensive to others (Lee & Oh, 1999). *Taijin kyofusho* is a Japanese form of social anxiety disorder that reflects an unreasonable fear of offending others with inappropriate behavior or an offensive physical appearance (Nagata et al., 2003). These cultural differences have been attributed to the collectivist orientation of Asian culture. Moreover, social anxiety disorder is more common among individuals with a collectivist orientation, regardless of culture (Dinnel, Kleinknecht, & Tanaka-Matsumi, 2002).

Social anxiety disorder seems to have its origins in childhood, with shy children more prone than outgoing children to develop social anxiety disorder in adulthood (Stein, Chavira, & Jang, 2001). Social anxiety disorder is maintained by increased self-focused attention in feared situations (Spurr & Stopa, 2003). Social anxiety disorder also is associated with perfectionism, making the person overly concerned with being evaluated (Rosser, Issakidis, & Peters, 2003). You have gotten a hint of this experience if you have noticed your mouth becoming dry, your palms sweating, and your heart beating strongly just before making an oral presentation in class.

Agoraphobia In 1992 former star football player Earl Campbell sat in his car listening to country music when suddenly he felt terrified, his heart racing out of control. After being hospitalized for a week for a suspected heart attack, he was diagnosed instead as suffering from panic disorder. His fear of having a panic disorder in public led him to stay home, afraid to venture outside even to check his mailbox. He had developed *agoraphobia*.

Agoraphobia, which affects about 3 percent of Americans (Kessler et al., 2012), is the fear of being in public. The word *agoraphobia*, from the Greek term for "fear of the marketplace," was coined in 1871 to describe the cases of four men who feared being in a city plaza (Boyd & Crump, 1991). People with agoraphobia typically have a history of panic attacks. They tend to avoid public places because they fear the embarrassment of having witnesses to their panic attacks (Amering et al., 1997). This fear makes them avoid parties, sporting events, shopping malls, and other public places. In extreme cases, the person can become a prisoner in her or his own home—terrified to leave for any reason. Because agoraphobia disrupts every aspect of the victim's life, including potentially destroying intimate relationships (McCarthy & Shean, 1996), it is a phobia commonly seen by psychotherapists.

agoraphobia A fear of being in public, usually because the person fears the embarrassment of a panic attack.

Causes of Phobias

Phobias have been the target of much scientific research into their causes. Whereas many researchers search for biological factors, many others look to possible psychological factors.

Biopsychological Factors Some people have a biological, possibly hereditary, predisposition to develop phobias. One bit of evidence for this finding is that identical twins have a higher concordance rate than do fraternal twins (Lichtenstein & Annas, 2000). Moreover, research on the human genome has found that specific genetic markers are associated with the tendency to develop specific phobias (Gelernter et al., 2003); however, the genetic correlations are modest at best. According to psychologist Martin Seligman (1971), evolution has biologically prepared us to develop phobias of potentially dangerous natural objects or situations, such as fire, snakes, and heights. Whereas infants have an innate fear of loud startling noises, no one is born with a phobia; phobias develop over time. Early humans who were predisposed to avoid these dangers were more likely to survive long enough to reproduce and, as a result, pass on this predisposition to their offspring in their genes. This hypothesis might explain why phobias that involve potentially dangerous natural objects, such as snakes, are more persistent than phobias that involve usually safe, natural objects, such as flowers (McNally, 1987).

Agoraphobia

People with agoraphobia suffer from an excessive and debilitating fear of being in public places or open spaces.
Source: Mr.Tobin/Shutterstock.com.

Chapter 14 Psychological Disorders

Though some researchers question the existence of inherited preparedness to fear specific objects or situations (de Jong & Merckelbach, 1997), there is experimental research supporting it. For example, a recent twin study that compared the heritability of different phobias found that heredity had a moderate effect on fear of animals, whereas heredity had no effect on common situational fears (Skre, Onstad, Torgersen, Lygren, & Kringlen, 2000). The idea that we are genetically predisposed to fear certain things has some commonality with Jung's concept of archetypes (see Chapter 13).

Psychological Factors Psychoanalytic theorists trace the origin of phobias to early childhood experiences. For example, agoraphobia has been associated with separation anxiety in childhood (Hayward, Killen, & Taylor, 2003). The psychoanalytic viewpoint holds that phobias might be caused by anxiety displaced from a feared object or situation onto another object or situation. By displacing the anxiety, the person keeps the true source unconscious. The classic psychoanalytic case is that of little Hans, a 5-year-old boy who was afraid to go outside because of his fear of horses. Sigmund Freud attributed the phobia to inadequate resolution of the Oedipus complex. Freud claimed that Hans had an incestuous desire for his mother and a fear of being punished for it by being castrated by his father. Hans displaced his fear from his father to horses, permitting him to keep his incestuous feelings unconscious.

Behavioral psychologists view phobias as learned responses to life situations. Phobias develop because of learning, either through personal experience, observation of people with phobias, or exposure to information about fearful situations. Little Hans's phobia, for example, might have been attributable to a horrifying incident that he witnessed in which horses harnessed to a wagon fell and then struggled to get to their feet (Stafford-Clark, 1965). More recently, a study found that children's dog phobias arose, as predicted, from personal experience with dogs, observation of other people's experiences with dogs, or exposure to information about the dangerousness of dogs (King, Clowes-Hollins, & Ollendick, 1997).

Cognitive-behavioral explanations of phobias implicate self-efficacy (see Chapter 13). That is, people with phobias may believe that they lack the ability to cope with stressful situations. Research findings indicate that a person's feeling of self-efficacy in regard to the feared situation is a more important factor in phobias than is the person's anxiety level or perception of danger (Williams, Turner, & Peer, 1985). Cognitive explanations of phobias also stress the importance of exaggerated beliefs about the harmfulness of the fear-inducing object or situation (Thorpe & Salkovskis, 1995). For example, people with social anxiety disorder are more vigilant to potential social threats, such as angry faces (Mogg, Philippot, & Bradley, 2004); are more pessimistic about social events (Taylor & Wald, 2003); are more likely to be overly critical of their social behavior; and ruminate about their self-perceived social blunders (Abbott & Rapee, 2004).

Section Review: Anxiety Disorders

1. Why does agoraphobia prompt people to seek therapy more than any other phobia does?
2. How have psychologists connected the fear of suffocation and panic disorder?

Obsessive-Compulsive Disorder

Have you ever been unable to keep an advertising jingle from continually running through your mind? If so, you have experienced a mild *obsession*, which is a persistent, recurring thought. If you have ever repeatedly checked your alarm clock to make sure it was set the night before an early morning exam, you have experienced a mild *compulsion*, which is an action that you feel compelled to perform repeatedly. An obsession is a thought, and a compulsion is a behavior.

Characteristics of Obsessive-Compulsive Disorder

People whose obsessions and compulsions interfere with their daily functioning suffer from **obsessive-compulsive disorder (OCD)**. Howie Mandel, a comedian and television host, became an unexpected mental health advocate in 2009 when he went public with his OCD diagnosis. His fist-bumps on the show *Deal or No Deal* may be his trademark, but they also are a hallmark of his symptoms of OCD. A very common feature of this disorder is irrational thoughts about contamination by germs. To avoid shaking hands, Mandel fist-bumps a person as an introduction. OCD is found in about 1 percent of the American population and is more common among women than men (Kessler et al., 2012). Cross-cultural research indicates that the prevalence of OCD is similar in Western and non-Western cultures (Al-Issa & Oudji, 1998), though symptoms may vary by culture (Lemelson, 2003). Obsessions can be self-perpetuating because the very act of trying to suppress a thought will make it more likely to enter consciousness (Wegner & Schneider, 2003). The most common compulsive symptoms include hoarding, checking, washing, cleaning, ordering, and desiring excessive symmetry (Leckman, Grice, Boardman, & Zhang, 1997). In some cases, OCD can be so intrusive that it has potentially dangerous consequences, as in the case of a U.S. Air Force missile launch officer whose symptoms kept him from performing his job efficiently (Bourgeois & Bunn, 1996).

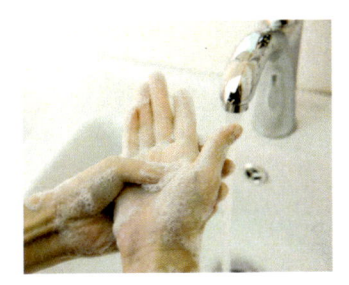

Obsessive-Compulsive Disorder

Compulsive hand washing is an example of a compulsive ritual a person might perform to relieve anxiety from obsessions about germs or contamination.
Source: hxdbzxy/Shutterstock.com.

obsessive-compulsive disorder (OCD) An anxiety disorder in which the person has recurrent, intrusive thoughts (obsessions) and recurrent urges to perform ritualistic actions (compulsions).

Causes of Obsessive-Compulsive Disorder

Some people appear to have a hereditary predisposition to develop OCD; this finding is based in part on research showing that OCD runs in families (Nestadt et al., 2000). Stronger support for the hereditary basis of OCD comes from a study of more than 400 pairs of twins, which found that heredity plays a role in the development of obsessions (Clifford, Murray, & Fulker, 1984). Heredity might predispose certain people to OCD because of its effects on the brain. OCD is associated with low levels of the neurotransmitter serotonin (Pogarell et al., 2003). Functional MRI and PET scans have found that people with OCD have abnormally high activity in the frontal lobes (Greenberg et al., 2000; Ursu, Stenger, Shear, Jones, & Carter, 2003). This brain activity might mean that compulsive behavior serves to prevent anxiety from rising to uncomfortable levels. You might have encountered this experience in a milder form when you felt anxious about schoolwork, spent an hour rearranging your room, and as a result, felt less anxious after doing so. Even more convincing evidence suggests a dysfunction between the frontal cortex and basal ganglia. Neuroimaging studies have focused on the size and function of this neural network (Saxena & Rauch, 2000). Though OCD is typically treated with antidepressants, neurosurgical interventions (such as lesions or deep brain stimulation) are used for intractable cases of OCD (Greenberg, Rauch, & Haber, 2010).

According to psychoanalysts, OCD is caused by fixation at the anal stage, resulting from harsh toilet training. This fixation causes repressed anger directed at the parents. The child defends against the guilt generated by these feelings of anger and later transgressions by repeating certain thoughts and actions over and over. The obsessions and compulsions often have symbolic meaning, as portrayed in Shakespeare's *Macbeth* when Lady Macbeth engages in compulsive hand washing after murdering King Duncan. A study found that people with OCD do, in fact, feel more guilt than people without OCD (Shapiro & Stewart, 2011). Children with OCD also tend to suffer from separation anxiety, which might contribute to the development of OCD symptoms to relieve their distress (de Mathis et al., 2013). This psychoanalytic viewpoint is disputed by biopsychosocial theorists. For example, there is evidence that cases of OCD that develop in childhood differ in several ways from cases that develop in adulthood. And some researchers believe that childhood OCD is related to a *tic disorder*, such as Tourette's syndrome (Eichstedt & Arnold, 2001).

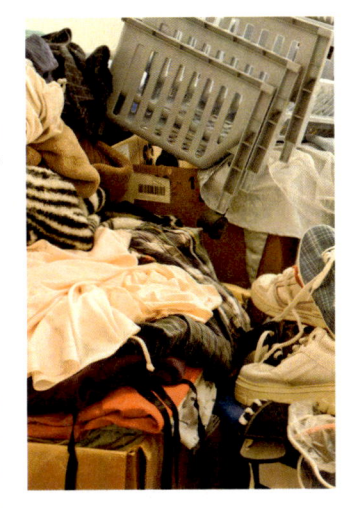

Behavioral theorists view obsessions and compulsions as ways of avoiding anxiety-inducing situations. So you might compulsively write and rewrite lists of things to do instead of studying for an upcoming final exam. Cognitive theorists note that OCD symptoms might be responses to imagined threats. In one study, for example, compulsive

OCD and Hoarding

One potential symptom of OCD is hoarding. This is manifested by people who have difficulty discarding items that appear to others to have little or no value.
Source: MCarper/Shutterstock.com.

Chapter 14 Psychological Disorders

washing, checking, and hoarding were associated with exaggerated perceptions of threat, and compulsive ordering was associated with perfectionism (Tolin, Woods, & Abramowitz, 2003). Humanistic theorists, like psychoanalytic theorists, note the relationship between guilt and OCD, but they stress the importance of the conscious, rather than the unconscious, experience of guilt. Despite these explanations for OCD, it is likely that biological, psychological, and social factors interact to initiate and maintain this devastating disorder.

> ### Section Review: Obsessive-Compulsive Disorder
>
> 1. What is the relationship between obsessive-compulsive disorder and anxiety?
> 2. What psychological factors are associated with obsessive-compulsive disorder?

Somatic Symptom and Related Disorders

somatic symptom and related disorder A psychological disorder characterized by physical symptoms in the absence of disease or injury.

Somatic means "bodylike." A **somatic symptom and related disorder** is characterized by heightened bodily sensations, such as back pain, joint pain, headache, and abdominal symptoms in the absence of disease or injury (Rief, Hessel, & Braehler, 2001). In previous versions of the *DSM*, these symptoms were thought to be caused, instead, by psychological factors or symptoms that were unable to be traced to a medical cause. Now, in the *DSM-5*, a person can be diagnosed with somatic symptom and related disorders with or without a diagnosis of a coexisting medical condition. This change now allows people suffering from both somatic symptom and related disorders and another medical diagnosis to get the help they need. Somatic symptom and related disorders run in families. The concordance rate for identical twins is three times greater than for fraternal twins (about 30 percent versus about 10 percent). But it is unclear whether the higher concordance rate for identical twins simply reflects greater genetic similarity or greater similarity in their life experiences (Torgersen, 1986). One particular challenge is diagnosing this disorder in pediatric patients.

Somatic symptom and related disorders affect less than 1 percent of the population, with women more likely to report somatic symptoms than men (Kroenke & Spitzer, 1998). Somatic symptom and related disorders also are more common among certain cultural groups. Chinese Americans, for example, report more somatic symptoms than do European Americans (Hsu & Folstein, 1997). Because of cultural differences in what is considered normal behavior and what is considered a symptom of a disorder, the diagnosis of somatic symptom and related disorders might be unreliable across cultures (Brown & Lewis-Fernández, 2011; Ono & Janca, 1999). Somatic symptom and related disorders include *illness anxiety disorder* and *conversion disorder*.

Illness Anxiety Disorder

illness anxiety disorder A somatic symptom and related disorder in which the person interprets the slightest physical changes as evidence of a serious illness.

A person with **illness anxiety disorder**, often called hypochondriasis, interprets the slightest physical change in her or his body as evidence of a serious illness. To the person with illness anxiety disorder, a headache might indicate a brain tumor, and indigestion might signal an imminent heart attack. People with this disorder are also focused on the idea of being sick.

Characteristics of Illness Anxiety Disorder

Many people with illness anxiety disorder go from physician to physician, searching for the one who will finally diagnose the disease that they are sure is causing their symptoms. Some medical students experience a mild form of illness anxiety disorder in the so-called "medical student disease," in which a mere cough might convince them they have lung cancer. As you read about the various psychological disorders, you should beware of developing a similar "psychology student syndrome," in which you interpret your normal variations in mood, thinking, and behavior as symptoms of a psychological disorder. Of course, if your symptoms become distressing, prolonged, or disruptive to your life, you should consider professional counseling.

Causes of Illness Anxiety Disorder

What accounts for illness anxiety disorder? Recent evidence demonstrates a remarkable similarity in the brain circuitry for people with illness anxiety disorder, OCD, and panic disorder. In one study, participants with all three anxiety disorders and a healthy control group were asked to perform a Tower of London Task, a widely used task of attentional and cognitive control, while undergoing fMRI scans. The researchers found reduced activity in the frontal cortex and basal ganglia in the anxiety disorder group versus the healthy control group (van den Heuvel et al., 2011). Psychoanalytic theorists see it as a defense against becoming aware of feelings of guilt or low self-esteem. Support for this view comes from the close association between fear of death, fear of separation, and illness anxiety disorder (Noyes, Stuarat, Longley, Langbehn, & Happel, 2002). Behavioral theorists point not only to positive reinforcement, such as being lavished with attention, and negative reinforcement, such as relief from work responsibilities, but also to parental modeling of bodily symptoms (Watt & Stewart, 2000).

Cognitive theorists note that people who develop illness anxiety disorder fear disease so much that they process normal physical symptoms through biased schema, thus noticing or exaggerating the slightest ones. In fact, this cognitive bias might generalize to other life experiences (Schwenzer & Mathiak, 2011). One study found that people with illness anxiety disorder were more likely to interpret ambiguous normal physical symptoms as indicative of disease (Schaefer, Egloff, & Witthöft, 2012). Explanations consistent with humanistic psychology see illness anxiety disorder as a form of self-handicapping. People with illness anxiety disorder, for example, are more likely to complain of symptoms when they know they are going to be evaluated (Smith, Snyder, & Perkins, 1983). There is evidence supporting each of these views, but none is clearly superior to the others.

Conversion Disorder

A girl whose legs were "paralyzed" for a year without any physical cause began walking again after simply being given biofeedback that provided her with evidence of activity in her leg muscles (Klonoff & Moore, 1986). She had been suffering from a **conversion disorder**.

Characteristics of Conversion Disorder

In typical cases, the person with conversion disorder experiences muscle paralysis, such as difficulty in speaking, or sensory loss, such as an inability to feel an object on the skin. But the apparently lost function is actually intact. Physicians suspect the presence of a conversion disorder when patients display *la belle indifférence*—a lack of concern about their symptoms. As illustrated in Figure 14-3, a conversion disorder might also be diagnosed by a physician who notices that a patient's symptoms are anatomically impossible.

Causes of Conversion Disorder

Theories explaining conversion disorder have a long and sometimes bizarre history. An Egyptian papyrus dating from 1900 B.C. attributed the disorder, which was believed to be limited to women, to a wandering uterus (Jones, 1980). Hippocrates accepted this explanation and called the disorder *hysteria*, from the Greek word for "uterus." Because Hippocrates believed that the uterus wandered when a woman was sexually frustrated, he prescribed marriage as a cure. The wandering-womb view lost credibility in the face of 19th-century science.

In the late 19th century, Sigmund Freud claimed that hysteria resulted from anxiety generated by repressed sexual impulses and conflicts (Huopainen, 2002). The anxiety was converted into symbolic physical symptoms, such as paralyzed legs, that enabled a woman to avoid acting on her sexual impulses. Freud called such disorders *conversion hysteria*. Today, to avoid the implication that the disorder is strictly a female problem, it is called *conversion disorder*. There is evidence that severe childhood trauma, such as

conversion disorder A somatic symptom and related disorder in which the person exhibits motor or sensory loss or the alteration of a physiological function without any apparent physical cause.

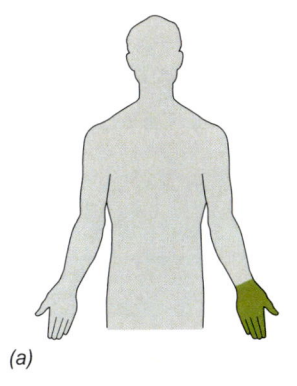

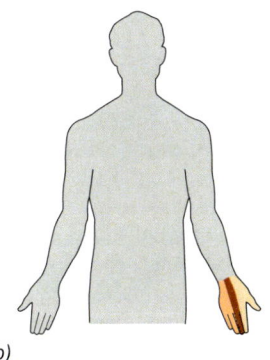

FIGURE 14-3
Conversion Disorder

(a) A person with "glove anesthesia" will complain of numbness in the hand from the wrist to the tips of the fingers. This condition is easily diagnosed as a conversion disorder because damage to the sensory nerves of the hand will not produce this pattern of sensory loss. (b) Different areas of the hand are served by the ulnar, radial, and median nerves. If a given nerve is injured, there will be numbness in only a portion of the hand. For example, damage to the ulnar nerve produces numbness only along the outer edge of the hand.

Chapter 14 Psychological Disorders

sexual or physical abuse, might contribute to the development of a conversion disorder (Roelofs, Keijsers, Hoogduin, Naering, & Moene, 2002).

Early biopsychological researchers conducted a case study of a 45-year-old woman with limb paralysis. They concluded that her paralysis might be associated with reduced activity in brain regions that stimulate movement in the affected limb and with increased activity in brain regions that inhibit movement of the affected limb (Marshall, Halligan, Fink, Wade, & Frackowiak, 1997). A more recent study using fMRI found a smaller left thalamus among participants with conversion disorder (Nicholson et al., 2014). As discussed in Chapter 3, the thalamus is a brain structure involved in relaying and integrating motor output (see Chapter 3). This study and only a handful of others indicate the brain structures that might be involved in conversion disorder.

Behavioral theorists assume that somatic symptom and related disorders occur because they are reinforced by increased attention or a reduction in responsibilities. Children may be prone to somatic symptom and related disorders after they observe other members of their family being reinforced for their physical symptoms (Mullins & Olson, 1990). And, as in the case of illness anxiety disorder, humanistic theorists may see conversion disorder as a form of self-handicapping. Whereas there is evidence supporting each of these views, none is clearly superior to the others.

Section Review: Somatic Symptom and Related Disorders

1. How would you determine whether a person was displaying a somatic symptom related disorder?
2. What is "la belle indifference" in regard to conversion disorder?

Dissociative Disorders

dissociative disorder A psychological disorder in which thoughts, feelings, and memories become separated from conscious awareness.

In a **dissociative disorder**, the person's conscious mind loses access to certain of his or her thoughts, feelings, and memories. The dissociative disorders include *dissociative amnesia*, *dissociative fugue*, and *dissociative identity disorder*. About 3 percent of North Americans show symptoms of dissociative disorders (Waller & Ross, 1997). Though dissociative symptoms appear in all cultures, they are not always considered signs of a psychological disorder. The diagnosis of dissociative disorders should be made within the individual's cultural context (Lewis-Fernandez, 1998).

Dissociative Amnesia and Fugue

dissociative amnesia The inability to recall personally significant memories.

dissociative fugue Memory loss characteristic of dissociative amnesia as well as the loss of one's identity and fleeing from one's prior life.

While being interrogated about his assassination of Robert F. Kennedy in 1968, Sirhan Sirhan was unable to recall the incident (Bower, 1981). He apparently suffered from **dissociative amnesia**, the inability to recall personally significant memories (Coons & Milstein, 1992). In September 1980, a young woman was found wandering in Birch State Park in Florida. She could not recall who she was or where she was from. After an appearance on a nationally televised morning talk show, she was reunited with her family in Illinois. She suffered from **dissociative fugue**, which is marked by the memory loss characteristic of dissociative amnesia as well as the loss of one's identity and fleeing from one's prior life. The word *fugue* comes from the Latin word meaning "to flee."

Characteristics of Dissociative Amnesia and Fugue

In dissociative amnesia, the lost memories are usually related to a traumatic event, such as witnessing a catastrophe. But the lost memories typically return within hours or days. However, prolonged or repeated traumas may be more likely to lead to dissociative amnesia, especially if they occur in childhood (Joseph, 1997). In dissociative fugue, the person may adopt a new identity, only to emerge from the fugue state days, months, or years later, recalling nothing that happened during the intervening period (Kopelman, Christensen, Puffett, & Stanhope, 1994). In one case a 15-year-old girl assumed a new identity, spoke a foreign language she had learned in school, adopted new dress and grooming habits, and showed new skills, interests, and personality traits. Six days later she returned to her normal self (Venn, 1984).

Causes of Dissociative Amnesia and Fugue

The psychoanalytic viewpoint assumes that the repression of painful memories causes dissociative amnesia. This view was supported by a study in which people who viewed slides of normal and disfigured faces accompanied by verbal descriptions had poorer recall of the descriptions associated with the disfigured faces (Christianson & Nilsson, 1984). The most common factors implicated in dissociative amnesia are combat, adult rape, criminal acts, attempted suicide, disasters and accidents, and the violent death of a parent during childhood (Arrigo & Pezdek, 1997). People with dissociative amnesia experience *hypomnesia*—memory loss. There are often significant gaps in memories that involve the traumatic event.

There also is emerging evidence that biopsychological processes may contribute to dissociative amnesia. Researchers investigating the role of trauma in memory loss point to the impact of chronic elevations of stress hormones on impaired memory functioning. In a recent study, 14 patients with dissociative amnesia that resulted from stressful or traumatic events submitted to PET scans. Researchers found decreased metabolism in the prefrontal cortex in this sample (Brand et al., 2009).The relationship of overwhelming stress and the resulting stress hormones to disrupted memory of traumatic events is complex, however, with some traumatized people displaying *hypermnesia*—stronger-than normal recall of the traumatic event—and others displaying dissociative amnesia (Nadel & Jacobs, 1998). For example, a study of survivors of World War II concentration camps found that those who experienced traumatic events rarely reported dissociative amnesia (Merckelbach, Dekkers, Wessel, & Roefs, 2003), though this seems to be rare.

Dissociative Identity Disorder

In 1812, Benjamin Rush, the founder of American psychiatry, reported the following case involving a minister's wife:

> In her paroxysms of madness, she resumed her gay habits, spoke French, and ridiculed the tenets and practices of the sect to which she belonged. In the intervals of her fits, she renounced her gay habits, became zealously devoted to the religious principles and ceremonies of the Methodists, and forgot everything she did and said during the fits of her insanity. (Carlson, 1981, p. 668)

This case was one of the first well-documented cases of **dissociative identity disorder** (formerly called *multiple personality disorder*) in which a person has two or more distinct personalities that alternate with one another, as in the story of Dr. Jekyll and Mr. Hyde (Garcia, 1990).

dissociative identity disorder A dissociative disorder, formerly known as multiple personality disorder, in which the person has two or more distinct personalities that alternate with one another.

Characteristics of Dissociative Identity Disorder

An individual's multiple personalities might include men and women, children and adults, and moral and immoral persons. A quiet, retiring, middle-aged woman might alternate with a flamboyant, promiscuous young man. Each personality might have its own way of walking, writing, and speaking (Hendrickson, McCarty, & Goodwin, 1990).

You might be familiar with two cases of dissociative identity disorder that were the subjects of popular movies: the story of Chris Cotner Sizemore, portrayed by Joanne Woodward in *The Three Faces of Eve*, and the story of Sybil Dorsett, portrayed by Sally Field in *Sybil*. According to her psychiatrists at the height of her disorder, Sizemore had 22 distinct personalities. Her personalities were finally integrated in 1975, and she went on speaking tours to discuss her experiences (Sizemore & Huber, 1988). Dissociative identity disorder has been popularized in more recent movies as well. In 2000, Jim Carrey starred in a slapstick comedy, *Me, Myself, and Irene*, in which he struggles with multiple personalities to control his shared body. More recently, in the 2014 movie, *The Lego Movie*, one Lego character played by Liam Neeson had two personalities—the good cop and bad cop.

Causes of Dissociative Identity Disorder

People who develop multiple personalities almost always have had traumatic experiences in early childhood, typically including sexual, physical, and emotional abuse, leading them to escape into their alternate personalities (Kluft, 1987). One longitudinal study followed 28 children with a history of sexual abuse and 71 nonabused children for one year. At the time of follow-up, the sexually abused children—especially boys—were far more likely to display dissociative symptoms, compared to the nonabused children (Bernier, Hébert, & Collin-Vézina, 2013). Psychoanalytic theorists believe that dissociative identity disorder arises from the child's impossible predicament—the need to escape intolerable abuse while maintaining emotional attachment to the abusive parent (Blizard, 1997).

Because of a marked increase in reported cases of dissociative identity disorder in the 1980s, some cognitive theorists believe that multiple personalities are being overdiagnosed and are simply the product of role-playing. This possibility was demonstrated in a study in which students were hypnotized and asked to reveal the hidden personality of an accused multiple murderer called Harry Hodgins or Betty Hodgins. Eighty percent did so (Spanos, Weekes, & Bertrand, 1985). A more recent study found that hypnotized participants who were asked to role-play patients with dissociative identity disorder were more likely to report incidents of sexual or satanic ritual abuse than were hypnotized participants who were asked to role-play patients with depression or personal adjustment problems (Stafford & Lynn, 2002). This finding indicates that at least some reputed cases of dissociative identity disorder may be no more than role-playing, whether intentional or not.

Despite these findings, a review of the research evidence found little support for the view that multiple personalities are induced by suggestions during psychotherapy (Gleaves, 1996). Clinical evidence supporting dissociative identity disorder comes from a survey of 425 psychotherapists, which found that most psychotherapists believe they had encountered a true case of dissociative personality disorder and that about one-third believed they had seen a feigned case (Cormier & Thelen, 1998). Even biopsychological evidence supports this view. One study found that when a middle-aged woman with dissociative identity disorder was switching from one personality to another, a functional MRI of her brain showed a distinctive pattern of changes in her hippocampus—the brain structure most important in memory for personal experiences and general information (Tsai, Condie, Wu, & Chang, 1999). In a well-designed fMRI study with multiple participants, results were similar. In this study, researchers were interested in adding to the biopsychological evidence that dissociative identity disorder is not an effect of fantasy or role-playing. One group of female actors and another group of female patients with dissociative identity disorder were scanned while viewing neutral and angry faces. The actors had different neural and behavioral reactions, compared to the patients with dissociative identity disorder (Schlumpf et al., 2013). Researchers have also determined that there can be distinct physiological attributes for each personality, ranging from subjective reactions to trauma-related memories, cardiovascular responses, and cerebral activation patterns (Reinders et al., 2006). Taken together, it is possible that individuals with this disorder regulate emotions and memory differently than do healthy people.

Section Review: Dissociative Disorders

1. What kind of life experiences are common among people who develop dissociative identity disorder?
2. Why do some psychologists doubt the existence of dissociative identity disorder?

Major Depressive Disorder and Related Disorders

We all experience periodic fluctuations in our emotions, such as becoming briefly depressed after failing an exam or briefly elated after getting an A. But people with **major depressive disorder (MDD)** experience prolonged periods of extreme depression, often unrelated to their current circumstances, that disrupt their everyday functioning. Psychologists who study major depressive disorder also are interested in the causes and prevention of suicide.

major depressive disorder (MDD) A disorder marked by depression so intense and prolonged that the person may be unable to function in everyday life.

Major Depressive Disorder

People normally feel depressed after personal losses or failures; the frequency and intensity of depressive episodes vary from person to person. Since World War II, MDD has become 10 times more common among Americans (Seligman, 1989) and is considered the common cold of psychological disorders. Major depressive disorder is so prevalent and distressing that when Ann Landers (who wrote a syndicated advice newspaper column from 1943–2002) offered a pamphlet on MDD to her readers, 250,000 persons wrote away for it (Holden, 1986). People with major depressive disorder struggle to feel happiness from activities they once enjoyed. This disorder can be as debilitating as other chronic medical conditions.

Characteristics of Major Depressive Disorder

People with major depressive disorder experience extreme distress that disrupts their lives for weeks or months at a time. They commonly express despondency, helplessness, and loss of self-esteem. Their depressed mood is usually worse in the morning (Graw, Krauchi, Wirz-Justice, & Poldinger, 1991). They also may suffer from an inability to fall asleep or to stay asleep, lose their appetite or overeat, feel constantly fatigued, abandon good grooming habits, withdraw from social relations, lose interest in sex, find it difficult to concentrate, and fail to perform up to their normal academic and vocational standards. Symptoms also may vary by ethnicity (Avalon & Young, 2003) and culture (Yen, Robins, & Lin, 2000). About 13 percent of men and about 20 percent of women suffer from major depressive disorder (Kessler et al., 2005), and this gender difference is consistent across cultures (Weissman & Olfson, 1995). Why is MDD more common in women? The gender difference in the rates of major depressive disorder is complex and is not simply a difference in sex hormones. More likely, it is due to differences in how men and women process emotional events, especially the cognitive processes associated with rumination (see "The Research Process" feature).

Stress is a major trigger for the development of major depressive disorder as well as relapse. Usually, a series of events over time can lead to depressive states; however, large-scale disasters also can lead to increased rates of major depressive disorder. For example, in the 6-month period after the September 11, 2001, attacks on the World Trade Center in New York City, there was a 9 percent increase in major depressive disorder diagnoses in the New York City metropolitan area (Person, Tracy, & Galea, 2006). The prevalence of MDD is also higher among racial and ethnic minorities in the United States, who also are more likely than European Americans to report difficulties in meeting their basic needs (Plant & Sachs-Ericsson, 2004), and problems with acculturation or perceptions of racism (Liu & Lau, 2013). Higher rates of MDD have been reported among male college undergraduates who reported unwanted sexual contact (Larimer, Lydum, Anderson, & Turner, 1999) and a multiethnic sample of women who experienced child sexual abuse (Roosa, Reinholtz, & Angelini, 1999).

Causes of Major Depressive Disorder

What accounts for major depressive disorder? Each of the major viewpoints offers its own explanation.

The Biopsychological Viewpoint Major depressive disorder has a biological basis, apparently influenced by heredity. Identical twins have higher concordance rates for MDD (Lyons et al., 1998) than do fraternal twins. The fact that identical twins have the same genetic inheritance, whereas fraternal twins are no more genetically alike than ordinary siblings, provides evidence of a hereditary predisposition to develop mood

Gender Differences in Depression

Women have higher rates of major depressive disorder, possibly due to rumination.
Source: Jochen Schoenfeld/Shutterstock.com.

FIGURE 14-4

Sleep and Major Depressive Disorder

The solid line in the graph shows a normal sleep EEG pattern for healthy people. The dotted line shows an EEG pattern for people with major depressive disorder. People with depressed mood enter REM (rapid eye movement) sleep sooner and have more awakenings, compared to healthy people.

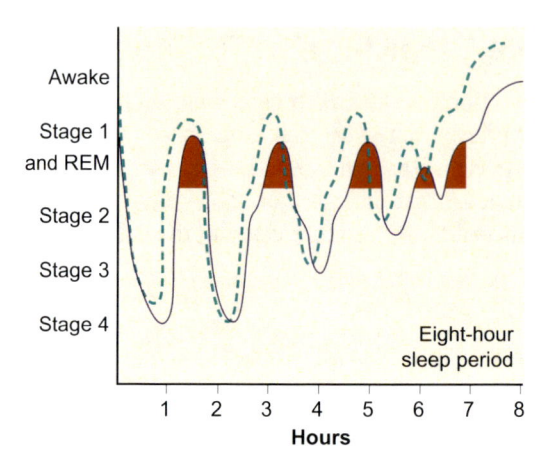

disorders. But it is important to note that the effect of the environment, as well as behavioral predispositions, might be affected by hereditary tendencies. In fact, our sensitivity to stressful events, our ability to mobilize social support, and our choice of stressful environments to expose ourselves to are affected by genetic factors (Wade & Kendler, 2000). Nearly all people with major depressive disorder experience disturbances in their quality sleep time. Researchers have found that people with major depressive disorder enter REM sleep faster than healthy people (see Figure 14-4). However, reporting sleep disturbances does not replace a valid clinical judgment for diagnosis of major depressive disorder (Arfken et al., 2014). More recent studies have pointed to potential breathing abnormalities experienced during sleep. People with major depressive disorder exhibit higher rates of sleep-disordered breathing and sleep apnea, compared with healthy people (Cheng, Casement, Hoffmann, Armitage, & Deldin, 2013).

The hereditary predisposition to develop mood disorders might manifest itself by its effect on neurotransmitters. Major depressive disorder is related to abnormally low levels of *serotonin* and *norepinephrine* in the brain (Fava, 2003). One study measured levels of a chemical by-product of serotonin in the cerebrospinal fluid of people with MDD who had attempted suicide. Of those with above-average levels, none subsequently committed suicide. Of those with below-average levels, 20 percent subsequently did attempt suicide (Traskman, Asberg, Bertilsson, & Sjostrand, 1981). Many antidepressant drugs act by increasing levels of serotonin or norepinephrine (Nutt, 2002). Fluoxetine (Prozac), a well-known antidepressant, is a selective serotonin reuptake inhibitor (SSRI) and increases serotonin levels (see Chapter 15).

The Psychoanalytic Viewpoint The classic psychoanalytic view holds that the loss of a parent or rejection by a parent early in childhood predisposes the person to experience MDD whenever she or he suffers a personal loss, such as a job or a lover, later in life. Because these children feel that it is unacceptable to express anger at the lost or rejecting parent, they learn to turn their anger on themselves, creating feelings of guilt and self-loathing (Freud, 1917/1963). But research studies have found that this view cannot explain all cases of major depressive disorder. For example, both adults with and without MDD are equally likely to have suffered the loss of a parent in childhood (Crook & Eliot, 1980).

The Cognitive-Behavioral Viewpoint Behavioral explanations of major depressive disorder stress the role of learning and environmental factors. One of the most influential of these explanations is Peter Lewinsohn's reinforcement theory, which assumes that people with MDD lack the social skills needed to gain normal social reinforcement from others and might instead provoke negative reactions from them. For example, people with MDD stimulate less smiling, fewer statements of support, more unpleasant facial expressions, and more negative remarks from others than do healthy people (Gotlib & Robinson, 1982). Lewinsohn points out that the person with major depressive disorder is caught in a vicious cycle in which reduced social reinforcement leads to MDD, and depressed behavior further reduces social reinforcement (Youngren & Lewinsohn, 1980).

An influential cognitive-behavioral theory of major depressive disorder is based on Martin Seligman's attributional theory of depression. People with major depressive disorder attribute negative events in their lives to internal, stable, and global factors (Abramson, Seligman, & Teasdale, 1978). An internal factor is a characteristic of one's self rather than of the environment. A stable factor is unlikely to change. And a global factor affects almost all areas of one's life. This attributional style is associated with pessimistic expectations for the future (Peterson & Vaidya, 2001). Yet, many individuals rely on defensive pessimism—expecting the worst—to prepare themselves for negative outcomes (and, perhaps, to gain greater pleasure from positive outcomes). This approach is particularly prevalent in academic settings (Yamawaki, Tschanz, & Feick, 2004), as in the case of students who always claim that they have failed an exam—only to discover, more often than not, that they have done well.

Research on major depressive disorder has tended to find that, as predicted, people suffering from MDD make internal, stable, and global attributions for negative events in their lives (Sweeney, Anderson, & Bailey, 1986). For example, college freshmen who attribute their poor academic performance to internal, stable, and global factors, such as intelligence, become more depressed than do those who attribute their own poor academic performance to external, unstable, and specific factors, such as being assigned difficult teachers (Peterson & Barrett, 1987).

Seligman's attributional theory has also been supported in other cultures, such as Egypt, Turkey, and India (Aydin & Aydin, 1992; Duddu, Chaturvedi, & Isaac, 2003; Emam, 2013). But there are cultural differences related to depression and attributions. A study of American and Chinese students found that Chinese students tended to experience MDD more than American students. Most notably, the Chinese students tended to blame themselves more for their failures and to credit themselves less for their successes than did the American students. This difference might reflect the relatively greater interdependence of people in Chinese culture and the relatively greater independence of people in American culture (Anderson, 1999). Researchers often wonder why the rate of major depressive disorder has increased. They often speculate that our modern environments could be a contributing factor. One review study found a correlation between lifetime risk of a mood disorder and modernization as measured by purchasing power and the national wealth of a country (Hidaka, 2012).

One of the most influential cognitive views of major depressive disorder is Aaron Beck's (1967) cognitive theory. Beck, known for his Beck Depression Inventory, has found that people with MDD exhibit what he calls a cognitive triad: They have a negative view of themselves, their current circumstances, and their future possibilities (Anderson & Skidmore, 1995). Moreover, this cognitive style appears to make people with major depressive disorder more reactive to day-to-day events than are healthy people (Nezlek & Gable, 2001). The cognitive triad is more common among people with MDD than among people with other psychological disorders (Jacobs & Joseph, 1997). This finding indicates that the triad is specific to major depressive disorder. The cognitive triad is maintained by the tendency of people with MDD to overgeneralize from negative events. For example, people with MDD tend to assume that a single failure means that they are incompetent (Carver & Ganellen, 1983).

As mentioned in the earlier section "Viewpoints on Psychological Disorders," people with psychological disorders may have more objective beliefs about themselves and the world than do people without such disorders. MDD researcher Lauren Alloy and her colleagues have found that this objectivity is especially true of people with major depressive disorder. Healthy people overestimate the likelihood of positive events and underestimate the likelihood of negative events (Crocker, Alloy, & Kayne, 1988). They also tend to have unrealistically positive self-evaluations (McKendree-Smith & Scogin, 2000). These findings lead to the surprising conclusion that if you have a healthy, positive mood, it might mean that you have an unrealistically positive view of reality and that people with MDD are more accurate in their view of their reality—so-called depressive realism (McKendree-Smith & Scogin, 2000). Nonetheless, some researchers have found that

Major Depressive Disorder and Failure

People with MDD often respond to a single failure with thoughts of incompetence.
Source: Ljupco Smokovski/Shutterstock.com.

this difference between people with MDD and healthy people holds more in laboratory studies than in real-life emotional situations (Pacini, Muir, & Epstein, 1998). Moreover, depressive realism is more likely to be associated with only mild levels of depressed mood (Soderstrom, Davalos, & Vázquez, 2011).

Another cognitive view of major depressive disorder, put forth by Susan Nolen-Hoeksema, implicates continual rumination about one's plight. People who constantly think about and brood over the sad state of their lives—especially at night—experience more severe and more chronic depressed mood than do people who take action to improve their lives or who distract themselves by pursuing enjoyable activities (Takano & Tanno, 2011; Treynor, Gonzalez, & Nolen-Hoeksema, 2003). Nolen-Hoeksema believes that this rumination may explain why, after age 15, women are about twice as likely as men to experience MDD (Nolen-Hoeksema, 2001). Whereas women with MDD tend to ruminate about their plight, men with MDD tend to distract themselves from it (Nolen-Hoeksema, 2012). Thus, gender differences in MDD may reflect different cognitive coping strategies employed by men and women. In fact, Nolen-Hoeksema found that among college undergraduates, rumination was the single most important predictor of how long depressed mood would last. Because female undergraduates tended to ruminate more than male undergraduates, depressed women tended to have longer-lasting bouts of MDD (Butler & Nolen-Hoeksema, 1994). Moreover, rumination appears to contribute to a vicious cycle of uncertainty, chronic strain, and low sense of mastery—all contributing to depressive symptoms (Nolen-Hoeksema, Larson, & Grayson, 1999; Ward, Lyubomirsky, Sousa, & Nolen-Hoeksema, 2003).

The rumination hypothesis also has been found to be related to biological factors. Researchers have looked at the protein BDNF as a variable that contributes to a predisposition to rumination. One study identified a sample of adolescent girls at risk for developing major depressive disorder because they had a mother with a diagnosis of MDD. They assessed levels of BDNF, tendencies to ruminate, and depressive symptoms in mothers and daughters. The results indicated that mutations in BDNF levels predicted rumination and depressive symptoms in the young adolescent girls with mothers with major depressive disorder (Hilt, Sander, Nolen-Hoeksema, & Simen, 2007). Nolen-Hoeksema's response-style theory was tested in the study discussed in "The Research Process" feature.

The Humanistic Viewpoint Psychologists who favor the humanistic viewpoint attribute depression to the frustration of self-actualization. More specifically, people with major depressive disorder suffer from incongruence between their actual self and their ideal self (Weilage & Hope, 1999). The actual self is the person's subjective appraisal of his or her own qualities. The ideal self is the person's subjective judgment of the person he or she would like to become. If the actual self has qualities that are too distinct from those of the ideal self, the person becomes depressed.

The Sociocultural Viewpoint There are some cross-cultural commonalities in the manifestation of major depressive disorder but also great variability in the symptoms of MDD. The symptoms of MDD are the result of the interaction of universal tendencies and cultural factors (Draguns, 1995). Among the kinds of sociocultural factors in MDD are variables correlated with ethnicity, such as socioeconomic status. A survey of more than 2,000 Americans found that African Americans were more likely to experience MDD than European Americans. But when socioeconomic status was factored in, there were no differences. That is, African Americans and European Americans of the same socioeconomic class had equal rates of MDD. Thus, because African Americans on average have lower socioeconomic status, it is poverty, not ethnicity, that probably accounts for the ethnic difference (Biafora, 1995).

Seasonal Affective Disorder

Norman Rosenthal (1993) and his colleagues identified a form of depression called **seasonal affective disorder**, or **SAD**, and pioneered the use of light therapy. People with SAD suffer from depressive symptoms during certain seasons, most commonly in the winter.

seasonal affective disorder (SAD) A mood disorder in which severe depressive symptoms occur during a particular season, usually the winter but sometimes the summer.

> **The Research Process**
>
> **Are People Who Ruminate About Their Problems More Likely to Develop Major Depressive Disorder?**
>
> **Rationale**
>
> Finding an association between rumination and major depressive disorder does not guarantee a causal relationship between them. This problem prompted Nolen-Hoeksema (Nolen-Hoeksema & Morrow, 1993) to conduct an experiment to determine whether rumination does, in fact, affect depressed mood.
>
> **Method**
>
> Nolen-Hoeksema randomly assigned 24 healthy undergraduates and 24 undergraduates with mild to moderately depressive symptoms to spend 8 minutes focusing their attention on their current feelings and personal characteristics (the rumination condition) or on descriptions of geographic locations and objects (the distraction condition).
>
> **Results and Discussion**
>
> Nolen-Hoeksema found that participants with depressive symptoms in the rumination condition became significantly more depressed. In contrast, participants with depressive symptoms in the distraction condition became significantly less depressed. Moreover, rumination and distraction did not affect the moods of healthy participants. Thus, the results supported her contention that depressed people who ruminate are prone to more intense depression, making them take longer to return to a normal mood. The results also supported her contention that people with MDD who try to distract themselves become less depressed, enabling them to return to normal moods faster (Nolen-Hoeksema & Morrow, 1993).

Characteristics of Seasonal Affective Disorder

SAD afflicts about 1 percent of Americans (Blazer, Kessler, & Swartz, 1998), though global population estimates vary by geographic latitude (Michalak & Lam, 2002). For example, the rate of SAD can be as high as 2.9 percent in Canada (Westrin & Lam, 2007). Typically, people develop SAD at latitudes with shorter days in the winter season. It is three to four times more common in women than in men (Lee & Chan, 1999b).

Causes of Seasonal Affective Disorder

Seasonal affective disorder might be caused by an inability to adjust physiologically to seasonal changes in light levels. Seasonal affective disorder is treated by *phototherapy*, which involves extending the day by exposing the afflicted person to artificial bright light before sunrise or after sunset. Depressive symptoms have been alleviated with as little as two one-hour sessions of exposure to bright light (Reeves et al., 2012). Stronger light intensity tends to produce more relief of typical symptoms (Lee & Chan, 1999a). The exact mechanism of its effect is unknown; however, some research has indicated that exposure to bright light in specific wavelengths promotes the skin's production of vitamin D. Researchers have suggested that low levels of vitamin D are associated with depressed mood (Berk et al., 2007). One mystery is that SAD is found even in countries, such as India (Srivastava & Sharma, 1998), that have little variation in sunlight across the year.

Research into the causes of SAD has implicated genes that regulate serotonin activity in the brain (Thierry et al., 2004). SAD is related to depletion of serotonin. This finding was demonstrated in a double-blind experiment that compared light therapy and fluoxetine (Prozac) therapy. Participants (average age 41 years) had SAD and were randomly assigned to the conditions. Each participant received 1 week of placebo treatment and 5 weeks of active treatment. The active treatment consisted of fluoxetine plus a placebo light condition versus bright light plus a placebo drug. There were 20 participants in each of the two conditions. The results indicated that both treatments were effective, with 14 of the bright-light participants improving and 13 of the fluoxetine participants improving. Fluoxetine produced a faster effect on typical SAD symptoms (Ruhrmann et al., 1998).

Whereas there is not one species that perfectly replicates attributes of any psychological disorder, Randy Nelson has found that Siberian hamsters are a model organism with which to study SAD. Compared to rats and mice, these hamsters display behavior related to depression and anxiety in response to short day length (Pyter & Nelson, 2006). Animal work also has helped us understand another mechanism that might contribute to the development of SAD. For example, some drugs that act on melatonin have been shown to produce antidepressant-like effects (Soumier et al., 2009). However many researchers speculate that there are many physiological processes that make an individual susceptible to SAD.

Suicide and Major Depressive Disorder

On January 22, 1987, at a televised news conference, Pennsylvania treasurer R. Budd Dwyer killed himself by putting the barrel of a pistol in his mouth and pulling the trigger. Dwyer had suffered from major depressive disorder after his conviction on charges of corruption. People who suffer from major depressive disorder are more susceptible to suicide.

Though some suicides are done for honor, as in the Japanese ritual of hara-kiri, or to escape intolerable pain, as in some cases of terminal illnesses, most are associated with major depressive disorder. There are more than 200,000 suicide attempts each year in the United States, with more than 25,000 fatalities. Though some suicide victims leave notes explaining why they killed themselves, the vast majority do not (O'Donnell, Farmer, & Catalan, 1993). The kinds of notes vary with age, with older victims citing factors associated with aging, such as illness and loneliness (Bauer et al., 1997). Overall, the most common issue addressed in suicide notes is the assignment of blame for the act (McClelland, Reicher, & Booth, 2000).

Factors in Suicide

Who commits suicide? Globally, more than one million people commit suicide every year, and it is the 13th leading cause of death (Bailey et al., 2011). Roy Baumeister (1990), a leading researcher on disorders of the self, believes that people commit suicide when their self-image becomes so negative that it is too painful to bear. Sex, ethnicity, and age are also factors. Women are much more likely than men to attempt suicide, yet many more men than women succeed (Spicer & Miller, 2000; Schmidtke et al., 1999). This difference is, in part, because men tend to use more lethal means, such as gunshots to the head, whereas women tend to use less lethal means, such as overdoses of depressants. This gender difference holds both in Western countries, such as the United States, and in Asian countries, such as China (He & Lester, 1998).

Widowed and divorced people are more likely to commit suicide than are single or married people (Canetto & Lester, 1995). There is some evidence that marriage has a stronger protective effect on men's risk of suicide relative to women's (Kposowa, 2000), possibly by reducing its acceptability (Stack, 1998). Traditionally, European Americans and Native Americans commit suicide more often than African Americans do, but in recent years, the suicide rate among young African Americans has increased (Willis, Coombs, Drentea, & Cockerham, 2003). There is increasing concern about the suicide rate among American military personnel, who are at risk of committing suicide only one month after being released from psychiatric care (Luxton, Trofimovich, & Clark, 2013). Elderly people have the highest suicide rate of any age group in the United States. The gender difference in suicide is dramatic among the elderly. Six out of seven suicides among those aged 65 or higher are men (Coren & Hewitt, 1999).

Though suicide rates are lower for high school and college students than for older people, suicide is one of the most common causes of death for the 15- to 24-year-old age group. Adolescent suicide often is associated with a dysfunctional family (Husain, 1990), blaming oneself for failure (Lester, 2003), and drug or alcohol abuse (Rowan, 2001). One study of 775 adolescents aged 12 to 19 living on the streets in San Francisco found that the mean number of suicide attempts was 6.2 for female and 5.1 for male participants. A history of sexual and physical abuse increased these adolescents' risk of suicide to 1.9 to 4.3 times the risk of nonabused adolescents (Molnar, Shade, Kral, Booth, & Watters, 1998). Because even young children commit suicide (Lester, 1995), parents and school personnel should be aware of the possibility in depressed, withdrawn children.

Seasonal Affective Disorder

Using Siberian hamsters, researchers have found a relationship between season and symptoms of depression and anxiety. Baby hamsters born to limited daylight were more likely to show signs of depression and anxiety later in life. Additionally, researchers found that adult hamsters housed in short artificial days, as one might find in the winter months, displayed more symptoms of depression and anxiety.
Source: Kuttelvaserova Stuchelova/Shutterstock.com.

Suicide Prevention

During your lifetime, you will probably know people whom you suspect are contemplating suicide. According to Edwin Shneidman (1994), a leading authority, at least 90 percent of people who attempt suicide give verbal or behavioral warnings before their attempts. People who have attempted suicide in the past are at especially high risk of trying again. A study of almost 400 youth suicides in Paris found that one-third of them had made earlier attempts (Lecomte & Fornes, 1998).

These statistics make it important to take threats seriously and to take appropriate actions to prevent suicide attempts. But a study of high school students found that few had knowledge of major warning signs and appropriate responses to suicidal threats by their peers (Norton, Durlak, & Richards, 1989). Major warning signs include changes in moods and habits associated with severe major depressive disorder, such as emotional apathy, social withdrawal, poor grooming habits, and loss of interest in recreational activities; giving away cherished belongings; tying up loose ends in their lives; and outright suicide threats (Shaughnessy & Nystul, 1985).

One of the obvious means of preventing suicide is to restrict access to means of suicide, especially guns (Brent & Bridge, 2003). But interpersonal action is also important. Shneidman suggests that because suicide attempts are usually cries for help, the simple act of providing an empathetic response might reduce the immediate likelihood of an actual attempt. Just talking about a problem may reduce its apparent dreadfulness and help the person realize possible solutions other than suicide. It may help to broaden the suicidal person's options to more than a choice between death and a hopeless, helpless life. An immediate goal should be to relieve the psychological pain of the person by intervening, if possible, with those who might be contributing to the pain, whether friends, lovers, teachers, or family members. You also should encourage the person to seek professional help, even if you have to make the appointment for the person and accompany him or her to it.

The U.S. Department of Health and Human Services sponsors a number of suicide prevention programs (DeMartino et al., 2003), as does the Canadian Association for Suicide Prevention (Leenaars, 2000), and 21 countries on 3 continents (Matsubayashi & Ueda, 2011). Many cities have 24-hour suicide hotlines or walk-in centers to provide emergency counseling. School systems also have begun to implement suicide-prevention programs (Kalafat, 2003). With the advent of the Internet, professionals are even developing email approaches to suicide prevention (Wilson & Lester, 1998). In some college programs, resident assistants are trained to recognize warning signs of suicide. They also are taught how to respond to suicide threats, how to make referrals to professional counselors, and how to support those who seek therapy (Grosz, 1990). In the United States, the presence of suicide-prevention centers in a state is associated with a lowering of suicide rates (Lester, 1993). A study in Japan found that the more suicide-prevention centers there are in a region and the longer they are open, the relatively lower will be the suicide rate (Lester, Saito, & Abe, 1997).

Section Review: Major Depressive Disorder and Related Disorders

1. How does Seligman's attributional theory explain major depressive disorder?
2. How does rumination affect major depressive disorder?
3. What are Shneidman's suggestions for preventing someone from committing suicide?

Bipolar Disorder

A biblical story describes how King Saul stripped off his clothes in public, exhibited alternating bouts of elation and severe depression, and eventually committed suicide. Though the story attributes his behavior to evil spirits, psychologists might attribute it to bipolar disorder.

Characteristics of Bipolar Disorder

bipolar disorder mood disorder marked by periods of mania alternating with longer periods of major depressive disorder.

mania A mood disorder marked by euphoria, hyperactivity, grandiose ideas, annoying talkativeness, unrealistic optimism, and inflated self-esteem.

Bipolar disorder, formerly called *manic depression*, is characterized by days or weeks of mania alternating with longer periods of major depressive disorder, typically separated by days or weeks of normal moods. **Mania** (from the Greek term for "madness") involves euphoria, hyperactivity, grandiose ideas, incoherent talkativeness, blind optimism, and inflated self-esteem. People with mania are sexually, physically, and financially reckless. They may also overestimate their own abilities, perhaps leading them to make rash business deals or to leave a sedentary job to train for the Olympics. At some time in their lives, about 4 percent of adults have bipolar disorder, which is equally common in men and women (Kessler et al., 2005), though there are gender differences in the nature of symptoms and the course of the disorder (Amsterdam, Brunswick, & O'Reardon, 2002).

Causes of Bipolar Disorder

There is compelling evidence that heredity plays a strong role in bipolar disorder. Identical twins have higher concordance rates for bipolar disorder (Mitchell, Mackinnon, & Waters, 1993) than do fraternal twins. A recent study in the United Kingdom of twins in which one twin was diagnosed with bipolar disorder found concordance rates of 67 percent among monozygotic twins and 19 percent among dizygotic twins (McGuffin et al., 2003). Additional evidence supportive of a hereditary basis for bipolar disorder was provided by a study by Janice Egeland of the Amish community in Lancaster County, Pennsylvania (Egeland et al., 1987). Because the Amish have an isolated community that includes descendants from 30 ancestors in the 18th century, only marrying among themselves, they provide an excellent opportunity to study the influence of heredity on psychological disorders. Egeland studied the families of Amish people with bipolar disorder, using blood tests to examine their chromosome structures.

Egeland found that Amish people who suffer from bipolar disorder share a defective gene on the 11th chromosome. But because only 63 percent of those with this defect develop the disorder, differences in life experience also play a role. Nonetheless, similar studies of families in which bipolar disorder follows a hereditary pattern have failed to find a genetic marker for it on the 11th chromosome. These include a study of two Australian families (Mitchell, Waters, Morrison, & Shine, 1991) and a study of three Icelandic families (Kelsoe, Kristbjanarson, Bergesch, & Shilling, 1993). These findings reinforce the importance of research replication, across different social groups, which was stressed in Chapter 2. Of course, it is possible that some cases of bipolar disorder are linked to the 11th chromosome, whereas others are linked to other chromosomes (Ewald, Mors, Flint, & Koed, 1995). More recent data from the National Institute of Mental Health study of more than 150 families with bipolar disorder implicate chromosomes 6, 10, 11, 16, and

The Amish Community

Members of the Amish community, because of their social and genetic isolation, may exhibit diseases likely to be seen in the general public, but at a higher rate.
Source: Arina P Habich/Shutterstock.com.

FIGURE 14-5

Brain Activity in Bipolar Disorder

These PET scans show the brain activity of a rapid-cycling bipolar patient. The patient cycled between mania and depression every 24 to 48 hours. The top and bottom sets of scans were obtained during periods when the patient was depressed. The middle set of scans was obtained during a manic period. Note that the red areas indicate significantly higher brain activity during the manic period.
Source: Phelps, M. E., & Maziotta, J. C. (1985). Positron-emission tomography: Human brain function and biochemistry. *Science, 228,* 799–809. Courtesy of Drs. Lewis Baxter and Michael Phelps, UCLA School of Medicine.

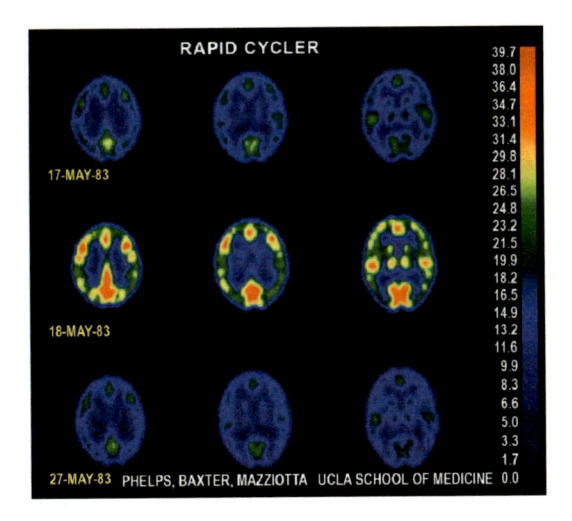

20, which suggests that a single genetic cause for bipolar disorder is unlikely (McInnis et al., 2003). Molecular genetics has taken this field a bit further. A mutation on the cell membrane of neurons that regulate calcium flow has been found to be a risk factor for developing bipolar disorder. Carriers of this mutation are also at risk for developing major depressive disorder or schizophrenia (Green et al., 2010). The degree of overlap in the biological underpinnings of these psychological disorders indicates the complexity of this disorder.

Whereas major depressive disorder is associated with a combination of low levels of both serotonin and norepinephrine, mania is associated with a combination of low levels of serotonin and high levels of norepinephrine. Figure 14-5 shows that mania also is associated with unusually high levels of brain arousal, perhaps related to these neurotransmitter levels. Imaging studies have pointed to certain brain structures involved in bipolar disorder. Whereas some results are inconsistent, the most consistent findings focus on brain structures related to emotional processing. Compared to healthy control groups, people with bipolar disorder show altered activity in the amygdala, cingulate, and cortex when viewing emotional stimuli. Moreover, this group had difficulty in identifying fearful faces (Sagar, Dahlgren, Gönenç, & Gruber, 2013). Imaging studies also are helpful to reveal brain activity during manic episodes. Despite its biological roots, the course of bipolar disorder also is affected by stressful life events interacting with a biological vulnerability (Post, Leverich, Xing, & Weiss, 2001). This combination of factors is in keeping with the biopsychosocial model of psychological disorders.

Section Review: Bipolar Disorder

1. What are the interpersonal consequences experienced by people with mania?
2. Explain one reason why major depressive disorder and bipolar disorder are distinct psychological disorders.

Schizophrenia

In middle age, Edvard Munch, the founder of modern expressionist painting referred to earlier in this chapter, began acting in odd ways. He became a social recluse, believed his paintings were his children, and claimed they were too jealous to be exhibited with other paintings (Wilson, 1967). Munch's actions were symptoms of **schizophrenia**, a severe psychological disorder characterized by impaired social, emotional, cognitive, and perceptual functioning.

schizophrenia A class of psychological disorders characterized by grossly impaired social, emotional, cognitive, and perceptual functioning.

The Nature of Schizophrenia

The modern classification of schizophrenia began in 1860 when the Belgian psychiatrist Benedict Morel used the Latin term *demence precoce* (meaning "premature mental deterioration") to describe the behavior of a brilliant, outgoing 13-year-old boy who gradually withdrew socially and deteriorated intellectually. The term was popularized by German psychiatrist Emil Kraepelin in his diagnostic system as *dementia praecox*. In 1911, the Swiss psychiatrist Eugen Bleuler (1857–1939) coined the term *schizophrenia* (from the Greek terms for "split mind") to refer to the disorder. This term reflected his belief that schizophrenia involved a splitting apart of the normally integrated functions of perceiving, feeling, and thinking. Whereas the *DSM-IV-TR* differentiated between discrete types of schizophrenia, the *DSM-5* considers schizophrenia to be a cluster of symptoms that can be demarcated by a series of stages of increasing psychosis (Häfner, Mauer, & vander Heiden, 2013). About 1 percent of the world's population are victims of schizophrenia, which is equally prevalent among men and women. Gender differences are apparent, though, in age of onset, psychosocial functioning, and the subtype of schizophrenia diagnosed (Tammings, 1997). Patients with schizophrenia occupy half the beds in American mental hospitals and cost the American economy billions of dollars each year. In contrast, there is some evidence that the course of schizophrenia is more favorable in developing countries, possibly due to a higher interdependence of the individual within the community and the role of the family in providing care and interpersonal support to mentally ill relatives (López & Guarnaccia, 2000).

Characteristics of Schizophrenia

Schizophrenia is associated with a diversity of potential symptoms. These include sensory-perceptual, cognitive, social-emotional, and motor symptoms. Particular kinds of brain dysfunctions might be associated with particular sets of schizophrenic symptoms. According to schizophrenia researcher Nancy Andreasen, there are two kinds of schizophrenic syndromes, characterized by either *positive symptoms* or *negative symptoms* (Andreasen & Flaum, 1991). Positive symptoms are psychotic behaviors that are not seen in healthy people and are active symptoms that include hallucinations, delusions, thought disorders, and bizarre behaviors. People with positive symptoms experience acute episodes and show progressively worsening symptoms. In contrast, negative symptoms are passive symptoms characterized by their absence in healthy people that include mutism, apathy, flat emotionality, social withdrawal, intellectual impairment, poverty of speech, and inability to experience pleasure.

Sensory-Perceptual Symptoms People with schizophrenia typically experience *hallucinations*, which are sensory experiences in the absence of sensory stimulation. Schizophrenic hallucinations are usually auditory, typically voices that may ridicule the person or order the person to commit harmful acts, perhaps violent ones (Zisook, Byrd, Kuck, & Jese, 1995). Researchers, however, have discovered that the type and prevalence of hallucinations can vary by culture (Bauer et al., 2011). Failure of the cognitive mechanism that normally helps people distinguish between experiences generated by the mind and experiences evoked by external stimuli can contribute to hallucinations (Beck & Rector, 2003). Researchers using fMRI and PET scans have demonstrated that schizophrenic hallucinations are associated with increased activity in the region of the cerebral cortex that normally processes the relevant sensory information. Auditory hallucinations, for example, are associated with increased activity in the temporal cortex, which processes sounds (Copolov et al., 2003).

Cognitive Symptoms Chief among the cognitive symptoms of schizophrenia is difficulty with attention. People with schizophrenia are easily distracted by irrelevant stimuli (Mirsky, Yardley, Jones, & Walsh, 1995) and have difficulty voluntarily switching their attention from one stimulus to another (Smith et al., 1998). This inability to control attention may account for the cognitive fragmentation that is a hallmark of schizophrenia. Because this fragmentation also is evident in schizophrenic speech, you might find it frustrating to converse with someone who suffers from schizophrenia. Schizophrenic speech might include invented words called *neologisms*, as in "The children have to have this 'accentuative' law so they don't go into the 'mortite' law of the church" (Vetter, 1969, p. 189). Schizophrenic speech might also include a meaningless jumble of words called a *word salad*, such as "The house burnt the cow horrendously always" (Vetter, 1969, p. 147).

Among the most distinctive cognitive disturbances in schizophrenia are delusions. A *delusion* is a belief that is held despite compelling evidence to the contrary, such as Edvard Munch's belief that his paintings were his children and were jealous of other paintings. The most common delusions are delusions of influence, such as the belief that one's thoughts are being beamed to all parts of the universe (*thought broadcasting*).

Less common are *delusions of grandeur*, in which the person believes that she or he is a famous or powerful person. The fascinating book *The Three Christs of Ypsilanti* (Rokeach, 1964/1981) describes the cases of three men in a mental hospital who had the same delusion of grandeur: Each claimed to be Jesus Christ. The workings of the schizophrenic mind are vividly illustrated when they meet, and each man tries to explain why he is Jesus and the others merely impostors.

Delusions vary from culture to culture, as demonstrated in a large-scale study of German and Japanese people with schizophrenia. The study found that Germans were more likely to have delusions of direct persecution, such as poisoning. The Japanese were more likely to have delusions of reference, such as being slandered (Tateyama, Asai, Kamisada, & Hashimoto, 1993). These and other cognitive symptoms make it difficult to interact with people who have schizophrenia and can cause great distress to caregivers.

Social-Emotional Symptoms People with schizophrenia typically have flat or inappropriate emotionality. Emotional flatness is shown by an unchanging facial expression, a lack of expressive gestures, and an absence of vocal inflections. For example, people with schizophrenia are less facially responsive to emotional films than other people are (Blanchard, Kring, & Neale, 1994). Emotional inappropriateness is shown by bizarre outbursts, such as laughing when someone is seriously injured. And, as in the case of Edvard Munch, people with schizophrenia tend to be socially withdrawn, with few, if any, friends. This withdrawal usually first appears in childhood.

Motor Symptoms Schizophrenia also is associated with unusual motor behavior. The person might rock incessantly, make bizarre faces, pace back and forth, hold poses for hours, or trace patterns in the air.

The Western media have sensationalized periodic cases in which people with schizophrenia have committed violent crimes. This sensationalism might lead to the public's overestimating the incidence of violence by the mentally ill (Angermeyer & Schulze, 2001). But some researchers insist that people with schizophrenia are more likely to be violent and that this tendency might be inherited (Tehrani, Brennan, Hodgins, & Mednick, 1998). Other researchers have found a weak link between schizophrenia and violence (Walsh, Buchanan, & Fahy, 2002). Thus, violence by people with schizophrenia often is a product of factors, such as a history of victimization, personality disorders, substance abuse, or a violent environment (Serper, 2011).

Causes of Schizophrenia

The variety, complexity, and diversity of schizophrenic symptoms make the discovery of the causes of schizophrenia one of the most challenging of all tasks facing those who study the disorder (Andreasen, 1997). No single viewpoint can explain all cases of schizophrenia or why some people with certain risk factors develop schizophrenia and others do not.

The Biopsychological Viewpoint
Biopsychological theories of schizophrenia consider genetic, biochemical, and neurological factors.

FIGURE 14-6
Heredity and the Risk of Schizophrenia

The concordance rates for schizophrenia between people become higher as their genetic similarity becomes greater. This finding provides evidence supportive of the hereditary basis of schizophrenia but cannot by itself rule out the influence of the degree of similarity in life experiences.
Source: Data from I. I. Gottesman and J. Shields (1982). *Schizophrenia: The epigenetic puzzle.* New York: Cambridge University Press.

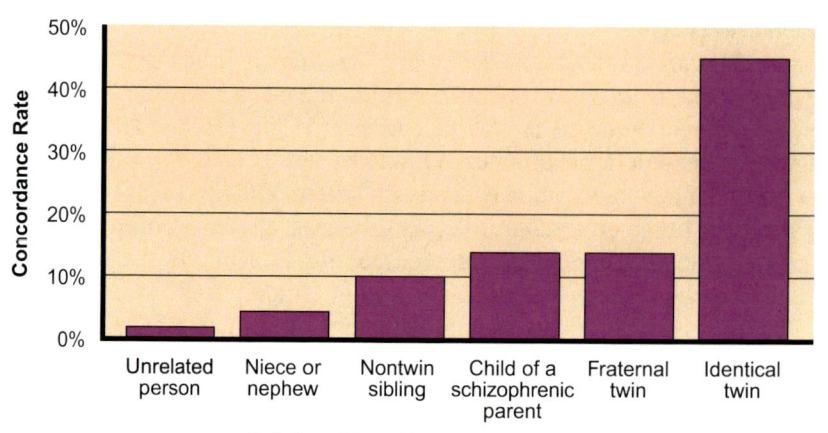

Hereditary Factors Schizophrenia runs in families; the closer the genetic relationship is to a family member with schizophrenia, the more likely a person is to develop schizophrenia (Kety, Wender, Jacobsen, & Ingraham, 1994). Figure 14-6 shows that the concordance rates for schizophrenia appear to have a strong hereditary basis. A major study found a concordance rate of 48 percent for identical twins and only 4 percent for fraternal twins (Onstad, Skre, Torgerson, & Kringlen, 1991). Yet, the higher concordance rate might be caused by the more similar treatment that identical twins receive rather than by their identical genetic endowment. A recent meta-analysis of 12 twin studies concluded that schizophrenia is a result of a complex relationship of genetic and environmental factors (Sullivan, Kendler, & Neale, 2003). Schizophrenia also frequently coexists with other psychological disorders. For example, a common problem for people with schizophrenia is substance abuse, especially alcohol abuse. The European Schizophrenia Cohort Survey, a large-scale survey, reported that about 35 percent of people with schizophrenia also abused alcohol and/or drugs (Carrà et al., 2012).

To assess the relative contributions of heredity and experience, researchers have turned to adoption studies. Many of these studies have been conducted in Denmark, where the government maintains excellent birth and adoption records. The studies support the genetic basis of schizophrenia. For example, schizophrenia is more common in the biological relatives of adoptees with schizophrenia than in their adoptive relatives, children adopted from parents with schizophrenia have a greater risk of schizophrenia than do children adopted from healthy parents, and children of healthy parents adopted by parents with schizophrenia do not show an increased risk of schizophrenia (Buchsbaum & Haier, 1983).

Consistent with the view that both heredity and experience contribute to the development of schizophrenia, it seems that schizophrenia is best explained by the biopsychological model, which sees it as the outcome of the interaction between a genetic predisposition and stressful life experiences (Conklin & Iacono, 2002). A review of research found that people with schizophrenia are predisposed to be more vulnerable to stressors, so stress that would hardly affect other people might cause them to develop symptoms of schizophrenia (Norman & Malla, 1993). For example, children who have both a genetic predisposition to develop schizophrenia and the stress of losing their father are more likely to develop schizophrenia than are children with only one of those factors (Walker, Hoppes, Emory, Mednick, & Schulsinger, 1981). The most convincing genetic information comes from a longitudinal family study. After studying a large Scottish family for decades, Millar et al. (2000) discovered a mutation in the gene called DISC1, abbreviated for *disrupted in schizophrenia-1*. This gene controls many cellular functions. However, as many advances were made as a result of this discovery, it is unlikely to be the sole explanation of the genetic effects on the risk of schizophrenia in every population (Bae et al., 2013).

Neurochemical Factors Given the apparent hereditary basis of schizophrenia, what biological differences might exist between people who develop schizophrenia and those who do not? One factor is the effect of genetic influences on activity of the neurotransmitter dopamine in the brain (Amin et al., 1999). Studies have found a relationship between schizophrenia and high levels of activity at synapses that use the neurotransmitters *dopamine* and *serotonin*.

What evidence is there of a dopamine basis for schizophrenia? First, drugs that are used to treat schizophrenia work by blocking dopamine (Silvestri et al., 2000) and serotonin receptors (Kapur & Remington, 1996). Second, drugs such as amphetamines, which increase dopamine levels in the brain, can induce schizophrenic symptoms in mentally healthy people (Adeyemo, 2002). Third, *L-dopa*, a drug used to treat Parkinson's disease because it increases dopamine levels in the brain, can induce schizophrenic symptoms in Parkinson's victims (Nicol & Gottesman, 1983). Fourth, brain-imaging studies have found overactivity of dopamine neurons in the brains of people with schizophrenia (Farde, 1997). And drugs that block both dopamine and serotonin receptors are effective in reducing symptoms of schizophrenia (O'Connor, 1998).

Season-of-Birth and Developmental Factors In seeking other factors in schizophrenia, biopsychological researchers are struck by one of the most well-replicated findings regarding schizophrenia: A disproportionate number of victims are born in the winter or early spring (Davies, Welham, Chant, Torrey, & McGrath, 2003). This finding has been confirmed in countries throughout the Northern Hemisphere, including Taiwan (Tam & Sewell, 1995), France (Amato, Rochet, Dalery, & Chauchat, 1994), Denmark (Mortensen et al., 1999), Holland (Pallast, Jongbloet, Straatman, & Zielhuis, 1994), and Switzerland (Modestin, Ammann, & Wurmle, 1995). But studies in the Southern Hemisphere, in countries such as Australia, have found that people with schizophrenia are born disproportionately in the Southern Hemisphere's spring and early summer (November, December, and January). Schizophrenia might be associated with certain months, not certain seasons (Berk, Terre-Blanche, Maude, & Lucas, 1996).

The observation that people are more likely to develop schizophrenia if they are born during certain months has inspired a search for a possible connection to influenza viruses prevalent during those months. These viruses might have infected the brains of people with schizophrenia prenatally, particularly during the second trimester, when brain development accelerates. The possible role of infections in the development of schizophrenia is supported by the tendency of the season-of-birth effect to hold more strongly in more crowded urban areas than in more sparsely populated rural areas (Verdoux et al., 1997).

Many studies have investigated the relationship between a worldwide influenza epidemic in 1957 and the development of schizophrenia in people born shortly afterward. Unfortunately, findings have been inconsistent. Some studies have found that people exposed to influenza prenatally, especially during the second trimester, have higher rates of schizophrenia (Takei, Mortensen, Klaening, & Murray, 1996). But other studies have found that they do not (Mino, Oshima, Tsuda, & Okagami, 2000). Moreover, efforts to find viruses in the brains of people with schizophrenia have had little success (Taller, Asher, Pomeroy, & Eldadah, 1996), though this dearth of evidence does not mean they do not exist. Perhaps the viruses do their damage before ultimately being destroyed by the immune system (Sierra-Honigmann, Carbone, & Yolken, 1995).

A viral basis for schizophrenia might help explain why identical twins do not have 100 percent concordance rate for schizophrenia. For example, identical twins who share the same placenta have a higher concordance rate for schizophrenia than do identical twins with separate placentas. It is reasonable to assume that if one twin is infected by a virus, the other twin will be more likely to become infected if it shares the same placenta than if it does not (Davis & Phelps, 1995). Maternal health habits also have been found to play a role in the development of schizophrenia. Mothers who smoke can alter both oxygen levels and hormone levels of the fetus. One study compared the smoking rates of mothers of offspring with schizophrenia and a control group of mothers of healthy offspring. Approximately 44 percent of the mothers of offspring with schizophrenia smoked, whereas only 22 percent of the mothers of healthy offspring smoked. Thus, smoking while being pregnant is correlated with the development of schizophrenia among offspring (Stathopoulou, Beratis, & Beratis, 2013). This and other studies suggest that we

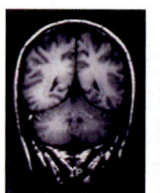

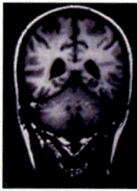

FIGURE 14-7
Schizophrenia and Neurological Abnormalities

CT scans of the brains of people with schizophrenia often show atrophy of brain tissue and enlarged ventricles. Notice that the ventricles (the dark areas) in the brain of the twin with schizophrenia *(right)* are much larger than those in the brain of the healthy twin *(left)*.
Source: Courtesy of Daniel R. Weinberger and E. Fuller Torrey.

cannot attribute the development of schizophrenia solely to genetics, but to a genetic/environment interaction.

Neurological Factors If viral infections play a role in schizophrenia, they would do so by affecting the brain. Brain-imaging studies have shown that schizophrenia is often associated with unusual brain activity. Schizophrenia is marked by greater abnormalities in activity in the left cerebral hemisphere than in the right cerebral hemisphere (Gur & Chin, 1999). In experiments that involve cognitive tasks, participants with schizophrenia also tend to have lower frontal-lobe activity than do healthy controls (Davidson & Heinrichs, 2003). As discussed in Chapter 3, the frontal lobes are important in thinking, planning, attention, and problem solving, each of which is likely to be deficient in schizophrenia.

As illustrated in Figure 14-7, some people with schizophrenia show atrophy of brain tissue, reducing the size of the amygdala and the hippocampus, as well as creating enlargement of the cerebral ventricles, the fluid-filled chambers inside the brain. A meta-analysis of MRI studies of biopsychological correlates of schizophrenia found that the largest difference between the brains of people with schizophrenia and healthy controls was found in the lateral ventricles (Wright et al., 2000). Because this enlargement can exist in people who have exhibited schizophrenic symptoms for only a brief time, it is not the consequence of prolonged drug treatments normally associated with chronic schizophrenia (Nopoulos, Torres, Flaum, & Andreasen, 1995). Andreasen and her associates have reported that some symptoms of schizophrenia are not consistently associated with ventricular enlargement (Andreasen, Flaum, Swayze, & Tyrrell, 1990). Moreover, it might be premature to divide schizophrenia into just two categories with either positive or negative symptoms. And the evidence is stronger for the existence of a syndrome of negative symptoms than for a syndrome of positive symptoms (Andreasen, Arndt, Alliger, & Miller, 1995).

The Psychoanalytic Viewpoint

According to the psychoanalytic viewpoint, people who develop schizophrenia fail to overcome their dependence on their mothers and, as a result, become fixated at the oral stage. This fixation gives them a weak ego that may fail to defend them against the anxiety caused by unconscious id impulses and external stressors. Instead, they cope with anxiety by resorting to behaviors characteristic of the oral stage, including fantasy, silly actions, incoherent speech, and irrational thinking.

Research in the spirit of the psychoanalytic viewpoint has found that parents high in what is known as *expressed emotion* might contribute to the maintenance or relapse of schizophrenia in their children. Parents who are high in expressed emotion criticize their children and become emotionally overprotective. Children's self-evaluations become more negative because of these critical attitudes, and the number of positive symptoms increases (Barrowclough, Tarrier, Humphreys, Ward, & Andrews, 2003). People with schizophrenia whose families are high in expressed emotion are more likely to suffer relapses (Hooley & Hiller, 2000). One study found that people with schizophrenia recalled more stressful memories about parents high in expressed emotion than parents low in expressed emotion (Cutting & Docherty, 2000). The notion of expressed emotion was developed in England and then in other Western countries, but the cross-cultural validity of the expressed emotion hypothesis is controversial (Cheng, 2002). Moreover, the relationship of expressed emotion to relapse varies by ethnicity (Subandi, 2011).

The Behavioral Viewpoint

Behavioral theories of schizophrenia, which stress the role of learning, assume that people with schizophrenia are rewarded for behaving in bizarre ways (Ullmann & Krasner, 1975). This situation was portrayed in the 1974 movie *A Woman Under the Influence*, in which a wife (played by Gena Rowlands) makes bizarre sounds to be rewarded with attention from her boorish husband (played by Peter Falk). Behavioral theorists also assume that a person who engages in bizarre behavior provokes social rejection from others, which in turn contributes to the suspiciousness and social withdrawal displayed by some people with schizophrenia.

The Cognitive Viewpoint

Proponents of the cognitive viewpoint point to disturbances of attention and thinking as the main factors in schizophrenia. As the leading schizophrenia researcher Eugen Bleuler observed early in the 20th century, people with schizophrenia seem "incapable of holding the train of thought in the proper channel" (Baribeau-Braun, Picton, & Gosselin, 1983). Children exposed to parents who communicate in confusing, irrational ways are predisposed to develop the disturbed cognitive activity of schizophrenia (Doane, West, Goldstein, Rodnick, & Jones, 1981).

The Humanistic Viewpoint

According to the humanistic viewpoint, schizophrenia is caused by extreme incongruence between the public self and the actual self. Psychologist R. D. Laing (1967) claimed that schizophrenia results when a person develops a false public self to confront an intolerable life situation. This retreat from reality permits the person to experience her or his actual self. The person's bizarre thinking, language, and behavior are indicative of this retreat from reality. In contrast to other humanistic psychologists, Laing recommended that family, friends, and professionals permit the person with schizophrenia to go on what he called a "voyage of self-discovery" into his or her actual self rather than interfering with that process through the administration of drugs or commitment to a mental hospital. According to Laing, traditional psychiatry and psychology unfairly try to force the person to conform to unfulfilling circumstances (Crossley, 1998).

Laing's critics claim that he romanticized schizophrenia, in the same way that 19th-century poets romanticized tuberculosis, by implying that it is somehow noble to have a serious psychological disorder. One of Laing's chief critics is Mark Vonnegut, son of the late novelist Kurt Vonnegut. Mark had been a follower of Laing's until he suffered several episodes of schizophrenia, as described in his autobiography *The Eden Express* (Vonnegut, 1975). When Mark recovered, he did not describe a voyage of self-discovery. Instead, he related a horrifying experience that he would have been better off without. Mark's disillusionment with Laing's view of schizophrenia led him to write a commentary for *Harper's* magazine entitled "Why I Want to Bite R. D. Laing" (Vonnegut, 1974).

The Sociocultural Viewpoint

Sociocultural factors can affect the precise pattern of symptoms in schizophrenia, but there is some cross-cultural universality in schizophrenic symptoms (Draguns & Tanaka-Matsumi, 2003). A study of French and North African participants with schizophrenia, for example, found little difference in their symptoms (Taleb, Rouillon, Petitjean, & Gorwood, 1996). Though the *DSM-5* considers sociocultural factors in schizophrenia more than prior editions did, critics insist that the *DSM* should pay even greater attention to them (Lake, 2012).

Section Review: Schizophrenia

1. What are the major symptoms of schizophrenia?
2. What evidence is there supporting the role of dopamine and serotonin in schizophrenia?
3. How do positive symptoms and negative symptoms of schizophrenia differ?

Personality Disorders

Personality disorders are long-standing, inflexible, maladaptive patterns of behavior. People with personality disorders exhibit certain personality traits to an inappropriate extreme. In essence, personality disorders are negative examples of what Alfred Adler called a style of life (see Chapter 13). Personality disorders are influenced by gender roles

personality disorder A psychological disorder characterized by enduring, inflexible, maladaptive patterns of behavior.

TABLE 14-3 Personality Disorders

Disorders	Symptoms
Cluster A: Disorders Characterized by Odd or Eccentric Behavior	
Paranoid personality disorder	Unrealistic mistrust and suspiciousness of people
Schizoid personality disorder	Problems in forming emotional relationships with others
Schizotypal personality disorder	Oddities of thinking, perception, communication, and behavior not severe enough to be diagnosed as schizophrenia
Cluster B: Disorders Characterized by Dramatic, Emotional, or Erratic Behavior	
Antisocial personality disorder	Continually violating the rights of others, being prone to impulsive behavior, and feeling no guilt for the harm done to others
Borderline personality disorder	Instability in mood, behavior, self-image, and social relationships
Histrionic personality disorder	Overly dramatic behavior, self-centeredness, and a craving for attention
Narcissistic personality disorder	Grandiose sense of self-importance, an insistence on being the center of attention, and a lack of empathy for others
Cluster C: Disorders Characterized by Anxious or Fearful Behavior	
Avoidant personality disorder	Hypersensitivity to potential rejection by others, causing social withdrawal despite a desire for social relationships
Dependent personality disorder	Failure to take responsibility for own life, instead relying too much on others to make decisions
Obsessive-compulsive personality disorder	Preoccupation with rules, schedules, organization, and trivial details, and inability to express emotional warmth

(Sprock, 2000), ethnicity (Chavira et al., 2003), and other sociocultural factors (Paris, 1998). Moreover, some critics assert that the *DSM-5* does not adequately represent the role of sociocultural factors in shaping personality disorders (Stone, 2012). Table 14-3 summarizes the personality disorders.

Borderline Personality Disorder

borderline personality disorder (BPD) A personality disorder marked by impulsivity, unstable moods, an inconsistent sense of identity, and difficulty maintaining intimate relationships.

A personality disorder of growing interest to psychologists is the **borderline personality disorder (BPD)**. This increase in interest is because BPD has become more prevalent, devastates the lives of its victims and their loved ones, and presents one of the greatest challenges to therapists. Though BPD occurs in all cultures, it is more prevalent in highly developed ones. This prevalence has been attributed in part to the breakdown of family ties (Paris, 1996).

Characteristics of Borderline Personality Disorder

The hallmark symptoms of BPD include impulsivity, unstable moods, an inconsistent sense of identity, and difficulty maintaining fulfilling intimate relationships. The impulsivity of people with BPD leads them into unwise behavior regarding sex, eating, driving, gambling, and spending (Hochhausen, Lorenz, & Newman, 2002). Such people can be in a friendly, lighthearted mood and suddenly become angry and vindictive for no apparent reason, reflecting their chronic emotional instability (Yen, Zlotnick, & Costello, 2002). Their sense of identity can be grandiose one moment and marked by suicidal self-loathing the next.

Perhaps of greatest pain to people with BPD and those close to them is their tendency to switch unpredictably between idealizing others and tearing them down, which professionals call splitting. People with BPD cannot retain a realistic view of people that combines positive and negative qualities. Instead, they rely on their latest interaction with the person to determine their feelings toward her or him.

People with BPD will desperately seek intimacy, only to run away when they find it. In romance, they can be charming and ingratiating at the first, superficial contact, only to become hostile and manipulative when true intimacy beckons. The author of the best-selling book on BPD, *I Hate You, Don't Leave Me*, stressed this problem by offering one intellectual's observation, "All is caprice. They love without measure those whom they will soon hate without reason" (Kreisman & Straus, 1989, p. 17). The chief reason for this behavior is that people with BPD desire love but are terrified at being engulfed by an intimate relationship. So they vacillate between clinging to their romantic partner and pushing their lover away (Chabrol, 1997). This inconsistency often leads to a romantic life marked by stormy, short-term relationships. Because of their inability to maintain healthy, intimate relationships, people with BPD tend to feel painfully alone. Given these feelings, experienced therapists know that most of their clients with BPD will call them repeatedly for support between therapy sessions (Gunderson, 1996).

Causes of Borderline Personality Disorder

Borderline personality disorder (BPD) affects 2 percent of the population. Many studies find that BPD is more common among women; however, these findings are controversial (Sansone & Sansone, 2011). This prevalence among women might reflect the greater incidence of childhood sexual abuse of infants and girls because there is a relationship between BPD and sexual abuse (Johnson et al., 2003). The child who experiences sexual, physical, or emotional abuse develops a powerful conflict between his or her normal need for closeness and attachment, and fear of the pain that it might bring (Sable, 1997). However, a recent 10-year longitudinal twin study found no causal relationship between child emotional, physical, and sexual abuse and BPD. Whereas child sexual abuse was correlated with BPD, it also was correlated with genetic factors and behavioral problems. The researchers concluded that genetic factors interact with behavioral disorders and make the child more susceptible to developing BPD (Bornovalova et al., 2013). There also is evidence of a biological basis for BPD. For example, BPD is associated with a reduction in the size of the hippocampus, amygdala, and frontal lobes (Tebartz van Elst et al., 2003) and less active frontal lobes (De la Fuente et al., 1997). How these differences might contribute to BPD is unknown.

Antisocial Personality Disorder

Until the recent surge of interest in BPD, the personality disorder of greatest interest to the general public was **antisocial personality disorder**, perhaps because it has been implicated in many notorious criminal cases. Between 1972 and 1978, a successful, civic-minded Chicago building contractor named John Wayne Gacy murdered 33 boys and young men and buried them under his house. After his capture, Gacy expressed no remorse and, instead, reported that his acts of cold-blooded murder had given him pleasure. Gacy's personal history indicated that he had an antisocial personality disorder.

antisocial personality disorder A personality disorder marked by impulsive, manipulative, often criminal behavior, without any feelings of guilt in the perpetrator.

Characteristics of Antisocial Personality Disorder

Antisocial personality disorder is found in about 3 percent of American men and less than 1 percent of American women. In the 19th century, it was called "moral insanity," and for most of the past century, it was called *psychopathy* or *sociopathy*. The disorder is characterized by maladaptive behavior beginning in childhood. This behavior includes lying, stealing, truancy, vandalism, fighting, drug abuse, physical cruelty, academic failure, and early sexual activity. Adults with antisocial personality disorder do not conform to social norms. They might fail to hold a job, to honor financial obligations, or to fulfill parental responsibilities. They also are more likely to become compulsive gamblers (Slutske et al., 2001).

Because people with antisocial personality disorder can be charming, lie with a straight face, and talk their way out of trouble, they may pursue careers as shyster lawyers, crooked politicians, or phony evangelists. Two hallmarks of the antisocial personality are impulsive behavior, such as reckless driving or promiscuous sexual relations, and a remarkable lack of guilt for the pain and suffering they inflict on others (Rogers, Duncan, Lynett, & Sewell, 1994). In extreme cases, people with an antisocial personality engage in criminal activities, yet fail to change their behavior even after being punished for it. Robert Hare, a noted researcher on antisocial personality disorder, has found that, fortunately for society, criminals with an antisocial personality tend to "burn out" after age 40 and commit fewer crimes than do other criminals (Hare, McPherson, & Forth, 1988).

Causes of Antisocial Personality Disorder

Antisocial personality disorder has been subjected to more research than any other personality disorder. Studies have provided evidence of a biological predisposition underlying it. Thomas Bouchard's University of Minnesota study of identical twins who were separated in infancy and then reunited years later (see Chapter 13) indicates that antisocial personality disorder has a genetic basis (Grove, Eckert, Heston, & Bouchard, 1990). Heredity seems to provide people who develop an antisocial personality disorder with an unusually low level of physiological reactivity to stress, most notably physical punishment (Arnett, Howland, Smith, & Newman, 1993). Given that people try to maintain an optimal level of physiological arousal (see Chapter 11), perhaps the unusually low level of arousal of people with an antisocial personality disorder motivates them to engage in behaviors that increase their level of arousal (Ellis, 1987). Whereas some people seek to increase their arousal by engaging in auto racing and similar socially acceptable activities, those with an antisocial personality disorder might learn to do so by committing bank robberies and similar antisocial activities. An MRI study found that men with antisocial personality disorder showed an 11 percent reduction in prefrontal gray matter, compared to healthy controls. The researchers believe that this deficit in the frontal lobe may underlie the low arousal, lack of conscience, and poor decision making that characterize antisocial personality disorder (Raine, Lencz, Bihrle, LaCasse, & Colletti, 2000).

But what makes one person with a low level of physiological arousal seek thrills through auto racing and another seek thrills through robbing banks? Behaviorists believe that antisocial personality disorder is caused by parents who reward, or fail to punish, their children for engaging in antisocial behaviors, such as lying, stealing, or aggression. However, a history of childhood conduct problems predicts antisocial personality disorder in adulthood independently of familial or social variables (Hill, 2003). There is some evidence that people with antisocial personality disorder, perhaps because of their low physiological reactivity, are less likely to learn from punishment for misdeeds. They do not show the normal increase in anxiety when exposed to punishment (Eysenck, 1982).

Section Review: Personality Disorders

1. Why do you think antisocial personality disorder at one time was called "moral insanity"?
2. What would be some signs that the person you are dating has a borderline personality disorder?

Developmental Disorders

developmental disorders
Psychological disorders originating in childhood that can be characterized by physical, learning, language, or behavioral impairments. The disorder can improve or persist throughout a person's lifetime.

Many theories address the origin of **developmental disorders**, which are psychological disorders originating in childhood that can be characterized by physical, learning, language, or behavioral impairments. None has been completely supported, but researchers ask question such as these: Do environmental factors disrupt normal development? Are the developmental abnormalities predetermined due to genetics? Could developmental disorders be a result of the combination of genetics and environment?

Autism Spectrum Disorder (ASD)

Autism spectrum disorder (ASD) is characterized by impaired social functioning that is present in early childhood. This disorder was first reported by Leo Kanner, when he published a case study in which he described three young children from his child psychiatry clinic at Johns Hopkins University "whose condition differs so markedly and uniquely from anything reported so far, that each case merits . . . a detailed consideration of its fascinating peculiarities" (Kanner, 1943, p. 217). He noted that these children had developmental delays in motor skills, extraordinary memory capabilities, poor verbal skills, and engaged in self-stimulating behavior, such as intense fascination with spinning blocks and other round objects.

Kanner used the word *autism*, previously associated with childhood schizophrenia, to describe these children. The term *autism* comes from the Greek word *autos*, or self. This term was coined to capture one of the core facets of autism: impaired social functioning. Kanner, in his original paper, called attention to what he observed as a lack of warmth among the fathers and mothers of autistic children. This promoted the misconception that this disorder was environmental in origin and caused by "refrigerator moms" who exhibited cold, distant, and insensitive parenting. Today, parents likely still feel a social stigma when their children diagnosed with ASD are perceived negatively by others in public settings. Social psychologists have found this to be the case when children with ASD are found to be high functioning intellectually yet still display noncompliant behaviors. Wales (2002) found that mothers feel the greatest impact from this social stigma.

Characteristics of Autism Spectrum Disorder (ASD)

The defining characteristics of ASD according to the *DSM-5* (APA, 2013) are:

1. Deficits in social communication and social interaction (across multiple contexts).
2. Repetitive patterns of behavior (including self-stimulating behavior, extreme adherence to routines, difficulty in making transitions, rigidity and lack of flexibility in thought, and unusual sensory processes).
3. Symptoms are first present in early childhood.

In addition to these core symptoms, children with ASD show a variety of other symptoms. In previous versions of the *DSM*, children could be diagnosed into four separate but related disorders with a strict requirement that symptoms develop before the age of 3: *autistic disorder*, *Asperger's disorder*, *childhood disintegrative disorder*, or *pervasive developmental disorder not otherwise specified (PDD-NOS)*. But now, to avoid inconsistencies and improve reliability in diagnosis and, ideally, treatment, people with the core symptoms noted are diagnosed with autism spectrum disorder (ASD). For example, Asperger's syndrome, which is characterized primarily by impaired social interactions, was once a subcategory of ASD. Now, it is diagnosed as ASD.

A recent study conducted by the Centers for Disease Control and Prevention estimated the prevalence of ASD in the United States as 11.3 in 1,000 (CDCP, 2012). ASD is approximately four times more common in boys than in girls, but girls appear to experience more disability from the disorder (Volkmar et al., 2014). Globally, there is more variation in prevalence rates. This is likely due to cultural differences and the fact that the *DSM* is still being revised. Fredrick Volkmar, a leading researcher who has spent decades improving diagnosis and treatment for individuals with ASD, suggests that the changes in the *DSM-5* will help practitioners differentiate between ASD and a variety of other disorders that develop in infancy and childhood. Many individuals with well-known genetic disorders, such as Down syndrome (see Chapter 10), display behaviors that mimic ASD. And these behaviors occasionally can coexist with a diagnosis of ASD (Moss, Richards, Nelson, & Oliver, 2013).

Developmental Characteristics of ASD

There is evidence that diagnosis of ASD can occur as early as age 2 (Moore & Goodson, 2003). Family studies have indicated that there is a strong genetic basis for ASD. Siblings of people with ASD are nearly 100 times more likely to be at risk of developing the disorder, compared to that of the general population (Bolton et al., 1994). Researchers

Developmental Disorders

Developmental disorders are caused by impaired development of the brain. Diagnosing psychological disorders in young children can be challenging.
Source: Marcin Pawinski/Shutterstock.com.

autism spectrum disorder (ASD) A psychological disorder characterized by poor social relationships, impaired communication, and repetitive behaviors.

Autism Spectrum Disorder (ASD)

Children with ASD often engage in repetitive, self-stimulating behavior.
Source: viki2win/Shutterstock.com.

have begun to study abnormal brain structures that are common in people with ASD. In one recent study, the brains of infants at risk for developing ASD were scanned in modified MRI machines at 6 months, 12 months, and 24 months of age. The scans of infants that were ultimately diagnosed with ASD at 24 months of age indicated abnormal development of the axons of the neurons (Wolff et al., 2012). These results support a finding that has been replicated many times; that is, individuals with ASD have surprisingly large heads and brains (White, O'Reilly, & Frith, 2009).

Abnormal connections among neurons are not the only biopsychological relationship. Postmortem studies of the brains of individuals who had lived with ASD have found a number of abnormal brain structures, regardless of the age at which the person died. For example, the number of abnormal neurons in areas of the brain associated with emotion is increased, whereas the number of abnormal neurons in the cerebellum is decreased (Bauman & Kemper, 2005). Other researchers have investigated the relationship of neurotransmitters in the development of ASD. One neurotransmitter—serotonin—has received special attention. High blood levels of serotonin are found in people with ASD, and high levels of serotonin during childhood development can, in turn, alter brain function and behavior (Whitaker-Azmitia, 2001).

Maternal exposure to teratogens (see Chapter 4) and complications of pregnancy and childbirth can contribute to the development of ASD. Thalidomide, a drug previously used to treat the nausea often associated with the morning sickness experienced by pregnant women, has a long and sometimes notorious history. Whereas exposure to thalidomide *later* in pregnancy has been found to be associated with a loss of limbs in offspring, exposure to thalidomide very *early* in pregnancy has been found to be associated with ASD. The late Patricia Rodier was critical in helping ASD researchers link exposure to thalidomide during critical periods of the development of the fetal nervous system. She found that women who ingested thalidomide 20 to 24 days after conception were more likely to give birth to offspring with ASD than women who were not exposed to thalidomide (Rodier, Ingram, Tisdale, & Croog, 1997). And though there is no credible evidence that vaccines can cause ASD, the influence of maternal immune system reactions on the developing fetus have not been ruled out (Pardo, Vargas, & Zimmerman, 2005). It has taken many years, but researchers have ruled out a causal relationship between the administration of vaccines that contain mercury in childhood and ASD (Hviid, Stellfeld, Wohlfahrt, & Melbye, 2003). Thus, genetic and environmental factors also can contribute to the development of this disorder.

Attention Deficit Hyperactivity Disorder (ADHD)

attention deficit hyperactivity disorder (ADHD)
A developmental disorder that begins in childhood and can persist into adulthood that is characterized by persistent lack of attention, distractibility when engaged in important tasks, impulsive behavior, hyperactivity, and failure to follow through with future plans.

Attention deficit hyperactivity disorder (ADHD) is a common childhood psychological disorder that can continue through adolescence and into adulthood. "Smart But Stuck" is how one leading clinical psychologist describes ADHD (Brown, 2014). This refers to bright children with ADHD who often must repeat grades in school (Kessler et al., 2013). It was not until 1968, when the *DSM-II* was published, that there was mention of a disorder that resembled ADHD, "hyperkinetic impulse disorder." Thus, this is a relatively new disorder listed in the DSM. Currently, there is no single test to diagnose ADHD and no cure. And many other psychological disorders can have symptoms that mimic those of ADHD. As described in "Smart But Stuck," people with ADHD can have high IQs (Antshel et al., 2010).

Characteristics of Attention Deficit Hyperactivity Disorder (ADHD)
The defining characteristics for diagnosing a person with ADHD according to the *DSM-5* (APA, 2013) are:

1. *Inattention that is not age appropriate* (for example, failure to pay close attention to details, difficulty in maintaining attention to task, seemingly not listening when spoken to directly, failure to follow through on instructions, difficulty organizing tasks and activities, reluctance to perform tasks that require mental effort over a sustained period of time, frequent losses of personal belongings, and frequently being distracted and forgetful).

2. *Hyperactivity and impulsivity that is disruptive and age inappropriate* (for example, a tendency to physically fidget, inability to remain seated when expected to, tendency to run or climb in inappropriate settings, chronic restlessness, inability to participate in quiet activities, excessive talking, difficulty in waiting turns, and a tendency to interrupt others).

These symptoms must be present before the age of 12 and occur in multiple settings, such as at school, home, or work. Depending on the age of the person, a certain number of the characteristics listed must occur. And these symptoms must interfere with or reduce the quality of the person's social interactions or school and work performance. There are three subtypes of ADHD: *combined presentation, predominantly inattentive presentation,* and *predominantly hyperactive-impulsive presentation.*

Globally, prevalence rates of ADHD have been reported to be between 8 and 12 percent of the population (Faraone, Sergeant, Gillberg, & Biederman, 2003). One contemporary trend is the increasing rate of diagnosis of ADHD among children. The National Survey on Children's Health has recently reported that 2 million children and adolescents were diagnosed with ADHD in 2011. And adolescent boys are more likely than girls to have ever been diagnosed with ADHD (Visser et al., 2014). Studies also show that people with ADHD also are often diagnosed with mood disorders, disruptive behaviors, and substance abuse disorders (Kessler et al., 2013). Another study in which researchers reviewed insurance claims found a pronounced shift in care from pediatricians to psychiatrists for children with ADHD (Garfield et al., 2012). This study, as well as others, leads to the conclusion that close to two-thirds of children and adolescents diagnosed with ADHD are taking medication (Visser et al., 2014). This trend toward increased medication of children with ADHD—and children with ASD—demonstrates a need for pediatric psychiatrists for their treatment.

Despite the core symptoms noted earlier, clinicians are puzzled by the inconsistency of inattention symptoms. A person diagnosed with ADHD can abandon a boring task, yet then intensely focus on an interesting task. This *attentional bias* can influence the emotional processing in people with ADHD. Brown notes that attentional bias can cause emotional flare-ups and may contribute to poor motivation for achieving goals. He likens this phenomenon to viewing a spectator sport:

> For those with ADHD, life can be like trying to watch a basketball game through a telescope, which allows them to see only a small fragment of the action at any specific time. Sometimes, that telescope stays too long on one part of the court, missing out completely on important events occurring elsewhere at the same time. At other times, the telescope may randomly flit from one bit of action to another, losing track of where the ball is and what various players are in a position to do. To follow what is going on in a basketball game, a person needs to be able to watch the whole court, noting movements of the ball and rapidly shifting positions of players as they present multiple risks and opportunities in the game. (Brown, 2014, pp. 9–10)

In fact, examining the brain structures involved in attentional, emotional, and motivational processing is one way researchers are attempting to understand the neurobiology of ADHD.

Developmental Causes of ADHD

Today, researchers are trying to identify the causes of ADHD. It is likely that there is more than one cause and more than one brain structure involved in the development of ADHD. Moreover, it is very likely that there are multiple causes that also might interact with each other. Nevertheless, research points to a very strong genetic link with high heritability rates (Larsson, Chang, D'Onofrio, & Lichtenstein, 2013). Children with parents or siblings with the disorder are two to eight times more likely to have ADHD (Faraone & Biederman). The average heritability estimates from 20 twin studies in the United States, Australia, Scandinavia, and the European Union are 76 percent (Faraone et al., 2005), indicating that ADHD is a highly heritable condition.

The brain areas researchers focus on are related to attention and cognitive control, particularly the *prefrontal cortex* (Carr, Henderson, & Nigg, 2010). The prefrontal cortex (see Chapter 3) is a sheet of cells covering our brain in the anterior portion of the frontal lobe. The prefrontal cortex is an important area that regulates attention, the planning of complex tasks, the shifting and dividing of attention in a task-appropriate manner, behavioral inhibition, and decision making. Typically, psychologists refer to this area as the "executive center." One famous neurobiologist—Patricia Goldman-Rakic—describes the prefrontal cortex as a "mental sketch pad" with special processing domains, allowing for the highest level of cognitive ability. She goes on to describe dysfunction in the domains as a "dysexecutive syndrome" characterized by disorganization, preservation, and distractibility (Goldman-Rakic, 1996).

Recently, fMRI studies have helped us understand the neural circuitry and structure of the prefrontal cortex. In one large study using fMRI, researchers scanned over 160 participants with ADHD. These scans were used to measure the thickness of the cortex across the brain. Children with ADHD had a general thinning of the cortex. This was most pronounced in regions associated with attention and cognition that were located in the prefrontal cortex (Shaw et al., 2006). This led researchers to question if development of the prefrontal cortex in people with ADHD is either delayed or dysfunctional. This same research group went on to scan over 200 more children and adolescents with ADHD and found that the cortical development in children with ADHD lagged behind that of a control group of healthy children. This lag in maturation was estimated to be equivalent to several years (Shaw et al., 2007a).

Genetic studies have identified genes in several neurotransmitter systems, including dopamine, norepinephrine, serotonin, and acetylcholine, that may be implicated in the development of ADHD (Gizer, Ficks, & Waldman, 2009). Particular attention has been paid to the dopamine system in the prefrontal cortex. Another study by Shaw and colleagues (2007) sought to examine the relationship between genetics and ADHD symptoms. In this longitudinal study, they looked at children with a particular version of a gene related to dopamine receptors and found, again, thinner cortical tissue in the prefrontal cortex. Interestingly, as the children grew up or took long-term medication, portions of their cortex developed to a normal thickness. This improvement in the cortical thickness was correlated with improved ADHD symptoms (Shaw et al., 2007b; Shaw, Gogtay, & Rapoport, 2010). Studies such as these highlight the plasticity of our brains and that ADHD might be a disorder related to this neuroplasticity.

Low doses of stimulants are effective in the treatment of ADHD. These medications enhance attention and cognitive skills. Stimulant medications that have been used in treating ADHD include *methyphenidate* (Ritalin), *mixed amphetamine salts* (Adderall), and the newer drug *lisdexamfetamine dimesylate* (Vyvanse). These medications work by increasing levels of dopamine in the neural synapses. Functional MRI studies demonstrate that stimulants reverse the underactivity found in the prefrontal cortex in people with ADHD (Bush, Valera, & Seidman, 2005). Animal studies also have confirmed the relationship between the effect of stimulants on the prefrontal cortex. Rats that have stimulants injected into their prefrontal cortex show improvements on cognitive tasks that are dependent on prefrontal cortex functioning (Spencer, Klein, & Berridge, 2012). Though it might seem counterintuitive to treat people with ADHD with stimulants, these medications work by improving focus and attention and reducing hyperactivity that is due to an understimulation of dopamine. The use of stimulants, especially those that have an extended release over the course of the day, help people with ADHD to improve their social functioning, school performance, behavior outside school, ability to drive, and to reduce disruptive behavior in general (Cox et al., 2006; Buitelaar & Medori, 2010; Swanson, Baler, & Volkow, 2011).

A noninvasive therapy that has received attention is neurofeedback. This technique uses biofeedback to help guide people with ADHD to regulate their brain activity, usually while playing video games. Some studies indicate that this treatment is effective (Butnik, 2005; Nazari, 2011), whereas others suggest that treatment efficacy was demonstrated to be less robust in randomized controlled and double-blinded studies (Moriyama et al.,

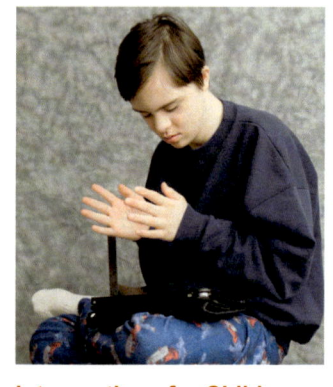

Interventions for Children with Developmental Disorders

In this photo, a boy diagnosed with both ASD and Down syndrome is clapping his hands as he plays with a tablet device. Tablet devices are powerful interventions that develop social interaction and communication skills. Touch-screen technology has been studied for intervention in developmental disorders such as ASD.

Source: wallybird/Shutterstock.com.

2012). Researchers continue to study the relationship between brain structure and function and ADHD to identify the causes of this disorder and to optimize treatment interventions.

> **Section Review:** Developmental Disorders
>
> 1. Why was ASD once considered a disorder caused by environmental influences?
> 2. What is a consistent neurological correlate of people with ASD?
> 3. What are the major symptoms of ADHD, and how long can this disorder last?

Experiencing Psychology

How Do the Media Portray Psychological Disorders?

Rationale

Psychological disorders are a favorite topic of the media. You cannot go a day without reading about them on the Internet or in a magazine or newspaper, seeing people with disorders on daytime talk shows and soap operas, hearing about them on radio talk shows, or watching reports on them on the nightly television news. This activity asks you to keep a record of media portrayals of psychological disorders.

Procedure

Keep a 2-week diary of every instance in which you encounter a media portrayal of a person with a psychological disorder. Note such instances on the Internet, in movies, on television, and in books, magazines, or newspapers. Also note how often particular topics or disorders are presented and whether they are portrayed in a casual, scientific, or sensational manner.

Results and Discussion

Discuss your impression of how the media portray psychological disorders. How does the information presented in the media compare with the information presented in this chapter? What should the media present concerning psychological disorders that they do not do well enough?

Chapter Summary

Characteristics of Psychological Disorders

- Researchers in the field of psychopathology study psychological disorders.
- The criteria for determining the presence of a psychological disorder include abnormality, maladaptiveness, and personal distress.
- The major viewpoints on the causes of psychological disorders include the biopsychological, psychoanalytic, behavioral, cognitive, humanistic, and sociocultural viewpoints.
- The more recent biopsychosocial viewpoint sees psychological disorders as the result of an interaction of biological, psychological, and social factors.
- *The Diagnostic and Statistical Manual of Mental Disorders–Fifth Edition (DSM-5)*, published by the American Psychiatric Association, is the accepted standard for classifying psychological disorders.
- Some psychologists and psychiatrists have questioned the reliability and validity of the *DSM-5*.
- Psychologist David Rosenhan and psychiatrist Thomas Szasz have noted certain dangers involved in diagnosing psychological disorders.
- Though the insanity defense is rarely used and is even more rarely successful in criminal cases, it has sparked controversy over concern that people guilty of violent crimes might escape punishment.

Anxiety Disorders

- Anxiety disorders are associated with anxiety that is intense and disruptive of everyday functioning.
- A generalized anxiety disorder is marked by a constant state of anxiety that exists independently of any particular stressful situation.
- A panic disorder is marked by sudden attacks of overwhelming anxiety accompanied by dizziness, trembling, cold sweats, heart palpitations, shortness of breath, fear of dying, and fear of going crazy.
- Phobias are excessive or inappropriate fears.
- A specific phobia involves a specific object or situation, a social anxiety disorder involves fear of social evaluation, and agoraphobia involves fear of being in public places.

Obsessive-Compulsive Disorder
- People with obsessions and compulsions that interfere with their daily functioning suffer from obsessive-compulsive disorder.
- An obsession is a persistent, recurring thought, and a compulsion is a repetitive action that one feels compelled to perform.

Somatic Symptom and Related Disorders
- The somatic symptom and related disorders are characterized by physical symptoms in the absence of disease or injury, with the symptoms caused instead by psychological factors.
- A person with illness anxiety disorder interprets the slightest physical changes in his or her body as evidence of a serious illness.
- A person with a conversion disorder exhibits loss or alteration of a physical function without any apparent physical cause.

Dissociative Disorders
- In a dissociative disorder, the person's conscious awareness becomes separated from certain aspects of her or his thoughts, feelings, and memories.
- A person with dissociative amnesia is unable to recall personally significant memories.
- A person with dissociative fugue suffers from dissociative amnesia and loss of identity and flees from home.
- A person with a dissociative identity disorder (formerly called multiple personality disorder) has two or more distinct personalities that may vie for dominance.

Major Depressive Disorder and Related Disorders
- People with major depressive disorder (MDD) experience depression that is so intense and prolonged that it causes severe distress and disrupts their lives.
- In cases of MDD, suicide is always a concern.
- People who attempt suicide usually give warnings, so suicidal threats should be taken seriously.

Bipolar Disorder
- In bipolar disorder, the person alternates between periods of mania and major depressive disorder.
- Mania is characterized by euphoria, hyperactivity, grandiose ideas, annoying talkativeness, inflated optimism, and inflated self-esteem.

Schizophrenia
- Schizophrenia is characterized by a severe disruption of perception, cognition, emotionality, behavior, and social relationships.
- The *DSM-5* considers schizophrenia to be a cluster of symptoms that can be demarcated by a series of stages of increasing psychosis.
- Biological theories of schizophrenia consider genetic, biochemical, developmental, and neurological factors.

Personality Disorders
- Personality disorders are long-standing, inflexible, maladaptive patterns of behavior.
- Of growing concern is the prevalence of the borderline personality disorder, marked by emotional instability and severely maladaptive social relationships.
- Of greatest concern is the antisocial personality disorder, associated with lying, stealing, fighting, drug abuse, physical cruelty, and lack of responsibility.

Developmental Disorders
- Developmental disorders are psychosocial disorders present in early childhood that can persist into adulthood
- Autism spectrum disorder (ASD) is characterized by poor social skills, poor communicative abilities, and repetitive behavior.
- People with attention deficit hyperactivity disorder (ADHD) have difficulty concentrating, remaining still, and staying on task at school or work.
- According to family studies, there is strong support for a genetic influence in both ASD and ADHD.

Key Terms

Characteristics of Psychological Disorders

biopsychosocial model (p. 482)
insanity (p. 486)
psychopathology (p. 481)

Anxiety Disorders

agoraphobia (p. 495)
anxiety disorder (p. 489)
generalized anxiety disorder (p. 491)
panic disorder (p. 493)
phobia (p. 494)
social anxiety disorder (p. 494)
specific phobia (p. 494)

Obsessive-Compulsive Disorder

obsessive-compulsive disorder (OCD) (p. 497)

Somatic Symptom and Related Disorder

conversion disorder (p. 499)
illness anxiety disorder (p. 498)
somatic symptom and related disorder (p. 498)

Dissociative Disorders

dissociative amnesia (p. 500)
dissociative disorder (p. 500)
dissociative fugue (p. 500)
dissociative identity disorder (p. 501)

Major Depressive Disorder and Related Disorders

major depressive disorder (MDD) (p. 503)
seasonal affective disorder (SAD) (p. 506)

Bipolar Disorder

bipolar disorder (p. 510)
mania (p. 510)

Schizophrenia

schizophrenia (p. 511)

Personality Disorders
antisocial personality disorder (p. 519)
borderline personality disorder (BPD) (p. 518)
personality disorder (p. 517)

Developmental Disorders
autism spectrum disorder (ASD) (p. 521)

attention deficit hyperactivity disorder (ADHD) (p. 522)
developmental disorders (p. 520)

Chapter Quiz

Note: Answers for the Chapter Quiz questions are provided at the end of the book.

1. The Swiss physician Paracelsus countered the supernatural view of psychological disorders by attributing them to
   a. neurotransmitters.
   b. phases of the moon.
   c. hallucinogenic substances.
   d. imbalances in body humors.

2. _____ involves the inability to develop normal social and communication skills and a tendency to be self-absorbed.
   a. Schizophrenia
   b. Parkinson's disease
   c. Autism spectrum disorder
   d. Attention deficit hyperactivity disorder

3. A woman subjected to horrible abuse from her husband suddenly loses her memory for herself, husband, and place of employment and begins a new life with a new identity in another state. This situation is most likely a case of
   a. hypermnesia.
   b. dissociative fugue.
   c. dissociative amnesia.
   d. conversion disorder.

4. A person likes to be by herself, laughs when she hears of tragedies, speaks gibberish, believes she is Catherine the Great, and hears voices that curse at her. This situation is most likely a case of
   a. schizophrenia.
   b. bipolar disorder.
   c. dissociative identity disorder.
   d. antisocial personality disorder.

5. Enlarged cerebral ventricles are associated with
   a. schizophrenia.
   b. bipolar disorder.
   c. conversion disorder.
   d. antisocial personality disorder.

6. Psychopathology is the study of
   a. psychopaths.
   b. schizophrenia.
   c. psychological disorders.
   d. physiological bases of mental illness.

7. Just before a major singing competition, one of the singers loses his voice. A physical examination reveals no medical cause for the condition. This situation is most likely a case of
   a. illness anxiety disorder.
   b. dissociative fugue.
   c. conversion disorder.
   d. obsessive-compulsive disorder.

8. According to R. D. Laing, whose belief was criticized by Mark Vonnegut, schizophrenia is a
   a. myth.
   b. mystical state.
   c. neurochemical disorder.
   d. voyage of self-discovery.

9. A friend of yours suddenly changes many of her habits. She stays in bed until late afternoon, rarely leaves her room, shows little appetite for food, no longer takes daily showers, and expresses no interest in spending time with friends. This situation is most likely a case of
   a. agoraphobia.
   b. schizophrenia.
   c. major depressive disorder.
   d. conversion disorder.

10. Parents high in expressed emotion may cause relapses in children with
    a. schizophrenia.
    b. major depressive disorder.
    c. dissociative amnesia.
    d. obsessive-compulsive disorder.

11. A young man enjoys getting into fights, has a history of stealing cars, and expresses no remorse for inflicting physical and emotional harm on others. This situation is most likely a case of
    a. mania.
    b. schizophrenia.
    c. dissociative identity disorder.
    d. antisocial personality disorder.

12. In 1843, Daniel M'Naghten became the first person to
    a. cure schizophrenia.
    b. use the insanity defense.
    c. demonstrate conversion hysteria in a man.
    d. be diagnosed with dissociative identity disorder.

13. According to research by Susan Nolen-Hoeksema, major depressive disorder is linked to
    a. chromosome 11.
    b. anger turned inward.
    c. ruminating about problems.
    d. faulty attributional processes.

14. According to the humanistic viewpoint, incongruence between the actual self and the ideal self causes
    a. major depressive disorder.
    b. schizophrenia.
    c. dissociative fugue.
    d. dissociative identity disorder.

15. According to Martin Seligman, depressed people tend to attribute negative events in their lives to
    a. stable, global, and internal factors.
    b. unstable, global, and internal factors.
    c. stable, specific, and external factors.
    d. unstable, specific, and external factors.

16. A psychological disorder in which depressive symptoms occur during particular times of the year is called
    a. neurosis.
    b. spring fever.
    c. bipolar disorder.
    d. seasonal affective disorder.

17. Janice Egeland and her colleagues (1987) found evidence, since disputed, that a defective gene on the 11th chromosome predisposed members of an extended Amish family to develop
    a. schizophrenia.
    b. bipolar disorder.
    c. seasonal affective disorder.
    d. antisocial personality disorder.

18. In regard to suicide,
    a. most attempters give warnings.
    b. most attempters leave notes explaining why.
    c. women tend to use more lethal means than men do.
    d. taking threats seriously will only instigate them.

19. The main criteria for diagnosing a psychological disorder are abnormality, personal distress, and
    a. insanity.
    b. delusions.
    c. maladaptiveness.
    d. auditory hallucinations.

20. A student who fails out of school becomes severely depressed and sees a psychologist for help. The psychologist attributes this depression to the frustration of the student's movement toward self-actualization. This situation indicates that the psychologist favors the
    a. cognitive viewpoint.
    b. behavioral viewpoint.
    c. humanistic viewpoint.
    d. psychoanalytic viewpoint.

21. A student who had been gloomy, unkempt looking, and socially aloof a week ago suddenly becomes wildly optimistic, impeccably groomed, and the "life of the party." This situation is most likely a case of
    a. agoraphobia.
    b. bipolar disorder.
    c. conversion disorder.
    d. disorganized schizophrenia.

22. David Rosenhan's (1973) study, in which pseudopatients had themselves admitted to mental hospitals, indicated that psychological diagnosis may be
    a. biased by preconceptions.
    b. more accurate than medical diagnosis.
    c. more accurate for psychoses than neuroses.
    d. affected by the socioeconomic status of the patient.

23. A college student faced with upcoming exams and term papers responds to his resulting feelings of anxiety by reorganizing his notes, rearranging his bookshelves, cleaning out his desk drawers, and straightening up his closet. He would be showing symptoms of
    a. claustrophobia.
    b. dissociative fugue.
    c. disorganized schizophrenia.
    d. obsessive-compulsive disorder.

24. While walking through a shopping mall, you suddenly have an intense feeling of dread, notice your heart beating strongly, feel as if you are suffocating, and find yourself running for the nearest exit. You would be exhibiting symptoms of
    a. mania.
    b. acrophobia.
    c. schizophrenia.
    d. panic disorder.

25. A student compulsively rearranges her room over and over. Her psychotherapist attributes this behavior to her desire to control an unconscious conflict over sex. The psychotherapist probably favors the
    a. cognitive viewpoint.
    b. behavioral viewpoint.
    c. humanistic viewpoint.
    d. psychoanalytic viewpoint.

Thought Questions

1. How would the three criteria for diagnosing psychological disorders be applied to agoraphobia?
2. Why might public concern about the use of the insanity defense in criminal cases be overblown?
3. A student becomes overwhelmed with anxiety when he is faced with major exams. How might the different viewpoints on psychological disorders explain this?

Therapy

CHAPTER 15

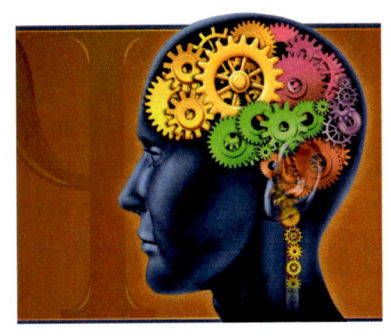

From 1880 to 1882, Austrian physician Josef Breuer (1842–1925) treated a wealthy, intelligent, young woman he called Anna O. who suffered from *conversion hysteria*—that is, physical symptoms without any apparent physical cause (Van der Kolk, 2000). Her symptoms apparently were triggered by her difficulty dealing with her father's terminal illness, but also may have been complicated by morphine and chloral hydrate dependence (de Paula Ramos, 2003). She displayed a variety of symptoms that came and went, including eye squinting, loss of speaking ability, and paralyzed arms and legs.

Breuer found that when Anna O. spoke freely about her condition—at times under hypnosis—her symptoms disappeared. She called this experience her "talking cure." As she spoke freely, she often recalled distressing childhood experiences that had been repressed, sometimes violently reexperiencing the emotions she had felt in childhood. By talking about her feelings and experiences, she obtained emotional release, typically followed by the disappearance of her physical symptoms. Breuer called this process of emotional release **catharsis**. His treatment of Anna O. marked the beginning of modern psychotherapy. Breuer related the story of Anna O. to his young friend Sigmund Freud, who was so impressed by Breuer's approach that he began to use it himself. His use of it led to the founding of psychoanalysis, which Freud always attributed to his mentor, Breuer.

As for Anna O., she led a rich, productive life under her real name, Bertha Pappenheim (1859–1936). She became a founder of the social work profession (Swenson, 1994), championing the rights of the poor. She stressed the influence of poverty on crime and illness. Pappenheim also was an early feminist and wrote *A Woman's Right*, a play that denounced the exploitation of women (Kimball, 2000). Bertha Pappenheim's life is testimony to the power of psychotherapy to help individuals overcome psychological disorders and live full lives. At some time in your life you might develop a psychological disorder that leads you to seek professional help. If so, you will be in good company. Since the 1950s, the percentage of Americans who seek psychotherapy during their lifetime has doubled (VandenBos, 1996).

Source: Lightspring/Shutterstock.com.

Chapter Outline

The History of Therapy
The Psychoanalytic Orientation
The Behavioral Orientation
The Cognitive Orientation
The Humanistic Orientation
The Social-Relations Orientation
The Biological Orientation
Community Mental Health
The Rights of the Therapy Client
Finding the Proper Therapy
The Effectiveness of Psychotherapy

catharsis In psychoanalysis, the release of repressed emotional energy as a consequence of insight into the unconscious causes of one's psychological problems.

529

The History of Therapy

The treatment of psychological disorders has come a long way since its ancient origins. Treatment practices have been influenced by their cultural, religious, and scientific contexts.

Ancient Practices

If you visit the Smithsonian Institution in Washington, D.C., you will encounter a display of Stone Age skulls with holes that were cut into them with stones—in the ancient practice of **trephining**. Some authorities assume that these ancient trephiners believed that they were releasing demons that caused abnormal behavior. Of course, without written records there is no way to know if demon release was the true reason. Perhaps, instead, trephining was performed for some unknown medical purpose.

The Greek philosopher Hippocrates (460–377 B.C.) turned away from supernatural explanations of psychological disorders, which attributed them to demons or punishment from the gods, in favor of naturalistic explanations. Hippocrates believed that many psychological disorders were caused by imbalances in fluids that he called humors, which included blood, phlegm, black bile, and yellow bile (see Chapter 14). For example, because Hippocrates believed that an excess of blood caused the agitated state of mania, he treated mania with bloodletting. As you would expect, people weakened by the loss of blood became less agitated.

Medieval and Renaissance Approaches

During the early Christian era, such naturalistic treatments existed side by side with supernatural ones. But by the late Middle Ages, treatments increasingly involved physical punishment. This inhumane treatment continued into the Renaissance, which also saw the advent of *insane asylums*. Though some of these institutions were pleasant communities in which residents received humane treatment, most were no better than prisons in which inmates lived under deplorable conditions. The most humane asylum was the town of Geel in Belgium, where people with mental disorders lived in the homes of townspeople, moved about freely, and worked to support themselves. In the 1990s, Geel continued to provide humane care for 800 individuals living with 600 families (Godemont, 1992).

Few Renaissance asylums were as pleasant as Geel. The most notorious one was St. Mary's of Bethlehem in London. In this nightmarish place, inmates were treated like animals in a zoo. On weekends, families would go on outings to the asylum, pay a small admission fee, and be entertained by the antics of the inmates. Visitors called the male inmates of St. Mary's "Tom Fools," contributing the word *tomfoolery* to our language. And the asylum became known as "Bedlam" (Harris, 2003b), reflecting the cockney pronunciation of Bethlehem.

18th- and 19th-Century Reforms

In 1792 inhumane conditions in French insane asylums and the positive model of Geel spurred physician Philippe Pinel (1745–1826) to institute what he called **moral therapy** at the Bicetre asylum in Paris (Harris, 2003a). Moral therapy was based on the premise that humane treatment, honest work, and pleasant recreation would promote mental well-being. Pinel had the inmates unchained, provided with good food, and treated with kindness. He even instituted the revolutionary technique of speaking with them about their problems. The first inmate released was a giant, powerful man who had been chained in a dark cell for 40 years after killing a guard with a blow from his manacles. Onlookers were surprised (and relieved) when he simply strolled outside, gazed up at the sky, and exclaimed, "Ah, how beautiful" (Bromberg, 1954, p. 83).

Pinel's moral therapy spread throughout Europe. It was introduced to the United States by Benjamin Rush (1745–1813), the founder of American psychiatry. As part of moral therapy, Rush prescribed work, music, and travel (Farr, 1944/1994). He also prescribed physical treatments that with hindsight we might view as barbaric, but which he believed

---

trephining An ancient technique in which sharp stones were used to chip holes in the skull, possibly to let out evil spirits that supposedly caused abnormal behavior.

moral therapy An approach to therapy, developed by Philippe Pinel, that provided mental patients with humane treatment.

Pinel Unchaining the Inmates of an Asylum

Philippe Pinel shocked and frightened many French citizens by freeing the inmates of an insane asylum and providing them with humane treatment. When opponents asked, "Citizen, are not you yourself crazy, that you would free these beasts?" Pinel replied, "I am convinced that these *people* are not incurable if they can have air and liberty" (Bromberg, 1954, p. 83).

Source: Anki Hoglund/Shutterstock.com.

had therapeutic value. For example, because Rush assumed that depressed people had too little blood in their brains, he whirled them around in special chairs to force blood from their bodies into their heads. One can imagine that, much as an amusement park ride can do today, this treatment induced a temporary feeling of elation.

In the 1840s, Dorothea Dix (1802–1887), a Massachusetts schoolteacher, shocked the U.S. Congress with reports of the brutal treatment of the inmates confined to insane asylums. Because of her efforts, many state mental hospitals were built throughout the United States, usually in rural settings, that provided good food, social activities, and employment on farms. Though Canadian asylums were influenced more by Britain and France (Sussman, 1998), Dix also influenced Canadian reforms, including the establishment of the first mental hospital in Nova Scotia (Goldman, 1990). Unfortunately, over time many of these mental hospitals became human warehouses, providing little more than custodial care. This result contradicted the humane treatment that Dix had envisioned for asylum residents.

The Mental Health Movement

In the early 20th century, public concern about the deplorable conditions in state mental hospitals grew after the publication of *A Mind That Found Itself* by a Yale University graduate named Clifford Beers (Beers, 1908/1970). The book described the physical abuse Beers suffered during his 3 years in the Connecticut State Hospital. Beers (1876–1943) founded the mental health movement, which promotes the humane treatment of people with mental disorders. The mental health movement has seen mental hospitals joined by group homes, private practices, and counseling centers as alternative treatment sites for psychological disorders.

Today, specially trained professionals offer therapy for psychological disorders. Psychological therapy, or **psychotherapy**, involves the therapeutic interaction of a professional therapist with one or more persons suffering from a psychological disorder. Though there are many approaches to psychotherapy, most psychotherapists favor an *eclectic orientation*, in which they select techniques from different kinds of therapy that they believe will help particular clients. The first formal orientation toward the practice of psychotherapy was psychoanalysis, the topic of the next section.

A recent trend in psychotherapy is increased attention to sociocultural factors that might influence the course of therapy. For example, the 1999 National Multicultural Conference and Summit was a collaborative attempt by psychologists to broaden the concept of multiculturalism to include other variables relevant to the practice of psychology—culture, ethnicity, gender, and sexual orientation. The focus of the conference was the implementation of *cultural competence* in psychological training, research, and clinical practice (Sue, 2003). According to Stanley Sue, **cultural competence** is the "belief that people should not only appreciate and recognize other cultural groups but also be able to effectively work with them" (Sue, 1998, p. 440). Thus, cultural competence consists of cultural knowledge and the interpersonal skills to effectively use this knowledge.

The need for cultural competence is driven in part by changing demographics—about 50 percent of Americans will be members of ethnic minority groups by the year 2050. Therapists need to be aware of cross-cultural differences in beliefs and behaviors that they may encounter in therapy. For example, members of Western cultures disclose intimate details more readily than do members of Asian cultures (Toukmanian & Brouwers, 1998). And, as discussed in Chapter 13, there are cross-cultural differences in the construal of self-schema related to the dimensions of independence and interdependence (Hall, 2003). Failure to understand these cultural differences could affect assessment, the development of an empathetic relationship, and the effective provision of treatment. The University of South Dakota's clinical psychology training program for Native Americans, The Four Winds, is an example of the ways in which cultural competence can be incorporated into the psychological curriculum and practice. It presents traditional training in psychotherapy within a Native American cultural context. The program aims to increase the number of Native American psychotherapists and the availability of culturally sensitive psychotherapists to serve that ethnic group (Yutrzenka, Todd-Bazemore, & Caraway, 1999).

psychotherapy The treatment of psychological disorders through psychological means generally involving verbal interaction with a professional therapist.

cultural competence The consideration of sociocultural factors such as gender, ethnicity, sexual orientation, and religion in psychological training and practice.

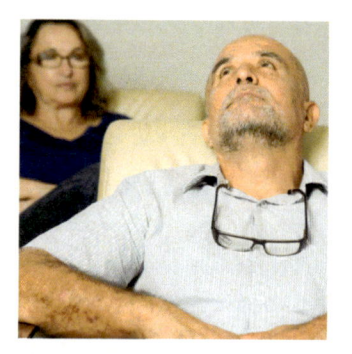

Psychoanalysis Today

Though most psychotherapists now favor seated, face-to-face interaction with their clients, some psychoanalytic psychotherapists still sit out of sight of the client, who reclines on a couch.

Source: Adam Gregor/Shutterstock.com.

psychoanalysis The early school of psychology that emphasized the importance of unconscious causes of behavior.

> ### Section Review: The History of Therapy
> 1. Does the existence of trephined skulls necessarily mean that trephining was performed to release evil spirits?
> 2. What were some of the basic techniques used in moral therapy?

The Psychoanalytic Orientation

As discussed at the beginning of the chapter, psychoanalysis grew out of Josef Breuer's case study of Anna O. Though Breuer was the first to describe this "talking cure," it was Sigmund Freud who elaborated it into a system of psychotherapy.

The Nature of Psychoanalysis

Freud believed that childhood emotional conflicts repressed into the unconscious mind cause the symptoms of psychological disorders, including conversion hysteria. Freud's aim was to make the person gain insight into his or her repressed conflicts, thereby inducing catharsis and relieving the underlying conflict. This approach led Freud to develop the form of therapy known as **psychoanalysis**. Traditional Freudian psychoanalysis takes place with the client reclining on a couch and the therapist sitting nearby, just out of sight. Freud claimed that this arrangement relaxes the client, thereby reducing inhibitions about discussing emotional topics. Traditional Freudian psychoanalysts might see clients three to five times a week for years.

Techniques in Psychoanalysis

An important goal of psychoanalytic techniques is to make the client's unconscious conflicts conscious. To accomplish this goal, the therapist actively *interprets* the significance of what the client says. The therapist's interpretations are based on the analysis of *free associations*, *resistances*, *dreams*, and *transference*.

Analysis of Free Associations

analysis of free associations In psychoanalysis, the process by which the therapist interprets the underlying meaning of the client's uncensored reports of anything that comes to mind.

The main technique of psychoanalysis is the **analysis of free associations**, which has much in common with Anna O.'s "talking cure." In free association, the client is urged to report any thoughts or feelings that come to mind—no matter how trivial or embarrassing they seem. Freud assumed, based on the principle of psychic determinism (see Chapter 1), that free association would unlock meaningful information related to the client's psychological disorder (Bronstein, 2002).

Analysis of Resistances

analysis of resistances In psychoanalysis, the process by which the therapist interprets client behaviors that interfere with therapeutic progress toward uncovering unconscious conflicts.

In the **analysis of resistances**, the psychoanalyst notes behaviors that interfere with therapeutic progress. Signs of resistance include arriving late, missing sessions, abruptly changing topics, and talking about insignificant things. The client holds on dearly to resistances to block awareness of painful feelings, conflicts, or memories. By interpreting the meaning of the client's resistances, the therapist helps the client uncover these unconscious memories and conflicts. Suppose a client changes the topic whenever the therapist asks him about his father. The therapist might interpret this action as a sign that the client has unconscious emotional conflicts regarding his father. But resistances also might indicate that the client simply believes that the therapist is not empathetic enough (Messer, 2002).

Analysis of Dreams

analysis of dreams In psychoanalysis, the process by which the therapist interprets the symbolic, manifest content of dreams to reveal their true, latent content to the client.

Freud believed that the **analysis of dreams** was the "royal road to the unconscious" (see Chapter 6). He claimed that dreams symbolized unconscious sexual and aggressive con-

532 Chapter 15 Therapy

flicts. Freud relied on his own dreams, as well as those of his clients, to illustrate his theory (Mautner, 1991). Having the client free-associate about the content of a series of dreams allows the psychoanalyst to interpret the symbolic, or *manifest*, content of the client's dreams to reveal the true, or *latent*, content—their true meaning.

Analysis of Transference

The key to a psychoanalytic cure is the **analysis of transference**. Transference is the tendency of the client to act toward the therapist in the way she or he acts toward important people in everyday life, such as a boss, spouse, parent, or teacher. Transference can be positive or negative. In *positive transference*, the client expresses feelings of approval and affection toward the therapist. In *negative transference*, the client expresses feelings of disapproval and rejection toward the therapist—such as criticizing the therapist's skill. By interpreting transference, the therapist helps the client gain insight into the earlier interpersonal origins of his or her current emotional problems.

Offshoots of Psychoanalysis

Traditional Freudian psychoanalysis inspired many offshoots. Nonetheless, psychoanalysis in its various forms went from being the choice of most therapists in the 1950s to being the choice of about 15 percent in the 1980s (Smith, 1982). One of the main reasons for this declining trend is that other less costly and less lengthy therapies are at least as effective as psychoanalysis (Fisher & Greenberg, 1985).

Today, few therapists are strict Freudians. Instead, many practice what is called *psychodynamic therapy*, which employs aspects of psychoanalysis in face-to-face, once-a-week therapy lasting months instead of years. Psychodynamic therapists also rely more on discussions of past and present social relationships than on trying to uncover unconscious emotional conflicts. Psychodynamic therapy has proved effective in the treatment of a variety of psychological disorders (Shedler, 2010), though this conclusion has been criticized by others citing methodological problems in comparing different therapeutic approaches (Anestis, Anestis, & Lilienfeld, 2011).

Analysis of Resistances

In analysis of resistances, behaviors that interfere with therapeutic progress are noted.
Source: Ambrophoto/Shutterstock.com.

analysis of transference In psychoanalysis, the process by which the therapist interprets the feelings expressed by the client toward the therapist as being indicative of the feelings typically expressed by the client toward important people in his or her personal life.

Section Review: The Psychoanalytic Orientation

1. How do psychoanalysts employ the analysis of free associations?
2. How do psychoanalysts employ the analysis of resistances?

The Behavioral Orientation

In 1952, British psychologist Hans Eysenck coined the term **behavior therapy** to refer to treatments that favor changing maladaptive behaviors rather than providing insight into unconscious conflicts. Unlike traditional psychoanalysts, behavior therapists ignore unconscious conflicts, emphasize present behavior, and assume that therapy can be accomplished in weeks or months instead of years. To behavior therapists, abnormal behavior—like normal behavior—is learned and therefore can be unlearned (Tryon, 2000). Behavior therapists change maladaptive behaviors by applying the principles of classical conditioning, operant conditioning, and social learning theory. In their practices, behavior therapists often combine various behavioral techniques. Some behavior therapists stress the need to consider the cultural context of a person's behavior when working with clients. Misinterpretation of behaviors because of cultural ignorance might lead to the inappropriate application of behavioral change techniques (LaRoche & Lustig, 2013).

behavior therapy The therapeutic application of the principles of learning to change maladaptive behaviors.

Classical Conditioning Therapies

Several kinds of behavior therapy have been derived from Ivan Pavlov's work on classical conditioning (Plaud, 2003). In classical conditioning, a stimulus associated with another stimulus that elicits a response may itself come to elicit that response (see Chapter 7). Therapies based on classical conditioning stress the importance of stimuli in controlling behavior. The goal of these therapies is the removal of the stimuli that control maladaptive behaviors or the promotion of more adaptive responses to those stimuli.

Counterconditioning

The classical conditioning technique of **counterconditioning** replaces unpleasant emotional responses to stimuli with pleasant ones, or vice versa. The procedure is based on the assumption that we cannot simultaneously experience an unpleasant feeling, such as anxiety, and a pleasant feeling, such as relaxation. Therapeutic counterconditioning was introduced by John B. Watson's student, Mary Cover Jones (1896–1987). Watson had conditioned a toddler he called Little Albert to fear a white rat by pairing the rat with a loud sound (see Chapter 7). Watson proposed that the fear could be eliminated by pairing the rat with a pleasant stimulus, such as pleasurable stroking. Jones (1924) took Watson's suggestion and, under his advisement, tried to rid a 3-year-old boy named Peter of a rabbit phobia (see Chapter 14). Jones used what she called "direct conditioning," which is now known as counterconditioning. Jones presented Peter with candy and then brought a caged rabbit closer and closer to him. This therapy was done twice a day for 2 months.

At first, Peter cried when the rabbit was within 20 feet of him. Over the course of the study, he became less and less fearful of it. On the last day, he asked for the rabbit, petted it, tried to pick it up, and finally played with it on a windowsill. Evidently, the pleasant feelings Peter experienced in response to the candy gradually became associated with the rabbit. This association reduced his fear of the rabbit. Jones cautioned, however, that this procedure was delicate. If performed too rapidly, it could produce the opposite effect—fear of the candy. More recently, counterconditioning has been used effectively to treat posttraumatic stress disorder (PTSD) (Paunovic, 2003) and to reduce distress associated with a hypodermic injection (Slifer, Eischen, & Busby, 2002). In one application of counterconditioning, participants with spider phobias who were asked to imagine scenes of spiders paired with humorous scenes showed a significant reduction in the intensity of their phobias (Ventis, Higbee, & Murdock, 2001).

Systematic Desensitization

Today, the most widely used form of counterconditioning is **systematic desensitization**, developed by Joseph Wolpe (1915–1997) for treating phobias (Wolpe, 1958). Systematic desensitization involves three steps. The first step is for the client to practice *progressive relaxation*, a technique developed in the 1930s by Edmund Jacobson to relieve anxiety. To learn progressive relaxation, clients sit in a comfortable chair and practice successively tensing and relaxing each of the major muscle groups—including those of the head, arms, torso, and legs—until they gain the ability to relax their entire body.

The second step is the construction of an *anxiety hierarchy* (see Table 15-1), consisting of a series of anxiety-inducing scenes related to the person's phobia. The client lists 10 to 20 scenes, rating them on a 100-point scale from least to most anxiety inducing. A rating of zero would mean that the scene induces no anxiety; a rating of 100 would mean that the scene induces abject terror. Suppose that you have *arachnophobia*—a spider phobia. You might rate a photo of a spider a 5, a spider on your arm a 60, and a spider on your face an 85.

The third step involves imagining each of the anxiety-inducing responses in the anxiety hierarchy while relaxing. The therapist would start with the scene with the lowest rating, moving along the hierarchy from least to most threatening. For example, you first would learn to relax while imagining holding a photo of a spider. Once the relaxation response had been reliably conditioned to this stimulus, the therapist would move to the next scene on the anxiety hierarchy. In this way the new response, relaxation, would become conditioned to each of the anxiety-inducing stimuli.

Counterconditioning
One of the first uses of counterconditioning was eliminating a rabbit phobia in a young boy.
Source: Nagy-Bagoly Arpad/Shutterstock.com.

counterconditioning A behavior therapy technique that applies the principles of classical conditioning to replace unpleasant emotional responses to stimuli with more pleasant ones.

systematic desensitization A form of counterconditioning that trains the client to maintain a state of relaxation in the presence of imagined anxiety-inducing stimuli.

TABLE 15-1 A Test-Anxiety Hierarchy

Initial Rating of Distress	Fear-Inducing Scene
10	Registering for next semester's courses
15	Going over the course outline in class
20	Hearing the instructor announce that the midterm exam will take place in three weeks
30	Discussing the difficulty of the exam with fellow students
45	Reviewing your notes one week before the exam
50	Attending a review session three days before the exam
60	Listening to the professor explain what to expect on the exam the day before
65	Studying alone the day before the exam
70	Studying with a group of students the night before the exam
75	Overhearing superior students expressing their self-doubts about the exam
80	Realizing that you are running out of study time at 1:00 A.M. the day of the exam
90	Entering the class before the exam and having the professor remind you that one-third of your final grade depends on it
95	Reading the exam questions and discovering that you do not recognize several of them
100	Answering the exam questions while hearing other students hyperventilating and muttering about them

In Vivo Desensitization

This type of therapy has a very high success rate in reducing an individual's fear of objects or places. Before this behavioral therapy an individual with ophidiophobia, or a fear of snakes, would not be able to be in close proximity to a snake.
Source: Siarhei Kasilau/Shutterstock.com.

Systematic desensitization has been successful in treating a wide variety of phobias. These phobias include fear of dentists (Klepac, 1986), choking (Millikin & Braun-Janzen, 2013), and public speaking (Rossi & Seiler, 1989–1990). Given the success of systematic desensitization in treating phobias, what accounts for its effectiveness? This question is the topic of "The Research Process" box.

Of course, the ultimate test of systematic desensitization is the ability to face the actual source of your phobia. One way of ensuring such success is to use **in vivo desensitization**, which physically exposes the client to successive situations on the client's anxiety hierarchy. This technique is a variation of systematic sensitization and is in contrast to *in vitro desensitization* in which the patient simply imagines the source of the phobia. In vivo desensitization has been successful in treating claustrophobia (Edinger & Radtke, 1993), school phobia (Houlihan & Jones, 1989), and many other kinds of phobias. In one case, a woman who had chronic nightmares about snakes was relieved of them by an in vivo procedure that had her move closer and closer to a live, harmless snake (Eccles, Wilde, & Marshall, 1988). A newer refinement of these techniques is to use virtual reality technology to help patients with phobias. A recent study looked at active-duty members of the military who were diagnosed with post-traumatic stress disorder (see Chapter 16) related to service in Iraq or Afghanistan. The patients provided experimenters with information related to their most traumatic events during combat tours. The experimenters then took these scripts and converted them to virtual reality simulations that approximated the traumatic experiences the patients described. The results of the study concluded that virtual reality therapy was more effective than the control group that received combinations of cognitive processing therapy, eye movement desensitization, drug therapy, and other PTSD-related services (McLay et al., 2011). The results of this study suggest virtual reality therapy as a useful adjunct therapy to already existing PTSD therapies.

in vivo desensitization A form of counterconditioning that trains the client to maintain a state of relaxation in the presence of anxiety-inducing stimuli.

The Research Process

Do Endorphins Mediate the Effect of Systematic Desensitization on Phobias?

Rationale

Might systematic desensitization exert its effects through the actions of endorphins? Perhaps pleasurable feelings induced by endorphins can counter phobic anxiety. This hypothesis was the rationale behind a study conducted by Kelly Egan, John Carr, Daniel Hunt, and Richard Adamson of the University of Washington (Egan, Hunt, Carr, & Adamson, 1988).

Method

Participants all suffered from specific phobias (see Chapter 14), such as fear of heights, fear of dogs, and fear of elevators. Participants were randomly assigned into two groups. Prior to sessions of systematic desensitization, 6 participants (the experimental group) received intravenous infusions of naloxone, a drug that blocks the effect of endorphins, and 5 participants (the control group) received intravenous infusions of a placebo, a saline solution with no specific effects. Because the study used the double-blind procedure, neither the participants nor the experimenter knew which participants received naloxone and which received the placebo. The double-blind procedure controlled for any participant or experimenter biases. Participants received 8 sessions over a period of 4 weeks.

Results and Discussion

The results indicated that participants who received the placebo experienced a significant decrease in the severity of their phobias, whereas those who received naloxone did not. Because naloxone blocks the effects of the endorphins, the results support the possible role of endorphins in the effects of systematic desensitization. The pleasant feelings produced by the endorphins may become conditioned to the formerly fear-inducing stimuli.

Aversion Therapy

aversion therapy A form of behavior therapy that inhibits maladaptive behavior by pairing a stimulus that normally elicits a maladaptive response with an unpleasant stimulus.

The goal of **aversion therapy** is to make a formerly pleasurable, but maladaptive, behavior unpleasant. In aversion therapy, a stimulus that normally elicits a maladaptive response is paired with an unpleasant stimulus, leading to a reduction in the maladaptive response. Aversion therapy has been used to treat a variety of behavioral problems, including smoking, bed-wetting, and overeating.

But aversion therapy was originally introduced in the 1930s to treat alcoholism by administering painful electric shocks to alcoholic patients in the presence of the sight, smell, and taste of alcohol. Today, aversion therapy for alcoholism uses drugs that make the individual feel deathly ill after drinking alcohol (see Figure 15-1). The drugs interfere with the metabolism of alcohol, leading to the buildup of a toxic chemical that induces nausea and dizziness. A study of more than 400 alcoholic patients who underwent a treatment program that included aversion therapy found that 60 percent were abstinent a year later (Smith & Frawley, 1993).

Operant-Conditioning Therapies

Treatments based on operant conditioning change maladaptive behaviors by controlling their consequences. Popular forms of behavior modification rely on the behavioral contingencies of positive reinforcement, punishment, and extinction.

Positive Reinforcement

token economy An operant conditioning procedure that uses tokens as positive reinforcers in programs designed to promote desirable behaviors, with the tokens later used to purchase desired items or privileges.

One of the most important uses of positive reinforcement has been in treating patients in mental hospitals. Residents of mental hospitals have traditionally relied on the staff to take care of all their needs. This reliance often leads to passivity, a decrease in self-care, and a general decline in dignified behavior. The development of the *token economy* provided a way to overcome this problem. The **token economy** provides tokens (often plastic poker chips) as positive reinforcement for desirable behaviors, such as making beds, taking showers, or wearing appropriate clothing. The patients use the tokens to purchase items such as books or candy and privileges such as television or passes to leave the hospital grounds. The use of token economies has proved successful, for example, in reducing self-injurious behavior and promoting positive social behavior by criminal inmates

FIGURE 15-1
Aversion Therapy in the Treatment of Alcoholism

In aversion therapy, when alcoholics drink alcohol mixed with the drug Antabuse, they experience extreme nausea. The Antabuse serves as an unconditioned stimulus (UCS) that naturally elicits nausea as an unconditioned response (UCR). After repeated pairings of Antabuse and alcohol, classical conditioning takes place and alcohol becomes a conditioned stimulus (CS) that elicits nausea as a conditioned response (CR). Thus, alcohol, which previously had elicited a pleasant state of intoxication, now elicits an unpleasant state of nausea. This response increases the likelihood that the individual will stop drinking alcohol.

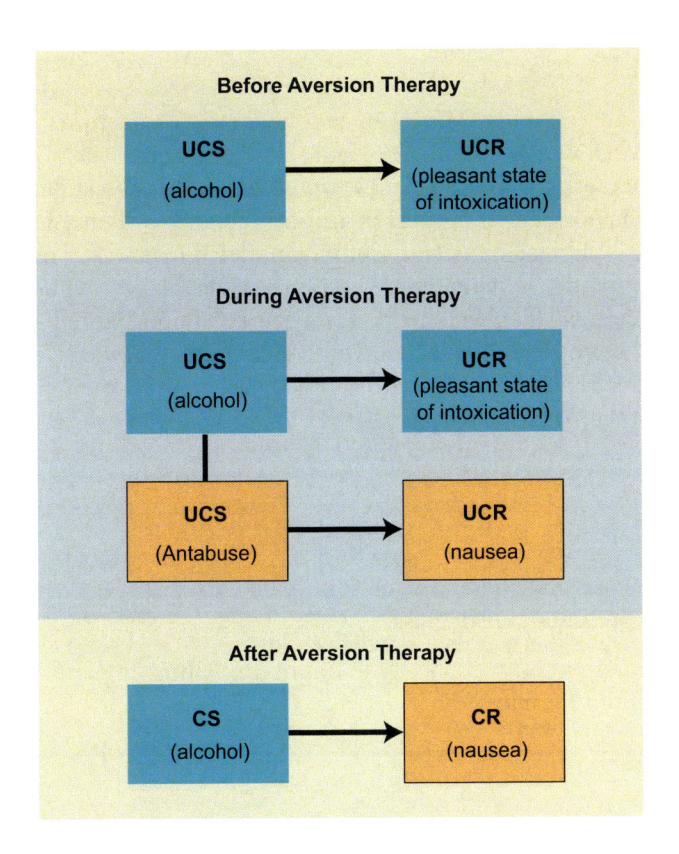

with psychological disorders (Seegert, 2003). Token economies also are employed in programs for people with intellectual disabilities. In one study, a token economy motivated a man with an intellectual disability to behave in a more socially appropriate manner (LeBlanc, Hagopian, & Maglieri, 2000).

Punishment

Though less desirable than positive reinforcement, punishment also can be effective in changing maladaptive behaviors. In fact, sometimes it may be the only way to prevent inappropriate, or even dangerous, behavior. In using punishment, the therapist provides aversive consequences for maladaptive behavior. A controversial application of punishment that was used in the past was mild electric shocks to reduce self-biting, head banging, and other self-destructive behaviors in children with autism spectrum disorder (ASD), who do not respond to talk therapy (see Chapter 14). Today, milder forms of punishment are used, such as sharply saying "no" when the child engages in the self-injurious behavior Once the behavior has stopped, the therapist uses positive reinforcement to promote more appropriate behaviors. The combination of punishment and positive reinforcement has been effective in improving the behavior of children with ASD (Ma, 2009).

Extinction

If a behavior—whether adaptive or maladaptive—is not reinforced, it will become extinguished. The technique of *flooding* takes advantage of this phenomenon in the elimination of intense fears and phobias. Unlike systematic desensitization, which trains the client to relax and experience a graded series of anxiety-inducing situations, **flooding** exposes the client to a situation that evokes intense anxiety. In *imaginal flooding*, the client is asked to hold in mind an image of the feared situation; in *in vivo flooding*, the client is placed in the actual feared situation. As clients experience the situation mentally or in reality, their anxiety diminishes because they are prevented from escaping and thereby negatively reinforcing their flight behavior through fear reduction. Of course, care must be taken to protect the client from being overwhelmed by fear. Flooding has helped clients overcome anxiety disorders such as panic disorder and agoraphobia (Siegmund et al., 2011), and PTSD (Foa et al., 1999).

Operant-Conditioning Therapy for Autism Spectrum Disorder (ASD)

The combination of punishment and positive reinforcement has been effective in reducing self-injurious behaviors in children with ASD and promoting appropriate behaviors.
Source: Pixel Memoirs/Shutterstock.com.

flooding An extinction procedure in which a phobic client is exposed to a stimulus that evokes intense anxiety.

Chapter 15 Therapy 537

Social-Learning Therapies

In treating Peter's rabbit phobia, Mary Cover Jones (1924) sometimes let Peter observe other children playing with a rabbit. By doing so, Jones made use of social learning (see Chapter 7). Therapists who use social learning have their clients watch other people model adaptive behaviors either in person or on videotape. Clients learn better social skills or to overcome phobias by performing the modeled behavior. Therapists also may use **participant modeling**, in which the therapist models the desired behavior while the client watches. The client then tries to perform the behavior. Participant modeling has been successful in helping individuals overcome their fears, including fear of dogs (May, Rudy, & Thomas, 2013) and post-traumatic stress disorder, even when the therapy is provided over the Internet (Mouthaan et al., 2011).

participant modeling A form of social-learning therapy in which the client learns to perform more adaptive behaviors by first observing the therapist model the desired behaviors.

> **Section Review:** The Behavioral Orientation
>
> 1. How would you use systematic desensitization to treat a student who is terrified of making oral presentations in class?
> 2. How would you use a token economy to improve spelling and arithmetic performance by third graders?

The Cognitive Orientation

The Greek Stoic philosopher Epictetus (A.D. ca. 60–ca. 120) noted that irrational people tend to become emotionally upset. His observation explains the kinship between Stoic philosophy and the cognitive orientation in psychotherapy (Still & Dryden, 2003). Cognitive therapists believe that events in themselves do not cause maladaptive emotions and behaviors. Instead, it is our interpretation of events that does so. Given this assumption, cognitive therapists believe that changes in thinking can produce changes in maladaptive emotions or behaviors. Because cognitive therapies can include aspects of behavior therapy, they are commonly called *cognitive-behavior therapies*. They have been effective in treating many kinds of disorders, including compulsive gambling (Jiminez-Murcia et al., 2012), panic disorder (Stuart, Treat, & Wade, 2000), major depressive disorder, generalized anxiety disorder, social anxiety disorder, and post-traumatic stress disorder (Butler, Chapman, Forman, & Beck, 2006). Still, some cognitive therapists believe that the assumptions and practice of cognitive therapy may not translate well to other cultures. Beliefs and interpretations of events might be adaptive in one culture and maladaptive in others (Dowd, 2003).

Rational-Emotive Behavior Therapy

Albert Ellis (1962) developed the first form of cognitive therapy, which he called *rational-emotive therapy (R-E-T)*. He more recently renamed it **rational-emotive behavior therapy (R-E-B-T)** to emphasize the interaction of thinking, feeling, and behaving in maintaining psychological well-being (Ellis, 1999). A survey of therapists found that Ellis has been second only to Carl Rogers in his influence on the field of psychotherapy (Smith, 1982). Ellis's therapy is based on his *A-B-C theory* of emotion (Ziegler, 2001), in which *A* is an activating event, *B* is an irrational belief, and *C* is an emotional consequence (see Figure 15-2). Ellis points out that most of us believe that *A* causes *C*, when, in fact, *B* causes *C*.

Imagine that you fail an exam *(A)* and become depressed *(C)*. Ellis would attribute your depression not to your failure but to an irrational belief, such as the belief *(B)* that you must be perfect. Thus, your irrational belief, not your failure, causes your depression—and the behaviors it produces. Ellis has pointed out similarities between the Western practice of R-E-B-T and the Eastern practice of Zen Buddhism and urged that the two practices be integrated into an effective means of improving psychological well-being (Kwee & Ellis, 1998).

rational-emotive behavior therapy (R-E-B-T) A type of cognitive therapy, developed by Albert Ellis, that treats psychological disorders by forcing the client to give up irrational beliefs.

FIGURE 15-2

The A-B-C Theory of Emotion

According to Albert Ellis's A-B-C theory of emotion, our emotions are caused by our beliefs about events, not the events themselves. That is, it is our cognitive interpretation of events that determines how they affect us emotionally.

Common Sense

Activating Event (A): A person you've been dating for a few weeks breaks up with you. → Emotional Consequence (C): You become depressed.

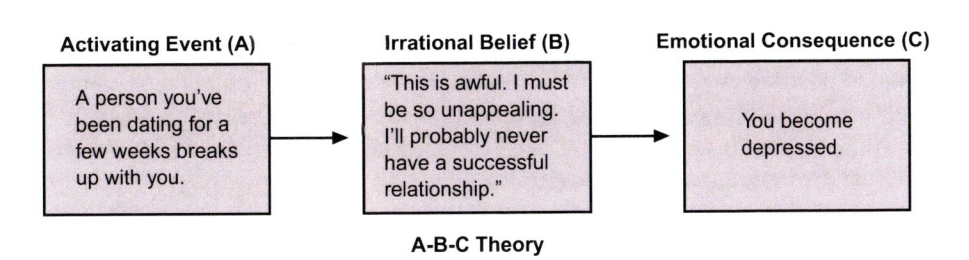

A-B-C Theory

Activating Event (A): A person you've been dating for a few weeks breaks up with you. → Irrational Belief (B): "This is awful. I must be so unappealing. I'll probably never have a successful relationship." → Emotional Consequence (C): You become depressed.

Though therapists who use R-E-B-T can develop warm, empathetic relationships with their clients, Ellis himself is more interested in demolishing, sometimes harshly, the irrational ideas of his clients (Johnson, DiGiuseppe, & Ulven, 1999). After identifying a client's irrational beliefs, Ellis challenges the client to provide evidence supporting them. Ellis then contradicts any irrational evidence, almost demanding that the client agree with him. Table 15-2 presents a verbatim transcript illustrating the use of R-E-B-T. Ellis (1997) has even described how R-E-B-T has helped him deal with a lifetime of physical disorders, including diabetes and deficient hearing.

TABLE 15-2 Rational-Emotive Behavioral Therapy

This transcript illustrates how the rational-emotive behavior therapist (T) challenges the client (C) to change irrational beliefs. The client is a 23-year-old young woman experiencing intense feelings of guilt for not living up to her parents' strict standards.

C: Well, this is the way it was in school, if I didn't do well in one particular thing, or even on a particular test—and little crises that came up—if I didn't do as well as I had wanted to do.

T: Right. You beat yourself over the head.

C: Yes.

T: But why? What's the point? Are you supposed to be perfect? Why the hell shouldn't human beings make mistakes, be imperfect?

C: Maybe you always expect yourself to be perfect.

T: Yes. But is that *sane*?

C: No.

T: Why do it? Why not give up that unrealistic expectation?

C: But then I can't accept myself.

T: But you're saying, "It's shameful to make mistakes." Why is it shameful? Why can't you go to somebody else when you make a mistake and say, "Yes, I made a mistake"? Why is that so awful? . . .

C: It might all go back to, as you said, the need for approval. If I don't make mistakes, then people will look up to me. If I do it all perfectly—

T: Yes, that's part of it. That is the erroneous belief; that if you never make mistakes everybody will love you and that it is necessary they do. That's right. That's a big part of it. But is it true, incidentally? Suppose you never did make mistakes—*would* people love you? They'd sometimes hate your guts, wouldn't they?

Source: Ellis, A. (1971). *Growth through reason.* Palo Alto, CA: Science & Behavior Books. Reprinted by permission.

Chapter 15 Therapy

A meta-analysis of research studies found that R-E-B-T is more effective than placebo treatment and as effective as other therapies (Engels, Garnefski, & Diekstra, 1993). It has helped people overcome depression (Macaskill & Macaskill, 1996), extreme jealousy (Ellis, 1996), and childhood sexual abuse (Rieckert & Moeller, 2000).

Cognitive Therapy

Psychiatrist Aaron Beck has found that depression is caused by negative beliefs about oneself, the world, and the future (Beck, 1997). Thus, depressed people tend to blame themselves rather than their circumstances for misfortunes, attend more to negative events than to positive events, and have a pessimistic view of the future (see Chapter 14). Depressed people also overgeneralize from rare or minor negative events in their lives. The goal of Beck's **cognitive therapy** is to change such exaggerated beliefs in treating psychological disorders, most notably depression.

Beck is less directive in his approach than is Ellis. Beck has clients keep a daily record of their thoughts and urges them to note irrational beliefs and replace them with rational ones. A client who claims, "I am an awful student and will never amount to anything," might be encouraged to think, instead, "I am doing poorly in school because I do not study enough. If I change my study habits, I will graduate and pursue a desirable career." To promote positive experiences, Beck might begin by giving the client homework assignments that guarantee success, such as having a client who feels socially incompetent speak to a close friend on the telephone. Cognitive therapy has been especially successful in treating depression, which was its original purpose (Scott, Palmer, Paykel, Teasdale, & Hayhurst, 2003). Moreover, cognitive therapy is being used nationally in the Department of Veteran Affairs to treat U.S. military and personnel who suffer from major depressive disorder (Karlin et al., 2012). Nonetheless, it also is effective in treating other disorders, such as panic disorder (Rathgeb-Feutsch, Kempter, Feil, Pollmächer, & Schuld, 2011) and obsessive-compulsive disorder (Sabine, 2000).

Cognitive Therapy
Cognitive therapy has been effective in treating the negative beliefs of depressed people.
Source: Burlingham/Shutterstock.com.

cognitive therapy A type of therapy, developed by Aaron Beck, that aims at eliminating exaggerated negative beliefs about oneself, the world, or the future.

> **Section Review:** The Cognitive Orientation
>
> 1. What are the basic assumptions and techniques of Ellis's rational-emotive behavior therapy?
> 2. What are the basic assumptions and techniques of Beck's cognitive therapy?

The Humanistic Orientation

Unlike the psychoanalytic orientation, the humanistic orientation stresses the present rather than the past, and conscious rather than unconscious experience. Unlike the behavioral orientation, the humanistic orientation stresses the importance of subjective cognitive experience rather than objective environmental circumstances. And unlike the cognitive orientation, the humanistic orientation encourages the expression of emotion rather than its control.

Person-Centered Therapy

person-centered therapy A type of humanistic therapy, developed by Carl Rogers, that helps clients find their own answers to their problems.

The most popular kind of humanistic therapy is **person-centered therapy**, originally called *client-centered therapy*. It was developed in the 1950s by Carl Rogers (1902–1987) as one of the first alternatives to psychoanalysis. Rogers has been the most influential of all contemporary psychotherapists (Smith, 1982). Unlike the rational-emotive behavior therapist, who is *directive* in challenging the irrational beliefs of clients, the person-centered therapist is *nondirective* in encouraging clients to find their own answers to their problems (Bozarth, 2002). This approach is in keeping with the humanistic concept of self-actualization and is reminiscent of the Socratic method of self-discovery. Japanese psychologists have noted the similarity between person-centered therapy and the nondirective aspects of Taoist philosophy (Hayashi et al., 1998).

Given that person-centered therapists offer no advice, how do they help their clients? Their goal is to facilitate the pursuit of self-actualization, not by offering expertise but by providing a social climate in which clients feel comfortable being themselves. Person-centered therapists do so by promoting self-acceptance. Humanistic psychologists assume that psychological disorders arise from an incongruence between a person's public self and her or his actual self (see Chapter 14). This incongruence makes the person distort reality or deny feelings, trying to avoid the anxiety caused by failing to act in accordance with those feelings. The goal of person-centered therapy is to help individuals reduce this discrepancy by expressing and accepting their true feelings. The person-centered therapist promotes self-actualization through reflection of feelings, genuineness, accurate empathy, and unconditional positive regard (Rogers, 1957). Note that a close friend or relative whom you consider a "good listener" and valued counselor probably exhibits these characteristics, too.

Reflection of feelings is the main technique of person-centered therapy. The therapist is an active listener who serves as a therapeutic mirror, attending to the emotional content of what the client says and restating it to the client. This mirroring helps clients recognize their true feelings. By being *genuine* the therapist acts in a concerned, open, and sincere manner rather than in a detached, closed, and phony manner. This genuineness makes clients more willing to disclose their true feelings. During his career, Rogers increasingly stressed the importance of genuineness (Bozarth, 1990). The client also becomes more willing to share feelings when the therapist shows *accurate empathy*, which means that the therapist's words and actions indicate a true understanding of how the client feels (Meissner, 1996).

Perhaps the most difficult task for the person-centered therapist is the maintenance of *unconditional positive regard*—acting in a personally warm and accepting manner. The therapist must remain nonjudgmental, no matter how distasteful she or he finds the client's thoughts, feelings, and actions to be. This unconditional positive regard encourages clients to freely express and deal with even the most distressing aspects of themselves. Unconditional positive regard also promotes positive therapeutic outcomes by encouraging the client and the therapist to develop a mutually empathic and genuine relationship throughout the process of therapy (Murphy, Cramer, & Joseph, 2012).

Gestalt Therapy

Fritz Perls (1893–1970), a former psychoanalytic psychotherapist and the founder of **Gestalt therapy**, claimed, "The idea of Gestalt therapy is to change paper people to real people" (Perls, 1973, p. 120). To Perls, paper people were people out of touch with their true feelings, which made them live "inauthentic lives." Like psychoanalysis, Gestalt therapy seeks to bring unconscious feelings into conscious awareness. Like person-centered therapy, Gestalt therapy tries to increase the client's emotional expressiveness. And like rational-emotive behavior therapy, Gestalt therapy may be confrontational in forcing clients to change maladaptive ways of thinking and behaving.

Gestalt therapy A type of humanistic therapy, developed by Fritz Perls, that encourages clients to become aware of their true feelings and to take responsibility for their own actions.

Despite its name, Gestalt therapy is not derived from Gestalt psychology, which is discussed in Chapter 1, except in stressing the need to achieve wholeness of the personality—meaning that one's emotions, language, and actions should be consistent with one another (Polster & Polster, 1993). Gestalt therapists insist that clients take responsibility for their own behavior rather than blame other people or events for their problems and that clients live in the here and now rather than being concerned about events occurring at other places and times. Gestalt therapists also assume that people who are aware of their feelings can exert greater control over their reactions to events. The Gestalt therapist notes any signs that the client is not being brutally honest about his or her feelings, at times by observing the client's nonverbal communication posture, gestures, facial expressions, and tone of voice. For example, a client who denies feeling anxious while tightly clenching his fists would be accused of lying about his emotions.

Though research studies have found that Gestalt therapy can be effective with certain psychological disorders, such as phobias (Martinez, 2002), there has been a lack of scientific research on its effectiveness. Moreover, Perls has been criticized for promoting self-centeredness and emotional callousness, as in his "Gestalt prayer" (Perls, 1972, p. 70): "I do my thing and you do your thing. I am not in this world to live up to your expectations. And you are not in this world to live up to mine. You are you and I am I. And if by chance we find each other, it's beautiful. If not, then it can't be helped."

Section Review: The Humanistic Orientation

1. What are the basic characteristics of client-centered therapy?
2. How does Gestalt therapy differ from R-E-B-T?

The Social-Relations Orientation

The therapeutic orientations that have been discussed so far involve a therapist and a client. In contrast, the *social-relations orientation* assumes that because many psychological problems involve interpersonal relationships, additional people must be brought into the therapy process. Many psychotherapists insist that ethnic differences (Maiello, 1999), sexual orientation (Hartwell, Serovich, Gravsky, & Kerr, 2012), social class differences (Storck, 1997), and religious differences (Gopaul-McNicol, 1997) must be considered in any group approach to psychotherapy.

Group Therapy

In 1905, Joseph Pratt, a Boston physician, found that his tuberculosis patients gained relief from emotional distress by meeting in groups to discuss their feelings. Pratt's discovery marked the beginning of group therapy (Allen, 1990). Because group therapy allows a therapist to see more people (typically six to twelve in a group) in less time, more people can receive help at less cost per person. Group therapy provides participants with a range of role models, encouragement from others with similar problems, feedback about their own behavior, assurance that their problems are not unique, and the opportunity to try out new behaviors. Group therapy has been used to improve the emotional well-being of people as varied as cancer patients (Harman, 1991), bereaved relatives (Zimpfer, 1991), and people with major depressive disorder (Feng et al., 2012). Group therapy also has been used effectively in Botswana to provide treatment for the children who have been orphaned due to the HIV/AIDS epidemic in the region (Thamaku & Daniel, 2013). The procedures used in group therapy depend on the theoretical orientation of the therapist.

Transactional Analysis

Group therapies derived from psychoanalysis emphasize insight and emotional catharsis. A form of group therapy inspired by psychoanalysis is **transactional analysis (TA)**, popularized in the 1960s by psychiatrist Eric Berne (1910–1970) in his best-selling book *Games People Play* (1964). Berne claimed that people act according to one of three roles: child, parent, or adult (Solomon, 2003). These roles resemble the Freudian personality structures of id, superego, and ego, respectively. The *child*, like the id, acts impulsively and demands immediate gratification. The *parent*, like the superego, is authoritarian and guides moral behavior. And the *adult*, like the ego, promotes rational and responsible behavior.

Each role is adaptive in certain situations and maladaptive in others. For example, acting childish might be appropriate at parties but not at job interviews. According to Berne, our relationships involve *transactions*—social interactions between these roles. *Complementary transactions*, in which both individuals act according to the same role, are usually best. *Crossed transactions*, as when one person acts as a child and the other acts as an adult, are

transactional analysis (TA) A form of psychoanalytic group therapy, developed by Eric Berne, that helps clients change their immature or inappropriate ways of relating to other people.

maladaptive. The goal of TA is to analyze transactions between group members. For example, a person might engage in transactions that support her or his feelings of worthlessness and continually provoke responses from others that support those feelings. TA has been used to treat various problems, including personality disorders (Haimowitz, 2000).

Social-Skills Training

Psychologists who favor behavioral group therapies assume that changes in overt behavior will bring relief from emotional distress. A popular form of behavioral group therapy, also used in individual therapy, is **social-skills training**. Its goal is to improve social relationships by enhancing social skills, such as cultivating friendships or carrying on conversations. Participants are encouraged to rehearse new behaviors in the group setting. Members of the group may model more effective behaviors. Social-skills training has been used to help people with intellectual disabilities improve their social competence (Travis & Sturmey, 2013) and also has been used in the treatment of social anxiety disorder (van Dam-Baggen & Kraaimaat, 2000).

A form of social-skills training called **assertiveness training** helps people learn to express their feelings constructively in social situations. Many people experience poor social relations because they are unassertive. They are unable to ask for favors, to say no to requests, or to complain about poor service. By learning to express their feelings, formerly unassertive people relieve their anxiety and have more rewarding social relations. Members of assertiveness-training groups try out assertive behaviors in the group situation. Assertiveness training has improved the social skills of visually impaired adolescents (Kim, 2003) and has enabled female undergraduates to successfully resist sexual coercion (Rowe, Jouriles, McDonald, Platt, & Gomez, 2012). It also has been used to reduce drug use and risky sexual behavior in male methamphetamine users who are HIV-positive and have sex with other men (Semple, Strathdee, Zians, McQuaid, & Patterson, 2013).

Self-Help Groups

In the 1950s Carl Rogers introduced the encounter group, which comprised strangers who met to honestly assess their emotional and behavioral issues. The encounter group movement died out but led to the emergence of *self-help groups* for drug abusers, phobia sufferers, and others with specific shared problems. A survey of directors of substance abuse programs affiliated with the U.S. Department of Veterans Affairs found that 79 percent of their patients were referred to Alcoholics Anonymous (Humphreys, 1997). Self-help groups are conducted by people who have experienced those problems. For example, self-help groups for the elderly often are run by older adults (Gottlieb, 2000).

Family Therapy

Group therapy usually brings together unrelated people; **family therapy** brings together members of the same family. The basic assumption of family therapy is that a family member with problems related to her or his family life cannot be treated apart from the family. The main goals of family therapy are the constructive expression of feelings and the establishment of rules that family members agree to follow. The therapist helps family members establish an atmosphere in which no individual is blamed for all the family's problems. Like other kinds of group therapy, family therapy is paying greater attention to sociocultural factors, including ethnicity, sexual orientation, and religion (Carr, 2011).

Family therapists who favor a *systems approach* may have family members draw diagrams of their relationships and discuss how certain of the relationships are maladaptive (Satir, Bitter, & Krestensen, 1988). Perhaps the family is too child-oriented, or perhaps a parent and child are allied against the other parent. The goal of the therapist is to have the family replace these maladaptive relationships with more effective ones. An offshoot of family therapy is *marital therapy*, which tries to improve relationships between married people. Because of the great number of committed couples who are not married, marital therapy has been joined by *couple therapy* (Gurman & Fraenkel, 2002). Research on couple therapy has found that it can have beneficial effects on both the couple's relationship

Assertiveness Training

Members of assertiveness-training groups practice assertive behaviors in the group situation. Assertiveness training can lower anxiety and improve social skills.
Source: wavebreakmedia/Shutterstock.com.

social-skills training A form of behavioral group therapy that improves the client's social relationships by improving her or his interpersonal skills.

assertiveness training A form of social-skills training that teaches clients to express their feelings constructively.

family therapy A form of group therapy that encourages the constructive expression of feelings and the establishment of rules that family members agree to follow.

and their individual emotional well-being. For example, when couple therapy reduces emotional depression, marital discord tends to decline. Likewise, when couple therapy improves marital discord, emotional depression tends to decline (Whisman & Beach, 2012).

> **Section Review:** The Social-Relations Orientation
>
> **1.** What are the basic assumptions and techniques of transactional analysis?
>
> **2.** What are the basic characteristics of assertiveness training?

The Biological Orientation

Though Sigmund Freud practiced psychoanalysis, he predicted that, as science progressed, therapies for psychological disorders would become more and more biological (Trotter, 1981). During the past few decades, the *biological orientation* has indeed become an important approach to therapy. It is based on the assumption that psychological disorders are associated with brain dysfunctions and consequently will respond to treatments that alter brain activity. Biological treatments, because they involve medical procedures, can be offered only by psychiatrists and other physicians. The biological treatments include *psychosurgery, electroconvulsive therapy,* and *drug therapy.*

Psychosurgery

psychosurgery The treatment of psychological disorders by destroying brain tissue.

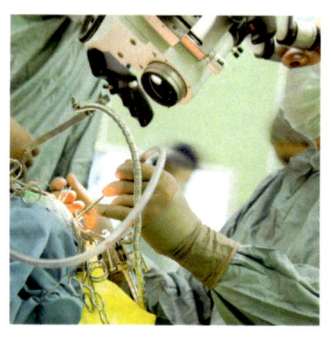

Psychosurgery

Today, psychosurgery is used less to destroy a region of the brain but more to modulate it. Psychosurgical techniques are much more refined as well. Instead of removing large sections of the frontal lobe, as in the early operations, neurosurgeons use computer-based magnetic resonance imaging to guide small electrodes to the brain region of interest.
Source: VILevi/Shutterstock.com.

While attending a professional meeting in 1935, Portuguese neurologist Egas Moniz was impressed by a report that agitated chimpanzees became calmer after undergoing brain surgery that separated their frontal lobes from the rest of their brain. Moniz wondered whether such **psychosurgery** might benefit agitated mental patients. Moniz convinced neurosurgeon Almeida Lima to perform a *prefrontal leucotomy* (also known as a *prefrontal lobotomy*) on anesthetized patients. Lima drilled holes in the patient's temples, inserted a scalpel through the holes, and cut away portions of the frontal lobes. Moniz reported many successes in calming agitated patients (Moniz, 1937/1994). As a result, he won a Nobel Prize in 1949 for inventing psychosurgery, which was considered a humane alternative to the common practice of locking agitated patients in padded rooms or restraining them in straitjackets.

Psychosurgery was introduced to the United States in 1936 by neurosurgeon Walter Freeman and psychiatrist James Watts. They favored a technique called *transorbital leucotomy* (Freeman, 1948). The patient's eye socket (the *orbit*) was anesthetized (the brain itself is insensitive to pain), and a mallet was used to drive a surgical pick into the frontal lobe. The pick was then levered back and forth to separate portions of the lobe from the rest of the brain. By 1979, psychosurgery had been performed on about 35,000 mental patients in the United States. But the use of psychosurgery declined markedly and rightfully so. One reason was its unpredictable effects (Swayze, 1995)—some patients improved, others became apathetic, still others became violent, and a small percentage died. A second reason for its decline was the advent of drug therapies in the 1950s and 1960s, which provided safer, more effective, and more humane treatment (Tierney, 2000). And a third reason was public opposition to what seemed to be a barbaric means of behavior control.

Today, psychosurgery rarely is used in the United States; when it is used, it involves the use of electrodes inserted into the brain's limbic system to treat problems such as self-mutilation (Price et al., 2001). In this case a direct current is sent through the electrodes, destroying small amounts of tissue in precise areas of that brain region. This technique has achieved some success in treating cases of obsessive-compulsive disorder that have not responded to other treatments (Sachdev et al., 2001). A more common modification of psychosurgery is deep brain stimulation (DBS). This procedure increases surgical

544 Chapter 15 Therapy

precision, minimizes risk of injury to the patient (Lapidus, Kopell, Ben-Haim, Rezai, & Goodman, 2013), and modulates the function of brain regions rather than destroying them. DBS is one of the treatments used for improving motor symptoms in patients with Parkinson's disease (Gervais-Bernard et al., 2009).

Electroconvulsive Therapy

In 1938, on a visit to a slaughterhouse, Italian psychiatrist Ugo Cerletti watched pigs being rendered unconscious by electric shocks. Cerletti reasoned that electric shock might be a safe alternative to drug-induced shock therapy in calming agitated patients with schizophrenia (Cerletti, 1954). This hypothesis inspired Cerletti and his fellow psychiatrist Lucio Bini to introduce **electroconvulsive therapy (ECT)**. ECT uses a brief electrical current to induce brain seizures. Though ECT originally was used for treating agitated patients, it proved more successful in elevating the mood of severely depressed patients who had failed to respond to drug therapy.

A psychiatrist administers ECT by attaching electrodes to one or both temples of a patient who is under general anesthesia and who has been given a muscle relaxant. The muscle relaxant prevents injuries that might otherwise be caused by violent contractions of the muscles. A burst of electricity of 70 to 150 volts is passed through the brain for about half a second. This electrical current induces a brain seizure, which is followed by a period of unconsciousness lasting up to 30 minutes. The patient typically receives three treatments a week for several weeks.

A major published review of the research literature found that it is unclear whether ECT or antidepressant drugs are best in the treatment of major depressive disorder (Piper, 1993). But because ECT produces more rapid improvement than antidepressant drugs, which can take several weeks, it is the treatment of choice for people with major depressive disorder in imminent danger of committing suicide (Persad, 1990). But ECT's mechanism of action in humans is unclear. For example, its antidepressant effect is unrelated to its induction of seizures (Sackeim, 1994). Because major depressive disorder is associated with reduced activity of serotonin and norepinephrine neurons in the brain, one explanation is that ECT stimulates an increase in the levels of those neurotransmitters. But a study found that the effectiveness of ECT in relieving major depressive disorder was unrelated to its effects on serotonin and norepinephrine neuronal activity (Markianos, Hatzimanolis, & Lykouras, 2002).

However, animal studies have offered a clue to the effectiveness of ECT. Researchers are studying *neurogenesis*, the birth of new neurons, which are identified by labeling them with a special compound. In one study, adult rats that were exposed to ECT experienced increased neurogenesis in the hippocampus (Scott, Wojtowicz, & Burnham, 2000). Adult-born neurons in the hippocampus have been linked to cognition and emotion (Snyder, Soumier, Brewer, Pickel, & Cameron, 2011). Because researchers are not able to

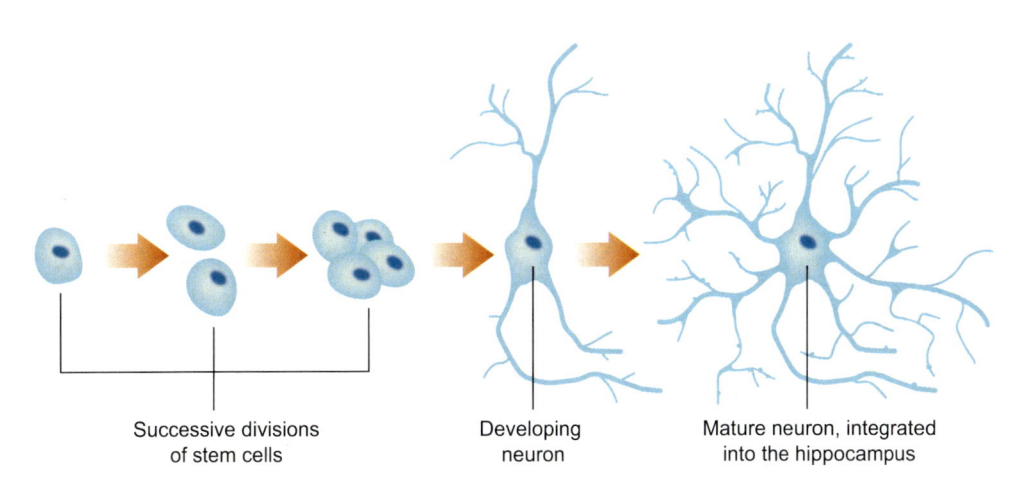

electroconvulsive therapy (ECT) A biological therapy that uses brief electric currents to induce brain seizures in victims of major depressive disorder.

Neurogenesis Theory of Depression

Neurogenesis is the process in which neurons are generated from stem cells. In mammals, neurogenesis has been shown to occur in the hippocampus and occasionally in certain species in the olfactory bulb. This theory is supported by animal studies. Researchers can induce depressive-like symptoms in rodents which correlates with decreased neurogenesis in the hippocampus. Then, rodents are given antidepressants and their behavior, along with increased neurogenesis, returned. Could antidepressant treatment trigger neurogenesis? Neurogenesis is the process in which neurons are generated from stem cells. In mammals, neurogenesis has been shown to occur in the hippocampus and subventricular zone and occasionally in certain species in the olfactory bulb.

| Successive divisions of stem cells | Developing neuron | Mature neuron, integrated into the hippocampus |

measure neurogenesis in the human brain, studies of these also do not provide a definitive explanation for the effectiveness of ECT.

Despite evidence of its effectiveness in relieving major depressive disorder, there has been controversy about ECT's safety and effectiveness. In the past, the violence of the convulsions induced by ECT often broke bones and tore muscles. Today, muscle relaxants prevent such injury. But ECT still causes *retrograde amnesia*—the forgetting of events that occurred from minutes to days prior to the treatment. There also is conflicting evidence regarding the possibility that ECT can produce brain damage (Reisner, 2003). The debate about the desirability of using ECT remains as much emotional and political as scientific.

Drug Therapy

Since its introduction in the 1950s, drug therapy has become the most widely used form of biological therapy. Because many psychological disorders are associated with abnormal levels of neurotransmitters (see Chapter 14), drug therapies generally work by restoring neurotransmitter activity to more normal levels. But a common criticism of drug therapies is that they may relieve symptoms without changing the person's ability to adjust to everyday stress. Concurrent psychotherapy is desirable to help clients learn more adaptive ways of thinking and behaving. The following discussion uses well-known brand names for drugs, with their generic names in parentheses.

Antianxiety Drugs

antianxiety drugs
Psychoactive drugs that are used to treat anxiety disorders.

Because of their calming effect, the **antianxiety drugs** were originally called *tranquilizers* or *anxiolytics*. Today the most widely prescribed are the *benzodiazepines*, such as Xanax (alprazolam) and Valium (diazepam). In fact, the prevalence of anxiety disorders has made the antianxiety drugs the most widely prescribed psychoactive drugs (Sand et al., 2000). In a double-blind study, participants received either Valium or a placebo. Those who received Valium showed a significantly greater reduction in their anxiety level than did those who received a placebo (Rickels, DeMartinis, & Aufdembrinke, 2000). The benzodiazepines act almost immediately and work by stimulating receptors in the brain that enhance the effects of the neurotransmitter GABA, which inhibits brain activity (Gorman, 2003). Benzodiazepines can also produce side effects, including drowsiness, depression, and dependence. A newer drug, Buspar (buspirone), is effective in relieving anxiety without the side effects of the older benzodiazepines, but it takes up to several weeks to have an effect. Buspar works by increasing serotonin levels in the brain (Haller, Halasz, & Makara, 2000).

Antidepressant Drugs

antidepressant drugs
Psychoactive drugs that are used to treat major depressive disorder.

The first **antidepressant drugs** were the *MAO inhibitors*, such as Nardil. Originally used to treat tuberculosis, they were prescribed as antidepressants after physicians noted that they induced euphoria in tuberculosis patients. The MAO inhibitors work by blocking enzymes that normally break down the neurotransmitters dopamine, serotonin, and norepinephrine. This blocking action increases the levels of those neurotransmitters in the brain, elevating the patient's mood. But the MAO inhibitors fell into disfavor because they can cause dangerously high blood pressure.

The MAO inhibitors gave way to the *tricyclic antidepressants*, such as Elavil (amitriptyline), Tofranil (imipramine), and Anafranil (clomipramine). The tricyclics increase serotonin and norepinephrine levels by preventing their reuptake by brain neurons that release them. Though the tricyclics are effective in treating major depressive disorder (Faravelli et al., 2003), they take 2 to 4 weeks to have an effect and also have undesirable side effects. This delay means that suicidal patients given antidepressants must be watched carefully during that period.

More recently, drugs known as *selective serotonin reuptake inhibitors (SSRIs)* have been added to the arsenal of antidepressants. These drugs relieve major depressive disorder by elevating serotonin levels by preventing its reuptake by neurons that release it. Among the most popular of these drugs are Zoloft (sertraline), Paxil (paroxetine), and most notably, Prozac (fluoxetine). A meta-analysis of studies with 10,706 participants found that SSRIs and tricyclic antidepressants are equally effective in the relief of major depressive disorder, with fewer patients discontinuing SSRIs due to side effects (Anderson, 2000).

But what is the relative effectiveness of drug therapy and psychotherapy for major depressive disorder? A meta-analysis compared the results of six studies evaluating the treatment outcomes of almost 600 depressed clients—some of whom received psychotherapy and some of whom received combined drug therapy and psychotherapy. In less severe cases of major depressive disorder, recovery rates for psychotherapy and combined therapy were not significantly different. However, in more severe cases, recovery rates for clients who received psychotherapy combined with drug therapy were higher (Thase et al., 1997). An alternative and noninvasive therapy that you have probably heard about is exercise. Exercise is inexpensive and does not require a doctor's prescription. Animal studies show that exercise increases neurogenesis in the hippocampus, and some researchers conclude that this might provide some relief to patients who suffer from psychological disorders, including major depressive disorder (DeCarolis & Eisch, 2010).

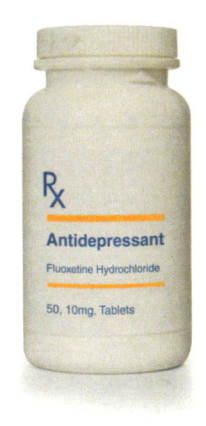

Antidepressant Medication
SSRIs such as Prozac (fluoxetine) are similar to tricyclic antidepressants but more specific in their effects.
Source: James Steidl/Shutterstock.com.

Mood Stabilizers

In the 1940s, Australian physician John Cade (1949) observed that the chemical lithium calmed agitated guinea pigs. Cade then tried lithium on patients and found that it calmed those suffering from mania—apparently because of its ability to reduce abnormal firing patterns of brain neurons (Lenox & Hahn, 2000). Psychiatrists now prescribe antimanic drugs, also known as **mood stabilizers**, such as *lithium carbonate*, to prevent the extreme mood swings of bipolar disorder (Kleindienst & Greil, 2003). It is important for patients to stay on the drug because, of those who discontinue its use, 50 percent relapse within 3 months (Baker, 1994). Psychiatrists must vigilantly monitor patients taking lithium because it can produce dangerous side effects, including seizures, brain damage, and irregular heart rhythms. Another reason for careful monitoring of these patients is the risk that mood stabilizers will be consumed along with alcohol and other drugs. Substance abuse is significantly more common among individuals with bipolar disorder than among individuals with major depressive disorder (Moreno et al., 2012).

mood stabilizers Psychoactive drugs, most notably lithium carbonate, that are used to treat bipolar disorder.

Antipsychotic Drugs

For centuries physicians in India prescribed the snakeroot plant for calming agitated patients. Beginning in the 1940s, a chemical derivative of the plant, *reserpine*, was used to reduce symptoms of mania and schizophrenia. But reserpine fell into disfavor because of its tendency to cause major depressive disorder and low blood pressure. The 1950s saw the development of safer **antipsychotic drugs** called *phenothiazines*, such as Thorazine (chlorpromazine), for treating people with schizophrenia. French physicians had noted that the drug, used to sedate patients before surgery, calmed psychotic patients.

antipsychotic drugs Psychoactive drugs that are used to treat schizophrenia.

The phenothiazines work by blocking brain receptor sites for the neurotransmitter dopamine (Schwartz et al., 2000). Unfortunately, long-term use of antipsychotic drugs can cause the motor side effects that characterize *tardive dyskinesia*, which include grimacing, lip smacking, and limb flailing. A newer antipsychotic drug, Clozaril (clozapine), produces fewer symptoms of tardive dyskinesia while effectively treating many cases of schizophrenia that have not responded well to the phenothiazines (Sachdev, 2000).

Section Review: The Biological Orientation

1. Why has the use of ECT been controversial?
2. How do the tricyclic antidepressants produce their results?

Community Mental Health

Since the 1960s psychologists have played a role in the community mental health movement. They have been involved in deinstitutionalization, community mental health centers, and the prevention of psychological disorders.

Deinstitutionalization

As discussed in the section, "The History of Therapy," for most of the 19th and 20th centuries, state mental hospitals served as the primary sites of treatment for people with serious psychological disorders. But since the 1950s there has been a movement toward **deinstitutionalization**, which promotes the treatment of people in community settings instead of in mental hospitals. Since the 1950s the number of occupied beds in state mental hospitals has decreased from 339 to just 29 per 100,000 members of the population (Lamb, 1998). What accounts for this trend?

deinstitutionalization The movement toward treating people with psychological disorders in community settings instead of mental hospitals.

- The introduction of drug treatments made it more feasible for mental patients to function in the outside world.
- Mental hospitals had become underfunded, understaffed, and overcrowded. Community-based treatment seemed to be a cheaper, superior alternative.
- Increasing concern for the legal rights of mental patients made it more difficult to have people committed to mental hospitals and to keep them there.
- The Community Mental Health Centers Act of 1963, sponsored by President John F. Kennedy, mandated the establishment of federally funded centers in every community in the United States. These centers were to provide services to prevent and treat psychological disorders, further reducing the need for mental hospitals.

Despite its noble intentions and the fact that many people have benefited from it (Goldman, 1998), deinstitutionalization has worked better in theory than in practice. In many communities, funding has been inadequate to establish and run community mental health centers and to provide needed services. Even when funding is available for treatment facilities, such as halfway houses, homeowners often oppose the placement of such facilities in their neighborhoods (Piat, 2000). As a consequence, former mental hospital patients who lack family support might have little choice but to live on the street. Others languish in prisons.

The potential benefits of adequately supported deinstitutionalization are evident in the results of a study that compared community care for former mental hospital patients in the comparable cities of Portland, Oregon, and Vancouver, British Columbia. At the time of the study, Portland provided few community mental health services, whereas Vancouver provided many private and public services. One year after their discharge, formerly hospitalized people with schizophrenia in Vancouver were less likely than those in Portland to have been readmitted and more likely to be employed and to report a greater sense of psychological well-being. Because the two groups were initially equivalent, the greater progress of the Vancouver group was attributed to community mental health services rather than to preexisting differences between the groups (Beiser et al., 1985). A more recent study assessed the effectiveness of a brief intervention focusing on psychosocial skills and continuity of care to people with schizophrenia living in a homeless shelter. Symptoms were assessed at the study's onset and six months after moving into the community. Men in the intervention group exhibited a significant decrease in some, but not all, symptoms of schizophrenia, compared to men in the control group (Herman et al., 2000). Thus, the provision of support services may have an impact on easing the transition of mental health patients into the community.

Prevention of Psychological Disorders

Community mental health centers have three main goals in the prevention of psychological disorders: primary prevention, secondary prevention, and tertiary prevention.

Primary prevention helps prevent psychological disorders by fostering social support systems, eliminating sources of stress, and strengthening individuals' ability to deal with stressors. These goals might be promoted, for example, by reducing unemployment and making low-cost housing available. Canada has instituted a community-based primary prevention program called *Better Beginnings, Better Futures* to prevent physical, cognitive, emotional, and behavioral problems in children from economically disadvantaged families (Peters, 1994). Primary prevention programs have, in fact, been effective in preventing social and behavioral problems in children (Leadbeater, Hoglund, & Woods, 2003), providing treatment to people affected by natural disasters (Bassilios, Reifels, & Pirkis, 2012), and immigrants and refugees (Kirmayer et al., 2011).

Secondary prevention provides early treatment for people at immediate risk of developing psychological disorders, sometimes through *crisis intervention*, as in the case of survivors of violence, natural disasters, or political terrorism (Everly, 2000). Secondary prevention has been used, for example, to prevent posttraumatic stress disorder in individuals who have experienced traumatic events (Pitman et al., 2002). A review of 130 secondary prevention programs for children and adolescents with early signs of maladjustment found that the programs were successful in preventing the development of full-blown psychological disorders (Durlak & Wells, 1998).

Tertiary prevention helps keep people who have full-blown psychological disorders from getting worse or having relapses after successful treatment for a disorder, such as drug dependence (Carroll, Tanneberger, & Monti, 1998). Tertiary prevention has been used in a Canadian program to prevent abusive parents from continuing to abuse their children. The program involves home visits by specially trained nurses who provide emotional support, education in proper child-rearing practices, and assistance to parents who are looking to obtain help from other human services (MacMillan & Thomas, 1993). Among the main community approaches to tertiary prevention are community residences that provide homelike, structured environments in which former mental hospital patients readjust to independent living. For example, tertiary prevention has been shown to reduce the rate of homelessness among people discharged from psychiatric care (Forchuk et al., 2013).

Primary Prevention Programs

Primary prevention programs have been employed to provide treatment to people affected by natural disasters, such as those who survived this devastating tornado that hit Joplin, Missouri, with winds greater than 200 mph in 2011.
Source: Melissa Brandes/Shutterstock.com.

Section Review: Community Mental Health

1. What accounted for the growth of the deinstitutionalization movement?
2. How do community mental health centers provide primary, secondary, and tertiary prevention?

The Rights of the Therapy Client

Does a resident of a mental hospital have the right to refuse treatment? Does a resident of a mental hospital have the right to receive treatment? Is what a client reveals to a therapist privileged information? These questions have generated heated debate during the past few decades.

The Rights of Hospitalized Patients

In the United States, people who are committed to mental hospitals lose many of their rights, including their rights to vote, to marry, to divorce, and to sign contracts. Revelations about past psychiatric practices in the former Soviet Union show the extent to which the commitment process can be abused. Soviet psychiatrists used diagnoses such as "reformist delusions" and "schizophrenia with religious delirium" to commit political or religious dissidents to mental hospitals (Faraone, 1982).

Legally, only people who are judged to be dangerous to themselves or others can be involuntarily committed to mental hospitals. The need to demonstrate that people are

The Crisis Intervention Center

The community mental-health system is aided by crisis intervention centers. These centers handle emergencies such as rape cases, physical abuse, suicide threats, or other problems that require immediate help.
Source: Albert Lozano/Shutterstock.com.

dangerous before they can be committed was formalized by the U.S. Supreme Court in 1979 in *Addington v. Texas* (Hays, 1989). Commitment typically requires that two psychiatrists document that the person is dangerous. During the commitment process, the person has the right to a lawyer, to call witnesses, and to a hearing or a jury trial. The final decision on commitment is made by a judge or jury, not a psychiatrist.

The Right to Receive Treatment

Court decisions also have ruled that people committed to mental hospitals have a right to receive treatment. In 1975, in *Donaldson v. O'Connor*, the U.S. Supreme Court ruled that mental patients have a right to more than custodial care (Behnke, 1999). If they are not given treatment, are not dangerous, and can survive in the community, they must be released. The case was brought by Kenneth Donaldson, who had been confined for 15 years in a Florida mental hospital without treatment. But the court ruling in his case may be difficult to put into practice in particular cases. For example, it is difficult to predict whether a person will be dangerous if released from custodial care (Bernard, 1977). Legal decisions such as *Donaldson v. O'Connor* contributed to the deinstitutionalization movement by making it more difficult to keep mental patients hospitalized against their will.

The Right to Refuse Treatment

In 1983, in *Rogers v. Commissioner of Mental Health*, the Massachusetts Supreme Court ruled that mental patients also have a right to *refuse* treatment unless a court judges them to be incompetent to make their own decisions (Hermann, 1990). A person committed to a mental hospital is not automatically considered incompetent. When the Rogers case was in court, critics claimed that such a ruling would merely give mental patients the right to "rot with their rights on" (Appelbaum & Gutheil, 1980). Some patients are so psychologically disordered that they are unable to make a rational decision about whether they will accept treatment (Johnson, 1998). In reality, the decision appears to have had little influence. A Massachusetts study found that few cases of involuntary treatment were reviewed in court, and the ones that were reviewed were usually decided in favor of those who had prescribed treatment for a patient who had refused it (Veliz & James, 1987). Recent legal cases in Canada have expanded the right to refuse treatment there as well (Gratzer & Matas, 1994).

The Right to Confidentiality

But what of the rights of individuals receiving therapy? One of the most important is the right to confidentiality. In general, therapists are ethically, but not always legally, bound to keep confidential the information revealed by their clients. The extent to which this information is privileged varies from state to state. There are also fears, based on the movement to control costs, that third-party payers might demand more and more information that has traditionally been confidential (Kremer & Gesten, 1998).

The Tarasoff Decision

In recent decades, the most significant legal decision concerning confidentiality was the *Tarasoff* decision, a ruling by the California Supreme Court that a therapist who believes that a client might harm a particular person must protect or warn that person. The ruling came in the case of Prosenjit Poddar, who murdered his former lover, Tatiana Tarasoff. In 1969 Poddar had informed his therapist at the counseling center of the University of California at Berkeley that he intended to kill Tarasoff. The therapist reported the threat to the campus police, who ordered Poddar to stay away from Tarasoff. Two months later Poddar murdered her, leading her parents to sue the therapist, the police, and the university. In 1976 the court ruled in favor of the parents; the therapist should have directly warned Tarasoff about Poddar's threat (Mangalmurti, 1994). The *Tarasoff* decision upholding the duty to warn influenced similar decisions in other states and has become an issue in other countries, including Canada (Birch, 1992) and Australia (McMahon, 1992).

Controversy About the Duty to Warn

The duty to warn has provoked concern among therapists for several reasons. First, no therapist can reliably predict whether a threat made by a client is a serious one (Rubin & Mills, 1983). If a student in a moment of anger about an unfair exam says to a therapist, "I could just *kill* my psychology professor," should the therapist immediately warn the professor?

Second, it can be impractical to warn potential victims. In one case, a client threatened to kill "rich people." He then murdered a wealthy couple. Considering the duty to warn, this case prompted a therapist to ask whether a sign should have been posted reading, "All rich people watch out!" (Fisher, 1985). Moreover, the spread of HIV/AIDS has exacerbated the conflict between confidentiality and the duty to warn. Should a therapist warn the potential sex partners of clients who are HIV-positive (Alghazo, Upton, & Cioe, 2011)? How about breaking confidentiality to protect the life of a person with anorexia nervosa (Werth, Wright, Archambault, & Bardash, 2003)? Critics of the duty to warn also wonder why therapists should be required to reveal confidential information when the same legal jurisdiction might not require laypersons to do so (Wallace, 1988).

Third, the duty to warn might keep people from discussing hostile feelings or even seeking therapy at all (Appelbaum, 1998). This possibility was the basis of a 1988 ruling by the Court of Appeals in North Carolina in the case of *Currie v. United States*. The court ruled that psychiatrists did not have a duty to commit people to mental hospitals for threatening acts of violence. The case concerned a 1982 murder in which a man, who was under the care of Veterans Administration psychiatrists, shot a fellow IBM employee after making threats against IBM. The victim's relatives sued, claiming that the psychiatrists should have committed the man after he made threats against IBM. The court ruled that such a duty would prevent psychiatrists and clients from discussing hostile feelings, perhaps *increasing* the probability of violence (Bales, 1988).

Canadian legal decisions restricting client confidentiality have provoked similar alarm about the potential negative effects of the duty to disclose information on the client-therapist relationship (Glancy, Regehr, & Bryant, 1998). The implications of the *Tarasoff* decision continue to perplex therapists, who must balance the need to serve their clients while protecting themselves from potential lawsuits if their clients harm third parties (Monahan, 1993).

Section Review: The Rights of the Therapy Client

1. What are the possible ramifications of the right to refuse treatment and the right to receive treatment?
2. Why has the *Tarasoff* decision been controversial?

Finding the Proper Therapy

At times in your life, you or someone you know might face psychological problems that require more than friendly advice. When personal problems disrupt your social, academic, or vocational life or when you experience severe and prolonged emotional distress, you might be wise to seek the help of a therapist. You could receive therapy from a psychologist, a psychiatrist, or a variety of other kinds of therapists. You might even choose to read one of the many self-help books for specific psychological problems—an approach called *bibliotherapy*.

Selecting the Right Therapist

Just as there is no single way to find a physician, there is no single way to find a therapist. As explained in the section "Factors in the Effectiveness of Psychotherapy," in general the personal qualities of the therapist matter more than the kind of therapy she or he practices. How might you find a therapist? Your college counseling center would be a good place to start. You may have a friend, relative, or professor who can recommend a therapist or counseling center to you. Other potential sources of help or referral include community mental health centers, psychological associations, and mental health associations. In keeping with the growing use of the Internet, a relatively new source of psychotherapy is *e-therapy*, which is provided by online therapists. A recent review indicates that e-therapy may be as effective as face-to-face therapy, but much more research is necessary to evaluate the effectiveness of e-therapy (Sucala et al., 2012).

After finding a therapist, try to assess her or his credentials, reputation, therapeutic approach, and interpersonal manner as best you can. Does the therapist have legitimate academic and clinical training? For example, is the therapist licensed or certified? Do you know anyone who will vouch for the therapist's competence? Does the therapist's approach make sense for your problem? The therapist should be warm, open, concerned, and empathetic. Clients prefer therapists whom they find helpful and likeable (Crosier, Scott, & Steinfeld, 2012).

Bibliotherapy as an Alternative

You can't visit a typical bookstore or shop online without noting the large section devoted to self-help books. Some traditional psychotherapists even have their clients read books relevant to their central problem. The use of books as a form of psychotherapy is called *bibliotherapy*. Many self-help books are written by people who make unrealistic claims about what they can offer you. Two task forces sponsored by the American Psychological Association found that perhaps the main weakness of bibliotherapy is that self-help books are rarely subjected to scientific research regarding their effectiveness and possible harmful consequences (Floyd, Scogin, McKendree-Smith, Floyd, & Rokke, 2004). Nonetheless, if you choose high-quality books written by credible authors, bibliotherapy can be effective. Bibliotherapy has been used to treat disorders such as insomnia (Mimeault & Morin, 1999), alcoholism (Apodaca & Miller, 2003), panic disorder (Carlbring et al., 2011), and sexual dysfunctions (Mintz, Balzer, Zhao, & Bush, 2012).

Bibliotherapy has been widely used in treating major depressive disorder. In one study, participants received either 16 weeks of cognitive therapy or read a book on how to overcome depression. Participants in both groups had a greater reduction in depression than did those in a control group who had received no treatment. A three-month follow-up found that participants in both treatment groups maintained an equal reduction in depression (Floyd, McKendree-Smith, & Scogin, 2004). Psychotherapists commonly use bibliotherapy as one component of therapy, rather than as a form of therapy in itself. For example, cognitive-behavior therapists may recommend that their clients read books that are relevant to their particular problems (Broder, 2000).

Bibliotherapy
Bibliotherapy can be effective if you choose high-quality books written by credible authors.
Source: kazoka/Shutterstock.com.

Section Review: Finding the Proper Therapy

1. What are the major kinds of psychotherapists?
2. How would you advise a friend to go about seeking a psychotherapist?

The Effectiveness of Psychotherapy

In 1952, Hans Eysenck published an article that sparked a debate on the effectiveness of psychotherapy that has continued to this day. Based on his review of 24 studies of psychotherapy with people suffering from disorders involving moderate anxiety or depression, Eysenck concluded that about two-thirds of those who received psychotherapy improved.

This analysis would have provided strong evidence in support of the effectiveness of psychoanalysis (then the dominant kind of psychotherapy), had Eysenck not also found that about two-thirds of control participants who had received *no* therapy also improved. He called improvement without therapy **spontaneous remission** and attributed it to beneficial factors that occurred in the person's everyday life. Because those who received no therapy were as likely to improve as those who received therapy, Eysenck concluded that psychotherapy is ineffective.

spontaneous remission The improvement of some persons with psychological disorders without their undergoing formal therapy.

Eysenck's article provoked criticisms of its methodological shortcomings. One shortcoming was that many of the untreated people were under the care of physicians who prescribed drugs for them and provided informal counseling. Another shortcoming was that the treated groups and untreated groups were not equivalent, differing in educational level, socioeconomic status, and motivation to improve. These differences meant that the control group might have had a better initial prognosis than the treatment group had. Still another shortcoming was that Eysenck overestimated the rate of spontaneous remission, which later researchers found to be closer to 40 percent than to 65 percent (Bergin & Lambert, 1978). Many years later, Eysenck (1994) still insisted that psychotherapy does not produce improvement beyond that of spontaneous remission.

Evaluation of Psychotherapy

During the decades since Eysenck's article, hundreds of studies have assessed the effectiveness of psychotherapy. This scientific endeavor is difficult. One of the basic issues concerns what criteria to use in evaluating the success of psychotherapy.

Criteria of Success

The definition of *effective* varies with the orientation to therapy. Thus, the criteria of therapeutic success must consider the theoretical orientation of the therapy being evaluated. Changing a specific target behavior, for example, might be a goal of behavioral therapy but not of humanistic therapy (Bohart, O'Hara, & Leitner, 1998).

Moreover, who is to judge whether desired changes have occurred? A survey of client satisfaction with psychotherapy found that most of those who responded said that they were pleased with their experience (Hollon, 1996). But clients as well as therapists can be biased in favor of reporting improvement. To avoid bias, friends, family members, teachers, or employers might also be asked for their assessment of the client's progress. Such examination provides cross-validation of client and therapist reports of improvement.

What has the admittedly imperfect research on the effectiveness of psychotherapy found? The general conclusion drawn from research conducted since Eysenck issued his challenge is that, overall, psychotherapy is more effective than placebo treatment, which in turn is more effective than no-treatment control conditions (Grissom, 1996). Placebo effects in psychotherapy are caused by factors such as the client's faith in the therapist's ability and the client's expectation of success.

Major Research Studies

Mary Lee Smith and her colleagues (1980) published a comprehensive meta-analysis that combined the results of 475 studies on the effectiveness of psychotherapy. They found that, on the average, the typical psychotherapy client is better off than 80 percent of untreated persons—and that there is little overall difference in the effectiveness of the various approaches to therapy (see Figure 15-3). So psychotherapy does work, but no single kind stands out as clearly more effective than the others. This finding has been supported by Lester Luborsky's more recent summary of meta-analyses of studies on the relative effectiveness of different kinds of psychotherapy (Luborsky et al., 2003).

Moreover, results of an ambitious $10 million U.S. government study—the National Institute of Mental Health (NIMH) Treatment of Depression Collaborative Research Program—in the 1980s have lent further support to the effectiveness of psychotherapy. The study randomly assigned 239 adult participants with major depressive disorder into

FIGURE 15-3
The Effectiveness of Psychotherapy

Research has found that psychotherapy is effective but that no kind of therapy is consistently better than any other kind. The figure shows the effectiveness of different kinds of therapy relative to no treatment. Overall, people given psychotherapy show, on the average, significantly greater improvement than about 80 percent of untreated people.

Source: Based on data from Smith, M. L., Glass, G. V., & Miller, T. I. (1980). *The benefits of psychotherapy.* Baltimore: Johns Hopkins University Press.

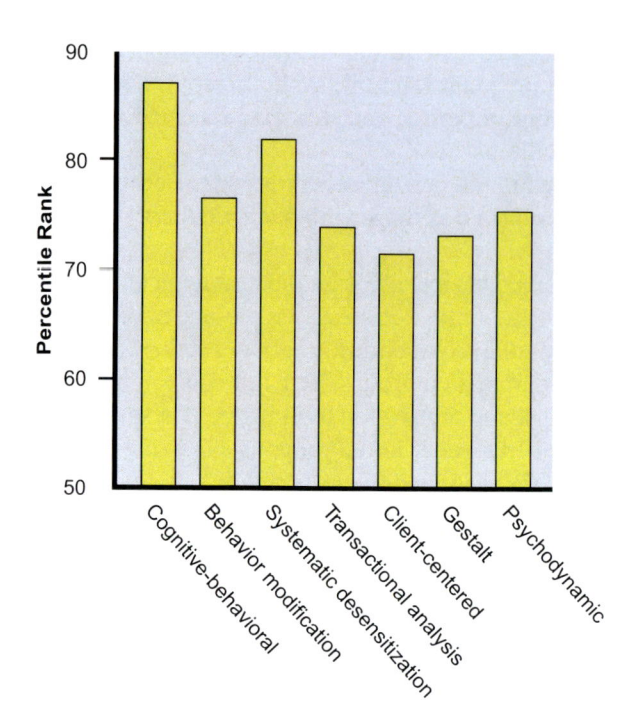

---

four groups. One group received Beck's cognitive therapy. A second group received interpersonal psychotherapy (a form of psychoanalytic therapy). A third group received the antidepressant drug Tofranil (imipramine) plus a minimal amount of social support from a therapist. And a fourth group received a placebo treatment consisting of an inactive pill plus a minimal amount of social support from a therapist (Stewart, Garfinkel, Nunes, Donovan, & Klein, 1998).

The participants were assessed after 16 weeks of therapy and again at a follow-up 18 months later. As expected, all the groups improved by the end of the 16 weeks; the three forms of active therapy eliminated depression in more than 50 percent of the participants, and the placebo therapy eliminated depression in 29 percent of the participants. There were no differences in effectiveness between the three active forms of therapy. Though drug therapy relieved symptoms more quickly, the two psychotherapies eventually caught up in their effectiveness (Mervis, 1986). But a follow-up study found that many of the participants relapsed, indicating that 16 weeks of therapy might be insufficient to produce lasting relief of depression (Shea, Elkin, Imber, & Sotsky, 1992).

Factors in the Effectiveness of Psychotherapy

Given the consensus that psychotherapy is usually effective and that no approach is significantly more effective than any other approach, researchers are faced with the question, What factors account for the effectiveness of psychotherapy? In trying to answer this question, researchers study the characteristics of therapies, clients, and therapists.

Therapy Characteristics

One of the first comprehensive reviews of therapy, client, and therapist factors, carried out by Lester Luborsky and his colleagues (1971), found that the poorest predictor of successful therapy was the nature of the therapy itself. More recent research studies have likewise found that the major kinds of psychotherapy are equally effective (Shapiro, 1995). Moreover, group therapy and individual psychotherapy are equally effective (McRoberts, Burlingame, & Hoag, 1998).

The inability to establish a reliable difference between psychotherapies in clinical outcomes has led some researchers to consider the *therapeutic alliance* to be a more important predictor of successful treatment. The therapeutic alliance refers to three aspects of the therapeutic context: the degree of collaboration, the quality of the emotional bond,

FIGURE 15-4

The Relationship Between the Length of Therapy and Therapy Effectiveness

As the number of therapy sessions increases, the percentage of clients who improve increases. But after the 26th session, additional sessions help relatively few clients. Note the difference between objective ratings of improvement given by therapists (green line) and subjective ratings given by the clients themselves (purple line), though the general trend is similar for both.

Source: From Howard, K. I., Kopta, S. M., Krausse, M. S., & Orlinsky, D. E. (1986). "The dose-effect relationship in psychotherapy" from *American Psychologist, 41,* 159–164. Copyright © 1986 by the American Psychological Association. Reproduced with permission.

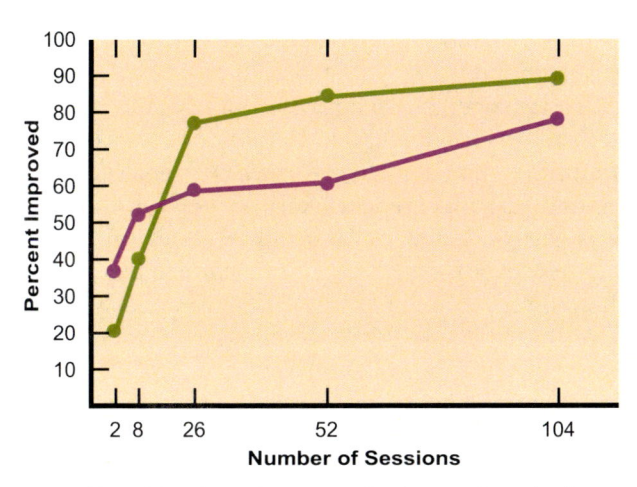

Note: Objective ratings at termination are shown by the top line; subjective ratings during therapy are shown by the bottom line.

and the ability of the client and the therapist to agree on the goals and means of treatment. A review of 79 studies found that the quality of the therapeutic alliance was positively correlated with therapeutic outcomes; the therapeutic alliance is a consistent predictor of therapeutic success regardless of the type of therapy (Martin, Garski, & Davis, 2000). These findings have led some researchers to argue that the therapeutic alliance is a common factor that underlies psychotherapeutic approaches—regardless of theoretical orientation.

The only important therapy characteristic seems to be the number of therapy sessions—the more sessions, the greater the improvement. A review of 15 studies of psychotherapy using more than 2,400 clients found that 50 percent of clients improved by the end of 8 weekly sessions and 75 percent improved by the end of 26 weekly sessions (Howard et al., 1986) (see Figure 15-4). A recent meta-analysis of more than 100 studies of clinical patients found that the effectiveness of psychotherapy continued to increase over time, with benefits leveling off at approximately one year (Shadish et al., 2000). Nonetheless, certain kinds of psychotherapy, particularly psychoanalytic therapy (Doidge, 1997), might require more therapy sessions to produce positive effects.

Client Characteristics

The classic review by Luborsky and his colleagues (1971) found that therapeutic success was related to client characteristics. Clients were more likely to improve if they were higher in education, intelligence, and socioeconomic status. Improvement also was greatest in clients with less severe disorders and disorders of recent onset. Other factors that promoted therapeutic success were a more adequate personality and greater motivation to change. Data from the NIMH Treatment of Depression Collaborative Research Program found greater success with participants who expected therapy to be effective, apparently because they participated more constructively in therapy sessions (Meyer et al., 2002).

Unfortunately, no client characteristics have been documented that can serve as a basis for the selection of a particular treatment (Dance & Neufeld, 1988). And studies have tended to use European American clients to the exclusion of African Americans and members of other ethnic minority groups (Matt & Navarro, 1997). This exclusion makes it difficult to generalize research findings from the participants in psychotherapy studies to the population in general.

Therapist Characteristics

Research findings indicate that the nature of the therapist might be more important than the nature of the therapy (Charman, 2003). Therapy is an intense, intimate, vulnerable relationship between two people. Though it might be logical to assume that therapy would be best when the client and therapist are similar, there is little evidence that similarity in their sex (Bowman, Scogin, Floyd, & McKendree-Smith, 2001) or personality (Rinaldi, 1987) is a crucial factor in therapeutic outcomes. But research investigating ethnic similarity of clients and therapists has found that therapists' ratings of client functioning are higher when both are of the same ethnicity (Russell, Fujino, Sue, Cheung, & Snowden, 1996). And ethnic minority clients are less likely to drop out of therapy when they use mental health services designed to meet the needs of ethnic minority clients (Takeuchi, Sue, & Yee, 1995). A recent meta-analysis of relevant studies reported, however, that the effect size of ethnic similarity on the length of therapy and symptom improvement is small (Erdur, Rude, & Baron, 2003). Moreover, the effect of ethnic similarity on treatment outcomes varies by ethnic group (Cabral & Smith, 2011).

Just what therapist characteristics *are* important, then? The client's perception of therapist empathy has been consistently identified as an important factor in the effectiveness of psychotherapy (Keijsers, Schaap, & Hoogduin, 2000). In fact, one of the main factors in negative effects of psychotherapy is a lack of empathy by the therapist (Mohr, 1995). But empathy is not enough. Personal warmth has been found to be a factor that differentiates successful and unsuccessful therapists (Keijsers, Schaap, & Hoogduin, 2000). And professional training also is important. A meta-analysis found that highly trained therapists are more successful than less well-trained therapists, particularly in having fewer clients drop out of therapy (Stein & Lambert, 1995).

Researchers have become interested in investigating the therapist characteristics that promote or disrupt the therapeutic alliance. A review of relevant research findings found that therapist personal characteristics that contribute positively to the therapeutic alliance include being warm, open, honest, confident, respectful, trustworthy, and interested (Ackerman & Hilsenroth, 2003). In contrast, another review of relevant research findings found that therapist personal characteristics that contribute negatively to the therapeutic alliance include being tense, rigid, distant, critical, uncertain, and distracted. Therapist techniques such as inappropriate self-disclosure, inappropriate use of silence, and over-structuring of therapy sessions likewise have negative effects on the therapeutic alliance (Ackerman & Hilsenroth, 2001).

Researchers, particularly those who favor an eclectic approach (Beutler & Consoli, 1993), are refining their methods to study the more precise question, What kind of therapy, offered by what kind of therapist, is helpful for what kind of client, experiencing what kind of problem, in what kind of circumstances? We must wait for future studies testing interactions among these factors to determine the most effective combinations. Currently, the best we can do is determine the effectiveness of two factors at a time, such as the kind of therapy and the kind of problem. For example, cognitive therapy is superior to other therapies in the treatment of depression (Gaffan, Tsaousis, & Kemp-Wheeler, 1995), and behavior therapy is usually superior to other therapies in the treatment of phobias (Goisman, 1983) and for treating children and adolescents (Weisz et al., 1995).

Section Review: The Effectiveness of Psychotherapy

1. Why did Eysenck claim that psychotherapy produces no better results than spontaneous remission?
2. Are any therapist factors important in the effectiveness of psychotherapy?

Experiencing Psychology

How Do the Media Portray Drug Therapy?

Rationale

Drug therapy is a major approach to the treatment of psychological disorders. Drugs such as Prozac have inspired abundant media coverage. In this activity, you will examine the nature of drug therapy coverage in popular magazines and newspapers.

Method

Use your library and the Internet to find articles in popular magazines and newspapers about drug therapy from the past five years. Possible sources to peruse are *Time*, *Newsweek*, *The Washington Post*, and *The New York Times*. Note which drugs are covered, the tone of the articles, and the positive and negative information presented.

Results and Discussion

Discuss the kinds of drugs that were covered, how sober or sensational the articles were, and any biases you came across. Based on what you read, what seem to be the disorders and drugs that are of greatest interest to the media? Why do you think this is so?

Chapter Summary

The History of Therapy

- In trephining, holes were cut in the skull, possibly to release evil spirits that were alleged to cause abnormal behavior.
- Hippocrates introduced a more naturalistic form of treatment, including procedures to restore the balance of body humors.
- The Renaissance saw the appearance of insane asylums; some, such as Bedlam, were awful places, but others, such as Geel, provided humane treatment.
- Near the end of the 18th century, Philippe Pinel released asylum inmates and championed moral therapy.
- Moral therapy was introduced to America by Benjamin Rush, who also used unusual devices for treating certain disorders.
- Through the efforts of Dorothea Dix, state mental hospitals were built throughout the United States.
- But the mental hospitals became crowded and deteriorated into mere human warehouses.
- In the early 20th century, a book by Clifford Beers, describing his horrible experiences in a mental hospital, led to the founding of the mental health movement, which promotes the prevention and humane treatment of psychological disorders.
- Increasing cultural diversity in the United States has prompted interest in developing cultural competence in psychological training and practice.

The Psychoanalytic Orientation

- After hearing Joseph Breuer's report of the benefits of catharsis in the case of Anna O., Sigmund Freud developed psychoanalysis.
- Psychoanalysis principally involves the analysis of free associations, dreams, resistances, and transference.
- The goal of these analyses is to have the client gain insight into unconscious conflicts and experience catharsis.

The Behavioral Orientation

- The behavioral orientation emphasizes the importance of learning and environmental influences.
- Two of the main kinds of behavioral therapy based on classical conditioning are systematic desensitization, which is useful in treating phobias, and aversion therapy, which makes formerly pleasurable but maladaptive behavior unpleasant.
- One of the main applications of the operant conditioning principle of positive reinforcement is the use of a token economy in institutional settings.
- The operant conditioning principle of punishment is useful in eliminating behaviors such as self-injurious behavior in autistic children.
- Social-learning theory has contributed participant modeling as a way to overcome phobias.

The Cognitive Orientation

- The cognitive orientation assumes that thoughts about events, rather than events themselves, cause psychological disorders.
- In Albert Ellis's rational-emotive behavior therapy, the client learns to change irrational thinking.
- Aaron Beck developed cognitive therapy to help depressed people think less negatively about themselves, the world, and the future.

The Humanistic Orientation

- The humanistic orientation emphasizes the importance of being aware of one's emotions and feeling free to express them.

- Carl Rogers's person-centered therapy, a form of nondirective therapy, helps clients find their own solutions to their problems.
- In contrast, Fritz Perls's Gestalt therapy is more directive in making clients face their true feelings and act on them.

The Social-Relations Orientation
- The social-relations orientation assumes that people cannot be treated as isolated individuals.
- In group therapy, people, usually strangers, are brought together for therapy.
- One form of group therapy derived from the psychoanalytic approach employs transactional analysis.
- Group therapy derived from the behavioral approach includes social-skills training and assertiveness training.
- In family therapy, family members gain insight into their unhealthy patterns of interaction and learn to change them.

The Biological Orientation
- The biological orientation uses medical procedures to treat psychological disorders.
- The main procedures include psychosurgery (rarely used today), modifications of psychosurgery such as deep brain stimulation, electroconvulsive therapy, and drug therapy.
- Psychiatrists may prescribe antianxiety drugs, antidepressant drugs, mood stabilizers, and antipsychotic drugs.

Community Mental Health
- The community mental health movement was stimulated by deinstitutionalization, the treatment of people in community settings instead of in mental hospitals.
- The failure to provide adequate housing and services for former mental hospital patients has contributed to the growing homelessness problem.
- Community mental health centers take a preventive approach to psychological disorders.

The Rights of the Therapy Client
- Laws require that formal procedures be followed before a person is committed to a mental hospital.
- Once in a mental hospital, patients have the right to refuse treatment and the right to receive treatment.
- What clients reveal in therapy sessions is normally confidential, but legal cases, most notably the *Tarasoff* decision, have led to the concept of the duty to warn.

Finding the Proper Therapy
- Most professional therapists are eclectic.
- You should be as careful in selecting a therapist as you are in selecting a physician.

The Effectiveness of Psychotherapy
- In 1952 Hans Eysenck challenged psychotherapists by claiming that people who received psychotherapy improved no more than did people who received no therapy.
- Subsequent research has shown that psychotherapy is better than no therapy and better than placebo therapy.
- No single kind of therapy stands out as clearly superior to the rest.
- More sophisticated research is required to determine the ideal combinations of therapy, therapist, and client factors for treating specific disorders.

Key Terms

catharsis (p. 529)

The History of Therapy
cultural competence (p. 531)
moral therapy (p. 530)
psychotherapy (p. 531)
trephining (p. 530)

The Psychoanalytic Orientation
analysis of dreams (p. 532)
analysis of free associations (p. 532)
analysis of resistances (p. 532)
analysis of transference (p. 533)
psychoanalysis (p. 532)

The Behavioral Orientation
aversion therapy (p. 536)
behavior therapy (p. 533)

counterconditioning (p. 534)
flooding (p. 537)
in vivo desensitization (p. 535)
participant modeling (p. 538)
systematic desensitization (p. 534)
token economy (p. 536)

The Cognitive Orientation
cognitive therapy (p. 540)
rational-emotive behavior therapy (R-E-B-T) (p. 538)

The Humanistic Orientation
Gestalt therapy (p. 541)
person-centered therapy (p. 540)

The Social-Relations Orientation
assertiveness training (p. 543)

family therapy (p. 543)
social-skills training (p. 543)
transactional analysis (TA) (p. 542)

The Biological Orientation
antianxiety drugs (p. 546)
antidepressant drugs (p. 546)
antipsychotic drugs (p. 547)
electroconvulsive therapy (ECT) (p. 545)
mood stabilizers (p. 547)
psychosurgery (p. 544)

Community Mental Health
deinstitutionalization (p. 548)

The Effectiveness of Psychotherapy
spontaneous remission (p. 553)

Chapter Quiz

Note: Answers for the Chapter Quiz questions are provided at the end of the book.

1. The duty to warn that a therapy client might be dangerous to another person was established in the
   a. *Tarasoff* decision.
   b. *Addington v. Texas* decision.
   c. *Donaldson v. O'Connor* decision.
   d. *Rogers v. Commissioner of Mental Health* decision.

2. An early hominid from the Stone Age claims he hears voices in his head, continually rants and raves, and makes bizarre movements with his hands. The tribe's medicine man treats him by using sharp rocks to cut holes in his head and release the evil spirits that are causing his behavior. This treatment is called
   a. trephining.
   b. aversion therapy.
   c. prefrontal lobotomy.
   d. transorbital leucotomy.

3. If a therapist noted that you tend to act childish when interacting with other adults and adult-like when playing with children, you are most likely undergoing
   a. counterconditioning.
   b. psychoanalysis.
   c. Gestalt therapy.
   d. transactional analysis.

4. In the 19th century, mental hospitals were built throughout the United States as a result of the work of
   a. Dorothea Dix.
   b. Benjamin Rush.
   c. Clifford Beers.
   d. Philippe Pinel.

5. The form of therapy that aims at contradicting exaggerated negative beliefs about oneself, the world, and the future is called
   a. moral therapy.
   b. cognitive therapy.
   c. counterconditioning.
   d. existential psychotherapy.

6. A therapist asks a client with a spider phobia to rate the degree of anxiety induced by imagined scenes involving spiders, such as a rubber spider, a spider on the wall, or a spider crawling on the client's arm. This procedure is most likely a component of
   a. flooding.
   b. aversion therapy.
   c. analysis of transference.
   d. systematic desensitization.

7. A community mental health center concerned with spousal abuse and child abuse institutes a stress management program for husbands and wives. This program is an example of
   a. primary prevention.
   b. tertiary prevention.
   c. secondary prevention.
   d. deinstitutionalization.

8. The token economy is based on principles derived from
   a. R-E-B-T.
   b. operant conditioning.
   c. transactional analysis.
   d. person-centered therapy.

9. During a therapy session, whenever the topic of the client's father arises, the client changes the topic and ridicules the therapist's ability. A psychoanalyst would consider this situation an example of
   a. catharsis.
   b. resistance.
   c. free association.
   d. counterconditioning.

10. Tardive dyskinesia is a side effect of long-term treatment with
    a. mood stabilizers,
    b. antianxiety drugs.
    c. antipsychotic drugs.
    d. antidepressant drugs.

11. A man who derives sexual pleasure from collecting used women's underwear is captured by police while stealing items from a laundromat. He enters therapy in which he is given a painful electric shock whenever he exhibits sexual arousal in the presence of women's underwear. This procedure is most likely a component of
    a. moral therapy.
    b. aversion therapy.
    c. in vivo desensitization.
    d. systematic desensitization.

12. A person who experiences intense anxiety in enclosed places is told by a therapist to imagine entering an elevator and remaining there even if terrified. This procedure is an example of
    a. flooding.
    b. catharsis.
    c. spontaneous remission.
    d. systematic desensitization.

13. Research (Egan et al., 1988) indicates that systematic desensitization might exert its effects through the actions of
    a. glycine.
    b. thyroxin.
    c. endorphins.
    d. epinephrine.

14. The American mental health movement was inspired by the publication of *A Mind That Found Itself* by
    a. Dorothea Dix.
    b. Benjamin Rush.
    c. Clifford Beers.
    d. Philippe Pinel.

15. The main technique of psychoanalysis is the analysis of
    a. dreams.
    b. resistances.
    c. transference.
    d. free association.

16. According to Albert Ellis's A-B-C theory of emotion, during therapy the client learns to change
    a. A.
    b. B.
    c. C.
    d. D.

17. A woman visits a therapist and complains that she is depressed because people criticize her. The therapist tries to convince the woman that her depression is caused by her unrealistic belief that she must be liked by everyone. The therapist's tactic is a component of
    a. moral therapy.
    b. counterconditioning.
    c. social-skills training.
    d. rational-emotive behavior therapy.

18. A client states, "I'm afraid to tell my parents that I didn't do too well this semester." The therapist replies, "It seems that you care very much what your parents think of you." The client adds, "I let them down." The therapist notes, "You seem to feel like a failure." This dialog would be most characteristic of
    a. R-E-B-T.
    b. participant modeling.
    c. assertiveness training.
    d. person-centered therapy.

19. A review of research studies on the effectiveness of psychotherapy (Luborsky et al., 1971) found that the most important therapy characteristic is the
    a. kind of therapy.
    b. location of therapy.
    c. number of therapy sessions.
    d. attention to unconscious conflicts.

20. The line from Shakespeare's *Hamlet*, "There is nothing either good or bad, but thinking makes it so," agrees with the basic premise of
    a. moral therapy.
    b. psychoanalysis.
    c. counterconditioning.
    d. rational-emotive behavior therapy.

21. The form of humanistic therapy that helps clients find their own answers to their problems by the reflection of feelings is called
    a. R-E-B-T.
    b. transactional analysis.
    c. person-centered therapy.
    d. existential psychotherapy.

22. A major review of 475 studies on the effectiveness of psychotherapy (Smith et al., 1980) found that the percentage of clients who improve more than untreated people is about
    a. 30 percent.
    b. 65 percent.
    c. 80 percent.
    d. 95 percent.

23. Research on therapy has found that an important therapist factor that promotes therapy's success is
    a. self-analysis.
    b. directiveness.
    c. accurate empathy.
    d. negative transference.

24. Tricyclic antidepressant drugs increase brain levels of
    a. GABA.
    b. glutamate.
    c. norepinephrine.
    d. monoamine oxidase.

25. A therapist accompanies a client with a fear of flying on several trips to the airport. They first simply go to the terminal, eventually sit in an airplane, and finally take off on a flight. This procedure is most likely a component of
    a. flooding.
    b. aversion therapy.
    c. in vivo desensitization.
    d. systematic desensitization.

Thought Questions

1. If a friend of yours had acrophobia (fear of heights), how would a therapist use systematic desensitization to treat it?

2. Why has deinstitutionalization not produced all the beneficial effects that were envisioned for it?

3. Why is the duty to warn a two-edged sword, with potentially both positive and negative consequences?

4. What criteria would you use to determine whether an approach to psychotherapy is effective?

Psychology, Health, and Stress

CHAPTER 16

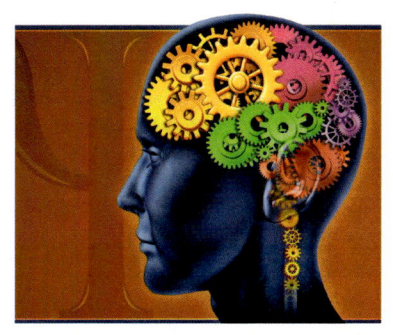

In 1991 Earvin "Magic" Johnson, one of the greatest of all basketball players, announced that he had contracted the human immunodeficiency virus (HIV), which causes acquired immune deficiency syndrome (AIDS), by engaging in unprotected, nonmonogamous, heterosexual sex. Johnson's statement contradicted the common belief that AIDS was a disease restricted to gay men. The case of actor Rock Hudson, who had kept his homosexuality secret for decades, further dramatized the fact that no one—not even a wealthy, talented, popular movie star—is immune to HIV infection. These cases, and the millions of other cases of HIV infection that have occurred worldwide since AIDS was first identified in the early 1980s, show that we are not always passive victims of disease. In many cases we inflict illness or injury on ourselves—and others—through our own behavior, whether through ignorance or carelessness.

A meta-analysis of studies on the effects of Magic Johnson's announcement that he was HIV-positive found that the announcement was associated with positive effects on the public. It was associated with more accurate knowledge about HIV and AIDS, an increase in the number of persons who sought HIV testing, and a greater desire for information about HIV and AIDS. The announcement also was associated with an increased realization among adults that any sexually active person could be at risk of contracting HIV (Casey et al., 2003).

HIV infection is just one of many health issues related to our own behavior. Do you overeat, smoke cigarettes, drive recklessly, exercise rarely, drink excessive amounts of alcohol, respond ineffectively to stressful situations, or fail to follow your physician's medical recommendations? If you engage in any of these maladaptive behaviors, which are among the leading causes of death in the United States, you might be reducing your life span. A recent meta-analysis that analyzed 21 studies that included more than 530,000 participants over a period of more than 13 years assessed the influence of five lifestyle factors (i.e., obesity, alcohol consumption, smoking, diet, and physical activity) on all causes of mortality. Avoidance of at least four of these lifestyle factors was associated with a 66 percent reduction in mortality. Thus, adherence to a healthy lifestyle substantially reduces one's risk of mortality (Loef & Walach, 2012).

This statement would not have been true at the beginning of the 20th century, when most North Americans died from infectious diseases such as influenza, pneumonia, or tuberculosis. But the development

Source: Lightspring/Shutterstock.com.

Chapter Outline

Psychological Stress and Stressors

The Biopsychology of Stress and Illness

Factors That Moderate the Stress Response

Coping with Stress

Health-Promoting Habits

Reactions to Illness

Behavioral Causes of Illness and Death

More than half the mortality from the leading causes of death in the United States is influenced by unhealthy or dangerous behaviors, such as overeating, physical inactivity, and overexposure to the sun.
Source: Nomad_Soul/Shutterstock.com.

health psychology The field that applies psychological principles to the prevention and treatment of physical illness.

stress The physiological response of the body to physical and psychological demands.

stressor A physical or psychological demand that induces physiological adjustment.

of vaccines and antibiotics, as well as improved hygiene and public sanitation practices, led to a decline in illness and mortality due to infectious diseases. This decline was accompanied by a surge in the prevalence of noninfectious diseases, especially those caused by dangerous or unhealthy behaviors. A century ago, cancer and cardiovascular disease, which are promoted by unhealthy lifestyles pursued over a span of decades, were relatively uncommon causes of death among Americans. Today, they are the two most common causes. We now are more likely to become ill or die because of our own actions than because of viruses or bacteria that invade our bodies. One of the main problems that psychologists who do research in *health psychology* study is the role of psychological factors in the onset and prevention of cancer, cardiovascular disease, and other illnesses that are affected by lifestyle and sociocultural variables associated with gender, ethnicity, and poverty.

Health psychology is the field that studies the role of biological, psychological, and sociocultural factors in the promotion of health and the prevention of illness. Health psychologists favor a *biopsychosocial model* of health and illness, which emphasizes the interaction of biological, psychological, and social factors (Suls, Krantz, & Williams, 2013). In contrast, the traditional *biomedical model* emphasizes biological factors and neglects psychological and social ones. The chief topics of interest to health psychologists are the relationship between stress and illness, the modification of health-impairing habits, and the promotion of adaptive reactions to illness.

Psychological Stress and Stressors

According to Canadian endocrinologist Hans Selye (1907–1982), the founder of modern stress research, **stress** is the physiological response of the body to physical and psychological demands. Such demands are known as **stressors**. Though stress has been implicated as a factor in illness, some degree of stress is normal, necessary, and unavoidable. Stress motivates us to adjust our behavior to meet changing demands, as when we study for an upcoming exam or seek companionship when lonely. Stress can even be pleasurable, as when we attend a party or shoot river rapids on a raft. Selye called unpleasant stress *distress* and pleasant stress *eustress* (Spector, 1997). *Eustress* comes from the Greek for "good stress." The major sources of stress include *life changes* and *daily hassles*.

Life Changes

Throughout life, each of us must adjust to life changes, both pleasant ones (such as moving into a new home) and unpleasant ones (such as the death of a loved one). Health psychologists who study the effects of life changes are mainly concerned with *life events* and *posttraumatic stress disorder*.

Life Events

Interest in the relationship between life changes and illness began when Thomas Holmes and Richard Rahe (1967) developed the Social Readjustment Rating Scale. Holmes and Rahe asked medical patients to report positive and negative life changes that they had experienced during the months before they became ill. This study generated a list of 43 kinds of life changes. (A recent revision of the Social Readjustment Rating Scale includes 51 life changes [Hobson & Delunas, 2001] but is only now beginning to be used by researchers.)

Participants in another sample were then asked to rate, on a 100-point scale, the degree of *adjustment* required by each of the 43 life changes. The scale includes both negative events, such as the foreclosure on a mortgage or loan, and positive events, such as Christmas. Your *life change score* is the sum of the scores for your life changes that occurred in a given period of time, generally the past year. Holmes and Rahe found that people who had a total life change score of more than 300 points in the preceding year were more than twice as likely to become ill as were people who had a total of less than 300 points. Similarly, a survey of adults found that the more life changes they had experienced, the more stress-related symptoms they had reported (Scully, Tosi, & Banning, 2000).

An important weakness of the Social Readjustment Rating Scale is that its very content might make researchers overestimate the relationship between life changes and illness. The scale contains some life changes that may be either causes or effects of illness (Zimmerman, 1983). The most obvious examples are "change in eating habits" and "personal injury or illness." Thus, a positive correlation between life changes and illness indicates only that there *might* be a causal relationship between the two.

But some experiments have provided evidence supporting the causal effect of life events on illness. One of these studies exposed 17 volunteers to a rhinovirus (which causes the common cold) and then isolated them individually for 5 days. The 12 participants who developed colds had experienced significantly more life changes in the previous year than had the 5 participants who did not (Stone, Bovberg, Neale, & Napoli, 1992). An explanation for this finding is provided by research studies that show that the greater the number of life changes that one experiences, the weaker one's immune response (Burns, Carroll, Drayson, Whitham, & Ring, 2003).

Though Holmes and Rahe assumed that adjustment to life changes induces stress, subsequent research has shown that it is the nature of the change, rather than change itself, that induces stress. Negative life changes induce more stress than neutral or positive life changes do (Monroe, 1982). One study of adolescent boys found that those with more positive changes in their lives had lower blood pressure than other adolescent boys had (Caputo, Rudolph, & Morgan, 1998). Moreover, there are gender and ethnic differences in the type of life events people experience. One study of children and adolescents found that girls reported more interpersonal stressors—such as parent-child conflicts—than did boys (Rudolph & Hammen, 1999). And a study of an ethnically diverse sample of undergraduates found that participants reported a number of ethnicity-related stressors. Whereas the type of stressors varied by ethnic group, participants reported stressors associated with perceived discrimination, stereotype confirmation concern, and conformity pressure from their own ethnic group (Contrada et al., 2001). These findings support Selye's distinction between distress and eustress.

Posttraumatic Stress Disorder

Traumatic events, such as wars or disasters, are particularly stressful and may lead to **posttraumatic stress disorder (PTSD)**, which can appear months or years after the event. As you might imagine, the suicide airline attacks on the World Trade Center and Pentagon on September 11, 2001, led to many studies on PTSD among the survivors as well as the rescuers and medical personnel who had worked to save lives after the attacks. For example, research studies have reported an unusually high incidence of PTSD among those who lived or worked near the World Trade Center or the Pentagon at the time of the attack. Moreover, survivors have reported symptoms up to 6 years after the attacks (Neria, DiGrande, & Adams, 2011).

The syndrome of symptoms that characterize posttraumatic stress disorder first was formally identified among American and Canadian veterans of the Vietnam War. Lifetime prevalence rates for U.S. veterans who served in the Vietnam War have been found to be close to 20 percent, with approximately 10 percent still suffering from symptoms. And a strong positive correlation was found between the amount of combat exposure and PTSD diagnosis (Dohrenwend et al., 2006). In other words, greater combat stress was related to a greater likelihood of being diagnosed with PTSD. More recent research has investigated

posttraumatic stress disorder (PTSD) A syndrome of physical and psychological symptoms that appears as a delayed response after exposure to an extremely emotionally distressing event.

Posttraumatic Stress Disorder (PTSD) and Military Service

PTSD is positively correlated with combat stress and sexual abuse among women and men.
Source: John Gomez/Shutterstock.com.

posttraumatic stress disorder among women and men who have served during the military conflicts in Iraq and Afghanistan. Tragically, this group of veterans—male and female—has reported the additional psychological burden associated with sexual abuse during their tours of duty (Worthen, 2011).

Emotional symptoms of PTSD include apathy, anxiety, and survivor guilt. Cognitive symptoms include hypervigilance, difficulty concentrating, recurring memories that are difficult to control, and flashbacks of the event. Behavioral symptoms include insomnia and social detachment. PTSD is especially common among rape survivors; those who were sexually abused as children are particularly vulnerable (Nishith, Mechanic, & Resick, 2000). Rape survivors initially experience intense anxiety and major depressive disorder, which tend to diminish gradually over the first year. Nonetheless, 20 percent of rape survivors have severe, long-lasting emotional scars (Hanson, 1990).

PTSD can affect children as well as adults. One factor that has been found to increase the risk of developing PTSD after trauma is growing up with parents who fail to cope effectively with trauma. For example, parents may express their distress and frustration by lashing out at others. One study was conducted of almost 400 families that were affected by Hurricane Katrina in New Orleans, Louisiana, in 2005. Researchers found that maladaptive coping by parents, such as resorting to physical punishment of their children, increased a child's risk for PTSD (Kelley et al., 2010). Perhaps providing positive support to parents experiencing stress from a traumatic event would protect their children from developing PTSD.

PTSD, along with anxiety disorders, has been linked to the amygdala, a brain structure that maintains our vigilance against potential threats (see Chapter 3). A study that used functional magnetic resonance imaging found that combat veterans with PTSD had greater amygdala activity in response to threatening stimuli than did combat veterans without PTSD (Rauch et al., 2000). In another study, participants were scanned in an fMRI and shown a series of negative, neutral, or positive photographs. When participants with PTSD were presented with the negative emotional photographs, the scans demonstrated an exaggerated response from the amygdala. One week later, the participants returned and were given a recognition memory task, where they were presented with half of the original photographs. Scans in this session demonstrated that the hippocampus—a brain structure that plays a critical role in the formation of long-term memory—was overactive for the negative images that participants remembered. There was no change in the hippocampus for the negative images that participants had forgotten (Brohawn, Offringa, Pfaff, Hughes, & Shin, 2010). Together, these fMRI studies suggest that heightened brain processing in brain areas is associated with learning and memory and processing of trauma-related information.

PTSD also is associated with an increased risk of physical illness. For example, in 1980, the state of Washington was struck by a natural disaster—the eruption of the Mount Saint Helens volcano in the Cascade Mountains. Though more than 100 miles from the volcano, the town of Othello was covered by volcanic ash. Residents of that farming community suffered the distress of their fields being covered with ash, the fear of the effects of the ash on their health, and the dread that the volcano would erupt again. During the 6 months that followed the disaster, a local medical clinic reported an almost 200 percent increase in stress-related illnesses among the residents of Othello. There also was an almost 20 percent increase in the local death rate (Adams & Adams, 1984). Though the long-term health effects of volcanic ash exposure have not been studied, it is conceivable that exposure to the ash itself posed an additional health hazard (Baxter et al., 1999).

Daily Hassles

Though major life changes are important stress-inducing events, they are not the sole ones. Richard Lazarus (1922–2002) and his colleagues found other important, though less dramatic, stress-inducing events: the *hassles* of everyday life. A typical day can be filled with dozens of hassles, such as forgetting one's keys, being stuck in traffic, or dealing with a rude salesclerk. People who experience the cumulative effect of many daily hassles are more likely to suffer from health problems, including headaches, sore throats, and influenza (DeLongis, Folkman, & Lazarus, 1988).

Life Changes and Daily Hassles

Life changes can promote illness indirectly by increasing daily hassles. Some studies have even found that there is a stronger association between hassles and illness than between life changes and illness (Ruffin, 1993). For example, a study that examined 930 victims of a devastating hurricane found that the stress they experienced was due less to the hurricane itself and more to the chronic physical, family, and financial hassles it created for them (Norris & Uhl, 1993).

Our adrenal glands respond to stress by increasing their secretion of the hormones cortisol, epinephrine, and norepinephrine (see Figure 16-3). Though these hormones help us adapt to stressors, they also impair the immune system's ability to protect us from illness. And increases in daily hassles are indeed associated with adverse effects on the immune response (Peters, Godaert, Ballieux, & Heijnen, 2003). Daily hassles also can indirectly impair health by triggering unhealthy behaviors, including smoking more, exercising less, and eating fattier foods (Twisk, Snel, Kemper, & van Mechelen, 1999). Prolonged exposure to stress can decrease immune function, increase the release of *cytokines* (molecules that move cells toward areas of inflammation), alter the ability to cope with stressors, and affect brain regions associated with learning and memory (McEwen, 2004).

Prospective Studies of Daily Hassles

Most research on the relationship between daily hassles and illnesses makes it difficult to determine whether the two are just correlated with each other or whether hassles actually promote illness. This difficulty is because few *prospective* studies have been conducted on the relationship between hassles and health. A prospective study would investigate whether a person's current level of hassles is predictive of his or her future health. Prospective studies contrast with *retrospective* studies, which simply find that people who are ill report more hassles in their recent past.

One of the few prospective studies of the effects of daily hassles found that hassles do, in fact, promote illness. On two occasions, adolescent girls who served as participants in the study were asked to indicate, for each of 20 commonly experienced circumstances, whether it had occurred in their lives and whether they rated its occurrence as positive or negative. They also completed an illness symptoms checklist and a measure of depression. The results indicated that negative circumstances were associated with depressed mood and poor health. But this finding was true only when the girls also reported low levels of positive circumstances, or *uplifts*. Apparently, uplifts can buffer the effects of hassles, making them have fewer negative effects (Siegel & Brown, 1988).

These results, again, are in keeping with Selye's distinction between distress (such as hassles) and eustress (such as uplifts). In fact, the immune system response can be activated during periods of eustress, as well as during periods of distress. This finding was demonstrated in a study in which healthy university students were exposed to an *antigen* (that is, a substance that evokes an immune response). Three weeks later, those students who had experienced more "good stress" had higher lymphocyte proliferation, a measure of the immune response, than did those who had experienced more "bad stress" (Snyder, Roghmann, & Sigal, 1993). During times of maximum hassles, such as the last few weeks of a semester, students might do well to seek compensatory uplifts, such as visiting a friend, seeing a movie, or going to a party. However, it is well known that the immune system is activated during periods of distress, and the adverse effects of psychological stress can also be examined. The wear and tear of caring for aging relatives who suffer from the neurocognitive disorders associated with Alzheimer's disease can cause stress. Kiecolt-Glaser and colleagues made small wounds in the forearms of caregivers of family members with Alzheimer's disease and a control group who were not providing care to family members. When compared to the control group, the caregivers had slower rates of healing and lower levels of helpful immune cells (Kiecolt-Glaser, Marucha, Malarkey, Mercado, & Glaser, 1995). A more recent meta-analysis examining 11 studies of the wound-healing literature confirmed a link between psychological stress and impaired healing of wounds (Walburn, Vedhara, Hankins, Rixon, & Weinman, 2009).

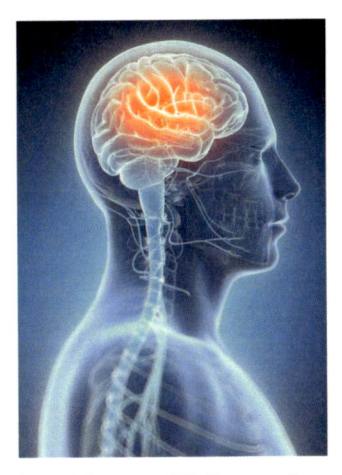

Cytokines and Inflammation

Chronic stress can lead to an increase in cytokine production in the nervous system. Elevated cytokine levels are thought to play a role in the development of psychological disorders related to stress and depression.
Source: Sebastian Kaulitzki/Shutterstock.com.

Together, these studies indicate that both high and chronic stress can impair the strength of your immune system.

Section Review: Psychological Stress and Stressors

1. Why are cancer and cardiovascular disease the most common causes of death today, though they were not a century ago?

2. Why do some researchers believe that life changes create stress through their effects on daily hassles?

3. What are the characteristics of posttraumatic stress disorder?

The Biopsychology of Stress and Illness

Whether it is caused by life changes or daily hassles, stress is marked by physiological arousal and, in some cases, diminished resistance to disease. In the 19th century, English physician Daniel Hack Tuke wrote one of the first books on the physiological effects of psychological stressors, *Illustrations of the Influence of the Mind on the Body* (Weiss, 1972). Today, Tuke's intellectual descendants study the effects of both physical and psychological stressors on physiological arousal. As explained in Chapter 12, physical and psychological stressors evoke the *fight-or-flight response*, first described by physiologist Walter Cannon (1915/1989). The fight-or-flight response involves activation of the sympathetic nervous system and secretion of stress hormones (including cortisol, epinephrine, and norepinephrine) by the adrenal glands.

The hormonal response to stress described in Chapter 12 does not vary significantly between the sexes. Recently, though, researchers have begun to investigate the role of one hormone produced in the hypothalamus and secreted by the pituitary gland—oxytocin—that might be related to gender differences in stress and coping. Both men and women under stress release oxytocin. However, oxytocin release is greater among women than men. Androgens appear to inhibit the release of oxytocin, and estrogens also modulate the effect of oxytocin, increasing its potential effect on women's stress response.

The differential effects of oxytocin in female and male stress responses have led Shelley Taylor and her colleagues (Taylor et al., 2000) to wonder whether the fight-or-flight response is more descriptive of the male stress response. According to this model, men are likely to respond to stress with hostile and aggressive behaviors, but women are more likely to respond to stress with a *tend-and-befriend* response. The results of animal and human studies suggest that the release of oxytocin in the female stress response is associated with three biopsychosocial outcomes: reduced anxiety, increased affiliative behaviors, and increased nurturing behaviors. More recently, Taylor found that women

Fight-or-Flight? Or Tend-and-Befriend?

Men and women are affected differently by stressful relationships.
Source: Iakov Filimonov/Shutterstock.com.

566   Chapter 16 Psychology, Health, and Stress

in distressed relationships have higher levels of plasma oxytocin, whereas men in distressed relationships do not (Taylor, Saphire-Bernstein, & Seeman, 2010). As described in Chapter 4, gender-role socialization and family responsibilities have a profound influence on women's social lives—particularly in the domains of caregiving and interpersonal relationships. However, this research points to a biological factor that may contribute to gender differences in stress and coping.

General Adaptation Syndrome

Cannon's work influenced that of Hans Selye. Selye (1936) hoped to discover a new sex hormone. As part of his research, he injected rats with extracts of ovarian tissue. He found that the rats developed stomach ulcerations, enlarged adrenal glands, and atrophied spleens, lymph nodes, and thymus glands. Selye later observed that rats displayed this same response to a variety of stressors. This observation indicated that his initial findings were not necessarily caused by a sex hormone.

Selye also found that animals and people, in reacting to stressors, go through three stages, which he called the **general adaptation syndrome**. During the first stage, the *alarm reaction*, the body prepares to cope with the stressor by increasing activity in the sympathetic nervous system and adrenal glands (the fight-or-flight response). For example, medical students experiencing the stress of a series of academic exams respond with increased cortisol secretion (Malarkey, Pearl, Demers, & Kiecolt-Glaser, 1995). Selye noted that, during the alarm reaction, different stressors produce similar symptoms, including fatigue, fever, headache, and loss of appetite.

If the body continues to be exposed to the stressor, it enters the *stage of resistance*, during which it becomes more resistant to the stressor. Yet, during the stage of resistance, the body's resistance to disease may decline. During final exams week, you might be able to cope well enough to study for all your exams, but soon after finals are over, you might come down with the flu. If you succumb to disease, you might have entered the *stage of exhaustion*. At this point, the body's resistance to disease collapses; in extreme cases, the person might die. Figure 16-1 illustrates the stages of the general adaptation syndrome.

The fight-or-flight response evolved because it helped animals and human beings cope with periodic stressors, such as wildfires or animal attacks. Unfortunately, in modern industrialized countries, we are subjected to continual, rather than periodic, stressors. The repeated activation of the fight-or-flight response takes its toll on the body, possibly causing or aggravating diseases. Stress-affected noninfectious diseases include asthma (Moran, 1991), diabetes (Fisher, Delamater, Bertelson, & Kirkley, 1982), gastric ulcers (Young, Richter, Bradley, & Anderson, 1987), and essential hypertension (Mellors, Boyle, & Roberts, 1994). Such diseases traditionally have been called *psychosomatic*, based on the assumption that they are caused or worsened by emotional factors (Fava & Sonino, 2000).

general adaptation syndrome As first identified by Hans Selye, the body's stress response, which includes the stages of alarm, resistance, and exhaustion.

Stress and Cardiovascular Disease

Of all the diseases that might be affected by stress, coronary heart disease has received the most attention from health psychologists. Researchers study the effects of stress on the cardiovascular system and coronary-prone (so-called Type A) behavior.

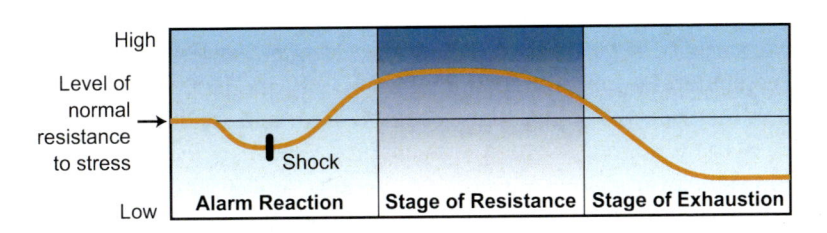

FIGURE 16-1 General Adaptation Syndrome

According to Hans Selye, when we react to stressors, we pass through one or more of the three stages of the general adaptation syndrome. These stages are the alarm reaction, the stage of resistance, and the stage of exhaustion.

Chapter 16 Psychology, Health, and Stress

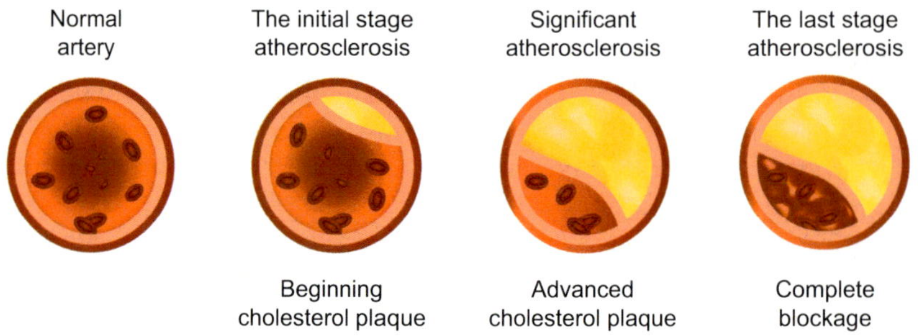

The Relationship of Stress to Atherosclerosis

Chronic stress can lead to overeating, which promotes glucose uptake. This promotes both an increase in body fat and atherosclerotic plaque buildup. Red blood cells are blocked as arteries narrow due to plaque buildup.
Source: Mrs_Bazilio/Shutterstock.com.

Normal artery

The initial stage atherosclerosis
Beginning cholesterol plaque

Significant atherosclerosis
Advanced cholesterol plaque

The last stage atherosclerosis
Complete blockage

Cardiovascular Effects of Stress

Coronary heart disease is caused by *atherosclerosis*, which is promoted by cholesterol deposits in the coronary arteries. Even the stress of everyday college life can affect the level of cholesterol in a person's blood. College students who merely anticipate an upcoming exam show significant increases in their levels of blood cholesterol (Van Doornen & van Blokland, 1987). Stress also can promote coronary heart disease by elevating heart rate and blood pressure, as well as by stimulating the release of stress hormones. These responses can damage the walls of the coronary arteries, making them more susceptible to the buildup of cholesterol plaques (Krantz & Manuck, 1984).

Type A Behavior and Cardiovascular Disease

On November 2, 1988, "Iron Mike" Ditka, the tough head coach of the Chicago Bears football team, was hospitalized with a mild heart attack. In a televised interview on ESPN, Ditka's physician reported that Ditka had none of the common physical risk factors for coronary heart disease. His only risk factor was a psychological one: *Type A behavior*. A published review of research on Type A behavior in middle-aged men (such as Mike Ditka) found that Type A behavior was present in 70 percent of those with coronary heart disease and in only 46 percent of those who were healthy (Miller, Turner, Tindale, Posavac, & Dugoni, 1991). And in men, Type A behavior is associated with an increased risk of cardiovascular disease, including strokes (Kim et al., 1998)—though its presence does not guarantee coronary heart disease, and its absence does not guarantee freedom from it.

Characteristics of Type A Behavior In the late 1950s, San Francisco cardiologist Meyer Friedman noticed that his patients were easily angered, highly competitive, and driven to do more and more in less and less time. Friedman, with his colleague Ray Rosenman, called this syndrome of behaviors **Type A behavior**. In contrast, *Type B behavior* is characterized by patience, an even temper, and willingness to do a limited number of things in a reasonable amount of time. The Type A person also might show time urgency by changing lanes to advance a single car length, chronic activation by staying busy most of every day, and *multiphasic activity* by texting, eating, and watching television at the same time. This lifestyle means that the Type A person is in a constant state of fight or flight. Would this lifestyle be associated with a greater risk of heart disease?

Friedman and Rosenman asked managers and supervisors of large companies to identify colleagues who fit the description of the Type A and Type B behavior patterns. They identified samples of men, including many executives, who fit each pattern. No women were included because, at the time, relatively few women were in executive positions. Participants were interviewed about their medical history and behavioral tendencies, such as being driven to succeed, feeling highly competitive, and feeling under chronic time pressure. They were observed for body movements, tone of voice, teeth clenching, and any observable signs of impatience. Based on the interview, 69 of the men were labeled pure Type A, and 58 of the men were labeled pure Type B.

Friedman and Rosenman found that the Type A participants had significantly higher levels of blood cholesterol than did the Type B participants. More important, 28 percent of the Type A participants had symptoms of coronary heart disease, but only 4 percent of the Type B participants had such symptoms. Before leaping to the conclusion that

Type A behavior A syndrome—marked by impatience, hostility, and extreme competitiveness—that is associated with the development of coronary heart disease.

the study definitely demonstrated that Type A behavior promotes heart disease, note two other findings: First, the Type A participants smoked much more than the Type B participants did. Today, we know that smoking is a major risk factor in heart disease. Second, the Type A participants' parents had a higher incidence of coronary heart disease than did the Type B participants' parents. Perhaps the Type A participants inherited a genetic tendency to develop heart disease (Vogler, Mcclearn, Snieder, & Boomsma, 1997). Of course, there could just as well be a genetic tendency toward Type A behavior, which in turn might promote heart disease. In any case, Friedman and Rosenman contributed one of the first formal studies demonstrating a possible link between behavior and heart disease. Later, based on subsequent research findings, Friedman and Rosenman boldly concluded:

> In the absence of Type A behavior pattern, coronary heart disease almost never occurs before 70 years of age, regardless of the fatty foods eaten, the cigarettes smoked, or the lack of exercise. But when this behavior pattern is present, coronary heart disease can easily erupt in one's thirties or forties. (Friedman & Rosenman, 1974, p. xi)

Multiphasic Activity

The Type A behavior pattern is associated with multiphasic activity, in which the person engages in several activities at once as part of a continual effort to do more and more in less and less time.
Source: fizkes/Shutterstock.com.

In 1975, Friedman, Rosenman, and their colleagues reported the results of a study on coronary heart disease that began in 1960 and lasted 9 years—the Western Collaborative Group Study (Rosenman et al., 1975). They studied more than 3,000 middle-aged men who were free of heart disease at the beginning of the study. Each of the men was categorized as Type A or Type B, based on an interview. The results indicated that, during the period of the study, the men classified as Type A were more than twice as likely to develop coronary heart disease as were the men classified as Type B.

The pattern of behavior shown by Type A participants indicates that they are overconcerned with control of their environment. This concern leads to repeated physiological arousal when other people, time constraints, or personal responsibilities threaten their sense of control. Type A behavior is not just a style of responding to the environment; it can induce the very environmental circumstances that evoke it. This finding was illustrated in a study that compared Type A and Type B police radio dispatchers during work shifts. Type A dispatchers generated more job pressures by initiating extra work for themselves and attending to multiple tasks at the same time. Moreover, their coworkers and supervisors looked to them when there were additional tasks to be performed. So, Type A people can help create work conditions that maintain their driven, time-urgent, impatient behavioral style (Kirmeyer & Biggers, 1988).

But the role of Type A behavior in coronary heart disease was brought into question by the results of a 22-year follow-up of participants in a large-scale study of Type A behavior and coronary heart disease mortality (Ragland & Brand, 1988). In fact, Type A participants who had suffered a heart attack had a somewhat *lower* risk of a second heart attack. Of course, this result might have been due to other factors, such as greater medical attention given to Type A than to Type B heart attack victims. Though this study indicated that the *overall* pattern of Type A behavior is unrelated to coronary heart disease, research findings have been converging on a specific component of the Type A behavior pattern—*hostility*—as the factor most related to coronary heart disease (Miller, Smith, Turner, Guijarro, & Hallet, 1996). According to researcher Redford Williams, hostility has emerged as an independent risk factor for cardiovascular disease (Suarez, Kuhn, Schanberg, Williams, & Zimmermann, 1998).

Effects of Type A Behavior Regardless of whether hostility or some other aspect of Type A behavior promotes coronary heart disease, how might it do so? One way might be by inducing a chronic stress response. In fact, people who display hostility are more physiologically reactive to physical and emotional stressors (Smith, Cranford, & Mann, 2000). One study investigated the relationship between hostility and cardiovascular reactivity in social interactions among male and female undergraduates. The participants discussed a controversial topic with a confederate who was instructed to disagree with the participant. Female and male participants who scored high on a measure of hostility had greater increases in blood pressure during the discussion than did participants who scored low on hostility (Davis, Matthews, & McGrath, 2000).

High physiological reactivity also might unleash harmful effects through the actions of stress hormones. This hypothesis was confirmed in a study in which Redford Williams and his colleagues (1982) had Type A and Type B male college students compete in a stressful laboratory task. The results indicated that the Type A students displayed a significantly greater increase in levels of the adrenal gland stress hormones cortisol, epinephrine, and norepinephrine. These stress hormones promote the buildup of cholesterol plaques on the walls of arteries, increasing the risk of heart attacks.

The results of a study conducted in northern Ireland suggests that Type A behavior also might indirectly contribute to cardiovascular disease by promoting the eating of fast foods, which are convenient but also have higher levels of fat, salt, and sugar than more healthful food (Barker, Thompson, & McClean, 1996). Another possible factor mediating the effect of Type A behavior on coronary heart disease is the tendency of Type A people to ignore symptoms of illness. Before being hospitalized with his heart attack, Mike Ditka had ignored pain earlier in the week until his assistant coaches forced him to seek medical attention. This tendency of Type A people to discount their symptoms first appears in childhood. Type A children are less likely to complain of symptoms of illness, and Type A children who have surgery miss fewer days of school than do Type B children (Leikin, Firestone, & McGrath, 1988).

Development of Type A Behavior Though there is only weak evidence of a hereditary basis for Type A behavior, there is strong evidence that the pattern runs in families. Karen Matthews, a leading researcher on Type A behavior, points to child-rearing practices as the primary origin of Type A behavior. Parents of Type A children encourage them to try harder even when they do well and offer them few spontaneous positive comments. Type A children might be given no standards except "Do better," which makes it difficult for them to develop internal standards of achievement. They may then seek to compare their academic performance with the best in their class. This reaction might contribute to the development of the hard-driving component of the Type A behavior pattern (Matthews & Woodall, 1988).

There also are sociocultural differences in Type A behavior tendencies. One study found that low socioeconomic status was associated with increased cardiovascular reactivity in response to stress among African American and European American children (Gump, Matthews, & Raeikkoenen, 1999). And African American participants who experience stereotype threat (see Chapter 10) while performing a laboratory task have greater increases in blood pressure than do European American or African American participants who do not experience stereotype threat (Blascovich, Spencer, Quinn, & Steele, 2001). In fact, the term *John Henryism* has been coined to describe the psychological effects of trying to actively cope with chronic stress in the face of insurmountable odds—as many poor and ethnic minority individuals must do. John Henryism appears to be particularly lethal for African American men (Merritt, Bennett, Williams, Sollers, & Thayer, 2004).

Modification of Type A Behavior Because of the possible association between Type A behavior and coronary heart disease, its modification might be wise. But a paradox of Type A behavior is that Type A persons are not necessarily disturbed by their behavior. Why change a behavior pattern that is rewarded in competitive Western society? Programs to modify the Type A behavior of those who are willing to participate try to alter specific components of the Type A behavior pattern, particularly impatience, hostility, and competitiveness. One hostility-reduction program reduced diastolic blood pressure in participants compared to nonparticipants (Gidron, Davidson, & Bata, 1999). And a Swedish intervention study reduced both hostility and time pressure in Type A participants (Karlberg, Krakau, & Unden, 1998).

Stress and Immune Functioning

In 1884, a physician reported in a British medical journal that the depressed mood experienced by mourners at funerals predisposed them to develop illnesses (Baker, 1987). A century later, a research study provided a scientific basis for this observation that stress,

FIGURE 16-2
Immune Response to Bereavement

During the first 2 months after the death of their wives, widowers showed a decrease in the proliferation of lymphocytes in response to doses of antigens.

Source: Data from S. J. Schleifer et al., Suppression of lymphocytic stimulation following bereavement, *Journal of the American Medical Association, 250*, 374–377.

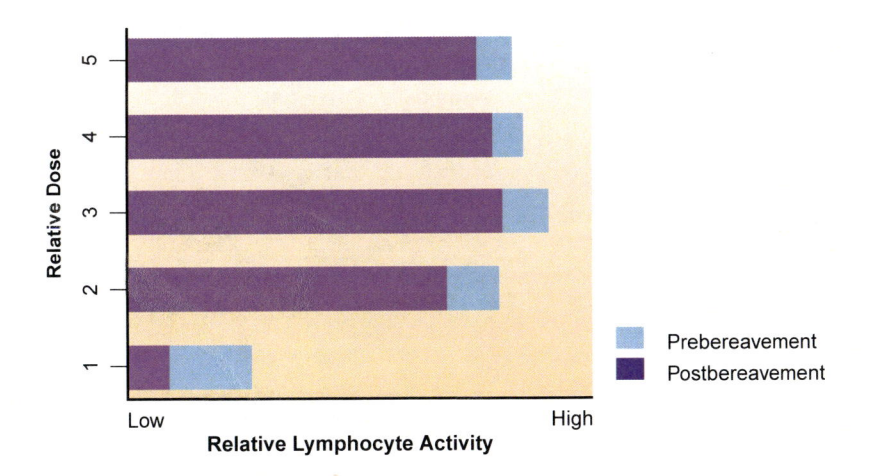

depressed mood, and immune functioning are linked. As shown in Figure 16-2, the study found that men whose wives had died of breast cancer showed impaired functioning of their immune systems during the first 2 months of their bereavement (Schleifer, Keller, Camerino, Thornton, & Stein, 1983). This finding agrees with research showing that major depressive disorder is associated with suppression of the immune system (McGuire, Kiecolt-Glaser, & Glaser, 2002). This research has led to the hypothesis that one cause of major depressive disorder is immunosuppression. More recent research has suggested that this can be extended to inflammation (Savitz, Tan, Taylor, Drevets, & Teague, 2013) and has led to the new field of psychoneuroimmunology.

psychoneuroimmunology The interdisciplinary field that studies the relationship between psychological factors and physical illness.

Psychoneuroimmunology

The realization that stressful events, such as the death of a loved one, can impair the immune system led to the emergence of **psychoneuroimmunology**, the interdisciplinary field that studies the relationship between psychological factors and illness, especially the effects of stress on the immune system (Ader, 2001). Though many of the mechanisms by which stress suppresses the immune system remain to be determined, one mechanism is well established (see Figure 16-3). Stress prompts the hypothalamus to secrete a hormone that stimulates the pituitary gland to secrete adrenocorticotropic hormone (ACTH), which then stimulates the adrenal cortex to secrete corticosteroids. The hypothalamus also increases activity in the sympathetic nervous system, which stimulates the adrenal medulla to secrete the hormones epinephrine and norepinephrine. As noted in the section

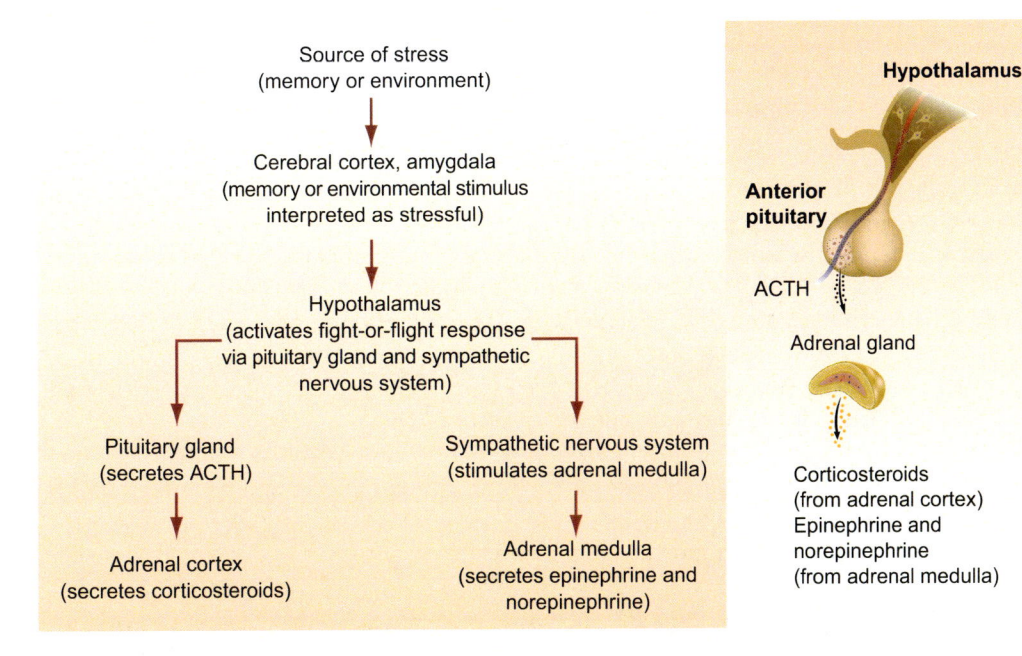

FIGURE 16-3
Stress Pathways

When the cerebral cortex processes stressful memories or stressful input from the immediate environment, it stimulates a physiological response by way of the endocrine system and the sympathetic nervous system. Both pathways involve the hypothalamus. The hypothalamus signals the pituitary gland, which secretes adrenocorticotropic hormone (ACTH). ACTH, in turn, stimulates the adrenal cortex to secrete corticosteroid hormones, which mobilize the body's energy stores, reduce tissue inflammation, and inhibit the immune response. The hypothalamus also sends signals through the sympathetic nervous system to the adrenal medulla, which in turn stimulates the release of epinephrine and norepinephrine. These hormones contribute to the physiological arousal characteristic of the fight-or-flight response.

Source: Alila Medical Media/Shutterstock.com.

Chapter 16 Psychology, Health, and Stress

FIGURE 16-4
The Role of T-Lymphocytes in the Immune Response

This figure reflects one of many normal processes of immune activation, when the body detects an antigen (a substance that evokes an immune response). Macrophages recruit helper and memory T cells to multiply. The killer cells recognize and destroy cells infected with the antigen. After the process slows down, a small number of T cells live on as memory cells. Chronic stress can alter this process and can suppress the immune responses.
Source: Designua/Shutterstock.com.

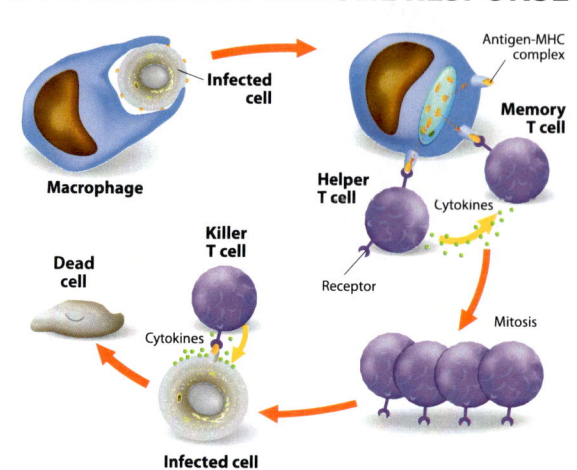

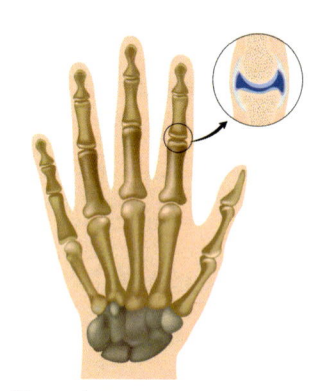

CELL-MEDIATED IMMUNE RESPONSE

Normal

Rheumatoid arthritis

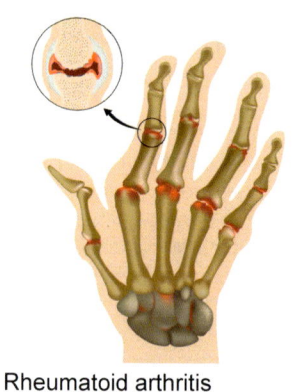

FIGURE 16-5
Stress and Rheumatoid Arthritis

Psychological stress aggravates rheumatoid arthritis. Though the exact mechanisms are unknown, cytokines are likely to play a role.
Source: Alila Medical Media/Shutterstock.com.

"Daily Hassles," though adrenal hormones might make us more resistant to stressors, they also can impair our immune systems (Kiecolt-Glaser & Glaser, 1995).

A review of research studies found that major depressive disorder is consistently associated with large decreases in natural killer cell activity (Herbert & Cohen, 1993). *Natural killer cells* are lymphocytes responsible for triggering cytokine release. More recent evidence suggests that other immune cells also are involved in major depressive disorder. One study of men diagnosed with major depressive disorder who were not taking antidepressants found an increase in the number of white blood cells and a decrease in the number of specialized T-lymphocytes (Savitz, Tan, Taylor, Drevets, & Teague, 2013).

The cells chiefly responsible for the immunological response to infections are white blood cells called B-lymphocytes and T-lymphocytes. *B-lymphocytes* attack invading bacteria, and *T-lymphocytes* attack viruses, cancer cells, and foreign tissues (see Figure 16-4). The immunosuppressive effects of stress hormones might explain why Apollo astronauts, after returning to Earth from stressful trips to the moon, had impaired immune responses (Jemmott & Locke, 1984). But you do not have to go to the moon to experience stress-induced suppression of your immune response, as revealed in a study of college students. After the students had given speeches that were evaluated for their merit, they showed impairment of their immune response (Marsland, Manuck, Fazzari, & Stewart, 1995). And the chronic stress experienced by women who care for husbands suffering from Alzheimer's disease is associated with impaired immune functioning (Wu et al., 1999). In addition, there is a positive relationship between stressful life events and the progression of HIV disease (Leserman, 2003).

Conditioning the Immune Response

Given that the immune system is affected by stressful life experiences, is it conceivable that learning could alter the immune response? This question inspired the experiment described in "The Research Process" feature.

Perhaps classical conditioning one day will be applied clinically to enhance immune responses in people who have low resistance to infections, such as people who are HIV-positive or living with AIDS. People with AIDS experience stress induced by their illness, as well as hostile social reactions. Such stress might further impair the functioning of their immune systems, making them even more vulnerable to infections that often prove fatal (Ironson, Schneiderman, Kumar, & Antoni, 1994).

Classical conditioning also might be used to suppress undesirable immune responses, such as those that occur in *autoimmune diseases*, in which the immune system attacks a person's own body tissues as though they were foreign. One candidate for such treatment is rheumatoid arthritis (see Figure 16-5), which is affected by stress (Evers, Kraaimaat, Geenen, Jacobs, & Bijlsma, 2003; McEwen, 2004). Preliminary research indicates that another beneficial application of conditioned immunosuppression might be in preventing

The Research Process

Can the Immune Response Be Altered by Classical Conditioning?

Rationale

Certain chemicals can enhance or suppress the immune response. Researcher Robert Ader wondered whether such a chemical could be used as the basis for classically conditioning the immune response. He reasoned that a neutral stimulus paired with the chemical might come to have the same effect on the immune response. This possibility inspired him to test his hypothesis experimentally.

Method

Ader and his colleague Nicholas Cohen (1982) used the drug cyclophosphamide, which suppresses the immune system, as the unconditioned stimulus. When mice were injected with the drug, they experienced both nausea and immunosuppression—dual effects of the drug. Ader and Cohen used saccharin-flavored water as the neutral stimulus. They hoped that if the mice drank the water before being injected with the drug, the taste of sweet water would suppress their immune response to an antigen.

Results and Discussion

As Ader and Cohen expected, the mice developed an aversion to sweet-tasting water because they associated it with nausea caused by the drug. But when some of the mice were later forced to drink sweet-tasting water, several developed illnesses and died. Ader and Cohen attributed this result to conditioned suppression of the mice's immune response, with the sweet-tasting water having become a conditioned stimulus after being paired with the drug (see Figure 16-6). Many subsequent studies have provided additional evidence that the immune response is subject to classical conditioning (Ader, 2003). Animal research indicates that epinephrine and norepinephrine mediate conditioned immunosuppression (Lysle, Cunnick, & Maslonek, 1991).

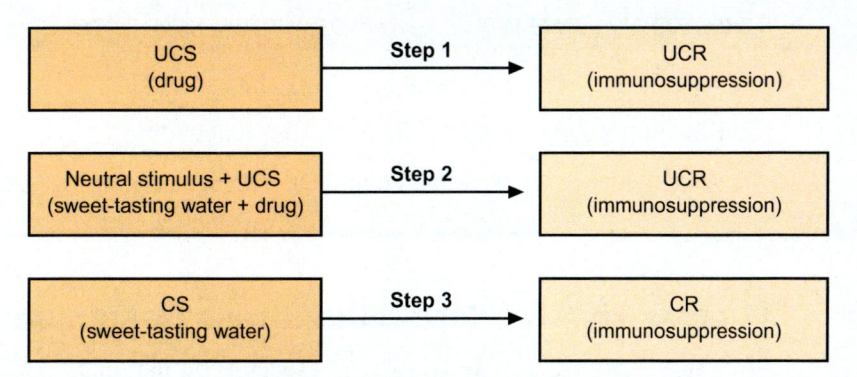

FIGURE 16-6 Conditioned Immunosuppression

When Ader and Cohen (1982) paired saccharin-sweetened water with cyclophosphamide, a drug that suppresses the immune response, they found that the sweet-tasting water itself came to elicit immunosuppression. (See Chapter 7 for a discussion of the relationship between the UCS, UCR, CS, and CR.)

---

the rejection of transplanted tissues and organs. In one study, heart transplants in rats were less likely to be rejected when the rats had been conditioned to suppress their immune response (Exton, Westermann, & Schedlowski, 2000).

Stress and Cancer

In the second century, the Greek physician Galen noted that depressed women were more likely than happy women to develop cancer. This relationship between emotionality and cancer has received support from modern research. Consider a study of medical students who were given personality tests in medical school and then assessed 30 years later. Of those participants who had been emotionally expressive, less than 1 percent had developed cancer. Those who had been loners, and presumably more emotionally controlled, were 16 times more likely to develop cancer than were those who were emotionally expressive (Shaffer, Graves, Swank, & Pearson, 1987). Other studies have supported the relationship between the tendency to suppress emotions and the development of cancer (Andersen, Kiecolt-Glaser, & Glaser, 1994), apparently because emotion suppression is associated with suppression of the immune response (Eysenck, 1994). A recent meta-analysis has found that psychosocial variables, such as personality, emotionality, and coping, have a modest but consistent relationship to the development of cancer (McKenna, Zevon, Corn, & Rounds, 1999). On the other hand, optimism appears to be associated with lower levels of stress, slower progression of disease, and improved survival rates in patients with certain cancers (Carver et al., 2005; de Moor et al., 2006).

Assuming that our emotions can affect the progress of cancer, what mechanisms might account for this relationship? Stress might indirectly promote cancer by affecting health behaviors, such as smoking tobacco, eating high-fat foods, and drinking too much alcohol. Stress also might directly interfere with the immune system's ability to defend against cancer. In fact, during periods when they are under intense academic pressure, medical students exhibit a reduction in the activity of natural killer cells, the lymphocytes responsible for detecting and destroying cancer cells (Glaser, Rice, Speicher, Stout, & Kiecolt-Glaser, 1986). And women who suffered repeated bouts of chronic depressed mood years earlier are more prone to developing breast cancer (Jacobs & Bovasso, 2000). Simply being diagnosed with cancer or being treated for cancer can induce stress-related suppression of the very immune responses that are needed to combat the cancer (Pompe, Antoni, & Heijnen, 1998). In reflecting on the link between psychological factors and cancer, note that though stress can *impair* the immune system's ability to destroy cancerous cells, there is little evidence that stress can directly *cause* normal cells to become cancerous (Levenson & Bemis, 1991).

Section Review: The Biopsychology of Stress and Illness

1. What is the relationship between stress and cancer?
2. How might stress impair immune system functioning?
3. What evidence is there that the immune response can be classically conditioned?

Factors That Moderate the Stress Response

More than 2,000 years ago, Hippocrates recognized the relationship between individual factors and physiological responses when he observed that it is more important to know what sort of person has a disease than to know what sort of disease a person has. Because of variability among individuals, a given stressor will not evoke the same response in every person. Our reactions to stress are moderated by a variety of factors. These factors include *physiological reactivity*, *cognitive appraisal*, *explanatory style*, *perceived control*, *psychological hardiness*, and *social support*.

Physiological Reactivity

People differ in their pattern of physiological responses to stressors (Walsh, Wilding, & Eysenck, 1994). **Physiological reactivity** refers to increased heart rate, blood pressure, stress hormone secretion, and other physiological activity in response to stressors. People with slower cardiovascular recovery after exposure to stress are more prone to develop high blood pressure (Hocking-Schuler & O'Brien, 1997). In one study, men with mild hypertension played a video game while their heart rate and blood pressure were measured. Those men who displayed greater increases in heart rate and blood pressure also had higher levels of blood cholesterol (Jorgensen, Nash, Lasser, Hymowitz, & Langer, 1988). This finding might help explain why people with greater physiological reactivity have a higher risk of atherosclerosis (Aheneku, Nwosu, & Aheneku, 2000). And men show greater increases than women in both cardiovascular activity and secretion of stress hormones such as cortisol in response to stressors. This difference might contribute to the greater vulnerability of men to coronary heart disease (Earle, Linden, & Weinberg, 1999).

physiological reactivity The extent to which a person displays increases in heart rate, blood pressure, stress hormone secretion, and other physiological activity in response to stressors.

More recent research supports the hypothesis that there is a genetic factor in physiological responses to stressors. Men who have a mutation in the receptor that responds to cortisol have enhanced cortisol secretion and heart rate responses to psychosocial stressors (DeRijk et al., 2006). Studying mutations in this receptor could help researchers understand physiological predispositions to psychological disorders related to stress and major depressive disorder.

Cognitive Appraisal

Though Hans Selye believed that all stressors produce similar patterns of physiological responses, more recent research indicates that different stressors may produce different patterns (Krantz & Manuck, 1984). Richard Lazarus, whose work on daily hassles was discussed earlier in the chapter, believed that one of the reasons that different stressors can produce different responses in the same person is that the person interprets the two stressors differently. This difference in interpretation is known as **cognitive appraisal** (Lazarus, 1993), which Lazarus also used as the basis of his theory of emotion (see Chapter 12).

Cognitive appraisal involves two stages: primary appraisal and secondary appraisal. In *primary appraisal*, you judge whether a situation requires a coping response. If you judge that a situation requires a coping response, you then engage in *secondary appraisal* by determining whether you have the ability to cope with the situation. The greater the perceived controllability of a stressful situation, the lower its perceived stressfulness (Peeters, Buunk, & Schaufeli, 1995). Consider final exams. Students who perceive their exams to be highly demanding and who lack confidence in their ability to perform well on them will experience greater stress than will students who perceive their upcoming exams as moderately demanding and are confident of their ability to perform well. This view has been supported by research finding more positive emotion and better coping among people who appraise stressors as challenging, rather than threatening (Folkman & Moskowitz, 2000).

cognitive appraisal The subjective interpretation of the severity of a stressor.

Explanatory Style

People diagnosed with major depressive disorder (see Chapter 14) tend to have a pessimistic **explanatory style**. They attribute unpleasant events to *internal*, *stable*, and *global* characteristics of themselves. In other words, depressed people attribute unpleasant events to their own unchanging, pervasive, and personal characteristics. The possible role of a pessimistic explanatory style in the promotion of illness was supported by a retrospective study of 99 graduates of the Harvard University classes of 1942–1944. Graduates who had had a pessimistic explanatory style at the age of 25 (based on questionnaires they had completed at that time) became less healthy between the ages of 45 and 60 than did graduates who did not have a pessimistic explanatory style. All the graduates had been healthy at age 25 (Peterson, Seligman, & Vaillant, 1988).

explanatory style The tendency to explain events optimistically or pessimistically.

The researchers hypothesized that pessimism might make people less likely to take actions to counter the effects of negative life events, leading to more severe stress in their lives. A pessimistic explanatory style might increase susceptibility to illness by leading to poor health habits, suppression of the immune system, and withdrawal from sources of social support. Each of these factors can promote illness. For example, one study found that older adults with a pessimistic explanatory style showed a weaker immune response to antigens than did older adults who did not exhibit a pessimistic explanatory style (Kamen-Siegel, Rodin, Seligman, & Dwyer, 1991).

One research study of male college students who were exposed to acute psychological stress found that higher levels of optimism were associated with smaller amounts of cytokines in their blood. Interestingly, there was no direct association between cytokine responses and negative mood. This finding suggests that the optimism-cytokine relationship is mediated by stress (Brydon, Walker, Wawrzyniak, Chart, & Steptoe, 2009). These findings were supported by a study in which college students with a pessimistic explanatory style were more likely to develop physical illnesses (Jackson, Sellers, & Peterson, 2002). Moreover, explanatory style is related to premature mortality. In particular, catastrophizing (operationally defined as making global attributions) has been found to predict mortality, especially among men (Peterson, Seligman, Yurko, Martin, & Friedman, 1998).

Fortunately, for many people, as demonstrated by health psychologist Shelley Taylor (Taylor, Lerner, Sherman, Sage, & McDowell, 2003), people with a more optimistic outlook on life—even a somewhat unrealistically positive one—are less susceptible to illness. For example, optimistic people are less likely than pessimistic people to develop cardiovascular disease (Kubzansky, Sparrow, Vokonas, & Kawachi, 2001).

Perceived Control

In a best-selling book describing his recovery from a massive heart attack, Norman Cousins, former editor of the *Saturday Review*, claimed that his insistence on taking personal responsibility for his recovery—including devising his own rehabilitation program—helped him regain his health. In contrast, as Cousins noted in his book, "good patients" (patients who remain passive) discover that "a weak body becomes weaker in a mood of total surrender" (Cousins, 1983, p. 223).

Research findings have supported Cousins's anecdotal report by converging on **perceived control** over stressors as one of the most important factors moderating the relationship between stress and illness. Perceived control over stressors reduces stress (Shirom, Melamed, & Nir-Dotan, 2000). People who work at demanding jobs and feel they have little control over job stressors are more likely to develop coronary heart disease (Krantz, Contrada, Hill, & Friedler, 1988). And consider impoverished residents of urban slums who are subjected to environmental factors out of their control, such as pollution, crowding, noise, and traffic. One study found that slum dwellers in Delhi, India, reported **learned helplessness**—the feeling that one has little control over events in one's life—in coping with these stressors (Siddiqui & Pandey, 2003) (see Chapter 7).

As mentioned in Chapter 13, there are cultural differences in perceived control (O'Connor & Shimizu, 2002). People with a sense of *primary control* believe that they can directly influence other people or the environment. People with a sense of *secondary control* accept and adjust to their environment. Whereas American culture emphasizes the importance of primary control, Japanese culture promotes secondary control (Weisz, Rothbaum, & Blackburn, 1984). For example, in one study American and Japanese participants in aerobics classes responded to a questionnaire assessing their reasons for choosing a class and their responses to being in a difficult class. American participants were more likely to choose a class based on convenience and to simplify moves they felt were too difficult. Japanese participants were more likely to choose classes based on their ability level and to work harder on moves that they felt were too difficult (Morling, 2000).

People in all walks of life benefit from a sense of control over the stressors that affect them. Residents of retirement homes who are given greater responsibility for self-care and everyday activities live longer and healthier lives than do residents whose lives are controlled by staff members (Langer & Rodin, 1976). People who feel a lack of control tend to secrete more adrenal hormones in response to stress (Peters et al., 1998), which in turn can impair their immune systems. In fact, people who lack a sense of control over their lives show reduced T helper cell (Brosschot et al., 1998) and natural killer cell (Reynaert, Janne, Bosly, & Staquet, 1995) activity in response to stressors. This reduction in cellular activity could impair their immunological defense against cancer.

Studying people's perceptions of stress is a complex task. Cognitive control does appear to decrease physiological responses to stress, and stressful events do appear to increase stress pathway responses (see Figure 16-3). Yet, successfully experiencing stressful events can help lead to a sense of cognitive control over future stressful events (Oldehinkel et al., 2011). Nevertheless, a potential consequence of exposure to uncontrollable stress is the state of physical and psychological exhaustion called **burnout**. Burnout is especially common among human-service providers, including university professors and other teachers (Watts & Robertson, 2011), police officers (Gana & Boblique, 2000), athletic coaches (Price & Weiss, 2000), and medical personnel (Peltzer, Mashego, & Mabeba, 2003).

---

perceived control The degree to which a person feels in control over life's stressors.

learned helplessness A feeling of futility caused by the belief that one has little or no control over events in one's life, which can make one stop trying and become depressed.

burnout A state of physical and psychological exhaustion associated with chronic exposure to uncontrollable stress.

Children who experience stress early in life, such as separation from the primary caregiver, maltreatment, or neglect, have been found to have difficulty in regulating cognitive processes and elevated stress-related hormones. One fMRI study of adolescents who experienced such early life stress found that brain areas associated with cognitive control were impaired (Mueller et al., 2010).

Psychological Hardiness

Psychologists Salvatore Maddi and Suzanne Kobasa were puzzled by the fact that while some people can work under chronic, intense pressure and remain healthy, others cannot. Maddi and Kobasa wondered whether this difference might be related to personality. To test this possibility scientifically, they gave a group of business executives a battery of personality tests and then conducted a 5-year, prospective study during which they periodically assessed the executives' health. Maddi and Kobasa found that those executives who were illness-resistant tended to share a set of personality characteristics that those who were illness-prone did not (Kobasa, Maddi, & Kahn, 1982).

Maddi and Kobasa called this set of personality characteristics **psychological hardiness**. They have found that people high in psychological hardiness are more resistant to stressors and, possibly as a result, are less susceptible to stress-related illness (Maddi, 2002). Other researchers have supported this finding as well. For example, a study of college undergraduates found that participants high in hardiness reported lower levels of stress and depression (Pengilly & Dowd, 2000). And a 10-week study of college students found a negative correlation between hardiness and visits to the college health center. That is, psychologically hardier students tended to be physically healthier than less hardy students (Mathis & Lecci, 1999). And psychological hardiness has been found to reduce burnout (Lo Bue, Taverniers, Mylle, & Euwema, 2013) and posttraumatic disorder symptoms among military personnel (Escolas, Pitts, Safer, & Bartone, 2013).

What characteristics do people high in psychological hardiness share? Kobasa found that hardy people face stressors with a sense of commitment, challenge, and control. People with a sense of *commitment* are wholeheartedly involved in everyday activities and social relationships, rather than being alienated from them. People with a sense of *challenge* view life's stressors as opportunities for personal growth rather than as burdens to be endured. And people with a sense of *control* believe they have the personal resources to cope with stressors, rather than being helpless in the face of them. Table 16-1 shows how individuals high or low in psychological hardiness might respond to stressors typically faced by college students.

But how does hardiness reduce susceptibility to illness? One way is by making hardy individuals less physiologically reactive to stressors, as demonstrated in a study of patients who were awaiting dental surgery (Solcova & Sykora, 1995). People who are higher in

> **psychological hardiness** A set of personality characteristics marked by feelings of commitment, challenge, and control that promotes resistance to stress.

TABLE 16-1 Psychological Hardiness

	Student High in Psychological Hardiness	Student Low in Psychological Hardiness
Commitment (vs. Alienation)	"Even though I'm a psychology major, I would like to learn all I can from my courses in English, history, and fine arts."	"I don't know why I have to waste my time taking courses that are not in my major."
Challenge (vs. Threat)	"My statistics course is difficult, but if I can master the material, I can do well in just about any course."	"My statistics course is too hard. Maybe I should drop the course so I don't get a low grade that hurts my GPA."
Control (vs. Helplessness)	"My Spanish professor wants us to make oral presentations of our term papers to the class. I suppose that if I practice enough, I should be able to do well."	"I can't believe that my Spanish professor wants us to make oral presentations of our term papers to the class. No matter how much I prepare, I'll just sound stupid."

psychological hardiness also have a stronger immune response to antigens (Dolbier et al., 2001) and miss work less frequently (Hystad, Eid, & Brevik, 2011). Another way that hardiness reduces susceptibility to illness is by affecting health habits. People high in psychological hardiness, compared to people low in it, are more likely to maintain good health habits in the face of stress (Wiebe & McCallum, 1986). Thus, hardy students may be more resistant to illness because they are more likely to eat well, take vitamins, exercise more, and seek medical attention for minor ailments, even when under stress. Stress-management programs aimed at enhancing psychological hardiness have achieved initial success in increasing job satisfaction and reducing the severity of physical illness (Maddi, Kahn, & Maddi, 1998).

Social Support

social support The availability of support from other people, whether tangible or intangible.

People who have **social support** are less likely to become ill. Social support can be tangible, in the form of money or practical help, or intangible, in the form of advice or encouragement about how to eliminate or cope with stress. Social support promotes health by reducing the effects of stressful life events, promoting recovery from illness, and increasing adherence to medical regimens (Heitzmann & Kaplan, 1988).

People show lower cardiovascular reactivity in the face of a stressful situation when someone else accompanies them (Kamarck, Peterman, & Raynor, 1998). Social support can retard the progress of atherosclerosis by reducing stress-related increases in heart rate, blood pressure, and stress hormones (Knox & Uvnaes-Moberg, 1998). And social support is associated with a stronger immune response in HIV-positive patients (Cruess et al., 2000). This finding is important because HIV-positive individuals show reductions in the activity of natural killer cells and certain other important lymphocytes when facing stressful life events (Evans, Leserman, Perkins, & Stern, 1995).

But what experimental evidence is there that social support boosts the immune response? In one study, saliva samples were taken from healthy college students 5 days before their first final exam, during the final-exams period, and 14 days after their last final exam. The samples were analyzed for the level of immunoglobulin A, an antibody that provides immunity against infections of the upper respiratory tract, gastrointestinal tract, and urogenital system. Salivary concentrations of immunoglobulin A after the final-exams period were lower than before it. But students who reported more adequate social support during the pre-exam period had consistently higher immunoglobulin A concentrations than did their peers who reported less adequate social support (Jemmott & Magloire, 1988). These results indicate that social support may promote health by directly strengthening the immune response.

Can social support be studied at the level of brain and behavior? Social exclusion is one way to experimentally study the influence of social support. Researchers scanned participants in an fMRI while the participants were playing a virtual ball-tossing game in which they first participated and then were eventually excluded by other players. One region of the brain—the anterior cingulate cortex—was active when the participant was excluded, which is a response similar to that of patients who experience pain (Eisenberger, Lieberman, & Williams, 2003). Another study showed that participants who interacted regularly with supportive individuals across a 10-day period had reduced activity in the anterior cingulate cortex and decreased cortisol reactivity in response to a social stressor (Eisenberger, Taylor, Gable, Hilmert, & Lieberman, 2007). Social support and its relation to health is an important area of research for health psychologists.

Another example of the importance of social support comes from the research on the consequences of bullying on children and adolescents. Bullies repeatedly make their victims feel sad, anxious, and unable to concentrate. Traditional or *direct bullying*, which might consist of hitting, name-calling, or social isolation among school-aged children, has been found to contribute to victims experiencing increased rates of depressed mood and poor academic grades (Hawker & Boulton, 2000), and this effect is more pronounced in boys (Rothon, Head, Klineberg, & Stansfeld, 2011). And Rothon and colleagues found that social support can have a protective effect against the negative consequences of bullying on school achievement and mental health. Cyberbullying is a form of *indirect bullying*. Cyberbullying involves the use of mobile phones and the Internet to bully a victim. In this modern form of bullying, women and girls are more likely to be both the bully and victim. Whereas social support has been found to be protective in direct forms of bullying, researchers are just beginning to examine the changing face of bullying (Law, Shapka, Olson, & Waterhouse, 2012) and the impact of cyberbullying on social interpersonal relationships and health.

There are sociocultural differences in the expressed need for social support in coping with illness. A study of European American, Chinese American, and Japanese American breast cancer patients found that European Americans desired more social support than the other two groups did (Wellisch et al., 1999). Another study found that European American participants tended to provide emotional social support, whereas Japanese participants not only provided emotional social support but also problem-focused support, such as helping a patient find a medical specialist. These findings were attributed to the cultural context, with Japanese support providers being motivated to maintain closeness with others, whereas European American support providers were motivated to maintain closeness but also to improve the self-esteem of others (Chen, Kim, Mojaverian, & Morling, 2012).

Social support groups are more likely to be sought out by people suffering from stigmatizing illnesses and health problems—such as AIDS, substance abuse, and cancer—than equally serious but less embarrassing disorders, such as heart disease (Davison, Pennebaker, & Dickerson, 2000). There also are gender differences in the effects of social support. In one study of 2,348 married or cohabiting heterosexual adults, social support from one's partner and family predicted psychological well-being among both women and men. However, women's psychological and physical health was more likely to suffer when their family was under stress. Moreover, whereas social support reduced stress among men and women in this sample, friends and family were more common sources of social support for women than for men (Walen & Lachman, 2000).

Cyberbullying

Cyberbullying is a new form of bullying that utilizes communication technologies and is becoming increasingly common. The bully's actions are repeated, hostile, and deliberate. Teenage girls engage in this behavior more often than do boys.
Source: SpeedKingz/Shutterstock.com.

Section Review: Factors That Moderate the Stress Response

1. What are the components of psychological hardiness?
2. How does social support moderate the stress response?

Coping with Stress

Given that stress is unavoidable and often harmful, coping with stress is an important part of everyday life. One approach to coping divides it into task-oriented, emotion-oriented, and avoidance-oriented coping (Higgins & Endler, 1995). For example, suppose that you find it distressing to make oral presentations. You might engage in task-oriented coping by preparing carefully for oral presentations, emotion-oriented coping by cognitively reappraising the possible negative consequences of peer responses to your presentations, or avoidance-oriented coping by not enrolling in courses that require oral presentations. And the coping strategy you choose when under stress may be influenced by sociocultural factors, such as culture and gender. One study found that, when faced with difficult interpersonal situations, Nepalese children were more likely to engage in emotion-oriented coping, whereas American children were more likely to engage in task-oriented coping (Cole, Bruschi, & Tamang, 2002). Likewise, a recent metaanalysis found that women were more likely to use emotion-oriented coping strategies, such as ruminating about their problems, engaging in positive self-talk, and seeking emotional support (Tamres, Janicki, & Helgeson, 2002). These results are consistent with cross-cultural differences in emotional expression (see Chapter 12) and gender differences in rumination (see Chapter 14).

Of course, some people pursue more formal ways of coping with stress. Among the most common of these are stress-management programs, which have been effective in reducing angina pectoris (Gallacher, Hopkinson, Bennett, Burr, & Elwood, 1997) and high blood pressure (Garcia-Vera, Labrador, & Sanz, 1997). And an 8-week stress-management

Cross-Cultural Differences in Coping

Compared to American children, these Nepalese girls are more likely to engage in emotion-oriented coping.
Source: nevenm/Shutterstock.com.

Chapter 16 Psychology, Health, and Stress

program for patients with multiple sclerosis resulted in decreased frequency and severity of physical symptoms, as well as reduced stress and depression (Artemiadis et al., 2012).

Emotional Release and Stress Management

Psychologist James Pennebaker and his colleagues have found that writing about our emotions is a stress-relieving practice that produces greater physical and psychological benefits than writing about superficial topics (Campbell & Pennebaker, 2003). Writing about stressful life experiences relieved symptoms in asthma and arthritis patients, when compared with patients who did not participate in writing (Stone, Smyth, Kaell, & Hurewitz, 2000). And undergraduates who wrote about traumatic experiences—the trauma itself, as well as how they grew or benefited from the experience—made fewer visits to the university health center compared to participants who did not write about their experiences (King & Miner, 2000). In contrast, suppressing our feelings while writing may adversely affect our immune system, as in a study in which participants wrote about their emotions or wrote while suppressing their emotions. Whereas those who wrote about their emotions showed increased lymphocyte activity, those who suppressed their emotions showed decreased lymphocyte activity (Petrie, Booth, & Pennebaker, 1998).

Stress-Inoculation Training

stress-inoculation training A type of cognitive therapy that helps clients change their pessimistic thinking into more positive thinking when in stressful situations.

A version of cognitive-behavior therapy called **stress-inoculation training**, introduced by Donald Meichenbaum (1985), helps clients change their pessimistic thinking into optimistic thinking when in stressful situations. A major review of 37 studies involving more than 1,800 participants found that stress-inoculation training is effective in reducing performance anxiety and improving work performance under stress (Saunders, Driskell, Johnston, & Salas, 1996). Stress-inoculation training also is effective in reducing anxiety in college students (Fontana, Diegman, Villeneuve, & Lepore, 1999) and law school students (Sheehy & Horan, 2004).

In a study of the effect of stress-inoculation training on anxiety and writing quality, participants were assigned to one of three conditions. The first condition combined stress-inoculation training with writing instruction, the second condition combined writing instruction with interpersonal attention, and the third condition (the control group) involved no treatment. Participants in the first two groups reported reductions in their anxiety levels that were greater than those reported by participants in the control group, but only the combination of stress-inoculation training and writing instruction improved writing quality—and significantly more of those in that group were able to pass a first-year college English equivalency examination (Salovey & Haar, 1990).

Stress-inoculation training also has proved effective in helping athletes during physical rehabilitation after arthroscopic surgery for torn cartilage, usually in a knee. A study of 60 athletes who underwent cartilage surgery found that those who received rehabilitation plus stress-inoculation training experienced less postsurgical pain and anxiety than did those who received rehabilitation alone. Those who received stress-inoculation training also regained use of their affected limbs more quickly (Ross & Berger, 1996).

Exercise and Stress Management

In the early 1960s, President John F. Kennedy, a physical fitness proponent, observed that "The Greeks knew that intelligence and skill can only function at the peak of their capacity when the body is healthy and strong—that hearty spirits and tough minds usually inhabit sound bodies" (Silva & Weinberg, 1984, p. 416). Kennedy would approve of the recent trend toward greater concern with personal fitness. The only way to achieve cardiovascular fitness is to maintain a program that includes regular aerobic exercise (exercise that markedly raises heart rate for at least 20 minutes). The possible beneficial effect of aerobic exercise was demonstrated in a longitudinal study (Brown & Siegel, 1988) that found that adolescents under high levels of stress who exercised regularly had a significantly lower incidence of illness than did adolescents who exercised little (see Figure 16-7).

FIGURE 16-7
Exercise and Illness

A study of the relationship between exercise and illness found that adolescents who exercised little and adolescents who exercised regularly did not differ in their incidence of illness when under low levels of stress. In contrast, when under high levels of stress, those who exercised regularly had a significantly lower incidence of illness than did those who exercised little (Brown & Siegel, 1988).

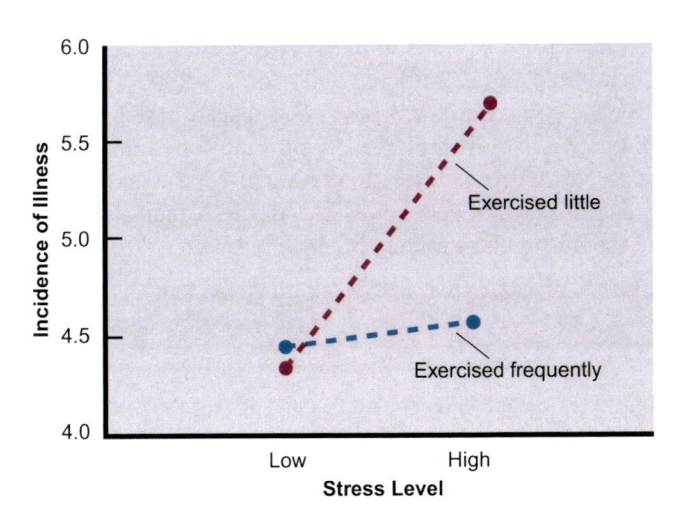

Experimental research likewise shows that aerobic exercise programs improve both cardiovascular fitness and psychological well-being, regardless of age, occupation, or gender (Garcia, Archer, Moradi, & Andersson-Arntén, 2012). People who exercise become less physiologically reactive to stressors (Throne, Bartholomew, Craig, & Farrar, 2000) and more confident in their ability to cope (Steptoe, Moses, Edwards, & Mathews, 1993). There also is evidence that exercise can enhance the functioning of the immune system (Hong, 2000). The results of animal studies have indicated that exercise increases the generation of new neurons in the hippocampus, a brain structure involved in learning and memory (DeCarolis & Eisch, 2010).

Relaxation and Stress Management

Because stress is associated with physiological arousal, health psychologists emphasize the importance of relaxation training. Several techniques have proved effective in reducing psychological or physiological arousal. These include massage (Zeitlin, Keller, Shiflett, Schleifer, & Bartlett, 2000); hypnosis (Kiecolt-Glaser, Marucha, Atkinson, & Glaser, 2001); meditation (Speca, Carlson, Goodey, & Angen, 2000); biofeedback (Critchley, Melmed, Featherstone, Mathias, & Dolan, 2001); deep, rhythmic breathing (Gilbert, 2003); and restricted environmental stimulation training, or REST (Schulz & Kaspar, 1994). Hypnosis is discussed in Chapter 6, biofeedback in Chapter 7, and REST in Chapter 11.

The most basic relaxation technique is **progressive relaxation** (see Chapter 15). This technique was developed by Edmund Jacobson, who was inspired to evaluate the effect of relaxation on anxiety after noticing years earlier how distressed his father had become after losing some of his real estate in a fire (Jacobson, 1977). Progressive relaxation has been effective in reducing high blood pressure (Anthony et al., 2003). And heart-attack patients who receive training in breathing and relaxation develop a slower breathing rate and more normal heart rate (van Dixhoorn, 1998).

progressive relaxation A stress-management procedure that involves the successive tensing and relaxing of each of the major muscle groups of the body.

Progressive relaxation can even enhance the immunological response (Lekander, Fuerst, Rostein, Hursti, & Fredrikson, 1997). A study that compared children who practiced relaxation to children who did not found that the relaxation group had an increase in immunoglobulins, a measure of immune system functioning (Hewson-Bower & Drummond, 1996). Consider the following experiment that involved medical students, conducted by Janice Kiecolt-Glaser, a leading researcher on psychoneuroimmunology. Blood samples were taken from students 1 month before midterm exams and then again on the day of the exams. Half the students were randomly assigned to participate in relaxation practice during the month between the two measurement days. The students who were not assigned to practice relaxation, compared to the students who were, displayed a significantly greater decrease in natural killer cell activity between the first and second measurements (Kiecolt-Glaser et al., 1986). You will recall that natural killer cells are one of the body's main defenses against cancer cells.

As discussed earlier in this chapter, caregivers for patients with Alzheimer's disease experience chronic stress. A sample of caregivers participated in a study of the effects of

Chapter 16 Psychology, Health, and Stress

Meditation and Stress

Recent evidence shows that daily structured meditation can help reverse the harmful effects of stress.
Source: Deborah Kolb/Shutterstock.com.

meditation. Meditation, a form of relaxation, has been used for stress reduction for centuries. One group meditated for 12 minutes daily for 8 weeks. The other group listened to relaxing music for the same period of time. The researchers found that after 8 weeks of meditation, participants displayed increased immune functioning (Black et al., 2013). Whereas it is difficult for the researchers to conclude what exact features of meditation (e.g., chanting or breathing) might be responsible for these changes, practicing meditation daily might reverse the detrimental effects of chronic stress.

Section Review: Coping with Stress

1. What did the study of adolescents by Brown and Siegel (1988) conclude about the relationship between exercise and health?
2. What did the study by Kiecolt-Glaser et al. (1986) find about the relationship between relaxation and the immune response?

Health-Promoting Habits

Habits as varied as smoking, overeating, a sedentary lifestyle, and failing to wear seat belts sharply increase the chances of illness, injury, or death. Yet, a study found that college students tended to have an "it can't happen to me" attitude. Their estimate of the probability that their own risky behaviors would lead to illness or injury underestimated the actual probability. This feeling of invulnerability accounts for the greater tendency of young drivers to not use seat belts (Matsuura, Ishida, & Ishimatsu, 2002). Because of our inability to estimate the true riskiness of our behaviors, programs aimed at changing health-impairing habits must not only point out risky behaviors but also make participants realize that those habits make them more susceptible to unhealthy consequences than they might believe (Weinstein, 1984). An ambitious community program in New Zealand called Superhealth Basic used brief group sessions to help participants improve their behaviors related to sleep, stress, weight, smoking, drinking, exercise, and nutrition. Participants showed significant improvements in their mental health, physical health, management of stress, and sense of well-being (Raeburn, Atkinson, Dubignon, & Fitzpatrick, 1994).

One of the most important factors influencing whether people are motivated to engage in health-promoting behavior is their feeling of self-efficacy (Kelly, Zyzanski, & Alemagno, 1991). People high in self-efficacy feel that their actions will be effective. Feelings of self-efficacy are positively related to important health-promoting behaviors, including maintenance of smoking cessation, control of diet and body weight, and adherence to preventive health behaviors and medical regimens (O'Leary, 1985). For example, young adults with diabetes who are high in self-efficacy are more likely to practice procedures for keeping their disease under control (Griva, Myers, & Newman, 2000). Among the most important health-promoting habits are practicing safe sex, keeping physically fit, maintaining a healthy diet and body weight, and avoiding tobacco products.

Practicing Safe Sex

Today many health psychologists have turned their attention to risky sexual practices that contribute to the spread of sexually transmitted diseases, including AIDS, syphilis, gonorrhea, chlamydia, genital warts (the human papillomavirus), and genital herpes (the herpes simplex virus). But because it is usually fatal, AIDS has become of greatest interest to them.

HIV and AIDS

Acquired immune deficiency syndrome (AIDS) kills its victims by impairing their immune systems, making them eventually succumb to cancer or opportunistic infections—that is, infections that rarely occur in people with healthy immune systems. Since 1981, when it was first identified, AIDS has spread through much of the world with alarming rapidity. AIDS afflicts people of all ages, sexes, ethnicities, and sexual orientations. AIDS is caused by the human immunodeficiency virus (HIV). A person with HIV does not necessarily have AIDS but could develop AIDS in the future. Today, the use of antiviral therapy has helped delay or eliminate the progression of HIV-positive status to AIDS and can prevent noninfected sex partners from developing the disease (Cohen et al., 2011).

HIV is spread by infected protein-rich body fluids, such as blood or semen (Catania, Gibson, Chitwood, & Coates, 1990). Drug addicts can acquire HIV by sharing hypodermic needles with infected addicts. The virus also can be transmitted through unprotected sexual activity, including anal sex and vaginal sex. Even infants born to HIV-positive mothers are at high risk of infection, especially if they are breast-fed. Transmission of the virus from infected dental or medical personnel to their patients, or from infected patients to dental or medical personnel, is much less likely. There is no evidence that kissing, simple touching, food handling, or other casual kinds of contact spread the virus.

Prevention of HIV Infection

Blood, vaginal fluid, breast milk, and semen are the fluids that transmit HIV. Safe sex through the use of latex condoms is the primary prevention approach.
Source: kaarsten/Shutterstock.com.

Promoting Safe Sex

Because there is no cure for AIDS, prevention of HIV infection is crucial. One of the primary means of prevention is educating people to avoid risky behaviors. Foremost among the suggestions has been to practice "safe" sex (or at least "safer" sex). In regard to HIV infection, the safest sex is abstinence or limiting oneself to an uninfected partner. Many people do not abstain, however, and may have a series of sexual partners, so the next best suggestions are to use latex condoms and limit the number of sex partners.

Efforts to reduce risky behaviors have achieved some success. Though elsewhere in the world AIDS is more prevalent among heterosexuals, especially women, in North America, it has been more prevalent among gay men, Latinos, and African Americans (Grossman, Purcell, Rotheram-Borus, & Veniegas, 2013). This prevalence has been attributed to the common practice of unprotected anal sex. The 10 percent of heterosexuals who practice anal sex also are at increased risk of infection (Voeller, 1991). Because AIDS has so ravaged the North American gay community, the earliest anti-AIDS programs were aimed at gay men. Cities with large gay and lesbian populations have instituted workshops on AIDS prevention for gay and bisexual men. For example, a survey of gay men in San Francisco, where there is a high level of AIDS education, found a significant increase in condom use (Catania, Coates, Stall, & Bye, 1991).

A review of research on the use of HIV-AIDS prevention videotapes found that they increase knowledge of HIV and AIDS and improve attitudes regarding risky sexual behavior. But it is unclear whether these changes translate into actual reductions in risky behavior (Kalichman, 1996). The National Institute of Mental Health conducted a program in 37 clinics across the United States that each had a high-risk population. The participants, compared to controls, showed a reduction in risky sexual behavior. They showed fewer acts of unprotected sex and increased use of condoms over a 12-month follow-up period (National Institute of Mental Health, 1998).

Keeping Physically Fit

People who exercise regularly are healthier and live longer than those who do not. Exercise promotes health and longevity, in part by boosting the immune system. A study found that HIV-positive people showed enhanced immunological responses after participating in an aerobic exercise program (Antoni, LaPerriere, Schneiderman, & Fletcher, 1991).

Beneficial Effects of Exercise

There is especially strong evidence for the effectiveness of exercise in preventing obesity and cardiovascular disease. Aerobic exercise (such as running, swimming, bicycling, brisk walking, or cross-country skiing) combats obesity by burning calories, raising the basal metabolic rate, and inhibiting the appetite. Aerobic exercise also reduces the cardiovascular risk factors of elevated cholesterol and high blood pressure.

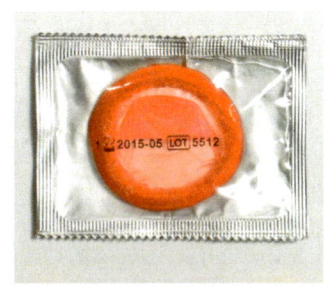

Chapter 16 Psychology, Health, and Stress

The health risks of physical inactivity and the health benefits of exercise have led many sedentary people to start exercising. Unfortunately, of those who begin formal exercise programs, about 50 percent will drop out within 6 months. This attrition rate is unfortunate because participants in weight-control programs who continue to exercise after the programs end regain less weight than do those who stop exercising (Wadden, Vogt, Foster, & Anderson, 1998). According to Rod Dishman, an authority on exercise adherence, people who are obese or who have symptoms of cardiovascular disease—the very people who might benefit most from exercise—are the least likely to exercise (Dishman & Gettman, 1980). Physical inactivity is a greater health problem among African Americans and Latinos, who engage in less physical activity during leisure time than do European Americans. Moreover, this difference appears to be unrelated to social class (Crespo, Smit, Andersen, Carter-Pokras, & Ainsworth, 2000).

Adhering to an Exercise Program

Common reasons for failing to adhere to exercise programs are a lack of time and a lack of motivation (McAuley, Poag, Gleason, & Wraith, 1990). Moreover, a 2-year prospective study found that exercise adherence was lower among people who had experienced more than one major life event (Oman & King, 2000). One study conducted by the Centers for Disease Control and Prevention assessed barriers to physical activity in a multiethnic sample of young and middle-aged women. Regardless of ethnicity, family priorities were the main barrier to physical activity. Participants with multiple roles, such as wife, daughter, mother, and community member, reported having little time or energy for exercise (Eyler et al., 2002). Because of these responsibilities, home training may promote adherence relative to group training at an exercise facility (Perri, Martin, Leermakers, & Sears, 1997).

Other factors influence exercise adherence. People who practice dissociation (that is, blocking their conscious feelings of pain and fatigue) while running can exercise longer (Masters & Ogles, 1998). Intrinsic motivation (see Chapter 11) promotes exercise adherence. That is, people who exercise for enjoyment, competence, and social interaction show greater adherence than those who exercise just to improve their fitness or appearance (Ryan, Frederick, Lepes, Rubio, & Sheldon, 1997). In addition, one study found that people tend to adhere more to exercise programs that involve more frequent, lower-intensity workouts than to less frequent, higher-intensity workouts (Perri et al., 2002). And people who fail to adhere to exercise programs may have low self-efficacy—that is, a lack of confidence in their ability to meet the demands of the program. One study measured the self-efficacy of participants in a step-aerobics exercise class who participated in an 8-week program. There was a positive relationship between their self-efficacy levels and their attendance (Fontaine & Shaw, 1995).

The failure of people to maintain exercise programs has prompted health psychologists to study ways of increasing exercise adherence. One of the best ways to improve the motivation to exercise is to make exercising enjoyable (Wankel, 1993). Perhaps enjoyment explains the popularity of kickboxing classes and similar approaches to exercise. But some programs aimed at increasing adherence are more formal. In one study, groups of people engaged in jogging, aerobic dancing, or conditioning for skiing for 10 weeks. Some of the participants in each of the three groups also took part in a special program to increase their motivation to exercise. The program made participants more aware of obstacles to exercise and taught them how to cope with periodic exercise lapses instead of having an all-or-none attitude. Rather than giving up after exercise lapses, exercisers were urged to return immediately to their exercise programs. The results showed that those who participated in the adherence program, compared to those who did not, were indeed more likely to adhere to their exercise programs (Belisle, Roskies, & Levesque, 1987). Similar results have been found in a recent study that found that exercise adherence among older women was increased when they were provided with regularly scheduled telephone calls that offered assistance in coping with the demands of physical exercise and strategies to maintain their exercise regimen (Evers, Klusmann, Ziegelman, Schwarzer, & Heuser, 2012).

Maintaining a Healthy Diet and Body Weight

Health psychologists recognize the importance of maintaining a healthy diet and body weight. They are especially concerned with the relationship between diet and both diabetes and cardiovascular disease (Vidal, 2002). As mentioned earlier in this chapter, a high-fat diet is one of the main risk factors in cardiovascular disease. High-fat diets contribute to high blood pressure and high levels of cholesterol in the blood, which promote atherosclerosis by the buildup of plaque deposits that narrow the arteries. The narrowing of cerebral arteries and coronary arteries reduces blood flow, promoting strokes and heart attacks. Health psychologists have developed programs that combine nutritional education and cognitive-behavior modification to help people reduce their risks of cardiovascular disease by adopting healthier eating habits. For example, programs that reduce caloric intake produce significant reductions in blood pressure in participants with elevated blood pressure (Steffen et al., 2001).

The Ideal Female Figure

In Western cultures the ideal female figure has changed over time, becoming leaner and more muscular.
Source: Maksim Toome/Shutterstock.com.

Sociocultural Influences on Desirable Physiques

A high-fat diet also contributes to obesity—an important risk factor in illness for both men and women. Yet, in Western cultures, a leaner figure has been stylish for women only since the early 20th century, and a toned, muscular figure only in the past few decades. For the preceding 600 years, cultural standards favored a more rounded figure (Bennett & Gurin, 1982). You probably have seen this standard in Renaissance paintings that depict the ideal woman as being plump. Thus, what we consider an ideal body weight is regulated by cultural as well as biological and behavioral factors (Brownell & Wadden, 1991). Today, cultures differ in what they view as ideal physiques. A study found that Singaporeans rated muscular physiques as more attractive than did British participants. All participants rated muscular physiques as more attractive in men than in women. There was no difference in ratings given by male and female raters (Furnham & Lim, 1997).

But current Western standards of beauty, and concern with the health-impairing effects of obesity, make weight loss a major North American preoccupation (Dorian & Garfinkel, 2002). Weight reduction seems deceptively easy: You simply make sure that you burn more calories than you ingest. Yet, as noted by obesity researcher Kelly Brownell (1982), fewer than 5 percent of obese people maintain their weight loss long enough to be considered "cured." Some obesity researchers argue that this pessimistic figure represents only people who have been in formal weight-loss programs. In contrast, most people who try to lose weight on their own succeed. Perhaps those who seek treatment for obesity are a select group of people who are the least likely to succeed (Schachter, 1982). In fact, negative results typically come from university-based treatment programs. A small percentage of participants in these programs lose weight—but they differ from the general population of obese people. They tend to be more overweight, more likely to engage in binge eating, and more prone to psychological disorders (Brownell, 1993).

Because of the great cultural variability in perceptions of ideal body types and the difficulty that obese people have in maintaining weight loss, some critics believe it might be better to help obese people learn to accept their body types. There are group counseling programs that try to accomplish this acceptance. Participants discuss ways of maintaining their self-respect and social relationships despite being fat in a culture that frowns on fat people (Tenzer, 1989). In keeping with this approach, some authorities believe it would be better to promote weight control as a way to improve health, rather than as a way to achieve a particular body weight (Foreyt & Goodrick, 1994).

Approaches to Weight Control

Though many people do, in fact, desire to lose weight for health reasons, others desire to do so for social or aesthetic reasons. But how can people control their weight? A common but ineffective approach is dieting. People who diet may drastically reduce their caloric intake for weeks or months. Unfortunately, as dieters lose weight, their basal metabolic rate slows (Foreyt, 1987), forcing them to diet indefinitely to maintain their lower level of weight—an impossible feat. Because dieting cannot last for a lifetime, dieters eventually return to the same eating habits that contributed to their obesity. Moreover, dieting is unhealthy; 25 percent of diet-induced weight loss consists of lean body tissue, including skeletal muscle (Brownell, 1982).

Formal psychological approaches to weight loss rely on cognitive-behavior therapy in conjunction with aerobic exercise. In cognitive-behavior therapy programs, participants monitor their eating behaviors, change maladaptive eating habits, and correct misconceptions about eating. Aerobic exercise promotes weight loss not only by burning calories during exercise but also by raising the metabolic rate for hours afterward. This increase counters dieting-induced decreases in the basal metabolic rate. Weight loss through aerobic exercise also is healthier than weight loss through dieting alone because only 5 percent of weight loss will be lean tissue (Brownell, 1982). Despite the effectiveness of aerobic exercise in weight control, most people who are trying to lose weight fail to increase their physical activity or engage in regular exercise (Gordon, Heath, Holmes, & Christy, 2000). Moreover, it is difficult for many obese people to maintain the intensity of exercise necessary to produce significant weight loss (Blix & Blix, 1995).

People who wish to lose weight often are impatient. But rapid weight loss does not guarantee long-term weight loss. Though the past few decades have demonstrated the short-term effectiveness of behavioral modification in helping mildly or moderately obese people lose weight, no program has been able to halt the inevitable return to obesity by the great majority of participants. The typical 15-week weight-loss program of dieting or dieting plus exercise, for example, produces a loss of about 22 pounds, with 60 to 80 percent of participants maintaining weight loss for one year. But few participants maintain their weight after 3 to 5 years (Miller, 1999). Longer treatment programs that emphasize the importance of physical activity are more successful in promoting long-term weight loss (Jeffery et al., 2000).

Avoiding Tobacco Products

During the 1996 presidential campaign, Senator Robert Dole provoked controversy when he declared that smoking was not addictive. Dole's proclamation went against an enormous amount of evidence that smoking tobacco is addictive and is perhaps the single worst health-impairing habit. Despite the harmful effects of smoking, governments permit it—and even profit from it. In 1565, King James I of England, though viewing smoking as a despicable habit, chose to tax cigarettes rather than ban them, a practice governments still follow today.

The Effects of Smoking

Contrary to Dole's claim, smokers can become addicted to the nicotine in tobacco—though a small minority of smokers remain "chippers" who are able to smoke intermittently without becoming addicted (Davies, Willner, & Morgan, 2000). Though many addicted smokers insist that they smoke to relieve anxiety or to increase alertness, they actually smoke to avoid the unpleasant symptoms of nicotine withdrawal, which include irritability, hand tremors, heart palpitations, and difficulty concentrating. Thus, addicted smokers smoke to regulate the level of nicotine in their bodies (Parrott, 1995) and reduce craving (Gilbert & Warburton, 2000). Smoking is especially difficult to stop because it can become a conditioned response to many everyday situations, as in the case of smokers who light a cigarette when answering the telephone, after eating a meal, or after leaving a class.

Smoking produces harmful side effects through the actions of tars and other substances in cigarette smoke. Smoking causes fatigue by reducing the blood's ability to carry oxygen, making smoking an especially bad habit for athletes. But more important, smoking contributes to the deaths of more than 300,000 Americans each year from stroke, cancer, emphysema, and heart disease. Thus, its prevention is paramount.

The Prevention of Smoking

The ill effects of smoking make it imperative to devise programs to prevent the onset of smoking. Children are more likely to start smoking if their parents and peers smoke

(Simons-Morton, 2002), especially boys (Nuño, Zhang, Harris, Wilkinson-Lee, & Wilhelm, 2011). Many smoking-prevention programs are based in schools and provide information about the immediate and long-term social and physical consequences of smoking (Ahmed, Ahmed, Bennett, & Hinds, 2002). But simply providing children with information about the ill effects of smoking is not enough to prevent them from starting. Smoking-prevention programs must also teach children how to resist peer pressure and advertisements that encourage them to begin smoking. Moreover, smoking prevention programs must address sociocultural factors that influence smoking in different ethnic groups. For example, culturally sensitive programs have been developed for Latinos (Gonzalez-Blanks, Lopez, & Garza, 2012), Native Americans (McKennitt & Currie, 2012), and Israeli Orthodox Jews (Knishkowi, Verbov, Amitai, Stein-Zamir, & Rosen, 2012). Overall, smoking-prevention programs have been effective, reducing the number of new smokers among participants by 50 percent (Flay, 1985).

The Treatment of Smoking

Though programs to prevent the onset of smoking are important, techniques to help people stop smoking are also essential. But quitting is difficult. A major University of Minnesota study followed 802 smokers for 2 years. Of those, 62 percent tried to quit, but only 16 percent succeeded, and 9 percent became chippers (Hennrikus, Jeffery, & Lando, 1995). People who do quit find it difficult to resist relapsing. The problem of relapse is such that the U.S. Public Health Service considers dependence on tobacco to be a chronic condition (Fiore, 2000). Moreover, relapse rates are higher among women. As yet, researchers are unable to account for this gender difference because women's relapse rates are not influenced by gender-related factors such as weight gain or weight concerns (Wetter et al., 1999).

Health psychologists use a variety of techniques to help people who cannot quit on their own. Participants are taught to expect the symptoms of nicotine withdrawal, which begin 6 to 12 hours after smoking cessation, peak in 1 to 3 days, and last 3 to 4 weeks (Hughes, Higgins, & Bickel, 1994). Even smoking non-nicotine (placebo) cigarettes reduces withdrawal symptoms (possibly because of classical conditioning) and might be useful in the transition period to total abstinence (Butschky, Bailey, Henningfield, & Pickworth, 1995). But certain consequences of quitting, including increased hunger, weight gain, and nicotine craving, may persist for 6 months or more (Hughes, Gust, Skoog, & Keenan, 1991). Nicotine prevents weight gain by reducing hunger and increasing metabolism (Winders & Grunberg, 1989). Thus, many smokers rightly fear that quitting will lead to weight gain.

Because tars and other chemicals in tobacco cause the harmful effects of smoking, some treatments aim at preventing smoking by providing participants with safer ways of obtaining nicotine. These nicotine-replacement techniques prevent some of the relapse caused by the desire to avoid weight gain (Nides, Rand, Dolce, & Murray, 1994) or withdrawal symptoms (Levin, Westman, Stein, & Carnahan, 1994).

Nicotine replacement therapy has proved successful. Though some smokers use nicotine nasal spray (Schneider et al., 2003), the two most common nicotine replacement techniques use *nicotine chewing gum* or a *nicotine patch*, which provides nicotine through the skin. A meta-analysis of well-controlled experiments found that, of participants who used a nicotine patch, 22 percent abstained from smoking after 6 months. Moreover, those who used a nicotine patch smoked less than those who used a placebo patch—that is, a patch without nicotine (Fiore, Smith, Jorenby, & Baker, 1994). Higher-dose nicotine patches produce greater long-term abstinence than do lower-dose nicotine patches (Daughton et al., 1999). However, men appear to benefit from the nicotine patch more than do women. In a double-blind study using the nicotine patch and a placebo patch, the rate of sleep disturbances—which are related to withdrawal symptoms—was higher among women than men (Wetter et al., 1999). Smokers who use the nicotine patch and chew nicotine gum are more successful in quitting than are those who use either technique alone (Fagerstrom, Schneider, & Lunell, 1993). A more recent trend in smoking cessation has been the use of electronic cigarettes as a form of nicotine replacement. However, the Food and Drug Administration has documented short- and long-term adverse health effects of electronic

A Safe Cigarette?

The safety of electronic cigarettes is currently under study, and their regulation is the subject of an ongoing debate.
Source: Tibanna 79/Shutterstock.com.

cigarettes (Chen, 2013), and studies of their use in formal smoking cessation programs need to be conducted to assess their efficacy (Odum, O'Dell, & Schepers, 2012).

Of course, though *replacement* therapy reduces the health risks of smoking, it does not help smokers overcome their *addiction* to nicotine. Those who wish to overcome their addiction do better if they are high in two of the factors that appear repeatedly as health promoters: a feeling of self-efficacy (Ockene et al., 2000) and the presence of social support (Nides, Rakos, Gonzales, & Murray, 1995). But a study of 210 smokers found that social support was more important in quitting for men than for women (Westmaas, Wild, & Ferrence, 2002).

Another approach to smoking cessation involves *self-management programs*, which employ behavior modification. The programs encourage smokers to avoid stimuli that act as cues for smoking, such as coffee breaks, alcoholic beverages, and other smokers. A potentially powerful way of teaching smokers self-management skills is to have their physicians educate them about how to quit. An ambitious study in England involved 1,200 heavy smokers and their primary-care physicians. The smokers received brief advice from their physician, a booklet on how to quit smoking, and nicotine patches or placebo patches that they wore for 16 hours a day for 18 weeks. A 1-year follow-up found that the nicotine patch was twice as effective as a placebo patch in promoting abstinence: 9.6 percent versus 4.8 percent, respectively (Stapleton, Russell, Feyerabend, & Wiseman, 1995). Effective smoking cessation involves behavioral change.

Section Review: Health-Promoting Habits

1. What behaviors can transmit HIV from one person to another?
2. What are the beneficial effects of regular aerobic exercise?
3. Why is it unwise to try to lose weight solely by dieting?

Reactions to Illness

Despite your best efforts to adapt to stress and to live a healthy lifestyle, you will periodically suffer from illness. Health psychologists study ways to encourage people to seek treatment for symptoms of illness, to reduce patient distress, and to increase patient adherence to medical regimens.

Seeking Treatment for Health Problems

What do you do when you experience a headache, nausea, diarrhea, dizziness, constipation, or nasal congestion? Your reaction would depend on your interpretation of the symptoms. This interpretation would depend, in turn, on your past experience with these symptoms, information you have received about them, their intensity, and their duration. Some people inappropriately seek medical attention for the most minor symptoms. However, many others deny, ignore, or misinterpret their symptoms, which might make them fail to seek help; as a consequence, many people let minor ailments become serious or delay treatment of serious ailments that might be cured by early treatment. Victims of heart attacks have a much better prognosis for recovery if they seek help within an hour of experiencing symptoms. But victims typically wait several hours from the time they first notice symptoms until they seek help (Walsh, Lynch, Murphy, & Daly, 2004).

Sociocultural factors influence the rates at which people make use of health-care services. A national survey of health attitudes and behaviors found that 33 percent of American men have no regular doctor, compared to 19 percent of American women. Moreover, women's greater tendency to seek regular medical care cannot be explained by medical visits due to pregnancy, reproductive health, and childbearing. Uninsured, younger, and less-educated men were especially likely to delay seeking treatment for a medical condition (Sandman, Simantov, & An, 2000). Many health psychologists believe that this gender difference in access to and use of medical care contributes to men's higher death rates and reduced longevity relative to women (Courtenay, 2000). Many ethnic groups, too, make use of home remedies, rituals, or folk practitioners, either alone or in conjunction with traditional medical treatment (Landrine & Klonoff, 1994).

The importance of seeking appropriate medical care has inspired health psychologists to study factors that motivate people to seek treatment. An important factor is social support. People with social support may be encouraged to seek treatment, may be referred to appropriate medical personnel, and may feel less anxious about seeking treatment (Roberts, 1988). Even one's explanatory style can affect the decision to seek medical treatment. A study of undergraduates found that those with a pessimistic explanatory style were less likely than optimistic students to seek medical treatment. Thus, the finding that pessimistic people are usually less healthy than optimistic ones might be caused by their greater passivity in the face of illness (Lin & Peterson, 1990).

One of the main factors in seeking treatment for symptoms is how one interprets them. A study of 366 older adults (average age 62 years) found that when they had ambiguous symptoms of illness, those who had experienced a stressful life event in the preceding 3 weeks were less likely to seek treatment than were those who had not experienced one. Evidently, those who did not seek treatment attributed their symptoms to stress instead of an illness. When the symptoms were not ambiguous, there was no difference in the likelihood of seeking treatment (Cameron, Leventhal, & Leventhal, 1995).

Relieving Patient Distress

Illness, especially chronic illness or illness that requires surgery or painful procedures, is distressing. Patients differ in their ability to cope with illness or stressful medical procedures. One important factor is self-efficacy. For example, patients high in self-efficacy cope better with painful dental procedures (Litt, Nye, & Shafer, 1995).

Some patients also can benefit from psychological techniques that encourage effective coping with pain or stressful procedures. These patients include cancer patients (Cohen, 2002), children who undergo prolonged hospitalizations (Yap, 1988), and burn victims who must undergo excruciatingly painful skin debridement (Fauerbach, Lawrence, Haythornthwaite, & Richter, 2002). A meta-analysis found that psychological preparation for surgery is effective in reducing pain, distress, and length of stay. Informing surgery patients about the procedures they will undergo is especially effective (Johnston & Vogele, 1993).

A sensitive, comprehensive orientation program is especially important for patients about to undergo cancer treatment. In one study, a group of 150 breast cancer patients seen at an outpatient oncology clinic were assigned to an orientation program or a usual-care control condition. Those in the orientation program were given a guided tour, information about clinic operations, and a question-and-answer session with an oncology counselor. The results showed that the orientation group had less distress, anxiety, and depression (McQuellon et al., 1998).

Modeling has been a useful technique for reducing patient distress during unpleasant medical procedures (O'Halloran & Altmaier, 1995). In keeping with this technique, observing a patient who has undergone successful surgery can be beneficial to a patient about to undergo surgery. Patients waiting to undergo coronary bypass surgery who have a hospital roommate who has just undergone successful surgery of any kind are less anxious before surgery, walk more after surgery, and go home sooner than are similar patients who have a roommate who is about to undergo surgery. Apparently, simply observing a person who has survived surgery has a calming effect on patients anticipating surgery. Moreover, people who have undergone surgery can reduce the distress of patients about to undergo surgery by letting them know what to expect and suggesting ways to cope with the situation (Kulik & Mahler, 1987).

In some cases, relatively simple procedures can reduce illness-related distress. In a study of children undergoing chemotherapy for cancer, the experimental group played

FIGURE 16-8
Controlling Patient Distress with Video Games

Children who played video games while undergoing cancer chemotherapy (the experimental group) showed a marked reduction in nausea. In contrast, children who did not play video games while undergoing cancer chemotherapy (the control group) showed little change in nausea.

Source: Data from W. H. Redd et al., "Cognitive/attentional distraction in the control of conditioned nausea in pediatric cancer patients receiving chemotherapy," in *Journal of Consulting and Clinical Psychology, 55,* 391–395.

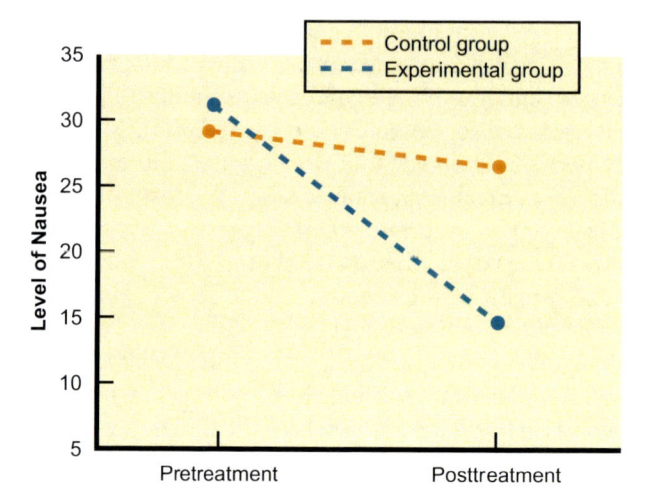

video games during their chemotherapy, and a control group did not. As shown in Figure 16-8, children in the experimental group reported less nausea. The children who played video games were apparently distracted from the unpleasant sensations caused by the chemotherapy (Redd et al., 1987).

There has been increasing interest in another factor related to patient distress: the quality of the relationship between patients and medical practitioners. A study found a negative correlation between the perceived empathy of nurses and patient anger, anxiety, and depression (Olson, 1995). Patients who perceive a lack of empathy in their physicians are more likely to sue them for malpractice (Frankel, 1995). There is a strong, positive correlation between the use of humor—both by physicians and their patients—and patient satisfaction (Sala, Krupat, & Roter, 2002). Research indicates that there are gender differences in the ways that physicians treat their patients. Female physicians tend to be more collaborative, rather than authoritarian, in relating to their patients. They are more likely to deal with feelings and emotions and to consider the patient's social and psychological context (Roter & Hall, 1998). Findings like these have prompted some health psychologists to suggest that health-care professionals receive education on improving patient interaction, including learning how to prepare patients for stressful medical and surgical procedures, as well as how to communicate with worried family members (Wilson-Barnett, 1994).

Encouraging Adherence to Medical Regimens

Recovery from illness often depends on following a medical regimen recommended by a physician. This regimen might include a prescription drug, a restricted diet, or an exercise program. Adherence is important in medical regimens aimed at controlling diabetes (DiMatteo, Sherbourne, Hays, & Ordway, 1993), treating obesity (Brownell & Cohen, 1995), controlling arthritis pain (Taal, Rasker, Seydel, & Wiegman, 1993), and lowering high blood pressure (Ibrahim, 2003). One of the main reasons that patients fail to follow treatment regimens is that they do not understand the physician's instructions (Glen & Anderson, 1989). The patient's personality also is a factor. A study based on the five-factor theory of personality (see Chapter 13) found that patients who scored high on the factor of conscientiousness were more likely to adhere to medication regimens (Christensen & Smith, 1995). A meta-analysis found that social support is an important factor in encouraging adherence to medical regimens (DiMatteo, 2004).

As is the case in the relief of patient distress, the relationship between the patient and the physician plays a key role in adherence to medical regimens. Patients are more likely to adhere to regimens prescribed by physicians they like. One of the most important factors determining whether a patient will be satisfied with a physician is the physician's emotional warmth during consultations. A longitudinal study of HIV-positive gay and bisexual men found that strong positive beliefs about their doctors and other health-care providers predicted adherence to protease inhibitor treatment regimens (Evans, Ferrando, Rabkin, & Fishman, 2000).

Sometimes, patients abandon their medical regimens prematurely because they no longer notice any symptoms. Consider a patient with essential hypertension (marked by chronic high blood pressure) who must take medication, watch her diet, and follow an exercise program. Because we have, at best, a slight ability to sense the level of our blood pressure (Pennebaker & Watson, 1988), the patient might assume, incorrectly, that because she does not feel like she has high blood pressure, she actually does not have high blood pressure—and abandon her prescribed medical regimen. This problem again points to the importance of adequate communication between the physician and the patient. Physicians need to communicate the risks and benefits of treatment and the specific details of the medical regimen (DiMatteo, Reiter, & Gambone, 1994). Even the simple act of asking patients to adhere to medical regimens can be effective. In one study, patients were put on 10-day antibiotic regimens to treat bacterial infections. The patients were divided into an experimental group and a control group. Those in the experimental group made oral and written commitments to adhere to the regimen. Those in the control group did not. The results showed that those in the experimental group were more likely than those in the control group to adhere to the regimen (Putnam, Finney, Barkley, & Bonner, 1994).

Health psychologists have demonstrated that we play an active role in maintaining our health, succumbing to disease, and recovering from illness. Though some diseases and injuries are unavoidable, we can no longer view ourselves as simply the passive victims of viruses, bacteria, or carcinogens. By learning to adapt effectively to stressors, to eliminate risky behaviors, to adopt health-promoting behaviors, and to respond appropriately to symptoms of disease, we can greatly reduce our chances of illness, injury, and death.

Section Review: Reactions to Illness

1. What are some factors that affect seeking treatment for symptoms of illness?
2. What role does the relationship between patient and health practitioner play in medical treatment?

Experiencing Psychology

Increasing Exercise Adherence

Rationale

Regular exercise is essential to physical health and stress management. But, as discussed in the section "Keeping Physically Fit," many people find it difficult to incorporate physical activity into their daily schedules. This activity asks you to keep a record of your physical activity and modify one variable that may be affecting your physical activity level.

Procedure

Keep a 1-week diary of your exercise habits. Note the date, time, and type of physical activity—for example, participation in an aerobics class, a brisk 20-minute walk, or a short spin on a bicycle, skateboard, or scooter. Note how long you exercised, whether you exercised alone or with others, and how you felt before, during, and after your exercise session. After 1 week, review the chapter section on exercise adherence and choose *one* variable that you feel might have influenced your physical activity during the preceding week. Identify the variable in your diary, and indicate how you will modify this variable. For example, if you feel that taking a walk by yourself is boring, indicate that you will recruit a friend to exercise with you. Then, continue to use your diary to monitor your physical activity for another week.

Results and Discussion

Compare your physical activity during the 2-week period recorded in your diary. Did manipulating the variable you identified increase the frequency and/or duration of your physical activity? What else could you do to increase your exercise adherence? If you are ambitious, review Chapters 7 and 15, and consider how you might employ cognitive-behavioral techniques to increase your physical activity.

Chapter Summary

Psychological Stress and Stressors

- Health psychology is the field that studies the role of psychological factors in the promotion of health and the prevention of illness and injury.
- One of the main topics of interest to health psychologists is stress, the physiological response of the body to physical and psychological demands.
- The chief psychological stressors are often categorized as either life changes or daily hassles.

The Biopsychology of Stress and Illness

- Hans Selye identified a pattern of physiological response to stress that he called the general adaptation syndrome, which includes the alarm reaction, the stage of resistance, and the stage of exhaustion.
- Stress has been linked to infectious and noninfectious diseases.
- The field that studies the relationship between psychological factors and illness is called psychoneuroimmunology.
- There is evidence that the immune response can be altered by classical conditioning.
- The main noninfectious diseases linked to stress are cardiovascular disease and cancer.

Factors That Moderate the Stress Response

- The relationship between stress and illness is mediated by the interaction of a variety of factors.
- The major factors include physiological reactivity, cognitive appraisal, explanatory style, perceived control, psychological hardiness, and social support.

Coping with Stress

- Health psychologists use stress-management programs to help people learn to cope with stress.
- Some of the main methods of reducing stress use stress-inoculation training, formal exercise, and relaxation techniques.

Health-Promoting Habits

- Most deaths in the United States are associated with unhealthy habits, including unsafe sexual practices, lack of exercise, poor nutrition, and smoking.
- Programs aimed at changing these habits hold promise for reducing the incidence of illness and death.

Reactions to Illness

- Health psychologists study aspects of how people cope with illness, including the seeking of treatment, patient distress, and adherence to medical regimens.
- The patient-practitioner relationship is an important factor in adherence.

Key Terms

health psychology (p. 562)

Psychological Stress and Stressors

posttraumatic stress disorder (PTSD) (p. 563)
stress (p. 562)
stressor (p. 562)

The Biopsychology of Stress and Illness

general adaptation syndrome (p. 567)

psychoneuroimmunology (p. 571)
Type A behavior (p. 568)

Factors That Moderate the Stress Response

burnout (p. 576)
cognitive appraisal (p. 575)
explanatory style (p. 575)
learned helplessness (p.576)
perceived control (p. 576)
physiological reactivity (p. 574)

psychological hardiness (p. 577)
social support (p. 578)

Coping with Stress

progressive relaxation (p. 581)
stress-inoculation training (p. 580)

Chapter Quiz

Note: Answers for the Chapter Quiz questions are provided at the end of the book.

1. A century ago, North Americans were most likely to die from
   a. influenza.
   b. lung cancer.
   c. heart attacks.
   d. cerebral vascular accidents.

2. Hans Selye called pleasant stress
   a. eustress.
   b. pressure.
   c. endorphogenic stress.
   d. psychological hardiness.

3. Hormones that are most likely to impair the immune system are secreted by the
   a. pancreas.
   b. pineal gland.
   c. adrenal gland.
   d. thyroid gland.

4. Research on stress and cancer (Glaser, Rice, Speicher, Stout, & Kiecolt-Glaser, 1986) indicates that stress may promote cancer by reducing the activity of
   a. epinephrine.
   b. B-lymphocytes.
   c. corticosteroids.
   d. natural killer cells.

5. Research on the reasons for smoking indicates that habitual smokers smoke mainly to
   a. enhance self-esteem.
   b. make them more alert.
   c. conform to the behavior of their peers.
   d. regulate the level of nicotine in their bodies.

6. Research findings indicate that the component of Type A behavior that is most highly correlated with coronary heart disease is
   a. hostility.
   b. time pressure.
   c. chronic activation.
   d. multiphasic activity.

7. The Canadian scientist who founded modern stress research was
   a. Hans Selye.
   b. Meyer Friedman.
   c. Karen Matthews.
   d. Suzanne Kobasa.

8. One of the main weaknesses of the Social Readjustment Rating Scale is that it
   a. includes only negative life changes.
   b. ignores family-related life changes.
   c. includes life changes that can be either causes or effects of illness.
   d. has stimulated no research on its relationship to actual health status.

9. A student majoring in psychology registers for a course in behavioral statistics, a course that he anticipates will be stressful. The student's level of stress is reduced when he realizes that he has good logical and mathematical abilities. This realization is an example of what Richard Lazarus called
   a. primary appraisal.
   b. tertiary appraisal.
   c. secondary appraisal.
   d. preconscious appraisal.

10. Stress prompts the hypothalamus to secrete a hormone that stimulates the pituitary gland to secrete
    a. ACTH.
    b. adrenaline.
    c. lymphocytes.
    d. corticosteroids.

11. A professor feels in complete control of her courses, challenged by the need to prepare lively lectures, and committed to the teaching profession. She would most likely be high in
    a. burnout.
    b. Type A behavior.
    c. psychological hardiness.
    d. physiological reactivity.

12. A man tests HIV-positive. He most likely
    a. kissed someone who is HIV-positive.
    b. ate food prepared by a cook who is HIV-positive.
    c. used a toilet after a person who is HIV-positive.
    d. used a hypodermic needle used previously by a person who is HIV-positive.

13. Posttraumatic stress disorder became widely publicized as a result of interest in
    a. rape survivors.
    b. Vietnam War veterans.
    c. survivors of child abuse.
    d. survivors of the Mount Saint Helens volcano eruption.

14. Walter Cannon called the body's stress response the
    a. fight-or-flight syndrome.
    b. general adaptation syndrome.
    c. posttraumatic stress disorder.
    d. tend-or-befriend syndrome.

15. In Ader and Cohen's (1982) study of the classical conditioning of the immune response, in which sweetened water was paired with the immunosuppressive drug cyclophosphamide, the conditioned stimulus was
    a. nausea.
    b. sweetened water.
    c. cyclophosphamide.
    d. immunosuppression.

16. Edmund Jacobson was an early contributor to stress management through his research on
    a. burnout.
    b. Type A behavior.
    c. progressive relaxation.
    d. transcendental meditation.

17. Research indicates that of those people who begin formal exercise programs, the proportion who will drop out within 6 months is about
    a. 25 percent.
    b. 50 percent.
    c. 65 percent.
    d. 90 percent.

18. A major weakness in assessing the effect of daily hassles on health is that there has been little research using
    a. case studies.
    b. prospective studies.
    c. retrospective studies.
    d. naturalistic observation.

19. The field that studies the relationship between psychological factors and physical illness is called
    a. biofeedback.
    b. biopsychology.
    c. psychophysiology.
    d. psychoneuroimmunology.

20. B-lymphocytes are the body's main defense against
    a. viruses.
    b. bacteria.
    c. cancer cells.
    d. foreign tissues.

21. Worldwide, most victims of AIDS are
    a. gay men.
    b. hemophiliacs.
    c. heterosexuals.
    d. heroin addicts.

22. Smoking contributes to a yearly death rate of more than
    a. 50,000 Americans.
    b. 100,000 Americans.
    c. 300,000 Americans.
    d. 900,000 Americans.

23. Karen Matthews has found that children who engage in Type A behavior tend to have parents who
    a. pass on "Type A genes" to them.
    b. frown on the expression of anger.
    c. urge them to do better and better.
    d. stress the importance of punctuality.

24. For most of the past 1,000 years in Western cultures, the standard for the most attractive female physique has been
    a. thin.
    b. rounded.
    c. muscular.
    d. grossly obese.

25. Nicotine chewing gum
    a. leads to cigarette smoking.
    b. has no more than a placebo effect.
    c. eliminates the addiction to nicotine.
    d. may motivate weight-conscious smokers to stop smoking.

Thought Questions

1. Students commonly experience intense stress during the final weeks of the academic semester due to such factors as research papers, final exams, and lack of money. What physiological pathway might explain how these stressors could impair your immune system and make you more susceptible to illness immediately after the end of the semester?

2. Some researchers believe that major life events exert their harmful health effects through the daily hassles and related problems they create. How might getting divorced induce stress by this route?

3. Imagine that a friend of yours exhibits a pattern of Type A behavior. Which aspects of this pattern might it be best for her to alter?

4. What five risky or unhealthy behaviors would you be wisest to avoid?

Social Psychology

CHAPTER 17

On March 26, 1997, millions around the world were shocked to learn of the mass suicide of 39 members of a cult known as Heaven's Gate in the wealthy California suburb of Rancho Santa Fe. In prearranged shifts over several days, cult members ingested lethal doses of phenobarbital, put plastic bags over their heads, and suffocated themselves. Their bodies were covered with identical purple shrouds. The chilling scene was made more so by its being meticulously neat and tidy, with identically clad people (down to their black Nike athletic shoes) lying peacefully on their backs, with their belongings (including lip balm and spiral notebooks) packed neatly in overnight bags stowed under their beds.

Cult members even left videotaped messages explaining why they took their lives. They committed suicide because their leader, Marshall Applewhite, had promised that they would be resurrected into a better life aboard a spaceship allegedly hidden behind the comet Hale-Bopp, which had appeared in the night sky. Applewhite, seeking more members to accompany the cult on its journey to Hale-Bopp, had taken out an advertisement in *USA Today* reading, "UFO Cult Resurfaces with Final Offer." The advertisement warned that it would be "the last chance to advance beyond human." Applewhite, an early advocate of the Internet as an advertising tool, also had created an elaborate Web page to entice others to join Heaven's Gate.

How could Applewhite, an outgoing former music teacher at the University of Alabama, transform himself into a charismatic cult leader? How could normal, intelligent adults be persuaded to forsake their families, abandon successful careers, and flee their "bodily containers" with a mere promise of a better life at the "Next Level"? The answers to these questions are sought by social psychologists, who study factors involved in human social interactions.

The scientific study of social psychology began more than a century ago. In the 1890s, bicycle racing was a major spectator sport in North America. As noted in Chapter 11, Norman Triplett (1898) observed that cyclists who raced against other riders rode faster than those who raced against the clock. He decided to study this phenomenon experimentally by having boys spin fishing reels as fast as they could while competing either against time or against another boy. He found that participants who competed against another boy performed faster. This study, the first experimental study of the relationship between psychological factors and sport performance, was possibly the first experiment in social psychology.

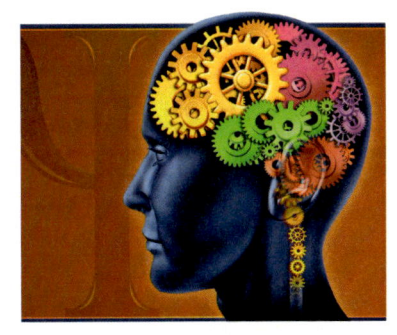

Source: Lightspring/Shutterstock.com.

Chapter Outline

Social Cognition
Interpersonal Attraction
Attitudes
Group Dynamics
Aggression
Prosocial Behavior

social psychology The field that studies how the actual, imagined, or implied presence of other people affects one's thoughts, feelings, and behaviors.

Social psychology is the field that studies behavior in its interpersonal context—that is, how the actual, imagined, or implied presence of other people affects one's thoughts, feelings, and behaviors. Though social-psychological research was conducted before the turn of the 20th century and the first social psychology textbooks were published in 1908 (Pepitone, 1981), social psychology did not become an important field of study until after World War II, when many psychologists became interested in the formal study of social behavior. This interest occurred largely through the earlier efforts of Floyd Allport, perhaps the leading pioneer in the development of social psychology (Parkovnick, 2000). The major topics of interest to social psychologists include social cognition, interpersonal attraction, attitudes, group dynamics, aggression, and prosocial behavior.

Social Cognition

social cognition The process of perceiving, interpreting, and predicting social behavior.

Psychologists who study **social cognition** are concerned with how we perceive, interpret, and predict social behavior. Though social cognition is usually accurate (Jussim, 1991), biases and subjectivity can distort it. Two of the main topics in social cognition are causal attribution and person perception.

Causal Attribution

causal attribution The cognitive process by which we infer the causes of both our own and other people's social behavior.

As first noted in the 1940s by social psychologist Fritz Heider (1944), when we engage in **causal attribution**, we determine the extent to which a person's behavior is caused by the person or by the person's circumstances. There was so much research on causal attribution in the 1970s that the decade became known as "the decade of attribution theory in social psychology" (Weiner, 1985b, p. 74). The most influential attribution theorist of that decade was Harold Kelley (1921–2003); he identified factors that determine how we explain people's behavior.

When you decide that someone is primarily responsible for his or her behavior, you are making a *dispositional* attribution. That is, you would be attributing the behavior to personal qualities such as emotions, abilities, or personality traits. When you decide that circumstances are primarily responsible for a person's behavior, you are making a *situational* attribution. Consider explanations given for poverty. Two research studies, one using university students and one using nonstudents, found that political liberals and political conservatives tended to make different attributions (Zucker & Weiner, 1993). Whereas liberals tended to make situational attributions for poverty (blaming it on factors such as discrimination and lack of opportunities), conservatives tended to make dispositional attributions (blaming it on factors such as a lack of effort or ability). Moreover, there is increasing evidence that there are cultural differences in people's tendencies to make dispositional or situational attribution. One study compared Korean and American undergraduates' explanations for criminal behavior. Korean undergraduates held more lenient attitudes toward criminals and made more situational attributions for crime than did American undergraduates (Na & Loftus, 1998). Whereas people in Asian cultures favor situational factors when making attributions, people in Western cultures favor dispositional factors when making attributions (Kitayama, Duffy, Kawamura, & Larsen, 2003; Norenzayan, Choi, & Nisbett, 2002).

Dimensions of Causal Attribution

Kelley's theory of attribution was soon joined by one devised by Bernard Weiner (1985a). Whereas Kelley's theory has been used primarily to explain the behavior of others, Weiner's has been used primarily to explain how we make causal attributions for our own behavior (Martinko & Thomson, 1998). Weiner and his colleagues found that estimating the relative impact of dispositional and situational factors is important but cannot by itself account for the nature of causal attribution. Weiner identified three dimensions that govern the attribution process. The *internal-external* dimension is akin to Kelley's distinction between dispositional and situational attribution. The *stable-unstable* dimension refers to the degree to which we attribute a behavior to a factor that is stable or unstable. And the *controllable-uncontrollable* dimension indicates the extent to which we attribute a behavior to a factor that is controllable or uncontrollable. Weiner has found that people in a variety of cultures around the world use these dimensions in making attributions for their successes and failures (Schuster, Forsterling, & Weiner, 1989). Figure 17-1 illustrates the interaction of two of Weiner's attributional dimensions.

Weiner's three attributional dimensions are commonly used by students in explaining their academic performance (Anazonwu, 1995). In fact, students may use the dimensions in making excuses that both maintain their self-esteem and prevent professors from becoming angry at them (Weiner, Figueroa-Munoz, & Kakihara, 1991). Suppose you wanted to make an excuse for submitting a term paper late. Your excuse would be more effective if you attributed your behavior to external, unstable, and uncontrollable factors, such as a family emergency, than if you attributed it to internal, stable, and controllable factors, such as a difficulty in budgeting your time.

	Internal	External
Stable	Ability	Task difficulty
Unstable	Effort	Luck

FIGURE 17-1
Two Dimensions of Causal Attribution

According to Bernard Weiner, we may explain our successes and failures by attributing them to internal or external causes that are either stable or unstable.

Biases in Causal Attribution

If human beings were as rational and objective as Mr. Spock in *Star Trek*, the causal attribution process would be straightforward. But being somewhat irrational and subjective, we exhibit biases in the causal attributions we make. These biases include the fundamental attribution error and the self-serving bias.

The Fundamental Attribution Error One bias is the tendency to attribute other people's behavior to dispositional factors. This bias is known as the **fundamental attribution error** (Nisbett & Ross, 1980). In one study, college undergraduates read descriptions of an expectant mother or father who was anticipating staying at home with the baby or being employed after its birth. Participants rated the parents who expected to remain at home to care for their child as being more nurturing and family oriented and less independent and competitive than parents who expected to return to work. Moreover, these ratings were unaffected by information about whether parents' employment was a matter of choice or necessity (Riggs, 1998). Thus, in explaining why parents work outside the home, we might commit the fundamental attribution error by overemphasizing the role of personality (dispositional attributions) rather than situational factors.

Cross-cultural research finds that the fundamental attribution error, like other cognitive biases reported in this chapter, is more common in Western cultures. Cross-cultural studies indicate that Asian participants are *less* likely to attribute people's behavior to dispositional factors. A study relevant to this distinction compared how American and Japanese newspapers treated "rogue trader" financial scandals. Whereas American newspapers tended to focus on the individual traders as being responsible, Japanese newspapers tended to focus on the traders' organizations as being responsible (Menon, Morris, Chiu, & Hong, 1999). These cultural differences are attributable to East Asians' tendency to see people—and their behavior—as being constrained by social situations or circumstances (Nisbett, Peng, Choi, & Norenzayan, 2001).

The Self-Serving Bias We also are subject to a **self-serving bias**, which is the tendency to make dispositional attributions for our own successes and situational attributions for our own failures, especially when our self-esteem is threatened (Campbell & Sedikides, 1999). For example, a study of college students found that those who received high grades (As or Bs) tended to make dispositional attributions for their own performance, attributing their success to their own efforts and abilities. In contrast, students who received lower grades (Cs, Ds, or Fs) tended to make situational attributions, attributing their lack of success to bad luck and difficult tests (Bernstein, Stephan, & Davis, 1979). People who tend to attribute negative events to dispositional qualities in themselves might

Attributions and Excuses

An effective strategy for making an excuse, such as being late, would include external, unstable, and uncontrollable factors, such as a personal emergency.
Source: Ljupco Smokovski/Shutterstock.com.

fundamental attribution error
The bias to attribute other people's behavior to dispositional factors.

self-serving bias The tendency to make dispositional attributions for one's successes and situational attributions for one's failures.

even induce physiological stress responses that impair their immune response. A study of HIV-positive gay men found that those who attributed negative events in their lives to aspects of themselves showed a more rapid decline in their immune response during the next 18 months than those who did not (Segerstrom, Taylor, Kemeny, Reed, & Visscher, 1996). The self-serving bias is in keeping with evidence (see Chapter 13) that psychological well-being is associated with the maintenance of an unrealistically positive view of oneself (Taylor & Brown, 1988).

But is psychological well-being achieved only by focusing on oneself? People also may derive a sense of well-being from their group identity or collective achievements. There is evidence that in collectivist cultures attributions may follow a self-effacing rather than self-enhancing pattern. In one study, Japanese participants were more likely to make dispositional attributions following failure and less likely to make dispositional attributions following success on some achievement tasks (Kashima & Triandis, 1986). Moreover, Japanese students have been found to attribute the successes of others to dispositional factors and the failures of others to situational factors (Yamaguchi, 1988). This cross-cultural difference is even stronger for successes that are meaningful in individualist versus collectivist cultures (Leung, Kim, Zhang, Tam, & Chiu, 2012). Markus and Kitayama (1991) have coined the term *modesty bias* for this apparent reversal of the self-serving bias, noting its prevalence in collectivist cultures.

Person Perception

In addition to making causal attributions about the causes of behavior, we spend a great deal of our time making judgments about the personal characteristics of people, or engaging in **person perception**. Researchers interested in person perception study topics such as impression management, stereotypes, first impressions, and self-fulfilling prophecy.

person perception The process of making judgments about the personal characteristics of others.

Impression Management

Do you know a student who is considered "phony" by other students? The students might be reacting to that student's obvious attempt to convey an impression that is at odds with his or her true self. The deliberate attempt to control the impressions that others form of us is called **impression management** (Leary & Kowalski, 1990). Impression management is a normal part of everyday social relations. Job applicants use impression management when they write their résumés (Knouse, 1994) and during job interviews (Ellis, West, Ryan, & DeShon, 2002). And British banking executives found themselves in a double-bind when engaged in impression management during the UK banking inquiry that followed the 2008 global economic crisis. In order to avoid being held accountable by the press, they were faced with appearing to be either unethical or having poor professional credibility (Stapleton & Hargie, 2011). People who are good at impression management even may adapt better than those who are not when they find themselves in other cultures (Montagliani & Giacalone, 1998).

impression management The deliberate attempt to control the impression that others form of us.

A common technique that we use in impression management is self-handicapping (see Chapter 13). When we self-handicap, we let others know that we are performing under a handicap. If we then do well, we look good to others. If we do poorly, others will attribute our poor performance to our "handicap." Consider a student who announces that he was too anxious to study for an exam. Success on the exam would reflect well on his ability; others would attribute failure on the exam to his anxiety rather than to lack of ability—thereby protecting his self-esteem. We would not be so lenient in judging his performance if he claimed he had not tried hard (Rhodewalt, Sanbonmatsu, Tschanz, & Feick, 1995).

Self-handicapping may protect self-esteem, but it also may have serious consequences for academic performance. One longitudinal study (see Chapter 4) found that undergraduates who scored high on a measure of self-handicapping had poorer academic records than low self-handicappers—in part due to poor study habits. Moreover, self-handicapping was correlated with poor adjustment and coping—which then led to even more self-handicapping (Zuckerman, Kiefer, & Knee, 1998). Thus, self-handicapping may lead to a vicious cycle of poor adjustment, ineffective coping, and increased self-handicapping.

Impression Management
Job applicants use impression management during job interviews.
Source: Africa Studio/Shutterstock.com.

Moreover, self-handicapping may not always be an effective impression management strategy—especially in relationships with women. In one study, male participants evaluated self-handicappers more positively and were more willing to accept excuses for their poor performance than were female participants. Female participants, however, were very critical of self-handicappers, viewing them with suspicion and believing that they were unmotivated. The researchers attributed these differences to women's tendency to value effort over ability when evaluating themselves and others (Hirt, McCrea, & Boris, 2003).

Stereotypes

College professor. Millenial. Johnny Depp. Latina. Each of these concepts involves a **social schema**, which comprises the presumed characteristics of a role, event, person, or group. Social schemas bring order to what might otherwise be a chaotic social world by permitting us to interpret and predict the behavior of others. A **stereotype** is a social schema that includes characteristics that are ascribed to almost all members of a group. Note that stereotypes, though usually negative, can be positive. For example, American television commercials portray Asian Americans as a "model minority" consisting of people with a universally high work ethic. A study that analyzed more than 1,300 television commercials found that Asian Americans were overrepresented, appearing in 8.4 percent of the commercials though comprising only 3.6 percent of the population. But they were more likely than members of other minorities to appear in the background of commercials, with Asian American women rarely appearing in major roles. Moreover, the commercials support the stereotype of the hard-working Asian American by generally showing them in business situations and rarely at social functions or in family settings (Taylor & Stern, 1997).

Stereotypes are reinforced in part by our tendency to view members of our own group (our in-group) as more variable than members of another group (an out-group). For example, a study of college sororities found that they judged their own members as more variable than those of another sorority (Ryan & Bogart, 2001). This effect is stronger for groups with which we have little experience (Linville, Fischer, & Yoon, 1996). One study compared views of South Africans and European Americans about their own group and the other group. The results showed that both groups held relatively complex views of their own group but a relatively simplistic view of the other group (Bartsch, Judd, Louw, Park, & Ryan, 1997).

Stereotypes are more likely to be activated in certain situations. For example, stereotypes have a strong influence when we have little information about people other than their group membership. And we can inhibit the activation of stereotypes when we want to avoid prejudice (Kunda & Spencer, 2003). Of course, few people assume that all members of an out-group share the same characteristics. Thus, when confronted with someone who violates a stereotype, they simply assimilate that person into their out-group schema as an exception to the rule (Wilder, Simon, & Faith, 1996).

First Impressions

When we first meet a person, we might have little information about the individual other than her or his sex, ethnicity, apparent age, and physical appearance. Each of these characteristics might activate a particular social schema, which in turn will create a first impression of that person. A first impression functions as a social schema to guide our predictions of a person's behavior and our desire to interact with that person. First impressions are important in many situations, such as in determining whether college roommates will become friends (Berg, 1984). One clever study had trained coders evaluate the firmness of undergraduates' handshakes. A firm handshake was defined by duration and completeness of grip, vigor, strength, and amount of eye contact. Participants—especially females—with firm handshakes received more positive first impression ratings than did participants with weaker handshakes (Chaplin, Phillips, Brown, Clanton, & Stein, 2000). And even our exercise habits may contribute to the impressions we make on others. An experiment found that college students rated students described as exercisers more positively than students described as nonexercisers (Kanarek, Mathes, & D'Anci, 2012).

social schema A cognitive structure comprising the presumed characteristics of a role, an event, a person, or a group.

stereotype A social schema that incorporates characteristics, which can be positive or negative, supposedly shared by almost all members of a group.

First Impressions

Do these men bring different thoughts and feelings to mind? Your first impression of them might determine how you initially act toward them.
Source: (top) vdovin_vn/Shutterstock.com; (bottom) kiuikson/Shutterstock.com.

A classic experiment by Harold Kelley (1950) demonstrated the importance of a first impression on our evaluation of a stranger. Undergraduates were given a written description of a guest lecturer as "a rather warm person, industrious, critical, practical, and determined" or the same description with the word *warm* replaced by the word *cold*. After the lecture, which provided the opportunity for questions and discussion, the students were asked for their impressions of the lecturer. Students who had been told that the lecturer was warm rated him as more informal, sociable, and humorous than did those who were told he was cold. Those who had been told the lecturer was warm also asked more questions and participated in more discussions with him. These findings indicated that the students assimilated the lecturer's behavior into the schema they had created on the basis of the written description. This study has been replicated successfully using similar methodology (Widmeyer & Loy, 1988).

Self-Fulfilling Prophecy

self-fulfilling prophecy The tendency for one person's expectations to influence another person to behave in accordance with them.

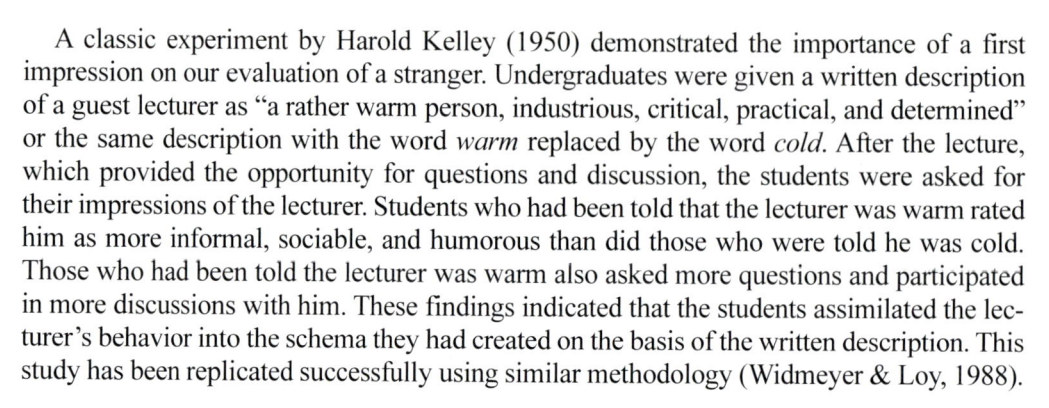

One of the important effects of first impressions is the **self-fulfilling prophecy**, which is the tendency for one person's expectations to make a second person behave in accordance with them. This phenomenon occurs because the social schema we have of the other person will make us act a certain way toward that person, which in turn will make the person respond in accordance with our expectations (Rosenthal, 2002). Thus, if you expect a person to be unfriendly and, as a result, act cold and aloof, you might elicit unfriendly behavior from that person—even if he or she would normally be inclined to be friendly. In fact, research shows that dating partners who expect to be rejected tend to behave in ways that provoke their partner to eventually reject them (Downey, Freitas, Michaelis, & Khouri, 1998). But in contrast, a 1-year longitudinal study found that dating partners who idealized each other at the beginning tended to create a self-fulfilling prophecy that produced the very relationship they sought (Murray, Holmes, & Griffin, 1996).

However, one recent longitudinal study found that chronically insecure college students' relationships can be enhanced by an intervention designed to influence their self-fulfilling prophecies of social rejection. At the beginning of the experiment, participants completed measures of relational security and also were rated by a trained nurse who rated their social demeanor (for example, calm/agitated, relaxed/anxious, and appreciative/unappreciative). Participants in the experimental condition engaged in a self-affirmation procedure in which they spent 15 minutes writing short paragraphs about why their values were important to them, their lives, and their self-image. Participants in the control condition spent 15 minutes writing about other people's values. This procedure was repeated approximately weekly over a period of 4 weeks. Results indicated that participants who wrote self-affirmations reported increased relational security and more positive social behavior ratings than participants in the control condition. Moreover, these effects persisted up to two months after the beginning of the experiment. Thus, a negative self-fulfilling prophecy can be mitigated by engaging in a process of positive self-affirmation (Stinson, Logal, Shepherd, & Zanna, 2011).

Stereotypes also may contribute to self-fulfilling prophecies. People perform better when they are unaware of negative stereotypes that others might hold. But what of positive stereotypes? Suppose you belong to two stereotyped groups, such as the case of Asian American women. As Asian Americans they are stereotypically viewed as good in mathematics. As women they are stereotypically viewed as poor in mathematics. In one study, Asian American women who completed a questionnaire that included items about their ethnicity then performed better on a mathematics test than did Asian American women who did not. But Asian American women who completed a questionnaire that included items about their gender then performed worse on a mathematics test than Asian American women who did not. Evidently, participants' performances depended on whether their ethnic or gender stereotype had been made salient to them (Shih, Pittinsky, & Ambady, 1999). And a replication study addressed the social costs of being a "model minority." In this study, Asians' *extremely* high performance in mathematics was made salient to Asian American women. Under these conditions, participants found it difficult to concentrate and performed more poorly. Hence, people's awareness of positive stereotypes that others might hold may lead to choking under pressure (Cheryan & Bodenhausen, 2000).

Self-Fulfilling Prophecy
Chronically insecure people may suffer from self-fulfilling prophecies of social rejection.
Source: Iakov Fiulimonov/Shutterstock.com.

> ### Section Review: Social Cognition
> 1. What are the three dimensions in Weiner's attribution model?
> 2. What is the self-serving bias?
> 3. How can a first impression create a self-fulfilling prophecy?

Interpersonal Attraction

While forming impressions of other people, we also develop interpersonal attraction toward some of them. By this point in the semester, you have probably become friendly with certain students; you might even have developed a romantic relationship with someone in particular. Social psychologists interested in interpersonal attraction seek answers to questions like these: Why do we like certain people more than others? What is the nature of romantic love?

Liking

Think of the students you have met this semester. Which ones do you like? Which ones do you not like? Among the factors that determine which ones you like are proximity, familiarity, physical attractiveness, similarity, and self-disclosure.

Proximity

You are more likely to develop a liking for someone who lives near you, works with you, or attends the same classes as you. Research has consistently supported the importance of proximity in the development of friendships, as in a classic study of the residents of apartments in a housing project for married students at the Massachusetts Institute of Technology. The closer that students lived to one another, the more likely they were to become friends. In fact, 41 percent of the students reported that their best friends lived next door. Because the students had been randomly assigned to apartments, their initial degree of liking for one another could not explain the findings (Festinger, Schachter, & Back, 1950). Proximity is important in dating relationships, too. But what effect does electronic communication and telecommuting have on people's friendships with coworkers? The Internet is quickly changing patterns of human interaction, especially inside the workplace. One study found that under these circumstances, physical proximity was the *least* important factor in friendship initiation. On the other hand, face-to-face communication in the workplace was the most important factor in maintaining satisfying friendships (Sias, Pedersen, Gallagher, & Kopaneva, 2012).

Familiarity

Proximity makes us more familiar with certain people. But contrary to the popular saying, familiarity tends to breed liking, not contempt. The more familiar we become with a stimulus, whether a car, a painting, or a professor, the more we will like it. So in general, the more we interact with particular people, the more we tend to like them (Moreland & Zajonc, 1982). In one study, participants who spoke with a person for a few minutes or simply waited quietly with a person were more likely to comply with a request from that person than were participants who were simply approached with a request (Burger, Soroka, Gonzago, Murphy, & Somervell, 2001). Of course, this tendency, called the *mere exposure effect*, holds only when people do not behave in negative ways. The effect of familiarity on liking is not lost on politicians, who enhance their popularity by making repeated television appearances. The more familiar we are with public figures (assuming they do nothing scandalous), the more we tend to like them (Harrison, 1969).

The mere exposure effect was supported by a clever experiment that used female college students as participants. For each participant, two photographs of the participant were presented to the participant and to a friend. One photograph was a direct image of

Physical Attractiveness

Cross-culturally, the results of research studies agree that "what is beautiful is good."
Source: Cheryl A. Rickabaugh.

the participant; the second was a mirror image—what the participant would see when looking at herself in a mirror. Mirror images and normal photographic images differ because our faces are not perfectly symmetrical—the left and right sides look different. Participants and friends were asked to choose which of the two photographs was preferable. Friends were more likely to choose the direct image, whereas participants were more likely to choose the mirror image. These results were evidence for the mere exposure effect because the friends were more familiar with the direct image, whereas the participants were more familiar with their own mirror image (Mita, Dermer, & Knight, 1977).

Physical Attractiveness

Proximity not only lets us become familiar with people, it also lets us note their appearance. We tend to like physically attractive people more than physically unattractive ones. For example, one study found that both adults and children preferred physically attractive avatars from the Nintendo Wii console (Principe & Langlois, 2013). Contemporary films promote this tendency by associating positive personal characteristics with more physically attractive actors and actresses. A study that examined a random sample of five decades of top-grossing films found that physically attractive characters were portrayed more positively than physically unattractive ones. Moreover, after people view films that portray physically attractive characters as more appealing, they become more likely to evaluate physically attractive people in their own lives more positively, as when considering someone for admission to graduate school. These studies provide consistent findings that we believe that "what is beautiful is good" (Smith, McIntosh, & Bazzini, 1999).

Sensitivity to physical attractiveness begins early in life, with infants as young as 4 months old preferring to look at attractive faces instead of unattractive ones (Samuels, Butterworth, Roberts, & Graupner, 1994). This bias can have practical benefits for attractive people—especially physically attractive girls and women (Maner et al., 2003). Attractive adults and children are judged more positively and treated more positively by others. In turn—consistent with the self-fulfilling prophecy—attractive adults and children also exhibit more positive behaviors and personality traits (Langlois et al., 2000). For example, physically attractive people are perceived to be more intelligent (Jackson, Hunter, & Hodge, 1995) and more socially competent (Hope & Mindell, 1994). They also are more likely to be hired than are less attractive applicants with equivalent qualifications (Hosoda, Stone-Romero, & Coats, 2003). Physically attractive defendants are less likely to be convicted of crimes and, if convicted, less likely to be subjected to severe punishment (Mazzella & Feingold, 1994). And physically attractive college students are less likely to be asked for proof of age by bartenders (McCall, 1997).

Judgments of facial attractiveness have strong cross-cultural consistency (Langlois et al., 2000). In one study, native-born European Americans and newly arrived Asian and Hispanic students rated the attractiveness of photographs of African American, European American, Asian, and Latina women. The correlation in ratings, .93, was almost perfect. In a companion study, African and European American men rated the attractiveness of photos of African American women. Ratings of facial attractiveness correlated .94, but African Americans and European Americans differed in their judgments of body attractiveness (Cunningham, Roberts, Barbee, & Druen, 1995). In regard to facial attractiveness, there is cross-cultural evidence that we find symmetrical faces more attractive than faces that are not symmetrical (Rhodes et al., 2001). Moreover, this effect has been found among American children as young as 9 years of age (Vingilis-Jaremko & Larissa, 2013). Some researchers interpret this attraction as having a hereditary basis, perhaps one that is the product of evolution (Fink & Penton-Voak, 2002).

Physical attractiveness is an important factor in dating relationships. In an early experiment on the effect of physical attractiveness, first-year students at the University of Minnesota took part in a computer dating study. They completed personality and aptitude tests and were told that they would be paired based on their responses. In reality, they were paired randomly. Independent judges rated the physical attractiveness of each student. The couples then attended a dance that lasted several hours and rated their partners on a questionnaire. The results showed that physical attractiveness was the most important factor in determining whether participants liked their partners and whether they desired to date them again (Walster et al., 1966). More recent research has replicated this finding; both men and women value physically attractiveness in dating relationships (Eastwick, Eagly, Finkel, & Johnson, 2011).

Though we may prefer to have relationships with very attractive people, social sorting usually leads us to have friends (Cash & Derlega, 1978) and romantic partners (Folkes, 1982) who are similar to us in physical attractiveness. That is, though we may prefer more attractive people, they may reject us—just as we may reject people who are less attractive than we are. These rejections leave us in relationships with people whose level of attractiveness is similar to our own.

Similarity

Though we tend to develop relationships with people who are similar to us in physical attractiveness, do we seek people who are similar to us in other ways? Do opposites attract? Or do birds of a feather flock together? You may recall the experiment discussed in Chapter 2 that showed that we are more attracted to people whose attitudes are similar to our own (Byrne, Ervin, & Lamberth, 1970). The findings of that classic study have been replicated in many research studies, including recent experiments (Klohnen & Luo, 2003), and a recent meta-analysis has reported a large effect size for both actual and perceived similarity on attraction (Montoya, Horton, & Kirchner, 2008). But this interpretation has been challenged by research showing that we are likely to associate with people who hold similar attitudes simply by default because we are repulsed by those who have dissimilar ones. Life's circumstances simply put us in religious, political, recreational, and educational settings where we are likely to associate with people who share our attitudes (Rosenbaum, 1986).

But the results of recent research studies indicate that attitude similarity plays a more important role in interpersonal attraction in some contexts and that attitude dissimilarity plays a role in preventing interpersonal attraction in others (Singh & Ho, 2000). For example, we are attracted to people with similar attitudes if we expect to enjoy each other's company (Michinov & Monteil, 2002). And other research indicates that we like people who share our activity preferences even more than we like people who share our attitudes (Lydon, Jamieson, & Zanna, 1988). Thus, you might enjoy playing sports or going to music concerts with someone whose sexual, religious, and political values differ from yours. And in certain cases we are, indeed, more attracted to people who are not similar to us, particularly if we find that their personal characteristics are fulfilling to us. Such attraction may occur, for example, when one person is dominant and the other is submissive. These partners are more satisfied with their relationship than are partners who are similar in those personality characteristics (Dryer & Horowitz, 1997).

Self-Disclosure

To determine whether we share similar attitudes and interests with someone else, we must engage in self-disclosure, in which we reveal our beliefs, feelings, and experiences. Reciprocation of self-disclosure is important because we tend to like people more if they have disclosed personal information to us and if we have disclosed personal information to them (Collins & Miller, 1994). In social relationships, self-disclosure is best if it is gradual. When people disclose highly personal information to us too early in a relationship, we may become uneasy, suspicious, and less attracted to them. If someone you have just met has ever regaled you with his or her whole life story, including intimate details, you might have felt uncomfortable and uninterested in pursuing the relationship. Moreover, we must consider the cultural background of the person with whom we are interacting. For example, a study found that American college students preferred to engage in more self-disclosure than did Taiwanese college students (Chen, 1995).

Romantic Love

Love might make the world go round, but there were few scientific studies of romantic love until the 1970s. Since then, the findings of such research have been used to help prevent and relieve the emotional and physical suffering that is produced by unhappy romantic relationships, including spouse abuse, child abuse, and relationship dissolution. What have researchers discovered about the nature of romantic love? For one thing, the concept of love has "fuzzy borders" (see Chapter 9). That is, we know love when we see it or experience it, but we cannot define it by a single set of features without finding exceptions to any definition we put forth (Fehr & Russell, 1991).

Theories of Love

Elaine Hatfield—undaunted by earning the first Golden Fleece Award (regularly bestowed by former U.S. Senator William Proxmire for the project that he believed was the greatest waste of government funding) for the research she conducted with her colleague, Ellen Berscheid—distinguishes between passionate love and companionate love (Hatfield, 1988). **Passionate love**, commonly known as sexual love, involves intense emotional arousal, including sexual feelings. **Companionate love** involves feelings of affection and commitment to the relationship. Over time, romantic relationships tend to decline in passionate love and increase in companionate love.

More research has been conducted on passionate love than on companionate love. According to Berscheid and Hatfield, passionate love depends on three factors. First, the culture must promote the notion of passionate love. Passionate love has been important in Western cultures for only a few centuries, and even today some cultures have no concept of it. Second, the person must experience a state of intense emotional arousal. Third, the emotional arousal must be associated with a romantic partner (Berscheid & Walster, 1974).

Berscheid and Hatfield's theory of romantic love incorporates aspects of Stanley Schachter and Jerome Singer's two-factor theory of emotion. As explained in Chapter 12, Schachter and Singer's theory assumes that you will experience a particular emotion when you perceive that you are physiologically aroused, and you will attribute that arousal to an emotionally relevant aspect of the situation in which you find yourself. The two-factor theory assumes that romantic love is the result of being physiologically aroused in a situation that promotes the labeling of that arousal as romantic love.

The two-factor theory of romantic love was supported by a clever experiment that took place on two bridges in Vancouver, British Columbia (Dutton & Aron, 1974). One, the Capilano River Bridge, was 5 feet wide, 450 feet long, and 230 feet above rocky rapids. It had low handrails and was constructed of wooden boards attached to wire cables, making it prone to wobble back and forth, inducing fear-related physiological arousal in those who walked across it. The other bridge, over a tiny tributary of the Capilano River, was wide, solid, immobile, and only 10 feet above the water. These characteristics made that bridge less likely to induce arousal in those who walked across it.

Whenever a man walked across one of the bridges, he was met by an attractive woman who was the experimenter's confederate. The woman asked each man to participate in a psychology course project about the effects of scenic attractions on creativity. Each man was shown a picture of a man and a woman in an ambiguous situation and was asked to write a brief dramatic story about the picture. The woman then gave the man her telephone number in case he wanted to ask her any questions about the study. The results showed that, compared with the men on the solid bridge, the men who were on the bridge that induced physiological arousal wrote stories with more sexual content and were more likely to call the woman later.

According to the two-factor theory of romantic love, the men on the bridge that induced arousal had attributed their arousal to the presence of the attractive woman, leading them to experience romantic feelings toward her. But this interpretation of the results has been rejected by some researchers, who offer an alternative interpretation that assumes that the presence of the woman reduced the men's fear of the bridge, which, as a consequence, conditioned them to find her more attractive (Riordan & Tedeschi, 1983).

Nonetheless, results of studies similar to the Capilano River study have supported the two-factor theory of romantic love. In one such study, female and male participants who had just ridden a roller coaster rated photographs of persons of the other sex as more attractive and desirable than did participants who were waiting to ride the roller

passionate love Love characterized by intense emotional arousal and sexual feelings.

companionate love Love characterized by feelings of affection and commitment to a relationship with another person.

Companionate Love

For romantic love to last after passionate love has waned somewhat, romantic partners must maintain the deep affection that characterizes companionate love.

Source: Monkey Business Images/Shutterstock.com.

coaster (Meston & Frolich, 2003). A recent meta-analysis also found consistent effects of arousal on attraction, with effect sizes ranging from small to moderate across a number of conditions. For example, sexual arousal increased physical attraction, but not liking or interpersonal attraction (Foster et al., 1998).

Another prominent theory of love has been put forth by Robert Sternberg (1986). His triangular theory of love presumes that the experience of love depends on the interaction of three components. Passion encompasses drives that lead to romance, physical attraction, and sexual relations. Intimacy encompasses feelings of closeness, bondedness, and connectedness. And decision/commitment encompasses, in the short term, the decision that one loves another and, in the long term, the commitment to maintain that love. The intensity of love depends on the individual strengths of these three components, whereas the kind of love that is experienced depends on the strengths of the three components relative to one another. For example, strong passion combined with little intimacy and weak decision/commitment is associated with infatuation, whereas strong passion and great intimacy combined with weak decision/commitment is associated with romantic love.

Romantic Love

According to the two-factor theory of romantic love, sexual arousal experienced by couples may be enhanced by visits to amusement parks.
Source: Lucky Business/Shutterstock.com.

Though the triangular theory of love has been with us for more than two decades, it has inspired surprisingly little empirical research until more recently. There is some research evidence supporting the three components of the theory (Lemieux & Hale, 2002), its relationship to commitment in romantic relationships (Campbell, Foster, & Finkel, 2002), and gender differences in beliefs about love (Sprecher & Toro-Morn, 2002). A recent survey found that passionate love was higher among younger couples and companionate love higher among older couples. That does not mean that passionate love is doomed to die as the relationship endures. Whereas passionate love indeed waned over the first 20 years of a relationship, there was a "rebound" effect in which it grew stronger among couples in relationships that lasted longer than 20 years. This finding was attributed to family and life cycle transitions that enable older couples to enjoy each other more (Sheets, 2013). There also is research evidence that passion and intimacy are intertwined, with increases in intimacy associated with strong passion. When intimacy is stable, whether high or low, passion will be low (Baumeister & Bratslavsky, 1999).

There also are culture-related differences in the definition of romantic love (Landis & O'Shea, 2000) and the importance and expression of emotional intimacy (Seki, Matsumoto, & Imahori, 2002). One study compared love songs in the United States and Hong Kong and mainland China. In Chinese songs love was expected to come to an unhappy end that involved intense suffering. Though songs from both cultures depicted similar levels of desire, Chinese songs depicted love as being less individualistic and more influenced by family relationships and even the environment—a reflection of the Taoist principle of harmony with nature and society (Rothbaum & Tsang, 1998). In traditional Chinese culture many women and men consider the wishes of their family when choosing a mate. Thus, the prevalence of arranged marriages in traditional Chinese culture, which benefit the extended family, may be at odds with the Western concept of romantic love (Hsu, 1981). Recent surveys, however, point to individualistic trends, with more Chinese men and women preferring a love-based marriage (Xiaohe & Whyte, 1990).

Promoting Romantic Love

What factors promote romantic love? As in the case of personal liking, similarity is an important factor. We tend to choose romantic partners who are similar to us in attractiveness (Yela & Sangrador, 2001) as well as in religion, ethnic background, and educational level (Buss, 1985). One factor is an exception to the similarity rule—chronological age. Gay and heterosexual men prefer younger partners than do lesbian and heterosexual women (Silverthorne & Quinsey, 2000). A survey found that when men and women were asked to rate the personal factors that would make someone attractive as a romantic partner, a sense of humor was the most important one (Buss, 1988). A more recent survey of heterosexual college students found that both men and women viewed humorous people as more appealing for serious relationships, including marriage, but only when they perceived them as physically attractive (Lundy, Tan, & Cunningham, 1998). We also prefer romantic partners who view us as we see ourselves but who also bolster our self-esteem (Katz & Beach, 2000). And a study of 18-year-old dating couples found that those who engaged in mutual self-disclosure early in the relationship were more likely to be together 4 months later (Berg & McQuinn, 1986).

Another important factor in romantic relationships is equity, the belief that each partner is contributing equally to the relationship, which promotes long-term contentment and commitment, especially among men and women with nontraditional gender roles (Donaghue & Fallon, 2003). Even the mere promise of equity might be important in promoting romantic relationships. This finding has been shown in archival research on personal advertisements. A survey of 800 advertisements placed by individuals seeking romantic partners found that the advertisers tended to seek equitable relationships. But heterosexual women and men differed in complementary ways in the rewards they sought and offered. Men tended to seek attractive women while offering financial security in return. In contrast, women tended to seek financially secure men while offering physical attractiveness in return (Harrison, 1977). These findings have been replicated in a laboratory experiment (Buunk, Dijkstra, Fetchenhauer, & Kenrick, 2002) and in more recent archival research studies (Cicerello & Sheehan, 1995). These findings also hold across cultures, as in a study of the marital preferences of more than 1,500 heterosexual college students in Japan, Russia, and the United States (Hatfield & Sprecher, 1995). But the content of personal advertisements may vary with the individual's gender identity or sexual orientation. Two studies found, for example, that heterosexuals mentioned financial security more frequently than did gay men or lesbians. Physical characteristics were mentioned the most by gay men and the least by lesbians (Gonzales & Meyers, 1993).

Evolutionary psychologists would claim that these findings are not surprising because they reflect millions of years of evolution. According to evolutionary psychologists' interpretation of these findings, men prefer younger, physically attractive women because they would be more likely to have the ability to bear children and, as a result, pass on the men's genes. Similarly, women prefer men of higher financial status—especially those with personalities that are kind, caring, and loyal—because they would probably be more able and willing to care for the women and their offspring (Buss, 2003). Of course, this evolutionary psychology viewpoint, as it usually is, is an after-the-fact explanation for behaviors that might be explained just as well by learned cultural differences in male and female gender roles. This interpretation is supported by the results of a recent study that compared heterosexual women's and men's mate preferences in 37 cultures. Women (but not men) preferred mates with greater financial resources in cultures that limited reproductive freedom and educational equality for women (Kasser & Sharma, 1999).

Section Review: Interpersonal Attraction

1. What evidence is there that the mere exposure effect contributes to liking?
2. How does the two-factor theory explain romantic love?
3. How do personal advertisements for romantic partners support equity as a factor in romantic relationships?

Attitudes

attitude An evaluation—containing cognitive, emotional, and behavioral components—of an idea, event, object, or person.

What are your opinions about the insanity defense? Surprise parties? Abstract art? Sorority members? Your answers to these questions would reveal your attitudes. **Attitudes** are evaluations of ideas (such as the insanity defense), events (such as surprise parties), objects (such as cellular phones), or people (such as sorority members). In the 1930s, the noted psychologist Gordon Allport claimed that the concept of attitude was the single most important concept in social psychology. It no longer maintains such a lofty position, but it is still one of the most widely studied concepts in social psychology.

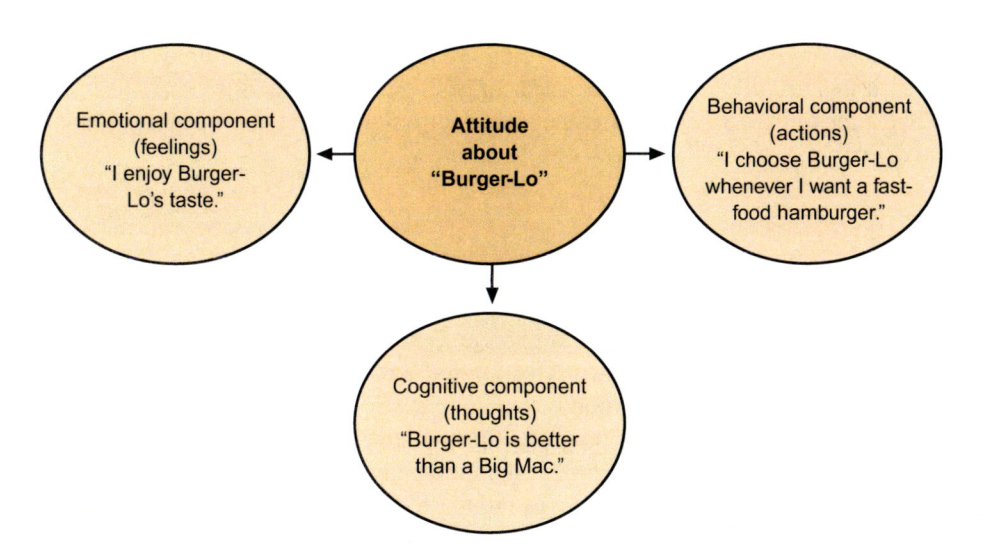

FIGURE 17-2
The Components of Attitudes

Attitudes have emotional, cognitive, and behavioral components.

- Emotional component (feelings) "I enjoy Burger-Lo's taste."
- Attitude about "Burger-Lo"
- Behavioral component (actions) "I choose Burger-Lo whenever I want a fast-food hamburger."
- Cognitive component (thoughts) "Burger-Lo is better than a Big Mac."

As shown in Figure 17-2, attitudes have emotional, cognitive, and behavioral components (Breckler, 1984). To appreciate these components, imagine that you have been asked to participate in a market research survey of attitudes toward a new low-cholesterol, fast-food hamburger called "Burger-Lo." The market researcher would determine your attitude toward Burger-Lo by measuring one or more of the three components of your attitude. Your emotional response might be measured by a questionnaire asking you to rate your feelings about Burger-Lo's taste, aroma, texture, and appearance. Your cognitive response might be measured by asking you to describe the thoughts that Burger-Lo brings to mind, such as "It's better than a Big Mac." And your behavioral response might be measured by observing whether you choose Burger-Lo over several other fast-food hamburgers in a blind taste test.

The Formation of Attitudes

How are our attitudes formed? Some are learned through classical conditioning (see Chapter 7) by the pairing of a desirable or undesirable feeling with the object of the attitude (Olson & Fazio, 2002). If Burger-Lo tastes good, you will associate that experience with Burger-Lo and develop a positive attitude toward it. Research indicates that our food preferences are, in fact, influenced by classical conditioning (Rozin & Zellner, 1985). Advertisers of foods and other products take advantage of classical conditioning by pairing them with stimuli that are already desirable (Grossman & Till, 1998). Thus, advertisers often try to sell automobiles to consumers by associating them with attractive men and women in media advertisements.

Attitudes also can be formed through operant conditioning (see Chapter 7), as in an experiment conducted at the University of Hawaii (Insko, 1965). Undergraduates, contacted by telephone, were asked whether they agreed or disagreed with statements that favored or opposed a proposed "Springtime Aloha Week." The caller positively reinforced certain statements by saying "good." For half the telephone calls, the caller said "good" whenever the student agreed with a statement favoring the proposal. For the other half, the caller said "good" whenever the student agreed with a statement opposing the proposal. One week later the students were given a "local issues questionnaire." Among the items on the questionnaire was a question asking whether they favored or opposed the proposed Springtime Aloha Week. The responses to that question showed that students who earlier had been reinforced for making statements that favored the Springtime Aloha Week were more likely to favor it, whereas students who earlier had been reinforced for making statements that opposed it were more likely to oppose it.

According to social-learning theory, many of our attitudes are learned through observing others—particularly our parents, our peers, and characters on television shows—being punished or positively reinforced for engaging in particular behaviors (Kanekar, 1976). For example, cross-cultural differences and similarities in attitudes toward favorite foods

Chapter 17 Social Psychology

are acquired through acculturation (Cervellon & Dube, 2002). Even our attitudes toward the use of drugs are affected by social learning. For example, adolescents have a more positive attitude toward alcohol use if they have consistently seen their peers, parents, and siblings drinking it (Ary, Tildesley, Hops, & Andrews, 1993).

The Art of Persuasion

In 1956, Edward Schein published an article that described the results of his interviews with United Nations soldiers who, as prisoners during the Korean War, had been subjected to so-called brainwashing, which in some cases made them express sympathy for the North Koreans and antipathy toward the United States. Publicity about brainwashing, and fears that it could be used by totalitarian governments to control citizens, stimulated further interest in studying factors that affect persuasion and resistance to it. **Persuasion** is the attempt to influence the attitudes of other people. Today, researchers have less interest in studying brainwashing than in studying the use of persuasion in everyday life, whether by friends, relatives, advertisers, or politicians.

According to the **elaboration likelihood theory** of Richard Petty and John Cacioppo (1990), persuasive messages may take a central route or a peripheral route. A message that takes a central route relies on clear, explicit arguments about the issue at hand. A central route encourages active consideration of the merits of the arguments. In contrast, a message that takes a peripheral route relies on factors other than the merits of the arguments, such as characteristics of the source or the situational context. The more elaborately we think about the merits of an argument, the more lasting will be any attitude change that occurs. The central and peripheral routes are related to the main factors in persuasion: the source, the message, and the audience. These three factors were first studied more than 2,000 years ago by Aristotle. He found that persuasion was most effective when the source had good character, the message was supported by strong evidence, and the audience was in a receptive frame of mind (Jones, 1985).

The Source and Persuasion

One of the important peripheral factors in persuasion is the source of the message. The greater the credibility of the source, the greater the persuasiveness of the message (Smith, De Houwer, & Nosek, 2013). Politicians realize this importance and gain votes by having credible supporters praise their merits and criticize their opponents' faults (Calantone & Warshaw, 1985). But what determines a source's credibility? Perhaps the most important factor is the source's expertise. A meta-analysis of 114 studies on the effects of source characteristics on persuasion found that expertise was the single most credibility-enhancing source characteristic (Wilson & Sherrell, 1993). For example, people who read stories about UFOs that include supportive statements from a scientific authority become more likely to express their belief in UFOs than people who read stories that do not include such statements (Sparks & Pellechia, 1997).

Another important factor in promoting source credibility is trustworthiness. When we perceive a source as trustworthy, we are less likely to critically scrutinize her or his message. Trust makes us more likely to be persuaded by the message (Priester & Petty, 2003). We perceive sources as especially trustworthy when their message is not an obvious attempt at persuasion, particularly when the message is contrary to the source's expected position (Wood & Eagly, 1981). For example, as noted in Chapter 10, Sir Cyril Burt's biographer concluded that Burt had fabricated data supporting a strong genetic basis for intelligence. The author of an article that discussed Burt's biography claimed, "The conclusion carries more weight because the author of the biography, Professor Leslie Hearnshaw, began his task as an admirer" (Hawkes, 1979, p. 673). If Hearnshaw had been a critic of Burt's work, his conclusion would have been less credible.

Sources who are attractive, because they are likable or physically appealing, also are more persuasive. Advertisers take advantage of this factor by having attractive actors appear in their commercials (Shavitt, Swan, Lowrey, & Wanke, 1994). Even the persuasiveness of politicians is affected by their attractiveness. Richard Nixon's unattractive appearance

---

persuasion The attempt to influence the attitudes of other people.

elaboration likelihood theory A theory of persuasion that considers the extent to which messages take a central route or a peripheral route.

The Power of Persuasion
Attempts at persuasion pervade our everyday lives, as in this protest against genetically modified organisms, or GMOs.
Source: Glynnis Jones/Shutterstock.com.

Credibility and Persuasion
The effectiveness of a doctor's medical advice is based on perceived expertise and trustworthiness.
Source: Stuart Jenner/Shutterstock.com.

during a debate with John F. Kennedy may have cost him the 1960 presidential election. Nixon's five-o'clock shadow and tendency to perspire made him less attractive to voters who watched the debate on television. Surveys found that people who watched the debate on television rated Kennedy the winner of the debate, whereas those who listened to it on the radio rated Nixon the debate's winner (Weisman, 1988). Having learned from Nixon's mistake, today's politicians make sure that they appear as attractive as possible on television.

The Message and Persuasion

It might surprise you to learn that it is not always desirable to present arguments that support only your position. Simply acknowledging the other side of an issue while strongly supporting your own is at times more effective. A meta-analysis of research studies found that two-sided messages are generally more effective than one-sided messages in changing attitudes (Allen, 1993). This finding was discovered by social psychologist Carl Hovland and his colleagues in the waning days of World War II, following the surrender of Germany (Hovland, Lumsdaine, & Sheffield, 1949). The military asked Hovland for advice on how to convince soldiers that the war against Japan would take a long time to win. The researchers presented soldiers with a 15-minute talk that presented either one-sided or two-sided arguments. In the one-sided argument, they presented only arguments about why the war would not be over soon, such as the fighting spirit of the Japanese. In the two-sided argument, they presented both that argument and arguments explaining why the war might end earlier, such as Allied air superiority. Before and after the message, participants were given surveys that included questions about how long they believed the war would last.

The results showed that those soldiers who originally believed that the war would take a long time to win were more influenced by the one-sided argument and became more extreme in their attitudes. But those who originally believed there would be an early end to the war were more influenced by the two-sided argument. As you can see, if the listener already favors your position or has no counterarguments handy, arguments that favor your position alone will be more persuasive. But if the listener opposes your position, arguments that acknowledge both sides of the issue will be more persuasive. Two-sided arguments are effective in part because they enhance the credibility of the source and decrease counterarguing by the listener (Bohner, Einwiller, Erb, & Siebler, 2003).

An intriguing aspect of persuasion is the **sleeper effect**. This effect occurs when a person initially fails to be convinced by a persuasive message, perhaps because the source lacks credibility, yet responds more favorably to it with the mere passage of time. A meta-analysis of research on the sleeper effect found that it is more likely to occur when the persuasive message had a strong initial impact but there was a strong reason for not responding positively to it (Kumkale & Albarracin, 2004). Thus, if you provide a well-presented argument that is initially rejected because, for example, you are perceived as lacking in expertise, it still might have a positive—though delayed—impact on its intended audience.

sleeper effect Responding favorably to a persuasive message following the mere passage of time after having initially rejected it because of a strong peripheral factor, such as not trusting the source of the message.

The Audience and Persuasion

Persuasion depends on the audience as well as the message and its source. An important audience factor is intelligence because it determines whether a message will be more effective using the central or the peripheral route. People of relatively high intelligence are more likely to be influenced by messages supported by rational arguments—the central route. People of relatively low intelligence are more likely to be influenced by messages supported by factors other than rational arguments—the peripheral route (Eagly & Warren, 1976). Overall, people of lower intelligence are more easily influenced than are people of higher intelligence (Rhodes & Wood, 1992).

Another important audience factor is whether the audience finds the message personally important (Zuwerink & Devine, 1996). A message's importance for a particular audience determines whether the central route or the peripheral route will be more effective (Petty & Cacioppo, 1990). When a message has high importance to an audience, the central route will be more effective. When a message has low importance, the peripheral route will be more effective. This finding came from a study that measured student attitudes toward recommended policy changes at a university. The changes would be instituted

Chapter 17 Social Psychology

either the following year (high importance) or in 10 years (low importance). Students who were asked to respond to arguments about policy changes of high importance were influenced more by the quality of the arguments (central route) than by the expertise of the source (peripheral route). In contrast, students who were asked to respond to arguments about policy changes of low importance were influenced more by the expertise of the source than by the quality of the arguments (Petty, Cacioppo, & Goldman, 1981).

Attitudes and Behavior

Common sense tells us that if we know a person's attitudes, we can accurately predict her or his behavior. But the relationship is not that simple. For one thing, our behavior might not always agree with our attitudes. Perhaps more surprisingly, our behavior can sometimes affect our attitudes.

The Influence of Attitudes on Behavior

Until the late 1960s, most social psychologists accepted the commonsense notion that our behavior is consistent with our attitudes. But since then researchers have found that attitudes are not as consistent with behavior as previously believed (Scott & Willits, 1994). You have seen this inconsistency exhibited dramatically, for example, by television evangelists who preach sexual denial to their audience while they themselves engage in extramarital sexual relations.

Though widespread interest in the inconsistency between attitudes and behaviors is only a few decades old, evidence supporting the inconsistency between attitudes and behaviors appeared as early as the 1930s, when sociologist Richard LaPiere (1934) traveled with a young Chinese couple for 10,000 miles throughout the United States. They ate at 184 restaurants and stayed at 66 hotels, motels, and other places. Though anti-Chinese feelings were strong at that time, only 1 of the 250 establishments refused them service. Six months after the journey, LaPiere wrote to each of the establishments, asking whether they would serve Chinese people. Of the 128 that replied, 118 (92 percent) said they would not. LaPiere's conclusion was that our behaviors do not always agree with our attitudes. But the study had a major flaw. The people who served the couple (servers and desk clerks) may not have been the same people who responded to LaPiere's letter (owners and managers). Nonetheless, LaPiere's study stimulated interest in research on the ability of attitude questionnaires to predict real-life behavior (Dockery & Bedeian, 1989).

But what determines whether our attitudes and behaviors will be consistent? Attitudes that are strongly held (Kraus, 1995) or personally important (Crano & Prislin, 1995) are better predictors of behavior. For example, in one study researchers measured the strength of participants' attitudes toward Greenpeace, an international environmental advocacy group. A week later the participants were given the opportunity to donate money to Greenpeace. The results showed that the strength of the participants' attitudes toward Greenpeace was positively correlated with the likelihood of their donating money. That is, participants who had strongly positive attitudes were more likely to donate money than were those with less positive attitudes. Likewise, participants who had strongly negative attitudes were less likely to donate money than were those with less negative attitudes (Holland, Verplanken, & van Knippenberg, 2002).

Attitude-behavior consistency also is affected by the specificity of the attitude and the behavior. Your attitudes and behaviors are more consistent with one another when they are at similar levels of specificity (Weigel, Vernon, & Tognacci, 1974). For example, your attitude toward safe driving might not predict whether you will obey the speed limit tomorrow morning, but it will predict your general tendency, over time, to engage in safe driving behaviors, such as checking your tire pressure, using turn signals, and obeying the speed limit.

The Influence of Behavior on Attitudes

In the mid-1950s, Leon Festinger (1919–1989) and his colleagues were intrigued by a sect whose members believed they would be saved by aliens in flying saucers at midnight prior to the day of a prophesized worldwide flood (Festinger, Riecken, & Schachter,

Attitudes and Behavior

Market researchers are interested in measuring consumer attitudes to predict behavior. For example, if customers rate customer service highly, it is assumed that they will return.
Source: Brian A Jackson/Shutterstock.com.

1956). But neither the aliens nor the flood ever arrived. Did the members lose their faith? Some did, but many reported that their faith was strengthened. They simply concluded that the aliens had rewarded their faith by saving the world from the flood. These members simply changed their belief in order to justify their action.

The ability of the sect's members to relieve the emotional distress they experienced when the prophecy failed to come true stimulated Festinger's interest in attitude change and his development of the **cognitive dissonance theory**. Cognitive dissonance is an unpleasant state of tension associated with increased physiological (Harmon-Jones, Brehm, Greenberg, & Simon, 1996) and psychological (Elliot & Devine, 1994) arousal, caused by the realization that one holds beliefs that are inconsistent with each other or a belief that is inconsistent with one's behavior. Cognitive dissonance would occur in people who believe that smoking is dangerous, yet find themselves to be smokers. We are motivated to reduce the unpleasant arousal associated with cognitive dissonance by making our cognitions consistent. Thus, a smoker might stop smoking, simply discount reports of the health risks of smoking, or estimate that the risk is lower in his or her own case. Consider a person who drinks alcohol despite believing that drinking is wrong. A study of drinkers found that those who had negative attitudes toward drinking were more likely than those with positive attitudes to claim that other people drank more than they did, apparently to reduce their cognitive dissonance in response to performing a behavior they believed was inappropriate (Maekelae, 1997).

The theory of cognitive dissonance has practical applications in promoting positive behaviors. One study aroused cognitive dissonance in undergraduates by making them feel hypocritical about their willingness to help those in need. Researchers accomplished this arousal by getting some of the participants to recall times when they failed to help others while inducing high levels of empathy for a child with cancer. This inconsistency between their beliefs, emotions, and behavior was expected to arouse cognitive dissonance and, as a consequence, make the students change their behavior. The results supported this hypothesis because participants in the hypocrisy condition were more willing to help than were participants who were reminded of their past failures to help but who did not experience high levels of empathy toward the child (Harmon-Jones, Peterson, & Vaughn, 2003). According to cognitive dissonance theory, the participants in the hypocrisy condition reduced their distress by changing their behavior.

The more we feel responsible for the inconsistencies between our cognitions, the stronger will be our feelings of cognitive dissonance and the more motivated we will be to change them. This was the finding of a classic experimental study of cognitive dissonance (Festinger & Carlsmith, 1959). Students were asked to perform boring tasks, one of which was to arrange small spools on a tray, dump the tray, and arrange the spools again and again for half an hour. Each student was paid either $1 or $20 to tell the next student that the task was enjoyable. After the experiment was over, the students were asked to express their attitude toward the task. Their responses violated what common sense predicted. As shown in Figure 17-3, those who were paid less ($1) tended to rate the task as interesting, whereas those who were paid more ($20) tended to rate the task as boring.

What could account for this finding? According to the theory of cognitive dissonance, the students experienced unpleasant arousal because their claim that the task was interesting did not agree with their belief that the task was boring. But those who were paid $20 to lie about the task experienced weaker cognitive dissonance because they could justify their lies by attributing them to the large payment they received. In contrast, those who were paid only $1 to lie experienced stronger cognitive dissonance because they could not attribute their lies to such a paltry sum. Consequently, those who were paid only $1 reduced the dissonance between their cognitions by changing their attitudes toward the task, rating it as more interesting than it actually was.

The cognitive dissonance interpretation of attitude change has been challenged by a theory put forth by Daryl Bem (1967). According to his **self-perception theory**, attitude change is not motivated by our need to reduce cognitive dissonance. Instead, we infer our attitudes from our behavior in the same way that we infer other people's attitudes from their behavior.

cognitive dissonance theory Leon Festinger's theory that attitude change is motivated by the desire to relieve the unpleasant state of arousal caused when one holds cognitions and/or behaviors that are inconsistent with each other.

self-perception theory The theory that we infer our attitudes from our behavior in the same way that we infer other people's attitudes from their behavior.

Chapter 17 Social Psychology

FIGURE 17-3
Cognitive Dissonance

In the classic study by Festinger and Carlsmith, participants who received $1 for telling other people that a boring task was interesting later rated the task as more enjoyable than did participants who received $20 for doing so.

Source: Data from L. Festinger and J. M. Carlsmith (1959), "Cognitive Consequences of Forced Compliance," *Journal of Abnormal and Social Psychology, 58*, 203–210.

Self-Perception Theory

Consider the predictions of self-perception theory and paying children to complete their homework or household chores. Is it wiser to pay large or small sums? Why?

Source: kitty/Shutterstock.com.

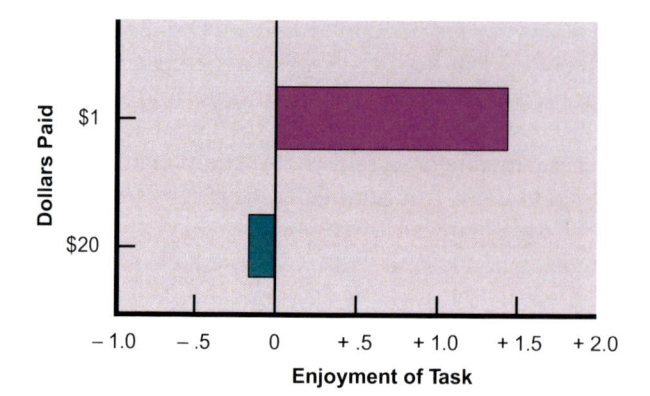

When we observe people behaving under no apparent external constraints, we use the behavior to make inferences about their attitudes. Likewise, when the situation we are in does not place strong constraints on our behavior, we might infer our attitudes from our behavior. Perhaps self-perception theory explains why we tend to favor our home sports teams. Because of our proximity to them, we are more likely to attend our home teams' games, watch our home teams on television, and read about them in the newspaper. When we observe ourselves engaging in these behaviors, we may infer that we like our home teams.

But how does self-perception theory explain why students who were paid $1 for lying showed greater attitude change than students who were paid $20? According to Bem, the students did not experience cognitive dissonance. Instead, they determined whether their behavior was attributable to themselves or to the situation. The students who were paid $20 attributed their behavior to being paid a relatively large sum of money. They had no reason to attribute their behavior to their attitude. In contrast, the students who were paid $1 could not attribute their behavior to such a small sum of money. Consequently, those students attributed their behavior to their attitude, perhaps saying to themselves, "If I told another student that the task was interesting and I was not induced to do so by a large amount of money, then the task must have been interesting to me."

Neither cognitive dissonance theory nor self-perception theory has emerged as the clearly superior explanation of the effect of behavior on attitudes. But each seems to be superior in certain circumstances. Whereas cognitive dissonance theory seems to be better at explaining the effect of behavior on well-defined attitudes, self-perception theory seems to be better at explaining the effect of behavior on poorly defined attitudes (Chaiken & Baldwin, 1981).

Prejudice

More than three decades ago, third-grade teacher Jane Elliott of Riceville, Iowa, gained national attention for a demonstration she gave of the devastating psychological effects of a particular kind of attitude: prejudice (Stewart, LaDuke, Bracht, Sweet, & Gamarel, 2003). She divided her students, who all were European American, into a blue-eyed group and a brown-eyed group. On the first day of the demonstration, Elliott declared that blue-eyed people were superior to brown-eyed people. The next day, she declared that brown-eyed people were superior to blue-eyed people.

Members of the superior group were given privileges, such as sitting where they wanted to in class, going to lunch early, and staying late at recess. Members of the inferior group were made to wear identification collars and were not permitted to play with members of the superior group. Elliott reported that during the two-day demonstration, students who were made to feel inferior became depressed and performed poorly on class work (Leonard, 1970). If prejudice could have this effect in an artificial, temporary situation, imagine the effect that prejudice has on children who are its targets in everyday life.

Fortunately, some forms of prejudice appear to be declining in North America. Surveys of European American adults have found that those born after World War II, compared to those born before the war, are less prejudiced toward people with Jewish, Asian,

African American, or Latino backgrounds (Wilson, 1996). Canadians have become more accepting of immigrant groups and multicultural diversity (Berry & Kalin, 1995). And sexual prejudice is declining as Americans have become more tolerant of bisexuals, gay men, and lesbians. However, a majority of adult Americans still believe that homosexual behavior is "wrong" (Yang, 1997). This lack of tolerance also is reflected in a high rate of violence. More than 1,100 hate crimes against lesbians, bisexuals, and gay men were reported to American law enforcement agencies in 1997 (Herek, 2000).

Prejudice is a positive or negative attitude toward a person based on her or his membership in a particular group. People vary in how aware they are about their own prejudiced attitudes. Some people are well aware of their prejudices; others may act in an explicitly prejudiced manner without even realizing they are implicitly prejudiced (Dovidio, Kawakami, & Gaertner, 2002). For example, a survey of four Western European countries found that respondents who scored high on a measure of blatant prejudice were more likely to endorse harsh exclusionary policies reducing immigration. In contrast, respondents who scored high on a measure of subtle prejudice shared exclusionary attitudes toward immigrants—however, they supported methods that were ostensibly nondiscriminatory (Meertens & Pettigrew, 1997). This *modern racism* is a subtle form of prejudice that could develop from social norms that discourage the expression of overt prejudice (McConahay, 1986). Modern racism is characterized by the beliefs that discrimination is no longer a problem, that ethnic minority groups' claims of inequality are unfounded, and that the gains ethnic minorities have made over the years may be unjustified.

The behavioral component of prejudice is discrimination, which involves treating persons differently, whether positively or negatively, based only on their group membership. For example, a study found that European American undergraduates who evaluated the employment applications of European American and African American candidates showed no racial discrimination in the case of strong or weak applications. However, European Americans did discriminate against African Americans in the case of ambiguous applications (Dovidio & Gaertner, 2000). Researchers who have applied the concept of modern racism to contemporary sexism believe that similar beliefs underlie negative attitudes toward affirmative action programs for women (Masser & Abrams, 1999). Moreover, this form of sexism is not unique to the United States. A cross-cultural study of 15,000 women and men found similar sexist beliefs in 19 countries (Glick et al., 2000).

Factors That Promote Prejudice

What factors account for the origin and maintenance of prejudice? As with all attitudes, learning plays an important role. Parents, peers, and the media all provide input, informing us of the supposed characteristics of particular groups. For example, an analysis of 1,699 television commercials found that they stereotyped European American men as powerful, European American women as sex objects, African American men as aggressive, and African American women as unimportant (Coltrane & Messineo, 2000). Even humor can promote prejudice. A Canadian study found that college students who were exposed to disparaging humor about an ethnic minority group became more prejudiced against that group than were students exposed to nondisparaging humor (Maio, Olson, & Bush, 1997).

prejudice A positive or negative attitude toward a person based on her or his membership in a particular group.

Prejudice and Social Learning

Adult models play a powerful role in determining whether children will become prejudiced against members of other groups.
Source: Monkey Business Images/Shutterstock.com.

Chapter 17 Social Psychology 613

authoritarian personality A personality type marked by the tendency to obey superiors while dominating subordinates, to favor one's own group while being prejudiced against other groups, and to be unwilling to admit one's own faults while projecting them onto members of other groups.

Research has been especially concerned with factors that promote prejudice. The horrors of Nazism in the 1930s and 1940s led to a major research program at the University of California at Berkeley aimed at identifying the personality characteristics associated with fascist tendencies (Adorno, Frenkel-Brunswik, Levinson, & Sanford, 1950). Based on the results of tests and interviews with adult Californians, the researchers discovered what they called the **authoritarian personality**. People with an authoritarian personality tend to be obedient toward their superiors and domineering toward subordinates (authoritarianism), prejudiced in favor of their own groups and against other groups (ethnocentrism), and unwilling to admit their own faults but willing to place them on members of other groups (projection). In fact, the higher one's self-esteem, the less prejudiced one will tend to be against members of stereotyped groups (Fein & Spencer, 1997). Authoritarians tend to be prejudiced against other ethnic groups (Heaven & St. Quintin, 2003) as well as other out-groups, including people with AIDS (Cunningham et al., 1991), gay men and lesbians (Goodnight, Cook, Parrott, & Peterson, 2013), and mental hospital patients (Morrison, de Man, & Drumheller, 1993).

As mentioned in the section "Liking," one of the most important factors in interpersonal attraction is attitude similarity. Prejudiced people perceive stereotyped groups as having attitudes that are different from those of their own groups. In fact, when there is little or no pressure to discriminate, ethnicity is less important than attitude similarity in determining racial or ethnic discrimination (Insko, Nacoste, & Moe, 1983). In a study of this phenomenon, participants were asked to choose a work partner. When they were given information about another's ethnicity and attitudes, their choices were influenced more by their similarity in attitudes than by their similarity in ethnicity (Rokeach & Mezei, 1966).

People also exhibit favoritism to their own kind. In a series of experiments, Henri Tajfel and Michael Billig (Tajfel, 1981; Tajfel & Billig, 1974) demonstrated that the social experience of becoming a member of a group can produce an in-group bias, or a tendency to exhibit favoritism toward members of one's group. Moreover, perceptions of threat to the in-group appear to increase this tendency. One study assessed the relationship between perceived threats to the in-group, intergroup anxiety, and negative stereotypes of Cuban, Mexican, and Asian immigrants in Florida, New Mexico, and Hawaii. Each of these factors was positively correlated with prejudice toward immigrants (Stephan, Ybarra, & Bachman, 1999). Similar results were found in a study of prejudice toward Moroccan, Russian, and Ethiopian immigrants in Spain and Israel (Stephan, Ybarra, Martinez, Schwarzwald, & Tur-Kaspa, 1998) and in a study of prejudice toward Turkish immigrants in Germany (Florack, Piontkowski, Bohman, Balzer, & Perzig, 2003). Likewise, a study of children and adults involved in the wars in the Republic of Georgia and Sierra Leone found that in-group biases were especially strong among individuals who were exposed to inter-ethnic conflict during middle childhood through early adulthood (Bauer, Cassar, Chytilová, & Heinrich, 2014).

Factors That Reduce Prejudice

Social psychologists also are concerned with finding ways to reduce prejudice. But this task is difficult because people are hesitant to revise personal judgments that are based on stereotypes. We modify the stereotypes we hold only gradually through individual experiences and by creating subtypes to accommodate instances that we cannot easily assimilate. As mentioned in the section "Person Perception," we do not necessarily revise our stereotypes after experiencing a few dramatic exceptions to them (Weber & Crocker, 1983). Nonetheless, exceptions to stereotypes do make the out-group seem more variable, which tends to weaken the stereotypes somewhat (Hamburger, 1994).

In the 1950s, Gordon Allport (1954) insisted that prejudice could be reduced by increasing social contact between members of different social groups. At about the same time, in 1954, in the landmark case of *Brown v. Board of Education of Topeka*, the U.S. Supreme Court ruled that "separate but equal" schools did not provide African American children with the same benefits as European American children. The Court's decision was influenced by research, most notably by Kenneth B. Clark and Mamie Phipps Clark, showing that segregated schools hurt the self-esteem of African American children, increased racial prejudice, and encouraged European Americans to view African Americans as inferior

(Benjamin & Crouse, 2002). For example, a study by the Clarks found that African American children believed European American dolls were better than African American ones and preferred to play with European American ones (Clark & Clark, 1947). A published review of studies of self-concept in African American children revealed that research findings differ according to whether the research was conducted before or after the civil rights movement of the 1960s. Earlier studies reported that African Americans had lower self-esteem than European Americans; more recent studies conducted after the civil rights movement have found that this conclusion is no longer true (Twenge & Crocker, 2002).

Events during the past few decades have shown that social contact alone might not produce the effects predicted by Allport and the Supreme Court. For contact between groups to reduce prejudice, the contact must be between group members of equal status (Spangenberg & Nel, 1983). If the contact is between group members of unequal status, then prejudice may actually increase. The effectiveness of equal-status contact in reducing racial prejudice was supported by a study of African American and European American high school athletes. European American athletes who played team sports with African American teammates had more positive attitudes toward African Americans as a group than did European American athletes who played individual sports (Brown, Brown, Jackson, Sellers, & Manuel, 2003). Contact with members of an out-group can weaken stereotypes by increasing the perceived heterogeneity of that group (Lee & Ottati, 1993).

Another way to reduce prejudice is to promote intergroup cooperation (Desforges et al., 1991). Unfortunately, cooperative efforts do not always increase liking. If cooperative efforts fail, members of one group may attribute responsibility for this failure to members of the other group. And if cooperative efforts succeed, members of one group will attribute responsibility for the success to a favorable situation rather than giving any credit to members of the other group (Brewer & Kramer, 1985). Thus, in certain situations, members of a cooperating group will be caught in a no-win situation.

Reducing Prejudice

For contact between groups to reduce prejudice, the contact must be between group members of equal status.
Source: Monkey Business Images/Shutterstock.com.

Section Review: Attitudes

1. What factors influence the consistency between attitudes and behaviors?
2. What factors determine whether the central route or the peripheral route will be more effective in persuasion?
3. What does research say about the effect of contact between in-group members and out-group members on prejudice?

Group Dynamics

In everyday life we refer to any collection of people as a "group." But social psychologists favor a narrower definition of a **group** as a collection of two or more persons who interact and have mutual influence. Examples of groups include a sorority, a softball team, and the board of trustees of your school. In the late 1940s, hoping to understand the social factors that contributed to the Great Depression, the rise of European dictatorships, and World War II, social psychologists became more interested in studying the factors that affect relationships between members of groups (Zander, 1979). Group dynamics remains an important area of research in social psychology and includes the topics of group decision making, group effects on performance, and social influence.

group A collection of two or more persons who interact and have mutual influence on each other.

Group Decision Making

As members of groups, we often are called on to make group decisions. A family must decide which new house to buy, a jury must agree upon a verdict, college administrators must decide which proposed new academic majors to approve, and government officials

Chapter 17 Social Psychology

must decide on air pollution standards. Decisions made by groups are not simply the outcome of rational give-and-take, with the wisest decision automatically emerging. They are affected by other factors as well.

Group Polarization

In the 1950s, social critic William H. Whyte (1956) claimed that groups, notably those within business and government organizations, tended to make safe, compromise decisions instead of risky, extreme decisions. Whyte assumed that this tendency explained why organizations failed to be as creative and innovative as individuals. In the 1960s, his view was challenged by studies that found a tendency for group decisions to be riskier than decisions made by individuals who composed those groups (Stoner, 1961). This tendency became known as the risky shift (Wallach, Kogan, & Bem, 1962). But later research found that groups tend to make decisions in either a risky or cautious direction, rather than in only a risky direction. The tendency for groups to make more extreme decisions than their individual members would make is called **group polarization**. For example, when groups of high school students either high or low in racial prejudice discussed racial issues, groups that were low in prejudice became even less prejudiced and groups that were high in prejudice became even more prejudiced (Myers & Bishop, 1970).

What accounts for group polarization? Persuasive-argumentation theory assumes that group members who initially hold a moderate position about an issue will move in the direction of the most persuasive arguments, which will eventually move the group toward either a risky or a cautious decision (Mongeau & Garlick, 1988). Simply repeating an attitude over and over will tend to polarize a group in that direction (Brauer, Judd, & Gliner, 1995).

Minority Influence

Does the majority always determine the outcome of group decision making? In general, the answer is yes. This tendency becomes stronger as the size of the majority increases relative to the size of the minority (Bassili, 2003). The majority has the power to convince group members to go along with its decision, in part because of its ability to criticize and ostracize those who dissent. Yet, under certain circumstances, minorities may influence group decisions.

If you are part of a minority and wish to influence group decisions, you should follow several well-established principles.

- You must present rational rather than emotional reasons for your position. That is, you must take the central rather than the peripheral route of persuasion to make the majority consider your position. If minority arguments are of relatively higher quality than majority arguments, the minority will be more likely to influence the majority (Gordijn, De Vries, & De Dreu, 2002).

- You must appear absolutely confident in your position, with no wavering at all. If you are unsure or apologetic about your position, majority members will discount it.

- You must be consistent in your position over time to make the majority wonder whether there might actually be something to what you're saying. Again, if you are inconsistent, your opponents will discredit you. In fact, a meta-analysis of 97 relevant research studies found that the ability of the minority to be consistent in its position is an especially powerful factor in minority influence (Wood, Lundgren, Ouellette, & Busceme, 1994).

- Try to bring at least one other person over to your side (Clark, 2001). A minority of two is much more credible and influential than a minority of one. Each of the two will embolden and give credibility to the other.

- You must be patient. Though majorities may initially dismiss minority positions, the passage of time might make them privately ponder the evidence you have provided and gradually change their positions (Nemeth, 1986).

Group Decision Making

Decisions made by groups, such as juries, are not simply the outcome of rational give-and-take, with the wisest decision automatically emerging. They are affected by other factors as well.
Source: bikeriderlondon/Shutterstock.com.

group polarization The tendency for groups to make more extreme decisions than their members would make as individuals.

Groupthink

On January 28, 1986, the space shuttle *Challenger* exploded shortly after taking off from Cape Canaveral, Florida, killing the crew and shocking the millions of television viewers excited by the presence of the first teacher-astronaut, Christa McAuliffe. The committee that investigated this tragedy reported that the explosion was caused by a faulty joint seal in one of the rocket boosters. The decision to launch the shuttle had been made despite warnings from engineers that the joint might fail in cold weather. This ill-fated decision has been attributed to groupthink, which in this case put safety second to currying favor with the public and Congress (Moorhead, Ference, & Neck, 1991).

The term **groupthink**, coined by psychologist Irving Janis (1918–1990), refers to a decision-making process in small, cohesive groups that places unanimity ahead of critical thinking and aims at premature consensus (Kerr & Tindale, 2004). Notice that groupthink is a form of group polarization. Groupthink is promoted by several factors: a charismatic leader, feelings of invulnerability, discrediting of contrary evidence, fear of criticism for disagreeing, the desire to maintain group harmony, isolation from outside influences, and disparaging outsiders as incompetent. A central factor in groupthink is a shared overestimate of the group's capabilities (Whyte, 1998). In criticizing the decision to launch the *Challenger*, Senator John Glenn of Ohio, the first American to orbit Earth, referred to feelings of invulnerability among the officials who made the decision: "The mindset of a few people in key positions at NASA had changed from an optimistic and supersafety conscious 'can do' attitude, when I was in the program, to an arrogant 'can't fail' attitude" (Zaldivar, 1986, p. 12-A). This change in attitudes was unfortunate because having dissenting views promotes consideration of alternatives (Nemeth, Connell, Rogers, & Brown, 2001).

Janis's concept of groupthink has received support from experimental studies on group decision making. Groups with directive leaders consider fewer alternatives than do groups with leaders who encourage member participation, especially if the leader expresses her or his opinion early in deliberation (Leana, 1985). Group cohesiveness also has an effect. A meta-analysis of the effect of group cohesiveness on decision making found that if other conditions conducive to groupthink are present, group cohesiveness will promote groupthink; if those conditions are not present, cohesiveness actually will improve decision making (Mullen, Anthony, Salas, & Driskell, 1994). Of course, the groupthink phenomenon does not always occur during group decision making, and when it does occur, it does not always produce negative outcomes (Aldag & Fuller, 1993; Choi & Kim, 1999). Though the concept of groupthink seems convincing, evidence for it has come primarily from after-the-fact interpretations of well-known, misguided group decisions. In fact, there has been relatively little support for the groupthink phenomenon from experimental research (Park, 2000). More experimental research is needed to determine whether groupthink is a robust phenomenon and, if it does exist, to identify the factors that account for it.

groupthink The tendency of small, cohesive groups to place unanimity ahead of critical thinking in making decisions.

Group Effects on Performance

One of the first topics to be studied by social psychologists was the influence of groups on the task performances of their members. Social psychologists have been especially interested in studying the effects of social facilitation and social loafing on performance.

Social Facilitation

As described at the beginning of the chapter, more than a century ago Norman Triplett (1898) observed that people performed faster when competing against other people than when competing against a clock. Two decades later, Floyd Allport (1920) found that people performed a variety of tasks better when working in the same room than when working in separate rooms. Allport used the term **social facilitation** to describe the improvement in performance caused by the presence of other people.

But later studies found that the presence of others sometimes may impair performance. A review of 241 studies involving almost 24,000 participants found that the presence of other people improves performance on simple or well-learned tasks and impairs performance on complex or poorly learned tasks (Bond & Titus, 1983). For example, in one

social facilitation The effect of the presence of other people on a person's task performance, with performance on simple or well-learned tasks improved and performance on complex or poorly learned tasks impaired.

Social Facilitation

Cyclists ride faster when they are competing with others than when they are competing against the clock.
Source: Pavel1964/Shutterstock.com.

study, children tried to balance on a teeterboard for as long as possible. Children who were highly skilled performed better in the presence of others; children who were poorly skilled performed better when alone (MacCracken & Stadulis, 1985). Even college students learning to use personal computers may perform better when working alone than when working in the presence of an instructor (Schneider & Shugar, 1990).

What would account for these findings? The most influential explanation for both social facilitation and social inhibition is the drive theory of Robert Zajonc (1965). According to Zajonc, the presence of other people increases physiological arousal, which energizes the performer's most likely responses to a task. For those who are good at a task, the most likely responses will be effective ones. Consequently, those people will perform better in the presence of others. In contrast, for those who are not good at a task, the most well-learned responses will be ineffective ones. Consequently, those people will perform worse in the presence of others.

Our drive level may increase in the presence of others because of evaluation apprehension. Consider a field study in which male and female runners were timed (without their being aware of it) as they ran along a 90-yard segment of a footpath. One-third of the participants ran alone, one-third encountered a woman facing them at the halfway point, and one-third encountered a woman seated with her back to them at the halfway point. Only the group who encountered a woman facing them (putting her in a position to evaluate them) showed a significant acceleration between the first and second halves of the segment (Worringham & Messick, 1983).

Social Loafing

Social facilitation is concerned with the effects of others on individual performance. But what of the effect of working in a group that has a common goal? In the 1880s, a French agricultural engineer named Max Ringelmann found that people exerted less effort when working in groups than when working alone. He had men pull on a rope attached to a meter that measured the strength of their pull. As the number of men pulling increased from one to eight, the average strength of each man's pull decreased. Ringelmann attributed this decrease to a loss of coordination when working with other people, a phenomenon that became known as the Ringelmann effect (Kravitz & Martin, 1986). His study has been replicated in other countries, including Japan (Kugihara, 1999) and Canada (Lichacz & Partington, 1996), but the effect diminishes markedly beyond a group size of three (Ingham, Levinger, Graves, & Peckham, 1974).

social loafing A decrease in the individual effort exerted by group members when working together on a task.

More recently, the Ringelmann effect has been attributed to a decrease in the effort exerted by individuals when working together, a phenomenon known as **social loafing**. This phenomenon supports the old saying "Many hands make light the work." In one experiment, high school cheerleaders cheered either alone or in pairs. Sound-level recordings found that individual cheerleaders cheered louder when alone than when cheering with a partner (Hardy & Latané, 1988). Social loafing has been demonstrated in sports such as elite rowing (Anshel, 1995) and high school swimming (Miles & Greenberg, 1993). A meta-analysis of 78 studies found that social loafing has been demonstrated across many different cultures, though it is more common in individualistic cultures such as Canada and the United States (Karau & Williams, 1993).

According to the concept of diffusion of responsibility, social loafing occurs when group members feel anonymous; believing that their individual performance will not be evaluated, they are less motivated to exert their maximum effort. Because of this lack of evaluation apprehension, group members often overestimate their contribution to the group's performance (Forsyth, Zyzniewski, & Giammanco, 2002). Ways to reduce social loafing include convincing group members that they will be held accountable (Weldon & Gargano, 1988), that their individual efforts will be evaluated (Hoeksema-van Orden, Gaillard, & Buunk, 1998), or that their individual effort will contribute to the group's performance (Shepperd & Taylor, 1999). Social loafing also can be overcome when a task is important to an individual and that person believes other group members lack the ability to perform better (Plaks & Higgins, 2000).

Social Loafing

Because of social loafing, these children will probably exert less individual effort than they would if they pulled by themselves.
Source: Diego Cervo/Shutterstock.com.

Social Influence

The groups we belong to influence our behavior in ways that range from subtle prodding to direct demands. We are influenced by police, bosses, clergy, parents, spouses, teachers, physicians, advertisers, politicians, salespersons, and a host of other people. Their influence is sometimes negative but often is positive, as, for example, in the case of exercise adherence. The influence of others tends to make us more likely to maintain a program of regular exercise (Carron, Hausenblas, & Mack, 1996). Among the most important kinds of social influence are conformity, compliance, and obedience.

Conformity

Do you dress the way you do because your friends dress that way? Do you hold certain religious beliefs because your parents hold them? If you answered yes to these questions, you would be exhibiting **conformity**, which means behaving in accordance with real or imagined group pressure. For example, a study of more than 100 men and 100 women found that people eating in a cafeteria were more likely to select a dessert if a dining companion did so (Guarino, Fridrich, & Sitton, 1994). And of greater importance, we are more likely to refuse to enter a vehicle with a drunk driver if a companion refuses than if the companion enters the vehicle (Powell & Drucker, 1997).

The power of conformity was demonstrated in a classic series of experiments conducted by psychologist Solomon Asch (1907–1996) in the 1950s. These experiments showed that even visual perception, something we take for granted, may be influenced by the social context (Gleitman, Rozin, & Sabini, 1997). In a typical experiment, a male college student who had volunteered to be a research participant was told that he would be taking part in a study of visual perception. He was seated at a table with six other "participants," who were actually the experimenter's confederates. As illustrated in Figure 17-4, the experimenter presented a series of trials in which he displayed two large white cards. One card contained three vertical lines of different lengths. The second card contained a single vertical line clearly equal in length to one of the three lines on the first card. On each of 18 trials, the participants were asked, one person at a time, to choose the line on the first card that was the same length as the line on the second card. The lengths of the lines varied from trial to trial. On the first 2 trials, each confederate chose the correct line. But on the 3rd trial, and on 11 of the succeeding trials, the confederates chose a line that was clearly not the same length as the single line.

On the first few bogus trials, the participant appeared uncomfortable but usually chose the correct line. Yet, over the course of the 12 bogus trials, the participant sometimes conformed to the erroneous choices made by the confederates. The results indicated that, overall, participants conformed on 37 percent of the bogus trials. Three-quarters of the participants conformed on at least one bogus trial. In other versions of the experiment, Asch varied the number of confederates from 1 to 15 persons. He found that the

conformity Behaving in accordance with group expectations with little or no overt pressure to do so.

FIGURE 17-4
The Asch Study

Participants in one of Solomon Asch's studies had to decide which of three lines was equal in length to another line.

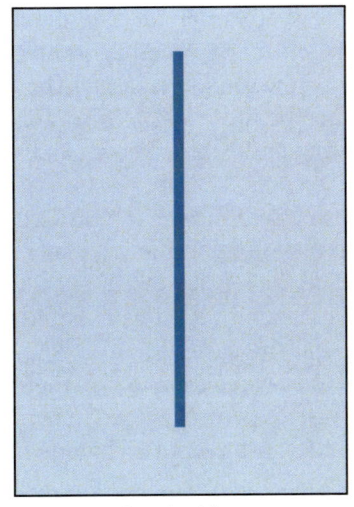

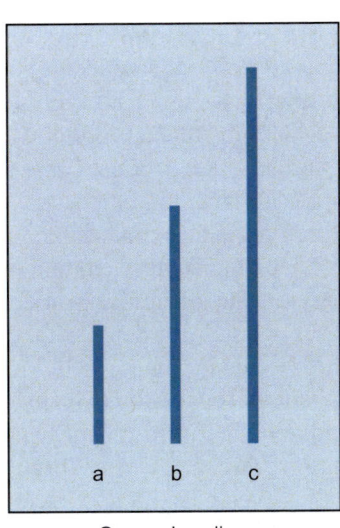

Standard line   Comparison lines

Chapter 17 Social Psychology   619

participants' tendency to conform increased dramatically until there were three confederates, with additional confederates inducing smaller increases in conformity (Asch, 1955).

Though some attempts to replicate Asch's study have failed (Lalancette & Standing, 1990), his research has been successfully replicated in different cultures, including studies using American (Larsen, 1990), Dutch (Vlaander & Van Rooijen, 1985), Kuwaiti (Amir, 1984), British (Nicholson, Cole, & Rocklin, 1985), and Australian (Walker & Andrade, 1996) participants. But a meta-analysis of 133 studies from 17 countries that used Asch's line-judgment task found that conformity has declined since the 1950s. And collectivist countries tended to show greater conformity than did individualistic countries (Bond & Smith, 1996). For example, Chinese college students tend to be more conforming than American college students (Zhang & Thomas, 1994).

These differences may be attributable to different cultural values related to uniqueness. In a series of experiments, East Asian and European American participants' preferences were assessed in a number of domains. In one version of the experiment, for example, participants were asked to select a ballpoint pen as a gift from a collection of five pens.

At least one of the five pens was a different color from the rest of the group. Participants' choices were coded for uniqueness if they chose one of the pens that was different from the rest of the pens in the group. Participants' choices were coded for conformity if they chose one of the pens that did not differ from the rest of the group. European Americans were more likely to choose the unique pen, whereas East Asians were more likely to choose a pen that did not differ from the group (Kim & Markus, 1999).

In Asch's study, why did the participants conform to the obviously erroneous judgments of strangers? A few claimed that they really saw the lines as equal, and others assumed that the confederates knew something they did not. But their main reason for conforming was their need for social approval—they feared social rejection. Participants found, as do many people, that it is difficult to be the lone dissenter in a group. In variations of the experiment in which one of the confederates joined the participant in dissenting, participants conformed on less than one-tenth, rather than on one-third, of the bogus trials (Asch, 1955). Thus, like one of the principles mentioned for minority influence, dissent is more likely when we have fellow dissenters.

Compliance

We are continually bombarded with requests. A friend might want to borrow your car. A professor might ask you to help move laboratory equipment. An advertiser might urge you to purchase a particular deodorant. The process by which a person agrees to a request that is backed by little or no threat of punishment is called **compliance**. As discussed in Chapter 16, compliance often is lifesaving when it comes to medical regimens, dieting, and exercise. Two of the major means of inducing compliance are the foot-in-the-door technique and the door-in-the-face technique.

The Foot-in-the-Door Technique Years ago, it was common for salespersons to go door-to-door trying to sell encyclopedias, vacuum cleaners, or other products. Every salesperson knew that a person who complied with the small request to be permitted inside to discuss or demonstrate a product would then be more likely to comply with the larger request to purchase the product. This phenomenon became known as the **foot-in-the-door technique** (Dillard, 1991).

This technique can produce extraordinary degrees of compliance. In one study, women were surveyed by telephone about the brand of soap they used. Three days later they were called again, as were a group of similar women who had not received the first call. This time the caller asked each woman for permission to send a team of men who would rummage through her cabinets to record the household items that she used. Of those who had complied with the first (small) request, 53 percent agreed to permit a team to visit their home. Of those who received only the second (large) request, just 22 percent agreed to permit a team to visit their home (Freedman & Fraser, 1966). The foot-in-the-door technique has proved so effective that it has even been used to encourage gynecological cancer check-ups (Dolin & Booth-Butterfield, 1995) and organ donations (Girandola, 2002). But the foot-in-the-

---

compliance Behaving in accordance with a request that is backed by little or no threat of punishment.

foot-in-the-door technique Increasing the likelihood that a person will comply with a request by first getting the person to comply with a smaller one.

door technique may fail if the larger request follows immediately after the smaller request. A delay between the two may be more effective (Chartrand, Pinckert, & Burger, 1999).

Why is the foot-in-the-door technique effective? Self-perception theory, which assumes that we infer our attitudes from observing our own behavior, provides an answer (Eisenberg, Cialdini, McCreath, & Shell, 1987). If you freely comply with a small, worthwhile request, you will view yourself as a person who has a positive attitude toward worthwhile requests. Because you wish to be consistent with your self-perception, you will be more likely to comply with other requests (Burger & Guadagno, 2003).

The Door-in-the-Face Technique Salespeople also know that customers who refuse to purchase a particular item will be more likely to comply with a request to purchase a less expensive item. Fostering compliance by presenting a smaller request after a larger request has been denied is called the **door-in-the-face technique** (Dillard, 1991). We resort to this technique in our everyday lives in situations such as negotiating salaries (perhaps asking for several thousand dollars more than we expect) or convincing professors to give us extra time to complete term papers (boldly asking for an extra week when we would gladly settle for two extra days). Even charities use the technique. In one study, potential volunteers were asked to commit themselves to serve as a Big Brother or Big Sister at a juvenile detention center for 2 hours a week for 2 years. After they all rejected this large request, they were subjected to a much smaller request—to chaperone a group of low-income children on a single 2-hour visit to a zoo. Participants were significantly more likely to comply with this request than were those who had not been asked earlier to serve as a Big Brother or Big Sister (Cialdini et al., 1975).

The door-in-the-face technique depends on social norms that require that concessions offered by one negotiating party be met by concessions from the other party. The willingness of one person to reduce the size of an initial request would be a concession, imposing social pressure on the person who had refused the first request to comply with the second one (Cann, Sherman, & Elkes, 1975). Another explanation for the effectiveness of the foot-in-the-door technique assumes that the recipient complies with the second request to reduce guilt at refusing the first request (Millar, 2002). The foot-in-the door technique generally is more effective than the door-in-the-face technique (Fern, Monroe, & Avila, 1986).

Obedience

Would you assist in the cold-blooded murder of innocent people if your superior ordered you to? This question deals with the limits of **obedience**—the following of orders given by an authority. The limits of obedience were at the heart of the Nuremberg war crime trials held after World War II. The defendants were Nazis accused of crimes against humanity for their complicity in the executions of millions of innocent people during World War II, most notably the genocide of 6 million Jews. The defendants claimed that they were only following orders. In his journal, Adolf Eichmann, who personally oversaw the deportation and murder of millions of Jews as a high-ranking Nazi official, described his role in the genocide as "the same as millions of others who had to obey" (Trounson, 2000, p. A1). The surprising extent to which people will obey orders to harm others was demonstrated in the classic study discussed in "The Research Process" box.

Foot-in-the-Door Technique
Salespeople know that a person who complied with the small request to be permitted inside to discuss or demonstrate a product would then be more likely to comply with the larger request to purchase the product.
Source: Iakov Filimonov/Shutterstock.com.

door-in-the-face technique Increasing the likelihood that a person will comply with a request by first getting the person to reject a larger one.

obedience Following orders given by an authority.

Section Review: Group Dynamics

1. How would you prevent groupthink in decision making?
2. How does social facilitation both enhance and impair performance?
3. How would you prevent social loafing during group performance?
4. How might the foot-in-the-door technique have contributed to the high rates of obedience in Milgram's experiments?

Chapter 17 Social Psychology

> **The Research Process**
>
> ### Would You Harm Someone Just Because an Authority Figure Ordered You To?
>
> **Rationale**
>
> Are people who obey orders to hurt innocent people unusually cruel, or are most human beings susceptible to obeying such orders? This question led psychologist Stanley Milgram (1933–1984) of Yale University to conduct perhaps the most famous—and controversial—of all psychology experiments (Milgram, 1963).
>
> **Method**
>
> Milgram's participants were adult men who had responded to an advertisement for volunteers to participate in a study of the effects of punishment on learning. On arriving at the laboratory, each participant was introduced to a pleasant, middle-aged man who also would participate in the experiment. In reality, the man was a confederate of the experimenter. The experimenter asked both men to draw a slip of paper out of a hat to determine who would be the "teacher" and who would be the "learner."
>
> The drawing was rigged so that the participant was always the teacher. The teacher communicated with the learner over an intercom as the learner performed a memory task while strapped to an electrified chair in another room. The teacher sat at a control panel with a series of switches with labels ranging from "Slight Shock" (15 volts) to "Danger: Severe Shock" (450 volts) in 15-volt increments. The experimenter instructed the participant to administer an increasingly strong electric shock to the learner's hand whenever he made an error. At higher shock levels, the learner cried out in pain or begged the teacher to stop. Many participants responded to the learner's distress with sweating, trembling, and stuttering. If the participant hesitated to administer a shock, the experimenter might say, "You have no other choice, you must go on," and remind the teacher that he, the experimenter, was responsible for any ill effects. Note the similarity between this incremental approach and the foot-in-the-door technique (Gilbert, 1981).
>
> **Results and Discussion**
>
> How far do you think you would have gone as the teacher in Milgram's study? Surveys of psychiatrists and Yale students had predicted that less than 2 percent of the participants would reach the maximum level. To Milgram's surprise, two-thirds of the participants reached the maximum level of shock, and none stopped before reaching 300 volts—the point at which the learner frantically banged on the wall and stopped answering questions. (By the way, the learner never received a shock. In fact, his "responses" were played on a tape recorder.)
>
> Could the prestige of Yale University and the apparent legitimacy of a laboratory study have affected the participants? Milgram replicated the study in a run-down office building in Bridgeport, Connecticut. The experimenter did not wear a laboratory coat, and he made no reference to Yale. He obtained impressive results nonetheless. Of those who participated, 48 percent reached the maximum level of shock. Would physically separating the teacher and the learner have an effect? Somewhat. When the participant sat near the learner, 40 percent reached the maximum. Even when the participant had to force the learner's hand onto a shock grid, 30 percent still reached the maximum (Milgram, 1974). No gender differences in obedience have been found in studies comparing male and female participants (Blass, 1999). Figure 17-5 shows how the results were affected by different experimental conditions. Milgram's original experiment also has been successfully replicated in other countries, which indicates that obedience to authority is common across cultures (Shanab & Yahya, 1977).

Aggression

aggression Verbal or physical behavior aimed at harming another person.

As much as people are capable of prosocial behavior, they are, unfortunately, just as capable of antisocial behavior. The most extreme form of antisocial behavior is **aggression**, which is verbal or physical behavior aimed at causing harm to another person. What accounts for the prevalence of aggression?

Theories of Aggression

One class of theories views aggression as the product of physiology. A second class of theories views aggression as the product of experience. Obviously, both are important, including their interaction.

Aggression as the Product of Physiology

The earliest theories of aggression claimed that it was instinctive. An instinct is an inborn tendency, unaffected by learning, to engage in a relatively complex behavior that charac-

The Research Process

Would You Harm Someone Just Because an Authority Figure Ordered You To? *continued*

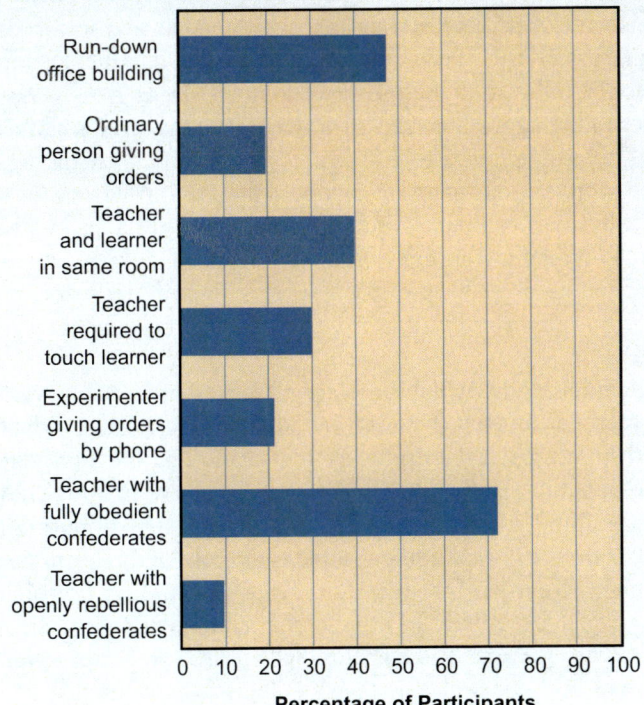

FIGURE 17-5
Variables That Affect Obedience to Authority

In his series of classic experiments, Stanley Milgram varied the location of the experiment, the proximity of the teacher to the learner and the experimenter, and the presence of confederates.

Sources: Data from S. Milgram, *Obedience to Authority: An Experimental View*, Harper and Row, Publishers, Inc., 1974; and S. Milgram, *The Individual in a Social World: Essays and Experiments*, Addison-Wesley Publishing Company, 1992.

Milgram's research has disturbing implications. The line that separates us from war criminals may be thinner than we would like to believe. Many of us, given orders by someone we consider to be a legitimate authority and who we assume will be responsible for our actions, might be willing to harm an innocent person. Despite the insight that Milgram's research provided into the nature of obedience, it provoked criticism, most notably from Diana Baumrind (1964). She claimed that Milgram's use of deception increased distrust of psychological researchers and that his participants' self-esteem was damaged by the realization that they might harm an innocent person simply because an authority figure ordered them to.

In response to these criticisms, Milgram reported that 84 percent of the participants in his study were debriefed, that participants were glad they had participated, that there was no evidence that any of them developed long-term emotional distress, and that the importance of the findings made the use of deception worthwhile (Milgram, 1964). Given today's increased concern with the rights of research participants, partly in response to studies like Milgram's, it is unlikely that any researchers would replicate his studies. Milgram's research still sparks interest today, particularly in regard to people who disobey despite threats to their life and well-being—such as those who smuggled slaves out of Southern states via the underground railroad in the mid-19th century. One lesson is that those who resist early are more likely to maintain their defiance. For example, a reanalysis of audio recordings of participants in one of Milgram's replications of his original study found that the sooner participants resisted, the more likely they were to become defiant and refuse to give any more shocks (Modigliani & Rochat, 1995).

---

terizes members of a species—such as nest building in birds. After observing the extraordinary violence of World War I, Sigmund Freud concluded that human aggression is caused by an instinct that he called Thanatos (Greek for "death"). According to Freud, Thanatos causes a buildup of aggressive energy, which must be released periodically through a process called catharsis. This release would prevent outbursts of extreme violence. You might experience catharsis by playing football, field hockey, or another aggressive sport.

Nobel Prize–winning ethologist Konrad Lorenz (1966) agreed with Freud that we have an instinct for aggression. He claimed that all animals have a powerful aggressive drive that, like the sex drive, promotes the survival of their species. But because animals have evolved natural weapons such as fangs and claws that can kill, they also have evolved ritualistic behaviors to inhibit aggression and prevent unnecessary injuries and deaths. In contrast, because people have not evolved natural weapons that can kill, they have not evolved ritualistic behaviors to inhibit aggression against their own species. As a consequence, people are less inhibited in using artificial weapons such as clubs, spears, guns, and missiles against one another. Lorenz, like Freud, believed that outbursts of aggression could be avoided only by providing outlets for the cathartic release of aggressive energy through

Chapter 17 Social Psychology

Catharsis and Violence

According to Freud, both the participants and the spectators of a violent sport, such as boxing or wrestling, should show a decrease in their tendencies toward violence as the result of catharsis. But research has found that, on the contrary, watching or taking part in violence will increase one's tendency to engage in it.
Source: Ersler Dmitry/Shutterstock.com.

means such as sports (Leakey & Lewin, 1977). But research has failed to support the belief that aggression can be reduced through catharsis. In fact, participants who hit a punching bag while thinking about a person who angered them were more angry and more aggressive than participants who distracted themselves or did nothing at all (Bushman, 2002).

Evolutionary psychologists assume that there is a strong hereditary basis for aggression and other social behaviors (Buss, 1999). Twin studies have provided evidence supporting this hypothesis. Psychologists who study twins might compare the aggressiveness of identical twins reared together to the aggressiveness of fraternal twins reared together. These researchers assume that if heredity plays a role in aggression, identical twins (who are genetically identical) will be more similar in aggressiveness than will fraternal twins (who are no more alike genetically than ordinary siblings). Twin studies have, indeed, found this correlation, providing evidence for the hereditary basis of aggressiveness (Beatty, Heisel, Hall, Levine, & LaFrance, 2002). Of course, this finding does not rule out the possibility that identical twins are more similar in aggressiveness because they are treated more alike than fraternal twins.

What might be the physiological means by which heredity affects aggression? Several brain structures play important roles, particularly the left frontal cortex (Hortensius, Schutter, & Harmon-Jones, 2012) and structures in the limbic system, including the amygdala (Gopal et al., 2013) and the hypothalamus (Haller, 2013). A review of brain-imaging studies using CT, MRI, and PET scans found a relationship between frontal lobe abnormalities and aggressiveness (Mills & Raine, 1994). Another factor is the role of the hormones cortisol and especially testosterone (Montoya, Terburg, Bos, & van Honk, 2012). Violent criminals have higher levels of testosterone than do nonviolent criminals (Rubin, Reinisch, & Haskett, 1981). Athletes who use anabolic steroids, which are synthetic derivatives of testosterone, become more anxious and aggressive (Oberlander & Henderson, 2012). Testosterone levels are positively correlated with self-reported verbal and physical aggression in women (von der Pahlen, Lindman, Sarkola, Maekisalo, & Eriksson, 2002). The combination of psychotherapy and the administration of medications that lower testosterone levels may reduce sex-crime recidivism (Turner, Basdeskis-Jozsa, & Briken, 2013). And transgender individuals, who undergo testosterone treatment during female-to-male sex reassignment, report experiencing more aggression after starting hormone treatment (Slabbekoorn, Van Goozen, Gooren, & Cohen-Kettenis, 2001).

But some research has failed to find a relationship between testosterone levels and aggression. A recent meta-analysis found a weak positive relationship between increased testosterone levels and increased likelihood of aggression in humans (Book, Starzyk, & Quinsey, 2001). Other studies have found that men who receive testosterone injections may become more aggressive because of an expectancy effect—they act more aggressively simply because they believe they have received testosterone (Bjorkqvist, Nygren, Bjorklund, & Bjorkqvist, 1994). These negative findings have led some researchers to study the effect of experience on aggression (Albert, Walsh, & Jonik, 1993).

Aggression as the Product of Experience

Whereas some researchers look to hereditary factors, most look to life experiences as the main determinants of aggression. In the late 1930s, a team of behaviorists concluded that aggression is caused by frustration (Dollard, Doob, Miller, Mowrer, & Sears, 1939). This hypothesis became known as the **frustration-aggression hypothesis**. We experience frustration when we are blocked from reaching a goal. But the frustration-aggression hypothesis is an inadequate explanation of aggression because experiences other than frustration can cause aggression and because frustration does not always lead to aggression.

The inadequacies of the frustration-aggression hypothesis inspired psychologist Leonard Berkowitz to develop the revised frustration-aggression hypothesis. According to Berkowitz (1974), frustration does not directly provoke aggression. Instead, it directly provokes anger or another unpleasant emotion, such as anxiety or depression. The unpleasant emotion, in turn, will provoke aggression—particularly when stimuli (such as guns) that have been associated with aggression are present. Berkowitz demonstrated his hypothesis in a study in which male college students gave electric shocks to other stu-

frustration-aggression hypothesis The assumption that frustration causes aggression.

dents to induce feelings of anger in the shock recipients. When students who had received shocks were given the opportunity to give shocks to those who had shocked them, they gave more shocks when an aggressive stimulus such as a revolver, rather than a neutral stimulus such as a badminton racket, was left on the table (Berkowitz & LePage, 1967). Though some studies have failed to support the revised frustration-aggression hypothesis (Buss, Booker, & Buss, 1972), many have found that anger in the presence of aggressive stimuli does tend to provoke aggression (Rule & Nesdale, 1976). Moreover, unexpected frustrations, because they evoke stronger unpleasant emotions, are more likely to provoke aggression than are expected frustrations (Berkowitz, 1989). For example, one study found that participants who lost in a competitive video game demonstrated increased negative affect and aggression (Breuer, Scharkow, & Quandt, 2013).

As described in Chapter 7, much of our behavior is the product of social learning—learning by observing the behavior of others. Aggression is no exception to this rule. We may learn to be aggressive by observing people who act aggressively. For example, women who observed their parents being aggressive are more likely to become aggressive themselves (White & Humphrey, 1994). And, as you read in Chapter 4, one explanation for the gender difference in aggression is gender-role socialization. However, many of the laboratory studies of aggression have relied on male samples and operational definitions of aggression based on physical aggression—like the application of electric shock to a stranger. When other measures of aggression are studied, levels of aggression observed among women and girls rise dramatically. In an extensive review of the literature, Jacquelyn White and Robin Kowalski (1994) found that gender differences in aggressive behavior reflect the social structure of women's and men's lives. For example, women are more likely to be verbally aggressive or sexually coercive within intimate relationships. In contrast, men are far more likely to be physically aggressive and to assault strangers in public places (Graham & Wells, 2001). Moreover, this gender difference is evident in childhood—across cultures. A cross-cultural study of American and Indonesian children aged 11 to 14 years found that boys were more likely to be engaged in physical aggression, whereas girls were more likely to be engaged in relational aggression involving the spread of malicious rumors, the manipulation of relationships, or social ostracism (French, Jansen, & Pidada, 2002).

Group Violence

In the year A.D. 59, opposing fans rioted at the Pompeii amphitheater during a gladiatorial contest, prompting the Roman Senate to ban such contests in Pompeii for 10 years. Contemporary society also has seen its share of riots at athletic events. In June 2000, hundreds of basketball fans spilled into the streets the night that the Los Angeles Lakers won the NBA playoff, torching or destroying more than half a dozen vehicles—including police cars and an MTA bus. Within an hour, the crowd had grown to more than 6,000. Police eventually fired rubber bullets into the crowd in an attempt to regain control. The riot was finally quelled almost two hours later (Hall & Briggs, 2000). Group violence also can arise under more mundane circumstances. Less than 2 weeks before the riot in Los Angeles, sexual violence erupted in Central Park, New York, following a local parade. Roving groups of men sexually assaulted at least 24 women by spraying them with water, stripping off their clothes, and fondling and molesting them (Getlin, 2000).

What makes normally peaceful individuals become violent when they are in groups? We are usually aware of our own thoughts, feelings, and perceptions and are concerned about being socially evaluated. But when in groups, we may become less aware of ourselves and less concerned about being socially evaluated. Leon Festinger named this process **deindividuation** (Festinger, Pepitone, & Newcomb, 1952). As the result of deindividuation, our behavior might no longer be governed by our social norms, which in turn can lead to the loss of normal restraints against undesirable behavior, making us more likely to conform to the behavior of the group (Postmes, Spears, Sakhel, & de Groot, 2001). Moreover, the anonymity provided by group membership can make us less concerned with how others are evaluating our behavior because we feel less accountable for our own actions (Prentice-Dunn & Rogers, 1982).

deindividuation The process by which group members become less aware of themselves as individuals and less concerned about being socially evaluated.

Deindividuation

Deindividuation might lead to violence when people in large groups experience anonymity.
Source: Pablo77/Shutterstock.com.

Even aggression by individuals who are not in groups is more likely when they feel anonymous. An experiment found that people driving convertibles with their tops up (high anonymity) will be more likely to honk their horns at cars that fail to proceed immediately at green lights than will people driving convertibles with their tops down (low anonymity). Those with tops up honk quicker, longer, and more frequently (Ellison, Govern, Petri, & Figler, 1995).

Deindividuation is most likely when the group is large and when the group members feel anonymous, have reduced self-awareness, and are emotionally aroused. These factors mean that large groups of people wearing masks, uniforms, or disguises and aroused by drugs, dancing, chanting, or oratory will be more likely to engage in violence. Disguised offenders engage in more acts of violence and vandalism than do nondisguised offenders (Silke, 2003). Despite theoretical support for deindividuation, research findings are far from convincing in supporting the existence of such a state of consciousness (Postmes & Spears, 1998).

Section Review: Aggression

1. What evidence is there for the role of testosterone in aggression?
2. What is the role of deindividuation in aggression?

prosocial behavior Behavior that helps others in need.

altruism The helping of others without the expectation of a reward.

Prosocial Behavior

On a spring day in 1986, 1-year-old Jennifer Kroll of West Chicago, Illinois, fell into her family's swimming pool. Jennifer's mother, after pulling Jennifer out of the pool and discovering that she was not breathing, ran outside and began screaming for help. Her screams were heard by James Patridge, who had been confined to a wheelchair since losing his legs in a land-mine explosion during the Vietnam War. Patridge responded by rolling his wheelchair toward the pool, until he encountered heavy brush, forcing him to crawl the final 20 yards. Patridge revived Jennifer by using cardiopulmonary resuscitation ("God's Hand," 1986). Patridge's heroic act led to offers of financial rewards, which he declined to accept, saying that saving Jennifer's life was reward enough.

Altruism

Is This Altruism?

This woman is providing first aid by applying a thermal blanket over the victim. Her actions could be explained by two perspectives. Some researchers have found that prosocial behavior associated with feelings of empathy is truly altruistic, whereas prosocial behavior associated with the desire to relieve one's own distress is not.
Source: Halfpoint/Shutterstock.com.

Patridge's act is an example of **prosocial behavior**—helping others in need. His behavior also is an example of **altruism**—helping others without the expectation of a reward in return. But are altruistic acts ever truly selfless? Perhaps people who engage in apparently altruistic behaviors do receive some kind of immaterial rewards. The most famous person to make this claim was Abraham Lincoln. During a train trip, Lincoln looked out his window and saw several piglets drowning. He ordered the train to stop so they could be saved. When praised for his action, Lincoln discounted altruism as his motive, claiming instead that his act was motivated by the selfish desire to avoid a guilty conscience (Batson et al., 1986).

Social psychologists interested in the study of altruism have been especially concerned with empathy, the ability to feel the emotions that someone else feels. Some researchers have found that prosocial behavior associated with feelings of empathy is truly altruistic (Batson, Bolen, Cross, & Neuringer-Benefiel, 1999), whereas prosocial behavior associated with the desire to relieve one's own distress is not (Maner et al., 2002). Research studies on the role of empathy in prosocial behavior have provided contradictory findings. In one study, participants completed a questionnaire that measured their level of sadness and their level of empathy for a person in need. Participants then were given the opportunity to help the person. The results indicated that the participants' willingness to help was related more to their sadness score than to their empathy score, indicating that they acted more out of a desire to reduce their own distress than out of a desire to reduce the distress of the other person. In fact, when the participants were given a "mood-fixing" placebo

Chapter 17 Social Psychology

that allegedly (but not actually) made it impossible for them to alter their moods, fewer participants were willing to help, even when they had high empathy scores (Cialdini et al., 1987). This study provided support for the **negative state relief theory** of prosocial behavior of Robert Cialdini (Schaller & Cialdini, 1988).

But what about people whose prosocial behavior is associated with helpers' feelings of both distress and empathy? In an experiment, participants were empathetically aroused and led to anticipate an imminent mood-enhancing experience. The experimenters reasoned that if the motivation to help was directed toward the goal of negative state relief, then empathetically aroused individuals who anticipate mood enhancement should help less than those who do not. The rate of helping among high-empathy participants was no lower when they anticipated mood enhancement than when they did not. Regardless of anticipated mood enhancement, high-empathy participants helped more than did low-empathy participants. The results supported the empathy-altruism hypothesis (Batson et al., 1989). Reviews of relevant research have produced inconsistent findings in regard to the existence of altruistic helping (Carlson & Miller, 1987; Cialdini & Fultz, 1990). So it still is unclear whether prosocial behavior is motivated more by empathy for others or by the desire to relieve one's own negative emotional states.

negative state relief theory The theory that we engage in prosocial behavior to relieve our own state of emotional distress at another's plight.

Bystander Intervention

Regardless of his motivation, James Patridge's rescue of Jennifer was an example of **bystander intervention**, the act of helping someone who is in immediate need of aid. Interest in the study of bystander intervention was stimulated by a widely publicized tragedy in which bystanders failed to help save a woman's life. At 3:20 A.M. on March 13, 1964, a 28-year-old woman named Kitty Genovese was returning home from her job as a bar manager. As she walked to her apartment building in the New York City borough of Queens, she was attacked by a mugger who repeatedly stabbed her. Thirty-eight of her neighbors reported that they had been awakened by her screams and had rushed to look out their windows but had not seen the attack. The assailant left twice, returning each time to continue his attack until, 30 minutes after her ordeal had begun, Kitty Genovese died.

bystander intervention The act of helping someone who is in immediate need of aid.

How would you have responded had you been one of her neighbors? The neighbors' responses might surprise you. At no time during these three separate attacks did any of the 38 persons try to help Kitty Genovese or even call the police. When questioned by police and reporters, the witnesses gave a variety of explanations for why they had not called the police. Their reasons included feeling tired, assuming it was a lovers' quarrel, and believing that "it can't happen here" (Gansberg, 1964). The murder of Kitty Genovese gained national attention, and the apparent apathy of her neighbors was taken as a sign of the callous, impersonal nature of the residents of big cities.

But social psychologists John Darley and Bibb Latané rejected this commonsense explanation as too simplistic. Instead, they conducted research studies to determine the factors that affect the willingness of bystanders to intervene in emergencies. This intervention is as important today as it was when Kitty Genovese was murdered. In fact, a survey of more than 500 undergraduates and faculty members found that only 25 percent of those who had witnessed children being abused in public had ever intervened to help (Christy & Voight, 1994). Darley and Latané found that bystander intervention involves a series of steps, which are presented in Figure 17-6. The intervention process may continue through each of these steps or be halted at any one.

Noticing the Victim

To intervene in an emergency, you must first notice the event or the victim. James Patridge heard the screams of Jennifer Kroll's mother, and neighbors heard the screams of Kitty Genovese.

Interpreting the Situation as an Emergency

People's interpretations of an event as an emergency or nonemergency are influenced by their perceptions and attributions about the situation (Hoefnagels & Zwikker, 2001).

Chapter 17 Social Psychology

FIGURE 17-6
Steps in Bystander Intervention

According to Latané and Darley (1968), bystanders go through certain steps before intervening in emergencies. The possibility of intervening can be inhibited at any of these steps.

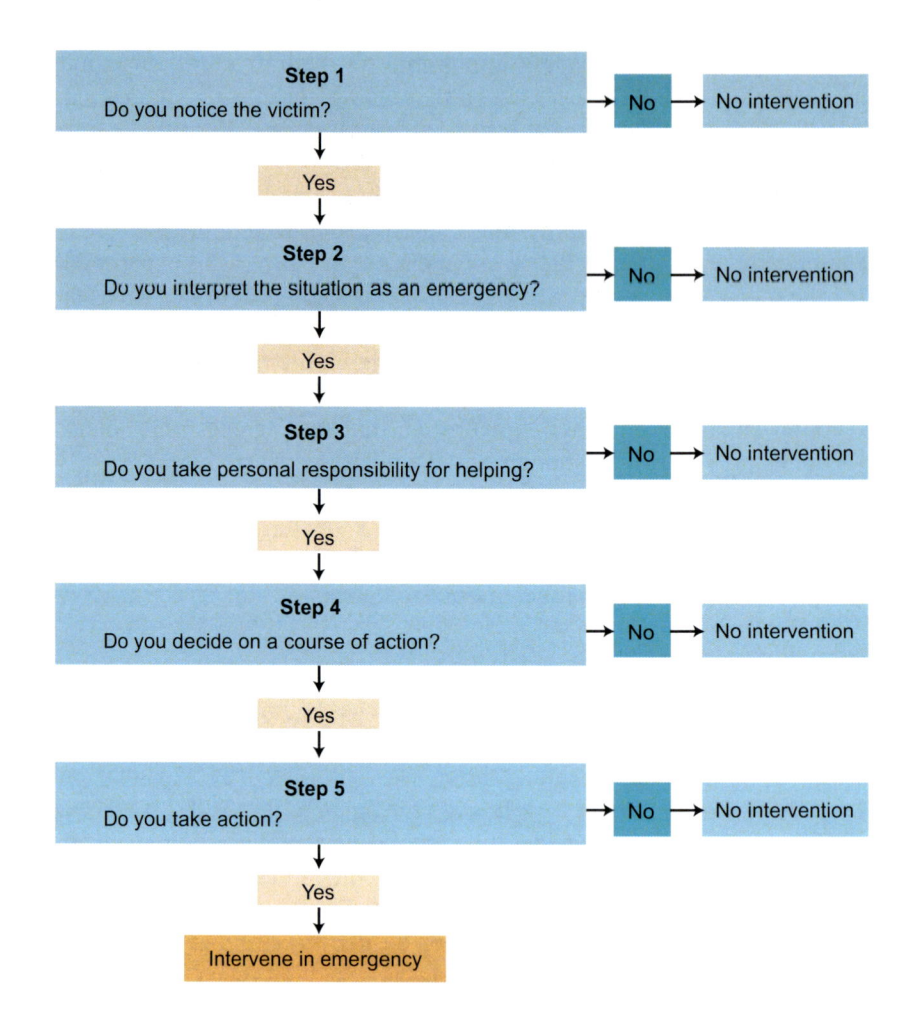

Step 1: Do you notice the victim? → No → No intervention
↓ Yes

Step 2: Do you interpret the situation as an emergency? → No → No intervention
↓ Yes

Step 3: Do you take personal responsibility for helping? → No → No intervention
↓ Yes

Step 4: Do you decide on a course of action? → No → No intervention
↓ Yes

Step 5: Do you take action? → No → No intervention
↓ Yes

Intervene in emergency

James Patridge was confronted by an unambiguous situation. He interpreted the screams of Jennifer's mother as the sign of an emergency. In contrast, there was some ambiguity in Kitty Genovese's situation. In fact, bystanders tend to assume that an apparent confrontation between a man and a woman is a lovers' quarrel rather than a true emergency (Shotland & Straw, 1976). Because almost all of Kitty Genovese's neighbors interpreted the situation as a nonemergency, at that point there was little likelihood that any neighbors would help.

Taking Personal Responsibility

After interpreting the situation as an emergency, Patridge took responsibility for intervening. But not even those neighbors who may have interpreted Kitty Genovese's situation as an emergency took responsibility for helping her. Darley and Latané discovered a surprising reason for this lack of responsibility. Contrary to what you might expect, as the number of bystanders increases, the likelihood of a bystander's intervening decreases (Forsyth, Zyzniewski, & Giammanco, 2002). Note that this decrease in intervention is true only in situations involving strangers. In emergencies involving highly cohesive groups of people, such as friends or relatives, the probability of intervention will increase as the number of bystanders increases (Rutkowski, Gruder, & Romer, 1983).

The influence of the number of bystanders on bystander intervention was demonstrated in an early study by Darley and Latané (1968). They had college students meet to discuss the problems they faced in attending school in New York City. Each student was led to a room and told to communicate with other students over an intercom. The students were told that two, three, or six students were taking part in the discussion, but all the other students were the experimenter's confederates; in fact, the remarks of the other students were tape recordings. Early in the session the participant (the nonconfederate) heard another student apparently having an epileptic seizure and crying out for help.

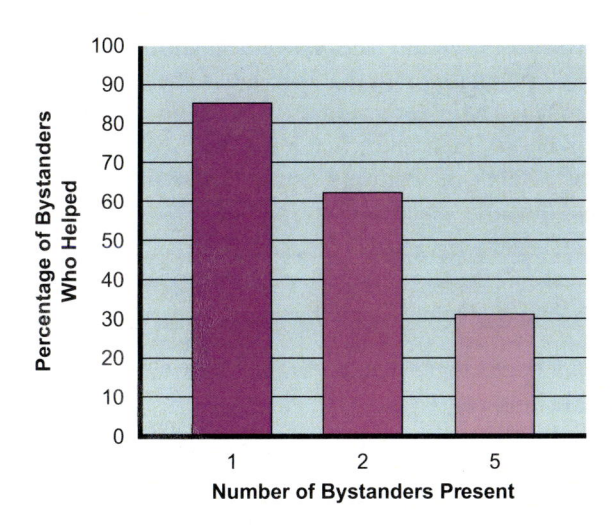

FIGURE 17-7
Diffusion of Responsibility

Darley and Latané found that as the number of bystanders increased, the likelihood of any of them going to the aid of a student apparently having an epileptic seizure decreased.

Source: Data from J. M. Darley and Bibb Latané, "Bystander Intervention in Emergencies: Diffusion of Responsibility," *Journal of Personality and Social Psychology, 8*, 377–383. Copyright © 1968 by the American Psychological Association.

Figure 17-7 shows that of those participants who believed they were a lone bystander, 85 percent sought help for the stricken person. Of those who believed they were one of two bystanders, 62 percent sought help. And of those who believed they were one of five bystanders, only 31 percent sought help. One reason for this decrease is the diffusion of responsibility: As the number of bystanders increases, the responsibility felt by each one decreases. So the students who were exposed to a mock epileptic seizure felt less responsibility for helping the victim when they believed other bystanders were present. In contrast to Kitty Genovese's neighbors, who assumed that other neighbors had been awakened, Patridge may have assumed that no one else could intervene, leaving him with the responsibility.

Deciding on a Course of Action

The decision to intervene depends in part on whether the bystander feels competent to meet the demands of the situation (Clark & Word, 1974). Patridge decided to wheel himself toward the pool and then crawl to it. Because Patridge had training in cardiopulmonary resuscitation, whereas Jennifer Kroll's mother did not, he felt more competent to try to revive Jennifer. Though none did so until after Kitty Genovese was dead, her neighbors might have at least considered calling the police when they heard her screams. A study that interviewed people who had intervened in violent crimes, such as muggings and armed robberies, found that they were usually larger and stronger than those who did not. Moreover, they typically were better trained to cope with crimes and emergencies, having had more police training or emergency medical training. Thus, they felt more competent to help (Huston, Ruggiero, Conner, & Geis, 1981).

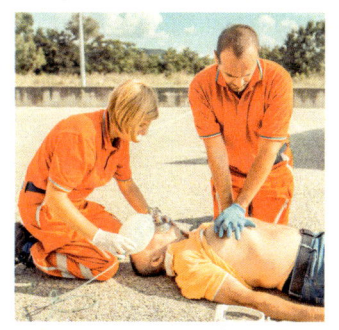

Taking Action

Patridge believed that the potential benefits of his intervention outweighed the potential costs. In one study, undergraduates reported the likelihood that they would help in a series of scenarios. The majority (76 percent) of their decisions reflected an assessment of the costs and benefits of each intervention (Fritzsche, Finkelstein, & Penner, 2000). This "bystander calculus" might explain why bystanders who believe that intervening in an emergency would place them in danger (as some might have believed in the case of Kitty Genovese) are less likely to intervene.

The characteristics of the victim also influence bystander intervention. One of the most important characteristics is the degree to which the victim appears responsible for his or her predicament. You might recognize this situation as an example of causal attribution. If we make dispositional attributions for a person's predicament, we will be less likely to help than if we make situational attributions for it (Weiner, 1980). We are more likely to help people in need when we perceive their situation to be the result of uncontrollable factors, such as a sudden illness, than when we perceive it to be the result of controllable factors, such as personal recklessness (Schmidt & Weiner, 1988).

As you can now appreciate, bystander intervention is not simply the product of a particular personality type. Instead, it is a complex process that depends on the interaction

Expertise and Bystander Intervention

In dangerous situations, bystanders will be more likely to intervene when they feel competent to do so. A person specially trained to rescue people experiencing a heart attack or drowning, such as these two rescuers, will be more likely to intervene than will someone who is not.
Source: William Perugini/Shutterstock.com.

Chapter 17 Social Psychology

between characteristics of the victim, the bystander, and the situation. For example, a recent study found that women reported that they would be more likely to intervene when a child is being hit than when a dog or a woman is being hit. In contrast, men reported that they would be more likely to intervene when a woman is being hit than when a dog or a child is being hit (Laner, Benin, & Ventrone, 2001). These findings are consistent with the gender-role analysis of altruism discussed in Chapter 2.

> ### Section Review: Prosocial Behavior
>
> 1. What research evidence is there to support the negative state relief theory of seemingly altruistic behavior?
> 2. What is the role of the diffusion of responsibility in bystander intervention?

Experiencing Psychology

A Study of Personal Advertisements

As noted in the section, "Romantic Love," there are gender differences in the characteristics that women and men prefer when they are seeking a romantic partner. In this exercise, you will record data about age preferences in mate selection, analyze it statistically, and discuss it in the context of what you learned from reading this chapter. You should work in a group of three to four students and should agree on hypotheses about what you will find.

Method
Materials
Choose one of the websites that follow to serve as a source for your data. Each of these sites is the home page of a metropolitan newspaper that provides access to the personal advertisement area of their classified section.

- *Atlanta Journal-Constitution*: www.accessatlanta.com
- *Chicago Tribune*: www.chicagotribune.com/
- *Denver Post*: www.denverpost.com/
- *Los Angeles Times*: www.latimes.com/
- *Miami New Times*: www.miaminewtimes.com
- *New York Times*: www.nytimes.com/
- *Phoenix New Times*: www.phoenixnewtimes.com/
- *San Francisco Chronicle*: www.sfgate.com/
- *Village Voice*: http://villagevoice.com/
- *Washington Post*: www.washingtonpost.com/

Select 15 to 20 advertisements in each of the following categories: men seeking women, women seeking men, men seeking men, and women seeking women. Each of your advertisements must contain the following information: the advertiser's age, the advertiser's sex, the sex of the desired partner, and the exact age range desired. Do not include any advertisement that is ambiguous on any of these criteria.

Prepare four coding sheets, one for each of the advertiser categories (i.e., heterosexual men and women, gay men, and lesbians). Each coding sheet should have three columns: one for the advertiser's age, one for average age of desired partner, and one for a difference score that you will compute.

Procedure
Record your data for each of the advertisements you selected using the following procedure. Record the advertiser's age. Then compute an average age of desired partner by adding the minimum and maximum age in the range and divide by 2. For example, if an advertiser specified an age range of 20 to 30, the average age of desired partner would be 25. Then compute a difference score, the advertiser's age minus the average age of desired partner, and record this score on your data sheet. A negative score indicates that the advertiser is seeking an older partner; a positive score indicates that the advertiser is seeking a younger partner.

Results
Calculate group means for the difference scores for each of the four advertiser categories. Group means should be used for drawing a graph showing the difference scores for each of the four advertiser categories. (See Chapter 2 and Appendix C in the Online Edition.)

Discussion
Discuss whether your results agree with your hypotheses. Do the results support what you read in the chapter? Do the results support any of the theories discussed in the chapter? Were there any differences between men and women? Were there any differences between the heterosexual women and men, gay men, and lesbians? Are there any other conclusions that can be reached from the data?

As a researcher, you should also note any shortcomings of the study and aspects that you would change to improve it. Finally, you should suggest a research study that would be a logical offshoot of this study.

Chapter Summary

Social Cognition

- Social psychology is the field that studies behavior in its interpersonal context.
- The process by which we try to explain social behavior is called causal attribution.
- When you decide that a person is responsible for her or his own behavior, you are making a dispositional attribution.
- When you decide that circumstances are responsible for a person's behavior, you are making a situational attribution.
- Bernard Weiner's attribution theory looks at the interaction of the internal-external, stable-unstable, and controllable-uncontrollable dimensions.
- Biases in causal attribution include the fundamental attribution error and the self-serving bias.
- Person perception is the process by which we make judgments about the personal characteristics of people.
- Sometimes we try to affect other people's perceptions of us by engaging in impression management.
- Person perception also is affected by social schemas, which comprise the presumed characteristics of a role, an event, a person, or a group.
- Social schemas that we believe can be applied to almost all members of a group are called stereotypes.
- Our first impressions play an important role in person perception, in some cases creating a self-fulfilling prophecy.

Interpersonal Attraction

- Psychologists interested in studying social attraction are concerned with the factors that make us like or love other people.
- Liking depends on the factors of proximity, familiarity, physical attractiveness, similarity, and self-disclosure.
- Researchers who study love distinguish between passionate love and companionate love.
- According to Ellen Berscheid and Elaine Hatfield, romantic love depends on cultural support for the concept of romantic love, a state of physiological arousal, and the presence of an appropriate person to love.
- Robert Sternberg's triangular theory of love has received little empirical evaluation.
- Among the most important factors in promoting love are similarity, self-disclosure, and equity.

Attitudes

- Attitudes are evaluations of ideas, events, objects, or people.
- Attitudes have emotional, cognitive, and behavioral components.
- Classical conditioning, operant conditioning, and social-learning theory explain how attitudes are learned.
- We often are subjected to persuasive messages aimed at getting us to change our attitudes.
- Persuasive messages can take a central route or a peripheral route.
- Persuasiveness depends on the message, the source, and the audience.
- Sources that are more credible and attractive are more persuasive.
- Under certain circumstances, two-sided messages will be more effective than one-sided messages.
- The intelligence of the receiver and the relevance of the message also determine the effectiveness of persuasive messages.
- Our attitudes might not always accurately predict our behavior.
- Our behavior sometimes can affect our attitudes, a phenomenon that is explained by cognitive dissonance theory and self-perception theory.
- Prejudice is a positive or negative attitude toward others based on their membership in particular groups.
- The behavioral component of prejudice is discrimination.
- Among the important factors promoting prejudice are stereotypes and the authoritarian personality.
- Prejudice can be reduced when there is equal-status contact and intergroup cooperation.

Group Dynamics

- Psychologists interested in group dynamics study the effects of social relationships on thinking, feeling, and behaving.
- Decision making in groups can be affected by group polarization, which is the tendency for groups to make more extreme decisions than their members would make as individuals.
- Group decisions sometimes are characterized by groupthink, in which group members place greater emphasis on unanimity than on critical thinking.
- A minority can affect group decisions by being rational, confident, consistent, and patient.
- Groups can affect task performance through social facilitation, which is the improvement of performance caused by the presence of other people.
- Our performance can also be affected by social loafing, which is the tendency of individuals to exert less effort when performing in groups.
- Human relationships are characterized by conformity, compliance, and obedience.
- Conformity is behaving in accordance with group norms with little or no overt pressure to do so.

- Compliance is agreeing to a request that is backed by little or no threat of punishment.
- Two of the chief techniques for inducing compliance are the foot-in-the-door technique and the door-in-the-face technique.
- Obedience is following orders given by an authority.
- Stanley Milgram found that most people are all too willing to harm other people when ordered to do so by a legitimate authority figure.

Aggression

- Aggression is behavior aimed at causing harm to someone else.
- Physiological theories view aggression as biologically based, perhaps inborn.
- Sigmund Freud and Konrad Lorenz believed that aggression is instinctive, meaning that we have no choice but to engage in it periodically.
- Today, most researchers reject the instinct theory of aggression but still study hormonal and hereditary influences on it.
- Most researchers look to life experiences as the main determinants of aggression.
- According to the frustration-aggression hypothesis, aggression becomes more likely after we have been blocked from reaching a goal.
- According to social-learning theory, we may learn to be aggressive by observing people who act aggressively.
- Group violence is promoted by deindividuation, which is the loss of self-awareness and the feeling of anonymity that comes from being part of a group.

Prosocial Behavior

- Prosocial behavior involves helping others in need.
- Altruism is helping others without the expectation of a reward in return.
- Some researchers have found that true altruism occurs only when prosocial behavior is done out of empathy rather than out of a desire to reduce one's own distress at the plight of another person.
- Other researchers have found, instead, that prosocial behavior is never truly altruistic—it always depends on the desire to reduce our own distress.
- Psychologists who study prosocial behavior are especially concerned with bystander intervention, the act of helping someone who is in immediate need of aid.
- Bystander intervention depends on noticing the victim, interpreting the situation as an emergency, taking personal responsibility, deciding on a course of action, and taking action to help.

Key Terms

social psychology (p. 596)

Social Cognition

causal attribution (p. 596)
fundamental attribution error (p. 597)
impression management (p. 598)
person perception (p. 598)
self-fulfilling prophecy (p. 600)
self-serving bias (p. 597)
social cognition (p. 596)
social schema (p. 599)
stereotype (p. 599)

Interpersonal Attraction

companionate love (p. 604)
passionate love (p. 604)

Attitudes

attitude (p. 606)
authoritarian personality (p. 614)
cognitive dissonance theory (p. 611)
elaboration likelihood theory (p. 608)
persuasion (p. 608)
prejudice (p. 613)
self-perception theory (p. 611)
sleeper effect (p. 609)

Group Dynamics

compliance (p. 620)
conformity (p. 619)
door-in-the-face technique (p. 621)
foot-in-the-door technique (p. 620)
group (p. 615)

group polarization (p. 616)
groupthink (p. 617)
obedience (p. 621)
social facilitation (p. 617)
social loafing (p. 618)

Aggression

aggression (p. 622)
deindividuation (p. 625)
frustration-aggression hypothesis (p. 624)

Prosocial Behavior

altruism (p. 626)
bystander intervention (p. 627)
negative state relief theory (p. 627)
prosocial behavior (p. 626)

Chapter Quiz

Note: Answers for the Chapter Quiz questions are provided at the end of the book.

1. Richard LaPiere's (1934) study of prejudice against Chinese citizens by hotels and restaurants indicated that
   a. attitudes predict behavior.
   b. behavior predicts attitudes.
   c. attitudes may not predict behaviors.
   d. self-monitoring mediated attitude-behavior consistency.

2. In 1898, Norman Triplett conducted one of the first experiments in social psychology, which was influenced by his interest in
   a. persuasion.
   b. advertising.
   c. bicycle racing.
   d. pornography's effect on violence.

3. The student government decides to sponsor a spring picnic for the entire student body. But the student-government president insists that one person, rather than a committee, be responsible for it. The president most likely wishes to avoid
   a. social loafing.
   b. social facilitation.
   c. cognitive dissonance.
   d. self-fulfilling prophecy.

4. Two college students decide to see a horror movie together. They are terrified by the movie, become physiologically aroused, and immediately after the movie are surprised to find that they have romantic feelings toward each other. In regard to the emotional experience of romantic love, this situation would give the strongest support to the
   a. two-factor theory.
   b. James-Lange theory.
   c. Cannon-Bard theory.
   d. opponent-process theory.

5. According to Richard Petty and John Cacioppo (1990), persuasive messages that rely on characteristics of the source, instead of the merits of the arguments, take the
   a. direct route.
   b. central route.
   c. indirect route.
   d. peripheral route.

6. You receive a free sample of a new toothpaste, which, in reality, is no different from other kinds. After a period of using it, though your oral health is the same as it has always been, you develop a positive attitude toward the toothpaste—simply because you have been using it. Your attitude would be explained best by
   a. self-perception theory.
   b. self-serving bias theory.
   c. cognitive dissonance theory.
   d. self-fulfilling prophecy theory.

7. A basketball player is a notoriously poor "practice player" but performs well during actual games. This behavior would most likely be attributable to
   a. social loafing.
   b. social facilitation.
   c. cognitive dissonance.
   d. self-fulfilling prophecy.

8. If you decide that a fellow student has performed well on an exam because she is intelligent and conscientious, you have made a
   a. free will attribution.
   b. situational attribution.
   c. deterministic attribution.
   d. dispositional attribution.

9. Social psychologists interested in the study of altruism have been especially concerned with its relationship to
   a. empathy.
   b. egocentrism.
   c. social facilitation.
   d. cognitive dissonance.

10. You are asked to promote the building of a nuclear power plant in a community where most people oppose it. Based on the research of Carl Hovland and his associates near the end of World War II on factors involved in persuasion, you would be most persuasive if you
    a. denied the possibility of a nuclear meltdown.
    b. tried to convince the residents that they were being irrational.
    c. presented the financial and environmental benefits of nuclear energy, but none of its potential harmful effects.
    d. admitted the small probability of a nuclear meltdown, but stressed that nuclear energy produced less pollution than other sources of energy.

11. A political campaign asks you to volunteer to be a poll watcher on election day. After you say yes, you are then asked to call 50 potential voters in support of your favored candidate. The political campaign is making use of the
    a. jigsaw method.
    b. self-serving bias.
    c. door-in-the-face technique.
    d. foot-in-the-door technique.

12. Research by Kenneth and Mamie Phipps Clark (1947) on the effects of racial discrimination influenced the U.S. Supreme Court decision that
    a. African Americans should be guaranteed the right to vote.
    b. African Americans should be granted the same civil rights as European Americans.
    c. IQ tests should be banned from use with African American children.
    d. separate education for African Americans and European Americans was inherently unequal.

13. While enrolled in a course, you notice that one student is consistently late to class and conclude that she is irresponsible and lazy. This situation is an example of
    a. the fundamental attribution error.
    b. prejudice.
    c. self-serving bias.
    d. self-fulfilling prophecy.

14. In Stanley Milgram's (1963) classic study of the administration of electric shocks to a "learner," the proportion of participants who reached the maximum level of shock was about
    a. one-half.
    b. one-tenth.
    c. two-thirds.
    d. three-quarters.

15. Research indicates that interpersonal attraction between two persons is enhanced when
    a. both engage in gradual rather than rapid self-disclosure.
    b. both engage in immediate rather than long-term self-disclosure.
    c. neither person engages in self-disclosure, because "familiarity breeds contempt."
    d. one person engages in rapid self-disclosure and the other does not, because it flatters the recipient of the self-disclosure.

16. The individual members of the academic affairs committee of a college would like to make minor revisions in the college's curriculum. Yet, after discussing the topic for several meetings, arguing every side of the issue, and working independently of any powerful administrator, they produce a radical revision that changes every aspect of the old curriculum. This situation would most likely be an example of
    a. groupthink.
    b. group polarization.
    c. social facilitation.
    d. self-fulfilling prophecy.

17. In a debate during the presidential campaign of 1960, Richard Nixon's less attractive appearance made many people determine that John F. Kennedy was the winner of the debate. In regard to Richard Petty and John Cacioppo's (1990) theory of persuasion, this example shows the power of the
    a. direct route.
    b. central route.
    c. indirect route.
    d. peripheral route.

18. The study of friendship among residents of apartments in a housing project for married students at the Massachusetts Institute of Technology (Festinger et al., 1950) demonstrated the importance of
    a. proximity.
    b. similarity.
    c. familiarity.
    d. physical attractiveness.

19. The deliberate attempt to control the attitudes that others have toward us is called
    a. self-serving bias.
    b. fundamental attribution error.
    c. impression management.
    d. self-fulfilling prophecy.

20. If you continually insist that other people's misfortunes are caused by their own lack of ability or effort, you would be committing the
    a. self-serving bias.
    b. stereotype bias.
    c. fundamental attribution error.
    d. self-fulfilling prophecy effect.

21. The study in which participants' photographs representing true images or mirror images were shown to the participants and to their friends (Mita et al., 1977) demonstrated that social attraction is affected by
    a. proximity.
    b. similarity.
    c. familiarity.
    d. physical attractiveness.

22. If you tend to blame your academic failures on unfair exams and biased grading and to credit yourself for your academic successes, you would be committing the
    a. self-serving bias.
    b. modesty bias.
    c. fundamental attribution error.
    d. self-fulfilling prophecy effect.

23. According to research by John Darley and Bibb Latané, a person who collapsed on the street would be most likely to be helped if
    a. there are many witnesses to the event.
    b. there is a single witness to the event.
    c. witnesses are strangers rather than acquaintances.
    d. witnesses assumed that the person was drunk rather than a diabetic suffering from insulin shock.

24. According to Konrad Lorenz, people engage in widespread violence because they
    a. are easily frustrated.
    b. suffer from original sin.
    c. observe other people being aggressive.
    d. lack inborn ritualistic ways to inhibit aggression.

25. A social schema that includes characteristics that are ascribed to almost all members of a group is an example of
    a. a stereotype.
    b. a first impression.
    c. a causal attribution.
    d. an attitude.

Thought Questions

1. How might the attributions you make about a failed romantic relationship make you feel better about yourself?

2. In trying to persuade other students that your school's core curriculum should be made more rigorous, how might you use research findings on the role of the source, the message, and the audience?

3. How might you keep your family from succumbing to groupthink in making a decision on whether to buy a particular house?

4. If you were asked to coordinate a group of students in running a special lecture series, how might you prevent social loafing?

Answers to Section Review Questions

Chapter 1: The Nature of Psychology

The Historical Context of Psychology

1. The structuralists tried to analyze the mind into its component elements and discover how the elements interact.
2. Functionalism stressed the importance of how the mind helps us adapt to reality, and it expanded the kinds of methods, subjects, and settings used in psychological research.
3. Structuralism was criticized as being "brick-and-mortar psychology" for its attempt to analyze mental experience into discrete elements.
4. Behaviorism emerged when John B. Watson and other psychologists, seeking to make psychology an objective science, rejected the study of the unobservable mind in favor of studying observable behavior.

Contemporary Perspectives in Psychology

1. Like Gestalt psychologists, cognitive psychologists stress the active role of the mind in organizing perceptions, processing information, and interpreting experiences. Like behavioral psychologists, cognitive psychologists stress the need for objective, well-controlled, laboratory studies.
2. The three areas of interest to psychologists who favor the biopsychological perspective are the brain, the hormonal system, and the effects of heredity on psychological functions.
3. The sociocultural perspective is a reaction against the tendency to presume that psychological research findings in Western cultures are automatically generalizable to other cultures.

The Scope of Psychology

1. Basic research aims at contributing to knowledge, and applied research aims at solving practical problems.
2. A psychiatrist is a physician who has served a residency in psychiatry, which takes a medical approach to the treatment of psychological disorders.
3. Peace psychologists conduct research and seek to apply their findings to help prevent violence, reduce conflict, and avoid war.

Chapter 2: Psychology as a Science

Sources of Knowledge

1. The basic assumptions of science are that the universe is orderly, determinism is the best approach to explaining events, and skepticism is the proper scientific attitude.
2. Critical thinking is the systematic evaluation of claims by identifying the claim being made, examining evidence in support of the claim, and considering alternative explanations of the claim.
3. The steps in the scientific method include providing a rationale, conducting the study, analyzing the data, communicating the research findings, and replicating the study.

Goals of Scientific Research

1. Scientists use operational definitions to provide precise, concrete, and often quantitative definitions of events or characteristics in their research.
2. Science involves probabilistic prediction because so many variables are at work at any given time that it usually is impossible to be certain about the accuracy of one's predictions.
3. Scientific explanation in psychology involves the discovery of the causes of overt behaviors, mental experiences, cognitive processes, and physiological changes.

Methods of Psychological Research

1. A random sample permits generalization of survey findings from the sample to the population it represents.
2. The validity of a test is the extent to which it measures what it is supposed to measure.
3. The independent variable is manipulated by the experimenter, who determines its values before the experiment begins.
4. Internal validity is the extent to which changes in the dependent variable are attributable to the independent variable.

Ans-1

Statistical Analysis of Research Data

1. Measures of central tendency, which are used to represent a set of scores, include the mode, median, and mean.
2. Measures of variability, which are used to describe the degree of dispersion of a set of scores, include the range, the variance, and the standard deviation.
3. Statistical significance involves deciding whether the size of the difference between group performances is of sufficiently low probability to occur by chance that it can be attributed to the independent variable.
4. Meta-analysis combines the results of a large number of published and unpublished studies. After collecting the studies, the researcher computes the average size of the effect of the independent variable on the dependent variable.

Ethics of Psychological Research

1. Critics argue that the methodological benefits of deception do not outweigh the mistrust of psychological research it might create and the distress it might cause in deceived participants.
2. Debriefing involves informing participants of the purpose of the research study in which they participated and any unusual aspects, such as the use of deception.
3. Animal rights advocates oppose all laboratory research using animals, regardless of its scientific merit or practical benefits. Animal welfare advocates would permit laboratory research on animals as long as the animals are given humane care and the potential benefits of the research outweigh any pain and distress experienced by the animals.

Chapter 3: Biopsychological Bases of Behavior

Nature versus Nurture

1. Evolutionary psychology views human behavior through concepts from the theory of evolution. It assumes that human behaviors that exist today evolved because they had survival value for generation after generation of people.
2. The closer two persons are related biologically, the more genetically similar they will be, but also, in general, the more similar they will be in life experiences. Thus, we have no more right to attribute personal similarities between two closely related people solely to heredity than we do to attribute them solely to common life experiences.

Biological Communication Systems

1. The nervous system is divided into the central nervous system (including the brain and spinal cord) and the peripheral nervous system (including the somatic nervous system and the autonomic nervous system).
2. Whereas the endocrine glands secrete hormones into the bloodstream, exocrine glands secrete their chemicals into the body surface or into the body cavities. Moreover, endocrine secretions have many behavioral effects, but exocrine secretions have relatively few.

Neuronal Activity

1. The major structures of the neuron are the cell body (soma), the dendrites, axon, and synaptic terminals.
2. Neural impulses depend on the flow of positively charged ions into the neuron, which produces an action potential.

Brain Functions

1. The brain stem regulates breathing, heart rate, motor coordination, brain arousal, attention, and other important life functions. The limbic system regulates processes related to emotion, motivation, and memory. And the cerebral cortex contains motor areas that control body movements, sensory areas that process sensory input, association areas that permit the integration of information from different brain areas, and in people, language areas that permit the production and comprehension of speech.
2. Broca's area selects the muscle movements necessary for the expression of words and communicates them to the motor cortex. Wernicke's area selects words that convey meaning and communicates them to Broca's area.
3. Split-brain research shows that the left hemisphere predominates in speech because split-brain patients can respond orally only when information is presented to the left hemisphere. Likewise, we know the right hemisphere predominates in spatial relations because split-brain patients perform better on tests of spatial relations using the left hand than using the right hand.

Chapter 4: Human Development

Research Methods in Developmental Psychology

1. Maturation is the sequential unfolding of inherited abilities, such as an infant's progression from crawling to walking to standing.
2. Cross-sectional research designs assess age differences at one point in time. However, it may not be possible to generalize the results of cross-sectional research to other cohorts. Longitudinal research designs assess how individuals change over time. However, longitudinal designs require considerable financial support, and participants often drop out. If the participants who drop out differ from the remaining participants, the results of such studies might not be generalizable to the population of interest.

Prenatal Development

1. Cell-adhesion molecules direct the movement of cells and determine which cells will adhere to one another, thereby determining the size, shape, and location of organs in the embryo.
2. The hallmarks of fetal alcohol syndrome are facial deformities, hearing disorders, intellectual disability, attentional deficits, and poor impulse control.

Infant and Child Development

1. Depth perception is present in human infants by 6 months of age, and generally it develops in animals about the time when they can move about on their own.
2. Piaget assumed that the child proceeds through qualitatively different stages of cognitive development during which cognitive schemas are altered by the processes of assimilation and accommodation.
3. Securely attached infants have more successful peer relationships and more secure romantic attachments later in life.
4. Permissive parents set few rules and rarely punish misbehavior; authoritarian parents set strict rules and rely on punishment; and authoritative parents tend to be warm and loving, yet insist that their children behave appropriately. Authoritative parenting is the most successful, and the preferred, style of parenting.

Adolescent Development

1. Cultural and historical factors that are unique to particular cohorts can make those cohorts somewhat different from cohorts that precede or succeed them.
2. The person who has reached the formal operational stage can apply abstract principles and make predictions about hypothetical situations.
3. Adolescents develop a sense of identity by adopting their own set of values and social behaviors. This is a normal part of finding answers to questions such as these: What do I believe is important? What are my goals in life?

Adult Development

1. A reduction in caloric intake is associated with increased longevity.
2. Research indicates that fluid intelligence declines in old age but that crystallized intelligence does not.
3. Adults who achieve generativity become less self-absorbed and more concerned about being a productive worker, spouse, or parent.

Chapter 5: Sensation and Perception

Sensory Processes

1. Sensation is the process that detects stimuli from one's body or environment. Perception is the process that organizes sensations into meaningful patterns.
2. Psychophysics is the study of the relationship between the physical characteristics of stimuli and the corresponding psychological responses to them.
3. Sensory adaptation is the tendency of sensory receptors to respond less and less to an unchanging stimulus.

Visual Sensation

1. Light waves pass through the cornea, pupil, lens, and photoreceptors.
2. Trichromatic theory assumes that the retina has three kinds of receptors, each of which is maximally sensitive to red, green, or blue light. The relative degree of activity of these receptors determines the colors that we perceive.

Visual Perception

1. These are the principles of proximity, closure, similarity, and continuity.
2. Two binocular cues are binocular disparity and convergence.

Hearing

1. The major structures of the outer ear are the pinna, auditory canal, and tympanic membrane; the major structures of the middle ear are the eustachian tube and ossicles; and the major structures of the inner ear are the oval window, cochlea, basilar membrane, hair cells, and auditory nerve.
2. Place theory assumes that particular points on the basilar membrane vibrate maximally in response to sound waves of particular frequencies.
3. Sound localization depends on sounds reaching one ear slightly before reaching the other, on sounds being slightly more intense at the closer ear, and on the irregular shape of the pinna altering sounds differently depending on their location.

Chemical Senses

1. Pheromones are odorous chemicals that affect animals' behavior. Recent research suggests that pheromones may have some effect on humans' behavior and emotions.
2. The enjoyment of flavors depends on not only the sense of taste but also the sense of smell, which is diminished by a head cold.

Skin Senses

1. The blind person wears a camera on special eyeglasses and a computer-controlled electronic vest covered with a grid of tiny Teflon cones. Outlines of images provided by the camera are impressed onto the skin by vibrations of the cones.
2. The gate-control theory of pain assumes that pain impulses from the limbs or body pass through a part of the spinal cord that provides a "gate" for pain impulses, perhaps

involving substance P neurons. Stimulation of neurons that convey touch sensations "closes" the gate, preventing input from neurons that convey pain sensations.

3. If human participants or animal subjects are given naloxone and the pain-relieving technique becomes less effective, it is assumed that the technique depends on the release of endorphins because naloxone blocks the effects of endorphins.

Body Senses

1. The kinesthetic sense informs you of the position of your joints, the tension in your muscles, and the movement of your arms and legs.

2. One of the major theories of motion sickness holds that it is produced by a conflict between sensory input to the eyes and sensory input to the vestibular organs.

Extrasensory Perception

1. The four paranormal abilities are mental telepathy, clairvoyance, precognition, and psychokinesis.

2. The major shortcomings of paranormal research are that it might involve poorly controlled demonstrations, chance events, fraud, or magic. Moreover, paranormal events cannot be explained by any known physical processes.

Chapter 6: Consciousness

The Nature of Consciousness

1. Automatic processing involves less conscious awareness and mental effort than controlled processing. As a result, it does not interfere with our performance of other activities.

2. The "cocktail party phenomenon" involves being engrossed in one conversation at a party yet noticing when your name is mentioned in another conversation.

3. Subliminal psychodynamic activation presents emotionally charged subliminal messages to alter the recipient's moods and behaviors by stimulating unconscious fantasies.

Sleep

1. The night typically involves four or five cycles in which the sleeper descends into the depths of NREM sleep, ascends to lighter stages of NREM sleep, and ends each cycle in REM sleep. During the second half of the night, the sleeper might not reach sleep deeper than stage 2 and will have longer REM periods.

2. The length of sleep varies negatively with how long it takes animals to find their daily food and positively with how secure they are from attack while asleep.

3. Persons with sleep-onset insomnia should avoid ingesting caffeine or doing exercise too close to bedtime. They also should avoid napping during the day; go to bed only when they feel sleepy; refrain from eating, reading, watching television, or listening to music while in bed; and get out of bed instead of tossing and turning.

Dreams

1. Among Calkins's findings were that we dream every night, that we have several dream periods each night, that we are more likely to dream during the second half of the night, that most dreams are mundane, that we can incorporate external stimuli into our dreams, that we can engage in "real thinking" while asleep, and that we can control our dreams.

2. Freud believed that dreams are often disguised forms of wish fulfillment in which the manifest content of the dream symbolically represents its true meaning; its latent content.

Hypnosis

1. During hypnotic induction you might have the person focus on a spot on the ceiling. You might then suggest that the person's eyelids are closing, feet are warming, muscles are relaxing, and breathing is slowing. You would gradually induce the person to relinquish more and more control of his or her perceptions, thoughts, and behaviors to you.

2. Hypnosis can help people recall memories but might make them overly confident in their recall of inaccurate "memories."

3. Some researchers believe that hypnosis is merely a state of heightened suggestibility in which people are willing to act out the suggestions given by the hypnotist. They also note that motivated nonhypnotized people can often perform the same feats as hypnotized people.

Psychoactive Drugs

1. The symptoms of physical drug dependency include tolerance and withdrawal symptoms.

2. Cocaine is a stimulant drug that induces a relatively brief state of euphoria. It can cause addiction, paranoia, hallucinations, and sudden death from cardiac arrest.

3. Marijuana alters sensory experiences and in higher doses can induce hallucinations. It impairs coordination, disrupts memory formation, and has been linked to a motivational syndrome.

4. Entactogens are a category of psychoactive drugs that induce altered perceptions, feelings of well-being, and interpersonal closeness and have been linked to memory impairment in chronic users.

Chapter 7: Learning

Classical Conditioning

1. You would repeatedly turn on the can opener just before presenting the cat with food. Eventually, the cat will come running at the sound of the can opener.
2. Bernstein suggests offering patients unusual, strange-tasting food before they have chemotherapy so that they will associate their resulting nausea with that food instead of with more common, nutritious foods.
3. Garcia found that rats have a tendency, apparently inborn, to associate nausea and dizziness with tastes, but not with sights and sounds, and to associate pain with sights and sounds, but not with tastes.

Operant Conditioning

1. Thorndike, like Skinner, found that behavior can be changed by altering its consequences.
2. You might train them by giving them a piece of cookie for looking at toys strewn on the floor, then for taking a step toward them, then for approaching them, then for touching one of them, then for picking it up, and finally for placing it in the toy box.
3. Both produce an increase in behavior, but whereas positive reinforcement involves the presentation of something appealing, negative reinforcement involves the removal of something unappealing.

Cognitive Learning

1. According to the cognitive explanation, blocking occurs because a new neutral stimulus adds nothing to the predictability of the UCS. The existing CS already predicts the occurrence of the UCS.
2. Latent learning and observational learning show that learning can take place without performing the relevant overt behavior.
3. Though the role of mirror neurons and their networks are still speculative, their functions have been observed in monkeys and humans. Mirror neurons fire when an animal learns to imitate the same action it just observed. This is thought to be an important physiological basis for observational learning and, thus, the phenomenon of empathy among humans.

Chapter 8: Memory

Information Processing and Memory

1. Some psychologists note that normal memory processes, such as thinking more often and more elaborately about certain experiences or being in a highly emotional state, can explain so-called flashbulb memories. Moreover, there is evidence that people are more confident in their flashbulb memories, even though those might be no more accurate than normal memories.
2. Sensory memory stores exact replicas of stimuli impinging on the senses for a brief period—from a fraction of second to several seconds. Short-term memory stores a limited amount of information in conscious awareness for about 20 seconds. And long-term memory stores a virtually unlimited amount of information for up to a lifetime.

Sensory Memory

1. By using partial report, Sperling demonstrated that iconic memory stores virtually all the information that strikes the photoreceptors, though the information fades so quickly that it seems that we store only a fraction of it.
2. Echoic memory helps us store speech sounds long enough to blend them with subsequent speech sounds, thereby letting us perceive a meaningful sequence of sounds.

Short-Term Memory

1. Research indicates that even when participants are tested on their short-term memory for letters presented visually, their errors indicate that they confuse letters based on their sounds more than on their appearance.
2. When they presented participants with trigrams to recall and prevented rehearsal of them, they found that after about 20 seconds participants could rarely recall the trigrams.

Long-Term Memory

1. Elaborative rehearsal involves processing the meaning of information instead of (as in maintenance rehearsal) its superficial qualities.
2. Procedural memory includes memories of how to perform behaviors, whereas declarative memory includes memories of facts.
3. In proactive interference, old memories interfere with new memories. In retroactive interference, new memories interfere with old ones.
4. Memories encoded while a person is in a specific state (such as a psychoactive drug-induced state) will be recalled better when the person is again in that state. There is also research showing that our recall of information that has been encoded in a particular mood will be best when we are in that mood again.

Memory, Forgetting, and Eyewitness Testimony

1. Children's eyewitness testimony is less accurate than that of adults, primarily because children are more suggestible and they are more likely to guess. The memories of preschool children are more fallible than the memories of older children.

2. Loftus believes that biased or leading questions can alter people's memory of past events. This becomes even more of an issue when hypnosis is used to recreate memories.

Improving Your Memory

1. You should set up a study schedule in a comfortable, nondistracting environment. You might also use the SQ3R method of studying. Other suggestions would be to use overlearning, distributed practice, and mnemonic devices.
2. You would memorize a list of concrete nouns that rhyme with numbers 1, 2, 3, 4, and so on. You would then imagine the objects to be recalled interacting with the objects represented by the concrete nouns. Then simply recall the concrete nouns associated with each number. This should automatically make you recall the interacting object.

The Biopsychology of Memory

1. After classically conditioning an eye-blink response in a rabbit, researchers found that electrical stimulation of a tiny site in the cerebellum of the rabbit elicited the conditioned eye blink and that destruction of the site eliminated it.
2. Since his hippocampus was removed decades ago, H. M. has been unable to form new long-term memories.
3. When participants are given a drug that blocks the effects of acetylcholine, they have trouble forming new long-term declarative memories. Other evidence comes from the loss of memory in victims of Alzheimer's disease, which is associated with the destruction of acetylcholine neurons in the brain.

Chapter 9: Thought and Language

Thought

1. Human development is characterized by critical periods during which the window for learning language is optimal.
2. Cognitive psychology combines William James's concern with mental processes and John B. Watson's concern with observable behavior.
3. Research indicates that we can think and form memories while our speech muscles are paralyzed; therefore, thought does not depend on subvocal speech.

Concept Formation

1. A logical concept is formed by identifying the specific features possessed by all things that the concept applies to. A natural concept is formed through everyday experience rather than by testing hypotheses about particular features that are common to all members of the concept.
2. They have fuzzy borders because it is difficult to identify their defining features.

Problem Solving

1. A heuristic can be more efficient because it rules out many useless alternatives before they are even attempted. But unlike an algorithm, a heuristic does not guarantee a correct solution.
2. Sometimes we are hindered by mental sets, which are commitments to problem-solving strategies that have succeeded in the past but that interfere with problem solving that requires a new strategy.

Creativity

1. Creative people tend to be above average in intelligence, imaginative, unconventional, and nonconforming; they also have a wide range of interests and are open to new experiences.
2. Amabile found that when students were given extrinsic reasons for writing poetry, they wrote less creative poems, whereas there was no decline in the creativity in poems by students who wrote for intrinsic reasons.

Decision Making

1. The availability heuristic is the tendency to estimate the probability of an event by how easily instances of it come to mind.
2. Leading questions affect people's decision making by the way in which they present the facts of a case, often as subtle as describing a 50 percent success rate versus a 50 percent failure rate.

Artificial Intelligence

1. Expert systems are using powerful computer programs that think more like world-class chess players rather than simply relying on brute calculation speed.
2. The study of neo-robotics is based on the belief that models of human problem solving must occur in a real-world context. AI researchers interested in this approach believe that problem solving must be modeled with a machine that operates within a physical environment and exhibits actions that are modifiable by feedback.

The Structure of Language

1. Semanticity is the conveying of the thoughts of the communicator in a meaningful way to those who understand the language. Generativity is the combining of language symbols in novel ways, without being limited to a fixed number of combinations. Displacement is the use of language to refer to objects and events that are not present.
2. In terms of transformational grammar, language comprehension involves transforming the surface structure, which is the verbal message, into its deep structure, which is its meaning.

The Acquisition of Language

1. Between 4 and 6 months of age, infants enter the babbling stage. When infants are about 1 year old, they begin to say their first words. Infants then begin using holophrastic speech, which is the use of single words to represent whole

phrases or sentences. Next, in the two-word stage, infants use telegraphic speech.
2. Skinner believes that all aspects of language are learned. Chomsky believes that we have an inborn language mechanism that makes us sensitive to the rules of grammar.

The Relationship Between Language and Thought
1. In 1984 Orwell portrays a society in which the government changes the meaning of words or invents words to limit citizen's ability to think rebellious thoughts.
2. Research indicates that when male pronouns are used to represent people generically, those who read or hear them tend to take them to refer to males rather than to both males and females.

Language in Apes
1. Some apes have been able to use words meaningfully, use words in novel ways, and use words to refer to things that are not physically present.
2. Some researchers believe that apes do not use language spontaneously but instead use it to get things they want or simply as responses to prompting by their trainers.

Chapter 10: Intelligence

Intelligence Testing
1. An autistic savant is a person with autism spectrum disorder with below-average intelligence but with an outstanding ability, typically in art, music, memory, or calculating.
2. Galton similarly assumed that people with superior physical abilities, especially sensory and motor abilities, are better adapted for survival and, therefore, more intelligent.

Extremes of Intelligence
1. The possible causes of intellectual disability include hereditary defects, sociocultural deprivation, and brain damage.
2. Terman's Genetic Studies of Genius showed that mentally gifted children tend to become socially, physically, vocationally, and academically superior adults.

Theories of Intelligence
1. Spearman found that intelligence depends on a general intelligence factor more than on separate kinds of intelligence. In contrast, Thurstone found that intelligence depends more on separate kinds of intelligence than on a general intelligence factor.
2. The seven types of intelligence are linguistic, logical-mathematical, spatial, musical, bodily-kinesthetic, intrapersonal, and interpersonal.

Nature, Nurture, and Intelligence
1. In terms of intelligence, adopted children are more like their biological parents than like their adoptive parents. Moreover, identical twins reared apart are more alike in intelligence than ordinary siblings reared together are.
2. The beneficial effects of intellectual enrichment programs include gains in IQ scores and improved cognitive skills.

Chapter 11: Motivation

The Nature of Motivation
1. Critics fear that acceptance of sociobiology would lend support to the status quo, making us less inclined to change what many people believe has been "ordained by God or nature," such as racial differences, differences in sexual behavior, child neglect and abuse, criminality, and social status.
2. According to Maslow, you must first satisfy your basic physiological needs before you will be motivated to move on up the needs hierarchy to your higher needs of safety and security, belongingness and love, through the need for esteem, and ultimately, self-actualization and transcendence.

The Hunger Motive
1. Stimulation of the lateral hypothalamus provokes eating, and stimulation of the ventromedial hypothalamus inhibits eating. Nonetheless, the hypothalamus is only part of a complex physiological system that regulates hunger and eating.

2. The role of heredity in obesity has been supported by studies showing that the correlation in the amount of body fat between identical twins stays roughly the same whether they are reared together or apart. Moreover, adopted children are more similar in weight to their biological parents than to their adoptive parents.
3. Factors may include cultural emphasis on thinness, dissatisfaction with their bodies, and concerns about physical attractiveness.

The Sex Motive
1. The four phases of the human sexual response cycle are excitement, plateau, orgasm, and resolution.
2. Kinsey's surveys found that people engaged in more sex and a greater variety of sexual activities than was popularly believed. Women are less likely than men to have masturbated, and men are more likely to approve of casual sex.
3. Biopsychological factors influencing sexual orientation include genetics and prenatal exposure to sex hormones.

The Arousal Motive
1. According to the Yerkes-Dodson law, performance will be best at a moderate level of arousal.
2. Flotation REST has proved useful in reducing chronic pain and high blood pressure.

The Achievement Motive
1. Goals should be specific, challenging, and paired with performance feedback. Moreover, goals you set yourself will be more motivating than goals others impose on you.
2. Overjustification theory assumes that an extrinsic reward decreases intrinsic motivation when a person attributes his or her performance to the extrinsic reward. Cognitive-evaluation theory holds that a reward perceived as providing information about a person's competence in an activity will increase her or his intrinsic motivation to perform that activity, but a reward perceived as an attempt to control a person's behavior will decrease that person's intrinsic motivation to perform that activity.

The Role of Motivation in Sport
1. An athlete might be underaroused or overaroused in practice and optimally roused during a competition—or optimally aroused during practice and underaroused or overaroused during a competition.
2. Opponents of much lower or much higher ability would not be a fair test of the athlete's ability.

Chapter 12: Emotion

The Biopsychology of Emotion
1. Studies measuring brain activity or the effects of brain damage have found that increased activity in the left hemisphere is associated with positive emotions and increased activity in the right hemisphere is associated with negative emotions.
2. Endorphin levels rise markedly after activities that induce euphoria.

The Expression of Emotion
1. Women are superior to men in the expression and detection of emotion. And studies have found that people perceive women and men to experience emotions with different frequency. And people perceive women to be expressing more sadness, whereas men are perceived as expressing more anger.
2. One line of research has found that even people who are blind from birth exhibit facial expressions for the basic emotions. A second line of research shows that young infants produce facial expressions for the basic emotions. Some studies also show that facial expressions for the basic emotions are universal across cultures.

The Experience of Emotion
1. Happiness is positively correlated with physical health, an outgoing and agreeable personality, a sense of personal control, intelligence, social skills, and family support. Physical attractiveness has a low to moderate correlation with happiness. Our happiness also depends on comparisons we make between ourselves and others and between our current circumstances and our past circumstances.
2. According to disparagement theory, we feel amused when humor makes us feel superior to other people. According to incongruity theory, incongruous humor brings together incompatible ideas in a surprising outcome that violates our expectations. And according to release theory, humor is a cathartic outlet for anxiety caused by repressed sexual or aggressive energy.

Theories of Emotion
1. Evidence for the theory comes from studies finding different patterns of physiological responses for different emotions. Evidence against the theory includes the findings that we are unable to perceive many of the subtle physiological changes induced by the sympathetic nervous system, that different emotions are associated with the same pattern of physiological arousal, and that physiological changes dependent on the secretion of hormones by the adrenal glands are too slow to be the basis of all emotions.
2. When participants alter their facial expressions, they report changes in their subjective emotional experience.
3. Participants who experience unexplained arousal will experience negative emotions, regardless of their social context, thereby contradicting the theory. The only consistent finding in favor of the theory is that misattribution of physiological arousal to an outside source will intensify an emotional experience.

Chapter 13: Personality

The Psychoanalytic Approach to Personality
1. The Barnum effect demonstrates that useful personality descriptions must distinguish one person from another.
2. The id is unconscious, consists of our inborn biological drives, and demands immediate gratification. The ego directs us to express sexual and aggressive impulses in socially acceptable ways. The superego, our moral guide, counteracts the id, which is concerned only with immediate gratification, and the ego, which is concerned only with adapting to reality.
3. Adler assumed that because children feel small, weak, and dependent on others, they develop an inferiority

complex. This motivates them to compensate by striving for superiority.
4. Horney emphasized the role of gender roles, interpersonal power, and sociocultural factors in personality development, especially women's. She also was a proponent of cross-cultural research.
5. Jung claimed that archetypes influence our dreams, religious symbols, and artistic creations.

The Dispositional Approach to Personality

1. Allport believed we are guided by the interaction among our cardinal traits, central traits, and secondary traits.
2. The MMPI was constructed by retaining only those questions that discriminate between people who differ on the characteristics of interest.
3. First, individuals do show consistency on certain traits. Second, cross-situational consistency in behavior depends on whether a person is a high self-monitor or a low self-monitor. Third, many of the studies that Mischel reviewed were guaranteed to find low cross-situational consistency because they either correlated trait test scores with single instances of behaviors or correlated single instances of behaviors with each other. Psychologists have achieved greater success in demonstrating cross-situational consistency by using behavioral aggregation.

The Cognitive-Behavioral Approach to Personality

1. It is different from operant conditioning theory in arguing that behavior is affected by cognitive processes.
2. Reciprocal determinism reflects Bandura's belief that neither personal dispositions nor environmental factors can by themselves explain behavior. Instead, Bandura assumes that personality traits, environmental factors, and overt behavior affect one another.
3. Cultural values and social experiences become integrated into the self, producing differences in the construal of self-schema. People in Western cultures value independent aspects of the self; people in Asian cultures value interdependent aspects of the self.
4. In experience sampling, participants carry a portable device that beeps at random times, and on hearing the beep, the person reports her or his experiences and behaviors at that time.

The Humanistic Approach to Personality

1. The humanistic approach tends to have a positive view of human nature, studies subjective mental experience, and assumes we have free will.
2. Some of the research topics include self-actualization, self-schema, self-concept, self-development, and self-esteem.
3. You would have the person sort the cards twice, first into piles of statements that are or are not characteristic of the actual self and then into piles of statements that are or are not characteristic of the ideal self.

The Biopsychological Approach to Personality

1. Because Sheldon rated participants' somatotype and temperament, his findings possibly were influenced by experimenter bias. Also, whereas Sheldon found a modest relationship between somatotype and personality, other researchers have been unable to replicate his findings.
2. Researchers have found amazing similarities in the personalities of identical twins reared apart and reunited later in life.

Chapter 14: Psychological Disorders

Characteristics of Psychological Disorders

1. The biopsychological viewpoint emphasizes the role of genetic and biological factors. The psychoanalytic perspective emphasizes the role of the unconscious mind. The behavioral perspective emphasizes the role of the environment and learning in the development of maladaptive behaviors. The cognitive viewpoint emphasizes maladaptive thoughts. The humanistic perspective emphasizes failure in reaching one's human potential. And the sociocultural viewpoint emphasizes the role of cultural factors.
2. The cognitive rule says that a person was insane at the time of a crime if the person did not know what he or she had done or did not know that it was wrong. The volitional rule says that the person was insane at the time of the crime if the person was not in voluntary control of his or her actions.
3. Rosenhan's findings indicate that the diagnosis of psychological disorders is influenced more by the label provided by the diagnosis and the treatment setting than by behavioral or psychological attributes of the person.

Anxiety Disorders

1. Agoraphobia prompts so many people to seek therapy because it disrupts every aspect of the sufferer's life, including intimate relationships
2. Some people with panic disorder are hypersensitive to carbon dioxide levels in their blood. Instead of breathing normally to reduce carbon dioxide levels, they might respond as if they are being suffocated and experience a panic attack.

Obsessive-Compulsive Disorder

1. Obsessions and compulsions might be seen as ways of avoiding anxiety-inducing situations and responses to imagined threats.
2. People with obsessive-compulsive disorder report higher levels of guilt and a history of separation anxiety,

Somatic Symptom and Related Disorders

1. A malingerer would have no physical ailment. A person with illness anxiety disorder would exaggerate minor ailments. A person with conversion disorder would display

Answers to Section Review Questions   **Ans-9**

sensory or motor loss or the alteration of a physiological function without any apparent physiological cause.
2. The person shows remarkable indifference to an apparently serious physical problem.

Dissociative Disorders

1. Most of them have suffered physical and sexual abuse as young children.
2. Some psychologists believe that people suffering from dissociative identity disorder are doing little more than role playing and do not, in fact, have more than one personality.

Major Depressive Disorder and Related Disorders

1. Seligman's theory explains major depressive disorder in terms of the attributions we make for events in our lives. According to this theory, people with major depressive disorder attribute negative events in their lives to stable, global, internal factors.
2. People who constantly think about and brood over the sad state of their lives experience more severe and more chronic major depressive disorder than do people who take action to improve their lives or who distract themselves by pursuing enjoyable activities.
3. Shneidman suggests that because suicide attempts are usually cries for help, the simple act of providing an empathetic response can reduce the immediate likelihood of an actual attempt. Just talking about a problem might reduce its apparent dreadfulness and help the person realize that solutions other than suicide are possible and that his or her options include more than a choice between death and a hopeless, helpless life. An immediate goal should be to relieve the person's psychological pain by intervening, if possible, with those who might be contributing to the pain, whether friends, lovers, teachers, or family members. You should also encourage the person to seek professional help, even if you have to make the appointment for the person and accompany him or her to it.

Bipolar Disorder

1. People with mania are sexually, physically, and financially reckless. They may also overestimate their own abilities, perhaps leading them to make poor decisions.
2. People with major depressive disorder do not have alternating periods of mania.

Schizophrenia

1. The major symptoms of schizophrenia are hallucinations, problems maintaining attention, language disturbances, delusions, flat or inappropriate emotionality, unusual motor behavior, and social withdrawal.
2. First, drugs that are used to treat schizophrenia work by blocking dopamine and serotonin receptors. Second, drugs such as amphetamines, which increase dopamine levels in the brain, can induce schizophrenic symptoms in healthy people. Third, L-dopa, a drug used to treat Parkinson's disease because it increases dopamine levels in the brain, can induce schizophrenic symptoms in Parkinson's victims. Fourth, brain-imaging studies have found that people with schizophrenia have overactive dopamine neurons.
3. Positive symptoms are active symptoms and include hallucinations, delusions, thought disorders, and bizarre behaviors. Negative symptoms are passive symptoms and include mutism, apathy, flat affect, social withdrawal, intellectual impairment, poverty of speech, and inability to experience pleasure.

Personality Disorders

1. People with antisocial personality disorder show an appalling lack of conscience and have no qualms about harming other people.
2. People with borderline personality disorder are impulsive, have unstable moods, and exhibit problems in establishing interpersonal relationships. At first, the person you are dating might seem to be pleasant and charming. As the relationship continues, though, she or he becomes hostile and manipulative—especially if the relationship is becoming more intimate.

Developmental Disorders

1. Early theories of autism spectrum disorder (ASD) that were driven by Leo Kanner's observations believed that ASD was acquired through interactions with parents who were cold and hostile toward their children. Hence, parents were blamed for their child's poor social skills and impaired communication. We now know that parents of children with ASD are just as warm and sociable as other parents.
2. People with ASD have larger brain volumes and an increased number of abnormal cells.
3. The major symptoms are inattention, hyperactivity, and impulsivity that can persist into adulthood.

Chapter 15: Therapy The History of Therapy

The History of Therapy

1. No, it might have been done for other purposes, perhaps medical, religious, or punitive.
2. Moral therapy used humane treatment, honest work, and pleasant recreation to promote mental well-being.

The Psychoanalytic Orientation

1. In free association, the client is urged to report any thoughts or feelings that come to mind—no matter how trivial or embarrassing they seem. This is supposed to reveal important information that can help the client gain self-knowledge.

2. In the analysis of resistances, the psychoanalyst notes behaviors that interfere with therapeutic progress toward self-awareness. These resistances are interpreted to uncover the unconscious conflicts that underlie them.

The Behavioral Orientation

1. You would first use progressive relaxation to train the student to relax. You would then set up a hierarchy of scenes related to oral presentation. Finally, you would have the student relax while first imagining low-anxiety scenes and gradually progressing to higher-anxiety scenes.
2. You would give the students tokens for doing well in spelling and arithmetic and let them trade in the tokens for things or activities they enjoy.

The Cognitive Orientation

1. Ellis assumes that maladaptive emotions and behaviors are caused by irrational thinking. Therefore, his therapeutic techniques are aimed at making his clients think more rationally.
2. Beck assumes that major depressive disorder is caused by negative beliefs about oneself, the world, and the future. Beck's cognitive therapy teaches clients to recognize their negative beliefs and replace them with positive beliefs.

The Humanistic Orientation

1. Client-centered therapy strives to create greater congruence between the client's actual self and the client's ideal self by encouraging clients to express and accept their true feelings. The person-centered therapist promotes self-actualization through reflection of feelings, genuineness, accurate empathy, and unconditional positive regard.
2. Gestalt therapy attempts to help clients become aware of their unconscious feelings, increase their emotional expressiveness, and change their maladaptive thoughts and behaviors.

The Social-Relations Orientation

1. transactional analysis (TA) assumes that there are basic roles we all play and that these are sometimes adaptive, sometimes maladaptive. TA teaches group members to recognize the roles they play in their interactions (their transactions, or the "games" they play) and to use this understanding to improve their social relations.
2. Assertiveness training is a form of social-skills training that teaches people to express their feelings constructively in social situations.

The Biological Orientation

1. Critics believe that Electroconvulsive therapy (ECT) is dangerous because it can cause brain damage, memory loss, and other problems. Others say its dangers are outweighed by its ability to induce neurogenesis to relieve major depressive disorder and prevent suicide.

2. The tricyclics increase the levels of serotonin and norepinephrine in the brain by preventing their re-uptake by brain neurons that release them.

Community Mental Health

1. Four factors brought this movement about: (1) new drug treatments, (2) the underfunding and overcrowding of mental hospitals, (3) an increased concern for the legal rights of mental patients, and (4) the Community Mental Health Centers Act of 1963, which mandated the establishment of federally funded mental health centers in every community in the United States.
2. Primary prevention helps prevent psychological disorders by fostering social support systems, eliminating sources of stress, and strengthening individuals' ability to deal with stressors. Secondary prevention provides early treatment for people at immediate risk of developing psychological disorders. Tertiary prevention helps people with psychological disorders from getting worse or relapsing after successful treatment.

The Rights of the Therapy Client

1. The right to refuse treatment has led to some mental hospital patients not receiving necessary therapy. The right to receive treatment assures that patients who do not receive treatment must be released from custodial care.
2. The *Tarasoff* decision has been praised because it might help protect individuals whom a therapy client has threatened to harm. It has been criticized because it might inhibit people who feel hostile toward others from dealing with those feelings honestly in therapy and because it creates a legal obligation to inform that conflicts with the therapist's ethical obligation to maintain confidentiality.

Finding the Proper Therapy

1. Psychological therapy may be provided by a psychologist, a psychiatrist, or other mental health professionals.
2. The college counseling center might be a good place to start. A friend, relative, or professor might be able to recommend a therapist or counseling center to you. Other potential sources of help or referral include community mental health associations.

The Effectiveness of Psychotherapy

1. He found that about two-thirds of people with psychological disorders improve with or without psychotherapy.
2. The client's perception of therapist empathy has been consistently identified as an important factor in the effectiveness of psychotherapy. Personal warmth has also been found to be a factor that differentiates successful and unsuccessful therapists.

Chapter 16: Psychology, Health, and Stress

Psychological Stress and Stressors

1. A century ago most people died young from infectious diseases. Today, with infectious diseases under control, people live longer and tend to succumb to behavior-related diseases, including cancer and cardiovascular disease.
2. Some studies have found that there is a stronger association between hassles and illness than between life changes and illness. Moreover, life changes might produce their negative effects by increasing daily hassles.
3. This is a disorder that appears months or years after a person experiences a traumatic event. It includes emotional, cognitive, and behavioral symptoms.

The Biopsychology of Stress and Illness

1. Stress can suppress the immune response, particularly natural killer cell activity, which might reduce the body's ability to destroy cancerous cells.
2. Stress stimulates the secretion of adrenal hormones, which have an immunosuppressive effect.
3. In animal studies, when a neutral stimulus is paired with a drug (an unconditioned stimulus) that alters the immune response (an unconditioned response), the neutral stimulus will become a conditioned stimulus that likewise alters the immune response (a conditioned response).

Factors That Moderate the Stress Response

1. Hardiness involves a sense of commitment, challenge, and control.
2. Social support promotes health by reducing the effects of stressful life events, promoting recovery from illness, and increasing adherence to medical regimens

Coping with Stress

1. The study found that adolescents under high levels of stress who exercised regularly had a significantly lower incidence of illness than did adolescents who exercised little.
2. The study found that the students who were not assigned to practice relaxation, compared to the students who were, displayed a significantly greater decrease in natural killer cell activity during final exams.

Health-Promoting Habits

1. HIV is most commonly transmitted by breastfeeding, the sharing of hypodermic needles by drug users, and unprotected anal and vaginal sex.
2. Aerobic exercise boosts the basal metabolic rate, promotes weight control, and reduces the risk of cardiovascular disease.
3. Dieting by itself slows the basal metabolic rate, cannot last a lifetime, promotes the loss of lean body tissue, and tends to result in greater weight gain from rebound eating when the diet ends.

Reactions to Illness

1. Important factors include social support, explanatory style, and interpretation of symptoms.
2. A study found a negative correlation between the perceived empathy of nurses and patient anger, anxiety, and major depressive disorder. Patients who perceive a lack of empathy in their physicians are more likely to sue them for malpractice. And practitioners must communicate so that patients will adhere to medical regimens.

Chapter 17: Social Psychology

Social Cognition

1. The three dimensions in Weiner's attribution model are internal-external, stable-unstable, and controllable-uncontrollable.
2. The self-serving bias is the tendency to make dispositional attributions for our positive behaviors and situational attributions for our negative behaviors.
3. This occurs because the social schema we have of the other person will make us act a certain way toward that person, which in turn can make the person respond in accordance with our expectations.

Interpersonal Attraction

1. Evidence includes the fact that we like people more the more we are exposed to them. We even like images of our own faces that we see in mirrors more than images of our faces as they are seen by other people.
2. According to two-factor theory, the experience of physiological aroused in a situation that promotes the labeling of this arousal as love results in the development of romantic love.
3. Men offer financial status and seek physical attractiveness. Women seek financially well-off men and note their own physical attractiveness.

Attitudes

1. Attitudes that are strongly held or personally important are better predictors of behavior. Attitude-behavior consistency is also affected by the specificity of the attitude and the behavior.
2. A message that takes a central route relies on clear, explicit arguments about the issue at hand. A message that takes a peripheral route relies on factors other than the merits of the arguments, such as characteristics of the source or the situational context.
3. For such contact to reduce prejudice, it must be between people of equal status.

Group Dynamics

1. Groupthink can be prevented by not assigning a group leader and by encouraging group members to consider as many alternatives as possible.
2. Social facilitation enhances performance on easy or well-learned tasks. Social facilitation impairs performance on difficult tasks or tasks that are not well learned.
3. A good way to reduce social loafing is to convince group members that their individual efforts will be evaluated or that they will be held accountable. Social loafing can also be overcome when a task is important to an individual and that person believes other group members lack the ability to perform better.
4. Participants in Milgram's experiments were asked to increase shock gradually, in 15-volt increments. Their initial compliance in administering mild shock might have contributed to their obedience to the experimenter's instructions to administer higher levels of shock

Aggression

1. Violent criminals have higher levels of testosterone than nonviolent criminals do. Athletes who use anabolic steroids become more aggressive.
2. When people feel anonymous, are emotionally aroused, and experience reduced self-awareness, they are more likely to take part in group aggression.

Prosocial Behavior

1. Some research indicates that people will be more likely to help other people if they believe it will relieve their own negative feelings, such as guilt.
2. When strangers notice someone in trouble, as the number of strangers increases, their probability of helping decreases, apparently because each feels less responsible for helping.

Answers to Chapter Quiz Questions

Chapter 1

1. B	4. B	7. C	10. B	13. B	16. C	19. C	22. B	25. B
2. A	5. D	8. D	11. C	14. A	17. A	20. C	23. D	
3. A	6. B	9. D	12. D	15. D	18.. B	21. C	24. A	

Chapter 2

1. D	4. A	7. D	10. D	13. D	16. A	19. C	22. A	25. B
2. B	5. C	8. B	11. C	14. B	17. A	20. D	23. B	
3. B	6. B	9. B	12. D	15. C	18. B	21. B	24. A	

Chapter 3

1. A	4. C	7. B	10. A	13. A	16. C	19. D	22. B	25. C
2. B	5. A	8. A	11. C	14. C	17. D	20. D	23. C	
3. A	6. C	9. C	12. D	15. B	18. B	21. A	24. B	

Chapter 4

1. B	4. B	7. A	10. D	13. B	16. A	19. A	22. C	
2. C	5. C	8. C	11. C	14. A	17. B	20. A	23. A	
3. C	6. B	9. B	12. B	15. B	18. C	21. C	24. B	

Chapter 5

1. B	4. B	7. D	9. D	12. D	15. A	18. B	21. D	24. C
2. B	5. A	8. C	10. C	13. D	16. B	19. B	22. D	25. B
3. C	6. B		11. C	14. A	17. C	20. B	23. C	

Chapter 6

1. A	4. C	7. C	10. B	13. D	16. D	19. C	22. A	25. A
2. A	5. A	8. D	11. D	14. D	17. D	20. B	23. D	
3. A	6. C	9. A	12. C	15. A	18. C	21. C	24. D	

Chapter 7

1. C	4. D	7. D	10. B	13. B	16. B	19. A	22. C	25. A
2. D	5. C	8. A	11. C	14. C	17. C	20. B	23. D	
3. B	6. C	9. A	12. A	15. A	18. B	21. B	24. B	

Chapter 8

1. A	4. D	7. B	10. A	13. C	16. A	19. C	22. B	25. A
2. D	5. A	8. C	11. D	14. C	17. B	20. B	23. D	
3. A	6. C	9. B	12. D	15. C	18. A	21. D	24. D	

Chapter 9

1. D	4. C	7. C	10. A	13. A	16. A	19. C	22. B	25. B
2. D	5. B	8. D	11. A	14. D	17. D	20. B	23. B	
3. B	6. D	9. B	12. A	15. C	18. C	21. B	24. B	

Chapter 10

1. D	4. D	7. D	10. B	13. B	16. C	19. A	22. D	25. C
2. B	5. A	8. A	11. B	14. D	17. B	20. D	23. C	
3. D	6. A	9. C	12. C	15. D	18. C	21. C	24. A	

Chapter 11

1. D	4. A	7. A	10. D	13. C	16. C	19. B	22. D	25. A
2. A	5. B	8. B	11. C	14. A	17. B	20. B	23. D	
3. B	6. C	9. A	12. C	15. C	18. D	21. B	24. C	

Chapter 12

1. A	4. A	7. C	10. A	13. C	16. A	19. D	22. B	25. D
2. B	5. D	8. A	11. B	14. D	17. B	20. C	23. C	
3. C	6. B	9. A	12. B	15. B	18. D	21. A	24. C	

Chapter 13

1. C	4. C	7. D	10. C	13. B	16. A	19. A	22. B	25. C
2. D	5. B	8. D	11. D	14. A	17. A	20. C	23. B	
3. A	6. B	9. A	12. C	15. D	18. B	21. C	24. A	

Chapter 14

1. B	4. A	7. C	10. A	13. C	16. D	19. C	22. A	25. D
2. D	5. A	8. D	11. D	14. A	17. A	20. C	23. D	
3. B	6. C	9. C	12. B	15. A	18. A	21. B	24. D	

Chapter 15

1. A	4. A	7. A	10. C	13. C	16. B	19. C	22. C	25. D
2. A	5. B	8. B	11. B	14. C	17. D	20. D	23. C	
3. D	6. D	9. B	12. A	15. D	18. D	21. C	24. C	

Chapter 16

1. A	4. D	7. A.	10. A	13. B	16. C	19. D	22. C	25. D
2. A	5. D	8. C	11. C	14. A	17. B	20. B	23. C	
3. C	6. A	9. C	12. D	15. B	18. B	21. C	24. B	

Chapter 17

1. C	4. A	7. B	10. D	13. A	16. B	19. C	22. A	25. A
2. C	5. D	8. D	11. D	14. C	17. D	20. C	23. B	
3. A	6. A	9. A	12. D	15. A	18. A	21. C	24. D	

Key Contributors

Chapter 1: The Nature of Psychology

The Historical Context of Psychology
Alfred Adler (p. 10)
Aristotle (p. 2)
Saint Augustine (p. 3)
Avicenna (p. 3)
Francis Bacon (p. 3)
Albert Bandura (p. 12)
Mary Whiton Calkins (p. 7)
James McKeen Cattell (p. 5)
Charles Darwin (p. 5)
René Descartes (p. 3)
John Dewey (p. 7)
Hermann Ebbinghaus (p. 5)
Gustav Fechner (p. 4)
Pierre Flourens (p. 4)
Anna Freud (p. 10)
Sigmund Freud (p. 9)
Francis Galton (p. 5)
Hermann von Helmholtz (p. 4)
William James (p. 7)
Carl Jung (p. 10)
Immanuel Kant (p. 4)
Melanie Klein (p. 10)
Kurt Koffka (p. 9)
Wolfgang Köhler (p. 9)
Christine Ladd-Franklin (p. 8)
John Locke (p. 4)
Hugo Münsterberg (p. 7)
Plato (p. 2)
B. F. Skinner (p. 12)
Edward Titchener (p. 6)
Margaret Floy Washburn (p. 7)
John B. Watson (p. 11)
Ernst Weber (p. 4)
Max Wertheimer (p. 8)
Wilhelm Wundt (p. 5)

Contemporary Perspectives in Psychology
Kenneth B. Clark (p. 17)
Mamie Phipps Clark (p. 17)
William E. Cross Jr. (p. 17)
Thomas Kuhn (p. 13)
Abraham Maslow (p. 13)
Wilder Penfield (p. 14)
Jean Piaget (p. 14)
Carl Rogers (p. 13)
Herbert Simon (p. 14)
Roger Sperry (p. 15)
Harry Triandis (p. 16)

Chapter 2: Psychology as a Science

Sources of Knowledge
Francis Bacon (p. 28)
René Descartes (p. 28)
William James (p. 27)
Harold Kelley (p. 26)

Goals of Scientific Research
Francis Galton (p. 31)

Methods of Psychological Research
Anne Anastasi (p. 36)
Jane Goodall (p. 33)
Marion McPherson (p. 38)
John Popplestone (p. 38)
Robert Rosenthal (p. 42)
Lewis Terman (p. 36)

Statistical Analysis of Research Data
Ronald Fisher (p. 49)
Florence Nightingale (p. 46)
Karl Pearson (p. 48)

Ethics of Psychological Research
Diana Baumrind (p. 54)
Bernard Rollin (p. 55)

Chapter 3: Biopsychological Bases of Behavior

Nature versus Nurture
Charles Darwin (p. 61)
Francis Galton (p. 65)

Neuronal Activity
Luigi Galvani (p. 73)
Stephen Hales (p. 71)
Alan Hodgkin (p. 73)
Andrew Huxley (p. 73)
Otto Loewi (p. 76)
Candace Pert (p. 78)
Santiago Ramón y Cajal (p. 75)
Charles Sherrington (p. 75)
Solomon Snyder (p. 78)

Brain Functions
Hans Berger (p. 81)
Paul Broca (p. 92)
Paul Bucy (p. 88)
Gustav Fritsch (p. 89)
Michael Gazzaniga (p. 98)
Heinrich Klüver (p. 88)
Hippocrates (p. 80)
Eduard Hitzig (p. 89)
Jerre Levy (p. 98)
Horace Magoun (p. 86)
Peter Milner (p. 87)
Giuseppe Moruzzi (p. 86)
James Olds (p. 87)
Wilder Penfield (p. 90)
Jacqueline Sagen (p. 101)
Roger Sperry (p. 98)
Karl Wernicke (p. 92)

Chapter 4: Human Development

G. Stanley Hall (p. 108)

Infant and Child Development
Mary Ainsworth (p. 120)
Diana Baumrind (p. 122)
Sandra Bem (p. 125)
John Bowlby (p. 119)
Marian Diamond (p. 112)
Erik Erikson (p. 118)

Tiffany Field (p. 114)
Sigmund Freud (p. 119)
Eleanor Gibson (p. 116)
Carol Gilligan (p. 128)
Harry Harlow (p. 119)
Lawrence Kohlberg (p. 126)
Eleanor Maccoby (p. 125)
Jean Piaget (p. 114)

Adult Development
Camilla Benbow (p. 138)
Alice Eagly (p. 141)
Janet Shibley Hyde (p. 141)
Daniel Levinson (p. 145)
Cicely Saunders (p. 146)
K. Warner Schaie (p. 137)
Julian Stanley (p. 138)

Chapter 5: Sensation and Perception

Sensory Processes
Gustav Fechner (p. 152)
Ernst Weber (p. 152)

Visual Sensation
Hermann von Helmholtz (p. 163)
Ewald Hering (p. 163)
Russell de Valois (p. 164)
George Wald (p. 163)
Thomas Young (p. 161)

Visual Perception
James J. Gibson (p. 165)
David Hubel (p. 167)
Max Wertheimer (p. 166)
Torsten Wiesel (p. 167)

Hearing
Georg von Békésy (p. 178)
Ernest Rutherford (p. 178)
Ernest Wever (p. 178)

Chemical Senses
Linda Bartoshuk (p. 182)

Skin Senses
Ronald Melzack (p. 185)
Patrick Wall (p. 185)

Extrasensory Perception
James Randi (p. 192)
J. B. Rhine (p. 192)
Louisa Rhine (p. 192)
Gertrude Schmeidler (p. 193)

Chapter 6: Consciousness

The Nature of Consciousness
Sigmund Freud (p. 203)
William James (p. 199)
John Locke (p. 199)

Sleep
Eugene Aserinsky (p. 207)
William Dement (p. 209)
Nathaniel Kleitman (p. 207)
Wilse Webb (p. 211)

Dreams
Mary Whiton Calkins (p. 215)
Rosalind Cartwright (p. 218)
Sigmund Freud (p. 215)
Calvin Hall (p. 216)
J. Allan Hobson (p. 215)
Stephen LaBerge (p. 217)
Robert McCarley (p. 219)

Hypnosis
Theodore Barber (p. 222)
James Braid (p. 220)
James Esdaile (p. 221)
Ernest Hilgard (p. 223)
Franz Anton Mesmer (p. 219)
Martin Orne (p. 222)
Nicholas Spanos (p. 224)

Chapter 7: Learning

Classical Conditioning
Ilene Bernstein (p. 245)
John Garcia (p. 244)
Carl Gustavson (p. 244)
Ivan Pavlov (p. 238)
John B. Watson (p. 239)

Operant Conditioning
Neal Miller (p. 258)
David Premack (p. 248)
Martin Seligman (p. 257)
B. F. Skinner (p. 247)
Edward Thorndike (p. 247)

Cognitive Learning
Albert Bandura (p. 263)
Robert Rescorla (p. 261)
Edward Tolman (p. 262)

Chapter 8: Memory

William James (p. 271)

Information Processing and Memory
Richard Atkinson (p. 271)
Richard Shiffrin (p. 271)

Sensory Memory
George Sperling (p. 273)

Short-Term Memory
George Miller (p. 275)
Lloyd and Margaret Peterson (p. 275)

Long-Term Memory
Frederic C. Bartlett (p. 281)
Fergus Craik (p. 277)
Hermann Ebbinghaus (p. 283)
Sigmund Freud (p. 286)

Elizabeth Loftus (p. 287)
Robert Lockhart (p. 277)
Ulric Neisser (p. 282)
Endel Tulving (p. 278)

The Biopsychology of Memory
Suzanne Corkin (p. 300)
Karl Lashley (p. 298)
Brenda Milner (p. 300)

Chapter 9: Thought and Language

Thought
Teresa Amabile (p. 318)
William James (p. 309)
Daniel Kahneman (p. 320)
Wolfgang Köhler (p. 313)
Allen Newell (p. 314)
Herbert Simon (p. 314)
E. Paul Torrance (p. 317)
Amos Tversky (p. 320)

Margaret Floy Washburn (p. 309)
John B. Watson (p. 309)

Language
Albert Bandura (p. 331)
Jean Berko (p. 330)
Noam Chomsky (p. 327)
Allen Gardner (p. 338)
Beatrix Gardner (p. 336)
Janet Shibley Hyde (p. 334)

Francine Patterson (p. 337)
Ann Premack (p. 336)
David Premack (p. 336)
Eleanor Rosch (p. 334)
Duane Rumbaugh (p. 336)
Sue Savage-Rumbaugh (p. 337)
B. F. Skinner (p. 330)
Herbert Terrace (p. 337)
Benjamin Lee Whorf (p. 332)
Robert Yerkes (p. 336)

Chapter 10: Intelligence

Intelligence Testing
Alfred Binet (p. 346)
James McKeen Cattell (p. 345)
Francis Galton (p. 345)
Henry Goddard (p. 346)
Theodore Simon (p. 346)
William Stern (p. 346)
Lewis Terman (p. 346)
David Wechsler (p. 344)
Richard Weinberg (p. 351)

Theories of Intelligence
Raymond Cattell (p. 359)
Howard Gardner (p. 360)
J.P. Guilford (p. 359)
John Horn (p. 359)
Charles Spearman (p. 357)
Robert Sternberg (p. 360)
Louis Thurstone (p. 359)

Nature, Nurture, and Intelligence
Anne Anastasi (p. 370)
Cyril Burt (p. 366)
Leta Stetter Hollingworth (p. 362)
Sandra Scarr (p. 367)
Helen Thompson Woolley (p. 362)
Robert Zajonc (p. 368)

Chapter 11: Motivation

The Nature of Motivation
Sigmund Freud (p. 376)
Clark Hull (p. 377)
Abraham Maslow (p. 378)
William McDougall (p. 376)

The Hunger Motive
Walter Cannon (p. 379)
Judith Rodin (p. 385)
Stanley Schachter (p. 384)

The Sex Motive
Alfred Kinsey (p. 392)
Virginia Johnson (p. 390)
William Masters (p. 390)
John Money (p. 394)

The Arousal Motive
Donald Hebb (p. 399)
Peter Suedfeld (p. 401)

The Achievement Motive
John Atkinson (p. 402)
David McClelland (p. 402)
Christiana Morgan (p. 403)
Henry Murray (p. 403)

Chapter 12: Emotion

The Biopsychology of Emotion
Richard Davidson (p. 420)
David Lykken (p. 416)

The Expression of Emotion
Charles Darwin (p. 425)
Carroll Izard (p. 425)

The Experience of Emotion
Edward Diener (p. 428)
Sigmund Freud (p. 431)
Robert Plutchik (p. 426)

Theories of Emotion
Phillip Bard (p. 432)
Walter Cannon (p. 432)

Paul Ekman (p. 435)
William James (p. 432)
Carl Lange (p. 432)
Richard Lazarus (p. 436)
Stanley Schachter (p. 436)
Jerome Singer (p. 436)
Richard Solomon (p. 434)
Robert Zajonc (p. 438)

Chapter 13: Personality

The Psychoanalytic Approach to Personality
Alfred Adler (p. 447)
Sigmund Freud (p. 444)
Erich Fromm (p. 447)
Karen Horney (p. 449)
Carl Jung (p. 449)
Hermann Rorschach (p. 450)
Harry Stack Sullivan (p. 447)

The Dispositional Approach to Personality
Gordon Allport (p. 454)
Hans Eysenck (p. 453)
Walter Mischel (p. 458)

The Cognitive-Behavioral Approach to Personality
Albert Bandura (p. 460)
Shinobu Kitayama (p. 462)
Hazel Markus (p. 461)

Julian Rotter (p. 460)
B. F. Skinner (p. 460)

The Humanistic Approach to Personality
Abraham Maslow (p. 466)
Carl Rogers (p. 467)

The Biopsychological Approach to Personality
Thomas Bouchard (p. 474)
William Sheldon (p. 471)

Chapter 14: Psychological Disorders

Characteristics of Psychological Disorders
Albert Bandura (p. 485)
Sigmund Freud (p. 484)
Hippocrates (p. 482)
Emil Kraepelin (p. 488)
Abraham Maslow (p. 485)
Carl Rogers (p. 485)
David Rosenhan (p. 490)
B. F. Skinner (p. 485)
Robert Spitzer (p. 490)
Thomas Szasz (p. 490)

Anxiety Disorders
Samuel Turner (p. 492)

Dissociative Disorders
Benjamin Rush (p. 501)

Major Depressive Disorder and Related Disorders
Lauren Alloy (p. 505)
Aaron Beck (p. 505)
Janice Egeland (p. 510)
Peter Lewinsohn (p. 504)

Susan Nolen-Hoeksema (p. 506)
Norman Rosenthal (p. 506)
Martin Seligman (p. 505)
Edwin Shneidman (p. 509)

Schizophrenia
Nancy Andreasen (p. 512)
R. D. Laing (p. 517)

Personality Disorders
Robert Hare (p. 520)

Chapter 15: Therapy

Bertha Pappenheim (Anna O.) (p. 529)

The History of Therapy
Clifford Beers (p. 531)
Dorothea Dix (p. 531)
Hippocrates (p. 530)
Philippe Pinel (p. 530)
Benjamin Rush (p. 530)

The Psychoanalytic Orientation
Josef Breuer (p. 532)
Sigmund Freud (p. 532)

The Behavioral Orientation
Mary Cover Jones (p. 534)
Joseph Wolpe (p. 534)

The Cognitive Orientation
Aaron Beck (p. 540)
Albert Ellis (p. 538)

The Humanistic Orientation
Fritz Perls (p. 541)
Carl Rogers (p. 540)

The Social-Relations Orientation
Eric Berne (p. 542)
Virginia Satir (p. 543)

The Biological Orientation
Ugo Cerletti (p. 545)
Egas Moniz (p. 544)

The Effectiveness of Psychotherapy
Hans Eysenck (p. 552)
Lester Luborsky (p. 553)
Mary Lee Smith (p. 553)

Chapter 16: Psychology, Health, and Stress

Psychological Stress and Stressors
Thomas Holmes (p. 562)
Richard Lazarus (p. 564)
Richard Rahe (p. 562)
Hans Selye (p. 562)

The Biopsychology of Stress and Illness
Robert Ader (p. 573)
Walter Cannon (p. 566)
Nicholas Cohen (p. 573)

Meyer Friedman (p. 568)
Karen Matthews (p. 570)
Ray Rosenman (p. 568)
Redford Williams (p. 569)

Factors That Moderate the Stress Response
Suzanne Kobasa (p. 577)
Salvatore Maddi (p. 577)
Shelley Taylor (p. 566)

Coping with Stress
Edmund Jacobson (p. 581)
Janice Kiecolt-Glaser (p. 581)
James Pennebaker (p. 580)

Health-Promoting Habits
Kelly Brownell (p. 585)
Rod Dishman (p. 574)

Chapter 17: Social Psychology

Social Cognition
Harold Kelley (p. 596)
Bernard Weiner (p. 596)

Interpersonal Attraction
Ellen Berscheid (p. 604)
Elaine Hatfield (p. 604)

Attitudes
Kenneth B. Clark (p. 614)

Mamie Phipps Clark (p. 614)
Leon Festinger (p. 610)

Group Dynamics
Solomon Asch (p. 619)
Irving Janis (p. 617)
Stanley Milgram (p. 622)
Robert Zajonc (p. 618)

Aggression
Leonard Berkowitz (p. 624)
Sigmund Freud (p. 623)

Prosocial Behavior
John Darley (p. 627)
Bibb Latané (p. 627)

Appendix B: Industrial/Organizational Psychology

History of Industrial/Organizational Psychology
Walter Dill Scott (p. B-1)

Hugo Münsterberg (p. B-1)
Walter VanDyke Bingham (p. B-2)
Frank Gilbreth (p. B-2)

Lillian Gilbreth (p. B-2)
Robert Yerkes (p. B-2)

Glossary

absolute threshold The minimum amount of stimulation that an individual can detect through a given sense.

accommodation 1. The cognitive process that revises existing schemas to incorporate new information. 2. The process by which the lens of the eye increases its curvature to focus light from close objects or decreases its curvature to focus light from more distant objects.

achievement motive The desire for mastery, excellence, and accomplishment.

achievement test A test that measures knowledge of a particular subject.

acronym A mnemonic device that involves forming a term from the first letters of a series of words that are to be recalled.

action potential A series of changes in the electrical charge across the axonal membrane that occurs after the axon has reached its firing threshold.

activation-synthesis theory The theory that dreams are the by-products of the cortex's attempt to make sense of the spontaneous changes in physiological activity generated by the brain stem during REM sleep.

acupuncture A pain-relieving technique that relies on the insertion of fine needles into various sites on the body.

adaptation-level theory The theory that happiness depends on comparing one's present circumstances with one's past circumstances.

adolescence The transitional period lasting from the onset of puberty to the beginning of adulthood.

adrenal gland An endocrine gland that secretes hormones that regulate the excretion of minerals and the body's response to stress.

adulthood The period beginning when the individual assumes responsibility for her or his own life.

afterimage An image that persists after the removal of a visual stimulus.

age regression A hypnotic state in which the individual apparently behaves as she or he did as a child.

aggression Verbal or physical behavior aimed at harming another person.

agoraphobia A fear of being in public, usually because the person fears the embarrassment of a panic attack.

algorithm A problem-solving rule or procedure that, when followed step by step, ensures that a correct solution will be found.

all-or-none law The principle that once a neuron reaches its firing threshold, a neural impulse travels at full strength along the entire length of its axon.

altruism The helping of others without the expectation of a reward.

Alzheimer's disease A brain disorder characterized by difficulty in forming new memories and by general mental deterioration.

amphetamines Stimulants used to maintain alertness and wakefulness.

amygdala A limbic system structure that evaluates information from the immediate environment, contributing to feelings of fear, anger, or relief.

anal stage In Freud's theory, the stage of personality development between ages 1 and 3, during which the child gains pleasure from defecation and faces a conflict over toilet training.

analysis of dreams In psychoanalysis, the process by which the therapist interprets the symbolic, manifest content of dreams to reveal their true, latent content to the client.

analysis of free associations In psychoanalysis, the process by which the therapist interprets the underlying meaning of the client's uncensored reports of anything that comes to mind.

analysis of resistances In psychoanalysis, the process by which the therapist interprets client behaviors that interfere with therapeutic progress toward uncovering unconscious conflicts.

analysis of transference In psychoanalysis, the process by which the therapist interprets the feelings expressed by the client toward the therapist as being indicative of the feelings typically expressed by the client toward important people in his or her personal life.

analysis of variance A statistical technique used to determine whether the difference between three or more sets of scores is statistically significant.

analytic introspection A research method in which highly trained participants report the contents of their conscious mental experiences.

andropause The gradual decline of testosterone experienced by men after the age of 40.

anorexia nervosa An eating disorder marked by self-starvation.

antianxiety drugs Psychoactive drugs that are used to treat anxiety disorders.

antidepressant drugs Psychoactive drugs that are used to treat major depressive disorder.

antipsychotic drugs Psychoactive drugs that are used to treat schizophrenia.

antisocial personality disorder A personality disorder marked by impulsive, manipulative, often criminal behavior, without any feelings of guilt in the perpetrator.

anxiety disorder A psychological disorder marked by persistent and unrealistic worry that disrupts everyday functioning.

applied research Research aimed at improving the quality of life and solving practical problems.

aptitude test A test designed to predict a person's potential to benefit from instruction in a particular academic or vocational setting.

archetypes In Jung's theory, inherited images that are passed down from our prehistoric ancestors and that reveal themselves as universal symbols in art, dreams, and religion.

archival research The systematic examination of collections of letters, manuscripts, tape recordings, video recordings, or other records.

arousal motive The motive to maintain an optimal level of physiological activation.

artificial intelligence (AI) The field that integrates computer science and cognitive psychology in studying information processing through the design of computer programs that appear to exhibit intelligence.

assertiveness training A form of social-skills training that teaches clients to express their feelings constructively.

assimilation The cognitive process that interprets new information in light of existing schemas.

association area Regions of the cerebral cortex that integrate information from the primary cortical areas and other brain areas.

attention The process by which the individual focuses awareness on certain contents of consciousness while ignoring others.

attention deficit hyperactivity disorder (ADHD) A developmental disorder that begins in childhood and can persist into adulthood that is characterized by persistent lack of attention, distractibility when engaged in important tasks, impulsive behavior, hyperactivity, and failure to follow through with future plans.

attitude An evaluation—containing cognitive, emotional, and behavioral components—of an idea, event, object, or person.

audition The sense of hearing.

auditory cortex The area of the temporal lobes that processes sounds.

auditory nerve The nerve that conducts impulses from the cochlea to the brain.

authoritarian personality A personality type marked by the tendency to obey superiors while dominating subordinates, to favor one's own group while being prejudiced against other groups, and to be unwilling to admit one's own faults while projecting them onto members of other groups.

authoritative parenting An effective style of parenting in which the parent is warm and loving yet sets well-defined limits that he or she enforces in an appropriate manner.

autism spectrum disorder (ASD) A group of psychological conditions characterized by poor social skills, impaired communication, and repetitive behaviors.

automatic processing Information processing that requires less conscious awareness and cognitive effort and that does not interfere with the performance of other ongoing activities.

autonomic nervous system The division of the peripheral nervous system that controls automatic, involuntary, physiological processes.

autonomy versus shame and doubt Erikson's developmental stage in which success is achieved by gaining a degree of independence from one's parents.

availability heuristic In decision making, the tendency to estimate the probability of an event by how easily relevant instances of it come to mind.

aversion therapy A form of behavior therapy that inhibits maladaptive behavior by pairing a stimulus that normally elicits a maladaptive response with an unpleasant stimulus.

avoidance learning Learning to prevent the occurrence of an aversive stimulus by giving an appropriate response to a warning stimulus.

axon The part of the neuron that conducts neural impulses to glands, muscles, or other neurons.

axonal conduction The transmission of a neural impulse along the length of an axon.

barbiturates Depressants used to induce sleep or anesthesia.

basal metabolic rate The rate at which the body burns calories just to keep itself alive.

basic research Research aimed at finding answers to questions out of theoretical interest or intellectual curiosity.

basilar membrane A membrane running the length of the cochlea that contains the auditory receptor (hair) cells.

behavior therapy The therapeutic application of the principles of learning to change maladaptive behaviors.

behavioral contingencies Relationships between behaviors and their consequences, such as positive reinforcement, negative reinforcement, extinction, and punishment.

behavioral genetics The study of the relative effects of heredity and life experiences on behavior.

behavioral neuroscience The field that studies the physiological bases of human and animal behavior and mental processes.

behavioral preparedness The degree to which members of a species are innately prepared to learn particular behaviors.

behaviorism The psychological viewpoint that rejects the study of mental processes in favor of the study of overt behavior.

benzodiazepines Depressants used to relieve anxiety and nervousness.

binocular cues Depth perception cues that require input from the two eyes.

biofeedback A form of operant conditioning that enables an individual to learn to control a normally involuntary physiological process or to gain better control of a normally voluntary one when provided with visual or auditory information indicating the state of that response.

biological rhythms Repeating cycles of physiological changes.

biopsychological perspective The psychological viewpoint that stresses the relationship of physiological factors to behavior and mental processes.

biopsychosocial model The model that considers that psychological disorders are the result of an interaction of biological, psychological, and social factors.

bipolar disorder A mood disorder marked by periods of mania alternating with longer periods of major depressive disorder.

blocking The process by which a neutral stimulus paired with a conditioned stimulus that already elicits a conditioned response fails to become a conditioned stimulus.

borderline personality disorder (BPD) A personality disorder marked by impulsivity, unstable moods, an inconsistent sense of identity, and difficulty maintaining intimate relationships.

brain The structure of the central nervous system that is located in the skull and plays important roles in sensation, movement, and information processing.

brain stem A group of brain structures that provide life-support functions.

brightness constancy The perceptual process that makes an object maintain a particular level of brightness despite changes in the amount of light reflected from it.

Broca's area The region of the frontal lobe responsible for the production of speech.

bulimia nervosa An eating disorder marked by binging and purging.

burnout A state of physical and psychological exhaustion associated with chronic exposure to uncontrollable stress.

bystander intervention The act of helping someone who is in immediate need of aid.

caffeine A stimulant used to increase mental alertness.

Cannon-Bard theory The theory that an emotion is produced when an event or object is perceived by the thalamus, which conveys this information simultaneously to the cerebral cortex and the skeletal muscles and sympathetic nervous system.

case study An in-depth study of an individual.

cataplexy A sudden and temporary loss of muscle tone in the body while conscious that is triggered by laughing or crying.

catharsis In psychoanalysis, the release of repressed emotional energy as a consequence of insight into the unconscious causes of one's psychological problems.

causal attribution The cognitive process by which we infer the causes of both our own and other people's social behavior.

causation An effect of one or more variables on another variable.

central nervous system The division of the nervous system consisting of the brain and the spinal cord.

central tendency error The tendency to rate everyone in the middle.

cerebellum A brain stem structure that controls the timing of well-learned movements.

cerebral cortex The outer covering of the brain.

cerebral hemispheres The left and right halves of the cerebrum.

cerebral palsy A movement disorder that is caused by brain damage and is often accompanied by intellectual disabilities.

chaining An operant conditioning procedure used to establish a desired sequence of behaviors by positively reinforcing each behavior in the sequence.

childhood The period that extends from birth until the onset of puberty.

circadian rhythms Twenty-four-hour cycles of physiological changes, most notably the sleep-wake cycle.

clairvoyance The alleged ability to perceive objects or events without any sensory contact with them.

classical conditioning A form of learning in which a neutral stimulus comes to elicit a response after being associated with a stimulus that already elicits that response.

clinical psychology The field that applies psychological principles to the prevention, diagnosis, and treatment of psychological disorders.

cocaine A stimulant used to induce cognitive alertness and euphoria.

cochlea The spiral, fluid-filled structure of the inner ear that contains the receptor cells for hearing.

coefficient of correlation A statistic that assesses the degree of association between two or more variables.

cognitive appraisal The subjective interpretation of the severity of a stressor.

cognitive appraisal theory The theory that our emotion at a given time depends on our interpretation of the situation we are in at that time.

cognitive dissonance theory Leon Festinger's theory that attitude change is motivated by the desire to relieve the unpleasant state of arousal caused when one holds cognitions and/or behaviors that are inconsistent with each other.

cognitive evaluation theory The theory that a person's intrinsic motivation will increase when a reward is perceived as a source of information but will decrease when a reward is perceived as an attempt to exert control.

cognitive neuroscience The study of the neurological bases of cognitive processes.

cognitive perspective The psychological viewpoint that favors the study of how the mind organizes perceptions, processes information, and interprets experiences.

cognitive psychology The field of psychology that studies cognitive processes such as thought and language.

cognitive therapy A type of therapy, developed by Aaron Beck, that aims at eliminating exaggerated negative beliefs about oneself, the world, or the future.

cohort A group of people of the same age group.

cohort-sequential research A research design that begins as a cross-sectional study by comparing different cohorts and then follows the cohorts longitudinally.

collateral sprouting The process in which branches from the axons of nearby healthy neurons grow into the pathways normally occupied by the axons of damaged neurons.

collective efficacy People's perception that with collaborative effort the group will obtain its desired outcome.

collective unconscious In Jung's theory, the unconscious mind that is shared by all people and that contains archetypal images passed down from our prehistoric ancestors.

color blindness The inability to distinguish between certain colors, most often red and green.

companionate love Love characterized by feelings of affection and commitment to a relationship with another person.

comparative psychology The field that studies similarities and differences in the physiology, behaviors, and abilities of different species of animals, including humans.

compliance Behaving in accordance with a request that is backed by little or no threat of punishment.

computed tomography (CT) A brain-scanning technique that relies on X-rays to construct computer-generated images of the brain or body.

computer-assisted instruction The use of computer programs to provide programmed instruction.

concept A category of objects, events, qualities, or relations that share certain features.

concrete operational stage The Piagetian stage, extending from 7 to 11 years of age, during which the child learns to reason logically about objects that are physically present.

conditioned response (CR) In classical conditioning, the learned response given to a particular conditioned stimulus.

conditioned stimulus (CS) In classical conditioning, a neutral stimulus that comes to elicit a particular conditioned response after being paired with a particular unconditioned stimulus that already elicits that response.

conditioned taste aversion A taste aversion induced by pairing a taste with gastrointestinal distress.

conduction deafness Hearing loss usually caused by blockage of the auditory canal, damage to the eardrum, or deterioration of the ossicles of the middle ear.

cones Receptor cells of the retina that play an important role in day vision and color vision.

confluence model Robert Zajonc's model of environmental influences on intelligence, which assumes that each child is born into an intellectual environment related to birth order and to the number and differences in age of her or his siblings.

conformity Behaving in accordance with group expectations with little or no overt pressure to do so.

confounding variable A variable whose unwanted effect on the dependent variable might be confused with that of the independent variable.

conscious mind The level of consciousness that includes the cognitive experiences that we are aware of at a given moment.

consciousness Awareness of one's own cognitive activity, including thoughts, feelings, and sensations.

conservation The realization that changing the form of a substance does not change its amount.

consideration Leader behaviors characterized by support and caring of the supervisor for subordinates.

constructive recall The distortion of memories by adding, dropping, or changing details to fit a schema.

context-dependent memory The tendency for recall to be best when the environmental context present during the encoding of a memory is also present during attempts at retrieving it.

continuous schedule of reinforcement A schedule of reinforcement that provides reinforcement for each instance of a desired response.

control group The participants in an experiment who are not exposed to the experimental condition of interest.

controlled processing Information processing that involves conscious awareness and cognitive effort and that interferes with the performance of other ongoing activities.

conventional level In Kohlberg's theory, the level of moral reasoning characterized by concern with upholding laws and conventional values and by favoring obedience to authority.

convergent thinking The cognitive process that focuses on finding conventional solutions to problems.

conversion disorder A somatic symptom and related disorder in which the person exhibits motor or sensory loss or the alteration of a physiological function without any apparent physical cause.

cornea The round, transparent area in the front of the sclera that allows light to enter the eye.

corpus callosum A thick bundle of axons that provides a means of communication between the cerebral hemispheres and that is severed in so-called split-brain surgery.

correlation The degree of relationship between two or more variables.

correlational research Research that studies the degree of relationship between two or more variables.

correlational statistics Statistics that determine the relationship between two variables.

counseling psychology The field that applies psychological principles to help individuals deal with problems of daily living, generally less serious ones than those treated by clinical psychologists.

counterconditioning A behavior therapy technique that applies the principles of classical conditioning to replace unpleasant emotional responses to stimuli with more pleasant ones.

creativity A form of problem solving that generates novel, socially valued solutions to problems.

critical period A period in childhood when experience with language produces optimal language acquisition.

cross-cultural psychology An approach that tries to determine the extent to which research findings about human psychology hold true across cultures.

cross-sectional research A research design in which groups of participants of different ages are compared at the same point in time.

crystallized intelligence The form of intelligence that reflects knowledge acquired through schooling and in everyday life.

cultural competence The consideration of sociocultural factors such as gender, ethnicity, sexual orientation, and religion in psychological training and practice.

cultural psychology An approach that studies how cultural factors affect human behavior and mental experience.

dark adaptation The process by which the eyes become more sensitive to light when under low illumination.

debriefing A procedure, after the completion of a research study, that informs participants of the purpose of the study and aims to remove any physical or psychological distress caused by participation.

decay theory The theory that forgetting occurs because memories naturally fade over time.

decision making A form of problem solving in which one tries to make the best choice from among alternative judgments or courses of action.

declarative memory The long-term memory system that contains memories of facts.

deep structure The underlying meaning of a statement.

defense mechanism In Freud's theory, a process that distorts reality to prevent the individual from being overwhelmed by anxiety.

deindividuation The process by which group members become less aware of themselves as individuals and less concerned about being socially evaluated.

deinstitutionalization The movement toward treating people with psychological disorders in community settings instead of mental hospitals.

déjà vu A feeling that you have experienced a present situation in the past and that you can anticipate what will happen next.

dendrites The branchlike structures of the neuron that receive neural impulses.

dependent variable A variable showing the effect of the independent variable.

depressants Psychoactive drugs that inhibit activity in the central nervous system.

depth perception The perception of the relative distance of objects.

descriptive research Research that involves the recording of behaviors that have been observed systematically.

descriptive statistics Statistics that summarize research data.

determinism The assumption that every event has physical, potentially measurable, causes.

developmental disorders Psychological disorders originating in childhood that can be characterized by physical, learning, language, or behavioral impairments. The disorder can improve or persist throughout a person's lifetime.

developmental psychology The field that studies physical, perceptual, cognitive, and psychosocial changes across the life span.

difference threshold The minimum amount of change in stimulation that can be detected.

differential psychology The field of psychology that studies individual differences in physical, personality, and intellectual characteristics.

discriminative stimulus In operant conditioning, a stimulus that indicates the likelihood that a particular response will be reinforced.

disparagement theory The theory that humor is amusing when it makes one feel superior to other people.

displacement The characteristic of language marked by the ability to refer to objects and events that are not present.

dissociation A state in which the mind is split into two or more independent streams of consciousness.

dissociative amnesia The inability to recall personally significant memories.

dissociative disorder A psychological disorder in which thoughts, feelings, and memories become separated from conscious awareness.

dissociative fugue Memory loss characteristic of dissociative amnesia as well as the loss of one's identity and fleeing from one's prior life.

dissociative identity disorder A dissociative disorder, more commonly known as multiple personality disorder, in which the person has two or more distinct personalities that alternate with one another.

distributed practice Spreading out the memorization of information or the learning of a motor skill over several sessions.

divergent thinking The cognitive process by which an individual freely considers a variety of potential solutions to artistic, literary, scientific, or practical problems.

door-in-the-face technique Increasing the likelihood that a person will comply with a request by first getting the person to reject a larger one.

double-blind technique A procedure that controls experimenter bias and participant bias by preventing experimenters and participants from knowing which participants have been assigned to particular conditions.

Down syndrome A form of intellectual disability, associated with certain physical deformities, that is caused by an extra, third chromosome on the 21st pair.

dream A storylike sequence of visual images, usually occurring during REM sleep.

drive A state of psychological tension induced by a need.

drive-reduction theory The theory that behavior is motivated by the need to reduce drives such as sex or hunger.

echoic memory Auditory sensory memory, which lasts up to 4 or more seconds.

educational psychology The field that applies psychological principles to help improve curriculum, teaching methods, and administrative procedures.

ego In Freud's theory, the part of the personality that helps the individual adapt to external reality by making compromises between the id, the superego, and the environment.

egocentrism The inability to perceive reality from the perspective of another person.

elaboration likelihood theory A theory of persuasion that considers the extent to which messages take a central route or a peripheral route.

elaborative rehearsal Actively organizing new information to make it more meaningful and integrating it with information already stored in long-term memory.

Electra complex A term used by some psychoanalysts, but not by Freud, to refer to the Oedipus complex in girls.

electroconvulsive therapy (ECT) A biological therapy that uses brief electric currents to induce brain seizures in victims of major depressive disorder.

electroencephalograph (EEG) A device used to record patterns of electrical activity produced by neuronal activity in the brain.

embryonic stage The prenatal period that lasts from the end of the second week through the tenth week.

emotion A motivated state marked by physiological arousal, expressive behavior, and cognitive experience.

empiricism The philosophical position that true knowledge comes through the senses.

encoding The conversion of information into a form that can be stored in memory.

encoding specificity The principle that recall will be best when cues that were associated with the encoding of a memory are also present during attempts at retrieving it.

endocrine system The physiological system whose glands secrete hormones into the bloodstream.

endorphins Neurotransmitters that play a role in pleasure, pain relief, and other functions.

engram A memory trace in the brain.

entactogens A new category of psychoactive drugs that have unique effects intermediate to those associated with hallucinogens and stimulants.

environmental psychology The field that applies psychological principles to help improve the physical environment, including the design of buildings and the reduction of noise.

episodic memory The subsystem of declarative memory that contains memories of personal experiences tied to particular times and places.

Equal Employment Opportunity Commission (EEOC) Commission established by the Civil Rights Act of 1991 that works to ensure fair employment practices.

escape learning Learning to perform a behavior that terminates an aversive stimulus, as in negative reinforcement.

ethnic psychology The field that employs culturally appropriate methods to describe the experience of members of groups that historically have been underrepresented in psychology.

ethology The study of animal behavior in the natural environment.

ethyl alcohol (ethanol) A depressant found in beverages and commonly used to reduce social inhibitions.

eugenics The practice of encouraging supposedly superior people to reproduce while preventing supposedly inferior people from reproducing.

evolutionary psychology The study of the evolution of behavior through natural selection.

existential psychology A branch of humanistic psychology that studies how individuals respond to the basic philosophical issues of life, such as death, meaning, freedom, and isolation.

expectancy 1. The strength of the individual's beliefs about whether a particular outcome is attainable. 2. The perceived probability of success in a particular area.

experimental group Participants in an experiment who are exposed to the experimental condition of interest.

experimental method Research that manipulates one or more variables, while controlling other factors, to determine the effects on one or more other variables.

experimental psychology The field primarily concerned with laboratory research on basic psychological processes, including perception, learning, memory, thinking, language, motivation, and emotion.

experimenter bias effect The tendency of experimenters to let their expectancies alter the way they treat their participants.

expert systems Computer programs that display expertise in specific domains of knowledge.

explanatory style The tendency to explain events optimistically or pessimistically.

explicit memory Conscious recollection of general information or personal experiences.

external validity The extent to which the results of a research study can be generalized to other people, animals, or settings.

extinction 1. In classical conditioning, the gradual disappearance of the conditioned response when the conditioned stimulus is repeatedly presented without being paired with the unconditioned stimulus. 2. In operant conditioning, the gradual disappearance of a response that is no longer followed by a reinforcer.

extrasensory perception (ESP) The alleged ability to perceive events without the use of sensory receptors.

extravert A person who is socially outgoing and prefers to pay attention to the external environment.

extrinsic motivation The desire to perform a behavior in order to obtain an external reward, such as praise, grades, or money.

eyewitness testimony Witnesses' recollections about events, most notably about criminal activity.

facial-feedback theory The theory that particular facial expressions induce particular emotional experiences.

factor analysis A statistical technique that determines the degree of correlation between performances on various tasks to determine the extent to which they reflect particular underlying characteristics, which are known as factors.

family therapy A form of group therapy that encourages the constructive expression of feelings and the establishment of rules that family members agree to follow.

feature-detector theory The theory that we construct perceptions of stimuli from activity in neurons of the brain that are sensitive to specific features of those stimuli.

fetal alcohol syndrome A disorder, marked by physical defects and intellectual disability, that can afflict the offspring of women who drink alcohol during pregnancy.

fetal stage The prenatal period that lasts from the end of the eighth week through birth.

field experiment An experiment that is conducted in real life as opposed to laboratory settings.

fight-or-flight response A state of physiological arousal that enables us to meet sudden threats by either confronting them or running away from them.

figure-ground perception The distinguishing of an object (the figure) from its surroundings (the ground).

fixed-interval schedule of reinforcement A partial schedule of reinforcement that provides reinforcement for the first desired response made after a set length of time.

fixed-ratio schedule of reinforcement A partial schedule of reinforcement that provides reinforcement after a set number of desired responses.

flashbulb memory A vivid, long-lasting memory of a surprising, important, emotionally arousing event.

flooding An extinction procedure in which a phobic client is exposed to a stimulus that evokes intense anxiety.

fluid intelligence The form of intelligence that reflects reasoning ability, memory capacity, and speed of information processing.

foot-in-the-door technique Increasing the likelihood that a person will comply with a request by first getting the person to comply with a smaller one.

forensic psychology The field that applies psychological principles to improve the legal system, including the work of police and juries.

forgetting The failure to retrieve information from memory.

forgetting curve A graph showing that forgetting is initially rapid and then slows.

formal operational stage The Piagetian stage, beginning at about age 11, marked by the ability to use abstract reasoning and to solve problems by testing hypotheses.

fovea A small area at the center of the retina that contains only cones and provides the most acute vision.

frame-of-reference training Assessing an employee's performance by referring to an agreed upon standard for each dimension being rated.

framing effects Biases introduced into the decision-making process by presenting an issue or situation in a certain manner.

frequency distribution A list of the frequency of each score or group of scores in a set of scores.

frequency histogram A graph that displays the frequency of scores as bars.

frequency polygon A graph that displays the frequency of scores by connecting points representing them above each score.

frequency theory The theory of pitch perception that assumes that the basilar membrane vibrates as a whole in direct proportion to the frequency of the sound waves striking the eardrum.

frontal lobe A lobe of the cerebral cortex responsible for motor control and higher mental processes.

frustration-aggression hypothesis The assumption that frustration causes aggression.

functional fixedness The inability to realize that a problem can be solved by using a familiar object in an unusual way.

functional magnetic resonance imaging (fMRI) A brain-scanning technique that relies on strong magnetic fields to construct computer-generated images of physiological activity in the brain or body.

functionalism The early psychological viewpoint that studied how the conscious mind helps the individual adapt to the environment.

fundamental attribution error The bias to attribute other people's behavior to dispositional factors.

gate-control theory The theory that pain impulses can be blocked by the closing of a neuronal gate in the spinal cord.

gender identity One's self-perceived sex.

gender roles Behaviors that are considered appropriate for women or men in a given culture.

gender schema theory A theory of gender-role development that combines aspects of social learning theory and the cognitive perspective.

general adaptation syndrome As first identified by Hans Selye, the body's stress response, which includes the stages of alarm, resistance, and exhaustion.

generalized anxiety disorder An anxiety disorder marked by a persistent state of worry that exists independently of any particular stressful situation and often interferes with daily functioning.

generativity The characteristic of language marked by the ability to combine words in novel, meaningful ways.

generativity versus stagnation Erikson's developmental stage in which success is achieved by becoming less self-absorbed and more concerned with the well-being of others.

genital stage In Freud's theory, the last stage of personality development, associated with puberty, during which the individual develops erotic attachments to others.

genotype An individual's genetic inheritance.

germinal stage The prenatal period that lasts from conception through the second week.

Gestalt psychology The early psychological viewpoint that claimed that we perceive and think about wholes rather than simply combinations of separate elements.

Gestalt therapy A type of humanistic therapy, developed by Fritz Perls, that encourages clients to become aware of their true feelings and to take responsibility for their own actions.

glial cell A kind of cell that provides a physical support structure for the neurons, supplies them with nutrition, removes neuronal metabolic waste materials, facilitates the transmission of messages by neurons, and helps regenerate damaged neurons in the peripheral nervous system.

global competition Business competition among countries around the globe.

goal setting The use of goals to increase motivation and improve performance by providing incentives.

goal-setting theory The theory that performance is improved by setting specific goals.

gonads The male and female sex glands.

grammar The set of rules that governs the proper use and combination of language symbols.

group A collection of two or more persons who interact and have mutual influence on each other.

group polarization The tendency for groups to make more extreme decisions than their members would make as individuals.

groupthink The tendency of small, cohesive groups to place unanimity ahead of critical thinking in making decisions.

Guilty Knowledge Test A method that assesses lying by comparing physiological arousal in response to information that is relevant to a transgression and physiological arousal in response to information that is irrelevant to that transgression.

gustation The sense of taste, which detects molecules of substances dissolved in the saliva.

hair cell A sensory receptor of the auditory system located in the organ of Corti of the cochlea.

hallucinogens Psychoactive drugs that induce extreme alterations in consciousness, including visual hallucinations, a sense of timelessness, and feelings of depersonalization.

halo effect A type of rating bias in which the overall evaluation of an individual and other specific ratings are based on a single notable aspect of the individual's performance.

haptic memory Tactile sensory memory, which lasts up to 2 seconds.

health psychology The field that applies psychological principles to the prevention and treatment of physical illness.

heritability The proportion of variability in a trait across a population attributable to genetic differences among members of the population.

heuristic A general principle that guides problem solving, though it does not guarantee a correct solution.

hidden observer Ernest Hilgard's term for the part of the hypnotized person's consciousness that is not under the control of the hypnotist but is aware of what is taking place.

hierarchy of needs Maslow's arrangement of needs in the order of their motivational priority, ranging from physiological needs to the needs for self-actualization and transcendence.

higher-order conditioning In classical conditioning, the establishment of a conditioned response to a neutral stimulus that has been paired with an existing conditioned stimulus.

hippocampus A limbic system structure that contributes to the formation of memories.

holophrastic speech The use of single words to represent whole phrases or sentences.

homeostasis A steady state of physiological equilibrium.

hormones Chemicals, secreted by endocrine glands, that play a role in a variety of functions, including synaptic transmission.

hospice movement The providing of care for the dying patient with attention to alleviating the patient's physical, emotional, and spiritual suffering.

humanistic perspective The psychological viewpoint that holds that the proper subject matter of psychology is the individual's subjective mental experience of the world.

Human Relations Movement A consequence of the Hawthorne Studies; researchers focused on worker attitudes toward their work group and the organization.

hypermnesia The hypnotic enhancement of recall.

hyperopia Visual farsightedness, which is caused by a shortened eyeball.

hypnosis An induced state of consciousness in which one person responds to suggestions by another person for alterations in perception, thinking, and behavior.

hypothalamus A limbic system structure that, through its effects on the pituitary gland and the autonomic nervous system, helps regulate aspects of motivation and emotion, including eating, drinking, sexual behavior, body temperature, and stress responses.

hypothesis A testable prediction about the relationship between two or more events or characteristics.

iconic memory Visual sensory memory, which lasts up to about a second.

id In Freud's theory, the part of the personality that contains inborn biological drives and that seeks immediate gratification.

identity versus role confusion Erikson's developmental stage in which success is achieved by establishing a sense of personal identity.

illness anxiety disorder A somatic symptom and related disorder in which the person interprets the slightest physical changes as evidence of a serious illness.

illusory contours The perception of nonexistent contours as if they were the edges of real objects.

implicit memory Recollection of previous experiences demonstrated through behavior rather than through conscious, intentional remembering.

impression management The deliberate attempt to control the impression that others form of us.

in vivo desensitization A form of counterconditioning that trains the client to maintain a state of relaxation in the presence of anxiety-inducing stimuli.

incentive An external stimulus that pulls an individual toward a goal.

incentive value The perceived rewards that accompany success in a particular area.

incongruity theory The theory that humor is amusing when it brings together incompatible ideas in a surprising outcome that violates one's expectations.

independent variable A variable manipulated by the experimenter to determine its effect on another, dependent, variable.

industrial/organizational psychology The field that applies psychological principles to improve productivity in businesses, industries, and government agencies.

industry versus inferiority Erikson's developmental stage in which success is achieved by developing a sense of competency.

infancy The period that extends from birth through 2 years of age.

inferential statistics Statistics used to determine whether changes in a dependent variable are caused by an independent variable.

information-processing model The view that the processing of memories involves encoding, storage, and retrieval.

initiating structure Leader behaviors that define and organize the group's tasks and activities.

initiative versus guilt Erikson's developmental stage in which success is achieved by behaving in a spontaneous but socially appropriate way.

insanity A legal term attesting that a person is not responsible for his or her own actions, including criminal behavior.

insight An approach to problem solving that depends on cognitive manipulation of information rather than overt trial and error and produces sudden solutions to problems.

insomnia Chronic difficulty in either falling asleep or staying asleep.

instinct A complex, inherited behavior pattern characteristic of a species.

instinctive drift The reversion of animals to behaviors characteristic of their species even when being reinforced for performing other behaviors.

instrumental conditioning A form of learning in which a behavior becomes more or less probable, depending on its consequences.

instrumentality The extent to which an individual believes that attaining a particular outcome will lead to other positively valued outcomes.

integrity versus despair Erikson's developmental stage in which success is achieved by reflecting back on one's life and finding that it has been meaningful.

intellectual disability Intellectual deficiency marked by an IQ of 70 or below and difficulties performing in everyday life.

intelligence The global capacity to act purposefully, to think rationally, and to deal effectively with the environment.

intelligence quotient (IQ) Originally, the ratio of mental age to chronological age; that is, mental age/chronological age $\times$ 100.

intelligence test A test that assesses overall mental ability.

interference theory The theory that forgetting results from some memories interfering with the ability to recall other memories.

internal validity The extent to which changes in a dependent variable can be attributed to one or more independent variables rather than to a confounding variable.

interneuron A neuron that conveys messages between neurons in the brain or spinal cord.

interval scale A scale of measurement that indicates the exact magnitude of scores but not their ratio to one another.

intimacy versus isolation Erikson's developmental stage in which success is achieved by establishing a relationship with a strong sense of emotional attachment and personal commitment.

intrinsic motivation The desire to perform a behavior for its own sake.

introvert A person who is socially reserved and prefers to pay attention to his or her private cognitive experiences.

James-Lange theory The theory that specific patterns of physiological changes evoke specific emotional experiences.

job analysis Defining a job in terms of the tasks and duties involved and the requirements needed to perform it.

job description A written statement of what a job entails and how and why it is done.

just noticeable difference (jnd) Weber and Fechner's term for the difference threshold.

kinesthetic sense The sense that provides information about the position of the joints, the degree of tension in the muscles, and the movement of the arms and legs.

language A formal system of communication involving symbols—whether spoken, written, or gestured—and rules for combining them.

latency stage In Freud's theory, the stage between age 5 and puberty, during which there is little psychosexual development.

latent content Sigmund Freud's term for the true, though disguised, meaning of a dream.

latent learning Learning that occurs without the reinforcement of overt behavior.

law of effect Edward Thorndike's principle that a behavior followed by a satisfying state of affairs is strengthened and a behavior followed by an annoying state of affairs is weakened.

leader-member exchange (LMX) theory Theory that proposes leaders often use different behaviors with individual subordinates, which then leads to qualitatively different relationships with subordinates.

learned helplessness A feeling of futility caused by the belief that one has little or no control over events in one's life, which can make one stop trying and experience depressed mood.

learning A relatively permanent change in knowledge or behavior resulting from experience.

leniency The tendency to rate an employee too positively.

lens The transparent structure behind the pupil that focuses light onto the retina.

levels of processing theory The theory that the "depth" at which we process information determines how well it is encoded, stored, and retrieved.

libido Freud's term for the sexual energy of the id.

limbic system A group of brain structures that, through their influence on emotion, motivation, and memory, promote the survival of the individual and, as a result, the continuation of the species.

line graph A graph used to plot data showing the relationship between independent and dependent variables in an experiment.

linguistic relativity hypothesis Benjamin Whorf's hypothesis that one's perception of the world is molded by one's language.

link method A mnemonic device that involves connecting, in sequence, images of items to be memorized, to make them easier to recall.

logical concept A concept formed by identifying the specific features possessed by all things to which the concept applies.

longitudinal research A research design in which the same group of participants is tested or observed repeatedly over a period of time.

long-term memory The stage of memory that can store a virtually unlimited amount of information relatively permanently.

long-term potentiation A phenomenon related to the facilitation of neural impulses in which synaptic transmission of impulses is made more efficient by brief electrical stimulation of specific neural pathways.

loudness perception The subjective experience of the intensity of a sound, which corresponds most closely to the amplitude of the sound waves composing it.

LSD A hallucinogen derived from a fungus that grows on rye grain.

lucid dreaming The ability to be aware that one is dreaming and to direct one's dreams.

magnetic resonance imaging (MRI) A brain-scanning technique that relies on strong magnetic fields to construct computer-generated images of the brain or body based on blood flow.

magnetoencephalography (MEG) A functional neuroimaging technique to measure brain activity using magnetic fields. MEG is useful to map brain changes across time and is often used together with fMRI.

maintenance rehearsal Repeating information to oneself to keep it in short-term memory.

major depressive disorder (MDD) A disorder marked by depression so intense and prolonged that the person may be unable to function in everyday life.

mania A mood disorder marked by euphoria, hyperactivity, grandiose ideas, annoying talkativeness, unrealistic optimism, and inflated self-esteem.

manifest content Sigmund Freud's term for the verbally reported dream.

massed practice Cramming the memorization of information or the learning of a motor skill into one session.

maturation The sequential unfolding of inherited predispositions in physical and motor development.

mean The arithmetic average of a set of scores.

mean length of utterance (MLU) A unit of measurement that assesses children's level of language maturation.

measure of central tendency A statistic that represents the "typical" score in a set of scores.

measure of variability A statistic describing the degree of dispersion in a set of scores.

measurement The use of numbers to represent events or characteristics.

median The middle score in a set of scores that have been ordered from lowest to highest.

medulla A brain stem structure that regulates breathing, heart rate, blood pressure, and other life functions.

memory The process by which information is acquired, stored in the brain, later retrieved, and eventually possibly forgotten.

menarche The beginning of menstruation, usually occurring between the ages of 11 and 13.

menopause The cessation of menstruation, usually occurring between the ages of 40 and 55.

mental giftedness Intellectual superiority marked by an IQ of 130 or above and exceptionally high scores on achievement tests in specific subjects, such as mathematics.

mental set A tendency to use a particular problem-solving strategy that has succeeded in the past but that may interfere with solving a problem requiring a new strategy.

mental telepathy The alleged ability to perceive the thoughts of others.

meta-analysis A technique that combines the results of many similar studies to determine the effect size of a particular kind of independent variable.

method of loci A mnemonic device in which items to be recalled are associated with landmarks in a familiar place and then recalled during a mental walk from one landmark to another.

method of savings The assessment of memory by comparing the time or number of trials needed to memorize a given amount of information and the time or number of trials needed to memorize it again at a later time.

mirror neurons Neurons that appear to be involved in the neural circuits responsible for observational learning.

mnemonic devices Techniques for organizing information to be memorized to make it easier to remember.

mode The score that occurs most frequently in a set of scores.

monocular cues Depth perception cues that require input from only one eye.

mood stabilizers Psychoactive drugs, most notably lithium carbonate, that are used to treat bipolar disorder.

moon illusion The misperception that the moon is larger when it is at the horizon than when it is overhead.

moral therapy An approach to therapy, developed by Philippe Pinel, that provided mental patients with humane treatment.

morpheme The smallest meaningful unit of language.

motivation The psychological process that arouses, directs, and maintains behavior toward a goal.

motor cortex The area of the frontal lobes that controls specific voluntary body movements.

motor neuron A neuron that sends messages from the central nervous system to smooth muscles, cardiac muscles, or skeletal muscles.

multicultural psychology The field that studies psychological similarities and differences across the subcultures that commonly exist within individual countries.

myelin A fatty white substance that forms sheaths around certain axons and increases the speed of neural impulses.

myopia Visual nearsightedness, which is caused by an elongated eyeball.

narcolepsy A condition in which an awake person suffers from repeated, sudden, and irresistible REM sleep attacks.

nativism The philosophical position that heredity provides individuals with inborn knowledge and abilities.

natural concept A concept, typically formed through everyday experience, whose members possess some, but not all, of a common set of features.

naturalistic observation The recording of the behavior of people or animals in their natural environments, with little or no intervention by the researcher.

need A motivated state caused by physiological deprivation, such as a lack of food or water.

negative correlation A correlation in which variables tend to change values in opposite directions.

negative reinforcement In operant conditioning, an increase in the probability of a behavior that is followed by the removal of an aversive stimulus.

negative skew A graph that has scores bunching up toward the positive end of the horizontal axis.

negative state relief theory The theory that we engage in prosocial behavior to relieve our own state of emotional distress at another's plight.

neodissociation theory The theory that hypnosis induces a dissociated state of consciousness.

nerve A bundle of axons that conveys information to or from the central nervous system.

nerve deafness Hearing loss caused by damage to the hair cells of the basilar membrane, the axons of the auditory nerve, or the neurons of the auditory cortex.

nervous system The chief means of communication in the body.

neural grafting The transplantation of healthy tissue into damaged nerves, brains, or spinal cords.

neural plasticity The brain's ability to learn from experience and to promote adaptive behavior.

neuron A cell specialized for the transmission of information in the nervous system.

neurotransmitter Chemicals secreted by neurons that provide the means of synaptic transmission.

nicotine A stimulant used to regulate physical and cognitive arousal.

night terror A frightening NREM experience, common in childhood, in which the individual may suddenly sit up, let out a bloodcurdling scream, speak incoherently, and quickly fall back to sleep, yet usually fails to recall it on awakening.

nightmare A frightening dream occurring during REM sleep.

nominal scale A scale of measurement that places objects, individuals, or characteristics into categories.

norm A score, based on the test performances of large numbers of participants, that is used as a standard for assessing the performances of test takers.

normal curve A bell-shaped graph representing a hypothetical frequency distribution for a given characteristic.

NREM sleep The stages of sleep not associated with rapid eye movements and marked by relatively little dreaming.

null hypothesis The prediction that the independent variable will have no effect on the dependent variable in an experiment.

obedience Following orders given by an authority.

obesity An unhealthy condition in men who have more than 25 percent body fat and women who have more than 30 percent body fat.

object permanence The realization that objects exist even when they are no longer visible.

observational learning Learning produced by observing the consequences that others receive for performing particular behaviors.

obsessive-compulsive disorder (OCD) An anxiety disorder in which the person has recurrent, intrusive thoughts (obsessions) and recurrent urges to perform ritualistic actions (compulsions).

occipital lobe A lobe of the cerebral cortex responsible for processing vision.

Oedipus complex In Freud's theory, a conflict, during the phallic stage, between the child's sexual desire for the parent of the other sex and fear of punishment from the same-sex parent.

olfaction The sense of smell, which detects molecules carried in the air.

operant conditioning B. F. Skinner's term for instrumental conditioning, a form of learning in which a behavior becomes more or less probable, depending on its consequences.

operational definition The definition of behaviors or qualities in terms of the procedures used to measure or produce them.

opiates Depressants, derived from opium, used to relieve pain or to induce a euphoric state of consciousness.

opponent-process theory 1. The theory that color vision depends on red-green, blue-yellow, and black-white opponent processes in the brain. 2. The theory that the brain counteracts a strong positive or negative emotion by evoking an opposite emotional response.

optic chiasm The point under the frontal lobes at which some axons from each of the optic nerves cross over to the opposite side of the brain.

optic nerve The nerve, formed from the axons of ganglion cells, that carries visual impulses from the retina to the brain.

oral stage In Freud's theory, the stage of personality development between birth and age 1 year, during which the infant gains pleasure from oral activities and faces a conflict over weaning.

ordinal scale A scale of measurement that indicates the relative, but not exact, magnitude of scores.

otolith organs The vestibular organs that detect horizontal or vertical linear movement of the head.

ovaries The female gonads, which secrete hormones that regulate the development of the female reproductive system and secondary sex characteristics.

overextension The tendency to apply a word to more objects or actions than it actually represents.

overjustification theory The theory that an extrinsic reward will decrease intrinsic motivation when a person attributes her or his performance to that reward.

overlearning Studying material beyond the point of initial mastery.

overregularization The application of a grammatical rule without making necessary exceptions to it.

panic disorder An anxiety disorder marked by sudden, unexpected attacks of overwhelming anxiety, often associated with the fear of dying or "losing one's mind."

parapsychology The study of extrasensory perception, psychokinesis, and related phenomena.

parasympathetic nervous system The division of the autonomic nervous system that calms the body and performs maintenance functions.

parietal lobe A lobe of the cerebral cortex responsible for processing bodily sensations and perceiving spatial relations.

Parkinson's disease A degenerative disease of the dopamine pathway, which causes marked disturbances in motor behavior.

partial schedule of reinforcement A schedule of reinforcement that reinforces some, but not all, instances of a desired response.

participant bias The tendency of people who know they are participants in a study to behave differently than they normally would.

participant modeling A form of social-learning therapy in which the client learns to perform more adaptive behaviors by first observing the therapist model the desired behaviors.

passionate love Love characterized by intense emotional arousal and sexual feelings.

peace psychology The field that applies psychological principles to reducing conflict and maintaining peace.

Pearson's product-moment correlation Perhaps the most commonly used correlational statistic.

pegword method A mnemonic device that involves associating items to be recalled with objects that rhyme with the numbers 1, 2, 3, and so on to make the items easier to recall.

perceived control The degree to which a person feels in control over life's stressors.

percentile The score at or below which a particular percentage of scores fall.

perception The process that organizes sensations into meaningful patterns.

perception without awareness The unconscious perception of stimuli that normally exceed the absolute threshold but fall outside our focus of attention.

performance appraisal Systematic review, evaluation, and feedback regarding an employee's job performance.

peripheral nervous system The division of the nervous system that conveys sensory information to the central nervous system and motor commands from the central nervous system to the skeletal muscles and internal organs.

person-centered therapy A type of humanistic therapy, developed by Carl Rogers, that helps clients find their own answers to their problems.

person perception The process of making judgments about the personal characteristics of others.

personal unconscious In Jung's theory, the individual's own unconscious mind, which contains repressed memories.

personality An individual's unique, relatively consistent pattern of thinking, feeling, and behaving.

personality disorder A psychological disorder characterized by enduring, inflexible, maladaptive patterns of behavior.

personality psychology The field that focuses on factors accounting for the differences in behavior and enduring personal characteristics among individuals.

persuasion The attempt to influence the attitudes of other people.

phallic stage In Freud's theory, the stage of personality development between ages 3 and 5, during which the child gains pleasure from the genitals and must resolve the Oedipus complex.

phase advance Shortening the sleep-wake cycle, as occurs when traveling from west to east.

phase delay Lengthening the sleep-wake cycle, as occurs when traveling from east to west.

phenomenological psychology A branch of humanistic psychology primarily concerned with the study of subjective mental experience.

phenotype The overt expression of an individual's genotype (genetic inheritance) in his or her appearance or behavior.

phenylketonuria (PKU) A hereditary enzyme deficiency that, if left untreated in the infant, causes intellectual disabilities.

pheromone An odorous chemical secreted by an animal that affects the behavior of other animals.

phi phenomenon Apparent motion caused by the presentation of different visual stimuli in rapid succession.

phobia An anxiety disorder marked by excessive or inappropriate fear.

phoneme The smallest unit of sound in a language.

phonology The study of the sounds that compose languages.

photopigments Chemicals, including rhodopsin and iodopsin, that enable the rods and cones to generate neural impulses.

phrenology A discredited technique for determining intellectual abilities and personality traits by examining the bumps and depressions of the skull.

physiological reactivity The extent to which a person displays increases in heart rate, blood pressure, stress hormone secretion, and other physiological activity in response to stressors.

pie graph A graph that represents data as percentages of a pie.

pineal gland An endocrine gland that secretes a hormone that has a general tranquilizing effect on the body and that helps regulate biological rhythms.

pitch perception The subjective experience of the highness or lowness of a sound, which corresponds most closely to the frequency of the sound waves that compose it.

pituitary gland An endocrine gland that regulates many of the other endocrine glands by secreting hormones that affect the secretion of their hormones.

place theory The theory of pitch perception that assumes that hair cells at particular points on the basilar membrane are maximally responsive to sound waves of particular frequencies.

placebo An inactive substance that might induce some of the effects of the drug for which it has been substituted.

pleasure principle The process by which the id seeks immediate gratification of its impulses.

polygraph test The lie detector test, which assesses lying by measuring changing patterns of physiological arousal in response to particular questions.

pons A brain stem structure that regulates the sleep-wake cycle.

population A group of individuals who share certain characteristics.

positive correlation A correlation in which variables tend to change values in the same direction.

positive reinforcement In operant conditioning, an increase in the probability of a behavior that is followed by a desirable consequence.

positive skew A graph that has scores bunching up toward the negative end of the horizontal axis.

positron-emission tomography (PET) A brain-scanning technique that produces color-coded pictures showing the relative activity of different brain areas.

postconventional level In Kohlberg's theory, the level of moral reasoning characterized by concern with obeying mutually agreed-upon laws and by the need to uphold human dignity.

posthypnotic suggestions Suggestions directing people to carry out particular behaviors or to have particular experiences after leaving hypnosis.

posttraumatic stress disorder (PTSD) A syndrome of physical and psychological symptoms that appears as a delayed response after exposure to an extremely emotionally distressing event.

pragmatics The relationship between language and its social context.

precognition The alleged ability to perceive events in the future.

preconscious mind The level of consciousness that contains feelings and memories that we are unaware of at the moment but can become aware of at will.

preconventional level In Kohlberg's theory, the level of moral reasoning characterized by concern with the consequences that behavior has for oneself.

predictors Tests that measure the attributes that an employee needs to be successful at a job.

prejudice A positive or negative attitude toward a person based on her or his membership in a particular group.

Premack principle The principle that a more probable behavior can be used as a reinforcer for a less probable one.

preoperational stage The Piagetian stage, extending from 2 to 7 years of age, during which the child's use of language becomes more sophisticated but the child has difficulty with the logical mental manipulation of information.

primary cortical area Regions of the cerebral cortex that serve motor or sensory functions.

primary reinforcer In operant conditioning, an unlearned reinforcer that satisfies a biological need such as food, water, or oxygen.

proactive interference The process by which old memories interfere with the ability to recall new memories.

problem solving The thought process by which an individual overcomes obstacles to reach a goal.

procedural memory The long-term memory system that contains memories of how to perform particular actions.

programmed instruction A step-by-step approach, based on operant conditioning, in which the learner proceeds at his or her own pace through more and more advanced material and receives immediate knowledge of the results of each response.

progressive relaxation A stress-management procedure that involves the successive tensing and relaxing of each of the major muscle groups of the body.

projective test A psychoanalytic personality test based on the assumption that individuals project their unconscious feelings when responding to ambiguous stimuli.

prosocial behavior Behavior that helps others in need.

prosody The vocal features of speech other than the words themselves.

prosopagnosia A condition in which an individual can recognize details in faces but cannot recognize faces as a whole.

prototype The best representative of a concept.

psychiatry The field of medicine that diagnoses and treats psychological disorders by using medical or psychological forms of therapy.

psychic determinism The Freudian assumption that all human behavior is influenced by unconscious motives.

psychoactive drugs Chemicals that induce changes in mood, thinking, perception, and behavior by affecting neuronal activity in the brain.

psychoanalysis The early school of psychology that emphasized the importance of unconscious causes of behavior.

psychokinesis (PK) The alleged ability to control objects with the mind alone.

psychological hardiness A set of personality characteristics marked by feelings of commitment, challenge, and control that promotes resistance to stress.

psychological test A formal sample of a person's behavior, whether written or performed.

psychology The science of behavior and cognitive processes.

psychoneuroimmunology The interdisciplinary field that studies the relationship between psychological factors and physical illness.

psychopathology The study of psychological disorders.

psychophysics The study of the relationship between the physical characteristics of stimuli and the conscious psychological experiences that are associated with them.

psychosurgery The treatment of psychological disorders by destroying brain tissue.

psychotherapy The treatment of psychological disorders through psychological means generally involving verbal interaction with a professional therapist.

puberty The period of rapid physical change that occurs during adolescence, including the development of the ability to reproduce sexually.

punishment In operant conditioning, the process by which an aversive stimulus decreases the probability of a response that precedes it.

pupil The opening at the center of the iris that controls how much light enters the eye.

random assignment The assignment of participants to experimental and control conditions so that each participant is as likely to be assigned to one condition as to another.

random sampling The selection of a sample from a population so that each member of the population has an equal chance of being included.

range A statistic representing the difference between the highest and lowest scores in a set of scores.

rational-emotive behavior therapy (REBT) A type of cognitive therapy, developed by Albert Ellis, that treats psychological disorders by forcing the client to give up irrational beliefs.

rationalism The philosophical position that true knowledge comes through correct reasoning.

ratio scale A scale of measurement that indicates the ratio of scores to one another.

reality principle The process by which the ego directs the individual to express sexual and aggressive impulses in socially acceptable ways.

reciprocal determinism Bandura's belief that cognitive factors, environmental factors, and overt behavior affect each other.

reflex An automatic, involuntary motor response to sensory stimulation.

release theory The theory that humor relieves anxiety caused by sexual or aggressive energy.

reliability The extent to which a test gives consistent results.

REM sleep The stage of sleep associated with rapid eye movements, an active brain-wave pattern, and vivid dreams.

replication The repetition of a research study, usually with some alterations in its methods or setting, to determine whether the principles derived from that study hold up under similar circumstances.

representativeness heuristic In decision making, the assumption that a small sample is representative of its population.

repression In psychoanalytic theory, the defense mechanism that involves banishing threatening thoughts, feelings, and memories into the unconscious mind.

resting potential The electrical charge of a neuron when it is not firing a neural impulse.

reticular formation A diffuse network of neurons, extending through the brain stem, that helps maintain vigilance and an optimal level of brain arousal.

retina The light-sensitive inner membrane of the eye that contains the receptor cells for vision.

retrieval The recovery of information from memory.

retroactive interference The process by which new memories interfere with the ability to recall old memories.

rods Receptor cells of the retina that play an important role in night vision and peripheral vision.

role-congruity theory In leadership research, perceiving women as less capable than men of being leaders, and when women occupy such roles, evaluating their behavior as less favorably than men enacting the same behaviors.

sample A group of participants selected from a population.

scatter plot A graph of a correlational relationship.

schema A cognitive structure that guides people's perception and information processing that incorporates the characteristics of particular persons, objects, events, procedures, or situations.

schema theory The theory that long-term memories are stored as parts of schemas, which are cognitive structures that organize knowledge about events or objects.

schizophrenia A class of psychological disorders characterized by grossly impaired social, emotional, cognitive, and perceptual functioning.

school psychology The field that applies psychological principles to improve the academic performance and social behavior of students in elementary, middle, and high schools.

scientific method A source of knowledge based on the assumption that knowledge comes from the objective, systematic observation and measurement of particular variables and the events they affect.

scientific paradigm A model that determines the appropriate goals, methods, and subject matter of a science.

sclera The tough, white, outer membrane of the eye.

seasonal affective disorder (SAD) A mood disorder in which depressive symptoms occur during a particular season, usually the winter but sometimes the summer.

secondary reinforcer In operant conditioning, a neutral stimulus that becomes reinforcing after being associated with a primary reinforcer.

self-actualization In Maslow's theory, the individual's predisposition to try to fulfill her or his potentials.

self-efficacy In Bandura's theory, a person's belief that she or he can perform behaviors that are necessary to bring about a desired outcome.

self-fulfilling prophecy The tendency for one person's expectations to influence another person to behave in accordance with them.

self-perception theory The theory that we infer our attitudes from our behavior in the same way that we infer other people's attitudes from their behavior.

self-schema In schema theory, specialized cognitive structures about the self.

self-serving bias The tendency to make dispositional attributions for one's successes and situational attributions for one's failures.

semantic conditioning In classical conditioning, the use of words as conditioned stimuli.

semantic memory The subsystem of declarative memory that contains general information about the world.

semantic network theory The theory that memories are stored as nodes interconnected by links that represent their relationships.

semanticity The characteristic of language marked by the use of symbols to convey thoughts in a meaningful way.

semantics The study of how language conveys meaning.

semicircular canals The curved vestibular organs of the inner ear that detect rotary movements of the head in any direction.

sensate focusing A technique, pioneered by Masters and Johnson, in which partners are urged to concentrate on their pleasurable feelings instead of striving for erections and orgasms.

sensation The process that detects stimuli from the body or surroundings.

sensation seeking The motivation to pursue sensory stimulation.

sensorimotor stage The Piagetian stage, from birth through the second year, during which the infant learns to coordinate sensory experiences and motor behaviors.

sensory adaptation The tendency of the sensory receptors to respond less and less to a constant stimulus.

sensory deprivation The prolonged withdrawal of normal levels of external stimulation.

sensory memory The stage of memory that briefly (for at most a few seconds) stores exact replicas of sensations.

sensory neuron A neuron that sends messages from sensory receptors to the central nervous system.

sensory receptors Specialized cells that detect stimuli and convert their energy into neural impulses.

sensory transduction The process by which sensory receptors convert stimuli into neural impulses.

serial-position effect The superiority of immediate recall for items at the beginning and end of a list.

set point A specific body weight that the brain tries to maintain through the regulation of diet, activity, and metabolism.

sexual dysfunction A chronic problem at a particular phase of the sexual response cycle.

sexual orientation A person's pattern of erotic attraction to persons of the same sex, other sex, or both sexes.

sexual response cycle During sexual activity, the phases of excitement, plateau, orgasm, and resolution.

shape constancy The perceptual process that makes an object appear to maintain its normal shape regardless of the angle from which it is viewed.

shaping An operant conditioning procedure that involves the positive reinforcement of successive approximations of an initially improbable behavior to eventually bring about that behavior.

short-term memory The stage of memory that can store a few items of unrehearsed information for up to about 20 seconds.

signal-detection theory The theory holding that the detection of a stimulus depends on both the intensity of the stimulus and the physical and psychological state of the individual.

simple phobia A phobia of a specific object or situation.

single photon emission computed tomography (SPECT) A brain-imaging technique that creates images of cerebral blood flow.

size constancy The perceptual process that makes an object appear to remain the same size despite changes in the size of the image it casts on the retina.

skepticism An attitude that doubts all claims not supported by solid research evidence.

skin senses The senses of touch, temperature, and pain.

Skinner box An enclosure that contains a bar or key that can be pressed to obtain food or water and that is used to study operant conditioning in rats, pigeons, or other small animals.

sleep apnea A condition in which a person awakens repeatedly in order to breathe.

sleeper effect Responding favorably to a persuasive message following the mere passage of time after having initially rejected it because of a strong peripheral factor, such as not trusting the source of the message.

smooth pursuit movements Eye movements controlled by the ocular muscles that keep objects focused on the fovea.

social anxiety disorder A phobia of situations that involve social evaluation.

social attachment A strong emotional relationship between an infant and a caregiver.

social clock The typical or expected timing of major life events in a given culture.

social cognition The process of perceiving, interpreting, and predicting social behavior.

social-comparison theory The theory that happiness is the result of estimating that one's life circumstances are more favorable than those of others.

social facilitation The effect of the presence of other people on a person's task performance, with performance on simple or well-learned tasks improved and performance on complex or poorly learned tasks impaired.

social learning theory A theory of learning that assumes that people learn behaviors mainly through observation and mental processing of information.

social loafing A decrease in the individual effort exerted by group members when working together on a task.

social psychology The field that studies how the actual, imagined, or implied presence of other people affects one another's thoughts, feelings, and behaviors.

social schema A cognitive structure comprising the presumed characteristics of a role, an event, a person, or a group.

social-skills training A form of behavioral group therapy that improves the client's social relationships by improving her or his interpersonal skills.

social support The availability of support from other people, whether tangible or intangible.

sociobiology The study of the hereditary basis of human and animal social behavior.

sociocultural perspective The psychological viewpoint that favors the scientific study of human behavior in its sociocultural context.

soma The cell body, which is the neuron's control center.

somatic nervous system The division of the peripheral nervous system that sends messages from the sensory organs to the central nervous system and messages from the central nervous system to the skeletal muscles.

somatic symptom and related disorder A psychological disorder characterized by physical symptoms in the absence of disease or injury.

somatosensory cortex The area of the parietal lobes that processes information from sensory receptors in the skin.

somatotype In Sheldon's theory, a physique associated with a particular temperament.

sound localization The process by which the individual determines the location of a sound.

specific phobia A phobia of a specific object or situation.

spermarche The first ejaculation, usually occurring between the ages of 13 and 15.

spinal cord The structure of the central nervous system that is located in the spine and plays a role in bodily reflexes and in communicating information between the brain and the peripheral nervous system.

split-brain research A research technique for the study of cerebral hemispheric lateralization that involves people whose hemispheres have been surgically separated from each other.

spontaneous recovery 1. In classical conditioning, the reappearance after a period of time of a conditioned response that has been subjected to extinction. 2. In operant conditioning, the reappearance after a period of time of a behavior that has been subjected to extinction.

spontaneous remission The improvement of some persons with psychological disorders without their undergoing formal therapy.

sport psychology The field that applies psychological principles to help amateur and professional athletes improve their performance.

SQ3R method A study technique in which the student surveys, questions, reads, recites, and reviews course material.

standard deviation A statistic representing the degree of dispersion of a set of scores around their mean.

standardization 1. A procedure ensuring that a test is administered and scored in a consistent manner. 2. A procedure for establishing test norms by giving a test to large samples of people who are representative of those for whom the test is designed.

state-dependent memory The tendency for recall to be best when one's emotional or physiological state is the same during the recall of a memory as it was during the encoding of that memory.

statistical significance A low probability (usually less than 5 percent) that the results of a research study are due to chance factors rather than to the independent variable.

statistics Mathematical techniques used to summarize research data or to determine whether the data support the researcher's hypothesis.

stereotype A social schema that incorporates characteristics, which can be positive or negative, supposedly shared by almost all members of a group.

stimulants Psychoactive drugs that increase central nervous system activity.

stimulus discrimination In classical conditioning, giving a conditioned response to the conditioned stimulus but not to stimuli similar to it.

stimulus generalization In classical conditioning, giving a conditioned response to stimuli similar to the conditioned stimulus.

storage The retention of information in memory.

stress The physiological response of the body to physical and psychological demands.

stress-inoculation training A type of cognitive therapy that helps clients change their pessimistic thinking into more positive thinking when in stressful situations.

stressor A physical or psychological demand that induces physiological adjustment.

structuralism The early psychological viewpoint that sought to identify the components of the conscious mind.

subliminal perception The unconscious perception of stimuli that are too weak to exceed the absolute threshold for detection.

subliminal psychodynamic activation The use of subliminal messages to stimulate unconscious fantasies.

superego In Freud's theory, the part of the personality that acts as a moral guide telling us what we should and should not do.

surface structure The word arrangements used to express meanings.

survey A set of questions related to a particular topic of interest administered to a sample of people through an interview or questionnaire.

sympathetic nervous system The division of the autonomic nervous system that arouses the body to prepare it for action.

synapse The junction between a neuron and a gland, muscle, sensory organ, or another neuron.

synaptic transmission The conveying of a neural impulse between a neuron and a gland, muscle, sensory organ, or another neuron.

synesthesia The process in which an individual experiences sensations in one sensory modality that are characteristic of another.

syntax The rules that govern the acceptable arrangement of words in phrases and sentences.

systematic desensitization A form of counterconditioning that trains the client to maintain a state of relaxation in the presence of imagined anxiety-inducing stimuli.

taste buds Structures lining the grooves of the tongue that contain the taste receptor cells.

telegraphic speech Speech marked by reliance on nouns and verbs while other parts of speech, including articles and prepositions, are omitted.

temperament A person's characteristic emotional state, first apparent in early infancy and possibly inborn.

temporal lobe A lobe of the cerebral cortex responsible for processing hearing.

teratogen A noxious substance, such as a virus or drug, that can cause prenatal defects.

testes The male gonads, which secrete hormones that regulate the development of the male reproductive system and secondary sex characteristics.

tetrahydrocannabinol (THC) The psychoactive ingredient found in the *Cannabis sativa* plant.

thalamus The brain stem structure that acts as a sensory relay station for taste, body, visual, and auditory sensations.

theory An integrated set of statements that summarizes and explains research findings and from which research hypotheses can be derived.

theory of multiple intelligences Howard Gardner's theory of intelligence, which assumes that the brain has evolved separate systems for seven kinds of intelligence.

thought The cognitive manipulation of words and images, as in concept formation, problem solving, and decision making.

timbre The subjective experience that identifies a particular sound and corresponds most closely to the mixture of sound waves composing it.

tip-of-the-tongue phenomenon The inability to recall information that one knows has been stored in long-term memory.

token economy An operant conditioning procedure that uses tokens as positive reinforcers in programs designed to promote desirable behaviors, with the tokens later used to purchase desired items or privileges.

toxic leadership Leaders who abuse their power and in doing so, inflict harm on their followers and organizations.

trait A relatively enduring, cross-situationally consistent personality characteristic that is inferred from a person's behavior.

transactional analysis (TA) A form of psychoanalytic group therapy, developed by Eric Berne, that helps clients change their immature or inappropriate ways of relating to other people.

transactional leadership Leaders who set expectations for followers and then reward or punish followers for fulfilling or failing to fulfill those expectations.

transcranial magnetic stimulation (TMS) An experimental manipulation of the brain that involves electrically stimulating the cerebral cortex of the brain by using pulsed magnetic fields administered near the scalp.

transcutaneous electrical nerve stimulation (TENS) The use of electrical stimulation of sites on the body to provide pain relief, apparently by stimulating the release of endorphins.

transfer of training Bringing back to the job environment what was learned in training.

transformational grammar The rules by which languages generate surface structures out of deep structures and deep structures out of surface structures.

transformational leadership Leaders who inspire, typically with charismatic and visionary influence, their followers to achieve beyond self-interest.

transitive inference The application of previously learned relationships to infer new relationships.

trephining An ancient technique in which sharp stones were used to chip holes in the skull, possibly to let out evil spirits that supposedly caused abnormal behavior.

trial and error An approach to problem solving in which the individual tries one possible solution after another until one works.

triarchic theory of intelligence Robert Sternberg's theory of intelligence, which assumes that there are three main kinds of intelligence: componential, experiential, and contextual.

trichromatic theory The theory that color vision depends on the relative degree of stimulation of red, green, and blue receptors.

trust versus mistrust Erikson's developmental stage in which success is achieved by having a secure social attachment with a caregiver.

t test A statistical technique used to determine whether the difference between two sets of scores is statistically significant.

turnover Relative to the total number of employees, the proportion of employees who leave an organization, either through dismissal or resignation.

two-factor theory The theory that emotional experience is the outcome of physiological arousal and the attribution of a cause for that arousal.

tympanic membrane The eardrum; a membrane separating the outer ear from the middle ear that vibrates in response to sound waves that strike it.

Type A behavior A syndrome—marked by impatience, hostility, and extreme competitiveness—that is associated with the development of coronary heart disease.

unconditioned response (UCR) In classical conditioning, an unlearned, automatic response to a particular unconditioned stimulus.

unconditioned stimulus (UCS) In classical conditioning, a stimulus that automatically elicits a particular unconditioned response.

unconscious mind The level of consciousness that contains thoughts, feelings, and memories that influence us without our awareness and that we cannot become aware of at will.

underextension The tendency to apply a word to fewer objects or actions than it actually represents.

unilateral neglect A disorder, caused by damage to a parietal lobe, in which the individual acts as though the side of her or his world opposite to the damaged lobe does not exist.

valence How much value an individual places on a particular outcome validation. A process that determines whether tests are accurate predictors of job performance.

validity The extent to which a test measures what it is supposed to measure.

variability hypothesis The prediction that men, as a group, are more variable than women.

variable An event, behavior, condition, or characteristic that has two or more values.

variable-interval schedule of reinforcement A partial schedule of reinforcement that provides reinforcement for the first desired response made after varying, unpredictable lengths of time.

variable-ratio schedule of reinforcement A partial schedule of reinforcement that provides reinforcement after varying, unpredictable numbers of desired responses.

variance A measure based on the average deviation of a set of scores from their group mean.

vestibular sense The sense that provides information about the head's position in space and helps in the maintenance of balance.

visible spectrum The portion of the electromagnetic spectrum that we commonly call light.

vision The sense that detects objects by the light reflected from them into the eyes.

visual agnosia A condition in which an individual can see objects and identify their features but cannot recognize the objects.

visual cortex The area of the occipital lobes that processes visual input.

visual illusion A misperception of physical reality usually caused by the misapplication of visual cues.

volley theory The theory of pitch perception that assumes that sound waves of particular frequencies induce auditory neurons to fire in volleys, with one volley following another.

Wada test A technique in which a cerebral hemisphere is anesthetized to assess hemispheric lateralization.

Weber's law The principle that the amount of change in stimulation needed to produce a just noticeable difference is a constant proportion of the original stimulus.

Wernicke's area The region of the temporal lobe that controls the meaningfulness of speech.

Yerkes-Dodson law The principle that the relationship between arousal and performance is best represented by an inverted U-shaped curve.

References

Abatzoglou, I., Anninos, P., Tsalafoutas, I., & Koukourakis, M. (2009). Multi-channel magnetoencephalogram on Alzheimer disease patients. *Journal of Integrative Neuroscience, 8,* 13–22.

Abbott, M. J., & Rapee, R. M. (2004). Post–event rumination and negative self–appraisal in social phobia before and after treatment. *Journal of Abnormal Psychology, 113,* 136–144.

Abel, M. H. (2002). Humor, stress, and coping strategies. *Humor: International Journal of Humor Research, 15,* 365–381.

Abelman, R. (1999). Preaching to the choir: Profiling TV advisory ratings users. *Journal of Broadcasting and Electronic Media, 43,* 529–550.

Abelson, R. P. (1981). Psychological status of the script concept. *American Psychologist, 36,* 715–729.

Abernethy, E. M. (1940). The effect of changed environmental conditions upon the results of college examinations. *Journal of Psychology, 10, 293–301.*

Abide, M. M., Richards, H. C., & Ramsay, S. G. (2001). Moral reasoning and consistency of belief and behavior: Decisions about substance abuse. *Journal of Drug Education, 31,* 367–384.

Abo, M., Chen, Z., Lai, L., Reese, T., & Bjelke, B. (2001). Functional recovery after brain lesioncontralateral neuromodulation: An fMRI study. *Neuroreport: For Rapid Communication of Neuroscience Research, 12,* 1543–1547.

Abokrysha, N. (2009). Ibn Sina (Avicenna) on pathogenesis of migraine compared with the recent theories. *Headache: Journal of Head and Neck Pain, 49,* 923–927.

Abou-Khalil, B. (2007). An update on determination of language dominance in screening for epilepsy surgery: The Wada test and newer noninvasive alternatives. *Epilepsia, 48,* 442–455.

Abrams, S. (1995). False memory syndrome versus total repression. *Journal of Psychiatry and the Law, 23,* 283–293.

Abramson, L. Y., Seligman, M. E. P., & Teasdale, J. D. (1978). Learned helplessness in humans: Critique and reformulation. *Journal of Abnormal Psychology, 87,* 49–74.

Ackerman, S. J., & Hilsenroth, M. J. (2001). A review of therapist characteristics and techniques negatively impacting the therapeutic alliance. *Psychotherapy: Theory, Research, Practice, Training, 38,* 171–185.

Ackerman, S. J., & Hilsenroth, M. J. (2003). A review of therapist characteristics and techniques positively impacting the therapeutic alliance. *Clinical Psychology Review, 23,* 1–33.

Ackil, J. K., & Zaragoza, M. S. (1998). Memorial consequences of forced confabulation; Age differences in susceptibility to false memories. *Developmental Psychology, 34,* 1358–1372.

Adams, P. R., & Adams, G. R. (1984). Mount Saint Helen's ashfall: Evidence for a disaster stress reaction. *American Psychologist, 39,* 252–260.

Adams, R. J., & Courage, M. L. (2002). A psychophysical test of the early maturation of infants' mid- and long-wavelength retinal cones. *Infant Behavior and Development, 25,* 247–254.

Adams, S. K., & Kisler, T. S. (2013). Sleep quality as a mediator between technology-related sleep quality, depression, and anxiety. *Cyberpsychology, Behavior, and Social Networking, 16,* 25–30.

Adams, W. L., Garry, P. J., Rhyne, R., & Hunt, W. C. (1990). Alcohol intake in the healthy elderly: Changes with age in a cross-sectional and longitudinal study. *Journal of the American Geriatrics Society, 38,* 211–216.

Adelmann, P. K., & Zajonc, R. B. (1989). Facial efference and the experience of emotion. *Annual Review of Psychology, 40,* 249–289.

Adelson, B. (1984). When novices surpass experts: The difficulty of a task may increase with expertise. *Journal of Experimental Psychology: Learning, Memory, and Cognition, 10,* 483–495.

Ader, R. (2001). Psychoneuroimmunology. *Current Directions in Psychological Science, 10,* 94–98.

Ader, R. (2003). Conditioned immunomodulation: Research needs and directions. *Brain, Behavior, and Immunity, 17,* S51–S57.

Ader, R., & Cohen, N. (1982). Behaviorally conditioned immunosuppression and murine systemic lupus erythematosus. *Science, 215,* 1534–1536.

Adeyemo, S. A. (2002). A review of the role of the hippocampus in memory. *Psychology and Education: An Interdisciplinary Journal, 39,* 46–63.

Adler, A. (1927). *Understanding human nature.* New York: Greenberg.

Adler, K. A. (1994). Socialist influences on Alderian psychology. *Individual Psychology: Journal of Adlerian Theory, Research, and Practice, 50,* 131–141.

Adler, T. (1991, November). Hypothalamus study stirs social questions. *APA Monitor,* pp. 8–9.

Adorno, T. W., Frenkel-Brunswik, E., Levinson, D. J., & Sanford, R. N. (1950). *The authoritarian personality.* New York: Harper & Row.

Afnan, S. M. (1958/1980). *Avicenna: His life and works.* Westport, CT: Greenwood.

Aghajanian, G. K. (1994). Serotonin and the action of LSD in the brain. *Psychiatric Annals, 24,* 137–141.

Agmo, A., & Berendfeld, R. (1990). Reinforcing properties of ejaculation in the male rat: Role of opioids and dopamine. *Behavioral Neuroscience, 104,* 177–182.

Agostino, H., Erdstein, J., & Di Meglio, G. (2013). Shifting paradigms: Continuous nasogastric feeding with high caloric intakes in anorexia nervosa. *Journal of Adolescent Health, 53,* 590–594.

Agras, W. S. (1997). Pharmacotherapy of bulimia nervosa and binge eating disorder: Long-term outcomes. *Psychopharmacology Bulletin, 33,* 433–436.

Agrawal, A., & Lynskey, M. T. (2008). Are there genetic influences on addiction? Evidence from family, adoption and twin studies. *Addiction, 103,* 1069–1081.

Aheneku, J. E., Nwosu, C. M., & Ahaneku, G. I. (2000). Academic stress and cardiovascular health. *Academic Medicine, 75,* 567–568.

Ahlberg, S. W., & Sharps, M. J. (2002). Bartlett revisited: Reconfiguration of long-term memory in young and older adults. *Journal of Genetic Psychology, 163,* 211–218.

Ahmed, N. U., Ahmed, N. S., Bennett, C. R., & Hinds, J. E. (2002). Impact of a Drug Abuse Resistance Education (D.A.R.E) program in preventing the initiation of cigarette smoking in fifth- and sixth-grade students. *Journal of the National Medical Association, 94,* 249–256.

Ahrendt, L. P., Christensen, J.-W., & Ladewig, J. (2012). The ability of horses to learn an instrumental task through social observation. *Applied Animal Behaviour Science, 139,* 105–113.

Aiken, L. R. (1982). *Psychological testing and assessment.* Boston: Allyn & Bacon.

Aisner, R., & Terkel, J. (1992). Ontogeny of pine cone opening behavior in the black rat, *Rattus rattus. Animal Behaviour, 44,* 327–336.

Akimova, I. M., Gurchin, F. A., Koroleva, N. Y., Melyucheva, L. A., Taits, E. A., & Khrakovskaya, M. G. (2000). Clinical use of the embryonic brain tissue grafts in epilepsy. *Human Physiology, 26,* 308–318.

Alaoui-Ismaieli, O., Vernet-Maury, E., Dittmar, A. Delhomme, G., & Chanel, J. (1997). Odor hedonics: Connection with emotional response estimated by autonomic parameters. *Chemical Senses, 22,* 237–248.

Alba, J. W., & Hasher, L. (1983). Is memory schematic? *Psychological Bulletin, 93,* 203–231.

Albert, D. J., Walsh, M. L., & Jonik, R. H. (1993). Aggression in humans: What is its biological foundation? *Neuroscience and Biobehavioral Reviews, 17,* 405–425.

Albright, T. D., Jessell, T. M., Kandel, E. R., & Posner, M. I. (2001). Progress in the neural sciences in the century after Cajal (and the mysteries that remain). *Annals of the New York Academy of Sciences, 929,* 11–40.

Aldag, R. J., & Fuller, S. R. (1993). Beyond fiasco: A reappraisal of the groupthink phenomenon and a new model of group decision processes. *Psychological Bulletin, 113,* 533–552.

Alden, D. L., Mukherjee, A., & Hoyer, W. D. (2000). The effects of incongruity, surprise, and positive moderators on perceived humor in television advertising. *Journal of Advertising, 29,* 1–15.

Alderfer, C. P. (2003). The science and nonscience of psychologists' responses to *The Bell Curve. Professional Psychology: Research and Practice, 34,* 287–293.

Aldrich, M. S. (1992). Narcolepsy. *Neurology, 42,* 34–43.

Alexy, B. B. (1991). Factors associated with participation or nonparticipation in a workplace wellness center. *Research in Nursing and Health, 14,* 33–40.

Alghazo, R., Upton, T. D., & Cioe, N. (2011). Duty to warn versus duty to protect confidentiality: Ethical and legal considerations relative to individuals with AIDS/HIV. *Journal of Applied Rehabilitation Counseling, 42,* 43–49.

Al-Issa, I., & Oudji, S. (1998). Culture and anxiety disorders. In S. S. Kazarian & D. R. Evans (Eds.), *Cultural clinical psychology: Theory, research, and practice* (pp. 127–151). New York: Oxford University Press.

Allalouf, A., & Ben-Shakhar, G. (1998). The effect of coaching on the predictive validity of scholastic aptitude tests. *Journal of Educational Measurement, 35,* 31–47.

Allen, J., & Walsh, J. A. (2000). A construct-based approach to equivalence: Methodologies for cross-cultural/multicultural personality assessment research. In R. H. Dana (Ed.), *Handbook of cross-cultural and multicultural personality assessment* (pp. 63–85). Mahwah, NJ: Erlbaum.

Allen, J. J., Iacono, W. G., Laravuso, J. J., Dunn, L. A. (1995). An event–related potential investigation of posthypnotic recognition amnesia. *Journal of Abnormal Psychology, 104,* 421–430.

Allen, J. J. B., & Iacono, W. G. (1997). A comparison of methods for the analysis of event-related potentials in deception detection. *Journal of Applied Psychology, 82,* 426–433.

Allen, M. (1993). Determining the persuasiveness of message sidedness: A prudent note about utilizing research summaries. *Western Journal of Communication, 57,* 98–103.

Allen, M. G. (1990). Group psychotherapy: Past, present and future. *Psychiatricannals, 20,* 358–361.

Allik, J., & McCrae, R. R. (2004). Toward a geography of personality traits: Patterns of profiles across 36 cultures. *Journal of Cross-Cultural Psychology, 35,* 13–28.

Allport, F. H. (1920). The influence of the group upon association and thought. *Journal of Experimental Psychology, 3,* 159–182.

Allport, G. W. (1954). *The nature of prejudice.* Reading, MA: Addison-Wesley.

Allport, G. W. (1967). Autobiography. In E. G. Boring & G. Lindzey (Eds.), *A history of psychology in autobiography* (Vol. 5, pp. 1–25). New York: Appleton-Century-Crofts.

Alpers, G. W., & Tuschen-Caffier, B. (2001). Negative feelings and the desire to eat in bulimia nervosa. *Eating Behaviors, 2,* 339–352.

Alpert, J. L., Brown, L. S., & Courtois, C. A. (1998). Symptomatic clients and memories of childhood abuse: What the abuse literature tells us. *Psychology, Public Policy, and Law, 4,* 941–995.

Althoff, R. R., Faraone, S. V., Rettew, D. C., Morley, C. P., & Hudziak, J. J. (2005). Family, twin, adoption, and molecular genetic studies of juvenile bipolar disorder. *Bipolar Disorders, 7,* 598–609.

Alto, L. T., Havton, L. A., Conner, J. M., Hollis II, E. R., Blesch, A., & Tuszynski, M. H. (2009). Chemotropic guidance facilitates axonal regeneration and synapse formation after spinal cord injury. *Nature Neuroscience, 12,* 1106–1115.

Alvarado, C. S. (1996). The place of spontaneous cases in parapsychology. *Journal of Broadcasting and Electronic Media, 41,* 345–359.

Alvarado, K. A., Templer, D. I., Bresler, C., & Thomas-Dobson, S. (1995). The relationship of religious variables to death depression and death anxiety. *Journal of Clinical Psychology, 51,* 202–204.

Amabile, T. M. (1989). *Growing up creative.* New York: Random House.

Amabile, T. M., Goldfarb, P., & Brackfield, S. C. (1990). Social influences on creativity: Evaluation, coaction, and surveillance. *Creativity Research Journal, 3,* 6–21.

Amato, P. R., & Keith, B. (1991). Parental divorce and the well-being of children: A meta-analysis. *Psychological Bulletin, 110,* 26–46.

d'Amato, T., Rochet, T., Dalery, J., & Chauchat, J. H. (1994). Seasonality of birth and ventricular enlargement in chronic schizophrenia. *Psychiatry Research: Neuroimaging, 55,* 65–73.

Ameis, S. H., Ducharme, S., Albaugh, M. D., Hudziak, J. J., Botteron, K. N., Lepage, C., . . . Karama, S., (2014). Cortical thickness, cortico-amygdalar networks, and externalizing behaviors in healthy children. *Biological Psychiatry, 75,* 65–72.

Amen, D. G. (2010). High resolution brain SPECT imaging in a clinical substance abuse practice. *Journal of Psychoactive Drugs, 42,* 153–160.

American Psychiatric Association. (2013). *Diagnostic and statistical manual of mental disorders* (5th ed.). Washington, DC: Author.

Amering, M., Katschnig, H., Berger, P., Windhaber, J., Baischer, W., & Dantendorfer, K. (1997). Embarrassment about the first panic attack predicts agoraphobia in disorder patients. *Behaviour Research and Therapy, 35,* 517–521.

Amin, F., Silverman, J. M., Siever, L. J., Smith, C. J., Knott, P. J., & Davis, K. L. (1999). Genetic antecedents of dopamine dysfunction in schizophrenia. *Biological Psychiatry, 45,* 1143–1150.

Amir, T. (1984). The Asch conformity effect: A study in Kuwait. *Social Behavior and Personality, 12,* 187–190.

Amorose, A. J., & Horn, T. S. (2001). Pre- to post-season changes in the intrinsic motivation of first year college athletes: Relationship with coaching behavior and scholarship status. *Journal of Applied Sport Psychology, 13,* 355–373.

Amsterdam, J. D., Brunswick, D. J., & O'Reardon, J. (2002). Bipolar disorder in women. *Psychiatric Annals, 32,* 397–404.

Anand, B. K., & Brobeck, J. R. (1951). Hypothalamic control of food intake in rats and cats. *Yale Journal of Biology and Medicine, 24,* 123–140.

Anastasi, A. (1958). Heredity, environment, and the question "How?" *American Psychologist, 65,* 197–208.

Anastasi, A. (1972). The cultivation of diversity. *American Psychologist, 27,* 1091–1099.

Anastasi, A. (1985). Psychological testing: Basic concepts and common misconceptions. In A. M. Rogers & C. J. Scheirer (Eds.), *The G. Stanley Hall Lecture Series* (Vol. 5, pp. 87–120). Washington, DC: American Psychological Association.

Anazonwu, C. O. (1995). Locus of control, academic self-concept, and attribution of responsibility for performance in statistics. *Psychological Reports, 77,* 367–370.

Andersen, B. L., Kiecolt-Glaser, J. K., & Glaser, R. A (1994). A biobehavioral model of cancer stress and disease course. *American Psychologist, 49,* 389–404.

Andersen, R. E., Crespo, C. J., Bartlett, S. J., Cheskin, L. J., & Pratt, M. (1998). Associations among physical activity, television watching, and obesity in adult Pima Indians. *JAMA: Journal of the American Medical Association, 279,* 938–942.

Andersen, S. M., & Ross, L. (1984). Self-knowledge and social inference: I. The impact of cognitive/ affective and behavioral data. *Journal of Personality and Social Psychology, 46,* 280–293.

Anderson, A. K., & Phelps, E. A. (2000). Expression without recognition: Contributions of the human amygdala to emotional communication. *Psychological Science, 11,* 106–111.

Anderson, B. L. (2003). The role of occlusion in the perception of depth, lightness, and opacity. *Psychological Review, 110,* 785–801.

Anderson, B. L., Cyranowski, J. M., & Aarestad, S. (2000). Beyond artificial, sex-linked distinctions to conceptualize female sexuality: Comment on Baumeister, 2000. *Psychological Bulletin, 126,* 380–384.

Anderson, C. A. (1999). Attributional style, depression, and loneliness: A cross–cultural comparison of American and Chinese students. *Personality and Social Psychology Bulletin, 25,* 482–499.

Anderson, D. C., Crowell, C. R., Doman, M., & Howard, G. S. (1988). Performance posting, goal setting, and activity-contingent praise as applied to a university hockey team. *Journal of Applied Psychology, 73,* 87–95.

Anderson, I. M. (2000). Selective serotonin reuptake inhibitors versus tricyclic antidepressants: A meta–analysis of efficacy and tolerability. *Journal of Affective Disorders, 58,* 19–36.

Anderson, J. R. (1983). Retrieval of information from long-term memory. *Science, 220,* 25–30.

Anderson, J. R. (2001). Obituary: Herbert A. Simon (1916–2001). *American Psychologist, 56,* 516–518.

Anderson, K. J., Revelle, W., & Lynch, M. J. (1989). Caffeine, impulsivity, and memory scanning: A comparison of two explanations for the Yerkes-Dodson effect. *Motivation and Emotion, 13,* 1–20.

Anderson, K. W., & Skidmore, J. R. (1995). Empirical analysis of factors in depressive cognition: The Cognitive Triad Inventory. *Journal of Clinical Psychology, 51,* 603–609.

Anderson, P. L., Price, M., Edwards, S. M., Obasaju, M. A., Schmertz, S. K., Zimand, E., Calamaras, M. R. (2013). Virtual reality exposure therapy for social anxiety disorder: A randomized controlled trial. *Journal of Consulting and Clinical Psychology, 81,* 751–760.

Anderson, R. A., Baron, R. S., & Logan, H. (1991). Distraction, control, and dental stress. *Journal of Applied Social Psychology, 21,* 156–171.

Anderson, S. W., & Rizzo, M. (1994). Hallucinations following occipital lobe damage: The pathological activation of visual representations. *Journal of Clinical and Experimental Neuropsychology, 16,* 651–663.

Anderson, U. S., Kelling, A. S., Pressley-Keough, R., Bloomsmith, M. A., & Maple, T. L. (2003). Enhancing the zoo visitor's experience by public animal training and oral interpretation at an otter exhibit. *Environment and Behavior, 35,* 826–841.

Anderson, W. S., Sheth, R. N., Bencherif, B., Frost, J. J., & Campbell, J. N. (2002). Naloxone increases pain induced by topical capsaicin in healthy human volunteers. *Pain, 99,* 207–216.

Andre, T. (1979). Does answering higher-level questions while reading facilitate productive learning? *Review of Educational Research, 49,* 280–318.

Andreasen, N. C. (1997). The evolving concept of schizophrenia: From Kraepelin to the present and future. *Schizophrenia Research, 28,* 105–109.

Andreasen, N. C., & Flaum, M. (1991). Schizophrenia: The characteristic symptoms. *Schizophrenia Bulletin, 17,* 27–49.

Andreasen, N. C., Arndt, S., Alliger, R., & Miller, D. (1995). Symptoms of schizophrenia: Methods, meanings, and mechanisms. *Archives of General Psychiatry, 52,* 341–351.

Andreasen, N. C., Flaum, M., Swayze, V. W., & Tyrrell, G. (1990). Positive and negative symptoms in schizophrenia: A critical reappraisal. *Archives of General Psychiatry, 47,* 615–621.

Andreassen, P. B. (1988). Explaining the price-volume relationship: The difference between price changes and changing prices. *Organizational Behavior and Human Decision Processes, 41,* 371–389.

Andrews, G., & Halford, G. S. (1998). Children's ability to make transitive inferences: The importance of premise integration and structural complexity. *Cognitive Development, 13,* 479–513.

Anestis, M. D., Anestis, J. C., & Lilienfeld, S. O. (2011). When it comes to evaluating psychodynamic therapy, the devil is in the details. *American Psychologist, 66,* 149–151.

Angermeyer, M. C., & Schulze, B. (2001). Reinforcing stereotypes: How the focus on forensic cases in news reporting may influence public attitudes towards the mentally ill. *International Journal of Law and Psychiatry, 24,* 469–486.

Anisfeld, M. (1996). Only tongue protrusion modeling is matched by neonates. *Developmental Review, 16,* 149–161.

Ansbacher, H. L. (1990). Alfred Adler's influence on the three leading cofounders of humanistic psychology. *Journal of Humanistic Psychology, 30,* 45–53.

Anshel, M. H. (1995). Examining social loafing among elite female rowers as a function of task duration and mood. *Journal of Sport Behavior, 18,* 39–49.

Anthony, B., Boudreaux, L., Dobbs, I., Jamal, S., Guerra, P., & Williamson, J. W. (2003). Can relaxation lower metaboreflex-mediated blood pressure elevations? *Medicine and Science in Sports and Exercise, 35,* 394–399.

Antoni, M. H., LaPerriere, A., Schneiderman, N., & Fletcher, M. A. (1991). Stress and immunity in individuals at risk for AIDS. *Stress Medicine, 7,* 35–44.

Antshel, K. M., Faraone, S. V, Maglione, K., Doyle, A. E., Fried, R., Seidman, L. J., & Biederman, J. (2010). Executive functioning in high-IQ adults with ADHD. *Psychological Medicine, 40,* 1909–1918.

Antunano, M. J., & Hernandez, J. M. (1989). Incidence of airsickness among military parachutists. *Aviation, Space, and Environmental Medicine, 60,* 792–797.

Apodaca, T. R., & Miller, William R. (2003). Metaanalysis of the effectiveness of bibliotherapy for alcohol problems. *Journal of Clinical Psychology, 59,* 289–304.

Appel, J., Potter, E., Shen, Q., Pantol, G., Greig, M. T., Loewenstein, D., & Duara, R. (2009). A comparative analysis of structural brain MRI in the diagnosis of Alzheimer's disease. *Behavioural Neurology, 21,* 13–19.

Appelbaum, P. S. (1998). A "Health Information Infrastructure" and the threat to confidentiality of health records. *Psychiatric Services, 49,* 27–28, 33.

Appelbaum, P. S., & Gutheil, T. G. (1980). The Boston State Hospital case: "Involuntary mind control," the Constitution, and the "right to rot." *American Journal of Psychiatry, 137,* 720–723.

Apperloo, M. J. A., Van Der Stege, J. G., Hoek, A., Schultz, W., & Willibrord, C. M. (2003). In the mood for sex: The value of androgens. *Journal of Sex and Marital Therapy, 29,* 87–102.

Araújo, D. (2007). Ecological validity, representative design, and correspondence between experimental task constraints and behavioral setting: Comment on Rogers, Kadar, and Costall (2005). *Ecological Psychology, 19,* 69–78.

Ardila, A., Montanes, P., & Gempeler, J. (1986). Echoic memory and language perception. *Brain and Language, 29,* 134–140.

Ares-Santos, S., Granado, N., & Moratalla, R. (2013). The role of dopamine receptors in the neurotoxicity of methamphetamine. *Journal of Internal Medicine, 273,* 1365–2796.

Arfken, C. L., Joseph, A., Sandhu, G. R., Roehrs, T., Douglass, A. B., Boutros, N. N. (2014). The status of sleep abnormalities as a diagnostic test for major depressive disorder. *Journal of Affective Disorders, 56,* 36–45.

Armario, A. (2006). The hypothalamic-pituitary-adrenal axis: What can it tell us about stressors? *CNS and Neurological Disorders: Drug Targets, 5,* 485–501.

Armstrong, G. B., & Chung, L. (2000). Background television and reading memory in context: Assessing TV interference and facilitative context effects on encoding versus retrieval processes. *Communication Research, 27,* 327–352.

Arndt, J., Schimel, J., & Goldenberg, J. L. (2003). Death can be good for your health: Fitness intentions as a proximal and distal defense against mortality salience. *Journal of Applied Social Psychology, 33,* 1726–1746.

Arnett, J. J. (1999). Adolescent storm and stress, reconsidered. *American Psychologist, 54,* 317–326.

Arnett, P. A., Howland, E. W., Smith, S. S., & Newman, J. P. (1993). Autonomic responsivity during passive avoidance in incarcerated psychopaths. *Personality and Individual Differences, 14,* 173–184.

Arnold, R. M., Miller, M., Mehta, R. S. (2012). Insomnia: Nonpharmacologic treatments #104. *Journal of Palliative Medicine, 15,* 242–243.

Arns, M., Heinrich, H., & Strehl, U. (2014). Evaluation of neurofeedback in ADHD: The long and winding road. *Biological Psychology, 95,* 108–115.

Aronson, S. C., Black, J. E., McDougle, C. J., & Scanley, B. E. (1995). Serotonergic mechanisms of cocaine effects in humans. *Psychopharmacology, 119,* 179–185.

Arrigo, J. M., & Pezdek, K. (1997). Lessons from the study of psychogenic amnesia. *Current Directions in Psychological Science, 6,* 148–152.

Artemiadis, A. K., Vervainioti, A. A., Alexopoulos, E. C., Rombos, A., Anagnostouli, M. C., & Darviri, C. (2012). Stress management and multiple sclerosis: A randomized controlled trial. *Archives of Clinical Neuropsychology, 27,* 406–416.

Ary, D. V., Tildesley, E., Hops, H., & Andrews, J. A. (1993). The influence of parent, sibling, and peer modeling and attitudes on adolescent use of alcohol. *International Journal of the Addictions, 28,* 853–880.

Asahina, M., Suzuki, A., Mori, M., Kanesaka, T., & Hattori, T. (2003). Emotional sweating response in a patient with bilateral amygdale damage. *International Journal of Psychophysiology, 17,* 87–93.

Asai, M., Ramachandrappa, S. Joachim, M., Shen, Y., Zhang, R. Nuthalapati, Ramanathan, Strolich, D. L., . . . Majzoub, J. A. (2013). Loss of function of the melanocortin 2 receptor accessory protein 2 is associated with mammalian obesity. *Science, 341,* 275–278.

Asch, S. E. (1955, November). Opinions and social pressure. *Scientific American,* pp. 31–35.

Aseltine, R. H., Jr. (1996). Pathways linking parental divorce with adolescent depression. *Journal of Health and Social Behavior, 37,* 133–148.

Aserinsky, E., & Kleitman, N. (1953). Regularly occurring periods of eye motility and concomitant phenomena during sleep. *Science, 118,* 273–274.

Aserinsky, E., Lynch, J. A., Mack, M. E., Tzankoff, S. P., & Hurn, E. (1985). Comparison of eye motion in wakefulness and REM sleep. *Psychophysiology, 22,* 1–10.

Ash, D. W., & Holding, D. H. (1990). Backward versus forward chaining in the acquisition of a keyboard skill. *Human Factors, 32,* 139–146.

Aslin, R. N., & Smith, L. B. (1988). Perceptual development. *Annual Review of Psychology, 39,* 435–474.

Aspen, V. A., Stein, R. I., & Wilfley, D. E. (2012). An exploration of salivation patterns in normal weight and obese children. *Appetite, 58,* 539–542.

Astin, G. R., & Garber, H. (1982). *The rise and fall of national test scores.* New York: Academic Press.

Atkinson, D. R. (1983). Ethnic similarity in counseling psychology: A review of research. *Counseling Psychologist, 11,* 79–92.

Atkinson, J. W. (1981). Studying personality in the context of an advanced motivational psychology. *American Psychologist, 36,* 117–128.

Atkinson, J. W., & Litwin, G. H. (1960). Achievement motive and test anxiety concerned as motive to approach success and motive to avoid failure. *Journal of Abnormal and Social Psychology, 60,* 52–63.

Attie, I., & Brooks-Gunn, J. (1989). Development of eating problems in adolescent girls: A longitudinal study. *Developmental Psychology, 25,* 70–79.

Atwood, G. E., & Tomkins, S. S. (1976). On the subjectivity of personality theory. *Journal of the History of the Behavioral Sciences, 12,* 166–177.

Austin, A. J., & Duka, T. (2012). Mechanisms of attention to conditioned stimuli predictive of a cigarette outcome. *Behavioural Brain Research, 232,* 183–189.

Avalon, L, & Young, M. A. (2003) A comparison of depressive symptoms in African Americans and Caucasian Americans. *Journal of Cross-Cultural Psychology, 34,* 111–124.

Axmacher, N., Lenz, S., Haupt, S., Elger, C. E., & Fell, J. (2010). Electrophysiological signature of working and long-term memory interaction in the human hippocampus. *European Journal of Neuroscience, 31,* 177–188.

Ayabe-Kanamura, S., Schicker, I., Laska, M., Hudson, R., Distel, H., Kobayakawa, T., & Saito, S. (1998). Differences in perception of everyday odors: A Japanese-German cross-cultural study. *Chemical Senses, 23,* 31–38.

Aydin, G., & Aydin, O. (1992). Learned helplessness and explanatory style in Turkish samples. *Journal of Social Psychology, 132,* 117–119.

Aydt, H., & Corsaro, W. A. (2003). Differences in children's construction of gender across culture: An interpretative approach. *American Behavioral Scientist, 46,* 1306–1325.

Babad, E., Bernieri, F., & Rosenthal, R. (1989). When less information is more informative: Diagnosing teacher expectations from brief samples of behavior. *British Journal of Educational Psychology, 59,* 281–295.

Baban, A., & Craciun, C. (2007). Changing health risk behaviors: A review of theory and evidence-based interventions in health psychology. *Journal of Cognitive and Behavioral Psychotherapies, 7,* 45–67.

Baddeley, A. D. (1982). Domains of recollection. *Psychological Review, 89,* 708–729.

Baddeley, A. D. (1994). The magical number seven: Still magic after all these years? *Psychological Review, 101,* 353–356.

Bae, J. S., Kim, J. Y., Park, B.-L., Cheong, H. S., Kim, J.-H., Shin, J.-G, Woo, S.-I. (2013). Lack of association between DISC1 polymorphisms and risk of schizophrenia in a Korean population. *Psychiatry Research, 208,* 189–190.

Baer, J. (1996). The effects of task-specific divergent-thinking training. *Journal of Creative Behavior, 30,* 183–187.

Bagati, D., Nizamie, S. H., & Prakash, R. (2009). Effect of augmentatary repetitive transcranialmagnetic stimulation on auditory hallucinations in schizophrenia: Randomized controlled study. *Australian and New Zealand Journal of Psychiatry, 43,* 386–392.

Bagozzi, R. P., Wong, N., & Yi, Y. (1999). The role of culture and gender in the relationship between positive and negative affect. *Cognition & Emotion, 13,* 641–672.

Bagwell, C. L., Newcomb, A. F., & Bukowski, W. M. (1998). Preadolescent friendship and peer rejection as predictors of adult adjustment. *Child Development, 69,* 140–153.

Bahill, A. T., & Karnavas, W. J. (1993). The perceptual illusion of baseball's rising fastball and breaking curveball. *Journal of Experimental Psychology: Human Perception and Performance, 19,* 3–14.

Bahill, A. T., & LaRitz, T. (1984). Why can't batters keep their eyes on the ball? *American Scientist, 72,* 249–253.

Bahrick, H. P., Bahrick, P. O., & Wittlinger, R. P. (1975). Fifty years of memory for names and faces: A cross-sectional approach. *Journal of Experimental Psychology: General, 104,* 54–75.

Bailey, C. J., Karhu, J., & Ilmoniemi, R. J. (2001). Transcranial magnetic stimulation as a tool for cognitive studies. *Scandinavian Journal of Psychology, 42,* 297–305.

Bailey, J. M., Dunne, M. P., & Martin, N. G. (2000). Genetic and environmental influences on sexual orientation and its correlates in an Australian twin sample. *Journal of Personality and Social Psychology, 78,* 524–536.

Bailey, J. M., Pillard, R. C., Dawood, K., Miller, M. B., Farrer, L. A., Trivedi, S., & Murphy, R. L. (1999). A family history study of male sexual orientation using three independent samples. *Behavior Genetics, 29,* 79–86.

Bailey, R. K., Patel, T. C., Avenido, J., Patel, M., Jaleel, M., Barker, N., . . . Jabeen, S. (2011). Suicide: Current trends. *Journal of the National Medical Association, 103,* 614–617.

Bailey, S. P., Hall, E. E., Folger, S. E., & Miller, P. C. (2008). Changes in EEG during graded exercise on a recumbent cycle ergometer. *Journal of Sports Science and Medicine, 7,* 505–511.

Bailis, D. S. (2001). Benefits of self-handicapping in sport: A field study of university athletes. *Canadian Journal of Behavioural Science, 33,* 213–223.

Baird, J. C., & Wagner, M. (1982). The moon illusion: I. How high is the sky? *Journal of Experimental Psychology: General, 111,* 296–303.

Baisden, R. H. (1995). Therapeutic uses for neural grafts: Progress slowed but not abandoned. *Behavioral and Brain Sciences, 18,* 47–48.

Baker, G. H. B. (1987). Psychological factors and immunity. *Journal of Psychosomatic Research, 31,* 1–10.

Baker, J. P. (1994). Outcomes of lithium discontinuation: A meta-analysis. *Lithium, 5,* 187–192.

Baker, L. M., & Dunbar, K. (2000). Experimental design heuristics for scientific discovery: The use of "baseline" and "known standard" controls. *International Journal of Human-Computer Studies. Special Issue: Machine Discovery, 53,* 335–349.

Bala, N., Kang, L., Lindsay, R. C. L., & Talwar, V. (2010). The competency of children to testify: Psychological research informing Canadian law reform. *International Journal of Children's Rights, 18,* 53–77.

Balanovski, E., & Taylor, J. G. (1978). Can electromagnetism account for extra sensory phenomena? *Nature, 276,* 64–67.

Balch, W. R., Myers, D. M., & Papotto, C. (1999). Dimensions of mood in mood-dependent memory. *Journal of Experimental Psychology: Learning, Memory, and Cognition, 25,* 70–83.

Baldwin, D., Woods, R., Lawson, R., & Taylor, D. (2011). Efficacy of drug treatments for generalised anxiety disorder: Systematic review and meta-analysis. *British Medical Journal Open, 342,* 1–11.

Baldwin, E. (1993). The case for animal research in psychology. *Journal of Social Issues, 49,* 121–131.

Baldwin, M. W. (1954). Subjective measurements in television. *American Psychologist, 9,* 231–234.

Bales, J. (1988, August). Pre-work polygraph ban signed by Reagan. *APA Monitor,* p. 5.

Bales, J. (1988, March). Court rules no duty to commit in N. C. *APA Monitor,* p. 20.

Balkany, T. J, Hodges, A. V., Eshraghi, A. A., Butts, S., Bricker, K., Lingvai, J., . . . King, J. (2002). Cochlear implants in children: A review. *Acta Oto-Laryngologica, 122,* 356–362.

Ball, C., Mann, L., & Stamm, C. (1994). Decision-making abilities of intellectually gifted and non-gifted children. *Australian Journal of Psychology, 46,* 13–20.

Ball, I. L., Farnill, D., Wangeman, J. F. (1984). Sex and age differences in sensation seeking: Some national comparisons. *British Journal of Psychology, 75,* 257–265.

Ball, K., & Lee, C. (2000). Relationship between psychological stress, coping, and disordered eating. *Psychology and Health, 14,* 1007–1035.

Ballard, C. G., O'Brien, J. T., Reichelt, K. P., & Elaine K. (2002). Aromatherapy as a safe and effective treatment for the management of agitation in severe dementia: The results of a double-blind, placebo-controlled trial with Melissa. *Journal of Clinical Psychiatry, 63,* 553–558.

Bancroft, J., Janssen, E., Strong, D., Carnes, L., Vukadinovic, Z., & Long, J. S. (2003). Sexual risk-taking in gay men: The relevance of sexual arousability, mood, and sensation seeking. *Archives of Sexual Behavior, 32,* 555–572.

Bandura, A. (1965). Influence of model's reinforcement contingencies on the acquisition of imitative responses. *Journal of Personality and Social Psychology, 1,* 589–595.

Bandura, A. (1977). *Social learning theory.* Englewood Cliffs, NJ: Prentice-Hall.

Bandura, A. (1982). The psychology of chance encounters and life paths. *American Psychologist, 37,* 747–755.

Bandura, A. (1986). *Social foundations of thought and action: A social-cognitive theory.* Englewood Cliffs, NJ: Prentice Hall.

Bandura, A. (1989). Human agency in social cognitive theory. *American Psychologist, 44,* 1175–1184.

Bandura, A. (2000). Exercise of human agency through collective efficacy. *Current Directions in Psychological Science, 9,* 75–78.

Bandura, A. (2001). Social-cognitive theory: An agentic perspective. *Annual Review of Psychology, 52,* 1–26.

Bandura, A. (2002). Social cognitive theory in cultural context. *Applied Psychology, 51,* 269–290.

Bandura, A., Blanchard, E. B., & Ritter, B. (1969). The relative efficacy of desensitization and modeling approaches for inducing behavioral, affective, and attitudinal changes. *Journal of Personality and Social Psychology, 13,* 173–199.

Bandura, A., & Locke, E. A. (2003). Negative self-efficacy and goal effects revisited. *Journal of Applied Psychology, 88,* 87–99.

Bandura, A., Caprara, G. V., Barbaranelli, C., Regalia, C., & Scabini, E. (2011). Impact of family efficacy beliefs on quality of family functioning and satisfaction with family life. *Applied Psychology: An International Review, 60,* 421–448.

Bandura, A., Reese, L., & Adams, N. E. (1982). Microanalysis of action and fear arousal as a function of differential levels of perceived self-efficacy. *Journal of Personality and Social Psychology, 43,* 5–21.

Bang, H., & Montgomery, D. (2013). Understanding international graduate students' acculturation using Q methodology. *Journal of College Student Development, 54,* 343–360.

Bangasser, D. A., & Valentino, R. J. (2014). Sex differences in stress-related psychiatric disorders: Neurobiological perspectives. *Frontiers in Neuroendocrinology, 35*(3), 303–319.

Bangerter, A., Grob, A., & Krings, F. (2001). Personal goals at age 25 in three generation of the twentieth century: Young adulthood in historical context. *Swiss Journal of Psychology—Schweizerische Zeitschrift fuer Psychologie—Revue Suisse de Psychologie, 60,* 59–64.

Banik, R. K., Kozaki, Y., Sato, J., Gera, L., & Mizumura, K. (2001). B2 receptor-mediated enhanced bradykinin sensitivity of rat cutaneous c-fiber nociceptors during persistent inflammation. *Journal of Neurophysiology, 86,* 2727–2735.

Banks, S. M., & Kerns, R. D. (1996). Explaining high rates of depression in chronic pain: A diathesis-stress framework. *Psychological Bulletin, 119,* 95–110.

Barako Arndt, K., & Schuele, C. M. (2012). Production of infinitival complements by children with specific language impairment. *Clinical Linguistics & Phonetics, 26,* 1–17.

Baraona, E., Abittan, C. S., Dohmen, K., Moretti, M., Pozzato, G., Chayes, Z. W., . . . Lieber, C. S. (2001). Gender differences in pharmacokinetics of alcohol. *Alcoholism, Clinical and Experimental Research, 25,* 502–507.

Barbalet, J. M. (1999). William James' theory of emotions: Filling in the picture. *Journal for the Theory of Social Behaviour, 29,* 251–266.

Barbara, J. G. (2007). Louis Ranvier (1835–1922): The contribution of microscopy to physiology and the renewal of French general anatomy. *Journal of the History of the Neurosciences, 16,* 413–431.

Barber, T. X. (2000). A deeper understanding of hypnosis: Its secrets, its nature, its essence. *American Journal of Clinical Hypnosis, 42,* 208–272.

Barbut, M. (1993). Comments on a pseudo-mathematical model in social psychology. *European Journal of Social Psychology, 23,* 203–210.

Barclay, N. L. & Gregory, A. M. (2013). Quantitative genetic research on sleep: A review of normal sleep, sleep disturbances and associated emotional, behavioural, and health-related difficulties. *Sleep Medicine Reviews, 17,* 29–40.

Bard, P. (1934). On emotional experience after decortication with some remarks on theoretical views. *Psychological Review, 41,* 309–329.

Bargh, J. A. (1992). The ecology of automaticity: Toward establishing the conditions needed to produce automatic processing effects. *American Journal of Psychology, 105,* 181–199.

Baribeau-Braun, J., Picton, T. W., & Gosselin, J. Y. (1983). Schizophrenia: A neuropsychological evaluation of abnormal information processing. *Science, 219,* 874–876.

Barker, L. (2006). Teaching evolutionary psychology: An interview with David M. Buss. *Teaching of Psychology, 33,* 69–76.

Barker, M. E., Thompson, K. A., & McClean, S. I. (1996). Do type As eat differently? A comparison of men and women. *Appetite, 26,* 277–286.

Barker, R. A., Barrett, J. B., Mason, S. L., & Björklund, A. (2013). Fetal dopaminergic transplantation trials and the future of neural grafting in Parkinson's disease. *Lancet Neurology, 12,* 84–91.

Barker-Collo, S., Read, J., & Cowie, S. (2012). Coping strategies in female survivors of childhood sexual abuse from two Canadian and two New Zealand cultural groups. *Journal of Trauma & Dissociation, 13,* 435–447.

Barnes, M. L., & Rosenthal, R. (1985). Interpersonal effects of experimenter attractiveness, attire, and gender. *Journal of Personality and Social Psychology, 48,* 435–446.

Barnes, R. C. (2000). Viktor Frankl's logotherapy: Spirituality and meaning in the new millennium. *TCA Journal, 28,* 24–31.

Barnett, L. B., & Corazza, L. (1998). Identification of mathematical talent and programmatic efforts to facilitate development of talent. *European Journal for Higher Ability, 9,* 48–61.

Barnett, Z. L., Robleda-Gomez, S., & Pachana, N. A. (2011). Viagra: The little blue pill with big repercussions. *Aging & Mental Health, 16,* 84–88.

Barrault, S., & Varescon, I. (2013). Impulsive sensation seeking and gambling practice among a sample of online poker players: Comparison between non pathological, problem, and pathological gamblers. *Personality and Individual Differences, 55,* 502–507.

Barrett, P. T., Daum, I., & Eysenck, H. J. (1990). Sensory nerve conduction and intelligence: A methodological study. *Journal of Psychophysiology, 4,* 1–13.

Barrowclough, C., Tarrier, N., Humphreys, L., Ward, G. L., & Andrews, B. (2003). Self-esteem in schizophrenia: Relationships between self-evaluation, family attitudes, and symptomatology. *Journal of Abnormal Psychology, 112,* 92–99.

Barry, T. D., Lochman, J. E., Fite, P. J., Wells, K. C., & Colder, C. R. (2012). The influence of neighborhood characteristics and parenting practices on academic problems and aggression outcomes among moderately to highly aggressive children. *Journal of Community Psychology, 40,* 372–379.

Bartholomew, D. J. (1995). Spearman and the origin and development of factor analysis. *British Journal of Mathematical and Statistical Psychology, 48,* 211–220.

Bartholomew, R. E., & Radford, B. (2003). *Hoaxes, myths, and manias: Why we need critical thinking.* Amherst, NY: Prometheus.

Bartlett, F. C. (1932). *Remembering: A study in experimental and social psychology.* Cambridge, England: Cambridge University Press.

Bartoshuk, L. M. (1991). Sensory factors in eating behavior. *Bulletin of the Psychonomic Society, 29,* 250–255.

Bartoshuk, L. M., & Beauchamp, G. K. (1994). Chemical senses. *Annual Review of Psychology, 45,* 419–449.

Bartoshuk, L. M., Cain, W. S., & Pfaffmann, C. (1985). Taste and olfaction. In G. A. Kimble & K. Schlesinger (Eds.), *Topics in the history of psychology* (Vol. 1, pp. 221–260). Hillsdale, NJ: Erlbaum.

Bartsch, R. A., Judd, C. M., Louw, D. A., Park, B., & Ryan, C. S. (1997). Cross-national outgroup homogeneity: United States and South African stereotypes. *South African Journal of Psychology, 27,* 166–170.

Bartussek, D., Becker, G., Diedrich, O., & Naumann, E. (1996). Extraversion, neuroticism, and event-related brain potentials in response to emotional stimuli. *Personality and Individual Differences, 20,* 301–312.

Basadur, S., Wakabayashi, M., & Takai, J. (1992). Training effects on the divergent thinking attitudes of Japanese managers. *International Journal of Intercultural Relations, 16,* 329–345.

Bassili, J. N. (2003). The minority slowness effect: Subtle inhibitions in the expression of views not shared by others. *Journal of Personality and Social Psychology, 84,* 261–276.

Bassilios, B., Reifels, L., & Pirkis, J. (2012). Enhanced primary mental health services in response to disaster. *Psychiatric Services, 63,* 868–874.

Bassuk, E. L. (1984, July). The homelessness problem. *Scientific American,* pp. 40–45.

Batson, C. D., Ahmad, N., Yin, J., Bedell, S. J., Johnson, J. W., Templin, C. M., & Whiteside, A. (1999).

Two threats to the common good: Self-interested egoism and empathy and empathy-induced altruism. *Personality and Social Psychology Bulletin, 25,* 3–16.

Batson, C. D., Batson, J. G., Griffitt, C. A., Barrientos, S., Brandt, J. R., Sprengelmeyer, P., & Bayly, M. J. (1989). Negative-state relief and the empathy-altruism hypothesis. *Journal of Personality and Social Psychology, 56,* 922–933.

Batson, C. D., Bolen, M. H., Cross, J. A., & Neuringer-Benefiel, H. E. (1986). Where is the altruism in the altruistic personality? *Journal of Personality and Social Psychology, 50,* 212–220.

Bauer, D. G. (2005). Review of the endocrine system. *Medsurg Nursing, 14,* 335–337.

Bauer, M., Cassar, A., Chytilová, J., & Heinrich, J. (2014). War's enduring effects on the development of egalitarian motivations and in-group biases. *Psychological Science, 25,* 47–57.

Bauer, M. N., Leenaars, A. A., Berman, A. L., Jobes, D. A., Dixon, J. F., & Bibb, J. L. (1997). Late adulthood suicide: A life-span analysis of suicide notes. *Archives of Suicide Research, 3,* 91–108.

Bauer, P. J., Stennes, L., & Haight, J. C. (2003). Representation of the inner self in autobiography: Women's and men's use of internal states language in personal narratives. *Memory, 11,* 27–42.

Bauer, S. M., Schanda, H., Karakula, H., Olajossy-Hilkesberger, L., Rudaleviciene, P., Okribelashvili, N., . . . Stompe, T. (2011). Culture and the prevalence of hallucinations in schizophrenia. *Comprehensive Psychiatry, 52,* 319–325.

Baum, A., Grunberg, N. E., & Singer, J. E. (1992). Biochemical measurements in the study of emotion. *Psychological Science, 3,* 56–60.

Bauman, K. E., Carver, K., & Gleiter, K. (2001). Trends in parent and friend influence during adolescence. The case of adolescent cigarette smoking. *Addictive Behaviors, 26,* 349–361.

Bauman, M. L., & Kemper, T. L. (2005). Neuroanatomic observations of the brain in autism: A review and future directions. *International Journal of Developmental Neuroscience, 23,* 183–187.

Baumeister, A. A. (1998). Intelligence and the "personal equation." *Intelligence, 26,* 255–265.

Baumeister, R. F. (1982). A self-presentational view of social phenomena. *Psychological Bulletin, 91,* 3–26.

Baumeister, R. F. (1984). Choking under pressure: Self-consciousness and paradoxical effects of incentives on skillful performance. *Journal of Personality and Social Psychology, 46,* 610–620.

Baumeister, R. F. (1988). Should we stop studying sex differences altogether? *American Psychologist, 43,* 1092–1095.

Baumeister, R. F. (1990). Suicide as escape from self. *Psychological Review, 97,* 90–113.

Baumeister, R. F. (2000). Gender differences in erotic plasticity: The female sex drive as socially flexible and responsive. *Psychological Bulletin, 126,* 347–374.

Baumeister, R. F., & Bratslavsky, E. (1999). Passion, intimacy, and time: Passionate love as a function of change in intimacy. *Personality and Social Psychology Review, 3,* 49–67.

Baumeister, R. F., Campbell, J. D., Krueger, J. I., & Vohs, K. D. (2003). Does high self-esteem cause better performance, interpersonal success, happiness, or healthier lifestyles? *Psychological Science in the Public Interest, 4,* 1–44.

Baumeister, R. F., Catanese, K. R., Vohs, K. D. (2001). Is there a gender difference in strength of sex drive? Theoretical views, conceptual distinctions, and a review of relevant evidence. *Personality and Social Psychology Bulletin, 5,* 242–273.

Baumeister, R. F., Dale, K., & Sommer, K. L. (1998). Freudian defense mechanisms and empirical findings in modern social psychology: Reaction formation, projection, displacement, undoing, isolation, sublimation, and denial. *Journal of Personality, 66,* 1081–1124.

Baumrind, D. (1964). Some thoughts on ethics of research: After reading Milgram's "Behavioral Study of Obedience." *American Psychologist, 19,* 421–423.

Baumrind, D. (1966). Effects of authoritative control on child behavior. *Child Development, 37,* 887–907.

Baumrind, D. (1983). Rejoinder to Lewis's reinterpretation of parental firm control effects: Are authoritative families really harmonious? *Psychological Bulletin, 94,* 132–142.

Baumrind, D. (1985). Research using intentional deception: Ethical issues revisited. *American Psychologist, 40,* 165–174.

Baumrind, D. (2010). Differentiating being confrontive and coercive kinds of parental power–assertive disciplinary practices. *Human Development, 55,* 35–51.

Bavelier, D., Corina, D., Jezzard, P., Clark, V., Karni, A., Lalwani, A., . . . Neville, H. J. (1998). Hemispheric specialization for English and ASL: Left invariance–right variability. *Neuroreport, 9,* 1537–1542.

Baxter, J., Tridgell, A., & Weaver, L. (2000). Learning to play chess using temporal differences. *Machine Learning, 40,* 243–263.

Baxter, P. J., Bonadonna, C., Dupree, R., Hards, D. L., Kohn, S. C., Murphy, M. D., . . . Vickers, B. P. (1999). Cristobalite in volcanic ash of the Soufriere Hills volcano, Montserrat, British West Indies. *Science, 19,* 1142–1145.

Bayley, N. (1955). On the growth of intelligence. *American Psychologist, 10,* 805–818.

Bayton, J. A. (1975). Francis Sumner, Max Meenes, and the training of black psychologists. *American Psychologist, 30,* 185–186.

Beal, C. R., Schmitt, K. L., & Dekle, D. J. (1995). Eyewitness identification of children: Effects of absolute judgments, nonverbal response options, and event encoding. *Law and Human Behavior, 19,* 197–216.

Beatty, M. J., Heisel, A. D., Hall, A. E., Levine, T. R., & LaFrance, B. H. (2002). What can we learn from the study of twins about genetic and environmental influences on interpersonal affiliation, aggressiveness, and social anxiety? A meta-analytic study. *Communication Monographs, 69,* 1–18.

Beatty, W. W. (1984). Discriminating drunkenness: A replication. *Bulletin of the Psychonomic Society, 22,* 431–432.

Beaver, K. M., Vaughn, M. G., DeLisi, M., & Wright, J. P. (2008). Anabolic-androgenic steroid use and involvement in violent behavior in a nationally representative sample of you adult males in the United States. *American Journal of Public Health, 98,* 2185–2187.

Becht, M. C., & Vingerhoets, J. J. M. (2002). Crying and mood change: A cross-cultural study. *Cognition and Emotion, 16,* 87–101.

Beck, A. T. (1967). *Depression: Clinical, experimental and theoretical aspects.* New York: Harper & Row.

Beck, A. T. (1997). The past and future of cognitive therapy. *Journal of Psychotherapy Practice and Research, 6,* 276–284.

Beck, A. T. (2002). Cognitive patterns in dreams and daydreams. *Journal of Cognitive Psychotherapy, 16,* 23–28.

Beck, A. T., & Rector, N. A. (2003). A cognitive model of hallucinations. *Cognitive Therapy and Research, 27,* 19–52.

Becker, A. E., Burwell, R. A., Herzog, D. B., Hamburg, P., & Gilman, S. E. (2002). Eating behaviors and attitudes following prolonged exposure to television among ethnic Fijian adolescent girls. *British Journal of Psychiatry, 180,* 509–514.

Becker, J. B., Curran, E. J., & Freed, W. J. (1990). Adrenal medulla graft-induced recovery of function in an animal model of Parkinson's disease: Possible mechanisms of action. *Canadian Journal of Psychology, 44,* 293–310.

Becker, P. (1999). Beyond the Big Five. *Personality and Individual Differences, 26,* 511–530.

Becona, E., & Garcia, M. P. (1993). Nicotine fading and smoke-holding methods to smoking cessation. *Psychological Reports, 73,* 779–786.

Beebe, L. H., & Smith, K. (2010). Informed consent to research in persons with schizophrenia spectrum disorders. *Nursing Ethics, 17,* 425–434.

Beer, J. M., Arnold, R. D., & Loehlin, J. C. (1998). Genetic and environmental influences on MMPI factor scales: Joint model fitting to twin and adoption data. *Journal of Personality and Social Psychology, 74,* 818–827.

Beers, C. W. (1908/1970). *A mind that found itself.* New York: Doubleday. Begley, S., & Hager, M. (1993, July 26). Does DNA make some men gay? *Newsweek,* p. 59.

Behnke, S. H. (1999). O'Connor v. Donaldson: Retelling a classic and finding some revisionist history. *Journal of the American Academy of Psychiatry and the Law, 27,* 115–126.

Behrend, D. A. (1988). Overextensions in early language comprehension: Evidence from a signal detection approach. *Journal of Child Language, 15,* 63–75.

Behrens, R. R. (2003). Thinking outside of the box: On Karl Duncker, functional fixedness, and the adaptive value of engaging in purposely deviant acts. *Gestalt Theory, 25,* 63–70.

Behrmann, M., & Kimchi, R. (2003). What does visual agnosia tell us about perceptual organization and its relationship to object perception? *Journal of Experimental Psychology: Human Perception and Performance, 29,* 19–42.

Beijersbergen, M. D., Juffer, F., Bakermans-Kranengurb, M. J., & van IJzendoorn, M. H. (2012). Remaining or becoming secure: Parental sensitive support predicts attachment continuity from infancy to adolescence in a longitudinal adoption study. *Developmental Psychology, 48,* 1277–1282.

Beiser, M., Shore, J. H., Peters, R., & Tatum, W. (1985). Does community care for the mentally ill make a difference? A tale of two cities. *American Journal of Psychiatry, 142,* 1047–1052.

Bekoff, M., Gruen, L., Townsend, S. E., & Rollin, B. E. (1992). Animals in science: Some areas revisited. *Animal Behaviour, 44,* 473–484.

Beleza-Meireles, A., & Al-Chalabi, A. (2009). Genetic studies of amyotrophic lateral sclerosis: Controversies and perspectives. *Amyotrophic Lateral Sclerosis, 10,* 1–14.

Belisle, M., Roskies, E., & Levesque, J. M. (1987). Improving adherence to physical activity. *Health Psychology, 6,* 159–172.

Bell, A. P., Weinberg, M. S., & Hammersmith, S. J. (1981). *Sexual preference: Its development in men and women.* Bloomington: Indiana University Press.

Bellisle, F. (1999). Glutamate and the Umami taste: Sensory, metabolic, nutritional and behavioural considerations. A review of the literature published in the last 10 years. *Neuroscience and Biobehavioral Reviews, 23,* 423–438.

Belmont, L., & Marolla, F. A. (1973). Birth order, family size, and intelligence. *Science, 182,* 1096–1101.

Belsky, J. (1988). The "effects" of infant day care reconsidered. *Early Childhood Research Quarterly, 3,* 235–272.

Belsky, J., & Hsieh, K. H. (1998). Patterns of marital change during the early childhood years: Parent personality, coparenting, and division-of-labor correlates. *Journal of Family Psychology, 12,* 511–528.

Belsky, J., & Pluess, M. (2009). The nature (and nurture?) of plasticity in early human development. *Perspectives on Psychological Science, 4,* 345–351.

Bem, D. J. (1967). Self-perception: An alternative interpretation of cognitive dissonance phenomena. *Psychological Review, 74,* 183–200.

Bem, D. J. (2000). Exotic becomes erotic: Interpreting the biological correlates of sexual orientation. *Archives of Sexual Behavior, 29,* 531–548.

Bem, D. J., & Allen, A. (1974). On predicting some of the people some of the time: The search for cross-situational consistencies in behavior. *Psychological Review, 81,* 506–520.

Bem, D. J., & Honorton, C. (1994). Does psi exist? Replicable evidence for an anomalous process of information transfer. *Psychological Bulletin, 115,* 4–18.

Bem, S. L. (1981). Gender schema theory: A cognitive account of sex typing. *Psychological Review, 88,* 354–364.

Benbow, C. P. (1988). Sex differences in mathematical reasoning ability in intellectually talented preadolescents: Their nature, effect, and possible causes. *Behavioral and Brain Sciences, 11,* 169–232.

Benbow, C. P., & Stanley, J. C. (1983). Sex differences in mathematical reasoning ability: More facts. *Science, 222,* 1029–1031.

Benbow, C. P., Lubinski, D., Shea, D. L., & Eftekhari-Sanjani, H. (2000). Sex differences in mathematical reasoning ability at age 13: Their status 20 years later. *Psychological Science, 11,* 474–480.

Bender, S. L., Ponton, L. E., Crittenden, M. R., & Word, C. O. (1995). For underprivileged children, standardized intelligence testing can do more harm than good: Reply. *Journal of Developmental and Behavioral Pediatrics, 16,* 428–430.

Benham, B. (2008). The ubiquity of deception and the ethics of deceptive research. *Bioethics, 22,* 147–156.

Benjamin, A. S., & Tullis, J. (2010). What makes distributed practice effective? *Cognitive Psychology, 61,* 228–247.

Benjamin, J., Ebstein, R. P., & Belmaker, R. H. (1997). Personality genetics. *Israel Journal of Psychiatry and Related Sciences, 34,* 270–280.

Benjamin, L. T., Jr. (1988). A history of teaching machines. *American Psychologist, 43,* 703–712.

Benjamin, L. T., Jr. (2002). Marion White McPherson (1919–2000). *American Psychologist, 57,* 62.

Benjamin, L. T., Jr., & Crouse, E. M. (2002). The American Psychological Association's response to *Brown v. Board of Education*: The case of Kenneth B. Clark. *American Psychologist, 57,* 38–50.

Benjamin, L. T., Jr., & Nielsen-Gammon, E. (1999). B. F. Skinner and psychotechnology: The case of the heir conditioner. *Review of General Psychology, 3,* 155–167.

Benjamin, L. T., Jr., & Shields, S. A. (1990). Leta Stetter Hollingworth (1886–1939). In A. N. O'Connell & N. F. Russo (Eds.), *Women in psychology: A bio-bibliographic sourcebook* (pp. 173–183). New York: Greenwood Press.

Benjamin, L. T., Jr., Durkin, M., Link, M., Vestal, M., & Acord, J. (1992). Wundt's American doctoral students. *American Psychologist, 47,* 123–131.

Benjamin, L. T., Jr., Henry, K. D., & McMahon, L. R. (2005). Inez Beverly Prosser and the education of African Americans. *Journal of the History of the Behavioral Sciences, 41,* 43–62.

Bennett, D. S., Bendersky, M., & Lewis, M. (2002). Facial expressivity at 4 months: A context by expression analysis. *Infancy, 3,* 97–113.

Bennett, W., & Gurin, J. (1982). *The dieter's dilemma.* New York: Basic Books.

Ben-Shakhar, G., & Dolev, K. (1996). Psychophysiological detection through the guilty knowledge technique: Effect of mental countermeasures. *Journal of Applied Psychology, 81,* 273–281.

Ben-Shakhar, G., & Elaad, E. (2003). The validity of psychophysiological detection of information with the Guilty Knowledge Test: A meta-analytic review. *Journal of Applied Psychology, 88,* 131–151.

Ben-Shakhar, G., Gronau, N., & Elaad, E. (1999). Leakage of relevant information to innocent examinees in the GKT: An attempt to reduce false-positive outcomes by introducing target stimuli. *Journal of Applied Psychology, 84,* 651–660.

Ben-Shlomo, Y., Smith, G. D., Shipley, M., & Marmot, M. G. (1993). Magnitude and causes of mortality differences between married and unmarried men. *Journal of Epidemiology and Community Health, 47,* 200–205.

Bentall, R. P., & Pilgrim, D. (1993). Thomas Szasz, "crazy talk" and the myth of mental illness. *British Journal of Medical Psychology, 66,* 69–76.

Benton, D., Owens, D. S., & Parker, P. Y. (1994). Blood glucose influences memory and attention in young adults. *Neuropsychologia, 32,* 595–607.

Benton, T. R., Ross, D. F., Bradshaw, E., Thomas, W. N., & Bradshaw, G. S. (2006). Eyewitness memory is still not common sense: Comparing jurors, judges and law enforcement to Eyewitness experts. *Applied Cognitive Psychology, 20,* 115–129.

Berenbaum, S. A., & Hines, M. (1992). Early androgens are related to childhood sex-typed toy preferences. *Psychological Science, 3,* 203–206.

Berg, J. H. (1984). Development of friendship between roommates. *Journal of Personality and Social Psychology, 46,* 346–356.

Berg, J. H., & McQuinn, R. D. (1986). Attraction and exchange in continuing and noncontinuing dating relationships. *Journal of Personality and Social Psychology, 50,* 942–952.

Berger, A. A. (1987). Humor: An introduction. *American Behavioral Scientist, 30,* 6–15.

Berger, R. E., & Persinger, M. A. (1991). Geophysical variables and behavior: LXVII. Quieter annual geomagnetic activity and larger effect size for experimental psi (ESP) studies over six decades. *Perceptual and Motor Skills, 73,* 1219–1223.

Berger, R. J., & Phillips, N. H. (1995). Energy conservation and sleep. *Brain Research, 69,* 65–73.

Bergeron, S. M., & Senn, C. Y. (1998). Body image and sociocultural norms: A comparison of heterosexual and lesbian women. *Psychology of Women Quarterly, 22,* 385–401.

Bergin, A. E., & Lambert, E. (1978). The evaluation of therapeutic outcome. In S. L. Garfield & A. E. Bergin (Eds.), *Handbook of psychotherapy and behavior change* (pp. 139–189). New York: Wiley.

Berk, M., Sanders, K. M., Pasco, J. A., Jacka, F. N., Williams, L. J., Hayles, A. L., & Dodd, S. (2007). Vitamin D deficiency may play a role in depression. *Medical Hypotheses, 69,* 1316–1319.

Berk, M., Terre-Blanche, M. J., Maude, C., & Lucas, M. D. (1996). Season of birth and schizophrenia: Southern hemisphere data. *Australian and New Zealand Journal of Psychiatry, 30,* 220–222.

Berko, J. (1958). The child's learning of English morphology. *Word, 14,* 150–177.

Berkowitz, L. (1974). Some determinants of impulsive aggression. *Psychological Review, 81,* 165–176.

Berkowitz, L. (1989). Frustration-aggression hypothesis: Examination and reformulation. *Psychological Bulletin, 106,* 59–73.

Berkowitz, L., & LePage, A. (1967). Weapons as aggression-eliciting stimuli. *Journal of Personality and Social Psychology, 7,* 202–207.

Berkowitz, M. W., Mueller, C. W., Schnell, S. V., & Padberg, U. (1986). Moral reasoning and judgments of aggression. *Journal of Personality and Social Psychology, 51,* 885–891.

Berlucchi, G. (2006). Revisiting the 1981 Nobel Prize to Roger Sperry, David Hubel, and Torsten Wiesel on the occasion of the centennial of the prize to Golgi and Cajal. *Journal of the History of the Behavioral Sciences, 15,* 369–375.

Bernard, J. L. (1977). The significance for psychology of *O'Connor v. Donaldson. American Psychologist, 32,* 1085–1088.

Berndt, T. J., & Hoyles, S. G. (1985). Stability and change in childhood and adolescent friendships. *Developmental Psychology, 21,* 1007–1015.

Berne, E. (1964). *Games people play.* New York: Grove Press.

Bernier, M.-J., Hébert, M., & Collin-Vézina, D. (2013). Dissociative symptoms over a year in a sample of sexually abused children. *Journal of Trauma & Dissociation, 14,* 455–472.

Berninger, V. W. (1988). Development of operational thought without a normal sensorimotor stage. *Intelligence, 12,* 219–230.

Bernstein, I. L. (1978). Learned taste aversions in children receiving chemotherapy. *Science, 200,* 1302–1303.

Bernstein, I. L. (1991). Aversion conditioning in response to cancer and cancer treatment. *Clinical Psychology Review, 11,* 185–191.

Bernstein, W. M., Stephan, W. G., & Davis, M. H. (1979). Explaining attributions for achievement: A path-analytic approach. *Journal of Personality and Social Psychology, 37,* 1810–1821.

Berry, J. W., & Kalin, R. (1995). Multicultural and ethnic attitudes in Canada: An overview of the 1991 national survey. *Canadian Journal of Behavioural Science, 27,* 301–320.

Bersagliere, A., & Achermann, P. (2010). Slow oscillations in human non-rapid eye movement sleep electroencephalogram: Effects of increased sleep pressure. *Journal of Sleep Research, 19,* 228–237.

Berscheid, E., & Walster, E. (1974). A little bit about love. In T. L. Houston (Ed.), *Foundations of interpersonal attraction.* (pp. 356–382). New York: Academic Press.

Bertelli, J. A., Orsal, D., & Mira, J. C. (1994). Median-nerve neurotization by peripheral nerve grafts directly implanted into the spinal cord: Anatomical, behavioral, and electrophysiological evidences of sensorimotor recovery. *Brain Research, 644,* 150–159.

Best, C. T., & Avery, R. A. (2000). Left-hemisphere advantage for click consonants is determined by linguistic significance and experience. *Psychological Science, 10,* 65–70.

Beutler, L. E., & Consoli, A. J. (1993). Matching the therapist's interpersonal stance to clients' characteristics: Contributions from systematic eclectic psychotherapy. *Psychotherapy, 30,* 417–422.

Bexton, W. H., Heron, W., & Scott, T. H. (1954). Effects of decreased variation in the sensory environment. *Canadian Journal of Psychology, 8,* 70–76.

Biafora, F. (1995). Cross-cultural perspective on illness and wellness: Implications for depression. *Journal of Social Distress and the Homeless, 4,* 105–129.

Bianchi, S. M. (1995). The changing demographic and socioeconomic characteristics of single parent families. *Marriage and Family Review, 20,* 71–97.

Bidzan, L., Mahableshwarkar, A. R., Jacobsen, P., Yan, M., & Sheehan, D. B. (2012). Vortioxetine (Lu AA21004) in generalized anxiety disorder: Results of an 8-week multinational, randomized, double-blind, placebo-controlled clinical trial. *European Neuropsychopharmacology, 22,* 847–857.

Binder, J. R., Rao, S. M., Hammeke, T. A., & Yetkin, F. Z. (1994). Functional magnetic resonance imaging of human auditory cortex. *Annals of Neurology, 35,* 662–672.

Binsted, G., & Elliott, D. (1999). The Mueller-Lyer illusion as a perturbation to the saccadic system. *Human Movement Science, 18,* 103–117.

Birch, D. E. (1992). Duty to protect: Update and Canadian perspective. *Canadian Psychology, 33,* 94–104.

Birch, J. (1997). Efficiency of the Ishihara test for identifying red-green colour deficiency. *Ophthalmic and Physiological Optics, 17,* 403–408.

Birchall, H. M. (1995). Reporting experiences of panic: Sex differences in a community sample. *Journal of Community and Applied Social Psychology, 5,* 167–172.

Bird, S. (2011). Effects of distributed practice on the acquisition of second language English syntax. *Applied Psycholinguistics, 32,* 437–452.

Birdsong, D., & Molis, M. (2001). On the evidence for maturational constraints in second-language acquisition. *Journal of Memory and Language, 44,* 235–249.

Bishop, D. V. M. (1990). *Handedness and developmental disorder.* Oxford, England: Mac Keith Press.

Bishop, D. V. M. (2001). Individual differences in handedness and specific speech and language impairment: Evidence against a genetic link. *Behavior Genetics, 31,* 339–351.

Bitgood, S. C. (2002). Environmental psychology in museums, zoos, and other exhibition centers. In R. B. Bechtel & A. Churchman (Eds.), *Handbook of environmental psychology* (pp. 461–480). New York: Wiley.

Bjork, D. W. (1988). *William James: The center of his vision.* New York: Columbia University Press.

Bjork, E. L., & Cummings, E. M. (1984). Infant search errors: Stage of concept development or stage of memory development. *Memory and Cognition, 12,* 1–19.

Bjorklund, D. F., & Buchanan, J. J. (1989). Developmental and knowledge-based differences in the acquisition and extension of a memory strategy. *Journal of Experimental Child Psychology, 48,* 451–471.

Bjorkqvist, K., Nygren, T., Bjorklund, A.-C., Bjorkqvist, S.-E. (1994). Testosterone intake and aggressiveness: Real effect or anticipation? *Aggressive Behavior, 20,* 17–26.

Bjorvatn, B., Grønli, J., & Pallesen, S. (2010). Prevalence of different parasomnias in the general population. *Sleep Medicine, 11,* 1031–1034.

Black, B., Herr, K., Fine, P., Sanders, S., Tang, X., Bergen–Jackson, K., Titler, M., & Forcucci, C. (2011). The relationships among pain, nonpain symptoms, and quality of life measures in older adults with cancer receiving hospice care. *Pain Medicine, 12,* 880–889.

Black, D. S., Cole, S. W., Irwin, M. R., Breen, E., St Cyr, N. M., Nazarian, N., Lavretsky, H. (2013). Yogic meditation reverses NF-Kb and IRF-related transcriptome dynamics in leukocytes of family dementia caregivers in a randomized controlled trial. *Psychoneuroendocrinology, 38,* 348–355.

Black, J. E., Isaacs, K. R., & Greenough, W. T. (1991). Usual vs. successful aging: Some notes on experiential factors. *Neurobiology of Aging, 12,* 325–328.

Blackford, J. U., Allen, A. H., Cowan, R. L., & Avery, S. N. (2013). Amygdala and hippocampus fail to habituate to faces in individuals with an inhibited temperament. *Social Cognitive and Affective Neuroscience, 8,* 143–150.

Blair, M. E., & Shimp, T. A. (1992). Consequences of an unpleasant experience with music: A second-order negative conditioning perspective. *Journal of Advertising, 21,* 35–43.

Blaisdell, A. P., Gunther, L. M., & Miller, R. R. (1999). Recovery from blocking achieved by extinguishing the blocking CS. *Animal Learning and Behavior, 27,* 63–76.

Blakemore, C. (1977). *Mechanics of the mind.* New York: Cambridge University Press.

Blakemore, C., & Cooper, G. F. (1970). Development of the brain depends on the visual environment. *Nature, 228,* 477–478.

Blanchard, J. J., Kring, A. M., & Neale, J. M. (1994). Flat affect in schizophrenia: A test of neuropsychological models. *Schizophrenia Bulletin, 20,* 311–325.

Blanchard, R., & Ellis, L. (2001). Birth weight, sexual orientation and the sex of preceding siblings. *Journal of Biosocial Science, 33,* 451–467.

Blanchard, R., Zucker, K. J., Siegelman, M., Dickey, R., & Klassen, P. (1998). The relation of birth order to sexual orientation in men and women. *Journal of Biosocial Science, 30,* 511–519.

Blanco-Centurion, C. A., & Salin-Pascual, R. J. (2001). Extracellular serotonin levels in the medullary reticular formation during normal sleep and after REM sleep deprivation. *Brain Research, 923,* 128–136.

Blaney, P. H. (1986). Affect and memory: A review. *Psychological Bulletin, 99,* 229–246.

Blankfield, R. P. (1991). Suggestion, relaxation, and hypnosis as adjuncts in the care of surgery patients: A review of the literature. *American Journal of Clinical Hypnosis, 33,* 172–186.

Blanton, H., & Jaccard, J. (2008). Representing versus generalizing: two approaches to external validity and their implications for the study of prejudice. *Psychological Inquiry, 19,* 99–105.

Blascovich, J., Spencer, S. J., Quinn, D., & Steele, C. (2001). African Americans and high blood pressure: The role of stereotype threat. *Psychological Science, 12,* 225–229.

Blasczyk-Schiep, S., Kazén, M., Kuhl, J., & Grygielski, M. (2011). Appraisal of suicidal risk among adolescents and young adults through the Rorschach Test. *Journal of Personality Assessment, 95,* 518–526.

Blass, T. (1999). The Milgram Paradigm after 35 years: Some things we now know about obedience to authority. *Journal of Applied Social Psychology, 29,* 955–978.

Blatt, I., Peled, R., Gadoth, N., & Lavie, P. (1991). The value of sleep recording in evaluating somnambulism in young adults. *Electroencephalography and Clinical Neurophysiology, 78,* 407–412.

Blazer, D. G., Kessler, R. C., & Swartz, M. S. (1998). Epidemiology of recurrent major and minor depression with a seasonal pattern: The National Comorbidity Survey. *British Journal of Psychiatry, 172,* 164–167.

Bleichrodt, N., Hoksbergen, R. A. C., & Khire, U. (1999). Cross-cultural testing of intelligence. *Cross-Cultural Research: The Journal of Comparative Social Science, 33,* 3–25.

Bliem, H. R., & Danek, A. (1999). Direct evidence for a consistent dissociation between structural facial discrimination and facial individuation in prosopagnosia. *Brain and Cognition, 40,* 48–52.

Blix, G. G., & Blix, A. G. (1995). The role of exercise in weight loss. *Behavioral Medicine, 21,* 31–39.

Blizard, R. A. (1997). The origins of dissociative identity disorder from an object relations and attachment theory perspective. *Dissociation: Progress in the Dissociative Disorders, 10,* 223–229.

Bloom, R., Przekop, A., & Sanger, T. D. (2010). Prolonged electromyogram biofeedback improves upper extremity function in children with cerebral palsy. *Journal of Child Neurology, 25,* 1480–1484.

Blume, H. K., Brockman, L. N, & Bruener, C. C. (2012). Biofeedback therapy for pediatric headache: Factors associated with response. *Headache: The Journal of Head and Face Pain, 52,* 1377–1386.

Blume-Marcovici, A. (2010). Gender differences in dreams: Applications to dream work with male clients. *Dreaming, 20,* 199–210.

Boake, C. (2002). From the Binet-Simon to the Wechsler-Bellevue: Tracing the history of intelligence testing. *Journal of Clinical and Experimental Neuropsychology, 24,* 383–405.

Boatwright, K., & Nolan, B. (2005). *Campaign for Mary Whiton Calkins: Update.* Paper presented at the Association of Women in Psychology National Conference, Tampa, FL.

Boddington, S. J., & Lavender, A. (1995). Treatment models for couples therapy: A review of the outcome literature and the Dodo's verdict. *Sexual and Marital Therapy, 10,* 69–81.

Bogaert, A. F., & Hershberger, S. (1999). The relation between sexual orientation and penile size. *Archives of Sexual Behavior, 28,* 213–221.

Bohannon, J. N., III, & Stanowicz, L. (1988). The issue of negative evidence: Adult responses to children's language errors. *Developmental Psychology, 24,* 684–689.

Bohart, A. C., O'Hara, M., & Leitner, L. M. (1998). Empirically violated treatments: Disenfranchisement of humanistic and other psychotherapies. *Psychotherapy Research, 8,* 141–157.

Bohner, G., Einwiller, S., Erb, H.-P., & Siebler, F. (2003). When small means comfortable: Relations between product attributes in two-sided advertising. *Journal of Consumer Psychology, 13,* 454–463.

Bolm-Audorff, U., Schwammle, J., Ehlenz, K., & Kaffarnik, H. (1989). Plasma level of catecholamines and lipids when speaking before an audience. *Work and Stress, 3,* 249–253.

Bolsover, S., Fabes, J., & Anderson, P. N. (2008). Axonal guidance molecules and the failure of axonal regeneration in the adult mammalian spinal cord. *Restorative Neurology and Neuroscience 26,* 117–130.

Bolte, S., & Poustka, F. (2004). Comparing the profiles of savant and non-savant individuals with autistic disorder. *Intelligence, 32,* 121–131.

Bolton, P., Macdonald, H., Pickles, A., Rios, P., Goode, S., Crowson, M., Bailey, A., & Rutter, M. (1994). A case-control family history study of autism. *Journal of Child Psychology and Psychiatry 35,* 877–900.

Bond, C. F., Jr., & Titus, L. J. (1983). Social facilitation: A meta-analysis of 241 studies. *Psychological Bulletin, 94,* 265–292.

Bond, R., & Smith, P. B. (1996). Culture and conformity: A meta-analysis of studies using Asch's (1952b, 1956) line judgment task. *Psychological Bulletin, 119,* 111–137.

Bonds, D. R., & Crosby, L. O. (1986). "An adoption study of human obesity": Comment. *New England Journal of Medicine, 315,* 128.

Boneau, C. A. (1974). Paradigm regained? Cognitive behaviorism revisited. *American Psychologist, 29,* 297–309.

Boneva, B., Frieze, I. H., Ferligoj, A., Pauknerova, D., & Orgocka, A. (1998). Achievement, power, and affiliation motive as clues to (e) migration desires: A four-countries comparison. *European Psychologist, 3,* 247–254.

Boniecki, K. A., & Moore, S. (2003). Breaking the silence: Using a token economy to reinforce classroom participation. *Teaching of Psychology, 30,* 224–227.

Bonilla, C., Zurita, M., Otero, L., Aguayo, C., & Vaquero, J. (2009). Delayed intralesional transplantation of bone marrow stromal cells increases endogenous neurogenesis and promotes functional recovery after severe traumatic brain injury. *Brain Injury, 23,* 760–769.

Bonnefond, A., Muzet, A., Winter-Dill, A. S., Bailloeuil, C., Bitouze, F., & Bonneau, A. (2001). Innovative working schedule: Introducing one short nap during the night shift. *Ergonomics, 44,* 937–945.

Book, A. S., Starzyk, K. B., & Quinsey, V. L. (2001). The relationship between testosterone and aggression: A meta-analysis. *Aggression and Violent Behavior, 6,* 579–599.

Boone, L., Soenens, B., Vansteenkiste, M., & Braet, C. (2012). Is there a perfectionist in each of us? An experimental study on perfectionism and eating disorder symptoms. *Appetite, 59,* 531–540.

Boone, R. T., & Cunningham, J. G. (1998). Children's decoding of emotion in expressive body movement: The development of cue attunement. *Developmental Psychology, 34,* 1007–1016.

Boot, B. P., McGregor, I. S., & Hall, W. (2000). MDMA (Ecstasy) neurotoxicity: assessing and communicating the risks. *Lancet, 355,* 1818–1821.

Boring, E. G. (1950). *A history of experimental psychology.* New York: Appleton-Century-Crofts.

Borkenau, P., Riemann, R., Angleitner, A., & Spinath, F. M. (2001). Genetic and environmental influences on observed personality: Evidence from the German Observational Study of Adult Twins. *Journal of Personality and Social Psychology, 80,* 655–668.

Bornovalova, M. A., Huibregtse, B. M., Hicks, B. M., Keyes, M., McGue, M., & Iacona, W. (2013). Tests of a direct effect of childhood abuse on adult borderline personality disorder: A longitudinal discordant twin design. *Journal of Abnormal Psychology, 122,* 180–194.

Bornstein, M. H., & Arterberry, M. E. (2003). Recognition, discrimination, and categorization of smiling by 5-month-old infants. *Developmental Science, 6,* 585–599.

Borod, J. C., Haywood, C. S., & Koff, E. (1997). Neuropsychological aspects of facial asymmetry during emotional expression: A review of the normal adult literature. *Neuropsychology Review, 7,* 41–60.

Bors, D. A., & Forrin, B. (1995). Age, speed of information processing, recall, and fluid intelligence. *Intelligence, 20,* 229–248.

Bortz, W. M. II, Wallace, D. H., & Wiley, D. (1999). Sexual function in 1,202 aging males: Differentiating aspects. *Journals of Gerontology: Series A: Biological Sciences and Medical Sciences, 54A,* M237–M241.

Bosl, W., Tierney, A., Tager-Rusberg, H., & Nelson, C. (2011). EEG complexity as a biomarker for autism spectrum disorder risk. *BMC Medicine, 9,* 18–33.

Bothwell, R. K., Brigham, J. C., & Malpass, R. S. (1989). Cross-racial identification. *Personality and Social Psychology Bulletin, 15,* 19–25.

Bouchard, T. J., Jr., & Hur, Y.-M. (1998). Genetic and environmental influences on the continuous scales of the Myers-Briggs Type Indicator: An analysis based on twins reared apart. *Journal of Personality, 66,* 135–149.

Bouchard, T. J., Jr., & Loehlin, J. C. (2001). Genes, evolution, and personality. *Behavior Genetics, 31,* 243–273.

Bouchard, T. J., Jr., Lykken, D. T., McGue, M., Segal, N. L., & Tellegen, A. (1990). Sources of human psychological differences: The Minnesota Study of Twins Reared Apart. *Science, 250,* 223–228.

Bouchard, T. J., Jr., & McGue, M. (1981). Familial studies of intelligence: A review. *Science, 212,* 1055–1059.

Bouchard, T. J., Jr., & McGue, M. (1990). Genetic and rearing environmental influences on adult personality: An analysis of adopted twins reared apart. *Journal of Personality, 58,* 263–292.

Bouchard, T. J., Jr., McGue, M., Hur, Y.-M., & Horn, J. M. (1998). A genetic and environmental analysis of the California Psychological Inventory using adult twins reared apart and together. *European Journal of Personality, 12,* 307–320.

Boudreaux, R. (2000, March 28). Spaniards are missing their naps. *Los Angeles Times,* p. A1.

Bourgeois, J. A., & Bunn, A. (1996). Obsessive-compulsive disorder symptoms associated with military duty. *Military Medicine, 161,* 358–359.

Bouton, M. E., & Swartzentruber, D. (1991). Sources of relapse after extinction in Pavlovian and instrumental learning. *Clinical Psychology Review, 11,* 123–140.

Bower, G. H. (1970). Analysis of a mnemonic device. *American Scientist, 58,* 496–510.

Bower, G. H. (1981). Mood and memory. *American Psychologist, 36,* 129–148.

Bower, G. H., & Clark, M. C. (1969). Narrative stories as mediators for serial learning. *Psychonomic Science, 14,* 181–182.

Bower, G. H., & Mayer, J. D. (1989). In search of mood-dependent retrieval. *Bulletin of the Psychonomic Society, 4,* 121–156.

Bowers, K. S. (1994). A review of Ernest R. Hilgard's books on hypnosis, in commemoration of his 90th birthday. *Psychological Science, 5,* 186–189.

Bowers, K. S., & Farvolden, P. (1996). Revisiting a century-old Freudian slip—From suggestion disavowed to the truth repressed. *Psychological Bulletin, 119,* 355–380.

Bowlby, J. (1988). *A secure base: Parent-child attachment and healthy human development.* New York: Basic Books.

Bowmaker, J. K. (1998). Visual pigments and molecular genetics of color blindness. *Physiology, 13,* 63–69.

Bowman, D., Scogin, F., Floyd, M., & McKendree-Smith, N. (2001). The effects of providing therapists with feedback on patient progress during psychotherapy: Are outcomes enhanced? *Psychotherapy Research, 11,* 49–68.

Boyce, B. A. (1992). The effects of goal proximity on skill acquisition and retention of a shooting task in a field-based setting. *Journal of Sport and Exercise Psychology, 14,* 298–308.

Boyce, W. T., Essex, M. J., Alkon, A., Smider, N. A., Pickrell, T., & Kagan, J. (2001). Temperament, tympanum and temperature: Four provisional studies of the biobehavioral correlates of tympanic membrane temperature asymmetries. *Child Development, 73,* 718–733.

Boyd, J. H. (1986). Use of mental health services for the treatment of panic disorder. *American Journal of Psychiatry, 143,* 1569–1574.

Boyd, J. H., & Crump, T. (1991). Westphal's agoraphobia. *Journal of Anxiety Disorders, 5,* 77–86.

Boynton, R. M. (1988). Color vision. *Annual Review of Psychology, 39,* 69–100.

Bozarth, J. D. (1990). The evolution of Carl Rogers as a therapist. *Person-Centered Review, 5,* 387–393.

Bozarth, J. D. (2002). Nondirectivity in the person-centered approach: Critique of Kahn's critique. *Journal of Humanistic Psychology, 42,* 78–83.

Brackbill, Y., & Nichols, P. L. (1982). A test of the confluence model of intellectual development. *Developmental Psychology, 18,* 192–198.

Bradbury, E. J., & McMahon, S. B. (2006). Spinal cord repair strategies: Why do they work? *Nature Reviews: Neuroscience, 7,* 644–653.

Bradley, B. P., & Baddeley, A. D. (1990). Emotional factors in forgetting. *Psychological Medicine, 20,* 351–355.

Bradley, M. T., & Warfield, J. F. (1984). Innocence, information, and the Guilty Knowledge Test in the detection of deception. *Psychophysiology, 21,* 683–689.

Bradley, M. T., MacLaren, V. V., & Carle, S. B. (1996). Deception and nondeception in guilty knowledge and guilty actions polygraph tests. *Journal of Applied Psychology, 81,* 153–160.

Bradshaw, M., & Ellison, C. G. (2009). The nature-nurture debate is over, and both sides lost! Implications for understanding gender differences in religiosity. *Journal for the Scientific Study of Religion, 48,* 241–251.

Brady, D. R., & Mufson, E. J. (1990). Amygdaloid pathology in Alzheimer's disease: Qualitative and quantitative analysis. *Dementia, 1,* 5–17.

Bramlett, R. K., Murphy, J. J., Johnson, J., Wallingsford, L., & Hall, J. D. (2002). Contemporary practices in school psychology: A national survey of roles and referral problems. *Psychology in the Schools, 39,* 327–335.

Branch, W. (1990). On interpreting correlation coefficients. *American Psychologist, 45,* 296.

Brand, G., & Millot, J. L. (2001). Sex differences in human olfaction: Between evidence and enigma. *Quarterly Journal of Experimental Psychology: Comparative and Physiological Psychology, 54B,* 259–270.

Brand, M., Eggers, C., Reinhold, N., Fujiwara, E., Kessler, J., Heiss, W., & Markowitsch, H. J. (2009). Functional brain imaging in 14 patients with dissociative amnesia reveals right inferolateral prefrontal hypometabolism. *Psychiatry Research: Neuroimaging, 174,* 32–39.

Brattico, E., Pallesen, K. J., Varyagina, O., Bailey, C., Anourova, I., Järvenpää, M., Eerola, T., & Tervaniemi, M. (2009). Neural discrimination of nonprototypical chords in music experts and laymen: An MEG study. *Journal of Cognitive Neuroscience, 21,* 2230–2244.

Brauer, M., Judd, C. M., & Gliner, M. D. (1995). The effects of repeated expressions on attitude polarization during group discussions. *Journal of Personality and Social Psychology, 68,* 1014–1029.

Braun, A., & Preiser, S. (2013). The impact of disparaging humor content on the funniness of political jokes. *Humor: International Journal of Humor Research, 26,* 249–275.

Braun, D. L., Sunday, S. R., Huang, A., & Halmi, K. A. (1999). More males seek treatment for eating disorders. *International Journal of Eating Disorders, 25,* 415–424.

Brawman-Mintzer, O., & Lydiard, R. B. (1997). Biological basis of generalized anxiety disorder. *Journal of Clinical Psychiatry, 58,* 16–26.

Bray, S. R., & Widmeyer, W. N. (2000). Athletes' perceptions of the home advantage: An investigation of perceived causal factors. *Journal of Sport Behavior, 23,* 1–10.

Breathnach, C. S. (1989). Validation of language localization by computer-assisted tomographic and topographic techniques. *Irish Journal of Psychological Medicine, 6,* 11–18.

Brébion, G., Stephan-Otto, C., Huerta-Ramos, E., Usall, J., Ochoa, S., Roca, M., . . . Haro, J.-M. (2013). Abnormal functioning of the semantic network in schizophrenia patients with thought disorganization: An examplar production task. *Psychiatry Research, 205,* 1–6.

Breckler, S. J. (1984). Empirical validation of affect, behavior, and cognition as distinct components of attitude. *Journal of Personality and Social Psychology, 47,* 1191–1205.

Breier, J. I., Randle, S., Maher, L. M., & Papanicolaou, A. C. (2010). Changes in maps of language activity activation following melodic intonation

therapy using magnetoencephalography: Two case studies. *Journal of Clinical and Experimental Neuropsychology, 32,* 309–314.

Breland, K., & Breland, M. (1961). The misbehavior of organisms. *American Psychologist, 16,* 681–684.

Brennan, C. (1997a, July 24). Killer's portrait "silly," profiler says. Former FBI agent says report issued by family "boilerplate 101." *Rocky Mountain News.*

Brennan, C. (1997b, July 25). Ramsey team distributes fliers of "profile." *Rocky Mountain News.*

Brent, D. A., & Bridge, J. (2003). Firearms availability and suicide: Evidence, interventions, and future directions. *American Behavioral Scientist, 46,* 1192–1210.

Bressan, P., Garlaschelli, L., & Barracano, M. (2003). Antigravity hills are visual illusions. *Psychological Science, 14,* 441–449.

Breuer, J., Scharkow, M., & Quandt, T. (2013). Sore losers? A reexamination of the frustration-aggression hypothesis for collocated video game play. *Psychology of Popular Media Culture,* December 23, 2013.

Brewer, M. B., & Kramer, R. M. (1985). The psychology of intergroup attitudes and behavior. *Annual Review of Psychology, 36,* 219–243.

Brewer, N., Keast, A., Sauer, J. D. (2010). Children's eyewitness identification and performance. Effects of a *Not Sure* response option and accuracy motivation. *Legal and Criminological Psychology, 15,* 261–277.

Bricklin, J. (1999). A variety of religious experience: William James and the non-reality of free will. *Journal of Consciousness Studies, 6,* 77–98.

Brickman, P., Coates, D., & Janoff-Bulman, R. (1978). Lottery winners and accident victims: Is happiness relative? *Journal of Personality and Social Psychology, 36,* 917–927.

Briggs, K. C., & Myers, I. B. (1943). *Myers-Briggs type indicator.* Palo Alto, CA: Consulting Psychologists Press.

Brigham, C. C. (1923). *A study of American intelligence.* Princeton, NJ: Princeton University Press.

Brigham, C. C. (1930). Intelligence tests of immigrant groups. *Psychological Review, 37,* 158–165.

Brigham, T. A. (1989). On the importance of recognizing the difference between experiments and correlational studies. *American Psychologist, 44,* 1077–1078.

Bringmann, M. W., Tyler, K. E., McAhren, P. E., & Bringmann, W. G. (1989). A successful and unsuccessful replication of William Stern's eyewitness research. *Perceptual and Motor Skills, 69,* 619–625.

Brinton, R. D., & Nilsen, J. (2003). Effects of estrogen plus progestin on risk of dementia. *JAMA: Journal of the American Medical Association, 290,* 1706.

Brittain, A. E., & Lerner, R. M. (2013). Early influences and later outcomes associated with developmental trajectories of Eriksonian fidelity. *Developmental Psychology, 49,* 722–735.

Broberg, D. J., & Bernstein, I. L. (1987). Candy as a scapegoat in the prevention of food aversions in children receiving chemotherapy. *Cancer, 60,* 2344–2347.

Broder, M. S. (2000). Making optimal use of homework to enhance your therapeutic effectiveness. *Journal of Rational and Cognitive Behavior Therapy, 18,* 3–18.

Brodnick, R. J., & Ree, M. J. (1995). A structural model of academic performance, socioeconomic status, and Spearman's g. *Educational and Psychological Measurement, 55,* 583–594.

Brody, N. (1999). What is intelligence? *International Review of Psychiatry, 11,* 19–25.

Brogaard, B. (2011). Are there unconscious perceptual processes? *Consciousness & Cognition: An International Journal, 20,* 449–463.

Brohawn, K. H., Offringa, R., Pfaff, D. L., Hughes, K. C., & Shin, L. M. (2010). The neural correlates of emotional memory in posttraumatic stress disorder. *Biological Psychiatry, 68,* 1023–1030.

Bromberg, W. (1954). *Man above humanity: A history of psychotherapy*. Philadelphia: Lippincott.

Bronstein, C. (2002). On free association and psychic reality. *British Journal of Psychotherapy, 18*, 477–489.

Brooks, K., & Siegel, M. (1991). Children as eyewitnesses: Memory, suggestibility, and credibility. *Australian Psychologist, 26*, 84–88.

Brooks, S. J., Savov, V., Allzen, E., Benedict, R., Fredriksson, R., & Schioth, H. B. (2012). Exposure to subliminal arousing stimuli induces robust activation in the amygdala, hippocampus, anterior cingulate, insular cortex and primary visual cortex: A systematic meta-analysis of fMRI studies. *NeuroImage, 59*, 2962–2973.

Brooks-Gunn, J., & Warren, M. P. (1989). Biological and social contributions to negative affect in young adolescent girls. *Child Development, 60*, 40–55.

Brooks-Gunn, J., Klebanov, P. K., & Duncan, G. J. (1996). Ethnic differences in children's intelligence test scores: Role of economic deprivation, home environment, and maternal characteristics. *Child Development, 67*, 396–408.

Brosschot, J. F, Godaert, G. L. R., Benschop, R. J., Olff, M., Ballieux, R. E., & Heijnen, C. J. (1998). Experimental stress and immunological reactivity: A closer look at perceived uncontrollability. *Psychosomatic Medicine, 60*, 359–361.

Broughton, R. S., & Perlstrom, J. R. (1992). PK in a competitive computer game: A replication. *Journal of Parapsychology, 56*, 291–305.

Brown, A. S. (1991). A review of the tip-of-the-tongue experience. *Psychological Bulletin, 109*, 204–223.

Brown, A. S. (2003). A review of the déjà vu experience. *Psychological Bulletin, 129*, 394–413.

Brown, D., Scheflin, A. W., & Whitfield, C. L. (1999). Recovered memories: The current weight of the evidence in science and the courts. *The Journal of Psychiatry and Law, 27*, 5–156.

Brown, D. A. (2006). Acetylcholine. *British Journal of Pharmacology, 147*, S120–S126.

Brown, J., Beard, E., Kotz, D., Michie, S., & West, R. (2014). Real-world effectiveness of e-cigarettes when used to aid smoking cessation: A cross-sectional population study. *Addiction, 109*, 1531–1540.

Brown, J. D., & Siegel, J. M. (1988). Exercise as a buffer of life stress: A prospective study of adolescent health. *Health Psychology, 7*, 341–353.

Brown, K. T., Brown, T. N., Jackson, J. S., Sellers, R. M., & Manuel, W. J. (2003). Teammates on and off the field? White student athletes. *Journal of Applied Social Psychology, 33*, 1379–1403.

Brown, R. (1973). *A first language: The early stages*. Oxford, England: Harvard University Press.

Brown, R. B., & Keegan, D. (1999). Humor in the hotel kitchen. *Humor: International Journal of Humor Research, 12*, 47–70.

Brown, R. J., & Lewis-Fernández, R. (2011). Culture and conversion disorder: Implications for *DSM-5*. *Psychiatry, 74*, 187–206.

Brown, R. T., Reynolds, C. R., & Whitaker, J. S. (1999). Bias in mental testing since *Bias in Mental Testing*. *School Psychology Quarterly, 14*, 208–238.

Brown, R., & Kulik, J. (1977). Flashbulb memories. *Cognition, 5*, 73–99.

Brown, R., Price, R. J., King, M. G., & Husband, A. J. (1989). Interleukin-1B and muramyl depeptide can prevent decreased antibody response associated with sleep deprivation. *Brain, Behavior, and Immunity, 3*, 320–330.

Brown, T. E. (2014). *Smart but stuck: emotions in teens and adults with ADHD*. San Francisco, CA: Wiley.

Brown, V. R., & Paulus, P. B. (2002). Making group brainstorming more effective: Recommendations from an associative memory perspective. *Current Directions in Psychological Science, 11*, 208–212.

Brownell, K. D. (1982). Obesity: Understanding and treating a serious, prevalent, and refractory disorder. *Journal of Consulting and Clinical Psychology, 50*, 820–840.

Brownell, K. D. (1993). Whether obesity should be treated. *Health Psychology, 12*, 339–341.

Brownell, K. D., & Cohen, L. R. (1995). Adherence to dietary regimens: 1. An overview of research. *Behavioral Medicine, 20*, 149–154.

Brownell, K. D., & Wadden, T. A. (1991). The heterogeneity of obesity: Fitting treatments to individuals. *Behavior Therapy, 22*, 153–177.

Brozek, J. (1999). From "psichiologia" to "psychologia": A graphically documented archival study across three centuries. *Journal of the History of the Behavioral Sciences, 35*, 177–180.

Bruce, M. L., Takeuchi, D. T., & Leaf, P. J. (1991). Poverty and psychiatric status: Longitudinal evidence from the New Haven Epidemiologic Catchment Area study. *Archives of General Psychiatry, 48*, 470–474.

Brugger, P., & Taylor, K. I. (2003). ESP: Extrasensory perception or effect of subjective probability? *Journal of Consciousness Studies, 10*, 221–246.

Brummett, B. H., Boyle, S. H., Kuhn, C. M., Siegler, J. C., & Williams, R. B. (2009). Positive affect is associated with cardiovascular reactivity, norepinephrine level, and morning rise in salivary cortisol. *Psychophysiology, 46*, 862–869.

Bruner, J. S. (1956). Freud and the image of man. *American Psychologist, 11*, 463–466.

Bruno, G. (2009). Film, aesthetics, science: Hugo Münsterberg's laboratory of moving images. *Grey Room, 36*, 88–113.

Bryant, D. M., & Maxwell, K. L. (1999). The environment and mental retardation. *International Review of Psychiatry, 11*, 56–67.

Bryck, R. L., & Fisher, P. A. (2012). Training the brain: Practical applications of neural plasticity from the intersection of cognitive neuroscience, developmental psychology and prevention science. *American Psychologist, 67*, 87–100.

Bryden, M. P. (1993). Perhaps not so sinister [Review of *The left-hander syndrome*]. *Contemporary Psychology, 38*, 71–72.

Bryden, M. P., Ardila, A., & Ardila, O. (1993). Handedness in native Amazonians. *Neuropsychologia, 31*, 301–308.

Brydon, L., Walker, C., Wawrzyniak, A. J., Chart, H., & Steptoe, A. (2009). Dispositional optimism and stress-induced changes in immunity and negative mood. *Brain, Behavior, and Immunity, 23*, 810–816.

Buchsbaum, M. S., & Haier, R. J. (1983). Psychopathology: Biological approaches. *Annual Review of Psychology, 34*, 401–430.

Buck, R. (1980). Nonverbal behavior and the theory of emotion: The facial-feedback hypothesis. *Journal of Personality and Social Psychology, 38*, 811–824.

Buck, R. (1985). Prime theory: An integrated view of motivation and emotion. *Psychological Review, 92*, 389–413.

Buckley, K. W. (1989). *Mechanical man: John Broadus Watson and the beginnings of behaviorism*. New York: Guilford.

Buckner, J. D., Heimberg, R. G., Ecker, A. H., & Vinci, C. (2013). A biopsychosocial model of social anxiety and substance use. *Depression & Anxiety, 30*, 276–284.

Buechel, C., Price, C., Frackowiak, R. S. J., & Friston, K. (1998). Different activation patterns in the visual cortex of late and congenitally blind subjects. *Brain, 121*, 409–419.

Buitelaar, J., & Medori, R. (2010). Treating attention deficit/hyperactivity disorder beyond symptom control alone in children and adolescents: A review of the potential benefits of long-acting stimulants. *European Child & Adolescent Psychiatry, 19*, 325–340.

Bulik, C. M., Sullivan, P. F., & Kendler, K. S. (1998). Heritability of binge-eating and broadly defined bulimia nervosa. *Biological Psychiatry, 44*, 1210–1218.

Bulik, C. M., Sullivan, P. F., & Kendler, K. S. (2003). Genetic and environmental contributions to obesity and binge eating. *International Journal of Eating Disorders, 33*, 293–298.

Bullough, V. L. (1998). Alfred Kinsey and the Kinsey Report: Historical overview and lasting contributions. *Journal of Sex Research, 35*, 127–131.

Bunge, M. (1992). The scientist's skepticism. *Skeptical Inquirer, 16*, 377–380.

Bunney, B., Li, J., Walsh, D., Stein, R., Vawter, M., Cartagena, P., … Bunney, W. (2015). Circadian dysregulation of clock genes: clues to rapid treatments in major depressive disorder HHS Public Access. *Molecular Psychiatry, 20138*, 48–55.

Burchinal, M. R., Bryant, D. M., Lee, M. W., & Ramey, C. T. (1992). Early day care, infant-mother attachment, and maternal responsiveness in the infant's first year. *Early Childhood Research Quarterly, 3*, 383–396.

Burgard, S. A., & Ailshire, J. A. (2013). Gender and time for sleep among U.S. adults, *American Sociological Review, 78*, 51–69.

Burger, J. M., & Guadagno, R. E. (2003). Self-concept clarity and the foot-in-the-door procedure. *Basic and Applied Social Psychology, 25*, 79–86.

Burger, J. M., Soroka, S., Gonzago, K., Murphy, E., & Somervell, E. (2001). The effect of fleeting attraction on compliance to requests. *Personality and Social Psychology Bulletin, 27*, 1578–1586.

Burman, B., & Margolin, G. (1992). Analysis of the association between marital relationships and health problems: An interactional perspective. *Psychological Bulletin, 112*, 39–63.

Burnham, T. C., Chapman, J. F., Gray, P. B., McIntyre, M. H., Lipson, S. F., & Ellison, P. T. (2003). Men in committed, romantic relationships have lower testosterone. *Hormones and Behavior, 44*, 119–122.

Burns, V. E., Carroll, D., Drayson, M., Whitham, M., & Ring, C. (2003). Life events, perceived stress, and antibody response to influenza vaccination in young, healthy adults. *Journal of Psychosomatic Research, 55*, 569–572.

Bursik, K. (1998). Moving beyond gender differences: Gender-role comparisons of manifest dream content. *Sex Roles, 38*, 203–214.

Burton, D., Gillham, A., Weinberg, R., Yukelson, D., & Weigand, D., (2013). Goal setting styles: Examining the role of personality factors on the goal practices of prospective Olympic athletes. *Journal of Sport Behavior, 36*, 23–44.

Bush, G., Valera, E. M., & Seidman, L. J. (2005). Functional neuroimaging of attention-deficit/hyperactivity disorder: A review and suggested future directions. *Biological Psychiatry, 57*, 1273–1284.

Bushman, B. J. (2002). Does venting anger feed or extinguish the flame? Catharsis, rumination, distraction, anger, and aggressive responding. *Journal of Personality and Social Psychology, 28*, 724–731.

Bushman, B. J., & Anderson, C. A. (2001). Media violence and the American public: Scientific facts versus media misinformation. *American Psychologist, 56*, 477–489.

Buss, A., Booker, A., & Buss, E. (1972). Firing a weapon and aggression. *Journal of Personality and Social Psychology, 22*, 296–302.

Buss, A. R. (1976). Galton and the birth of differential psychology and eugenics: Social, political, and economic forces. *Journal of the History of the Behavioral Sciences, 12*, 47–58.

Buss, D. M. (1985). Human mate selection. *American Scientist, 73*, 47–51.

Buss, D. M. (1988). The evolution of human intrasexual competition. *Journal of Personality and Social Psychology, 54*, 616–628.

Buss, D. M. (1995). Psychological sex differences: Origins through sexual selection. *American Psychologist, 50*, 164–168.

Buss, D. M. (1999). *Evolutionary psychology: The new science of the mind*. Boston: Allyn & Bacon.

Buss, D. M. (2003). Sexual strategies: A journey into controversy. *Psychological Inquiry, 14*, 219–226.

Buss, D. M. Abbott, M., Angleitner, A., Asherian, A., Biaggio, A., Blanco-Villasenor, A. . . . Yang, K.-S. (1990). International preferences in selecting

Buss, D. M., Sarsen, R. J., Westen, D., & Semmelroth, J. (1992). Sex differences in jealousy: Evolution, physiology, and psychology. *Psychological Science, 3*, 251–255.

Bussey, K., & Bandura, A. (1999). Social cognitive theory of gender development and differentiation. *Psychological Review, 106*, 676–713.

Butler, A. C., Chapman, J. E., Forman, E. M., & Beck, A. T. (2006). The empirical status of cognitive-behavioral therapy: A review of meta-analyses. *Clinical Psychology Review, 26*, 17–31.

Butler, B. E., & Petrulis, J. (1999). Some further observations concerning Sir Cyril Burt. *British Journal of Psychology, 90*, 155–160.

Butler, L. D., & Nolen-Hoeksema, S. (1994). Gender differences in responses to depressed mood in a college sample. *Sex Roles, 30*, 331–346.

Butnik, S. M. (2005). Neurofeedback in adolescents and adults with attention deficit hyperactivity disorder. *Journal of Clinical Psychology, 61*, 621–625.

Butschky, M. F., Bailey, D., Henningfield, J. E., Pickworth, W. B. (1995). Smoking without nicotine delivery decreases withdrawal in 12-hour abstinent smokers. *Pharmacology, Biochemistry, and Behavior, 50*, 91–96.

Buunk, B. P., Angleitner, A., Oubaid, V., & Buss, D. M. (1996). Sex differences in jealousy in evolutionary and cultural perspective: Tests from the Netherlands, Germany, and the United States. *Psychological Science, 7*, 359–363.

Buunk, B. P., Dijkstra, P., Fetchenhauer, D., & Kenrick, D. T. (2002). Age and gender differences in mate selection criteria for various involvement levels. *Personal Relationships, 9*, 271–278.

Byars, K. C., Yolton, K., Rausch, J., Lanphear, B., Beebe, D. W. (2012). Prevalence, patterns, and persistence of sleep problems in the first 3 years of life. *Pediatraics, 129*, e276–e284.

Bylsma, W. H., Cozzarelli, C., & Sumer, N. (1997). Relation between adult attachment styles and global self-esteem. *Basic and Applied Social Psychology, 19*, 1–16.

Byne, W. (1997). Why we cannot conclude that sexual orientation is primarily a biological phenomenon. *Journal of Homosexuality, 34*, 73–80.

Byrne, D., Ervin, C. R., & Lamberth, J. (1970). Continuity between the experimental study of attraction and real-life computer dating. *Journal of Personality and Social Psychology, 16*, 157–165.

Byrne, W. L., and 22 cosigners. (1966). Memory transfer. *Science, 153*, 658–659.

Byrnes, J. P., Miller, D. C., & Schafer, W. D. (1999). Gender differences in risk taking: A metaanalysis. *Psychological Bulletin, 125*, 367–383.

Byron, K., & Khazanchi, S. (2011). A meta-analytic investigation of the relationship of state and trait anxiety to performance on figural and verbal creative tasks. *Personality & Social Psychological Bulletin, 37*, 269–283.

Cabral, R. R., & Smith, T. B. (2011). Racial/ethnic matching of clients and therapists in mental health services: A meta-analytic review of preferences, perceptions and outcomes. *Journal of Counseling Psychology, 58*, 537–554.

Cacioppo, J. T. Berntson, G. G., & Nusbaum, H. C. (2008). Neuroimaging as a new tool in the toolbox of psychological science. *Current Directions in Psychological Science, 17*, 62–67.

Cade, J. F. J. (1949). Lithium salts in the treatment of psychotic excitement. *Medical Journal of Australia, 2*, 349–352.

Cadet, J. L., Jayanthi, S., & Deng, X. (2005). Methamphetamine-induced neuronal apoptosis involves the activation of multiple death pathways. *Neurotoxicity Research, 8*, 199–206.

Cadoret, R. J., Yates, W. R., Troughton, E., & Woodworth, G. (1995). Adoption study demonstrating two genetic pathways to drug abuse. *Archives of General Psychiatry, 52*, 42–52.

Cadwallader, E. H. (1984). Values in Fritz Perls' Gestalt Therapy: On the dangers of half-truths. *Counseling and Values, 28*, 192–201.

Cahan, D. (2006). The "imperial chancellor of the sciences": Helmholtz between science and politics, *Social Research, 73*, 1093–1128.

Cahan, E. D., & White, S. H. (1992). Proposals for a second psychology. *American Psychologist, 47*, 224–235.

Cahill, L., Prins, B., Weber, M., & McGaugh, J. L. (1994). B-Adrenergic activation and memory for emotional events. *Nature, 371*, 702–704.

Calantone, R. J., & Warshaw, P. R. (1985). Negating the effects of fear appraisals in election campaigns. *Journal of Applied Psychology, 70*, 627–633.

Caldwell, J. L. (2000). The use of melatonin: An information paper. *Aviation, Space, and Environmental Medicine 71*, 238–244.

Calkins, M. W. (1893). Statistics of dreams. *American Journal of Psychology, 5*, 311–343.

Calkins, M. W. (1901). *An introduction to psychology.* New York: Macmillan.

Calkins, M. W. (1930). Mary Whiton Calkins. In C. Murchison (Ed.), *A history of psychology in autobiography* (Vol. 1, pp. 31–62). New York: Russell & Russell.

Camel, J. E., Withers, G. S., & Greenough, W. T. (1986). Persistence of visual cortex dendritic alterations induced by postweaning exposure to a "superenriched" environment in rats. *Behavioral Neuroscience, 100*, 810–813.

Cameron, J., Banko, K. M., & Pierce, W. D. (2001). Pervasive negative effects of rewards on intrinsic motivation: The myth continues. *Behavior Analyst, 24*, 1–44.

Cameron, L., Leventhal, E. A., & Leventhal, H. (1995). Seeking medical care in response to symptoms and life stress. *Psychosomatic Medicine, 57*, 37–47.

Cameron, M. J., & Cappello, M. J. (1993). "We'll cross that hurdle when we get to it": Teaching athletic performance within adaptive physical education. *Behavior Modification, 17*, 136–147.

Caminiti, R. (2009). Replacement of animals in research will never be possible. *Nature, 457, 147*.

Campbell, R. S., & Pennebaker, J. W. (2003). The secret life of pronouns: Flexibility in writing style and physical health. *Psychological Science, 14*, 60–65.

Campbell, W. K., Foster, C. A., & Finkel, E. J. (2002). Does self-love lead to love for others? A story of narcissistic game playing. *Journal of Personality and Social Psychology, 83*, 340–354.

Campbell, W. K., & Sedikides, C. (1999). Self-threat magnifies the self-serving bias: A meta-analytic integration. *Review of General Psychology, 3*, 23–43.

Campione, J. E., & Brown, A. L. (1979). Toward a theory of intelligence: Contributions from research with retarded children. *Intelligence, 2*, 279–304.

Camras, L. A., Oster, H., Campos, J., Campos, R., Ujiie, T., Miyake, K., ... Meng, Z. (1998). Production of emotional facial expressions in European American, Japanese, and Chinese infants. *Developmental Psychology, 34*, 616–628.

Canel-Çınarba?, D., Cui, Y., & Lauridsen, E. (2011). Cross-cultural validation of the Beck Depression Inventory-II across U.S. and Turkish samples. *Measurement and Evaluation in Counseling and Development, 44*, 77–91.

Canetto, S. S., & Lester, D. (1995). Gender and the primary prevention of suicide mortality. *Suicide and Life-Threatening Behavior, 25*, 58–69.

Cann, A., Sherman, S. J., & Elkes, R. (1975). Effects of initial request size and timing of a second request on compliance: The foot in the door and the door in the face. *Journal of Personality and Social Psychology, 32*, 774–782.

Cannon, D. S., & Baker, T. B. (1981). Emetic and electric shock alcohol aversion therapy: Assessment of conditioning. *Journal of Consulting and Clinical Psychology, 49*, 20–33.

Cannon, W. B. (1915/1989). *Bodily changes in pain, hunger, fear, and rage.* Birmingham, AL: Gryphon.

Cannon, W. B. (1927). The James-Lange theory of emotions: A critical examination and an alternative. *American Journal of Psychology, 39*, 106–124.

Cannon, W. B., & Washburn, A. L. (1912). An explanation of hunger. *American Journal of Physiology, 29*, 444–454.

Caplan, L. J., & Barr, R. A. (1989). On the relationship between category intensions and extensions in children. *Journal of Experimental Child Psychology, 47*, 413–429.

Capraro, R. M., & Capraro, M. M. (2002). Myers-Briggs Type Indicator score reliability across studies: A meta-analytic reliability generalization study. *Educational and Psychological Measurement, 62*, 590–602.

Caputo, J. L., Rudolph, D. L., & Morgan, D. W. (1998). Influence of positive life events on blood pressure in adolescents. *Journal of Behavioral Medicine, 21*, 115–129.

Caqueret, A., Yang, C., Duplin, S., & Boucher, F. (2005). Looking for trouble: A search for developmental defects of the hypothalamus. *Hormone Research, 64*, 222–230.

Carlbring, P., Maurin, T., Sjömark, J., Maurin, L., Westling, B. E., Ekselius, L., ... Anderssen, G. (2011). All at once or one at a time? A randomized controlled trial comparing two ways of delivering bibliotherapy for panic disorder. *Cognitive Behaviour Therapy, 40*, 228–235.

Carlson, D. (2011). Benefits of student-generated note packets: A preliminary investigation of SQ3R implementation. *Teaching of Psychology, 38*, 142–146.

Carlson, E. T. (1981). The history of multiple personality in the United States: I. The beginnings. *American Journal of Psychiatry, 138*, 666–668.

Carlson, M., & Miller, N. (1987). Explanation of the relation between negative mood and helping. *Psychological Bulletin, 102*, 91–108.

Carlsson, C. P. O., & Sjoelund, B. H. (2001). Acupuncture for chronic low back pain: A randomized placebo-controlled study with long-term follow-up. *Clinical Journal of Pain, 17*, 296–305.

Carmichael, L., Hogan, H. P., & Walter, A. (1932). An experimental study of the effect of language on the reproduction of visually perceived form. *Journal of Experimental Psychology, 15*, 73–86.

Carney, R. N., & Levin, J. R. (2001). Remembering the names of unfamiliar animals: Keywords as keys to their kingdom. *Applied Cognitive Psychology, 15*, 133–143.

Carney, R. N., & Levine, J. R. (2011). Delayed mnemonic benefits for a combined pegword strategy, time after time, rhyme after rhyme. *Applied Cognitive Psychology, 25*, 204–211.

Caron, S. L., Halteman, W. A., & Stacy, C. (1997). Athletes and rape: Is there a connection? *Perceptual and Motor Skills, 85*, 1379–1393.

Carpenter, C. R. (1955). Psychological research using television. *American Psychologist, 10*, 606–610.

Carr, A. (2011). Thematic review of family therapy journals 2010. *Journal of Family Therapy, 33*, 429–447.

Carr, A. S., Cardwe, C. R., McCarron, P. O., & McConville, J. (2010). A systematic review of population based epidemiological studies in myasthenia gravis. *BMC Neurology, 10*, 10–46.

Carr, L., Henderson, J., & Nigg, J. T. (2010). Cognitive control and attentional selection in adolescents with ADHD versus ADD. *Journal of Clinical Child and Adolescent Psychology, 39*, 726–740.

Carrà, G., Johnson, S., Bebbington, P., Angermeyer, M. C., Heider, D., Brugha, T., ... Toumi, M. (2012). The lifetime and past-year prevalence of dual diagnosis in people with schizophrenia across Europe: Findings from the European Schizophrenia Cohort (EUROSC). *European Archives of Psychiatry and Clinical Neuroscience, 262*, 607–616.

Carretero, M., Escames, G., López, L. C., Venegas, C., Dayoub, J. C., Garcia, L., & Acuña-Castroviejo, D. (2009). Long-term melatonin administration protects brain mitochondria from aging. *Journal of Pineal Research, 47*, 192–200.

Carroll, J. (1999). The deep structure of literary representations. *Evolution and Human Behavior, 20,* 159–173.

Carroll, J. B. (1997). Psychometrics, intelligence, and public perception. *Intelligence, 24,* 25–52.

Carroll, J. F. X., Tanneberger, M., & Monti, T. C. (1998). Tertiary prevention strategy for drug–dependent clients completing residential treatment. *Alcoholism Treatment Quarterly, 16,* 51–61.

Carroll, J. M., & Russell, J. A. (1996). Do facial expressions signal specific emotions? Judging emotion from the face in context. *Journal of Personality and Social Psychology, 70,* 205–218.

Carroll, M. (1998). But fingerprints don't lie, eh? Prevailing gender ideologies and scientific knowledge. *Psychology of Women Quarterly, 22,* 739–749.

Carroll, M. E., & Overmier, J. B. (Eds.). (2001). *Animal research and human health: Advancing human welfare through behavioral science.* Washington, DC: American Psychological Association.

Carron, A. V., Hausenblas, H. A., & Mack, D. (1996). Social influence and exercise: A meta-analysis. *Journal of Sport and Exercise Psychology, 18,* 1–16.

Carson, R. C., & Butcher, J. N. (1992). *Abnormal psychology* (9th ed.). New York: HarperCollins.

Carson, S. H., Peterson, J. B., & Higgins, D. M. (2003). Decreased latent inhibition is associated with increased creative achievement in high-functioning individuals. *Journal of Personality and Social Psychology, 85,* 499–506.

Carter, M. M., Mitchell, F. E., & Sbrocco, T. (2012). Treating ethnic minority adults with anxiety disorders: Current status and future recommendations. *Journal of Anxiety Disorders, 26*(4), 488–501.

Carton, J. S. (1996). The differential effects of tangible rewards and praise on intrinsic motivation: A comparison of cognitive evaluation theory and operant theory. *Behavior Analyst, 19,* 237–255.

Cartwright, R. D. (1978). *A primer on sleep and dreaming.* Reading, MA: Addison–Wesley.

Cartwright, R. D. (1991). Dreams that work: The relation of dream incorporation to adaptation to stressful events. *Dreaming: Journal of the Association for the Study of Dreams, 1,* 3–9.

Carver, C. (1998). Premature ejaculation: A common and treatable concern. *Journal of the American Psychiatric Nurses Association, 4,* 199–204.

Carver, C. S., & Ganellen, R. J. (1983). Depression and components of self-punitiveness: High standards, self-criticism, and overgeneralization. *Journal of Abnormal Psychology, 92,* 330–337.

Carver, C. S., Smith, R. G., Antoni, M. H., Petronis, V. M., Weiss, S., & Derhagopian, R. P. (2005). Optimistic personality and psychosocial well-being during treatment predict psychosocial well-being among long-term survivors of breast cancer. *Health Psychology, 24,* 508–516.

Case, L., & Smith, T. B. (2000). Ethnic representation in a sample of the literature of applied psychology. *Journal of Consulting and Clinical Psychology, 68,* 1107–1110.

Casey, M. K., Allen, M., Emmers-Sommer, T., Sahlstein, E., Degooyer, D., Winters, A. M., Wagner, . . . Dun, T. (2003). When a celebrity contracts a disease: The example of Earvin "Magic" Johnson's announcement that he was HIV positive. *Journal of Health Communication, 8,* 249–265.

Cash, T. F., & Derlega, V. J. (1978). The matching hypothesis: Physical attractiveness among same-sexed friends. *Personality and Social Psychology Bulletin, 4,* 240–243.

Casto, S. D., DeFries, J. C., & Fulker, D. W. (1995). Multivariate genetic analysis of Wechsler Intelligence Scale for Children-Revised (WISC-R) factors. *Behavior Genetics, 25,* 25–32.

Catania, J. A., Coates, T. J., Stall, R., & Bye, L. (1991). Changes in condom use among homosexual men in San Francisco. *Health Psychology, 10,* 190–199.

Catania, J. A., Gibson, D. R., Chitwood, D. D., & Coates, T. J. (1990). Methodological problems in AIDS behavioral research: Influences on measurement error and participation bias in studies of sexual behavior. *Psychological Bulletin, 108,* 339–362.

Catherwood, D. (1993). The haptic processing of texture and shape by 7- to 9-month-old infants. *British Journal of Developmental Psychology, 11,* 299–306.

Cattell, J. M. (1890). Mental tests and measurements. *Mind, 15,* 373–381.

Cattell, R. B. (1940). A culture free intelligence test: I. *Journal of Educational Psychology, 31,* 161–179.

Ceci, S. J., & Bruck, M. (1993). Suggestibility of the child witness: A historical review and synthesis. *Psychological Bulletin, 113,* 403–439.

Ceci, S. J., & Liker, J. J. (1986). A day at the races: A study of IQ, expertise, and cognitive complexity. *Journal of Experimental Psychology: General, 115,* 255–266.

Ceci, S. J., Huffman, M. L. C., & Smith, E. (1994). Repeatedly thinking about a non-event: Source misattributions among preschoolers. *Consciousness and Cognition: An International Journal, 3,* 388–407.

Ceci, S. J., Ross, D. F., & Toglia, M. P. (1987). Suggestibility of children's memory: Psychological implications. *Journal of Experimental Psychology: General, 116,* 38–49.

Cecil, J. E. (2001). Oral, gastric and intestinal influences on the control of appetite and feeding in humans. *Appetite, 36,* 235–236.

Centers for Disease Control and Prevention (2012). Prevalence of autism spectrum disorders—Autism and developmental disabilities monitoring network, 14 sites, United States, 2008. *Morbidity and Mortality Weekly Report, 61,* 1–19.

Centers for Disease Control and Prevention. (2011). CDC grand rounds. Childhood obesity in the United States. *JAMA:Journal of the American Medical Association, 305,* 988–991.

Cerf-Ducastel, B., & Murphy, C. (2003). FMRI brain activation in response to odors is reduced in primary olfactory areas of elderly subjects. *Brain Research, 986,* 39–53.

Cerletti, U. (1954). Electroshock therapy. *Journal of Clinical and Experimental Psychopathology, 15,* 191–227.

Cervellon, M.-C., & Dube, L. (2002). Assessing the cross-cultural applicability of affective and cognitive components of attitude. *Journal of Cross-Cultural Psychology, 33,* 346–357.

Cha, K., Horch, K. W., & Normann, R. A. (1992). Mobility performance with a pixelized vision system. *Vision Research, 32,* 1367–1372.

Chabal, C., Fishbain, D. A., Weaver, M., & Heine, L. W. (1998). Long-term transcutaneous electrical nerve stimulation (TENS) use: Impact on medication utilization and physical therapy costs. *Clinical Journal of Pain, 14,* 66–73.

Chabrol, H. (1997). Abandonment and intrusion fears in borderline personality disorder. *American Journal of Psychiatry, 154,* 1329.

Chadwick, H. (1986). *Augustine.* New York: Oxford University Press.

Chaiken, S., & Baldwin, M. W. (1981). Affective-cognitive consistency and the effect of salient behavioral information on the self-perception of attitudes. *Journal of Personality and Social Psychology, 41,* 1–12.

Challis, B. H., Velichovsky, B. M., & Craik, F. I. M. (1996). Levels-of-processing effects on a variety of memory tasks: New findings and theoretical implications. *Consciousness and Cognition: An International Journal, 5,* 142–164.

Chan, A. S., Salmon, D. P., & De La Pena, J. (2001). Abnormal semantic network for "animals" but not "tools" in patients with Alzheimer's disease. *Cortex, 37,* 197–217.

Chandler, M. J. (2009). Piaget on Piaget. *British Journal of Psychology, 100,* 225–228.

Chao, R. K. (1994). Beyond parental control and authoritarian parenting style: Understanding Chinese parenting through the cultural notion of training. *Child Development, 65,* 1111–1119.

Chao, R. K. (2001). Extending research on the consequences of parenting style for Chinese Americans and European Americans. *Child Development, 72,* 1832–1843.

Chaplin, W. F., Phillips, J. B., Brown, J. D., Clanton, N. R., & Stein, J. L. (2000). Handshaking, gender, personality, and first impressions. *Journal of Personality and Social Psychology, 79,* 110–117.

Charlton, H. (2008). Hypothalamic control of anterior pituitary function: A history. *Journal of Neuroendocrinology, 20,* 641–646.

Charman, D. (2003). Paradigms in current psychotherapy research: A critique and the case for evidence-based psychodynamic psychotherapy research. *Australian Psychologist, 38,* 39–45.

Charness, N. (1992). The impact of chess research on cognitive science. *Psychological Research, 54,* 4–9.

Chartrand, T., Pinckert, S., & Burger, J. M. (1999). When manipulation backfires: The effects of time delay and requester on the foot-in-the-door technique. *Journal of Applied Social Psychology, 29,* 211–221.

Chase, W. G., & Simon, H. A. (1973). Perception in chess. *Cognitive Psychology, 4,* 55–81.

Chaves, J. F. (1994). Recent advances in the application of hypnosis to pain management. *American Journal of Clinical Hypnosis, 37,* 117–129.

Chavira, D. A., Grillo, C. M., Shea, M. T., Yen, S., Gunderson, J. L. C., Skodol, . . . Mcglashan, T. (2003). Ethnicity and four personality disorders. *Comprehensive Psychiatry, 44,* 483–491.

Chen, C., Kasof, J., Himsel, A. J., Greenberger, E., Dong, Q., & Xue, G. (2002). Creativity in drawings of geometric shapes: A cross-cultural examination with the consensual assessment technique. *Journal of Cross-Cultural Psychology, 33,* 171–187.

Chen, C., Lee, S.-Y., & Stevenson, H. W. (1995). Response style and cross-cultural comparisons of rating scales among East Asian and North American students. *Psychological Science, 6,* 170–175.

Chen, G.-M. (1995). Differences in self-disclosure patterns among Americans versus Chinese: A comparative study. *Journal of Cross-Cultural Psychology, 26,* 84–91.

Chen, I.-L. (2013). FDA summary of adverse events on electronic cigarettes. *Nicotine & Tobacco Research, 15,* 615–616.

Chen, J. M., Kim, H. S., Mojaverian, T., & Morling, B. (2012). Culture and social support provision: Who gives what and why? *Personality & Social Psychology Bulletin, 38,* 3–13.

Cheng, A. T. A. (2002). Expressed emotion: Across-culturally valid concept? *British Journal of Psychiatry, 181,* 466–467.

Cheng, C., Cheung, S.-F., Chio, J. H. M., & Chan, M.-P. S. (2013). Cultural meaning of perceived control: A meta-analysis of locus of control and psychological symptoms across 18 cultural regions. *Psychological Bulletin, 139,* 152–188.

Cheng, P., Casement, M. D., Hoffmann, R. F., Armitage, R., & Deldin, P. J. (2013). Sleep-disordered breathing in major depressive disorder. *Journal of Sleep Research, 22,* 459–462.

Cherek, D. R., Lane, S. D., & Dougherty, D. M. (2002). Possible amotivational effects following marijuana smoking under laboratory conditions. *Experimental and Clinical Psychopharmacology, 10,* 26–38.

Cherney, I. D., & Ryalls, B. O. (1999). Gender-linked differences in the incidental memory of children and adults. *Journal of Experimental Child Psychology, 72,* 305–328.

Cherrier, M. M., Asthana, S., Plymate, S., Baker, L., Matsumoto, A. M., Peskind, E., . . . Craft, S. (2001). Testosterone supplementation improves spatial and verbal memory in healthy older men. *Neurology, 57,* 80–88.

Cherry, E. C. (1953). Some experiments on the recognition of speech with one and two ears. *Journal of the Acoustical Society of America, 25,* 975–979.

Cheryan, S., & Bodenhausen, G. V. (2000). When positive stereotypes threaten intellectual performance:

The psychological hazards of "model minority" status. *Psychological Science, 11,* 399–402.

Chi, M. T. H., & Koeske, R. D. (1983). Network representation of a child's dinosaur knowledge. *Developmental Psychology, 19,* 29–39.

Chiao, J. Y., Iidaka T., Gordon H. L., Nogawa, J., Bar, M., Aminoff, E., Sadato, N., & Ambady, N. (2008). Cultural specificity in amygdala response to fear faces. *Journal of Cognitive Neuroscience, 20,* 2167–2174.

Chichilnisky, E. J., & Wandell, B. A. (1999). Trichromatic opponent color classification. *Vision Research, 39,* 3444–3458.

Child, I. L. (1985). Psychology and anomalous observations: The question of ESP in dreams. *American Psychologist, 40,* 1219–1230.

Chipuer, H. M., Rovine, M. J., & Plomin, R. (1990). LISREL modeling: Genetic and environmental influences on IQ revisited. *Intelligence, 14,* 11–29.

Chodorow, N. (1978). *The reproduction of mothering.* Berkeley: University of California Press.

Choi, J. N., & Kim, M. U. (1999). The organizational application of groupthink and its limitations in organizations. *Journal of Applied Psychology, 84,* 297–306.

Chongde, L., & Tsingan, L. (2003). Multiple intelligence and the structure of thinking. *Theory and Psychology, 13,* 829–845.

Choudhury, N., & Gorman, K. S. (1999). The relationship between reaction time and psychometric intelligence in a rural Guatemalan adolescent population. *International Journal of Psychology, 34,* 209–217.

Christ, T. J. (2007). Experimental control and threats to internal validity of concurrent and nonconcurrent multiple baseline designs. *Psychology in the Schools, 44,* 451–459.

Christensen, A. J., & Smith, T. W. (1995). Personality and patient adherence: Correlates of the five-factor model in renal analysis. *Journal of Behavioral Medicine, 18,* 305–313.

Christensen, L. (1988). Deception in psychological research: When is its use justified? *Personality and Social Psychology Bulletin, 14,* 664–675.

Christensen, T. M., & Brooks, M. C. (2001). Adult children of divorce and intimate relationships: A review of the literature. *Family Journal-Counseling and Therapy for Couples and Families. 9,* 289–294.

Christianson, S. A., & Loftus, E. F. (1987). Memory for traumatic events. *Applied Cognitive Psychology, 1,* 225–239.

Christianson, S. A., & Nilsson, L. (1984). Functional amnesia as induced by a psychological trauma. *Memory and Cognition, 12,* 142–155.

Christie, D. J. (2006). What is peace psychology the psychology of ? *Journal of Social Issues, 62,* 1–17.

Christie, I. C., & Friedman, B. H. (2004). Autonomic specificity of discrete emotion and dimensions of affective space: A multivariate approach. *International Journal of Psychophysiology, 51,* 143–153.

Christman, S. (2010). Eclectic lefty-hand: Conjectures on Jimi Hendrix, handedness, and Electric Ladyland. *Laterality, 15,* 253–269.

Christmann, E. P., & Badgett, J. L. (2003). A meta-analytic comparison of the effects of computer-assisted instruction on elementary students' academic achievement. *Information Technology in Childhood Education Annual, 15,* 91–104.

Christy, C. A., & Voigt, H. (1994). Bystander responses to public episodes of child abuse. *Journal of Applied Social Psychology, 24,* 824–847.

Church, A. T., Katigbak, M. S., Del Prado, A. M., Ortiz, F. A., Mastor, K. A., Harumi, Y., . . . Cabrera, H. F. (2006). Implicit theories and self-perceptions of traitedness across cultures: Toward integration of cultural and trait psychology perspectives. *Journal of Cross-Cultural Psychology, 37,* 694–716.

Cialdini, R. B., & Fultz, J. (1990). Interpreting the negative mood-helping literature via "mega"analysis: A contrary view. *Psychological Bulletin, 107,* 210–214.

Cialdini, R. B., Schaller, M., Houlihan, D., Arps, K., Fultz, J., & Beaman, A. L. (1987). Empathy-based helping: Is it selflessly motivated? *Journal of Personality and Social Psychology, 52,* 749–758.

Cialdini, R. B., Vincent, J. E., Lewis, S. J., Catalan, J., Wheeler, D., & Darley, B. L. (1975). Reciprocal concessions procedure for inducing compliance: The door-in-the-face technique. *Journal of Personality and Social Psychology, 31,* 206–215.

Ciarrochi, J. V., Chan, A. Y.-C., & Caputi, P. (2000). A critical evaluation of the emotional intelligence construct. *Personality and Individual Differences, 28,* 539–561.

Cicerello, A., & Sheehan, E. P. (1995). Personal advertisements: A content analysis. *Journal of Social Behavior and Personality, 10,* 751–756.

Cicerone, C. M., & Hayhoe, M. M. (1990). The size of the pool for bleaching in human rod vision. *Vision Research, 30,* 693–697.

Ciffone, J. (2007). Suicide prevention: An analysis and replication of a curriculum-based high school program. *Social Work, 52,* 41–49.

Ciftci Uruk, A., & Demir, A. (2003). The role of peers and families in predicting the loneliness level of adolescents. *Journal of Psychology, 137,* 179–193.

Cipolli, C., Bolzani, R., Tuozzi, G., & Fagioli, I. (2001). Active processing of declarative knowledge during REM-sleep dreaming. *Journal of Sleep Research, 10,* 277–284.

Claassen, D. O., & Rao, S. C. (2008). Locked-in or comatose? Clinical dilemma in acute pontine infarct. *Mayo Clinic Proceedings, 83,* 1197.

Claassen, N. C. W. (1997). Cultural differences, politics and test bias in South Africa. *European Review of Applied Psychology, 47,* 297–316.

Clancy, S. A. (2007). *Abducted: How people come to believe that they were kidnapped by aliens.* Cambridge, MA: Harvard University Press.

Clark, K. B., & Clark, M. P. (1947). Racial identification and preference in Negro children. In T. M. Newcomb & E. L. Hartley (Eds.), *Readings in social psychology* (pp. 169–178). New York: Holt.

Clark, L. A., Watson, D., & Reynolds, S. (1995). Diagnosis and classification of psychopathology: Challenges to the current system and future directions. *Annual Review of Psychology, 46,* 121–153.

Clark, R. D., III. (2001). Effects of majority defection and multiple minority sources on minority influence. *Group Dynamics, 5,* 57–62.

Clark, R. D., & Word, L. E. (1974). Where is the apathetic bystander? Situational characteristics of the emergency. *Journal of Personality and Social Psychology, 29,* 279–287.

Clark, S. A., McNally, R. J., Schachter, D. L., Lenzenweger, M. F., & Pitman, R. K. (2002). Memory distortion in people reporting abduction by aliens. *Journal of Abnormal Psychology, 111,* 455–461.

Clarke, P. G. H. (2010). Determinism, brain function, and free will. *Science and Christian Belief, 22,* 133–149.

Cliffe, M. J. (1991). Behaviour modification by successive approximation: Saxon age examples from Bede. *British Journal of Clinical Psychology, 30,* 367–369.

Clifford, C. A., Murray, R. M., & Fulker, D. W. (1984). Genetic and environmental influences on obsessional traits and symptoms. *Psychological Medicine, 14,* 791–800.

Clutton-Brock, T. H., & Parker, G. A. (1995). Punishment in animal societies. *Nature, 373,* 209–216.

Cobos, P., Sanchez, M., Garcia, C., Vera, M. N., & Vila, J. (2002). Revisiting the James versus Cannon debate on emotion: Startle and autonomic modulation in patients with spinal cord injuries. *Biological Psychology, 61,* 251–269.

Cochran, D. Q. (1999). Alabama v. Clarence Simmons: FBI "Profiler" testimony to establish an essential element of capital murder. *Law and Psychology Review, 23,* 69–89.

Cofer, C. N. (1985). Drives and motives. In G. A. Kimble & K. Schlesinger (Eds.), *Topics in the history of psychology* (Vol. 2, pp. 151–190). Hillsdale, NJ: Erlbaum.

Cofer, L. F., Grice, J. W., Sethre-Hofstad, L., Radi, C. J., Zimmerman, L. K., Palmer, Seal, D., & Santa Maria, G. (1999). Developmental perspectives on morningness-eveningness and social interactions. *Human Development, 42,* 169–198.

Cogan, D., & Cogan, R. (1984). Classical salivary conditioning: An easy demonstration. *Teaching of Psychology, 11,* 170–171.

Cohen, D. B. (1979). *Sleep and dreaming: Origins, nature and functions.* New York: Pergamon.

Cohen, J. (1969). *Statistical power analysis for the behavioral sciences.* New York: Academic Press.

Cohen, M. (2002). Coping and emotional distress in primary and recurrent breast cancer patients. *Journal of Clinical Psychology in Medical Settings, 9,* 245–251.

Cohen, M. S., Chen, Y. Q., McCauley, M., Gamble, T., Hosseinipour, M. C., Kumarasamy, N., & Fleming, T. R. (2011). Prevention of HIV-1 infection with early antiretroviral therapy. *New England Journal of Medicine, 365,* 493–505.

Cohen, N. J., & Squire, L. R. (1980). Preserved learning and retention of pattern-analyzing skill in amnesia: Dissociation of knowing how and knowing that. *Science, 210,* 207–210.

Cohen, S. L., Chelland, S., Ball, K. T., & LeMura, L. M. (2002). Effects of fixed ratio schedules on reinforcement on exercise by college students. *Perceptual and Motor Skills, 94,* 1177–1186.

Coke-Pepsi slugfest. (1976, July 26). *Time,* pp. 64–65.

Cokley, K., & Rosales, R. (2005). Book review: Handbook of multicultural competencies in counseling and psychology. *Measurement and Evaluation in Counseling and Development, 38,* 176–182.

Colace, C. (2003). Dream bizarreness reconsidered. *Sleep and Hypnosis, 5,* 105–128.

Colapinto, J. (2001). *As nature made him: The boy who was raised as a girl.* New York: HarperCollins.

Collaer, M. L., & Hines, M. (1995). Human behavioral sex differences: A role for gonadal hormones during early development? *Psychological Bulletin, 118,* 55–107.

Colcombe, S., & Kramer, A. F. (2003). Fitness effects on the cognitive function of older adults: A meta-analytic study. *Psychological Science, 14,* 125–130.

Cole, P. M., Bruschi, C. J., & Tamang, B. L. (2002). Cultural differences in children's emotional reactions to difficult situations. *Child Development, 73,* 983–996.

Colegrove, F. W. (1899). Individual memories. *American Journal of Psychology, 10,* 228–255.

Coleman-Mesches, K., & McGaugh, J. L. (1995). Differential involvement of the right and left amygdalae in expression of memory for aversively motivated training. *Brain Research, 670,* 75–81.

Collaer, M. L., Geffner, M. E., Kaufman, F. R., Buckingham, B., & Hines, M. (2002). Cognitive and behavioral characteristics of Turner syndrome: Exploring a role for ovarian hormones in female sexual differentiation. *Hormones and Behavior, 41,* 139–155.

Colligan, J. (1983). Musical creativity and social rules in four cultures. *Creative Child and Adult Quarterly, 8,* 39–44.

Collins, A. M., & Loftus, E. F. (1975). A spreading-activation theory of semantic processing. *Psychological Review, 82,* 407–428.

Collins, N. L., & Miller, L. C. (1994). Self-disclosure and liking: A meta-analytic review. *Psychological Bulletin, 116,* 457–475.

Colom, R., & Garcia-Lopez, O. (2003). Secular gains in fluid intelligence: Evidence from the Culture-Fair Intelligence Test. *Journal of Biosocial Science, 35,* 33–39.

Colom, R., Burgaleta, M., Román, F. J., Karama, S., Álvarez-Linera, J., Abad, F. J., . . . Haier, R. J.

(2013). Neuroanatomic overlap between intelligence and cognitive factors: Morphometry methods provide support for the key role of the frontal lobes. *NeuroImage, 72,* 143–152.

Colon-Ramos, D. A., & Shen, K. (2008). Cellular conductors: Glial cells as guideposts during neural circuit development. *PLOS Biology, 6,* 672–674.

Coltrane, S., & Messinco, M. (2000). The perpetuation of subtle prejudice: Race and gender imagery in 1990s television advertising. *Sex Roles, 42,* 363–389.

Colvin, C. R., Block, J., & Funder, D. C. (1995). Overly positive evaluations and personality: Negative implications for mental health. *Journal of Personality and Social Psychology, 68,* 1152–1162.

Conklin, H. M., & Iacono, W. G. (2002). Schizophrenia: A neurodevelopmental perspective. *Current Directions in Psychological Science, 11,* 33–37.

Connie, F. O. Y., Kelvin, L. K. H., Chung, A, C., Diana, C. M. K., & Gilberto, L. K. K. (2008). Knowledge, acceptance and perception towards brainstem death among medical students in Hong Kong: A questionnaire survey on brainstem death. *Medical Teacher, 30,* 125–130.

Connors, A. (1988, February 5). At 91, she's stepping up in class. *Los Angeles Times,* p. 2.

Conrad, R. (1962). An association between memory errors and errors due to acoustic masking of speech. *Nature, 193,* 1314–1315.

Contrada, R. J., Ashmore, R. D., Gary, M. L., Coups, E., Egeth, J. D., Sewell, A., ... Chasse, V. (2001). Measures of ethnicity-related stress: Psychometric properties, ethnic group differences, and associations with well-being. *Journal of Applied Social Psychology, 31,* 1775–1820.

Cook, M., & Mineka, S. (1989). Observational conditioning of fear to fear-relevant versus fear-irrelevant stimuli in rhesus monkeys. *Journal of Abnormal Psychology, 98,* 448–459.

Coolidge, F. L., Moor, C. J., Yamazaki, T. G., Stewart, S. E., & Segal, D. L. (2001). On the relationship between Karen Horney's tripartite neurotic type theory and personality disorder features. *Personality and Individual Differences, 30,* 1387–1400.

Coon, D. J. (1982). Eponymy, obscurity, Twitmyer, and Pavlov. *Journal of the History of the Behavioral Sciences, 18,* 255–262.

Coon, D. J. (2000). Salvaging the self in a world without soul: William James's The Principles of Psychology. *History of Psychology, 3,* 83–103.

Coon, H., Fulker, D. W., DeFries, J. C., & Plomin, R. (1990). Home environment and cognitive ability of seven-year-old children in the Colorado Adoption Project: Genetic and environmental etiologies. *Developmental Psychology, 26,* 459–468.

Coons, E. E. (2002). Neal Elgar Miller (1909–2002). *American Psychologist, 57,* 784–786.

Coons, P. M., & Milstein, V. (1992). Psychogenic amnesia: A clinical investigation of 25 cases. *Dissociation: Progress in the Dissociative Disorders, 5,* 73–79.

Cooper, J., & Cooper, G. (2002). Subliminal motivation: A story revisited. *Journal of Applied Social Psychology, 32,* 2213–2227.

Copolov, D. L., Seal, M. L., Maruff, P., Ulusoy, R., Wong, M. T. H., Tochon-Danguy, H. J., & Egan, G. F. (2003). Cortical activation associated with the human experience of auditory hallucinations and perception of human speech in schizophrenia: A PET correlation study. *Psychiatry Research: Neuroimaging, 122,* 139–152.

Coram, G. J. (1995). A Rorschach analysis of violent murderers and nonviolent offenders. *European Journal of Psychological Assessment, 11,* 81–88.

Corballis, M. C. (2001). Is the handedness gene on the X chromosome? Comment on Jones and Martin (2000). *Psychological Review, 108,* 805–810.

Corbetta, M., Kincades, M. J., Lewis, C., Snyder, A. Z., & Sapir, A. (2005). Neural basis and recovery of spatial attention deficits in spatial neglect. *Nature Neuroscience, 8,* 1603–1610.

Coren, S. (1996). *Sleep thieves: An eye-opening exploration into the science and mysteries of sleep.* New York: Free Press.

Coren, S., & Halpern, D. F. (1991). Left-handedness: A marker for decreased survival fitness. *Psychological Bulletin, 109,* 90–106.

Coren, S., & Hewitt, P. L. (1999). Sex differences in elderly suicide rates: Some predictive factors. *Aging and Mental Health, 3,* 112–118.

Coren, S., & Previc, F. H. (1996). Handedness as a predictor of increased risk of knee, elbow, or shoulder injury, fractures, and broken bones. *Laterality: Asymmetries of Body, Brain and Cognition, 1,* 139–152.

Coren, S., & Searleman, A. (1987). Left sidedness and sleep difficulty: The alinormal syndrome. *Brain and Cognition, 6,* 184–192.

Corkin, S. (2004, July 23). *Personal communication.*

Corkin, S., Amaral, D. G., Gonzalez, R. G., Johnson, K. A., & Hyman, B. T. (1997). H. M.'s medial temporal lobe lesion: Findings from magnetic resonance imaging. *Journal of Neuroscience, 17,* 3964–3979.

Cormier, J. F., & Thelen, M. H. (1998). Professional skepticism of multiple personality disorder. *Professional Psychology: Research and Practice, 29,* 163–167.

Corrigan, N. M., Richards, T. L., Treffert, D. A., Dager, S. R. (2012). Toward a better understanding of the savant brain, *Comprehensive Psychiatry, 53,* 706–717.

Cosgrove, L. (2007). Humanistic psychology and the contemporary crisis of reason. *Humanistic Psychologist, 35,* 15–25.

Costello, E. J., Compton, S. N., Keeler, G., & Angold, A. (2003). Relationships between poverty and psychopathology. A natural experiment. *JAMA: Journal of the American Medical Association, 290,* 2023–2029.

Cotgrove, A. J., Zirinsky, L., Black, D., & Weston, D. (1995). Secondary prevention of attempted suicide in adolescence. *Journal of Adolescence, 18,* 569–577.

Courtenay, W. H. (2000). Engendering health: A social constructionist examination of men's health beliefs and behaviors. *Psychology of Men and Masculinity, 1,* 4–15.

Courtin, J., Karalis, N., Gonzalez-Campo, C., Wurtz, H., & Herry, C. (2013). Persistence of amygdala gamma oscillations during extinction learning predicts spontaneous fear recovery. *Neurobiology of Learning and Memory, 113,* 82–89.

Cousins, N. (1983). *The healing heart: Antidotes to panic and helplessness.* New York: W. W. Norton.

Cowan, N. (1988). Evolving conceptions of memory storage, selective attention, and their mutual constraints within the human information-processing systems. *Psychological Bulletin, 104,* 163–191.

Cowles, M. (1989). *Statistics in psychology: An historical perspective.* Hillsdale, NJ: Erlbaum.

Cowley, G. (1995, November 6). Melatonin mania. *Newsweek,* pp. 60–63.

Cox, D. J., Merkel, R. L., Moore, M., Thorndike, F., Muller, C., & Kovatchev, B. (2006). Relative benefits of stimulant therapy with OROS methylphenidate versus mixed amphetamine salts extended release in improving the driving performance of adolescent drivers with attention-deficit/hyperactivity disorder. *Pediatrics, 118,* 704–710.

Cox, K. S., Wilt, J, Olson, B., & McAdams, D. P. (2010). Generativity, the Big Five, and psychosocial adaptation in midlife adults. *Journal of Personality, 78,* 1185–1208.

Cox, W. E. (1984). Magicians and parapsychology. *Journal of the Society for Psychical Research, 52,* 383–386.

Cox, W. J., & Kenardy, J. (1993). Performance anxiety, social phobia, and setting effects in instrumental music students. *Journal of Anxiety Disorders, 7,* 49–60.

Coxon, P., & Valentine, T. (1997). The effects of the age of eyewitnesses on the accuracy and suggestibility of their testimony. *Applied Cognitive Psychology, 11,* 415–430.

Craft, S., Asthana, S., Cook, D. G., Baker, L. D., Cherrier, M., Purganan, K., ... Kroohn, A. J. (2003). Insulin dose–response effects on memory and plasma amyloid precursor protein in Alzheimer's disease: Interactions with apolipoprotein E genotype. *Psychoneuroendocrinology, 28,* 809–822.

Craig, C. L. (1994). Limits to learning: Effects of predator pattern and colour on perception and avoidance-learning by prey. *Animal Behaviour, 47,* 1087–1099.

Craik, F. I. M., & Lockhart, R. S. (1972). Levels of processing: A framework for memory research. *Journal of Verbal Learning and Verbal Behavior, 11,* 671–684.

Craik, F. I. M., & Tulving, E. (1975). Depth of processing and the retention of words in episodic memory. *Journal of Experimental Psychology: General, 104,* 268–294.

Crain, W. (2009). Jane Goodall. *Encounter: Education for Meaning and Social Justice, 22,* 2–6.

Cramer, D. (2003). Acceptance and need for approval as moderators of self-esteem and satisfaction with a romantic relationship or closest friendship. *Journal of Psychology, 137,* 495–505.

Cramer, P. (1999). Future directions for the Thematic Apperception Test. *Journal of Personality Assessment, 72,* 74–92.

Cramer, P. (2000). Development of identity: Gender makes a difference. *Journal of Research in Personality, 34,* 42–72.

Cramer, P. (2003). Defense mechanisms and physiological reactivity to stress. *Journal of Personality, 71,* 221–244.

Crandall, J. E. (1980). Adler's concept of social interest: Theory, measurement, and implications for adjustment. *Journal of Personality and Social Psychology, 39,* 481–495.

Crano, W. D., & Prislin, R. (1995). Components of vested interest and attitude-behavior consistency. *Basic and Applied Social Psychology, 17,* 1–21.

Cranwell-Bruce, L. A. (2010). Drugs for Parkinson's disease. *Nursing Pharmacology, 19,* 347–355.

Cras, P. (2008). Glial neurobiology. *Spinal Cord, 46,* 463.

Crawford, H. J., Knebel, T., & Vendemia, J. M. C. (1998). The nature of hypnotic analgesia: Neurophysiological foundation and evidence. *Contemporary Hypnosis, 15,* 22–33.

Crepeau-Hobson, M. F., FiLaccio, M., & Gottfried, L. (2005). Violence prevention after Columbine: A survey of high school mental health professionals. *Children and Schools, 27,* 157–165.

Crespo, C. J., Smit, E., Andersen, R. E., Carter-Pokras, O., & Ainsworth, B. E. (2000). Race/ethnicity, social class, and their relation to physical inactivity during leisure time: Results from the Third National Health and Nutrition Examination Survey, 1988–1994. *American Journal of Preventive Medicine, 18,* 46–53.

Crews, F. (1994). Amyloid b protein disruption of cholinergic and growth factor phospholipase C signals could underlie cognitive and neurodegenerative aspects of Alzheimer's disease. *Neurobiology of Aging, 15,* S95–S96.

Critchley, H. D., Melmed, R. N., Featherstone, E., Mathias, C. J., & Dolan, R. J. (2001). Brain activity during biofeedback relaxation: A functional neuroimaging investigation. *Brain, 124,* 1003–1012.

Critchlow, S. (1998). False memory syndrome: Balancing the evidence for and against. *Irish Journal of Psychological Medicine, 15,* 64–67.

Crocker, J., Alloy, L. B., & Kayne, N. T. (1988). Attributional style, depression, and perceptions of consensus for events. *Journal of Personality and Social Psychology, 54,* 840–846.

Croft, G. P., & Walker, A. E. (2001). Are the Monday blues all in the mind? The role of expectancy in the subjective experience of mood. *Journal of Applied Social Psychology, 31,* 1133–1145.

Crohan, S. E. (1992). Marital happiness and spousal consensus on beliefs about marital conflict: A longitudinal investigation. *Journal of Social and Personal Relationships, 9*, 89–102.

Crook, T., & Eliot, J. (1980). Parental death during childhood and adult depression: A critical review of the literature. *Psychological Bulletin, 87*, 252–259.

Crosier, M., Scott, J., & Steinfeld, B. (2012). Improving satisfaction in patients receiving mental health care. A case study. *Journal of Behavioral Health Services & Research, 39*, 42–54.

Cross, S., & Markus, H. (1991). Possible selves across the life span. *Human Development, 34*, 230–255.

Crossley, N. (1998). R. D. Laing and the British anti-psychiatry movement: A socio-historical analysis. *Social Science and Medicine, 47*, 877–889.

Crowe, R. R. (1990). Panic disorder: Genetic considerations. *Journal of Psychiatric Research, 24*, 129–134.

Crowley, J. J., & Lucki, I. (2006). Opportunities to discover genes regulating depression and antidepressant response from rodent behavioral genetics. *Current Pharmaceutical Design, 11*, 157–169.

Crowley, S. J., & Eastman, C. I. (2013). Melatonin in the afternoons of a gradually advancing sleep schedule enhances the circadian rhythm phase advance. *Psychopharmacology, 225*, 825–837.

Croy, I., Olgun, S., & Joraschky, P. (2011). Basic emotions elicited by odors and pictures. *Emotion, 11*, 1331–1335.

Crozier, J. B. (1997). Absolute pitch: Practice makes perfect, the earlier the better. *Psychology of Music, 25*, 110–119.

Cruess, S., Antoni, M., Cruess, D., Fletcher, M. A., Ironson, G., Kumar, M., . . . Schneiderman, N. (2000). Reductions in herpes simplex virus type 2 antibody titers after cognitive behavioral stress management and relationships with neuroendocrine function, relaxation skills, and social support in HIV-positive men. *Psychosomatic Medicine, 62*, 828–837.

Crum, B. (2009). It should be possible to replace animals in research. *Nature, 457*, 657.

Cruz, C., Boquet, A., Detwiler, C., & Nesthus, T. (2003). Clockwise and counterclockwise rotating shifts: Effects on vigilance and performance. *Aviation, Space, and Environmental Medicine, 74*, 606–614.

Cubit, K. (2010). Informed consent for research involving people with dementia: A grey area. *Contemporary Nurse, 34*, 230–236.

Cuellar, I., Roberts, R. E., Nyberg, B., & Maldonado, R. E. (1997). Ethnic identity and acculturation in a young adult Mexican-origin population. *Journal of Community Psychology, 25*, 535–549.

Culpepper, L. (2003). Use of algorithms to treat anxiety in primary care. *Journal of Clinical Psychiatry, 64*, 30–33.

Cunningham, J. A., Dollinger, S. J., Satz, M., & Rotter, N. S. (1991). Personality correlates of prejudice against AIDS victims. *Bulletin of the Psychonomic Society, 29*, 165–167.

Cunningham, M. R., Roberts, A. R., Barbee, A. P., & Druen, P. B. (1995). "Their ideas of beauty are, on the whole, the same as ours": Consistency and variability in the cross-cultural perception of female physical attractiveness. *Journal of Personality and Social Psychology, 68*, 261–279.

Cunningham, S. (1981, July). Chimps use sign language to talk to each other. *APA Monitor*, p. 11.

Cunningham, W. A., Preacher, K. J., & Banaji, M. R. (2001). Implicit attitude measures: Consistency, stability, and convergent validity. *Psychological Science, 12*, 163–170.

Cuntz, U., Enck, P., Frühauf, E., Lehnert, P., Riepl, R. L., Fichter, M. M., & Otto, B. (2013). Cholecystokinin revisited: CCK and the hunger trap in anorexia nervosa. *PLOS ONE, 8*, 454–457.

Curcio, C. A., Sloan, K. R., Jr., Packer, O., Hendrickson, A. E., & Kalina, R. E. (1987). Distribution of cones in human and monkey retina: Individual variability and radial asymmetry. *Science, 236*, 579–582.

Currie, C., Ahluwalia, N., Godeau, E., Gabhainn, S. N., Due, P., & Currie, D. B. (2012). Is obesity at individual and national level associated with lower age at menarche? Evidence from 34 countries in the Health Behaviour in School-aged Children Study. *Journal of Adolescent Health, 50*, 621–626.

Curzon, G. (1982). Transmitter amines in depression. *Psychological Medicine, 12*, 465–470.

Cutler, W. B., Friedmann, E., & McCoy, N. L. (1998). Pheromonal influences on sociosexual behavior in men. *Archives of Sexual Behavior, 27*, 1–13.

Cutting, L. P., & Docherty, N. M. (2000). Schizophrenia outpatients' perceptions of their parents: Is expressed emotion a factor? *Journal of Abnormal Psychology, 109*, 266–272.

Cytowic, R. E. (1989). Synesthesia and mapping of subjective sensory dimensions. *Neurology, 39*, 849–850.

Czeisler, C. A., Moore-Ede, M. C., & Coleman, R. M. (1982). Rotating shift work schedules that disrupt sleep are improved by applying circadian principles. *Science, 217*, 460–463.

Czyzewska, M. A. (2001). Implicit learning: Theoretical and methodological controversies. *Polish Psychological Bulletin, 32*, 45–52.

da C. Menezes Costa, L., Maher, C. G., McAuley, J. H., Hancoci, M. J., & Smeets, R. J. E. M. (2011). Self-efficacy is more important than fear of movement in mediating the relationship between pain and disability in chronic low back pain. *European Journal of Pain, 15*, 213–219.

Dabbs, J. M., Jr. (1997). Testosterone and puillary response to auditory sexual stimuli. *Physiology and Behavior, 62*, 909–912.

Dahlstrom, W. G. (1993). Tests: Small samples, large consequences. *American Psychologist, 48*, 393–399.

Daigen, V., & Holmes, J. G. (2000). Don't interrupt! A good rule for marriage? *Personal Relationships, 7*, 185–201.

Dale, K., & Collett, T. S. (2001). Using artificial evolution and selection to model insect navigation. *Current Biology, 11*, 1305–1316.

Dammann, E. J. (1997). "The myth of mental illness": Continuing controversies and their implications for mental health professionals. *Clinical Psychology Review, 17*, 733–756.

Dance, K. A., & Neufeld, R. W. J. (1988). Aptitude-treatment interaction research in the clinical setting: A review of attempts to dispel the "patient uniformity" myth. *Psychological Bulletin, 104*, 192–213.

Daniels, M. (1982). The development of the concept of self-actualization in the writings of Abraham Maslow. *Current Psychological Reviews, 2*, 61–75.

Danko, S. G., Bechtereva, N. P., Shemyakina, N. V., & Antonova, L. V. (2003). Electroencephalographic correlates of mental performance of emotional personal and scenic situations: I. Characteristics of local synchronization. *Human Physiology, 29*, 263–272.

Dantzer, J. M. (2006). Bursting on the scene: How thalamic neurons grab your attention. *PLOS Biology, 4*, 1100–1101.

Danziger, K. (1994). Does the history of psychology have a future? *Theory and Psychology, 4*, 467–484.

Darch, C. B., Carnine, D. W., & Kameenui, E. J. (1986). The role of graphic organizers and social structure in content area instruction. *Journal of Reading Behavior, 18*, 275–295.

Darley, J. M., & Latané, B. (1968). Bystander intervention in emergencies: Diffusion of responsibilities. *Journal of Personality and Social Psychology, 8*, 377–383.

Darling, C. A., Davidson, J. K., & Jennings, D. A. (1991). The female sexual response revisited: Understanding the multiorgasmic experience in women. *Archives of Sexual Behavior, 20*, 527–540.

Darling, N., & Steinberg, L. (1993). Parenting style as context: An integrative model. *Psychological Bulletin, 113*, 487–496.

Darlington, R. B. (1996). On race and intelligence: A commentary on affirmative action, the evolution of intelligence, the regression analyses in *The Bell Curve*, and Jensen's two-level theory. *Psychology, Public Policy, and Law, 2*, 635–645.

Darwin, C. (1859/1975). *The origin of species*. New York: W. W. Norton.

Darwin, C. (1872/1965). *The expression of the emotions in man and animals*. Chicago: University of Chicago Press.

Datko, M., Pineda, J. A., & Müller, R.-A. (2017). Positive effects of neurofeedback on autism symptoms correlate with brain activation during imitation and observation. *European Journal of Neuroscience*, 1–42.

Datta, S. (2002). Evidence that REM sleep is controlled by the activation of brain stem pedunculopontine tegmental kainate receptor. *Journal of Neurophysiology, 87*, 1790–1798.

Daughton, D. M., Fortmann, S. P., Glover, E. D., Hatsukami, D. K., Heatley, S. A., Lichtenstein, E., . . . Rennard, S. I. (1999). The smoking cessation efficacy of varying doses of nicotine patch delivery systems 4 to 5 years post-quit day. *Preventive Medicine: An International Journal Devoted to Practice and Theory, 28*, 113–118.

David, A. S., Woodruff, P. W. R., Howard, R., & Mellers, J. D. C. (1996). Auditory hallucinations inhibit exogenous activation of auditory association cortex. *Neuroreport: An International Journal for the Rapid Communication of Research in Neuroscience, 7*, 932–936.

David, S. S., Foot, H. C., & Chapman, A. J. (1990). Children's sensitivity to traffic hazard in peripheral vision. *Applied Cognitive Psychology, 4*, 471–484.

Davidson, D. (1995). The representativeness heuristic and the conjunction fallacy effect in children's decision making. *Merrill-Palmer Quarterly, 41*, 328–346.

Davidson, D. J., Zacks, R. T., & Williams, C. C. (2003). Stroop interference, practice, and aging. *Aging, Neuropsychology, and Cognition, 10*, 85–98.

Davidson, L. L., & Heinreichs, R. W. (2003). Quantification of frontal and temporal lobe brain-imaging findings in schizophrenia: A metaanalysis. *Psychiatry Research: Neuroimaging, 122*, 69–87.

Davies, G., & Alonso-Quecuty, M. (1997). Cultural factors in the recall of a witnessed event. *Memory, 5*, 601–614.

Davies, G., Welham, J., Chant, D., Torrey, E. F., & McGrath, J. (2003). A systematic review and meta-analysis of northern hemisphere season of birth studies in schizophrenia. *Schizophrenia Bulletin, 29*, 587–593.

Davies, G. M., Willner, P., & Morgan, M. J. (2000). Smoking-related cues elicit craving in tobacco "chippers": A replication and validation of the two-factor structure of the Questionnaire of Smoking Urges. *Psychopharmacology, 152*, 334–342.

Davies, I. R. L. (1998). A study of colour grouping in three languages: A test of linguistic relativity hypothesis. *British Journal of Psychology, 89*, 433–452.

Davies, M., Stankov, L., & Roberts, R. D. (1998). Emotional intelligence: In search of an elusive construct. *Journal of Personality and Social Psychology, 75*, 989–1015.

Davies, P. T., & Cummings, E. M. (1994). Marital conflict and child adjustment: An emotional security hypothesis. *Psychological Bulletin, 116*, 387–411.

Davis, A., & Eels, K. (1953). *Davis-Eels games*. Yonkers, NY: World Book.

Davis, C., & Katzman, M. A., (1999). Perfection as acculturation: Psychological correlates of eating problems in Chinese male and female students living in the United States. *International Journal of Eating Disorders, 25*, 65–70.

Davis, H., & Memmott, J. (1982). Counting behavior in animals: A critical evaluation. *Psychological Bulletin, 92*, 547–571.

Davis, J. M., Sargent, R. G., Brayboy, T. D., & Bartoli, W. P. (1992). Thermogenic effects of pre-prandial and post-prandial exercise in obese females. *Addictive Behaviors, 17*, 185–190.

Davis, J. O., & Phelps, J. A. (1995). Twins with schizophrenia: Genes or germs? *Schizophrenia Bulletin, 21*, 13–18.

Davis, J., Schiffman, H. R., & Greist-Bousquet, S. (1990). Semantic context and figure-ground organization. *Psychological Research, 52*, 306–309.

Davis, K. D., Lozano, A. M., Manduch, M., Tasker, R. R., Kiss, Z. H. T., & Dostrovsky, J. O. (1999). Thalamic relay site for cold perception in humans. *Journal of Neurophysiology, 81*, 1970–1973.

Davis, K. L., Price, C. C., Kaplan, E., & Libon, D. J. (2002). Error analysis of the nine-word California Verbal Learning Test (CVLT-9) among older adults with and without dementia. *Clinical Neuropsychologist, 16*, 81–89.

Davis, M. C., Matthews, K. A., & McGrath, C. E. (2000). Hostile attitudes predict elevated vascular resistance during interpersonal stress in men and women. *Psychosomatic Medicine, 62*, 17–25.

Davis, P. J. (1999). Gender differences in autobiographical memory for childhood emotional experiences. *Journal of Personality and Social Psychology, 76*, 498–510.

Davis, R. (1986). Knowledge-based systems. *Science, 231*, 957–963.

Davis, R. (1993). Biological tests of intelligence as culture fair. *American Psychologist, 48*, 695–696.

Davis, S. F., Thomas, R. L., & Weaver, M. S. (1982). Psychology's contemporary and all-time notables: Student, faculty, and chairperson viewpoints. *Bulletin of the Psychonomic Society, 20*, 3–6.

Davison, K. P., Pennebaker, J. W., & Dickerson, S. S. (2000). Who talks? The social psychology of illness support groups. *American Psychologist, 55*, 205–217.

De Castro, J. M. (1999). Heritability of hunger relationships with food intake in free-living humans. *Physiology and Behavior, 67*, 249–258.

de Gelder, B., & Rouw, R. (2000). Structural encoding precludes recognition of face parts in prosopagnosia. *Cognitive Neuropsychology, 17*, 89–102.

de Graaf, C., Polet, P., & van Staveren, W. A. (1994). Sensory perception and pleasantness of food flavors in elderly subjects. *Journals of Gerontology, 49*, P93–P99.

De Jesus, S. N., Rus, C. L., Lens, W., & Imaginário, S. (2013). Intrinsic motivation and creativity related to product: A meta-analysis of the studies published between 1990–2010. *Creativity Research Journal, 25*, 80–84.

de Jong, P. J., & Merckelbach, H. (1997). No convincing evidence for a biological preparedness explanation of phobias. *Behavioral and Brain Sciences, 20*, 362–363.

De la Fuente, J. M., Goldman, S., Stanus, E., Vizuete, C., Morlan, I., Bobes, J., & Mendlewicz, J. (1997). Brain glucose metabolism in borderline personality disorder. *Journal of Psychiatric Research, 31*, 531–541.

de Mathis, M. A., Diniz, J. B., Hounie, A. G., Shavitt, R. G., Fossaluza, V., Ferrão, Y., . . . Eurípedes, C. M. (2013). Trajectory in obsessive-compulsive disorder comorbidities. *European Neuropschopharmacology, 23*, 594–601.

De Moor, J. S., de Moor, C. A, Basen-Engquist, K., Kudelka, A., Bevers, M. W., & Cohen, L.(2006). Optimism, distress, health-related quality of life, and change in cancer antigen 125 among patients with ovarian cancer undergoing chemotherapy. *Psychosomatic Medicine, 68*, 555–562.

de Paula Ramos, S. (2003). Revisiting Anna O.: A case of chemical dependence. *History of Psychology, 6*, 239–250.

de Valois, R. L., Abramov, I., & Jacobs, G. H. (1966). Analysis of response patterns of LGN cells. *Journal of the Optical Society of America, 56*, 966–977.

De Wolff, M., & van Ijzendoorn, M. H. (1997). Sensitivity and attachment: A meta-analysis on parental antecedents of infant attachment. *Child Development, 68*, 571–591.

Deahl, M. (1991). Cannabis and memory loss. *British Journal of Addiction, 86*, 249–252.

Deaux, K. (1985). Sex and gender. *Annual Review of Psychology, 36*, 49–81.

Deaux, K., & Major, B. (1987). Putting gender into context: An interactive model of gender-related behavior. *Psychological Review, 94*, 369–389.

Debski, J., Spadafore, C. D., Jacob, S., Poole, D. A., & Hixson, M. D. (2007). Suicide intervention: training, roles, and knowledge of school psychologists. *Psychology in the Schools, 44*, 157–170.

DeCarolis, N. A, & Eisch, A. J. (2010). Hippocampal neurogenesis as a target for the treatment of mental illness: A critical evaluation. *Neuropharmacology, 58*, 884–893.

DeCharms, R., & Moeller, G. H. (1962). Values expressed in American children's readers: 1800–1950. *Journal of Abnormal and Social Psychology, 64*, 136–142.

Deci, E. L., Koestner, R., & Ryan, R. M. (1999). A meta-analytic review of experiments determining the effects of extrinsic rewards on intrinsic motivation. *Psychological Bulletin, 125*, 627–668.

Deci, E. L., Nezlek, J., & Sheinman, L. (1981). Characteristics of the rewarder and intrinsic motivation of the rewardee. *Journal of Personality and Social Psychology, 40*, 1–10.

Deffner-Rappold, C., Azorlosa, J., & Baker, J. D. (1996). Acquisition and extinction of context-specific morphine withdrawal. *Psychobiology, 24*, 219–226.

Degel, J., & Koester, E. P. (1999). Odors: Implicit memory and performance effects. *Chemical Senses, 24*, 317–325.

DeHart, T., Murray, S. L., Pelham, B. W., & Rose, P. (2003). The regulation of dependency in parent-child relationships. *Journal of Experimental Social Psychology, 39*, 59–67.

Del Giudice, M. (2011). Sex differences in romantic attachment: A meta-analysis. *Personality and Social Psychology Bulletin, 37*, 193–214.

Delamater, A. R. (2011). At the interface of learning and cognition: An associative learning perspective. *International Journal of Comparative Psychology, 24*, 389–411.

Delanoë, D., Hajri, S., Bachelot, A., Mahfoudg, D., Hassoun, D., Marsicano, E., & Ringa, V. (2012). Class, gender and culture in the experience of menopause: A comparative survey in Tunisia and France. *Social Science & Medicine, 75*, 401–409.

DeLongis, A., Folkman, S., & Lazarus, R. S. (1988). The impact of daily stress on health and mood: Psychological and social resources as mediators. *Journal of Personality and Social Psychology, 54*, 486–495.

DeMartino, R. E., Crosby, A. E., EchoHawk, M., Litts, D. A., Pearson, J., Reed, G A., & West, M. (2003). A call to collaboration: The federal commitment to suicide prevention. *Suicide and Life-Threatening Behavior, 33*, 101–110.

Dement, W. C. (1960). The effect of dream deprivation. *Science, 131*, 1705–1707.

Dement, W. C. (1976). *Some must watch while some must sleep.* New York: Norton.

Dement, W. C., & Wolpert, E. (1958). The relation of eye movements, body motility, and external stimuli to dream content. *Journal of Experimental Psychology, 53*, 543–553.

Dempster, F. N. (1985). Proactive interference in sentence recall: Topic similarity effects and individual differences. *Memory and Cognition, 13*, 81–89.

DeNeve, K. M. (1999). Happy as an extraverted clam? The role of personality for subjective well-being. *Current Directions in Psychological Science, 8*, 141–144.

DeNeve, K. M., & Cooper, H. (1998). The happy personality: A meta-analysis of 137 personality traits and subjective wellbeing. *Psychological Bulletin, 124*, 197–229.

Denmark, F. L. (1998). Women and psychology: An international perspective. *American Psychologist, 53*, 465–473.

Dennerstein, L., Dudley, E., & Guthrie, J. (2002). Empty nest or revolving door? A prospective study of women's quality of life during the phase of children leaving and re-entering the home. *Psychological Medicine, 32*, 545–550.

Denney, N. W., Field, J. K., & Quadagno, D. (1984). Sex differences in sexual needs and desires. *Archives of Sexual Behavior, 13*, 233–245.

Denny, K. (2009). Handedness and depression: Evidence from a large population survey. *Laterality, 14*, 246–255.

Derbyshire, S. W. G., Whalley, M. G., Stenger, V. A., & Oakley, D. A. (2004). Cerebral activation during hypnotically induced and imagined pain. *NeuroImage, 23*, 392–401.

DeRijk, R. H., Wüst, S., Meijer, O. C., Zennaro, M.-C., Federenko, I. S., Hellhammer, D. H., . . . de Kloet, E. R. (2006). A common polymorphism in the mineralocorticoid receptor modulates stress responsiveness. *Journal of Clinical Endocrinology and Metabolism, 91*, 5083–5090.

Desforges, D. M., Lord, C. G., Ramsey, S. L., Manson, J. A., van Leeuwen, M. D., West, S. C., & Lepper, M. R. (1991). Effects of structured cooperative contact on changing negative attitudes toward stigmatized social groups. *Journal of Personality and Social Psychology, 60*, 531–544.

DeShon, R. P., Smith, M. R., Chan, D., & Schmitt, N. (1998). Can racial differences in cognitive test performance be reduced by presenting problems in a social context? *Journal of Applied Psychology, 83*, 438–451.

DeSousa, E. A., Albert, R. H., & Kalman, B. (2002). Cognitive impairments in multiple sclerosis: A review. *American Journal of Alzheimer's Disease, 17*, 23–29.

Detterman, D. K. (1999). The psychology of mental retardation. *International Review of Psychiatry, 11*, 26–33.

Deuser, W. E., & Anderson, C. A. (1995). Controllability attributions and learned helplessness: Some methodological and conceptual problems. *Basic and Applied Social Psychology, 16*, 297–318.

Deutsch, D. (2002). The puzzle of absolute pitch. *Current Directions in Psychological Science. 11*, 200–204.

Devine, P. G., & Malpass, R. S. (1985). Orienting strategies in differential face recognition. *Personality and Social Psychology Bulletin, 11*, 33–40.

Deweer, B., Ergis, A. M., Fossati, P., & Pillon, B. (1994). Explicit memory, procedural learning and lexical priming in Alzheimer's disease. *Cortex, 30*, 113–126.

Dewsbury, D. A. (1990). Early interactions between animal psychologists and animal activists and the founding of the APA Committee on Precautions in Animal Experimentation. *American Psychologist, 45*, 315–327.

Dewsbury, D. A. (1996). Beatrix Tugendhat Gardner (1933–1995). *American Psychologist, 51*, 1332.

Dewsbury, D. A. (2000). Comparative cognition in the 1930s. *Psychonomic Bulletin and Review, 7*, 267–283.

Dhami, M. K. (2003). Psychological models of professional decision making. *Psychological Science, 14*, 175–180.

Di Nuovo, A. G., Nuovo, S. D., & Buono, S. (2012). Intelligent quotient estimation of mental retarded people from different psychometric instruments using artificial neural networks. *Artificial Intelligence in Medicine, 54*, 135–145.

Diaconis, P. (1978). Statistical problems in ESP research. *Science, 201*, 131–136.

Diamanduros, T., Downs, E., & Jenkins, S. J. (2008). The role of school psychologists in the assessment, prevention, and intervention of cyber bullying. *Psychology in the Schools, 45*, 693–704.

Diamond, L. M. (1998). Development of sexual orientation among adolescent and young adult women. *Developmental Psychology, 34*, 1085–1095.

Diamond, L. M. (2003a). Was it a phase? Young women's relinquishment of lesbian/bisexual identities over a 5-year period. *Journal of Personality & Social Psychology, 84*, 352–364.

Diamond, L. M. (2003b). What does sexual orientation orient? A biobehavioral model distinguishing romantic love and sexual desire. *Psychological Review, 110*, 173–192.

Diamond, M. C. (1988). *Enriching heredity: The impact of the environment on the anatomy of the brain.* New York: Free Press.

Diamond, M., & Sigmundson, H. K. (1997). Sex reassignment at birth: A long term review and clinical implications. *Archives of Pediatric & Adolescent Medicine, 151*, 298–304.

Dickson, D. (1984). Edinburgh sets up parapsychology chair. *Science, 223*, 1274.

Diego, M. A., Jones, N. A., Field, T., Hernandez-Reif, M., Schanberg, S., Kuhn, C., . . . Galamaga, M. (1998). Aromatherapy positively affects mood, EEG patterns of alertness and math computations. *International Journal of Neuroscience, 96*, 217–224.

Diener, E. (1984). Subjective well-being. *Psychological Bulletin, 95*, 542–575.

Diener, E. (2013). The remarkable changes in the science of subjective well-being. *Perspectives on Psychological Science, 8*, 663–666.

Diener, E., & Diener, C. (1996). Most people are happy. *Psychological Science, 7*, 181–185.

Diener, E., & Fujita, F. (1995). Resources, personal strivings, and subjective well-being: A nomothetic and idiographic approach. *Journal of Personality and Social Psychology, 68*, 926–935.

Diener, E., Colvin, C. R., Pavot, W. G., & Allman, A. (1991). The psychic costs of intense positive affect. *Journal of Personality and Social Psychology, 61*, 492–503.

Diener, E., Gohm, C. L., Suh, E., & Oishi, S. (2000). Similarity of the relations between marital status and subjective well-being across cultures. *Journal of Cross-Cultural Psychology, 31*, 419–436.

Diener, E., Lucas, R. E., Oishi, S., & Suh, E. M. (2002). Looking up and down: Weighting good and bad information in life satisfaction judgments. *Personality and Social Psychology Bulletin, 28*, 437–445.

Diener, E., Oishi, S., & Lucas, R. E. (2003). Personality, culture, and subjective well-being: Emotional and cognitive evaluations of life. *Annual Review of Psychology, 54*, 403–425.

Diener, E., Sandvik, E., Seidlitz, L., & Diener, M. (1993). The relationship between income and subjective well-being: Relative or absolute? *Social Indicators Research, 28*, 195–223.

Diener, E., Suh, E. M., Lucas, R. E., & Smith, H. L. (1999). Subjective well-being: Three decades of progress. *Psychological Bulletin, 125*, 276–302.

Diener, E., Tay, L., & Oishi, S. (2013). Rising income and the subjective well-being of nations. *Journal of Personality and Social Psychology, 104*, 267–276.

Diener, E., Wolsic, B., & Fujita, F. (1995). Physical attractiveness and subjective well-being. *Journal of Personality and Social Psychology, 69*, 120–129.

Digiuni, M., Jones, F. W., & Camic, P. M. (2013). Perceived social stigma and attitudes towards seeking therapy in training: A cross-national study. *Psychotherapy, 50*, 213–223.

DiLalla, D. L., Carey, G., Gottesman, I. I., & Bouchard, T. J., Jr. (1996). Heritability of MMPI personality indicators of psychopathology in twins reared apart. *Journal of Abnormal Psychology, 105*, 491–499.

Dillard, J. P. (1991). The current status of research on sequential-request compliance techniques. *Personality and Social Psychology Bulletin, 17*, 283–288.

Dillon, K. M., & Totten, M. C. (1989). Psychological factors, immunocompetence, and health of breast-feeding mothers and their infants. *Journal of Genetic Psychology, 150*, 155–162.

DiMatteo, M. R. (2004). Social support and patient adherence to medical treatment: A meta-analysis. *Health Psychology, 23*, 207–218.

DiMatteo, M. R., Reiter, R. C., & Gambone, J. C. (1994). Enhancing medication adherence through communication and informed collaborative choice. *Health Communication, 6*, 253–265.

DiMatteo, M. R., Sherbourne, C. D., Hays, R. D., & Ordway, L. (1993). Physicians' characteristics influence patients' adherence to medical treatment: Results from the Medical Outcomes Study. *Health Psychology, 12*, 93–102.

Dimberg, U., Thunberg, M., & Elmehed, K. (2000). Unconscious facial reactions to emotional facial expressions. *Psychological Science, 11*, 86–89.

Dimitrov, M., Phipps, M., Zahn, T. P., & Grafman, J. (1999). A thoroughly modern Gage. *Neurocase, 5*, 345–354.

Dindia, K., & Allen, M. (1992). Sex differences in self-disclosure: A meta-analysis. *Psychological Bulletin, 112*, 106–124.

Dinnel, D. L., Kleinknecht, R. A., & Tanaka–Matsumi, J. (2002). A cross-cultural comparison of social phobia symptoms. *Journal of Psychopathology and Behavioral Assessment, 24*, 75–84.

Dipietro, J. A., Bornstein, M. H., Costigan, K. A., Pressman, E. K., Hahn, C.-S., Painter, K., Smith, B. A., & Yi, L. J. (2002). What does fetal movement predict about behavior during the first two years of life? *Developmental Psychobiology, 40*, 358–371.

DiPietro, J. A., Hilton, S. C., Hawkins, M., Costigan, K. A., & Pressman, E. K. (2002). Maternal stress and affect influence fetal neurobehavioral development. *Developmental Psychology, 38*, 659–668.

Dishman, R. J., & Gettman, L. R. (1980). Psychobiologic influences on exercise adherence. *Journal of Sport Psychology, 2*, 295–310.

Distal, H., Ayabe-Kanamura, S., Martinez-Gomez, M., Schicker, I., Kobayakawa, T., Saito, S., & Hudson, R. (1999). Perception of everyday odors: Correlations between intensity, familiarity and strength of hedonic judgement. *Chemical Senses, 24*, 191–199.

Ditunno, P. L., Patrick, M., Stineman, M., Morganti, B., Townson, A. F., & Ditunno, J. F. (2006). Cross-cultural differences in preference for recovery of mobility among spinal cord injury rehabilitation professionals. *Spinal Cord, 44*, 567–575.

Dixon, N. F., & Henley, S. H. (1991). Unconscious perception: Possible implications of data from academic research for clinical practice. *Journal of Nervous and Mental Disease, 179*, 243–252.

Dixson, A. F., Halliwell, G., East, R., Wignarajah, P., & Anderson, M. J. (2003). Masculine somatotype and hirsuteness as determinants of sexual attractiveness to women. *Archives of Sexual Behavior, 32*, 29–39.

Doane, J. A., West, K. L., Goldstein, M. J., Rodnick, E. H., & Jones, J. E. (1981). Parental communication deviance and affective style: Predictors of subsequent schizophrenia spectrum disorders in vulnerable adolescents. *Archives of General Psychiatry, 38*, 679–685.

Dobbins, A. C., Jeo, R. M., Fiser, J., & Allman, J. M. (1998). Distance modulation of neural activity in the visual cortex. *Science, 281*, 552–555.

Dockery, T. M., & Bedeian, A. G. (1989). "Attitudes versus actions": LaPiere's (1934) classic study revisited. *Social Behavior and Personality, 17*, 9–16.

Dodd, D. K., Russell, B. L., & Jenkins, C. (1999). Smiling in school yearbook photos: Gender differences from kindergarten to adulthood. *Psychological Record, 49*, 543–554.

Doell, R. G. (1995). Sexuality in the brain. *Journal of Homosexuality, 28*, 345–354.

Dohrenwend, B. P., Turner, J. B., Turse, N. A, Adams, B. G., Koenen, K. C., & Marshall, R. (2006). The psychological risks of Vietnam for U.S. veterans: A revisit with new data and methods. *Science, 313*, 979–82.

Doi, Y., & Minowa, M. (2003). Gender differences in excessive daytime sleepiness among Japanese workers. *Social Science & Medicine, 56*, 883–894.

Doidge, N. (1997). Empirical evidence for the efficacy of psychoanalytical psychotherapies and psychoanalysis: An overview. *Psychoanalytic Inquiry [supplement]*, 102–150.

Dolbier, C. L., Cocke, R. R., Leiferman, J. A., Steinhardt, M. A., Schapiro, S. J., Nehete, P. N., Perlman, J. E., & Sastry, J. (2001). Differences in functional immune responses of high vs. low hardy healthy individuals. *Journal of Behavioral Medicine, 24*, 219–229.

Dolin, D. J., & Booth-Butterfield, S. (1995). Foot-in-the-door and cancer prevention. *Health Communication, 7*, 55–66.

Dollard, J., Doob, I. W., Miller, N. E., Mowrer, O. H., & Sears, R. R. (1939). *Frustration and aggression.* New York: McGraw-Hill.

Dolliver, R. H. (1995). Carl Rogers's personality theory and psychotherapy as a reflection of his life and personality. *Journal of Humanistic Psychology, 35*, 111–128.

Dominguez, M. M., & Carton, J. S. (1997). The relationship between self-actualization and parenting style. *Journal of Social Behavior and Personality, 12*, 1093–1100.

Domino, E. F. (1999). Cannabinoids and the cholinergic system. In G. G. Nahas et al. (Eds.), *Marihuana and medicine* (pp. 223–226). Totowa, NJ: Humana Press.

Donaghue, N., & Fallon, B. J. (2003). Gender-role self-stereotyping and the relationship between equity and satisfaction in close relationships. *Sex Roles, 48*, 217–230.

Donaldson, K. D. (1976). *Insanity inside out: The personal story behind the landmark Supreme Court decision.* New York: Crown.

Donderi, D. C. (1994). Visual acuity, color vision, and visual search performance at sea. *Human Factors, 36*, 129–144.

Dong, Y. T., & Church, A. T. (2003). Cross-cultural equivalence and validity of the Vietnamese MMPI-2: Assessing psychological adjustment of Vietnamese refugees. *Psychological Assessment, 15*, 370–377.

Donovan, J. J., & Radosevich, D. J. (1999). A metaanalytic review of the distribution of practice effect: Now you see it, now you don't. *Journal of Applied Psychology, 84*, 795–805.

Donovan, R. J., & Jalleh, G. (1999). Positively versus negatively framed product attributes: The influence of involvement. *Psychology and Marketing, 16*, 613–630.

Donovan, W. L., Leavitt, L. A., & Walsh, R. O. (1997). Cognitive set and coping strategy affect mother's sensitivity to infant cries. *Child Development, 68*, 760–772.

Dorian, L., & Garfinkel, P. E. (2002). Culture and body image in Western culture. *Eating and Weight Disorders, 7*, 1–19.

Dorn, L. D., Susman, E. J., & Ponirakis, A. (2003). Pubertal timing and adolescent adjustment and behavior: Conclusions vary by rater. *Journal of Youth and Adolescence, 32*, 157–167.

Dougherty, D. M., Cherek, D. R., & Bennett, R. H. (1996). The effects of alcohol on the aggressive responding of women. *Journal of Studies on Alcohol, 57*, 178–186.

Dovidio, J. F., & Gaertner, S. L. (2000). Aversive racism and selection decisions: 1989 and 1999. *Psychological Science, 11*, 315–319.

Dovidio, J. F., Kawakami, K., & Gaertner, S. L. (2002). Implicit and explicit prejudice and interracial integration. *Journal of Social and Personality Psychology, 82*, 62–68.

Dowd, E. T. (2003). Cultural differences in cognitive therapy. *Behavior Therapist, 26*, 247–249.

Downey, G., Freitas, A. L., Michaelis, B., & Khouri, H. (1998). The self-fulfilling prophecy in close relationships: Rejection sensitivity and rejection by romantic partners. *Journal of Personality and Social Psychology, 75*, 545–560.

Doyle, A. C. (1930). *The complete Sherlock Holmes.* Garden City, NY: Doubleday.

Doyle, J. (1995). *The male experience* (3rd ed.). Madison, WI: Brown & Benchmark.

Dozois, D. J. A., & Dobson, K. S. (2003). The structure of the self-schema in clinical depression: Differences related to episode recurrence. *Cognition and Emotion, 17,* 933–941.

Draguns, J. G. (1995). Cultural influences upon psychopathology: Clinical and practical implications. *Journal of Social Distress and the Homeless, 4,* 79–103.

Draguns, J. G., & Tanaka-Matsumi, J. (2003). Assessment of psychopathology across and within cultures: Issues and findings. *Behaviour Research and Therapy, 41,* 755–776.

Dremencov, E., el Mansari, M., & Blier, P. (2009). Brain norepinephrine system as a target for antidepressant and mood stabilizing medications. *Current Drug Targets, 10,* 1061–1068.

Drews, F. A., Yazdani, H., Godfrey, C. N., Cooper, J. M., & Strayer, D. L. (2009). Text messaging during simulated driving. *Human Factors: The Journal of the Human Factors and Ergonomics Society, 51,* 762–770.

Drigotas, S. M. (2002). The Michelangelo phenomenon and personal well-being. *Journal of Personality, 70,* 59–77.

Driskell, J. E., Willis, R. P., & Copper, C. (1992). Effect of overlearning on retention. *Journal of Applied Psychology, 77,* 615–622.

Droesler, J. (2000). An n-dimensional Weber law and the corresponding Fechner law. *Journal of Mathematical Psychology, 44,* 330–335.

Drummond, T. (1999a, May 10). Battling the Columbine copycats. *Time.*

Dryer, D. C., & Horowitz, L. M. (1997). When do opposites attract? Interpersonal complementarity versus similarity. *Journal of Personality and Social Psychology, 72,* 592–603.

Dube, L., & Le Bel, J. L. (2003). The content and structure of laypeople's concept of pleasure. *Cognition & Emotion, 17,* 263–295.

Duddu, V., Chaturvedi, S. K., & Isaac, M. K. (2003). Amplification and attribution styles in somatoform and depressive disorders: A study from Bangalore, India. *Psychopathology, 36,* 98–103.

Dudycha, G. J. (1936). An objective study of punctuality in relation to personality and achievement. *Archives of Psychology, 29,* 1–53.

Duffy, J. F. (2000, May 9). New Hope bids farewell to "Mother." *Intelligencer Record,* pp. A1, A4.

Dufresne, T. (Ed.). (2007). *Against Freud: Critics talk back.* Stanford: Stanford University Press.

Duncan, J., Burgess, P., & Emslie, H. (1995). Fluid intelligence after frontal lobe lesions. *Neuropsychologia, 33,* 261–268.

Duncan, J., Seitz, R. J., Kolodny, J., Bor, D., Herzog, H., Ahmed, A., . . . Emslie, H. (2000). A neural basis for general intelligence. *Science, 289,* 457–460.

Dunn, R. L., & Schwebel, A. I. (1995). Meta-analytic review of marital therapy outcome research. *Journal of Family Psychology, 9,* 58–68.

Durand, K., & Lecuyer, R. (2002). Object permanence observed in 4-month-old infants with a 2D display. *Infant Behavior and Development, 35,* 269–278.

Durlak, J. ., & Wells, A. M. (1998). Evaluation of indicated preventive intervention (secondary prevention) mental health programs for children and adolescents. *American Journal of Community Psychology, 26,* 775–802.

Durstewitz, D., Vittoz, N. M., Floresco, S. B., & Seamans, J. K. (2010). Abrupt transitions between prefrontal neural ensemble states accompany behavioral transitions during rule learning. *Neuron, 66,* 438–448.

Dushanova, J., & Donoghue, J. (2010). Neurons in primary motor cortex engaged during action observation. *European Journal of Neuroscience, 31,* 386–398.

Dutton, D. G., & Aron, A. P. (1974). Some evidence for heightened sexual attraction under conditions of high anxiety. *Journal of Personality and Social Psychology, 30,* 510–517.

Duyme, M. (1988). School success and social class: An adoption study. *Developmental Psychology, 24,* 203–209.

Dworkin, B. R., & Miller, N. E. (1986). Failure to replicate visceral learning in the acute curarized rat preparation. *Behavioral Neuroscience, 100,* 299–314.

Dyer, C. A. (1999). Pathophysiology of phenylketonuria. *Mental Retardation and Developmental Disabilities Research Reviews, 5,* 104–112.

Dyer, F. C. (2002). When it pays to waggle. *Nature, 419,* 885–886.

Dym, R. J., Burns, J., Freeman, K., & Lipton, M. L. (2011). Is functional MR imaging assessment of hemispheric language dominance as good as the Wada Test? A meta-analysis. *Radiology 261,* 446–455.

Eagle, M. (1997). Contributions of Erik Erikson. *Psychoanalytic Review, 84,* 337–347.

Eagly, A., & Steffen, V. J. (1983). Gender stereotypes stem from the distribution of women and men into social roles. *Journal of Personality and Social Psychology, 46,* 735–754.

Eagly, A. H. (1983). Gender and social influence: A social psychological analysis. *American Psychologist, 38,* 971–981.

Eagly, A. H. (1994). On comparing women and men. *Feminism and Psychology, 4,* 513–522.

Eagly, A. H. (1995). The science and politics of comparing women and men. *American Psychologist, 50,* 145–158.

Eagly, A. H., & Crowley, M. (1986). Gender and helping behavior: A meta-analytic review of the social psychology literature. *Psychological Bulletin, 100,* 283–308.

Eagly, A. H., & Steffen, V. J. (1986). Gender and aggressive behavior: A meta-analytic review of the social psychological literature. *Psychological Bulletin, 100,* 309–330.

Eagly, A. H., & Warren, R. (1976). Intelligence, comprehension, and opinion change. *Journal of Personality and Social Psychology, 44,* 226–242.

Earle, T. L., Linden, W., & Weinberg, J. (1999). Differential effects of harassment on cardiovascular and salivary cortisol stress reactivity and recovery in women and men. *Journal of Psychosomatic Research, 46,* 125–141.

Eastwick, P. W., Eagly, A. H., Finkel, E. J., & Johnson, S. E. (2011). Implicit and explicit prefeences for physical attractiveness in a romantic partner: A double dissociation in predictive validity. *Journal of Personality & Social Psychology, 101,* 993–1011.

Eaves, L. J., Silberg, J. L., Maes, H. H., Simonoff, E., Pickles, A., Rutter, M., . . . Hewitt, J. K. (1997). Genetics and developmental psychopathology: 2. The main effects of genes and environment on behavioral problems in the Virginia Twin Study of Adolescent Behavioral Development. *Journal of Child Psychology and Psychiatry and Allied Disciplines, 38,* 965–980.

Ebbeck, V., & Weiss, M. R. (1988). The arousal-performance relationship: Task characteristics and performance measures in track and field athletics. *Sport Psychologist, 2,* 13–27.

Ebbinghaus, H. (1885/1913). *Memory: A contribution to experimental psychology.* New York: Columbia University Press.

Eccles, A., Wilde, A., & Marshall, W. L. (1988). In vivo desensitization in the treatment of recurrent nightmares. *Journal of Behavior Therapy and Experimental Psychiatry, 19,* 285–288.

Eccles, J. S., & Wigfield, A. (1995). In the mind of the actor: The structure of adolescents' achievement task values and expectancy-related beliefs. *Personality & Social Psychology Bulletin, 21,* 215–225.

Ecenbarger, W. (1987, June 4). The forgotten sense. *Philadelphia Inquirer Magazine,* pp. 24–26, 34–35.

Eckert, E. D., Bouchard, T. J., Bohlen, J., & Heston, L. L. (1986). Homosexuality in monozygotic twins reared apart. *British Journal of Psychiatry, 148,* 421–425.

Edeline, J. M., & Weinberger, N. M. (1991). Subcortical adaptive filtering in the auditory system: Associative receptive field plasticity in the dorsal medial geniculate body. *Behavioral Neuroscience, 105,* 154–175.

Edinger, J. D., & Radtke, R. A. (1993). Use of in vivo desensitization to treat a patient's claustrophobic response to nasal CPAP. *Sleep, 16,* 678–680.

Egan, K. J., Carr, J. E., Hunt, D. D., & Adamson, R. (1988). Endogenous opiate system and systematic desensitization. *Journal of Consulting and Clinical Psychology, 56,* 287–291.

Egeland, J. A., Gerhard, D. S., Pauls, D. L., Sussex, J. N., Kidd, K. K., Allen, C. R., . . . Housman, D. E. (1987). Bipolar affective disorders linked to DNA markers on chromosome 11. *Nature, 325,* 783–787.

Egeth, H. (1992). Dichotic listening: Long-lived echoes of Broadbent's early studies. *Journal of Experimental Psychology: General, 121,* 124.

Ehara, T. H. (1980, December). On the electronic chess circuit. *Science, 80,* 78, 80.

Ehrlichman, H., & Halpern, J. N. (1988). Affect and memory: Effects of pleasant and unpleasant odors on retrieval of happy and unhappy memories. *Journal of Personality and Social Psychology, 55,* 769–779.

Eich, E., Macaulay, D., & Ryan, L. (1994). Mood-dependent memory for events of the personal past. *Journal of Experimental Psychology General, 123,* 201–215.

Eich, J. E. (1980). The cue-dependent nature of state-dependent retrieval. *Memory and Cognition, 8,* 157–173.

Eich, J. E. (1995). Searching for mood-dependent memory. *Psychological Science, 6,* 67–75.

Eich, J. E., Weingartner, H., Stillman, R. C., & Gillin, J. C. (1975). State-dependent accessibility of retrieval cues in the retention of a categorized list. *Journal of Verbal Learning and Verbal Behavior, 14,* 408–417.

Eichenbaum, H. (1997). Declarative memory: Insights from cognitive neurobiology. *Annual Review of Psychology, 48,* 547–572.

Eichstedt, J. A., Arnold, S. L. (2001). Childhood-onset obsessive-compulsive disorder: A tic-related subtype of OCD? *Clinical Psychology Review, 21,* 137–157.

Eiden, R. D., Schuetze, P., & Coles, C. D. (2011). Maternal cocaine use and mother-infant interactions: Direct and moderated associations. *Neurotoxicology & Teratology, 33,* 120–128.

Eisdorfer, C. (1983). Conceptual models of aging: The challenge of a new frontier. *American Psychologist, 38,* 197–202.

Eisenberg, N., Cialdini, R. B., McCreath, H., & Shell, R. (1987). Consistency-based compliance: When and why do children become vulnerable? *Journal of Personality and Social Psychology, 52,* 1174–1181.

Eisenberg, N., & Lennon, R. (1983). Sex differences in empathy and related capacities. *Psychological Bulletin, 94,* 100–131.

Eisenberger, N. I., Lieberman, M. D., & Williams, K. D. (2003). Does rejection hurt? An fMRI study of social exclusion. *Science, 302,* 290–292.

Eisenberger, N. I., Taylor, S. E., Gable, S. L., Hilmert, C. J., & Lieberman, M. D. (2007). Neural pathways link social support to attenuated neuroendocrine stress responses. *NeuroImage, 35,* 1601–1612.

Eisenman, R. (1993). Belief that drug usage in the United States is increasing when it is really decreasing: An example of the availability heuristic. *Bulletin of the Psychonomic Society, 31,* 249–252.

Ekbia, H. R. (2008). *Artificial dreams: The quest for non-biological intelligence.* New York: Cambridge University Press.

Ekman, P. (1992a). An argument for basic emotions. *Cognition and Emotion, 6,* 169–200.

Ekman, P. (1992b). Facial expressions of emotion: New findings, new questions. *Psychological Science, 3,* 34–38.

Ekman, P. (1993). Facial expression and emotion. *American Psychologist, 48,* 384–392.

Ekman, P., & Friesen, W. V. (1971). Constants across cultures in the face and emotion. *Journal of Personality and Social Psychology, 17,* 124–129.

Ekman, P., & O'Sullivan, M. (1991). Who can catch a liar? *American Psychologist, 46,* 913–920.

Ekman, P., Davidson, R. J., & Friesen, W. V. (1990). The Duchenne smile: 2. Emotional expression and brain physiology. *Journal of Personality and Social Psychology, 58,* 342–353.

Ekman, P., Friesen, W. V., O'Sullivan, M., Chan, A., Diacoyanni-Tarlatzis, I., Heider, K., . . . Tzavaras, A. (1987). Universals and cultural differences in the judgments of facial expressions of emotion. *Journal of Personality and Social Psychology, 53,* 712–717.

Ekman, P., Levenson, R. W., & Friesen, W. V. (1983). Autonomic nervous system activity distinguishes among emotions. *Science, 221,* 1208–1210.

Ekman, P., O'Sullivan, M., & Frank, M. G. (1999). A few can catch a liar. *Psychological Science, 10,* 263–266.

Elaad, E. (1990). Detection of guilty knowledge in real-life criminal investigations. *Journal of Applied Psychology, 75,* 521–529.

Elaad, E. (1994). The accuracy of human decisions and objective measurements in psychophysiological detection of knowledge. *Journal of Psychology, 128,* 267–280.

Elaad, E. (1997). Polygraph examiner awareness of crime-relevant information and the Guilty Knowledge Test. *Law and Human Behavior, 21,* 107–120.

Elder, W. B., Brooks, G. R., & Morrow, S. L. (2012). Sexual self-schemas of heterosexual men. *Psychology of Men & Masculinity, 13,* 166–179.

Elfenbein, H. A., & Ambady, N. (2002). On the universality and cultural specificity of emotion recognition: A meta-analysis. *Psychological Bulletin, 128,* 203–235.

Elkind, D. (1996). Inhelder and Piaget on adolescence and adulthood: A postmodern appraisal. *Psychological Science, 7,* 216–220.

Elkins, R. L. (1987). An experimenter effect on place avoidance learning of selectively-bred taste-aversion prone and resistant rats. *Medical Science Research: Psychology and Psychiatry, 15,* 1181–1182.

Ellenberger, H. F. (1970). *The discovery of the unconscious: The history and evolution of dynamic psychiatry.* New York: Basic Books.

Elliot, A. J., & Devine, P. G. (1994). On the motivational nature of cognitive dissonance: Dissonance as psychological discomfort. *Journal of Personality and Social Psychology, 67,* 382–394.

Elliott, R. (1988). Tests, abilities, race, and conflict. *Intelligence, 12,* 333–350.

Ellis, A. (1962). *Reason and emotion in psychotherapy.* New York: Lyle Stuart.

Ellis, A. (1996). The treatment of morbid jealousy: A rational emotive behavior therapy approach. *Journal of Cognitive Psychotherapy, 10,* 23–33.

Ellis, A. (1997). Using Rational Emotive Behavior Therapy techniques to cope with disability. *Professional Psychology: Research and Practice, 28,* 17–22.

Ellis, A. (1999). Why rational-emotive therapy to rational emotive behavior therapy? *Psychotherapy, 36,* 154–159.

Ellis, A. P. J., West, B. J., Ryan, A. M., & DeShon, R. P. (2002). The use of impression management tactics in structured interviews: A function of question type? *Journal of Applied Psychology, 87,* 1200–1208.

Ellis, H. C. (1987). Recent developments in human memory. In V. P. Makosy (Ed.), *The G. Stanley Hall Lecture Series* (Vol. 7, pp. 161–206). Washington, DC: American Psychological Association.

Ellis, L. (1987). Relationships of criminality and psychopathy with eight other apparent behavioral manifestations of sub-optimal arousal. *Personality and Individual Differences, 8,* 905–925.

Ellis, L. (1998). The evolution of attitudes about social stratification: Why many people (including social scientists) are morally outraged by *The Bell Curve. Personality and Individual Differences, 24,* 207–216.

Ellis, L., & Ames, M. A. (1987). Neurohormonal functioning and sexual orientation: A theory of homosexuality-heterosexuality. *Psychological Bulletin, 101,* 233–258.

Ellis, L., & Engh, T. (2000). Handedness and age of death: New evidence on a puzzling relationship. *Journal of Health Psychology, 5,* 561–565.

Ellis, R. R., & Lederman, S. J. (1998). The golf-ball illusion: Evidence for top-down processing in weight perception. *Perception, 27,* 193–201.

Ellison, P. A., Govern, J. M., Petri, H. L., & Figler, M. H. (1995). Anonymity and aggressive driving behavior: A field study. *Journal of Social Behavior and Personality, 10,* 265–272.

Ellison, W. J. (1987). State execution of juveniles: Defining "youth" as a mitigating factor for imposing a sentence of less than death. *Law and Psychology Review, 11,* 1–38.

Else-Quest, N. M., Hyde, J. S., & Linn, M. C. (2010). Cross-national patterns of gender differences in mathematics: A meta-analysis. *Psychological Bulletin, 136,* 103–127.

Else-Quest, N. M., Hyde, J. S., Goldsmith, H. H., Van Hulle, C. A. (2006). Gender differences in temperament: A meta-analysis. *Psychological Bulletin, 132,* 33–72.

Emam, M. M. (2013). Problem-solving orientation and attributional style as predictors of depressive symptoms in Egyptian adolescents with visual impairment. *British Journal of Visual Impairment, 31,* 150–163.

Emde Boas, W. van (1999). Juhn A. Wada and the sodium amytal test: The first (and last?) 50 years. *Journal of the History of the Neurosciences, 8,* 286–292.

Emmons, R. A. (2000). Is spirituality an intelligence? Motivation, cognition, and the psychology of ultimate concern. *International Journal for the Psychology of Religion, 10,* 3–26.

Emonson, D. L., & Vanderbeek, R. D. (1995). The use of amphetamines in U.S. Air Force tactical operations during Desert Shield and Storm. *Aviation, Space, and Environmental Medicine, 66,* 260–263.

Enders, C. K., Laurenceau, J. P., & Stuetzle, R. (2006). Teaching random assignment: A classroom demonstration using a deck of playing cards. *Teaching of Psychology, 33,* 239–242.

Enea, V., & Dafinoiu, I. (2013). Flexibility in processing visual information: Effects of mood and hypnosis. *International Journal of Clinical and Experimental Hypnosis, 61,* 55–70.

Engel, S. A. (1999). Using neuroimaging to measure mental representations: Finding color-opponent neurons in visual cortex. *Current Directions in Psychological Science, 8,* 23–27.

Engels, G. I., Garnefski, N., & Diekstra, R. F. W. (1993). Efficacy of rational-emotive therapy: A quantitative analysis. *Journal of Consulting and Clinical Psychology, 61,* 1083–1090.

Engstrom, M., & Söderfeldt, B. (2010). Brain activation during compassion meditation: A case study. *Journal of Alternative and Complementary Medicine, 16,* 597–599.

Epstein, M. H., & Synhorst, L. (2008). Preschool Behavioral and Emotional Rating Scale (PreBERS): Test-retest reliability and inter-rater reliability. *Journal of Child and Family Studies, 17,* 853–862.

Epstein, R. (1991). Skinner, creativity, and the problem of spontaneous behavior. *Psychological Science, 2,* 362–370.

Epstein, R., Kirshnit, C. E., Lanza, R. P., & Rubin, I. C. (1984). "Insight" in the pigeon: Antecedents and determinants of an intelligent performance. *Nature, 308,* 61–62.

Epstein, S. (1994). Integration of the cognitive and the psychodynamic unconscious. *American Psychologist, 49,* 709–724.

Epstein, S., & Feist, G. J. (1988). Relation between self- and other-acceptance and its moderation by identification. *Journal of Personality and Social Psychology, 54,* 309–315.

Epstein, S., & O'Brien, E. J. (1985). The person-situation debate in historical and current perspective. *Psychological Bulletin, 98,* 513–537.

Er, N. (2003). A new flashbulb memory model applied to the Marmara earthquake. *Applied Cognitive Psychology, 17,* 503–517.

Erdur, O., Rude, S. S., & Baron, A. (2003). Symptom improvement and length of treatment in ethnically similar and dissimilar client–therapist pairings. *Journal of Counseling Psychology, 50,* 52–58.

Erel, O., & Burman, B. (1995). Interrelatedness of marital relations and parent-child relations: A meta-analytic review. *Psychological Bulletin, 118,* 108–132.

Erez, A., & Judge, T. A. (2001). Relationship of core self-evaluations to goal setting, motivation, and performance. *Journal of Applied Psychology, 86,* 1270–1279.

Ericsson, K. A., & Polson, P. G. (1988). An experimental analysis of the mechanisms of a memory skill. *Journal of Experimental Psychology: Learning, Memory, and Cognition, 14,* 305–316.

Erikson, E. (1963). *Childhood and society.* New York: W. W. Norton.

Erwin, P. G. (1994). Effectiveness of social skills training with children: A meta-analytic study. *Counselling Psychology Quarterly, 7,* 305–310.

Escolas, S. M., Pitts, B. L., Safer, M. A., & Bartone, P. T. (2013). The protective value of hardiness on military posttraumatic stress symptoms. *Military Psychology, 25,* 116–123.

Espejo, E. F., Gonzalez-Albo, M. C., Moraes, J. P., El Banoua, F., Flores, J. A., & Caraballo, I. (2001). Functional regeneration in a rat Parkinson's model after intrastriatal grafts of glial cell line-derived neurotrophic factor and transforming growth factor beta-sub-1-expressing extra-adrenal chromaffin cells of the Zuckerkandl's organ. *Journal of Neuroscience, 21,* 9888–9895.

Estrada, C. A., Isen, A. M., & Young, M. J. (1994). Positive affect improves creative problem solving and influences reported source of practice satisfaction in physicians. *Motivation and Emotion, 18,* 285–299.

Etkin, A., & Wager, T. D. (2007). Functional neuroimaging of anxiety: A meta-analysis of emotional processing in PTSD, social anxiety disorder, and specific phobia. *American Journal of Psychiatry, 164*(10), 1476–1488.

Evans, D. L., Leserman, J., Perkins, D. O., & Stern, R. A. (1995). Stress-associated reductions of cytotoxic T lymphocytes and natural killer cells in asymptomatic HIV infection. *American Journal of Psychiatry, 152,* 543–550.

Evans, K. C., Wright, C. I., Wedig, M. M., Gold, A. L., Pollack, M. H., & Rauch, S. L. (2008). A functional MRI study of amygdala responses to angry schematic faces in social anxiety disorder. *Depression and Anxiety, 25,* 496–505.

Evans, S., Ferrando, S. J., Rabkin, J. G., & Fishman, B. (2000). Health locus of control, distress, and utilization of protease inhibitors among HIV-positive men. *Journal of Psychosomatic Research, 49,* 157–162.

Everly, G. S., Jr. (2000). Crisis management briefings (CMB): Large group crisis intervention in response to terrorism, disasters, and violence. *International Journal of Emergency Mental Health, 2,* 53–57.

Evers, A., Klusmann, V., Ziegelmann, J. P., Schwarzer, R., & Heuser, I. (2012). Long-term adherence to a physical activity intervention: The role of telephone-assisted vs. self-administered coping plans and strategy use. *Psychology & Health, 27,* 784–797.

Evers, A. W. M., Kraaimaat, F. W., Geenen, R., Jacobs, J. W. G., & Bijlsma, J. W. J. (2003). Stress-vulnerability factors as long-term predictors of disease activity in early rheumatoid arthritis. *Journal of Psychosomatic Research, 55,* 293–302.

Eviatar, Z. (2000). Culture and brain organization. *Brain and Cognition, 42,* 50–52.

Ewald, H. Mors, O., Flint, T., & Koed, K. (1995). A possible locus for manic depressive illness on chromosome 16p13. *Psychiatric Genetics, 5,* 71–81.

Ewin, D. M. (1994). Many memories retrieved with hypnosis are accurate. *American Journal of Clinical Hypnosis, 36,* 174–176.

Exton, M. S., Westermann, J., & Schedlowski, M. (2000). Behaviorally conditioned immunosuppression: Mechanisms and biological relevance. *Psychologische Beitrage, 42,* 118–129.

Eyler, A. A., Matson-Koffman, D., Vest, J. R., Evenson, K. R., Sanderson, B., Thompson, J. L., . . . Young, D. R. (2002). Environmental, policy, and cultural factors related to physical activity in a diverse sample of women: The Women's Cardiovascular Health Network Project—Summary and discussion. *Women and Health, 36,* 123–134.

Eysenck, H. J. (1982). *Personality, genetics, and behavior: Selected papers.* New York: Praeger.

Eysenck, H. J. (1988). Skinner, Skinnerism, and the Skinnerian in psychology. *Counseling Psychology Quarterly, 1,* 299–301.

Eysenck, H. J. (1990). Genetic and environmental contributions to individual differences: The three major dimensions of personality. *Journal of Personality, 58,* 245–261.

Eysenck, H. J. (1994). Cancer, personality, and stress: Prediction and prevention. *Advances in Behaviour Research and Therapy, 16,* 167–215.

Eysenck, H. J. (1994). The outcome problem in psychotherapy: What have we learned? *Behaviour Research and Therapy, 32,* 477–495.

Eysenck, S. B., Barrett, P. T., & Barnes, G. E. (1993). A cross-cultural study of personality: Canada and England. *Personality and Individual Differences, 14,* 1–9.

Ezzo, J., Berman, B., Hadhazy, V. A., Jadad, A. R., Lao, L., & Singh, B. B. (2000). Is acupuncture effective for the treatment of chronic pain? A systematic review. *Pain, 86,* 217–225.

Fabbro, F. (2000). Introduction to language and cerebellum. *Journal of Neurolinguistics, 13,* 83–94.

Fagan, J. F., & Holland, C. R. (2002). Equal opportunity and racial differences in IQ. *Intelligence, 30,* 361–387.

Fagan, M. M., & Ayers, K. (1983). Levinson's model as a predictor of the adult development of policemen. *International Journal of Aging and Human Development, 16,* 221–230.

Fagerstrom, K. O., Schneider, N. G., & Lunell, E. (1993). Effectiveness of nicotine patch and nicotine gum as individual versus combined treatments for tobacco withdrawal symptoms. *Psychopharmacology, 111,* 271–277.

Fairburn, C. G., Cowen, P. J., Harrison, P. J. (1999). Twin studies and the etiology of eating disorders. *International Journal of Eating Disorders, 26,* 349–358.

Fairburn, C. G., Shafran, R., & Cooper, Z. (1999). A cognitive behavioural theory of anorexia nervosa. *Behaviour Research and Therapy, 37,* 1–13.

Faith, M. S., Rha, S. S., Neale, M. C., & Allison, D. B. (1999). Evidence for genetic influences on human energy intake: Results from a twin study using measured observations. *Behavior Genetics, 29,* 145–154.

Falbo, T., & Polit, D. F. (1986). Quantitative review of the only-child literature: Research evidence and theory development. *Psychological Bulletin, 100,* 176–189.

Falk, J. L. (1994). The discriminative stimulus and its reputation: Role in the instigation of drug abuse. *Experimental and Clinical Psychopharmacology, 2,* 43–52.

Falk, R. (1998). Replication: A step in the right direction [Commentary on Sohn]. *Theory and Psychology, 8,* 313–321.

Fallace, T. D. (2010). The mind at every stage has its own logic: John Dewey as genetic psychologist. *Educational Theory, 60,* 129–146.

Fallon, A. E., & Rozin, P. (1985). Sex differences in perceptions of desirable body shape. *Journal of Abnormal Psychology, 94,* 102–105.

Fals-Stewart, W. (2003). The occurrence of partner physical aggression on days of alcohol consumption: A longitudinal diary study. *Journal of Consulting and Clinical Psychology, 71,* 41–52.

Fancher, R. E. (1984). Not Conley, but Burt and others: A reply. *Journal of the History of the Behavioral Sciences, 20,* 186.

Fancher, R. E. (1987). Henry Goddard and the Kallikak Family photographs: "Conscious skulduggery" or "Whig history"? *American Psychologist, 42,* 585–590.

Fani, L., Bak, S., Delhanty, P., van Rossum, E. F. C., & van den Akker, E. L. T. (2014). The melanocortin-4 receptor as target for obesity treatment: A systematic review of emerging pharmacological therapeutic options. *International Journal of Obesity, 38,* 163–169.

Fantoni-Salvador, P., & Rogers, R. (1997). Spanish versions of the MMPI-2 and PAI: An investigation of concurrent validity with Hispanic patients. *Assessment, 4,* 29–39.

Faraone, S. (1982). Psychiatry and political repression in the Soviet Union. *American Psychologist, 37,* 1105–1112.

Faraone, S. V., Perlis, R. H., Doyle, A. E., Smoller, J. W., Goralnick, J. J., Holmgren, M. A., & Sklar, P. (2005). Molecular genetics of attention-deficit/hyperactivity disorder. *Biological Psychiatry, 57,* 1313–1323.

Faraone, S. V., Sergeant, J., Gillberg, C., & Biederman, J. (2003). The worldwide prevalence of ADHD: Is it an American condition? *World Psychiatry, 2,* 104–113.

Faravelli, C., Cosci, F., Ciampelli, M., Scarpato, M. A., Spiti, R., & Ricca, V. (2003). A self-controlled, naturalistic study of selective serotonin reuptake inhibitors versus tricyclic antidepressants. *Psychotherapy and Psychosomatics, 72,* 95–101.

Farde, L. (1997). Brain imaging of schizophrenia: The dopamine hypothesis. *Schizophrenia Research, 28,* 157–162.

Farr, C. B. (1944/1994). Benjamin Rush and American psychiatry. *American Journal of Psychiatry, 151,* 65–73.

Farrimond, T. (1990). Effect of alcohol on visual constancy values and possible relation to driving performance. *Perceptual and Motor Skills, 70,* 291–295.

Farthing, G. W., Venturino, M., & Brown, S. W. (1984). Suggestion and distraction in the control of pain: Test of two hypotheses. *Journal of Abnormal Psychology, 93,* 266–276.

Fassbender, P. (1997). Parapsychology and the neurosciences: A computer-based content analysis of abstracts in the database "Medline" from 1975 to 1995. *Perceptual and Motor Skills, 84,* 452–454.

Fauerbach, J. A., Lawrence, J. W., Haythornthwaite, J. A., & Richter, L. (2002). Coping with the stress of a painful medical procedure. *Behaviour Research and Therapy, 40,* 1003–1015.

Faust, J., Olson, R., & Rodriguez, H. (1991). Same-day surgery preparation: Reduction of pediatric patient arousal and distress through participant modeling. *Journal of Consulting and Clinical Psychology, 59,* 475–478.

Fava, G. A., & Sonino, N. (2000). Psychosomatic medicine: Emerging trends and perspectives. *Psychotherapy and Psychosomatics, 69,* 184–197.

Fava, M. (2003). The role of the serotonergic and noradrenergic neurotransmitter systems in the treatment of psychological and physical symptoms of depression. *Journal of Clinical Psychiatry, 64,* 26–29.

Fava, M., & Rankin, M. (2002). Sexual functioning and SSRIs. *Journal of Clinical Psychiatry, 63,* 13–16.

Favreau, O. E. (1997). Sex and gender comparisons: Does null hypothesis testing create a false dichotomy? *Feminism and Psychology, 7,* 63–81.

Feather, S. R. (1983). Something different: A biographical sketch of Louisa Rhine. *Journal of Parapsychology, 47,* 293–302.

Fedoroff, I. C., Polivy, J., & Herman, C. P. (1997). The effect of pre-exposure to food cues on the eating behavior of restrained and unrestrained eaters. *Appetite, 28,* 33–47.

Feest, U. (2005). Operationism in psychology: What the debate is about, what the debate should be about. *Journal of the History of the Behavioral Sciences, 41,* 131–149.

Feest, U. (2007). Science and experience/science of experience: Gestalt psychology and the anti-metaphysical project of the auf bau. *Perspectives on Science, 15,* 1–25.

Fehr, B. (1999). Laypeople's conceptions of commitment. *Journal of Personality and Social Psychology, 76,* 90–103.

Fehr, B., & Russell, J. A. (1984). Concept of emotion viewed from a prototypic perspective. *Journal of Experimental Psychology: General, 113,* 464–486.

Fehr, B., & Russell, J. A. (1991). The concept of love viewed from a prototype perspective. *Journal of Personality and Social Psychology, 60,* 425–438.

Fein, D. (1990). Cerebral lateralization: A dominant question in developmental research [Review of Brain lateralization in children: Developmental implications]. *Contemporary Psychology, 35,* 676–677.

Fein, S., & Spencer, S. J. (1997). Prejudice as self-image maintenance: Affirming the self through derogating others. *Journal of Personality and Social Psychology, 73,* 31–44.

Feingold, A. (1994). Gender differences in personality: A meta-analysis. *Psychological Bulletin, 116,* 429–456.

Feingold, A., & Mazzella, R. (1998). Gender differences in body image are increasing. *Psychological Science, 9,* 190–195.

Feinstein, J. S., Rudrauf, D., Khalsa, S. S., Cassell, M. D., Bruss, J., Grabowski, T. J., & Tranel, D. (2010). Bilateral limbic system destruction in man. *Journal of Clinical and Experimental Neuropsychology, 32,* 88–106.

Feng, C.-Y., Chu, H., Chen, C.-H., Chang, Y.-S., Chen, T. H., Chou, Y.-H., . . . Chou, K. R. (2012). The effect of cognitive behavioral group therapy for depression: A meta-analysis. *World Views on Evidence-Based Nursing, 9,* 2–17.

Feng, D., Silverstein, M., Giarrusso, R., McArdle, J. J., & Bengtson, V. L. (2006). Attrition of older adults in longitudinal surveys: Detection and correction of sample selection bias using multigenerational data. *The Journals of Gerontology: Series B: Psychological Sciences and Social Sciences, 61,* S323–S328.

Feng, L. R., & Maguire-Zeiss, K. A. (2010). Gene therapy in Parkinson's disease: Rationale and current status. *CNS Drugs, 24,* 177–192.

Fenn, K. M., Nusbaum, H. C., & Margoliash, D. (2003). Consolidation during sleep of perceptual learning of spoken language. *Nature, 425,* 614–616.

Ferchiou, A., Schürhoff, F., Bulzacka, E., Leboyer, M., & Szöke, A. (2010). Selective attention impairment in schizophrenia: Can it explain source monitoring failure? *Journal of Nervous and Mental Disease, 198,* 779–781.

Ferlazzo, F., Conte, S., & Gentilomo, A. (1993). Event-related potentials and recognition memory within the "levels of processing" framework. *Neuroreport: An International Journal for the Rapid Communication of Research in Neuroscience, 4,* 667–670.

Fern, E. F., Monroe, K. B., & Avila, R. A. (1986). Effectiveness of multiple request strategies: A synthesis of research results. *Journal of Marketing Research, 23,* 144–152.

Ferrari, M. (1996). Observing the observer: Self-regulation in the observational learning of motor skills. *Developmental Review, 16,* 203–240.

Ferris, A. M., & Duffy, V. B. (1989). Effect of olfactory deficits on nutritional status: Does age predict persons at risk? *Annals of the New York Academy of Sciences, 561,* 113–123.

Fery, Y. A. (2003). Differentiating visual and kinesthetic imagery in mental practice. *Canadian Journal of Experimental Psychology, 57,* 1–10.

Festinger, L., & Carlsmith, J. M. (1959). Cognitive consequences of forced compliance. *Journal of Abnormal and Social Psychology, 58,* 203–210.

Festinger, L., Pepitone, A., & Newcomb, T. (1952). Some consequences of deindividuation in a group. *Journal of Abnormal and Social Psychology, 47,* 382–389.

Festinger, L., Riecken, H. W., & Schachter, S. (1956). *When prophecy fails.* New York: Harper & Row.

Festinger, L., Schachter, S., & Back, K. (1950). *Social pressures in informal groups: A study of a housing community.* Stanford, CA: Stanford University Press.

Fieckenstein, L. (1996, May 20). Trailblazing Hulda Crooks, 100: Loma Linda resident publishes memoirs. *Press-Enterprise,* p. B03.

Fiedler, K., Schmid, J., & Stahl, T. (2002). What is the current truth about polygraph lie detection? *Basic and Applied Social Psychology, 24,* 313–324.

Field, T. M. (1991). Quality infant day-care and grade school behavior and performance. *Child Development, 62,* 863–870.

Field, T. M. (1996). Attachment and separation in young children. *Annual Review of Psychology, 47,* 541–561.

Field, T. M., Woodson, R., Greenberg, R., & Cohen, D. (1982). Discrimination and imitation of facial expressions by neonates. *Science, 218,* 179–181.

Field, T., Hernandez-Reif, M., Diego, M., Schanberg, S., & Kahn, C. (2005). Cortisol decreases and serotonin and dopamine increase following massage therapy. *International Journal of Neuroscience, 115,* 1397–1413.

Filsinger, E. E., Braun, J. J., Monte, W. C., & Linder, D. E. (1984). Human (Homo sapiens) responses to the pig (Sus scrofa) sex pheromone 5 alpha-androst-16en-3-one. *Journal of Comparative Psychology, 98,* 219–222.

Fine, A., Meldrum, B. S., & Patel, S. (1990). Modulation of experimentally induced epilepsy by intracerebral grafts of fetal GABAergic neurons. *Neuropsychologia, 28,* 627–634.

Fink, B., & Penton-Voak, I. (2002). Evolutionary psychology of facial attractiveness. *Current Directions in Psychological Science, 11,* 154–158.

Finkelstein, E. A., Trogdon, J. G., Cohen, J. W., & Dietz, W. (2009). Annual medical spending attributable to obesity: Payer-and-service-specific estimates. *Health Affairs, 28,* 822–831.

Finzi, R., Har-Even, D., & Weizman, A. (2003). Comparisons of ego defenses among physically abused children, neglected, and non-maltreated children. *Comprehensive Psychiatry, 44,* 388–395.

Fiore, M. C. (2000). A clinical practice guideline for treating tobacco use and dependence: A US Public Health Service Report. *JAMA: Journal of the American Medical Association, 283,* 3244–3254.

Fiore, M. C., Smith, S. S., Jorenby, D. E., & Baker, T. B. (1994). The effectiveness of the nicotine patch for smoking cessation: A meta-analysis. *JAMA: Journal of the American Medical Association, 271,* 1940–1947.

Fiorito, G., & Scotto, P. (1992). Observational learning in *Octopus vulgaris. Science, 256,* 545–547.

Fischer, A. R., Jome, L. M., & Atkinson, D. R. (1998). Back to the future of multicultural psychotherapy with a common factors approach. *Counseling Psychologist, 26,* 602–606.

Fischer, H., Wik, G., & Fredrikson, M. (1997). Extraversion, neuroticism, and brain function: A PET study of personality. *Personality and Individual Differences, 23,* 345–352.

Fischer, K. W., & Hencke, R. W. (1996). Infants' construction of actions in context: Piaget's contribution to research on early development. *Psychological Science, 7,* 204–210.

Fischer, K. W., & Silvern, L. (1985). Stages and individual differences in cognitive development. *Annual Review of Psychology, 36,* 613–648.

Fisher, C. B., & Fyrberg, D. (1994). Participant partners: College students weigh the costs and benefits of deceptive research. *American Psychologist, 49,* 417–427.

Fisher, C. B., Fried, A. L., & Feldman, L. G. (2009). Graduate socialization in the responsible conduct of research: A national survey on the research ethics training experiences of psychology doctoral students. *Ethics and Behavior, 19,* 496–518.

Fisher, E. B., Delamater, A. M., Bertelson, A. D., & Kirkley, B. G. (1982). Psychological factors in diabetes and its treatment. *Journal of Consulting and Clinical Psychology, 50,* 993–1003.

Fisher, K. (1983, February). TV violence. *APA Monitor,* pp. 7, 9.

Fisher, K. (1985, November). Duty to warn: Where does it end? *APA Monitor,* pp. 24–25.

Fisher, S., & Greenberg, R. P. (1985). *The scientific credibility of Freud's theories and therapy.* New York: Columbia University Press.

Fiske, D. W., Conley, J. J., & Goldberg, R. P. (1987). E. Lowell Kelly (1905–1986). *American Psychologist, 42,* 511–512.

Fitzgerald, P. B., Hoy, K., Daskalakis, Z. J., & Kulkarni, J. (2009). A randomized trial of the anti-depressant effects of low-and high-frequency transcranial magnetic stimulation in treatment-resistant depression. *Depression and Anxiety, 26,* 229–234.

Flack, W. F., Jr., Laird, J. D., & Cavallaro, L. A. (1999). Separate and combined effects of facial expressions and bodily postures on emotional feelings. *European Journal of Social Psychology, 29,* 203–217.

Flannagan, D. A., & Blick, K. A. (1989). Levels of processing and the retention of word meanings. *Perceptual and Motor Skills, 68,* 1123–1128.

Flay, B. R. (1985). Psychosocial approaches to smoking prevention: A review of findings. *Health Psychology, 4,* 449–488.

Fleckenstein, J., Irnich, D., Goldman, N., Chen, M., Fujita, X., Xu, Q., . . . Nedergaard, M. (2010). Adenosine A1 receptors mediate local anti-nociceptive effects of acupuncture. *Deutsche Zeitschrift Fur Akupunktur, 5,* 38–39.

Fleming, V. M. (2002). Improving students' exam performance by introducing study strategies and goal setting. *Teaching of Psychology, 29,* 115–119.

Flesher, M. M., Butt, A. E., & Kinney-Hurd, B. L. (2011). Differential acetylcholine release in the prefrontal cortex and hippocampus during Pavlovian trace and delay conditioning. *Neurobiology of Learning and Memory, 96,* 181–191.

Florack, A., Piontkowski, U., Bohman, A., Balzer, T., & Perzig, S. (2003). Perceived intergroup threat and attitudes of host community members toward immigrant acculturation. *Journal of Social Psychology, 143,* 633–648.

Flores, S. A., & Hartlaub, M. G. (1998). Reducing rape-myth acceptance in male college students: A meta-analysis of intervention studies. *Journal of College Student Development, 39,* 438–448.

Flor-Henry, P. (1983). Mood, the right hemisphere, and the implications of spatial information-perceiving systems. *Research Communications in Psychology, Psychiatry, and Behavior, 8,* 143–170.

Floyd, M., McKendree-Smith, N. L., & Scogin, F. R. (2004). Remembering the 1978 and 1990 task forces on self-help therapies: A response to Gerald Rosen. *Journal of Clinical Psychology, 60,* 115–117.

Floyd, M., Scogin, F., McKendree-Smith, N. L., Floyd, D. L., & Rokke, P. D. (2004). Cognitive therapy for depression: A comparison of individual psychotherapy and bibliotherapy for depressed older adults. *Behavior Modification, 28,* 297–318.

Flynn, J. R. (1987). Massive IQ gains in 14 nations: What IQ tests really measure. *Psychological Bulletin, 101,* 171–191.

Foa, E. B., Dancu, C. V., Hembree, E. A., Jaycox, L. H., Meadows, E. A., & Street, G. P. (1999). Comparison of exposure therapy, stress inoculation training, and their combination for reducing posttraumatic stress disorder in female assault victims. *Journal of Consulting and Clinical Psychology, 67,* 194–200.

Foerstl, J. (1989). Early interest in the idiot savant. *American Journal of Psychiatry, 146,* 566.

Fogarty, G. J. (1994). Using the Personal Orientation Inventory to measure change in student self-actualization. *Personality and Individual Differences, 17,* 435–439.

Fogel, R. B., Malhotra, A., Dalagiorgou, G., Robinson, M. K., Jakab, M., Kikinis, R., . . . White, D. P. (2003). Anatomic and physiologic predictors of apnea severity in morbidly obese subjects. *Sleep: Journal of Sleep and Sleep Disorders Research, 26,* 150–155.

Folkes, V. S. (1982). Forming relationships and the matching hypothesis. *Personality and Social Psychology Bulletin, 8,* 631–636.

Folkes, V. S. (1988). The availability heuristic and perceived risk. *Journal of Consumer Research, 15,* 13–23.

Fontaine, K. R., & Shaw, D. F. (1995). Effects of self-efficacy and dispositional optimism on adherence to step aerobic exercise classes. *Perceptual and Motor Skill, 81,* 251–255.

Fontana, A. M., Diegman, T., Villeneuve, A., & Lepore, A. J. (1999). Nonevaluative social support reduces cardiovascular reactivity in young women during acutely stressful performance situations. *Journal of Behavioral Medicine, 22,* 75–91.

Folkman, S., & Moskowitz, J. T. (2000). Stress, positive emotion, and coping. *Current Directions in Psychological Science, 9,* 115–118.

Foltin, R. W., Fischman, M. W., & Levin, F. R. (1995). Cardiovascular effects of cocaine in humans: Laboratory studies. *Drug and Alcohol Dependence, 37,* 193–210.

Forchuk, C., Godin, M., Hoch, J. S., Kingston-MacClure, S., Jeng, M. S., Puddy, L., . . . Jensen, E. (2013). Preventing homelessness after discharge from psychiatric wards: Perspectives of consumers and staff. *Journal of Psychosocial Nursing & Mental Health Services, 51,* 25–31.

Ford, B. D. (1993). Emergenesis: An alternative and a confound. *American Psychologist, 48,* 1294.

Forehand, M. R., Deshpanda, R., & Reed, A. (2002). Identity salience and the influence of the social self-schema on advertising response. *Journal of Applied Psychology, 87,* 1086–1099.

Foret, A., Quertainmont, R., Botman, O., Bouhy, D., Amabili, P., Brook, G., . . . Franzen, R. (2010). Stem cells in the adult rat spinal cord: Plasticity after injury and treadmill training exercise. *Journal of Neurochemistry, 112,* 762–772.

Foreyt, J. P. (1987). Issues in the assessment and treatment of obesity. *Journal of Consulting and Clinical Psychology, 55,* 677–684.

Foreyt, J. P., & Goodrick, G. K. (1994). Impact of behavior therapy on weight loss. *American Journal of Health Promotion, 8,* 466–468.

Forgas, J. P., Dunn, E., & Granland, S. (2008). Are you being served. . .? An unobtrusive experiment of affective influences on helping in a department store. *European Journal of Social Psychology, 38,* 333–343.

Forsyth, D. R., Zyzniewski, L. E., & Giammanco, C. A. (2002). Responsibility diffusion in cooperative collectives. *Personality and Social Psychology Bulletin, 28,* 54–65.

Foster, J. K., Lidder, P. G., & Suenram, S. I. (1998). Glucose and memory: Fractionation of enhancement effects? *Psychopharmacology, 137,* 259–270.

Foster-Schubert, K. E., Alfano, C. M., Duggan, C. R., Xiao, L., Campbell, K. L., Kong, A., . . . McTiernan, A. (2012). Effect of diet and exercise, alone or combined, on weight and body composition in overweight-to-obese postmenopausal women. *Obesity, 20,* 1628–1638.

Fox, B. H., & Farrington, D. P. (2012). Creating burglary profiles using latent class analysis: A new approach to offender profiling. *Criminal Justice and Behavior, 39,* 1582–1611.

Fox, E., Lester, V., Russo, R., Bowles, R. J., Pichler, A., & Dutton, K. (2000). Facial expressions of emotion: Are angry faces detected more efficiently? *Cognition and Emotion, 14,* 61–92.

Fox, L. H. (1981). Identification of the academically gifted. *American Psychologist, 36,* 1103–1111.

Fox, N. A., & Davidson, R. J. (1988). Patterns of brain electrical activity during facial signs of emotion in 10-month-old infants. *Developmental Psychology, 24,* 230–236.

Fox, S. E., & Burns, D. J. (1993). The mere exposure effect for stimuli presented below recognition threshold: A failure to replicate. *Perceptual and Motor Skills, 76,* 391–396.

Fraley, C. R., Roisman, G. I., Booth-LaForce, C., Owen, M. T., & Holland, A. S. (2013). Interpersonal and genetic origins of adult attachment styles: A longitudinal study from infancy to early adulthood. *Journal of Personality and Social Psychology, 104,* 817–838.

France, C. R., France, J. L., al'Absi, M., Ring, C., & McIntyre, D. (2002). Catastrophizing is related to pain ratings, but not nociceptive flexion reflex threshold. *Pain, 99,* 459–463.

Frank, D. A., Brown, J., Johnson, S., & Cabral, H. (2002). Forgotten fathers: An exploratory study of mothers' report of drug and alcohol problems among fathers of urban newborns. *Neurotoxicology & Teratology, 24,* 339–347.

Frank, E., & Brandstaetter, V. (2002). Approach versus avoidance: Different types of commitment in intimate relationships. *Journal of Personality and Social Psychology, 82,* 208–221.

Frank, M. G., & Stennett, J. (2001). The forced-choice paradigm and the perception of facial expressions of emotion. *Journal of Personality and Social Psychology, 80,* 75–85.

Frankel, R. M. (1995). Emotion and the physician-patient relationship. *Motivation and Emotion, 19,* 163–173.

Franklin, B., et al. (1784/2002). Report of the commissioners charged by the King with the examination of animal magnetism [reprint]. *International Journal of Clinical and Experimental Hypnosis, 50,* 332–363.

Franko, D. L., & Herrera, I. (1997). Body image differences in Guatemalan-American and White college women. *Eating Disorders: The Journal of Treatment and Prevention, 5,* 119–127.

Fraser, S. (Ed.). (1995). *The bell curve wars: Race, intelligence, and the future of America.* New York: Basic Books.

Frederick, C. M., & Ryan, R. M. (1995). Self-determination in sport: A review using cognitive evaluation theory. *International Journal of Sport Psychology, 26,* 5–23.

Frederiksen, N. (1986). Toward a broader conception of human intelligence. *American Psychologist, 41,* 445–452.

Fredrikson, M., Annas, P., Fischer, H., & Wik, G. (1996). Gender and age differences in the prevalence of specific fears and phobias. *Behaviour Research and Therapy, 34,* 33–39.

Freedman, J. L. (1984). Effect of television violence on aggressiveness. *Psychological Bulletin, 96,* 227–246.

Freedman, J. L., & Fraser, S. C. (1966). Compliance without pressure. *Journal of Personality and Social Psychology, 4,* 195–202.

Freedman, M. A. (2002). Quality of life and menopause: The role of estrogen. *Journal of Women's Health, 11,* 703–718.

Freedman, R., Lewis, D. A., Michels, R., Pine, D. S., Schultz, Tamminga, C. A., . . . Yager, J. (2013). The initial field trials of *DSM-5*: New blooms and old thorns. *American Journal of Psychiatry, 170,* 1–5.

Freeman, A. (1999). Will increasing our social interest bring about a loss of our innocence? *Journal of Individual Psychology, 55,* 130–145.

Freeman, C. (1998). Drug treatment for bulimia nervosa. *Neuropsychobiology, 37,* 72–79.

Freeman, J., Palk, J., & Davey, J. (2010). Sex offenders in denial: A study into a group of forensic psychologists' attitudes regarding the corresponding impact upon risk assessment calculations and parole eligibility. *Journal of Forensic Psychiatry and Psychology, 21,* 39–51.

Freeman, R., Barabasz, A., Barabasz, M., & Warner, D. (2000). Hypnosis and distraction differ in their effects on cold pressor pain. *American Journal of Clinical Hypnosis, 43,* 137–148.

Freeman, W. (1948). Transorbital leucotomy. *Lancet, 255,* 371–373.

Freivalds, A., & Horii, K. (1994). An oculomotor test to measure alcohol impairment. *Perceptual and Motor Skills, 78,* 603–610.

French, D. C., Jansen, E. A., & Pidada, S. (2002). United States and Indonesian children's and adolescents' reports of relational aggression by disliked peers. *Child Development, 73,* 1143–1150.

French, S. E., & Holland, K. J. (2013). Condom negotiation strategies as a mediator of the relationship between self-efficacy and condom use. *Journal of Sex Research, 50,* 48–59.

Frenda, S. J., Nichols, R. M., & Loftus, E. F. (2011). Current issues and advances in misinformation research. *Current Directions in Psychological Science, 20,* 20–23.

Freud, S. (1900/1990). *The interpretation of dreams.* New York: Basic Books.

Freud, S. (1901/1965). *Psychopathology of everyday life.* New York: W. W. Norton.

Freud, S. (1901/2011). *The psychopathology of everyday life.* Eastford, CT: Martino.

Freud, S. (1905). *Jokes and their relationship to the unconscious.* London: Hogarth Press.

Freud, S. (1914/1957). On the history of the psychoanalytic movement. In J. Strachey (Ed.), *The standard edition of the complete psychological works of Sigmund Freud* (Vol. 14, pp. 7–66). London: Hogarth Press.

Freud, S. (1917/1963). Mourning and melancholia. In J. Strachey (Ed.), *The standard edition of the complete psychological works of Sigmund Freud* (Vol. 14, pp. 243–258). London: Hogarth Press.

Freud, S. (1974). *Cocaine papers* (R. Byck, Ed.). New York: Stonehill.

Freund, A. M., & Baltes, P. B. (1998). Selection, optimization, and compensation as strategies of life management: Correlations with subjective indicators of successful aging. *Psychology of Aging, 13,* 531–543.

Frick, R. W. (1985). Communicating emotion: The role of prosodic features. *Psychological Bulletin, 97,* 412–429.

Friedman, M., & Rosenman, R. H. (1974). *Type A behavior and your heart.* New York: Knopf.

Frisco, M. L., & Williams, K. (2003). Perceived housework equity, marital happiness, and divorce in dual-earner households. *Journal of Family Issues, 24,* 51–73.

Fritsch, G., & Hitzig, E. (1870/1960). *On the electrical excitability of the cerebrum.* Springfield, IL: Thomas

Fritzsche, B. A., Finkelstein, M. A., & Penner, L. A. (2000). To help or not to help: Capturing individuals' decision policies. *Social Behavior and Personality, 28,* 561–578.

Froming, W. J., Nasby, W., & McManus, J. (1998). Prosocial self-schemas, self-awareness, and children's prosocial behavior. *Journal of Personality and Social Psychology, 75,* 766–777.

Fromm, E. (1941). *Escape from freedom.* New York: Holt, Rinehart & Winston.

Froufe, M., & Schwartz, C. (2001). Subliminal messages for increasing self-esteem: Placebo effect. *Spanish Journal of Psychology, 4,* 19–25.

Fuchs, A. H. (1998). Psychology and "The Babe." *Journal of the History of the Behavioral Sciences, 34,* 153–165.

Fuchs, A. H., & Viney, W. (2002). The course in the history of psychology: Present status and future concerns. *Journal of the History of the Behavioral Sciences, 5,* 3–15.

Fuchs-Beauchamp, K. D., Karnes, M. B., & Johnson, L. J. (1993). Creativity and intelligence in preschoolers. *Gifted Child Quarterly, 37,* 113–117.

Fudin, R. (2001). Problems in Silverman's work indicate the need for a new approach to research on subliminal psychodynamic activation. *Perceptual and Motor Skills, 92,* 611–622.

Fujita, K. (1996). Linear perspective and the Ponzo illusion: A comparison between rhesus monkeys and humans. *Japanese Psychological Research, 38,* 136–145.

Fujita, K., Blough, D. S., & Blough, P. M. (1993). Effects of the inclination of context lines on perception of the Ponzo illusion by pigeons. *Animal Learning and Behavior, 21,* 29–34.

Fulker, D. W., DeFries, J. C., & Plomin, R. (1988). Genetic influence on general mental ability increases between infancy and middle childhood. *Nature, 336,* 767–769.

Fullerton, A. S., & Dixon, J. C. (2010). Generational conflict or methodological artifact? Reconsidering the relationship between age and policy attitudes in the U.S., 1984–2008. *Public Opinion Quarterly, 74,* 643–673.

Fundytus, M. E. (2001). Glutamate receptors and nociception: Implications for the drug treatment of pain. *CNS Drugs, 15,* 29–58.

Furman, W. (2002). The emerging field of adolescent romantic relationships. *Current Directions in Psychological Science, 11,* 177–180.

Furnham, A., & Lim, A.-N. (1997). Cross-cultural differences in the perception of male and female body shapes as a function of exercise. *Journal of Social Behavior and Personality, 12,* 1037–1053.

Furnham, A., & Strbac, L. (2002). Music is as distracting as noise: The differential distraction of background music and noise on the cognitive test performance of introverts and extraverts. *Ergonomics, 45,* 203–217.

Furnham, A., & Thompson, J. (1991). Personality and self-reported delinquency. *Personality and Individual Differences, 12,* 585–593.

Furumoto, L. (1980). Mary Whiton Calkins (1863–1930). *Psychology of Women Quarterly, 5,* 94–102.

Gabrieli, J. D. E., Fleischman, D. A., Keane, M. M., & Reminger, S. L. (1995). Double dissociation between memory systems underlying explicit and implicit memory in the human brain. *Psychological Science, 6,* 76–82.

Gaffan, E. A., Tsaousis, J., & Kemp-Wheeler, S. M. (1995). Researcher allegiance and meta-analysis: The case of cognitive therapy for depression. *Journal of Consulting and Clinical Psychology, 63,* 966–980.

Galak, J., LeBoeuf, R. A., Nelson, L. D., & Simmons, J. P. (2012). Correcting the past: Failures to replicate psi. *Journal of Personality & Social Psychology, 103,* 933–948.

Galanter, E. (1962). *New directions in psychology.* New York: Holt, Rinehart & Winston.

Galati, D., Miceli, R., & Sini, B. (2001). Judging and coding facial expression of emotions in congenitally blind children. *International Journal of Behavioral Development, 25,* 268–278.

Galef, B. G. (1993). Functions of social learning about food: A causal analysis of effects of diet novelty on preference transmission. *Animal Behaviour, 46,* 257–265.

Galef, B. G., Jr. (1980). Diving for food: Analysis of a possible case of social learning in wild rats

(*Rattus norvegicus*). *Journal of Comparative and Physiological Psychology, 94,* 416–425.

Gallacher, J. E. J., Hopkinson, C. A., Bennett, P., Burr, M. L., & Elwood, P. C. (1997). Effect of stress management on angina. *Psychology and Health, 12,* 523–532.

Galton, F. (1869). *Hereditary genius*. London: Macmillan.

Gamaro, G. D., Denardin, J. D., Michalowski, M. B., Catelli, D., Correa, J. B., Xavier, M. H., & Dalmaz, C. (1997). Epinephrine effects on memory are not dependent on hepatic glucose release. *Neurobiology of Learning and Memory, 68,* 221–229.

Gana, K., & Boblique, C. (2000). Coping and burnout among police officers and teachers: Test of a model. *European Review of Applied Psychology, 50,* 423–430.

Ganchrow, J. R., Steiner, J. E., & Daher, M. (1983). Neonatal facial expressions in response to different qualities and intensities of gustatory stimuli. *Infant Behavior and Development, 6,* 189–200.

Gandour, J., Larsen, J., Dechongkit, S., & Ponglorpisit, S. (1995). Speech prosody in affective contexts in Thai patients with right hemisphere lesions. *Brain & Language, 51,* 422–443.

Gangestad, S., & Snyder, M. (1985). "To carve nature at its joints": On the existence of discrete classes in personality. *Psychological Review, 92,* 317–349.

Gannon, L., Luchetta, T., Rhodes, K., Pardie, L., & Segrist, D. (1992). Sex bias in psychological research: Progress or complacency? *American Psychologist, 47,* 389–396.

Ganong, L., Coleman, M., Fine, M., & Martin, P. (1999). Stepparents' affinity-seeking and affinity-maintaining strategies with stepchildren. *Journal of Family Issues, 20,* 299–327.

Gansberg, M. (1964, March 27). Thirty-seven who saw murder didn't call the police. *New York Times,* pp. 1, 38.

Garcia, D., Archer, T., Moradi, S., & Andersson-Arntén, A.-C. (2012). Exercise frequency, high activation positive affect, and psychological well-being: Beyond age, gender, and occupation. *Psychology, 3,* 328–336.

Garcia, E. E. (1990). A brief note on "Jekyll and Hyde" and MPD. *Dissociation: Progress in the Dissociative Disorders, 3,* 165–166.

Garcia, J. (1981). Tilting at the paper mills of academe. *American Psychologist, 36,* 149–158.

Garcia, J., & Gustavson, A. R. (1997, January). Carl R. Gustavson (1946–1996): Pioneering wildlife psychologist. *APS Observer,* pp. 34–35.

Garcia, J., & Koelling, R. A. (1966). The relation of cue to consequence in avoidance learning. *Psychonomic Science, 4,* 123–124.

Garcia, J., Kimeldorf, D. J., Hunt, E. L., & Davies, B. P. (1956). Food and water consumption of rats during exposure to gamma radiation. *Radiation Research, 4,* 33–41.

Garcia, L. T., & Hoskins, R. (2001). Actual-ideal self discrepancy and sexual esteem and depression. *Journal of Psychology and Human Sexuality, 13,* 49–61.

Garcia-Bajos, E., & Migueles, M. (2003). False memories for script actions in a mugging account. *European Journal of Cognitive Psychology, 15,* 195–208.

Garcia-Larrea, L., Perchet, C., Perrin, F., & Amenedo, E. (2001). Interference of celular phone conversations with visuomotor tasks: An ERP study. *Journal of Psychophysiology, 15,* 14–21.

Garcia-Vera, M. P., Labrador, F. J., & Sanz, J. (1997). Stress-management training for essential hypertension: A controlled study. *Applied Psychophysiology and Biofeedback, 22,* 261–283.

Gardener, H., Munrer, K., Chitnis, T., Spiegelman, D., & Ascherio, A. (2009). The relationship between handedness and risk of multiple sclerosis. *Multiple Sclerosis, 15,* 587–592.

Gardner, D. G. (1986). Activation theory and task design: An empirical test of several new predictions. *Journal of Applied Psychology, 71,* 411–418.

Gardner, H. (1983). *Frames of mind: The theory of multiple intelligences*. New York: Basic Books.

Gardner, H. (2000). A case against spiritual intelligence. *International Journal for the Psychology of Religion, 10,* 27–34.

Gardner, R. A., Gardner, B. T., & Van Cantfort, T. E. (Eds.). (1989). *Teaching sign language to chimpanzees*. Albany: State University of New York Press.

Garfield, C. F., Dorsey, E. R., Zhu, S., Huskamp, H. A, Conti, R., Dusetzina, S. B., . . . Alexander, G. C. (2012). Trends in attention deficit hyperactivity disorder ambulatory diagnosis and medical treatment in the United States, 2000–2010. *Academic Pediatrics, 12,* 110–116.

Garmon, L. C., Basinger, K. S., Gregg, V. R., & Gibbs, J. C. (1996). Gender differences in stage and expression of moral judgment. *Merrill-Palmer Quarterly, 42,* 418–437.

Garonzik, R. (1989). Hand dominance and implications for left-handed operation of controls. *Ergonomics, 32,* 1185–1192.

Garrison, D. W., & Foreman, R. D. (1994). Decreased activity of spontaneous and noxiously evoked dorsal horn cells during transcutaneous electrical nerve stimulation (TENS). *Pain, 58,* 309–315.

Gater, R., Tansella, M., Korten, A., Tiemens, G. B., Mavreas, V. G., & Olatawura, M. O. (1998). Sex differences in the prevalence and detection of depressive and anxiety disorders in general health care settings: Report from the World Health Organization collaborative study on psychological problems in general health care. *Archives of General Psychiatry, 55,* 405–413.

Gathercole, S. E., & Conway, M. A. (1988). Exploring long-term modality effects: Vocalization leads to best retention. *Memory and Cognition, 16,* 110–119.

Gates, G. J. (2013). Demographics and LGBT health. *Journal of Health and Social Behavior, 54,* 72–74.

Gates, G. J., & Newport, F. (2012). *Gallup special report: The US LGBT adult population*. Washington, DC: Gallup, Inc.

Gaukroger, S. (2009). The role of natural philosophy in the development of Locke's empiricism. *British Journal for the History of Philosophy, 17,* 55–83.

Gauld, A. O. (1990). The early history of hypnotic skin marking and blistering. *British Journal of Experimental and Clinical Hypnosis, 7,* 139–152.

Gawin, F. H. (1991). Cocaine addiction: Psychology and neurophysiology. *Science, 251,* 1580–1586.

Gay, P. (1988). *Freud: A life for our time*. New York: W. W. Norton.

Gay, V. (1986). Augustine: The reader as self-object. *Journal for the Scientific Study of Religion, 25,* 64–76.

Gazzaniga, M. S. (1967, August). The split brain in man. *Scientific American,* pp. 24–29.

Gazzaniga, M. S. (1983). Right hemisphere language following brain bisection: A 20-year perspective. *American Psychologist, 38,* 525–537.

Gazzaniga, M. S. (2005). Forty-five years of split-brain research and still going strong. *Nature Reviews; Neuroscience, 6,* 653–659.

Gazzola, N., & Stalikas, A. (1997). An investigation of counselor interpretations in client–centered therapy. *Journal of Psychotherapy Integration, 7,* 313–327.

Geen, R. G. (1984). Preferred stimulation levels in introverts and extraverts: Effects on arousal and performance. *Journal of Personality and Social Psychology, 46,* 1303–1312.

Gelb, S. A. (1986). Henry H. Goddard and the immigrants, 1910–1917: The studies and their social context. *Journal of the History of the Behavioral Sciences, 22,* 324–332.

Gelernter, J., Page, G. P., Bonvicini, K., Woods, S. W., Pauls, D. L., & Kruger, S. (2003). A chromosome 14 risk locus for simple phobia: Results from a genomewide linkage scan. *Molecular Psychiatry, 8,* 71–82.

Geller, L. (1982, Spring). The failure of self-actualization theory: A critique of Carl Rogers and Abraham Maslow. *Journal of Humanistic Psychology, 22,* 56–73.

Gelman, D., Foote, D., Barrett, T., & Talbot, M. (1992, February 24). Born or bred? *Newsweek,* pp. 46–53.

Geracioti, T. D., & Liddle, R. A. (1988). Impaired cholecystokinin secretion in bulimia nervosa. *New England Journal of Medicine, 319,* 683–688.

Gerra, G., Zaimovic, A., Timpano, M., Zambelli, U., Delsignore, R., & Brambilla, F. (2000). Neuroendocrine correlations of temperamental traits in humans. *Psychoneuroendocrinology, 25,* 479–496.

Gerrard, M. (1987). Sex, sex guilt, and contraceptive use revisited: The 1980s. *Journal of Personality and Social Psychology, 52,* 975–980.

Gershoff, E. T. (2002). Corporal punishment by parents and associated child behaviors and experiences: A meta-analytic and theoretical review. *Psychological Bulletin, 128,* 539–579.

Gervais-Bernard, H., Xie-Brustolin, J., Mertens, P., Polo, G., Klinger, H., Adamec, D., . . . Thobois, S. (2009). Bilateral subthalamic nucleus stimulation in advanced Parkinson's Disease: Five year follow-up. *Journal of Neurology, 256,* 225–233.

Gescheider, G. A., Beiles, E. J., Checkosky, C. M., & Bolanowski, S. J. (1994). The effects of aging on information processing channels in the sense of touch: II. Temporal summation in the P channel. *Somatosensory and Motor Research, 11,* 359–365.

Geschwind, N. (1979, September). Specializations of the human brain. *Scientific American,* pp. 180–199.

Getlin, J. (2000, June 15). Outrage in N.Y. over assaults: Giuliani says videotapes will be used to identify attackers of women in Central Park, and allegedly uncaring police. *Los Angeles Times,* p. A5.

Gfellner, B. M., & Hundleby, J. D. (1994). Developmental and gender differences in drug use and problem behaviour during adolescence. *Journal of Child and Adolescent Substance Abuse, 3,* 59–74.

Giannakoulas, G., Katramados, A., Melas, N., Diamantopoulos, I., & Chimonas, E. (2003). Acute effects of nicotine withdrawal syndrome in pilots during flight. *Aviation, Space, and Environmental Medicine, 74,* 247–251.

Gibbons, B. (1986). The intimate sense of smell. *National Geographic, 170,* 324–361.

Gibbons, P., Mulryan, N., & O'Connor, A. (1997). Guilty but insane: The insanity defence in Ireland, 1850–1995. *British Journal of Psychiatry, 170,* 467–472.

Gibbs, E. D., Teti, D. M., & Bond, L. A. (1987). Infant-sibling communication: Relationships to birth-spacing and cognitive and linguistic development. *Infant Behavior and Development, 10,* 307–323.

Gibson, B., Sachau, D., Doll, B., & Shumate, R. (2002). Sandbagging in competition: Responding to the pressure of being the favorite. *Personality and Social Psychology Bulletin, 28,* 1119–1130.

Gibson, E. J., & Walk, R. D. (1960, April). The visual cliff. *Scientific American,* pp. 67–71.

Gibson, H. B. (1991). Can hypnosis compel people to commit harmful, immoral and criminal acts? A review of the literature. *Contemporary Hypnosis, 8,* 129–140.

Gibson, J. J. (1979). *The ecological approach to visual perception*. Boston: Houghton Mifflin.

Gidron, Y., Davidson, K., & Bata, I. (1999). The short-term effects of a hostility-reduction intervention on male coronary heart disease patients. *Health Psychology, 18,* 416–420.

Giesler, G. J., Katter, J. T., & Dado, R. J. (1994). Direct spinal pathways to the limbic system for nociceptive information. *Trends in Neurosciences, 17,* 244–250.

Gilbert, A. K. (2003). The contribution of descending fibers from the rostral ventromedial medulla to nociception, and to opioid and non-opioid analgesia. *Dissertation Abstracts International: Section B: The Sciences and Engineering, 63,* 3507.

Gilbert, C. (2003). Clinical applications of breathing regulation: Beyond anxiety management. *Behavior Modification, 27,* 692–709.

Gilbert, H. M., & Warburton, D. M. (2000). Craving: A problematic concept in smoking research. *Addiction Research, 8,* 381–397.

Gilbert, S. J. (1981). Another look at the Milgram obedience studies: The role of the graduated series of shocks. *Personality and Social Psychology Bulletin, 7,* 690–695.

Gilbert, T., Martin, R., & Coulson, M. (2010). Attentional biases using the body in the crowd task: Are angry body postures detected more rapidly? *Cognition and Emotion, 25,* 700–708.

Gilchrist, H., Povey, R., Dickinson, A., & Povey, R. (1995). The Sensation Seeking Scale: Its use in a study of the characteristics of people choosing "adventure holidays." *Personality and Individual Differences, 19,* 513–516.

Gillam, B. (1980, January). Geometrical illusions. *Scientific American,* pp. 102–111.

Gillam, B. (1992). The status of perceptual grouping 70 years after Wertheimer. *Australian Journal of Psychology, 44,* 157–162.

Gilligan, C. (1982). *In a different voice: Psychological theory and women's development.* Cambridge, MA: Harvard University Press.

Gilman, S., Chervin, R. D., Koeppe, R. A., Consens, F. B., Little, R., An, H., . . . Heumann, M. (2003). Obstructive sleep apnea is related to a thalamic cholinergic deficit in MSA. *Neurology, 61,* 35–39.

Ginandes, C., Brooks, P., Sando, W., Jones, C., & Aker, J. (2003). Can medical hypnosis accelerate post-surgical wound healing? Results of a clinical trial. *American Journal of Clinical Hypnosis, 45,* 333–351.

Girandola, F. (2002). Sequential requests and organ donation. *Journal of Social Psychology, 142,* 171–178.

Ginis, K. A. M., Jetha, A., Dack, D. E., & Hetz, S. (2010). Physical activity and subjective well-being among people with spinal cord injury: A meta-analysis. *Spinal Cord, 48,* 65–72.

Giovanni, G. D. (2008). Will it ever become possible to prevent dopaminergic neuronal degeneration? *CNS and Neurological Disorders, 7,* 28–44.

Giovannini, D., & Ricci Bitti, P. E. (1981). Culture and sex effect in recognizing emotions by facial and gestural cues. *Italian Journal of Psychology, 8,* 95–102.

Gisiner, R., & Schusterman, R. J. (1992). Sequence, syntax, and semantics: Responses of a language-trained sea lion *(Zalophus californianus)* to novel sign combinations. *Journal of Comparative Psychology, 106,* 78–91.

Gitau, R., Modi, N., Gianakoulopoulos, X., Bond, C., Glover, V., & Stevenson, J. (2002). Acute effects of maternal skin-to-skin contact and massage on saliva cortisol in preterm babies. *Journal of Reproductive and Infant Psychology, 20,* 83–88.

Gizer, I. R., Ficks, C., & Waldman, I. D. (2009). Candidate gene studies of ADHD: A meta-analytic review. *Human Genetics, 126,* 51–90.

Glancy, G. D., Regehr, C., & Bryant, A. G. (1998). Confidentiality in crisis: Part II—Confidentiality of treatment records. *Canadian Journal of Psychiatry, 43,* 1006–1011.

Gläscher, J., Adolphs, R., Damasio, H., Bechara, A., Rudrauf, D., Calamia, M., . . . Trane, D. (2012). Lesion mapping of cognitive control and value-based decision making in the prefrontal cortex. *Proceedings of the National Academy of Sciences, 109,* 14681–14686.

Glaser, R., Rice, J., Speicher, C. E., Stout, J. C., & Kiecolt-Glaser, J. K. (1986). Stress depresses interferon production by leukocytes concomitant with a decrease in natural killer cell activity. *Behavioral Neuroscience, 100,* 675–678.

Gleaves, D. H. (1996). The sociocognitive model of dissociative identity disorder: A reexamination of the evidence. *Psychological Bulletin, 120,* 42–59.

Gleitman, H., Rozin, P., & Sabini, J. (1997). Solomon E. Asch (1907–1996): Obituary. *American Psychologist, 52,* 984–985.

Glen, L., & Anderson, J. A. (1989). Medication and the elderly: A review. *Journal of Geriatric Drug Therapy, 4,* 59–89.

Glenn, C. R., Klein, D. N., Lissek, S., Britton, J. C., Pine, D. S., & Hajcak, G. (2012). The development of fear learning and generalization in 8–13-year-olds. *Developmental Psychobiology, 54,* 675–684.

Glenn, S. S., & Ellis, J. (1988). Do the Kallikaks look "menacing" or "retarded"? *American Psychologist, 43,* 742–743.

Glennon, R. A. (1990). Do classical hallucinogens act as 5-HT-sub-2 agonists or antagonists? *Neuropsychopharmacology, 3,* 509–517.

Glick, P., Fiske, S. T., Mladinic, A., Saiz, J. L., Abrams, D., Masser, B., . . . Lopez, W. L. (2000). Beyond prejudice as simple antipathy: Hostile and benevolent sexism across cultures. *Journal of Personality and Social Psychology, 79,* 763–775.

Glickstein, M., Waller, J., Baizer, J. S., Brown, B., & Timmann, D. (2005). Cerebellar lesions and finger use. *Cerebellum, 4,* 189–197.

Gliedman, J. (1983, November). Interview with Noam Chomsky. *Omni,* pp. 112–118, 171–174.

Gloor, P. (1994). Is Berger's dream coming true? *Electroencephalography and Clinical Neurophysiology, 90,* 253–266.

Glover, E., & Ginsberg, M. (1934). A symposium on the psychology of peace and war. *British Journal of Medical Psychology, 14,* 274–293.

Gluck, M. A., & Myers, C. E. (1995). Representation and association in memory: A neurocomputational view of hippocampal function. *Current Directions in Psychological Science, 4,* 23–29.

Glucksberg, S., & Danks, J. H. (1968). Effects of discriminative labels and of nonsense labels upon availability of novel functions. *Journal of Verbal Learning and Verbal Behavior, 7,* 72–76.

Gobet, F., & Simon, H. A. (1998). Expert chess memory: Revisiting the chunking hypothesis. *Memory, 6,* 225–255.

Goddard, C. (2003). Thinking across language and cultures: Six dimensions of variation. *Cognitive Linguistics, 14,* 109–140.

Goddard, H. H. (1912). *The Kallikak family: A study in the heredity of feeblemindedness.* New York: Macmillan.

Goddard, H. H. (1917). Mental tests and the immigrant. *Journal of Delinquency, 2,* 243–277.

Godden, D. R., & Baddeley, A. D. (1975). Context-dependent memory in two natural environments: On land and under water. *British Journal of Psychology, 66,* 325–331.

Godemont, M. (1992). Six hundred years of family care in Geel, Belgium: 600 years of familiarity with madness in town life. *Community Alternatives: International Journal of Family Care, 4,* 155–168.

"God's hand": Legless veteran crawls to save life of a baby. (1986, June 6). *Philadelphia Inquirer,* pp. 1-A, 24-A.

Goebel, B. L., & Boeck, B. E. (1987). Ego integrity and fear of death: A comparison of institutionalized and independently living older adults. *Death Studies, 11,* 193–204.

Goebel, B. L., & Brown, D. R. (1981). Age differences in motivation related to Maslow's need hierarchy. *Developmental Psychology, 17,* 809–815.

Goisman, R. M. (1983). Therapeutic approaches to phobia: A comparison. *American Journal of Psychotherapy, 37,* 227–234.

Gold, M. S., Pottash, A. L. C., Sweeney, D. R., Martin, D. M., & Davies, R. K. (1980). Further evidence of hypothalamic-pituitary dysfunction in anorexia nervosa. *American Journal of Psychiatry, 137,* 101–102.

Gold, P. E. (2003). Acetylcholine modulation of neural systems involved in learning and memory. *Neurobiology of Learning & Memory, 80,* 194–210.

Goldberg, M. A., & Remy-St. Louis, G. (1998). Understanding and treating pain in ethnically diverse patients. *Journal of Clinical Psychology in Medical Settings, 5,* 343–356.

Goldbloom, D. S., Olmsted, M., Davis, R., Clewes, J., Heinmaa, M., Rockert, W., & Shaw, B. (1997). A randomized controlled trial of fluoxetine and cognitive behavioral therapy for bulimia nervosa: Short-term outcome. *Behaviour Research and Therapy, 35,* 803–811.

Goldin-Meadow, S., & Mylander, C. (1998). Spontaneous sign systems created by deaf children in two cultures. *Nature, 391,* 279–281.

Golding, J. F., Bles, W., Bos, J. E., Haynes, T., & Gresty, M. A. (2003). Motion sickness and tilts of the inertial force environment: Active suspension systems vs. active passengers. *Aviation, Space, and Environmental Medicine, 74,* 220–227.

Goldman, D. L. (1990). Dorothea Dix and her two missions of mercy in Nova Scotia. *Canadian Journal of Psychiatry, 35,* 139–143.

Goldman, H. H. (1998). Deinstitutionalization and community care: Social welfare policy as mental health policy. *Harvard Review of Psychiatry, 6,* 219–222.

Goldman, M., & Fordyce, J. (1983). Prosocial behavior as affected by eye contact, touch, and voice expression. *Journal of Social Psychology, 121,* 125–129.

Goldman-Rakic, P. S. (1996). The prefrontal landscape: implications of functional architecture for understanding human mentation and the central executive. *Philosophical Transactions of the Royal Society of London. Series B, Biological Sciences, 35,* 1445–1453.

Goldstein, A. (1980). Thrills in response to music and other stimuli. *Physiological Psychology, 8,* 126–129.

Goldstein, S. R., & Hall, D. (1990). Variable ratio control of the spitting response in the archer fish *(Toxotes jaculator)*. *Journal of Comparative Psychology, 104,* 373–376.

Golombok, S., & Tasker, F. (1996). Do parents influence the sexual orientation of their children? Findings from a longitudinal study of lesbian families. *Developmental Psychology, 32,* 3–11.

Gonzalez, A. B., Salas, D., & Umpierrez, G. E. (2011). Special considerations on the management of Latino patients with type 2 diabetes mellitus. *Current Medical Research and Opinion, 27,* 969–979.

Gonzales, M. H., & Meyers, S. A. (1993). "Your mother would like me": Self-presentation in the personals ads of heterosexual and homosexual men and women. *Personality and Social Psychology Bulletin, 19,* 131–142.

Gonzalez, R. (1989). Ministering intelligence: A Venezuelan experience in the promotion of cognitive abilities. *International Journal of Mental Health, 18,* 5–18.

Gonzalez-Blanks, A. G., Lopez, S. G., & Garza, R. T. (2012). Collectivism in smoking prevention programs for Hispanic preadolescents: Raising the ante on cultural sensitivity. *Journal of Child & Adolescent Substance Abuse, 21,* 427–439.

Goodall, J. (1990). *Through a window: My thirty years with the chimpanzees of Gombe.* Boston: Houghton Mifflin.

Goode, E. (2002). Mental retardation is dead: Long live mental retardation! *Mental Retardation, 40,* 57–59.

Goodenough, F. L. (1932). Expression of the emotions in a blind-deaf child. *Journal of Abnormal and Social Psychology, 27,* 328–333.

Goodman, G. S., & Schaaf, J. M. (1997). Over a decade of research on children's eyewitness testimony: What have we learned? Where do we go from here? *Applied Cognitive Psychology, 11,* S5–S20.

Goodnight, B. L., Cook, S. L., Parrott, D. J., & Peterson, J. L. (2013). Effects of masculinity, authoritarianism, and prejudice on anti-gay aggression: A path analysis of gender-role enforcement. *Psychology of Men & Masculinity, 16,* 3–17.

Goodwin, C. J. (1985). On the origins of Titchener's experimentalists. *Journal of the History of the Behavioral Sciences, 21,* 383–389.

Gopal, A., Clark, E., Allgair, A., Amato, C. D., Furman, M., Gansler, D. A., & Fulwiler, C. (2013). Dorsal/ventral parcellation of the amygdala: Relevance to impulsivity and aggression. *Psychiatry Research: Neuroimaging, 211,* 24–30.

Gopaul-McNicol, S. (1997). The role of religion in psychotherapy: A cross-cultural examination. *Journal of Contemporary Psychotherapy, 27,* 37–48.

Gordijn, E. H., De Vries, N. K., & De Dreu, C. K. W. (2002). Minority influence on focal and related attitudes: Change in size, attributions, and information processing. *Personality and Social Psychology Bulletin, 28,* 1315–1326.

Gordon, I. E., & Earle, D. C. (1992). Visual illusions: A short review. *Australian Journal of Psychology, 44,* 153–156.

Gordon, P. M., Heath, G. W., Holmes, A., & Christy, D. (2000). The quantity and quality of physical activity among those trying to lose weight. *American Journal of Preventive Medicine, 18,* 83–86.

Gorelick, P. B., & Ross, E. D. (1987). The aprosodias: Further functional-anatomical evidence for the organization of affective language in the right hemisphere. *Journal of Neurology, Neurosurgery, and Psychiatry, 50,* 553–560.

Gorman, J. (1985, February). My fair software. *Discover,* pp. 64–65.

Gorman, J. M. (2003). New molecular targets for antianxiety interventions. *Journal of Clinical Psychiatry, 64,* 28–35.

Gorrese, A., & Ruggieri, R. (2012). Peer attachment: A meta-analytic review of gender and age differences and associations with parent attachment. *Journal of Youth & Adolescence, 41,* 650–672.

Gorunescu, F., Gorunescu, M., Saftoiu, A., Vilmann, P., & Belciug, S. (2011). Competitive/collaborative neural computing system for medical diagnosis in pancreatic cancer detection. *Expert Systems: International Journal of Knowledge Engineering & Neural Networks, 28,* 33–48.

Gosnell, B. A., & Hsiao, S. (1984). Effects of cholecystokinin on taste preference and sensitivity in rats. *Behavioral Neuroscience, 98,* 452–460.

Gosselin, P., Kirouac, G., & Dore, F. Y. (1995). Components and recognition of facial expression in the communication of emotion by actors. *Journal of Personality and Social Psychology, 68,* 83–96.

Goswami, M. (1998). The influence of clinical symptoms on quality of life in patients with narcolepsy. *Neurology, 50,* S31–S36.

Gotlib, I. H., & Robinson, L. A. (1982). Responses to depressed individuals: Discrepancies between self-report and observer-rated behavior. *Journal of Abnormal Psychology, 91,* 231–240.

Gottlieb, B. H. (2000). Self-help, mutual aid, and support groups among older adults. *Canadian Journal on Aging, 19,* 58–74.

Gould, S. J. (1981). *The mismeasure of man.* New York: W. W. Norton.

Gouzoulois-Mayfrank, E., Becker, S., Pelz, S., Tuchtenhagen, F., & Daumann, J. (2002). Neuroendocrine abnormalities in recreational ecstasy (MDMA) users: Is it ecstasy or cannabis? *Biological Psychiatry, 51,* 766–769.

Gouzoulis-Mayfrank, E., Thelen, B., Habermeyer, E., Kunert, H. J., Kovar, K. A., Lindenblatt, H., . . . Sass, H. (1999). Psychopathological, neuroendocrine and autonomic effects of 3,4-methylenedioxyethylamphetamine (MDE), psilocybin, and d-methamphetamine in healthy volunteers. *Psychopharmacology, 142,* 41–50.

Grace, M. S., Woodward, O. M., Church, D. R., & Calisch, G. (2001). Prey targeting by the infrared-imaging snake python: Effects of experimental and congenital visual deprivation. *Behavioural Brain Research, 119,* 23–31.

Graham, A. L., Papandonatos, G. D., DePue, J. D., Pinto, B. M., Borrelli, B., Neighbors, C. J. . . . Abrams, D. B. (2008). Lifetime characteristics of participants and non-participants in a smoking cessation trial: implications for external validity and public health impact. *Annals of Behavioral Medicine, 35,* 295–307.

Graham, K., & Wells, S. (2001). The two worlds of aggression for men and women. *Sex Roles, 45,* 595–622.

Graham, M. J., Larsen, U., & Xu, X. (1999). Secular trend in age at menarche in China: A case study of two rural counties in Anhui province. *Journal of Biosocial Science, 31,* 257–267.

Grant, H. M., Bredahl, L. C., Clay, J., Ferrie, J., Groves, J. E., McDorman, T. A., & Dark, V. J. (1998). Context-dependent memory for meaningful material: Information for students. *Applied Cognitive Psychology, 12,* 617–623.

Grant, I., Gonzalez, R., Carey, C. L., Natarajan, L., & Wolfson, T. (2003). Non-acute (residual) neurocognitive effects of cannabis use: A meta-analytic study. *Journal of the International Neuropsychological Society, 9,* 679–689.

Grattan, D. R., Pi, X. J., Jasoni, C. L., Andrews, Z. B., Augustine, R. A., Kokay, I. C., Summerfield, M. R., . . . Bunn, S. J. (2001). Prolactin and receptors in the brain during pregnancy and lactation: Implications for behavior. *Hormones and Behavior, 40,* 115–124.

Gratzer, T. G., & Matas, M. (1994). The right to refuse treatment: Recent Canadian developments. *Bulletin of the American Academy of Psychiatry and the Law, 22,* 249–256.

Graves, R., & Landis, T. (1990). Asymmetry in mouth opening during different speech tasks. *International Journal of Psychology, 25,* 179–189.

Gravius, A., Pietraszek, M., Dekundy, A., & Danysz, W. (2010). Metabotropic glutamate receptors as therapeutic targets for cognitive disorders. *Current Topics in Medicinal Chemistry, 10,* 187–206.

Graw, P., Krauchi, K., Wirz-Justice, A., & Poldinger, W. (1991). Diurnal variation of symptoms in seasonal affective disorder. *Psychiatry Research, 37,* 105–111.

Gray, D. E., (2002). Everybody just freezes. Everybody is just embarrassed: Felt and enacted stigma among parents of children with high functioning autism. *Sociology of Health and Illness, 24,* 734–749.

Greeff, A. P., & de Bruyne, Tanya (2000). Conflict management style and marital satisfaction. *Journal of Sex and Marital Therapy, 26,* 321–334.

Green, A. J. K., & Gilhooly, K. J. (1990). Individual differences and effective learning procedures: The case of statistical computing. *International Journal of Man-Machine Studies, 33,* 97–119.

Green, C. D., & Powell, R. (1990). Comment on Kimble's generalism. *American Psychologist, 45,* 556–557.

Green, E. K., Grozeva, D., Jones, I., Jones, L., Kirov, G., Caesar, S., . . . Craddock, N. (2010). The bipolar disorder risk allele at CACNA1C also confers risk of recurrent major depression and of schizophrenia. *Molecular Psychiatry, 15,* 1016–1022.

Green, J. P., Lynn, S. J., & Malinoski, P. (1998). *Applied Cognitive Psychology, 12,* 431–444.

Greenberg, B. D., Ziemann, U., Cora-Locatelli, G., Harmon, A., Murphy, D. L., Keel, J. C., & Wassermann, E. M. (2000). Altered cortical excitability in obsessive-compulsive disorder. *Neurology, 54,* 142–147.

Greenberg, B. D., Rauch, S. L., & Haber, S. N. (2010). Invasive circuitry-based neurotherapeutics: Stereotactic ablation and deep brain stimulation for OCD. *Neuropsychopharmacology. 35,* 317–336.

Greene, E., Flynn, M. S., & Loftus, E. F. (1982). Inducing resistance to misleading information. *Journal of Verbal Learning and Verbal Behavior, 21,* 207–219.

Greene, R. L. (1987). Effects of maintenance rehearsal on human memory. *Psychological Bulletin, 102,* 403–413.

Greeno, J. G. (1980). Psychology of learning, 1960–1980: One participant's observations. *American Psychologist, 35,* 713–728.

Greenough, A., Cole, G., Lewis, J., Lockton, A., & Blundell, J. (1998). Untangling the effects of hunger, anxiety, and nausea on energy intake during intravenous cholecystokinin octapeptide (CCK-8) infusion. *Physiology and Behavior, 65,* 303–310.

Greenwood, J. D. (1999). Understanding the "cognitive revolution" in psychology. *Journal of the History of the Behavioral Sciences, 35,* 1–22.

Gregory, A. M., Light-Häusermann, J. H., Rijsdijk, F., & Eley, T. C. (2009). Behavioral genetic analyses of prosocial behavior in adolescents. *Developmental Science, 12,* 165–174.

Gregory, C. M., Bowden, M. G., Jayaraman, A., Shah, P., Behrman, A., Kautz, S. A., & Vandenborne, K. (2007). Resistance training and locomotor recovery after incomplete spinal cord injury: A case series. *Spinal Cord, 45,* 522–530.

Greskoo, R. B., & Karlsen, A. (1994). The Norwegian program for the primary, secondary, and tertiary prevention of eating disorders. *Eating Disorders: The Journal of Treatment and Prevention, 2,* 57–63.

Grey, W. (1994). Philosophy and the paranormal, Part 1: The problem of "psi." *Skeptical Inquirer, 18,* 142–149.

Gribble, J. R. (2000). The psychosocial crisis of industry versus inferiority and self-estimates of vocational competence in high school students. *Dissertation Abstracts International: Section B. The Sciences and Engineering, 60,* 3618.

Griffies, W. S. (2010). Believing in the patient's capacity to know his mind: A psychoanalytic case study of fibromyalgia. *Psychoanalytic Inquiry, 30,* 390–404.

Grimshaw, G. M., Adelstein, A., Bryden, M. P., & MacKinnon, G. E. (1998). First-language acquisition in adolescence: Evidence for a critical period for verbal language development. *Brain and Language, 63,* 237–255.

Grisaru, N., Budowski, D., & Witztum, E. (1997). Possession by the "Zar" among Ethiopian immigrants to Israel: Psychopathology or culture-bound syndrome? *Psychopathology, 30,* 223–233.

Grissom, R. J. (1996). The magical number 7 +−2: Meta-meta-analysis of the probability of superior outcome in comparisons involving therapy, placebo, and control. *Journal of Consulting and Clinical Psychology, 64,* 973–982.

Griva, K., Myers, L. B., & Newman, S. (2000). Illness perceptions and self-efficacy beliefs in adolescents and young adults with insulin dependent diabetes mellitus. *Psychology and Health, 15,* 733–750.

Gross, C. G. (2007). The discovery of motor cortex and its background. *Journal of the History of the Neurosciences, 16,* 320–331.

Gross, M., & Lavie, P. (1994). Dreams in sleep apnea patients. *Dreaming: Journal of the Association for the Study of Dreams, 4,* 195–204.

Grossman, C. I., Purcell, D. W., Rotheram-Borus, M. J., & Veniegas, R. (2013). Opportunities for HIV combination prevention to reduce racial and ethnic health disparities. *American Psychologist, 68,* 237–246.

Grossmann, K., Grossmann, K. E., Fremmer-Bombik, E., Kindler, H., Scheuerer-Englisch, H., & Zimmerman, P. (2002). The uniqueness of the child-father attachment relationship: Fathers' sensitive and challenging play as a pivotal variable in a 16-year longitudinal study. *Social Development, 11,* 307–331.

Grossman, R. P., & Till, B. D. (1998). The persistence of classically conditioned brand attitudes. *Journal of Advertising, 27,* 23–31.

Grosz, R. D. (1990). Suicide: Training the resident assistant as an interventionist. *Journal of College Student Psychotherapy, 4,* 179–194.

Grouios, G., Tsorbatzoudis, H., Alexandris, K., & Barkoukis, V. (2000). Do left-handed competitors have an innate superiority in sports? *Perceptual and Motor Skills, 90,* 1273–1282.

Grove, W. M., Eckert, E. D., Heston, L., & Bouchard, T. J. (1990). Heritability of substance abuse and antisocial behavior: A study of monozygotic twins reared apart. *Biological Psychiatry, 27,* 1293–1304.

Grover, B. L. (2011). The validity of MMPI-2 scores with a correctional population and convicted sex offenders. *Psychology, 2,* 638–642.

Grutzendler, J., Kasthuri, N., & Gan, W. B. (2002). Long-term dendritic spine stability in the adult cortex. *Nature, 420,* 812–816.

Guarino, M., Fridrich, P., & Sitton, S. (1994). Male and female conformity in eating behavior. *Psychological Reports, 75,* 603–609.

Guay, F., Boggiano, A. K., & Vallerand, R. J. (2001). Autonomy support, intrinsic motivation, and perceived competence. *Personality & Social Psychology Bulletin, 27,* 643–650.

Gubernskaya, Z. (2010). Changing attitudes toward marriage and children in six countries. *Sociological Perspectives, 53,* 179–200.

Guègen, N. (2002). The effects of a joke on tipping when it is delivered at the same time as the bill. *Journal of Applied Social Psychology, 32,* 1955–1963.

Guhu, N., Sönksen, P. H., & Holt, R. I. G. (2010). Growth hormone abuse: A threat to elite sport. *The Biologist, 57,* 185–190.

Guilford, J. P. (1959). Three faces of intellect. *American Psychologist, 14,* 469–479.

Guilford, J. P. (1984). Varieties of divergent production. *Journal of Creative Behavior, 18,* 1–10.

Guilford, J. P. (1985). The structure of intellect model. In B. B. Wolman (Ed.), *Handbook of intelligence* (pp. 225–266). New York: Wiley.

Gulevich, G., Dement, W., & Johnson, L. (1966). Psychiatric and EEG observations on a case of prolonged (264 hours) wakefulness. *Archives of General Psychiatry, 15,* 29–35.

Gump, B. B., Matthews, K. A., & Raeikkoenen, K. (1999). Modeling relationships among socioeconomic status, hostility, cardiovascular reactivity, and left ventricular mass in African American and White children. *Health Psychology, 18,* 140–150.

Gunderson, J. G. (1996). Borderline patient's intolerance of aloneness: Insecure attachments and therapist availability. *American Journal of Psychiatry, 153,* 752–758.

Gunderson, V. M., Yonas, A., Sargent, P. L., & Grant-Webster, K. S. (1993). Infant macaque monkeys respond to pictorial depth. *Psychological Science, 4,* 93–98.

Gunter, T. D., Vaughn, M. G., & Philibert, R. A. (2010). Behavioral genetics in antisocial spectrum disorders and psychopathy: A review of the recent literature. *Behavioral Sciences and the Law, 28,* 148–173.

Gur, R. E., & Chin, S. (1999). Laterality in functional brain imaging studies of schizophrenia. *Schizophrenia Bulletin, 25,* 141–156.

Gurman, A. S., & Fraenkel, P. (2002). The history of couple therapy: A millennial review. *Family Process, 41,* 199–260.

Gustavson, C. R., Garcia, J., Hawkins, W. G., & Rusiniak, K. W. (1974). Coyote predation control by aversive conditioning. *Science, 184,* 581–583.

Guttler, F., Guldberg, P., & Henriksen, K. F. (1993). Mutation genotype of mentally retarded patients with phenylketonuria. *Developmental Brain Dysfunction, 6,* 92–96.

Guttman, S. R. (2006). Hysteria as a concept: A survey of its history in the psychoanalytic literature. *Modern Psychoanalysis, 31,* 182–228.

Haase, A. M., Prapavessis, H., & Owens, R. G. (2002). Perfectionism, social physique anxiety, and disordered eating: A comparison of male and female elite athletes. *Psychology of Sport and Exercise, 3,* 209–222.

Haber, R. N. (1980). How we perceive depth from flat pictures. *American Scientist, 68,* 370–380.

Habert, M. O., Cruz de Souza, L., Lamari, F., Daragon, N., Desarnaud, S., Jardel, C., . . . Sarazin, M. (2010). Brain perfusion SPECT correlates with CSF biomarkers in Alzheimer's disease. *European Journal of Nuclear Medicine and Molecular Imaging, 37,* 589–593.

Hadjikhani, N., & de Gelder, B. (2002). Neural basis of prosopagnosia: An fMRI study. *Human Brain Mapping, 16,* 176–182.

Hadjikhani, N., & Tootell, R. B. H. (2000). Projection of rods and cones within human visual cortex. *Human Brain Mapping, 9,* 55–63.

Hadley, J. (2009). Animal rights extremism and the terrorism question. *Journal of Social Philosophy, 40,* 363–378.

Häffner, H., Maurer, K., & an der Heiden, W. (2013). ABC schizophrenia study: An overview of results since 1996. *Social Psychiatry and Psychiatric Epidemiology, 48,* 1021–1031.

Hagan, L. D., & Hagan, A. C. (2008). Custody evaluations without psychological testing: Prudent practice or fatal flaw? *Journal of Psychiatry and Law, 36,* 67–106.

Hagerty, M. R. (1999). Testing Maslow's hierarchy of needs: National quality-of-life across time. *Social Indicators Research, 46,* 249–271.

Hagopian, L. P., Farrell, D. A., & Amari, A. (1996). Treating total liquid refusal with backward chaining and fading. *Journal of Applied Behavior Analysis, 29,* 573–575.

Haidt, J., & Keltner, D. (1999). Culture and facial expression: Open-ended methods find more expressions and a gradient of recognition. *Cognition and Emotion, 13,* 225–266.

Haight, B. K., Michel, Y., & Hendrix, S. (2000). The extended effects of the life review in nursing home residents. *International Journal of Aging and Human Development, 50,* 151–168.

Haimowitz, C. (2000). Maybe it's not "kick me" after all: Transactional analysis and schizoid personality disorder. *Transactionalanalysis Journal, 30,* 84–90.

Haist, F., Song, A. W., Wild, K., Faber, T. L., Popp, C. A., & Morris, R. D. (2001). Linking sight and sound: fMRI evidence of primary auditory cortex activation during visual word recognition. *Brain and Language, 76,* 340–350.

Hall, C., & Briggs, J. (2000, June 20). NBA Championship: Lakers 116–Pacers 111: Vandalism mars L. A.'s euphoria. *Los Angeles Times,* p. A1.

Hall, C. S. (1966). *The meaning of dreams.* New York: McGraw-Hill.

Hall, G. C. N. (2003). The self in context: Implications for psychopathology and psychotherapy. *Journal of Psychotherapy, 13,* 66–82.

Hall, G. C. N., Bansal, A., & Lopez, I. R. (1999). Ethnicity and psychopathology: A meta-analytic review of 31 years of comparative MMPI/MMPI-2 research. *Psychological Assessment, 11,* 186–197.

Hall, G. S. (1904). *Adolescence.* New York: Appleton.

Hall, H. K., & Byrne, A. T. J. (1988). Goal setting in sport: Clarifying recent anomalies. *Journal of Sport and Exercise Psychology, 10,* 184–198.

Hall, M., Baum, A., Buysse, D. J., Prigerson, H. G., Kupfer, D., & Reynolds, C. F. III (1998). Sleep as a mediator of the stress-immune relationship. *Psychosomatic Medicine, 60,* 48–56.

Hall, T. E., Hughes, C. A., & Filbert, M. (2000). Computer-assisted instruction in reading for students with learning disabilities: A research synthesis. *Education and Treatment of Children, 23,* 173–193.

Hallenbeck, B. A., & Kauffman, J. M. (1995). How does observational learning affect the behavior of students with emotional or behavioral disorders? A review of research. *Journal of Special Education, 29,* 45–71.

Haller, J. (2013). The neurobiology of abnormal manifestations of aggression—A review of hypothalamic mechanisms in cats, rodents, and humans. *Brain Research Bulletin, 93,* 97–109.

Haller, J., Halasz, J., & Makara, G. B. (2000). Housing conditions and the anxiolytic efficacy of buspirone: The relationship between main and side effects. *Behavioural Pharmacology, 11,* 403–412.

Halligan, P. W., & Oakley, D. A. (2013). Hypnosis and cognitive neuroscience: Bridging the gap. *Cortex, 49,* 359–364.

Halpern, D. F. (1994). Stereotypes, science, censorship, and the study of sex differences. *Feminism & Psychology, 4,* 523–530.

Halpern, D. F. (1995). Cognitive gender differences: Why diversity is a critical research issue. In H. Landrine (Ed.), *Bringing cultural diversity to feminist psychology* (pp. 77–92). Washington, DC: American Psychological Association.

Halpern, D. F. (2000). *Sex differences in cognitive abilities* (3rd ed.). Mahwah, NJ: Erlbaum.

Halpern, D. F., & Coren, S. (1988). Do right-handers live longer? *Nature, 333,* 213.

Halpern, D. F., & Coren, S. (1993). Left-handedness and life span: A reply to Harris. *Psychological Bulletin, 114,* 235–241.

Halpern, D. F., & LeMay, M. L. (2000). The smarter sex: A critical review of sex differences in intelligence. *Educational Psychology Review, 12,* 229–246.

Halpern, D. F., Gilbert, R., & Coren, S. (1996). PC or not PC? Contemporary challenges to unpopular research findings. *Journal of Social Distress and the Homeless, 5,* 251–271.

Halpern, L., Blake, R., & Hillerbrand, J. (1986). Psychoacoustics of a chilling sound. *Perception and Psychophysics, 39,* 77–80.

Hamann, S. B., Ely, T. D., Hoffman, J. M., & Kilts, C. D. (2002). Ecstasy and agony: Activation of human amygdala in positive and negative emotion. *Psychological Science, 13,* 135–141.

Hamarman, S., Pope, K. H., & Czaja, S. J. (2002). Emotional abuse in children: Variations in legal definitions and rates across the United States. *Child Maltreatment: Journal of the American Professional Society on the Abuse of Children, 7,* 303–311.

Hamburger, Y. (1994). The contact hypothesis reconsidered: Effects of the atypical outgroup member on the outgroup stereotype. *Basic and Applied Social Psychology, 15,* 339–358.

Hamel, R., & Elshout, J. J. (2000). On the development of knowledge during problem solving. *European Journal of Cognitive Psychology, 12,* 289–322.

Hamer, D. H., Hu, S., Magnuson, V. L., & Hu, N. (1993). A linkage between DNA markers on the X chromosome and male sexual orientation. *Science, 261,* 321–327.

Hamill, R., Wilson, T. D., & Nisbett, R. E. (1980). Insensitivity to sample bias: Generalizing from atypical cases. *Journal of Personality and Social Psychology, 39,* 578–589.

Hammack, S. E., Cooper, M. A., & Lezak, K. R. (2012). Overlapping neurobiology of learned helplessness and conditioned defeat: Implications for PTSD and mood disorders. *Neuropharmacology, 62,* 565–575.

Hammer, A. L., & Mitchell, W. D. (1996). The distribution of MBTI types in the U.S. by gender and ethnic group. *Journal of Psychological Type, 37,* 2–15.

Hammersley, R., Ditton, J., Smith, I., & Short, E. (1999). Patterns of ecstasy use by drug users. *British Journal of Criminology, 39,* 625–647.

Hammond, G. (2002). Correlates of human-handedness in primary motor cortex: A review and hypothesis. *Neuroscience and Biobehavioral Reviews, 26,* 285–292.

Hampstead, B. M., & Koffler, S. P. (2009). Thalamic contributions to anterograde, retrograde, and implicit memory: A case study. *Clinical Neuropsychologist, 23,* 1232–1249.

Hamson-Utley, J. J., Martin, S., & Walters, J. (2009). Athletic trainers' and physical therapists' perceptions of the effectiveness of psychological skills within sport injury rehabilitation programs. *Journal of Athletic Training, 43,* 258–264.

Han, D. H., Kim, Y. S., Lee, Y. S., Min, K. J., & Renshaw, P. F. (2010). Changes in cue-induced, prefrontal cortex activity with video-game play. *Cyberpsychology, Behavior, and Social Networking, 13,* 655–661.

Han, J. S. (2003). Acupuncture: Neuropeptide release produced by electrical stimulation of different frequencies. *Trends in Neurosciences, 26,* 17–22.

Hancock, D. J., Rymal, A. M., & Ste-Marie, D. M. (2011). A triadic comparison of the use of observational learning amongst team sport athletes, coaches, and officials. *Psychology of Sport & Exercise, 12,* 236–241.

Haney, P., & Durlak, J. A. (1998). Changing self-esteem in children and adolescents: A meta-analytic review. *Journal of Clinical Child Psychology, 27,* 423–433.

Hanley, S. J., & Abell, S. C. (2002). Maslow and relatedness: Creating an interpersonal model of self-actualization. *Journal of Humanistic Psychology, 42,* 37–56.

Hanna, G., Kundiger, E., & Larouche, C. (1990). Mathematical achievement of grade 12 girls in fifteen countries. In L. Burton (Ed.), *Gender and mathematics: An international perspective* (pp. 87–98). New York: Cassell.

Hansen, L., Bakken, M., & Braastad, B. O. (1997). Failure of LiCl-conditioned taste aversion to prevent dogs from attacking sheep. *Applied Animal Behaviour Science, 54,* 251–256.

Hansen, C. H., & Hansen, R. D. (1988). Finding the face in the crowd: An anger superiority effect. *Journal of Personality and Social Psychology, 54,* 917–924.

Hanson, R. K. (1990). The psychological impact of sexual assault on women and children: A review. *Annals of Sex Research, 3,* 187–232.

Harbach, H., Hell, K., Gramsch, C., Katz, N., Hempelmann, G., & Teschemacher, H. (2000). Beta-endorphin (1-31) in the plasma of male volunteers undergoing physical exercise. *Psychoneuroendocrinology, 25,* 551–562.

Harbin, G., Durst, L., & Harbin, D. (1989). Evaluation of oculomotor response in relationship to sports performance. *Medicine and Science in Sports and Exercise, 21,* 258–262.

Hardy, C. J., & Latané, B. (1988). Social loafing in cheerleaders: Effects of team membership and competition. *Journal of Sport and Exercise Psychology, 10,* 109–114.

Hardy, L., & Callow, N. (1999). Efficacy of external and internal visual imagery perspectives for the enhancement of performance on tasks in which form is important. *Journal of Sport and Exercise Psychology, 21,* 95–112.

Hare, R. D., McPherson, L. M., & Forth, A. E. (1988). Male psychopaths and their criminal careers. *Journal of Consulting and Clinical Psychology, 56,* 710–714.

Hariri, A. R., Bookheimer, S. Y., & Mazziotta, J. C. (2000). Modulating emotional responses: Effects of a neocortical network on the limbic system. *Neuroreport: For Rapid Communication of Neuroscience Research, 11,* 43–48.

Harlow, H. F., & Zimmerman, R. R. (1959). Affectional responses in the infant monkey. *Science, 130,* 421–432.

Harlow, J. M. (1993). Recovery from the passage of an iron bar through the head. *History of Psychiatry, 4,* 271–281.

Harman, M. J. (1991). The use of group psychotherapy with cancer patients: A review of recent literature. *Journal for Specialists in Group Work, 16,* 56–61.

Harmer, C. J., Hill, S. A., Taylor, M. J., Cowen, P. J., & Goodwin, G. M. (2003). Toward a neuropsychological theory of antidepressant drug action: Increase in positive emotional bias after potentiation of norepinephrine activity. *American Journal of Psychiatry, 160,* 990–992.

Harmon-Jones, E., Brehm, J. W., Greenberg, J., & Simon, L. (1996). Evidence that the production of aversive consequences is not necessary to create cognitive dissonance. *Journal of Personality and Social Psychology, 70,* 5–16.

Harmon-Jones, E., Peterson, H., & Vaughn, K. (2003). The dissonance-inducing effects of an inconsistency between experienced empathy and knowledge of past failures to help: Support for the action-based model of dissonance. *Basic and Applied Social Psychology, 25,* 69–78.

Harrington, D. M., Block, J. H., & Block, J. (1987). Testing aspects of Carl Rogers' theory of creative environments: Childrearing antecedents of creative potential in young adolescents. *Journal of Personality and Social Psychology, 52,* 851–856.

Harrington, R., & Loffredo, D. A. (2001). The relationship between life satisfaction, self-consciousness, and the Myers-Briggs Type Inventory dimensions. *Journal of Psychology, 135,* 439–450.

Harris, C. R. (2003). A review of sex differences in sexual jealousy, including self-report data, psychophysiological responses, interpersonal violence, and morbid jealousy. *Personality and Social Psychology Review, 7,* 102–128.

Harris, E. G., & Mowen, J. C. (2001). The influence of cardinal-, central-, and surface-level personality traits on consumers' bargaining and complaint intentions. *Psychology and Marketing, 18,* 1155–1185.

Harris, J. C. (2003a). Pinel orders the chains removed from the insane at Bicetre. *Archives of General Psychiatry, 60,* 442.

Harris, J. C. (2003b). A rake's progress: "Bedlam." *Archives of General Psychiatry, 60,* 338–339.

Harris, L. J. (1993). Do left-handers die sooner than right-handers? Commentary on Coren and Halpern's (1991) "Left-handedness: A marker for decreased survival fitness." *Psychological Bulletin, 114,* 203–234.

Harris, L. J. (1999). Early theory and research on hemispheric specialization. *Schizophrenia Bulletin, 25,* 11–39.

Harris, M. J. (1994). Self-fulfilling prophecies in the clinical context: Review and implications for clinical practice. *Applied and Preventive Psychology, 3,* 145–158.

Harris, R. L., Ellicott, A. M., & Holmes, D. S. (1986). The timing of psychosocial transitions and changes in women's lives: An examination of women aged 45 to 60. *Journal of Personality and Social Psychology, 51,* 409–416.

Harrison, A. A. (1969). Exposure and popularity. *Journal of Personality, 37,* 359–377.

Harrison, A. A. (1977). Let's make a deal: An analysis of revelations and stipulations in lonely hearts advertisements. *Journal of Personality and Social Psychology, 35,* 257–264.

Harrison, D. W., Gavin, M. R., & Isaac, W. (1988). A portable biofeedback device for autonomic responses. *Journal of Psychopathology and Behavioral Assessment, 10,* 217–224.

Hart, D. (1998). Can prototypes inform moral developmental theory? *Developmental Psychology, 34,* 420–423.

Hartley, J., & Homa, D. (1981). Abstraction of stylistic concepts. *Journal of Experimental Psychology: Human Learning and Memory, 7,* 33–46.

Hartmann, E., & Basile, R. (2003). Dream imagery becomes more intense after 9/11/01. *Dreaming: Journal of the Association for the Study of Dreams, 13,* 61–66.

Hartshorne, H., & May, M. A. (1928). *Studies in deceit.* New York: Macmillan.

Hartup, W. W. (1989). Social relationships and their developmental significance. *American Psychologist, 44,* 120–126.

Hartwell, E. E., Serovich, J. M., Gravsky, E. L., & Kerr, Z. Y. (2012). Coming out of the dark: Content analysis of articles pertaining to gay, lesbian, and bisexual issues in couple and family therapy journals. *Journal of Marital & Family Therapy, 38,* 227–243.

Harwood, C., & Swain, A. (2002). The development and activation of achievement goals within tennis: II. A player, parent, and coach intervention. *Sport Psychologist, 16,* 111–137.

Hasebe, S., Graf, E. W., & Schor, C. (2001). Fatigue reduces tonic accommodation. *Ophthalmic and Physiological Optics, 21,* 151–160.

Haslam, N. (1997). Evidence that male sexual orientation is a matter of degree. *Journal of Personality and Social Psychology, 73,* 862–870.

Hassett, J. (1978). *A primer of psychophysiology.* San Francisco: Freeman.

Hatfield, E. (1988). Passionate and companionate love. In R. J. Sternberg & M. L. Barnes (Eds.), *The psychology of love* (pp. 191–218). New Haven, CT: Yale University Press.

Hatfield, E., & Sprecher, S. (1995). Men's and women's preferences in marital partners in the United States, Russia, and Japan. *Journal of Cross-Cultural Psychology, 26,* 728–750.

Hatfield, G. (2002). Psychology, philosophy, and cognitive science: Reflections on the history and philosophy of experimental psychology. *Mind and Language, 17,* 207–232.

Hathaway, S. R., & McKinley, J. C. (1943). *Minnesota Multiphasic Personality Inventory.* New York: Psychological Corporation.

Hatton, C. (1998). Pragmatic language skills in people with intellectual disabilities: A review. *Journal of Intellectual and Developmental Disability, 23,* 79–100.

Hatzichristou, D. G., Bertero, E. B., & Goldstein, I. (1994). Decision making in the evaluation of impotence: The patient profile–oriented algorithm. *Sexuality and Disability, 12,* 29–37.

Hawker, D. S., & Boulton, M. J. (2000). Twenty years' research on peer victimization and psychosocial maladjustment: A meta-analytic review of cross-sectional studies. *Journal of Child Psychology and Psychiatry, and Allied Disciplines, 41,* 441–455.

Hawkes, N. (1979). Tracing Burt's descent to scientific fraud. *Science, 205,* 673–675.

Hawkins, D. L., Pepler, D. J., & Craig W. M. (2001). Naturalistic observations of peer interventions in bullying. *Social Development, 10,* 512–527.

Hawkins, M. J., Hawkins, W. E., & Ryan, E. R. (1989). Self-actualization as related to age of faculty members at a large midwestern university. *Psychological Reports, 65,* 1120–1122.

Hawkins, R. F. M. (2001). A systematic meta-review of hypnosis as an empirically supported treatment for pain. *Pain Reviews, 8,* 47–73.

Hay, P. J., Touyz, S., & Sud, R. (2012). Treatment for severe and enduring anorexia nervosa: A review. *Australian and New Zealand Journal of Psychiatry, 46,* 1136–1144.

Hayashi, S., Kuno, T., Morotomi, Y., Osawa, M., Shimizu, M., & Suetake, Y. (1998). Client-centered therapy in Japan: Fujio Tomoda and taoism. *Journal of Humanistic Psychology, 38,* 103–124.

Hayden, T., & Mischel, W. (1976). Maintaining trait consistency in the resolution of behavioral inconsistency: The wolf in sheep's clothing? *Journal of Personality, 44,* 109–132.

Hayes, D. S. (1999). Young children's exposure to rhyming and nonrhyming stories: A structural analysis of recall. *Journal of Genetic Psychology, 160,* 280–293.

Hayes, D. S., Chemelski, B. E., & Palmer, M. (1982). Nursery rhymes and prose passages: Preschoolers' liking and short-term retention of story events. *Developmental Psychology, 18,* 49–56.

Hayes, R. L., Pechura, C. M., Katayama, Y., Povlishuck, J. T., Giebel, M. L., & Becker, D. P. (1984). Activation of pontine cholinergic sites implicated in unconsciousness following cerebral concussions in the cat. *Science, 223,* 301–303.

Hayflick, L. (1980, January). The cell biology of human aging. *Scientific American,* pp. 58–65.

Haykin, S., & Chen, Z. (2005). The cocktail party problem. *Neural Computation, 17,* 1875–1902.

Hays, J. R. (1989). The role of Addington v. Texas on involuntary civil commitment. *Psychological Reports, 65,* 1211–1215.

Hays, P. J., Touyz, S., & Sud, R. (2012). Treatment for severe and enduring anorexia nervosa: A review. *Australian & New Zealand Journal of Psychiatry, 46,* 1136–1144.

Hays, W. S. T. (2003). Human pheromones: Have they been demonstrated? *Behavioral Ecology and Sociobiology, 54,* 89–97.

Hayward, C., Killen, J. D., & Taylor, C. B. (2003). The relationship between agoraphobia symptoms and panic disorder in a non-clinical sample of adolescents. *Psychological Medicine, 33,* 733–738.

Haywood, H. C., Meyers, C. E., & Switzky, H. N. (1982). Mental retardation. *Annual Review of Psychology, 33,* 309–342.

Hazelrigg, P. J., Cooper, H., & Strathman, A. J. (1991). Personality moderators of the experimenter expectancy effect: A reexamination of five hypotheses. *Personality and Social Psychology Bulletin, 17,* 569–579.

Hazlett-Stevens, H., & Craske, M. G. (2003). The catastrophizing worry process in generalized anxiety disorder: A preliminary investigation of an analog population. *Behavioral and Cognitive Psychotherapy, 31,* 387–401.

He, Z.-X., & Lester, D. (1998). Methods for suicide in mainland China. *Death Studies, 22,* 571–579.

Hearne, K. M. (1989). A nationwide mass dream-telepathy experiment. *Journal of the Society for Psychical Research, 55,* 271–274.

Hearnshaw, L. S. (1979). *Cyril Burt: Psychologist.* Ithaca: Cornell University Press.

Hearnshaw, L. S. (1985). Francis Bacon: Harbinger of scientific psychology. *Revista de Historia de la Psicologia, 6,* 5–14.

Hearst, E. (1999). After the puzzle boxes: Thorndike in the 20th century. *Journal of the Experimental Analysis of Behavior, 72,* 441–446.

Heath, D. T., & Orthner, D. K. (1999). Stress and adaptation among male and female single parents. *Journal of Family Issues, 20,* 557–587.

Heaton, P., Hermelin, B., & Pring, L. (1998). Autism and pitch processing: A precursor for savant musical ability. *Music Perception, 15,* 291–305.

Heaven, P. C., L., & St. Quintin, D. (2003). Personality factors predict racial prejudice. *Personality and Individual Differences, 34,* 625–634.

Heavey, L., Pring, L., & Hermelin, B. (1999). A date to remember: The nature of memory in savant calendrical calculators. *Psychological Medicine, 29,* 145–160.

Hebb, D. O. (1955). Drives and the C.N.S. (conceptual nervous system). *Psychological Review, 62,* 243–254.

Hebb, D. O. (1958). The motivating effects of exteroceptive stimulation. *American Psychologist, 13,* 109–113.

Hebl, M. R., & Heatherton, T. F. (1998). The stigma of obesity in women: The difference is black and white. *Personality and Social Psychology Bulletin, 24,* 417–426.

Hechinger, N. (1981, March). Seeing without eyes. *Science, 81,* 38–43.

Hedges, L. V. (1987). How hard is hard science, how soft is soft science? The empirical cumulativeness of research. *American Psychologist, 42,* 443–455.

Hedges, L. V., & Nowell, A. (1999). Changes in the Black-White gap in achievement test scores. *Sociology of Education, 72,* 111–135.

Heffner, H. E. (1983). Hearing in large and small dogs: Absolute thresholds and size of the tympanic membrane. *Behavioral Neuroscience, 97,* 310–318.

Heidelberger, M. (2004). *Nature from within: Gustav Theodor Fechner and his psychophysical worldview.* Pittsburgh: University of Pittsburgh Press.

Heider, F. (1944). Social perception and phenomenal causality. *Psychological Review, 51,* 358–374.

Heine, M. K., Ober, B. A., & Shenaut, G. K. (1999). Naturally occurring and experimentally induced tip-of-the-tongue experiences in three adult age groups. *Psychology and Aging, 14,* 445–457.

Heine, S. H., Lehman, D. R., Markus, H. R., & Kitayama, S. (1999). Is there a universal need for positive self-regard? *Psychological Review, 106,* 766–794.

Heinrichs, J., Heine, S. J., & Norenzayan, A. (2010). The weirdest people in the world? *Behavioral and Brain Sciences, 33,* 61–135.

Heitzmann, C. A., & Kaplan, M. (1988). Assessment of methods for measuring social support. *Health Psychology, 7,* 75–109.

Hellekant, G., Ninomiya, Y., & Danilova, V. (1998). Taste in chimpanzees. I: Labeled-line coding in sweet taste. *Physiology and Behavior, 65,* 191–200.

Helmes, E., & Reddon, J. R. (1993). A perspective on developments in assessing psychopathology: A critical review of the MMPI and MMPI-2. *Psychological Bulletin, 113,* 453–471.

Hendrick, C. (1990). Replications, strict replications, and conceptual replications: Are they important? *Journal of Social Behavior and Personality, 5,* 41–49.

Hendrickson, K. M., McCarty, T., & Goodwin, J. M. (1990). Animal alters: Case reports. *Dissociation: Progress in the Dissociative Disorders, 3,* 218–221.

Hendriks, A. A. J., Hofstee, W. K. B., & De Raad, B. (1999). The Five-Factor Personality Inventory (FFPI). *Personality and Individual Differences, 27,* 307–325.

Henle, M. (1978). One man against the Nazis: Wolfgang Köhler. *American Psychologist, 33,* 939–944.

Henle, M. (1993). Man's place in nature in the thinking of Wolfgang Köhler. *Journal of the History of the Behavioral Sciences, 29,* 3–7.

Hennig, J., Laschefski, U., & Opper, C. (1994). Biopsychological changes after bungee jumping: b-Endorphin immunoreactivity as a mediator of euphoria? *Neuropsychobiology, 29,* 28–32.

Hennrikus, D. J., Jeffery, R. W., & Lando, H. A. (1995). The smoking cessation process: Longitudinal observations in a working population. *Preventive Medicine: An International Journal Devoted to Practice and Theory, 24,* 235–244.

Hepper, P. G., Shahidulla, S., & White, R. (1991). Handedness in the human fetus. *Neuropsychologia, 29,* 1107–1111.

Herbert, T. B., & Cohen, S. (1993). Depression and immunity: A meta-analytic review. *Psychological Bulletin, 113,* 472–486.

Herbert, W. (1983). MMPI: Redefining normality for modern times. *Science News, 134,* 228.

Herbert, W. (1983). Remembrance of things partly. *Science News, 124,* 378–381.

Herek, G. M. (2000). The psychology of sexual prejudice. *Current Directions in Psychological Science, 9,* 19–22.

Hergenhahn, B. R. (1984). *An introduction to theories of personality.* Englewood Cliffs, NJ: Prentice-Hall.

Hergovich, A., & Olbrich, A. (2002). What can artificial intelligence do for peace psychology? *Review of Psychology, 9,* 3–11.

Herkenhahn, M., Lynn, A. B., deCosta, B. R., & Richfield, E. K. (1991). Neuronal localization of cannabinoid receptors in the basal ganglia of the rat. *Brain Research, 547,* 267–274.

Herman, D., Opler, L., Felix, A., Valencia, E., Wyatt, R. J., & Susser, E. (2000). A critical time intervention with mentally ill homeless men: Impact on psychiatric symptoms. *Journal of Nervous and Mental Disease, 188,* 135–140.

Herman, L. M., & Uyeyama, R. K. (1999). The dolphin's grammatical competency: Comments on Kako (1999). *Animal Learning and Behavior, 27,* 18–23.

Hermann, D. H. (1990). Autonomy, self determination, the right of involuntarily committed persons to refuse treatment, and the use of substituted judgment in medication decisions involving incompetent persons. *International Journal of Law and Psychiatry, 4,* 361–385.

Hernandez, M., & Iyengar, S. S. (2001). What drives whom? A cultural perspective on human agency. *Social Cognition, 19,* 269–294.

Herning, R. I. (1985). Cocaine increases EEG beta: A replication of Hans Berger's historic experiments. *Electroencephalography and Clinical Neurophysiology, 60,* 470–477.

Herrero, J. V., & Hillix, W. A. (1990). Hemispheric performance in detecting prosody: A competitive dichotic listening task. *Perceptual and Motor Skills, 71,* 479–486.

Herrnstein, R. J. (1994). *The bell curve: Intelligence and class structure in American life.* New York: Free Press.

Herrnstein, R. J., Nickerson, R. S., de Sanchez, M., & Swets, J. A. (1986). Teaching thinking skills. *American Psychologist, 41,* 1279–1289.

Hersen, M., Kazdin, A. E., & Bellack, A. S. (Eds.). (1983). *The clinical psychology handbook.* New York: Pergamon.

Hershberger, S. L. (1997). A twin registry study of male and female sexual orientation. *Journal of Sex Research, 34,* 212–222.

Hershenson, D. B. (2008). Ahead of its time: Career counseling's roots in phrenology. *Career Development Quarterly, 57,* 181–190.

Hertenstein, M. J. (2002). Touch: Its communicative functions in infancy. *Human Development, 45,* 70–94.

Herter, C. J., & Rhine, J. B. (1945). An exploratory investigation of the PK effect. *Journal of Parapsychology, 9,* 17–25.

Hertwig, R., & Ortmann, A. (2008). Deception in experiments: Revisiting the arguments in its defense. *Ethics and Behavior, 18,* 59–92.

Hertz, L., & Chen, Y. (2016, September). Editorial: All 3 types of glial cells are important for memory formation. *Frontiers in Integrative Neuroscience, 10,* 31.

Herz, R. S., & Cupchik, G. C. (1992). An experimental characterization of odor-evoked memories in humans. *Chemical Senses, 17,* 519–528.

Hetherington, A. W., & Ranson, S. W. (1942). The spontaneous activity and food intake of rats with hypothalamic lesions. *American Journal of Physiology, 136,* 609–617.

Hettema, J. M., Prescott, C. A., & Kendler, K. S. (2001). A population-based twin study of generalized anxiety disorder in men and women. *Journal of Nervous and Mental Disease, 189,* 413–420.

Hewitt, J. K. (1997). Behavior genetics and eating disorders. *Psychopharmacology Bulletin, 33,* 355–358.

Hewitt, J. K. (1997). The genetics of obesity: What have genetic studies told us about the environment? *Behavior Genetics, 27,* 353–358.

Hewlett, B. S., Lamb, M. E., Shannon, D., Leyendecker, B., & Schoelmerich, A. (1998). Culture and early infancy among central African foragers and farmers. *Developmental Psychology, 34,* 653–661.

Hewson-Bower, B., & Drummond, P. D. (1996). Secretory immunoglobulin A increases during relaxation in children with and without recurrent upper respiratory tract infections. *Journal of Developmental and Behavioral Pediatrics, 17,* 311–316.

Heyes, C. M., Dawson, G. R., & Nokes, T. (1992). Imitation in rats: Initial responding and transfer evidence. *Quarterly Journal of Experimental Psychology Comparative and Physiological Psychology, 45B,* 229–240.

Heywood, C., & Beale, I. L. (2003). EEG biofeedback vs. placebo treatment for attention-deficit/hyperactivity disorder: A pilot study. *Journal of Attention Disorders, 7,* 43–55.

Hiatt, S. W., Campos, J. J., & Emde, R. N. (1980). Facial patterning and infant emotional expression: Happiness, surprise, and fear. *Annual Progress in Child Psychiatry and Child Development,* 95–121.

Hickok, G. (2009). Eight problems for the mirror neuron theory of action understanding in monkeys and humans. *Journal of Cognitive Neuroscience, 21,* 1229–1243.

Hicks, A. U., Lappalainen, R. S., Narkilahti, S., Suuronen, R., Corbett, D., Sivenius, J., . . . Jolkkonen, J. (2009). Transplantation of human embryonic stem cell-derived neural precursor cells and enriched environment after cortical stroke in rats: Cell survival and functional recovery. *European Journal of Neuroscience, 29,* 563–574.

Hicks, R. A., Johnson, C., Cuevas, T., & Debaro, D. (1994). Do right-handers live longer? An updated assessment of baseball player data. *Perceptual and Motor Skills, 78,* 1243–1247.

Hicks, R. A., Johnson, C., & Pellegrini, R. J. (1992). Changes in the self-reported consistency of normal habitual sleep duration of college students (1978 and 1992). *Perceptual and Motor Skills, 75,* 1168–1170.

Hidaka, B. (2012). Depression as a disease of modernity: Explanations for increasing prevalence. *Journal of Affective Disorders, 140,* 205–214.

Higashiyama, A., & Kitano, S. (1991). Perceived size and distance of persons in natural outdoor settings: The effects of familiar size. *Psychologia: An International Journal of Psychology in the Orient, 34,* 188–199.

Higgins, E. T. (1987). Self-discrepancy: A theory relating self and affect. *Psychological Review, 94,* 319–340.

Higgins, E. T. (1990). Self-state representations: Patterns of interconnected beliefs with specific holistic meanings and importance. *Bulletin of the Psychonomic Society, 28,* 248–253.

Higgins, J. E., & Endler, N. S. (1995). Coping, life stress, and psychological and somatic distress. *European Journal of Personality, 9,* 253–270.

Highet, A. (1998). Casablanca, Humphrey Bogart, the Oedipus complex, and the American male. *Psychoanalytic Review, 85,* 761–774.

Hilgard, E. (1987). *Psychology in America: A historical survey.* San Diego: Harcourt Brace Jovanovich.

Hilgard, E. R. (1973). A neodissociative interpretation of pain reduction in hypnosis. *Psychological Review, 80,* 403–419.

Hilgard, E. R. (1978, January). Hypnosis and consciousness. *Human Nature,* pp. 42–49.

Hill, C. E., & Stephany, A. (1990). Relation of nonverbal behavior to client reactions. *Journal of Counseling Psychology, 37,* 22–26.

Hill, J. (2003). Early identification of individuals at risk for antisocial personality disorder. *British Journal of Psychiatry, 182,* S11–S14.

Hill, J. L., Waldfogel, J., Brooks-Gunn, J., & Han, W. J. (2005). Maternal employment and child development: A fresh look using newer methods. *Developmental Psychology, 41,* 833–850.

Hill, J. O., & Peters, J. C. (1998). Environmental contributions to the obesity epidemic. *Science, 280,* 1371–1374.

Hill, R. D., Allen, A. C., & McWhorter, P. (1991). Stories as a mnemonic aid for older learners. *Psychology and Aging, 6,* 484–486.

Hillson, T. R., & Martin, R. A. (1994). What's so funny about that? The domains-interaction approach as a model of incongruity and resolution in humor. *Motivation and Emotion, 18,* 1–29.

Hilt, L. M., Sander, L. C., Nolen-Hoeksema, S., & Simen, A. A. (2007). The BDNF Val66Met polymorphism predicts rumination and depression differently in young adolescent girls and their mothers. *Neuroscience Letters, 429,* 12–16.

Hilts, V. L. (1982). Obeying the laws of hereditary descent: Phrenological views on inheritance and eugenics. *Journal of the History of the Behavioral Sciences, 18,* 62–77.

Hinchy, J., Lovibond, P. F., & Ter-Horst, K. M. (1995). Blocking in human electrodermal conditioning. *Quarterly Journal of Experimental Psychology Comparative and Physiological Psychology, 48,* 2–12.

Hines, T. M. (1998). Comprehensive review of biorhythm theory. *Psychological Reports, 83,* 19–64.

Hinney, A., & Volckmar, A. L. (2013). Genetics of eating disorders. *Current Psychiatry Reports, 15,* 17–33.

Hinton, D. E., & Lewis-Fernández, R. (2011). The cross-cultural validity of posttraumatic stress disorder: Implications for *DSM-5. Depression & Anxiety, 28,* 783–801.

Hirata, Y., Kuriki, S., & Pantev, C. (1999). Musicians with absolute pitch show distinct neural activities in the auditory cortex. *Neuroreport: For Rapid Communication of Neuroscience Research, 10,* 999–1002.

Hirsch, H. V. B., & Spinelli, D. N. (1970). Visual experience modifies distribution of horizontally and vertically oriented receptive fields in cats. *Science, 168,* 869–871.

Hirt, E. R., McCrea, S. M., & Boris, H. I. (2003). "I know you self-handicapped last exam": Gender differences in reactions to self-handicapping. *Journal of Personality and Social Psychology, 84,* 177–193.

Hobson, C. J., & Delunas, L. (2001). National norms and life-event frequencies for the revised Social Readjustment Rating Scale. *International Journal of Stress Management, 8,* 299–314.

Hobson, J. A. (1988). *The dreaming brain.* New York: Basic Books.

Hobson, J. A., & McCarley, R. W. (1977). The brain as a dream state generator: An activation-synthesis hypothesis of the dream process. *American Journal of Psychiatry, 134,* 1335–1348.

Hobson, J. A., Pace-Schott, E. F., & Stickgold, R. (2000). Dream science 2000: A response to commentaries on "Dreaming and the brain." *Behavioral and Brain Sciences, 23,* 1019–1035, 1083–1121.

Hochhausen, N. M., Lorenz, A. R., & Newman, J. R. (2002). Specifying the impulsivity of female inmates with borderline personality disorder. *Journal of Abnormal Psychology, 111,* 495–501.

Hocking-Schuler, J. L., & O'Brien, W. H. (1997). Cardiovascular recovery from stress and hypertension risk factors: A meta-analytic review. *Psychophysiology, 34,* 649–659.

Hodgins, H. S., & Zuckerman, M. (1990). The effect of nonverbal sensitivity on social interaction. *Journal of Nonverbal Behavior, 14,* 155–170.

Hoefnagels, C., & Zwikker, M. (2001). The bystander dilemma and child abuse: Extending the Latané and Darley model to domestic violence. *Journal of Applied Social Psychology, 31,* 1158–1183.

Hoek, H. W., & Van Hoeken, D. (2003). Review of the prevalence and incidence of eating disorders. *International Journal of Eating Disorders, 34,* 383–396.

Hoeksema-van Orden, C. Y. D., Gaillard, A. W. K., & Buunk, B. P. (1998). Social loafing under fatigue. *Journal of Personality and Social Psychology, 75,* 1179–1190.

Hoemann, H. W., & Keske, C. M. (1995). Proactive interference and language change in hearing adult students of American Sign Language. *Sign Language Studies, 86,* 45–61.

Hoffman, C., Lau, I., & Johnson, D. R. (1986). The linguistic relativity of person cognition: An English-Chinese comparison. *Journal of Personality and Social Psychology, 51,* 1097–1105.

Hoffman, N. (1995). The social "instinct." *Journal of the American Academy of Psychoanalysis and Dynamic Psychiatry, 23,* 197–206.

Hofmann, A. (1983). *LSD: My problem child.* Los Angeles: Tarcher.

Hogan, J. D. (2003). Anne Anastasi: Master of differential psychology and psychometrics. In G. Kimble & M. Wertheimer (Eds.), *Portraits of pioneers in psychology* (Vol. 5, pp. 263–296). Mahwah, NJ: Erlbaum.

Hogben, M. (1998). Factors moderating the effect of televised aggression on viewer behavior. *Communication Research, 25,* 220–247.

Holahan, C. K., Holahan, C. J., & Wonacott, N. L. (1999). Self-appraisal, life satisfaction, and retrospective life choices across one and three decades. *Psychology and Aging, 14,* 238–244.

Holden, C. (1980, November). Twins reunited: More than the faces are familiar. *Science, 80,* 55–59.

Holden, C. (1983). Insanity defense reexamined. *Science, 222,* 994–995.

Holden, C. (1986). Depression research advances, treatment lags. *Science, 233,* 723–726.

Holden, C. (1986). Researchers grapple with problems of updating classic psychological test. *Science, 233,* 1249–1251.

Holden, C. (1987). Animal regulations: So far, so good. *Science, 237,* 598–601.

Holden, C. (1987). The genetics of personality. *Science, 237,* 598–601.

Holland, L. N., Goldstein, B. D., & Aronstam, R. S. (1993). Substance P receptor desensitization in the dorsal horn: Possible involvement of receptor-G protein complexes. *Brain Research, 600,* 89–96.

Holland, R. W., Verplanken, B., & van Knippenberg, A. (2002). On the nature of attitude-behavior relations: The strong guide, the weak follow. *European Journal of Social Psychology, 32,* 869–876.

Hollender, M. H. (1983). The 51st landmark article. *Journal of the American Medical Association, 250,* 228–229.

Hollingworth, L. S. (1914). Variability as related to sex differences in achievement. *American Journal of Sociology, 19,* 510–530.

Hollins, M., Delemos, K. A., & Goble, A. K. (1991). Vibrotactile adaptation on the face. *Perception and Psychophysics, 49,* 21–30.

Hollist, C. S., Miller, R. B., Falceto, O. G., & Fernandes, C. L. C. (2007). Marital satisfaction and depression: A replication of the marital discord model in a Latino sample. *Family Process, 46,* 485–498.

Hollon, S. D. (1996). The efficacy and effectiveness of psychotherapy relative to medications. *American Psychologist, 51,* 1025–1030.

Holm, L., Ullén, F., & Madison, G. (2011). Intelligence and temporal accuracy of behavior: Unique and shared associations with reaction time and motor timing. *Experimental Brain, Research, 214,* 175–183.

Holmes, D. S. (1974). Investigations of repression: Differential recall of material experimentally or naturally associated with ego threat. *Psychology Bulletin, 81,* 632–653.

Holmes, J. D., & Beins, B. C. (2009). Psychology is a science: At least some students think so. *Teaching of Psychology, 36,* 5–11.

Holmes, T. H., & Rahe, R. H. (1967). The Social Readjustment Rating Scale. *Journal of Psychosomatic Research, 11,* 213–218.

Holroyd, J. (1996). Hypnosis treatment of chronic pain: Understanding why hypnosis is useful. *International Journal of Clinical and Experimental Hypnosis, 44,* 33–51.

Holtgraves, T. (1997). Styles of language use: Individual and cultural variability in conversational indirectness. *Journal of Personality and Social Psychology, 73,* 624–637.

Holtgraves, T., & Skeel, J. (1992). Cognitive biases in playing the lottery: Estimating the odds and choosing the numbers. *Journal of Applied Social Psychology, 22,* 934–952.

Holton, R. (2009). Determinism, self-efficacy, and the phenomenology of free will. *Inquiry, 52,* 412–428.

Honchar, M. P., Olney, J. W., & Sherman, W. R. (1983). Systematic cholinergic agents induce seizures and brain damage in lithium-treated rats. *Science, 220,* 323–325.

Hong, S. (2000). Exercise and psychoneuroimmunology. *International Journal of Sport Psychology, 31,* 204–227.

Honts, C. R., Hodes, R. L., & Raskin, D. C. (1985). Effects of physical countermeasures on the physiological detection of deception. *Journal of Applied Psychology, 70,* 177–187.

Hood, K. E. (1995). Social psychology and sociobiology: Which is the metatheory? *Psychological Inquiry, 6,* 54–56.

Hooley, J. M., & Hiller, J. B. (2000). Personality and expressed emotion. *Journal of Abnormal Psychology, 109,* 40–44.

Hope, D. A., & Mindell, J. A. (1994). Global social skill ratings: Measures of social behavior or physical attractiveness? *Behaviour Research and Therapy, 32,* 463–469.

Hopkins, J. R. (1995). Erik Homburger Erikson (1902–1994). *American Psychologist, 50,* 796–797.

Horesh, N., Amir, M., Kedem, P., Goldberger, Y., & Kotler, M. (1997). Life events in childhood, ad-

Hormuth, S. E. (1986). The sampling of experiences in situ. *Journal of Personality, 54,* 262–293.

Horn, J. L., & Cattell, R. C. (1966). Refinement and test of the theory of fluid and crystallized general intelligences. *Journal of Educational Psychology, 57,* 253–270.

Horn, J. L., & Donaldson, G. (1976). On the myth of individual decline in adulthood. *American Psychologist, 31,* 701–719.

Horne, J. A., & Reyner, L. A. (1996). Counteracting driver sleepiness: Effects of napping, caffeine, and placebo. *Psychophysiology, 33,* 306–309.

Horner, M. D. (1990). Psychobiological evidence for the distinction between episodic and semantic memory. *Neuropsychology Review, 1,* 281–321.

Horney, K. (1924). On the genesis of the castration complex in women. *International Journal of Psychoanalysis, 5,* 50–65.

Horney, K. (1926/1967). The flight from womanhood. In K. Horney, *Feminine psychology* (pp. 54–70). New York: W. W. Norton.

Horney, K. (1950). *Neurosis and human growth.* New York: W. W. Norton.

Hornstein, S. L., Brown, A. S., & Mulligan, N. W. (2003). Long-term flashbulb memory for learning of Princess Diana's death. *Memory, 11,* 293–306.

Horowitz, F. D. (1992). John B. Watson's legacy: Learning and environment. *Developmental Psychology, 28,* 360–367.

Horowitz, S. W., Kircher, J. C., Honts, C. R., & Raskin, D. C. (1997). The role of comparison questions in physiological detection of deception. *Psychophysiology, 34,* 108–115.

Horrey, W. J., & Wickens, C. D. (2006). Examining the impact of cell phone conversations on driving using meta-analytic techniques. *Human Factors: The Journal of the Human Factors and Ergonomics Society, 48,* 196–205.

Horsley, R. R., Osborne, M., Norman, C., & Wells, T. (2012). High-frequency gamblers show increased resistance to extinction following partial reinforcement. *Behavioural Brain Research, 229,* 438–442.

Hortensius, R., Schutter, D. J. L. G., & Harmon-Jones, E. (2012). When anger leads to aggression: Induction of relative left frontal cortical activity with transcranial direct current stimulation increases the anger-aggression relationship. *Social Cognitive & Affective Neuroscience, 7,* 342–347.

Hosoda, M., Stone-Romero, E. F., & Coats, G. (2003). The effects of physical attractiveness on job-related outcomes: A meta-analysis of experimental studies. *Personnel Psychology, 56,* 431–462.

Hou, C., Miller, B. L., Cummings, J. L., Goldberg, M., Mychack, P., Bottino, V., & Benson, D. F. (2000). Artistic savants. *Neuropsychiatry, Neuropsychology, and Behavioral Neurology, 13,* 29–38.

Houlihan, D. D., & Jones, R. N. (1989). Treatment of a boy's school phobia with in vivo systematic desensitization. *Professional School Psychology, 4,* 285–293.

House, J. D. (1998). High school achievement and admissions test scores as predictors of course performance of American Indian and Alaska Native students. *Journal of Psychology, 132,* 680–682.

Hovland, C. I., Lumsdaine, A., & Sheffield, F. (1949). *Experiments on mass communication.* Princeton, NJ: Princeton University Press.

Howard, K. I., Kopta, S. M., Krausse, M. S., & Orlinsky, D. E. (1986). The dose-effect relationship in psychotherapy. *American Psychologist, 41,* 159–164.

Howarth, H. V. C., & Griffin, M. J. (2003). Effect of roll oscillation frequency on motion sickness. *Aviation, Space, and Environmental Medicine, 74,* 326–331.

Howe, M., Toth, S. L., & Cicchetti, D. (2011). Can maltreated children inhibit true and false memories for emotional information? *Child Development, 82,* 967–981.

Howe, M. J., & Smith, J. (1988). Calendar calculating in "idiot savants": How do they do it? *British Journal of Psychology, 79,* 371–386.

Hsu, F. L. K. (1981). *Americans and Chinese: Passage to differences* (3rd ed.). Honolulu: The University of Hawaii Press.

Hsu, L. G., Chester B. E., & Santhouse, R. (1990). Bulimia nervosa in eleven sets of twins: A clinical report. *International Journal of Eating Disorders, 9,* 275–282.

Hsu, L. G., & Sobkiewicz, T. A. (1991). Body image disturbance: Time to abandon the concept for eating disorders? *International Journal of Eating Disorders, 10,* 15–30.

Hsu, L. K. G., & Folstein, M. F. (1997). Somatoform disorders in Caucasian and Chinese Americans. *Journal of Nervous and Mental Disease, 185,* 382–387.

Hu, L. W., Gorenstein, C., & Fuentes, D. (2007). Portuguese version of Corah's Dental Anxiety Scale: Transcultural adaptation and reliability analysis. *Depression and Anxiety, 24,* 467–471.

Hu, S., & Stern, R. M. (1999). The retention of adaptation to motion sickness eliciting stimulation. *Aviation, Space, and Environmental Medicine, 70,* 766–768.

Hu, S., Xu, D., Peterson, B. S., Wang, Q., He, X., Hu, J., . . . Xu, Y. (2013) Association of cerebral networks in resting state with sexual preference of homosexual men: A study of regional homogeneity and functional connectivity. *PLOS ONE 8(3),* e59426.

Huang, W., & Cuvo, A. J. (1997). Social skills training for adults with mental retardation in job-related settings. *Behavior Modification, 21,* 3–44.

Hubel, D. H., & Wiesel, T. N. (1979, September). Brain mechanisms of vision. *Scientific American,* pp. 130–144.

Huber, A., Lui, F., Porro, C. A. (2013). Hypnotic susceptibility modulates brain activity related to experimental placebo analgesia, *Pain, 154,* 1509–1518.

Huberfeld, G., Habert, M. O., Clemenceau, S., Maksud, P., Baulac, M., & Adam, C. (2006). Ictal brain hyperperfusion contralateral to seizure onset: The SPECT mirror image. *Epilepsia, 47,* 123–133.

Hublin, C., Partinen, M., Koskenvuo, M., & Kaprio, J. (2013). Genetic factors in evolution of sleep length—A longitudinal twin study in Finnish adults. *Journal of Sleep Research, 22,* 513–518.

Hudesman, J., Page, W., & Rautiainen, T. (1992). Use of subliminal stimulation to enhance learning mathematics. *Perceptual and Motor Skills, 74,* 1219–1224.

Hugdahl, K., Satz, P., Mitrushina, M., & Miller, E. N. (1993). Left-handedness and old age: Do lefthanders die earlier? *Neuropsychologia, 31,* 325–333.

Hughes, B. M. (2001). Just noticeable differences in 2D and 3D bar charts: A psychophysical analysis of chart readability. *Perceptual and Motor Skills, 92,* 495–503.

Hughes, J., Gabbay, M., Funnell, E., & Dowrick, C. (2012). Exploratory review of placebo characteristics reported in randomized placebo controlled antidepressant drug trials. *Pharmacopsychiatry, 45,* 20–27.

Hughes, J., Smith, T. W., Kosterlitz, H. W., Fothergill, L. A., Morgan, B. A., & Morris, H. R. (1975). Identification of two related pentapeptides from the brain with potent opiate agonistic activity. *Nature, 258,* 577–579.

Hughes, J. R., & Callas, P. W. (2010). Data to assess the generalizability of samples from studies of adult smokers. *Nicotine and Tobacco Research, 12,* 73–76.

Hughes, J. R., Gust, S. W., Skoog, K., & Keenan, R. (1991). Symptoms of tobacco withdrawal: A replication and extension. *Archives of General Psychiatry, 48,* 52–59.

Hughes, J. R., Higgins, S. T., & Bickel, W. K. (1994). Nicotine withdrawal versus other drug withdrawal syndromes: Similarities and dissimilarities. *Addiction, 89,* 1461–1470.

Hughes, J. R., Higgins, S. T., Bickel, W. K., Hunt, W. K., Fenwick, J. W., Gulliver, S. B., & Mireault, G. C. (1991). Caffeine self-administration, withdrawal, and adverse effects among coffee drinkers. *Archives of General Psychiatry, 48,* 611–617.

Hui, K. K. S., Liu, J., Makris, N., Gollub, R. L., Chen, A. J. W., Moore, C. I., . . . Kwong, K. K. (2000). Acupuncture modulates the limbic system and subcortical gray structures of the human brain: Evidence from fMRI studies in normal subjects. *Human Brain Mapping, 9,* 13–25.

Hull, C. L. (1943). *Principles of behavior.* New York: Appleton-Century-Crofts.

Hull, J. G., & Bond, C. F., Jr. (1986). Social and behavioral consequences of alcohol consumption and expectancy: A meta-analysis. *Psychological Bulletin, 99,* 347–360.

Hulme, C., & Roodenrys, S. (1995). Verbal working memory development and its disorders. *Journal of Child Psychology and Psychiatry and Allied Disciplines, 36,* 373–398.

Hultsch, D. F., Hertzog, C., Small, B. J., & Dixon, R. A. (1999). Use it or lose it: Engaged lifestyle as a buffer of cognitive decline in aging? *Psychology and Aging, 14,* 245–263.

Humphreys, K. (1997). Clinicians' referral and matching of substance abuse patients to self-help groups after treatment. *Psychiatric Services, 48,* 1445–1449.

Humphreys, M. S., & Revelle, W. (1984). Personality, motivation, and performance: A theory of the relationship between individual differences and information processing. *Psychological Review, 91,* 153–184.

Hunsberger, B., Pratt, M., & Pancer, S. M. (2001). Adolescent identity formation: Religious exploration and commitment. *Identity, 1,* 365–386.

Hunt, E. (1997). The status of the concept of intelligence. *Japanese Psychological Research, 39,* 1–11.

Hunter, J. E., & Schmidt, F. L. (2000). Racial and gender bias in ability and achievement tests: Resolving the apparent paradox. *Psychology, Public Policy, and Law, 6,* 151–158.

Huopainen, H. (2002). Freud's view of hysteria in light of modern trauma research. *Scandinavian Psychoanalytic Review, 25,* 92–107.

Hur, J., & Osborne, S. (1993). A comparison of forward and backward chaining methods used in teaching corsage making skills to mentally retarded adults. *British Journal of Developmental Disabilities, 39,* 108–117.

Hur, Y.-M., Bouchard, T. J., Jr., & Eckert, E. (1998). Genetic and environmental influences on self-reported diet: A reared-apart twin study. *Physiology and Behavior, 64,* 629–636.

Hur, Y.-M., McGue, M., & Iacono, W. G. (1998). The structure of self-concept in female preadolescent twins: A behavioral genetic approach. *Journal of Personality and Social Psychology, 74,* 1069–1077.

Hurst, L. C., & Mulhall, D. J. (1988). Another calendar savant. *British Journal of Psychiatry, 152,* 274–277.

Hurvich, L. M. (1969). Hering and the scientific establishment. *American Psychologist, 24,* 497–514.

Husain, S. A. (1990). Current perspective on the role of psychosocial factors in adolescent suicide. *Psychiatric Annals, 20,* 122–127.

Huston, A. C., Watkins, B. A., & Kunkel, E. (1989). Public policy and children's television. *American Psychologist, 44,* 424–433.

Huston, A. C., Wright, J. C., Marquis, J., & Green, S. B. (1999). How young children spend their time: Television and other activities. *Developmental Psychology, 35,* 912–925.

Huston, T. L., Ruggiero, M., Conner, R., & Geis, G. (1981). Bystander intervention into crime: A study based on naturally-occurring episodes. *Social Psychology Quarterly, 44,* 14–23.

Huttenlocher, P. R. (1990). Morphometric study of human cerebral-cortex development. *Neuropsychologia, 28,* 517–527.

Huxley, A. F. (1959). Ion movements during nerve activity. *Annals of the New York Academy of Sciences, 81,* 221–246.

Hviid, A., Stellfeld, M., Wohlfahrt, J., & Melbye, M. (2003). Association between thimerosalcontaining vaccine and autism. *Journal of the American Medical Association, 290,* 1763–1766.

Hyde, J. S. (1984). Children's understanding of sexist language. *Developmental Psychology, 20,* 697–706.

Hyde, J. S. (1994). Can meta-analysis make feminist transformations in psychology? *Psychology of Women Quarterly, 18,* 451–462.

Hyde, J. S. (2007). New directions in the study of gender similarities and differences. *Current Directions in Psychological Science, 16,* 259–263.

Hyde, J. S., & Durik, A. M. (2000). Gender differences in erotic plasticity—Evolutionary or sociocultural forces? Comment on Baumeister, 2000. *Psychological Bulletin, 126,* 375–379.

Hyde, J. S., Fennema, E., & Lamon, S. J. (1990). Gender differences in mathematics performance: A meta-analysis. *Psychological Bulletin, 107,* 139–155.

Hyde, J. S., & Linn, M. C. (1988). Gender differences in verbal ability: A meta-analysis. *Psychological Bulletin, 104,* 53–69.

Hyde, J. S., & Plant, E. A. (1995). Magnitude of psychological gender differences: Another side of the story. *American Psychologist, 50,* 159–161.

Hyland, B. (1998). Neural activity related to reaching and grasping in rostral and caudal regions of rat motor cortex. *Behavioural Brain Research, 94,* 255–269.

Hyman, R. B. (1988). Four stages of adulthood: An exploratory study of growth patterns of inner-direction and time-competence in women. *Journal of Research in Personality, 22,* 117–127.

Hynan, D. J. (1990). Client reasons and experiences in treatment that influence termination of psychotherapy. *Journal of Clinical Psychology, 46,* 891–895.

Hystad, S. W., Eid, J., & Brevik, J. I., (2011). Effects of psychological hardiness, job demands, and job control on sickness absence: A prospective study. *Journal of Occupational Health Psychology, 16,* 265–278.

Ibrahim, S. A. (2003). Hypertension and medication adherence among African Americans: A potential factor in cardiovascular disparities. *Journal of the National Medical Association, 95,* 28–29.

Ickes, W., Gesn, P. R., & Graham, T. (2000). Gender differences in empathic accuracy: Differential ability or differential motivation? *Personal Relationships, 7,* 95–109.

Iijima, M., Osawa, M., Nishitan, N., & Iwata, M. (2009). Effects of incense on brain function: Evaluation using electroencephalograms and event-related potentials. *Neuropsychobiology, 59,* 80–86.

Ilies, R., & Judge, T. A. (2003). On the heritability of job satisfaction: The mediating role of personality. *Journal of Applied Psychology, 88,* 750–759.

Imada, T., & Ellsworth, P. C. (2011). Proud Americans and lucky Japanese: Cultural differences in appraisal and corresponding emotion. *Emotion, 11,* 329–345.

Immergluck, L. (1964). Determinism-freedom in contemporary psychology: An ancient problem revisited. *American Psychologist, 19,* 270–281.

Ingelfinger, F. J. (1944). The late effects of total and subtotal gastrectomy. *New England Journal of Medicine, 231,* 321–327.

Ingham, A. G., Levinger, G., Graves, J., & Peckham, V. (1974). The Ringelmann effect: Studies of group size and group performance. *Journal of Experimental Social Psychology, 10,* 371–384.

Ingram, D. H. (1985). Karen Horney at 100: Beyond the frontier. *American Journal of Psychoanalysis, 45,* 305–309.

Inman, M. L., & Baron, R. S. (1996). Influence of prototypes on perceptions of prejudice. *Journal of Personality and Social Psychology, 70,* 727–739.

Inouye, S., Honda, K., & Komoda, Y. (1995). Sleep as neuronal detoxification and restitution. *Behavioural Brain Research, 69,* 91–96.

Insko, C. A. (1965). Verbal reinforcement of attitude. *Journal of Personality and Social Psychology, 2,* 621–623.

Insko, C. A., Nacoste, R. W., & Moe, J. L. (1983). Belief congruence and racial discrimination: Review of the evidence and critical evaluation. *European Journal of Social Psychology, 13,* 153–174.

Invernizzi, M. A., & Abouzeid, M. P. (1995). One story map does not fit all: A cross-cultural analysis of children's written story retellings. *Journal of Narrative & Life History, 5,* 1–19.

Iqbal, H. M., & Shayer, M. (2000). Accelerating the development of formal thinking in Pakistan secondary school students: Achievement effects and professional development issues. *Journal of Research in Science Teaching, 37,* 259–274.

Irnich, D., Behrens, N., Gleditsch, J. M., Stor, W., Schreiber, M. A., Schops, P., . . . Beyer, A. (2002). Immediate effects of dry needling and acupuncture at distant points in chronic neck pain: Results of a randomized, double-blind, sham-controlled crossover trial. *Pain, 99,* 83–89.

Ironson, G., Schneiderman, H., Kumar, M., & Antoni, M. H. (1994). Psychosocial stress, endocrine, and immune response in HIV-1 disease. *Homeostasis in Health and Disease, 35,* 137–148.

Irwin, M., Mascovich, A., Gillin, J. C., & Willoughby, R. (1994). Partial sleep deprivation reduced natural killer cell activity in humans. *Psychosomatic Medicine, 56,* 493–498.

Ishai, A., Ungerleider, L. G., Martin, A., & Haxby, J. V. (2000). The representation of objects in the human occipital and temporal cortex. *Journal of Cognitive Neuroscience, 12,* 35–51.

Ishizawa, Y., Ma, H.-C., Dohi, S., & Shimonaka, H. (2000). Effects of cholinomimetic injection into the brain stem reticular formation on halothane anesthesia and antinociception in rats. *Journal of Pharmacology and Experimental Therapeutics, 293,* 845–851.

Ispa, J. M., Thornburg, K. R., & Gray, M. M. (1990). Relations between early childhood care arrangements and college students' psychosocial development and academic performance. *Adolescence, 25,* 529–542.

Isurin, L., & McDonald, J. L. (2001). Retroactive interference from translation equivalents: Implications for first language forgetting. *Memory and Cognition, 29,* 312–319.

Iversen, I. H. (1993). Techniques for establishing schedules with wheel running as reinforcement in rats. *Journal of the Experimental Analysis of Behavior, 60,* 219–238.

Ivry, G. B., Ogle, C. A., & Shim, E. K. (2006). Role of sun exposure in melanoma. *Dermatological Surgery, 32,* 481–492.

Ivtzan, I., Gardner, H. E., Bernard, I., Sekhon, M., & Hart, R. (2013). Wellbeing through self-fulfillment: Examining developmental aspects of self-actualization. *Humanistic Psychologist, 41,* 119–132.

Iyengar, S. S., & Lepper, M. R. (1999). Rethinking the value of choice: A cultural perspective on intrinsic motivation. *Journal of Personality and Social Psychology, 76,* 349–366.

Izard, C. E. (1990a). Facial expressions and the regulation of emotions. *Journal of Personality and Social Psychology, 58,* 487–498.

Izard, C. E. (1990b). The substrates and functions of emotion feelings: William James and current emotion theory. *Personality and Social Psychology Bulletin, 16,* 626–635.

Izard, C. E. (1993). Four systems for emotion activation: Cognitive and noncognitive processes. *Psychological Review, 100,* 68–90.

Izard, C. E. (1994). Innate and universal facial expressions: Evidence from developmental and cross-cultural research. *Developmental Psychology, 115,* 288–299.

Izard, C. E., & Haynes, O. M. (1988). On the form and universality of the contempt expression: A challenge to Ekman and Friesen's claim of discovery. *Motivation and Emotion, 12,* 1–16.

Izard, C. E., Huebner, R. R., Risser, D., McGinnes, G. C., & Dougherty, L. M. (1980). The young infant's ability to produce discrete emotion expressions. *Developmental Psychology, 16,* 132–140.

Jack, S. J., & Ronan, K. R. (1998). Sensation seeking among high- and low-risk sports participants. *Personality and Individual Differences, 25,* 1063–1083.

Jacklin, C. N. (1989). Female and male: Issues of gender. *American Psychologist, 44,* 127–133.

Jackson, B., Sellers, R. M., & Peterson, C. (2002). Pessimistic explanatory style moderates the effect of stress on physical illness. *Personality and Individual Differences, 32,* 567–573.

Jackson, G. R., Owsley, C., & McGwin, G., Jr. (1999). Aging and dark adaptation. *Vision Research, 39,* 3975–3982.

Jackson, L. A., Hunter, J. E., & Hodge, C. N. (1995). Physical attractiveness and intellectual competence: A meta-analytic review. *Social Psychology Quarterly, 58,* 108–122.

Jackson, R. R., Carter, C. M., & Tarsitano, M. S. (2001). Trial-and-error solving of a confinement problem by a jumping spider, Portia fimbriata. *Behaviour, 138,* 1215–1234.

Jacobs, G. H., Neitz, M., Deegan, J. F., & Neitz, J. (1996). Trichromatic colour vision in New World monkeys. *Nature, 382,* 156–158.

Jacobs, J. R., & Bovasso, G. B. (2000). Early and chronic stress and their relation to breast cancer. *Psychological Medicine, 30,* 669–678.

Jacobs, L., & Joseph, S. (1997). Cognitive Triad Inventory and its association with symptoms of depression and anxiety in adolescents. *Personality and Individual Differences, 22,* 769–770.

Jacobs, W. J., & Blackburn, J. R. (1995). A model of Pavlovian conditioning: Variations in representations of the unconditional stimulus. *Integrative Physiological and Behavioral Science, 30,* 12–33.

Jacobsen, P. B., Bovbjerg, D. H., Schwartz, M. D., & Hudis, C. A. (1995). Conditioned emotional distress in women receiving chemotherapy for breast cancer. *Journal of Consulting and Clinical Psychology, 63,* 108–114.

Jacobson, E. (1977). The origins and development of progressive relaxation. *Journal of Behavior Therapy and Experimental Psychiatry, 8,* 119–123.

Jaencke, L., Shah, N. J., & Peters, M. (2000). Cortical activations in primary and secondary motor areas for complex bimanual movements in professional pianists. *Cognitive Brain Research, 10,* 177–183.

Jaffee, S., & Hyde, J. S. (2000). Gender differences in moral orientation: A meta-analysis. *Psychological Bulletin, 126,* 703–726.

James, W. (1884). What is an emotion? *Mind, 9,* 188–205.

James, W. (1892/1985). *Psychology: Briefer course.* Cambridge, MA: Harvard University Press.

James, W. (1902/1992). *The varieties of religious experience.* New York: Gryphon.

Jancke, L., & Steinmetz, H. (2003). Brain size: A possible source of interindividual variability in corpus callosum morphology. In E. Zaidel & M. Iacoboni (Eds.), *The parallel brain: The cognitive neuroscience of the corpus callosum* (pp. 51–63). Cambridge, MA: MIT Press.

Jang, K. L., McCrae, R. R., Angleitner, A., Riemann, R., & Livesley, W. J. (1998). Heritability of facet-level traits in a cross-cultural twin sample: Support for a hierarchical model of personality. *Journal of Personality and Social Psychology, 74,* 1556–1565.

Jason, L. A., & Brackshaw, E. (1999). Access to TV contingent on physical activity: Effects on reducing TV-viewing and body weight. *Journal of Behavior Therapy and Experimental Psychiatry, 30,* 145–151.

Jeffery, R. W., Epstein, L. H., Wilson, G. T., Drewnowski, A., Stunkard, A. J., & Wing, R. R.

(2000). Long-term maintenance of weight loss: Current status. *Health Psychology, 19,* 5–16.

Jeffrey, S. A., & Adomdza, G. K. (2011). Incentive salience and improved performance. *Human Performance, 24,* 47–59.

Jeffries, S., & Konnert, C. (2002). Regret and psychological well-being among voluntarily and involuntarily childless women and mothers. *International Journal of Aging and Human Development, 54,* 89–106.

Jegede, J. O., Jegede, R. T., & Ugodulunwa, C. A. (1997). Effects of achievement motivation and study habits on Nigerian secondary school students' academic performance. *Journal of Psychology, 131,* 523–529.

Jemmott, J. B., & Locke, S. E. (1984). Psychosocial factors, immunologic mediation, and human susceptibility to infectious diseases: How much do we know? *Psychological Bulletin, 95,* 78–108.

Jemmott, J. B., & Magloire, K. (1988). Academic stress, social support, and secretory immunoglobulin A. *Journal of Personality and Social Psychology, 55,* 803–810.

Jenkins, J. G., & Dallenbach, K. M. (1924). Obliviscence during sleep and waking. *American Journal of Psychology, 35,* 605–612.

Jensen, A. R. (1969). How much can we boost IQ and scholastic achievement? *Harvard Educational Review, 39,* 1–123.

Jensen, A. R. (1980). *Bias in mental testing.* New York: Free Press.

Jensen, K. P, Stein, M. B., Kranzler, H. R., Yang, B. Z., Farrer, L. A., & Gelernter, J. (2014). The α-endomannosidase gene (*manea*) is associated with panic disorder and social anxiety disorder. *Translational Psychiatry, 4,* 1–6.

Jensvold, M. L. A., & Gardner, R. A. (2000). Interactive use of sign language by cross-fostered chimpanzees (*Pan troglodytes*). *Journal of Comparative Psychology, 114,* 335–346.

Jeynes, W. H. (2002). The relationship between the consumption of various drugs by adolescents and their academic achievement. *American Journal of Drug and Alcohol Abuse, 28,* 15–35.

Jiminez-Murcia, S., Ayamí, N., Gómez-Peña, M., Santamaría, J. J. Álvarez-Moya, E., Fernández-Aranda, F., . . . Menchón, J. M. (2012). Does exposure and response prevention improve the results of group cognitive-behavioral therapy for male slot-machine gamblers? *British Journal of Clinical Psychology, 51,* 54–71.

Jocklin, V., McGue, M., & Lykken, D. T. (1996). Personality and divorce: A genetic analysis. *Journal of Personality and Social Psychology, 71,* 288–299.

Joensson, E. G., Cichon, S., Gustavsson, J. P., Gruenhage, F., Forslund, K., Mattila-Evenden, M., . . . Noethen, M. M. (2003). Association between a promoter dopamine D-sub-2 receptor gene variant and the personality trait detachment. *Biological Psychiatry, 53,* 577–584.

Johnson, A. (2002). Prevalence and characteristics of children with cerebral palsy in Europe. *Developmental Medicine and Child Neurology, 44,* 633–640.

Johnson, C., & Flach, A. (1985). Family characteristics of 105 patients with bulimia. *American Journal of Psychiatry, 142,* 1321–1324.

Johnson, D. L. (1998). The right to refuse medication: Freedom and responsibility. *Psychiatric Rehabilitation Journal, 21,* 252–254.

Johnson, D. L., Swank, P. R., Owen, M. J., Baldwin, C. D., Howie, V. M., & McCormick, D. P. (2000). Effects of early middle ear effusion on child intelligence at three, five, and seven years of age. *Journal of Pediatric Psychology, 25,* 5–13.

Johnson, D. L., Wiebe, J. S., Gold, S. M., Andreasen, N. C., Hichwa, R. D., Watkins, G. L., & Ponto, L. L. B. (1999). Cerebral blood flow and personality: A positron emission tomography study. *American Journal of Psychiatry, 156,* 252–257.

Johnson, D. M., Shea, M. T., Yen, S., Battle, C. L., Zlotnick, C., Sanislow, C. A., . . . McGlashan, T. (2003). Gender differences in borderline personality disorder: Findings from the Collaborative Longitudinal Personalitiy Disorders Study. *Comprehensive Psychiatry, 44,* 284–292.

Johnson, M. E., & Hauck, C. (1999). Beliefs and opinions about hypnosis held by the general public. *American Journal of Clinical Hypnosis, 42,* 10–20.

Johnson, P., Smith, A. J., & Nelson, M. D. (2003). Predictors of social interest in young adults. *Journal of Individual Psychology, 59,* 281–292.

Johnson, S. B. (2013). Increasing psychology's role in health research and health care. *American Psychologist, 68,* 311–321.

Johnson, T. J., & Cropsey, K. L. (2000). Sensation seeking and drinking game participation in heavy-drinking college students. *Addictive Behaviors, 25,* 109–116.

Johnson, W., McGue, M., Krueger, R. F., & Bouchard, T. J., Jr. (2004). Marriage and personality: A genetic analysis. *Journal of Personality and Social Psychology, 86,* 285–294.

Johnson, W. B., Digiuseppe, R., & Ulven, J. (1999). Albert Ellis as mentor: National survey results. *Psychotherapy: Theory, Research, Practice, Training, 36,* 305–312.

Johnston, M., & Vogele, C. (1993). Benefits of psychological preparation for surgery: A metaanalysis. *Annals of Behavioral Medicine, 15,* 245–256.

Johnston, M. V. (2009). Plasticity in the developing brain: Implications for rehabilitation. *Developmental Disabilities Research Reviews, 15,* 94–101.

Jonah, B. A. (1997). Sensation seeking and risky driving: A review and synthesis of the literature. *Accident Analysis and Prevention, 29,* 651–665.

Jonas, G. (1972). *Visceral learning: Toward a science of self-control.* New York: Viking.

Jones, C. J., & Meredith, W. (2000). Developmental paths of psychological health from early adolescence to later adulthood. *Psychology and Aging, 15,* 351–360.

Jones, E. E. (1985). History of social psychology. In G. A. Kimble & K. Schlesinger (Eds.), *Topics in the history of psychology* (Vol. 2, pp. 371–407). Hillsdale, NJ: Erlbaum.

Jones, E. E., & Berglas, S. (1978). Control of attributions about the self through self-handicapping strategies: The appeal of alcohol and the role of underachievement. *Personality & Social Psychology Bulletin, 4,* 200–206.

Jones, J. H. (1997, August 25/September 1). Dr. Yes. *New Yorker,* pp. 98–113.

Jones, K. D. (2012). A critique of the *DSM-5* field trials. *Journal of Nervous & Mental Disease, 200,* 517–519.

Jones, K. M., & Friman, P. C. (1999). A case study of behavioral assessment and treatment of insect phobia. *Journal of Applied Behavior Analysis, 32,* 95–98.

Jones, L. (1900). Education during sleep. *Suggestive Therapeutics, 8,* 283–285.

Jones, L. V. (1984). White-black achievement differences: The narrowing gap. *American Psychologist, 39,* 1207–1213.

Jones, M. C. (1924). The elimination of children's fears. *Journal of Experimental Psychology, 7,* 383–390.

Jones, M. M. (1980). Conversion disorders: Anachronism or evolutionary form? A review of the neurologic, behavioral, and psychoanalytic literature. *Psychological Bulletin, 87,* 427–441.

Jones, R. B. (2003). Have cholinergic therapies reached their clinical boundary in Alzheimer's disease? *International Journal of Geriatric Psychiatry, 18,* S7–S13.

Jones, S. (2008). Nature and nurture in the development of social smiling. *Philosophical Psychology, 21,* 349–357.

Jorgensen, R. S., Nash, J. K., Lasser, N. L., Hymowitz, N., & Langer, A. W. (1988). Heart rate acceleration and its relationship to total serum cholesterol, triglycerides, and blood pressure. *Psychophysiology, 25,* 39–44.

Joseph, R. (1997). Traumatic amnesia, repression, and hippocampus injury due to emotional stress, corticosteroids, and enkephalins. *Child Psychiatry and Human Development, 29,* 169–185.

Jousselin-Hosaja, M., Venault, P., Tobin, C., Joubert, C., Delacour, J., & Chapouthier, G. (2001). Involvement of adrenal medulla grafts in the open field behavior. *Behavioural Brain Research, 121,* 29–37.

Joyce, J. (1916/1967). *A portrait of the artist as a young man.* New York: Viking.

Joynson, R. B. (2003). Selective interest and psychological practice: A new interpretation of the Burt affair. *British Journal of Psychology, 94,* 409–426.

Judge, S. J., & Cumming, B. G. (1986). Neurons in the monkey midbrain with activity related to convergence eye movement and accommodation. *Journal of Neurophysiology, 55,* 915–930.

Judge, T. A., & Bono, J. E. (2001). Relationship of core self-evaluation traits—self-esteem, generalized self-efficacy, locus of control, and emotional stability—with job satisfaction and job performance: A meta-analysis. *Journal of Applied Psychology, 86,* 80–92.

Julien, R. M. (1981). *A primer of drug action.* San Francisco: Freeman.

Jung, C. G. (1959/1969). *Flying saucers: A modern myth of things seen in the sky.* New York: Signet.

Jussim, L. (1991). Social perception and social reality: A reflection-construction model. *Psychological Review, 98,* 54–73.

Kagan, J. (1997). Temperament and the reactions to unfamiliarity. *Child Development, 68,* 139–143.

Kagan, J. (2002). Empowerment and education: Civil rights, expert-advocates, and parent politics in Head Start, 1964–1980. *Teachers College Record, 104,* 516–562.

Kahan, T. L., & LaBerge, S. (1994). Lucid dreaming as metacognition: Implications for cognitive science. *Consciousness and Cognition: An International Journal, 3,* 246–264.

Kahneman, D. (2003). A perspective on judgment and choice: Mapping bounded rationality. *American Psychologist, 58,* 697–720.

Kahneman, D., & Tversky, A. (1973). On the psychology of prediction. *Psychological Review, 80,* 237–251.

Kahneman, D., & Tversky, A. (1982, January). The psychology of preferences. *Scientific American,* pp. 160–173.

Kail, R., & Hall, L. K. (2001). Distinguishing short-term memory from working memory. *Memory and Cognition, 29,* 1–9.

Kako, E. (1999). Elements of syntax in the systems of three language-trained animals. *Animal Learning and Behavior, 27,* 1–14.

Kalafat, J. (2003). School approaches to youth suicide prevention. *American Behavioral Scientist, 46,* 1211–1223.

Kalakoski, V., & Saariluoma, P. (2001). Taxi drivers' exceptional memory of street names. *Memory & Cognition, 29,* 634–638.

Kalbfleisch, M. L. (2008). Introduction to the special issues on the cognitive neuroscience of giftedness. *Roeper Review, 30,* 159–161.

Kalichman, S. C. (1996). HIV-AIDS prevention videotapes: A review of empirical findings. *Journal of Primary Prevention, 17,* 259–280.

Kalish, C. (2002). Gold, jade, and emeruby: The value of naturalness for theories of concepts and categories. *Journal of Theoretical and Philosophical Psychology, 22,* 45–66.

Kaltiala-Heino, R., Koivisto, A.-M., Marttunen, M., & Fröjd, S. (2011). Pubertal timing and substance use in middle adolescence: A 2-year follow-up study. *Journal of Youth and Adolescence, 40,* 1288–1301.

Kalueff, A. V., & Nutt, D. J. (2007). Role of GABA in anxiety and depression. *Depression and Anxiety, 24,* 495–517.

Kamarck, T. W., Peterman, A. H., & Raynor, D. A. (1998). The effects of the social environment on stress-related cardiovascular activation: Current findings, prospects, and implications. *Annals of Behavioral Medicine, 20,* 247–256.

Kamen-Siegel, L., Rodin, J., Seligman, M. E., & Dwyer, J. (1991). Explanatory style and cell-mediated immunity in elderly men and women. *Health Psychology, 10,* 229–235.

Kamin, L. J. (1974). *The science and politics of IQ.* New York: Wiley.

Kamp-Becker, I., Ghahreman., M., Heinzel-Gutenbrunner, M., Peters, M., Remschmidt, H., & Becker, K. (2013). Evaluation of the revised algorithm of Autism Diagnostic Observation Schedule (ADOS) in the diagnostic investigation of high-functioning children and adolescents with autism spectrum disorders. *Autism, 17,* 87–102.

Kanarek, R. B., Mathes, W. F., & D'Anci, K. E. (2012). Exercise promotes positive first impression formation towards both men and women. *Appetite, 58,* 786–789.

Kanda, M., Nagamine, T., Ikeda, A., Ohara, S., Kunieda, T., Fujiwara, N., . . . Shibasaki, H. (2000). Primary somatosensory cortex is actively involved in pain processing in human. *Brain Research, 853,* 282–289.

Kandel, E. R. (2001). The molecular biology of memory storage: A dialogue between genes and synapses. *Science, 294,* 1030–1038.

Kandel, E. R., & Schwartz, J. H. (1982). Molecular biology of learning: Modulation of transmitter release. *Science, 218,* 433–443.

Kanekar, S. (1976). Observational learning of attitudes: A behavioral analysis. *European Journal of Social Psychology, 6,* 5–24.

Kanner, L. (1943). Autistic disturbances of affective contact. *Nervous Child, 2,* 217–250.

Kansaku, K., & Kitazawa, S. (2001). Imaging studies on sex differences in lateralization of language. *Neuroscience Research, 41,* 333–337.

Kapur, S., & Remington, G. (1996). Serotonin-dopamine interaction and its relevance to schizophrenia. *American Journal of Psychiatry, 153,* 466–476.

Karama, S., LeCours, A. R., Leroux, J.-M., Bourgouin, P., Beaudoin, G., Joubert, S., & Beauregard, M. (2002). Areas of brain activation in males and females during viewing of erotic film excerpts. *Human Brain Mapping, 16,* 1–13.

Karau, S. J., & Williams, K. D. (1993). Social loafing: A meta-analytic review and theoretical integration. *Journal of Personality and Social Psychology, 65,* 681–706.

Karcher, M. J., & Lindwall, J. (2003). Social interest, connectedness, and challenging experiences: What makes high school mentors persist? *Journal of Individual Psychology, 59,* 293–315.

Karlberg, L., Krakau, I., & Unden, A.-L. (1998). Type A behavior intervention in primary health care reduces hostility and time pressure: A study in Sweden. *Social Science and Medicine, 46,* 397–402.

Karlin, B. E., Brown, G. K., Trockel, M., Cunning, D., Zeiss, A. M., & Taylor, C. B. (2012). National dissemination of cognitive behavioral therapy for depression in the Department of Veteran Affairs health care system: Therapist and patient-level outcomes. *Journal of Consulting & Clinical Psychology, 80,* 707–718.

Karmel, R. (2003). Freud's "Cocaine Papers" (1884–1887): A commentary. *Canadian Journal of Psychoanalysis, 11,* 161–169.

Karney, B. R., & Bradbury, T. N. (2000). Attributions in marriage: State or trait? A growth curve analysis. *Journal of Personality and Social Psychology, 78,* 295–309.

Karnovsky, M. L. (1986). Progress in sleep. *New England Journal of Medicine, 315,* 1026–1028.

Karon, B. P., & Widener, A. J. (1998). Repressed memories: The real story. *Professional Psychology: Research and Practice, 29,* 482–487.

Kasai, H., Fukuda, M., Watanabe, S., Hayashi-Takagi, A., & Noguchi, J. (2010). Structural dynamics of dendritic spines in memory and cognition. *Trends in Neurosciences, 33,* 121–129.

Kashima, E. S., & Kashima, Y. (1998). Culture and language: The case of cultural dimensions and personal pronoun use. *Journal of Cross-Cultural Psychology, 29,* 461–486.

Kashima, Y., & Triandis, H. C. (1986). The self-serving bias in attributions as a coping strategy: *Journal of Cross-Cultural Psychology, 17,* 83–97.

Kassel, J. D., & Unrod, M. (2000). Smoking, anxiety, and attention: Support for the role of nicotine in attentionally mediated anxiolysis. *Journal of Abnormal Psychology, 109,* 161–166.

Kasser, T., & Sharma, Y. S. (1999). Reproductive freedom, educational equality, and females' preference for resource-acquisition characteristics in mates. *Psychological Science, 10,* 374–377.

Kassin, S. M., Tubb, V. A., Hosch, H. M., & Memon, A. (2001). On the "general acceptance" of eyewitness testimony research. *American Psychologist, 56,* 405–416.

Katata, K., Sakai, N., Doi, K., Kawamitsu, H., Fujii, M., Sugimura K., & Nibu, K. I. (2009). Functional MRI of regional brain responses to "pleasant" and "unpleasant" odors. *Acta Oto-Lryngologica, 129,* 85–90.

Katz, J., & Beach, S. R. H. (2000). Looking for love? Self-verification and self-enhancement effects on initial romantic attraction. *Personality and Social Psychology Bulletin, 26,* 1526–1539.

Katz, J., & Schneider, M. E. (2013). Casual hook-up sex during the first year of college: Prospective associations with attitudes about sex and love relationships. *Archives of Sexual Behavior, 42,* 1451–1462.

Kaufman, I., & Rock, I. (1962, July). The moon illusion. *Scientific American,* 120–130.

Kaufman, J. C. (2010). Editor's introduction. *The International Journal of Creativity & Problem Solving, 20,* 5.

Kavšek, M., Yonas, A., & Granrud, C. E. (2012). Infants' sensitivity to pictorial depth cues: A review and meta-analysis of looking studies. *Infant Behavior & Development, 35,* 109–128.

Kazemi-Bajestani, S. M. R., Amirsadri, A., Samari, S. A. A., & Akbar, J. A. (2011). Lunar phase cycle and psychiatric hospital emergency visits, inpatient admissions and aggressive behavior. *Asian Journal of Psychiatry, 4,* 45–50.

Kebbell, M. R. (2000). The law concerning the conduct of lineups in England and Wales: How well does it satisfy the recommendations of the American Psychology-Law Society? *Law and Human Behavior, 24,* 309–315.

Kebbell, M. R., & Wagstaff, G. F. (1997). An investigation into the influence of hypnosis on the confidence and accuracy of eyewitness recall. *Contemporary Hypnosis, 14,* 157–166.

Kebbell, M. R., & Wagstaff, G. F. (1998). Hypnotic interviewing: The best way to interview eyewitnesses? *Behavioral Sciences and the Law, 16,* 115–129.

Keegan, J., Parva, M., Finnegan, M., Gerson, A., & Beldon, M. (2010). Addiction in pregnancy. *Journal of Addictive Diseases, 29,* 175–191.

Keen, R., Carrico, R. L., Sylvia, M. R., & Berthier, N. E. (2003). How infants use perceptual information to guide action. *Developmental Science, 6,* 221–231.

Keesey, R. E., & Powley, T. L. (1986). The regulation of body weight. *Annual Review of Psychology, 37,* 109–133.

Keijsers, G. P. J., Schaap, C. P. D. R., & Hoogduin, C. A. L. (2000). The impact of interpersonal patient and therapist behavior on outcome in cognitive-behavioral therapy: A review of empirical studies. *Behavior Modification, 24,* 264–297.

Keillor, J. M., Barrett, A. M., Crucian, G. P., Kortenkamp, S., & Heilman, K. M. (2002). Emotional experience and perception in the absence of facial feedback. *Journal of the International Neuropsychological Society, 8,* 130–135.

Keith, J. R., & McVety, K. M. (1988). Latent place learning in a novel environment and the influences of prior training in rats. *Psychobiology, 16,* 146–151.

Keller, F. S. (1991). Burrhus Frederic Skinner (1904–1990). *Journal of the History of the Behavioral Sciences, 27,* 3–6.

Kelley, H. H. (1950). The warm-cold variable in first impressions of personality. *Journal of Personality, 18,* 431–439.

Kelley, H. H. (1992). Commonsense psychology and scientific discovery. *Annual Review of Psychology, 43,* 1–23.

Kelley, M. L., Self-Brown, S., Le, B., Bosson, J. V., Hernandez, B. C., & Gordon, A. T. (2010). Predicting posttraumatic stress symptoms in children following Hurricane Katrina: A prospective analysis of the effect of parental distress and parenting practices. *Journal of Traumatic Stress 23,* 582–590.

Kelly, J. F., & Greene, M. C. (2013). Where there's a will there's a way: A longitudinal investigation of the inter play between recovery motivation and self-efficacy in predicting treatment outcome. *Psychology of Addictive Behaviors,* Retrieved from http://psycnet.apa.org/ psycinfo/2013-40800-001/, 4/20/14.

Kelly, M. P., Strassberg, D. S., & Kircher, J. R. (1990). Attitudinal and experiential correlates of anorgasmia. *Archives of Sexual Behavior, 19,* 165–177.

Kelly, R. B., Zyzanski, S. J., & Alemagno, S. A. (1991). Prediction of motivation and behavior change following health promotion: Role of health beliefs, social support, and self-efficacy. *Social Science and Medicine, 32,* 311–320.

Kelly, S. J., Macaruso, P., & Sokol, S. M. (1997). Mental calculation in an autistic savant: A case study. *Journal of Clinical and Experimental Neuropsychology, 19,* 172–184.

Kelly, W. E., Kelly, K. E., & Clanton, R. C. (2001). The relationship between sleep length and grade point average among college students. *College Student Journal, 35,* 84–86.

Kelsoe, J. R., Kristbjanarson, H., Bergesch, P., & Shilling, P. (1993). A genetic linkage study of bipolar disorder and 13 markers on chromosome 11 including the D-sub-2 dopamine receptor. *Neuropsychopharmacology, 9,* 293–301.

Kemp, B., Krause, J. S., & Adkins, R. (1999). Depression among African Americans, Latinos, and Caucasians with spinal cord injury: An exploratory study. *Rehabilitation Psychology, 44,* 235–247.

Kendler, K. S., Gardner, C. O., & Prescott, C. A. (1998). A population-based twin study of self-esteem and gender. *Psychological Medicine, 28,* 1403–1409.

Kendzierski, D., Sheffield, A., & Morganstein, M. S. (2002). The role of schema in attributions for own versus other's exercise lapse. *Basic and Applied Social Psychology, 24,* 251–260.

Kenneally, S. M., Bruck, G. E., Frank, E. M., & Nalty, L. (1999). Language intervention after thirty years of isolation: A case study of a feral child. *Education and Training in Mental Retardation and Developmental Disabilities, 33,* 13–23.

Kennedy, P., & Rogers, B. A. (2000). Anxiety and depression after spinal cord injury: A longitudinal analysis. *Archives of Physical Medicine and Rehabilitation, 8,* 932–937.

Kenrick, D. T., & Dantchik, A. (1983). Interactionism, idiographics, and the social psychological invasion of personality. *Journal of Personality, 51,* 286–307.

Kenrick, D. T., & Funder, D. C. (1988). Profiting from controversy: Lessons from the person-situation debate. *American Psychologist, 43,* 23–34.

Keppel, R. D., & Walter, R. (1999). Profiling killers: A revised classification model for understanding sexual murder. *International Journal of Offender Therapy and Comparative Criminology, 43,* 417–437.

Kerkhoff, G., & Rossetti, Y. (2006). Plasticity in spatial neglect—Recovery and rehabilitation. *Restorative Neurology and Neuroscience, 24,* 201–206.

Kerr, N. L., & Tindale, R. S. (2004). Group performance and decision making. *Annual Review of Psychology, 55,* 623–655.

Kessler, R. C., Adler, L. A., Berglund, P., Green, J. G., McLaughlin, K. A., Fayyad, J., . . . Zaslavsky, A. M. (2013). The effects of temporally secondary co-morbid mental disorders on the associations of *DSM-IV* ADHD with adverse outcomes in the U.S. National Comorbidity Survey Replication Adolescent Supplement (NCS-A). *Psychological Medicine/FirstView*, 1–14.

Kessler, R. C., Berglund, P., Demler, O., Jin, R., Merikangas, K. R., & Walters, E. E. (2005). Lifetime prevalence and age-of-onset distributions of *DSM–IV* disorders in the National Comorbidity Survey Replication. *Archives of General Psychiatry, 62*, 593–602.

Kessler, R. C., Chiu, W. T., Demler, O., Merikangas, K. R., & Walters, E. E. (2005). Prevalence, severity, and comorbidity of twelve-month *DSM-IV* disorders in the National Comorbidity Survey Replication (NCS-R). *Archives of General Psychiatry, 62*, 617–627.

Kessler, R. C., Petukhova, M., Sampson, N. A., Zaslavsky, A. M., & Wittchen, H.-U. (2012). Twelve-month and lifetime prevalence and lifetime morbid risk of anxiety and mood disorders in the United States. *International Journal of Methods in Psychiatric Research, 21*, 169–184.

Kessler, R. C., Stang, P. E., Wittchen, H.-U., Ustun, T. B., Roy-Burne, P. P., & Walters, E. E. (1998). Lifetime panic-depression comorbidity in the National Comorbidity Survey. *Archives of General Psychiatry, 55*, 801–808.

Kessler, R. C., Stein, M. B., & Berglund, P. (1998). Social phobia subtypes in the National Comorbidity Survey. *American Journal of Psychiatry, 155*, 613–619.

Kessler, S. (1984). The myth of mythical disease [Review of *Schizophrenia: Medical diagnosis or moral verdict?*]. *Contemporary Psychology, 29*, 380–381.

Kety, S. S., Wender, P. H., Jacobsen, B., & Ingraham, L. J. (1994). Mental illness in the biological and adoptive relatives of schizophrenic adoptees: Replication of the Copenhagen study in the rest of Denmark. *Archives of General Psychiatry, 51*, 442–455.

Kevles, D. J. (1995, April 3). The X factor: The battle over the ramifications of the gay gene. *New Yorker*, pp. 85–90.

Kidd, J. A. (2003). The need for improved operational definition of suicide attempts: Illustrations from the case of street youth. *Death Studies, 27*, 449–455.

Kiecolt-Glaser, J. K., & Glaser, R. (1995). Psychoneuroimmunology and health consequences: Data and shared mechanisms. *Psychosomatic Medicine, 57*, 269–274.

Kiecolt-Glaser, J. K., Glaser, R., Strain, E. C., Stout, J. C., Tarr, K. L., Holliday, J. E., & Speicher, C. E. (1986). Modulation of cellular immunity in medical students. *Journal of Behavioral Medicine, 9*, 5–21.

Kiecolt-Glaser, J. K., Marucha, P. T., Atkinson, C., & Glaser, R. (2001). Hypnosis as a modulator of cellular immune dysregulation during acute stress. *Journal of Consulting and Clinical Psychology, 69*, 674–682.

Kiecolt-Glaser, J. K., Marucha, P. T., Malarkey, W. B., Mercado, A M., & Glaser, R. (1995). Slowing of wound healing by psychological stress. *Lancet, 346*, 1194–1196.

Kiecolt-Glaser, J. K., Newton, T., Cacioppo, J. T., MacCallum, R. C., Glaser, R., & Malarkey, W. (1996). Marital conflict and endocrine function: Are men really more physiologically affected than women? *Journal of Consulting and Clinical Psychology, 64*, 324–332.

Kiernan, B. D., Dane, J. R., Phillips, L. H., & Price, D. D. (1995). Hypnotic analgesia reduces R-III nociceptive reflex: Further evidence concerning the multifactorial nature of hypnotic analgesia. *Pain, 60*, 39–47.

Kihlstrom, J. F., & McConkey, K. M. (1990). William James and hypnosis: A centennial reflection. *Psychological Science, 1*, 174–178.

Kilborn, L. C., & Labbe, E. E. (1990). Magnetic resonance imaging scanning procedures: Development of phobic response during scan and at one-month follow-up. *Journal of Behavioral Medicine, 13*, 391–401.

Kilmartin, C. T., & Dervin, D. (1997). Inaccurate representation of the Electra complex in psychology textbooks. *Teaching of Psychology, 24*, 269–271.

Kim, D., Adipudi, V., Shibayama, M., Giszter, S., Tessler, A., Murray, M., & Simansky, K. J. (1999). Direct agonists for serotonin receptors enhance locomotor function in rats that received neural transplants after neonatal spinal transection. *Journal of Neuroscience, 19*, 6213–6224.

Kim, E., Zeppenfeld, V., & Cohen, D. (2013). Sublimation, culture, and creativity. *Journal of Personality & Social Psychology, 105*, 639–666.

Kim, H., & Markus, H. R. (1999). Deviance or uniqueness, harmony or conformity? A cultural analysis. *Journal of Personality and Social Psychology, 77*, 785–800.

Kim, J., Lim, J.-S., & Bhargava, M. (1998). The role of affect in attitude formation: A classical conditioning application. *Journal of the Academy of Marketing Science, 26*, 143–152.

Kim, J. E., & Moen, P. (2001). Is retirement good or bad for subjective well-being? *Current Directions in Psychological Science, 10*, 83–86.

Kim, J. S., Yoon, S. S., Lee, S. I., Yoo, H. J., Kim, C. Y., Choi-Kwon, S., & Lee, B. C. (1998). Type A behavior and stroke: High tenseness dimension may be a risk factor for cerebral infarction. *European Neurology, 39*, 168–173.

Kim, Y. I. (2003). The effects of assertiveness training on enhancing the social skills of adolescents with visual impairments. *Journal of Visual Impairment and Blindness, 97*, 285–297.

Kim-Cohen, J., Caspi, A., Taylor, A., Williams, B., Newcombe, R., Craig, I. W., Moffitt, T. E. (2006). MAOA, maltreatment, and gene-environment interaction predicting children's mental health: New evidence and a meta-analysis. *Molecular Psychiatry 11*, 903–913.

Kimball, M. M. (1989). A new perspective on women's math achievement. *Psychological Bulletin, 105*, 198–214.

Kimball, M. M. (1995). *Gender and math: What makes a difference? Feminist visions of gender similarities and differences*. New York: Harrington Park Press.

Kimball, M. M. (2000). From "Anna O." to Bertha Pappenheim: Transforming private pain into public action. *History of Psychology, 3*, 20–43.

Kimble, G. A. (1981). Biological and cognitive constraints on learning. In L. T. Benjamin, Jr. (Ed.), *The G. Stanley Hall Lecture Series* (Vol. 1, pp. 11–60). Washington, DC: American Psychological Association.

Kimura, D. (1987). Are men's and women's brains really different? *Canadian Psychology, 28*, 133–147.

Kimura, D., & Hampson, E. (1994). Cognitive pattern in men and women is influenced by fluctuations in sex hormones. *Current Directions in Psychological Science, 3*, 57–61.

Kimura, R., MacTavish, D., Yang, J., Westaway, D., & Jhamandas, J. H. (2012). Beta amyloid-induced depression of hippocampal long-term potentiation is mediated through the amylin receptor. *Journal of Neuroscience, 32*, 17401–17406.

King, D. B., Raymond, B. L., & Simon-Thomas, J. A. (1995). History of sport psychology in cultural magazines of the Victorian era. *Sport Psychologist, 9*, 376–390.

King, L. A., & Miner, K. N. (2000). Writing about the perceived benefits of traumatic events: Implications for physical health. *Personality and Social Psychology Bulletin, 26*, 220–230.

King, N. J., Clowes-Hollins, V., & Ollendick, T. H. (1997). The etiology of childhood dog phobia. *Behaviour Research and Therapy, 35*, 77.

King, R. (1998). Evidence-based practice: Where is the evidence? The case of cognitive behaviour therapy and depression. *Australian Psychologist, 33*, 83–88.

Kinsey, A. C., Pomeroy, W. D., & Martin, C. E. (1948). *Sexual behavior in the human male*. Philadelphia: Saunders.

Kinsey, A. C., Pomeroy, W. D., Martin, C. E., & Gebhard, T. H. (1953). *Sexual behavior in the human female*. Philadelphia: Saunders.

Kirmayer, L. J., Narasiah, L., Munoz, M., Rashid, M., Ryder, A. G., Guzder, J., . . . Pottie, K. (2011). Common mental health problems in immigrants and refugees: General approach in primary care. *Canadian Medical Association Journal, 183*, e959–e967.

Kirmeyer, S. L., & Biggers, K. (1988). Environmental demand and demand engineering behavior: An observational analysis of the Type A patterns. *Journal of Personality and Social Psychology, 54*, 997–1005.

Kirsch, I. (1996). Hypnotic enhancement of cognitive-behavioral weight loss treatments: Another metareanalysis. *Journal of Consulting and Clinical Psychology, 64*, 517–519.

Kirschner, S. M., & Galperin, G. J. (2001). Psychiatric defenses in New York County: Pleas and results. *Journal of the American Academy of Psychiatry and the Law, 29*, 194–201.

Kisch, J., & Erber, J. (1999). Operant conditioning of antennal movements in the honey bee. *Behavioural Brain Research, 99*, 93–102.

Kisilevsky, B. S., & Hains, S. M. J. (2011). Onset and maturation of fetal heart rate response to the mother's voice over late gestations. *Developmental Science, 14*, 214–223.

Kisner, M. J. (2005). Scepticism and the early Descartes. *British Journal for the History of Philosophy, 13*, 207–235.

Kitayama, S., Duffy, S., Kawamura, T., & Larsen, J. T. (2003). Perceiving object and its context in different cultures. *Psychological Science, 14*, 201–206.

Kitayama, S., Markus, H. R., & Kurokawa, M. (2000). Culture, emotion, and well-being: Good feelings in Japan and the United States. *Cognition and Emotion, 14*, 93–124.

Kittlerova, P., & Valouskova, V. (2000). Retinal ganglion cells regenerating through the peripheral nerve graft retain their electroretinographic responses and mediate light-induced behavior. *Behavioural Brain Research, 112*, 187–194.

Kittrell, D. (1998). A comparison of the evolution of men's and women's dreams in Daniel Levinson's theory of adult development. *Journal of Adult Development, 5*, 105–115.

Kjellgren, A., Sundequist, U., Norlander, T., & Archer, T. (2001). Effects of flotation-REST on muscle tension pain. *Pain Research & Management, 6*, 181–189.

Klahr, A. M., Rueter, M. A., McGue, M., Iacono, W. G., & Alexandra, B. S. (2011). The relationship between parent-child conflict and adolescent antisocial behavior: Confirming shared environmental mediation. *Journal of Abnormal Child Psychology, 39*, 683–694.

Klar, Y., & Giladi, E. E. (1999). Are most people happier than their peers, or are they just happy? *Personality and Social Psychology Bulletin, 25*, 585–594.

Kleiber, C., & Harper, D. C. (1999). Effects of distraction on children's pain and distress during medical procedures: A meta-analysis. *Nursing Research, 48*, 44–49.

Klein, A. G. (2000). Fitting the school to the child: The mission of Leta Stetter Hollingworth, founder of gifted education. *Roeper Review, 23*, 97–103.

Klein, P. D. (1997). Multiplying the problems of intelligence by eight: A critique of Gardner's theory. *Canadian Journal of Education, 22*, 377–394.

Klein, S. B. (1982). *Motivation: Biosocial approaches*. New York: McGraw–Hill.

Kleindienst, N., & Greil, W. (2003). Lithium in the long-term treatment of bipolar disorders. *European Archives of Psychiatry and Clinical Neuroscience, 253,* 120–125.

Kleinke, C. L., Peterson, T. R., & Rutledge, T. R. (1998). Effects of self-generated facial expressions on mood. *Journal of Personality and Social Psychology, 74,* 272–279.

Kleinmuntz, B., & Szucko, J. J. (1984a). A field study of the fallibility of polygraph lie detection. *Nature, 308,* 449–450.

Kleinmuntz, B., & Szucko, J. J. (1984b). Lie detection in ancient and modern times: A call for contemporary scientific study. *American Psychologist, 39,* 766–776.

Klepac, R. K. (1986). Fear and avoidance of dental treatment in adults. *Annals of Behavioral Medicine, 8,* 17–22.

Klimesch, W., (2012). Alpha-band oscillations, attention, and controlled access to stored information. *Trends in Cognitive Sciences, 16,* 606–617.

Kling, K. C., Hyde, J. S., Showers, C. J., & Buswell, B. N. (1999). Gender differences in self-esteem: A meta-analysis. *Psychological Bulletin, 125,* 470–500.

Kling, K. C., Hyde, J. S., Showers, C. J., & Buswell, B. N. (1999). Gender differences in self-esteem: A meta-analysis. *Psychological Bulletin, 125,* 470–500.

Klohnen, E. C., & Luo, S. (2003). Interpersonal attraction and personality: What is attractive—Self similarity, ideal similarity, complementarity, or attachment security? *Journal of Personality and Social Psychology 85,* 709–722.

Klonoff, E. A., Janata, J. W., & Kaufman, B. (1986). The use of systematic desensitization to overcome resistance to magnetic resonance imaging (MRI) scanning. *Journal of Behavior Therapy and Experimental Psychiatry, 17,* 189–192.

Klonoff, E. A., & Moore, D. J. (1986). "Conversion reactions" in adolescents: A biofeedback-based operant approach. *Journal of Behavior Therapy and Experimental Psychiatry, 17,* 179–184.

Klosterhalfen, W., & Klosterhalfen, S. (1983). A critical analysis of the animal experiments cited in support of learned helplessness. *Psychologische Beitrage, 25,* 436–458.

Kluft, R. P. (1987). An update on multiple personality disorder. *Hospital and Community Psychiatry, 38,* 363–373.

Klump, K. L., McGue, M., & Iacono, W. G. (2002). Genetic relationship between personality and eating attitudes and behaviors. *Journal of Abnormal Psychology, 111,* 380–389.

Klump, K. L., Miller, K. B., Keel P. K., McGue, M., & Iacono, W. G. (2001). Genetic and environmental influences on anorexia nervosa syndromes in a population-based twin sample. *Psychological Medicine, 31,* 737–740.

Klüver, H., & Bucy, P. C. (1937). "Psychic blindness" and other symptoms following bilateral temporal lobectomy in rhesus monkeys. *American Journal of Physiology, 119,* 352–353.

Kmiecik-Małecka, E., Małecki, A., Pawlas, N., Woźniakova, Y., & Pawlas, K. (2009). The effect of blood lead concentration on EEG, brain electrical activity mapping and psychological test results in children. *Polish Journal of Environmental Studies, 18,* 1021–1027.

Knapp, T. J., & Shodahl, S. A. (1974). Ben Franklin as a behavior modifier: A note. *Behavior Therapy, 5,* 656–660.

Knee, C. R., & Boon, S. D. (2001). When the glass is half-empty: Framing effects and evaluations of a romantic partner's attributes. *Personal Relationships, 8,* 249–263.

Knishkowy, B., Verbov, G., Amitai, Y., Stein-Zamir, C., & Rosen, L. (2012). Reaching Jewish ultra-orthodox adolescents: Results from a targeted smoking prevention trial. *International Journal of Adolescent Medicine & Health, 24,* 173–179.

Knouse, S. B. (1994). Impressions of the resume: The effects of applicant education, experience, and impression management. *Journal of Business and Psychology, 9,* 33–45.

Knox, S. S., & Uvnaes-Moberg, K. (1998). Social isolation and cardiovascular disease: An atherosclerotic pathway? *Psychoneuroendocrinology, 23,* 877–890.

Knudsen, E. I. (1981, December). The hearing of the barn owl. *Scientific American,* pp. 112–113, 115–116, 118–125.

Kobasa, S. C., Maddi, S. R., & Kahn, S. (1982). Hardiness and health: A prospective study. *Journal of Personality and Social Psychology, 42,* 168–177.

Kobayakawa, T., Ogawa, H., Kaneda, H., Ayabe-Kanamura, S., Endo, H., & Saito, S. (1999). Spatio-temporal analysis of cortical activity evoked by gustatory stimulation in humans. *Chemical Senses, 24,* 201–209.

Koch, G., Di Lorenzo, F., Bonnì, S., Ponzo, V., Caltagagirone, C., & Martorana, A. (2012). Impaired LTP-but not LTD-like cortical plasticity in Alzheimer's Disease patients. *Journal of Alzheimer's Disease, 31,* 593–599.

Kocsis, R. N. (2013). The criminal profiling reality: What is actually behind the smoke and mirrors? *Journal of Forensic Psychology Practice, 13,* 79–91.

Kocsis, R. N., Hayes, A. F., & Irwin, H. J. (2002). Investigative experience and accuracy in psychological profiling of a violent crime. *Journal of Interpersonal Violence, 17,* 811–823.

Kocsis, R. N., Irwin, H. J., & Hayes, A. F. (1998). Organised and disorganised criminal behaviour syndromes in arsonists: A validation study of a psychological profiling concept. *Psychiatry, Psychology, and Law, 5,* 117–131.

Koehler, J. J., & Conley, C. A. (2003). The "hot hand" myth in professional basketball. *Journal of Sport and Exercise Psychology, 25,* 253–259.

Kohlberg, L. (1981). *Essays on moral development.* New York: Harper & Row.

Köhler, W. (1925). *The mentality of apes.* New York: Harcourt Brace Jovanovich.

Köhler, W. (1959). Gestalt psychology today. *American Psychologist, 14,* 727–734.

Kohnken, G., & Maass, A. (1988). Eyewitness testimony: False alarms on biased instructions. *Journal of Applied Psychology, 73,* 363–370.

Kolata, G. (1985). Why do people get fat? *Science, 227,* 1327–1328.

Kolata, G. (1987). Associations or rules in learning language? *Science, 237,* 133–134.

Koltko-Rivera, M. E. (2006). Rediscovering the later version of Maslow's hierarchy of needs: Self-transcendence and opportunities for theory, research, and unification. *Review of General Psychology, 10,* 302–317.

Komisaruk, B. R., & Whipple, B. (2005). Functional MRI of the brain during orgasm in women. *Annual Review of Sex Research, 16,* 62–86.

Koole, S. L., Greenberg, J., & Pyszczynski, T. (2006). Introducing psychology to the science of the soul: Experimental existential psychology. *Current Directions in Psychological Science, 15,* 212–216.

Koopmans, J. R., Boomsma, D. I., Heath, A. C., & van Doornen, L. J. P. (1995). A multivariate genetic analysis of sensation seeking. *Behavior Genetics, 25,* 349–356.

Kopelman, M. D., Christensen, H., Puffett, A., & Stanhope, N. (1994). The great escape: A neuropsychological study of psychogenic amnesia. *Neuropsychologia, 32,* 675–691.

Koppe, S. (1983). The psychology of the neuron: Freud, Cajal, and Golgi. *Scandinavian Journal of Psychology, 24,* 1–12.

Koretz, J., & Gutheil, T. G. (2009). "I can't let anything go": A case study with psychological testing of a patient with pathologic hoarding. *American Journal of Psychotherapy, 63,* 257–266.

Korpi, E. R. (1994). Role of GABA-sub(A) receptors in the actions of alcohol and in alcoholism: Recent advances. *Alcohol and Alcoholism, 29,* 115–129.

Korsnes, M. S., Magnussen, S., & Reinvang, I. (1996). Serial position effects in visual short-term memory for words and abstract spatial patterns. *Scandinavian Journal of Psychology, 37,* 62–73.

Kosmicki, F. X., & Glickauf–Hughes, C. (1997). Catharsis in psychotherapy. *Psychotherapy, 34,* 154–159.

Kossowsky, J., Pfaltz, M. C., Schneider, S., Taeymans, J., Locher, C., & Gaab, J. (2013). The separation anxiety hypothesis of panic disorder revisited: A meta-analysis. *American Journal of Psychiatry, 170,* 768–781.

Kotani, H. (1999). Aspects of intrapsychic, interpersonal and cross-cultural dynamics in Japanese group psychotherapy. *International Journal of Group Psychotherapy, 49,* 93–104.

Kotz, S. A., Meyer, M., Alter, K., Besson, M., von Cramon, D. Y., & Friederici, A. D. (2003). On the lateralization of emotional prosody: An event-related functional MR investigation. *Brain and Language, 86,* 366–376.

Kouider, S., & Dehaene, S. (2007). Levels of processing during non-conscious perception: A critical review of visual masking. *Philosophical Transactions of the Royal Society of London. Series B, Biological Sciences, 362,* 857–875.

Kovac, S. H., & Range, L. M. (2000). Writing projects: Lessening undergraduates' unique suicidal bereavement. *Suicide and Life-Threatening Behavior, 30,* 50–60.

Kovar, K. A. (1998) Chemistry and pharmacology of hallucinogens, entactogens, and stimulants. *Pharmacopsychiatry, 31,* 69–72.

Kozub, S. A., & McDonnell, J. F. (2000). Exploring the relationship between cohesion and collective efficacy in rugby teams. *Journal of Sport Behavior, 23,* 120–129.

Kposowa, A. J. (2000). Marital status and suicide in the National Longitudinal Mortality Study. *Journal of Epidemiology and Community Health, 54,* 254–261.

Krafka, C., & Penrod, S. (1985). Reinstatement of context in a field experiment on eyewitness identification. *Journal of Personality and Social Psychology, 49,* 58–69.

Krakow, B., Schrader, R., Tandberg, D., Hollifield, M., Koss, M. P., Yau, C. L., & Cheng, D. T. (2002). Nightmare frequency in sexual assault survivors with PTSD. *Journal of Anxiety Disorders, 16,* 175–190.

Kralikova, E., Kozak, J. T., Rasmussen, T., Gustavsson, G., & Le Houezec, J. (2009). Smoking cessation or reduction with nicotine replacement therapy: A placebo-controlled double blind trial with nicotine gum and inhaler. *BMC Public Health, 9,* 433–440.

Kramer, D. E., & Bayern, C. D. (1984). The effects of behavioral strategies on creativity training. *Journal of Creative Behavior, 18,* 23–24.

Krantz, D. S., Contrada, R. J., Hill, D. R., & Friedler, E. (1988). Environmental stress and biobehavioral antecedents of coronary heart disease. *Journal of Consulting and Clinical Psychology, 56,* 333–341.

Krantz, D. S., & Manuck, S. B. (1984). Acute psychophysiologic reactivity and risk of cardiovascular disease: A review and methodologic critique. *Psychological Bulletin, 96,* 435–464.

Kraus, S. J. (1995). Attitudes and the prediction of behavior: A meta-analysis of the empirical literature. *Personality and Social Psychology Bulletin, 21,* 58–75.

Krause, E. D., Vélez, C. E., Woo, R., Hoffmann, B., Freres, D. R., Abenavoli, R. M., & Gillham, J. E. (2017). Rumination, depression, and gender in early adolescence: A longitudinal study of a bidirectional model. *Journal of Early Adolescence.*

Krause, J. S. (1998). Subjective well-being after spinal-cord injury: Relationship to gender, race-ethnicity, and chronologic age. *Rehabilitation Psychology, 43,* 282–296.

Kravitz, D. A., & Martin, B. (1986). Ringelmann rediscovered: The original article. *Journal of Personality and Social Psychology, 50*, 936–941.

Kreisman, J. J., & Straus, H. (1989). *I hate you—Don't leave me: Understanding the borderline disorder.* New York: Avon Books.

Kremer, J. F., & Dietzen, L. L. (1991). Two approaches to teaching accurate empathy to undergraduates: Teacher-intensive and self-directed. *Journal of College Student Development, 32*, 69–75.

Kremer, T. G., & Gesten, E. L. (1998). Confidentiality limits of managed care and clients' willingness to self-disclose. *Professional Psychology: Research and Practice, 29*, 553–558.

Kreppner, K. (1992). William L. Stern, 1871–1938: A neglected founder of developmental psychology. *Developmental Psychology, 28*, 539–547.

Kretch, K. S., & Adolph, K. E. (2013). Cliff or step? Posture-specific learning at the edge of a drop-off. *Child Development, 84*, 226–240.

Kretschmer, E. (1925). *Physique and character.* New York: Harcourt, Brace.

Krichmar, J. L., & Edelman, G. M. (2002). Machine psychology: Autonomous behavior, perceptual categorization and conditioning in a brain-based device. *Cerebral Cortex, 12*, 818–830.

Krinsky, R., & Krinsky, S. G. (1994). The peg-word mnemonic facilitates immediate but not long-term memory in fifth-grade children. *Contemporary Educational Psychology, 19*, 217–229.

Krippner, S. (1995). Psychical research in the postmodern world. *Journal of the American Society for Psychical Research, 89*, 1–18.

Krippner, S., Braud, W., Child, I. L., & Palmer, J. (1993). Demonstration research and meta-analysis in parapsychology. *Journal of Parapsychology, 57*, 275–286.

Krippner, S., & Thompson, A. (1996). A 10-factor model of dreaming applied to dream practices of 16 Native-American cultural groups. *Dreaming: Journal of the Association for the Study of Dreams, 6*, 71–96.

Krippner, S., Vaughan, A., & Spottiswoode, S. J. P. (2000). Geomagnetic factors in subjective precognitive dream experiences. *Journal of the Society for Psychical Research, 64*, 109–117.

Krishnan, H. S., & Chakravarti, D. (2003). A process analysis of the effects of humorous advertisng executions on brand claims memory. *Journal of Consumer Psychology, 18*, 230–245.

Krishnan, R. V., Sankar, V., & Muthusamy, R. (2001). Recovery of locomotor function in adult paraplegic frogs by inductive lability in the distal isolated spinal cord neural networks. *International Journal of Neuroscience, 108*, 43–54.

Kroenke, K., & Spitzer, R. L. (1998). Gender differences in the reporting of physical and somatoform symptoms. *Psychosomatic Medicine, 60*, 150–155.

Kropp, P., Brecht. I.-B., Niederberger, U., Kowalski, J., Schröder, D., Thome, J., . . . Gerber, W. D. (2012). Time-dependent post-imperative negative variation indicates adaptation and problem-solving in migraine patients. *Journal of Neural Transmission, 119*, 1213–1221.

Krueger, T. H. C., Haake, P., Hartmann, U., Schedlowski, M., & Exton, M. S. (2002). Orgasm-induced prolactin secretion: Feedback control of sexual drive? *Neuroscience and Biobehavioral Reviews, 26*, 31–44.

Krupa, D. J., Thompson, J. K., & Thompson, R. F. (1993). Localization of a memory trace in the mammalian brain. *Science, 260*, 989–991.

Krupnick, J. L., Sotsky, S. M., Simmens, S., & Moyer, J. (1996). The role of the therapeutic alliance in psychotherapy and pharmacotherapy outcome: Findings in the National Institute of Mental Health Treatment of Depression Collaborative Research Program. *Journal of Consulting and Clinical Psychology, 64*, 532–539.

Kubzansky, L. D., Sparrow, D., Vokonas, P., & Kawachi, I. (2001). Is the glass half empty or half full? A prospective study of optimism and coronary heart disease in the normative aging study. *Psychosomatic Medicine, 63*, 910–916.

Kudo, F. T., Longhofer, J. L., & Floersch, J. E. (2012). On the origins of early leadership: The role of authoritative parenting practices and mastery orientation. *Leadership, 8*, 345–375.

Kuehberger, A. (1998). The influence of framing on risky decisions: A meta-analysis. *Organizational Behavior and Human Decision Processes, 75*, 23–55.

Kuelbelbeck, A. (1991, August 23). A real high point. *Los Angeles Times*, p. E1.

Kugel, W. (1990–91). Amplifying precognition: Two experiments with roulette. *European Journal of Parapsychology, 8*, 85–97.

Kugihara, N. (1999). Gender and social loafing in Japan. *Journal of Social Psychology, 139*, 516–526.

Kuhlman, T. L. (1985). A study of salience and motivational theories of humor. *Journal of Personality and Social Psychology, 49*, 281–286.

Kuhlmann, H. (2005). *Living Walden Two: B. F. Skinner's behaviorist utopia and experimental communities.* Champaign, IL: University of Illinois Press.

Kuhn, T. S. (1970). *The structure of scientific revolutions.* Chicago: University of Chicago Press.

Kukla, A. (1989). Nonempirical issues in psychology. *American Psychologist, 44*, 785–794.

Kulik, J. A., & Mahler, H. I. M. (1987). Effects of preoperative roommate assignment and preoperative anxiety and recovery from coronarybypass surgery. *Health Psychology, 6*, 525–543.

Kumar, A. (2000). Interference effects of contextual cues in advertisements on memory for ad content. *Journal of Consumer Psychology, 9*, 155–166.

Kumar, K. B., Ramalingam, S., & Karanth, K. S. (1994). Phenytoin and phenobarbital: A comparison of their state-dependent effects. *Pharmacology, Biochemistry, and Behavior, 47*, 951–956.

Kumari, V., Hemsley, D. R., Cotter, P. A., Checkley, S. A., & Gray, J. A. (1998). Haloperidol-induced mood and retrieval of happy and unhappy memories. *Cognition and Emotion, 12*, 437–508.

Kumkale, G. T., & Albarracin, D. (2004). The sleeper effect in persuasion: A meta-analytic review. *Psychological Bulletin, 130*, 143–172.

Kuncel, N. R., Hezlett, S. A., & Ones, D. S. (2001). A comprehensive meta-analysis of the predictive validity of the graduate record examinations: Implications for graduate student selection and performance. *Psychological Bulletin, 127*, 162–181.

Kunda, Z., & Schwartz, S. H. (1983). Undermining intrinsic moral motivation: External reward and self-presentation. *Journal of Personality and Social Psychology, 45*, 763–771.

Kunda, Z., & Spencer, S. J. (2003). When do stereotypes come to mind and when do they color judgment? A goal-based theoretical framework for stereotype activation and application. *Psychological Bulletin, 129*, 522–544.

Kuo, L. E., Kitlinska, J. B., Tilan, J. U., Li, L., Baker, S. B., Johnson, M. D., . . . Zukowska, Z. (2007). Neuropeptide Y acts directly in the periphery on fat tissue and mediates stress-induced obesity and metabolic syndrome. *Nature Medicine, 1*, 803–811.

Kupán, K., Miklósi, Á., Gergely, G., & Topál, J. Why do dogs (*Canis familiaris*) select the empty container in an observational learning task? *Animal Cognition, 14*, 259–268.

Kupfer, D. J., Kuhl, E. A., & Regier, D. A. DSM-5—The future arrived. *JAMA: Journal of the American Medical Association, 309*, 1691–1692.

Kurdek, L. A. (1998). Relationship outcomes and their predictors: Longitudinal evidence from heterosexual married, gay cohabiting, and lesbian cohabiting couples. *Journal of Marriage and the Family, 60*, 553–568.

Kurdek, L. A. (1999). The nature and predictors of the trajectory of change in marital quality for husbands and wives over the first 10 years of marriage. *Developmental Psychology, 35*, 1283–1296.

Kwee, M., & Ellis, A. (1998). The interface between rational emotive behavior therapy (REBT) and Zen. *Journal of Rational-Emotive and Cognitive Behavior Therapy. 16*, 5–43.

La Roche, M., & Lustig, K. (2013). Being mindful about the assessment of culture: A cultural analysis of culturally adapted acceptance-based behavior therapy approaches. *Cognitive and Behavioral Practice, 20*, 60–63.

La Vaque, T. J. (1999). History of EEG Hans Berger: Psychophysiologist. A historical vignette. *Journal of Neurotherapy, 3*, 1–9.

LaBar, K. S., & Cabeza, R. (2006). Cognitive neuroscience of emotional memory. *Nature Reviews, 7*, 54–64.

Lader, M. (1991). History of benzodiazepine dependence. *Journal of Substance Abuse Treatment, 8*, 53–59.

LaFrance, M., Hecht, M. A., & Paluck, E. L. (2003). The contingent smile: A meta-analysis of sex differences in smiling. *Psychological Bulletin, 129*, 305–334.

Laing, R. D. (1967). *The politics of experience.* New York: Ballantine Books.

Laitinen, J., Ek, E., & Sovio, U. (2001). Stress-related eating and drinking behavior and body mass index and predictors of this behavior. *Preventive Medicine, 34*, 29–39.

Lake, A. E., III, & Saper, J. R. (2002). Chronic headache: New advances in treatment strategies. *Neurology, 59*, S8–S13.

Lake, C. R. (2012). *Schizophrenia is a misdiagnosis: Implications for the DSM-5 and ICD-11.* New York: Springer.

Lakkis, J., & Ricciardelli, L. A., & Williams, R. J. (1999). Role of sexual orientation and gender-related traits in disordered eating. *Sex Roles, 41*, 1–16.

Lal, S. (2002). Giving children security: Mamie Phipps Clark and the racialization of child psychology. *American Psychologist, 57*, 20–28.

Lalancette, M. F., & Standing, L. G. (1990). Asch fails again. *Social Behavior and Personality, 18*, 7–12.

Lalumiere, M. L., Blanchard, R., & Zucker, K. J. (2000). Sexual orientation and handedness in men and women: A meta-analysis. *Psychological Bulletin, 126*, 575–592.

Lam, D. C. K., Salkovskis, P. M., & Warwick, H. M. C. (2005). An experimental investigation of the impact of biological versus psychological explanations of the cause of "mental illness." *Journal of Mental Health, 14*, 453–464.

Lamb, M. E. (1996). Effects of nonparental child care on child development: An update. *Canadian Journal of Psychiatry, 41*, 330–342.

Lamb, M. E. (2012). Mothers, fathers, families and circumstances: Factors affecting children's adjustment. *Applied Developmental Science, 16*, 98–111.

Lamb, R. H. (1998). Deinstitutionalization at the beginning of the new millennium. *Harvard Review of Psychiatry, 6*, 1–10.

Lamb, T. (1999). Obituary: Alan Hodgkin (1914–98). *Nature, 397*, 112.

Lambdin, J. R., Greer, K. M., Jibotian, K. S., Wood, K. R., & Hamilton, M. C. (2003). The animal = male hypothesis: Children's and adults' beliefs about the sex of non-sex-specific stuffed animals. *Sex Roles, 48*, 471–482.

Lambert, M. J. (1989). The individual therapist's contribution to psychotherapy process and outcome. *Clinical Psychology Review, 9*, 469–485.

Lambert, N. M. (1981). Psychological evidence in *Larry P. v. Wilson Riles. American Psychologist, 36*, 937–952.

Lambert, S. M., Moore, D. W., & Dixon, R. S. (1999). Gymnasts in training: The differential effects of self- and coach-set goals as a function of locus of control. *Journal of Applied Sport Psychology, 11*, 72–82.

Lamme, V. A. F. (1995). The neurophysiology of figure-ground segregation in primary visual cortex. *Journal of Neuroscience, 15*, 1605–1615.

Lanciano, T., Curci, A., & Semin, G. R. (2010). The emotional and reconstructive determinants of emotional memories: An experimental approach to flashbulb memory investigation. *Memory, 18,* 473–485.

Landers, S. (1987, December). Aversive device sparks controversy. *APA Monitor,* p. 15.

Landesman, S., & Ramey, C. (1989). Developmental psychology and mental retardation: Integrating scientific principles with treatment practices. *American Psychologist, 44,* 409–415.

Landis, D., & O'Shea, W. A. (2000). Cross-cultural aspects of passionate love: An individual differences analysis. *Journal of Cross-Cultural Psychology, 31,* 752–777.

Landolt, A. S., & Milling, L. S. (2011). The efficacy of hypnosis as an intervention for labor and delivery pain: A comprehensive methodological review. *Clinical Psychology Review, 31,* 1022–1031.

Landolt, H. P., Werth, E., Borbely, A. A., & Dijk, D. J. (1995). Caffeine intake (200 mg) in the morning affects human sleep and EEG power spectra at night. *Brain Research, 675,* 67–74.

Landrine, H. (1987). On the politics of madness: A preliminary analysis of the relationship between social roles and psychopathology. *Psychology Monographs, 113,* 341–406.

Landrine, H. (1989). The politics of personality disorder. *Psychology of Women Quarterly, 13,* 325–339.

Landrine, H., & Klonoff, E. A. (1994). Cultural diversity in causal attributions for illness: The role of the supernatural. *Journal of Behavioral Medicine, 17,* 181–194.

Landy, F. J. (1997). Early influences on the development of industrial and organizational psychology. *Journal of Applied Psychology, 86,* 467–477.

Laner, M. R., Benin, M. H., & Ventrone, N. A. (2001). Bystander attitudes toward victims of violence: Who's worth helping? *Deviant Behavior, 22,* 23–42.

Lang, A. J., Craske, M. G., Grown, M., & Ghaneian, A. (2001). Fear–related state dependent memory. *Cognition and Emotion, 15,* 695–703.

Lang, P. J. (1994). The varieties of emotional experience: A meditation on James-Lange theory. *Psychological Review, 101,* 211–221.

Lang, P. J., Bradley, M. M., & Cuthbert, B. N. (1998). Emotion, motivation, and anxiety: Brain mechanisms and psychophysiology. *Biological Psychiatry, 44,* 1248–1263.

Langenbucher, J. W., & Nathan, P. E. (1983). Psychology, public policy, and the evidence for alcohol intoxication. *American Psychologist, 38,* 1070–1077.

Langer, E. J., & Rodin, J. (1976). The effects of choice and enhanced personal responsibility for the aged: A field experiment in an institutional setting. *Journal of Personality and Social Psychology, 34,* 191–198.

Langlois, J. H., Kalakanis, L., Rubenstein, A. J., Larson, A., Hallam, M., & Smoot, M. (2000). Maxims or myths of beauty? A meta-analytic and theoretical review. *Psychological Bulletin, 126,* 390–423.

Langone, J. (1983, September). B. F. Skinner: Beyond reward and punishment. *Discover,* pp. 38–46.

Lantz, J., & Gregoire, T. (2000). Existential psychotherapy with couples facing breast cancer: A twenty-year report. *Contemporary Family Therapy, 22,* 315–327.

Lapidus, K. A. B., Kopell, B. H., Ben-Haim, S., Rezai, A. R., & Goodman, W. K. (2013). History of psychosurgery: A psychiatrist's perspective. *World Neurosurgery, 80,* 1–16.

LaPiere, R. T. (1934). Attitudes versus action. *Social Forces, 13,* 230–237.

Larimer, M. E., Lydum, A. R., Anderson, B. K., & Turner, A. P. (1999). Male and female recipients of unwanted sexual contact in a college student sample: Prevalence rates, alcohol use, and depression symptoms. *Sex Roles, 40,* 295–308.

Lariviere, W. R., Wilson, S. G., Laughlin, T. M., Kokayeff, A., West, E. E., Adhikari, S. M., Wan, Y., & Mogil, J. S. (2002). Heritability of nociception. III. Genetic relationships among commonly used assays of nociception and hypersensitivity. *Pain, 97,* 75–86.

Laroche, M., Nepomuceno, M. V., Huang, L., & Richard, M. (2011). What's so funny? The use of humor in magazine advertising in the United States, China, and France. *Journal of Advertising Research, 51,* 404–416.

Larsen, K. S. (1990). The Asch conformity experiment: Replication and transhistorical comparisons. *Journal of Social Behavior and Personality, 5,* 163–168.

Larsson, H., Chang, Z., D'Onofrio, B. M., & Lichtenstein, P. (2013). The heritability of clinically-diagnosed attention deficit hyperactivity disorder across the lifespan. *Psychological Medicine/FirstView,* 1–7.

Lashley, K. S. (1950). In search of the engram. In *Symposium of the Society for Experimental Biology* (Vol. 4, pp. 454–482). New York: Cambridge University Press.

Laska, M., Scheuber, H.-P., Sanchez, E. C., & Luna, E. R. (1999). Taste difference thresholds for sucrose in two species of nonhuman primates. *American Journal of Primatology, 48,* 153–160.

Lassonde, M., & Sauerwein, H. C. (2003). Agenesis of the corpus callosum. In K. Hugdahl & R. J. Davidson (Eds.), *The asymmetrical brain* (pp. 619–649). Cambridge, MA: MIT Press.

Latané, B., & Darley, J. M. (1968). Group inhibition of bystander intervention in emergencies. *Journal of Personality and Social Psychology, 10,* 215–221.

Lattal, K. A. (1995). Contingency and behavior analysis. *Behavior Analyst, 18,* 209–224.

Laumann, E. O., Gagnon, J. H., Michael, R. T., & Michaels, S. (1994). *The social organization of sexuality.* Chicago: University of Chicago Press.

Laumann, E. O., Paik, A., & Rosen, R. C. (1999). Sexual dysfunction in the United States: Prevalence and predictors. *Journal of the American Medical Association, 281,* 537–544.

Laurence, J. R., & Perry, C. (1983). Hypnotically created memory among highly hypnotizable subjects. *Science, 222,* 523–524.

Laursen, B., Coy, K. C., & Collins, W. A. (1998). Reconsidering changes in parent-child conflict across adolescence: A meta-analysis. *Child Development, 69,* 817–832.

Laver, A. B. (1972). Precursors of psychology in ancient Egypt. *Journal of the History of the Behavioral Sciences, 8,* 181–195.

Lavie, P. (2000). Sleep-wake as a biological rhythm. *Annual Review of Psychology, 52,* 277–303.

Lavin, C. (1996). The Wechsler Intelligence Scale for Children—third edition and the Stanford-Binet Intelligence Scale–fourth edition: A preliminary study of validity. *Psychological Reports, 78,* 491–496.

Lavoisier, P., Aloui, R., Schmidt, M. H., & Watrelot, A. (1995). Clitoral blood flow increases following vaginal pressure stimulation. *Archives of Sexual Behavior, 24,* 37–45.

Law, D. M., Shapka, J. D., Hymel, S., Olson, B. F., & Waterhouse, T. (2012). The changing face of bullying: An empirical comparison between traditional and internet bullying and victimization. *Computers in Human Behavior, 28,* 226–232.

Lawson, T. J. (1999). Assessing psychological critical thinking as a learning outcome for psychology majors. *Teaching of Psychology, 26,* 207–209.

Lawton, C. A. (2001). Gender and regional differences in spatial referents used in direction giving. *Sex Roles, 44,* 321–337.

Lazarus, A. A. (1989). Brief psychotherapy: The multimodal model. *Professional Psychology, 26,* 6–10.

Lazarus, R. S. (1993a). Coping theory and research: Past, present, and future. *Psychosomatic Medicine, 55,* 234–247.

Lazarus, R. S. (1993b). From psychological stress to the emotions: A history of changing outlooks. *Annual Review of Psychology, 44,* 1–21.

Lazarus, R. S. (1995). Cognition and emotion from the RET viewpoint. *Journal of Rational-Emotive and Cognitive Behavior Therapy, 13,* 29–54.

Leadbeater, B., Hoglund, W., & Woods, T. (2003). Changing contents? The effects of a primary prevention program on classroom levels of peer relational and physical victimization. *Journal of Community Psychology, 31,* 397–418.

Leaf, R. C., Krauss, D. H., Dantzig, S. A., & Alington, D. E. (1992). Educational equivalents of psychotherapy: Positive and negative mental health benefits after group therapy exercises by college students. *Journal of Rational Emotive and Cognitive Behavior Therapy, 10,* 189–206.

Leakey, R. E., & Lewin, R. (1977, November). Is it our culture, not our genes, that makes us killers? *Smithsonian,* pp. 56–64.

Leana, C. R. (1985). A partial test of Janis' groupthink model: Effects of group cohesiveness and leader behavior on defective decision making. *Journal of Management, 11,* 5–17.

Leaper, C., Anderson, K. J., & Sanders, P. (1998). Moderators of gender effects on parents' talk to their children: A meta-analysis. *Developmental Psychology, 34,* 3–27.

Leary, M. R., & Kowalski, R. M. (1990). Impression management: A literature review and two-component model. *Psychological Bulletin, 107,* 34–47.

Leary, M. R., Kowalski, R. M., Smith, L., & Phillips, S. (2003). Teasing, rejection, and violence: Case studies of the school shootings. *Aggressive Behavior, 29,* 202–214.

LeBlanc, L. A, Hagopian, L. P., & Maglieri, K. A. (2000). Use of a token economy to eliminate excessive inappropriate social behavior in an adult with developmental disabilities. *Behavioral Interventions, 15,* 135–143.

Lebow, J. (2000). What does the research tell us about couple and family therapy? *Journal of Clinical Psychology, 56,* 1083–1094.

Leckman, J. F., Grice, D. E., Boardman, J., & Zhang, H. (1997). Symptoms of obsessive-compulsive disorder. *American Journal of Psychiatry, 154,* 911–917.

Leclerc, G., Lefrancois, R., Dube, M., Hebert, R., & Gaulin, P. (1998). The self-actualization concept: A content validation. *Journal of Social Behavior and Personality, 13,* 69–84.

Lecomte, D., & Fornes, P. (1998). Suicide among youth and young adults, 15 through 24 years of age: A report of 392 cases from Paris, 1989–1996. *Journal of Forensic Sciences, 43,* 964–968.

Ledezma, E., & Monroig, R. (1997). Parapsychology in Mexico. *Journal of the American Society for Psychical Research, 91,* 122–132.

LeDoux, J. E. (1986). Sensory systems and emotion: A model of affective processing. *Integrative Psychiatry, 4,* 237–243.

LeDoux, J. E. (1995). Emotion: Clues from the brain. *Annual Review of Psychology, 46,* 209–235.

LeDoux, J. E., Romanski, L., & Xagoraris, A. (1989). Indelibility of subcortical emotional memories. *Journal of Cognitive Neuroscience, 1,* 238–243.

Lee, C. S., Therriault, D. J., & Linderholm, T. (2012). On the cognitive benefits of cultural experience: Exploring the relationship between studying abroad and creative thinking. *Applied Cognitive Psychology, 26,* 768–778.

Lee, E. H., Kim, J. H., & Yu, B. H. (2009). Reliability and validity of the self-report version of the panic disorder severity scale in Korea. *Depression and Anxiety, 26,* E120–E123.

Lee, G. P., Loring, D. W., Meader, K. J., & Brooks, B. B. (1990). Hemispheric specialization for emotional expression: A reexamination of results from intracarotid administration of sodium amobarbital. *Brain and Cognition, 12,* 267–280.

Lee, H., & Kim, J. J. (1998). Amygdalar NMDA receptors are critical for new fear learning in previously fear-conditioned rats. *Journal of Neuroscience, 18,* 8444–8454.

Lee, J.-H., & Beitz, A. J. (1992). Electroacupuncture modifies the expression of c-fos in the spinal cord induced by noxious stimulation. *Brain Research, 577,* 80–91.

Lee, M. G., Hassani, O. K., & Jones, B. E. (2005). Discharge of identified orexin/hypocretin neurons across the sleep-wakingcycle. *Journal of Neuroscience, 25,* 6716–6720.

Lee, M. S., Choi, J., Posadzki, P., & Ernst, E. (2012). Aromatherapy for health care: An overview of systematic reviews. *Maturitas, 71,* 257–260.

Lee, S., & Lee, A. M. (2000). Disordered eating in three communities of China: A comparative study of female high school students in Hong Kong, Shenzhen, and rural Hunan. *International Journal of Eating Disorders, 27,* 317–327.

Lee, S. H., & Oh, K. S. (1999). Offensive type of social phobia: Cross-cultural perspectives. *International Medical Journal, 6,* 271–279.

Lee, T. M. C., & Chan, C. C. H. (1999a). Dose-response relationship of phototherapy for seasonal affective disorder: A meta-analysis. *Acta Psychiatrica Scandinavica, 99,* 315–323.

Lee, T. M. C., & Chan, C. C. H. (1999b). Vulnerability by sex to seasonal affective disorder. *Perceptual and Motor Skills, 87,* 1120–1122.

Lee, T. M. C., Liu, H. L., Tan, L. H., Chan, C. C. H., Mahankali, S., Feng, C. M., . . . Gao, J. H. (2002). Lie detection by functional magnetic resonance imaging. *Human Brain Mapping, 15,* 157–164.

Lee, V. E., & Loeb, S. (1995). Where do head start attendees end up? One reason why preschool effects fade out. *Educational Evaluation and Policy Analysis, 17,* 62–82.

Lee, V. E., Brooks-Gunn, J., Schnur, E., & Liaw, F.-R. (1990). Are Head Start effects sustained? A longitudinal follow-up comparison of disadvantaged children attending Head Start, no preschool, and other preschool programs. *Child Development, 61,* 495–507.

Lee, Y. T., & Ottati, V. (1993). Determinants of in-group and out-group perceptions of heterogeneity: An investigation of Sino-American stereotypes. *Journal of Cross-Cultural Psychology, 24,* 298–318.

Leenaars, A. A. (2000). Suicide prevention in Canada: A history of a community approach. *Canadian Journal of Community Mental Health, 19,* 57–73.

Leeson, F. J., & Nixon, R. D. V. (2011). The role of children's appraisals on adjustment following psychological maltreatment: A pilot study. *Journal of Abnormal Child Psychology, 39,* 759–771.

Lei, T. (1994). Being and becoming moral in a Chinese culture: Unique or universal? *Cross-Cultural Research: The Journal of Comparative Social Science, 28,* 58–91.

Leibowitz, H. W., & Pick, H. A., Jr. (1972). Cross-cultural and educational aspects of the Ponzo perspective illusion. *Perception and Psychophysics, 12,* 430–432.

Leigland, S. (2000). On cognitivism and behaviorism. *American Psychologist, 55,* 273–274.

Leikin, L., Firestone, P., & McGrath, P. (1988). Physical symptom reporting in Type A and Type B children. *Journal of Consulting and Clinical Psychology, 56,* 721–726.

Leit, R. A., Pope, H. G., & Gray, J. J. (2001). Cultural expectations of muscularity in men: The evolution of Playgirl centerfolds. *International Journal of Eating Disorders, 29,* 90–93.

Leitenberg, H. (1995). Cognitive-behavioural treatment of bulimia nervosa. *Behaviour Change, 12,* 81–97.

Lekander, M., Fuerst, C. J., Rostein, S., Hursti, T. J., & Fredrikson, M. (1997). Immune effects of relaxation during chemotherapy for ovarian cancer. *Psychotherapy and Psychosomatics, 66,* 185–191.

Lemelson, R. (2003). Obsessive-compulsive disorder in Bali: The cultural shaping of a neuropsychiatric disorder. *Transcultural Psychiatry, 40,* 377–408.

Lemere, F. (1993). "Homeless mentally ill or mentally ill homeless?": Comment. *American Journal of Psychiatry, 150,* 989.

Lemieux, R., & Hale, J. L. (2002). Cross-sectional analysis of intimacy, passion, and commitment: Testing the assumptions of the triangular theory of love. *Psychological Reports, 90,* 1009–1014.

Lenox, R. H., & Hahn, C. G. (2000). Overview of the mechanism of action of lithium in the brain: Fifty-year update. *Journal of Clinical Psychiatry, 61,* 5–15.

Leonard, J. (1970, May 8). Ghetto for blue eyes in the classroom. *Life,* p. 16.

Leong, T. T. L., Zachar, P., Conant, L., & Tolliver, D. (2007). Career specialty preferences among psychology majors: Cognitive processing styles associated with scientist and practitioner interests. *Career Development Quarterly, 55,* 328–338.

Lepper, M. R., Greene, D., & Nisbett, R. E. (1973). Undermining children's intrinsic interest with extrinsic reward: A test of the "overjustification" hypothesis. *Journal of Personality and Social Psychology, 28,* 129–137.

Lerman, D. C., & Iwata, B. A. (1995). Prevalence of the extinction burst and its attenuation during treatment. *Journal of Applied Behavior Analysis, 28,* 93–94.

Lerner, A. G., Gelkopf, M., Skladman, I., Oyffe, I., Finkel, B., Sigal, M., & Weizman, A. (2002). Flashback and hallucinogen persisting perception disorder: Clinical aspects and pharmacological treatment approach. *Israel Journal of Psychiatry and Related Sciences, 39,* 92–99.

Lerner, B. S., Ostrow, A. C., Yura, M. T., & Etzel, E. F. (1996). The effects of goal-setting and imagery training programs on the free-throw performance of female collegiate basketball players. *Sport Psychologist, 10,* 382–397.

Lerner, E. (1943). Preface to the psychology of peace and reconstruction. *Journal of Psychology, 15,* 3–25.

Lerner, G. H., & Takagi, T. (1999). On the place of linguistic resources in the organization of talk-in-interaction: A co-investigation of English and Japanese grammatical practices. *Journal of Pragmatics, 31,* 49–75.

Lescaudron, L., & Stein, D. G. (1990). Functional recovery following transplants of embryonic brain tissue in rats with lesions of visual, frontal, and motor cortex: Problems and prospects for future research. *Neuropsychologia, 28,* 588–599.

Leserman, J. (2003). HIV disease progression: Depression, stress, and possible mechanisms. *Biological Psychiatry, 54,* 295–306.

Leslie, K., & Ogilvie, R. (1996). Vestibular dreams: The effect of rocking on dream mentation. *Dreaming, 6,* 1–16.

Lester, D. (1990). Maslow's hierarchy of needs and personality. *Personality and Individual Differences, 11,* 1187–1188.

Lester, D. (1993). The effectiveness of suicide prevention centers. *Suicide and Life-Threatening Behavior, 23,* 263–267.

Lester, D. (1995). Myths about childhood suicide. *Psychological Reports, 77,* 330.

Lester, D. (2003). Adolescent suicide from an international perspective. *American Behavioral Scientist, 46,* 1157–1170.

Lester, D., Kaminsky, S., & McGovern, M. (1993). Sheldon's theory of personality in young children. *Perceptual and Motor Skills, 77,* 1330.

Lester, D., Saito, Y., & Abe, K. (1997). The effect of suicide prevention centers on suicide in Japan. *Crisis, 18,* 48.

Lester, D., & Wosnack, K. (1990). An exploratory test of Sheldon's theory of personality in neonates. *Perceptual and Motor Skills, 71,* 1282.

Leung, A. K.-Y., Kim, Y.-H., Zhang, Z.-X., Tam, K. P., & Chiu, C.-Y. (2012). Cultural construction of success and epistemic motives moderate American-Chinese differences in reward allocation biases. *Journal of Cross-Cultural Psychology, 43,* 46–52.

LeVay, S. (1991). A difference in hypothalamic structure between heterosexual and homosexual men. *Science, 253,* 1034–1037.

Levenson, J. L., & Bemis, C. (1991). The role of psychological factors in cancer onset and progression. *Psychosomatics, 32,* 124–132.

Levenson, R. W., Ekman, P., Heider, K., & Friesen, W. V. (1992). Emotion and autonomic nervous system activity in the Minangkabau of West Sumatra. *Journal of Personality and Social Psychology, 62,* 972–988.

Leventhal, H., & Tomarken, A. J. (1986). Emotion: Today's problems. *Annual Review of Psychology, 37,* 565–610.

Levin, B. E. (2009). Synergy of nature and nurture in the development of childhood obesity. *International Journal of Obesity, 33,* 553–556.

Levin, E. D., & Simon, B. B. (1998). Nicotinic acetylcholine involvement in cognitive function in animals. *Psychopharmacology, 138,* 217–230.

Levin, E. D., Westman, E. C., Stein, R. M., & Carnahan, E. (1994). Nicotine skin patch treatment increases abstinence, decreases withdrawal symptoms, and attenuates rewarding effects of smoking. *Journal of Clinical Psychopharmacology, 14,* 41–49.

Levin, I. P., Schnittjer, S. K., & Thee, S. L. (1988). Information framing effects in social and personal decisions. *Journal of Experimental Social Psychology, 24,* 520–529.

Levin, R. B., & Gross, A. M. (1985). The role of relaxation in systematic desensitization. *Behaviour Research and Therapy, 23,* 187–196.

Levine, J. S., & MacNichol, E. F., Jr. (1982, February). Color vision in fishes. *Scientific American,* pp. 140–149.

Levine, M. (1976). The academic achievement test: Its historical context and social functions. *American Psychologist, 31,* 228–238.

Levine, S. C., Huttenlocher, J., Taylor, A., & Langrock, A. (1999). Early sex differences in spatial skill. *Developmental Psychology, 35,* 940–949.

Levinson, D. J. (1978). *The seasons of a man's life.* New York: Knopf.

Levinson, D. J. (1986). A conception of adult development. *American Psychologist, 41,* 3–13.

Levinthal, C. F. (1988). *Messengers of paradise.* New York: Anchor/Doubleday.

Levis, D. J. (1999). The negative impact of the cognitive movement on the continued growth of the behavior therapy movement: A historical perspective. *Genetic, Social, and General Psychology Monographs, 125,* 157–171.

Levitt, D. H. (2001). Anorexia nervosa: Treatment in the family context. *Family Journal. 9,* 159–163.

Levy, G. D. (1999). Gender-typed and non-gender-typed category awareness in toddlers. *Sex Roles, 41,* 851–873.

Levy, J. (1983). Language, cognition, and the right hemisphere: A response to Gazzaniga. *American Psychologist, 38,* 538–541.

Levy, N. (2002). Reconsidering cochlear implants: The lessons of Martha's Vineyard. *Bioethics, 16,* 134–153.

Lew, A. S., Allen, R., Papouchis, N., & Ritzler, B. (1998). Achievement orientation and fear of success in Asian American college students. *Journal of Clinical Psychology, 54,* 97–108.

Lew, M. W., Kravits, K., Garberoglio, C., & Williams, A. C. (2011). Use of preoperative hypnosis to reduce postoperative pain and anesthesia-related side effects. *International Journal of Clinical & Experimental Hypnosis, 59,* 406–423.

Lewicki, P. (1985). Nonconscious biasing effects of single instances on subsequent judgments. *Journal of Personality and Social Psychology, 48,* 563–574.

Lewinsohn, P. M., Gotlib, I. H., Lewinsohn, M., Seeley, J. R., & Allen, N. B. (1998). Gender differences in anxiety disorders and anxiety symptoms in adolescents. *Journal of Abnormal Psychology, 107,* 109–117.

Lewis, D. (1899/1983). The gynecologic consideration of the sexual act. *Journal of the American Medical Association, 250,* 222–227.

Lewis, J. (1981). *Something hidden: A biography of Wilder Penfield.* New York: Doubleday.

Lewis-Fernandez, R. (1998). A cultural critique of the *DSM–IV* dissociative disorders section. *Transcultural Psychiatry, 35,* 387–400.

Leyendecker, B., Lamb, M. E., Fracasso, M. P., Schölmerich, A., & Larson, C. (1997). Playful interaction and the antecedents of attachment. A longitudinal study of Central American and Euro-American mothers and infants. *Merrill-Palmer Quarterly, 43,* 24–47.

Li, J., & Zheng, F. (2015). "The craziness for extra-sensory perception: Qigong fever and the science–pseudoscience debate in China. *Zygon: Reviews on Religion and Science Around the World, 50,* 877–892.

Li, J. Z., Bunney, B. G., Meng, F., Hagenauer, M. H., Walsh, D. M., Vawter, M. P., … Bunney, W. E. (2013). Circadian patterns of gene expression in the human brain and disruption in major depressive disorder. *Proceedings of the National Academy of Sciences of the United States of America, 110,* 9950–9955.

Lichacz, F. M., & Partington, J. T. (1996). Collective efficacy and true group performance. *International Journal of Sport Psychology, 27,* 146–158.

Lichtenstein, P., & Annas, P. (2000). Heretability and prevalence of specific fears and phobias in childhood. *Journal of Child Psychology and Psychiatry and Allied Disciplines, 41,* 927–937.

Lieberman, D. A. (1979). Behaviorism and the mind: A (limited) call for a return to introspection. *American Psychologist, 34,* 319–333.

Liechti, M. E., & Vollenweider, F. X. (2001). Which neuroreceptors mediate the subjective effects of MDMA in humans? A summary of mechanistic studies. *Human Psychopharmacology: Clinical and Experimental, 16,* 589–598.

Liegois, M. J. (1899). The relation of hypnotism to crime. *Suggestive Therapeutics, 6,* 18–21.

Lightdale, J. R., & Prentice, D. A. (1994). Rethinking sex differences in aggression: Aggressive behavior in the absence of social roles. *Personality and Social Psychology Bulletin, 20,* 34–44.

Lilienfeld, S. O., & Loftus, E. F. (1998). Repressed memories and World War II: Some cautionary notes. *Professional Psychology: Research and Practice, 29,* 471–475.

Lilienfeld, S. O., Marshall, J., Todd, J. T., & Shane, H. C. (2014). The persistence of fad interventions in the face of negative scientific evidence: Facilitated communication for autism as a case example. *Evidence-Based Communication Assessment and Intervention, 8,* 62–101.

Lilienfeld, S. O., Wood, J. M., & Garb, H. N. (2000). The scientific status of projective techniques. *Psychological Science in the Public Interest, 1,* 27–66.

Lin, E. H., & Peterson, C. (1990). Pessimistic explanatory style and response to illness. *Behaviour Research and Therapy, 28,* 243–248.

Lindberg, A. C., Kelland, A., & Nicol, C. J. (1999). Effects of observational learning on acquisition of an operant response in horses. *Applied Animal Behaviour Science, 61,* 187–199.

Lindberg, S. M., Hyde, J. S., Petersen, J. L., & Linn, M. C. (2010). New trends in gender and mathematics performance: A meta-analysis. *Psychological Bulletin, 136,* 1123–1135.

Linden, D. J. (2003). From molecules to memory in the cerebellum. *Science, 301,* 1682–1683, 1685.

Lindholm, T., & Christianson, S.-A. (1998). Intergroup biases and eyewitness testimony. *Journal of Social Psychology, 138,* 710–723.

Lindsay, D. S. (1993). Eyewitness suggestibility. *Current Directions in Psychological Science, 2,* 86–89.

Lindsay, D. S. (1994). Contextualizing and clarifying criticisms of memory work. *Consciousness and Cognition: An International Journal, 3,* 426–437.

Lindsay, G. (2007). Educational psychology and the effectiveness of inclusive education/mainstreaming. *British Journal of Educational Psychology, 77,* 1–24.

Lindsay, R. C. L., & Pozzulo, J. D. (1999). Sources of eyewitness identification error. *International Journal of Law and Psychiatry, 22,* 347–360.

Lindvall, O., Brundin, P., Widner, H., Rehncrona, S., Gustavii, B., Frackowiak, R., … Bjorklund, A. (1990). Grafts of fetal dopamine neurons survive and improve motor function in Parkinson's disease. *Science, 247,* 574–577.

Link, S. W. (1994). Rediscovering the past: Gustav Fechner and signal detection theory. *Psychological Science, 5,* 335–340.

Linn, R. L. (1982). Admissions testing on trial. *American Psychologist, 37,* 279–291.

Linville, P. W., Fischer, G. W., & Yoon, C. (1996). Perceived covariation among the features of ingroup and outgroup members: The outgroup covariation effect. *Journal of Personality and Social Psychology, 70,* 421–436.

Liossi, C., & Hatira, P. (2003). Clinical hypnosis in the alleviation of procedure-related pain in pediatric oncology patients. *International Journal of Clinical and Experimental Hypnosis, 51,* 4–28.

Lipman, J. J., Miller, B. E., Mays, K. S., & Miller, M. N. (1990). Peak B endorphin concentration in cerebrospinal fluid: Reduced in chronic pain patients and increased during the placebo response. *Psychopharmacology, 102,* 112–116.

Lippa, R. A., & Tan, F. D. (2001). Does culture moderate the relationship between sexual orientation and gender-related personality traits? *Cross-Cultural Research: The Journal of Comparative Social Science, 35,* 65–87.

Lips, H. M. (2000). College students' visions of power and possibility as moderated by gender. *Psychology of Women Quarterly, 24,* 39–43.

Lipton, R. B., Stewart, W. F., Diamond, S., Diamond, M. L., & Reed, M. (2001). Prevalence and burden of migraine in the United States: Data from the American Migraine Study II. *Headache, 41,* 646–657.

Litchfield, R. C., Fan, J., & Brown, V. R. (2011). Directing idea generation using brainstorming with specific novelty goals. *Motivation & Emotion, 35,* 135–143.

Litt, M. D., Nye, C., & Shafer, D. (1995). Preparation for oral surgery: Evaluating elements of coping. *Journal of Behavioral Medicine, 18,* 435–459.

Littner, M., Johnson, S. F., McCall, W. V., Anderson, W. M., Davila, D., Hartse, K., … Woodson, B. T. (2001). Practice parameters for the treatment of narcolepsy: An update for 2000. *Sleep: Journal of Sleep and Sleep Disorders Research, 24,* 451–466.

Liu, H., Bravata, D. M., Olkin, I., Friedlander, A., Liu, V., Roberts, B., … Hoffman, A. R. (2008). Systematic review: The effects of growth hormone on athletic performance. *Annals of Internal Medicine, 148,* 747–758.

Liu, L. L., & Lau, A. S. (2013). Teaching about race/ethnicity and racism matters: An examination of how perceived ethnic racial socialization processes are associated with depression symptoms. *Cultural Diversity & Ethnic Minority Psychology, 19,* 383–394.

Liu, X., Uchiyama, M., Kim, K., Okawa, M., Shibui, K., Kudo, Y., … Ogihara, R. (2000). Sleep loss and daytime sleepiness in the general adult population of Japan. *Psychiatry Research, 93,* 1–11.

Ljungvall, A., & Zimmerman, F. J. (2012). Bigger bodies: Long-term trends and disparities in obesity and body-mass index among U.S. adults, 1960–2008. *Social Science & Medicine, 75,* 109–119.

Llorente, M. D., Currier, M. B., Norman, S. E., & Mellman, T. A. (1992). Night terrors in adults: Phenomenology and relationship to psychopathology. *Journal of Clinical Psychiatry, 53,* 392–394.

Lo Bue, S., Taverniers, J., Mylle, J., & Euwema, M. (2013). Hardiness promotes work engagement, prevents burnout, and moderates their relationship. *Military Psychology, 25,* 105–115.

LoBello, S. G., & Gulgoz, S. (1991). Factor analysis of the Wechsler Preschool and Primary Scale of Intelligence–Revised. *Psychological Assessment, 3,* 130–132.

Lockart, R. S., & Craik, F. I. (1990). Levels of processing: A retrospective commentary on a framework for memory research. *Canadian Journal of Psychology, 44,* 87–112.

Locke, E. A., & Latham, G. P. (2002). Building a practically useful theory of goal setting and task motivation: A 35-year odyssey. *American Psychologist, 57,* 705–717.

Locke, J. (1690/1959). *An essay concerning human understanding.* New York: Dover.

Lockhart, R. S., & Craik, F. I. (1990). Levels of processing: A retrospective commentary on a framework for memory research. *Canadian Journal of Psychology, 44,* 87–112.

Locurto, C. (1990). The malleability of IQ as judged from adoption studies. *Intelligence, 14,* 275–292.

Locurto, C. (1991). Beyond IQ in preschool programs? *Intelligence, 15,* 295–312.

Loef, M., & Walach, H. (2012). The combined effects of healthy lifestyle behaviors on all-cause mortality. *Preventive Medicine: An International Journal Devoted to Practice & Theory, 55,* 163–170.

Loehlin, J. C., Horn, J. M., & Willerman, L. (1990). Heredity, environment, and personality change: Evidence from the Texas Adoption Project. *Journal of Personality, 58,* 221–243.

Loehlin, J. C., & Martin, N. G. (2001). Age changes in personality traits and their heritabilities during the adult years: Evidence from Australian twin registry samples. *Personality and Individual Differences, 30,* 1147–1160.

Loewi, O. (1960). An autobiographical sketch. *Perspectives in Biology and Medicine, 3,* 3–25.

Loftus, E., Joslyn, S., & Polage, D. (1998). Repression: A mistaken impression? *Development and Psychopathology, 10,* 781–792.

Loftus, E. F. (1993). The reality of repressed memories. *American Psychologist, 48,* 518–537.

Loftus, E. F., & Burns, T. E. (1982). Mental shock can produce retrograde amnesia. *Memory and Learning, 10,* 318–323.

Loftus, E. F., & Hoffman, H. G. (1989). Misinformation and memory: The creation of new memories. *Journal of Experimental Psychology: General, 118,* 100–104.

Loftus, E. F., & Palmer, J. C. (1974). Reconstruction of automobile destruction: An example of the interaction between language and memory. *Journal of Verbal Learning and Verbal Behavior, 13,* 585–589.

Loftus, G. R., Duncan, J., & Gehrig, P. (1992). On the time course of perceptual information that results from a brief visual presentation. *Journal of Experimental Psychology: Human Perception and Performance, 18,* 530–549.

Logan, C. (2002). When scientific knowledge becomes scientific discovery: The disappearance of classical conditioning before Pavlov. *Journal of the History of the Behavioral Sciences, 38,* 393–403.

Logie, R. H. (1999). Working memory. *Psychologist, 12,* 174–178.

Logie, R. H. The functional organization and capacity limits of working memory. *Current Directions in Psychological Science, 20,* 240–245.

Lombardo, G. P., & Foschi, R. (2002). The European origins of "personality psychology." *European Psychologist, 7,* 134–145.

Long, M. E., Hammons, M. E., Davis, J. L., Frueh, B. C., Khan, M. M., Klhai, J. D., & Teng, E. J. (2011). Imagery rescripting and exposure group treatment of posttraumatic nightmares in veterans with PTSD. *Journal of Anxiety Disorders, 25,* 531–535.

Lonner, W. J., & Malpass, R. S. (Eds.). (1994). *Psychology and culture.* Boston: Allyn & Bacon.

Lonsdale, A. J., & North, A. C. (2012). Musical taste and the representativeness heuristic. *Psychology of Music, 40,* 131–142.

Lonsway, K. A., Klaw, E. L., Berg, D. R., Waldo, C. R., Kothari, C., Mazurek, C. J., & Hegeman, K. E. (1998). Beyond "no means no": Outcomes of an intensive program to train peer facilitators for campus acquaintance rape education. *Journal of Interpersonal Violence, 13,* 73–92.

Loomis, A. L., Harvey, E. N., & Hobart, G. A. (1937). Electrical potentials of the human brain. *Journal of Experimental Psychology, 21,* 127–144.

Loomis, M., & Saltz, E. (1984). Cognitive styles as predictors of artistic styles. *Journal of Personality, 52,* 22–35.

Loose, R., Kaufmann, C., Auer, D. P., & Lange, K. W. (2003). Human prefrontal and sensory cortical activity during divided attention tasks. *Human Brain Mapping, 18,* 249–259.

López, S. R., & Guarnaccia, P. J. J. (2000). Cultural psychopathology: Uncovering the social world of mental illness. *Annual Review of Psychology, 51,* 571–598.

Lord, C. G. (1982). Predicting behavioral consistency from an individual's perception of situational similarities. *Journal of Personality and Social Psychology, 42,* 1076–1088.

Lorenz, K. Z. (1966). *On aggression.* New York: Harcourt Brace Jovanovich.

Lorist, M. M., & Tops, M. (2003). Caffeine, fatigue, and cognition. *Brain and Cognition, 53,* 82–94.

Lottes, I. L. (1993). Nontraditional gender roles and the sexual experiences of heterosexual college students. *Sex Roles, 29,* 645–669.

Lou, L., & Chen, J. (2003). Attention and blind-spot phenomenology. *Psyche: An Interdisciplinary Journal of Research on Consciousness, 9,* 02.

Lovell, P. G., Bloj, M., & Harris, J. M. (2012). Optimal integration of shading and binocular disparity for depth perception. *Journal of Vision, 12,* 1–18.

Lovie, A. D., & Lovie, P. (1993). Charles Spearman, Cyril Burt, and the origins of factor analysis. *Journal of the History of the Behavioral Sciences, 29,* 308–321.

Loving, T. J., Gleason, M. J., & Pope, M. T. (2009). Transition novelty moderates daters' cortisol responses when talking about marriage. *Personal Relationships, 16,* 187–2003.

Lowe, G. (1982). Alcohol-induced state-dependent learning: Differentiating stimulus and storage hypotheses. *Current Psychological Research, 2,* 215–222.

Lowe, M. R., Foster, G. D., Kerzhnerman, I., Swain, R. M., & Wadden, T. A. (2001). Restrictive dieting vs. "undieting": Effects on eating regulation in obese clinic attenders. *Addictive Behaviors, 26,* 253–266.

Lozano, D. I., Crites, S. L., Jr., & Aikman, S. N. (1999). Changes in food attitudes as a function of hunger. *Appetite, 32,* 207–218.

Lu, L., & Shih, J. B. (1997). Personality and happiness: Is mental health a mediator? *Personality and Individual Differences, 22,* 249–256.

Lu, Z. L., Williamson, S. J., & Kaufman, L. (1992). Behavioral lifetime of human auditory sensory memory predicted by physiological measures. *Science, 258,* 1668–1670.

Lubar, J. F. (1991). Discourse on the development of EEG diagnostics and biofeedback for attention-deficit/hyperactivity disorders. *Biofeedback and Self-Regulation, 16,* 201–225.

Lubart, T. I. (1999). Creativity across cultures. In R. J. Sternberg (Ed.), *Handbook of creativity* (pp. 339–350). NY: Cambridge University Press.

Lubek, I., Innis, N. K., Kroger, R. O., McGuire, G. R., Stam, H. J., & Herrmann, T. (1995). Faculty genealogies in five Canadian universities: Historiographical and pedagogical concerns. *Journal of the History of the Behavioral Sciences, 31,* 52–72.

Lubinski, D., Benbow, C. P., Shea, D. L., Eftekhari-Sanjani, H., & Halvorson, B. J. (2001). Men and women at promise for scientific excellence: Similarity not dissimilarity. *Psychological Science, 12,* 309–317.

Luborsky, L., Chandler, M., Auerbach, A. H., Cohen, J., & Bachrach, H. M. (1971). Factors influencing the outcome of psychotherapy: A review of quantitative research. *Psychological Bulletin, 75,* 145–185.

Luborsky, L., Rosenthal, R., Diguer, L., Andrusyna, T. P., Levitt, J. T., Seligman, D. A., . . . Krause, E. D. (2003). Are some psychotherapies much more effective than others? *Journal of Applied Psychoanalytic Studies, 5,* 455–460.

Luce, G. G., & Segal, J. (1966). *Sleep.* New York: Coward McCann.

Luchins, A. (1946). Classroom experiments on mental sets. *American Journal of Psychology, 59,* 295–298.

Luders, E., Narr, K. I., Bilder, R. M., Szeszko, P. R., Gurbani, M. N., Hamilton, L., . . . Gaser, C. (2008). Mapping the relationship between cortical convolution and intelligence: Effects of gender. *Cerebral Cortex, 18,* 2019–2026.

Luhmann, M., Lucas, R. E., Eid, M., & Diener, E. (2013). The prospective effect of life satisfaction on life events. *Social Psychological & Personality Science, 4,* 39–45.

Lukas, K. E., Marr, M. J., & Maple, T. L. (1998). Teaching operant conditioning at the zoo. *Teaching of Psychology, 25,* 112–116.

Lundqvist, L.-O. (1995). Facial EMG reactions to facial expressions: A case of facial emotional contagion? *Scandinavian Journal of Psychology, 36,* 130–141.

Lundstrom, J. N., Goncalves, M., Esteves, F., & Olsson, M. J. (2003). Psychological effects of subthreshold exposure to the putative human pheromone 4,16-androstadien-3-one. *Hormones and Behavior, 44,* 395–401.

Lundy, D. E., Tan, J., & Cunningham, M. R. (1998). Heterosexual romantic preferences: The importance of humor and physical attractiveness for different types of relationships. *Personal Relationships, 5,* 311–325.

Luo, J., Phan, T. X., Yang, Y., Garelick, M. G., & Storm, D. R. (2013). Increases in cAMP, MAPK activity, and CREB phosphorylation during REM sleep: Implications for REM sleep and memory consolidation. *Journal of Neuroscience, 33,* 6460–6468.

Lutz, J., Means, L. W., & Long, T. E. (1994). Where did I park? A naturalistic study of spatial memory. *Applied Cognitive Psychology, 8,* 439–451.

Luxton, D. D., Trofimovich, L., & Clark, L. L. (2013). Suicide risk among U.S. service members after psychiatric hospitalization, 2002–2011. *Psychiatric Services, 64,* 626–629.

Lydon, J. E., Jamieson, D., & Zanna, M. P. (1988). Interpersonal similarity and the social and intellectual dimensions of first impressions. *Social Cognition, 6,* 269–286.

Lykken, D. T. (1974). Psychology and the lie detector industry. *American Psychologist, 29,* 725–739.

Lykken, D. T. (1981). *A tremor in the blood: Uses and abuses of the lie detector.* New York: McGraw-Hill.

Lykken, D. T. (1982). Research with twins: The concept of emergenesis. *Psychophysiology, 19,* 361–373.

Lykken, D. T. (1988). Detection of guilty knowledge: A comment on Forman and McCauley. *Journal of Applied Psychology, 73,* 303–304.

Lykken, D. T., Bouchard, T. J., Jr., McGue, M., & Tellegen, A. (1993). Heritability of interests: A twin study. *Journal of Applied Psychology, 73,* 303–304.

Lykken, D. T., McGue, M., Tellegen, A., & Bouchard, T. J., Jr. (1992). Emergenesis: Genetic traits that may not run in families. *American Psychologist, 47,* 1565–1577.

Lymburner, J. A., & Roesch, R. (1999). The insanity defense: Five years of research (1993–1997). *International Journal of Law and Psychiatry, 22,* 213–240.

Lynch, P. S., Kellow, J. T., & Willson, V. L. (1997). The impact of deinstitutionalization on the adaptive behavior of adults with mental retardation: A meta-analysis. *Education and Training in Mental Retardation and Developmental Disabilities, 32,* 255–261.

Lynn, R. (1982). IQ in Japan and the United States shows a growing disparity. *Nature, 297,* 222–223.

Lynn, S. J., Rhue, J. W., & Weekes, J. R. (1990). Hypnotic involuntariness: A social-cognitive analysis. *Psychological Review, 97,* 169–184.

Lyons, J. (2002). Factors contributing to low back pain among professional drivers: A review of current literature and possible ergonomic controls. *Work: Journal of Prevention, Assessment and Rehabilitation, 19,* 95–102.

Lyons, M. J., Eisen, S. A., Goldberg, J., True, W., Lin, N., Meyer, J. M., . . . Tsuang, M. T. (1998). A registry-based twin study of depression in men. *Archives of General Psychiatry, 55,* 468–472.

Lysle, D. T., Cunnick, J. E., & Maslonek, K. A. (1991). Pharmacological manipulation of immune alterations induced by an aversive conditioned stimulus: Evidence for a-adrenergic receptor-mediated Pavlovian conditioning process. *Behavioral Neuroscience, 105,* 443–449.

Lytton, H., & Romney, D. M. (1991). Parents' differential socialization of boys and girls: A meta-analysis. *Psychological Bulletin, 109,* 267–296.

Ma, H.-H. (2009). The effectiveness of intervention on the behavior of individuals with autism: A meta-analysis using percentage of data point exceeding the median of baseline phase (PEM). *Behavior Modification, 33,* 339–359.

Ma, H. K., Shek, D. T. L., Cheung, P. C., Oi Bun Lam, C. (2000). Parental, peer, and teacher influences on the social behavior of Hong Kong Chinese adolescents. *Journal of Genetic Psychology, 161,* 65–78.

Maag, U., Vanasse, C., Dionne, G., & Laberge-Nadeau, C. (1997). Taxi drivers' accidents: How binocular vision problems are related to their rate and severity in terms of the number of victims. *Accident Analysis and Prevention, 29,* 217–224.

Maass, A., & Russo, A. (2003). Directional bias in the mental representation of spatial events: Nature or culture? *Psychological Science, 14,* 296–301.

Macaskill, N. D., & Macaskill, A. (1996). Rational-emotive therapy plus pharmacotherapy versus pharmacotherapy alone in the treatment of high cognitive dysfunction depression. *Cognitive Therapy and Research, 20,* 575–592.

Macchi, M. M., Boulos, Z., Ranney, T., Simmons, L., & Campbell, S. S. (2002). Effects of an afternoon nap on nighttime alertness and performance in long-haul drivers. *Accident Analysis and Prevention, 34,* 825–834.

Maccoby, E. E., & Jacklin, C. N. (1974). *The psychology of sex differences* (2 vols.). Stanford, CA: Stanford University Press.

Maccoby, E. E., & Lewis, C. C. (2003). Less day care or different day care? *Child Development, 74,* 1069–1075.

MacCracken, M. J., & Stadulis, R. E. (1985). Social facilitation of young children's dynamic balance performance. *Journal of Sport Psychology, 7,* 150–165.

MacDonald, D. A., & Holland, D. (2003). Spirituality and the MMPI-2. *Journal of Clinical Psychology, 59,* 399–410.

MacDonald, D. J., & Standing, L. G. (2002). Does self-serving bias cancel the Barnum effect? *Social Behavior and Personality, 30,* 625–630.

MacDonald, T. K., MacDonald, G., Zanna, M. P., Fong, G. (2000). Alcohol, sexual arousal, and intentions to use condoms in young men: Applying alcohol myopia theory to risky sexual behavior. *Health Psychology, 19,* 290–298.

Macera, M. H., Cohen, S. H. (2006). Psychology as a profession: An effective career exploration and orientation course for undergraduate psychology majors. *Career Development Quarterly, 54,* 367–371.

MacFarlane, J. G., Cleghorn, J. M., Brown, G. M., & Streiner, D. L. (1991). The effects of exogenous melatonin on the total sleep time and daytime alertness of chronic insomniacs: A preliminary study. *Biological Psychiatry, 30,* 371–376.

Mack, A., Heuer, F., Villardi, K., & Chambers, D. (1985). The dissociation of position and extent in Müller-

Lyer figures. *Perception and Psychophysics, 37,* 335–344.

Mack, S. (1981). Novel help for the handicapped. *Science, 212,* 26–27.

Macklin, M. C. (1994). The effects of an advertising retrieval cue on young children's memory and brand evaluations. *Psychology and Marketing, 11,* 291–311.

MacLean, H. N. (1993). *Once upon a time: A true story of memory, murder, and the law.* New York: HarperCollins.

MacLeod, C. M. (1988). Forgotten but not gone: Savings for pictures and words in long-term memory. *Journal of Experimental Psychology: Learning, Memory, and Cognition, 14,* 195–212.

MacMillan, H. L., & Thomas, B. H. (1993). Public health nurse home visitation for the tertiary prevention of child maltreatment: Results of a pilot study. *Canadian Journal of Psychiatry, 38,* 436–442.

Macmillan, M. (2000). Nineteenth-century inhibitory theories of thinking: Bain, Ferrier, Freud (and Phineas Gage). *History of Psychology, 3,* 187–217.

Maddi, S. R. (2002). The story of hardiness: Twenty years of theorizing, research, and practice. *Consulting Psychology Journal: Practice and Research, 54,* 175–185.

Maddi, S. R., Kahn, S., & Maddi, K. L. (1998). The effectiveness of hardiness training. *Consulting Psychology Journal: Practice and Research, 50,* 78–86.

Maekelae, K. (1997). Drinking, the majority fallacy, cognitive dissonance, and social pressure. *Addiction, 92,* 729–736.

Maenner, M. J., Blumberg, S. J., Kogan, M. D., Christensen, D., Yeargin-Allsopp, M., & Schieve, L. A. (2016). Prevalence of cerebral palsy and intellectual disability among children identified in two U.S. National Surveys, 2011–2013. *Annals of Epidemiology, 26*(3), 222–226.

Maganaris, C. N., Collins, D., & Sharp, M. (2000). Expectancy effects and strength training: Do steroids make a difference? *Sport Psychologist, 14,* 272–278.

Magee, W. J., Eaton, W. W., Wittchen, H.-W., McGonagle, K. A., & Kessler, R. C. (1996). Agoraphobia, simple phobia, and social phobia in the national comorbidity survey. *Archives of General Psychiatry, 53,* 159–168.

Mah, K., & Binik, Y. M. (2002). Do all orgasms feel alike? Evaluating a two-dimensional model of the orgasm experience across gender and sexual context. *Journal of Sex Research, 39,* 104–113.

Maiello, S. (1999). Encounter with an African healer: Thinking about the possibilities and limits of cross-cultural psychotherapy. *Journal of Child Psychotherapy, 25,* 217–238.

Maier, N. R. (1931). Reasoning in humans. *Journal of Comparative Psychology, 12,* 181–194.

Maier, S. F. (1984). Learned helplessness and animal models of depression. *Progress in Neuro-Psychopharmacology and Biological Psychiatry, 8*(3), 435–446.

Maio, G. R., Olson, J. M., & Bush, J. E. (1997). Telling jokes that disparage social groups: Effects on the joke teller's stereotypes. *Journal of Applied Social Psychology, 27,* 1986–2000.

Majde, J. A., Krueger, J. M. (2005). Links between the innate immune system and sleep. *Journal of Allergy and Clinical Immunology, 116,* 188–1198.

Majeres, R. L. (1999). Sex differences in phonological processes: Speeded matching and word reading. *Memory and Cognition, 27,* 246–253.

Majhi, P., Bagga, R., Kalra, J., & Sharma, M. (2009). Intravaginal use of natural micronised progesterone to prevent pre-term birth: A randomised trial in India. *Journal of Obstetrics and Gynaecology, 29,* 493–498.

Mäkinen, M., Puukko-Viertomies, L.-R, Lindberg, N., Siimes, M. A., & Aalberg, V. (2012). Body dissatisfaction and body mass in girls and boys transitioning from early to mid-adolescence: Additional role of self-esteem and eating habits. *BMC Psychiatry, 12,* 1–8.

Malamuth, N. M., Hald, G. M., & Koss, M. (2012). Pornography, individual differences in risk and men's acceptance of violence against women in a representative sample. *Sex Roles, 66,* 427–439.

Malarkey, W. B., Pearl, D. K., Demers, L. M., & Kiecolt-Glaser, J. K. (1995). Influence of academic stress and season on 24-hour mean concentrations of ACTH, cortisol, and b-endorphin. *Psychoneuroendocrinology, 20,* 499–508.

Malik, R., Paraherakis, A., Joseph, S., & Ladd, H. (1996). The method of subliminal psychodynamic activation: Do individual thresholds make a difference? *Perceptual and Motor Skills, 83,* 1235–1242.

Malinowski, C. I., & Smith, C. P. (1985). Moral reasoning and moral conduct: An investigation prompted by Kohlberg's theory. *Journal of Personality and Social Psychology, 49,* 1016–1027.

Malmberg, A. B., & Basbaum, A. I. (1998). Partial sciatic nerve injury in the mouse as a model of neuropathic pain: Behavioral and neuroanatomical correlates. *Pain, 76,* 215–222.

Man, D. W. K., Tam, S. F., & Hui-Chan, C. W. Y. (2003). Learning to live independently with expert systems in memory rehabilitation. *NeuroRehabilitation, 18,* 21–29.

Mandai, O., Guerrien, A., Sockeel, P., & Dujardin, K. (1989). REM sleep modifications following a Morse code learning session in humans. *Physiology and Behavior, 46,* 639–642.

Mandel, D. R., Jusczyk, P. W., & Pisoni, D. B. (1995). Infants' recognition of the sound patterns of their own names. *Psychological Science, 6,* 314–317.

Mandler, G. (2002). Origins of the cognitive (r)evolution. *Journal of the History of the Behavioral Sciences, 38,* 339–353.

Maner, J. K., Kenrick, D. T., Becker, D. V., Delton, A. W., Hofer, B., Wilbur, C. J., & Neuberg, S. L. (2003). Sexually selective cognition: Beauty captures the mind of the beholder. *Journal of Personality and Social Psychology, 85,* 1107–1120.

Maner, J. K., Luce, C. L., Neuberg, S. L., Cialdini, R. B., Brown, S., & Sagarin, B. J. (2002). The effects of perspective taking on motivations for helping: Still no evidence for altruism. *Personality and Social Psychology Bulletin, 28,* 1601–1610.

Mangalmurti, V. S. (1994). Psychotherapists' fear of a Tarasoff: All in the mind? *Journal of Psychiatry and Law, 22,* 379–409.

Manley, R. S., Smye, V., & Srikameswaran, S. (2001). Addressing complex ethical issues in the treatment of children and adolescents with eating disorders: Application of a framework for ethical decision-making. *European Eating Disorders Review, 9,* 144–166.

Mann, M., Pankok, J., Connemann, B., & Roeschke, J. (2003). Temporal relationship between nocturnal erections and rapid eye movement episodes in healthy men. *Neuropsychobiology, 47,* 109–114.

Manning, B. H. (1990). A categorical analysis of children's self-talk during independent school assignments. *Journal of Instructional Psychology, 17,* 208–217.

Manning, C. A., Parsons, M. W., & Gold, P. E. (1992). Anterograde and retrograde enhancement of 24-hour memory by glucose in elderly humans. *Behavioral and Neural Biology, 58,* 125–130.

Mansell, W., & Carey, T. A. (2009). A century of psychology and psychotherapy: Is an understanding of "control" the missing link between theory, research, and practice? *Psychology and Psychotherapy: Theory, Research, and Practice, 82,* 337–353.

Mansfield, N. J., & Griffin, M. J. (2000). Difference thresholds for automobile seat vibration. *Applied Ergonomics, 31,* 255–261.

Maragos, W. F., Greenamyre, J. T., Penney, J. B., & Young, A. B. (1987). Glutamate dysfunction in Alzheimer's disease: A hypothesis. *Trends in Neuroscience, 10,* 65–68.

Maranto, G. (1984, December). Aging: Can we slow the inevitable? *Discover,* pp. 17–21.

Maratsos, M. (2000). More overregularizations after all: New data and discussion on Marcus, Pinker, Ullman, Hollander, Rosen and Xu. *Journal of Child Language, 27,* 183–212.

Marchand, S., Charest, J., Li, J., & Chenard, J. R. (1993). Is TENS purely a placebo effect? A controlled study on chronic low back pain. *Pain, 54,* 99–106.

Marcus, G. F. (1995). Children's overregularization of English plurals: A quantitative analysis. *Journal of Child Language, 22,* 447–459.

Marcus, G. F., & Fisher, S. E. (2003). FOXP2 in focus: What can genes tell us about speech and language? *Trends in Cognitive Sciences, 7,* 257–262.

Marder, S. R., Wirshing, W. C., Mintz, J., & McKenzie, J. (1996). Two-year outcome of social skills training and group psychotherapy for outpatients with schizophrenia. *American Journal of Psychiatry, 153,* 1585–1592.

Maren, S., & Baudry, M. (1995). Properties and mechanisms of long–term synaptic plasticity in the mammalian brain: Relationships to learning and memory. *Neurobiology of Learning and Memory, 63,* 1–18.

Margolis, R. B., & Mynatt, C. R. (1986). The effects of external and self-administered reward on high base rate behavior. *Cognitive Therapy and Research, 10,* 109–122.

Marken, R. S., & Powers, W. T. (1989). Random-walk chemotaxis: Trial and error as a control process. *Behavioral Neuroscience, 103,* 1348–1355.

Markianos, M., Hatzimanolis, J., & Lykouras, L. (2002). Serotonergic and dopaminergic neuroendocrine responses of male depressive patients before and after a therapeutic ECT course. *European Archives of Psychiatry and Clinical Neuroscience, 252,* 172–176.

Markowitsch, H. J. (1998). Cognitive neuroscience of memory. *Neurocase: Case Studies in Neuropsychology, Neuropsychiatry, and Behavioural Neurology, 4,* 429–435.

Marks, I. M. (1995). Advances in behavioral-cognitive therapy of social phobia. *Journal of Clinical Psychiatry, 56,* 25–31.

Markus, E., Lange, A., & Pettigrew, T. F. (1990). Effectiveness of family therapy: A meta-analysis. *Journal of Family Therapy, 12,* 205–221.

Markus, H. (1977). Self-schemata and processing information about the self. *Journal of Personality and Social Psychology, 35,* 63–78.

Markus, H. (1983). Self-knowledge: An expanded view. *Journal of Personality, 51,* 543–565.

Markus, H. R., & Kitayama, S. (1991). Culture and the self: Implications for cognition, emotion, and motivation. *Psychological Review, 98,* 224–253.

Maron, E., Tõru, I. Must, A., Tasa, G., Toover, E., Vasar, V., . . . Shlik, J. (2007). Association study of tryptophan hydroxylase 2 gene polymorphisms in panic disorder. *Neuroscience Letters, 411,* 180–184.

Marosi, E., Bazan, O., Yanez, G., Bernal, J., Fernandez, T., Rodriguez, M., . . . Reyes, A. (2002). Narrow-band spectral measurements of EEG during emotional tasks. *International Journal of Neuroscience, 112,* 871–891.

Marsa, F., O'Reilly, G., Carr, A., Murphy, P., O'Sullivan, M., Cotter, A., & Hevey, D. (2004). Attachment styles and psychological profiles of child sex offenders in Ireland. *Journal of Interpersonal Violence, 19,* 228–251.

Marsden, J. (2011). Cerebellar ataxia: Pathophysiology and rehabilitation. *Clinical Rehabilitation, 25,* 195–216.

Marsh, A. A., Finger, E. C., Fowler, K. A., Jurkowitz, I., Schechter, J. C., Yu, H. H., . . . Blair, R. J. R., (2011). Reduced amygdala–orbitofrontal connectivity during moral judgments in youths with disruptive behavior disorders and psychopathic traits. *Psychiatry Research: Neuroimaging, 194,* 279–286.

Marshall, G. D., & Zimbardo, P. G. (1979). Affective consequences of inadequately explained physiological arousal. *Journal of Personality and Social Psychology, 37,* 970–988.

Marshall, J. C., Halligan, P. W., Fink, G. R., Wade, D. T., & Frackowiak, R. S. J. (1997). The functional anatomy of a hysterical paralysis. *Cognition, 64,* B1–B8.

Marshall, M. (1990). The theme of quantification and the hidden Weber in the early work of Gustav Theodor Fechner. *Canadian Psychology, 31,* 45–63.

Marsland, A. L., Manuck, S. B., Fazzari, T. V., & Stewart, C. J. (1995). Stability of individual differences in cellular immune responses to acute psychological stress. *Psychosomatic Medicine, 57,* 295–298.

Martin, A. J., Nejad, H. G., Colmar, S., & Liem, G. A. D. (2013). Adaptability: How students' responses to uncertainty and novelty predict their academic and nonacademic outcomes. *Journal of Educational Psychology, 105,* 728–746.

Martin, D. J., Garske, J. P., & Davis, M. K. (2000). Relation of the therapeutic alliance with outcome and other variables: A meta-analytic review. *Journal of Consulting and Clinical Psychology, 68,* 438–450.

Martin, R. A., Kuiper, N. A., Olinger, L. J., & Dance, K. (1993). Humor, coping with stress, self-concept, and psychological well-being. *Humor: International Journal of Humor Research, 6,* 89–104.

Martin, S. J., & Morris, R. G. M. (2002). New life in an old idea: The synaptic plasticity and memory hypothesis revisited. *Hippocampus, 12,* 609–636.

Martinez, H. R., Gonzalez-Garza, M. T., Moreno-Cuevas, J. E., Caro, E., Gutierrez-Jimenez, E., & Segura, J. J. (2009). Stem-cell transplantation into the frontal motor cortex in amyotrophic lateral sclerosis patients. *Cytotherapy, 11,* 26–34.

Martinez, J. L., Jr., & Derrick, B. E. (1996). Long-term potentiation and learning. *Annual Review of Psychology, 47,* 173–203.

Martínez, K., Burgaleta, M., Román, F. J., Escorial, S., Shih, P. C., Ángeles Quiroga, M., & Colom, 2011. Can fluid intelligence be reduced to "simple" short-term storage? *Intelligence, 39,* 473–480.

Martinez, M., Brezun, J. M., Zennou-Azogui, Y., Baril, N., & Xerri, C. (2009). Sensorimotor training promotes functional recovery and somatosensory cortical map reactivation following cervical spinal cord injury. *European Journal of Neuroscience, 30,* 2356–2367.

Martinez, M. E. (2002). Effectiveness of operationalized Gestalt therapy role playing in the treatment of phobic behaviors. *Gestalt Review, 6,* 148–167.

Martinez-Pons, M. (1997). The relation of emotional intelligence with selected areas of personal functioning. *Imagination, Cognition and Personality, 17,* 3–13.

Martinko, M. J., & Thomson, N. F. (1998). A synthesis and extension of the Weiner and Kelley attribution models. *Basic and Applied Social Psychology, 20,* 271–284.

Martins, I. P., & Parriera, E. (2001). Behavioral response to headache: A comparison between migraine and tension-type headache. *Headache, 41,* 546–553.

Marx, B., Gross, A. M., & Adams, H. E. (1999). The effect of alcohol on the responses of sexually coercive and noncoercive men to an experimental rape analog. *Sexual Abuse: Journal of Research and Treatment, 11,* 131–145.

Marx, J. L. (1980). Ape-language controversy flares up. *Science, 207,* 1330–1333.

Masling, J., Bornstein, F. R., Fishman, I., & Davila, J. (2002). Can Freud explain women as well as men? A meta-analytic review of gender differences in psychoanalytic research. *Psychoanalytic Psychology, 19,* 328–347.

Maslow, A. H. (1970). *Motivation and personality.* New York: Harper & Row.

Masoro, E. J., Shimokawa, I., Higami, Y., & McMahan, C. A. (1995). Temporal pattern of food intake not a factor in the retardation of aging processes by dietary restriction. *Journals of Gerontology: Series A: Biological Sciences and Medical Sciences, 50A,* B48–B53.

Masserano, J. M., Takimoto, G. S., & Weiner, N. (1981). Electroconvulsive shock increases tyrosine hydroxylaseactivity via the brain and adrenal gland of the rat. *Science, 214,* 662–665.

Masser, B., & Abrams, D. (1999). Contemporary sexism: The relationships among hostility, benevolence, and neosexism. *Psychology of Women Quarterly, 23,* 503–517.

Masters, K. S. (1992). Hypnotic susceptibility, cognitive dissociation, and runner's high in a sample of marathon runners. *American Journal of Clinical Hypnosis, 34,* 193–201.

Masters, K. S., & Knestel, A. (2011). Religious orientation among a random sample of community-dwelling adults: Relations with health status and health-relevant behaviors. *International Journal for the Psychology of Religion, 21,* 63–76.

Masters, K. S., & Ogles, B. M. (1998). Associative and dissociative cognitive strategies in exercise and running: 20 years later, what do we know? *Sport Psychologist, 12,* 253–270.

Masters, W. H., & Johnson, V. E. (1966). *Human sexual response.* Boston: Little, Brown.

Mastropieri, M. A., Scruggs, T. E., & Whedon, C. (1997). Using mnemonic strategies to teach information about U.S. presidents: A classroom-based investigation. *Learning Disability Quarterly, 20,* 13–21.

Mathew, R. J., Wilson, W. H., Turkington, T. G., Hawk, T. C., Coleman, R. E., DeGrado, T. R., & Provenzale, J. (2002). Time course of tetrahydrocannabinol-induced changes in regional cerebral blood flow measured with positron emission tomography. *Psychiatry Research: Neuroimaging, 116,* 173–185.

Mathis, M., & Lecci, L. (1999). Hardiness and college adjustment: Identifying students in need of services. *Journal of College Student Development, 40,* 305–309.

Matlock, J. G. (1991). Records of the Parapsychology Laboratory: An inventory of the collection in the Duke University library. *Journal of Parapsychology, 55,* 301–314.

Matson, J. L., DiLorenzo, T. M., & Esveldt-Dawson, K. (1981). Independence training as a method of enhancing self-help skills acquisition of the mentally retarded. *Behaviour Research and Therapy, 19,* 399–405.

Matsubayashi, T., & Ueda, M. (2011). The effect of national suicide prevention programs on suicide rates in 21 OECD nations. *Social Science & Medicine, 73,* 1395–1400.

Matsumoto, D. (1987). The role of facial response in the experience of emotion: More methodological problems and a meta-analysis. *Journal of Personality and Social Psychology, 52,* 769–774.

Matsumoto, D. (1999). Culture and self: An empirical assessment of Markus and Kitayama's theory of independent and interdependent self-construal. *Asian Journal of Social Psychology, 2,* 289–310.

Matsuura, T., Ishida, T., & Ishimatsu, K. (2002). Changes in seatbelt use after licensing: A developmental hypothesis for novice drivers. *Transportation Research Part F: Traffic Psychology and Behaviour, 5,* 1–13.

Matt, G. E., & Navarro, A. M. (1997). What meta-analyses have and have not taught us about psychotherapy effects: A review and future directions. *Clinical Psychology Review, 17,* 1–32.

Matt, G. E., Vazquez, C., & Campbell, W. K. (1992). Mood-congruent recall of affectively toned stimuli: A meta-analytic review. *Clinical Psychology Review, 12,* 227–255.

Mattai, P. R. (2002). The multifaceted needs, concerns and responses to educating all children: Editor's comments. *Child Study Journal, 32,* 1–3.

Mattanah, J. F., Pratt, M. W., Cowan, P. A., & Cowan, C. P. (2005). Authoritative parenting, parental scaffolding of long-division mathematics, and children's academic competence in fourth grade. *Journal of Applied Developmental Psychology, 26,* 85–106.

Matthews, D. B., Best, P. J., White, A. M., Vandergriff, J. L., & Simon, P. E. (1996). Ethanol impairs spatial cognitive processing: New behavioral and electrophysiological findings. *Current Directions in Psychological Science, 5,* 111–115.

Matthews, K. A., & Woodall, K. L. (1988). Childhood origins of overt Type A behaviors and cardiovascular reactivity to behavioral stressors. *Annals of Behavioral Medicine, 10,* 71–77.

Mautner, B. (1991). Freud's Irma dream: A psychoanalytic interpretation. *International Journal of Psycho-Analysis, 72,* 275–286.

May, R. (1982, Summer). The problem of evil: An open letter to Carl Rogers. *Journal of Humanistic Psychology,* pp. 10–21.

Mayer, B., & Merckelbach, H. (1999). Unconscious processes, subliminal stimulation, and anxiety. *Clinical Psychology Review, 19,* 571–590.

Mazzella, R., & Feingold, A. (1994). The effects of physical attractiveness, race, socioeconomic status, and gender of defendants and victims on judgments of mock jurors: A meta-analysis. *Journal of Applied Social Psychology, 24,* 1315–1344.

McAdams, D. P., de St. Aubin, E., & Logan, R. L. (1993). Generativity among youth, midlife, and older adults. *Psychology and Aging, 8,* 221–230.

McAllister, D. E., & McAllister, W. R. (1994). Extinction and reconditioning of classically conditioned fear before and after instrumental learning: Effects of depth of fear extinction. *Learning and Motivation, 25,* 339–367.

McAlpine, D., & Grothe, B. (2003). Sound localization and delay lines: Do mammals fit the model? *Trends in Neurosciences, 26,* 347–350.

McAuley, E., Poag, K., Gleason, A., & Wraith, S. (1990). Attrition from exercise programs: Attributional and affective perspectives. *Journal of Social Behavior and Personality, 5,* 591–602.

McCabe, K. O., & Fleeson, W. (2012). What is extraversion for? Integrating trait and motivational perspectives and identifying the purpose of extraversion. *Psychological Science, 23,* 1498–1505.

McCaffrey, T. (2012). Innovation relies on the obscure: A key to overcoming the classic problem of functional fixedness. *Psychological Science, 23,* 215–218.

McCall, M. (1997). The effects of physical attractiveness on gaining access to alcohol: When social policy meets social decision making. *Addiction, 92,* 597–600.

McCalley, L. T., & Midden, C. J. H. (2002). Energy conservation through product-integrated feedback: The roles of goal-setting and social orientation. *Journal of Economic Psychology, 23,* 589–603.

McCallister, C., Nash, W. R., & Meckstroth, E. (1996). The social competence of gifted children: Experiments and experience. *Roeper Review, 18,* 273–276.

McCammon, S., Durham, T. W., Allison, E. J., & Williamson, J. E. (1988). Emergency workers' cognitive appraisal and coping with traumatic events. *Journal of Traumatic Stress, 1,* 353–372.

McCanne, T. R., & Anderson, J. A. (1987). Emotional responding following experimental manipulation of facial electromyographic activity. *Journal of Personality and Social Psychology, 52,* 759–768.

McCarthy, L., & Shean, G. (1996). Agoraphobia and interpersonal relationships. *Journal of Anxiety Disorders, 10,* 477–487.

McCauley, C., & Forman, R. F. (1988). A review of the Office of Technology Assessment report on polygraph validity. *Basic and Applied Social Psychology, 9,* 73–84.

McCauley, C., Woods, K., Coolidge, C., & Kulick, W. (1983). More-aggressive cartoons are funnier. *Journal of Personality and Social Psychology, 44,* 817–823.

McClelland, J. L., Fiez, J. A., & McCandliss, B. D. (2002). Training the /r/-/l/ discrimination to Japanese adults: Behavioral and neural aspects. *Physiology & Behavior, 77,* 657–662.

McClelland, J. L., McNaughton, B. L., & O'Reilly, R. C. (1995). Why there are complementary learning systems in the hippocampus and neocortex: Insights from the successes and failures of connectionist models of learning and memory. *Psychological Review, 102*, 419–437.

McClelland, L., Reicher, S., & Booth, N. (2000). A last defence: The negotiation of blame within suicide notes. *Journal of Community and Applied Social Psychology, 10*, 225–240.

McCloskey, M., & Egeth, H. E. (1983). Eyewitness identification: What can a psychologist tell a jury? *American Psychologist, 38*, 550–563.

McCloskey, M., Wible, C. G., & Cohen, N. J. (1988). Is there a special flashbulb-memory mechanism? *Journal of Experimental Psychology: General, 117*, 171–181.

McClure, E. B. (2000). A meta-analytic review of sex differences in facial expression processing and their development in infants, children, and adolescents. *Psychological Bulletin, 126*, 424–453.

McComas, A., & Upton, A. (2009). Therapeutic transcranial magnetic stimulation in migraine and its implications for a neuroinflammatory hypothesis. *Inflammopharmacology, 17*, 68–75.

McConahay, J. B. (1986). Modern racism, ambivalence, and the Modern Racism Scale. In J. F. Dovidio & S. L. Gaertner (Eds.), *Prejudice, discrimination, and racism* (pp. 91–125). London: Academic Press.

McConaghy, N., & Blaszczynski, A. (1991). Initial stages of validation by penile volume assessment that sexual orientation is distributed dimensionally. *Comprehensive Psychiatry, 32*, 52–58.

McConnell, J. V., Cutler, R. L., & McNeil, E. B. (1958). Subliminal stimulation: An overview. *American Psychologist, 13*, 229–242.

McConnell, J. V., Jacobson, A. L., & Kimble, D. P. (1959). The effects of regeneration upon retention of a conditioned response in the planarian. *Journal of Comparative and Physiological Psychology, 52*, 1–5.

McCrae, R. R., & Costa, P. T., Jr. (1995). Trait explanations in personality psychology. *European Journal of Personality, 9*, 231–252.

McCrae, R. R., & Costa, P. T., Jr. (1997). Personality trait structure as a human universal. *American Psychologist, 52*, 509–516.

McCrae, R. R., Costa, P. T., Jr., Del Pilar, G. H., Rolland, J.-P., & Parker, W. D. (1998). Cross-cultural assessment of the five-factor model: The Revised NEO Personality Assessment. *Journal of Cross-Cultural Psychology, 29*, 171–188.

McCrea, D. A. (1992). Can sense be made of spinal interneuron circuits? *Behavioral and Brain Sciences, 15*, 633–643.

McCrea, S. M., & Hirt, E. R. (2001). The role of ability judgments in self-handicapping. *Personality and Social Psychology Bulletin, 27*, 1378–1389.

McCullough, M. E., Tsang, J.-A., & Brion, S. (2003). Personality traits in adolescence as predictors of religiousness in early adulthood: Findings from the Terman longitudinal study. *Personality and Social Psychology Bulletin, 29*, 980–991.

McDonald, D. N. (2007). Differing conceptions of personhood within the psychology and philosophy of Mary Whiton Calkins. *Transactions of the Charles S. Peirce Society, 43*, 753–768.

McDonald, M. S. (1980, September 10). Emperor Norton. *American West*, pp. 30–32, 51, 61.

McDougal, Y. B., Crowe, G. W., & Holland, S. M. (2003). Motion parallax: Is it presented accurately in textbooks? *Teaching of Psychology, 30*, 256–258.

McDougall, W. (1908). *Social psychology*. New York: G. Putnam & Sons.

McDowell, M. J. (2001). Principle of organization: A dynamic-systems view of the archetype-as-such. *Journal of Analytical Psychology, 46*, 637–654.

McEwen, B. S. (2004). Protection and damage from acute and chronic stress: Allostasis and allostatic overload and relevance to the pathophysiology of psychiatric disorders. *Annals of the New York Academy of Sciences, 1032*, 1–7.

McFadden, D. (1998). Sex differences in the auditory system. *Developmental Neuropsychology, 14*, 261–298.

McFadden, D. (2002). Masculinization effects in the auditory system. *Archives of Sexual Behavior, 31*, 99–111.

McFadden, D., & Pasanen, E. G. (1999). Spontaneous otoacoustic emissions in heterosexuals, homosexuals, and bisexuals. *Journal of the Acoustical Society of America, 105*, 2403–2413.

McGaha, A. C., & Korn, J. H. (1995). The emergence of interest in the ethics of psychological research with humans. *Ethics and Behavior, 5*, 147–159.

McGaugh, J. L., & Roozendaal, B. (2002). Role of adrenal stress hormones in forming lasting memories in the brain. *Current Opinion in Neurobiology, 12*, 205–210.

McGrady, A. (2002). A commentary on "Problems inherent in assessing biofeedback efficacy studies." *Applied Psychophysiology and Biofeedback, 27*, 111–112.

McGrady, A., Turner, J. W., Fine, T. H., & Higgins, J. T. (1987). Effects of biobehaviorally assisted relaxation training on blood pressure, plasma renin, cortisol, and aldosterone levels in borderline essential hypertension. *Clinical Biofeedback and Health, 10*, 16–25.

McGue, M., Bacon, S., & Lykken, D. T. (1993). Personality stability and change in early adulthood: A behavioral genetic analysis. *Developmental Psychology, 29*, 96–109.

McGuffin, P., Rijsdijk, F., Andrew, M., Sham, P., Katz, R., & Cardno, A. (2003). The heritability of bipolar affective disorder and the genetic relationship to unipolar depression. *Archives of General Psychiatry, 60*, 497–502.

McGuigan, F. J. (1970). Covert oral behavior during the silent performance of language tasks. *Psychological Bulletin, 74*, 309–326.

McGuire, L., Kiecolt-Glaser, J. K., & Glaser, R. (2002). Depressive symptoms and lymphocyte proliferation in older adults. *Journal of Abnormal Psychology, 111*, 192–197.

McInnis, M. G., Dick, D. M., Willour, V. L., Avramopoulos, D., MacKinnon, D. F., Simpson, S., . . . Foroud, T. M. (2003). Genome-wide scan and conditional analysis in bipolar disorder: Evidence for genomic interaction in the National Institute of Mental Health genetics initiative bipolar pedigrees. *Biological Psychiatry, 54*, 1265–1273.

McIntosh, D. N. (1996). Facial feedback hypotheses: Evidence, implications, and directions. *Motivation and Emotion, 20*, 121–147.

McIntosh, D. N., Zajonc, R. B., Vig, P. S., & Emerick, S. W. (1997). Facial movement, breathing, temperature, and affect: Implications of the vascular theory of emotional efference. *Cognition and Emotion, 11*, 171–195.

McKelvie, S. J., & Drumheller, A. (2001). The availability heuristic with famous names: A replication. *Perceptual & Motor Skills, 92*, 507–516.

McKendree-Smith, N., & Scogin, F. (2000). Depressive realism: Effects of depression severity and interpretation time. *Journal of Clinical Psychology, 56*, 1601–1608.

McKenna, M. C., Zevon, M. A., Corn, B., & Rounds, J. (1999). Psychosocial factors and the development of breast cancer: A meta-analysis. *Health Psychology, 18*, 520–531.

McKennitt, D. S., & Currie, C. L. (2012). Does a culturally sensitive smoking prevention program reduce smoking intentions among aboriginal children? A pilot study. *American Indian and Alaska Native Mental Health Research, 19*, 55–63.

McKenzie, J. (1998). Fundamental flaws in the Five Factor Model: A re-analysis of the seminal correlation matrix from which the "openness-to-experience" factor was extracted. *Personality and Individual Differences, 24*, 475–480.

McKinney, M., & Richelson, E. (1984). The coupling of the neuronal muscarinic receptor to responses. *Annual Review of Pharmacology and Toxicology, 24*, 121–146.

McKown, C., & Weinstein, R. S. (2003). The development and consequences of stereotype consciousness in middle childhood. *Child Development, 74*, 498–515.

McLay, R. N., Wood, D. P., Webb-Murphy, J., Spira, J. L., Wiederhold, M. D., Pyne, J. M., & Wiederhold, B. K. (2011). A randomized, controlled trial of virtual reality-graded exposure therapy for post-traumatic stress disorder in active duty service members with combat-related post-traumatic stress disorder. *Cyberpsychology, Behavior and Social Networking, 14*, 223–229.

McLeod, D. M., & Detenber, B. H. (1999). Framing effects of television news coverage of social protest. *Journal of Communication, 49*, 3–23.

McLure, J., Walkey, F., & Allen, M. (1999). When earthquake damage is seen as preventable: Attributions, locus of control, and attitudes to risk. *Applied Psychology: An International Review, 48*, 239–256.

McMahon, M. (1992). Dangerousness, confidentiality, and the duty to protect. *Australian Psychologist, 27*, 12–16.

McManus, C., Nicholls, M., & Vallortigara, G. (2009). Editorial commentary: Is LRRTM1 the gene for handedness? *Laterality, 14*, 1–2.

McMillan, D. E., & Katz, J. L. (2002). Continuing implications of the early evidence against the drive–reduction hypothesis of the behavioral effects of drugs. *Psychopharmacology, 163*, 251–264.

McMinn, M. R., Vogel, M. J., & Heyne, L. K. (2010). A place for the church within professional psychology. *Journal of Psychology and Theology, 38*, 267–274.

McNatt, D. B. (2000). Ancient Pygmalion joins contemporary management: A meta-analysis of the result. *Journal of Applied Psychology, 85*, 314–322.

McNelles, L. R., & Connolly, J. A. (1999). Intimacy between adolescent friends: Age and gender differences in intimate affect and intimate behaviors. *Journal of Research on Adolescence, 9*, 143–159.

McPherson, K. S. (1985). On intelligence testing and immigration legislation. *American Psychologist, 40*, 242–243.

McQuellon, R. P., Wells, M., Hoffman, S., Craven, B., Russell, G., Cruz, J., . . . Savage, P. (1998). Reducing distress in cancer patients with an orientation program. *Psycho-Oncology, 7*, 207–217.

McRoberts, C., Burlingame, G. M., & Hoag, M. J. (1998). Comparative efficacy of individual and group psychotherapy: A meta-analytic perspective. *Group Dynamics, 2*, 101–117.

McWilliams, S. A., & Tuttle, R. J. (1973). Long-term psychological effects of LSD. *Psychological Bulletin, 79*, 341–351.

Meana, M., & Binik, Y. M. (1994). Painful coitus: A review of female dyspareunia. *Journal of Nervous and Mental Disease, 182*, 264–272.

Mecacci, L., & Rocchetti, G. (1998). Morning and evening types: Stress-related personality aspects. *Personality and Individual Differences, 25*, 537–542.

Medin, D. L. (1989). Concepts and conceptual structure. *American Psychologist, 44*, 1469–1481.

Medland, S. E., Geffen, G., & McFarland, K. (2002). Lateralization of speech production using verbal/manual dual tasks: Meta-analysis of sex differences and practice effects. *Neuropsychologia, 40*, 1233–1239.

Meehan, J. W., & Day, R. H. (1995). Visual accommodation as a cue for size. *Ergonomics, 38*, 1239–1249.

Meehl, P. E. (1956). Wanted: A good cookbook. *American Psychologist, 11*, 263–272.

Meeker, W. B., & Barber, T. X. (1971). Toward an explanation of stage hypnosis. *Journal of Abnormal Psychology, 77*, 61–70.

Meert, T. F., Vissers, K., Geenen, F., & Kontinen, V. K. (2003). Functional role of exogenous administration of substance P in chronic constriction injury model of neuropathic pain in gerbils.

Meertens, R. W., & Pettigrew, T. F. (1997). Is subtle prejudice really prejudice? *Public Opinion Quarterly, 61,* 54–71.

Mehu, M, & Dunbar, R. I. M. (2008). Naturalistic observations of smiling and laughter in human group interactions. *Behaviour, 145,* 1747–1780.

Meichenbaum, D. (1985). *Stress-inoculation training.* New York: Pergamon.

Meichenbaum, D. H., Bowers, K. S., & Ross, R. R. (1969). A behavioral analysis of teacher expectancy effect. *Journal of Personality and Social Psychology, 13,* 306–316.

Meisenzahl, E. M., Schmitt, G. J., Scheuerecker, J., & Möller, H. J. (2007). The role of dopamine for the pathophysiology of schizophrenia. *International Review of Psychiatry, 19,* 337–345.

Meissner, W. W. (1996). Empathy in the therapeutic alliance. *Psychoanalytic Inquiry, 16,* 39–53.

Melanoma risk and socio-economic class (1983). *Science News, 124,* 232.

Mellon, M. W., & McGrath, M. L. (2000). Empirically supported treatments in pediatric psychology: Nocturnal enuresis. *Journal of Pediatric Psychology, 25,* 193–214.

Mellors, V., Boyle, G. J., & Roberts, L. (1994). Effects of personality, stress, and lifestyle on hypertension: An Australian twin study. *Personality and Individual Differences, 16,* 967–974.

Melmed, S. (2009). Acromegaly pathogenesis and treatment. *Journal of Clinical Investigation, 119,* 3189–3202.

Melville, J. D., & Naimark, D. (2002). Punishing the insane: The verdict of guilty but mentally ill. *Journal of the American Academy of Psychiatry and the Law, 30,* 553–555.

Melzack, R. (1993). Pain: Past, present and future. *Canadian Journal of Experimental Psychology, 47,* 615–629.

Melzack, R., & Wall, P. D. (1965). Pain mechanisms: A new theory. *Science, 150,* 971–979.

Men, W., Falk, D., Sun, T., Chen, W., Li, J., Yin, D., ... Fan, M. (2014). The corpus callosum of Albert Einstein's brain: Another clue to his high intelligence? *Brain, 137.*

Menachemi, N. (2011). Assessing response bias in a web survey at a university faculty. *Evaluation and Research in Education, 24,* 5–15.

Menchettil, M., Bortolottil, B., Rucci, P., Scocco, P., Bombil, A., & Berardi, D. (2010). Depression in primary care: Interpersonal counseling vs selective serotonin reuptake inhibitors. The DEPICS Study: A multicenter randomized controlled trial— Rationale and design. *BMC Psychiatry, 10,* 97–105.

Mendelson, W. B., Maczaj, M., & Holt, J. (1991). Buspirone administration to sleep apnea patients. *Journal of Clinical Psychopharmacology, 11,* 71–72.

Menéndez-Colino, L. M., Falco, C., Traserra, J., Berenguer, J., Pujo, T., Doménech, J., & Bernal-Prekelsen, M. (2007). Activation patterns of the primary auditory cortex in normal-hearing subjects: a functional magnetic resonance imaging study. *Acta Oto-Laryngologica, 127,* 1283–1291.

Mengel, M. K. C., Stiefenhofer, A. E., Jyvasjarvi, E., & Kniffki, K. D. (1993). Pain sensation during cold stimulation of the teeth: Differential reflection of Ad and C fibre activity? *Pain, 55,* 159–169.

Menon, T., Morris, M. W., Chiu, C.-Y., & Hong, Y.-Y. (1999). Culture and the construal of agency: Attribution to individual versus group dispositions. *Journal of Personality and Social Psychology, 76,* 701–717.

Menzel, C. R., Savage-Rumbaugh, E. S., & Menzel, E, W. (2002). Bonobo *(Pan paniscus)* spatial memory and communication in a 20-hectare forest. *International Journal of Primatology, 23,* 601–619.

Mercier, M., Schwartz, S., Michel, C. M., & Blanke, O. (2009). Motion direction tuning in human visual cortex. *European Journal of Neuroscience, 29,* 424–434.

Merckelbach, H., Arntz, A., & de Jong, P. (1991). Conditioning experiences in spider phobics. *Behaviour Research and Therapy, 29,* 333–335.

Merckelbach, H., Dekkers, T., Wessel, I., & Roefs, A. (2003). Dissociative symptoms and amnesia in Dutch concentration camp survivors. *Comprehensive Psychiatry, 44,* 65–69.

Merckelbach, H., Muris, P., & Kop, W. J. (1994). Handedness, symptom reporting, and accident susceptibility. *Journal of Clinical Psychology, 50,* 389–392.

Merewether, F. C., & Alpert, M. (1990). The components and neuroanatomical bases of prosody. *Journal of Communication Disorders, 23,* 325–336.

Merikle, P. M., Smilek, D., & Eastwood, J. D. (2001). Perception without awareness: Perspectives from cognitive psychology. *Cognition, 79,* 115–134.

Merrick, J. (2000). Aspects of Down syndrome. *International Journal of Adolescent Medicine and Health, 12,* 5–17.

Merritt, M. M., Bennett, G. G., Williams, R. B., Sollers, J. J., III, & Thayer, J. F. (2004). Low educational attainment, John Henryism, and cardiovascular reactivity to and recovery from personally relevant stress. *Psychosomatic Medicine, 66,* 49–55.

Mervis, J. (1984, March). Council ends forums trial, opens way for new divisions. *APA Monitor,* pp. 10–11.

Mervis, J. (1986, July). NIMH data point way to effective treatment. *APA Monitor,* pp. 1, 13.

Messer, S. B. (2002). A psychodynamic perspective on résistance in psychotherapy: Vive la resistance. *Journal of Clinical Psychology, 58,* 157–163.

Messer, W. S., & Griggs, R. A. (1989). Student belief and involvement in the paranormal and performance in introductory psychology. *Teaching of Psychology, 16,* 187–191.

Messick, S., & Jungeblut, A. (1981). Time and method in coaching for the SAT. *Psychological Bulletin, 89,* 191–196.

Messier, C. (1997). Object recognition in mice: Improvement of memory by glucose. *Neurobiology of Learning and Memory, 67,* 172–175.

Messier, C., Pierre, J., Desrochers, A., & Gravel, M. (1998). Dose-dependent action of glucose on memory processes in women: Effect on serial position and recall priority. *Cognitive Brain Research, 7,* 221–233.

Meston, C. M., & Frolich, P. F. (2003). Love at first fright: Partner salience moderates roller-coaster–induced excitation transfer. *Archives of Sexual Behavior, 32,* 537–544.

Metcalfe, J., & Wiebe, D. (1987). Intuition in insight and noninsight problem solving. *Memory and Cognition, 15,* 238–246.

Mettetal, G., Jordan, C., & Harper, S. (1997). Attitudes toward a multiple intelligences curriculum. *Journal of Educational Research, 91,* 115–122.

Metz, M. E., & Epstein, N. (2002). Assessing the role of relationship conflict in sexual dysfunction. *Journal of Sex & Marital Therapy, 28,* 139–164.

Meuret, A. E., Wilhelm, F. H., & Roth, W. T. (2001). Respiratory biofeedback-assisted therapy in panic disorder. *Behavior Modification, 25,* 584–605.

Meyer, B., Pilkonis, P., Krupnick, J. L., Egan, M. K., Simmens, S. J., & Sotsky, S. M. (2002). Treatment expectancies, patient alliance and outcome: Further analyses from the National Institute of Mental Health Treatment of Depression Collaborative Research Program. *Journal of Consulting and Clinical Psychology, 70,* 1051–1055.

Meyer-Bahlburg, H. F. L., Ehrhardt, A. A., Rosen, L. R., Guren, R. S., Veridiano, N. P., Vann, F. H., & Neuwalder, H. F. (1995). Prenatal estrogens and the development of homosexual orientation. *Developmental Psychology, 31,* 12–21.

Meyer-Bisch, C. (1996). Epidemiological evaluation of hearing damage related to strongly amplified music (personal cassette players, discotheques, rock concerts): High-definition audiometric survey on 1364 subjects. *Audiology, 35,* 121–142.

Mezzacappa, E. S., Katkin, E. S., & Palmer, S. N. (1999). Epinephrine, arousal, and emotion: A new look at two-factor theory. *Cognition and Emotion, 13,* 181–199.

Miaskowski, C. (1999). The role of sex and gender in pain perception and response to treatment. In R. J. Gatchel et al. (Eds.), *Psychosocial factors in pain: Critical perspectives* (pp. 401–411). New York: Guilford Press.

Michalak, E. E., & Lam, R. W. (2002). Seasonal affective disorder: The latitude hypothesis revisited. *Canadian Journal of Psychiatry, 47,* 787–788.

Michel, C., & Cabanac, M. (1999). Lipectomy, body weight, and body weight set point in rats. *Physiology and Behavior, 66,* 473–479.

Michinov, E., & Monteil, J.-M. (2002). The similarity-attraction relationship revisited: Divergence between the affective and behavioral facets of attraction. *European Journal of Social Psychology, 32,* 485–500.

Miczek, K. A., Thompson, M. L., & Shuster, L. (1982). Opioid-like analgesia in defeated mice. *Science, 215,* 1520–1523.

Middlebrooks, J. C., & Green, D. M. (1991). Sound localization by human listeners. *Annual Review of Psychology, 42,* 135–159.

Midgley, N. (2006). The "inseparable bond between cure and research": Clinical case study as a method of psychoanalytic inquiry. *Journal of Child Psychotherapy, 32,* 122–147.

Miklosi, A., Polgardi, R., Topal, J., & Csanyi, V. (2000). Intentional behavior in dog-human communication: An experimental analysis of "showing" behavior in the dog. *Animal Cognition, 3,* 159–166.

Mikulincer, M., & Florian, V. (2000). Exploring individual differences in reactions to mortality salience: Does attachment style regulate terror management mechanisms? *Journal of Personality and Social Psychology, 79,* 260–273.

Mikulincer, M., Florian, V., & Hirschberger, G. (2003). The existential function of close relationships: Introducing death into the science of love. *Personality and Social Psychology Review, 7,* 20–40.

Milan, R. J., Kilmann, P. R., & Boland, J. P. (1988). Treatment outcome of secondary orgasmic dysfunction: A two- to six-year follow-up. *Archives of Sexual Behavior, 17,* 463–480.

Milar, K. S. (2000). The first generation of women psychologists and the psychology of women. *American Psychologist, 55,* 616–619.

Miles, C., & Hardman, E. (1998). State-dependent memory produced by aerobic exercise. *Ergonomics, 41,* 20–28.

Miles, J. A., & Greenberg, J. (1993). Using punishment threats to attenuate social loafing effects among swimmers. *Organizational Behavior and Human Decision Processes, 56,* 246–265.

Miletic, M. P. (2002). The introduction of a feminine psychology to psychoanalysis: Karen Horney's legacy. *Contemporary Psychoanalysis, 38,* 287–299.

Milgram, S. (1963). Behavioral study of obedience. *Journal of Abnormal and Social Psychology, 67,* 371–378.

Milgram, S. (1964). Issues in the study of obedience: A reply to Baumrind. *American Psychologist, 19,* 848–852.

Milgram, S. (1974). *Obedience to authority.* New York: Harper & Row.

Millar, J. K., Wilson-Annan, J. C., Anderson, S., Christie, S., Taylor, M. S., Semple, C. A., ... Porteous, D. J. (2000). Disruption of two novel genes by a translocation co-segregating with schizophrenia. *Human Molecular Genetics, 9,* 1415–1423.

Millar, M. (2002). Effects of a guilt induction and guilt reduction on door in the face. *Communication Research, 29,* 666–680.

Miller, B. D., & Wood, B. L. (1997). Influence of specific emotional states on autonomic reactivity and pulmonary function in asthmatic children. *Journal of the American Academy of Child and Adolescent Psychiatry, 36,* 669–677.

Miller, C. (2003). Ethical guidelines in research. In J. C. Thomas & M. Hersen (Eds.), *Understanding research in clinical and counseling psychology* (pp. 271–293). Mahwah, NJ: Erlbaum.

Miller, D. L., & Kelley, M. L. (1994). The use of goal setting and contingency contracting for improving children's homework performance. *Journal of Applied Behavior Analysis, 27,* 73–84.

Miller, E. (1996). Phrenology, neuropsychology, and rehabilitation. *Neuropsychological Rehabilitation, 6,* 245–255.

Miller, E. M. (1994). Intelligence and brain myelination: A hypothesis. *Personality and Individual Differences, 17,* 803–832.

Miller, G. A. (1956). The magical number seven, plus or minus two: Some limits on our capacity for processing information. *Psychological Review, 63,* 81–97.

Miller, G. A. (2003). The cognitive revolution: A historical perspective. *Trends in Cognitive Sciences, 7,* 141–144.

Miller, H. A., Watkins, R. J., & Webb, D. (2009). The use of psychological testing to evaluate law enforcement leadership competencies and development. *Police Practice and Research, 10,* 49–60.

Miller, J. (1983). Three constructions of transference in Freud, 1895–1915. *Journal of the History of the Behavioral Sciences, 19,* 153–172.

Miller, L. K. (1999). The Savant syndrome: Intellectual impairment and exceptional skill. *Psychological Bulletin, 125,* 31–46.

Miller, N. E. (1985). The value of behavioral research on animals. *American Psychologist, 40,* 423–440.

Miller, N. S., & Gold, M. S. (1994). LSD and Ecstasy: Pharmacology, phenomenology, and treatment. *Psychiatric Annals, 24,* 131–133.

Miller, S. C., Mor, V., Wu, N., Gozalo, P., & Lapane, K. (2002). Does receipt of hospice care in nursing homes improve the management of pain at the end of life? *Journal of the American Geriatrics Society, 50,* 507–515.

Miller, T. Q., Smith, T. W., Turner, C. W., Guijarro, M. L., & Hallet, A. J. (1996). Meta-analytic review of research on hostility and physical health. *Psychological Bulletin, 119,* 322–348.

Miller, T. Q., Turner, C. W., Tindale, R. S., Posavac, E. J., & Dugoni, B. L. (1991). Reasons for the trend toward null findings in research on Type A behavior. *Psychological Bulletin, 110,* 469–485.

Miller, W. C. (1999). How effective are traditional dietary and exercise interventions for weight loss? *Medicine and Science in Sports and Exercise, 31,* 1129–1134.

Miller-Jones, D. (1989). Culture and testing. *American Psychologist, 44,* 360–366.

Millikin, C., & Braun-Janzen, C. (2013). Collaborative treatment of choking phobia in an older adult. *Clinical Case Studies, 12,* 263–277.

Milling, L. S. (2012). The Spanos Attitudes Toward Hypnosis Questionnaire: Psychometric characteristics and normative data. *American Journal of Clinical Hypnosis, 54,* 202–212.

Millon, T. (2003). It's time to rework the blueprints: Building a science for clinical psychology. *American Psychologist, 58,* 948–961.

Mills, E., Wu, P., Seely, D., & Guatt, G. (2005). Melatonin in the treatment of cancer: A systematic review of randomized controlled trials and meta-analysis. *Journal of Pineal Research, 39,* 360–366.

Mills, E. J., Wu, P., Lockhart, I., Thorlund, K., Puhan, M., & Ebbert, J. O. (2012). Comparisons of high-dose and combination nicotine replacement therapy, varenicline, and bupropion for smoking cessation: A systematic review and multiple treatment metaanalysis. *Annals of Medicine, 44,* 588–597.

Mills, S., & Raine, A. (1994). Neuroimaging and aggression. *Journal of Offender Rehabilitation, 21,* 145–158.

Milosevic, M., & McConville, K. M. V. (2011). Audiovisual biofeedback system for postural control. *International Journal on Disability and Human Development, 10,* 321–324.

Mimeault, V., & Morin, C. M. (1999). Self-help treatment for insomnia: Bibliotherapy with and without professional guidance. *Journal of Consulting & Clinical Psychology, 67,* 511–519.

Mindell, J. A., & Barrett, K. M. (2002). Nightmares and anxiety in elementary-aged children: Is there a relationship? *Child: Care, Health and Development, 28,* 317–322.

Mineka, S., & Cook, M. (1993). Mechanisms involved in the observational conditioning of fear. *Journal of Experimental Psychology General, 122,* 23–38.

Minini, L., Parker, A. J., & Bridge, H. (2010). Neural modulation by binocular disparity in human dorsal visual stream. *Journal of Neurophysiology, 104,* 169–178.

Mino, Y., Oshima, I., Tsuda, T., & Okagami, K. (2000). No relationship between schizophrenic birth and influenza epidemics in Japan. *Journal of Psychiatric Research, 34,* 133–138.

Mintz, L. B., Balzer, A. M., Zhao, X., & Bush, H. E. (2012). Bibliotherapy for low sexual desire: Evidence for effectiveness. *Journal of Counseling Psychology, 59,* 471–478.

Minuchin, S. (1974). *Families and family therapy.* Cambridge, MA: Harvard University Press.

Mirsky, A. F., Yardley, S. L., Jones, B. P., & Walsh, D. (1995). Analysis of the attention deficit in schizophrenia: A study of patients and their relatives in Ireland. *Journal of Psychiatric Research, 29,* 23–42.

Mischel, W., & Peake, P. J. (1982). Beyond déjà vu in the search for cross-situational consistency. *Psychological Review, 89,* 730–755.

Mischel, W., Shoda, Y., & Mendoza-Denton, R. (2002). Situation-behavior profiles as a locus of consistency in personality. *Current Directions in Psychological Science, 11,* 50–54.

Miserandino, M. (1991). Memory and the seven dwarfs. *Teaching of Psychology, 18,* 169–171.

Mishkin, M., & Appenzeller, T. (1987). The anatomy of memory. *Scientific American,* pp. 80–89.

Misra, G., Sahoo, F. M., & Puhan, B. N. Cultural bias in testing: India. *European Review of Applied Psychology, 47,* 309–317.

Mita, T. H., Dermer, M., & Knight, J. (1977). Reversed facial images and the mere-exposure hypothesis. *Journal of Personality and Social Psychology, 35,* 597–601.

Mitchell, P., Mackinnon, A. J., & Waters, B. (1993). The genetics of bipolar disorder. *Australian and New Zealand Journal of Psychiatry, 27,* 560–580.

Mitchell, P., & Taylor, L. M. (1999). Shape constancy and theory of mind: Is there a link? *Cognition, 70,* 167–190.

Mitchell, P., Waters, B., Morrison, N., & Shine, J. (1991). Close linkage of bipolar disorder to chromosome 11 markers is excluded in two large Australian pedigrees. *Journal of Affective Disorders, 21,* 23–32.

Mitte, K. (2005). Meta-analysis of cognitive-behavioral treatments for generalized anxiety disorder: A comparison with pharmacotherapy. *Psychological Bulletin, 5,* 785–795.

Modestin, J., Ammann, R., & Wurmle, O. (1995). Season of birth: Comparison of patients with schizophrenia, affective disorders, and alcoholism. *Acta Psychiatrica Scandinavica, 91,* 140–143.

Modigliani, A., & Rochat, F. (1995). The role of interaction sequences and the timing of resistance in shaping obedience and defiance to authority. *Journal of Social Issues, 51,* 107–123.

Moen, M. D. (2010). Bevacizumab in previously treated glioblastoma. *Drugs, 70,* 181–189.

Mogg, K., Philippot, P., & Bradley, B. P. (2004). Selective attention to angry faces in clinical social phobia. *Journal of Abnormal Psychology, 113,* 160–165.

Mohanty, A. K., & Perregaux, C. (1997). Language acquisition and bilingualism. In J. W. Berry, P. R. Dasen, & T. S. Saraswathi (Eds.), *Handbook of cross-cultural psychology: Basic processes and human development* (Vol. 2, 2nd ed., pp. 217–253). Boston: Allyn & Bacon.

Mohr, C. D., Armeli, S., Tennen, H., Carney, M. A., Affleck, G., & Hromi, A. (2001). Daily interpersonal experiences, context, and alcohol consumption: Crying in your beer and toasting good times. *Journal of Personality and Social Psychology, 80,* 489–500.

Mohr, D. C. (1995). Negative outcome in psychotherapy: A critical review. *Clinical Psychology: Science and Practice, 2,* 1–27.

Molchan, G., & Keilis-Borok, V. (2008). Earthquake prediction: Probabilistic aspect. *Geophysical Journal International, 173,* 1012–1017.

Molina, M., & Jouen, F. (1998). Modulation of the palmar grasp behavior in neonates according to texture property. *Infant Behavior and Development, 21,* 659–666.

Molnar, B. E., Shade, S. B., Kral, A. H., Booth, R. E., & Watters, J. K. (1998). Suicidal behavior and sexual/physical abuse among street youth. *Child Abuse and Neglect, 22,* 213–222.

Monahan, J. (1993). Limiting therapist exposure to Tarasoff liability: Guidelines for risk containment. *American Psychologist, 48,* 242–250.

Money, J. (1986). *Venuses penuses: Sexology, sexosophy, and exigency theory.* Buffalo, NY: Prometheus.

Money, J. (1987). Sin, sickness, or status? Homosexual gender identity and psychoneuroendocrinology. *American Psychologist, 42,* 384–399.

Money, J., & Ehrhardt, A. A. (1972). *Man and woman, boy and girl: Differentiation and dimorphism of gender identity from conception to maturity.* Oxford, England: Johns Hopkins University Press.

Mongeau, P. A., & Garlick, R. (1988). Social comparison and persuasive arguments as determinants of group polarization. *Communication Research Reports, 5,* 120–125.

Moniz, E. (1937/1994). Prefrontal leucotomy in the treatment of mental disorders. *American Journal of Psychiatry, 151,* 237–239.

Monroe, S. M. (1982). Life events and disorder: Event-symptom associations and the course of disorder. *Journal of Abnormal Psychology, 91,* 14–24.

Monson, T. C., Hesley, J. W., & Chernick, L. (1982). Specifying when personality traits can and cannot predict behavior: An alternative to abandoning the attempt to predict single-act criteria. *Journal of Personality and Social Psychology, 43,* 385–399.

Montag, I., & Comrey, A. L. (1987). Internality and externality as correlates of involvement in fatal driving accidents. *Journal of Applied Psychology, 72,* 339–343.

Montagliani, A., & Giacalone, R. A. (1998). Impression management and cross-cultural adaptation. *Journal of Social Psychology, 138,* 598–608.

Montague, H., & Hollingworth, L. S. (1914). The comparative variability of the sexes at birth. *American Journal of Sociology, 20,* 335–370.

Monte, C. F. (1980). *Beneath the mask: An introduction to theories of personality.* New York: Holt, Rinehart & Winston.

Montgomery, G., & Kirsch, I. (1996). Mechanisms of placebo pain reduction: An empirical investigation. *Psychonomic Science, 7,* 174–176.

Montgomery, G. H., DuHamel, K. N., & Redd, W. H. (2000). A meta-analysis of hypnotically induced analgesia: How effective is hypnosis? *International Journal of Clinical & Experimental Hypnosis, 48,* 138–153.

Montour, K. (1977). William James Sidis: The broken twig. *American Psychologist, 32,* 265–279.

Montoya, E. R., Terburg, D., Bos, P. A., & van Honk, J. (2012). Testosterone, cortisol, and serotonin as key regulators of social aggression: A review and theoretical perspective. *Motivation & Emotion, 36,* 65–73.

Montoya, R. M., Horton, R. S., & Kirchner, J. (2008). Is actual similarity necessary for attraction? A metaanalysis of actual and perceived similarity. *Journal of Social & Personal Relationships, 25,* 889–922.

Mooney, G., Speed, J., & Sheppard, S. (2005). Factors related to recovery after mild traumatic brain injury. *Brain Injury, 19,* 975–987.

Moore, C., & Engel, S. A. (1999). Visual perception: Mind and brain see eye to eye. *Current Biology, 9,* R74–R76.

Moore, J. (1990). On mentalism, privacy, and behaviorism. *Journal of Mind and Behavior, 11,* 19–36.

Moore, M. S. (2002). Psychophysical measurement and prediction of digital video quality. *Dissertation Abstracts International: Section B. The Sciences and Engineering, 63,* 2955.

Moore, V., & Goodson, S. (2003). How well does early diagnosis of autism stand the test of time? Follow-up study of children assessed for autism at age 2 and development of an early diagnostic service. *Autism, 7,* 47–63.

Moorhead, G., Ference, R., & Neck, C. P. (1991). Group decision fiascoes continue: Space shuttle Challenger and a revised groupthink framework. *Human Relations, 44,* 539–550.

Moran, M. G. (1991). Psychological factors affecting pulmonary and rheumatologic diseases: A review. *Psychosomatics, 32,* 14–23.

Morawski, J. G. (1982). Assessing psychology's moral heritage through our neglected utopias. *American Psychologist, 37,* 1082–1095.

Moreland, R. L., & Zajonc, R. B. (1982). Exposure effects in person perception: Familiarity, similarity, and attraction. *Journal of Experimental Social Psychology, 18,* 395–415.

Moreno, C., Hasin, D. S., Arango, C., Oquendo, M. A, Vieta, E., Liu, S., . . . Blanco, C. (2012). Depression in bipolar disorder versus major depressive disorder: Results from the National Epidemiologic Survey on Alcohol and Related Conditions. *Bipolar Disorders, 14,* 271–282.

Moreno, M., Estevez, A. F., Zaldivar, F., Montes, J. M. G., Guttiérez–Ferre, V. E., Esteban, L., . . . Flores, P. (2012). Impulsivity differences in recreational cannabis users and binge drinkers in a university population. *Drug & Alcohol Dependence, 124,* 355–362.

Morfei, M. Z., Hooker, K., Fiese, B. H., & Cordeiro, A. M. (2001). Continuity and change in parenting possible selves: A longitudinal follow-up. *Basic and Applied Social Psychology, 23,* 217–223.

Morgan, C., & Murray, H. A. (1935). A method of investigating fantasies. *Archives of Neurology and Psychiatry, 4,* 310–329.

Morgan, W. G. (2002). Origin and history of the earliest thematic apperception test pictures. *Journal of Personality Assessment, 79,* 422–445.

Mori, T., Sugimura, T., & Minami, M. (1996). Effects of prior knowledge and response bias upon recognition memory for a story: Implications for children's eyewitness testimony. *Japanese Psychological Research, 38,* 39–46.

Morin, A. (2001). The split-brain debate revisited: On the importance of language and self-recognition for right hemispheric consciousness. *Journal of Mind and Behavior, 22,* 107–118.

Morisse, D., Batra, L., Hess, L., & Silverman, R. (1996). A demonstration of a token economy for the real world. *Applied and Preventive Psychology, 5,* 41–46.

Moriyama, T. S., Polanczyk, G., Caye, A., Banaschewski, T., Brandeis, D., & Rohde, L. A. (2012). Evidence-based information on the clinical use of neurofeedback for ADHD. *Neurotherapeutic, 9,* 588–598.

Morley, J. E. (2001). Androgens and aging. *Maturitas, 38,* 61–73.

Morley, J. E., & Levine, A. S. (1980). Stress-induced eating is mediated through endogenous opiates. *Science, 209,* 1259–1261.

Morley, J. E., & Perry, H. M. (2003). Andropause: An old concept in new clothing. *Clinics in Geriatric Medicine, 19,* 507–528.

Morling, B. (2000). "Taking" an aerobics class in the U.S. and "entering" an aerobics class in Japan: Primary and secondary control in a fitness context. *Asian Journal of Social Psychology, 3,* 73–85.

Morris, S. (1980, April). Interview: James Randi. *Omni,* pp. 76–78, 104, 106, 108.

Morris, W., & Morris, M. (1985). *Harper dictionary of contemporary usage.* New York: Harper & Row.

Morrison, A. R. (1983, April). A window on the sleeping brain. *Scientific American,* pp. 94–102.

Morrison, M., de Man, A. F., & Drumheller, A. (1993). Correlates of socially restrictive and authoritarian attitudes toward mental patients in university students. *Social Behavior and Personality, 21,* 333–338.

Morrongiello, B. A., Fenwick, K. D., & Chance, G. (1990). Sound localization acuity in very young infants: An observer-based testing procedure: Correction. *Developmental Psychology, 26,* 1003.

Morry, M. M., & Staska, S. L. (2001). Magazine exposure: Internaliation, self-objectification, eating attitudes, and body satisfaction in male and female university students. *Canadian Journal of Behavioural Science, 33,* 269–279.

Morse, C. K. (1999). Age and variability in Francis Galton's data. *Journal of Genetic Psychology, 160,* 99–104.

Mortensen, P. B., Pedersen, C. B., Westergaard, T., Wohlfahrt, J., Ewald, H., Mors, O., . . . Melbye, M. (1999). Effects of family history and place and season of birth on the risk of schizophrenia. *New England Journal of Medicine, 340,* 603–608.

Moruzzi, G., & Magoun, H. W. (1949). Brain-stem reticular formation and activation of the EEG. *Electroencephalography and Clinical Neurophysiology, 1,* 455–473.

Morvay, Z. (1999). Horney, Zen, and the real self: Theoretical and historical connections. *American Journal of Psychoanalysis, 59,* 25–35.

Moscovitch, M. (1995). Recovered consciousness: A hypothesis concerning modularity and episodic memory. *Journal of Clinical and Experimental Neuropsychology, 17,* 276–290.

Moshinsky, A., & Bar-Hillel, M. (2002). Where did 1850 happen first—in America or in Europe? A cognitive account for a historical bias. *Psychological Science, 13,* 20–26.

Moss, J., Richards, C., Nelson, L., & Oliver, C. (2013). Prevalence of autism spectrum disorder symptomatology and related behavioural characteristics in individuals with Down syndrome. *Autism: The International Journal of Research and Practice, 17,* 390–404.

Mouratidis, A., & Michou, A. (2011). Self-determined motivation and social achievement goals in children's emotions. *Educational Psychology, 31,* 67–86.

Mouthaan, J., Sijbrandij, M., Reitsma, J. B., Luitse, J. S. K., Goslings, J. C., & Olff, M. (2011). Trauma tips: An Internet-based intervention to prevent posttraumatic stress disorder in injured trauma patients. *Journal of CyberTherapy & Rehabilitation, 4,* 331–340.

Mowrer, O. H. (1947). On the dual nature of learning—A reinterpretation of "conditioning" and "problem solving." *Harvard Educational Review, 17,* 102–148.

Mowrer, O. H., & Mowrer, W. M. (1938). Enuresis: A method for its study and treatment. *American Journal of Orthopsychiatry, 8,* 436–559.

Moy, S. S., & Nadler, J. J. (2008). Advances in behavioral genetics: Mouse models of autism. *Molecular Psychiatry, 13,* 4–25.

Muccio, C. F., De Simone, M., Esposito, G., De Blasio, E., Vittori, C., & Cerase, A. (2009). Reversible post-traumatic bilateral extensive restricted diffusion of the brain. A case study and review of the literature. *Brain Injury, 23,* 466–472.

Muehlbach, M. J., & Walsh, J. K. (1995). The effects of caffeine on simulated night-shift work and subsequent daytime sleep. *Sleep, 18,* 22–29.

Mueller, C. G. (1979). Some origins of psychology as a science. *Annual Review of Psychology, 30,* 9–29.

Mueller, S. C., Maheu, F. S., Dozier, M., Peloso, E., Mandell, D., Leibenluft, E., & Ernst, M. (2010). Early-life stress is associated with impairment in cognitive control in adolescence: An fMRI study. *Neuropsychologia, 48,* 3037–3044.

Muir-Broaddus, J., King, T., Downey, D., & Petersen, M. (1998). Conservation as a predictor of individual differences in children's susceptibility to leading questions. *Psychonomic Bulletin and Review, 5,* 454–458.

Muldoon, K. A., Duff, P. K., Fielden, S., & Anema, A. (2013). Food insufficiency is associated with psychiatric morbidity in a nationally representative study of mental illness among food insecure Canadians. *Social Psychiatry and Psychiatric Epidemiology, 48,* 795–803.

Mullen, B., Anthony, T., Salas, E., & Driskell, J. E. (1994). Group cohesiveness and quality of decision making: An integration of tests of the groupthink hypothesis. *Small Group Research, 25,* 189–204.

Mulligan, T., & Moss, C. R. (1991). Sexuality and aging in male veterans: A cross-sectional study of interest, ability, and activity. *Archives of Sexual Behavior, 20,* 17–25.

Mullins, L. L., & Olson, R. A. (1990). Familial factors in the etiology, maintenance, and treatment of somatoform disorders in children. *Family Systems Medicine, 8,* 159–175.

Mumenthaler, M. S., Taylor, J. L., O'Hara, R., & Yesavage, J. A. (1999). Gender differences in moderate drinking effects. *Alcohol Research and Health, 23,* 55–61.

Mumford, M. D., & Gustafson, S. B. (1988). Creativity syndrome: Integration, application, and innovation. *Psychological Bulletin, 103,* 27–43.

Mumme, D. L., & Fernald, A. (2003). The infant as onlooker: Learning from emotional reactions observed in a television scenario. *Child Development, 74,* 221–237.

Munakata, Y., McClelland, J. L., Johnson, M. H., & Siegler, R. S. (1997). Rethinking infant knowledge: Toward an adaptive process account of successes and failures in object permanence tasks. *Psychological Review, 104,* 686–713.

Münsterberg, H. (1908). *On the witness stand.* New York: Doubleday.

Murnen, S. K., Smolak, L., Mills, J. A., & Good, L. (2003). Thin, sexy women and strong, muscular men: Grade-school children's responses to objectified images of women and men. *Sex Roles, 49,* 427–437.

Murphy, D., Cramer, D., & Joseph, S. (2012). Mutuality in person-centered therapy: A new agenda for research and practice. *Person-Centered and Experiential Psychotherapies, 11,* 109–123.

Murphy, G. L., & Medin, D. L. (1985). The role of theories in conceptual coherence. *Psychological Review, 92,* 289–316.

Murphy, P. J., & Campbell, S. S. (1997). Nighttime drop in body temperature: A physiological trigger for sleep onset? *Sleep, 20,* 505–511.

Murray, H. A. (1938). *Explorations in personality.* New York: Oxford University Press.

Murray, J. B. (1990). Review of research on the Myers-Briggs Type Indicator. *Perceptual and Motor Skills, 70,* 1187–1202.

Murray, S. L., Holmes, J. G., & Griffin, D. W. (1996). The self-fulfilling nature of positive illusions in romantic relationships: Love is not blind, but prescient. *Journal of Personality and Social Psychology, 71,* 1155–1180.

Muse, L. A., Harris, S. G., & Feild, H. S. (2003). Has the inverted-U theory of stress and job performance had a fair test? *Human Performance, 16,* 349–364.

Musikantow, R. (2011). Thinking in circles: Power and responsibility in hypnosis. *American Journal of Clinical Hypnosis, 54,* 83–85.

Mussone, L., Ferrari, A., & Oneta, M. (1999). An analysis of urban collisions using an artificial intelligence model. *Accident Analysis and Prevention, 31,* 705–718.

Myers, D. G. (2000). The funds, friends, and faith of happy people. *American Psychologist, 55,* 56–67.

Myerscough, R., & Taylor, S. (1985). The effects of marijuana on human physical aggression. *Journal of Personality and Social Psychology, 49,* 1541–1546.

Myers, D. G., & Bishop, G. D. (1970). Discussion effects on racial attitudes. *Science, 169,* 778–779.

Na, E. U., & Loftus, E. F. (1998). Attitudes toward law and prisoners, conservative authoritarianism, attribution, and internal-external locus of control: Korean and American law students and undergraduates. *Journal of Cross-Cultural Psychology, 29,* 595–615.

Nadel, L., & Jacobs, W. J. (1998). Traumatic memory is special. *Current Directions in Psychological Science, 7,* 154–156.

Nagata, T., Oshima, J., Wada, A., Yamada, H., Iketani, T., & Kiriike, N. (2003). Open trial of milnacipran for Taijin-Kyofusho in Japanese patients with social anxiety disorder. *International Journal of Psychiatry in Clinical Practice, 7,* 107–112.

Nagata, T., Yamada, H., Teo, A. R., Yoshimura, C., Nakajima, T., & van Vliet, I. (2013). Comorbid social withdrawal (hikikomori) in outpatients with social anxiety disorder: Clinical characteristics and treatment response in a case series. *International Journal of Social Psychiatry, 59,* 73–78.

Nahas, G., Harvey, D. J., Sutin, K., Turndorf, H., & Cancro, R. (2002). A molecular basis of the therapeutic and psychoactive properties of cannabis (Delta-sup-9 tetrahydrocannabinol). *Progress in Neuro-Psychopharmacology and Biological Psychiatry, 26,* 721–730.

Najavits, L. M., & Strupp, H. H. (1994). Differences in the effectiveness of psychodynamic therapists: A process-outcome study. *Psychotherapy, 31,* 114–123.

Naka, M., Itsukushima, Y., & Itoh, Y. (1996). Eyewitness testimony after three months: A field study on memory for an incident in everyday life. *Japanese Psychological Research, 38,* 14–24.

Nakagawa, Y., & Iwasaki, T. (1996). Ethanol-induced state-dependent learning is mediated by 5hydroxytryptamine-sub-3 receptors but not by Nmethyl-D-aspartate receptor complex. *Brain Research, 706,* 227–232.

Nakamura, K., Kawashima, R., Ito, K., Sugiura, M., Kato, T., Nakamura, A., . . . Kojima, S. (1999). Activation of the right inferior frontal cortex during assessment of facial emotion. *Journal of Neurophysiology, 82,* 1610–1614.

Nakayama, K. (1994). James J. Gibson: An appreciation. *Psychological Review, 101,* 329–335.

Narash-Eisikovits, O., Dierberger, A., & Westen, D. (2002). A multidimensional meta-analysis of pharmacotherapy for bulimia nervosa: Summarizing the range of outcomes in controlled clinical trials. *Harvard Review of Psychiatry, 10,* 193–211.

Narita, E., Echizenya, M., Takeshima, M., Inomata, Y., & Shimizu, T. (2011). Core body temperature rhythms in circadian rhythm sleep disorder, irregular sleep-wake type. *Psychiatry & Clinical Neurosciences, 65,* 679–680.

Narita, M., Hashimoto, K., Amano, T., Narita, M., Niikura, K., Nakamura, A., & Suzuki, T. (2008). Post-synaptic action of morphine on glutamatergic neuronal transmission related to the descending antinociceptive pathway in the rat thalamus. *Journal of Neurochemistry, 104,* 469–478.

Narrow, W. E., Clarke, D. E., Kuramoto, S. J., Kraemer, H. C., Kupfer, D. J., Greiner, L., & Regier, D. A. (2013). DSM-5 field trials in the United States and Canada. Part III: Development and reliability testing of a cross-cutting symptom assessment for *DSM-5. American Journal of Psychiatry, 170,* 71–82.

NAS calls tests fair but limited. (1982, April). *APA Monitor,* p. 2.

Nash, M. (1987). What, if anything, is regressed about hypnotic age regression? A review of the empirical literature. *Psychological Bulletin, 102,* 42–52.

National Drug Intelligence Center. (2011). *National Drug Threat Assessment 2011.* Washington, DC: Author.

National Institute of Mental Health. (1998). The NIMH Multisite HIV Prevention Trial: Reducing HIV sexual risk behavior. *Science, 280,* 1889–1894.

National Institute on Drug Abuse. (2014). *Prescription opioids and heroin.* Retrieved from https://www.drugabuse.gov/sites/default/files/rx_and_heroin_rrs_layout_final.pdf

National Science Foundation. (2014). Science and technology: Public attitudes and understanding. In *Science and engineering indicators 2014* (pp. 1–53). Arlington, VA: Author.

National Sleep Foundation. (2011). *2011 Sleep in America Poll: Communications technology in the bedroom.* Retrieved from http://www.sleepfoundation.org/article/sleep-america-polls/2011-communication-stechnology-use-and-sleep. Retrieved 11/17/2013.

Natsoulas, T. (1997–1998). The stream of consciousness, XVII: James in recent context (1991–1996). *Imagination, Cognition, and Personality, 17,* 345–364.

Nava, F., Carta, G., Colombo, G., & Gessa, G. L. (2001). Effects of chronic Delta-sup-9tetrahydrocannabinol treatment on hippocampal extracellular acetycholine concentration and alternation performance in the T-maze. *Neuropharmacology, 41,* 392–399.

Navarro, M., Fernandez-Ruiz, J. J., de Miguel, R., & Hernandez, M. L. (1993). Motor disturbances induced by an acute dose of d-sup-9tetrahydrocannabinol: Possible involvement of nigrostriatal dopaminergic alterations. *Pharmacology, Biochemistry, and Behavior, 45,* 291–298.

Nayak, S., Shiflett, S. C., Eshun, S., & Levine, F. M. (2000). Culture and gender effects in pain beliefs and the prediction of pain tolerance. *Cross-Cultural Research, 34,* 135–151.

Nazari, M. A. (2011). Effectiveness of EEG biofeedback as compared with methylphenidate in the treatment of attention-deficit/hyperactivity disorder: A cinical outcome study. *Neuroscience & Medicine, 2,* 78–86.

Nazzi, T., Floccia, C., & Bertoncini, J. (1998). Discrimination of pitch contours by neonates. *Infant Behavior and Development, 21,* 779–784.

Neher, A. (1996). Jung's theory of archetypes: A critique. *Journal of Humanistic Psychology, 36,* 61–91.

Neisser, U. (1981). John Dean's memory: A case study. *Cognition, 9,* 1–22.

Neisser, U. (1984). Interpreting Harry Bahrick's discovery: What confers immunity against forgetting? *Journal of Experimental Psychology: General, 113,* 32–35.

Neisser, U., & Becklen, R. (1975). Selective looking: Attending to visually specified events. *Cognitive Psychology, 7,* 480–494.

Neisser, U., Boodoo, G., Bouchard, T. J., Jr., Boykin, A. W., Brody, N., Ceci, S. J., . . . Urbina, S. (1996). Intelligence: Knowns and unknowns. *American Psychologist, 51,* 77–101.

Nejime, Y., & Moore, B. C. J. (1998). Evaluation of the effect of speech rate slowing on speech intelligibility in noise using a simulation of cochlear hearing loss. *Journal of the Acoustical Society of America, 103,* 572–576.

Nelson, K. E. (1977). Facilitating children's syntax acquisition. *Developmental Psychology, 18,* 101–107.

Nelson, T. O. (1996). Consciousness and metacognition. *American Psychologist, 51,* 102–116.

Nelson, T. O., Leonesio, R. J., Shimamura, A. P., Landwehr, R. F., & Narens, L. (1982). Overlearning and the feeling of knowing. *Journal of Experimental Psychology: Learning, Memory, and Cognition, 8,* 279–288.

Nemeth, C. J. (1986). Differential contributions of majority and minority influence. *Psychological Review, 93,* 23–32.

Nemeth, C. J., Connell, J. B., Rogers, J. D., & Brown, K. S. (2001). Improving decision making by means of dissent. *Journal of Applied Social Psychology, 31,* 48–58.

Nenty, H. J. (1986). Cross-culture bias analysis of Cattell Culture-Fair Intelligence Test. *Perspectives in Psychological Researches, 9,* 1–16.

Neria, Y., DiGrande, L., & Adams, B. G. (2011). Postraumatic stress disorder following the September 11, 2001 terrorist attacks: A review of the literature among highly exposed populations. *American Psychologist, 66,* 429–466.

Nesheim, B. I., Kinge, R., Berg, B., Alfredsson, B., Allgot, E., Hove, G., . . . Solberg, S. (2003). Acupuncture during labor can reduce the use of meperidine: A controlled clinical study. *Clinical Journal of Pain, 19,* 187–191.

Nestadt, G., Samuels, J., Riddle, M., Bienvenu, J., Liang, K.-Y., LaBuda, M., Walkup, J., . . . Hoehn-Saric, R. (2000). A family study of obsessive-compulsive behavior. *Archives of General Psychiatry, 57,* 358–363.

Neubauer, A. C., Riemann, R., Mayer, R., & Angleitner, A. (1997). Intelligence and reaction times in the Hick, Sternberg and Posner paradigms. *Personality and Individual Differences, 22,* 885–894.

Neugebauer, V., Schaible, H. G., Weirretter, F., Freudenberger, U. (1994). The involvement of substance P and neurokinin-1 receptors in the responses of rat dorsal horn neurons to noxious but not to innocuous mechanical stimuli applied to the knee joint. *Brain Research, 666,* 207–215.

Neumann, R. (2000). The causal influences of attributions on emotions: A procedural priming approach. *Psychological Science, 11,* 179–182.

Nevo, O. (1985). Does one ever really laugh at one's own expense? *Journal of Personality and Social Psychology, 49,* 799–807.

Nevo, O., & Nevo, B. (1983). What do you do when asked to answer humorously? *Journal of Personality and Social Psychology, 44,* 188–194.

Newcomb, A. F., & Bagwell, C. L. (1995). Children's friendship relations: A meta-analytic review. *Psychological Bulletin, 117,* 306–347.

Newcomb, A. F., Bukowski, W. M., & Pattee, L. (1993). Children's peer relations: A meta-analytic review of popular, rejected, neglected, controversial, and average sociometric status. *Psychological Bulletin, 113,* 99–128.

Newcombe, N. S. (2002). The nativist-empiricist controversy in the context of recent research on spatial and quantitative development. *Psychological Science, 13,* 395–401.

Newell, A., & Simon, H. A. (1972). *Human problem solving.* Oxford, England: Prentice-Hall.

Newman, A. J., Bavelier, D., Corina, D., Jezzard, P., & Neville, H. J. (2002). A critical period for right hemisphere recruitment in American Sign Language processing. *Nature Neuroscience, 5,* 76–80.

Newman, B., O'Grady, M. A., Ryan, C. S., & Hemmes, N. S. (1993). Pavlovian conditioning of the tickle response of human subjects: Temporal and delay conditioning. *Perceptual and Motor Skills, 77,* 779–785.

Newman, J., & Layton, B. D. (1984). Overjustification: A self-perception perspective. *Personality and Social Psychology Bulletin, 10,* 419–425.

Nezlek, J. B., & Gable, S. L. (2001). Depression as a moderator of relationships between positive daily events and day-to-day psychological adjustment. *Personality and Social Psychology Bulletin, 27,* 1692–1704.

Nezu, A. M., Nezu, C. M., & Blissett, S. E. (1988). Sense of humor as a moderator of the relation between stressful events and psychological distress: A prospective analysis. *Journal of Personality and Social Psychology, 54,* 520–525.

Ng, W.-J., & Lindsay, R. C. L. (1994). Cross-race facial recognition: Failure of the contact hypothesis. *Journal of Cross-Cultural Psychology, 25,* 217–232.

NICHD Early Child Care Research Network (1997). The effects of infant child care on infant-mother attachment security: Results of the NICHD study of early child care. *Child Development, 68,* 860–879.

Nicholls, J. G. (1972). Creativity in the person who will never produce anything original and useful: The concept of creativity as a normally distributed trait. *American Psychologist, 27,* 717–727.

Nicholls, J. G. (1984). Achievement motivation: Conceptions of ability, subjective experience, task choice, and performance. *Psychological Review, 91,* 328–346.

Nichols, A. L., & Maner, J. K. (2008). The good-subject effect: Investigating participant demand characteristics. *Journal of General Psychology, 135,* 151–165.

Nichols, M. P., & Efran, J. S. (1985). Catharsis in psychotherapy: A new perspective. *Psychotherapy, 22,* 46–58.

Nicholson, N., Cole, S. G., & Rocklin, T. (1985). Conformity in the Asch situation: A comparison between contemporary British and U.S. university students. *British Journal of Social Psychology, 24,* 59–63.

Nicholson, T. R., Aybek, S., Kempton, M. J., Daly, E. M., Murphy, D. G., David, D. G., & Kanaan, R. A. (2014). A structural MRI study of motor conversion disorder: evidence of reduction in thalamic volume. *Journal of Neurology and Neuropsychiatry, 85,* 227–229.

Nickerson, R. S., & Adams, M. J. (1979). Long-term memory for a common object. *Cognitive Psychology, 11,* 287–307.

Nicol, S. E., & Gottesman, I. I. (1983). Clues to the genetics and neurobiology of schizophrenia. *American Scientist, 71,* 398–404.

Nicoll, R. A., & Madison, D. V. (1982). General anesthetics hyperpolarize neurons in the vertebrate nervous system. *Science, 217,* 1055–1057.

Nicolson, P. (2002). Psychology, evolution, and gender: Editorial. *Psychology, Evolution, and Gender, 4,* 1–2.

Nides, M. A., Rakos, R. F., Gonzales, D., & Murray, R. P. (1995). Predictors of initial smoking cessation and relapse through the first 2 years of the Lung Health Study. *Journal of Consulting and Clinical Psychology, 63,* 60–69.

Nides, M., Rand, C., Dolce, J., & Murray, R. (1994). Weight gain as a function of smoking cessation and 2-mg nicotine gum use among middle-aged smokers with mild lung impairment in the first 2 years of the Lung Health Study. *Health Psychology, 13,* 354–361.

Niedeggen, M., & Roesler, F. (1999). N400 effects reflect activation spread during retrieval of arithmetic facts. *Psychological Science, 10,* 271–276.

Nielsen, T. A. (1993). Changes in the kinesthetic content of dreams following somatosensory stimulation of leg muscles during REM sleep. *Dreaming: Journal of the Association for the Study of Dreams, 3,* 99–113.

Niemann, Y. F., O'Connor, E., & McClorie, R. (1998). Intergroup stereotypes of working class Blacks and Whites: Implications for stereotype threat. *Western Journal of Black Studies, 22,* 103–108.

Niles, S. (1998). Achievement goals and means: A cultural comparison. *Journal of Cross-Cultural Psychology, 29,* 656–667.

Nisbett, R. E., Aronson, J., Blair, C., Dickens, W., Flynn, J., Halpern, D. F., & Turkheimer, E. (2012). Intelligence: New findings and theoretical developments. *American Psychologist, 67,* 130–159.

Nisbett, R. E., Peng, K., Choi, I., & Norenzayan, A. (2001). Culture and systems of thought: Holistic versus analytic cognition. *Psychological Review, 108,* 291–310.

Nisbett, R. E., & Ross, L. (1980). *Human inference: Strategies and shortcomings of social judgment.* Englewood Cliffs, NJ: Prentice-Hall.

Nishikawa, T., Okuda, J., Mizuta, I., Ohno, K., Jamshidi, J., Tokunaga, H., . . . Takeda, M. (2001). Conflict of intentions due to callosal disconnection. *Journal of Neurology, Neurosurgery, and Psychiatry, 71,* 462–471.

Nishimura, H., Hashikawa, K., Doi, K., Iwaki, T., Watanabe, Y., Kusuoka, H., Nishimura, T., & Kubo, T. (1999). Sign language "heard" in the auditory cortex. *Nature, 397,* 116.

Nishith, P., Mechanic, M. B., & Resick, P. A. (2000). Prior interpersonal trauma: The contribution to current PTSD symptoms in female rape victims. *Journal of Abnormal Psychology, 109,* 20–25.

Nissen, M. J., Knopman, D. S., & Schacter, D. L. (1987). Neurochemical dissociation of memory systems. *Neurology, 37,* 789–794.

Niu, W., & Sternberg, R. (2002). Contemporary studies on the concept of creativity. The East and the West. *Journal of Creative Behavior, 36,* 269–288.

Nolen-Hoeksema, S. (2001). Gender differences in depression. *Current Directions in Psychological Science, 10,* 173–176.

Nolen-Hoeksema, S. (2012). Emotion regulation and psychopathology: The role of gender. *Annual Review of Clinical Psychology, 8,* 61–87.

Nolen-Hoeksema, S., & Morrow, J. (1993). Effects of rumination and distraction on naturally occurring depressed mood. *Cognition and Emotion, 7,* 561–570.

Nolen-Hoeksema, S., Larson, J., & Grayson, C. (1999). Explaining the gender difference in depression. *Journal of Personality and Social Psychology, 77,* 1061–1072.

Nopoulos, P., Torres, I., Flaum, M., & Andreasen, N. C. (1995). Brain morphology in first-episode schizophrenia. *American Journal of Psychiatry, 152,* 1721–1723.

Norcross, J. C., Strausser, D. J., & Faltus, F. J. (1988). The therapist's therapist. *American Journal of Psychotherapy, 42,* 53–66.

Nordblom, J. Persson, J. K. E., Svensson, M.,.& Mattsson, P. (2009). Peripheral nerve grafts in a spinal cord prosthesis result in regeneration and motor evoked potentials following spinal cord resection. *Restorative Neurology and Neuroscience 27,* 285–295.

Nordstrom, R., Lorenz, P., & Hall, R. V. (1990). A review of public posting of performance feedback in work settings. *Journal of Organizational Behavior Management, 11,* 101–123.

Norenzayan, A., Choi, I., & Nisbett, R. E. (2002). Cultural similarities and differences in social inferences: Evidence from behavioral predictions and lay theories of behavior. *Personality and Social Psychology Bulletin, 28,* 109–120.

Norlander, T., Bergman, H., & Archer, T. (1999). Primary process in competitive archery performance: Effects of flotation REST. *Journal of Applied Sport Psychology, 11,* 194–209.

Norlander, T., Kjellgren, A., & Archer, T. (2000–2001). The experience of flotation-rest as a function of setting and previous experience of altered state of consciousness. *Imagination, Cognition & Personality, 20,* 161–178.

Norman, K. A., & O'Reilly, R. C. (2003). Modeling hippocampal and neocortical contributions to recognition memory: A complementary-learningsystems approach. *Psychological Review, 110,* 611–646.

Norman, R. M., & Malla, A. K. (1993). Stressful life events and schizophrenia: I. A review of the research. *British Journal of Psychiatry, 162,* 161–166.

Norris, F. H., & Uhl, G. A. (1993). Chronic stress as a mediator of acute stress: The case of Hurricane Hugo. *Journal of Applied Social Psychology, 23,* 1263–1284.

Norris, N. P. (1978). Fragile subjects. *American Psychologist, 33,* 962–963.

Northrup, T., & Mulligan, N. (2013). Conceptual implicit memory in advertising research. *Applied Cognitive Psychology, 27,* 127–136.

Norton, E. M., Durlak, J. A., & Richards, M. H. (1989). Peer knowledge of and reactions to adolescent suicide. *Journal of Youth and Adolescence, 18,* 427–437.

Nosofsky, R. M. (1991). Relation between the rational model and the context model of categorization. *Psychological Science, 2,* 416–421.

Notz, W. W. (1975). Work motivation and the negative effects of extrinsic rewards: A review with implications for theory and practice. *American Psychologist, 30,* 884–891.

Novick, L. R., & Sherman, S. J. (2003). On the nature of insight solutions: Evidence from skill differences in anagram solution. *Quarterly Journal of Experimental Psychology: Human Experimental Psychology, 56A,* 351–382.

Nowicki, S., & Duke, M. P. (1992). The association of children's nonverbal decoding abilities with their popularity, locus of control, and academic achievement. *Journal of Genetic Psychology, 153,* 385–393.

Noyes, R., Jr., Stuart, S., Longley, S. L., Langbehn, D. R., & Happel, R. L. (2002). Hypochondriasis and fear of death. *Journal of Nervous and Mental Disease, 190,* 503–509.

Nunn, J., & Hodges, H. (1994). Cognitive deficits induced by global cerebral ischaemia: Relationship to brain damage and reversal by transplants. *Behavioral Brain Research, 65,* 1–31.

Nuño, V. L., Zhang, Q., Harris, R. B., Wilkinson- Lee, A. M., & Wilhem, M. S. (2011). Smoking susceptibility among students followed from grade six to eight. *Addictive Behaviors, 36,* 1261–1266.

Nutt, D. J. (2002). The neuropharmacology of serotonin and noradrenaline in depression. *International Clinical Psychopharmacology, 17,* S1–S12.

Nutt, D. J., Ballenger, J. C., Sheehan, D., & Wittchen, H.-U. (2002). Generalized anxiety disorder: Comorbidity, comparative biology, and treatment. *International Journal of Neuropsychopharmacology, 5,* 315–325.

Nyberg, L. (2002). Levels of processing: A view from functional brain imaging. *Memory, 10,* 345–348.

O'Brien, L. T., & Crandall, C. S. (2003). Stereotype threat and arousal: Effects on women's math performance. *Personality and Social Psychology Bulletin, 29,* 782–789.

O'Carroll, R. E., Masterton, G., Dougall, N., Ebmeier, K. P., & Goodwin, G. M. (1995). The neuropsychiatric sequelae of mercury poisoning: The Mad Hatter's disease revisited. *British Journal of Psychiatry, 167,* 95–98.

O'Connell, A. N. (1990). Karen Horney (1885–1952). In A. N. O'Connell & N. F. Russo (Eds.), *Women in psychology: A bio-bibliographic sourcebook* (pp. 184–185). New York: Greenwood Press.

O'Connell, A. N., & Russo, N. F. (Eds.). (1990). *Women in psychology: A bio-bibliographic sourcebook.* New York: Greenwood.

O'Connor, D. B., & Shimizu, M. (2002). Sense of personal control, stress, and coping style: A cross-cultural study. *Stress and Health, 18,* 173–183.

O'Connor, F. L. (1998). The role of serotonin and dopamine in schizophrenia. *Journal of the American Psychiatric Nurses Association, 4,* S30–S34.

O'Connor, P. J., Lewis, R. D., & Kirchner, E. M. (1995). Eating disorder symptoms in female college gymnasts. *Medicine and Science in Sports and Exercise, 27,* 550–555.

O'Donnell, I., Farmer, R., & Catalan, J. (1993). Suicide notes. *British Journal of Psychiatry, 163,* 45–48.

O'Halloran, C. M., & Altmaier, E. M. (1995). The efficacy of preparation for surgery and invasive medical procedures. *Patient Education and Counseling, 25,* 9–16.

O'Leary, A. (1985). Self-efficacy and health. *Behaviour Research and Therapy, 23,* 437–451.

O'Leary, K. D., & Smith, D. A. (1991). Marital interactions. *Annual Review of Psychology, 42,* 191–212.

O'Malley, R. C., Wallauer, W., Murray, C. M., & Goodall, J. (2012). The appearance and spread of ant fishing among the Kasekela chimpanzees of Gombe: A possible case of intercommunity cultural transmission. *Current Anthropology, 53,* 650–663.

O'Neil, W. M. (1995). American behaviorism: A historical and critical analysis. *Theory and Psychology, 5,* 285–305.

O'Neill, S. K. (2003). African American women and eating disturbances: A meta-analysis. *Journal of Black Psychology, 29,* 3–16.

O'Shea, R. P., Govan, D. G., & Sekuler, R. (1997). Blur and contrast as pictorial depth cues. *Perception, 26,* 599–612.

Oberlander, J. G., & Henderson, L. P. (2012). The *Sturm und Drang* of anabolic steroid use: Angst, anxiety, and aggression. *Trends in Neurosciences, 35,* 382–392.

Obozova, T. A., Smirnova, A. A., & Zorina, Z. A. (2011). Observational learnng in a glaucous-winged gull natural colony. *International Journal of Comparative Psychology,24,* 226–234.

Ochs, E. P. P., & Binik, Y. M. (1998). A sex-expert computer system helps couples learn more about their sexual relationship. *Journal of Sex Education and Therapy, 23,* 145–155.

Ockene, J. K., Mermelstein, R. J., Bonollo, D. S., Emmons, K. M., Perkins, K. A., Voorhees, C. C., & Hollis, J. F. (2000). Relapse and maintenance issues for smoking cessation. *Health Psychology, 19,* 17–31.

Oden, G. C. (1984). Dependence, independence, and emergence of word features. *Journal of Experimental Psychology: Human Perception and Performance, 10,* 394–405.

Oden, M. H. (1968). The fulfillment of promise: 40-year followup of the Terman gifted group. *Genetic Psychology Monographs, 77,* 3–93.

Odum, L. E., O'Dell, K. A., & Schepers, J. S. (2012). Electronic cigarettes: Do they have a role in smoking cessation? *Journal of Pharmacy Practice, 25,* 611–614.

Ogden, C. L., Carroll, M. D., Kit, B. K., & Flegal, K. M. (2012). *Prevalence of obesity in the United States 2009–2010. NCHS Data Brief, no. 82.* Hyattsville, MD: National Center for Health Statistics.

Ogilvie, R. D., McDonagh, D. M., Stone, S. N., & Wilkinson, R. T. (1988). Eye movements and the detection of sleep onset. *Psychophysiology, 25,* 81–91.

Ohayon, M. M., Guilleminault, C., & Priest, R. G. (1999). Night terrors, sleepwalking, and confusional arousals in the general population. *Journal of Clinical Psychiatry, 60,* 268–276.

Öhman, A. (2009). Of snakes and faces: An evolutionary perspective on the psychology of fear. *Scandinavian Journal of Psychology, 50,* 543–552.

Oishi, S. (2002). The experiencing and remembering of well-being: A cross-cultural analysis. *Personality and Social Psychology Bulletin, 28,* 1398–1406.

Okano, H., Sakaguchi, M., Ohki, K., Suzuki, N., & Sawamoto, K. (2007). Regeneration of the central nervous system using endogenous repair mechanisms. *Journal of Neurochemistry, 102,* 1459–1465.

Oku, Y., & Okada, M. (2008). Periodic breathing and dysphagia associated with a localized lateral medullary infarction. *Respirology, 13,* 608–610.

Okwumabua, T. M. (1985). Psychological and physical contributions to marathon performance: An exploratory investigation. *Journal of Sport Behavior, 8,* 163–171.

Oldehinkel, A. J., Ormel, J., Bosch, N. M., Bouma, E. M. C., Van Roon, A. M., Rosmalen, J. G. M., & Riese, H. (2011). Stressed out? Associations between perceived and physiological stress responses in adolescents: The TRAILS study. *Psychophysiology, 48,* 441–452.

Olds, J. (1956, October). Pleasure centers in the brain. *Scientific American,* pp. 105–116.

Olds, J., & Milner, P. (1954). Positive reinforcement produced by electrical stimulations of septal area and other regions of rat brain. *Journal of Comparative and Physiological Psychology, 47,* 419–427.

Oliver, M. B., & Hyde, J. S. (1993). Gender differences in sexuality: A meta-analysis. *Psychological Bulletin, 114,* 29–51.

Oller, D. K., & Eilers, R. E. (1988). The role of audition in infant babbling. *Child Development, 59,* 441–449.

Olmo, R. J., & Stevens, G. L. (1984, August). Chess champs: Introverts at play. *Psychology Today,* pp. 72, 74.

Olsen, S., Smith, S. S., Oei, T. P. S., & Douglas, J. (2012). Motivational interviewing (MINT) improves continuous positive airway pressure (CPAP) acceptance and adherence: A randomized controlled trial. *Journal of Consulting and Clinical Psychology, 80,* 151–163.

Olson, J. K. (1995). Relationships between nurse-expressed empathy, patient-perceived empathy and patient distress. *IMAGE: Journal of Nursing Scholarship, 27,* 317–322.

Olson, M. A., & Fazio, R. H. (2002). Implicit acquisition and manifestation of classically conditioned attitudes. *Social Cognition, 20,* 89–104.

Oman, R. F., & King, A. C. (2000). The effect of life events and exercise program formation on the adoption and maintenance of exercise behavior. *Health Psychology, 19,* 605–612.

Ono, Y., & Janca, A. (1999). Rethinking somatoform disorders. *Journal of Psychosomatic Research, 46,* 537–539.

Onstad, S., Skre, I., Torgerson, S., & Kringlen, E. (1991). Twin concordance for *DSM-III-R* schizophrenia. *Acta Psychiatrica Scandinavica, 83,* 395–401.

Oosterveld, W. J. (1987). The combined effect of Cinnarizine and domperidone on vestibular susceptibility. *Aviation, Space, and Environmental Medicine, 58,* 218–223.

Oppliger, P. A., & Sherblom, J. C. (1992). Humor: Incongruity, disparagement, and David Letterman. *Communication Research Reports, 9,* 99–108.

Orange, C. (1997). Gifted students and perfectionism. *Roeper Review, 20,* 39–41.

Orenstein, P. A., Ceci, S. J., & Loftus, E. F. (1998). Adult recollections of childhood abuse: Cognitive and developmental perspectives. *Psychology, Public Policy, and Law, 4,* 1025–1051.

Orne, M. T. (1951). The mechanisms of hypnotic age regression: An experimental study. *Journal of Abnormal and Social Psychology, 46,* 213–225.

Orne, M. T., & Evans, F. J. (1965). Social control in the psychological experiment: Antisocial behavior and hypnosis. *Journal of Personality and Social Psychology, 1,* 189–200.

Osawa, A., & Maeshima, S. (2010). Family participation can improve unilateral spatial neglect in patients with acute right hemispheric stroke. *European Neurology, 63,* 170–175.

Osberg, T. M. (1993). Psychology is not just common sense: An introductory psychology demonstration. *Teaching of Psychology, 20,* 110–111.

Osiel, S., Golombek, D. A., & Ralph, M. R. (1998). Conservation of locomotor behavior in the golden hamster: Effects of light cycle and a circadian period mutation. *Physiology and Behavior, 65,* 123–131.

Oswald, D. L., & Harvey, R. D. (2003). A Q-methodological study of women's subjective perspectives on mathematics. *Sex Roles, 49,* 133–142.

Oudiette, D., & Paller, K. A. (2013). Upgrading the sleeping brain with targeted memory reactivation. *Trends in Cognitive Sciences, 17,* 142–149.

Ouimet, J., & De Man, A. F. (1998). Correlates of attitudes toward the application of eugenics to the treatment of people with intellectual disabilities. *Social Behavior and Personality, 26,* 69–74.

Overton, D. A. (1991). Historical context of state dependent learning and discriminative drug effects. *Behavioural Pharmacology, 2,* 253–264.

Owen, P. R., & Laurel-Seller, E. (2000). Weight and shape ideals: Thin is dangerously in. *Journal of Applied Social Psychology, 30,* 979–990.

Ozbay, H., Goka, E., Ozturk, E., & Gungor, S. (1993). Therapeutic factors in an adolescent psychodrama group. *Journal of Group Psychotherapy, Psychodrama,and Sociometry, 46,* 3–11.

Pacini, R., Muir, F., & Epstein, S. (1998). Depressive realism from the perspective of cognitive-experiential self-theory. *Journal of Personality and Social Psychology, 74,* 1056–1068.

Paddock, J. R., & Nowicki, S. (1986). Paralanguage and the interpersonal impact of dysphoria: It's not what you say but how you say it. *Social Behavior and Personality, 14,* 29–44.

Padian, K. (2008). Darwin's enduring legacy. *Nature, 451,* 632–634.

Page, S. J., Martin, S. B., & Wayda, V. K. (2001). Attitudes toward seeking sport psychology consultation among wheelchair basketball athletes. *Adapted Physical Activity Quarterly, 18,* 183–192.

Page-Voth, V., & Graham, S. (1999). Effects of goal setting and strategy use on the writing performance and self-efficacy of students with writing and learning problems. *Journal of Educational Psychology, 91,* 230–240.

Paik, H., & Comstock, G. (1994). The effects of television violence on antisocial behavior: A meta-analysis. *Communication Research, 21,* 516–546.

Paikoff, R. L., & Brooks-Gunn, J. (1991). Do parent-child relationships change during puberty? *Psychological Bulletin, 110,* 47–66.

Palaniappan, A. K., & Torrance, E. P. (2001). Comparison between regular and streamlined versions of scoring of Torrance Tests of Creative Thinking. *Korean Journal of Thinking and Problem Solving, 11,* 5–7.

Palencik, J. T. (2007). William James and the psychology of emotion: From 1884 to the present. *Transactions of the Charles S. Peirce Society, 43,* 769–786.

Palermo, G. B. (2002). Criminal profiling: The uniqueness of the killer. *International Journal of Offender Therapy and Comparative Criminology, 46,* 383–385.

Pallast, E. G. M., Jongbloet, P. H., Straatman, H. M., & Zielhuis, G. A. (1994). Excess seasonality of births among patients with schizophrenia and seasonal ovopathy. *Schizophrenia Bulletin, 20,* 269–276.

Palmer, J. A., Honorton, C., & Utts, J. (1989). Reply to the National Research Council Study on parapsychology. *Journal of the American Society for Psychical Research, 83,* 31–49.

Pan, Y., Chen, M., Yin, J., An, X., Zhang, X., Lu, Y., . . . Wang, W. (2012). Equivalent representation of real and illusory contours in macque V4. *The Journal of Neuroscience, 32,* 6760–6770.

Panksepp, J., & Panksepp, J. B. (2013). Toward a cross-species understanding of empathy. *Trends in Neurosciences, 36,* 489–496.

Pantev, C., Roberts, L. E., Schulz, M., Engelien, A., & Ross, B. (2001). Timbre-specific enhancement of auditory cortical representations in musicians. *Neuroreport: For Rapid Communication of Neuroscience Research, 12,* 169–174.

Paradis, M. (1998). The other side of language: Pragmatic competence. *Journal of Neurolinguistics, 11,* 1–10.

Pardo, C. A., Vargas, D. L., & Zimmerman, A. W. (2005). Immunity, neuroglia and neuroinflammation in autism. *International Reviews of Psychiatry, 17,* 485–495.

Pare, D., Collins, D. R., & Guillaume Pelletier, J. (2002). Amygdala oscillations and the consolidation of emotional memories. *Trends in Cognitive Sciences, 6,* 306–314.

Paris, J. (1996). Cultural factors in the emergence of borderline pathology. *Psychiatry: Interpersonal and Biological Processes, 59,* 185–192.

Paris, J. (1998). Personality disorders in sociocultural perspective. *Journal of Personality Disorders, 12,* 289–301.

Park, D. C., Smith, A. D., & Cavanaugh, J. C. (1990). Metamemories of memory researchers. *Memory and Cognition, 18,* 321–327.

Park, R. L. (2008). Fraud in science. *Social Research, 75,* 1135–1150.

Park, W. W. (2000). A comprehensive empirical investigation of the relationship among variables of the groupthink model. *Journal of Organizational Behavior, 21,* 873–887.

Parker, A., & Gellatly, A. (1997). Moveable cues: A practical method for reducing context-dependent forgetting. *Applied Cognitive Psychology, 11,* 163–173.

Parker, K. C. H., Hanson, R. K., & Hunsley, J. (1988). MMPI, Rorschach, and WAIS: A meta-analytic comparison of reliability, stability, and validity. *Psychological Bulletin, 103,* 367–373.

Parker, S. (1990). A note on the growth of the use of statistical tests in perception and psychophysics. *Bulletin of the Psychonomic Society, 28,* 565–566.

Parker, W. D. (1996). Psychological adjustment in mathematically gifted students. *Gifted Child Quarterly, 40,* 154–157.

Parkovnick, S. (2000). Contextualizing Floyd Allport's social psychology. *Journal of the History of the Behavioral Sciences, 36,* 429–441.

Parra, A. (1997). Parapsychological developments in Argentina (1990–1995). *Journal of the American Society for Psychical Research, 91,* 103–109.

Parron, D. L. (1997). The fusion of cultural horizons: Cultural influences on the assessment of psychopathology on children. *Applied Developmental Science, 1,* 156–159.

Parrott, A. C. (1995). Smoking cessation leads to reduced stress, but why? *International Journal of the Addictions, 30,* 1509–1516.

Parsons, M. W., & Gold, P. E. (1992). Glucose enhancement of memory in elderly humans: An inverted-U dose-response curve. *Neurobiology of Aging, 13,* 401–404.

Partala, T., & Surakka, V. (2003). Pupil size variation as an indication of affective processing. *International Journal of Human-Computer Studies, 59,* 185–198.

Parten, M. B. (1932). Social participation among preschool children. *Journal of Abnormal and Social Psychology, 27,* 243–269.

Pates, J., Maynard, I., & Westbury, T. (2001). An investigation into the effects of hypnosis on basketball performance. *Journal of Applied Sport Psychology, 31,* 84–102.

Patra, J., & Rath, P. K. (2000). Computer and pedagogy: Replacing telling with computer assisted instruction for teaching arithmetic skills to mentally retarded children. *Journal of Adolescent Health, 26,* 244–251.

Pattatucci, A. M. L., & Hamer, D. H. (1995). Development and familiality of sexual orientation in females. *Behavior Genetics, 25,* 407–420.

Patterson, D. R., Adcock, R. J., & Bombardier, C. H. (1997). Factors predicting hypnotic analgesia in clinical burn pain. *International Journal of Clinical and Experimental Hypnosis, 45,* 377–395.

Patterson, D. R., & Jensen, M. P. (2003). Hypnosis and clinical pain. *Psychological Bulletin, 129,* 495–521.

Patterson, F. G., Patterson, L. H., & Brentari, D. K. (1987). Language in child, chimp, and gorilla. *American Psychologist, 42,* 270–272.

Patton, J. E., Routh, D. K., & Stinard, T. A. (1986). Where do children study? Behavioral observations. *Bulletin of the Psychonomic Society, 24,* 439–440.

Paul, M. A., Miller, J. C., Gray, G. W., Love, R. J., Lieberman, H. R., & Arendt, J. (2010). Melatonin treatment for eastward and westward travel preparation. *Psychopharmacology, 208,* 377–386.

Paulsen, F. (1899/1963). *Immanuel Kant: His life and doctrine.* New York: Ungar.

Paunonen, S. V. (2003). Big Five factors of personality and replicated predictions of behavior. *Journal of Personality and Social Psychology, 84,* 411–422.

Paunovic, N. (2003). Prolonged exposure counterconditioning as a treatment for chronic posttraumatic stress disorder. *Journal of Anxiety Disorders, 17,* 479–499.

Pavlov, I. P. (1928). *Lectures on conditioned reflexes.* New York: Liveright.

Pawlak, J. L., & Klein, H. A. (1997). Parental conflict and self-esteem: The rest of the story. *Journal of Genetic Psychology, 158,* 303–313.

Pear, J. J., & Crone-Todd, D. E. (1999). Personalized system of instruction in cyberspace. *Journal of Applied Behavior Analysis, 32,* 205–209.

Pearce, J. M. S. (2007). Corpus callosum. *European Neurology, 57,* 249–250.

Pearce, J. M. S. (2009). Marie-Jean-Pierre Flourens (1794–1867) and cortical localization. *European Neurology, 61,* 311–314.

Pearson, E. S. (2012). Goal setting as a health behavior change strategy in overweight and obese adults: A systematic literature review examining intervention components. *Patient Education and Counseling, 87,* 32–42.

Pedersen, W., & Skrondal, A. (1999). Ecstasy and new patterns of drug use: A normal population study. *Addiction, 94,* 1695–1706.

Peeters, M. C. W., Buunk, B. P., & Schaufeli, W. B. (1995). A micro-analysis exploration of the cognitive appraisal of daily stressful events at work: The role of controllability. *Anxiety, Stress, and Coping: An International Journal, 8,* 127–139.

Peisner-Feinberg, E. S., Burchinal, M. R., Clifford, R. M., Culkin, M. L., Howes, C., Kagan, S. L., & Yazejian, N. (2001). The relation of preschool child-care quality to children's cognitive and social developmental trajectories through second grade. *Child Development, 72,* 1534–1553.

Pejovic, S., Basta, M., Vgontzas, A. N., Kritikou, I., Shaffer, M. L., Tsaoussoglou, M., . . . Chrousos, G. P. (2013). Effects of recovery sleep after one work week of mild sleep restriction on interleukin-6 and cortisolsecretion and daytime sleepiness and performance. *American Journal of Physiology—Endocrinology and Metabolism, 305,* 890–896.

Pell, M. D. (1998). Recognition of prosody following unilateral brain lesion: Influence of functional and structural attributes of prosodic contours. *Neuropsychologia, 36,* 701–715.

Pell, M. D., Jaywant, A., Monetta, L., & Kotz, S. A. (2011). Emotional speech processing: Disentangling the effects of prosody and semantic cues. *Cognition and Emotion, 25,* 834–853.

Peltzer, K., Mashego, T. A., & Mabeba, M. (2003). Occupational stress and burnout among South African medical practitioners. *Psychology and Health, 18,* 677–684.

Penfield, W. (1975). *The mystery of the mind.* Princeton, NJ: Princeton University Press.

Pengilly, J. W., & Dowd, E. T. (2000). Hardiness and social support as moderators of stress. *Journal of Clinical Psychology, 56,* 813–820.

Penido, A. B., Rezende, G. H., Abreu, R. V., Oliveira, A. C., Guidine, P. A., Schenatto-Pereira G., . . . Moraes, M. F. (2012). Malnutrition during central nervous system growth and development impairs permanently the subcortical auditory pathway. *Nutritional Neuroscience, 15,* 31–36.

Pennebaker, J. W., & Watson, D. (1988). Blood pressure estimation and beliefs among normotensives and hypertensives. *Health Psychology, 7,* 309–328.

Pepitone, A. (1981). Lessons from the history of social psychology. *American Psychologist, 36,* 972–985.

Peregrine, P. N., Ember, C. R., & Ember, M. (2003). Cross-cultural evaluation of predicted associations between race and behavior. *Evolution and Human Behavior, 24,* 357–364.

Perelman, M. A. (1998). Commentary: Pharmacological agents for erectile dysfunction and the human sexual response cycle. *Journal of Sex and Marital Therapy, 24,* 309–312.

Peretz, I., Kolinsky, R., Tramo, M., & Labrecque, R. (1994). Functional dissociations following bilateral lesions of auditory cortex. *Brain, 117,* 1283–1301.

Perfetto, F., Piluso, A., Cagnacci, A., & Tarquini, R. (2002). Circadian pattern of serum leptin and beta-endorphin levels in obese and non obese women. *Biological Rhythm Research, 33,* 287–302.

Perl, D. P. (2010). Neuropathology of Alzheimer's disease. *Mount Sinai Journal of Medicine, 77,* 32–42.

Perlman, D. (1999, October 15). Odds on the big one. *The San Francisco Chronicle,* p. A1.

Perlmutter, D. D. (2002). On incongruities and logical inconsistencies in humor: The delicate balance. *Humor: International Journal of Humor Research, 15,* 155–168.

Perls, F. (1972). Interview with Frederick Perls. In A. Bry (Ed.), *Inside psychotherapy* (pp. 58–70). New York: Basic Books.

Perls, F. (1973). *The Gestalt approach and eyewitness to therapy.* Palo Alto, CA: Science & Behavior Books.

Perosa, S. L., & Perosa, L. M. (1993). Relationships among a Minuchin's structural family model, identity achievement, and coping style. *Journal of Counseling Psychology, 40,* 479–489.

Perri, M. G., Anton, S. D., Durning, P. E., Ketterson, T. U., Sydeman, S. J., Berlant, N. E., . . . Martin, A. D. (2002). Adherence to exercise prescriptions: Effects of prescribing moderate versus higher levels of intensity and frequency. *Health Psychology, 21,* 452–458.

Perri, M. G., Martin, A. D., Leermakers, E. A., & Sears, S. F. (1997). Effects of group-versus home-based exercise in the treatment of obesity. *Journal of Consulting and Clinical Psychology, 65,* 278–285.

Perronia, B. F., Tessitorea, C. A., Cibellid, G., Lupoa, C., D'Artibalea. E., Cortisa, E. C., . . . Capranica, L. (2009). Effects of simulated firefighting on the responses of salivary cortisol, alpha-amylase and psychological variables. *Ergonomics, 52,* 484–491.

Persad, E. (1990). Electroconvulsive therapy in depression. *Canadian Journal of Psychiatry, 35,* 175–182.

Person, C., Tracy, M., & Galea, S. (2006). Risk factors for depression after a disaster. *Journal of Nervous and Mental Disease, 194,* 659–666.

Pert, C. B., & Snyder, S. H. (1973). Opiate receptor: Demonstration in nervous tissue. *Science, 179,* 1031–1034.

Peters, M. L., Godaert, G. L., Ballieux, R. E., & Heijnen, C. J. (2003). Moderation of physiological stress responses by personality traits and daily hassles: Less flexibility of immune system responses. *Biological Psychology, 65,* 21–48.

Peters, M. L., Godaert, G. L., Ballieux, R. E., van Vliet, M., Willemsen, J. J., Sweep, F. C. G. J., & Heijnen, C. J. (1998). Cardiovascular and endocrine responses to experimental stress: Effects of mental effort and controllability. *Psychoneuroendocrinology, 23,* 1–17.

Peters, R., & McGee, R. (1982). Cigarette smoking and state-dependent memory. *Psychopharmacology, 76,* 232–235.

Peters, R. D. (1994). Better beginnings, Better futures: A community-based approach to primary prevention. *Canadian Journal of Community Mental Health, 13,* 183–188.

Petersen, J. L., & Hyde, J. S. (2010). A meta-analytic review of research on gender differences in sexuality: 1993–2007. *Psychological Bulletin, 136,* 21–38.

Peterson, B. E., & Gerstein, E. D. (2005). Fighting and flying: Archival analysis of threat, authoritarianism, and the North American comic book. *Political Psychology, 26,* 887–904.

Peterson, C., & Barrett, L. C. (1987). Explanatory style and academic performance among university freshmen. *Journal of Personality and Social Psychology, 53,* 603–607.

Peterson, C., Seligman, M. E. P., & Vaillant, G. E. (1988). Pessimistic explanatory style is a risk factor for physical illness: A 35-year longitudinal study. *Journal of Personality and Social Psychology, 55,* 23–27.

Peterson, C., Seligman, M. E. P., Yurko, K. H., Martin, L. R., & Friedman, H. S. (1998). Catastrophizing and untimely death. *Psychological Science, 9,* 127–130.

Peterson, C., & Vaidya, R. S. (2001). Explanatory style, expectations, and depressive symptoms. *Personality and Individual Differences, 31,* 1217–1223.

Peterson, C. C. (1996). The ticking of the social clock: Adults' beliefs about the timing of transition events. *International Journal of Aging and Human Development, 42,* 189–203.

Peterson, I. (1983). Playing chess bit by bit. *Science News, 124,* 236–237.

Peterson, J. L., & Hyde, J. S. (2010). A meta-analytic review of research on gender differences in sexuality: 1993–2007. *Psychological Bulletin, 136,* 21–38.

Peterson, L. R., & Peterson, M. (1959). Short-term retention of individual verbal items. *Journal of Experimental Psychology, 58,* 193–198.

Peterson, M. A., & Gibson, B. S. (1994). Must figure-ground organization precede object recognition? An assumption in peril. *Psychological Science, 5,* 253–259.

Petitto, L. A., Holowka, S., Sergio, L. E., & Ostry, D. (2001). Language rhythms in baby hand movements. *Nature, 413,* 35–36.

Petrie, K. J., Booth, R. J., & Pennebaker, J. W. (1998). The immunological effects of thought suppression. *Journal of Personality and Social Psychology, 75,* 1264–1272.

Pettersen, L., Yonas, A., & Fisch, R. O. (1980). The development of blinking in response to impending collision in preterm, full-term, and postterm infants. *Infant Behavior and Development, 3,* 155–165.

Pettijohn, T. F., II. (1996). Perceived happiness of college students measured by Maslow's hierarchy of needs. *Psychological Reports, 79,* 759–762.

Petty, R. E., & Cacioppo, J. T. (1990). Involvement and persuasion: Tradition versus integration. *Psychological Bulletin, 107,* 367–374.

Petty, R. E., Cacioppo, J. T., & Goldman, R. (1981). Personal involvement as a determinant of argument-based persuasion. *Journal of Personality and Social Psychology, 41,* 847–855.

Pfeffer, K., & Barnecutt, P. (1996). Children's auditory perception of movement of traffic sounds. *Child: Care, Health & Development, 27,* 129–137.

Phelps, E. A., & LeDoux J. E. (2005). Contributions of the amygdala to emotion processing: From animal models to human behavior. *Neuron, 48,* 175–187.

Phillips, R. D., Wagner, S. H., Fells, C. A., & Lynch, M. (1990). Do infants recognize emotion in facial expressions? Categorical and "metaphorical" evidence. *Infant Behavior and Development, 13,* 71–84.

Phinney, J. S. (1990). Ethnic identity in adolescents and adults: Review of research. *Psychological Bulletin, 108,* 499–514.

Phinney, J. S., Cantu, C. L., & Kurtz, D. A. (1997). Ethnic and American identity as predictors of self-esteem among African American, Latino, and White adolescents. *Journal of Youth and Adolescence, 26,* 165–185.

Phinney, J. S., Ong, A., & Madden, T. (2000). Cultural values and intergenerational value discrepancies in immigrant and nonimmigrant families. *Child Development, 71,* 528–539.

Phinney, J. S., & Ong, A. D. (2002). Adolescent-parent disagreements and life satisfaction in families from Vietnamese- and European-American backgrounds. *International Journal of Behavioral Development, 26,* 556–561.

Piaget, J. (1932). *The moral judgment of the child.* New York: Harcourt, Brace & World.

Piaget, J. (1952). *The origins of intelligence in children.* New York: International Universities Press.

Piat, M. (2000). The NIMBY phenomenon: Community residents' concerns about housing for deinstitutionalized people. *Health and Social Work, 25,* 127–138.

Pichika, R., Buchsbaum, M. S., Bailer, U., Hoh, C., DeCastro, A., Buchsbaum, B. R., & Kaye, W. (2012). Serotonin transporter binding after recovery from bulimia nervosa. *International Journal of Eating Disorders, 45,* 345–352.

Pichon, S., & Kell, C. A. (2013). Affective and sensorimotor components of emotional prosody generation. *Journal of Neuroscience, 33,* 1640–1650.

Pickles, A., Hill, J., Breen, G., Quinn, J., Abbott, K., Jones, H., & Sharp, H. (2013). Evidence for interplay between genes and parenting on infant temperament in the first year of life: Monoamine oxidase a polymorphism moderates effects of maternal sensitivity on infant anger proneness. *Journal of Child Psychology and Psychiatry 54,* 1308–1317.

Pierce, E. F., & Daleng, M. L. (1998). Distortion of body image among elite female dancers. *Perceptual and Motor Skills, 87,* 769–770.

Pierce, E. F., Eastman, N. W., Tripathi, H. L., & Olson, K. G. (1993). B-endorphin response to endurance exercise: Relationship to exercise dependence. *Perceptual and Motor Skills, 77,* 767–770.

Pieri, L. F., & Campbell, D. A. (1999). Understanding the genetic predisposition to anorexia nervosa. *European Eating Disorders Review, 7,* 84–95.

Pierrehumbert, B., Santelices, M. P., Ibáñez, M., Alberdi, M., Ongari, B., Roskam, I., . . . Borghini, A., (2009). Gender and attachment representations in the preschool years: Comparisons between five countries. *Journal of Cross-Cultural Psychology, 40,* 543–566.

Pierson, A., le Houezec, J., Fossaert, A., Dubal, S., & Jouvent, R. (1999). Frontal reactivity and sensation seeking an ERP study in skydivers. *Progress in Neuro-Psychopharmacology & Biological Psychiatry, 23,* 447–463.

Pieters, R. G. M., & Bijmolt, T. H. A. (1997). Consumer memory for television advertising: A field study of duration, serial position, and competition effects. *Journal of Consumer Research, 23,* 362–372.

Pietsch, J., Walker, R., & Chapman, E. (2003). The relationship between self-concept, self-efficacy, and performance in mathematics during secondary school. *Journal of Educational Psychology, 95,* 589–603.

Piko, B. F., & Balázs, M. Á. (2012). Authoritative parenting style and adolescent smoking and drinking. *Addictive behaviors, 37,* 353–356.

Pilcher, J. J., Lambert, B. J., & Huffcutt, A. I. (2000). Differential effects of permanent and rotating shifts on self-report sleep length: A meta-analytic review. *Sleep: Journal of Sleep and Sleep Disorders Research, 23,* 155–163.

Piliavin, J. A., Callero, P. L., & Evans, E. E. (1982). Addiction to altruism: Opponent-process theory and habitual blood donation. *Journal of Personality and Social Psychology, 43,* 1200–1213.

Pincus, T., & Morley, S. (2001). Cognitive-processing bias in chronic pain: A review and integration. *Psychological Bulletin, 127,* 599–617.

Pinel, J. P. J., Assanand, S., & Lehman, D. R. (2000). Hunger, eating, and ill health. *American Psychologist, 55,* 1105–1116.

Piner, K. E., & Kahle, L. R. (1984). Adapting to the stigmatizing label of mental illness: Foregone but not forgotten. *Journal of Personality and Social Psychology, 47,* 805–811.

Pines, M. (1981, September). The civilizing of Genie. *Psychology Today,* pp. 28–34.

Pinkofsky, H. B. (1997). Mnemonics for *DSM–IV* personality disorders. *Psychiatric Services, 48,* 1197–1198.

Pinquart, M. (2003). Loneliness in married, widowed, divorced, and never-married older adults. *Journal of Social and Personal Relationships, 20,* 31–53.

Pinquart, M., & Soerensen, S. (2003). Differences between caregivers and noncaregivers in psychological health and physical health: A metaanalysis. *Psychology and Aging, 18,* 250–267.

Piper, A. (1993). Tricyclic antidepressants versus electroconvulsive therapy: A review of the evidence for efficacy in depression. *Annals of Clinical Psychiatry, 5,* 13–23.

Piper, B. J., Gray, H. M., & Birkett, M. A. (2012). Maternal smoking cessation and reduced academic and behavioral problems in offspring. *Drug and Alcohol Dependence, 121,* 62–67.

Pitman, R. K., Sanders, K. M., Zusman, R. M., Healy, A. R., Cheema, F., Lasko, N. B., . . . Orr, S. P. (2002). Pilot study of secondary prevention of posttraumatic stress disorder with propranolol. *Biological Psychiatry, 51,* 189–192.

Pittenger, D. J. (1996). Reconsidering the overjustification effect: A guide to critical resources. *Teaching of Psychology, 23,* 234–236.

Pittenger, D. J. (2002). Deception in research: Distinctions and solutions from the perspective of utilitarianism. *Ethics and Behavior, 12,* 117–142.

Plaks, J. E., & Higgins, E. T. (2000). Pragmatic use of stereotyping in teamwork: Social loafing and compensation as a function of inferred partner-situation fit. *Journal of Personality and Social Psychology, 79,* 962–974.

Plant, E. A., & Sachs-Ericsson, N. (2004). Racial and ethnic differences in depression: The roles of social support and meeting basic needs. *Journal of Consulting and Clinical Psychology, 72,* 41–52.

Plant, E. A., Hyde, J. S., Keltner, D., & Devine, P. G. (2000). The gender stereotyping of emotion. *Psychology of Women Quarterly, 24,* 81–92.

Plass, J. A., & Hill, K. T. (1986). Children's achievement strategies and test performance: The role of time pressure, evaluation, anxiety, and sex. *Developmental Psychology, 22,* 31–36.

Platz, S. J., & Hosch, H. M. (1988). Cross-racial/ethnic eyewitness identification: A field study. *Journal of Applied Social Psychology, 18,* 972–984.

Plaud, J. J. (2003). Pavlov and the foundation of behavior therapy. *Spanish Journal of Psychology, 6,* 147–154.

Ploeger, A., van der Maas, H. L. J., & Raijmakers, M. E. J. (2008). Is evolutionary psychology a metatheory for psychology? A discussion of four major issues in psychology from an evolutionary developmental perspective. *Psychological Inquiry, 19,* 1–18.

Plomin, R., & Asbury, K. (2001). Nature and nurture in the family. *Marriage and Family Review, 33,* 273–281.

Plomin, R., Asbury, K., & Dunn, J. (2001). Why are children in the same family so different? Nonshared environment a decade later. *Canadian Journal of Psychiatry, 46,* 225–233.

Plomin, R., Corley, R., Caspi, A., Fulker, D. W., & DeFries, J. (1998). Adoption results for self-reported personality: Evidence for nonadditive genetic effects? *Journal of Personality and Social Psychology, 75,* 211–218.

Ploog, B. O., Scharf, A., Nelson, D., & Brooks, P. J. (2013). Use of computer-assisted technologies (CAT) to enhance social communicative, and language development in children with autism spectrum disorders. *Journal of Autism and Developmental Disorders, 43,* 301–322.

Plotkin, W. B. (1979). The alpha experience revisited: Biofeedback in the transformation of psychological state. *Psychological Bulletin, 86,* 1132–1148.

Plous, S. (1991). An attitude survey of animal rights activists. *Psychological Science, 2,* 194–196.

Plucker, J. A., Callahan, C. M., & Tomchin, E. M. (1996). Wherefore art thou, multiple intelligences? Alternative assessments for identifying talent in ethnically diverse and low income students. *Gifted Child Quarterly, 40,* 81–92.

Plutchik, R. (1980, February). A language for the emotions. *Psychology Today,* pp. 68–78.

Podlesny, J. A., & Raskin, D. C. (1978). Effectiveness of techniques and physiological measures in the detection of deception. *Psychophysiology, 15,* 344–359.

Pogarell, O., Hamann, C., Popperi, G., Juckel, G., Chouker, M., Zaudig, M., . . . Tatsch, K. (2003). Elevated brain serotonin transporter availability in patients with obsessive-compulsive disorder. *Biological Psychiatry, 54*, 1406–1413.

Poincaré, H. (1948, August). Mathematical creation. *Scientific American*, pp. 14–17.

Poldrack, R. A., & Wagner, A. D. (2008). The interface between neuroscience and psychological science. *Current Directions in Psychological Science, 17*, 61.

Politis, M. (2010). Dyskinesias after neural transplantation in Parkinson's disease: What do we know and what is next? *BMC Medicine, 8*, 80–84.

Polivy, J., & Herman, C. P. (2002). Causes of eating disorders. *Annual Review of Psychology 53*, 187–213.

Pollack, M. H., Otto, M. W., Kaspi, S. P., & Hammerness, P. G. (1994). Cognitive behavior therapy for treatment-refractory panic disorder. *Journal of Clinical Psychiatry, 55*, 200–205.

Pollak, S. D., & Tolley-Schell, S. A. (2003). Selective attention to facial emotion in physically abused children. *Journal of Abnormal Psychology, 112*, 323–338.

Pollard, I. (2000). Substance abuse and parenthood: Biological mechanisms—Bioethical challenges. *Women and Health, 30*, 1–24.

Polster, E., & Polster, M. (1993). Frederick Perls: Legacy and invitation. *Gestalt Journal, 16*, 23–25.

Pomerantz, J. R., & Portillo, M. C. (2011). Grouping and emergent features in vision: Toward a theory of basic gestalts. *Journal of Experimental Psychology: Human Perception & Performance, 37*, 1331–1349.

Pomerleau, O. F. (1995). Individual differences in sensitivity to nicotine: Implications of genetic research on nicotine dependence. *Behavior Genetics, 25*, 161–177.

Pompe, G. van der, Antoni, M. H., & Heijnen, C. J. (1998). The effects of surgical stress and psychological stress on the immune function of operative cancer patients. *Psychology and Health, 13*, 1015–1026.

Ponpaipan, M., Srisuphan, W., Jitapunkul, S., Panuthai, S., Tonmukayakul, O., & White, A. (2011). Multimedia computer-assisted instruction for carers on exercise for older people: Development and testing. *Journal of Advanced Nursing, 67*, 308–316.

Poole, D. A., & White, L. T. (1993). Two years later: Effect of question repetition and retention interval on the eyewitness testimony of children and adults. *Developmental Psychology, 29*, 844–853.

Poppen, P. J. (1994). Adolescent contraceptive use and communication: Changes over a decade. *Adolescence, 29*, 503–514.

Popplestone, J. A., & McPherson, M. W. (1976). Ten years at the Archives of the History of American Psychology. *American Psychologist, 31*, 533–534.

Populin, L. C., & Yin, T. C. T. (1998). Pinna movements of the cat during sound localization. *Journal of Neuroscience, 18*, 4233–4243.

Porac, C., & Coren, S. (1981). *Lateral preferences and human behavior*. New York: Springer-Verlag.

Porreca, F., & Gebhart, G. F. (2002). Chronic pain and medullary descending facilitation. *Trends in Neurosciences, 25*, 319–325.

Porro, C. A., Baraldi, P., Pagnoni, G., Serafini, M., Facchin, P., Maieron, M., & Nichelli, P. (2002). Does anticipation of pain affect cortical nociceptive systems? *Journal of Neuroscience, 22*, 3206–3214.

Porsch, R. M., Middeldorp, C. M., Cherny, S. S., Krapohl, E., van Beijsterveldt, C. E. M., et al. (2016). Longitudinal heritability of childhood aggression. *Journal of Medical Genetics Part B: Neuropsychiatric Genetics, 171*, 697–707.

Post, R. M., Leverich, G. S., Xing, G., & Weiss, S. R. B. (2001). Developmental vulnerabilities to the onset and course of bipolar disorder. *Development and Psychopathology, 13*, 581–598.

Postman, L. (1985). Human learning and memory. In G. A. Kimble & K. Schlesinger (Eds.), *Topics in the history of psychology* (Vol. 1, pp. 69–134). Hillsdale, NJ: Erlbaum.

Postmes, T., & Spears, R. (1998). Deindividuation and antinormative behavior: A meta-analysis. *Psychological Bulletin, 123*, 238–259.

Postmes, T., Spears, R., Sakhel, K., & de Groot, D. (2001). Social influence on computer-mediate communication: The effects of anonymity on group behavior. *Personality and Social Psychology Bulletin, 27*, 1243–1254.

Poston, W. S. II, & Winebarger, A. A. (1996). The misuse of behavioral genetics in prevention research, or for whom the "Bell Curve" tolls. *Journal of Primary Prevention, 17*, 133–147.

Poulson, R. L. (1990). Mock juror attribution of criminal responsibility: Effects of race and the guilty but mentally ill (GBMI) verdict option. *Journal of Applied Social Psychology, 20*, 1596–1611.

Pourtois, G., Schwartz, S., Seghier, M. L., Lazeyras, F., & Vuilleumier, P. (2005). Portraits or people? Distinct representations of face identity in the human visual cortex. *Journal of Cognitive Neuroscience, 17*, 1043–1057.

Powell, D. J., & Fuller, R. W. (1983). Marijuana and sex: Strange bedpartners. *Journal of Psychoactive Drugs, 15*, 269–280.

Powell, J. L., & Drucker, A. D. (1997). The role of peer conformity in the decision to ride with an intoxicated driver. *Journal of Alcohol and Drug Education, 43*, 1–7.

Powers, D. E., & Rock, D. A. (1999). Effects of coaching on SAT I: Reasoning Test scores. *Journal of Educational Measurement, 36*, 93–118.

Prados, J., Chamizo, V. D., & MacKintosh, N. J. (1999). Latent inhibition and perceptual learning in a swimming-pool navigation task. *Journal of Experimental Psychology: Animal Behavior Processes, 25*, 37–44.

Prasinos, S., & Tittler, B. I. (1981). The family relationships of humor-oriented adolescents. *Journal of Personality, 47*, 295–305.

Pratkanis, A. R. (1992). The cargo-cult science of subliminal persuasion. *Skeptical Inquirer, 16*, 260–272.

Pratto, F., & Hegarty, P. (2000). The political psychology of reproductive strategies. *Psychological Science, 11*, 57–62.

Premack, D. (1965). Reinforcement theory. In D. Levine (Ed.), *Nebraska symposium on motivation* (pp. 123–188). Lincoln: University of Nebraska Press.

Prentice-Dunn, H., & Prentice-Dunn, S. (2012). Physical activity, sedentary behavior, and childhood obesity: A review of cross-sectional studies. *Psychology, Health & Medicine, 17*, 255–273.

Prentice-Dunn, S., & Rogers, R. W. (1982). Effects of public and private self-awareness on deindividuation and aggression. *Journal of Personality and Social Psychology, 3*, 503–513.

Prepeliczay, S. (2002). Socio-cultural and psychological aspects of contemporary LSD use in Germany. *Journal of Drug Issues, 32*, 431–458.

Price, B. H., Baral, I., Cosgrove, G. R., Rauch, S. L., Nierenberg, A. A., Jenike, M. A., & Cassem, E. H. (2001). Improvement in severe self-mutilation following limbic leucotomy: A series of 5 consecutive cases. *Journal of Clinical Psychiatry, 62*, 925–932.

Price, M. S., & Weiss, M. R. (2000). Relationships among coach burnout, coach behaviors, and athletes' psychological responses. *Sport Psychologist, 14*, 391–409.

Price, R., & Gottesman, I. I. (1991). Body fat in identical twins reared apart: Roles for genes and environment. *Behavior Genetics, 21*, 1–7.

Price-Williams, E., Gordon, W., & Ramirez, M. (1969). Skill and conservation: A study of pottery-making children. *Developmental Psychology, 1*, 769.

Priester, J. R., & Petty, R. E. (2003). The influence of spokesperson trustworthiness on message elaboration, attitude strength, and advertising effectiveness. *Journal of Consumer Psychology, 13*, 408–421.

Principe, C. P., & Langlois, J. H. (2013). Children and adults use attractiveness as a social cue in real people and avatars. *Journal of Experimental Child Psychology, 115*, 590–597.

Pritchard, W. S., Robinson, J. H., deBethizy, J. D., & Davis, R. A. (1995). Caffeine and smoking: Subjective, performance, and psychophysiological effects. *Psychophysiology, 32*, 19–27.

Prochaska, J. O. (1984). *Systems of psychotherapy: A transtheoretical approach*. Homewood, IL: Dorsey.

Proctor, R. W., & Kim-Phuong, L. V. (2006). The cognitive revolution at age 50: Has the promise of the human information-processing approach been fulfilled? *International Journal of Human-Computer Interaction, 21*, 253–284.

Prud'homme, M. J. L., Cohen, D. A. D., & Kalaska, J. F. (1994). Tactile activity in primate primary somatosensory cortex during active arm movements: Cytoarchitectonic distribution. *Journal of Neurophysiology, 71*, 173–181.

"A psychic Watergate." (1981, June). *Discover*, p. 8.

Puccio, G. J. (1991). William Duff's eighteenth century examination of original genius and its relationship to contemporary creativity research. *Journal of Creative Behavior, 25*, 1–10.

Pukall, C. F., Payne, K. A., Binik, Y. M., & Khalife, S. (2003). Pain measurement in vulvodynia. *Journal of Sex & Marital Therapy, 29*, 111–120.

Pullum, G. K. (1991). *The great Eskimo vocabulary hoax*. Chicago: University of Chicago Press.

Pulsifer, M. B. (1996). The neuropsychology of mental retardation. *Journal of the International Neuropsychological Society, 2*, 159–176.

Punamaki, R.-L., & Joustie, M. (1998). The role of culture, violence, and personal factors affecting dream content. *Journal of Cross-Cultural Psychology, 29*, 320–342.

Punamaki, R.-L., Kanninen, K., Quota, S., & El-Sarraj, E. (2002). The role of psychological defences in moderating between trauma and post-traumatic symptoms among Palestinian men. *International Journal of Psychology, 37*, 286–296.

Purdy, J. E., Harriman, A., & Molitorisz, J. (1993). Contributions to the history of psychology: XCV. Possible relations between theories of evolution and animal learning. *Psychological Reports, 73*, 211–223.

Purselle, D. C., & Nemeroff, C. B. (2003). Serotonin transporter: A potential substrate in the biology of suicide. *Neuropsychopharmacology, 28*, 613–619.

Putnam, D. E., Finney, J. W., Barkley, P. L., & Bonner, M. J. (1994). Enhancing commitment improves adherence to a medical regimen. *Journal of Consulting and Clinical Psychology, 62*, 191–194.

Putnam, F. W. (2003). Ten-year research update review: Child sexual abuse. *Journal of the American Academy of Child and Adolescent Psychiatry, 42*, 269–278.

Putnam, K. T., Harris, W. H., & Putnam, F. W. (2013). Synergistic childhood adversities and complex adult psychopathology. *Journal of Traumatic Stress, 26*, 435–442.

Pyszczynski, T., Greenberg, J., Solomon, S., Arndt, J., & Schimel, J. (2004). Why do people need self-esteem? A theoretical and empirical review. *Psychological Bulletin, 130*, 435–468.

Pyter, L. M., & Nelson, R. J. (2006). Enduring effects of photoperiod and affective behaviors in Siberian hamsters. *Behavioral Neuroscience, 120*, 125–134.

Qian, Y., Zeng, B. F., Zhang, X. L., & Jiang, Y. (2008). High levels of substance P and CGRP in pseudosynovial fluid from patients with aseptic loosening of their hip prosthesis. *Acta Orthopaedica, 79*, 342–345.

Qin, S., Young, C. B., Duan, X., Chen, T., Supekar, K., & Menon, V. (2014). Amygdala subregional structure and intrinsic functional connectivity predicts individual differences in anxiety during early childhood. *Biological Psychiatry, 75*(11), 892–900.

Quadflieg, S., Vermeulen, N., & Rossion, B. (2013). Differential reliance on the Duchenne marker during smile evaluations and person judgments. *Journal of Nonverbal Behavior, 37,* 69–77.

Quigley, N., Green, J. F., Morgan, D., Idzikowski, C., & King, D. J. (2000). The effect of sleep deprivation on memory and psychomotor function in healthy volunteers. *Human Psychopharmacology: Clinical and Experimental, 15,* 171–179.

Quintana, S. M., Aboud, F. E., Chao, R. K., Contreras-Grau, J., Cross, W. E. Jr., Hudley, C., . . . Vietze, D. L. (2006). Race, ethnicity, and culture in child development: Contemporary research and future directions. *Child Development, 77,* 1129–1141.

Quirk, G. J. (2002). Memory for extinction of conditioned fear is long-lasting and persists following spontaneous recovery. *Learning and Memory, 9,* 402–407.

Rabin, J., & Wiley, R. (1994). Switching from forward-looking infrared to night vision goggles: Transitory effects on visual resolution. *Aviation, Space, and Environmental Medicine, 65,* 327–329.

Rabinowitz, F. M. (1984). The heredity-environment controversy: A Victorian legacy. *Canadian Psychology, 25,* 159–166.

Racagni, G., & Brunello, N. (1999). Physiology to functionality: The brain and neurotransmitter activity. *International Clinical Psychopharmacology, 14,* S3–S7.

Rachman, S. (1991). Neo-conditioning and the classical theory of fear acquisition. *Clinical Psychology Review, 11,* 155–173.

Rachman, S. J. (1993). Statistically significant difference or probable nonchance difference. *American Psychologist, 48,* 1093.

Racine, M., Tousignant-Laflamme, Y., Kloda, L. A., Dion, D., Dupuis, G., & Choiniere, M. (2012). A systematic literature review of 10 years of research on sex/gender and pain perception—Part 2: Do biopsychosocial factors alter pain sensitivity differently in women and men? *Pain, 153,* 619–635.

Radin, D. (2007). Review of C. Carter (2007), Parapsychology and the skeptics: A scientific argument for the existence of ESP. *Journal of Parapsychology, 71,* 184–185.

Raeburn, J. M., Atkinson, J. M., Dubignon, J. M., & Fitzpatrick, J. (1994). Superhealth basic: Development and evaluation of a low-cost community-based lifestyle change programme. *Psychology and Health, 9,* 383–395.

Ragland, D. R., & Brand, R. J. (1988). Type A behavior and mortality from coronary heart disease. *New England Journal of Medicine, 318,* 65–69.

Rahim-Williams, B., Riley, J. L., Williams, A. K. K., & Fillingham, R. (2012). A quantitative review of ethnic group differences in experimental pain response: Do biology, psychology, and culture matter? *Pain Medicine, 13,* 522–540.

Raine, A., Lencz, T., Bihrle, S., LaCasse, L., & Colletti, P. (2000). Reduced prefrontal gray matter volume and reduced autonomic activity in antisocial personality disorder. *Archives of General Psychiatry, 57,* 119–127.

Rainville, P., Hofbauer, R. K., Bushnell, M. C., Duncan, G. H., & Price, D. D. (2002). Hypnosis modulates activity in brain structures involved in the regulation of consciousness. *Journal of Cognitive Neuroscience, 14,* 887–901.

Rajan, R. (2000). Centrifugal pathways protect hearing sensitivity at the cochlea in noisy environments that exacerbate the damage induced by loud sound. *Journal of Neuroscience, 20,* 6684–6693.

Raloff, J. (1982). Noise can be hazardous to your health. *Science News, 121,* 377–381.

Ramón y Cajal, S. (1937/1966). *Recollections of my life.* Cambridge, MA: MIT Press.

Randall, J. L. (1998). Physics, philosophy and precognition: Some reflections. *Journal of the Society for Psychical Research, 63,* 1–11.

Range, L. M., Kovac, S. H., & Marion, M. S. (2000). Does writing about the bereavement lessen grief following sudden, unintentional death? *Death Studies, 24,* 115–134.

Rapee, R. M. (1991). Generalized anxiety disorder: A review of clinical features and theoretical concepts. *Clinical Psychology Review, 11,* 419–440.

Rapp, D. (1988). The reception of Freud by the British press: General interest and literary magazines, 1920–1925. *Journal of the History of the Behavioral Sciences, 24,* 191–201.

Raskin, D. C., & Podlesny, J. A. (1979). Truth and deception: A reply to Lykken. *Psychological Bulletin, 86,* 54–59.

Rasmussen, T., & Penfield, W. (1947). Further studies of the sensory and motor cerebral cortex of man. *Federation Proceedings, 6,* 452–460.

Rassuli, A. (2012). Engagement in classroom learning: Creating temporal participation incentives for extrinsically motivated students through bonus credits. *Journal of Education for Business, 87,* 86–93.

Rathgeb-Feutsch, M., Kempter, G., Feil, A., Pollmächer, T., & Schuld, A. (2011). Short- and long-term efficacy of cognitive behavioral therapy for *DSM–IV* panic disorder in patients with and without severe psychiatric morbidity. *Journal of Psychiatric Research, 45,* 1264–1268.

Rauch, S. L., Whalen, P. J., Shin, L. M., McInerney, S. C., Macklin, M. L., Lasko, N. B., . . . Pitman, R. K. (2000). Exaggerated amygdala response to masked facial stimuli in posttraumatic stress disorder: A functional MRI study. *Biological Psychiatry, 47,* 769–776.

Raufaste, E., Eyrolle, H., & Marine, C. (1998). Pertinence generation in radiological diagnosis: Spreading activation and the nature of expertise. *Cognitive Science, 22,* 517–546.

Ravelli, G. P., Stein, Z. A., & Susser, M. W. (1976). Obesity in young men after famine exposure in utero in early infancy. *New England Journal of Medicine, 295,* 349–353.

Raw, S. (2003). Professional and legislative issues. *Behavior Therapist, 26,* 322–324.

Rawdon, V. A., Willis, F. N., & Ficken, E. J. (1995). Locus of control in young adults in Russia and the United States. *Perceptual and Motor Skills, 80,* 599–604.

Rawlings, D., & Ciancarelli, V. (1997). Music preference and the five-factor model of the NEO Personality Inventory. *Psychology of Music, 25,* 120–132.

Ray, C. G., & Finley, J. K. (1994). Did CMHCs fail or succeed? Analysis of the expectations and outcomes of the community mental health movement. *Administration and Policy in Mental Health, 21,* 283–293.

Ray, O. (1983). *Drugs, society, and human behavior.* St. Louis: Mosby.

Read, P. P. (1974). *Alive: The story of the Andes survivors.* Philadelphia: Lippincott.

Reason, J. (2000). The Freudian slip revisited. *Psychologist, 13,* 610–611.

Rebeta, J. L., Brooks, C. I., O'Brien, J. P., & Hunter, G. A. (1993). Variations in trait-anxiety and achievement motivation of college students as a function of classroom seating position. *Journal of Experimental Education, 61,* 257–267.

Redd, W. H., Jacobsen, P. B., Die-Trill, M., Dermatis, H., McEvoy, M., & Holland, J. C. (1987). Cognitive/attentional distraction in the control of conditioned nausea in pediatric cancer patients receiving chemotherapy. *Journal of Consulting and Clinical Psychology, 55,* 391–395.

Reddon, J. R., Whippler, S. M., & Reddon, J. E. (2007). Seemingly anomalous WISC-IV full scale IQ scores in the American and Canadian standardization samples. *Current Psychology, 26,* 60–69.

Reddy, A. V., & Reddy, P. B. (1983). Creativity and intelligence. *Psychological Studies, 28,* 20–24.

Redfern, S., Dancey, C. P., & Dryden, W. (1993). Empathy: Its effect on how counsellors are perceived. *British Journal of Guidance and Counselling, 21,* 300–309.

Reed, D. R., Bachmanov, A. A., Beauchamp, G. K., & Tordoff, M. G. (1997). Heritable variation in food preferences and their contribution to obesity. *Behavior Genetics, 27,* 373–387.

Reeder, K., & Shapiro, J. (1993). Relationship between early literate experience and knowledge and children's linguistic pragmatic strategies. *Journal of Pragmatics, 19,* 1–22.

Reese, E. P. (1986). Learning about teaching from teaching about learning: Presenting behavioral analysis in an introductory survey course. In V. P. Makosky (Ed.), *The G. Stanley Hall Lecture Series* (Vol. 6, pp. 65–127). Washington, DC: American Psychological Association.

Reeve, J. M., Bolt, E., & Cai, Y. (1999). Autonomy-supportive teachers: How they teach and motivate students. *Journal of Educational Psychology, 91,* 537–548.

Reeves, G. M., Nijjar, G. V., Langenberg, P., Johnson, M. A., Khabazghazvini, B., Sleemi, A., . . . Snitker, S. (2012). Improvement in depression scores after 1 hour of light therapy treatment in patients with seasonal affective disorder. *Journal of Nervous and Mental Disease, 200,* 51–55.

Regan, P. C., Kocan, E. R., & Whitlock, T. (1998). Ain't love grand! A prototype analysis of the concept of romantic love. *Journal of Social and Personal Relationships, 15,* 411–420.

Regan, T., & Woods, K. (2000). Teachers' understandings of dyslexia: Implications for educational psychology practice. *Educational Psychology in Practice, 16,* 333–347.

Regehr, C., Edward, M., & Bradford, J. (2000). Research ethics and forensic patients. *Canadian Journal of Psychiatry, 45,* 892–898.

Reggiani, P., & Weerts, A. H. (2008). Probabilistic quantitative precipitation forecast for flood prediction: An application. *Journal of Hydrometeorology, 9,* 76–95.

Rehbein, F., Kleimann, M., & Mödle, T. (2010). Prevalence and risk factors of video gamedependency in adolescence: Results of a German nationwide survey, *Cyberpsychology, Behavior, and Social Networking, 13,* 269–277.

Reifman, A., Villa, L. C., Amans, J. A., Rethinam, V., & Telesca, T. Y. (2001). Children of divorce in the 1990s: A meta-analysis. *Journal of Divorce and Remarriage, 36,* 27–36.

Reilly, R. R., & Chao, G. R. (1982). Validity and fairness of some alternative employee selection procedures. *Personnel Psychology, 35,* 1–62.

Reinders, A. A. T., Nijenhuis, E. R. S., Quak, J., Korf, J., Haaksma, J., Paans, A. M. J., . . . den Boer, J. A. (2006). Psychobiological characteristics of dissociative identity disorder: A symptom provocation study. *Biological Psychiatry, 60,* 730–740.

Reiner, W. G., & Gearhart, J. P. (2004). Discordant sexual identity in some genetic males with cloacal exstrophy assigned to female sex at birth. *New England Journal of Medicine, 350,* 333–341.

Reis, S. (1989). Reflections on policy affecting the education of gifted and talented students: Past and future perspectives. *American Psychologist, 44,* 399–408.

Reisenzein, R. (1983). The Schachter theory of emotion: Two decades later. *Psychological Bulletin, 94,* 239–264.

Reisner, A. D. (2003). The electroconvulsive therapy controversy: Evidence and ethics. *Neuropsychology Review, 13,* 199–219.

Reissing, E. D., Binik, Y. M., Khalife, S., Cohen, D., & Amsel, R. (2004). Vaginal spasm, pain, and behavior: An empirical investigation of the diagnosis of vaginismus. *Archives of Sexual Behavior, 33,* 5–17.

Renart, A., Parga, N., & Rolls, E. T. (1999). Backward projections in the cerebral cortex: Implications for memory storage. *Neural Computation, 11,* 1349–1388.

Renn, J. A., & Calvert, S. L. (1993). The relation between gender schemas and adults' recall of stereotyped and countersterotyped televised information. *Sex Roles, 28,* 449–459.

Renner, J. W., Abraham, M. R., Grzybowski, E. B., & Marek, E. A. (1990). Understandings and misunderstandings of eighth graders of four physics concepts found in textbooks. *Journal of Research in Science Teaching, 27,* 35–54.

Rescorla, R. A. (1968). Probability of shock in the presence and absence of CS in fear conditioning. *Journal of Comparative and Physiological Psychology, 66,* 1–5.

Rescorla, R. A. (1988). Pavlovian conditioning: It's not what you think it is. *American Psychologist, 43,* 151–160.

Rescorla, R. A. (2003). Contemporary study of Pavlovian conditioning. *Spanish Journal of Psychology, 6,* 185–195.

Rescorla, R. A., & Holland, P. C. (1982). Behavioral studies of associative learning in animals. *Annual Review of Psychology, 33,* 265–308.

Resendes, J., & Lecci, L. (2013). Comparing the MMPI-2 scale scores of parents involved in parental competency and child custody assessments. *Psychological Assessment, 24,* 1054–1059.

Ressler, R. K., & Shachtman, T. (1992). *Whoever fights monsters.* New York: St. Martin's Press.

Reynaert, C., Janne, P., Bosly, A., & Staquet, P. (1995). From health locus of control to immune control: Internal locus of control has a buffering effect on natural killer cell activity decrease in major depression. *Acta Psychiatrica Scandinavica, 92,* 294–300.

Rheingold, H. L., & Adams, J. L. (1980). The significance of speech to newborns. *Developmental Psychology, 16,* 397–403.

Rhine, J. B. (1974). Security versus deception in parapsychology. *Journal of Parapsychology, 38,* 99–121.

Rhodes, G., Yoshikawa, S., Clark, A., Lee, K., McKay, R., & Akamatsu, S. (2001). Attractiveness of facial averageness and symmetry in non-Western cultures: In search of biologically based standards of beauty. *Perception, 30,* 611–625.

Rhodes, N., & Wood, W. (1992). Self-esteem and intelligence affect influenceability: The mediating role of message reception. *Psychological Bulletin, 111,* 156–171.

Rhodewalt, F., Sanbonmatsu, D. M., Tschanz, B., & Feick, D. L. (1995). Self-handicapping and interpersonal trade-offs: The effects of claimed self-handicaps on observers' performance evaluations and feedback. *Personality and Social Psychology Bulletin, 21,* 1042–1050.

Rice, M. L. (1989). Children's language acquisition. *American Psychologist, 44,* 149–156.

Rickels, K., DeMartinis, N., & Aufdembrinke, B. (2000). A double-blind, placebo-controlled trial of abecarniland diazepam in the treatment of patients with generalized anxiety disorder. *Journal of Clinical Psychopharmacology, 20,* 12–18.

Rieber, R. W. (Ed.). (1980). *Wilhelm Wundt and the making of a scientific psychology.* New York: Plenum.

Rieckert, J., & Moeller, A. T. (2000). Rational-emotive behavior therapy in the treatment of adult victims of childhood sexual abuse. *Journal of Rational-Emotive and Cognitive Behavior Therapy, 18,* 87–102.

Ried, K., Sullivan, T., Fakler, P., Frank, O. R., & Stocks, N. P. (2010). Does chocolate reduce blood pressure? A meta-analysis. *BMC Medicine, 8,* 39–49.

Rief, W., Hessel, A., & Braehler, E. (2001). Somatization symptoms and hypochondriacal features in the general population. *Psychosomatic Medicine, 63,* 595–602.

Ries, M. L., Carlsson, C. M., Rowley, H. A., Sager, M. A., Gleason, C. E., Asthana, S., & Johnson, S. C. (2008). Magnetic resonance imaging characterization of brain structure and function in mild cognitive impairment: A review. *Journal of the American Geriatrics Association, 56,* 920–934.

Riggs, J. M. (1998). Social roles we choose and don't choose: Impressions of employed and unemployed parents. *Sex Roles, 39,* 431–443.

Riggs, L. A. (1985). Sensory processes: Vision. In G. A. Kimble & K. Schlesinger (Eds.), *Topics in the history of psychology* (Vol. 1, pp. 165–220). Hillsdale, NJ: Erlbaum.

Riley, J. L., Robinson, M. E., Wise, E. A., Myers, C. D., & Fillingim, R. B. (1998). Sex differences in the perception of noxious experimental stimuli: A meta-analysis. *Pain, 74,* 181–187.

Riley, K., Snowdon, D. A., & Markesbery, W. R. (2002). Alzheimer's neurofibrillary pathology and the spectrum of cognitive function: Findings from the Nun Study. *Annals of Neurology, 51,* 567–577.

Rilling, M. (1996). The mystery of the vanished citations: James McConnell's forgotten 1960s quest for planarian learning, a biochemical engram, and celebrity. *American Psychologist, 51,* 589–598.

Rinaldi, R. C. (1987). Patient-therapist personality similarity and the therapeutic relationship. *Psychotherapy in Private Practice, 5,* 11–29.

Rinn, W. E. (1984). The neuropsychology of facial expression: A review of the neurological and psychological mechanisms for producing facial expressions. *Psychological Bulletin, 95,* 52–77.

Riordan, C. A., & Tedeschi, J. T. (1983). Attraction in aversive environments: Some evidence for classical conditioning and negative reinforcement. *Journal of Personality and Social Psychology, 44,* 683–692.

Risch, N., Squires-Wheeler, E., & Keats, B. J. B. (1993). Male sexual orientation and genetic evidence. *Science, 262,* 2063–2065.

Rittenhouse, C. D., Stickgold, R., & Hobson, J. A. (1994). Constraint on the transformation of characters, objects, and settings in dream reports. *Consciousness and Cognition: An International Journal, 3,* 100–113.

Rivera-Tovar, L. A., & Jones, R. T. (1990). Effect of elaboration on the acquisition and maintenance of cardiopulmonary resuscitation. *Journal of Pediatric Psychology, 15,* 123–138.

Robazza, C., Bortoli, L., & Nougier, V. (1998). Physiological arousal and performance in elite archers: A field study. *European Psychologist, 3,* 263–270.

Robbins, S. B., Lauver, K., Le, H., Davis, D., Langley, R., & Carlstrom, A. (2004). Do psychological and study skill factors predict college outcomes? A metaanalysis. *Psychological Bulletin, 130,* 261–288.

Robert, M. (1990). Observational learning in fish, birds, and mammals: A classified bibliography spanning over 100 years of research. *Psychological Record, 40,* 289–311.

Roberts, M., & Shapiro, M. (2002). NMDA receptor antagonists impair memory for nonspatial, socially transmitted food preferences. *Behavioral Neuroscience, 116,* 1059–1069.

Roberts, M. C., & Fanurik, D. (1986). Rewarding elementary school children for their use of safety belts. *Health Psychology, 5,* 185–196.

Roberts, R. E., Phinney, J. S., Masse, L. C., Chen, Y. R., Roberts, C. R., & Romero, A. (1999). The structure of ethnic identity of young adolescents from diverse ethnocultural groups. *Journal of Early Adolescence, 19,* 301–322.

Roberts, R. E. L., & Bengtson, V. L. (1996). Affective ties to parents in early adulthood and self-esteem across 20 years. *Social Psychology Quarterly, 59,* 96–106.

Roberts, S. J. (1988). Social support and help seeking: Review of the literature. *Advances in Nursing Science, 10,* 1–11.

Robins, R. W., Gosling, S. D., & Craik, K. H. (1999). An empirical analysis of trends in psychology. *American Psychologist, 54,* 117–128.

Robinson, D. L. (1993). The EEG and intelligence: An appraisal of methods and theories. *Personality and Individual Differences, 15,* 695–716.

Robinson, D. L. (2001). How brain arousal systems determine different temperament types and the major dimensions of personality. *Personality and Individual Differences, 31,* 1233–1259.

Robinson, F. P. (1970). *Effective study.* New York: Harper & Row.

Robinson, J., & Briggs, P. (1997). Age trends and eyewitness suggestibility and compliance. *Psychology, Crime and Law, 3,* 187–202.

Robinson, M. D. (1998). Running from William James' bear: A review of preattentive mechanisms and their contributions to emotional experience. *Cognition and Emotion, 12,* 667–696.

Robison, R., Keltner, D., Ward, A., & Ross, L. (1995, March). Actual Versus Assumed Differences in Construal: "Naive Realism" in Intergroup Perception and Conflict. *Journal of Personality and Social Psychology, 68,* 404–417.

Robinson, S. J., & Rollings, L. J. L. (2011). The effect of mood-context on visual recognition and recall memory. *Journal of General Psychology, 138,* 66–79.

Roccas, S., Sagiv, L., Schwartz, S. H., & Knafo, A. (2002). The Big Five personality factors and personal values. *Personality and Social Psychology Bulletin, 28,* 789–801.

Rock, I., Gopnik, A., & Hall, S. (1994). Do young children reverse ambiguous figures? *Perception, 23,* 635–644.

Rockwell, T. (1979). Pseudoscience or pseudocriticism? *Journal of Parapsychology, 43,* 221–231.

Rodgers, J. E. (1982, June). The malleable memory of eyewitnesses. *Science, 82,* 32–35.

Rodgers, J. L., Cleveland, H. H., van den Oord, E., & Rowe, D. C. (2000). Resolving the debate over birth order, family size, and intelligence. *American Psychologist, 55,* 599–612.

Rodgers, R., & Hunter, J. E. (1991). Impact of management by objectives on organizational productivity. *Journal of Applied Psychology, 76,* 322–336.

Rodier, P. M., Ingram, J. L., Tisdale, B., & Croog, V. J. (1997). Linking etiologies in humans and animal models: Studies of autism. *Reproductive Toxicology, 11,* 417–422.

Rodin, J. (1981). Current status of the internal-external hypothesis for obesity: What went wrong? *American Psychologist, 36,* 361–372.

Rodin, J. (1985). Insulin levels, hunger, and food intake: An example of feedback loops in body weight regulation. *Health Psychology, 4,* 1–23.

Roelofs, K., Keijsers, G. P. J., Hoogduin, K. A. L., Naering, G. W. B., & Moene, F. C. (2002). Childhood abuse in patients with conversion disorder. *American Journal of Psychiatry, 159,* 1908–1913.

Rogers, A. E., Aldrich, M. S., & Lin, X. (2001). A comparison of three different sleep schedules for reducing daytime sleepiness in narcolepsy. *Sleep: Journal of Sleep and Sleep Disorders Research, 24,* 385–391.

Rogers, C. R. (1957). The necessary and sufficient conditions of therapeutic personality change. *Journal of Consulting Psychology, 21,* 95–103.

Rogers, C. R. (1961). *On becoming a person: A therapist's view of psychotherapy.* Boston: Houghton Mifflin.

Rogers, C. R. (1968). Interpersonal relationships. *Journal of Applied Behavioral Science, 4,* 1–12.

Rogers, C. R. (1985). Toward a more human science of the person. *Journal of Humanistic Psychology, 25,* 7–24.

Rogers, K. B. (1996). What *The Bell Curve* says and doesn't say: Is a balanced view possible? *Roeper Review, 18,* 252–255.

Rogers, L. J. (2000). Evolution of hemispheric specialization: Advantages and disadvantages. *Brain and Language, 73,* 236–253.

Rogers, R. (1987). APA's position on the insanity defense: Empiricism versus emotionalism. *American Psychologist, 42,* 840–848.

Rogers, R., Duncan, J. C., Lynett, E., & Sewell, K. W. (1994). Prototypical analysis of antisocial personality disorder: *DSM-IV* and beyond. *Law and Human Behavior, 18,* 471–484.

Rogers, R., Sewell, K. W., Martin, M. A., & Vitacco, M. J. (2003). Detection of feigned mental disorders: A meta-analysis of the MMPI-2 and malingering. *Assessment, 10,* 160–177.

Rogers, R. L., & Petrie, T. A. (2001). Psychological correlates of anorexia and bulimic symptomatology. *Journal of Counseling and Development, 79,* 178–187.

Rogers, R. L., Meyer, J. S., & Mortel, K. F. (1990). After reaching retirement age physical activity sustains cerebral perfusion and cognition. *Journal of the American Geriatrics Society, 38,* 123–128.

Rogge, R. D., & Bradbury, T. N. (1999). Till violence does us part: The differing roles of communication and aggression in predicting adverse marital outcomes. *Journal of Consulting and Clinical Psychology, 67,* 340–351.

Rogoff, B., & Chavajay, P. (1995). What's become of research on the cultural basis of cognitive development? *American Psychologist, 50,* 459–477.

Röhl, M., Kollmeier, B., & Uppenkamp, S. (2011). Spectral loudness summation takes place in the primary auditory cortex. *Human Brain Mapping, 32,* 1483–1496.

Rohsenow, D. J. (2005). Understanding the interactions of nicotine and alcohol: How basic research can help guide treatment for alcoholic smokers. *Brown University Digest of Addiction Theory and Application, 24,* 8.

Roig, M. (1993). Summarizing parapsychology in psychology textbooks: A rejoinder to Kalat and Kohn. *Teaching of Psychology, 20,* 174–175.

Rokeach, M. (1964/1981). *The three Christs of Ypsilanti.* New York: Columbia University Press.

Rokeach, M., & Mezei, L. (1966). Race and shared belief as factors in social choice. *Science, 151,* 167–172.

Roll, R., Kavounoudias, A., & Roll, J. P. (2002). Cutaneous afferents from human plantar sole contribute to body posture awareness. *Neuroreport: For Rapid Communication of Neuroscience Research, 13,* 1957–1961.

Rollman, G. B. (1998). Culture and pain. In S. S. Kazarian, D. R. Evans (Eds.). *Cultural clinical psychology: Theory, research, and practice* (pp. 267–286). NY: Oxford University Press.

Rondall, J. A. (1994). Pieces of minds in psycholinguistics: Steven Pinker, Kenneth Wexler, and Noam Chomsky. *International Journal of Psychology, 29,* 85–104.

Rook, K. S., Catalano, R., & Dooley, D. (1989). The timing of major life events: Effects of departing from the social clock. *American Journal of Community Psychology, 17,* 233–258.

Roosa, M. W., Reinholtz, C., & Angelini, P. J. (1999). The relation of child sexual abuse and depression in young women: Comparisons across four ethnic groups. *Journal of Abnormal Child Psychology, 27,* 65–76.

Roozendaal, B., McEwen, B. S., & Chattarji, S. (2009). Stress, memory and the amygdala. *Nature Reviews: Neuroscience, 10,* 423–433.

Rosch, E. (1975). Cognitive representation of semantic categories. *Journal of Experimental Psychology: General, 104,* 192–233.

Rose, D. (2011) Growing our kids in "Healthy Soil": New research on environmental influences on children's food intake. *Journal of Adolescent Health, 48,* 3–4.

Rose, J. E., & Fantino, E. (1978). Conditioned reinforcement and discrimination in second-order schedules. *Journal of the Experimental Analysis of Behavior, 29,* 393–418.

Rosen, G. M., Sageman, M., & Loftus, E. (2004). A historical note on false traumatic memories. *Journal of Clinical Psychology, 60,* 137–139.

Rosenbaum, M. E. (1986). The repulsion hypothesis: On the nondevelopment of relationships. *Journal of Personality and Social Psychology, 51,* 1156–1166.

Rosenberg, M. (1965). *Society and the adolescent self-image.* Princeton, NJ: Princeton University Press.

Rosenbloom, T., & Wolf, Y. (2002). Signal detection in conditions of everyday life traffic dilemmas. *Accident Analysis and Prevention, 34,* 763–772.

Rosenhan, D. L. (1973). On being sane in insane places. *Science, 179,* 250–258.

Rosenkoetter, L. I. (1999). The television situation comedy and children's prosocial behavior. *Journal of Applied Social Psychology, 29,* 979–993.

Rosenman, R. H., Brand, R. J., Jenkins, D., Friedman, M., Straus, R., & Wurm, M. (1975). Coronary heart disease in the Western Collaborative Group Study: Final follow-up experience of 8 1/2 years. *Journal of the American Psychological Association, 233,* 872–877.

Rosenthal, N. E. (1993). *Winter blues: Seasonal affective disorder—What it is and how to overcome it.* New York: Guilford.

Rosenthal, R. (1995). Ethical issues in psychological science: Risk, consent, and scientific quality. *Psychological Science, 6,* 322–323.

Rosenthal, R. (2002). Covert communication in classrooms, clinics, courtrooms, and cubicles. *American Psychologist, 57,* 839–849.

Rosenthal, R., & DiMatteo, M. R. (2002). Meta-analysis. In H. Pashler & J. Wixted (Eds.), *Stevens' handbook of experimental psychology: Methodology in experimental psychology* (Vol. 4, 3rd ed., pp. 391–428). New York: Wiley.

Rosenthal, R., & Fode, K. L. (1963). The effect of experimenter bias on the performance of the albino rat. *Behavioral Science, 8,* 183–189.

Rosenthal, R., & Jacobson, L. (1968). *Pygmalion in the classroom.* New York: Holt, Rinehart & Winston.

Rosenwald, R. R. (2009). The future of research into growth hormone responsiveness. *Hormone Research, 71,* 71–74.

Rosenzweig, M. R., & Bennett, E. L. (1996). Psychobiology of plasticity: Effects of training and experience on brain and behavior. *Behavioral Brain Research, 78,* 57–65.

Ross, E. (1999, June 18). Einstein's brain was exceptional. *Philadelphia Inquirer,* p. A-1.

Ross, E. D., Edmondson, J. A., Seibert, G. B., & Homan, R. W. (1988). Acoustic analysis of affective prosody during right-sided Wada test: A within-subjects verification of the right hemisphere's role in language. *Brain and Language, 33,* 128–145.

Ross, E. D., Thompson, R. D., & Yenkosky, J. (1997). Lateralization of affective prosody in brain and the callosal integration of hemispheric language functions. *Brain and Language, 56,* 27–54.

Ross, M. J., & Berger, R. S. (1996). Effects of stress inoculation training on athletes' postsurgical pain and rehabilitation after orthopedic injury. *Journal of Consulting and Clinical Psychology, 64,* 406–410.

Ross, S. R., Rausch, M. K., & Canada, K. E. (2003). Competition and cooperation in the five-factor model: Individual differences in achievement orientation. *Journal of Psychology, 137,* 323–337.

Rosser, S., Issakidis, C., & Peters, L. (2003). Perfectionism and social phobia: Relationship between the constructs and impact on cognitive behavior therapy. *Cognitive Therapy and Research, 27,* 143–151.

Rossi, A. F., Rittenhouse, C. D., & Paradiso, M. A. (1996). The representation of brightness in primary visual cortex. *Science, 273,* 1104–1107.

Rossi, A. M., & Seiler, W. J. (1989–1990). The comparative effectiveness of systematic desensitization and an integrative approach in treating public speaking anxiety: A literature review and a preliminary investigation. *Imagination, Cognition, and Personality, 9,* 49–66.

Rossi, B., & Creatti, L. (1993). The sensation seeking in mountain athletes as assessed by Zuckerman's Sensation Seeking Scale. *International Journal of Sport Psychology, 24,* 417–431.

Rossi, F. (1988, November 8). Stress test. *Philadelphia Inquirer,* pp. 1-E, 10-E.

Roter, D. L., & Hall, J. A. (1998). Why physician gender matters in shaping the physician-patient relationship. *Journal of Women's Health, 7,* 1093–1097.

Roth, L. W., & Polotsky, A. J. (2012). Can we live longer by eating less? A review of caloric restriction and longevity. *Maturitas, 71,* 315–319.

Roth, T. (1995). An overview of the report of the National Commission on Sleep Disorders Research. *European Psychiatry, 10,* 109s–113s.

Rothbart, M. K., Ahadi, S. A., & Evans, D. E. (2000). Temperament and personality: Origins and outcomes. *Journal of Personality and Social Psychology, 78,* 122–135.

Rothbaum, F., & Tsang, B. Y. P. (1998). Love songs in the United States and China: On the nature of romantic love. *Journal of Cross-Cultural Psychology, 29,* 306–319.

Rothon, C., Head, J., Klineberg, E., & Stansfeld, S. (2011). Can social support protect bullied adolescents from adverse outcomes? A prospective study on the effects of bullying on the educational achievement and mental health of adolescents at secondary schools in East London. *Journal of Adolescence, 34,* 579–588.

Rothschild, A. J. (2000). New directions in the treatment of antidepressant–induced sexual dysfunction. *Clinical Therapeutics: The International Journal of Drug Therapy, 22,* A42–A57.

Rotter, J. B. (1966). Generalized expectancies for internal versus external control of reinforcement. *Psychological Monographs, 80,* 1–28.

Rotter, J. B. (1990). Internal versus external control of reinforcement: Case history of a variable. *American Psychologist, 45,* 489–493.

Rotton, J., & Kelly, I. W. (1985). Much ado about the full moon: A meta-analysis of lunar-lunacy research. *Psychological Bulletin, 97,* 286–306.

Roug, L., Landberg, I., & Lundberg, L. J. (1989). Phonetic development in early infancy: A study of four Swedish children during the first eighteen months of life. *Journal of Child Language, 16,* 19–40.

Rouillon, F. (1997). Epidemiology of panic disorder. *Human Psychopharmacology: Clinical and Experimental, 12,* S7–S12.

Routh, D. K. (1969). Conditioning of vocal response differentiation in infants. *Developmental Psychology, 1,* 219–226.

Rowan, A. B. (2001). Adolescent substance abuse and suicide. *Depression and Anxiety, 14,* 186–191.

Rowe, L. S., Jouriles, E. N., McDonald, R., Platt, C. G., & Gomez, G. S. (2012). Enhancing women's resistance to sexual coercion: A randomized controlled trial of the DATE program. *Journal of American College Health, 60,* 211–218.

Rowe, R., Pickles, A., Simonoff, E., Bulik, C. M., & Silberg, J. L. (2002). Bulimic symptoms in the Virginia twin study of adolescent behavioral development: Correlates, comorbidity, and genetics. *Biological Psychiatry, 51,* 172–182.

Rowsell, H. C. (1988). The status of animal experimentation in Canada. *International Journal of Psychology, 23,* 377–381.

Rozin, P. (2005). The meaning of food in our lives: A cross-cultural perspective on eating and well-being. *Journal of Nutrition Education and Behavior, 37,* S107–S112.

Rozin, P., & Fallon, A. E. (1987). A perspective on disgust. *Psychological Review, 94,* 23–41.

Rozin, P., & Zellner, D. (1985). The role of Pavlovian conditioning in the acquisition of food likes and dislikes. *Annals of the New York Academy of Sciences, 443,* 189–202.

Rubin, D. H., Althoff, R. R., Ehli, E. A., Davies, G. E., Rettew, D. C., Crehan, E. T., Walkup, J. T., & Hudziak, J. J. (2013). Candidate gene associations with withdrawn behavior. *Journal of Child Psychology and Psychiatry, 54,* 1337–1345.

Rubin, J. R., Provenzano, F. J., & Luria, Z. (1974). The eye of the beholder: Parents' views on sex of newborns. *American Journal of Orthopsychiatry, 44,* 512–519.

Rubin, L. C., & Mills, M. J. (1983). Behavioral precipitants to civil commitment. *American Journal of Psychiatry, 140,* 603–606.

Rubin, R. T., Reinisch, J. M., & Haskett, R. F. (1981). Postnatal gonadal steroid effects on human behavior. *Science, 211,* 1318–1324.

Rubin, Z. (1985). Deceiving ourselves about deception: Comment on Smith and Richardson's "Amelioration of deception and harm in psychological research." *Journal of Personality and Social Psychology, 48,* 252–253.

Ruch, W., & Forabosco, G. (1996). A cross-cultural study of humor appreciation: Italy and Germany. *Humor: International Journal of Humor Research, 9,* 1–18.

Ruch, W., McGhee, P. E., & Hehl, F. J. (1990). Age differences in the enjoyment of incongruity-resolution and nonsense humor during adulthood. *Psychology and Aging, 5,* 348–355.

Ruda, M. A. (1982). Opiates and pain pathways: Demonstration of enkephalin synapses on dorsal horn projection neurons. *Science, 215,* 1523–1525.

Rudolph, K. D., & Hammen, C. (1999). Age and gender as determinants of stress exposure, generation, and reactions in youngsters: A transactional perspective. *Child Development, 70,* 660–677.

Rudy, D., & Grusec, J. E. (2001). Correlates of authoritarian in individualistic and collectivist cultures and implications for understanding the transmission of values. *Journal of Cross-Cultural Psychology, 32,* 202–212.

Ruedl, G., Abart, M., Ledochowski, L., Burtscher, M., & Kopp, M. (2012). Self-reported risk taking and risk compensation in skiers and snowboarders are associated with sensation seeking. *Accident Analysis and Prevention, 48,* 292–296.

Ruffin, C. L. (1993). Stress and health: Little hasslers vs. major life events. *Australian Psychologist, 28,* 201–208.

Ruffman, T. K., & Olson, D. R. (1989). Children's ascriptions of knowledge to others. *Developmental Psychology, 25,* 601–606.

Ruhrmann, S., Kasper, S., Hawellek, B., Martinez, B., Hoeflich, G., Nickelsen, T., & Moeller, H.-J. (1998). Effects of fluoxetine versus bright light in the treatment of seasonal affective disorder. *Psychological Medicine, 28,* 923–933.

Ruiter, M. E., DeCoster, J., Jacobs, L., & Lichstein, K. L. (2011). Normal sleep in African-Americans and Caucasian-Americans: A meta-analysis. *Sleep Medicine, 12,* 209–214.

Ruiz, G., & Baños, J. E. (2009). Heat hyperalgesia induced by endoneurial nerve growth factor and the expression of substance p in primary sensory neurons. *International Journal of Neuroscience, 119,* 185–203.

Rujescu, D., Giegling, I., Gietl, A., Hartmann, A. M., & Moeller, H. J. (2003). A functional single nucleotide polymorphism (V158M) in the COMT gene is associated with aggressive personality traits. *Biological Psychiatry, 54,* 34–39.

Rule, B. G., & Nesdale, A. R. (1976). Emotional arousal and aggressive behavior. *Psychological Bulletin, 83,* 851–863.

Rummel, R., & Feinberg, R. (1988). Cognitive evaluation theory: A meta-analytic review of the literature. *Social Behavior and Personality, 16,* 147–164.

Runco, M. A. (1993). Divergent thinking, creativity, and giftedness. *Gifted Child Quarterly, 37,* 16–22.

Runco, M. A., & Johnson, D. J. (2002). Parents' and teachers implicit theories of children's creativity: A cross-cultural perspective. *Creativity Research Journal, 14,* 427–438.

Rungger-Brändle, E., Ripperger, J. A., Steiner, K., Conti, A., Stieger, A., Soltanieh, S., & Rungger, D. (2010). Retinal patterning by Pax6-dependent cell adhesion molecules. *Developmental Neurobiology, 70,* 764–780.

Rury, J. L. (1988). Race, region, and education: An analysis of Black and White scores on the 1917 Army Alpha Intelligence Test. *Journal of Negro Education, 57,* 51–65.

Ruscio, A. M., Stein, D. J., Chiu, W. T., & Kessler, R. C. (2010). The epidemiology of obsessive-compulsive disorder in the National Comorbidity Survey Replication. *Molecular Psychiatry, 15,* 53–63.

Rushton, J. P. (1990). Creativity, intelligence, and psychoticism. *Personality and Individual Differences, 11,* 1291–1298.

Rushton, J. P. (1997). Race, IQ, and the APA report on *The Bell Curve. American Psychologist, 52,* 69–70.

Rushton, J. P., & Ankney, C. D. (2009). Whole brain size and general mental ability: A review. *International Journal of Neuroscience, 119,* 692–732.

Rushton, J. P., & Jensen, A. R. (2003). African-White IQ differences from Zimbabwe on the Wechsler Intelligence Scale for Children-Revised are mainly on the g factor. *Personality and Individual Differences, 34,* 177–183.

Russell, G. F. M. (2001). Involuntary treatment in anorexia nervosa. *Psychiatric Clinics of North America, 24,* 337–349.

Russell, G. L., Fujino, D. C., Sue, S., Cheung, M.-K., & Snowden, L. R. (1996). The effects of therapist-client ethnic match in the assessment of mental health functioning. *Journal of Cross-Cultural Psychology, 27,* 598–615.

Russell, J. A. (1991). In defense of a prototype approach to emotion concepts. *Journal of Personality and Social Psychology, 60,* 37–47.

Russell, J. A. (1994). Is there universal recognition of emotion from facial expressions? A review of the cross-cultural studies. *Psychological Bulletin, 115,* 102–141.

Russell, M. J. (1976). Human olfactory communication. *Nature, 260,* 520–522.

Rust, J., Golombok, S., Hines, M., Johnston, K., & Golding, J. (2000). The role of brothers and sisters in the gender development of preschool children. *Journal of Experimental Child Psychology, 77,* 292–303.

Rutherford, A. (2000). Radical behaviorism and psychology's public: B. F. Skinner in the popular press, 1934–1990. *History of Psychology, 3,* 371–395.

Rutkowski, G. K., Gruder, C. L., & Romer, D. (1983). Group cohesiveness, social norms, and bystander intervention. *Journal of Personality and Social Psychology, 44,* 545–552.

Ruys, K. K., & Aarts, H. (2012). I didn't mean to hurt you! Unconscious origins of experienced self-agency over others' emotions. *Emotion, 12,* 132–141.

Ryan, C. S., & Bogart, L. M. (2001). Longitudinal changes in the accuracy of new group members' in-group and out-group stereotypes. *Journal of Experimental Social Psychology, 37,* 118–133.

Ryan, E. D. (1980). Attribution, intrinsic motivation, and athletics: A replication and extension. In C. H. Nadeau, W. R. Halliwell, K. M. Newell, & G. C. Roberts (Eds.), *Psychology of motor behavior and sport-1979* (pp. 19–26). Champaign, IL: Human Kinetics.

Ryan, J. J., Sattler, J. M., & Lopez, S. J. (2000). Age effects in Wechsler Adult Intelligence Scale-III subtests. *Archives of Clinical Neuropsychology, 15,* 311–317.

Ryan, K. M., & Kanjorski, J. (1998). The enjoyment of sexist humor, rape attitudes, and relationship aggression in college students. *Sex Roles, 38,* 743–756.

Ryan, R. H., & Geiselman, R. E. (1991). Effects of biased information on the relationship between eyewitness confidence and accuracy. *Bulletin of the Psychonomic Society, 29,* 7–9.

Ryan, R. M., Frederick, C. M., Lepes, D., Rubio, N., & Sheldon, K. M. (1997). Intrinsic motivation and exercise adherence. *International Journal of Sport Psychology, 28,* 335–354.

Sabatini, B. L., & Regehr, W. G. (1999). Timing of synaptic transmission. *Annual Review of Psychology, 61,* 521–542.

Sabbagh, M., & Cunnings, J. (2011). Progressive cholinergic decline in Alzheimer's disease: Consideration for treatment with donepezil 23 mg in patients with moderate to severe symptomatology. *BMC Neurology, 11,* 21–26.

Sabine, W. (2000). Cognitive therapy for obsessive-compulsive disorder. *Journal of Cognitive Psychotherapy, 14,* 245–259.

Sable, P. (1997). Attachment, detachment, and borderline personality disorder. *Psychotherapy, 34,* 171–181.

Sachdev, P. (2000). The current status of tardive dyskinesia. *Australian and New Zealand Journal of Psychiatry, 34,* 355–369.

Sachdev, P., Trollor, J., Walker, A., Wen, W., Fulham, M., Smith, J. S., & Matheson, J. (2001). Bilateral orbitomedial leucotomy for obsessive-compulsive disorder: A single-case study using positron emission tomography. *Australian and New Zealand Journal of Psychiatry, 35,* 684–690.

Sachdeva, S., Singh, P., & Medin, D. (2011). Culture and the quest for universal principles in moral reasoning. *International Journal of Psychology, 46,* 161–176.

Sackeim, H. A. (1994). Central issues regarding the mechanisms of action of electroconvulsive therapy: Directions for future research. *Psychopharmacology Bulletin, 30,* 281–308.

Sacks, O. (1985). *The man who mistook his wife for a hat and other clinical tales.* New York: Summit.

Saczynski, J. S. (2002). Cognitive training gains in the Seattle longitudinal study: Individual predictors and mediators of training effects. *Dissertation Abstracts International: Section B. The Sciences and Engineering, 62,* 6001.

Sadeh, A., Raviv, A., & Gruber, R. (2000). Sleep patterns and sleep disruptions in school-age children. *Developmental Psychology, 36,* 291–301.

Sadigh-Lindell, B., Sylven, C., Hagerman, I., Berglund, M., Terenius, L., Franzen, O., & Eriksson, B. E. (2001). Oscillation of pain intensity during adenosine infusion: Relationship to beta-endorphin and sympathetic tone. *Neuroreport: For Rapid Communication of Neuroscience Research, 12,* 1571–1575.

Sagar, K. A., Dahlgren, M. K., Gönenç, A., & Gruber, S. A. (2013). Altered affective processing in bipolar disorder: an fMRI study. *Journal of Affective Disorders, 150,* 1192–1196.

Sagie, A., Elizur, D., & Yamauchi, H. (1996). The structure and strength of achievement motivation: A cross-cultural comparison. *Journal of Organizational Behavior, 17,* 431–444.

Sakamoto, N., Gozal, D., Smith, D. L., Yang, L., Morimoto, N., Wada, H., ... Tanigawa, T. (2017). Sleep duration, snoring prevalence, obesity, and behavioral problems in a large cohort of primary school students in japan. *Sleep, 40.*

Sala, F., Krupat, E., & Roter, D. (2002). Satisfaction and the use of humor by physicians and patients. *Psychology and Health, 17,* 269–280.

Salanova, M., Llorens, S., Cifre, E., Martinez, I. M., & Schaufeli, W. B. (2003). Perceived collective efficacy, subjective well-being, and task performance among electronic work groups: An experimental study. *Small Group Research, 34,* 43–73.

Salerian, A. J., Deibler, W. E., Vittone, B. J., Geyer, S. P., Drell, L., Mirmirani, N., ... Fleisher, S. (2000). Sildenafil for psychotropic-induced sexual dysfunction in 31 women and 61 men. *Journal of Sex and Marital Therapy, 26,* 133–140.

Sales, B. D., & Folkman, S. (2000). *Ethics in research with human participants.* Washington, DC: American Psychological Association.

Salfati, C. G., & Canter, D. V. (1999). Differentiating stranger murders: Profiling offender characteristics from behavioral styles. *Behavioral Sciences and the Law, 17,* 391–406.

Sallis, J. F., Carlson, J. A., Mignano, A. M., Lemes, A., & Wagner, N. (2013). Trends in presentations of environmental and policy studies related to physical activity, nutrition, and obesity at society of behavioral medicine, 1995–2010: A commentary to accompany the Active Living Research supplement to *Annals of Behavioral Medicine. Annals of Behavioral Medicine, 45,* S14–S17.

Salovey, P., & Haar, M. D. (1990). The efficacy of cognitive-behavior therapy and writing process training for alleviating writing anxiety. *Cognitive Therapy and Research, 14,* 513–526.

Salthouse, T. A. (1991). Mediation of adult age differences in cognition by reductions in working memory and speed of processing. *Psychological Science, 2,* 179–183.

Salvatore, J., & Maracek, J. (2010). Gender in the gym: Evaluation concerns as barriers to women's weight lifting. *Sex Roles, 63,* 556–567.

Samelson, F. (1997). On the uses of history: The case of *The Bell Curve. Journal of the History of the Behavioral Sciences, 33,* 129–133.

Sameroff, A. (2010). A unified theory of development: A dialectic integration of nature and nurture. *Child Development, 81,* 6–22.

Samms, M., Hari, R., Rif, J., & Knuutila, J. (1993). The human auditory sensory memory trace persists about 10 sec: Neuromagnetic evidence. *Journal of Cognitive Neuroscience, 5,* 363–370.

Samuels, C. A., Butterworth, G., Roberts, T., & Graupner, L. (1994). Facial aesthetics: Babies prefer attractiveness to symmetry. *Perception, 23,* 823–831.

Sand, P., Kavvadias, D., Feineis, D., Riederer, P., Schreier, P., Kleinschnitz, M., . . . Beckmann, H. (2000). Naturally occurring benzodiazepines: Current status of research and clinical implications. *Journal of Clinical Psychopharmacology, 20,* 12–18.

Sanday, L., Zanin, K. A., Patti, C. L., Tufik, S., & Frussa-Filho, R. (2012). Role of state-dependency in memory impairment inducted by acute administration of midazolam in mice. *Progress in Neuro-Psychophamalogy & Biological Psychiatry, 37,* 1–7.

Sander, K., Brechmann, A., & Scheich, H. (2003). Audition of laughing and crying leads to right amygdala activation in a low-noise fMRI setting. *Brain Research Protocol, 11,* 81–91.

Sandman, D., Simantov, E., & An, C. (2000). *Out of touch: American men and the health care system* (Publication No. 374). New York: The Commonwealth Fund.

Sanghvi, C. (1995). Efficacy of study skills training in managing study habits and test anxiety of high test anxious students. *Journal of the Indian Academy of Applied Psychology, 21,* 71–75.

Sansone, R. A., & Sansone, L. A. (2011). Gender patterns in borderline personality disorder. *Innovations in Clinical Neuroscience, 8,* 16–20.

SantaCruz, K. S., Sonnen, J. A., Pezhough, M. K., Desrosiers, M. F., Nelson, P., & Tyas, S. L. (2011). Alzheimer disease pathology in subjects without dementia in 2 studies of aging: The Nun Study and the Adult Changes in Thought Study. *Journal of Neuropathology & Experimental Neurology, 70,* 832–840.

Santucci, A. C., Gluck, R., Kanof, P. D., & Haroutunian, V. (1993). Induction of memory and cortical cholinergic neurochemical recovery with combined fetal transplantation and GMI treatments in rats with lesions of the NBM. *Dementia, 4,* 272–281.

Saper, C. B., & Lowell, B. B. (2014). The hypothalamus. *Current Biology, 24,* R111–R116.

Sapp, M., Farrell, W. C., Jr., Johnson, J. H., Jr., & Hitchcock, K. (1999). Attitudes toward rape among African American male and female college students. *Journal of Counseling and Development, 77,* 204–208.

Sarason, S. (1984). If it can be studied or developed, should it be? *American Psychologist, 39,* 477–485.

Sargent-Cox, K. A., Anstey, K. J., & Luszcz, M. A. (2010). Patterns of longitudinal change in older adults' self-rated health, the effect of the point of reference. *Health Psychology, 29,* 143–152.

Satapathy, B. (2001). Getting the best out of your people: The Indian way. *Social Science International, 17,* 37–45.

Satir, V., Bitter, J. R., & Krestensen, K. K. (1988). Family reconstruction: The family within—A group experience. *Journal for Specialists in Group Work, 13,* 200–208.

Sato, T., & Beidler, L. M. (1997). Broad tuning of rat taste cells for four basic taste stimuli. *Chemical Senses, 22,* 287–293.

Satoh, M., Takeda, K., Nagata, K., Hatazawa, J., & Kuzuhara, S. (2001). Activated brain regions in musicians during an ensemble: A PET study. *Cognitive Brain Research, 12,* 101–108.

Saum, C. A., & Inciardi, J. A. (1997). Rohypnol misuse in the United States. *Substance Use and Misuse, 32,* 723–731.

Saunders, C. (1996). Hospice. *Mortality, 1,* 317–322.

Saunders, T., Driskell, J. E., Johnston, J. H., & Salas, E. (1996). The effect of stress-inoculation training on anxiety and performance. *Journal of Occupational Health Psychology, 1,* 170–186.

Savage-Rumbaugh, E. S., Rumbaugh, D. M., Smith, S. T., & Lawson, J. (1980). Reference: The linguistic essential. *Science, 210,* 922–925.

Savitz, J., Tan, C., Taylor, A., Drevets, W., & Teague, K., (2013). Abnormalities in regulatory T cells and natural killer cells in major depressive disorder (P3127). *Journal of Immunology, 190,* 25–43.

Sawatzky, J. V., & Naimark, B. J. (2002). Physical activity and cardiovascular health in aging women: A health-promotion perspective. *Journal of Aging and Physical Activity, 10,* 396–412.

Saxe, L., Dougherty, D., & Cross, T. (1985). The validity of polygraph testing: Scientific analysis and public controversy. *American Psychologist, 40,* 355–366.

Saxena, S., & Rauch, S. L. (2000). Functional neuroimaging and the neuroanatomy of obsessive-compulsive disorder. *Psychiatric Clinics of North America, 23,* 563–586.

Saygin, A. P., & Cicekli, I. (2002). Pragmatics in human-computer conversations. *Journal of Pragmatics, 34,* 227–258.

Scammell, T. E. (2001). Wakefulness: An eye-opening perspective on orexin neurons. *Current Biology, 11,* R769–R771.

Scammell, T. E. (2003). The neurobiology, diagnosis, and treatment of narcolepsy. *Annals of Neurology, 53,* 154–166.

Scarborough, H. S., Rescorla, L., Tager-Flusberg, H., Fowler, A. E., & Sudhalter, V. (1991). The relation of utterance length to grammatical complexity in normal and language-disordered groups. *Applied Psycholinguistics, 12,* 23–45.

Scarr, S. (1998). American child care today. *American Psychologist, 53,* 95–108.

Scarr, S., & Carter-Saltzman, L. (1979). Twin method: Defense of a critical assumption. *Behavior Genetics, 9,* 527–542.

Scarr, S., & Weinberg, R. A. (1976). IQ test performance of black children adopted by white families. *American Psychologist, 31,* 726–739.

Scarr, S., & Weinberg, R. A. (1983). The Minnesota Adoption Studies: Genetic differences and malleability. *Child Development, 54,* 260–267.

Schaal, B., Marlier, L., & Soussignan, R. (1998). Olfactory function in the human fetus: Evidence from selective neonatal responsiveness to the odor of amniotic fluid. *Behavioral Neuroscience, 112,* 1438–1449.

Schaap, J., & Meijer, J. H. (2001). Opposing effects of behavioural activity and light on neurons of the suprachiasmatic nucleus. *European Journal of Neuroscience, 13,* 1955–1962.

Schachter, S. (1971). Some extraordinary facts about obese humans and rats. *American Psychologist, 26,* 129–144.

Schachter, S. (1982). Recidivism and self-cure of smoking and obesity. *American Psychologist, 37,* 436–444.

Schachter, S., & Singer, J. E. (1962). Cognitive, social, and physiological determinants of emotional state. *Psychological Review, 69,* 379–399.

Schacter, D. L. (1983). Amnesia observed: Remembering and forgetting in a natural environment. *Journal of Abnormal Psychology, 92,* 236–242.

Schacter, D. L. (1992). Understanding implicit memory: A cognitive neuroscience approach. *American Psychologist, 47,* 559–569.

Schacter, D. L., Norman, K. A., & Koutstaal, W. (1998). The cognitive neuroscience of constructive memory. *Annual Review of Psychology, 49,* 289–318.

Schaefer, G. B., & Bodensteiner, J. B. (1999). Developmental anomalies of the brain in mental retardation. *International Review of Psychiatry, 11,* 47–55.

Schaefer, M., Egloff, B., & Witthöft, M. (2012). Is interoceptive awareness really altered in somatoform disorders? Testing competing theories with two paradignms of heartbeat perception. *Journal of Abnormal Psychology, 121,* 719–724.

Schafe, G. E., Sollars, S. I., & Bernstein, I. L. (1995). The CS-US interval and taste aversion learning: A brief look. *Behavioral Neuroscience, 109,* 799–802.

Schaie, K. W. (1989). Perceptual speed in adulthood: Cross-sectional and longitudinal studies. *Psychology and Aging, 4,* 443–453.

Schaie, K. W., & Hertzog, C. (1983). Fourteen-year cohort-sequential analyses of adult intellectual development. *Developmental Psychology, 19,* 531–543.

Schaie, K. W., Labouvie, G. V., & Barrett, T. J. (1973). Selective attrition effects in a 14-year study of adult intelligence. *Journal of Gerontology, 28,* 328–334.

Schaller, M., & Cialdini, R. B. (1988). The economics of empathic helping: Support for a mood management motive. *Journal of Experimental Social Psychology, 24,* 163–181.

Schaubroeck, J., Lam, S. S. K., & Xie, J. L. (2000). Collective efficacy versus self-efficacy in coping responses to stressors and control: A cross-cultural study. *Journal of Applied Psychology, 85,* 512–525.

Schechter, E. (2012). The switch model of split-brain consciousness. *Philosophical Psychology, 25,* 203–226.

Scheffler, T. S., & Naus, P. J. (1999). The relationship between fatherly affirmation and a woman's self-esteem, fear of intimacy, comfort with womanhood, and comfort with sexuality. *Canadian Journal of Human Sexuality, 8,* 39–45.

Scheflin, A. W., & Brown, D. (1996). Repressed memory or dissociative amnesia: What the science says. *Journal of Psychiatry and Law, 24,* 143–188.

Scherer, K. R. (1997). Profiles of emotion-antecedent appraisal: Testing theoretical predictions across cultures. *Cognition and Emotion, 11,* 113–150.

Scherer, K. R., & Ceschi, G. (1997). Lost luggage: A field study of emotion-antecedent appraisal. *Motivation and Emotion, 21,* 211–235.

Scherer, K. R., & Wallbott, H. G. (1994). Evidence for universality and cultural variation of differential emotion response patterning. *Journal of Personality and Social Psychology, 66,* 310–328.

Schiff, M., Duyme, M., Dumaret, A., & Tomkiewicz, S. (1982). How much could we boost scholastic achievement and IQ scores? A direct answer from a French adoption study. *Cognition, 12,* 165–196.

Schiffman, S. S., Sattely-Miller, E. A., Suggs, M. S., & Graham, B. G. (1995). The effect of pleasant odors and hormone status on mood of women at midlife. *Brain Research Bulletin, 36,* 19–29.

Schill, T., & O'Laughlin, M. S. (1984). Humor preference and coping with stress. *Psychological Reports, 55,* 309–310.

Schimel, J., Greenberg, J., & Martens, A. (2003). Evidence that projection of a feared trait can serve a defensive function. *Personality and Social Psychology Bulletin, 29,* 969–979.

Schlegel, P. A., & Roth, J. (1997). Tuning of electroreceptors in the blind cave salamander, *Proteus anguinus L. Brain, Behaviour, and Evolution, 49,* 132–136.

Schleifer, S. J., Keller, S. E., Camerino, M., Thornton, J. C., & Stein, M. (1983). Suppression of lymphocytic stimulation following bereavement. *Journal of the American Medical Association, 250,* 374–377.

Schlenker, B. R., Phillips, S. T., Boniecki, K. A., & Schlenker, D. R. (1995). Championship pressures: Choking or triumphing in one's own territory?

Schlesinger, L. B., & Revitch, E. (1999). Sexual burglaries and sexual homicide: Clinical, forensic, and investigative considerations. *Journal of the American Academy of Psychiatry and the Law, 27,* 227–238.

Schlumpf, Y. R., Nijenhuis, E. R. S., Chalavi, S., Weder, E. V, Zimmermann, E., Luechinger, R., . . . Jäncke, L. (2013). Dissociative part-dependent biopsychosocial reactions to backward masked angry and neutral faces: An fMRI study of dissociative identity disorder. *NeuroImage. Clinical, 3,* 54–64.

Schmader, T., & Johns, M. (2003). Converging evidence that stereotype threat reduces working memory capacity. *Journal of Personality & Social Psychology, 85,* 440–452.

Schmeidler, G. R. (1985). Belief and disbelief in psi. *Parapsychology Review, 16,* 1–4.

Schmeidler, G. R. (1993). William James: Pioneering ancestor of modern parapsychology. In M. E. Donnelly (Ed.), *Reinterpreting the legacy of William James* (pp. 339–352). Washington, DC: American Psychological Association.

Schmeidler, G. R. (1997). Psi-conducive experimenters and psi-permissive ones. *European Journal of Parapsychology, 13,* 83–94.

Schmid, H. (2003). The mystery of the moon illusion. Exploring size perception. *Swiss Journal of Psychology, 62,* 200–201.

Schmidt, G., & Weiner, B. (1988). A attribution-affect-action theory of behavior: Replications of judgments of help-giving. *Personality and Social Psychology Bulletin, 14,* 610–621.

Schmidt, H. G., Peeck, V. E., Paas, F., & Van Breukelen, G. J. P. (2000). Remembering the street names of one's childhood neighbourhood: A study of very long-term retention. *Memory, 8,* 37–49.

Schmidt, L. A., Trainor, L. J., & Santesso, D. L. (2003). Development of frontal electroencephalogram (EEG) and heart rate (ECG) responses to affective musical stimuli during the first 12 months of postnatal life. *Brain and Cognition, 52,* 27–32.

Schmidt, N. B., Lerew, D. R., & Jackson, R. J. (1999). Prospective evaluation of anxiety sensitivity in the pathogenesis of panic: Replication and extension. *Journal of Abnormal Psychology, 108,* 532–537.

Schmidt, S., & Walach, H. (2000). Electrodermal activity (EDA): State-of-the-art measurement and techniques for parapsychological purposes. *Journal of Parapsychology, 64,* 139–163.

Schmidtke, A., Weinacker, B., Apter, A., Batt, A., Berman, A., Bille-Brahe, U., . . . Wasserman, D. (1999). Suicide rates in the world: Update. *Archives of Suicide Research, 5,* 81–89.

Schmitt, I., Bitoun, E. I., & Manto, M. (2009). PTPRR, cerebellum, and motor coordination. *Cerebellum, 8,* 71–73.

Schmitt-Rodermund, E., & Vondracek, F. W. (1999). Breadth of interests, exploration, and identity development in adolescence. *Journal of Vocational Behavior, 55,* 298–317.

Schneider, B. H., Atkinson, L., & Tardif, C. (2001). Child-parent attachment and children's peer relatins: A quantitative review. *Developmental Psychology, 37,* 86–100.

Schneider, C. J. (1987). Cost effectiveness of biofeedback and behavioral medicine treatments: A review of the literature. *Biofeedback and Self-Regulation, 12,* 71–92.

Schneider, H. G., & Shugar, G. J. (1990). Audience and feedback effects in computer learning. *Computers in Human Behavior, 6,* 315–321.

Schneider, M. P., van Melle, G., Uldry, C., Huynh-Ba, M., Stubi, C. L. F., Iorillo, D., . . . Zellweger, J. P. (2003). Electronic monitoring of long-term use of the nicotine nasal spray and predictors of success in a smoking cessation program. *Nicotine and Tobacco Research, 5,* 719–727.

Schneider, P., Scherg, M., Dosch, H. G., Specht, H. J., Gutschalk, A., & Rupp, A. (2002). Mor phology of Heschl's gyrus reflects enhanced activation in the auditory cortex of musicians. *Nature Neuroscience, 5,* 688–694.

Schneider, T. R., Salovey, P., Pallonen, U., Mundorf, N., Smith, N. F., & Steward, W. T. (2001). Visual and auditory message framing effects on tobacco smoking. *Journal of Applied Social Psychology, 31,* 667–682.

Schneider-Rosen, K., & Burke, P. B. (1999). Multiple attachment relationships within families: Mothers and fathers with two young children. *Developmental Psychology, 35,* 436–444.

Schoen, L. M. (1996). Mnemopoly: Board games and menomics. *Teaching of Psychology, 23,* 30–32.

Schonemann, P. H., & Schonemann, R. D. (1994). Environmental versus genetic models for Osborne's personality data on identical and fraternal twins. *Cahiers de Psychologie, 13,* 141–167.

Schooler, C., Mulatu, M. S., & Oates, G. (1999). The continuing effects of substantively complex work on the intellectual functioning of older workers. *Psychology and Aging, 14,* 483–506.

Schott, R. L. (1995). The childhood and family dynamics of transvestites. *Archives of Sexual Behavior, 24,* 309–327.

Schotte, C. K. W., Van Den Bossche, B., De Doncker, D., Claes, S., & Cosyns, P. (2006). A biopsychosocial model as a guide for psychoeducation and treatment of depression. *Depression & Anxiety, 23,* 312–324.

Schretlen, D., Pearlson, G. D., Anthony, J. C., Aylward, E. H., Augustine, A. M., Davis, A., & Barta, P. (2000). Elucidating the contributions of processing speed, executive ability, and frontal lobe volume to normal age-related differences in fluid intelligence. *Journal of the International Neuropsychological Society, 6,* 52–61.

Schroth, M. L. (1995). A comparison of sensation seeking among different groups of athletes and nonathletes. *Personality and Individual Differences, 18,* 219–222.

Schroth, M. L., & McCormack, W. A. (2000). Sensation seeking and need for achievement among study-abroad students. *Journal of Social Psychology, 140,* 533–535.

Schrut, A. H. (1994). The Oedipus complex: Some observations and questions regarding its validity and universal existence. *Journal of the American Academy of Psychoanalysis, 22,* 727–751.

Schull, W. J., Norton, S., & Jensh, R. P. (1990). Ionizing radiation and the developing brain. *Neurotoxicology and Teratology, 12,* 249–260.

Schulz, D., Mirrione, M. M., & Henn, F. A. (2010). Cognitive aspects of congenital learned helplessness and its reversal by the monoamine oxidase (MAO)-B inhibitor deprenyl. *Neurobiology of Learning and Memory, 93,* 291–301.

Schulz, P., & Kaspar, C. H. (1994). Neuroendocrine and psychological effects of restricted environmental stimulation technique in a flotation tank. *Biological Psychology, 37,* 161–175.

Schulz, R., & Curnow, C. (1988). Peak performance and age among superathletes: Track and field, swimming, baseball, tennis, and golf. *Journal of Gerontology, 43,* 113–120.

Schuster, B., Forsterling, F., & Weiner, B. (1989). Perceiving the causes of success and failure: A cross-cultural examination of attributional concepts. *Journal of Cross-Cultural Psychology, 20,* 191–213.

Schuster, D. T. (1990). Fulfillment of potential, life satisfaction, and competence: Comparing four cohorts of gifted women at midlife. *Journal of Educational Psychology, 82,* 471–478.

Schutte, N. S., Malouff, J. M., Bobik, C., Coston, T. D., Greeson, C., Jedlicka, C., . . . Wendorf, G. (2001). Emotional intelligence and interpersonal relations. *Journal of Social Psychology, 141,* 523–536.

Schwartz, B. L., & Smith, S. M. (1997). The retrieval of related information influences tip-of-the-tongue states. *Journal of Memory and Language, 36,* 68–86.

Schwartz, C. E., Wright, C. I., Shin, L. M., Kagan, J., & Rauch, S. L. (2003). Inhibited and uninhibited infants "grown up": Adult amygdalar responses to novelty. *Science, 300,* 1952–1953.

Schwartz, J. C., Diaz, J., Pilon, C., & Sokoloff, P. (2000). Possible implications of the dopamine D-sub-3 receptor in schizophrenia and in antipsychotic drug actions. *Brain Research Reviews, 31,* 277–287.

Schwarz, T., Loewenstein, J., & Isenberg, K. E. (1995). Maintenance ECT: Indications and outcome. *Convulsive Therapy, 11,* 14–23.

Schweizer, T. A., Alexander, M. P., Gillingham, S., Cusimano, M., & Stuss, D. T. (2010). Lateralized cerebellar contributions to word generation: A phonemic and semantic fluency study. *Behavioral Neurology, 23,* 31–37.

Schwenzer, M., & Mathiak, K. (2011). Hypochondriacal attitudes may reflect a general cognitive bias that is not limited to illness-related thoughts. *Psychology & Health, 26,* 965–973.

Schyns, P. (1998). Cross-national differences in happiness: Economic and cultural factors explored. *Social Indicators, 43,* 3–26.

Scopesi, A., Zanobini, M., & Carossino, P. (1997). Childbirth in different cultures: Psychophysical reactions of women delivering in U.S., German, French, and Italian hospitals. *Journal of Reproductive and Infant Psychology, 15,* 9–30.

Scott, B. W., Wojtowicz, J. M., & Burnham, W. M. (2000). Neurogenesis in the dentate gyrus of the rat following electroconvulsive shock seizures. *Experimental Neurology, 165,* 231–236.

Scott, D., & Willits, F. K. (1994). Environmental attitudes and behavior: A Pennsylvania survey. *Environment and Behavior, 26,* 239–260.

Scott, J., Palmer, S., Paykel, E., Teasdale, J., & Hayhurst, H. (2003). Use of cognitive therapy for relapse prevention in chronic depression: Cost-effectiveness study. *British Journal of Psychiatry, 182,* 221–227.

Scott, K. G., & Carran, D. T. (1987). The epidemiology and prevention of mental retardation. *American Psychologist, 42,* 801–804.

Scott, M. S., Deuel, L. L. S., Jean-Francois, B., & Urbano, R. C. (1996). Identifying cognitively gifted ethnic minority children. *Gifted Child Quarterly, 40,* 147–153.

Scott, R. L., Butcher, J. N., Young, T. L., & Gomez, N. (2002). The Hispanic MMPI-A across five countries. *Journal of Clinical Psychology, 58,* 407–417.

Scoville, W. B., & Milner, B. (1957). Loss of recent memory after bilateral hippocampal lesions. *Journal of Neurology, Neurosurgery, and Psychiatry, 20,* 11–21.

Scully, J. A., Tosi, H., & Banning, K. (2000). Life events checklists: Revisiting the Social Readjustment Rating Scale after 30 years. *Educational and Psychological Measurement, 60,* 864–876.

Sears, R. R. (1977). Source of life satisfaction of the Terman gifted men. *American Psychologist, 32,* 119–128.

Sechrest, L. (1984). Review of the development and application of social language theory: Selected papers. *Journal of the History of the Behavioral Sciences, 20,* 228–230.

Sedlacek, K., & Taub, E. (1996). Biofeedback treatment of Raynaud's disease. *Professional Psychology: Research and Practice, 27,* 548–553.

Seegert, C. R. (2003). Token economies and incentive programs: Behavioral improvement in mental health inmates housed in state prisons. *Behavior Therapist, 208,* 210–211.

Segal, N. L. (2000). Virtual twins: New findings on within-family environmental influences on intelligence. *Journal of Educational Psychology, 92,* 442–448.

Segall, M. H., Dasen, P. R., Berry, J. W., & Poortinga, Y. H. (1990). *Human behavior in global perspective: An introduction to cross-cultural psychology.* New York: Pergamon.

Segerstrom, S. C., Taylor, S. E., Kemeny, M. E., Reed, G. M., & Visscher, B. R. (1996). Causal attributions predict rate of immune decline in HIV-seropositive gay men. *Health Psychology, 15,* 485–493.

Segovia, C., Hutchinson, I., Laing, D, G., & Jinks, A. L. (2002). A quantitative study of fungiform papillae and taste pore density in adults and children. *Developmental Brain Research, 138,* 135–146.

Seidenbecher, T., Laxmi, T. R., Stork, O., & Pape, H. C. (2003). Amygdalar and hippocampal theta rhythm synchronization during fear memory revisited. *Science, 301,* 846–850.

Seidlitz, L., & Diener, E. (1998). Sex differences in the recall of affective experiences. *Journal of Personality and Social Psychology, 74,* 262–271.

Seidman, S. M. (2003). The aging male: Androgens, erectile dysfunction, and depression. *Journal of Clinical Psychiatry, 64,* 31–37.

Seifert, L. S. (1996). On the use of concept formation tasks to educate naive observers about the visual arts. *Visual Arts Research, 22,* 11–19.

Seki, K., Matsumoto, D., & Imahori, T. T. (2002). The conceptualization and expression of intimacy in Japan and the United States. *Journal of Cross-Cultural Psychology, 33,* 303–319.

Selcuk, E., & Ong, A. D. (2013). Perceived partner responsiveness moderates the association between received emotional support and all-cause mortality. *Health Psychology, 32,* 231–235.

Self, D. J., & Baldwin, D. C., Jr. (1998). Does medical education inhibit the development of moral reasoning in medical students? A cross-sectional study. *Academic Medicine, 73,* S91–S93.

Seligman, M. E. P. (1970). On the generality of the laws of learning. *Psychological Review, 77,* 406–418.

Seligman, M. E. P. (1971). Phobias and preparedness. *Behavior Therapy, 2,* 307–320.

Seligman, M. E. P. (1989). Research in clinical psychology: Why is there so much depression today? In I. S. Cohen (Ed.), *The G. Stanley Hall Lecture Series* (Vol. 9, pp. 75–96). Washington, DC: American Psychological Association.

Seligman, M. E. P., & Maier, S. F. (1967). Failure to escape traumatic shock. *Journal of Experimental Psychology, 74,* 1–9.

Selye, H. (1936). A syndrome produced by diverse nocuous agents. *Nature, 138,* 32.

Semendeferi, K., Lu, A., Schenker, N., & Damasio, H. (2002). Humans and great apes share a large frontal cortex. *Nature Neuroscience, 5,* 272–276.

Semple, S. J., Strathdee, S. A., Zians, J., McQuaid, J. R., & Patterson, T. L. (2013). Drug assertiveness and sexual risk-taking behavior in a sample of HIV-positive, methamphetamine-using men who have sex with men. *Journal of Substance Abuse Treatment, 41,* 265–272.

Seo, D., Ahluwalia, A., Potenza, M. N., & Sinha, R. (2017). Gender differences in neural correlates of stress-induced anxiety. *Journal of Neuroscience Research, 95*(1–2), 115–125.

Serebriakoff, V. (1985). *Mensa: The society for the highly intelligent.* New York: Stein & Day.

Serok, S., & Levi, N. (1993). Application of Gestalt therapy with long-term prison inmates in Israel. *Gestalt Journal, 16,* 105–127.

Serper, M. R. (2011). Aggression in schizophrenia. *Schizophrenia Bulletin, 37,* 897–898.

Servan-Schreiber, D., & Perlstein, W. M. (1998). Selective limbic activation and its relevance to emotional disorders. *Cognition and Emotion, 12,* 331–352.

Setlow, B. (1997). Georges Ungar and memory transfer. *Journal of the History of the Neurosciences, 6,* 181–192.

Seto, M. C., Lalumiere, M. L., & Quinsey, V. L. (1995). Sensation seeking and males' sexual strategy. *Personality and Individual Differences, 19,* 669–675.

Seyfarth, R. M., Cheney, D. L., & Marler, P. (1980). Monkey responses to three different alarm calls: Evidence of predator classification and semantic communication. *Science, 210,* 801–803.

Seymour, T. L., Seifert, C. M., Shafto, M. G., & Mosmann, A. L. (2000). Using response time measures to assess "guilty knowledge." *Journal of Applied Psychology, 85,* 30–37.

Shackelford, T. K., Buss, D. M., & Weekes-Shackelford, V. A. (2003). Wife killings committed in the context of a lover's triangle. *Basic and Applied Social Psychology, 25,* 137–143.

Shadish, W. R., Navarro, A. M., Matt, G. E., & Phillips, G. (2000). The effects of psychological therapies under clinically representative conditions: A meta-analysis. *Psychological Bulletin, 126,* 512–529.

Shaffer, J. W., Graves, P. L., Swank, R. T., & Pearson, T. A. (1987). Clustering of personality traits in youth and the subsequent development of cancer among physicians. *Journal of Behavioral Medicine, 10,* 441–447.

Shah, M., & Jeffery, R. W. (1991). Is obesity due to overeating and inactivity, or to a defective metabolic rate? A review. *Annals of Behavioral Medicine, 13,* 73–81.

Shahab, L., West, R., & McNeill, A. (2011). A randomized, controlled trial of adding expired carbon monoxide feedback to brief stop smoking advice: Evaluation of cognitive and behavioral effects. *Health Psychology, 30,* 49–57.

Shaham, Y., Singer, J. E., & Schaeffer, M. H. (1992). Stability/instability of cognitive strategies across tasks determine whether stress will affect judgmental processes. *Journal of Applied Social Psychology, 22,* 691–713.

Shammi, P., & Stuss, D. T. (1999). Humour appreciation: A role of the right frontal lobe. *Brain, 122,* 657–666.

Shanab, M. E., & Yahya, K. A. (1977). A behavioral study of obedience in children. *Journal of Personality and Social Psychology, 35,* 530–536.

Shanker, S. G., Savage-Rumbaugh, E. S., & Taylor, T. J. (1999). Kanzi: A new beginning. *Animal Learning and Behavior, 27,* 24–25.

Shapiro, C. M., Bortz, R., Mitchell, D., Bartel, P., & Jooste, P. (1981). Slow-wave sleep: A recovery period after exercise. *Science, 214,* 1253–1254.

Shapiro, D. (1995). Finding out how psychotherapies help people change. *Psychotherapy Research, 5,* 1–21.

Shapiro, J. K. (1995). Dr. Kohlberg goes to Washington: Using congressional debates to teach moral development. *Teaching of Psychology, 22,* 245–247.

Shapiro, L. A. (2005). Can psychology be a unified science? *Philosophy of Science, 72,* 953–963.

Shapiro, L. J., & Stewart, S. E. (2011). Pathological guilt: A persistent yet overlooked treatment factor in obsessive-compulsive disorder. *Annals of Clinical Psychiatry, 23,* 63–70.

Sharpe, D., & Faye, C. (2009). A second look at debriefing practices: Madness in our method? *Ethics and Behavior, 19,* 432–447.

Sharpley, A. L. (2002). Sleep: Slow wave and non-REM stages. In E. Perry et al. (Eds.), *Neurochemistry of consciousness: Neurotransmitters in mind* (pp. 105–122). Amsterdam, Netherlands: John Benjamins.

Shaughnessy, M. F., & Nystul, M. S. (1985). Preventing the greatest loss—Suicide. *Creative Child and Adult Quarterly, 10,* 164–169.

Shavitt, S., Swan, S., Lowrey, T. M., & Wanke, M. (1994). The interaction of endorser attractiveness and involvement in persuasion depends on the goal that guides message processing. *Journal of Consumer Psychology, 3,* 137–162.

Shaw, J. S. III, Garcia, L. A., & McClure, K. A. (1999). A lay perspective on the accuracy of eyewitness testimony. *Journal of Applied Social Psychology, 29,* 52–71.

Shaw, P., Eckstrand, K., Sharp, W., Blumenthal, J., Lerch, J. P., Greenstein, D., . . . Rapoport, J. L. (2007). Attention-deficit/hyperactivity disorder is characterized by a delay in cortical maturation. *Proceedings of the National Academy of Sciences of the United States of America, 104,* 19649–19654.

Shaw, P., Gogtay, N., & Rapoport, J. (2010). Childhood psychiatric disorders as anomalies in neurodevelopmental trajectories. *Human Brain Mapping, 31,* 917–925.

Shaw, P., Gornick, M., Lerch, J., Addington, A., Seal, J., Greenstein, D., . . . Rapoport, J. L. (2007). Polymorphisms of the dopamine D4 receptor, clinical outcome, and cortical structure in attention-deficit/hyperactivity disorder. *Archives of General Psychiatry, 64,* 921–931.

Shaw, P., Lerch, J., Greenstein, D., Sharp, W., Clasen, L., Evans, A., . . . Rapoport, J. (2006). Longitudinal mapping of cortical thickness and clinical outcome in children and adolescents with attention-deficit/hyperactivity disorder. *Archives of General Psychiatry, 63,* 540–549.

Shea, J. D. (2003). Hypnosis with cancer patients. *Australian Journal of Clinical Hypnotherapy and Hypnosis, 24,* 98–111.

Shea, M. T., Elkin, I., Imber, S. D., & Sotsky, S. M. (1992). Course of depressive symptoms over follow-up: Findings from the National Institute of Mental Health Treatment of Depression Collaborative Research Program. *Archives of General Psychiatry, 49,* 782–787.

Shear, M. K., Feske, U., & Greeno, C. (2000). Gender differences in anxiety disorders: Clinical implications. In E. Frank (Ed.), *Gender and its effects on psychopathology* (pp. 151–165). Washington, DC: American Psychiatric Publishing.

Shedler, J. (2010). The efficacy of psychodynamic psychotherapy. *American Psychologist, 65,* 98–109.

Sheehan, P. W., & Tilden, J. (1983). Effects of suggestibility and hypnosis on accurate and distorted retrieval from memory. *Journal of Experimental Psychology: Learning, Memory, and Cognition, 9,* 283–293.

Sheehy, R., & Horan, J. J. (2004). Effects of stress inoculation training for 1st-year law students. *International Journal of Stress Management, 11,* 41–55.

Sheets, V. L. (2013). Passion for life: Self-expansion and passionate love across the life span. *Journal of Social & Personal Relationships, 28,* 748–771.

Shefler, G., Dasberg, H., & Ben-Shakhar, G. A. (1995). A randomized controlled outcome and follow-up study of Mann's limited psychotherapy. *Journal of Consulting and Clinical Psychology, 63,* 585–593.

Sheikh, J. I., Leskin, G. A., & Klein, D. F. (2002). Gender differences in panic disorder: Findings from the National Comorbidity survey. *American Journal of Psychiatry, 159,* 55–58.

Sheiner, E. K., Sheiner, E., Shoham-Vardi, I., Mazor, M., & Katz, M. (1999). Ethnic differences influence care giver's estimates of pain during labour. *Pain, 81,* 299–305.

Sheldon, W. H., & Stevens, S. S. (1942). *The varieties of temperament: A psychology of constitutional differences.* New York: Harper.

Shepard, R. N. (1984). Ecological constraints on internal representation: Resonant kinematics of perceiving, imagining, and dreaming. *Psychological Review, 91,* 417–447.

Sheppard, L. C., & Teasdale, J. D. (2004). How does dysfunctional thinking decrease during recovery from major depression? *Journal of Abnormal Psychology, 113,* 64–71.

Shepperd, J. A., & Taylor, K. M. (1999). Social loafing and expectancy-value theory. *Personality and Social Psychology Bulletin, 25,* 1147–1158.

Sherwood, S. J., & Roe, C. A. (2003). A review of dream ESP studies conducted since the Maimonides dream ESP studies. *Journal of Consciousness Studies, 10,* 85–109.

Shettleworth, S. J. (2012). Do animals have insight, and what is insight anyway? *Canadian Journal of Experimental Psychology, 66,* 217–226.

Shettleworth, S. J., & Juergensen, M. R. (1980). Reinforcement of the organization of behavior in golden hamsters: Brain stimulation reinforcement for seven action patterns. *Journal of Experimental Psychology: Animal Behavior Processes, 6,* 352–375.

Shevell, S. K., & He, J. C. (1997). The visual photopigments of simple deuteranomalous trichromats inferred from color matching. *Vision Research, 37,* 1115–1127.

Shields, S. A. (1975). Functionalism, Darwinism, and the psychology of women: A study in social myth. *American Psychologist, 30,* 739–754.

Shields, S. A. (1982). The variability hypothesis. *Signs, 7,* 769–797.

Shiffrin, R. M., & Atkinson, R. C. (1969). Storage and retrieval processes in long-term memory. *Psychological Review, 76,* 179–193.

Shih, M., Pittinsky, T. L., & Ambady, N. (1999). Stereotype susceptibility: Identity salience and shifts in quantitative performance. *Psychological Science, 10,* 80–83.

Shimada-Sugimoto, M., Otowa, T., & Hettema, J. M. (2015). Genetics of anxiety disorders: Genetic epidemiological and molecular studies in humans. *Psychiatry and Clinical Neurosciences, 69*(7), 388–401.

Shinskey, J. L. (2012). Disappearing décalage: Object search in light and dark at 6 months. *Infancy, 17,* 272–294.

Shioiri, T., Murashita, J., Kato, T., & Fujii, K. (1996). Characteristic clinical features and clinical course in 270 Japanese outpatients with panic disorder. *Journal of Anxiety Disorders, 10,* 163–172.

Shiraishi, T. (1990). CCK as a central satiety factor: Behavioral and electrophysiological evidence. *Physiology and Behavior, 48,* 879–885.

Shirom, A., Melamed, S., & Nir-Dotan, M. (2000). The relationships among objective and subjective environmental stress levels and serum uric acid: The moderating effect of perceived control. *Journal of Occupational Health Psychology, 5,* 374–385.

Shneidman, E. (1987, March). At the point of no return. *Psychology Today,* pp. 54–58.

Shneidman, E. S. (1994). Clues to suicide reconsidered. *Suicide and Life-Threatening Behavior, 24,* 395–397.

Shockley, W. (1972). Dysgenics, geneticity, raceology: A challenge to the intellectual responsibility of educators. *Phi Delta Kappan, 53,* 297–307.

Shook, N. J., Gerrity, D. A., Jurich, J., & Segrist, A. E. (2000). Courtship violence among college students: A comparison of verbally and physically couples. *Journal of Family Violence, 15,* 1–22.

Short, A., Vandelanotte, C., Rebar, A., & Duncan, M. J. (2013). A comparison of correlates associated with adult physical activity behavior in major cities and regional settings. *Health Psychology.*

Shostrom, E. L. (1962). *Personal orientation inventory.* San Diego: EDITS.

Shotland, R. L., & Straw, M. J. (1976). Bystander response to an assault: When a man attacks a woman. *Journal of Personality and Social Psychology, 34,* 990–999.

Shumaker, S. A., Legault, C., Rapp, S. R., Thal, L., Wallace, R. B., Ockens, J. K., . . . Wactawski-Wende, J. (2003). Estrogen plus progestin and the incidence of dementia and mild cognitive impairment in postmenopausal women: The Women's Health Initiative Memory Study: A randomized controlled trial. *JAMA: Journal of the American Medical Association, 289,* 2651–2662.

Shurcliff, A. (1968). Judged humor, arousal, and the relief theory. *Journal of Personality and Social Psychology, 8,* 360–363.

Sias, P. M., Pedersen, H., Gallagher, E. B., & Kopaneva, I. (2012). Workplace friendship in the electronically connected organization. *Human Communication Research, 38,* 253–279.

Siddiqui, R. N., & Pandey, J. (2003). Coping with environmental stressors by urban slum dwellers. *Environment and Behavior, 35,* 589–604.

Siegel, J. M., & Brown, J. D. (1988). A prospective study of stressful circumstances, illness symptoms, and depressed mood among adolescents. *Developmental Psychology, 24,* 715–721.

Siegel, S., & Allan, L. G. (1996). The widespread influence of the Rescorla-Wagner model. *Psychonomic Bulletin and Review, 3,* 314–321.

Siegel, S., Baptista, M. A. S., & Kim, J. (2000). Pavlovian psychopharmacology: The associative basis of tolerance. *Experimental and Clinical Psychopharmacology, 8,* 276–293.

Siegmund, A., Köster, L., Meves, A. M., Plag, J., Stoy, M., & Ströhe, A. (2011). Stress hormones during flooding therapy and their relationship to therapy outcomes in patients with panic disorder and agoraphobia. *Journal of Psychiatric Research, 45,* 339–346.

Sierra-Honigmann, A. M., Carbone, K. M., & Yolken, R. H. (1995). Polymerase chain reaction (PCR) search for viral nucleic acid sequences in schizophrenia. *British Journal of Psychiatry, 166,* 55–60.

Siever, M. D. (1994). Sexual orientation and gender as factors in socioculturally acquired vulnerability to body dissatisfaction and eating disorders. *Journal of Consulting and Clinical Psychology, 62,* 252–260.

Signorella, M. L., Bigler, R. S., & Liben, L. S. (1997). A meta-analysis of children's memories for own-sex and other-sex information. *Journal of Applied Developmental Psychology, 18,* 429–445.

Silinsky, E. M. (1989). Adenosine derivatives and neuronal function. *Seminars in the Neurosciences, 1,* 155–165.

Silke, A. (2003). Deindividuation, anonymity, and violence: Findings from Northern Ireland. *Journal of Social Psychology, 143,* 493–499.

Silva, J. M. III, & Weinberg, R. S. (1984). *Psychological foundations of sport.* Champaign, IL: Human Kinetics.

Silverman, I. W. (2003). Gender differences in delay of gratification: A meta-analysis. *Sex Roles, 49,* 451–463.

Silverstein, L. B., & Auerbach, C. F. (1999). Deconstructing the essential father. *American Psychologist, 54,* 397–407.

Silverthorne, Z. A., & Quinsey, V. L. (2000). Sexual partner age preferences of homosexual and heterosexual men and women. *Archives of Sexual Behavior, 29,* 67–76.

Silvestri, S., Seeman, M. V., Negrete, J.-C., Houle, S., Shammi, C. M., Remington, G. J., . . . Seeman, P. (2000). Increased dopamine D-sub-2 receptor binding after long-term treatment with antipsychotics in humans: A clinical PET study. *Psychopharmacology, 152,* 174–180.

Simon, H. A. (1995). The information-processing theory of mind. *American Psychologist, 50,* 507–508.

Simon, N. (1979). Kaspar Hauser's recovery and autopsy: A perspective on neurological and sociological requirements for language development. *Annual Progress in Child Psychiatry & Child Development, 215*–228.

Simon, R. I. (1997). Video voyeurs and the covert videotaping of unsuspecting victims: Psychological and legal consequences. *Journal of Forensic Sciences, 42,* 884–889.

Simonoff, E., Bolton, P., & Rutter, M. (1996). Mental retardation: Genetic findings, clinical implications and research agenda. *Journal of Child Psychology and Psychiatry and Allied Disciplines, 37,* 259–280.

Simons, D. A., & Wurtele, S. K. (2010). Relationship between parents' use of corporal punishment and their children's endorsement of spanking and hitting other children. *Child Abuse & Neglect, 34,* 639–646.

Simons-Morton, B. G. (2002). Prospective analysis of peer and parent influences on smoking initiation among early adolescents. *Prevention Science, 3,* 275–283.

Simonton, D. K. (1984). *Genius, creativity, and leadership: Historimetric inquiries.* Cambridge, MA: Harvard University Press.

Simonton, D. K. (1999). Creativity and genius. In L. Pervin & O. John (Eds.), *Handbook of personality theory and research* (2nd ed., pp. 629–652). NY: Guilford.

Simonton, D. K. (2000). Creativity: Cognitive, personal, developmental, and social aspects. *American Psychologist, 55,* 151–158.

Simpson, B. A. (1986). The polygraph: Concept, usage, and validity. *Psychology: A Quarterly Journal of Human Behavior, 23,* 42–45.

Simpson, D. (2005). Phrenology and the neurosciences: contributions of F. J. Gall and J. G. Spurzheim. *Australian and New Zealand Journal of Surgery, 75,* 472–482.

Singer, A. G., & Macrides, F. (1990). Aphrodisin: Pheromone or transducer? *Chemical Senses, 15,* 199–203.

Singer, J. D., Fuller, B., Keiley, M. K., & Wolf, A. (1998). Early child-care selection: Variation by geographic location, maternal characteristics, and family structure. *Developmental Psychology, 34,* 1129–1144.

Singer, J. L., & Kolligian, J., Jr. (1987). Personality: Developments in the study of private experience. *Annual Review of Psychology, 38,* 533–574.

Singh, A. K., Mahlios, J., & Mignot, E. (2013). Genetic association, seasonal infections and autoimmune basis of narcolepsy. *Journal of Autoimmunity, 43,* 26–31.

Singh, R., & Ho, S. Y. (2000). Attitudes and attraction: A new test of the attraction, repulsion and similarity-dissimilarity hypotheses. *British Journal of Social Psychology, 39,* 197–211.

Sinha, R., & Jastreboff, A. M. (2013). Stress as a common risk factor for obesity and addiction. *Biological Psychiatry, 73,* 827–835.

Sinson, J. C. (1994). Normalization and community integration of adults with severe mental handicap relocated to group homes. *Journal of Developmental and Physical Disabilities, 6,* 255–270.

Sirridge, M. (2005). Dream bodies and dream pains in Augustine's "De natura et orgine animae." *Vivarium, 43,* 213–249.

Sizemore, C. C., & Huber, R. J. (1988). The 22 faces of Eve. *Individual Psychology: Journal of Adlerian Theory, Research, and Practice, 44,* 53–62.

Skinner, B. F. (1945, October). Baby in a box. *Ladies Home Journal,* pp. 30–31.

Skinner, B. F. (1948). *Walden two.* New York: Macmillan.

Skinner, B. F. (1953). *Science and human behavior.* New York: Macmillan.

Skinner, B. F. (1956). A case history in scientific method. *American Psychologist, 11,* 221–233.

Skinner, B. F. (1957). *Verbal behavior.* New York: Appleton-Century-Crofts.

Skinner, B. F. (1960). Pigeons in a pelican. *American Psychologist, 15,* 28–37.

Skinner, B. F. (1974). *About behaviorism.* New York: Knopf.

Skinner, B. F. (1984). The shame of American education. *American Psychologist, 39,* 947–954.

Skinner, B. F. (1986). What is wrong with daily life in the Western world? *American Psychologist, 41,* 220–222.

Skinner, B. F. (1989). Teaching machines. *Science, 243,* 1535.

Skinner, N., & Brewer, N. (2002). The dynamics of threat and challenge appraisals prior to stressful achievement events. *Journal of Personality and Social Psychology, 83,* 678–692.

Skinner, N. F. (1983). Switching answers on multiple-choice questions: Shrewdness or shibboleth? *Teaching of Psychology, 10,* 220–222.

Skoe, E. E. A., Cumberland, A., Eisenberg, N., Hansen, K., & Perry, J. (2002). The influence of sex and gender-role identity on moral cognition and prosocial personality traits. *Sex Roles, 46,* 295–309.

Skoe, E. E. A., Hansen, K. L., Morch, W.-T., Bakke, I., Hoffmann, T., Larsen, B., & Aasheim, M. (1999). Care-based moral reasoning in Norwegian and Canadian early adolescents: A cross-national comparison. *Journal of Early Adolescence, 19,* 280–291.

Skre, I., Onstad, S., Torgersen, S., Lygren, S., & Kringlen, E. (2000). The heritability of common phobic fear: A twin study of a clinical sample. *Journal of Anxiety Disorders, 14,* 549–562.

Slabbekoorn, D., Van Goozen, S. H. M., Gooren, L. J. G., & Cohen-Kettenis, P. T. (2001). Effects of cross-sex hormone treatment on emotionality in transsexuals. *International Journal of Transgenderism, 5,* 2.

Slater, A. (1992). The visual constancies in early infancy. *Irish Journal of Psychology, 13,* 412–425.

Slater, C. L. (2003). Generativity versus stagnation: An elaboration of Erikson's adult stage of human development. *Journal of Adult Development, 10,* 53–65.

Slavik, S., & Croake, J. (2006). Individual psychology perspectives on the phenomenology of depression. *Journal of Individual Psychology, 62,* 429–442.

Slayton, J. M. (1998). Treatment algorithms: Bane or boon to mental health? *Harvard Review of Psychiatry, 6,* 225–227.

Slife, B. D. (2005). The Kant of psychology: Joseph Rychlak and the bridge to postmodern psychology, *Journal of Constructivist Psychology, 18,* 297–306.

Slifer, K. J., Eischen, S. E., & Busby, S. (2002). Using counterconditioning to treat behavioural distress during subcutaneous injections in a paediatric rehabilitation patient. *Brain Injury, 16,* 901–916.

Slišković, A., Seršić, D. M., & Burić, I. (2011). Work locus of control as a mediator of the relationship between sources and consequences of occupational stress among university teachers. *Review of Psychology, 18,* 109–118.

Slob, A. K., Steyvers, C. L., Lottman, P. E. M., van der Werften Bosh, J. J., & Hop, W. C. J. (1998). Routine psychophysiological screening of 384 men with erectile dysfunction. *Journal of Sex and Marital Therapy, 24,* 273–279.

Slutske, W. S., Eisen, S., Xian, H., True, W. R., Lyons, M. J., Goldberg, J., & Tsuang, M. (2001). A twin study of the association between pathological gambling and antisocial personality disorder. *Journal of Abnormal Psychology, 110,* 297–308.

Small, S. L., Buccino, G., & Solodkin, A. (2012). The mirror neuron system and treatment of stroke. *Developmental Psychobiology, 54,* 293–310.

Smith, A. L., & Tart, C. T. (1998). Cosmic consciousness experience and psychedelic experiences: A first-person comparison. *Journal of Consciousness Studies, 5,* 97–107.

Smith, B. D., Cranford, D., & Mann, M. (2000). Gender, cynical hostility, and cardiovascular function: Implications for differential cardiovascular disease risk? *Personality and Individual Differences, 29,* 659–670.

Smith, B. M., Schumaker, J. B., Schaeffer, J., & Sherman, J. A. (1982). Increasing participation and improving the quality of discussion in seventh-grade social studies classes. *Journal of Applied Behavior Analysis, 15,* 97–110.

Smith, C. T., De Houwer, J., & Nosek, B. A. (2013). Consider the source: Persuasion of implicit evaluations is moderated by source credibility. *Personality & Social Psychology Bulletin, 39,* 193–205.

Smith, D. (1982). Trends in counseling and psychotherapy. *American Psychologist, 37,* 802–809.

Smith, D. G., Standing, L., & de Man, A. (1992). Verbal memory elicited by ambient odor. *Perceptual and Motor Skills, 74,* 339–343.

Smith, D. V., & Margolis, F. L. (1999). Taste processing: Whetting our appetites. *Current Biology, 9,* R453–R455.

Smith, G. L., Large, M. M., Kavanagh, D. J., Karayanidis, F., Barrett, N. A., Michie, P. T., & O'Sullivan, B. T. (1998). Further evidence for a deficit in switching attention in schizophrenia. *Journal of Abnormal Psychology, 107,* 390–398.

Smith, H. V. (1992). Is there a magical number 7 ± 2? The role of exposure duration and information content in immediate recall. *Irish Journal of Psychology, 13,* 85–97.

Smith, H. F. (1995). Introduction: Gedo and Freud on working through. *Journal of the American Psychoanalytic Association, 43,* 331–392.

Smith, J. D. (1988). Fancher on Gould, Goddard, and historical interpretation: A reply. *American Psychologist, 43,* 744–745.

Smith, J. L., & White, P. H. (2002). An examination of implicitly activated, explicitly activated, and nullified stereotypes on mathematical performance: It's not just a woman's issue. *Sex Roles, 47,* 179–191.

Smith, J. W., & Frawley, P. J. (1993). Treatment outcome of 600 chemically dependent patients treated in a multimodal inpatient program including aversion therapy and pentothal interviews. *Journal of Substance Abuse Treatment, 10,* 359–369.

Smith, K. K. (2000). Symptom management in the adult headache population. *Dissertation Abstracts International: Section B: The Sciences and Engineering, 60,* 50–52.

Smith, L. D. (2002). On prediction and control: B. F. Skinner and the technological ideal of science. In W. E. Pickren & D. A. Dewsburgy (Eds.), *Evolving perspectives on the history of psychology* (pp. 255–272). Washington, DC: American Psychological Association.

Smith, L. T. (1974). The interanimal transfer phenomenon: A review. *Psychological Bulletin, 81,* 1078–1095.

Smith, M. C. (1983). Hypnotic memory enhancement of witnesses: Does it work? *Psychological Bulletin, 94,* 387–407.

Smith, M. C., & Phillips, M. R., Jr. (2001). Age differences in memory for radio advertisements: The role of mnemonics. *Journal of Business Research, 53,* 103–109.

Smith, M. L., Glass, G. V., & Miller, T. I. (1980). *The benefits of psychotherapy.* Baltimore: Johns Hopkins University Press.

Smith, S. M. (1984). A comparison of two techniques for reducing context-dependent forgetting. *Memory and Cognition, 12,* 477–482.

Smith, S. M., Brown, H. O., Toman, J. E. P., & Goodman, J. S. (1947). The lack of cerebral effects of d-tubercurarine. *Anesthesiology, 8,* 1–14.

Smith, S. M., McIntosh, W. D., & Bazzini, D. G. (1999). Are the beautiful good in Hollywood? An investigation of the beauty-and-goodness stereotype on film. *Basic and Applied Social Psychology, 21,* 69–80.

Smith, S. M., & Vela, E. (1992). Environmental context-dependent eyewitness recognition. *Applied Cognitive Psychology, 6,* 125–139.

Smith, S. S., & Richardson, D. (1983). Amelioration of deception and harm in psychological research: The important role of debriefing. *Journal of Personality and Social Psychology, 44,* 1075–1082.

Smith, T., Snyder, C. R., & Perkins, S. (1983). The self-serving function of hypochondriacal complaints: Physical symptoms as self-handicapping strategies. *Journal of Personality and Social Psychology, 44,* 787–797.

Smits, M. G., Nagtegaal, E. E., van der Heijden, J., Coenen, A. M. L., & Kerkhof, G. A. (2001). Melatonin for chronic sleep onset insomnia in children: A randomized placebo-controlled trial. *Journal of Child Neurology, 16,* 86–92.

Smolak, L., Murnen, S. K., & Ruble, A. E. (2000). Female athletes and eating problems: A meta-analysis. *International Journal of Eating Disorders, 27,* 371–380.

Snarey, J. R., Reimer, J., & Kohlberg, L. (1985). Development of social-moral reasoning among kibbutz adolescents: A longitudinal cross-cultural study. *Developmental Psychology, 21,* 3–17.

Sneed, J. R., Whitbourne, S. K., Schwartz, S. J., & Huang, S. (2012). The relationship between identity, intimacy, and midlife well-being: Findings from the Rochester Adult Longitudinal Study. *Psychology and Aging, 27,* 318–323.

Snow, C. E. (1981). The uses of imitation. *Journal of Child Language, 8,* 205–212.

Snow, D. S. (2000). The emotional basis of linguistic and nonlinguistic intonation: Implications for hemispheric specialization. *Developmental Neuropsychology, 17,* 1–28.

Snow, W. G., & Sheese, S. (1985). Lateralized brain damage, intelligence, and memory: A failure to find sex differences. *Journal of Consulting and Clinical Psychology, 33,* 940–941.

Snyder, B. K., Roghmann, K. J., & Sigal, L. H. (1993). Stress and psychosocial factors: Effects on primary cellular immune response. *Journal of Behavioral Medicine, 16,* 143–161.

Snyder, J. S., Soumier, A., Brewer, M., Pickel, J., & Cameron, H. A. (2011). Adult hippocampal neurogenesis buffers stress responses and depressive behaviour. *Nature, 476,* 458–461.

Snyder, M. (1983). The influence of individuals on situations: Implications for understanding the links between personality and social behavior. *Journal of Personality, 51,* 497–516.

Snyder, R. F. (2000). The relationship between learning styles/multiple intelligences and academic achievement of high school students. *High School Journal, 83,* 11–20.

Snyder, S. H. (2002). Forty years of neurotransmitters: A personal account. *Archives of General Psychiatry, 59,* 983–994.

Snyderman, M., & Herrnstein, R. J. (1983). Intelligence tests and the Immigration Act of 1924. *American Psychologist, 38,* 986–995.

Soderstrom, N. C., Davalos, D. B., & Vázquez, S. M. (2011). Metacognition and depressive realism: Evidence for the level-of-depression account. *Cognitive Neuropsychiatry, 16,* 461–472.

Soffer-Dudek, N., & Shahar, G. (2010). Effect of exposure to terrorism on sleep-related experiences in Israeli young adults. *Psychiatry: Interpersonal & Biological Processes, 73,* 264–276.

Sogon, S., & Izard, C. E. (1987). Sex differences in emotion recognition by observing body movements: A case of American students. *Japanese Psychological Research, 29,* 89–93.

Solcova, I., & Sykora, J. (1995). Relation between psychological hardiness and physiological response. *Homeostasis in Health and Disease, 36,* 30–34.

Solomon, C. (2003). Transactional analysis theory: The basics. *Transactional Analysis Journal, 33,* 15–22.

Solomon, P. R., & Morse, D. L. (1981). Teaching the principles of operant conditioning through laboratory experience: The rat Olympics. *Teaching Psychology, 8,* 111–112.

Solomon, R. L. (1980). The opponent-process theory of acquired motivation: The costs of pleasure and the benefits of pain. *American Psychologist, 35,* 691–712.

Solomon, S., & Guglielmo, K. M. (1985). Treatment of headache by transcutaneous electrical stimulation. *Headache, 25,* 12–15.

Solowij, N., Michie, P. T., & Fox, A. M. (1995). Differential impairments of selective attention due to frequency and duration of cannabis use. *Biological Psychiatry, 37,* 731–739.

Sommer, B., Avis, N., Meyer, P., Ory, M., Madden, T, Kagawa-Singer, M., . . . Adler, S. (1999). Attitudes toward menopause and aging across ethnic/racial groups. *Psychosomatic Medicine, 61,* 868–875.

Sommers, S. (1984). Reported emotions and conventions of emotionality among college students. *Journal of Personality and Social Psychology, 46,* 207–215.

Sonino, N., Navarrini, C., Ruini, C., Fallo, F., Boscaro, M., & Fava, G. A. (2004). Life events in the pathogenesis of hyperprolactinemia. *European Journal of Endocrinology, 151,* 61–65.

Sonstroem, R. J., & Bernardo, P. (1982). Intraindividual pregame state anxiety and basketball performance: A re-examination of the inverted-U curve. *Journal of Sport Psychology, 4,* 235–245.

Soumier, A., Banasr, M., Lortet, S., Masmejean, F., Bernard, N., Kerkerian-Le-Goff, L., . . . Daszuta, A. (2009). Mechanisms contributing to the phase-dependent regulation of neurogenesis by the novel antidepressant, agomelatine, in the adult rat hippocampus. *Neuropsychopharmacology, 34,* 2390–2403.

Sourkes, T. L. (2009). Acetylcholine: From vagusstoff to cerebral neurotransmitter. *Journal of the History of the Neurosciences, 18,* 47–58.

Soussignan, R. (2002). Duchenne smile, emotional experience, and autonomic reactivity: A test of the facial feedback hypothesis. *Emotion, 2,* 52–74.

Sowislo, J. F., & Orth, U. (2013). Does low self-esteem predict depression and anxiety? A meta-analysis of longitudinal studies. *Psychological Bulletin, 139,* 213–240.

Spangenberg, E. R., Crowley, A. E., & Henderson, P. W. (1996). Improving the store environment: Do olfactory cues affect evaluations and behaviors? *Journal of Marketing, 60,* 67–80.

Spangenberg, J., & Nel, E. M. (1983). The effect of equal-status contact on ethnic attitudes. *Journal of Social Psychology, 121,* 173–180.

Spangler, W. D. (1992). Validity of questionnaire and TAT measures of need for achievement: Two meta-analyses. *Psychological Bulletin, 112,* 140–154.

Spanos, N., Weekes, J. R., & Bertrand, L. (1985). Multiple personality: A social psychological perspective. *Journal of Abnormal Psychology, 94,* 362–376.

Spanos, N. P., Burgess, C. A., Burgess, M. F., Samuels, C., & Blois, W. G. (1999). Creating false memories of infancy with hypnotic and nonhypnotic procedures. *Applied Cognitive Psychology, 13,* 201–218.

Spanos, N. P., & Hewitt, E. C. (1980). The hidden observer in hypnotic analgesia: Discovery or experimental creation? *Journal of Personality and Social Psychology, 49,* 1201–1214.

Spanos, N. P., McNeil, C., & Stam, H. J. (1982). Hypnotically "reliving" a prior burn: Effects on blister formation and localized skin temperature. *Journal of Abnormal Psychology, 91,* 303–305.

Sparks, G. G., & Pellechia, M. (1997). The effect of news stories about UFOs on readers' UFO beliefs: The role of confirming or disconfirming testimony from a scientist. *Communication Reports, 10,* 165–172.

Sparks, G. G., Pellechia, M., & Irvine, C. (1999). The repressive coping style and fright reactions to mass media. *Communication Research, 26,* 176–192.

Speca, M., Carlson, L. E., Goodey, E., & Angen, M. (2000). A randomized, wait-list controlled clinical trial: The effect of a mindfulness meditation-based stress reduction program on mood and symptoms of stress in cancer outpatients. *Psychosomatic Medicine, 62,* 613–622.

Spector, I. P., & Carey, M. P. (1990). Incidence and prevalence of the sexual dysfunctions: A critical review of the empirical literature. *Archives of Sexual Behavior, 19,* 389–408.

Spector, N. H. (1997). The great Hans Selye and the great "stress" muddle. *Developmental Brain Dysfunction, 10,* 538–542.

Spector, P. E., Sanchez, J. I., Sui, O. L., Salgado, J., & Ma., J. (2004). Eastern versus Western control beliefs at work: An investigation of secondary control, socioinstrumental control, and work locus of control in China and the US. *Applied Psychology, 53,* 38–60.

Speisman, J. C., Lazarus, R. S., Mordkoff, A., & Davison, L. (1964). Experimental reduction of stress based on ego-defense theory. *Journal of Abnormal and Social Psychology, 68,* 367–380.

Spencer, R. C., Klein, R. M., & Berridge, C. W. (2012). Psychostimulants act within the prefrontal cortex to improve cognitive function. *Biological Psychiatry, 72,* 221–227.

Spengler, F., Godde, B., & Dinse, H. R. (1995). Effects of ageing on topographic organization of somatosensory cortex. *Neuroreport: An International Journal for the Rapid Communication of Research in Neuroscience, 6,* 469–473.

Sperling, G. (1960). The information available in brief visual presentations. *Psychological Monographs, 74* (498).

Sperry, R. W. (1982). Some effects of disconnecting the cerebral hemispheres. *Science, 217,* 1223–1226.

Sperry, R. W. (1984). Consciousness, personal identity, and the divided brain. *Neuropsychologia, 22,* 661–673.

Spicer, R. S., & Miller, T. R. (2000). Suicide acts in 8 states: Incidence and case fatality rates by demographics and method. *American Journal of Public Health, 90,* 1885–1891.

Spiegel, A. D., & Suskind, P. B. (1998). Chloroform-induced insanity defense confounds lawyer Lincoln. *History of Psychiatry, 8,* 487–500.

Spierings, E. L. H. (2003). Pathogenesis of the migraine attack. *Clinical Journal of Pain, 19,* 255–262.

Spillmann, J., & Spillmann, L. (1993). The rise and fall of Hugo Münsterberg. *Journal of the History of the Behavioral Sciences, 29,* 322–338.

Spinella, M., Znamensky, V., Moroz, M., Ragnauth, A., & Bodnar, R. J. (1999). Actions of NMDA and cholinergic receptor antagonists in the rostral ventromedial medulla upon beta-endorphin analgesia elicited from the ventrolateral periaqueductal gray. *Brain Research, 829,* 151–159.

Spitzer, R. L. (1975). On pseudoscience in science, logic in remission, and psychiatric diagnosis: A critique of Rosenhan's "On being sane in insane places." *Journal of Abnormal Psychology, 84,* 442–452.

Spotts, E. L., Lichtenstein, P., Pedersen, N., Neiderhiser, J. M., Hansson, K., Cederblad, M., & Reiss, D. (2005). Personality and marital satisfaction: A behavioural genetic analysis. *European Journal of Personality, 19,* 205–227.

Sprecher, S., & Toro-Morn, M. (2002). A study of men and women from different sides of earth to determine if men are from Mars and women are from Venus in their beliefs about love and romantic relationships. *Sex Roles, 46,* 131–147.

Springer, S. P., & Deutsch, G. (1998). *Left brain, right brain* (5th ed.). New York: Freeman.

Sprock, J. (2000). Gender-typed behavioral examples of histrionic personality disorder. *Journal of Psychopathology and Behavioral Assessment, 22,* 107–122.

Spurr, J. M., & Stopa, L. (2003). The observer perspective: Effects on social anxiety and performance. *Behaviour Research and Therapy, 41,* 1009–1028.

Spyer, K. M. (1989). Neural mechanisms involved in cardiovascular control during affective behavior. *Trends in Neurosciences, 12,* 506–513.

Squire, L. R. (1992). Declarative and nondeclarative memory: Multiple brain systems supporting learning and memory. *Journal of Cognitive Neuroscience, 4,* 232–243.

Srivastava, S., & Sharma, M. (1998). Seasonal affective disorder: Report from India (latitude 26" 45' N). *Journal of Affective Disorders, 49,* 145–150.

Staats, A. W. (1994). Psychological behaviorism and behaviorizing psychology. *Behavior Analyst 17,* 93–114.

Stack, S. (1998). Gender, marriage, and suicide acceptability: A comparative analysis. *Sex Roles, 38,* 501–520.

Stack, S., & Eshleman, J. R. (1998). Marital status and happiness: A 17-nation study. *Journal of Marriage and the Family, 60,* 527–536.

Stafford, J., & Lynn, S. J. (2002). Cultural scripts, memories of childhood abuse, and multiple identities: A study of role-played enactments. *International Journal of Clinical and Experimental Hypnosis, 50,* 67–85.

Stafford-Clark, D. (1965). *What Freud really said.* New York: Schocken Books.

Stairs, A. (1992). Self-image, world-image: Speculations on identity from experiences with Inuit. *Ethos, 20,* 116–126.

Stajkovic, A. D., & Luthans, F. (1998). Self-efficacy and work-related performance: A meta-analysis. *Psychological Bulletin, 124,* 240–261.

Stamps, J. J., Bartoshuck, L. M., & Heilman, K. M. (2013). A brief olfactory test for Alzheimer's disease. *Journal of the Neurological Sciences, 333,* 19–24.

Stankov, L., & Roberts, R. D. (1997). Mental speed is not the "basic" process of intelligence. *Personality and Individual Differences, 22,* 69–84.

Stanley C. Krippner: Award for Distinguished Contributions to the International Advancement of Psychology. (2003). *American Psychologist, 57,* 960–962.

Stapleton, J. A., Russell, M. A. H., Feyerabend, C., & Wiseman, S. M. (1995). Dose effects and predictors of outcome in a randomized trial of transdermal nicotine patches in general practice. *Addiction, 90,* 31–42.

Stapleton, K., & Hargie, O. (2011). Double-bind accountability dilemmas: Impression management and accountability strategies used by senior banking executives. *Journal of Language & Social Psychology, 30,* 266–289.

Stark, E. (1981, September). Pigeon patrol. *Science, 81,* 85–86.

Stark, E., Drori, R., Asher, I., Ben-Shaul, Y., & Abeles, M. (2007). Distinct movement parameters are represented by different neurons in the motor cortex. *European Journal of Neuroscience, 26,* 1055–1066.

Stark-Wroblewski, K., Wiggins. T. L., & Ryan, J. J. (2006). Assessing student interest and familiarity with professional psychology specialty areas. *Journal of Instructional Psychology, 33,* 273–277.

Stathopoulou, A., Beratis, I. N., & Beratis, S. (2013). Prenatal tobacco smoke exposure, risk of schizophrenia, and severity of positive/negative symptoms. *Schizophrenia Research, 148,* 105–106.

Steel, P., & Ones, D. S. (2002). Personality and happiness: A national-level analysis. *Journal of Personality and Social Psychology, 83,* 767–781.

Steele, C. M., & Aronson, J. (1995). Stereotype threat and the intellectual test performance of African Americans. *Journal of Personality and Social Psychology, 69,* 797–811.

Steele, C. M., & Aronson, J. A. (2004). Stereotype threat does not live by Steele and Aronson (1995) alone. *American Psychologist, 59,* 47–48.

Steele, C. M., & Josephs, R. A. (1990). Alcohol myopia: Its prized and dangerous effects. *American Psychologist, 45,* 921–933.

Steele, R. J., Stewart, M. G., & Rose, S. P. R. (1995). Increases in NMDA receptor binding are specifically related to memory formation for a passive avoidance task in the chick: A quantitative autoradiographic study. *Brain Research, 674,* 352–356.

Steeves, R., Kahn, D., Ropka, M. E., & Wise, C. (2001). Ethical considerations in research with bereaved families. *Family and Community Health, 23,* 75–83.

Steffen, P. R., Sherwood, A., Gullette, E. C. D., Georgiades, A., Hinderliter, A., & Blumenthal, J. A. (2001). Effects of exercise and weight loss on blood pressure during daily life. *Medicine and Science in Sports and Exercise, 33,* 1635–1640.

Steiger, H., Gauvin, L., Jabalpurwala, S., Séguin, J. R., & Stotland, S. (1999). Hypersensitivity to social interactions in bulimic syndromes. Relationship to binge eating. *Journal of Consulting and Clinical Psychology, 67,* 765–775.

Stein, D. M., & Lambert, M. J. (1995). Graduate training in psychotherapy: Are therapy outcomes enhanced? *Journal of Consulting and Clinical Psychology, 63,* 182–196.

Stein, M. B., Chavira, D. A., & Jang, K. L. (2001). Bringing up bashful baby: Developmental pathways to social phobia. *Psychiatric Clinics of North America, 24,* 661–675.

Stein, M. B., Jang, K. L., & Livesley, W. J. (1999). Heritability of anxiety sensitivity: A twin study. *American Journal of Psychiatry, 156,* 246–251.

Stein, M. B., Jang, K. L., & Livesley, W. J. (2002). Heritability of social anxiety-related concerns and personality characteristics: A twin study. *Journal of Nervous and Mental Disease, 19,* 219–224.

Steiner, S. S., & Dince, W. M. (1981). Biofeedback efficacy studies: A critique of critiques. *Biofeedback and Self-Regulation, 6,* 275–288.

Steinkamp, F. (2000). Acting on the future: A survey of precognitive experiences. *Journal of the American Society for Psychical Research, 94*, 37–59.

Steinkamp, F., Milton, J., & Morris, R. L. (1998). A meta-analysis of forced-choice experiments comparing clairvoyance and precognition. *Journal of Parapsychology, 62*, 193–218.

Stelmack, R. M. (1990). Biological bases of extraversion: Psychophysiological evidence. *Journal of Personality, 58*, 293–311.

Stelmack, R. M., & Stalikas, A. (1991). Galen and the humour theory of temperament. *Personality and Individual Differences, 12*, 255–263.

Stemmer, N. (1990). Skinner's verbal behavior, Chomsky's review, and mentalism. *Journal of the Experimental Analysis of Behavior, 54*, 307–315.

Stephan, K. E., Marshall, J. C., Friston, K. J., Rowe, J. B., Ritzl, A., Zilles, K., & Fink, G. R. (2003). Lateralized cognitive processes and lateralized task control in the human brain. *Science, 301*, 384–386.

Stephan, W. G., Stephan, C. W., & de Vargas, M. C. (1996). Emotional expression in Costa Rica and the United States. *Journal of Cross-Cultural Psychology 27*, 147–160.

Stephan, W. G., Ybarra, O., & Bachman, G. (1999). Prejudice toward immigrants. *Journal of Applied Social Psychology, 29*, 2221–2237.

Stephan, W. G., Ybarra, O., Martinez, C. M., Schwarzwald, J., & Tur-Kaspa, M. (1998). Prejudice toward immigrants to Spain and Israel: An integrated threat theory analysis. *Journal of Cross-Cultural Psychology, 29*, 559–576.

Stephan, Y., & Maiano, C. (2007). On the social nature of global self-esteem: A replication study. *Journal of Social Psychology, 147*, 573–575.

Steptoe, A., Moses, J., Edwards, S., & Mathews, A. (1993). Exercise and responsivity to mental stress: Discrepancies between the subjective and physiological effects of aerobic training. *International Journal of Sport Psychology, 24*, 110–129.

Sterling, R. C. (2002). Researching the treatment of drinking problems: A call for external as well as internal validity. *Addiction, 97*, 294–295.

Sternberg, R. J. (1986). A triangular theory of love. *Psychological Review, 93*, 119–135.

Sternberg, R. J. (1996). The sound of silence: A nation responds to its gifted. *Roeper Review, 18*, 168–172.

Sternberg, R. J. (1999). A triarchic approach to the understanding and assessment of intelligence in multicultural populations. *Journal of School Psychology, 37*, 145–159.

Sternberg, R. J. (2000). Patterns of giftedness: A triarchic analysis. *Roeper Review, 22*, 231–235.

Sternberg, R. J. (2003). A broad view of intelligence: The theory of successful intelligence. *Consulting Psychology Journal: Practice and Research, 55*, 139–154.

Sternberg, R. J., Castejon, J. L., Prieto, M. D., Hautamaeki, J., & Grigorenko, E. L. (2001). Confirmatory factor analysis of the Sternberg Triarchic Abilities Test in three international samples: An empirical test of the triarchic theory of intelligence. *European Journal of Psychological Assessment, 17*, 1–16.

Sternberg, R. J., & Clinkenbeard, P. B. (1995). The triarchic model applied to identifying, teaching, and assessing gifted children. *Roeper Review, 17*, 231–235.

Sternberg, R. J., Conway, B. E., Ketron, J. L., & Bernstein, M. (1981). People's conceptions of intelligence. *Journal of Personality and Social Psychology, 41*, 37–55.

Sternberg, R. J., Torff, B., & Grigorenko, E. L. (1998). Teaching triarchically improves school achievement. *Journal of Educational Psychology, 90*, 374–384.

Sternberg, R. J., & Wagner, R. K. (1993). The geocentric view of intelligence and job performance is wrong. *Current Directions in Psychological Science, 2*, 1–5.

Sterrenberg, P., & Thunnissen, M. M. (1995). Transactional analysis as a cognitive treatment for borderline personality disorder. *Transactional Analysis Journal, 25*, 221–227.

Stessman, J., Maaravi, Y., Hammerman-Rozenberg, R, & Cohen, A. (2000). The effects of physical activity on mortality in the Jerusalem 70-year-olds longitudinal study. *Journal of the American Geriatrics Society, 48*, 499–504.

Stevens, P. (1998–99). Remote psychokinesis. *European Journal of Parapsychology, 14*, 68–79

Steward, O., & Worley, P. (2002). Local synthesis of proteins at synaptic sites on dendrites: Role in synaptic plasticity and memory consolidation? *Neurobiology of Learning & Memory, 78*, 508–527.

Stewart, J. W., Garfinkel, R., Nunes, E. V., Donovan, S., & Klein, D. F. (1998). Atypical features and treatment response in the National Institute of Mental Health Treatment of Depression Collaborative Research Program. *Journal of Clinical Psychopharmacology, 18*, 429–434.

Stewart, M. G., Lowndes, M. Hunter, A., & Doubell, T. (1992). Memory storage in chicks involves an increase in dendritic spine number and synaptic density. *Brain Dysfunction, 5*, 50–64.

Stewart, T. L., LaDuke, J. R., Bracht, C., Sweet, B. A. M., & Gamarel, K. E. (2003). Do the "eyes" have it? A program evaluation of Jane Elliott's "blue-eyes/brown-eyes" diversity training exercise. *Journal of Applied Social Psychology, 33*, 1898–1921.

Still, A., & Dryden, W. (2003). Elli sand Epictetus: Dialogue vs. method in psychotherapy. *Journal of Rational-Emotive and Cognitive Behavior Therapy, 21*, 37–55.

Stinson, D. A., Logel, C., Shepherd, S., & Zanna, M. P. (2011). Rewriting the self-fulfilling prophecy of social rejection: Self-affirmation improves relational security and social behavior up to 2 months later. *Psychological Science, 22*, 1145–1149.

Stoiber, K. C., & Waas, G. A. (2002). A contextual and methodological perspective on the evidence-based movement within school psychology in the United States. *Educational and Child Psychology, 19*, 7–21.

Stolerman, I. P., & Jarvis, M. J. (1995). The scientific case that nicotine is addictive. *Psychopharmacology, 117*, 2–10.

Stone, A. A., Bovberg, D. H., Neale, J. M., & Napoli, A. (2002). Development of common cold symptoms following experimental rhinovirus infection is related to prior stressful life events. *Behavioral Medicine, 18*, 115–120.

Stone, A. A., & Brownell, K. D. (1994). The stress-eating paradox: Multiple daily measurements in adult males and females. *Psychology and Health, 9*, 425–436.

Stone, A. A., Hedges, S. M., Neale, J. M., & Satin, M. S. (1985). Prospective and cross-sectional mood reports offer no evidence of a "blue Monday" phenomenon. *Journal of Personality and Social Psychology, 49*, 129–134.

Stone, A. A., Schneider, S., & Harter, J. K. (2012). Day-of-week mood patterns in the United States: On the existence of "Blue Monday," "Thank God It's Friday," and weekend effects. *Journal of Positive Psychology, 7*, 306–314.

Stone, A. A., Smyth, J. M., Kaell, A., & Hurewitz, A. (2000). Str uctured writing about stressful events: Exploring potential psychological mediators of positive health effects. *Health Psychology, 19*, 619–624.

Stone, M. H. (2012). Disorder in the domain of personality disorders. *Psychodynamic Psychiatry, 40*, 23–46.

Stoner, J. A. F. (1961). *A comparison of individual and group decisions involving risk.* Unpublished master's thesis, Massachusetts Institute of Technology, Cambridge.

Storck, L. E. (1997). Cultural psychotherapy: A consideration of psychosocial class and cultural differences in group treatment. *Group, 21*, 331–349.

Storey, A. E., Walsh, C. J., Quintin, R. L., & Wynne-Edwards, K. E. (2000). Hormonal correlates of paternal responsiveness in new and expectant fathers. *Evolution and Human Behavior, 21*, 79–95.

Storm, L., Tressoldi, P. E., & DiRisio, L. (2010). Metaanalysis of free-response studies, 1992–2008: Assessing the noise reduction model in parapsychology. *Psychological Bulletin, 136*, 471–485

Storms, M. D. (1981). A theory of erotic orientation development. *Psychological Review, 88*, 340–353.

Strack, F., Schwarz, N., Chassein, B., & Kern, D. (1990). Salience of comparison standards and the activation of social norms: Consequences for judgements of happiness and their communication. *British Journal of Social Psychology, 29*, 303–314.

Straneva, P. A., Maixner, W., Light, K. C., Pedersen, C. A., Costello, N. L., & Girdler, S. S. (2002). Menstrual cycle, beta-endorphins, and pain sensitivity in premenstrual dysphoric disorder. *Health Psychology, 21*, 358–367.

Strang, J., McCambridge, J., Best, D., Beswick, T., Bearn, J., Rees, S., & Gossop, M. (2003). Loss of tolerance and overdose mortality after inpatient opiate detoxification: Follow up study. *BMJ: British Medical Journal, 326*, 959–960.

Strassman, R. J. (1984). Adverse reactions to psychedelic drugs: A review of the literature. *Journal of Nervous and Mental Disease, 172*, 577–595.

Strauman, T. J., & Higgins, E. T. (1988). Self-discrepancies as predictors of vulnerability to distinct syndromes of chronic emotional distress. *Journal of Personality, 56*, 685–707.

Strauman, T. J., & Higgins, E. T. (1988). Self-discrepancies as predictors of vulnerability to distinct syndromes of chronic emotional distress. *Journal of Personality, 56*, 246–253.

Straus, M. A. (1991). Discipline and deviance: Physical punishment of children and violence and other crime in adulthood. *Social Problems, 38*, 133–154.

Straus, M. A., & Kantor, G. K. (1994). Corporal punishment of adolescents by parents: A risk factor in the epidemiology of depression, suicide, alcohol abuse, child abuse, and wife beating. *Adolescence, 29*, 543–561.

Strayer, D. L., & Kramer, A. F. (1990). Attentional requirements of automatic and controlled processing. *Journal of Experimental Psychology: Learning, Memory, and Cognition, 16*, 67–82.

Strecher, V. J., Seijts, G. H., Kok, G. J., & Latham, G. P. (1995). Goal setting as a strategy for health behavior change. *Health Education Quarterly, 22*, 190–200.

Streitmatter, J. (1993). Gender differences in identity development: An examination of longitudinal data. *Adolescence, 28*, 55–66.

Stricker, E. M., & McCann, M. J. (1985). Visceral factors in the control of food intake. *Brain Research Bulletin, 14*, 687–692.

Stricker, E. M., & Verbalis, J. G. (1987). Biological bases of hunger and satiety. *Annals of Behavioral Medicine, 9*, 3–8.

Strickland, B. R. (1989). Internal-external control expectancies: From contingency to creativity. *American Psychologist, 44*, 1–12.

Striegel-Moore, R. H., Silberstein, L. R., & Rodin, J. (1986). Toward an understanding of risk factors in bulimia. *American Psychologist, 41*, 246–263.

Stroebe, M. S. (1994). The broken heart phenomenon: An examination of the mortality of bereavement. *Journal of Community and Applied Social Psychology, 4*, 47–61.

Stroebe, W., Stroebe, M. S., & Abakoumkin, G. (1999). Does differential social support cause sex differences in bereavement outcome? *Journal of Community and Applied Social Psychology, 9*, 1–12.

Struch, N., Schwartz, S. H., & van der Kloot, W. A. (2002). Meanings of basic values for women and men: A cross-cultural analysis. *Personality and Social Psychology Bulletin, 28,* 16–28.

Stuart, G. L., Treat, T. A., & Wade, W. A. (2000). Effectiveness of an empirically based treatment for panic disorder delivered in a service clinic setting: 1 year follow-up. *Journal of Consulting and Clinical Psychology, 68,* 506–512.

Stumbrys, T., & Daniels, M. (2010). An exploratory study of creative problem-solving in lucid dreams: Preliminary findings and methodological considerations. *International Journal of Dream Research, 3,* 121–129.

Stunkard, A. J., Stinnett, J. L., & Smoller, J. W. (1986). Psychological and social aspects of the surgical treatment of obesity. *American Journal of Psychiatry, 143,* 417–429.

Sturgeon, R. S., Cooper, L. M., & Howell, R. J. (1989). Pupil response: A psychophysiological measure of fear during analogue desensitization. *Perceptual and Motor Skills, 69,* 1351–1367.

Stuss, D. T., Gow, C. A., & Hetherington, C. R. (1992). "No longer Gage": Frontal lobe dysfunction and emotional changes. *Journal of Consulting and Clinical Psychology, 60,* 349–359.

Suarez, E., Kuhn, C. M., Schanberg, S. M., Williams, R B., Jr., & Zimmermann, E. A. (1998). Neuroendocrine, cardiovascular, and emotional responses of hostile men: The role of interpersonal challenge. *Psychosomatic Medicine, 60,* 78–88.

Subandi, M. A. (2011). Family expressed emotion in a Javanese cultural context. *Culture, Medicine, & Psychiatry, 35,* 331–346.

Subotnik, R, F., Karp, D. E., & Morgan, E. R. (1989). High IQ children at midlife: An investigation into the generalizability of Terman's genetic studies of genius. *Roeper Review, 11,* 139–144.

Sucala, M., Schnur, J. B., Constantino, M. J., Miller, S. J., Brackman, E. H., & Montgomery, G. H. (2012). The therapeutic relationship in e-therapy for mental health: A systematic review. *Journal of Medical Internet Research, 14,* 175–187.

Sue, S. (1998). In search of cultural competence in psychotherapy and counseling. *American Psychologist, 53,* 440–448.

Sue, S. (1999). Science, ethnicity, and bias: Where have we gone wrong? *American Psychologist, 54,* 1070–1077.

Sue, S. (2003). In defense of cultural competency in psychotherapy and treatment. *American Psychologist, 58,* 964–970.

Sue, S., Fujino, D., Hu, L., Takeuchi, D., & Zane, N. (1991). Community mental health services for ethnic minority groups: A test of the cultural responsiveness hypothesis. *Journal of Clinical and Consulting Psychology, 59,* 533–540.

Sue, S., & Okazaki, S. (1990). Asian-American educational achievements: A phenomenon in search of an explanation. *American Psychologist, 45,* 913–920.

Suedfeld, P. (1990). Restricted environmental stimulation and smoking cessation: A 15-year progress report. *International Journal of the Addictions, 25,* 861–888.

Suedfeld, P., & Bruno, T. (1990). Flotation REST and imagery in the improvement of athletic performance. *Journal of Exercise and Exercise Psychology, 12,* 82–85.

Suedfeld, P., & Coren, S. (1989). Perceptual isolation, sensory deprivation, and REST: Moving introductory psychology texts out of the 1950s. *Canadian Psychology, 30,* 17–29.

Suedfeld, P., & Steel, G. D. (2000). The environmental psychology of capsule habitats. *Annual Review of Psychology, 51,* 227–253.

Sufka, K. J., & Price, D. D. (2002). Gate control theory reconsidered. *Brain and Mind, 3,* 277–290.

Suh, E., Diener, E., & Fujita, F. (1996). Events and subjective well-being: Only recent events matter. *Journal of Personality and Social Psychology, 70,* 1091–1102.

Sulik, K., Johnston, M., & Webb, M. (1981). Fetal alcohol syndrome?: Embryogenesis in a mouse model. *Science, 214,* 936–938.

Sullins, E. S., Hernandez, D., Fuller, C., & Tashiro, J. S. (1995). Predicting who will major in a science discipline: Expectancy-value theory as part of an ecological model for studying academic communities. *Journal of Research in Science Teaching, 32,* 99–119.

Sullivan, H. S. (1953). *An interpersonal theory of psychiatry.* New York: W. W. Norton.

Sullivan, J. E., & Chang, P. (1999). Review: Emotional and behavioral functioning in phenylketonuria. *Journal of Pediatric Psychology, 24,* 281–299.

Sullivan, P. F., Kendler, K. S., & Neale, M. C. (2003). Schizophrenia as a complex trait: Evidence from a meta-analysis of twin studies. *Archives of General Psychiatry, 60,* 1187–1192.

Suls, J., Krantz, D. S., & Williams, G. C. (2013). Three strategies for bridging different levels of analysis and embracing the biopsychosocial model. *Health Psychology, 32,* 597–601.

Sumerlin, J. R., & Bundrick, C. M. (1996). Brief index of self-actualization: A measure of Maslow's model. *Journal of Social Behavior and Personality, 11,* 253–271.

Superkids? A sperm bank for Nobelists. (1980, March 10). *Time,* p. 49.

Sussan, T. A. (1990). How to handle the process litigation effectively under the Education for All Handicapped Children Act of 1975. *Journal of Reading, Writing, and Learning Disabilities International, 6,* 63–70.

Sussman, S. (1998). The first asylums in Canada: A response to neglectful community care and current trends. *Canadian Journal of Psychiatry, 43,* 260–264.

Swann, W. B., Jr., Hixon, J. G., & De La Ronde, C. (1992). Embracing the bitter "truth": Negative self-concepts and marital commitment. *Psychological Science, 3,* 118–121.

Swanson, J., Baler, R. D., & Volkow, N. D. (2011). Understanding the effects of stimulant medications on cognition in individuals with attention-deficit hyperactivity disorder: A decade of progress. *Neuropsychopharmacology, 36,* 207–226.

Swartz, S. (2013). Feminism and psychiatric diagnosis: Reflections of a feminist practitioner. *Feminism & Psychology, 23,* 41–48.

Swayze, V. W. (1995). Frontal leucotomy and related psychosurgical procedures in the era before antipsychotics (1935–1954): A historical overview. *American Journal of Psychiatry, 152,* 505–515.

Sweat, J. A., & Durm, M. W. (1993). Psychics: Do police departments really use them? *Skeptical Inquirer, 17,* 148–158.

Sweeney, P. D., Anderson, K., & Bailey, S. (1986). Attributional style in depression: A meta-analytic review. *Journal of Personality and Social Psychology, 50,* 974–991.

Swenson, C. R. (1994). Freud's "Anna O.": Social work's Bertha Pappenheim. *Clinical Social Work Journal, 22,* 149–163.

Swenson, R. S., Danielsen, E. H., Klausen, B. S., & Erlich, E. (1989). Deficits in beam walking after neonatal motor cortical lesions are not spared by fetal cortical transplants in rats. *Journal of Neural Transplantation, 1,* 129–133.

Swiatek, M. A. (1993). A decade of longitudinal research on academic acceleration through the study of mathematically precocious youth. *Roeper Review, 15,* 120–124.

Swiatek, M. A., & Lupkowski-Shoplik, A. (2003). Elementary and middle school student participation in gifted programs: Are gifted students underserved? *Gifted Child Quarterly, 47,* 118–130.

Swickert, R. J., Rosentreter, C. J., Hittner, J. B., & Mushrush, J. E. (2002). Extraversion, social support processes, and stress. *Personality and Individual Differences, 32,* 877–891.

Swiezy, N. B., Matson, J. L., & Box, P. (1992). The Good Behavior Game: A token reinforcement system for preschoolers. *Child and Family Behavior Therapy, 14,* 21–32.

Swindale, N. V. (1982). The development of columnar systems in the mammalian visual cortex: The role of innate and environmental factors. *Trends in Neurosciences, 5,* 235–241.

Swindale, N. V. (2000). How many maps are there in visual cortex? *Cerebral Cortex, 10,* 633–643.

Szabo, A. (2003). The acute effects of humor and exercise on mood and anxiety. *Journal of Leisure Research, 35,* 152–162.

Szasz, T. (1960). The myth of mental illness. *American Psychologist, 15,* 113–118.

Szasz, T. (1980). "J'Accuse": Psychiatry and the diminished American capacity for justice. *Journal of Mind and Behavior, 1,* 111–120.

Taal, E., Rasker, J. J., Seydel, E. R., & Wiegman, O. (1993). Health status, adherence with health recommendations, self-efficacy and social support in patients with rheumatoid arthritis. *Patient Education and Counseling, 20,* 63–76.

Tafarodi, R. W., & Walters, P. (1999). Individualism-collectivism, life events, and self-esteem: A test of two trade-offs. *European Journal of Social Psychology, 29,* 797–814.

Taits, I. (2011). Learning lucid dreaming and its effect on depression in undergraduates. *International Journal of Dream Research, 4,* 117–126.

Tajfel, H. (1981). *Human groups and social categories: Studies in social psychology.* London: Cambridge University Press.

Tajfel, H., & Billig, M. (1974). Familarity and categorization in intergroup behavior. *Journal of Experimental Social Psychology, 10,* 159–170.

Takagi, M., Toda, H., Yoshizawa, T., & Hara, N. (1992). Ocular convergence-related neuronal responses in the lateral suprasylvian area of alert cats. *Neuroscience Research, 15,* 229–234.

Takahata, Y., Hasegawa, T., & Nishida, T. (1984). Chimpanzee predation in the Mahale Mountains from August 1979 to May 1982. *International Journal of Primatology, 5,* 213–233.

Takano, K., & Tanno, Y. (2011). Diurnal variation in rumination. *Emotion, 11,* 1046–1058.

Takei, N., Mortensen, P. B., Klaening, U., & Murray, R. M. (1996). Relationship between in utero exposure to influenza epidemics and risk of schizophrenia in Denmark. *Biological Psychiatry, 40,* 817–824.

Takei, Y., Kumano, S., Hattori, S., Uehara, T., Kawakubo, Y., Kasai, K., Fukuda, M., & Mikuni, M. (2009). Preattentive dysfunction in major depression: A magnetoencephalography study using auditory mismatch negativity. *Psychophysiology, 46,* 52–61.

Takeuchi, D. T., Sue, S., & Yeh, M. (1995). Return rates and outcomes from ethnicity-specific mental health programs. *American Journal of Public Health, 85,* 638–643.

Takeuchi, M. S., Miyaoka, H., Tomoda, A., Suzuki, M., Liu, Q., & Kitamura, T. (2010). The effect of interpersonal touch during childhood on adult attachment and depression: A neglected area of family and developmental psychology? *Journal of Child and Family Studies, 19,* 109–117.

Talarczyk, M. (2011). The authorial model of the therapy used in night terrors and sleep disorders in children. *Archives of Psychiatry & Psychotherapy, 13,* 45–51.

Talarico, J. M., & Rubin, D. C. (2003). Confidence, not consistency, characterizes flashbulb memories. *Psychological Science, 14,* 455–461.

Taleb, M., Rouillon, F., Petitjean, F., & Gorwood, P. (1996). Cross-cultural study of schizophrenia. *Psychopathology, 29,* 85–94.

Taller, A. M., Asher, D. M., Pomeroy, K. L., & Eldadah, B. A. (1996). Search for viral nucleic acid sequences in brain tissues of patients with schizophrenia using nested polymerase chain reaction. *Archives of General Psychiatry, 53,* 32–40.

Tam, W.-C. C., & Sewell, K. W. (1995). Seasonality of birth in schizophrenia in Taiwan. *Schizophrenia Bulletin, 21,* 117–127.

Tammings, C. A. (1997). Gender and schizophrenia. *Journal of Clinical Psychiatry, 58,* 33–37.

Tamres, L. K., Janicki, D., & Helgeson, V. S. (2002). Sex differences in coping behavior: A meta-analytic review and examination of relative coping. *Personality and Social Psychology Review, 6,* 2–30.

Tan, G., Jensen, M. P., Robinson-Whelen, S., Thornby, J. I., Monga, T., Taylor, W. R., & Vaney, D. I. (2003). New directions in retinal research. *Trends in Neurosciences, 26,* 379–385.

Tang, S. H., & Hall, V. C. (1995). The overjustification effect: A meta-analysis. *Applied Cognitive Psychology, 9,* 365–404.

Tankard, J. W. (1984). *The statistical pioneers.* Cambridge, MA: Schenkman.

Tardieu, D., & McAdams, S. (2012). Perceptions of dyads of impulsive and sustained instrument sounds. *Music Perception, 30,* 117–128.

Tarricone, B. J., Simon, J. R., Li, Y. J., & Low, W. C. (1996). Neural grafting of cholinergic neurons in the hippocampal formation. *Behavioural Brain Research, 74,* 25–44.

Tateyama, M., Asai, M., Kamisada, M., & Hashimoto, M. (1993). Comparison of schizophrenic delusions between Japan and Germany. *Psychopathology, 26,* 151–158.

Taubes, G. (1998). As obesity rates rise, experts struggle to explain why. *Science, 280,* 1367–1370.

Tauer, C. A. (1994). The NIH trials of growth hormone for short stature. *IRB: A Review of Human Subjects Research, 16,* 1–9.

Taulbee, P. (1983). Solving the mystery of anxiety. *Science News, 124,* 45.

Taylor, B. A., Levin, L., & Jasper, S. (1999). Increasing play-related statement in children with autism toward their siblings: Effects of video modeling. *Journal of Development and Physical Disabilities, 11,* 253–264.

Taylor, C. R., & Stern, B. B. (1997). Asian-Americans: Television advertising and the "model minority" stereotype. *Journal of Advertising, 26,* 47–61.

Taylor, D. J., & Roane, B. M. (2010). Treatment of insomnia in adults and children: A practice-friendly review of research. *Journal of Clinical Psychology, 66,* 1137–1147.

Taylor, J., Iacono, W. G., & McGue, M. (2000). Evidence for a genetic etiology of early-onset delinquency. *Journal of Abnormal Psychology, 109,* 634–643.

Taylor, R. L. (1990). The *Larry P.* decision a decade later: Problems and future directions. *Mental Retardation, 28,* iii–vi.

Taylor, S., & Goritsas, E. (1994). Dimensions of identity diffusion. *Journal of Personality Disorders, 8,* 229–239.

Taylor, S., & Wald, J. (2003). Expectations and attributions in social anxiety disorder: Diagnostic distinctions and relationship to general anxiety and depression. *Cognitive Behaviour Therapy, 32,* 166–178.

Taylor, S. A., & Mudford, O. C. (2012). Improving behavior in a residential service for youth in drug and alcohol rehabilitation. *Behavioral Intervention, 27,* 109–128.

Taylor, S. E., & Brown, J. D. (1988). Illusion and well-being: A social psychological perspective on mental health. *Psychological Bulletin, 103,* 193–210.

Taylor, S. E., Klein, L. C., Lewis, B. P., Gruenewald, T. L., Gurung, R. A. R., & Updegraff, J. A. (2000). Biobehavioral responses to stress in females: Tend-and-befriend, not fight-or-flight. *Psychological Review, 107,* 411–429.

Taylor, S. E., Lerner, J. S., Sherman, D. K., Sage, R. M., & McDowell, N. K. (2003). Are self-enhancing cognitions associated with healthy or unhealthy biological profiles? *Journal of Personality and Social Psychology, 85,* 605–615.

Taylor, S. E., Saphire-Bernstein, S., & Seeman, T. E. (2010). Are plasma oxytocin in women and plasma vasopressin in men biomarkers of distressed pair-bond relationships? *Psychological Science, 21,* 3–7.

Teasdale, N., Forget, R., Bard, C., & Paillard, J. (1993). The role of proprioceptive information for the production of isometric forces and for handwriting tasks. *Acta Psychologica, 82,* 179–191.

Tebartz van Elst, L., Hesslinger, B., Thiel, T., Geiger, E., Haegele, K., Lemieux, L., ... Ebert, D. (2003). Frontolimbic abnormalities in patients with borderline personality disorder: A volumetric magnetic resonance imaging study. *Biological Psychiatry, 54,* 163–171.

Tehrani, J. A., Brennan, P. A., Hodgins, S., & Mednick, S. A. (1998). Mental illness and criminal violence. *Social Psychiatry and Psychiatric Epidemiology, 33* (Suppl. 1), S81–S85.

Teichman, Y., & Teichman, M. (1990). Interpersonal view of depression: Review and integration. *Journal of Family Psychology, 3,* 349–367.

Teigen, K. H. (1984). A note on the origin of the term "nature and nurture": Not Shakespeare and Galton, but Mulcaster. *Journal of the History of the Behavioral Sciences, 20,* 363–364.

Teigen, K. H. (1994). Yerkes-Dodson: A law for all seasons. *Theory and Psychology, 4,* 525–547.

Teipel, S. J., Bayer, W., Alexander, G. E., Bokde, A. L. W., Zebuhr, Y., Teichberg, D., ... Hampel, H. (2003). Regional pattern of hippocampus and corpus callosum atrophy in Alzheimer's disease in relation to dementia severity: Evidence for early neocortical degeneration. *Neurobiology of Aging, 24,* 85–94.

Telford, C., McCarthy-Jones, S., Corcoran, R., & Rowse, G. (2012). Experience sampling methodology studies of depression: The state of the art. *Psychological Medicine, 42,* 1119–1129.

Tellegen, A., Lykken, D. T., Bouchard, T. J., Jr., Wilcox, K. J., Segal, N. L., & Rich, S. (1988). Personality similarity in twins reared apart and together. *Journal of Personality and Social Psychology, 54,* 1031–1039.

Templeton, L. M., & Wilcox, S. A. (2000). A tale of two representations: The misinformation effect and children's developing theory of mind. *Child Development, 71,* 402–416.

Tenenbaum, H. R., & Leaper, C. (2002). Are parents' gender schemas related to their children's gender-related cognitions? A meta-analysis. *Developmental Psychology, 38,* 615–630.

Teng, E., & Squire, L. R. (1999). Memory for places learned long ago is intact after hippocampal damage. *Nature, 400,* 675–677.

Tenzer, S. (1989). Fat acceptance therapy (F.A.T.): A non-dieting group approach to physical wellness, insight, and self-acceptance. *Women and Therapy, 8,* 39–47.

Terman, L. (1925). *Genetic studies of genius, Vol. I: Mental and physical traits of a thousand gifted children.* Stanford, CA: Stanford University Press.

Terman, L. M. (1917). The intelligence quotient of Francis Galton in childhood. *American Journal of Psychology, 28,* 209–215.

Terman, L. M. (1918). Expert testimony in the case of Alberto Flores. *Journal of Delinquency, 3,* 145–164.

Terrace, H. S., Petitto, L. A., Sanders, R. J., & Bever, T. G. (1979). Can an ape create a sentence? *Science, 206,* 891–902.

Terry-McElrath, Y. M., & O'Malley, P. M. (2011). Substance use and exercise participation among young adults: Parallel trajectories in a national cohort-sequential study. *Addiction, 106,* 1855–1865.

Thakker, J., Ward, T., & Strongman, K. T. (1999). Mental disorder and cross-cultural psychology: A constructivist perspective. *Clinical Psychology Review, 19,* 843–874.

Thamaku, M., & Daniel, M. (2013). Exploring responses to transformative group therapy for orphaned children in the context of mass orphaning in Botswana. *Death Studies, 37,* 413–447.

Thase, M. E., Greenhouse, J. B., Frank, E., Reynolds, C. F., Pilkonis, P. A., Hurley, K., ... Kupfer, D. J. (1997). Treatment of major depression with psychotherapy or psychotherapy-pharmacotherapy combinations. *Archives of General Psychiatry, 54,* 1009–1015.

Thierry, N., Willeit, M., Praschak-Rieder, N., Zill, P., Hornik, K., Neumeister, A., ... Kasper, S. (2004). Serotonin transporter promoter gene polymorphic region (5-HTTLPR) and personality in female patients with seasonal affective disorder and in healthy controls. *European Neuropsychopharmacology, 14,* 53–58.

Thiessen, D., & Umezawa, Y. (1998). The sociobiology of everyday life: A new look at a very old novel. *Human Nature, 9,* 293–320.

Thomas, E. (1988). Forebrain mechanisms in the relief of fear: The role of the lateral septum. *Psychobiology, 16,* 36–44.

Thomas, H. (1993). A theory explaining sex differences in high mathematical ability has been around for some time. *Behavioral and Brain Sciences, 16,* 187–189.

Thomas, T. N. (1997). Sleepwalking disorder and *mens rea*: A review and case report. *Journal of Forensic Sciences, 42,* 17–24.

Thompson, A., Hollis, C., & Richards, D. (2003). Authoritarian parenting attitudes as a risk for conduct problems: Results from a British national cohort study. *European Child and Adolescent Psychiatry, 12,* 84–91.

Thompson, B. (2002). "Statistical," "practical," and "clinical": How many kinds of significance do counselors need to consider? *Journal of Counseling and Development, 80,* 64–71.

Thompson, B., Diamond, K. E., McWilliam, R., Snyder, P., & Snyder, S. W. (2005). Evaluating the quality of evidence from correlational research for evidence-based practice. *Exceptional Children, 71,* 181–194.

Thompson, J. K., & Heinberg, L. J. (1999). The media's influence on body image disturbance and eating disorders: We've reviled them, now can we rehabilitate them? *Journal of Social Issues, 55,* 339–353.

Thompson, J. K., & Stice, E. (2001). Thin-ideal internalization: Mounting evidence for a new risk factor for body-image disturbance and eating pathology. *Current Directions in Psychological Science, 10,* 181–183.

Thompson, K., Biddle, K. R., Robinson-Long, M., Poger, J., Wang, J., Yang, Q. X., & Eslinger, P. J. (2009). Cerebral plasticity and recovery of function after childhood prefrontal cortex damage. *Developmental Neurorehabilitation, 12,* 298–312.

Thompson, L. (1995, June 12). Search for a gay gene. *Time,* 60–61.

Thompson, N. J., Coker, J., Krause, J. S., & Henry, E. (2003). Purpose in life as a mediator of adjustment after spinal cord injury. *Rehabilitation Psychology, 48,* 100–108.

Thompson, R. F. (1991). Are memory traces localized or distributed? *Neuropsychologia, 29,* 571–582.

Thompson, S. M. (2000). Synaptic plasticity: Building memories to last. *Current Biology, 10,* R218–R221.

Thordardottir, E. T., & Weismer, S. E. (1998). Mean length of utterance and other language sample measures in early Icelandic. *First Language, 18,* 1–32.

Thorndike, E. L. (1898). Animal intelligence: An experimental study of the associative processes in animals. *Psychological Review Monograph Supplement, 2*(4).

Thorndike, E. L. (1961). Edward Lee Thorndike. In C. Murchison (Ed.), *A history of psychology in autobiography* (Vol. 1, pp. 263–270). New York: Russell & Russell.

Thorpe, S. J., & Salkovskis, P. M. (1995). Phobia beliefs: Do cognitive factors play a role in specific phobias? *Behaviour Research and Therapy, 33,* 805–816.

Throne, L. C., Bartholomew, J. B., Craig, J., & Farrar, R. P. (2000). Stress reactivity in fire fighters: An exercise intervention. *International Journal of Stress Management, 7,* 235–246.

Thurstone, L. L. (1938). *Primary mental abilities.* Chicago: University of Chicago Press.

Tiedt, A. D. (2013). Cross-national comparisons of gender differences in late-life depressive symptoms in Japan and the United States. *Journals of Gerontology: Series B: Psychological Sciences and Social Sciences, 68,* 443–454.

Tiefer, L. (1995). *Sex is not a natural act.* Boulder, Co: Westview Press.

Tierney, A. J. (2000). Egas Moniz and the origins of psychosurgery: A review commemorating the 50th anniversary of Moniz's Nobel Prize. *Journal of the History of the Neurosciences, 9,* 22–36.

Tiffany, S. T., Martin, E. M., & Baker, T. B. (1986). Treatments for cigarette smoking: An evaluation of the contributions of aversion and counseling procedures. *Behaviour Research and Therapy, 24,* 437–452.

Till, B. D., & Priluck, R. L. (2000). Stimulus generalization in classical conditioning: An initial investigation and extension. *Psychology and Marketing, 17,* 55–72.

Tilley, A. J., & Empson, J. A. (1978). REM sleep and memory consolidation. *Biological Psychology, 6,* 293–300.

Timberlake, W. (2003). Marian Breland Bailey: Many lives (SQAB, May 25, 2002, Toronto, Canada). *Behavioural Processes, 62,* 1–4.

Timberlake, W., & Farmer-Dougan, V. A. (1991). Reinforcement in applied settings: Figuring out ahead of time what will work. *Psychological Bulletin, 110,* 379–391.

Timberlake, W., & Melcer, T. (1988). Effects of poisoning on predatory and ingestive behavior toward artificial prey in rats (*Rattus norvegicus*). *Journal of Comparative Psychology, 102,* 182–187.

Timm, H. W. (1982). Effect of altered outcome expectancies stemming from placebo and feedback treatments on the validity of the guilty knowledge technique. *Journal of Applied Psychology, 67,* 391–400.

Timmann, D., Lee, P., Watts, S., & Hore, J. (2008). Kinematics of arm joint rotations in cerebellar and unskilled subjects associated with the inability to throw fast. *Cerebellum, 7,* 366–378.

Timney, B., & Keil, K. (1996). Horses are sensitive to pictorial depth cues. *Perception, 25,* 1121–1128.

Tobach, E. (2006). Identity of comparative psychology: Its status and advances in evolutionary theory and genetics. *International Journal of Comparative Psychology, 19,* 129–150.

Todd, L. K. (1996). A computer-assisted expert system for clinical diagnosis of eating disorders: A potential tool for practitioners. *Professional Psychology: Research and Practice, 27,* 184–187.

Todman, D. (2008). Henry Dale and the discovery of chemical synaptic transmission. *European Neurology, 60,* 162–164.

Tolin, D. F., Woods, C. M., & Abramowitz, J. S. (2003). Relationship between obsessive beliefs and obsessive-compulsive symptoms. *Cognitive Therapy and Research, 27,* 657–669.

Tolman, E. C. (1932). *Purposive behavior in animals and man.* New York: Appleton-Century-Crofts.

Tolman, E. C., & Honzik, C. H. (1930). Introduction and removal of reward, and maze performance in rats. *University of California Publications in Psychology, 4,* 257–275.

Tomfohr, L., Pung, M. A., Edwards, K. M., & Dimsdale, J. E. (2012). Racial differences in sleep architecture: The role of ethnic discrimination. *Biological Psychology, 89,* 34–38.

Tomlinson-Keasey, C. (1990). The working lives of Terman's gifted women. In H. Y. Grossman & N. L. Chester (Eds.), *The experience and meaning of work in women's lives* (pp. 213–240). Hillsdale, NJ: Erlbaum.

Tonello, G. (2008). Seasonal affective disorder: Lighting research and environmental psychology. *Lighting Research and Technology, 40,* 103–110.

Topolinski, S., & Reber, R. (2010). Gaining insight into the "aha" experience. *Current Directions in Psychological Science, 19,* 402–405.

Topp, L., Hando, J., Dillon, P., Roche, A., & Solowij, N. (1999). Ecstasy use in Australia: Patterns of use and associated harm. *Drug and Alcohol Dependence, 55,* 105–115.

Torgersen, S. (1983). Genetic factors in anxiety disorders. *Archives of General Psychiatry, 40,* 1085–1089.

Torgersen, S. (1986). Genetics of somatoform disorders. *Archives of General Psychiatry, 43,* 502–505.

Törnroos, M., Hintsanen, M., Hintsa, T., Jokela, M., Pulkki-Råback, L., & Hutri-Kähönen, N. (2013). Associations between five-factor model traits and perceived job strain: A population-based study. *Journal of Occupational Health Psychology, 18,* 492–500.

Torri, G., Cecchettin, M., Bellometti, S., & Galzigna, L. (1995). Analgesic effect and beta-endorphin and substance P levels in plasma after short-term administration of a ketoprofen-lysine salt or acetylsalicylic acid in patients with osteoarthrosis. *Current Therapeutic Research, 56,* 62–69.

Toth, C., McNeil, S., & Feasby, T. (2005). Peripheral nervous system injuries in sport and recreation. *Sports Medicine, 35,* 717–738.

Toth, L. A., & Krueger, J. M. (1990). Somnogenic, pyrogenic thermatologic effects of experimental pasteurellosis in rabbits. *American Journal of Physiology, 258,* R536–R542.

Toufexis, A. (1990, December 17). Drowsy America. *Time,* pp. 78–85.

Toukmanian, S. G., & Brouwers, M. C. (1998). Cultural aspects of self-disclosure and psychotherapy. In S. S. Kazarian & D. R. Evans (Eds.), *Cultural clinical psychology: Theory, research, and practice* (pp. 106–124). New York: Oxford University Press.

Tourney-Jetté, E., Dupuis, G., Denault, A., Carter, R., & Bherer, L. (2012). The benefits of cognitive training after a coronary artery bypass graft surgery. *Journal of Behavioral Medicine, 35,* 557–568.

Towell, A., Muscat, R., & Willner, P. (1989). Noradrenergic receptor interactions in feeding elicited by stimulation of the paraventricular hypothalamus. *Pharmacology, Biochemistry, and Behavior, 32,* 133–139.

Tracey, I., Ploghaus, A., Gati, J. S., Clare, S., Smith, S., Menon, R. S., & Matthews, P. M. (2002). Imaging attentional modulation of pain in the periaqueductal gray in humans. *Journal of Neuroscience, 22,* 2748–2752.

Tranel, D. (1995). Where did my arm go? [Review of *Unilateral neglect: Clinical and experimental studies*]. *Contemporary Psychology, 40,* 885–887.

Tranel, D., & Damasio, A. R. (1985). Knowledge without our awareness: An automatic index of facial recognition by prosopagnosics. *Science, 228,* 1453–1454.

Trappey, C. (1996). A meta-analysis of consumer choice and subliminal advertising. *Psychology and Marketing, 13,* 517–530.

Traskman, L., Asberg, M., Bertilsson, L., & Sjostrand, L. (1981). Monoamine metabolites in CSF and suicidal behavior. *Archives of General Psychiatry, 38,* 631–636.

Travis, R. W., & Sturmey, P. (2013). Using behavioural skills training to treat aggression in adults with mild intellectual disability in a forensic setting. *Journal of Applied Research in Intellectual Disabilities, 26,* 481–488.

Treede, R. D. (2002). Spinothalamic and thalamocortical nociceptive pathways. *Journal of Pain, 3,* 109–112.

Treffert, D. A. (1989). *Extraordinary people: Understanding savant syndrome.* New York: Harper & Row.

Trevethan, C. T., & Sahraie, A. (2003). Spatial and temporal processing in a subject with cortical blindness following occipital surgery. *Neuropsychologia, 41,* 1296–1306.

Treynor, W., Gonzalez, R., & Nolen-Hoeksema, S. (2003). Rumination reconsidered: A psychometric analysis. *Cognitive Therapy and Research, 27,* 247–259.

Triandis, H. C. (1989). The self and social behavior in differing cultural contexts. *Psychological Review, 96,* 506–520.

Triandis, H. C. (1990). Theoretical concepts that are applicable to the analysis of ethnocentrism. In R. W. Brislin (Ed.), *Applied cross-cultural psychology* (pp. 34–55). Newbury Park, CA: Sage.

Triarhou, L. C. (1995). The cerebellar model of neural grafting: Str uctural integration and functional recovery. *Brain Research Bulletin, 39,* 127–138.

Trice, A. D., & Ogden, E. P. (1987). Informed consent: Effects of the withdrawal clause in longitudinal research. *Perceptual and Motor Skills, 65,* 135–138.

Triplet, R. G. (1992). Discriminatory biases in the perception of illness: The application of availability and representativeness heuristics to the AIDS crisis. *Basic and Applied Social Psychology, 13,* 303–322.

Triplett, N. (1898). The dynamogenic factors in pacemaking and competition. *American Journal of Psychology, 9,* 507–553.

Troster, H., & Bambring, M. (1992). Early social-emotional development in blind infants. *Child Care, Health, and Development, 18,* 207–227.

Trotter, R. J. (1981). Psychiatry for the 80's. *Science News, 119,* 348–349.

Trotter, R. J. (1986, August). Three heads are better than one. *Psychology Today,* pp. 56–62.

Trounson, R. (2000, March 1). Eichmann rationalizes his Nazi role in jail notebooks. *Los Angeles Times,* p. A1.

Truax, C. B. (1966). Reinforcement and nonreinforcement in Rogerian psychotherapy. *Journal of Abnormal Psychology, 71,* 1–9.

Tryon, W. W. (1998). A neural network explanation of posttraumatic stress disorder. *Journal of Anxiety Disorders, 12,* 373–385.

Tryon, W. W. (2000). Behavior therapy as applied learning theory. *Behavior Therapist, 23,* 131–133.

Tsai, D. C., & Pike, P. L. (2000). Effects of acculturation on the MMPI-2 scores of Asian American students. *Journal of Personality Assessment, 74,* 216–230.

Tsai, G. E., Condie, D., Wu, M.-T., & Chang, I.-W. (1999). Functional magnetic resonance imaging of personality switches in a woman with dissociative identity disorder. *Harvard Review of Psychiatry, 7,* 119–122.

Tsao, J. C. I., Fanurik, D., & Zeltzer, L. K. (2003). Long-term effects of a brief distraction intervention on children's laboratory pain reactivity. *Behavior Modification, 27,* 217–232.

Tsutsui, K. I., Sakata, H., Naganuma, T., & Taira, M. (2002). Neural correlates for perception of 3D surface orientation from texture gradient. *Science, 298,* 409–412.

Tucker, L. A. (1983). Muscular strength: A predictor of personality in males. *Journal of Sports Medicine and Physical Fitness, 23,* 213–220.

Tucker, W. H. (1994). Fact and fiction in the discovery of Sir Cyril Burt's flaws. *Journal of the History of the Behavioral Sciences, 30,* 335–347.

Tucker, W. H. (1997). Re-reconsidering Burt: Beyond a reasonable doubt. *Journal of the History of the Behavioral Sciences, 33,* 145–162.

Tuckey, M. R., & Brewer, N. (2003). The influence of schemas, stimulus ambiguity, and interview schedule on eyewitness memory over time. *Journal of Experimental Psychology: Applied, 9,* 101–118.

Tulsky, F. N. (1986, March 28). $988,000 is awarded in suit over lost psychic power. *Philadelphia Inquirer,* p. 1-A.

Tulving, E. (1985). How many memory systems are there? *American Psychologist, 40,* 385–398.

Tulving, E. (1993). What is episodic memory? *Current Directions in Psychological Science, 2,* 67–70.

Tulving, E., & Markowitsch, H. J. (1998). Episodic and declarative memory: Role of the hippocampus. *Hippocampus, 8,* 198–204.

Tulving, E., & Thomson, D. M. (1973). Encoding specificity and retrieval processes in episodic memory. *Psychological Review, 80,* 352–373.

Turk, C. L., Heimberg, R. G., Orsillo, S. M., Holt, C. S., Gitow, A., Street, L. L., . . . Liebowitz, M. R. (1998). An investigation of gender differences in social phobia. *Journal of Anxiety Disorders, 12,* 209–223.

Turkheimer, E. (1991). Individual and group differences in adoption studies of IQ. *Psychological Bulletin, 110,* 392–405.

Turkheimer, E. (1998). Heritability and biological explanation. *Psychological Review, 105,* 782–791.

Turnbull, C. M. (1961). Some observations regarding the experiences of the Bambuti Pygmies. *American Journal of Psychology, 74,* 304–308.

Turner, D., Basdekis-Jozsa, R., & Briken, P. (2013). Prescription of testosterone-lowering medications for sex offender treatment in German forensic-psychiatric institutions. *Journal of Sexual Medicine, 10,* 570–578.

Turner, S. M., Beidel, D. C., & Costello, A. (1987). Psychopathology in the offspring of anxiety disorder patients. *Journal of Consulting and Clinical Psychology, 55,* 229–235.

Turner, S. M., Beidel, D. C., Roberson-Nay, R. (2005). Offspring of anxious parents: Reactivity, habituation, and anxiety-proneness. *Behavioral Research Therapy, 10,* 1263–1279.

Turner, S. M., Beidel, D. C., Roberson-Nay, R., & Tervo, K. (2003). Parenting behaviors in parents with anxiety disorders. *Behavioral Research Therapy, 5,* 541–554.

Twenge, J. M., & Crocker, J. (2002). Race and self-esteem: Meta-analyses comparing Whites, Blacks, Hispanics, Asians, and American Indians and comment on Gray-Little and Hafdahl, 2000. *Psychological Bulletin, 128,* 371–408.

Twisk, J. W. R., Snel, J., Kemper, H. C. G., & van Mechelen, W. (1999). Changes in daily hassles and life events and the relationship with coronary heart disease risk factors: A 2-year longitudinal study in 27–29-yr-old males and females. *Journal of Psychosomatic Research, 46,* 229–240.

Twitmyer, E. B. (1974). A study of the knee jerk. *Journal of Experimental Psychology, 103,* 1047–1066.

Ullman, M., Krippner, S., & Vaughan, A. (1973). *Dream telepathy.* New York: Macmillan.

Ullmann, L. P., & Krasner, L. (1975). *Psychological approaches to abnormal behavior.* Englewood Cliffs, NJ: Prentice-Hall.

Ulrich, R. E., Stachnik, T. J., & Stainton, N. R. (1963). Student acceptance of generalized personality interpretations. *Psychological Reports, 13,* 831–834.

Unal, E., Koksal, Y., Baysal, T., Energin, M., Aydin, K., & Caliskan, U. (2007). Klüver-Bucy syndrome in a boy with non-Hodgkin lymphoma. *Pediatric Hematology and Oncology, 24,* 149–152.

Underwood, G. (1994). Subliminal perception on TV. *Nature, 370,* 103.

Unger, G., Desiderio, D. M., & Parr, W. (1972). Isolation, identification and synthesis of a specific behavior-inducing brain peptide. *Nature, 238,* 198–202.

Ursu, S., Stenger V. A., Shear, M. K., Jones, M. R., & Carter, C. S. (2003). Overactive action monitoring in obsessive-compulsive disorder: Evidence from functional magnetic resonance imaging. *Psychological Science, 14,* 347–353.

Urushihara, K., & Miller, R. R. (2010). Backward blocking in first-order conditioning. *Journal of Experimental Psychology: Animal Behavior Processes, 36,* 281–295.

Usher, J. A., & Neisser, U. (1993). Childhood amnesia and the beginnings of memory for four early life events. *Journal of Experimental Psychology General, 122,* 155–165.

Vaidya, C. J., & Stollstorff, M. (2008). Cognitive neuroscience of attention deficit hyperactivity disorder: Current status and working hypotheses. *Developmental Disabilities, 14,* 261–267.

Vaillant, G. E., & Milofsky, E. (1980). Natural history of male psychological health: IX. Empirical evidence for Erikson's model of the life cycle. *American Journal of Psychiatry, 137,* 1348–1359.

Vakil, E., Blachstein, H., Sheinman, M., & Greenstein, Y. (2009). Developmental changes in attention test norms: Implications for the structure of attention. *Child Neuropsychology, 15,* 21–39.

Valentine, C. W. (1930). The innate bases of fear. *Journal of Genetic Psychology, 37,* 485–497.

Vallerand, R. J., & Losier, G. F. (1999). An integrative analysis of intrinsic and extrinsic motivation in sport. *Journal of Applied Sport Psychology, 11,* 142–169.

van Beek, N., Perna, G., Schruers, K., Verburg, K., Cucchi, M., Bellodi, L., & Griez, E. (2003). Vulnerability to 35% CO2 of panic disorder patients with a history of respiratory disorders. *Psychiatry Research, 120,* 125–130.

Van Boven, R. W., Hamilton, R. H., Kauffman, T., Keenan, J. P., & Pascual-Leone, A. (2000). Tactile spatial resolution in blind Braille readers. *Neurology, 54,* 2230–2236.

Van Dam-Baggen, R., & Kraaimaat, F. W. (2000). Social skills training in two subtypes of psychiatric inpatients with generalized social phobia. *Scandinavian Journal of Behaviour Therapy, 29,* 14–21.

Van de Water, T. J. (1997). Psychology's entrepreneurs and the marketing of industrial psychology. *Journal of Applied Psychology, 82,* 486–499.

van den Heuvel, O. A., Mataix-Cols, D., Zwitser, G., Cath, D. C., van der Werf, Y. D., Groenewegen, H. J., . . . Veltman, D. J. (2011). Common limbic and frontal-striatal disturbances in patients with obsessive-compulsive disorder, panic disorder and hypochondriasis. *Psychological Medicine, 41,* 2399–2410.

Van der Heijden, E., Klein, T. J., Müller, W., & Potters, J. (2012). Framing effects and impatience: Evidence from a large-scale experiment. *Journal of Economic Behavior & Organization, 84,* 701–711.

Van der Kolk, B. A. (2000). Trauma, neuroscience, and the etiology of hysteria: An exploration of the relevance of Breuer and Freud's 1893 article in light of modern science. *Journal of the American Academy of Psychoanalysis, 28,* 237–262.

Van Der Werf, Y. D., Jolles, J., Witter, M. P., & Uylings, H. B. M. (2003). Contributions of thalamic nuclei to declarative memory functioning. *Cortex, 39,* 1047–1062.

Van Dixhoorn, J. (1998). Cardiorespiratory effects of breathing and relaxation instruction in myocardial infarction patients. *Biological Psychology, 49,* 123–135.

Van Doorn, M. D., Branje, S. J. T., & Meeus, W. H. J. (2011). Developmental changes in conflict resolution styles in parent-adolescent relationships: A four-wave longitudinal study. *Journal of Youth & Adolescence, 40,* 97–107.

Van Doornen, L. J. P., & van Blokland, R. (1987). Serum-cholesterol: Sex specific psychological correlates during rest and stress. *Journal of Psychosomatic Research, 31,* 239–249.

van Grootheest, D. S., Cath, D. C., Beekman, A. T., & Boomsma, D. I. (2005). Twin studies on obsessive-compulsive disorder: A review. *Twin Research and Human Genetics, 8,* 450-458.

van Lankveld, J. J. D. M. (1998). Bibliotherapy in the treatment of sexual dysfunctions: A meta-analysis. *Journal of Consulting & Clinical Psychology, 66,* 702–708.

van Ommen, G. J. B. (2005). The human genome, revisited. *European Journal of Human Genetics, 13,* 265–270.

Van Wyk, P. H., & Geist, C. S. (1995). Biology of bisexuality: Critique and observations. *Journal of Homosexuality, 28,* 357–373.

VandenBos, G. R. (1996). Outcome assessment of psychotherapy. *American Psychologist, 51,* 1005–1006.

VanderZee, K., Buunk, B., & Sanderman, R. (1996). The relationship between social comparison processes and personality. *Personality and Individual Differences, 201,* 551–565.

Vargas, E. A., & Vargas, J. S. (1991). Programmed instruction: What it is and how to do it. *Journal of Behavioral Education, 1,* 235–251.

Varner, L. J., & Ellis, H. C. (1999). Cognitive activity and physiological arousal: Processes that mediate mood-congruent memory. *Memory and Cognition, 26,* 939–950.

Vecera, S. P., & O'Reilly, R. C. (1998). Figure-ground organization and object recognition processes: An interactive account. *Journal of Experimental Psychology: Human Perception and Performance, 24,* 441–462.

Vein, A. M., Sidorov, A. A., Martazaev, M. S., & Karlov, A. V. (1991). Physical exercise and nocturnal sleep in healthy humans. *Human Physiology, 17,* 391–397.

Veissier, I. (1993). Observational learning in cattle. *Applied Animal Behaviour Science, 35,* 235–243.

Veliz, J., & James, W. S. (1987). Medicine court: Rogers in practice. *American Journal of Psychiatry, 144,* 62–67.

Vella-Zarb, R. A., & Elgar, F. J. (2009). The "freshman 5": A meta-analysis of weight gain in the freshman year of college. *Journal of American College Health, 58,* 161–166.

Veneroso, C., Tuñón, M. J., González-Gallego, J., & Collado, P. S. (2009). Melatonin reduces cardiac inflammatory injury induced by acute exercise. *Journal of Pineal Research, 47,* 184–191.

Venn, J. (1984). Family etiology and remission in a case of psychogenic fugue. *Family Process, 23,* 429–435.

Ventis, W. L., Higbee, G., & Murdock, S. (2001). Using humor in systematic desensitization to reduce fear. *Journal of General Psychology, 128,* 241–253.

Verbaten, M. N. (2003). Specific memory deficits in ecstasy users? The results of a meta-analysis. *Human Psychopharmacology: Clinical and Experimental, 18,* 281–290.

Verdoux, H., Takei, N., Cassou de Saint-Mathurin, R., Murray, R. M., & Bourgeois, M. L. (1997). Seasonality of birth in schizophrenia: The effect of regional population density. *Schizophrenia Research, 23,* 175–180.

Verissimo, M., Santos, A. J., Vaughn, B. E., Torres, N., Monteiro, L., & Santos, O. (2011). Quality of attachment to father and mother and number of reciprocal friends. *Early Child Development and Care, 181,* 27–38.

Vermetten, E., & Bremner, J. D. (2003). Olfaction as a traumatic reminder in posttraumatic stress disorder: Case reports and review. *Journal of Clinical Psychiatry, 64,* 202–207.

Vernon, P. A. (1998). From the cognitive to the biological: A sketch of Arthur Jensen's contributions to the study of g. *Intelligence, 26,* 267–271.

Vernon, P. A., Jang, K. L., Harris, J. A., & McCarthy, J. M. (1997). Environmental predictors of personality differences: A twin and sibling study. *Journal of Personality and Social Psychology, 72,* 177–183.

Veroff, J., Depner, C., Kulka, R., & Douvan, E. (1980). Comparison of American motives: 1957 versus 1976. *Journal of Personality and Social Psychology, 39,* 1249–1262.

Verschuere, B., Crombez, G., & Koster, E. H. W. (2004). Orienting to guilty knowledge. *Cognition and Emotion, 18,* 265–279.

Vertes, R. P., & Eastman, K. E. (2000). The case against memory consolidation in REM sleep. *Behavioral and Brain Sciences, 23,* 867–876, 904–1018, 1083–1121.

Vetter, H. J. (1969). *Language behavior and psychopathology.* Chicago: Rand McNally.

Viard, A., Chételat, G., Lebreton, K., Desgranges, B., Landeau, B., de la Sayette, V., . . . Piolino, P.

(2011). Mental time travel into the past and future in healthy aged adults: An fMRI study. *Brain & Cognition, 75,* 1–9.

Vidal, J. (2002). Updated review on the benefits of weight loss. *International Journal of Obesity and Related Metabolic Disorders, 26,* S25–S28.

Vigliocco, G., Vinson, D. P., Martin, R. C., & Garrett, M. F. (1999). Is "count" and "mass" information available when the noun is not? An investigation of tip-of-the-tongue states and anomia. *Journal of Memory and Language, 40,* 534–558.

Vincent, K. R. (1991). Black/white IQ differences: Does age make the difference? *Journal of Clinical Psychology, 47,* 266–270.

Viney, W. (1993). *A history of psychology: Ideas and context.* Boston: Allyn & Bacon.

Vingilis-Jaremo, L., & Maurer, D. (2013). The influence of symmetry on children's judgments of facial attractiveness. *Perception, 42,* 302–320.

Visser, S. N., Danielson, M. L., Bitsko, R. H., Holbrook, J. R., Kogan, M. D., Ghandour, R. M., . . . Blumberg, S. J. (2014). Trends in the parent-report of health care provider-diagnosed and medicated attention-deficit/hyperactivity disorder: United States, 2003–2011. *Journal of the American Academy of Child and Adolescent Psychiatry, 53,* 34–46.

Vitiello, B. (2008). Effectively obtaining informed consent for child and adolescent participation in mental health research. *Ethics and Behavior, 18,* 182–198.

Vlaander, G. P., & Van Rooijen, L. (1985). Independence and conformity in Holland: Asch's experiment three decades later. *Gedrag: Tijdschrift voor Psychologie, 13,* 49–55.

Voeller, B. (1991). AIDS and heterosexual anal intercourse. *Archives of Sexual Behavior, 20,* 233–276.

Vogel, J. J., Bowers, C. A., & Vogel, D. S. (2003). Cerebral lateralization of spatial abilities: A meta-analysis. *Brain and Cognition, 52,* 197–204.

Vogler, G. P., Mcclearn, G. E., Snieder, H., & Boomsma, D. I. (1997). Genetics and behavioral medicine: Risk factors for cardiovascular disease. *Behavioral Medicine, 22,* 141–149.

Vokey, J. R., & Read, J. D. (1985). Subliminal messages: Between the devil and the media. *American Psychologist, 40,* 1231–1239.

Volkmar, F., Siegel, M., Woodbury-Smith, M., King, B., McCracken, J., & State, M. (2014). Practice parameter for the assessment and treatment of children and adolescents with autism spectrum disorder. *Journal of the American Academy of Child and Adolescent Psychiatry, 53,* 237–257.

Vollenweider, F. X., Gamma, A., Liechti, M., & Huber, T. (1998). Psychological and cardiovascular effects and short-term sequelae of MDMA ("Ecstasy") in MDMA-naive healthy volunteers. *Neuropsychopharmacology, 19,* 241–251.

von Békésy, G. (1957, August). The ear. *Scientific American,* pp. 66–78.

von der Pahlen, B., Lindman, R., Sarkola, T., Maekisalo, H., & Eriksson, C. J. P. (2002). An exploratory study on self-evaluated aggression and androgens in women. *Aggressive Behavior, 28,* 273–280.

von Hofsten, C., Kellman, P., & Putaansuu, J. (1992). Young infants' sensitivity to motion parallax. *Infant Behavior and Development, 15,* 245–264.

von Mayrhauser, R. T. (1989). Making intelligence functional: Walter Dill Scott and applied psychological testing in World War I. *Journal of the History of the Behavioral Sciences, 25,* 60–72.

von Senden, M. (1960). *Space and sight: The perception of space and shape in the congenitally blind before and after operation.* Oxford, England: Free Press of Glencoe.

Vonnegut, M. (1974, April). Why I want to bite R. D. Laing. *Harper's Magazine,* pp. 90–92.

Vonnegut, M. (1975). *The Eden express.* New York: Bantam Books.

Vosburg, S. K. (1998). The effects of positive and negative mood on divergent-thinking performance. *Creativity Research Journal, 11,* 165–172.

Votruba-Drzal, E., Coey, R. L., Maldonado-Carreño, Li-Grining, C. P., & Chase-Lansdale, P. L. (2010). Child care and the development of behavior problems among economically disadvantaged children in middle childhood. *Child Development, 81,* 1460–1474.

Voyer, D., & Flight, J. (2001). Gender differences in laterality on a dichotic task: The influence of report strategies. *Cortex, 37,* 345–362.

Voyer, D., & Rodgers, M. A. (2002). Reliability of laterality effects in a dichotic listening task with nonverbal material. *Brain and Cognition, 48,* 602–606.

Voyer, D., Voyer, S., & Bryden, M. P. (1995). Magnitude of sex differences in spatial abilities: A meta-analysis and consideration of critical variables. *Psychological Bulletin, 117,* 250–270.

Vrbova, G., Mehra, N., Shanmuganathan, H., Tyreman, N., Schachner, M., & Gordon, T. (2009). Chemical communication between regenerating motor axons and Schwann cells in the growth pathway. *European Journal of Neuroscience, 30,* 366–375.

Vuksic-Mihaljevic, Z., Mandic, N., Barkic, J., & Mrdenovic, S. (1998). A current psychodynamic understanding of panic disorder. *British Journal of Medical Psychology, 71,* 27–45.

Vulliemoz, S., Lemieux, L., Daunizeau, J., Michel, C. M., & Duncan, J. S. (2010). The combination of EEG source imaging and EEG-correlated functional MRI to map epileptic networks. *Epilepsia, 51,* 491–505.

Wadden, T. A., Foster, G. D., & Letizia, K. A. (1994). One-year behavioral treatment of obesity: Comparison of moderate and severe caloric restriction and the effects of weight maintenance therapy. *Journal of Consulting and Clinical Psychology, 62,* 165–171.

Wadden, T. A., Vogt, R. A., Foster, G. D., & Anderson, D. A. (1998). Exercise and the maintenance of weight loss: 1-year follow-up of a controlled clinical trial. *Journal of Consulting and Clinical Psychology, 66,* 429–433.

Wade, A. G., Ford, I., Crawford, G., McConnachie, A., Nir, T., Laudon, M., & Zisapel, M. (2010). Nightly treatment of primary insomnia with prolonged release melatonin for 6 months: A randomized placebo controlled trial on age and endogenous melatonin as predictors of efficacy and safety. *BMC Medicine, 8,* 51–69.

Wade, T. D., Bulik, C. M., Sullivan, P. F., Neale, M. C., & Kendler, K. S. (2000). The relation between risk factors for binge eating and bulimia nervosa: A population-based female twin study. *Health Psychology, 19,* 115–123.

Wade, T. D., & Kendler, K. S. (2000) The relationship between social support and major depression: Cross-sectional, longitudinal, and genetic perspectives. *Journal of Nervous and Mental Disease, 188,* 251–258.

Wagar, B. M., & Cohen, D. (2003). Culture, memory, and the self: An analysis of the personal and collective self in long-term memory. *Journal of Experimental Social Psychology, 39,* 468–475.

Wagemans, J. Elder, J. H., Kubovy, M., Palmer, S. E., Peterson, M. A., Singh, M., & von der Heyt, R. (2012). A century of Gestalt psychology in visual perception: I. Perceptual grouping and figure-ground organization. *Psychological Bulletin, 138,* 1172–1217.

Wagemans, J., Feldman, J., Gepshtein, S., Kimchi, R., Pomerantz, J. R., van der Helm, P. A., & van Leeuwen, C. (2012). A century of Gestalt psychology in visual perception: II. Conceptual and theoretical foundations. *Psychological Bulletin, 138,* 1218–1252.

Wagner, A. M., & Houlihan, D. D. (1994). Notes and shorter communications: Sensation seeking and trait anxiety in hang-glider pilots and golfers. *Personality and Individual Differences, 16,* 975–977.

Wagner, R. V. (2006). Terrorism: A peace psychological analysis. *Journal of Social Issues, 62,* 155–171.

Wagner, U., Gais, S., & Born, J. (2001). Emotional memory formation is enhanced across sleep intervals with high amounts of rapid eye movement sleep. *Learning and Memory, 8,* 112–119.

Wagstaff, G. F., & Frost, R. (1996). Reversing and breaching posthypnotic amnesia and hypnotically created pseudomemories. *Contemporary Hypnosis, 13,* 191–197.

Wagstaff, G. F., Vella, M., & Perfect, T. (1992). The effect of hypnotically elicited testimony on jurors' judgments of guilt and innocence. *Journal of Social Psychology, 132,* 591–595.

Wahlsten, D. (1999). Single-gene influences on behavior. *Annual Review of Psychology, 50,* 599–624.

Wai, J., Lubinski, D., Benbow, C. P., & Steiger, J. H. (2010). Accomplishment in science, technology, engineering, and mathematics (STEM) and its relation to STEM educational dose: A 25-year longitudinal study. *Journal of Educational Psychology, 102,* 860–871.

Waid, W. M., & Orne, M. T. (1982). The physiological detection of deception. *American Scientist, 70,* 402–409.

Waid, W. M., Wilson, S. K., & Orne, M. T. (1981). Cross-modal physiological effects of electrodermal ability in the detection of deception. *Journal of Personality and Social Psychology, 40,* 1118–1125.

Wainright, J. L., Russell, S. T., & Patterson, C. J. (2004). Psychosocial adjustment, school outcomes, and romantic relationships of adolescents with same-sex parents. *Child Development, 75,* 1886–1898.

Wakeman, D. R., Dodiya, H. B., & Kordower, J. H. (2011). Cell transplantation and gene therapy in Parkinson's disease. *Mount Sinai Journal of Medicine, 78,* 126–158.

Walburn, J., Vedhara, K., Hankins, M., Rixon, L., & Weinman, J. (2009). Psychological stress and wound healing in humans: A systematic review and meta-analysis. *Journal of Psychosomatic Research, 67,* 253–271.

Walczyk, J. J. (2000). The interplay between automatic and control processes in reading. *Reading Research Quarterly, 35,* 554–566.

Wald, G. (1964). The receptors of human color vision. *Science, 145,* 1007–1017.

Waldhauser, F., Saletu, B., & Trinchard, L. I. (1990). Sleep laboratory investigations on hypnotic properties of melatonin. *Psychopharmacology, 100,* 222–226.

Waldrop, M. M. (1984). Artificial intelligence in parallel. *Science, 225,* 608–610.

Walen, H. R., & Lachman, M. E. (2000). Social support and strain from partner, family, and friends: Costs and benefits for men and women in adulthood. *Journal of Social and Personal Relationships, 17,* 5–30.

Walk, R. D., & Homan, C. P. (1984). Emotion and dance in dynamic light displays. *Bulletin of the Psychonomic Society, 22,* 437–440.

Walker, E., Hoppes, E., Emory, E., Mednick, S., & Schulsinger, F. (1981). Environmental factors related to schizophrenia in psychophysiologically labile high-risk males. *Journal of Abnormal Psychology, 90,* 313–320.

Walker, L. (1986). Experiential and cognitive sources of moral development in adulthood. *Human Development, 29,* 113–124.

Walker, L. J. (1989). A longitudinal study of moral reasoning. *Child Development, 60,* 157–166.

Walker, M. B., & Andrade, M. G. (1996). Conformity in the Asch task as a function of age. *Journal of Social Psychology, 136,* 367–372.

Walker, M. M., Dennis, T. E., & Kirschvink, J. L. (2002). The magnetic sense and its use in long-distance navigation by animals. *Current Opinion in Neurobiology, 12,* 735–744.

Wallace, R. E. (1988). Abolish the duty to protect: It's time to release the scapegoats. *Psychotherapy in Private Practice, 6,* 55–63.

Wallace, W. (2003). The vibrating nerve impulse in Newton, Willis, and Gassendi: First steps in a mechanical theory of communication. *Brain and Cognition, 51,* 66–94.

Wallach, H., & Marshall, F. J. (1986). Shape constancy in pictorial representation. *Perception and Psychophysics, 39,* 233–235.

Wallach, M. A., Kogan, N., & Bem, D. J. (1962). Group influence on individual risk taking. *Journal of Abnormal and Social Psychology, 65,* 75–86.

Waller, N. G., & Ross, C. A. (1997). The prevalence and biometric structure of pathological dissociation in the general population: Taxometric and behavior genetic findings. *Journal of Abnormal Psychology, 106,* 499–510.

Waller, N. G., Kojetin, B. A., Bouchard, T. J., & Lykken, D. T. (1990). Genetic and environmental influences on religious interests, attitudes, and values: A study of twins reared apart and together. *Psychological Science, 1,* 138–142.

Wallis, C. (1984, June 11). Unlocking pain's secrets. *Time,* pp. 58–66.

Walsh, B. T., & Devlin, M. J. (1998). Eating disorders: Progress and problems. *Science, 280,* 1387–1390.

Walsh, E., Buchanan, A., & Fahy, T. (2002). Violence and schizophrenia: Examining the evidence. *British Journal of Psychiatry, 180,* 490–495.

Walsh, J. (1981). A plenipotentiary for human intelligence. *Science, 214,* 640–641.

Walsh, J. (1983). Wide world of reports. *Science, 220,* 804–805.

Walsh, J. C., Lynch, M., Murphy, A. W., & Daly, K. (2004). Factors influencing the decision to seek treatment for symptoms of acute myocardial infarction: An evaluation of the self-regulatory model of illness behaviour. *Journal of Psychosomatic Research, 56,* 67–73.

Walsh, J. J., Wilding, J. M., & Eysenck, M. W. (1994). Stress responsivity: The role of individual differences. *Personality and Individual Differences, 16,* 385–394.

Walsleben, J. A., Norman, R. G., Novak, R. D., O'Malley, E. B., Rapoport, D. M., & Strohl, K. P. (1999). Sleep habits of Long Island Railroad commuters. *Sleep, 22,* 728–734.

Walster, E., Aronson, V., Abrahams, D., & Rottman, L. (1966). Importance of physical attractiveness in dating behavior. *Journal of Personality and Social Psychology, 4,* 508–516.

Walters, G. C., & Grusec, J. E. (1977). *Punishment.* San Francisco: Freeman.

Waltz, D. L. (1982, October). Artificial intelligence. *Scientific American,* pp. 118–133.

Wang, C. L., Briston, T., Mowen, J. C., & Chakraborty, G. (2000). Alternative modes of self-construal: Dimensions of connectedness-separateness and advertising appeals to the cultural and gender-specific self. *Journal of Consumer Psychology, 9,* 107–115.

Wang, J. Q., Mao, L., & Han, J.-S. (1992). Comparison of the antinociceptive effects induced by electroacupuncture and transcutaneous electrical nerve stimulation in the rat. *International Journal of Neuroscience, 65,* 117–129.

Wang, L., Li, X., Hsiao, S. S., Lenz, F. A., Bodner, M., Zhou, Y.-D., & Fuster, J. M. (2015). Differential roles of delay-period neural activity in the monkey dorsolateral prefrontal cortex in visual-haptic crossmodal working memory. *Proceedings of the National Academy of Sciences of the United States of America, 112,* E214-9.

Wang, M. Q., Nicholson, M. E., Mahoney, B. S., & Li, Y. (1993). *Perceptual and Motor Skills, 77,* 83–88.

Wang, W., & Viney, L. L. (1997). The psychosocial development of children and adolescents in the People's Republic of China: An Eriksonian approach. *International Journal of Psychology, 32,* 139–153.

Wang, W., Wu, Y. X., Peng, Z. G., Lu, S. W., Yu, L., Wang, G. P., . . . Wang, Y. H. (2000). Test of sensation seeking in a Chinese sample. *Personality and Individual Differences, 28,* 169–179.

Wang, X. T., & Johnston, V. S. (1995). Perceived social context and risk preference: A re-examination of framing effects in a life-death decision problem. *Journal of Behavioral Decision Making, 8,* 279–293.

Wankel, L. M. (1993). The importance of enjoyment to adherence and psychological benefits from physical activity. Special Issue: Exercise and psychological well-being. *International Journal of Sport Psychology, 24,* 151–169.

Wanzer, M. B., & Frymier, A. B. (1999). The relationship between student perceptions of instructor humor and student's reports of learning. *Communication Education, 48,* 48–62.

Ward, A., Lyubomirsky, S., Sousa, L., & Nolen-Hoeksema, S. (2003). Can't quite commit: Rumination and uncertainty. *Personality and Social Psychology Bulletin, 29,* 96–107.

Ward, L. C., & Perry, M. S. (1998). Measurement of social introversion by the MMPI-2. *Journal of Personality Assessment, 70,* 171–182.

Ward, P., & Carnes, M. (2002). Effects of posting self-set goals on collegiate football players' skill execution during practice and games. *Journal of Applied Behavior Analysis, 35,* 1–12.

Wardle, J., Guthrie, C., Sanderson, S., Birch, L., & Plomin, R. (2001). Food and activity preferences in children of lean and obese parents. *International Journal of Obesity & Related Metabolic Disorders, 25,* 971–977.

Warwick-Evans, L. A., Symons, N., Fitch, T., & Burrows, L. (1998). Evaluating sensory conflict and postural instability: Theories of motion sickness. *Brain Research Bulletin, 47,* 465–469.

Washburn, D. A., & Rumbaugh, D. M. (1997). Faster is smarter, so why are we slower? A comparative perspective on intelligence and processing speed. *American Psychologist, 52,* 1147–1148.

Washburn, M. F. (1916). *Movement and mental imagery.* Oxford, England: Houghton Mifflin.

Washio, Y., Hayes, L. J., Hunter, K. W., & Pritchard, J. K. (2011). Backward conditioning of tumor necrosis factor-cc in a single trial. Changing intervals between exposures to lipopolysaccharide and saccharin taste. *Physiology & Behavior, 102,* 239–244.

Wasserman, E. A. (1997). What's elementary about associative learning? *Annual Review of Psychology, 48,* 573–607.

Watanabe, S., & Sato, K. (1999). Discriminative stimulus properties of music in Java sparrows. *Behavioural Processes, 47,* 53–57.

Waterhouse, J., Reilly, T., Atkinson, G., & Edwards, B. (2007). Jet lag: Trends and coping strategies. *Lancet, 369,* 1117–1129.

Waters, E., Merrick, S., Treboux, D., Crowell, J., & Albersheim, L. (2000). Attachment security in infancy and early adulthood: A twenty-year longitudinal study. *Child Development, 71,* 684–689.

Waters, E., Weinfield, N. S., & Hamilton, C. E. (2000). The stability of attachment security from infancy to adolescence and early adulthood: General discussion. *Child Development, 71,* 703–706.

Waters, R. S., Samulack, D. D., Dykes, R. W., & McKinley, P. A. (1990). Topographic organization of baboon primary motor cortex: Face, hand, forelimb, and shoulder representation. *Somatosensory and Motor Research, 7,* 485–514.

Watson, J. B. (1913). Psychology as the behaviorist views it. *Psychological Review, 20,* 158–177.

Watson, J. B. (1930). *Behaviorism.* New York: W. W. Norton.

Watson, J. B., & Rayner, R. (1920). Conditioned emotional reactions. *Journal of Experimental Psychology, 3,* 1–14.

Watt, M. C., & Stewart, S. H. (2000). Anxiety sensitivity mediates the relationships between childhood learning experiences and elevated hypochondriacal concerns in young adulthood. *Journal of Psychosomatic Research, 49,* 107–118.

Watten, R. G., Lie, I., & Birketvedt, O. (1994). The influence of long-term visual near-work on accommodation and convergence: A field study. *Journal of Human Ergology, 23,* 27–39.

Watters, P. A., Martin, F., & Schreter, Z. (1997). Caffeine and cognitive performance: The nonlinear Yerkes-Dodson Law. *Human Psychopharmacology Clinical and Experimental, 12,* 249–257.

Watts, B. L. (1982). Individual differences in circadian activity rhythms and their effects on roommate relationships. *Journal of Personality, 50,* 374–384.

Watts, J., & Robertson, N. (2011), Burnout in university teaching staff: A systematic literature review. *Educational Research, 53,* 33–50.

Watts, R. E., & Critelli, J. W. (1997). Roots of contemporary cognitive theories in the individual psychology of Alfred Adler. *Journal of Cognitive Psychotherapy, 11,* 147–156.

Watts, R. E., & Holden, J. M. (1994). Why continue to use "fictional finalism"? *Individual Psychology: Journal of Adlerian Theory, Research, and Practice, 50,* 161–163.

Wax, M. L. (1999). The angel of dreams: Toward an ethnology of dream interpreting. *Journal of the American Academy of Psychoanalysis, 27,* 417–429.

Weaver, C. A. (1993). Do you need a "flash" to form a flashbulb memory? *Journal of Experimental Psychology: General, 122,* 39–46.

Weaver, J. B., Masland, J. L., Kharazmi, S., & Zillman, D. (1985). Effect of alcoholic intoxication on the appreciation of different types of humor. *Journal of Personality and Social Psychology, 49,* 781–787.

Webb, W. B. (1981). An essay on consciousness. *Teaching of Psychology, 8,* 15–19.

Webb, W. B. (1985). Sleep and dreaming. In G. A. Kimble & K. Schlesinger (Eds.), *Topics in the history of psychology* (Vol. 2, pp. 191–217). Hillsdale, NJ: Erlbaum.

Webb, W. B. (1992). *Sleep: The gentle tyrant* (2nd ed.). Boston: Anker.

Weber, M. M., & Engstrom, E. J. (1997). Kraepelin's "diagnostic cards": The confluence of clinical research and preconceived categories. *History of Psychiatry, 8,* 375–385.

Weber, R., & Crocker, J. (1983). Cognitive processes in the revision of stereotype beliefs. *Journal of Personality and Social Psychology, 45,* 961–977.

Webster, S., & Coleman, S. R. (1992). The reception of Clark L. Hull's behavior theory, 1943–1960. *Psychological Reports, 70,* 1063–1071.

Wechsler, D. (1958). *Measurement and appraisal of adult intelligence.* Baltimore: Williams & Wilkins.

Weekes, J. R., Lynn, S. J., Green, J. P., & Brentar, J. T. (1992). Pseudomemory in hypnotized and task-motivated subjects. *Journal of Abnormal Psychology, 101,* 356–360.

Wegner, D. M., & Schneider, D. J. (2003). The white bear story. *Psychological Inquiry, 14,* 326–329.

Weidman, N. (1997). Heredity, intelligence and neuropsychology; or, why *The Bell Curve* is good science. *Journal of the History of the Behavioral Sciences, 33,* 141–144.

Weigel, R. H., Vernon, D. T. A., & Tognacci, L. N. (1974). Specificity of the attitude as a determinant of attitude-behavior congruence. *Journal of Personality and Social Psychology, 30,* 724–728.

Weilage, M., & Hope, D. A. (1999). Self-discrepancy in social phobia and dysthymia. *Cognitive Therapy and Research, 23,* 637–650.

Weinberg, R. A. (1989). Intelligence and IQ: Landmark issues and great debates. *American Psychologist, 44,* 98–104.

Weinberg, R. A., Scarr, S., & Waldman, I. D. (1992). The Minnesota Transracial Adoption Study: A follow-up of IQ test performance at adolescence. *Intelligence, 16,* 117–135.

Weinberger, J., & Silverman, L. H. (1990). Testability and empirical verification of psychoanalytic dynamic propositions through subliminal psychodynamic activation. *Psychoanalytic Psychology, 7,* 299–339.

Weinberger, J., & Smith, B. (2011). Investigating merger: Subliminal psychodynamic activation and oneness motivation research. *Journal of the American Psychoanalytic Association, 59,* 553–570.

Weiner, B. (1980). A cognitive (attribution)-emotionaction model of motivated behavior: An analysis of judgments of help-giving. *Journal of Personality and Social Psychology, 39,* 186–200.

Weiner, B. (1985a). An attributional theory of achievement motivation and emotion. *Psychological Review, 92,* 548–573.

Weiner, B. (1985b). "Spontaneous" causal thinking. *Psychological Bulletin, 97,* 74–84.

Weiner, B., Figueroa-Munoz, A., & Kakihara, C. (1991). The goals of excuses and communication strategies related to causal perceptions. *Personality and Social Psychology Bulletin, 17,* 4–13.

Weinstein, L., & Almaguer, L. L. (1987). "I'm bored!" *Bulletin of the Psychonomic Society, 25,* 389–390.

Weinstein, N. D. (1984). Reducing un realistic optimism about illness susceptibility. *Health Psychology, 3,* 431–457.

Weisfeld, G. E., Czilli, T., Phillips, K. A., Gall, J. A., & Lichtman, C. M. (2003). Possible olfaction-based mechanisms in human kin recognition and inbreeding avoidance. *Journal of Experimental Child Psychology, 85,* 279–295.

Weisman, J. (1988, November 19–25). Remembering JFK: Our first TV president. *TV Guide,* pp. 2–4, 6–8.

Weiss, J. M. (1972, June). Psychological factors in stress and disease. *Scientific American,* pp. 104–113.

Weiss, M. G. (1995). Eating disorders and disordered eating in different cultures. *Psychiatric Clinics of North America, 18,* 537–553.

Weiss, S. J., Panlilio, L. V., & Schindler, C. W. (1993). Single-incentive selective associations produced solely as a function of compound-stimulus conditioning context. *Journal of Experimental Psychology Animal Behavior Processes, 19,* 284–294.

Weisskirch, R. S., & Murphy, L. C. (2004). Friends, porn, and punk: Sensation seeking in personal relationships, Internet activities and music preference among college students. *Adolescence, 39,* 189–201.

Weissman, M. M., Bland, R. C., Canino, G. J., & Faravelli, C. (1997). The cross-national epidemiology of panic disorder. *Archives of General Psychiatry, 54,* 305–309.

Weissman, M. M., Bland, R. C., Canino, G. J., Greenwald, S., Lee, C.-K., Newman, S. C., . . . & Wick ramaratne, P. J. (1996). The cross-national epidemiology of social phobia: A preliminary report. *International Clinical Psychopharmacology, 11,* 9–14.

Weissman, M. M., & Olfson, M. (1995). Depression in women: Implications for health care research. *Science, 269,* 799–801.

Weisz, J. R., Rothbaum, F. M., & Blackburn, T. C. (1984). Standing out and standing in: The psychology of control in America and Japan. *American Psychologist, 39,* 955–969.

Weisz, J. R., Weiss, B., Han, S. S., & Granger, D. (1995). Effects of psychotherapy with children and adolescents revisited: A meta-analysis of treatment outcome studies. *Psychological Bulletin, 117,* 450–468.

Weitzenhoffer, A. M., & Hilgard, E. R. (1962). *Stanford Scale of Hypnotic Susceptibility, Form C.* Palo Alto, CA: Consulting Psychologists Press.

Welch, S. L., Doll, H. A., & Fairburn, C. G. (1997). Life events and the onset of bulimia nervosa: A controlled study. *Psychological Medicine, 27,* 515–522.

Welch-Ross, M. K., & Schmidt, C. R. (1996). Gender-schema development and children's constructive story memory: Evidence for a developmental model. *Child Development, 67,* 820–835.

Weldon, E., & Gargano, G. M. (1988). Cognitive loafing: The effects of accountability and shared responsibility on cognitive effort. *Personality and Social Psychology Bulletin, 14,* 159–171.

Weller, S. (2012). Evolving creativity in qualitative longitudinal research with children and teenagers, *International Journal of Social Research Methodology: Theory & Practice, 15,* 119–133.

Wellisch, D., Kagawa-Singer, M., Reid, S. L., Lin, Y. J., Nishikawa-Lee, S., & Wellisch, M., (1999). An exploratory study of social support: A cross-cultural comparison of Chinese-, Japanese-, and Anglo-American breast cancer patients. *Psycho-Oncology, 8,* 207–219.

Wells, G. L., & Lindsay, R. C. L. (1985). Methodological notes on the accuracy-confidence relation in eyewitness identification. *Journal of Applied Psychology, 70,* 413–419.

Wenderoth, P. (1994). On the relationship between the psychology of visual perception and the neurophysiology of vision. *Australian Journal of Psychology, 46,* 1–6.

Wendorf, C. A. (2001). History of American morality research, 1894–1932. *History of Psychology, 4,* 272–288.

Wermter, A. K., Laucht, M., Schimmelmann, B. G., Banaschewski, T., Sonuga-Barke, E. J. S., Rietschel, M., & Becker, K. (2010). From nature versus nurture, via nature and nurture, to gene 3 environment interaction in mental disorders. *European Child and Adolescent Psychiatry, 19,* 199–210.

Werth, J. L. Jr., Wright, K. S., Archambault, R. J., & Bardash, R. (2003). When does the "duty to protect" apply with a client who has anorexia nervosa? *Counseling Psychologist, 31,* 427–450.

Wertheimer, M. (1978). Humanistic psychology and the humane but tough-minded psychologist. *American Psychologist, 33,* 739–745.

Wertheimer, M., & King, D. B. (1994). Max Wertheimer's American sojourn, 1933–1943. *History of Psychology Newsletter, 26,* 3–15.

Wesp, R., & Montgomery, K. (1998). Developing critical thinking through the study of paranormal phenomena. *Teaching of Psychology, 25,* 275–278.

Wesson, G. (1997, November 25). Mountain climber Hulda Crooks dies at 101. *Press-Enterprise,* p. B06A.

Westen, D., DeFife, J. A., Bradley, B., & Hilsenroth, M. J. (2010). Prototype personality diagnosis in clinical practice: A viable alternative for *DSM-5* and *ICD-11. Professional Psychology: Research & Practice, 41,* 482–487.

Westermeyer, J. F. (2004). Predictors and characteristics of Erikson's life cycle model among men: A 32-year longitudinal study. *The International Journal of Aging & Human Development, 58,* 29–48.

Westmaas, J. L., Wild, T. C., & Ferrence, R. (2002). Effects of gender in social control of smoking cessation. *Health Psychology, 21,* 368–376.

Westrin, A., & Lam, R. W. (2007). Seasonal affective disorder: A clinical update. *Annals of Clinical Psychiatry: Official Journal of the American Academy of Clinical Psychiatrists, 19,* 239–246.

Wetter, D. W., Fiore, M. C., Young, T. B., McClure, J. B., deMoor, C. A., & Baker, T. B. (1999). Gender differences in response to nicotine replacement therapy: Objective and subjective indexes of tobacco withdrawal. *Experimental and Clinical Psychopharmacology, 7,* 135–144.

Wetter, D. W., Kenford, S. L., Smith, S. S., Fiore, M. C., Jorenby, D. E., & Baker, T. B. (1999). Gender differences in smoking cessation. *Journal of Consulting and Clinical Psychology, 67,* 555–562.

Wever, E. G., & Bray, C. W. (1937). The perception of low tones and the resonance volley theory. *Journal of Psychology, 3,* 101–114.

Whaley, D. E. (2003). Future-oriented self-perceptions and exercise behavior in middle-aged women. *Journal of Aging and Physical Activity, 11,* 1–17.

Wheat, A. L., & Larkin, K. T. (2010). Biofeedback of heat rate variability and related physiology: A critical review. *Applied Psycholphysiology & Biofeedback, 35,* 229–242.

Wheeler, R. E., Davison, R. J., & Tomarken, A. J. (1993). Frontal brain asymmetry and emotional reactivity: A biological substrate of affective style. *Psychophysiology, 30,* 82–89.

Whelan, B. M., Murdoch, B. E., Theodoros, D. G., Silburn, P., & Hall, B. (2002). A role for the dominant thalamus in language? A linguistic comparison of two cases subsequent to unilateral thalamotomy procedures in the dominant and nondominant hemispheres. *Aphasiology, 16,* 1213–1226.

Wheldall, K., & Benner, H. (1993). Conservation without conversation revisited: A replication and elaboration of the Wheldall-Poborca findings on the nonverbal assessment of conservation of liquid quantity. *Educational Psychology, 13,* 49–58.

Whisman, M. A., & Beach, S. R. H. (2012). Couple therapy for depression. *Journal of Clinical Psychology, 68,* 526–535.

Whissell, C. M. (1984). Emotion: A classification of current literature. *Perceptual and Motor Skills, 59,* 599–609.

Whitaker-Azmitia, P. M. (2001). Serotonin and brain development: Role in human developmental diseases.'

Whitbourne, S. K., & Hulicka, I. M. (1990). Ageism in undergraduate psychology texts. *American Psychologist, 45,* 1127–1136.

White, G. L., & Taytroe, L. (2003). Personal problem-solving using dream incubation: Dreaming, relaxation, or waking cognition? *Dreaming: Journal of the Association for the Study of Dreams, 13,* 193–209.

White, J. W., & Humphrey, J. A. (1994). Women's aggression in heterosexual conflicts. *Aggressive Behavior, 20,* 195–202.

White, J. W., & Kowalski, R. M. (1994). Deconstructing the myth of the nonaggressive woman: A feminist analysis. *Psychology of Women Quarterly, 18,* 487–508.

White, S. H. (1990). Child study at Clark University. *Journal of the History of the Behavioral Sciences, 26,* 131–150.

White, S. H. (1994). Hilgard's vision of psychology's history. *Psychological Science, 5,* 192–194.

White, S., O'Reilly, H., & Frith, U. (2009). Big heads, small details and autism. *Neuropsychologia, 47,* 1274–81.

Whitehurst, G. J., Falco, F. L., Lonigan, C. J., Fischel, J. E., DeBaryshe, B. D., Valdez-Menchaca, M. C., & Caulfield, M. (1988). Accelerating language development through picture book reading. *Developmental Psychology, 24,* 552–559.

Whitlock, F. A. (1987). Addiction. In R. L. Gregory (Ed.), *Oxford companion to the mind* (pp. 3–5). New York: Oxford University Press.

Whittal, M. L., Agras, W. S., & Gould, R. A. (1999). Bulimia nervosa: A meta-analysis of psychosocial and pharmacological treatments. *Behavior Therapy, 30,* 117–135.

Whorf, B. L. (1956). Science and linguistics. In J. B. Carroll (Ed.), *Language, thought, and reality: Selected writings of Benjamin Lee Whorf* (pp. 202–19). Cambridge, MA: MIT Press.

Whyte, G. (1998). Recasting Janis's groupthink model: The key role of collective efficacy in decision fiascoes. *Organizational Behavior and Human Decision Processes, 73,* 185–209.

Whyte, W. H. (1956). *The organization man.* New York: Simon & Schuster.

Wichstrom, L. (2001). The impact of pubertal timing on adolescents' alcohol use. *Journal of Research on Adolescence, 11,* 131–150.

Wickelgren, I. (1998). Obesity: How big a problem? *Science, 280,* 1364–1367.

Wicker, F. W., Barron, W. L., & Willis, A. C. (1980). Disparagement humor: Dispositions and resolutions. *Journal of Personality and Social Psychology, 39,* 701–709.

Wickramasekera, I. E., II, & Szlyk, J. P. (2003). Could empathy be a predictor of hypnotic ability? *International Journal of Clinical and Experimental Hypnosis, 51,* 390–399.

Widen, S. C., & Russell, J. A. (2003). A closer look at preschoolers' freely produced labels for facial expressions. *Developmental Psychology, 39,* 114–128.

Widiger, T. A., & Trull, T. J. (1991). Diagnosis and clinical assessment. *Annual Review of Psychology, 42,* 109–133.

Widmeyer, W. N., & Loy, J. W. (1988). When you're hot, you're hot: Warm-cold effects in first impressions of persons and teaching effectiveness. *Journal of Educational Psychology, 80,* 118–121.

Wiebe, D. J., & McCallum, D. M. (1986). Health practices and hardiness as mediators in the stress-illness relationship. *Health Psychology, 5,* 425–438.

Wiederman, M. W. (1999). A classroom demonstration of potential biases in the subjective interpretation of projective tests. *Teaching of Psychology, 26,* 37–39.

Wiederman, M. W. (1999). Volunteer bias in sexuality research using college student participants. *Journal of Sex Research, 36,* 59–66.

Wiederman, M. W., & Kendall, E. (1999). Evolution, sex, and jealousy: Investigation with a sample from Sweden. *Evolution and Human Behavior, 20,* 121–128.

Wiesmann, U., & Hannich, H.-J. (2011). A salutogenic analysis of developmental tasks and ego integrity vs. despair. *The International Journal of Aging & Human Development, 73,* 351–369.

Wightman, D. C., & Lintern, G. (1984, August). Part-task training of tracking in manual control. *NAVTRAEQUIPCEN* (Technical Report 81-C-0105-2).

Wijk, R. G., van (2009). From statistical significance to clinical relevance. *Clinical and Experimental Allergy, 40,* 197–199.

Wilcox, J. A. (1990). Fluoxetine and bulimia. *Journal of Psychoactive Drugs, 22,* 81–82.

Wilder, D. A., Simon, A. F., & Faith, M. (1996). Enhancing the impact of counterstereotypic information: Dispositional attributions for deviance. *Journal of Personality and Social Psychology, 71,* 276–287.

Wildgruber, D., Riecker, A., Hertrich, I. Erb, M., Grodd, W., Ethoger T., & Ackerman, H. (2005). Identification of emotional intonation evaluated by fMRI. *Neuroimage, 24,* 1233–1241.

Wilding, J., Rashid, W., Gilmore, D., & Valentine, E. (1986). A comparison of two mnemonic methods in learning medical information. *Human Learning: Journal of Practical Research and Applications, 5,* 211–217.

Wiles, R., Crow, G., Heath, S., & Charles, V. (2008). The management of confidentiality and anonymity in social research. *International Journal of Social Research Methodology, 11,* 417–428.

Wiley, J. (1998). Expertise as mental set: The effects of domain knowledge in creative problem solving. *Memory and Cognition, 26,* 716–730.

Wilhelm, F. H., Trabert, W., & Roth, W. T. (2001). Physiologic instability in panic disorder and generalized anxiety disorder. *Biological Psychiatry, 49,* 596–605.

Wilkins, P. (2000). Unconditional positive regard reconsidered. *British Journal of Guidance and Counselling, 28,* 23–36.

Williams, C. D. (1959). The elimination of tantrum behavior by extinction procedures. *Journal of Abnormal and Social Psychology, 59,* 269.

Williams, J., Merritt, J., Rittenhouse, C., & Hobson, J. A. (1992). Bizarreness in dreams and fantasies: Implications for the activation-synthesis hypothesis. *Consciousness and Cognition: An International Journal, 1,* 172–185.

Williams, J. D., & Klug, M. G. (1996). Aging and cognition: Methodological differences in outcome. *Experimental Aging Research, 22,* 219–244.

Williams, J. E., & Best, D. L. (1990). *Measuring sex stereotypes: A multination study.* Newbury Park, CA: Sage.

Williams, L., Forster, G., & Petrak, J. (1999). Rape attitudes amongst British medical students. *Medical Education, 33,* 24–27.

Williams, R. B. Jr., Kuhn, C. M., Melosh, W., White, A. D., & Schonberg, S. M. (1982). Type A behavior and elevated physiological and neuroendocrine responses to cognitive tasks. *Science, 218,* 483–485.

Williams, S. L., Brakke, K. E., & Savage-Rumbaugh, E. S. (1997). Comprehension skills of language-competent and nonlanguage-competent apes. *Language and Communication, 17,* 301–317.

Williams, S. L., Turner, S. M., & Peer, D. F. (1985). Guided mastery and performance desensitization treatments for severe acrophobia. *Journal of Consulting and Clinical Psychology, 53,* 237–247.

Williams, T. J., Pepitone, M. E., Christensen, S. E., Cooke, B. M., Huberman, A. D., Breedlove, N. J., . . . Breedlove, S. M. (2000). Finger length patterns and human sexual orientation. *Nature, 404,* 455–456.

Williams, T. L., Clarke, V., & Borland, R. (2001). Effects of message framing on breast-cancer-related beliefs and behaviors: The role of mediating factors. *Journal of Applied Social Psychology, 31,* 925–950.

Willis, L. A., Coombs, D. W., Drentea, P., & Cockerham, W. C. (2003). Uncovering the mystery: Factors of African American suicide. *Suicide and Life-Threatening Behavior, 33,* 412–429.

Wilson, B. J., Smith, S. L., Potter, W. J., Kunkel, D., Linz, D., Colvin, C. M., & Donnerstein, E. (2002). Violence in children's television programming: Assessing the risks. *Journal of Communication, 52,* 5–35.

Wilson, C., Boni, D., & Hogg, A. (1997). The effectiveness of task clarification, positive reinforcement, and corrective feedback in changing courtesy among police staff. *Journal of Occupational Behavior Management, 17,* 65–99.

Wilson, E. J., & Sherrell, D. L. (1993). Source effects in communication and persuasion research: A meta-analysis of effect size. *Journal of the Academy of Marketing Science, 21,* 101–112.

Wilson, E. O. (1975). *Sociobiology: The new synthesis.* Cambridge, MA: Harvard University Press.

Wilson, G., & Lester, D. (1998). Suicide prevention by e-mail. *Crisis Intervention and Time–Limited Treatment, 4,* 81–87.

Wilson, G. D. (1987). Male-female differences in sexual activity, enjoyment, and fantasies. *Personality and Individual Differences, 8,* 125–127.

Wilson, G. T., Fairburn, C. C., Agras, W. S., Walsh, B. T., & Kraemer, H. (2002). Cognitive-behavioral therapy for bulimia nervosa: Time course and mechanisms of change. *Journal of Consulting and Clinical Psychology, 70,* 267–274.

Wilson, J. R. (1967). *The mind.* New York: Time.

Wilson, T. C. (1996). Cohort and prejudice: Whites' attitudes toward Blacks, Hispanics, Jews, and Asians. *Public Opinion Quarterly, 60,* 253–274.

Wilson-Barnett, J. (1994). Preparing patients for invasive medical and surgical procedures: III. Policy implications for implementing specific psychological interventions. *Behavioral Medicine, 20,* 23–26.

Winders, S. E., & Grunberg, N. E. (1989). Nicotine, tobacco smoke, and body weight: A review of the animal literature. *Annals of Behavioral Medicine, 11,* 125–133.

Windholz, G. (1992). Pavlov's conceptualization of learning. *American Journal of Psychology, 105,* 459–469.

Windholz, G., & Kuppers, J. R. (1990). Pavlov and the Nobel Prize award. *Pavlovian Journal of Biological Science, 25,* 155–162.

Winefield, A. H. (1982). Methodological difficulties in demonstrating learned helplessness in humans. *Journal of General Psychology, 107,* 255–266.

Winer, R. S. (1999). Experimentation in the 21st century: The importance of external validity. *Journal of the Academy of Marketing Science, 27,* 349–358.

Winnepenninckx, B., Rooms, L., & Kooy, R. F. (2003). Mental retardation: A review of the genetic causes. *British Journal of Developmental Disabilities, 49,* 29–44.

Winner, E. (2000). The origins and ends of giftedness. *American Psychologist, 55,* 159–169.

Winsky-Sommerer, R. (2009). Role of GABAA receptors in the physiology and pharmacology of sleep. *European Journal of Neuroscience, 29,* 1779–1794.

Winter, Y., Lopez, J., & von Helversen, O. (2003). Ultraviolet vision in a bat. *Nature, 425,* 612–614.

Winton, W. M. (1990). Jamesian aspects of misattribution research. *Personality and Social Psychology Bulletin, 16,* 652–664.

Wittmann, A., Schlagenhauf, F., Guhn, A., Lueken, U., Gaehlsdorf, C., Stoy, M., . . . Ströhle, A. (2014). Anticipating agoraphobic situations: The neural correlates of panic disorder with agoraphobia. *Psychological Medicine/First View,* 1–12.

Wittmann, A., Schlagenhauf, F., Guhn, A., Lueken, U., Gaehlsdorf, C., Stoy, M., . . . Ströhle, A. (2014). Anticipating agoraphobic situations: The neural correlates of panic disorder with agoraphobia. *Psychological Medicine, 44*(11), 2385–2396.

Wixted, J. T. (1991). Conditions and consequences of maintenance rehearsal. *Journal of Experimental Psychology: Learning, Memory, and Cognition, 17,* 963–973.

Wixted, J. T., & Ebbesen, E. B. (1991). On the form of forgetting. *Psychological Science, 2,* 409–415.

Wolfe, J. (1936). Effectiveness of token rewards for chimpanzees. *Comparative Psychology Monographs, 12*(5).

Wolfensberger, W. (1972). *Normalization.* Toronto: National Institute on Mental Retardation.

Wolfensohn, S., & Maguire, M. (2010). What has the animal rights movement done for animal welfare? *Biologist, 57,* 22–27.

Wolff, J. J., Gu, H., Gerig, G., Elison, J. T., Styner, M., Gouttard, S., . . . Piven, J. (2012). Differences in white matter fiber tract development present from 6 to 24 months in infants with autism. *American Journal of Psychiatry, 169,* 589–600.

Wolgast, M., Lundh, L.-G., & Viborg, G. (2011). Cognitive reappraisal and acceptance: An experimental comparison of two emotion regulation strategies. *Behaviour Research & Therapy, 49,* 858–866.

Wolkowitz, O. M., Gertz, B., Weingartner, H., & Beccaria, L. (1990). Hunger in humans induced by MK-329, a specific peripheral-type cholecystokinin receptor antagonist. *Biological Psychiatry, 28,* 169–173.

Wollen, K. A., Weber, A., & Lowry, D. H. (1972). Bizarreness versus interaction of mental images as determinants of learning. *Cognitive Psychology, 3,* 518–523.

Wolpe, J. (1958). *Psychotherapy by reciprocal inhibition.* Stanford, CA: Stanford University Press.

Wolpe, J. (1988). Obituary: Mary Cover Jones 1896–1987. *Journal of Behavior Therapy and Experimental Psychiatry, 19,* 34.

Wolpin, M., Marston, A., Randolph, C., & Clothier, A. (1992). Individual difference correlates of reported lucid dreaming frequency and control. *Journal of Mental Imagery, 16,* 231–236.

Wood, J. M., Bootzin, R. R., Kihlstrom, J. F., & Schacter, D. L. (1992). Implicit and explicit memory for verbal information presented during sleep. *Psychological Science, 3,* 236–239.

Wood, J. M., Bootzin, R. R., Rosenhan, D., Nolen-Hoeksema, S., & Jourden, F. (1992). Effects of the 1989 San Francisco earthquake on frequency and content of nightmares. *Journal of Abnormal Psychology, 101,* 219–224.

Wood, W., & Eagly, A. H. (1981). Stages in the analysis of persuasive messages: The role of causal attributions and message comprehension. *Journal of Experimental and Social Psychology, 40,* 246–259.

Wood, W., & Eagly, A. H. (2000). A call to recognize the breadth of evolutionary perspectives: Sociocultural theories and evolutionary psychology. *Psychological Inquiry, 11,* 52–55.

Wood, W., Lundgren, S., Ouellette, J. A., & Busceme, S. (1994). Minority influence: A meta-analytic review of social influence processes. *Psychological Bulletin, 115,* 323–345.

Woodruff-Pak, D. S. (1993). Eyeblink classical conditioning in H. M.: Delay and trace paradigms. *Behavioral Neuroscience, 107,* 911–925.

Woods, C. J. P. (1996). Gender differences in moral development and acquisition: A review of Kohlberg's and Gilligan's models of justice and care. *Social Behavior and Personality, 24,* 375–384.

Woolley, H. T. (1910). A review of recent literature on the psychology of sex. *Psychological Bulletin, 7,* 335–342.

Worringham, C. J., & Messick, D. M. (1983). Social facilitation of running: An unobtrusive study. *Journal of Social Psychology, 121,* 23–29.

Worthen, M. (2011). The anger between traumatic exposures, posttraumatic stress disorder, and anger in male and female veterans. *23,* 188–201.

Wright, D. B., Gaskell, G. D., & O'Muircheartaigh, C. A. (1998). Flashbulb memory assumptions: Using national surveys to explore cognitive phenomena. *British Journal of Psychology, 89,* 103–121.

Wright, I. C., Rabe-Hesketh, S., Woodruff, P. W. R., David, A. S., Murray, R. M., & Bullmore, E. T. (2000). Meta-analysis of regional brain volumes in schizophrenia. *American Journal of Psychiatry, 157,* 16–25.

Wright, S., Grogan, S., & Hunter, G. (2000). Motivations for anabolic steroid use among bodybuilders. *Journal of Health Psychology, 5,* 566–571.

Wu, H., Wang, J., Cacioppo, J. T., Glaser, R., Kiecolt-Glaser, J. K., & Malarkey, W. B. (1999). Chronic stress associated with spousal caregiving of patients with Alzheimer's dementia is associated with downregulation of B-lymphocyte GH mRNA. *Journals of Gerontology, 54A,* M212–M215.

Wu, J., Witkiewitz, K., McMahon, R. J., & Dodge, K. A. (2010). A parallel process growth mixture model of conduct problems and substance use with risky sexual behavior. *Drug and Alcohol Dependence, 111,* 207–214.

Wyatt, J. W. (1993). Identical twins, emergenesis, and environments. *American Psychologist, 48,* 1294–1295.

Wyatt, J. W., Posey, A., Walker, W., & Seamonds, C. (1984). Natural levels of similarities between identical twins and between unrelated people. *Skeptical Inquirer, 9,* 62–66.

Wynn, K. (1995). Infants possess a system of numerical knowledge. *Current Directions in Psychological Science, 4,* 172–177.

Wysocki, C. J., & Preti, G. (1998). Pheromonal influences. *Archives of Sexual Behavior, 27,* 627–629.

Xantidis, L., & McCabe, M. P. (2000). Personality characteristics of male clients of female commercial sex workers. *Archives of Sexual Behavior, 29,* 165–176.

Xiao, Q., & Frost, B. J. (2013). Motion parallax processing in pigeon (*Columba livia*) pretectal neurons. *European Journal of Neuroscience, 37,* 1103–1111.

Xiaohe, X., & Whyte, M. K. (1990). Love matches and arranged marriages: A Chinese replication. *Journal of Marriage and the Family, 52,* 709–722.

Xie, L., Kang, H., Xu, Q., Chen, M. J., Liao, Y., Thiyagarajan, M., . . . Nedergaard, M. (2013). Sleep drives metabolite clearance from the adult brain. *Science 342,* 373–377.

Yaccarino, M. E. (1993). Using Minuchin's structural family therapy techniques with Italian–American families. *Contemporary Family Therapy: An International Journal, 15,* 459–466.

Yaffe, K. (2003). Hormone therapy and the brain: Déjà vu all over again? *JAMA: Journal of the American Medical Association, 289,* 2717–2719.

Yamagishi, T., Kikuchi, M., & Kosugi, M. (1999). Trust, gullibility, and social intelligence. *Asian Journal of Social Psychology, 2,* 145–161.

Yamaguchi, H. (1988). Effects of actor's and observer's roles on causal attribution by Japanese subjects for success and failure in competitive situations. *Psychological Reports, 63,* 619–626.

Yamamiya, Y., Shroff, H., & Thompson, J. K. (2008). The tripartite influence model of body image and eating disturbance: A replication with a Japanese sample. *International Journal of Eating Disorders, 41,* 88–91.

Yamawaki, N., Tschanz, B. T., & Feick, D. L. (2004). Defensive pessimism, self-esteem instability, and goal strivings. *Cognition and Emotion, 18,* 233–249.

Yanchar, S. C. (1997). William James and the challenge of methodological pluralism. *Journal of Mind and Behavior, 18,* 425–442.

Yang, A. (1997). Trends: Attitudes toward homosexuality. *Public Opinion Quarterly, 61,* 477–507.

Yang, C. M., & Spielman, A. J. (2001). The effect of a delayed weekend sleep pattern on sleep and morning functioning. *Psychology and Health, 16,* 715–725.

Yap, J. N. (1988). The effects of hospitalization and surgery on children: A critical review. *Journal of Applied Developmental Psychology, 9,* 349–358.

Yarmey, A. D. (1973). I recognize your face but I can't remember your name: Further evidence on the tip-of-the-tongue phenomenon. *Memory and Cognition, 1,* 287–290.

Yates, D. (2016). Astrocytic go-betweens. *Nature Reviews Neuroscience, 17,* 401–409.

Yela, C., & Sangrador, J. L. (2001). Perception of physical attractiveness throughout loving relationships. *Current Research in Social Psychology, 6,* 57–75.

Yen, S., Robins, C. J., & Lin, N. (2000). A cross-cultural comparison of depressive symptom manifestation: China and the United States. *Journal of Consulting and Clinical Psychology, 68,* 993–999.

Yen, S., Zlotnick, C., & Costello, E. (2002). Affect regulation in women with borderline personality disorder traits. *Journal of Nervous and Mental Disease, 190,* 693–696.

Yerkes, R. M., & Dodson, J. D. (1908). The relation of strength of stimulus to rapidity of habit formation. *Journal of Comparative Neurology and Psychology, 18,* 459–482.

Young, L. D., Richter, J. E., Bradley, L. A., & Anderson, K. O. (1987). Disorders of the upper gastrointestinal system: An overview. *Annals of Behavioral Medicine, 9,* 7–12.

Young, R. L., & Nettelbeck, T. (1995). The abilities of a musical savant and his family. *Journal of Autism and Developmental Disorders, 25,* 231–248.

Youngren, M. A., & Lewinsohn, P. M. (1980). The functional relation between depression and problematic interpersonal behavior. *Journal of Abnormal Psychology, 89,* 333–341.

Yu, S., & Ho, I. K. (1990). Effects of acute barbiturate administration, tolerance and dependence on brain GABA system: Comparison to alcohol and benzodiazepines. *Alcohol, 7,* 261–272.

Yuan, W., Ming, Z., Rana, N., Hail, L., Chen-Wang, J., & Shao-Hui, M. (2010). A functional magnetic resonance imaging study of human brain in pain-related areas induced by electrical stimulation with different intensities. *Neurology India, 58,* 922–927.

Yurek, D., Farrar, W., & Andersen, B. L. (2000). Breast cancer surgery: Comparing surgical groups and determining individual differences in postoperative sexuality and body change stress. *Journal of Consulting and Clinical Psychology, 68,* 697–709.

Yutrzenka, B. A., Todd-Bazemore, E., & Caraway, S. J. (1999). Four winds: The evolution of culturally inclusive clinical psychology training for Native Americans. *International Review of Psychiatry, 11,* 129–135.

Zach, U., & Keller, H. (1999). Patterns of the attachment-exploration balance of 1-year-old infants from the United States and northern Germany. *Journal of Cross-Cultural Psychology, 30,* 381–388.

Zadra, A. L., O'Brien, S. A., & Donderi, D. C. (1998). Dream content, dream recurrence, and well-being: A replication with a younger sample. *Imagination, Cognition, and Personality, 17,* 293–311.

Zadra, A. L., & Pihl, R. O. (1997). Lucid dreaming as a treatment for recurrent nightmares. *Psychotherapy and Psychosomatics, 66,* 50–55.

Zajecka, J., Dunner, D. L., Gelenberg, A. J., Hirschfeld, R. M. A., Kornstein, S. G., Ninan, P. T., . . . Keller, M. B. (2002). Sexual function and satisfaction in the treatment of chronic major depression with nefazodone, psychotherapy and their combination. *Journal of Clnical Psychiatry, 63,* 709–716.

Zajonc, R. B. (1965). Social facilitation. *Science, 149,* 269–274.

Zajonc, R. B. (1976). Family configuration and intelligence. *Science, 192,* 227–236.

Zajonc, R. B. (1984). On the primacy of affect. *American Psychologist, 39,* 117–123.

Zajonc, R. B. (1985). Emotion and facial efference: A theory revisited. *Science, 228,* 15–21.

Zajonc, R. B. (1986). The decline and rise of scholastic aptitude scores: A prediction derived from the confluence model. *American Psychologist, 41,* 862–867.

Zajonc, R. B. (1993). The confluence model: Differential or difference equation. *European Journal of Social Psychology, 23,* 211–215.

Zajonc, R. B., & Mullally, P. R. (1997). Birth order: Reconciling conflicting effects. *American Psychologist, 52,* 685–699.

Zaldivar, R. A. (1986, June 10). Panel faults NASA on shuttle. *Philadelphia Inquirer,* pp. 1-A, 12-A.

Zander, A. (1979). The psychology of group processes. *Annual Review of Psychology, 30,* 417–451.

Zangariand, W., & Machado, F. R. (2001). Parapsychology in Brazil: A science entering young adulthood. *Journal of Parapsychology, 65,* 351–356.

Zanoto de Luca, M. C., Brandao, M. L., Motta, V. A., & Landeira-Fernandez, J. (2003). Antinociception induced by stimulation of ventrolateral periaqueductal gray at the freezing threshold is regulated by opioid and 5-HT-sub(2A) receptors as assessed by the tail-flick and formalin tests. *Pharmacology, Biochemistry and Behavior, 75,* 459–466.

Zatorre, R. J., Belin, P., & Penhune, V. B. (2002). Structure and function of auditory cortex: Music and speech. *Trends in Cognitive Sciences, 6,* 37–46.

Zatorre, R. J., Bouffard, M., Ahad, P., & Belin, P. (2002). Where is "where" in the human auditory cortex? *Nature Neuroscience, 5,* 905–909.

Zec, R. F., & Trivedi, M. A. (2002). The effects of estrogen replacement therapy on neuropsychologial functioning in postmenopausal women with and without dementia: A critical and theoretical review. *Neuropsychology Review, 12,* 65–109.

Zentall, T. R., Sutton, J. E., & Sherburne, L. M. (1996). True imitative learning in pigeons. *Psychological Science, 7,* 343–346.

Zeitlin, D., Keller, S. E., Shiflett, S. C., Schleifer, S. J., & Bartlett, J. A. (2000). Immunological effects of massage therapy during acute academic stress. *Psychosomatic Medicine, 62,* 83–84.

Zerbo, O., Qian, Y., Yoshida, C., Grether, J. K., Van de Water, J., & Croen, L. A. (2013). Maternal infection during pregnancy and autism spectrum disorders. *Journal of Autism and Developmental Disorders, 40,* 1423–1430.

Zhang, J., & Thomas, D. L. (1994). Modernization theory revisited: A cross-cultural study of adolescent conformity to significant others in mainland China, Taiwan, and the USA. *Adolescence, 29,* 885–903.

Zhang, X., & Nurmi, J.-E. (2012). Teacher-child relationships and social competence: A two-year longitudinal study of Chinese preschoolers. *Journal of Applied Developmental Psychology, 33,* 125–135.

Zhou, Q., Wang, Y., Deng, X., Eisenberg, N., Wolchik, S. A., & Tein, J.-Y. (2008). Relations of temperament and temperament to Chinese children's experience of negative life events, coping efficacy, and externalizing problems. *Child Development, 79,* 493–513.

Zhou, X., & Li, P. (2013), Simulating cross-language priming with a dynamic computational model of the lexicon. *Bilingualism: Language & Cognition, 16,* 288–303.

Zhou, Y. D., & Fuster, J. M. (2004). Somatosensory cell response to an auditory cue in a haptic memory task. *Behavioural Brain Research, 153,* 573–578.

Zhu, A. J., & Walsh, B. T. (2002). In review: Pharmacologic treatment of eating disorders. *Canadian Journal of Psychiatry, 47,* 227–234.

Zhu, Z., Disbrow, E. A., Zumer, J. M., McGonigle, D. J., & Nagarajan, S. S. (2007). Spatiotemporal integration of tactile information in human somatosensory cortex. *BMC Neuroscience, 8,* 21–34.

Zickar, M. J. (2003). Remembering Arthur Kornhauser: Industrial psychology's advocate for worker wellbeing. *Journal of Applied Psychology, 88,* 363–369.

Ziegler, D. J. (2001). The possible place of cognitive appraisal in the ABC model underlying Rational-Emotive Behavior Therapy. *Journal of Rational-Emotive and Cognitive Behavior Therapy, 19,* 137–152.

Zigler, E. (1999). Head Start is not child care. *American Psychologist, 54,* 142.

Zigler, E., Abelson, W. D., Trickett, P. K., & Seitz, V. (1982). Is an intervention program necessary in order to improve economically disadvantaged children's IQ scores? *Child Development, 33,* 340–348.

Zimmerman, M. (1983). Methodological issues in the assessment of life events: A review of issues and research. *Clinical Psychology Review, 3,* 339–370.

Zimpfer, D. G. (1991). Groups for grief and survivorship after bereavement: A review. *Journal for Specialists in Group Work, 16,* 46–55.

Zimprich, D., & Martin, M. (2002). Can longitudinal changes in processing speed explain longitudinal age changes in fluid intelligence? *Psychology and Aging, 17,* 690–695.

Zinn, T. E., & Lilienfeld, S. (2010). The pleasures and lessons of academic mythbusting: An interview with Scott Lilienfeld. *Teaching of Psychology, 37,* 287–293.

Zisook, S., Byrd, D., Kuck, J., & Jeste, D. V. (1995). Command hallucinations in outpatients with schizophrenia. *Journal of Clinical Psychiatry, 56,* 462–465.

Ziv, A. (1987). The effect of humor on aggression catharsis in the classroom. *Journal of Psychology, 121,* 359–364.

Zohar, D., Tzischinski, O., & Epstein, R. (2003). Effects of energy availability on immediate and delayed emotional reactions to work events. *Journal of Applied Psychology, 88,* 1082–1093.

Zola-Morgan, S. M., & Squire, L. R. (1990). The primate hipppocampal formation: Evidence for a time-limited role in memory storage. *Science, 250,* 288–290.

Zomlaiski, N., Dyrborg, J., Rasmussen, H., Schumann, T., Koch, S. V., & Bilenberg, N. (2010). Validity and clinical feasibility of the ADHD rating scale (ADHD-RS): A Danish nationwide multicenter study. *Acta Pediatrica, 98,* 397–402.

Zucker, G. S., & Weiner, B. (1993). Conservatism and perceptions of poverty: An attributional analysis. *Journal of Applied Social Psychology, 23,* 925–943.

Zuckerman, M. (1990). The psychophysiology of sensation seeking. *Journal of Personality, 58,* 313–345.

Zuckerman, M., Eysenck, S. B., & Eysenck, H. J. (1978). Sensation seeking in England and America: Cross-cultural, age and sex comparisons. *Journal of Consulting and Clinical Psychology, 46,* 139–149.

Zuckerman, M., Joireman, J., Kraft, M., & Kuhlman, D. M. (1999). Where do motivational and emotional traits fit within three-factor models of personality? *Personality and Individual Differences, 26,* 487–504.

Zuckerman, M., Kieffer, S. C., & Knee, C. R. (1998). Consequences of self-handicapping: Effects on coping, academic performance, and adjustment. *Journal of Personality and Social Psychology, 74,* 1619–1628.

Zuckerman, M., Koestner, R., DeBoy, T., Garcia, T., Maresca, B. C., & Sartoris, J. M. (1988). To predict some of the people some of the time: A reexamination of the moderator variable approach in personality theory. *Journal of Personality and Social Psychology, 54,* 1006–1019.

Zuroff, D. C. (1986). Was Gordon Allport a trait theorist? *Journal of Personality and Social Psychology, 51,* 983–1000.

Zuwerink, J. R., & Devine, P. G. (1996). Attitude importance and resistance to persuasion: It's not just the thought that counts. *Journal of Personality and Social Psychology, 70,* 931–944.

Zwislocki, J. J. (1981). Sound analysis in the ear: A history of discoveries. *American Scientist, 69,* 184–192.

Appendix References

Arthur, W., Day, E. A., McNelly, T. L., & Edens, P. S. (2003). A meta-analysis of the criterion-related validity of assessment center dimensions. *Personnel Psychology, 56,* 125–153.

Baltes, B. B., Briggs, T. E., Huff, J. W., Wright, J. A., & Neuman, G. A. (1999). Flexible and compressed workweeks schedules. A meta-analysis of their effects on work-related criteria. *Journal of Applied Psychology, 84,* 496–513.

Bandura, A. (1986). *Social foundations of thought and action: A social-cognitive theory.* Englewood Cliffs, NJ: Prentice Hall.

Bandura, A. (2012). On the functional properties of perceived self-efficacy revisited. *Journal of Management, 38,* 9–44.

Barrick, M. R., Mount, M. K., & Judge, T. A. (2001). The FFM personality dimensions and job performance: Meta-analysis of meta-analyses. *International Journal of Selection and Assessment, 9,* 9–30.

Bass, B. M. (1985). *Leadership and performance beyond expectations.* New York: Free Press.

Bass, B. M. (1997). Does the transactional-transformational leadership paradigm transcend organizational and national boundaries? *American Psychologist, 52,* 130–139.

Bass, B. M. (1999). Two decades of research and development in transformational leadership. *European Journal of Work and Organizational Psychology, 8,* 9–32.

Bowling, N. A., Eschleman, K. J., & Wang, Q. (2010). A meta-analytic examination of the relationship between job satisfaction and subjective well-being. *Journal of Occupational and Organizational Psychology, 83,* 915–934.

Bramel, D., & Friend, R. (1981). Hawthorne, the myth of the docile worker, and class bias in psychology. *American Psychologist, 36,* 867–878.

Brown, S. P. (1996). A meta-analysis and review of organizational research in job involvement. *Psychological Bulletin, 120,* 235–255.

Bryan, L. L. K. & Vinchur, A. (2013). Industrial-organizational psychology. In D. K. Freedheim (Vol. Ed.), *History of psychology, Vol. 1, Handbook of psychology* (pp. 407–428).

Callinan, M., & Robertson, I. T. (2000). Work sample testing. *International Journal of Selection and Assessment, 8,* 248–260.

Campion, M. A., Palmer, D. K., & Campion, J. E. (1998). Structuring employment interviews to improve reliability, validity, and users' reactions. *Current Directions in Psychological Science, 7,* 77–82.

Cascio, W. F. (1991). *Applied psychology in personnel management* (4th ed.). Englewood Cliffs, NJ: Prentice-Hall.

Cascio, W. F. (1995). Whither industrial and organizational psychology in a changing work of work? *American Psychologist, 50,* 928–939.

Chhokar, J. S., Brodbeck, F. C., & House, R. J. (Eds.). (2013). *Culture and leadership across the world: The GLOBE book of in-depth studies of 25 societies.* New York: Routledge.

Clarke, N. (2003). The politics of training needs analysis. *Journal of Workplace Learning, 15,* 141–153.

Connolly, J. J., & Viswesvaran, C. (2000). The role of affectivity in job satisfaction: A meta-analysis. *Personality and Individual Differences, 29,* 265–281.

Dansereau, F., Graen, G. B., & Haga, W. J. (1975). A vertical dyad linkage approach to leadership within formal organizations. *Organizational Behavior and Human Performance, 13,* 46–78.

Dean, M. A. (2013). Examination of ethnic group differential responding on a biodata instrument. *Journal of Applied Social Psychology, 43,* 1905–1917.

DeNisi, A. S. (2011). Managing performance to change behavior. *Journal of Organizational Behavior Management, 31,* 262–276.

DeNisi, A. S., & Peters, L. H. (1996). Organization of information in memory and the performance appraisal process: Evidence from the field. *Journal of Applied Psychology, 81,* 717–737.

DeRue, D. S., Nahrgang, J. D., Wellman, N. E. D., & Humphrey, S. E. (2011). Trait and behavioral theories of leadership: An integration and meta-analytic test of their relative validity. *Personnel Psychology, 64,* 7–52.

DeShon, R. P., Kozlowski, S. W., Schmidt, A. M., Milner, K. R., & Wiechmann, D. (2004). A multiple-goal, multilevel model of feedback effects on the regulation of individual and team performance. *Journal of Applied Psychology, 89,* 1035–1056.

DiClemente, D. F. & Hantula, D. A. (2000, April). John Broadus Watson, I-O psychologist. *The Industrial-Organizational Psychologist.* Retrieved online April 30, 2014 from https://www.siop.org/tip/backissues/TipApril00/7Diclemente.aspx.

Dulebohn, J. H., Bommer, W. H., Liden, R. C., Brouer, R. L., & Ferris, G. R. (2012). A meta-analysis of antecedents and consequences of leader-member exchange integrating the past with an eye toward the future. *Journal of Management, 38,* 1715–1759.

Eagly, A. H., Johannesen-Schmidt, M. C., & Van Engen, M. L. (2003). Transformational, transactional, and laissez-faire leadership styles: a meta-analysis comparing women and men. *Psychological Bulletin, 129,* 569–591.

Eagly, A. H., & Karau, S. J. (2002). Role congruity theory of prejudice toward female leaders. *Psychological Review, 109,* 573–598.

Fiedler, F. E. (1967). *A theory of leader effectiveness.* New York: McGraw-Hill.

Froese, F. J., & Peltokorpi, V. (2013). Organizational expatriates and self-initiated expatriates: differences in cross-cultural adjustment and job satisfaction. *International Journal of Human Resource Management, 24,* 1953–1967.

Gaddis, B. H., & Foster, J. L. (2013). Meta-analysis of dark side personality characteristics and critical work behaviors among leaders across the globe: Findings and implications for leadership development and executive coaching. *Applied Psychology.* Advance online publication.

Gaugler, B. B., Rosenthal, D. B., Thornton, G. C., & Bentson, C. (1987). Meta analysis of assessment center validity. *Journal of Applied Psychology, 72,* 493–511.

Glick, P., Fiske, S. T., Mladinic, A., Saiz, J. L., Abrams, D., Masser, B., . . . & López, W. L. (2000). Beyond prejudice as simple antipathy: Hostile and benevolent sexism across cultures. *Journal of Personality and Social Psychology, 79,* 763–775.

Goldstein, I. L. (1993). *Training in organizations* (3rd ed.). Pacific Grove, CA: Brooks/Cole.

Greenhaus, J. H., & Kossek, E. E. (2014). The contemporary career: A work–home perspective. *Annual Review of Organizational Psychology and Organizational Behavior, 1,* 361–388.

Griffeth, R. W., Hom, P. W., & Gaertner, S. (2000). A meta-analysis of antecedents and correlates of employee turnover: Update, moderator tests, and research implications for the next millennium. *Journal of Management, 26,* 463–488.

Gutman, A., Koppes, L. L., & Vodanovich, S. J. (2010). *EEO law and personnel practices.* New York: Routledge.

Hackett, R. D., Bycio, P., & Guion, R. M. (1989). Absenteeism among hospital nurses: An idiographic-longitudinal analysis. *Academy of Management Journal, 32,* 424–453.

Harter, J. K., Schmidt, F. L., & Hayes, T. L. (2002). Business-unit-level relationship between employee satisfaction, employee engagement, and business outcomes: A meta-analysis. *Journal of Applied Psychology, 87,* 268–279.

Hersey, P., & Blanchard, K. H. (1969). Life cycle theory of leadership. *Training & Development Journal, 23,* 26–34.

Hom, P. W., Mitchell, T. R., Lee, T. W., & Griffeth, R. W. (2012). Reviewing employee turnover: focusing on proximal withdrawal states and an expanded criterion. *Psychological Bulletin, 138,* 831–858.

Hough, L. M., & Oswald, F. L. (2000). Personnel selection: Looking toward the future—Remembering the past. *Annual Review of Psychology, 51,* 631–664.

House, R. J. (1971). A path-goal theory of leadership. *Administrative Science Quarterly, 16,* 321–338.

Howell, J. M., & Avolio, B. J. (1993). Transformational leadership, transactional leadership, locus of control, and support for innovation: Key predictors of consolidated-business-unit performance. *Journal of Applied Psychology, 78,* 891–902.

Hui, H., & Luk, C. L. (1997). Industrial/organizational psychology. In J W. Berry, M. H. Segall, & C. Kagitçibasi (Eds.), *Handbook of cross-cultural psychology: Social behavior and applications* (Vol. 3, pp. 371–411). Boston: Allyn & Bacon.

Hulsman, R. L., Ros, W. J. G., Winnubst, J. A. M., & Bensing, J. M. (2002). The effectiveness of a computer-assisted instruction program on communication skills of medical specialists in oncology. *Medical Education, 36,* 125–134.

Ilgen, D. R., Barnes-Farrell, J. L., & McKellin, D. B. (1993). Peformance appraisal process research in the 1980s: What has it contributed to appraisals in use? *Organizational Behavior and Human Decision Processes, 54,* 321–368.

Johns, G. (1997). Contemporary research on absence from work: Correlates, causes and consequences. In C. L. Cooper & I. T. Robertson (Eds.), *International review of industrial and organizational psychology* (Vol. 12, pp. 115–173). Chichester: Wiley.

Johnson, R. E., Chang, C. H., & Lord, R. G. (2006). Moving from cognition to behavior: What the research says. *Psychological Bulletin, 132,* 381–415.

Judge, T. A., Thoresen, C. J., Bono, J. E., & Patton, G. K. (2001). The job satisfaction–job performance relationship: A qualitative and quantitative review. *Psychological Bulletin, 127,* 376–407.

Kanfer, R. (1990). Motivation theory and industrial organizational psychology. In M. E. Dunnette and L. M. Hough (Eds.), *Handbook of industrial and organizational psychology* (2nd ed., pp. 75–124). Palo Alto, CA: Consulting Psychologists Press.

Katzell, R. A., & Austin, J. T. (1992). From then to now: The development of industrial-organizational psychology in the United States. *Journal of Applied Psychology, 77,* 803–835.

Kirkpatrick, D. L. (1959). Techniques for evaluating training programs. I. *Journal of the American Society of Training Directors, 13,* 3–9, 21–26.

Kirkpatrick, D. L. (1960). Techniques for evaluating training programs. II. *Journal of the American Society of Training Directors, 14,* 13–18, 28–32.

Koenig, A. M., Eagly, A. H., Mitchell, A. A., & Ristikari, T. (2011). Are leader stereotypes masculine? A meta-analysis of three research paradigms. *Psychological Bulletin, 137,* 616–642.

Koppes, L. L. (1997). American female pioneers of industrial and organizational psychology during the early years. *Journal of Applied Psychology, 82,* 500–515.

Landy, F. J., & Farr, J. L. (1980). Performance rating. *Psychological Bulletin, 87,* 72–107.

Latham, G. P., & Wexley, K. N. (1977). Behavioral observation scales for performance appraisal purposes. *Personnel Psychology, 30,* 255–268.

Lefkowitz, J. (2000). The role of interpersonal affective regard in supervisory performance ratings: A literature review and proposed causal model. *Journal of Occupational and Organizational Psychology, 73,* 67–85.

Levy, P. E., & Williams, J. R. (2004). The social context of performance appraisal: A review and framework for the future. *Journal of Management, 30,* 881–905.

Locke, E. A. (1976). The nature and causes of job satisfaction. In M. D. Dunnette (Ed.), *Handbook of industrial and organizational psychology* (pp. 1297–1349). Chicago: Rand McNally.

Locke, E. A., & Latham, G. P. (1990). *A theory of goal setting and task performance.* Englewood Cliffs, NJ: Prentice Hall.

Locke, E. A., & Latham, G. P. (2006). New directions in goal-setting theory. *Current Directions in Psychological Science, 15,* 265–268.

Lord, R. G., & Levy, P. E. (1994). Control theory: Moving from cognition to action. *Applied Psychology: An International Review, 43,* 335–367.

Lowry, P. E. (1997). The assessment center process: New directions. *Journal of Social Behavior and Personality, 12,* 53–62.

Mathieu, J. E., & Zajac, D. M. (1990). A review and meta-analysis of the antecedents, correlates, and consequences of organizational commitment. *Psychological Bulletin, 108,* 171–194.

McDaniel, M. A., Whetzel, D. L., Schmidt, F. L., & Maurer, S. D. (1994). The validity of employment interviews: A comprehensive review and metaanalysis. *Journal of Applied Psychology, 79,* 599–616.

McHenry, J. J., Hough, L. M., Toquam, J. L., Hanson, M. A., & Ashworth, S. (1990). Project A validity results: The relationship between predictor and criterion domains. *Personnel Psychology, 43,* 335–354.

Methot, L. L., & Phillips-Grant, K. (1998). Technological advances in the Canadian workplace: An I-O perspective. *Canadian Psychology, 39,* 133–141.

Meyer, J. P., Allen, N. J., & Smith, C. A. (1993). Commitment to organizations and occupations: Extension and test of a three-component conceptualization. *Journal of Applied Psychology, 78,* 538–551.

Meyer, J. P., Stanley, D. J., Herscovitch, L., & Topolnytsky, L. (2002). Affective, continuance, and normative commitment to the organization: A meta-analysis of antecedents, correlates, and consequences. *Journal of Vocational Behavior, 61,* 20–52.

Meyer, J. P., Stanley, D. J., Jackson, T. A., McInnis, K. J., Maltin, E. R., & Sheppard, L. (2012). Affective, normative, and continuance commitment levels across cultures: A meta-analysis. *Journal of Vocational Behavior, 80,* 225–245.

Miller, D. L. (2001). Reexamining teamwork KSAs and team performance. *Small Group Research, 32,* 745–766.

Miner, J. B. (2003). The rated importance, scientific validity, and practical usefulness of organizational behavior theories: A quantitative review. *Academy of Management Learning & Education, 2,* 250–268.

Mowday, R. T., Steers, R. M., & Porter, L. W. (1979). The measurement of organizational commitment. *Journal of Vocational Behavior, 14,* 224–247.

Nagengast, B., Marsh, H. W., Scalas, L. F., Xu, M. K., Hau, K. T., & Trautwein, U. (2011). Who took the "?" out of expectancy-value theory? A psychological mystery, a substantive-methodological synergy, and a cross-national generalization. *Psychological Science, 22,* 1058–1066.

Noe, R. A., Clarke, A. D., & Klein, H. J. (2014). Learning in the twenty-first-century workplace. *Annual Review of Organizational Psychology and Organizational Behavior, 1,* 245–275.

O'Boyle, E. H., Jr., Forsyth, D. R., Banks, G. C., & McDaniel, M. A. (2012). A meta-analysis of the dark triad and work behavior: A social exchange perspective. *Journal of Applied Psychology, 97,* 557–579.

Olivares, O. J. (2001). Student interest, grading leniency, and teacher ratings: A conceptual analysis. *Contemporary Educational Psychology, 26,* 382–399.

Owens, R. A. (1976). Background data. In M. D. Dunnette (Ed.), *Handbook of industrial and organizational psychology.* Chicago: Rand McNally.

Padilla, A., Hogan, R., & Kaiser, R. B. (2007). The toxic triangle: Destructive leaders, susceptible followers, and conducive environments. *Leadership Quarterly, 18,* 176–194.

Parkes, L., Bochner, S., & Schneider, S. (2001). Person–organization fit across cultures: An empirical investigation of individualism and collectivism. *Applied Psychology, 50,* 81–108.

Paulhus, D. L., & Williams, K. M. (2002). The dark triad of personality: Narcissism, Machiavellianism, and psychopathy. *Journal of Research in Personality, 36,* 556–563.

Pelletier, K. L. (2010). Leader toxicity: An empirical investigation of toxic behavior and rhetoric. *Leadership, 6,* 373–389.

Peters, L. H., Hartke, D. D., & Pohlmann, J. T. (1985). Fiedler's contingency theory of leadership: An application of the meta-analysis procedures of Schmidt and Hunter. *Psychological Bulletin, 97,* 274–285.

Pichler, S. (2012). The social context of performance appraisal and appraisal reactions: A meta-analysis. *Human Resource Management, 51,* 709–732.

Porter, L. W., & Schneider, B. (2014). What was, what is, and what may be in OP/OB. *Annual Review of Organizational Psychology and Organizational Behavior, 1,* 1–21.

Raymond, M. R. (2001). Job analysis and the specification of content for licensure and certification examinations. *Applied Measurement in Education, 14,* 369–415.

Rhea, M. R., Alvar, B. A., & Gray, R. (2004). Physical fitness and job performance of firefighters. *The Journal of Strength & Conditioning Research, 18,* 348–352.

Roberts, G. E. (2003). Employee performance appraisal system participation: A technique that works. *Public Personnel Management, 32,* 89–97.

Rockstuhl, T., Dulebohn, J. H., Ang, S., & Shore, L. M. (2012). Leader–member exchange (LMX) and culture: A meta-analysis of correlates of LMX across 23 countries. *Journal of Applied Psychology, 97,* 1097–1130.

Roethlisberger, F. J., & Dickson, E. J. (1939). *Management and the worker.* Cambridge: Harvard University Press.

Rothstein, H. R., Schmidt, F. L., Erwin, F. W., Owens, W. A., & Sparks, C. P. (1990). Biographical data in employment selection: Can validities be made generalizable? *Journal of Applied Psychology, 75,* 175–184.

Ryan, A. M., & Ployhart, R. E. (2014). A century of selection. *Annual Review of Psychology, 65,* 693–717.

Sagie, A. (1998). Employee absenteeism, organizational commitment, and job satisfaction: Another look. *Journal of Vocational Behavior, 52,* 156–171.

Schmidt, F. L. & Hunter, J. E. (1998). The validity and utility of selection methods in personnel psychology: Practical and theoretical implications of 85 years of research findings. *Psychological Bulletin, 124,* 262–274.

Schriesheim, C. A., Castro, S. L., Zhou, X. T., & DeChurch, L. A. (2006). An investigation of path-goal and transformational leadership theory predictions at the individual level of analysis. *The Leadership Quarterly, 17,* 21–38.

Schyns, B., & Schilling, J. (2013). How bad are the effects of bad leaders? A meta-analysis of destructive leadership and its outcomes. *Leadership Quarterly, 24,* 138–158.

Shuffler, M. L., DiazGranados, D., & Salas, E. (2011). There's a science for that: Team development interventions in organizations. *Current Directions in Psychological Science, 20,* 365–372.

Silzer, R., & Parson, C. (2013, April). Trends in SIOP membership, graduate education and member satisfaction. *Industrial-Organizational Psychologist, 50,* 135–149.

Sitzmann, T. (2011). A meta-analytic examination of the instructional effectiveness of computer-based simulation games. *Personnel Psychology, 64,* 489–528.

Smith, P. C., & Kendall, L. M. (1963). Retranslation of expectations: An approach to the construction of unambiguous anchors for rating scales. *Journal of Applied Psychology, 47,* 149–155.

Spence, J. R., & Keeping, L. (2011). Conscious rating distortion in performance appraisal: A review, commentary, and proposed framework for research. *Human Resource Management Review, 21,* 85–95.

Stanley, L., Vandenberghe, C., Vandenberg, R., & Bentein, K. (2013). Commitment profiles and employee turnover. *Journal of Vocational Behavior, 82,* 176–187.

Steers, R. M., Mowday, R. T., & Shapiro, D. L. (2004). Introduction to special topic forum: The future of work motivation theory. *Academy of Management Review,* 379–387.

Steers, R. M., & Porter, L. W. (Eds.). (1991). *Motivation and work behavior* (5th ed.). New York: McGraw-Hill.

Steers, R. M., Porter, L. W., & Bigley, G. A. (Eds.). (1996). *Motivation and leadership at work* (6th ed.). New York: McGraw-Hill.

Steers, R. M., & Rhodes, S. R. (1978). Major influences on employee attendance: A process model. *Journal of Applied Psychology, 63,* 391–407.

Stogdill, R. M. (1948). Personal factors associated with leadership: A survey of the literature. *Journal of Psychology, 25,* 35–71.

Strong, E. K. (1918). Work of the committee on classification of personnel in the Army. *Journal of Applied Psychology, 2,* 130–139.

Suemer, H. C., Suemer, N., Demirutku, K., & Cifci, O., & Sinan (2001). Using a personality-oriented job analysis to identify attributes to be assessed in officer selection. *Military Psychology, 13,* 129–146.

Sundstrom, E., McIntyre, M., Halfhill, T., & Richards, H. (2000). Work groups: From the Hawthorne studies to work teams of the 1990s and beyond. *Group Dynamics, 4,* 44–67.

Taylor, P. J., & Small, B. (2002). Asking applicants what they would do versus what they did do: A meta-analytic comparison of situational and past behaviour employment interview questions. *Journal of Occupational and Organizational Psychology, 75,* 277–294.

Thompson, G., & Vecchio, R. P. (2009). Situational leadership theory: A test of three versions. *Leadership Quarterly, 20,* 837–848.

Thoroughgood, C. N., Tate, B. W., Sawyer, K. B., & Jacobs, R. (2012). Bad to the bone empirically defining and measuring destructive leader behavior. *Journal of Leadership & Organizational Studies, 19,* 230–255.

Tubbs, M. E. (1986). Goal setting: A meta-analytic examination of the empirical evidence. *Journal of Applied Psychology, 71,* 474–483.

Valentine, S., Godkin, L., Fleischman, G. M., & Kidwell, R. (2011). Corporate ethical values, group creativity, job satisfaction and turnover intention: The impact of work context on work response. *Journal of Business Ethics, 98,* 353–372.

Van Eerde, W., & Thierry, H. (1996). Vroom's expectancy models and work-related criteria: A meta-analysis. *Journal of Applied Psychology, 81,* 575–586.

Vinchur, A. J., Schippmann, J. S., Switzer III, F. S., & Roth, P. L. (1998). A meta-analytic review of predictors of job performance for salespeople. *Journal of Applied Psychology, 83,* 586–597.

Vinkenburg, C. J., van Engen, M. L., Eagly, A. H., & Johannesen-Schmidt, M. C. (2011). An exploration of stereotypical beliefs about leadership styles: is transformational leadership a route to women's promotion? *Leadership Quarterly, 22,* 10–21.

Vroom, V. H. (1964). *Work and motivation.* New York: Wiley.

Wang, G., Oh, I. S., Courtright, S. H., & Colbert, A. E. (2011). Transformational leadership and performance across criteria and levels: A metaanalytic review of 25 years of research. *Group & Organization Management, 36,* 223–270.

Wang, X. M., Wong, K. F. E., & Kwong, J. Y. (2010). The roles of rater goals and ratee performance levels in the distortion of performance ratings. *Journal of Applied Psychology, 95,* 546–561.

Wasti, S. A. (2003). Organizational commitment, turnover intentions and the influence of cultural values. *Journal of Occupational and Organizational Psychology, 76,* 303–321.

Whitney, D. J., & Schmitt, N. (1997). Relationship between culture and responses to biodata employment items. *Journal of Applied Psychology, 82,* 113–129.

Woehr, D. J., & Huffcutt, A. I. (1994). Rater training for performance appraisal: A quantitative review. *Journal of Occupational and Organizational Psychology, 67,* 189–205.

Wofford, J. C., & Liska, L. Z. (1993). Path-goal theories of leadership: A meta-analysis. *Journal of Management, 19,* 857–876.

Wonderlic, Inc. (2002). *Wonderlic Personnel Test & Scholastic Level Exam User's Manual.* Libertyville, IL: Author.

Yukl, G. (2013). *Leadership in organizations,* 8th ed. Upper Saddle River, NJ: Prentice Hall.

Yukl, G., Wall, S., & Lepsinger, R. (1990). Preliminary report on validation of the managerial practices survey. In K. E. Clark & M. B. Clark (Eds.), *Measures of leadership* (pp. 223–238). West Orange, NJ: Leadership Library of America.

Zaccaro, S. J., Foti, R. J., & Kenny, D. A. (1991). Self-monitoring and trait-based variance in leadership: An investigation of leader flexibility across multiple group situations. *Journal of Applied Psychology, 76,* 308–315.

Zhou, J., & Hoever, I. J. (2013). Research on workplace creativity: A review and redirection. *Annual Review of Organizational Psychology and Organizational Behavior, 1,* 333–359.

Name Index

Aalberg, V., 386
Aarestad, S., 398
Aarts, H., 203
Abakoumkin, G., 146
Abart, M., 401
Abatzoglou, I., 83
Abbott, M. J., 496
Abe, K., 509
Abel, M. H., 429
Abeles, M., 89
Abell, S. C., 378, 470
Abelman, R., 264
Abelson, R. P., 323
Abelson, W. D., 369
Abernethy, E. M., 289
Abide, M. M., 128
Abo, M., 100
Abokrysha, N., 3
Abou-Khalil, B., 95
Abouzeid, M. P., 281
Abraham, M. R., 132
Abramov, I., 164
Abramowitz, J. S., 498
Abrams, D., 613
Abrams, S., 288
Abramson, L. Y., 505
Achermann, P., 83
Ackerman, S. J., 556
Ackil, J. K., 292
Acord, J., 6
Adams, B. G., 563
Adams, G. R., 564
Adams, H. E., 227
Adams, J. L., 329
Adams, M. J., 276
Adams, N. E., 460
Adams, P. R., 564
Adams, R. J., 152
Adams, S. K., 212
Adams, W. L., 109
Adamson, R., 536
Adcock, R. J., 188
Adelmann, P. K., 435
Adelson, B., 315
Adelstein, A., 308
Ader, R., 571, 573
Adeyemo, S. A., 78, 230, 301, 515
Adkins, R., 68
Adler, A., 10, 447, 448, 451–452
Adler, K. A., 447
Adler, T., 397
Adolph, K. E., 116
Adomdza, G. K., 378

Adorno, T. W., 614
Afnan, S. M., 3
Aghajanian, G. K., 231
Agostino, H., 388
Agras, W. S., 389
Agrawal, A., 66
Ahad, P., 180
Ahadi, S. A., 471
Ahaneku, G. I., 574
Aheneku, J. E., 574
Ahlberg, S. W., 281
Ahmed, N. S., 587
Ahmed, N. U., 587
Ahrendt, L. P., 263
Aiken, L. R., 349
Aikman, S. N., 385
Ailshire, J. A., 208
Ainsworth, B. E., 584
Ainsworth, M., 120
Aisner, R., 263
Akbar, J. A., 482
Aker, J., 221
Akimova, I. M., 101
al'Absi, M., 186
Alaoui-Ismaieli, O., 433
Alba, J. W., 281
Albarracin, D., 609
Albert, D. J., 624
Albert, R. H., 75
Albert, S. M., 213
Albright, T. D., 75
Al-Chalabi, A., 71
Aldag, R. J., 617
Alden, D. L., 430
Alderfer, C. P., 364
Aldrich, M. S., 214
Alemagno, S. A., 582
Alessi, C., 213
Alexander, M. P., 86
Alexandra, B. S., 123
Alexandris, K., 94
Alghazo, R., 551
Alington, D. E., 469
Al-Issa, I., 497
Allalouf, A., 349
Allan, L. G., 261
Allen, A., 458
Allen, A. C., 298
Allen, A. H., 471
Allen, J. J. B., 418
Allen, J., 37
Allen, J. J., 223
Allen, M., 140, 463, 609

Allen, M. G., 542
Allen, R., 491
Alliger, R., 516
Allik, J., 455
Allison, D. B., 382
Allison, E. J., 436
Allman, A., 427
Allman, J. M., 160
Alloy, L. B., 505
Allport, F. H., 617
Allport, G. W., 454, 459, 606, 614–615
Almaguer, L. L., 401
Alonso-Quecuty, M., 291
Aloui, R., 390
Alpers, G. W., 389
Alpert, J. L., 287
Alpert, M., 422
Althoff, R. R., 65
Altmaier, E. M., 589
Alto, L. T., 99
Alvarado, C. S., 193
Alvarado, K. A., 146
Amabile, T. M., 318
Amans, J. A., 124
Amari, A., 250
Amato, P. R., 124
Ambady, N., 426, 600
Ameis, S. H., 474
Amen, D. G., 84
Amenedo, E., 201
Amering, M., 495
Ames, M. A., 396
Amin, F., 515
Amir, M., 493
Amir, T., 620
Amirsadri, A., 482
Amitai, Y., 587
Ammann, R., 515
Amorose, A. J., 408
Amsel, R., 393
Amsterdam, J. D., 510
An, C., 589
Anand, B. K., 381
Anastasi, A., 29, 36, 370
Anazonwu, C. O., 597
Anchimbe, E. A., 327
Andersen, B. L., 462, 584
Andersen, R. E., 384
Andersen, S. M., 469
Anderson, A. K., 419
Anderson, B. L., 169, 255, 472
Anderson, C. A., 503, 505

Anderson, I. M., 547
Anderson, J. A., 435, 567
Anderson, J. R., 14, 39, 124, 282
Anderson, K., 505
Anderson, K. J., 329, 400, 584, 590
Anderson, K. W., 257, 505
Anderson, P. N., 100
Anderson, R. A., 188
Anderson, S. W., 91
Anderson, W. S., 185
Andersson-Arntén, A.-C., 581
Andrade, M. G., 620
Andre, T., 295
Andreasen, N. C., 512, 513, 516
Andreassen, P. B., 321
Andrews, B., 516
Andrews, G., 117
Andrews, J. A., 608
Anema, A., 487
Anestis, J. C., 533
Anestis, M. D., 533
Angelini, P. J., 503
Angen, M., 581
Angermeyer, M. C., 513
Angleitner, A., 63, 358, 475
Angold, A., 485
Anisfeld, M., 114
Ankney, C. D., 83
Annas, P., 495
Anninos, P., 83
Ansbacher, H. L., 451
Anshel, M. H., 618
Anstey, K. J., 108
Anthony, B., 581
Anthony, T., 617
Antoni, M. H., 574, 583
Antonova, L. V., 420
Antshel, K. M., 522
Antunano, M. J., 189
Apodaca, T. R., 552
Appel, J., 84
Appelbaum, P. S., 550, 551
Apperloo, M. J. A., 70
Applewhite, M., 595
Araújo, D., 43
Archambault, R. J., 551
Archer, T., 401, 407, 581
Archimedes, 312–313
Ardila, A., 94, 273
Ardila, O., 94
Ares-Santos, S., 230
Arfken, C. L., 504
Aristotle, 3, 62, 80, 217, 238

I-1

Armario, A., 87
Armitage, R., 504
Armstrong, G. B., 276
Arndt, J., 469
Arndt, S., 516
Arnett, J. J., 134
Arnett, P. A., 520
Arnold, R. D., 475
Arnold, R. M., 213
Arnold, S. L., 497
Arntz, A., 265
Aron, A. P., 604
Aronson, J., 351
Aronson, J. A., 350
Aronson, S. C., 230
Aronstam, R. S., 185
Arrigo, J. M., 501
Artemiadis, A. K., 580
Arterberry, M. E., 424
Ary, D. V., 608
Asahina, M., 88
Asai, M., 383, 513
Asberg, M., 504
Asbury, K., 62
Asch, S. E., 619–620
Ascherio, A., 96
Aseltine, R. H., Jr., 123
Aserinsky, E., 207–208
Ash, D. W., 250
Asher, D. M., 515
Asher, I., 89
Aslin, R. N., 114, 116
Aspen, V. A., 384
Assanand, S., 381
Astin, G. R., 368
Atkinson, C., 221, 581
Atkinson, G., 205
Atkinson, J., 402
Atkinson, J. M., 582
Atkinson, J. W., 376, 407
Atkinson, R. C., 271, 284
Attie, I., 388
Atwood, G. E., 444
Auer, D. P., 200
Auerbach, C. F., 123
Aufdembrinke, B., 546
Augustine, 3
Austin, A. J., 243
Avalon, L., 503
Avery, R. A., 326
Avery, S. N., 471
Avicenna, 3, 183
Avila, R. A., 621
Axmacher, N., 88
Ayabe-Kanamura, S., 181
Aydin, G., 505
Aydin, O., 505
Aydt, H., 124
Ayers, K., 145
Azorlosa, C., 243

Babad, E., 423
Baban, A., 20
Bachman, G., 614

Bachmanov, A. A., 382
Back, K., 601
Bacon, F., 3, 7, 28, 31
Bacon, S., 66
Baddeley, A. D., 275, 288, 289
Badgett, J. L., 257
Badr, M. S., 213
Bae, J. S., 514
Baer, J., 319
Bagati, D., 81
Bagga, R., 70
Bagozzi, R. P., 427
Bagwell, C. L., 124
Bahill, A. T., 162
Bahill, T., 162
Bahrick, H. P., 295
Bahrick, P. O., 295
Bailey, C. J., 81
Bailey, D., 587
Bailey, J. M., 65, 395
Bailey, R. K., 508
Bailey, S., 505
Bailey, S. P., 83
Bailis, D. S., 408
Baird, J. C., 172
Baisden, R. H., 102
Baizer, J. S., 86
Bak, S., 382
Baker, D., 243
Baker, G. H. B., 570
Baker, J. P., 547
Baker, L. M., 314
Baker, R., 155
Baker, T. B., 587
Bakermans-Kranengurb, M. J., 121
Bakken, M., 238
Bala, N., 21
Balanovski, E., 193
Balázs, M. Á., 122
Balch, W. R., 290
Baldwin, D., 492
Baldwin, D. C., Jr., 109
Baldwin, E., 55
Baldwin, M. W., 5, 612
Baler, R. D., 524
Bales, J., 417, 551
Balkany, T. J., 180
Ball, C., 360
Ball, I. L., 401
Ball, K., 387
Ball, K. T., 251
Ballard, C. G., 181
Ballieux, R. E., 565
Baltes, P. B., 146
Balzer, A. M., 552
Balzer, T., 614
Bambring, M., 425
Banaji, M. R., 203
Bancroft, J., 402
Bandura, A., 12, 125, 142, 263, 264, 331, 460–461, 464, 485
Bang, H., 469
Bangerter, A., 129
Banik, R. K., 186

Banko, K. M., 405
Banks, S. M., 185
Banning, K., 563
Bansal, A., 457
Baptista, M. A. S., 244
Barabasz, A., 188
Barabasz, M., 188
Baraona, A., 227
Barbalet, J. M., 433
Barbara, J. G., 75
Barbaranelli, C., 461
Barbee, A. P., 602
Barber, T. X., 222, 223–224
Barbut, M., 368
Barclay, N. L., 208
Bard, C., 189
Bard, P., 432
Bardash, R., 551
Bargh, J. A., 202
Bar-Hillel, M., 320
Baribeau-Braun, J., 517
Baril, N., 100
Barker, L., 15
Barker, M. E., 570
Barker, R. A., 101
Barker-Collo, S., 45
Barkic, J., 493
Barkley, P. L., 591
Barkoukis, V., 94
Barnecutt, P., 180
Barnes, G. E., 457
Barnes, M. L., 42
Barnett, L. B., 357
Barnett, Z. L., 394
Barnum, P. T., 443
Baron, A., 556
Baron, R. S., 188, 311
Barr, R. A., 328
Barrault, S., 401
Barrett, A. M., 216, 435
Barrett, J. B., 101
Barrett, L. C., 505
Barrett, P. T., 358, 457
Barrett, T. J., 109
Barron, F., 317
Barron, W. L., 430
Barrowclough, C., 516
Bartel, P., 210
Bartholomew, D. J., 357
Bartholomew, J. B., 580
Bartholomew, R. E., 29
Bartlett, F. C., 281
Bartlett, J. A., 581
Bartlett, S. J., 384
Bartoli, W. P., 384
Bartone, P. T., 577
Bartoshuk, L. M., 181, 182, 183, 184
Bartsch, R. A., 599
Bartussek, D., 474
Basadur, M. S., 320
Basbaum, A. I., 78
Basdekis-Jozsa, R., 624
Basile, R., 216
Basinger, K. S., 128

Bassili, J. N., 616
Bassilios, B., 549
Bata, I., 570
Batra, L., 258
Batson, C. D., 626, 627
Bauer, D. G., 68
Bauer, M., 614
Bauer, M. N., 508
Baucr, P. J., 281
Bauer, S. M., 512
Baum, A., 420
Bauman, K. E., 135
Bauman, M. L., 522
Baumeister, A. A., 358, 451
Baumeister, R. F., 141, 398, 406, 470, 508, 605
Baumrind, D., 54, 121, 623
Bavelier, D., 95, 308
Baxter, J., 323
Baxter, P. J., 564
Bayern, C. D., 312
Bayley, N., 348
Bazzini, D. G., 602
Beach, S. R. H., 544, 606
Beal, C. R., 292
Beale, I. L., 259
Beard, E., 229
Beatty, M. J., 624
Beatty, W. W., 28
Beauchamp, G. K., 182, 382
Beaver, K. M., 70
Becht, M. C., 426
Bechtereva, N. P., 420
Beck, A. T., 505, 512, 538, 540
Becker, A. E., 232, 387
Becker, G., 474
Becker, J. B., 101
Becker, P., 457
Becklen, R., 200
Bedeian, A. G., 610
Beebe, D. W., 216
Beekman, A. T., 65
Beer, J. M., 475
Beers, C. W., 531
Begley, S., 397
Behnke, S. H., 550
Behrend, D. A., 328
Behrens, R. R., 315
Behrmann, M., 151
Beidel, D. C., 492
Beidler, L. M., 183
Beijersbergen, M. D., 121
Beiles, E. J., 184
Beins, B. C., 2
Beiser, M., 548
Beitz, A. J., 186
Békésy, G., 175, 178
Bekoff, M., 55
Belciug, S., 323
Beldon, M., 112
Belenky, G., 213
Beleza-Meireles, A., 71
Belin, P., 91, 180
Belisle, M., 584

I-2   Name Index

Bell, A. G., 178
Bell, A. P., 398
Bellisle, F., 184
Bellometti, S., 185
Belmaker, R. H., 475
Belmont, L., 368
Belsky, J., 108, 144
Bem, D. J., 191, 399, 458, 611, 612, 616
Bem, S. L., 125–126
Bemis, C., 574
Benbow, C. P., 138, 141, 355, 357
Bencherif, B., 186
Bender, S. L., 349
Bendersky, M., 424
Bengtson, V. L., 109, 468
Ben-Haim, S., 545
Benham, B., 54
Benin, M. H., 630
Benjamin, A. S., 296
Benjamin, J., 475
Benjamin, L. T., Jr., 6, 38, 256, 363, 615
Benner, H., 118
Bennett, D. S., 424, 587
Bennett, G. G., 570
Bennett, P., 579
Bennett, R. H., 99, 227
Bennett, W., 585
Ben-Shakhar, G., 349, 418
Ben-Shaul, Y., 89
Ben-Shlomo, Y., 143
Bentall, R. P., 490
Benton, D., 303
Benton, T. R., 26
Beratis, I. N., 515
Beratis, S., 515
Berenbaum, S. A., 140
Berg, J. H., 599, 606
Berger, A. A., 430
Berger, H., 81–82, 90
Berger, K., 81
Berger, R. J., 211
Berger, R. S., 580
Bergeron, S. M., 387
Bergesch, P., 510
Bergin, A. E., 553
Berglas, S., 467
Berglund, P., 491, 494
Bergman, H., 407
Berk, M., 507, 515
Berko, J., 330
Berkowitz, L., 624–625
Berkowitz, M. W., 127
Berlucchi, G., 15
Bernard, I., 469
Bernard, J. L., 550
Bernardo, P., 407
Berndt, T. J., 124
Bernheim, H., 287
Bernier, M.-J., 502
Bernieri, F., 423
Berninger, V. W., 115
Bernstein, I. L., 245, 246

Bernstein, W. M., 597
Berntson, G. G., 84
Berridge, C. W., 524
Berry, J. W., 115, 613
Bersagliere, A., 83
Berscheid, E., 604
Bertelli, J. A., 101
Bertelson, A. D., 567
Bertero, E. B., 314
Berthier, N. E., 115
Bertilsson, L., 504
Bertoncini, J., 114
Bertrand, L., 502
Best, C. T., 326
Best, D. L., 424
Best, P. J., 227
Beutler, L. E., 556
Bever, T. G., 337
Bexton, W. H., 400
Bhargava, M., 240
Bherer, L., 297
Biafora, F., 506
Bianchi, S. M., 144
Bickel, W. K., 587
Bidzan, L., 41
Biederman, J., 523
Biggers, K., 569
Bigler, R. S., 281
Bihrle, S., 520
Bijlsma, J. W. J., 572
Bijmolt, T. H. A., 283
Bilder, R. M., 95
Billig, M., 614
Binder, J. R., 91
Binet, A., 290, 346, 357
Binik, Y. M., 324, 391, 393
Binsted, G., 173
Birch, D. E., 550
Birch, J., 164
Birch, L., 382
Birchall, H. M., 493
Bird, S., 296
Birdsong, D., 330
Birkett, M. A., 112
Birketvedt, O., 168
Bishop, D. V. M., 94, 96
Bishop, G. D., 616
Bitgood, S. C., 21
Bitoun, E. I., 86
Bitter, J. R., 543
Bjelke, B., 100
Bjork, D. W., 61
Bjork, E. L., 117
Björklund, A., 101
Bjorklund, A. C., 624
Bjorklund, D. F., 280
Bjorkqvist, K., 624
Bjorkqvist, S.-E., 624
Bjorvatn, B., 207
Blachstein, H., 36
Black, B., 146
Black, D. S., 582
Black, J. E., 137, 230
Blackburn, J. R., 239

Blackburn, T. C., 576
Blackford, J. U., 471
Blair, M. E., 240
Blaisdell, A. P., 261
Blake, R., 180
Blakemore, C., 173, 493
Blanchard, J. J., 513
Blanchard, R., 396
Blanco-Centurion, C. A., 86
Bland, R. C., 493
Blanke, O., 91
Blanton, H., 43
Blascovich, J., 570
Blaszczyk-Schiep, S., 450
Blass, T., 622
Blaszcynski, A., 398
Blatt, I., 207
Blazer, D. G., 507
Bleichrodt, N., 350
Bles, W., 189
Bleuler, E., 512
Blick, K. A., 295
Blix, A. G., 586
Blix, G. G., 586
Blizard, R. A., 502
Block, J., 319, 470
Block, J. H., 319
Blois, W. G., 222
Bloj, M., 169
Bloom, R., 258
Bloomsmith, M. A., 255
Blough, D. S., 174
Blough, P. M., 174
Blume, H. K., 258
Blume-Marcovici, A., 216
Blundell, J., 380
Boake, C., 347
Boardman, J., 497
Boatwright, K., 8
Bobbitt, L., 487
Bobbitt, W., 487
Boblique, C., 576
Bodenhausen, G. V., 600
Bodensteiner, J. B., 352
Bodnar, R. J., 79
Boeck, B. E., 146
Bogaert, A. F., 396
Bogart, L. M., 599
Bogen, J., 98
Boggiano, A. K., 406
Bohannon, J. N., III, 332
Bohart, A. C., 553
Bohlen, J., 397
Bohman, A., 614
Bohner, G., 609
Bolanowski, S. J., 184
Bolen, M. H., 626
Bolm-Audorff, U., 421
Bolsover, S., 100
Bolt, E., 121
Bolte, S., 343
Bolton, P., 352, 521
Bolzani, R., 218
Bombardier, C. H., 188

Bombel, G., 451
Bond, C. F., 617
Bond, C. F., Jr., 227
Bond, L. A., 368
Bond, R., 620
Bonds, D. R., 383
Boneau, C. A., 260
Boneva, B., 403
Boni, D., 248
Boniecki, K. A., 256
Bonilla, C., 102
Bonnefond, A., 209
Bonner, M. J., 591
Bono, J. E., 463
Book, A. S., 624
Booker, A., 625
Bookheimer, S. Y., 419
Boomsma, D. I., 65, 569
Boon, S. D., 322
Boone, L., 387, 389
Boone, R. T., 423
Boot, B. P., 232
Booth, N., 508
Booth, R. E., 508, 580
Booth-Butterfield, S., 620
Booth-LaForce, C., 121
Bootzin, R. R., 201
Boquet, A., 205
Borbely, A. A., 229
Boring, E. G., 5
Boris, H. I., 599
Borkenau, P., 475
Borland, R., 322
Born, J., 218
Bornovalova, M. A., 519
Bornstein, M. H., 10, 424
Borod, J. C., 420
Bortoli, L., 400
Bortz, R., 210
Bortz, W. M., II, 136
Bos, J. E., 189
Bos, P. A., 624
Bosl, W., 83
Bosly, A., 576
Bothwell, R. K., 291
Bouchard, T. J., 397
Bouchard, T. J., Jr., 65, 66, 366, 367, 379, 473, 474, 475, 484, 520
Boucher, F., 87
Boudreaux, R., 209
Bouffard, M., 180
Boulos, Z., 209
Boulton, M. J., 578
Bourgeois, J. A., 497
Bouton, M. E., 242
Bovasso, G. B., 574
Bovbjerg, D. H., 563
Bovbjerg, D. H., 243
Bower, G. H., 297, 298, 500
Bowers, C. A., 95
Bowers, K. S., 45, 223, 451
Bowlby, J., 119
Bowmaker, J. K., 165
Bowman, D., 556

Box, P., 256
Boyce, B. A., 408
Boyce, W. T., 175
Boyd, J. H., 493, 495
Boyle, G. J., 567
Boyle, S. H., 70
Boynton, R. M., 165
Bozarth, J. D., 540, 541
Braastad, B. O., 238
Bracht, C., 612
Brackbill, Y., 368
Brackfield, S. C., 318
Brackshaw, E., 384
Bradbury, E. J., 100
Bradbury, T. N., 143, 144
Bradford, J., 53
Bradley, B., 311
Bradley, B. P., 288, 496
Bradley, L. A., 567
Bradley, M. M., 414
Bradley, M. T., 418
Bradshaw, E., 26
Bradshaw, G. S., 26
Bradshaw, M., 66
Braehler, E., 498
Braet, C., 387
Brakke, K. E., 335, 338
Bramlett, R. K., 20
Branch, W., 48
Brand, G., 181
Brand, M., 501
Brand, R. J., 569
Brandao, M. L., 185
Brandstaetter, V., 144
Branje, S. J. T., 134
Bratslavsky, E., 605
Brattico, E., 83
Brauer, M., 616
Braun, A., 430
Braun, D. L., 387
Braun-Janzen, C., 535
Brawman-Mintzer, O., 492
Bray, C. W., 178
Bray, S. R., 461
Brayboy, T. D., 384
Breathnach, C. S., 92
Brébion, G., 280
Brechmann, A., 87
Breckler, S. J., 607
Brehm, J. W., 611
Breier, J. I., 83
Breland, K., 260
Breland, M., 260
Bremner, J. D., 182
Brennan, C., 465
Brennan, P. A., 513
Brent, D. A., 509
Brentar, J. T., 222
Brentari, D. K., 337
Bresler, C., 146
Breuer, J., 444, 529, 532, 625
Brevik, J. I., 578
Brewer, M., 545
Brewer, M. B., 615

Brewer, N., 291, 292, 436
Brezun, J. M., 100
Briad, J., 220
Bricklin, J., 28
Brickman, P., 429
Bridge, H., 168
Bridge, J., 509
Briggs, J., 625
Briggs, K. C., 455
Brigham, C. C., 363–364
Brigham, J. C., 38, 291
Briken, P., 624
Brinton, R. D., 303
Brion, S., 455
Briston, T., 462
Brittain, A. E., 133
Brobeck, J. R., 381
Broberg, D. J., 245
Broca, P., 92
Brockman, L. N., 258
Broder, M. S., 552
Brody, N., 344
Brogaard, B., 202
Brohawn, K. H., 564
Brokaw, T., 464
Bromberg, W., 530
Bronstein, C., 532
Brooks, B. B., 420
Brooks, G. R., 462
Brooks, K., 293
Brooks, L. J., 213
Brooks, M. C., 123
Brooks, P., 221
Brooks, P. J., 257
Brooks, S. J., 154
Brooks-Gunn, J., 123, 130, 131, 349, 365, 369, 388
Brosschot, J. F., 576
Broughton, R. S., 192
Brouwers, M. C., 531
Brown, A. L., 354
Brown, A. S., 50, 192, 270, 315
Brown, B., 86
Brown, D., 287, 350, 429
Brown, D. A., 76
Brown, D. R., 379
Brown, H. O., 309
Brown, J., 229
Brown, J. D., 470, 485, 565, 580, 581, 598
Brown, K. S., 617
Brown, K. T., 615
Brown, L. S., 287
Brown, R., 212, 270, 329
Brown, R. J., 319, 498
Brown, S. W., 221
Brown, T. E., 522, 523
Brown, T. N., 615
Brown, V. R., 112, 319
Brownell, K. D., 385, 585, 586, 590
Brozek, J., 2
Bruce, M. L., 485
Bruck, G. E., 308
Bruck, M., 291

Bruener, C. C., 258
Brugger, P., 192
Brummett, B. H., 70
Brunello, N., 78
Bruner, J. S., 10
Bruni, O., 213
Bruno, G., 7
Bruno, T., 407
Brunswick, D. J., 510
Bruschi, C. J., 579
Bryant, A. G., 551
Bryant, D. M., 123, 352
Bryck, R. L., 113
Bryden, M. P., 94, 138, 308
Brydon, L., 575
Buccino, G., 264
Buchanan, A., 513
Buchanan, J. J., 280
Buchsbaum, M. S., 514
Buck, R., 414, 435
Buckingham, B., 111
Buckley, K. W., 11
Buckner, J. D., 483
Bucy, P. C., 88
Budowski, D., 487
Buechel, C., 160
Buitelaar, J., 524
Bukowski, W. M., 124
Bulik, C. M., 382, 389
Bullough, V. L., 392
Bulzacka, E., 200
Bundrick, C. M., 469
Bunge, M., 28–29
Bunn, A., 497
Bunney, B., 204
Buono, S., 323
Burchinal, M. R., 123
Burgard, S. A., 208
Burger, J. M., 601, 621
Burgess, A. (Allen), 464
Burgess, A. (Ann), 464
Burgess, C. A., 222
Burgess, M. F., 222
Burgess, P., 359
Buric, I., 34
Burke, P. B., 120
Burlingame, G. M., 554
Burman, B., 123
Burnham, W. M., 545
Burns, J., 95
Burns, T. E., 288
Burns, V. E., 563
Burr, M. L., 579
Burrows, L., 190
Bursik, K., 216
Burt, C., 366, 608
Burton, D., 408
Burtscher, M., 401
Burwell, R. A., 387
Busby, S., 534
Buscene, S., 616
Bush, G., 524
Bush, G. H. W., 107
Bush, H. E., 552

Bush, J. E., 613
Bushman, B. J., 39, 624
Bushnell, M. C., 223
Buss, A., 624
Buss, A. R., 5, 138
Buss, D. M., 25, 62, 63, 140, 143, 605, 606, 624
Bussey, K., 125
Buswell, B. N., 139, 468
Butcher, J. N., 457, 486
Butler, A. C., 538
Butler, B. E., 366
Butler, L. D., 506
Butnik, S. M., 524
Butschky, M. F., 587
Butt, A. E., 241
Butterworth, G., 602
Buunk, B. P., 63, 428, 575, 606, 618
Byars, K. C., 216
Bye, L., 583
Bylsma, W. H., 468
Byne, W., 397
Byrd, D., 512
Byrne, D., 30, 31, 53, 603
Byrne, W. L., 301
Byrnes, J. P., 140
Byron, K., 320

Cabanac, M., 381
Cabeza, R., 15
Cabral, H., 112
Cabral, R. R., 556
Cacioppo, J. T., 84, 608, 609, 610
Cade, J. F. J., 547
Cadet, J. L., 230
Cadoret, R. J., 65
Cagnacci, A., 385
Cahan, D., 4
Cahan, E. D., 16
Cahill, L., 303
Cai, Y., 121
Cain, W. S., 183
Calantone, R. J., 607
Caldwell, J. L., 205
Calisch, G., 157
Calkins, M. W., 7–8, 215–216, 217, 233
Callahan, C. M., 361
Callas, P. W., 43
Callero, P. L., 434
Callow, N., 409
Calvert, S. L., 126
Camel, J. E., 114
Camerino, M., 571
Cameron, H. A., 545
Cameron, J., 405
Cameron, L., 589
Cameron, M. J., 249
Camic, P. M., 26
Caminiti, R., 55
Campbell, D. A., 597
Campbell, J. D., 470, 580
Campbell, J. N., 186, 209, 605
Campbell, S. S., 204

Campione, J. E., 354
Camras, L. A., 425
Canada, K. E., 455
Canel-Çinarbas, D., 37
Canetto, S. S., 508
Canino, G. J., 493
Cann, A., 621
Cannon, W. B., 380, 432, 433, 566
Canter, D. V., 465
Cantu, C. L., 133
Caplan, L. J., 328
Cappello, M. J., 249
Caprara, G. V., 461
Capraro, M. M., 455
Capraro, R. M., 455
Caputi, P., 361
Caputo, J. L., 563
Caqueret, A., 87
Caraway, S. J., 531
Carbone, K. M., 515
Cardwe, C. R., 77
Carey, C. L., 232
Carey, G., 484
Carey, M. P., 393
Carey, T. A., 32
Carlbring, P., 552
Carle, S. B., 418
Carlsmith, J. M., 611, 612
Carlson, D., 294
Carlson, E. T., 501
Carlson, J. A., 384
Carlson, L. E., 581
Carlson, M., 627
Carlsson, C. P. O., 187
Carlstrom, A., 461
Carmichael, L., 333
Carnahan, E., 587
Carnes, M., 408
Carney, R. N., 298
Carnine, D. W., 293
Carossino, P., 187
Carpenter, C. R., 264
Carr, A., 543
Carr, A. S., 77, 524
Carr, J. E., 536
Carrà, G., 514
Carretero, M., 26
Carrey, J., 501–502
Carrico, R. L., 115
Carroll, D., 563
Carroll, J. B., 365
Carroll, J. M., 423
Carroll, M., 398, 549
Carroll, M. E., 55
Carron, A. V., 619
Carson, J., 430
Carson, R. C., 486
Carson, S. H., 317
Carta, G., 232
Carter, C. M., 312
Carter, C. S., 497
Carter, M. M., 493
Carter, R., 297
Carter-Pokras, O., 584

Carter-Saltzman, L., 367
Carton, J. S., 406, 466
Cartwright, R. D., 207, 218
Carver, C., 393
Carver, C. S., 505, 574
Carver, K., 135
Case, L., 45
Casement, M. D., 504
Casey, M. K., 561
Cash, T. F., 603
Caspi, A., 475
Cassar, A., 614
Castejon, J. L., 360
Casto, S. D., 365
Catalan, J., 508
Catalano, R., 129
Catanese, K. R., 398
Catania, J. A., 583
Cath, D. C., 65
Cattell, J. M., 5, 6, 8, 345–346
Cattell, R. B., 350
Cattell, R. C., 359
Caulfield, M., 331
Cavallaro, L. A., 435
Cavanaugh, J. C., 298
Cavellucci, J., 375–376
Cecchettin, M., 185
Ceci, S. J., 287, 291, 292, 357
Cecil, J. E., 380
Cerletti, U., 545
Cervellon, M.-C., 608
Ceschi, G., 438
Cézanne, P., 316–317
Chabal, C., 187
Chabrol, H., 519
Chadwick, H., 311
Chaiken, S., 612
Chakraborty, G., 462
Chakravarti, D., 429
Challis, B. H., 278
Chambers, D., 173
Chamizo, V. D., 263
Chan, A. S., 280
Chan, A. Y.-C., 361
Chan, C. C. H., 507
Chan, D., 350
Chan, M. P., 463
Chance, G., 114
Chandler, M. J., 14
Chanel, J., 433
Chang, P., 352, 502
Chang, Z., 523
Chant, D., 515
Chao, G. R., 352
Chao, R. K., 122
Chaplin, W. F., 599
Chapman, A. J., 159
Chapman, J. E., 538
Chapman, J. F., 464
Charcot, J., 444
Charest, J., 187
Charles, V., 53
Charlton, H., 68
Charman, D., 555

Charness, N., 323
Chart, H., 575
Chartrand, T., 621
Chase, W. G., 275
Chase-Lansdale, P. L., 123
Chassein, B., 428
Chaturvedi, S. K., 505
Chauchat, J. H., 515
Chavajay, P., 132
Chavira, D. A., 518
Checkley, S. A., 78
Checkosky, C. M., 184
Chelland, S., 251
Chemelski, B. E., 296
Chen, C., 35, 319, 603
Chen, J., 160
Chen, M., 579
Chen, M. J., 588
Chen, Y., 71
Chen, Z., 86, 100
Chenard, J. R., 187
Cheney, D. L., 325
Cheng, A. T. A., 516
Cheng, C., 463, 504
Cherek, D. R., 227, 232
Cherney, I. D., 281
Chernick, L., 459
Cherrier, M. M., 303
Cherry, E. C., 201
Cheryan, S., 600
Cheskin, L. J., 384
Chesterfield, P. D., 423
Chételat, G., 279
Cheung, M.-K., 556
Cheung, P. C., 133
Cheung, S.-F., 463
Chi, M. T. H., 280
Chiao, J. Y., 88
Chichilnisky, E. J., 163
Child, I. L., 193
Chimonas, E., 229
Chin, S., 516
Chio, J. H.-M., 463
Chipuer, II. M., 65
Chitnis, T., 96
Chitwood, D. D., 583
Chiu, C.-Y., 597, 598
Chiu, W. T., 45, 481
Chodorow, N., 452
Choi, I., 596
Choi, J., 181
Choi, J. N., 617
Chomsky, N., 327, 331–332
Chongde, L., 361
Choudhury, N., 358
Christ, T. J., 41
Christensen, A. J., 590
Christensen, H., 501
Christensen, J.-W., 263
Christensen, L., 54
Christensen, T. M., 123
Christianson, S. A., 288, 501
Christie, D. J., 21

Christie, I. C., 433
Christmann, E. P., 257
Christy, C. A., 627
Christy, D., 586
Chung, A. C., 86
Chung, L., 276
Church, A. T., 457, 458
Church, D. R., 157
Chytilová, J., 614
Cialdini, R. B., 621, 627
Ciancarelli, V., 455
Cicchetti, D., 287
Cicekli, I., 327
Cicerello, A., 606
Cicerone, C. M., 159
Ciffone, J., 45
Cifre, E., 461
Ciftci Uruk, A., 134
Cioe, N., 551
Cipolli, C., 218
Claassen, D. O., 86
Claassen, N. C. W., 350
Claes, S., 483
Clancy, S. A., 283
Clanton, N. R., 599
Clanton, R. C., 210
Clark, K. B., 17, 614–615
Clark, L. A., 488
Clark, L. L., 508
Clark, M. C., 298
Clark, M. P., 17, 614–615
Clark, R. D., 629
Clark, R. D., III, 616
Clarke, P. G. H., 28
Clarke, V., 322
Cleghorn, J. M., 50
Cleveland, H. H., 369
Cliffe, M. J., 249
Clifford, C. A., 497
Clinkenbeard, P. B., 360
Clinton, B., 416
Clothier, A., 217
Clouser, R., 290
Clowes-Hollins, V., 496
Clutton-Brock, T. H., 254
Coates, D., 429
Coates, T. J., 583
Coats, G., 602
Cobos, P., 432
Cochran, D. Q., 465
Cockerham, W. C., 508
Coenen, A. M. L., 41
Cofer, C. N., 377
Cofer, L. F., 204
Cogan, D., 240
Cogan, R., 240
Cohen, A., 137
Cohen, D., 114, 393, 446, 462
Cohen, D. A. D., 188
Cohen, D. B., 211
Cohen, J., 50
Cohen, J. W., 382
Cohen, L. R., 590
Cohen, M. S., 583

Cohen, N., 573
Cohen, N. J., 270
Cohen, S., 572
Cohen, S. H., 17
Cohen, S. L., 251, 589
Cohen-Kettenis, P. T., 624
Coker, J., 68
Cokley, K., 26
Colace, C., 219
Colapinto, J., 394
Colcombe, S., 136
Colder, C. R., 122
Cole, G., 380
Cole, P. M., 579
Cole, S. G., 620
Colegrove, F. W., 270
Coleman, M., 121
Coleman, R. M., 205
Coleman, S. R., 377
Coleridge, S. T., 228
Coles, C. D., 112
Collado, P. S., 26
Collaer, M. L., 111, 140
Collett, T. S., 323
Colletti, P., 520
Colligan, J., 318
Collins, A. M., 280
Collins, D., 70
Collins, D. R., 299, 419
Collins, N. L., 603
Collins, W. A., 134
Collin-Vézina, D., 502
Colmar, S., 467
Colom, R., 350, 358
Colombo, G., 232
Colon-Ramos, D. A., 71
Coltrane, S., 613
Colvin, C. M., 264
Colvin, C. R., 427, 470
Compton, S. N., 485
Comrey, A. L., 463
Comstock, G., 264
Conant, L., 17
Condie, D., 502
Conklin, H. M., 514
Conley, C. A., 36
Conley, J. J., 168
Connell, J. B., 617
Connemann, B., 207
Conner, R., 629
Connie, F. O. Y., 86
Connolly, J. A., 135
Connors, A., 107
Conrad, R., 275
Consoli, A. J., 556
Conte, S., 278
Contrada, R. J., 563, 576
Conway, M. A., 295
Cook, M., 265, 266
Cook, S. L., 614
Coolidge, C., 431
Coolidge, F. L., 449
Coombs, D. W., 508
Coon, D. J., 7, 239

Coon, H., 367
Coons, E. E., 258
Coons, P. M., 500
Cooper, G., 154
Cooper, G. F., 173
Cooper, H., 43, 428
Cooper, J., 154
Cooper, J. M., 201
Cooper, L. M., 158
Cooper, M. A., 257
Cooper, Z., 388
Copolov, D. L., 512
Copper, C., 295
Coram, G. J., 451
Corazza, L., 357
Corballis, M. C., 96
Corbetta, M., 60
Corcoran, R., 463
Cordeiro, A. M., 462
Coren, S., 94, 96–97, 198, 508
Corina, D., 308
Corkin, S., 300–301
Corley, R., 475
Cormier, J. F., 502
Corn, B., 574
Corrigan, N. M., 343, 344
Corsaro, W. A., 124
Cosgrove, L., 13
Costa, P. T., Jr., 454, 457
Costello, A., 492
Costello, E. J., 485
Costello, N. L., 518
Cosyns, P., 483
Cotter, P. A., 78
Coulson, M., 425
Courage, M. L., 152
Courtenay, W. H., 589
Courtin, J., 419
Courtois, C. A., 287
Cousins, N., 576
Cowan, C. P., 122
Cowan, N., 272
Cowan, P. A., 122
Cowan, R. L., 471
Cowen, P. J., 387
Cowie, S., 45
Cowles, M., 31, 32, 46
Cowley, G., 25
Cox, D. J., 524
Cox, K. S., 145
Cox, W. E., 193
Cox, W. J., 494
Coy, K. C., 134
Cozzarelli, C., 468
Craciun, C., 20
Craig, C. L., 253
Craig, J., 581
Craig, W. N., 33
Craik, F. I. M., 277–278
Craik, K. H., 14
Crain, W., 33
Cramer, D., 446, 468, 541
Cramer, P., 133, 451
Crandall, C. S., 351

Crandall, J. E., 466
Cranford, D., 569
Crano, W. D., 610
Cranwell-Bruce, L. A., 78
Cras, P., 71
Craske, M. G., 492
Crawford, H. J., 188
Crepeau-Hobson, M. F., 1
Crespo, C. J., 384, 584
Crews, F. T., 302
Critchley, H. D., 581
Critchlow, S., 287
Critelli, J. W., 451
Crites, S. L., Jr., 385
Crittenden, M. R., 349
Croake, J., 13
Crocker, J., 505, 614, 615
Croft, G. P., 427
Crohan, S. E., 143
Crombez, G., 418
Crone-Todd, D. E., 257
Croog, V. J., 522
Crook, T., 504
Crooks, H., 107–108
Crosby, L. O., 383
Crosier, M., 552
Cross, J. A., 626
Cross, S., 464
Cross, T., 417
Cross, W. E., 17
Crossley, N., 517
Crouse, E. M., 615
Crow, G., 53
Crowe, G. W., 168
Crowe, R. R., 493
Crowley, A. E., 181
Crowley, J. J., 15
Crowley, M., 50
Crowley, S. J., 205
Croy, I., 182
Crozier, J. B., 178
Crucian, G. P., 435
Cruess, S., 578
Crum, B., 55
Crump, T., 495
Cruz, C., 205
Csanyi, V., 325
Cubit, K., 53
Cuellar, I., 134
Cuevas, T., 96
Cui, Y., 37
Culpepper, L., 314
Cumberland, A., 128
Cumming, B. G., 168
Cummings, E. M., 117, 123
Cunnick, J. E., 573
Cunningham, J. A., 614
Cunningham, J. G., 423, 429, 605
Cunningham, M. R., 602
Cunningham, S., 336
Cunningham, J., 78
Cunningham, W. A., 203
Cuntz, U., 388
Cupchik, G. C., 182

Curci, A., 270
Curcio, C. A., 159
Curnow, C., 136
Curran, E. J., 101
Currie, C., 131, 587
Currier, M. B., 216
Curzon, G., 420
Cusimano, M., 86
Cuthbert, B. N., 414
Cutler, R. L., 154
Cutting, L. P., 516
Cuvo, A. J., 355
Cyranowski, J. M., 398
Cytowic, R. E., 231
Czaja, S. J., 122
Czeisler, C. A., 205
Czilli, T., 182
Czyzewska, M. A., 201

d'Amato, T., 515
D'Ambrosio, C., 213
D'Anci, K. E., 599
D'Onofrio, B. M., 523
da Menezes Costa, L., 461
da Vinci, L., 158
Dack, D. E., 68
Dado, R. J., 185
Dafinoiu, I., 220
Dager, S. R., 343, 344
Daher, M., 425
Dahlgren, M. K., 511
Dahlstrom, W. G., 37
Daigen, V., 143
Dale, H., 76
Dale, K., 323, 451
Daleng, M. L., 388
Dalery, J., 515
Dallenbach, K. M., 285, 286
Daly, K., 588
Damasio, A. R., 202
Damasio, H., 91
Dammann, E. J., 490
Dance, K. A., 555
Dane, J. R., 188
Daniel, M., 542
Daniels, M., 218, 470
Danielsen, E. H., 102
Danilova, V., 183
Danko, S. G., 420
Danks, J. H., 316
Dantchik, A., 470
Dantzer, J. M., 87
Dantzig, S. A., 469
Danysz, W., 78
Danziger, K., 2
Darch, C. B., 294
Darley, J., 627–629
Darling, C. A., 391
Darling, N., 122
Darlington, R. B., 364
Darwin, C., 5, 6, 9, 15, 61, 62, 108, 138, 238, 345, 362, 376, 425, 426
Dasen, P. R., 115
Daskalakis, Z. J., 81

I-6 Name Index

Datko, M., 264
Datta, S., 86
Daughton, D. M., 587
Daum, I., 358
Daumann, J., 232
Daunizeau, J., 83
Davalos, D. B., 506
Davey, J., 21
Davi, R., 464
David, A. S., 177
David, S. S., 159
Davidson, D., 320
Davidson, D. J., 203, 516
Davidson, J. K., 302, 391
Davidson, K., 570
Davidson, R. J., 420, 424
Davies, B. P., 244
Davies, G., 291, 515
Davies, G. M., 586
Davies, I. R. L., 334, 361
Davies, P. T., 123, 321
Davila, J., 10
Davis, A., 350, 555, 569
Davis, D., 461
Davis, J., 166
Davis, J. M., 384
Davis, J. O., 515
Davis, K. L., 87, 281, 299, 387
Davis, M. H., 597
Davis, R., 323
Davis, S. F., 10, 335
Davison, K. P., 579
Davison, L., 438
Dawson, G. R., 263
Day, R. H., 168
de Bruyne, T., 143
De Castro, J. M., 379
De Doncker, D., 483
De Dreu, C. K. W., 616
de Gelder, B., 151, 152
de Graaf, C., 183
de Groot, D., 625
De Houwer, J., 607
de Jesus, S. N., 317
de Jong, P., 265
de Jong, P. J., 246, 496
De la Fuente, J. M., 519
De La Pena, J., 280
De La Ronde, C., 144
de la Sayette, V., 279
de Man, A., 288
de Man, A. F., 362, 614
de Mathis, M. A., 497
de Miguel, R., 232
de Moor, C. A., 574
de Paula Ramos, S., 529
De Raad, B., 455
de Sanchez, M., 370
de St. Aubin, E., 145
de Valois, R. L., 164
de Vargas, M. C., 422
De Vries, N. K., 616
De Wolff, M., 120
Dean, J., 282

Deaux, K., 126, 141
Debaro, D., 96
DeBaryshe, B. D., 331
Debski, J., 20
DeCarolis, N. A., 547, 581
DeCharms, R., 402
Dechongkit, S., 422
Deci, E. L., 405
deCosta, B. R., 231
DeCoster, J., 208
Deegan, J. F., 163
Deffner-Rappold, C., 243
DeFife, J. A., 311
DeFries, J., 475
DeFries, J. C., 365, 367
Degel, J., 279
Dehaene, S., 154
DeHart, T., 468
Dekkers, T., 501
Dekle, D. J., 292
Dekundy, A., 78
Del Giudice, M., 51
Del Pilar, G. H., 457
Delamater, A. M., 567
Delamater, A. R., 238
Delanoë, D., 136
Deldin, P. J., 504
Delemos, K. A., 156
Delhanty, P., 382
Delhomme, G., 433
DeLisi, M., 70
DeLongis, A., 564
Delunas, L., 562
DeMartinis, N., 546
DeMartino, R. E., 509
Dement, W., 209, 210, 216, 217
Demers, L. M., 567
Demir, A., 134
Demler, O., 481, 491
Dempster, F. N., 286
Denault, A., 297
DeNeve, K. M., 428
Deng, X., 230
Denmark, F. L., 8
Dennerstein, L., 145
Denney, N. W., 391
Dennis, T. E., 152
Denny, K., 96
Depner, C., 403
DeRijk, R. H., 575
Derlega, V. J., 603
Dermer, M., 602
Derrick, B. E., 299
Dervin, D., 447
Descartes, R., 3, 28, 72, 335
Desforges, D. M., 615
Desgranges, B., 279
DeShon, R. P., 350, 598
Deshpanda, R., 462
Desiderio, D. M., 301
DeSousa, E. A., 75
Detenber, B. H., 322
Detterman, D. K., 352
Detwiler, C., 205

Deuel, L. L. S., 355
Deuser, W. E., 257
Deutsch, D., 178
Deutsch, G., 93, 95, 141
Devine, P. G., 291, 424, 609
Devlin, M. J., 387
Dewey, J., 7
Dewsbury, D. A., 54, 262, 336
Dhami, M. K., 320
Di Meglio, G., 388
Di Nuovo, A. G., 323
Diaconis, P., 193
Diamanduros, T., 20
Diamantopoulos, I., 229
Diamond, K. E., 38
Diamond, L. M., 398, 399
Diamond, M., 112, 394
Diamond, M. L., 185
Diamond, S., 185
Diana, C. M. K., 86
Dickerson, S. S., 579
Dickson, D., 192
Diedrich, O., 474
Diegman, T., 580
Diego, M., 70
Diego, M. A., 181
Diekstra, R. F. W., 540
Diener, C., 429
Diener, E., 143, 281, 427, 428, 429
Diener, M., 429
Dierberger, A., 389
Dietz, O., 382
Digiuni, M., 26
DiGiuseppe, R., 539
DiGrande, L., 563
Dijk, D. J., 229
Dijkstra, P., 606
DiLalla, D. L., 484
Dillard, J. P., 620, 621
Dillon, P., 232
DiLorenzo, T. M., 355
DiMatteo, M. R., 50, 590, 591
Dimberg, U., 438
Dimitrov, M., 92
Dince, W. M., 259
Dindia, K., 140
Dinnel, D. L., 495
Dinse, H. R., 184
Dionne, G., 167
Dipietro, J. A., 471
DiRisio, L., 193
Disbrow, E. A., 89
Dishman, R. J., 584
Disraeli, B., 47–48
Distal, H., 181
Ditka, M., 568
Dittmar, A., 433
Ditton, J., 232
Ditunno, P. L., 100
Dix, D., 531
Dixon, J. C., 109
Dixon, N. F., 451
Dixon, R. A., 141, 408
Dixson, A. F., 472

Doane, J. A., 517
Dobbins, A. C., 160
Dobson, K. S., 485
Docherty, N. M., 516
Dockery, T. M., 610
Dodd, D. K., 425
Dodge, K. A., 135
Dodiya, H. B., 102
Dodson, J. D., 399
Doell, R. G., 396
Dohi, S., 86
Dohrenwend, B. P., 563
Doi, Y., 209
Doidge, N., 555
Dolan, R. J., 581
Dolbier, C. L., 578
Dolce, J., 587
Dole, R., 586
Dolev, K., 418
Dolin, D. J., 620
Doll, B., 467
Doll, H. A., 389
Dollard, J., 624
Dolliver, R. H., 467
Dominguez, M. M., 466
Domino, E. F., 77
Donaghue, N., 606
Donaldson, K., 550
Donderi, D. C., 162, 216
Dong, Y. T., 457
Donnerstein, E., 264
Donoghue, J., 71
Donovan, J. J., 296, 322
Donovan, S., 554
Donovan, W. L., 153
Doob, I. W., 624
Dooley, D., 129
Dore, F. Y., 424
Dorian, L., 585
Dorn, L. D., 131
Dorsett, S., 501
Dougall, N., 484
Dougherty, D., 417
Dougherty, D. M., 227, 232
Dougherty, L. M., 425
Douglas, J., 214, 464, 465
Douvan, E., 403
Dovidio, J. F., 613
Dowd, E. T., 538, 577
Down, J. L., 344
Downey, D., 118, 600
Downs, E., 20
Dowrick, C., 41
Doyle, A. C., 31, 230, 450
Dozois, D. J. A., 485
Draguns, J. G., 486, 506, 517
Drayson, M., 563
Dremencov, E., 78
Drentea, P., 508
Drevets, W., 571, 572
Drews, F. A., 201
Drigotas, S. M., 467
Driskell, J. E., 295, 580, 617
Droesler, J., 155

Name Index   I-7

Drori, R., 89
Drucker, A. D., 619
Druen, P. B., 602
Drumheller, A., 321, 614
Drummond, E., 486
Drummond, P. D., 581
Drummond, T., 464
Dryden, W., 538
Dryer, D. C., 603
Dubal, S., 402
Dube, L., 311, 608
Dube, M., 469
Dubignon, J. M., 582
Duddu, V., 505
Dudley, E., 145
Dudycha, G. J., 459
Duff, P. K., 487
Duffy, J. F., 375–376
Duffy, S., 596
Duffy, V. B., 184
Dufresne, T., 10
Dugoni, B. L., 568
DuHamel, K. N., 221
Dujardin, K., 219
Duka, T., 243
Duke, M. P., 423
Dumaret, A., 367
Dumitrascu, N., 451
Dunbar, K., 314
Dunbar, R. I. M., 44
Duncan, G. H., 223
Duncan, G. J., 349, 365
Duncan, J., 274, 358, 359
Duncan, J. C., 520
Duncan, J. S., 83
Duncan, M. J., 460
Dunn, E., 40
Dunn, J., 62
Dunn, L. A., 223
Dunne, M. P., 65, 395
Duplin, S., 87
Dupuis, G., 297
Durham, T. W., 436
Durik, A. M., 398
Durkin, M., 6
Durlak, J. A., 468, 509, 549
Durm, M. W., 191
Durst, L., 162
Durstewitz, D., 313
Dushanova, J., 71
Dutton, D. G., 604
Duyme, M., 367, 368
Dworkin, B. R., 258
Dwyer, B. D., 508
Dwyer, J., 575
Dyer, C. A., 352
Dyer, F. C., 325
Dykes, R. W., 91
Dym, R. J., 95

Eagle, M., 119
Eagly, A. H., 51, 63, 140, 141, 603, 608, 609
Earle, D. C., 172

Earle, T. L., 574
East, R., 472
Eastman, C. I., 205
Eastman, K. E., 219
Eastman, N. W., 79
Eastwick, P. W., 603
Eastwood, J. D., 201
Eaves, L. J., 484
Ebbeck, V., 400
Ebbesen, E. B., 284
Ebbinghaus, H., 5, 283, 284, 285
Ebmeier, K. P., 484
Ebstein, R. P., 475
Eccles, A., 535
Eccles, J. S., 404
Ecenbarger, W., 181
Echizenya, M., 211
Ecker, A. H., 483
Eckert, E., 379
Eckert, E. D., 397, 520
Edeline, J. M., 177
Edelman, G. M., 324
Edinger, J. D., 535
Edmondson, J. A., 422
Edson, C. L., 430
Edward, M., 53
Edwards, B., 205
Edwards, S., 581
Eels, K., 350
Eftekhari-Sanjani, H., 141, 357
Egan, K. J., 536
Egeland, J. A., 510
Egeth, H. E., 293
Egloff, B., 499
Ehara, T. H., 323
Ehlenz, K., 421
Ehrhardt, A. A., 394
Eich, J. E., 289
Eichenbaum, H., 279
Eichmann, A., 621
Eichstedt, J. A., 497
Eid, J., 578
Eid, M., 143
Eiden, R. D., 112
Eilers, R. E., 328
Einstein, A., 27, 82, 83
Einwiller, S., 609
Eisch, A. J., 547, 581
Eischen, S. E., 534
Eisdorfer, C., 145
Eisenberg, N., 140, 621
Eisenberg, P. R., 128
Eisenberger, N. I., 578
Eisenman, R., 321
Ek, E., 385
Ekbia, H. R., 324
Ekman, P., 413, 416, 424, 425–426, 433, 435
el Mansari, M., 78
Elaad, E., 418
Elaine, K., 181
Eldadah, B. A., 515
Elder, W. B., 462
Eley, T. C., 62

Elfenbein, H. A., 426
Elgar, F. J., 51
Elger, C. E., 88
Eliot, J., 504
Elkes, R., 621
Elkin, I., 554
Elkind, D., 115
Elkins, R. L., 44
Ellenberger, H. F., 221
Ellicott, A. M., 145
Elliot, A. J., 611
Elliott, D., 173
Elliott, R., 350
Ellis, A., 538–540
Ellis, A. P. J., 598
Ellis, H. C., 396, 520
Ellis, L., 96, 189, 365
Ellison, C. G., 66
Ellison, P. A., 626
Ellison, W. J., 117
Ellsworth, P. C., 438
Elmehed, K., 438
El-Sarr, E., 445
Else-Quest, N. M., 139
Elshout, J. J., 313
Elwood, P. C., 579
Ely, T. D., 419
Emam, M. M., 505
Ember, C. R., 377
Ember, M., 377
Emde Boas, W. van., 95
Emerick, S. W., 435
Emmons, R. A., 361
Emonson, D. L., 229
Emory, E., 514
Empson, J. A., 218
Emslie, H., 360
Enders, C. K., 42
Endler, N. S., 579
Enea, V., 220
Engel, S. A., 160
Engelien, A., 180
Engels, G. I., 540
Engh, T., 96
Engstrom, E. J., 488
Engstrom, M., 84
Epictetus, 485
Epstein, M. H., 37
Epstein, N., 393
Epstein, R., 313, 316, 463
Epstein, S., 459, 470, 506
Er, N., 270
Erb, H.-P., 609
Erber, J., 248
Erdstein, J., 388
Erdur, O., 556
Erel, O., 123
Erez, A., 463
Ericsson, K. A., 280
Erikson, E., 118–121, 132, 133, 145, 452
Eriksson, C. J. P., 624
Erlich, E., 102
Ernst, E., 181

Ervin, C. R., 30, 603
Escolas, S. M., 577
Esdaile, J., 221
Eshleman, J. R., 428
Eshun, S., 186
Espejo, E. F., 101
Esteves, F., 183
Estrada, C. A., 320
Esveldt-Dawson, K., 355
Etkin, A., 493
Eustache, F., 279
Euwema, M., 577
Evans, D. E., 471, 590
Evans, D. L., 578
Evans, E. E., 434
Evans, F. J., 222
Evans, K. C., 88
Everly, G. S., 549
Evers, A., 584
Evers, A. W. M., 572
Eviatar, Z., 95
Ewald, H., 510
Ewin, D. M., 222
Exton, M. S., 391, 573
Eyler, A. A., 584
Eyrolle, H., 282
Eysenck, H. J., 358, 401, 453, 454, 455, 463, 471, 520, 533, 552–553
Eysenck, J. J., 453
Eysenck, M. W., 574
Eysenck, S. B., 401, 453, 457
Ezzo, J., 187

Fabbro, F., 86
Fabes, J., 100
Fagan, J. F., 349
Fagan, M. M., 145
Fagerstrom, K. O., 587
Fagioli, I., 218
Fahy, T., 513
Fairburn, C. C., 389
Fairburn, C. G., 387, 388, 389
Faith, M., 599
Faith, M. S., 382
Fakler, P., 51
Falceto, O. G., 45
Falco, F. L., 331
Falk, J. L., 249
Falk, R., 50
Fallace, T. D., 7
Fallon, A. E., 386, 426
Fallon, B. J., 606
Fals-Stewart, W., 227
Fan, J., 319
Fancher, R. E., 362
Fani, L., 382
Fantino, E., 261
Fantoni-Salvador, P., 457
Fanurik, D., 188, 255
Faraone, S., 549
Faraone, S. V., 65, 523
Faravelli, C., 493, 546
Farde, L., 515

Farmer, R., 508
Farmer-Dougan, V. A., 248
Farnill, D., 401
Farr, C. B., 530
Farrar, W., 462, 581
Farrell, D. A., 250
Farrimond, T., 171
Farrington, D. P., 465
Farthing, G. W., 221
Farvolden, P., 451
Fassbender, P., 193
Fauerbach, J. A., 589
Fava, G. A., 567
Fava, M., 504
Favreau, O. E., 51
Fay, F., 417
Faye, C., 54
Fazio, R. H., 607
Fazzari, T. V., 572
Feasby, T., 68
Feather, S. R., 192
Featherstone, E., 581
Fechner, G., 4–5, 95, 152, 155, 283
Feest, U., 9, 31
Fehr, B., 311, 414, 604
Feick, D. L., 505, 598
Feil, A., 540
Feild, H. S., 400
Fein, D., 94
Fein, S., 614
Feinberg, R., 406
Feingold, A., 139, 387, 602
Feinstein, J. S., 87
Feist, G. J., 470
Feldman, L. G., 52
Fell, J., 88
Fells, C. A., 114
Feng, C.-Y., 542
Feng, D., 109
Feng, L. R., 78
Fenn, K. M., 218
Fennema, E., 50, 138, 139
Fenwick, K. D., 114
Ferchiou, A., 200
Ference, R., 617
Ferlazzo, F., 278
Ferligoj, A., 403
Fern, E. F., 621
Fernald, A., 263
Fernandes, C. L. C., 45
Fernandez-Ruiz, J. J., 232
Ferrando, S. J., 590
Ferrari, A., 323
Ferrari, M., 263
Ferrence, R., 588
Ferris, A. M., 184
Fery, Y. A., 189
Feske, U., 492
Festinger, L., 601, 610, 611, 612, 625
Fetchenhauer, D., 606
Feyerabend, C., 588
Ficken, E. J., 463
Ficks, C., 524
Fieckenstein, L., 107

Fiedler, K., 417
Field, J. K., 391
Field, S., 501
Field, T., 70
Field, T. M., 114, 120, 123
Fielden, S., 487
Fiese, B. H., 462
Fiez, J. A., 326
Figler, M. H., 626
Figueroa-Munoz, A., 597
Filaccio, M., 1
Filbert, M., 257
Fillingim, R. B., 186
Fine, A., 101
Fine, M., 121
Fine, T. H., 401
Fink, B., 602
Fink, G. R., 500
Finkel, B., 605
Finkel, E. J., 603
Finkelstein, E. A., 382
Finkelstein, M. A., 629
Finnegan, M., 112
Finney, J. W., 591
Finzi, R., 446
Fiore, M. C., 587
Fiorito, G., 263
Firestone, P. T., 570
Fisch, R. O., 111
Fischel, J. E., 331
Fischer, B., 453
Fischer, H., 474
Fischer, K. W., 115, 599
Fischman, M. W., 230
Fiser, J., 160
Fishbain, D. A., 187
Fisher, C. B., 52, 53
Fisher, E. B., 567
Fisher, K., 264
Fisher, P. A., 113
Fisher, R., 49
Fisher, S., 218, 451, 533, 551
Fisher, S. E., 331
Fishman, B., 590
Fishman, I., 10
Fiske, D. W., 169
Fitch, T., 190
Fite, P. J., 122
Fitzgerald, P. B., 81
Fitzpatrick, J., 582
Flack, W. F., Jr., 435
Flannagan, D. A., 295
Flaum, M., 512, 516
Flay, B. R., 587
Fleckenstein, J., 187
Fleeson, W., 453
Flegal, K. M., 382
Fleischman, D. A., 279
Fleming, V. M., 404
Flesher, M. M., 241
Fletcher, M. A., 583
Flight, J., 95
Flint, T., 510
Floccia, C., 114

Floersch, J. E., 122
Florack, A., 614
Flor-Henry, P., 420
Florian, V., 468
Flourens, P., 4, 80
Floyd, M., 552, 556
Flynn, J. R., 370
Flynn, M. S., 293
Foa, E. B., 537
Fode, K. L., 44
Foerstl, J., 344
Fogarty, G. J., 469
Fogel, R. B., 214
Folkes, V. S., 321, 603
Folkman, S., 53, 564, 575
Folstein, M. F., 498
Foltin, R. W., 230
Fong, G., 227
Fontaine, K. R., 584
Fontana, A. M., 580
Foot, H. C., 159
Forabosco, G., 430
Forchuk, C., 549
Ford, B. D., 66
Fordyce, J., 423
Forehand, M. R., 462
Foreman, R. D., 188
Foret, A., 100
Foreyt, J. P., 585
Forgas, J. P., 40
Forget, R., 189
Forman, E. M., 538
Forman, R. F., 418
Fornes, P., 509
Forsterling, F., 597
Forsyth, D. R., 618, 628
Forth, A. E., 520
Foschi, R., 454
Fossaert, A., 402
Foster, C. A., 605
Foster, G. D., 385, 584
Foster, J. K., 584, 605
Foster-Schubert, K. E., 384
Fowler, A. E., 329
Fox, A. M., 232
Fox, B. H., 465
Fox, L. H., 345, 355
Fox, N. A., 420
Fracasso, M. P., 120
Frackowiak, R. S. J., 160, 500
Fraenkel, P., 543
Fraley, C. R., 121
France, C. R., 186
France, J. L., 186
Frank, D. A., 112
Frank, M. G., 308, 416, 426
Frank, O. R., 51
Frankel, R. M., 590
Franklin, B., 220, 434
Franklin, G., 287
Franklin-Lipster, E., 287
Franko, D. L., 387
Fraser, S., 364
Fraser, S. C., 620

Frawley, P. J., 536
Frederick, C. M., 408, 584
Frederiksen, N., 360
Fredrikson, M., 474, 581
Freed, W. J., 101
Freedman, J. L., 39, 620
Freedman, M. A., 136
Freedman, R., 489
Freeman, A., 451
Freeman, C., 389
Freeman, J., 21
Freeman, K., 95
Freeman, R., 188
Freeman, W., 544
Freitas, A. L., 600
Freivalds, A., 160
Fremmer-Bombik, E., 120
French, D. C., 625
French, S. E., 34
Frenda, S. J., 291
Frenkel-Brunswik, E., 614
Freud, A., 10, 132
Freud, S., 3, 9–10, 11, 12, 34, 119, 124–125, 132, 203, 215, 217–218, 220, 230, 286, 288, 299, 431, 444–447, 449, 451, 454, 460, 484, 496, 499, 504, 529, 532, 623
Freund, A. M., 146
Frick, R. W., 422
Fridrich, P., 619
Fried, A. L., 52
Friedler, E., 576
Friedman, B. H., 433
Friedman, H. S., 576
Friedman, M., 568–569
Friesen, W. V., 424, 425, 433, 435
Frieze, I. H., 403
Friman, P. C., 494
Frisco, M. L., 144
Friston, K., 160
Frith, U., 522
Fritsch, G., 88
Fritzsche, B. A., 629
Fröhlich, A., 380
Fröjd, S., 131
Frolich, P. F., 605
Froming, W. J., 462
Fromm, E., 447
Frost, B. J., 168
Frost, J. J., 186
Frost, R., 287
Froufe, M., 154
Frussa-Filho, R., 289
Frymier, A. B., 429
Fuchs, A. H., 2, 406
Fuchs-Beauchamp, K. D., 317
Fuentes, D., 37
Fuerst, C. J., 581
Fujii, K., 493
Fujino, D. C., 556
Fujita, F., 428
Fujita, K., 174, 429
Fukuda, M., 72

Fulker, D. W., 365, 367, 475, 497
Fuller, B., 123
Fuller, C., 404
Fuller, R. W., 231
Fuller, S. R., 617
Fullerton, A. S., 109
Fultz, J., 627
Funder, D. C., 458, 470
Fundytus, M. E., 185
Funnell, E., 41
Furman, W., 135
Furnham, A., 453, 585
Furumoto, L., 8
Fuster, J. M., 273
Fyrberg, D., 53

Gabbay, M., 41
Gable, S. L., 505, 578
Gabriel, P., 155
Gacy, J. W., 482, 519
Gadoth, N., 207
Gaertner, S. L., 613
Gaffan, E. A., 556
Gage, P., 80, 92
Gagnon, J. H., 395
Gaillard, A. W. K., 618
Gais, S., 218
Galak, J., 193
Galanter, E., 153
Galati, D., 425
Galea, S., 503
Galef, B. G., 263
Galef, B. G., Jr., 249, 250
Galen, 470
Gall, F. J., 82
Gall, J. A., 182
Gallacher, J. E. J., 579
Gallagher, E. B., 601
Galperin, G. J., 487
Galton, F., 5, 37, 65, 138, 345, 355, 362, 363
Galvani, L., 73
Galzigna, L., 185
Gamarel, K. E., 612
Gamaro, G. D., 303
Gambone, J. C., 591
Gamma, A., 232
Gan, W. B., 72
Gana, K., 576
Ganchrow, J. R., 425
Gandhi, M., 379
Gandour, J., 422
Ganellen, R. J., 505
Gangestad, S., 458
Ganong, L., 121
Gansberg, M., 627
Garb, H. N., 452
Garber, H., 368
Garberoglio, C., 221
Garcia, C., 432
Garcia, D., 581
Garcia, E. E., 501
Garcia, J., 237, 244, 246
Garcia, L. A., 292

Garcia, L. T., 467
Garcia-Bajos, E., 282
Garcia-Larrea, L., 201
Garcia-Lopez, O., 350
Garcia-Vera, M. P., 579
Gardener, H., 96
Gardner, A., 336, 338–339
Gardner, B., 336
Gardner, B. T., 336
Gardner, C. O., 473
Gardner, D. G., 407
Gardner, H., 359, 361–362
Gardner, H. E., 469
Gardner, R., 210
Gardner, R. A., 336
Garelick, M. G., 218
Garfield, C. F., 523
Garfinkel, P. E., 585
Garfinkel, R., 554
Gargano, G. M., 618
Garlick, R., 616
Garmon, L. C., 128
Garnefski, N., 540
Garonzik, R., 94
Garrett, M. F., 288
Garrison, D. W., 188
Garry, P. J., 109
Garske, J. P., 555
Garza, R. T., 587
Gaskell, G. D., 271
Gater, R., 491
Gathercole, S. E., 295
Gaukroger, S., 4
Gauld, A. O., 221
Gaulin, P., 469
Gauvin, L., 389
Gavin, M. R., 259
Gawin, F. H., 230
Gay, P., 9
Gay, V., 3
Gazzaniga, M. S., 98–99
Gearhart, J. P., 395
Gebhard, T. H., 392
Gebhart, G. F., 86
Geen, R. G., 457
Geenen, F., 185, 572
Geffen, G., 95
Geffner, M. E., 111
Gehrig, P., 274
Geis, G., 629
Geiselman, R. E., 293
Gelb, S. A., 363
Gelernter, J., 495
Gellatly, A., 289
Geller, L., 470
Gempeler, J., 273
Genovese, K., 627–629
Gentilomo, A., 278
Gera, L., 185
Gergely, G., 263
Gerra, G., 471
Gerrard, M., 392
Gershoff, E. T., 254
Gerson, A., 112

Gerstein, E. D., 38
Gervais-Bernard, H., 545
Gescheider, G. A., 184
Geschwind, N., 92, 93
Gesn, P. R., 140
Gessa, G. L., 232
Gesten, E. L., 550
Getlin, J., 625
Gettman, L. R., 584
Gfellner, B. M., 135
Giacalone, R. A., 598
Giammanco, C. A., 618, 628
Giannakoulas, G., 229
Giarrusso, R., 109
Gibbons, B., 182
Gibbons, P., 487
Gibbs, E. D., 368
Gibbs, J. C., 128
Gibson, B., 467
Gibson, B. S., 165
Gibson, D. R., 583
Gibson, E. J., 116
Gibson, H. B., 222
Gibson, J. J., 165
Gidron, Y., 570
Giegling, I., 475
Giesler, G. J., 185
Gietl, A., 475
Giladi, E. E., 429
Gilbert, A. K., 186, 581
Gilbert, H. M., 586
Gilbert, R., 97
Gilbert, S. J., 622
Gilbert, T., 425
Gilberto, L. K. K., 86
Gilhooly, K. J., 312
Gill, T. V., 336
Gillam, B., 166
Gillberg, C., 523
Gillham, A., 408
Gilligan, C., 128, 133
Gillin, J. C., 289
Gillingham, S., 86
Gilman, S., 214
Gilman, S. E., 387
Ginandes, C., 221
Ginis, K. A. M., 68
Ginsberg, M., 21
Giovanni, G. D., 78
Giovannini, D., 424
Girandola, F., 620
Gisiner, R., 335
Gitau, R., 70
Gizer, I. R., 524
Glancy, G. D., 551
Gläscher, J., 320
Glaser, R., 221, 565, 571, 572, 573, 581
Glass, G. V., 554
Gleason, A., 584
Gleason, M. J., 70
Gleaves, D. H., 502
Gleiter, K., 135
Gleitman, H., 619

Glen, L., 590
Glenn, C. R., 241
Glenn, J., 617
Glennon, R. A., 230
Glick, P., 613
Glickstein, M., 86
Gliedman, J., 327
Gliner, M. D., 616
Gloor, P., 82
Glover, E., 21
Gluck, R., 101
Glucksberg, S., 316
Gobet, F., 275
Goble, A. K., 156
Godaert, G. L., 565
Goddard, C., 335
Goddard, H., 346, 352
Goddard, H. H., 363
Godde, B., 184
Godden, D. R., 289
Godemont, M., 530
Godfrey, C. N., 201
Goebel, B. L., 146, 379
Gogtay, N., 524
Gohm, C. L., 143
Goisman, R. M., 556
Gold, M. S., 231
Gold, P. E., 302, 303
Goldberg, M. A., 186
Goldberg, R. P., 169
Goldberger, Y., 493
Goldbloom, D. S., 389
Goldenberg, J. L., 469
Goldfarb, P., 318
Golding, J., 125
Golding, J. F., 189
Goldin-Meadow, S., 332
Goldman, D. L., 531
Goldman, H. H., 548
Goldman, M., 423
Goldman, R., 610
Goldman-Rakic, P. S., 524
Goldsmith, H. H., 139
Goldstein, A., 421
Goldstein, B. D., 185
Goldstein, I., 314
Goldstein, M. J., 517
Goldstein, S. R., 251
Golgi, C., 75
Golombek, D. A., 204
Golombok, S., 125, 398
Gomez, G. S., 543
Gomez, N., 457
Goncalves, M., 183
Gönenç, A., 511
Gonzago, K., 601
Gonzales, D., 588
Gonzales, M. H., 606
Gonzalez, A. B., 32
Gonzalez, R., 232, 369, 506
Gonzalez-Blanks, A. G., 587
Gonzalez-Campo, C., 419
González-Gallego, J., 26
Good, L., 385

Goodall, J., 33–34
Goodenough, F. L., 425
Goodey, E., 581
Goodman, G. S., 293
Goodman, J. S., 309
Goodman, W. K., 545
Goodnight, B. L., 614
Goodrick, G. K., 585
Goodson, S., 521
Goodwin, C. J., 7
Goodwin, G. M., 484
Goodwin, J. M., 501
Gooren, L. J. G., 624
Gopal A., 624
Gopaul-McNicol, S., 542
Gopnik, A., 166
Gordijn, E. H., 616
Gordon, I. E., 172
Gordon, P. M., 586
Gordon, W., 118
Gore, A., 155
Gorelick, P. B., 422
Gorenstein, C., 37
Goritsas, E., 133
Gorman, J., 328
Gorman, J. M., 546
Gorman, K. S., 358
Gorrese, A., 120
Gorunescu, F., 323
Gorunescu, M., 323
Gorwood, P., 517
Gosling, S. D., 14
Gosnell, B. A., 380
Gosselin, J. Y., 517
Gosselin, P., 424
Goswami, M., 214
Gotlib, I. H., 491, 504
Gottesman, I. I., 382, 484, 514
Gottfried, L., 1
Gottlieb, B. H., 543
Gould, R. A., 389
Gould, S. J., 354, 363, 364, 365
Gouzoulis-Mayfrank, E., 232
Govan, D. G., 169
Govern, J. M., 626
Gow, C. A., 92
Grace, M. S., 157
Graf, E. W., 158
Grafman, J., 92
Graham, A. L., 43
Graham, K., 625
Graham, M. J., 130, 404
Graham, T., 140
Granado, N., 230
Granland, S., 40
Granrud, C. E., 169
Grant, H. M., 289
Grant, I., 232
Grant-Webster, K. S., 174
Grattan, D. R., 69
Gratzer, T. G., 550
Graupner, L., 602
Graves, J., 618
Graves, P. L., 573

Graves, R., 422
Gravius, A., 78
Gravsky, E. L., 542
Graw, P., 503
Gray, H. M., 112
Gray, J. A., 78
Gray, J. J., 135, 385
Gray, M. M., 123
Grayson, C., 506
Greeff, A. P., 143
Green, C. D., 30, 312
Green, D. M., 180
Green, E. K., 511
Green, J. F., 210
Green, J. P., 222, 294
Green, S. B., 264
Greenberg, B. D., 497
Greenberg, J., 14, 446, 468, 611, 618
Greenberg, R., 114
Greenberg, R. P., 218, 451, 533
Greene, D., 405
Greene, E., 293
Greene, M. C., 461
Greene, R. L., 277
Greeno, C., 492
Greeno, J. G., 262
Greenough, A., 380
Greenough, W. T., 113, 137
Greenstein, Y., 36
Greenwood, J. D., 309
Greer, K. M., 334
Gregg, V. R., 128
Gregory, A. M., 62, 208
Gregory, C. M., 100
Greil, W., 547
Greist-Bousquet, S., 166
Gresty, M. A., 189
Grey, W., 194
Gribble, J. R., 121
Grice, D. E., 497
Griffies, W. S., 34
Griffin, D. W., 600
Griffin, M. J., 155, 189
Griggs, R. A., 190
Grigorenko, E. L., 360
Grimshaw, G. M., 308
Grisaru, N., 487
Grissom, R. J., 553
Griva, K., 582
Grob, A., 129
Grogan, S., 70
Gronau, N., 418
Grønli, J., 207
Gross, A. M., 227
Gross, C. G., 89
Gross, M., 217
Grossman, C. I., 583
Grossman, K. E., 120
Grossman, R. P., 607
Grossmann, K., 120
Grosz, R. D., 509
Grothe, B., 180
Grouios, G., 94
Grove, W. M., 520

Grover, B. L., 457
Gruber, R., 208
Gruber, S. A., 511
Gruder, C. L., 628
Gruen, L., 55
Grunberg, N. E., 420, 587
Grusec, J. E., 122, 254
Grutzendler, J., 72
Grygielski, M., 450
Grzybowski, E. B., 132
Guadagno, R. E., 621
Guarino, M., 619
Guarnaccia, P. J. J., 487, 491, 512
Guatt, G., 26
Guay, F., 406
Gubernskaya, Z., 142
Guègen, N., 429
Guerrien, A., 219
Guglielmo, K. M., 187
Guhu, N., 69
Guijarro, M. L., 569
Guilford, J. P., 319, 359
Guilford, P., 316
Guillaume Pelletier, J., 299
Guilleminault, C., 216
Guillotin, J. I., 220
Gulevich, G., 210
Gulgoz, S., 347
Gump, B. B., 570
Gunderson, J. G., 519
Gunderson, V. M., 174
Gunter, T. D., 62
Gunther, L. M., 261
Gur, R. E., 516
Gurbani, M. N., 95
Gurin, J., 585
Gurman, A. S., 543
Gust, S. W., 587
Gustafson, S. B., 316
Gustavson, A. R., 237
Gustavson, C. R., 237
Gustavsson, G., 43
Gutheil, T. G., 34, 550
Guthrie, C., 382
Guthrie, J., 145
Guttman, S. R., 9

Haake, P., 391
Haar, M. D., 580
Haber, R. N., 169
Haber, S. N., 497
Habert, M. O., 84
Hadjikhani, N., 152, 158
Hadley, J., 54
Häffner, H., 512
Hagan, A. C., 36
Hagan, L. D., 36
Hager, M., 397
Hagerty, M. R., 379
Hagopian, L. P., 250, 537
Hahn, C. G., 547
Haidt, J., 426
Haier, R. J., 514
Haight, B. K., 145

Haight, J. C., 281
Haimowitz, C., 543
Hains, S. M. J., 111
Haist, F., 177
Halasz, J., 545
Hald, G. M., 35
Hale, J. L., 605
Hales, S., 71–72
Halford, G. S., 117
Hall, C. S., 216
Hall, D., 251, 404
Hall, G. C. N., 457, 531
Hall, G. S., 6, 54, 108, 129, 192
Hall, J. D., 20, 87, 624
Hall, L. K., 275
Hall, M., 212, 590
Hall, S., 166, 192
Hall, V. C., 405
Hall, W., 232, 257, 625
Hall, W. A., 213
Hallenbeck, B. A., 263
Haller, J., 545, 624
Hallet, A. J., 569
Halligan, P. W., 223, 500
Halliwell, G., 472
Halmi, K. A., 387
Halpern, D., 94
Halpern, D. F., 50, 96–97, 138, 141
Halpern, L., 180
Halvorson, B. J., 141
Hamann, S. B., 419
Hamarman, S., 122
Hamburg, P., 387
Hamburger, Y., 614
Hamel, R., 313
Hamer, D. H., 395, 396
Hamill, R., 321
Hamilton, L., 95
Hamilton, M. C., 334
Hamilton, R. H., 121, 184
Hammack, S. E., 257
Hammeke, T. A., 91
Hammen, C., 563
Hammer, A. L., 455
Hammerman-Rozenberg, R., 137
Hammersley, R., 232
Hammersmith, S. J., 398
Hammond, G., 93
Hampson, E., 140
Hampstead, B. M., 87
Hamson-Utley, J. J., 20
Han, D. H., 92
Han, J.-S., 187
Han, W.-J., 123
Hancock, D. J., 263, 461
Hando, J., 232
Haney, P., 468
Hankins, M., 565
Hanley, S. J., 378, 470
Hanna, G., 137
Hannich, H.-J., 145
Hansen, C. H., 425
Hansen, K., 128
Hansen, L., 238

Hansen, R. D., 425
Hanson, R. K., 456, 564
Happel, R. L., 499
Hara, N., 168
Harbach, H., 79
Harbin, D., 162
Harbin, G., 162
Hardman, E., 289
Hardy, C. J., 618
Hardy, L., 409
Hare, R. D., 520
Har-Even, D., 446
Hargie, O., 598
Hari, R., 273
Hariri, A. R., 419
Harlow, H. F., 119–120
Harlow, J. M., 92
Harman, M. J., 542
Harmon-Jones, E., 611, 624
Haroutunian, V., 101
Harper, D. C., 188
Harper, S., 361
Harriman, A., 238
Harrington, D. M., 317, 319
Harrington, R., 455
Harris, C. R., 63, 400, 530
Harris, E., 1
Harris, E. G., 454
Harris, J. A., 475
Harris, J. M., 169
Harris, L., 96
Harris, L. J., 94
Harris, M. J., 42
Harris, R. B., 587
Harris, R. L., 145
Harris, W. H., 485
Harrison, A. A., 601, 606
Harrison, D. W., 259
Harrison, P. J., 387
Hart, D., 311
Hart, R., 469
Harter, J. K., 427
Hartley, J., 311
Hartmann, E., 216, 475
Hartmann, U., 391
Hartshorne, H., 458
Hartup, W. W., 124
Hartwell, E. E., 542
Harvey, E. N., 206
Harvey, R. D., 213, 462
Harvey, T., 83
Harwood, C., 408
Hasebe, S., 158
Hasegawa, T., 34
Hasher, L., 281
Hashimoto, M., 513
Haskett, R. F., 624
Haslam, N., 398
Hassani, O. K., 208
Hassett, J., 73
Hatazawa, J., 84
Hatfield, E., 604, 606
Hatfield, G., 2, 39
Hathaway, S. R., 455

Hatira, P., 188
Hatton, C., 352
Hattori, T., 88
Hatzichristou, D. G., 314
Hatzimanolis, J., 545
Hauck, C., 222
Haupt, S., 88
Hausenblas, H. A., 619
Hauser, K., 308
Hautamaeki, J., 360
Hawker, D. S., 578
Hawkes, N., 607
Hawkins, D. L., 33, 188
Hawkins, M. J., 469
Hawkins, W. E., 469
Hawkins, W. G., 237
Haxby, J. V., 160
Hay, P. J., 388
Hayashi, S., 541
Hayashi-Takagi, A., 72
Hayden, T., 458
Hayes, A. F., 465
Hayes, C., 335–336
Hayes, D. S., 296
Hayes, K., 335–336
Hayes, L. J., 241
Hayes, R. L., 86
Hayflick, L., 137
Hayhoe, M. M., 159
Hayhurst, H., 540
Haykin, S., 86
Haynes, O. M., 425
Haynes, T., 189
Hays, J. R., 550
Hays, R. D., 590
Hays, W. S. T., 183
Haythornthwaite, J. A., 589
Hayward, C., 496
Haywood, C. S., 420
Haywood, H. C., 351
Hazelrigg, P. J., 43
Hazlett-Stevens, H., 492
He, J. C., 164
He, Z.-X., 508
Head, J., 578
Hearne, K. M., 191
Hearnshaw, L., 608
Hearnshaw, L. S., 3, 366
Hearst, E., 247
Heath, D. T., 144
Heath, G. W., 586
Heath, S., 53
Heatherton, T. F., 387
Heaton, P., 343
Heaven, P. C. L., 614
Heavey, L., 344
Hebb, D. O., 399–400
Hébert, M., 502
Hebert, R., 469
Hebl, M. R., 387
Hechinger, N., 185
Hecht, M. A., 50–51
Hedges, L. V., 32
Hedges, S. M., 427

Heffner, H. E., 178
Hegarty, P., 63
Hehl, F. J., 431
Heidelberger, M., 5
Heider, F., 596
Heider, K., 433
Heijnen, C. J., 565, 574
Heilman, K. M., 181, 435
Heimberg, R. G., 483
Heinberg, L. J., 385
Heine, L. W., 187
Heine, M. K., 288, 470
Heine, S. J., 174
Heinrich, H., 614
Heinrichs, R. W., 516
Heisel, A. D., 624
Heitzmann, C. A., 578
Helgeson, V. S., 579
Hellekant, G., 183
Helmes, E., 457
Helmholtz, H. von, 4, 163, 165, 167, 178
Hemmes, N. S., 240
Hemsley, D. R., 78
Henderson, J., 524
Henderson, L. P., 624
Henderson, P. W., 181
Hendrick, C., 45
Hendrickson, A. E., 159
Hendrickson, K. M., 501
Hendriks, A. A. J., 455
Hendrix, S., 145
Henle, M., 9
Henley, S. H., 451
Hennig, J., 79, 421
Henningfield, J. E., 587
Hennrikus, D. J., 587
Henrich, J., 174
Henry, E., 68
Hepper, P. G., 94
Herbert, T. B., 572
Herbert, W., 456, 485
Herek, G. M., 613
Hergenhahn, B. R., 447
Hergovich, A., 323
Hering, E., 163
Herkenhahn, M., 231
Herman, C. P., 388, 389
Herman, D., 548
Herman, L. M., 335
Hermann, D. H., 550
Hermelin, B., 343, 344
Hernandez, D., 404
Hernandez, J. M., 189
Hernandez, M., 464
Hernandez, M. L., 232
Hernandez-Reif, M., 70
Herning, R. I., 82
Heron, W., 401
Herrera, I., 387
Herrero, J. V., 422
Herrmann, T., 7
Herrnstein, R. J., 363, 364, 370
Herry, C., 419

Hershberger, S., 396
Hershenson, D. B., 82
Hertenstein, M. J., 184
Herter, C. J., 192
Hertwig, R., 54
Hertz, H., 175
Hertz, L., 71
Hertzog, C., 137, 141
Herz, R. S., 182
Herzog, D. B., 387
Hesley, J. W., 459
Hess, L., 258
Hessel, A., 498
Heston, L., 520
Heston, L. L., 397
Hetherington, A. W., 381
Hetherington, C. R., 92
Hettema, J. M., 492, 493
Hetz, S., 68
Heuer, F., 173
Heuser, I., 584
Hewitt, E. C., 224
Hewitt, J. K., 384
Hewitt, P. L., 508
Hewlett, B. S., 119
Hewson-Bower, B., 581
Heyes, C. M., 263
Heywood, C., 258
Hezlett, S. A., 37
Hickok, G., 263
Hicks, A. U., 101
Hicks, R. A., 96, 209
Hidaka, B., 505
Higami, Y., 137
Higashiyama, A., 169
Higbee, G., 534
Higgins, D. M., 317
Higgins, E. T., 401, 469, 492, 618
Higgins, J. E., 579
Higgins, S. T., 587
Highet, A., 451
Hilgard, E., 5, 472
Hilgard, E. R., 220, 223
Hill, C. E., 423
Hill, D. R., 576
Hill, J. L., 123
Hill, J. O., 384
Hill, K. T., 400
Hill, R. D., 298
Hill, S. A., 520
Hiller, J. B., 516
Hillerbrand, J., 180
Hillix, W. A., 422
Hillson, T. R., 430
Hilmert, C. J., 578
Hilsenroth, M. J., 311, 556
Hilt, L. M., 506
Hilts, V. L., 471
Hinchy, J., 262
Hinckley, J. Jr., 486, 487
Hinds, J. E., 587
Hines, M., 111, 125, 140
Hines, T. M., 204
Hinton, D. E., 489

I-12 Name Index

Hippocrates, 80, 470, 482, 530, 574
Hirata, Y., 177
Hirsch, H. V. B., 173
Hirschberger, G., 468
Hirshkowitz, M., 213
Hirt, E. R., 468, 599
Hitler, A., 27
Hittner, J. B., 457
Hitzig, E., 88
Hixon, J. G., 144
Hixson, M. D., 20
Ho, I. K., 228
Ho, S. Y., 603
Hoag, M. J., 554
Hobart, G. A., 206
Hobbes, T., 430
Hobson, C. J., 562
Hobson, J. A., 214, 215, 219, 220
Hochhausen, N. M., 518
Hocking-Schuler, J. L., 574
Hodes, R. L., 417
Hodge, C. N., 602
Hodges, H., 101
Hodgins, H. S., 423
Hodgins, S., 513
Hodgkin, A., 73
Hoefnagels, C., 627
Hoek, A., 70, 387, 388
Hoeksema-van Orden, C. Y. D., 618
Hoemann, H. W., 286
Hofbauer, R. K., 223
Hoffman, C., 335
Hoffman, D., 343, 344
Hoffman, H. G., 293
Hoffman, J. M., 419
Hoffman, N., 377
Hoffmann, R. F., 504
Hofmann, A., 230–231
Hofstee, W. K. B., 455
Hogan, H. P., 333
Hogan, J. D., 36
Hogben, M., 264
Hogg, A., 248
Hoglund, W., 549
Hoksbergen, R. A. C., 350
Holahan, C. J., 356
Holahan, C. K., 356
Holden, C., 55, 455, 473, 474, 485, 503
Holden, J. M., 449
Holding, D. H., 250
Holland, C. R., 349, 610
Holland, D., 168, 457
Holland, K. J., 34, 121
Holland, L. N., 185
Holland, P. C., 241
Hollender, M. H., 392
Hollingworth, L. S., 138, 355, 362
Hollins, M., 156
Hollis, C., 122
Hollist, C. S., 45
Hollon, S. D., 553
Holm, L., 358
Holmes, A., 586

Holmes, D. S., 145
Holmes, J. D., 2
Holmes, J. G., 143, 600
Holmes, T. H., 562, 563
Holowka, S., 332
Holroyd, J., 221
Holt, J., 214
Holt, R. I. G., 69
Holtgraves, T., 321, 327
Holton, B., 203
Holton, R., 27
Homa, D., 311
Homan, C. P., 423
Homan, R. W., 422
Homburger, E., 132
Homburger, T., 132
Homer, 217
Honda, K., 210
Hong, S., 581
Hong, Y.-Y., 597
Honorton, C., 192
Honts, C. R., 417, 418
Honzik, C. H., 263
Hood, K. E., 377
Hooduin, C. A. L., 556
Hooduin, K. A. L., 500
Hooker, K., 462
Hooley, J. M., 516
Hoover, J. E., 392
Hope, D. A., 506, 602
Hopkins, J. R., 132
Hopkinson, C. A., 579
Hoppes, E., 514
Hops, H., 608
Horan, J. J., 580
Hore, J., 86
Horesh, N., 493
Horii, K., 160
Hormuth, S. E., 463
Horn, J. L., 359
Horn, J. M., 66, 367, 473
Horn, T. S., 408
Horne, J. A., 209
Horner, M. D., 280
Horney, K., 449, 451–452
Hornstein, S. L., 270
Horowitz, F. D., 11
Horowitz, S. W., 418, 603
Horrey, W. J., 201
Horsley, R. R., 251
Hortensius, R., 624
Horton, R. S., 603
Hosch, H. M., 291
Hoskins, R., 467
Hosoda, M., 602
Hou, C., 343
Houlihan, D. D., 535
House, J. D., 350
Hovland, C. I., 609
Howard, K. I., 555
Howard, R., 177
Howarth, H. V. C., 189
Howe, M., 287
Howell, R. J., 158

Howland, E. W., 520
Hoy, K., 81
Hoyer, W. D., 430
Hoyles, S. G., 124
Hsiao, S., 380
Hsieh, K. H., 144
Hsu, F. L. K., 605
Hsu, L. G., 386
Hsu, L. K. G., 498
Hu, L. W., 37
Hu, S., 189, 396, 397
Huang, A., 387
Huang, L., 431
Huang, S., 108, 142
Huang, W., 354
Hubbard, L. R., 155
Hubel, D., 173
Hubel, D. H., 167
Huber, A., 223
Huber, R. J., 501
Huber, T., 232
Huberfeld, G., 84
Hublin, C., 209
Hudis, C. A., 243
Hudziak, J. J., 65
Huebner, R. R., 425
Huffcutt, A. I., 205
Huffman, M. L. C., 292
Hugdahl, K., 97
Hughes, B. M., 155
Hughes, C. A., 257
Hughes, J., 41, 79
Hughes, J. R., 43, 229, 564, 587
Hui, K. K. S., 186
Hui-Chan, C. W. Y., 324
Hulicka, I. M., 146
Hull, C. L., 377
Hull, J. G., 227
Hultsch, D. F., 141
Hume, D., 238
Humphrey, J. A., 625
Humphreys, K., 543
Humphreys, L., 516
Humphreys, M. S., 404
Hundleby, J. D., 135
Hunsberger, B., 133
Hunsley, J., 456
Hunt, D. D., 536
Hunt, E., 359
Hunt, E. L., 244
Hunt, W. C., 109
Hunter, G. A., 308
Hunter, J. E., 70, 349, 404, 602
Hunter, K. W., 241
Huopainen, H., 499
Hur, J., 250
Hur, Y.-M., 66, 379, 475
Hurewitz, A., 579
Hurst, L. C., 344
Hursti, T. J., 581
Hurvich, L. M., 163
Husain, S. A., 508
Husband, A. J., 212
Huston, A. C., 264

Huston, T. L., 629
Hutchinson, I., 183
Huttenlocher, J., 138
Huttenlocher, P. R., 99
Huxley, A., 242
Huxley, A. F., 73
Hviid, A., 522
Hyde, J. S., 50, 128, 135, 138, 139, 141, 334, 393, 398, 424, 468
Hyland, B., 89
Hyman, R. B., 469
Hymowitz, N., 574
Hystad, S. W., 578

Iacono, W. G., 62, 123, 223, 387, 388, 418, 475, 514
Ibrahim, S. A., 590
Ickes, W., 140
Idzikowski, C., 210
Iijima, M., 83
Ilies, R., 475
Ilmoniemi, R. J., 81
Imada, T., 438
Imaginário, S., 317
Imahori, T. T., 605
Imber, S. D., 554
Immergluck, L., 27
Inciardi, J. A., 228
Ingelfinger, F. J., 380
Ingham, A. G., 618
Ingraham, L. J., 514
Ingram, D. H., 451
Ingram, J. L., 522
Innis, N. K., 7
Inomata, Y., 211
Inoue, D., 282
Inouye, S., 210
Insko, C. A., 607, 614
Invernizzi, M. A., 281
Iqbal, H. M., 132
Irnich, D., 186
Ironson, G., 572
Irvine, C., 451
Irwin, H. J., 465
Irwin, M., 212
Isaac, M. K., 505
Isaac, W., 259
Isaacs, K. R., 137
Isen, A. M., 320
Ishai, A., 160
Ishida, T., 582
Ishimatsu, K., 582
Ishizawa, Y., 86
Ispa, J. M., 123
Issakidis, C., 495
Isurin, L., 286
Itard, J., 308
Itoh, Y., 291
Itsukushima, Y., 291
Iversen, I. H., 248
Ivry, G. B., 39
Ivtzan, I., 469
Iwasaki, T., 289
Iwata, B. A., 253

Name Index I-13

Iwata, M., 83
Iyengar, S. S., 405, 464
Izard, C. E., 422, 423, 425, 435, 438

Jabalpurwala, S., 389
Jaccard, J., 43
Jack, S. J., 406
Jacklin, C. N., 125, 138, 141
Jackson, B., 575
Jackson, G. R., 162, 493
Jackson, J. S., 615
Jackson, L. A., 602
Jackson, R. R., 312
Jacob, S., 20
Jacobs, G. H., 163
Jacobs, J. R., 574
Jacobs, J. W. G., 572
Jacobs, L., 208, 505
Jacobs, W. J., 239, 501
Jacobsen, B., 514
Jacobsen, P., 41
Jacobsen, P. B., 243
Jacobson, A. L., 301
Jacobson, E., 581
Jacobson, L., 42
Jaencke, L., 89
Jaffee, S., 128
Jalleh, G., 322
James, W., 2, 7, 8, 10, 11, 13, 27–28, 35, 61, 113, 114, 192, 199, 200, 201, 203, 239, 247, 271, 276, 280, 281, 282, 283, 294, 296, 309, 376, 404, 432, 466
James, W. S., 550
James I, 586
Jamieson, D., 603
Janca, A., 498
Jancke, L., 95
Jang, K. L., 475, 493, 495
Janicki, D., 579
Janis, I., 617
Janne, P., 576
Janoff-Bulman, R., 429
Jansen, E. A., 625
Jarvis, M. J., 229
Jason, L. A., 384
Jasper, S., 250
Jastreboff, A. M., 385
Jayanthi, S., 230
Jaywant, A., 422
Jean-Francois, B., 355
Jeffery, R. W., 383, 586, 587
Jeffrey, S. A., 378
Jeffries, S., 144
Jegede, J. O., 403
Jegede, R. T., 403
Jemmott, J. B., 572, 578
Jenkins, C., 425
Jenkins, J. G., 285, 286
Jenkins, S. J., 20
Jennings, D. A., 391
Jensen, A. J., 369
Jensen, A. R., 350, 364–365
Jensen, K. P., 492, 493

Jensh, R. P., 352
Jensvold, M. L. A., 339
Jeo, R. M., 160
Jeste, D. V., 512
Jetha, A., 68
Jewell, R., 464
Jeynes, W. H., 135
Jezzard, P., 308
Jhamandas, J. H., 300
Jiang, Y., 78
Jibotian, K. S., 334
Jiminez-Murcia, S., 538
Jin, R., 491
Jinks, A. L., 183
Jocklin, O., 473
Joensson, E. G., 475
Johns, M., 351
Johnson, C., 96, 209
Johnson, D. L., 176, 222, 474, 539, 550
Johnson, D. M., 447, 519
Johnson, E., 561
Johnson, J., 20, 112, 352
Johnson, J. S., 330
Johnson, K. A., 117
Johnson, L., 210, 364
Johnson, L. J., 317
Johnson, S. B., 482
Johnson, S. E., 603
Johnson, V. E., 335, 390–391, 393–394
Johnson, W., 475
Johnston, J. H., 580
Johnston, K., 125
Johnston, M., 112, 589
Johnston, M. V., 100
Johnston, V. S., 322
Joireman, J., 457
Jonas, G., 258
Jones, B. E., 208
Jones, B. P., 512
Jones, C., 221, 497
Jones, C. J., 469
Jones, E. E., 467, 607
Jones, F. W., 26
Jones, J. E., 517
Jones, J. H., 392
Jones, K. D., 489
Jones, L., 201
Jones, L. V., 369
Jones, M. C., 243, 534, 538
Jones, M. M., 499
Jones, P., 494
Jones, R. N., 535
Jones, R. T., 277
Jones, S., 66
Jongbloet, P. H., 515
Jonik, R. H., 624
Jooste, P., 210
Joraschky, P., 182
Jordan, C., 361
Jordan, M., 423
Jorenby, D. E., 587
Jorgensen, R. S., 574

Joseph, S., 500, 505, 541
Josephs, R. A., 227
Joslyn, S., 446
Jouen, F., 114
Jouriles, E. N., 543
Jousselin-Hosaja, M., 102
Joustie, M., 216
Jouvent, R., 402
Joyce, J., 199–200
Joynson, R. B., 366
Judd, C. M., 599, 616
Judge, S. J., 168
Judge, T. A., 463, 475
Juergensen, M. R., 260
Juffer, F., 121
Julien, R. M., 231
Jung, C., 10, 447, 449–450, 453
Jungeblut, A., 349
Jusczyk, P. W., 114
Jussim, L., 596
Jyvasjarvi, E., 185

Kaell, A., 580
Kaffarnik, H., 421
Kagan, J., 364, 471
Kahan, T. L., 217
Kahle, L. R., 490
Kahn, C., 70
Kahn, D., 53
Kahn, S., 577, 578
Kahneman, D., 320, 321, 322
Kail, R., 275
Kakihara, C., 597
Kako, E., 338
Kalafat, J., 509
Kalakoski, V., 294
Kalaska, J. F., 188
Kalbfleisch, M. L., 15
Kalichman, S. C., 583
Kalin, R., 613
Kalina, R. E., 159
Kalish, C., 310
Kallikak, M., 352
Kalman, B., 75
Kalra, J., 70
Kaltiala-Heino, R., 131
Kalueff, A. V., 78
Kamarck, T. W., 578
Kameenui, E. J., 294
Kamen-Siegel, L., 575
Kamin, L. J., 366
Kaminsky, S., 475
Kamisada, M., 513
Kamp-Becker, I., 314
Kanarek, R. B., 599
Kanda, M., 185
Kandel, E. R., 298–299
Kanekar, S., 607
Kanesaka, T., 88
Kang, L., 21
Kanjorski, J., 431
Kanner, L., 521
Kanninen, K., 445
Kanof, P. D., 101

Kansaku, K., 95
Kant, I., 4, 430
Kantor, G. K., 255
Kaplan, M., 578
Kaprio, J., 209
Karalis, N., 419
Karama S., 87
Karanth, K. S., 289
Karau, S. J., 618
Karcher, M. J., 449
Karhu, J., 81
Karkow, B., 216
Karlberg, L., 570
Karlin, B. E., 540
Karlov, A. V., 210
Karmel, R., 230
Karnavas, W. J., 162
Karnes, M. B., 317
Karney, B. R., 144
Karnovsky, M. L., 212
Karon, B. P., 287
Karp, D. E., 356
Kasai, H., 72
Kashima, E. S., 335
Kashima, Y., 335, 598
Kaspar, C. H., 401, 581
Kasparov, G., 323
Kassel, J. D., 229
Kasser, T., 606
Kassin, S. M., 291
Kasthuri, N., 72
Katata, K., 84
Katkin, E. S., 437
Kato, T., 493
Katramados, A., 229
Katter, J. T., 185
Katz, J., 109
Katz, J. L., 377
Katz, M., 187
Katz, N., 606
Katzman, M. A., 387
Kauffman, J. M., 263
Kauffman, T., 184
Kaufman, F. R., 111
Kaufman, I., 172
Kaufman, J. C., 316
Kaufman, L., 273
Kaufmann, C., 200
Kavounoudias, A., 184
Kavšek, M., 169
Kawachi, I., 576
Kawakami, K., 613
Kawamura, T., 596
Kayne, N. T., 505
Kazemi-Bajestani, S. M. R., 482
Kazén, M., 450
Keane, M. M., 279
Keast, A., 292
Keats, B. J. B., 396
Kebbell, M. R., 21
Kedem, P., 493
Keegan, D., 429
Keegan, J., 112
Keel, P. K., 388

I-14   Name Index

Keeler, G., 485
Keen, R., 115
Keenan, J. P., 184
Keenan, R., 587
Keesey, R. E., 381
Keijsers, G. P. J., 500, 556
Keil, K., 174
Keiley, M. K., 123
Keilis-Borok, V., 32
Keillor, J. M., 435
Keith, B., 124
Keith, J. R., 263
Keller, F. S., 12
Keller, H., 120
Keller, L., 376
Keller, S. E., 571, 581
Kelley, H. H., 26, 596, 597, 600
Kelley, M., 564
Kelling, A. S., 255
Kellogg, J. H., 392
Kellogg, L., 335
Kellogg, W., 335
Kellow, J. T., 355
Kelly, I. W., 482
Kelly, J. F., 461
Kelly, K. E., 210
Kelly, M. P., 393
Kelly, R. B., 582
Kelly, S. J., 343
Kelly, W. E., 210
Kelsoe, J. R., 510
Keltner, D., 424, 426
Kelvin, L. K. H., 86
Kemeny, M. E., 598
Kemp, B., 68
Kemper, H. C. G., 565
Kemper, T. L., 522
Kempter, G., 540
Kemp-Wheeler, S. M., 556
Kenardy, J., 494
Kendall, E., 63
Kendler, K. S., 382, 473, 492, 504, 514
Kendzierski, D., 464
Kenneally, S. M., 308
Kennedy, J. F., 270, 580, 608–609
Kennedy, J. F., Jr., 270
Kennedy, P., 67
Kennedy, R. F., 500
Kenrick, D. T., 458, 470, 606
Keppel, R. D., 465
Kerkhoff, G., 60
Kern, D., 428
Kerns, R. D., 185
Kerr, N. L., 617
Kerr, Z. Y., 542
Kerzhnerman, I., 385
Keske, C. M., 286
Kessler, R. C., 45, 481, 489, 491, 493, 494, 495, 497, 503, 507, 510, 522, 523
Kessler, S., 490
Kety, S. S., 514
Kevles, D. J., 397

Khalife, S., 393
Kharazmi, S., 430
Khazanchi, S., 320
Khire, U., 350
Khouri, H., 600
Kidd, J. A., 31
Kiecolt-Glaser, J. K., 70, 221, 565, 571, 572, 573, 574, 581
Kiefer, S. C., 598
Kiernan, B. D., 188
Kihlstrom, J. F., 201, 223
Kikuchi, M., 361
Kilborn, L. C., 494
Killen, J. D., 496
Kilmartin, C. T., 447
Kilts, C. D., 419
Kim, D., 68
Kim, H. S., 579
Kim, J., 240, 302, 568
Kim, J. E., 145
Kim, J. H., 37
Kim, J. Y., 446
Kim, K., 244
Kim, M. U., 617, 620
Kim, Y. H., 598
Kim, Y. I., 543
Kim, Y. S., 92
Kimball, M. M., 139, 529
Kimble, D. P., 301
Kimble, G. A., 245
Kimchi, R., 151
Kim-Cohen, J., 473
Kimeldorf, D. J., 244
Kim-Phuong, L. V., 14
Kimura, D., 140, 141
Kimura, R., 300
Kincades, M. J., 60
King, D. B., 8, 406
King, D. J., 210, 579, 584
King, M. G., 212
King, N. J., 496
King, T., 118
Kinney-Hurd, B. L., 241
Kinsey, A. C., 392–393
Kirchner, J., 603
Kircher, J. C., 418
Kircher, J. R., 393
Kirkley, B. G., 567
Kirmayer, L. J., 549
Kirmeyer, S. L., 569
Kirouac, G., 424
Kirsch, I., 186
Kirschner, S. M., 487
Kirschvink, J. L., 152
Kirshnit, C. E., 313
Kisch, J., 248
Kisilevsky, B. S., 111
Kisler, T. S., 212
Kisner, M. J., 3
Kit, B. K., 382
Kitano, S., 169
Kitayama, S., 428, 462, 470, 596, 598
Kitazawa, S., 95
Kittlerova, P., 101

Kittrell, D., 145
Kjellgren, A., 401
Klaening, U., 515
Klahr, A. M., 123
Klar, Y., 429
Klausen, B. S., 102
Klebanov, P. K., 349, 365
Klebold, D., 1
Kleiber, C., 188
Kleimann, M., 34
Klein, A. G., 355
Klein, D. F., 493, 554
Klein, D. N., 322, 524
Klein, M., 10
Klein, P. D., 468
Klein, S. B., 391
Kleindienst, N., 547
Kleinke, C. L., 435
Kleinknecht, R. A., 495
Kleinmuntz, B., 416–418
Kleitman, N., 207–208
Klepac, R. K., 535
Klimesch, W., 279
Klineberg, E., 578
Kling, K. C., 139, 468
Klohnen, E. C., 603
Klonoff, E. A., 499, 589
Klosterhalfen, S., 257
Klosterhalfen, W., 257
Kluft, R. P., 502
Klug, M. G., 110
Klump, K. L., 387, 388, 389
Klusmann, V., 584
Klüver, H., 88
Kmiecik-Malecka, E., 36
Knafo, A., 455
Knapp, T. J., 248
Knebel, T., 188
Knee, C. R., 322, 598
Knestel, A., 35
Kniffki, K. D., 185
Knight, J., 601
Knishkowy, B., 587
Knopman, D. S., 302
Knouse, S. B., 598
Knox, S. S., 578
Knudsen, E. I., 180
Knuutila, J., 273
Kobasa, S. C., 577
Kobayakawa, T., 184
Kocan, E. R., 311
Koch, G., 300
Kocsis, R. N., 465
Koed, K., 510
Koehler, J. J., 26
Koelling, R. A., 246
Koeske, R. D., 280
Koester, E. P., 279
Koestner, R., 405
Koff, E., 420
Koffka, K., 9, 166
Kogan, N., 616
Kohlberg, L., 126–128
Köhler, W., 9, 14, 166, 313

Kohnken, G., 293
Koivisto, A.-M., 131
Kojetin, B. A., 65
Kolata, G., 330, 383
Kolinsky, R., 177
Kolligian, J., Jr., 469
Kollmeier, B., 178
Komisaruk, B. R., 84
Komoda, Y., 210
Konnert, C., 144
Kontinen, V. K., 185
Koole, S. L., 14
Kooy, R. F., 352
Kop, W. J., 96
Kopaneva, I., 601
Kopell, B. H., 545
Kopelman, M. D., 501
Kopp, M., 401
Koppe, S., 75
Kopta, S. M., 555
Kordower, J. H., 102
Koretz, J., 34
Korn, J. H., 53
Korpi, E. R., 227
Korsnes, M. S., 283
Kortenkamp, S., 435
Koskenvuo, M., 209
Koss, M., 35
Kossowsky, J., 493
Koster, E. H. W., 418
Kosterlitz, H., 79
Kosugi, M., 361
Kotagal, S., 213
Kotler, M., 493
Kotz, D., 229
Kotz, S. A., 422, 423
Kouider, S., 154
Koukourakis, M., 83
Koutstaal, W., 282
Kovac, S. H., 146
Kovar, K. A., 232
Kowalski, R. M., 34, 598, 625
Kozak, J. T., 43
Kozaki, Y., 185
Kozub, S. A., 461
Kposowa, A. J., 508
Kraaimaat, F. W., 543, 572
Kraemer, H., 389
Kraeplin, E., 488, 512
Krafka, C., 293
Kraft, M., 457
Krakau, I., 570
Kral, A. H., 508
Kralikova, E., 43
Kramer, A. F., 136, 202
Kramer, D. E., 312
Kramer, R. M., 615
Krantz, D. S., 562, 568, 575
Krasner, L., 516
Krauchi, K., 503
Kraus, S. J., 610
Krause, J. S., 68
Krauss, D. H., 469
Krausse, M., 555

Name Index I-15

Kravits, K., 221
Kravitz, D. A., 618
Kreisman, J. J., 519
Kremer, T. G., 550
Kreppner, K., 346
Krestensen, K. K., 543
Kretch, K. S., 116
Kretschmer, E., 471
Krichmar, J. L., 324
Kring, A. M., 513
Kringlen, E., 496, 514
Krings, F., 129
Krinsky, R., 297
Krinsky, S. G., 297
Krippner, S., 191, 193, 217
Krishnan, H. S., 429
Krishnan, R. V., 99
Kristbjanarson, H., 510
Kroenke, K., 498
Kroger, R. O., 7
Kroll, J., 626, 627, 629
Kropp, P., 257
Krueger, J. I., 470
Krueger, J. M., 212
Krueger, T. H. C., 391
Krupa, D. J., 299
Krupat, E., 429, 590
Kubzansky, L. D., 576
Kuck, J., 512
Kudo, F. T., 122
Kuehberger, A., 322
Kuelbelbeck, A., 107
Kugihara, N., 618
Kuhl, E. A., 489
Kuhl, J., 450
Kuhlman, D. M., 457
Kuhlman, T. L., 431
Kuhlmann, H., 12
Kuhn, C., 569
Kuhn, C. M., 70
Kuhn, T. S., 13
Kukla, A., 31
Kulick, W., 431
Kulik, J., 270
Kulik, J. A., 589
Kulka, R., 403
Kulkarni, J., 81
Kumar, A., 285
Kumar, K. B., 289, 572
Kumari, V., 78
Kumkale, G. T., 609
Kuncel, N. R., 47
Kunda, Z., 599
Kundiger, E., 139
Kunkel, D., 264
Kunkel, E., 264
Kuo, L. E., 78
Kupán, K., 263
Kupfer, D. J., 489
Kuppers, J. R., 239
Kurdek, L. A., 143, 144
Kuriki, S., 177
Kurokawa, M., 428
Kurtz, D. A., 133

Kuzuhara, S., 84
Kwee, M., 538

La Roche, M., 533
La Vaque, T. J., 81
Labar, K. S., 15
Labbe, E. E., 494
LaBerge, S., 217
Laberge-Nadeau, C., 167
Labouvie, G. V., 109
Labrador, F. J., 579
Labrecque, R., 177
LaCasse, L., 520
Lachman, M. E., 579
Ladd-Franklin, C., 8
Lader, M., 228
Ladewig, J., 263
LaDuke, J. R., 612
LaFrance, B. H., 624
LaFrance, M., 50–51
Lai, L., 100
Laing, D. G., 183
Laing, R. D., 517
Laird, J. D., 435
Laitinen, J., 385
Lake, A. E., III, 185
Lake, C. R., 517
Lakkis, J., 387
Lal, S., 17
Lalancette, M. F., 620
Lalumiere, M. L., 396
Lam, D. C. K., 32
Lam, R. W., 507
Lam, S. S. K., 461
Lamb, M. E., 119, 120, 123, 124, 548
Lamb, T., 73
Lambdin, J. R., 334
Lambert, B. J., 205
Lambert, E., 553
Lambert, M. J., 184, 556
Lambert, N. M., 349
Lambert, S. M., 408
Lamberth, J., 30, 603
Lamme, V. A. F., 165
Lamon, S. J., 50, 138, 139
Lanciano, T., 270
Landberg, I., 328
Landeau, B., 279
Landeira-Fernandez, J., 185
Landers, A., 503
Landesman, S., 352
Landis, D., 605
Landis, T., 422
Lando, H. A., 587
Landolt, A. S., 221
Landolt, H. P., 229
Landon, A., 36
Landrine, H., 490, 589
Landwehr, R. F., 295
Landy, F. J., 5
Lane, S. D., 232
Laner, M. R., 630
Lang, P. J., 414, 433
Langbehn, D. R., 499

Lange, C., 432
Lange, K. W., 200
Langenbucher, J. W., 28
Langer, A. W., 574
Langer, E. J., 576
Langley, R., 461
Langlois, J. H., 602
Langone, J., 256
Langrock, A., 138
Lanphear, B., 216
Lanza, R. P., 313
LaPerriere, A., 583
Lapidus, K. A. B., 545
LaPiere, R. T., 610
Laravuso, J. J., 223
Larimer, M. E., 503
Larkin, K. T., 258
Laroche, M., 431
Larouche, C., 139
Larsen, J. T., 596
Larsen, J., 422
Larsen, K. S., 620
Larsen, R., 62
Larsen, U., 130
Larson, C., 120
Larson, J., 506
Larsson, H., 523
Laschefski, U., 79, 421
Lashley, K. S., 298
Laska, M., 152
Lasser, N. L., 574
Lassonde, M., 98
Latané, B., 618, 627–629
Latham, G. P., 404
Lattal, K. A., 248
Lau, A. S., 503
Lau, I., 335
Laumann, E. O., 393
Laurel-Seller, E., 385
Laurence, J. R., 222
Laurenceau, J. P., 42
Lauridsen, E., 37
Laursen, B., 134
Lauver, K., 461
Laver, A. B., 80
Lavie, P., 205, 207, 217
Lavin, C., 348
Lavoisier, A., 220
Lavoisier, P., 390
Law, D. M., 579
Lawrence, J. W., 589
Lawson, J., 337
Lawson, R., 492
Lawson, T. J., 29
Lawton, C. A., 138
Layton, B. D., 405
Lazarus, R. S., 436, 438, 564, 575
Lazeyras, F., 91
Le Bel, J. L., 311
Le Houezec, J., 43, 402
Leadbeater, B., 549
Leaf, P. J., 485

Leaf, R. C., 469
Leakey, R. E., 624
Leana, C. R., 617
Leaper, C., 126, 329
Leary, M. R., 34, 598
Leavitt, L. A., 153
LeBlanc, L. A., 537
LeBoeuf, R. A., 193
Leboyer, M., 200
Lebreton, K., 279
Lecci, L., 457, 577
Leckman, J. F., 497
Leclerc, G., 469
Lecomte, D., 509
Lederman, S. J., 189
Ledezma, E., 190
Ledochowski, L., 401
LeDoux, J. E., 62, 87, 415, 432, 438
Lee, C., 387
Lee, C. S., 181, 317
Lee, E. H., 37
Lee, G. P., 369, 420
Lee, H., 302
Lee, M. G., 208
Lee, M. W., 123, 186
Lee, P., 86
Lee, S. H., 495
Lee, S. Y., 35, 369
Lee, T. M. C., 418, 507
Lee, W. H., 464
Lee, Y. S., 92
Lee, Y. T., 615
Leenaars, A. A., 509
Leermakers, E. A., 584
Leeson, F. J., 122
Lefrancois, R., 469
Lehman, D. R., 381, 470
Lei, T., 128
Leibowitz, H. W., 174
Leigland, S., 12
Leikin, L., 570
Leit, R. A., 385
Leitner, L. M., 553
Lekander, M., 581
LeMay, M. L., 138
Lemelson, R., 497
Lemes, A., 384
Lemieux, L., 83
Lemieux, R., 605
LeMura, L. M., 251
Lencz, T., 520
Lennon, R., 140
Lenox, R. H., 547
Lens, W., 317
Lenz, S., 88
Leonard, J., 612
Leonesio, R. J., 295
Leong, T. T. L., 17
LePage, A., 625
Lepes, D., 408, 584
Lepore, A. J., 580
Lepper, M. R., 405
Lerew, D. R., 493
Lerman, D. C., 253

Lerner, A. G., 231
Lerner, B. S., 408
Lerner, E., 21
Lerner, G. H., 327
Lerner, J. S., 576
Lerner, R. M., 133
Lescaudron, L., 101
Leserman, J., 572, 578
Leskin, G. A., 493
Leslie, K., 217
Lester, D., 378, 466, 475, 508, 509
Letterman, D., 430
Leung, A. K.-Y., 598
LeVay, S., 396, 397
Levenson, J. L., 574
Levenson, R. W., 433, 435
Leventhal, E. A., 589
Leventhal, H., 420, 589
Leverich, G. S., 511
Levesque, J. M., 584
Levin, B. E., 66
Levin, E. D., 77, 587
Levin, F. R., 230
Levin, I. P., 322
Levin, J. R., 297, 298
Levin, L., 250
Levine, A. S., 385
Levine, F. M., 186
Levine, J. S., 163
Levine, M., 346
Levine, S. C., 138
Levine, T. R., 624
Levinger, G., 618
Levinson, D. J., 136, 145, 614
Levinthal, C. F., 79, 228
Levitt, D. H., 388
Levy, D., 323
Levy, G. D., 126
Levy, J., 98
Levy, N., 180
Lew, A. S., 403
Lew, M. W., 221
Lewicki, P., 321
Lewin, R., 624
Lewinsky, M., 416
Lewinsohn, P. M., 491, 504
Lewis, C., 60
Lewis, C. C., 123
Lewis, D., 392
Lewis, J., 380
Lewis, M., 424
Lewis-Fernández, R., 489, 498, 500
Leyendecker, B., 119, 120
Lezak, K. R., 257
Li, J., 189
Li, J. Z., 204
Li, P., 282
Li, Y. J., 102
Liaw, F.-R., 369
Liben, L. S., 281
Lichacz, F. M., 618
Lichstein, K. L., 208
Lichtenstein, P., 495, 523
Lichtman, C. M., 182

Lie, I., 168
Lieberman, D. A., 6
Lieberman, M. D., 578
Liechti, M., 232
Liechti, M. E., 232
Liegois, M. J., 222
Lightdale, J. R., 140
Light-Häusermann, J. H., 62
Liker, J. J., 357
Lilienfeld, S. O., 287, 452, 533
Lim, A.-N., 585
Lim, J.-S., 240
Lima, A., 544
Lin, E. H., 589
Lin, N., 503
Lin, X., 214
Lincoln, A., 270, 378, 466, 486, 626
Lindberg, N., 386
Lindberg, S. M., 139, 141
Linden, D. J., 299
Linden, W., 574
Linderholm, T., 317
Lindman, R., 624
Lindsay, D. S., 287, 291, 293
Lindsay, G., 21
Lindsay, R. C. L., 21, 291, 294
Lindvall, O., 101
Lindwall, J., 449
Link, M., 6
Linn, M. C., 50, 138, 139, 141
Linn, R. L., 348
Lintern, G., 250
Linville, P. W., 599
Linz, D., 264
Liossi, C., 188
Lipman, J. J., 186
Lippa, R. A., 395
Lips, H. M., 464
Lipton, M. L., 95
Lipton, R. B., 185
Litchfield, R. C., 319
Litt, M. D., 589
Littner, M., 214
Litwin, G. H., 407
Liu, H., 69
Liu, J., 209
Liu, L. L., 503
Livesley, W. J., 475, 493
Ljungvall, A., 382
Llorens, S., 461
Llorente, M. D., 216
Lloyd, R. M., 213
Lo Bue, S., 577
LoBello, S. G., 347
Lochman, J. E., 122
Locke, E. A., 404, 460
Locke, J., 4, 11, 199, 238, 242
Locke, S. E., 572
Lockhart, R. S., 277
Lockton, A., 380
Locurto, C., 368, 369
Loeb, S., 369
Loef, M., 561
Loehlin, J. C., 66, 367, 453, 473, 475

Loewi, O., 76
Loffredo, D. A., 455
Loftus, E. F., 274, 280, 282, 287, 288, 291, 292–293, 446, 596
Loftus, G. R., 274
Logan, C., 239
Logan, H., 188
Logan, R. L., 145
Logel, C., 600
Logie, R. H., 275
Lombardo, G. P., 454
Long, M. E., 216
Long, T. E., 33
Longhofer, J. L., 122
Longley, S. L., 499
Lonigan, C. J., 331
Lonner, W. J., 16
Lonsdale, A. J., 321
Loomis, A. L., 206
Loomis, M., 452
Loose, R., 200
Lopez, I. R., 457
Lopez, J., 157
Lopez, S. G., 587
Lopez, S. J., 137
López, S. R., 487, 491, 512
Lord, C. G., 458
Lorenz, A. R., 518
Lorenz, K. Z., 623
Lorenzi, P., 404
Loring, D. W., 420
Lorist, M. M., 229
Losier, G. F., 408
Lou, L., 160
Louis XIII, 72
Louis XVI, 220
Louw, D. A., 599
Lovell, P. G., 169
Lovibond, P. F., 262
Loving, T. J., 70
Low, W. C., 102
Lowe, M. R., 385
Lowrey, T. M., 607
Lowry, D. H., 297
Loy, J. W., 600
Lozano, A. M., 385
Lu, A., 91
Lu, L., 428
Lu, Z. L., 273
Lubart, T. I., 318
Lubek, I., 7
Lubinski, D., 141, 357
Luborsky, L., 553, 554, 555
Lucas, M. D., 515
Lucas, R. E., 143, 427, 428
Luce, G. G., 198
Luchins, A., 314, 315, 338
Lucki, I., 15
Luders, E., 95
Luhmann, M., 143
Lui, F., 223
Lukas, K. E., 255
Lumsdaine, A., 609
Luna, E. R., 152

Lundberg, L. J., 328
Lundgren, S., 616
Lundh, L.-G., 438
Lundqvist, L.-O., 424
Lundstrom, J. N., 183
Lundy, D. E., 429, 605
Lunell, E., 587
Luo, J., 218
Luo, S., 603
Lupkowski-Shoplik, A., 355
Luria, Z., 125
Lustig, K., 533
Luszcz, M. A., 108
Luthans, F., 464
Lutz, J., 33
Luxton, D. D., 508
Lydiard, R. B., 492
Lydon, J. E., 603
Lydum, A. R., 503
Lygren, S., 496
Lykken, D. T., 65, 66, 366, 416, 418, 473
Lykouras, L., 545
Lymburner, J. A., 487
Lynch, M., 114, 588
Lynch, M. J., 400
Lynch, P. S., 355
Lynett, E., 520
Lynn, A. B., 231
Lynn, R., 370
Lynn, S. J., 220, 294, 502
Lynskey, M. T., 66
Lyons, J., 185
Lyons, M. J., 503
Lysle, D. T., 573
Lytton, H., 125
Lyubomirsky, S., 506

M'Naghten, D., 486
Ma, H.-C., 86, 133
Ma, H.-H., 537
Ma, J., 463
Maag, U., 167
Maaravi, Y., 137
Maass, A., 95, 293
Mabeba, M., 576
Macaruso, P., 343
Macaskill, A., 540
Macaskill, N. D., 540
Macchi, M. M., 209
Maccoby, E. E., 123, 125, 138
MacCracken, M. J., 618
MacDonald, D. A., 457
MacDonald, D. J., 443
MacDonald, G., 227
MacDonald, T. K., 227
Macera, M. H., 18
MacFarlane, J. G., 50
Machado, F. R., 190
Mack, D., 619
Mack, M. E., 173
Mack, S., 255
Mackinnon, A. J., 510
MacKinnon, G. E., 308

MacKintosh, N. J., 263
Macklin, M. C., 282
MacLaren, V. V., 418
MacLean, H. N., 287
MacLeod, C. M., 284
MacMillan, H. L., 549
Macmillan, M., 92
MacNichol, E. F., Jr., 163
Macrides, F., 183
MacTavish, D., 300
Maczaj, M., 214
Madden, T., 134
Maddi, K. L., 578
Maddi, S. R., 577, 578
Madison, D. V., 74
Madison, G., 358
Maekelae, K., 611
Maekisalo, H., 624
Maenner, M. J., 353
Maeshima, S., 60
Maganaris, C. N., 70
Maglieri, K. A., 537
Magloire, K., 578
Magnuson, V. L., 397
Magnussen, S., 283
Magoun, H. W., 86
Maguire, M., 55
Maguire-Zeiss, K. A., 78
Mah, K., 391
Mahableshwarkar, A. R., 41
Maher, C. G., 461
Maher, L. M., 83
Mahler, H. I. M., 589
Mahlios, J., 214
Mahoney, B. S., 189
Maiano, C., 45
Maiello, S., 542
Maier, N. R., 315
Maier, S. F., 257
Maio, G. R., 613
Majde, J. A., 212
Majeres, R. L., 326
Majhi, P., 70
Major, B., 126
Makara, G. B., 546
Mäkinen, O., 386
Malamuth, N. M., 35
Malarkey, W. B., 565
Maldonado, R. E., 134
Malecki, A., 36
Malinoski, P., 294
Malinowski, C. I., 128
Malla, A. K., 514
Malmberg, A. B. 78
Malpass, R. S., 26, 291
Malvo, L. B., 486–487
Man, D. W. K., 324
Mandai, O., 219
Mandel, D. R., 114
Mandel, H., 497
Mandic, N., 493
Mandler, G., 309
Maner, J. K., 42, 602, 626
Mangalmurti, V. S., 550

Manley, R. S., 53
Mann, K., 207
Mann, L., 360
Mann, M., 569
Manning, B. H., 463
Manning, C. A., 303
Mansell, W., 32
Mansfield, N. J., 155
Manto, M., 86
Manuck, S. B., 568, 572, 575
Manuel, W. J., 615
Mao, L., 188
Maple, T. L., 255
Maracek, J., 38
Maragos, W. F., 303
Maranto, G., 136
Maratsos, M., 329
Marchand, S., 187
Marcus, G. F., 330, 331
Marek, E. A., 132
Margoliash, D., 218
Margolis, F. L., 183
Marine, C., 282
Marion, M. S., 146
Mariotte, E., 159
Marken, R. S., 312
Markianos, M., 545
Markus, H., 461–462, 464
Markus, H. R., 428, 470, 620
Marler, P., 325
Marlier, L., 114
Marmot, M. G., 143
Marolla, F. A., 368
Maron, E., 493
Marosi, E., 420
Marquis, J., 264
Marr, M. J., 255
Marsa, F., 465
Marsden, J., 86
Marsh, A. A., 474
Marshall, F. J., 171
Marshall, G. D., 437
Marshall, J. C., 500
Marshall, M., 4
Marshall, W. L., 535
Marsland, A. L., 572
Marston, A., 217
Martazaev, M. S., 210
Martens, A., 446
Martin, A. J., 467
Martin, B., 618
Martin, C. E., 392
Martin, F., 400, 584
Martin, L. R., 576
Martin, N. G., 20, 65, 160, 395, 453, 555
Martin, P., 121, 288
Martin, R., 425
Martin, R. A., 431
Martin, S., 20
Martin, S. J., 137, 299
Martinez, B., 614
Martinez, H. R., 100, 101
Martinez, I. M., 461

Martinez, J. L., Jr., 299
Martinez, M. E., 542
Martinez-Pons, M., 361
Martinko, M. J., 596
Martins, I. P., 185
Marttunen, M., 131
Marucha, P. T., 221, 565, 581
Marx, B., 227
Marx, J. L., 337
Mashego, T. A., 576
Masland, J. L., 430
Masling, J., 10
Maslonek, K. A., 573
Maslow, A. H., 13, 378, 466, 470, 485
Mason, S. L., 101
Masoro, E. J., 137
Masser, B., 613
Masters, K. S., 35, 222, 584
Masters, W. H., 390–391, 393–394
Masterton, G., 484
Mastropieri, M. A., 296
Matas, M., 550
Mathes, W. F., 599
Mathew, R. J., 84
Mathews, A., 581
Mathiak, K., 499
Mathias, C. J., 581
Mathis, M., 577
Matlock, J. G., 192
Matson, J. L., 256, 355
Matsubayashi, T., 509
Matsumoto, D., 435, 464, 605
Matsuura, T., 582
Matt, G. E., 555
Mattai, P. R., 37
Mattanah, J. F., 122
Matthews, D. B., 227
Matthews, K. A., 569, 570
Mattsson, P., 101
Maude, C., 515
Maurer, K., 512
Mautner, B., 533
Maxwell, K. L., 352
May, M. A., 458, 459
May, R., 470
Mayer, B., 433
Mayer, R., 358
Mayrhauser, R. T., 347
Maziotta, J. C., 511
Mazor, M., 187
Mazzella, R., 387, 602
Mazziotta, J. C., 419
McAdams, D. P., 145
McAdams, S., 180
McAllister, D. E., 243
McAllister, W. R., 243
McAlpine, D., 180
McArdle, J. J., 109
McAuley, E., 584
McAuley, J. H., 461
McAuliffe, C., 617
McCabe, K. O., 453
McCabe, M. P., 402

McCaffrey, T., 316
McCall, M., 602
McCalley, L. T., 404
McCallister, C., 356
McCallum, D. M., 578
McCammon, S., 436
McCandliss, B. D., 326
McCann, M. J., 380
McCanne, T. R., 435
McCarley, R. W., 219, 220
McCarron, P. O., 77
McCarthy, J. M., 475
McCarthy, L., 495
McCarthy-Jones, S., 463
McCarty, T., 501
McCauley, C., 418, 431
McClean, S. I., 570
Mcclearn, G. E., 569
McClelland, D., 402
McClelland, J. L., 117, 326
McClelland, L., 508
McCloskey, M., 270, 293
McClure, E. B., 424
McClure, K. A., 292
McComas, A., 81
McConaghy, N., 398
McConahay, J. B., 613
McConkey, K. M., 223
McConnell, J. V., 154, 301
McConville, J., 77
McConville, K. M. V., 258
McCormack, W. A., 401
McCrae, R. R., 454, 457, 475
McCrary, G., 465
McCrea, D. A., 72
McCrea, S. M., 468, 599
McCreath, H., 621
McCullough, M. E., 455
McDonagh, D. M., 206
McDonald, D. N., 8
McDonald, J. L., 286
McDonald, M. S., 481
McDonald, R., 543
McDonnell, J., 192–193
McDonnell, J. F., 461
McDougal, Y. B., 168
McDougall, W., 95–96, 376
McDougle, C. J., 230
McDowell, M. J., 450
McDowell, N. K., 576
McEwen, B. S., 87, 565, 572
McFadden, D., 174, 396
McFarland, K., 95
McGaha, A. C., 53
McGaugh, J. L., 303
McGhee, P. E., 431
McGinnes, G. C., 425
McGonigle, D. J., 89
McGovern, M., 475
McGrady, A., 259, 401
McGrath, C. E., 569
McGrath, J., 515
McGrath, M. L., 241
McGrath, P., 570

I-18 Name Index

McGregor, I. S., 232
McGue, M., 62, 65, 66, 123, 366, 367, 387, 388, 473, 474, 475
McGuffin, P., 510
McGuigan, F. J., 309
McGuire, G. R., 7
McGuire, L., 571
McGwin, G., Jr., 162
McInnis, M. G., 511
McIntosh, D. N., 435
McIntosh, W. D., 602
McIntyre, D., 186
McKelvie, S. J., 321
McKendree-Smith, N., 505, 556
McKendree-Smith, N. L., 552
McKenna, M. C., 574
McKennitt, D. S., 587
McKenzie, J., 457
McKinley, J. C., 455
McKinley, P. A., 91
McKinney, M., 302
McKown, C., 350
McLay, R. N., 535
McLeod, D. M., 322
McLure, J., 463
McMahan, C. A., 137
McMahon, M., 550
McMahon, R. J., 135
McMahon, S. B., 100
McManus, C., 94
McManus, J., 462
McMillan, D. E., 377
McNally, R. J., 495
McNatt, D. B., 43
McNeil, C., 221
McNeil, E. B., 154
McNeil, S., 68
McNeill, A., 259
McNelles, L. R., 135
McPherson, K. S., 363
McPherson, L. M., 520
McPherson, M. W., 38
McQuaid, J. R., 543
McQuellon, R. P., 589
McQuinn, R. D., 606
McRoberts, C., 554
McVety, K. M., 263
McWhorter, P., 298
McWilliam, R., 38
McWilliams, S. A., 231
Meader, K. J., 420
Means, L. W., 33
Mecacci, L., 452
Mechanic, M. B., 564
Meckstroth, E., 356
Medin, D., 128
Medin, D. L., 310, 311
Medland, S. E., 95
Mednick, S., 514
Mednick, S. A., 513
Medori, R., 524
Meehan, J. W., 168
Meehl, P. E., 443
Meeker, W. B., 222

Meert, T. F., 185
Meertens, R. W., 613
Meeus, W. H. J., 134
Mehta, R. S., 213
Mehu, M., 33
Meichenbaum, D., 580
Meichenbaum, D. H., 45
Meijer, J. H., 204
Meisenzahl, E. M., 78
Meissner, W. W., 541
Melamed, S., 576
Melas, N., 229
Melbye, M., 522
Melcer, T., 238
Meldrum, B. S., 101
Mellers, J. D. C., 177
Mellman, T. A., 216
Mellon, M. W., 239
Mellors, V., 567
Melmed, R. N., 581
Melmed, S., 69
Melville, H., 216
Melville, J. D., 485
Melzack, R., 185, 186
Memmott, J., 335
Memon, A., 291
Menachemi, N., 35
Mendelson, W. B., 214
Mendoza-Denton, R., 459
Menéndez-Colino, L. M., 91
Mengel, M. K. C., 185
Menon, T., 597
Menzel, C. R., 338
Menzel, E., 338
Mercado, A. M., 565
Mercier, M., 91
Merckelbach, H., 96, 246, 265, 433, 496, 501
Meredith, W., 469
Merewether, F. C., 422
Merikangas, K. R., 481, 491
Merikle, P. M., 201
Merrick, J., 352
Merritt, J., 219
Merritt, M. M., 570
Mervis, J., 485, 554
Mesmer, F. A., 219–220
Messer, S. B., 532
Messer, W. S., 190
Messick, D. M., 618
Messick, S., 349
Messineo, M., 613
Meston, C. M., 605
Metcalfe, J., 313
Mettetal, G., 361
Metz, M. E., 393
Meuret, A. E., 258
Meyer, B., 55
Meyer, G. J., 451
Meyer, J. S., 137
Meyer-Bahlburg, H. F. L., 396
Meyer-Bisch, C., 179
Meyers, C. E., 351
Meyers, S. A., 606

Mezei, L., 614
Mezzacappa, E. S., 437
Miaskowski, C., 186
Miceli, R., 425
Michael, R. T., 394
Michaelis, B., 600
Michaels, S., 394
Michalak, E. E., 507
Michel, C., 381
Michel, C. M., 83, 91
Michel, Y., 145
Michie, P. T., 232
Michie, S., 229
Michinov, E., 603
Michou, A., 121
Miczek, K. A., 79
Midden, C. J. H., 404
Middlebrooks, J. C., 180
Midgley, N., 34
Mignano, A. M., 384
Mignot, E., 214
Migueles, M., 282
Mihura, J. L., 451
Miklósi, Á., 263, 325
Mikulincer, M., 468
Milar, K. S., 362
Miles, C., 289
Miles, J. A., 618
Miletic, M. P., 449
Milgram, S., 622–623
Milk, H., 486
Millar, J. K., 514
Millar, M., 621
Miller, B. D., 433
Miller, B. E., 331
Miller, B. L., 508
Miller, C., 52, 309, 552
Miller, D. L., 231, 603
Miller, D., 430, 516
Miller, E., 82, 569
Miller, E. N., 97
Miller, G. A., 275
Miller, H. A., 21, 36
Miller, K. B., 388
Miller, M., 213
Miller, M. B., 140, 343, 586
Miller, N., 627
Miller, N. E., 54, 258, 624
Miller, R. B., 45
Miller, R. R., 261, 262
Miller, T. I., 554
Miller, T. Q., 154, 568
Millikin, C., 535
Milling, L. S., 220
Millon, T., 377
Millot, J. L., 181
Mills, E., 36
Mills, J. A., 385
Mills, M. J., 551
Mills, S., 624
Milner, B., 88, 300
Milner, P., 87
Milofsky, E., 119
Milosevic, M., 258

Milstein, V., 500
Milton, J., 191
Mimeault, V., 552
Min, K. J., 92
Mindell, J. A., 216, 602
Mineka, S., 265, 266
Miner, K. N., 580
Minini, L., 168
Mino, Y., 515
Minowa, M., 209
Mintz, L. B., 552
Mira, J. C., 101
Mirsky, A. F., 512
Mischel, W., 458, 459, 460
Miserandino, M., 288
Misra, G., 350
Mita, T. H., 602
Mitchell, D., 210
Mitchell, F. E., 493
Mitchell, P., 171, 510
Mitchell, W. D., 455
Mitrushina, M., 97
Mitte, K., 492
Mizumura, K., 185
Modestin, J., 515
Modigliani, A., 623
Mödle, T., 34
Moe, J. L., 614
Moeller, A. T., 540
Moeller, G. H., 402
Moeller, H. J., 475
Moen, M. D., 71
Moen, P., 145
Moene, F. C., 500
Mogg, K., 496
Mohanty, A. K., 329
Mohr, C. D., 453
Mohr, D. C., 556
Mojaverian, T., 579
Molaison, H., 271
Molaison, H. G., 88, 300
Molchan, G., 32
Molina, M., 114
Molis, M., 330
Molitorisz, J., 238
Möller, H. J., 78
Molnar, B. E., 508
Monahan, J., 551
Monetta, L., 422
Money, J., 392, 394, 399
Mongeau, P. A., 616
Moniz, E., 544
Monroe, K. B., 621
Monroe, S. M., 563
Monroig, R., 190
Monson, T. C., 459
Montag, I., 463
Montagliani, A., 598
Montague, H., 362
Montanes, P., 273
Monte, C. F., 450
Monteil, J.-M., 603
Montesquieu, C., 428
Montgomery, D., 469

Name Index I-19

Montgomery, G., 186
Montgomery, G. H., 221
Montgomery, K., 192
Monti, T. C., 549
Montoya, E. R., 624
Montoya, R. M., 603
Mooney, G., 100
Moor, C. J., 449
Moore, B. C. J., 152, 153
Moore, D. J., 499
Moore, D. W., 160, 408
Moore, J., 11
Moore, M. S., 152
Moore, S., 256, 521
Moore-Ede, M. C., 205
Moorhead, G., 617
Moradi, S., 581
Moran, M. G., 567
Moratalla, R., 230
Morawski, J. G., 11
Mordkoff, A., 438
Moreland, R. L., 601
Moreno, M., 401, 547
Morfei, M. Z., 462
Morgan, C., 403, 451
Morgan, D. W., 563
Morgan, D., 210, 586
Morgan, E. R., 356
Morgan, W. G., 451
Morganstein, M. S., 464
Mori, M., 88
Morin, A., 99
Morin, C. M., 552
Morisse, D., 258
Moriyama, T. S., 524
Morley, C. P., 65
Morley, J. E., 136, 186, 303, 385, 464
Morling, B., 576, 579
Moroz, M., 79
Morris, M., 446
Morris, M. W., 597
Morris, R. G. M., 299
Morris, R. L., 191
Morris, S., 192
Morris, W., 446
Morrison, A. R., 211, 614
Morrison, N., 510
Morrongiello, B. A., 114
Morrow, J., 507
Morrow, S. L., 462
Morry, M. M., 385
Mors, O., 510
Morse, C. K., 345
Mortel, K. F., 137
Mortensen, P. B., 515
Moruzzi, G., 86
Morvay, Z., 449
Moscone, G., 486
Moses, J., 581
Moshinsky, A., 320
Moskowitz, J. T., 575
Mosmann, A. L., 418
Moss, C. R., 109
Moss, J., 521

Motta, V. A., 185
Mouratidis, A., 121
Mouthaan, J., 538
Mowen, J. C., 454, 462
Mowrer, O. H., 240, 253, 624
Mowrer, W. M., 240
Moy, S. S., 15
Mrdenovic, S., 493
Muccio C. F., 80
Mudford, O. C., 256
Muehlbach, M. J., 229
Mueller, C. G., 11
Mueller, C. W., 127
Mueller, S. C., 577
Muhammad, A., 486–487
Muir, F., 506
Muir-Broaddus, J., 118
Mukherjee, A., 430
Mulatu, M. S., 137
Muldoon, K. A., 487
Mulhall, D. J., 344
Mullally, P. R., 368
Mullen, B., 617
Müller, R.-A., 264
Müller, W., 322
Müller-Lyer, F., 172–173
Mulligan, N., 279
Mulligan, N. W., 270
Mulligan, T., 109
Mullins, L. L., 500
Mulryan, N., 485
Mumenthaler, M. S., 227
Mumford, M. D., 316
Mumme, D. L., 263
Munakata, Y., 117
Munch, E., 492
Munrer, K., 96
Münsterberg, H., 7, 8, 290
Murashita, J., 493
Murdoch, B. E., 87
Murdock, S., 534
Muris, P., 96
Murnen, S. K., 385, 388
Murphy, D., 541
Murphy, G. L., 310
Murphy, J., 338
Murphy, J. J., 20
Murphy, L. C., 401, 588
Murphy, P. J., 204
Murphy, T., 601
Murray, C., 364
Murray, C. M., 33
Murray, H. A., 402, 403, 451
Murray, J. B., 455
Murray, R., 587
Murray, R. M., 497, 515, 600
Murray, R. P., 186, 588
Murray, S. L., 468
Muscat, R., 380
Muse, L. A., 400
Mushrush, J. E., 457
Musikantow, R., 220
Mussone, L., 323
Muthusamy, R., 99

Myers, C. D., 186
Myers, D. G., 428, 582, 616
Myers, D. M., 290
Myers, I. B., 455
Myerscough, R., 231
Mylander, C., 332
Mylle, J., 577

Na, E. U., 596
Nacoste, R. W., 614
Nadel, L., 501
Nadler, J. J., 15
Naering, G. W. B., 500
Naganuma, T., 169
Nagarajan, S. S., 89
Nagata, K., 84
Nagata, T., 37, 495
Nagtegaal, E. E., 41
Nahas, G., 231
Naimark, D., 136, 485
Naka, M., 291
Nakagawa, Y., 289
Nakajima, T., 37
Nakamura, K., 419
Nakayama, K., 165
Nalty, L., 308
Napoli, A., 563
Narash-Eisikovits, O., 389
Narens, L., 295
Narita, E., 211
Narita, M., 87
Narr, K. I., 95
Narrow, W. E., 488
Nasby, W., 462
Nash, J. K., 574
Nash, M., 223
Nash, W. R., 356
Nason, S., 287
Natarajan, L., 232
Nathan, P. E., 28
Natsoulas, T., 199
Naumann, E., 474
Naus, P. J., 468
Nava, F., 232
Navarro, A. M., 55
Navarro, M., 232
Nayak, S., 186
Nazari, M. A., 524
Nazzi, T., 114
Neale, J. M., 427, 513, 563
Neale, M. C., 382, 514
Neck, C. P., 617
Neeson, L., 502
Neher, A., 452
Neisser, U., 200, 282, 300, 364
Neitz, J., 163
Neitz, M., 163
Nejad, H. G., 467
Nejime, Y., 153
Nel, E. M., 615
Nelson, C., 83
Nelson, K. E., 331
Nelson, L., 257, 521
Nelson, L. D., 193

Nelson, M. D., 447
Nelson, R. J., 507
Nelson, T. O., 201, 295
Nemeroff, C. B., 78
Nemeth, C. J., 616, 617
Nepomuceno, M. V., 431
Neria, Y., 563
Nesdale, A. R., 625
Nesheim, B. I., 186
Nestadt, G., 497
Nesthus, T., 205
Nettelbeck, T., 344
Neubauer, A. C., 358
Neufeld, R. W. J., 555
Neumann, R., 437
Neuringer-Benefiel, H. E., 626
Neville, H. J., 308
Nevo, B., 431
Nevo, O., 430, 431
Newcomb, A. F., 124
Newcomb, T., 625
Newcombe, N. S., 4
Newell, A., 314
Newman, J., 405
Newman, J. P., 240, 520
Newman, J. R., 308, 518
Newman, S., 582
Newport, E. L., 330
Newton, Isaac, 73
Nezlek, J., 405
Nezlek, J. B., 505
Ng, W.-J., 291
Nicholls, J. G., 317, 407
Nicholls, M., 94
Nichols, A. L., 42
Nichols, P. L., 368
Nichols, R. M., 291
Nicholson, M. E., 189
Nicholson, N., 620
Nicholson, T. R., 500
Nickerson, R. S., 276, 370
Nicol, S. E., 515
Nicoll, R. A., 74
Nicolson, P., 15
Nides, M. A., 588
Nides, M., 587
Niedeggen, M., 282
Nielsen, T. A., 217
Nielsen-Gammon, E., 256
Nigg, J. T., 524
Nightingale, F., 46
Niles, S., 403
Nilsen, J., 303
Nilsson, L., 501
Ninomiya, Y., 183
Nir-Dotan, M., 576
Nisbett, R. E., 321, 349, 405, 596, 597
Nishida, T., 34
Nishikawa, T., 98
Nishimura, H., 177
Nishitan, N., 83
Nishith, P., 564
Nissen, M. J., 302
Niu, W., 318

I-20   Name Index

Nixon, R., 282, 608–609
Nixon, R. D. V., 122
Nizamie, S. H., 81
Noguchi, J., 72
Nokes, T., 263
Nolan, B., 8
Nolen-Hoeksema, S., 506, 507
Nopoulos, P., 516
Nordblom, J., 101
Nordstrom, R., 404
Norenzayan, A., 174, 596, 597
Norlander, T., 401, 407
Norman, C., 251
Norman, K. A., 282, 299
Norman, R. G., 209
Norman, R. M., 514
Norman, S. E., 216
Norris, F. H., 565
Norris, N. P., 53
North, A. C., 321
Northrup, T., 279
Norton, E. M., 509
Norton, J., 480–481
Norton, S., 352
Nosek, B. A., 607
Nosofsky, R. M., 311
Nougier, V., 400
Novak, R. D., 209
Novick, L. R., 313
Nowicki, S., 422, 423
Noyes, R., Jr., 499
Nunes, E. V., 554
Nunn, J., 101
Nuño, V. L., 587
Nuovo, S. D., 323
Nurmi, J.-E., 121
Nusbaum, H. C., 84, 218
Nutt, D. J., 78, 504
Nwosu, C. M., 574
Nyberg, B., 134
Nyberg, L., 277
Nye, C., 589
Nygren, T., 624
Nystul, M. S., 509

O'Brien, E. J., 459
O'Brien, J. T., 181
O'Brien, L. T., 351
O'Brien, S. A., 216
O'Brien, W. H., 574
O'Carroll, R. E., 484
O'Connell, A. N., 8, 449
O'Connor, A., 485
O'Connor, D. B., 576
O'Connor, F. L., 515
O'Dell, K. A., 588
O'Donnell, I., 508
O'Grady, M. A., 240
O'Halloran, C. M., 589
O'Hara, M., 553
O'Hara, R., 227
O'Laughlin, M. S., 431
O'Leary, A., 582
O'Leary, K. D., 143

O'Malley, E. B., 209
O'Malley, P. M., 109
O'Malley, R. C., 33
O'Muircheartaigh, C. A., 271
O'Neil, W. M., 11
O'Neill, E., 10
O'Neill, S. K., 387
O'Reardon, J., 510
O'Reilly, H., 522
O'Reilly, R. C., 299
O'Shea, R. P., 169
O'Shea, W. A., 605
O'Sullivan, M., 416
Oakley, D. A., 223
Oates, G., 137
Ober, B. A., 288
Oberlander, J. G., 624
Obozova, T. A., 263
Ochs, E. P. P., 324
Ockene, J. K., 588
Odbert, H., 454
Oden, G. C., 167
Oden, M. H., 356
Odum, L. E., 588
Oei, T. P. S., 214
Offit, P., 228
Offringa, R., 564
Ogden, C. L., 382
Ogden, E. P., 53
Ogilvie, R., 217
Ogilvie, R. D., 206
Ogle, C. A., 39
Ogles, B. M., 584
Oh, K. S., 495
Ohayon, M. M., 216
Ohki, K., 100
Öhman, A., 62
Ohrwall, O., 183
Oi Bun Lam, C., 133
Oishi, S., 143, 428, 463
Okada, M., 86
Okagami, K., 515
Okano, H., 100
Okazaki, S., 370
Oku, Y., 86
Okwumabua, T. M., 464
Olbrich, A., 323
Oldehinkel, A. J., 576
Olds, J., 87
Olfson, M., 503
Olgun, S., 182
Oliver, C., 521
Ollendick, T. H., 496
Oller, D. K., 328
Olmo, R. J., 453
Olsen, S., 214
Olson, B., 145
Olson, B. F., 579
Olson, D. R., 117
Olson, J. K., 590
Olson, J. M., 613
Olson, K. G., 79
Olson, M. A., 607
Olson, R. A., 500

Olsson, M. J., 183
Oman, R. F., 584
Ones, D. S., 37, 428
Oneta, M., 323
Ong, A., 134
Ong, A. D., 134, 143
Ono, Y., 498
Onstad, S., 496, 514
Opper, C., 79, 421
Oppliger, P. A., 430
Orange, C., 356
Ordway, L., 590
Orenstein, P. A., 287
Orgocka, A., 403
Orlinsky, D. E., 555
Ormsby, K., 407
Orne, M. T., 222, 223, 417
Orsal, D., 101
Orth, U., 468
Orthner, D. K., 144
Ortmann, A., 54
Orwell, G., 332
Osawa, A., 60
Osawa, M., 83
Osberg, T. M., 35
Osborne, M., 251
Osborne, S., 250
Oshima, I., 515
Osiel, S., 204
Ostry, D., 332
Oswald, D. L., 462
Otowa, T., 493
Ottati, V., 615
Oubaid, V., 63
Oudiette, D., 219
Oudji, S., 497
Ouellette, J. A., 616
Ouimet, J., 362
Overmier, J. B., 55
Overton, D. A., 289
Owen, M. J., 385
Owen, M. T., 121
Owens, D. S., 303
Owsley, C., 162

Pace-Schott, E. F., 214
Pachana, N. A., 394
Pacini, R., 506
Packer, O., 159
Padberg, U., 127
Paddock, J. R., 422
Padian, K., 5
Pagano, B., 290, 291
Page, S. J., 20
Page-Voth, V., 404
Paik, A., 393
Paik, H., 264
Paikoff, R. L., 130
Paillard, J., 189
Palaniappan, A. K., 317
Palencik, J. T., 7
Palermo, G. B., 465
Palk, J., 21
Pallast, E. G. M., 515

Paller, K. A., 219
Pallesen, S., 207
Palmer, J. A., 192
Palmer, J. C., 292
Palmer, M., 296
Palmer, S. N., 437
Palmer, S., 540
Paluck, E. L., 51
Pan, Y., 167
Pancer, S. M., 133
Pandey, J., 576
Pankok, J., 207
Panksepp, J., 313
Panksepp, J. B., 313
Panlilio, L. V., 246
Pantev, C., 177, 180
Papanicolaou, A. C., 83
Papotto, C., 290
Pappenheim, B., 529
Paradis, M., 327
Paradiso, M. A., 160
Pardo, C. A., 522
Pare, D., 299, 419
Paris, J., 518
Park, B., 599
Park, D. C., 298
Park, R. L., 52
Park, W. W., 617
Parker, A., 289
Parker, A. J., 168
Parker, G. A., 254
Parker, K. C. H., 456
Parker, P. Y., 303
Parker, S., 46
Parker, W. D., 356, 456
Parkinson, J., 78
Parkovnick, S., 596
Parr, W., 301
Parra, A., 190
Parriera, E., 185
Parron, D. L., 487
Parrott, A. C., 586
Parrott, D. J., 614
Parsons, M. W., 303
Partala, T., 157
Parten, M. B., 124
Partinen, M., 209
Partington, J. T., 618
Paruthi, S., 213
Parva, M., 112
Pasanen, E. G., 396
Pascual-Leone, A., 184
Patel, S., 101
Patra, J., 257
Patridge, J., 626, 627–629
Pattatucci, A. M. L., 395
Pattee, L., 124
Patterson, C. J., 121
Patterson, D. R., 188
Patterson, F. G., 337
Patterson, L. H., 337
Patterson, T. L., 543
Patti, C. L., 289
Patton, J. E., 400

Pauknerova, D., 403
Paul, M. A., 26
Paulsen, F., 4
Paulus, P. B., 319
Paunonen, S. V., 455
Paunovic, N., 534
Pavlov, I. P., 11, 238–239, 246, 312, 534
Pavot, W. G., 427
Pawlak, J. L., 468
Pawlas, K., 36
Pawlas, N., 36
Paykel, E., 540
Payne, K. A., 393
Peake, P. J., 458
Pear, J. J., 257
Pearce, J. M. S., 4, 98
Pearl, D. K., 567
Pearson, K., 48
Pearson, T. A., 573
Peckham, R., 349
Peckham, V., 618
Pedersen, C. B., 232
Pedersen, H., 601
Peel, R., 486
Peer, D. F., 496
Peeters, M. C. W., 575
Peisner-Feinberg, E. S., 123
Pejovic, S., 212
Peled, R., 2-7
Pelham, B. W., 468
Pell, M. D., 422, 423
Pellechia, M., 451, 607
Pellegrini, R. J., 209
Pelletier, J., 419
Peltzer, K., 576
Pelz, S., 232
Pemberton, J., 230
Penfield, W., 14–15, 80, 81, 90–91
Peng, K., 597
Pengilly, J. W., 577
Penhune, V. B., 91
Penido, A. B., 352
Pennebaker, J. W., 580, 591
Penner, L. A., 629
Penrod, S., 293
Penton-Voak, I., 602
Pepitone, A., 596, 625
Pepler, D. J., 33
Perchet, C., 201
Peregrine, P. N., 377
Peretz, I., 177
Perfect, T., 222
Perfetto, F., 385
Perkins, D. O., 578
Perkins, S. C., 499
Perl, D. P., 88
Perlman, D., 32
Perlmutter, D. D., 430
Perls, F., 541, 542
Perlstein, W. M., 419
Perlstrom, J. R., 192
Perregaux, C., 329
Perri, M. G., 584

Perrin, F., 201
Perronia, B. F., 70
Perry, C., 222
Perry, H. M., 303
Perry, J., 128
Perry, M. S., 457
Persad, E., 545
Person, C., 503
Persson, J. K. E., 101
Pert, C., 78–79
Perzig, S., 614
Peterman, A. H., 578
Peters, J. C., 384, 576
Peters, L., 495, 565
Peters, M., 89
Peters, R. D., 549
Petersen, J. L., 135
Petersen, M., 118
Peterson, B. E., 38
Peterson, B. S., 614
Peterson, C., 505, 575, 589
Peterson, C. C., 129
Peterson, I., 323
Peterson, J. B., 317, 611
Peterson, J. L., 139, 141
Peterson, L. R., 275, 276
Peterson, M. A., 165
Peterson, M. J., 275, 276
Peterson, T. R., 435, 576
Petitjean, F., 517
Petitto, L. A., 332, 337
Petri, H. L., 626
Petrie, K. J., 580
Petrie, T. A., 388
Petrulis, J., 366
Pettersen, L., 111
Pettigrew, T. F., 613
Pettijohn, T. F., II, 379
Petty, R. E., 608, 609, 610
Petukhova, M., 488, 491
Pezdek, K., 501
Pfaff, D. L., 564
Pfaffmann, C., 183
Pfeffer, K., 180
Pfungst, O., 335
Phan, T. X., 218
Phelps, E. A., 62, 87, 419
Phelps, J. A., 515
Phelps, M. E., 511
Philibert, R. A., 62
Philippot, P., 496
Phillips, J. B., 599
Phillips, L. H., 188, 211
Phillips, M. R., Jr., 296
Phillips, N. H., 211
Phillips, R. D., 114
Phillips, S., 34, 182
Phinney, J. S., 133
Phipps, M., 92
Piaget, J., 14, 114–118, 126
Piat, M., 548
Pichika, R., 389
Pick, H. A., Jr., 174
Pickel, J., 545

Pickles, A., 389, 473
Pickworth, W. B., 587
Picton, T. W., 517
Pidada, S., 625
Pierce, E. F., 79
Pierce, W. D., 405
Pierrehumbert, B., 120
Pierson, A., 402
Pieters, R. G. M., 283
Pietraszek, M., 78
Pietsch, J., 464
Pihl, R. O., 217
Pike, P. L., 457
Pilcher, J. J., 205
Pilgrim, D., 490
Piliavin, J. A., 434
Piluso, A., 385
Pinckert, S., 621
Pincus, T., 186, 464
Pineda, J. A., 264
Pinel, J. P. J., 381
Pinel, P., 530
Piner, K. E., 490
Pines, M., 308
Pinkofsky, H. B., 296
Pinquart, M., 50, 146
Piolino, P., 279
Piontkowski, U., 614
Piper, A., 545
Piper, B. J., 112
Pirkis, J., 549
Pisoni, D. B., 114
Pitman, R. K., 549
Pittenger, D. J., 54, 405
Pittinsky, T. L., 600
Pitts, B. L., 577
Plaks, J. E., 618
Plant, E. A., 138, 141, 424, 503
Plass, J. A., 400
Plato, 2–3, 62, 486
Platt, C. G., 543
Platz, S. J., 291
Plaud, J. J., 534
Ploeger, A., 62
Plomin, R., 62, 65, 367, 382, 475
Ploog, B. O., 257
Plotkin, W. B., 259
Plous, S., 54
Plucker, J. A., 361
Pluess, M., 108
Plutchik, R., 426
Poag, K., 584
Podlesny, J. A., 418
Poe, E. A., 322
Pogarell, O., 497
Poincaré, H., 317
Polage, D., 446
Poldinger, W., 503
Poldrack, R. A., 15
Polet, P., 183
Polgardi, R., 325
Politis, M., 102
Polivy, J., 388, 389

Pollak, S. D., 200
Pollard, I., 112
Pollmächer, T., 540
Polotsky, A. J., 137
Polson, P. G., 280
Polster, E., 541
Polster, M., 541
Pomerantz, J. R., 166
Pomerleau, O. F., 229
Pomeroy, K. L., 515
Pomeroy, W. D., 392
Pompe, G., 574
Ponglorpisit, S., 422
Ponirakis, A., 131
Ponpaipan M., 257
Ponton, L. E., 349
Poole, D. A., 20, 293
Poortinga, Y. H., 115
Pope, H. G., 385
Pope, K. H., 122
Pope, M. T., 70
Popplestone, J. A., 38
Populin, L. C., 175
Porreca, F., 86
Porro, C. A., 186, 223
Porsch, R. M., 65
Portillo, M. C., 166
Posadzki, P., 181
Posavac, E. J., 568
Posey, A., 476
Post, R. M., 511
Postman, L., 283, 291
Postmes, T., 625, 626
Poston, W. S., II, 364
Potter, W. J., 264
Potters, J., 322
Poulson, R. L., 485
Pourtois, G., 91
Poustka, F., 343
Powell, D. J., 231
Powell, J. L., 619
Powell, R., 30
Powers, D. E., 348
Powers, W. T., 312
Powley, T. L., 381
Pozzulo, J. D., 291
Prados, J., 263
Prakash, R., 81
Prasinos, S., 430
Pratkanis, A. R., 154
Pratt, M., 133, 384
Pratt, M. W., 122
Pratto, F., 63
Preacher, K. J., 203
Preiser, S., 430
Premack, A., 336
Premack, D., 248, 336
Prentice, D. A., 140, 335
Prentice-Dunn, H., 384
Prentice-Dunn, S., 384, 625
Prepeliczay, S., 231
Prescott, C. A., 473, 492
Pressley-Keough, R., 255
Previc, F. H., 96

Price, B. H., 544
Price, C., 160
Price, C. C., 186, 223
Price, D. D., 188
Price, M. S., 576
Price, R., 382
Price, R. J., 212
Price-Williams, E., 118
Priest, R. G., 216
Priester, J. R., 607
Prieto, M. D., 360
Priluck, R. L., 241
Principe, C. P., 602
Pring, L., 343, 344
Prislin, R., 610
Pritchard, J. K., 241
Pritchard, W. S., 229
Proctor, R. W., 14
Provenzano, F. J., 125
Prud'homme, M. J. L., 188
Przekop, A., 258
Puccio, G. J., 319
Puffett, A., 501
Puhan, B. N., 350
Pukall, C. F., 393
Pullum, G. K., 333
Pulsifer, M. B., 352
Punamacki, R. L., 216
Punamaeki, R.-L., 445
Purcell, D. W., 583
Purdy, J. E., 238
Purselle, D. C., 78
Putnam, D. E., 591
Putnam, F. W., 122, 484
Putnam, K. T., 484
Puukko-Viertomies, L.-R., 386
Pyszczynski, T., 14, 468
Pyter, L. M., 507

Qian, Y., 78
Qin, S., 492
Quadagno, D., 391
Quadflieg, S., 424
Quandt, T., 625
Quigley, N., 210
Quinn, D., 570
Quinsey, V. L., 605, 624
Quintana, S. M., 17
Quintin, R. L., 69
Quirk, G. J., 242
Quota, S., 445

Rabin, J., 157
Rabinowitz, F. M., 362
Rabkin, J. G., 590
Racagni, G., 78
Rachman, S. J., 51
Rachman, S., 265
Racine, M., 186
Radford, B., 29
Radin, D., 29
Radosevich, D. J., 296
Radtke, R. A., 535
Raeburn, J. M., 582

Raeikkoenen, K., 570
Ragland, D. R., 569
Ragnauth, A., 79
Rahe, R. H., 562, 563
Rahim-Williams, B., 186
Raijmakers, M. E. J., 62
Raine, A., 520, 624
Rainville, P., 223
Rakos, R. F., 588
Raloff, J., 179
Ralph, M. R., 204
Ramalingam, S., 289
Ramey, C., 352
Ramey, C. T., 123
Ramirez, M., 118
Ramón y Cajal, S., 75, 299
Ramsay, S. G., 128
Ramsey, J. (John), 465
Ramsey, J. (JonBenet), 464–465
Ramsey, P., 465
Rand, C., 587
Rand, T., 192
Randall, J. L., 191
Randi, J., 192–193
Randle, S., 83
Randolph, C., 217
Range, L. M., 146
Ranney, T., 209
Ranson, S. W., 381
Ranvier, L., 75
Rao, S. C., 86
Rao, S. M., 91
Rapee, R. M., 491, 496
Rapoport, D. M., 209
Rapoport, J., 524
Rapp, D., 444
Rasker, J. J., 590
Raskin, D. C., 417, 418
Rasmussen, T., 91
Rassuli, A., 378
Rath, P. K., 257
Rathgeb-Feutsch, M., 540
Rauch, S. L., 471, 497, 564
Raufaste, E., 282
Rausch, J., 216
Rausch, M. K., 455
Rautiainen, J., 203
Ravelli, G. P., 383
Raviv, A., 208
Raw, S., 20
Rawdon, V. A., 463
Rawlings, D., 455
Ray, F., 221
Ray, O., 229
Raymond, B. L., 406
Rayner, R., 242–243, 246
Raynor, D. A., 578
Read, J., 45
Read, J. D., 155
Read, P. P., 378
Reagan, R., 192, 417, 486
Reason, J., 445
Rebar, A., 460
Reber, R., 313

Rector, N. A., 512
Redd, W. H., 221, 590
Reddon, J. E., 36
Reddon, J. R., 36, 457
Reddy, A. V., 319
Reddy, P. B., 319
Reed, A., 462
Reed, D. R., 382
Reed, G. M., 598
Reed, M., 185
Reeder, K., 327
Reese, E. P., 237, 253
Reese, L., 460
Reese, T., 100
Reeve, C., 100
Reeve, J. M., 121
Reeves, G. M., 507
Regalia, C., 461
Regan, P. C., 311
Regan, T., 20
Regehr, C., 53, 551
Regehr, W. G., 75
Reggiani, P., 32
Regier, D. A., 489
Rehbein, F., 34
Reichelt, K. P., 181
Reicher, S., 508
Reifels, L., 549
Reifman, A., 124
Reilly, R. R., 351
Reilly, T., 205
Reimer, J., 128
Reinders, A. A. T., 502
Reiner, W. G., 395
Reinholtz, C., 503
Reinisch, J. M., 624
Reinvang, I., 283
Reisenzein, R., 437
Reisner, A. D., 546
Reissing, E. D., 393
Reiter, R. C., 591
Reminger, S. L., 279
Remington, G., 515
Remy-St. Louis, G., 186
Renaud, S, 324
Renn, J. A., 126
Renner, J. W., 132
Renshaw, P. F., 92
Rescorla, L., 329
Rescorla, R. A., 241, 260–261
Resendes, J., 457
Resick, P. A., 564
Ressler, R. K., 464–465
Rethinam, V., 124
Rettew, D. C., 65
Revelle, W., 400, 404
Revitch, E., 465
Reynaert, C., 576
Reyner, L. A., 209
Reynolds, C. R., 350
Reynolds, S., 488
Rezai, A. R., 545
Rha, S. S., 382
Rheingold, H. L., 329

Rhine, J. B., 192
Rhine, L., 192
Rhodes, E., 602
Rhodes, K., 609
Rhodewalt, F., 598
Rhue, J. W., 220
Rhyne, R., 109
Ricci Bitti, P. E., 424
Ricciardelli, L. A., 387
Rice, J., 574
Rice, M. L., 328
Richard, M., 431
Richards, C., 521
Richards, D., 122
Richards, H. C., 128
Richards, M. H., 508
Richards, T. L., 343, 344
Richardson, B., 413, 416
Richardson, D., 54
Richelson, E., 302
Richfield, E. K., 231
Richter, J. E., 567
Richter, L., 589
Rickels, K., 546
Rieber, R. W., 200
Riecken, H. W., 610
Rieckert, J., 540
Ried, K., 51
Rief, W., 498
Riemann, R., 358, 475
Ries, M. L., 84
Rif, J., 273
Riggs, J. M., 597
Riggs, L. A., 159, 161
Rijsdijk, F., 62
Riley, J. L., 186
Rilling, M., 301
Rinaldi, R. C., 556
Ring, C., 186, 563
Ringelmann, M., 618
Rinn, W. E., 416
Riordan, C. A., 604
Ripperger, J. A., 110
Risch, N., 396
Risser, D., 425
Rittenhouse, C., 219
Rittenhouse, C. D., 160, 219
Rivera-Tovar, L. A., 277
Rixon, L., 565
Rizzo, M., 91
Roane, B. M., 213
Robazza, C., 400
Robbins, S. B., 461
Roberson-Nay, R., 492
Robert, M., 263
Roberts, A. R., 602
Roberts, L., 567
Roberts, L. E., 180
Roberts, M., 303
Roberts, M. C., 255
Roberts, R. D., 361
Roberts, R. E., 133, 358
Roberts, R. E. L., 468
Roberts, S. J., 589

Name Index I-23

Roberts, T., 602
Robertson, N., 576
Robins, C. J., 503
Robins, R. W., 14
Robinson, D. L., 471
Robinson, F. P., 294
Robinson, L. A., 504
Robinson, M. E., 186, 433
Robinson, S. J., 290
Robleda-Gomez, S., 394
Roccas, S., 455
Rocchetti, G., 452
Rochat, F., 623
Roche, A., 232
Rochet, T., 515
Rock, D. A., 348
Rock, I., 166, 172
Rocklin, T., 620
Rockwell, T., 193
Rodgers, J. E., 290
Rodgers, J. L., 369
Rodgers, M. A., 201
Rodgers, R., 404
Rodier, P. M., 522
Rodin, J., 380, 381, 385, 389, 576
Rodnick, E. H., 517
Roe, C. A., 191
Roefs, A., 501
Roelofs, K., 500
Roesch, R., 485
Roeschke, J., 207
Roesler, F., 282
Rogers, A. E., 214, 388
Rogers, B. A., 67
Rogers, C., 13, 14, 467, 470, 485, 538, 540
Rogers, J. D., 617
Rogers, K. B., 365
Rogers, L. J., 93
Rogers, R., 456, 457, 485, 520
Rogers, R. L., 137
Rogers, R. W., 625
Rogge, R. D., 143
Roghmann, K. J., 565
Rogoff, B., 132
Röhl, M., 178
Rohsenow, D. J., 18
Roig, M., 193
Roisman, G. I., 121
Roisson, B., 424
Rokeach, M., 513, 614
Rokke, P. D., 552
Roll, J. P., 184
Roll, R., 184
Rolland, J.-P., 457
Rollin, B. E., 55
Rollings, L. J. L., 290
Rollman, G. B., 186
Romanski, L., 432
Romer, D., 628
Romney, D. M., 125
Ronan, K. R., 406
Rondall, J. A., 331
Rook, K. S., 129

Rooms, L., 352
Roosa, M. W., 503
Roosevelt, E., 378, 466
Roosevelt, F., 36
Roozendaal, B., 87, 303
Ropka, M. E., 53
Rorschach, H., 450
Rosales, R., 26
Rosch, E., 311, 334
Rose, D., 34
Rose, J. E., 261
Rose, P., 468
Rose, S. P. R., 302
Rosen, G. M., 287
Rosen, L., 587
Rosen, R. C., 393
Rosenbaum, M. E., 603
Rosenberg, M., 468
Rosenbloom, T., 153
Rosenhan, D. L., 490
Rosenkoetter, L. I., 264
Rosenman, R. H., 568–569
Rosenthal, N. E., 506–507
Rosenthal, R., 42–43, 44, 50, 53, 423, 600
Rosentreter, C. J., 457
Rosenwald, R. R., 69
Rosenzweig, M. R., 99
Roskies, E., 584
Ross, B., 180
Ross, D. F., 26, 291, 422
Ross, E., 83
Ross, E. D., 94, 422, 500
Ross, L., 469, 597
Ross, M. J., 580
Ross, R. R., 45
Ross, S. R., 455
Rosser, S., 495
Rossetti, Y., 60
Rossi, A. F., 160
Rossi, A. M., 535
Rostein, S., 581
Roter, D., 429, 590
Roter, D. L., 590
Roth, A., 152
Roth, L. W., 137
Roth, T., 211
Roth, W. T., 258, 492
Rothbart, M. K., 471
Rothbaum, F. M., 576
Rothbaum, F., 605
Rotheram-Borus, M. J., 583
Rothon, C., 578
Rotter, J. B., 460, 463
Rotton, J., 482
Roug, L., 328
Rouillon, F., 517
Rounds, J., 574
Routh, D. K., 331, 400
Rouw, R., 151
Rovine, M. J., 65
Rowan, A. B., 508
Rowe, D. C., 369
Rowe, L. S., 543

Rowe, R., 389
Rowse, G., 463
Rowsell, H. C., 55
Rozin, P., 26, 386, 426, 607, 619
Rubin, D. C., 271
Rubin, D. H., 454
Rubin, E., 166
Rubin, I. C., 313
Rubin, J. R., 125
Rubin, L. C., 551
Rubin, R. T., 624
Rubin, Z., 54
Rubio, N., 408, 584
Ruble, A. E., 388
Ruch, W., 430, 431
Ruda, M. A., 186
Rude, S. S., 556
Rudolph, D. L., 563
Rudolph, K. D., 563
Rudy, D., 122
Ruedl, G., 401
Rueter, M. A., 123
Ruffin, C. L., 565
Ruffman, T. K., 117
Ruggieri, R., 120
Ruggiero, M., 629
Ruhrmann, S., 507
Ruiter, M. E., 208
Ruiz, G., 78
Rujescu, D., 475
Rule, B. G., 625
Rumbaugh, D. M., 336, 337, 358
Rummel, A., 406
Runco, M. A., 319
Rungger, D., 110
Rungger-Brändle, E., 110
Rury, J. L., 364
Rus, C. L., 317
Ruscio, A. M., 45
Rush, B., 501, 530–531
Rushton, J. P., 83, 317, 365
Rusiniak, K. W., 237
Russell, B. L., 425
Russell, G. F. M., 388
Russell, G. L., 423, 556
Russell, J. A., 311, 414, 424, 426, 604
Russell, M. A. H., 588
Russell, M. J., 182
Russell, S. T., 121
Russo, A., 95
Russo, N. F., 8
Rust, J., 125
Ruth, B., 406
Rutherford, A., 12
Rutherford, E., 178
Rutkowski, G. K., 628
Rutledge, T. R., 435
Rutter, M., 352
Ruys, K. K., 203
Ryalls, B. O., 281
Ryan, A. M., 598
Ryan, C. S., 240, 599
Ryan, E. D., 408
Ryan, E. R., 469

Ryan, J. J., 19, 137
Ryan, K. M., 431
Ryan, R. H., 293
Ryan, R. M., 405, 408, 584, 599
Rymal, A. M., 263

Saariluoma, P., 294
Sabatini, B. L., 75
Sabbagh, M., 78
Sabine, W., 540
Sabini, J., 619
Sable, P., 519
Sachau, D., 467
Sachdev, P., 544, 547
Sachdeva, S., 128
Sachs-Ericsson, N., 503
Sackeim, H. A., 545
Sacks, O., 151, 189
Saczynski, J. S., 137
Sadeh, A., 208
Sadigh-Lindell, B., 186
Safer, M. A., 577
Saftoiu, A., 323
Sagar, K. A., 511
Sage, R. M., 576
Sageman, M., 287
Sagiv, L., 455
Sahoo, F. M., 350
Sahraie, A., 91
Saito, Y., 509
Sakaguchi, M., 100
Sakata, H., 169
Sakhel, K., 625
Sala, F., 429, 590
Salanova, M., 461
Salas, D., 32
Salas, E., 580, 617
Salerian A. J., 394
Sales, B. D., 53
Saletu, B., 50
Salfati, C. G., 465
Salgado, J., 463
Salin-Pascual, R. J., 86
Salkovskis, P. M., 32, 496
Sallis, J. F., 384
Salmon, D. P., 280
Salovey, P., 580
Salthouse, T. A., 137
Saltz, E., 452
Salvatore, J., 38
Samari, S. A. A., 482
Samelson, F., 364
Sameroff, A., 62
Samms, M., 273
Sampson, N. A., 489, 491
Samuels, C., 222
Samuels, C. A., 602
Samulack, D. D., 91
Sanbonmatsu, D. M., 598
Sanchez, E. C., 152
Sanchez, J. I., 463
Sanchez, M., 432
Sand, P., 546
Sanday, L., 289

Sander, K., 87
Sander, L. C., 506
Sanderman, R., 428
Sanders, P., 329
Sanders, R. J., 337
Sanderson, S., 382
Sandman, D., 589
Sando, W., 221
Sandvik, E., 429
Sanford, E. C., 215
Sanford, R. N., 614
Sanger, T. D., 258
Sanghvi, C., 294
Sangrador, J. L., 605
Sankar, V., 99
Sansone, L. A., 519
Sansone, R. A., 519
Santa Cruz, K. S., 141
Santesso, D. L., 83
Santucci, A. C., 101
Sanz, J., 579
Saper, J. R., 185
Saphire-Bernstein, S., 567
Sapir, A., 60
Sarason, S., 370
Sargent, P. L., 174
Sargent, R. G., 384
Sargent-Cox, K. A., 108
Sarkola, T., 624
Satapathy, B., 378
Satin, M. S., 427
Satir, V., 543
Sato, J., 185
Sato, K., 312
Sato, T., 183
Satoh, M., 84
Sattely-Miller, E. A., 181
Sattler, J. M., 137
Satz, P., 97
Saudino, K. J., 475
Sauer, J. D., 292
Sauerwein, H. C., 98
Saum, C. A., 228
Saunders, C., 146, 580
Savage-Rumbaugh, E. S., 335, 337–339, 338
Savitz, J., 571, 572
Sawatzky, J. V., 136
Saxe, L., 417
Saygin, A. P., 327
Sbrocco, T., 493
Scabini, E., 461
Scammell, T. E., 208, 214
Scanley, B. E., 230
Scarborough, H. S., 329
Scarr, S., 123, 367, 368
Schaaf, J. M., 293
Schaal, B., 114
Schaap, C. P. D. R., 556
Schaap, J., 204
Schachter, S., 384, 436, 437, 585, 601, 610
Schacter, D. L., 201, 279, 282, 302
Schaefer, G. B., 352

Schaefer, M., 499
Schaeffer, J., 256
Schaeffer, M. H., 320
Schafe, G. E., 246
Schafer, W. D., 140
Schaie, K. W., 109, 137
Schaller, M., 627
Schanberg, S., 70, 569
Scharf, A., 257
Scharkow, M., 625
Schaubroeck, J., 461
Schaufeli, W. B., 461, 575
Schechter, E., 99
Schedlowski, M., 391, 573
Scheffler, T. S., 468
Scheflin, A. W., 287
Scheich, H., 87
Schein, E., 608
Schenker, N., 91
Schepers, J. S., 588
Scherer, K. R., 426, 436, 438
Scheuber, H.-P., 152
Scheuerecker, J., 78
Scheuerer-Englisch, H., 120
Schiff, M., 367
Schiffman, H. R., 166
Schiffman, S. S., 181
Schill, T., 431
Schimel, J., 446, 469
Schindler, C. W., 246
Schlegel, P. A., 152
Schleifer, S. J., 571, 581
Schlesinger, L. B., 465
Schlumpf, Y. R., 502
Schmader, T., 351
Schmeidler, G. R., 193
Schmid, H., 172
Schmid, J., 417
Schmidt, F. L., 192, 285, 349
Schmidt, G., 629
Schmidt, L. A., 83
Schmidt, M. H., 390
Schmidt, N. B., 493
Schmidtke, A., 508
Schmitt, G. J., 78
Schmitt, I., 86
Schmitt, K. L., 292
Schmitt, N., 350
Schmitt-Rodermund, E., 133
Schneider, B. H., 322
Schneider, C. J., 259
Schneider, D. J., 497, 587
Schneider, H. G., 618
Schneider, M. E., 109
Schneider, N. G., 587
Schneider, P., 91
Schneider, S., 427
Schneiderman, H., 572
Schneiderman, N., 583
Schneider-Rosen, K., 120
Schnell, S. V., 127
Schnittjer, S. K., 322
Schnur, E., 369
Schoelmerich, A., 119

Schoen, L. M., 297
Schölmerich, A., 120
Schonemann, P. H., 473
Schonemann, R. D., 473
Schooler, C., 137
Schor, C., 158
Schotte, C. K. W., 483
Schreter, Z., 400
Schretlen D., 359
Schroth, M. L., 401, 406
Schrut, A. H., 451
Schuetze, P., 112
Schuld, A., 540
Schull, W. J., 352
Schulsinger, F., 514
Schultz, W., 70
Schulz, M., 180
Schulz, P., 401, 581
Schulz, R., 136
Schulze, B., 513
Schumaker, J. B., 256
Schürhoff, F., 200
Schuster, B., 597
Schuster, D. T., 356
Schusterman, R. J., 335
Schutte, N. S., 361
Schutter, D. J. L. G., 624
Schwammle, J., 421
Schwartz, B. L., 288
Schwartz, C., 154
Schwartz, C. E., 471
Schwartz, J. C., 547
Schwartz, J. H., 298
Schwartz, M. D., 243
Schwartz, S., 91
Schwartz, S. H., 140, 455
Schwartz, S. J., 108, 142
Schwarz, N., 428
Schwarzer, R., 584
Schwarzwald, J., 614
Schweizer, T. A., 86
Schwenzer, M., 499
Schyns, P., 428
Scogin, F., 505, 556
Scogin, F. R., 552
Scopesi, A., 187
Scott, B. W., 545
Scott, D., 610
Scott, J., 540, 552
Scott, M. S., 355
Scott, R. L., 457
Scott, T. H., 401
Scotto, P., 263
Scoville, W. B., 88, 300
Scruggs, T. E., 296
Scully, J. A., 563
Seamonds, C., 476
Searleman, A., 96
Sears, P., 356
Sears, R. R., 356, 624
Sears, S. F., 584
Sechrest, L., 463
Sedikides, C., 597
Sedlacek, K., 258

Seegert, C. R., 537
Seeley, J. R., 491
Seely, D., 26
Seeman, T. E., 567
Segal, D. L., 449
Segal, J., 198
Segal, N. L., 65, 367
Segall, M. H., 115
Segerstrom, S. C., 598
Seghier, M. L., 91
Segovia, C., 183
Séguin, J. R., 389
Seibert, G. B., 422
Seidenbecher, T., 299
Seidlitz, L., 281, 429
Seidman, L. J., 524
Seidman, S. M., 393
Seifert, C. M., 418
Seifert, L. S., 311
Seiler, W. J., 535
Seitz, V., 369
Sekhon, M., 469
Seki, K., 605
Sekuler, R., 169
Selcuk, E., 143
Self, D. J., 109
Seligman, M. E., 575
Seligman, M. E. P., 257, 260, 495, 503, 505, 575, 576
Sellers, R. M., 575, 615
Selye, H., 567
Semendeferi, K., 91
Semin, G. R., 270
Semmelroth, J., 62
Semple, S. J., 543
Senn, C. Y., 387
Serebriakoff, V., 355
Sergeant, J., 523
Sergio, L. E., 332
Serovich, J. M., 542
Serper, M. R., 513
Seršic, D. M., 34
Servan-Schreiber, D., 419
Setlow, B., 301
Sevic, R. A., 338
Sewell, K. W., 515, 520
Seydel, E. R., 590
Seyfarth, R. M., 325
Seyle, H., 562
Seymour, T. L., 418
Shachtman, T., 464
Shackelford, T. K., 63
Shade, S. B., 508
Shadish, W. R., 555
Shafer, D., 589
Shaffer, J. W., 573
Shafran, R., 388
Shafto, M. G., 418
Shah, M., 383
Shah, N. J., 89
Shahab, L., 259
Shaham, Y., 320
Shahar, G., 216
Shahidulla, S., 94

Name Index I-25

Shakespeare, 80, 436
Shammi, P., 430
Shanab, M. E., 622
Shanker, S. G., 338
Shannon, D., 119
Shapiro, C. M., 210
Shapiro, J., 327
Shapiro, J. K., 127, 554
Shapiro, L. A., 13
Shapiro, L. J., 497
Shapiro, M., 303
Shapka, J. D., 579
Sharma, M., 70, 507
Sharma, Y. S., 606
Sharp, M., 70
Sharpe, D., 54
Sharpley, A. L., 208
Sharps, M. J., 281
Shaughnessy, M. F., 509
Shavitt, S., 607
Shaw, D. F., 584
Shaw, J. S., III, 292
Shaw, P., 524
Shayer, M., 132
Shea, D. L., 141, 357
Shea, M. T., 221, 554
Shean, G., 495
Shear, M. K., 492, 497
Shedler, J., 533
Sheehan, D. B., 41
Sheehan, E. P., 606
Sheehan, P. W., 222
Sheehy, R. A., 580
Sheese, S., 141
Sheets, V. L., 605
Sheffield, A., 464
Sheffield, F., 609
Sheikh, J. I., 493
Sheiner, E. K., 187
Sheiner, E., 187
Sheinman, L., 405
Sheinman, M., 36
Shek, D. T. L., 133
Sheldon, K. M., 408, 584
Sheldon, W. H., 471–472, 475
Shell, R., 621
Shelley, M., 73
Shemyakina, N. V., 420
Shen, K., 71
Shenaut, G. K., 288
Shepherd, S., 600
Sheppard, L. C., 485
Sheppard, S., 100
Shepperd, J. A., 618
Sherblom, J. C., 430
Sherbourne, C. D., 590
Sherburne, L. M., 263
Sherman, J. A., 256
Sherman, S. J., 313, 576, 621
Sherrell, D. L., 607
Sherrington, C., 75
Sherwood, S. J., 191
Sheth, R. N., 185
Shettleworth, S. J., 260, 313

Shevell, S. K., 164
Shields, J., 514
Shields, S. A., 362
Shiffrin, R. M., 271, 284
Shiflett, S. C., 186, 581
Shih, J. B., 428
Shih, M., 600
Shilling, P., 510
Shim, E. K., 39
Shimada-Sugimoto, M., 493
Shimamura, A. P., 295
Shimizu, M., 576
Shimizu, T., 211
Shimokawa, I., 137
Shimonaka, H., 86
Shimp, T. A., 240
Shin, L. M., 471
Shin, L. M., 564
Shine, J., 510
Shinskey, J. L., 117
Shioiri, T., 493
Shipley, M., 143
Shiraishi, T., 381
Shirom, A., 576
Shneidman, E., 145
Shneidman, E. S., 509
Shockley, W., 365
Shoda, Y., 459
Shodahl, S. A., 248
Shoham-Vardi, I., 187
Shook, N. J., 227
Short, A., 460
Short, E., 232
Shostrom, E. L., 468
Shotland, R. L., 628
Showers, C. J., 139, 468
Shroff, H., 45
Shugar, G. J., 618
Shumaker, S. A., 303
Shumate, R., 467
Shurcliff, A., 431
Shuster, L., 79
Sias, P. M., 601
Siddiqui, R. N., 576
Sidis, W. J., 357
Sidorov, A. A., 210
Siebler, F., 609
Siegel, J. M., 565, 580, 581
Siegel, M., 293
Siegel, S., 244, 261
Siegler, J. C., 70
Siegler, R. S., 117
Siegmund, A., 537
Sierra-Honigmann, A. M., 515
Siever, M. D., 387
Sigal, L. H., 565
Sigmundson, H. K., 394
Signorella, M. L., 281
Siimes, M. A., 386
Silberg, J. L., 389
Silberstein, L. R., 389
Silburn, P., 87
Silinsky, E. M., 229
Silke, A., 626

Silva, J. M., 580
Silverman, I. W., 140
Silverman, R., 258
Silvern, L., 115
Silverstein, L. B., 123
Silverstein, M., 109
Silverthorne, Z. A., 605
Silvestri, S., 515
Simantov, E., 589
Simen, A. A., 506
Simmons, J. P., 193
Simmons, L., 209
Simon, H., 322
Simon, H. A., 14, 77, 275, 314
Simon, J. R., 102, 227, 599, 611
Simon, N., 308
Simon, T., 346
Simonides, 297
Simonoff, E., 352, 389
Simons, D. A., 255
Simons-Morton, B. G., 135, 587
Simon-Thomas, J. A., 406
Simonton, D. K., 316, 317
Simpson, B. A., 417
Simpson, D., 82
Simpson, O. J., 416
Sina, Abu Ibn, 3
Singer, A. G., 183
Singer, J. D., 123
Singer, J. E., 320, 420, 436, 437
Singer, J. L., 469
Singh, A. K., 214
Singh, B. B., 603
Singh, P., 128
Sinha, R., 385
Sini, B., 425
Sinson, J. C., 355
Sirhan, S., 500
Sirridge, M., 3
Sitton, S., 619
Sizemore, C. C., 501
Sjoelund, B. H., 187
Sjostrand, L., 504
Skeel, J., 321
Skidmore, J. R., 505
Skinner, B. F., 11, 247–249, 251, 253,
 255, 256–257, 260, 330, 460,
 463, 485
Skinner, N., 436
Skinner, N. F., 27
Skoe, E. E. A., 128
Skoog, K., 587
Skre, I., 496, 514
Skrondal, A., 232
Slabbekoorn, D., 624
Slater, A., 169
Slater, C. L., 145
Slavik, S., 13
Slayton, J. M., 314
Slife, B. D., 4
Slifer, K. J., 534
Sliškovic, A., 34
Sloan, K. R., Jr., 159
Slutske, W. S., 519

Small, B. J., 141
Small, S. L., 264
Smeets, R. J. E. M., 461
Smilek, D., 201
Smirnova, A. A., 263
Smit, E., 584
Smith, A. D., 298
Smith, A. J., 34, 447
Smith, B., 556
Smith, B. A., 32, 139, 264
Smith, B. D., 569
Smith, B. M., 256, 533, 538, 540
Smith, C. J., 183, 232, 427, 602
Smith, C. P., 128
Smith, C. T., 607
Smith, D. A., 143
Smith, D. G., 288
Smith, E., 292, 587
Smith, H. V., 275
Smith, L. B., 114, 116
Smith, L. T., 301
Smith, M. C., 54, 221, 499
Smith, M. L., 553, 554
Smith, M. R., 231, 350, 512
Smith, N. F., 296
Smith, P. B., 332, 620
Smith, S. M., 288, 289, 309
Smith, S. S., 143, 214, 520, 536
Smith, S. T., 337
Smith, T. B., 45
Smith, T. W., 569, 590
Smits, M. G., 41
Smolak, L., 385, 388
Smoller, J. W., 382, 383
Smye, V., 53
Smyth, J. M., 580
Snarey, J. R., 128
Sneed, J. R., 108, 142
Snel, J., 565
Snieder, H., 569
Snow, C. E., 331
Snow, D. S., 93
Snow, W. G., 141
Snowden, L. R., 556
Snyder, A. Z., 60
Snyder, B. K., 565
Snyder, C. R., 499
Snyder, J. S., 545
Snyder, M., 458
Snyder, P., 38
Snyder, R. F., 361
Snyder, S., 78–79
Snyder, S. H., 76, 79
Snyder, S. W., 38
Snyderman, M., 363
Sobkiewicz, T. A., 386
Sockeel, P., 219
Söderfeldt, B., 84
Soderstrom, N. C., 506
Soenens, B., 387
Soerensen, S., 50
Soffer–Dudek, N., 216
Sogon, S., 423
Sokol, S. M., 343

Solcova, I., 577
Sollars, S. I., 246
Sollers, J. J., 570
Solodkin, A., 264
Solomon, C., 542
Solomon, R. L., 434
Solomon, S., 187, 468
Solowij, N., 232
Soltanieh, S., 110
Somervell, E., 601
Sommer, B., 136
Sommer, K. L., 451
Sommers, S., 427
Sonino, N., 69, 567
Sönksen, P. H., 69
Sonstroem, R. J., 407
Soroka, S., 601
Sotsky, S. M., 554
Soumier, A., 508, 545
Sourkes, T. L., 76
Sousa, L., 506
Soussignan, R., 114, 435
Sovio, U., 385
Sowell, T., 364–365
Sowislo, J. F., 468
Spadafore, C. D., 20
Spangenberg, E. R., 181
Spangenberg, J., 615
Spangler, W. D., 451
Spanos, N., 502
Spanos, N. P., 221, 222, 224
Sparks, G. G., 451, 607
Sparrow, D., 576
Spearman, C., 357
Spears, R., 625, 626
Speca, M., 581
Spector, I. P., 393
Spector, N. H., 562
Spector, P. E., 463
Speed, J., 100
Speicher, C. E., 574
Speisman, J. C., 438
Spencer, R. C., 524
Spencer, S. J., 570, 599, 614
Spengler, F., 184
Sperling, G., 274
Sperry, R., 15
Sperry, R. W., 98
Spicer, R. S., 509
Spiegel, A. D., 486
Spiegelman, D., 96
Spielman, A. J., 209
Spierings, E. L. H., 185
Spillman, L., 7
Spillmann, J., 7
Spinath, F. M., 475
Spinella, M., 79
Spinelli, D. N., 173
Spitzer, R. L., 490, 498
Spottiswoode, S. J. P., 193
Spotts, E. L., 62
Sprecher, S., 605
Springer, S. P., 93, 95, 141
Sprock, J., 518

Spurr, J. M., 495
Spyer, K. M., 419
Squire, L. R., 299
Squires-Wheeler, E., 396
Srikameswaran, S., 53
Srivastava, S., 507
St. Quintin, D., 614
Staats, A. W., 460
Stachnik, T. J., 443
Stack, S., 428, 508
Stadulis, R. E., 618
Stafford, J., 502
Stafford-Clark, D., 496
Stahl, T., 417
Stainton, N. R., 443
Stairs, A., 134
Stajkovic, A. D., 464
Stalikas, A., 471
Stall, R., 583
Stam, H. J., 7, 221
Stamm, C., 360
Stamps, J. J., 181
Standing, L., 288
Standing, L. G., 443, 620
Stanhope, N., 501
Stankov, L., 358, 361
Stanley, J. C., 138, 355, 357
Stanowicz, L., 332
Stansfeld, S., 578
Stapleton, J. A., 588
Stapleton, K., 598
Staquet, P., 576
Stark, E., 89, 255
Stark-Wroblewski, K., 19
Starzyk, K. B., 624
Staska, S. L., 385
Stathopoulou, A., 515
Steel, G. D., 21
Steel, P., 428
Steele, C., 570
Steele, C. M., 227, 302, 350, 351
Steeves, R., 53
Steffen, P. R., 585
Steffen, V. J., 140
Steiger, H., 389
Steiger, J. H., 110, 357
Stein, D. G., 101
Stein, D. J., 45
Stein, D. M., 556
Stein, J. L., 599
Stein, M., 571
Stein, M. B., 475, 493, 494
Stein, R. I., 385
Stein, R. M., 587
Stein, Z. A., 383
Steinberg, L., 122
Steiner, J. E., 425
Steiner, S. S., 259
Steinfeld, B., 552
Steinkamp, F., 191
Steinmetz, H., 95
Stein-Zamir, C., 587
Stellfeld, M., 522
Stelmack, R. M., 453, 471

Ste-Marie, D. M., 263
Stemmer, N., 332
Stenger, V. A., 497
Stennes, L., 281
Stennett, J., 426
Stephan, C. W., 422
Stephan, K. E., 95
Stephan, W. G., 422, 597, 614
Stephan, Y., 45
Stephany, A., 423
Steptoe, A., 575, 581
Sterling, R. C., 43
Stern, B. B., 599
Stern, R. A., 578
Stern, R. M., 189
Stern, W., 346
Sternbach, L., 227
Sternberg, R. J., 318, 355, 357, 359, 360, 605
Stessman, J., 137
Stevens, G. L., 453
Stevens, S. S., 472, 475
Stevenson, H. W., 35
Stevenson, R. L., 230
Steward, O., 299
Stewart, J. W., 554
Stewart, M. G., 302, 572
Stewart, S. E., 185, 449, 497
Stewart, S. H., 499
Stewart, T. L., 612
Stice, E., 385
Stickgold, R., 214, 219
Stiefenhofer, A. E., 185
Still, A., 538
Stillman, R. C., 289
Stinard, T. A., 400
Stinnett, J. L., 382, 383
Stinson, D. A., 600
Stocks, N. P., 51
Stohr, O., 474
Stoiber, K. C., 20
Stolerman, I. P., 229
Stollstorff, M., 15
Stone, A. A., 385, 427, 518, 563, 580
Stone, S. N., 206
Stoner, J. A. F., 616
Stone-Romero, E. F., 602
Stopa, L., 495
Storck, L. E., 542
Storey, A. E., 69
Storm, D. R., 218
Storm, L., 193
Stotland, S., 389
Stout, J. C., 574
Straatman, H. M., 515
Strack, F., 428
Straneva, P. A., 79
Strang, J., 225
Strassberg, D. S., 393
Strassman, R. J., 230
Strathdee, S. A., 543
Strathman, A. J., 43
Strauman, T. J., 469, 492
Straus, H., 519

Straus, M. A., 255
Straw, M. J., 628
Strayer, D. L., 201, 202
Strbac, L., 454
Streiner, D. L., 50
Streitmatter, J., 133
Stricker, E. M., 380, 381
Strickland, B. R., 463
Striegel-Moore, R. H., 389
Stroebe, W., 146
Strohl, K. P., 209
Strongman, K. T., 486
Stroop, J. R., 203
Struch, N., 140
Stuart, G. L., 538
Stuart, S., 499
Stuetzle, R., 42
Stunkard, A. J., 382, 383
Sturgeon, R. S., 158
Sturmey, P., 543
Stuss, D. T., 86, 92, 430
Suarez, E., 569
Subandi, M. A., 516
Subotnik, R. F., 356
Sucala, M., 552
Sud, R., 388
Sudhalter, V., 329
Sue, S., 45, 370, 531, 556
Suedfeld, P., 21, 401, 407
Sufka, K. J., 186
Suggs, M. S., 181
Suh, E., 143, 429
Suh, E. M., 427
Sui, O. L., 463
Sulik, K., 112
Sullins, E. S., 404
Sullivan, H. S., 447
Sullivan, J. E., 352
Sullivan, P. F., 382, 514
Sullivan, T., 51
Suls, J., 562
Sumer, N., 468
Sumerlin, J. R., 469
Sunday, S. R., 387
Sundequist, U., 401
Surakka, V., 157
Suskind, P. B., 486
Susman, E. J., 131
Sussan, T. A., 354
Susser, M. W., 383
Sussman, S., 531
Sutton, J. E., 263
Suzuki, A., 88
Suzuki, N., 100
Svensson, M., 101
Swain, A., 408
Swain, R. M., 385
Swan, S., 607
Swank, R. T., 573
Swann, W. B., Jr., 144
Swanson, J., 524
Swartz, M. S., 507
Swartz, S., 489
Swartzentruber, D., 242

Swayze, V. W., 516, 544
Sweat, J. A., 191
Sweeney, P. D., 505
Sweet, B. A. M., 612
Swenson, C. R., 529
Swenson, R. S., 102
Swets, J. A., 370
Swiatek, M. A., 355, 357
Swickert, R. J., 457
Swiezy, N. B., 256
Swindale, N. V., 91, 174
Switzky, H. N., 351
Sykora, J., 577
Sylvia, M. R., 115
Symons, N., 190
Synhhorst, L., 37
Szabo, A., 429
Szasz, T., 486, 490
Szaszko, P. R., 95
Szlyk, J. P., 220
Szöke, A., 200
Szucko, J. J., 416–418

Taal, E., 590
Tafarodi, R. W., 468
Tager-Flusberg, H., 329
Tager-Rusberg, H., 83
Taira, M., 169
Taits, I., 217
Tajfel, H., 614
Takagi, M., 168
Takagi, T., 327
Takahata, Y., 34
Takai, J., 320
Takano, K., 506
Takeda, M., 84
Takei, N., 515
Takei, Y., 83
Takeshima, M., 211 [
Takeuchi, D. T., 485, 556
Takeuchi, M. S., 19
Talarczyk, M., 216
Talarico, J. M., 271
Taleb, M., 517
Taller, A. M., 515
Talwar, V., 21
Tam, K. P., 598
Tam, S. F., 324
Tam, W.-C. C., 515
Tamang, B. L., 579
Tammings, C. A., 512
Tamres, L. K., 579
Tan, C., 571, 572
Tan, F. D., 395
Tan, G., 186
Tan, J., 429, 605
Tanaka-Matsumi, J., 486, 495, 517
Tang, S. H., 405
Tankard, J. W., 49
Tanneberger, M., 549
Tanno, Y., 506
Tardieu, D., 180
Tarquini, R., 385
Tarricone, B. J., 101, 102

Tarrier, N., 516
Tarsitano, M. S., 312
Tart, C. T., 231
Tashiro, J. S., 404
Tasker, F., 398
Tateyama, M., 513
Taub, E., 258
Taubes, G., 382
Tauer, C. A., 69
Taulbee, P., 484
Taverniers, J., 577
Tay, L., 428
Taylor, A., 138, 171, 227, 250, 338, 571, 572, 618
Taylor, C. R., 599
Taylor, D., 492
Taylor, D. J., 213
Taylor, J. G., 193
Taylor, K. I., 159, 192, 496
Taylor, M. S., 62
Taylor, R. L., 349
Taylor, S., 133, 231
Taylor, S. A., 256
Taylor, S. E., 470, 485, 566–567, 576, 578, 598
Taytroe, L., 218
Teague, K., 571, 572
Teasdale, J., 540
Teasdale, J. D., 485, 505
Teasdale, N., 189
Tebartz van Elst, L., 519
Tedeschi, J. T., 604
Tehrani, J. A., 513
Teichman, M., 460
Teichman, Y., 460
Teigen, K. H., 399
Teipel, S. J., 299
Telesca, T. Y., 124
Telford, C., 463
Tellegen, A., 65, 66, 474
Templer, D. I., 146
Templeton, L. M., 291
Tenenbaum, H. R., 126
Teng, E., 301
Tenzer, S., 585
Teo, A. R., 37
Terburg, D., 624
Teresa, M., 27, 454
Ter-Horst, K. M., 262
Terkel, J., 263
Terman, L., 346
Terman, L. M., 36–37, 355, 356
Terrace, H. S., 337
Terre-Blanche, M. J., 515
Terry-McElrath, Y. M., 109
Tervo, K., 492
Teti, D. M., 368
Thakker, J., 486
Thamaku, M., 542
Thase, M. E., 547
Thayer, J. F., 570
Thee, S. L., 322
Thelen, M. H., 502
Theodoros, D. G., 87

Therriault, D. J., 317
Thierry, N., 507
Thiessen, D., 377
Thomas, D. L., 620
Thomas, E., 419
Thomas, H., 138, 549
Thomas, R. L., 10
Thomas, T. N., 207, 486
Thomas, W. N., 26
Thomas-Dobson, S., 146
Thompson, A., 68, 122, 217, 570
Thompson, B., 38, 51
Thompson, H. T., 362
Thompson, J., 453
Thompson, J. K., 45, 299, 385
Thompson, K., 100
Thompson, L., 184, 397
Thompson, M. L., 79
Thompson, R. D., 94
Thompson, R. F., 299
Thompson, S. M., 299
Thomson, D. M., 288
Thomson, N. F., 596
Thordardottir, E. T., 329
Thornburg, K. R., 123
Thorndike, E. L., 247, 259–260, 404–405
Thornton, J. C., 571
Thorpe, S. J., 496
Throne, L. C., 581
Thunberg, M., 438
Thurstone, L. L., 359
Tiedt, A. D., 26
Tiefer, L., 391, 394
Tierney, A., 83
Tierney, A. J., 544
Tilden, J., 222
Tildesley, E., 608
Till, B. D., 241, 607
Tilley, A. J., 218
Timberlake, W., 238, 248, 260
Timm, H. W., 418
Timmann, D., 86
Timney, B., 174
Tindale, R. S., 568, 617
Tisdale, B., 522
Titchener, E., 6, 7
Tittler, B. I., 430
Titus, L. J., 617
Tobach, E., 19
Todd, L. K., 323
Todd-Bazemore, E., 531
Todman, D., 76
Toglia, M. P., 291
Tognacci, L. N., 610
Tolin, D. F., 498
Tolley-Schell, S. A., 200
Tolliver, D., 17
Tolman, E. C., 262–263
Toman, J. E. P., 309
Tomarken, A. J., 420
Tomchin, E. M., 361
Tomkiewicz, S., 368
Tomkins, S. S., 444

Tomlinson-Keasey, C., 356
Tonello, G., 21
Tönroos, M., 455
Tootell, R. B. H., 158
Topál, J., 263, 325
Topolinski, S., 313
Topp, L., 232
Tops, M., 229
Tordof, M. G., 382
Torff, B., 360
Torgersen, S., 492, 496, 498
Torgerson, S., 514
Toro-Morn, M., 605
Torrance, E. P., 317
Torres, I., 516
Torrey, E. F., 515
Torri, G., 185
Tosi, H., 563
Toth, C., 68
Toth, L. A., 212
Toth, S. L., 287
Toufexis, A., 209
Toukmanian, S. G., 531
Tourney-Jetté, E., 297
Touyz, S., 388
Towell, A., 380
Townsend, S. E., 55
Trabert, W., 492
Tracey, I., 188
Tracy, M., 503
Trainor, L. J., 83
Tramo, M., 177
Tranel, D., 60, 202
Trappey, C., 154
Traskman, L., 504
Travis, R. W., 543
Travolta, J., 155
Treat, T. A., 538
Treede, R. D., 185
Treffert, D. A., 343, 344
Tressoldi, P. E., 193
Trevethan, C. T., 91
Treynor, W., 506
Triandis, H. C., 26, 462, 598
Triarhou, L. C., 102
Trice, A. D., 53
Trickett, P. K., 369
Tridgell, A., 323
Trinchard, L. I., 50
Tripathi, H. L., 79
Triplet, R. G., 321
Triplett, N., 406, 595, 617
Tripp, P., 198–199
Trivedi, M. A., 302
Trofimovich, L., 508
Trogdon, J. G., 382
Troster, H., 425
Trotter, R. J., 360, 544
Trounson, R., 621
Trull, T. J., 482
Tryon, W. W., 533
Tsai, D. C., 457
Tsai, G. E., 502
Tsalafoutas, I., 83

I-28 Name Index

Tsang, B. Y. P., 605
Tsang, J.-A., 455
Tsao, J. C. I., 188
Tsaousis, J., 556
Tschanz, B., 598
Tschanz, B. T., 505
Tsingan, L., 361
Tsorbatzoudis, H., 94
Tsuda, T., 515
Tsutsui, K. I., 169
Tubb, V. A., 291
Tuchtenhagen, F., 232
Tucker, L. A., 475
Tucker, W. H., 52
Tuckey, M. R., 291
Tufik, S., 289
Tuke, D. H., 566
Tullis, J., 296
Tulsky, F. N., 191
Tulving, E., 278, 279, 288
Tuñón, M. J., 26
Tuozzi, G., 218
Turk, C. L., 494
Tur-Kaspa, M., 614
Turkheimer, E., 64, 362, 370
Turnbull, C. M., 174
Turner, A. P., 503
Turner, C. W., 568
Turner, D., 624
Turner, J. W., 401, 492
Turner, S. M., 492, 496
Tuschen-Caffier, B., 389
Tutankhamen, 80
Tuttle, R. J., 231
Tversky, A., 320, 321, 322
Twain, M., 192
Twenge, J. M., 615
Twisk, J. W. R., 565
Twitmyer, E. B., 239
Tyrrell, G., 516
Tzischinski, O., 463

Ueda, M., 509
Ugodulunwa, C. A., 403
Uhl, G. A., 565
Ullén, F., 358
Ullman, M., 191
Ullmann, L. P., 516
Ulrich, R. E., 443
Ulven, J., 539
Umezawa, Y., 377
Umpierrez, G. E., 32
Unal, E., 88
Unden, A.-L., 571
Unger, G., 301
Ungerleider, L. G., 160
Unrod, M., 229
Uppenkamp, S., 178
Upton, A., 81
Upton, T. D., 551
Urbano, R. C., 355
Ursu, S., 497
Urushihara, K., 262
Usher, J. A., 300

Utts, J., 192
Uvnaes-Moberg, K., 578
Uyeyama, R. K., 335

Vaidya, C. J., 15
Vaidya, R. S., 505
Vaillant, G. E., 119, 575
Vakil, E., 36
Valdez-Menchaca, M. C., 331
Valentine, C. W., 246
Valera, E. M., 524
Vallerand, R. J., 406, 408
Vallortigara, G., 94
Valouskova, V., 101
van Beek, N., 493
van Blokland, R., 568
Van Boven, R. W., 184
Van Cantfort, T. E., 336
Van Dam-Baggen, R., 543
Van de Water, T. J., 7
van den Akker, E. L. T., 382
Van Den Bossche, B., 483
van den Heuvel, O. A., 499
van den Oord, E., 369
van der Heiden, W., 512
van der Heijden, E., 322
van der Heijden, J., 41
van der Kloot, W. A., 140
Van der Kolk, B. A., 529
van der Maas, H. L. J., 62
Van Der Stege, J. G., 70
Van Der Werf, Y. D., 299
van Dixhoorn, J., 581
Van Doom, M. D., 134
Van Doornen, L. J. P., 568
Van Dyke, H., 429
Van Goozen, S. H. M., 624
van Grootheest, D. S., 65
van Hoeken, D., 387, 388
van Honk, J., 624
Van Hulle, C. A., 139
van IJzendoorn, M. H., 120
van Knippenberg, A., 610
van Mechelen, W., 565
van Ommen, G. J. B., 64
Van Rooijen, L., 620
van Rossum, E. F. C., 382
van Staveren, W. A., 183
Vanasse, C., 167
Vandelanotte, C., 460
VandenBos, G. R., 529
Vanderbeek, R. D., 229
Vandergriff, J. L., 227
VanderZee, K., 428
Vaney, D. I., 159
Vansteenkiste, M., 387
Varescon, I., 401
Vargas, D. L., 522
Vargas, E. A., 256
Vargas, J. S., 256
Vaughan, A., 191, 193
Vaughn, K., 611
Vaughn, M. G., 62, 70
Vázquez, S. M., 506

Vedhara, K., 565
Vein, A. M., 210
Veissier, I., 263
Vela, E., 289
Velichovsky, B. M., 278
Veliz, J., 550
Vella, M., 222
Vella-Zarb, R. A., 51
Vendemia, J. M. C., 188
Veneroso, C., 26
Veniegas, R., 583
Venn, J., 501
Ventis, W. L., 534
Ventrone, N. A., 630
Venturino, M., 221
Vera, M. N., 432
Verbalis, J. G., 381
Verbaten, M. N., 232
Verbov, G., 587
Verdoux, H., 515
Verissimo, M., 124
Vermetten, E., 182
Vermeulen, N., 424
Vernet-Maury, E., 433
Vernon, D. T. A., 610
Vernon, P. A., 358, 475
Veroff, J., 403
Verplanken, B., 610
Verschuere, B., 418
Vertes, R. P., 219
Vestal, M., 6
Vetter, H. J., 513
Viard, A., 279
Viborg, G., 438
Vidal, J., 585
Vig, P. S., 435
Vigliocco, G., 288
Vila, J., 432
Villa, L. C., 124
Villa, L., 323
Villardi, K., 173
Villeneuve, A., 580
Vilmann, P., 323
Vincent, K. R., 369
Vinci, C., 483
Viney, W., 2, 46
Vingerhoets, J. J. M., 426
Vingilis-Jaremo, L., 602
Vinson, D. P., 288
Visscher, B. R., 598
Visser, S. N., 523
Vissers, K., 185
Vitiello, B., 53
Vlaander, G. P., 620
Voeller, B., 583
Vogel, D. S., 95
Vogel, J. J., 95
Vogel, P., 98
Vogele, C., 589
Vogler, G. P., 569
Vogt, R. A., 584
Vohs, K. D., 398, 470
Voigt, H., 627
Vokey, J. R., 155

Vokonas, P., 576
Volckmar, A. L., 388
Volkmar, F., 521
Volkow, N. D., 524
Vollenweider, F. X., 232
von der Pahlen, B., 624
von Glasersfeld, E. C., 336
von Helversen, O., 157
von Kempelen, W., 322
von Senden, M., 174
Vondracek, F. W., 133
Vonnegut, K., 517
Vonnegut, M., 517
Vosburg, S. K., 320
Votruba-Drzal, E., 123
Voyer, D., 95, 138, 201
Vrbova, G., 99
Vuilleumier, P., 91
Vuksic-Mihaljevic, Z., 493
Vulliemoz, S., 83

Waas, G. A., 20
Wada, J., 95
Wadden, T. A., 385, 584, 585
Wade, A. G., 26
Wade, D. T., 500
Wade, T. D., 504, 538
Wagar, B. M., 462
Wagemans J., 165, 166, 167
Wager, T. D., 493
Wagner, A. D., 15
Wagner, M., 172
Wagner, N., 384
Wagner, R. K., 357
Wagner, R. V., 21
Wagner, S. H., 114
Wagner, U., 218
Wagstaff, G. F., 222, 287
Wahlsten, D., 64
Wai, J., 357
Waid, W. M., 417
Wainright, J. L., 121
Wakabayashi, M., 320
Wakeman, D. R., 102
Walach, H., 192
Walach, H. J., 561
Walburn, J., 565
Walczyk, J. J., 202
Wald, G., 163
Wald, J., 496
Waldfogel, J., 123
Waldhauser, F., 50
Waldman, I. D., 367, 524
Waldrop, M. M., 443
Walen, H. R., 579
Walk, R. D., 116, 423
Walker, A. E., 427
Walker, C., 575
Walker, E., 514
Walker, L. J., 126, 128
Walker, M. B., 620
Walker, M. M., 152
Walker, R., 464
Walker, W., 476

Name Index I-29

Walkey, F., 463
Wall, P., 185
Wallace, A. R., 5
Wallace, D. H., 136
Wallace, R. B., 73
Wallace, R. E., 551
Wallach, H., 171
Wallach, M. A., 616
Wallauer, W., 33
Wallbott, H. G., 426
Waller, J., 86
Waller, N. G., 65, 500
Wallingsford, L., 20
Walsh, B. T., 387
Walsh, D., 229, 512
Walsh, E., 389, 513
Walsh, J., 264, 370
Walsh, J. A., 37, 69
Walsh, J. C., 588
Walsh, J. J., 574
Walsh, M. L., 624
Walsh, R. O., 153
Walsleben, J. A., 209
Walster, E., 603, 604
Walter, A., 333
Walter, R., 465
Walters, E. E., 481, 491
Walters, G. C., 254
Walters, J., 20
Walters, P., 468
Waltz, D. L., 314
Wandell, B. A., 163
Wang, C. L., 401, 462
Wang, J. Q., 188
Wang, L., 273
Wang, M. Q., 189
Wang, X. T., 322
Wangeman, J. F., 401
Wanke, M., 607
Wankel, L. M., 584
Wanzer, M. B., 429
Warburton, D. M., 586
Ward, G. L., 506, 516
Ward, L. C., 457
Ward, P., 408
Ward, T., 486
Wardle, J., 382
Warfield, J. F., 418
Warner, D., 188
Warren, M. P., 131
Warren, R., 609
Warshaw, P. R., 607
Warwick, H. M. C., 32
Warwick-Evans, L. A., 190
Washburn, A. L., 379–380
Washburn, D. A., 358
Washburn, M. F., 7–8, 309
Washington, G., 229
Washio, Y., 241
Wasserman, E. A., 261
Watanabe, S., 72
Watanabe, Y., 312
Waterhouse, J., 205
Waterhouse, T., 579

Waters, B., 510
Waters, E., 121
Waters, R. S., 91
Watkins, B. A., 264
Watkins, R. J., 21, 36
Watrelot, A., 390
Watson, D., 488, 591
Watson, J. B., 11, 12, 54, 201, 239, 242–243, 246, 309, 376, 534
Watson, N. F., 213
Watt, M. C., 499
Watten, R. G., 168
Watters, J. K., 508
Watters, P. A., 400
Watts, B. L., 204
Watts, J., 544, 576
Watts, R. E., 449, 451
Watts, S., 86
Wawrzyniak, A. J., 575
Wax, M. L., 217
Wayda, V. K., 20
Waynbaum, I., 435
Weaver, J. B., 430
Weaver, L., 323
Weaver, M., 187
Weaver, M. S., 10
Webb, D., 21, 36
Webb, M., 112
Webb, W. B., 6, 205, 208, 211
Weber, A., 297
Weber, E., 4, 152
Weber, M. M., 488
Weber, R., 614
Webster, S., 377
Wechsler, D., 344–345, 347
Weekes, J. R., 220, 502
Weekes-Shackelford, V. A., 63
Weerts, A. H., 32
Wegner, D. M., 497
Weidman, N., 365
Weigand, D., 408
Weigel, R. H., 610
Weilage, M., 506
Weinberg, J., 574
Weinberg, M. S., 398
Weinberg, R., 408
Weinberg, R. A., 351, 367, 368
Weinberg, R. S., 580
Weinberger, N. M., 177
Weiner, B., 596–597, 629
Weinfield, N. S., 121
Weingartner, H., 289
Weinman, J., 565
Weinstein, L., 401
Weinstein, N. D., 582
Weinstein, R. S., 350
Weisfeld, G. E., 182
Weisman, J., 609
Weismer, S. E., 329
Weiss, J. M., 566
Weiss, M. R., 400, 576
Weiss, S. J., 246
Weiss, S. R. B., 511
Weisskirch, R. S., 401

Weissman, M. M., 493, 495, 503
Weisz, J. R., 556, 576
Weitzenhoffer, A. M., 220
Weizman, A., 446
Welch, S. L., 389
Weldon, E., 618
Welham, J., 515
Weller, S., 108
Wellisch, D., 579
Wells, A. M., 549
Wells, G. L., 294
Wells, S., 625
Wells, T., 122, 251
Wender, P. H., 514
Wenderoth, P., 167
Wendorf, G., 126
Wermter, A. K., 66
Wernicke, C., 92–93
Werth, E., 229
Werth, J. L., Jr., 551
Wertheimer, M., 8–9, 13, 166
Wesp, R., 192
Wessel, I., 501
West, E. E., 598
West, K. L., 517
West, R., 229, 259
Westaway, D., 300
Westen, D., 62, 311, 389
Westermann, J., 573
Westermeyer, J. F., 145
Westheimer, G., 166
Westmaas, J. L., 588
Westman, E. C., 587
Westrin, A., 507
Wetter, D. W., 587
Wever, E. G., 178
Whaley, D. E., 462
Wheat, A. L., 258
Whedon, C., 296
Wheeler, R. E., 420
Whelan, B. M., 87
Wheldall, K., 118
Whipple, B., 84
Whipplet, S. M., 36
Whisman, M. A., 544
Whissell, C. M., 427
Whitaker, J. S., 350
Whitaker-Azmitia, P. M., 522
Whitbourne, S. K., 108, 142, 146
White, A. M., 227
White, D., 486, 487
White, D. P., 218
White, J. W., 6, 321, 625
White, L. T., 293
White, P. H., 139
White, R., 94
White, S., 522
White, S. H., 16, 108
Whitehurst, G. J., 331
Whitfield, C. L., 287
Whitham, M., 563
Whitlock, F. A., 227, 228
Whitlock, T., 311
Whiton, K., 213

Whittal, M. L., 389
Whorf, B. L., 332, 333, 334
Whyte, G., 617
Whyte, M. K., 605
Whyte, W. H., 616
Wible, C. G., 270
Wickelgren, I., 384
Wickens, C. D., 201
Wicker, F. W., 430
Wickramasekera, I. E., II, 220
Widen, S. C., 424
Widener, A., 287
Widiger, T. A., 482
Widmeyer, W. N., 461, 600
Wiebe, D. J., 578
Wiebe, D., 313
Wiederman, M. W., 45, 63, 450
Wiegman, O., 591
Wiesel, T., 173
Wiesel, T. N., 167
Wiesmann, U., 145
Wigfield, A., 404
Wiggins, T. L., 19
Wightman, D. C., 250
Wignarajah, P., 472
Wijk, R. G., 50
Wik, G., 474
Wilcox, J. A., 389
Wilcox, S. A., 291
Wild, T. C., 588
Wilde, A., 535
Wilder, D. A., 599
Wildgruber, D., 423
Wilding, J. M., 574
Wiles, R., 53
Wiley, D., 136
Wiley, J., 315
Wiley, R., 157
Wilfley, D. E., 385
Wilhelm, F. H., 258, 492
Wilhelm, M. S., 587
Wilkinson, R. T., 206
Wilkinson-Lee, A. M., 587
Willerman, L., 367, 473
Williams, A. C., 221
Williams, A. K. K., 186
Williams, C. C., 144, 203, 578
Williams, C. D., 256
Williams, G. C., 562
Williams, J., 219, 570
Williams, J. D., 110
Williams, J. E., 424
Williams, K. D., 618
Williams, L., 387
Williams, R. B., 70, 569, 570
Williams, S. L., 335, 496
Williams, T., 162
Williams, T. J., 396
Williams, T. L., 322
Williamson, J. E., 436
Williamson, S. J., 273
Willibrord, C. M., 70
Willis, A. C., 430
Willis, F. N., 463

Willis, L. A., 508
Willis, R. P., 295
Willits, F. K., 610
Willner, P., 380, 586
Willson, V. L., 355
Wilson, C., 248
Wilson, E. J., 607
Wilson, E. O., 377
Wilson, G., 511
Wilson, J. R., 511
Wilson, S. G., 264, 389
Wilson, S. K., 417
Wilson, T. C., 613
Wilson, T. D., 321
Wilson-Barnett, J., 590
Wilt, J., 145
Winders, S. E., 587
Windholz, G., 239, 312
Winebarger, A. A., 364
Winefield, A. H., 257
Winer, R. S., 43
Winnepenninckx, B., 352
Winner, E., 356
Winsky-Sommerer, R., 78
Winter, Y., 157
Winton, W. M., 437
Wirz-Justice, A., 503
Wise, C., 53
Wise, E. A., 186
Wiseman, S. M., 588
Witelson, S., 83
Withers, G. S., 113
Witkiewitz, K., 135
Wittchen, H.-U., 489, 491
Witthöft, M., 499
Wittlinger, R. P., 295
Wittmann, A., 484
Witztum, E., 487
Wixted, J. T., 277, 284
Wohlfahrt, J., 522
Wojtowicz, J. M., 545
Wolf, A., 123
Wolf, Y., 152
Wolfe, J., 249
Wolfensberger, W., 354
Wolfensohn, S., 55
Wolff, J. J., 522
Wolfson, T., 232
Wolgast, M., 438
Wollen, K. A., 297
Wolpe, J., 534
Wolpert, E., 216
Wolpin, M., 216
Wolsic, B., 428
Wonacott, N. L., 356
Wong, N., 427
Wood, B. L., 433
Wood, J. M., 63, 201, 452, 609

Wood, K. R., 334
Wood, W., 607, 616
Woodall, K. L., 570
Woodruff, P. W. R., 177
Woodruff-Pak, D. S., 301
Woods, C. J. P., 128
Woods, K., 20, 431
Woods, R., 492
Woods, S. W., 498, 549
Woodson, R., 114
Woodward, J., 501
Woodward, O. M., 157
Woolley, H. T., 362
Word, C. O., 349
Word, L. E., 629
Worley, P., 299
Worringham, C. J., 618
Worthen, M., 564
Wosnack, K., 475
Woźniakowa, Y., 36
Wraith, S., 584
Wright, C. I., 471, 551
Wright, D. B., 271
Wright, I. C., 70, 516
Wright, J. C., 264
Wright, J. P., 70
Wu, J., 135
Wu, M.-T., 502, 572
Wu, P., 25
Wundt, W., 5–6, 7
Wurmle, O., 515
Wurtele, S. K., 255
Wurtz, H., 419
Wyatt, J. W., 66, 475, 476
Wynn, K., 114
Wynne-Edwards, K. E., 69

Xagoraris, A., 432
Xantidis, L., 402
Xerri, C., 100
Xiao, Q., 168
Xiaohe, X., 605
Xie, J. L., 461
Xie, L., 210
Xing, G., 511
Xu, X., 130

Yaffe, K., 303
Yahya, K. A., 622
Yamada, H., 37
Yamagishi, T., 361
Yamaguchi, H., 598
Yamamiya, Y., 45
Yamawaki, N., 505
Yamazaki, T. G., 449
Yan, M., 41
Yanchar, S. C., 7
Yang, A., 613

Yang, C., 87
Yang, C. M., 209
Yang, J., 300
Yang, Y., 218
Yap, J. N., 589
Yardley, S. L., 512
Yarmey, A. D., 288
Yates, D., 71
Yazdani, H., 201
Ybarra, O., 614
Yeh, M., 556
Yela, C., 605
Yen, S., 503, 518
Yenkosky, J., 94
Yerkes, R., 336, 363
Yerkes, R. M., 399
Yesavage, J. A., 227
Yetkin, F. Z., 91
Yi, Y., 427
Yin, T. C. T., 175
Yolken, R. H., 515
Yolton, K., 216
Yonas, A., 111, 169, 174
Yoon, C., 599
Yoshimura, C., 37
Yoshizawa, T., 168
Young, A. B., 567
Young, M. A., 503
Young, M. J., 320
Young, R. L., 344
Young, T., 163
Young, T. L., 457
Youngren, M. A., 504
Yu, B. H., 37
Yu, S., 228
Yuan, W., 84
Yufe, J., 474
Yukelson, D., 408
Yurek, D., 462
Yurko, K. H., 576
Yutrzenka, B. A., 531

Zach, U., 120
Zachar, P., 17
Zacks, R. T., 203
Zadra, A. L., 216, 217
Zahn, T. P., 92
Zajecka, J., 394
Zajonc, R. B., 368, 435, 438, 601, 618
Zaldivar, R. A., 617
Zander, A., 615
Zangariand, W., 190
Zanin, K. A., 289
Zanna, M. P., 227, 600, 603
Zanobini, M., 187
Zanoto de Luca, M. C., 185
Zaragoza, M. S., 292

Zaslavsky, A. M., 489, 491
Zatorre, R. J., 91, 180
Zec, R. F., 302
Zeineh, M. M., 301
Zeitlin, D., 581
Zellner, D., 607
Zeltzer, L. K., 188
Zeng, B. F., 78
Zennou-Azogui, Y., 100
Zentall, T. R., 263
Zeppenfeld, V., 446
Zerbo, O., 352
Zevon, M. A., 574
Zhang, H., 497
Zhang, J., 620
Zhang, Q., 587
Zhang, X., 121, 598
Zhang, X. L., 78
Zhao, X., 552
Zhou, Q., 122
Zhou, X., 282
Zhou, Y. D., 273
Zhu, A. J., 389
Zhu, Z., 89
Zians, J., 543
Zickar, M. J., 20
Ziegelmann, J. P., 584
Ziegler, D. J., 538
Zielhuis, G. A., 515
Zigler, E., 369
Zillman, D., 430
Zimbardo, P. G., 437
Zimmerman, A. W., 522
Zimmerman, F. J., 382
Zimmerman, M., 563
Zimmerman, P., 121
Zimmerman, R. R., 119
Zimmermann, E. A., 569
Zimpfer, D. G., 542
Zimprich, D., 137
Zisook, S., 512
Ziv, A., 431
Zlotnick, C., 518
Znamensky, V., 79
Zohar, D., 463
Zola-Morgan, S. M., 299
Zorina, Z. A., 263
Zucker, G. S., 596
Zucker, K. J., 396
Zuckerman, M., 401, 423, 457, 458, 598
Zumer, J. M., 89
Zuroff, D. C., 459
Zuwerink, J. R., 609
Zwikker, M., 627
Zwislocki, J. J., 178
Zyzanski, S. J., 582
Zyzniewski, L. E., 618, 628

Subject Index

Note: Page numbers in italics identify illustrations. An italic *t* next to a page number (e.g., 517*t*) indicates information that appears in a table.

A

A-B-C theory of emotion, 538, *539*
Abnormality criterion, 481
Absolute pitch, 178
Absolute threshold, 152–154
Abu ibn Sina, 3
Abuse (physical). *See also* Sexual abuse; Substance abuse
  borderline personality disorder and, 519
  children's testimony, 293–294
  dissociative identity disorder and, 502
  effect on children's psychosocial development, 122
  recovered memories, 287
  suicide and, 508
Academic achievement, drug use and, 135
Academic fields of specialization, in psychology, 18–19
Accommodation, 115, 158, 168
Accurate empathy, 541
Acetylcholine, 76, 76–78, 101, 302, 414
Achievement motive, 402–406
  sports and, 407–408
Achievement tests, 345
Acoustic level of encoding, 278, *278*
Acquired immune deficiency syndrome (AIDS). *See* HIV-AIDS
Acromegaly, 69
Acronyms, 296
Action potentials, 73–75, *74*
Activation-synthesis theory, 219
Actual self, 467, *467*, 469, 506, 517
Acupuncture, 186–187
Adaptation, 61–62
  dark, 161–162
  sensory, 155–156
Adaptation-level theory, 429
Adaptive inactivity, sleep as, 211
Addiction, 225, 227, 228, 586–588
Addington v. Texas, 549–550
Additive color processes, 163
A-delta fibers, 185
Adler, Alfred, 10, 447–449, 451–452
Admissions tests, 348–349
Adolescence, defined, 129
Adolescent development, 129–135
Adoption studies, 65, 367–368, 473, 514

Adrenal cortex, 70
Adrenal glands, 69–70
Adrenal medulla, 70
Adrenocorticotropic hormone (ACTH), 571
Adult development, 136–146
Adulthood
  defined, 136
  early, 142–144
  middle, 144
  late, 145–146
Aerial perspective, 169, *170*
Aerobic exercise, 580–581, 583–584. *See also* Exercise
African Americans
  body image, 387
  impact of segregation on, 614–615
  influence of environment on intelligence, 367, 369–370
  on IQ tests, 365
  stereotype threat, 350–351
  suicide and, 508
  test bias against, 349–350
  Type A behavior and, 570
Afterimages, 162–163
  color, *164*
Age regression, 223
Aggression. *See also* Violence
  alcohol intoxication and, 227
  defined, 623
  evolutionary explanations, 15
  gender differences, 140
  school shootings, 1, 34
  steroid use and, 70
  television viewing and, 264
  theories, 622–625
Aging. *See also* Adult development
  alcohol use and, 109
  effects on sleep duration, 208–209
  physical effects, 136–137
  physical fitness and, 107–108, 136–137
  sexual desire and, 109, 136
  suicide and, 508
Agoraphobia, 482, 495
Agreeableness, 455
AIDS. *See* HIV-AIDS
Ainsworth, Mary, 120
Air crib, 256
Aka culture, 119

Alarm reaction, 567
Alcoholism, aversion therapy for, 536, *537*
Alcohol myopia, 227
Alcohol use
  aging and, 109
  effect on academic achievement, 135
  effects on vision, 160, 169, 171
  impact on prenatal development, 112
  psychoactive effects, 224, 227–228
  state-dependent memory, 289
Aldosterone, 70
Algorithms, 313–314
Alice in Wonderland, 484
All-or-none law, 74–75
Allport, Floyd, 596, 617
Allport, Gordon, 454, 606, 614
Alpha rhythm, 82
Alpha waves, *206*, 206
Altruism, 626–627
Alzheimer's disease
  caregiver stress and, 565, 581–582
  features of, 77
  memory studies from, 279, 299–300, 302
  neural transplant treatment, 101
  sleep disorders and, 210
  smell sensation, 181
Amabile, Teresa, 318
American Bar Association, 487
American intelligence testing, 346–347
American Law Institute standard of insanity, 486
American Psychiatric Association, 487
American Psychological Association
  human treatment standards, 53
  position on insanity defense, 487
American Sign Language (ASL), 95, 336, 337
Amino acids, 78, 302
Amish people, 510
Amnesia
  dissociative, 500–501
  infantile, 300
  retrograde, 546
  surgically caused, 300–301
Amotivational syndrome, 232
Amphetamines, 226*t*, 229–230, 515
Amplitude
  of light waves, 157
  of sound waves, 175, *175*
Amygdala, 87–88, 299, *300*, 301, 419

I-32

Amyotrophic lateral sclerosis, 71
Anabolic steroids, 70
Anafranil (clomipramine), 546
Anal sex, 583
Anal stage, 447, 449*t*
Analysis. *See also* Psychoanalysis; Therapy
  of dreams, 532–533
  free associations, 532
  resistances, 532, 533
  transference, 533
Analytical psychology, 449–450
Analytic introspection, 6
Anastasi, Anne, 29, 36
Androcentrism of psychoanalytic theory, 449
Andropause, 136
Androstadienone, 183
Angel dust, 230
Anima, 450
Animal Behavior Enterprises, 260
Animal magnetism, 219–220
Animals
  communication by, 325–326, 335–339
  ethical treatment, 54–55
  experimenter effects on, 44
  insight studies, 313
  research on, reasons for, 55
  rights and welfare advocates, 54–55
  training techniques, 247–248, 255–256, 260
Animus, 450
Anna O., 529
Anorexia nervosa, 387–388
Anosmia, 184
Anterograde amnesia, 300–301
Anthropometry, 345–346
Antianxiety drugs, 546
Antidepressants, 78, 389, 394, 546–547
Antigravity hills, 171–172
Antimania drugs, 547
Antipsychotic drugs, 547
Antisocial personality disorder, 490, 518*t*, 519–520
Anxiety disorders, 489–496, 546
Anxiety hierarchies, 534
Anxiolytics, 546
Apes, language in, 335–339
Aphrodisin, 182–183
Aplysia, 298–299
Apnea, 211, 213–214
Apparent-distance hypothesis, 172
Applewhite, Marshall, 595
Applied research, 18
Applied science, 3
Approach commitment, 144
Aptitude tests, 345
Arachnophobia, 534
Archetypes, 450, 452
Archimedes, 312–313
Archival research, 37–38
Archives of the History of American Psychology, 38
Aristotle, 2–3, 62, 80, 238
Army Alpha Test, 346–347, 363–364
Army Beta Test, 346–347
Aromatherapy, 181
Arousal motive. *See also* Emotions
  in antisocial personality disorder, 520

  need for achievement and, 403–404
  overview, 399–402
  personality and, 457
  sport and, 406–407
Artificial concepts. *See* Logical concepts
Artificial intelligence (AI), 322–324
Artistic styles, 311–312
Asch, Solomon, 619
Asch study, *619*
Asian American IQ scores, 370
Asian cultures
  behavioral attributions in, 596
  collective orientation, 462
  social anxiety disorders, 495
Asperger's syndrome, 521
Assertiveness training, 543
Assimilation, 115
Association areas, 89
Association cortex, 91–92
Associationists, 238
Associative learning, 238, 261–262
Astrocytes, 71
Astrological profiles, 443
Atherosclerosis, 568, 578, 585
Athletes
  eating disorders among, 387–388
  motivations, 406, 407–408
  peak performance age, 136
  smooth pursuit eye movements, 162
Attachment, 119–121
Attention, 200–201, 512
  view, 191–192
Attention deficit hyperactivity disorder (ADHD), 522–252
Attitudes
  components, 606–607, *607*
  defined, 606
  formation, 607–608
  implicit, 203
  interactions with behavior, 610–612
  interpersonal attraction and, 603
  persuasion and, 608–610
  prejudiced, 612–615
Attraction, 30, 601–606
Attractiveness, 602–603, 608–609
Attributional theory, of depression, 505
Attribution theory, in social psychology, 596–598
Audience effects, on persuasion, 606–610
Audition. *See* Hearing
Auditory cortex, 91, 177, 178, 180
Auditory nerve, 177
Auditory sensory memory, 273
Auditory system anatomy, 175–177
Augustine, 3
Auras, 90
Austin (chimpanzee), 337
Authoritarian parenting, 122
Authoritarian personality, 614
Authoritative parenting, 122
Authority, obedience to, 621, 622–623, *623*
Autism spectrum disorder (ASD), 343–344, 489, 521–522
  operant-conditioning therapy for, 537
Autistic savants, 343–344

Autobiographical memory, 281
Autoimmune diseases, 572
Automatic processing, 202–203, *203*
Autonomic nervous system (ANS), 68, 414–415, *415*
Autonomy versus shame and doubt, 119*t*, 121
Availability heuristic, 320, 321
Averages, 47
Aversion therapy, 536, 588
Aversive stimulus, 253, 254
Avicenna, 3, 183
Avoidance commitment, 144
Avoidance learning, 253
Avoidance-oriented coping, 579
Avoidant personality disorder, 518*t*
Awareness, perception without, 201–203
Axonal conduction, 73
Axons
  of nerve cells, 72, 73–74
  of optic nerves, 160
  regeneration, 99–100

B

Babbling, 328
Backmasking, 155
Back pain, 185
Backward chaining, 250
Backward conditioning, 241
Bacon, Francis, 3–4
Bad trips, 231
Bahill, Terry, 162
Bandura, Albert, 263, 264, 331, 460–461, 485
Barbiturates, 226*t*, 228, 289
Barnum effect, 443
Basal ganglia, 484, 497, 499
Basal metabolic rate, 136, 383–384
Baseball players, 162
Basic anxiety, 449
Basic hostility, 449
Basic research, 18
Basilar membrane, *176*, 177–178
Basketball, motivation in, 406–407, 408
Baumrind, Diana, 623
Beauty, 602
Beck, Aaron, 540
Beck Depression Inventory, 505
Bed-wetting, in childhood, 240–241
Bee communications, 325
Beers, Clifford, 531
Behavioral aggregation, 459
Behavioral contingencies, 248, 255*t*
Behavioral effects, of hypnosis, 222
Behavioral genetics, 15, 62–66, 473, 475
Behavioral neuroscience, 18, 61
Behavioral perspective. *See also* Skinner, B. F.
  on antisocial personality disorder, 520
  on anxiety disorders, 492, 495
  disinterest in study of thought, 309
  elements of, 11–13
  on major depressive disorder, 504
  on obsessive-compulsive disorder, 497
  on psychological disorders, in general, 485
  on schizophrenia, 516

Subject Index I-33

on somatic symptom and related disorder, 499, 500
  therapy, 533–538
Behavioral preparedness, 260
Behaviorism, 8, 11–12
Behavior modification, 258, 354–355
The Behavior of Organisms, 12
Behavior therapy, 533
Békésy, Georg von, 178
The Bell Curve debate, 364–365
Bell, Alexander Graham, 178
Belle computer, 323
Bell-shaped curve. *See* Normal curve
Belongingness, 259, 378
Benzedrine, 229
Benzodiazepines, 289, 546
Bereavement, 146, 571, *571*
Berger, Hans, 81–82
Berkeley Growth Study, 348
Berkowitz, Leonard, 624
Berne, Eric, 543
Bernheim, Hippolyte, 287
Berscheid, Ellen, 604
Beta amyloid, 210, 299–300
Beta rhythm, 82
Beta waves, *206*, 206
Better Beginnings, Better Futures program, 549
"Between the Wars" cohort, 129
Bias
  in causal attribution, 597–598
  effects on dependent variables, 42
  in testing, 349–350
Biased samples, 36
Bibliotherapy, 551
Biculturalism, 134
Binet, Alfred, 290–291, 346
Binet-Simon scale, 346, 347
Binocular depth cues, 167–168
Binocular disparity, 167–168
Biofeedback, 258–259, *259*
Biological constraints, on classical conditioning, 246
Biological rhythms
  defined, 204
  sleep-wake cycle and, 204–205
Biomedical model, 562
Biopsychological perspective
  on anxiety disorders, 493, 495–496
  on dissociative disorders, 501, 502
  elements of, 14–16
  emotion theory, 432–434
  on major depressive disorder, 503–504
  on personality, 470–475
  on psychological disorders in general, 484
  on schizophrenia, 513–516
  on somatic symptom and related disorder, 500
  on stress and illness, 566–574
  therapies, 544–547
Biopsychosocial model, 482, *483*
Biorhythms, 204–205
Bipolar cells, 158
Bipolar disorder, 509–511, 547
  brain activity in, *511*
Bisexuality, 395

Blastocyst, 110
Bleuler, Eugen, 512, 517
Braille system, 184
Blindsight, 202
Blind spot, 159–160, *160*
Block-design tasks, 98
Blocking, 261, 262*t*
Blue Monday effect, 427
B-lymphocytes, 572
BMI. *See* Body mass index
Bobbitt, Lorena, 487
Bodily-kinesthetic intelligence, 361
Body mass index (BMI), *382*
Body movements, emotions and, 423
Body satisfaction, 385–386
Body senses, 188–190
Bogen, Joseph, 98
Books, therapeutic, 551–552
Borderline personality disorder (BPD), 518–519
Bottom-up processing, 166
Bouchard, Thomas, 474, 475
Bowlby, John, 119
Bradykinin, 185
Braille system, 184
Brain
  bipolar disorder and, 511, *511*
  central nervous system role, 67–68
  cerebral cortex, 88–93
  development in infancy, 112–113
  hemispheric lateralization, 93–99
  lesioning, 80
  limbic system, 87–88
  lobes of, *89*
  memory structures in, 299
  methods of studying, 80–84
  neural plasticity, 99–102
  processing speeds, 358
  psychoactive drugs and, 226*t*
  regulating hunger, 380–381
  role in vision, 160
  schizophrenia and, 514–514, 516
  speech and, *93*
  stem functions, 86–87
  structure of, *85*
Brain damage
  case studies, 80, 91
  early studies, 4
  effects on sensation and perception, 151, 202
  evidence of lateralization from, 94
  intellectual disabilities and, 353
  memory studies, 279
  recovery from, 99–100
  unilateral neglect from, 60
Brain hemispheres, Sperry's studies on, 15
Brain-imaging techniques
  lateralization evidence from, 93
  for memory research, 301
  overview, 84
  personality studies, 474
Brain stem, 84, 86–87
Brainstorming, 319
Brainwashing, 400, 608
Brave New World, 242
Breuer, Josef, 444, 529

Brick and mortar psychology, 8
Brightness constancy, 171
Brightness of light, 157
Broca, Paul, 92, 94
Broca's aphasia, 92
Broca's area, 92–93
Brown v. Board of Education of Topeka, 614
Bulimia nervosa, 388–389
Bullying, consequences of, 578–579
Burger-Lo, 607
Burnout, 576
Burt, Cyril, 366, 608
Buspar (buspirone), 545
Byrne, Donn, 30
Bystander intervention, 627–630
  steps in, *628*

C

Caffeine, 226*t*, 228–229
Calkins, Mary Whiton, 7–8, 215–217
Callosal agenesis, 98
Caloric intake, 137
Canadian Association for Suicide Prevention, 509
Cancer, 589–590
  stress and, 573–574
Cannabis sativa, 231
Cannon-Bard theory of emotion, 432, *432*
Cannon, Walter, 379
Cannot say scale, 456*t*
"Can States of Mind Be Unconscious?" 201
Capilano River Bridge, 604
Cardinal traits, 454
Cardiovascular disease, stress and, 567–570
Careers in psychology, 17–21
Care reasoning, 128
Carpenter, Karen, 387
Case studies
  brain damage and behavior, 80, 91
  brain damage and memory, 88, 300–301
  language acquisition, 309
  method described, 34
Castration anxiety, 447
Cataplexy, 214
Catharsis
  in Breuer's therapy, 529
  Freud's theory, 444
  humor as, 431
  research findings on, 624
  violence and, 623–624
Cattell, James McKeen, 5–6, 6–8, 345
Causal attribution, 596–598
  two dimensions of, *597*
Causation, 38, 39
Cavellucci, Joseph, 375–376
Cell-adhesion molecules, 110
Cell phones, 200–201
Central nervous system, 67–68
Central-route arguments, 608, 609–610
Central tendency measures, 46–48
Central traits, in Allport's theory, 454
Cerebellum, 4, 86, 299, *300*
Cerebral cortex, 88–93, 419

Cerebral hemispheres
　divisions of, 88
　lateralization, 93–99, 419–420
Cerebral palsy, 353
Cerebrotonia, 472
Cerebrum, 88
Cerletti, Ugo, 545
Cézanne, Paul, 316
C fibers, 185
Chaining, 249–250, 255
Challenge, hardiness and, 577
Challenger explosion, 617
Charcot, Jean, 444
Chemical senses, 181–184
Chemotherapy patients, 243, 245, 589–590
Chess, 314, 322–323
Chesterfield, Philip D., 423
Chiao shun, 122
Child abuse, 122, 287, 293–294
Childbirth pain, cultural differences, 187
Child development. *See* Infant and child development
Childhood, defined, 112
Childhood geniuses, 356
Childhood upbringing and sexual orientation, 398
Childlessness, 144
Child psychology, 108
Child rearing, 256, 570
Children, as eyewitnesses, 291–294
Chimpanzees, 33–34, 335–339
Chocolate, 228–229
Choking in competition, 406–407
Cholecystokinin, 380, 381
Cholesterol, 568
Choline, 302
Chomsky, Noam, 327, 331–332
Chowchilla case, 221–222
Chromosomes, 62, *64*, 110, 353
Chronic pain, 186–187
Chunking, 275
Cialdini, Robert, 627
Circadian rhythms, 204
Clairvoyance, 191
Clark, Kenneth B., 614–615
Clark, Mamie Phipps, 614–615
Classical conditioning, *240*
　advertising and, *243*
　to alter immune response, 572, 573
　applications of, 242–246
　attitude formation by, 607
　biological constraints on, 246
　cognitive factors, 261–262
　neurochemical transmission, 301
　origins, 238–239
　principles, 239–242
　processes in, *242*
　therapies, 534–536
Classification of psychological disorders, 488–489
Claustrophobia, 494
Clever Hans, 335
Click consonants, 326
Client-centered therapy. *See* Person-centered therapy
Client characteristics, therapy success and, 555

Clinical case studies. *See* Case studies
Clinical psychology, 19–20
Close Encounters of the Third Kind, 450
Closure principle, 166–167, *166, 167*
Clouser, Ronald, 290
Clozaril (clozapine), 547
Club drugs, 232
Coca-Cola, 41, 154, 230
Cocaine, 226*t*, 230
Cochlea, 176–177, *176*, 178
Cochlear implants, 179–180
Cocktail party phenomenon, 86, 200
Code of ethics, APA, 53
Coefficient of correlation, 48
Cognitive abilities, gender differences, 138
Cognitive appraisal, 574, 575
Cognitive-appraisal theory of emotion, 436–438
Cognitive-behavioral approach
　to anxiety disorders, 492, 496
　to major depressive disorder, 504–506
　personality, 460–465
Cognitive-behavioral therapy
　for eating disorders, 388, 389
　types, 538–540
　for weight loss, 585, 586
Cognitive behaviorism, 11–12
Cognitive development
　in adolescence, 131–132
　in adulthood, 137, 141
　in infancy and childhood, 114–118, *116*
　Piaget's states of, 115*t*
Cognitive dissonance theory, 611, *612*
Cognitive effects of hypnosis, 221–222
Cognitive-evaluation theory, 405–406
Cognitive learning, 260–266
Cognitive linguistics, 334
Cognitive maps, 263
Cognitive neuroscience, 309
Cognitive perspective
　on anxiety disorders, 492, 493, 496
　on dissociative disorders, 502
　elements of, 14
　on major depressive disorder, 505
　on obsessive-compulsive disorder, 497–498
　on psychological disorders in general, 485
　on schizophrenia, 517
　on somatic symptom and related disorder, 499
　therapies, 538–540
Cognitive psychology, 309
Cognitive rule, insanity defense, 486
Cognitive schemas, 278, 280–281
Cognitive symptoms, in schizophrenia, 512–513
Cognitive theories of emotion, 436–438
Cognitive therapy, 540
Cognitive triad, 505
Cohen's *d*, 50
Cohorts, 109, 129
Cohort-sequential research, 109–110
Cold pressor test, 223
Coleridge, Samuel Taylor, 228
Collateral sprouting, 100, *100*
Collective efficacy, 461
Collective unconscious, 449–450
Collectivist cultures, 462, 468, 598

College admissions tests, 348–349
College students' sleep patterns, 209
Colorado Adoption Project, 367
Color afterimages, *164*
Color, 164–165
Color perception, language and, 334
Color vision, 158–159, 162–165
Columbine High School shootings, 1
Commitment, 311
　hardiness and, 577
Common sense, 25–27
　psychology versus, 28
Communication benefits for marriage, 143
Communication systems, 67–70. *See also* Language
Community mental health, 548–549
Community Mental Health Centers Act of 1963, 548
Companionate love, 604
Comparative psychology, 18–19
Complementary colors, 164
Complementary transactions, 542
Compliance, 620–621
Componential intelligence, 360
Computed tomography (CT), 84
Computer-assisted instruction, 256–257
Computers
　algorithm concept from, 313–314
　artificial intelligence and, 323–324
　influence on psychology, 14
　memory compared to, 272
　speech comprehension by, 327–328
Concept formation, 310–312, *311*
Conception, human, 110
Concordance rates, 492, 493, 496, 498, 503, 510, 514, *514*, 515
Concrete operational stage, 115*t*, 117–118
Conditional positive regard, 485
Conditioned immunosuppression, 572–573, *573*
Conditioned reinforcer, 248–249
Conditioned response (CR), 239–241, 261, 262*t*
Conditioned stimulus (CS), 238–241, 260, 261–262, 262*t*
Conditioned taste aversion, 244–246
Conditions of worth, 467
Conduction deafness, 179
Cones, 158, 162–163, 164–165
Confederate, 40
Confessions of Augustine, 3
Confidence of eyewitnesses, 294
Confidentiality, 53, 550–551
Confluence model, 368
Conformity, 619–620
Confounding variables, 41
Conscience, 445
Conscientiousness, 455
Conscious mind, in Freud's theory, 203, 444–445
Consciousness
　dreaming, 207–208, 214–219
　hypnosis, 219–224
　levels of, *204*
　nature of, 199–203
　psychoactive drug effects, 224–232
　role of pons, 86
　sleep functions, patterns, and disorders, 204–214

Conservation, in Piaget's theory, 117–118, *118*
Consistency
    of attitudes with behavior, 610
    effect on influence, 616
    of personality, 458–459
    of punishment, 254
    test reliability, 37, 348
Constitutional theory of personality, 472
Constructionist theory, of visual perception, 165
Constructive recall, 281, 282–283
Consumer psychology, 41
Context-dependent memory, 288–289
Contextual intelligence, 360
Contiguity, 238, 261
Continuity principle, 166–167, *166*, *167*
Continuous positive airway pressure, 214
Continuous schedules of reinforcement, 251
Contralateral control, 89
Contraprepared species, 260
Control groups, 39–40
Control, hardiness and, 577
Controlled processing, 202–203, *203*
Control, locus of, 463
Control questions, 416–417, *417*
Controls, in research, 32
Conventional level, of moral development, 127
Convergence, 168
Convergent thinking, 319–320
Conversion disorder, *499*, 499–500
Conversion hysteria, 9, 444, 499, 529
Convolutions of cerebral cortex, 88
Cooperation, intergroup, 615
Coping styles, in Horney's theory, 449
Coping with stress and distress, 579–582, 589
Coren, Stanley, 94, 96–97
Corkin, Suzanne, 300–301
Cornea, 157
Coronary heart disease, 567–570
Corpus callosum, 98
Correction scale, 456*t*
Correlation
    causation and, 38, 39
    coefficient of, 48
    defined, 38
    kinds of, 38
    negative, 38, 48, *49*
    positive, 38, 48, *49*
    zero, 48, *49*
Correlational research, 38–39
Correlational statistics, 48–49
Cortisol, 70, 421
Counseling psychology, 19–20
Counterconditioning, 534
Couple therapy, 543
Cousins, Norman, 576
Cramming, 296
Creativity, 316–320, 356, 360
Credibility of source, 608
Crime
    antisocial personality disorder and, 520
    insanity defense, 486–487
    psychological profiling and, 464–465
Crisis intervention center, 549
Criteria, in testing, 37

Critical period for language acquisition, 308, 330
Critical thinking, 28–29
Crooks, Hulda, 107–108
Cross-cultural psychology, 16
Crossed transactions, 542–543
Cross-sectional research, 109
Crying, culture and, 426
Crystallized intelligence, 137, 359, *359*
Cue-dependence theory, 288
Cultural competence, of psychotherapy, 531
Culturally unbiased tests, 350
Cultural psychology, 16–17
Cultural schemas, 281
Culture
    attachment behavior and, 119, 120
    behavioral attributions and, 596
    conformity and, 620
    creativity and, 317–319
    effects on identity achievement, 133–134
    effects on survey responses, 35
    emotional experience and, 427
    external validity of experiments and, 45
    eyewitness testimony and, 291
    facial attractiveness and, 602
    facial expressions and, 425–426
    impact on dominant hand, 94
    impact on psychology, 16–17
    impact on sense of smell, 181
    influence on personality, 455, 462, 468
    influence on play behavior, 124
    influence on sleep patterns, 208
    influence on visual perception, 174
    intelligence and, 349–351, 358, 364
    intrinsic motivation and, 405
    language effects on, 334–335
    moral reasoning and, 128
    pain perception and, 186
    parenting styles and, 122
    physiques and, 585
    psychological disorders and, 486–488, 495, 505
    romantic love and, 606
    sexual behavior and, 391–392, 398
    social clocks, 129
    social support and, 579
Curare, 76–77
Currie v. United States, 551
Cyberbullying, 578–579
Cytokines, 565

D

Daily hassles, 564–566
Dale, Henry, 76
Dallenbach, Karl, 285
Dani language, 334
Dark adaptation, 161–162
Darley, John, 627, 628
Darwin, Charles
    on emotions, 426
    evolutionary psychology, 15
    on facial expressions, 425
    influence on Freud, 9
    influence on Galton, 5, 138, 345, 362
    influence on G. Stanley Hall, 108

    nature vs. nurture, 61, 62, 362
    theory of evolution, 5, 6, 138, 238, 376
Darwin VII, 324
Data, ethical treatment of, 52
Dating relationships, 601, 602–603
Davidson, Richard, 420
The Da Vinci Code, 315
da Vinci Surgical System, 324
Day care, 123
The Day the Earth Stood Still, 450
Deafness, 179
Dean, John, 282
Death, 136–137, 146
    leading causes in United States, 561–562
Debriefing, 53–54
Decay theory, 285
Deception
    detecting, 413, 416–418, 424
    in research, 53–54
Decibels, 178
Decision making, 320–322, 615–617
Declarative memory, 278–279, *279*, 300–301, 302
Deep Blue program, 323
Deep brain stimulation (DBS), 544–545
Deep structure of language, 327
Defense mechanisms, 445–446, 451, 484
Defensive pessimism, 505
Deindividuation, 625–626
Deinstitutionalization, 548
Déjà vu, 191–192
Delayed conditioning, 241
Delta waves, *206*, 206
Delusions, 198–199, 513
Delusions of grandeur, 513
Demence precoce (premature mental deterioration), 512
Dementia praecox, 512
Dement, William, 209, 210
Dendrites, 72, 113
Dendritic spines, 72, 299
Denial, 446
Denial group, 438
Deoxyribonucleic acid (DNA), 62, *64*
Dependence on psychoactive drugs, 225, 230, 243–244
Dependent personality disorder, 518*t*
Dependent variables, 39
Depolarization, 73
Depressants, 225, 226*t*, 227–228
Depression. *See also* Bipolar disorder; Major depressive disorder
    explanatory style and, 575–576
    immunosuppression and, 571
    learned helplessness and, 257
    MMPI-2 scale, 456*t*
    reciprocal determinism in, 460
    therapies, 540, 546–547, 552, 553–554
Depressive realism, 505–506
Depth perception, 116, 167–169, *170*, *171*
Descartes, René, 3–4, 72–73
Description, as goal of research, 30–31
Descriptive research methods, 33–38
Descriptive statistics, 46–48
Determinism, 27–28, 460

de Valois, Russell, 164
Developmental disorders, 520–525
Developmental psychology, 19, 108
Deviation IQ, 347
Dewey, John, 7
Dexedrine, 229
Diagnostic and Statistical Manual of Mental Disorders, 488–489
  DSM-I, 488
  DSM-II, 488
  DSM-III, 488
  DSM-IV, 488
  DSM-5, 488–489, 490, 512, 517
Dianetics, 155
Dichotic listening, 201–202, *202*
Dichromats, 164
Diener, Edward, 428–429
Diet, 585–586
Difference threshold, 154–155
Differential psychology, 5, 345
Diffusion of responsibility, 618, *629*
Dipmeter (expert system), 323
Direct bullying, 578
Direct conditioning, 534
Direct perception theory, of vision, 165
DISC1 (disrupted in schizophrenia-1) gene, 514
Discrimination (social), 613
Discriminative stimulus, 249
Diseases. *See* Illness
Disparagement theory, 430
Displacement
  as defense mechanism, 446
  of language, 325
Dispositional approach to personality, 452–457
Dispositional attributions, 596–597
Disraeli, Benjamin, 48–49
Dissociation, 222, 584
Dissociative amnesia, 500–501
Dissociative disorders, 500–502
Dissociative fugue, 500–501
Dissociative identity disorder, 501–502
Distal stimulus, 167
Distracting stimuli, 188
Distress, 562, 589–590
  criterion, 481, 482
Distributed practice, 294, 296
Ditka, Mike, 568
Divergent thinking, 319–320
Divorce, 123–124, 143–144
Dix, Dorothea, 531
Dizygotic twins, 65
Doctors, 590
Dominant genes, 64
Dominant hands, 94
Donaldson v. O'Connor, 550
Door-in-the-face technique, 620, 621
Dopamine, 78, 514–515
Double-blind technique, 43, 421
Down, John Langdon, 344
Down syndrome, 111, 344, 353–354, 521, 524
Dreams
  analysis of, 532–533
  association with REM sleep, 207–208, 214–219
  content of, 215–217
  purposes, 217–219
  sleep and, 233
Drive-reduction theory, 377
Drives, motivation and, 377–378
Drive theory, 618
Drug abuse. *See* Substance abuse
Drug dependence, classical conditioning in, 243–244
Drug effects
  on brain functions, 80–81
  on consciousness, 224–232
  nervous system and, 76–78
  on prenatal development, 112
Drug overdose, 225
Drugs, experimentation with, 135
Drug therapies, 546–547
Drunk driving, 227
Drunkenness, detection of, 28. *See also* Alcohol use; Intoxication
DSM. *See Diagnostic and Statistical Manual of Mental Disorders*
D statistic, 50
Dual-processing view, 191
Duchenne smile, 424, 435
Duncker, Karl, 315
Duration of sleep, 208–209
Duty to warn, 551
Dwarfism, 69
Dwyer, R. Budd, 508
Dysexecutive syndrome, 524
Dyspareunia, 393
Dysphoria, 485

E

Ear anatomy, 175–177, *176*
Eardrum, 175–176, *176*
Early adulthood, 142–144
"Early Baby Boomers" cohort, 129
Early maturation, 131
Eating. *See also* Hunger
  disorders, 385–389
  regulation of, 379
Ebbinghaus, Hermann, 5, 283–284, *285*
Echoic memory, 273
Eclectic orientation to psychotherapy, 531
Ecstasy. *See* MDMA
Ectomorphs, 472
The Eden Express, 517
Education, 256–257. *See also* Learning
  of people with intellectual disabilities, 354–355
Educational psychology, 20
Education for All Handicapped Children Act of 1975, 354
Ego, 445
Egocentrism, 117
Eichmann, Adolf, 621
Einstein, Albert, 82, 83
Elaboration likelihood theory, 608
Elaborative rehearsal, 277
Elavil (amitriptyline), 546
Electra complex, 124, 447, 451
Electrical activity, recording, 81–83
Electrical stimulation of the brain (ESB), 81
Electricity, in neural impulses, 73
Electric shock therapy, 537
Electroconvulsive therapy (ECT), 545–546
Electrodes, 81
Electroencephalograph (EEG), 81–83, 206
Electromagnetic spectrum, 156
Elements of Psychophysics, 152
Elevation, 169, *170*
Elimination hypothesis, 95
Elliott, Jane, 612
Ellis, Albert, 538
Embryonic stage, 110–111
Emergencies, interpreting events as, 627–628
Emotional intelligence, 361
Emotional jealousy, 63
Emotion-oriented coping, 580
Emotions
  A-B-C theory, 538, *539*
  association with tympanic membrane temperature, 175
  autonomic nervous system role, 414–415
  body movements and, 423
  brain's role in, 87, 182, 415, 419–420
  chemistry of, 420–421
  creativity and, 320
  defining, 414
  endorphins and, 421
  experiencing, 426–431
  expression of, 422–426
  facial expressions and, 423–426
  hormones and, 420–421
  pathways for, *439*
  with schizophrenia, 513
  stress-relieving effects, 580
  theories of, 431–438, *432*, 604–605
  vocal qualities and, 422–423
Empathogens. *See* Entactogens
Empathy
  altruistic behavior and, 626–627
  gender differences, 140
  of medical practitioners, 590
  in person-centered therapy, 540–541
  therapist success and, 556
Emperor Norton, 480–481
Empirical method of test construction, 455
Empiricism, 3
Empty nest syndrome, 145
Encoding
  in information-processing model of memory, 272
  long-term memory, 276–278, 288–290
  specificity, 288–290
Encounter groups, 543
Endocrine system, 68–70, *69*
Endomorphs, 472
Endorphins
  discovery, 78–79
  emotion and, 421
  in gate-control theory, 185–186
  obesity and, 385
  placebo effect on, 186
  systematic desensitization and, 536
Energy conservation role of sleep, 211
Enkephalin, 79
Enriched environments, 112–113

Entactogens, 226t, 232
Environment
  effects on brain development, 112–113
  influence on intelligence, 366–370
  influence on personality, 460, 463, 475
  memory cues, 289
  role in hunger, 379
Environmental determinism, 460
Environmental psychology, 21
Enzymes, 76
Epictetus, 485, 538
Epilepsy victims
  hippocampus removal, 88, 300
  split-brain studies of, 98
  surgery on brains of, 14–15
  tissue transplant treatments, 101
Epinephrine
  basic functions, 70
  role in emotion, 421, 437
  role in memory, 303
Episodic memory, 278–279
Equity, 606
Erectile dysfunction, 393
Erection during sleep, 207
Erikson, Erik
  adolescent development stages, 132–133
  adult development stages, 142, 144
  infant and child development stages, 118–119, 119t, 121
Erogenous zones, 446
Eros, 444
Erotic stimuli, 87
Errors
  fundamental attribution, 597
  trial and, 312
Escape learning, 253
Esdaile, James, 221
ES-MR (expert system), 323–324
Essential hypertension treatment, 591
Esteem, in Maslow's hierarchy of needs, 378
Estrogens
  aging effects, 136
  basic functions, 70
  effects in puberty, 130
  e-therapy, 552
  role in embryonic formation, 110–111
  role in memory, 303
Ethics in research, 52–55
Ethnicity. *See also* Culture
  external validity of experiments and, 45
  eyewitness testimony and, 291
  identity development and, 133–134
  intelligence and, 349–351, 363, 364
Ethnic psychology, 17
Ethnocentrism, 16
Ethology, 33
Ethyl alcohol (ethanol), 227
Eugenics, 362
Euphoria, 421, 434, 435
European Americans
  bias in testing, 349
  body image, 387
  influence of environment on intelligence, 367–368, 369–370

on IQ tests, 365
  stereotype threat, 350–351
  Type A behavior and, 570
Eustachian tubes, 176
Eustress, 562
Evaluation apprehension, 618
Eve. *See* MDE
Evolution
  Darwin's theory, 5, 6, 9, 15, 61, 62
  as explanation for phobias, 495
  facial expressions and, 425
  human development and, 108
  influence on learning theory, 238
Evolutionary psychology, 15, 62, 606
Excessive punishment, 254
Excitatory neurotransmitters, 76
Excitement phase, 390
Exercise
  effect on endorphin levels, 79
  effect on sleep patterns, 210
  illness and, 580–581, 581
  increasing adherence to, 591
  intrinsic motivation for, 408
  longevity and, 107–109, 137
  obesity and, 384, 583, 586
  overall health effects, 583–584
  stress management effects, 580–581
Exhaustion stage, 567
Existential psychology, 13
Exocrine glands, 68
Expectancy, 404
Expectations, effect on visual perception, 166
Experience, influence on visual perception, 173–174
Experience sampling, 462–463
Experiential intelligence, 360
Experimental groups, 39–40
Experimental manipulation of brain, 80–81
Experimental psychology, 18
Experimental research method, 39–46
Experimenter bias effect, 42, 43
Experimenter effects on dependent variables, 42–43
Expertise, credibility and, 608
Expert systems, 323–324
Explanation, as goal of research, 32
Explanatory style, 574, 575–576, 589
Explicit memory, 278–279, 279, 284
Expressed emotion, 516
External auditory canal, 175
External locus of control, 463
External validity, 43–46
Extinction
  in classical conditioning, 241–242
  in operant conditioning, 251, 253–254, 255t
  in therapy, 537
Extracellular fluid, 73
Extrasensory perception (ESP), 190–194
Extraversion
  in Eysenck's model, 453–454, 455
  in five-factor model, 454–455
  happiness and, 428
  humor and, 430
  in Jung's theory, 450, 452

Extrinsic motivation, 405
  for creativity, 318
Eye anatomy, 157–160. *See also* Vision
Eye movements, 160
Eyewitness testimony, 290–294
Eysenck, Hans, 453, 533, 552–553

F

Facial attractiveness, 602
Facial expressions
  assessing emotions from, 419, 420
  as cause of emotion, 435
  conveying emotion with, 423–426
  culture and, 425–426
  deception cues from, 416
  heredity and, 425
  infant perceptions, 114, 424
  universality of, 426
Facial-feedback theory, 435
  of emotion, 434–436
Factor analysis, 357
Factor-analytic intelligence theories, 357–359
Fallon, April, 386
Fallopian tubes, 110
False memory syndrome, 287
False positives, 418
Familiarity, interpersonal attraction and, 601–602
Family configuration studies, 368–369
Family obligations, adolescent conflicts over, 134
Family studies, 65
  of intelligence, 366–369
Family therapy, 543–544
Farsightedness, 158
Fathers, attachment to, 120–121
Fats, dietary, 585
Fay, Floyd, 417
Fear, 241, 242, 265–266, 494–496
Feature analysis, 167, 168
Feature-detector cells, 167, 168
Feature-detector theory, 167, 168, 173
Fechner, Gustav, 4–5, 95, 98, 152
Feeblemindedness, 363
Female impersonators, 375–376
Feminine psychology, 449
Festinger, Leon, 610–611
Fetal alcohol syndrome, 112
Fetal stage, 111–112
Fetal stem cells, 102
Fictional finalism, 449
Field experiments, 30, 40
Fields of specialization, in psychology, 17
  academic, 18–19
  professional, 19–22
Fight-or-flight response, 379, 414–415, 566, 567
Figure-ground perception, 165–166
Firing threshold, 73
First impressions, 599–600
Fisher, Ronald, 49
Fitness. *See* Exercise; Physical fitness
Five-factor model of personality, 454–455
Fixation, 446–447
Fixed-interval schedules of reinforcement, 251
Fixed-ratio schedules of reinforcement, 251

I-38   Subject Index

Flashbacks, 231
Flashbulb memories, 270–271
Flavor, taste versus, 184
Flooding, 537
Flotation REST, 401, 407
Flourens, Pierre, 4
Fluid intelligence, 137, 359
Fluoxetine (Prozac), 78, 492, 504, 507, 546–547
Folk Psychology, 16
Food cues, 384–385
Foot-in-the-door technique, 620–621
Forensic psychology, 21
Foreplay, 391
Fore tribe, 425
Forgetting
    curve, 284–285, *285*
    explanations for, 285–290
    eyewitness testimony, 290–294
    in information-processing model of memory, 272
    measurement of, 283–286
    long-term memory, 283–290
Formal operational stage, 115*t*, 127, 131
Form perception, 165–167
Forward chaining, 250
The Four Winds, 531
Fovea, 159
FOXP2 gene, 331
Framing effects, in decision making, 321–322
Franklin, Benjamin, 146
Fraternal twins, 65
Free associations, 532
Freeman, Walter, 544
Free nerve endings, 185
Free will, determinism versus, 27–28
Frequency of sound waves, 175, *175*, 178
Frequency scale, 456*t*
Frequency theory, 178
Freud, Anna, 10, 132
Freudian slips, 10, 203, 445
Freud, Sigmund
    on aggression, 623
    attachment assumptions, 119
    cocaine use, 230
    gender-role development theory, 124–126
    memory formation, 299
    personality theory, 444–447, 449, 451
    psychoanalytic theory, 9–10, 484–485, 496
    psychotherapy of, 532–533
    psychological disorders, 484–485, 496, 499
    theory of dreaming, 214, 217–218
    theory of humor, 431
    theory of unconscious, 203–204
Friedman, Meyer, 568–569
Friendships, 124, 134–135
Fröhlich, Alfred, 380
Fromm, Erich, 447
Frontal lobes, 89, 90–91, 200
Frustration-aggression hypothesis, 624–625
Fugue, 500
Functional fixedness, 314, 315–316
Functionalism, 6–8
Functional magnetic resonance imaging (fMRI), 84, *85*, 94–95, 200, 471, 474, 499
Fundamental attribution error, 597

G

Gabriel, Peter, 155
Gacy, John Wayne, 482, 519
Gage, Phineas, 92
Galen, 470
Gall, Franz Joseph, 82
Galton, Francis, 473
    application of Darwin's theories, 5, 138, 345, 362
    correlation concept, 48
    intelligence studies, 345–346, 362
    mental giftedness studies, 355
    predictive validity studies, 37
    twin studies, 65
Galvani, Luigi, 73
Galvanism, 73
Gamma aminobutyric acid (GABA), 78
Ganglion cells, 158–159, 164
Garcia, John, 244, 246
Gardner, Howard, 360–361
Gardner, Randy, 210
Gate-control theory, 185–186
Gays and lesbians. *See also* Homosexuality
    HIV-AIDS and, 583
    prejudice against, 613
    relationship dissolution, 143
Gazzaniga, Michael, 98
Geel, 530
Gender differences
    attempts to explain, 15, 138–141
    in body images, *386*
    cognitive abilities, 138
    in depression, 503
    development of sexual orientation, 398
    early studies, 362–363
    in effects of social support, 579
    emotional expression, 424–425
    in friendships, 134–135
    hemispheric lateralization, 95
    language effects on, 334
    memory, 281
    psychosocial development, 133, 138–141
    reporting research findings of, *51*, 51–52
    in romantic jealousy, 63
    in self-esteem, 468
    sexual behavior, 393
    smoking relapse, 587
    suicide, 508
Gender dysphoria, 489
Gender identity, 394–395
Gender roles
    childhood development, 124–126
    Horney's analysis, 449
    language effects on, 334
Gender schema theory, 125
General adaptation syndrome, 567, *567*
General intelligence factor (*g*), 357–358
Generalized anxiety disorder, 489, 491–492
General paresis, 484
Generation X cohort, 129
Generativity
    of language, 325
    stagnation stage versus, 119*t*, 145
Genes, 62–65, 376–377. *See also* Heredity

Genetic defects, 353
Genetics, behavioral, 15, 62–66
Genetic Studies of Genius, 356
Genie case study, 308
Genital stage, 447, 449*t*
Genius, 356
Genotypes, 64, *64*
Genovese, Kitty, 627–629
German measles, 112
Germinal stage, 110
Gestalt principles, 166–167, *166*, *167*
Gestalt psychology, 8–9
Gestalt therapy, 541–542
Ghrelin, 380
Giantism, 69
Gibson, Eleanor, 116
Giftedness, mental, 355–357
Gilligan, Carol, 128, 133
Glenn, John, 617
Glial cells, 71, *71*, 75, 99–100
Glioblastoma, 71
Global factors, in Seligman's attributional theory, 505
Glove anesthesia, 499
Glucose, 302, 303, 380
Glutamate, 78, 184, 185
Goal setting, 404
    sports and, 408
Goddard, Henry, 346, 352, 363, 370
Golgi, Camillo, 75
Gonads
    defined, 70
    embryonic formation, 110–111
    role in sexual motivation, 390
Goodall, Jane, 33
Gore, Al, 155
Graduate Record Examination (GRE), 37
Grammar, 326
Graphology, 450
Greenpeace, 610
Group contact, prejudice and, 615
Group, defined, 615
Group differences, 51–52
Group dynamics, 615–621
Group polarization, 616
Group therapy, 542–543
Groupthink, 617
Group violence, 625–626
Growth hormone, 69, 210
Growth spurts, 129–130, *130*
Gua (chimpanzee), 335
Guilford, J. P., 316, 359
Guilty but mentally ill rule, 487
Guilty Knowledge Test, 418, 419
Gustation, 183–184
Gustavson, Carl, 237–238, 244

H

Habits, health-promoting, 582–588
Habituation, 114
Hair cells, 177, 178–179, 189, *190*
Hales, Stephen, 71
Hall, G. Stanley, 6, 108, 134, 192

Hallucinations, 198, 512
Hallucinogens, 230
Halpern, Diane, 94, 96–97
Handedness, 94
   longevity and, 95
Handicaps in competition, 407–408
Handshakes, 599
Happiness, 427–429
Hardiness, 577–578
Hare, Robert, 520
Harlow, Harry, 119–120
Harm, preventing, 53
Harrison Narcotic Act, 228
Hashish, 231
Hassles, 564–566
Hatfield, Elaine, 604
Hauser, Kaspar, 308
Headaches, 185
Head Start, 364, 369
Health habits, 582–588
Health problems, seeking treatment for, 588–589
Health psychology, 20, 562. *See also* Stress
Health, sleep and, 212, 213
Hearing, 114, 174–180
   sound waves and, *175*
Hearnshaw, Leslie, 608
Heart, as location of mind in early belief, 80
Heart attacks, 570, 585, 588
Heaven's Gate cult, 595
Heinz dilemma, 126
Heir Conditioner, 256
Helmholtz, Hermann von, 4, 163, 178
Hemispheres of brain. *See* Cerebral hemispheres
Hemispheric lateralization
   from damaged brain, 94
   and emotion, 419–420
   from intact brain, 94–95
   from split brain, 95–99
Heredity
   aggression and, 624
   antisocial personality disorder and, 520
   anxiety disorders and, 492, 496
   bipolar disorder and, 510
   color blindness and, 165
   eating behavior and, 379, 387
   environment versus, *366*
   facial expressions and, 425
   influence on behavior studied, 62
   influence on intelligence, 364–370
   intellectual disabilities and, 353
   major depressive disorder and, 503
   motivation and, 376–377
   obesity and, 382–383, *383*
   personality and, 473
   potential role in homosexuality, 395–396
   schizophrenia and, 514, *514*
Hering, Ewald, 163–164
Heritability, 64–65, 364–365, 367, 475
Heroin, 228, 243–244
Herrnstein, Richard, 364
Hertz (Hz), 175
Heterosexuality, 395
HIV-AIDS and, 582–583
Heuristics, 312, 314, 320–321, 323

Hidden observer, 223, 224
Hierarchy of needs, 378–379, *378*
Higher-order conditioning, 239–241
High-fat diets, 585
High-quality day care, 123
High self-monitors, 458
Hilgard, Ernest, 223
Hippocampus, 88, 299–301, *300*
Hippocrates, 80, 470, 482, 499, 530, 574
History of psychology
   growth of, 8–13
   origins, 2–13
Histrionic personality disorder, 518*t*
HIV-AIDS
   celebrity victims, 561
   infection prevention, 582–583
   among LeVay's subjects, 397
   stress and, 572
H. M. case study, 88, 300–301
Hobbes, Thomas, 430
Hodgkin, Alan, 73
Hofmann, Albert, 230–231
Hollingworth, Leta Stetter, 138, 355, 362
Holophrastic speech, 328–329
Holton, Brian, 203
Homeostasis, 377
Homosexuality
   defined, 395
   Kinsey's view, 392
   prejudice against, 613
Hormone replacement therapy, 303
Hormones
   defined, 68
   effects in puberty, 130
   effects of stress on, 565, 566, 570, 571–572
   influence on biological rhythms, 204–205
   relating to hunger and body weight, 380*t*
   role in embryonic formation, 110–111
   role in emotion, 420–421
   role in gender differences, 140
   role in memory, 303
Horney, Karen, 449, 451–452
Hospice movement, 146
Hospitalized patients' rights, 549–550
Hostility, 569
"Hot hands," 25–26
Hubbard, L. Ron, 155
Hue, 156
Human development. *See also* Developmental psychology
   adolescence, 129–135
   adulthood, 136–146
   infancy and childhood, 112–128
   prenatal period, 111
   research methods in, 108–110
Human Genome Project, 64, 331
Human immunodeficiency virus. *See* HIV-AIDS
Humanistic perspective, 13–14
   on anxiety disorders, 492
   on major depressive disorder, 506
   on obsessive-compulsive disorder, 498
   on personality, 465–470
   on psychological disorders in general, 485
   on schizophrenia, 517

   on somatic symptom and related disorder, 499
   therapies, 540–542
Human sexual response cycle, 390–391, *390*
Human subjects, ethical treatment of, 52–54
Humor, 429–431, 470, 613
Humoral theory, 471, 530
Hunger
   bodily factors and, 379–380
   brain factors and, 380–381
   eating disorders and, 385–389
   insulin and, 380
   mental experience of, 11
   obesity and, 381–385
   physiology of, 379–381
   regulation of eating, 380
   sociocultural influences, 381
Huxley, Andrew, 73
H-Y antigens, 396
Hyde, Janet Shibley, 50, 141
Hyperkinetic impulse disorder, 522
Hypermnesia, 222, 501
Hyperopia, 158
Hypertension treatment, 591
Hypnosis, 188, 219–224
   consciousness and, 224
   as dissociated state, 223
   effects of, 221–222
   nature of, 222–224
   as role playing, 223–224
Hypnotism, 220
Hypochondriasis, 456, 456*t*, 498
Hypocretin, 208
Hypomania, 456*t*
Hypomnesia, 501
Hypothalamic-pituitary-adrenal (HPA) axis, 385
Hypothalamus
   basic control functions, 68, 87, 419
   effects of stress, 571
   experimental manipulations, 80
   hunger and, *381*
   role in biological rhythms, 204–205
   sexual orientation, 396, 397
Hypothesis, 29
Hypoxia, 353
Hysteria, 456*t*, 499

I

Iconic memory, 273
Id, 445
Ideal body weight, 585
Ideal self, *467*, 467, 469, 506
Identical twins. *See also* Heredity; Twin studies
   intelligence studies, 366, 367
   personality studies, 473, 474, 475, 476
   sexual orientation, 395–396
   studying, reared apart, 65, 66
Identification, in Freud's theory, 447
Identity development, 132–134, 142
Identity versus role confusion stage, 119*t*, 132
Illness
   behavioral causes of, 562
   biopsychological factors, 566–574
   exercise and, 580–581, *581*

reactions to, 588–591
stress and, 562, 563, 564
Illness anxiety disorder, 498–499
Illusions, visual, 171–173
Illusory contours, 167, *168*
Imaginal flooding, 537
Immigrants
   early studies of intelligence, 363–364
   family conflicts, 134
   prejudice against, 614
Immigration Act of 1924, 363
Immune system. *See also* HIV-AIDS
   effects of hypnosis, 221
   effects of stress, 565, 570–573
   importance of sleep to, 212
Implicit attitudes, 203
Implicit memory, 201, 278–279, *279*, 284
Impoverished environments, 112–113
Impression management, 598–599
Inactivity, obesity and, 384
INAH-3, 396
Incentives, 377–378
Incentive value, 404
Incongruity theory, 430–431
Incus, 176, *176*
Independent variables, 39
Indirect bullying, 578–579
Individual differences, 51–52
Individualistic cultures, 462, 468
Individual psychology, 447–449
Industrial/organizational (I/O) psychology, 20
Industry versus inferiority, 119*t*, 121
Infancy, defined, 112
Infant and child development
   cognitive, 114–118, 115*t*, *116*, *118*
   language acquisition, 328–332
   motor milestones, *113*
   perceptual, 113–114
   physical, 112–113
   psychosocial, 118–128, 119*t*
   temperament, 470–471
Infantile amnesia, 300
Infectious diseases, 561–562
Inferences, transitive, 117
Inferential statistics, 49–52
Inferiority complex, 447
Influenza viruses, 515
Information-processing model of memory, 271–272
Informed consent, 53
Infrared light, 157
In-groups, 599, 614
Inhibitory neurotransmitters, 76
Initiative versus guilt, 119*t*, 121
Inkblot tests, 450
Innate goodness, 470
Inner ear, 175, 176–177
Insane asylums, 530
Insanity defense, 486–487
Insanity, defined, 486
Insecure attachment, 120
Insight, 312–313
Insomnia, 40–41, 211–213
Instinctive drift, 260

Instincts
   aggression and, 622–623
   learning versus, 238
   motivation as, 376–377
Institutional Review Board (IRB), 52–53
Instrumental conditioning, 247
Insulin, 380, 381
Integrity versus despair stage, 119*t*, 145
Intellectual disabilities
   causes of, 351–355
   classification of, 351–352
   defined, 351
   education of people with, 354–355
   psychological research, 37
Intellectual enrichment programs, 369–370
Intellectualization, 446
Intellectualization group, 438
Intelligence
   aging effects, 137
   artificial, 322–324
   attempts to defining, 344–345
   of audiences for persuasive messages, 609
   evolution of testing methods, 345–351
   extremes of, 351–357
   heritability, 64–65
   life-span change in, *359*
   nature-nurture issues, 362–370
   theories of, 357–361
Intelligence quotient (IQ), 346, 347, *348*. *See also* Intelligence; Intelligence testing
Intelligence testing
   bias in, 364–365
   development, 345–347
   history, 345–347
   standardization in, 347, 351
   types, 345
   use of norms, 36
Interference
   proactive and retroactive, *286*
   recall and, *286*
   theory, 285–286
Intergenerational conflicts, 134
Intermittent schedules, 251
Internal-External Locus of Control Scale, 463
Internal factors, in Seligman's attributional theory, 505
Internal validity, 41–43
International Classification of Diseases (ICD), 488–489
Interneurons, 72
Interpersonal attraction, 30, 601–606
Interpersonal intelligence, 361
Interpersonal similarity, attraction and, 30
The Interpretation of Dreams, 215, 449
Interval schedules of reinforcement, 251–252
Intimacy versus isolation stage, 119*t*, 142
Intimate relationships, 142–144
Intoxication, 28, 224, 227–228. *See also* Alcohol use
Intracellular fluid, 73
Intrapersonal intelligence, 361
Intrinsic motivation
   cognitive-evaluation theory, 405–406
   exercise adherence and, 584
   overjustification theory, 405

overview, 404–406
sport and, 408
Introspection, analytic, 6
Introversion, 450, 452, 456*t*, 457
Inuits, 134, 333
In vivo desensitization, 535
In vivo flooding, 537
Involuntary commitment, 550
Involuntary responses, operant conditioning of, 258–259
Iodopsin, 160, 161, 164
Ions, 73
IQ, 346, 347, *348*. *See also* Intelligence; Intelligence testing
Iris of eye, 157
Ishihara color test, 164
Islamic science, 3
Isolation, language acquisition and, 308
Israeli Psychometric Entrance Exam, 349

J

James-Lange theory of emotion, *432*, 432, 433
James, William
   on consciousness, 199–200, 202, 203
   determinism versus free will, 27–28
   emotion theory, 432
   emphasis on biology, 61
   on memory, 271, 276, 280, 283, 294, 296
   motivation for writing, 404–405
   overview of contributions, 7–8
   paranormal studies, 192
   skepticism about unconscious motivations, 10, 11
Janis, Irving, 617
Japanese IQ scores, 370
Jealousy, 63
Jefferson, Thomas, 193
Jenkins, John, 285
Jensen, Arthur, 358, 364–365
Jet lag, 205
Jewell, Richard, 464
John Henryism, 570
Johnson, Samuel, 446
Jones, Mary Cover, 534
Jung, Carl, 10, 449–450, 452
Justice reasoning, 128
Just noticeable difference (jnd), 155

K

Kahneman, Daniel, 320
Kallikak, Martin, 352
Kamin, Leon, 366
Kanner, Leo, 521
Kant, Immanuel, 4, 9, 430
Kanzi (pygmy chimpanzee), 337–338
Kasparov, Gary, 323
Keller, Helen, 181
Kelley, Harold, 26, 596–597
Kempelen, Wolfgang von, 322
Kiecolt-Glaser, Janice, 581
Kinesthetic sense, 188–189
Kinsey, Alfred, 392–393
Kitayama, Shinobu, 462

Subject Index I-41

Klein, Melanie, 10
Klüver-Bucy syndrome, 88
Knee jerk reflex, 239
KnightCap, 323
Koffka, Kurt, 9
Kohlberg, Lawrence, 126–128
Köhler, Wolfgang, 9, 313
Koko (gorilla), 337
Kraepelin, Emil, 488, 512
Krippner, Stanley, 191

L

Labeled lines, 183
La belle indifference, 499
Labels effect, on recall, *333*
Ladd-Franklin, Christine, 7–8
Laing, R. D., 517
Lana (chimpanzee), 337
Lancet, The, 82
Lange, Carl, 432
Language
    acquisition of, 308–309, 328–332
    ape communications, 335–339
    case studies, 308
    cortex, 92–93
    development in childhood, 117
    elements of, 324–326
    hemispheric lateralization and, 95
    impact of intellectual disability, 352
    relation to thought, 332–335
    structure of, 326–328
Language acquisition device, 331
LaPiere, Richard, 610
LaRitz, Tom, 162
Larry P. v. Wilson Riles, 349
Lashley, Karl, 298
Latané, Bibb, 627, 628
Late adulthood, 145–146
Late maturation, 131
Latency stage, 447, 449*t*
Latent content, of dreams, 217–218, 533
Latent learning, 262–263
Lateral hypothalamus (LH), 381
Lateralization of cerebral hemispheres, 93–99, 419–420
Law of effect, 247
Lazarus, Richard, 436, 438, 564, 575
L-dopa, 78, 101, 515
Leading questions, 292–293, 322
Learned helplessness, 257, 576
Learning
    classical conditioning, 238–247
    cognitive, 260–266
    defined, 238
    language acquisition as, 330–331
    operant conditioning, 247–260
Led Zeppelin, 155
Left cerebral hemisphere, 92, 419–420, 422–423
Left-handedness, 93, 96–97
Lens of eye, 158
Leptin, 381, 388
Lesbians' body image, 387

LeVay, Simon, 397
Levels of consciousness, 203
Levels of processing theory, 277–278, *278*
Levodopa (L-dopa), 78, 101, 515
Levy, David, 323
Levy, Jerre, 98
Lewis, Denslow, 392
Libido, 446
Lie detectors, 413, 416–418
Lie scale, 456, 456*t*
Life changes
    daily hassles and, 565
    score, 563
    stress and, 562–564
Life events, stress and, 562–563
Life reviews, 145
Light, 156–157
    therapy, 506, 507
    three primary colors of, *163*
Liking, 601–603
Lima, Almeida, 544
Limbic system, *419*. See also Hypothalamus
    basic functions, 87–88
    emotion and, 419
    olfactory functions, 182
    role in emotion, 432
Limb-withdrawal reflex, 71–72
Limen, 152
Linear perspective, 169, *170*, *171*
Linguistic intelligence, 361
Linguistic relativity
    hypothesis, 332–335
    sexist language and, 335
Link method, 298
Links, in semantic network theory, 280
Lisdexamfetamine dimesylate (Vyvanse), 524
Listening, dichotic, 201–202, *202*
Literary Digest poll, 36
Lithium carbonate, 547
Lithium chloride, 237–238
Little Albert study, 242–243
Lobes of cerebral cortex, *89*
Localization of sound, 180
Locke, John, 4, 10
Locus of control, 463
Loewi, Otto, 76
Loftus, Elizabeth, 292–293
Logical concepts, 310
Logical-mathematical intelligence, 361
Lombroso, Cesare, 416
Longevity
    handedness and, 95
    limits, 137
    physical fitness and, 107–109, 137
Longitudinal research, 108–109
Long-term memory
    defined, 272
    encoding in, 276–278, 288–290
    forgetting, 283–290
    retrieval, 281–283
    storage, 278–281
Long-term potentiation, 299
Lorazepam (Ativan), 78
Lorenz, Konrad, 623

Loudness perception, 178–180
Lou Gehrig's disease, 71
Loulis (chimpanzee), 336
Love, 378, 603–606
Low-calorie diets, 137
Low self-monitors, 458
LSD, 226*t*, 230–231
Luborsky, Lester, 553, 554
Lucid dreaming, 217
Lunacy, 482
Lykken, David, 416, 418
Lysergic acid diethylamide (LSD), 226*t*, 230–231

M

Mad Hatter, 484
Maezel Chess Automaton, 322
Magnetic resonance imaging (MRI), 84, 301
Magnetoencephalography (MEG), 83
Maimonides studies, 191
Mainstreaming, 354–355
Maintenance rehearsal, 275, 277
Major depressive disorder (MDD), 503–509
    drug therapy and, 546–547
    prevalence in United States, *491*, 503
    suicide and, 508–509
Maladaptiveness criterion, 481, 482
Malleus, 176, *176*
Malnutrition, during pregnancies, 353
Malvo, Lee Boyd, 486–487
Management by objectives, 404
Mandala, 450
MANEA gene, 492, 493
Mania, 510, 547
Manic depression. *See* Bipolar disorder
Manifest content, of dreams, 217–218, 533
The Man Who Mistook His Wife for a Hat, 151
MAO inhibitors, 546
Marijuana, 112, 226*t*, 231–232, 289–290
Mariotte, Edmé, 159–160
Marital conflict, impact on children, 123–124
Marital therapy, 543
Markus, Hazel, 462
Marmara earthquake, 270
Marriage, 142–144, 428
Masculine pronouns, 335
Masculinity-femininity scale, 456*t*
Maslow, Abraham
    hierarchy of needs, 378–379, *378*
    overview of contributions, 13
    personality theory, 466
Massed practice, 296
Masters and Johnson studies, 390–391, 392, 393–394
Masturbation, 391–392
Mathematical abilities, 138–139
Mathematically Precocious Youth study, 141
Matthews, Karen, 570
Maturation, 107, 238
McAuliffe, Christa, 617
McDonnell, James, 192
McDougall, William, 95, 98, 376
McPherson, Marion, 38
MDE (methylenedioxyethylamphetamine), 226*t*, 232

MDMA (methylenedioxymethamphetamine), 226t, 232
Mean, 46–47
Mean length of utterance (MLU), 329
Measurement
 central tendency, 46–48
 of forgetting, 283–285
 intelligence, 345–351
 language maturation, 329
 need for achievement, 403–404
 personality, 450–451, 455–457, 462–463, 468–469
 use in research, 31
 variability, 48
Media coverage of psychology, 25, 26
Median, 46
"Medical student disease," 498
Medical treatment
 regimens, 590–591
 seeking, 588–589
Meditation, and stress, 581–582
Medulla, 86
Melanocortin, 380, 382–383, 388
Melanoma risk, 39
Melatonin
 media reports, 26
 sleep effects, 40–41, 42, 47t, 48–49, 204–205
Memory
 anatomy of, 300
 biopsychology of, 298–303
 defined, 271
 dreaming and, 218–219
 effects of hypnosis, 222
 encoding in, 272, 276–278, 288–290
 eyewitness testimony, 290–294
 flashbulb, 270–271
 forgetting, 272, 283–290
 improving, 294–298
 information-processing model of, 271–272
 processes, 272
 retrieval, 272, 281–283
 role of hippocampus, 88
 sensory, 271–272, 272, 272–275
 short-term, 272, 273–276, 276
 storage, 272, 278–281
 systems, 278–280, 279
 trace, 298–299
 transfer studies, 301
 view, 191
Menarche, 130
Menopause, 136
MENSA, 355
Mental age, 346
Mental distress, protecting research subjects from, 53
Mental giftedness, 355–357
Mental health movement, 531
Mental illness. See Psychological disorders
Mental retardation. See Intellectual disabilities
Mental sets, 314–315, 315, 338
Mental telepathy, 81–82, 191
Mental tests, 5
Mere exposure effect, 601
Mescaline, 230

Mesmer, Franz Anton, 219–220
Mesmerism, 219–220
Mesomorphs, 472
Meta-analyses, 50–51
Metcalfe, Janet, 313
Methamphetamines, 226t, 230
Methedrine, 229
Method of loci, 296, 297
Method of savings, 284
Methyphenidate (Ritalin), 524
Miami Project to Cure Paralysis, 101
Microglia, 71
Microsleeps, 210
Middle adulthood, 145
Middle ear, 175, 176, 176
Midlife crises, 145
Migraine headaches, 185
Mild intellectual disability, 352
Milgram, Stanley, 622, 623
Miller, Neal, 54
Milner, Peter, 87
Mind, 11, 80, 98. See also Cognitive perspective
Minnesota Adoption Study, 367
Minnesota Multiphasic Personality Inventory (MMPI), 452, 455–457
Minnesota Study of Twins Reared Apart, 366, 379, 474
Minority influence, 616
Mirror neurons, 71, 263–264
Mischel, Walter, 458
Misleading information, effects on eyewitness testimony, 291, 293
Mixed amphetamine salts (Adderall), 524
MMPI. See Minnesota Multiphasic Personality Inventory
M'Naghten rule, 486
Mnemonic devices, 296–298
Moby Dick, 216
Mode, 46
Modeling language, 331
Modeling technique, for reducing distress, 589
Moderate intellectual disability, 352
Modern racism, 613
Modesty bias, 598
Modification hypothesis, 96
Molaison, Henry, 88, 271, 300–301
Money, John, 394, 399
Mongolism, 353
Moniz, Egas, 544
Monkeys, 358
 communications, 325
Monoamine Oxidase A (MAO-A), 473
Monochromats, 165
Monocular depth cues, 167, 168–169
Monozygotic twins, 65
Montesquieu, Charles, 428
Montreal Neurological Institute, 90
Montreal procedure, 90
Mood-dependent memory, 290
Moods, effect of odors on, 181
Mood stabilizers, 547
Moon, effects on behavior debunked, 482
Moon illusion, 172
Moral development, 126–128, 127t

Moral insanity, 519
Moral therapy, 530
Morel, Benedict, 512
Morgan, Christiana, 451
Morphemes, 326
Morphine, 228
Mother, 375–376
Mothers, attachment to, 119–120
Motion parallax, 168
Motion sickness, 189–190
Motivation
 achievement, 402–406
 arousal, 399–402, 406–407, 457
 for creativity, 318
 defined, 376
 for exercise adherence, 584
 for forgetting, 286, 288
 hunger, 379–389
 for prosocial behavior, 626–627
 sexual, 389–399
 sources, 376–378
 in sport, 406–408
Motor behavior, with schizophrenia, 513
Motor cortex, 89, 90
Motor homunculus, 89
Motor milestones, 113
Motor neurons, 71
Motor skill development, 112–113
Motor theory of thought, 309
Mount Saint Helens eruption, 564
Muhammad, John Allen, 486–487
Mulika (pygmy chimpanzee), 337
Müller-Lyer illusion, 172–173, 173
Multicultural psychology, 16
Multiphasic activity, 568–569
Multiple-choice tests, 27
Multiple intelligences, 360–361
Multiple personality disorder. See Dissociative identity disorder
Multiple sclerosis (MS), 75
Munch, Edvard, 511
Münsterberg, Hugo, 7–8, 290
Murray, Charles, 364
Murray, Henry, 451
Musical intelligence, 361
Musicians, timbre perception, 180
Myasthenia gravis, 77
Mycin (expert system), 323
Myelin, 75, 353
 damaged and healthy sheaths, 75
Myers-Briggs Type Indicator, 455
Myopia, 158

N

Naloxone, 78–79, 81, 186, 188, 421
Naps, 209, 210, 214
Narcissistic personality disorder, 518t
Narcolepsy, 211, 214
Narcotics, 78
Nardil, 546
Narrative method, 298
National Comorbidity Survey Replication (NCS-R), 481, 484

National Institute of Child Health and Human Development Study of Early Child Care, 123
National Institute of Health (NIH), 55
National Institute of Mental Health (NIMH) Treatment of Depression Collaborative Research Program, 553
National Sleep Foundation, 212, 213
Nativism, 3
Natural concepts, 310–312, 344
Naturalistic observation, 33–34
Natural killer cells, 212, 572
Natural selection, 5, 15, 62
Nature-versus-nurture debate
  early theorists, 4
  evolutionary psychology and, 61
  on intelligence, 362–370
Nazi war crimes, 621
Nearsightedness, 158
Need for achievement, 402–404
  sports and, 407–408
Needs, 377, 378–379
Negative correlations, 38, 48, *49*
Negative incentives, 378
Negative reinforcement, 253, 254–255, 255*t*
Negative state relief theory, 627
Negative symptoms, of schizophrenia, 512, 516
Negative transference, 533
Neil v. Biggers, 294
Nelson, Randy, 507
Neodissociation theory, 223
Neo-Freudians, 10, 447
Neologisms, 513
Nerve deafness, 179
Nerve growth factor, 99
Nerve impulses, 4
Nerves, 68
Nervous system overview, 67–68, *67*
Neural grafting, 101
Neural networks, 323
Neural plasticity, 99–102
Neural transplantation, 101–102
Neuroanatomy of memory, 298–301
Neurological factors, in schizophrenia, 516
Neurological view, 191
Neuromodulators, 79
Neuronal membrane, 73
Neuron doctrine, 75
Neurons, 67, 71–79, *72*
Neuropeptides, 78
Neuropeptide Y, 78
Neuroses, 451–452, 488
Neuroticism, 453, *453*, 455
Neurotransmitters
  basic functions, 76
  bipolar disorder and, 511
  developmental disorders and, 522
  drug effects on, 76–78, 227, 229, 232
  major depressive disorder and, 504
  memory functions, 301
  pain, 185
  role in emotion, 420–421
  schizophrenia and, 514–515
  sleep regulation, 208
Newborns. *See* Infant and child development

Newspeak, 332
Newsweek magazine, 26
Newton, Isaac, 72–73
Ngandu culture, 119
Nicotine, 226*t*, 229, 586–588
Nicotine chewing gum, 587
Nicotine replacement therapy, 587–588
Nightingale, Florence, 46
Nightmares, 216–217
Night terrors, 216
Nim Chimpsky (chimpanzee), 337
Nintendo, 602
Nixon, Richard, 608–609
NMDA receptors, 302–303
N-methyl-D-aspartate (NMDA) receptors, 302–303
Nociceptors, 185
Nocturnal emissions, 130
Nocturnal enuresis, 240–241
Nodes, in semantic network theory, 280
Nodes of Ranvier, 75
Nolen-Hoeksema, Susan, 506, 507
Nonsense syllables, 283, *285*, 285
Nonverbal behavior, 423
Norepinephrine, 414
  bipolar disorder and, 511
  major depressive disorder and, 78, 504, 545, 546
  role in emotion, 420–421
  source, 70
Normal curve, 347
Normalization, 355
Norms, in testing, 36
Norton, Joshua, 480–481
NREM sleep, *206, 207*, 207–208
Nun Study, 141
Nuremberg war crimes trials, 621
Nutrition, prenatal, 383

O

Obedience, 621
Obesity
  behavioral factors in, 384–385
  biopsychological factors in, 382–384
  causes, 381–385
  cultural influences, 585
  health risks, 583
  heredity and, *383*
  weight control approaches, 585–586
Objective tests, 455
Object permanence, 115, 117
Observational learning, 263–266, 331
Observation, naturalistic, 33–34
Obsessive-compulsive disorder (OCD), 487, 496–498, 540, 544
Obsessive-compulsive personality disorder, 518*t*
Occipital lobes, 91, 160
Occlusion, 169, *170*
Odors, sensing, 181–183
Oedipus complex, 124, 447, 451
Offensive social anxiety disorders, 495
Ohrwall, Hjalmar, 183
Olds, James, 87
Olfaction, 181–183
Olfactory nerves, 182, *182*

Oligodendrocytes, 71
One-sided messages, 609
Online therapy, 552
Open-minded skepticism, 28
Openness to experience, 455
Operant conditioning
  applications, 255–259
  attitude formation by, 607
  for autism spectrum disorder (ASD), 537
  biological constraints, 259–260
  cognitive factors, 261–262
  origins, 247
  principles, 247–255
  therapies, 536–538
Operational definitions, 31
Operations, in Piaget's theory, 117
Opiate receptors in brain, 79
Opiates, 226*t*, 228
Opium poppy, 228
Opponent-process theory, 434
  of color vision, 163–164
Optic chiasm, 160, *161*
Optic nerves, 158, 159, *160*
Optimal arousal, 399–400, 404, 406–407, 408
Oral stage, 446–447, 449*t*, 516
Orexin, 208
Orgasmic disorder, 393
Orgasm phase, 390–391
Orientation programs, for cancer patients, 589
Origin of Species, 5
Ormsby, Kathy, 407
Orne, Martin, 222
Oscilloscope, *168*
Ossicles, 176, *176*, 179
Othello, Washington, 564
Otolith organs, 189, *190*
Ought self, 469
Outer ear, 175, *176*
Out-groups, 599
Oval window, 175, *176*, 178
Ovaries, 70, 110
Overextension, 328
Overjustification theory, 405
Overlearning, 294, 295
Overregularization, 328–329
Ovum, 110
Oxytocin, 566–567

P

Pagano, Bernard, 290–291
Pain perception, 185–188, 221
Pain relief, 79
Panic disorder, 492–493
Papillae, 183
Pappenheim, Bertha, 529
Paracelsus, 482
Paradoxical intention, 213
Paradoxical sleep, 207
Parallel play, 124
Paranoia scale, 456, 456*t*
Paranoid personality disorder, 518*t*
Parapsychology, 190–194
Parasympathetic nervous system, 68, 414, *415*

I-44 Subject Index

Parental conflict, 123–124
Parent-child relationships, 121–124
Parenting influences, 144
Parenting styles, 122, 466
Parents, adolescent relationships with, 134
Parietal lobes, 82, 83, 89
Parkinson's disease, 78, 101–102
Partial schedules of reinforcement, 251
Participant bias, 42
Participant modeling, 538
Participant variables, 42
Partly empty nest syndrome, 145
Passionate love, 604
Patient distress, relieving, 589–590
Patridge, James, 626, 627–629
Patterns of sleep, 205–209
Patterson, Francine, 337
Pavlov, Ivan, 11, 44, 238–240, 312
Paxil (paroxetine), 546–547
PCP, 230
Peace psychology, 21
Pearson, Karl, 48
Pearson's r, 48
Peckham, Robert, 349–350
Peer relationships, 124, 134–135
Pegword method, 296, 297–298, *297*, 304
Penfield, Wilder, 14–15, 81, 90
Penis envy, 447, 449
Pentothal, 228
Pepsi Challenge taste tests, 41
Perceived control, 574, 576–577
Perception
  auditory, 177–180
  without awareness, 201–203
  effects of brain damage, 151–152, 202
  extrasensory, 190–194
  hypnosis and, 221
  pain and touch, 185–188
  paranormal, 190–194
  sensation versus, 152
  smell and taste, 181–184
  subliminal, 153–154
  visual, 165–174
Perceptual constancies, 169–171
Perceptual development, 113–114
Performance, group effects on, 617–618
Periaqueductal gray, 185, 188
Peripheral nervous system, 68
Peripheral-route arguments, 608, 609–610
Peripheral vision, 158–159
Perls, Fritz, 541–542
Permissive parenting, 122
Persona, 450
Personal advertisements, 630
Personal distress criterion, 481, 482
Personal importance of messages, persuasion and, 609
Personality
  cognitive-behavioral approach, 460–465
  creativity and, 317
  defined, 443
  dispositional approach, 452–457
  eating disorders and, 387

Eysenck's dimensions, *453*
  gender differences, 139
  hardy, 577–578
  heritability, 66
  humanistic approach, 465–470
  psychoanalytic approach to, 444–452
  structure of, *445*, 445
Personality development theories, 10
Personality disorders, 517–520, 518*t*
Personality psychology, 19
Personal Orientation Inventory (POI), 468–469
Personal responsibility, taking, 628–629
Personal unconscious, 450
Person-centered therapy, 13, 540–541
Personnel psychology. *See* Industrial psychology
Person perception, 598–600
Persuasion, 608–610, 616
Persuasive-argument theory, 616
Pert, Candace, 78–79
Pessimistic explanatory style, 575–576
Pfungst, Oskar, 335
Phallic stage, 447, 449*t*
Phase advance, 205
Phase delay, 205
Phencyclidine, 230
Phenomenological experience, 466
Phenomenological psychology, 13
Phenomenon, 155
Phenothiazines, 547
Phenotypes, 64
Phenylalanine, 353
Phenylketonuria (PKU), 353–354
Pheromones, 182–183
Philosophy, roots of psychology in, 2–5
Phi phenomenon, 8
Phobias
  causes of, 495–496
  characteristics of, 494–495
  classes of, 494
  classical conditioning and, 242–243
  defined, 494
  learning by observing, 265
  specific, 494
  treatments for, 534–536
Phonemes, 326
Phonology, 326
Photopigments, 160–161
Photoreceptors, 158
Phototherapy, 507
Phrenology, 82, 471–472
Physical attractiveness, 602–603, 608–609
Physical dependence, 225
Physical development in
  adolescence, 129–131
  adulthood, 136–137
  infancy and childhood, 112–113
Physical effects of hypnosis, 221
Physical fitness. *See also* Exercise
  aging and, 107–109, 136–137
  overall health effects, 583–584
  stress management effects, 580–581
Physical punishment, 254–255
Physical restoration, sleep as, 209–210

Physicians, 590
Physiognomy, 471
Physiological arousal, 437, 461
Physiological explanations for gender differences, 140
Physiological needs, 378
Physiological reactivity, 574–575
Physiological responses, operant conditioning of, 258–259
Physiological roots of psychology, 4–5
Physique, personality and, 471–473, 474–475
Piaget, Jean
  cognitive development theory, 114–118, 115*t*, 131–132
  cognitive perspective, 14
  moral development theory, 126
Pictorial cues, 169, *170*
Picture-description test, 290
Pineal gland, 204
Pinel, Philippe, 530
Pinnae, 175
Pitch perception, 177–178
Pituitary gland, 68–69
Placebos, 40, 42, 43, 186, 289–290
Place theory, 178
Plasticity of brain, 99–102
Plateau phase, 390–391
Plath, Sylvia, 318
Plato, 2–3, 62
Play behavior, 124
Pleasure centers, 87
Pleasure principle, 445
Plomin, Robert, 66
Poe, Edgar Allen, 322
Poincaré, Henri, 316–317
Polarization, 73, 616
Polygenic traits, 64
Polygraph Protection Act, 417
Polygraph testing, 413, 416–418, 419
Pons, 86
Ponzo illusion, 172, *172*, 174
Popplestone, John, 38
Populations, 35
Po River, *250*
A Portrait of the Artist as a Young Man, 199
Positive correlations, 38, 48, *49*
Positive incentives, 377–378
Positive reinforcement
  impact on language acquisition, 330–331
  in operant conditioning, 248–252, 255*t*
  in therapy, 536–537
Positive symptoms of schizophrenia, 512, 516
Positive transference, 533
Positron-emission tomography (PET), 84, 279
Postconventional level, of moral development, 127
Posthypnotic amnesia, 223
Posthypnotic suggestions, 223
Posttraumatic stress disorder (PTSD), 563–564
Poverty, 485
Practice, 202–203
  distributed, 294, 295
Pragmatics, 327, 352
Pratt, Joseph, 542

Precognition, 191, 192
Preconscious mind, 203, 444
Preconventional level, of moral development, 127
Predator control, 237–238
Prediction, 31–32, 261
Predictive validity, 37, 348–349
Prefrontal cortex, 524
Prefrontal leucotomy, 544
Prejudice, 612–615
Premack principle, 248
Premarital sexual activity, 392
Premature ejaculation, 393
Premature infants, 111
Prenatal development, 110–112, *111*
  and sexual orientation, 396–398
Prenatal exposure, 353
Prenatal nutrition, 383
Preoperational stage, 115*t*, 117
Preschool Behavioral and Emotional Rating Scale, 37
Preschool enrichment programs, 369
Prevention of psychological disorders
  primary, 548–549
  secondary, 548, 549
  tertiary, 548, 549
Previous success, 461
Primacy effect, 283–284
Primary appraisal, 575
Primary control, 576
Primary cortical areas, 88–89
Primary mental abilities, 359
Primary prevention, of psychological disorders, 548–549
Primary reinforcer, 248
Primary reinforcers, 261
Primary sex characteristics, 130
The Principles of Psychology, 7, 61, 280
Proactive interference, 285–286, *286*
Probabilistic prediction, 31–32
Problem solving, 312–316
  dreaming as, 218
Procedural memory, 278–280, 302
Prodigious savants, 344
Professional psychology, 19–21
Profiling, criminal, 464–465
Profound intellectual disability, 352
Progesterone, 70, 110–111
Programmed instruction (PI), 256
Progressive relaxation, 212–213, 534, 581
Project Head Start, 364, 369
Projection, 446
Projective tests, 450, 452
Project Pigeon, 255
Project Sea Hunt, 255
Prolactin, 391
  levels, 69
Prophetic dreams, 217
Prosocial behavior, 264, 626–630
Prosody, 422
Prosopagnosia, 80, 151–152, 202
Prospective studies, of daily hassles, 565–566
Prospector (expert system), 323
Prototypes, 311

Proximal stimulus, 167
Proximity
  interpersonal attraction and, 601
  principle, 166–167, *166, 167*
Proxmire, William, 604
Prozac (fluoxetine), 78, 492, 504, 507, 546–547
Pseudoscience, 26
Psilocybin, 230
Psychasthenia scale, 456*t*
Psychiatry, 20
Psychic blindness, 88
Psychic determinism, 10, 203, 445, 460
Psychoactive drugs, 224–232
  effects on brain and, 226*t*
Psychoanalysis, 8, 9–10, 532–533
Psychoanalytic approach to personality
  Adler's theory, 447–449
  assessment tools, 450–451
  Freud's theory, 444–447, 449*t*
  Horney's theory, 449
  Jung's theory, 449–450
  status, 451–452
Psychoanalytic perspective on
  anxiety disorders, 492, 493, 496
  dissociative disorders, 501, 502
  major depressive disorder, 504
  obsessive-compulsive disorder, 498
  psychological disorders in general, 484–485
  schizophrenia, 516
  somatic symptom and related disorder, 499
Psychodynamic therapy, 533
Psychokinesis (PK), 192
Psychological Abstracts, 427
Psychological Corporation, 5
Psychological dependence, 225
Psychological disorders. *See also* Therapy
  anxiety, 489–496
  bipolar disorder, 509–511
  causes of, 482, 483*t*
  characteristics of, 481–489
  classifying, 488–489
  criteria for, 481–482
  criticisms of diagnosis of, 489
  developmental disorders, 520–525
  dissociative, 500–502
  major depressive disorder, 503–509
  obsessive-compulsive disorder, 496–498
  operant conditioning and, 257–258
  personality, 517–520
  prevalence in United States, *491*
  schizophrenia, 511–517
  somatic symptom and related disorder, 498–500
  testing for, 455–457
  viewpoints on, 482–487, 483*t*
Psychological hardiness, 574, 577–578, 577*t*
Psychological profiling, 464–465
Psychological research, 52–55
Psychological testing, 36–37
Psychology
  brick and mortar, 8
  common sense versus, 28
  contemporary perspectives in, 13–17
  defining, 1–2

  fields of specialization in, *17*
  founding schools of, 5–8
  goals and methods of, 33*t*
  growth of, 8–12
  historical context of, 2–13
  perspectives of, *12*
  roots of, 2–5
  scope of, 17–21
Psychology: Briefer Course, 7
Psychology student syndrome, 498
Psychoneuroimmunology, 571–572, 581
Psychopathic deviate scale, 456*t*
Psychopathology, 481
The Psychopathology of Everyday Life, 10
Psychopathy, 519
Psychophysics, 4–5, 152
Psychoses, 488
Psychosexual development, 446–447
  stages of, 449*t*
Psychosocial development
  in adolescence, 132–135
  in adulthood, 141–146
  gender differences, 133, 138–141
  in infancy and childhood, 118–128, 119*t*
Psychosomatic diseases, 567
Psychosurgery, 544–545
Psychotherapy. *See also* Therapy
  drug therapy with, 546, 547
  effectiveness, 552–556, *554, 555*
  trends in, 531
Psychoticism, 453
Ptolemy, 172
Pubertal change, *130*
Puberty, 129–130
Public self, 517
Punishment, 254–255, 255*t*, 537
Pupil of eye, 157–158
Puzzle boxes, 247, *247*
Pygmalion effect, 42–43, 45
Pygmy chimpanzees, 337, 339

Q

Q-sort, 469
Qualitatively abnormal behavior, 481
Quantitatively abnormal behavior, 481
Questioning eyewitnesses, 294

R

Racism, 613
Rain Man, 343–344
Rakic, Patricia-Goldman, 524
Ramón y Cajal, Santiago, 75
Ramsey murder case, 465
Randi, James, 192–193
Random assignment, 42
Random sampling, 35
Rand, Tamara, 192
Range, 48
Rational-emotive behavior therapy (R-E-B-T), 538–539, 539*t*
Rationalism, 3

I-46 Subject Index

Rationalization, 446
Ratio schedules of reinforcement, 251–252
Rats, experimenter effects on, 44
Raven Progressive Matrices, 350, *350*
Reaction formation, 446
Reaction times, 358
Reading, therapeutic, 551–552
Reality principle, 445
Recall ability, aging effects, 141
Recall tests, 284, 289
Recency effect, 283–284
Receptor fields, 159
Receptors. *See* Sensory receptors
Receptor sites, 76
Recessive genes, 64
Reciprocal determinism, 460, *460*
Recognition tests, 284, 289
Recovered memories, 287
Red-green color blindness, 164–165
Reeve, Christopher, 100
Reflection of feelings, 541
Reflexes
  classical conditioning of, 239
  defined, 67
  discovery, 71–72
  of infants, 112
  learning versus, 238
Refractory period, 391
Regression, 446
Regulatory functions of hypothalamus, 87
Rehabilitation, stress-inoculation training during, 580
Rehearsal, 275, 277
Reinforcement
  impact on language acquisition, 330–331
  negative, 253, 254–255
  positive, 248–252
  schedules of, 251–252, *252*
  Skinner's focus on, 12
Reinforcement theory, 504
Relative size, 169
Relativism, 16
Relaxation
  progressive, 212–213, 534, 581
  and stress management, 581–582
Relearning, 284
Release theory, 431
Relevant questions, 416–417, *417*
Reliability, 37, 489
  of intelligence tests, 348, 349
REM rebound effect, 217
REM sleep, 207–208, 211, 214–219
Renaissance psychology, 3
Replacement therapy, 587–588
Replication, 29–30, 45
Repolarization, 74
Representational thought, 117
Representativeness heuristic, 320–321
Repression
  in Freud's theory, 286, 288, 444–446
  of painful memories, 287, 501
  research findings on, 451
Republic of Georgia, 614

Research
  correlational, 38–39
  descriptive methods, 33–38
  developmental psychology methods, 108–110
  ethics, 52–55
  experimental, 39–46, 40*t*
  goals, 30–32, 33*t*
  scientific method and, 29–30
  statistics, 29, 46–52
Reserpine, 547
Resistances, analysis of, 532, 533
Resistance stage, 567
Resolution phase, 390–391
Response bias, 153
Responsibility
  diffusion of, 618, *629*
  taking, 628–629
Ressler, Robert, 464–465
Resting potential, 73, 74, 75
Restorative function of sleep, 210
Reticular formation, 86
Retina
  basic processes in, 160–161
  cells of, *159*
  defined, 158
  depth perception role, 167–168
  structure of, 158–160
Retrieval, 272, 281–283
Retroactive interference, 286, *286*, 288
Retrograde amnesia, 546
Retrospective studies, of daily hassles, 565
Reuptake, 76
Rewards, 262, 318, 405
Rheumatoid arthritis, 572, *572*
Rhine, J. B. and Louisa, 192
Rhodopsin, 160, 161
Rhymes, 296
Ribonucleic acid (RNA), 62–63
Richardson, Bill, 413
Right cerebral hemisphere, 92, 419–420, 422–423, 430
Right-handedness, 94
Rights of therapy clients, 549–451
Ringelmann effect, 618
Riots, 625
Risky behavior, 401–402
Risky shift, 616
Robotics, 324
Rochester Adult Longitudinal study, 142
Rods, 158, 161
Rogers, Carl, 13–14, 467, 540
Rogers v. Commissioner of Mental Health, 550
Role playing, hypnosis as, 223–224
Rollin, Bernard, 55
Romantic love, 603–606
Romantic relationships, 63, 134–135, 603–606
Rorschach, Hermann, 450
Rorschach test, 450–451, 452
Rosenhan, David, 490
Rosenman, Ray, 568–569
Rosenthal, Robert, 42, 44
Rotating shifts, 205
Rotter, Julian, 463

Rozin, Paul, 386
Rubella virus, 112, 353
Rubin, Edgar, 166
Rumbaugh, Duane, 337
Rumination, 506, 507
Rush, Benjamin, 501, 530–531
Rutherford, Ernest, 178

S

Sacks, Oliver, 80, 151
Safe sex, 582–583
Safety and security needs, 378
Sagen, Jacqueline, 101
Samples, 35
Sarah (chimpanzee), 336
Satiation, 249
Saturation of light, 156
Saunders, Cicely, 146
Savage-Rumbaugh, Sue, 337–338
Savant syndrome, 343–344
Savings in memory, 284
"Scapegoat" food, 245
Schachter, Stanley, *436*, 436, 437
Schedules of reinforcement, 251–252, *252*
Schein, Edward, 608
Schemas
  development in infancy, 115
  in eyewitness testimony, 291
  gender-role, 125
  social, 599
Schema theory of
  memory organization, 280–281, 282–283
  personality, 461–462, 464
Schizoid personality disorder, 518*t*
Schizophrenia, 64, 65, 78, 511–517
  auditory cortex activity, 177
  of Emperor Norton, 481
  erroneous diagnoses of, 490
  MMPI-2 scale, 456*t*
  treatments for, 548
Schizotypal personality disorder, 518*t*
Scholastic Aptitude Test (SAT), 138
Scholastic Assessment Test (SAT), 348, 349, 368
School psychology, 20
School shootings, 1, 34
Science, assumptions of, 27–29
Science fiction, 450
Scientific method, 2, 29–30. *See also* Research
  formal steps in, 29–30
Scientific paradigms, 13
Sclera, 156
Scotophobin, 301
The Scream, 492–493
Seasonal affective disorder (SAD), 506–508
Season-of-birth factors, in schizophrenia, 515–516
Seattle Longitudinal Study, 109, 137
Seconal, 228
Secondary appraisal, 575
Secondary control, 576
Secondary prevention, of psychological disorders, 548–549
Secondary reinforcer, 248–249, 261

Secondary sex characteristics, 130
Secondary traits, 454
Second language acquisition, 330
Secure attachment, 120, 124
Sedatives, 211–212
Selective permeability of neuronal membrane, 73
Selective serotonin reuptake inhibitors (SSRIs), 78, 546–547
Selectivity of consciousness, 200
Self-actualization
  defined, 13
  in Maslow's hierarchy of needs, 378
  of personality, 466
  in person-centered therapy, 540–541
  research findings on, 469–470
Self-concepts, 144
Self-descriptions, 133
Self-disclosure, interpersonal attraction and, 603
Self-efficacy
  adhering to exercise program, 584
  defined, 460–461
  health-promoting behavior and, 582
  research findings on, 464
Self-esteem
  effect of peer relationships on, 124
  in humanistic personality theory, 468, 470
  impression management and, 598
  relation to attitudes about ethnicity, 133
Self-fulfilling prophecy, 42, 43, 350, 356, 600
Self-handicapping, 227–228, 407–408, 467–468, 598–599
Self-help audiotapes, 154
Self-help books, 551–552
Self-help groups, 543
Self-management programs, 588
Self-perception theory, 611–612, 621
Self-schemas, 461–462, *462*
Self-serving bias, 597–598
Self theory of personality, 467–468
Seligman, Martin, 257, 505
Selye, Hans, 562, 567
Semantic conditioning, 240
Semanticity of language, 324–325, 327–328
Semantic level of encoding, 278, *278*
Semantic memory, *279*, 279–280
Semantic network, 278, 280, *280*
Semantic network theory, 280, *280*, 282, 283
Semicircular canals, 189, *190*
Senden, Marius von, 174
Sensate focusing, 394
Sensation
  body senses, 188–190
  effects of brain damage, 151–152
  hearing, 174–180
  perception versus, 152
  processes in, 152–156
  role of thalamus, 87, 160, *161*, 164–165
  skin senses, 184–188
  smell and taste, 181–184
  vision, 156–165
Sensation seeking, 399, 401–402, 406
Sensorimotor stage, 115t, 115
Sensory adaptation, 155–156

Sensory cortex, 89–91
Sensory deprivation, 399, 400–401
Sensory homunculus, 90
Sensory memory, 271–272, *272*, 272–275
Sensory neurons, 71
Sensory-perceptual symptoms, in schizophrenia, 512–513
Sensory receptors
  defined, 152
  hearing, 174–180
  kinesthetic and vestibular, 188–190, *190*
  pain and touch, 185–188
  smell, 181–183
  taste, 183–184
  vision, 156–165
Sensory thresholds, 152–155, 182
Sensory transduction, 152
Separation anxiety, 493, 496, 497
September 11 attacks, 270, 563
Septum, 419
Serial-position effect, *283*, 283–284
Serotonin
  bipolar disorder and, 511
  developmental disorders and, 522
  entactogen effects, 232
  major depressive disorder and, 78, 504, 507, 545, 546–547
  potential link to eating disorders, 389
  schizophrenia and, 515
Set point, 381
  obesity and, 383
Severe intellectual disability, 352
Sex determination in human embryo, 110–111
Sex hormones, 70
Sexism, 613
Sexist humor, 431
Sexist language, 335
Sex-linked traits, 165
Sexpert, 323–324
Sex reassignment surgery, 393
Sex research, 45
Sexual abuse
  borderline personality disorder and, 519
  children's testimony, 293–294
  dissociative identity disorder and, 502
  effect on children's psychosocial development, 122
  posttraumatic stress disorder and, 564
  recovered memories, 287
  suicide and, 508
Sexual assault, 625
Sexual behavior
  in adolescence, 134–135
  aging effects, 109, 136
  safety in, 582–583
Sexual dysfunctions, 393–394
Sexual jealousy, 63
Sexual love. *See* Passionate love
Sexually transmitted diseases, 392
Sexual motivations
  biopsychological factors, 390–391
  dysfunctions and, 393–394
  Freud's theory, 10, 444

  gender identity, 394–395
  psychosocial factors, 391–393
  sexual orientation, 395–399
Sexual organ development, 110–111
Sexual orientation
  biopsychological factors in, 395–398
  body image and, 387
  childhood upbringing and, 398
  current status of theories, 398–399
  defined, 394
  gender and, 398
  heredity and brain, 395–396, 397
  Kinsey's view, 392–393
  prenatal development and, 396–398
  psychosocial factors in, 398
Sexual response cycle, 390–391, *390*
Shading patterns, 169, *170*
Shape constancy, 171
Shaping, 249, *250*, 255, 265
Sheldon, William, 471–472, 474–475
Sherman (chimpanzee), 337
Sherrington, Charles, 75
Shift work, 205
Shockley, William, 365–366
Short-term memory, 272, 273–276, *276*
Siblings, 124
Sidis, William James, 357
Sierra Leone, 614
Siestas, 209
Signal-detection theory, 153
Sign language, 336, 337
Sildenafil, 394
Silent group, 438
Similarity, interpersonal attraction and, 30, 603, 605, 614
Similarity principle, 166–167, *166, 167*
Simon, Herbert, 14, 322–323
Simonides, 297
Simon, Theodore, 346
The Simpsons, 154
Simultaneous conditioning, 241
Singer, Jerome, *436*, 436, 437
Single parenthood, 123–124, 144
Single photon emission computed tomography (SPECT), 84
Situational attributions, 596–597
Situational variables, 41
Six Arts, 361
Size constancy, 169–171, 174
Sizemore, Chris, 501
Skepticism, 28–29
Skinner, B. F.
  child-rearing practices, 256
  language acquisition views, 330
  operant conditioning discoveries, 251, 255, 463
  overview of contributions, 12
  support for programmed instruction, 256
  Thorndike's influence on, 247
  view of personality, 460
Skinner boxes, 247–248, *248*, 249, 251
Skin senses, 184–188
Sleep
  across life span, *208*

biological rhythms and, 204–205
caffeine ingestion and, 229
deprivation, *208*
disorders, 211–214
dreaming, 207–208, 214–219, 233
effects on melatonin, 40–41, 42, 47*t*, 48–49, 204–205
effects on memory, 285
functions, 209–211
major depressive disorder and, 504, *504*
patterns, 205–209
stages of, *206*
typical night's, 205–208, *207*
Sleep apnea, 211, 213–214
Sleep deprivation, 198–199, *208*, 210, 212
Sleeper effect, 609
Sleep-maintenance insomnia, 211
Sleep-onset insomnia, 211
Sleep-wake cycle, 204–205
Sleepwalking, 208
Smell, 114, 181–183
Smith, Scott, 309
Smoking effects and treatment programs, 586–588
Smooth pursuit eye movements, 160, *162*
Snow, words for, 332–333
Snyder, Solomon, 78–79
Social anxiety disorder, 494–495
Social attachment, 119
Social clock, 129, 142
Social cognition, 596–600
Social-cognitive theory of personality, 460–461
Social-comparison theory, 428–429
Social-emotional symptoms, in schizophrenia, 513
Social facilitation, 617–618
Social factors in pain perception, 186
Social influence, 619–621
Social interest, in Adler's theory, 447
Social introversion, 456*t*
Social learning theory
  of aggression, 625
  of attitude formation, 607–608
  elements of, 263
  of gender-role development, 125
  therapies, 538
Social loafing, 618
Social play, 124
Social psychology
  aggression, 622–625
  attitudes, 606–615
  defined, 19, 596
  group dynamics, 615–621
  interpersonal attraction, 601–606
  origins, 595–596
  prosocial behavior, 626–630
  social cognition, 596–600
Social Readjustment Rating Scale, 562–563
Social relationships, 134–135
Social-relations orientation to therapy, 542–544
Social-skills training, 543
Social support, 574, 578–579, 589
Society for Psychical Research, 192

Society of Experimentalists, 7
Sociobiology, 377
Sociocultural explanations for gender differences, 141
Sociocultural perspective. *See also* Culture
  elements of, 16–17
  on major depressive disorder, 506
  on psychological disorders in general, 485–488
  on schizophrenia, 517
Sociopathy, 519
Soma of nerve cell, 72
Somatic nervous system, 68
Somatic symptom and related disorder, 498–500
Somatosensory cortex, 89–90, *90*, 184
Somatotonia, 472
Somatotypes, 472, 474
Somnambulism, 208
Sound
  decibel levels, 179*t*
  infant perceptions, 114
  localization, 180
  short-term memories encoded as, 275
  wave form, 175
Source credibility, 608
Spanos Attitudes Toward Hypnosis Questionnaire, 220
Spanos, Nicholas, 224
Spatial abilities, gender differences, 138
Spatial intelligence, 361
Spearman, Charles, 357–358, 359
Specializations in psychology, 17–21, *17*
Specific phobias, 494, 494*t*
Spectrum of visible light, 156–157
Speech center of brain, 92–93
Sperling, George, 274
Sperm, 110
Spermarche, 130
Sperry, Roger, 15, 98
Spinal cord, 67–68, 71–72
  injuries, 67–68, 99–100, 101, 432
Spiritual intelligence, 361
Split-brain research, 98–99, *99*
Splitting, 518
Spontaneous recovery, 242, 254
Spontaneous remission, 553
Sport, motivation in, 406–408
Sport psychology, 20, 406
Spouses' death, 146
Spreading activation, 281–282
SQ3R method, 294–295
Stability/instability, 453, *453*
Stable extraversion, 428
Stable factors, in Seligman's attributional theory, 505
Stage of exhaustion, 567
Stage of resistance, 567
Stages of sleep, 205–208, *206*
Standard deviation, 48, 347, *348*
Standardization in intelligence testing, 347–351
Standardization of tests, 36–37
Stanford-Binet Intelligence Scale, 36, 347
Stanford Hypnotic Susceptibility Scale, 220
Stapes, 176, *176*

State-dependent memory, 215, 288, 289–290
Statistical significance, 49–50
Statistics, 29, 46–52
Stepparents, 121
Stereotypes
  features of, 599
  gender role, 424
  influence on diagnoses, 490
  prejudice and, 614
  as self-fulfilling prophecies, 600
Stereotype threat, 350–351, 570
Sternberg, Robert, 359, 360, 605
Stern, William, 291, 346, 347
Stevenson, Robert Louis, 230
Stimulants, 226*t*, 228–230
Stimulus control, 213
Stimulus discrimination, 241
Stimulus generalization, 241
St. Mary's of Bethlehem, 530
Stomach, role in hunger, 379–380
Storage, of memories, 272, 278–281
Strange Situation, 120
Stream of consciousness, 7, 199–200
Stress, 504
  biopsychology of, 566–574
  cardiovascular disease and, 567–570
  coping with, 579–582
  eating disorders and, 387
  moderating factors, 574–579
  obesity and, 385
  overview, 562–566
  pathways, *571*
Stress-inoculation training, 580
Stressors, 562
Stroke damage, unilateral neglect from, 60
Stroop effect, 202, *202*
Structuralism, 6
Studies of twins reared apart, 66
Study habits, 294–296
Study of Mathematically Precocious Youth, 355, 357
Subjective well-being, 427
Sublimation, 446
Subliminal perception, 153–154, 201
Subliminal stimulation, 155
Substance abuse
  aversion therapy for, 536
  drug therapy and, 547
  intoxication, 28, 227
  prevalence in United States, *491*
  psychoactive effects, 227, 225*t*
  with schizophrenia, 514
Substance P, 78, 185–186
Subtractive color processes, 163
Subvocal speech, thought as, 309
Success criteria for therapy, 553, 554–555
Successful intelligence theory, 360
Sue, Stanley, 370
Suicide, 595
  major depressive disorder and, 508–509
Sullivan, Harry Stack, 447
Superego, 445
Superhealth Basic program, 582

Superior colliculus, *161*
Superiority, striving for, 447
Suprachiasmatic nucleus, 204–205
Suproxin, 437
Surface structure of language, 327
Surveys, 34–36
Sympathetic nervous system, 68, 414, *415*
Synapse, 75, 299
Synaptic terminals, 76
Synaptic transmission, 75–79, 299
    mechanisms of, *77*
Synaptic vesicles, 76
Synesthesia, 231
Syntax, 327
Systematic desensitization, 534–536
Systems approach to family therapy, 543
Szasz, Thomas, 490

T

Tabula rasa, 4
Tachistoscopes, 8–9
Taijin kyofusho, 495
The Tale of Genji, 377
Talkativeness, 138
Tarasoff decision, 550
Tardive dyskinesia, 547
Task-oriented coping, 579
Taste aversions, 244–246
Taste buds, 183
Taste, sense of, 6, 183–184, *183*
Taylor, Shelley, 576
Teaching machines, 256–257
Telegraphic speech, 329
Television, 264
    obesity and, 384
Temperament, 470–471, 472, 473, 474–475
Temporal lobes, 91, 177
Tend-and-befriend response, 566
Teratogens, 111–112
Terman, Lewis, 36–37, 346–347, 355, 356, 362–363
Terrace, Herbert, 337
Terror management theory, 468
Tertiary prevention, of psychological disorders, 548–549
Test-anxiety hierarchy, 535*t*
Testes, 70, 110
Testing
    for creativity, 317
    for deception, 413, 416–417
    as descriptive research method, 36–37
    intelligence, 345–351
    memory and, 284
    need for achievement, 402–403
    personality, 450–451, 455–457, 462–463, 468–469
Testosterone
    aggression and, 624
    aging effects, 136
    basic functions, 70
    effects in puberty, 130
    role in embryonic formation, 110–111

    role in memory, 303
    role in sexual motivation, 390
Test-retest method, 37
Tetrahydrocannabinol (THC), 231
Texas Adoption Project, 367, 473
Texture gradient, 169, *170*
Thalamus, 87, 160, *161*, 164, 165, 299, *300*
Thalidomide, 522
Thanatos, 444, 623
"The Big Five," 454–455
Thematic Apperception Test (TAT), 403, 450, 451, 452
Theology, roots of psychology in, 3
Theophrastus, 452
Theories, 31
Theory of multiple intelligences, 360–361
Therapeutic alliance, 554–555
Therapist characteristics, therapy success and, 555–556
Therapy. *See also* Psychological disorders
    behavioral, 533–538
    biopsychological, 544–547
    client rights, 549–551
    cognitive, 540
    community mental health, 548–549
    effectiveness, 552–556
    history of, 530–531
    humanistic, 540–542
    obtaining, 551–552
    operant, 536–538
    person-centered, 13
    psychoanalytic, 532–533
    social-relations orientation, 542–544
Theta waves, *206*, 206
Thorazine (chlorpromazine), 547
Thorndike, Edward, 247, 259–260
Thought
    artificial intelligence, 322–324
    behaviorists' disinterest in studying, 309
    broadcasting, 513
    concept formation, 310–312
    creativity of, 316–320
    decision making, 320–322
    defined, 309
    problem solving, 312–316
    relation to language, 332–335
Threats, nervous system response to, 414
The Three Christs of Ypsilanti, 513
Three-factor theory of personality, 453, 457
Thresholds, 182
    sensory, 152–155
Thurstone, Louis, 359
Tic disorder, 497
Timbre perception, 180
Tip-of-the-tongue phenomenon, 288
Titchener, Edward, 6, 7
T-lymphocytes, 572, *572*
Tobacco
    classical conditioning of dependence, 243
    health effects, 586
    nicotine effects, 229
    smoking prevention programs, 586–587
Tofranil (imipramine), 546, 554

Token economies, 256, 536–537
Tolerance
    for drugs, 225, 232, 244
    to motion, 189
Tolman, Edward, 262–263
Tongue, 183, *183*
Top-down processing, 166
Torrance, E. Paul, 317
Torrance Tests of Creative Thinking, 317
Touch, 184–185
Tough-mindedness/tender-mindedness, 453
Trace conditioning, 241
Trace decay, 285
Traits, 64
Trait theories
    of personality, 454–455
Tranquilizers, 78, 546
Transactional analysis (TA), 542–543
Transcendence, 378
Transcranial magnetic stimulation (TMS), 81
Transcutaneous electrical nerve stimulation (TENS), 187–188
Transference, analysis of, 533
Transformational grammar, 327
Transitive inferences, 117
Transorbital leucotomy, 544
Transplantation of neural tissue, 99, 101–102
Trauma group, 438
Travolta, John, 155
Treatment, right to receive or refuse, 550
Trench Coat Mafia group, 1
Trephining, 530
Trial and error, 312
Triandis, Harry, 16
Triangular theory of love, 605
Triarchic theory of intelligence, 360
Trichromatic theory, 163
Trichromats, 164
Tricyclic antidepressants, 546–547
Triplett, Norman, 595
Tripp, Peter, 198–199, 210
Trust versus mistrust stage, 119, 119*t*
Trustworthiness, 608
Truth serum, 228
Tryptophan hydroxylase, 493
Tuke, Daniel Hack, 566
Tulving, Endel, 278–279
Turner, Samuel, 492
Tversky, Amos, 320
Twain, Mark, 192
Twin studies. *See also* Heredity
    of aggression, 624
    anxiety disorders and, 496
    on bipolar disorder, 510
    dietary preference findings, 379
    on intelligence, 366, 367
    on major depressive disorder, 503
    obesity, 382
    overview, 65, 66
    of psychological disorders, 484
    on schizophrenia, 514, 515
    sexual orientation, 395–396
Twitmyer, Edwin, 239

Two-factor theory, *436*
 of emotion, 436, 437, 604–605
 of intelligence, 359
Two-sided messages, 609
Tympanic membrane, 175–176, *176*
Type A behavior, 451, 568–570
Type B behavior, 568–570
Type theories of personality, 452–454

U

UFO sightings, 450
Ultraviolet light, 156–157
Umami, 183–184
Unconditional positive regard, 467, 541
Unconditioned response (UCR), 239–241
Unconditioned stimulus (UCS), 239–241, 260, 261–262, 262*t*
Unconscious conflicts, 9
Unconscious, features of, 201–203
Unconscious inferences, 165
Unconscious mind in
 Freud's theory, 10, 203, 444
 Jung's theory, 449–450
Underextension, 328
Unilateral neglect, 60
Universal grammar, 331
Universalism, 16
University of Minnesota study of twins reared apart, 66
Uplifts, 565
Utopianism, 12

V

Vaginismus, 393
Vagus nerve, 76
Validity
 external, 43–46
 internal, 41–43
 of DSM-5, 488–489
 of intelligence tests, 348–351
 scales, 456, 456*t*
 of tests, 37
Valium (diazepam), 546
Variability hypothesis, 362–363
Variability measures, 48
Variable-interval schedules of reinforcement, 252, *252*
Variable-ratio schedules of reinforcement, 251
Variables, 38, 39, 41–42
Variance, 48
Vascular theory, 435
Ventromedial hypothalamus (VMH), 381
Verbal abilities, 138
Verbal persuasion, 461
Vestibular sense, 189–190, *190*
Viagra, 393
Vicarious experience, 461
Victor case study, 308
Viewmaster, 167–168
Vigilance, 86

Viki (chimpanzee), 335–336
Villa, Luigi, 323
Violence
 alcohol intoxication and, 227
 effect on children's psychosocial development, 122
 of groups, 625–626
 with schizophrenia, 513
 school shootings, 1, 34
 television viewing and, 264
Virtual twin studies, 366–367
Viscerotonia, 472
Visible spectrum, 156–157
Vision
 brain and, 160–165
 depth perception, 167–169, *170*, *171*
 effects of experience and culture, 173–174
 eye anatomy, 157–160
 form perception, 165–167
 illusions, 171–173
 perceptual constancies, 169–171
 properties of light and, 156–157
 role of brain in, 160
Visual acuity, *158*
Visual agnosia, 151–152
Visual cliff study, 114, 116
Visual cortex, 91, 160
Visual illusions, 171–173
Visual imagery, 409
Visual level of encoding, 278, *278*
Visual pathway, *161*
Visual referencing, 120
Visual sensory memory, 273
Vocal qualities, and emotion, 422–423
Vogel, Phillip, 98
Volitional rule, 486
Volkmar, Fredrick, 521
Volley theory, 178
Volunteer participants, effects on validity of experiments, 45
Vonnegut, Mark, 517
Voyage of self-discovery, 517

W

Wada test, 95, 420
Walden Two, 12
Wald, George, 163
Walk, Richard, 116
Wallace, Alfred Russell, 5
Warm glow effect, 434
Warning signs of suicide, 509
Washburn, Arthur, 379–380
Washburn, Margaret Floy, 7–8, 309
Washoe (chimpanzee), 336, 336–337, 338–339
Watergate investigation, 282
Watson, John B., 376
 learning study, 239
 Little Albert study, 241–242, 534
 overview of contributions, 11–13
 on thought, 309
Watts, James, 544

Wavelengths of visible light, 156–157
Waynbaum, Israel, 435
Wealth, happiness and, 428–429
Weber, Ernst, 4, 152
Weber's law, 155
Wechsler, David, 344, 347
Wechsler intelligence scales, 347, *348*
Weight control, 585–586
Weiner, Bernard, 596–597
Wen Ho Lee, 464
Wernicke, Karl, 92
Wernicke's aphasia, 92–93
Wernicke's area, 92–93
Wertheimer, Max, 8–9
Western Collaborative Group Study, 569
Western cultures, 462
Whorf, Benjamin Lee, 332–333
Wild Boy of Aveyron, 308
Williams, Redford, 569–570
Wish fulfillment, dreaming as, 217–218
Withdrawal symptoms, 225, 587
A Woman's Right, 529
A Woman Under the Influence, 516
Womb envy, 449
Women. *See also* Gender differences
 in psychology, 38
Women's Health Initiative Memory Study, 303
Women's intelligence, early studies, 362–363
Wooley, Helen Thompson, 362
Word salad, 513
Work
 impact on longevity, 137
Working memory, 275
World Trade Center attacks, 563
World Values Survey, 142
Wug test, 330
Wundt, Wilhelm, 5–6, 7, 16

X

Xanax (alprazolam), 546
X chromosomes, 110, 165
X rays, 353

Y

Y chromosomes, 110, 165
Yerkes-Dodson law, *399*, 399–400
Yerkes, Robert, 336, 363
Yerkish, 336, 337–338
Young-Helmholtz theory, 163
Young, Thomas, 163

Z

Zajonc, Robert, 368, 618
Zar, 487
Zen, 449
Zero correlation, 48, 49
Zoloft (sertraline), 546–547
Zygotes, 110